Footprint

Caribbean Islands

The travel guide

Handbook 2001

Sarah Cameron

A good holiday is one spent among people whose notions of time are vaguer than yours.

JB Priestley

Caribbean Islands Handbook 2001

Published by Footprint Handbooks
6 Riverside Court
Lower Bristol Road
Bath BA2 3DZ. England
T +44 (0)1225 469141
F +44 (0)1225 469461
Email info@footprintbooks.com
Web www.footprintbooks.com

ISBN 1 900949 62 8
ISSN 0967-4748
CIP DATA: A catalogue record for this
book is available from the British Library.

In USA, published by
NTC/Contemporary Publishing Group
4255 West Touhy Avenue, Lincolnwood
(Chicago), Illinois 60712-1975, USA
T 847 679 5500 F 847 679 24941
Email NTCPUB2@AOL.COM

ISBN 0-658-01153-7
Library of Congress Catalog Card
Number: 00-132905

© Footprint Handbooks Ltd 2000
12th edition

Credits

Series editor
Patrick Dawson and Rachel Fielding
Editorial
Editor: Stephanie Lambe
Maps: Sarah Sorensen
Production
Manager: Jo Morgan
Typesetting: Emma Bryers
Maps: Kevin Feeney (colour), Robert
Lunn, Claire Benison

Design
Mytton Williams

Photography
Front cover: Images Colour Library.
Back cover: Axiom.
Inside colour section: Art Directors &
Trip Photo Library, Getty One Stone, Eye
Ubiquitous, James Davies Worldwide,
Life File Photographic Library, Impact
Photos and The Travel Library.

Print
Manufactured in Italy by LEGOPRINT

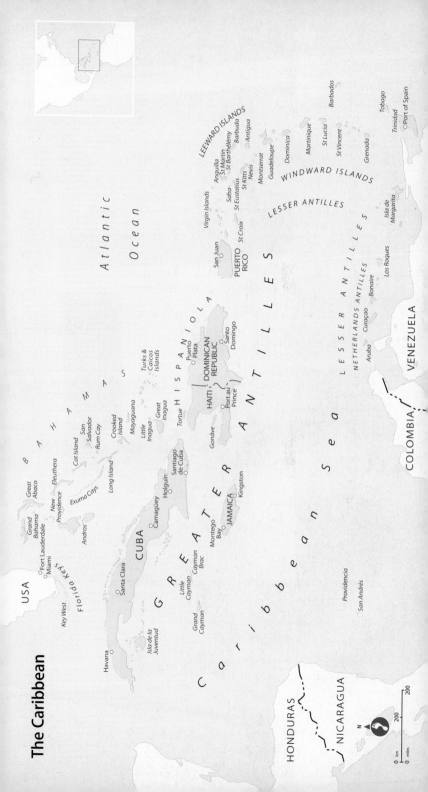

The Caribbean

USA
Florida
Fort Lauderdale
Miami
Key West
Havana
Santa Clara
CUBA
Isla de la Juventud

Atlantic Ocean

BAHAMAS
Grand Bahama
Great Abaco
Eleuthera
New Providence
Andros
Cat Island
San Salvador
Rum Cay
Long Island
Exuma Cays
Crooked Island
Little Inagua
Great Inagua
Mayaguana
Turks & Caicos Islands

Tortue
HISPANIOLA
HAITI
Gonâve
Port au Prince
Puerto Plata
Santo Domingo
DOMINICAN REPUBLIC

GREATER ANTILLES
Camaguey
Holguin
Santiago de Cuba
Montego Bay
JAMAICA
Kingston
Little Cayman
Cayman Brac
Grand Cayman

Providencia
San Andrés

HONDURAS
NICARAGUA

Caribbean Sea

PUERTO RICO
San Juan
St Croix
Virgin Islands
Saba
St Eustatius
Anguilla
St Martin
St Barthélemy
Barbuda
St Kitts
Nevis
Antigua
Montserrat
Guadeloupe
Dominica
Martinique
St Lucia
St Vincent
Barbados
Grenada
Tobago
Trinidad
Port of Spain

LEEWARD ISLANDS
WINDWARD ISLANDS
LESSER ANTILLES

Isla de Margarita
Los Roques
Aruba
Curaçao
Bonaire
NETHERLANDS ANTILLES
LESSER ANTILLES

COLOMBIA
VENEZUELA

N

0 km 200
0 miles 200

Contents

Left: brightly painted wooden houses in Tortola, British Virgin Islands.

4

Right: a lined seahorse holding fast in the Netherland Antilles

6

Right: a way of life - everyone joins in to
play cricket in the Anglo islands on any
patch of bare ground.
Below: St John's, Antigua, a functional town
transformed by a lick of paint.

Above: centuries of waves have crashed against
the rocks to form this natural stone bridge in
Aruba. *Right*: Crop Over in Barbados, parades
and calypso to celebrate the traditional end of
the sugar harvest.

The Caribbean in a conch shell

Finding your way around the Caribbean can seem like a daunting task – so many islands to choose from and not enough time to see them all? Here's a handy five minute A-Z trip around them all to help you decide where to start, finish, or just lounge, depending upon how energetic you are feeling.

Anguilla

Anguilla is known for its luxury hotels and extensive sandy beaches. Its high standard of living makes it one of the safest islands and consequently one of the most relaxing. Visitors amuse themselves in the water during the day and eat at excellent restaurants and bars at night, taking in a weekend beach party with live music. There's not much else to do on this low-lying coral island, but that's why people come here.

Antigua

A family holiday destination with great beaches, watersports and safe swimming. Direct, non-stop flights from Europe and North America make this island ideal for introducing children to the Caribbean. Good transport links with other islands facilitate two-centre holidays or more extensive island hopping. English Harbour is particularly picturesque, with yachts filling a historic bay that has been a popular staging post for centuries. Nelson's Dockyard and ruined forts are overlooked by the old battery on Shirley Heights, now better known for Sunday jump-ups and reggae bands.

Aruba

Aruba is the smallest of the 'ABC' group of islands, only 25 km north of Venezuela. It has been closely linked with the Venezuelan oil industry for most of the 20th century, but when times were hard a decision was made to diversify into mass tourism. The coastal strip on the leeward side of the island with the best beaches is now wall-to-wall hotels, with all those of more than 300 rooms allowed to have a casino. A wide range of watersports are on offer, including excellent windsurfing, which is world class. On land there is a golf course among the sand dunes in the north and efforts are being made to tempt visitors away from the beach and develop ecotourism.

The Bahamas

Hundreds of flat, sandy islands, specks of green set in ever changing hues of aquamarine. Cruise ships bring customers for casinos and shopping malls in Freeport and Nassau, but elsewhere the islands are quiet, often deserted, places to chill out. There are fabulous opportunities for all watersports in crystal clear water and hotels have a variety of water toys. Reefs and walls offer spectacular diving while the islands are world famous for bonefishing and deep sea fishing adventures. Formerly a haven for pirates, smugglers and bootleggers, the islands' proximity to the USA has shaped their development.

Barbados

Barbados has a long-established tourist industry and is highly experienced in providing efficient service to a wide clientele. It hasn't got the best beaches in the Caribbean, there are no volcanoes, no rainforest, no virgin coral reef, but visitors come back time and time again. You can pay hundreds of dollars for a hotel room and be truly cosseted or rent a moderate apartment and look after yourself. You can play golf (the courses are very highly rated), tennis, squash and any number of other sports, or you can watch cricket, horseracing or polo. There is lovely walking along the rugged north and east coasts on the Atlantic side, while watersports are offered along the more protected west and south coasts on the Caribbean. For sightseeing, there are fortifications, plantation houses, museums, rum distilleries and gardens. Barbados' history as a British colony is evident in its political system and place names, but times are changing. You can no longer stand in Trafalgar Square and look at Nelson's statue; the Lord High Admiral has been moved and the square now honours National Heroes.

8

Right: fresh fruit and vegetables from Venezuela
brought to the floating market in Curaçao.
Below: a barracuda glides by - one of the thrills
of diving in the Cayman Islands.

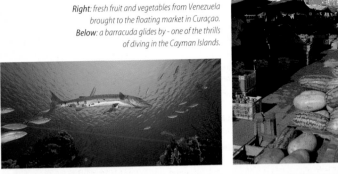

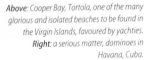

Above: Cooper Bay, Tortola, one of the many
glorious and isolated beaches to be found in
the Virgin Islands, favoured by yachties.
Right: a serious matter, dominoes in
Havana, Cuba.

The diving here is among the best in the Caribbean, with pristine reefs and wonderful visibility as there are no rivers to muddy the waters and it is out of the hurricane belt. The climate is dry and the vegetation little more than scrub and cactus but it is prized by birdwatchers. Once important as a salt producer, this Dutch island now makes its living out of tourism. **Bonaire**

The British Virgin Islands have a reputation for excellent sailing and there are many charter companies offering crewed or bareboat yachts. Windsurfing is also top quality and both sports organize races and regattas which attract competitors of international standard. Races are accompanied by lots of parties and related activities typical of the yachtie fraternity. There are plenty of hotels, and a few really special places – popular with newly weds or the seriously rich. **British Virgin Islands**

These three low lying little islands south of Cuba are green with pine and mangroves. Seven Mile Beach along the west side of Grand Cayman provides a welcome break for workers in the offshore financial centre. Conservation is top priority here, both on land and under water and there are a number of sanctuaries in the ponds and wetlands. Cayman Brac and Little Cayman are quiet, unhurried places where you can escape the crowds and relax without giving up your creature comforts. A dive resort ranked among the world's best, the islands offer a variety of thrilling dive sites. **Cayman Islands**

The largest island in the Caribbean, Cuba is blessed with varied and picturesque scenery, from the rolling green sugar cane land or flat cattle plains to forested mountains, lakes, caves, beaches and swamps. Travellers come for the vibrant culture, music, dance, art and the people who make it. The island's turbulent political past and its current communist stability is of interest to many. Colonial towns and cities are unspoilt by advertising or neon and American influence is minimal: Cuba is Cuban. You can laze on a beach, hike up a mountain, cycle the deserted roads, wander around fortresses, historical monuments and museums or take to the water. Deep sea fishing was made famous here by Hemingway and both the inland waters and the sea have always been a great attraction. Long, sandy beaches on the north coast, such as Varadero, or picture book coves and bays offer excellent swimming, while the reefs and cays offshore attract divers and snorkellers. **Cuba**

Curaçao is the largest of the Netherlands Antilles and its capital, Willemstad, has some very fine Dutch colonial architecture painted in a variety of pastel colours, while in the countryside there are several beautiful plantation houses, called *landhuisen*. It also has one of the most important historical sites in the Caribbean: a synagogue dating back to 1732, which is the oldest in continuous use in the Western Hemisphere. For most of the 20th century the island's fortunes, like Aruba, depended on its oil refinery, which processes Venezuelan crude oil, but more recently tourism also has become more important. Diving has grown very popular since the establishment of an underwater park to preserve the reef and there are dive sites all along the leeward side of the island. **Curaçao**

Known as the 'Nature Island' of the Caribbean, this is the place to come for dense forests, volcanic hills, rivers, waterfalls and the Boiling Lake, providing good hiking and birdwatching opportunities. It is also a highly regarded diving destination, with a good marine park system, and for much of the year you can see whales and dolphins offshore. Hotels around the island are small, intimate and low-key, greater development being deterred by the lack of beaches. It is the only island where Caribs have survived and they still retain many of their traditions such as canoe carving. The island's culture and language are an amalgam of the native and immigrant peoples; Carib, French, English, African. **Dominica**

Dominican Republic This is the Hispanic side of Hispaniola, with some exceptionally fine colonial towns set in stunning scenery. It contains the highest mountain in the Caribbean and some of the most beautiful beaches. It is green and fertile except in the southwest, which is a dry zone, and the southeast where huge cacti grow. The capital, Santo Domingo, was the first in Spanish America and it boasts the first cathedral and the first university. Hotels sprawl along the coast for sun, sea and sand worshippers, but development is also taking place inland where sugar plantations have made way for golf courses and adventure tourism is increasingly popular. Mountain biking, white water rafting, hiking, canyoning, horse riding and other sports are available in the hills and forests. If you've still got any energy after all that for nightlife, the discos are throbbing and you must try the merengue.

Grenada Known as the spice island because of the nutmeg, mace and other spices it produces, Grenada, the most southerly of the Windward Islands, is volcanic in origin, has a beautiful mountainous interior and is well endowed with lush forests and cascading rivers. Hikers and nature lovers enjoy the trails in the national parks, where many different ecosystems are found, from dry tropical forest and mangroves on the coast, through lush rainforest on the hillsides, to elfin woodland on the peaks. St George's, the capital, is widely acknowledged as the prettiest harbour city in the West Indies, blending the architectural styles of the French and English with a picturesque setting on steep hills overlooking the bay. The southern coast, with its sandy beaches, protected bays and rocky promontories, is being developed for tourism and there is a wide range of places to stay.

Guadeloupe This is France in the tropics, the French islands having the same status as any French *département* on the mainland. They have many of the same smells too: coffee, croissants, baguettes and other French foods, which you can wash down with French wines (or opt for some very fine Caribbean rum). Créole food is often spicy and delicious. Guadeloupe is really two islands: the western Basse-Terre, which is mountainous and forested, with a huge national park on and offshore, and Grand-Terre, to the east, which is smaller, flatter and more densely populated. Hiking on Basse-Terre is very popular and there are rivers and pools, some warm, some cold, to refresh you on a long, hot walk. Large areas are used for growing sugar cane, bananas and other fruits and flowers, but there are also good beaches which attract tourists, mostly from France. The outer islands of Les Saintes, La Désirade and Marie Galante are easily reached from Guadeloupe but are quiet and untouched by mass tourism.

Haiti The only country to have successfully carried out a slave rebellion, Haiti's religious beliefs, music, dance and art stem directly from Africa. French Créole, rather than Spanish, is nearly everybody's first language. Fortifications and other historical landmarks dot the countryside, but the most impressive is the massive La Citadelle, built on top of a 900-metre peak to deter any French invasion. The capital, Port-au-Prince, is a seething mass of humanity where everyone plies their trade in the streets to eke out a living. This is the most mountainous island in the Caribbean, but pressure for the land has led Haitians to cut down all their trees for fuel, leaving the hillsides bare. Haiti is the poorest country in the Western Hemisphere and there is no mass tourism. Occupying the western third of the island of Hispaniola, it has little in common culturally with its neighbour, the Dominican Republic.

Left: the local bus service, tap taps, loaded with people and produce at the Iron Market in Port-au-Prince, Haiti.
Below: St George's, Grenada, one of the most attractive capital cities with buildings clinging to the hillsides around a horseshoe-shaped bay.
Next page: music on the move in Jamaica where rhythm goes with you everywhere.

Above: One of the many idyllic sandy beaches around the Dominican Republic. *Left*: the oldest fortress in the Americas, Fortaleza Ozama and the Torre del Homenaje, one of the sights in the colonial city of Santo Domingo, Dominican Republic.

SWING A LING
mobile RECORD SHACK

GIVE * THANKS ALWAYS GOD IS LOVE

RECORDS

DISCO FOR

Gospel ♫

OLDIES

* PEACE * LOVE *

O DE. REGGAE * FUNKY

SOUL

NATTY

A beautiful island with rolling hills and steep gullies, the spectacular Blue Mountains overlook **Jamaica** a coastline indented with bays and coves. Rain falls freely, water is abundant, the vegetation is luxuriant and colours are vibrant. The people have a culture to match, from reggae and rastafarianism to English plantation houses and cricket. Music is everywhere and Jamaica is a hub of creativity in the Caribbean. The advent of cruise ships and package tourism has led to overdevelopment of some coasts, but it is easy to escape the crowds. Every conceivable watersport is on offer in the resort areas on the north coast, where the beaches are safe for swimming. The south coast has fewer beaches but important mangrove areas which are home to manatee and crocodiles.

Like Guadeloupe, this is a piece of France transported to the tropics, where language and **Martinique** customs have adapted to the climate. There is something for everybody here: a variety of hotels; good beaches; watersports; historical attractions; beautiful scenery; hiking; birdwatching and countless other activities. Tourism is well-developed in the south, but a large part of the more mountainous north is taken up by protected rainforest. The volcano, Pelée, last erupted in 1902, when it destroyed the former capital, St-Pierre, killing all but one of its 26,000 inhabitants. The ruins and vulcanology museum are a fascinating insight into island life before 1902. It was on Martinique at the turn of the 18th century that the Dominican friar, Père Labat, perfected the process of making rum, an enterprise that continues today, with great success.

The 'Emerald Isle', with its Irish influences, is not currently offering many tourist facilities, its **Montserrat** visitors being mostly scientists and aid workers helping the island recover after the eruption of the volcano in 1995. As an illustration of the volatility of the region's geology, Montserrat is incomparable, but that is little comfort to those who have been evacuated from the southern part of the island, including the capital, Plymouth, which is under a blanket of ash. Construction is taking place in the north and evacuees are returning from abroad, but it will be some time before life returns to normal.

The smallest of the Greater Antilles, Puerto Rico is Spanish American; its inhabitants descended **Puerto Rico** from Taino Indians, their Spanish colonial masters and African slaves. San Juan, the island's capital, was founded in 1510 and the old city still stands within its walls on a spit of land jutting out to sea. The sprawling new city is US-influenced, with shopping malls, industrial zones and wide highways. Mass tourism is encouraged with large resorts, casinos, marinas and golf courses, but it is easy to escape from this if you want to find a quieter Puerto Rico. Inland, there are mountains, rainforest, country inns, caves and archaeological sites, while offshore there are the unspoilt islands of Vieques and Culebra or the even smaller Mona Island where facilities are limited to a camp site.

This tiny Dutch island rises out of the sea, green and lush. An extinct volcano, its peak is aptly **Saba** named Mount Scenery. Underwater, the landscape is equally spectacular and divers treasure the marine park, noted for its 'virginity'. When not under water, visitors find walking challenging and rewarding. Ancient trails weave their way around the island, the most stunning being the 1,064 irregular steps up Mount Scenery through different types of tropical vegetation according to altitude. Lodging is in small, friendly hotels, guest houses and cottages, where you won't need a key – there is no crime.

Only 35km from St-Martin, tiny St-Barths is easily reached by boat or a short air hop. It has **St-Barthélémy** gained a reputation as the place to go for the rich and famous. It is chic and expensive and its many beautiful beaches are dotted with luxury hotels and villas, designed for those who appreciate privacy. Gourmet French restaurants and créole bistros can be found all over the island. This is a place to indulge yourself and be a part of the jet set.

Only 2,100 people live on this Dutch outpost and very few tourists make the effort to visit. It **Sint Eustatius** has a rich colonial history and a prosperous past, when there were 8,000 inhabitants (mostly slaves) and some 3,500 ships visited each year. Having made its fortune in the 18th century out of the slave trade and commerce in plantation crops, it lost it in the 19th century with the abolition of slavery and has never really recovered. The main town, Oranjestad, still has the fortifications and remains of warehouses from its heyday, parts of which are being restored as hotels and restaurants, but the island is generally underdeveloped. There are walking trails up into the rainforest of the extinct volcano, the Quill, and diving is good in the marine park.

St Kitts & Nevis Slightly off the beaten track, neither island is overrun with tourists. St Kitts is developing its southern peninsula where there are golden sandy beaches, but most of the island is untouched by tourism. Rugged volcanic peaks, forests and old fortresses produce spectacular views and hiking is very rewarding. Two miles away, the conical island of Nevis is smaller, quieter and very desirable. Here, plantation houses have been converted into some of the most romantic hotels in the Caribbean, very popular with honeymooners.

St Lucia Very popular as both a family holiday destination and a romantic paradise for honeymooners, St Lucia offers something for everyone. Its beaches are golden or black sand, some with the spectacular setting of the Pitons as a backdrop, and many are favoured by turtles as a nesting site. Offshore there is good diving and snorkelling along the west coast, with a marine park along part of it. Rodney Bay is one of the best harbours in the West Indies, with a marina for 1,000 yachts, and windsurfing and other watersports are available. The mountainous interior is outstandingly beautiful and there are several forest reserves to protect the St Lucian parrot and other wildlife. Sightseeing opportunities include sulphur springs, colonial fortifications and plantation tours. St Lucia has a rich cultural heritage, having alternated between the French and English colonial powers, both of whom used African slaves, and has produced some of the finest writers and artists in the region, including two Nobel prize winners.

Sint Maarten/ St-Martin Shared amicably between Holland and France, this island offers you two cultures within easy reach of each other. Good international air transport links have encouraged the construction of large resort hotels with casinos and duty free shopping in the Dutch part. The French part is considered more 'chic' and crowded with restaurants dedicated to the serious business of eating well. Both sides have good harbours and marinas and are popular with the sailing crowd. Heavily populated, there are not many places on the island where houses have not been built, so this is not a place to come to get away from it all, but it is ideal for a fun beach holiday perhaps in combination with another quieter island nearby.

St Vincent & the Grenadines St Vincent is green and fertile and very pretty, with its fishing villages, coconut groves, banana plantations and volcanic interior. However, it is widely known for the superb sailing conditions provided by its 32 sister islands and cays and most visitors spend some time on a yacht, even if only for a day. Bareboat and crewed yachts are available for as long as you require, wherever you want to go. There are also very competitive regattas and yacht races held throughout the year, accompanied by a lot of parties and social events. The Grenadines have a certain exclusivity, some of the smaller islands are privately owned and Mustique is known for its villas owned by the rich, royal and famous. There are some fabulously expensive and luxurious places to stay, but there are also more moderate hotels, guest houses and rental homes for those who don't want to spend all their time afloat.

Trinidad & Tobago Tourism is not highly developed in Trinidad, which has traditionally depended on its industrial base for wealth and employment. However, its attractions are now becoming better known. The island has a rich culture, largely a mixture of the traditions of African slaves and Indian indentured labourers, which are brought together so spectacularly in the island's carnival, one of the best in the world. Tobago, on the other hand, is a laid back island where visitors appreciate the clear, calm sea, the sandy beaches, the diving and snorkelling and the small, friendly hotels and guest houses. The two islands together are home to more species of birds than any other island in the Caribbean and birdwatchers have long been attracted to the forests of the Northern Range, the Caroni Swamp and the Nariva Swamp on Trinidad and the Forest Reserve on Tobago.

Left: you too can look like this! Join in the fun in Trinidad's carnival with one of the Mas' camps, get this year's costume and 'tramp' through town. *Below*: Marigot Bay, St Lucia, a haven for yachts and one of the prettiest anchorages in the West Indies.

Above: a period of calm, during rosaries at the Roman Catholic church in Soufrière, St Lucia. *Left*: the red roofs of Charlotte Amalie, mecca for cruise ship shoppers and capital of St Thomas, US Virgin Islands.

The Turks & Caicos Islands Similar to the southern Bahamas islands, to which they are geographically linked, these flat, coral islands are a British Dependent Territory. Miles of sandy beaches attract sun-loving tourists to a water playground. Diving and snorkelling are superb among coral gardens, wrecks and walls which drop dramatically to the floor of the ocean. Most hotels are on the island of Providenciales, spread along Grace Bay on the north shore, and there are lots of facilities for sailing, diving and fishing. Grand Turk is the seat of government but is a quiet, unhurried place with a few small hotels and some pleasant colonial buildings. Other inhabited islands, North Caicos, Middle Caicos, South Caicos and Salt Cay have tiny populations – good places to escape the crowds.

US Virgin Islands The three US Virgin Islands are very different from each other but are all very American. St Thomas attracts cruise ships and when several are in port the streets of town are heavily congested with shoppers. St John is dominated by the Virgin Islands National Park, which has been in existence since 1956 and has some excellent trails for walkers. St Croix is the poorest of the three but has a great deal to offer in the way of tourist attractions. All three have good hotels and are popular with sailors.

The Venezuelan Islands Isla de Margarita is the largest of Venezuela's 72 islands in the Caribbean. It first became popular with Venezuelan tourists taking advantage of its duty free status to go on a shopping spree but, following a property boom, foreign tourists are now also attracted by low prices as hotels struggle to fill their rooms. The beaches are long, sandy and varied, those facing east having excellent surfing and windsurfing. More difficult to get to, Islas Los Roques are a national park, treasured for long stretches of white beaches, snorkelling and diving on the reef and many nesting sites for sea birds. Other islands are even more remote and are best visited by yacht, giving you the freedom to explore without worrying where you are going to sleep.

Essentials

Essentials

Planning your trip

Holiday companies and travel agents tend to market the Caribbean as a homogenous tropical destination, but in reality each island has its own personality and what suits one person will not suit another. Here is a run down of what is on offer.

As a general rule, the low-lying coral islands have the best beaches, with miles of white sand and good swimming. A reef offshore usually provides calm seas and great snorkelling and diving. Away from the beach, however, the landscape is flat, covered with scrub, cactus and maybe pine trees. These islands include the Bahamas, The Turks and Caicos, Anegada in the British Virgin Islands, Anguilla, St Martin, Aruba, Bonaire and Curaçao and the islands off the Venezuelan coast. The volcanic or mountainous islands have beaches, but these are usually fairly narrow and can be black or grey sand or even shingle. On the other hand, they can be stunningly beautiful, with steep, forested hills falling into the sea, horse shoe shaped bays with picturesque headlands and palm trees providing shade on the shore. The Windward Islands are typical of this scenery: Dominica, Martinique, St Lucia, St Vincent and Grenada. The larger islands in the Greater Antilles: Cuba, Hispaniola (Haiti and the Dominican Republic), Jamaica and Puerto Rico are big enough to have everything. You just need to decide which end of the island you want to be, or how long it will take you to see it all. Wherever you are, remember that the Atlantic coast will be more rugged and have rougher seas than the Caribbean coast. There are few Atlantic beaches where it is safe to swim, although they can be fascinating to beachcomb for flotsam and jetsam from Africa.

Sun, sea & sand

Watersports are available everywhere, with hotels providing a wide variety of toys for entertainment on the water. Places like Cabarete in the Dominican Republic, Aruba, Bonaire and the Virgin Islands have the best winds for **windsurfing** and excellent equipment and instruction. **Sailing** is one of the most popular activities and all islands have craft of varying sizes, from hobie cats and dinghies to large liveaboard yachts for charter. Two of the nicest places for sailing are the Virgin Islands and the Grenadines, where there are pretty clusters of small islands where you can anchor safely and take advantage of the bars and restaurants dotted among the bays. **Regattas** and races are organized by local yacht clubs throughout the year in all islands (see inside the back cover for dates), great if you want to participate or just spectate. **Scuba diving** and **snorkelling** are popular everywhere, sometimes too popular if you are on a boat with dozens of other people. Marine parks have been established in many islands keen to protect their underwater charms, but the best places are usually the more remote where there are not so many tourists anyway. Try Bonaire, Tobago, Saba, Dominica, Grand Turk, Little Cayman or the Isla de la Juventud off Cuba, where there are reefs, walls and drop-offs to trenches many miles deep, the coral is in good condition and there is plenty of marine life, from multicoloured fishes to tiny worms and crustaceans. Small, intimate lodges cater to divers' needs and are cheerful and relaxed places to stay. For those who like to catch, rather than watch or photograph, **fishing** is well-established in the Bahamas, Cuba, Puerto Rico and many other islands, both deep sea and shore fishing, for fun, for the pot or competitively. The biggest creatures in the sea are, however, now more protected, and seasonal **whale watching** is becoming a big tourist attraction. The Dominican Republic has boat excursions to see the hump backed whales during the breeding season, the Turks Passage off Grand Turk is a good place to see them on their migration and boats with sonar tracking equipment take visitors out off the coast of Dominica.

A drop in the ocean

Not everyone wants to sit on the beach or play in the water for all, or even part of, their holiday. Despite being relatively small, the Caribbean islands have a lot to offer in terms of land-based sports. **Hiking** is rewarding in places like Dominica, Grenada and Jamaica in the mountains and rainforests. **Birdwatching** is superb in Trinidad and increasingly popular in Bonaire, Cuba and elsewhere. **Cycling** is a great way to get around Cuba, while off-road and downhill mountain biking is brilliant in the Dominican Republic. Almost anywhere you can hire bikes and explore but remember this can be a hot and sweaty activity. For some people,

Outward bound

Essentials

of course, their only reason for going to the Caribbean is to watch **cricket** in the former English islands, although **baseball** in the Hispanic islands commands equally enthusiastic support.

A cultural mix Colonial architecture varies according to whether the islands were once Spanish, English, French or Dutch, but the best **colonial cities** are Havana, Santo Domingo and San Juan, all once part of the Spanish Empire. Willemstad in Curaçao is a charming example of Dutch architecture in the tropics, remnants of Danish building can be seen in St Croix, while the French islands retain the gingerbread style with intricate fretwork, and elegant plantation houses can be seen in the former British islands. Cultural life in the Caribbean is varied, depending on the tastes of former colonial rulers and the customs of other immigrants such as East Indians and Chinese, but is overwhelmingly influenced by the African traditions brought to the islands by thousands of slaves from hundreds of tribes. Their **religions** have been adapted and preserved, particularly in Haiti (voodoo) and Cuba (santería), but it is rhythm which makes the greatest impact on a visitor. Caribbean **music and dance** are cultural exports of tremendous worldwide importance, whether reggae, calypso, jazz, rumba, zouk, salsa, merengue or any number of other styles. **Carnival** is the best way for a visitor to experience local talent and while all the islands have their own celebrations at different times of the year, carnival in Trinidad is second to none. However, if this doesn't appeal, you can always go to the opera in Barbados or the ballet in Cuba.

Before you travel

Getting in

Documents North Americans, British and Commonwealth citizens in some cases need only show proof of
Individual island identity, but it is always best to carry a **passport**. Immigration authorities are not keen on
entry requirements driver's licences or voter registration cards, even if technically they are adequate forms of
are given in the identification. If intending to visit Puerto Rico or the US Virgin Islands, or making connections
relevant chapters through Miami or another US gateway, a **visa** for the United States will not be necessary if
under Essentials your home country and the airline on which you are travelling are part of the US Visa Waiver Program. A US consulate will supply all relevant details. An **onward ticket** is a common prerequisite for entry (see below). Australians and New Zealanders should note that many islands impose strict entry laws on holders of the above passports. Satisfying visa and other requirements, if not done at home, can take at least a day, usually involve expense, and passport photographs will be needed: be prepared.

On all forms, refer to yourself as a 'visitor' rather than a 'tourist'. If asked where you are staying and you have not booked in advance, say any hotel (they do not usually check), but do not say you are going to camp and do not say that you are going to arrange accommodation later.

Onward ticket Many islands insist that visitors have an air ticket to their home country before being allowed to enter; for non-US citizens travelling to the Caribbean from the USA, this means a ticket from the USA to their home country, not a ticket back to the USA. Tickets to other countries will not suffice. This becomes a problem if you are not going home for 12 months since airline tickets become void after a year. Some airlines sell tickets on the six to 12 month extended payment plan; these can be credited when you have left the islands with restrictive entry requirements. Even if you propose to take some boat trips between islands, we recommend that you purchase flights in advance and refund those that have not been used later.

Passport You should always carry your passport in a safe place about your person, or if not going far, leave it in the hotel safe. If staying in a place for several weeks, it is worth while registering at your embassy or consulate. Then, if your passport is stolen or lost, the process of replacing it is quicker. Keeping photocopies of essential documents, and some additional passport-sized photographs, is recommended.

Money

The Caribbean is not a cheap area to visit. Transport is expensive (unless you are staying in   Cost of visiting
one place and using only buses), but if you book your flights in advance, taking advantage of
whatever air pass or stopovers are suitable, that expenditure at least will be out of the way.

Accommodation is generally expensive, too, even at the lower end of the market. There is
no shortage of luxury resorts and beach hotels throughout the price range. In a number of
instances you can book all-inclusive packages which are often good value and let you know
in advance almost exactly what your expenditure will be. However, you will not see much of
your chosen island outside your enclave and organized excursions can work out costly. To
find cheaper accommodation you need mobility, probably a hired car. One option is renting a
self-catering apartment, villa or house, the range of which is also vast, and here the advantage is
that a group of people can share the cost (not so economical for single travellers).

Since, on a number of islands, resort-type hotels form the majority, turning up at a cheaper
place may not always yield a room because competition is great. The term guest house is
usually applied to places at the lower end of the market; they tend, but by no means in all
cases, to be basic. Note also that, if booking ahead, tourist office lists may not include the
cheapest establishments, so you may have to reserve a dearer room, then look around. This is
probably what you will have to do in any event, time permitting, to find the best value. In the
main, tourist offices publish accurate, up-to-date lists of accommodation, which are a great
help for making preliminary bookings. Remember that the Dominican Republic and Cuba
have the most hotel rooms in the Caribbean, so there is no real problem in finding a space
there. Some islands, such as the French Antilles, have well-organized camp sites, but on many
camping is actually prohibited.

Essentials

Essentials

👉 Exchange rates (July 2000)

Country	Currency	Abbreviation	Exchange RATE/US$
Anguilla	East Caribbean dollar	EC$	2.66
Antigua & Barbuda	East Caribbean dollar	EC$	2.66
Aruba	Aruban florin	Afl	1.78
Bahamas	Bahamian dollar	B$	0.98
Barbados	Barbados dollar	B$	1.98
Bonaire	Guilder	Naf	1.77
British Virgin Islands	US dollar	US$	1.00
Cayman Islands	Cayman dollar	CI$	0.83
Cuba	Cuban peso	$	1.00
		Market rate	21.00
Curaçao	Guilder	Naf	1.77
Dominica	East Caribbean dollar	EC$	2.66
Dominican Rep	Dominican peso	RD$	16.15
Grenada	East Caribbean dollar	EC$	2.66
Guadeloupe	French franc	F	7
Haiti	Gourde		19.8
Jamaica	Jamaican dollar	J$	42
Martinique	French franc	F	7
Montserrat	East Caribbean dollar	EC$	2.66
Puerto Rico	US dollar	US$	1.00
Saba	Guilder	Naf	1.77
St Barthélémy	French franc	F	7
St Kitts & Nevis	East Caribbean dollar	EC$	2.66
St Lucia	East Caribbean dollar	EC$	2.66
St Martin	French franc	F	7
St Vincent & the Grenadines	East Caribbean dollar	EC$	2.66
Sint Eustatius	Guilder	Naf	1.77
Sint Maarten	Guilder	Naf	1.77
Trinidad & Tobago	Trinidad dollar	TT$	6.24
Turks & Caicos	US dollar	US$	1.00
US Virgin Islands	US dollar	US$	1.00
Venezuela	Bolivar	Bs	683.25

The following tips on economizing were sent by Steve Wilson and Debra Holton of San Francisco: look out bunk rentals on boats (see below, page 27); happy hours in bars often have free food; couples sharing costs can often take advantage of Ladies' Night in a bar or nightclub, which either permits free entry or cheap drinks.

Currency In general, the US dollar is the best currency to take, in cash or travellers' cheques. The latter are the most convenient and, if you follow the issuer's instructions, can be replaced if lost or stolen. On the most frequently-visited holiday islands, eurocurrencies can be exchanged without difficulty but at a poor rate and US dollars are preferred. In some places, the US dollar is accepted alongside local currency (but make sure in which currency prices are being quoted). In others, only the local currency is accepted. On the French islands dollars are accepted, but the franc is the preferred currency. Credit cards are widely used. Remember to keep your money, credit cards, etc, safely on your person, or in a hotel safe. If your guesthouse has no safe in which to store money, passport, tickets, etc, try local banks.

Getting there

Air

In addition to the scheduled flights listed, there are a great many charter flights from Europe and North America. For details on both types of service, you are advised to consult a good travel agent. An agent will also be able to tell you if you qualify for any student or senior citizen discount on offer. From the USA, Puerto Rico and Antigua are the only islands to which student fares are available; it is worth checking these out since it may be cheaper to take a student flight then continue to your destination rather than flying direct to the island of your choice (contact CIEE in the USA). For those over 65, **Delta Airlines** has a Senior Citizen Young at Heart programme, which offers a 10% discount on published fares on Delta between any US cities (except in Alaska or Hawaii) including San Juan, Puerto Rico, and the US Virgin Islands. You can carry on from there on another airline. If buying tickets routed through the USA, check that US taxes are included in the price. At certain times of the year, **Air France** and **AOM** have flights at very advantageous prices from several southern French cities and Paris to Guadeloupe and Martinique; travellers from France, Switzerland and southern Germany should be able to use them. **Air France** flights can also be combined with **Liat** air passes.

Airlines
See individual islands for major airlines flying to each island

Airlines will only allow a certain weight of luggage without a surcharge; this is normally 30 kg for first class and 20 kg for business and economy classes, but these limits may not be strictly enforced if the plane is not going to be full. **JMC Airways** (year round charter from the UK) allows 40 kg, which is very popular with travellers visiting friends and relatives in the Caribbean. Weight limits for inter-island flights are often much lower; it is best to enquire beforehand.

Baggage allowance

In Switzerland, **Globetrotter Travel Service**, Rennweg, 8001 Zürich, has been recommended for arranging cheap flights to the region. In the UK, **The Caribbean Experience** (ATOL 5149), 70 Pembroke Road, Kensington, London W8 6NX, T0207-6024021, F0207-6036101, www.caribbean-ex.co.uk, specialize in the Eastern Caribbean, booking accommodation or flights for independent travellers, or package deals.

Specialist operators

If you are in full-time education you will be entitled to an ISIC, which is distributed by student travel offices and travel agencies in 77 countries. The ISIC gives you special prices on all forms of transport (air, sea, rail, etc), and access to a variety of other concessions and services. If you need to find the location of your nearest ISIC office contact: The ISIC Association, Box 15857, 1001 NJ Amsterdam, Holland T+45-33939303.

International Student Identity Card (ISIC)

Essentials

Sea

Cruise lines & cargo ships The most popular way of visiting the Caribbean by ship is on a cruise liner, as the figures given in the Economy sections below attest. There are also sailing cruisers (eg the Windjammer and Star Clipper fleets) which allow flexible itineraries for cruising between the islands; very spectacular when under sail. A travel agent will advise on these modes of transport. *Windjammer Barefoot Cruises*, which operates five tall-masted ships (*Flying Cloud*, British Virgin Islands; *Legacy*, US and British Virgin Islands; *Mandalay*, Leeward and Windward Islands; *Polynesia*, French West Indies; *Yankee Clipper*, Grenadines) and a supply ship (*Amazing Grace*, see below), can be contacted direct at PO Box 190120, Miami Beach, Florida 33119-0120, USA, T305-6726453, F305-6741219, www.windjammer.com

For cargo ships which carry passengers, it is best to enquire in your own country. In general it is very difficult to secure a passage on a cargo ship from Europe to the Caribbean without making full arrangements in advance. Full details on this type of travel are available in the UK from **Strand Voyages**, Charing Cross Shopping Concourse, The Strand, London WC2N 4HZ, T020-78366363, F020-74970078; *Cargo Ship Voyages Ltd*, Hemley, Woodbridge, Suffolk, IP12 4QF, T/F01473-736265. In Switzerland, *Wagner Frachtshiffreisen*, Stadlerstrasse 48, CH-8404, Winterthur, T052-2421442, F2421487. In the USA, contact *Freighter World Cruises*, 180 South Lake Av, Pasadena, CA 91101, T818-4493106, or *Travltips Cruise and Freighter Association*, 163-07 Depot Road, PO Box 188, Flushing, NY 11358, T800-8728584.

From Europe: *Strand Voyages* can also advise on the *Compagnie Générale Maritime's* three sailings a month from Dunkerque or Le Havre to Fort-de-France and Pointe-à-Pitre, 23 days' voyage. CGM's *Cap Blanco* (on charter to Furness Withy) calls at Kingston, Jamaica, on its sailings from Felixstowe, via various North European ports, to the west coast of South America. CGM's *Caravelle* sails from Rotterdam to Ponce (Puerto Rico), Port of Spain (Trinidad), Willemstad (Curaçao), Aruba, Puerto Cabello (Venezuela), Santa Marta (Colombia), Cartagena (Colombia), Puerto Limón (Costa Rica), Kingston (Jamaica), and sometimes unscheduled ports. *Safmarine's* *Author*, on a 42-day round trip, sails Felixstowe, Rotterdam, Le Havre, Ponce (Puerto Rico), Port-of-Spain, La Guaira and Puerto Cabello (Venezuela), Willemstad, Oranjestad, Cartagena (Colombia), Puerto Limón (Costa Rica), Santa Marta (Colombia), Kingston (Jamaica), Rotterdam, Hamburg, Felixstowe. The *Horn Line* has regular sailings on the following route: Hamburg, Le Havre, Fort-de-France, Pointe-à-Pitre, Willemstad, Cartagena (Colombia), Chiriquí Grande (Panama), Moín (Costa Rica), Antwerp, Hamburg. From Felixstowe, *Projex Line's* *EWL West Indies* sails to Paramaribo, Georgetown, Port of Spain, La Guaira and Puerto Cabello (Venezuela), Willemstad, Oranjestad, Cartagena and Santa Marta (Venezuela), Bremen, Rotterdam to Felixstowe, 44-day round trip. *Fyffes* banana boats carry passengers from Portsmouth and Flushing direct to Paramaribo, Suriname, and occasionally to Georgetown. From Livorno, a German consortium sails via Valencia (Spain) to San Juan (Puerto Rico), Cartagena (Colombia), Panama Canal, Guayaquil (Ecuador), Panama Canal, Cartagena, Santa Marta, San Juan, Livorno, 35-day round trip. A German consortium sails Hamburg, Bilbao, San Juan, Río Haina (Dominican Republic), Veracruz or Tampico, La Guaira, Río Haina, San Juan, Bilbao, Antwerp, Hamburg on a 55-day round trip. There is a 45-day round-trip sailed by a German consortium from Liverpool, via Hamburg, Rotterdam and Bilbao, to Havana, Tampico and Veracruz, then back to Liverpool. Another German consortium makes a seven-day round trip Río Haina, San Juan, Puerto Cabello, Port-of-Spain, Río Haina.

From the USA: *Ivaran Lines'* container ship, *Americana*, carries 80 passengers in luxury accommodation: New Orleans to Houston, Altamira and Veracruz in Mexico, Puerto Limón, Cartagena, Puerto Cabello, La Guaira, San Juan, Río Haina, New Orleans, 21 days round trip. The *Sven Oltmann* makes an 11-14 day round trip Port Everglades (Florida), Fernandina Beach, back to Port Everglades, then Oranjestad, La Guaira and Puerto Cabello (Venezuela), Port Everglades. The supply ship, MV *Amazing Grace*, sails every month from West Palm Beach, picking up southbound passengers in Freeport, Bahamas and visiting lots of islands as it meets up with the *Windjammer* tall ships, delivering monthly supplies, before turning round in Trinidad after two weeks and stopping at different ports from the southbound trip.

Windward Lines basic itinerary

Port		Day	Arrival	Departure
St Lucia	(SLT)	Sun	-	1900
Barbados	(BDS)	Mon	0600	0830
St Vincent	(SVG)	Mon	1630	2000
Trinidad	(TRD)	Tue	1000	1800
*(Guiria)	(VEN)	-	(2200)	-
Margarita	(VEN)	Wed	0600	1800
*(Guiria)	(VEN)	-	-	(2300)
Trinidad	(TRD)	Thu	0800	1600
St Vincent	(SVG)	Fri	0730	1000
Barbados	(BDS)	Fri	1900	2230
St Lucia	(SLT)	Sat	0800	-

*NB Guiria alternates with Margarita and Trinidad every other week.

Yacht crewing For those with 1,000 miles offshore sailing experience, a cheap way to get to the Caribbean is crewing on a yacht being delivered from Europe or the USA to the region.

Where to stay

See inside front cover for hotel price grades & abbreviations

High season in the Caribbean is usually called 'winter'; in other words it comes in the Northern Hemisphere's colder months. Dates vary a little but the season is roughly from mid-December to mid-April. 'Summer' is low season, the remainder of the year. In high season air fares, room rates and other costs rise. In addition, air fares are also increased at European and US holiday times, ie July and August from the USA, etc. Flights to the Caribbean from the UK are at a premium in the pre-Christmas period. The cheapest time is September-November, when hurricane risk is greatest. Rates are subject to change without notice and therefore those given in this book should only be taken as representative.

Getting around

Air

The most extensive links between islands are by air, either with the scheduled flights on the regional and international carriers (again given in the text), or by chartered plane. If you are in a group, or family, the latter option may not cost very much more than a scheduled flight. It often has the advantage of linking the charter direct to your incoming or homeward flight.

Air passes The regional carriers with most routes in the Caribbean are *LIAT* (with its headquarters in Antigua), *BWIA* (based in Trinidad) and *ALM* (of the Netherlands Antilles).

LIAT LIAT has two passes called *Explorer tickets*: the *LIAT Explorer* costs US$279, valid for 21 days, maximum three stops between San Juan, Puerto Rico and Trinidad; the *LIAT Super Explorer* costs US$475 for a 30-day ticket, allowing unlimited stop overs in 23 destinations between San Juan and Caracas and Georgetown as well (do not overload your itinerary, a lot of time can be spent waiting at airports for flights). LIAT also operates an *Eastern Caribbean* airpass in which each flight costs US$85, valid for 21 days; minimum three stop overs, maximum six. These tickets may only be issued in conjunction with an international flight to a Caribbean gateway, the itinerary must be settled in advance, with no changes permitted, and no child discounts. A specialist travel agency may be able to book a return ticket with stopovers cheaper than the airpass, so it is worth enquiring. The Eastern Caribbean airpass is

Essentials

Essentials

Windward Lines government head-tax

Tax In	Out	To	From VEN	TRD	SVG	BDS	SLT
11.90	0.00	**VEN**	-	16.90	29.30	41.30	48.70
5.00	0.00	**TRD**	16.90	-	12.40	24.40	31.80
3.70	3.70	**SVG**	25.60	8.70	-	15.70	23.10
6.00	6.00	**BDS**	35.30	18.40	9.70	-	13.40
5.20	5.20	**STL**	45.00	28.10	23.10	15.70	-

Head tax added to ticket fare. Single way calculated from left column. If passenger is staying off until another voyage, the out tax for that port is added to the round-trip fare. In addition to the Head-tax: passenger staying off in Trinidad pays directly to ship's agent departure tax, cash TT$75. St Lucia environmental tax US$1.50.

only sold in Europe (including the UK and Eire), while the *Explorer* is sold worldwide except for the Caribbean area and Venezuela, and the *Super Explorer* is sold worldwide except Venezuela. In the USA, contact a specialist travel agent. LIAT's telephone number on Antigua is (268) 462 0700, or 462 2682 for fax.

For those who fly regularly within the Caribbean, LIAT runs a frequent flyer club, organized in Antigua. Try to book LIAT flights as far in advance as possible; planes are not large and fill up quickly. A golden rule when flying with LIAT: just because you are *not* booked on a flight it does not mean you will not get on (be patient and sweet-talking); just because you *are* booked on a flight it does not mean you will get on (never be last in the queue). Note also that LIAT is in financial difficulties and travel companies are warning clients that there can be no refunds once a ticket is issued, some also charge a booking fee.

Windward Lines rates

To/From	VEN	TRD	SVG	BDS	STL
Venezuela	-	60	138	148	148
Trinidad	60	-	90	90	95
St Vincent	138	90	-	71	60
Barbados	148	90	71	-	60
St Lucia	148	95	60	60	-

NB *Rates may change without notice. To/from Margarita add US$10. Rates are for round-trip in US$. One way is 65% of round-trip. One way ticket can only be sold if passenger has an onward ticket to his/her country of residence.*

For information on LIAT airpasses contact *The Caribbean Experience* (ATOL 5149), 70 Pembroke Road, Kensington, London W8 6NX, T020-76024021, F020-76036101, www.caribbean-ex.co.uk, who specialize in the Eastern Caribbean.

BWIA BWIA's intra-Caribbean unlimited mileage fare is US$399 (often US$499 if you do not fly transatlantic with BWIA); no destination may be visited more than once, except for making a connection and the entire journey must be fixed at the time of payment (changes are subject to a US$20 surcharge); dates may be left open. This airpass is valid for 30 days, no refunds are given for unused sectors. It may not be used between 19 December and 6 January.

American Airlines American Airlines includes its Caribbean destinations in its Visit USA air pass (minimum three, maximum 10 coupons). This is available to transatlantic passengers using American, British Airways, Virgin Atlantic or any non-US carrier.

Sea

Island-hopping by boats with scheduled services is fairly limited. Boat services are more common between dependent islands, eg St Vincent and the Grenadines, Trinidad and Tobago. Again, full details are given in the relevant sections below. *The Windward Lines*, www.infinetworx.com/windward/ run a weekly passenger and cargo ferry service: St Lucia-Barbados-St Vincent-Trinidad-Güiria or Isla Margarita-Trinidad-St Vincent-Barbados- St Lucia, an excellent way of seeing the southern Caribbean. Cabins are available. Their local agents for ticket sales are: **Barbados** *Windward Agencies Ltd*, Brighton Warehouse Complex, Brighton, T246 4257402, F246 4257399, windward@sjds.net; **St Lucia** *Mendes Shipping*, Valco Building, Cadet Street, Castries, T758-4521364, F758-4531654, mendesshipslu@candw.lc; **St Vincent** *Perry's Customs & Shipping*, Sharpe St, Kingstown, T784-4572920, F784-4562619, dhlsvg@caribsurf.com; **Trinidad** *Global Steamship Agencies*, Mariners Club, Wrightson Road, Port of Spain, T868-6242279, F868-6275091, globalship@carib-link.net; **Venezuela** *Acosta Asociados SA*, Calle Bolívar, Guiria, Estado Sucre, T58(0)94 820058, F58(0)94 81112, grupoacosta@cantv.net

Departure tax is payable on leaving every island; make sure you know what this is in advance so you do not get caught out

Irregular passenger services on cargo boats (with basic accommodation, usually a hammock on deck, no meals supplied), schooners, crewing or hitching on yachts can only be discovered by asking around when you are in port. Crewing on yachts is not difficult in winter (in the hurricane season yachtsmen stay away). If you are looking for a job on a yacht, or trying to hitch a ride, it will be easier to make contact if you are living at the yacht harbour. Boat owners often advertise bunks for rent, which is a very cheap form of accommodation (US$10-30); ask around, or look on the bulletin boards. If arriving by sea, make sure you are aware of the island's entry requirements before setting out.

Road

Buses are cheap, but services tend not to be very convenient, in the sense that they often involve a night away from the point of departure, even on small islands. This is because buses

Bus

start in outlying towns in the early morning and return from the capital in the afternoon. Another limiting factor to public transport is a shortage of funds for spare parts, so buses may be scarce and crowded. Many smaller islands do not even have a bus service.

Taxi   Taxis are plentiful, but generally not cheap. Some islands, eg Trinidad, have route taxis, which are inexpensive and travel only on set routes. On many islands, taxi fares are set by the tourist office or government.

Car hire   Renting a car gives the greatest flexibility, but is also hardest on the pocket. You can expect to pay more than in the USA or Europe. A number of islands require drivers to take out a temporary, or visitor driver's licence (these are mentioned in the text), but some places will not issue a licence to those over 70 years of age without a medical certificate. In small places, to rent a motorcycle, scooter or bicycle is a good idea.

Keeping in touch

Language   In the majority of cases, English is widely spoken and understood (although non-native speakers of English may have difficulty understanding some of the local dialects). In the French Antilles and Haiti, French is the main language. However, in these last, and on English islands which at one time belonged to France, Créole is spoken. The population is bilingual, so on English islands the English-speaking traveller will have no problems with communication and on the French islands, knowledge of French is of great benefit. The Netherlands Antilles speak Dutch, English and Papiamento. English and Spanish are both spoken on Puerto Rico. The principal language in the Dominican Republic, Cuba and the Venezuelan islands is Spanish. If visiting non-English islands, a basic knowledge of the main language is a great advantage.

Language courses in Spanish, plus volunteer programmes and travel advice, are run in Puerto Rico and the Dominican Republic by *AmeriSpan Unlimited*, PO Box 40007, Philadelphia, PA 19106-0007, USA, T215-7511100, (800-8796640 in USA and Canada), F215-7511986.

There are Post Offices in all the main towns but you can often buy stamps in hotels. Islands like Montserrat, the Caymen Islands and Nevis pride themselves on their philatelic issues, which are collectors' items. Postal service is not very efficient and for sending packages or parcels a courier service is recommended for speed and security.

Post

Many airport lounges and phone companies in the region have *AT&T*'s USA Direct phones by which the USA and Canada may be called using a charge card (which bills your home phone account), or by calling collect. The service is not available to Europe, but the BT chargecard, for example, can be used on many of the islands (check with your phone company). Public card phones have been introduced by *Cable and Wireless* on those islands where it operates. This company offers discounts on evening rates for IDD calls from cardphones: 1800-2300 15%, 2300-0500 40%. Discounts do not apply to credit card calls (1-800-877-8000). Phone cards usually come in several denominations, with a tax added on, and can be useful for local and international calls, particularly as you then avoid the extra charges made by hotels on phone calls. Communicating by fax is a convenient way of sending messages home. Places with public fax machines may receive messages as well as send. Cybercafés are springing up but are not yet widespread. Often the local telephone office will have a terminal you can use to send emails, but don't rely on it actually working. Countries such as Haiti and Dominica have cybercafés but you won't find one in Cuba yet.

Telephone
See inside front cover for a list of the phone codes for all the islands

Essentials

Sports

Information on sport is given under each island, but for those visiting the former British colonies, British dependencies and even the US Virgin Islands, an understanding of **cricket** is an advantage. It is more than a national game, having become a symbol of achievement and a unifying factor (**baseball** and **basketball** serve much the same function in the Dominican Republic, Cuba and Puerto Rico). Spectating at a match is entertaining both for the cricket itself and for the conversation that arises.

Watersports

The crystal clear waters of the sunny Caribbean combined with the constant northeast trade winds make the islands a paradise for watersports enthusiasts. The great increase in tourism in the area has brought a corresponding development in watersports and every conceivable watersport is now available. For a full range of watersports with all arrangements, if not at hotel reception at only a short walk down the beach, some of the best islands to head for are Barbados, Jamaica, Antigua, Martinique, the Bahamas, Cayman Islands, Puerto Rico and the Virgin Islands. On these islands you can find hobie-cats and sunfishes for rent, windsurfers, water skiing, glass-bottomed boats plying the reefs, charter yachts and booze cruises, scuba diving, snorkelling and deep sea fishing. Prices for such watersports vary from island to island and often increase by about 30% in the peak tourist season (December to April). It is worth knowing that prices can often be reduced for regular or long term rentals and that bargaining with individual beach operators is definitely worth trying.

See individual islands for detailed information

If all you want is sea and sand, these abound on nearly every island. The coral islands have the white postcard-perfect beaches and some of the islands of the Grenadines are nothing more than this. Swimming is safe on almost all Caribbean coasts, but do be careful on the exposed Atlantic coasts where waves are big at times and currents rip. Swimming in the Atlantic can be dangerous and in some places it is actually forbidden.

Swimming

Cricket in the Caribbean

Test matches in the Caribbean are played, to date, in five countries: Jamaica, Barbados, Guyana, Trinidad and Antigua. Other first-class and one-day matches may be played in some of the smaller islands, part of either the Windward Islands or Leeward Islands teams, such as Grenada, Dominica, St Lucia, St Vincent, St Kitts and Nevis or Anguilla. The six first class teams are: Jamaica, Trinidad and Tobago, Barbados, Guyana, Windward Islands and Leeward Islands. Antigua is hoping to play separately from the Leeward Islands at some time in the future.

Huge and more relaxed entertainment can also be enjoyed by going to inter-island matches. Currently the one-day competition is being played before Christmas; it has suffered a lot of disruption from rain and this might not be the best time to go. The four-day competition, currently called the BUSTA Cup, runs from January to March. Unless West Indies are on tour at the time all the international players are required to play in the competition, so it is high standard.

Large numbers of visitors go to the Caribbean to watch international matches. Book accommodation well in advance, particularly in Antigua. Note that it frequently rains in Guyana and that Barbados is expensive.

Information about international matches can be obtained in the UK from the Test and County Cricket Board, Lord's Cricket Ground, St John's Wood, London NW8 8QN,

T0207-4321200. However, finding out about the first class matches between the islands is difficult. First ring the International Cricket Council (ICC), also at Lord's Cricket Ground (the Clock Tower) in London, T0207-2661818, F0207-2661777 (no resources for email queries). They may give you the address and number of the West Indies Cricket Board which is based in Antigua. This is of little use, however, because the board does not answer letters and their number does not accept international calls! The best ploy is to ask someone at the ICC if they can help. (Don't ring up when a test match is being played.) They may give you the number of one of the local organizations, eg the Trinidad and Tobago or Windward Islands Board, or may even be prepared to ring themselves. If all else fails, a hotel or other organization in the Caribbean may be able to find out for you.

It is a lot of trouble but well worth it!

Some useful websites for news, scores and statistics:

www.caribinfo.com
www.caribbeansports.com
www.candw.cricket.bb/ (schedule for the Cable & Wireless Test Series, toll free West Indies ticket line 1-800-744-GAME)
www.caribcentral.com/cricket.htm
www.cricket.org

Water-skiing This is almost always available in developed resort areas and beginners are looked after well. If you are a serious water skier it may be worth bringing your own slalom ski as many boats only cater for beginners.

Surfing Good breaks for surfing and boogey-boarding can be found on the north shores of Puerto Rico, the Dominican Republic, Tobago and in Barbados. In both Puerto Rico and Barbados, custom-made surfboards can be bought and several competitions are organized every year. There are several good surf spots in Puerto Rico and the most consistent break in Barbados is at Bathsheba. In the Dominican Republic and Tobago, the sport is less developed. Waves tend to be bigger and more consistent in winter.

Fishing Sportfishing is excellent in many of the islands of the North Caribbean. Almost every variety of deep-sea game fish: marlin, swordfish, tuna, mackerel and dorado abound in the waters. Over 50 world record catches have been made off the Bahamas alone. In the reefs and shallows there are big barracuda, tarpon and bonefish. There are areas for all methods of fishing: surf fishing, bottom fishing or trolling. Spearfishing, however, is banned in many islands. Although most fish seem to run between November and March, there is really no off-season in most islands and a good local captain will always know where to find the best fishing grounds. Note, fishermen should beware of eating large predators (eg grand barracuda) and other fish which accumulate the ciguatera toxin by eating coral-browsing smaller fish.

Fishing is very well organized in such islands as the Bahamas where Bimini, lying close to the Gulf Stream, is devoted entirely to game fishing. Exciting game fishing is also available very close to the shore off Puerto Rico, especially in the area which has become known to the enthusiasts as Blue Marlin Alley. Fishing is also very good off the Cayman Islands, Jamaica and the US Virgin Islands. In many islands there are annual fishing tournaments open to all, such as the International Fishing Tournament held in April in the Caymans. Deep-sea fishing boats can be chartered for a half or full day and some are available on a weekly basis. Anglers can also pay individually on split charters. When arranging a charter, be careful to clarify all details in advance.

Exploring the Caribbean by boat has never been easier. New marinas and local communities near popular anchorages are catering to the increasing number of yachts which have made the Caribbean their home. The Caribbean islanders have coined the name 'yachties' to refer to those people who live and travel on their own boats as contrasted with those who visit the islands on their vacations on chartered boats, cruise ships or landbased resorts. While this information is directed toward the yachties, bareboat charterers will also find it useful.

Sailing
See individual islands for detailed information

From Europe to the Caribbean For boats crossing the Atlantic along the trade wind route, Barbados is the first landfall. Boats have the option of going on to Venezuela and Central America or through the Windward Islands of Grenada, St Vincent and the Grenadines. The Atlantic Rally for Cruisers offers support and entertainment for any sailors contemplating an Atlantic crossing. Departure is from Gran Canaria at the end of November and the yachts arrive in St Lucia to a warm welcome for Christmas.

From the USA to the Caribbean The two routes from the USA to the Caribbean are (a) from New England or Norfolk directly to the US Virgin Islands with the possibility of a stop in

Bermuda or (b) island-hopping from Florida through the Bahamas across the 'Thornless Path' to windward described by Bruce Van Sant in his book *Passages South*. The Caribbean 1500 Rally organizes cruisers wishing to travel in a group to the Caribbean and depart from Newport, Rhode Island or Norfolk, Virginia, in late October arriving in St Thomas in the US Virgin Islands.

Ports of entry Arrive during weekday working hours to avoid overtime fees. Have the sun at your back to navigate through reefs, sand bars or other water hazards even if it means a midnight or late afternoon departure and an overnight sail. When making windward passages, overnight trips often mean lighter winds and seas.

Customs and immigration Yachties cross many countries and have to deal with more officials and procedures than tourists aboard cruise ships or travelling to resorts. No matter how many guidebooks are available, there will be at least one country with a change in procedures. Be careful to clear immigration on arrival as there are heavy fines for failing to do so. Plan to pay fees and to fill out paperwork in all countries. Occasionally,

Essentials

☞ Hurricane Season

June too soon
July stand by
August it must
September remember
October all over
If only! In recent years there have been several late storms and the 'October all over' proved a myth. There was little hurricane activity in the region from the 1950s until the late 1980s. Many of the islands were not affected by hurricanes and residents thought little of them. Homes were not built to withstand severe storms. In 1989 this all started to change when several violent storms roared through the islands and Hurricane Hugo did untold damage in the US Virgin Islands. The next few years were relatively quiet but 1995 struck with a bang (three names were 'retired' in deference to the dead and injured) and was the start of a five-year cycle that has gone down in history as the most active stretch on record for hurricanes: 41 developed with 20 major ones (Category 3 at 111 mph or more). 1996 brought nine hurricanes; 1997 gave the islands a breather with only three. 1998 was another active season with 10, one of which did much damage. On 25 September 1998 there were a record four hurricanes at the same time. 1999 brought eight hurricanes, five of which were Category 4 (130mph or over) and two came late in the season, in October and November.

In the daily weather forecasts, a **tropical depression** is an organized system of clouds and thunderstorms with a defined circulation and maximum sustained winds of 38 mph (33 knots) or less; a **tropical storm** is an organized system of strong thunderstorms with a defined circulation and maximum sustained winds of 39 to 73 mph (34 –63 knots); a **hurricane** is an intense tropical weather system with a well-defined circulation and maximum sustained winds of 74 mph (64 knots) or more.

A hurricane develops in warm waters and air, which is why the tropics are known for hurricanes. Powered by heat from the sea they are steered by the easterly trade winds and the temperate westerly winds, as well as their own ferocious energy. In the Atlantic, these storms form off the African coast and move west, developing as they come into warmer water. Around the core, winds grow to great velocity, generating violent seas. The process by which a disturbance forms and strengthens into a hurricane depends on at least three conditions: warm water, moisture and wind pattern near the ocean surface that spirals air inward. Bands of thunderstorms form and allow the air to warm further and rise higher into the atmosphere. If the winds at these higher levels are light, the structure remains intact and allows for further strengthening. If the winds are strong, they will shear off the top and stop the development. If the system develops, a definite eye is formed around which the most violent activity takes place; this is known as the eyewall. The center of the eye is relatively calm. When the eye passes over land those on the ground are often misled that the hurricane is over; some even abandon safe shelter, not aware that as the eye passes the other side of the eyewall will produce violent winds and the other half of the hurricane. At the top of the eyewall (around 50,000 ft), most of the air is propelled outward, increasing the air's upward motion. Some of the air however, moves inward and sinks into the eye and creates a cloud-free area.

The word 'hurricane' is derived from the Amerindian 'Hurakan', both the Carib god of evil and also one of the Maya creator gods who blew his breath across the chaotic water and brought forth dry land. In the North Atlantic, Gulf of Mexico, Caribbean and the Eastern Pacific they are called hurricanes, in Australia, cyclones or 'willy willy', and in the

there are no fees; however, most countries have airport departure taxes and most have realized that these fees are another source of income. Different fees are often charged for charter boats and cruisers on their own boats who may wish to stay for a longer period of time.

Q Flag and courtesy flags Fly your 'Q' or quarantine flag until paperwork is completed. The captain should take ship's papers, passports and a list of the places you wish to stop and visit as in some countries you must be given specific clearance to stop and anchor. All crew should remain aboard until they have received clearance from the port authorities. Even though

Philippines, 'baguio'. In the Western North Pacific tropical cyclones of hurricane force are called typhoons. The first time hurricanes were named was by an Australian forecaster in the early 1900s who called them after political figures he disliked. During World War II US Army forecasters named storms after their girlfriends and wives. Between 1950-52 they were given phonetic names (able, baker, charlie). In 1953 the Weather Bureau started giving them female names again. Today individual names (male and female) are chosen by the National Hurricane Center in Miami and submitted to the World Meteorology Organization in Geneva, Switzerland. If approved these become the official names for the upcoming hurricane season. As a system develops and becomes a tropical depression (TD), it is assigned a name in alphabetical order from the official list.

There is very good information before hurricanes hit any land, thanks to accurate weather data gathered by the Hurricane Hunters from Keesler Airforce Base in the USA. During the storm season they operate out of St Croix in the US Virgin Islands, where they are closer to storms. This elite group of men and women actually fly through the eye of a hurricane in C130 airplanes gathering critical information on the wind speeds and directions and other data. This is sent to the Miami Hurricane Center where a forecast is made and sent to all islands in the potential path so they can prepare for the storm. Most of the island governments are now well prepared to cope with hurricanes and have disaster relief teams in place, while many of the island resorts, especially the larger ones, have their own generators and water supplies.

While a hurricane can certainly pose a threat to life, in most cases if precautions are taken the risks are reduced. Some of the main hazards are storm surge, heavy winds and rains. There is usually disruption of services such as communications, internal transport and airline services. The tourist may be left stranded while the roads and power lines are cleared and airline service is renewed. Communications home may be impossible for some days. Ideally, if a hurricane is approaching, it is better for the tourist to evacuate the island. During the hurricane, which is usually 6-36 hours, you have to be shut up inside a closed area, often with little ventilation or light, which can be stressful. Some tourists think a hurricane will be "fun" and want to remain on island to see the storm. This is short sighted and foolish. If you do remain you should register with your local consulate or embassy. You should also be prepared to be inconvenienced in the ways already mentioned and even to help out in the clearing up afterwards.

When there is potentially violent weather approaching, the local government met office issues advisories:

A tropical storm watch is an announcement to be on alert for a storm (winds of 39-73 mph) which may pose threats to coastal areas within 36 hours.

A tropical storm warning is issued if the storm is expected within 24 hours.

A hurricane watch is given if hurricane conditions could be coming in 36 hours.

A hurricane warning is issued if the hurricane is expected within 24 hours.

One of the best internet sites for information and data from reporters on the islands during an actual hurricane is Storm 2001 **www.gopbi.com/weather/storm**

The Web site of the Hurricane Hunters is **www.hurricanehunters.com** (virtual reality flight with them into the eye of a hurricane on this site).

Miami National Hurricane Center **www.nhc.noaa.gov/**

Essentials

many of the islands are still a part of the British Commonwealth, they prefer to see their country's courtesy flag flown. (And fly it the right side up!)

Liveaboard community anchorages are found with a good, well protected anchorage, provisions, water, laundry available in Marsh Harbour in the Abacos, Georgetown in the Exumas, Luperón, Samaná and Puerto Plata in the Dominican Republic, Boquerón in Puerto Rico, Phillipsburg in Sint Maarten, Bequia in the Grenadines, Secret Harbour and Prickly Bay in Grenada, Chaguaramas in Trinidad, Porlamar, Margarita and Puerto la Cruz in Venezuela.

Cruisers Net in Puerto la Cruz, Venezuela VHF 72 0745, during hurricane season in Porlamar, Margarita VHF 72 0800. Radio nets provide information about social activities, including ladies lunches and especially Carnival activities in Trinidad, that might be of interest to tourists with extra time as well as cruisers.

Yacht charters Charter fleets operate from the US and British Virgin Islands, in the Abacos in the Bahamas, Antigua, St Martin, Martinique, Guadeloupe, St Lucia, St Vincent and Grenada. One way charters can often be arranged for an additional fee. Yachts can be chartered on a daily or term basis, either bareboat or with skipper and crew. Skippered day charters are now found in almost any area where there are landbased tourists.

Marinas Dry dock facilities for long term boat storage are found in the Turks and Caicos, Puerto Rico, the Virgin Islands, St Martin, St Lucia, St Vincent, Antigua, Grenada, Trinidad and Venezuela. Marinas with slips of different types (slips, stern-to, pilings) are found in the majority of the islands and new ones are opening frequently. Most marinas will hold mail addressed to yachts for pickup.

Hitching rides Hitching and working on yachts is another way to see the islands for the adventurous person with time on his/her hands. Many yachts charter in the Caribbean in winter and go north to the USA or Mediterranean for the charter season there. Other yachts are cruisers passing on their way around the world. Yachties are friendly people and if you ask in the right places, frequent the yachtie bars and put up a few notices, crew positions can often be found. Bulletin boards are found in Georgetown (Bahamas), Turtle Cove Marina (Turks and Caicos), Great Bay and Marina in the Lagoon (Sint Maarten), Fort-de-France, Trois-Ilets and Le Marin (Martinique), Rodney Bay and Marigot Bay (St Lucia), English Harbour (Antigua), Admiralty Bay (Bequia) and Anchorage (Union Island) in the Grenadines, Secret Harbour and Spice Island Marina (Grenada), Porlamar (Margarita), any of the marinas in El Morro complex in Puerto la Cruz (Venezuela) where foreign yachties hang out, and any marina or yacht club in Chaguaramas in Trinidad. If you want to crew, check you have all necessary visas and documentation and confirm with the skipper that your paperwork is in order. Puerto Rico and the US Virgin Islands require visas for boat travellers as though you were travelling to the USA. To visit the USA from the Caribbean by yacht, many yachts leave Trinidad after Carnival in late February; boat deliveries back to the USA are also possible.

Weather Information SSB US weather broadcasts, US Ham net (east coast of USA & Bahamas), in the Caribbean, David on SV *Mystine* is on SSB kHz 6224 at 0800, with weather summaries covering the Dominican Republic, Puerto Rico, Virgin Islands, Leewards and Windwards, Trinidad and Tobago, northern Venezuela, central Caribbean basin, Colombia and Honduras. In case of marine advisory, he will come up on 6224 at 1815 with updates. Cruisers are invited to call in their location and current information. Alex from SV *Albatross* operates a morning 'chat net' on 5104 from 0700-0800 out of Venezuela. He reads weather forecasts from earlier hamnet reports. Caribbean weather is found on SSB4003, 0815-0830 and 8104 0830-0900 Caribbean time and has been handled by volunteers since 1996; however, it is anticipated that David Jones, author of *A Concise Guide to Caribbean Weather* will take over the net in the near future from the British Virgin Islands. Yachts crossing the Atlantic use Herb from *Southbound II* 1600-1700, 12359. Weather information is critical before making long passages or during hurricane season (June-November). This is also the rainy season as tropical waves cross over the Caribbean bringing rain and squalls.

VHF Nets In those areas where there are a substantial number of liveaboard sailors, VHF nets seem to spring up with volunteers taking turns providing weather information, arrivals and departures, information about services and announcements about local activities, sharing taxis or tours; guests returning home often offer to take mail back to the USA or Europe. Email is becoming a popular means of communication. Local access can be obtained by boats staying in a marina.

Fishing permits, park rules The Caribbean islands are becoming more ecoconscious. They are interested in preserving their natural resources and beauty and have established parks, marine preserves or national trust foundations. Some have mooring buoys, no-anchoring or anchoring limitations. Most prohibit taking of coral or live creatures in shells; many prohibit taking of shells. Don't anchor in areas where coral may be growing. Don't dispose of rubbish in enclosed anchorages. **Rubbish** is a problem on many of the smaller islands; don't give rubbish to boat boys as they often just take the money and throw the waste into the water. Try to dispose of edible waste at sea while travelling between islands in deep water; take paper, cans and bottles ashore to the town dump or a marina where they have waste disposal facilities.

Scuba diving Saba and Dominica require special permits and St Eustatius requires divers to go with a local dive group. Do not assume you can dive wherever you like even if you have all your own tanks and equipment. A marine park has been established and is run by the Soufrière Marine Management Association in St Lucia and requires diving with a local dive company.

Weapons Some countries want weapons and ammunition checked in ashore until you are ready to depart. Others will let you keep them locked on board and others don't really ask questions. Make sure clearance papers have the correct serial numbers and ammunition counts to avoid confusion when it comes time to pick up the weapons that were checked ashore. Some areas even consider spearguns weapons and require them to be turned in until you leave.

Regattas or special activities Sailboat races of all types are held throughout the Caribbean during the entire year. Spectator boats may go out to watch the races, there may be crew-sign-up lists for those who would like to sail and best of all, there are usually parties and activities on shore. Most regattas have various different types of classes, even including liveaboard classes.

Guidebooks cover most areas of the Caribbean and are updated periodically. Julius Wilensky's guides have good sketch charts that are still useful even if not updated. *Yachtsman's Guide to the Bahamas and Turks and Caicos, Cruising Guide to Abaco,* Steve Dodge; *Cruising Guide to the Abacos* (2nd edition) Julius Wilensky; *Yachtsman's Guide to the Virgin Islands, Southern Waterway Guide* (covers Bahamas and Turks & Caicos), *Passages South,* Bruce Van Sant; *Guide to the Leeward Islands,* Chris Doyle; *VIP Cruising Guide* (Sint Maarten area), *Guide to the Windward Islands,* Chris Doyle; *Guide to Venezuela, Trinidad & Tobago,* Chris Doyle; *Guide to Trinidad and Tobago,* Chris Doyle; *Guide to Venezuela,* Chris Doyle; *Donald Street's Guides to the Caribbean* (Volumes I, II, III, IV). There are several 'yachting newspapers' that are distributed free around the Caribbean that have things to do, reports on regattas, tourist and sailing events: *Nautical Scene* (St Thomas to Venezuela), *The Compass* (Bequia and southern Caribbean), *All at Sea* (northern Caribbean), *The Boca* (Trinidad and Tobago) and *Mar y Tierra* (Venezuela).

Scuba diving has become the 'in sport' with the numbers of divers having increased dramatically in recent years. The epitome of a scuba dive is in clear, tropical waters on a colourful reef abounding with life. The Caribbean is a scuba diver's paradise, for there is a conglomeration of islands surrounded by living reefs providing different types of diving to suit everyone's dreams. Unfortunately, some of the islands have turned into a 'diving circus', as in some of the more developed northern Caribbean islands where 30 or 40 divers are herded onto large dive boats and dropped on somewhat packaged dive sites where 'tame' fish come for handouts. Other islands in the region are still virginal in the diving sense, which can lead to an exciting undersea adventure. Nevertheless, this can also be frustrating on a diving holiday as on the more remote islands facilities are not often available and diving can be more difficult and basic.

Scuba diving
See individual islands for detailed information

Cayman Islands These are among the most developed for scuba diving and there is a fine organization of over 20 dive operations, including liveaboard boats. There is also a well-run

Essentials

Caribbean festivals at a glance

	Jan	Feb	Mar	Easter	April
Aruba	Festival	Carnival			
Anguilla			Music and arts festival, Trophy		
Antigua					Sailing
Bahamas					
Barbados		Festival, Sailing	Music and arts festival	Festival	
Bonaire		Carnival			
British Virgin Islands			Sailing, Sailing	Festival	
Carriacou		Carnival		Festival	
Cayman Islands					Carnival
Cuba	Festival				Sailing
Curaçao	Sailing	Carnival	Fish	Festival	Sailing
Dominica		Carnival			Sailing
Dominican Republic		Carnival			
Grenada	Fish, Sailing, Trophy		Festival	Sailing	
Guadeloupe		Carnival			
Haiti	Festival	Carnival			
Isla de Margarita		Carnival		Festival	
Jamaica					Carnival
Martinique	Sailing/Sailing	Carnival	Sailing	Festival	Festival
Montserrat			Festival	Festival	Festival
Nevis					
Puerto Rico			Sailing		Carnival
Saba					
Sint Maarten		Sailing			Carnival, Festival
St Eustatius					
St Kitts					
St Lucia		Carnival, Festival			
St Vincent & the Grenadines			Fish	Sailing	
Bequia				Sailing, Trophy	
Union Island					
St-Barthélémy		Carnival			
St-Martin		Carnival, Sailing			
Tobago		Carnival, Fish		Festival	
Trinidad		Carnival, Festival			
Turks & Caicos					
Grand Turk					
Providenciales					
South Caicos					
North Caicos					
Middle Caicos					
USVI St Thomas			Sailing		Carnival
St John					
St Croix	Sailing	Trophy	Festival, Trophy		

Carnival (usually means pre-Lenten)   Festival   Music and arts festival
/ = two types of event combined; without / = two separate events fall within same month.

May   Jun   Jul   Aug   Sep   Oct   Nov   Dec

Essentials

Angling tournament   Regatta   Windsurf races   Other sports

Where an event begins in one month and ends in another, the month of commencement is given.
See Festivals, Watersports, Culture and Public holidays sections.

decompression facility on Grand Cayman, which is an added safety factor. The Caymans are very conservation minded and it is a criminal offence to take ANY form of marine life while scuba diving. In fact, it is illegal on Cayman Brac, the smaller sister island, even to wear gloves while scuba diving. This helps ensure that divers will not hold or damage the delicate coral formations and other marine life.

British Virgin Islands With some 50 coral islands, these islands are well worth a mention as the diving is exciting and varied. Both liveaboard and land-based operations are available with well-developed facilities for divers. Popular diving sites include the wreck of the *HMS Rhone*, a 310 ft British mail ship sunk in 1867 in a hurricane. She was the site for the Hollywood movie *The Deep*. Other interesting sites include Turtle Cave in Brewers Bay which offers a spiral arch divers can swim through beginning at a depth of 45 ft and winding up to 15 ft. Many sites lie in the string of islands to the south between Tortola and the island of Virgin Gorda. To the north lies Mosquito Island, the site of The Cousteau Society's Project Ocean Search. Hosted annually by Jean-Michel Cousteau, the expedition gives a small number of participants the chance to find out what it is like to be on a Cousteau expedition (The Cousteau Society, 870 Greenbrier Circle, Suite 402, Chesapeake, Virginia 23320, T1-800-4414395, www.cousteausociety.org).

Other especially spectacular diving destinations with abundant marine life include Saba, Dominica and the Turks and Caicos. **Saba**, a tiny Dutch island, only five miles long, is truly one of the most protected places for divers. The entire reef surrounding the island was established as a marine park in 1987 and this conservation effort has led to an abundance of 'tame' fish. Saba diving is known for several deep pinnacles including Third Encounter, Twilight Zone and Shark Shoal. For the less adventurous and experienced, sites like Diamond Rock and Tent Reef offer the thrill of seeing large French Angels swimming up to the divers. The sport has been developing with both land-based and liveaboard diving boat facilities available, as well as a recompression chamber facility.

Dominica 'The Nature Island', or 'The Water Island', is a lush, mountainous island with rugged topside and underwater terrain. It is diving for the adventurous and not for the diver who wants easy diving although there are a few beginner sites. This is one of few islands left where black coral abounds and can be seen along the wall drop-offs starting at 60 ft. For the more experienced the Atlantic east coast offers some spectacular wall dives.

Turks and Caicos Islands They consist of over 40 lovely sand islands and cays and are located on the Turks Island Passage, a 22-mile channel which is 7,000 ft deep connecting the Atlantic Ocean and the Caribbean Sea. This contributes to the abundance of marine life and large pelagic fish seen in these waters and spectacular wall diving in the channel. The islands are surrounded by coral reefs that cover over 200 square miles. Visibility is usually 100 ft or more and marine life plentiful. A wild Atlantic bottle nosed dolphin, JoJo, occasionally interacts with swimmers, snorkellers, divers and boaters and has actually been made a national treasure of the TCI. There is also a dolphin rehabilitation project, Into the Blue, in Providenciales, which has so far released three dolphins from UK zoos, but they have no contact now with people. The strong attitude towards conservation is reinforced by *Protection of Reefs and Islands from Degradation and Exploitation* (PRIDE), based at the Sea Island Centre, a commercial conch farm. PRIDE is a US-based foundation which has helped in numerous conservation projects. There are several dive shops on Providenciales and Grand Turk, mostly catering for small groups of divers, and there are three or four liveaboard boats in the islands' waters at any one time.

Grenadines Lying in the South Eastern Caribbean they offer pristine diving, although facilities are limited. Grenada and tiny sister island of Carriacou offer limited diving facilities, as does Bequia, although nearby St Vincent is more developed for scuba diving.

Tobago An unspoiled destination well worth visiting. This small island is close to the South American coast and large marine life is encouraged by the flow of plankton-rich water from the continent's rivers. Manta ray are especially attracted by the plankton and at Speyside (also called Manta City) where currents meet they are seen on nearly every dive. Most diving is along the west and north coast.

Barbados Among the more developed islands in the Caribbean though the surrounding reef life is not as unspoiled as on some of the less developed islands. However, there are some thriving reefs and within the last few years the island has become known as a wreck diving destination. Five shipwrecks have been intentionally sunk as diving sites, offering interesting underwater photography. In addition, the island is the base for the regional organization, *The Eastern Caribbean Safe Diving Association*. This association helps to maintain a decompression facility for the Leeward and Windward islands and is attempting to establish minimum safe operating standards for dive shops, initially in the East Caribbean and eventually, regionally. For more information write ECSDA, Box 86 WRD, Welches Post Office, Barbados.

Bonaire Just off the South American coast Bonaire has long been known as a 'hot spot' for diving, and is one of the few islands (like the Caymans) which has devoted itself to scuba diving. A far-sighted government established a marine park way back in 1979 when conservation was not even being discussed by most diving destinations. Neighbouring Curaçao has now joined her in this reputation, with an expansion of diving facilities and exciting diving sites. Aruba is not likely to equal her sister islands as she lacks the reefs which surround Bonaire and Curaçao, although diving is available. Bonaire, being very experienced in offering diving, has a wide selection of about a dozen dive operations, including photo and marine life education facilities. Diving sites are also varied with reef, wreck and wall dives. In fact, the Marine Park Guide for Bonaire lists over 50 dive sites. The town pier, right off the capital, has long been a favourite night dive and the pilings are covered in soft sponges and invertebrate life.

Curaçao Offers the reef diving of Bonaire and a couple of wreck dives of interest. The freighter, *Superior Producer* (rather deep at 100 ft) is intact and has a variety of growth including beautiful orange tubastera sponges.

Aruba While the reefs may not be as prolific as her sister islands, there is an interesting wreck site, with which few other sites around the island compare in marine life. The *Antilla*, a 400 ft German ship, is in 70 ft (and less) of water. Her massive hull has provided a home for an amazing variety and size of fish life and night dives are truly a thrill.

Most Caribbean destinations offer some form of scuba diving, although not all operations are safety minded. While scuba diving is exciting and thrilling, it can also be dangerous, particularly for beginners who are not aware of what to look for in a safe diving operation. Proper instruction from a recognized scuba instructor is a must. Not all diving shops in the Caribbean adhere to the recommended safety standards, so it is important to ensure the level of training an instructor has and request to see certificates of instructor training if they are not displayed.

Good health is a must, but the myth that one needs to be a super man or super woman is not true. Important health aspects are healthy lungs, sinus and the ability to equalize your ears (by gently blowing air into the eustachian tube while blocking your nose). A medical exam by a physician trained in hyperbaric (diving) medicine is recommended and required by many instructors. A good basic swimming ability is necessary, although you do not need to be an Olympic swimmer. For female divers, smaller, lighter scuba tanks are available at some dive shops which makes the cumbersome, heavy gear easier to handle.

Most scuba training organizations offer several types of diving courses. A 'resort course' provides diving instruction in a condensed version (about three hours) with a minimum of academic knowledge, one confined water session (usually in a swimming pool) and one scuba dive. This type of course is done by many tourists who do not have the time to do a full certification course, which requires written exams, classroom lectures, several confined water sessions and several scuba dives. For the serious diver, however, a full certification course should be taken.

For information on the liveaboard boats mentioned for the Cayman Islands, contact The Aggressor Fleet, PO Drawer K, Morgan City, LA 70881-000K, T504-3852416, F504-3840817 or (USA & Canada) 800-3482628, www.aggressor.com

Windsurfing

Whether you are an accomplished windsurfer or merely wishing to give it a try the Caribbean offers the windsurfer warm clear water, trade winds and a wealth of locations to choose from. Throughout the Caribbean there are hundreds of pristine windsurfing locations, many undeveloped. Bring your own gear and have an adventure, or sail with the many schools across the islands. The strongest steadiest winds are June and July, this is when the trades are

For operators & associations, see individual islands

Essentials

Hurricanes

On 17 September 1989, Hurricane Hugo ripped across St Croix causing damage or destruction to 90% of the buildings and leaving 22,500 people homeless. In September 1995 the islands escaped the worst of Hurricane Luis but were hit by Hurricane Marilyn, causing damage estimated at

US$3.5bn. St Thomas was the worst hit, with five deaths and a quarter of all homes destroyed. In July 1996 the hurricane season came early with the arrival of Bertha, but the 80 mile per hour winds caused only relatively minor damage.

at their most constant. Winter brings either howling winds or flat calm and is unpredictable. In summer the gentle breezes provide good learning conditions. Each island has different winds and conditions, there is something for everyone, even if you just want to sit on the beach and watch.

Antigua Steady winds and lots of good locations, at present there is only one dedicated school, although hotels often have learner boards. Best wind November-February, June-July.

Aruba Well known as a centre for great windsurfing, flat waist deep water on the leeward side with strong wind make this an ideal location for learners and advanced windsurfers, the perfect family windsurf vacation. Best wind May-July.

Barbados Sun, sand, wind and waves make Barbados one of the favourite locations for many pro windsurfers on the World Tour. For those not willing to try the waves, flat water can be found at Oistins Bay. Best wind and wave conditions December-January and June.

Bequia Bequia is a beautiful island, but though the wind blows and the sun shines, there is only one windsurf school run by Basil, a Bequian with a big smile. Good location for learners or advanced sailors with flat water and wave sailing, well off the beaten track. Best winds November-February, June-July.

Bonaire Good winds and locations for all levels of sailors from flat water to gentle waves. Best winds December-August.

British Virgin Islands The centre for windsurf cruising, with over 50 small islands scattered within 40 miles and steady trades, the islands are perfect for flat water cruising and blasting. Already a popular yachting centre, the two sports fuse with international events such as the Hi Ho (hook in and hold on), a week long windsurf race and yacht cruise. Good sailing for all levels. Best winds December-January, June-July.

Grand Cayman Famous for its diving, Grand Cayman also offers good windsurfing, the east end is popular for beginners to advanced and everything in between, flat water on the inside and bump and jump further out. Best wind November-March.

Dominican Republic Voted by many top sailors as one of the most exciting places to sail in the Caribbean, Cabarete, on the north coast, offers everything a windsurfer could want: flat water for beginners and great wavesailing on the outside with thermally affected winds that mean you can take the morning off. Lots of schools and hotels on the strip of beach and some of the best gear in the Caribbean. Best wind January-March and June-August.

Grenadines Great location with no facilities, take your own gear and hire a yacht out of Grenada or St Vincent, or visit Basil at Bequia (see above) the only rental centre in the area.

Nevis A windsurfer's paradise waiting to be discovered, good flat water and wavesailing, definitely no crowds, the island is small enough to offer all conditions for every skill level. Best wind December-January, June-July.

Puerto Rico Great wave sailing spot, the Caribbean's answer to Maui. The location is The Shacks at Isabela on the northwest point of the island. Thermal winds make this a winter spot for the committed wave sailor, gentler sailing is offered in the San Juan area and in the summer. Best waves and wind December-April, slalom July-September.

St Barts Small exclusive island with some good windsurf spots for beginners and advanced, and it is quiet. Best wind December-February.

St Croix A great sailing spot and often overlooked, the guys here are good wave sailors and slalom racers as the island boasts all conditions at many locations. Best wind January-February and July.

St Lucia A beautiful destination for any visitor and for the windsurfer it offers uncrowded sailing and plenty to do on no wind days. Best to bring your own gear if you are an advanced sailor, although there is limited good gear to rent at Windsurf Cas-en-Bas. Best winds December-June.

St Martin Ever fancied windsurfing naked across flat tropical waters? Orient Bay (Baie Orientale) is probably the only place in the world you can do this without getting arrested. Aside from the novelty of sailing naked, St Martin offers good learning and advanced slalom sailing. Best winds December-January and July.

St Thomas Everything you expect from a Caribbean windsurf vacation, with shopping malls. St Thomas boasts a lively local windsurfing community, flat water and lots of races and events to attend. Best wind December-January and July, join the fun at the Caribbean Team Boardsailing Championships in July.

Trinidad & Tobago Situated in the prime trade wind zone, Tobago's Pigeon Point is the place to go, unexplored and beautiful with some excellent sailing spots. You will probably need to take your own gear. Best wind December-May.

Turks & Caicos Flat turquoise waters and steady winds make this an ideal learner and intermediate destination, perfect for a family diving and windsurf vacation. Best winds February-March intermediate, October-November for beginners.

Walking

The Caribbean provides ideal conditions for medium-distance walking in the tropics. Small islands avoid the very high temperatures which are common in India, Africa, or the South American mainland. Distances are manageable; a hard day's walk will take you from coast to coast on the smaller islands, and a few days is enough for a complete circuit. The scenery is varied: peasant farms with fruit trees, rain forests, and high mountains. Mountain streams and waterfalls which would be ice-cold in temperate countries are perfect for bathing. The sea is never far away. Nor are road transport, comfortable accommodation, rum shops and restaurants. Nevertheless, the illusion of remoteness can sometimes be complete. And much of the nastier *mainland* wildlife can't swim, so there are no large carnivores and few poisonous snakes on the islands.

See individual islands for further details

Good large scale maps (1:25,000 or 1:50,000) are available for all the Commonwealth islands. These can be obtained from the local Lands and Surveys department on each island; and usually from *Stanfords*, 12/14 Long Acre, London WC2E 9LP (T020-78361321, F020-78360189), sales@stanfords.co.uk, or *The Map Shop*, 15 High Street, Upton-upon-Severn, Worcestershire, WR8 0HJ (T01684-593146), www.themapshop.co.uk The Ordnance Survey (Romsey Road, Southampton, UK, T01703-792763, F01703-792404) publishes a series of colourful world maps including some holiday destinations. They contain comprehensive tourist information ranging from hotels and beaches to climbing and climate. Each map is produced in association with the country concerned. Relevant titles so far are: Barbados, St Lucia, Cayman Islands, British Virgin Islands, St Vincent, Dominica. There are also good large scale Serie Bleu maps of Guadeloupe and Martinique (1:25,000, seven maps of Guadeloupe, No 4601G-4607G) issued by the Institut Géographique National, Paris, which include all hiking trails. Footpath information on maps is not always reliable, however.

Maps

Clothing Lightweight cotton clothing, with a wide brimmed hat to keep off the sun. Shorts are more comfortable, but can leave the legs exposed to sunburn or sharp razor grasses; ditto short sleeved shirts. It is best to carry short and long, and change en route as appropriate. Rain comes in intense bursts. Raincoats are not particularly comfortable. A better technique is to strip down to light clothes and dry off when the rain stops. (A small, collapsible umbrella may be useful and can also provide protection against the sun.) In the rainy season leather footwear is of little use as it will be permanently wet. Use trainers instead.

Hints

Essentials

Timing An early start is ideal, preferably just before sunrise. This will give several hours walking before the sun becomes too hot. Public transport starts running surprisingly early in most places.

Water Carry a large thermos. This can keep water ice-cold through a full day. Refilling from mountain streams is generally safe if purification tablets are used, but be careful of streams *below* villages especially in islands like St Lucia and Martinique where there is some bilharzia, and of springs in cultivated areas where generously applied pesticides may have leached into the groundwater.

Sunburn Remember that the angle of the sun in the sky is what counts, not the temperature. So you may get burnt at midday even if you feel cool, but are unlikely to have trouble before 1000 or after 1500. Forearms can get burnt, and so can the back of your legs if you are walking away from the sun. It is a good idea to walk west in the morning and east in the afternoon to avoid strong sun on the face.

Snakes The only islands where these are a worry are Trinidad, St Lucia, and Martinique. Trinidad has several dangerous species, and also has African killer bees. All three islands have the venomous Fer de Lance. This snake, however, is usually frightened off by approaching footsteps, so snakebites are rare, but they can be fatal. The Fer de Lance prefers bush country in dry coastal areas. Ask and accept local advice on where to go, and stick to well marked trails. Some other islands have boa constrictors, which can bite but are not poisonous. In Trinidad, beware of the coral snake; visitors with children should take care because the snake looks like a colourful bracelet coiled on the ground. Snakes are also found in the interior jungles of the Guianas; walk with a guide. Most snakes will only attack in the breeding season if they feel the nest is threatened. Large centipedes (sometimes found in dry coastal areas) can also give a very nasty bite.

Marijuana farmers In remote mountain areas in most islands these people are likely to assume that outsiders have come either to steal the crop or as police spies. On most islands they are armed, and on some they set trap guns for the unwary. Again, the best way to avoid them is to keep to well marked trails, and accept local advice about where to go.

Around the islands

Jamaica Spectacular scenery especially in the Blue Mountains and in the Cockpit country. Marijuana growers are a real problem in the remote areas, but the main trails in the Blue Mountains are safe. Jamaica Camping and Hiking Association and Ministry of Tourism have a useful *Hikers Guide to the Blue Mountains*.

Dominican Republic Home to the two highest peaks in the Caribbean (Pico Duarte and Pico La Pelona) in addition to many smaller mountains, it is being discovered as one of the great places for hiking. For information contact the Dirección Nacional de Parques, Av Independencia 539 esq Cervantes, Santo Domingo, Apartado Postal 2487.

Haiti Another story altogether. Walking is the normal means of transport in rural areas, so there are masses of well-trodden trails, but it is better to walk with a group. Maps are rudimentary and small scale. Few people speak French in remote areas – try to pick up some Créole. Make sure you carry basic supplies, particularly water. Hiring a guide should be no problem.

Guadeloupe Network of waymarked trails on the mountainous half (Basse Terre) in the Parc Naturel and up La Soufrière. Contact the Organisation des Guides de Montagne de la Caraïbe (Maison Forestière, 97120 Matouba, T590-800579) for a guide and/or the booklet *Promenades et Randonnées*.

Martinique The *Parc Naturel Régional* (9 Boulevard Géneral-de-Gaulle, T596-731930) organizes group hikes, usually on Sundays, and publishes a useful *Guide des Sentiers Pedestres à la Martinique*. Good trails on Mont Pelée and along the north coast.

Dominica Probably has the best unspoiled mountain scenery in the Caribbean. Some of the long distance trails are hard to follow, though. Guides readily available. Try the path via Laudat to the Boiling Lake.

St Lucia Very well marked east-west trail through Quillesse forest reserve. Other walks organized by the Forestry Department. Also a good trail up Gros Piton. See St Lucia chapter for details.

St Vincent Spectacular but sometimes difficult trail across the Soufrière volcano from Orange Hill to Richmond. Guide advisable. North coast trail past Falls of Baleine is spectacular, but hard to follow. Marijuana growers.

Grenada Very accessible mountain and rainforest scenery. Good network of signposted trails linking Grand Etang, Concord waterfall, and other points. The mountains to the southeast of the Grand Étang Forest Reserve are less well marked and you may need a local guide, but the walking is spectacular with marvellous views.

Barbados Very safe and pleasant walking, especially on the east coast, but little really wild scenery. Barbados National Trust (T246-4262421/4369033) organizes regular Sunday hikes, morning at 0600, afternoon at 1500.

Trinidad Some fine scenery, but marijuana growers are a problem, particularly in the Northern Range and you are advised always to walk in a group. Well marked trails are safe. Those at the Asa Wright Nature Centre are recommended (T868-6674655, F6670493). Trinidad Field Naturalists Club (PO Box 642, Port of Spain, T868-6248017, evenings only) organizes long distance hikes, and visits to caves etc.

Tobago Safe and pleasant walking; distances are not too great. The scenery is varied: hills, woodland and unspoilt beaches.

Useful Addresses For groups organizing a serious hiking/camping expedition in the Caribbean, contact the Duke of Edinburgh's Award Scheme, Bridge House, Cavans Lane, Bridgetown, Barbados (T246-4369763). They may be able to provide advice and to supply the address of a local organization on most islands with expedition experience.

Cycling

Mountain biking is a sport that originated in California and has made its way to the Caribbean. You can rent bikes on almost every island and because of the mountainous terrain and cool breezes, it is quite a comfortable way to get around and visit Caribbean villages. There has even been a Caribbean cup bike race, with bike clubs from each island travelling to different islands for the competition. Some of the islands have mountains as high as 3,000 m towering above the ocean, making the Caribbean one of the most exciting new mountain bike destinations in the world.

Antigua Has good bike shops and great single track, in addition to a local bike club.

Barbados Mountain biking on back country roads with bike rental available.

Cuba Mountain Bike tour companies, good terrain. Charity sponsored tours frequently organized.

Dominica A new attraction, with bike rental and tours offered by *Nature Island Dive*.

Dominican Republic Coined as the mountain bike mecca of the Caribbean, has a bicycle club with over 300 members with both mountain bike and road bike races held monthly. Bike shops throughout the island. *Iguana Mama* for tours.

Grenada Bike rental available.

Jamaica Bike rental and tour operators offering trips, excellent terrain.

Puerto Rico Bike touring companies and rentals throughout the island, excellent terrain.

St Croix Cycling tours of the forest or beach are offered by *St Croix Bikes & Tours*, while *VI Cycling* organize weekly rides and races.

St Kitts Bike rental and tours available.

St Martin *Frogs Legs* is a good bike shop in town, the owner David will take you out on great rides.

Flora and fauna

For many travellers, a trip to the Caribbean offers a first glimpse of the tropics, complete with luxuriant vegetation and exotic wildlife. Images of untouched beaches and rainforest form a

Essentials

major selling point of many travel brochures. In fact there is very little 'untouched' wilderness left and what visitors see is an environment that has been affected by the activities of man. Forestry, agriculture, fisheries and increasingly tourism have all helped to mould the modern landscape and natural heritage of the Caribbean. However, there is still much of interest to see, and it is true to say that small islands can combine a variety of habitats within a limited area. On many islands, it is possible to move between the coastal reefs and beaches through thorn scrub and plantation into rainforest within a matter of miles. Increasingly, the complexity and fragility of island ecosystems is being appreciated and fortunately most countries have recognized the value of balancing development and the protection of the natural environment and have begun to develop national parks and protected areas programmes. Many islands also have active conservation societies or national wildlife trusts (see page 51 below).

Wildlife

Over long periods of time, islands tend to develop their own unique flora and fauna. These endemic species add to the interest of wildlife and natural history tours. The St Lucia parrot and Dominica's sisserou have become a regular part of the tour circuit of these islands, and have undoubtedly benefited from the interest that tourists have shown in their plight. Details of National Parks and wildlife are included under the specific island chapter headings (Fauna and Flora). This section provides a broad overview of the range of animals, plants and habitats that are to be found in the region.

Mammals   Mammals are not particularly good colonizers of small islands and this has resulted in a general scarcity of species in the Caribbean. Many of the more commonly seen species (mongoose, agouti, opossum, and some of the monkeys) were introduced by man. Bats are the one exception to this rule and most islands have several native species. Again, in the forested interior of the Guianas there are many mammals associated with rain forest habitats. There are also the animals of the south savannas and mountains.

Mongoose were introduced to many islands to control snakes, they have also preyed on many birds, reptiles and other animals and have had a devastating effect on native fauna.

Of the monkeys, the green monkeys of Barbados, Grenada and St Kitts and Nevis were introduced from West Africa in the 17th century. Similarly, rhesus monkeys have been introduced to Desecheo Island off Puerto Rico. The red howler monkeys on Trinidad are native to the island as are several other mammals including the brocket deer, squirrel and armadillo. These species have managed to colonize from nearby Venezuela.

Sailors may encounter marine mammals including dolphin, porpoise and whales. Between November and December hump back whales migrate through the Turks and Caicos Passage on their way to the Silver Banks breeding grounds off the Dominican Republic. The ungainly manatee, or sea cow, can still be seen in some coastal areas in the Greater Antilles (especially Jamaica, Cuba – Zapata Peninsula – and Puerto Rico) although it is becoming increasingly uncommon.

Birds   It is the birds perhaps more than any other group of animals that excite the most interest from visitors to the region. Many islands have their own endemic species such as the Grenada dove, yellow-billed parrot and 24 other species in Jamaica and Guadeloupe woodpecker. The islands also act as important stepping stones in the migration of many birds through the Americas. As a result, the region is highly regarded by ornithologists and there are several important nature reserves.

Trinidad and Tobago demonstrate the influence of the nearby South American mainland. While they have no endemic species they still support at least 433 species and the Asa Wright Centre is regarded as one of the premier bird watching sites in the world. At the other end of the Caribbean, Inagua (Bahamas) is the site of the world's largest flamingo colony at Lake Windsor. There is also an important flamingo colony on Bonaire in the southern Caribbean.

Many of the endemic species have become rare as a result of man's activities. Habitat destruction, introduction of new species (especially the mongoose) and hunting for food and the international pet trade have all had an effect. Parrots in particular have suffered as a result of these activities. Fortunately, measures are now being undertaken to protect the birds and their habitats on many islands (eg Bahamas, Jamaica, Dominica, Puerto Rico and St Lucia).

Lizards and geckos are common on virtually all the islands in the region and may even be seen on very small offshore islets. There are also a number of species of snakes, iguanas and turtles scattered throughout the region. Many are restricted to one island and Jamaica has at least 27 island endemics including several species of galliwasp. The vast majority of reptiles found in the region are completely harmless to man although there are strong superstitions about the geckos (*mabouya*) and of course the snakes. For example, the skin and fat of boa constrictors (*tête chien*) are used for bush remedies on some of the Windward Islands.

Reptiles

The fer de lance snake (St Lucia, Martinique and also South America), deserves to be treated with extreme caution; although the bite is not usually lethal, hospitalization is required. It is found in isolated areas of dry scrubland and river valley. The best protection is to wear long trousers and stout boots and to avoid walking in these areas at night. Local advice should be sought if in doubt.

Iguanas are still found on many islands although they have declined as a result of hunting throughout the region. Although of fearsome appearance, they are herbivorous and spend much of their time in trees and low scrub feeding on leaves and trying to avoid man.

Marine turtles including the loggerhead, leatherback, hawksbill and green turtles are found throughout Caribbean waters and on the coasts of the Guianas and they may occasionally be seen by divers and snorkellers. Females come ashore on isolated sandy beaches between the months of May and August to lay eggs. There may be opportunities for assisting natural history and wildlife societies (St Lucia Naturalists Society, Fish and Wildlife Dept in the US Virgin Islands) in their turtle watches, to record numbers and locations of nests and to protect the turtles from poachers. There is a large commercial breeding programme for green turtles in the Cayman Islands. Freshwater turtles are also found on some islands including Jamaica and Cat Island (Bahamas). Caiman have been introduced to Puerto Rico and are also found on Cuba and the Dominican Republic.

Many species of reptile are now protected in the region (especially the marine turtles and iguana) and reserves have been specifically established to protect them. For example, the Maria Islands Nature Reserve on St Lucia is home to the St Lucia ground lizard and grass snake. The latter is possibly the rarest snake in the world with an estimated population of 150 individuals.

Frogs and toads are common in a variety of shapes and colours. There are generally more species on the larger islands (Greater Antilles and Trinidad; there are also many in the Guianas). The Cuban pygmy frog is described as the world's smallest frog, while at the other end of the scale, the mountain chicken of Dominica and Montserrat is probably the largest frog in the region. Its name relates to its supposed flavour. The call of the piping frogs (*eleutherodactylus spp*) is often mistaken for a bird and these small animals are common throughout the Lesser Antilles, becoming especially vocal at night and after rain. The largest and most visible amphibian is probably the marine toad which has been introduced to islands throughout the region in an attempt to control insects and other invertebrate pests. The male toads use flat exposed areas from which to display, often roads. Unfortunately, they have not evolved to deal with the car yet and as a result many are killed.

Amphibians

This group includes the insects, molluscs, spiders and a host of other animals that have no backbones. For first time travellers to the tropics, the huge range of invertebrates can seem daunting and it is estimated that there are at least 290 species of butterfly in the Caribbean. No one knows how many species of beetles, bugs or mollusc there are.

Invertebrates

Of the butterflies, the swallowtails are perhaps the most spectacular, with several species being found in the Greater Antilles (especially Cuba). However the other islands also have large colourful butterflies including the monarch and flambeau which are present throughout the region. Another insect of note is the hercules beetle, reportedly the world's second largest beetle with a large horn that protrudes from its thorax, occasionally found in rainforest in the Lesser Antilles.

Land and freshwater crabs inhabit a range of environments from the rainforest (eg bromeliad crab from Jamaica) to the dry coastal areas (many species of hermit crab). Tarantula spiders are also fairly common, although they are nocturnal and rarely seen. Their bite is painful but, in most of the species found in the region, no worse than a bee sting. Of far more concern are the large centipedes (up to 15cm long) that can inflict a nasty and painful bite with their pincers. They are mostly restricted to the dry coastal areas and are most active at night. Black widow spiders are also present on some of the islands in the Greater Antilles. Fortunately they are rarely encountered by the traveller.

Environments

Beaches, coral reef, sea cliffs A diving or snorkelling trip over a tropical reef allows a first hand experience of this habitat's diversity of wildlife. There are a number of good field guides to reef fish and animals (see book list) and some are even printed on waterproof paper. Alternatively, glass bottomed boats sail over some sites (Buccoo Reef, Tobago), and there are underwater trails which identify types of corals and marine habitats.

Amongst the commonest fish are the grunts, butterfly, soldier, squirrel and angel fish. Tiny damsel fish are very territorial and may even attempt to nip swimmers who venture too close to their territories (more surprising than painful).

There are over fifty species of hard coral (the form that builds reefs) with a variety of sizes and colours. Amongst the most dramatic are the stagshorn and elkhorn corals which are found on the more exposed outer reefs. Brain coral forms massive round structures up to 2 m high and Pillar coral forms columns that may also reach 2 m in height. Soft corals, which include black corals, sea fans and gorgonians, colonize the surface of the hard coral adding colour and variety. Associated with these structures is a host of animals and plants. Spiny lobsters may be seen lurking in holes and crevices along with other crustaceans and reef fish. The patches of sand between outcrops of coral provide suitable habitat for conch and other shellfish. Some islands now restrict the collection and sale of corals (especially black corals) and there are also legal restrictions on the sale of black corals under CITES. Overfishing has affected conch and lobster in places and there are reports of them being taken from the sea too small.

The delights of swimming on a coral reef need to be tempered by a few words of caution. Many people assume the water will be seething with sharks, however these animals are fairly uncommon in nearshore waters and the species most likely to be encountered is the nurse shark, which is harmless unless provoked or cornered. Other fish to keep an eye open for include the scorpion fish with its poisonous dorsal spines; it frequently lies stationary on coral reefs onto which the incautious can blunder. Finally moray eels may be encountered, a fearsome looking fish, but harmless unless provoked at which point they can inflict serious bites. Of far more concern should be the variety of stinging invertebrates that are found on coral reefs. The most obvious is fire coral which comes in a range of shapes and sizes but is recognizable by the white tips to its branches. In addition, many corals have sharp edges and branches that can graze and cut. Another common group of stinging invertebrates are the fire worms which have white bristles along the sides of their bodies. As with the fire coral, these can inflict a painful sting if handled or brushed against. Large black sea urchins are also common on some reefs and their spines can penetrate unprotected skin very easily. The best advice when observing coral reefs and their wildlife is to look, not touch.

Other coastal habitats that may have interesting wildlife include beaches and sea cliffs. Some islands, especially those in the southern part of the Caribbean, have spectacular cliffs and offshore islets. These are home to large flocks of sea birds including the piratical frigate bird which chases smaller birds, forcing them to disgorge their catch; another notable species is the tropic bird with its streamer like tail feathers. The cliffs may also provide dry sandy soils for the large range of Caribbean cacti, including prickly pear (*opuntia sp*) and the Turks head cactus.

Rivers, swamps, mangroves Wetlands include a wide range of fresh and brackish water habitats such as rivers, marsh and mangroves. They are important for many species of bird, as well as fish. Unfortunately they are also home to an array of biting insects, including mosquitos which are unpleasant and a serious problem where malaria or dengue are present.

Important coastal wetlands include the Baie de Fort de France (Martinique), the Cabrits Swamp (Dominica), Caroni and Nariva Swamps (Trinidad), Negril and Black Morass (Jamaica). These sites all support large flocks of migratory and resident birds including waders, herons, egrets and ducks. In addition, some of the mangroves in the Greater Antilles also provide habitats for manatee, and the Negril and Black Morass has a population of American crocodiles. Large freshwater lakes are less common although Grenada, Dominica and St Vincent all have volcanic crater lakes and these are used by migratory waders and ducks as well as kingfishers.

There is little if any primary rainforest left in the Caribbean Islands, although there may be small patches in Guadeloupe. Nevertheless, many of the islands still have large areas of good secondary forest which has only suffered from a limited amount of selective felling for commercially valuable wood (eg gommier, balata and blue mahoe). **Thorn scrub, plantations, rainforest**

Martinique has some of the largest tracts of forest left in the Caribbean (eg rainforest at Piton du Carbet, cloud forest on Mt Pelée, dry woodland in the south). Many other islands also have accessible forest, although you should always use a local guide if venturing off the beaten track.

The Caribbean rainforests are not as diverse as those on the South and Central American mainland, however they still support a very large number of plant species many of which are endemic (Jamaica has over 3,000 species of which 800 are endemic). The orchids and bromeliads are particularly impressive in many forests and it is not unusual to see trees festooned with both these groups. The wildlife of the rainforest includes both native and introduced species, although they are often difficult to see in the rather shady conditions. Agouti, boa constrictor, monkeys and opossum may be seen, but it is the bird life that is most evident. Hummingbirds, vireos, thrashers, todies and others are all found along with parrots, which are perhaps the group most associated with this habitat. Early morning and evening provide the best times for birdwatching.

Plantations of commercial timber (blue mahoe, Caribbean pine, teak, mahogany and others) have been established in many places. These reduce pressure on natural forest and help protect watersheds and soil. They are also valuable for wildlife and some species have adapted to them with alacrity.

Closer to the coasts, dry scrub woodland often predominates. The trees may lose their leaves during the dry season. One of the most recognizable of the trees in this woodland is the turpentine tree, also known as the tourist tree because of its red peeling bark! Bush medicines and herbal remedies are still used in the countryside although less so than previously. Leaves and bark can be seen for sale in markets.

Books

There are not many good books on Caribbean wildlife. Look out for the following: **Field guides** C C Chaplin, *Fishwatchers Guide to West Atlantic Coral Reefs* (Horowood Books – some printed on plastic paper for use underwater); **I Greenberg**, *Guide to Corals and Fishes of Florida, the Bahamas and the Caribbean* (Seahawk Press); **J Bond**, *Birds of the West Indies* (Collins); **P Bacon**, *Flora and Fauna of the Caribbean* (Key Caribbean Publications, PO Box 21, Port of Spain, Trinidad); **P Honeychurch**, *Caribbean Wild Plants and their Uses* (Macmillan); **Richard ffrench**, *A Guide to the Birds of Trinidad and Tobago* (Horowood); **V E Graham**, *Tropical Wild Flowers* (Hulton Educational Publications).

Macmillan also produce short field guides on *The Flowers of the Caribbean*, *The Fishes of the Caribbean*, *Fishes of the Caribbean Reefs*, *Marine Life of the Caribbean*, *Butterflies and Other Insects of the Caribbean*; and the *Ephemeral Isles, a Natural History of the Bahamas*.

Margaret Mee, *In Search of Flowers of the Amazon Forest* (Nonesuch Expeditions Ltd, 48 Station Road, Woodbridge, Suffolk, UK). **R Meyer de Schauensee and W H Phelps Jr**, *A Guide to the Birds of Venezuela* (Princeton).

For the more serious naturalist, there are several detailed reviews of the natural history and conservation of wildlife in the Caribbean. Among the best and most widely available are the **Specialist reading**

Floristic Inventory of Tropical Countries (World Wide Fund for Nature) which contains a short report on the Caribbean; *Biodiversity and Conservation in the Caribbean, Profiles* of selected islands (includes Cozumel, Dominica, Grenada, Guadeloupe, Jamaica, Martinique, Montserrat, Puerto Rico, St Lucia, St Vincent, San Andrés) published by the International Council for Bird Preservation, ISBN 0 946888 14 0; *Fragments of Paradise* which covers conservation issues in the UK dependencies (Pisces Publications, ISBN 0 9508245 5 0). *A Field Guide to the Coral Reefs of the Caribbean and Florida including Bermuda and the Bahamas,* Peterson Field Guides Series no 27 (Houghton Mifflin Company). *Coral Reefs of the World* – Volume I, S Wells et al (IUCN). The Natural History Book Service (T UK 01803 865913) holds a very large stock of wildlife and conservation books on the Caribbean.

Whale and dolphin watching

Whale and dolphin watching, long popular around North America, is starting to take off in the Caribbean too. There are three main attractions. The humpback whales, the acrobatic whale-watchers' favourite, who come to the Caribbean during the winter to mate, raise their calves and sing. The sperm whales are resident in various spots around the Caribbean but are easiest to see along the west coast of Dominica and Martinique. Spotted and other dolphin species travel in large herds and are resident around many of the reefs, mangrove forests and offshore fishing banks. It is possible to see whales and dolphins from land and on some regular ferries, and even on air flights between the islands, but the best way to encounter them close-up is on boat tours. Some of these are general marine nature or even birding tours that include whales and dolphins. Others are specialized tours offered by diving, sportfishing or new eco-tourism ventures. Following is a guide to the best of whale and dolphin watching in the waters covered by this *Handbook*.

Look outs   **Bahamas** Tours to meet and sometimes swim with Atlantic spotted dolphins are offered May to September. The tours leave either from East Florida ports, North Bimini, or from West End, on Grand Bahama Island. Cost starts at about US$1,500 for a week on the 62 ft catamaran *Stenella* and various other boats. Some trips last 10 days. Tour operators include *Wild Dolphin Project*, PO Box 8436, Jupiter, FL 33468 USA, T407-5755660 or *Oceanic Society Expeditions*, Fort Mason Center, Building E, San Francisco, CA 94123 USA, T415-4411106. Others include: *Bottom Time Adventures*, PO Box 11919, Fort Lauderdale, FL 33339 USA, T800-2348464; *Windward Adventures*, PO Box 1713, Dania, FL 33004-1713, USA T/F954-9222351; *Dream Team*, PO Box 12714, Lake Park, FL 33403, USA, T888-2778181, F561-8407946; *Sea Fever Diving Cruises*, PO Box 21725, Fort Lauderdale, FL 33335, T954-2025608, F954-3519740; *Natural Habitat Adventures*, 2945 Center Green Court, Suite H, Boulder, Colorado 80301-9539, USA, T303-4493711, 800-5438917, F303-4493712; *Discover the World Ltd*, 29 Nork Way, Banstead, Surrey SM7 1PB, UK, T01737-218800, 016977-48361/56, F01737-362341; *Wild Oceans/Wild Wings*, International House, Bank Road, Kingswood, Bristol BS15 2LX, UK, T0117-9848040, F0117-9674444. Various excellent wildlife and dolphin tours, led by scientist Diane Claridge, are offered on Abaco by *Bahamas Naturalist Expeditions* (BNE), Marsh Harbour, Great Abaco, Bahamas, T242-3674505. Extended whale-watching trips with researchers and a chance to help on whale surveys to determine the abundance and distribution of large whales in the Bahamas are offered by *Earthwatch*, 680 Mount Auburn Street, PO Box 403, Watertown, MA 02272 USA, T617-9268200.

Turks & Caicos Islands Humpbacks can be found offshore January-March with bottlenose and other dolphins which are also seen close to shore. Boats can be chartered from Leeward Marina on Providenciales, but there are organized tours from Grand Turk. Contact *Blue Water Divers*, Grand Turk, T649-9462432; *Sea Eye Diving*, T649-9461407, F649-9461408; *Oasis Divers*, T/F649-9461128, www.oasisdivers.com

Puerto Rico Humpback whales and dolphins can be seen from land and occasional tours, particularly out of Rincón on the west coast of the island. Best lookouts are Aguadilla and from an old lighthouse near Punta Higuera, outside Rincón.

Dominican Republic The most popular and well-established whale watching in the Caribbean is found here. The industry is centred on humpback whales, but pilot whales and spotted dolphins can also be seen in Samaná Bay, and bottlenose, spinner, and spotted dolphins, Bryde's and other whales on Silver Bank. The season for both locales is January through March with whale watching tours in Samaná Bay 15 January-15 March. In recent years, more than 32,000 people a year have gone whale watching in the 20,000 sq km marine sanctuary, most of them to Samaná Bay where the trips last two to four hours. The trips to Silver Bank are more educational and are usually arranged by specialist groups. In Samaná Bay, Whale Samaná is the oldest tour operator in the region and highly rated. There are about 40 registered boats; some specialize in speed, some in mass tourism and some in education and information. You will get a better view of the whales from a big boat, the smaller ones can get dwarfed by the waves. For more information there is a general Samaná website, samana.org.do. The national parks whale watch co-ordinator in Samaná can be contacted at T809-5382042, dnpballenas@yahoo,com Contact: Kim Beddall, Whale Samaná, Victoria Marine, PO Box 53-2, Samaná, Dominican Republic, T/F809-5382494, Kim.Beddall@usa.net Miguel Bezi, another operator, has five boats of different sizes. Contact: Transporte Marítimo Minadiel, Samaná Bay, Dominican Republic, T809-5382556. For tours to see humpbacks on Silver Bank, some 50 miles (33 km) north of Puerto Plata, contact: *Bottom Time Adventures*, PO Box 11919, Ft Lauderdale, FL 33339-1919, USA, T954-9217798, F954-9207798.

For whale watching from land from January to March, but especially in February, try Cabo Francés Viejo, east along the coast from Puerto Plata, near Cabrera, as well as Punta Balandra light and Cabo Samaná (near Samaná). At Cueva de Agua there is a volunteer land-based whale watching project.

US Virgin Islands and **British Virgin Islands** They have periodic trips to see the 60-100 humpback whales that winter north of the islands. There are also spinner and other dolphins to be seen. The season is January through March. For a full-day catamaran sail contact Grethelyn Piper, Environmental Association of St Thomas and St John (EAST), PO Box 12379, St Thomas, USVI 00801, T340-7761976. On Tortola in the BVIs, air tours are offered by *Fly BVI*, Beef Island Airport, British Virgin Islands, T284-4951747, F284-4951973.

Guadeloupe There are tours to see sperm and pilot whales and spotted dolphins offered by Caroline and Renato Rinaldi by *Evasion Tropicale*. The whale watch runs from the dive centre Les Heures Saines in Malendure, about 4 km north of Bouillant on Basse-Terre. Contact: *Les Heures Saines*, Rocher de Malendure, 97132 Pigeon, Guadeloupe, T590-988663, F590-987776.

Dominica Eight to 12 resident sperm whales delight visitors almost year-round. You can also see spinner and spotted dolphins, pilot whales, false killer whales, and pygmy sperm whales. Occasional sightings are made of bottlenose, Risso's and Fraser's dolphins, orcas, dwarf sperm whales and melon-headed whales. The tours are run out of the *Anchorage Hotel*. Hydrophones are used to find and listen to the whales. The tours are three to four hours. *Anchorage Hotel & Dive Centre*, PO Box 34, Roseau, Dominica, T 767-4482638, F767-4485680. Tours are also offered by a well-equipped diving operator, Derek Perryman, next to the *Anchorage* at the *Castle Comfort Lodge* near Roseau. *Dive Dominica Ltd*, PO Box 2253, Roseau, Dominica, T767-4482188, F767-4486088. For land-based whale watching of sperm whales and others, Scotts Head, at the southwest tip of Dominica, overlooking Martinique Passage, is good most of the year.

Martinique Sperm and the other whales and dolphins found off Dominica can also be seen off the west side. At St-Pierre, whale- and dolphin-watching tours are part of the varied activities of a large diving club. Using Boston Whalers and other motor boats, they see spinner and spotted dolphins year-round and sperm whales and humpbacks mainly in the winter high season. Contact: *Carib Scuba Club*, Villa Populo Bel Event, Morne Verte, Carbet, Martinique 97221, T596-555944.

St Vincent Off the west coast, large herds of spinner and spotted dolphins are seen regularly. Sometimes bottlenose dolphins and pilot whales are also found and, sporadically, humpback whales. Tours go aboard the 36-ft sloop, *Sea Breeze*, or on a 21-ft power boat. Snorkelling and a trip to Baleine Falls are also included. Almost year-round but avoid windy weather months of mid-December to mid-February. Best April to September when there is

Essentials

an 80% success rate. Trips depart from Calliaqua Lagoon on Indian Bay, southeast of Kingstown and Arnos Vale Airport. Cost for tours is US$30-40. Contact: Hal Daize, Arnos Vale Post Office, St Vincent, T784-4584969.

Petit Nevis Off Bequia, nine miles (15 km) south of St Vincent is the site of the old whaling station, once the hub of Caribbean whaling in this century. Access will require making arrangements locally as Petit Nevis is currently for sale.

Grenada From St George's Marina, Mosden Cumberbach offers whale watching from his reliable 44 ft sloop or 34 ft power boat. He takes people off the south coast and to the Grenada Bank where humpbacks are often sighted from January through March, as well as up the coast to meet various dolphins and sometimes pilot whales. US$50 includes lunch and snorkelling. Contact: *Starwind Enterprise*, PO Box 183, St George's, Grenada, T4403678.

Carriacou Twenty-three miles (37 km) northeast of Grenada, humpbacks are often seen between December and April, as well as various dolphins and pilot whales year-round. Tours are offered aboard a catamaran by researchers working on wildlife conservation. Tour options are visiting bird sanctuaries, pristine coral reefs and Ile de Ronde, the submarine volcano north of Grenada. The catamaran, *Hokule'a*, is docked in North Hillsborough Bay. Contact: Dario Sandrini, Kido Project, Carriacou, T/F473-4437936.

St Lucia Sperm whales and various dolphins can be seen and on occasions humpback and pilot whales, Bryde's whales and orcas. The St Lucia Whale and Dolphin Watching Association is helping to organize and field enquiries for tours and to make sure that the whale watching is conducted with appropriate regulations. Contact St Lucia Whale and Dolphin Watching Association, c/o PO Box 1114, Castries, St Lucia, T758-4529708/0321, F758-4529806.

Conservation By watching whales and dolphins in the Caribbean, you can actually contribute to saving them. Many dolphins are still killed, mainly by fishermen, for food or fish bait. As well, pilot whales and even rare beaked whales are commonly harpooned, particularly in the eastern Caribbean. In March 1998 and then again in February 1999, a humpback mother and calf were killed off Bequia. Whale and dolphin watching provides local people with another way to look at these intriguing animals – as well as a potentially more sustainable source of income.

Your support of whale watching may have the biggest impact in countries of the eastern Caribbean: Dominica, Grenada, St Lucia, and St Vincent and the Grenadines. Over the past few years, Japan has contributed to the development of these nations, by helping to build airports and adding fish docks and piers. In exchange, Japan has counted on the support of these four governments, all members of the International Whaling Commission (IWC), in its attempt to re-open commercial whaling. You can help conservation here by simply saying you enjoy seeing whales and dolphins in local waters. However, when referring to dolphins, use the word 'porpoises'. In most parts of the Caribbean, the word 'dolphin' means the dolphin fish. Best to specify that it is the mammal and not the fish that you want to see. And if you see whales and dolphins being killed at sea, express your views to local and national tourism outlets of the country concerned.

For more information contact the Whale and Dolphin Conservation Society, Alexander House, James Street West, Bath, BA1 2BT, UK, www.wdcs.org

Responsible travel

Travel to the furthest corners of the globe is now commonplace and the mass movement of people for leisure and business is a major source of foreign exchange and economic development in many parts of the Caribbean. In many areas it is the most significant economic activity.

The benefits of international travel are self-evident for both hosts and travellers: employment; increased understanding of different cultures; business and leisure opportunities. At the same time there is clearly a downside to the industry. Where visitor pressure is high and/or poorly regulated, adverse impacts to society and the natural environment may be apparent. Paradoxically, this is as true in undeveloped and pristine areas (where culture and the natural environment are less 'prepared' for even small numbers of visitors) as in major resort destinations.

A few ideas

Where possible choose a destination, tour operator or hotel with a proven ethical and environmental commitment; if in doubt, ask. Spend money on locally produced (rather than imported) goods and services and use common sense when bargaining, your few dollars saved may be a week's salary to someone else.

Use water and electricity carefully, travellers may receive preferential supply while the needs of local communities are overlooked.

Learn about local etiquette and culture, consider local norms of behaviour and dress appropriately for local cultures and situations.

Protect wildlife and other natural resources: don't buy souvenirs or goods made from wildlife unless they are clearly sustainably produced and are not protected under CITES legislation (CITES controls trade in endangered species).

Don't give money or sweets to children (it encourages begging), instead give to a recognized project, charity or school.

Always ask before taking photographs or videos of people.

Consider staying in local accommodation rather than foreign owned hotels, the economic benefits for host communities are far greater and there are far greater opportunities to learn about local culture.

Essentials

The travel industry is growing rapidly and increasingly the impacts of this supposedly 'smokeless' industry are becoming apparent. These impacts can seem remote and unrelated to an individual trip or holiday (for example air travel is clearly implicated in global warming and damage to the ozone layer, resort location and construction can destroy natural habitats and restrict traditional rights and activities), but individual choice and awareness can make a difference in many instances, and collectively, travellers are having a significant effect in shaping a more responsible and sustainable industry.

In an attempt to promote awareness of and credibility for responsible tourism, organizations such as **Green Globe** (UK), T44-020-79308333, greenglobe@compuserve.com and the **Centre for Environmentally Sustainable Tourism (CERT)** (UK), T44-1268-795772, now offer advice on destinations and sites that have achieved certain commitments to conservation and sustainable development. Generally these are larger mainstream destinations and resorts, but they are still a useful guide and increasingly aim to provide information on smaller operations.

Of course travel can have beneficial impacts and this is something to which every traveller can contribute. Many national parks are part funded by receipts from visitors. Similarly, travellers can promote patronage and protection of important archaeological sites and heritage through their interest and contributions via entrance and performance fees. They can also support small-scale enterprises by staying in locally run hotels and hostels, eating in local restaurants and by purchasing local goods, supplies and arts and crafts.

Since the early 1990's there has been a phenomenal growth in tourism that promotes and supports the conservation of natural environments and is also fair and equitable to local communities. This 'ecotourism' segment is probably the fastest growing sector of the travel industry and provides a vast and growing range of destinations and activities in the Caribbean. While the authenticity of some ecotourism operators claims need to be interpreted with care, there is clearly both a huge demand for this type of activity and also significant opportunities to support worthwhile conservation and social development initiatives.

Organizations such as **Conservation International**, T1-202-4295660, www.ecotour.org, **The Eco-Tourism society**, T1-802-4472121, http://ecotourism.org **Planeta**, www2.planeta.com/mader and **Tourism Concern**, (UK) T44-020-77533330, www.gn.apc.org/ tourism-concern have begun to develop and/or promote ecotourism projects and destinations, and their websites are an excellent source of information and details for sites and initiatives throughout Latin America and the Caribbean. Additionally, organizations such as **Earthwatch**, (UK) T44-1865-311601, www.earthwatch.org and **Discovery International**, (UK) T44-020-

72299881, www.discoveryinitiatives.com offer opportunities to participate directly in scientific research and development projects throughout the region.

The Caribbean offers unique and unforgettable experiences – often based on the natural environment, cultural heritage and local society. These are the reasons many of us choose to travel and why many more will want to do so in the future. Shouldn't we provide an opportunity for future travellers and hosts to enjoy the quality of experience and interaction that we take for granted?

Health

Staying healthy in the Caribbean is straightforward. With the following advice and precautions you should keep as healthy as you do at home and most travellers experience no problems at all beyond an upset stomach. Obviously this in part depends on how you are travelling: the beach tourist who stays in good hotels is much less at risk than the backpacker who slings his hammock in the back of beyond. Most of the islands have a tropical climate but this does not mean that tropical diseases as such are a great problem or even the main problem for visitors. Should you fall ill, remember that throughout the islands there are well qualified doctors who speak good English (or French or Spanish). Medical practices may vary from those you are used to but there is likely to be better experience in dealing with locally occurring diseases. Most of the better hotels have a doctor on standby; ask at reception.

Before travelling

Take out medical insurance. Make sure it covers all eventualities especially evacuation to your home country by a medically equipped plane, if necessary. You should have a dental check up, obtain a spare glasses prescription, a spare oral contraceptive prescription (or enough pills to last) and, if you suffer from a chronic illness (such as diabetes, high blood pressure, ear or sinus troubles, cardio-pulmonary disease or a nervous disorder) arrange for a check-up with your doctor, who can at the same time provide you with a letter explaining the details of your disability in English or, if necessary, French or Spanish. Check the current practice in countries you are visiting for malaria prophylaxis (prevention) if you are going to the Dominican Republic or Haiti.

Children More preparation is probably necessary for babies and children than for an adult and perhaps a little more care should be taken when travelling to remote areas where health services are primitive. This is because children can become more rapidly ill than adults (on the other hand they often recover more quickly). Diarrhoea and vomiting are the most common problems, so take the usual precautions, but more intensively. Breastfeeding is best and most convenient for babies, but powdered milk is generally available and so are baby foods. Papaya, bananas and avocados are all nutritious and can be cleanly prepared. The treatment of diarrhoea is the same as for adults, except that it should start earlier and be continued with more persistence. Children get dehydrated very quickly in hot countries and can become drowsy and unco-operative unless cajoled to drink water or juice plus salts. Upper respiratory infections, such as colds, catarrh and middle ear infections are also common and if your child suffers from these normally take some antibiotics against the possibility. Outer ear infections after swimming are also common and antibiotic eardrops will help. 'Wet wipes' are always useful and sometimes difficult to find in the Caribbean, as in some places such as Cuba, are disposable nappies.

What to take There is little control on the sale of drugs and medicines in some of the Caribbean. You may be able to buy any and every drug in pharmacies without a prescription. Be wary of this because pharmacists can be poorly trained and might sell you drugs that are unsuitable, dangerous or old. Many drugs and medicines are manufactured under licence from American or European companies, so the trade names may be familiar to you. This means you do not have to carry a whole chest of medicines with you (except in Cuba, where there are shortages) but remember that the shelf life of some items, especially vaccines and antibiotics, is markedly reduced in hot conditions. Buy your supplies at the better outlets where there are refrigerators, even though more expensive and check the expiry date of all preparations you buy. Immigration officials occasionally confiscate scheduled drugs (Lomotil is an example) if they are not accompanied by a doctor's prescription.

Self-medication may be forced on you by circumstances so the following text does include the names of drugs and medicines which you may find useful in an emergency or in out-of-the-way places and you may like to take some of the following items with you from home: sunglasses designed for intense sunlight; earplugs for sleeping on aeroplanes and in noisy hotels; suntan cream with high protection factor; insect repellent containing DET for preference; mosquito net lightweight permethrin-impregnated for choice; tablets for travel sickness; tampons can be expensive in some countries; condoms; contraceptives; water sterilizing tablets; antimalarials; anti-infective cream eg Cetrimide; dusting powder for feet etc containing fungicide; antacid tablets for indigestion; sachets of rehydration salts plus anti-diarrhoea preparations; painkillers such as paracetamol or aspirin; antibiotics for diarrhoea etc; a simple first aid kit; small pack containing a few sterile syringes and needles and disposable gloves. The risk of catching hepatitis etc from a dirty needle used for injection is now negligible in the Caribbean but some may be reassured by carrying their own supplies, available from camping shops and often at airports.

Smallpox vaccination is no longer required anywhere in the world. Neither is yellow fever vaccination unless you are going to or are coming from South America. The cholera epidemic in South and Central America has not spread to any of the Caribbean islands but they are all on the alert for the possibility. Although cholera vaccination is largely ineffective, immigration officers may ask for proof of such vaccination if coming from a country where the epidemic has occurred.

Vaccination & immunization

Typhoid A disease spread by the insanitary preparation of food. A number of new vaccines against this condition are now available; the older TAB and monovalent typhoid vaccines are being phased out. The newer, eg Typhim Vi, cause fewer side effects, but are more expensive. For those who do not like injections, there are now oral vaccines. **Poliomyelitis** Despite its decline in the world this remains a serious disease if caught and is easy to protect against. There are live oral vaccines and in some countries injected vaccines. Whichever one you choose it is a good idea to have a booster every three to five years if visiting developing countries regularly. **Tetanus** One dose should be given with a booster at six weeks and another at six months and 10 yearly boosters thereafter are recommended. Children should already be properly protected against diphtheria, poliomyelitis and pertussis (whooping cough), measles and HIB, all of which can be more serious infections in the Caribbean than at home. Measles, mumps and rubella vaccine is also given to children throughout the world, but those teenage girls who have not had rubella (German measles) should be tested and vaccinated. Hepatitis B vaccination for babies is now routine in some countries. Consult your doctor for advice on tuberculosis innoculation: the disease is still present on some of the Islands – BVI, Grenada, Guadeloupe, Haiti and Martinique. **Infectious Hepatitis** Less of a problem for travellers than it used to be because of the development of two extremely effective vaccines against the A and B form of the disease. It remains common, however, in some of the islands. A combined hepatitis A and B vaccine is now licensed – one jab covers both diseases. **Other vaccinations** Might be considered in the case of epidemics, eg meningitis. There is an effective vaccination against rabies which should be considered by all travellers, especially those going through remote areas or if there is a particular occupational risk, eg for zoologists or veterinarians.

Further information on health risks abroad, vaccinations etc, may be available from a local travel clinic. If you wish to take specific drugs with you such as antibiotics these are best prescribed by your own doctor. Bear in mind that not all doctors can be experts on the health problems of remote countries. More detailed or more up-to-date information than local doctors can provide are available from various sources. In the UK there are hospital

Further information

departments specializing in tropical diseases in London, Liverpool, Birmingham and Glasgow and the Malaria Reference Laboratory at the *London School of Hygiene and Tropical Medicine* provides free advice about malaria, T0891-600350. In the USA the local Public Health Services can give such information and information is available centrally from the Centres for Disease Control (CDC) in Atlanta, T404-3324559.

There are in addition computerized databases which can be accessed for destination-specific up-to-the-minute information. In the UK there is *MASTA* (Medical Advisory Service to Travellers Abroad) T020-76314408, Tx8953473, F020-74365389 and *Travax* (Glasgow, telephone 0141 946 7120 extension 247). Other information on medical problems overseas can be obtained from the book by Richard Dawood (Editor) – *Travellers' Health, How to Stay Healthy Abroad,* Oxford University Press 1992 £7.99 (new edition imminent). We strongly recommend the revised and updated edition, especially to the intrepid traveller heading for the more out of the way places. General advice is also available in the UK in 'Health Information for Overseas Travel' published by the Department of Health and available from HMSO and 'International Travel and Health' published by WHO Handbooks on First Aid are produced by the British & American Red Cross and by St John's Ambulance (UK).

On the road

If a trip to the Caribbean crosses time zones then jetlag can be a problem where your body's biological clock gets out of synchrony with the real time at your destination. The main symptoms are tiredness and sleepiness at inconvenient times and, conversely, a tendency to wake up in the middle of the night feeling like you want your breakfast. Most find that the problem is worse when flying in an easterly direction. The best way to get over jetlag is probably to try to force yourself into the new time zone as strictly as possible which may involve, on a westward flight, trying to stay awake until your normal bedtime and on an eastward flight forgetting that you have lost some sleep on the way out and going to bed relatively early but near your normal time the evening after you arrive. The symptoms of jetlag may be helped by keeping up your fluid intake on the journey, but not with alcohol. The hormone melatonin seems to reduce the symptoms of jetlag but is not presently licensed in most of Europe although can be obtained from health food stores in the USA.

On long-haul flights it is also important to stretch your legs at least every hour to prevent slowing of the circulation and the possible development of blood clots. Drinking plenty of non-alcoholic fluids will also help.

If travelling by boat then sea sickness can be a problem – dealt with in the usual way by taking anti-motion sickness pills.

Intestinal upsets The thought of catching a stomach bug worries visitors to the Caribbean but there have been great improvements in food hygiene and most such infections are preventable. Travellers' diarrhoea and vomiting is due, most of the time, to food poisoning, usually passed on by the insanitary habits of food handlers. As a general rule the cleaner your surroundings and the smarter the restaurant, the less likely you are to suffer.

Foods to avoid Uncooked, undercooked, partially cooked or reheated meat, fish, eggs. Raw vegetables and salads, especially when they have been left out and exposed to flies. Stick to fresh food that has been cooked from raw just before eating and make sure you peel fruit yourself. Wash and dry your hands before eating – disposable wet-wipe tissues are useful for this. Shellfish eaten raw are risky and at certain times of the year some fish and shellfish concentrate toxins from their environment and cause various kinds of food poisoning. The local authorities notify the public not to eat these foods. Do not ignore the warning. Heat treated milk (UHT) pasteurized or sterilized is becoming more available in the Caribbean as is pasteurized cheese. On the whole matured or processed cheeses are safer than the fresh varieties. Fresh unpasteurized milk from whatever animal can be a source of food poisoning germs, tuberculosis and brucellosis. This applies equally to ice cream, yoghurt and cheese made from unpasteurized milk, so avoid these homemade products – the factory made ones are probably safer.

Water Tap water is rarely safe outside the major cities, especially in the rainy season and stream water, if you are in the countryside, is often contaminated by communities living surprisingly high in the mountains. Filtered or bottled water is usually available and safe, although you must make sure that somebody is not filling such bottles from the tap and hammering on a new crown cap. If your hotel has a central hot water supply this water is safe to drink after cooling. Ice for drinks should be made from boiled water, but rarely is so stand your glass on the ice cubes, rather than putting them in the drink. The better hotels have water purifying systems.

This is usually caused by eating food which has been contaminated by food poisoning germs. Drinking water is rarely the culprit. Sea water or river water is more likely to be contaminated by sewage and so swimming can also be a cause. Infection with various organisms can give rise to travellers' diarrhoea. They may be viruses, bacteria, eg Escherichia coli (probably the most common cause worldwide), protozoal (such as amoebas and giardia) salmonella and cholera. The diarrhoea may come on suddenly or rather slowly. It may or may not be accompanied by vomiting or by severe abdominal pain and the passage of blood or mucus when it is called dysentery.

How do you know which type you have caught and how to treat it? If you can time the onset of the diarrhoea to the minute ('acute') then it is probably due to a virus or a bacterium and/or the onset of dysentery. The treatment in addition to rehydration is Ciprofloxacin 500 mg every 12 hours; the drug is now widely available and there are many similar ones. If the diarrhoea comes on slowly or intermittently ('sub-acute') then it is more likely to be protozoal, ie caused by an amoeba or giardia. Antibiotics such as Ciprofloxacin will have little effect. These cases are best treated by a doctor as is any outbreak of diarrhoea continuing for more than three days. Sometimes blood is passed in amoebic dysentery and for this you should certainly seek medical help. If this is not available then the best treatment is probably Tinidazole (Fasigyn) one tablet four times a day for three days. If there are severe stomach cramps, the following drugs may help but are not very useful in the management of acute diarrhoea: Loperamide (Imodium) and Diphenoxylate with Atropine (Lomotil). They should not be given to children.

Any kind of diarrhoea, whether or not accompanied by vomiting, responds well to the replacement of water and salts, taken as frequent small sips, of some kind of rehydration solution. There are proprietary preparations consisting of sachets of powder which you dissolve in boiled water or you can make your own by adding half a teaspoonful of salt (3.5 grammes) and four tablespoonsful of sugar (40 grammes) to a litre of boiled water.

Thus the linchpins of treatment for diarrhoea are rest, fluid and salt replacement, antibiotics such as Ciprofloxacin for the bacterial types and special diagnostic tests and medical treatment for the amoeba and giardia infections. Salmonella infections and cholera, although rare, can be devastating diseases and it would be wise to get to a hospital as soon as possible if these were suspected.

Fasting, peculiar diets and the consumption of large quantities of yoghurt have not been found useful in calming travellers' diarrhoea or in rehabilitating inflamed bowels. Oral rehydration has on the other hand, especially in children, been a life saving technique and should always be practised, whatever other treatment you use. As there is some evidence that alcohol and milk might prolong diarrhoea they should be avoided during and immediately after an attack.

Diarrhoea occurring day after day for long periods of time (chronic diarrhoea) is notoriously resistent to amateur attempts at treatment and again warrants proper diagnostic tests.

There are ways of preventing travellers' diarrhoea for short periods of time by taking antibiotics, but this is not a foolproof technique and should not be used other than in exceptional circumstances. Doxycycline is possibly the best drug. Some preventatives such as Enterovioform can have serious side effects if taken for long periods.

Paradoxically constipation is also common, probably induced by dietary change, inadequate fluid intake in hot places and long bus journeys. Simple laxatives are useful in the short-term and bulky foods such as maize, beans and plenty of fruit are also useful.

Heat & cold Full acclimatization to high temperatures takes about two weeks. During this period it is normal to feel a bit apathetic, especially if the relative humidity is high. Drink plenty of water (up to 15 litres a day are required when working physically hard in the tropics) use salt on your food and avoid extreme exertion. Tepid showers are more cooling than hot or cold ones. Large hats do not cool you down, but do prevent sunburn. Remember that, especially in the highlands, there can be a large and sudden drop in temperature between sun and shade and between night and day, so dress accordingly. Warm jackets or woollens are essential after dark at high altitude. Loose cotton is still the best material when the weather is hot.

Insects These are mostly more of a nuisance than a serious hazard and if you try, you can prevent yourself entirely from being bitten. Some, such as mosquitoes are, of course, carriers of potentially serious diseases, so it is sensible to avoid being bitten as much as possible. Sleep off the ground and use a mosquito net or some kind of insecticide. Preparations containing pyrethrum or synthetic pyrethroids are safe. They are available as aerosols or pumps and the best way to use these is to spray the room thoroughly in all areas (follow the instructions rather than the insects) and then shut the door for a while, re-entering when the smell has dispersed. Mosquito coils release insecticide as they burn slowly. They are widely available and useful out of doors. Tablets of insecticide which are placed on a heated mat, and plugged into a wall socket are probably the most effective. They fill the room with insecticidal fumes in the same way as aerosols or coils.

You can also use insect repellents, most of which are effective against a wide range of pests. The most common and effective is diethyl metatoluamide (DET). DET liquid is best for arms and face (care around eyes and with spectacles – DET dissolves plastic). Aerosol spray is good for clothes and ankles and liquid DET can be dissolved in water and used to impregnate cotton clothes and mosquito nets. Some repellents now contain DET and permethrin insecticide. Impregnated wrist and ankle bands can also be useful.

If you are bitten or stung, itching may be relieved by cool baths, antihistamine tablets (care with alcohol or driving) or mild corticosteroid creams, eg hydrocortisone (great care, never use if any hint of infection). Careful scratching of all your bites once a day can be surprisingly effective. Calamine lotion and cream have limited effectiveness and antihistamine creams are not recommended – they can cause allergies themselves.

Bites which become infected should be treated with a local antiseptic or antibiotic cream, such as Cetrimide as should any infected sores or scratches.

When living rough, skin infestations with body lice (crabs) and scabies are easy to pick up. Use whatever local commercial preparation is recommended for lice and scabies. Crotamiton cream (Eurax) alleviates itching and also kills a number of skin parasites. Malathion lotion 5% (Prioderm) kills lice effectively, but avoid the use of the toxic agricultural preparation of Malathion.

Ticks Usually attach themselves to the lower parts of the body, often after walking in areas where cattle have grazed. They take a while to attach themselves strongly, but swell up as they start to suck blood. The important thing is to remove them gently, so that they do not leave their head parts in your skin because this can cause a nasty allergic reaction some days later. Do not use petrol, vaseline, lighted cigarettes etc. to remove the tick, but, with a pair of tweezers remove the beast gently by gripping it at the attached (head) end and rock it out in very much the same way that a tooth is extracted. Certain tropical flies which lay their eggs under the skin of sheep and cattle also occasionally do the same thing to humans with the unpleasant result that a maggot grows under the skin and pops up as a boil or pimple. The best way to remove these is to cover the boil with oil, vaseline or nail varnish so as to stop the maggot breathing, then to squeeze it out gently the next day.

Sunburn The burning power of the tropical sun, especially at altitude, is phenomenal. Always wear a wide brimmed hat and use some form of suncream lotion on untanned skin. Normal temperate zone suntan lotions (protection factor up to seven) are not much good; you need to use the types designed specifically for the tropics or for mountaineers or skiers with protection factors up to 15 or above. These may be available in all the islands. Glare from the sun can cause conjunctivitis, so wear sunglasses, especially on tropical beaches, where high protection factor sunscreen should also be used.

In the Caribbean AIDS is increasing and is not wholly confined to high risk sections of the population, ie homosexual men, intravenous drug users and children of infected mothers. Heterosexual transmission is now the dominant mode and so the main risk to travellers is from casual sex. The same precautions should be taken as with any sexually transmitted disease. The AIDS virus (HIV) can be passed by unsterilized needles which have been previously used to inject an HIV positive patient, but the risk of this is negligible. It would, however, be sensible to check that needles have been properly sterilized or disposable needles have been used. If you wish to take your own disposable needles be prepared to explain what they are for. The risk of receiving a blood transfusion with blood infected with the HIV virus is greater than from dirty needles because of the amount of fluid exchanged. Supplies of blood for transfusion should now be screened for HIV in all reputable hospitals, so again the risk is very small indeed. Catching the AIDS virus does not always produce an illness in itself (although it may do). The only way to be sure if you feel you have been put at risk is to have a blood test for HIV antibodies on your return to a place where there are reliable laboratory facilities. The test does not become positive for some weeks.

AIDS

Essentials

In the West Indies, malaria is confined to the island of Hispaniola, being more prevalent in Haiti than the Dominican Republic. It remains a serious disease and you are advised to protect yourself against mosquito bites as above, and to take prophylactic (preventive) drugs. Start taking the tablets a few days before exposure and continue to take six weeks after leaving the malaria zone. Remember to give drugs to babies and children also. The subject of malaria prevention is becoming more complex as the malaria parasite becomes immune to some of the older drugs. However, at the present time Chloroquine should give sufficient protection. You can catch malaria even when taking these drugs, though it is unlikely. If you do develop symptoms (high fever, shivering, headaches), seek medical advice immediately. If this is not possible and the likelihood of malaria is high the treatment is Chloroquine, a single dose of four tablets (600 milligrammes) followed by two tablets (300 milligrammes) in six hours and 300 milligrammes each day following. Pregnant women are particularly prone to malaria and should stick to Proguanil for prophylaxis. The risk of malaria is obviously greater the further you move from cities and into rural areas with primitive facilities and standing water.

Malaria

The main symptoms are pains in the stomach, lack of appetite, lassitude and yellowness of the eyes and skin. Medically speaking there are two main types. The less serious, but more common is hepatitis A for which the best protection is the careful preparation of food, the avoidance of contaminated drinking water and scrupulous attention to toilet hygiene. The other, more serious, version is hepatitis B which is acquired usually as a sexually transmitted disease or by blood transfusion. It can less commonly be transmitted by injections with unclean needles and possibly by insect bites. The symptoms are the same as for hepatitis A. The incubation period is much longer (up to six months compared with six weeks) and there are more likely to be complications.

Infectious Hepatitis (Jaundice)

Hepatitis A can be protected against with gamma globulin. It should be obtained from a reputable source and is certainly useful for travellers who intend to live rough. You should have a shot before leaving and have it repeated every six months. The dose of gamma globulin depends on the concentration of the particular preparation used, so the manufacturers advice should be taken. The injection should be given as close as possible to your departure and as the dose depends on the likely time you are to spend in potentially affected areas. Again follow the manufacturer's instructions. Gamma globulin has really been superseded now by a proper vaccination against hepatitis A (Havrix), which gives immunity lasting up to 10 years. After that boosters are required. Havrix monodose is now widely available as is junior Havrix. The vaccination has negligible side effects and is extremely effective. Gamma globulin injection can be a bit painful, but it is cheaper than Havrix and may be more available in some places.

Hepatitis B can be effectively prevented by a specific vaccine (Engerix) – three shots over six months before travelling. If you have had jaundice in the past it would be worthwhile having a blood test to see if you are immune to either of these two types, because this might obviate the necessity and cost of vaccination or gamma globulin. There are other kinds of viral hepatitis (C, E, etc) which are very similar to A and B, but vaccines are not available as yet.

Snake bite This is a very rare event indeed for travellers. If you are unlucky (or careless) enough to be bitten by a venomous snake, spider, scorpion or sea creature, try to identify the creature, but do not put yourself in further danger. Snake bites in particular are very frightening, but in fact rarely poisonous – even venomous snakes bite without injecting venom. What you might expect if bitten are: fright, swelling, pain and bruising around the bite and soreness of the regional lymph glands, perhaps nausea, vomiting and a fever. Signs of serious poisoning would be the following symptoms: numbness and tingling of the face, muscular spasms, convulsions, shortness of breath and bleeding. Victims should be got to a hospital or a doctor without delay. Commercial snake bite and scorpion kits are available, but usually only useful for the specific type of snake or scorpion for which they are designed. Most serum has to be given intravenously so it is not much good equipping yourself with it unless you are used to making injections into veins. It is best to rely on local practice in these cases, because the particular creatures will be known about locally and appropriate treatment can be given.

Treatment Reassure and comfort the victim frequently. Immobilize the limb by a bandage or a splint or by getting the person to lay still. Do not slash the bite area and try to suck out the poison because this sort of heroism does more harm than good. If you know how to use a tourniquet in these circumstances, you will not need this advice. If you are not experienced, do not apply a tourniquet.

Precautions Avoid walking in snake territory in bare feet or sandals – wear proper shoes or boots. If you encounter a snake stay put until it slithers away, and do not investigate a wounded snake. Spiders and scorpions may be found in the more basic hotels. If stung, rest and take plenty of fluids and call a doctor. The best precaution is to keep beds away from the walls and look inside your shoes and under the toilet seat every morning.

Certain tropical sea fish when trodden upon inject venom into bathers' feet. This can be exceptionally painful. Wear plastic shoes when you go bathing if such creatures are reported. The pain can be relieved by immersing the foot in extremely hot water for as long as the pain persists.

Other afflictions **Prickly heat** A very common intensely itchy rash is avoided by frequent washing and by wearing loose clothing. Cured by allowing skin to dry off through use of powder and spending two nights in an air-conditioned hotel!! **Athletes foot** This and other fungal skin infections are best treated with Tolnaftate or Clotrimazole. **Dengue Fever** This is increasing worldwide including in South and Central American countries and the Caribbean. It can be completely prevented by avoiding mosquito bites in the same way as malaria. No vaccine is available. Dengue is an unpleasant and painful disease, presenting with a high temperature and body pains, but at least visitors are spared the more serious forms (haemorrhagic types) which are more of a problem for local people who have been exposed to the disease more than once. There is no specific treatment for dengue – just pain killers and rest. **Typhus** Can still occur carried by ticks but is exceptionally rare in the Caribbean. There is usually a reaction at the site of the bite and a fever. Seek medical advice. **Intestinal worms** These are common and the more serious ones such as hookworm can be contracted from walking barefoot on infested earth or beaches. Some cause an itchy rash on the feet 'cutaneous larva migrans'. **Leptospirosis** Various forms of leptospirosis occur throughout the Caribbean, transmitted by a bacterium which is excreted in rodent urine. Fresh water and moist soil harbour the organisms which enter the body through cuts and scratches. If you suffer from any form of prolonged fever consult a doctor.

When you return home Remember to take your antimalarial tablets for six weeks after leaving the malarial area. If you have had attacks of diarrhoea it is worth having a stool specimen tested in case you have picked up amoebas. If you have been living rough, blood tests may be worthwhile to detect worms and other parasites. If you have been exposed to bilharzia (schistosomiasis) by swimming in lakes etc check by means of a blood test when you get home, but leave it for six

Surfing the Caribbean

Nearly all the tourist offices have their own websites and are also linked to:
Caribbean Tourism Organization www.caribtourism.com

Each country has its own pages on the CTO website and it is a good place to start a general search for information.

The following is a list of general sites for each country, a combination of official tourist office and private sector sites:

Anguilla www.anguilla-vacation.com
http://net.ai
Antigua
www.interknowledge.com/ antigua-barbuda
Aruba www.aruba.com
Bahamas www.bahamas.com
www.bahama-out-islands.com
www.bahamasvg.com
Barbados www.barbados.org
Bonaire www.InfoBonaire.com
British Virgin Islands www.b-v-i.com
www.bviwelcome.com
www.ultimatebvi.com
www.britishvirginislands.com
Cayman Islands www.caymanislands.ky
Cuba www.dtcuba.com
Curaçao www.curacao-tourism.com
Dominica www.dominica.dm
Dominican Republic www.hispaniola.com
www.dominicana.com.do
www.domrep-hotels.com.do
Grenada www.grenada.org
www.travelgrenada.com
www.grenadines.net
Guadeloupe
www.antilles-info-tourism.com/guadeloupe
Haiti www.haititourisme.com

Jamaica www.jamaicatravel.com
www.jamaicans.com
Martinique http://martinique.org
Montserrat www.visitmontserrat.com
Puerto Rico www.prtourism.com
www.travelandsports.com
www.culebra.org
www.vieques-island.com
www.viequespr.net
Saba www.turq.com/saba
St-Barthélémy www.st.barths.com
www.saint-barths.com
St Kitts and Nevis www.stkitts-nevis.com
www.nevisweb.kn
www.nevis1.com
St Lucia www.stlucia.org
St-Martin www.st-martin.org
www.destination.st-martin.com
St Vincent and the Grenadines
http://stvincentandgrenadines.com
www.vincy.com
www.svgtourism.com
www.grenadines.net
Sint Eustatius www.turq.com/statia
Sint Maarten www.st-maarten.com
Trinidad and Tobago www.visittnt.com
Turks and Caicos Islands
www.turksandcaicostourism.com
www.tcimall.tc
US Virgin Islands www.usvi.net
Venezuelan Islands www.chevere.com
www.infoguia.net

Useful general websites and search engines for the Caribbean include:
www.caribbean-online.com
www.turq.com
www.caribseek.com
www.caribsurf.com

Essentials

weeks because the test is slow to become positive. Report any untoward symptoms to your doctor and tell the doctor exactly where you have been and, if you know, what the likelihood of disease is to which you were exposed.

Further reading

By no means all the writers of history, fiction, poetry and other topics will be found below. There is no room to talk of the many authors who have been inspired by aspects of the Caribbean for their fiction such as Robert Louis Stevenson, Graham Greene, Ernest Hemingway, Gabriel García Márquez. Nor have travel writers, such as Patrick Leigh Fermor, *The Traveller's Tree*, Quentin Crewe, *Touch the Happy Isles*, Trollope, *Travels in the West Indies and the*

Other books have been suggested in culture, tourist information & other sections. See individual islands & page 41 for maps

Spanish Main, Alec Waugh, *The Sugar Isles*, James Pope-Hennessy, *West Indian Summer*, among others. This list is not exhaustive, concentrating mainly on books in English, published (or readily available) in the UK. For any favourites omitted, we apologize.

History Of the histories of the region, **James Ferguson**, *A Traveller's History of the Caribbean*, (1998), The Windrush Press. Concise and easy to dip in to. More academic is **J H Parry, P M Sherlock and Anthony Maingot**, *A Short History of The West Indies*, (1987) Macmillan. Very accessible. Also **Eric Williams**, *From Columbus to Castro: The History of the Caribbean 1492-1969*, (1970) Harper and Row.

Geography For an introduction to the geography of the Caribbean, **Mark Wilson**, *The Caribbean Environment*, (1989) Oxford University Press. Prepared for the Caribbean Examinations Council, a fascinating text book. Another introductory book is **James Ferguson**, *Far from Paradise, An Introduction to Caribbean Development*, (1990) Latin American Bureau.

Economics An economic study is **Clive Y Thomas**, *The Poor and the Powerless, Economic Policy and Change in the Caribbean* (1988) Latin American Bureau. A recent study of tourism in the Caribbean and its impact on the economies and people is **Polly Pattullo**'s *Last Resort, The Cost of Tourism in the Caribbean* (1996) Cassell and Latin American Bureau.

Literature For an introduction to Caribbean writers and writers on the Caribbean, with extracts from numerous literary works, **James Ferguson**, *Traveller's Literary Companion to the Caribbean*, with chapters on Cuba and Puerto Rico by Jason Wilson, (1997) In Print. Highly recommended. The work of a great many English-speaking poets is collected in *The Penguin Book of Caribbean Verse in English*, edited by **Paula Burnett** (1986) see also *Hinterland: Caribbean Poetry From the West Indies and Britain*, edited by **E A Markham** (1990) Bloodaxe, and *West Indian Poetry*, edited by **Kenneth Ramchand and Cecil Gray** (1989) Longman Caribbean. For a French verse anthology, see *La Poésie Antillaise*, collected by **Maryse Condé** (1977) Fernand Nathan. There are a number of prose anthologies of stories in English, eg *The Oxford Book of Caribbean Short Stories*, **Stewart Brown and John Wickham** (1999), *Stories from the Caribbean*, introduced by **Andrew Salkey** (1972) Paul Elek, or *West Indian Narrative: an Introductory Anthology*, **Kenneth Ramchand** (1966) Nelson. Heinemann's Caribbean Writers series publishes works of fiction by well-established and new writers. The *Story of English*, by **Robert McCrumb**, **William Cran** and **Robert MacNeil** (1986) Faber and Faber/BBC, has an interesting section on the development of the English language in the Caribbean.

Caribbean Insight, published weekly by the Caribbean Council for Europe (Suite 18, Westminster Palace Gardens, 1-7 Artillery Row, London SW1P 1RR, T020-77991521, insight@caribbean- council.com) is an informative on-line newsletter covering the entire region. Finally, a generally excellent series of Caribbean books is published by Macmillan

Caribbean; this includes island guides, natural histories, books on food and drink, sports and pirates, and wall maps (for a full catalogue, write to Macmillan Caribbean, Houndmills, Basingstoke, Hampshire, RG21 2XS, England). An excellent source of maps is *Stanfords* at 12-14 Long Acre, London WC2, T020-78361321, F020-78360189.

Background

Pre-columbian civilizations

Today's visitors to the Caribbean find an arc of islands whose culture has been determined by its immigrants: colonists, slaves, indentured labourers, from Europe, Africa and the East. It is easy to forget that there was a well-developed Amerindian society which was obliterated by Europeans in the 16th century.

The recorded history of the Caribbean islands begins with the arrival of Christopher Columbus' fleet in 1492. Our knowledge of the native peoples who inhabited the islands before and at the time of his arrival is largely derived from the accounts of contemporary Spanish writers and from archaeological examinations as there is no evidence of indigenous written records.

The Amerindians encountered by Columbus in the Greater Antilles had no overall tribal name **Tribes** but organized themselves in a series of villages or local chief-doms, each of which had its own tribal name. The name now used, 'Arawak', was not in use then. The term was used by the Indians of the Guianas, a group of whom had spread into Trinidad, but their territory was not explored until nearly another century later. The use of the generic term 'Arawak' to describe the Indians Columbus encountered, arose because of linguistic similarities with the Arawaks of the mainland. It is therefore surmised that migration took place many centuries before Columbus' arrival, but that the two groups were not in contact at that time. The time of the latest migration from the mainland, and consequently the existence of the island Arawaks, is in dispute, with some academics tracing it to about the time of Christ (the arrival of the Saladoids) and others to 1000 AD (the Ostionoids).

The inhabitants of the Bahamas were generally referred to as Lucayans, and those of the Greater Antilles as Tainos, but there were many sub-groupings. The inhabitants of the Lesser Antilles were, however, referred to as Carib and were described to Columbus as an aggressive tribe which sacrificed and sometimes ate the prisoners they captured in battle. It was from them that the Caribbean gets its name and from which the word cannibal is derived.

The earliest known inhabitants of the region, the 'Siboneys', migrated from Florida (some say Mexico) and spread throughout the Bahamas and the major islands. Most archaeological evidence of their settlements has been found near the shore, along bays or streams, where they lived in small groups. The largest discovered settlement has been one of 100 inhabitants in Cuba. They were hunters and gatherers, living on fish and other seafood, small rodents, iguanas, snakes and birds. They gathered roots and wild fruits, such as guava, guanabana and mamey, but did not cultivate plants. They worked with primitive tools made out of stone, shell, bone or wood, for hammering, chipping or scraping, but had no knowledge of pottery. The Siboneys were eventually absorbed by the advance of the Arawaks migrating from the south, who had made more technological advances in agriculture, arts and crafts.

The people now known as Arawaks migrated from the Guianas to Trinidad and on through the island arc to Cuba. Their population expanded because of the natural fertility of the islands and the abundance of fruit and seafood, helped by their agricultural skills in cultivating and improving wild plants and their excellent boat-building and fishing techniques. They were healthy, tall, good looking and lived to a ripe old age. It is estimated that up to eight million may have lived on the island of Hispaniola alone, but there was always plenty of food for all.

Their society was essentially communal and organized around families. The smaller islands **Society** were particularly egalitarian, but in the larger ones, where village communities of extended

Essentials

families numbered up to 500 people, there was an incipient class structure. Typically, each village had a headman, called a 'cacique', whose duty it was to represent the village when dealing with other tribes, to settle family disputes and organize defence. However, he had no powers of coercion and was often little more than a nominal head. The position was largely hereditary, with the eldest son of the eldest sister having rights of succession, but women could and did become caciques. In the larger communities, there was some delegation of responsibility to the senior men, but economic activities were usually organized along family lines, and their power was limited.

The division of labour was usually based on age and sex. The men would clear and prepare the land for agriculture and be responsible for defence of the village, while women cultivated the crops and were the major food producers, also making items such as mats, baskets, bowls and fishing nets. Women were in charge of raising the children, especially the girls, while the men taught the boys traditional customs, skills and rites.

Food & farming

The Tainos hunted for some of their food, but fishing was more important and most of their settlements were close to the sea. Fish and shellfish were their main sources of protein and they had many different ways of catching them – from hands, baskets or nets to poisoning, shooting or line fishing. Cassava was a staple food, which they had successfully learned to leach of its poisonous juice. They also grew yams, maize, cotton, arrowroot, peanuts, beans, cocoa and spices, rotating their crops to prevent soil erosion. It is documented that in Jamaica they had three harvests of maize annually, using maize and cassava to make bread, cakes and beer.

Cotton was used to make clothing and hammocks (never before seen by Europeans), while the calabash tree was used to make ropes and cords, baskets and roofing. Plants were used for medicinal and spiritual purposes, and cosmetics such as face and body paint. Also important, both to the Arawaks and later to the Europeans, was the cultivation of tobacco, as a drug and as a means of exchange.

Arts & crafts

They had no writing, no beasts of burden, no wheeled vehicles and no hard metals, although they did have some alluvial gold for personal ornament. The abundance of food allowed them time to develop their arts and crafts and they were skilled in woodwork and pottery. They had polished stone tools, but also carved shell implements for manioc preparation or as fish hooks. Coral manioc graters have also been found. Their boatbuilding techniques were noted by Columbus, who marvelled at their canoes of up to 75 ft in length, carrying up to 50 people, made of a single tree trunk in one piece. It took two months to fell a tree by gradually burning and chipping it down, and many more to make the canoe.

Religion

The Arawaks had three main deities, evidence of which have been found in stone and conch carvings in many of the Lesser Antilles as well as the well populated Greater Antilles, although their relative importance varied according to the island. The principal male god was Yocahú, yoca being the word for cassava and hú meaning 'giver of'. It is believed that the Indians associated this deity's power to provide cassava with the mystery of the volcanoes, for all the carvings, the earliest out of shells and the later ones of stone, are conical. The Yocahú cult was wiped out in the Lesser Antilles by the invading Caribs, and in the Greater Antilles by the Spaniards, but it is thought to have existed from about 200AD.

The main female deity was a fertility goddess, often referred to as 'Atabeyra', but she is thought to have had several names relating to her other roles as goddess of the moon, mother of the sea, the tides and the springs, and the goddess of childbirth. In carvings she is usually depicted as a squatting figure with her hands up to her chin, sometimes in the act of giving birth.

A third deity is a dog god, named Opiyel-Guaobiran, meaning 'the dog deity who takes care of the souls of the immediately deceased and is the son of the spirit of darkness'. Again, carvings of a dog's head or whole body have been found of shell or stone, which were often used to induce narcotic trances. Many of the carvings have holes and Y-shaped passages which would have been put to the nose to snuff narcotics and induce a religious trance in the shaman or priest, who could then ascertain the status of a departed soul for a recently bereaved relative.

One custom which aroused interest in the Spaniards was the ball game, not only for the sport and its ceremonial features, but because the ball was made of rubber and bounced, a phenomenon which had not previously been seen in Europe. Catholicism soon eradicated the game, but archaeological remains have been found in several islands, notably in Puerto Rico, but also in Hispaniola. Excavations in the Greater Antilles have revealed earth embankments and rows of elongated upright stones surrounding plazas or courts, pavements and stone balls. These are called *bateyes, juegos de indios, juegos de bola, cercados* or *corrales de indios*. Batey was the aboriginal name for the ball game, the rubber ball itself and also the court where it was played. The word is still used to designate the cleared area in front of houses in the country.

The ball game had religious and ceremonial significance but it was a sport and bets and wagers were important. It was played by two teams of up to 20 or 30 players, who had to keep the ball in the air by means of their hips, shoulders, heads, elbows and other parts of their body, but never with their hands. The aim was to bounce the ball in this manner to the opposing team until it hit the ground. Men and women played, but not usually in mixed sex games. Great athleticism was required and it is clear that the players practised hard to perfect their skill, several, smaller practice courts having been built in larger settlements. The game was sometimes played before the village made an important decision, and the prize could be a sacrificial victim, usually a prisoner, granted to the victor.

In 1492 Arawaks inhabited all the greater islands of the Caribbean, but in Puerto Rico they were being invaded by the Caribs who had pushed north through the Lesser Antilles, stealing their women and enslaving or killing the men. The Caribs had also originated in South America, from around the Orinoco delta. In their migration north through the Caribbean islands they proved to be fierce warriors and their raids on the Arawak settlements were feared. Many of their women were captured Arawaks, and it was they who cultivated the land and performed the domestic chores. Polygamy was common, encouraged by the surplus of women resulting from the raids, and the Arawak female influence on Carib culture was strong.

Despite rumours of cannibalism reported to Columbus by frightened Arawaks, there appears to be no direct evidence of the practice, although the Spaniards took it seriously enough to use it as an excuse to justify taking slaves. After some unfortunate encounters, colonizers left the Caribs alone for many years. The Arawaks, on the other hand, were soon wiped out by disease, cruelty and murder. The Spanish invaders exacted tribute and forced labour while allowing their herds of cattle and pigs to destroy the Indians' unfenced fields and clearings. Transportation to the mines resulted in shifts in the native population which could not be fed from the surrounding areas and starvation became common. Lack of labour in the Greater Antilles led to slave raids on the Lucayans in the Bahamas, but they also died or committed collective suicide. They felt that their gods had deserted them and there was nowhere for them to retreat or escape. Today there are no full-blooded Arawaks and only some 2,000 Caribs are left on Dominica (there has been no continuity of Carib language or religious belief on Dominica). The 500 years since Columbus' arrival have served to obliterate practically all the evidence of the indigenous civilization.

The Bahamas

3

The Bahamas

The Bahamas is a coral archipelago consisting of some 700 low-lying islands, and over 2,000 cays (pronounced "keys"). The highest hills, on Cat Island, are less than 400 ft and most islands have a maximum height of 100 ft. The total area of the islands is about 5,400 square miles, roughly the same as Jamaica. The whole archipelago extends for about 600 miles southeast from the Mantanilla shoal off the coast of Florida to 50 miles north of Haiti. Some of the smaller cays are privately owned but most of them are uninhabited. The main tourist areas are Paradise Island and Cable Beach, on New Providence, and Freeport, on Grand Bahama, where huge resorts attract mass tourism. Most cruise ships come in to Nassau, the capital, on New Providence, and its main shopping street can be packed when several ships are in port. The other islands, known as the "Family Islands", or "Out Islands", are largely unspoilt and include Bimini, the Berry Islands, Abaco, Eleuthera (these two are particularly attractive), the Exumas, Andros, Cat Island, Long Island, San Salvador, Rum Cay, Inagua, Acklins and Crooked Island. The water around these islands and the smaller cays changes from deep blue to pale turquoise according to depth and underwater features, producing spectacularly beautiful colour schemes when seen from the air and a huge playground for all manner of watersports: sailing, fishing, diving, snorkelling and anything else you can think of.

Essentials

Before you travel

Documents All visitors to the Bahamas must have a **passport** valid for at least six months and a return ticket. Visitors from EU member countries and South Africa do not require a **visa** for stays of up to three months. Citizens of Russia, Czech Republic, Hungary, Poland, Ukraine and Slovakia may stay one month without a visa. Visas are not required by nationals of Commonwealth countries, South Korea, Israel and Japan (length of permitted stay varies between three and eight months), nor by most Latin American nationals if staying no longer than 14 days. Colombians without a US visa need a Bahamian visa. Nationals of Haiti and communist countries need a visa. You will need a certificate of vaccination against yellow fever if you are coming from an infected area. To enter the Bahamas for business purposes the permission of the Immigration Department, Nassau, must be obtained. Apply in writing to: Director of Immigration, Immigration Department, PO Box N3002, Nassau. No expatriate can be employed in a post for which a suitably qualified Bahamian is available, nor can a permit be considered if the prospective employee is in the country, having come in as a visitor.

Money **Banks** There are several hundred banks licensed to do banking or trust business in the Bahamas. Some of the largest commercial banks are *Royal Bank of Canada* at Nassau, the airport, Abaco, Andros (Fresh Creek), Bimini, Grand Bahama, Harbour Island, Long Island, Lyford Cay, and Spanish Wells; *Lloyds Bank* (Bahamas); *Barclays Bank Plc*, at Nassau, Grand Bahama, Eleuthera, Abaco; *Scotiabank*, at Nassau, Abaco, Grand Bahama, Exuma, Long Island; *Canadian Imperial Bank of Commerce* also at Nassau, Grand Bahama, Andros (Nicholl's Town), Abaco; *Bank of the Bahamas Ltd,* Nassau, Grand Bahama, Andros and Inagua; *Citibank*.

Currency The unit of currency is the Bahamian Dollar (B$) which is at par with the US dollar. Both currencies are accepted everywhere. There is no restriction on foreign currency taken in or out; Bahamian currency may be exported up to B$70 per person. Notes of B$ 100, 50, 20, 10, 5, 3, 1 and 50c; coins of B$5, 2, 1, 50c, 25c, 15c, 10c, 5c and 1c.

Credit cards All major credit cards are accepted on New Providence and Grand Bahama. Not all the hotels and restaurants on the Family Islands take credit cards, although most take American Express, Mastercard and Visa.

Climate
Jun-Nov is the official hurricane season

The sunshine and warm seas attract visitors throughout the year but winter, from December to April, is the high season. Temperatures are around 68°F. Summer temperatures average 86°F. Humidity is fairly high, particularly in the summer. The rainy season is May to October, when the showers are usually short but heavy. The weather can be pleasant in the winter season although cold fronts from the North American continent can bring strong north winds, heavy rain and surprisingly low temperatures. The summer months are hot, humid and often windless, with frequent thunderstorms. In August 1992 Hurricane Andrew hit the Bahamas, making over 1,200 homeless, killing four people and causing damage of over US$250 mn. North Eleuthera was badly damaged. In October 1996 Hurricane Lili destroyed houses and crops and cut power lines in Exuma, Long Island and other islands after passing over Cuba. In June 1997 unprecedented rainfall and a spring tide caused flooding in New Providence while a tornado struck Hope Town, damaging boats and power supplies. In August 1999 the islands were again hit, by Hurricane Floyd. Businesses soon get back to normal, however, and there is usually little evidence of storm damage by the time the tourist high season is in full swing.

Getting there

Air Most flights to the Bahamas originate in the USA. Connecting flights by *Bahamasair* go out from Nassau like spokes of a wheel to the Family Islands although many airlines now fly direct from Florida to the Family Islands.

To Nassau From the USA: from Atlanta (*Delta*), Charleston (*Delta*), Charlotte (*US Air*), Cincinnati (*Delta Connection*), Columbus (*Delta*), Fort Lauderdale (*American Eagle, Continental Connection/Gulfstream International, Chalks, Bahamasair*), Key West (*Continental Connection/Gulfstream*), Manchester, New Hampshire (*US Air*), Miami (*Continental Connection/Gulfstream, American Eagle, Pan Am Airbridge, Chalks, Bahamasair*), Milwaukee (*US Air*), New York (*TWA, Continental, Delta*), Orlando (*Delta Connection, Comair, Continental Connection/Gulfstream, American Eagle, Bahamasair*), Philadelphia (*US Air*), St Louis (*Delta Connection*), Tallahassee (*Gulfstream*), Tampa/St Petersburg (*Gulfstream/Continental Connection*), West Palm Beach (*Gulfstream/ Continental Connection, Bahamasair*). **From Canada**: *Air Canada* flies from Montréal and Toronto. **From Europe**: *British Airways* have three flights a week from London (Gatwick); *AOM French Airlines* fly twice a week from Paris and Condor have charters from Germany. **From the Caribbean**: *Bahamasair* connects Providenciales with Nassau, *British Airways* flies from San José, Costa Rica and Grand Cayman on its way back to London, *AOM* from Havana, *Air Jamaica* from Montego Bay.

To Freeport From the USA: *TWA* flies from New York (La Guardia). *American Eagle, Gulfstream International* and *Bahamasair* fly from Miami. *LB Limited* from Baltimore, Chicago, Cincinnati, Cleveland, Fort Lauderdale, Hartford, Raleigh/Durham, Richmond and West Palm Beach; *Gulfstream International Airlines* from Fort Lauderdale, Fort Myers, Gainesville, Jacksonville, Key West, Orlando, Miami, West Palm beach and Tampa. *Grand Bahama Vacations* flies two weekly non-stop jets from 10 US cities including Pittsburgh and Memphis, and daily from Fort Lauderdale.

There are also several commuter airlines serving some of the Family Islands direct from airports in Florida including *Gulfstream International Airlines* (in Miami T305-8711200, F305-8713540), *Island Express* (T3673597, in USA 954-3590380, F954-3592752), *Walkers International* (T954-3591405, F954-3591414), *US Air Express* (T800-6221015), *Chalk's International* (T800-4242557), (Miami T305-3718628, Bimini T3473024, Nassau T3632845), *Air Sunshine* (T800-4358900), *Continental, American Eagle, Lynx Air* and *Pan Am Airbridge*. Also in Miami, *Bahamasair*, T305-5931910, 800-2224262. Tickets can be booked through computer systems but are normally purchased on the spot at the airport, routing and timing subject to last minute alteration depending on demand. See text for details of services to each island. *LB Limited* (T3523389) has charter flights to Freeport from Florida with some flights timed so that gamblers can do a day-trip to the casino. Other charter airlines including *Cleare Air* (T3770341, F3770342), *Congo Air* (T3778329, F3777413, Fort Lauderdale T305-4565611, F305-9850855) and *Island Air Charters* (T305-3599942, 800-4449904). Private pilots should ask the tourist office for the Air Navigation Chart or contact the Private Pilot Briefing Centre, T800-3277678 in the USA.

To Freeport From the USA *Sea Jets* have two 250-passenger jet foils from Palm Beach **Sea** twice daily, Thu-Mon, 1½ hours, US$99 return (US$49 for children under 16), plus arrival and departure tax of US$25.

Ports of entry (Own flag) **Abaco**: Walker's Cay, Green Turtle Cay, Marsh Harbour, Sandy Point. **Andros**: Morgan's Bluff, Fresh Creek, Mangrove Cay, Congo Town. **Berry Islands**: Great Harbour Cay, Chub Cay. **Bimini**: Alice Town, Cat Cay, Gun Cay. **Eleuthera**: Harbour Island, Hatchet Bay, Governor's Harbour, Rock Sound. **Exuma**: George Town. **Grand Bahama**: West End, Freeport Harbour, Port Lucaya, Lucaya Marina, Xanadu Marina. **Inagua**: Matthew Town. **Long Island**: Stella Maris. **New Providence**: Nassau (any yacht basin). **Ragged Island**: Duncan Town. **San Salvador**: Cockburn Town.

Boat documents Complete duplicate copies of Maritime Declaration of Health, Inwards Report for Pleasure Vehicles and crew/passengers lists required. The vessel will be issued with a one-year cruising permit, US$10. During regular working hours, the only charge is for

The Bahamas

Touching down

Business hours Banks: in Nassau, Monday-Thursday 0930-1500, Friday 0930-1700; in Freeport, Monday-Friday 0900-1300 and Friday 1500-1700. **Shops:** 0900-1700 Monday-Saturday. **Government offices:** 0900-1730 Monday-Friday.

Emergency numbers on New Providence Police: T3224444. **Ambulance:** T3222221. Hospital: T3222861. **Med Evac:** T3222881. **BASRA:** T3223877. The Police have offices at East Bay T3221275, Paradise Island T3633160, Cable Beach T3278800 and downtown T3223114.

Official time Bahamas time is five hours behind GMT, except in summer when Eastern Daylight Time (GMT – four hours) is adopted.

Voltage 120 volt/60 cycles.

Safety Nassau is less dangerous than Kingston or Port of Spain. However visitors should be extremely careful, particularly at night or when venturing off the beaten track. Do not be lulled into a false sense of security. Vigilance is also advised in Freeport. Never leave screen doors open at night, there have been a number of armed robberies and sexual assaults where intruders have just walked in through screen doors left open.

Tipping The usual tip is 15%, including for taxi drivers. Hotels and restaurants include a service charge on the bill, sometimes a flat rate per day, or a percentage.

transportation for the clearing officer. Individuals will be given 60 days clearance with extensions obtained at a port of entry. A boat with a cruising permit may import parts duty-free.

Radio communications Morning ham net 0745-0845 7268; Nassau and George Town have VHF net. Exuma Markets in George Town will accept and hold faxes and mail for visiting boats. Marinas also hold mail, be sure the name of the vessel is clearly marked.

Touching down

Airport information

Airlines American Airlines, T1800-4337300. Air Canada, T3278411. Bahamasair, T3773223 in Nassau, T3528341 in Freeport, 800-2224262 in the USA. Delta Airlines/Comair, T3771043, 800-2211212. Gulfstream International, T3528532. Air Jamaica, T800-5235585. AOM, T3777035. Chalk's International, T3632845. Condor, T800-5246975. Continental, T800-2310856. United, T3524511.

Departure tax Airport and security tax is US$15 from Nassau and US$18 from Freeport except for children under the age of three. US immigration and customs formalities for those going to the USA are carried out at Nassau airport. Harbour departure tax is US$15.

Tourist information

Local tourist offices The Bahamas Ministry of Tourism, Market Plaza, Bay Street, Nassau, Bahamas, T3227500, F3255835, www.bahamas.com There are representatives of the Bahamas Tourist Office on Abaco, Eleuthera, Exuma and throughout the USA. **Maps** The Lands and Surveys Department on East Bay Street, Nassau, PO Box 592, has an excellent stock of maps, including a marine chart of the whole archipelago for US$10 and a 1:25,000 maps covering most of the islands for US$1 per sheet (several sheets per island). These are also available from Fairey Surveys, Maidenhead, Berks, UK. A good, up-to-date street map of New Providence is available from most Bahamian bookstores for US$2.95.

Religion There are about 20 denominations represented in the Bahamas, of which those with the largest congregations are the Baptists, Roman Catholics and Anglicans. There is a synagogue in Nassau and Freeport and a Mosque in Nassau. The Tourist Office publishes a leaflet called Bahamas Places of Worship, with a full list of addresses and services.

Tourist offices overseas

Canada *1255 Phillips Sq, Montreal, T514-8616797; 121 Bloor Street E, Toronto, T416-3634441.*

France *60 rue Saint Lazare, 75009 Paris, T1-45-266262, F-1-48-740605.*

Germany *Leipziger Strasse 67d, D 60487, Frankfurt am Main, T069-9708340, F069-97083434, info-line T01030-813118. Italy, Via Cusani 7, 20121, Milano, T02-72022526, Toll free 02-1678-77225, F02-72023123.*

Japan *4-9-17 Akasaka, Minato-Ku, Tokyo, T813-4706162.*

Sweden *Gumshornsgatan 7, S-11460 Stockholm, T8-6632850, F8-6605780.*

UK *3 The Billings, Walnut Tree Close, Guildford, Surrey, T01483-448900, F01483-571846.* **USA** *150 East 52nd Street, 28th floor N, NY 10022, T212-7582777; also in other major US cities.*

The Bahama Out Islands Promotion Board offices:

Germany, *Am Schleifweg 16, D-55128 Mainz, T0049-613199330, F0049-61319931 www.bahama-out-islands.com* **USA**, *1100 Lee Wagener Boulevard, Suite 204, Fort Lauderdale, FLB3315, T305-3598099, 800-6884752, F305-3598098.*

The Nassau/Paradise Island Promotion Board:

USA, *T800-3279019, in the* **UK** *at Suite 31, Parkway House, Sheen Lane, East Sheen, London, SW14 8LS, T020-88785569, F020-88787854, in* **Canada** *T800-6673777.*

The Bahamas Reservation Service:

UK *79 Dean Street, London W1V 6HY, T020-74349915, F020-7346460 sales@bahamasreservations.co.uk Bahamasair is at the same address, T020-74378766, F020-77346460.*

Where to stay

Accommodation ranges from luxury hotels and resorts with every conceivable facility, to modest guest houses or self-catering apartments and villas. Some of the larger properties have T800 reservations numbers in the USA and Canada. You will often get a cheaper package if you book from abroad. These packages often include restaurants, tours, day trips and airfare and are cheap enough for you to discard the bits you do not want. In restaurants, visitors on a package can pay 25-50% less than locals.

Getting around

Air — *Bahamasair* operates scheduled flights between Nassau and the Family Islands. Charter flights and excursions available through them and several private companies, see Prestel for details. Seaplanes fly to those islands which have no landing strip. Inter-island travel is difficult given that nearly all flights originate in Nassau. To fly from Abaco to Eleuthera with Bahamasair, for example, you have to change planes in Nassau, often with a wait of several hours and thus waste a day. Each island has developed direct transport links with the USA rather than with each other. *Bahamasair* now has a scheme for multiple island destinations (*Discover the Bahamas*) from Miami, Orlando or Nassau, based on the number of flights you want to take, valid 21 days, for example from Miami, four flights US$180; from Orlando eight flights US$380; from Nassau six flights US$125.

Road — Visitors are permitted to drive on a valid foreign licence or International Permit for up to three months. Beyond that they need a local licence issued by the Road Traffic Department in Nassau. Traffic keeps left, although most cars are left-hand drive. Strict speed limits: Nassau and Freeport 30 miles per hour; elsewhere 40 miles per hour. The roads are in good condition but are congested in town; drivers pay scant attention to the laws.

On many of the Family Islands bicycles and mopeds are appropriate. These can be hired in Nassau, Freeport and in many other places through hotels; helmets should be worn. Approximate rates: bicycles US$10 per day, US$40 per week; mopeds: US$30-45 per day. Scooters and light motorcycles can also be hired. Helmets are mandatory. Remember, though, that rates for car and bike hire tend to vary, according to season. Minimum age for hiring in Exuma is 25 years.

Sea **Ferries** In 1999 a high-speed 177-passenger a/c catamaran ferry was launched. The *Bo Hengy* makes daily crossings from Nassau/Paradise Island to Eleuthera, Harbour Island and Spanish Wells, US$90 return (US$50 for children), or US$139 (US$89) for a 'day away', which includes a walking historical tour, lunch and cabana privileges on the pink sand beach. Reported efficient, always on time, excellent value and has virtually replaced Bahamasair as the best way of getting to Eleuthera. A colourful way of travelling between the islands is on the **mail boats**, which also carry passengers and merchandise. They leave from Potter's Cay Dock, just below the Paradise Island Bridge in Nassau, and Woodes Rogers Walk; their drawback is that they are slow and accommodation on board is very basic, but they do go everywhere, usually once a week. The Bahamas Family Islands Association has a helpful brochure listing fares (US$20-50) and schedules, but do not expect the boats to leave according to the timetable. For the latest information listen to the radio on ZNS, which lists the daily schedule with last minute changes broadcast at lunchtime, or ask for information at the Dock Master's office on Potter's Cay, T3931064.

We give here the name of the boat, its destination and travel time: *Bahamas Daybreak III*, to North Eleuthera, Spanish Wells, Harbour Island, Bluff, 5½ hours; *Captain Moxey*, to South Andros, Kemp's Bay, Long Bay Cays, Bluff, 7½ hours; *Central Andros Express*, to Fresh Creek, Staniard Creek, Blanket Sound, Bowne Sound, 3½ hours; *Sea Hauler*, to Cat Island, Bluff, Smith's Bay, 10 hours; *North Cat Island Special*, to North Cat Island, Arthur's Town, Bennet's Harbour, 14 hours; *Maxine*, to San Salvador, United Estates, Rum Cay, 18 hours; *Grand Master, Seahauler, Lady Roslyn, Captain Moxey*, to Exuma, George Town, Mt Thompson, 14 hours; *Abilin*, to Long Island, Clarence Town, 18 hours; *Champion II*, to Abaco, Sandy Point, Bullock Harbour, Moore Island, 11 hours; *Lisa J II*, to North Andros, Nichol's Town, Mastic Point, Lowe Sound, five hours; *Lady Francis*, to Exuma Cays, Staniel Cay, Black Point, Farmer's Cay, Barraterre; *Deborah K*, Abaco, Marsh Harbour, Hope Town, Treasure Cay, Green Turtle Cay, Coopers Town, 12 hours; *Mangrove Cay Express* to Mangrove Cay, Lisbon Creek, 5½ hours; *Lady Gloria* to Mangrove Cay, Behring Point, Cargill Creek, five hours; *Current Pride* to Current Island, Upper and Lower Bogue, Eleuthera, five hours; *Emmette and Cephas* to Ragged Island, 21 hours; *Bahamas Daybreak III*, to Rock Sound, Davis Harbour, South Eleuthera, seven hours; *Nay Dean*, to North Long Island, Salt Pond, Deadman's Cay, Stella Maris, 14 hours; *Marcella III*, to Grand Bahama, Freeport, High Rock, Eight Mile Rock, West End, 12 hours; *Windward Express*, to Crooked Island, Acklins, Mayaguana, Inagua; *Spanish Rose*, to Spanish Wells, 5½ hours; *Eleuthera Express*, to Rock Sound, five hours; *Challenger*, to North Andros; *Lady Margo*, also to North Andros; *Eleuthera Express*, Spanish Wells, Harbour Island, five hours; *Bimini Mack*, to Bimini, Cat Cay, 12 hours.

Yacht charter A pleasant way of seeing the islands is to charter your own yacht and several companies offer boats with or without crews. *Abaco Bahamas Charters* (ABC) is based in Hope Town. *Bahamas Yachting Service* (BYS) is based in Marsh Harbour, Abaco, T305-4678644 or toll free 800-3272276 in North America, prices start from about US$50 per person per day. *Moorings* bases its bareboat charters at Marsh Harbour and has crewed yacht charters in George Town, Exuma. Contact the Bahamas Reservation Service for the Bahamas Marina Guide, marina reservations, known as 'book-a-slip', with details of over 50 marinas in the Bahamas and confirmation of boat slip reservations down as far as Grand Turk. Most resort islands have boats to rent.

Keeping in touch

Post Main post office is at East Hill Street, Nassau. Letters to North America and the Caribbean US$0.65, to Europe and South America US$0.60; to Africa, Asia and Australia US$0.70. All postcards US$0.40. Air mail to Europe takes 4-8 days, surface mail takes a couple of months. There is no door to door mail delivery in the Bahamas, everything goes to a PO Box. Parcels must be opened at the Post Office with customs officials present. Stamp collectors can contact the Bahamas Philatelic Bureau at East Hill Street, PO Box N8302, Nassau, for current mint stamps and first day covers.

There is a public telephone and cable open 24 hours in the *Batelco* office on East Street, near the BITCO building in Nassau. *Batelco* also provides internet services. International calls can be made and faxes sent/received from here; also Prince George Dock, Shirley Street, Blue Hill Road, Mall at Marathon, Golden Gates and Fox Hill (0700-2000). *Batelco's* mailing address is PO Box N3048, Nassau (T3234911). Grand Bahama, New Providence and most of the other islands have automatic internal telephone systems. Direct dialling is available from New Providence and most of the other islands all over the world. International calls are expensive: US$5 per minute to the UK through the operator, US$2.50 to the Caribbean. Pay phones can be used to contact USA Direct (1-800-2822881) for more economical rates than *Batelco*. Credit card facilities. Phone cards are now quite widely available in denominations of US$5, US$10 and US$20. A call to the UK with a phone card is US$4 per minute. Not all phones take cards. Facilities are available at most Batelco offices in Nassau and Freeport, Nassau and Freeport airports and several of the Family Islands. Videoconferencing facilities at Batelco's offices in the Mall at Marathon, Nassau and in Freeport. Cellular service is available for most islands. Check with *Batelco* to see if they have reciprocal agreements with your cellular company, otherwise sign up for a roaming agreement.

Telephone
International code: 242

Newspapers There are three daily newspapers: the *Nassau Guardian*, *The Tribune* and the *Bahama Journal*. There are lots of tourist magazines, for example *What's On, Dining and Entertainment Guide, Nassau, Cable Beach, Paradise Island*; *What-To-Do, Freeport Lucaya*; *Getaway, Bahamas Out Islands*; *The Cruising Guide to Abaco, Bahamas* (annual); *Abaco Life*. **Radio** The local commercial radio stations are ZNS1, owned by the Government and covering all the Bahamas, ZNS2 and ZNS3 covering New Providence and the North Bahamas. There are also Radio Abaco, Cool 96 (Freeport), More FM (Nassau) and Love 97 (Nassau). The local commercial television station is ZNS TV 13. Transmissions from Florida can be picked up and satellite reception is common.

Media

The People-to-People programme is a recommended way to meet local Bahamians. Fill in a form from the Ministry of Tourism giving age, occupation and interests and you will be matched with a Bahamian. Each experience is different but it might lead to a meal in a Bahamian home, a tour of out of the way places or a trip to church. They also hold a tea party at Government House in January to August on the last Friday of each month and can arrange weddings. T3265371, F3280945 in Nassau or 3528044, F3522714 in Freeport, or ask at your hotel. The programme is also available in Eleuthera (T3322142, F3322480), Abaco (T3673067, F3673068), San Salvador, Exuma (T3362430, F3662431) and Bimini.

People-to-People

Food and drink

Conch is the staple diet of many Bahamians. It is considered an aphrodisiac and a source of virility, especially the small end part of the conch which is bitten off and eaten from the live conch for maximum effect. Conch is prepared in a variety of ways; conch fritters and cracked conch are both coated in batter and fried, while conch salad is made from raw, shredded conch, onion, lime, lettuce and tomatoes. It can be bought daily from vendors who let you choose your conch from their truck and will 'jewk' it from the shell and prepare it for you in salad. Although delicious, conch has been linked to major outbreaks of food poisoning, so treat with caution. Bahamian cuisine is tasty, if a little predictable. The standard fare at most parties/cookouts is peas'n'rice, barbecue ribs and chicken wings, conch salad or fritters, potato salad, coleslaw and macaroni. Bahamian potato salad and macaroni are far richer than their English/Italian counterparts. The Bahamas have some good fruit: sapodilla, mango, breadfruit, sugar apple and pawpaw. Try soursop ice cream, coconut tarts and sugar bananas,

Conch, crab, grouper, snapper, dolphin (not the Flipper variety) & other seafood are on all the menus

The Bahamas

which have an apple flavour. Guava duff is a popular sweet, a bit like jam roly poly pudding topped with guava sauce (often flavoured with rum). Tap water can be salty; Bahamians drink bottled water, bought at the supermarket. The local beer brewed in Nassau, Kalik, is worth trying, it has won several international prizes. The local rum is Bacardi; the Anejo variety is OK. Bahama Mammas, Yellowbirds and Island Woman are all popular rum-based cocktails. Many bars have their own special cocktails.

Shopping

For those who want to pick up a bargain, prices of crystal, china and jewellery are cheaper than in the USA. You can find designer clothes and other goods from all over the world at the International Bazaar in Freeport. Local products including straw items, Androsia batik printed silk and cotton, shell jewellery and wood carvings. Bargaining is expected in the markets. Duty-free shopping was introduced on 11 categories of goods on 1 January 1992; the Bahamas Duty-Free Promotion Board was formed to monitor the system and ensure that merchants participating in the scheme sell authentic goods.

Sport

Fishing   Annual fishing permits: US$20 per boat for hook and line. Lobster season from 1 August to 31 March. Conch must have fully formed lip to be taken. Hawaiian slings are permitted but spearfishing is not. Within Bahamas National Parks you may not fish, take lobster, conch, coral or shells, etc. Fishing is good all year with peak times for bonefish in March to April, permit March to August, snapper Spring to Summer, barracuda June to August, blue marlin March to July, white marlin March to June, sailfish March to June, broadbill swordfish May to September, Allison tuna March to May, blackfin tuna May to July, bluefin tuna April to June. The best flats for reef fishing are found off Andros, the Abacos, Eleuthera, the Exumas, Grand Bahama and San Salvador. The best big game fishing is off Bimini, also good off Cat Island, Chub Cay, Nassau, the Abacos and many other islands. Contact the tourist office for lists of operators, fishing lodges and prices.

Scuba diving   In addition to the land-based dive operators mentioned in the text for each island, there are several liveaboard boats which cruise the Bahamas and offer less crowded and unspoilt sites: *Blackbeard's Cruises*, contact Bruce Purdy, PO Box 66-1091, *Miami Springs*, FL 33266, T800-3279600, 305-8881226, F305-8844214, sales@blackbeard-cruises.com; *Bottom Time Adventures Inc*, contact AJ Bland, Elizabeth Longtin, PO Box 11919, Fort Lauderdale, FL 33339-1919, T800-2348464, F954-9205578; *Nekton Diving Cruises*, contact Lynn A Oetzman, 520 SE 32nd Street, Fort Lauderdale, FL 33316, T954-4639324, F954-4638938; the first Bahamian owned and operated boat, *MV Ballymena*, *Out Island Voyages*, contact James or Marilynn Nottage, PO Box N-7775, Nassau, T242-3940951, F3940948; *Sea Fever Diving Cruises*, contact Tom Guarino, Cynthia Herod, PO Box 398 276, Miami Beach, FL 33239, T954-12025608, www.seafever.com, *Sea Dragon*, contact Dan Doyle, Sue Ford, 717SW Coconut Drive, Fort Lauderdale, FL 33315, T954-5220161. All the above are BDA members. There are hyperbaric chambers in Freeport, Lyford Cay and Andros. All dive operators should carry oxygen and a first aid kit. Diving can be enjoyed all year round although the waters are cooler in the winter months: about 76°F in the northern Bahamas. In the summer the water temperature rises to about 84°F throughout the island chain. Possession of spearguns is illegal.

Holidays and festivals

Public holidays   New Year's Day, Good Friday, Easter Monday (very busy at the airport), Whit Monday, Labour
See individual island   Day (first Friday in June, a parade is organized by the trade unions), Independence Day (10
listings for local   July), Emancipation Day (first Monday in August), Discovery Day (12 October), Christmas Day,
festivals   Boxing Day.

Further reading

Out-island Doctor by **Evans Cottman** (Hodder and Stoughton) gives a picture of the 1940s; an interesting comparison can be made with *Cocaine Wars* by **Paul Eddy** et al (Bantam), a fascinating study of the 1980s. *Talkin' Bahamian*, by **Patricia Glinton Meicholas**, is a charming collection of tongue-in-cheek definitions of popular Bahamian sayings, complete with cartoon illustrations. *The Bahamas Handbook*, Dupuch Publications, is an annual publication for residents and visitors with detailed information on government, the economy, finance, history, investment and tourism. For a history of Paradise Island, read *Paradise Island Story*, by **Paul Albury** (Macmillan Caribbean).

New Providence

New Providence is in the centre of the Bahamas archipelago and is one of the smallest major islands, at only 80 square miles, yet two thirds of the population live here. The centre of Nassau has some fine historic buildings and there are some good beaches, but most of the island is covered by sprawling suburbia, scrubby woodland or swamp. Paradise Island, just off the north coast, is 826 acres of tourist resort. Once known as Hog Island, because it reminded Governor Nicholas Trott of his pig farm in Bermuda, it was developed in the 1950s by Huntington Hartford as a resort. The name was changed after a bridge was built to connect the island with Nassau and the first casino licence was granted.

Population: 180,000

The Bahamas

Ins and outs

Nassau International Airport (NAS), is about 14 miles from Nassau. Taxi to Cable Beach US$12, to Nassau US$17-20 and to Paradise Island US$20-25. Third and subsequent extra passengers should be charged US$3, but drivers sometimes try to charge everyone a separate full fare, which is illegal. Make sure meter is turned on and used. There is no public bus service to or from the airport, though some hotels have buses. For the return journey there is a bus from Nassau to Clifton (US$1.50); it leaves on the hour from Bay and Frederick Sts (Western Transportation Company) and will drop you 1½ miles from the airport, not recommended option. Left luggage space is available in lockers outside the doors mid-way between the domestic and international ends of the terminal, they take 4 US quarter coins.

Getting there

See transport, page 86, for further information

Buses called 'jitneys', are mostly a/c and good value at US$0.75, carrying from 9-44 people and going all over New Providence Island between 0630 and 2000. Have the exact fare, by

Getting around

New Providence

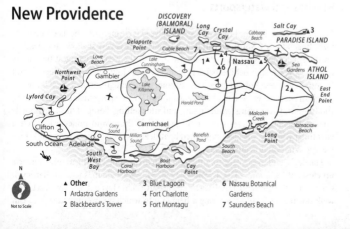

N
Not to Scale

▲ Other	3 Blue Lagoon	6 Nassau Botanical
1 Ardastra Gardens	4 Fort Charlotte	Gardens
2 Blackbeard's Tower	5 Fort Montagu	7 Saunders Beach

law the driver keeps the change. If you want to see some of the island catch any bus in town and it will bring you back about an hour later. They can be crowded but service is regular. To cross to Paradise Island from Woodes Rogers Walk take the Paradise Express boat for US$2, it leaves when full and stops at several docks on Paradise Island. A small rental **car** can cost US$70 a day or US$400-450 a week. Prices depend on the model and features. **Bicycles** can be hired for US$10 per day with US$10 deposit. Traffic for such a small island is busy and roads are not well maintained. Take care.

Diving and marine life

Dive sites Wrecks have been planted by film crews off the southwest corner of New Providence, which attract scuba divers eager to see the underwater scenes of James Bond films (the James Bond wreck was damaged by Hurricane Andrew and the front part collapsed, but it is still being dived), or Walt Disney's *20,000 Leagues Under the Sea* was filmed. Just off Paradise Island there is a series of caves and a 19th-century wreck, there is a Blue Hole 10 miles east of Nassau, while to the west of New Providence there are dramatic walls and drops leading to the mile-deep 'Tongue of the Ocean'. Marine conservation is not as highly developed as in some of the other Bahamian islands where dive tourism is promoted, although there are 50 permanent moorings and seven dive operations, all offering PADI certification courses and trips to wrecks, reefs and walls, as well as other activities. Shark feeding and swimming with dolphins are two popular dives. The former involves sitting on the ocean floor and watching a dive master, clad in chain mail or other protective gear, feed several large sharks. Critics claim that more sharks are attracted to the dive site than is natural and are becoming dependent upon daily handouts.

Dive centres On the south coast, Stuart Cove's *Dive South Ocean* is particularly recommended (T3624171, F3625227), but the others include *Bahama Divers Ltd* (T3935644/1466, F3936078, www.bahamadivers.com, East Bay Street, in the Nassau Yacht Haven Marina), *Dive, Dive, Dive Ltd* (T3621143/1401, F3621994, Coral Harbour, Nitrox certification available), *Diver's Haven* (T3933285, F3933695, East Bay Street), *Nassau Scuba Centre* (T3621964/1379, F3621198, Coral Harbour) and *Sunskiff Divers Ltd* (T/F3621979, Coral Harbour, speciality diving). The cost of a two-tank scuba dive with all equipment and transport included is about US$70. A learn-to-dive package costs much the same and enables you to dive with the same company throughout your stay on the island. Snorkelling trips for non-divers are US$25-35. Shark dives cost US$75 or more; you can see silky sharks, bull sharks and reef sharks. Stuart Cove's *Dive South Ocean* also offers a Shark Awareness certification course for US$210.

Beaches and watersports

Beaches are best near the hotels where the seaweed is cleaned off. The nicest ones are **Love Beach** (west), **South Ocean Beach** (the sea here is very shallow) and beaches on the small islands off New Providence. One of the best and longest beaches is **Lyford Cay**, which is behind barriers in an exclusive housing area for the rich and famous in the west, but not impossible to enter with enough confidence. It is unwise to go to a beach where you might be on your own. Watersports include **waterskiing** (no tuition), **parasailing**, **windsurfing** and **snorkelling**. Some of the larger hotels offer full facilities to guests and non-guests. For those who prefer a less active encounter with the sea, glass-bottomed boats leave several times a day from Prince George Wharf in downtown Nassau.

Hartley's Undersea Walk, for those not keen to dive but wanting to see coral reefs up close, at 0930 and 1330, US$40 (T3938234, www.bahamasnet.com/hartleys). Check in at the houseboat, *Full Circle*, at Nassau Yacht Haven, East Bay Street. You walk down a 12 ft ladder wearing a helmet into which air is pumped so you can breath normally. The *Seaworld Explorer* is a semi-submarine which descends 10-15 ft and is reached by a shuttle boat which leaves from Captain Nemo's dock. Two trips daily except Sunday and Wednesday of 1½ hours, 1100 and 1500, US$33 adults, US$19 children under 12, T3238426, 3562548. Stuart Cove's (see above) offers a 40-minute underwater trip in a sub (scenic underwater bubble), which is a submersible scooter with a clear dome allowing a 180° view of the undersea world. No scuba or snorkelling experience is necessary, just US$89, which includes pilot guides, T3624171.

For **island cruises**, the Calypso Blue Lagoon trip and Rose Island excursions aboard large MVs with three decks are recommended (daily at 1000 except Wednesday, T3633577, US$35 for the day with lunch, although it is unlikely to be as good as in the brochure pictures, no complimentary snorkelling equipment). The *Swim With The Dolphins Experience* is at Blue Lagoon, Salt Cay, reached by tender from several cruise ships or on a day excursion with Calypso 1 and 11, reservations required, T3631003, www.dolphinswims.com You get a 15-minute lecture on the dolphins, then you wade or swim with the dolphins; a full-day trip including lunch, drinks, beach, equipment, is US$75 or US$145. *Flying Cloud* catamaran cruises depart from Paradise Island West Dock for sunset, half-day, dinner or Sunday cruises for US$35-50 including snorkelling gear and transport from hotels (T3931957). *Sea Island Adventure* also do boat trips to Rose Island with lunch, snorkelling etc (T3253910, 3282581, www.bahamasnet.com/seaisland), while *Yellow Bird* (250 passengers) and *Tropic Bird* (170 passengers) catamarans cater to cruise ships with three-hour cruises. *Top Sail Yacht Charters* (T3930820) have three boats and offer an all-day cruise from *British Colonial Hilton Hotel* dock 0945, Paradise Island ferry dock 1015, arriving Rose Island 1200, depart 1400, snorkelling included, US$49, private charters from US$370.

Powerboat Adventures go further in a high-speed boat; day trip departing from Captain Nemo's dock 0900, with lavish picnic to the Exuma Cays for US$159, including seeing iguanas on Allan's Cay, a nature trail walk and drift snorkelling (T3261936, 3275385, Monday-Friday 0800-2000). *Out Island Safaris* (seaplane and boat, Captain Paul Harding, T3932522/1179) also offers day trips to other islands, for example Harbour Island, the Exumas, Hope Town, with scuba, snorkelling and lunch. A captained boat for **fishing** trips is US$300 for four hours or US$600 for a day for up to six people (T3632335, Captain Jesse Pinder, or T3228148, F3264140, Captain Mike Russell of Chubasco Charters, or T3934144, 3632003, Captain Philip Pinder, excellent), or arranged through hotel tour desks for US$60 per person for a half day.

The most popular and well-developed sport on dry land is probably **golf**. There are four world class courses on New Providence: *Cable Beach Golf Course* (T3278617), *South Ocean Golf Club* (T3624391), *Ocean Club Golf Course* on Paradise Island (T3633000) and the private *Lyford Cay Golf Course*. Green fees vary and hotel guests can get package deals or discounts. **Other sports**

There are over 100 **tennis** courts in the Nassau/Cable Beach/Paradise Island area and many of them are lit for night-time play until 2200 (with an extra charge). Most of the larger hotels have tennis courts, usually free for guests. *The Racquets Club*, on Independence Drive (T3231854) has **squash** courts at about US$7 per hour. Very popular with Bahamians, it has European-sized courts. *The Radisson Resort Sports Centre* charges US$6 an hour for guests, US$10 for others, and has racquet-ball, squash and tennis available. Smarter, but the squash courts are smaller, being converted racquet-ball courts.

You can go **horse riding** for US$45 an hour, including transport, along the beach at *Happy Trails*, Coral Harbour (T3621820).

Cricket is played every Saturday and Sunday during the cricket season (5 March to 27 November) at Haynes Oval, West Bay Street, Nassau. Matches begin at 1200. For further details contact Sydney Deveaux of the Bahamas Cricket Association, T3221875.

The Bahamas

Gambling at *Paradise Island and Crystal Palace* casinos, 1000-0400. Enquire about lessons free of charge. Fascinating to see the massed ranks of flashing fruit machines and the many games tables. Bahamians and permanent residents are not allowed to gamble in the casinos.

Nassau

Nassau is the capital of the Bahamas. It looks comfortably old-fashioned with its white and pink houses: by-laws forbid skyscrapers. Bay Street is the main shopping street, which is packed with cruise ship visitors seeking duty-free bargains during the day, but deserted at night. Parliament Square is typical of the colonial architecture with the Houses of Assembly, the old Colonial Secretary's Office and the Supreme Court clustered around a statue of Queen Victoria.

On the north side of the Parliament Square, government buildings overlook the bust of Sir Milo B Butler, the first Bahamian Governor-General. To the right, 25-minute surrey rides can be taken through the town. ■ *US$10 per person (horses rest 1300-1500 May-Oct, 1300-1400 Nov-Apr)*. Walking up Parliament Street you pass the Cenotaph on the left and the *Parliament Inn*, built in the 1930s, on the right. The octagonal pink building bordering on Shirley Street is the **Public Library**, built in 1798, which was once used as a prison. Inside you can climb stairs and look out from the balcony, but unfortunately the old dungeons below are no longer open to the public. ■ *T3224907. Mon-Thu 1000-2000, Fri 1000-1700, Sat 1000-1600*. Opposite the library is the site of the *Royal Victoria Hotel*, the first hotel in the Bahamas, built in 1859-61, which closed in 1971. It was built by the Government to accommodate the influx of visitors during the American Civil War, but sold in 1898, after when it changed hands several times. There is not much to see and it looks like a park with some lovely tall trees providing shade, while much of it is used as a car park.

Nassau

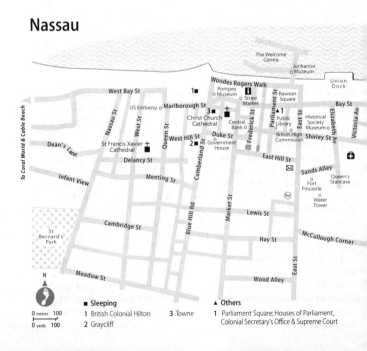

■ Sleeping		▲ Others
1 British Colonial Hilton	3 Towne	1 Parliament Square; Houses of Parliament,
2 Graycliff		Colonial Secretary's Office & Supreme Court

The Bahamas

On Elizabeth Av on the corner with Shirley Street is the **Bahamas Historical Society**, which organizes monthly talks and houses a small museum. There is a collection of old pictures, historical documents, a few old household items and things brought up from the sea, not all of which are well-labelled; it is an old-fashioned display with little information. ■ *Mon-Fri 1000-1600, Sat 1000-1200, closed Thur, T3224231.* Nearby is the **Queen's Staircase**. The 65 steps (102 ft climb) at the end of a gorge (thought to have been cut out of the limestone by slaves in 1790, the canyon is now lined with palm trees and there is an attractive waterfall alongside the steps) lead to the ruined **Fort Fincastle**. Ignore men offering information on the history of the area unless you want to pay for it. They are very persistent. The fort itself was built in 1789 in the shape of a ship's bow. The Water Tower beside the fort was declared a water landmark in 1993. Take the lift (US$0.50) or the stairs to the top to see the shape of the fort. This is the highest point on the island (216 ft above sea level) and gives some lovely views of the island. There is another guide at the top who also expects a tip. The area is heavily visited by cruise ship tours and there are many souvenir stalls.

Government House in traditional Bahamian pink (built 1801) is pretty. Gregory's Arch is an overpass to Government House. On alternate Saturday mornings at 1000, the Royal Bahamian Police Force Band plays in front of the **Christopher Columbus Statue** at the top of the flight of stairs. **Balcony House** on Market Street is the oldest wooden residence in Nassau, built in the 18th century. ■ *T3262568. Mon, Wed, Fri, 1000-1600, closed 1300-1400, donations required.* On West Hill Street is a plaque set in the rock which claims the site as being that of the oldest church in Nassau. Further along the street you pass several old houses including the Postern Gate on the left and the Sisters of Charity Convent on the right. Turning down the steps to Queen Street you pass by some of the oldest and prettiest houses in Nassau (no 16 is said to be 200 years old). The **St Francis Xavier Catholic Cathedral** is on West Street and down the hill is the quaint **Greek Orthodox Church** in blue and white. **Christ Church Cathedral** (built 1837) stands on the corner of George's Street and immediately to the south is **Lex House**, thought to have housed the Spanish Garrison in 1782-83.

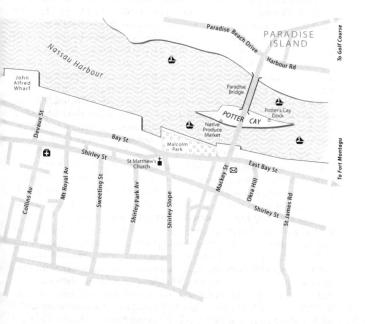

The Bahamas

Vendue House on Bay Street, close to the *British Colonial Hilton Hotel*, was the site of slave auctions, and has now been restored (with a grant from Bacardi to commemorate 1492) and converted into the **Pompey Museum**. It has drawings, artefacts and documents relating to slavery and emancipation in the Bahamas. The collection is limited but well displayed and interesting. Upstairs there is a permanent art exhibition of paintings by Mr Amos Ferguson, who uses house paints. ■ *Mon-Fri 1000-1630, Sat 1000-1300, adults US$1, children under 12, US$0.50.* The renowned **Straw Market** has the offices of the Ministry of Tourism above. Almost all the straw work is imported from East Asia and is no longer native (better prices upstairs); they also sell carvings, jewellery and T-shirts. Bargain with the saleswomen but do not expect to get more than 15% off the originally stated price. Running behind the market is the enormous **Wellcome Centre** (formerly **Prince George Wharf**) which can take up to 11 big cruise ships at once (peak time Saturday). A multi-million dollar renovation programme has been completed and it now has brightly painted and covered seating areas, a hair braiding area and sidewalk stalls where vendors have wares similar to the main straw market on Bay Street, just a few hundred yards away. Enlargement of the terminal allows the mega-cruise ships to come to Nassau. The **Junkanoo Museum** on the waterfront, also renovated, shows the colourful costumes used in the parades. Highly recommended, good chance to see the workmanship up close. ■ *0900-1700 daily, closed on holidays, US$2 for adults, US$0.50 children, T3562731.* Guided **walking tours** of old Nassau start from Rawson Square, daily at 1000 and 1400, US$2, contact the Tourist Information Centre, T3269772.

Around the island

Go west along Bay Street, past Nassau Street and continue to the Road Traffic Centre where you turn left to **Fort Charlotte**, built in 1787-89 out of limestone. It has a dry moat and battlements. The fort was manned during the Napoleonic Wars but never saw action. The soldiers left some interesting graffiti. Look down on the cricket field, the guns (not original cannon), Arawak Cay and the west end of Paradise Island. Guides will fill you in on the history for a small tip or just wander at leisure. The guides have Ministry of Tourism name badges and are not as pushy as at Fort Fincastle.

Arawak Cay, along West Bay St, opposite the cricket pitch, is now the site of the annual Junkanoo in June at the weekends. It is also home to the Arawak Cay Fish Fry, where, from 0900-2300 every day, you can sample fried fish and conch salad, freshly prepared at a collection of some 20 wooden frame eateries painted in bright Junkanoo colours. Initially a small entrepreneurial effort by a few out of work fishermen, it has slowly won the approval of the Ministry of Tourism. The buildings have expanded their menus to include salads and other hot and cold seafood dishes, while some have added a second storey, with balconies providing great views of the neighbourhood. Locals play dominoes or checkers, or you can catch the sports news on TV. Live bands perform on the patios during the weekend evenings.

Crystal Cay Marine Park and Observatory is on a 16-acre island, reached by a bridge from the manmade Arawak Cay (made when the harbour was dredged to allow cruise ships in), which is in turn reached by a bridge. Highlights include descending the observatory tower to view the sea below (lots of fish and masses of lobsters), wandering through the excellent indoor exhibits of reef ecology, watching sting ray and sharks feed and selecting your own oyster with a pearl inside. The only drawback is the small size of the pools housing turtles, rays and sharks. A snorkelling trail has been added, US$12 for hire of mask, snorkel and fins, and mandatory life jacket. It is open 0930-1600, off a small beach overlooking Arawak Cay, where there are plenty of rest rooms and sun beds. Allow half a day for a visit. There is a restaurant, gift shops and also stands with sea biscuits and sand dollars for sale. ■ *T3281036. 0900-1800, US$16 adults, US$11 children, annual membership US$21 adults, US$15 children, under 4s free. A US$3 bus runs from Cable Beach, a US$3 boat* goes from Woodes Rodgers dock (daily except Thur, 1015, 1230, 1530, return 1200, 1500, 1700), or a US$3 bus from Paradise Island.

Going up Chippingham Road you come to the **Nassau Botanic Gardens** where there are 18 acres of tropical plants. ■ *Mon-Fri, 0800-1600, Sat-Sun 0900-1600, adults US$1, children US$0.50.* Also **The Ardastra Gardens and Zoo**. Trained, parading flamingos march just after 1100, 1400, and 1600, but can be a disappointment. There are also parrots and some other animals, but not really enough to warrant the term zoo. ■ *T3235806. 0900-1700, last admission 1630, adults US$7.50, children US$3.75.*

Going west along the coast, Saunders Beach is bordered by casuarina trees and Brown's Point looks across to the *Nassau Marriott Resort and Crystal Casino* (and *Radisson Resort*) at **Cable Beach**, which at night is a multi-coloured sight when the dayglo lights are switched on. Leaving Cable Beach you soon come to Delaporte Point (once a slave village) and Sandy Port residential areas. Further on are some local bars (*Nesbits* is very popular in the evenings) where you can buy drinks and native conch salad before you get to some limestone caves. There is an inscription commemorating the first visit by the British Royal Family in 1841. Just beyond is **Conference Corner** where Macmillan, Kennedy and Diefenbaker planted trees in 1962. At this point Blake Road leads to the airport while West Bay Street continues past Orange Hill Beach and Gambier Village, another slave village. *Travellers Rest*, a bar and restaurant, overlooks the sea, and is very pleasant to watch the sunset (excellent daiquiris and minced lobster). **Love Beach** further on the right is probably one of the best beaches on New Providence. Park on the side of the road and walk down between the apartments, you can not see the beach from the road. *Compass Point Beach Club* is on this stretch of coast. You can walk along the beach at the trendy *Club*, and across the street is the Compass Point Recording Studio, both of which are Chris Blackwell properties, brightening up the oldest community on New Providence Island.

Continuing as far west as you can go you reach **Lyford Cay**, a private residential area for the rich, protected by barriers. Turn left at the roundabout for Clifton, a stretch of rocky coast now being developed for a power station and industry. In 2000 **Clifton** was the site of some controversy when a US$400 mn tourism project was proposed for a 600-acre beachfront location. Environmentalists and locals campaigned against the planned digging of canals for boats because it would remove sand, destroy the habitat of turtles, and three endangered bird species, and threaten two Lucayan Indian villages and the remains of a walled slave plantation. The luxury gated estate would also restrict public access to the beach. The road then leads to South West Bay where you can turn off to visit the *Clarion Hotel* and beachfront (a good stop for a swim and a drink) before returning east. After two miles there is a signpost to **Adelaide Village**. This settlement is one of the oldest, founded when illegal slave traders were intercepted by the British Navy in the 19th century and the human cargo was taken to the Bahamas. The traditional houses are brightly painted, the beach is quite good, though the water is shallow, and the bars prepare fresh fish or conch salad. Continue east on Adelaide Road and you come to the Coral Harbour roundabout. To the right, the Bahamas Defence Force has its base. Coral Harbour was designed as a second Lyford Cay, exclusive, with security barriers, but when it was built in the 1960s there was considerable local opposition to it becoming a select ghetto. The development company went bankrupt leaving it incomplete. The shell of the hotel still stands and the area is now an upper middle class subdivision. At the roundabout you can turn off for the airport or join Carmichael Road and you will pass the Bacardi Company, open weekdays until 1600. At the end of Carmichael Road turn left to go along Blue Hill Road and join Independence Drive at the roundabout (with the cock on top). Here on the north side is the Town Centre Shopping Mall. In this area you will see many examples of the Government's low-cost housing. Rows of rectangular houses have been painted and adapted by their owners to make each one individual. Notice also that cemeteries are built on hills, where you can dig

The Bahamas

down 6 ft and not hit water; elsewhere water is too close to the surface.

Continue east on Independence until you come to traffic lights with another mall. At Marathon Mall turn right on to Prince Charles Drive and follow this to the sea. Turn left and you will be on Eastern Road, which hugs the coast and has many impressive homes overlooking the sea. **Blackbeard's Tower**, an old lookout point, is now closed. **Fort Montagu** (and beach), constructed in 1741, is famous for having been captured briefly by Americans during the Revolution. It is a rather smelly area where conch and fish are sold. If you turn left into Shirley Street and immediately left again into Village Road, you will come to **The Retreat** (opposite Queen's College), the headquarters of the Bahamas National Trust and an 11-acre botanical park. ■ *Guided tours (20 min) US$2, Tue-Thu at 1150*. Members of the BNT (PO Box N4105) are entitled to discounts at several tourist destinations locally (for example Crystal Cay, Power Boat Adventures, Ardastra Gardens) and free admission to National Trust properties worldwide. The BNT was set up in 1959. It publishes a quartely newsletter, *Currents*.

Returning to East Bay Street you will pass the *Club Waterloo* and the *Nassau Yacht Club* before reaching the toll bridge which crosses over to **Paradise Island**. A new bridge was opened at the end of 1998 and traffic now crosses over to Paradise Island on the new bridge (US$1 per car), returning to Nassau via the old bridge. Alternatively there is a water taxi, US$2, to the Calypso Dock on Paradise Island. Stop at the **Versailles Gardens and Cloisters** on the way to the Ocean Club golf course. The gardens with various statues were allowed to fall into disrepair for a while, but have been restored. The Augustinian cloisters were brought in pieces from France and date back to the 14th century. The gazebo looking across to Nassau is a favourite spot for weddings. The *Atlantis Resort* with its aquarium and waterscapes is worth a visit; you could spend half a day walking the pathways among turtle habitats, the predator pool and the aquarium (see the huge jewfish), including one with a glass tunnel where sharks swim all round you (all for free). Paradise had some lovely stretches of beach on the north side, but most of the island has now been gobbled up by *Atlantis* construction crews adding condos on one side of the island and more hotel rooms on the other. Unless you are an *Atlantis* hotel guest, you'll look long and hard before finding a stretch of accessible beach.

Potters Cay, next to the old Paradise Island toll bridge, has the main fish and produce market. Try freshly made conch salad or scorched conch, very spicy and fresh.

Essentials

Sleeping
You can usually pick up a cheaper package deal in the USA than by arranging a hotel on arrival

The two main resort areas on New Providence are **Cable Beach**, which stretches 3 miles west of Nassau along the north coast, and **Paradise Island**, 5 mins across Nassau harbour. The benefit of staying at Cable Beach is that the jitney service into town is very easy to use, while from Paradise Island you need a taxi. Other hotels are in the town and suburbs. There is a great variety of accommodation, ranging from small guest houses, offering only rooms, to luxury hotels and sprawling resorts. *Small Treasures* are a collection of small hotels which have been inspected by the Ministry of Tourism, T800-3279019 for directory and comments, T800-5233782 for reservations. Prices vary according to the season. Standards at hotels are good, helped by the privatization of state hotels, greater competition and huge refurbishment programmes, but even so, service is slow at reception desks. Watch out for tax (8-10%), resort levies (10%), fuel surcharges and compulsory maid gratuities which are added to the basic price quoted. Up to date rates available at the Tourist Information Centres in Nassau, or write to the Tourist Offices listed on page 86.

Nassau The most expensive hotel is **LL-AL** *Graycliff*, West Hill, PO Box N-10246, T3222796, F3266110. 14 large rooms in an 18th-century mansion, some suites, some balconies, Olympic sized swimming pool, jacuzzi, sauna, elegant gourmet restaurant boasting the largest wine cellar in the Caribbean, cigars a speciality, produced by Graycliff Cigar Co using Cuban cigar rollers. The largest hotel is **L-AL** *British Colonial Hilton Hotel* conveniently located at the beginning of Bay St, PO Box N-7148, T3223301, F3222286. Built in 1923 on site of Fort Nassau, the cannon outside were found when the foundations were dug, being restored to its former glory, small beach, complimentary non-motorized watersports, view of cruise ships. **L** *Holiday Inn Junkanoo Beach Hotel*, opposite the Western Esplanade, 5-min walk from town centre, PO Box SS-19055, T3560000, F3231408. Good value, small but nicely appointed dining room. **D** *Diplomat Inn*, Delancey St on top of the hill, PO Box N-4, T3252688, F3562138. Budget hotel in a less salubrious area.

Nearby on West Bay St close to the junction with Nassau St, are middle range hotels along the road overlooking Long Walk Beach: **A-C** *El Greco*, PO Box N4187, West Bay and Augusta Sts, T3251121, F3251124. Pool, restaurant, 26 rooms. **B-C** *Ocean Spray*, PO Box N-3035, T3228032, F3255731. 28 rooms, restaurant. A 10-min walk from the beach in the same area is the *Plumbago House*, 17 West St, T3222643, F3222644, PO Box N-4930. Formerly the *Parthenon*, 10 deluxe suites. Guest houses include **A-B** *Dillet's*, Dunmore Av and Strachan St, PO Box N-204, Chippingham, T3251133, F3257183. 7 a/c suites, non-smoking, some have cooking facilities, includes continental breakfast, bicycles for hire, parking, internet café, Pop Pop Studios, a fine arts gallery. **D** *Mignon* 12 Market St, PO Box N-786, T/F3224771. 6 rooms. **A-B** *Towne Hotel*, 40 George St, PO Box N-4808, T3228452, F3281512. **E** *Olive's* on Blue Hill Rd, PO Box GT-2130, T3235298.

Cable beach **LL** *Breezes*, PO Box CB13049, T3275356, F3275155. A SuperClubs resort for singles and couples over 16, 392 rooms and suites expanding to 492, a/c, TV, phone, pool, games room, fitness centre, outdoor sports and watersports. **LL-L** *Nassau Beach Hotel*, PO Box N-7756, T3277711, F3278829. 408 rooms, lots of restaurants, 2 pools, free tennis and non-motorized watersports, *King & Knights* native show club. Next door is the sister resort, **LL-AL** *Nassau Marriott Resort and the Crystal Palace Casino*, PO Box N-8306, T3276200, F3276459. (Suites up to US$25,000 per night), this huge landmark hotel is usually lit up in dayglo orange, yellow, purple and magenta at night and contains shops, bars, 12 restaurants and a casino the size of a football pitch, Rainforest Theatre with Caribe dinner show. **LL-L** *Radisson Cable Beach Casino and Golf Resort*, next door, adjacent to the casino, PO Box N-4914, T3276000, F3376987. 2 wings extend from central lobby area (from where you can see the beach), curving around lagoons and pools, long walk to some rooms down dark corridors, lots of packages, children's activities, all facilities. Further along the beach **LL** *Sandals Royal Bahamian Resort and Spa*, PO Box CB-13005, T3276400, F3272009. Couples only, 406 rooms, all-inclusive, minimum 2 nights, lots of sports, every luxury, 3 pools, spa, further pool on private island, 8 gourmet restaurants.

West of Cable Beach Close to the airport: **LL-L** *Compass Point Beach Club*, on Love Beach, PO Box CB-13842, West Bay St, Nassau, T3274500, F3273299, www.islandlife.com 18 rooms in wooden cabanas, cottages on stilts or huts, all brightly painted in multi colours, fan, TV, CD, radio, bathrobes, mini bar, kitchens, restaurant, pool, diving, part of Chris Blackwell's Island Outpost chain. Most popular small property on the island drawing a big crowd to its restaurant, gorgeous waterfront patio for lunch and dinner at sunset. **AL-B** *Orange Hill Beach Inn*, PO Box N-8583, T3277157, F3275186, www.orangehill.com 32 rooms, pool, near beach, restaurant, bar, balconies, popular with divers, packages available, long term rates on request.

Paradise Island Sun International Hotels owns the huge **LL-L** *Atlantis*, PO Box N-4777, T3633000, F3633524. The feature of the new 2,355-room resort is the 14-acre waterscape and free form pool area with aquarium, 30,000 sq ft casino, 18-hole golf course, tennis courts, lots of restaurants including *Lagoon Bar and Grill* reached by underwater glass walkway with fish swimming all round you, a waterslide actually takes you via a perspex tunnel through the shark tank, lots of package deals available, including golf, air fares. Expansion and construction continues. Other large hotels include **LL-L** *Sheraton Grand Resort*, PO Box SS-6307, T3632011, F3633900, www.sheratongrand.com Refurbished 2000, 340 rooms, tennis, pool. **LL** *Club Mediterranée*, PO Box N-7137, T3632640, F3633496, www.clubmed.com 310 rooms, children from 12 years, large tennis centre with 20 courts, watersports. **LL** *Ocean Club*, T3636000, 800-3213000. Renovated and expanded in 2000 with new rooms and

The Bahamas

suites, work also being done to renew the beautiful Versailles gardens and Augustinian clois-ter in the grounds, fitness and tennis centre, former Paradise Island Golf Club redesigned by Tom Weiskopf as the new Ocean Club Golf Course, clubhouse and spa. Along Cabbage Beach, Smugglers Beach and other coastal strips by the golf course are the *Ocean Club Estates*, with 110 properties available. **B-C** *The Pink House*, PO Box SS-19157, T3633363, F3773383, pinkhouse@batelnet.bs Includes breakfast, a very small 4-roomed smart hotel in the grounds of the *Club Med*. **LL** *Club Land'Or*, T3632400, F3633403. Good suites and time share hotel, with good restaurant, shares *Atlantis* facilities. **LL-AL** *Paradise Harbour Club and Marina*, T800-7424276, phc@bahamas.net.bs 23 apartments and rooms, specializes in watersports for active guests. At the opposite end of the spectrum the **B** *Yoga Retreat*, PO Box N-7550, T3632902, F3633783. 40 rooms, very strict, no onions, not allowed to skip medi-tation, guests cook and wash up.

Crystal Cay **LL-L** *Villas on Crystal Cay*, PO Box N-7797, T3281036, F3233202. Built in a row along rocky coastline but very private and enclosed, renovated in 1999, each of the 22 suites has small pool, bed sitting room, small kitchenette/dining area, large bathroom, luxury fur-nishings, leafy surroundings, unlimited access to the marine park.

South coast **LL-A** *Clarion South Ocean Beach Resort*, PO Box N-8191 (Adelaide Rd) South Ocean, T3624391, F3624810. Set in 195 acres, with the main hotel attractively situated in the middle of the 18-hole, PGA-rated, par 72, 6,707yd golf course, ocean front rooms with jacuzzi in a separate section between main hotel and sea convenient for dive shop, several restau-rants and bars, nightclub, 2 pools, exercise room, games, jogging trail, watersports, tennis, under new management and renovated, casino to be built in 2000.

Eating

A 15% gratuity will be added to every food & drink bill although service can be very slow & poor

Lunch is always cheaper than dinner and can be taken until 1700. The large hotels often offer free snack buffets during happy hours. Most hotels have expensive and formal restaurants but they also have good value buffets (US$12-20).

For al fresco dining try **Passin' Jacks** or the **Poop Deck** on East Bay, **Traveller's Rest** near Gambier Village (always enjoyable). Middle range places with bars and open-air meals including **Coconuts** (indoors) and **Le Shack** (same place but outside), East Bay St between Paradise Bridge and Nassau backing onto the harbour, T3252148. Where you can get exotic cocktails, Bahamian food and hamburgers. Cheap, cheerful and Bahamian are **The Shoal**, on Nassau St, **Briteleys**, and **Three Queens** on Wulff Rd, the first 2 are better than the *Three Queens*. Opposite the Central Bank, through arch down Market St is **Palm Tree**, which has very good native cooking and does takeaway. Both the **Blue Lagoon** (a trio) on Paradise Island and the **Cellar** in town have music. **Café Matisse**, Bank Lane, off Parliament Square. Classy, specializes in home made pasta and real Italian pizza, Impressionist art on the walls and classical music in the background, courtyard for outdoor dining. **The Bahamian Kitchen**, Trinity Plaza, opposite the Central Bank. No frills, neighbourhood restaurant special-izing in the stick-to-the-ribs meals Bahamian mothers make, run by Mena Wallace. **Chez Willie**, West Bay Street. Serves fine Bahamian and French cuisine, management and execu-tive chef trained at the 5-star Graycliff, just down the road. **Vesuvio's** on West Bay St. Good Italian restaurant. **East Villa** on East Bay St, T393-3377/3385. Chinese restaurant. **Blue Mar-lin**, T3632660. One of only 2 restaurants on Paradise Island not owned by a hotel, lunch and dinner, steel band most nights, cheaper than hotels. For a special meal visitors are often encouraged to go to **Graycliff**, West Hill St. In a colonial mansion (also a hotel, see above), but service and food are not always up to the prices charged. **Blue Lagoon** in *Club Land'Or* for fish. Recommended (over US$50 per person). Also expensive but good are **Ocean Club** on Paradise Island and **Buena Vista**, on Delancey St, T322-2811/4039. Reservations required, men wear jackets, popular with business people, pianist, also 10-12 guest rooms.

The Joker's Wild Comedy Club, T3633000. Mostly US comedians and entertainers perform Tue-Sat. The *King and Knights* at *Nassau Beach Hotel* has a good native show, with steel drums etc. Native shows generally do not mean native to the Bahamas, but borrow from the culture of Trinidad and Jamaica with Junkanoo added. *Blue Marlin*, a restaurant/bar and nightclub on Paradise Island, offers a native revue similar to that at *King and Knights*, every night except Mon, starts 2115, lasts about 1½ hrs. *Club 601*, Bay Street. Live bands every evening, decor reminiscent of *Studio 54* (minus the glitter ball), it has the best Bahamian live music in town. Live bands can be heard at the *Waterloo*, East Bay (where you can bungee jump from 40 ft over the indoor swimming pool). Several restaurants have live music, see above. *We Place*, Thompson Av, US$4, is full of Bahamians and very lively at weekends. *Bahama Boom Beach Club*, down town on Elizabeth Av, T3257733. New dance nightclub, combination of techno pop and Caribbean. *The Zoo*, West Bay St. Tue-Sat, 2 restaurants, dancing areas, state of the art private lounges, theme bar, multi-faceted club caters for wide clientèle, from young parties to the sophisticated executive. Discos can be found in most of the larger hotels. Dinner cruises in the harbour on the *Majestic Lady*, Bay St, T3222606. Nightly for US$35pp. The *Dundas Centre for the Performing Arts*, Mackey St, T3222728. Regularly has shows and plays by local groups.

Nightlife
Some clubs have a cover charge or a 2-drink minimum

Junkanoo is a loud and boisterous national festivity loosely derived from African customs, celebrated on New Providence at 0300 on *26 December* and *1 January* (see further page 80) and, since 1999, in *June*. Every weekend in June there is live entertainment by Bahamian recording artists, dancers and performance artists, at an outdoor bandstand by the Arawak Cay Fish Fry. Festivities also include storytelling sessions and poetry readings on a porch patio, demonstrations of Junkanoo costume making and cowbell creations. An instant hit with locals and visitors alike, it has enlivened an otherwise quiet month. While the exact origins of Junkanoo are unknown, it is thought to have its roots in slave celebrations on their only days off in the year, at Christmas. John Canoe is said to have been a popular slave leader. Wild costumed rushers dance in Bay Street until dawn beating cowbells and shak-shaks, and blowing whistles. As in Carnival in many countries, local businesses sponsor groups who spend the whole year making their costumes. There is a Junkanoo Museum at the Wellcome Centre, by the cruise ships, where previous years' costumes are stored. Small Junkanoo displays can be seen on certain days in many of the large hotels. Parades with a military spirit and fireworks celebrate **Independence Day** on *10 July*.

Festivals

Shops are open 0900-1700, Monday to Saturday, but some close at 1200 on Thursday. As there is no sales tax and many items are duty-free, buying imported goods can save you about 20-50%, but shop around. The *English Shops* have Irish linen and gifts from England. Look in the *Perfume Shop* for French perfume. Try *John Bull* for watches and cameras. For unusual gifts look in *Marlborough Antiques*, West Bay, *Coin of the Realm*, Charlotte St, or *Best of the Bahamas*, east of the square. For clothing see the *Androsia* boutique in *Mademoiselle's* and Radisson Mall, Cable Beach, batik fashions from Andros. There are also international names like *St Michael*, *The Body Shop*, *Benetton*, *Gucci* and *Colombian Emeralds* all in Nassau. In general, however, buy everything you could possibly need before you arrive as regular import duties are high. Most of the smarter, tourist-oriented shops are on (or just off) Bay St. For everyday shopping most people use suburban centres, of which the most convenient is in the Mackey St-Madeira St area. *Super Value* supermarkets have good variety of breads and salad bar (sold by the pound). The main fish and produce market is on Potters Cay (see above). Other fresh fish markets are Montague Foreshore, next to the Sailing Club and on West Bay St, opposite Fort Charlotte and at the entrance to Crystal Cay. The best book shop is *Logos Bookstore*, at the East Bay Shopping Centre, just past the Paradise Island Bridge, good selection and good quality. Also reasonable is the book department of the *Island Shop* on Bay St, but most cater for 'holiday reading'. Service in shops is often poor, be prepared to wait. Film developing at the *Island Colour Lab* in the Island shop, opposite the Straw Market, on Bay St or *Mr Photo* chain on the Market Range off Bay St.

Shopping

The Bahamas

The Bahamas

Transport **Local Bus**: most buses run on one-way circular routes, which can be confusing. Route 10 goes out to Cable Beach along the coast road (leaving from beside *British Colonial Hilton Hotel*), route 16 goes along Eastern Rd to Fox Hill and Western Transportation buses go to the *Clarion* from Queen St (US$1.75). A bus runs between hotels and the golf course on Paradise Island (blue and white striped bus, US$0.50, 30-min intervals between 0800-0130) but no buses go over the bridge. **Car hire**: *Avis* (T3266380 or 3777121 at airport, avis@batelnet.bs); *Hertz* (T3778684); *Dollar* (T3778300) and *Budget* (T3777406) have offices at the airport and at other locations but local firms can be cheaper. *Orange Creek Rent-a-Car* has Suzuki run-abouts for US$39 (T3234967). Large cash deposits can be required if you have no credit card. Scooters can be hired, *Gibson's Scooter Rentals*, T3252963, US$30-45. Helmets are provided and it is mandatory that you wear them. **Taxi**: taxis are abundant but expensive. The rates are government-controlled and are for two people. Zoned taxi fares: airport to Cable Beach, US$14, airport to downtown, US$20, airport to Paradise Island, US$24 (not including US$1 bridge toll), Cable Beach to downtown, US$10. You will be charged US$3 extra for additional passengers and for more than two pieces of luggage. To avoid overcharging, agree a price beforehand, or check that the meter is used. Taxi drivers in Nassau may "take you for a ride" otherwise. Taxis can be hired by the hour, US$20 per hour for up to 5 passengers, larger taxis for seven or more cost US$23 per hour. Tipping is not necessary but 15% is normally expected. For a limousine service, Romeo's Executive Limousine Service is highly recommended. Run by Bahamahost guide, Romeo Farrington, who has a white stretch limo and a fleet of lovely Bentleys, used for official visitors, special occasions or just sightseeing tours in style, T3276400, PO Box GT-2280. For radio-dispatched taxis T3235111 or 3234555.

Anchorage At West Bay at west end of island is protected in most weather and you can stop there if it is too late to enter Nassau. Cruise ships, commercial shipping and yachts make Nassau harbour very busy. All vessels must check in and out with Harbour Control, VHF 16, when entering or leaving harbour. There is a VHF net for cruising boats. Anchorage in Nassau is limited and holding is poor. Theft and other security problems make it preferable to take a slip in one of the many marinas: West Bay, Lyford Cay Club and Marina, Great Harbour Cay Marina, East Bay Yacht Basin, Nassau Yacht Haven, Nassau Harbour Club Hotel & Marina, Paradise Harbour Club and Marina. If you need to clear customs, enter with quarantine flag raised and contact marina; customs and immigration staff will come to your vessel.

Directory **Banks** See page 68. **Communications** See page 72. **Embassies & consulates** *British High Commission*, Bitco Building, East Street, T3257471. *Canada*, T3932123. *US* Embassy, Mosmar Building, Queen Street, PO Box N-8197, T3221181. Honorary consulates: *Denmark* and *Norway*, T3221340, F3288779. *France*, T3265061. *Germany*, T3228032 (office), T3243780 (residence). *Israel*, T3224130. *Japan*, T3228560. *The Netherlands*, T3235275. *Spain*, T3621271. *Sweden*, T3277944. *Switzerland*, T3221412. There is a *Haitian* Embassy, East and Bay Sts, T3260325. Consulate of the *Dominican Republic*, T3255521. **Tour companies & travel agents** *Majestic Tours*, PO Box N-1401, Hillside Manor, Cumberland St, T3222606, F3261995. One of the main agents for trips to Cuba, although *Havanatur*, T3947195, F3945196, is better. *Happy Tours* (T3224011) arrange day trips to 'deserted' islands or cays, although the Blue Lagoon trip (see page 77) is probably better value. Many organized excursions offer the visitor an easy way of getting about but you can sometimes do the same thing by yourself for a lot less. As well as drives to places of interest, tours include visits to beaches on the Family Islands and trips aboard a catamaran with stops for swimming and sunbathing. **Tourist office** In the straw market, extremely helpful. Ask for the monthly *What's On* (www.whatsonbahamas.com) and the *Tourist News*. Another, *Best-Buys*, is in your hotel or at the airport. There is also an information booth in Rawson Square (T3269772) and at the airport which will help you find accommodation. A Ministry of Tourism hotline for urgent assistance or complaints is T3256694, Mon-Sat 0900-1700, T3256694, Sun and holidays 0900-1300. The tourist office has a list of churches (and church services).

Grand Bahama

The nearest to the USA, this is where the most spectacular development has taken place. Nearly all the hotels are in Freeport/Lucaya, where golf and gambling are major attractions. The Freeport/Lucaya area is isolated from the rest of the island and most tourists never venture into the settlements. There is a marked division between the wealthy, Americanized and manicured tourist area and the rest of the island which looks like a Family Island, less developed, almost forgotten, with holes in the roads and a laid-back atmosphere.

*Population: 40,898
1990 census*

Ins and outs

For flights and ferries to Freeport see page 69. Taxis are available at the airport; expect to share, they leave when full and they are big. To Port Lucaya it costs US$10.50 for two people, tip at your discretion. Establish the fare before you set off.

Getting there

Getting to see most of Grand Bahama without a car is difficult. Cars can be rented at the airport or in Freeport on a daily basis (US$70 for a compact car, plus insurance of about US$12 a day) or weekly (US$420), as can jeeps (US$90 per day), mopeds (US$20 per day) and bicycles. Public buses run from Freeport to Lucaya (US$0.75) and less frequently from Freeport to High Rock, Eight Mile Rock (US$1), Holmes Rock (US$2), West End (US$3) and East End. Check for timetable details. Buses drive fast and recklessly. There are routed stops with pink and white bus shelters in Freeport/Lucaya, but usually drivers will stop wherever you shout "bus stop coming up" loud enough to be heard over the music. Buses do not generally leave the bazaar or centre until full. Many hotels have a complimentary bus service for guests to the beach or in to Freeport. Taxi fares are fixed and cabs are metered but expect additional charges for extra passengers and more than two pieces of luggage.

Getting around
See transport, page 97, for further details

Be careful of wild dogs. If out walking or jogging carry a stick. If bothered, local people stoop as if to pick up a stone. This gives some breathing space

History

Thanks to a freshwater table under the island it has no water problem. The pinewoods which this natural irrigation supports were, indirectly, the beginning of the present prosperity. Early in the 1940s, an American millionaire financier, Wallace Groves, bought a small timber company and developed it into an enterprise employing 2,000 people. In 1955, the Bahamas Government entered into an agreement with him as president of the Grand Bahama Port Authority Ltd, granting to the specific area, called **Freeport**, owned by the Port Authority, certain rights and privileges which apply to that area only and to no other section of the Colony. Most important, the area was to be free of taxes and with certain concessions on several

Grand Bahama

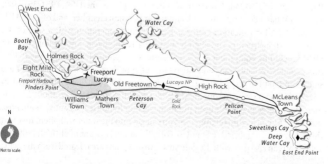

imported goods. In return, Groves would pay for government services within the area, promote industry and dredge a deepwater harbour. By 1961 a large cement works was under construction and the harbour housed a thriving ship bunkering terminal. Seeing the potential for a tourist industry, Groves made a further agreement with the Government in 1960. He formed the Grand Bahama Development Company and purchased a large area of land which was to become **Lucaya**. He also built a luxury hotel and casino, the first of its kind in the Bahamas.

So successful was this that the population of the island grew from 9,500 in 1963 to 35,250 in 1967. In the same period, the total investment rose from US$150 mn to US$577 mn and the tonnage of cargo handled increased 10 times to 1.25 mn tonnes. In 1969, however, the Government decided to introduce controls on the expansion of Freeport, and the vertiginous growth process slowed down. However, construction and sustained activity at the container port have begun affecting the fresh water table as well as the coral reefs and blue holes around the island.

Flora and fauna

Common fruit trees include avocado, lime, grapefruit, mango & custard apple

Grand Bahama is mostly covered in scrub or Caribbean pines. The Royal and Cabbage palms found on the island have been imported, the former coming originally from Cuba. In the north there are marsh and mangrove swamps. Much of the coast supports the attractive sea-grape tree and it is not unusual to see children collecting grapes from the trees. Common flowers and trees are the yellow elder, the national flower of the Bahamas, the lignum vitae, the national tree, hibiscus, bougainvillea, oleander, poinciana and poinsettia. There is not a great deal of wildlife on Grand Bahama, although you may see racoons, snakes, lizards and frogs. Birds include pelicans, herons, egrets, owls, woodpeckers, magpies, humming birds (mostly Cuban Emeralds), the rare olive-capped warbler, cranes and ospreys. Watch out for poison wood which is found in the bush and pine copses around beaches and causes a very unpleasant rash over the body.

Diving and marine life

The paucity of wildlife on land is compensated by the richness of the marine life offshore. Rays often spring from the water in pairs, but be careful not to stand on them when snorkelling as they have a powerful whiplash sting. The spotted eagle rays are particularly beautiful when seen from above. Sea horses and moray eels are also common along the coral reef. It is illegal to break off coral or harvest starfish and there are fines for offenders. Shell collectors will find sand dollars and sea biscuits on the beaches. Conch usually has to be dived for but the beaches are often littered with empty shells.

UNEXSO   Scuba diving is popular, with attractions such as **Treasure Reef**, where more than US$1 mn in sunken treasure was discovered in 1962, and **Theo's Wreck**, a deliberately sunk steel hulled freighter. The Underwater Explorers Society (UNEXSO) in Port Lucaya (T3731244, F3738956, PO Box F-42433, in the USA T954-3519889, F3519740) has a deep training tank and recompression chamber, and offers PADI, SSI and NAUI certification courses. This is a huge operation with a staff of 80, including 16 instructors and eight boats taking 10-30 divers. Snorkelling trips are US$15 including equipment. They rent underwater photographic equipment, film processing is available daily and video tapes of your dive or dolphin encounter are sold. The Dolphin Experience is a popular programme, usually booked well in advance. You take a boat from the UNEXSO dock to Sanctuary Bay, about 25 minutes, where large pens have been put in the lagoon to house the captive bottlenose dolphins. After a lecture on dolphins you can get into the water with them to touch them. Very well organized so as not to worry the animals. Sessions at 1000, 1100 and 1400. You can also dive with the dolphins. Two dolphins are released from the pens, follow the dive boat out to the ocean, where they swim with the divers and return home afterwards. You can also enrol as a dolphin trainer for a day. Membership of UNEXSO is US$50 (discounts for students or families) and US$25 a year thereafter, entitling you to a newsletter, various discounts and invitations to participate in diving expeditions (PO Box 22878, Fort Lauderdale, FL 33335).

Other dive operators include Xanadu Undersea Adventures at the *Xanadu Hotel* **Dive centres** (T3523811, F3524731), which offers certification courses (PADI, SSI, NAUI) and resort courses. Both UNEXSO and Xanadu offer shark dives. They take it in turns to dive the same site, so the sharks are fed nearly every day with frozen fish from Canada, just like the dolphins. The fish is free of parasites, but not their natural diet. *Caribbean Divers* are at *Bell Channel Inn*, across from Port Lucaya Marina, T3739111-2; *Sun Odyssey Divers*, T3734014. There is also the *Deep Water Cay Club* at East End, with no certification courses available. The *Deep Water Cay Club* is primarily a bone fishing lodge. Their boats fish over 200 square miles of flats and creeks. Accommodation is in cottages and cabins, there is a restaurant and private air strip, PO Box F-40039, T3533073, F3533095)

For the non-diver, there is a snorkelling cruise run by Paradise Water Sports, T3522887. You snorkel over the coral reefs and then over *Winky's* 40ft wreck, US$25 adults, US$18 children, equipment included.

Beaches and watersports

The island has several natural advantages over others in the group. It has miles of south-facing beaches sheltered from northerly winds and enjoys the full benefit of the Gulf Stream. Generally, beaches can be classed as tourist or local, the former having sports and refreshment facilities as well as security and regular cleaning. The more remote beaches, on the other hand, are usually completely empty, unspoiled by commercialism and very peaceful, their only drawback being that there is often considerable domestic waste and rubbish washed ashore, probably emanating from the garbage collection ships on their way to Florida.

Do exercise caution on the beaches as crime is common and most beaches have a security guard because of the high incidence of robbery and assault. Walking on beaches at night is definitely not a good idea and there is not necessarily safety in numbers. Also theft from parked cars is common so do not leave valuables in your car. Fortune Beach and the National Park Beach are both areas in which to be careful. Topless sunbathing is frowned upon by the Bahamians and skinny dipping is against the law.

Coral Beach is popular with windsurfers, cleaned regularly and has a small bar. Beach facilities are for hotel residents only and this policy is sporadically enforced with vigour. **Xanadu Beach** serves the *Bahamia and Xanadu Hotels* and various watersports are available through Paradise Watersports (T3522887), including jet skis, water-skiing, paddle boats, catamarans, snorkelling equipment (there is a good reef here within easy reach), fishing and parasailing. Use of jet skis and boats is limited to a cordoned area. Hair braiding is done on the beach by local children who have fixed prices according to the number of plaits and length of hair. Watch out for scalp burn afterwards. There is a straw market and a bar which has very loud live music on Sunday. Drinks or conch salad can be bought more cheaply if you walk just beyond the boundary fence where locals bring ice boxes of cold sodas. The *Glass Bottom Boat* operates from Xanadu Marina, tickets on sale on the beach. Make sure the sea is calm, it can be very rough outside the marina and then water visibility is poor and most passengers get seasick.

The **Lucayan Beach** area includes the beaches for the big resort hotels which are clean, with bar and sports facilities. Windsurfers, hobie cats, Boston whalers, snorkelling equipment, water skis and wave runners can all be hired here. At nearby Port Lucaya, Reef Tours operate the *Mermaid Kitty*, a glass bottomed boat which sails several times a day. They also have two-hour snorkelling trips, US$15 per person.

The Bahamas

Various booze cruises depart daily as well as a trimaran sunset trip.

On the road to West End past Eight Mile Rock are two good beaches for shelling, **Bootle Bay** and **Shell Bay**. At West End, the beach is rather small. There are good coral heads here, close enough to wade to.

One of the nicest beaches on the island with attractive palms and a few broken down old umbrellas is **Taino Beach**, which is over a mile long and has an excellent stretch of coral for snorkelling very close to the shore. The *Taino Beach Resort* on the first part of the beach has expensive condominiums which can be rented on a short term basis. The *Club Viva Fortuna Beach Resort* has been built with Italian investment in this area. **Fortune Beach** is sometimes used for tourist beach parties which are noisy and to be avoided. The main attraction of the beach is the restaurant *Bahama Bay*. The beach is a bit rocky especially at low tide. Take care in this area, it is best to park near the restaurant as there have been many cars broken into in the rather lonely car park further along. The walk from William's Town along the beach is very pleasant, the vegetation being lush, mostly mangrove, sea grapes and tall grasses along the shore. The beach is used by Pinetree Riding Stables and occasionally local churches hold services here. Other beaches on the island include **Smith's Point** and **Mathers Town** just outside Freeport. Here you will find two popular bars: *Club Caribe* (Mathers Town) and the *White Wave Club* (Smith's Point).

Peterson's Cay is the archetypal one tree desert island and because of this can be crowded. Some tour companies run day trips to snorkel and eat lunch here. You can hire a boat to get there from Port Lucaya, the approach is a bit tricky because of the reef. Directly opposite is **Barbary Beach**, pleasant and backed by a wide pine copse (good for hanging hammocks). An old church here called the Hermitage was built in 1901 by an ex-trappist monk,

Of the less commercial beaches, **Gold Rock Beach** is probably the most beautiful on the island, about 20 miles east of Freeport and part of the Bahamas National Trust. *En route* to it you cross the Grand Lucayan Waterway, a canal built in the 1960s when development was booming. Barely used today, the canal bisects the island and the abandoned building sites are a reminder of what Freeport could have become had the planned development taken place. Once past the canal turn right and further along this road is a deserted, never-used film studio. If you take the left turn before the studio you come to a signposted road for the crossing to **Water Cay**. It is not always easy to get a boat across. If you take the left turn but carry on, the road becomes overgrown and pot holed, and the area is littered with small planes shot down by drug enforcement officers or abandoned by drug traffickers. Fat Albert, a barrage balloon full of radar equipment is supposed to have put a stop to aircraft landing on the road undetected. Another detour before reaching Gold Rock is to take the first turning after the film studio to Old Free Town, where there are blue holes and Mermaid's Lair, an opening to an underwater cave system. Further inland is a sink hole, the Owl Hole. Back on the road, turn off when you see the sign for the **Lucayan National Park**. There is a car park and a map. The 50-acre park was set up by workers from Operation Raleigh and a subsequent expedition laid the foundations (but nothing more) for a visitors centre. A Lucayan village and burial ground have been found here. The park contains the largest charted underwater cave system in the world. You can see two caves and climb to a lookout point. As well as bromeliads and orchids there are hundreds of bats in the first cave in the breeding season; also a rare water centipede found only in these waters. Across the road from the caves is a 1,000yd board walk through mangrove swamp which leads to Gold Rock Beach. The beach is best seen at low tide as the sea goes out a long way and there is not much room to sit when the tide is in. The beach stretches for over a mile and is usually deserted. There are dunes and a large rock sticks out of the water giving the beach its name. It is excellent for shell collecting, but horseflies are very persistent so bring insect repellent. The picnic area is often too strewn with rubbish to be pleasant. Occasionally the area is cleaned.

Another wide, beautiful beach is **Pelican Point**, at the east end of the island, backed by Royal Palms and a very pretty and colourful village. There are fishing boats on the beach and it is not uncommon to see people gutting or cooking fish here. Pelicans can be seen flopping by. Roads out to the East End are poor and in places four-wheel drive is preferable.

Kayaking can be done with Kayak Nature Tours run by Mrs Moultrie from Hawksbill Creek, Queen's Cove, along north shore through mangrove creeks or Gold Rock Creek in the National Park, US$75 for all-day trip including lunch and transport; 16ft kayaks, single or double, no experience necessary, minimum age 10, T3732485.

There is no shortage of **golf** courses on Grand Bahama. The *Country Club at the Bahamia* has there are two heavily wooded, well-conditioned, PGA championship courses, the 6,679yd Emerald and the 6,750yd Ruby, with 162 bunkers between them (also tennis courts and a six-mile jogging trail). The length of each hole is changed daily by moving the holes on the putting green. Reservations for starting times are essential and in peak season, winter, times are often booked a month in advance, T3526721, ext 4600. Carts are mandatory. The *Fortune Hills Golf and Country Club* is a 3,458yd, 9-hole scenic par 36 course (T3732222). A challenging third hole (par 4) requires a difficult second shot over water. Friday night outdoor fish fry. The oldest is the *Lucaya Golf and Country Club*, built in 1963 where there is an 18-hole, 6,488yd PGA-rated championship course (PO Box F-40333, Lucaya, T3731066, F3736659), discounts are available through the large hotels and there is a booking booth at Port Lucaya. The *Lucayan Reef Golf and Country Club* is a brand new 18-hole course designed by the Robert Trent Jones II Group and opened summer 2000, T3731333. You can play **tennis** at the large resort hotels, courts often open to non-guests. The Grand Bahama Tennis and Squash Club (T3734567) has courts available from 0930-2400 but you have to be a member.

Horse riding is available at Pinetree Stables (T3733600, PO Box F-2915), US$35 for 1½-hours trail and beach ride with guide (20 horses, rider's weight limit 200 pounds), lessons can also be arranged with BHS and AIRA instructor (no credit cards). There is a Rugby and Hockey Club (Pioneers Way), which organizes various social events. The YMCA next to the Rugby Club can give information about watching local **basketball** and **softball** matches. **Volleyball** is a popular sport and many beaches and residential street corners have nets. **Bowling** at Sea Surf Lanes, Queen's Highway, was not available in 2000 because of hurricane damage. There is a Super-Cross **Motor Cycle** dash in the autumn. **Aerobics** classes are available at most of the major hotels. There are several **jogging** routes but watch out for dogs. The Conchman Triathlon (swim/cycle/jog) is held in November. The GB5000 road race is in February, a 5 km flat race from *Bahamia Country Club*, with a one-mile fun run/walk and a run for children. Contact the Grand Bahama Island Promotion Board, T3528356, for information and registration. UNEXSO organizes a conch diving competition for locals at Port Lucaya.

Other sports

The Bahamas

Freeport

Avenues are large and buildings are spaced far apart, there are few corner shops or neighbourhood bars and it is hard to go anywhere without a car. Freeporters have a reputation of being less friendly than other Bahamians, but this is often blamed on the design of the town and the lack of community spirit. In downtown Freeport there are a few small shopping malls. If you take East Mall Drive out of town towards the airport you will pass the Rand Memorial Hospital and the excellent **Wallace Groves Library**. On the other side of the road is a bright pink pseudo classical building which is the Grand Bahama Port Authority Building. East Mall Drive connects with the Ranfurly Circle (named after 1950s British Colonial Governor) and the **International Bazaar**, a 10-acre integrated shopping complex on East Mall and

West Sunrise Highway, with streets built in various assorted national styles with international merchandise and food. There is also a straw market and an Arts and Crafts Village behind it. ■ *Both open Mon-Sat 0900-1600, some stores on Sun.* To the rear of the International Bazaar, the other side of the street from Colombian Emeralds International and the Straw Market, is a perfume factory in a replica of an old Bahamian mansion, which you can tour briefly and even mix your own perfume. ■ *T3529391, F3529040, orders in USA 1-800-6289033, PO Box F-770, Freeport, open Mon-Fri, 1000-1730.* Just over a mile east of Ranfurly Circle you come to another roundabout. Turn right to get to the Lucaya area, where there is the **Port Lucaya** shopping and entertainment complex and a number of hotels, casino, marinas with lots of construction going on in 2000. At the Market place there is another straw and crafts market, open daily. UNEXSO is based here. In the evenings live music is played at the bandstand by the waterwalk.

Around the island

Excursions from Freeport

The Hydroflora Gardens on East Beach Drive, five minutes' drive from Ranfurly Circle, contain four acres of tropical plants grown hydroponically. Although the garden is on pure oolite rock, growth of up to 5 ft a year is achieved by this method. ■ *T3526052. Mon-Sat 0900-1730, US$1 or US$2 guided tour.*

The Garden of Groves is a 12-acre botanical garden of flowers, birds (the flamingos have been killed by dogs), pools and waterfalls. The centrepiece is a stone replica of the original church built for the loggers on Pine Ridge, and is a popular place for weddings. A children's petting zoo has pygmy goats and pot-bellied pigs and a jerk pit and picnic area has been added to give a family appeal. ■ *1000-1700 except Wed. Closed holidays. Free. T3524045 for up to date information. Times subject to change according to how much voluntary help is available. Gardens located on Magellan Drive, 8 miles out of Freeport.*

The Rand Nature Centre, East Settlers Way, opposite the Catholic High School, two miles out of town, is a 100-acre forest with a few flamingos, hummingbirds and

Freeport/Lucaya

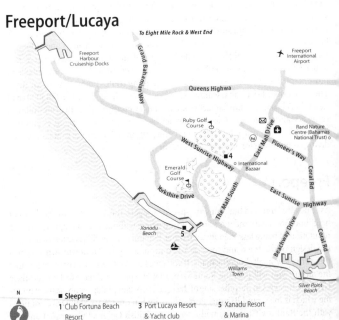

■ **Sleeping**
1 Club Fortuna Beach Resort
2 Lucayan
3 Port Lucaya Resort & Yacht club
4 The Bahamia
5 Xanadu Resort & Marina

Not to scale

the rare olive capped warbler. Highly recommended for its explanation of the ecology of a Bahamian forest. Run by the Bahamas National Trust since 1992, work is being done on more educational programmes, more trail development and an improved self-guided tour. A replica of a Lucayan village is under construction. Special birdwatching walks are offered on the first Saturday of each month at 0700, 1½ hours, US$5 unless you are a BNT member, bring binoculars and field guide. ■ *Mon-Fri 0900-1600, guided tours 1000 and 1400, US$5 (children US$3), T3525438, randnature@batelnet.bs, PO Box F-3441, Freeport.*

Eight Mile Rock (eight miles from Freeport) is the name given to eight miles of rock stretching east and west of Hawksbill Creek. The name refers to the town west of the creek. The Rock, as locals call it, has a strong sense of community not found in Freeport. The coastal road is prettier than the road directly through EMR although if you pass through the town you can see the original wooden clapboard dwellings raised off the ground, some with verandas where the inhabitants sit chillin' and rapping. Local bar, *The Ritz*, very friendly, see further page 96. Sample Mr Wildgoose's tequila. Along the coastal road is a boiling hole and the Catholic church in Hepburn Town with walls shaped like praying hands. East of Hawksbill Creek are the settlement areas of Pinders Point, Lewis Yard and Hunters. Off Pinders Point is a boiling hole called the Chimney, which causes a vortex. Below is a large cave system but you need to go with a very experienced cave diver to see it.

West of Freeport

  West End, 21 miles from Freeport, was supposedly the first settlement on Grand Bahama. It enjoyed prosperity as a haven for rum-runners during the American prohibition era. The coastal road is pleasant with local fishermen hooking conch from their boats on one side and bars, shops and houses in pastel shades on the other. At the most westerly point is new *Old Bahama Bay Hotel*, built on the site of the *Jack Tar Hotel Village*, brainchild of Sir Billy Butlin, which was closed in 1990.

Driving east from Freeport, you can see evidence of the aborted development plans, with many half-built plots, now mostly covered by bush, and roads which lead to

East of Freeport

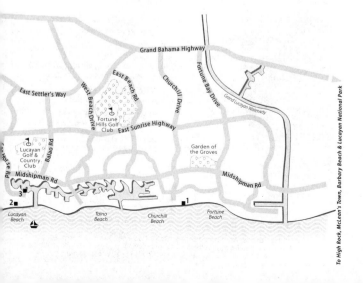

nowhere. Fifteen miles east of Freeport, towards High Rock, is the 42-acre **Lucaya National Park**, with about 250 plant species, caves, plus a path through a mangrove swamp, built in March 1985 by volunteers from 'Operation Raleigh'. Continuing east you get to High Rock (20 miles) (*Ezekiel Pinder's Restaurant* has an ocean view – almost) and Pelican Point (10 miles further), excellent deserted beach. The road on to **McLean's Town** (see page 96 for details of the festival) and East End is poor, but passable. From McLean's Town you can get a boat across to Sweetings or Deep Water Cay. Neither has vehicular traffic. There is the *Traveller's Rest Bar* on Sweetings Cay. *Deep Water Cay Club* was established in 1958 and now has seven ocean front cottages and two 2-bedroomed houses for rent with packages for fishermen, T800-6884752, 954-3599488, Bahamabone@aol.com East End Adventures run four-wheel drive tours to Sweetings Cay and Lightbourne's Cay via the Lucaya National Park and McLean's Town, ■ *US$100 per person, US$50 for children under 12, including lunch.*T3736662, 3526222 (after hrs).

Essentials

Sleeping
See also note on page 82

Price lists can be obtained from the tourist office in the Bazaar or in Lucaya. There has been considerable development over the last few years with many of the large resorts sold, merged or rebuilt. Still in limbo is the former *Bahamas Princess Resort and Casino*, comprising the *Princess Tower* and the *Princess Country Club*, which were known in 2000 as the *Resorts at Bahamia* but up for sale again.

Self-catering apartments are available at many resorts. To stay with a Bahamian family, write to the Grand Bahama Island Promotion Board, Freeport, see page 97 (tourist offices), and for details of the People-To-People Program me, see page 73 .

Port Lucaya **LL-AL** *The Lucayan*, Royal Palm Way, across the street from Port Lucaya Market Place, T3731333, F3738804, www.thelucayan.com A merger and rebuilding of 3 hotels has created this huge 1,350-room resort with 7 ½ acres of private white sand beach, 2 swimming pools with water slides and waterfalls, spa, gym, full service conference centre, 15 restaurants and lounges, casino, lots of packages. **LL-AL** *Royal Palm*, Port Lucaya Marina

Village, PO Box F-42654, Port Lucaya, T3739550, F3739551. 48 rooms, superior and deluxe all with balconies, a/c, phone, TV, pool, hot tub, restaurant, bar. **LL-A** *Port Lucaya Resort and Yacht Club*, PO Box F-42452, T3736618, F3736652, www.portlucaya.com/resort Pool, jacuzzi, bars, restaurant, on reclaimed land jutting out into harbour, rooms and 1-2 bedroom suites, slips for 50 boats of 40-125 ft surround the resort, the adjoining marina caters for all sizes of yachts including a luxury, private dock, all services and facilities, for information on dockage call Jack Chester, T3739090, F3735884.

West along the coast LL-A *Xanadu Beach Resort and Marina*, PO Box F-42438, T3526782, F3525799, Xanadu@batelnet.bs Where Howard Hughes, the recluse, used to live on the top floors, there is a small study/library dedicated to him on the ground floor of the tower, which has a ring of apartments on top. Alongside is a lower rise block of rooms and restaurants, small pool, bar, 3 tennis courts with pro, dive shop and watersports centre on site, nice beach, 67 slips in marina. **AL** *Royal Islander Hotel*, close to *Bahamia*, T3516000, F3513546. 100 rooms. **LL** *Ocean Reef Yacht Club & Resort*, T3734662, F3738261, geltex@batelnet.bs 63 waterfront suites. **A** *Running Mon Marina & Resort*, T3526834, F3526835, runmon@batelnet.bs 32 waterfront rooms, meeting room. Less expensive hotels are **B** *The New Victoria Inn* off Midshipman Rd, PO Box F-41261, T3733040, F3733874, 40 rooms, 2-bedroom suite, pool, transport to beach, shops, casino and **A-B** *Cast-aways* next to the Bazaar off the Ranfurly Circle, PO Box F-42629, T3526682, F3525087. 130 rooms on 4 floors, poolside or noisy roadside, TV, a/c, phone, small bathroom, courtesy transport to beach, avoid overpriced excursions, but none can be recommended for service.

Fortuna Beach LL-L *Club Viva Fortuna Beach Resort*, on south side of island, 4 miles east of Port Lucaya, PO Box F-42398, T3734000, F3735555, www.vivaresorts.com Italian resort on 26 acres, all-inclusive, 276 rooms with garden or ocean view, a/c, phone, cable TV, 2 big beds, sailing, windsurfing, kayaking, tennis, archery, bicycles, aerobics, golf putting green, volley ball, children's playground, scuba diving at extra cost, dive shop on site, nightly entertainment. Also *Club Viva Dominicus* in the Dominican Republic.

The hotels have several expensive restaurants which serve native/international cuisine. Buffet brunches on Sunday are recommended, you can eat as much as you like at some of the major hotels (US$18 including as much champagne as you can drink). Many restaurants, particularly those in hotels, do Early Bird Specials from 1730-1830. Although some restaurants are efficient and friendly, be prepared for indifferent service and long waits in many. A poll showed that 51% of tourists were dissatisfied with service in local hotels and restaurants. A cheap alternative is to go to one of the many cook outs, usually of a high standard. Often the proceeds go to a good cause, such as someone's hospital bills. Taino Beach hosts cook outs but best to look in local press for details.

Eating
Restaurants open & close with alarming speed, check the local newspapers for new ones or special offers

Beach front restaurants *Pier One*, at Freeport Harbour, where they feed the sharks around 2100, and *The Stoned Crab* on Taino Beach are both expensive, romantic, with good views. *Bahama Bay* on Fortune Beach, friendly, reasonably priced menu, mosquitoes and no see'ums can be troublesome if you eat outside. *The Buccaneer Club* at Deadman's Reef has a courtesy bus (call 349 3794) but if you use it you will be presented with a higher priced menu on arrival, about 40-mins' drive from Freeport, Wed night specials, closed in Oct, interesting guest signature book.

Other popular restaurants *The Traveller's Rest*, Williams Town. Good cheap breakfasts, Johnny Cake and soused fish are popular. *The Outriggers* at Smith's Point, just outside Lucaya at the far end of Taino Beach, T3734811. Distinctly Bahamian flavour, phone to check menu, fish fry outdoors on Wed night. Nearby is *Mama Flo's*, similar, even more popular for fish fry on Wed when there is lots of loud music and barbecues. *The Ole Native Hut*, Sergeant Major Drive, pea soup. *Scorpios*, Explorers Way, reasonably priced native food, favourable reports. *Silvano's* on Ranfurly Circus, serves Italian. *Luciano's* in Port Lucaya, good, book a table outside to see fireworks over the square on Sat evenings at 2030-2100, noisy music though.

The Bahamas

Port Lucaya area *Islander's Roost*, opposite International Bazaar, open-air dining patio, live entertainment, variety of Bahamian and American dishes, mascot Bella the parrot oversees all. For oriental dishes there are at least 3 Chinese restaurants in the International Bazaar, the one at the entrance is not recommended. The *Phoenix* (*Silver Sands Hotel*) serves kebabs and curries and has an unusual bar. The *Ruby Swiss Restaurant* on West Sunrise (seafood) is expensive but service is good. *Fat Man's Nephew* in Port Lucaya, T3738520. Reasonably priced, good view of bandstand, open 1200-2400 except Tue 1700-2400 and Sun 1700-2300. (*Fat Man* in Pinder's Point used to be popular but the owner, Fat Man, was gunned down by an armed robber.) *The Bahama Beach Club*, just west of the *Xanadu Hotel*, has a superb view of the sea, usually only bar snacks available, but watch newspapers for specials, eg Fish Fry on Fri, barbecue on Sat at 1900, nice local atmosphere. For sandwiches and salads at lunchtime, *Kristi's* in the Bain Building, West Atlantic Drive, Downtown, T3523149. Takeaway or eat in, open Mon-Sat 0800-1600.

Nightlife **Bars** There are many in Freeport, most have a Happy Hour between 1700-1900, and most of the restaurants mentioned above have bars. The *Pub on the Mall, Britannia Pub* and the *Winston Churchill* are all English style pubs. The *Winston Churchill* sells draught Courage, T3528866. Serves pizzas, fish 'n' chips, and hosts the Gong Show on Wed (starts around 2330, open 1100-0200). *Pussers Pub* in Port Lucaya with an English-style pub menu is in a very pleasant location overlooking the waterfront and band stand where live calypso music is played most nights. Pussers Painkiller is recommended. For cheaper drinks in a less touristy environment, *Outriggers, Surfside* and *The Traveller's Rest* are recommended. *The Ritz* in Eight Mile Rock has a number of hammocks outside which overlook the sea (rubbish spoils the view), there has been some night-time violence at the bar, better to go during the day. *The Ruby Swiss* on East Sunrise Highway, lively 0100-0400 when casino workers gather there after their shift ends. *The Bahama Mama* in the east corner of the Port Lucaya complex is one of the most popular bars, attracting local, expatriate and tourist customers giving it a lively, cosmopolitan atmosphere, interesting music, busy from 2300 onwards.

Shows Most hotels have native shows. The *Yellow Bird Club* close to the International Bazaar, T3522325. Limbo, drums, fire dancing and a glass eater, 3737368. The casino show at the *Bahamia* is good, with a large cast, well-choreographed, bright and lively. The huge casino has 20,000 sq ft of gaming space. At the *Bahamia Country Club* there is *Goombaya*, a dinner and island music review, culminating in a Junkanoo rush-out. At the *Yellowbird Show Club* in the International Bazaar, the *Yellowbird Island Review* features fire and limbo dancers. The *Bahamian Native Cultural Show* is held at the Port Lucaya Market Place, with dancing, singing and fire eating.

Discos At most of the large hotels, with two drinks in entrance fee. If you want to know which disco is flavour of the month, ask the croupiers at the casino as they closely monitor the nightlife. *Goombay Land* behind *The Party Palace* has roller skating and go-karts, very popular with local youth, entrance US$5.

Festivals **Junkanoo** is held on *1 January* in Freeport. Beginning from the Ranfurly Circle, dancing outside *Bahamia Hotel* 0400 onwards with drums, cowbells, whistles, brass instruments and foghorns. Scrap gangs, impromptu groups, join in with the rushin'. Much smaller than Nassau's but worth seeing. Go to Ranfurly Circle early to see the participants flame heating their goat skin drums to stretch them. On *10 July*, **Independence Day**, a Junkanoo parade is held at 0400 in West End and also on the first Monday in *August*, which is a holiday to commemorate the emancipation of the slaves. Many of the hotels include a small Junkanoo as part of their native show. Other events are publicized in a calendar of events from the tourist office in the bazaar or major hotels.

On **Discovery Day**, *12 October*, a fair is held at McLean's Town, including a conch-cracking competition started by a British couple in the 1940s. The aim is to see who can remove the most conch from their shell in 10 mins. The women's competition has many machete-wielding experts who bring a lot of partisan support. There is also a swimming race to a nearby islet and back, which attracts a lot of local competition. The plaiting of the

Maypole is an interesting Caribbean version of the English tradition, with children dancing round the pole to the beat of Reggae songs. Although much of the road to McLean's Town has been paved, the road is very poor in parts. Minibuses run regularly from Ranfurly Circle (US$2). If you rent a car it is sometimes difficult to park. Look out for details of local fairs in the Freeport News and at the Ranfurly Circle.

Shopping

Many items are tax exempt in the bonded area of Freeport/Lucaya and bargains include perfume, linens, sweaters, china, cameras, emeralds, watches, leather goods and alcoholic drinks. The two main shopping areas are the International Bazaar and Port Lucaya. The **International Bazaar** is off Ranfurly Circle. Built in 1967, the 10-acre complex was designed by a film special effects expert, with shops designed in national styles and selling corresponding food and goods, although the overall effect is very American. The entrance is a giant Torri gate, the Japanese symbol of welcome. **Port Lucaya** was the brainchild of Count Basie, who used to live on Grand Bahama. The atmosphere is usually friendly and there is live music most evenings. There are many different shops to buy souvenirs as well as a straw market. The Rastafarian Shop has some interesting souvenirs and there is a Bahamian Arts and Crafts stall in the centre of the complex, one row back from the central bandstand. In downtown Freeport there are a few small shopping malls; Regency has a Marks & Spencers, 17 Centre behind the main Post Office. Close by are a Winn Dixie and a Woolley's which have a virtual monopoly of the grocery supplies.

A Vendors Committee has been set up for hair braiders, conch sellers and peddlers, to control and regulate their operation and prevent complaints of hassling by tourists. A photo identification card is to be worn by all vendors and they will generally wear Androsia batik tops. They must have a permit and to have completed a Bahamahost programme. Hair braiding is US$2-3 per braid.

Transport

Car hire *Five Wheels Car Hire*, T3527001; *Hertz*, T3522977; *Dollar Rent A Car*, T3529325 at the airport, T3739139 at Lucaya. Check the telephone yellow pages for many more. Rates are US$49-119 for 24 hrs, with unlimited mileage. **Taxi** From the Harbour to the International Bazaar cost US$10 and to Port Lucaya US$14, for 2 people, tip at your discretion. Be sure to establish the fare in advance especially when there are people going to different destinations. Report any problems to the Ministry of Tourism. A strict rotation system is used and **buses** are not allowed into the harbour area.

Directory

Banks See beginning of the chapter page 68. **Communications** See page 73. **Tourist office** In Freeport, Bazaar, Port Lucaya Market Place, as well as in any large hotel. The Tourist Information Centres in Freeport/Lucaya can give a brochure listing all licensed hotels in the Bahamas and their rates. *The Grand Bahama Island Promotion Board* can be contacted through PO Box F-40251, Freeport, T3528044, F3527840, or in Florida, PO Box 22857, Fort Lauderdale, FL33335, T800-4483386.

The Family Islands

The Family Islands, often called the Out Islands, are very different in atmosphere from New Providence and Grand Bahama. The larger islands are up to 100 miles long, but have only a few thousand inhabitants. Sea and sky come in every possible shade of blue, there are wild cliffs and miles of white sand beaches. Inland, pine forests grow in the northern islands, dry woodland in the central islands and sparse scrub vegetation in the southern islands. Red-coloured salt ponds were once the basis of a thriving salt industry on the south islands, but the land offered few other economic possibilities, though one other product was Cascarilla bark, used to flavour Vermouth and Campari. Thousands of yachts visit the islands, mainly during the winter season. The sea is clean and clear and ideal for swimming, snorkelling and scuba diving. Most of the islands have relatively few tourists, although Eleuthera and one or two others have big, resort-type hotels with marinas and sports facilities.

The Bahamas

Ins & outs **Getting there** Most islands have at least one *Bahamasair* flight a day and at least one mailboat a week. If you are travelling in a group, a small charter plane may be much more convenient and only a little more expensive. Some islands also have a direct flight from Miami or another Florida airport; this cuts out the need for an unreliable, time-consuming connection in Nassau. **Getting around** Travel is restricted to one main road per island, usually called the Queen's Highway. Car, jeep or bike rental is generally available; there are taxis and water taxis but no bus service.

Abaco

Population: 10,034
1990 census

The Abaco islands, a chain of islands and cays within the Family Islands, are covered in pine forests, stretching in a curve for 130 miles. Great Abaco covers 776 square miles and is the second largest island in the Bahamas after Andros. The main centre on Abaco is Marsh Harbour, of much of Greater Abaco. The scrub and swamp give the island a rather desolate appearance, but like many islands, life revolves around the offshore cays and the coastal settlements. The area south of Marsh Harbour owes its development and particularly its roads to lumber companies. There are miles and miles of pine forests, secondary growth after the heavy logging earlier this century. Nobody lives south of Sandy Point although there is a lighthouse at Hole in the Wall. Roads are better in the north, where they are mostly paved, while in the south they are dirt. Resorts are small and the atmosphere is casual and friendly even in the most luxurious hotels.

Ins and outs

Getting there There are airstrips at Marsh Harbour (MHH), Treasure Cay (TCB) and Walker's Cay (WKR). American (T800-4337300), Island Express (T3673597). Several airlines fly to Marsh Harbour and/or Treasure Cay from Fort Lauderdale, Key West, Miami, Orlando, Tampa and West Palm Beach in Florida. *Bahamasair* provides domestic air services to Nassau, Freeport and on to other islands. Walker's Cay is served by Pan Am Air Bridge from Fort Lauderdale. Look out for package deals to the various resorts with Bahamasair. Charter planes including *Abaco Air*, T3672266, 3672205, PO Box 492, Marsh Harbour, VHF 74; *Cherokee Air*, T3672089, 3672613, 3672530, PO Box 485, Marsh Harbour; *Zig Zag Airplane Charter*, T3672889, Marsh Harbour.

Getting around
For ferry information see transport, page 107

A **taxi** from Marsh Harbour airport to the ferry dock costs US$12 for two; from Treasure Cay airport to the ferry for Green Turtle Cay US$3 per person, minimum US$5. Unmetered taxis charge US$1.50 per mile. **Car rental** can be arranged in Marsh Harbour or Treasure Cay with a number of companies: *H & L Car Rental* (Marsh Harbour, T3672840); *Wilmac Rent-a-Car* (Marsh Harbour Airport, T3674314); *Carl's Car Rentals* (Marsh Harbour Airport, T3672493, Visa/MC accepted); *Cornish Car Rental* (Treasure Cay, T3658623); *McKenzies Car Rental* (Treasure Cay, T3658849/3652249).

History

The Taino name for Abaco was Lucayoneque, although the first Spanish reference to it was Habacoa, a name also used for Andros. The Spanish did not settle, but by 1550 they had kidnapped all the Indian inhabitants for slavery elsewhere and the islands remained uninhabited for 200 years, despite a brief French attempt at settlement in 1625 and visits by pirates and fishermen. In 1783 over 600 loyalists left New York for Abaco, settling first at Carleton (north of Treasure Cay beach but no longer visible) and then moving to Marsh Harbour. Other groups settled further south but all found it hard to make a living on the small pockets of soil and of the 2,000 who arrived in the 1780s, only about 400 (half white and half black) were left in 1790.

Wrecking was a profitable pastime and Abaco was ideally placed on a busy shipping route to take advantage of its reefs and sand banks. Sponge, pineapple, sisal, sugar and lumber were later developed but never became big business. Wrecking also declined after the construction of lighthouses. The lighthouse on Elbow Cay at Hope Town was built in 1863, after the wreck in 1862 of the *USS Adirondack*, despite sabotage attempts by local people. By 1900 Hope Town was the largest town in the Abacos, with a population of 1,200 engaged in fishing, sponging, shipping and boat building. The boats made in Abaco were renowned for their design and the builders became famous for their construction skills. Boats, though made of fibreglass, are still made on Man-O-War Cay today.

The inhabitants of Abaco continued to live barely at subsistence levels until after the Second World War, when the Owens-Illinois Corporation revived the lumber business, built roads and introduced cars. An airport was built at Marsh Harbour and banks arrived. When the pulpwood operation ended in the 1960s sugar replaced it but was short lived. Nowadays the major agribusiness is citrus from two huge farms which export their crop to Florida. Abaco has developed its tourist industry slowly and effectively and has a high employment rate.

The Bahamas

Abaco Islands

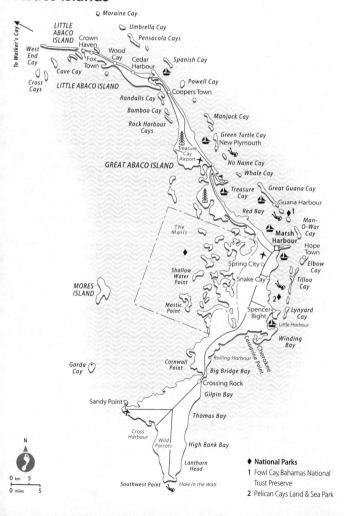

♦ **National Parks**
1 Fowl Cay, Bahamas National Trust Preserve
2 Pelican Cays Land & Sea Park

Flora and fauna

Like other northern Family Islands, Abaco is mostly covered by secondary growth stands of Caribbean pine, interspersed with hammocks or coppices of hardwoods such as mahogany and wild coffee. The Bahama parrot, extinct on all other islands bar Inagua, survives in these coppices, 42 breeding pairs have been counted. A captive breeding programme is now in progress and fledglings will be released back into these areas. In the wild, the parrots nest around Hole in the Wall and the area is to be made a reservation for them. A herd of wild horses roams the citrus groves and pine forests in the north. They are a hardy breed of work horses descended from those used in the sawmills which closed in the 1920s and 1930s.

Diving and marine life

Dive sites Many areas are now officially protected and fish life is abundant, green turtles and porpoises numerous in and around harbour areas. Fishing is strictly controlled in reef areas although the coral still shows signs of previous damage by bleaching and careless sailors. Three of the best reefs for diving or snorkelling are **Sandy Cay Reef** (part of Pelican Cay Park), **Johnny's Cay Reef** and **Fowl Cay Reef** at each of which there are several dive sites and a few permanent moorings for small boats. Don't miss **Pelican Cay Land and Sea Park**, which is an underwater wildlife sanctuary, fishing or spear fishing allowed and **Fowl Cay Bahamas National Trust Preserve** with similar restrictions. If you like exploring wrecks, the 110-year old *USS Adirondack* with her rusting cannon is worth a visit. If it is windy or the sea rough there is unlikely to be any diving because of poor visibility in the shallow waters. Inland you can dive into Devil's Hole.

For offshore **snorkelling**, *Captain Nick's Tours*, from the *Jib Room* marina and restaurant, runs trips out to local reefs and beauty spots, including Pelican Cay. Snorkel gear is available for hire. For **dolphin-watching** and other nature tours, Diane Claridge, T3674545. Marsh Harbour lacks good beaches, but **Mermaid's Cove** on the road to the Point is a pretty little beach with excellent snorkelling. The best beach on Great Abaco is probably that at **Treasure Cay**, there is a large, sandy bay backed by casuarina trees and a friendly beach bar. On the cays there are lots of sandy beaches, many of which are best reached by boat. Boat rental, *Rich's Boat Rentals*, across from the fish house, Marsh Harbour, T3672742; *Blue Wave Boat Rentals*, at Harbour View Marina between *Tiki Hut* and *Mangoes*, T3673910; *The Moorings*, at the *Conch Inn Marina*, T3674000; *Pier One Boat Rentals*, at the *Jib Room*, Marsh Harbour Marina, T3672700 and *Sea Horse Boat Rentals*, at *Abaco Beach Resort*, T3672513.

Dive centres Specialist dive operations include: *Dive Abaco* at Marsh Harbour (*Conch Inn Marina*, T3672787, VHF 16, F3674779, dives in the morning, one boat, two instructors but often only one member of staff per dive; *Abaco Beach Resort Dive Centre*, T3674646, offers day trips, reef dives, wrecks, snorkelling; *Divers Down* at Treasure Cay (T3658465, F3658508, one tank US$50, two tanks US$70, snorkelling US$30); *Brendal's Dive Shop* at Green Turtle Cay, who can offer introductory courses, wreck, catacomb and cavern dives, and a wide variety of facilities, T/F3654411; *Green Turtle Divers*, T3654271, is a PADI International Resort member and a NAUI Dream Resort, with a wide range of offerings, from PADI Bubble makers for children to blue hole diving for experts, Mark Knowles runs the facility and his pet nurse shark, Bandit, is a featured attraction; *Dave's Dive Shop*, Hope Town, T3660029, is a fully equipped dive shop with dive gear and boat rentals, and guided snorkelling and scuba; *Froggies Out Island Adventure*, next to the Post Office, Hope Town, T3656494, PADI dive instructor, all day scuba and snorkel trips to Fowl Cay and Sandy Cay.

Revolution Abaco style

The 1967 elections resulted in a victory for Lynden Pindling's party the Progressive Liberal Party (PLP), which represented the black majority of the Bahamas. Abaco, which was 50% white, voted for the opposition.

In the early 1970s some Abaco residents formed the Greater Abaco Council which was opposed to Bahamian independence. When independence became a reality in 1973, the Abaco Independence Movement tried to assert Abaco's independence from the rest of the Bahamas. This breakaway movement by white residents caused the islanders to split into two camps and there were bitter conflicts.

According to local storytellers, there was going to be a revolution, but there was confusion over whether it was planned for Wednesday or Thursday, then some men went fishing and, well ....

Support for the main opposition party, the Free National Movement (FNM), remained strong in Abaco. In 1992, and again in 1997, it was elected to government and its Prime Minister, Hubert Ingraham, lives near Coopers Town.

The Bahamas

Sailing Life revolves around the sea and Abaco is sometimes called the 'sailing capital of the world', with good marina facilities at the *Treasure Cay Marina*, one of the largest tourist resorts in the Family Islands, the *Conch Inn Resort and Marina* (a 75-slip marina can accommodate boats up to 140ft), the Boat Harbour Marina by the *Great Abaco Beach Hotel* (160 slips, boat hire, services, showers, laundromat, will hold mail, T3672736, VHF 16) and the *Green Turtle Yacht Club and Marina*. Winter (December-March) can be harsh with strong cold fronts and gale-force northerly winds making sailing and other watersports uncomfortable. Spring and summer are better. Most yachts prefer to winter further south in the Exumas and return to the Abacos later in the year. Marsh Harbour Regatta is 22 June to 4 July. Marsh Harbour is the starting place/drop off for many sailing charter companies. Charters can be arranged by the day or week, through numerous agencies (such as Sun Sail at Marsh Harbour, ABC at Hope Town or JIC Boat Rentals and Charter at Treasure Cay, T3672507), or more cheaply by private arrangement with boat owners. Ask at local marinas such as the *Jib Room*. Fishing charters can also be arranged.

Other sports You can play tennis at *Bluff House*, *Great Abaco Beach Hotel*, *Green Turtle Club* or *Walker's Cay Hotel and Marina*. *Treasure Cay Beach Hotel and Villas*, has a 6,972yd, 18-hole championship golf course (T3672570) and tennis.

Marsh Harbour

The town straggles along the flat south shore of a good and busy yachting harbour. It has the major airport about three miles from the town and is the commercial centre of Abaco. As you drive in from the airport you pass government offices, supermarkets and lots of churches and liquor stores. The town has a large white population, but at the last census 40% were found to be Haitian, most of whom lived in the districts of Pigeon Pea and The Mud and worked as domestic servants in the white suburbs. Many Haitians have since been repatriated however. Shops are varied and well stocked and international banks are represented. The only traffic lights on the island are outside Barclays. Batelco is a yellow building off Queen Elizabeth Drive. The Tourist Office is nearby. The main food stores are *Golden Harvest*; *A&A Food Store* (T3674521), *Boat Harbour Mini Market* (T3674711), *Roderick's Convenience Store* (T3673237) and *Wilson's Quick Trip* (T3672653). The Bahamas Family Market on Front Street sells mainly fruit and vegetables grown on Abaco.

The Bahamas

Around the island

The roads are better in the northern half of the island and it is easy to drive the 26 miles to **Treasure Cay**, a self-contained resort approached by a long drive through the grounds, past the golf course. There is a nice beach here and lots of watersports available at the marina. The main road continues past Treasure Cay airport and several small communities, where most of the workers for *Treasure Cay* live, to **Coopers Town**. Twenty miles from Treasure Cay, it has lots of little painted wooden houses and an air of bustling importance. It is the seat of the commissioner for North Abaco and about 900 people live here. The Prime Minister, Hubert Ingraham, was raised here, but now lives in Nassau. In 1993-94 a new health clinic was built, the biggest on the island with doctors, dentists and nurses working there. There is no harbour but along the waterfront are wooden jetties where fishermen clean their catch, leaving piles of conch shells. Offshore on Powell Cay (uninhabited), there are some lovely beaches, good shelling and the *Shipwreck Bar and Grill*. The paved road carries on another 15 miles to Crown Haven, the end of the island.

South of Marsh Harbour it is 56 miles to **Sandy Point**, through citrus groves, or you can fork left to Hole in the Wall, the area where parrots breed. On the way you can visit Spencer Bight and the abandoned Wilson City, a company town founded in 1906 by the Bahamas Timber Company but closed in 1916. In its heyday there was a saw mill and dock facilities and it boasted electricity and an ice plant, both rarities at that time. At **Little Harbour** you find the highest point in Abaco, which is 120 ft. Little Harbour is a small, pretty and protected anchorage, famed for the Johnston family's artwork in bronze, ceramics and jewellery. Their work is on display in two galleries. ■ *1030-1200, 1400-1500 or by appointment, closed Sun.* Pete Johnston also has *Pete's Pub*, where there are moorings and you can eat at the open-air bar on the beach (hot dogs, hamburgers, lobster). There is a nice walk to the old lighthouse and snorkelling is good over the small reef at the east entrance to the harbour. There are caves where the Johnstons lived when they first came to Little Harbour. If you go on Independence Day, 10 July, there is a free for all on the beach, everyone chips in, roast wild pig a feature.

Elbow Cay The name Elbow Cay is rarely used, people refer to the settlement as Hope Town, the main town. It is marked by a striped lighthouse from the top of which you can get lovely views. Built by the

Elbow Cay

0 metres 500
0 yards 500

■ **Sleeping**
1 Club Soleil Resort & Hope Town Hideaways
2 Hope Town Harbour Lodge
3 Abaco Inn
4 Sea Spray Villas & Marinas

● **Eating**
1 Captain Jack's Bar
2 Harbour's Edge Restaurant

British Imperial Lighthouse Service in 1863, it is one of the last hand-powered Kerosene-fuelled beacons still in use. ■ *Mon-Fri 1000-1600*. **White Sound**, southwest of the town, has a couple of resorts. **Hope Town** is very picturesque, set around a charming harbour, cluttered with jetties and brightly painted wooden houses. Cars are not allowed along the narrow streets edged by white picket fences and saltbox cottages. Visit the Wyannie Malone Historical Museum which has a collection of old furniture, genealogies and memorabilia from the town. The museum is staffed by volunteers. If it is not open, call Peggy Thompson at *Hope Town Hideaways*. The town's jail is no longer used as such, but is filled with visitor's brochures. There are several places to eat and drink in the town, there are grocery stores, bakeries and gift shops. A lovely beach runs along the ocean side of the island and **Tahiti Beach** is at the extreme end in the southwest. Bicycles can be hired but it is a rough ride down to the south. Dave's Boat Rentals, T3660029, VHF 16, next to Hope Town Lower Ferry Dock, rents Boston Whalers or larger boats, which are an easier way of getting around. Dave also rents diving gear and tanks. Hopetown marina has fuel, moorings, dockage.

Man-O-War Cay

This cay is a boat building and repair centre with New England Loyalist origins, where, until recently, blacks were not allowed to stay overnight. Nearly everyone on the island can trace their family back to Pappy Ben and Mammy Nellie, a young couple who settled there in the 1820s. There are two boatyards now, Edwin's Boat Yard, which specializes in boat repair and building fibreglass outboard boats, and Albury Brothers Boat Building, which makes smaller, fibreglass runabouts. Albury's Ferry is based here. It is very pretty, with a good beach on the east side and snorkelling at the north point. The Marina offers full services, T3656008, VHF 16, and a gift shop. There are a couple of small places to eat, but they really cater for the takeaway trade, and a couple of grocery stores. No alcohol is sold on the island, you have to go to Marsh Harbour for that. The CIBC bank is open Thursday only. There are no cars, people use golf carts and scooters. Sundays are graveyard quiet.

Green Turtle Cay

Great Guana Cay

The population of Great Guana Cay is about 100. There are a few shops, including a grocery and a liquor store, and most services are available. A wide, sandy beach extends nearly the length of the ocean side of the island, about 5½ miles, although the north end has been developed for use of Treasure Cay visitors. For snorkellers there is a reef just off the beach at High Rocks, southeast of Guana Harbour.

Green Turtle Cay

The picturesque and quaint village of **New Plymouth** can be reached from Treasure Cay airport by a short taxi ride (US$3 per person, minimum US$5) and then a ferry from Treasure Cay Dock (US$8, children 2-11yr, US$4, one-way, to Black Sound, White Sound, Bluff Cay or Coco Bay, ferry is three times a day, timed to meet planes, but can be chartered any time, VHF 16). The **Albert Lowe Museum** chronicles the British settlers who came in the 18th century and their shipbuilding skills. The **Memorial Sculpture Garden** is also

The Bahamas

4 Roosters Rest
5 New Plymouth Inn

■ **Sleeping**
Green Turtle Club & Marina
Bluff House Club
Linton Cottages

▲ **Other**
1 Albert Lowe
Museum & Post Office

worth a visit. The island has some lovely beaches, ideal for shelling, and boats are easily rented for exploring other cays. On New Year's Day, the inhabitants celebrate the capture of Bunce, a legendary figure said to have lived in Abaco's pine forests.

Spanish Cay Spanish Cay is a private 185-acre island off Cooper's Town which has recently been developed as a resort. There is a 5,000 ft runway and a full-service marina with a dive shop, *Spanish Cay Diving*. Transport on the island is by golf cart or walking. **LL-L** *Spanish Cay Inn and Marina* has five villas and seven apartments, a restaurant and store overlook the marina, another restaurant is at the tip of one of the five beaches, tennis, snorkelling, diving and fishing available, T3650083, F3650466, PO Box 882, Cooper's Town, reservations essential. The cay can be reached from Abaco at Coopers Town, where the resort's ferry will pick you up from the government dock.

Walker's Cay Walker's Cay was named after Judge Thomas Walker, who was banished to the island in the 18th century. It is the furthest north of all the Abaco cays and is dominated by the **L-AL** *Walker's Cay Hotel and Marina*, which offers sailors and fishermen lots of facilities and hosts several fishing tournaments. Yachtsmen approaching Abaco from the north clear customs and immigration here. There are restaurants, bars, tennis and two pools for when you are on land, 62 rooms, four suites and four villas. Enquire about package deals with airfares from Fort Lauderdale if you do not want to tour other cays, T3525252, F3523301, or write to 700 SW 34 Street, Ft Lauderdale, FL 33315. You can visit the fish farm on Walker's Cay, the Aqua Life Mariculture Project, the largest in the world breeding tropical fish.

Essentials

Sleeping: **Marsh Harbour** **LL-AL** *Abaco Towns By the Sea*, PO Box 20486, T3672227, F3673927,
Abaco canam@bigsky.net 2-bedroom villas, timeshare resort, short walk to water, convenient for restaurants, tennis. **L** *Abaco Beach Resort*, 52 rooms and 6 villas, 2 pools, tennis, beach, attached to *Boat Harbour Marina*, T3672158, F3672819, PO Box AB-20511. With 180 slips, nice location, comfortable rooms. **A** *Conch Inn Hotel and Marina*, PO Box AB-20469, T3674000, F3674004. 9 rooms, full marina facilities, pool, restaurant, dockside bar and cable TV, well located and a yachtie meeting place. **LL-L** *Pelican Beach Villas*, PO Box AB-20304, T3673600, F912-4376223, pelican@g-net.net 5 villas, 2 bedroom, 2 bath, fully equipped, a/c, phone, on beach, need car to get to shops, boat dock, hammocks. **AL-A** *Lofty Fig*, PO Box AB-20437, T/F3672681. 6 villas, nice looking, opposite water, near *Conch Inn*. **B** *Ambassador Motel*, PO Box AB-20484, T3672022, F3672113. Cheaper but not well located. **A** *D's Guest House*, T/F3673980. 5 mins from airport, weekly rates cheaper, cable TV, pool, designed for couples. **Casuarina Point** (18 miles south of Marsh Harbour) **LL-AL** *Different of Abaco*, VHF 16, PO Box AB-20092, T3662150, F3278152, www.oii.net/different A bonefishing lodge and home of Great Abaco Bone Fishing Club, in a nature park with flamingos, iguanas and donkeys, 8 rooms, 15 huts, 8 bonefishing boats, good restaurant open from 0900. **Sandy Point** **B** *Oeisha's Motel*, T3664139, F3664283, and **C** *Pete and Gay's Guest House* T3664119, F3664007, which cater to an increasing number of bonefishermen using local fishermen as guides, very casual, all doors left unlocked. **Treasure Cay**, a peninsula 26 miles north of Marsh Harbour, **LL-A** *Treasure Cay Hotel*, PO Box AB-22183, T3658535, F3658847, info@treasurecay.com 96 rooms, 7 villas, there are also 600 homes owned by non-residents, 18-hole golf course, tennis, fishing, watersports on site, marina, restaurants, bars, shops, bank, doctor, pleasant resort, lovely beach close by, a 54-room hotel and 12 acres which were once part of the resort have been sold for redevelopment to Sandals. **LL** *Banyan Beach Club*, Treasure Cay, T3654181, www.banyanbeach.com. 2-3 bedroom luxury beachfront condos. **Wood Cay**, off Little Abaco, **B** *Tangelo Hotel*, PO Box 830, T3652222, F3652200. 12 rooms, TV, a/c, fans, restaurant, bar, taxi from Treasure Cay airport will cost US$50 for 2 people, but if you call the hotel in advance they will provide a bus for US$10 for 2 people.

Marsh Harbour There are several restaurants within walking distance of each other, look out for special menus and happy hours on different days. *Mangoes* restaurant and marina, T3672366. Patio bar from 1130, lunch 1130-1430, dinner 1830-2100, good food, about US$25 for dinner. *Wally's*, nearby, other side of road, T3672074. Good Bahamian food, popular happy hour, Wed 1600-1800, open lunch Mon 1130-1400, Tue-Sat 1130-1500, dinner Mon by reservation only, Sat 1800-2100, bar daily except Sun 1100-1700, music, boutique. The *Jib Room* at Marsh Harbour Marina on north side of harbour, PO Box AB 20518, T3672700, F3672033. Very long walk, coffee and croissants from 0830, lunch daily 1130-1500, daily special activities for dinner, huge ribs on Wed US$12 recommended, happy hour Thur 1830-1930 all drinks US$1, closed Tue. *Sapodilly's*, T3673498, VHF 19. Waterfront, deli, beer and wine, picnic baskets, provisioning, breakfast and lunch from 0830 Mon-Sat, 0930 Sun. *Angler's Restaurant* , Boat Harbour Marina, T3672158. Serves breakfast, lunch, dinner, with a lovely view of the harbour. *George 'Sho Bo' Wilmore* makes fresh conch salad before your eyes, adjacent to the Harbour View Marina. *Kool Scoops Ice Cream Parlour* , Stratton Drive, T3673880, also serves sandwiches. *Mavis Country Restaurant*, Don McKay Blvd, T3672002. Specializes in Bahamian and Jamaican dishes. **Casaurina Point** *Nettie's Different of Abaco*, south of Marsh Harbour, T3662150. Interesting and unusual lunch and dinner prepared in traditional Bahamian style. **Treasure Cay** There are several restaurants and bars here. *Island Boil*, a yellow wooden shack near Treasure Cay ferry serves Bahamian dishes, fish for breakfast, cheap, used by locals, tourists, air arrivals. **Coopers Town**, *M & M,* restaurant and disco serves local dishes with peas 'n' rice. A converted van, *Mac's Rolling Kitchen*, goes out to Treasure Cay and nearby settlements for lunches. *Conch Crawl*, T3650423. A shack and pier, the fresh conch salad is made in front of you, fish fries and barbecues on different nights, sit inside or outside; there are lots of jetties along this stretch of coast, all with piles of conch shells underneath.

L-AL *Hope Town Harbour Lodge*, T3660095, F3660286, www.hopetownlodge.com Bar and pool the Atlantic side of the hill overlooking beach, lunch by pool, no pre-booking in restaurant, rooms with harbour view in main hotel, or with ocean view, lovely location, friendly. *Hope Town Villas*, T3660030, F3660377, htvillas@batelnet.bs Run by Michael Myers, clapboard cottages, overlooking lighthouse, or nearer the beach, US$950-1,500 per week, fully equipped. On the other side of the water, reached by boat, is **AL** *Club Soleil Resort*, T3660003, F3660254. Restaurant on waterfront, good menu, fish, chicken, champagne Sun brunch, always full, reservations needed, try their drink Tropical Shock, 6 rooms, bright, cheerful, TV, VCR, a/c, fridge, all overlook harbour, balcony, German and Dutch also spoken, own boat for deep sea fishing. A walkway connects with **LL-L** *Hope Town Hideaways and Marina*, T3660224, F3660434, www.hopetown.com An attractive cluster of 4 villas, run by Chris and Peggy Thompson, very friendly, lovely location but you have to go everywhere by boat, each villa has 2 master bedrooms, full kitchen/diner, a/c, fans, TV, music centre, telephone, videos, games, beautifully decorated, small pool, manmade beach and infants' sand play area, rental boats US$75-95 per day, cheaper for longer, 12 large slips, power and water, no restaurant but local cooks can be contracted if you do not want to go next door. On White Sound, **AL** *Abaco Inn* overlooks the calm water and also the ocean, T3660133, F3660113. There is a dirt road from Hope Town, or you can hire a boat or charter a ferry, small rooms harbour side or ocean side, wonderful view, a/c, fan, hammocks, restaurant and pool overlook ocean, bar overlooks harbour, nude bathing area, snorkelling gear and bicycles free for guests, small children not encouraged, no evening entertainment, owned by John Goodloe, usually full. *Seaspray Resort and Marina*, also on White Sound, T3660065, F3660383, www.seasprayresort.com Boats for hire, 1-2 bedroom villas US$910-1,235 per week, have spacious living area, full kitchen, small bedrooms, a/c, minimum 3-nights, run by Monty and Ruth Albury, Monty's mother runs a bakery and will cook Bahamian meals if required, pool, windsurfing, sunfish, motorboats US$65-95 per day, snorkelling, sailing and fishing trips, freshwater pool, games room with pool table, quiet, villas spread out, free Hope Town shuttle. There are several bars and restaurants: *Captain Jack's*, T3660247. Tables on its own jetty, lovely views across the water to the mangroves, breakfast 0830-1030, lunch and dinner 1100-2100, happy hour 1700-1830. *Harbour's Edge*, T3660087. Bar open from 1000, free transport for dinner, good food, open-air or indoors, Sat night live band, weather permitting, pool table, satellite TV, bicycle rental US$8 per day, friendly, happy hour 1700-1800, VHF 16, closed around Oct for 6 weeks.

Sleeping: **L** *Schooner's Landing Resort*, T3656072, F3656285. 2-bedroom condos on the beach, a/c, **Man-O-War** tennis, minimum 3 nights' stay, manageress Brenda Sawyer can arrange sailing, diving, snor- **Cay** kelling, fishing, boat rentals etc. Contact Bill and Sherry Albury for rental cottages, US$450-650 per week, T3656009.

Sleeping **LL-AL** *Guana Beach Resort and Marina*, PO Box AB-20474, T3655133, F3655134, **& eating:** guanabeach@guanabeach.com Small, informal, 11 rooms, 8 suites, in villas, own beach off **Great Guana** the harbour cove and 5 mins' walk from ocean beach, pool, docks and marina offering full **Cay** service and yacht management programme. The restaurant is open 0730-1000 for indoor or outdoor dining. Guests are picked up by boat from *Conch Inn*, Marsh Harbour, at 0930 and 1600 or by arrangement. **L-AL** *Guana Seaside Village*, T3655106, F3655146, guanaseaside @oii.net 4 villas, fully equipped, pool, beach, restaurant, diving. **L-AL** *Dolphin Beach Resort*, T/F3655137, www.dolphinbeachresort.com 4 rooms, 3 cottages, breakfast included, pool, beach, kitchenette. *Mermaid Café*, at *Dolphin Beach Resort*, T3655137. Serves breakfast, lunch, dinner, adjoining Potcakes Boutique. *Coco Paradise* , T3655197. Over-looking gorgeous beach, complimentary transport from the main dock, offers selections like garlic shrimp, scampi, coconut shrimp, crab meat quiche, free coffee.

Sleeping In the village the only place to stay is the **L-A** *New Plymouth Inn*, T3654161, F3654138. A **& eating:** restored colonial building with 9 rooms, pool, restaurant and bar, good food, Bahamian **Green Turtle** dishes, cocktails 1830, dinner 1945, also breakfast, lunch and Sun brunch. Further east along **Cay** the coast, are **LL-L** *Linton's Beach and Harbour Cottages*, PO Box 158601, T3654003, F365-4002/4261. 1-2 bedrooms, on the ocean, fans. Overlooking White Sound and beauti-fully sheltered is **LL-AL** *Green Turtle Club and Marina*, PO Box AB-22792, T3654271, F3654272, www.greenturtleclub.com Deluxe accommodation with diveshop and all watersports, 32 rooms and cottages, in yellow wooden villas, beautifully furnished in hard-woods, clean, fresh, the beach at Coco Bay is a 5-min walk, lots of repeat guests, Brendal's Dive Shop on site does scuba, snorkelling, island excursions, and bicycle rentals, T3654411, VHF 16, there is also a gym, boat rental, bone fishing and deep sea fishing, PO Box 462, New Plymouth. **LL-A** *Bluff House Beach Hotel*, T3654247, F3654248, www.bluffhouse.com A marvellous view of the sea, fully renovated and remodelled after 1999 hurricane damage, pool, tennis, Boston whalers and sailboats US$50-80 per day, bicycles, relaxed atmosphere, 23 rooms in 3 rustic, painted villas on small beach, suites and cottages 1-3 bedrooms, 6 high seasons, lots of repeat business, great food and view at new beach bar and deck overlooking ocean, reservations needed for candlelit dinners at excellent restaurant up the hill, no locks, no TV. Boat rides to New Plymouth 3 mornings a week and for Sat night dance. Day trips to other cays with Lincoln Jones, barbecued lobster on the beach for lunch. Fishing and diving arranged. 20-min walk to Coco Bay, a 3-mile beach. Popular with honeymooners, a secluded and friendly resort. **LL-L** *Coco Bay Cottages*, PO Box AB-22795, T3655464, F3655465, cocobay@oii.net 4 cottages, each with 2 bedrooms, comfortably furnished, in 5 acres of beach front property, fruit trees, snorkelling equipment available. **AL** *Treehouse By The Sea*, T/F3654258, www.oii.net/treehouse 3 cottages, minimum 3 nights, beach nearby, solitude, relaxation. To rent cottages sleeping up to 8 people/cottage, phone Sid's Grocery Store in New Plymouth, but take mosquito repellent in summer and autumn. *Miss Emily's Blue Bee Bar*, T3654181, is worth a visit, located in the centre of the settlement, next to the netball pitch, it is bursting with memorabilia of previous famous and infamous customers and serves unforgettable and very strong cocktails. *Laura's Kitchen*, near the ferry dock, open 1100-1500, 1830-2100, T3654287, VHF 16. *Rooster's Restaurant & Pub*, T3654066, on the outskirts, painted red, is a bar, restaurant and club, Gully's Roosters play there 2-3 nights a week, going to other clubs on other nights. Nearby, on Black Sound, the Alton Lowe art gal-lery is open to the public.

Guy Fawkes Day is celebrated on *5 November* with parades through the streets led by the **Festivals**
Guy to a big bonfire in the evening (no fireworks).

Boat *Albury's Ferry Service* (T3656010, F3656487, www.oii.net/AlburysFerry) runs from **Transport**
Sandy Crossing, 2 miles east of Marsh Harbour to Hope Town and Man-O-War Cay, US$8 single, US$12 day return. Separate boats leave each cay at 0800 and 1330, returning from the
mainland at 1030 and 1600. Albury's boats can also be chartered to these 2 cays and to other
islands. For 5 or more, a charter to Hope Town or Man-O-War works out at US$10 per person
each way, to Guana Cay for 6 or more US$12 per person, or US$70 for 1-5 pax. All day excursions to Treasure Cay, Guana Cay, Hope Town, Man-O-War, Little Harbour and Green Turtle
Cay. Green Turtle Cay (see above) is reached from the ferry dock at Treasure Cay, US$8 per
person, you can be dropped off wherever you are staying. Great Guana Cay can be reached
by ferry, US$8 per person, or the *Guana Beach Resort* boat from *Conch Inn*, Marsh Harbour.
The *Spanish Cay Inn* ferry picks up guests from Coopers Town.

Tourist office *Ministry of Tourism*, Abaco Tourist Office, PO Box AB 0464, Marsh Harbour, Abaco, **Directory**
T3673067, F3673068. Most businesses in the Abacos can be found at www.oii.net, which runs a
noticeboard service and helpful forums.

Andros

Andros is the largest island in the Bahamas, with pine and mahogany forests, creeks   Population: 8,187
and prolific birdlife. According to Indian legend, the forests house the 'chickcharnie', a   1990 census
mythical, three-fingered, three-toed, red-eyed creature who hangs upside down and
can cause good or bad luck. It is also blamed when tools or other things go missing. In
fact, a large, three-toed, burrowing owl of this description did inhabit the forests until
the early 16th century when it became extinct. More recent legend has it that the pirate,
Sir Henry Morgan, lit a beacon on the top of Morgan's Bluff, the highest point on the
island at 67ft. This lured passing ships on to the treacherous reef close by. Sir Henry and
his pirates then ransacked the ships and hid their treasure in the caves below. The Span-
ish called the island La Isla del Espíritu Santo, but its present name is said to come from
the British commander Sir Edmund Andros.

Getting there *Bahamasair* has daily flights to all four from Nassau. *Small Hope Bay Lodge*   **Ins & outs**
runs its own charter flights from Fort Lauderdale to Fresh Creek/Andros Town, US$220 per   See transport,
person round trip, minimum 2 people, children under 12 half price, 1 hr, T305-3598240,   page 112, for
F305-3598241 or phone the Lodge on Andros. Airports are at Fresh Creek/Andros Town   further details
(ASD), Mangrove Cay (MAY) (both central), San Andros (SAQ) and Congo Town/South
Andros (TZN). **Getting around** There are two separate islands, North and South Andros,
with the central regions (middle bights) accessible by boat from either direction. No roads
connect the different parts and unless you have a boat you have to fly between them. Cars
and scooters can be rented.

Flora and fauna

Andros has an extensive creek system which is largely unexplored. In South Andros
the 40-square-mile area beyond the half mile long ridge is also uninhabited and
rarely visited. The large pine forests and mangrove swamps are home to a variety of
birds and animals. In the south there are wild bird reserves which allow hunting in
the season (September-March). Sightings of the Bahamian parrot have been
reported in South Andros, while rare terns and whistling tree ducks, roseatte spoonbills and numerous different herons have been seen in the north and central areas.
Green Cay, one of the many small islands off Andros (20 miles east of Deep Creek)
has the world's second largest population of white crowned pigeons. These pigeons
are prey to hunters from September to March each year. The west side of Andros is

The Bahamas

Andros & Berry Islands

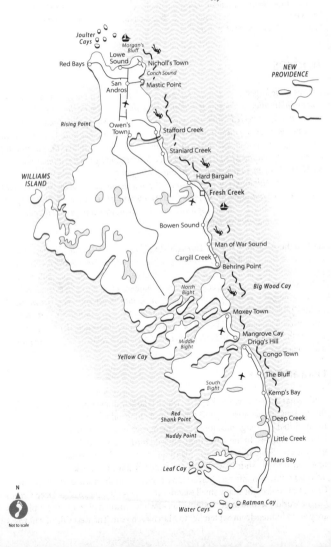

Great Sturrup Cay

Great Harbour Cay

BERRY ISLANDS

Hoffman's Cay

Bonds Cay

Chub Cay

Whale Cay

Joulter Cays

Morgan's Bluff

Lowe Sound

Red Bays

Nicholl's Town

Conch Sound

San Andros

Mastic Point

NEW PROVIDENCE

Rising Point

Owen's Town

Stafford Creek

Staniard Creek

Hard Bargain

WILLIAMS ISLAND

Fresh Creek

Bowen Sound

Man of War Sound

Cargill Creek

Behring Point

North Bight

Big Wood Cay

Moxey Town

Mangrove Cay

Drigg's Hill

Middle Bight

Congo Town

Yellow Cay

The Bluff

South Bight

Kemp's Bay

Red Shank Point

Deep Creek

Nuddy Point

Little Creek

Mars Bay

Leaf Cay

N

Not to scale

Water Cays

Ratman Cay

undeveloped and other than Red Bays in the northwest corner there are no settlements on this side, making it ideal for wildlife; large rock iguanas up to 6 ft long and hundreds of flamingos live here. During May to August the Andros land crabs migrate from the pine forests to the sea. These enormous crabs are to be found everywhere during this time. Many are caught and exported to Nassau.

Diving and marine life

Visitors mostly come for the unspoiled beaches, the diving on pristine reefs in 80°F water with excellent visibility and extraordinary bonefishing. Development has been concentrated on the east coast facing one of the world's largest underwater reefs. This huge barrier reef, the second largest in the Western Hemisphere, plunges 6,000 ft to the Tongue of the Ocean, an exciting drop-off dive. **Wreck** dive sites include the *Lady Gloria*, an old mailboat sunk recently off Morgan's Bluff, and the *Potomac*, a steel-hulled barge which sank just after the war and is now home to many huge, friendly grouper and parrot fish, as well as some impressive barracuda. Andros has 197 **blue holes**, of these 50 are oceanic, the rest inland. Formed by water erosion then flooded at the end of the last ice-age, the oceanic holes actually connect to the intricate inland underwater cave system. As tide rushes in and out ideal feeding grounds are created and consequently the oceanic blue holes harbour prolific and diverse marine life and are excellent dive sites at slack tide. The inland blue holes can be very deep (up to 350 ft) and contain a lens of freshwater 40-100ft deep floating on seawater, which is beautiful to swim in. **Charlie's blue hole**, near Nicholl's Town is clearly signposted as is **Church's blue hole**, just north of Fresh Creek. Marine life in the inland blue holes is limited, though the rare crustacean *Remepedidia* and the blind cave fish *Lucifuga* have been found. Earthwatch is currently conducting a detailed study on the mosquito fish, one of the few colonists of the blue holes on North Andros. On South Andros two popular blue holes are the **Giant Doughnut** near Deep Creek, south of Kemps Bay, and Inland Blue Hole **Lissy** near the Bluff, South Andros. Legends abound about blue holes, serpents known as *Luska*, originally a part of Seminole Indian legends are thought to drag unsuspecting swimmers and fishermen below. Caution should be exercised at some of the holes as they are extremely deep. A 1991 expedition discovered remains of a Lucayan burial site in one of the blue holes of South Andros. Intact Lucayan skulls were recovered, as well as femurs and hip bones.

Dive sites
The underwater cave system on Andros is considered to have some of the world's longest, deepest & most stunning caves

Small Hope Bay Lodge is the place to go for diving, just north of Fresh Creek and a short boat journey from the barrier reef, wrecks, caves and an ocean blue hole. A well-run operation with several decades of experience in Andros, they cater for beginners as well as specialty divers and have an excellent safety record. Most guests are on all-inclusive packages, otherwise diving is US$45 for a single tank dive, US$10 for a second tank, US$50 night dive, US$5 snorkelling boat trip. Specialty diving is tailored to individual requirements. This dive operation is one of the more conservation-minded in the Bahamas. There are also daily snorkel trips to the reef and snorkel trails from the shore. Dive Propulsion Vehicles are available for wall riding (scuba) or reef riding (snorkel). Liveaboard dive boats also cruise around Andros and Stuart Cove's Dive South Ocean occasionally come over from Nassau and dive in Andros waters. For ecological tours *Forfar Field Station*, at Blanket Sound north of Fresh Creek, runs guided diving, snorkelling and inland excursions, mainly for high school students or college groups from the USA, T3682014, F3682015 for details. Accommodation sometimes available.

Dive centres

Small Hope Bay Lodge also does **bonefishing** (US$325 per day boat and guide for two people or US$380-480 per day reef fishing for up to four), but the best place for serious fishermen and women is the **Cargill Creek** area, where there are lots of guides. You can stay at *Grassy Camp* further south, or do a one-day Grassy Cay trip

Fishing
All sportfishing is catch & release

The Bahamas

for US$800 (maximum five people). There is also *Andros Island Bonefish Club* (known locally as Rupert's Place) where deep sea fishing can be arranged.

The usual weight of bonefish is 5-7 pounds but on most days you will find fish of 12 pounds and over. There are around 100 square miles of flats in the north and middle bights which are fished by Cargill Creek resorts. Most are fished infrequently and you see hardly anyone else. The west side of the island can also be fished, depending on the weather and tide, but it will cost an extra US$50 per day for fuel as it is 1½ hours from Cargill Creek. You can still see traditional Bahamian wooden sailboats here, made by local craftsman Ronald Young, although nowadays he makes mostly fishing boats. On Christmas Day, Columbus' Discovery Day and Easter Monday sailboat races, featuring locally made Bahamian sloops, are held at Lowe Sound, Nicholl's Town and sometimes Conch Sound. Ask locals for details. Regattas also combine cook-outs, local music and dancing. On Independence Day there is a sailboats race in the Regatta.

Beaches and watersports

In the north, **Nicholl's Town** has the best beach. A wide, golden beach runs the length of the north coast, almost to Morgan's Bluff. It is ideal for swimming and excellent snorkelling spots are to be found directly off the beach. **Lowe Sound**, **Conch Sound** and **Mastic Point** all have good beaches. A very pleasant, 2½-mile walk from Nicholl's Town to Morgan's Bluff along a leafy overgrown road (in fact the first road built on this part of the island) leads to the caves at Morgan's Bluff and offers beautiful views of this part of the coast. Further south near Fresh Creek is **Staniard Creek** where there is an attractive palm-fringed beach with white sand and pleasant settlement close by. Sand bars, exposed at the mouth of Staniard Creek at low tide, are excellent shelling spots. **Somerset beach** is just south of Fresh Creek, signposted from the main highway. It is a spectacular spot, especially at low tide and another excellent shelling beach. At **Victoria Point** in central Andros there is a graveyard right on the water's edge. In some parts of Andros on Easter Monday at 0200-0600 there is a candlelight vigil by gravesites at which Easter hymns are sung. The east side of Mangrove Cay has spectacular beaches all lined with coconut groves. In South Andros along the 28-mile stretch from Mars Bay to Drigg's Hill are beautiful palm-lined beaches with occasional picturesque settlements.

Around the island

The main settlements in the north are **Nicholl's Town**, **Lowe Sound**, **Conch Sound**, **Red Bays**, **Mastic Point** and **Fresh Creek** (previously known as Andros Town and Coakley Town). **Mangrove Cay** is in central Andros, while in the south are **Congo Town**, **Deep Creek** and ex-Prime Minister Sir Lynden Pindling's constituency at **Kemp's Bay**.

Near Fresh Creek, you can visit the Androsia clothing factory which makes batik fabrics in tropical colours and watch the whole process from the wax painting to the drying of the dyed cloth. Ask in the shop for a factory tour. Henry Wallace is a rastafarian wood carver, usually to be found chipping away to the beat of reggae music. He is also the curator of a small museum of the island's culture and history, near the mailboat dock in Fresh Creek (the old health clinic buildings), worth a visit. South of Fresh Creek is the Atlantic Underwater Testing and Evaluation Center (Autec), a joint venture between the USA and the UK for underwater testing of weapons and consequently top secret.

Nicholl's Town has a lively Junkanoo on Boxing Day (very early morning) and New Year's Eve, and Goombay Festival on every Thursday in July and August from 1900 onwards on Seaview Square. There are many government administration buildings, schools, clinic, Batelco office, in what is a straggling, spread-out town with no apparent centre. **Conch Sound** is very close, almost an extension of

Nicholl's Town; between the two are shops, a bakery, auditorium, laundry and disco. At **Morgan's Bluff** you can visit the caves where pirates were rumoured to have hidden their treasure. Both the Bluff and the caves are signposted; the caves are in fact quite small and rather a disappointment. The area nowadays is more important for the docks, from where water is barged to Nassau. The mailboat comes in at the old harbour.

Red Bays (population under 200) is the only settlement on the west coast of the island and is about five minutes' drive from Red Bays beach, where there are a few small motor boats moored but nothing else. Long isolated and reached only by boat it is now connected by a good paved road cutting across the wild interior of the island. Originally a Seminole Indian settlement many of the people have distinctly Indian features and a true out island lifestyle. The village welcomes visitors. Contact Rev Bertram A Newton for his history of Red Bays. Locally caught sponges and hand made baskets can all be bought very cheaply. The straw work here is excellent. Mrs Marshall is the local bush granny and community celebrity. Usually found weaving in the centre of the village she will show how baskets are made, and explain local culture, politics and bush medicine to visitors. Mr Russell always has plenty of sponges for sale (and illegally caught turtle and iguanas, don't buy these) and also works as a bonefishing guide. There is only one telephone in Red Bays, T3292369 and leave a message for the person you want to contact.

Essentials

A-B *Green Windows Inn*, PO Box 23076, T3292194, F3292016. 5 mins' walk to beach, pool, 12 rooms, bar, restaurant. **B** *Conch Sound Resort Inn*, Conch Sound, Nicholl's Town, T3292060. 6 rooms, restaurant, bar. Staniard Creek is a settlement of small, mostly single storey houses with a clinic and school, reached by rutted road across swamp (turn off main road by Batelco). **B-C** *Quality Inn*, T3686217. Also known as *Dicky's Place*, owned by Richard Riley, remote, small, jetty, on creek short way from sea, cheaper rooms in main house, or better rooms in new annex, food and drinks available, fishing. **L** *Small Hope Bay Lodge*, between Staniard Creek and Fresh Creek, T3682014, F3682015, Box CB11 817, Nassau, or PO Box 21667, Ft Lauderdale, Fl 33335-1667, T305-3598240, F3598241, www.SmallHope.com The nicest place to stay and highly recommended, specializes in diving and fishing but still good if only one partner dives/fishes, informal, cabin accommodation among trees right on seafront, all inclusive with 3 hearty meals, drinks, taxes, service and scuba lesson, child and teen discounts, rustic but comfortable, good beds and lots of towels, fans, no phones, TV or a/c, sailboat, windsurfers, hot tub, bicycles, books, games, children's toys, birdwatching, yoga, run by Birch family since 1960s, very friendly, staff and guests mingle at meals and after dinner, excellent service. In Fresh Creek, **B** *Chickcharnie's Hotel*, T3682025. Overlooks harbour, lovely view, 75ft dock, restaurant, bar, foodstore, rooms with shared bath and fan, or with bath and a/c, or new rooms with view, Bahamian decor. **AL** *Andros Lighthouse Yacht Club and Marina*, T3682305-8, F3682300. The other side of the creek, government owned, up for sale, appalling service, unfriendly and usually empty but otherwise lovely location on waterfront, attractive buildings with luxury yachts moored at dock, big, tiled rooms, a/c, cool, TV, fridge, phones, bar, restaurant, tennis, bicycles, pool, ping pong, 12 rooms, 2 villas, 18 boat slips with fuel available.

Around Behring Point and Cargill Creek the lodges offer fishing and nothing else, all guests are expected to be anglers: **L** *Andros Island Bonefishing Club* (*Rupert's Place*), 368-5167/5200, F3685235, www.bahamas.com/hotels/abone Owned by Rupert Leadon, 12 rooms with 2 double beds, a/c, some with fan and fridge, includes meals, 4-night package with fishing US$960 per person double occupancy, 2-3 months reservation needed, 80-90% repeat guests, comfortable but not luxurious, friendly, most fishermen go out by 0730, return 1500, shower, cocktails, supper 1900, bed by 2100. **LL** *Cargill Creek Fishing Lodge*, next door, PO Box N-1882, Cargill Creek, T3685129, F3685046. 7 double rooms, 4 singles, 3 cottages with 2 bedrooms (sleep 4), TV, pool, 10% discount for Autec employees, boats and guides for fishing. **LL-AL** *Tranquillity Hill Bone Fish Lodge*, T/F3684132. All-inclusive, 9

Sleeping
Listed from north to south

rooms, bar, restaurant, TV. On Mangrove Cay, **AL-B** *Mangrove Cay Inn*, T3690069, F3690014. 8 rooms, restaurant, fishing. **AL-A** *Seascape Inn*, PO Box 023824, T/F3690342, www.seascapeinn.com. 5 rooms, fishing, diving, restaurant, breakfast included, transfer to hotel included. **AL** per person *Moxey's Guest House*, Little Harbour, T/F3690023. All-inclusive, 10 rooms, diving. On the border of Congo Town and Long Bay, **L-A** *Emerald Palms-By-The-Sea*, PO Box N-9520, T3692661, F3692667. Modern with balconies facing the sea, swimming pool, tennis court and boats for charter.

Eating   Andros has an exportable surplus of crabs, so crab dishes are very popular. May to July is the crab season. Try baked Andros crab, which uses the crab's own fat to cook it in, also Vetol's crab'n'rice and stewed crab cooked with conch. Andros is relatively undeveloped and some restaurants may need advance warning. For a cheap meal look out for cook outs.

Rupert's Fish Camp, Cargill Creek, very good local game fish, candlelit veranda overlooks sea. *Seaview Restaurant and Bar* at the *Andros Island Bone Fishing Club* is nearby. *Dig Dig's* is an excellent restaurant at Cargill Creek, on side of main road, T3685097 for reservations in evening. 1 hr notice enough at lunchtime. The *Small Hope Bay Lodge* serves large, filling meals, well cooked. *Chickcharnie Hotel* in Fresh Creek. **Nicholl's Town** *Rolle's* takeaway serves best local food on island, cracked conch, chicken etc; *Rumours* restaurant, T3292398. Bar and disco, Fri, Sat, 2100-0300. **Kemps Bay**, *Dudley's Pink Pussy Cat Club* has a rake'n'scrape band and traditional stepping dancing with Rosita on saw and Ben on drums.

Transport   **Car hire** In Kemps Bay Mr Rahming rents cars and also provides a charter service to any of the Family Islands (T3691608). At San Andros airport *Cecil Gaitor* has cars for hire. *Small Hope Bay Lodge* will organize car hire for US$50-75 per day. It is often possible to hire cars for the day from private individuals, ask locally, taxi drivers have details. Most settlements are linked by paved roads with plenty of potholes to keep you awake. **Taxis** are available. A taxi from the airport at Fresh Creek to *Small Hope Bay Lodge* is US$20 (fare usually included in all-inclusive package), to Cargill Creek US$37. **Boat** Boats can dock at Mastic Point (north), Fresh Creek (central) and Congo Town (south). For mailboat schedules and fares see ferries in the Essentials section at the front of the chapter.

Berry Islands

Population: 628   *There are thirty Berry Islands, all of which offer wonderful opportunities for divers and*
1990 census   *snorkellers. Most are the private homes of the wealthy or inhabited only by wildlife.*

Ins & outs   Great Harbour Cay (GHC) and Chub Cay (CCZ) have airports served by Island Express from Fort Lauderdale (T954-3590380). *Southern Pride Aviation/Bimini Island Air* fly daily to Chub Cay from Fort Lauderdale's Executive Airport. Other carriers include *Island Air Charters*, T954-3599942, and *Pan Am Air Bridge*, T800-4242557.

Around the   **Bullock's Harbour** in **Great Harbour Cay** is the main settlement in the area, Great
islands   Harbour Cay is the largest cay in the Berry chain at just two miles across. First settled by ex-slaves in 1836, the cay proved difficult to farm. **LL-A** *The Great Harbour Cay Club* is here, with 28 rooms and villas, T954-9219084, F954-9211044. There are facilities for yachts and a nine-hole golf course. Cruise ships drop anchor off Great Sturrup Cay and passengers can spend the day on the deserted beach there.

The only other spot in the Berry Islands which caters for tourists is **Chub Cay** which has been extensively rebuilt since Hurricane Andrew in 1992. The **LL-L** *Chub Cay Club* (PO Box 661067, Miami Springs, FL 33266, www.chubcay.com, T3251490, F3225199), has rooms and villas, its own airstrip, tennis courts, restaurant, 96-slip marina and extensive dive facilities offered by Chub Cay Undersea Adventures T4623400, F4624100, www.chubcaydive. com Chub Cay is a port of entry and has a surge-proof harbour. There is a US$2 charge to use the marina docks to clear customs and immigration unless you take

Chalk's

Chalk's seaplanes are a popular and exciting feature of travelling to Bimini and conjure up a certain nostalgia for pre-war adventure travel. Founded in 1919 by Arthur B 'Pappy' Chalk on the docks of the Royal Palm Hotel in Miami, the company is now the largest seaplane airline in the world. Famous passengers in the 1930s included Ernest Hemingway, who travelled frequently to Bimini along with many other Americans escaping Prohibition, and the Cuban dictator, Gerardo Machado, who fled a coup in 1933 in a chartered Chalk's plane. His occupation on the manifest was listed as 'retired'.

slip. It is a good place to stop and clean off the salt after a hard crossing. There is a deep water canyon at Chub Cay where you can find a variety of colourful reef fish and open water marine life. Schools of up to 300 Nassau groupers have been seen. Staghorn coral can be seen in the shallow waters near Mamma Rhoda Rock. Less natural, but still fascinating is the submarine deliberately sunk in 90 ft of water off Bond Cay, named after James himself.

Many of the cays do not welcome uninvited guests. Interesting wildlife can be found on Frozen Cay and Alder Cay. Terns and pelicans can be seen here and although they are privately owned, sailors may anchor here to observe the birds. Hoffman's Cay, now deserted, was originally home to a thriving farming settlement. Ruins of houses, a church and a graveyard still stand. Paths also lead to a deep blue hole. A golden beach runs along the length of the east coast of the island. On Little Whale Cay, Wallace Groves, the founder of Freeport, has his own home and airstrip.

Bimini

Once thought to be the site of the lost city of Atlantis, the Bimini chain of islands, only 50 miles from Florida, is divided into North and South Bimini and a series of cays. There are more bars than shops on Bimini and service is minimal. It is not a glamorous resort, although there are plenty of luxury yachts moored there. The big attraction on Bimini is the deep sea fishing, which has drawn sportsmen to its waters for generations. The theme of big game fishing is reflected in the bars and restaurants, which also have Hemingway associations.

Population: 1,639
1990 census

Getting there Pan Am Air Bridge flies from Fort Lauderdale, Miami and Nassau. Chalk's International (T800-4242557, in Alice Town T3473024, in Bailey Town T3473131) flies into the harbour from Florida. For mailboat details see Essentials sections at the beginning of the chapter. Bimini is the port of entry for most boats coming from Florida. **Getting around** There is no car rental. People use golf carts and boats to get around.

Ins & outs

Ernest Hemingway lived on Bimini in 1931-37 at Blue Marlin Cottage and his novel *Islands in the Stream* was based on Bimini. A display of Hemingway memorabilia can be seen at Compleat Angler Hotel and Museum. On South Bimini is the legendary site of the Fountain of Youth, sought by Ponce de León in 1512. The pool known as the Healing Hole is claimed to have some beneficial effects. In 1994, a Spanish treasure ship, believed to be the Santiago El Grande, which sank in 1766 while heading for Spain laden with gold, silver and emeralds, was discovered off the southern tip of Bimini.

Background

Bimini is famous for **big game fishing**. Fishing is excellent all year round although 7 May to 15 June is the tuna season (blue fin), June and July are best for blue marlin, winter and spring for white marlin. Blue marlin are the favourite target, averaging between 150 and 500 pounds, but which can exceed 1,000 pounds. The South Biminis, Cat Cay and Gun Cay are the places to catch billfish and bluefin. There are lots of fishing tournaments and the Ministry of Tourism promotes over 40 annually,

Diving & marine life

The Bahamas

including the Bacardi Billfish Tournament, the Bimini Benefit Tournament, the Bahamas Championship Tournament and the Bahamas Billfish Championship series. *The Bimini Big Game Fishing Club* caters for most fishermen's needs and can arrange fishing trips with guides. It has 180 slips, charter/boat rental, all supplies and a large walk-in freezer for daily catches. Fishing can also be arranged through the *Compleat Angler Hotel*, Brown's Marina or Weech's Bimini Dock.

Scuba diving is recommended, particularly over the Bimini Wall with its black coral trees, or at the lovely reefs off Victory Cay. *Bimini Undersea*, run by Bill and Nowdla Keefe, has a comprehensive list of facilities and can also offer **dolphin excursions**, **sailing**, **sea kayaking**, **fishing** and **tennis**, T3473089, F3473079, in the USA T305-6535572, info@biminiundersea.com

Around the island **Alice Town** is the capital of Bimini although most people live in **Bailey Town** to the north along the King's Highway. Alice Town has a lot of bars and a straw market, and little else. Heading north from Alice Town you come to *The Anchorage*, a restaurant on the highest point on the island with good views of the sea. The beach in either direction is excellent with white sand and good surfing waves. Above the beach is a pathway which passes the picturesque Methodist Church (1858) and leads to Bailey Town.

The airplane wrecks at the edge of the airfield at **Alice Town** on North Bimini are mostly the results of unsuccessful drugs running attempts en route from Colombia to Miami. Bimini has been claimed as an important success in the fight against drug running to the US mainland; **Gun Cay** has become the centre for drug interdiction operations and is full of US DEA personnel. Bimini suffered flood damage caused by Hurricane Andrew in 1992 but soon recovered.

Cat Cay, to the south, was hit by Hurricane Andrew in August 1992, with winds of 180 miles per hour, gusting to 250 miles per hour. Damage to island property was estimated at US$100mn. First developed in 1932 it had a golf course, 68 houses for the rich and their staff, and lots of expensive yachts. The private club here accepts transient yachts except on big holiday weekends when members converge. There is a marina fee for customs and immigration.

In 1997, the government signed a controversial agreement with a US company for development of a five-mile strip of land at Bimini Bay. The US$400mn project will include a 225-room hotel and casino, a marina, golf course and residential development. Local people are concerned that proposed in-filling of mangroves will damage spawning grounds for shrimp, conch and fish, with a consequent impact on the fishing industry.

Sleeping & eating **LL-L** *The Bimini Big Game Club* (T3473391, F3473392, www.bimini-big-game-club.com, PO Box 699, Alice Town), owned by Bacardi, this is the main hotel (rooms, suites and cottages) and social centre (beware the Beastwhacker, a cocktail of champagne and Bacardi rum) and has swimming pool and tennis courts as well as a marina with charter boats and all facilities for deep sea fishing or bonefishing. **LL-A** *Bimini Blue Water*, PO Box 601, T3473166, F3473293. Rooms, 3-bedroomed cottage, suites also include Hemingway's Marlin Cottage, private beach, swimming pool and 32-slip marina. **A-B** *Compleat Angler Hotel*, PO Box 601, T3473122, F3473293. In town, popular bar. **LL-AL** *All My Children Hotel*, T3473334, F3473333. Owned by Glen Rolle, 33 rooms, bar, restaurant (see below). **L-A** *Sea Crest*, PO Box 654, Alice Town, T3473071, F3473495. Managed by Alfred Sweeting.

Nightlife After dark activities consist of drinking and dancing. *The Red Lion Pub*, T3473259, is recommended for its seafood, as is *Captain Bob Smith's*, T3473260, and *The Big Game Restaurant* on the sea front in Alice Town. The *Calypsonians* play weekly at *The Compleat Angler*, worth seeing, and *Glen Rolle and the Surgeons* provide musical entertainment at *All My Children Hotel*.

Cat Island

Named after Arthur Catt, a British pirate who was in league with Henry Morgan and Edward Teach (Blackbeard), Cat Island boasts Lucayan Indian caves near Port Howe, as well as the usual underwater sites of interest and beauty. Fifty miles long, it was once called San Salvador, and is a contender for the site of Columbus' first landfall. It has rolling hills and the highest point in the Bahamas, Mount Alvernia, 206 ft above sea level. The island is a centre for the practice of Obeah, a Bahamian voodoo incorporating both bush medicine and witchcraft, which is indicated by bottles and other small objects hanging from the branches of the trees.

*Population: 1,698
1990 census*

Getting there *Bahamasair* has flights to Arthur's Town (ATC) from Nassau 3 times a week. There is also an airport at New Bight which is more convenient for most hotels but there are no scheduled services. Some hotels have their own airstrips. For details on mailboats page 72 at the beginning of this chapter. **Getting around** Transport is difficult in the north as there are no taxis or buses and few cars for hitching lifts.

Ins & outs

The Bahamas

Flora and fauna

Uninhabited **Conception Island** and its adjoining reefs, between Cat Island and Long Island, is a land and sea park visited by migrating birds and nesting turtles, protected by the Bahamas National Trust. Many great and little blue herons can be seen at Hawksnest Creek bird sanctuary. In inland ponds it is possible to find the Cat Island turtle (*pseudyms felis*). Unfortunately, the turtles are a source of very rich meat and their numbers have recently dwindled. Near the settlements of Gaitors and Stephenson you can visit large caves full of bats. There are more bat caves south of Gaitors, near Stephenson. Farming is mostly subsistence, using slash and burn to grow crops such as red corn, guinea corn, cassava, okra, peas, beans, sugarcane, watermelons, pineapples, coconuts and bananas. Pot hole farming uses small amounts of soil in deep limestone holes to cultivate plants like the banana tree.

Cat Island

Around the island

New Bight is the capital and shares an impressive bay with the quaint Old Bight, the site of an early 19th-century attempt to establish a cotton plantation. You can see the ruins of Pigeon Bay Cottage, an old plantation house just outside Old Bight. New Bight has a few shops. The annual regatta is held here in August. Above the village you can climb **Mount Alvernia** and visit Father Jerome's Hermitage. The **Stations of the Cross** are carved along a winding path leading to the Hermitage, built by Father Jerome, an Anglican priest who converted to Roman Catholicism and designed several churches on Cat Island and Long Island.

Most development has taken place in the south

Fernandez Bay, three miles north of New Bight and home to *The Fernandez Bay Village Resort*, has one of the island's best beaches, a secluded cove with excellent sands. On the most southerly tip of the island are two beaches with facilities: *The Cutlass Bay Club* (tennis, water-skiing) has its own airstrip and a good restaurant. World famous **bonefishing** flats are within wading distance of the beach. Close by along the crumbling cliff tops are the impressive ruins of the **Richman Hill plantation**, with ruins of slave quarters, an overseer's house and a plantation house. The original plantation stretched from the ocean to the inland lake. Another interesting ruin is Colonel Andrew Deveaux' mansion at **Port Howe**. Granted land on Cat Island for delivering Nassau from the Spanish, he set up a briefly prosperous cotton plantation here. Early settlers in Port Howe lured ships on to the rocks in order to loot their cargoes. Today Port Howe is famous for its coconuts and pineapples, while the bread, cooked in Dutch or Rock wood-fuelled ovens, is said to be the Bahamas' tastiest. The *Greenwood Dive Centre* at The Greenwood Beach Resort, Port Howe offers **scuba diving** and **snorkelling**. Run by Waldemar Illing, the hotel attracts German and other European visitors (T/F3423053). There are two boats taking 4-20 passengers on diving or snorkelling trips, but diving can also be done from the shore. Yachting facilities and activities are found at Hawks Nest Marina.

The main settlement in the north of the island is **Arthur's Town**, but other than an airstrip there is not much else; there are no restaurants and only one shop which does not sell much. Local people rely on the weekly mailboat from Nassau for groceries. There are bars but none serves food. Two miles inland is a small lake surrounded by mangrove thickets. Islanders refer to it as a blue hole and tell stories of its supernatural inhabitants. The beaches in the north are excellent. Northside Beach, reached by dirt road, stretches for 20 miles but has no facilities at all and has the ubiquitous debris. Orange Creek is an attractive inlet three miles north of Arthur's Town. Along the nearby shores are the 'white sand farms' with small scale farming of beets, potatoes and carrots.

Essentials

Sleeping **LL-L** *Fernandez Bay Village*, New Bight, T3423043, F3423051, www.fernandezbayvillage.com 1-2 bedroomed cottages, kitchens in larger ones, built of stone and tile, garden showers, fans, private terrace, meal plans available, most watersports available, diving arranged, snorkelling, fishing, sailing, paddle tennis, volley ball, waterskiing, boat rental with or without captain, canoes and kayaks complimentary, bicycles, beach bar, restaurant, hammocks, relaxed, unpretentious, flights can be arranged, US$100 per person one way from Nassau. **LL** *Cutlass Bay Club*, Port Howe, T3423085, F3425048. All-inclusive, 3 nights minimum, pool, beach, in USA, PO Box 273767, Tampa, FL33688, F813-2690556. **AL-B** *Greenwood Beach Resort*, at Port Howe, T3423053, F3425053, www.hotelgreenwoodinn.com German-run, good snorkelling, scuba diving from the beach, pool, satellite TV, bicycles, fishing, car and scooter rental. **LL** *Hawks Nest Resort & Marina*, T3427050, half board, 10 rooms. **LL-AL** *Pigeon Cay Beach Club*, T3544116, F3544161. Reservations T800-6884752, 5 cottages, 4 day minimum, reduced rates for longer stays. **AL** *The Bridge Inn*, New Bight, T3423013, F3423041. With disco, reasonable accommodation, good food, bar, fishing. **B** *Orange Creek Inn*, T3544110, F3544042. 3 mins from airport, free transport, 16 rooms with kitchenettes, laundromat, store. **B** *Sea Spray Hotel*, Orange Creek, T3544116. 15 rooms.

Eating The Bahamas' biggest goat farm is near New Bight. Goat meat is used in a local dish called 'souce stew', cooked with potatoes, onions and a lemon lookalike fruit called souce. The restaurant at the *Fernandez Bay Resort* is elegant and expensive. *Greenwood Inn* has Bahamian and European menu. *Blue Bird*, open air restaurant in New Bight, T3423095. Dinner from US$16, access by boat. *Pilot Harbour* on waterfront at Old Bight, T3424066, VHF 16, Bahamian specials, cocktails. **Bars in Arthur's Town**: *Miss Nelly's* (pool table), the *Hard Rock Oasis Restaurant and Bar* (T3427050) and *Mr Pratt's Bar* (dominoes). Also *Lovers' Boulevard Disco and Satellite Lounge* (T3542207) is popular and has a good local band playing Rake'n'Scrape.

Crooked Island, Long Cay and Acklins

Crooked Island, Long Cay and Acklins comprise Crooked Island District, stretching three sides round the Bight of Acklins and bordered by 45 miles of treacherous barrier reef. At Crooked Island Passage, coral reefs can be found in very shallow water, falling sharply in walls housing sponges of every shape and colour. Although at 92 square miles, Crooked Island is larger than New Providence the population is sparce and still declining because of emigration. Tourism is not very developed and there is no electricity or running water in most of the settlements.

Crooked Island population: 412
Acklins population: 405
1990 census

Getting there The main airport (Crooked Island – CRI) is at Major Cay; Acklins has an airport at Spring Point (AXP). *Bahamasair* has two flights a week from Nassau, one goes to Major Cay first, the other lands first at Spring Point. The *Windward Express* mailboat docks at the harbour in Landrail Point once a week, see page 72. **Getting around** The two islands are linked by a ferry, which runs twice a day between Lovely Bay and Richmond.

Ins & outs

Around the islands

Once as many as 40 plantations thrived here, but as in other islands, the crops failed because of poor soil and the industry declined. Nowadays, two valuable exports from the Crooked Island and Acklins District are aloe vera for use in skin preparations and the cascarilla bark which is sold to Italy for the production of Campari. Remains of the plantation era can be seen in Marine Farm and at Hope Great House in the north of the island. **Bird Rock Lighthouse** in the north is said to be the site of one of Columbus' original anchor spots on his first voyage. Close by is **Pittstown** where you can see the Bahamas' first General Post Office built in the era of William Pitt. It is now the restaurant of the hotel **A** *Pittstown Point Landings* (14 rooms in

Crooked Island

The Bahamas

Crooked Island and Acklins

cottages, T3362507, www.pittstownpointlandings.com), which has its own airstrip, beaches, fishing, snorkelling, windsurfing and diving facilities. **Gun Bluff**, near the hotel was thought to have been a pirate's lookout, cannons have been found close by. In the surrounding area many North Americans have winter residences. Two miles away is **Landrail Point**, the main centre of the island, which has *Landrail Point* (T3444233, 12 rooms, simply furnished, neighbourly atmosphere, home cooking, inexpensive, a restaurant and store). The people here are Seventh Day Adventists so no pork or alcohol is sold and everything closes on Saturday. *Mrs Gibson's Lunch Room* is recommended for its freshly baked bread and simple Bahamian dishes.

Further south at **Cabbage Hill B-C** *Crooked Island Beach Inn* and the 6-room *Cabbage Hill* (both at T3442321, F3442502 at Batelco, fishing available), the former is near the beach and airport, owned by Rev Ezekiel Thompson, who is the Bahamasair representative. The capital of Crooked Island is **Colonel Hill**. There is a restaurant/baker's/guesthouse here run by Mrs Deleveaux, called *Sunny Lea*. Rooms have a good view of Major Cay Harbour. Close to the sheltered lagoon near Major Cay is a large cave; bromeliads can be seen at its entrance.

Acklins

Atwood Bay is recommended as one of the Family Islands' most beautiful curved bays

Acklins is a few miles from Crooked Island and a ferry operates between the two islands, docking at **Lovely Bay** twice a day. The island is 192 square miles and was named La Isabella by Columbus before being known as Acklins Cay and then just Acklins. Archaeological evidence points to a large Indian community once existing between Jamaica Cay and Delectable Bay (possibly the largest in the Bahamas). Today, Acklins is not very developed; there are roads but they are not paved.

The main settlement on Acklins is **Spring Point**, which has an airport. The *Airport Inn* run by Curtis Hanna is a popular meeting place, with rooms to rent and a restaurant/bar. **B** *Nae's Guest House*, T3443089, run by Mrs Naomi Hanna, five rooms, restaurant, beach. At nearby **Pompey Bay** it is still possible to see rock walls which were plantation demarcation boundaries. Pompey was once prosperous and busy; today most of the town is deserted and a tall church on the coast is abandoned. There is also a guesthouse at Pinefield run by the Williams family.

Long Cay

To the south of Acklins is a group of uninhabited cays sometimes referred to as the **Mira Por Vos Cays**. The most southerly is called **Castle Island** and is distinguished easily from afar by its tall battery operated lighthouse. There is a large seabird population here. South, North Guana and Fish Cay are all noted as havens for wildlife. **Long Cay** is the largest of the cays in this area and is inhabited. Long Cay was once known as Fortune Island and enjoyed great prosperity in the 19th century as a clearing house for ships between Europe and the Americas. The advent of the steamship made the use of Long Cay port redundant. Today you can see reminders of its former prosperity in the large unused Catholic church, various civic buildings and the relics of a railway system. On the south end of this island there is a large nesting ground for the West Indian flamingo.

Eleuthera

Population: 7,993 1990 census

Eleuthera is 110 miles long but thin, two miles at its widest and only the width of a car at its narrowest. It has lovely pink sand beaches, particularly on the Atlantic side, coves and cliffs. This was the first permanent settlement in the Bahamas when Eleutheran Adventurers came from Bermuda and American colonial loyalists fled the mainland during the American Revolution. Their descendants still live here, living in houses painted in pastel colours. The first black settlers were slaves and free Africans from Bermuda.

Ins and outs

Getting there

There are airports at **Governor's Harbour** (GHB) (8 miles from the town, US$20 taxi fare for 2 people), **North Eleuthera** (ELH) and **Rock Sound** (RSD). *Bahamasair* have scheduled flights daily from Nassau to all three. Governor's Harbour and North Eleuthera are served also by *Gulfstream International* in conjunction with *Continental Connection*, *Island Express*, *US Airways Express*, *Air Sunshine*, *Twin Air*, *Sandpiper Air*, *Bel Air Transport* and *American Eagle* from Fort Lauderdale, Miami, Key West and/or Orlando. Four mailboats and a very efficient ferry from Nassau call at Eleuthera. See page 72. The harbour master or shopkeepers will also tell you about mailboat sailings.

Getting around

The main road which runs down the backbone of the island is called the Queen's Highway and makes exploring by car easy and direct. Car hire from all 3 airports and in town costs US$45-50 per day, **ASA Rent-A-Car Service** (T3322575); **Hilton Johnson** (near Hatchet Bay, T3320241); also **Ethel Knowles** at *Ethel's Cottages*, at Tarpum Bay. You can also hire mopeds. There are some public buses.

Flora and fauna

Eleuthera is visited by many migrant birds. At **Hatchet Bay**, a few miles south of the Glass Window, there are ring necked pheasants. The Schooner and Kinley Cays in the **Bight of Eleuthera** are uninhabited but have large populations of white crowned pigeons. On **Finlay Cay** there are also sooty terns and noddy terns. The cays are protected by the Wild Bird Act. Local indigenous flowers include yellow elder, poincianas and hibiscus. Lizards, chicken snakes and feral goats and pigs are common. North of Hatchet Bay you can visit a bat cave where there are thousands of roosting leaf-nosed bats.

Eleuthera

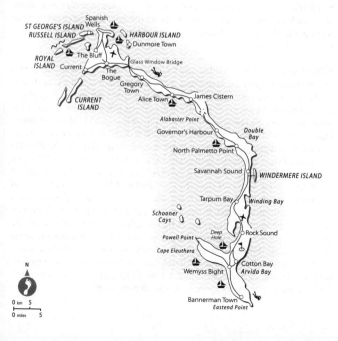

The Bahamas

Diving and marine life

Dive sites The **Plateau** became an underwater national park in 1993. It is a pretty site with mini walls, ledges, fissures and lots of fish in an area about ¾ mile by ½ mile. The usual regulations apply, with no fish feeding, no reef touching, no collecting and no spear fishing. The Plateau is about a mile from the Glass Window, seven miles from Harbour Island. If you like exciting diving, try riding the **Current Cut** on the incoming tide, which propels you between islands at a speed of about seven knots. Surfing is also good here. A 300-year old shipwreck at **Yankee Channel** lies in only 10 ft of water, while on the shallow, sharp reefs to the north called the **Devil's Backbone**, there is the wreck of a train where a barge once sank with its cargo on its way to Cuba, and a 19th-century passenger steamship. Four miles south of Royal Island is an old freighter, sunk by fire while loaded with a cargo of bat guano, now used as a landmark by sailors. The guano is an excellent fish food and the wreck is home to enormous fish, with Angel fish weighing up to 15 pounds and parrot fish of 20-30 pounds. A remarkable dive or snorkel site. Unfortunately, illegal bleach used by craw fishermen has spoiled many west side reefs.

Dive centres Diving and other watersports can be arranged with *Romora Bay Club* (T3332323, T/F3332500, PO Box 146, Harbour Island), where the dive operation is run by Jeff Fox and his diving dog. There is one boat taking out groups of 12-14 divers for single tank dives only, US$28 including tank and weights, resort course US$55-65, full PADI certification available. Individual specialized trips can be arranged. If the wind is north-northeast there is no diving.

Beaches and watersports

Beaches There are excellent beaches on the east side of southern Eleuthera. The west coast, however, is a little rocky. Many of the easterly beaches are backed by coconut palms or rocky cliffs with cedars. Three miles north of Alice Town in North Eleuthera there is a bushy and bumpy road off the main road which leads to **Surfers Beach**. It has the best surfing waves in the Bahamas and is frequently visited by surfing enthusiasts. **Harbour Island** has a beautiful pink sand beach which is said to be one of the most photographed beaches in the world. **Lighthouse Beach** at Cape Eleuthera has three miles of good beach.

Sailing Sailing boats are recommended to use a local pilot along the notoriously dangerous stretch of coast between Harbour Island and Spanish Wells. Valentine's Yacht Club, Harbour Island, has a 50-slip marina taking boats of up to 140ft and offering full services but no charter yachts. A regatta held to celebrate Discovery Day in November results in Valentine's bursting at the seams. Also on Harbour Island is the *Harbour Island Club and Marina* with 32 slips for 50-60 ft boats. Full service facilities are gradually coming on stream, contact Roger Ironside for details (T/F3332427, VHF 16, PO Box 43). At Spanish Wells there is the *Spanish Wells Yacht Haven* (T3334255, VHF 16), with 30 slips, and several boatyards for repairs. On the west side of Eleuthera, *Marine Services* of Eleuthera (T/F3350186, VHF 16), with 20 slips, and *Hatchet Bay Yacht Club* are at Hatchet Bay. The grassy bottom at Hatchet Bay makes anchoring difficult, so it is best to take a mooring or dock. Round Cape Eleuthera is *Davis Harbour Marina*, with 40 slips (T3134-6303/6101, VHF 16). This is also the centre for the deep sea and bonefishing charter companies. *Cape Eleuthera Marina* has docks, sometimes with water and electricity and rubbish collection, which yachts may use for a nominal fee. Redevelopment of the resort has been rumoured for years but nothing has happened yet. Harbour Island, Hatchet Bay, Governor's Harbour, Rock Sound and Cape Eleuthera are all ports of entry.

Around the island

In 1999 Hurricane Floyd hit the island, causing extensive damage. Some resorts stayed closed for the winter season, some went out of business, while others soon reopened. Many homes were destroyed and they took longer than the resorts to be repaired. On Harbour Island some homes were badly damaged. To a visitor now, however, there is little evidence of the hurricane. The southern part of the island was hardest hit economically, as many foreign-owned properties have been slow to get round to repairs, although Bahamian-run hotels have received government assistance. Both *Club Med* and *Venta Club* have closed, while *Cape Eleuthera* is dormant.

Just north of Gregory Town is the **Glass Window Bridge**, where you can compare the blue Atlantic Ocean with the greenish water of the Caribbean on the other side, separated by a strip of rock just wide enough to drive a car across. Nearby are two small farming communities, Upper and Lower Bogue. **The Bogue** was once known as 'the bog' because of its marshy ground. During the hurricane in 1965 the sea flooded the land and now there are saltwater pools where you can find barracuda, grouper and snapper which were washed there by the tide. Also in the north is **The Cave**, which contains some impressive stalagmites and stalactites and the **Preacher's Cave**, where the Adventurers took shelter. The latter is reached by a rough unpaved track about 10 miles north of North Eleuthera; there is a pulpit carved out of rock from when the cave became a place of worship. **Rock Sound Water Hole Park** is an ocean or blue hole well stocked with grouper and yellowtail, while the walls are encrusted with flat oysters. Swimming is dangerous. Fishing is restricted.

Gregory Town is the main settlement in the north of the island. Pineapples here take 18 months to grow, making them sweeter than plants grown in six months with the help of commercial chemicals. All the farms are small and there are no large plantations. There is a beach with good surfing. It is 20 minutes drive from the airport. Locally-made stained glass can be seen and bought at the Simba studio gallery and shop.

Home of pineapple rum where a pineapple festival is held annually in Jun/Jul

Governor's Harbour is one of the oldest settlements in the Bahamas with several interesting colonial period houses. The harbour is picturesque and is linked by a causeway to Cupid's Cay, the original settlement. A new cruise ship pier was built in 1991 but is unusable as no deep water channel was dredged. On 10 November a Guy Festival celebrates Guy Fawkes Day and parades are held, culminating in an evening bonfire. Tourism used to be dominated here by *Club Med Eleuthera*, on the Atlantic beachfront.

In the south, **Windermere Island**, linked to the mainland by a small bridge, was an exclusive resort popular with the British Royal Family. The resort is closed now but opulent holiday homes remain. **Tarpum Bay** is the home of MacMillan-Hughes' Art Gallery and Castle. It used to be a big pineapple centre and there are many examples of wooden colonial houses in good repair.

Further south is **Rock Sound**, the largest settlement on the island with a population of about 1,100. It was first known as New Portsmouth and then Wreck Sound. Rock Sound is surrounded by limey, bush covered hills. It has a large modern shopping centre, three churches and many bars.

A few farming villages exist in the extreme south with more stretches of beach and fishing. One such is **Bannerman Town**, once known as the Pearl of the South. In the 1930s it was a prosperous sponge fishing centre with 20 or more sponging schooners anchored off the west shore. Today the settlement is like a ghost town with large churches in ruins and few people. Those who have stayed eke out a living by farming goats and pineapples and catching land crabs to send to Nassau. At the most southerly point of the island, **Cape Eleuthera** and **Point Eleuthera** are sometimes likened to the opposite points on the tail of a fish. On Cape Eleuthera there is a lighthouse which was repaired by the Raleigh Expedition in 1988. At one time the keeper, Captain Finby, was also the local obeah man. Legend has it that he slept with a ghost

The Bahamas

The Bahamas

called the White Lady, who visited him nightly. Lighthouse Beach is three miles long. At Eleuthera Point there is a good cliff top view of Cat Island and Little San Salvador. Be careful as the edges are badly eroded. From here you can also see nesting stacks of fairy terns, shark and barracuda channels and the spectacular blues, greens, yellows, reds and browns of fringing reefs. A lone tarpon known as Tommy cruises off this beach often in less than 4 ft of water.

Spanish Wells
Population: 1,372
1990 census

On St George's Cay, an island off the north of Eleuthera (a short ferry ride), Spanish Wells gets its name from the use of the cay by Spanish ships as a water supply. One and three quarter miles long and half a mile wide, until the hurricane disaster of 1992 it was reputed to have the highest per capita income of the Bahamas islands, with the wealth coming from fishing the spiny Bahamian lobster (known locally as bugs) as well as tourism. Most of the boats were wrecked by the storm and the fishermen lost their livelihoods. The population are descended from the original settlers, the Eleutheran Adventurers from Bermuda and the British Loyalists from the mainland, and are all white. The Spanish Wells Museum in a restored wooden house with shutters has exhibits of the island's history and culture. ■ *1000-1200, 1300-1500, Mon-Sat. To get to Spanish Wells from North Eleuthera airport, take a Pinders Taxi to the ferry dock, then ferry to the island (US$10).*

A number of local fishermen can be hired as fishing guides off nearby **Russell** and **Royal Islands** (inhabited by a group of Haitians), payment by negotiation. Royal Island was once developed as a sheep farm by an estranged English dignitary. The old house still stands and paths weave through the overgrown grounds and gardens. Visitors can hire bicycles, but there are no cars.

Harbour Island
Population: 1,219
1990 census

This is the most desirable place to stay in North Eleuthera. From the airport it is a quick taxi ride, US$3 per person, to the dock and from there water taxis wait to take passengers on a 10-minute ride to the island (US$4 per person one-way or US$8 for only one person). Taxis from the harbour to most resorts cost US$3 per person. **Dunmore Town**, named after Lord Dunmore, Governor 1786-1797, is a mixture of pastel coloured cottages, white picket fences and a number of small hotels and restaurants. It was the capital of the Bahamas for a time and once an important shipyard and sugar refining centre. Rum making was particularly popular during Prohibition. The three mile pink sand beach is popular. Bicycles can be rented at the dock. Fishing trips are easily arranged (US$85 per half day). Reggie does taxi tours of the island for day trippers and he and his wife Jena run a regular taxi service, recommended, T3332116. Access by yacht should be done with a hired local guide as you have to pass by a reef called the Devil's Backbone and the trip appears to take the yacht almost on the beach.

Essentials

Sleeping
All the major hotels close in the autumn for some weeks so plan ahead if visiting Sep-Nov

Gregory Town B *Cambridge Villas*, in Gregory Town, PO Box GT-1548, T3355080, F3355308. Run by Mr and Mrs Cambridge, painted yellow, 21 rooms of different sizes, pool, transport to Golden Key beach for swimming or elsewhere for surfing, bar/restaurant, music some nights, rental cars available. **AL-A** *The Cove Eleuthera*, also known as *Pineapple Cove*, PO Box GT-1548, T3355142, F3355338, www.thecoveeleuthera.com Rooms in scattered cottages on headland with rocky cove one side, sandy cove the other. Triples available, children under 12 free, large airy dining room, rather spartan but relaxed, small pool, tennis, snorkelling, sea kayaks, volley ball, badminton, hammocks, is just outside the town within walking distance.

Hatchet Bay, L-AL *Rainbow Inn*, PO Box EL 25053, T/F3350294, www.Rainbowinn.com A/c rooms with fan, deck, kitchenette, or 2-3-bedroomed villa, tennis, swimming pool and a good restaurant, rocky outlook, good snorkelling, caves, fantastic view, Rainbow beach 1 mile, two beaches just other side of hill, bicycles for guests, live entertainment Wed evenings in nautical bar, popular, run by Ken Keene, friendly host, closed mid-Sep to mid-Nov. Nearby is *Hilton & Elsie Island House*, T3356241, 3320241. 1-2 bedroom apartments US$500-700 per week, rental car US$200 per week, on hill, great view of island, Rainbow beach close or walk 1 mile to Eden beach on other side if rough, good kitchens, ideal for families, food stores in nearby Hatchet Bay or Rainbow Bay, Hilton is a taxi driver and does car rentals.

Governor's Harbour and the south *Club Med Eleuthera*, www.clubmed.com, closed in 2000. North of the town near North Palmetto Point on the ocean beach is **L-AL** *Unique Village*, PO Box 187, T3321830, F3321838. Rooms, apartments or 2-bedroom villas, restaurant, bar, satellite TV, children under 18 free in summer, under 12 in winter, all with seaviews. **A-B** *Laughing Bird Apartments*, PO Box EL-25076, T3322012, F3322358, ddavies@grouper. batelnet.bs Efficiency units and a guesthouse for 1-4 people, in town, overlooking the beach, owned and managed by nurse Jean Davies and her British architect husband Dan. **A** *Buccaneer Club*, T3322000, F3322888. Formerly a farmhouse, converted to 5 modern double rooms, pool. **AL-A** *Duck Inn Cottages*, T3322608, F3322160. Rooms or full house sleeps 8, 2-night minimum. **Tarpum Bay**: **B-C** *Hilton's Haven* near beach and Rock Sound airport, T3344231, F3344020. Owned and managed by nurse Mary Hilton, bicycles, car rental, bar/restaurant with Bahamian specials. **L-A** *Cartwrights Ocean View*, T3344215. Room or cottage with full kitchen, run by Iris Cartwright. **B** *Ethel's Cottages*, on the waterfront, PO Box 27, T3344233. Families welcomed, Mrs Ethel Knowles also rents out cars. **Rock Sound**: **B** *Edwina's Place*, PO Box 30, T3342094, F3342280. Run by Edwina Burrows, modest accommodation but good. **AL-A** *Palmetto Shores Vacation Villas*, at South Palmetto Point, 12 miles south of the airport, PO Box EL25131, T/F3321305. 1-3 bedroom villas, a/c, snorkelling gear, watersports, rental cars or scooters.

Spanish Wells **AL-B** *Spanish Wells Yacht Haven*, PO Box EL-27427, T3334255, F3334649. 5 rooms, pool, beach.

Harbour Island **L-A** *Romora Bay Club*, PO Box 146, T3332325, F3332500. Wide variety of units scattered around the property, all decorated differently, dive packages available with dive shop on site, sailing, tennis, fishing available, day trips for couples with picnic hamper to deserted Jacob or Man Island, bicycles, bar, restaurant on hill top, one sitting for dinner. **LL** *Dunmore Beach Club*, PO Box EL-27122, T3332200, F3332429. Very expensive, 12 rooms, tennis, fishing, scuba equipment, a hideaway hotel. **LL-A** *The Landing*, PO Box 190, T3332707, F3332650. Run by former Miss Bahamas, Brenda Berry and her daughter Tracey, 6 rooms in colonial wooden house, balcony overlooking sea, Australian chef serves varied international menu. **LL-AL** *Coral Sands Hotel*, T3332320, F3332368, www.coralsands.com Right on the beach with 14 acres stretching over the hill to Dunmore Town, concrete block painted blue and yellow, cottages in gardens, 23 rooms and 8 suites, beach bar, restaurant, twice weekly evening entertainment, tennis lit for night play, watersports, games room, library. **AL-A** *Valentine's*

Yacht Club and Inn, PO Box 1, T3332080, F3332135, T800-3235655. In town, has rooms which get heavily booked during regatta, pool side or garden side, pool, jacuzzi, tennis, 2 restaurants and all the facilities of the marina and dive shop, friendly. On the other side of the island overlooking the pink sand beach, there are several lovely places to stay. **LL-L** *Runaway Hill*, PO Box EL 27031, PO Box EL 27031, T3332150, F3332420. Built as a private home in the 1940s, now extended, lovely bar, restaurant, pool and deck all overlooking the sea, 10 luxury rooms, all different in size and character, casual but smart, men wear jackets for candlelit dinner. **LL** *Ocean View Club*, PO Box 134, T3332276, F3332459. Only open for winter season, split level overlooking sea, 10 rooms, those upstairs are larger, lovely old furniture, designer decorated, lower rooms smaller, children under 12 half price, meals US$60 per person, large chessmen on patio. **LL-L** *Pink Sands*, PO Box 87, T3332030, F3332060. A Chris Blackwell hotel, high luxury 26 1, 2 and 3 bedroom cottages, a/c, fans, stereo and CD player, tennis, on the beach, lovely location, although the US$70pp dinner is overrated and overpriced.

Eating

Pineapple upside down pudding is a common dish

The pineapples on Eleuthera are said to be the world's sweetest. In Gregory Town they produce a pineapple rum called 'Gregory Town Special' which is highly recommended. Other local dishes include Cape Eleuthera's conch chowder, which is a substantial meal, the best is from Mary Cambridge in Gregory Town, hulled bonavas (a type of bean which tastes like split pea soup) or hulled corn soup with dumplings of rice. This is eaten traditionally after a special church service on Good Friday. On New Year's Eve traditional fare includes Benny Cake, pig's feet or mutton souse, or cassava/potato bread. In many of the smaller settlements such as James Cistern, outdoor or Dutch ovens are still used to bake bread.

Most of the resorts have their own restaurants. Others which have been recommended are *Cambridge Villas*, in Gregory Town, good seafood, fairly expensive. In Governor's Harbour there are plenty of Bahamian places to eat, fairly smart are *Buccaneer* (open Mon-Sat, no credit cards, T3322500, on New Bond St on top of hill) and *Sunset Inn* (on water, open daily from 0800, pool table, satellite TV, juke box). *Lady Blanche's Lifesaver Restaurant* in Upper Bogue serves the best cracked conch in the area, run by hospitable family, prices reasonable; for very cheap, tasty food try a takeaway meal of barbecue ribs or chicken for less than US$5 at roadside stands in James Cistern. *Blue Room* (T3322736) is a restaurant/bar/disco, as is *Ronnie's* in Cubid's Cay, free transport to yacht or hotel at night. *Big Sally's Disco*, just north of Rock Sound, cocktails, bar snacks, dancing. *Cush's Place* (between Gregory Town and Hatchet Bay) does cookouts Sat and Sun afternoons with music and dancing, US$10; Lida Scavella in Hatchet Bay does cheap food, her pastries are recommended; a popular bar in the Palmetto Point area is *Mate and Jenny's Pizza*, T3322504, try conch pizza, good cocktails. In Rock Sound, *Edwina Burrows'* restaurant is highly recommended, good food reasonably priced, popular barbecue dishes. *Sammy's Place*, T3342121. Another recommended restaurant and bar, open daily 0800-2200. Several bars in Wemyss Bight and Green Castle sell spirits in half pint glasses very cheaply; recommended in Deep Creek are *Bab's Place* and *Mr Pratt's Bar*. *The Waterfront Bar* in Rock Sound is cheap, no food, while *The Ponderosa* and *The Dark Side* are bars and cheap fast food restaurants. In Harbour Island, *The Landing*, serves a blend of sumptuous gourmet and nouvelle cuisine in a delightful setting, get a patio table facing the dock and catch the sunset on the water at dinner. A nice place to eat is *Harbour Lounge*, T3332031. In an old wooden building overlooking the ferry dock with a bar and indoor or outdoor dining, good food but not cheap, bar food all day and late, Sun brunch in high season. *Arthur's Bakery* does lunch and breakfast as well as being a bakery. *Miss Mae's Tearoom* is principally a gift shop selling prints, textiles etc but you can get salads and other food in the courtyard at lunchtime. There is an ice cream parlour and also a 2-bedroom apartment to rent upstairs, US$750 per week, contact through *Ocean View Club*. *Ma Rubie's* restaurant at *Tingum Village*, PO Box 61, T/F3332161. Good for native food but is particularly noted for its cheeseburgers, apparently among the world's top 10, there are also 12 rooms **B** and a 3-bedroom, 2-bath cottage **L**, under 12s free, 3 mins from beach.

Directory   **Tourist office** *Ministry of Tourism*, Eleuthera Tourist Office, Governors Harbour, Eleuthera, T3322142, F3322480.

The Exumas

The chain of 365 Exuma cays and islands stretches for 90 miles although the majority of the inhabitants live on Great Exuma and Little Exuma at the south end. Great Exuma is long and narrow, covered with scrub and dry woodland. The soil is pitifully thin but there are aromatic shrubs, curly-tailed lizards and songbirds and a few wild peacocks. Around the villages are a few patches of what the Lands and Surveys map accurately calls 'casual cultivation'. The main industry is tourism, based on yachting and a few hundred winter visitors who own houses on the island.

Population: 3,556
1990 census

Ins and outs

There is an international airport at Moss Town with an 8,000ft runway, 2 miles from George Town, and another airport at George Town with an 8,000ft runway but closed to commercial traffic. Confusingly the **Exuma International Airport** at Moss Town carries the (GGT) George Town code. **American Eagle** flies daily from Miami in high season, 5 times a week in summer. **Bahamasair** flies from Fort Lauderdale, Nassau and Stella Maris, Long Island. **Air Sunshine** flies from Fort Lauderdale and Sarasota/Bradenton, Florida, 4 times a week. **Lynx Air** also fly non-stop from Fort Lauderdale. Mr Harry Nixon runs a charter service, **Nixon Aviation** (PO Box 3, Airport, George Town, T3362104). For flight information to Staniel Cay, Capt Dennis Rotolo, Executive Air Travel, T2246002, F9795103. For details on mailboat sailings see page 72.

Getting there

The Bahamas

Taxis are expensive but plentiful. The fare from the airport to George Town is US$22. **Hitching** is easy. **Cars** can be rented at the airport and from George Town, ask at *Peace and*

Getting around

The Exumas

Plenty Hotel. **Buses** run between Rolleville and George Town. Christine Rolle runs *Island Tours* from George Town, leaving at 1000 and 1400, including a native lunch, visits to various settlements and to Gloria, the 'shark lady,' on Little Exuma, who catches sharks and sells the teeth as souvenirs. **Bicycles** can be rented from *Two Turtles* shop or several hotels. The island of Barreterre (pronounced Barra Terry) can be reached from Great Exuma by a bridge. There is a **ferry** to Stocking Island from Great Exuma and another to Lee Stocking Island from Barreterre, but otherwise the cays are difficult to visit unless you have a boat or small plane.

History

The islands were virtually uninhabited until after the American Revolution, when Loyalists from the south colonies were given land and brought their slaves to grow cotton. During the late 18th century the British Crown granted Denys Rolle, an Englishman, 7,000 acres of land and he set up cotton plantations at Rolletown, Rolleville, Mt Thompson, Steventon and Ramsey. Following the emancipation of the slaves and poor cotton harvests because of the exhaustion of the soil, it was believed that Rolle's son gave away his lands to his former slaves, who were also called Rolle as was customary at the time. However, no deeds have been found confirming transfer of title and longstanding squatter's rights provide an adequate title to the land for many. Today, half the population bears the surname Rolle and two of the largest settlements are Rolleville and Rolletown.

The Exuma cays are in general isolated communities which are difficult to get to (the exception being Staniel Cay). Their inaccessibility has attracted undesirable attention; Norman's Cay was for some time the drug smuggling centre of Carlos Lehder, the Colombian drug baron deported from the Bahamas in 1982 and now in prison in the USA. In 1993 the cay was confiscated by the Government and put up for sale. Recent attempts to control drug smuggling include mooring Fat Albert, an airship full of radar equipment, over Great Exuma, and low flying helicopters also monitor activity.

In 1994 the government approved a US$90mn residential and resort development covering 518 acres on Exuma. A US$35mn hotel was to be built in the first phase and there would eventually be a marina, golf course and casino as well. In 1997 it was again announced that a 200-room hotel, casino, marina and golf course would be built, but at a cost of US$70mn.

Diving and marine life

Dive sites
At Stocking Island is the oldest evidence of life on earth

The Exuma Cays begin at Sail Rocks about 35 miles from Nassau. On the northerly Allen Cays can be seen the protected Rock Iguanas which grow up to 2 ft long and are known as Bahamian Dragons, but they are extremely tame. Much of the Exuma chain is encompassed in the **Exuma Cays Land and Sea Park**, an area of some 176 square miles set up by the Bahamas National Trust to conserve all underwater life for boating, diving and observation of wildlife. Moorings (US$15 per two nights) have been placed in the main area of the park and anchoring is not allowed. There is a warden's residence on Waderick Wells Cay. The park stretches between Wax Cay and Conch Cut, 22 miles away and offers more delights for underwater explorers, with beautiful coral and limestone reefs, blue holes and shipwrecks. *Sampson Cay Club and Marina*, south of Waderick Wells, offers a 500ft dock and 30 full-service slips. Get in touch with marine biologist, Johnny Dye (*Exuma Dive*) for information on a stromatolite reef on the east (Atlantic) shore of **Stocking Island**. This is a growing reef of layered limestone, a living fossil and the oldest evidence of life on earth. Worth visiting are the underwater valley at **Ocean Rock**, the huge caves filled with black coral called the **Iron Curtain**, or **Thunderball Grotto** at Staniel Cay, where part of the James Bond film and the Disney film *Splash*, were made. Watch out for dangerous currents; you can snorkel here at slack tide, in a giant fishbowl with sunlight shining in through a hole.

Individual and package diving can be arranged with *Exuma Dive Centre and Watersports* **Dive centres**
in Georgetown, PO Box EX-29238, T3362390, F3362391, www.bahamasvg.com/
exumadive. Dive trips start at US$60 and three-hour snorkelling trips at US$35, with
rental equipment available, maximum six divers on board. Instruction from resort
course to advanced scuba on offer with NAUI, IDEA, IANTD and PADI instructors and
dive masters. Scooters can be rented for US$35 per day and 17-ft boats for use in the har-
bour, US$80 per day.

Beaches and watersports

Stocking Island is a long thin island about a mile from the mainland at Elizabeth
Harbour, George Town. Its shape and position provide a natural protection for the
harbour. It has good beaches and a burger bar and is famous for its **Mysterious
Cave**, but this can only be reached by divers. A boat leaves the *Peace and Plenty Hotel*
in George Town at 1000 and 1300, roundtrip US$8, free for guests, or boats can be
hired from Exuma Dive Centre and Watersports in George Town to visit the reefs off
Stocking Island. **The Three Sisters Rocks** which rise out of the water some 100 ft
from the shore, are situated between two very good beaches: Jimmy Hill, which is a
long empty beach good for swimming, and the beautiful bay of Ocean Bight. Other
recommended beaches are the **Tropic of Cancer Beach**, 15 miles east of George
Town, **Cocoplum Beach**, 20 miles north of George Town and **Jollie Hall Beach**,
two miles west of George Town (no land access).

The **Visiting Yachts Regatta** is held in early March and on the fourth Thursday
in April the Family Island Regatta is held at George Town when working boats compete for the title of 'Best in the Bahamas'. During August there is a series of smaller
regattas at Black Point, Barreterre and Rolleville.

For details of **sportfishing**, contact Bob Hyde, Director of Sportfishing at Staniel
Cay's *Peace and Plenty, the Bonefish Lodge*, T3455556, who runs a bonefishing
school and trains flyfishing guides; there are certified guides and three areas to fish.
In October the Bonefish Bonanza Tournament is held at *Peace and Plenty Hotel*,
George Town. In November a second Bonefish Bonanza Tournament is held at the
Peace and Plenty.

There are several **marinas** in the Exumas. Exuma Docking Service, 52 slips, usual
services, bar, fuel, showers etc, T3362578, VHF 16; Happy People Marina, Staniel
Cay, six slips, 6ft depth, showers, laundry, grocery, restaurant, T3552008; Staniel
Cay Yacht Club, four slips, all services, tackle and bait, hotel, repairs, T3552024,
VHF 16; Highborne Cay, fuel, electricity, supplies, restaurant, bar, VHF 16;
Sampson Cay Colony, 30 slips, 7ft depth, all services, charters and boat rentals,
hotel, wet and dry storage, T3552034, VHF 16.

Around the islands

The main town on Great Exuma is **George Town**, a pleasant little town built on a strip **Great Exuma**
of land between a round lake and the sea. A narrow channel allows small boats to use
the lake as a harbour but yachts moor offshore, often several hundred at a time in the
peak winter months. The large and beautiful bay is called **Elizabeth Harbour** and is
yet another contender for the site of Columbus' harbour that could "hold all the ships
in Christendom." The main building is the Government Administration Building,
pseudo colonial, pink and modelled on Nassau's Government House. Opposite is a
large tree under which women plait straw and sell their wares. There are several pretty
buildings, St Andrew's Church (Anglican), blue and white on the top of a little hill and
the *Peace and Plenty Hotel* in an old cotton warehouse which was formerly the site of a
slave market. There is a good range of shops and the supermarket is well stocked. The
Sandpiper shop has an interesting array of clothes and souvenirs.

To the south of George Town is **Rolletown**, a small village on a hill overlooking
the sea. Many old houses are painted in bright blues, yellows and pinks. There is a

The Bahamas

small cemetery in which are buried settlers from the 18th century in three family tombs: husband, wife and small child of the Mackay family. **The Ferry** is a small settlement by the beautiful strait which separates Great and Little Exuma, but there is a bridge there now, not a ferry.

North of George Town there is a thin scatter of expatriate holiday houses and a few shops along the Queen's Highway. East of the road are several fine beaches, including **Hoopers Bay** and **Tar Bay**. The airport turning is north of George Town. Small villages are Moss Town, Mount Thompson, Steventon and Rolleville. Moss Town was once an important sponging centre. Close by you can see The Hermitage, brick tombs dating back to just after the American War of Independence, not to be confused with the Hermitage or Cotton House close to Williams Town on Little Exuma. Mt Thompson was once the farming centre of Exuma and is important for its onion packing house. Some of the cottages in **Rolleville**, 16 miles northwest of George Town, were originally slave quarters. The town overlooks a harbour and was the base of a group of rebellious slaves who attempted to escape and thereafter refused to work except in the mornings, until emancipation. Unfortunately, quite a large area of North Exuma is disfigured by roads which were laid out as part of a huge speculative land development scheme in the 1960s. Almost all the lots are still empty, but **Cocoplum Beach** and the coastal scenery are unspoilt. At the north end of the island is a bridge to Barreterre, with more fine scenery and places to eat lunch. At **Lee Stocking Island**, just offshore, the Caribbean Marine Research Centre is involved in research into the tilapia, a freshwater fish brought from Africa which can grow in saltwater. This can be visited by prior appointment.

Little Exuma

On Good Friday a tree near the fort is said to give off a substance the colour of blood

A bridge leads to Little Exuma, which is 12 miles long and one mile wide. An attractive cove is Pretty Molly Bay, next to the abandoned *Sand Dollar Hotel*. A mermaid story is based on Pretty Molly, a slave girl who sat on the rocks at night and gazed by the light of the moon towards Africa. Near Forbes Hill is the 'fort', built in 1892 and said to be haunted. **Williams Town** is the most southerly of the settlements on Exuma. Salt used to be made in the lagoon. Perched on the cliff top here is a tall white obelisk which not only guided passing ships safely in the 19th century, but was an advertisement that salt and freshwater could be picked up here. The Cotton House, near Williams Town, is the only plantation owner's house still standing in the Exumas. It is at the end of a driveway marked by a pair of trees, but is tiny, not grand. Slave quarters can be seen close by.

The Cays

Staniel Cay has excellent beaches with a half mile of sand dunes on the ocean side of the cay and good watersports facilities. *Staniel Cay Yacht Club* and *Happy People Marina* have dockage, water and restaurants, but beware of bad weather. On Staniel Cay during Bahamian Independence Day weekend on 10 July, there is a bonefishing festival, entrance fee US$20. The Staniel Cay Yacht Club provides free food in the evening and a rake'n'scrape band plays traditional music. The morning before the contest there is a sailing regatta for working Bahamian sailboats. A Bahamian sailboat regatta is held on New Year's Day. The Royal Entertainers Lounge serves food and drinks.

Farmer's Cay to the south of Staniel Cay has a lively annual festival called The Farmer's Cay First Friday in February Festival at which there are races, dancing games and the Bahamas' only Hermit Crab Race. *Farmer's Cay Yacht Club and Marina* has dockage, moorings and a restaurant. *Ocean Cabin* restaurant has a mooring for diners. Further south on **Darby Island** is an old mansion which is probably the remains of a large coconut plantation.

Off Staniel Cay on the edge of the Tongue of the Ocean is **Green Cay**, home to the world's second largest population of white crowned pigeons.

Essentials

LL-AL *Coconut Cove*, PO Box EX 29299, T3362659, F3362658. A mile west of George Town. Newest hotel, 9 beach or garden rooms, one suite, about 20% less in summer, diving/honeymoon/pilots packages available, a/c and fans, minibar, beach towels and robes provided, dirty beach reported with lots of mosquitoes, transport to town and to Stocking Island costs extra, boat rentals, pool, popular Mon barbecue. **AL-B** *Two Turtles Inn*, T3362545, F3362528. 200 yds from harbour in George Town, 12 rooms, rooms large enough for 4, a/c, TV, some have kitchenettes, barbecue on Fri nights. **AL** *Club Peace and Plenty*, PO Box 29055, T3362551/2, F3362093, www.peaceandplenty.com Dive, fishing, photography, honeymoon packages available, 300 yds from harbour, the pink building was once the slave market and sponge warehouse, 35 rooms/suites, a/c, all rooms have balcony overlooking harbour, entertainment some evenings, pool, sailboats, bicycles, restaurant, bar. The hotel also has a *Bonefish Lodge*, PO Box 29173, T3455556. 8 rooms in a timber building close to the fishing grounds overlooking blue hole, 10 miles east of *Peace and Plenty*, restaurant/bar, games room, all fishing facilities, certified guides. **L-AL** *Regatta Point*, PO Box 29173. On a point just outside George Town, private beach, 5 apartments and 1 house for 2-4 people, kitchens, bicycles, sunfish, dock, run by Nancy Bottomlea. **LL** *Hotel Higgins Landing*, PO Box EX-29146, T3362460, F3570008, www.higginslanding.com The only hotel on Stocking Island, 5 luxury rooms with antique furniture, 3 nights minimum, all-inclusive, complimentary kayaks, sailboats, snorkelling gear, also rental boats, diving, fishing, award-winning eco-resort. **A-B** *The Palms At Three Sisters Beach Resort*, Mount Thompson, PO Box EX 29215, T3584040, F3584043, 800-2532711. 12 rooms, on beach, tennis, satellite TV, live music Fri, Sat nights, restaurant. **C** *Marshall's Guesthouse*, PO Box 29027, T3362328, F3362081. John Marshall (grocery shop in George Town) has apartments to rent by week/month.

Staniel Cay **LL-A** *Staniel Cay Yacht Club*, T3552011, F3552044, www.stanielcay.com Own private airstrip, accommodation in waterfront cottages sleep 2-7, packages available, including all meals and use of Boston whalers and golf carts, beach, marina, scuba diving gear available. *Staniel Cay Yacht Club* restaurant is open to non-guests if prior notice is given, VHF 16, breakfast 0800, lunch 1300, dinner 1900 one sitting, box lunches available.

The main hotels in George Town have good restaurants, *Peace and Plenty* (dance with local band Sat nights), and *Two Turtles* (barbecue Fri nights, very lively and good value but take your own cutlery if you want to cut up your steak, plastic only provided, happy hour 1700-2300, US$1.50 for spirit and mixer, frequented by visitors and ex-pats). For sandwiches and light meals, *Ruth's Deli*, in George Town, T3362596. Open Mon-Sat 0900-1700, no credit cards. *Marshall's Restaurant*, George Town. Small, homely, good home made bread. *Eddy's Edgewater*, T3362050. Specializes in Bahamian food, fried conch is recommended, open Mon-Sat 0730-2300, no credit cards. *Sam's Place*, T3362579, at dock. Run by Mr Sam Gray, manager of the marina, open daily from 0730 (expensive). *La Shante*, Forbes Hill, T3454136. Good, open daily 1000-0200, happy hour Sun 1800-1900, 3 a/c rooms to rent, guided bonefishing. *Silver Dollar*, George Town, T3362615. Traditional Bahamian cooking, no credit cards. *Central Highway Inn*, T3457014. On the road 6 miles northwest of George Town, Bahamian specialities. *Rodriguez Neighbourhood Bar/Restaurant & Lounge*, at Harts, a settlement 13 miles outside George Town. Largest nightclub on Exuma, on waterfront, live band Fri, disco Sat, Sun, famous for its conch fritters. Others doing mainly peas'n'rice type dishes are *Iva Bowes* and *Three Sisters* in Mount Thompson, *Kermit Rolle's*, in Rolleville is by appointment only but he also has a good restaurant opposite the airport building, *Kermit's Airport Lounge*, T3450002, VHF 16. For breakfast, lunch or dinner, takeaway service; and *Fisherman's Inn*, Barreterre, very good. Discos at *Paramount Club* (Moss Town), *Oasis* (Queen's Highway near Mt Thompson), *Flamingo Bay* (George Town).

Tourist office *Ministry of Tourism*, Exuma Tourist Office, Cousins Building, Queens Highway, George Town, Exuma, T3362430, F3662431.

Inagua

Population: 985
1990 census

Inagua (Great and Little) is the most southerly of the Bahamas Islands and the third largest. Little Inagua is uninhabited now, but the 49-square mile island is reputed to hide the treasure of Henri Christophe, one-time ruler of Haiti. On a clear day, Great Inagua is visible from both Cuba and Haiti.

Ins and outs

Getting there
Mosquitoes can be a problem at some times of the year, avoid May

The airport (IGA) is 2 miles from town. *Bahamasair* have 3 scheduled flights a week from Nassau. *Air Sunshine* flies 4 times a week from Fort Lauderdale and from Sarasota/Bradenton, Florida. The mailboat takes 2 days from Nassau, see page 72.

Getting around
See transport, page 131, for more details

A **taxi** from the airport to Matthew Town costs about US$4. There are taxis but no buses. Mr Harry Ingraham runs a fleet of three **tour buses** called *Great Inagua Tours*, rates negotiable. Most roads are paved, except for those leading into the interior. Taxis cannot be used for birdwatching tours because of the state of the roads. If you want to see the island properly you will need transport, particularly if you travel to the north side of the island. Local people are very friendly and helpful and will organize sightseeing/wildlife trips.

Flora and fauna

The southeast side of the island is rocky and because of the effects of the sea and wind, the trees do not grow more than a foot tall. Further inland trees have a better chance of maturing. Many cactii are found in this rocky part of Inagua, in particular the dildo cactus and the woolly-nipple. On Little Inagua, although it is largely overgrown, it is possible to see some of the only natural palms in the Bahamas. The whole of Little Inagua is a Land and Sea Park and is a Bird Sanctuary.

Inagua has a restricted access national park which is home to a wide range of birds including the world's largest flamingo colony on Lake Rosa (sometimes called Lake Windsor), a 12-mile stretch of marshy wildlife sanctuary. Almost half of Great Inagua is included in the 287-square-mile park. Visitors should contact the Bahamas National Trust in Nassau (PO Box N-4105, T3931317). A basic but comfortable camp has been established on the west side, 23 long miles by jeep from Matthew Town. National Trust wardens will accompany you on tours of the area and it is possible to view the flamingos close up. At certain times of the year they cannot be approached. Jimmy Nixon, one of the original wardens, is recommended as a guide. Early spring is the breeding season when large numbers of flamingos congregate on the lake. At the Union Creek camp on the northwest side of the island is a breeding and research area for Green and Hawksbill turtles, called Turtle Sound. It is ideal for observing sea turtles at close quarters. On the east side of the island are mangrove swamps which are the nesting grounds for many birds including cormorants, pelicans and the rare reddish egret. Here you can also see the white tailed tropic bird and inland, the Bahamas parrot, the most northerly species of parrot in the world.

Inagua

Beaches and sports

Beaches that are used by locals include **Cartwright's beach**, with bar/restaurant, within easy reach of Matthew Town, **Farquharson's Beach** and **Matthew Town Beach**, which is pleasant and conveniently located. **Man of War Bay** has a lovely beach with some shade.

Apart from the rocky SE side of the island, Inagua has many deserted & unspoiled beaches

It is possible to play **tennis** and **basketball** in Matthew Town, but the most popular pastime is **hunting**. You can arrange to go on a wild boar hunt with Herman Bowe (known as the Crocodile Dundee of the Bahamas, who prefers to hunt barefoot) or Jimmy Nixon (the excellent National Trust guide). On Emancipation Day (1 August) and other holidays, wild boar is roasted on the beach and there are wild donkey races. Rodeos take place on an ad hoc basis.

Around the island

Vegetation is sparse because of low rainfall, the buffetting trade winds and lack of freshwater, but this has granted ideal conditions for salt production leading to a development and prosperity not enjoyed by any of the surrounding islands. It is thought that the name Inagua comes from the Spanish *lleno* (full) and *agua* (water): *henagua*. This was apparently the name of the island when the first salt farmers settled there. In 1803 records show only one inhabitant, but the success of the salt industry meant that by 1871 the population had risen to 1,120. Although trade barriers in the USA caused the decline of the salt trade in Inagua for many years, the industry was revitalized in the 1930s with the establishment of the Morton Salt Company, which now utilizes 12,000 acres. Morton Bahamas Ltd installed a power plant which supplies electricity to all homes in **Matthew Town**. Inagua has the best telecommunications system in the Family Islands and nearly everyone has a telephone. For a while the island supported a cotton plantation; although a shortlived enterprise, wild cotton can still be found growing on Inagua today. Outside Matthew Town you can still see the ruins of the cotton mill and the narrow plantation roads, as well as the ruins of a prison from the days when the community was large enough to need one. The highest points on the island are Salt Pond Hill at 102 ft and East Hill at 132 ft.

Essentials

There are several guesthouses in Matthew Town. The **C** *Main House*, T3391267, F3391265. 6 rooms. **B-C** *Walkine's*, T3391612. 5 rooms, satellite TV, fishing. *Crystal Beach View Hotel*, T3391550. *Pour More Hotel*, T3391659.

Sleeping

Eating out is cheaper than Nassau or Grand Bahama. For a typical Bahamian meal of macaroni, coleslaw, ribs or chicken and potato salad, expect to pay US$6-7. Local dishes include roast wild boar, baked box fish, crab meat 'n rice and roast pigeon and duck. A popular local drink is gin and coconut, which is made with fresh coconuts on special occasions. *Topps Restaurant and Bar*, run by the Palacious brothers is recommended for its seafood dishes, fresh boiled fish is served for breakfast. Nightlife revolves around the local bars, which periodically have live music and dancing.

Eating

Car hire Jeeps for hire from Mr Burrows at Matthew Town Service Station, rates negotiable but expect to pay at least US$40 per day. To get out to the camps arrange transport with the warden in Matthew Town (about US$10). To arrange fishing expeditions or trips around the island contact the local repair man, Cecil Fawkes (nicknamed the old Red Fox), whose boat is called *The Foxy Lady*, or Mr Cartwright. There is no set rate, prices are negotiated. There is a marina and boats can moor here and refuel.

Transport

Banks Matthew Town has a *Bank of the Bahamas Ltd* (open 0930-1430 Mon-Thu, 1030-1830 Fri) and 6 churches. Credit cards are not generally accepted, take plenty of cash with you.

Directory

The Bahamas

Long Island

Population: 2,954
1990 census

Long Island lies southeast of Little Exuma and is 57 miles long and four miles across at its widest. Columbus made a stop here and changed its name from the Arawak name Yuma to Fernandina, after Ferdinand, the King of Spain. The island has a variety of communities from different ethnic backgrounds, from Europe, Africa and North America.

Ins and outs

Getting there There are 2 airports, **Stella Maris** (SML) and **Deadman's Cay** (LGI). *Island Express* flies several times a week from Fort Lauderdale to Stella Maris, while *Bahamasair* flies there from Deadman's Cay, George Town, Fort Lauderdale (via Exuma) and Nassau. Deadman's Cay only receives Bahamasair flights from Nassau and Stella Maris.

Getting around **Taxis** are available and **private cars** often negotiate to carry passengers too. Taxis are generally expensive. If you are going to Stella Maris it is better to get a flight to the airport there if possible, (Deadman's Cay to Stella Maris is a 2 hrs' drive) from where it is only 20 mins, US$3 per person, to the resort. The main road connecting all the main settlements on the island is the Queen's Highway. Avoid night driving.

Diving and marine life

The *Stella Maris Marina* is the only full-service marina in the area and is a port of entry. There are 12 slips and all facilities including repairs, VHF 16, and facilities for diving, snorkelling, reef, bone and deep sea fishing and boat charters, T3382050. Dive instruction (PADI, SSI) is in English or German. This was where shark dives started; reef sharks wait for the boat anchor to be dropped and the divers to be lined up against the reef before their feeding frenzy begins. At Clarence Town dock you can get fuel, water, ice and supplies. At Harding's Supplies Center on Salt Pond you can also find showers and a laundry. There are safe anchorages at Cape Santa Maria, Salt Pond and Little Harbour. Cape Santa Maria has lovely beaches, caves and bays but do not anchor there if there is a strong north or west wind. A lagoon just beyond the west end of the cape can accommodate boats of 60 ft with depths of 6 ft. Diving and snorkelling are also good in this area and the Cape Santa Maria Fishing Club operates from here. On the east coast, good anchorages are at Clarence Town (groceries and other supplies) and Little Harbour (no facilities). The annual **Long Island Regatta** at Salt Pond is held in May. Locals compete for best seaman award, the fastest boat and the best kept boat over five years old. The Regatta is popular and accompanied by authentic Bahamian food and traditional rake'n'scrape music.

Long Island

Around the island

Most islanders live on the west side where the hills and dunes offer some protection from the sea. There are paths and dirt tracks to the east side, mostly used by fishermen. Villages to the south are rather neglected. The landscape is diverse, with tall white cliffs at Cape

Santa Maria with caves below, old salt pans near Clarence Town, dense bush over much of the island and scattered areas of cactii. It has a rocky coastline on one side and lovely beaches and crystal clear water on the other, with the usual friendly fish and lots of convenient wrecks. One, a German freighter sunk in 1917, lies in 25ft of water only 200 yds from the beach at Guana Cay, south of Salt Pond. Beaches in the south are good but rather hard to get to. Long Island is a major producer of vegetables and cattle and is known for its pot-hole farming which gives hearty supplies of tomatoes, bananas and onions. The *Stella Maris Resort Club* in the north is the biggest employer, but there are not enough jobs and most young people leave to work in Nassau or Grand Bahama.

The main settlements are **Deadman's Cay** and **Clarence Town** further south. Most tourists stay at **Stella Maris**, which is supposed to have the best yachting marina in the southern Bahamas. From a lookout tower here it is possible to see right across the island and to see the nearby ruins of the Adderly Plantation House. The town of **Simms** is the home of some of the best straw work in the Bahamas, made by Ivy Simms and her workers. The mailboat calls here and there is a high school, magistrate's court and Commissioner's office. The settlement of Clarence Town in the south half of the island is very pretty and boasts two white, twin-spired churches built on opposite hilltops by Father Jerome (see under Cat Island). St Paul's is the Anglican church and St Peter's the Catholic. Both are still in use today. There are many caves to explore and ruins of old plantation houses: Adderly's near Stella Maris and the remains of a cotton gin and plantation gate posts at Dunmore. At Glenton's, north of Stella Maris, archaeologists have found the remains of an Arawak village, and at Hamilton, south of Deadman's Cay, caves have been discovered with Arawak drawings and carvings.

Essentials

The **LL-AL** *Stella Maris Resort Club*, PO Box LI-33105, T3382051, F3382052, www.stella **Sleeping**
marisresort.com It has 47 rooms, suites, 1-4-bedroom villas. A shopping centre has a bank and post office. There are 3 pools and 8 beaches along with tennis, volley ball, table tennis, bicycles, diving, windsurfing (guests free) and water-skiing (US$25). Bicycles are free for guests; cars and scooters can be rented. Full service marina, free daily snorkelling and land excursions. Glass bottom boat trips can be taken for US$20. Cave parties, Rum Punch party and other weekly entertainment. 25 different diving areas offer a lot of variety for the experienced or the beginner and there is a shark reef with shark feeding. Fishing trips can be arranged: during Nov and Dec huge shoals of grouper make fishing easy in the waters around Long Island. Bone fishing US$200 per day. The blue hole close to the harbour at Clarence Town is good for line fishing. **LL-L** *Cape Santa Maria Beach Resort* on the island's north point, PO Box LI-30117, T3385273, F3386013, www.obmg.com Full board, closed mid-Sep to mid-Nov, taxi from Stella Maris airport about US$20, arguably the best beach hotel on the island, new restaurant with great ocean view added in 1999. There are a few private guesthouses but these are unregistered. Ask around, we have heard of places to stay at Hardings, Clarence Town, Hamilton, Deadman's Cay and Simms, about **C**.

Two island dishes to try are wild hog with onion and spices and grouper roe with liver. **Eating**
Thompson's Bay Inn has a good restaurant but reservations essential. *The Blue Chip Restaurant and Bar* in Simms is recommended. *The Harbour Bar and Restaurant* at Clarence Town has Bahamian dishes. *Sabrina's*, at Burnt Ground Village, is by appointment only, cheap and simple, occasional disco. In Hard Bargain in the south, the *Forget Me Not Club* has a popular bar and restaurant. In Mangrove Bush the Knowles family run the hillside tavern and bar. They also sell fresh fish at *Summer Seafood* close by.

Mayaguana

Population: 312
1990 census

Mayaguana (an Arawak name), located 50 miles east of Acklins and 60 miles north of Inagua, is the least developed and most isolated of the Family Islands although there are now three Bahamasair flights a week (Monday, Wednesday and Friday) from Nassau, via Inagua. The main settlement is **Abraham's Bay**, a small town with a few shops and one bar/restaurant run by the Brown family who also own the guest-house (Batelco T3393065). There are two other settlements, **Betsy Bay** and **Pirate's Well**, which are both very isolated. Several people will rent you a room in their homes for US$30-60; freshwater and food can sometimes be hard to come by, young coconuts are recommended if short of water. Take mosquito repellent. Most people earn their living from fishing or farming and many leave for Nassau and Freeport to look for work. In 1993 the Government approved a tourist development by a Californian group in East Mayaguana. About half of the 50,000-acre project will be a botanical garden and park. If it is implemented it will provide employment but no doubt change the island considerably.

The island is on a direct route to the Caribbean and as such is sometimes visited by yachtsmen, although it is not a port of entry. There is a very large reef around the northwest side of the island and excellent diving, although a liveaboard dive boat is necessary. 20 miles from Mayaguana are the Plana and Samana Cays, notable for their interesting wildlife, where you can see the Bahama hutia, thought to be extinct until the mid-1960s. A cross between a rat and a rabbit, this rodent's flesh is said to be similar to pork.

Rum Cay

Population: 53
1990 census

Some 35 miles south of San Salvador, this small island is approximately 20 miles square. First known as Mamana by the Lucayan Indians, the cay was later renamed Santa María de la Concepción by Columbus. Spanish explorers once found a lone rum keg washed up on a shore and changed the name again to Rum Cay. In the north there is an interesting cave which has Lucayan drawings and carvings. Various artefacts from the Arawak period have been found by farmers in the fertile soil which the Indians enriched with bat guano. In common with other islands, Rum Cay has experienced a series of booms and busts. Pineapple, salt and sisal have all been important industries, but competition and natural disasters, such as the 1926 hurricane, have all taken their toll and today tourism is the main source of employment. Plantation boundaries known as 'margins' can be seen all over the island, which date from the beginning of the 19th century when Loyalists settled here. Nearly everybody lives in **Port Nelson** where cottages can be rented. Settlements such as Port Boyd, Black Rock and Gin Hill are now deserted and overgrown.

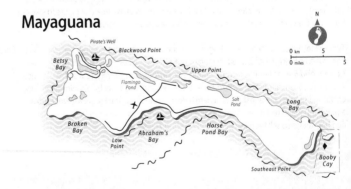

Mayaguana

This former pirates' haven is surrounded by deep reefs and drop-offs. There is stag-horn coral at Summer Point Reef and good diving at Pinder's Point. At the Grand Canyon, huge 60ft coral walls almost reach the surface. Summer Point Marina has dockage, moorings, bar and restaurant. There is a small guesthouse available from Constable Ted Bain. The Last Chance Yacht Supply has groceries. Batelco office for phone calls closes at lunchtime. Yachts wait here before sailing to Mayaguana or the Turks and Caicos Islands, or before returning to Georgetown and points north.

San Salvador

San Salvador is famous for being the probable site of Columbus' first landing in the New World in 1492. Nowadays it is also noted for its reefs, beautiful bays, creeks and lakes. Fishing, diving and sailing are all popular. There are shallow reefs, walls, corals and several wrecks to interest scuba divers and underwater life here is said to be some of the most spectacular in the Bahamas. The entire east coastline, with the exception of the creek areas, is uninhabited and has fine beaches of white sand. East of Dixon Lighthouse past the sand dunes is East Beach, a mile-long stretch of excellent sands. The island is about 12 miles long and six miles wide with a network of inland lakes (with names like Granny Lake and Old Granny Lake) which were once the main transport routes.

Population: 950 est 1998

Ins and outs

There are daily scheduled Bahamasair flights from Nassau to San Salvador (ZSA). Bahamasair also has 3 flights a week from Miami and Air Sunshine flies from Fort Lauderdale. For details of mailboat sailings see Ferries section in Essentials at the beginning of this chapter.

Getting there

If you avoid the bush and water it is perfectly feasible to walk around San Salvador. The Queen's Highway encircles the island and there are no other main roads. You can hire cars, enquire in Cockburn Town. Mopeds are not available. There is a bus tour which visits the main points of interest, ask at *Riding Rock Inn*.

Getting around

Background

Known as Guanahani by the original Lucayan inhabitants, this island claims to be the first place that Columbus landed after crossing the Atlantic in search of the East Indies. Four sites vie for recognition as the first landing place and celebrations marked the quincentennial anniversary in 1992. One of the sites where Columbus may have come ashore is **Long Bay**. There is a bronze monument under the sea where he was supposed to have anchored and a white cross on the shore where he was said to have landed. Close by is the **Mexican Monument** commemorating the handing over of the Olympic flame to the New World for the 1968 Olympics in Mexico. At **Crab Cay** in the east is the Chicago Herald Monument, erected in 1892 to commemorate the 400th anniversary of Columbus' landing.

Flora and fauna

At **Pigeon Creek** in the southeast there is a large lagoon, edged by mangroves, which is a nursery for many different kinds of large fish, including sharks. White Cay and Green Cay, off Graham's Harbour, are designated land and sea parks. **White Cay** has tall white cliffs on one side where there are large numbers of Brown Boobies. They are docile and you can get very close (once making them easy prey for hunters). **Green Cay** also has a large bird population. **Manhead Cay** off the northeast is home to a rare species of iguana over 1ft in length. There are large rock formations on the north side of the cay, access is possible from the south but is not easy,

The Bahamas

involving a climb up a rocky hill. Frigate birds can sometimes be seen here. Some subsistence farming using old slash and burn methods is still done on San Salvador.

Diving and marine life

The wall to the south and west of the island is very impressive, dropping from only 12 m to thousands of metres deep. *Club Med Columbus Isle* offers scuba diving. *Riding Rock Inn* has a full range of watersports activities on offer, an eight slip marina and daily scuba excursions. There are facilities for taking and developing underwater colour photographs (T3312631, F3312020). On Discovery Day, 12 October, there is a dinghies race.

French Bay is a popular beach with excellent shelling and snorkelling. There are large reefs of elk and staghorn coral in less than 50 ft of water, some of which are exposed at low tide. Overlooking French Bay are the ruins of **Watling's Castle**, now better known as the Sandy Point Estate. Going south following the Queen's Highway along the bay you come to the **Government Dock** and further on Sandy Point. Both spots are recommended for their privacy and good reefs for scuba divers and snorkellers.

Around the island

For a good view, climb the lookout tower east of the airport on Mount Kerr, at 140ft the highest point on the island. Until the 1920s San Salvador was known as Watling's Island after the legendary pirate John Watling, who was said to have built Watling's Castle on French Bay in the 17th century. Archaeologists have now proven that the

San Salvador

ruins are the remains of a loyalist plantation. You can see the stone ruins including the master's house, slave quarters and a whipping post. Access to the ruins is via the hill to the west of the Queen's Highway near the bay.

In the 1950s and 1960s, the US military leased land from the British Crown and built a submarine tracking station at **Graham's Harbour** in the north. Roads, an airport, a Pan American Base and a US Coast Guard Station were also built. The withdrawal of the military in the late 1960s led to unemployment and emigration. The building at Graham's Harbour is now occupied by the Bahamian Field Station, a geological and historical research institute. Further development took place under the Columbus Landing Development Project, which built houses, condominiums, roads and a golf course around Sandy Point. In the 1990s, *Club Med* built a resort near Cockburn Town, known as *Columbus Isle*, which has provided some jobs. In 1995, *Club Med* was granted a casino licence, the first ever to be awarded to any of the Family Islands. The largest settlement is **Cockburn** in the northwest.

North of Cockburn on the Queen's Highway is the small settlement of **Victoria Hill** where the New World Museum is owned by the local historian Ruth Wolper. There are interesting Lucayan artefacts, most of which came from the remains of an Indian settlement at Palmetto Grove, named after the silver top palmettos found there. **Dixon Hill Lighthouse**, which was built in Birmingham in the 19th century and rebuilt in 1930 is on the northeast coast, still on the Queen's Highway. Mrs Hanna, the keeper, gives tours of the lighthouse, which is run by candle power and clockwork and is one of the few remaining hand operated lighthouses. South of the lighthouse and past East Beach you get to Crab Cay and the Chicago Herald Monument.

Essentials

L-AL per person *Club Med Columbus Isle*, PO Box N-7525 Nassau, T3312000, F3312458, www.clubmed.com One of the nicer *Club Med* resorts, comfortable, well-integrated into surroundings, usual facilities and more, 286 rooms, a/c, TV, phone, mini-fridge, no children under 12, casino approved, tennis, horse riding, sailing, massage, fishing and diving at extra cost. **L-AL** *Riding Rock Inn Resort and Marina*, north of Cockburn Town, T3312631, F3312020, www.ridingrock.com 30 rooms, 6 villas, swimming pool and a restaurant overlooking the bay, tennis, beach, diving, bicycles to rent, island tours, weekly charter flights from Fort Lauderdale, write to 1170 Lee Wagner Blvd 103, Fort Lauderdale, FL 33315 for details, T800-2721492, F305-3598254.

Riding Rock Inn is considered expensive at US$30, but it has a rake'n'scrape band once a week featuring Bernie the Band Leader (also Bernie the airport manager). *Dixie Hotel and Restaurant*, Dixon Hill and *Ocean Cabin*, Cockburn Town, are both reasonable. *Harlem Square Rip Club* is recommended, friendly, Fri night disco. The local dish is crab'n'rice, made from the plentiful land crabs found on the island, average cost US$5-7.

Sleeping

Eating

Background

History

The first inhabitants were probably the Siboneys, fishermen who migrated from Florida and the Yucatán. The Indians Columbus found in the southern Bahamas were Arawaks, practising a culture called Tainan. They called themselves Lukku-cairi, island people, and became known as Lucayans. They were primitive farmers and fishermen, but produced the best cotton known to the Arawaks. The island of Guanahani is generally credited with Columbus' first landfall in the New World on 12 October 1492. Columbus called Guanahani San Salvador but it was not until 1926 that the Bahamas Parliament officially renamed Watling Island, an island which best fitted his rather vague description, as San Salvador. Columbus visited

The Bahamas

Rum Cay, which he named Santa María de la Concepción, Long Island, which he called Fernandina, and several other islands and cays, but finding no gold he set off for brighter horizons. The lack of mineral deposits meant that the islands held little interest for the Spanish and there is no evidence of permanent settlement. However, the development of Hispaniola and Cuba led to shortages of labour on those islands and to the depopulation of the Bahamas as the Lucayans were captured and carried off as slaves. By 1520 about 20,000 had been captured for use in the plantations, mines or pearl fisheries in the Spanish colonies and the Bahamas were uninhabited. The islands and cays became feared by navigators and many ships were wrecked there, including a whole fleet of 17 Spanish ships off Abaco in 1595.

It was after founding their first colonies in Virginia that the English realized the strategic importance of the Bahamas, and in 1629 the islands received their first constitution as part of the Carolinas. In fact, the first settlers came from Bermuda with the aim of founding a colony free from the religious and constitutional troubles of Charles I's England. Then William Sayle, who had been Governor of Bermuda, published in London in 1647 *A Broadside Advertising Eleuthera and the Bahama Islands*. As a result of this publicity, a company of Eleutherian Adventurers was formed and a party of about 70 settlers and 28 slaves, led by Sayle himself, set out for Eleuthera. Their ship was wrecked on the reefs. The party managed to land but most of the stores were lost and the settlers barely managed to survive by trading ambergris.

From this time on, the life of the Bahamas was largely influenced by their proximity to the North American mainland and their place on the sea routes. Piracy, buccaneering and the slave trade were features of the next two centuries. Pirates began to make the Bahamas their base after 1691 when they were thrown out of Tortuga. Conditions there were perfect, with creeks, shallows, headlands, rocks and reefs for hiding or making surprise attacks. By 1715 there were about 1,000 pirates active in the Bahamas, of whom the most notorious was Blackbeard, who wore his beard in plaits and was renowned for his cruelty. The colony was very poor and survived on the fortunes of shipping, both legal and illicit. In 1739 during the War of Jenkins' Ear, privateering brought a boom in trading activity but peace returned to the islands to poverty. A revival of trade during the Seven Years' War was welcomed but peace once more brought depression to Nassau. When not involved in piracy or privateering, many of the inhabitants lived off wrecks, and great was their enthusiasm when whole fleets were destroyed.

A new form of piracy began after the abolition of the British slave trade, when illegal slave traders used the Bahamas as a base to supply the southern states of the mainland. This was followed during the 1861-65 American Civil War by the advent of blockade runners, shipowners and adventurers drawn by the prospect of vast profits. New, fast ships were developed which were unable to carry large cargoes and needed to find a safe, neutral port within two or three days' steaming. Nassau was again ideal, and the port prospered, the harbour and shops being packed with merchandise. The captains and pilots of the blockade running ships became as famous as their pirate predecessors. The end of the war provoked a severe and prolonged recession, with the cotton warehouses lying empty for 50 years. The inhabitants turned again to wrecking but even this livelihood was denied them when lighthouses and beacons were introduced, leaving few stretches of dangerous waters.

In 1919, with the advent of Prohibition in the United States, Nassau became a bootleggers' paradise, but with the repeal of Prohibition, this source of wealth dried up and the islands had little to fall back on. The Thirties, a time of severe depression, ended in disaster in 1939 when disease killed off the sponges which had provided some means of livelihood. Once again, it was war which brought prosperity back. This time, however, foundations were laid for more stable conditions in the future and the two bases of prosperity, tourism and offshore finance, became firmly established. Nevertheless, the Bahamas' location and the enormous difficulty in policing thousands of square miles of ocean has attracted both drug trafficking and the laundering of the resulting profits. About 11 of the cocaine entering the USA has been officially estimated to pass through the Bahamas. The Bahamas Government, in full co-operation with the US anti-narcotics agencies, has stepped up efforts to eradicate the trade.

For three centuries the merchant class elite of Nassau, known as the 'Bay Street Boys', influenced government and prevented universal adult suffrage until 1961. In the 1967 elections, an administration supported by the black majority came to power, led by Lynden (later Sir Lynden) Pindling, of the Progressive Liberal Party (PLP), who retained power until 1992. In the first half of the 1980s allegations were made that he was involved in the drugs trade, but they were never conclusively proven. This and subsequent scandals led to the resignation or removal of a number of public officials, and contributed, together with economic decline, to the growing distrust and unpopularity of the Government.

General elections were held in August 1992 and a landslide victory was won by the Free National Movement (FNM), led by Hubert Ingraham. Mr Ingraham, a former PLP minister, had been dismissed from his post as Housing Minister after he supported a move for the resignation of Sir Lynden in 1984. Subsequently expelled from the party, he was elected as an Independent in 1987, joining the FNM in 1990. The new Prime Minister promised an improved climate for investment and tourism and an end to political patronage. A series of inquiries were held into the finances of state corporations including Bahamasair, and the Hotel Corporation, where corruption and misuse of public funds were alleged.

Legal challenges delayed the inquiry into the Bahamas Hotel Corporation, but the Commission resumed its hearings in January 1997. Sir Lynden Pindling returned to the islands after cancer treatment in the USA to face questions about deposits of US$3.9mn in his bank accounts in 1978-93. The Commission found that Sir Lynden acted improperly in accepting loans from businessmen and in dealing with a transaction involving the *Emerald Palms* hotel in his constituency. The report cited 'gross mismanagement' of the corporation and major projects leading to an accumulated loss of US$46mn which was written off in 1991. No action was taken against Sir Lynden. Two former cabinet members were found to have accepted illegal payments during their terms as chairman of Bahamasair; Philip Bethel and Darrell Rolle both stood down from their seats in the House of Assembly at the 1997 elections.

A general election was called on 14 March 1997, six months early. The number of seats in the House of Assembly was reduced from 49 to 40 because of new boundaries designed to give a more equitable distribution of voters per constituency. The FNM won a resounding victory with 57.6 of the vote and 34 seats. The turn out was high, at 91.7 of the electorate. The Bahamian Freedom Alliance's eight candidates and 11 independents failed to win any seats and the PLP won only six, despite gaining nearly 42 of the vote. After the elections Perry Christie became leader of the opposition PLP when Sir Lynden Pindling resigned. The new government announced legislation to establish a stock exchange, improve regulation of the insurance industry and management of pension funds and increase the role of the Bahamas Development Bank. A by-election for Sir Lynden Pindling's South Andros seat was held in September 1997 and won by the FNM candidate who had failed to unseat Sir Lynden at the general elections.

Geography

The islands are made up of limestone over 5,000 m deep, most of it Oolite, laid down for more than 150 million years on a gradually sinking sea bed. New material accumulated constantly and the seas of the Bahamas Platform remained remarkably shallow, often only a few metres deep. From the air, the different shades of turquoise, ultramarine and blue in these shallow waters are spectacular. On land, the soil is thin and infertile except for a few pockets of fertile soil. In many places, bare limestone rock is exposed at the surface while much land is swampy, impenetrable and uninhabitable. There are many large cave systems, including the impressive blue holes, formed when sea levels were lower and since flooded. There are no rivers or streams on any of the islands, but there is some freshwater, found close to the surface but resting on underlying saltwater. If wells are drilled too deep, they produce brackish or saltwater. Andros has a surplus of freshwater, which is barged to Nassau. Most people drink bottled water. Desalination plants are being built.

About 15 island areas have been developed. They have a total population of about 287,000; about two thirds live in New Providence and 16% in Grand Bahama. The weather can be pleasant in the winter season although cold fronts from the North American continent can bring strong north winds, heavy rain and surprisingly low temperatures. The summer months are hot, humid and often windless, with frequent thunderstorms. In August 1992 Hurricane Andrew hit the Bahamas, making over 1,200 homeless, killing four people and causing damage of over US$250mn. North Eleuthera was badly damaged. In October 1996 Hurricane Lili destroyed houses and crops and cut power lines in Exuma, Long Island and other islands after passing over Cuba. In June 1997 unprecedented rainfall and a spring tide caused flooding in New Providence while a tornado struck Hope Town, damaging boats and power supplies. In 1999 Hurricane Floyd hit Abaco, Cat Island and Eleuthera before heading for Grand Bahama and Florida. Wind speeds of 100 mph were recorded on Nassau, where coastal areas were flooded and power cut off, but on Eleuthera winds reached 155 mph and about 25% of houses were damaged. Businesses soon got back to normal, however, and there is little evidence of storm damage now.

Government

The Bahamas became independent, within the Commonwealth, in July 1973. The new Constitution provided for a Governor General to represent the British monarch who is head of state, a nominated 16-member Senate and an elected 49-member, now 40-member House of Assembly, with a parliamentary life of a maximum of five years. The Free National Movement (FNM) holds 35 seats while the Progressive Liberal Party (PLP) holds four. A new party, the Coalition for Democratic Reform, has one seat, held by a former PLP member who resigned from the party in 1999. Sir Orville Turnquest, former Attorney General and Minister of Foreign Affairs, was appointed Governor General at the end of 1994.

The economy

The economy of the Bahamas is based on tourism, financial services and shipping registration. Visitors are attracted throughout the year and since 1986, total arrivals have exceeded three million a year, mostly from the USA, of whom over half are cruise ship passengers or day trippers. Also, since 1986, annual total visitor expenditure has exceeded US$1,100 mn. Stopover tourists spend an average of US$794 per head while cruise ship passengers average US$60-70. In 1990 and 1991 the Gulf war and US recession took their toll on the Bahamian tourist industry with many airlines and hotels shedding staff and fiscal problems becoming more acute. Average hotel occupancy fell to 62 in 1990, 57 in 1993 and 62 in 1994, as US stopover visitors (82 of the total) declined. Room rates fell as over capacity in the hotel industry became critical. By 1994 prospects for the industry were improving, with a 5% increase in North American stopover visitors. In 1996, combined stopover and cruise visitors increased to 3.4 mn, a rise of 5.5% over 1995 and the first rise since 1992 but by 1998 the total was down to 3.3 million again. The sale of most of the state-run hotels to private investors improved quality and revenue. In 1997 there were 13,398 hotel rooms in the Bahamas, with up to 5,000 more planned by 2002. Expansion and new construction works led to a decline in visitor arrivals as many rooms were out of action. There were also fears that the growth was over-ambitious and that supply would exceed demand.

Agriculture is much less important than tourism, contributing only 2.9% of gdp. A third of farmers are women, the average age is 59, and half of all farm labourers are Haitian. Emphasis is on fruit farming, taking advantage of the lack of frost and competing with the Florida citrus growers. Economic activity is principally restricted to the two main islands although on the Family Islands tourist facilities are being developed and agriculture extended.

Some steps have been taken to encourage light industries, notably salt, pharmaceuticals, rum and beer production, and substantial investment has taken place in the free-trade zone of Freeport, Grand Bahama where a major expansion was under way in 1998-99. The financial sector, with its banks, insurance companies and finance companies, has developed since the 1920s, but since the mid-1980s has suffered from competition from other offshore centres such as the Cayman Islands and Barbados and from pressure from US bank regulators to reduce secrecy. In 1998 there were 77,531 registered international business companies (IBCs), who pay an annual licence fee of US$250. The Bahamas shipping registry is the fifth largest in the world, with 1,500 vessels and a gross tonnage of 25.6 million at end-1995 compared with one million in 1983. As far as foreign trade is concerned, exports are mostly re-exports of oil products and there are also sales of rum, pharmaceuticals, crawfish, fishery products, fruits and vegetables. Imports are of food, consumer goods and crude oil (mainly kept in bunkers for re-export).

The FNM government elected in 1992 aimed to reform and revive the economy. Of immediate importance was public finance and efforts were made to put the Treasury in order. Government expenditure had previously been allowed to expand unrestrained and many accounts were found to be overdrawn without proper documentation. Salaries and allowances of MPs and Senators were cut and several other reforms were instituted into public sector pay and conditions. In an attempt to attract foreign investment, the Government joined the World Bank affiliate, the Multilateral Investment Guaranty Agency, and began studies into the establishment of a securities market to aid the divestment of state enterprises.

The Bahamas

Cuba

Cuba

Cuba has something for everyone and its charms are as varied as they are fascinating. Most people spend some time relaxing and enjoying the sun and sand on Cuba's extensive beaches, but there is so much more to do. Go before Castro dies and see one of the last bastions of Communism and a culture which has denied itself the influences of the USA. Visit the Spanish colonial cities, where the architecture is being beautifully preserved, go hiking or cycling in the countryside and see rural life in Cuba, take a ride in one of those famous fifties cars, go birdwatching or scuba diving, the list is endless. No one will leave the island without being affected by the pulsating rhythms of the music and dance, the racial mixture which has produced such creativity and exuberance in the arts and entertainment, without being diverted into advertising bill boards and neon lighs. And of course, you haven't lived until you've learned to dance the rumba.

Essentials

Before you travel

Documents Visitors from the majority of countries need only a **passport**, **return ticket** and 30-day **tourist card** to enter Cuba, as long as they are going solely for tourist purposes and are staying in hotels. Tourist cards may be obtained from Cuban embassies, consulates, airlines, or approved travel agents (price in the UK £15 from the consulate, or from travel agents, some other countries US$15 or Can$15). To get a tourist card at a consulate you have to fill in an application form, photocopy the main pages of your passport (valid for more than six months after departure from Cuba), submit confirmation of your accommodation booking and your return or onward flight ticket. Immigration in Havana airport will only give you 30 days on your tourist card, but you can get it extended for a further 30 days at Immigration in Miramar (see below) and some other towns.

Travellers who will be staying with friends or in any type of private accommodation are not normally granted a tourist card unless they have a pre-booked hotel voucher for part of their stay. If you have not you will be asked to pay for a minimum of three nights in a hotel upon arrival in Cuba. Officially you have to request authorization from the Immigration Office if you want to stay outside hotels, but no one ever does as far as we know.

Nationals of countries without visa-free agreement with Cuba, journalists, students and those visiting on other business must check what visa requirements pertain and, if relevant, apply for an **official/business visa**. For this you must submit two application forms, two passport photos, your passport and a letter from the Cuban organization or company which has invited you. A business visa is issued for one entry into Cuba and can take at least 10 days to process.

There is also a **family visa**, for those who are visiting relatives, valid for one entry into Cuba. You have to fill in an application form naming the relative who has invited you (in duplicate), submit your passport (which must be valid for six months after your departure from Cuba) and pay a fee of £45.

The **US** government does not normally permit its citizens to visit Cuba. US citizens should have a US licence to engage in any transactions related to travel to Cuba, but tourist or business travel are not licensable, even through a third country such as Mexico or Canada. For further information on entry to Cuba from the US and customs requirements, US travellers should contact the *Cuban Interests Section*, an office of the Cuban government, at 2630 16th St NW, Washington DC 20009, T202-7978518. They could also contact *Marazul Tours*, New York, T212-5829570, or Miami, T305-2328157, (information also from *Havanatur*, C 2 No 17 Miramar, Havana, T332121/2318). The Cuban Interests Section in Washington DC will process applications for visas. Visas can take several weeks to be granted, and are apparently difficult to obtain for US citizens other than businessmen, guests of the Cuban Government or Embassy officials. Many travellers conceal their tracks by going via Mexico, the Bahamas, or Canada, when only the tourist card is stamped, not the passport. The Cuban Consulate in Mexico City refuses to issue visas unless you have pre-arranged accommodation and book through a travel agent; even then, only tourist cards are available, US$20. In Mérida or at Cancún airport, a travel agent will arrange your documents so you do not need to go to a consulate.

Visitors travelling on a visa must go in person to the Immigration Office for registration the day after arrival. The office is on the corner of C 22 and Av 3, Miramar. When you register you will be given an exit permit. Travellers coming from or going through infected areas must have certificates of vaccination against **cholera** and **yellow fever**. The Cuban authorities do not insist on stamping your passport in and out but they often do so. They will stamp your tourist card instead if you ask.

Customs Personal baggage and articles for personal use are allowed in free of duty; so are one carton of cigarettes and two bottles of alcoholic drinks. Visitors importing new goods worth between US$100 and US$1,000 will be charged 100% duty, subject to a limit of two items a year. No duty is payable on goods valued at under US$100. You may take in up to 10kg of medicine. It is prohibited to bring in fresh fruit and vegetables, which will be confiscated if

Cuban embassies overseas

Australia *The embassy is shared with, and located in, the Philippines, but there is a consulate: 18 Manwaring Ave, Maroubra NSW, 2035, T61-2-93114611, F931155112*

Austria *Himmelhofgasse 40 A-C, A-1130, Vienna, T43-1-8778198/8778159, F8777703*

Canada *388 Main Street, Ottawa, Ontario, K11E3, T1-613-5630141/5630326/5630136/5630209*

Denmark *See Sweden*

France *16 Rue de Presles 75015, Paris, T33-1-45675535, F45658092*

Germany *Kennedyallee 22-24, Bad Godesberg 53175, Bonn, T49-228-3090, F309244*

Israel *Cuba has no diplomatic relations*

Italy *Via Licinia No 7, 00153, Rome, T39-06-5742347/5755984, F5745445*

Netherlands *Mauritskade 49, 2514 HG The Hague, T31-70-3606061, F3647586*

Norway *See Sweden*

Portugal *Rua Pero Da Covilha No 14, Restelo, 1400, Lisbon, T351-1-3015318, F3011895*

South Africa *45 Mackenzie St, Brooklyn 0181, Pretoria, PO Box 11605, Hatfield 0028, T27-12-3462215, F3462216*

Spain *Paseo de La Habana No 194 entre Calle de la Macarena y Rodríguez, Pinilla, 28036, Madrid, T34-91-3592500, F3596145*

Sweden *Karlavagen 49, 11449 Stockholm, T46-8-6630850, F6611418*

Switzerland *Gesellsschaftsstrasse 8, CP 5275, 30112, Berne, T41-31-3022111/3029830 (Tourist Office), F3022111*

UK *167 High Holborn, London WC1 6PA, T020-72402488/8367886, F78362602*

found. On departure you may take out tobacco worth US$1,000 with a receipt, or only 50 cigars without a receipt, up to six bottles of rum and personal jewellery. To take out works of art you must have permission from the Registro Nacional de Bienes Culturales de la Dirección de Patrimonio del Ministerio de Cultura.

Currency The monetary unit is the **peso Cubano**. The official exchange rate is US$1=1 peso. Watch out for pre-1962 peso notes, which are no longer valid. There are notes for 3, 5, 10 and 20 pesos, and coins for 5, 20 and 40 centavos and 1 peso. You must have a supply of 5 centavo coins if you want to use the local town buses (20 or 40 centavos) or pay phones (very few work). The 20 centavo coin is called a *peseta*. In 1995 the government introduced a new freely 'convertible peso' on a par with the US dollar, with a new set of notes and coins. It is fully exchangeable with authorized hard currencies circulating in the economy. Remember to spend or exchange any *pesos convertibles* before you leave the country as they are worthless outside Cuba.

Money

Exchange As a result of currency reforms the black/street exchange rate fell from 130 pesos Cubanos = US$1 in May 1994 to 20 pesos = US$1 in May 1997 and it has stayed at around that level since then. Official Casas de Cambio (CADECA) rates fluctuate between 19-23 pesos to the dollar and there is now virtually no black market. The 'peso convertible' is equal to the dollar and can be used freely in the country. Cubans are allowed to hold US$ and to have a bank account. There will be very little opportunity for you to spend pesos Cubanos unless you are self-catering or travelling off the beaten track. Food in the markets (*agromercados*), at street stalls, on trains, books, popular cigarettes, but not in every shop, can be bought in pesos. You will need pesos for the toilet, rural trains, trucks, food at roadside cafeterías during a journey and drinks and snacks for a bus or train journey. Away from tourist hotels, in smaller towns there are very few dollar facilities and you will need pesos for everything. Visitors on pre-paid package tours are best advised not to acquire any pesos at all. Bring US$ in small denominations for spending money. US dollars are the only currency accepted in all tourist establishments. **Travellers' cheques** expressed in US or Canadian dollars or sterling are valid in Cuba. Travellers' cheques issued on US bank paper are not accepted so it is best to take Thomas Cook or Visa. Commission ranges from 2-4%. Don't enter the place or date when signing cheques, or they may be refused. There are **banks** and CADECAS (exchange houses) for changing money legally. Non-dollar currencies can be changed into dollars. Commission charges vary widely between banks and

Banks & money changers are listed in individual town directories

Cuba

Touching down

Hours of business *Government offices:*
0830-1230 and 1330-1730 Monday to Friday.
Some offices open on Saturday morning.
Banks: 0830-1200, 1330-1500 Monday to
*Friday. **Shops**: 0830-1800 Monday to*
Saturday, 0900-1400 Sunday. Hotel tourist
(hard currency) shops generally open
1000-1800 or 1900.

Official time *Eastern Standard Time, five*
hours behind GMT; Daylight Saving Time, four
hours behind GMT.

Voltage *110 Volts, 3 phase 60 cycles, AC. Plugs*
are usually of the American type.

Weights and measures *The metric system is*
compulsory, but exists side by side with
*American and old Spanish systems.**Public***
Holidays *Liberation Day (1 January), Labour*
Day (1 May), Revolution Day (26 July and the
day either side), Beginning of War of

Independence (10 October) and Christmas
*Day (25 December). Other **festive days***
which are not public holidays are 28 January
(birth of José Martí 1853), 24 February
(anniversary of renewal of War of
Independence, 1895), 8 March (International
Women's Day), 13 March (anniversary of 1957
attack on presidential palace in Havana by a
group of young revolutionaries), 19 April
(anniversary of defeat of mercenaries at Bay
of Pigs, 1961), 30 July (martyrs of the
Revolution day), 8 October (death of Che
Guevara, 1967), 28 October (death of Camilo
Cienfuegos, 1959), 27 November (death by
firing squad of eight medical students by
Spanish colonial government, 1871), 7
December (death of Antonio Maceo in battle
in 1896).

can be different from one town to the next, or even on different days of the week. Visitors have difficulties using torn or tatty US dollar notes.

Many restaurants are often reluctant to take credit cards

Credit cards The following credit cards are acceptable in most places: *Visa, MasterCard, Access, Diners, Banamex* (Mexican) and *Carnet*. No US credit cards are accepted so a Visa card issued in the USA will not be accepted. *American Express*, no matter where issued, is unacceptable. A master list of stolen and rogue cards is kept at the *Habana Libre* and any transaction over US$50 must be checked there; this can take up to three hours. You can obtain cash advances with a credit card at branches of the *Banco Financiero Internacional* and several other banks, but it is best to bring plenty of cash as there will often be no other way of paying for what you need. For Visa or MasterCard problems go to Av 23 entre L y M, Vedado, or phone the credit card centre on T344444, F334001. If you get really stuck and need money sent urgently to Cuba, you can get money transferred from any major commercial bank abroad direct to Asistur (see page 152) immediately for a 10% commission.

Climate The high season is mid-December to mid-April, when there are more dry days, more sunshine and less humidity. The season for hurricanes and tropical storms begins in August and can go on until the end of November. In the last few years there have been several storms which have caused flooding and damage to houses and crops. There are also variations in climate: it is hotter and drier in Santiago than in Havana, and wetter and cooler in the mountains than in the lowlands. Northeast trade winds temper the heat, but summer shade temperatures can rise to 33°C (91°F) in Havana, and higher elsewhere. In winter, day temperatures drop to 20°C (68°F) and there are a few cold days, 8°-10°C (45°-50°F), with a north wind. Average rainfall is from 860mm in Oriente to 1,730mm in Havana; it falls mostly in the summer and autumn, but there can be torrential rains at any time. Walking is uncomfortable in summer but most offices, hotels, leading restaurants and cinemas are air-conditioned.

Festivals *July* is a good time to visit Santiago if you want to catch the **carnival**, although **New Year** is also lively with parades and street parties (Havana's **carnival** is in *February*, but it is not such an exciting affair). New Year is celebrated everywhere as the anniversary of the **Revolution**, so you can expect speeches as well as parties. Throughout the year there are lots of excuses for music and dancing in the street, washed down with quantities of rum and local food. Some towns even do it weekly, called a **Noche Cubana**.

Bring all medicines you might need as they can be difficult to find. You might not be offered even a painkiller if you have an accident, as they are in very short supply. Many other things are scarce or unobtainable in Cuba, so take in everything you are likely to need other than food: razor blades; medicines and pills; heavy duty insect repellent; strong sun protection and after-sun preparations; toilet paper; tampons; disposable nappies; materials; photographic supplies; torch and batteries. **What to take**

Finding out more

UK Agents who sell holidays in Cuba include: *Regent Holidays*, 15 John St, Bristol BS1 2HR, **Travel agents** T0117-9211711, F0117-9254866, ABTA and AITO members, holding ATOL and IATA Licences; *Trips Worldwide*, 9 Byron Pl, Clifton, Bristol BS8 1JT, T0117-9872626, F0117-9872627, enquires@trips.demon.co.uk, ATOL, member of IATA, specialists in holidays to help you get off the beaten track; *South American Experience Ltd*, 47 Causton St, Pimlico, London SW1P 4AT, T0207-9765511, F0207-9766908, IATA, ATOL; *Progressive Tours*, 12 Porchester Pl, Marble Arch, London W2 2BS, T020-72621676, F020-77246941, ABTA, ATOL, IATA; *Scuba en Cuba*, 7 Maybank Gardens, Pinner, Middlesex HA5 2JW, www.scuba_ en_cuba.com, T01895- 624100, F01895-624377; *Interchange*, Interchange House, 27 Stafford Rd, Croydon, Surrey CR0 4NG, T020-86813612, F020-87600031; *Journey Latin America*, 14-16 Devonshire Rd, Chiswick, London W4 2HD, T020-87478315, F020-87421312; *Regal Diving*, T01353-778950, F01353-777897; *Steamond-Latin American Travel*, T0207-7308646, F0207-7303024; *Travelcoast Captivating Cuba*, T0870-8870123, F0870-8870128, www.captivating_ cuba.co.uk; *Cubanacan UK Ltd*, Skylines, Unit 49, Limeharbour Docklands, London E14 9TS, T020-75377909, F020-75377747; *The Holiday Place*, T020-74310670, F020-74313657; *Havanatour UK Ltd*, 3 Wyllyotts Pl, Potters Bar, Hertfordshire EN6 2JD, T01707-646463, F01707-663139, havanatour@compuserve.com Check with these agents for special deals combined with jazz or film festivals. **Eire** Cubatur agent is *Cubatravel*, T016-713422, F016-798006. See page 146 under *Marazul Tours* with regard to documents.

Mexico Many agencies in the Yucatán peninsula offer packages which are very good value and popular with travellers wanting to avoid Mexico City. There are several daily flights from Cancún. In 1999 Aerocaribe charged US$274 return to Havana, Mexicana US$265, Aviacsa US$208 and Cubana US$175. Flights are heavily booked. A recommended agency is *Viñales Tours*, in Mexico City at Oaxaca 80, Col Roma, T525-2089900, F2083704, www.spin.com. mx/vinales; in Guadalajara at Avenida Adolfo López Mateos Norte 1038-9, Plaza Florencia, T523-8172860, F8172983, vinales@infosel.net.mx; in Cancún at Av Coba 5, local A6, Plaza América, Super Manzana 4, T529-8840326, F8840396, adiel@cancun.rce.com.mex; and in Havana at Av 3 B 9207 entre 92 y 94, Miramar, T331051/5, F331054, vintours@ceniai.inf.cu

Canada *World of Vacations* has package tours to Varadero, Santiago de Cuba, Holguín, Cayo Coco, Cayo Guillermo all year round from Toronto, or Nov-Apr from Vancouver, Calgary, Edmonton and Halifax with connecting flights from other cities. *Signature Vacations* offers similar deals from the same cities, as does the popular *Air Transat Holidays*. *Fiesta West* has tours and packages from the western part of Canada Nov-Apr and the same or expanded destinations from Toronto and the Maritimes all year round. *Sunquest* and *Alba Tours* are also big tour operators with similar arrangements. All of these companies offer flights if you want them, for mostly one or two weeks. For longer stays, independent travel needs to be arranged with an agent who is familiar with this procedure, such as *Cubana* or charter airlines, for example *Canada 3000*, *Air Transat*. Some of these companies use Cubanacán to offer eco-tours. *Friendship Tours*, run by Joyce Holmes, 12883-98th Ave, Surrey, BC, V3T 1B1, T1604-5814065, F5810785, friendship@ home.com, offer tours in conjunction with conferences in Cuba, bird watching or other eco-tours, beach retreats of May Day tours with farm or factory visits. For more details, members.home.com/friendship

USA *AdventureCuba.com*, 4492 Camino de la Plaza, San Diego, California 92173, T310-8424148, www.adventurecuba.com a full service online travel agency. The site contains

Cuba

Cuban tourist offices overseas

Argentina, T541-3267810, 541-3267995, F541-3263325, oturcuar@tournet.com.ar

Belgium, Robert Jones Straat 77, Brussels 18, T32-2-3430022

Canada, 440 Blvd René Levesque, Suite 1402, Montréal, Quebec H2Z 1V7, T1-514-8758004/5, F8758006, mintur@generation.net

55 Queen Street E, Suite 705, Toronto, M5C 1R5, T1-416-3620700/2, F3626799, cuba.tbtor@simpatico.ca

China, T86-10-65322129, F65322017, menendez@public.bta.net.cn

France, 280 Bd Raspail, 75014 Paris, T33-14-5389010, F5389930, ot.cuba@wanadoo.fr

Germany, Frankfurt, T49-69-288322/3, F296664, gocuba@compuserve.com

Italy, Via General Fara 30, Terzo Plano, 20124 Milan, T39-2-66981463, F6690042, ufficioturisticodicuba@interbusiness.it

Mexico, T52-5-2555897, 2507974, F2555866, otcumex@mail.internet.com.mex

Russia, T/F7-095-2430383

Spain, Paseo de la Habana No 28 iro derecha, 28036 Madrid, T34-91-4113097, F5645804, otcuba@octocuba.esp.com

Switzerland, Gesellschaststrasse 8, 3012 Berne, Case Postale 52725, T/F41-31-3022111

UK, 154 Shaftesbury Avenue, London WC2H 8JT, T020-72406655, F778369265, cubatouristboard.london@virgin.net

over 80 pages of useful information on hotels, transportation as well as travel tips and practical advice. *Cuban Adventures*, call toll free from US/Canada T1-877-2822386, specialist tours (cigar, scuba, culture/music etc), www.cubanadventures.com

Venezuela, *Ideal Tours*, Centro Capriles, Plaza Venezuela, Caracas, T582-7930037, package tours depending on the season, flight only available. **Jamaica**, *UTAS Tours* offer weekends in Cuba for US$199 including flight, hotel etc, PO Box 429, Montego Bay, T9790684, F9793465.

Bahamas, *Havanatur* in Nassau, T242-3947195, F3945196 (ask for Joba), sells package tours and charter flights to Havana or Holguín (see page 150). Havanatur's Havana based reps for the Nassau-Havana route are efficient and helpful, Iris and Laura speak excellent English, C 2 17 entre 1 y 3, Miramar, T247413. A package includes the tourist card, hotel, breakfast, transfers and city tour of Havana, prices start at US$239 for return flight plus two nights at *Hotel Inglaterra*. You can use these two nights at the beginning and end of your visit, and travel on your own in between. Less efficient is the Nassau agency, *Majestic*, T242-3222606, F3261995, whose staff are on commission. Get a name, then ensure that all subsequent dealings are with the same person, otherwise multiple bookings/cancellations may result. Weekly charter flights from **Martinique** via **Guadeloupe**, which can be booked through *Laroc Voyages SA*, Zijambette, BP 292-97286 Lamentin, Cedex 02, Martinique, T596-603701, F603898. **Haiti**, *La Citadelle*, 17 Rue des Miracles, Place du Marron Inconnu in Port-au-Prince, T509-2235900, F2221792, has flights if you book two weeks in advance for US$300 return to Havana or US$190 return to Santiago.

Getting there

Air   There are **charters** from London, Frankfurt, Toronto, Vancouver, Montréal, Quebec, Halifax, Buenos Aires, Cancún, and between Santiago de Cuba and Montego Bay, Jamaica. There are also regular charters between Cayo Largo and Grand Cayman and occasional charters between Providenciales, Turks and Caicos Islands and Santiago de Cuba. The Cuban air charter line *AeroCaribbean* has an arrangement with *Bahamasair* for a (nearly) daily service Miami-Nassau-Havana, changing planes in Nassau; the Cuban tourist agency *Amistur* organizes the service. This route is probably the cheapest and quickest from the USA (see page 149). In July 1998 *ABC* charters started direct flights Miami-Havana. *Havanatur* has eight weekly charter flights, five to Cancún and three to Nassau. At certain times of the year there are special offers available from Europe; enquire at specialist agents. There are also many combinations of flights involving Cuba and Mexico, Venezuela, Colombia and the Dominican Republic; again ask a specialist agent. *AeroCaribbean* flies from Port-au-Prince, Haiti, to Santiago and Havana on

Thursdays, US$100 one-way to Santiago if paid for 14 days in advance, otherwise US$200. The cheapest flight from Santo Domingo to Santiago is US$150.

Touching down

On arrival Immigration can be very slow if you come off a busy Iberia DC10 flight but speedy off smaller *Cubana* aircraft. At Havana airport there are taxi dispatchers who can get you in a taxi or minibus for US$18. **NB** remember to reconfirm your onward or return flight as soon as you arrive in Cuba and certainly 48 hours before departure, otherwise you will lose your reservation. Cuba has several airports classified as international, but only Havana is of any size. Havana now has three terminals, the third and newest one being for international flights, with exchange facilities, snack bars, shops etc.

Airport information

On departure It is advisable to book your flight out of Cuba before actually going there, as arranging it there can be time-consuming. The airport departure tax is US$20 at Havana and Varadero airports, US$15 at other international airports. The seating in the Havana departure lounge is uncomfortable. The restaurant is OK for sandwiches or full meals, which will be welcome after your three-hour check-in and this will be your last chance to hear a live Cuban band while eating. The selection of shops is limited but there is lots of rum, coffee, a few books and magazines on sale. The selection of cigars is poor and overpriced. The Cubita coffee, on the other hand, is marginally cheaper than in the dollar shops in town.

Internet www.dtcuba.com has lots of details and addresses of hotels, tour companies, car hire etc. They also have a weekly newsletter, *Boletín Semanal DTC News*, listmaster@ dtcuba.com www.cubaweb.cu, has sections on news, travel, politics, business, internet and technology, health, science, art and culture, festivals and events.

Tourist information

Local tours Several state-owned tour companies offer day trips or excursion packages including accommodation to many parts of the island, as well as tours of colonial and modern Havana. Guides speak Spanish, English, French, Italian or German; the tours are generally recommended as well-organized and good value. A common complaint from individual tourists is that, when they sign up for day trips and other excursions (eg Cayo Largo), they are not told that actual departure depends on a minimum number of passengers (usually 6). The situation is made worse by the fact that most tourists are on pre-arranged package tours. They are often subject to long waits on buses and at points of departure and are not informed of delays in departure times. Always ask the organizers when they will know if the trip is on or what the real departure time will be.

Tour companies *Rumbos*, O 108 entre 1 y 3, Miramar, Havana, T249626-8, F247167, director@rumvia.rumb.cma.net, organize excursions and run bars and cafés. *Horizontes*, 23 156 entre N y O, Vedado, Havana, T662004, 662160, F333161, www.horizontes.cu Their hotels tend to be on the outskirts of towns and the chain provides activities for 'eco' tourists and hunters. Fly-drive tours can be arranged. *Cubanacán Recreación y Ocio* (for fishing, hunting), Dirección Comercial, T336868, 330345, F336986, gerente@cubasol.cha.cyt.cu *Cubanacán Agencia de Viajes*, T337952, 330607, www.cubanacan.cu In Santiago, T356156, or for Recreación y Ocío T39317. *Sol y Son*, 23 64, La Rampa, Vedado, T333271, 335159, F333385, solyson@ceniai.inf.cu The travel company of *Cubana* airlines. (Also has offices in some hotels.) *Cubamar Viajes*, Paseo 306 entre 13 y 15, Vedado, T662523-4, F333111, www.cubamar. cubaweb.cu Some camping resorts, student groups. *Gaviota Tours*, Hotels *Kohly* and *El Bosque* in Havana, T244781, 294528, 247683, F249470, gavitour@gavitur.gav.cma.net. Also Guardalavaca, Varadero, and in Topes de Collantes near Trinidad. Tours of the Oriente have been recommended, they include two nights in *Hotel Porto Santo*, Baracoa. *Havanatur*, Edif Sierra Maestra, Av 1 entre 0 y 2, Miramar, T247541, 241549, F242074, 242877, recommended for independent travellers who want tailor-made but reasonably priced tours. *Islazul*, Malecón y G, Vedado, T325152, 320571, F333458, 324410, cmazul@Teda.get.cma.net *Cuba Deportes*, C 29 710 entre 7 y 9, Miramar, T240945, F241914. Arranges all-inclusive sporting holidays.

Agencies specializing in **marinas** and **diving**, including packages with accommodation and transfers, are: *Cubamar* (see above); *Ecotur*, 98 y Av 5, Playa, T/F290230; *Gaviota* (see above), Av del Puerto 102, Edif La Marina, La Habana Vieja, T339780-1, 666777, F332780, 330742, gaviota@nwgaviot.gav.cma.net; *Horizontes* (see above); *Marlin*, 184 123, Reparto Flores, Playa, T336675, 339436, F337020; *Marsub*, B 310 esq 15, Vedado, T333055, 334638, F333481; *Puertosol*, Edif Focsa, 17 y M, Vedado, T334705-8, F334703.

Travel assistance *Asistur*, in *Hotel Casa del Científico*, Paseo del Prado 254, entre Animas y Trocadero, Habana Vieja, for 24-hour service T338527, F338088, cellular Asis 2747, linked to overseas insurance companies, can help with emergency hospital treatment, robbery, direct transfer of funds to Cuba etc. Also office in *Hotel Casa Granda*, Santiago.

Sex tourism Cuba had a reputation for prostitution before the Revolution and after a gap of some decades it has resurfaced. Despite government crackdowns and increased penalties, everything is available for both sexes if you know where to look. Be warned, you are likely to be fleeced. The age of consent is 18 in Cuba, so if you are introduced to a young girl you are in danger of being led into a blackmail trap. Hotels are not allowed to let Cubans enter the premises in the company of foreigners, so sexual encounters now often take place in *casas particulares*, private homes where there is little security and lots of risk. If you or your travelling companion are dark skinned, you may suffer from the exclusion policy in hotels as officials will assume he/she is Cuban until proved otherwise. If you are a man out alone at night in Havana you will find the market very active and you will be tugged at frequently, mostly by females, but around *Coppelia* the prostitutes are mostly males. Cubans who offer their services (whether sexual or otherwise) in return for dollars are known as *jineteros*, or *jineteras* ('jockeys', because they 'ride on the back' of the tourists).

Safety In general the Cuban people are very hospitable. The island is generally safer than many of its Caribbean and Latin neighbours, but certain precautions should be taken. Visitors should never lose sight of their luggage or leave valuables in hotel rooms (most hotels have safes). Do not leave your things on the beach when going swimming. Guard your camera closely. Pickpocketing and purse-snatching on buses is quite common in Havana and Santiago. Also beware of bag-snatching by passing cyclists. In the capital, street lighting is poor so care is needed when walking or cycling the city at night. Some people recommend walking in the middle of the street. Old Havana is now much safer, with police on nearly every street corner. The police are very helpful and thorough when investigating theft, ask for a stamped statement for insurance purposes.

Getting around

Air There are *Cubana de Aviación* services between most of the main towns. **From Havana** (October 1999 prices): to Camagüey (US$72 one-way); Holguín (US$82); Trinidad (US$74); Baracoa (US$108); Guantánamo (US$100); Manzanillo (US$82); Moa (US$100); Nueva Gerona/Isla de Juventud (US$22); Bayamo (US$82); Ciego de Avila (US$60); Las Tunas (US$80); Santiago (US$90); Cayo Largo (US$56); Cayo Coco (US$80); Varadero (US$32); all have airports. Santa Clara and some places with airstrips are reached by Aerotaxi. Tourists must pay air fares in US$; it is advisable to prebook flights at home as demand is very heavy, although you can get interprovincial flights from hotel tour desks if you are on a package deal. It is difficult to book flights from one city to another when you are not at the point of departure, except from Havana; the computers are not able to cope. Airports are usually a long way from the towns, so extra transport costs will be necessary. Delays are common. **NB** Cubana flights are very cold, take warm clothes and possibly some food for a long flight. Aerotaxi flights can also be cold, they are flying buses and you often get wooden bench seating in an old Soviet aircraft. Although theoretically possible to get a scheduled flight as listed above, it is often only possible for tourists to travel on excursions: day trips or packages with flights, accommodation, meals and sightseeing.

Return fare is twice the single fare

Cuba

• •

Where to stay

Tourists to Cuba often stay in private houses, known as *casas particulares*. Cubans may offer you their house, apartment or a room and cook for you and you pay for the service (US$). A taxation system for this form of 'self-employment' was introduced in 1997 so that it is now legal. Private homes vary considerably and can be extremely comfortable or very basic. Because of shortages things often don't work, there may be cold water only, once a day, and the lights often go off. A torch is useful. The families will usually offer you cheap transport too. Remember that rates are likely to be negotiable if you go direct to the owners, or stay for several nights. The owners pay US$5 per night per room for each client brought to them by a tout, and taxes and licences are high at US$60-200 per room per month, depending on the region, plus 10% of earnings to be paid at the end of each year, so profit margins are tight and prices have risen. To offer food, Cubans have to buy a licence, US$30 per month, although many do not. All *casas particulares* should have a yellow registration book you have to sign, and a sticker on their door of a blue triangle on a white background, if they are legal. An unlicensed casa owner will face a huge dollar fine if caught, which is quite likely given the neighbourhood watch system.

Cuba

• •

Bicycle

For people who really want to explore the country in depth and independently, cycling around is excellent, although you are advised to bring your own bike and all spare parts. *Iberia* and *Cubana* airlines both accept bicycles as normal luggage as long as you do not take more than 20 kg, but some charters, such as *Martinair*, charge extra. A good quality bicycle is essential if you are going to spend many hours in the saddle, although that does not mean it has to be very sophisticated. We have heard from cyclists who have toured Cuba without gears, although they did have plenty of muscle. Most of Cuba is flat, the road network is good and there is little traffic. In cities there are *parqueos bicicletas*, where you can store your bike while walking around. Cycling can get very hot, so you are advised to do long distances early in the morning.

For organized cycling tours of Cuba contact *Blazing Saddles*, in the UK, T020-84240483, saddles100@aol.com; *Bike Tours*, in the UK, T01225-480130, F01225-480132; *Fietsvakan tiewinkel*, Spoorlaan 19, 3445 AE Woerden, Holland, T31-3480-21844, F31-3480-23839. You may also be able to join a group of Cuban bikers (mostly English speaking) through the *Club Nacional de Cicloturismo* (National Bike Club), Gran Caribe, Transnico Internacional, Lonja del Comercio Oficina 6d, La Habana Vieja, T969193, F669908, trans@mail.infocom.etecsa.cu. They run tours of 1-28 days in all parts of the country, some with political themes.

Bus

The local word for bus is *guagua*. In Havana there are huge double jointed buses pulled by a truck, called *camellos* (camels) because of their shape, also irreverently known as 'Saturday night at the cinema' because they are full of 'sex, crime and alcohol'. In the rush hours they are filled to more than capacity, making it hard to get off if you have managed to get on. Buses are running but fuel shortages limit services. Urban tickets can only be bought in pesos Cubanos.

The urban bus fare throughout Cuba is 20 centavos for camellos & 40 centavos for all others; it helps to have the exact fare

For bus transport to other provinces from Havana there is a dollar ticket office in the Terminal de Omnibus Nacional, Boyeros y 19 de Mayo (third left via 19 de Mayo entrance), T703397, open daily 0700-2100, very helpful staff. You don't have to book in advance but it might be wiser to do so. There may be cancellations. Another service is Víazul (Viajes Azul), at Av 26 entre Av Zoológico y Ulloa, Nuevo Vedado, T811413/811108/815652, F666092, open 0900-2300, with long distance buses and minibuses. Other offices: Santiago, Av Libertadores esq Yarayó, T28484; Trinidad, Viro Guinart entre Antonio Maceo y Gustavo Izquierdo 224, T2597; Varadero, Calle 36 y Autopista, T614886; Viñales, Salvador Cisneros 63A. There is a weight limit for luggage of 20 kilos on all long distance bus journeys and the bus-hoverfoil to Isla de la Juventud.

It is theoretically possible to pay for tickets in pesos but, apart from all the complications of doing so, you will be depriving a Cuban of a seat. If you don't want the hassle, tickets between towns must be purchased in advance from: *Oficina Reservaciones Pasajes*, C 21, esquina 4,

Vedado (main booking office for buses and trains from Havana to anywhere in the country, one-way only, open Monday-Friday 1200-1745, organized chaos); *Plazoleta de la Virgen del Camino*, San Miguel del Padrón; Calzada 10 de Octubre y Carmen, Centro; *Terminal de Omnibus Nacional*, Boyeros y 19 de Mayo (all in Havana). Look for notices in the window for latest availabilities, find out who is last in the queue (separate queues for buses and trains, sometimes waiting numbers issued), and ask around for what is the best bet. Maximum three tickets sold per person. Seat reservations are only possible on a few long distance routes (for example Havana-Trinidad Express) but you still need pesos Cubanos, or a Cuban entrepreneur to obtain one. Cubans queue professionally and make a profit out of selling places near the top of the queue. You may end up paying the same as if you'd gone to the dollar ticket office. Away from the capital and off the beaten track, it is not so controversial to pay in pesos, in fact you may have no option.

Car

Shortage of fuel & decline in public transport has meant Cubans have taken to organized hitching

Car hire Through state rental companies at the International Airport and most large hotels, www.dtcuba.com/esp/transporte_tierra.asp Minimum US$40 a day (or US$50 for air conditioning) with limited mileage of 100 km a day, and US$8-20 a day optional insurance, or US$50-88 per day unlimited mileage; cheaper rates over seven days. Visa, Mastercard, Eurocard, Banamex, JCB and Carnet accepted for the rental, or cash or traveller's cheques paid in advance, guarantee of US$200-250 required; you must also present your passport and home driving licence. In practice, you may find car hire rates prohibitively expensive when small cars are 'unavailable' and a four-door sedan at US$93, unlimited km, insurance included, is your only option. Staff have been reported as 'unhelpful' in finding what you want. It pays to shop around, even between offices of the same company. Cubans are not allowed to hire cars (although they may drive them), so even if you have organized a local driver you will have to show a foreign driving licence. If you want to drive from Havana to Santiago and return by air, try *Havanautos.* They will charge at least US$80 to return the car to Havana, but most companies will not even consider it. Fly and drive packages can be booked from abroad through *Cubacar*, part of the Grupo Cubanacán, who have a wide range of jeeps and cars all

Motorway
Motorway under construction
Main road
Minor road

over the country and can even arrange a driver (pmando@cubacar.cha.cyt.cu). Most vehicles are Japanese or Korean makes, Suzuki jeeps can be hired for six to 12 hours in beach areas, US$11-22, plus US$8 insurance, extra hours US$5. Watch out for theft of the radio and spare tyre; you will have to pay about US$350 if stolen unless you take out the costly extra insurance. **Moped** rental at resorts is around US$8-10 per hour, cheaper for longer, US$25-30 per day, US$80 per week.

There are three types of taxi: tourist taxis, Cuban taxis and private taxis (*particulares*). **Dollar tourist taxis** can be hired for driving around; you pay for the distance, not for waiting time. On short routes, fares are metered. From the airport to Havana (depending on destination) costs US$12-18 with *Panataxi*, to Playas del Este US$30, to Varadero US$90; Cuban taxis, or *colectivos*, also operate on fixed routes and pick you up only if you know where to stand for certain destinations. Travelling on them is an adventure and a complicated cultural experience. Cubans are not allowed to carry foreigners in their vehicles, but they do; private taxis, *particulares*, are considerably cheaper than other taxis, for example airport to Havana centre US$8-12, from Santiago to the airport US$5. A *particular* who pays his tax will usually display a 'taxi' sign, which can be a hand-written piece of board, but have a private registration plate. Some have meters, in others you have to negotiate a price in either pesos or dollars, although as a foreigner you will be urged to pay in dollars. If not metered, 10 km should cost around US$5. For long distances you can negotiate with official taxis as well as *particulares*, and the price should be around US$10 per hour. As a general rule, the cost will depend on the quality of your Spanish and how well you know the area.

Taxi
See also page 180

Cuba

Train

Travel between provinces is usually booked solid several days or weeks in advance. If you are on a short trip you may do better to go by Viazul bus or on a package tour with excursions

This form of transport is recommended whenever possible, although delays and breakdowns must be expected. Be at the station at least one hour before the scheduled departure time. Fares are reasonable but have to be paid for in dollars, which will usually entitle you to a waiting area, seat reservation and to board the train before the big rush starts. There is a dollar ticket office in every station. Alternatively, the tourist desks in some of the larger hotels sell train tickets to foreigners, in dollars. Long distance trains allow only seated passengers, they are spacious and comfortable, but extremely cold unless the air conditioning is broken, so take warm clothes. All carriages are smoking areas. Bicycles can be carried as an express item only and often cost more than the fare for a person (see Cycling, page 153). There is no food service except on the *especial*, when a trolley passes through once with sandwiches and juice, followed later by coffee (pay in pesos). Sometimes there are additional sandwiches and drinks for sale at a bar (dollars only), but it is advisable to take food with you.

Keeping in touch

Telephone

International code: 53

Most hotels have facilities for international calls and faxes which you can use even if you are not staying there. Phone cards are now used elsewhere and can be quite economical. Cuba does not have a reputation for good communications; it can take time to get a line and email is rare, but things are gradually improving with help from foreign telecommunications companies. The downside is that numbers and codes are frequently changing.

Local telephone calls can be made from public telephones for five centavos. To phone abroad on a phone with international dialling facility, dial 119 followed by the country and regional codes and number. Many hotels and airports have telephone offices where international calls can be made at high prices. Look for the *Telecorreos* or *Etecsa* signs. No 'collect' calls allowed and only cash accepted. Collect calls to some places, are possible from private Cuban telephones. In a few top class hotels you can direct dial foreign countries from your room. The *Golden Tulip Plaza Central* has a business centre from where you can send emails and faxes, as well as make phone calls. Phonecards are in use at Etecsa call boxes, in different denominations from US$10-50, much cheaper for phoning abroad, for example US$2 per minute to USA and Canada, US$2.60 per minute to Central America and the Caribbean, US$3.40 to South America, US$4 to Europe and US$4.40 to the rest of the world. Telephone sockets (for computer users) are standard US type. The cost of these calls is high, connections are hard to make and you will be cut off frequently. Mobile phones are commonly used in Cuba. Cybercafés for internet access by the public do not exist yet. The only public service we know of is in the Capitol building in Havana, but it is slow.

Media

Newspapers *Granma*, mornings except Sunday and Monday; *Trabajadores*, Trade Union weekly; *Tribuna* and *Juventud Rebelde*, also only weekly. *Opciones* is a weekly national and international trade paper. *Granma* has a weekly edition, *Granma International*, published in Spanish, English, French and Portuguese, and a monthly selected German edition; all have versions on the Internet, www.granma.cu. Main offices: Av Gen Suárez y Territorial, Plaza de la Revolución, La Habana 6, T816265, F335176, Tx0511355; in UK 928 Bourges Blvd, Peterborough PE1 2AN. *El País* is the Mexican edition of the Spanish newspaper, available daily, two days late. Foreign magazines and newspapers are sometimes on sale at the telex centre in *Habana Libre* and in the *Riviera* (also telex centre, open 0800-2000). The previous day's paper is available during the week. Weekend editions on sale Tuesday.

Television There are two national channels: Cubavisión and Tele Rebelde, which broadcast morning and evening. The Sun Channel can be seen at hotels and broadcasts a special programme for tourists 24 hours a day. Some of the upmarket hotels also have satellite TV. The most watched programme is the Colombian telenovela, *Café con la aroma de mujer*, about a love triangle between Sebastián, his wife Lucía and his mistress, Gaviota. People gossip about the latest instalment in the street and a number of pets have been named Gaviota.

Language

Spanish, with local variants in pronunciation and vocabulary. English, German, Italian and French are spoken by those in the tourist industry. There are **language courses** available at the universities of Havana, Cienfuegos and Santiago. They generally start on the first Monday of the month and you study 20 hours a week, Monday-Friday 0900-1300. There are different levels of study and Cuban cultural courses are also available. At Havana, latest prices are US$250 for two weeks, US$650 full board. In Santiago, university accommodation is available for US$21 per person per day, including breakfast and evening meal. In Havana, contact Damaris Valdez, T335842, 704667; in Santiago, Enrique Vallejo, T43186. Information also from Eddy González, Mercado SA, 13 951 esq 8, Vedado, T333893, F333028.

Food and drink

Food is not Cuba's strong point, although the supply of fresh food has improved. Hotels tend to serve buffet meals which can get tedious after a while, but breakfast is usually good and plentiful and you can stock up for the day. The best meals at reasonable prices are to be had in the private restaurants, known as *paladares*, where you can get items paid for in dollars which are not available to Cubans on their ration cards. *Paladares* are licensed and taxed and limited to 12 chairs, as well as having employment restrictions. Some very good family-run businesses have been set up, offering a three-course meal in Havana for US$10-15 per person, half that outside the capital, excellent value. They are not allowed to have lobster or shrimp on the menu as these are reserved for the dollar hotels and the export market. However, if you ask, there are often items available which are not on the menu. Many families who rent out rooms also provide food in plentiful proportions. This is generally of excellent quality with the advantage that they will cook whatever you want. Remember, however, that it is not always strictly legal as many families provide meals without paying the required tax. State-owned 'dollar' restaurants are recognizable by the credit card stickers on the door, where meals are about US$15-25, paid only in US dollars.

Food

The **national dish** is *congrís* (rice mixed with black beans), roast pork and yuca (cassava) or fried plantain. Pork is traditionally eaten for the New Year celebrations, so before then all the pigs which have been fattened up on people's balconies or smallholdings are on the move (in various forms) in the backs of trucks, cars and bicycles, to be sold privately or at the markets. Salads in restaurants are mixed vegetables which are slightly pickled and not to everyone's taste. For **vegetarians** the choice is very limited, normally only cheese sandwiches, spaghetti, pizzas, salads, bananas and omelettes. Even beans (and *congris*) are usually cooked with meat or in meat fat. If you are staying at a *casa particular* licensed to serve food, or eating in a *paladar*, they will usually prepare meatless meals for you with advance warning. Always ask for beans to be cooked in vegetable oil.

Rum is the national drink and all cocktails are rum-based. There are several brand names and each has a variety of ages, so you have plenty of choice. Beer is good and there are regional varieties which come in bottles or cans. The locally grown coffee is good, although hotels often manage to make it undrinkable in the mornings.

Drink

The most widely available **beer** throughout the island is *Cristal*, made by Cervecería Mayabe, in Holguín. From the same brewery is *Mayabe*, also popular. *Hatuey*, made in Havana, is reckoned by some to be the best of Cuba's many beers, named after an Indian chief ruling when the Spanish arrived. It is becoming more widely available after a lengthy patent battle. *Bucanero*, from Holguín, is easily bought in the east of the island. *Tinimo* and *Lagarto* beer are difficult to find. The former can be bought in pesos and the latter at the airport.

Cuba now also produces **wines** under the *Soroa* label, grown and produced in Pinar del Río and sold for about US$3.15 in shops. There is also a more expensive range sold for about US$8, including Cabernet Sauvignon, Chardonnay, Tempranillo and other grapes, produced with the help of a Spanish company in a joint venture.

Tobacco is of course excellent, but remember that all the best leaves go into cigar making rather than cigarettes. Make sure you buy the best to take home and don't get tricked into buying fakes, you may not get them through customs. Buying cigars on the street is not legal, but they are often not genuine and may be confiscated at customs if you cannot produce an official receipt of purchase.

Tobacco

Cuba

Flora and fauna

When the Spanish arrived at the end of the 15th century more than 90% of Cuba was covered with forest. However, clearance for cattle raising and sugar cane reduced this proportion: 75% of the land is now savannah or plains, 18% mountains and 4% swamps. A reforestation programme aims to increase Cuba's forests to 27% of the total area by 2000. Besides semi-deciduous woodland, vegetation types include rainforest, coastal and upland scrub, distinctive limestone vegetation found in the Sierra de los Organos and similar areas, savannah vegetation found on nutrient-deficient white silica sands, pine forests, xerophytic coastal limestone woodland, mangroves and other coastal wetlands.

Cuba is characterized by extraordinarily high rates of biodiversity and endemism, particularly in four regions: the Montañas de Moa-Nipe-Sagua-Baracoa, which have the greatest diversity in all the Caribbean and are among the highest in the world, and 30% of the endemic species on the island; Parque Nacional Sierra de los Organos, the Reserva de la Biósfera Sierra del Rosario and the Reserva Ecológica del Macizo de Guamuhaya.

There are over 7,000 plant species in Cuba, of which around 3,000 are endemic. 950 plant species are endangered, rare, or have become extinct in the last 350 years. Oddities in the plant world include the **Pinguicola lignicola**, the world's only carniverous epiphytic plant; the **cork palm** (*Microcycas colocoma*), an endemic living fossil which is a threatened species; and the **Solandra grandiflora**, one of the world's largest flowers, 10 cm across at the calyx and 30 cm at the corolla. There are around 100 different palm trees in Cuba, of which 90 are endemic. The **Royal palm** is the national tree and can be seen in the countryside throughout the island. Cubans use the small, purple fruits to feed pigs, as they are oily and nutritious. There is one tiny orchid, *Pleurothallis shaferi*, which is only one centimetre, with leaves measuring five millimetres and flowers of only two millimetres.

Animal life is also varied, with nearly 14,000 species of fauna, of which 10 % could be on the verge of extinction. There are no native large mammals but some genera and families have diversified into a large number of distinct island species. These include mammals such as the **hutia**, **bats** and the protected **manatee** with more than 20 breeding groups, mostly in the Ciénaga de Zapata and north of Villa Clara. Reptiles range from three types of crocodiles including the **Cuban crocodile** now found only in the Ciénaga de Zapata (there is a farm on the Zapata Peninsula) to iguanas to tiny salamanders. Cuba claims the smallest of a number of animals, for example the **Cuban pygmy frog**, 12 mm long, the **almiquí**, a shrew-like insectivore, the world's smallest mammal, the **butterfly** or **moth bat** and the **bee hummingbird**, 63 mm long, called locally the *zunzuncito*. The latter is an endangered species, like the **carpintero real woodpecker**, the **cariara** or **caracara**, the **pygmy owl**, the **Cuban green parrot** and the *fermina*, or **Zapata wren**. Less attractively, there is also a **dwarf scorpion**, *alacrán*, 10 mm long.

The best place for birdwatching on the island is the Zapata Peninsula, where 170 species of Cuban birds have been recorded, including the majority of endemic species. In winter migratory waterbirds, swallows and others visit the marshes. The national bird is the forest-dwelling **Cuban trogon**, the *tocororo*, partly because of its blue head, white chest and red underbelly, the colours of the Cuban flag.

Protected areas cover 30% of Cuba including its marine platform. There are 14 national parks and four UNESCO biosphere reserves: **Guanahacabibes** in the extreme western tip of the island; the **Sierra del Rosario**, 60 km west of Havana; **Baconao** in the east and **Cuchillas del Toa**. However, not all legally established conservation areas have any infrastructure, personnel or administration in place.

Sport

Trekking, **hiking**, **rafting** and **bird watching** are elements of adventure or nature travel which are still in their infancy in Cuba but are likely to be heavily promoted in the near future. The island's plentiful fauna and flora, its mountains, cays and wetlands, and its expanding system of national parks and other protected areas, are perfect for getting close to nature. Hunting lodges still attract those who enjoy blasting ducks out of the sky and sport fishing is available in many marinas, but in the last few years the emphasis has been on looking and not touching, as in bird watching and scuba diving. The state travel agencies are opening specialist operations for organized tours, with expert staff on hand to advise on biology, botany or forestry (see page 151). Facilities are limited and many sports are simply unavailable. Traditionally, tourists have been expected to spend their time on the beach, with sightseeing excursions to colonial cities and night time forays into bars and clubs. More activities are now being developed though those seeking water sports are unlikely to be disappointed.

Cuba has an extensive network of tarmac and concrete roads, covering nearly 17,600 km. This impressive infrastructure means that the vast majority of the country is accessible to the cyclist, and there are some dramatic roads to climb and descend. There is total freedom of movement and the rewards can be immense. However, many of the roads are in a poor condition, particularly in the rural areas. See page 153.

Cycling
An integral part of local culture with an estimated 2 mn bicycles in Cuba

Cuba's marine environment is pristine compared with many Caribbean islands, where there has often been overharvesting and overdevelopment of the dive industry. The majority of coral reefs are alive and healthy and teeming with assorted marine life. The government has established a marine park around the **Isla de la Juventud** and much marine life is protected around the entire island, including turtles, the manatee and coral. There are three main marine platforms, the **Archipiélago del Rey** (Sabana-Camagüey), the **Archipiélago de la Reina** and the **Archipiélago de los Canarreos**. The first one has the greatest diversity of marine species and is being explored and classified with the aim of making it a protected zone. There are believed to be some 900 species of fish, 1,400 species of molluscs, 60 species of coral, 1,100 species of crustaceans, 67 species of sharks and rays and four types of marine turtles around the island, as well as the manatee. The main dive areas are Isla de la Juventud, Varadero, Faro de Luna, María La Gorda, Santa Lucía and Santiago de Cuba.

Diving

Cuba has been a fisherman's dream for many decades, not only for its deep sea fishing, popularized by Ernest Hemingway, but also for its freshwater fishing in the many lakes and reservoirs spread around the island. **Freshwater fishing** is mostly for the largemouth bass (*trucha*), which grow to a great size in the Cuban lakes. *Horizontes* is the travel company to contact for accommodation and fishing packages, which can be arranged all year round. The main places are Maspotón, in Pinar del Río, where you can fish in La Juventud reservoir or in the mouth of the Río Los Palacios or Río Carraguao; Laguna del Tesoro in the Ciénaga de Zapata, where there is a wide variety of fish; Presa Alacranes in Villa Clara province, which is the second largest reservoir in the country; Presa Zaza, in Sancti Spíritus, the largest artificial lake in Cuba, where the record catch of *trucha* is 16.5 lbs; Lago La Redonda, near Morón in Ciego de Avila province, where the clear waters hold such a concentration of fish that a group of US fishermen were able to catch 5,078 *trucha* in five days. **Deep sea fishing** can be organized at most marinas around the island, although most of the tournaments and the best facilities are at the Marina Hemingway, just west of Havana. The waters are home to a variety of beaked fish: marlin, swordfish, tarpon, sawfish, yellowfin tuna, dorado, wahoo, shark and a host of others are all caught here. Varadero is a good point from which to go fishing and take advantage of the Gulf Stream which flows between Key West in Florida and Cuba, but records have been broken all along the northern coast in the cays of the Archipiélago de Sabana and the Archipiélago de Camagüey. There is also good fishing off the south coast around the Isla de la Juventud and Cayo Largo. **Bonefishing** is best done off the south coast in the Archipiélago de los Jardines de la Reina, or off Cayo Largo.

Fishing
Equipment can be hired, but serious fishermen will prefer to bring their own & large quantities of insect repellent

There are 18 marinas around the country offering moorings, boat rental and a variety of services. Diving and fishing are on offer at many. The largest is the Marina Hemingway in Havana, see page 182. For technical specifications, see www.dtcuba.com/esp/naturaleza_marinas.asp. Marinas are owned by Cubanacán Náutica (formerly Marlin Marinas), Puertosol and Gaviota. Not many 'yachties' (people who live and travel on their own boats) visit the island because of the political difficulties between Cuba and the USA. The US administration

Sailing

Cuba

forbids any vessel, such as a cruise ship, cargo ship or humble yacht from calling at a US port if it has stopped in Cuba. This effectively prohibits anyone sailing from the US eastern seaboard calling in at a Cuban port on their way south through the Caribbean islands, or vice versa. It is better to rent a bareboat yacht from a Cuban marina and sail around the island, rather than include it in a Caribbean itinerary. It would be worthwhile to invest in *The Cruising Guide to Cuba*, by Simon Charles (Cruising Guide Publications, Box 1017, Dunedin, FL 34697-1017, USA, T813-7335322, F813-7348179) before embarking.

Walking

A good pair of hiking books are essential

The three main mountain ranges are excellent for hill walking in a wide range of tropical vegetation, where many national parks are being established and trails demarcated. The highest peaks are in the **Sierra Maestra** in the east, where there are also many historical landmarks associated with the Wars of Independence and the Revolution. A three day walk will take you from Alto del Naranjo up the island's highest peak, Pico Turquino, and down to the Caribbean coast at Las Cuevas, giving you fantastic views of the mountains and the coastline. The **Sierra del Escambray**, in the centre of the island, is conveniently located just north of the best preserved colonial city, Trinidad, and there are some lovely walks in the hills, along trails beside rivers, waterfalls and caves. The mountains of the west of the island, the **Sierra del Rosario** and the **Sierra de los Organos**, have some of the most unusual geological features, notably the large number of caves and the limestone *mogotes*, straight sided, flat topped hills rising from the midst of tobacco fields and looking almost Chinese, particularly in the early morning mist. Good large scale maps are non-existent and you are advised to take a guide when embarking on long walks.

Health

Local health facilities are listed in individual town directories

Cuba has a high quality national health service and is one of the healthiest countries in Latin America and the Caribbean. Travel in Cuba poses no health risk to the average visitor provided sensible precautions are taken. Visit your GP before you travel to get the latest up to date advice and information. Medical service is no longer free for foreign visitors in Havana, Santiago de Cuba and Varadero, where there are international clinics that charge in dollars (credit cards accepted). Visitors requiring medical attention will be sent to them. Emergencies are handled on an ad hoc basis. Check with your national health service or health insurance on coverage in Cuba and take a copy of your insurance policy with you. Remember you cannot dial any toll-free numbers abroad so make sure you have a contact number. Charges are generally lower than those in Western countries. According to latest reports, visitors are still treated free of charge in other parts of the country, with the exception of tourist enclaves with on-site medical services.

The most common affliction of travellers to any country is probably diarrhoea and the same is true of Cuba. Tap water is safe in most areas of the country, but bottled water is widely available if you prefer. Doctors will advise you to get hepatitis A and typhoid inoculations. Always carry toilet paper with you, it is not often available in public toilets and even some hotels do not have it.

The climate is hot; Cuba is a tropical country and protection against the sun will be needed. Take a high factor sun screen, apply it regularly and stay out of the midday sun. Children need to be particularly well protected and wear a hat. The breeze at the beach is deceptive, you may not feel hot, but the sun will burn very quickly. Between May and October, the risk of sunburn is high, sun blocks are recommended when walking around the city as well as on the beach. In the cooler months, limit beach sessions to two hours.

Havana

Of all the capital cities in the Caribbean, Havana has the reputation for being the most splendid and sumptuous. Before the Revolution, its casinos and nightlife attracted the megastars of the day in much the same way as Beirut and Shanghai, and remarkably little has changed (architecturally) since then. There have been no tacky modernizations, partly because of lack of finance and materials. Low level street lighting, relatively few cars (and many of those antiques), no (real) estate agents or Wendyburgers, no neon and very little advertising (except for political slogans), all give the city plenty of scope for nostalgia. Restoration works in the old part of the city are revealing the glories of the past, although most of the city is fighting a losing battle against the sea air – many of the finest buildings along the sea front are crumbling.

Population: 2,204,300

Havana is not a modern city in the materialist sense and is no good for people for whom shopping and eating well are the central leisure activities. It is, however, probably the finest example of a Spanish colonial city in the Americas. Many of its palaces were converted into museums after the Revolution and more work has been done (with millions of dollars of foreign aid and investment) since the old city was declared a UNESCO World Heritage Site in 1982. Away from the old city, there is some stunning modern architecture from the first half of the 20th century.

Cuba

Ins and outs

The **José Martí international airport** is 18 km from Havana. The most expensive **taxis** are *Turistaxi*, while the cheapest are *Panataxi*. Fares range from US$15-20, but US$18 is commonly asked to the old city. On the way back to the airport it is possible to arrange a private taxi, which may work out cheaper, if you negotiate with the driver. To get to the airport by bus, it is difficult with luggage, and it will take forever. The main **bus** terminal is very near the Plaza de la Revolución in Vedado, central and convenient for accommodation. Víazul dollar buses stop much further out and a taxi will be arranged for you by the company. The **train** station is at the southern end of the old city, within walking distance of any of the hotels there or in Centro Habana, although if you arrive at night, take a taxi.

Getting there

Buses involve complicated queuing procedures and a lot of pushing and shoving. A dollar bus, *Vaivén*, runs on a huge circular route and allows you to get on and off as often as you like. **Bicitaxi**, bicycle taxi, rates negotiable but generally only a fraction of what you would pay a normal taxi. Havana is very spread out along the coast. Those with really good walking boots

Getting around
See transport, page 180, for further details

Havana orientation

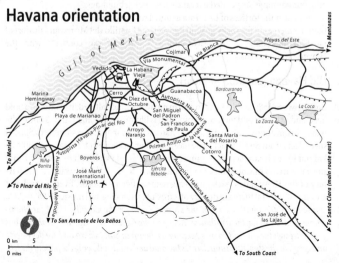

can cover much of the city on foot, but the average visitor will be content with one district at a time, eg Old Havana one day, Vedado the next, and still feel well-exercised.

Orientation The centre is divided into five sections, three of which are of most interest to visitors, **Old Havana** (Habana Vieja), **Central Havana** (Centro) and **Vedado**. The oldest part of the city, around the **Plaza de Armas**, is quite near the docks. Here are the former **Palace of the Captains-General**, the temple of **El Templete**, and **Castillo de La Real Fuerza**, the oldest of all the forts. From Plaza de Armas run two narrow and picturesque streets, Calles Obispo and O'Reilly (there are several old-fashioned pharmacies on Obispo with traditional glass and ceramic medicine jars and decorative perfume bottles on display in shops that gleam with polished wood and mirrors). These two streets go west to the heart of the city to **Parque Central**, with its laurels, poincianas, almonds, palms, shrubs and gorgeous flowers. To the southwest rises the golden dome of the **Capitol**. From the northwest corner of Parque Central a wide, tree-shaded avenue with a central walkway (where small boys wizz up and down on homemade skateboards and other vehicles), the **Paseo del Prado**, runs to the fortress of **La Punta**. At its north sea-side end is the **Malecón**, a splendid highway along the coast to the west residential district of Vedado. The sea crashing along the seawall here is a spectacular sight when the wind blows from the north. On calmer days, fishermen lean over the parapet, lovers sit in the shade of the small pillars, and joggers sweat along the pavement. On the other side of the six-lane road, buildings which from a distance look stout and grand, with arcaded pavements, balconies, mouldings and large entrances, are salt-eroded, faded and sadly decrepit inside. Restoration is progressing slowly, but the sea is destroying old and new alike and creating a mammoth renovation task.

Further west, Calle San Lázaro leads directly from the monument to **General Antonio Maceo** on the Malecón to the magnificent central stairway of **Havana University**. A monument to **Julio Antonio Mella**, founder of the Cuban Communist Party, stands across from the stairway. Further out, past **El Príncipe** castle, is **Plaza de la Revolución**, with the impressive monument to **José Martí** at its centre. The large buildings surrounding the square were mostly built in the 1950s and house the principal government ministries. The long grey building behind the monument is the former Justice Ministry (1958), now the headquarters of the Central Committee of the Communist Party, where Fidel Castro has his office. The Plaza is the scene of massive parades (May Day) and speeches marking important events. It was completely transformed for an open air mass held by the Pope in January 1998 with huge religious paintings suspended over the surrounding buildings.

From near the fortress of **La Punta** a tunnel runs east under the mouth of the harbour; it emerges in the rocky ground between the **Castillo del Morro** and the fort of **La Cabaña**, some 550m away, and a 5 km highway connects with the Havana-Matanzas road.

Old Havana (La Habana Vieja)

Castillo del Morro Built between 1589 and 1630, with a 20 m moat, but much altered. It stands on a bold headland, with the best view of Havana and is illuminated at night. It was one of the major fortifications built to protect the natural harbour and the assembly of Spain's silver fleets from pirate attack. The flash of its lighthouse, built in 1844, is visible 30 km out to sea. It now serves as a museum with a good exhibition of Cuban history since the arrival of Columbus. On the harbour side, down by the water, is the **Battery of the 12 Apostles**, each gun being named after an Apostle. Every Saturday at around 1000-1100 there is a display of AfroCuban dancing and music. ■ *0830-2030 (museum, 1000-1800). US$1 for the parque, US$3 for the Castillo, US$2 for photographs and US$2 for the lighthouse. Access to the Castillo del Morro is from any bus going through the tunnel (24 or 40 centavos), board at San Lázaro and Av del Puerto and get off at the stop after tunnel, cross the road and climb following the path to the left.*

Alternatively take a taxi, or a 20-min walk from the Fortaleza de la Cabaña (see Casablanca below).

Fronting the harbour is a high wall; the ditch on the landward side, 12 m deep, has a **Fortaleza de** drawbridge to the main entrance. Inside are **Los Fosos de los Laureles** where politi- **la Cabaña** cal prisoners were shot during the Cuban fight for independence. Every night the cannons are fired in an historical ceremony recalling the closing of the city walls in the 17th century to protect it from pirates; this starts at 2045 so that the walls are closed at 2100. There are two museums here, one about Che Guevara and another about fortresses with pictures and models, some old weapons and a replica of a large catapult and battering ram. ■ *Open to visitors 0830-2200, US$3, extra charge for camera or video. Access as for Castillo del Morro or via Casablanca.*
     The **National Observatory** and the station for trains to Matanzas are on the same side of the Channel as the forts, at **Casablanca**. This charming town is also the site of a statue of a very human Jesus Christ, erected during the Batista dictatorship as a pacifying exercise. Go up a steep, twisting flight of stone steps, starting on the other side of the plaza in front of the landing stage, and you can walk from the statue to the Fortaleza (10 minutes) and then on to the Castillo del Morro. ■ *Left-hand ferry queue next to the Customs House, opposite Calle Santa Clara, 10 centavos.*

Built at the end of the 16th century, a squat building with 250cm thick walls. ■ *Open* **Castillo de** *daily. Free.* Opposite the fortress, across the Malecón, is the **monument to Máximo** **la Punta** **Gómez**, the independence leader.

Cuba's oldest building and the second oldest fort in the New World. Built in 1558 **Castillo de la** after the city had been sacked by buccaneers and rebuilt in 1582. It is a low, long **Real Fuerza** building at the end of O'Reilly entre Av del Puerto y Tacón, with a picturesque tower from which there is a grand view. Inside the castle is a museum with armour and Cuban ceramic art dating from the 1940s onwards. ■ *Open daily, 0800-1900, US$2, T615010. Art exhibitions downstairs. Shop upstairs.* There are two other old forts in Havana: **Atarés**, finished in 1763, on a hill overlooking the southwest end of the harbour; and **El Príncipe**, on a hill at the far end of Avenida Independencia (Avenida Rancho Boyeros), built 1774-94, now the city gaol. There are amazing views of Havana from this hill.

Construction of a church on this site was begun by Jesuit missionaries at the beginning **Cathedral** of the 18th century. After the Jesuits were expelled in 1767, the church was converted into a cathedral. On either side of the Spanish colonial baroque façade are bell towers, the left one (west) being half as wide as the right (east),which has a grand view. The church is officially dedicated to the Virgin of the Immaculate Conception, but is better known as the church of Havana's patron saint, San Cristóbal, and as the Columbus cathedral. The bones of Christopher Columbus were sent to this cathedral when Santo Domingo was ceded by Spain to France in 1795; they now lie in Santo Domingo (Dominican Republic). ■ *Mon-Tue, Thu-Sat 0930-1230, Sun 0830-1230, Mass at 1030.*

The statue in the centre is of Carlos Manuel de Céspedes. In the northeast corner of **Plaza de** the square is the church of **El Templete**; a column in front of it marks the spot where **Armas** the first mass was said in 1519 under a ceiba tree. A sapling of the same tree, blown down by a hurricane in 1753, was planted on the same spot, and under its branches the supposed bones of Columbus reposed in state before being taken to the cathedral. This tree was cut down in 1828, the present tree planted, and the Doric temple opened. There are paintings by Vermay, a pupil of David, inside. On the north side of the Plaza is the **Palacio del Segundo Cabo**, the former private residence of the Captains General, now housing the Feria Cubana del Libro. Its patio is worth a look. On the east side is the small luxury hotel, the *Santa Isabel*, and on the south side the modern **Museo Nacional de Historia Natural**. Outside in the Plaza de Armas there

Cuba

Cuba

Central & Old Havana

Caleta de San Lázaro

To Havana University & Julio Antonio Mella Monument

A

■ 8

Calzada de Infanta

Humbolt

Príncipe

Vapor

B CAYO HUESO

Monumento General Antonio Maceo o

San Lázaro

Oquendo

Márquez González

Lucena

Padre Varela (Belascoaín)

Casa de la Trova

San Lázaro

Lagunas

Ánimas

Perseverancia

7 ■

Virtudes

Concordia

Neptuno

San Miguel

San Rafael

Nuestra Señora de Monserrate ✝ ■

C

San Martín

Gervasio

Escobar

Lealtad

Av de Italia (Galiano)

Boulevard

Zanja

Salud

CENTRO

Chinese Market o

Barcelona

Jesús Peregrino

Pocito

Chávez

Nuestra Señora de la Caridad del Cobre ✝ ■

Av Salvador Allende (Carlo III)

✉

D

Enrique Barnet (Estrella)

Maloja

Sitio

Peñalver

✝ ■ Sagrado Corazón de Jesús

Escobar

Lealtad

Campanario

Manrique

San Nicolás

Rayo

Ángeles

Av Simón Bolívar ✉

To Castillo del Príncipe

Desague

Benjumeda

Concepción de la Villa

Peñalver

Condesa

Figuras

Santo Tomás

Carmen

To Plaza de la Revolución

E

Clavel

Rastro

Santa Marta

Corrales

Gloria

Esperanza

Av de España (Vives)

Alambique

Arroyo (Av Manglar)

Puerta Cerrada

Diaria

1

2

3

N

0 metres 200
0 yards 200

■ **Sleeping**

1 Caribbean *B4*
2 Deauville *B4*
3 Golden Tulip Parque Central *C4*
4 Inglaterra *C4*

5 La Casa del Científico *C4*
6 Lido *C4*
7 Lincoln *C3*
8 Nacional de Cuba *A1*
9 Plaza *C4*

10 Residencia Santa Clara *D5*
11 Sevilla *C4*

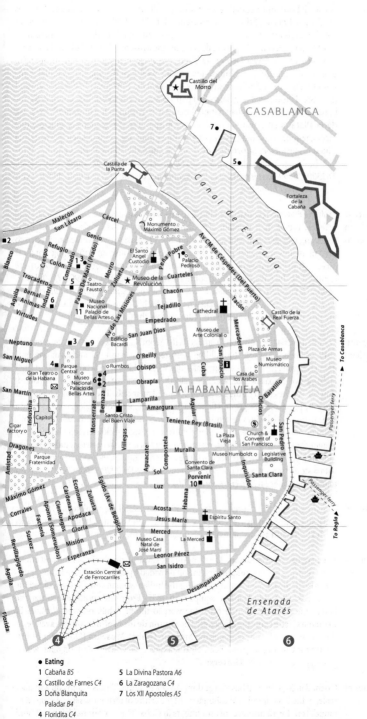

Cuba

● Eating

1 Cabaña *B5*
2 Castillo de Farnes *C4*
3 Doña Blanquita
  Paladar *B4*
4 Floridita *C4*

5 La Divina Pastora *A6*
6 La Zaragozana *C4*
7 Los XII Apostoles *A5*

is a small **book market** daily except Monday. On the west side of Plaza de Armas is the former **Palace of the Captains General**, built in 1780, a charming example of colonial architecture. The Spanish Governors and the Presidents lived here until 1917, when it became the City Hall. It is now the **Museo de la Ciudad**, the Historical Museum of the city of Havana. There are no explanations, even in Spanish. Nineteenth-century furnishings illustrate the wealth of the Spanish colonial community. The building was the site of the signing of the 1899 treaty between Spain and the USA. The arcaded and balconied patio is well worth a visit. The courtyard contains royal palms, the Cuban national tree. An extension to the museum is the **Casa de la Plata**, a silverware collection on Obispo entre Mercaderes y Oficios, fine pieces, jewellery and old frescoes on the upper floor, free with ticket to Museo de la Ciudad. The former **Supreme Court** on the north side of the Plaza is another colonial building, with a large patio. ■ *Open daily 0930-1830, camera fee US$3, T615001, 639981. It is possible to buy a combined one-day ticket which, allows access to several other museums.*

The church & convent of San Francisco
Built in 1608 and reconstructed in 1730, this is a massive, sombre edifice suggesting defence, rather than worship. The three-storey tower was both a landmark for returning voyagers and a look-out for pirates. The Basílica Menor de San Francisco de Asís is now a concert hall and the convent is a museum containing religious pieces. Restoration work is still going on. Most of the treasures, however, were removed by the government and some are in museums. ■ *Daily 0900-1900, US$2, photos US$2, video US$10, guide US$1, bell tower with stunning views of the city and port an extra US$1.* The Corinthian white marble building on Calle Oficios, south of the post office was the legislative building before the Capitol was built.

The Convento de Santa Clara
Founded in 1644 by nuns from Cartagena in Colombia, it was in use as a convent until 1919, when the nuns sold the building. Restoration began in 1982, and is still continuing. The convent occupies four small blocks in Old Havana, bounded by Calles Habana, Sol, Cuba and Luz, and originally there were three cloisters and an orchard. You can see the cloisters, the nuns' cemetery and their cells. The first cloister has been carefully preserved; the ground floor is a grand porticoed stone gallery surrounding a large patio packed with vegetation, in it are the city's first slaughterhouse, first public fountain and public baths. The Sailor's House in the second cloister, reputedly built by a sailor for his love-lorn daughter, is now a *Residencia Académica* for student groups (and independent travellers if room). The convent is topped by an extensive tiled roof with a stone turret next to the church choir. ■ *Mon-Fri 0900-1500, US$2 for guided tour in Spanish or French, entrance on Cuba.*

La Merced
Construction of this church began in 1755, and was still incomplete in 1792, when work stopped. Building was completed late in the 19th century. It has an unremarkable exterior and a redecorated lavish interior.

Parque Fraternidad
The park has been landscaped to show off the **Capitol**, north of it, to the best effect. At its centre is a ceiba tree growing in soil provided by each of the American republics. Also in the park is a famous statue of the Indian woman who first welcomed the Spaniards: La Noble Habana, sculpted in 1837. From the southwest corner the handsome Avenida Allende runs due west to the high hill, on which stands **El Príncipe Castle** (now the city gaol). The **Quinta de los Molinos**, on this avenue, at the foot of the hill, now contains the **Máximo Gómez Museum** (Dominican-born fighter for Cuban Independence). North, along Calle Universidad, on a hill which gives a good view, is the **University**.

The Capitol
Opened in May 1929, it has a large dome over a rotunda. This is a copy, on a smaller scale, of the US Capitol in Washington. At the centre of its floor is set a 24-carat diamond, zero for all distance measurements in Cuba. The interior has large halls and

stately staircases, all most sumptuously decorated. ■ *Entrance for visitors is to the left of the stairway, US$3 to go in the halls, tours available, restaurant.*

Partagas, on Calle Industria behind the Capitolio, gives tours, in theory, at 1000, US$10. The tour lasts for about an hour and is very interesting. You are taken through the factory and shown the whole production process from storage and sorting of leaves, to packaging and labelling (explanation in Spanish only). Four different brand names are made here; *Partagas, Cubana, Ramón Allones* and *Bolívar*. These and other famous cigars (and rum) can be bought at their shop here: open 0900-1700. Cigars are also made at many tourist locations.

Cigar factory

A very pleasant park with a monument to **José Martí** in the centre. On its west side are the *Hotel Telégrafo* (being restored in 2000), the historic *Hotel Inglaterra* and the **Gran Teatro de la Habana**, a beautiful building with tours of the inside. The north side is entirely occupied by the *Golden Tulip Parque Central*, while the *Hotel Plaza* is in the northeast corner. Restoration of one of the sites of the Museo Nacional Palacio de Bellas Artes is taking place on the east side of the park.

Parque Central

Cuba

The Jesuits built this church in 1672 on the slight elevation of **Peña Pobre** hill. The original church was largely destroyed by a hurricane in 1844 and rebuilt in its present neo-Gothic style in 1866-71. It has 10 tiny chapels, no more than kneeling places and some interesting stained glass depicting conquistadors.

Church of El Santo Angel Custodio

This is a beautiful Arab building housing shops and a restaurant/bar. It is now the **Palacio de la Artesanía**. ■ *0900-0200 Fri-Sun, with traditional dance at 2200.*

Palacio Pedroso

An 18th-century plaza, undergoing restoration since February 1996 as part of a joint project by UNESCO and Habaguanex, a state company responsible for the restoration and revival of old Havana. The former house of the Spanish Captain General, **Conde de Ricla**, who retook Havana from the English and restored power to Spain in 1763, can be seen on the corner of San Ignacio and Muralla. As restoration continues, 18th-century murals are being uncovered on the external walls of the buildings, many of which boast elegant balconies overlooking the plaza. The newly-restored Cuban Stock Exchange building, **La Lonja**, Oficios and Plaza San Francisco, is opposite the cruise ship terminal.

La Plaza Vieja

This huge, ornate building, topped by a dome, on Refugio entre Monserrate y Zulueta, facing Avenida de las Misiones, was once the Presidential Palace, but now contains the **Museo de la Revolución**. The history of Cuban political development is charted, from the slave uprisings to joint space missions with the ex-Soviet Union. The liveliest section displays the final battles against Batista's troops, with excellent photographs and some bizarre mementoes from the Sierra Maestra campaign. The yacht *Granma*, from which Dr Castro disembarked with his companions in 1956 to launch the Revolution, has been installed in the park facing the south entrance, surrounded by planes, tanks and other vehicles involved, as well as a Soviet-built tank used against the Bay of Pigs invasion and a fragment from a US spy plane shot down in the 1970s. ■ *T624091. Open Tue-Sun 1000-1700, US$3, guided tour 1030, US$10, cameras allowed, US$3 extra. Allow several hours to see it all, explanations mostly in Spanish.*

Museo de la Revolución
Look out for the bullet holes as you walk up the stairs to the stuffed mule & stuffed horse used by Che Guevara & Camilo Cienfuegos

For US$15 you can buy a one-day ticket from any of the museums, allowing you entrance to the Museo de la Ciudad, its Casa de la Plata and the following: **Casa de los Arabes** (with bar and restaurant, *Al Medina*), on Oficios between Obispo and Obrapía, a lovely building with vines trained over the courtyard for shade, includes a mosque, jewels and rugs. Open daily 0930-1830, US$1; **Casa de Africa**, on Obrapía 157 between San Ignacio and Mercaderes (Monday-Saturday 1030-1730, Sunday 0930-1230, US$2), small gallery of carved wooden artefacts and handmade

Museum tour

costumes; **Vintage Car Museum**, Oficios y Jústiz (just off Plaza de Armas, open daily 0900-1900, US$1). There are a great many museum pieces, pre-Revolutionary US models, still on the road especially outside Havana, in among the Ladas, VWs and Nissans; **Casa de Guayasimín**, Obrapía 111 entre Mercaderes y San Ignacio, exhibition of works donated to Cuba by the late Ecuadorean artist Oswaldo Guayasimín (paintings, sculpture and silkscreens) occasionally other exhibitions. Guayasimín painted a famous portrait of Fidel Castro for his 70th birthday with his hands raised; **Casa de México**, opposite the above, also called La Casa de Benito Juárez, Obrapía entre Mercaderes y Oficios, a museum of Mexico in a pink building marked with the Mexican flag, open Tuesday-Saturday 1030-1730, Sunday 0930-1230, entrance US$1; **Casa de Simón Bolívar**, Mercaderes entre Obrapía y Lamparilla, contains exhibits about the life of the South American liberator and some Venezuelan art, open Monday-Saturday 1030-1030, Sunday 1030-1300, US$1; and **Casa de Asia**, Mercaderes entre Obrapía y Obispo, converted from a solar, a multi-family dwelling with a central courtyard, into an exhibition space of art, furniture and other artefacts donated from the Asian subcontinent.

Sights outside Old Havana

Plaza de la Revolución
Museo José Martí, Plaza de la Revolución, in base of memorial. Beautifully restored and impressive museum, with lookout accessed by mirrored lift. ■ *Mon-Sat 0900-1600, lookout US$5 extra.* **Museo Postal Cubano**, Ministry of Communications, Plaza de la Revolución. History of the postal service and stamps and the story books of José Antonio de Armona (1765). ■ *Mon-Fri 0900-1600, US$1, T705193.*

Vedado
Museo Napoleónico, San Miguel 1159 esquina Ronda. Houses 7,000 pieces from the private collection of sugar baron, Julio Lobo: paintings and other works of art, a specialized library and a collection of weaponry. Check out the tiled fencing gallery. ■ *Mon-Sat 1000-1800, Sun 0900-1230, US$3, T791460.* The **Cuban pavilion** (Pabellón Cuba), a large building on Calle 23, is a combination of a tropical glade and a museum of social history. It tells the nation's story by a brilliant combination of objects, photography and the architectural manipulation of space. ■ *Closed Mon. Music and dancing from 2100 on Wed (reggae), Thu (son), Fri-Sun (disco).* **Casa de la Amistad**, Paseo 406, entre 17 y 19. A former mansion, a beautiful building with gardens, now operated by ICAP (Cuban Institute for Friendship among the Peoples) and housing the *Amistur* travel agency (see page 179). It has a reasonably priced bar, cafetería and tourist shop (0930-1800). Cuban music nights are US$5 for tourists; good traditional music in a nice setting. Lots of Cubans go there too, but there is no soliciting. You can eat in the garden, the food is consistently good with large portions. Two menus: one has lobster and shrimp, the other is a house menu. ■ *The bar and cafetería are open Mon-Fri 1100-2300 (with sextet), Sat 1100-0200 (with Cuban bands).* **Museo de la Danza**, G (Presidentes) esq Línea. Items from Alicia Alonso's personal collection and from the Ballet Nacional de Cuba. ■ *Tue-Sat 1100-1830, US$2.* **Galería Haydée Santamaría**, G esq 5, alongside Casa de las Américas. Work of Latin American artists, good representation of mostly 20th-century styles. The gallery was renovated with the help of the city of Seville and reopened in 1999. ■ *Tue-Sat 1000-1700, Sun 0900-1300, US$2.* The **Cementerio Colón** should be visited to see the wealth of funerary sculpture, including Carrara Marbles; Cubans visit the sculpture of Amelia de Milagrosa and pray for miracles. ■ *US$1.* The Chinese cemetery is at Avenida 26 y 31.

Miramar
Maqueta de la Ciudad (scale model of Havana) on Calle 28 113 entre 1 y 3. ■ *Tue-Sat 1000-1800, US$3.* Opened in 1995, this is fast becoming a great attraction. The model covers Havana and its suburbs as far out as Cojímar and the airport. Colonial buildings are in red, post-colonial pre-Revolution buildings in yellow and post-Revolution buildings in white. Good fun with every building represented and recommended for the end of your stay so that you can pick out the places you visited.

Excursions

You can take a ferry from nearby the Customs House, opposite Calle Santa Clara in **Regla**
Old Havana (or the Ruta 6 bus from Zulueta y Virtudes inland), to Regla, which has
a largely black population and a long, rich and still active cultural history of the
Yoruba and *santería*. The extension room of the **Museo Municipal de Regla** (Martí
158 entre Facciolo y La Piedra, on the left side of the church), houses information
and objects of Yoruba culture. ■ *Mon-Sat 0930-1830, Sun 0900-1300, US$2,
T906989, phone to check it is open.* Three blocks further on is the **Casa de la Cultura**,
which has very occasional cultural activities.

The former seaside village, now a concrete jungle, featured in Hemingway's *The Old* **Cojímar**
Man and the Sea, is an easy excursion (15 minutes by taxi) from central Havana. He
celebrated his Nobel prize here in 1954 and there is a bust of him opposite a small
fort. The coastline (no beach) is covered in sharp rocks and is dirty because of effluent from tankers.

Hemingway fans may wish to visit his house, 11 km from the centre of Havana, **San Francisco**
where he lived from 1939 to 1960 (called the **Museo Ernest Hemingway**). The sign- **de Paula**
post is opposite the post office, leading up a short driveway. Visitors are not allowed
inside the plain whitewashed house, which has been lovingly preserved with all
Hemingway's furniture and books, just as he left it. But you can walk all around the
outside and look in through the windows and open doors. The garden is beautiful
and tropical, with many shady palms. Next to the swimming pool (empty) are the
gravestones of Hemingway's pet dogs. ■ *0930-1600, US$3, T910809, closed Tue.
Hemingway tours are offered by hotel tour desks for US$35. No toilets. Photos US$5.*

The **Jardín Botánico Nacional de Cuba** is well-maintained with excellent collections, **Parks & zoos**
including a Japanese garden with tropical adaptations. There are only a few signs and
so not as informative as it might be. There is a good **organic vegetarian restaurant**
(the only one in Cuba) using solar energy for cooking. There is only one sitting for
lunch, but you can eat as much as you like from a selection of hot and cold vegetarian
dishes and drinks for US$12. Water and waste food is recycled and the restaurant
grows most of its own food. ■ *Wed-Sun 1000-1745, but in practice you may not be
allowed in after 1530, US$5, T442516/18. Getting there: Km 3.5, Carretera Rocío, south
of the city in Arroyo Naranjo, beyond Parque Lenín. Many hotel tour desks now organize
day trips including lunch for US$25, better value than going independently and probably
less effort. Taxi from Old Havana US$15-18 one-way.* **Parque Zoológico Nacional**,
Km 3, Carretera de Capdevila. ■ *Wed-Sun, 0900-1515, T447613.* **Parque Zoológico
de la Habana**, Avenida 26 y Santa Teresa, Nuevo Vedado. ■ *Tue-Sun 0930-1730,
US$2, T818915.* A jungle-like wood, **El Bosque de la Habana**, is worth visiting.
■ *From the entrance to the City Zoo, cross Avenida 26 and walk a few blocks until you
reach a bridge across the Almendares. Cross this, turn right at the end and keep going
north.* **National Aquarium**, Calle 60 and Avenida 1, Miramar, specializes in salt water
fish and dolphins. It was modernized in 1999 with a new section with interactive displays. ■ *Tue-Sun 1000-1745, T236401-6, F241242.* The **Parque Lenín aquarium** has
freshwater fish on show.

Essentials

Sleeping

Payment for hotels used by tourists is in US$. Always tell the hotel each morning if you intend ■ *on maps*
to stay on another day. Do not lose your 'guest card' which shows your name, meal plan and
room number. Tourist hotels are a/c, with 'tourist' TV (US films, tourism promotion), restaurants

with reasonable food, but standards are not comparable with Europe and plumbing is often faulty or affected by water shortages. Several important hotel renovation projects have been completed in Old Havana and these are now elegant places to stay.

Vedado

Gulf of Mexico

Monumento a Calixto García

Casa de las Américas

Galería Haydée Santamaría

CVD José Martí

Malecón

Calzada

Boca de la Chorrera

Malecón

Paseo

Línea

Museo de la Danza

Presidentes

Sagrado Corazón de Jesús

Teatro Mella

To Jardines 1830

Maxim

Casa de la Cultura de Plaza

Línea

7 (Calzada)

Museo de Artes Decorativas

Iglesia del Carmelo

Catedral Episcopal

Av 2

Av 4

Paseo

Amistur

Market

VEDADO

Italian Embassy

Castillo del Príncipe

Zapata

Museo del Deporte

Teatro Nacional & Café Cantante

Museo Postal Cubano

Cementerio de Colón

Paseo

Plaza de la Revolución

Monumento José Martí

San Antonio Chiquito

NUEVO VEDADO

San Pedro

Av de Carlos M de Céspedes

Av de Rancho Boyeros

Independencia

Ermita

Calzada de Ayestarán

Panchit

To Zoo, Botanical Gardens & Airport

N

0 metres 200
0 yards 200

■ **Sleeping**
1 Capri
2 Colina
3 Habana Riviera

4 Meliá Cohiba
5 Morro
6 Nacional de Cuba
7 Presidente

8 Tryp Habana Libre
9 Vedado
10 Victoria

Cuba

LL-L*Golden Tulip Parque Central* (Cubanacán), Neptuno entre Prado y Zulueta, T6066279, F606630, www.gt-parquecentral.com, on north side of Parque Central. 281 rooms of international standard, excellent bathrooms, separate shower and bathtub, business centre, 2 restaurants, 2 bars, great view of Havana from pool on 9th floor, fitness centre, charming and helpful multilingual staff, efficient Dutch management, good breakfast but pricey, US$12.50. **LL-L** *Santa Isabel* (Habaguanex), Baratillo 9 entre Obispo y Narciso López, Plaza de Armas, T338201, F338391. Five-star, only 27 rooms, 10 of them suites, busy with groups, height of luxury, very well-equipped bathrooms, rooms on 3rd floor have balcony overlooking plaza, pool, restaurant, central patio with fountain and greenery and lobby bar, good view of the Palacio de los Capitanes Generales, El Templete and other local sights, great location. **L-A** *Conde de Villanueva, Hostal del Habano* (Habaguanex), Mercaderes 202 esq Lamparilla, T6292934, F629682, hconde@ ip.etecsa.cu 9 rooms and suites around peaceful courtyard, attractive red and green colour scheme, cigar theme with cigar shop, café, bar, good restaurant, highly regarded, friendly staff, named after Claudio Martínez del Pinillo, Conde de Villanueva (1789-1853), a notable personality who promoted tobacco abroad and helped to bring the railway to Cuba. **L-A** *Florida* (Habaguanex), Obispo 252 esq Cuba, T624127, F624117. Restored building dates from 1885, cool oasis, elegant restaurant, bar just off the street, serves great daiquirís, marble floors and pillars in courtyard, beautiful rooms with high ceilings, quiet a/c, TV, some balconies, some singles, small continental breakfast, parking. **AL-A** *Sevilla* (Gran Caribe), Trocadero 55 y Prado, T338560, F338582. Recently restored, 188 rooms of 1937 vintage on edge of Old Havana, most have no view, noisy a/c, pool, shops, sauna and massage, tourism bureau, elegant restaurant and bar on top floor with great night time views over Vedado and the Malecón, huge windows are flung open to let in the breeze. **AL-B** *Inglaterra* (Gran Caribe), Prado 416 entre San Rafael y San Miguel, T335937, F338254. 86 rooms, built in 1875 next to the Teatro Nacional, famous former foreign guests style, regal atmosphere, but a bit drab, balconies overlook Parque Central, some single rooms have no windows but at least you won't get woken by the traffic, reasonable breakfast, lovely old mosaic tiled dining room, 1 of 4 cafés or restaurants with a variety of services and cuisines.

Cuba

A-B *Ambos Mundos* (Habaguanex), Obispo 153 esq Mercaderes, T66952931, F669532. Beautifully restored, Hemingway lived here for 10 years before moving to La Vigia in 1939, you can see his room on 5th floor where there is a nice terrace bar with jolly Cuban music, rooms small, some smell damp. **A-B** *Plaza* (Gran Caribe), Zulueta 267 esq Neptuno, or Ignacio Agramonte 267, T608583, F608591. 186 rooms, comfortable, high ceilings, noisy a/c, reasonable bathrooms, don't rely on toilet paper being provided, street front rooms very noisy, ask for one in the inner courtyard, good breakfast on 5th floor with fine view, poor dinner, service generally poor. **C** *Hostal Valencia* (Habaguanex), Oficios 53 esquina Obrapía, T623201, F335628. Joint Spanish/Cuban venture modelled on the Spanish *paradores*, rooms named after Valencian towns, tastefully restored building, nicely furnished, pleasant courtyard with vines, music, good restaurant (see below), the *Comendador*, next door, opened in 1999, separate but using the facilities of the *Valencia*. **D-E** *Residencia Santa Clara*, in convent buildings, entrance on Sol y Cuba, T613335, F335696, see page 166. Lovely, can be noisy early morning, nice café, poor breakfast.

Central Havana **C** *Caribbean* (Horizontes), Paseo Martí 164 esquina Colón, T338241/233. Remodelled, nice lobby, good security, convenient, 36 rooms, try and get one on 5th floor, fan and TV, popular with budget travellers, but avoid noisy rooms at front and lower floors at back over deafening water pump. **C** *Deauville* (Horizontes), Galiano y Malecón, T338812, F338148. 148 rooms, noise from Malecón, renovated 1999, breakfast included, pool. **C-D** *La Casa del Científico*, Prado 212 esquina Trocadero, T624511. Beautiful colonial building, charmingly old-fashioned, shared or private bathroom, cheap breakfast, luxurious dining room and lounge in classic style, very pleasant atmosphere, friendly staff, reservations essential, often booked by groups, best budget option in old city, Asistur office on site. **D** *Lincoln* (Islazul), Galiano 164 esquina Virtudes, T628061. 135 rooms, friendly, TV, hot water, a/c, radio, clean, good value, guests are mostly Cuban honeymooners. **D-E** *Lido* (Horizontes), Consulado 210 entre Animas y Trocadero, T571102, F338814. 65 rooms, a/c, some with TV, not bad for the price, but don't expect hot water in the shower, laundry expensive, done by hand and charged per item, central, friendly reception, restaurant downstairs, food bland and overpriced, bar and café on roof terrace much better, excellent views.

Vedado **LL-L** *Meliá Cohiba* (Cubanacán), Paseo entre 1 y 3, T333636, F334555, www.solmelia.es International grand luxury, high rise and dominating the neighbourhood, 342 rooms, 120 suites, shops, gym, healthclub, pool, gourmet restaurant, piano bar. **LL-AL** *Nacional de Cuba* (Gran Caribe), O esquina 21, T333564, F335054. 467 rooms, some renovated, good bathrooms with lots of bottles of goodies, some package tours use it at bargain rates, generally friendly and efficient service, faded grandeur, dates from 1930, superb reception hall, note the vintage Otis high speed lifts, steam room, 2 pools, restaurants, bars, shops, business desk in lobby for emails, faxes etc, exchange bureau, gardens with old cannons on hilltop overlooking the Malecón and harbour entrance, great place to watch people and vehicles. **AL** *Victoria* (Gran Caribe), 19 y M, T333510, F333109, reserva@gcvictoria.gca.cma.net 31 rooms, small, quiet and pleasant, tasteful if conservative, good bathrooms, small pool, parking, good cooking, in good order. **AL-B** *Presidente* (Gran Caribe), Calzada y G (Presidentes), T334394, F333753. Oldest hotel in Havana, refurbished, 160 rooms, 10 suites, pool. **A** *Habana Riviera* (Gran Caribe), Paseo y Malecón, T334051, F333154. 330 rooms, 1950s block, Mafia style, appearance suffers from being so close to the glitzy *Meliá Cohiba*, desolate square outside, which together with the hotel entrance is awash with prostitutes after dark, does a good breakfast, no need to eat again all day. **A** *Tryp Habana Libre* (Gran Caribe), L y 23, T334011, F333141, comer@rllibre.com.cu 606 rooms in huge block, prices depend on the floor number, most facilities are here, eg hotel reservations, excursions, Polynesian restaurant, buffet, 24-hr coffee shop, *Cabaret Turquino* 2200-0400, US$20 per couple, shopping mall, includes liquor store, cigar shop, jewellery and perfume, handicrafts, shoe shop, Air Jamaica, Photoservice, Banco Financiero Internacional, postal service. **B** *Capri* (Horizontes), 21 y N, T333571, F320525. 215 rooms, showing their age, public areas also with signs of wear and tear, a/c, pool, cabaret, shops, currency exchange, parking, car rental. **B** *Vedado* (Horizontes), O 244 entre 23 y 25, T334072, F334186. 194 rooms, a/c, pool, restaurants, nightclub, lacking in atmosphere, renovated 1999. **D** *Colina* (Horizontes), L y 27, T323535, F334104. 79 rooms, hot water, street noise, small rooms, excellent buffet breakfast, open to non-residents US$3, popular with airport Cubatur desk. **D** *Morro* (Horizontes), 3 entre C y D, T329507. 20 rooms, restaurant and bar.

There is a string of 4-star hotels west along the coast that are used by package tour operators; guests are often here for the first and last nights of their stay; not particularly convenient for visiting the old city, but you do get a sea view. **Miramar & further west**

Private accommodation

E *Gustavo Enamorado Zamora*, Teniente Rey (Brasil) 115 entre Cuba y San Ignacio, T626287. Two double rooms, shared bathroom, nice patio, warm atmosphere, kind and helpful. **E-F** *Marta y Israel*, Compostela 359 entre Lamparilla y Obrapía, T626862. Two rooms, fans, clean showers, breakfast. **Old Havana**

E *Dr Antonio E Clavero Machado*, Lealtad 262, Neptuno y Concordia. A nice single room with a/c, private bath with hot shower. **E** *Julio Massagué Barranco*, Escobar 413 entre San Rafael y San Martín, T631731. An English teacher and very friendly. **E** *Carlos Serrano*, Consulado 158, Apto 54, entre Colón y Trocadero, T616291. B&B, English spoken, a/c, showers, airport pickup. **E-F** *Eduardo y Bruno*, Industria 8 entre Genio y Refugio, Apto 4, T637605. 1 room, breakfast, very close to Malecón, superb location. **E-F** *Juan R Laborde*, San Lázaro 24 entre Cárcel y Prado. Good position, bakery next door, friendly, food available. **E-F** *Elsa Hernández Marcial*, Lealtad 415, Apto 38, esq San Rafael, T631501. Friendly owner, 1 room sleeps 3. **F** *Nancy*, Apto 25, Máximo Gómez 456, One room sleeps 3, fan, clean bathroom, breakfast. **F** *Dr Alejandro Oses*, Av Malecón 163, p 1, entre Aguila y Crespo, T637359. No a/c, helpful family, best view in city from balcony of entire Malecón, from El Morro to *Hotel Nacional*, nice place to stay. **F** *Ricardo Martín y María Esther Pérez*, San Lázaro 109 entre Genios y Crespo (bajos), very near Paseo del Prado and Malecón, phone the neighbour, Monga, T617009. A/c, comfortable, functional. *Maritza*, Príncipe 140 entre Espada y Hospital, T786842. Also contact for other rooms and apartments in the area. **Central Havana**

C *Bienvenido y Sara*, 36 22 esq Kohly, Nuevo Vedado, T813069. A/c rooms, worth it for the garden and Sara's traditional Cuban cooking. **E** *Aleida Ruga Sánchez*, 3 652, Apto 1 A, entre 12 y Malecón, T309578. **E** *Don Pepe*, Línea 58, ground floor, beside Japanese Embassy, T326183. A/c bedroom, doctor and dentist couple. **E** *Iraída Carpio*, 19 376 p10A, entre G y H, Elevador A, T324084. No English, breakfast US$3, a/c, good bed, hot water, good shower, friendly family. **E** *Jorge Coalla Potts*, I 456 apto 11 entre 21 y 23, T329032. Friendly, helpful, contacts throughout the island, hot water, comfortable, no meals. **E** *Luís y Alicia*, Línea 53 Apto 9 entre M y N, T328439. Friendly couple, both doctors, Spanish speaking only, rooms cleaned daily, long stays possible, good view from 9th floor. **E** *Marina Madán Bugarín*, K 508, left entrance, entre 25 y 27, T321629. **E** *Marta Vitorte*, G 301, Apartamento 14, 14th floor, entre 13 y 15, T326475, high rise building near corner with Línea. Spacious, en-suite bathroom, balcony, great sea view, Marta is a retired civil servant and speaks some English. **E** *Mercedes González*, 21 360 Apto 2A entre G y H, T325846. Two rooms, a/c, fan, good bathroom, hot water, airy rooms, balcony, smart, airport transfers. **E** *Suzanna*, 26 1060 entre 45 y 47, T811670. Two blocks from old zoo. Speaks good English. **E** *Villa Babi*, 27 965 entre 6 y 8, T306373. Beautiful old home, room with own entrance, includes breakfast, a/c, near Cementerio Colón. *Casa Jom*, 8 560 entre 23 y 25, p 2, T302341. Four bedrooms. *Casavera*, 18 (308 altos) entre 19 y 21, T312784. Friendly, relaxed, Italian, Russian and English spoken, wife is excellent guide, husband great cook, meals on request, a/c, clean, twin beds, terrace, TV. **F** *Casa Blanca*, C 13 917, entre 6 y 8, T35697. Run by Jorge Luis Duany and his mother, book through internet, www.caspar.net/casa/, English spoken, room with 2 double beds, private bathroom, a/c, parking, great breakfast. **Vedado**

Playa **D-E** *Nelson A Pérez Gutiérrez*, 68 1504 entre 15 y 17, T236685. Nice setting in pleasant area, old style building, beautiful furniture, a/c, away from the city centre. **E** *Carmen Batista y Reinaldo Acosta*, Av 35 5804 entre 58 y 58B, T238887. Self-catering or homestay, airport pickup available, long stays possible. **E** *María Elena Rodríguez*, 74 2118, entre 21 y 23, T237506. Two rooms, a/c, hot water, excellent food, helpful, friendly, pleasant verandah.

Eating

There are many **street stalls** and places where you can pick up snacks, pizza etc. Note that their prices are listed in pesos even though there is a $ sign posted. These can work out very cheap and are good for filling a hole at lunchtime, but don't expect a culinary masterpiece.

Paladares

Paladares are privately owned restaurants in Cuban houses

Old Havana *Doña Eutimia*, Callejón del Chorro, just off Plaza Catedral, by entrance to Taller Experimental de Gráfica, rather obscured by a vine. Tiny, no window, no menu, open daily 1200-2400. *Alhambra*, Virtudes esquina Consulado. Open 0800-2400, good meals for US$2-3. *Sevilla's*, Obispo 465, altos, entre Villegas y Aguacate. Open from 1130, good seafood but expensive. *La Julia*, O'Reilly 506A, T627438. Meals US$10, large portions, creole food, can help with finding accommodation or bicycles. *Doña Blanquita*, Prado 153 entre Colón y Refugio. Run by English-speaking lawyer, simple food, pork, chicken or eggs, US$7-9, upstairs, inside with fan or on balcony if dry, neon sign. *La Moneda* at San Ignacio 77. Limited choice, good for fish with salad, beans and rice with fried banana, around US$8. *Don Lorenzo*, Acosta 260A, entre Habana y Compostela. Good, not far from *Santa Clara*.

Central Havana *La Guarida*, Concordia 418 entre Gervasio y Escobar, T624940. Film location for *Fresa y Chocolate*, good food, fish a speciality, slow service. *Bellomar*, Virtudes 169A esq Amistad. Good, US$6 for fish, salad, rice, friendly and obliging.

Chinese market At Zanja and Rayo, 1 block west of Galiano, there are several *paladares* in a small street. Tables inside or outside, menus on view, you will be pestered for your custom. Do not expect authentic Chinese cuisine. Chop suey or chow mein is about the most Oriental you can get. Meals around US$5. *El Flamboyán*; opposite is *Tien Tan*. Open 1200-2100, always full. *Tong Po Laug*, No 10. Cheap, pesos accepted. *El Pacífico*. Impressive, looks like a Chinese temple, food can be very good if it is open, if there is water, if there is cooking gas and if there is any food, problems which affect all the restaurants around here, all prices in pesos, therefore very cheap, around US$3-4 for 2, eg lobster chop suey for 13 pesos, lemonade 60 centavos etc.

Vedado *Marpoly*, K 154, T322471. Meat, poultry and very fresh seafood, large portions, lovely ambiance, house filled with antiques. *La Fuente*, 10 303, T292836. No menu but excellent food, international style, elegant dining room. *El Balcón del Edén*, K 361 entre 19 y 21, T329113. Dining room on 2nd floor balcony, no menu, good seafood, large portions, English spoken. *La Palma*, 27 de Noviembre 303 entre M y N, T783488. Courtyard dining, local cooking, large portions. *Le Chansonnier*, 15 entre H y I, T323788. Cheap and cheerful, good. *Doña Nieves*, 19, entre 2 y 4, T306282. Open Tue-Sun 1200-2400. *El Helecho*, 6 entre Línea y 11. *El Moro*, 25 1003, entre Paseo y 2. *Los Amigos*, M y 19, opposite *Victoria*. Good, US$12 including drinks. *El Escorpión*, nearby, even better.

Near the university *La Reina*, San Lázaro 1214, apto 1, entre M y N. Open 1230-0100, T781260. A plate of food with salad and rice will cost US$5. Opposite is *Casa Karlita*, San Lázaro 1207, T783182. Both have small signs on street.

Nuevo Vedado *Acapulco*, 26 659 entre 35 y 37, T300197. *El Palenque*, Zoológico 110 entre 36 y 38, T811392. Cuban and Chinese. *Romeo y Julieta*, Ulloa 349, esquina Zoológico, T811170. Italian.

Miramar *Le Cocina de Liliam*, 48 1311, entre 13 y 15. Open Sun-Fri 1200-1600, 1900-2300, good Cuban food in lovely garden, fish, crab, popular with locals. *La Fontana*, Av 3 305 esq

48, T228337. Open 1200-2400, good Cuban food, extremely popular, ask for *menu de la casa* for non-inflated prices, arrive early or make a reservation. *Mi Jardín*, 66 517 esq Av 5, T234627. Good Mexican and Italian food for under US$15. *El Palio*, Av 1 entre 24 y 26. Open air, Italian, wonderful fresh fish with choice of creative sauces. *La Esperanza*, 16 105 entre 1 y 3, T224361. Open 1200-1600, 1900-2330, closed Thur. Small sign, gay restaurant, very popular, traditional Cuban food, reservations advisable, run by Hubert and Manolo.

Old Havana *La Bodeguita del Medio*, Empedrado 207, near the Cathedral, open 1030-0100, T338857. Made famous by Hemingway and should be visited if only for a drink (*mojito* – rum, crushed ice, mint, sugar, lemon juice and carbonated water – is a must, US$6), food poor, expensive at US$35-40 for 2 but very popular. *Floridita*, on the corner of Obispo and Monserrate, next to the Parque Central, T338856. Open 1200-0100, another favourite haunt of Hemingway. Recent face-lift and now a very elegant bar and restaurant reflected in the prices (US$6 for a daiquiri), but well worth a visit if only to see the sumptuous decor and 'Bogart atmosphere'. *La Zaragozana*, almost next door, Monserrate entre Obispo y Obrapía. Oldest restaurant in Havana, international cuisine, good seafood and wine, expensive, good service but generally food nothing special. *Castillo de Farnés*, Monserrate 361 y Obrapía, T631260. Tasty Spanish food, reasonable prices, good for garbanzos and shrimp, open 24 hrs, Castro came here at 0445, 9 January 1959, with Che and Raúl. *A Prado y Neptuno*, address of the same name, opposite *Hotel Parque Central*. Trendy, popular with ex-pats, overrated food but excellent tiramisu. *El Patio*, San Ignacio 54 esquina Empedrado, Plaza Catedral, T618504. Expensive, but has selection of national dishes, open 24 hrs, tables outside take up most of the square. *La Mina*, on Obispo esquina Oficios, Plaza de Armas, T620216. Open 1200-2400, also expensive, traditional Cuban food, sandwiches, pasta, lots of liqueur coffees, tables and chairs outside with live Cuban music. *Dominica*, O' Reilly esq Mercaderes, T662917. Italian, very smart, set menus US$25-30, pasta from US$6, pizza US$4.50-12 depending on size, vegetarian options, credit cards. *Café Literario* (Habaguanex), bar/café in the Palacio del Segundo Cabo, O'Reilly 4 esq Tacón. Open 1000-2000. *D'Giovanni*, Italian, Tacón entre Empedrado y O'Reilly, lovely old building with patio and terrace, interesting tree growing through the wall, overpriced pizza and spaghetti. Handicrafts shop in doorway specializes in miniature ornaments. *Gentiluomo*, Bernaza esq Obispo. Pasta, pizza, US$3-6, very tasty food, a/c. *Al Medina*, Oficios, entre Obrapía y Obispo, T630862. Arab food in lovely colonial mansion, dishes priced between US$4-11, try chicken in sesame, lovely fresh fruit juices US$1, good coffee, some seating on large cushions, show at 2130 Fri, Sat, also Mosque and Arab cultural centre off beautiful courtyard, open 1200-2300. *Torre de Marfil*, Mercaderes, entre Obispo y Obrapía. Good, inexpensive Cantonese menu, chop suey US$4, open 1200-2200, T623466, *Hostal Valencia* restaurant *La Paella* features the best paella in Havana, good food, charming, open 1200-2300. *Cabaña* (Habaguanex), Cuba 12 esq Peña Pobre, T335670, facing Av del Puerto. Bar and restaurant open 24 hrs. *Café del Oriente*, Oficios y Amargura. High class food, pleasant. Next door is *Café El Mercado*, more informal, pleasant terrace, open 24 hrs. *Café O' Reilly* (Habaguanex), O'Reilly 203 entre Cuba y San Ignacio. Coffee, snacks, pizza, spaghetti, sandwiches or the usual chicken and pork. *Café París*, Obispo y San Ignacio. Serves good and reasonably priced chicken for US$3.50, beer US$1, snacks and pizza around the clock, live music, lively in evenings. *Hanoi*, Av Brasil 507 y Bernaza, T631681. Open daily 1200-2300, Cuban food, 3 courses for US$5, plenty of food, live music sometimes, nice atmosphere. *Cafetería Torre La Vega*, Obrapía 114, next to the Casa de México. Open 0900-2100, does cheap breakfast, bland chicken and chips US$1.70, better value spaghetti US$0.65, beer US$1.

Vedado *El Conejito*, M esquina 17, T324671. Open 1800-2400, specializes in rabbit in several different sauces, quite expensive but worth it, nightclub attached used by sex tourists. *La Torre*, 17 y M, at top of Edif Fosca, T325650. Open 1200-2400, French chef, best French food in Havana, about US$40 per person but worth it. In the *Habana Libre Hotel*, try *El Barracón*, traditional Cuban with good fish and seafood at lobby level, open 1200-midnight, T305011, and *Sierra Maestra* restaurant and *Bar Turquino* on the 25th floor (spectacular views of Havana which makes the food acceptable, service bad). Cabaret 2230-0430. Along and near La Rampa there are some cheaper pizzerías and self-service restaurants. *La Azucena China* on

Restaurants
Restaurants are state-owned

Restaurants

Cuba

Cienfuegos. Chinese food, charges US$1-2 for a main course. *Casa de la Amistad*, Paseo entre 17 y 19. 1100-2300, for chicken, snacks and pizza. *Centro de Prensa Internacional*, 23 2502 esq O. Basement bar open until 1900, good hamburgers for US$1.

Miramar *El Tocororo* (national bird of Cuba), 18 y Av 3, T242209. Excellent food at US$40-60 a head, open Mon-Sat 1230-2400, old colonial mansion with nice terrace, great house band, no menu, ostrich steak, prices fluctuate widely but one of the best restaurants in town. *La Cecilia*, 5 entre 110 y 112, T241562. Good international food, mostly in open air setting, good salsa from 2200, dancing outside until 0300, US$20 cover charge.

Casablanca *La Divina Pastora*, Fortaleza de la Cabaña, open 1230-2300, T338341. Expensive, fish restaurant, food praised. *La Bodega* is a nice tapas bar in the fort, US$5 for a mixed plate, go there before the cannon firing. *Los XII Apostoles*, nearby on Vía Monumental. Fish and good criollo food, good views of the Malecón.

Parque Lenín *Las Ruinas*, 100 esquina Cortina Presa in Parque Lenín, open 1200-2400, T443336. One of the best restaurants in Havana, the ruined plantation house has been incorporated into a modern structure, mosquitoes at dusk, tours of Parque Lenín often include a meal here, otherwise take a taxi, US$15, try to persuade the driver to come back and fetch you, as otherwise it is difficult to get back.

Playa *La Ferminia*, Av 5, entre 182 y 184, T336555. International, elegant, lovely gardens, expensive. *El Rancho Palco* (Cubanacán), Av 19 y 140, Playa, T235838. Set in lovely jungle garden near the Palacio de las Convenciones, very popular with ex-pats for its Argentine steaks, good barbecued chicken, meats, typical *criolla* cuisine, expensive, good live music. *Palenque*, beside Expocuba pavillions 17 y 190, Siboney, T218167. Cheap, good food, speciality suckling pig US$6, open air, popular with locals and ex-pats.

Vegetarians There is little choice – fill up at breakfast and top up with street snacks. Your best bet is the restaurant in the Jardín Botánico, *El Bambú*, see above, where lunch is served at around 1400. The cafetería at the *Hotel Nacional* serves a big bowl of spaghetti for US$4.50 and the *Golden Tulip Parque Central* has a vegetarian option, eg vegetable lasagne. Italian restaurants such as *Dominica*, in Old Havana, see above, offer meatless pizza and pasta. Some *paladares* will serve meatless meals with advance notice, but always ask for the *congris* to be cooked in vegetable oil.

A visit to the *Coppelia* open-air **ice cream parlour**, 23 y L, Vedado, is recommended, open 1000-midnight, payment in pesos, you might have to queue for an hour or so, not unpleasant in the shade, or pay in dollars to avoid the queue, US$2 for small portion. The parlour found movie fame in *Strawberry and Chocolate*. The building is a good example of the architectural creativity of the post-Revolutionary years, by Mario Girona, 1966. Alternatively, sample the Coppelia ice-cream in the tourist hotels and restaurants and some dollar food stores.

Bars

Visitors find that ordinary bars *not* on the tourist circuit will charge them in dollars, if they let foreigners in at all. If it is a local bar and the Cubans are all paying in pesos, you will have to pay in US dollars. Even so, the prices in most places are not high by Caribbean standards.

The bar not to miss in Old Havana for Hemingway fans is *La Bodeguita* (see above, also for *La Floridita*), a favourite for tour parties. *Lluvia de Oro*, Obispo esq Habana. Good place to drink rum and listen to loud rock music or salsa, also food, open 24 hrs. Try a *mojito* in any bar. Tour groups are often taken to *O'Reilly*, on the street of the same name, for a *mojito*, pleasant upstairs, with balcony and musicians. *Bar Monserrate*, Av Bélgica y Obrapía. Beer US$1, *mojito* US$2, plenty of flavour but not very generous shot of rum, hot dogs US$2.50, filling meal featuring unidentifiable meat in breadcrumbs US$4, interesting to sit and watch comings and goings, high level of prostitutes/girls, though bar staff seem to have unwritten agreement whereby girls are allowed in with a foreigner, or if they buy a drink, but if girl to punters ratio gets too high, some of the girls have to leave, hustling is not excessive though, good atmosphere (a *Hard Rock Café* equivalent). The trendy new place to go is the *Habana Café* in the *Meliá Cohiba*, a 1950s theme place with old cars, small Cubana plane hanging from the ceiling, memorabilia on the walls, Benny Moré music and large screen showing brilliant film of old Cuban musicians and artistes, expensive and meals not recommended, turkey burger or veggie burger US$6, *limonada* US$2, beer US$1.75, entrance to the left of the main hotel entrance, open 1200-0100, live music at weekends 2230-0100, cover charge US$5-10 depending on the band. *Casa de la Amistad*, Paseo 406 (see above), bar with a beautiful garden extension, tasty cheap light meals optional, very peaceful surroundings. For Graham Greene *aficionados*, go to the *Hotel Sevilla*, have a drink and tapas in the courtyard by the fountain and fantasize about Wormold from *Our Man in Havana* being recruited into MI6 in the gents (which have unfortunately been modernized).

Entertainment

Casa De La Trova, San Lázaro, entre Belascoán y Gervasio, where locals go to hear traditonal Cuban music, US$5, especially on Fri from 1800, thoroughly recommended. Both here and at the *Casa de la Amistad* (see 'Museums in Vedado'), you are very unlikely to be hustled. *Casa de la Cultura de Plaza*, Calzada y 8, Vedado. Concerts and shows, different artistes, different times. For bolero admirers, try *Dos Gardenias*, with popular Chinese restaurant and bar, Av 7, esquina 26, Miramar, Playa, T242353. Traditonal boleros 2230-0300. *UNEAC*, 17 entre G y H, rumba Sat and other Cuban band performances. Events listed at entrance. At the *Teatro Nacional* there is a piano bar upstairs where you can hear quality music, nueva trova, bolero etc, beer US$2.50, downstairs in the theatre there are live concerts such as a Nueva Trova show for 10 pesos. You can find rumba on Wed at the *Teatro Mella*, Línea entre A y B. Also *Palmares*, Malecón y E, for rumba performances and disco dancing, 2100 until late. *Holá Ola*, Malecón, occasionally has big national groups, entry in pesos. The *Casa de la Música* in Miramar is a great place with a disco and stage in a beautiful old house, but expensive at US$20 and people have complained about the rampant sex trade, band comes on at 0200, so this is a real late night place. *Jardines 1830*, Malecón y 20, beside the road tunnel to Miramar, T334521, 553090. Top salsa bands play here, music daily 2200-0400, US$20, also a restaurant, you will be mobbed at the door by desperate Cubans. Comedy shows every night from 2300 at *Club Almendares*, Márgenes del Río Almendares, 49 C y 28. Cubans love slapstick and Benny Hill-style humour, minorities such as gays get hammered. *Café Gato Tuerto*, O entre 17 y 19, Vedado, T552696, 662224. Son, trova and boleros performed 2400-0500. Bohemian people and post-modern décor, funky, no cover charge, good restaurant on 1st floor, eat on balcony overlooking Malecón and *Hotel Nacional*.

Jazz *Coparrun*, *Hotel Riviera* (big names play there), jazz in the bar recommended. Fri nights at *Meliá Cohiba* from 2100. *La Zorra y el Cuervo*, 23 y O, Vedado. Entry US$5, opens 2130 for 1st set, 2nd set 2330, T662402. UNEAC, H y 17, Thur nights, but check listings on gate. *Jazz Café*, Galería Primera y Paseo, Vedado, top floor of blue glass building. Live jazz bands from 2300 every night, including *Irakere*, US$5 cover charge, bar and restaurant, very popular, can be hard to get a table.

Nightclubs *Tropicana* (closed Mon, Línea del Ferrocarril y 72 No 4504, Marianao, 2200-0200) is internationally famous and open-air (entry refunded if it rains). It costs US$70 for the show and a 3-course meal, or US$60 for the show and a quarter bottle of rum and coke. Best to take a tour, which will include transport, as a taxi from Old Havana costs US$12. Reservations are recommended, T270110 between 1000 and 1600. If you fancy a cheap drink or snack go to *Rodneys*, a pseudo 1950s bar and restaurant designed by Cuban painter, Nelson Domínguez, just beyond the entrance to the show. All the main hotels have their own cabarets, eg *Parisien* at *Hotel Nacional*, excellent long show for US$30, make a reservation. *Capri* is recommended, at US$15 and longer show than *Tropicana* but the drinks are expensive at US$40 for a bottle of best rum. *Aché* in the *Meliá Cohiba*. The *Habana Libre* cabaret

Cuba

Music & dance
Radio Taino FM 93.3, English & Spanish language tourist station, gives regular details of wide range of Cuban bands playing & venues, particularly in the programme at 1700-1900. The newspaper, Opciones, also has a listing of what's on

and disco is on the 25th floor, amazing views, the roof opens and you can dance under the stars, US$10, if you are in a group 1 person needs a passport, drinks expensive. Also *Havana Club*, the *Comodoro* disco (US$10), crowded, Western-style, US$5 for *Hotel Comodoro* guests. *Café Cantante*, Teatro Nacional, Paseo y 39, Plaza de la Revolución. Open nightly from 2200, 3 bands, US$10, sometimes it is US$15, although this place is well regarded, it is popular with *jinetero/as* and lone travellers have commented on feeling uncomfortable. *La Finca* at Playas del Este. The *Cabaret Nacional*, San Rafael y Prado, is a cheap version of the *Tropicana*, US$5 entry but expensive drinks. Shows at 2330 and 0030. Lots of prostitutes.

Cinemas The best are *Yara* (opposite *Habana Libre* hotel, T329430). *Acapulco*, 26 entre 35 y 37, Nuevo Vedado, T39573, from 1630. *Chaplin*, 23 entre 10 y 12, T311101. Arty films at 1700 and 2000, shop good for film memorabilia. *Payret*, Prado 503, esquina San José, T633163. Films shown continuously from 1230, and *La Rampa*, Rampa esquina O, T786146, from 1630. Many others, 2 pesos.

Theatres *Teatro Mella*, Línea entre A y B, Vedado, T38696. Specializes in modern dance; more traditional programmes at *Gran Teatro de la Habana* on Parque Central next to *Hotel Inglaterra*, T6130769. Claims to be the oldest working theatre in the world, opened in 1837, wonderful baroque building which seats 2,000. The Conjunto Folklórico Nacional and Danza Contemporánea dance companies sometimes perform here. Highly recommended. US$0.60. In Miramar, *Teatro Karl Marx*, Av 1 entre 8 y 10, T300720, 305521. *Amadeo Roldán*, Calzada y D, Vedado. Newly renovated concert hall where you can hear the Orquesta Sinfonía Nacional. Pay in pesos. *Opus* bar, open 1500-0300, serves light meals. Havana has some very lively theatre companies. Fringe theatres include *Teatro El Sótano*, K entre 25 y 27, Vedado; *Sala Herbert de Blanck*, Calzada entre A y B, Vedado; *Teatro Trianón*, Línea entre Paseo y A, Vedado; *Teatro Fausto*, Prado y Colón, Habana Vieja. *Amistur* travel agency can help with theatre and nightclub bookings.

Shopping

Shopaholics should be aware that Cuba is not going to satisfy your urges. There is little to spend your money on without a great deal of effort.

Works of art Original lithographs and other works of art can be purchased or commissioned directly from
& handicrafts the artists at the *Galería del Grabado*, at the back of the *Taller Experimental de Gráfica de la Habana*, Callejón del Chorro 62, Plaza de la Catedral (open all day, closed Sun, T620979, F338121). You can watch the prints and engravings being made and specialist courses are available, for 1 month, US$250, or 3 months, US$500. The *Taller Serigrafía* is another big workshop, on Cuba 513, making screen prints; again, you can watch them being made and buy things. *La Victoria*, Obispo 366 entre Compostela y Habana, T627914. Open 1000-1900, is an art gallery with a large choice of paintings at good prices, and books, owned by artist Natividad Scull Marchena. Reproductions of works of art are sold at *La Exposición*, San Rafael 12, Manzana de Gómez, in front of Parque Central. Handicraft and tourist souvenir markets have sprung up, especially the *feria de artesanías* (see below), on D and Av 1, Vedado, and on the Rampa, open Tue-Sun 0900-1600; Che Guevara and religious *Santería* items lead the sales charts. The *feria de artesanías* along Av del Puerto by Castillo de la Real Fuerza is a platform for many talented young artists to show off their skills, you may pick up a bargain, or you may be asked to pay Miami-type prices. You need documentation to take works of art out of the country or you may have them confiscated at the airport; galleries will provide the necessary paperwork and even vendors in the market can give you the necessary stamp. Also sold here are carvings, crochet, ceramics, boxes, jewellery, T-shirts, baseball bats and black coral (illegal to bring in to many countries, so avoid). There is a special boutique, the *Palacio de la Artesanía*, in the Palacio Pedroso (built 1780) at Cuba 64 (opposite Parque Anfiteatro), where the largest selection of Cuban handicrafts is available; the artisans have their workshops in the back of the same building (open Mon-Sat 0900-1900).

In the Palacio del Segundo Cabo, O'Reilly 4 y Tacón, is the Instituto Cubano del Libro and 3 **Bookshops** bookshops: *Librería Grijalba Mondadori*, excellent selection of novels, dictionaries, art books, children's books from around the world, all in Spanish; *Librería Bella Habana*, T628091-3, Cuban and international publications, and *Librería UNESCO Cultura*, which stocks UNESCO publications, books on Cuba, a few thrillers in English and postcards. There are second-hand bookstalls outside on the Plaza de Armas where you can pick up a treasure if you know what to look for. *Casa Editorial Abril*, at end of El Prado, opposite Capitol. English, French, German books, but selection poor, lots of scientific and cultural books on Cuba, in Spanish. Other good bookshops near Parque Central: *Ediciones Cubanas* on Obispo 527 esquina Bernaza, T38942, 631989. Books on Cuba, also some stationery. *Fernando Ortíz*, 27 160 esq L, T329653. Quite a wide selection, mostly in Spanish, and some beautiful postcards. *El Siglo de las Luces*, Neptuno esq Aguila, T635321, near Capitolio. Good place to buy *son*, *trova* and jazz (rock) records. *Instituto Hidrográfico*, Mercaderes entre Oficios y Obispo, T613625, F332869. Maps and charts, both national and regional, also prepaid phone cards.

Artex shop on L esq 23 has excellent music section and tasteful T-shirts and postcards, **Music & other** T320632, open Mon-Sat 0900-2100, Sun 1000-1600. The *Caracol* chain, in tourist hotels (eg **souvenirs** Habana Libre) and elsewhere, sell tourists' requisites and other luxury items such as chocolates, biscuits, wine, clothes, require payment in US$ (or credit cards: Mastercard, Visa).

Calle Monte is being redeveloped, with a variety of shops operating in dollars or Cuban **Food** pesos, starting from the Capitolio end with a food supermarket. At the other end is Cuatro Caminos market (see 'Markets', below). In Miramar there is a dollar shopping complex on Av 5 y 42 and a large diplomatic store, *Diplomercado* (Av 5 esquina 24 y 26), with a bakery next door. Bread is also available at the new French bakery on 42 y 19 and in the Focsa shopping complex on 17 entre M y N. For food shopping, there is the *Focsa Supermarket*, or the *Amistad*, on San Lázaro, just below Infanta. The *Isla de Cuba* supermarket on Máximo Gómez entre Factoría y Suárez has the best selection of food in Old Havana, with prices stamped on the goods to prevent overcharging. There are tourist mini-stores in most hotels, but they do not sell fresh food. The International Press Centre (open to the public) on La Rampa sells items like chocolate for dollars in a shop to the right of the entrance.

Markets Farmers are allowed to sell their produce (root and green vegetables, fruit, grains and meat) in free-priced city *agromercados*. You should pay for food in pesos. There are markets in Vedado at 19 y B; in Nuevo Vedado, Tulipán opposite Hidalgo; in the Cerro district at the Monte and Belascoaín crossroads; and in Central Havana, the Chinese market at the junction of Zanja and Av Italia where you can eat at street food stalls (avoid Mon, not a good day).

Bureaux in all the major hotels. Tours can be arranged all over Cuba by bus or air, with partici- **Tour operators** pants picked up from any hotel in Havana at no extra charge. Examples include a tour of the *See page 151* city's colonial sites (US$15, 4 hrs); a trip to the *Tropicana* cabaret (US$60, 4 hrs, US$70 with supper); Cayo Largo for the day by air with boat trip, snorkelling, optional diving, lunch (US$119, 12 hrs); Cayo Largo overnight (US$119); Guamá and the Península de Zapata with a stop en route at the *Finca Fiesta Campesina*, tour of crocodile farm, lunch (US$44, 9 hrs); Viñales and Pinar del Río, visiting *mogotes*, caves and tobacco factory, lunch (US$44, 9 hrs); a day on the beach at Varadero (US$35 or US$45 with lunch, 10 hrs); Trinidad and Cienfuegos overnight, visiting the colonial city and the Valle de los Ingenios (US$115); ecological tour of Las Terrazas with walking and river bathing, lunch (US$44, 10 hrs). In practice, prices vary between agencies and you can negotiate a reduction without meals. *Amistur*, Paseo 646, entre 19 y 17, T333544, F333515, is more geared towards independent travellers and can book you into good hotels in all the major cities at reduced rates. They are helpful with transport and tours and can also book excursions, restaurants, theatre and nightclubs, or help you find a guide. They arrange sociocultural tours with specific interest groups if contacted in advance.

Guides Many Cubans in Havana tout their services in their desperate quest for dollars, but in Old Havana this is now less of a problem since Castro's crackdown in 1999 which put police on every street corner. Elsewhere, they are a considerable nuisance and nearly all tourists complain of being hassled. If you feel you trust someone as a guide, make sure you state exactly what you want, eg private car, *paladar*, accommodation, and fix a price in advance to avoid shocks when it is too late. *Casas particulares* can often be a good source of information on reputable guides. You may find, however, that the police will assume your guide is a prostitute and prohibit him or her from accompanying you into a hotel.

Transport

Local
See also page 155

Bicycle hire Check the bicycle carefully (take your own lock, pump, even a bicycle spanner and puncture repair kit; petrol stations have often been converted into bicycle stations, providing air and tyre repairs). Cycling is a good way to see Havana, especially the suburbs; some roads in the Embassy area are closed to cyclists. The tunnel underneath the harbour mouth has a bus designed specifically to carry bicycles and their riders. Take care at night as there are few street lights and bikes are not fitted with lamps.

Buses The easiest way of getting around Havana is with *Vaivén*, a Rumbos service which covers many places of interest. For US$4 per day you can get on and off a 30-seater bus along the route; buses pass every 55 mins and there are 23 stops, several of which are hotels. There is a regular service on the *camellos*, long articulated buses on a truck bed, 20 centavos. They cover the main suburbs, M1 to Playa, M2 to the airport, M6 to Alamar, and mostly leave from Parque de la Fraternidad. Ask for the right queue. With all urban buses, there is a queuing ritual. Discover who is last (*última*) for the bus you want; when identified, ask him/her who they are behind (*detrás de*), as people mark their places and then wander off until the bus comes. Other than the *camellos*, buses cost 40 centavos.

Car hire Hiring a car is not recommended for getting around Havana, roads are badly signed and there have been many accidents with tourists driving rental cars.

Taxis A fleet of white '*Turistaxis*' with meters has been introduced for tourists' use; payment in US$: sample fare, Ciudad Vieja to Vedado US$4. A cheaper way of getting around is via *Panataxi*, a company set up for the 1992 Pan American Games. Basically a call-out service, T555555, Panataxis also wait just outside the Plaza de la Catedral, the *Meliá Cohiba*, on 17 entre L y M, and at the airport, or ask your hotel to call one. They are identified by their navy and yellow colour and have a new fleet of Citröen cars, so they are the most comfortable service as well as being the most reliable and still the cheapest dollar service, at under US$15 from the airport to Vedado. *Habanataxi* is a call-out taxi service, T419600. Others include *Gaviota*, T331730, *Taxi OK*, T249518-9, 241226, *MiCar*, T242444, and *Fénix*, T639720/639580. The cheapest taxis are the very smallest. Ask for the '*oferta especial*' and you will be charged only US$0.45 per km, T335539-42. For longer trips some companies charge by the hour and some by the km, eg for an excursion including Cojímar, Santa María del Mar and Regla, Panataxi quoted US$25 while Habanataxi quoted US$35. Licensed **Cuban peso taxis** are mostly reserved for hospital runs, funerals etc, but after completing their quotas they can now freelance, see page 155. Beware of private moonlighters (yellow licence plates, often identifiable by their harassment); they could charge you over the odds, generally are not paying any taxes and you have no come-back in the case of mishaps. In Habana Vieja and Vedado, bicycle or tricycle taxis are cheap and readily available, a pleasant way to travel. A short journey will cost US$1, Old Havana to Vedado US$3, or pay around US$5 per hour, bargaining is acceptable.

Long distance

Buses Terminal de Omnibus Interprovinciales, Av Rancho Boyeros (Independencia) by the Plaza de la Revolución. There are two ticket offices, the one painted blue is for foreigners and you pay in dollars. There is also a dollar tourist service, Víazul, which leaves from Av 26 entre Av Zoológico y Ulloa, Nuevo Vedado, T811413, 811108, 815652, F666092.

Ferries There are ferries from Habana Vieja to Casablanca and Regla, which depart from San Pedro opposite Calle Santa Clara. If you are facing the water, the Casablanca ferry docks on the left side of the pier and goes out in a left curve towards that headland, and the Regla ferry docks on the right side and goes out in a right curve.

Trains Estación Central in Av Egido (de Bélgica), Havana, to the larger cities. The Estación Central has what is claimed to be the oldest engine in Latin America, *La Junta*, built in Baltimore in 1842. Get your tickets in advance as destinations vary, the departure time is very approximate. Tickets are easily purchased from LADIS office on Esperanza y Bélgica, ground floor entrance at the side, open 0800-1700 daily, T614259, pay in US$, spacious, food and drink on board. The El Trece train leaves Estación Central daily at 1640, arrives Santiago de Cuba 0700, US$30.50, stopping at lots of places and cheaper than the Locura Azul train, which departs 1930 Mon, Wed, Thur, Sat and Sun, 11½ hrs theoretically. A long distance bus or dollar taxi may well do the same journey in a fraction of the time, eg Havana-Pinar del Río, 2 hrs or less by taxi, 7-8 hrs by train. It is not unusual for the trains to break down, in fact Cubans refer to this as 'normal service'. It will be mended and carry on, but be prepared to spend a serious amount of time travelling.

Airlines Most are in Havana, at the seaward end of Calle 23 (La Rampa), Vedado. *Cubana*, www.cubana.cu, for international sales, 23 64, esq Infanta, T3344469/334950, for national sales, Infanta esq Humboldt, T706714 and phone numbers above; *Cubana Express* is at Av 5 entre 82 y 84, Miramar, just before the turning to the *Hotel Comodoro*, T242331/242833, open weekdays only. *Aerocaribbean*, 23 esq P, T334543, F335016, or at the airport, T453013, 451135, F335017. *Aeroflot*, 23 64, esq Infanta, T333200/333759, F333288, at the airport, T335432. *Air Jamaica*, *Hotel Tryp Habana Libre*, T334011. *ALM*, 23 64 entre Infanta y P, T333730, F333729. *AOM French Airlines*, 23 64, Interior, T334098, 333997, F333783, at the airport, F335464. *British Airways* has a representative office in bungalow 719, *Hotel Comodoro*, but flights should be confirmed with *Cubana*. *Copa*, 23 64, Interior, esq Infanta, T331758, 333657, F333951. *Iberia*, 23 74 esq P, T3350412, 335064, F335061, at the airport T335063. *LTU*, 23 64 esq Infanta, T333549/333525/333590, F332789, at the airport F335359. *Martinair Holland*, 23 esq P, T334364, 333730, F333729. *Mexicana de Aviación*, 23 esq P, T3335312, F333077, at the airport F335051.

Banks *Banco Nacional* and its branches. For dollar services, credit card withdrawals, TCs and exchange, *Banco Financiero Internacional*, Línea esq O, T333003/333148, F333006, open Mon-Fri 0800-1500, last day of the month until 1200, branch in *Habana Libre* complex, T333429, F333795, same times, and another branch in Miramar, 18 111 entre 1 y 3, T332058, F332458, charges 3% commission for foreign exchange deals. Exchange bureau in *Hotel Nacional*, open 0800-1200, 1230-1930, credit card cash advances. Buró de Turismo in *Tryp Habana Libre* also gives credit card cash advances. *Banco Metropolitano*, Línea 63 y O, T5531168, open Mon-Fri 0830-1500, cheapest (2%) for changing TCs, most hotels and airport cambios charge 4% for changing TCs.

Communications Post: Oficios 102, opposite the Lonja, and in the *Hotel Nacional*, *Hotel Plaza* (5th floor, walk through dining area and turn right on to the terrace, open 0700-1900) and in the *Hotel Habana Libre* building. Also on Calle Ejido, next to central railway station and under the Gran Teatro de La Habana. Telephones: *The Empresa Telecomunicaciones de Cuba* (Etecsa) is on Av 33 1427 entre 18 y 14, Miramar, T332476, F332504. *Cubacel Telefonía Celular* is at 28 510 entre 5 y 7, Miramar, T332222, F331737. The large hotels of 4 or 5 stars such as the *Habana Libre*, *Plaza Central* and *Nacional* have international telephone, email and fax facilities. At the *Habana Libre* email is available 0700-1500. The *Parque Central* has an efficient business centre. At the *Hotel Plaza*, 5th floor, you can send faxes, US$5 to USA, US$7.50 to UK per min. **Email** is also available at the Bilblioteca de Ciencias in the Capitolio. There are 8 very slow terminals, US$5 per hour, open Mon-Fri 0900-1700, subject to frequent breakdowns.

Embassies & consulates All in Miramar, unless stated otherwise: *Argentina*, 36 511 entre 5 y 7, T242972/2549, F242140. *Austria*, 4 101, esquina 1, T242852, F241235. *Belgium*, Av 5 7406 esquina 76, T242410, F241318. *Brazil*, Lamparilla, Habana Vieja, T6690512. *Canada*, 30 518, esquina 7, T2425167, F241069. *France*, 14 312 entre 3 y 5, T242132, 2422380, F241439. *Germany*, 13 652, F331586. *Greece*, Av 5, 7802, esquina 78, T242854, F241784. *Japan*, Office 501-512, Miramar Trade Centre, Av 3 esq 80, T333453, F248902. *Mexico*, 12 518 entre 5 y 7, T242498, F242294, open 0900-1200, Mon-Fri. *Netherlands*, 8 307 entre 3 y 5, T242511/2, F242059. *Peru*, 30 109 entre 1 y 3, T242477, F242636. *Sweden*, Av 31A, 1411, T242563, F241194. *Switzerland*, Av 5, 2005, T242611, F241148. *UK*, 34, 702 y 704, T241771, F248104, 249214. embrit@ceniai.inf.cu. Commercial Section, open Mon-Fri 0800-1530. *Venezuela*, 36A 704 esquina 42, T242662, F242773. *The US Interests Section* of the Swiss Embassy,

Directory

Cuba

Calzada entre L y M, Vedado, T333551, 334401. *Spain*, Cárcel 51 esquina Zulueta, Habana Vieja, T3380256, F338006.

Medical facilities *The Cira García Clinic*, 20 4101 esquina 41, Miramar, T242811/14, F241633, payment in dollars, also the place to go for emergency dental treatment, the pharmacy (T24051, open 24 hrs) sells prescription and patent drugs and medical supplies that are often unavailable in other pharmacies, as does the *Farmacia Internacional*, Av 41, esq 20, Miramar (T245051, open Mon-Fri 0900-1700, Sat 0900-1200). *Camilo Cienfuegos Pharmacy*, L and 13, Vedado, T333599, open daily 0800-2000. *Optica Miramar*, 43 1803 entre 18 y 18A, T242590, ophthalmology consultants, contact lenses, photochromic brown and grey lenses, lightweight glasses, plastic and metal frames. *Servimed* (turismo de salud) is at 18 4304 entre 43 y 47, Playa, T332658, F332948, with information on special treatments, spas and health facilities around the country. All hotels have a doctor on permanent duty, US$25 per consultation.

Useful addresses Police: T820116. Fire: T811115, 798561-69. Asistur: in the *Casa del Científico* hotel, Prado esq Trocadero, Old Havana, T625519, 638284, F338087, for medical and dental emergencies, repatriations, financial and legal problems, travel insurance claims, reservations.

Beaches around Havana

The beaches in Havana, at Miramar and Playa de Marianao are rocky, polluted and generally very crowded in summer. The beach clubs belong to trade unions and may not let non-members in. Those to the east, El Mégano, Santa María del Mar and Bacuranao, for example, are much better. To the west of Havana are Arena Blanca and Bahía Honda, which are good for diving and fishing but difficult to get to unless you have a car.

Marina Hemingway Off Avenida 5, 20 minutes by taxi from Havana, is the Marina Hemingway tourist complex, in the fishing village of **Santa Fe**. Fishing and scuba diving trips can be arranged here as well as other watersports and land-based sports. The Offshore Class 1 World Championship and the Great Island speedboat Grand Prix races have become an annual event in Havana, usually held during the last week in April, attracting power boat enthusiasts from all over the world. In May and June the marina hosts the annual Ernest Hemingway International Marlin Fishing Tournament, and in August and September the Blue Marlin Tournament. There are 140 slips with electricity and water and space for docking 400 recreational boats. The resort includes the hotel *El Viejo y El Mar*, restaurants, bungalows and villas for rent, shopping, watersports, facilities for yachts, sports and a tourist bureau.

Sleeping and eating *El Viejo y El Mar* (Cubanacán), 248 y Av 5, Santa Fe, T336336, F336823. Pleasant enough hotel on seafront but out of the way and nothing to do unless you are busy at the marina, package tourists come here before going off on excursions, small pool, restaurant with buffet meals, lobby bar, clean, bath tub, tricky shower. **A** *Residencial Turístico*, T331150-6. Rooms overlook canals, pool, snack bar, good supermarket, noisy motorized watersports. Several restaurants and a grocery store at the Marina. Two popular *paladares*, just over 1 km from the marina overlooking the canals: *El Canal*, Av 5 26402 entre 264 y 266, Santa Fe, T297448. Open 1200-2300, closed Thu, low green house, famous for enormous portions and pork dishes; *El Laurel*, nearby. Specializes in seafood, very good, mosquitoes at dusk, restaurant in the garden, open late.

Watersports *Club Náutico Internacional 'Hemingway'*, Residencial Turístico 'Marina Hemingway', Av 5 y 248 Playa, T/F241689, 246653. *Cubanacán Náutica 'Marina Hemingway'*, same address, T241150-57, F241149, VHF 16 and 72. Open Mon-Fri 0800-1700, boat trips, sport fishing, US$450 half day, motorized sports (waterskiing, banana boat), catamarans, sailing lessons in dinghies, windsurfing, diving and snorkelling. The dive centre, *Centro de Buceo La Aguja*, takes up to 8 divers on the boat.

Playas del Este

This is the all-encompassing name for a string of beaches within easy reach of Havana. East of the city is the pleasant little beach of **Bacuranao**, 15 km from Havana. At the far end of the beach is a villa complex with restaurant and bar. Then come **Tarará** (famous for its hospital where the Chernobyl victims have been treated), **El Mégano** and **Santa María del Mar**, with a long, open beach which continues eastwards to the intimate, pretty beach at **Boca Ciega** and **Guanabo** (four train departures daily in July and August from Estación Cristal, Havana, and buses from Havana), a pleasant, non-touristy beach 27 km from Havana, but packed with Habaneros at weekends. Cars roll in from Havana early on Saturday mornings, line up and deposit their cargo of sun worshippers at the sea's edge. The quietest spot is **Brisas del Mar**, at the east end. As a general rule, facilities for foreigners are at Santa María del Mar and for Cubans at Guanabo. The latter is therefore cheaper and livelier. Tourism bureaux offer day excursions (minimum six people) for about US$15 per person to the Playas del Este, but for two or more people its worth hiring a private car for the day for US$20-25.

LL-B *Villa Tarará*, T335510, F335499. 121 a/c units in villas with 2-5 rooms, TV, fridge, porch and parking, at the marina, restaurant, snack bar, grill, disco, watersports. **LL-L** *Villa Los Pinos* (Gran Caribe), Av de las Terrazas 21 entre 4 y 5, Santa María del Mar, T971361, F971524, informatica@pinos.gca.cma.net 26 houses, 2 rooms, sleep 4, most with pools or near the beach, grill restaurant, popular with Italians, Spanish and French in that order, lots of repeat guests, comfortable, private, good for entertaining friends, very flexible management, multilingual staff. **B-C** *Tropicoco Beach Club*, Av Sur y Las Terrazas, Santa María del Mar, T971371. Price includes beer, rum, 3 meals, wonderful view of beach but food boring after 2 days, nothing to do but drink and bathe, 188 rooms. **B-E** *Aparthotel Las Terrazas*, Av de las Terrazas entre 10 y Rotonda, T971344. 154, 1-3 bedroomed apartments, each with cooking facilities, fridge, radio and TV, in rather unattractive block opposite the beach, 2-tier swimming pool with children's area, restaurant, bar, tourist bureau, disco in separate building, car and moped rental, great location but rather run down. **C** *Sea Club Arenal* (Horizontes), Laguna Itabo entre Santa María del Mar y Boca Ciega, T971272, F971287. All-inclusive, 198 a/c rooms, good accommodation in 4, 2-storey, buildings around large pool with terrace bar and barbecue, beach reached by footbridge over Itabo lagoon, non-motorized watersports and bicycles included, restaurant, disco, shop. **E** *Villa Playa Hermosa* (Islazul), 5 Av y 470, T962774, Guanabo. 33 rooms or chalets, good value, often used by party faithful and honeymooners. **E** *Gran Vía* (Islazul), 5 Av y 462, T962271, between Boca Ciega and Guanabo. Friendly service, better food than at the Horizontes hotels, US$3 for TV, US$5 key charge, live music. **E-F** *Miramar*, 478 esq 7B, T962507. A/c, no hot water, TV, dirty pool, water switched off after 2200, cheap and basic but perfectly adequate. **Casas particulares**: *Sra Eyda Iglesias Mora*, 494 A 5B10 entre 5B y 5C, T2903. **E-F** *Hugo Puig Roque*, 5 Av 47203 entre 472 y 474, T963426. Choice of rooms, bathrooms fair, good location, friendly. Prices negotiable, depending on season and length of stay. **E** *Aimé*, 472, Guanabo. Apartment with 2 double rooms, bathroom, living room, kitchen, porch. It may be possible to find privately rented apartments in Guanabo for US$15 a night with kitchen, ask around.

Sleeping

Restaurante Chino, Via Blanco Km 19, one of the best Chinese restaurants in Cuba. There are many *paladares* in Guanabo and elsewhere along the coast, reasonable prices. If you are self-catering, there is a farmers' market in Guanabo selling fresh fruit and vegetables 6 days a week and a supermarket for bread and tinned goods. Hotels in Guanabo have good, cheap food, with live music. *Cafetería Pinomar*, Santa María del Mar, fried chicken, US$2.50 for a half, open 24 hrs, attractive. *Pizzería Al Mare*, 482, Guanabo, for pizza. *Café River Ristorante*, behind *Villa Playa Hermosa* entre 472 y 474. All dishes under US$3, beer US$0.85, open 1200-0200, cozy, funky.

Eating

Cuba

Watersports The hotels provide some non-motorized watersports. *Marina Tarará*, run by Marinas Puertosol, Vía Blanca Km 19, T971462, F971333, VHF16, 19, 08, 72, has moorings for 50 boats, VHF communications and provisioning, yacht charters, deep sea fishing (US$250-450 per day depending on type of boat) and scuba diving, all of which can be arranged through the hotel tour desks. Note the advertising: the sea is funnier at Tarará.

Transport The 400 bus from near the Estación Central de Trenes can get you there, but getting back to Havana is problematic the longer you stay. The standard private taxi price is US$10, but getting a return taxi is more difficult. Cycling is a good way to get there. Use the *cyclobus* from the end of Zulueta to go through the tunnel under Havana Bay, or the 1 peso ferry from the Aduanas building, and cycle through Regla and Guanabacoa.

Directory **Medical facilities** *Clínica Internacional Habana del Este*, Av de las Terrazas, between *Aparthotel Las Terrazas* and *Hotel Tropicoco* in Santa María del Mar, T06872689.

West from Havana

A dual carriage highway has been completed almost to **Pinar del Río**, the major city west of Havana. It takes two hours to get to Pinar del Río on the autopista, a rather surreal experience, with modern motorway junctions but virtually no traffic using them except horse-drawn buses to nearby villages. The autopista passes through flat or gently rolling countryside, with large stretches of sugar cane, tobacco fields and some rice fields, scattered royal palms and distant views of the Cordillera de Guaniguanico. An alternative route is to leave the autopista at **Candelaria** or **Santa Cruz de los Pinos** for the Carretera Central, quite a good road which adds only 20 minutes to the journey. It passes through more intensively farmed countryside, with citrus and other fruit trees. Villages straggle along the road, with colonnaded single storey traditional houses and newer post-Revolution concrete block structures.

Las Terrazas On the autopista, 51 km west of Havana, the Sierra del Rosario appears on the right *Phone code: 8* and a roadside billboard announces the turning to **Las Terrazas/Moka**, 4 km north of the autopista. However, after that there is little signposting; you will have to ask the way. There is a barrier at the entrance to the **Biosphere Reserve** which covers 260 sq km of the eastern Sierra del Rosario. ■ *Admission to the Reserve, US$3 (diplomats US$1, other residents US$2), unless you have a reservation at the hotel.* Las Terrazas was built in 1971 as a forestry and soil conservation station, with nearby slopes terraced to prevent erosion. It is a pleasant settlement of white-painted houses and a long apartment block overlooking the lake of San Juan, which now houses an ecological research centre. In Las Terrazas there is a *paladar* (US$7), craft workshops, a gym, a cinema and a museum which sometimes holds *canturías* or folk music sessions. The hills behind the hotel rise to the **Loma del Salón** (564m). There are several easy hiking trails of 3-8 km or more demanding whole-day hikes. The cost of a day hiking with a professional ecologist as guide is US$33-41 for one person, falling to US$14-18 with six people. Other activities include riding (US$6 per hour), mountain bikes (US$1 per hour), rowing on the lake (US$2 per hour) and fishing.

Sleeping Above the village is the 26-room **B** *Hotel Moka*, run in co-operation with the Cuban Academy of Sciences as an ecotourism centre, breakfast US$5, other meals US$15, transfer from Havana US$32, a/c, satellite TV, T852921, 802694, Havana marketing office, Sr Falcón, T333814/3900, F335516. The hotel complex is beautifully designed and laid out, in Spanish colonial style with tiled roofs, staff are friendly and knowledgeable, gardens behind the hillside site have a tennis court and a pleasant swimming pool where you can have food and drinks. This is an unusual opportunity to stay in a nature reserve with tropical evergreen forests, 850 plant species, 82 bird species, an endemic water lizard, the world's 2nd smallest frog and world-class experts on tap. Even the hotel receptionist is an ecology PhD.

If travelling by car, you can make a detour to Soroa, a spa and resort in the Sierra del Rosario, 81 km southwest of the capital, either by continuing 18 km west then southeast from Moka through the Sierra del Rosario, or directly from the autopista, driving northwest from Candelaria. As you drive into the area from the south, a sign on the right indicates the **Mirador de Venus** and **Baños Romanos**. Past the baths is the *Bar Edén* (open till 1800), where you can park before walking up to the Mirador (25 minutes, free on foot, US$3 on a horse). Fine views of the southern plains, the forest-covered Sierra and Soroa itself. Lots of birds, butterflies, dragonflies and lizards around the path; many flowers in season.

Soroa
Phone code: 8

Further north is an **Orchidarium** with over 700 species of which 250 are native to Cuba, as well as ferns and begonias (check if the orchids are in bloom before visiting). ■ *Guided tours between 0830-1140, 1340-1555 daily, US$3 and the Castillo de las Nubes restaurant (1200-1900, US$5-6).*

Sleeping At the resort, **C-D** *Horizontes Villa Soroa*, T852122. 49 cabins and 10 self-catering houses, a/c, phone, radio, some have VCR and private pool, restaurant *El Centro* (quite good), lunch US$8, dinner US$10, disco, bar, Olympic-sized swimming pool, bike rental, riding nearby and handicrafts and dollar shop. A peaceful place. The hotel runs 1 day, gently paced hikes around the main sights of the area with picnic for US$10, to caves for US$12. **E** *Pepe*, at Km 5.5 north of autopista junction on the west of the main road into Soroa, is a *casa particular*. Not bad, Pepe drinks too much rum but his wife is nice. There is no officially licensed *paladar*.

Pinar del Río

The capital of Pinar del Río province is lively and attractive, and it gives a good taste of provincial Cuba. The centre consists of single-storey neo-classical houses with columns, some with other interesting architectural detail.

Phone code: 82

There is a **cigar factory**, one of the town's main tourist attractions, which reputedly makes the best cigars in Cuba. ■ *Mon-Sat 0800-1700, US$5 for a short visit, avoid the youngsters selling cigars outside.* Also worth a visit, if you're interested, is the **rum factory** (Fábrica de Guayabita) on Isabel Rubio which makes a special rum flavoured with miniature wild guavas, *Guayabita del Pinar*, which comes in either dry or sweet varieties. Between the two is the pretty cream-coloured cathedral of **San Rosendo**. The **Museo Provincial de Historia**, which details the history of the town and displays objects from the wars of independence. ■ *Martí 58, Mon-Sat 0800-1700, US$0.25.* Further along Martí is the **Museo de Ciencias Naturales Sandalio de Noda**, with geological and natural history. ■ *Mon-Sat 0800-1700.*

As you leave the autopista on the north side of José Martí, but in walking distance of the city centre, is the **C** *Hotel Pinar del Río*, José Martí final, T50707. Staff friendly and helpful, swimming pool, nightclub, car hire, in need of updating, beds too soft, sheets too short, hot water evenings only, poor lighting, no bedside light, poor TV reception, poor breakfast. There are a few licensed *casas particulares* and a mafia of young men on bicyles who will pester to take you to a *casa particular, paladar*, or whatever. They are after a commission, set by them at US$5 per person per night. A *casa particular* in the centre is more likely to have 24-hr water and electricity than one further out. **F** *Traveller's Rest*, 20 de Mayo 29 entre Isidro de Armas y Antonio Rubio, Apartment 16, T5681. Hot shower, a/c or fan, 2 rooms, good meals available, bicycle rental, excursions, parking US$1 a day. Run by Juan Carlos Otaño, also known as 'The Teacher', he speaks good English, some French and German, very friendly and helpful. **F** *Eloina*, on Isabel Rubio, no phone, is also good, central and not far from bus station. **F** *Villa Celeida*, Frank País (Sol), Pasaje A 4, entre Isabel Rubio y Gerardo Medina, T3633, 1 block from rum factory. Run by Sra Celeida Ramos Llano, a/c room.

Sleeping

The state-run *Rumayor*, 2 km on Viñales road. Specializes in *pollo ahumado* (smoked chicken), overpriced at US$6.50, grim toilets, open 1200-2200, closed Thur, cabaret at night,

Eating

see below. *Nuestra Casa* a *paladar* on Colón 161 entre Ceferino Fernández y Vandama. Pleasant, nicely decorated roof terrace, enormous meal for US$7, pork or chicken with 2 salads, yuca, masses of *papas fritas* and *congris*. *Mar Init*, José Martí, opposite Parque de la Independencia, T4952. Open Tue-Sun 1930-2130, pay in pesos, fish is the speciality of the house. *Vueltabajo*, Martí y Rafael Morales. Open 0930-2000, food available, also bar selling rum, beer, soft drinks. *Coppelia*, Gerardo Medina. Open daily 0800-2330, ice cream can be bought in pesos, very cheap. *Terrazina*, Antonio Rubio y Primero de Mayo. Open 1130-1500, 1800-2200, pay in pesos, pizza, spaghetti, beer, you can eat for less than US$1. *Doña Yuya*, José Martí 68, entre Isabel Rubio y Colón. Open 1130-1430, 1830-2130, pay in pesos, beautiful architecture but terrible food. *Pinar Café*, Gerardo Medina, opposite *Coppelia*. Open daily 1800-0200, expensive restaurant, US$5 for soft drink, beers, bottle of rum and potato chips, also a show at 2130.

Entertainment The town is very lively on Sat nights, and to a lesser extent on Fri. There is live music everywhere, salsa, son, Mexican music, international stuff. During the day in Parque Roberto Amarán you can hear traditional music (Mambo, Rumba, Cha, Cha, Cha, Danzón) Wed and Sat 1400-1520, Sun 0900. The *Casa de la Música* on Gerardo Medina next to *Coppelia* has live music daily except Mon, 1 peso, no drinks. *Disco Rita*, on González Coro, is an open-air venue popular with teenagers, where they play loud, US-style disco music, entry 2 pesos, the only drink on sale is neat rum at 25 pesos a bottle. *Bar La Esquinita*, on Isabel Rubio, 2000-0200, has live music, usually guitarist. *Rumayor* has a cabaret show at 2230-2400, followed by recorded music, US$5. The classy night life, however, is the disco in the *Hotel Pinar del Río*, US$1, 2000-0400, Thur-Sun, very popular, full every night, young crowd, nice atmosphere.

Transport **Local Car hire**: Havanautos and Transautos both have offices in *Hotel Pinar del Río*. Distances from Pinar del Río are 157 km to Havana, 159 km to María La Garda, 103 km to Las Terrazas, 88 km to Soroa, 25 km to Viñales.

Long distance Air: Alvaro Barba airport is northeast of the town, T63248. To Isla de la Juventud, 2 flights Mon and Fri, 1 flight Tue and Sat, US$22 1-way, rather like a flying bus. Reservations at the bus station at an office downstairs, only 2 seats for tourists. **Bus**: *Viazul* daily from Havana to Viñales at 0900. It stops on request at Las Terrazas (US$6) and San Diego de los Banos (US$8), and gets to Pinar del Río (US$11) at around 1120 with no stops. The return bus leaves Viñales at 1330, stopping in Pinar del Río around 1400 and getting to Havana at 1645. There is also a daily bus provided by *Astro*, which is cheaper but unreliable. The bus station is on Colón, north of José Martí, near Gómez. Pinar del Río to Viñales in a state taxi is US$10, although locals can hire a taxi for the same distance for about US$5. **Train**: Overnight train from Havana at 2140. Take a torch, hang on to your luggage, don't sleep, noisy, train stops about 29 times, very slow, should get in about 0300 but often doesn't arrive until 0600. The line continues to Guane, 3 pesos or US$3. The railway station in Pinar del Río is on Av Comandante Pinares. Trains to Havana leave at 0900 on alternate days, and cost US$7.

Directory **Banks** *Banco Financiero Internacional* (BFI), Gerardo Medina, opposite *Coppelia*, T78183, F78213. Open Mon-Fri 0800-1500. *Cadeca*, Gerardo Medina, next to *Coppelia*. Open 0830-1800. *Banco Popular de Ahorro*, Martí 113, opposite the chess academy. Mon-Fri 0800-1700, cash on credit cards. **Communications** Etecsa is at Av Alameda IIA, T4585-7, Parque de la Independencia. For calls abroad go to Etecsa Centro Telefónico, Marti 33, open 24 hrs. Telecorreos in *Hotel Pinar del Río*. **Post Office:** Martí esq Isabel Rubio, Mon-Sat 0800-1700. Fax service abroad US$8 per page. At Telecorreos in *Hotel Pinar del Río* US$10.20 a page. **Medical facilities** Dentist, Martí 162, T3348. Open 0800-1700. Pharmacy, *Camacho*, Martí 62. Open daily 0800-2300. *Piloto*, under *El Globo Hotel*, open daily 0800-2400 with emergency service. Policlínico Turcios Lima, opposite Cathedral, Gerardo Medina 112, open Mon-Sat 0800-1700. **Tour agency** Cubatur, Martí 51, esq Ormani Arenado, T78405, open 0800-1700, tour guide Dora Pendas.

Peninsula de Guanahacabibes

The Peninsula de Guanahacabibes, which forms the western tip of Cuba, is a Natural Biosphere Reserve and there is a scientific station at La Bajada. Guides can be hired here for walks into the Reserve. The reserve covers 1,175 sq km but has not yet been developed for ecotourism. The peninsula is formed of very recent limestone, with an irregular rocky surface and patchy soil cover. There are interesting fossil coastlines, caves and blue holes; but with dense woodland on the south coast and mangrove on the north, the peninsula is uninviting for the casual hiker. However, for keen naturalists there are 12 amphibian species, 29 reptiles including iguana species, 10 mammals (including *carabalí* and *jutia conga*) and 147 bird species, including nine of the 22 which are endemic to Cuba.

Phone code: 8

The main road continues 12 km south, hugging the coast, to **María La Gorda**, in the middle of nowhere, reputedly the best diving centre in Cuba and an idyllic spot for relaxing or doing nothing but **diving**. *Cubamar* and *Puertosol* organize a package including accommodation, food, diving and transfers from Havana. The sea is very clear, very warm and calm, even when it is too rough to dive anywhere else in Cuba. There is good snorkelling with small coral heads close to the white sand beach, or you can go out on the dive boat.

C-D *María La Gorda*, T/F5382. July-August are most expensive, November-Easter high season, 3 meals US$31 per person, nowhere else to eat. Lovely location, rooms open onto the beach, hammocks between palm trees, excellent value, renovated 1999, nicely decorated, simple but comfortable, a/c, hot water, minibar, TV, good service, friendly staff, buffet meals poor and dull, bar, shop, Telecorreos, dive shop on site with doctor specializing in hyperbaric medicine, US$30 per dive if not on a package.

Sleeping

A package tour or rented car are the only practical ways to visit by land. Private taxis charge around US$28 from Pinar del Río to La Bajada, where they have to leave you at the checkpoint. For visitors arriving by yacht, María La Gorda is a port of entry. There are 4 moorings, maximum draft 2m, VHF channels 16, 19, 68 and 72.

Transport

Viñales

North of Pinar del Río, the road leads across pine-covered hills and valley for 25 km to Viñales, a delightful, small town in a dramatic valley in the **Sierra de los Organos**. The valley has a distinctive landscape, with steep-sided limestone mountains called *mogotes* rising dramatically from fertile flat-floored valleys, where farmers cultivate the red soil for tobacco, fruits and vegetables. As in so much of rural Cuba, horses, pigs, oxen, zebu cattle and chickens are everywhere, including on the main road. An area of 132 sq km around Viñales has been declared a National Monument. Viñales itself is a pleasant town, with trees and wooden colonnades along the main street, red tiled roofs and a main square with a little-used church and a **Casa de Cultura** with an art gallery. Two km west is the **Mural de la Prehistoria**, painted by **Lovigildo González**, a disciple of the Mexican Diego Rivera, between 1959 and 1976, generally disliked as a monstrous piece of graffiti. One hundred metres before the Mural is *Restaurant Jurásico*, from where you can see the paintings and there is a swimming pool nearby. Bar open 0800-1630. Six km north of Viñales is the **Cueva del Indio**, a cave which you enter on foot, then take a boat (US$3 for foreigners) with a guide who gives you a description, very beautiful. There is a restaurant nearby where tour parties are given a lunch of suckling pig (*lechón*).

Phone code: 8

C *Los Jazmines* (Horizontes), Carretera de Vinales Km 23.5, 3 km before the town, in a superb location with travel brochure view of the valley, T936205, F936215, book through Horizontes in Havana, T334042, F333722. 62 nice rooms and 16 *cabañas*, nightclub, breakfast buffet US$5 if not already included, lunch US$10, dinner US$12, unexciting restaurant, bar with

Sleeping

snacks available, shops, swimming pool (US$5 including towels for day visitors and US$5 in vouchers for bar drinks), riding, easy transport. **C** *Horizontes La Ermita*, Carretera de la Ermita Km 2, 3 km from town with magnificent view, T893204. 62 rooms, a/c, phone, radio, shop, tennis court, wheelchair access, pool (not always usable), nicer public areas and food better than at *Los Jazmines*, breakfast included, lunch US$10, dinner US$12. **D** *Horizontes Rancho San Vicente*, Valle de San Vicente, near Cueva del Indio, T893200. 20 a/c *cabañas*, bar, restaurant, breakfast included, lunch US$8, dinner US$10, nightclub, shop, tourist information desk, nice pool, open to day visitors, good for lunch after visit to Caves, spa with warm sulphurous waters, mud baths, a full-body massage is US$20, with mud pack on the face US$5, mineral baths US$3 with use of pool. **Casas particulares F** *Caridad Chirino*, Rafael Trejo 38. Good food available. **F** *Doña Inesita*, Salvador Cisneros 40, T93297. Inés Núñez Rodríguez and her husband, both in their 80s, offer an upstairs apartment with own entrance, 2 bedrooms each sleep 3, sitting room, bathroom, cold water, balcony, terrace, a/c, but cheaper without, breakfast US$3, dinner US$5-6, fruit, eggs and meat from their own garden, even coffee is home grown and roasted, the energetic couple are friendly and welcoming. **F** *Roberto Valle González* (El Macho), Adela Azcuy 2 Norte, T93112. One room, a/c, excellent food, home grown fruit. **F** *Emilia Diaz Serrat* (Nenita), Salvador Cisnero Interior No 6-1, behind the clinic. A/c, private bathrooms but no hot water, delightful family, superb food. **F** *Luisia Crespo Crespo*, Carretera a Puerto Esperanza Km 27, T93323. Extended family, friendly, helpful, breakfast US$3, dinner US$5, huge, good. **F** *Osvaldo y Ana Díaz González*, Joaquín Pérez, interior s/n. Lovely terrace at the back overlooking fields. **F** *Eugenia Torres Valdes* (Gena), Salvador Cisnero 209, T93320. Not in the centre, but very nice people.

Eating *Paladar Restaurant*, or *Valle Bar*, T93183, on the main street. Small, friendly, recommended, *pollo frito* US$4, spaghetti US$2.50, steak, or just have a beer, US$1, and listen to the live music in the evening, can find you local accommodation with private families. Also licensed is *Casa Cocero*, which takes pesos. *Casa de Don Tomás* is the oldest house in Viñales (1879), state owned, features in Horizontes brochure. Unexciting paella, OK for US$8 but cocktails a bargain at US$0.90. *Casa Dago*, popular restaurant/bar with good jazz salsa band, run by extraordinary character with impressive 1927 Ford Chevrolet, food indifferent, but once the music gets going and the rum starts flowing you could be dancing all night.

Transport **Bus**: Bus terminal at Salvador Cisneros 63A. *Viazul* daily from Havana via Pinar del Río at 0900, US$12, arrives 1215, returns 1330, arrives in Havana at 1645 depending on the number of stops. *Astro* from Havana 0900 via Pinar del Río, returns 1430, arrives in Havana 1820, US$8, cheaper but less comfortable and unreliable. Local buses from Pinar del Río to Puerto Esperanza, La Palma and Bahía Honda all pass through Viñales. Tour buses from Havana will drop you off if you want to stay more than a day and collect you about 1600 on the day you want to return. Truck to Pinar del Río 2 pesos.**Car hire**: *Transtur*, Ceferino Fernández 6 entre Salvador Cisneros y Final, T936060, cars from US$45 a day, fuel extra. Transtur also rents **bicycles**, US$2 per hour, US$0.75 for more than 5 hrs or US$10.10 per day, and **scooters**, US$23 per day plus fuel. Moped hire from *Casa de Don Tomás* US$20 per day. **Taxi**: *Transtur* has a taxi service, US$0.40 per km, with waiting time of US$4 per hr. Viñales to Cayo Jutías US$40, Palma Rubia for Cayo Levisa US$22, Cuevas de Santo Tomás US$8.

Directory **Banks** *Bandec* does not do card transactions, but next door is *Banco Popular de Ahorro*, which does, open Mon-Fri 0800-1200, 1330-1630.

North coast The coast north of Viñales is worth a visit if you have transport. The best and closest, 50 km, beach is at **Cayo Jutías**, near Santa Lucía. A 6.7 km cay reached by a causeway, it is open to foreigners only, US$2 entrance, *Rumbos* bar/restaurant. Further east is **Cayo Levisa**, part of the **Archipiélago de los Colorados**, with a long, sandy beach and reef running parallel to the shore, with good snorkelling and scuba diving (lots of fish). Cayo Levisa is 15 minutes by boat from Palma Rubia. The jetty is on the south side and you follow a boardwalk through the mangroves to get to the hotel on the north side. Take insect repellent. Day trips or longer stays are organized by Horizontes; you can even visit by helicopter.

Sleeping AL *Cayo Levisa*, T335030 in Havana. Packages include transport from Havana, some or all meals and often watersports, book in Havana through any tour agency which deals with Horizontes or Cubamar. 20 cabins on beach, thatched, with verandahs, a/c, TV, comfortable but not luxurious, spacious, restaurant, bar, live music.

East of Havana

The main road along the coast towards Matanzas and Varadero is called the **Vía Blanca**. There are some scenic parts, but you also drive through quite a lot of industry. The **Hershey Railway** runs inland from the Casablanca station in eastern Havana, more or less parallel to the Vía Blanca, and is an interesting way to get to Matanzas. This electric line was built by the Hershey chocolate family in 1917 to service their sugar mill, at what is now the Central Camilo Cienfuegos.

Some 60 km east of Havana is **Jibacoa** beach, which is good for snorkelling as the reefs are close to the beach and it is also a nice area for walking. It is pretty, with hills coming down to the sea, and a pleasant place to go for a weekend away from Havana.

B *Superclubs Breezes (Jibacoa)*, Playa Arrojo Bermejo, Vía Blanca Km 60, T69285122, F69285150. Price per person, all-inclusive, no children under 16, 250 rooms and suites in 2-storey buildings, attractive setting with hilly backdrop and curved, sandy bay, well-equipped, comfortable, good food, vegetarian options, no motorized watersports to protect reef, excursions available, indoor games room, pool, lots of sports, wheelchair accessible, evening entertainment disappointing. **E-F** *Campismo El Abra*, further along rough track T83344, 83612. Cheaper if booked through Cubamar, 87, 2-3-bed cabins with fan or a/c, small rooms, very basic, hot, small shower, bicycles, small horses, badminton, pelota, bar, restaurant, Post Office and Cambio, enormous but murky pool, small, rocky beach, best to walk east or west, extensive grounds, lots of greenery and mosquitoes. 70% of guests are Cuban.

Sleeping

Matanzas

Matanzas is a sleepy town with old colonial buildings and a busy, ugly industrial zone. Both the rivers Yumurí and San Juan flow through the city. Most of the old buildings are between the two rivers, with another colonial district, Versalles, to the east of the Río Yumurí. This area was colonized in the 19th century by French refugees from Haiti after the revolution there. The newer district, Pueblo Nuevo, also has many colonial houses. The industrial zone runs along the north shore of the bay, with railways running inland and around the bay.

Phone code: 52
Population: 115,000

The town dates from 1693, but became prosperous with the advent of sugar mills in the 1820s, followed by the railway in 1843. Most of the buildings date from this time and by the 1860s it was the second largest town in Cuba after Havana. The **Galería de Arte Provincial** is on the **Plaza de la Vigía**. ■ *Mon 0900-1700, Tue-Sat 0900-1800, US$2.* Next door is **Ediciones Vigía**, where you can see books being produced. These are all handmade and in first editions of only 200 copies, so they are collectors' items, particularly if you get one signed. Also on Plaza de la Vigía is **Teatro Sauto**, a magnificent neo-classical building dating from 1862-63 and seating 775 people in three-tiered balconies the floor can be raised to convert the auditorium into a ballroom. ■ *Tue-Sun, US$2.*

Although you will now find numbers written on the streets, locals still refer to names. Streets running N-S in the old town have even numbers, while streets running E-W have odd numbers

Visit the **Museo Farmacéutico**, which contains the original equipment, porcelain jars, recipes and furnishings of the Botica La Francesa, opened in 1882 by the Triolet family. It was a working pharmacy until 1964, when it was converted into a

Museums

Cuba

fascinating museum, believed to be unique in Latin America. ■ *Milanés 4951 entre Santa Teresa y Ayuntamiento, on the south side of Parque Libertad, T23197. Mon-Sat 1000-1700, Sun 0800-1200, US$2.* The **Museo Provincial** is a large museum in the former **Palacio del Junco**, built by a wealthy plantation owner and dating from 1840. The historical exhibits include an archaeological display and the development of sugar and slavery in the province. ■ *Milanés entre Magdalena y Ayllón, T23195. Mon-Sat 1000-1700, Sun 0800-1200, US$1.*

Sleeping **D-E** *Hotel Canimao*, Km 4 Carretera Matanzas a Varadero, T668021. 120 rooms on hill above Río Canímar, pool, nightclub, good restaurant, excursions offered on the river or to caves. Another hotel outside town is **D-E** *El Valle*, T53300/53118, 7 km northwest of Matanzas, in woodland in the Valle del Yumurí. Built 1985, 42 rooms, some with shared bath, pool, bowling alley, riding, good walking. **E-F** *Hotel Louvre*, 19th-century building on south side of Parque Libertad, T4074. Variety of rooms and prices, opt for the a/c room with bathroom and balcony overlooking the square, beautiful mahogany furniture, rather than the small, dark, cupboard room in the bowels of the hotel, water shortages, no toilet paper, friendly, lush garden in patio. Several *casas particulares* near the beach. Ask a tout in Parque Libertad, or try **E** *Laurita*, T62333, hot water, TV, if she is booked she will know of somewhere else.

Eating *La Ruina*. Very attractive *Rumbos* restaurant converted from sugar warehouse, open 24 hrs, dinner US$2.5-10, delicious pastries, great ice cream, pesos and dollars accepted, live music at weekends. *Pekin*, 83 entre 292 y 294. Open daily 1200-1400, 1800-2100, foreigners pay in dollars. *Año 30*, 272 entre 75 y 77. Open Mon-Sat 1200-1400. *Café Atenas*, 83 y 272 on Plaza La Vigía. Open 24 hrs, snack food, modern design, strong lighting. *Paladar El Reloj*, 135 y 298. Collection of old clocks, big criollo meal US$5. Cheap food at Mercado Central, complete meal for less than US$2, pay in pesos, eg *Parillada Las Mariposas*, C 300 entre 95 y 97. Outdoor tables. Around the corner, *Shanghai*, standard cheap Chinese. These and others serve whatever the market is selling, seasonal fruit and vegetables.

Nightlife The Plaza Vigía is the place to go in the evenings; locals congregate here to chat, play dominoes or draughts, or make music. The *Casa de la Trova* here, near the bridge, was where the *Muñequitas de Matanzas*, a famous rumba band, was formed. The *Sala de Conciertos José White de Matanzas*, on 79 entre 288 y 290, was formerly the *Lyceum Club* and is famous for being the place where the *danzón* was danced for the first time in 1879; music is performed here and all events are free. *Teatro Sauto* usually has live performances at the weekends.

Transport **Bus** The long distance bus station is at 131 y 272, while the interprovincial terminal is at 298 y 127, both in Pueblo Nuevo. **Train** The 3-4 hr journey via the Hershey Railway, the only electric train in Cuba, is memorable and scenic if you are not in a hurry. Those who wish to make it a day trip from Havana can do so, long queues for return tickets, best to get one as soon as you arrive. Four trains daily, 3-4 hrs, from the Casablanca station to a station north of the Río Yumurí in Versalles. The station south of the town at C 181, Miret receives regular and *especial* trains from Havana en route to Santiago.

Directory **Banks** *Banco Financiero Internacional* at 85 y 298 for exchange facilities and cash advances on credit cards. *Banco Nacional* at 83 (Milanés) y 282. **Communications** Post Office: at 85 y 290. **Telephone:** office on 83 y 288, open 0630-2200 every day. **Medical facilities** Facilities for foreigners are available in Varadero, but there is a pharmacy here, open 24 hrs, at 85 y 280.

Varadero

Phone code: 5 *Cuba's chief beach resort, Varadero is built on the Península de Hicacos, a 20-km sandspit, the length of which run two roads lined with dozens of large hotels. Development of the peninsula began in 1923 but the village area was not built until the 1950s. The Du Pont family bought land, sold it for profit, then bought more, constructed roads and built a large house, now the Xanadú clubhouse for the new golf course. Varadero is still undergoing large-scale development with the aim of expanding capacity to 30,000 rooms. Despite the building in progress it is not over-exploited and is a good place for a family beach holiday. The beaches are quite empty, if a bit exposed, and you can walk for miles along the sand, totally isolated from the rest of Cuba.*

Museo Municipal, with some Indian artefacts and paintings. ■ *57 y Av de la Playa. Tue-Sat 0900-1800, Sun 0900-1200, US$1.* The **Parque Josone**, Avenida 1 y Calle 59, is a large park with pool, bowling, other activities and a café. Towards the end of the peninsula, half way between Marina Chapelín and Marina Gaviota, is a cave, **Cueva de Ambrosio**, where dozens of Indian drawings were discovered in 1961. ■ *Tue-Sun 1000-1200, 1400-1600, US$2, but may be unattended unless a tour party is booked in to visit.* At the far end of the peninsula the land has been designated the **Parque Natural de Varadero**. It is an area of scrub and cactus, with a lagoon where salt was once made, and several km of sandy beach.

Varadero's sandy beach stretches the length of the peninsula, broken only occasionally by rocky outcrops which can be traversed by walking through a hotel's grounds. Some parts are wider than others and as a general rule the older hotels have the best bits of beach. However, the sand is all beautifully looked after and cleaned daily. The water is clean and nice for swimming but for good **snorkelling** take one of the many boat trips out to the cays. There are three **marinas** (see below), all full service with sailing tours, restaurants, fishing and diving. All their services can be booked through the tour desks in hotels. **Deep sea fishing** costs around US$250 for four people for half a day, but prices vary according to what exactly is on offer. The dive operators are *Barracuda* (Cubanacán), Av 1 entre 58 y 59, T667072, *Marina Gaviota* (Gaviota Group), T667755, and *Dársena de Varadero* (Puertosol), T668063. Average prices are US$35 for a single dive, US$70 for two tanks. A five-day ACUC certification course costs US$365. Varadero's **Dolphinarium** is at Autopista Km 12, beyond the Marina Chapelín, but the one on Cayo Macho (see 'Excursions' below) is a nicer location. You can indulge in almost any form of watersports, including windsurfing, parasailing, waterskiing, jet skiing and non-motorized pedalos and water bikes.

Beaches & watersports

Beach vendors will try to sell you T-shirts, crochet work & wooden trinkets. Don't buy the black coral, it is protected internationally & you may not be allowed to take it into your country

The large hotels all offer **tennis** courts, some have **squash** courts and **volleyball** is played on the beach, usually organized by the hotel entertainment staff. **Table tennis**, **billiards** and other indoor games are available if the weather deteriorates or you have had enough sun. There is a Canadian-designed **golf** course on Av Las Américas Km 8.5, upgraded in 1996-98 to 18 holes, par 72. The original nine holes were set out by the Du Ponts around their mansion, built in 1928-30, which is now the *Xanadú Club House*, and the new ones extend along the Sol Meliá resorts. Golf lessons are offered and there are two putting greens, and a driving range. Packages of 3-8 days are available with accommodation in the clubhouse. Pro-shop and equipment rental at Caddie House. International Amateur Golf Week will be held 1-8 April 2000. ■ *T667788, F668481/180. Bookings can be made through hotel tour desks or direct. Open daily, make reservations 24 hrs in advance.*

Other sports

There are many **sailing tours** to the offshore cays. The *Jolly Roger*, T667565, is a comfortable catamaran, US$70 including lunch and open bar, good food, several stops for snorkelling or beaches. Ask for a detour to the **dolphinarium** on Cayo Macho if it is not already included and if your fellow passengers agree. It is isolated, apparently in the middle of nowhere, with large pens for the dolphins. ■ *US$5 for a show, US$5 to swim with them.*

  Cayo Mono lies five nautical miles north northeast of Punta de Morlas. During the nesting season in mid-year it becomes a seagull sanctuary for the 'Gaviota Negra' (*Anous stolidus*) and the 'Gaviota Monja' (*Sterna fuscata* and *Annaethetus*), during which time you can only pass by and watch them through binoculars.

Excursions

All hotels, restaurants & excursions must be paid in US dollars. Don't bother to buy any pesos for your stay here. Book excursions at any hotel with a Tour Agency office

Cuba

Varasub I, a Japanese semi-submersible carrying 48 passengers, has six daily departures, adults US$25, children US$20. Reservations can be made with Havanatur representatives or the Varasub offices: Avenida Playa 3606, entre 36 y 37, T667279, and others. The *Mundo Mágico* submarine goes down to a depth of 35m with 46 passengers for 55 minutes. It leaves from the Dársena Marina, T668060-5. You can also see underwater by taking a trip on the glass-bottomed boat, *Martín*, which does a three-hour tour over the reef, open bar and snorkelling equipment.

Sleeping
■ *on maps*

There is no private accommodation in Varadero

Hotels can be booked in the tourist office. Many offer all- inclusive rates but they can be disappointing with a lack of variety in food and drink. A Cuban-Spanish joint venture has a group of resort hotels managed by *Sol/Meliá Hotels* of Spain, www.solmelia.es **LL-L** *Meliá Las Américas* (Cubanacán), Autopista Sur Km 7, T667600, F667625. Five stars, 250 rooms, suites, 125 luxury bungalows, comfortable, glitzy public areas, restaurants, breakfast recommended, nice pool but cold, good beach, golf, tennis, watersports, disco, Plaza América shopping centre alongside, new, shops still opening up. **LL-AL** *Sol Club Palmeras* (Cubanacán), T667009, F667008. 375 rooms, 32 suites, 200 comfortable bungalows, well-landscaped, quiet, shady, attractive, cool lobby bar, 4 stars, same facilities. **LL-L** *Meliá Varadero* (Cubanacán), T667013, F667012. 490 rooms, 5 stars, on rocky promontory, tennis, watersports, disco, nightclub, spa, sauna, jacuzzi. *Sol Club Coral*, Carretera Las Américas entre H y K, T667009, F667008. 324 rooms, same facilities. There is a shuttle service through the Sol/Meliá complex 0730-2300. **AL** *Cuatro Palmas Coralia* (Gran Caribe), Av 1 entre 60 y 61, T667640, F667583. 343 a/c rooms, also in bungalows and villas hacienda style, on beach, opposite Centro Comercial Caiman in heart of hotel strip, very pleasant, pool, tennis, bicycle and moped hire, tourism bureau, post office, lots of services. **L-AL** *Arenas Blancas* (Gran Caribe), 64 entre Av 1 y Autopista, T612299, 614492/99, F614490. New, 5-star, 354 standard rooms, facilities for disabled people, 76 more rooms in smaller blocks, restaurants, snack bar, 2 pools, tennis, watersports, archery, mini golf, lots of facilities. **AL** *LTI Bella Costa Resort Hotel & Villas* (Cubanacán), Carretera Las Américas, Km 4.5, T667210/010, F667205. Good 4-star hotel at end of one section of sandy beach with rocky ironshore, landscaped gardens, attractive, well run, good service. Pool with swim up bar, watersports, tennis, lovely fish restaurant on small cliff overlooking sea. **AL** *LTI Tuxpán* (Cubanacán), Carretera Las Américas, Km 4, T667560, F667561. Also with very good facilities. *Varadero Internacional* (Gran Caribe), Av Las Américas, T667038, F667246. Formerly the *Hilton*, closed for renovation 1999, will have 163 rooms in main hotel and 149 rooms in 64 cabañas, tennis, pool, sauna, massage, watersports, restaurant, cabaret, Cuban art gallery, Porto Carrero original painting on tiles in lobby, best bit of beach on whole peninsula.

Varadero

Jamaican investors have built the 160-room, all-inclusive **A** (pp) *Superclubs Club Varadero* (Cubanacán), soon to become *Breezes*, Carretera de las Americas Km 3, T667030, F667005, clubvar@clubvar.var.cyt.cu For singles and couples, no children under 16, a/c, phone, satellite TV, lots of activities and sports, plenty of equipment, free sunbeds for guests, 5 bars, 3 restaurants, disco, theme parties, indoor games room, gym, sauna, jacuzzis, Olympic size pool, tennis, diving and other watersports, such as sailing and waterskiing, popular, crowded even in low season. Superclubs have taken over the *Paradiso* and *Puntarenas* hotels at the end of Av Kawama to make a family resort, *Superclubs Puntarena* (Gran Caribe), T667120-9, lots of activities. Sandals also opened a resort in 1999, *Beaches Varadero* (Cubanacán), Carretera Las Morlas Km 14.5, T668470, F668335, varadero@beaches.var.cyt.cu Ultra all-inclusive, 350 rooms, buffet and 3 other restaurants, 4 bars, no under 16s, diving, fitness centre, sauna, tennis, car rental, shuttle bus, lots of services and entertainment. *Club Med Varadero* (Gaviota), Autopista Sur Km 11, T668288/341, F668340. All-inclusive for ages 12 and up, 266 rooms including 18 suites, a/c, phone, TV, safety box, 3 restaurants and 3 bars, of which 1 is reserved for cigar smokers, lots of sports including catamarans, windsurfing, kayaks, aerobics, gymnasium, volleyball, basketball, 8 tennis courts, circus school, pool, dancing lessons, pétanque and indoor games. **AL-A** pp *Brisas del Caribe* (Cubanacán), Carretera Las Morlas Km 12, T668030, F668005. Another new and comfortable all-inclusive, 266 a/c rooms with satellite TV, phone, terrace or balcony and sea or garden view, 4 suites have jacuzzis, 2 restaurants, grill on the beach, 6 bars, lots of sporting facilities, pool, gym, games room, entertainment. *Sol Club Las Sirenas*, Av Las Américas y K, T668070, F668075. An all-inclusive in the Sol/Meliá chain, on the beach with the usual emphasis on sports and evening entertainment, restaurants, large curving pool, children welcome, very comfortable. **AL-A** pp *Gran Hotel* (Cubanacán), Carretera Las Morlas, 1 km west of Punta Francés, T668243, F668230, sistema@granhot.var.cyt.cu All-inclusive, 317 rooms, 24-hr drinks and snacks, non-motorized watersports, day and night entertainment, well-run, 4-star, 40 km from airport, taxi to town US$12, hourly bus US$1, lots of building works nearby in 1999. **A-C** *Kawama* (Gran Caribe), Carretera de Kawama y O, T614416. 202 rooms, all-inclusive, refurbished older hotel.

B *Acuazul*, Av 1 entre 13 y 14, T667132. 156 rooms, with pool, older style, not on beach, blue and white, lots of concrete. **B** *Villa Punta Blanca* (Gran Caribe), Reparto Kawama, T668050, F667004. All-inclusive, 4-star, 320 rooms, made up of a number of former private residences with some new complexes. **C** *Herradura*, Av Playa entre 35 y 36, T613725. Well-equipped suites, balcony, restaurant, bar, shop etc. **C** *Villa La Caleta* (Gaviota), 20 y Av 1, T667080, F3291. 46 a/c rooms with baths, phone, TV, minibar, restaurant, room service, pizzería, grill, bar, pool, scooter and bike hire, parking, convenient for nightlife. **D** *Caribe*, Av de la Playa y 30, T613310. 124 rooms, 2-star, not to be confused with the 4-star *Caribe* on K, T667280. **D** *Los Delfines*, Av

Cuba

Playa y 39, T667720, F667496. **D** *Varazul*, Av 1 entre C 14 y 15, T667132, F667229. Aparthotel, 69 rooms, quiet. **D** *Villa Sotavento*, dependency of *Acuazul*, 13 between Av 1 and Av Playa, T667132-4. 130 rooms, next to beach, clean, with bath, breakfast, US$5, buffet, very good.

Eating

All between US$9 & US$15 for a main dish

Mi Casita (book in advance), Camino del Mar entre 11 y 12, T63787. Meat and seafood, open 1800-2300. *La Cabañita* Camino del Mar esquina 9, T62215. Meat and seafood, open 1900-0100. *Oshin*, Chinese, in grounds of *Sol Palmeras*. Open 1200-1500, 1800-2300, popular, reservations essential. *Habana Café*, at *Club Las Sirenas*, T668070, copy of *Habana Café* at *Meliá Cohiba* in Havana. 1950s atmosphere, car, photos, music, open 1800-0200, snacks, cocktails, international food. *Halong*, Camino del Mar esquina 12, T63787. Chinese, open 1900-2300. *El Mesón del Quijote* at *Villa Cuba*, Carretera Las Américas, T63522. Spanish, open 1200-2300. *Albacora*, Av Playa y 59. Open 1200-2400, seafood, terrace with sea views, room available for changing if you've been on the beach, food described as disappointing, all dishes except *pescado*, US$12-18, but if you want fish you may be told '*no hay*'. *Lai-Lai* Av 1 y 18, T667793. Bar/restaurant, Oriental, Open 1200-0300. *Castelnuovo*, Av 1 y 11, T667794. Open 1200-2345, Italian. *La Fondue*, Av 1 y 64. Open 1200-2300, Swiss-French menu. *El Aljibe*, Av 1 y 36, T614019. Open 1200-2400, chicken and more chicken. *Las Américas*, Av Las Américas, T63856. Open 1200-2215, international food, beautiful setting, food good one night, inedible the next. *El Mirador*, at *LTI Bella Costa Resort*, on cliff overlooking the sea. Lovely fish restaurant, lobster US$18.50, shrimp US$14, open 1200-2300. *Bodegón Criollo*, Av Playa esquina 40, T667795. Open 1200-0100, pleasant atmosphere, copy of *Bodeguita del Medio* in Havana with graffiti on walls, popular, music, no vegetarian food. *Deportivo Kiki's Club*, Av 1 y 8. Open 1200-2345, sports theme, Italian food, sports shop and sporting exhibitions. *La Sangría*, snack bar on sea front, Av 1 entre C 8 y 9, T62025, open 24 hrs. In Parque Josone are: *El Retiro*, T667316, international; *Dante*, T667738, Italian; *La Campana*, T667224, criollo and *La Casa de las Antigüedades*, T667329, meat and seafood. *Coppelia*, Av 1 entre 44 y 46, T612866, open 1000-2245, in town centre, ice cream US$0.90.

Nightlife

Cinema: *Cine Varadero*, Av Playa entre 42 y 43. **Discos**: Most large hotels have one including: *La Patana*, Canal de Paso Malo, T667791, open 2200-0500, floating disco at entrance to the balneario; *La Bamba*, hottest in town at *LTI-Tuxpán*, biggest, most popular, T667560, open 2200-0400. **Nightclubs**: *Cabaret Continental* at *Hotel Internacional*. US$40 with dinner, 2000, show and disco US$25, open Tue-Sun, 2100-0330, reservations T667038. *Cabaret Cueva del Pirata*, show in a cave, Autopista Sur Km 11, T613829. Open 2200-0300, closed Sun. *Mambo Club*, next to *Gran Hotel*. The Orquesta Tarafa plays here, they were famous in the 1950s. *Palacio de la Rumba*, Av Las Américas, Km 4, T668210. Open daily 2200-0500, US$10 entrance, includes bar, live salsa bands at weekends.

Tour operators

Most hotels have a tour agency on-site offering local and national excursions, boat trips, multilingual guides, transfers, booking and confirmation of air tickets, air charters, car rentals, reception and representation service. Flights to Trinidad can be booked through *Inter*, T614845, or *Cubatur*, T667401. Main offices of agencies: *Cubanacán*, T667061/834; *Gaviota*, T667684, 613465; *Rumbos*, T666666, 667630; *Cubatur*, T667269/217.

Marinas

Marina Chapelin is at Carretera Las Morlas, Km 12.5, T667550/565, VHF 16 and 72. Moorings for 20 boats, maximum draft 30m, boat rental, laundry, fishing. *Marina Dársena de Varadero*, is at Carretera de Vía Blanca Km 31, T63730, 63133, 62363, VHF 16, 19, 68, 72. Moorings for 70 boats, maximum draft 5m, boat rental, showers, laundry, restaurants, bars, fishing, shops, day charters, diving, liveaboard for 20 people. *Marina Gaviota Varadero*, Peninsula de Hicacos Km 21, T667550/565, VHF 16. Ten moorings, 3m draft, showers, laundry, restaurant, bar, seafaris, yacht rental, fishing, dolphinarium, diving.

Transport

Local Car hire: *Havanautos*, agency in Varadero at Av 1 y 31, T63733, F667029, T63630 at airport, or through many hotels. *Cubacar* (Cubanacán) at: *Hotel Sol Palmeras*, T667359; *Hotel LTI-Tuxpan*, T667639; *Hotel Meliá Varadero*, T667013 ext 8191. *Transautos*, Av 2 y 64, T667336, or Av 1 entre 21 y 22. *Nacional* (Gaviota) at 13 entre Av 2 y Av 4, T63706,

T/F667663. Hot tip: hire a car rather than jeep to avoid having your spare wheel stolen, insurance covers 4 wheels, not the spare (see page 154). **Moped rental**: US$9 per hr, US$15 for 3 hrs, extra hours US$5, a good way to see the peninsula but you will have no insurance and no helmet. **Bicycle hire**: from hotels, US$1 per hr. **Horse drawn vehicles** act as taxis, usually just for a tour around town. **Taxis** (cars) charge US$0.50 per km. The best place to hail a taxi is at any hotel as they usually wait there for fares. *Transagaviota*, T619761-2; *Turistaxi*, T613763/377; *Taxi OK*, T612827.

Long distance Air The *Juan Gualberto Gómez* airport (VRA), T613016, 23 km from the beginning of the hotel strip, receives international scheduled and charter flights. *Cubana* or *Sansa* have domestic flights from Baracoa, Cayo Coco, Cayo Largo, Havana, Holguín, Santiago and Trinidad. Bus from airport to hotels US$10pp. Flights to Trinidad, 0900, 1630, leave from Kawama airstrip, just across the bridge on the mainland. **Bus** The interprovincial bus station is at Autopista Sur y 36, T63254, 62626. Víazul has 3 daily buses Havana-Varadero via Varadero airport, US$10, and there is a regular Astro bus twice a day (0805 and 1600) from Havana bus terminal to Varadero, which stops off at Varadero airport, US$8, reserve 1-2 days in advance. The Víazul a/c bus Varadero-Trinidad runs on alternate days, US$20, with stops in Santa Clara, US$11 and Sancti Spíritus, US$16, 6 hrs.

Airlines All at the airport: *Aerocaribbean*, T53616; *Aerogaviota*, T63018, 62010; *Air Canada*, T612010; *Air Europa*, T613016; *AOM*, T613016; *Cubana*, T63612-14; *LTU*, T53611; *Martinair*, T53624. *Aerotaxi* is at 24 y Av 1, T62929. *Cubana* has an office at 9 esq 1, T667593. **Banks** *Banco Financiero Internacional*, Av Playa y 32, cash advance service with credit cards, open 0900-1900 daily. **Communications** Most hotels have post offices where you can buy stamps for use and in packets for collectors. Phone and fax services are also usually available but prices vary. The *Centro Internacional de Comunicaciones* is at 64 entre Av 1 y Av 3, T62103/, 62356, F667020. For cellular phones, *Cubacel* is at 25 y Av 1, Edif La Cancha, T667222/198, F667222. *Etecsa* is at 18 y Av 3, T667070, F667050. *DHL* is on 10 next to *Hotel Barlovento*, T/F667330. **Medical facilities** *Policlínico Internacional*, Av 1 y 61, T668611, 667710-1, F667226, clinica@clinica.var.cyt.cu International clinic, doctor on duty 24 hrs, a medical consultation in your hotel will cost US$25. The clinic has an excellent international pharmacy attached, T667226. Recompression chamber at the Centro Médico Sub Acuática at the *Hospital Julio M Arístegui*, just outside Cárdenas. **Useful addresses** Immigration and **Police**: 39 y Av 1, T116. Immigration is open Mon-Fri 0800-1130, 1300-1600, Sat 0800-1130 for visa extensions.

Directory

Cárdenas

Cárdenas is usually visited as a day trip from Varadero and is empty of tourists, friendly and a good place to meet Cubans. There is no hustling and no police harassment of Cubans associating with foreigners. The town is 18 km southeast of Varadero on the Bahía de Cárdenas. It was founded in 1828 and attractive, in the traditional 19th century Spanish colonial style of houses with tall windows, intricate lattices, high ceilings inside, ceramic tiled floors and interior gardens. Cárdenas was a wealthy sugar town in the 19th century. Its main claim to fame is that the Cuban flag was first raised here in 1850 by the revolutionary **General Narciso López**, a Venezuelan who tried unsuccessfully to invade Cuba by landing at Cárdenas with an army of 600 men (only six of whom were Cuban). There is a plaque at the *Hotel Dominica*, which Narciso López occupied with his men and is now a National Monument and a flagpole monument on Avenida Céspedes. **Plaza Molokoff** is worth a visit to see the decaying iron market building, put up in the 19th century on Avenida 3 oeste and Calle 12. It was built in the shape of a cross and the two-storey building is surmounted by a 15 m dome made in the USA. On Calle 2, overlooking the water, is the *Fábrica de Ron Arrechabala*, which makes both the Varadero and Bucanero label rums. The site has been a rum factory since 1878, when the Havana Club company was founded here.

Phone code: 5
Population: 75,000

E *Dominica*, Av Céspedes y 9, T521502. 25 rooms in old sugar warehouse, converted to hotel in neo-classical style in 1919 and now a National Monument, big rooms and suites, some

Sleeping

Cuba

with balconies. *Dirección Municipal de Vivienda*, Laborde 18, T522852/414, Lanexys Abreu Guerra, has a list of legally registered **Casas particulares**, or just ask around. Most places have high ceilings, which are cool, but insect repellent is needed.

Eating *Café Espriú*, Rumbos, Plaza Echavarría, 2 blocks east of Céspedes. Popular, attractive, criollo food, great ice cream, reasonable prices, main course less than US$4, open 0800-2400, best place in town. *Café Cárdenas*, Av Céspedes. Club atmosphere, balcony overlooking street, terrace at the back or indoor tables, prices up to US$5.50, mainly criollo food, karaoke weekdays, live salsa or tríos at weekends. Cárdenas is not a great culinary experience; ask around for *paladares*. The public market has plenty of fresh fruit and vegetables.

Transport Bicycles or horses are the only carriers, 1 peso. Cárdenas is an easy bike ride from Varadero and a guard will watch your bike for 1 peso. The **bus** station is on Av Céspedes y 22, with services to Matanzas, Colón, Jagüey Grande, Havana and Santa Clara. To get to Varadero catch a bus from the corner of Av 13 oeste y 13, they should leave every hour, but as the principal demand is from hotel workers they are more likely to run according to shifts. *Víazul* will drop you here on request on their Havana-Varadero route. Alternatively, *Astro* from Havana 0845, US$6, or *colectivo* taxi, US$15. Astro returns to Havana 1340 via Varadero and Matanzas. There are no facilities to charge in dollars and if you show your ticket stub from your arrival they will charge you only 6 pesos for your return. Get there early, the bus soon fills up, or buy a reserved seat ticket early in the morning.

Zapata Peninsula

The whole of the south coast of Matanzas province is taken up with the **Zapata Peninsula**, an area of swamps, mangroves and beaches. It is the largest ecosystem in the island and contains the **Laguna del Tesoro**, a 9.1 sq km lagoon over 10 m deep, an important winter home for flocks of migrating birds. There are 16 species of reptiles, including crocodiles. Mammals include the jutia and the manatee, while there are over 1,000 species of invertebrate, of which more than 100 are spiders.

There is a **crocodile farm** (Criadero de Cocodrilos) at the Zapata Tourist Institute in **Boca de Guamá**, where they breed the native Rhombifer (*cocodrilo*). They also have tortoises, jutia and what they call a living fossil, the manjuari fish/alligator, on the farm. There are lots of shops, a bar and restaurant, occasional live bands and a ceramics factory. This is all a bit touristy; hotels and tourist agencies from Varadero, Havana and other places organize day excursions including lunch, a multilingual guide and a boat ride on the lagoon through the swamps to **Villa Guamá**, a replica Indian village. On one of the islets a series of life-size statues of Indians going through their daily routines has been carved by Cuban sculptor Rita Longa.

Zapata Peninsula

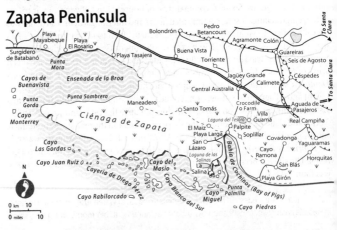

Birdwatchers are advised to spend a few nights, or go on a tour one day and return with the next tour the following day. You will see most at dawn before the tour buses arrive. Take insect repellent. ■ *Entrance to the crocodile farm 0900-1800, US$3; boat trip from Boca de Guamá to Villa Guamá US$10, 45 mins.*

The road south across the peninsula meets the coast at **Playa Larga**, at the head of the **Bahía de Cochinos**, commonly known as the **Bay of Pigs**. The US-backed invasion force landed here on 17 April 1961 but was successfully repelled. There is a small monument but most of the commemorative paraphernalia is at Playa Girón (see below). The beach is open and better than that at Playa Girón. The **Laguna de las Salinas**, 25 km southwest, is the temporary home of huge numbers of migratory birds from December-April. The rest of the year it is empty. ■ *Tours go from the Hotel Playa Larga, Mon and Wed mornings, US$15.*

West of Playa Larga, a track leads to **Santo Tomás** where, in addition to waterfowl, you can see the Zapata wren, the Zapata rail and the Zapata sparrow. The Park also runs a number of rare bird (Cuban parrots and Cuban parakeets), turtle and fish breeding programmes. Not far from the *Hotel Playa Larga* there is a good site for watching birds such as hummingbirds and the Cuban trogon. ■ *Park headquarters are near the Hotel Playa Larga, in the Empresa Municipal Agropecuaria, Oficina Parque Nacional, Carretera Principal, Playa Larga, T7249. Here you can get permission to enter and pay the admission fee of US$10 per person as well as find a guide (obligatory), about US$50. Insect repellent essential.*

The resort at **Playa Girón** is isolated and small. The beach is walled in and therefore protected, but the sea is rocky. The **diving** and **snorkelling** is excellent and you can walk to the reef from the shore. There is a **museum** at the site of national pilgrimage where, in 1961 at the **Bay of Pigs**, the disastrous US-backed invasion of Cuba was attempted. ■ *The museum is open daily 0800-1700, US$2.*

Sleeping

D *Horizontes Villa Guamá*, Laguna del Tesoro, T592979. 59 a/c rooms in thatched cabañas on several little islands in the style of a Taino village, with bath, phone, TV, restaurant, bar, *cafetería*, nightclub, shop, tourist information desk, excursions, fishing for largemouth bass in the lake. **E** *Villa Horizontes Playa Larga*, at Playa Larga, T597219. Sometimes fully booked with tour groups, 59 a/c spacious rooms in fairly basic 1- or 2-bedroomed bungalows with bath, Russian fridges, some of which work, radio, TV, water goes off at night, restaurant, bar, nightclub, shop, tour desk open 0800-1300, birdwatching and watersports. Most people prefer to travel on to stay at Playa Girón. **C-E** *Villa Horizontes Playa Girón*, T594118. 292 rooms in bungalows or blocks of rooms, a/c with bath, buffet meals, bar, pool, diving, disco, tourist information desk, shop, car rental (make sure they give you a full tank of fuel as there is no gas station nearby).

Casas particulares **E** *Roberto Mesa Pujol*, Caletón, Playa Larga, T7210. Double rooms, a/c, bathroom shared, hot water, garage, marvellous waterfront location, garden opens onto white sand beach where you can swim, palm trees, volleyball net. **E** *Ernesto Herreras*, Roberto's cousin, another waterfront property, same details. There are 15 in houses and 2 blocks of apartments in Playa Girón. Coming from Cienfuegos, the 1st block is edif 2, the one behind, at an angle, is edif 1. **E** *Hostal Luís*, Carretera a Cienfuegos esq Carretera a Playa Larga, www.cuba.tc/cuplayagiron.html Owned by Luís A García Padrón, 1 bedroom, a/c, hot water, parking, very clean and friendly. **E** *José García Mesa (Tito) y Yaquelín Ulloa Pérez*, Frente al edif 2. Room with bathroom, hot and cold water 24 hrs, parking, secure, very nice people. **E-F** *Mayra Ortega Mejías*, edif 1, Apto 19, neighbour's phone T4252. Only person legally renting 2 rooms, 1 triple, a/c, TV, 1 with 2 double beds, no a/c, share family bathroom. **F** *Maritza López Flores*, edif 1, Apto 21, neighbour's phone T4266. Double bed, clean, nice lady, share her bathroom. **F** *Miguel A Padrón y Odalys Figueredo*, behind edif 1, T4100. Brand new house, exceptionally clean, fan, helpful.

Eating

On the road to Playa Larga is *Rumbos' La Casa del Mar*, bar and grill, open 1000-1800, near here is a place to swim. Ask at the *casa particulares*, about eating in private homes. Lobster and crocodile on the menu.

Cuba

Transport **Taxi** An illegal taxi will charge about US$70 to Havana. Better to get a lift with a tour bus returning to Havana or Varadero, US$25-30. Alternatively, the Playa Larga hotel runs day trips to Havana on Mon and Thu, a 1-way ride will cost about US$25. **Bus** Guagua to Playa Larga from edif 2, 0630, 30-40 mins, 1.45 pesos. To Havana, Fri, Sat, Sun, 10.50 pesos, passes through Playa Larga. Playa Girón and the Bay of Pigs can also be reached by truck or taxi from Cienfuegos (1½ hrs). If you do not want to stay overnight, ask the driver to wait while you visit the beach and tourist complex, and the site of national pilgrimage.

Cienfuegos

Phone code: 432   *Cienfuegos, on the south coast, is an attractive seaport and industrial city, sometimes described as the pearl of the south, and there is a very Caribbean feel to the place. French immigrants at the beginning of the 19th century influenced the development and architecture of the city, which is a fascinating blend of styles.*

Sights There are interesting colonial buildings around the Parque José Martí. On the east side on Calle 29 is **La Catedral Purísima Concepción**, built in 1868, which has a somewhat neo-gothic interior with silvered columns. ■ *Mass is at 0730 and the church is open until 1200.* On the north side, on Avenida 56, is the **Teatro Tomás Terry**, built in 1889 after the death of the Venezuelan Tomás Terry, with the proceeds of a donation by his family. It was inaugurated in 1890 with an audience of 1,200. The lobby has an Italian marble statue of Terry and is decorated with fine paintings and ornate gold work. The interior is largely original with wooden seats. Note the ceiling with exquisite paintings. ■ *Open daily 0900-1800, US$1 including guided tour.* The most notable building on the west side is the **Palacio de Ferrer**, now the **Casa de Cultura Benjamín Duarte**. It is a beautiful building dating from 1894, with a magnificent tower on the corner designed to keep an eye on the port and shipping. Worth seeing for the marble floor, staircases and walls, carved in Italy and assembled at the palace. ■ *Mon-Sat 0830-1900, US$0.50 (including the tower, great views), guided tours in Spanish.*

Excursions On the road to Trinidad between the villages of San Antón and Guaos, 15 km east of Cienfuegos, is the **Jardín Botánico de Cienfuegos**, a national monument founded in 1901 by Edwin F Atkins, the owner of a sugar plantation called Soledad, nowadays Pepito Tey. Atkins turned over 4.5 ha of his sugar estates to study sugar cane, later including other trees and shrubs which could be used as raw materials for industry. Different sections of the gardens are devoted to areas such as medicinal plants, orchids, fruit trees, bamboos and one of the world's most complete collection of palm trees. ■ *0800-1700 every day, US$2.50, children US$1, bar for drinks. The entrance is not well signed, look out for 2 rows of palm trees leading to the garden from the entrance at the road.* **Playa Rancho Luna** is about 18 km from Cienfuegos, near the *Hotel Rancho Luna*. The beach is quite nice but nothing special. The Centro de Buceo Faro Luna runs the diving here. If you continue along the road past the beach you get to the *Hotel Pasacaballo*. There is a jetty here and another further along a rough track to the left, from where you can get a little ferry (US$1) across the mouth of the Bahía de Cienfuegos to the village on the western side, site of the **Castillo de Jagua**. The castle was built at the entrance to the bay in 1733-45 by Joseph Tantete, of France. There is only one entrance via a still-working drawbridge across a dry moat. ■ *0800-1700 every day, entrance US$1 includes a tour.*

Sleeping **A-D** *Mercure Coralia Jagua* (Gran Caribe), Punta Gorda, C 37 No 1, T451003, F667454. 145 a/c rooms with view over bay, singles, doubles and triples available, 4-star, being renovated in 2000 and only half full, comfortable, *Palacio de Valle* restaurant next door, gorgeous decor, live piano music, simple but good food in snack bar, small pool, DHL office in hotel. **D-E** *Hotel Pasacaballo* (Islazul), Carretera a Rancho Luna, Km 22, T96280/90. 150 rooms, not many foreign guests, seaside complex, cafetería. **D-E** *Rancho Luna* (Horizontes), Km 16, T48120/3,

F335057. 225 rooms with balcony, poor service, salt water pool, scuba diving, popular with Canadians in winter. **C** *Faro Luna* (Cubanacán), Carretera Pasacaballo Km 18, Playa Faro Luna, T48162/65. 70 rooms, 4-star, nice, clean, hot water, TV, some staff friendly, aimed at individual travellers who want to dive and sail. **D** *Villa Guajimico*, Carretera a Trinidad Km 42, Cumanayagua, T/F04328125, best to book through Cubamar, in Havana, T662523-4, F333111, cubamar@cubamar.mit.cma.net. Overlooks mouth of Río La Jutía, surrounded by cliffs, caves, coral reefs and small beaches accessible only by boat. Three-star, 51 cabins, some triples, white with red tiled roofs, a/c, bathroom, pool, restaurant, bar, parking, hobicats, good for excursions, but more than anything it is a great dive resort, 3 meals US$31, diving US$25, sailing US$10.

Casas particulares   **E** *Norberto Díaz*, Av 60 3910, entre 39 y 41, T5570. Renovated, turn of the 20th-century house, 3 rooms, a/c, private bath, 24-hr hot water, breakfast US$3, dinner US$6, friendly family, informative. **E** *Raúl Martínez*, Av 54 4923, T9056. Clean, nice courtyard. **E** *Arístides Martínez Pérez*, Av 14 5306, T5397. Room or apartment, hot shower. **E-F** *Delíz y Pedro Sierra*, C 37 3806. 5 a/c rooms, private bathroom, TV, fridge, 24-hr hot and cold water, meals on request, parking, English spoken by well-educated health professionals who are very knowledgeable about their country. **F** *Fela y Pepe*, 35 4605 entre 46 y 48, T9681. Room with 2 beds in spacious annex, a/c, hot water, fridge with drinks, large and tasty dinner US$5, very friendly family. **F** *Dr R Figueroa*, 35 4210, entre 42 y 44, T9108. Price negotiable. Also his brother, *Dr A Figueroa*, Av 56 3927, entre 39 y 41, T6107. Hot shower, nice family, excursions offered, will take you anywhere as long as you pay for the gasoline. **F** *Berta Linares*, 43 3402, T9926. A/c, hot and cold water, parking. **F** *Clara López*, Av 60 4707, entre 47 y 49, T3245. Clean, nice rooms, fan, hot water, good food. Numerous *casas* all down 37 to Punta Gorda, too many to list here. **F** *María Núñez Suárez*, Av 58 3705 Altos entre 37 y 39, T7867. A/c room with adjoining bathroom. Ask her husband and friends to tell you stories about when they were young, fighting with Che in the Sierra Maestra, at the Bay of Pigs or working in Ethiopia.

Eating

The place to go for its style, if not for the food, is *Palacio de Valle*, by *Hotel Jagua*, a building dating from 1894 in a mixture of architectural styles but with Arab influences predominating, incredibly ornate ceilings and other decorations. Open 1145-2300 for food, from 1000 for drinks, meals US$10-22, speciality seafood, upstairs on the roof is a bar with good views and another restaurant in the garden. In the same area on Calle 37, adjacent to the hotel, is *Los Laureles*, where meals are cheaper. Also on 37, opposite the hotel, is *Cueva del Camarón*. Nice place to eat, clean, open 1200-2300, meals around US$10-25. Nearby is *Coradonga*, on 37. Paella restaurant. *37 y 42*, 37 4204 entre 42 y 44, T6027. Open 1100-0100 or 0200, meals around US$6-10. *El Criollito*, 33 5603 entre 56 y 58, T5540. Open 24 hrs, meals US$7-8 include salad, chips, rice and coffee, tasty fish, live music. *La Verja*, Boulevard (Av 54) entre 33 y 35. Open 1200-1800 daily, quite a nice setting but food unappetizing, no fish or chicken, meals around US$6. *El Cochinto*, Prado y 4, near *Hotel Jagua*. Not a great choice but you pay in pesos, open 1900-2100. *1819*, Av Prado. Limited choice, menu in dollars or pesos. Plenty of *paladares* on the Prado. *Coppelia* ice cream, on Prado y 53, open Tuesday-Sunday 1100-2300. *Helados Alondria*, known as *Terry Sodería*, between Terry Theatre and Colegio San Lorenzo. Open 0900-2300, usual full range of ice cream delights.

Transport

Local   Coches: horse-drawn carriages operate in Cienfuegos. **Car hire**: RentaCar is in *Hotel Jagua* car park. *Havanautos* and *Servi Cupet Cimex* is at 37 entre 15 y 17. **Long distance Bus** Terminal at 49 esq Av 56. Tickets may be purchased 1 hr or so in advance from the small office with a brown door, next to the Salón Reservaciones. To **Havana**, daily, 0600, 1000, 1230, 1500, 2350, 5 hrs, US$14. From Havana, 0630, 1220, 1630, 1945, 2130. To **Santiago de Cuba**, every other day, 1700, US$31. To **Camagüey**, every other day, 0800, 1400. To **Trinidad**, 0630, arrive 1200, US$3. To **Santa Clara**, 0700, 0900, 1¼ hrs, US$1.50. The bus station will tell you that there is a bus to **Playa Girón** at 0430 and 1330, but it only goes to Yaguaramas, which is a long way from Playa Girón. It would be unwise to take this hoping for onward transport. There is a daily *Camión* from Av 56, 51, 1 block from bus station, at 1230, unreliable. An illegal taxi can be bargained down to US$25. **Train** Terminal at 49 esq Av 58. To **Havana**, direct or via

Cuba

Santa Clara, on alternate days, 1030, 9 hrs, US$9.50, or 1430, arrive Santa Clara 1700, US$2.10, Havana 2300, US$12.10, all services generally slow and uncomfortable.

Directory   **Banks** The *Banco Financiero Internacional* is on Av 54 esq 29, T/F335603, open 0800-1500 Mon-Fri, 3% commission on TCs. Cash advances on credit cards. **Medical facilities** *International Clinic*, Punta Gorda on C 37 202, opposite the *Hotel Jagua*, T/F8959, offering 24-hr emergency care, consultations, laboratory services, X-rays, pharmacy and other services. Pharmacy on Prado esq Av 60, open 24 hrs.

Santa Clara

Phone code: 422
Population: 200,000
Altitude: 112m

Santa Clara is a pleasant university city in the centre of the island best known for being the site of the last and definitive battle of the Revolution and the last resting place of Che Guevara. It is 300 km from Havana and 196 km from Varadero.

History   In December 1958, before Castro entered Havana, Batista sent an armoured train with military supplies including guns, ammunition and soldiers, to Santiago de Cuba to counter-attack the revolutionaries. However, **Che Guevara** and his troops were hiding in the outskirts of Santa Clara (on the Loma de Capiro and in the university), waiting for the train. On 28 December 1958 it was ambushed in the afternoon. The soldiers on the train surrendered quickly and the fighting for the train was soon over. However, the battle for the city lasted nearly four days, until 1 January 1959 when news spread that Batista had fled the country.

Sights   Heading east on Calle Independencia towards Camajuaní, between Río Cubanicay and the railway line, is the **Monumento a la Toma del Tren Blindado**, where four of the carriages of Batista's troop train are preserved. There is a museum inside the wagons showing weapons and other things carried on the train. ■ *Tue-Sat 0900-1200, 1500-1900, Sun 0900-1200.* There is also a monument on top of **El Capiro**, the hill where Che and his troops waited to attack the train. You can get an excellent view of the city from here, just as Che did in 1958.

A monument to Che has been built in the **Plaza de la Revolución Ernesto Guevara**, with a huge bronze statue of Che on top of a large concrete plinth, a bas-relief scene depicting Che in battle and an inscription of a letter from Che to Fidel. The remains of Che and his comrades who fell in Bolivia have been interred here. It is on Prolongación Marta Abreu after the Carretera Central forks to the north; look out for La Victoria service station, entrance on Calle Rafael Tristá, which runs parallel. Under the monument is a museum, the **Museo Histórico de la Revolución**, with good displays in Spanish and a video about Che's life and role in the Revolution, as well as displays of the battle in Santa Clara. Recommended. ■ *Tue-Sun 0900-1200, 1400-1700, US$2. Bicitaxi US$1 per person from the centre.*

Sleeping   **C** *Villa La Granjita* (Cubanacán), outside town at Km 2.5 on Maleza road, T26053, F28192. 75 rooms in thatched cabañas among fruit trees, cable TV, a/c, phone, pool, bar, shop, buffet restaurant, horses, night-time entertainment around the pool. **D** *Los Caneyes* (Horizontes), Av de los Eucaliptos y Circunvalación, T4512/5, F335009 (outside the city). Thatched public areas with 91 cabins, a/c, hot showers, TV, facilities for disabled people, pool, disco, evening entertainment by the pool, good buffet, supper US$12, breakfast US$4, excellent value, car rental, medical services, shop, tourism bureau, hairdresser, game shooting and fishing can be arranged, popular hotel for tour parties and hunters. **E** *Santa Clara Libre*, central, 1956 concrete building on Parque Vidal with bullet holes on the façade, preserved from the December 1958 battle when some of the police were using the building to defend the city from the revolutionaries, T27548, F5171. A/c and fans, phones, some rooms have TV, water shortages, lifts also erratic, noisy, car rental, observation deck with bar on top of the building, from where you get a great view of the city, cinema and disco, see entertainment.

Casas particulares **E-F** *Santiago Martínez y Lidia Viera*, Bonifacio Martínez 58A altos entre Síndico y Caridad, T26754. One room, hot shower, a/c, fridge, breakfast and dinner US$7 available. **E-F** *Martha Artiles Alemán*, Marta Abreu 56 (altos), entre Villuendas y Zayas, T5008, central but quiet, velo taxi outside. A/c, laundry, clean, breakfast US$3, dinner US$7, parking, watch out for extras on the bill. **E-F** *María and Jorge García Rodríguez*, Cuba 209, Apdo 1, entre Serafín García (Nazareno) y E P Morales (Síndico), T22329. Two a/c rooms, clean, comfortable, within walking distance of the memorial, owners very helpful and informative. **F** *José A Barón Bravo*, San Pedro 103 entre Independencia y Martí, T27937. 2 a/c rooms with private bathroom, José has a video recorder he may lend you to film in and around Santa Clara. **F** *Mercedes*, Máximo Gómez 51 altos, entre Independencia y Martí, contact her son Rafael, T4810, igbautsc@quantum.inf.cu, for collection from bus or train. Central, 3 rooms, each with own bathroom, 2 with own terrace, friendly family, high standard, good cooking. Rafael can give you addresses for houses in Remedios, Caibarién and Trinidad, but he will charge them commission and you will pay US$5 extra.

1878 Colonial, Máximo 8, near the Boulevard, T22428. Offers a variety of creole dishes, **Eating** mainly pork in different styles, bar in the patio. *El Marino*, Paseo de la Paz y Carretera Central, T5594. Seafood, *paellas* a speciality. *La Carreta*, Carretera Central. Creole food in cosy environment. *Mandarín*, Chinese, Carretera Central beyond bus stations, reservations needed with Islazul on Calle Lorda, or T91010, open 1830-2230. *Florida Centre*, southeast of Parque. US$7 for a meal, huge plate of prawns. *Sol de Cuba* on Machado (Candelaria) entre Alemán y Carretera Central, up spiral staircase. Limited menu, US$6-8 for main dish, make sure rice and salad are included, not charged extra, slightly overpriced. *Rincón Criollo*, Cuba 410, entre Serafín Sánchez y Estrada Palma, T71309. Chicken and pork dishes US$2-3, others can be ordered, lunch 1200-1500 by reservation, dinner 1800-2400, food OK, nice surroundings, clean. *La Casona*, Carretera Central 6 entre Padre Chao y Marta Abreu, just by Río Bélico, T5027. Very tasty, nice old house with beautiful tiled floor but no tables or chairs, food served at standing counter to avoid *paladar* regulations, like a takeaway service, friendly hosts, open 1200-2400, very clean, proprietor Orlando Molina is a manager at the nearby *Los Caneyes* hotel restaurant. *La Terraza*, Serafín Sánchez 5 entre Cuba y Colón, T73117. Open 1200-2400, tables on upper storey terrace, main dishes US$10 including rice and salad. *El Rápido* café, on Lorda near Plaza, hot dogs, pizzas, sandwiches, beer, billiards table, only US dollars, also on Marta Abreu, opposite interprovincial bus station, if you have a wait. *Coppelia* ice cream, Colón just off Parque Vidal, corner of Mujica, 1000-2330. *La Marquesina*, 24-hr café next to theatre, pleasant place for a drink, popular with young people at night.

Club Mejunje (mishmash), 2½ blocks west from Parque Vidal, Marta Abréu 107 entre Fabián y **Nightlife** Juan Bruno Zayas, cultural centre and *Casa de la Trova* in a backyard full of artefacts and graffiti-covered walls, opens 1700, Wed-Sun, free, pay for rum in pesos, composers, singers, musicians and friends sing, play and drink together, friendly, welcoming, enjoyable. Larger events are staged in the courtyard, wide variety ranging from concerts to theatre, from shows for kids to shows for gays, 5 pesos for Cubans, US$1 for foreigners. Comedians, rock bands and other entertainers can be seen at Parque del Humor, Chaflán, off Parque Vidal, open Tues-Sun at 1500 and 2000, and on Sun also at 0900. There is a cinema on the ground floor of the *Hotel Santa Clara Libre* on Parque Vidal and the best local disco is in the basement, *Disco Basement*, opens Tuesday-Sunday 2230-0400, US$5. The disco on the 10th floor has a reputation for prostitution; pimps entice tourists with underage prostitutes and then blackmail them.

Islazul is at Lorda 6 entre Parque Vidal y Boulevard, just off Parque Vidal by the theatre, deal- **Tour operators** ing mainly with Cubans, open Mon-Fri 0800-1130, 1300-1545, mostly hotel and restaurant reservations. *Rumbos Cuba* desk in *Café Europa* Independencia y Luís Estévez, tours arranged. Their main office is in *Hotel Los Caneyes*.

Local Horse-drawn **coches**, or **taxi-buses**, go all over town and down Marta Abreu to the **Transport** bus stations, 1 peso. There are also some **buses**, 40 centavos. Bicitaxi costs US$1 to most places in town, fix a price beforehand or they will overcharge you. For **taxi** service call T26856/956, or pick up a private car. **Cars** can be hired from the hotels.

Long distance Bus The municipal bus station for destinations within Villa Clara is on Marta Abreu, T26284, 1 km from centre, on corner with Calle Pichardo, white building. The intermunicipal bus station for long distances is on the same road with Oquendo, T92114, 1 km further out, in blue building. *Víazul* 3 a week, US$18 from Havana, US$33 from Santiago, also on alternate days on the route Varadero-Trinidad. *Astro* to **Havana** 2 daily, at 2350 (arrives 0430) and 1400 (1800), US$12; to **Santiago** alternate days 1900, 12 hrs, US$22.50; to **Cienfuegos** daily at 0710 (arrives 0900), US$2, 1120 (1230), US$2.50, and alternate days at 1440 (1600) US$2.50; to **Trinidad**, 1320, 3½ hrs, US$6; to **Varadero**, daily 0910 (arrives 1300), US$8; to **Camagüey**, alternate days, 1900, 5 hrs, US$10; to **Matanzas**, 1210, 4 hrs; to **Sancti Spíritus**, 0825, 2 hrs. To **Remedios**, 0700, 1435, 1 peso; to **Caibarién**, 1050, 1520, 1.50 pesos, or change at Remedios. Frequent delays, get numbered ticket then stay near departure gates until bus is ready and then join the scrum. **Train** The railway station, T22895, is north of Parque Vidal on Estévez and is much more central than either of the bus stations. There are 4 daily trains to Havana and 1 to Santiago; the *especial* stops here, heading east at 2048 (US$24, 10 hrs), and west at 0253 (US$12, 4 hrs). There is a train to Bayamo/Manzanillo at 0418 (US$18, 8 hrs), which on the return journey to Havana leaves Santa Clara at 0843. Similarly a train to Camagüey leaves at 2327 (US$9, 4 hrs), returning to Havana and passing through Santa Clara at 2338; a slow train, *lechero*, goes to Camagüey at 1415, 6 hrs or so; to Sancti Spíritus at 1319 (US$4, 2 hrs), returning to Havana at 0025. Two daily trains run Cienfuegos-Sancti Spíritus, passing through Santa Clara around 0700 and 1730. None of these times is reliable and the train may not even appear at any time.

Directory **Banks** The *Cadeca* office for changing currency and TCs (4% commission) is at Parque Vidal on the corner of Rafael Tristá and Cuba, T5690. *Bandec*, on the corner of Vidal and Tristá and Cuba, Visa and MC, open Mon-Fri 0800-1400, Sat 0800-1100. *Banco Financiero Internacional*, on Cuba just down from Parque Vidal, is open Mon-Fri 0800-1500, also Visa and MC. **Medical facilities** The best hospital for foreigners is the *Arnaldo Milián Castro Hospital*, at Circunvalación and Av Escambray in the Residencial Escambray area to the south of the town, T72016, 71234. If you need a taxi to take you there, T26956. Ambulance T22259, 23965. There is a 24-hr pharmacy at Luis Estévez 8 on the corner with Boulevard.

Trinidad

Phone code: 419
Population: 60,000

Trinidad, 133 km south of Santa Clara, is a perfect relic of the early days of the Spanish colony: beautifully preserved streets and buildings and hardly a trace of the 20th century anywhere. It was founded in 1514 by Diego Velázquez as a base for expeditions into the 'New World'and Cortés set out from here for Mexico in 1518. The five main squares and four churches date from the 18th and 19th centuries and the whole city, with its fine palaces, cobbled streets and tiled roofs, is a national monument and since 1988 has been a UNESCO World Heritage Site.

Sights On the Plaza Mayor is the cathedral, **Iglesia Parroquial de la Santísima Trinidad**, built between 1817 and 1892. It is the largest church in Cuba and is renowned for its acoustics. On the left of the altar is a crucifix of the brown-skinned Christ of Veracruz, who is the patron of Trinidad. ■ *1130-1300, 1930-2000, mass daily at 2000-2100 when tourists are excluded.*

The **Museo Romántico** has an excellent collection of romantic-style porcelain, glass, paintings and ornate furniture, which belonged to the Conde de Brunet family and dates from 1830-60. ■ *Hernández 52, next to the church of Santísima Trinidad on the main square, T4363. Tue, Thu 0800-2200, Sat-Mon, Wed, Fri 0800- 1800, US$2, no cameras allowed.* **Museo Municipal de Historia**, an attractive building but rather dull displays in eight rooms of scientific, historical and cultural displays, walk up the tower for a good view of Trinidad. ■ *Simón Bolívar 423, T4460.*

Sun-Tue, Thur 0900- 1800, Wed, Fri 0900-2200, US$2. Other museums worth visiting include: the **Museo de Arqueología Guamuhaya**, a general view of developments from precolumbian to post-conquest times, ■ *Simón Bolívar 457, esquina Villena, Plaza Mayor, T3420, Mon, Wed 0900- 2200, Sun, Tue, Thur, Fri 0900-1700, US$2.* **Museo de Arquitectura Colonial** exhibits specifically on the architecture of Trinidad, particularly aspects of the 18th and 19th centuries. ■ *Desengaño 83, T3208, Mon, Thur 0900-2200, Sat, Sun, Tue, Wed 0900-1700, US$2;* **Museo Nacional de Lucha Contra Bandidos,** housed in the old San Francisco convent, exhibits about the campaign in the Escambray mountains. ■ *Hernández esquina Piro Guinart, T4121, Tue, Fri 0900-2200, Wed, Thur, Sat, Sun 0900-1700, US$2.*

Inland from Trinidad are the beautiful, wooded Escambray mountains, whose highest point is **Pico San Juan**, also known as La Cuca, at 1,140m. Rivers have cut deep valleys, some of which, such as the Caburní and the Guanayara, have attractive waterfalls and pools where you can swim. The **Parque Natural Topes de Collantes**

Excursions

Cuba

Trinidad

is a 110 sq km area of the mountains which contains many endemic species of fauna and flora. There are several paths in the area and walking is very rewarding with lovely views and lush forest. There is no public transport but day trips are organized to Topes de Collantes by *Cubatur* or *Rumbos* by jeep or truck, which take in swimming in a waterfall. You can see lots of wildlife, butterflies, hummingbirds and the tocororo, the national bird of Cuba. A great day out. Private tours do not go to the same places as jeep tours, whatever anybody tells you.

Rumbos will also take you to the **Torre de Manaca Iznaga** in the village of the same name about 15 km from Trinidad on the road to Sancti Spíritus, or you can hire a private car to take you for about US$10 or you can catch a train heading to Meyor or Condado, US$7 return, to Manaca Iznaga. The tower, built between 1835 and 1845 is 43.5m high, has seven floors and 136 steps to the top. It was built as a lookout to watch the slaves working in the valley at the sugar mills. It has UNESCO World Heritage status alongside Trinidad city, because of its historical importance. There is a great view of the surrounding countryside, including the **Valle de los Ingenios** (Valley of the Sugar Mills) and the Escambray Mountains as well as the roof tops of the village below. ■ *0900-1600 or 1700, US$2.*

Sleeping
■ *on maps*

C-D *Motel Las Cuevas* (Horizontes), Finca Santa Ana, T4194013/9. On a hill 10 mins' walk from town (good road), with caves in the grounds, nice view of the sea, 114 very comfortable rooms in 60 chalets and apartments with a/c, phone, radio, hot water, and very clean, 2 swimming pools, bar, discotheque from 2200 in cave below reception, entrance US$5, dollar shop, post office, exchange facilities, car and motorbike rental, tour agencies (*Cubatur* and *Rumbos*), restaurant with buffet meals, breakfast US$4, evening meal US$12, not bad. **E** *Finca María Dolores*, Carretera Circuito Sur, T3581, also called *Casa de Campesino*, 3 km from Trinidad on the road to Cienfuegos. In a nice garden setting near Río Guaurabo, 20 brick cabañas, 2 single beds, a/c, shower, clean, restaurant, shop, bar, quiet spot but sometimes noisy in the evening as it is an all-dancing, all-singing tour group destination, horse riding, cock fighting, milk the cows.

Look for the blue triangle symbol on the doors of the registered houses

Casas particulares E-F *Hugo P Bastida Saenz de Buruaga*, Maceo 529, T3186. 1 lovely room, hot shower, breakfast and dinner available. **F** *Casa Colonial Muñóz*, José Martí 401 entre Fidel Clara y Santiago Escobar. Very friendly, English speaking, great house. **E** *Clara M Hernández López*, Antonio Maceo 430 entre Colón y Zerquera, T3531. Triple room, colonial house with courtyard, a/c, bathroom, breakfast US$3, filling, dinner US$5-6, 3 courses, fish feast. **E** *Víctor Valmuseda Díaz*, Frank País 381 entre Simón Bolívar y Zerquera, T4157 (same as Teresa Lería Echerrí). Self contained apartment, kitchen, bathroom, 2 bedrooms, balcony, terrace, sitting room, a bargain for 4 people, clean, central, good.

F *Casa Arandia*, Maceo 438 entre Colón y Rosario Trinidad, T3240. Very nice restored house, guest room has own courtyard and garage, breakfast included. **F** *Gisela Borrell Bastida*, Frank País 486 entre Fidel Claro y Santiago Escobar. Bedroom, dining room, sitting room, own entrance, breakfast included, lots of space. **F** *Dr Rogelio Inchauspi Bastida*, Simón Bolívar 312, T4107. Room with 2 beds, fans, US$6 for meat dinner. **F** *Hildeliza Borrell Faría*, Colón 312 entre Maceo y Jesús Menéndez. 2 rooms each with bathroom, huge house in historic centre, friendly, good English. **F** *Casa Hospedaje Lic Balbina Cadahía Benavente*, Maceo 355 entre Lino Pérez y Colón, CP 62600, T2585. Breakfast US$2, meals US$6, extremely nice family, old colonial house, hot water shower, will arrange trips, friendly, good reports. **F** *Sra Carmelina de la Paz*, Planta Alta, Zona Monumento, Piro Guinart 239, T3620. 1 big room, sleeps 5, plans for more rooms, clean, comfortable, cheap and excellent meals. **F** *Sra Teresa Lería Echerri*, Frank País 389 entre Simón Bolívar y Fco J Zerquera, T4157. 3 blocks from bus terminal, 3 rooms with bathrooms, 2 with noisy a/c, 1 with fan and cooking facilities, some French and English spoken, breakfast and dinner available, huge portions, several good reports. **F** *Maritza Hernández*, Francisco Cadahía 223 entre Colón y Lino Pérez, T3160. She speaks only Spanish, but is fluent in sign language. Family atmosphere, pleasant courtyard, excellent meals, US$7 for dinner, king prawns, huge whole fish etc, fruit and veg from family farm. **F** *Familia Gil Lemes*, José Martí

263 entre Colón y Fco J Zerquera, T3142, next to library. Beautiful colonial house with sumptuous tile decoration, 2 rooms with shared bath, hot water, fans. **F** *Casa de Huésped Mercedes Albalat Milord*, José Martí 330 entre Rosario y Desengaño, T3350. Large house full of antiques, quiet, good food on request, lobster, will guide if you want. **F** *Martha Puig Jiménez*, Francisco Cadahía 236, T2361. Speaks fluent English, meals arranged, free coffee, house and courtyard spotlessly clean, fans, shared bathroom, hot water, friendly, informative, car parking arranged. **F** *Alberto Duarte Reyes*, Ernesto Valdés Muñoz 75A entre Fco Javier Zerquera y P Lumumba, opposite Casa de la Cultura, T3721/3898. Four rooms, 3 bathrooms, friendly. **F** *Bárbara Vásquez* hostal, Simón Bolívar 312 entre José Martí y Maceo, T4107. Clean room, fan, hot water, not far from historic centre. **F** *Rafael Soler Valdés*, *Casa de Huéspedes El Rústico*, Juan M Martínez 54A entre Piro Guinart y Simón Bolívar, 1 block from Plaza Mayor, T2343. 3 rooms, a/c, bathroom shared by all 3, very clean. Rooms on top floor private, roof terrace, view over town, table for breakfast. Rafael was a professional chef and makes fantastic meals on request. Cousins in Santiago, Irma and Umberto, also rent rooms. **F** *Fernando Valero*, José Martí 317, T2107. Two rooms upstairs in separate part of the house, shared bathroom for visitors only, excellent views across rooftops to hills, nice family, good meals US$5, breakfast included. **F** *Sra María Eugenia Vilarino Pedraja*, Camilo Cienfuegos 359 entre Julio Antonia Mella y Jesús Menéndez, T2283. 2 rooms in large house, 1 a/c, shared bathroom, hot water, quiet, comfortable, clean, large meals available, US$3-6, friendly family, tours available. **F** *Hospedaje Yolanda*, Piro Guinart 227 entre Izquierdo y Maceo, opposite the bus station. Very nice rooms in enormous colonial house including 1 up a spiral staircase with 2 double beds, terrace and views of sea and mountains, hot water shower, a/c.

Plaza Mayor, Villena 15, just off Plaza Mayor. Elegant setting with pink tablecloths, lobster US$19, steak and seafood, buffet dinner US$9, open 0830-2400. *El Jigüe*, Real 69 esq Guinart, T4316. Open 1100-1700 only unless a group comes in and then they open at night, live music, good food and atmosphere, most dishes US$7-8, chicken special US$12, lower prices for groups of over 10 people. A *Rumbos* restaurant is *El Mesón del Regidor*, Simón Bolívar 424, opposite Toro, T3756. Open 0900-1800 daily, US$7-8. *Santa Ana*, on Plaza Santa Ana. Open 0900-2200 every day, house special pork US$12, other dishes US$5-8. The price of beer in some restaurants drops from US$2 to US$0.60 after 1700 when the tourist tours leave, but all the state-run places shut then too. *Paladares* include *Daniel's*, Camilo Cienfuegos 20, T4395. Open 1100 until everyone leaves, some courtyard tables, US$5-6 including side dishes, also rooms, a/c, but may be noisy from restaurant music downstairs. *Colonial*, Maceo 402, esquina Colón. Open daily 0900-2200, US$5-6, nice place, locally popular. *La Coruña*, Martí 430. Nice, shady courtyard, good food, pleasant atmosphere. *Sol y Son*, Simón Bolívar 283 entre Frank País y José Martí. Run by English-speaking ex-architect Lázaro, open 1200-2400, in 19th century house, nice décor, courtyard, vegetarian special, excellent pork, tasty stuffed fish around US$10 with drinks, but all meals cost US$3 extra if you go with a guide. *Ruinas de Leonci*, Gustavo Izquierdo entre Simón Bolívar y Piro Guinart. Bar and restaurant, cosy small garden, pleasant wooden tables and chairs inside, live music every night. *Restaurante Don Antonio*, Izquierdo entre Piro Guinart y Simón Bolívar. Open 0800-late, in nice old colonial house with ornate columns and tiled floor, meals around US$6-8. Sit-down pizza restaurant where tourists can pay in pesos on Martí at Parque Céspedes. Lots of pizza stalls on Lino Pérez entre Martí y Maceo, but the best on Francisco Cadahía y Lino Pérez.

Eating

Casa Fisher, Lino Pérez entre Cadahía y José Martí. In a nice old colonial house built in 1870, open 0900-0100. *Bar Daiquirí*, Lino Pérez entre Cadahía y José Martí. Open 24 hrs, also gallery of local art, kicks into life around 0200 when *Las Cuevas* nightclub closes. Unaccompanied Cuban women hanging around outside, beer US$1, mojito US$2, zombie US$4. *Bar Las Ruinas de Segarta*, Alameda entre Márquez y Galdós, in ruined courtyard. Open 24 hrs, also does fried chicken for US$1.50. *La Bodeguita de Trinidad*, Colón entre Martí y Maceo. Not as legendary as its Havana namesake, but a nice little music bar, open courtyard and with quaint sheltered booths for couples, trova group every night, entry free, beer US$1, cocktails US$2. Opposite is *El Jazmín*, bar in leafy courtyard, open late. The *Círculo Social de Obreros*, on Martí, serves rum in pesos, tourists welcome, an authentic drinking experience.

Bars

Cuba

Nightlife **Music and dance** One block from the church is the *Casa de la Trova*, open weekend lunchtimes and evenings, entry US$1 at night, but sometimes free. Excellent live Cuban music with a warm, lively atmosphere. There are mostly Cubans here, of all age groups, and it's a great place to watch, and join in with, the locals having a good time. All drinks paid for in dollars, quite expensive. Another venue for live music is *La Canchanchara*, Villena 70, T4345. Open 0900-1900, cocktails, no food, serves a drink of the same name in small earthenware pots created out of rum, sugar, honey and lime. More touristy than Casa de La Trova (cigar and souvenir shop), but good traditional music at lunchtimes. The disco at *Las Cuevas* (see above) is good, dance merengue and salsa with Cubans between the stalactites. *Casa de la Música*, up the steps past the church in Plaza Mayor, popular disco, full of tourists and Cubans. There is also a nice outdoor bar on the terrace leading up the steps, open till 0200. *Las Ruinas de Bruné*, Maceo entre Colón y Francisco Javier Zerquera. Nightly Afro-Cuban show for tourists in ruined colonial courtyard, very tacky and inauthentic, but worth seeing for the unintentionally hilarious red teletubby running around the stage, who is supposed to be a devil. US$1, open 2100-2400. *La Parranda*, Villena, just off Plaza Mayor. An outdoor bar/music venue, very ad hoc farmyard atmosphere, but excellent live music every night, watched from semi-circle of seats, cocktails US$2, dancing, open from 2200 till late.

Tour operators *Rumbos Cuba* office is on Simón Bolívar 430, T4414, 2264, open daily, can arrange tours and excursions and find out any information for travellers, will renew tourist cards, book flights from Trinidad and deal with Cubana enquiries. Staff speak French, English, German and Italian. *Cubatur*, Maceo esq Zerquera, open 0900-1200, 1300-1800, much the same tours and prices as *Rumbos*.

Transport **Local Car hire:** *Artex*, Lino Pérez y Martí, T2179, hires out microbuses. *Transtur*, Maceo esq Zerquera, T5314, cars and buses. *Transgaviota*, Frank País entre Escobar y Bolívar, T2282, buses, coaches and jeeps. *Nacional Rent A Car* is on José Martí 164 entre Cienfuegos y Lino Pérez, T4101, open 0800-2200 every day, but if all the cars are hired out then it closes, there is only a tiny sign on the door. There is also car hire at *Hotel Las Cuevas* and *Hotel Ancón*.

Long distance Air Daily flights to Havana 1355, US$60, with *Inter-Taca*, in Trinidad reservations can be made through *Rumbos* or *Cubatur*. In Havana, *Taca* is at *Hotel Habana Libre*, T662702, F333728, lacsa@teleda.get.cma.net Flights to Cayo Largo de Sur, US$50. Two daily flights to Varadero. **Bus** Terminal on Piro Guinart entre Izquierdo y Maceo. Bus for **Havana** leaves 1330 every other day, arrives 2230, US$21 a/c, US$17 without a/c; also *Víazul* a/c buses via Cienfuegos (US$6), at 1500, US$25, comfortable, buy tickets in advance if possible. To **Sancti Spíritus**, daily, 0400, 1230, 2000, 2 hrs 40 mins, US$2.50. To **Cienfuegos**, daily, 0900, 1415, US$3. *Camión* (truck) leaves every other day, 0700, 1300, 2 hrs, 2.30 pesos. To **Santa Clara**, daily, 1715, arrive 2030, US$6. Ticket office open daily, 0800-1200, 1330-1700. **Train** The station is south of the town, walk south straight down Lino Pérez until you get to the railway line, turn left and you will see a shelter and an old building, beyond which is the 'office', T3348. Local services only.

Directory **Banks** *Bandec* is on José Martí 264 entre Zerquera y Colón, open Mon-Fri 0800-1700, Sat 0800-1600, will change TCs for dollars and cash advances on credit cards. Cadeca on Martí 164, half a block east of Parque Céspedes, open weekdays 0830-1800, Sun 0830-1200. There are *cambios* in *Hotel Las Cuevas*, *Hotel Ancón* and *Hotel Costa Sur*, where you can change TCs for dollars. **Medical facilities** The *Clínica Internacional*, run by Servimed, is on Lino Pérez 103 esq Anastasio Cárdenas, T3391, modern, with out-patient consultations, laboratory tests, X-rays, pharmacy, dentistry and 24-hr emergency care. A consultation fee is US$25, a call out fee US$40.

Playa Ancón The best beach resort near Trinidad is Playa Ancón, not a town as such, just two resort hotels, with two more under construction. The beach is white sand and clean turquoise water, but sand flies appear after 1600. The best part of the beach is right in front of the *Hotel Ancón*, where there are straw sunshades and beach loungers. The rest of the beach has little shade. People are sometimes disappointed when they come here and expect something more spectacular. There is good **diving** less than 300m offshore.

Sleeping **B** *Ancón* (Gran Caribe), F6120/26. Price room only, though they encourage you to go all-inclusive, including 3 meals, drinks and such extras as snorkels, bicycles and horse riding, 279 rooms, hexagonal pool, good restaurant, snack bar by the pool does filling pizzas US$3-4, hot dogs US$2.50, disco and many facilities, including scuba diving and watersports, best beach here, popular with families. **B-C** *Costa Sur* (Horizontes), T6172. 131 rooms and chalets, run down and shabby, occasional hot water, a/c, bath, phone, balconies with mostly broken chairs, restaurant, good value breakfast buffet for US$3.50, dinner buffet US$10, not bad, bar, beer US$2, mojito US$2, nightclub, pool, shop, car rental and taxis, lovely beach if a bit narrow. The rainforest tour to Topes de Collantes offered by both hotels for US$30 per person is superb (minimum 3 people, but can negotiate higher price for 2), knowledgeable and adaptable guides (see page 203). *Trinidad del Mar*, A new *Cabañas* complex built by Cubanacán, was due to open early 2000 at Punta Mulas, while a large hotel is being built northeast of the *Hotel Costa Sur*.

Eating Apart from the hotels above, there is the *Grill del Caribe* along the beach northwest of the *Hotel Ancón*, which makes a change from hotel food but is poor value, a salad (plate of tomatoes) is US$1.

Sancti Spíritus

Phone code: 41
Population: 80,000

Sancti Spíritus, the provincial capital, is about 80 km northeast of Trinidad and 90 km southeast of Santa Clara. Like Trinidad, the town was founded by Diego Velázquez in 1514 and is one of Cuba's seven original Spanish towns and has a wealth of buildings from the colonial period.

The **Iglesia Parroquial Mayor del Espíritu Santo**, on Plaza Honorato, dates from 1522 when it was a wooden construction. Fray Bartolomé de las Casas gave his famous sermon here, marking the start of his campaign to help the indigenous people. The present building, of stone, replaced the earlier one in 1680, but it is acknowledged as the oldest church in Cuba because it still stands on its original foundations. The church has been declared a National Monument, but it is not always open so you may not be able to look inside. The **Puente Yayabo** is considered a particular feature of Sancti Spíritus and is the only one of its type left on the island. The bridge was built in 1815 with five arches made of lime, sand and bricks. It is now also a National Monument. The river itself has given its name to the *guayaba*, or guava, which grows along its banks, and also to the *guayabera*, a loose man's shirt without a tail worn outside the trousers and without a tie. The former **Teatro Principal** next to the bridge was built in 1839 and was the scene of all the major cultural, social and political events of the city. **Calle Llano** is a twisty street, with cobblestones right to the edge of the Yayabo River. **Parque Serafín Sánchez** is the centre of activity in the city where all major roads converge.

Embalse Zaza is a popular excursion for hiking, birdwatching, shooting and fishing, or just to go to the hotel (see below) and laze around the pool. The hotel can get busy at weekends.

Sleeping There are three hotels in town around Parque Serafín Sánchez which are being refurbished to take foreigners: **E** *Plaza* (Islazul), T27102. 27 rooms in old colonial building, high-ceilings, refurbished in colonial style, some with balconies overlooking plaza, triples available, a/c, TV, bar, restaurant. **F** *Colonial*, Máximo Gómez Norte 23, T25123. 20 rooms, was being renovated 1999 so phone number may change. *Perla de Cuba* (Cubanacán). Beautiful colonial building takes up the whole of the north side of the Parque, under renovation. **Casas particulares** **F** *Sergio Orihuela Ruíz*, room in apartment, Agramonte 61, Apto 5 Altos entre Jesús Menéndez y Llano, CP 60 100, T23828. Opposite Iglesia Parroquial Mayor del Espíritu Santo, English spoken, meets most trains. **F** *Casa du Juan Riscgo*, Independencia 56 entre

Agramonte y Onorato. Two rooms, good bathroom, fan, meals, convenient location. **F** *Ricardo Rodríguez*, Independencia Norte 28. Local taxi driver, friendly, good price. Ask around in the Parque or in restaurants for other accommodation, mostly **E-F**.

Out of town B-C *Rancho Hatuey* (Cubanacán), on hill 4 km north of town, just off Carretera Central at Km 384, T26015, 28315. Modern hotel with 38 overpriced rooms in main building or in cabaña, pool, restaurant, bar, quiet, hunting (shooting ducks and doves). **D-E** *Zaza* (Horizontes), T26012, F668001, 10 km outside the town on the Zaza artificial lake, at Finca San José. 128 a/c rooms with bath, phone, restaurant, bar, nightclub, pool (check quality of water), games room, shop, car rental, medical services, tourism bureau, rather run down but pleasant and good value, shooting and fishing can be arranged. **E** *Los Laureles*, T23913, 5 km north of town. 50 rooms, in semi-detached a/c chalets with solar power, large pool with bar, loud music day and night at weekends, almost exclusively Cuban guests, foreigners are stared at, extravagant Tropicana-style show Sat nights, overpriced, restaurant staff unwelcoming, occasional buses for workers going into town, taxis difficult to organize, private taxi US$10, reasonably convenient for Guayos railway station.

Eating *El Mesón*, on Plaza Honorato del Castillo, in a building which was the first post office, closed Mon. *Rumbos* has the *Saratoga* café on the plaza, serving drinks and snacks, and in 2000 will be opening a restaurant overlooking the river. *El Conquistador*, Agramonte 52 Ote. Delightful building, friendly staff, mainly Cuban dishes, moderate prices, open until 2200, closed Mon. *Shanghai*, Independencia, just off plaza. Chinese, mostly Cuban clientèle. Several *paladares* just across Puente Yayabo, then turn left or right. One of the best is *El Sótano*, Eduardo R Chivas 18C entre 26 de julio y Jesús Menéndez. One of the tables is on a balcony overlooking river (mosquitoes), ask in advance for vegetarian food, large portions, good food, nice family. Street stalls also sell snacks including pizza, which are good value.

Nightlife The *Casa de la Trova Miguel Companioni* is at Máximo Gómez Sur 26, for music. *Bar La Hermina*, over Puente Yayabo on the left, on a boat on the river with tables on the grass. *Bar La Quinta Helena*, on the left just before Puente Yayabo. Large, pleasant terrace, garden, patio, live music and concerts. There is a *Rumbos* Bar on Independencia Norte 32. Most night time activity happens around the Parque.

Transport **Local Taxi**: you can negotiate a private taxi (*particular*) to take you to Trinidad for about US$25 or less, and to Santa Clara for around US$30, depending on the quality of your Spanish. Find a driver outside the bus station.

Long distance Bus: The bus station is 2 km east of town on the Carretera Central. Walk out of town along Cervantes, follow signs to Ciego de Avila along Carretera Central, about 3 blocks past the zoo the bus station is on your right. Buses to **Trinidad** several daily, 70 km, 2 hrs, trucks are often used, crowded and uncomfortable; **Ciego de Avila** 2 daily, 75 km, 2 hrs; **Santa Clara** several daily, 86 km, 2 hrs; also long distance buses to **Havana**, **Holguín** and **Santiago** daily. **Train**: Station at Guayos, 15 km north. Taxi into town US$10. Touts offer transport and accommodation. Daily trains to Camagüey 0900, 1510, 1930, 2-3 hrs, US$6.50. The 'especial' to Havana at 2145, 9 hrs, US$14 and to Santiago at 2213, 8 hrs, US$22.

Directory **Banks** *Banco de Crédito* on the plaza, cash advance on credit cards, open Mon-Fri 0800-1500. *Cadeca*, Independencia 31, just off plaza, for TCs and currency exchange, open Mon-Sat 0830-1800, Sun 0830-1230, commission on TCs is 3% weekdays and 4% at weekends. **Medical facilities** Pharmacy at Independencia Sur 15 opposite the Post Office. **Tour companies & travel agents** On the square, at Cervantes 1, are *Havanatur*, T28308, for flights and tours, *Havanautos*, T28403, for car hire, and *Islazul*, T26390, for hotels and tours, but mostly for Cubans.

Ciego de Avila

Ciego de Avila was founded in 1849, and consequently is short of fine historical buildings and monuments. It is an agricultural market town with a large thermal electricity plant. The main road from Havana to Camagüey passes straight through the middle of town; most people just keep going. The main square is the **Parque Martí**, with a church and the former town hall, **Ayuntamiento**, built in 1911, and now the provincial government headquarters.

Phone code: 33
Population: 85,000

E *Hotel Ciego de Avila*, Carretera de Ceballos, T28013, 2 km out of town. 144 rooms in a modern, 5-storey block, pool, taxis, Havanautos car hire, good food. E *Santiago-Habana*, Chicho Valdés y Honorato del Castillo, T25703. 76 rooms on the main road through town, run down but convenient.

Sleeping

Usual crop of low quality state run restaurants, including: *Mesón El Fuerte*, Av Las Palmas on Plaza Camilo Cienfuegos; *Moscú*, Chicho Valdés 78, closed Wed; *Solaris*, on west side of Parque Martí, top floor of 12-storey building; *El Colonial*, Independencia 110, nice courtyard; *La Romagnola*, Chicho Valdés y Marcial Gómez, Italian; *Cafetería 12 Plantas*, Parque Martí, same building as *Solaris*, 24-hr *Rumbos* bar serving fried chicken and cold beer. *Paladares* are springing up and it would be best to investigate some of these. *Casa de la Trova*, at Libertad 130 y Simón Reyes.

Eating

Car hire: *Havanautos* is at *Hotel Ciego de Avila*. **Air** There is an airport at **Ceballos**, 24 km north of Ciego de Avila, Aeropuerto Máximo Gómez (AVI), which receives weekly scheduled flights from European cities, as well as twice weekly flights from Havana with *Cubana*. Charter flights also use this airport to get holiday-makers out to the resort hotels on Cayo Coco. **Bus** The bus station is on the Carretera Central just east of the zoo. Two daily buses to **Sancti Spíritus**, 1¼ hrs, US$3. There are buses to all the places on the main road from Havana to Santiago and a lot of others besides, such as Manzanillo, Holguín and Niquero. However, by the time the long distance buses get here they are nearly always full. **Train** Three trains daily to Havana. Most trains go through at night to **Holguín**, **Matanzas** and **Santiago**.

Transport

Airlines *Aerotaxi*, airport, T23937. *Cubana* Chicho Valdés 83 entre Maceo y Simón Reyes, T25316.

Directory

Cayo Coco

Cayo Coco is a large island, 374 sq km, of mostly mangrove and bush, which shelter many migratory birds as well as permanent residents. The island is connected to the mainland just north of Morón by a 27 km causeway across the Bahía de Perros. There is an airstrip for an air taxi service from Havana, but international flights and other large aircraft come in to the airport north of Ciego de Avila. The Atlantic side of the island has excellent beaches, particularly **Playa Los Flamencos**, with some 5 km of white sand and shallow, crystalline water. At certain times of the year you will see flamingos, after whom the beach is named. Cayo Coco is very isolated and nearly all foreigners are here on a package of a week or so and do not go far. Marina Puertosol offers deep sea fishing and there is good diving. There are large, luxury resorts and plans to build an average of 1,000 hotel rooms a year, all four- or five-star, until Cayo Coco has 16,000 and the other cays have a further 6,000.

Phone code: 33

    Cayo Guillermo, a 13 sq km cay with 5 km of beach, is connected to Cayo Coco by a causeway and there are plans to build a 35-km causeway to link it with Cayo Santa María to the west. Cayo Guillermo is protected by a long coral reef which is good for diving with plentiful fish and crustaceans, while on land there are lots of birds. Sand dunes, covered in palms and other vegetation, are believed to be in the highest in the Caribbean.

Cuba

Sleeping **On Cayo Coco AL-A** pp *Hotel Club Tryp Cayo Coco*, T301311 (locally), 333202, F333292 (in Havana), tryp@teleda.get.cma.net, www.tryp.es Spanish and Cuban, all-inclusive, the largest complex in Cuba, 1,000 rooms including a club, with a 250-room aparthotel and convention centre, like a village, shops, supermarket, pharmacy, disco, bowling alley, restaurants, bars, piano bar, snack bars, pools, watersports (extra charge for motorized watersports), volleyball, floodlit tennis, badminton, beach a bit disappointing but facilities well planned. *Sol Club Cayo Coco* (Cubanacán), T301280, F301285. All-inclusive, 270 rooms, lots of sports and entertainment for adults and children, several restaurants, disco, gym, pool. *Meliá Cayo Coco* 250 rooms, some round a lagoon, 5-star hotel. **On Cayo Guillermo** *Venta Club Gayo Guillermo*, Italian run, 220 rooms, all-inclusive, gourmet restaurant, *Bodeguita de Guillermo* overlooking beach. *Sol Club Cayo Guillermo* (Gran Caribe), T301760, F301748. 264 rooms in cabins with red tiled roofs, all the same facilities and all-inclusive luxury. *Iberostar Daiquirí* (Gran Caribe), T301650. Opened end-1998, 312 rooms. *Meliá Cayo Guillermo*, 318 rooms, opened 1999.

Transport Only tour buses go to Cayo Coco, there are no public buses and a checkpoint at the beginning of the causeway effectively prevents Cubans without permission from visiting the cay. The airport receives flights from Havana and Varadero. A new, international airport is under construction.

Camagüey

Phone code: 322
Population: 772,000

Camagüey has been politically and historically important since the beginning of the 16th century and still has a lot of well-preserved colonial buildings, most dating from the 18th and 19th centuries. Many generations of revolutionaries have been associated with Camagüey and several key figures are commemorated, the most notable being Ignacio Agramonte, who was killed in action in 1873.

History It was originally called Puerto Príncipe, until 9 June 1903. The village of Santa María de Puerto del Príncipe was first founded in 1515 at Punta del Guincho in the Bahía de Nuevitas but moved several times until it was finally established between the Río Tínima and the Río Hatibonico. Moving inland was no protection against pirate attacks. It was the target of the Englishman Henry Morgan in 1668 and of French pirates led by François Granmont in 1679. Architects took the precaution of designing the layout to foil pirate attacks. No two streets run parallel, to create a maze effect, which is most unlike other colonial towns built on the grid system.

Sights **Nuestra Señora de la Merced**, a National Monument on Av Agramonte on the edge of the Plaza de los Trabajadores, was built in 1747 as a church and convent, the catacomb can still be seen. The original wooden cross on the bell tower was moved into the catacombs in 1999. On the walls are 17th and 18th-century paintings, but the most important treasure in the church is the Santo Sepulcro constructed in 1762 with the donation of 23,000 silver coins. **San Juan de Dios**, another National Monument, was built in 1728 as a church with a hospital attached, the first hospital in the village for men which also contained a home for the aged. Apparently this is the only church in Latin America which has the Holy Trinity as its central image. On 12 May 1813 the body of Ignacio Agramonte was deposited in the hospital for identification before being taken to the cemetery. There are plans to turn it into a luxury hotel.

    Museo Provincial Ignacio Agramonte, first built as a cavalry barracks in 1848 was inaugurated on 23 December 1955 (the anniversary of Agramonte's birth). There are exhibitions of history, natural history, paintings and furniture of the 17th and 18th centuries, but nothing special. ■ *Av de los Mártires 2 esquina Ignacio Sánchez. Tue-Sat 0900-1700, Sun 0800-1200, US$2.* At the **Museo Casa Natal Ignacio Agramonte** you have an obligatory guided tour in Spanish with exhaustive explanation of every single document on display. Only for serious students of revolutionary history. Ignacio Agramonte y Loynaz, a cattle rancher, one of the national heroes of the struggle against the Spanish, was born here on 23 December 1841. ■ *Av Ignacio Agramonte 49, T97116. Tue-Sat 1000-1800, US$2.*

Sleeping

C *Villa Maraguán* (Cubanacán), Circunvalación Este, on outskirts, T72017, 72170. Three-star, 32 rooms and 2 suites with terrace, 3 bars, restaurant, cafetería, car rental, pool, open air night time entertainment when tour parties are staying, video and games room, squash, billiards, table tennis, volleyball, children's playground, horse riding, medical services.

D *Hotel Camagüey* (Horizontes), Av Ignacio Agramonte, T72015/82490. Good condition, modern, Soviet influenced architecture, pool, disco show, bar in the lobby and on 2nd floor, cafetería, buffet restaurant US$10, car hire. **D-E** *Gran Hotel* (Islazul), Maceo 67, entre Ignacio Agramonte y General Gómez, T92093/4, comazul@ teleda.get.cma.net. Colonial style, built 1939, renovated 1997, central, swimming pool, restaurant on top floor, good view, also cafetería and snack bar.

E *Plaza* (Islazul), Van Horne 1, entre República y Avellaneda, T82413, 82457. 67 rooms with TV, fridge, colonial building right by railway station, the nicest, more expensive rooms face the front, with balcony, but rooms at the back are away from traffic noise, mediocre restaurant, bar, Altamira travel agency. **E-F** *Puerto Príncipe*, Av de los Mártires 60 y Andrés Sánchez, La Vigía (in town), T82469/82403, near museum and railway station. 77 rooms, a/c, bar, very slow restaurant, choose a room away from the nightclub on roof open until 0130 every night.

F *Colón*, República 472 entre San José y San Martín, T83346, 83368. Old style built in 1920s, central, average restaurant, snack bar better, 2 grades of rooms, the better ones have a/c, ice box, TV, friendly staff. **F** *Isla de Cuba*, República y San Estéban, T91515. In the heart of the city, 43 rooms, 2 grades.

Casas particulares F *Casa Blanca*, San Ramón 201 altos, entre Heredia y Santa Rita, T93542. Family of 3 generations, English spoken, 2 rooms, good bathroom but poor water pressure, noisy but efficient a/c, 5 mins' walk to railway station, meals and drinks available at good prices, laundry service. **F** *El Hostal de Lita*, Padre Olallo (Pobre) 524, entre Ignacio Agramonte y Montera, T53322. Beautiful colonial house, US$7 for huge meal. **F** *Cachita*, Santa Rosa 7 entre Santa Rita y San Martín, T97782. Nice colonial house near the centre, friendly family. **F** *Deysi Leyva*, Santa Rita 16A, 1st floor, entre República y Santa Rosa, T93348. Extremely nice. **F** *Teresa Santana Ortega*, Santa Rita 37 entre Santa Rosa y San Ramón, T97214. Large a/c room with shared bathroom welcoming, friendly, large busy house with pleasant patio, great breakfast.

Eating

State-run restaurants, apart from those in hotels, include *Rancho Luna*, on Plaza Maceo, open 1200-1400, 1800-2200, and *La Volanta*, on Parque Agramonte, open 1200-2300, both of which offer Cuban food and you will be asked to pay in dollars. You can pay in pesos at *Pizzería La Piazza* on Agramonte on the corner with Maceo, but there may be a queue. On the Plaza de San Juan there are the *Parador de los Tres Reyes* and the *Campana de Toledo*, 2 small colonial-style restaurants serving Spanish food, pleasant, live music, meals from US$8. Near the railway station there is *El Paradero* cafetería and bar open 24 hrs and a bakery and cafetería also open 24 hrs. *Bar El Cambio* on Parque Agramonte is good.

Nightlife

Every Sat night a *Noche Camagueya* is held along República, when the street is closed to traffic and there is music everywhere and traditional food. The **Ballet de Camagüey**, ranked 2nd in the country after Havana's ballet company, often performs at the Teatro Principal, on Padre Valencia 64, T93048. Folk music is played at the *Casa de la Trova*, on the west side of Parque Agramonte between Martí and Cristo, closed Mon.

Tour operators

Rumbos, López Recio 108, T94807, 97229, Mon-Fri 0800-1800. Many tours available, including to Cayo Sabinal and Santa Lucía.

Transport

Local Car hire: *Havanautos* is at *Hotel Camagüey*. There are Servi Cupet gas stations by the river on Carretera Central with Av de la Libertad, and a couple of blocks further south on the other side of the Carretera Central. **Taxi**: service T81247/98721. For a tourist taxi T72428. Bicitaxis charge about US$1 per person, fix price in advance.

Long distance Air Ignacio Agramonte International Airport (CMW) is 9 km from the centre on the road to Nuevitas, T61010. *Cubana* flies daily from Havana and once a week from London Gatwick. There are also charter flights from Toronto and Europe depending on the season. **Bus** Ticket agency, T71602. The Interprovincial bus station is southwest of the centre along the Carretera Central. Three buses a day to **Havana**, daily to **Holguín, Manzanillo, Santiago de Cuba, Cienfuegos, Guantánamo, Matanzas, Sancti Spíritus, Las Tunas, Bayamo, Ciego de Avila** and **Baracoa**. **Train** Railway station, T92633/81525. Train ticket agency, T83214. Foreigners pay in dollars at Ladis office upstairs above the main ticket office opposite *Hotel Plaza*. Trains to **Havana** daily at 2219 and Mon, Wed and Fri at 1933, 10 hrs, US$21, stopping at **Guayos** (for Sancti Spíritus and Trinidad) at 2230, US$6.50. To **Bayamo** and **Manzanillo** at 0527. To **Holguín** at 2322. To **Morón** at 1208. The 'special' from Havana gets in to Camagüey at 0048 on its way to Santiago, 6 hours, US$12.50 and Guantánamo.

Directory **Airlines** *Cubana* is at República 400 esq Correa, open Mon-Fri 0700-1500, Sat 0700-1100, T92156/91338. **Banks** The *Banco Financiero Internacional* is on Plaza Maceo. There is a *cadeca* on República entre Primelles y Santa Rita. **Medical facilities** 24-hr pharmacy on the corner of Avellaneda y Primelles.

Playa Santa Lucía

Phone code: 32 **Santa Lucía** is a beach resort 112 km northeast, or two hours by bus, from Camagüey, where the sand stretches some 20 km along the northern coast near the **Bahía de Nuevitas**. This is a beautiful beach, protected by an offshore reef which contains over 50 species of coral and is much sought after by divers. The water is clear and warm, with an average temperature of 24°C. Diving is run by Marlin, which also has an underwater photo and video centre, T36404. There are 37 dive sites at depths of 5-40m in the area including a daily shark feeding site where up to 20 sharks congregate; some of them swim in between the divers. Contact Shark's Friends dive centre. It is a lovely place to come and relax but be aware that it is remote, there is no real town as such, and people who stay here are on all-inclusive package tours for a week or so and see little of Cuba. 8 km from Santa Lucía is **Playa Los Cocos**, which is even better than Santa Lucía. The sand here is very white and the water crystal clear. There are some bars and seafood restaurants. Across the channel, west of Playa Los Cocos, is **Cayo Sabinal**, reached by road from Nuevitas or by boat, with *Seafaris*, from Santa Lucía. There are beautiful beaches of white sand which are practically deserted and the cay is a wildlife reserve housing the largest colony of pink flamingos in the Caribbean, plus many other birds which are rare or endangered elsewhere.

Sleeping The resort is part of the Cubanacán group (www.cubanacan.cu), including joint venture hotels, restaurants, shopping centre, watersports, discos and other amenities. All the hotels are all-inclusive and prices are per person sharing a double room. **A-C** *Cuatro Vientos*, T36160, F334533, aloja@cvientos.stl.cyt.cu 404 rooms and 8 suites, 4-star, a/c, TV, all facilities, night club, tennis, volleyball, bicycles, marina, scuba diving. **B** *Club Mayanabo*, T36184-5, F365176, aloja@mayanabo.stl.cyt.cu Three-star, 212 rooms and 13 suites, a/c, pool, daily organized activities, night club on the jetty, restaurant, bars, cafeteria, car and bicycle hire, tennis, gym, games room, beach volleyball, watersports include windsurfing, catamarans and snorkelling, fishing or horse riding can be arranged. **B-C** *Vita Club Caracol*, T365158-9. Three-star, sea front in large gardens, 150 2-storey cabañas with sea view, a/c, TV, ice box, phone, free form pool with children's area, jacuzzi, disco, buffet restaurant, snack bar, tennis, volleyball, aerobics, bicycles, table games, watersports. **B** *Gran Club Santa Lucía*, T365146-8, aloja@coral.stl.cyt.cu Joint venture with La Cascina of Italy, 3-star, 108 rooms on the beach, 144 garden rooms and 108 suites, a/c, TV, buffet and à la carte restaurant, snack bar, disco, pool with children's area and swim-up bar, games room, bicycle and scooter hire, lots of activities and trying to cater for all ages. **D** *Villa Tararaco*, T36262/36310. Two-star, 30 rooms, TV, restaurant, bar, live music, car hire, diving and watersports.

State-run restaurants: *Las Brisas*, T36109, Creole; *Bonsai*, T36109, Chinese; and *Luna Mar*, **Eating**
T36284, Italian. There are also *paladares* where you can eat for a more reasonable price.

Air International flights use the airport near Camagüey, but there is a small airstrip, Joaquín **Transport**
de Agüero, for Aerotaxi services.

Medical services *Clínica Internacional*, T36203. **Tour operators** *Cubatur*, T36291. *Rumbos*, T36106. **Directory**

Holguín

Holguín was founded in 1545. It is known as the 'city of the parks', four of which, *Phone code: 24*
Parque Infantil, **Parque Carlos Manuel de Céspedes**, the **Plaza Central** and *Population: 250,000*
Parque José Martí, lie between the two main streets: Antonio Maceo and Libertad
(Manduley). There is a statue of **Carlos Manuel de Céspedes** in the park named
after him: he is remembered for having freed his slaves on 10 October 1868 and start-
ing the war of independence. The Plaza Central is named after **General Calixto
García Iñiguez** (statue in the centre), who was born in Holguín in 1837 and took
part in both wars of independence. He captured the town from the Spanish in 1872
and again occupied it in 1898 after helping the US forces defeat the colonial power in
Santiago de Cuba. His birthplace on Calle Miró 147, one block from the plaza, is now
a museum, **Casa Natal de Calixto García**. ■ *Mon-Fri 0800-1700, Sat 0800-1300,
US$1*. On the north side of the square is the **Museo Provincial**, built between
1860-1868 and now a National Monument. The most important item on display
here is the Hacha de Holguín, a precolumbian axe head carved with the head of a
man, found in 1860 on one of the hills around the city and believed to be about 500
years old. It has become the symbol of Holguín. ■*Mon-Fri 0900-1700, Sat
0900-1300, US$1, US$3 with camera.*
 Above the city is **La Loma de la Cruz**, a strategic hill which used to have a cross on
top until Hurricane Georges blew it down in 1998. On 3 May 1790, a Franciscan priest,
Antonio de Alegría, came with a group of religious people and put up the cross. In
1929 stone steps were begun up the hill, which were finished 3 May 1950. Every 3 May
locals celebrate the Romerías de la Cruz de Mayo. They light candles and offer coins.

D-E *Pernik* (Islazul), T481011. Near Plaza de la Revolución on Av Jorge Dimitrov y Av XX **Sleeping**
Aniversario. 202 rooms, mostly overnighters passing through, shops, bar, restaurant, empty
swimming pool, TV, a/c, nice view from top floor rooms, blue furniture, small bathrooms,
adequate. **D-E** *Villa El Bosque* (Islazul), T481012, just off Av Jorge Dimitrov. 69 rooms in
spread out villas, patio garden, fridge, basic shower room, TV, a/c, also 2 suites, **C**, good security, car rental, large pool, *El Pétalo* disco, popular. **D-E** *El Mirador de Mayabe* (Islazul),
T422160, T/F425347, outside the town, 24 rooms in cabins under the trees, tiled floors, a/c,
TV, wooden furniture, fridge, hot water, adequate bathroom, quiet, also a suite and **C** 4
rooms in a house at the top of the hill with a fantastic view.

Casa particular E *Barbara Cuenca Sánchez*, Narciso López 48B entre Luz Caballero y
Aricochea, walking distance from town centre. **F** *Eddy G Osorio*, Frexes 166 entre Morales
Lemus y Narciso López. With bath, very good breakfast for US$1.50. **F** *Rolando Torres
Cardet*, José Antonio Cardet 202 entre Frexes y Aguilera, T425619. Very clean, a/c, small
breakfast included, free coffee, central. **F** *Rosalía Días V*, Frexes 176 entre Miró y Morales
Lemus, T423395. Excellent location, big room with bathroom, a/c, run by charming elderly
lady, food available. **F** *Evaristo Bofill and Mirtha Lago*, Luz Caballero 78 Altos entre Miró y
Morales Lemus. 2 large rooms, very clean, private bathroom, a/c, terrace, friendly and helpful
family who make you feel at home and like a good laugh.

There are several *paladares*. *Aurora*, on Martí, has a good reputation and is popular. *Jelly* **Eating**
Boom, also on Martí, near the cemetery, is supposed to be the best in town; ask around for
others as they change quickly. *Pizzería Roma* on Maceo with Agramonte at the corner of

Parque Céspedes, is state-run. *La Begonia*, is a Rumbos *cafetería* on the Plaza Central. Outdoors under a flowering creeper, very pretty, good for a Mayabe beer, meeting place for *jineteras*. *El Tocororo*, across the square, also Rumbos but toasted sandwiches are cheaper here, open 24 hrs, wooden sculpture above door. *Cafetería Cristal*, corner of plaza with Libertad. Open 24 hrs, usual range of fastish food. For ice cream, **Coppelia** is on Parque Peralta. The 2 main hotels are rather far away from the restaurants and their own food is not recommended. *Taberna Pancho* is in the area, though, on Av Jorge Dimitrov, round the corner from the *Pernik* and serves beer and a reasonable burger.

Transport **Local** There is very little motorized public transport. The city is choked with *bicitaxis*, bicycles with an extra wheel and seat on the side, or cart behind, or horse drawn buses and taxis, charging 50-80 centavos. Out of town people wait at junctions for the *Amarillos* (traffic wardens dressed in yellow) to stop any truck or large vehicle and bundle on as many passengers as possible. **Long distance** **Bus**: The interurban bus terminal, notable for the number of horses, rather than vehicles, is on Av de los Libertadores after the coffee roasting plant and opposite the turning to Estadio Calixto García. The interprovincial bus terminal is west of the centre on the Carretera Central. A *colectivo* to Las Tunas costs 20 pesos.

Directory **Airlines** *Aerotaxi*, T462512. *Cubana* is in Edif Pico de Cristal, Libertad esquina Martí, Policentro, T425707, F46811. *LTU* at the airport, F335360. **Banks** *Bandec*, Arias 159, open Mon-Fri 0800-1500. **Medical facilities** The main hospital is west of the town centre on Av V I Lenin. There are medical services at the hotels *Pernik* and *El Bosque*.

Guardalavaca

Phone code: 24 Guardalavaca has been developed as a tourist resort along a beautiful stretch of coastline, indented with horseshoe bays and sandy beaches. The resort is in two sections: the older part is rather like a village, apartments for workers are here and there are a few shops, discos, bank, restaurant and bus stop, while newer hotels further west on the beach Estero Ciego (also referred to as Playa Esmeralda), are very isolated and there is nothing to do outside the hotels. There is a reef offshore for diving, which is very unspoilt and has a lot to offer.

Excursions The lagoon in the **Bahía de Naranjo** has a small marina, where sailing trips and fishing expeditions can be arranged. Near the mouth of the lagoon is an aquarium, 10 minutes by boat from the dock, with dolphins and a sea lion, and a restaurant.

West along the coast, **Playa Pesquero** is a lovely sandy beach, the east end is better for children as there are strong currents and deceptive sand bars to the west. There is a lifeguard on duty even out of season. The 309-room LTI *Costa Verde Beach Resort* (Gaviota), and the *Sol Club Playa Pesquero*, opened in 1999-2000.

A few km from Guardalavaca on a hill with a wonderful view, is the **Museo Aborigen Chorro de Maita**, a small but well-presented museum displaying a collection of 56 skeletons dating from 1490-1540, exactly as they were found. One is of a young Spaniard of about 22 years of age with his arms crossed for a Christian burial, but the rest are Amerindians, buried in the Central American style, lying flat with their arms folded across their stomachs. ■ *Tue-Sat 0900-1700, Sun 0900-1300, US$1 per photo, plus US$5 per film, small shop with souvenirs.*

The **Museo Indocubano Bani**, Gen Marrero 305 y Av José Martí, in **Banes** has a good collection of pre-columbian artifacts, probably the best in Cuba. ■ *Tue-Sat 0900-1700, Sun 0800-1200, US$1.* The town of Banes was originally the site of the Bani chieftancy and the museum contains treasures discovered by the many archaeological digs in the area.

Sleeping **L-B** *Delta Las Brisas* (Cubanacán), T30218, F30018, reserva@deltsbsa.gvc.gyt.cu All-inclusive, 349 good sized sea view or inland rooms, a/c, satellite TV, phone, balcony, and 84 mini-suites, 3 restaurants, 3 bars, non-motorized watersports, small man-made beach, nice pool, organized entertainment, gym, tennis, bicycles, kids kamp, tour desk, car rental. **AL-C** *Atlántico* (Cubanacán), T30180/30280, F30200, recep@hatlant.gvc,cyt.cu Best position right on beach, 264 rooms with shower, long dark corridors, adequate but nothing special for the price, good food, set meal times, OK for vegetarians, bicycles, windsurfing, pedalos, sailing, diving, snorkelling, gym, entertainment, shops, pool, tennis. **A** *Villa Turey*, opposite bus stop. Not on beach, spread out villas and apartments around pool, 136 rooms, 3 suites (with 2 bedrooms, 2 bathrooms upstairs, sitting room, kitchenette and toilet downstairs), large rooms, cupboards, TV, safe box, balconies, 2 restaurants, shop, short walk to beach through other hotels. **AL-C** *Club Amigo Guardalavaca* (Cubanacán), T30121, F30221, recep@hguard.gvc.cyt.cu 234 smallish rooms, TV, basic bathroom, shower, outside a/c, run down, tennis courts but no balls.

Meliá Río de Oro, T30090-4. All-inclusive, 5-star, 292 junior suites, a/c, TV, balcony, several restaurants, snack bars and bars, pool, tennis, football (grass pitch), beach volley ball, bicycles, scooters and cars for rent, windsurfing, catamarans, sailing school, snorkelling, dive centre, gym, sauna, massage, lots of organized entertainment. *Sol Club Río de Luna* (all-inclusive), T300304, F30035. Four-star and sister hotel next door, *Sol Río de Mares*, T337013, 30060-4 F30065. Four-star, half board only, most people on discounted packages, comfortable, open, well-designed for ventilation, not so good when it rains, pool, restaurants, bars, organized entertainment, lovely beach, diving and other watersports, shade, sunbeds US$2.

6 km along the coast at Estero Ciego are the best hotels in the area

Eating *El Cayuelo*, short walk along coast from *Las Brisas*, good for lobster, open daily 0900-2300. Most hotel restaurants in the hotels offer buffet meals which get very dull after a few days. There are restaurants in the Centro Comercial but no *paladares* in the area.

Watersports There are dive shops on the beach near the *Atlántico* and the *Sol Río de Mares*, offering courses and fun dives, no jetty so you have to swim and carry tank and gear out to boat. Good, well-maintained equipment and safety record. Safety not so good with other watersports, where life-jackets are not always offered or worn. The lifeguard on duty is not always in his chair. Hobie cats US$10 per hour, windsurfers and kayaks US$5 per hour, pedalo bikes US$2 per hour.

Santiago de Cuba

Santiago de Cuba is one of the oldest towns on the island, protected from the sea in an attractive bay surrounded by mountains. It is a lively city with plenty of music and other cultural activities. It is the place to come for carnival in July but there is lots going on at other times of the year too. It is easy to get out of the city for excursions to beaches, historical or interesting geological sites. Santiago, Cuba's second city, is not a colonial gem along the lines of Havana or Trinidad, but it does have an eclectic range of architectural styles from colonial to art deco. The city centre is cluttered, featuring many beautiful pastel coloured buildings in better condition than many of those in the capital.

Phone code: 226

Ins and outs

Getting there Santiago can be reached by air, train or bus. All major transport routes may be fully booked.
See page 224 for International and domestic *Cubana* flights arrive at the **Antonio Maceo airport** (SCU), 8 km
further details south of the city on the coast. Official and unofficial taxis around US$5-8, depending on the company and the distance. The long distance bus terminal is to the north of the city, by the Plaza de la Revolución. Outside are taxis, *colectivos*, trucks, buses and horse-drawn *coches*. The new railway station is more central, opposite the rum factory on Av Jesús Menéndez, and within walking distance of many **casas particulares** and some hotels in the centre.

Getting around Urban buses run until about 0100 and cost 20 centavos. There are also coches, 1 peso, motorbikes, US$1, and *bicitaxis*, US$0.50, for short journeys around town. Plaza Marte is a central hub for lots of local transport. For excursions there are buses and/or trucks on some routes out of town but it is easier to negotiate a day trip with a driver who can take you exactly where you want to go. Make sure everything is agreed and clear before you set off, as drivers have a reputation for moving the goalposts when you are a long way from base. Car hire is available if you want to drive yourself.

History Santiago de Cuba was one of the seven towns (*villas*) founded by Diego Velázquez. It was first built in 1515 on the mouth of the Río Paradas but moved in 1516 to its present location in a horseshoe valley surrounded by mountains. It was Cuba's capital city until replaced by Havana in 1553 and capital of Oriente province until 1976. During the 17th century Santiago was besieged by pirates from France and England, leading to the construction of the Castillo del Morro, still intact and now housing the piracy museum. Because of its location, Santiago has been the scene of many migratory exchanges with other countries; it was the first city in Cuba to receive African slaves, many French fled here from the slaves' insurrection in Haiti in the 18th century and Jamaicans have also migrated here from the neighbouring island. Santiago is more of a truly ethnic blend than many other towns in Cuba. It is known as the 'heroic city' (*Ciudad Héroe*) or '*capital moral de la Revolución Cubana*'. One of Cuba's foremost revolutionaries of the 19th century, **General Antonio Maceo**, is honoured in the **Plaza de la Revolución**, to the northeast of the centre, with a dramatic monument made of galvanized steel in searing, solid Soviet style, and a gargantuan bronze statue of the general on horseback surrounded by huge iron machetes.

Sights **Parque Céspedes** is in the centre of town and everything revolves around it. Most of the main museums are within easy walking distance. The *Hotel Casa Granda* flanks the entire east side of the small park. The **Cathedral**, Santa Iglesia Basílica Metropolitana, is on the south side, entrance on Félix Peña. The first building on the site was completed in 1524, but four subsequent disasters, including earthquakes and pirate attacks meant that the cathedral was rebuilt four times. ■ *0800-1200 daily, services Mon, Wed 1830, Sat 1700, Sun 0900, 1830.*

The **Cementerio Santa Ifigenia**, northwest of the city, features **José Martí's** mausoleum, a huge structure with a statue of Martí inside, designed to receive a shaft of sunlight all morning. Martí is surrounded by six statues of women, representing the six Cuban provinces of the 19th century. Also in the cemetery is the grave of **Frank País**, a prime mover in the revolutionary struggle and other notable figures such as Céspedes, the Bacardí family and the mother and widow of Maceo. There is a monument to the Moncada fallen and the tomb of Cuba's first president, Tomás Estrada Palma. Well worth a visit. ■ *Av Crombel, Reparto Juan G Gómez. US$1, extra US$1 to take pictures, price includes guided tour in Spanish and English.*

Museums Of the several museums, the best is the **Museo de Ambiente Histórico Cubano**, located in Diego Velázquez' house (the oldest in Cuba, started in 1516, completed 1530). Velázquez lived on the top floor, while the ground floor was used as a contracting house and a smelter for gold. Each room shows a particular period, featuring furniture, china, porcelain, crystal. ■ *At the northwest corner of Parque Céspedes, Félix Peña 612. Mon-Sat 0900-1700, Sun 0900-1300, US$2, with guided tour in English or German, camera fee US$1.*

The **Museo Emilio Bacardí**, was named after industrialist Emilio Bacardí Moreau, its main benefactor and collector of much of the museum's contents. This was the second museum founded in Cuba and has exhibits from prehistory to the Revolution downstairs, one of the most important collections of Cuban colonial paintings and the archaeology hall has mummies from Egypt and South America. ■ *Two blocks east of the Parque, opposite the Palacio Provincial, entrance on Pío Rosado esquina Aguilera, T28402. Tue-Sat 0900-1800, Sun 0900-1300. US$2.*

The **Museo Histórico 26 de Julio**, formerly the Moncada Garrison, was attacked (unsuccessfully) by Castro and his revolutionaries on 26 July 1953. When the revolution triumphed in 1959, the building was turned into a school. To mark the 10th anniversary of the attack, one of the buildings was converted to a museum, featuring photos, plans and drawings of the battle. All commentaries are in Spanish. Bullet holes, filled in by Batista, have been reconstructed on the outer walls. ■ *Av Moncada esquina General Portuondo. Mon-Sat 0800-1800, Sun 0800-1200, US$1.* The **Museo Casa Natal de Frank País**, is in the birthplace of the leader of the armed uprising in Santiago on 30 November 1956, who was shot in July 1957. ■ *General Banderas 226 y Los Maceos, T52710.* The **Museo de la Lucha Clandestina** highlights the support given by the local urban population during the battle in the Sierra Maestra. Exhibits revolve around Frank País, from his early moves to foment a revolutionary conscious-ness to his integration into the Movimiento 26 de Julio under Fidel Castro. ■ *At the top of picturesque Padre Pico (steps) and corner of Santa Rita and Jesús Rabí, T24689. 0900-1700 Tue-Sun, US$2, a guide speaking 'Spanlish' will take you round if you can't read Spanish.* The **Casa Natal de Antonio Maceo**, built between 1800-1830, was the birthplace, on 14 June 1845, of Antonio Maceo y Grajales, one of the greatest military commanders of the 1868 and 1895 wars of independence. The museum houses his biography and details of his 32 years' devotion to the struggle for independence. ■ *Los Maceo 207 entre Corona y Rastro. Mon-Sat 0800-1830.*

The **Museo del Carnaval** exhibits a collection of instruments, drums and costumes from Santiago's famous July carnival. If you are not going to be there in July, this is the best way to get a flavour of the celebrations. ■ *On Heredia esquina Pío Rosado. Tue-Sat 0900-1800, Sun 0900-1200, US$2.* The **Casa del Caribe** is a world renowned cultural centre. If you are interested in *Santería*, there is a musical and religious cere-mony at 0930 on Wednesdays. ■ *Off Av Manduley on 13 esquina 8.* The **Museo de la Religión** displays religious items particularly concerning *Santería*, but there are no written explanations of the exhibits, best to ask for a guide. ■ *13 206, esquina 10. Mon-Sat 0830-1700, free.*

South of Santiago The Ruta Turística runs along the shore of the Bahía de Santiago to the **Castillo del Morro**, a clifftop fort with the **Museo de la Piratería**, a museum of the sea, piracy and local history, charting the pirate attacks made on Santiago during the 16th cen-tury. Pirates included the Frenchman Jacques de Sores and the Englishman Henry Morgan, and you can see many of the weapons used in both attack and defence of the city (closed for renovations, T91569). You can wander around the fort, US$3, even if the museum is still closed. From the roof you can admire the thrilling views over the Bay of Santiago and Cayo Granma and you can follow some 16th-century steps almost down to the waterline. There is a good restaurant on a terrace with a great view, main dish US$6. *Turistaxi to El Morro, US$10 round trip with wait.*

East of Santiago Excellent excursions can be made to the **Gran Piedra** (26 km east) a viewpoint from which it is said you can see Haiti and Jamaica on a clear day, more likely their lights on a clear night. It is a giant rock weighing 75,000 tonnes, 1,234-m high, and reached by climbing 454 steps from the road (only for the fit). The view is tremendous and buzzards circle you. US$1 to climb. There are no buses but a private car will charge you about US$15 there and back (hotel tour desks will arrange a tour, good value).

Some 2 km before La Gran Piedra are the **Jardines de la Siberia**, on the site of a former coffee plantation, an extensive botanical garden; turn right and follow the track for about 1 km to reach the gardens. The **Museo La Isabelica** is at Carretera de la Gran Piedra Km 14, a ruined coffee plantation once owned by French emigrés from Haiti, the buildings of which are now turned into a museum housing the for-mer kitchen and other facilities on the ground floor with farming tools and archaeo-logical finds. Upstairs is the owners' house in authentic 19th-century style. ■ *Tue-Sat 0900-1700, Sun 0900-1300, US$2.*

On the Carretera Siboney at Km 13½ is **La Granjita Siboney**, the farmhouse used as the headquarters for the revolutionaries' attack on the Moncada barracks on 26 July 1953. It now has a museum of uniforms, weapons and artefacts used by the 100 men who gathered here the night before, as well as extensive newspaper accounts of the attack. ■ *Tue-Sun 0900-1700, T9836, entry US$2.*

Santiago de Cuba

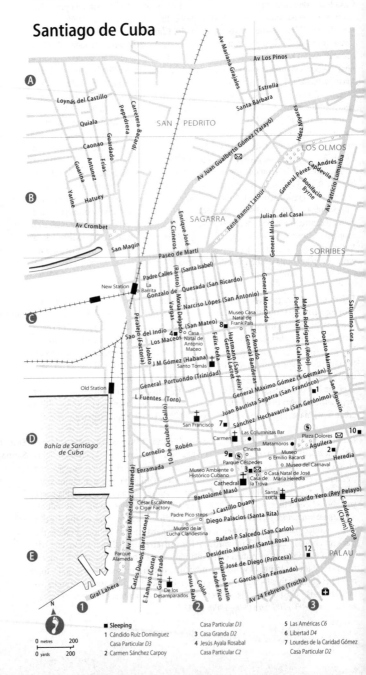

■ **Sleeping**
1 Cándido Ruíz Domínguez
  Casa Particular *D3*
2 Carmen Sánchez Carpoy

3 Casa Granda *D2*
4 Jesús Ayala Rosabal
  Casa Particular *C2*

5 Las Américas *C6*
6 Libertad *D4*
7 Lourdes de la Caridad Gómez
  Casa Particular *D2*

Siboney, 16 km east of the city, is the nearest beach to Santiago with a reef just offshore which is great for snorkelling. ■ *Take bus 214 from near bus terminal. Very crowded at weekends.* At Km 24 is the **Valle de la Prehistoria**, a huge park filled with life-size carved stone dinosaurs and stone age men. Great for the kids but due to the total absence of shade it is like walking around a desert. Take huge supplies of water and try to go early or late. ■ *Entrance US$2, extra US$1 to take photos.*

Daiquirí beach (turn right at Km 25) is beautiful and quiet but the resort there is now reserved for the military. The next beach, 1 km after Daiquirí, is **Culebrín**, featuring a seawater swimming pool and a few tourist facilities like cabins. Continuing east at Km 35 is **Comunidad Artística Verraco**, a small artists' community, where you can buy original artwork.

An **Aquarium and Dolphinarium** on this stretch of the coast has three sea-lion and dolphin shows daily, at 1000, 1130, 1445, however small the audience. The show is of a high standard and visitors are invited to dive in and play with the dolphins for an extra US$20, for about 10 minutes. The aquarium has many species of fish as well as turtle and sharks (feeding time is spectacular). There is a basic refreshment bar where you can get a sandwich for US$1 and a beach with trees for shade but no facilities. ■ *US$5.* **Laguna Baconao** is a large murky lake in a beautiful setting. Flanking the lake is a crocodile sanctuary, but they are kept in small enclosures with barely enough water to drink. ■ *US$1 to enter the Laguna Baconao area, which includes a boat ride to a floating bar in the middle of the lake.*

C *Club Coralia Santiago* (Gran Caribe), formely *Club Amigo Bucanero*, 3-star, Carretera Baconao Km 4, Arroyo La Costa, T54596, 28130, under renovation in 1999. **C** *Costa Morena*, Carretera Baconao, km 38.5, T56127. **C** *Balneario del Sol* (Cubanacán), Carretera Baconao Km 39, T398113, 398124. Three-star, all-inclusive resort with 123 rooms, car hire, Visa accepted, scuba diving. **AL** *LTI Los Corales – Carisol* (Cubanacán), T86177, 28519, F335216, reserva@carisol.scu.cyt.cu. Three-star, 120 rooms and 46 junior suites, a/c, minibar, TV, all-inclusive, buffet and à la carte restaurant and cafetería, pool tennis, dive centre, beach volleyball, tennis, car and bicycle hire, child care, near **Playa Cazonal**, which is a very high quality beach for this area. Wear something on your feet when swimming and avoid standing on the coral reef.

West of Santiago

Ten km west of Santiago is **El Sanctuario de Nuestra Señora de la Caridad del Cobre ('El Cobre')** where the shrine of Cuba's patron saint, the Virgen de la Caridad del Cobre, is built over a working copper mine. The story goes that in the 17th century, three fishermen were about to capsize in Nipe Bay, when they found a wooden statue of the Virgin Mary floating in the sea. Their lives were saved and they brought the statue to its current resting place above the altar. Downstairs there are many tokens of gratitude left by Cubans who have been helped by the Virgin in some way. There is a pilgrimage here on 12 September. Watch out for the touts; probably best to take a bit of copper and offer 50 cents or some pesos, otherwise they will be waiting for you when you leave the church. ■ *There is no bus, so either hire a car and driver, about US$8, or get on a truck at the bus station for a few pesos.*

West from Santiago runs a coastal road along the Sierra Maestra with beautiful bays and beaches, completely deserted, some with black sand. It is only possible to visit by car. Many of the villages have connections with revolutionary events. **El Uvero**, about 60 km from Santiago, has a monument marking the attack by Castro and his men on the Batista troop HQ on 28 May 1957. The building which was attacked is now a small museum. About 20 km further west is a turning for **Pico Turquino** (1,974m), just before the village of Ocujal. You can drive a short distance and park and walk. This is the highest peak in the Sierra Maestra.

At **Pilón** (population 12,000) a small town with a harbour, the road turns inland towards the Golfo de Guacanayabo past **Ojo de Agua**. After the village there are three separate signs and plaques marking the spots where three groups of men who disembarked from *Granma* crossed the road in underground water conduits, before heading into the Sierra Maestra. The road follows the Río Sevilla to join up with the Manzanillo-Niquero road running down the other side of the peninsula to **Cabo Cruz** at the tip. Turn left to **Niquero** from where a dirt road leads to the spot where Castro's 82 revolutionaries disembarked from the yacht, *Granma*, on 2 December 1956 in a mangrove swamp just southwest of **Playa Las Coloradas**. By the road is a small park where a replica of *Granma* can be seen and a 2 km concrete path through the swamp takes you to a rather ugly concrete jetty and a plaque marking the occasion. The dirt road ends at **Cabo Cruz** at the tip of the peninsula.

Chivirico 2 all-inclusive *SuperClubs* hotels: **AL-B** per person *Sierra Mar* (Cubanacán), on   **Sleeping**
Playa Sevilla, Carretera de Chivirico Km 60, T29101, F29007, sierrmar@smar.scu.cyt.cu 200
rooms, modern resort in terraced style, a/c, satellite TV, small beach, watersports, freeform
pool on terrace with bar and good sea view, 2 restaurants, 3 bars, shop, rental bikes, many
activities such as horse rental, helicopter ride into the mountains, sports, gymnasium, kids'
club, the only SuperClubs resort in Cuba where children are welcome, tours and car hire; 12
km further west past Chivirico is the smaller *Los Galeones* (Cubanacán), Carretera Chivirico,
T29110, F26160, galeones@smar.scu.cyt.cu For singles and couples over 16 only, marketed
to honeymooners, weddings arranged free of charge, 32 rooms including 1 suite on a cliff
overlooking the Caribbean, a/c and fan, satellite TV, 300 winding steps lead down to the sea,
restaurant, bar, sauna, massage, gym, special scuba training pool, bowling, volleyball, car
and bike rental, courtesy bus to *Sierra Mar*, a taxi from the airport costs about US$50.

Marea del Portillo before you get to Pilón, there are 2 more resort hotels popular with
Canadian package tours: **C-D** per person *Marea del Portillo*, (Cubanacán), Carretera Granma
Km 12.5, T594001/2. All-inclusive, 3-star, 130 rooms, hot water, phone, tennis, beach volleyball, watersports, car rental, shop. **A-B** per person *Farallón del Caribe*, (Cubanacán), Km 14,
T5974081, F597080, dsk@hfarcar.ma.grm.cyt.cu All-inclusive, 4-star, 140 rooms, a/c, TV, hot
water, phone for international calls, diving, watersports, tennis, car and bicycle rental, nice
position. **D** *Villa Punta Piedra*, (Cubanacán), Carretera Pilón, T59442. Two-star, further west
along the coast. Watersports, scuba diving, snorkelling and sailing can be arranged at all the
resorts. Scuba diving is with *Centro de Buceo Albacora* who take up to 8 divers to 17 sites at
depths of 5-40m.

Essentials

L-B *Casa Granda* (Gran Caribe) Heredia 201 entre San Pedro y San Félix, near Parque   **Sleeping**
Phone code: 226
Céspedes, T86600, F86035. Elegant building opened in 1914 and patronized by many
famous people. 4-star, 58 renovated rooms and suites, expansion in 2000 will bring more
rooms and a pool. A/c, fax service, laundry, car hire, satellite TV, nanny service, post office, disabled access and 1 room for handicapped people, *Havanatur* and *Asistur* offices. Excellent
central location with terrace bar, poor service, overlooking park, 5th floor bar with even
better views over city (US$1.50 to go up if you are not staying at the hotel but that buys your
first cocktail), restaurant, snack bar, café, open 2000-0300, good. **AL** *Sol Meliá Hotel Santiago* (Cubanacán), Av Las Américas entre 4 y M, T87070, 87270, F41756. Five-star, 302 rooms,
clean, good service, excellent breakfast buffet US$7, good. *La Cubana* restaurant, open
1200-2100, good view of city from roof top bar, swimming pool open to day visitors for US$5,
tennis, sauna, car hire, has post office and will change almost any currency into dollars.

B *Versalles* (Cubanacán), Carretera del Morro Km 1, T91014/91016/91504. US$2 taxi from
centre, 3-star, 61 rooms, takes Visa, very near airport, US$1 for visitors to use pool, expensive
pool side snack bar. **D** *Balcón del Caribe* (Islazul), next to Castillo del Morro, T91011.
Three-star, 72 rooms overlooking the sea, quiet, pool, tourist office, simple Cuban food, cold
water in bungalows, pleasant but inconvenient for the town. **D** *Las Américas* (Horizontes),
T42011, F86075, Av de las Américas esquina Gen Cebreco, easy bus/truck access to centre, private cars around bus stop in plaza opposite hotel. Three-star, 68 rooms, lively, restaurant not
recommended except for breakfast, hustlers on terrace café, fills up with *jineteras*,
non-residents may use swimming pool, helpful Rumbos agent, nice reception staff, safety
deposit, Havanautos in front of hotel, bicycle hire. **D** *Motel San Juan* (Horizontes), Km 1
Carretera a Siboney, T42478/42490, F86137, out of town but nice location, turistaxi US$3.95,
private car US$2. A complex with cabins, 112 very nice rooms, large and clean, intermittent hot
water, pool, bar and several restaurants, good breakfast, high quality by Cuban standards,
accepts pesos, queues at weekends and during festivals, car hire, private car into town US$2.

Cuba

D *Villa Santiago de Cuba* (Gaviota), Av Manduley 502, entre 19 y 21, Reparto Vista Alegre, T41368/41346, F87166. Three-star, car hire, tourist office, nearby pool for guests, quiet, no credit cards. **E** *Rancho Club Motel* (Islazul), Carretera Central Km 4.5, Altos de Quintero, T33202/33280. 29 rooms. **E-F** *MES* (Horizontes), L esquina 7, Reparto Terrazas (about 5 blocks north of *Las Américas*), T42398. Two-star, 16 rooms, clean, TV and fan, 2 rooms share bath and fridge, food OK. **E-F** *Libertad* on Plaza Marte, T23080. Good central location, good value if slightly downmarket, very noisy fans. There is an annex, *Rex* nearby on Av Garzón 10, T26314, where the rooms are better. Clean, with soap, toilet paper and towels, but the a/c is still noisy and the water is not always on, you have to register at the *Libertad* first.

Casas particulares Touts around Parque Céspedes, also near all hotels. **D** *María Gámez Gámez*, San Félix 211 entre San Mateo y Los Maceo, T54398. Central, 10 mins' walk from Plaza Céspedes, friendly landlady Toña, good cook, breakfast US$2.50, dinner US$5, 1 room with own shower (warm water) and toilet, sitting room with rocking chairs, TV, stereo, laundry on request. A recommended family is **E** *Hermes Domínguez and Dalgis López Sablón*, Féliz Peña 455 (altos), CP 90100, T20060. Some rooms a/c, breakfast US$3, dinner US$5, large portions, good. *Grethel Suárez Sánchez*, Alfredo Zayas 513 entre 13 y Anacaona, Santa Bárbara, CP 90300, T43177. Room with double bed and private bathroom. **E** *Nardys Aguilera Rodríguez*, Aguilera 565 entre San Agustín y Barnado Santiago, T22409. A/c, clean, very central, large apartment, very helpful. **E** *Carmen Sánchez Carpoy*, Clarín 6 entre Heredia y Aguilera, T28239. Bathroom next to bedroom, balcony, friendly, central and convenient. **E** *Milagros González Rivera*, Anacaona 104 entre Aguilera y Centro Gallego, T41364. Triple room, a/c, hot water, parking, near *La Maison* (see shopping) where spaghetti is good, US$1. **E** *Orestes González y Teresa Exposito*, Gen Portuondo 651¼ esq Moncada, to the left of the Iglesia de la Santísima Trinidad opposite Parque Moncada, T26305, sergio@ ebm.vo.edu.cu **E** *Pura Sabori y Juan Carlos*, Princesa 581½ altos entre Calvario y Carnicería, T29025, F86131 c/o Pura Sabori. **E** *Margarita Roca Serrano y Daniel del Pino Naranjo*, 10 407 entre 15 y 17, Vista Alegre, T42142. Retired doctors, 2 rooms with breakfast, shared bathroom, other meals available, also apartment, 2 bedrooms, US$150 month. **E** *Rubén Rodes Estrada*, 10 410 entre 15 y 17, Vista Alegre, T42611. Run by gay couple, house painted red and yellow, giant cactus outside and inside, hot water. **E-F** *Cándido Ruíz Domínguez*, Mayia Rodríguez 317A entre San Gerónimo y San Francisco, T54493, 27490. One room, hot shower, breakfast and dinner available. *Mujeres de Arena*, Félix Peña 554 entre Aguilera y Enramada. Used to be a *paladar*, now more profitable renting rooms but food still available. **E-F** *Jesús Ayala Rosabal*, Rastro 208 entre Los Maceo y San Mateo, T51694. Three rooms, 1 has terrace, hot water, a/c, fridge. **F** *Belkis Rodríguez*, Montenegro 6, T53734. Breakfast US$1-2. **F** *Lourdes de la Caridad Gómez*, Félix Peña 454 entre San Francisco y San Gerónimo, T54468. Good views over city, charming Señora, interesting conversationalist, excellent breakfast and dinner. **F** *Irma and Umberto*, Santa Lucía 303 entre San Pedro y San Félix, T22391, close to Parque Céspedes. Brother and sister, live in huge house with their respective families, large room sleeps 3, private bathroom, patio. Umberto has a taxi although he used to be a radiologist, very hospitable, caring people.

Eating
Hotels have restaurants & mostly serve buffet meals

Three restaurants run by Rumbos (*Combinado* is the collective name) on Plaza Dolores (known as Búlevar locally), Italian, Chinese and creole food, quite expensive and low on local atmosphere; opposite them on Búlevar is *Matamoros*, which is better although prices are quite high with a system of US$1=1 peso; also *Las Enramadas*, Búlevar. Good atmosphere, cheap, basic food, nice setting. *Las Acacias* in Hotel Villa Santiago de Cuba, Av Manduley 502, T41368. Open 1900-2300, Creole Cuban food; *La Taberna de Dolores*, Aguilera esquina Reloj, T23913. Spanish food, open 1900-2400, prices in pesos but tourists pay 1:1 in dollars. The *Terrace Coffee Bar* at the *Casa Granda* is open 24 hrs and is a nice place for a drink, look out for Tony, the deaf-mute magician who is there in the evening, the *Roof Garden* at the top of the same hotel is open 2000-0300, *mojitos* US$1.65, appalling service. *Coppelia* ice cream on Félix Peña under the cathedral, open Mon-Fri 1000-2100, Sat-Sun 1100-2200, no queuing if you have dollars. *Isabelica*, Aguilera esquina Plaza Dolores. Open 24 hrs, serves only coffee, US$0.85, cigars rolled, bohemian hangout, watch out for hustlers, serious hassling by jineteros/as. *Casa del Té*, Aguilera esquina Lacret. Grow their own herbs, cheap herbal tea available. *Café Ajedrez*, Enramada y Santo Tomás. Open air café in cool architectural structure designed by Cuban architect, Walter A Betancourt Fernández.

Lots of good *paladares* (official ones have a sign outside) around Calles Heredia and Aguilera, and in Reparto Vista Alegre, near the hotels *Santiago*, *Las Américas* and *San Juan*. *Paladar Mireya*, Padre Pico 368-A, Frente a la Escalinata. US$5-6 including rice and salad, open 1200-2400, in smokey back room. *Doña Cristina*, Padre Pico. Good reports. *El Balcón*, Independencia 253, Reparto Sueño, T27407. Good food, US$3, open 24 hrs, popular with locals. *Terrazas*, 5 50 entre M y Terraza, Ampliación de Terraza, T41491. *Paladar* on the upper floor open daily 1000-2400, tasty food, nicely presented, chicken US$6, pork US$5. If the gate is locked, whistle. *Casa Pita*, 8 208 entre 7 y 9, Vista Alegre. Open 1200-1500, 1900-2300, maximum US$10, good food. Street stalls sell snacks in pesos, usually only open until early evening, some only at lunchtime. Most things cost 1 peso. Avoid *fritos*, they are just fried lumps of dough; most reliable thing is cheese, pork or egg sandwich; pizza is usually dry bit of dough with a few gratings of cheese. Lots of stalls along 'Ferreiro' or Av Victoriano Garzón, these are open later than others, especially up near *Hotel Las Américas*. Also lots around bus station on Libertadores and a few along the bottom part of Aguilera, between Parque Céspedes and Plaza Dolores.

Nightlife *Club Tropicana Santiago*, local version of Havana show, on Autopista Nacional Km 1.5, T43036/43610, open 2000-0300, book direct or through a travel agent in any hotel, eg Rumbos US$50 including transport. *Cabaret San Pedro del Mar*, Carretera del Morro, Islazul-run, US$5 taxi, US$5 entrance, reasonable food. *Casa de la Trova*, Heredia 206 around the corner from *Casa Granda*. Two daily shows of music, morning and evening, traditional, acoustic Son music, open until 2400, US$1 and worth it, nice venue in beautiful building with patio where the bands play at night, also bar. *Grupo Folklórico del Oriente*, San Francisco y San Félix, folk groups play daytime till lunchtime, then again in the evening. *Ballet Folkórico Cutatumba*, Enramada, 2 blocks west of Plaza Céspedes. Superb show Sun 1030, US$3. *Casa de los Estudiantes*, Heredia, near *Casa Granda*. Live music Sun 1330, US$1. *Sala de Dolores* on Plaza Dolores has classical and choral concerts. Lively nightly disco in *Santiago* and *Las Américas* hotels, to which Cubans are welcome, American disco music, hardly any salsa, *jinetera* pick-up places. Two discos on Heredia, 1 of them opposite the Casa de la Trova, mostly for the under-20s. *Buró de Información Cultural* on Plaza Marte has live music in its patio bar every night. *Casa del Caribe* on 13 154 esquina 8, T42285, live Afro-Cuban music and dance at weekends. *El Patio de Artex*, Heredia 304. Home of painters, Félix and José Joaquín Tejada Revilla, often live music with fantastic local bands, lots of dancing.

Festivals The **Festival del Caribe** begins in the 1st week in Jul with theatre, dancing and conferences, and continues later in Jul to coincide with the Moncada celebrations on 26 Jul. The **Carnival**, already in full swing by then (as it was in 1953, the date carefully chosen to catch Batista's militia drunk and off-guard and use the noise of the carnival to drown the sound of gunfire), traditionally stops for a day of more serious celebration, then continues on 27 Jul. Carnival is the third week of Jul, taking in Santiago's patron saint's day, 25 Jul. This carnival is regaining its former glory and is well worth seeing.

On **New Year's Eve** you will find son bands playing in Plaza Marte and surrounding streets. Just before midnight everyone moves toward Parque Céspedes and sings the National Anthem. Then on the stroke of midnight the Cuban flag is raised on the Casa de Gobierno, commemorating the anniversary of the first time it was flown in 1902 when the Republic of Cuba was proclaimed.

Shopping *Casa de la Artesanía*, under the cathedral in Parque Céspedes, T23924. Open 0800-1730, also on Lacret 724 entre San Basilio y Heredia, T24027. *Cubartesana* on Félix Peña esquina Masó under the cathedral. *Salón Artexanda* on Heredia 304 entre Pío Rosado y Calvario. Handicrafts are sold on the street on Heredia entre Hartmann y Pío Rosado. **Music** *Casa de la Trova* sells CDs and tapes. *Artex* on Aguilera sells CDs, tapes and videos for dollars.

Cuba

Enramadas and *Siglo XX*, both on Enramada, are large stores with stalls inside selling records, books, clothes, jewellery, ornaments etc in pesos. On Enramada there is a second hand record shop. Several dollar stores can be found in the Parque Céspedes area, ask for 'shopping', especially on Saco. There is a good **bread** shop (dollars) called *Doña Neli* on Aguilera at Plaza Marte, just down from *Hotel Libertad*. *Panadería El Sol* is on Plaza Marte entre Saco y Aguilera. *Casa de Miel*, Gen Lacret, sells honey. *La Bombonera* is a dollar store selling **food** very near Parque Céspedes on Aguilera entre Gen Lacret y Hartmann, open Mon-Sat 0900-1800, Sun 0900-1200. Food market on Ferreiro opposite *Hotel Las Américas*.

Tour operators   *Rumbos Cuba* is on Heredia opposite *Casa Granda* hotel, open 0800-1700 for tours and later for car hire. Organized city tours with guide, also day trips to all destinations around Santiago. Prices vary according to season and number of people; also flights and trips to Jamaica and Santo Domingo. *Havanatur* main office is near La Maison on Av Manduley, T43603, with another office under the *Hotel Casa Granda*, offering the same as Rumbos but slightly more expensive. All the main hotels have tour agencies, usually outlets of Rumbos or Havanatur, and you can save time by using them rather than going to the main office. Islazul only deals with tourism for Cubans.

Transport   **Local Bus:** Buses run until about 0100 and the fare is always 20 centavos. If there is no sign of a bus, catch a truck, ask driver the destination, pay flat rate 1 peso. Horse drawn coches are also 1 peso. **Car hire**: At the airport: *Transautos*, T92245; *Havanautos*, T91873, 86161; *Vía Rent a Car*, T91014. These and other agencies in *Hotel Casa Granda, Hotel Santiago, Villa Santiago de Cuba, Hotel San Juan, Hotel Las Américas*. *Havanautos* also has an agency at La Punta service station, T39328. **Taxis**: there are 3 types: *Turistaxi* most expensive, eg US$8 from airport to town centre; *Taxis OK* also expensive; *Cubataxi*, T51038/9, cheapest (name on windscreen), eg airport to town US$5. You can also get a private taxi, lots of them hanging around Parque Céspedes and Plaza Marte, but they will charge about the same as a Cubataxi. For a longer journey, you can negotiate a price. However, get a written quote if possible as even Cubataxis have been known to renegue on their agreements and demand more and/or return to Santiago. You will be continually offered private taxis every time you go out. Motorbike transport can be arranged at Plaza Marte for about US$1. Bicitaxis cost US$0.50.

Long distance Bus: Terminal near Plaza de la Revolución at the top of Av de los Libertadores/Carretera Central. Buy ticket in advance at office on Yarayo (the 1st street on the left going north from the terminal), open daily 0600-1400. *Víazul*, T28484, is in an office to the left of the bus departure area, with a dark brown wooden door, for timetable, for an overnight journey wear trousers and a fleece if you have one, as the a/c is very cold and even Víazul is not comfortable at night. Trucks are available outside terminal to most destinations, drivers shout destination prior to departure, pay in pesos. For a long journey avoid trucks without any kind of cover, or you will burn. **Train**: The new station is opposite the rum factory on Av Jesús Menéndez. Book tickets in advance from basement office in new terminal. Train travel is not as reliable or comfortable as bus travel. Take sweater for Havana journey, freezing a/c.

Directory   **Airlines** *Cubana* office on Félix Peña 673 entre Heredia y San Basilio, near the cathedral, open Mon-Fri 0900-1700, Sat 0900-1400, T24156/51579/22290. *Aerotaxi* at the airport, T91410 ext 2019. *Aerocaribbean* office under *Hotel Casa Granda*. Local and inter-Caribbean (some destinations) flights can also be booked in the Rumbos Havanatur. **Banks** *Banco Financiero Internacional*, Parque Céspedes at Santo Tomás y Aguilera, T22101, open Mon-Fri 0800-1600, dollar cash on Visa, change foreign currency and TCs. *BICSA*, Enramada opposite Plaza Dolores, for changing foreign currency and TCs. *Banco Popular de Ahorro*, Plaza Dolores, 0800-1500, Visa and Mastercard, prompt service. TCs can be changed in any hotel except those in the Islazul chain; commission is usually 2-3%. *Hotel Santiago* will change virtually any cash currency into dollars. TCs can be changed in the Havanatur office in *Casa Granda*. In the Asistur office under *Casa Granda* you can get cash advance on all major credit cards including American Express and Diners Club; they will also change American Express TCs, the only place who will do so in all Cuba. **Medical facilities** *Clínica Internacional*, 13 y 14, Reparto Vista Alegre, T42589, along Av Raúl Pujol away from the city, opposite *Motel San Juan*, especially for tourists, has a dentist as well and pharmacy on site, everything payable in dollars, US$25 per consultation, the best clinic to visit to be sure of immediate treatment. There is a *pharmacy* next door to the *Casa de la Trova* on Heredia and another, open 24 hrs, on Victoriano Garzón y 10.

Useful addresses Immigration: Inmigración y Extranjería on Av Raúl Pujol y 1, Reparto Santa Bárbara, open Mon, Fri 0900-1200, 1330-1630, Tue, Wed, Thu 0900-1200, in summer holiday mornings only. Go to Bandec on Parque Céspedes y Aguilera and buy special stamp (sello) for US$25, then return to Immigration for paper work (15 mins). **Police:** T116. The central police station is Unidad 2, Corona y San Gerónimo. Near to the hotels *Santiago* and *Las Américas* is Unidad 4, on Aguilera near the hospital and the market. **Fire:** Martí 517, T23242. **Asistur:** *Hotel Casa Granda*, Heredia esquina San Pedro, T86600, for all health, financial, legal and insurance problems for foreign tourists.

Bayamo

Bayamo is the capital of the province of Granma. It was the second town founded by Diego Velázquez in November 1513 and has been declared a Ciudad Monumento Nacional. However, it was burned to the ground by its own population in 1869 as an act of rebellion against the colonial Spanish; consequently the town has little to offer in the way of colonial architecture and is really rather uninteresting.

Phone code: 23

The **Iglesia de Santísimo Salvador** in the Plaza del Himno Nacional is a 16th-century church which was badly damaged by the 1869 fire, but is currently under restoration. **Casa Natal de Carlos Manuel de Céspedes**, is a museum dedicated to the life of the main campaigner of the 1868 independence movement, who was born here. ■ *On Maceo. Tue-Sat 0900-1700, Sun 0900-1200, US$1.*

Manzanillo, is a small seaside town and principal port of Granma province. Outside Manzanillo in the hills are the ruins of the **Demajagua sugar mill**. This is the place where, in 1868, Carlos Manuel de Céspedes cast the first stone in the First War of Independence by liberating his slaves. The **Parque Nacional de Demajagua** is 10 km south of Manzanillo. The mill was named after the bell formerly used to call the slaves to work, which then became the symbol of the call to revolution.

Phone code: 23
Population: 100,000

C *Sierra Maestra* (Islazul), Carretera Central via Santiago de Cuba, T481013, 2 km from city centre. 204 rooms, delightful post-revolution 1960s building, thoroughly kitsch interior, avoid rooms overlooking noisy pool, plenty of nightlife, 3 bars, disco, mostly Cubans, helpful staff, car hire, credit cards accepted. Cheaper is *Villa Bayamo* (2-star) on the Carretera Manzanillo Km 5.5, T423102/423124. 34 rooms, 1 km from city centre. New in 1998. **E** *Royalton* (Islazul), on Maceo y Joaquín Palma, very central location, T422224/90/46/68. 33 rooms, a/c, private bathrooms, phones, restaurant, lobby bar and terrace bar open each night, toilets just beyond reception. *Hotel Central*, Av General García, is a basic, peso hotel, very central. **Casa particular F** *Ramón Enrique Alvarez Sánchez*, Pío Rosado 22 entre Ramírez y Av Fco Vte Aguilera, T423984. Enormous rooms, a/c, private bathroom, wife Carolina is a good cook.

Sleeping

Restaurante 1513, Gen García esquina General Lora, T425921. Open 1200-2200, small but recommended by many Bayameros. *La Casona*, Plaza del Himno Nacional, behind the church in a corner. Nice wooden bar, pizzas or spaghetti for 5 pesos, courtyard at the back completely covered at head height with flowering vine, lots of little green lizards, delightful, open 1300-2200. Lots of *paladares* and bars along Gen García, all charge in pesos, best every Sat night during *Noche Cubana*, some only open on Sat. *Sagitario*, Marmol 107, across the street is *Bartería*, on Av Francisco V Aguilera. Both recommended by locals. *Tropicrema*, Parque Céspedes. Cake and 2 scoops of ice cream, 1.80 pesos, very good and popular.

Eating

Casa de la Trova on the corner of Maspote and José Martí has shows during the afternoon and every night, quite touristy in high season. *Cabaret Bayamo* opposite *Hotel Sierra Maestra*, on Carretera Central, T421698. Open 2100-0200. Every Sat there is a *Noche Cubana*, when the whole of General García fills with stalls, ad hoc bars, pigs on spits, and the

Nightlife

restaurants all put tables on the road. Everything is sold in pesos, even in the established bars along this street.

Tour operators *Islazul* office on Gen García 207. Open 0830-1700, also tourist information in *Hotel Sierra Maestra* and occasionally maps, but it is difficult to get information about day trips as they do not cater for many foreign visitors.

Transport **Local** Horse and cart, 7 pesos from bus station to *Hotel Sierra Maestra*. **Car hire:** the *Havanautos* office is in Cupet Cimex gas station next to the bus station, on road to Jiguaní, T423223. Long distance **Air** Carlos Manuel de Céspedes airport is 4 km out of town; flight to Havana 3 times a week. **Bus** The terminal is on the corner of Carretera Central and Jesús Rabi, T424036. Bus to **Santiago** 0900, US$10; to **Guantánamo** US$12, sometimes there is a direct bus, otherwise change at Santiago. To **Manzanillo**, 2 daily, US$2.50, bus station 2 km outside Manzanillo. **Train** Station is at Saco y Línea. Daily trains to Santiago and Havana; 4 daily to Manzanillo, 2 hrs, 1.35 pesos.

Directory **Banks** *Banco Nacional de Cuba*, Saco y Gen García. *Bandec*, Gen García 101. Visa and MC, open Mon-Fri 0800-1500. **Medical facilities** *Farmacia Principal Municipal*, 24-hr at Gen García 53.

Guantánamo

Phone code: 21
Population: 205,000

Guantánamo is the most easterly and most mountainous province on the island. The range of the Montañas de Nipe-Sagua-Baracoa runs through the province, ending in the Atlantic Ocean on the northern coast and the Caribbean Sea to the south. The area is notable for its many endemic species of fauna and flora, and also for the US naval base housing the rare species of US 'imperialists' in Cuba.

Guantánamo, the provincial capital, had a large influx of Haitian, French and Jamaican immigrants in the 19th century. The architecture has much less of a Spanish colonial feel; the narrow, brightly coloured buildings with thin wooden balconies and wrought ironwork are more reminiscent of New Orleans than Madrid. This is also reflected in the local musical rhythms, notably the Tumba Francesa.

The central square, **Plaza Martí**, has a church in the centre. The **Casa de la Cultura** is on the west side and the *Tumba Francesa* on the east. Two km north, the **Plaza de la Revolución** has a modernist carved stone monument to the heroes of all the wars of independence. The **Museo Municipal**, for local history is in a former prison. ■ *José Martí. Tue-Sat 0800-1800, Sun 0800-1200.*

The **US naval base** of Guantánamo (which cannot be easily visited from Cuba) was established at the beginning of the 20th century in the area known as Caimanera. The base is so little a part of the town that you will not, come across it unless you make a specific trip to Mirador de Malones to view it through binoculars.

The **Zoológico de Piedra** is an outdoor museum of stone animals, just outside of town, set in a beautiful hillside location with tropical vegetation. Many are bizarre, from tiny stone lizards to huge bison. All are carved directly from the rocks in their natural setting and you can buy miniature replicas from the sculptor on the way out.

Sleeping **E** *Guantánamo* (Islazul), Ahogados, esq 13 Norte, Plaza Mariana Grajales, Reparto Caribe, T381015, F382406, 15 mins' walk from the centre. Three-star, 112 rooms, 12 cabins, pool, clean, a/c, 2 bars and busy restaurant, food average, disco, mostly Cuban clientèle, staff pleasant and helpful. **E** *La Lupe* (Islazul), Carretera del Salvador Km 2, T326168/326180. Two-star but much nicer than *Guantánamo*, a bit far out of town, nice pool, peaceful atmosphere, 50 rooms, mostly cabins, sports area, a/c, restaurant, bar. **E** *Casa de Los Ensueños*, Ahogados esq 15 Norte, Reparto Caribe, T326304. Three rooms, a/c, TV, bar, 24-hr room service.

Eating *Restaurante Caribe*, on top of a tower block near *Hotel Guantánamo*. Local food, pay in pesos. Plenty of *paladares*, most of whom charge in pesos but will accept dollars. Price should be about 45 pesos per person, but some raise it for tourists. Two *paladares* on Av de los

Estudiantes (Paseo) and a number of street stalls selling pork sandwiches for 5 pesos, some are there every day, all of them at weekends. Other *paladares* off Plaza Martí in the centre.

Peter Hope, Public Relations Officer at the *Hotel Guantánamo* (Room 117, Mon-Sat), is the fount of all tourist information in the area and runs guided Islazul and Havanatur tours for foreigners, including to Mt Malones, to see the US base through Soviet binoculars. He speaks English, German and French. Islazul office is on Los Maceo entre Narciso López y Paseo. **Tour operators**

Local Car hire: *Havanautos* office is at Cupet Cimex gas station at the beginning of the Baracoa road. **Long distance Air** Aeropuerto Mariana Grajales (GAO) is 16 km from Guantánamo, off the Baracoa road. Daily (except Mon) scheduled flight at 0600 from Havana, returning 0855, plus a Sat flight at 0845 (1140). **Bus** The bus terminal, T326016, is 5 km southwest from the centre. Private cars and taxis run from the train and bus station to *Hotel Guantánamo*/town centre, US$1. Daily bus to **Havana**, 4 buses to **Santiago**, 1 bus to **Baracoa. Camiones** to Baracoa leave from La Punta, 7 km from bus station (take a taxi) 4-5 hrs, 5 pesos. **Train** The station is in the centre on Calixto García. Daily trains to **Santiago**, **Havana** and **Holguín**. **Transport**

Banks *Banco de Crédito* at Calixto García esquina Carretera, changes TCs into dollars. **Directory**

Baracoa

Close to the most easterly point of the island, Baracoa is an attractive place surrounded by rich, tropical vegetation and the perfect place to come and spend a few relaxing days on the beach. It was the first town founded in 1512 by Diego Velázquez, and for three years it was the capital of Cuba. Up until the 1960s it was really only accessible by sea until the viaduct, La Farola was built. This is a spectacular road, 30 km long, joined to the mountain on one side and supported by columns on the other. It is well worth the trip from Santiago (150 km, four hours' drive) for the scenery of this section of road, which winds through lush tropical mountains and then descends steeply to the coast. *Phone code: 21*

The area is a UNESCO biosphere, with more than 10 rivers, including the **Río Toa**, 120 km long and the widest river in Cuba. White water rafting is possible down the Río Toa, with different levels of difficulty. The **Río Yumurí** is 30 km east of Baracoa. This is the most spectacular of Baracoa's rivers, running through two deep canyons. You can take an organized tour (US$28), rent a private car (US$10) or take a *colectivo* taxi or truck to the Río Yumurí where the road ends. A canoe will ferry you across or you can hire one to take you upriver for US$1. You can continue walking upriver and swim, very quiet and peaceful. **Sights**

Christopher Columbus arrived in Baracoa on 27 November 1492. He planted a cross, now housed in the church, **Iglesia de la Asunción**, and described a mountain in the shape of an anvil (*yunque*) which was thereafter used as a point of reference for sailors. The first maps of Cuba drawn by an Englishman showed the **Yunque de Baracoa** mountain, copies of which can be seen in the museum. Between 1639 and 1742, Baracoa's three forts were built. The oldest, **El Castillo**, was destroyed in 1652 by the French. The others were **Fuerte de la Punta**, now restaurant *La Punta*, and **Fuerte Matachín**, now the **Museo Municipal**. ■ *Daily 0800-1800, US$2.*

Baracoa has 56 archaeological sites, with many traces of the three Indian groups who lived there: the Siboney, the Taino and the Guanturabey. There is one surviving community of 300 Indians, called the **Yateras**, dating back to the Spaniards' arrival. They are integrated with the rest of society but only marry among themselves and maintain their traditions. They live in an isolated region along the shores of the Río Toa, but a visit can be organized through the Museo Municipal.

C-D *El Castillo* (Gaviota), Calixto García, Loma del Paraíso, T42147, F86074. 35 a/c rooms with bath, phone, TV in lobby lounge, pool (US$2 for use by non-residents), parking, friendly **Sleeping**

staff, food OK, excellent views, very good breakfast. **A-D** *Porto Santo* (Gaviota), T43511, F86074. 53 rooms, 3 suites, a/c, bath, TV, restaurant, bar, shop, beautiful swimming pool, car hire, next to airport, beach, peaceful atmosphere, friendly. **E-F** *La Rusa* (Islazul), a bright yellow building on the Malecón, Máximo Gómez 13, T43011, islazul@gtmo.cu Named after the Russian lady, Magdalena Menasse, who used to run the hotel and whose photos adorn the walls, famous guests have included Fidel Castro, accommodation now basic, food average, nice location, good *paladar* opposite.

Casas particulares *Ikira Mahíquez Machado*, Maceo 168-A entre Céspedes y Ciro Frías, T42466. 2 rooms, also a separate part of the house with kitchen and garage, nice building. **F** *Nelia y Yaquelín*, Mariana Grajales 11 entre Julio A Mella y Calixto García, T42652. Three generations of a delightful family offer a simple but comfortable place to stay, sea views, breakfast US$2, dinner US$5, both delicious and more than you can eat. **F** *Rosa y Alicia*, Emiliano Corrales 11 entre Mariano Grajales y Libertad, T42652. Two small rooms, a/c or fan, extremely nice family, outstanding food, will cook whatever you want, excellent cocoa for breakfast. **F** *Ana y Armando*, R López 79 entre Limbano Sánchez y Roberto Reyes T43169. Two rooms, comfortable, clean, cheap and excellent meals. **E-F** *El Mirador*, Sra Iliana, Maceo 86, entre 24 de Febrero y 10 de Octubre, T43592, 43671. Two rooms, lovely family, meals available. **F** *Neida Cuenca Prada*, Flor Crombet 194 esq Céspedes, T43178. Upstairs rooms better than the one downstairs, kind and generous family, also a *paladar* which serves wonderful food and is reasonably priced. **F** *Ana Elbyn Torres*, Calixto García 162 entre Céspedes y Coronel Galano, T42754. Good.

Eating   The isolation of Baracoa has led to an individual local cuisine, mostly featuring coconut milk and fish. 80% of Cuba's coconuts are grown here. Don't miss the *cucurucho*, a delicious mixture of coconut, fruit and sugar served in a cone of palm leaves and sold at roadsides for about 3 pesos. Lots of *paladares*, many of which are well-established, most offer pork, chicken, fish, turtle, some offer lobster, all of a high standard. One of the best is **Walter's**, on R López 47, T43380. US$5-7 for a good dinner. *La Colonial*, José Martí 123, T43161. Excellent subdued candlelit atmosphere, extensive menu. *Tropical*, José Martí 175. Good local specialities, calalú, vegetarian options, fish in coconut, book ahead for advance preparation of some dishes. The fort at La Punta, which juts out into the bay west of the town, has been converted to a pleasant, breezy, open air restaurant, *La Guama*, although everyone refers to it as La Punta. Nice setting, creole food, main courses (described on the menu as 'mean' plates) US$3-5.50. *Casa de Chocolate*, José Martí, near bus terminal. Local version of hot chocolate with water and salt.

Nightlife   *Casa de la Trova*, José Martí 149. Traditional music, Tue-Sun from 2100, US$1, good *son* and friendly atmosphere. *Casa de la Cultura*, Maceo 122. Live music in its patio. Nightly show of Afro-Cuban music by Yambú Akalé at *Restaurante La Punta*, highly recommended, US$4, very interesting to see all the costumes and instruments. *Dancing Light* on Maceo just before Parque Central, disco for young Cubans although tourists will not feel out of place, drinks in dollars for tourists, small but lively, check out breakdancing show nightly by local youths. *Cuatro ochenta cinco (485)*, Félix Ruenes, bar with live band every night, US$1, great fun, everyone gets up to dance. Disco playing western music next door. Nightly dancing and live music at *Porto Santo* and *El Castillo*, the former is livelier. *Noche Cubana* on Sat, when Antonio Maceo fills up with food and drink stalls and there is dancing to street musicians.

Tour operators   All organized excursions are best arranged through Wilder Laffita, a very efficient Public Relations Officer at the *Hotel Porto Santo*, T43590, who works for Gaviota and is also the guide for all local ecotourism walks. Antonio (Tony) Mas at *Hotel El Castillo* also organizes local excursions, speaks perfect English and can sort out just about anything. A city tour, minimum six people, will cost US$8 per person. A day trip with lunch to **Playa Maguana**, a beautiful white sand beach 22 km from Baracoa is US$28.

Cuba

Local Car hire: at the Servi Cupet station, Guantánamo road Km 4. **Long dis-**
tance Air: Airport 100m from *Hotel Porto Santo. Cubana* flight to Havana Tue, Sat 0950, to
Havana via Santiago Sun, 1030, US$18 to Santiago. All times subject to frequent change.
Bus: Main bus terminal at the end of Martí near Av de los Mártires, T42239, 43670, for buses
to **Havana, Santiago, Camagüey, Guantánamo**. Make sure you reserve in advance at busy
times and that your name is down on the list, *plano*, otherwise your reservation will not be
valid. Trucks to Guantánamo, Moa and other destinations from 2nd bus terminal on
Coroneles Galana.

Banks *Banco Nacional de Cuba* is on Maceo but will change only TCs, you can not get cash advance
on credit cards. *Porto Santo* and *El Castillo* hotels both change TCs. **Medical facilities** *Hospital*
Octavio de la Concepción y de la Pedraja, on Carretera Guantánamo. Policlínica in the small barrio next
to *Hotel Porto Santo*, where you pay in pesos, there is also a dentist here. *Clínica Dental* in Barrio de la
Punta, near the fort. 24-hr pharmacy on Maceo 132.

Isla de la Juventud

There are three good reasons for visiting the Isla de la Juventud: diving, birdwatching
and checking out Cuban provincial life away from tourist resorts. The island is a good
place to go for a weekend out of Havana, although if you plan to see the whole island
you will need more time.

In recent decades its population has been swelled by tens of thousands of Cuban and
Third World students, giving rise to the modern name of **Isle of Youth**. Early
aboriginal inhabitants called it **Camaraco**, **Ahao** or **Siguanea**. The abundant pine
and later casuarina (Australian pine) trees gave rise to the name **Isla de Pinos** (Isle of
Pines). From the 19th century until the Revolution its main function was as a prison
and both José Martí and Fidel Castro served time there.

The capital, Nueva Gerona, dates from the 19th century and remains the only sub-   **Nueva Gerona**
stantial settlement. Surrounded by small rounded hills, it is a pleasantly laid-back   *Phone code: 61*
country town with a slow pace. As most development has taken place post-1959, there
are few historically interesting buildings. The **Río Las Casas** runs through the
town heading northwards out to sea, and this has traditionally been the main route
to the Cuban mainland. The boat which served as a ferry from the 1920s until 1974,
El Pinero, has been preserved by the river at the end of Calle 28.

The **Museo Municipal** is in the building which was once the Casa de Gobierno,
built in 1853, one of the oldest on the island. It is on the south side of the Parque Central and has a small historical collection of items of local interest. ■ *Calle 30.*
0800-1700, Sun 0900-1300. The **Museo de la Lucha Clandestina**, near *Coppelia*, has a
collection of photos and other material relating to the Revolution. ■ *Calle 37 y 30.*
Tue-Sat, 0900-1700, Sun 0800-1200. The **Planetario y Museo de Historia Natural**,
has exhibits relating to the natural history, geology and archaeology of the island, with
a replica of the cave painting. ■ *Calle 41 y 52. Tue-Thu 0800-1900, Fri 1400-2200, Sat*
1300-1700, Sun 0900-1300, US$2. Outside the town, 3 km west just off the road to La
Demajagua, is **Museo Finca El Abra**. This is where José Martí came on 17 October
1870, to spend nine weeks of exile and hard labour quarrying marble in the Sierra de
las Casas before being deported to Spain. You can see the contents of the house and
kitchen and some of Martí's belongings. ■ *Tue-Sun 0900-1700.*

The **Presidio Modelo** (the Model Prison), 4 km east of Nueva Gerona in Reparto   **Excursions**
Chacón, was built by the dictator Machado to a high-security 'panopticon' design first
developed by Jeremy Bentham in 1791 to give total surveillance and control of the
inmates. It is a sinister and impressive sight; wander around the guard towers and circular cell blocks, and see the numbered, tiered cells. Inmates have included many
fighters in the independence struggle, Japanese Cuban internees in the Second World

Cuba

War, and Fidel Castro and fellow Moncada rebels imprisoned 1953-55. He closed the prison in 1967. ■ *Open Mon-Sat 0800-1700, Sun 0800-1300, US$2, cameras US$1.*

The **Cueva del Punta del Este** contains paintings attributed to the original Siboney inhabitants. They were discovered in 1910 by a shipwrecked French sailor and contain 235 pictures on the walls and ceilings, painted long before the arrival of the Spanish. They are considered the most important pictographs in the Caribbean and have been declared a national monument. It is believed that they might represent a solar calendar. ■ *The only way to get there is by organized excursion. US$92 flat rate divided between however many passengers there are.*

The **Cocodrilo** crocodile farm is a one-hour drive (any car) south and west from Nueva Gerona, including several km of dirt road. Guided tour (in Spanish) of the hatchery and the breeding pens where the crocodiles stay for 4-5 years until they are released. ■*Entry US$3.*

Sleeping

Hotels can be booked through Amistur

Main tourist hotel is **C-E** *El Colony*, T98282. 40 mins by road from Nueva Gerona's small airport, very isolated, established as a diving hotel before Cuba reappeared on the world tourist map, diving centre with access to 56 buoyed diving locations. Swimming and snorkelling not great because of shallow water and sea urchins, you have to wade a long way before it is deep enough to swim, but beach is white sand. 77 a/c rooms in main block and cabañas, in need of renovation, single and triple available, discounts for stays of over a week, TV. Lovely setting, pool, 3 restaurants, snack bar, store, basket ball, volleyball, tennis and squash courts, horse riding, disco Sat 2100-0600, busy with package tourists, so accommodation could be hard to find. **E** *Villa Gaviota* (3-star) on the outskirts of Nueva Gerona on the road to La Fe beside the river, T23290. 20 rooms, single and triple available, extra cots for children, a/c, fridge, TV, phone, pool where national swimming team trains, good service at poolside bar, restaurants, squash court and gymnasium, disco Thur-Sun 2130-0400, techno music, young crowd, dance and aerobics classes advertised, the nicest dollar place to stay if you are not diving or on a package, Havanautos for car and motorcycle rental. 1 km south of *Gaviota* is **F** *Rancho del Tesoro*, T24069, in woods close to the Río Las Casas. 60 rooms in blocks. In Nueva Gerona, **F** *La Cubana*, 39 y 16 above *Cubana*. 17 rooms with bath, but basic, formerly for Cubans only. Other peso places to stay include **F** *Los*

Isla de la Juventud

Codornices, T24981, on the way to the airport. 40 rooms in a block or in cabañas, pool, own transport needed. **Casas particulares** *Roberto Figuerero Rodríguez*, 35 1809, entre 18 y 20, Apto 1, T4892. Friendly, help with cars and drivers and information in general. **F** *Andrés Corbello Pino*, 24 5305 entre 53 y 55. A/c, food available, US$7 dinner including drinks.

If you are on a package you will probably take all your meals in hotels. Private restaurants are few and aimed mainly at locals. The best bet is to eat in people's homes, where you can get an excellent meal for US$5-6, with lobster, rice, beans, fried plantain extra. *El Tocororo*, opposite the park on Calles 39 y 16. Cuban dishes, pay in pesos, breakfast 0700-0900, lunch 1200-1400, dinner 1800-2000, but times seem flexible. *El Cochinito*, 39 y 24. State run, open 1400-2200, specializes in pork. *Cabaret El Dragón*, 39 y 26. Also state run but Chinese and Cuban food, restaurant and bar, open 1600-2200, Mon-Thur, 1600-0030 Fri-Sun, cabaret at weekends, deluxe atmosphere, upscale crowd; there is a *Mercado Agropecuario* at 41 y 40, fresh fruit and vegetables, and there are a few basic places to eat in this area where you can pay in pesos. For ice cream, *Coppelia* is at 37 y 32. **Eating**

Casa de los Vinos, 20 y 41. Open Mon-Wed 1400-2200, Fri-Sun 1400-2400, popular peso drinking spot with grapefruit, melon, tomato and grape wines in earthenware jugs, drink orders finish at 2300, advisable to take glasses, avoid the snacks. *Taberna Gerona*, 39 y 22. Open daily 1100-2100, Cuban food and pub atmosphere, very friendly, strictly pesos. **Bars**

El Patio, 24 entre 37 y 39. Open 2100-0300, cabaret, 2 shows nightly at weekends, at 2200 and 0100, entry US$3, lots of Cubans and popular. *La Movida* disco, 34 entre 18 y 20. Outdoors, US$3, Cubans pay in pesos, young student crowd, starts at 2200. *Villa Gaviota* disco, Thur-Sun, 2130-0400, entry US$1, cave-like atmosphere, picks up after midnight, young crowd, techno music. *Casa de la Cultura*, 37 y 24, check the schedule posted outside for dance events; beside the Servi Cupet petrol station on 39 y 30, no sign outside, café where you can dance, open 24 hrs, total mix of music, comfortable and friendly, best place. **Nightlife**

Local Travel to anywhere on the island can be difficult although nearly every car will turn into a taxi on request. Fares within Nueva Gerona and to main hotels are about US$2. The best way to see the island is to hire a private car with a driver/guide, which costs about US$40-60 a day. Motorbike hire from the hotels is US$7 per hour. Local transport is often by horse and cart. **Car hire**: *Havanautos* C 32 y 39, T24432, but the dollar hotels also have car hire desks. **Bus** Buses run to **La Fe**, the *Hotel Colony*, **Playa Bibijagua**, and bus marked 'Servicio Aereo', between the airport and the cinema, but don't rely on any of these to run on a regular basis. **Transport**

Long distance Air The Rafael Cabrera airport (GER) is nearly 5 km from town and there are 2 or 3 scheduled 40-min flights a day from Havana so you could do a day trip if you wanted. Fare US$22 1-way, book in advance. Aerotaxi to Pinar del Río US$22, like a flying bus. **Sea** An interesting way of getting to the island is by the 106-passenger *kometa* (a vintage Soviet hydrofoil), from Surgidero de Batabanó on the mainland south coast. There is a morning crossing and an evening crossing, which take 2 hrs, US$15. Connecting bus from **Havana** to Surgidero de Batabanó, 1 hr, from bus terminal on Boyeros at 0700 and 1300. Book a couple of days in advance at the terminal at the far end of the Boyeros entry, between 0600-1200, 2 pesos, at the office in the terminal. Snacks available at the terminal. On the *kometa* try for Salón A, the only one with a view. Those paying in dollars are usually directed to Salón C, with freezing air conditioning. Snacks available in pesos and beer at US$1. Customs entry both ways, remember 20-kilo weight limit. Alternatively, a ferry crosses on the same route Wed, Fri and Sun at 1930 from Havana train station and takes 6 hrs, US$10. In Havana tickets are sold at the station office. In Nueva Gerona the terminal is on the Río Las Casas at the end of Calle 22 and the ticket office is open daily 0600-1300. Fares in dollars, take your passport.

Airlines *Cubana* at 39 1415 entre 16 y 18, Nueva Gerona, T061-22531/24259. *Aerotaxi* at Siguanea airport, T98282, 98181. **Banks** *Banco Nacional*, 39 y 18, open Mon-Fri 0800-1400, Sat 1300-1500; Caja Popular de Ahorro, 39 y 26, open Mon-Fri 0800-1700. Best to bring enough cash from the **Directory**

Cuba

mainland. **Medical services** Pharmacy at 39 y 24, open Mon-Fri 0800-2200, Sat 0800-1600. Take plenty of insect repellent, particularly for the Ciénaga or the *Hotel Colony*.

Cayo Largo

Phone code: 5

Cayo Largo is at the eastern end of the Archipiélago de los Canarreos, 114 km east of Isla de la Juventud and 80 km south of the Península de Zapata. It is a long, thin, coral island, 26 km long and no more than 2 km wide. There are beautiful white sandy beaches all along the southern coast which, together with the cristal clear, warm waters of the Caribbean, make it ideal for tourism. A string of hotels lines the southern tip of the island. The northern coast is mostly mangrove and swamp, housing hungry mosquitoes as well as numerous birds (pelicans being the most visible) and iguanas. Turtles lay their eggs at Playa Tortuga in the northeast, and there is a turtle farm at Combinado northwest of the airstrip.

Beaches & watersports

The best beach on the island is the 2 km white sand **Playa Sirena**, which faces west and is spared any wind or currents which sometimes affect the southern beaches. Snorkelling and scuba diving can be done at Playa Sirena, 10 minutes' boat ride from the hotels and at **Playa Los Cocos**, which you can reach by bicycle. **Scuba diving** is good around the island. There is an extensive reef with gorgonians, sponges and lots of fish, while north of the island you will find large pelagics. **Sailing** is popular and there is a bareboat yacht charter fleet. The Marina Cayo Largo del Sur at Combinado has 50 moorings for visiting yachts, who don't have to buy a tourist card to come here if they are not going on to anywhere else in Cuba, because the island is a free port. To clear customs, call the marina on VHF 6, or maritime security (*seguridad marítima*) on VHF 16. There is **deep sea fishing** for marlin and other big fish, with international fishing tournaments held here. Other watersports include windsurfing, kayaking, jet skis, catamarans, and banana rides.

Sleeping

There are several hotels here at present, all in the Gran Caribe chain and grouped together under the name of the *Isla del Sur Hotel Resort*, T548111-8, F548201. All facilities shared and included in the package cost, which can be as low as US$400 per person for 4 nights, including air and ground transport from Havana, breakfast and dinner buffet. Prices include 3 meals and free use of all water sports and other activities such as tennis, horse riding and volleyball. Always check what is included in your package. Medical facilities, evening entertainment, disco, laundry, post office and fax services are all available. *Villa Capricho*, 75 rooms in thatched A-frame *cabañas*. *Hotel Isla del Sur*, 57 rooms. *Villa Coral*, 60 bungalows. *Villa Iguana*, 52 bungalows. *Villa Lindamar*, 63 cabañas. *Villa Soledad*, 43 bungalows. *Hotel Pelícano*, T548333-6, F548166. 230 rooms including 12 suites, set apart from the others and more isolated. The hotels and the thatched *cabañas* are low-lying and pleasantly spread out in gardens by the beach, all rooms are a/c, with private bath, telephone and satellite TV. There is no private accommodation on the island and you will not need any pesos.

Eating

There are several buffet restaurants and thatched snack bars (*ranchones*) attached to the hotels, as well as a seafood restaurant at the *Pelícano* which has to be booked, a highly recommended Italian place at the *Villas* and a good pizzería. Food is reported to be plentiful and fresh. You will not find any *paladares* here but there is lots of lobster.

Transport

Local Car hire: *Havanautos* and *Transautos* at the *Hotel Pelícano*. Motorcycles, bicycles, and jeeps are also available. **Long distance Air** There are several charters and scheduled international flights to Cayo Largo del Sur airport (CYO). *Aerogaviota* flies from Aeropuerto Playa Baracoa, **Havana**, a former military air base. There are also flights from **Varadero**, or by light plane or boat from **Isla de la Juventud**. *Aerotaxi* at the airport, T793255.

Background

History

Cuba was visited by Cristóbal Colón (Christopher Columbus) during his first voyage to find a westerly route to the Orient on 27 October 1492, and he made another brief stop two years later on his way from Hispaniola to Jamaica. Columbus did not realize it was an island when he landed; he hoped it was Japan. He arrived on the north coast of 'Colba', but found little gold. He did, however, note the Indians' practice of puffing at a large, burning roll of leaves, which they called 'tobacos'. Cuba was first circumnavigated by Sebastián de Ocampo in 1508, but it was Diego de Velázquez who conquered it in 1511 and founded several towns, called *villas*, including Havana.

The first African slaves were imported to Cuba in 1526. Sugar was introduced soon after. Tobacco was made a strict monopoly of Spain in 1717. The coffee plant was introduced in 1748. The British, under Lord Albemarle and Admiral Pocock, captured Havana and held the island in 1762-63, but it was returned to Spain in exchange for Florida.

Towards the end of the 18th century Cuba became a slave plantation society. By the 1860s Cuba was producing about a third of the world's sugar and was heavily dependent on slaves to do so, supplemented by indentured Chinese labourers in the 1850s and 1860s. An estimated 600,000 African slaves were imported by 1867.

Independence from Spain became a burning issue in Cuba as Spain refused to consider political reforms which would give the colony more autonomy. The first war of independence was in the eastern part of the island between 1868 and 1878, but it gained little save a modest move towards the abolition of slavery; and complete abolition was not achieved until 1886. Many national heroes were created during this period who have become revolutionary icons in the struggle against domination by a foreign power. One consequence of the war was the ruin of many sugar planters. US interests began to take over the sugar plantations and the sugar mills, and Cuba became more dependent on the US market.

From 1895 to 1898 rebellion flared up again in the second war of independence under the young poet and revolutionary, José Martí, together with the old guard of Antonio Maceo and Máximo Gómez. José Martí was tragically killed in May 1895 and Maceo in 1896. Despite fierce fighting throughout the island, neither the Nationalists nor the Spanish could gain the upper hand. However, the USA was now concerned for its investments and its strategic interests. When the US battleship *Maine* exploded in Havana harbour on 15 February 1898, killing 260 crew, the USA declared war on Spain. American forces were landed, a squadron blockaded Havana and defeated the Spanish fleet at Santiago de Cuba. In December peace was signed and US forces occupied the island for four years.

The Republic of Cuba was proclaimed in 1902 and the Government was handed over to its first president. However, the Platt Amendment to the constitution, passed by the US Congress, clearly made Cuba a protectorate of the USA. The USA retained naval bases and reserved the right of intervention in Cuban domestic affairs but, to quell growing unrest, repealed the Platt Amendment in 1934. The USA formally relinquished the right to intervene but retained its naval base at Guantánamo.

Around two thirds of sugar exports went to the USA under a quota system at prices set by Washington; two thirds of Cuba's imports came from the USA; foreign capital investment was largely from the USA and Cuba was effectively a client state. Yet its people suffered from grinding rural poverty, high unemployment, illiteracy and inadequate health care. Politics was a mixture of authoritarian rule and corrupt democracy.

Spanish conquest

Independence movement

Dictatorship

Cuba

From 1924 to 1933 the 'strong man' Gerardo Machado ruled Cuba. He was elected in 1924 on a wave of popularity but a drastic fall in sugar prices in the late 1920s led to strikes; nationalist popular rebellion was harshly repressed. The USA tried to negotiate a deal but nationalists called a general strike in protest at US interference, and Machado finally went into exile. The violence did not abate, however, and there were more strikes, mob attacks and occupations of factories. In September 1933 a revolt of non-commissioned officers including Sergeant Fulgencio Batista, deposed the government. He then held power through presidential puppets until he was elected president himself in 1940. Batista pursued nationalist and populist policies, set against corruption and political violence. In 1940 a new Constitution was passed by a constituent assembly dominated by Batista, which included universal suffrage and benefits for workers such as a minimum wage, pensions, social insurance and an eight-hour day. In 1944 Batista lost the elections but corruption continued. Batista, by then a self-promoted general, staged a military coup in 1952. Constitutional and democratic government was at an end. His harshly repressive dictatorship was brought to a close by Fidel Castro in January 1959, after an extraordinary and heroic three-year campaign, mostly in the Sierra Maestra, with a guerrilla force reduced at one point to 12 men.

Revolution Fidel Castro, the son of immigrants from Galicia and born in Cuba in 1926 saw José Martí as his role model and aimed to follow his ideals. In 1953, the 100th anniversary of José Martí's birth, Castro and a committed band of about 160 revolutionaries attacked the Moncada barracks in Santiago de Cuba on 26 July. The attack failed and Castro and his brother Raúl were later captured and put on trial. Fidel used the occasion to make an impassioned speech denouncing corruption in the ruling class and the need for political freedom and economic independence. In 1955 the Castros were given an amnesty and went to Mexico. There Fidel continued to work on his essentially nationalist revolutionary programme, called the 26 July Movement, which called for radical social and economic reforms and a return to the democracy of Cuba's 1940 constitution. He met another man of ideas, an Argentine doctor called Ernesto (Che) Guevara, who sailed with him and his brother Raúl and a band of 82 like-minded revolutionaries, back to Cuba on 2 December 1956. Their campaign began in the Sierra Maestra in the east of Cuba and after years of fierce fighting Batista fled the country on 1 January 1959. Fidel Castro, to universal popular acclaim, entered Havana and assumed control of the island.

Communism From 1960 onwards, in the face of increasing hostility from the USA, Castro led
& the 1960s Cuba into socialism and then communism. Officials of the Batista régime were put on trial in 'people's courts' and executed. The promised new elections were not held. The judiciary lost its independence when Castro assumed the right to appoint judges. The free press was closed or taken over. Trade unions lost their independence and became part of government. The University of Havana, a former focus of dissent, and professional associations all lost their autonomy. The democratic constitution of 1940 was never reinstated. In 1960 the sugar centrales, the oil refineries and the foreign banks were nationalized, all US property was expropriated and the Central Planning Board (Juceplan) was established. The professional and property-owning middle classes began a steady exodus which drained the country of much of its skilled workers. CIA-backed mercenaries and Cuban exiles kept up a relentless barrage of attacks, but failed to achieve their objective.

1961 was the year of the Bay of Pigs invasion, a fiasco which was to harden Castro's political persuasion. Some 1,400 Cuban emigrés, trained by the CIA landed in the Bahía de Cochinos (Bay of Pigs), but the men were stranded on the beaches when the Cuban air force attacked their supply ships. 200 were killed and the rest surrendered within three days. In his May Day speech, Fidel Castro confirmed that the Cuban Revolution was socialist. The US reaction was to isolate Cuba, with a full trade embargo. Cuba was expelled from the Organization of American States

(OAS) and the OAS imposed economic sanctions. In March 1962 rationing had to be imposed.

In April 1962, President Kruschev of the USSR decided to send medium-range missiles to Cuba, which would be capable of striking anywhere in the USA. This episode, which became known as the 'Cuban Missile Crisis', brought the world to the brink of nuclear war, defused only by secret negotiations between John F Kennedy and Kruschev. Without consulting Castro and without his knowledge, Kruschev eventually agreed to have the missiles dismantled and withdrawn on condition that the west would guarantee a policy of non-aggression towards Cuba.

Economic policy during the 1960s was largely unsuccessful in achieving its aims. The government wanted to industrialize rapidly to reduce dependence on sugar. However, the crash programme, with help from the USSR, was a failure and had to be abandoned. The whole nation was called upon to achieve a target of 10 million tonnes of sugar by 1970 and everyone spent time in the fields helping towards this goal. It was never reached and never has been. Rationing is still fierce, and there are still shortages of consumer goods. However, the Revolution's social policies have largely been successful and it is principally these achievements which have ensured the people's support of Castro and kept him in power. Education, housing and health services have been greatly improved and the social inequalities of the 1940s and 1950s have been wiped out.

During the second decade of the Revolution, Cuba became firmly entrenched as a member of the Soviet bloc, joining COMECON in 1972. The Revolution was institutionalized along Soviet lines and the Party gained control of the bureaucracy, the judiciary and the local and national assemblies. A new socialist constitution was adopted in 1976.

1970s Soviet domination

Cuba's foreign policy changed from actively fomenting socialist revolutions abroad (such as Guevara's forays into the Congo and Bolivia in the 1960s) to supporting other left wing or third world countries with combat troops and technical advisers including Angola, Ethiopia, Nicaragua, Jamaica and Grenada. In September 1979, Castro hosted a summit conference of the non-aligned nations in Havana, a high point in his foreign policy initiatives.

By the 1980s, the heavy dependence on sugar and the USSR, coupled with the trade embargo, meant that the expected improvements in living standards were not being delivered as fast as hoped and the people were tiring of being asked for ever more sacrifices. In 1980, the Peruvian embassy was overrun by 11,000 people seeking political asylum. Castro let them go and he opened the port of Mariel for a mass departure of some 125,000 by sea in anything they could find which would float.

1980s dissatisfaction

This was the decade of the Latin American debt crisis, and Cuba was unable to escape. Development projects in the 1970s had been financed with loans from western banks, in addition to the aid from the USSR. When interest rates went up in 1982, Cuba was forced to renegotiate its US$3.5 bn debt to commercial banks, and in 1986 its debt to the USSR. The need to control public finances brought more austerity.

Before the collapse of the Soviet system, aid to Cuba from the USSR was traditionally estimated at about 25% of gnp. Cuba's debt with the USSR was a secret; estimates ranged from US$8.5 bn to US$34 bn. Apart from military aid, economic assistance took two forms: balance of payments support (about 85%), under which sugar and nickel exports were priced in excess of world levels, and assistance for development projects. About 13 million tonnes of oil were supplied a year by the USSR, allowing three million to be re-exported, providing a valuable source of foreign earnings. By the late 1980s up to 90% of Cuba's foreign trade was with centrally planned economies.

The collapse of the Communist system in Eastern Europe, followed by the demise of the USSR, very nearly brought the end of Castro's Cuba as well. There were signs that a power struggle was taking place at the top of the Communist Party. In 1989,

Cuba

Gen Arnaldo Ochoa, a hero of the Angolan campaign, was charged with drug trafficking and corruption. He was publicly tried and executed along with several other military officers allegedly involved.

1990s crisis & change In an effort to broaden the people's power system of government introduced in 1976, the central committee of the Cuban Communist Party adopted resolutions in 1990 designed to strengthen the municipal and provincial assemblies and transform the National Assembly into a genuine parliament. In February 1993, the first direct, secret elections for the National Assembly and for provincial assemblies were held.

Economic difficulties in the 1990s brought on by the loss of markets in the former USSR and Eastern Europe, together with higher oil prices because of the Gulf crisis, forced the Government to impose emergency measures and declare a special period in peace time. Rationing was increased, petrol became scarce, the bureaucracy was slashed. In 1993, Cuba was hit by a storm which caused an estimated US$1bn in damage. In mid-1994, economic discontent boiled up and Cubans began to flee for Florida in a mass exodus similar to that of Mariel in 1980. It was estimated that between mid-August and mid-September 30,000 Cubans had left the country. Eventually the crisis forced President Clinton into an agreement whereby the USA was committed to accepting at least 20,000 Cubans a year, plus the next of kin of US citizens, while Cuba agreed to prevent further departures.

As the economic crisis persisted, the government adopted measures which opened up many sectors to private enterprise and recognized the dependence of much of the economy on dollars. The partial reforms did not eradicate the imbalances between the peso and the dollar economies, and shortages remained for those without access to hard currency. Cuba intensified its economic liberalization programme, allowing farmers to sell at uncontrolled prices once their commitments to the state procurement system were fulfilled. Importantly, the reforms also allowed middlemen to operate. Markets in manufactured goods and handicrafts also opened and efforts were made to increase the number of self-employed.

US pressure in the 1990s Before the Revolution of 1959 the USA had investments in Cuba worth about US$1,000mn, covering nearly every activity from agriculture and mining to oil installations. Today all American businesses, have been nationalized; the USA has cut off all imports from Cuba, placed an embargo on exports to Cuba, and broken off diplomatic relations. Prior to the 1992 US presidential elections, President Bush approved the Cuban Democracy Act (Torricelli Bill) which forbade US subsidiaries from trading with Cuba. Many countries, including EC members and Canada, said they would not allow the US bill to affect their trade with Cuba and the UN General Assembly voted in favour of a resolution calling for an end to the embargo.

In 1996, US election year, Cuba faced another crackdown by the US administration. In February, Cuba shot down two light aircraft piloted by Miami exiles allegedly over Cuban air space and implicitly confirmed by the findings of the International Civil Aviation Organization (ICAO) report in June. The attack provoked President Clinton to tighten and internationalize the US embargo on Cuba and on 12 March he signed into law the (Helms-Burton) Cuban Freedom and Democratic Solidarity Act. The new legislation allows legal action against any company or individual benefiting from properties expropriated by the Cuban government after the Revolution. It brought universal condemnation: Canada and Mexico (Nafta partners), the EU, Russia, China, the Caribbean Community and the Río Group of Latin American countries all protested that it was unacceptable to extend sanctions outside the USA to foreign companies and their employees who do business with Cuba.

Recent events 1997 was the 30th anniversary of the death of Che Guevara in Bolivia, whose remains were returned to Cuba in July. During a week of official mourning for Che and his comrades in arms, vast numbers filed past their remains in Havana and Santa Clara, where they were laid to rest on 17 October. In December 1998 the remains of 10 more guerrillas killed in Bolivia in 1967 were also interred in the Che Guevara memorial in Santa Clara. They included Haydée Tamara Bunke, known as Tania.

In January 1998 the Pope visited Cuba for the first time. During his four-day visit he held open-air masses around the country. The Pope preached against Cuba's record on human rights and abortion while also condemning the US trade embargo preventing food and medicines reaching the needy. The visit was a public relations success for both Castro and the Pope. Shortly afterwards, 200 prisoners were pardoned and released and more were expected.

In 1999 the UN Human Rights Commission expressed concern about 'continued repression' in Cuba, following the conviction of four Cubans for sedition. They were jailed for receiving funds and instructions from the USA aimed at obstructing foreign investment. Two Salvadoreans were sentenced to death for a bombing campaign in 1997 in which six Havana hotels and restaurants were attacked and an Italian killed. In a crackdown against crime, the National Assembly approved amendments to 25 articles of the penal code, increasing sentences and extending the death penalty. Police presence increased noticeably on the streets of Havana.

In November 1999 a six-year-old boy, Elián González, was rescued from the sea off Florida, the only survivor from a boatload of illegal migrants which included his mother and her boyfriend. He was looked after by distant relatives in Miami and quickly became the centrepiece of a new row between Cuban exiles, supported by right wing Republicans, and Cuba. The US Attorney General, Janet Reno, supported the decision by the US Immigration and and Naturalization Service (INS) on 5 January 2000, that the boy should be repatriated and reunited with his father in Cuba by 14 January, but she postponed the deadline to allow for legal challenges. Mass demonstrations were held in Havana in support of Elián's return but legal manoeuvres by US politicians stalled progress and caused further disputes. Amid enormous controversy, the US authorities siezed Elián on 22 April and reunited him with his father, who had travelled to the USA earlier in the month with his second wife and baby. The family remained in the USA, while more legal wranglings took place.

Geography

The island of Cuba, 1,250 km long, 191 km at its widest point, is the largest of the Caribbean islands and only 145 km south of Florida. The name is believed to derive from the Arawak word 'cubanacan', meaning central. Gifted with a moderate climate, afflicted only occasionally by hurricanes, not cursed by frosts, blessed by an ample and well distributed rainfall and excellent soils, it has traditionally been one of the largest exporters of cane sugar in the world.

Geologically at least, Cuba is part of North America; the boundary between the North American and Caribbean plates runs east-west under the Caribbean Sea to the south of the island. Along the plate margin is a deep underwater rift valley, which runs between Cuba and Jamaica. This feature is quite close to the Cuban coast to the south of the Sierra Maestra, with water plunging to 6,000 metres deep only a few km offshore.

The northern coastline is gradually emerging from the sea. Old coral reefs have been brought to the surface, so that much of the northern coast consists of coral limestone cliffs and sandy beaches. By contrast the southern coastline is being gradually submerged, producing wetlands and mangroves, with fewer sandy beaches than the north of the island. Limestones of various types cover about two-thirds of the island. In most areas, there is a flat or gently rolling landscape.

There are three main mountain areas in the island. In the west, the Cordillera de Guaniguanico is divided into the Sierra del los Organos in the west, with thick deposits of limestone which have developed a distinctive landscape of steep-sided flat-topped mountains; and the Sierra del Rosario in the east, made up partly of limestones and partly of lavas and other igneous rocks. Another mountainous area in central Cuba includes the Escambray mountains north of Trinidad, a double dome structure made up of igneous and metamorphic rocks, including marble.

The Sierra Maestra in east Cuba has Cuba's highest mountains, rising to Pico Turquino (1,974 metres) and a rather different geological history, with some rocks formed in an arc of volcanic activity around 50 million years ago. Older rocks include marble, and other metamorphics. Important mineral deposits are in this area; nickel is mined near Moa.

Constitution and government

In 1976 a new constitution was approved by 97.7% of the voters, setting up municipal and provincial assemblies and a National Assembly of People's Power. The membership of the Assembly is now 595, candidates being nominated by the 169 municipal councils, and elected by direct secret ballot. Similarly elected are members of the 14 provincial assemblies, both for five-year terms. The number of Cuba's provinces was increased from six to 14 at the First Congress of the Communist Party of Cuba in December 1975. Dr Fidel Castro was elected President of the Council of State by the National Assembly and his brother, Major Raúl Castro, was elected First Vice-President. There are five other Vice-Presidents.

The economy

Following the 1959 revolution, Cuba adopted a Marxist-Leninist system. Almost all sectors of the economy were state controlled and centrally planned, the only significant exception being agriculture, where some 12% of arable land was still privately owned. The country became heavily dependent on trade and aid from other Communist countries, principally the USSR (through its participation in the Council of Mutual Economic Aid), encouraged by the US trade embargo. It relied on sugar, and to a lesser extent nickel, for nearly all its exports. While times were good, Cuba used the Soviet protection to build up an impressive, but costly, social welfare system, with better housing, education and health care than anywhere else in Latin America and the Caribbean. The collapse of the Eastern European bloc, however, revealed the vulnerability of the island's economy and the desperate need for reform. A sharp fall in gdp of 35% in 1990-93, accompanied by a decline in exports from US$8.1bn (1989) to US$1.7bn (1993), forced the Government to take remedial action and the decision was made to change to a mixed economy.

Transformation of the heavily centralized state apparatus has progressed in fits and starts. The Government is keen to encourage self-employment to enable it to reduce the public sector workforce, but Cuban workers are cautious about relinquishing their job security. Some small businesses have sprung up, particularly in tourism. Free farm produce markets were permitted in 1994 and these were followed by similar markets at deregulated prices for manufacturers, including goods produced by state enterprises and handicrafts. Cubans are now allowed to hold US dollars and in 1995 a convertible peso at par with the US dollar was introduced.

The US trade embargo and the associated inability to secure finance from multilateral sources has led the Government to encourage foreign investment, principally in joint ventures. All sectors of the economy are now open to foreign investment and in some areas majority foreign shareholdings are allowed. 374 joint ventures are now established in Cuba, with capital from 46 countries. The leading investors are from Spain, Canada, France, Italy and Mexico, in that order.

Sugar is the major crop, and the second most important earner of foreign exchange after tourism. However, the industry has consistently failed to reach the targets set. Cuba's dream of a 10 mn tonne raw sugar harvest has never been reached and by 1998 output had fallen steadily to 3.2 mn tonnes, the lowest for 50 years. Poor weather and shortages of fertilizers, oil and spare parts cut output. The 1999/2000 harvest achieved its target of 4 mn tonnes, but world prices were low.

Structure of production

Citrus is an important agricultural export. Production in 1998 rose by 6% to 1,850,000 tonnes. Cuba became a member of the International Coffee Agreement in 1985 and produces about 22,000 tonnes of **coffee** a year but exports are minimal. **Tobacco** is a traditional crop with Cuban cigars world famous, but this too has suffered from lack of fuel, fertilizers and other inputs. Production is recovering with the help of Spanish credits and importers from France and Britain.

Diversification away from sugar is a major goal, with the emphasis on production of **food** for domestic use because of the shortage of foreign exchange for imports. The beef herd declined to four million in the first half of the 1990s because of the inability to pay for imports of grains, fertilizers and chemicals. Production is now less intensive and numbers are beginning to rise again. Similarly, milk production is also increasing. In 1993, in a new agricultural reform process, the Cuban state handed over more than 28,250 sq km of land in usufruct to workers in state enterprises. The newly created basic units of cooperative production (UBPCs) now possess approximately 42% of Cuba's arable land. Taking into account the longer-running cooperative systems and land given to *campesino* families to cultivate coffee and tobacco, the total non-state utilization of land has risen to 67.3%. The opening of farmers markets in 1994 has helped to stimulate diversification and greater availability of foodstuffs, although shortages still remain. Drought in the east in 1998 reached crisis proportions and was followed by Hurricane Georges and flooding, all affecting crops of beans, grains, vegetables and fruit.

The sudden withdrawal of **oil** supplies when trade agreements with Russia had to be renegotiated and denominated in convertible currencies, was a crucial factor in the collapse of the Cuban economy. Although trade agreements involving oil and sugar remain, Cuba has had to purchase oil from other suppliers with limited foreign exchange. As a result, Cuba has stepped up its own production: foreign companies explore for oil on and offshore and investment has borne fruit. In 1998 production of oil was 1,678,000 tonnes and gas was 117 mn cu m, but over 7 mn tonnes of hydrocarbons are imported, at a cost of US$1bn, and shortages of fuel remain.

Mining is attracting foreign interest and in 1994 a new mining law was passed. A Mining Authority was created and a tax system set up. 40,000 sq km have been allocated for mining ventures. Major foreign investors included Australian (nickel), Canadian (gold, silver and base metals) and South African (gold, copper, nickel) companies. Nickel and cobalt production rose to a record 68,000 tonnes in 1998, nearly half of which came from the Moa Bay plant run as a joint venture between Canadian interests and the Cuban state. Cuba has one small gold mine at Castellanos in Pinar del Río province. New, Canadian-backed projects in Pinar del Río at the Hierro Mantua site will produce gold and copper, and on Isla de la Juventud, gold and silver.

Tourism is now a major foreign exchange earner and has received massive investment from abroad with many joint ventures. New hotel projects are coming on stream and many more are planned. Most of the development has been along the Varadero coast, where large resort hotels attract package tourism, but Cayo Coco and Cayo Guillermo are now earmarked for major construction. Cuba has around 32,000 hotel rooms, of which two thirds are in beach resorts and a third in cities, although this is to rise to over 60,000 by 2006. Despite political crises, numbers of visitors have risen steadily from 546,000 in 1993 to 2 mn in 1999. Gross income reached US$2.1 bn. 15% of visitors come from Canada, 13% from Italy, 11% from Germany and 10% from Spain. The target is for 7 mn tourists a year by 2010, bringing earnings of about US$11.8 bn.

Cuba

Recent trends There has been considerable success in reducing the fiscal deficit, which was bloated by subsidies and inefficiencies. A deficit of 5,000 million pesos in 1993 was cut to 570 million in 1996, only 2.4% of gdp, reflecting subsidy reductions. More reforms are planned, which may include the removal of subsidies from almost all state enterprises, new legislation on property ownership and commercial practice, development of the tax system and restructuring of the banking system. Financial services will be overhauled to cater for the accumulation of capital by owners of small businesses, who currently have to operate in cash. In 1997 legislation was approved to transform the Banco Nacional de Cuba; the Banco Central de Cuba was established to assume the central banking functions of the Banco Nacional, which will continue as a commercial bank. There are signs that the Cuban economy has turned the corner, although these have yet to be felt by the population in general. The external accounts remain weak. Foreign debt was US$11bn in 1998 (excluding debt to former members of Comecon), and Cuba's dependence on high-interest, short-term trade finance is a burden. Cuba is ineligible for long-term development finance from multilateral lending agencies because of the US veto. Renegotiation of debt to some European countries and Japan is progressing.

Culture

Religion The major characteristic of Cuban culture is its combination of the African and European. Black African traditions persist, inevitably mingled with Hispanic influence, in religion: for instance *santería*, a cult which blends popular Catholicism with the Yoruba belief in the spirits which inhabit all plant life. This now has a greater hold than orthodox Catholicism. Church and State were separated at the beginning of the 20th century. The domination of the USA after that time encouraged the spread of Protestantism, although Catholicism remained the religion of the majority. Nevertheless, Catholicism was not as well supported as in some other Latin American countries. After the Revolution relations between the Catholic Church and Castro were frosty. Most priests left the country. By the late 1970s the Vatican's condemnation of the US embargo helped towards a gradual reconciliation. A ban on religious believers joining the Communist Party has been lifted and Protestant, Catholic and other Church leaders have reported rising congregations. In 1996 Fidel visited Pope John Paul II at the Vatican and the Pope visited Cuba in January 1998. Castro has stated in the past that there is no conflict between Marxism and Christianity and has been sympathetic towards supporters of liberation theology in their quest for equality and a just distribution of social wealth.

Afro Cuban religion From the mid-16th century to the late 19th, hundreds of thousands of African slaves were brought to Cuba. The most numerous and culturally most influential group were the Yoruba-speaking agriculturalists from of Southeast Nigeria, Dahomey and Togo, who became known collectively in Cuba as *lucumí*. It is their pantheon of deities or *orishas*, and the legends (*pwatakis*) and customs surrounding these, which form the basis of the syncretic **Regla de Ocha** cult, better known as **Santería**. Though slaves were ostensibly obliged to become Christians, their owners turned a blind eye to their rituals. The Catholic saints thus spontaneously merged or syncretised in the *lucumí* mind with the *orishas* whose imagined attributes they shared. Some two dozen regularly receive tribute at the rites known as *toques de santo*. Santería is non-sectarian and non-proselytizing, co-existing peacefully with both Christianity and the **Regla Conga** or **Palo Monte** cult brought to Cuba by *congos*, slaves from various Bantu-speaking regions of the Congo basin. Indeed many people are practising believers in both or all three. The **Abakuá Secret Society** is not a religion but a closed sect. Open to men only, and upholding traditional *macho* virtues, it has been described as an Afro-Cuban freemasonry, though it claims many non-black devotees. Also known as **ñañiguismo**, the sect originated among slaves brought from the Calabar region of southern Nigeria and Cameroon, whose Cuban descendants are called *carabalí*.

The Cuban Revolution had perhaps its widest cultural influence in the field of **litera-** **Literature**
ture. Many now famous Latin American novelists (like Gabriel García Márquez,
Mario Vargas Llosa and Julio Cortázar) visited Havana and worked with the Prensa
Latina news agency or on the *Casa de las Américas* review. Not all have maintained
their allegiance, just as some Cuban writers have deserted the Revolution. One such
Cuban is Guillermo Cabrera Infante, whose most celebrated novel is *Tres tristes
tigres* (1967). Other established writers remained in Cuba after the Revolution: Alejo
Carpentier, who invented the phrase 'marvellous realism' (*lo real maravilloso*) to
describe the different order of reality which he perceived in Latin America and the
Caribbean and which influenced many other writers from the region (his novels
include *El reino de este mundo, El siglo de las luces, Los pasos perdidos*, and many
more); Jorge Lezama Lima (*Paradiso*, 1966); and Edmundo Desnoes (*Memorias del
subdesarrollo*). Of post-revolutionary writers, the poet and novelist Miguel Barnet is
worth reading, especially for the use of black oral history and traditions in his work.
After 1959, Nicolás Guillén, a black, was adopted as the national poet; his poems of
the 1930s (*Motivos de son, Sóngoro cosongo, West Indies Ltd*) are steeped in popular
speech and musical rhythms. In tone they are close to the work of the *négritude* writers (see under Martinique), but they look more towards Latin America than Africa.
The other poet-hero of the Revolution is the 19th-century writer and fighter for freedom from Spain, José Martí. Even though a US radio and TV station beaming pro-
paganda, pop music and North American culture usurped his name, Martí's
importance to Cuba remains undimmed.

Music is incredibly vibrant on the island. It is, again, a marriage of African rhythms, **Music**
expressed in percussion instruments (batá drums, congas, claves, maracas, etc), and
the Spanish guitar. Accompanying the music is an equally strong tradition of dance.
A history of Cuban music is beyond the scope of this book, however there are certain
styles which deserve mention. There are four basic elements out of which all others
grow. The *rumba* (drumming, singing about social preoccupations and dancing) is
one of the original black dance forms. By the turn of the century, it had been transferred from the plantations to the slums; now it is a collective expression, with Saturday evening competitions in which anyone can partake. Originating in eastern
Cuba, *son* is the music out of which *salsa* was born. *Son* itself takes many different
forms and it gained worldwide popularity after the 1920s when the National Septet
of Ignacio Piñeiro made it fashionable. The more sophisticated *danzón*, ballroom
dance music which was not accepted by the upper classes until the end of the last
century, has also been very influential. It was the root for the *cha-cha-cha* (invented
in 1948 by Enrique Jorrin). The fourth tradition is *trova*, the itinerant troubadour
singing ballads, which has been transformed, post-Revolution, into the *nueva trova*,
made famous by singers such as Pablo Milanés and Silvio Rodríguez. The new tradition adds politics and everyday concerns to the romantic themes. There are many
other styles, such as the *guajira*, the most famous example of which is the song
'Guantanamera'; *tumba francesa* drumming and dancing; and Afro-Cuban jazz,
performed by internationally renowned artists like Irakere and Arturo Sandoval.
Apart from sampling the recordings of groups, put out by the state company Egrem,
the National Folklore Company (Conjunto Folklórico Nacional) gives performances of the traditional music which it was set up to study and keep alive.

242

Cayman Islands

5

Cayman Islands

The British Crown Colony of the Cayman Islands consists of Grand Cayman and the sister islands of Cayman Brac and Little Cayman, in the Caribbean Sea. None of the islands has any rivers, but vegetation is luxuriant, the main trees being coconut, thatch palm, seagrape and Australian pine.

The islands were first sighted by Columbus in May 1503 when he was blown off course on his way to Hispaniola. He found two small islands (Cayman Brac and Little Cayman) which were full of turtles, and he therefore named the islands Las Tortugas. A 1523 map of the islands referred to them as Lagartos, meaning alligators or large lizards, but by 1530 they were known as the Caymanas after the Carib word for the marine crocodile which also lived there.

World-famous for their underwater scenery, there are tropical fish of all kinds in the waters surrounding the islands, especially in the coral reefs, and green turtles are now increasing in numbers, having been deliberately restocked by excess hatchings at the Cayman Turtle Farm.

Essentials

Before you travel

Documents

Passports but not visas are required for citizens of USA, Canada, EU and Commonwealth countries, Israel, Japan, Argentina, Bahrain, Brazil, Chile, Costa Rica, Ecuador, El Salvador, Guatemala, Mexico, Oman, Panama, Peru, Saudi Arabia and Venezuela. If you are from any of these countries you may be admitted to the Cayman Islands for a period of up to six months providing you have proof of citizenship, sufficient resources to maintain yourself during your stay, and a return ticket to your country of origin or another country in which you will be accepted. Married women using their husband's name should also show their marriage certificate. **Visas** are required by all countries not included in the above list. Luggage is inspected by customs officials on arrival; no attempt should be made to take drugs into the country.

Money

The legal **currency** is the Cayman Islands dollar (CI$). The **exchange rate** is fixed at CI$1 to US$1.20, or CI$0.80 to US$1, although officially the exchange rate is CI$0.84 to US$1. US currency is readily accepted throughout the Islands (although all change will be returned in CI$) and Canadian and British currencies can be exchanged at all banks. There is no exchange control. **Credit cards** are not accepted everywhere; do not assume that your hotel will accept them. Personal cheques are not generally welcome. Travellers' cheques are preferred. Most of the major international **banks** are represented in George Town, Grand Cayman but not all are licensed to offer normal banking facilities. Those which do include *Bank of Nova Scotia*, *Barclays Bank International, Canadian Imperial Bank of Commerce* and *Royal Bank of Canada*. Commercial banking hours are 0900 to 1600 Monday to Thursday, and 0900 to 1630 on Friday. The *Cayman National Bank* has a branch on Cayman Brac.

Climate
Average temperatures in winter are about 24°C & in summer are about 26°-29°C

The Cayman Islands lie in the trade-wind belt and the prevailing northeast winds moderate the temperatures, making the climate delightful all year round. Most rain falls between May and October, but even then it only takes the form of short showers. Hurricane season is June to October but the Cayman Islands have had little trouble from severe storms since Hurricane Gilbert in 1988. Hurricane Mitch passed by in 1998 and took away a few jetties and some sand, but there was no major damage.

Getting there

Air

From Europe *British Airways* has two scheduled flights a week from London Gatwick via Nassau, so two-centre visits are possible. **From North America** The national flag carrier, *Cayman Airways,* has regular services between Grand Cayman and Cayman Brac and Miami, Houston, Orlando and Tampa in the USA. *Northwest Airlines* flies from Detroit. *American Airlines* flies from Chicago and Miami. *US Air* flies from Charlotte and Philadelphia. *Delta* flies from Atlanta. *Sunworld* from Cincinnati. **From the Caribbean** *Air Jamaica* and *Cayman Airways* share a service to Kingston; *Air Jamaica* also has services from Montego Bay. *Isleña* flies to La Ceiba, Honduras.

Sea
30 major cruise lines visit Grand Cayman with 600 calls to port each year bringing over 1 million visitors

No more than four ships may be in port at any given time, or 6,500 passengers, whichever is greater. The islands are not served by any scheduled passenger ships but there are cargo services between the islands, Kingston in Jamaica, Honduras and Costa Rica and Miami and Tampa in the USA. The port at George Town comprises the south-wharf, with a depth of 24 ft, and the west wharf, with a depth of 20 ft. The port at Creek, Cayman Brac, is equipped to handle the same class of vessels but Little Cayman has only a small facility. There is a small jetty at Spotts, Grand Cayman, which caters for cruise ships when the weather is too bad to land at George Town.

Tourist offices overseas

Canada Travel Marketing Consultants, 234 Eglinton Ave East, Suite 306, Toronto, Ontario, M4P IK5 T416-4851550, F416-4857578.

France/Benelux/Scandinavia Horwath Axe Consultants, 12 Rue de Madrid, 75008, Paris, France, T53-424136, F43-873285.

Germany/Austria/Switzerland Marketing Services International, Walter Sthrer and Partner GmbH, Johanna-Melber-Weg 12, D-60599, Frankfurt, T69-6032094, F69-629264.

Italy G & A Martinengo, Via Fratelli Ruffini 9, 20123 Milano, T02-48012068, F02-463532.

Spain Sergat España SL, Pau Casals 4, 08021 Barcelona, T93-4140210, F93-2018657.

UK 6 Arlington St, London SW1A 1RE, T020-74917771, F020-74097773, infouk@caymanislands.uk The Cayman

Turtle newsletter is produced twice a year, primarily for travel agents, but also for anyone interested in visiting the islands. The London office is also the European headquarters for Cayman Airways, providing air reservations and tickets as well as a hotel reservations service (free). The Public Relations office for both organizations is McCluskey and Associates, 50 Sulivan Rd, London SW6 3DX, T020-73718900, F020-73718116.

USA 6100 Blue Lagoon Drive, Suite 150, Miami, Fl 33126-2085, T305-2662300, F305-2672932; 9525 W Bryn Mawr, Suite 160, Rosemont, Illinois 60018, T847-6786446, F847-6786675; Two Memorial City Plaza, 820 Gessner, Suite 170, Houston, Texas 77024, T713-4611317, F713-4617409; 420 Lexington Ave, Suite 2733, New York, NY 10170, T212-6825582, F212-9865123; 3440 Wilshire Blvd, Suite 1202, Los Angeles, California 90010, T213-7381968, F213-7381829.

Touching down

Air communications are good and there are two international airports, the **Owen Roberts International Airport** on Grand Cayman and the **Gerrard Smith Airport** on Cayman Brac. **Owen Roberts International Airport** is situated less than two miles from the centre of George Town and only 10 minutes' drive from most of the hotels on Seven Mile Beach. In a plaza outside the terminal there are car hire companies and a café, open from 0700. | **Airport information**

Airlines *Cayman Airways*, T9492311. For information on flights to Cayman Brac, T9481221. *Island Air*, for flights to the sister islands, T9490241. *Air Jamaica*, T9492300. *American Airlines*, T9498799. *Island Air*, T9490241/5252, F9497044. *Northwest Airlines*, T9492955/6. *United Airlines*, T9497724. *US Air*, T9497488. Charter companies: *Executive Air Services*, T9497766.

Cable and Wireless, in conjunction with the Department of Tourism, provide a Tourist Hotline. By dialling 9498989 you can find out the week's events and local information. Further information may be obtained from the Cayman Islands Department of Tourism, The Pavilion, Cricket Square, Elgin Avenue, George Town, PO Box 67, George Town, Grand Cayman, BWI, T345-9490623, F9494053, toll free 1800-3463313, 0830-1700, www.caymanislands.ky | **Tourist information**

Privilege Card From 15 April to 15 December, more than 90 tourist industry companies participate in a discount programme. With your Privilege Card you can get discounts on accommodation, restaurants (10% on food), watersports (20%), car rentals (20%), golf (10-25%), shopping (15%) and attractions on all three islands. Ask a travel agent for details.

Weddings There is no residency requirement, so you can get married on a day trip to the Cayman Islands, provided you obtain a special licence from the Administrative Secretary, Room 46, Government Administration Building, George Town, or from the District Commissioner's office at Stake Bay, Cayman Brac, for US$200. Contact the tourist office for more information.

Cayman Islands

● ●

 Touching down

Official time *Eastern Standard Time, 5 hours behind GMT, for the whole year.*

Departure tax *US$12.50 for all visitors aged 12 and over payable either in Cayman or US currency when you leave the Islands (includes US$2.50 environmental tax).*

Safety *The Cayman Islands are safe to visit and present no need for extra security precautions. However, drugs related offences have increased. The islands remain a major trans-shipment point. Care must be taken when walking on a road, especially at night; they are narrow and vehicles move fast.*

Newspapers *The* Caymanian Compass *is published Monday to Friday with a circulation of 25,000. Online you can get news and information with Cayman Net News at www.caymannetnews.com The television station CITN has its own website at www.caymanews.com.ky*

Public holidays *New Year's Day, Ash Wednesday, Good Friday, Easter Monday, Discovery Day (third Monday in May), the Monday following the Queen's official birthday (June), Constitution Day (first Monday in July), the Monday after Remembrance Sunday (November), Christmas Day and Boxing Day.*

● ●

Further reading The Cayman Islands Government Information Services (The Pavilion, Cricket Square, Grand Cayman, T9498092, F9498487) publishes a series of booklets including *Marine Parks Rules and Sea Code in The Cayman Islands* and several on banking, captive insurance, company registration, residential status, work permits, living in the Cayman Islands etc. The Department of Tourism publishes *The Rates & Facts Guide to the Cayman Islands* annually, giving hotel and transport prices as well as other useful information. The tourist office also has a list of books about the Cayman Islands which can be bought in the islands. The Ordnance Survey produces a 1:50,000 scale map of the Cayman Islands with an inset map of George Town in its World Map Series. For information contact Ordnance Survey, Romsey Rd, Maybush, Southampton SO9 4DH, T0703-792000, F0703-792404.

Where to stay

The winter season, running from 16 December to 15 April, is the peak tourist season. Visitors intending to come to the islands during this period are advised to make hotel and travel arrangements well in advance. There are substantial reductions during the rest of the year (see Privilege Card above), with cut rates or even free accommodation for children under 12. Most hotels offer watersports, scuba diving and snorkelling, and many have tennis courts, swimming pools and other facilities. Accommodation is plentiful and varied, ranging from resort hotels on the beach to small, out of the way, family-run guest houses. There is also a wide variety of cottages, apartments (condominiums) and villas available for daily, weekly or monthly rental. A full list of tourist accommodation and prices, including hotels, cottages, apartments and villas, is available from Cayman Islands Department of Tourism. The Cayman Islands Hotel Reservations Service, T305-2666742, F305-2672931, represents 67 properties in the Cayman Islands and can be contacted abroad direct or through the tourist office. A government tax of 6% is added to the room charge and most hotels also add a 15% service charge to the bill in lieu of tipping.

Getting around

Air *Cayman Airways* and *Island Air* provide inter-island services from Grand Cayman to Cayman Brac and Little Cayman and return (US$110 day return, or US$149 to both sister islands). Reservations for *Island Air* are not possible through any CRS systems. You can have a full day on either sister island by booking *Island Air's* daily flight 6131, departing Grand Cayman 0745, arriving Cayman Brac at 0825 and Little Cayman at 0845. The last return flight 6314 departs Cayman Brac at 1725, Little Cayman at 1745, arriving back in Grand Cayman at 1830. A child's day trip fare is US$89, T9495252.

Keeping in touch

The Philatelic Bureau releases six stamp issues a year. Stamps are sold separately or as a First Day Cover from CI$0.10 to 2.00. Airmail postal rates are divided into three groups. **Group A**: the Caribbean, USA, Canada, Central America and Venezuela, first class 30 cents, second class, post cards, airletters 20 cents. **Group B**: Europe, Scandinavia, West Africa, South America, first class 40 cents, others 25 cents. **Group C**: East Africa, the Arabian sub-continent, Asia and the Far East, first class 55 cents, others 30 cents. Post Box suffixes are now required for mail delivery in the sister islands as well as Grand Cayman: Stake Bay post office, SPO; West End, WPO; Watering Place, WP; Creek, CK; Spot Bay, SB; Little Cayman, LC. A sample address would be: *Brac Reef Beach Resort*, PO Box 56 WE, Cayman Brac.

The Cayman Islands have a modern automatic telephone system operated by *Cable and Wireless*, which links them with the rest of the world by satellite and by submarine cable. International telephone, email and facsimile facilities are available and about 108 countries can be dialled directly. There is also a telephone route to the UK via Mercury. Public international telephone booths and a telegram counter are at the Cable and Wireless offices at Anderson Square. ■ *0815-1700*. **Communication Station** is behind Colombian Emeralds Internation in George Town by the harbour. There are 32 telephones, 5 internet kiosks, a photocopier, fax machine and phone cards for sale. The international code is followed by a seven-digit local number. For overseas credit card calls (Visa and Mastercard) dial 110.

Food and drink

The range of restaurants is wide and all international styles are available from fast food to gourmet. Check your bill, gratuities are sometimes added, sometimes not. Cayman-style fish is sautéed with tomato, onion, pepper and piquant seasoning. Conch is available as chowder, fritters, marinated etc. Try Caymanian Rum Cake for dessert. The *Tortuga Rum Company*, T9497701, has 17 retail outlets plus a 2,500 sq ft bakery (open to visitors) where up to 5,000 rum cakes are baked daily for shipment worldwide. While the recipe remains a family secret, a key component is the use of oak-aged private label Tortuga Gold Rum, which is not sold to the public. You can visit and sample the varieties of rum cake, purchase the 10 registered rum blends or other locally made items such as fudge, hot pepper sauce, steak sauce or flavoured coffee. The *Stingray Brewery*, Red Bay, east of George Town, T9476699, can also be visited. This microbrewery makes 1,500 barrels of beer annually for island consumption. ■ *The gift shop and brewery are open Mon-Sat 0900-1800*. Tours on request with free samples of dark and premium beer. *Icoa Chocolates*, Church Street, George Town, T9451915, is the only chocolate shop, making handcrafted delicacies blended with local ingredients such as key limes, Caribbean spice, Cayman honey and coconut. ■ *Mon-Sat 0900-1800.*

Shopping

As a free port, there is duty-free shopping and a range of British glass, crystal, china, woollens, perfumes and spirits are available. US citizens are entitled to a US$400 exemption after being away from the USA for 48 hours.

Black coral carvings and **jewellery** are widely available. Note that since the 1978 Cayman Islands Marine Conservation Law prohibited the removal of coral from local waters, manufacturers turned to Belize and Honduras for their supply. All the Central American countries are now members of CITES, so if you must buy it, it would be worth checking the source of the coral in case it has been procured illegally. **Caymanite** is a semi-precious gem stone with layers of various colours found only in the Cayman Islands. Local craftspeople use it to make jewellery.

At *Churchill's Cigar Store*, T9456141, you can buy Cuban seed tobacco, which is rolled and packaged in the Cayman Islands so it can be legally imported into the USA, look for Cayman Crown and Cayman Premium. The day's **fish** catch can be bought from the fishermen most afternoons opposite the Tower Building just outside central George Town. Otto Watler makes and sells **honey** in Savannah, sign on the right just after the speed limit notice.

Useful for arts and **crafts** is the *National Gallery of the Cayman Islands* (T9458111) comprehensive 'Art Trail' map which highlights the location of artists, studios, galleries, craftsmen's homes and retail outlets, related establishments and points of interest in the Cayman Islands. *Pure Art*, on South Church St (also at *Hyatt Regency*), sells the work of over 100 local artists and craftsmen and women; paintings, prints, sculptures, crafts, rugs, wallhangings etc. Open Monday-Saturday 1000-1600. *The National Gallery of the Cayman Islands* has a stall at Rum Point, Grand Cayman, selling work by local artists and craftsmen, run as a co-operative called *Native Done*. *The National Museum* on the waterfront in George Town has a popular, well-stocked gift shop for prints, posters, books and crafts. Open Monday-Saturday, 1000-1600, T9498368. The *National Trust House* headquarters on Courts Rd, T9490121, ntrust@candw.ky, open Monday-Friday 0900-1700, has a new gift shop featuring locally made gifts, Cayman-related books and Trust materials, including posters of the red-footed booby and the endangered blue iguana. *Caribbean Charlie*'s in Northside, near Rum Point, offers a wide assortment of tropical crafts with handmade, custom designed and signed work, T9479452. The *Glassblowing Studio* on the waterfront in George Town is open Monday-Saturday 0830-2100, T9497020, and you can watch the artisans creating glassware and figurines for sale. Interesting if not to everyone's taste. They have two other stores: *Flameworks*, in the Anchorage Centre across from the Port Authority and in the Regency Court, next to the *Hyatt Hotel*. Caymanian artist Kara Julian has a gallery in Galleria Plaza, T9465272, where you can buy her art glass paintings in vivid colours and tropical designs, ranging from champagne flutes to soap dispensers. *Tropical L'Attitude Islands Gifts and Apparel*, T9451233, in Butterfield Square across from the main post office in George Town, sells gifts and clothing from around the world, batik, bags, baskets, jewellery, paintings, carvings and furniture. On Cayman Brac, *NIM Things* sells items made locally, including caymanite jewellery, straw bags and crochet. Open 0900-1800 at Spot Bay, east-end of the Main North Side Rd, but not always open.

Joe Tourist is the newest 'Made in Cayman' casual wear and accessory line. The children's range is decorated with stingrays, blue iguanas and green sea turtles. Adult **clothing** is in earth tones and Caribbean colours and uses natural fibres and textures in locally-made products such as straw hats, leather bags and burlap knapsacks made from recycled croaker sacks. Joe Tourist products are available only in the Cayman Islands, although you can order them on-line at www.joetourist.com.

The Book Nook (which sells *Caribbean Islands Handbook* among other **books, toys, gifts** and games), is at Galleria Plaza, West Bay Rd, T9474686, and Anchorage Centre, T9497392, PO Box 1551, Grand Cayman, F9475053.

Flora and fauna

There are around 200 species of birds on the islands

Birds that inhabit the islands include the Antillean grackle, the smooth-billed ani, the green-backed heron, the yellow-crowned night heron and many other heron species, the snowy egret, the common ground dove, the bananaquit and the Cayman parrot. The endangered West Indian whistling duck can be seen on Grand Cayman and Little Cayman. If you are interested in birdwatching, go to the mosquito control dykes on the West Bay peninsula of Grand Cayman, or walk to the Cistern at East End. A former Governor was a keen birdwatcher and in 1993 he set up a fund to establish the **Governor Michael Gore Bird Sanctuary** on 3½ acres of wetland on Grand Cayman, where you can see 60 local species. There are nesting colonies of the red-footed booby and the magnificent frigate bird on Little Cayman. There is a parrot reserve on Cayman Brac on 197 acres of land donated to the National Trust by Donald Pennie. The **Brac Parrot Reserve** is the nesting ground for the endangered endemic Cayman Brac parrot, numbering about 400 birds. The reserve covers pristine ancient woodlands on a very rough and rocky terrain with a diversity of native trees, including species not present on Grand Cayman or Little Cayman. A 1-mile nature trail has been established through part of the reserve. The trail forms a loop which passes through several different types of terrain, from old farm land now under grass, past mango trees on red soil and through thickets and mature woodlands, a startling mixture of hardwoods and cacti. Signs and information boards are placed at strategic points along the trail and a brochure is available. *Birds of the Cayman Islands*, published by Bradley, is a photographic record; it costs £22. **Cardinal D's Park** on the outskirts of George Town, and the beginning of Seven Mile Beach, has four acres of natural lakes and woodlands. The bird sanctuary includes parrots, macaws, whistling duck and turtles. ■ *T9498855. Adults US$5, children US$2.50.*

Oncidium calochilum, a rare orchid, indigenous to Grand Cayman with a small yellow flower about ½in long, is found only in the rocky area off Frank Sound Drive. Several other orchid species have been recorded as endemic but are threatened by construction and orchid fanciers. There is protection under international and local laws for several indigenous species, including sea turtles, iguanas, Cayman parrots, orchids and marine life. For a full description of the islands' flora see George R Proctor, *Flora of the Cayman Islands*, Kew Bulletin Additional Series XI, HMSO (1984), 834 pp, which list 21 endemic plant taxa including some which are rare, endangered or possibly extinct. The **Queen Elizabeth II Botanic Park** (officially opened by the Queen in 1994), is off Frank Sound Rd, Grand Cayman. A mile-long woodland trail has been cleared and an entrance garden created. In 1997 a second phase brought a Floral Colour Garden and a Heritage Garden, with endemic plants within the park. The gardens are very beautiful now that they have become well-established and are recommended for a day away from the beach even for those who know nothing about botany. Over 200 plants have been labelled so far, several of which are rare. Orchids bloom in May-June and there are breeding areas for the Grand Cayman Blue Iguana, the Grand Cayman parrot, the Cayman rabbit and the Cayman anole lizard. More gardens and sections are planned. Special events are sometimes held, such as an orchid show, with the local orchid society in February, and a mango morning in August. There is a Visitor Centre, café and giftshop and a typical Caymanian cottage and garden has been built. ■ *T9473558 (information line), 9479462, F9477873, www.botanic-park.ky. Adults US$6.25, children 6-12 half price. Daily 0900-1830, last admission 1730.*

Indigenous animals on the islands are few. The most common are the agouti, non-poisonous snakes, iguana and other small lizards, freshwater turtle, the hickatee and two species of tree frog. Several animal sanctuaries have been established, most of which are RAMSAR sites where no hunting or collecting of any species is allowed. On Grand Cayman there are sanctuaries at Booby Cay, Meagre Bay Pond and Colliers Bay Pond; on Cayman Brac at the ponds near the airport and on Little Cayman at Booby Rd and Rookery, Tarpon Lake and the Wearis Bay Wetland, stretching east along the south coast to the Easterly Wetlands. The National Trust, T9490121, ntrust@candw.ky, has set up a Land Reserves Fund to buy environmentally sensitive land and protect natural resources. The first priority is the mountain area in North Side where the government donated 130 acres; another 200 acres need to be bought.

The Department of Tourism (T9490623) has produced a map of Cayman Brac depicting the location and full descriptions of 35 nature tourism sites as part of the Cayman Brac Development Project, funded by a grant from the European Union. The sites are either hiking trails, woodland walks, boardwalks out to wetlands, panoramic views including the Bluff and pristine beach sites, historic sites, swimming holes and areas, as well as the Brac Museum. All sites have proper signs so you do not have to hire a guide.

Diving and marine life

Since 1986, a Marine Parks plan has been implemented to preserve the beauty and marine life of the islands. Even before then, however, a moorings project was in place. This has been highly successful in marine conservation and critical in protecting Cayman's fragile coral reefs and marine life from destruction by boat anchors. Permanent moorings have been installed along the west coast of Grand Cayman where there is concentrated diving, and also outside the marine parks in order to encourage diving boats to disperse and lessen anchor damage to the reefs. There are now 281 single and double-pin mooring sites around all three islands, 177 around Grand Cayman, 47 around Cayman Brac and 57 around Little Cayman. These parks and protected areas are clearly marked and strictly enforced by a full-time Marine

The best months for diving are Apr to Oct

Cayman Islands

Conservation Officer who has the power to arrest offenders. Make sure you check all rules and regulations as there have been several prosecutions and convictions for offences such as taking conch or lobsters. The import of spearguns or speargun parts and their use without a licence is banned. Divers and snorkellers must use a flag attached to a buoy when outside safe swimming areas. For further information call Natural Resources, T9498469.

Many of the better reefs & several wrecks are found in water shallow enough to require only mask, snorkel & fins; the swimming is easy & fish friendly

Although boats take snorkellers to many sites, you can snorkel quite happily from the shore. However, each island has a wall going down to extraordinary depths: the north wall of Cayman Brac drops from 60 to 14,000ft, while the south wall drops to 18,000ft. The deepest known point in the Caribbean is the Cayman Trench, 40 miles south of Cayman Brac, where soundings have indicated a depth of 24,724ft. *The Dive Sites of the Cayman Islands*, by Lawson Wood, published by New Holland (Publishers) Ltd in 1995 (ISBN 1 85368 767 7) describes 145 dive sites around Grand Cayman, 47 around Cayman Brac and 56 around Little Cayman, together with beautiful underwater photographs mostly taken by the author. One site it does not mention in this edition is the Russian frigate (a Brigadier Type II Class), brought from Cuba and deliberately sunk in 1996 to provide good wreck diving off Cayman Brac. The 95m relic of the Cold War was sunk on a sloping bed of sand 9-24m deep and only 30m from the shore, good for snorkellers as well as divers. It has been renamed the MV Captain Keith Tibbetts, after a popular resident of Cayman Brac, and its sinking was supervised by Jean Michel Cousteau, who stood on the bridge and 'went down with the ship.' Mounted underwater cameras will monitor the growth of coral etc.

The dive-tourism market is highly developed in the Cayman Islands and there is plenty of choice, but it is frequently described as a cattle market with dive boats taking very large parties. Many companies offer full services to certified divers as well as courses designed to introduce scuba diving to novices; there are many highly qualified instructor-guides. There is a firm limit of a depth of 100ft for visiting divers, regardless of training and experience and the 69 member companies of the CIWOA will not allow you to exceed that. A complete selection of diving and fishing tackle, underwater cameras and video equipment is available for hire. The tourist office has a full price list for all operators. There is also the liveaboard *Cayman Aggressor IV* (US$1,695 per week all-inclusive), which accommodates 18 divers and cruises around Grand Cayman and Little Cayman. Contact Aggressor Fleet Limited, PO Drawer K, Morgan City, LA 70381, or PO Box 1882GT, Grand Cayman, T9495551, 1800-3482628, F504-3840817. A smaller liveaboard taking 10 divers maximum (US$1,295-1,595 per week all-inclusive) is the *Little Cayman Diver II*, which operates only around Little Cayman, T1800-458 BRAC, 813-9321993, F813-9352250, PO Box 280058, Tampa, FL33682.

Beaches and watersports

The beaches of the Cayman Islands are said to be among the best in the Caribbean. Various companies offer glass-bottomed boats, sailing, snorkelling, windsurfing, water skiing, water tours and a host of other activities. You can hire wave runners, aqua trikes and paddlecats, take banana rides and go parasailing. When waterskiing, there must be a minimum of two people in the boat so that one person can look out for hazards. There is year-round deep sea game fishing for blue marlin, white marlin, wahoo, yellow fin tuna and smaller varieties, and shorefishing in all three islands. Good fly fishing spots with local guides can be found on both Grand Cayman and Little Cayman.

Festivals

Pirates' Week is the islands' national festival and takes place in the last week of October. Parades, regattas, fishing tournaments, treasure hunts, historical and cultural 'district days' in Grand Cayman's five districts and on Little Cayman, are all part of the celebrations, which commemorate the days when the Cayman Islands were the haunt of pirates and buccaneers (T9495078). *Batabano* is Grand Cayman's costume carnival weekend, with street parades, music and dancing, which takes place in the last week of April or beginning of May. Cayman Brac has a similar celebration, known as *Brachanal*, which takes place in June. Everyone is invited to dress up and participate, and there are several competitions. *Cayfest*, the islands' national arts festival, takes place through most of April, with exhibitions, displays, dance and drama. The *Queen's Birthday* is celebrated in mid-June with a full-dress uniform parade, marching bands and a 21-gun salute. At the end of April is an eight-day *International Fishing Tournament* (replacing Million Dollar Month), with big prizes, contact the Cayman Islands Angling Club, T9497099, for details. In mid-June, *International Aviation Week* attracts private pilots and flight demonstrations over Seven Mile Beach. The first weekend in July the Cayman Islands Restaurant Association holds an annual food festival: the *Taste of Cayman*, with lots of food and outdoor activities. Towards the end of October, baby turtles, bred at the Turtle Farm, are released into the wild. Christmas brings the Parade of Lights by boat on the waterfront, the Rotary Club's Annual Christmas Tree Lighting and Radio 3-99's 'Wacky House Light Tour'.

Health

Medical care on Grand Cayman is good and readily available. There is a new 128-bed Cayman Islands Hospital in George Town, with a state of the art accident and emergency unit, maternity, surgical and paediatric units, physiotherapy, radiology and laboratory services, dental clinic, eye clinic and pharmacy. For 24-hour ambulance and paramedic service on Grand Cayman, T911 or 555. The hospital is affiliated with the Baptist Hospital of Miami for patient referrals involving advanced care or treatment. All hospital beds are in single rooms. A two-person, double-lock recompression chamber is located by the hospital and supervised by a physician experienced in hyperbaric medicine. Out-patients pay a fixed charge per visit. Primary care is provided through four district health centres in Grand Cayman. There is a 12-bed hospital in Cayman Brac (T9482243/2245). There is also a clinic on Little Cayman staffed by a registered nurse. Open Mon-Fri 0900-1300, or on call 24 hours. A doctor visits Wed, T9480072.

Grand Cayman is sprayed frequently though it is advisable to bring insect repellent to combat mosquitoes & sandflies. Little Cayman is sprayed every 2 weeks

Grand Cayman

Grand Cayman is a prosperous island with a very British feel. The island is green with luxuriant vegetation, especially at the East End where there are pastures and grazing cows. North Sound is a 40-square mile lagoon with mangroves, although dredging schemes and urban growth threaten the mangrove habitat and the reefs. Some low-key but sophisticated development has taken place along the north coast around Cayman Kai, a very attractive area with lovely beaches and good swimming and snorkelling. Most of the tourist development, however, is along Seven Mile Beach on West Bay, where there are hotels, condominiums, clubs, sports facilities, banks, restaurants and supermarkets.

Grand Cayman

Cayman Islands

Ins & outs
Driving is on the left & the roads are in good order. See transport section page 262 for more details

Getting there See page 246. **Getting around** The Public Transportation Board offers a recorded information service at T9455100, giving details on buses, taxis, limousines and tour buses, including routes and fares. There is an hourly bus service all over the island with marked stops, CI$1.50. If you stand by the road minibuses will toot their horns to see if you want a ride. Be careful of buses whose doors open into the centre of the road. Island tours can be arranged at about US$60 for a taxi, or US$10 per person on a bus with a minimum of 20 persons. Check with your hotel for full details.

Diving and marine life

Dive sites
Snorkelling and dive sites abound all round the island and include shallow dives for beginners as well as highly challenging and deeper dives for the experienced. Off the westcoast there are three wrecks, arches, tunnels, caves, canyons and lots of reef sites close to shore which can be enjoyed by snorkellers and divers. Along the southcoast the coral reefs are rich and varied with depths ranging from 15 ft to thousands of feet. The **East End wall** has pinnacles, tunnels and a coral formation known as **The Maze**, a 500-ft coral formation of caverns, chimneys, arches and crevices. There are several wrecks here also. Snorkelling is good near the *Morritts Tortuga Club* at the East End, also all along **Seven Mile Beach**, **North Sound**, **Smith Cove** in South Sound and off **Eden Rock**, near George Town. Along the north coast you can dive the **North Wall**. Near **Rum Point Channel** experienced divers can dive the Grand Canyon, where depths start at 70ft. The canyons, collapsed reefs, are 150ft wide in places. Other sites in this area towards **Palmetto Point** include the aptly-named **Eagle Ray Pass**, **Tarpon Alley** and **Stingray City**.

Dive centres
The tourist office lists 32 dive operations on Grand Cayman, offering a wide range of courses and dive sites. Many are at more than one location, attached to hotels. All are of a high standard but you may want to make your choice according to the number of divers per boat. One of the newer operators, *Ocean Frontiers*, in the East End, has been highly praised in magazine surveys. The most popular and accessible dive sites are off South Sound or North West Point, where the wall or mini walls are close to shore and an easy swim. Boat dives go to the many sites along Seven Mile Beach or the North Wall, which is much more dramatic but generally a little rougher. Prices for a certification course start at US$300, rising to US$500; for qualified divers, a two-tank dive costs US$50-75 and a Stingray City dive US$40-60, depending on how far the boat has to come. Snorkelling trips are also available, US$20-40. The British Sub-Aqua Club is represented, T9490685.

Grand Cayman is host to a revolutionary product for youngsters under 12 who are too young to use standard scuba equipment. Children as young as four years old can now snorkel with a SASY (approved by PADI and NAUI). Jean Michel Cousteau is a member of the Advisory Board. Supplied Air Snorkelling for Youth (SASY) is a scuba unit customised to fit children, but it is used only for snorkelling. The device consists of a small regulator attached to a pony tank and buoyancy vest which allows the child to float safely on the surface and view the marine world below without danger of being submerged. SASY units are available at all Red Sail Sports locations in Grand Cayman at the *Hyatt*, the *Westin* and the *Marriott* hotels (www.redsail.com). A non-profit foundation, Oceans for Youth, has been established to direct income from licensing and sales of SASY into an education programme about the marine environment.

An additional refinement, *Atlantis Research Submersibles Ltd*, PO Box 1043GT, Grand Cayman, T9497700, F9498574, operates a 20-ft research submarine, (two passengers, fare US$295 per person, five dives a day Monday to Saturday) to the 800ft deep Cayman Wall or to the wreck of the *Kirk Pride* at 780 ft. A larger submarine, with room for 48 passengers, is operated by *Atlantis Submarine*, PO Box 1043GT, Grand Cayman, T9497700; fares are US$55 for a one-hour day or night dive (children 4 to 12 half price), both to 100 ft along Cayman Wall. For US$29 you

Stingray City

Stingray City is a popular local phenomenon, where it is possible to swim with and observe large groups of extremely tame rays in only 12ft of water. Stingray City is better dived but half a mile away is the sandbar where sting rays also congregate, usually over 30 at a time, although there are thought to be around 250 in the area. The water here is only 1 to 3ft deep and crystal clear, so you hop out of your boat and the rays brush past you waiting to be fed. Their mouths are beneath their head and the rays, 3ft across, swim into your arms to be fed on squid. They can give your arm quite a suck if they miss the food in your hand. A glass bottom boat leaves from the Rum Point Club to the sandbar and a nearby reef, 1100-1230, 1500-1630, US$28. From Morgan's Harbour boats charge US$35.

can take a one-hour ride in *Seaworld Explorer*, an underwater observatory which feels like a submarine but you are down only 4 ft. A diver will attract fish within view by feeding them (Don Foster's (Subsee) Ltd, T9498534, F9497538, PO Box 1544). The Nautilus Semi-Submersible is a 110-ft submarine which seats 80 people. Snorkelling trips to view the harbour at 30 ft are available, plus special cruises: sunset dinner cruise, comedy cruise and the island's only murder mystery cruise, US$29-35 including food and drinks, T9451355.

Fishing There are at least 14 companies on Grand Cayman offering fishing. The tourist office can give you a full list with prices, which depend on the type of boat you choose. Deep sea fishing boats can be chartered for a half day (US$350-700) or full day (US$500-1,500). Reef and bone fishing is about US$400-700 for a full day including all equipment, bait and lunch. There is an Angling Club, call Donna Sjostrom, T9497099.

Beaches and watersports

West Bay Beach, now known as **Seven Mile Beach**, has dazzling white sand and is lined by hotels, tall Australian pines and silver thatch palms, the national tree. Beaches on the east and north coasts are equally good, and are protected by an offshore barrier reef. On the north coast, at **Cayman Kai**, there is a superb public beach with changing facilities; from here you can snorkel along the reef to **Rum Point**. The beaches around Rum Point are recommended for peace and quiet, with shallow water safe for children. *Red Sail Sports* at Rum Point also ensure lots of entertainment, with wind surfers, sail boats, wave runners and water skiing as well as glass bottomed boat tours to see the sting-rays and scuba diving. There are hammocks, sunbeds, lockers, changing rooms, showers, restaurants, bar and Thomas the tabby cat. You can cross the North Sound by ferry from the *Hyatt Regency* to *Rum Point Club* (also under Hyatt management). ■ *T9499098. US$15 round trip, children 5 to12yrs half price, under 5yrs free. 120 passengers, 30 minutes, departs 1000, 1200, 1600 Mon-Thur, 1000, 1200, 1800 Fri-Sun, returns 1100, 1500, 1830 Mon-Thur, 1100, 1530, 2115 Fri-Sun.* Around Rum Point at Water Cay and Finger Cay there are picnic sites on the lagoon. Take insect repellent. South of George Town there are good beaches for swimming and snorkelling at **Smith's Cove** and **Sand Cay**. In Frank Sound, **Heritage Beach**, just west of Cottage Point, is owned by the National Trust.

Sailing For information about sailing contact the *Cayman Islands Yacht Club*, PO Box 30 985 SMB, Grand Cayman, T9454322, F9454432, with docking facilities for 154 boats, 7ft maximum draft. *Aquanauts* at Morgan's Harbour, PO Box 30147SMB, T9451953, F9451954, also offers 15 slips accommodating boats of 6½ft draft and the usual facilities. For a social sailing club there is the *Grand Cayman Yacht Club*, Red Bay Estates, where the sailing pro is Matthew Whittaker, T9477913, PO Box 30513 SMB.

Cayman Islands

Windsurfing   *Cayman Windsurf*, a BiC Centre, is at *Morritt's Tortuga Club*, East End, T9477492, F9476763, with a full range of BiC boards and UP sails and instruction available. *Sailboards Caribbean* (T/F9491068, windsurf@candw.ky) also offer rental and instruction, this is a Mistral certified school. Windsurfing at the East End is highly rated for people of all abilities. Beginners are safe within the reef, while outside the reef experienced sailors can try wave jumping or wave riding. Winds are brisk nearly all the year, with speeds of 15-25 knots. Lots of hotels' watersports operators offer windsurfing, sunfish, wave runners and other equipment.

Golf   Jack Nicklaus has designed the Britannia **golf** course for the *Hyatt-Regency Grand Cayman Resort & Villas*. ■ *T9498020 for starting times.* There is a nine-hole Championship course, an 18-hole executive course and an 18-hole Cayman course played with a special short-distance Cayman ball, but it can only be laid out for one course at a time; the executive has 14 par threes and four par fours, so it is short, while the short-distance ball with local winds is a tourist gimmick. ■ *To play the executive course with hire of clubs and compulsory buggie will cost you about US$70, the regulation course US$100 for 18 holes.* The Links, the 18-hole championship golf course is at Safehaven, with a par 71 course and a total yardage of 6,605 from the championship tees, although every hole has five separate tee areas to accommodate all levels of players. ■ *18 holes with cart/buggie costs US$110.* The club house is open daily with restaurant and bar open to golfers and non-golfers. Practice facilities include an aqua range, two putting greens, sand trap and pitching green (night lights). ■ *T9495988, F9495457, 0700-1800. You can hire clubs, US$1, take lessons or just practice, US$10 per 100 balls (you can buy balls at the bar if the clubhouse is closed).* Sunrise Golf Centre is a nine-hole par 3 layout ideally suited for junior and beginning golfers looking to sharpen their iron and short-game skills. Located at the end of Hirst Road in Savannah, the longest hole is 160yds while the shortest is 57yds. There is also a 300yd driving range, practice chipping and putting green. Rental clubs and PGA professional on site for lessons. ■ *Daily 0730-1800, US$15 for 9 holes, US$22 for 18 holes. Buckets for the driving range are US$4 small and US$6 large. T9474653.*

Other sports   There are three **squash** courts at the *Cayman Islands Squash Racquets Association* at South Sound, also courts at *Downtowner Squash Club* in George Town. For information on matches contact John MacRury (T9492269). Most of the larger hotels have their own **tennis** courts but the *Cayman Islands Tennis Club* next door to the squash courts at South Sound has six floodlit tennis courts and a club pro. For match information contact Scott Smith (T9499464). For **soccer**, contact Tony Scott (T9497339) of the *Cayman Islands Football Association*. **Cricket** matches are played at the Smith Road Oval near the airport (although location may change with extension of runway); there are five teams in the *Cayman Islands Cricket Association's* league, details on matches from Jimmy Powell (T9493911) of the Cayman Islands Cricket Association. **Rugby** is played every Saturday between September and May at the *Cayman Rugby Football Club* at South Sound, for information phone Campbell Law (T9452387). **Horseriding** with *Nicki's Beach Rides*, T9455839, on trails and beaches in the northwest, or with *Pampered Ponies*, T9452262. *Eagles Nest Cycles* runs *The Harley Davidson Club*, T9494866, specializing in Harley Davidson motorcycles and souvenirs.

Motocross is popular in Grand Cayman and **stock car races** are held on the first Sunday of each month at the *Lakeview Raceway* (also known as Jay Bodden's Marl Pit) in George Town at 1300, CI$5 admission. The Cayman Motorsports Association's annual International Challenge Cup attracts racing drivers from Jamaica, Colombia, Canada and the USA. The association is building a new 30-acre racetrack, with a 20-acre family recreation area and 15-acre nature reserve, expected to open at the end of 2000, T9497135. No alcoholic beverages allowed.

You can go **bowling** at the *Stingray Bowling Centre and Arcade*, T9454444, at the Greenery on Seven Mile Beach, just north of the Strand Shopping Centre on West

Bay Road. The centre has 10 lanes with Qubica automatic scoring, CI$4 per game with adult rental shoes for CI$3 and junior rental shoes for CI$2.50. Up to six people can play each lane and lanes can be rented by the hour for CI$24. There is also a pro-shop, you can have lessons, there is a snack bar, four satellite TVs and an arcade with video games. No alcohol, children under 12 must be accompanied by an adult.

If you want to entertain small children out of the sun (or rain), there are two indoor **play centres**: *O2B Kidz*, Merren's Shopping Centre on West Bay Road has 1,600 sq ft of play equipment, toddler area, ride-on games, small café, party room, height restrictions on play equipment. ■ *Daily from 0900 weekdays, 1000 on Sat and 1100 on Sun, US$6 per child, must be accompanied by an adult, T9465439. Smyles,* at the Islander complex just off the Harquail Bypass, more than 3,200 sq ft of tunnels, ball pit, snack bar, soft play area, arcade, games, event room, the largest indoor play centre. ■ *Daily, T9465800.*

George Town

The largest town and capital of the islands is George Town, which is principally a business centre dominated by modern office blocks. However, many of the older buildings are being restored and the government is trying to promote museums and societies to complement beach and watersports tourism.

Population: over 18,000

The **Cayman Islands National Museum**, in the restored Old Courts Building in George Town, opened in 1990 and is well worth a visit. There are exhibits portraying the nation's seafaring history, an audio visual presentation and a natural history display, as well as temporary exhibitions. The newest feature is a CD-ROM interactive exhibit, where you can touch the screen and access nearly 400 images of traditional sand yards, provision gardens and other features of typical Caymanian life as it used to be. Also audio segments where you can touch and hear accounts by older Caymanians about backing sand, caboose cooking, tending provision gardens, making grounds and sharing the harvest with neighbours. ■ *www.museum.ky T9498368. CI$4 adults, CI$2 children 6-18 years. Mon-Fri 0900-1700, Sat 1000-1400. There is a museum shop and The Cool Caboose for refreshments.*

Four of the older buildings which are being preserved are the work of a local boat-builder, Captain Rayal Brazley Bodden, MBE, JP (1885-1976). He was called upon to build the **Elmslie Memorial Church** (Presbyterian, on Harbour Drive, opposite the docks) in 1923. He put in a remarkable roof, with timbers largely salvaged from shipwrecks. Such was the general admiration that he was asked to design the **Town Hall**, a peace memorial for the First World War. It now looks tiny, but when it was opened in 1926 it was considered a grandiose folly, far too big for the island. Then came the **Public Library** nearby, with its beautiful hammer-beam roof and painted British university heraldic shields. Lastly the **General Post Office**,1939, which once housed all the colony's departments of government. Bodden surrounded the main façades of the building with art deco tapered columns. All his buildings have an inter-war flavour. They are one-storey, made of carefully shaped concrete blocks, poured to give a rustic, deep-grooved effect.

An archaeological dig on the waterfront on the site of **Fort George** has been sponsored by the Cayman National Trust. Unfortunately only a small part of the walls remain, much was demolished in 1972 by a developer who would have destroyed the lot if residents had not prevented him. The National Trust has designed a walking tour of George Town to include 28 sites of interest, such as Fort George, built around 1790, the Legislative Assembly, the war and peace memorials and traditional Caymanian architecture. A brochure and map (free) is available from the National Trust, PO Box 10, T9490121, F9497494, or the tourist office. Walking tours are also available for West Bay and Bodden Town.

Cayman Islands

Around the island

Some of the many things of interest to visit in Grand Cayman include a tour round **Cayman Turtle Farm**, which houses over 17,000 green turtles. Located at North West Point, this is the only commercial turtle farm in the world. Most of the turtles are used for meat locally since the USA banned the import of turtle meat, but an average 1,700 hatchlings and year-old turtles are released into the wild each year to replenish native stocks. Those at the farm range in size from two-ounce hatchlings to breeding stock weighing around 2 oz. You can also see loggerhead, hawksbill and ridley sea turtles, but the kemp's ridley are being transferred back to Cancún, Mexico. Polished turtle shells are sold here for about US$100, but their import into the USA is prohibited. A flora and fauna section of the farm includes the Cayman green parrot, a macaw called Crackers, a freshwater turtle, ground iguanas and agouti (known as the Cayman rabbit). ■ *PO Box 645GT, T9493893/4, F9491387, www.turtle.ky US$6 adults, US$3 children aged 6-12. Daily 0830-1700.*

West Bay is a colourful area with pretty old houses dating back to the seafaring days. The National Trust has a self-guided walkers' booklet of the area, directing you along lanes and paths and giving illustrated information about the district. The Pink House, built in 1912, is included in all tour itineraries as a typical Caymanian home.

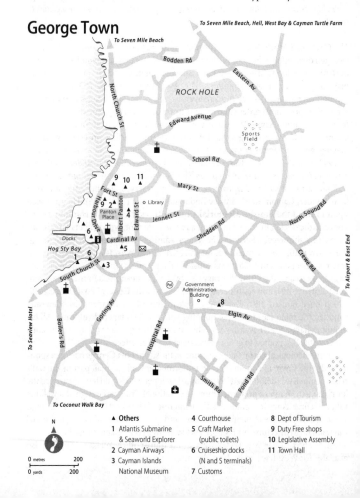

George Town

To Seven Mile Beach, Hell, West Bay & Cayman Turtle Farm

▲ **Others**
1 Atlantis Submarine & Seaworld Explorer
2 Cayman Airways
3 Cayman Islands National Museum
4 Courthouse
5 Craft Market (public toilets)
6 Cruiseship docks (N and S terminals)
7 Customs
8 Dept of Tourism
9 Duty Free shops
10 Legislative Assembly
11 Town Hall

Cayman Islands

Originally home to the Bothwell family, it is now open to the public. Its traditional sand yard is raked every morning according to custom. The **Caymanian Heritage Museum** at the Four Way Shop on West Bay Road in West Bay is home to all sorts of artefacts. Next door is a cooking caboose where you can feast on Caymanian cooking of fish tea, fritters and fried fish. ■ *Fri 1200-2400, Sat 1000-2400, Sun 1200-1600.* **Hell**, situated near West Bay, is a bizarre rock formation worth visiting. Have your cards and letters postmarked at the sub-post office there. ■ *The post office is open Mon-Fri 0830-1300, 1400-1530, Sat 0830-1130.*

On the south coast at Savannah, just off the main coastal road, **Pedro St James** has been restored and developed into a national landmark. On 4 December 1831 an historic meeting was held here at which it was decided to split the island into districts with representation, and democracy was introduced. The site has the oldest known existing stone structure in the Cayman Islands. The original building is believed to have been built of quarried native rock around 1780 by William Eden, a plantation owner, and is the only known remains of a late 18th-century residence on the island. The upper floors are of mahogany with a fine balcony. There are a number of outbuildings and traditional activities which recreate plantation life. The Steadman Bodden house, a 100-year-old wattle and daub cottage was relocated in 1995 from the cruise ship landing at Spotts. An impressive Visitors' Centre has been built as a gateway to the Great House and grounds, offering the opportunity to learn about the history of the site before beginning the tour. The main attraction is a state-of-the-art multimedia theatre featuring a 20-minute show that brings to life the people, their dramas and the conditions in which they struggled, including a storm. ■ *T9473329. US$7.50 adults, US$3.75 children. Daily 0800-1700.*

There are caves in **Bodden Town**, believed to have been used by pirates, where you can see bones and stocks, and a line of unmarked graves in an old cemetery on the shore opposite, said to be those of buccaneers. Bodden Town was once the capital of the island and all shipping came here. Continuing east just after Half Moon Bay you will see blow-holes: waterspouts that rise above the coral rock in unusual patterns as a result of water being funnelled along passages in the rock as the waves come rolling in. At the east end of the island there is a good viewing point at the **Goring Bluff lighthouse**. A trip to **Gun Bay** at the east end of the island will show you the scene of the famous 'Wreck of the Ten Sails', which took place in 1788 (see page 268).

A drive along the north coast to **Rum Point** (see page 255) is picturesque, with views of the sea through the vegetation. There are lots of villas and plots of land for sale along the coast and all development is upmarket. The return journey can be made via the Botanic Park (see page 251) to make a circular trip.

The National Trust organizes guided village walks and has opened a nature trail, the **Mastic Trail**, a two-mile walk through farmlands, woodlands and mangroves. It starts near the south coast and ends near the north coast, from where a van will carry you back to the start. It takes about 2½ hours, moderate fitness recommended, US$30 per person. *Silver Thatch Excursions* is the only tour operator offering the National Trust escorted hikes along the trail and is highly recommended, T9456588.

For a pleasurable day's outing, arrange a boat trip to **North Sound** for US$35 or so. This will include snorkelling, fishing and a good look at marine life on a barrier reef. Your guide will cook fish, fresh marinated conch or lobster for you, delicious and highly recommended. You can also take a moonlit cruise aboard the *Jolly Roger* or the *Valhalla*, T9498988, with a sunset buffet dinner cruise. ■ *US$50; a cocktail cruise on Tue, US$30, or a happy hour cruise on Fri, US$15. Mon, Wed, Thu, Sat.*

Cayman Islands

Essentials

Sleeping

There are about 50 hotels along Seven Mile Beach. All the major chains are represented, offering all types of luxury accommodation

Seven Mile Beach **LL** *Grand Cayman Marriott Beach Resort*, PO Box 30371, T9490088, F9490288, marriott@candw.ky Right on the beach, 309 rooms, comfortable, pleasant, friendly service, 2 miles from George Town, watersports, tennis. **LL** *Westin Casuarina Resort*, PO Box 30620, T9453800, F9495825. 341 rooms, a/c, TV, phone, mini-bar, fan, marble bath, 2 pools, swim-up bar, tennis, dive shop, watersports, next to golf course. Nearby, **LL-L** *Hyatt Regency Grand Cayman*, PO Box 1588GT, T9497440, F9498032, britania@ candw.ky 236 rooms, 55 villas, overlooking golf course and private waterway, lots of facilities, access for the disabled, in 1999 an all-suite 5-storey tower was opened directly across the road from the main Hyatt complex, 53 one or two bedroom apartments, lots of amenities, all with seaviews and concierge, www.britanniavillas.com **LL-L** *Sunshine Suites*, at the entrance to the *Links* at *Safe Haven* golf course, T9493000, www.sunshinesuites.com 132 suites with plantation shutters, ceiling fans, Caribbean-style decor, full kitchens, 3 room sizes, cable TV, laundry, pool. **LL-L** *Treasure Island*, PO Box 1817GT, T9497777, F9498672. 278 rather plain rooms, few extras, good beds, showers erratic, good service, fun steel band in lobby, poor buffet breakfast, better in *Hook's*, walk through condos to get to beach. **LL-L** *Comfort Suites and Resort*, West Bay Road, just south of the *Marriott*, PO Box 30238 SMB, T9457300, F9457400, www.comfortinn.com On the beach side of the road but not beachfront, about 300 ft from sea behind condos, 110 suites, studios and 1-2 bedroom suites with full kitchens, some accessible for wheelchair guests, phones, restaurant, meeting room, fitness centre, pool, scuba and watersports rental on site. A new, 5-storey *Holiday Inn*, is being built on the beach just south of *Indies Suites*, West Bay Road, and should open in 2001 with 230 standard rooms and 1 penthouse suite, 2 pools, shops, restaurant and meeting room.

There are lots of guest houses catering for divers in the suburbs south of George Town

Elsewhere **At North Sound: LL-L** *Grand Caymanian Beach Club and Resort*, T9494403, www.grandcaymanian.com 5-star, full-service resort, studios, one to two bedroom suites, grand villas, all with lots of luxury facilities, kitchens, jacuzzis, pool, barbecues, children's playground, Kid's Club, fitness centre, gift shop, concierge, watersports. **At East End: LL-AL** *Morritt's Tortuga Club*, PO Box 496GT, T9477449, F9477669, reservations@morritt's.com. Upmarket, suites and town houses, on beach, excellent windsurfing, pool with waterfalls and bar, full dive operation, packages available. **L-AL** *Cayman Diving Lodge*, PO Box 11, T9477555, F9477560, www.caymandivelodge.com 10 rooms, including 2-tank boat dive and 3 meals, photo centre, great diving, snorkelling. **At West Bay: LL** *Breadfruit House*, Northwest Point Rd, T9491700. Same owner as *Divetech*, quaint Caymanian-style, opened 1999, apartments sleep 4, a/c, fans, kitchens, satellite TV, sound system, maid service, price includes 2-tank daily boat dive, night dive and unlimited shore diving. **At Bodden Town: L** *Turtle Nest Inn*, T9478665, situated on a quiet, protected beach with excellent snorkelling, 8 one bedroom apartments with sofa beds, TV, phone, a/c, fans, laundry room, maid service, gas barbecue. **South of George Town: L-AL** *Coconut Harbour*, South Church St, south of George Town, T3229921, F3221885. 35 rooms, pool, a/c, fans, kitchenette, dive shop, reef 20yds offshore. **L-AL** *Sunset House*, PO Box 479, T9497111, F9497101, www.sunsethouse.com. 59 rooms, dedicated dive hotel on rocky shoreline, good shore diving. **A-B** *Adam's Guest House*, PO Box 312, on Melmac Av, ½ mile south of George Town, T9492512, F9490919. Run by Tom and Olga Adams, excellent accommodation, US$10 additional person, a/c or fan, very helpful, about 300yds from *Parrots Landing* dive shop, travellers cheques or credit cards accepted. Recommended. **AL-A** *Seaview Hotel and Dive Centre*, PO Box 260, T9450558, F9450559, seadive@candw.ky. Pleasant small hotel, 15 rooms, a/c, fans, saltwater pool, piano bar, award-winning restaurant, *Cayman Diving School* on site, excellent snorkelling and off-shore diving, credit cards accepted. **AL-B** *Eldemire's Guest House*, PO Box 482GT, South Church St, T9495387, F9496987. Room, studio or apartment, 1 mile from town, ½ mile from beach.

Self-catering Basic cottages may cost US$600-700 a week per week not per person. For those wishing to stay longer, two bedroom, furnished houses can be found away from the tourist areas in areas such as Breakers or Bodden Town for US$600-1,000 a month. Luxury villas and apartments, beachfront properties, can be rented through *Cayman Villas* (**L**), PO Box 681, George Town, T9454144, F9497471, www.ltravel.com/caymanvillas/, situated all round the island, along Seven Mile Beach and North Side, including the exclusive resort area of Cayman Kai.

There are dozens of restaurants on Grand Cayman ranging from gourmet standards, to smaller places serving native dishes. In George Town, there are many restaurants catering for the lunchtime trade of the office workers and a number of fast-food places, takeaways and delicatessens. Prices obviously vary according to the standard of restaurant, but for dinner, main courses start at about US$10 and range upward to US$60 or more for a full meal including wine. Lunch prices can be around US$7 to 10 and breakfast from about US$5. Excellent Sun brunch buffets, all you can eat, with orange juice and sparkling wine, at the *Hyatt* (recommended for meat, spit roasts) and the *Westin* (recommended for fish and sushi) for about US$44 per person. During the high season it is advisable to reserve tables for dinner. People tend to eat early so if you reserve a table after 2000 you are likely to finish with the restaurant to yourself. There is a restaurant delivery service called Fine Dine-In, T9463463, which you can call daily 1800-2300 for all sorts of cuisines from *Bed, Big Daddy's, Billy's Place, Café Mozart, Café Tabu, Chicken! Chicken!, China Village, Deckers, Grannie Mae's, Ragazzi Ristorante, West Bay Polo Club, Mount Fuji Sushi, Thai Orchid* and *Benjamin's Roof*.

George Town: *The Bed Restaurant*, near Harquail Bypass, just opposite cinemas, T9497199, whimsically appointed like a lady's boudoir, popular, continental food with Thai and Mediterranean influences, the adjoining lounge is a favourite late night hang-out. *Breadfruit Tree Café*, Eastern Av and Coconut Place. Best spot for local delicacies, Mon-Sat, 1100-0300, only place open that late, no alcohol, busiest very late, serves cowfoot, fish tea, curry goat, jerk pork, jerk chicken etc, quaint, garden-like atmosphere in décor, best prices in town. *Casanova Restaurant*, old Fort Building, T9497633. Excellent, Italian, on the waterfront. *Champion House, I* and *II*, both on Eastern Av, George Town, T9492190 (*I*), T9497882 (*II*), cheap, local food. Recommended. *Grand Old House*, South Church St, T9499333. Restored waterfront home, top notch service and seafood specialities. *Island Taste*, South Church St, T9494945. Upstairs outdoor patio overlooking harbour, excellent food. Recommended. *Lobster Pot*, North Church St, T9492736. *Maxin's*, Fort St, T9495747. French dining, moderately priced. *Paradise Bar & Grill* on waterfront, South Church St, T9451444. Good outdoor dining and regular drink specials. *Seymour's* has two 'stands', one in front of *The Planet*, off West Bay Rd, the other outside the Raquet Club near Cricket Square. Both open 2000-0100 for late crowds, sells Mannish Water, a local concoction of goats' parts rumoured to give a man extra potency, not sold to women, popular Fri, Sat night, couples line up to get a taste and eat great jerk pork and chicken. *The Brasserie*, Cricket Square, T9451815. Off the beaten path, undiscovered by many visitors, sophisticated menu, excellent wine selection, tapas bar daily, open for lunch and dinner, quite expensive. *Welly's Cool Spot*, North Sound Rd, T9492541. Native food at reasonable prices. *The Wharf*, on the outskirts of George Town on the way to Seven Mile Beach, T9492231. Bar open for happy hour 1700-1900, dinner daily 1800-2200, beautiful waterfront setting, quite a large restaurant, tarpon feeding nightly at 2100. *Pirate's Den*, Galleria Plaza, T9497144. Popular with ex-pats, breakfast, lunch and dinner, great Sun brunch buffet, open daily. *Benjamin's Roof*, Coconut Place, T9454080. Upstairs, continental and seafood specialities, live music downstairs, piano bar, oyster bar, moderately priced pastas, pizzas and entrées. For inexpensive fast food, *Chicken! Chicken!*, West Shore Centre, T9452290. Tasty spit-roasted chicken with assorted accompaniments, CI$20 for whole chicken plus 'fixin's', eat in or takeaway.

  West Bay Road: *Bamboo Lounge*, at the *Hyatt*, T9491234. Not your normal hotel restaurant, but great for sushi, shashimi, riqiri and specials, Japanese chef with flair, creative, generous portions, intimate and relaxing atmosphere, staff professional and friendly, popular with locals and visitors. *Coffee Grinder*, Seven Mile Shops, T9494833, a bakery. *Decker's 269*, T9456600. Built around a double decker bus, which serves as the bar, moderate prices, bistro style, nightly music, daily happy hours. *Eats Diner*, Cayman Falls, West Bay Road, T9475288. For breakfast. *Lantana's*, at the *Caribbean Club* on West Bay Rd. Fine, sophisticated dining, excellent food, featured by *Gourmet* magazine and *Bon Appetit*, who said the honey ginger salmon was the 'best of the year', also try the garlic soup, T9475595 for reservations. *Hook's Seafood Grotto*, next to *Treasure Island Resort*, T9497777. Looks like pirate's hideaway, breakfast, lunch and dinner, cheerful. *Pirate's Buffet* at the *Marriott*, T9490088. Fri nights, all you can eat, music, fire eater, limbo dancer, reservations required. *Reef Grille*, at *Royal Palms Beach Club*. One of the hottest dining and entertainment spots, dinner Mon to Sat 1730-2200, inside or out on the patio, wheelchair-accessible, American bistro, live bands at weekends and special occasions at the *Royal Palms*, also watersports centre and beach facility open daily.

North: *Calypso Grill* , Morgan's Harbour, T9493948. Lunch and dinner, 3-tiered dining area with panoramic view of North Sound, innovative menu, seafood and beef or salads and amazing desserts. *Caribbean Bakery and Pastry Shop*. *Cracked Conch*, Northwest Point Rd, T9475217. Near Turtle Farm, popular stopping place for excursions, very nice setting and atmosphere, lively, takeaways very popular. *Pappagallo*, Barkers, right in the north, see map, T9473479. Italian cuisine, expensive, on 14-acre bird sanctuary overlooking natural lagoon, eat inside the haphazardly thatched building or in outside screened patio, excellent food and extensive wine list, reservations essential, open daily 1800-2300.

South coast: *Crow's Nest*, about 4 miles south of George Town, T9499366. Open lunch Mon-Sat, 1130-1430, dinner daily 1800-2200, a local's favourite, small, glorious position, dining on the patio overlooking the sea or inside, moderate prices, reservations essential. *The Lighthouse* at Breakers T9472047. 20 minutes' drive east of George Town, good place to stop during island tour, light lunches, open air dining by sea, or smart dinners, moderately expensive.

North coast: *Cecil's Restaurant*, *Kaibo Yacht Club* at Cayman Kai, T9479975. Cajun and New Orleans food, beach bar downstairs open daily 1100-1800, upstairs open Tue-Sat 1800-2230 for dinner and Sun for brunch featuring New Orleans classics like crawfish etouffe, jambalaya, red beans and rice, shrimp creole plus fresh Louisiana oysters, fresh local seafood always on the menu.

Bars   **George Town**: for local colour visit *Farmers*, off Eastern Av, near the school. *The Landmark* on Harbour Drive is fairly typical 'pub', popular with expatriates, food not recommended but great for drinks. Open-air bars are *Sunset House* and *Blue Parrot* on South Church St. In down town George Town, *Captain Bryan's Seaside Patio*, T9496163. With a patio overlooking the harbour. *Rackham's Pub*, North Church St, T9453860. Good rum based drinks, light meals, view of harbour, food good value. *The Tree House* is an open-air bar right on the beach on North Church St. Thatched hut, pleasant tropical atmosphere. *West Bay Polo Club*, T9499892. Sports bar, speciality nights, eg sushi on weekdays, always popular. *Royal Palms* Seven Mile Beach, bar, food, the 'in' spot and *Lone Star Bar and Grill*, next to the *Hyatt Hotel*, West Bay Rd, T9495575. Favourites with sports fans, showing international sporting events nightly.

Nightlife   Curt Booker performs romantic favourites and Broadway Tunes at *Benjamin's Roof*, Coconut Place, Tue-Sat 1930-2300, T9454080. Paraguayan harpists play for dinner guests Mon-Sat at *The Wharf*, T9492231. Hear jazz at *The Bed Restaurant*, Mon evenings, T9497199. *Sharkey's* nightclub, Cayman Falls on West Bay Rd, T9475366, www.sharkeys.ky Popular Mon nights, dancing to disco and reggae. *Apollo II Club*, North Side, T9479568, local groups such as Cayman Edition, as well as rock, reggae and other Caribbean music. *McDoom's Club Inferno*, Hell, West Bay, T9493263. *The Barefoot Man*, calypso and a dash of country music is at Rum Point on Mon and Fri nights. *Coconuts Comedy Club*, is at *Sharkey's* and Hook's Seafood Grotto. There is also a comedy cruise aboard the *Nautilus*, Tue, 1700-1930, US$18, cash bar. The Cayman National Cultural Foundation, T9495477, puts on plays and musicals at the Harquail Theatre on West Bay Rd, T9495477. The Cayman Drama Society uses the Prospect Play House, a small theatre on the road to Bodden Town. There is a **cinema** on West Bay Rd with 2 screens, 2 showings a night Mon-Sat, CI$6 adults, CI$2.75 children, T9494011.

Transport   **Car hire**   *Avis*, *National* and *Hertz* are represented and there are a number of good local companies as well, many of which are at the airport. Rental firms issue visitors with driving permits on production of a valid driving licence from the visitor's country of residence. The minimum driving age is 21 at some places, 25 at other companies, check. Most car hire firms have boxes in the airport departure lounge where you can drop off your car keys prior to departure, having left the car in the company's car park. *Ace Hertz*, PO Box 53GT, T9492280, F9490572, standard jeep US$52 a day in winter, US$45 in summer, compact car US$27-34; *Andy's Rent A Car Ltd*, PO Box 277 WB, West Bay, T9498111, F9498385, cheapest automatic car US$35 in winter, US$25 in summer, weekly rates US$210 or US$150; *Just Jeeps*, PO Box 30497 SMB, West Bay Rd, T9497263, F9490216, US$45-65; *Cico Avis*, PO Box 400, T9492468, F9497127, smallest standard car US$40 winter/summer, jeeps, automatics and mini vans available, minimum 2 day rental, 1 day rental 25% extra, if paid in US dollars, add 25% for conversion; *Coconut Car Rentals Ltd*, PO Box 1991 GT, T9494037, F9497786, from US$40/30 a day winter/summer or US$240/180 a week, jeeps US$52/47, US$312/282. Collision damage waiver ranges from US$8-15 a day. **Bicycles** (cheapest US$10 per day), scooters (US$20-25 per day) can also be rented, from *Bicycles Cayman*, North Church St, T9495572, or *Cayman Cycle Rentals*, PO Box 31219 SMB, T9474021, at *Coconut Place*, *Hyatt Regency* and *Treasure Island*. *Soto Scooters & Car Rentals*, PO Box 1081, Seven Mile Beach, T9454652, F9454465, at Coconut Place, scooters US$25 per day, bicycles US$15 per day, mountain bikes and tandems available. Bicycles are also available at Rum Point. **Taxi**: taxis are readily obtainable at hotels and restaurants. In George Town there are always lots of taxis at the dock when the cruise ships come in, otherwise hailing a taxi is most easily done in the vicinity of the post office. Fares are based on a fixed place-to-place tariff rather than a meter charge and vary according to how many people there are and how much luggage there is. For going a long distance (ie across the island) they are expensive. From the airport to George Town is US$12, based on up to 4 passengers with 2 pieces of luggage each; to West Bay US$23-29; to East End, US$49; to Rum Point US$60.

Cayman Brac

Settlement on Cayman Brac has been determined by the Bluff, which rises from sea level at the west end to a sheer cliff at the east end. Most building first took place on the flatter land in the west, where the sea is a little calmer, and then spread along the north coast where the Bluff gives shelter. Cayman Brac is blessed with spectacular reef and wall diving with excellent visibility.

Getting there *Cayman Airways* and *Island Air* fly from Grand Cayman and Little Cayman. There is no inter-island ferry service, you have to catch a small plane, used like a bus service. **Getting around** An island tour by taxi costs about CI$15, *Elo's Taxi and Tours*, T9480220, recommended, *Hill's Taxi and Tours*, T9480540, *Maple Edward's Taxi and Tours*, T9480448.

Ins & outs
There is no bus service

The first three families of settlers arrived in 1833, followed by two more families in 1835. These five families, Ritch, Scott, Foster, Hunter and Ryan, are still well-represented on the island today. They made a living from growing coconuts and selling turtle shells and from the 1850s started building boats to facilitate trading. In 1886 a Baptist missionary arrived from Jamaica and introduced education and health care.

History

Most of the sites are around the west end, with both shallow reef snorkelling, with beautiful coral gardens and lots of fish, and diving and deeper wall diving a bit further out. There are also a few wrecks among the 40 or so named dive sites including a newly-sunk Russian frigate (see page 252), which is within snorkelling distance of the beach and rises to about 10ft from the surface. On the north coast road, go west past the airport turning to Robert Foster Lane, which leads to the sea. You can locate the wreck by the buoys for dive boats.

Two dive operations are based on Cayman Brac, offering diving at both Cayman Brac and Little Cayman sites, certification and resort courses, photo/video services and equipment rental. Reef Divers is at *Brac Reef Beach Resort* (T3238727, PO Box 56, West End) and Peter Hughes Dive Tiara, a full service PADI five-star dive and

Diving & marine life

photo operation, is at the *Divi Tiara Beach Resort* (T9481553, F9481563, PO Box 238, Stake Bay). Both offer PADI, NAUI, NASDS and SSI training. A two-tank dive costs US$50 with Reef Divers and US$55 with Dive Tiara. Snorkelling trips are US$20 with Reef Divers and US$10 with Dive Tiara. Nice snorkelling under *Brac Reef* dock, but watch out everywhere for sea urchins; bootees or fins recommended.

Around the island

It is not possible to drive all round the island because of the Bluff. The road linking the north and south coasts is roughly half way along the island. There are three roads running east-west, one along the north shore, one along the south coast and a third (unpaved) in the middle which runs along the top of the Bluff to the lighthouse. Although lots of roads have been built up on the Bluff, they are to service houses which have not yet been built, and do not lead anywhere. There are several, rather poor, farms and cows wander on the road. At the top of the Bluff it is sometimes possible to spot various orchids and there is a 197-acre **Parrot Reserve** (see page 250). A hiking trail has been cleared by the Cayman Brac National Trust, only for the able bodied as it is rocky, but there is a great view from the Bluff at the end of the path. You are only likely to see parrots at dawn or dusk, but it is a nice walk anyway through the bush.

From the airport the north shore road leads to **Cotton Tree Bay**, where in 1932 a hurricane flooded the area, killing more than 100 people and destroying virtually every house. The coconut groves were devastated and many people left the island at this time. Demand for turtle shell went into decline as the use of plastic increased and many men found that the only opportunities open to them were as sailors, travelling around the world on merchant ships.

Stake Bay is the main village on the north coast and it is well worthwhile visiting the small, but interesting **Cayman Brac Museum**. ■ *T9482622. Free. Mon-Fri 0900-1200, 1300-1600.* Further east at Creek, *La Esperanza* is a good place to stop for refreshment, in a glorious setting with good views and welcome sea breeze. At **Spot Bay** at the extreme east, follow a track up towards the lighthouse. Here you will find Peter's Cave and a good viewpoint. From the end of the north coast road you can walk through the almond trees to the beach, from where you get an excellent view of the Bluff from below.

Rock climbing is popular along this coastline. There are 66 recognized climbing sites

Along the south coast, the best beaches are at the west end, where there are two dive resorts. There is a pleasant public beach with shade and toilets at **South East Bay**. Bat Cave and Rebecca's Cave are in this vicinity and can be visited. When you get to the end of the road, walk along the ironshore to the end of the island. There is a blow hole, lots of beachcombing opportunities and if you look for stripes in the cliff you may find caymanite, which is only found here and at the east end of Grand Cayman. Holiday homes have been built along this coast. Tourism is now the

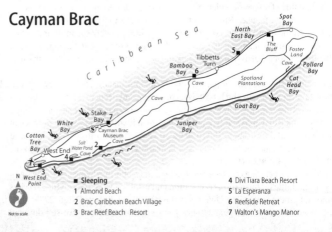

Cayman Brac

■ **Sleeping**
1 Almond Beach
2 Brac Caribbean Beach Village
3 Brac Reef Beach Resort

4 Divi Tiara Beach Resort
5 La Esperanza
6 Reefside Retreat
7 Walton's Mango Manor

Not to scale

mainstay of the economy but construction of homes for foreigners has pushed up the price of land out of the reach of many local families. Most young adults leave the island for a career in financial services or government on Grand Cayman or other jobs further afield.

LL-L *Brac Caribbean Beach Village*, on the south coast, West End, PO Box 4 SPO, T9482265, F9482206, in USA 800-7917911. A condominium development, a/c, fans, on beach, reef protected, credit cards accepted, 10 units all 2-bedroomed, restaurant, pool, dive packages, laundry, maid service available, satellite TV, child and teenage discounts, Cayman Villas, T9474144, F9497471, have a cottage for rent, **LL-AL** *Reefside Retreat*, sleeps 4, ocean front, excellent snorkelling; other apartments and/or cottages at **L** *Almond Beach*, Spot Bay, T/F541-4264863, www.almondbeach.com On beach, good snorkelling. At West End Point: **AL** *Brac Reef Beach Resort*, PO Box 56 WE, T3238727, F3238827, www.braclittle.com 40 rooms, packages available, run by English couple, afternoon tea a speciality, also hot cocoa for night divers on their return, comfortable, nice beach, some sea grass, lovely dock with lookout tower, buffet food poor, conference centre opened 2000 for large and small groups; and **AL** *Divi Tiara Beach Resort*, T9481553, F9481316, T800-3673484, www.diviresorts.com. 70 rooms, facilities for the handicapped, packages available. **AL-B** *La Esperanza*, PO Box 28 SPO, Stake Bay, T9480531, F9480525. Beachfront, snorkelling, hammocks. **A-B** *Walton's Mango Manor*, PO Box 56 SPO, Stake Bay, T/F9480518, waltons@candw.ky CP, 5 rooms, antiques, verandah, hammocks, a/c, fans, TV. | **Sleeping**

On Cayman Brac there are a few restaurants; *The Captain's Table*, at *Brac Caribbean Beach Village*. The best dining on the island, lobster, seafood and steaks. Recommended. *Blackie's*, at the Youth Centre, South Side, T9480232. Good ice cream. *La Esperanza*, T9480531, seafood, one of the nicest, tables at water's edge as well as a/c dining room, transport available, open Mon-Fri, 0900-0100, Sat 0900-2400, Sun 1200-2400 and *Lagoon*, T9487523, both at Stake Bay. *Sonia's*, White Bay, T9481214. Island food, open Mon-Sat 0900-1500. *Aunt Sha's Kitchen*, T9481581. Island style, local dishes, open breakfast, lunch, dinner. For groceries, *Billy's Supermarket*, T9481321. At the Point, meat, fish, vegetables, etc. | **Eating**

Bike and **moped hire** *B&S Motor Ventures* for moped and bike hire, T9481546. **Car hire** *Brac Hertz*, T9481515, F9481380, *T & D*, T9482847, F9482329 and *Four D's*, T/F9481599, about US$35-40 per day for a car. | **Transport**

Cayman Islands (side margin)

Little Cayman

Little Cayman is small and low-lying with large areas of dense mangrove swamps, ponds, lagoons and lakes. The diving is excellent. Underwater visibility averages 100-150 ft all year. Bloody Bay wall, a mile-deep vertical drop, is one of the major dive sites worldwide and is highly rated by marine biologists and photographers.

Getting there *Island Air* has small planes for island hopping from Grand Cayman and Cayman Brac (see page 248). The airport consists of a wooden shack and a grass runway. **Getting around** Jeep hire (US$62-65 per day) is available here with *McLaughlin Rentals*, T9481000, F9481001, daily and weekly rates, best to book in advance as last minute prices can be high. The office is 100yds away from airport. Roads are unpaved around the east half of the island but the main road goes all the way round the edge. You can not often see the sea because of seagrape and other vegetation lining the shore. | **Ins & outs** *There is no public transport, a 25 mph speed limit & frequent signs for iguana or duck crossings*

The first inhabitants of Little Cayman were turtlers who made camp on the southshore. After them, at the beginning of the 20th century, the population exploded to over 100 Caymanians living at Blossom on the southwest coast and farming coconuts. Attacks of blight killed off the palms and the farmers moved to the other two islands. In the 1950s, some US sport fishermen set up a small fishing | **History** camp on the south-coast known as the *Southern Cross Club*, which is still in operation today as a diving/fishing lodge. A handful of similar small resorts and holiday villas have since been built but the resident population remains tiny.

Diving & marine life
There are dive sites all round the island, but the most popular spot is in the Marine Park in **Bloody Bay**, a two-mile stretch between Spot Bay and Jackson's Point off the north coast. Unlike the walls around the other islands, which begin at a depth of about 65 ft and drop down about a mile, the Bloody Bay wall begins at only 15-20 ft, which means you can snorkel over the drop-off. This is spectacular, with coral canyons and caves before you get to the outer reef. Shore diving from **Jackson's Point** is also spectacular, with coral heads rising from a 40-ft sandy bottom to about 10ft of the surface. Along the south coast you can snorkel or kayak out to **Owen Island**.

Sam McCoy's Dive Lodge is at the west end of Spot Bay. They have two dive boats of 28ft and 30ft. There is also a Marine Park off the south-coast opposite the airport, with *Pirate's Point Dive Resort* at one end. Diving can be arranged with *Pirate's Point*, *Sam McCoy's* or *Southern Cross Club* (Terry and John are popular instructors with both novices and experienced divers). Newer dive operations are *Paradise Divers* (T9480001, F9480002), *Reef Divers Little Cayman Beach Resort*, South Sound (T3238727, F3238827) and *Blue Water Divers* (T9480032, F9480095). A two-tank dive costs US$50-73. There is also a liveaboard, *Little Cayman Diver II*, which takes 10 divers for US$1,690 per week all-inclusive (T813-932/1993, F813-9352250, PO Box 280058, Tampa, Fl 33682).

The bonefishing around Little Cayman is some of the best and just offshore. The 15-acre Tarpon Lake is home to the game fish from which the pond gets its name. Fishing is offered at *Sam McCoy's* (T9480026, F9480057), where bonefishing and tarpon is US$60 per half day and deep sea fishing is US$350 per half day and US$550 per full day on the 32-ft *Reel McCoy* fishing boat. At *Southern Cross Club* (T9481099) deep sea fishing is US$300 per half day and US$500 per day, while a half day of bonefishing for two people with guide is US$150. *Blue Water Divers* also offers bonefishing at US$180 per half day and deep sea fishing for US$500 per day.

Around the island
Little Cayman's swamps, ponds, lagoons and lakes make an ideal habitat for red-footed boobies and numerous iguanas. **Booby Pond Nature Reserve** attracts about 3,500 nesting pairs of red-footed boobies and 100 pairs of frigate birds. On the edge of the pond, the other side of the road from the museum, is the **National Trust House**, with an extensive veranda where you can look through a telescope or strong binoculars to watch the birds. ■ *The house is open Mon-Sat 1500-1800, but you can use the veranda any time.* Further east is **Tarpon Lake** (small sign on road), another

Little Cayman

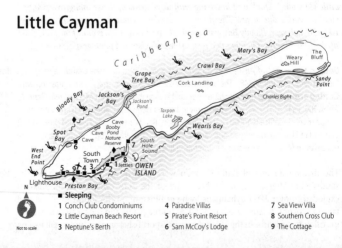

■ **Sleeping**
1 Conch Club Condominiums
2 Little Cayman Beach Resort
3 Neptune's Berth
4 Paradise Villas
5 Pirate's Point Resort
6 Sam McCoy's Lodge
7 Sea View Villa
8 Southern Cross Club
9 The Cottage

Not to scale

good spot for seeing wildlife. A boardwalk has been built out into the lake and if you are lucky you might see some tarpon in the brown water.

The beaches by the hotels on the south coast are good, with fine sand, but the swimming is marred by huge swathes of sea grass in the shallow water. Many of the other beaches around the island are more gritty, but you will have them to yourself. The best beach for swimming and snorkelling is at **Sandy Point** at the east-tip of the island. Look for a red and white marker opposite a pond, a sandy path leads down to the beach. Other beaches are at **Jackson's Point** on the north-side and on **Owen Island** in South Hole Sound. This privately owned island 200yds offshore, is freely used by residents and visitors alike and is accessible by row boat or kayak. Snorkelling is good just to the west of *Pirate's Point Resort*, where the water is shallow just within the reef.

Blossom is by the airstrip, and there you will find the post office. ■ *Mon-Fri 0900-1100, 1300-1500, Sat 0900-1100.* Car hire, a grocery and hardware store, bank (open Wednesday) and the Little Cayman Museum. The museum is in a typical wooden house and has a small, but nicely presented, collection of local artefacts and antiques. ■ *T9481072. Free. Mon-Fri 1500-1700. Little Cayman Baptist Church is the only church. Services Sun 1100, 1930, Wed 1930.*

Sleeping
Accommodation consists of small hotels, diving lodges, a few private cottages & homes

LL *Conch Club Condominiums*, PO Box 51, Blossom Village, T813-3238723, F813-3238827, www.conchclub.com. 8 units with 2 or 3 bedrooms, beachfront, pool, jacuzzi, diving, snorkelling, tennis, photo centre, restaurant. **LL-L** *Pirates Point*, PO Box 43, Sefton Bay, T9481010, F9481011. Rooms in cabins, simple luxury, lovely big bathrooms, all inclusive with or without diving, fishing, a/c, fan, TV, phone, small deep pool and 10-person jacuzzi, bar decorated with driftwood signs made by guests, owned by a cordon bleu chef, very relaxing, friendly. Highly recommended. **LL-L** *Suzy's Cottage*, contact Cayman Villas, T9474144, F9497471. Sleeps 6, beachfront in own grounds, weekly rates available. Also through Cayman Villas: **LL** *Little Cayman Cottage*, sleeps 6, shaded by palm trees and seagrape, on beach and **LL** *Neptune's Berth*, sleeps 6, on beach, jetty, walking distance from village. **LL-AL** *Little Cayman Beach Resort*, PO Box 51, Blossom Village, T813-3238727, F813-3238827, T1800-3273835, www.littlecayman.com. The only real hotel on the island and seems huge, 40 rooms, a/c, TV, on beach, dock facilities, spa, tennis, basketball, volleyball, pool, jacuzzi, diving, facilities for the handicapped, all-inclusive dive packages available, recommended staff and restaurant. **L** *Sam McCoy's*, T9480026, F9490057, mccoy@candw.ky Includes transport, diving, 3 meals, fishing costs extra (see above), small scale, simple and low key, 8 rooms, tiny pool with jacuzzi jets, hammocks, not much of a beach. **L-AL** *Paradise Villas*, PO Box 30, T9480001, F9480002, iggy@candw.ky. Small, duplex, 1-2-bedroom cottages with kitchens, on the shore, restaurant *Hungry Iguana* next door. **L-AL** *Southern Cross Club*, T9481099, F9481098, scc@candw.ky. Includes all meals, scuba, fishing, cabins on sandy beach, view of Owen Island, friendly, excellent staff, good food served family-style, indoor and outdoor bar, pool, one of the nicest places to stay. **A-B** *The Cottage*, PO Box 35, Blossom Village, T/F9480095. Restored turn-of-the-century Caymanian house, now a CP, 2 bedrooms, beachfront, a/c, fans, diving and fishing arranged.

Eating

Hungry Iguana, in the village at *Paradise Villas*, is the only independent restaurant, indoor or outdoor dining, good food, pizza on Sat, popular, shrimp, lobster often on menu, open breakfast (Sat, Sun only), lunch and dinner, takeaway available.

Cayman Islands

Background

History

The first recorded English visitor to the Caymans was Sir Francis Drake in 1586, when he reported that the *caymanas* marine crocodile (after which the islands are named) were edible. But it was the turtles which really attracted ships in search of fresh meat for their crews. The islands were ceded to the English Crown under the Treaty of Madrid in 1670, after the first settlers came from Jamaica in 1661-71 to Little Cayman and Cayman Brac. The first settlements were abandoned after attacks by Spanish privateers, but British privateers often used the Cayman Islands as a base and in the 18th century they became an increasingly popular hideout for pirates, even after the end of legitimate privateering in 1713. In November 1794, a convoy of 10 ships was wrecked on the reef in Gun Bay, on the East End of Grand Cayman, but with the help of the local residents there was no loss of life. Legend has it that there was a member of the Royal Family on board and that in gratitude for their bravery, King George III decreed that Caymanians should never be conscripted for war service and Parliament legislated that they should never be taxed.

From 1670, the Cayman Islands were dependencies of Jamaica, although there was considerable self-government. In 1832, a legislative assembly was established, consisting of eight magistrates appointed by the Governor of Jamaica and 10 (later increased to 27) elected representatives. In 1959 dependency ceased when Jamaica became a member of the Federation of the West Indies, although the Governor of Jamaica remained the Governor of the Cayman Islands. When Jamaica achieved independence in 1962 the islands opted to become a direct dependency of the British Crown.

In 1991 a review of the 1972 constitution recommended several constitutional changes to be debated by the Legislative Assembly (see Government). The post of Chief Secretary was reinstated in 1992 after having been abolished in 1986. Three teams with a total of 44 candidates contested the general election held on 20 November 1996: the governing National Team, Team Cayman and the Democratic Alliance Group. The National Team were returned to office but with a reduced majority, winning nine of the 15 seats. The Democratic Alliance won two seats in George Town, Team Cayman won one in Bodden Town and independents won seats in George Town, Cayman Brac and Little Cayman. The next election is in late-2000.

A British Government White Paper on the future of its overseas territories, released in March 1998, caused a stir in financial circles and pricked the national conscience. The White Paper called for tighter regulations for tax havens which should be brought into line with EU standards. It also called for the country to reverse the law prohibiting homosexual activity in private between consenting adults, to conform with human rights legislation worldwide. In 2000 an opinion poll was to be conducted among a sample of residents to gauge their views on the reforms. These will then be forwarded to the parliamentary select committee.

Geography

Grand Cayman, the largest of the three islands, lies 150 miles south of Havana, Cuba, about 180 miles northwest of Jamaica and 480 miles south of Miami. Grand Cayman is low-lying, 22 miles long and four miles wide, but of the total 76 square miles about half is swamp. A striking feature is the shallow, reef-protected lagoon, North Sound, 40 miles square and the largest area of inland mangrove in the Caribbean. George Town, the capital of the islands, is located on the west side of Grand Cayman. Cayman Brac (Gaelic for 'bluff') gets its name from the high limestone bluff rising from sea level in the west to a height of 140ft in the east. The island lies about 89 miles east northeast of Grand Cayman. It is about 12 miles long and a little more than a mile wide. Little Cayman lies five miles west of Cayman Brac and is 10 miles long and just over a mile

Sir Turtle

Turtles have always played a large part in the islands' folklore, dating back to 1503 when Columbus named them Las Tortugas. Generations of sailors stocked up on turtle meat while in the area and today there is a turtle farm, designed to replenish wild stocks and satisfy demand for the table.

In 1963 Suzy Soto designed the 'Sir Turtle' logo, of a peg-leg, swashbuckling, pirate turtle.

She sold it in the 1970s to the Department of Tourism for the grand sum of US$1, and it is now used intensively as a mascot and symbol for the Cayman Islands.

There was even a racehorse in the UK called 'Sir Turtle' (now sadly deceased), a hurdler sponsored by the Department of Tourism's British office and owned by Adrian Pratt, who had a good time on holiday in the islands.

wide with its highest point being only 40 ft above sea level. Owen Island, an islet off the southwest coast of Little Cayman, is uninhabited but visited by picnickers.

The people

The total population of mixed African and European descent is estimated at 38,000, of which nearly 36,000 live on Grand Cayman, most of them in George Town, or the smaller towns of West Bay, Bodden Town, North Side and East End. The population of Cayman Brac has fallen to 1,400. Little Cayman is largely undeveloped with only about 120 residents and frequented by sports fishermen. The Cayman Islands are very exclusive, with strict controls on who is allowed to settle, although the proportion of Caymanians in the resident population fell from 79% in 1980 to 58% by 1997. Consequently the cost of living is extremely high. On the other hand, petty crime is rare and the islands are well looked after (described as "a very clean sandbank"). Although Caymanians have considerable affection for Britain and do not seek independence, their way of life is Americanized. Higher education and advanced health care are usually sought in the USA and their geographical proximity influences travel choices. Many visitors to the islands never meet a Caymanian. To get to know local people you will have to get off the beach and drive into the districts. The high standard of living has deterred Caymanians from going into the hotel trade, regarding it as servitude, not service, and preferring the financial services industry.

District days during Cayfest in Apr & Pirates' Week in Oct are good times to meet local people

Government

A Governor appointed by the British Crown is the head of Government. The present Constitution came into effect in 1993 and provides for an Executive Council to advise the Governor on administration of the islands. The Council is made up of five Elected and three Official Members and is chaired by the Governor. The former, called Ministers from February 1994, are elected from the 15 elected representatives in the Legislative Assembly and have a range of responsibilities allocated by the Governor, while the latter are the Chief Secretary, the Financial Secretary, and the Attorney General. The Legislative Assembly may remove a minister from office by nine votes out of the 15. There is no Chief Minister. There have been no political parties since the mid-1960s but politicians organize themselves into teams. The Chief Secretary is the First Official Member of the Executive Council, and acts as Governor in the absence of the Governor.

Cayman Islands

The economy

Structure of production

The Cayman Islands is the largest offshore centre & the 5th largest financial centre in the world

The original settlers earned their living from the sea, either as turtle fishermen or as crew members on ships around the world. In 1906 more than a fifth of the population of 5,000 was estimated to be at sea, and even in the 1950s the government's annual report said that the main export was of seamen and their remittances the mainstay of the economy. Today the standard of living is high, with the highest per capita income in the Caribbean. The islands' economy is based largely on offshore finance and banking, tourism, real estate and construction, and a little local industry. Apart from a certain amount of meat, turtle, fish and a few local fruits and vegetables, almost all foodstuffs and other necessities are imported. The cost of living therefore rises in line with that of the main trading partners.

In 1999 there were 584 licensed banks and trust companies, 473 captive insurance companies and 1,928 registered mutual funds; the banking sector employs more than a tenth of the labour force and contributes 15.5% of gdp. The Cayman Islands Stock Exchange began operating in January 1997 at the same time as the establishment of a Monetary Authority, formed by the amalgamation of the government's financial services supervision department and currency board. As well as funds based in the Cayman Islands, the exchange hopes to attract overseas clients. By 1999 209 issuers of securities with a market capital of US$20 billion were listed, of which 60% were mutual funds. In 1990 the Cayman Islands signed a mutual legal assistance treaty with the USA and in 1996 the Islands enacted the UK's 'proceeds of criminal conduct' law. There is now an exchange of information with the USA regarding the perpetrators of commercial crime, while banks now alert authorities to suspicious transactions by clients without breaching the confidentiality law. It is an offence for banks to conceal money laundering although tax crimes or tax evasion are excluded because of the Cayman's tax free status. There is also a large shipping registry, with 1,200 ships on the register in 1999.

Tourism revenues have risen sharply in recent years. The slowdown in the US economy in 1991 brought a sharp drop in air arrivals and hotel occupancy fell to 60% from 68% in 1990, although cruise ship visitors soared by 31% to 474,747, with the introduction of calls by the cruise liner *Ecstasy* which carries 2,500 passengers. Since 1991 the market has improved. By 1998 cruise ship passenger arrivals were 852,527. Stopover visitors numbered a record 404,205 in 1998 having risen steadily each year. Nearly three quarters of all stayover visitors are from the USA. Total spending by tourists was US$508mn in 1997, of which stayover visitors accounted for US$456 mn.

Recent trends

There was a rapid rise in construction activity in the 1980s to meet demand and tourist accommodation doubled in 10 years. As a result, spectacular rates of economic growth were recorded: 15.6% in 1987, 15.2% in 1988, 10.6% in 1989, slowing to 8.0% in 1990. There was full employment and labour had to be imported to meet demand. The slowdown of the 1990s brought a huge fall in public and private construction projects and unemployment rose to a record 7.6% by 1992. The government budget went into deficit and the public debt rose from US$7mn at end-1990 to US$21.3mn at end-1991. The new Government elected in 1992 curbed public spending and brought the fiscal accounts back into surplus, helped by high gdp growth rates as US demand picked up again.

Jamaica

6

Jamaica

Jamaica has been called the Island of Springs, and its Arawak name, Xaymaca, meant land of wood and water. The luxuriance of the vegetation is indeed striking. Like other West Indian islands, it is an outcrop of a submerged mountain range. It is crossed by a spectacular range of mountains reaching 7,402 ft at the Blue Mountain Peak in the east and descending towards the west, with a series of spurs and forested gullies running north and south. Tropical beaches surround the island, the best being on the north and west coasts, though there are some good bathing places on the south coast too.

The island is a fascinating blend of cultures from colonial Britain, African slavery and immigrants from China, India and the Middle East. Reggae and Rastafariansim have become synonymous with Jamaica; Bob Marley and Peter Tosh among the greats to have been born here. The place lives and breathes rhythym, music is everywhere.

Essentials

Before you travel

Documents Canadian and US citizens do not need passports or visas for a stay of up to six months, if they reside in their own countries and have some proof of citizenship (for example a birth certificate or certificate of citizenship with photo ID). Residents of Commonwealth countries (except Nigerians, who need a visa), Austria, Belgium, Denmark, Finland, France, Iceland, Eire, Israel, Italy, Luxembourg, Mexico, Netherlands, Norway, Spain, Sweden, Switzerland, Turkey and Germany, need a passport and an onward ticket for a stay not exceeding six months. Japanese visitors need a passport and a visa if staying more than 30 days. Citizens of all other countries must have a **visa**, **passport** and **onward ticket**. Immigration may insist on your having an address, prior to giving an entry stamp. Otherwise you will have to book a hotel room in the airport tourist office (friendly and helpful). For visa extensions, apply to Ministry of Social Security and Justice, Kingston Mall, 12 Ocean Boulevard, Kingston, T9220800. No vaccinations are required unless you have visited Asia, Africa, Central and South America, Dominican Republic, Haiti, Trinidad and Tobago within six weeks of going to Jamaica.

Money **Currency** The Jamaican dollar (J$) is the local currency but foreign currency up to US$100 is legal tender for purchases of goods and services, with change given in J$.

Rates in Negril can be worse than in Montego Bay **Exchange** The Jamaican dollar floats on the foreign exchange market. The only legal exchange transactions are those carried out in commercial banks, or in official exchange bureaux in major hotels and the international airports. It is illegal to buy, sell or lend foreign currency without a licence. Banks pay slightly more for US$ travellers cheques than for cash. Retain your receipt so you can convert Jamaican dollars at the end of your stay. Most banks and exchange bureaux, including at the airport, will not accept US$100 bills because of forgeries. If using credit cards the transaction will be converted from the agreed J$ rate into US$ before you sign, be sure to verify exact rate that is being used, often a 5-10% downward adjustment can be instantly obtained by this enquiry.

Jamaica

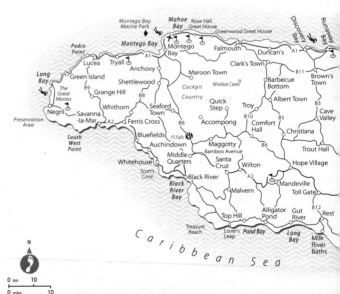

In the mountains, the temperature can fall to as low as 7°C during the winter season. **Climate** Temperatures on the coast average 27°C, rising occasionally to 32°C in July and August and never falling below 20°C. The humidity is fairly high. The best months are December to April. Rain falls intermittently from about May, with daily short tropical showers in September, October and November.

Getting there

From Europe *British Airways* (Gatwick) and *Air Jamaica* (Heathrow) fly direct, between **Air** London and Kingston and Montego Bay with lots of connections from other European cities. *LTU International Airways* has a weekly flight to Montego Bay from Dusseldorf. *Martinair Holland* flies from Amsterdam to Montego Bay. *Air Europe* flies weekly from Milan. *Condor* flies weekly from Frankfurt to Montego Bay. There are many charter flights from Europe which change according to the season, check with travel agent. **From North America** *Air Jamaica* has services to Kingston and/or Montego Bay from Atlanta, Baltimore, Chicago, Fort Lauderdale, Los Angeles, Miami, New York, Orlando, Philadelphia. *Air Canada* flies from Toronto to Kingston and from Halifax, Montréal, Toronto and Winnipeg to Montego Bay. *American Airlines* flies from Boston, New York and Miami daily to Montego Bay and from New York, Miami and Raleigh/Durham daily to Kingston, with lots of connections from other cities through Miami. *TWA* flies from Minneapolis and St Louis, Missouri to Montego Bay. *US Air* flies to Montego Bay from Charlotte, New York, Philadelphia and St Louis. *Northwest Airlines* from Los Angeles, Memphis and Tampa to Montego Bay. Enquire in Florida about cheap flights from Fort Lauderdale and Orlando. **From the Caribbean & Latin America** *Cayman Airways* and *Air Jamaica* connect the Caymans and Jamaica. *BWIA* flies to Kingston from Antigua, Barbados, Trinidad and Sint Maarten, while *ALM* flies to Kingston from Curaçao. There are *Cubana* flights from Havana to Kingston and Montego Bay. *TCI SkyKing* flies from Providenciales to Kingston. *Copa* flies Panama City-Kingston and Montego Bay. *Air Jamaica* now uses Montego Bay as its regional hub, with flights from Barbados, Bonaire, Grand Cayman, Grenada, Havana (also to Kingston), Miami, Nassau, St Lucia and Trinidad. Flights are timed to connect with intercontinental arrivals and departures.

Jamaica

Touching down

Departure tax *Airport departure tax of J$750, payable in Jamaican or US dollars by those who have stayed on the island for 24 hours or more. Cruise ship passengers pay a US$15 tax.*

Hours of business *Offices: usually open from 0830-1630 Monday to Friday.* **Shop:** *hours vary between 0830 and 0930 to 1600 and 1730, depending on area, Monday to Saturday; there is half-day closing (at 1200) on Wednesday in Down Town Kingston, on Thursday in uptown Kingston and Montego Bay, and on Friday in Ocho Rios.* **Banks:** *are 0900-1400 Monday to Thursday, 0900-1600 on Friday (there may be some local variations).*

Official time *Eastern Standard Time, five hours behind GMT and an hour behind the Eastern Caribbean.*

Voltage *110 volts, 50 cycles AC; some hotels have 220 volts.*

Weights and measures *Metric.*

Emergency numbers: *Fire/Ambulance 110, Police 119.*

Clothing *Light summer clothing is needed all the year round, with a sweater for cooler evenings. Some hotels expect casual evening wear in their dining rooms and nightclubs, but for the most part dress is informal. Bathing costumes, though, are only appropriate by the pool or on the beach.*

Tipping *Hotel staff, waiters at restaurants, barmen, taxi drivers, cloakroom attendants, hairdressers get 10-15% of the bill. In places where the bill already includes a service charge, often personal tips are nonetheless expected. In some areas you may be expected to give a tip when asking for local information.*

Drugs *Marijuana (ganja) is widely grown in remote areas and frequently offered to tourists. Cocaine (not indigenous to Jamaica) is also peddled. Possession of either drug is a criminal offence. On average over 50 foreigners are serving prison sentences in Jamaica at any given moment for drug offences. The police stop taxis, cars etc in random road checks and search you and your luggage. Airport security is being continually tightened (sniffer dogs, etc).*

Boat It is extremely difficult to book a passage by ship to other Caribbean islands. About nine cruise lines call at Ocho Rios or Montego Bay weekly, mostly out of Miami, but some from Tampa, Ft Lauderdale or New Orleans.

Touching down

Airport information
See pages 283 & 301 for further details

There are two international airports in Kingston and Montego Bay. Montego Bay airport is the only one really within walking distance of most hotels. The Kingston airstrip is at Tinson Pen which is two miles from the centre of town on Marcus Garvey Drive, those at Ocho Rios and Port Antonio are a long way out of town. At Kingston's Norman Manley airport you can change back excess Jamaican dollars into US$ at the bank in the departure lounge. There are also several reasonable shops there which will accept Jamaican currency (except for duty free goods). Allow plenty of time to check in for a flight; there are four separate security, baggage or documentation checks before you board.

Airlines *Air Jamaica* and *Air Jamaica Express*: The Towers, Dominica Drive, Kingston 5, T9224661 (opens at 0830), offices in Montego Bay, T888-9524300, Negril, T9574210, Ocho Rios, T9742566. Montego Bay is its regional hub. *British Airways* is also in The Towers, T9299020, 9400890 (Montego Bay). *BWIA*, 19 Dominica Drive, Kingston 5, T9293770, 9248364 (airport), 9524100 (Montego Bay). *American Airlines*, T9208887 (Kingston), 888-3592247 (Montego Bay).

Tourist information **Local tourist offices** Helpline T0888-995-9999, www.jamaicatravel.com Head office at ICWI Building, 2 St Lucia Avenue, Kingston 5, PO Box 360, T9299200, F9299375. Circulates

Jamaica (side tab)

Tourist offices overseas

Canada 1 Eglington Avenue East, Suite 616 Toronto, Ontario M4P 3A1, T416-4827850, F4821730.

France c/o Target International, 32 rue de Ponthieu, 75008 Paris, T331-45634201, F42256640.

Germany Postfach 900437, 60444 Frankfurt, T4961-84990044, F84990046.

Italy c/o Sergat Italia SRL, Piazza dei Cenci 7/A, 00186 Roma, T396-6875693, F6873644.

Japan 3 Mori Building, 1-4-10 Nishi-Shinbashi Minato-ku, Tokyo 105, T813-35913841, F813-35913845.

Taiwan 11F-8, No 200, Section 1, Tun Hwa S Road, Taipei, T8862-87738175, F877-35240.

UK 1-2 Prince Consort Rd, London, SW7 2BZ, T020-72240505, F72240551, jtb_@compuserve.com

USA New York: 801 Second Ave, 20th Floor, New York, NY10017, T212-8569727, F8569730; Suite 1101, 1320 South Dixie Highway, Coral Gables, Miami, FL 33146, T305-6650557, F6667239; 3440 Wilshire Blvd, Suite 805, Los Angeles, CA 900010, T213-3841123, F3841780.

detailed hotel lists and plenty of other information. Other offices in Jamaica: at the international airports; Cornwall Beach, Montego Bay, PO Box 67, T9524425 or T9522462, airport, nights, holidays, F9523587; Ocean Village Shopping Centre, Ocho Rios, PO Box 240, T9742582, F9742559; City Centre Plaza, Port Antonio, PO Box 151, T9933051, F9932117; Coral Seas Plaza, Negril PO, Westmoreland, T9574243, F9574489; Hendricks Building, 2 High Street, Black River PO, T9652074, F9652076. The 'Meet the People' programme can introduce you to Jamaicans with your interests and hobbies for different activities.

Local travel agents UTAS Tours, T9523820, F9793465, offer weekends in Havana. *Juta Jamaica*, T9520813, F9525355. *Caribic Vacations*, T9529874, F9533463. *Sun Venture Tours*, T9606685, F9208348, www.sunventuretours.com, a tour operator. Activities for nature lovers away from the beach, hiking, caving, safaris, birdwatching and educational tours, run by Robert Kerr. For scheduled or charter flights to neighbouring islands, for example Cuba, Dominican Republic, try *Apollo Travel Services*, 14 Dominica Drive, New Kingston, T9298483, F9687214, also at 28 Main Street, May Pen, T9864270, and Shop No 3, Spanish Town Shopping Centre, T9845040, IATA members, recommended.

Maps The *Discover Jamaica* road map (American Map Corporation) costs US$1 but is widely available free from tourist offices. It has plans of Kingston, Montego Bay, Negril, Mandeville, Ocho Rios, Port Antonio and Spanish Town. The *ITM Road Map of Jamaica* (1:250,000, International Travel Maps, 345 West Broadway, Vancouver, BC, V5Y 1P8, Canada) also includes plans of Kingston, Montego Bay, Spanish Town, Mandeville, Port Antonio and Ocho Rios. Good clear series of 1:50,000 maps covering Jamaica in 20 sheets from Survey Department, 23½ Charles Street, PO Box 493, Kingston.

The per capita crime rate is lower than in most North American cities, but there is much **Security** violent crime. This is particularly concentrated in downtown Kingston (90% of violent crime takes place in four Kingston police districts), but can be encountered anywhere on the island. You are advised not to walk any street in Kingston after dark. There are large areas of west Kingston where you should not go off the main roads even by day and even in a locked car. The motive is robbery so take sensible precautions with valuables. Gang warfare has been exacerbated by the US policy of deporting Jamaican criminals, who return to Kingston to shoot it out with local gangs. In the depressed areas of southwest Kingston, drug gangs now control territory previously demarcated as political party enclaves. There were 1,038 murders in 1997, the highest number since 1980, also an election year, but 1998 and 1999 showed improvement with 953 and 849 murders respectively.

Beware of pickpockets in the main tourist areas and be firm but polite with touts. Do not wear jewellery. Do not go into the downtown areas of any towns especially at night. Avoid arriving in a town at night. Take a taxi from bus stations to your hotel. Travellers have reported being threatened for refusing to buy drugs and incidents where Jamaicans have become aggressive over traffic accidents, however minor. Observe the obvious precautions and you should have no problem. The vast majority of Jamaicans welcome tourists and want to be helpful but the actions of the minority can leave you with the impression that tourists are not wanted. Crimes against tourists fell from over 600 in 1992 to 185 in 1998, but the hold up and robbery of two busloads of tourists led to the deployment of military patrols to reinforce the police in tourist areas. The disappearance of an American travel guide writer in Negril in 2000 was further cause for concern.

Where to stay

Larger hotels have introduced strict security to prevent guests being bothered by hustling

Because Jamaica is a major tourist destination there are a great many hotels and restaurants, particularly in the tourist areas. Full and up to date information is available at all tourist information centres. We only mention those which have recently been recommended or in the news for whatever reason. The brochure *Elegant Resorts* features most of the hotels in the top price-range which have reciprocal arrangements. All-inclusive resorts are extremely popular in Jamaica and development has been led by *SuperClubs* (www.superclubs.com) and *Sandals* (www.sandals.com), with hotels mainly along the north coast; some allow children but most are for couples. As a result of their popularity, other hotels have been forced to discount their rates, so bargains can be found. *Unique Vacations* is the worldwide representative for *Sandals* and *International Lifestyles* represents *SuperClubs*. Chris Blackwell's *Island Outpost* now has several small, luxury hideaways, popular with the rich and famous; in the UK at 421a Finchley Road, London NW3 6HJ, T0800-614790, in Jamaica 8 Worthington Av, Kingston 8, T968679214, F9686779.

Visitors on a low budget should aim to arrive at Montego Bay rather than Kingston because the former is the island's tourism capital with more cheap accommodation. Get hold of the tourist board's list of hotels and guest houses offering rates and addresses, and also a copy of *Jamaica Vacation Guide* (both free). Many small hotels and inns have grouped themselves as the 'Insider's Jamaica'. The tourist board has their brochure, or visit www.insidersjamaica.com

Information/reservations for self-catering villas and apartments can be done through the *Jamaica Association of Villas and Apartments* (JAVA), Pineapple Place, Ocho Rios, Box 298, T9742508, F9742967, who represent over 300 private houses. Renting a villa may be an attractive option if you do not intend to do much travelling and there are 4/6 of you to share the costs (about US$1,000-1,500 per week for a nice villa with private swimming pool and fully staffed). You will, however, probably have to rent a car as you will have to take the cook shopping, et cetera. You can go ever more upmarket and pay US$2,000-14,000 a week for a fully staffed luxury villa through *Elegant Resorts Villas International*, T9932287.

Accommodation is subject to a 15% value added tax called the General Consumption Tax, check whether it is included in a quoted room rate.

The Jamaica Association of Villas and Apartments at1501 W Fullerton, Chicago, IL60614, USA, T312-8831020, F8835140 or toll free 800-2218830 and *JAVA*, c/o ***Uncle Sam Travel***, 295 Soho Rd, Birmingham B21 9SA, UK, T0990-329623, F0121-5547315, both handle accommodation and car rental.

Getting around

Air *Air Jamaica Express* (T9224661) flies to anywhere with a landing field out of Kingston and Montego Bay daily. Charges are reasonable (US$50 Kingston-Montego Bay return) but using this method of travel is not very satisfactory unless you can arrange to be met at your destination.

Bus Public road transport is mostly by minibus. This is cheap but overcrowded and generally chaotic and only to be recommended for the young and fit ("Step Up!" shouted by the

Crime and tourism

The impact of tourism on a population of around two and a half million is massive, both economically and socially. Bad publicity abroad or a natural disaster, such as Hurricane Gilbert, can have a devastating effect. The crime rate is high but most of the serious crime is around Kingston, principally in West Kingston. Many country districts and north coast resorts are fairly safe and in fact less dangerous than US tourist cities such as Miami, Orlando and Washington DC. However, harassment of cruise ship passengers and other visitors by unsavoury vendors of drugs and services have contributed to the island's poor image abroad. Partly because of crime, all-inclusive resorts have become particularly important in Jamaica. A large proportion of tourists never leave these hotels except on an organized tour or to return to the airport.

conductors means please move down the bus, there is plenty of room at the back!). Be prepared also for a certain amount of physical abuse from the bus company front men as they compete for your custom. Country buses are slow and sometimes dangerous. There are also minibuses which ply all the main routes and operate on a 'colectivo' basis, leaving only when full.

Car

Petrol stations often close on Sun; note that fuel is paid for in cash

Driving times and distances of major routes: Kingston to Montego Bay 117 miles (3 hrs), to Ocho Rios 55 miles (2 hrs), to Port Antonio 68 miles (2 hrs); Montego Bay to Negril 50 miles (1½ hrs), to Ocho Rios 67 miles (2 hrs); Ocho Rios to Port Antonio 67 miles (2½ hrs). A new road linking Kingston with Montego Bay and Ocho Rios is to be built in 2000-2002, which may affect journey times. The speed limit is 30 mph in built up areas, 50 mph on highways. A North American driving licence is valid for up to three months per visit, a British licence 12 months and a Japanese licence 1 month. Drive on the left. Try to avoid driving outside towns at night. Roads, even on the coast, are twisty and in the mountains extremely so, add potholes and Jamaican drivers and you are an accident waiting to happen. Plan ahead because it gets dark early. Daylight driving isn't safety assured; the coastal road from Kingston to Port Antonio is in a particularly bad condition and the drivers awful. Breath tests from drunk driving are being considered. Traffic jams, especially between Kingston and Spanish Town and in the centre of Montego Bay, have been exacerbated by an influx of cheap, Japanese, second-hand vehicles: 'deportees' in popular parlance.

Car hire Undoubtedly a rented car is the most satisfactory, and most expensive, way of getting about. All the major car rental firms are represented both at the airports and in the major resort areas. There are also numerous local car rental firms which are mostly just as good and tend to be cheaper. The tourist board has a list of members of the Jamaica U-Drive Association, Newlin Street, Ocho Rios, T9742852. Be prepared to pay considerably more than in North America or Europe (starting from about US$65 per day plus CDW of US$12 and tax of 12½%). Many companies operate a three-day minimum hire policy. *Island Car Rentals* is a well known firm, airport office T9248075, Montego Bay T9255771, Kingston T9268861. *Praise Tours & Auto Rentals Ltd*, 72 Half Way Tree Road, Kingston 10, T9293580, F9293555, good deals on longer rentals, no trouble with refunds, airport transfers, recommended. *Don's Car Rental*, headquarters 1 Worthington Avenue, New Kingston, Kingston 5, T9262181, F9260866, also offices at Negril Aerodrome, T9574366, *Trident Hotel*, Port Antonio, T9932241. In the resort areas of Montego Bay, Ocho Rios and Negril, jeeps are available for about US$90 a day, motorbikes and scooters from US$30 and bicycles from US$5. Watch out for sunburn.

Taxi

There are taxis, with red PPV (Public Passenger Vehicle) licence plates, in all the major resort areas and at the airports. Some have meters, some do not. Only the JUTA taxis have officially authorized charges to all destinations, with others (Yellow Cab, Checker Cab etc), the important point is to ask the fare before you get in. It can be around US$3-4 for a short hop, US$5-6 from New Kingston to Down Town, US$7 from Down Town to Mona Campus. All taxis should charge the same to the airport, US$15-21 from New Kingston. The tourist information centres should also be able to help in this respect. Some 'non-tourist' taxis operate like minibuses, that is have a set route and can be flagged down. They will cram about six passengers into a small Nissan, Hyundai or Lada, but if you do not want to share you can hire it all to yourself. Negotiate the fare in advance. To take a taxi for long distance is expensive; a JUTA taxi from Kingston to Ocho Rios for example could cost US$100-120, rather more than a day's car hire, although you could negotiate a fare less than half that with a smaller taxi company.

Keeping in touch

Post There are post offices in all main towns. Post offices handle inland and overseas telegrams. The sorting office on South Camp Road, Down Town Kingston, has a good and helpful philatelic bureau.

Telephone Cable, telephone and fax services are operated by *Cable & Wireless Jamaica Ltd*. It has main
International phone offices in Kingston and Montego Bay, but calls can easily be made from hotels. 'Time and
code: 876 charge' phone calls overseas cost the same in hotels as at the phone company, but there is a 15% tax and a J$2 service charge. In fact, making an international call is often easier from a hotel. The only other method is a card phone, if you can find one which is working and you are prepared to queue. You can buy telephone cards at supermarkets J$50 but check that it is valid for the year you want to use it, several people have been sold out of date cards (particularly around January/February) and there is no refund. In 1999 the Government and Cable & Wireless signed an aggreement for a three-year transition to a fully competitive telecommunications sector. During that time, new lines will be installed, internet access will be provided at 60 post offices around the country and a world class call centre will be built in eastern Jamaica.

Newspapers The daily paper with the largest circulation is *The Daily Gleaner*, which also publishes an evening paper, *The Star* and the *Sunday Gleaner*. *The Jamaica Herald* is a livelier daily than *The Gleaner*, also the *Sunday Herald*. The other daily is the *Observer*. *Money Index* is a financial weekly, in Montego Bay *The Western Mirror* is weekly. *Lifestyle* is a monthly glossy magazine, *Jamaica Journal* is a quarterly with interesting but academic articles.

Food and drink

Food There are many unusual and delicious vegetables and fruits such as sweetsop, soursop and sapodilla. National specialities include codfish ('stamp-and-go' are crisp pancakes made with salt cod) and ackee; curried goat; and jerked pork, highly spiced pork which has been cooked in the earth covered by wood and burning coals. Chicken is cooked in the same way. Patties, sold in specialist shops and bars, are seasoned meat or lobster in pastry; normally very good value. Curried lobster is a delightful local speciality. Stew peas is chunks of beef stewed with kidney beans and spices and served with rice. Along the coast, fish tea is a hotch potch of the day's catch made into a soup, US$1 a cup.

Drink Local rum (white or brown, overproof and underproof), and the cocktails which combine it with local fruit juices, or mixed with Ting, the carbonated grapefruit soft drink; Tia Maria, the coffee liqueur and quite a lot of other liqueurs; Red Stripe lager, with which, the locals say, no other Caribbean beer compares, about US$1.10 at road side bar, considerably more in a hotel. Try the Irish Moss soft drink. All rums are very cheap duty free, typically US$13 for a three-pack.

Shopping

In the craft markets and stores you can find items of wood (by Rastafarians and Maroons), straw, batik (from a number of good textile companies) and embroidery; the hand-knitted woollen gold, red, green Rasta caps (with or without black dreadlocks affixed) are very cheap. Jewellery from Blue Mountain Gems, near Rose Hall, Montego Bay area. For art and ceramics, Devon House gallery, Chelsea Galleries on Chelsea Road, Gallery 14, Old Boulevard Gallery,

Grosvenor Gallery, Contemporary Art Centre in Liguanea. Blue Mountain coffee is excellent, cheaper at airport duty free shop than in supermarkets or tourist shops.

Please remember to check with legislation (and your conscience) before buying articles made from tortoiseshell, crocodile skin, and certain corals, shells and butterflies. Many such animals are protected and should not be bought as souvenirs. It is illegal to take or possess black or white coral in Jamaica; sea turtles are protected and you should refuse to buy products made from their shells. The closed season for lobster fishing is April-June, so if lobster is on the menu check where it has come from.

Some shopkeepers offer a 10-15% discount on all goods but in fact merely refrain from adding the tax when payment is made. Street vendors never add tax.

Photographic film is reasonably easily obtained but take spares of essentials such as Lithium batteries as they are difficult to find and expensive. Glare and UV light is constant, take suitable filters. Do not photograph Jamaicans without their permission, the men, particularly in Kingston, can get aggressive.

Flora and fauna

The 'land of wood and water' has resulted in a botanist's paradise. There are reported to be about 3,000 species of flowering plants alone, 827 of which are not found anywhere else. There are over 550 varieties of fern, 300 of which can be found in Fern Gully. The national flower is the dark blue bloom of the lignum vitae. There are many orchids, bougainvillea, hibiscus and other tropical flowers. Tropical hardwoods like cedar and mahogany, palms, balsa and many other trees, besides those that are cultivated, can be seen. Cultivation, however, is putting much of Jamaica's plant life at risk. Having been almost entirely forested, now an estimated 6% of the land is virgin forest. A great many species are now classified as endangered.

This is also a land of hummingbirds and butterflies; sea cows and the Pedro seal are found in the island's waters, although only about 50 sea cows, or manatee, survive. There are crocodiles, but no large wild mammals apart from the hutia, or coney (a native of the island and now an endangered species), the mongoose (considered a pest since it has eliminated snakes and now eats chickens) and, in the mountains, wild pig. There are, however, lots of bats, with 25 species recorded. Most live in caves or woods and eat fruit and insects, but there is a fish-eating bat which can sometimes be seen swooping over the water in Kingston Harbour. The Jamaican iguana (*Cyclura collei*), of the lizard family Iguonidae, subspecies Iguaninae, was thought to have died out in the 1960s, but in 1990 a small group was found to be surviving in the Hellshire Hills. There are five species of snakes, all harmless and rare, the largest of which is the yellow snake, which can grow up to 3 m.

Good sites for birdwatching are given in the text below; the three main areas are the Cockpit Country, the Blue Mountains and Marshall's Pen. The national bird is the red-billed streamertail hummingbird (*Trochilus polytmus*), also known as the doctor bird or swallow tail hummingbird. The male has a long, sweeping tail much longer than its body, and is one of Jamaica's endemic species. Other endemic birds are the yellow-billed parrot and the black-billed parrot, found in the Cockpit Country or Hope Zoo. There are 25 species and 21 subspecies of birds which are found nowhere else. A good place to see Jamaica's birds is the Rocklands Feeding Station, near Montego Bay. On weekday evenings you can watch the birds being fed and even offer a hummingbird a syrup and get really close. Many migratory birds stop on Jamaica on their journeys north or south. *Birds of Jamaica: a photographic field guide* by Audrey Downer and Robert Sutton with photos by Yves-Jacques Rey Millet, was published in 1990 by Cambridge University Press.

In 1989 the Government established two pilot national parks, the first in Jamaica, under the Protected Areas Resource Conservation (PARC) project. The Blue Mountain/John Crow Mountain National Park encompasses almost 200,000 acres of mountains, forests and rivers. Efforts are being made to stem soil erosion and restore woodland lost in Hurricane Gilbert, while developing the area for ecotourism and provide a livelihood for local people. The other national park is the Montego Bay Marine Park, which aims to protect the offshore reef from urban waste, over-fishing and hillside erosion leading to excessive soil deposition. All coral

Jamaica

reefs are now protected and the sale of both black and white coral is banned. Also forbidden is the hunting of the American crocodile, the yellow and black-billed parrot and all species of sea turtle.

Diving and marine life

There are now marine parks in Montego Bay, Port Antonio and Negril, which are resulting in increased numbers of fish and other marine life. Although established in 1989, the Montego Bay Marine Park was officially opened in July 1992. It stretches from the east end of the airport to the Great River and contains three major ecosystems, seagrass bed, mangroves and coral reefs. Non-motorized watersports such as diving, snorkelling and glass bottom boat tours are permitted, but do not touch or remove anything.

There are several conservation groups involved in marine ecology. In St Ann, *Friends of the Sea* is a non-profit, non-governmental organization, formed in 1992, which concentrates on education and public awareness and draws attention to what is happening on land which might affect what happens underwater. The *Negril Coral Reef Preservation Society* was formed in 1990. It has installed permanent mooring buoys for recreational boats and works on educational programmes with schools with slide shows, videos and environmental fun days. Together with the National Resource Conservation Authority and the Negril community, it has formed a marine park in conjunction with protected coastal and terrestrial habitats, aimed at protecting the coral reefs and improving fish stocks for fishermen.

Around Negril there are many reef sites and a huge variety marine life: coral, sponges, invertebrates, sea turtles, octopus, starfish and lots of fish. Off Montego Bay and Ocho Rios there is wall diving quite close to shore and a few wrecks. Off Port Antonio fish are attracted to freshwater springs which provide good feeding grounds. The best wreck diving is off Port Royal and Kingston where, in addition to ships, you can explore the city which slid into the sea in the 1692 earthquake.

Dive centres Nearly all dive operators are based along the north coast at hotels. They must be licensed by the Jamaica Tourist Board and most are members of the Jamaica Association of Dive Operators (JADO). They offer introductory and certification courses at all levels. Dive packages are available with the hotels where they are located. Contact the tourist board for a full list of operators and map of dive sites. Diving can be included in a hotel package, but if you are doing it independently, a two-tank dive costs on average US$65. Dives are limited to 100 ft. There are hyperbaric chambers at Discovery Bay and Port Royal.

Fishing Deep sea fishing for white marlin, wahoo, tuna and dolphin (not the mammal) can be arranged at north coast hotels. There is a famous Blue Marlin tournament at Port Antonio in October. A half-day charter costs US$400 for up to six people, plus a 10% tip for the crew, who will also expect to keep half the catch.

Other sports **Golf** is played at the Constant Spring (18 holes, green fee US$35, T9241610) and Caymanas Clubs (18 holes, green fee US$53, T9223386, c/o Liguanea Club) (Kingston), the Manchester Country Club (Mandeville, nine-hole, first opened in the middle of the 19th century, green fee US$14, T9622403), Sandals Ocho Rios Resort & Golf Club, formerly known as Upton (Ocho Rios, 18 holes, green fee US$70, golf and restaurant free for Sandals guests, T9750119/22), Breezes Golf Beach Resort (18 holes, green fee US$58, free for guests at *Breezes Runaway Bay*, the only golf school open to the public, T9732561), Ironshore Golf and Country Club (another Sandals course, free for guests, 18 holes, green fee US$45, T9532800), Half Moon Golf Club (advance booking necessary for this championship course, 18 holes, green fee US$95, T9532731, also **tennis** and **squash**) and Wyndham Rose Hall Golf Club (18 holes, green fee US$60, T9532650) (all east of Montego Bay) and Tryall Golf, Tennis and Beach Resort (Par 71, 6,920yds in 2,200-acre resort complex, green fee US$125, between Montego Bay and Negril, T9565681/3). The Tryall course is probably the best known and hosts the annual Johnny Walker World Championship. Advance bookings are essential. A new course near Negril is the Negril Hills Golf Club (T9574638), Par 72, 6,333yds, 18 holes in the hills, green fees US$58.

Jamaica

The island's main spectator sport is **cricket**, although overtaken by soccer in 1998 when Jamaica qualified for the World Cup. Test matches are played in Kingston. For details on matches ring Jamaica Cricket Association, T9670322. For **football** phone Jamaica Football Federation, T9290484. **Tennis** can be played at the Eric Bell Tennis Centre, Kingston. For **track and field** meets phone Jam Amateur Athletics Association. **Horse racing** at Caymanas Park, T9257780/9253312, every Wednesday and Saturday and most public holidays. **Polo** is played on Saturday afternoons at Drax Hall, near Ocho Rios, entrance free, and there are several polo clubs, for example Polo and Equestrian Club of Oakbrook, T9228581 for match details. International tournaments at Chukka Cove, Runaway Bay and Caymanas Polo Club, Kingston. **Riding** lessons and trail rides also available at Chukka Cove, which has probably the best facilities, T9722506. Hotels can arrange riding with local stables too and there are good facilities at the Equestrian Centre at *Half Moon Club*, Montego Bay, and *Good Hope*, where you can ride along the banks of the Martha Brae River. A three-hour beach ride costs about US$50, while a 2-3 day trek into the mountains costs US$285-500.

Holidays and festivals

Carnival has come only recently to Jamaica and is held around *Easter* time with floats, bands and mass dances, at various locations around the islands, attended by thousands. Dancing for six hours a night for seven nights, the best way to get fit! Byron Lee, the leading Jamaican calypsonian, spends a lot of time in Trinidad over Carnival period and then brings the Trinidad calypsoes back to Jamaica. Some Trinidadian costumes, although not the really spectacular ones (logistically impossible), are recycled for Jamaica's carnival. The annual reggae festival, **Sun Splash**, is held in *February*, usually in Montego Bay, in the Bob Marley Centre, but also at Reggae Park, White River, Ocho Rios (T9601904). In August, the celebrations around **Independence Day** (*1 August*) last a week and are very colourful. The annual **International Marlin Tournament** at Port Antonio in *October* attracts anglers from all over the world and includes festivities other than fishing. The tourist board publishes a twice-yearly calendar of events which covers the whole spectrum of arts and sports festivals.

Kingston

The capital since 1870 and the island's commercial centre, Kingston has one of the largest and best natural harbours in the world. Following the earthquake of 1907 much of the lower part of the city (Down Town) was rebuilt in concrete. On the waterfront there are some notable modern buildings including the Bank of Jamaica and the Jamaica Conference Centre which also houses the National Gallery. Most of the new shops and offices are scattered over a wide area of north and east Kingston. Crossroads and Halfway Tree are referred to as midtown areas. Many shopping plazas are further north again along the Constant Spring Road. The old racecourse was redeveloped in the 1960s as the New Kingston district, which contains most of the big hotels and many banks and financial institutions. Kingston is a busy city with traffic congestion at major junctions. It is a place to work rather than holiday, although there are some important places of interest. Reggae lovers will visit the Bob Marley Museum, but anywhere you may receive blasts of music from buses, bars and cars.

Population: 750,000

Ins and outs

The international airport for Kingston is the **Norman Manley** (restaurant, good tourist office), 11 miles away, up to 30 mins' drive, on the peninsula opposite Kingston across the bay. An exchange desk in the arrivals lounge changes cash and travellers' cheques (at a slightly lower rate than banks). Buses and shared taxis to/from North Parade for the airport, US$0.35, but the service is infrequent, so allow for waiting time. To get to New Kingston by bus involves a change of bus (to No 27) Down Town. The recognized service to/from town from airport is JUTA, taxi/minibus, which charges US$17 to New Kingston (taxi despatcher gives

Getting there
See transport, page 275, for further details

Jamaica

you a note of fare before you leave, can be shared). Alternatively, if you have not got much luggage, take taxi to Port Royal, US$9, ferry to Kingston (see below, Port Royal) and then taxi to New Kingston, US$5-6. There is also an airstrip on Tinson Pen, 2 miles from the centre, Wed for international flights, 10 mins' drive.

Getting around
You are recommended to go into a hotel & order a taxi, rather than hail one in the street

Bus travel in Kingston costs between US$0.20 and US$0.30. A free map of Kingston bus routes is available from Jamaica Omnibus Services Ltd, 80 King Street. Travelling by bus is not safe after dark or even during daytime in certain areas. Take a taxi to the bus station although you will still get hassled and pestered during the short walk to the bus. Do not walk out of the bus station; the area is notorious. Crossroads, Pechon Street and Half Way Tree are the main bus stops, but buses coming from town are usually full by the time they reach Crossroads or Half Way Tree.

Kingston orientation

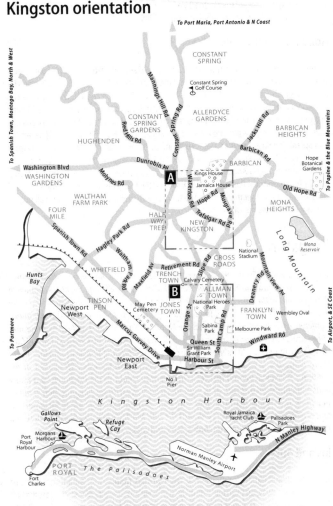

Related maps:
A. New Kingston, page 286
B. Downtown, Kingston, page 287

0 km 1
0 miles 1

Sights

Among older buildings of note in the Down Town area are **Gordon House** (on Duke Street), which dates from the mid-18th century and houses the Jamaican legislature. Visitors are allowed into the Strangers' Gallery but must be suitably dressed (jackets for men and dresses for women). There is also the early 18th century parish church south of Parade, where Admiral Benbow is buried. **Parade** (Sir William Grant Park) is at the heart of the city centre; it is an open oasis amid the densely-packed surroundings. The name derives from the British soldiers' parades here during colonial rule. Now it is at the junction of the main east-west route through the Down Town area (Windward Road/East Queen Street-West Queen Street/Spanish Town Road) and King Street/Orange Street which runs north to Cross Roads. At Cross Roads, the main route forks, left to Half Way Tree (recently renamed Nelson Mandela Park), straight on up Old Hope Road to Liguanea. These two roads encompass New Kingston.

The Parish Church at St Andrew at **Half Way Tree** dates from 1700. Half Way Tree, so called because it was a half-way stage on the road between the harbour and the hills, is a busy traffic junction which takes some negotiating in a car. Hope Road, on the north edge of New Kingston, runs east from Half Way Tree. Just off it are **Devon House**, a former 'great house', built by Jamaica's first millionaire in the 1880s, at the corner of Trafalgar and Hope Roads, now renovated, complete with antique furniture, with craft shops and refreshment stalls. ■ *Small admission fee to look inside the main house, US$3 for a guided tour, but the shops and restaurants in the grounds are open to all and well worth a visit. Tue-Sat, 1000-1700.* The **African Museum**, with exhibits on Jamaica's African heritage, is part of the Devon House complex. Not far away is **King's House**, the official residence of the Governor-General and, nearby, **Jamaica House**, the Prime Minister's residence.

About 10 blocks east of Devon House, off Hope Road, is the **Bob Marley Museum**. The house where Marley used to live traces back to his childhood and family, with paintings, newspaper cuttings, posters and other memorabilia. He died tragically of brain cancer in 1981 at the age of 36, having survived a controversial assassination attempt (the bullet-holes in the walls have been left as a reminder). There is an Ethiopian restaurant in the garden serving some of his favourite vegetarian dishes and a gift shop selling Jamaican and African artifacts. Marijuana plants grow profusely throughout the grounds and ganja is smoked openly in and around the restaurant and bar by staff. Photography is totally banned within the museum and grounds. ■ *0900-1700, Mon, Tue, Thu, Fri, 1230-1730, Wed, Sat. US$10 including obligatory guided tour, which takes 1 hr, including 20-min audio visual presentation. T9782991, 56 Hope Rd.*

Further east, along Old Hope Road, are the **Hope Botanical Gardens**. The land was first acquired by Major Richard Hope in 1671 and 200 years later the Governor of Jamaica, Sir John Peter Grant, bought 200 acres and created a botanical gardens. In 1961 a zoo was opened alongside the gardens (J$10, 1000-1700 daily). After extensive damage in 1988 by Hurricane Gilbert, plans have been made to transform the small, traditional zoo into a showcase for the different natural habitats of Jamaica and its indigenous animals. ■ *Free. 0830-1830.*

Beaches The swimming at Kingston is not very good. The sea at Gunboat beach, near the airport, is dirty. Better at Port Royal (see below). 'Hellshire', south of Port Henderson, is a locals' favourite, but is difficult to reach.

Essentials

Sleeping **Morgan's Harbour** is conveniently close to the airport and has complimentary transport there and back, 10 mins (see Port Royal); all the other main hotels are in or near **New Kingston**.

A full list is available from tourist board

LL-L *Le Meridien Jamaica Pegasus*, 81 Knutsford Blvd, PO Box 333, T9263690, F9295855, www.meridienjamaica.com 350 rooms, pleasant service and atmosphere but nothing special. **LL-L** *Hilton Kingston*, 77 Knutsford Blvd, PO Box 112, Kingston 5, T9265430, F9297439. 303 rooms, usual Hilton facilities. **L** *Terra Nova*, 17 Waterloo Rd, T9269334, F9294933, www.cariboutpost.com/terra_nova 35 rooms, popular with business travellers, pool, bar, café and restaurant. **L-AL** *Crowne Plaza*, 211 Constant Spring Rd, Kingston 8, T9257674, F9054425. 132 rooms, high rise, business hotel with executive floor, gym, sauna, exercise facilities, tennis, squash, jogging trail, pool. **AL-A** *Christar Villas*, 99A Hope Rd, Kingston 6, T9787864, F9788068, christar@n5.com.jm 32 1-2 bedroom suites and studios with kitchenettes, pool, bar, restaurant, small gym. **A** *Altamont Court*, 1-5 Altamont Terr, T9294497, F9292118. 55 rooms, pool, restaurant, close to *Pegasus* and *Hilton*. **A-B** *Four Seasons*, 18 Ruthven Rd, PO Box 190, T9297655, F9295964, www.hotelfourseasonsja.com Run by Mrs Stocker, German, long-time knowledgeable resident, in a converted Edwardian house and gardens, 76 rooms, pool, bar, conference room, business centre, good cooking. **B-C** *Mayfair*, 4 West King's House Close, Kingston 10, PO Box 163, T9261610, F9297741. Beautiful setting (adjoining the Governor General's residence), balconies look towards mountains, 32 good rooms, also 8 houses, pool, food and service. Among the cheaper hotels is **B** *The Indies*, 5 Holborn Rd, T9262952, F9262879. 15 rooms, television US$6 extra, breakfast and lunch available, comfortable, pleasant patio, garden, helpful owners. Next door is the popular

New Kingston

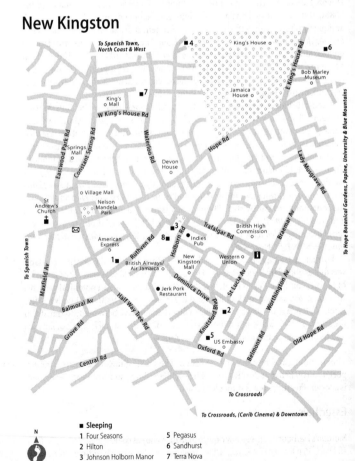

■ Sleeping

1 Four Seasons	5 Pegasus
2 Hilton	6 Sandhurst
3 Johnson Holborn Manor	7 Terra Nova
4 Mayfair	8 The Indies

N

Not to scale

D *Johnson Holborn Manor*, 3 Holborn Rd, with breakfast and shower. Fan, clean, safe and quiet, very convenient for business in New Kingston, 3 good places to eat within 50 yds, luggage storage available, friendly, new annex. **B** *Sandhurst*, 70 Sandhurst Cres, Kingston 6, T9277239. 35 rooms, a/c or fan, restaurant. **D-E** *Retreat Guest House*, 8 Devon Rd, T9262565. 4 rooms, among the cheapest, safe area after dark. About 25 mins from Kingston is **AL-A** *Ivor Guest House* and restaurant, Jack's Hill, Kingston 6, T9271460, F9770033, www.cariboutpost/ivor High up in the hills overlooking Kingston and set in its own extensive grounds, 10 rooms, free transport to/from Kingston, charge for airport pickup, lunches US$12, dinners US$16 by reservation only. Highly recommended. About 40 mins from Kingston is *Pine Grove*, see under Eastern Jamaica and the Mountains. The YMCA, opposite Devon House on Hope Road, has a good swimming pool, many sports facilities and a cheaply priced restaurant. The tourist board can arrange B&B for you, which usually costs US$25-60 a night.

Up in the hills overlooking Kingston Bay is Island Outpost's *Strawberry Hill*, now a 12-villa luxury retreat but formerly a coffee and fruit plantation house, sadly destroyed by Hurricane Gilbert in 1988. Recommended weekend brunch of jerk meats, salt fish etc washed down with champagne and orange juice, US$25 per person, T9448400, F9448408, or contact Island Outpost in UK, 421a Finchley Rd, London NW3 6HJ, T0800 614790.

There are a great many places to eat in Down Town Kingston, New Kingston and the Half **Eating** Way Tree area. There are plush establishments, inside and outside the hotels, and small places. For the impecunious, meat patties may be had at US$0.25 each. Be warned that

Jamaica

Downtown Kingston

Both Orange Street & Marescaux Rd converge at Cross Roads becoming respectively Old Hope Rd & Halfway Tree Rd

To Cross Roads

Orange Street

Jewish Cemetery

National Heroes Park

Marescaux Road

South Camp Road

TRENCH TOWN/ JONES TOWN AREA

To Spanish Town

Sabina Park

North Street

Spanish Town Rd

West Queen St

Orange Street

King Street

Ward Theatre

N Parade

Sir William Grant Park

S Parade

Pechon St

Parish Church

King Street

Duke Street

East Street

East Queen Street

Barry Street

Harbour Street

Crafts Market

National Gallery

Port Royal Street

Conference Centre

Ocean Blvd

To Norman Manley Airport, Bath & Morant Bay

N

Not to scale

around the waterfront most places close at 1700. On Holborn Rd, opposite the *Indies Hotel* is the *Indies Pub*, which is reasonable, and next door is the *Three Little Bears* with patisserie attached, cheap cakes and coffee, excellent lobster in the main restaurant and quite palatable Jamaican wine, main course for lunch under US$4, evening meal US$8-18, buffet Fri and Sun excellent value at US$8. *Akbar*, 11 Holborn Rd. Very good Indian food, good service, nice atmosphere, US$20 for 3-course dinner and drinks for 2. On Chelsea Av (in the same area) is *Jerk Pork*, popular with locals. Nearby are Mexican and Indian restaurants, both very good but not cheap. *The Lychee Gardens*, shop 34 in the New Kingston Shopping Mall, on Dominica Drive, T9298619. Serves excellent Chinese food, moderately priced, several other eating places here, from takeaway pattie bakery to upmarket restaurant, popular lunch spot for office workers. *Heathers*, Haining Rd, T9607739. Very pleasant to sit outside, Middle Eastern and Jamaican dishes, US$3.25-9. Around the corner at 2 Altamont Terr, *Hot Pot*, T9293906. Very cheap, serves good Jamaican food in a pleasant patio, also a take-out box for just over US$1, difficult to find it without asking for directions. *Red Bones*, 21, Braemar Av, T9788262. 'Nouvelle Jamaican cuisine', quite expensive but lovely garden and blues music. *Lyn's Vegetarian Restaurant* and Performing Arts Auditorium, 7 Tangerine Pl, Kingston 10, T9293842, 9683487. *Guilt Trip*, 20 Barbican Rd, T9775130. Delicious pastries and desserts. *Susie's Bakery*, Southdale Plaza, T9685030. Recommended for light lunches and coffee. On Knutsford Blvd there are lots of vans selling a satisfying lunch for US$1-1.50, often less, depending on what you eat. Many outlets of international takeaway chains all over the city, *Burger King* and *Kentucky Fried Chicken*, etc, as well as Jamaica's own variation, *Mothers*, also widespread; *The Tastees*, chain serves good value takeaway patties and cakes, branches on Knutsford Blvd, Liguanea, Manor Park and Papine. At *Devon House* (see page 285), there is a plush expensive restaurant, a reasonably priced snack bar and delicious ice cream at *I Scream*. In the grounds of the University of Technology at Papine is *Lillian's*, T9271615. Staffed by trainees, good cheap lunch for about US$3.

Nightlife
Most hotels have dancing at weekends

Tourists are strongly advised not to try, unless they have Jamaican friends, to probe deeply into real Jamaican nightlife, at least in towns. For genuine local dances and songs, see the advertizements in the local press. The *Jamaica Vacation Guide* (at hotels, tourist offices) has the latest information. Clubs and discos include *Asylum* Knutsford Blvd (above *Jam Rock*), *Mirage*, Sovereign Shopping Centre, Liguanea, *Turntable*, Red Hills Rd, *Mingles* at *Courtleigh Hotel*, *Peppers* on Waterloo Rd, a good open air drinking spot, *the* place to go at night. *Half Time*, and *Jam Rock*, both on Knutsford Blvd. Young crowd, sports bars, music, TV, pool. *Devon House* is a good place for a quiet evening drink under the trees. *Centre Pole* at Mary Brown's Corner on Constant Spring Rd is rowdy and raunchy but fairly safe too.

Entertainment

Amusements in Kingston include cinemas and theatres. There is a good School of Drama and several theatre and dance companies. Jamaica Dance Theatre is well known. Theatres include Ward Theatre (North Parade), Little Theatre (St Andrew), The Barn, New Kingston Playhouse, Green Gables, Creative Arts Centre. Watch the press for details of performances.

Shopping

In Down Town Kingston, the Jamaica Crafts Market and many shops at west end of Port Royal Street have local crafts. Off West Queen Street is an interesting local market, selling fish, fruit and general produce. Down Town is where Jamaicans shop for bargains, but be careful, particularly in the market, it can be dangerous and you need to be thick skinned to get through, even if you do not get robbed. Most shops are in the plazas along Constant Spring Road and in Liguanea. There is a smart little shopping centre in New Kingston. Reggae music shops can be found close together along Orange Street, just north of Parade. The best bookshop, particularly for Caribbean fiction, is *The Book Shop*, The Springs, 15-17 Constant Spring Rd, T9261800. Also very good is the *Kingston Bookshop* at 70B King Street, T9224056, and at the Pavilion Shopping Mall, Half Way Tree, T9684591. *Bookland* on Knutsford Blvd. Wide range of US magazines and newspapers and also *The Times*. There are various dutyfree concessions for visitors. There is a laundry in Chelsea Ave.

Bus   Fares from Kingston are: US$1.40 to Mandeville, US$2.75 to Montego Bay, US$1.50 to   **Transport**
Negril, US$1.25 to Ocho Rios, US$2 to Port Antonio, 3 hrs, you are lucky if you get a seat. The
buses are invaded by touts as they approach the bus station.

Banks   *National Commercial Bank of Jamaica*, 77 King St, Kingston and branches all over the island;   **Directory**
the same applies to the *Bank of Nova Scotia Jamaica Ltd*, head office: Duke and Port Royal Sts,
Kingston. *Citibank*, 63-67 Knutsford Blvd, Kingston; and other local banks. A string of **ATM's** has been
installed in main centres from which you can withdraw cash from Visa and Mastercards. Immediate
money transfers can be made via the Western Union Bank, behind the National Commercial Bank at
the top of Knutsford Blvd. **Cultural centres**   *The British Council* has an office in the First Life Building,
64 Knutsford Blvd, PO Box 575, Kingston 5, T9296915, F9297090. Information library, mainly on
education, British newspapers available. **Embassies & consulates**   British High Commission is at 26
Trafalgar Rd, Kingston 5, T9269050, F9297869, PO Box 575. 26 other countries represented. **Tourist
office**   2 St Lucia Av, T9299200.

Port Royal

Port Royal, the old naval base, lies across the harbour from Kingston. It was founded   *Population: 2,000*
in 1650, captured by the English and turned into a strategic military and naval base.
Merchant shipping developed under naval protection and the town soon became
prosperous. It also attracted less reputable shipping and in 1660-92 became a haven
for pirates such as Henry Morgan, with gambling and drinking dens and brothels
protected by the six forts and 145 guns. The 'wickedest city in the world', with a population of 8,000, soon provoked what was thought to be divine retribution. On 7
June 1692 an earthquake hit east Jamaica, coursing along the Port Royal fault line
and bringing with it massive tidal waves. The port, commercial area and harbour
front were cut away and slid down the slope of the bay to rest on the sea bed, while
much of the rest of the town was flooded for weeks. About 5,000 people died (of
drowning, injuries or subsequent disease) and the naval, merchant and fishing fleets
were wrecked. The town was gradually rebuilt as a naval and military post but has
had to withstand 16 hurricanes, nine earthquakes, three fires and a storm (which in
1951 left only four buildings undamaged).

Nelson served here as a post-captain from 1779 to 1780 and commanded **Fort
Charles**, built in 1655, key battery in the island's fortifications. The former British
naval headquarters are now the **Fort Charles Maritime Museum**, with a scale
model of the fort and ships. ■ *1000-1700 Mon-Thu, 1000-1600 Fri, US$1*. Part of
the ramparts, known as Nelson's Quarterdeck, still stands. ■ *US$2*. The Giddy
House was the Royal Artillery store, built in 1888 but damaged by the 1907 earthquake which caused it to tilt at an angle of 45°. The Victoria Albert battery complex
was a boiler house and underground armoury with late 19th century guns to protect
the harbour and tunnels. The old Naval Hospital was built in 1819 of prefabricated
cast iron sections brought all the way from England, one of the earliest constructions
of this type and built on a raft foundation. The old gaol can also be seen. This dates
from the early 18th century and was used as a women's prison in the 19th century. **St
Peter's Church**, though the restoration is unfortunate, is of historic interest, as is the
National Museum of Historical Archaeology. The museum is little more than one
room and the Fort Charles remains are more informative and substantive.
■ *US$0.30*. A US$60 mn tourist project for Fort Royal was announced in 1998, to
include renovation of the town, construction of a new museum, concert hall and
shopping centre. ■ *Getting there: beyond the international airport, some 15 miles by
excellent road. Can also be reached by boat from Victoria Pier; they leave 7 times a day,
take 20 mins and cost US$0.30.*

L *Morgan's Harbour* at Port Royal is a favourite holiday centre, T9678030, F9678073. 40   **Sleeping**
rooms, 5 suites, a/c, TV, balcony, sea view, seminar rooms, gift shop, scuba diving (packages
available with Buccaneer Scuba Club at the marina, T9678061, F9678073), with waterskiing,
fresh and saltwater swimming pools, beach cabins, a good seafood restaurant, and dancing,

closest hotel to airport. Boats may be hired for picnic bathing lunches on the numerous nearby cays or at Port Henderson. There is a full service marina at *Morgan's Harbour* with customs clearance, 24-hr security and fishing boats for hire.

Spanish Town

Spanish Town, the former capital founded in 1534, some 14 miles west of Kingston (bus from Half Way Tree and from Orange Street), is historically the most interesting of Jamaica's towns and in desperate need of funds for renovation. Its English-style architecture dates from the 18th century. Well worth seeing are the **Cathedral Church of St James**, the oldest in the anglophone West Indies dating back to 1714. Also in need of renovation is the fine Georgian main square which houses the ruins of the **King's House** built in 1762 (Governor's residence until 1872 when Kingston became the capital) that burnt down in 1925. The façade has been rebuilt and within it is the **Archaeological Museum**, containing exhibits excavated here and a site history of 1534-1872. In the old stables is the **Jamaican People's Museum of Craft and Technology**. ■ *Mon-Fri, 1000-1700, US$0.20*. Also on the square are a colonnade (paint peeling off) and statue commemorating Rodney's victory at the Battle of the Saints (see under Guadeloupe and Dominica); the **House of Assembly** and the **Court House**. There is a museum with interesting relics of Jamaican history and accurate portrayal of life of the country people. The **park** in the centre is overgrown with weeds and the gates are padlocked. Outside town, on the road to Kingston is the **White Marl Arawak Museum**. ■ *US$0.10. Mon-Fri, 1000-1600*. Restaurant: *Miami*, Cumberland Rd, near the market area; food is delicious, especially the pumpkin soup.

Eastern Jamaica and the mountains

North from Kingston Behind Kingston lie the Blue Mountains with Blue Mountain Peak rising to a height of 7,402 ft (2,256 m). This is undoubtedly one of the most spectacular and beautiful parts of Jamaica and an area which must be visited by keen bird watchers and botanists and also by those who like mountain walking. It is possible to explore some of the Blue Mountains by ordinary car from Kingston. Drive towards **Papine** and just before arriving there visit the **Botanical Gardens** at **Hope** with a splendid collection of orchids and tropical trees and plants, but rather run down and reported dangerous at dusk. After leaving Papine and just after passing the *Blue Mountain Inn* (good restaurant and nightclub), turn left to Irish Town and thence to **Newcastle**, a Jamaica Defence Force training camp at 4,000 ft with magnificent views of Kingston and Port Royal. If energetic you may climb the road to **Catherine's Peak** directly behind the camp (about one hour for the moderately fit).

Holywell National Park to Buff Bay Beyond Newcastle lies **Hardwar Gap** and **Holywell National Park**. *The Gap Café*, at Hardwar, T9237078, has spectacular views and serves real Blue Mountain coffee. This whole area is full of mountain trails with innumerable birds, some unique to Jamaica. The road then winds down to Buff Bay with a turning off to the right to **Clydesdale** and the **Cinchona botanical garden**. Unfortunately you are unlikely to be able to get an ordinary car past Clydesdale and perhaps not even to Clydesdale. From Clydesdale to Cinchona is about an hour's walk uphill but well worth it.

Around Blue Mountain If you wish to go towards **Blue Mountain Peak**, you drive straight on at *Blue Mountain Inn* (instead of turning left), through Gordon Town and on through **Mavis Bank** four miles to **Hagley Gap** (if the Mahogany Vale ford is passable). Again, however, you will almost certainly not be able to get a car up to the starting point for the walk to the Peak. Public transport up the Blue Mountains is infrequent. There are some buses to Mavis Bank from the square in Papine on the outskirts of Kingston,

US$0.60 but you will need to ask. To get to Papine, take a 70 or 75 bus along Hope Road. Taxis from Papine to Mavis Bank about US$7.50. Only four-wheel drive vehicles are advisable after Mavis Bank (no shortage of people offering to take you), and there are no petrol stations *en route*. There are two walking possibilities from Mavis Bank: either look for a four-wheel drive to Hagley Gap and walk from there to the starting point of the trail to the Peak (3½ miles uphill through villages), or walk the short cut from Mavis Bank. You may need to be guided for the first part (plenty of guides, Linford Morrison recommended, lives near Police Station), across two small rivers and on to the path, which is then straight forward, a reasonably hard but lovely walk for two hours. Keep going when you eventually reach the village. Ask for *Whitfield Hall* or *Wildflower Lodge* (see below), the turning for which is just beyond Penlyne Castle School, by the Post Office. It is then a few minutes' walk.

An alternative solution is to stay at **B** *Pine Grove Hotel*, c/o 62 Duke Street, Kingston, T9228708, F9225895, about half an hour's drive beyond Gordon Town. This consists of a series of cottages with central feeding and the atmosphere of a ski lodge with double rooms with bathroom, kitchen area and couch. The proprietors, Barbara and Radwick, live there and are extremely welcoming and helpful. Apart from giving advice they will also provide four-wheel drive vehicles at very moderate cost to take guests to Cinchona and the start of the trail to Blue Mountain Peak, et cetera. They will also pick up guests from the airport (US$50) or from Kingston.

Mountain lodges

Another possible solution for the active is to contact the *Jamaican Alternative Tourism, Camping and Hiking Association* (JATCHA) at Maya Lodge and Hiking Centre, Juba Spring, Peter's Rock Road, Jack's Hill, Kingston, T7020314. To get to Maya Lodge by public transport take the 76 or 76A bus from Duke Street (down town) or Knutsford Boulevard (New Kingston) to Barbican. From there take a shared taxi round the corner on Jack's Hill Road opposite the Texaco station, US$0.90, the taxis are sometimes very shared indeed. Alternatively, it is a 3½ mile walk uphill, not to be attempted after dark. A room or cabin at *Maya Lodge*, **E**, hostel style, camping in own tent or in hired tent all **F** (all plus 12½% to fund projects), restaurant, vegetarian options, menu repetitive, 15 acres of land in jungle setting, many paths for hikes around area. Highly recommended. A day's walk with a guide costs US$50. For a short tour of an organic farm ask for Willy, who will show you round his farm, interesting, reasonable rates, but only attempt it if you can walk up and down a steep hill and have old shoes. Willy is often used as a guide and will take you up into the forest on Mount Horeb giving you details of local lore and bush medicine as you go.

There are two lodges close to the point where the Blue Mount Peak trail begins. John Algrove (8 Almon Crescent, Kingston 6, T9270986) owns *Whitfield Hall Hostel*, a large wooden lodge with no electricity but gas for the kitchen and paraffin lamps, **F** per person, capacity 40, hostel or **D** private room accommodation, cold showers only. No meals unless you order them in advance, but kitchen with stoves and crockery, for guests' use. Very peaceful and homely with comfortable lounge, log fire and library (visitors' books dating back to the 1950s), staff friendly and helpful. If the hostel is full, camping is permitted. A couple of minutes' walk before *Whitfield Hall* is *Wildflower Lodge*, known locally as the White House. It charges the same prices for dormitory or private room as *Whitfield Hall*, but is a bit more modern and the food is better, breakfast US$3, evening meals US$5 but hard to tell the difference, substantial and excellent vegetables from the garden, T9295394/5 or write 10 Ellesmere Road, Kingston 10. Both lodges will arrange four-wheel drive transport from Kingston or Mavis Bank and offer guides and horses for walking or riding excursions.

The walk to **Blue Mountain Peak** (6½ miles from Whitfield Hall) takes three to four hours up and two to three hours down. The first part is the steepest. Some start very early in the morning in the hope of watching the sunrise from the Peak. As often as

Climbing the peak

Jamaica

not, though, the Peak is shrouded in cloud and rain in the early morning making it a depressing experience. You can leave in early daylight and almost certainly reach the top before it starts clouding over again (mid to late morning). In this case you do not need a guide as the path is straightforward. The trail winds through a fascinating variety of vegetation, coffee groves and banana plantations on the lower, south slopes, to tree ferns and dwarf forest near the summit (with some explanatory and mileage signposts). The doctor bird (national bird of Jamaica) is quite common, a beautiful swallow-tailed hummingbird. Quite hard to spot at first but recognizable by its loud buzz, especially near the many flowering bushes. You must take your own food and torch, sweater and rainproof if you set out in the darkness. There are two huts on the peak where one can stay overnight in some discomfort (empty concrete buildings with no door). There is a campsite with cabins, water and a shower at Portland Gap, about one hour up. Snacks and drinks are available at the ranger station; the rangers are very helpful. Another trail, to **Mossman Peak**, starts at Portland Gap, but is currently overgrown after 15 minutes, having not recovered from Hurricane Gilbert. In high season up to 500 people walk up Blue Mountain Peak every day, while in low season there will be only a handful. Considering the numbers, it is remarkably unspoiled and the views are spectacular.

John Crow mountains **Bath** at the east end of the island is another place from which one can make attractive trips into the **John Crow Mountains** (named after the ubiquitous turkey buzzards). There is a modest but cheap hotel, *Bath Spa,* dating from 1727 whose main attraction is that it contains natural hot water spring baths which are most relaxing at the end of a long day. There are two passes above Bath, called the **Cuna Cuna Pass** and the **Cornpuss Gap**, which lead down to the source of the Rio Grande River on the nrth slopes of the mountain range. Both are tough going particularly the Cornpuss

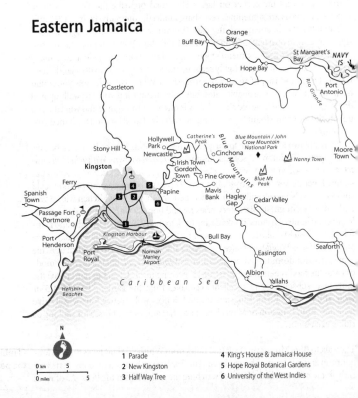

Eastern Jamaica

1 Parade
2 New Kingston
3 Half Way Tree
4 King's House & Jamaica House
5 Hope Royal Botanical Gardens
6 University of the West Indies

0 km 5
0 miles 5

Gap. It is absolutely essential to take a local guide. The north slopes of the mountain range are the home of the unique and extremely rare Jamaican butterfly, *papilio homerus*, a large black and yellow swallowtail. It can best be seen in May/June. Near Bath, but not easily accessible, is the magnificent **Pera** beach between Port Morant and Morant Lighthouse. Near the lighthouse is another good beach but, like nearly all the beaches along the east coast round to Port Antonio, there is a dangerous undertow in certain spots. Just before reaching Manchioneal from Bath there is a road off to the left which leads to the **Reach Falls** or **Manchioneal Falls** (about three miles). Well worth a visit if you have a car or are prepared to walk (45 minutes with views of rolling forested hills) from the main road. No facilities at the falls, there may be an entry charge. Pretty tiers of smooth boulders, the highest fall about 15 ft, through a lush, green gorge. Buses from main road to Port Antonio infrequent, every 1-2 hours. Further northwest along the coast from Manchioneal to Long Bay cottages and guest houses have been built on the beach.

Port Antonio

Once the major banana port where many of the island's first tourists arrived, on banana boats, Port Antonio dates back to the 16th century. Its prosperity has for many years been in gentle decline and it is now run down, but it has an atmosphere unlike any other town in Jamaica with some superb old public buildings. It is an excellent base from which to explore inland or along the coast. The rainfall in this part of the island is very high and in consequence the vegetation very lush. Boston Bay, Fairy Hill Beach, San San Beach, the Blue Lagoon (also known as the Blue Hole) and Frenchman's Cove Beach are notable beauty spots to the east of the town. **Boston Bay** is renowned for its local jerk food pits; several unnamed places by the roadside serving hot spicy chicken, pork or fish, chopped up and wrapped in paper, cooked on planks over a pit of hot coals, very good and tasty. Also worth visiting is **Nonsuch Cave**, a few miles to the southeast, where there are fossils and evidence of Arawak occupation, **Somerset Falls** and **Folly**, an elaborate, turn of the century mansion built in the style of Roman and Greek architecture, now in ruins (partly because the millionaire American's wife took an instant dislike to it). The Folly is about half an hour's walk around the bay from the town. Take a right fork off the path before going into a clump of trees on the peninsula (leading towards lighthouse inside military camp). It is a ghostly, crumbling old mansion in an open field with lovely views shared with grazing cows. ■ *0900-1600 daily, US$5. Stalactites, gift shop and lunch area. Getting there: there is no public transport to Nonsuch Cave, return taxi fare US$10 including waiting time. For Somerset Falls, 0900-1700 daily, US$3. Take a bus to Buff Bay (any westbound Kingston bus) and walk 5 mins from there.*

Population: 14,000

Jamaica

Navy Island In the harbour it is possible to visit the 68-acre **Navy Island**, at one time owned by Errol Flynn, which has beaches (one nudist) and a moderately expensive restaurant. Return boat fare US$3, ferry operates 0700-2200 daily. Accommodation at the **AL** *Navy Island Marina Resort*, reservations, T9932667, F9932041. Rooms (14) or individual villas, restaurant, pool and bar open to non-guests, open view of bay. 'Errol Flynn Gallery' has display of movie stills and screenings of his golden oldies. The beaches on the island all belong to the resort but are open to non-guests. Snorkelling available (at the nudist beach), US$2 for half-day hire, but there are strong currents and not many fish. Many other sports and other activities on offer, including a complete wedding ceremony in the resort chapel.

Rafting on the Flynn also saw the potential as a tourist attraction for the bamboo rafts which used to
Rio Grande bring bananas down the Rio Grande. Expert raftsmen now take tourists on these rafts down the river. One boatman is Keith Allen, with a registered licence, who can be contacted in Port Antonio at the Huntress Marina, but if you just turn up at Berrydale there are always rafters ready and willing to take you. Each raft (US$45 per raft from the ticket office, but if you arrive before it opens at 0830 or if you arrive by local bus, you can sometimes negotiate a fare of as little as US$25 with a rafter) takes two passengers and the trip takes 1½-2 hours (depending on the river flow) through magnificent scenery and with an opportunity to stop en route. Before you start make it clear who is buying the drinks. A driver will take your car down from the point of embarkation to the point of arrival. This is known as Rafter's Rest and is on the main coastal road. Recommended as a place to have a moderately priced lunch or drink in pleasant surroundings even if you are not proposing to raft. The return taxi fare is US$10, there are also buses, US$0.25, to Berrydale, the setting-off point, though infrequent. Returning from St Margaret's, downstream, is easier as there are plenty of buses passing between Annotto Bay and Port Antonio.

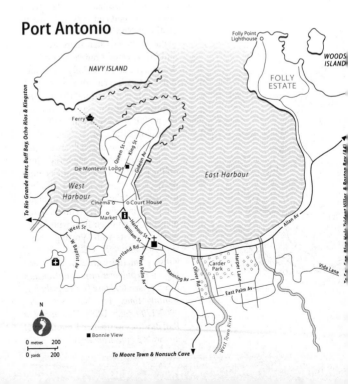

Port Antonio

The Rio Grande valley is also well worth exploring, including a trip to the Maroons (descendants of escaped slaves) at **Moore Town**, but the roads are rough and public transport minimal. Ask for Colonel Harris there who is the leader of the Maroons and is recommended for guided tours. There is no telephone contact nor accommodation, return taxi fare US$15. To the west of the Rio Grande lie the north slopes of the Blue Mountains, many parts of which are still virtually unexplored. **Nanny Town**, the home of the Maroons, was destroyed by the British in 1734 and then 'lost' until the 1960s. There is recent archaeological evidence at Nanny Town to suggest that the Maroons originally took to the mountains and lived with (and possibly later absorbed) Arawak peoples. There have been some dramatic discoveries of Arawak wooden carvings which are now on display at the National Gallery.

The Maroons

Port Antonio LL *Trident Villas and Hotel*, PO Box 119, T9932602, F9932960. 26 rooms/suites with sea view, MAP, antique furniture, private, tennis, croquet, pools, restaurants, afternoon tea. **L** *Jamaica Palace*, Williams Field, PO Box 277, T9932020, F9933459. 65 rooms, a/c, beach, pool, wheelchair accessible, watersports. On top of a hill overlooking both bays is **L-A** *Bonnie View*, set in its own working plantation, PO Box 82, T9932752, F9932862. Charming rooms, many with excellent views, bar and restaurant, horse riding and other activities also available. Titchfield Hill, 5 mins' walk from the town are **C-D** *De Montevin Lodge*, 21 Fort George St, PO Box 85, T9932604. Includes breakfast, shared bath, more expensive rooms have private bath, old Victorian house, restaurant serves set meals, US$8-10, very good value, and **C-E** *Ivanhoe* nearby. Some rooms with shared bath, patio with bay view. These are licensed but not recommended by the Tourist Board. Several nearby private houses also take guests. In the town centre **D** *Triff's Inn*, 1 Bridge St, T9932162, F9932062. Modern, clean, pleasant lounge area, 17 rooms, restaurant, bars.

Sleeping

Outside Port Antonio LL-L *Goblin Hill Villas* at San San, reservations c/o 11 East Av, Kingston 10, T9258108, F9256248. 44 rooms in 1 or 2 bedroomed villas, kitchen, restaurant or housekeepers available for shopping and cooking, cheaper with no sea view, tennis, short walk to beach, pool, car hire, bar, TV room. **LL-AL** *Dragon Bay Beach Resort*, PO Box 176, T9938514, F9933284. Attractive resort, villas or rooms on secluded bay, diving, snorkelling, pool, beach volleyball, tennis, good restaurant. **L-B** *Fern Hill Club* at San San, T9937374, F9937373. 31 rooms and spa suites, cottages, all-inclusive available including tours, 4 pools, jacuzzi, restaurant, golf, tennis, windsurfing, sailing, diving, snorkelling, horseriding. At Frenchman's Cove, **LL-L** *Hotel Mocking Bird Hill*, PO Box 254, Port Antonio, T9937134, F9937133, mockbrd@cwjamaica.com 15 mins from town, 5 mins' walk from beach, 10 rooms in Caribbean style villa in 7 acres of parkland, pool, gardens, nature

Jamaica

trail, restaurant with Jamaican international and cuisine, Gallery Carriacou and gift shop exhibits owner's art, German, French, English and Spanish spoken. 12 miles west of Port Antonio just after Hope Bay at Rodney Hall, Black Hill, is **C-D** *I-tal Village*, T9130917, F9130987, www.italvillage.com 5 rooms with shared facilities, breakfast included, dinner, fruit and juices all day US$15-20, Jamaican and Italian organic vegetarian food, locally grown, weekly rates available. Port Antonio has a Guest House Association offering good value lodging, excursions and transfers, www.go-jam.com

Eating *Blue Lagoon*, Fairy Hill, T9938491. Built over the water, great swimming in the deep blue water, Jamaican food, jerk specialities, fresh lobster, try the blue cocktail, live music and entertainment at weekends, open Mon-Wed 1100-1700, Thu-Sun 1100-2200. *Huntress Marina* on a jetty in the harbour. Mainly a bar popular with yachting fraternity, but good breakfast, evening meals also served, cold beer. *Coronation Bakery*, near Musgrave Market on West St. Good for cheap patties and spice buns. *Cream World*, good for ice cream, cakes and cheap snacks. *Stop Group Jerk Centre* on the bay out of town towards the folly. Bar and jerk pork, chicken and fish, also music and dance until late. *Roof Club* , dance shack with sign outside saying 'no drugs, no firecrackers, don't destroy furniture'.

Directory **Tourist office** Upstairs in City Centre Plaza on Harbour St, T9933051/2587, F9932117. Quite helpful, have timetables for local buses ("soon come"), which leave regularly when full, but at uncertain hours, from seafront behind Texaco station.

Port Antonio to Buff Bay Between Port Antonio and the Buff Bay area there are several roads into the interior from such places as Hope Bay and Orange Bay. It is worth a detour if you have a car being well off the beaten track. Just to the east of Buff Bay is **Crystal Springs** with beautifully laid out gardens, a variety of fish in the clear waters of the streams, an aviary, a bird sanctuary and masses of orchids. There is a moderately priced restaurant, three cottages to rent (**L**) and camping sites, T9961400. Take any bus between Port Antonio and Kingston (US$0.40, about 45 minutes from Port Antonio), signposted at a turn-off between Orange Bay and Buff Bay (marked Spring Garden on Discover Jamaica road map). About 1½ miles along a flat paved road there is a small **swimming pool** surrounded by palms and flowering tropical plants. An idyllic spot, not busy during the week. Well worth a visit and a good base for exploring the foothills of the Blue Mountains. ■ *0900-1700 daily, US$3.*

From Crystal Springs the road goes on to Chepstow and thence to **Claverty Cottage** and **Thompson Gap**; spectacular scenery, waterfalls in the valleys and very remote. It is possible to walk from Thompson Gap over the Blue Mountains via Morces Gap and down to Clydesdale, but this is a full day's trip and only to be undertaken with an experienced local guide and there is a problem of getting transport to meet you at Clydesdale. It is also possible to take a bus for part of the way up the Buff Bay valley and then walk on either to Clydesdale or over the Hardwar Gap to Newcastle. Both very long trips and only for the really fit.

The north coast

The Kingston to Port Maria road (the Junction Road) passes through **Castleton Botanical Gardens** (in a very tranquil setting, well worth a visit, ask Roy Bennett to be your guide if available). The journey takes about two hours and there are plenty of minibuses. **Port Maria** itself is a sleepy and decaying old banana port but not without charm and lots of goats. East of Port Maria in **Robin's Bay** there is a camping and cottage resort on the beach, **AL-C** *Sonrise Beach Retreat* (formerly Strawberry Fields), standard or 'deluxe' cabins (sleep 5-6) with or without bath and tent sites, **F**, bath house, T/F9997169, two miles from village, transport essential or arrange pick-up with resort, meal plans and ecotour packages available, restaurant, nature trails, trampoline, volley ball, ping pong. A few miles to the west of Port Maria lies the attractive looking **D** *Casa Maria* hotel which has seen better days, PO Box 10, T9942323, F9942324, 20 rooms, beach, restaurants, bars.

Close by the hotel is *Firefly*, Noel Coward's Jamaican home, now owned by the Jamaican National Trust. It is evocative of a stylish era and a highlight if you are interested in the theatre or film stars of that period and worth a visit if only for the magnificent view. ■ *0830-1700 daily except Fri, US$10, T9940920.* Noel Coward's other property, *Blue Harbour*, is half a mile from the hotel, and is where he used to entertain film stars, royalty etc. It is now a guest house with accommodation for up to 15 in the two-bedroomed Villa Grande, the one-bedroomed Villa Chica and the four-roomed Villa Rose, all much as Coward left it although there has been some hurricane damage and it is dilapidated. Prices range from **B-C** depending on season and number of guests, fans, saltwater pool, coral beach, good snorkelling and scuba, gardens, lovely views, PO Box 50, Port Maria, St Mary, T9942262.

Noel Coward's homes

Oracabessa is another old banana port with a half completed marina and *Golden Eye*, the house where **Ian Fleming** wrote all the James Bond books. The house has been recently restored and is now a retreat owned by Chris Blackwell's Island Outpost. The James Bond beach lies in front of the house, small but highly recommended as safe and child friendly. Bars and fish meals available. **LL** *Goldeneye*, three bedroom villa with full time staff. *Goldeneye Village*, has a further six bedrooms, cottage-style, for rent as a whole or individually, all-inclusive. To the west of Oracabessa is Boscobel, where the air strip for Ocho Rios is located. Opposite the air strip are numerous houses for rent.

Ian Fleming's home

Ocho Rios

On a bay sheltered by reefs and surrounded by coconut groves, sugar cane and fruit plantations, is Ocho Rios. The town has become very popular, with many cruise ships making a stop here. It is 64 miles east of Montego Bay and claims some of the best beaches on the island. The beach in town is safe and well-organized with facilities, 200 yds from Main Street where most of the shops and vehicle hire companies can be found. **Shaw Park Gardens** are an easy walk from the town centre, being up the hill on the edge of town. Nice gardens, recommended. ■ *0800-1700 daily, US$4, T9748888.*

The scenery of the surrounding area is an added attraction. Most spectacular are the beauty spots of **Fern Gully**, a marvel of unspoilt tropical vegetation, **Roaring River Falls**, which has been partially exploited for hydroelectric power, and **Dunn's River Falls**, tumbling into the Caribbean with invigorating salt and freshwater bathing at its foot. ■ *0900-1700 daily. US$6, locker US$1, bath shoes US$5 (rental) but not necessary if you move with care. Getting there: get there early before the coach parties arrive. Five-minute bus ride, US$0.20, from Ocho Rios, or 1-hr drive from Montego Bay (beware of pseudo guides who hang around and take you somewhere totally different, then try to sell you marijuana).* The minibus from Kingston to Ocho Rios costs US$2 and follows a spectacular route, up the gorge of the **Rio Cobre**, then across Mount Diablo. **Faith's Pen**, right on the top, is an enormous collection of huts selling food and drink, great for a stop but you may not get on another bus as they normally pass full. Near Moneague is *Café Aubergine*, T9730527, an upmarket and tasteful restaurant in an 18th-century house, about US$25 per person. The last section of road whizzes round a series of blind corners as you go through Fern Gully. Driving time is one hour 50 minutes once the bus has started. Alternatively, take a minibus from the Texaco petrol station on Da Costa Drive, Ocho Rios, for US$0.30 to Fern Gully. Lots of minibuses for return journey.

Excursions

Historical attractions in the area include **Sevilla Nueva**, some nine miles to the west, which was where the Spanish first settled in 1509. The ruins of the fort still

Jamaica

remain. The site is being investigated by the University of California at Los Angeles and the Spanish Government. Offshore, marine archaeologists, from the Institute of Nautical Archaeology at Texas A & M University, are investigating the **St Ann's Bay** area for sunken ships. Salvaged timbers are believed to have come from two disabled caravels, the *Capitana* and the *Santiago de Palos*, abandoned at Sevilla Nueva probably in 1503 during Columbus' last visit to Jamaica.

There are numerous **plantation tours** available to tourists all along the north coast. Details are widely publicized. Probably the most attractive, informative and certainly most accessible, is the *Prospect Plantation Tour*, a short distance to the east of Ocho Rios nearly opposite the *Sans Souci Lido*. ■ *1030, 1400, and 1530 daily. US$12. T9742058.* Another, just southwest of St Ann's Bay, is *Circle B*, owned by former senator, Bob Miller. Very good tour of working plantation, recommended. ■ *Welcome drink and sample fruits of Jamaica, lunch can be included, T9722988.* **Harmony Hall** art gallery just east of Ocho Rios is worth a visit. There are frequent exhibitions of paintings and sculpture in a classic gingerbread house, as well as crafts, clothes and other gifts to buy. ■ *T9754222, www.harmonyhall.com, open 1000-1800. There is also an Italian restaurant,* Toscanini's*, open 1000-2200, closed Mon evenings, T9754785.* Wassi Art pottery workshop (Great Pond, T9745044) is delightful; there is a good selection in the salesroom and you can visit each artist. Ask your taxi driver to wait as it is several miles away.

West of Ocho Rios is **Mammee beach**, which is beautiful and less crowded than Ocho Rios, though there is no shade there.

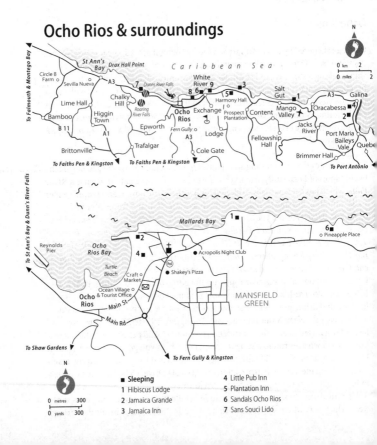

Ocho Rios & surroundings

■ **Sleeping**
1 Hibiscus Lodge
2 Jamaica Grande
3 Jamaica Inn
4 Little Pub Inn
5 Plantation Inn
6 Sandals Ocho Rios
7 Sans Souci Lido

LL *Jamaica Inn*, PO Box 1, T9742514, F9742449, www.jamaicainn.com 45 rooms, sea- **Sleeping**
view, FAP, pool, private beach, elegant, men wear jackets and ties in the evenings, Winston
Churchill used to stay here and Noel Coward drank here. **LL** *Plantation Inn*, PO Box 2,
T9745601, F9745912. 63 rooms, 15 suites, 2 cottages, pool, beach, tennis, facilities for disabled, watersports, diving, fishing etc. **LL-L** *Renaissance Jamaica Grande Resort*, PO Box
100, T9742201/9, F9742289. 720 rooms, all-inclusive or room only, pool complex with
waterfalls, children's programmes, convention facilities, singles packages, watersports,
yacht charter, fishing, diving. **LL** *Sans Souci Lido*, PO Box 103, T9742353, F9941544. A
SuperClubs all-inclusive resort for couples, lots of facilities, watersports, 146 rooms and
suites. There are also **LL** *Sandals Ocho Rios Resort & Golf Club*, Main St, PO Box 771,
T9745691, F9745700, and **LL** *Sandals Dunn's River Resort & Golf Club*, Mammee Bay,
T9720563, F9721611. Mid-price inns include: **AL-A** *Hibiscus Lodge*, 83 Main St, PO Box 52,
T9742676, F9741874. 26 rooms in gardens on cliff overlooking sea, manmade beach, pool,
jacuzzi, tennis. **B-C** *Little Pub Inn*, 59 Main St, T9742324, F9745825. Includes breakfast,
small, nice rooms, a/c, nightly entertainment, games room, shopping arcade, restaurants
and bars. **C** *La Penciano Guest House*, 3 Short Lane, T9745472, run by Lloyd Thomas.
Rooms with shared or private bath, fan, TV, in town centre and therefore noisy, but clean
and safe, friendly, helpful, bar open Fri and Sat night has nice view over Ocho Rios. About 1
mile from town centre, you can camp at Milford Falls, **F**, right by the waterfall, take
Kingston road out of Ocho Rios, turn right at sign to Shaw Park Gardens then fork left up
Milford Rd, stop at *George Barnes' shop* on right, he will take you there and provide you with
information, food and drink, he has a tent or a rustic cabin with 1 bed to rent, good place to
get away from city hustle.

Jamaica

Sleeping
1 Boscobel
2 Casa Maria
3 Couples
4 Firefly
5 Jamaica Inn
6 Plantation Inn
7 Sandals Dunns River
8 Sandals Ocho Rios
9 Sans Souci Lido

East of Ocho Rios there are all-inclusive
resorts which are very good if you want that
sort of holiday: **LL** *Boscobel Beach* is a
SuperClubs resort set up for family holidays
(PO Box 65, T9757330, F9757370). **LL** *Cou-*
ples is for honeymooners (T9754271,
F9754439). **LL** *Club Jamaica Beach Resort*
another all-inclusive is on Turtle Beach in
Ocho Rios, PO Box 342, T97466329,
F9746644, in USA T1-800-8182964. 95 rooms,
a/c, TV, phone, pool, watersports, diving, lots
of games, exercise facilities, nightclub.

On Main Street there are lots of restaurants **Eating**
offering Jamaican, international, seafood
cuisine, including *The Lobsterpot*, Chinese,
US$12-15 for lobster supper. *Jerk Pork*,
same price for barbecued pork, fish or
chicken. *Shakey's Pizza*, Main St. Nice bar
and patio, fast, friendly service, smallest
pizza from US$5.50. *Little Pub*, 59 Main St.
Jamaican food and entertainment. *Bill's*
Place on Main St. *The Acropolis* nightclub is
lively and fairly safe.

The *Lion's Den* is a friendly club frequented **Nightlife**
by Rastafarians; rooms available, good food,
clean. There is much fashionable nightlife in
and around Ocho Rios.

Tourist office *Ocean Village*, Shopping Centre, **Directory**
T9742582/3. **Cycling:** *Blue Mountain Bicycle*

Tours, Main St, T9747075, F9740635, bmtours@infochan.com, tours include an 18-mile downhill trip through the forest to a waterfall, no pedalling, food and drink and transfers included, don't expect much from the bikes.

West to Falmouth Continuing west along the coast is **Runaway Bay**, an attractive and friendly resort. It is named for the Spanish governor Ysasi, who left quickly for Cuba in a canoe when he saw the English coming. Only five miles away is **Discovery Bay** where Columbus made his first landing. The **Columbus Park**, an outdoor museum, has exhibits and relics of Jamaican history. From Runaway Bay, the Runaway Caves can be visited where there is an underground lake in the Green Grotto. However, you can no longer take a boat ride (as shown in their advert) and the place is littered with beer bottles; not recommended. ■ *0900-1700.* Among the hotels in this area is the **A** *Runaway Bay HEART Hotel*, PO Box 98, T9732671, F9732693, runaway.heart@cwjamaica.com, which has an adjoining hotel training centre and overlooks a golf course. The **LL** *Club Ambiance*, T9732066, F9732067, has been described as adequate for fine weather but lacking in indoor facilities when it rains. Golf is available at Runaway Bay Golf Club. There are several **LL** all-inclusive resorts here too, including *Breezes Runaway Bay* (SuperClubs, lots of activities, golf, tennis, scuba diving, for couples and singles, 238 rooms and suites, PO Box 58, Runaway Bay, T9732436, F9732352).

Falmouth Falmouth is a charming small town about 20 miles east of Montego Bay. It is the best example of a Georgian town and the Jamaica National Heritage Trust has declared the whole town a National Monument. It has a fine colonial court house, a church, some 18th-century houses with wrought iron balconies, and Antonio's, a famous place to buy beach shirts. There is good fishing (tarpon and kingfish) at the mouth of the Martha Brae, near Falmouth, and no licence is required. It is possible to go rafting from **Martha Brae** village. Expert rafters guide the craft very gently for the one-hour trip to the coast. ■ *US$36 from Montego Bay includes 2-person raft, lunch and transfers, 0900-1600, or take local bus from Montego Bay to Falmouth, US$0.50, hitchhike or walk 6 miles to upper station; end station is about 3 miles from Falmouth.* **Jamaica Swamp Safaris** is a crocodile farm where you can see lazy crocodiles with equally laid back guides. Bar and restaurant. Two James Bond films were made here. ■ *US$6 for adults.* Some 10 miles inland is the 18th-century plantation guest house of **Good Hope** amongst coconut palms. Deluxe accommodation in the superb setting of a working plantation, as well as day tours and horse riding – some of the best riding in Jamaica – and its own beach on the coast. ■ *Daily 1200-1600. US$10. T9543289.*

Cockpit Country This is a strange and virtually uninhabited area to the south of Falmouth and to the southwest of Montego Bay. It consists of a seemingly endless succession of high bumps made of limestone rock. The tourist office and hotels in Montego Bay organize day trips (about US$50) to **Maroon Town** (no longer occupied by Maroons) and **Accompong**, the headquarters of the Maroons who live in the Cockpit Country area. An annual festival is held here at the beginning of January with traditional music and dance, T9524546, Kenneth Watson. Older locals can accurately describe what happened at the last battle between the Maroons and the British forces. Ask to see the **'Wondrous Caves'** at Elderslie near Accompong. If you have a car take the road on the east side of the Cockpit Country from Duncans (near Falmouth) to Clark's Town. From there the road deteriorates to a track, impassable after a few miles even for four-wheel drive vehicles, to **Barbecue Bottom** and on to Albert Town. The views from Barbecue Bottom are truly spectacular (the track is high above the Bottom) and this is wonderful birding country. If you wish to walk in the Cockpit Country make your way, either by car or on foot (no public transport), to the **Windsor Caves** due south of Falmouth. They are full of bats which make a spectacular mass exit from the caves at dusk. There are local guides to hand. The underground rivers in the caves (as elsewhere in much of Jamaica) run for miles, but are only for the experienced and properly equipped potholer. There is a locally published book called *Jamaica Underground*; many caves and good walks in the area. For caving, contact Mike Schwartz of *Windsor Great House*, T9973832, windsor@cwjamaica.com It is possible to walk from the Windsor Caves across the middle of the Cockpit Country to Troy on the south side (about eight hours). It is essential to have a local guide and to make a preliminary trip to the Windsor Caves to engage him. Convince yourself that he really does know the way because these days this crossing is very rarely made even by the locals. It is also vastly preferable to be met with transport at Troy because you will still be in a pretty remote area.

Montego Bay

About 120 miles from Kingston, situated on the northwest coast, is Montego Bay, Jamaica's principal tourist centre with all possible watersport amenities. Known familiarly as Mo' Bay, it has superb natural features, sunshine most of the year round, a beautiful coastline with miles of white sand, deep blue water never too cold for bathing and gentle winds which make sailing a favourite sport. Doctor's Cave is the social centre of beach life. Gloucester Avenue, by Doctor's Cave, is one of the busiest streets for tourists, lined with duty-free shops, souvenir arcades, hotels and restaurants. In 2000, Montego Bay accepted an invitation to be twinned with another internationally famous, sprawling tourist resort: Varadero in Cuba.

Population: 92,000

Getting there The **Donald Sangster international airport** is only 2 miles from the town centre. Taxi from airport to town US$7 or 20-min walk airport to Doctor's Cave. JUTA and JCAL are licensed taxis. **Getting around** The **Soon Come Shuttle** bus is operated on 2 routes: Central Route (every 15 mins) and Eastern Route (every 45 mins) stopping at hotels and some shops, tokens (US$1) purchased at hotels and special outlets, costs 2 tokens on Eastern Route, 1 on Central Route 1000-2400.

Ins & outs
See page 275 for further details

Jamaica

Sights

Of interest to the sightseer are the remaining battery, cannons and powder magazine of an old British fort, **Fort Montego**, with landscaped gardens and crafts market, free, and the 18th-century church of **St James** in Montego Bay, built in 1778 and restored after earthquake damage in 1957. There are a few Georgian buildings, such as the *Town House Restaurant*, 16 Church Street (good local art gallery next door), and the Georgian Court at the corner of Union and Orange Streets. The centre of town is Sam Sharpe Square, named after the slave who led a rebellion in 1831-2. The Burchell Memorial Church, established in 1824 by the Baptist missionary, Thomas Burchell, was where Samuel Sharpe served as a deacon.

Forts & churches

Doctor's Cave for the underwater coral gardens, so clear that they can be seen without effort from glass-bottomed boats. ■ *US$1.70, children under 12 half price. 0900-1800 daily*. Doctor's Cave is the beach for relaxed sunbathing, while **Cornwall** is more sun 'n' fun, or beach 'n' boogie, with beach contests etc. ■ *US$1. 0900-1700 daily*. Scuba diving can be arranged through about a dozen operators, several of which have outlets at more than one hotel. A single dive costs about US$45, a snorkelling trip US$25.

Beaches

If you are staying in town, rather than at the hotel strip, there are beaches close by, either public ones with no services or private (US$0.50-2.00) with food, drinks, tennis, boat hire, snorkelling, shower, changing rooms et cetera. Walk from the traffic circle in the middle of town towards the hotels and the beach will be on your left. Mosquitoes can be a problem at certain times of the year or when the drains need cleaning out. Take repellent and coils.

Excursions

Out of town, to the east, are the great houses of **Rose Hall** and **Greenwood**. The latter was built by the forefathers of the poet, Elizabeth Barrett Browning, in 1780-1800. It has a colourful avenue of bougainvillea and mimosa and a panoramic view over the coast from the verandah. ■ *0900-1800 daily, US$10*. Rose Hall was

Montego Bay

Sleeping
1 Breezes
2 Coral Cliff
3 El Greco
4 Ocean View Guest House
5 Sandals Inn

Eating
1 Greenhouse
2 Marguerite's
3 Shakey's Pizza
4 Toby Inn
5 Town House

N
Not to scale

Jamaica

started 10 years earlier, in 1770, by John Palmer. A lively legend of witchcraft sur-rounds the wife of one of his descendants, Anne Palmer. ■ *US$15 adults. 0900-1800 daily, Rose Hall Beach Club US$55 includes lunch, drinks, entertainment, watersports, 1000-1730 daily.*

Inland, seven miles from Montego Bay off the Maroon Town road (turn off east half a mile before the village of Johns Hall), is the recommended **C-F** *Orange River Lodge*, an old Great House overlooking the **Orange River Valley**, which has guest rooms, hostel accommodation in bunk beds, and camping, bring own tent, beauti-ful location, excellent food, friendly staff, excursions arranged, also shuttle service to Montego Bay. Good walking in the area, you can swim in the river or go canoeing and birdwatching is good, T9792688 at Lodge or PO Box 822, 34 Fort Street, Montego Bay, T9527208, F9526241. Southeast of Montego Bay is the Arawak rock carving at **Kempshot**, while to the southwest is the bird sanctuary at **Anchovy**: Rocklands Feeding Station, don't miss this, the doctor bird humming birds will even perch on your finger, knowledgeable guides. ■ *US$8.50, 1400-1700 daily, but mem-bers of birdwatching societies will be admitted any time. Children under five are not admitted.* The road to Anchovy is too rough for ordinary cars. Three miles to the west of Anchovy is **Lethe**, the starting point for rafting down the Great River. Ten miles from Montego Bay on the Savanna-La-Mar road is the **Montpelier Great House**, on the site of the old Montpelier sugar factory which was destroyed during the 1831 rebellion, call Pat Ottey, T9524299, for bed and breakfast, **E-F**, children welcome. South of Anchovy, about 25 miles from Montego Bay, is **Seaford Town**, which was settled by Germans in the 1830s. Only about 200 of their descendants sur-vive. Write to Francis Friesen, Lamb's River Post Office.

Lucea is a charming spot on the north coast where the *Tamarind Lodge* serves excellent Jamaican food. Visit the Rusea School, endowed by a refugee Frenchman in the 18th century, in a lovely location but badly damaged by Hurricane Gilbert. Between here and Montego Bay (bus, US$0.88) is **Tryall**, with one of the best (and certainly the most expensive) golf courses on the island (see above, Sport). **LL** *Tryall Golf Tennis and Beach Club*, T9565600/5, F9565673, expensive, deluxe villas, one to two bedrooms. Continuing around the island's west end, the road passes through **Green Island** before reaching Negril (29 miles from Lucea). There are several pretty fishing villages between Lucea and Green Island, such as Cousins Cove, with small guest houses and seaside cottages for rent.

Essentials

In the super-luxury range are **LL** *Round Hill Hotel and Villas*, 10 mins west of Montego Bay on 98-acre peninsula, T9567050, www.roundhilljamaica.com Originally a coconut and pineapple plantation, it opened in the 1950s with the help of Noel Coward, popular with the rich and famous, celebrity owners include Paul McCartney, Ralph Lauren, Lord Rothermere. **LL** *Half Moon Golf, Tennis and Beach Club*, on 400 acres adjoining beach, T9532615. 340 rooms and 5-7 bedroomed villas with staff, golf, tennis, riding stables, squash, fitness centre, spa, theatre etc. **LL-L** *Coyaba Beach Resort and Club*, T9539150, F9532244, coyaba@ n5.com.jm 50 rooms and suites with a/c, TV, VCR, phones and balconies, beach, gardens, pool, jacuzzi, private dock, tennis, fitness room, watersports, restaurants, bar, hammocks on the shore, family-owned, 'elegantly relaxed'. There are several large, lavish resorts in the area, including a 523-room **LL-L** *Holiday Inn Sunspree*, all-inclusive or accommodation only. While Sandals have 3 all-inclusive resorts, **LL** *Sandals Inn*, **LL** *Sandals Montego Bay* and **LL** *Sandals Royal Caribbean*. SuperClubs have **LL** *Breezes Montego Bay* on Doctor's Cave Beach, T9401150, F9401160. 124 rooms and suites, tennis, watersports, fitness centre, enter-tainment, scuba and golf at extra cost. If you are looking for a self-catering resort in the heart of the beach strip, try **AL** *El Greco*, Queens Drive, PO Box 1624, T9406116, F9406115, www.montego-bay-jamaica.com/jhta/elgreco/ 64 1-bedroom and 32 2-bedroom suites on hillside overlooking bay, direct elevator access to Gloucester Av and Doctor's Cave Beach, grocery store, pool, beach towels, tennis, laundry, cook and nanny on request.

Sleeping
There are over 40 hotels, guest houses & apartment hotels listed by the tourist board & many more which are not

Jamaica

Warnings

Security Constant importuning is a major problem downtown and tourists are constantly hassled and hustled. Knife attacks and other muggings by thieves have been reported to us. Avoid the area ENE of Union Street. The unfortunate consequence of this is that tourists avoid the town centre and stay in the tourist strip, where the selling is not unpleasant, or, worse, stay confined to the all-inclusive resorts. If you do go into town, do not be fooled by those who 'just want to talk', nor by 'do you recognize me? Its Tony from the hotel'. Answer, 'which hotel?'

Health St James parish, which includes Montego Bay, has the highest incidence of AIDS in the country, with 198 cases per 100,000 population, compared with the national average of 83 per 100,000.

L-A *Cariblue* , Ironshore, T9532180, F9532550, www.jamaicaway.com A dedicated dive resort, lots of packages, 20 a/c rooms, pool, deep sea fishing, sailing, snorkelling, windsurfing, glass bottom boats, day sails. **A-B** *Coral Cliff*, 365 Gloucester Av, PO Box 253, T9524130, F9526532. Remodelled to allow slot machines, rooms variable, food reasonable, bar, pool and friendly service. **B** *The Guest House*, 29 Gloucester Av, T9523121, F9793176. Beautiful house with wide balcony overlooking sunset in the bay, get room at back to avoid traffic noise, includes huge nutritious breakfast, run by Irish and Canadian, very friendly. **AL-A** *Montego Bay Club*, Gloucester Av, T9524310, F9524639. Dominant 12-storey apartment hotel in centre of tourist area overlooking Doctor's Cave Beach, pool, tennis. There is a YMCA at Mount Salem with sports facilities available to members. **C-D** *Ocean View Guest House*, 26 Sunset Blvd, PO Box 210, T9522662. 10 mins' easy walk from the airport, cheaper without a/c, many rooms overlook the bay, all clean, with bath, back-breaking mattresses, no advance bookings, but on arrival, ask tourist board to phone the hotel who will arrange free transport from the airport. **E** *Ridgeway Guest House*, 34 Queen's Drive, PO Box 1237, T9522709, F9791740. 5 mins' walk from airport, with bath and fan, friendly, clean, family atmosphere, cheaper rates for longer stays.

Eating

Most restaurants are happy for guests to bring wine & provide chillers & glasses. Rum is cheaper here than at airport duty free shops

Service at restaurants can be begrudging but the food is excellent. On the way into town from the airport there are several reasonably-priced restaurants. Recommended is the **Pork Pit** next to *The Guest House*, 27 Gloucester Ave, T9521046. Jerk chicken, pork and ribs sold by weight, service basic, and the **Toby Inn**, very good for cheap barbecued chicken and pork, cheap drinks, live band, romantic atmosphere. *Baba Joe's* (Barbara Joe's), Kent Av, near airport on way to Whitehouse Village, just past Sandals. Excellent fish, local style, about US$8 for meal with beer. *Orlan Caribe Vegetarian Restaurant*, 71 Barnett St. Tidy, comfortable, low prices, rather out of the way, open 1000-1600, vegetarian restaurant. There are several restaurants along Gloucester Av, including *Shakey's*, for pizza and breakfasts, deliveries T9522665. Not too good. The *Pelican*, T9523171. Excellent breakfasts, good value. *Patsy's Place*, 100 m from *The Guest House*. Small, good local dishes, excellent curried goat, cheap. *Walter's Bar and Grill*, 39 Gloucester Av, T9529391. Local food, nice garden, good value; *The Greenhouse*, T9527838, opposite St James Place shopping arcade. Good food and inexpensive, Jamaican/American. *Marguerite's*, T9524777. On the seafront, 2 restaurants, one posh with a/c and *Margueritaville* next door on a patio. Sports bar and grill; *Le Chalet*, 32 Gloucester Av, T9525240. Clean, friendly, Chinese, Jamaican (good curried goat), European menu at a quarter of the price of neighbouring restaurants, free hotel transfers; *Town House*, 16 Church St (see above), T9522660. Mildly pungent, tasty stuffed lobster US$30, other dishes also good, US$12.50-27. *Natives Jerk Centre*, Market St. Garden, outside bar, jerk chicken or pork, fish dishes with rice 'n' peas, about US$7 for meal with beer. *Smokey Joe's*, St James St, just beyond Woolworths towards Courts. Good local restaurant, about US$6 for soup, main course and beer.

Nightlife *Margueritaville Caribbean Bar & Grill*, Gloucester Av, T9524777. Now quite an institution, very popular, 52 flavours of Margaritas and 32 oz 'bong of beer', sport on big TVs, Nintendo and kids' menu, waterslide from roof to sea, DJ at night, open daily from 1000, cover charge US$9 Fri-Sat. Disco on Cornwall Beach with volleyball on beach at night. Lots of hotels have discos and clubs.

Air The **Donald Sangster international airport** is *Air Jamaica*'s regional hub and there are good connections with lots of airlines landing here. For those landing here who want to go to Kingston, there is a transfer service by Martins minibus which takes 5 hrs. It is also possible to get to the **Norman Manley airport**, Kingston, by taking the minibus from the town centre to Pechon Street, Kingston, from where the airport buses leave; US$4.50, 3 hrs. Do not buy at the airport duty free shop; everything is half the price at ordinary shops in town.

Road Bicycle rentals through *Montego Bike Rentals*, T9524984, and *Tropic Ride Car & Bike Rental*, T9527096.

Bus There is no need to take the expensive tourist buses, except that the regular buses get crowded. They depart when full. The regular buses are fast, very frequent and cheap, about US$2 from Montego Bay to Negril with a 30-second transfer in Lucea. There are more buses Montego Bay-Lucea than Lucea-Negril, which often causes a bottleneck. Buses from Kingston depart from Pechon Street, near the railway station, roughly every hour from 0600 to 1500, US$2.80. It is possible to get to Montego Bay from Port Antonio all along the north coast, a scenic journey involving changes in Annotto Bay (then shared taxi, US$1 per person, mad rush to squeeze into clapped-out Ladas, the locals give no quarter to slow tourists), Port Maria US$1, and Ocho Rios. Ochos Rios-Montego Bay by bus takes 2 hrs, US$1.50. The bus station for Kingston and Ocho Rios is behind Courts (Electrical). The bus station for Negril is off Barnett Street (beware pickpockets). *UTAS Tours*, T9523820, F9793465, offer 12-hr day trip to Kingston via Dunns River Falls and Ocho Rios, US$60 for driver in a/c car; also 9-hr tour to Negril, US$21, with sunset drink at *Rick's Café*, Negril.

Taxi *JUTA* are usually found outside hotels. *JCAL*, T952-7574/8277, charges US$10 to Gloucester Av from *Sandals Montego Bay*, US$15 from *Wyndham*. A taxi Lucea-Negril costs about US$20.

Tourist office Cornwall Beach, T9524425.

Negril

Negril, on a seven-mile stretch of pure white sand on the west end of the island, is far less formal than other tourist spots but is still a one-industry town. The town is at the south end of Long Bay; at the north is the smaller Bloody Bay, where whalers used to carve up their catch. The Negril Area Environmental Protection Trust (NEPT) hopes to have the coastal area declared a national marine park and a grant has been awarded by the European Union (for information T9574473). The main part of the town has resorts and beaches but no snorkelling and you have to take a boat. In the West End of the village are beautiful cliffs and many fine caves, with great snorkelling but no beaches. In between is an area with neither beaches nor cliffs. Behind the bay is the Great Morass, which is being drained for development but remains a protected area as a natural wetland.

There is clothes optional bathing at certain hotels, which is still quite rare in non-French Caribbean islands. Watersports are a particular attraction and there are facilities for tennis and riding at *Babo's Horseback Riding Stable* and *Country Western Riding Stables*, ■ *US$30-35. 0800-1700 daily*. There is a dive shop at *Hedonism II*, T9574200, free for guests, and Sundivers Negril, a PADI five-star facility at *Poinciana Beach Resort*, diving lessons 0900 and 1200, resort course US$60, guided boat dives three times daily, US$30 single tank, US$45 for two tanks (also at *Rock Cliff Resort*). Negril Scuba Centre is at *Negril Beach Club* (T9574425, neg.scuba.centre@toj.com), while there are dive operations at *Swept Away* and *Sandals*.

By the *Poinciana Beach Resort* is the Anancy Park with boating lake, minigolf, go-karts, fishing pond, nature trail, video arcade and historical exhibitions. ■ *US$1-3. Tue-Sun 1300-2200.*

Hawkers ('higglers') are annoying and reported to be worse than at Montego Bay. They will interrupt whatever you are doing to push their drugs, hair braiding, aloe etc. Politely decline whatever they are offering (if you do not want it), they do not want to be shrugged off or ignored, but neither do they want to hold a long conversation with you. Fruit is readily available although not ready to eat; ask the vendor to cut it up and put it in a bag for you. To avoid the worst of the higglers go to the end of the beach near the crafts market where there are no stalls or bars. There are toilets and showers (US$0.30).

Inland, up in the hills, a golf course has been built: the *Negril Hills Golf Club* (T9574638, F9570222) is an 18-hole, Par 72, 6,333 yd course, with clubhouse, restaurant, pro shop and tennis.

Sleeping

A local rule is that no hotel should be taller than the tallest palm tree to minimize the visual & environmental impact of tourism

LL *Hedonism II*, PO Box 25, T9575200, F9575289. 280-room all-inclusive adult resort. **LL** *Grand Lido Negril*, SuperClubs resort at south end of 2-mile sandy beach of Bloody Bay, PO Box 88, T9575010, F9575517. All-inclusive, couples only, superb food, service and setting, clothes optional, pool and jacuzzi beside its nude beach area, guests can also use the facilities at Hedonism II, a short walk across Rutland Point. **LL** *Sandals Negril*, T9575216, F9575338. All-inclusive. Sandals also has **LL** *Beaches Negril*, an upmarket all-inclusive, T9579270, F9579269. **LL** *Swept Away*, all-inclusive, sports complex, T9574061, F9574060. **L-AL** *Negril Gardens Hotel*, PO Box 58, T9574408, F9574374. 64 suites with balconies, gardenside or beach, a/c, TV, good for families. **LL-A** *Foote Prints on the Sands*, PO Box 100, T9574300, F9574301. 30 rooms, a/c, on beach, all-inclusive or room only, cheaper packages sometimes available. **LL** *Poinciana Beach Resort*, PO Box 44, T9575100, F9575229. All-inclusive, 130 rooms and villas, scuba diving at extra cost, bicycle rental, 2 pools, gym, jacuzzi, tennis, ping pong, basketball and lots of other sports and watersports, children's programmes, free pass to the Anancy Family Fun and Nature Park opposite the resort. **L-AL** *Charela Inn*, on the beach, PO Box 33, T957-4648, F9574414. 49 rooms, family owned and run, kayaks, sunfish, sailboards, restaurant, bar. **L-AL** *Negril Cabins*, Norman Manley Blvd, on Bloody Bay, across the road from the beach, PO Box 118, T9575350, F9575381. 70 rooms in cabins on stilts, or more expensive rooms, pool, swim-up bar, private beach, restaurant, piano bar, beach parties, children's programme, security guards keep away 'higglers'. **LL-E** *Firefly Beach Cottages*, Norman Manley Blvd, on the beach and therefore not very private, PO Box 54, T9574358, F9573447. From a basic cabin for 2, to studios, or 1-3 bedroomed cottages, or luxury villa, prices reduced in summer, gymnasium, minimum 1 week rental in winter, 3 nights in summer. **B** *Llantrissant*, T305-6689877 (in Miami), www.beachcliff.com A fully staffed, 5-bedroomed beachhouse on 2 acres with tennis courts and beaches, kayaks and snorkelling.

Negril

Orange Bay

To Montego Bay

North Negril Point

Bloody Bay

Rutland Point
Point Village Resort
Booby Cay

Grand Lido
Hedonism II

Sandals Negril

Poinciana Resort
Beaches
Swept Away

The Great Morass

Long Bay

Norman Manley Blvd

Foote Prints on the Sands

Negril Beach

Charela Inn

Negril Inn

Negril Gardens

S Negril River

Negril
Crafts Market

Sheffield Rd

Mariner's Inn

WEST END

WHITE HALL

Rick's Café

West End Rd

White Hall Rd

Negril Hill

N

0 metres 800
0 yards 800

Negril Lighthouse

Mount Airy

Jamaica

C-E *Tigress 1*, West End Rd. Cheaper rooms with fan, no hot water, shared bathrooms, higher priced rooms with a/c, hot water, private bath, all with kitchen facilities, good security, bar and pool in nice gardens, 20 mins' walk to beach and walking distance from town centre, friendly, clean, well-maintained, lots of repeat business. **LL-AL** *Rock Cliff*, West End, PO Box 67, T9574331, F9574108, on rocky promontory. **L-A** *Rockhouse*, West End Road, PO Box 24, T/F9574373, www.rockhousehotel.com On cliffs at Pristine Cove, just north of *Rick's Café*, 11 octagonal villas by the sea with fans, indoor bathrooms, outdoor showers, built of timber, stone and thatch, or 17 studios in thatched blocks in the garden, cliff-edge pool, restaurant above the water serving 'new Jamaican cuisine', open 0700-2300, no beach but steps down to sea, snorkelling and kayak rental, quiet, restful, Australian-owned, no children under 12 because of potentially dangerous cliffs. **AL-B** *Mariner's Inn and Diving Resort*, West End, T9570393, F9570391. On cliffs, 52 rooms, PADI and NAUI instructors for diving, kayaking, riding, volleyball. **A-C** *Ocean Edge Resort*, also on cliffs, PO Box 71, T9574362, F9570086. 30 rooms. **A-C** *Heart Beat*, PO Box 95, T9574329, F9570069, heartbeat@cwjamaica.com, on West End cliffs. 9 rooms, 1, 2, or 3-bed cottages and efficiencies, run by Valerie Brewis, cafés and music nearby, great sunset watching from veranda. **C** *Emerald Hotel*, Westland Mountain Rd, c/o Negril PO, T9574814, F9570708. Chalets, small pool, includes breakfast, TV, gardens with hammocks, short walk to beach. Accommodation **D** is available at the Yacht Club, West End Rd, PO Box 34, T9995732. **D-F** *Lighthouse Park* on Negril's cliffs. Campsite, cabins, tent site.

Hotels to the west of centre, about 10-20 mins' walk, are better for mixing with locals

The northern end is the more expensive part of town, but there are a few cheap cabins: **E** *Roots Bamboo* is very neat. **F** *Coconut International*, on the beach. Basic cabin, dirty, no fan. Next door is *Gloria's Sunset*, Jamaican family-run, clean, friendly, helpful, security guards at night, variety of accommodation, bar, restaurant. This whole beach is lined with clubs and is noisy. None of the cabins has any services, nor do they provide blankets, but they are right on the beach. When choosing a cabin check to see whether it has a fan, whether

Jamaica

there is a mesh or screen to keep out mosquitoes (if not, buy 'Destroyers', 8-hr incense to keep bugs away) and whether it looks safe (many get broken into). Locals living along the beach will often let you camp on their property.

Eating *Rick's Café*, the 'trendy' place to watch the sunset, full ocean view from cliff top setting but pricey with it, Red Stripe beer or cocktail US$3, plastic bead money used, full restaurant next door, expensive, with even better view of sunset. *Cool Runnings*, with a chef/owner, is also recommended. *The Office*, on the beach. Open 24 hrs, provides a good choice of Jamaican food, reasonably priced and friendly service, a good place to meet the locals. *The Pickled Parrot* , West End Road, T9574864, on the cliffs, call for free pick-up. Serves Mexican, Jamaican and American food, large portions, also offers snorkelling and catamaran cruises and waterslide over the rocks into the sea, US$1. Eating cheaply is difficult but not impossible. The native restaurant-food stalls are good and relatively cheap; the local patties are delicious. Street hawkers will sell you jerk chicken for US$4-5, which is good but barely enough to whet your appetite. *The Bread Basket*, next to the banks at the mall in town is recommended, but even better is the *Fisherman's Club* supermarket, just off the beach in the main part of town near *Pete's Seafood*, which is a restaurant as well as a market and serves good local, filling meals for about US$4.

Nightlife Live reggae shows in outdoor venues most nights, featuring local and well known stars. Entrance is usually US$5-7, good fun, lively atmosphere, very popular. Nice bars are located along the beach, usually with music, unnamed bar next to *Coconut International* recommended, friendly service. For beautiful surroundings try the bar at the *Rock Cliff Hotel* on the West End Rd, friendly barman who mixes great fruit punches and cocktails.

Transport Licensed, unmetered taxis have red license plates with the designation, PP before the numbers. Avoid unlicensed taxis. Local buses operate between Negril and Montego Bay stopping frequently. JUTA operated tour buses typically charge US$20 per person with a minimum charge US$60 per trip (1 passenger only) between Montego Bay and Negril. From the Donald Sangster airport minibuses run to Negril; you must bargain with the driver to get the fare to US$5-7. Lots of companies do bike rental. Gasoline is more than US$3 per gallon.

Directory **Banks** Two banks *National Commercial Bank* and *Nova Scotia* and several cambios in town including one at the *Hi-lo- Supermarket*. **Tourist office** In Coral Seas Plaza, T9574243.

The south coast

Savanna-La-Mar About 18 miles east of Negril, on the coast, is Savanna-la-Mar, a busy, commercial town with shopping, banks and so on, but no major attractions for tourists. It does not have a good beach, nor good quality restaurants and accommodation. Regular concerts are held at the remodelled St Joseph's Catholic Church, T9552648. Talented local musicians play under the auspices of Father Sean Lavery, formerly a professor of music at Dublin University, recommended. It can easily be reached by minibus from Negril and there are hourly buses from Montego Bay (US$2). The Frome sugar refinery, five miles north of Savanna-la-Mar, will often allow visitors to tour their facilities during sugar cane season (generally November-June). Another interesting and unusual outing in this part of Jamaica is to the six-mile long **Roaring River** and the **Ital Herbs and Spice Farm**, two miles north of Petersfield, from where it is remarkably well signposted. The farm, owned by an American, Ed Kritzler, employs organic methods. There is a cave at Roaring River and the farm is about half a mile further on. It is a very scenic area with interesting walks and tumbling streams suitable for bathing. A good restaurant serves fish and vegetable dishes at the Farm, best to order lunch before exploring. Totally basic accommodation in a hut available, popular but it is suggested you look before you book.

Outside Savanna-la-Mar, the main south coast road (A2) passes by Paradise Planta- **Bluefields**
tion, a huge private estate with miles of frontage on **Bluefields Bay**, a wide protected
anchorage with unspoiled reefs and wetlands teeming with birds. Just after Paradise,
you come to Ferris Crossroads, where the A2 meets up with the B8 road, a
well-maintained north-south connection and about 40 minutes' drive to Montego
Bay via Whithorn and Anchovy. For the next four miles the A2 hugs the coast along a
beautiful stretch of road to Bluefields, where there is a lovely white sand beach
mainly used by local Jamaicans and guests of the upmarket *Villas on Bluefields Bay*.
There is no mass tourism either in Bluefields or in the adjacent village of **Belmont**,
where plenty of reggae is always playing at the numerous fishermen's bars.

Sleeping In Belmont there are a few expatriate homes which might sometimes be available for
rent: *Oristano*, the oldest home in west Jamaica, dating back to the 1700s, owned by the Hon
William Fielding, an Englishman who does beautiful drawings of the Jamaican greathouses, PO
Box 1, Bluefields, Westmoreland Parish. **A-D** *Ashton Great House*, higher up hillside, T/F9652036.
Pool, restaurant, free ride from Bluefields, 24 rooms. **C-D** *Casa Marina*, in Cave, 2 miles from
Bluefields. Friendly owner Manley Wallace, restaurant, small, private pier and gazebo.

The south coast is known as the best part of Jamaica for deep sea fishing and boat **East of**
trips go out from Belmont to the reefs or to off-shore banks. Snorkelling is also good **Bluefields**
because the sea is almost always very calm in the morning. The **Bluefields Great
House**, now privately owned, was the place where Philip Gosse lived in the 1830s
when he wrote his famous book, *Birds of Jamaica*, and reportedly contains the first
breadfruit tree planted in Jamaica by Captain Bligh after his expedition to the South
Pacific. The next six miles of coast southeast of Bluefields is one of the most beautiful, unspoiled coasts in Jamaica, but a 258-room *Sandals South Coast* resort is being
built at **Auchindown** due to open in 2000. However, much of the land is being left
untouched on the resort's property. A bird sanctuary has been designated and a section of beach set aside as a turtle nesting area. Just beyond here, **B** *Natania's*, a guest
house and seafood restaurant at Little Culloden, Whitehouse, has been praised. It is
on the sea and has eight rooms (16 beds), food extra but good and at reasonable
prices. The owner is Peter Probst; address: *Natania's*, Little Culloden, Whitehouse
PO, Westmoreland, T/F9635342. Transport from Montego Bay can be arranged, as
also local tours, deep sea fishing and watersports.

The A2 road passes through Scotts Cove, where you leave Westmoreland and
enter the parish of St Elizabeth. It proceeds to the town of Black River, travelling
inland from there to Middle Quarters, YS Falls and Bamboo Avenue, after which it
ascends to the old hill station of Mandeville.

Black River

Black River is one of the oldest towns in Jamaica. It had its heyday in the 18th century
when it was the main exporting harbour for logwood dyes. The first car imported
into Jamaica landed here. Along the shore are some fine early 19th-century
mansions, some of which are being restored.

At Black River, you can go by boat from across the bridge up the lower stretches of
the Black River, the longest river in Jamaica. ■ *Daily 0900, 1100, 1230, 1400, 1600,
US$15 per person, drinks included, 10 miles, 1½-2 hrs, 3 boats, 25 people per boat*. You
should see crocodiles (called alligators in Jamaica, most likely at midday when they
bask on the river banks) and plenty of birdlife in beautifully tranquil surroundings
with a very knowledgeable guide. Contact *South Coast Safaris*, run by Charles Swaby
in Black River, T9620220, F9652086. If you want to avoid large tour parties, go with
a local, whose boats are through the fish market. The boats are smaller, open, slower,
quieter and go further up river, which means you see more. They stop at a 'countryside bar' rather than the one the tour companies use. ■ *The trip takes about 2 hrs and
costs US$27 for 2 including boatman and guide*.

Sleeping **D-E** *Waterloo Guest House*, in a Georgian building (the first house in Jamaica with electric light). Old rooms in the main house, or more expensive in the new annex, all with showers, very good restaurant (lobster in season). Two miles east of Black River is the **D** *Port of Call Hotel*, 136 Crane Rd, T965-2360. A bit spartan but on the sea, a/c, pool. **D** *Bridge House Inn*, Crane Rd, T9652361, F2652081. 14 rooms, a/c, fan, kitchen facilities, shady garden with hammocks leads down to beach, good Jamaican food, US$8-10 for a meal, staff friendly, bar, TV, lounge, ask for odd numbered room at front to avoid noise from club down beach.

Eating *Bayside*, near bridge. Excellent steamed fish with rice and peas for US$6, usually all gone by 1300. *Caribbe*, near bus station. Very good steamed fish and curried goat for US$6 with beer. *Superbus*, an old bus near bus station. Good cheap food, eg fried chicken with trimmings and beer for US$3.

Transport **Road** To get to Black River from Mandeville by bus involves a change in Santa Cruz.

Directory **Tourist office** Hendricks Building, 2 High St, T9562074.

The road to Mandeville

On the south coast past Black River is **Treasure Beach**, a wide dark sand beach with body surfing waves, it is one of the most beautiful areas on the island. It is largely used by local fishermen as it is the closest point to the Pedro Banks. There is one small grocery shop and a bakery. A van comes to the village every day with fresh fruit and vegetables. This area is quite unlike any other part of Jamaica and still relatively unvisited by tourists. The local people are very friendly and you will be less hassled by higglers than elsewhere.

Sleeping On the beach is **AL** *Treasure Beach Hotel*, T9650110, F9652544, 36 rooms. **A** *Jake's Place*, T9650635, F9650552, www.islandlife.com, part of Island Outpost chain, run by Jason Henzell. 7 rooms in small and exclusive, brightly painted cottages, arty, includes breakfast, good food, salt water pool, riding, cycling and hiking can be arranged, music everywhere. **D** *Four M's Cottage*, Box 4, Mountainside PO, T/F9652472, T9650131. 4 rooms. Several houses can be rented: *Sparkling Waters*, *Folichon*, *Caprice*, and *Siwind* (PO Box 73, Black River), with its own cove.

To the east of Treasure Beach lies **Lovers' Leap**, a beauty spot named after the slave and his lover (his owner's daughter) who jumped off the cliff in despair ■ *US$3. 1000-1800 daily*, and Alligator Pond.

If you stay on the A2 instead of turning off at Black River, the road comes to **Middle Quarters**, on the edge of the Black River Morass (a large swamp); hot pepper shrimp are sold by the wayside, but insist that they are fresh (today's catch). Just after Middle Quarters is the left turn which takes you to the beautiful **YS Falls** (pronounced Why-Ess), an unspoiled spot in the middle of a large private plantation well worth visiting. ■ *US$9. 0930-1530, Tue-Sun, closed public holidays.* There is a 15-minute walk from where you park your car. You can bathe but there are no changing rooms or other facilities; plan a morning visit as there is no shelter in case of afternoon rain. Further along the main road is the impressive 2½-mile long **Bamboo Avenue**. North of Bamboo Avenue is **Maggotty**, on the (closed) railway line from Montego Bay to Kingston and close to the **Appleton Estate**, where tours of the rum factory are offered. ■ *For information contact Jamaica Estate Tours Ltd, T9976077, F9632243, or T9526606, Montego Bay. Regular tour parties come from Montego Bay and Negril hotels. US$12. 0900-1600, Mon-Fri.* Opposite the Maggotty train depot is the *Sweet Bakery*, run by Patrick and Lucille Lee, who can arrange accommodation in a Great House (**D**) or at a rustic campsite (**F**), very friendly and helpful, local trips organized, Mrs Lee is an excellent cook.

Mandeville

After Bamboo Avenue, the A2 road goes through Lacovia and Santa Cruz, an expanding town on the St Elizabeth Plain, and on up to Mandeville, a peaceful upland town with perhaps the best climate on the island. It is very spread out, with building on all the surrounding hills and no slums. In recent years, Mandeville has derived much of its prosperity from being one of the centres of the bauxite/alumina industry (though industrial activity is outside the town). There are lots of expensive homes and the town is congested.

Population: 50,000

The town's centre is the village green, now called **Cecil Charlton Park** (after the ex-mayor, whose opulent mansion, Huntingdon Summit, can be visited with prior arrangement). The green looks a bit like New England; at its northeast side stands a Georgian courthouse and, on the southeast, **St Mark's parish church** (both 1820). By St Mark's is the **market** area (busiest days are Monday, Wednesday and Friday – the market is supposed to be moved elsewhere) and the area where buses congregate. West of the green, at the corner of Ward Avenue and Caledonia Road, is the Manchester Club (T9622403), one of the oldest country clubs in the West Indies (1868) and the oldest in Jamaica. It has a nine-hole golf course (18 tee boxes, enabling you to play 18 holes) and tennis courts (you must be introduced by a member). Also, horse riding can be arranged, Ann Turner on T9622527.

AL-C *Astra Country Inn*, 62 Ward Av, PO Box 60, T9623265, F9621461. Reported for sale and run down, some way from the town centre, 22 rooms, pool, sauna, entertainment. In the centre is the **AL** *Mandeville Hotel*, 4 Hotel St, PO Box 78, T9622138, F9620700. TV, spacious, pool, restaurant, excursions arranged, good. **C** *Kariba Kariba*, Atkinson's Drive, near New Green roundabout on Winston Jones highway, first right off New Green Rd, 45 mins' walk from centre, on bus route, T9623039. Bath, fan, 5 rooms or suites, including breakfast, TV lounge, bar, dining room. The owners, Derrick and Hazel O'Conner, are friendly, knowledgeable and hospitable, they can arrange for you to meet local people with similar interests and offer tours. Derrick is developing a 12-acre farm at Mile Gully (opportunity for work if you wish) and plans to develop a small campsite, bar, accommodation and other facilities.

Sleeping

Jamaica

Mandeville

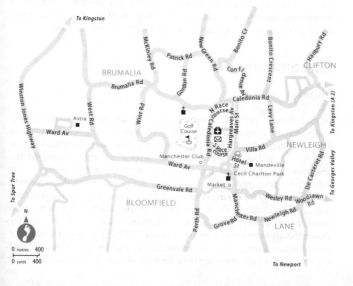

Eating Technically a restaurant, but also recommended for its décor (of old cars and licence plates) and atmosphere is *Bill Laurie's Steak House & Museum*, 600 ft above the town. Good for views, steaks, conversation (closed Sun); *Pot Pourri*, on 2nd floor of the Caledonia Mall, just north of the Manchester Club. Clean and bright, good food and service. *International Chinese Restaurant*, Newport Rd. *Hungry Hut*, 45 Manchester Rd. Cheap, excellent food and service (owner, Fay, grew up in England and likes a chat).

Shopping *Westico Health Foods*, by the West Indies College, run by Seventh Day Adventists. They also run a vegetarian restaurant behind the church in the town centre, Mon-Fri. Craft Centre, sponsored by the Women's Club of Manchester, on Manchester Rd.

Excursions Although some way inland, Mandeville is a good place from which to start exploring both the surrounding area and the south coast. In fact, by car you can get to most of Jamaica's resorts, except those east of Ocho Rios or Kingston, in two hours or less. Birdwatchers and those interested in seeing a beautiful 'great house' in a cattle property should contact Robert Sutton at **Marshall's Pen**. Robert is the island's top ornithologist (23 of Jamaica's endemic bird species have been observed here). ■ *T9622260, US$10 for Great House tour by appointment only. The Astra Hotel can arrange a visit.* Also around the town you can visit the High Mountain Coffee. ■ *Free. Mon-Fri.* Also Pioneer Chocolate Factories, a factory making bammy (a delicacy from cassava root), the Alcan works, and local gardens.

There are interesting excursions north to **Christiana** (at about 2,800 ft, **B** *Hotel Villa Bella*, PO Box 473, Christiana, T9642243, F9642765, 18 rooms and suites, restaurant, in six acres with orchard of ortaniques and bananas, nature walks, riding, special interest groups catered for), southwest to the Santa Cruz mountains, and south to **Alligator Pond** on the coast. Eat on the beach at Blackie's *Little Ochie* , fish restaurant, everything freshly caught, six ways of cooking lobster, US$10. East of Alligator Pond is Gut River, where you can sometimes see alligators and manatees; cottages can be rented near the very picturesque river flowing into the sea (contact through *Astra Hotel*). Boat and fishing trips can be made to Pigeon Island, with a day on the island for swimming and snorkelling.

From Mandeville it is about 55 miles east to Kingston on the A2, bypassing May Pen, through Old Harbour then on to Spanish Town and Kingston. Before the May Pen bypass, a road branches south to **Milk River Bath**, the world's most radioactive spa. The baths are somewhat run down, but the medical properties of the water are among the best anywhere. ■ *0700-2100, daily, US$1.40, 15 mins.* About three miles from the baths is a marine conservation area, **Alligator Hole**, where manatees (sea cows) can sometimes be seen. Local boatmen will do their best to oblige.

Background

History

The colony When Columbus landed on Jamaica in 1494 it was inhabited by peaceful Arawak Indians. Evidence collected by archaeologists suggests that the tribe had not lived on the island much before the year 1000. Under Spanish occupation, which began in 1509, the race died out and gradually African slaves were brought in to provide the labour force. In 1655 an English expeditionary force landed at Passage Fort and met with little resistance other than that offered by a small group of Spanish settlers and a larger number of African slaves who took refuge in the mountains. The Spaniards abandoned the island after about five years, but the slaves and their descendants, who became known as Maroons, waged war against the new colonists for 80 years until the 1730s although there was another brief rebellion in 1795. The Cockpit Country, or 'Look Behind Country,' where the Leeward Maroons hid and around Nanny Town where the Windward Maroons hid is still the home of some of their descendants.

"He huffed and he puffed ..."

Most of the earlier historical landmarks have been destroyed by hurricanes and earthquakes. Very few traces, apart from place names, therefore remain of the Spanish occupation. In 1692 an earthquake destroyed Port Royal which, because of being the base for English buccaneers such as Henry Morgan, had become famed as the most splendid town in the West Indies. In 1907 another earthquake damaged much of Kingston. Some of the historic buildings which are still standing, including the 18th-century churches at Port Royal, St Ann's Bay and Montego Bay, are now in the care of the

National Trust Commission. The Great Houses are a reminder of the British settlers; some have been converted into hotels or museums. Jamaica has the best preserved historical records in the Caribbean, held at the Institute of Jamaica, Kingston, and the Spanish Archives, Spanish Town. The copperplate slave returns (officially required from 1817) make fascinating reading, recommended for tracing family history, access free. In September 1988, Hurricane Gilbert travelled the length of the island causing extensive damage in all areas. There is hardly any sign of Gilbert now.

After a short period of military rule, the colony was organized with an English-type constitution and a Legislative Council. The great sugar estates, which still today produce an important part of the island's wealth, were planted in the early days of English occupation when Jamaica also became the haunt of buccaneers and slave traders. In 1833 emancipation was declared for slaves (although a system of apprenticeship remained until 1838) and modern Jamaica was born. The framework for Jamaica's modern political system was laid in the 1930s with the foundation in 1938 of the People's National Party (PNP) by Norman W Manley, and the Jamaica Labour Party (JLP) by his cousin, Sir Alexander Bustamante in 1944. These two parties had their roots in rival trade unions and have dominated Jamaican politics since universal adult suffrage was introduced in 1944.

Independence

In 1958, Jamaica joined the West Indies Federation with nine other British territories but withdrew following a national referendum on the issue in 1961. On 6 August 1962, Jamaica became an independent member of the Commonwealth.

The Manley Legacy

After 23 years as leader of the PNP, eight of them as Prime Minister in the 1970s and three as Prime Minister from 1989, Michael Manley, son of the party's founder, retired in March 1992 because of ill health. During Manley's first two terms in office between 1972 and 1980 he endorsed socialist policies at home and encouraged South-South relations abroad. He antagonized the USA by developing close economic and political links with Cuba. State control of the economy failed to produce the desired results and Mr Manley was rejected by the electorate. The conservative JLP led by Edward Seaga, held office for the next nine years. By 1989 however, Manley's political thinking had changed dramatically and he was re-elected with policies advocating the free market. Before his retirement he oversaw the reduction in the size of the state, deregulation of the economy and close relations with the IMF. He was succeeded by the Party Chairman, former deputy Prime Minister and Finance Minister P J Patterson who overwhelmingly defeated his only rival in an election at a special party meeting. Mr Patterson promised to maintain Mr Manley's policies and deepen the restructuring of the economy. Michael Manley died of cancer on 6 March 1997, aged 72. He is buried in Heroes' Park and his funeral was attended by many world leaders. Political figures from the Caribbean region included Fidel Castro (who was cheered by the crowds lining the funeral route), René Préval of Haiti, and former Venezuelan president Carlos Andrés Pérez.

The 1990s

General elections were held early on 30 March 1993 and the incumbent PNP was returned for a second term with a larger than expected majority, winning 55 of the 60

Jamaica

seats. Despite the landslide victory, the elections were marred by violence in which 11 people died, malpractices and a turnout of only 58%. The JLP boycotted parliament for four months while it demanded electoral reform and an inquiry into the election day events. It also refused to contest by-elections, two of which were held in the next 12 months and won by the PNP. Some concessions were made by the Government, such as reorganization of the police force to remove direct political control and the postponement of local government elections pending electoral reform. The reform drafted by the Electoral Advisory Committee was repeatedly delayed but eventually completed in time for general elections in December 1997.

The traditional two-party system was shaken up in 1995 by the launch of a third party, the National Democratic Movement (NDM), by Bruce Golding, the former chairman of the JLP. Mr Golding called for constitutional reform and the introduction of a republican system, arguing that the Westminster system concentrated too much power in the hands of the Prime Minister. Many JLP members defected to the new party and political tension increased with confrontations between JLP and NDM supporters. In 1999 there was a move by a faction of the JLP to persuade Mr Golding to return to the JLP, with the hope that he would assume the leadership in succession to Edward Seaga. This brought further divisions within the JLP, which had just re-elected Seaga unopposed as leader. Seaga, who has been leader since 1974, showed no signs of relinquising power over his party.

The 1997 elections gave the PNP a third consecutive term in office. The PNP won 50 seats while the JLP won 10 and the NDM failed to win any. There was less violence than in previous campaigns, with only two deaths, but there were some electoral inefficiencies because of the new register and a few irregularities leading to re-run elections in a couple of constituencies. When he was sworn into office, Prime Minister P J Patterson promised that it would be the last time that the government would swear allegiance to the British monarchy. The PNP proposes an executive president but the JLP advocates a ceremonial president with a Prime Minister.

Geography and people

Jamaica lies some 90 miles south of Cuba and a little over 100 miles west of Haiti. With an area of 4,244 square miles, it is the third largest island in the Greater Antilles. It is 146 miles from east to west and 51 miles from north to south at its widest, bounded by the Caribbean. Over 90% of Jamaicans are of West African descent, the English settlers having followed the Spaniards in bringing in slaves from West Africa. Because of this, Ashanti words still figure very largely in the local dialect, which is known as Jamaica Talk. There are also Chinese, East Indians and Christian Arabs as well as those of British descent and other European minorities. The population is approximately 2.5 million. There is considerable poverty on the island, which has created social problems and some tension. Jamaicans are naturally friendly, easy going and international in their outlook (more people of Jamaican origin live outside Jamaica than inside). There is a 'Meet the People' programme which enables visitors to meet Jamaicans on a one-to-one basis.

Government

Jamaica is a constitutional monarchy. A Governor-General represents the British monarch, who is Head of State, and the Government is made up of a Prime Minister (who nominates the Cabinet), a 60-seat House of Representatives and a 21-seat Senate. All citizens over 18 are eligible for the vote. The judicial system is on British lines.

The economy

Once one of the more prosperous islands in the West Indies, Jamaica went into recession in 1973 and output declined steadily throughout the 1970s and 1980s. At the core of Jamaica's economic difficulties lay the collapse of the vital bauxite mining and alumina refining industries. Nevertheless, Jamaica is the world's third largest producer of bauxite after Australia and Guinea. In 1997 bauxite production rose to its highest level since 1981, with a further increase in 1998 to 12.7 million tonnes and alumina production increased to 3.44 million tonnes but lower prices brought a 6% fall in earnings. In 1999 job losses were announced by three bauxite and alumina companies, to cut costs as prices slumped.

Structure of production

Manufacturing, which contributes over 18% to gdp, is mostly agricultural processing, such as rum, beer, cigarettes and foodstuffs. Garments exported to the USA and other miscellaneous manufactured articles have seen considerable expansion, rising by 23.2% to US$262 mn in 1994. However, several manufacturing plants have since closed because of competition from Mexico for the US market and from imports as markets have been liberalized. The number employed in the garments industry fell from 36,000 in 1994 to 20,000 in 1998. That year a further 525 workers were made redundant when a factory moved to Mexico after repeated shipments of drugs were found in its exports to the USA.

By comparison with manufacturing, agriculture is a less important sector in terms of contribution to gdp, though it generates far more employment. Sugar is the main crop, and most important export item after bauxite and alumina. Four state-owned sugar mills were sold in 1993 to the Sugar Company of Jamaica, in which the government had a 24% shareholding. However, drought and floods hit the privatized industry, additionally struggling under high interest rates. Despite government grants so that they would improve efficiency and reduce production costs, currently around US$0.24 per lb, the industry remained insolvent and in 1998-99 four mills were repossessed. Other export crops include bananas, coffee, cocoa and citrus fruits. Jamaica is famous for its Blue Mountain coffee, first produced in 1757, which commands a high premium in the world market.

Tourism is the second foreign exchange earner and contributes about 15% of gdp. Stopover arrivals grew by an annual average of 8% and cruise visitors by 14% in the first half of the 1980s until, in 1987, combined stopover and cruise arrivals passed the million mark for the first time. In the early 1990s numbers continued to rise and hotel capacity increased but occupancy is only 60%, with many tourists put off by stories of crime and harassment. In 1999, stopover tourists increased by 1.9% to 1,248,000, including 101,262 Jamaicans living overseas, while the number of cruise ship passengers rose by 13.5% to 764,341, of whom 583,623 landed at Ocho Rios and 180,161 at Montego Bay.

The Government turned to the IMF for support in 1976 and was a regular customer until 1995. In compliance with IMF agreements, the Government had to reduce domestic demand commensurate with the fall in export earnings, by devaluing the currency and reducing the size of its fiscal deficits. Jamaica has rescheduled its debt to creditor governments and also to foreign commercial banks. Some debt forgiveness has also been granted. By the end of 1999 debt had fallen to US$3.2 bn, through repayments, renegotiations and cancellations. Representing 48% of gdp, this was a considerable improvement on debt levels of 142% of gdp in 1990. The Jamaican dollar has been devalued, the foreign exchange market deregulated, and interest rates and credit ceilings kept high to reduce consumption, close the trade gap and rebuild foreign reserves.

Recent trends

The economy showed signs of growth but recovery was fragile. During the political leadership handover, uncertainties caused the currency to fall rapidly, but tighter monetary policies and private business sector support enabled it to recover soon afterwards and hold steady. Inflation was cut from an annual rate of 105% at the end

☞ *Dreadlocks to reggae*

Followers of the Rastafarian cult are easily recognizable by their long dreadlocks. They are non-violent, do not eat pork and believe in the divinity of the late Emperor of Ethiopia, Haile Selassie (Ras Tafari). Haile Selassie's call for the end of the superiority of one race over another has been incorporated into a faith which holds that God, Jah, will lead the blacks out of oppression (Babylon) back to Ethiopia (Zion, the Promised Land). The Rastas regard the ideologist, Marcus Garvey (born 1887, St Ann's Bay), as a prophet of the return to Africa (he is now a Jamaican national hero). In the early part of the twentieth century, Garvey founded the idea of black nationalism, with Africa as the home for blacks, be they living on the continent or not.

The music most strongly associated with Rastafarianism is reggae. According to O R Dathorne, "it is evident that the sound and words of Jamaican reggae have altered the life of the English-speaking Caribbean. The extent of this alteration is still unknown, but this new sound has touched, more than any other single art medium, the consciousness of the people of this region" (Dark Ancestor, page 229, Louisiana State University Press, 1981). The sound is a mixture of African percussion and up-to-the-minute electronics; the lyrics a blend of praise of Jah, political

comment and criticism and the mundane. The late Bob Marley, the late Peter Tosh, Dennis Brown and Jimmy Cliff are among the world-famous reggae artists, and many, many more can be heard on the island. Over the last few years, traditional reggae has been supplanted by Dance Hall, which has a much heavier beat, and instead of Marley's rather thoughtful lyrics, it is all about guns and sex, Shabba Ranks, Buju Banton and so on. Closely related to reggae is dub poetry, a chanted verse form which combines the musical tradition, folk traditions and popular speech. Its first practitioner was Louise Bennett, in the 1970s, who has been followed by poets such as Linton Kwesi Johnson, Michael Smith, Oku Onora and Mutabaruka. Many of these poets work in the UK, but their links with Jamaica are strong.

Two novels which give a fascinating insight into Rasta culture (and, in the latter, Revival and other social events) are Brother Man, *by Roger Mais, and* The Children of Sysiphus, *by H Orlando Patterson. These writers have also published other books which are worth investigating, as are the works of Olive Senior (eg Summer Lightning), and the poets Mervyn Morris, the late Andrew Salkey and Dennis Scott (who is also involved in the theatre).*

of 1991 to only 17% in 1992, but cuts in fiscal spending led to a reduction in health and education services as well as in the size of the civil service and the poor were worst hit. The lack of adequate housing is a perennial problem, commonly solved by poor Jamaicans by squatting.

Taxes were raised in each annual budget in the 1990s with tight fiscal and monetary policies. The Government faced pressure for higher spending on wages, with public sector disputes in 1994-97. Nevertheless, targets set by the IMF were met. Despite the results confidence at home deteriorated. The exchange rate again showed volatility as labour disputes became widespread and inflation jumped to 25.6% in 1995, twice the official target. The Government was forced to bail out ailing financial companies to avoid a crisis in the banking sector. Almost J$75 bn was spent in rescuing banks and insurance companies by its Financial Sector Adjustment Company (Finsac) set up in February 1997. Depositors, rather than shareholders, were protected. About half the amount was expected to be recovered through bank sales.

Debt servicing remains a heavy burden, with amortization and interest payments accounting for 58% of budget expenditure. The economy went into decline in 1996 and gdp has fallen every year since then. Gdp growth in the 1999 fiscal year was initially forecast at 2% but rioting in protest at a 31% fuel tax increase in April was expected to cost the country about J$14 bn, or 4-5% of gdp, in infrastructural damage, loss of production and government revenue. The Government finally agreed to halve the tax rise after many days of violence which left nine people dead and 450 were arrested. The impact on the tourist industry was considerable: airports were closed, cruise ships could not dock and guests were stranded in their hotels. Some commentators forecast further unrest in the light of high unemployment (16%), low wages (16% of households are below the poverty line of J$700 income per adult per month), high interest rates and low economic activity. In 1999 13,299 Jamaicans emigrated to the USA and Canada (10,064 in 1998), while over 2,000 people per month became unemployed. Nevertheless, the Government forecasts better economic prospects for the new century, with positive gdp growth in 2000 and lower interest rates. some 21,800 new housing units were to be built, providing Some 36,000 jobs, by the government, the National Housing Trust and the private sector, to relieve social pressures.

Culture

The predominant religion is Protestantism, but there is also a Roman Catholic community. There are followers of the Church of God, Baptists, Anglicans, Seventh Day Adventists, Pentecostals and Methodists. The Jewish, Moslem, Hindu and Bahai religions are also practised. It is said that Jamaica has more churches per square mile than anywhere else in the world. To a small degree, early adaptations of the Christian faith, Revival and Pocomania, survive, but the most obvious local minority sect is Rastafarianism (see box above).

Kingston is the main cultural centre of Jamaica. There are two important institutes which can be visited: the African Caribbean Institute (ACI), on Little North Street) is involved in research into African traditions in Jamaica and the Caribbean; the Institute of Jamaica (East Street) has historical sections, including Arawak carvings, the National Library, science museum and occasional lectures and exhibitions. The National Gallery of Jamaica (Orange Street and Ocean Boulevard) has a large collection of Jamaican art; there are about a dozen other galleries in the city. The National Dance Theatre has an annual summer season; throughout the year plays and concerts are staged. The local press has full details of events in Kingston and other centres.

Jamaica

Turks and Caicos Islands

7

Turks and Caicos Islands

The Turks and Caicos islands comprise about 40 low-lying islands and cays covering 193 square miles, surrounded by one of the longest coral reefs in the world. They are separated by the Columbus Passage, a 22-mile channel over 7,000 ft deep which connects the Atlantic and the Caribbean, contributing to the area's profusion of marine life. Generally, the windward sides of the islands are made up of limestone cliffs and sand dunes, while the leeward sides have more lush vegetation. The south islands of Grand Turk, Salt Cay and South Caicos are very dry, having had their trees felled by salt rakers long ago to discourage rain. The other islands have slightly more rain but very little soil and most of the vegetation is scrub and cactus. The islands lie 575 miles southeast of Miami, Florida, directly east of Inagua at the south tip of the Bahamas and north of Hispaniola.

Turks & Caicos Islands

Essentials

Before you travel

Documents US and Canadian citizens need only a birth certificate or some other proof of identity to enter the Turks and Caicos. Other nationalities need a valid passport; a visa is not necessary except for nationals of communist countries. An onward ticket is officially required. Visitors are allowed to stay for 30 days, renewable once only.

Money The official **currency** is the US dollar. Most banks will advance cash on **credit cards.** Most hotels, restaurants and taxi drivers will accept travellers' cheques, but personal cheques are not widely accepted. Take small denomination US dollars when visiting an island without a bank, as it is often difficult to get change from big notes. There are **banks** on Grand Turk and Providenciales. On Grand Turk, *Barclays Bank*, T9462831, F9462695, at Butterfield Square, PO Box 236, Provo, T9464245, F9464573. *Barclays Offshore Banking Centre*, Box 236, Providenciales, T9413606, F9413430. *Bordier International Bank & Trust Ltd*, T9464535, F9464540, Box 5, Providenciales. *Canadian Imperial Bank of Commerce*, PO Box 698, Providenciales, T9465303. *Turks & Caicos Banking Co Ltd*, Box 123, Grand Turk, T9462368, F9462365. *Scotiabank* is at the Town Centre Mall, PO Box 15, Provo, T9464750, F9464755, and at Harbour House, PO Box 132, Grand Turk, T9462506, F9462667.

Climate
There is no recognized rainy season. Hurricane season is normally Jun-Oct

Temperatures average 75-85°F from November to May, reaching into the 90°s from June to October, but constant tradewinds keep life comfortable. Average annual rainfall is 21 ins on Grand Turk and South Caicos but increases to 40 ins as you travel westwards through the Caicos Islands where more lush vegetation is found. Hurricane Kate swept through the islands November 1985; Hugo and Andrew missed in 1992; there were several near misses in

Turks & Caicos Islands

1995 and Bertha passed through in 1996. El Niño upset the weather pattern in 1997/98 with more rainy days and rougher seas.

Getting there

Ports of entry for aircraft are Providenciales, South Caicos and Grand Turk, but the major international airport is on Providenciales. There are also airstrips on North Caicos, Middle Caicos, Pine Cay and Salt Cay. **To Providenciales** *American Airlines* flies twice daily from Miami to Provo with one flight originating in New Orleans. *Bahamasair* flies from Nassau and Miami. *TWA* has a weekly charter flight from New York and is in negotiation to start a scheduled flight in 2000. TCI *Sky King* flies from Freeport, Kingston, Nassau, Puerto Plata (Dominican Republic) and Cap Haitiën into Provo and provides connecting flights to Grand Turk and South Caicos. *Turks and Caicos Airways* also flies from Cap Haitiën to Providenciales and on to Grand Turk, Middle Caicos, North Caicos and South Caicos. **To Grand Turk** *Lynx Air* flies three days a week from Fort Lauderdale, T305-7729808, 1995 West Commercial Boulevard, Ft Lauderdale. *TCA* flies from Cap Haitiën. *Sky King* will fly to Cuba, the Dominican Republic, Bahamas and Haiti on request.

Air
There are no direct flights from Europe

There is no scheduled passenger service (cargo comes in regularly from Florida) and no port is deep enough to take cruise ships although some occasionally stop outside the reef and shuttle in passengers for half a day.

Boat
Evening weather radio report on VHF from Blue Water Divers on Grand Turk; Mystine on SSB

Ports of entry (British flag) Providenciales: Turtle Cove Marina, Caicos Shipyard, Leeward Marina, South Dock/Sapodilla Bay; Grand Turk; South Caicos; Salt Cay. Clear in and out with customs and immigration, VHF 16. On arrival, customs will grant seven days immigration clearance. Go to town to the Immigration Office (closed 1230-1430) to obtain a 30 day extension. Fuel and alcoholic drink may be purchased duty free with clearance to leave the country. The Customs Office is at South Dock, Provo, and there are Customs Officers at the airport all day too.

Marinas There are five marinas on Provo. **Leeward Marina** at Leeward Going Through, T9465553, F9465674, marina@tciway.tc, gas/diesel sales only, restaurant; **Turtle Cove Landing**, Sellar's Pond, Provo, T9464307, F9464771, long term dockage for boats up to 70 ft, 5 ft draft; **Turtle Cove Marina**, Sellar's Pond, Provo, T9464303, F9464326, turtlecovemarina@provo.net, full service, all weather anchorage, 6 ft draft, 35 new slips (still under construction), RO, water and ice, premium prices; **South Side Marina**, T9464747, dockside T9464200, F9415776, hamilton&pratt@tciway.tc, diesel, gas, oil, water, 4½ft controlling depth, call for reservations; **Caicos Marina and Shipyard**, Long Bay, Provo, T9465600, F9465390, SSB 4143.6, (fuel, ice, dry storage, cabinet maker on the premises, Southwind Millworks, T9465700, and a machinist/diesel mechanic). South Caicos also has a marina. There are no bareboat charters.

(map)

Drum Point

EAST CAICOS

SOUTH CAICOS

g Cay

Atlantic Ocean

Columbus passage

GRAND TURK

Cockburn Town

Gibbs Cay

Long Cay

Cotton Cay

East Cay

Balfour Town

Salt Cay

Big Sand Cay

Endymion Rock

uth Rock

Turks & Caicos Islands

Touching down

Departure tax US$15.

Voltage 110 volts, 60 cycles, the same as in the USA.

Useful addresses Chief Secretary (Grand Turk), T9462702 (Provo), T9464258, 9415123; Customs (Grand Turk), T9462993/4, (Provo), T9464214; Immigration (Grand Turk), T9462939, (Provo), T9464233; time/weather, T141.

Clothing Dress is informal and shorts are worn in town as well as on the beach. Nudity is illegal although condoned by local hoteliers at Club Med and Le Deck, both on Grace Bay. The islanders find it offensive and flaunting local protocol may elicit unwelcome stares and remarks. Islanders love to dress up in the evenings when they frequent live band nights at hotels or discos.

Safety Providenciales is no longer as safe as it was before being discovered as a tourist and off-shore banking destination, but still safer than most Caribbean islands. It is not advisable to walk around alone at night or on deserted beaches. On Provo, take precautions about leaving valuables in your room or on the beach. Crime is on the increase. Traffic is fast and aggressive causing many accidents. Personal security is much better on Grand Turk and the other islands and a haven compared with most other Caribbean countries. Should you need it, the **police station** on Grand Turk is T9462299 and on Salt Cay, T9466929. In an **emergency** anywhere T999.

Touching down

Airport information
It is worth checking in early when returning to Miami from Provo, to avoid long queues

Scheduled service airlines are *TCA* (T9464255, F9462081, domestic emergency T9415353); *American Airlines* (T1-800-4337300, T9415700); *TCI Sky King* (T9461520 on Grand Turk, T9415461/4 on Provo, F9415127, King@tciway.tc); *Bahamasair* and *Lynx Air* (to Grand Turk only from Provo). Charter airlines are *Global Airways* (T9413222 on Provo, T9467093 on North Caicos, F9467290, www.globalairways.com, run by the Gardiner family); *Inter Island Airways* (Provo T9465481, F9464040, after hours T9464466, Lyndon Gardiner); *Flamingo Air Services* (Grand Turk T9462109/8); *Provo Air Charter* (T9465578, F9465040).

Tourist information

Local tourist office Turks and Caicos Islands Tourist Board, PO Box 128, Grand Turk, Turks & Caicos Islands, T9462321/2322, T800-2410824, F9462733, www.turksandcaicostourism.com On Provo the tourist office is at Turtle Cove, PO Box 174, T9464970, F9415494. Various maps and guidebooks have been published including *Where, When, How, Providenciales; Your Monthly Entertainment Guide*, placed in hotels and selected shops, free of charge; *Times of the Islands; International Magazine of the Turks and Caicos*, quarterly, US$4. Special Edition publishes a large, user-friendly road map of Providenciales each year, indicating the location of advertisers, pay/card phones, fuel stations and other information, contact Kathi Barrington, F9465122, MINX@Provo.net A useful website with lots of information on lodgings, particularly on the smaller islands is www.tcimall.tc

Local travel agents *Marco Travel Services*, Down Town, T9464393, F9464048, for reconfirmation of tickets, emergency check cashing, travel services, travellers' cheque sales, Amex representative. *Provo Travel Ltd*, run by Althea Ewing, at Central Square, Leeward Highway, T9464035, F9464081, helpful. *Island Travel*, T9415195, Down Town, near Shell station, specializes in travel and shopping packages for TCI residents, international bookings and tours. On Grand Turk: *T & C Travel Ltd*, at Hotel Osprey Beach, Box 42, T9462592, F9462877, run by Daphne James, friendly, reliable.

Tourist offices overseas

France *T01-42363660, F01-42364835, mkifr@easynet.fr*

Germany *T06131-337929, F06131-99331, 101514.3543@compuserve.com*
Italy *T0296-451071, F0296-56487, elysian@login.it*

UK *c/o Morris Kevan International Ltd, Mitre House, 66 Abbey Road, Bush Hill Park, Enfield,*

Middlesex, EN1 2RQ, T020-83501017, F020-83501000, www.mki.ltd.uk

USA *Trombone Associates Inc, 420 Madison Avenue, New York NY 10017, T212-2232323, F2230260, T1-800-2410824. TCI Tourist Board, 11645 Biscayne Boulevard, Suite 302, North Miami, FL 33181, T305-8914117, F305-8917096, T800-2410824, tcitrsm@bellSouth.net*

Where to stay

Hotels on Provo are aiming for North American standards and so they are expensive. Rack rates will not include tax and service, be sure to check what you are quoted. Most hotels on Provo are all-inclusive or condominium-style. Grand Turk, Salt Cay, South Caicos and North Caicos are better bets for inexpensive, charming, more 'islandy' lodgings. **Camping** is possible on beaches on most islands, but no water or sewage facilities and not encouraged. Contact the District Commissioner's office on each island for permission. If planning to stay on a deserted island take everything with you and leave nothing behind.

There is a 10-15% service charge & 9% bed tax added to the bill

Getting around

Flight time from Grand Turk to the furthest island (Provo) is 35 minutes. **Turks & Caicos Airways** provides a twice daily service Provo to Grand Turk via the out-islands, US$120 round trip. **SkyKing** and **Inter Island Airways** also provide frequent flights between the islands. Private charters are readily available within the island group and can easily be arranged by asking around at Grand Turk or Provo airport, as charter pilots meet incoming international flights and wait to see if they can fill a plane in the mornings. They often hold up boards showing which island they are flying to. Do not pre-book as you may sit for 2-3 hours waiting for a particular plane; similarly if travelling to the out islands, do not buy a return ticket, whatever the airlines tell you, as you may have to pay twice if you come back with someone else. Your hotel or guest house can help you arrange your return flight when you are ready to leave (this does not include package tours). Private pilots fly seven days a week, *TCA* does not fly on Sunday.

Air
See page 342 for telephone numbers of charter companies

Bicycles and motor scooters can be rented from some hotels but can be relatively expensive compared with cars. Helmets are not mandatory but should be worn. Tourists invite trouble riding in bathing suits and bare feet and at night.

Bicycle

Rental cars are available on Grand Turk, North and South Caicos and Provo although demand often exceeds supply on Provo. Most roads are fairly basic, although those on Provo have been upgraded and paved, and all parts are easily accessible. Maximum speed in urban areas is 20 mph and outside villages 40 mph, but on Provo driving is erratic and no one (except visitors) pays heed to speed limits, not even the Traffic Department. There is no control. Local drivers do not dim their headlights at night. Pedestrians and cyclists should be especially careful on the roads because of speeding, dangerous drivers and heavy construction vehicles.

Car
Drive on the left. Watch out for donkeys on Grand Turk

On-island transport is restricted to expensive taxi service with a basic fare of US$2 per mile, although drivers are not always consistent. Complaints are frequent. Taxis can be hired for island tours, agree the price before hand.

Taxi
There are a few private buses

Turks & Caicos Islands

Keeping in touch

Post On Grand Turk the post office is on Front Street near Barclays Bank, T9462801. *Federal Express*, T9462542 (Grand Turk), T9464682 (Provo); *DHL*, T9464352 (Provo); *UPS* agent, T9462030, F9462995, incoming only package delivery, Cee's Building, Pond Street, Grand Turk and on Provo through ***Provo Travel***, T9464080, F9464081. Postage for postcards US$0.50 to USA, US$0.60 Canada/UK, US$0.80 Europe, US$1.10 Africa. Letters each half an ounce US$0.60, US$0.80, US$1, US$1.25 respectively.

Telephone Grand Turk, Provo and South Caicos have a modern local and international telephone service, *International code: 649* with Cable and Wireless offices in Grand Turk and Provo. Telephone services on the North and Middle Caicos and Salt City are improving. There are two exchanges, 946 and 941. Local directory assistance T118, international operator T115; credit card calls T111, 1-800-8778000. The small volume of international calls means that costs are higher than in the USA. The local phone book has a list of charges to anywhere in the world. Phone cards are available from Cable and Wireless and from many outlets including Provo airport in US$5, US$10 and US$20 denominations plus 10%. The Cable and Wireless Public Sales Office in Grand Turk and Provo has a public fax service, F9462497/4210. Credit card calling, dial 111, three minutes minimum. Paging service is popular among businesses and cell phones are widely used. Many visitors bring their own cell phones, or you can rent one while on the islands. International calls from cell phones cost the same as from a regular phone. Internet service is also available. There is a telephone directory published by Olympia Publishing (saunders@tciway.tc) with lots of useful information about the TCI, more useful than the Cable & Wireless directory.

Food and drink

Seafood, lobster, conch Good, moderate to expensive meals in restaurants and bars are good quality. Watch out for *with peas 'n' rice is* specials with no posted prices. The local beer is Caya, Pilsner or West Indies Pale Ale, in bottles *standard island fare* or draft. Wine by the glass is US$5. With over 50 restaurants and delis on Provo alone, prices are variable but local restaurants with native cuisine are reasonable. Many restaurants feature vegetarian meals and low fat cooking. All food is imported (except seafood) from Miami, occasionally from the Dominican Republic, and therefore not cheap. Many restaurants charge a 10% gratuity and/or 9% government tax. Restaurants owned and operated by belongers do not have to charge tax because they serve the local market. Some do not charge for service. Check your bill carefully and tip, or not, accordingly.

Entertainment

Local bands play mostly calypso, reggae and the traditional island music with its Haitian and African influences. On Provo, ask hoteliers and residents when and where live bands are playing. Latin influence in discos such as *Club Latino* (Downtown-Provo) and *Caribbean Macks* in Blue Hills, featuring soca, reggae and latino, loudly! Live entertainment, Friday nights, Ports of Call courtyard. *Club Med* has nightly dinner/show for guests and visitors who phone for reservations (T9465500). Nightlife does not start until 2200-2300. On Grand Turk, the *Salt Raker Inn* for music on Wednesday and Sunday nights.

Flora and fauna

The islands support 175 resident and migrant species of birds, including flocks of greater flamingos, frigate birds, ospreys, brown pelicans, the ruby throated humming bird, the belted kingfisher, white billed tropic birds, black-necked stilts, snowy plovers, peregrine falcons, red-tailed hawks, northern harriers, Baltimore orioles and scarlet tanagers and many others. There are lizards, iguanas, two species of snake, including a pygmy boa, and two species of bat. The Turks and Caicos National Trust (in Providenciales, T9415710, Director, Mrs Ethlyn Gibbs-Williams) plans to develop and protect the Princess Alexandra National Park on Providenciales' north shore. The south parts of North, Middle and East Caicos have been designated an internationally important wetland under the Ramsar Convention for the protection of waterbirds, lobster, conch, flora and a fish nursery.

A system of conservation has been set up: the islands boast 11 national parks, 4 sanctuaries, 10 nature reserves & 7 historical sites: entrance to sanctuaries by permit only

In 1998 the British Government approved an allocation of US$1.6mn for the Turks and Caicos to implement a Coastal Resource Management Programme. Its aim is to conserve the natural resources of the islands by more effective management of protected areas, revitalizing the National Parks Service, setting up a headquarters and a National Environment Centre on Provo. A public awareness programme will educate people about the benefits of national parks and a scientific monitoring programme will be initiated for the Marine Parks. The Government will work in collaboration with the National Trust to implement the programme and a 1% tax on food, drinks and accommodation goes into a special fund.

Diving and marine life

Marine life is varied and beautiful and can be enjoyed by snorkellers & sailors as well as scuba divers. Colourful fish and grouper can be seen on the coral and close to the shore there are green and loggerhead turtles and manta and spotted eagle rays. In January-March, humpback whales migrate through the deep Turks Island Passage on their way south to the Silver and Mouchoir Banks breeding grounds north of the Dominican Republic. Whale watching is co-ordinated by the Department of Environmental Heritage and Parks, who have drawn up rules to protect the whales. On Grand Turk contact Everette Freites of Oasis Divers, he has swum with the humpbacks. Beyond the reef are the game fish such as tuna, blue marlin, wahoo, snapper, bill fish and barracuda. Great care is being taken to conserve the reefs and the coral is in very good condition. The islands have become one of the most highly regarded diving locations in the region. Some of the best diving is off the wall at Northwest Point, West Caicos and French Cay. Do not take live coral, sea fans or other marine life. The use of spearguns is prohibited.

Because there is no soil run off from the islands, water visibility is excellent. The best months for diving are Apr to Nov

All divers must have a valid certificate; there are plenty of training courses for novices. The sea is often rough in February-March. For detailed descriptive information consult the *Diving, Snorkelling, Visitor's Guide to the Turks and Caicos Islands*, by Captain Bob Gascoine.

Dive centres

There is a recompression chamber at Menzies Medical Practice on Provo, T9464242, DAN insurance is accepted

On **Provo** there are nine land based dive operations offering courses (resort course approximately US$130, full certification US$400) and dive packages. The standard cost of a two-tank dive is US$70. Several companies are based at **Turtle Cove**: *Flamingo Divers*, at the *Erebus Inn*, PO Box 322, Providenciales, T/F9464193, T800-2049282, www.Provo.net/flamingo, caters for small groups of experienced or novice divers, PADI and SSI instruction; *Provo Turtle Divers*, PO Box 219, T9464232, 1-800-3285285, F9415296, provoturtledivers@provo.net; *Turtle Cove Inn* at Turtle Cove marina and at *Ocean Club Resort*, and *Comfort Suites*, Grace Bay, run by Art Pickering, is also recommended for small groups of experienced divers at similar prices; *Caicos Adventures*, by Banana Boat, T/F9413346, www.caicosadventures.tc, 36 ft custom boat trips to West Caicos, French Cay for small groups, full service, NAUI/CMAS.

There are three live-aboard boats based in Provo for those who want to spend a week doing nothing else but diving. *Sea Dancer* (Peter Hughes Diving, T800-9-DANCER or 305-6699475, whatever@tciway.tc) operates from the Caicos Marina Shipyard, has accommodation for 18 people and offers five dives a day around French Cay, West Caicos and Northwest Point. *Tao*, a 56 ft trimaran takes groups of nine for up to two weeks' sailing, diving and fishing in the Turks and Caicos and Bahamas, T9416767, F9415510, TAO@provo.net *The*

Turks and Caicos Aggressor, contact the Aggressor Fleet Limited, PO Drawer K, Morgan City, LA 70381, T800-3482628, F504-3840817, www.aggressor.com

On **Grace Bay** there are: *Dive Provo*, located at the *Allegro Resort*, PO Box 350, T9465029/5040, F9465936, www.diveprovo.com, three boats, windsurfing, kayaks, shop in Ports of Call; *Big Blue Unlimited*, which specializes in eco-adventures, small groups, private charters, T9465034, F9465033, www.bigblue.tc; *Club Med* which also has a dive boat for in-house guests, T9465500, but caters for large parties; and *Beaches Turks & Caicos Resort & Spa* includes PADI and NAUI, scuba and all watersports in its all-inclusive packages, T9468000, F9468001.

At **Leeward Marina** is *J & B Tours*, T9465047, F9465288, 24 ft dive boat, courses, one tank US$60, two tanks US$85 and *Silver Deep*, T9465612, F9464527, www.silverdeep.com, private dives, three divers US$280 including tanks, 4-6 divers US$85 per person including tanks.

On **Grand Turk** there are three dive organizers. *Blue Water Divers Ltd* is on Front Street, next to the museum, PO Box 124, Grand Turk, T/F9462432, www.microplan.com/b104000.htm Mitch Rolling offers a complete range of courses and special day trips with two small boats (bimini tops for shade). *Sea Eye Diving*, run by Cecil Ingham and Connie Rus, is a larger operation in a beautifully renovated building with underwater photography and a range of watersports on offer as well as a shop selling diving equipment and beach wear. They have three boats, maximum 12 divers per boat, NAUI and PADI instruction, US$55 per dive, frequent cay trips, dive packages with accommodation available, PO Box 67, T/F9461407, www.reefnet.on.ca /grandturk *Oasis Divers* is run by Everette Freites and Dale Barker, PO Box 137, Grand Turk, T9461128, www.oasisdivers.com, offering a complete range of courses to small groups aboard 28ft dive boats. They also have a small shop. The highlight of diving here is the wall off Cockburn Town, which drops suddenly from 40ft to 7,000ft only a quarter of a mile offshore. There are 25 moored sites along the wall where you can find coral arches, tunnels, canyons, caves and overhangs.

On **Salt Cay**, *Salt Cay Divers*, operated by Debbie Manos and Oliver Been is based at the *Mount Pleasant Guest House*, run by Brian Sheedy, T9466906, www.saltcaydivers.com (see under Salt Cay). The dive boat is a 24ft Carolina skiff which takes you to the main dive site in five minutes. A two-tank dive is US$50, but most people stay at the guest house and take a five day package for US$914 which includes three meals, transfers and unlimited day and night diving. There are seven moored dive sites and off Great Sand Cay there is an 18th century British shipwreck, now a National Monument, the *Endymion*, still loaded with cannon. A wall chart telling her story is on sale at gift shops on the islands and at the Museum on Grand Turk. She was found in 1991 by Brian Sheedy with the help of a local historian, Josiah Marvel, and the only way to visit her is with Salt Cay Divers. It is thought that this is the only unsalvaged 18th century wreck in the world which the diving public can visit and explore. The wreck lies in about 25ft of water with the remains of two other ships nearby: a Civil War steamer and a ship dating from around 1900. The coral is prolific and the fish plentiful and huge. The best time for a visit is May-November.

On the west side of the Columbus Passage the wall along the east shores of **South Caicos** and **Long Cay** also drops gradually or steeply from a depth of about 50 ft, with many types of coral and a variety of fish of all sizes. Snorkelling is rewarding with several shallow reefs close to the shore. On South Caicos *Club Carib Dive and Watersports* offers excellent diving and snorkelling with eagle rays 5-10 minutes offshore, T9463444, F9463446, packages available. On **North Caicos** *Club Vacanze* will arrange diving and snorkelling, T9467119, F9467114.

Beaches and watersports

230 miles of white sand beaches & coral reefs surround the islands

Grace Bay on Provo is the longest stretch of sand, at 12 miles, and despite the hotels it is possible to find plenty of empty space, but *no* shade. There is rarely any shade on the beaches. Most watersports can be arranged through the hotels or tour operators.

Day sails Several tour operators represent all **day sails**, **scuba dives** or **snorkelling trips** or you can contact the captains direct or through your hotel. Sailing and beach cruising trips include: *Sail the Trade Winds Schooner, Atabeyra*, anchored at Leeward Marina, offering Pirates Cay full and a half day sails and ecology tours, cold drinks and snorkelling gear included, call **Sun Charters** T9415363 or the tour desk at your hotel; *Beluga*, Leeward Going Through, T/F9464396, VHF 68, 37ft catamaran, private full and half day sails; **Sand Dollar Cruises**, T946-5238/5407, F9465407, "cruise in comfort" to Little Water Cay, beach and snorkel half day trips, secluded island getaway with umbrella, snorkel, picnic and cold drinks. **Minx**, Turtle Cove Marina, T/F9465122, www.Provo.net/Minx, 41 ft trimaran, private charters only, up to six people, day, sunset, overnight trips, Captain Mike has 30 years' sailing experience, 10 doing charters in TCI; *Tao*, T9464783, F9415510, VHF 77, 56 ft trimaran, four double cabins, 1-2 week cruises in TCI and Bahamas, Captain Dave Matthews has 20 years' sailing experience, half day cruise, sunset or glow worm; **Caicos Cat Cruises**, 'conk out on de big boat', 45ft catamaran, island exploration under shade, from Turtle Cove Marina next to *Banana Boat*, T9415389; *Two Fingers*, T9464783, F9415510, VHF 77, 36ft catamaran, and *Arielle*, 52ft catamaran, full and half day cruises, snorkelling, trips arranged by **Sail Provo**, T9464783, F9465527, sailprovo@tciway.tc Also at Leeward Marina, **Catch the Wave Charters**, T/F9413047, catchthewaveprovo@yahoo.com, 26 ft Bowrider, comfortable and roomy, specialize in private charters and offer bonefishing, waterskiing, beach cruising, reggae sunset cruises; **J & B Tours**, T9465067, F9465288, offers beach and snorkelling excursions, barbecues, waterskiing, island getaways, trips to Conch Farm, caves on Middle Caicos, glow worm cruises, fishing and scuba. **Silver Deep** (see page 328), offers similar beach cruises, glow worm charters, secluded getaways, trips to Middle and North Caicos. Exclusively at Sapodilla Bay, **Ocean Outback**'s 'Ultimate Getaway', all day adventure by 18 ft or 24 ft runabouts visiting settlers' ruins, pirate caves and rock carvings, snorkelling, beach BBQ, snacks, beers, round trip transportation included, T9410824, www.Provo.net/OceanOutback or contact tour desk at your hotel. **Windsurfing Provo** at *Ocean Club*, Grace Bay, T9465649 and evenings T9465490, windpro@tciway.tc, offers hobie waves, hobie cats, small motor boats and kayaking as well as **windsurfing**.

Fishing is popular. Provo and Pine Cay have the best bonefishing though it is also possible at South Caicos, Middle Caicos, North Caicos and Salt Cay. May is the prime time. Fishermen have not organized themselves into offering packages, so you have to find your own accommodation and fishing guide. Shop around before committing US$250-300 per day because experienced visitor fishermen have reported a lack of skill, professionalism and simple amenities among local guides.

Fishing

An international billfishing tournament is held annually coinciding with the full moon in Jul, T9464106, F9464771. It is a big event with lots of parties

On **Providenciales**, the choices are: *Captain Barr Gardiner's Bonefish Unlimited* (Box 241, T9464874, F9464960), *Light Tackle and 'Black Diamond' Fishing and Boat Tours* (T9464451), Earl Musgrove. Leeward Going Through Marina is the best place to find and talk to fishermen, or try to reach them on the radio, VHF 16. *J & B Tours* (see above) will arrange full and half day fishing. *Gilley's* restaurant will cook your catch. **Silver Deep** (see above) includes bone, fly, light tackle and night fishing in his itinerary. The most experienced sports fishing operation on Provo is **Captain Bob Collins' Sakitumi Charters**, he has been fishing these waters on his 43ft Hatteras since 1989, T9464065, F9464141, US$650 per full day, US$350 per half day, VHF Channel 16 'Sakitumi'. There are four deep sea sport fishing operators in Turtle Cove Marina; *Sakitumi* (see above); **Gwod Phrienz** (Good Friends) contact Algie Dean, T9464342, F9415144, reservations@tciway.tc; **Gwendolyn**, 45ft Hatteras sportfisher, T9410412, 9465321, www.Provo.net/Gwendolyn/ Rates approximately US$400 half day, US$750 full day. On **Grand Turk** fishing can be arranged through Ossie (Oswald) Virgil, of Virgil's Taxis at the airport, or PO Box 78, T9462018. Ossie also arranges an annual Game Fishing Tournament in August. On **Middle Caicos** fishing and boating is arranged through the District Commissioner's Office, T9466100, with Dotis Arthur and her husband, Cardinal. On **South Caicos** a bonefish specialist is Julius 'Goo the Guide' Jennings, US$20 per hour, who can be contacted through the *Club Caribe*, T9463444, F9463446.

A US$10 sport fishing licence, for pole fishing only, is required from the Fisheries Department, Grand Turk, T9462970, or South Caicos, T9463306, or Provo, T9464017. Ask your guide whether the fishing licence is included in his package. Spear fishing is not allowed.

Turks & Caicos Islands

Other activities **Parasailing** with *Turtle Parasailing*, *Turtle Cove Inn*, costs US$60 a fly, T/F9415389, parasail@tciway.tc Provo now also offers **tandem skydiving** with *Skydive Provo*, T9410901. Visit the landing zone on the beach southwest of *Club Med*. Exclusive **scooter** getaway to North Caicos with *Provo Fun Cycles*, T9465868. **Jetskis** are banned from any of the marine parks, although they may be used in parts of Leeward Channel and on the Banks and can be rented from *Sun and Fun Seasports* at Leeward Marina, T9465724.

Other sports An 18-hole championship **golf** course opened November 1992 (black tees 3,202yds, white tees 2,865yds). Owned by the water company, it is located within walking distance of the *Club Med*, *Allegro Resort*, *Grace Bay Club* and *Ocean Club*. Most hotels offer 3-5 day packages of green fees and mandatory carts, T9465991, F9465992, www.provogolfclub.com, licensed snackbar. An amateur open golf championship is held in October. The former Governor created a nine-hole golf course on Grand Turk in the grounds of his residence (see box on 333). There are **tennis** courts on Grand Turk at the *Coral Reef* and on Provo at *Club Med*, *Erebus Inn*, T9413527 and the *Allegro Resort*. There are also courts on Pine Cay and at the *Parrot Cay Resort* and on North Caicos at *Club Vacanze*. A small but active squash community welcomes visitors and can be contacted at *Johnston Apartments*, Kings Court, T9465683. *Island Network* sports and **fitness centre** with aqua/land aerobics is at Ports of Call across from *Allegro Resort*, contact Darlene, T9464240. *Fun & Fit Health Club*, at the *Erebus Inn*, offers weights and machines, aerobics, pool, tennis, personal training and nutrition advice. There is a certified fitness trainer, T9413527, ask for Lisa. On Grand Turk there is a small fitness centre next to South Primary School. **Horse-riding** on Grand Turk can be arranged by phoning Gail Johnston at *Arawak Inn*, T9462276, and on Salt Cay by contacting Brian Sheedy at *Mount Pleasant Guest House*.

Holidays and festivals

Public holidays New Year's Day, Commonwealth Day, Good Friday, Easter Monday, National Heroes Day (end May), the Queen's birthday (second week in June), Emancipation Day (beginning of August), National Youth Day (end-September), Columbus' Day and Human Rights Day (both in October), Christmas Day and Boxing Day.

Festivals Most events are linked to the sea and land-based activities are tacked on to regattas or fishing tournaments. In Providenciales the billfishing tournament (see above) is a big event with lots of parties every night. Provo Day festivities follow Emancipation Day in August. Festivities culminate in the choosing and inauguration of Miss Turks and Caicos Islands, who competes in international beauty pagents. On Grand Turk a fishing tournament and the Cactus Fest are held in August, with competitions for sports, costumes, bands and gospel; there is a float parade, dancing and an art exhibition. On North Caicos, Festarama is in July; on Middle Caicos, Expo is in August; on South Caicos the Regatta with associated activities is in May.

Health

There are no endemic tropical diseases & no malaria, no special vaccinations are required prior to arrival. Aids exists On Provo, MBS Group Medical Practice, Leeward Highway, Jon Delisser Building, open 0830-1700 Monday-Friday, 0830-1200 Saturday, recompression chamber. Dr Euan Menzies, T9464242. Dr Sam Slattery, T9415252. Optometrist, T9415842. Dentist, Dr Robert McIntosh, T9464321 and Dr Steve Bourne. Chiropractor Dr Kathleen Kopping. The government clinic on Provo is Myrtle Rigby Health Complex, Leeward Highway, near Down Town, T9413000. They have three doctors and 15 nurses and midwives, open daily. Ambulance services available and emergency medical air charter to USA or Nassau, full life support can be arranged, T999 or any doctor. There is no anaesthetist on Provo so surgery is done on Grand Turk, Nassau or Miami. On Grand Turk there is a small, understaffed hospital on the north side of town, T9462333, and a government clinic in town, T9462328, open 0800-1230, 1400-1630. Dr D O Astwood, T9462451, Dr L Astwood, T9463287. The other islands organize emergency air evacuation to Grand Turk hospital. Island Pharmacy, T9464150, F9461942.

Grand Turk

Grand Turk is not a resort island although there are hotels and dive operations which concentrate mostly on the wall just off the west coast. The vegetation is mostly scrub and cactus, among which you will find wild donkeys and horses roaming. Behind the town are old salt pans, with crumbling walls and ruined windmills, where pelicans and other waterbirds fish. More abandoned salt pans can be seen around the island, particularly towards the south. The east coast is often littered with tree trunks and other debris which have drifted across from Africa, lending credence to the claim that Columbus could have been carried here, rather than further north in the Bahamas chain. Grand Turk is the seat of government and the second largest population centre, although it has an area of only seven square miles.

Population: 2,000

Getting there Airlines and schedules tend to change frequently. Most visitors to Grand Turk arrive with *American Airlines* to Provo and then shuttle over on a small aircraft, this works quite smoothly. *Bahamasair* began flying from Miami twice a week in 1999 but there was little confidence locally that it would last long. Alternatively, *Lynx Air* flies direct from Ft Lauderdale, comfortable, many advantages but lengthy flight. *TCA*, *Sky King* and *Inter Island Airways* operate frequent inter-island flights and it is often possible to turn up on the day you want to travel and catch the next flight. Reservations are recommended, however, particularly when going to Provo. **Getting around** Taxis are the only form of public transport (US$4 from the airport to the *Osprey Beach*, the nearest). Jeeps, cars and bicycles can be rented.

Ins & outs
See transport, page 335, for further details

Around the island

Cockburn Town, the capital and financial centre, has some very attractive colonial buildings, mostly along Duke Street, or Front Street, as it is usually known. The government offices are in a nicely restored, small square with cannons facing the sea. The town had a facelift in 1996-97: new stone planters were built along Front Street and trees planted; the post office and government buildings were painted in a combination of blues, ranging from deep turquoise to almost white, nicely matching the ocean; the Victoria Library was stripped and repainted and local landowners and householders were encouraged to clean up their property. Those who own old houses have been offered duty free import of materials for renovation and conservation work. New benches along Pond Street came complete with a litter bin beside them. However, in 1997/98 El Niño brought bad weather which caused damage to the sea walls. Holes opened up on Front Street and the sea started to fill them from the bottom. The trees on the west side lost all their leaves in the storms and the beaches were eroded. The rebuilding of the sea wall on Front Street started in 1999 to ensure that the old buildings will not suffer further sea damage and erosion.

The oldest church on Grand Turk is **St Thomas' Anglican church** (inland, near the water catchment tanks), built by Bermudan settlers. After a while it was considered too far to walk to the centre of the island and **St Mary's Anglican church** was built in 1899 on Front Street overlooking the water. This is now a pro-Cathedral with the southern Bahamas and is the first cathedral in the islands. The **Victoria Library**, built to commemorate 50 years of Queen Victoria's reign, is also an interesting building, with shutters. Walking north along Front Street you come to **Odd Fellows Lodge**, opposite the salt pier, which is thought to be one of the oldest buildings on the island and was probably the place where the abolition of slavery was proclaimed in 1832.

A new Tourist Board office was opened in 1999 in a renovated old town customs building and warehouse that sits right on the water at the north end of Cockburn Town. The work has been done sympathetically, in keeping with the old Bermudian architectural style and is a pleasant place to stop off during a walk round town.

Continue north to the **Turks and Caicos National Museum** opened in 1991 in the beautifully renovated Guinep Lodge. The exhibition on the ground floor is of the early 16th-century wreck of a Spanish caravel found on the Molasses Reef between

Turks & Caicos Islands

Grand Turk

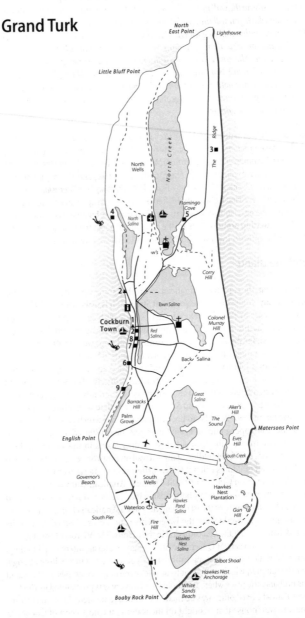

North East Point

Lighthouse

Little Bluff Point

The Ridge

North Creek

3

North Wells

Flamingo Cove

5

North Salina

4

w's

Corry Hill

2

Town Salina

Cockburn Town

1
2
8
7

Red Salina

Colonel Murray Hill

6

Back Salina

9

Great Salina

Aker's Hill

Barracks Hill

The Sound

Eves Hill

Matersons Point

Palm Grove

South Creek

English Point

Governor's Beach

South Wells

Hawkes Nest Plantation

Waterloo

Hawkes Pond Salina

Gun Hill

South Pier

Fire Hill

Hawkes Nest Salina

Talbot Shoal

1

Hawkes Nest Anchorage

White Sands Beach

Boaby Rock Point

N

0 metres 500
0 yards 500

■ **Sleeping**
1 Arawak
2 Beachcomber
3 Coral Reef
4 Guanahani Beach
5 Island House
6 Osprey Beach
7 Salt Raker Inn
8 Turks Head Inn
9 Water's Edge Townhomes

▲ **Other**
1 Harbour Master,
Anglican Church,
Telecommunications
& Post Office
2 Museum

The Battle of Waterloo

Governor John Kelly is a keen golfer and when he took over the Governor's residence, Waterloo, in 1996, he soon had designs on the 20 acres of wilderness surrounding his new home. The overgrown land was attacked by a battalion of volunteer kindred spirits to create a nine-hole, par three course. The acacia thorn bushes and vines fought back as trees not seen for years were exposed and park land appeared. The wilderness was finally dominated by a team from Her Majesty's Prison and some heavy equipment operators who uprooted the big thorn trees. The opening of the golf club was planned for June 1997, the anniversary of the Battle of Waterloo, but actually took place in January 1998 with 43 players in the Governor's Trophy competition. Visitors may pay their green fee at the Governor's office – a slightly unusual arrangement. T9462308 and speak to the secretary, Cynara John.

West Caicos and French Cay in only 20ft of water. The ship is believed to have been on an illegal slaving mission in the islands, as evidenced by locked leg irons found on the site. A guided tour is highly recommended although not essential. Upstairs there is an exhibition of local artefacts, photos, stamps, coins, a few Taino beads, figures and potsherds. A local historian, the late Herbert Sadler, compiled many volumes on the theory of Columbus' landfall and local history, some of which are on sale at the museum. A **Science Building** has been completed beside the museum, which houses a conservation laboratory, the only one of its kind in the English-speaking Caribbean. It has a climate-controlled storage space and classroom and the aim is to demystify archaeology and introduce the islanders to their history. The most recent find was a Taino paddle buried in the peat bottom of North Creek, which has been carbon dated to 1100 AD. Also beside the museum is a new and delightful garden. All the plants are native to the islands and carry a code number so that you can identify them from a booklet. The original building on the site was destroyed by fire, but the oven from the old slave kitchen and the water catchment tank have been renovated and preserved as garden features. The museum is working on the reconstruction of a windmill to illustrate the impact of the salt industry on the islands. ■ *US$5 for non-residents, US$2 residents, US$0.50 students. Mon-Fri 1000-1600, Sat 1000-1300. For further information contact the curator, Brian Riggs, Box 188, Grand Turk, T9462160.*

There is now an attractive walkway beside the salinas behind the town. There is a shaded viewing spot for birdwatchers and trees have been planted all along Pond Street to improve the view. Elaine Huard runs an animal sanctuary (United Humanitarians) at her home on Duke Street, where she usually has up to 40 dogs and cats. She brings vets from Canada three times a year to provide free sterilizations, medicines and general care for the domestic and stray animals on the island. Her dedicated voluntary work has made her something of a national institution and she is always pleased to receive visitors. Donations welcome.

The Governor's residence, **Waterloo**, south of the airport, was built in 1815 by a Bermudian salt merchant as a private residence and acquired for the head of government in 1857. Successive governors and administrators have modified and extended it, prompted partly by hurricane damage in 1866 and 1945, and by the Queen's visit in 1966. In 1993 the building was again renovated and remodelled; the works were so extensive they constituted a near rebuilding of the historic residence. Governor's Beach is one of the nicest beaches and excellent for snorkelling, with isolated coral heads rising out of the sand and a wide variety of fish and invertebrates.

Further south is an ex-USAF base, known as **South Base**, which is now used as government offices, and beyond there some pleasant beaches on the south coast, with good snorkelling at White Sands beach by the point. US Navy, NASA and Coast Guard bases were once important for the economy of Grand Turk; John Glenn, the first American to orbit the earth, splashed down off Grand Turk in the 1960s.

Turks & Caicos Islands

The cays southeast of Grand Turk are a land and sea national park, sheltering Turks Head cacti on **Martin Alonza Pinzon Cay**, frigate birds on **Penniston Cay** and breeding sooty terns, noddy terns and other seabirds on **Gibbs Quay**. The lagoons and red mangroves of South Creek are also a national park, serving as a nursery for fish, crabs and other sea life, as well as a reserve for birds.

North of Cockburn Town a paved road leads along The Ridge up the east side of the island to the 1852 lighthouse and another abandoned US base, from where there are good views out to sea. This is to be refurbished and converted into a Community College. A channel at the north point gives access to North Creek, an excellent hurricane shelter for boats.

Essentials

Sleeping **LL** *Water's Edge Townhomes*, south of town, T9462055, F9462911, 3 2-storey houses on beach. **L** *Osprey Beach*, PO Box 42, T9462232, F9462877. Rooms on ground floor, open directly onto the sand, suites available with kitchenette. **L-AL** *Turks Head Inn* on Duke St, PO Box 58, T9462466, F9461716, tophotel@grand-turk.com, is recommended. Built in 1869 by Jonathon Glass first as a private house and later used as a doctor's dispensary, the American Consulate and a guest house for the British Government, it is set back from the beach surrounded by tall trees. Renovated and decorated in period style, 7 rooms, with wooden floors, beds and balconies, phone, minibar, two family rooms, outside dining and upstairs dining deck, pizza ovens, barbecue night with live local music, weekly dive slide show (Oasis Divers), dive packages, expansion planned, Austrian management, Werner and Doris Koeder, both head chefs. **L-A** *Salt Raker Inn*, PO Box 1, T9462260, F9462817, www.microplan.com /bluerake.htm/ is an old Bermuda-style building on Duke St, also built by Bermudan ship-wright Jonathon Glass in the 1840s, facing the beach. Run by Jenny Smith, it is very friendly, relaxed and unpretentious. 10 rooms, 3 suites, sea or garden view, balconies or patios, a/c, fan, fridge, TV, dive packages with *Bluewater Divers*.

AL *Arawak Inn*, right on the beach at southwest end of island, PO Box 190, T9462277, F9462279, www.4arawak.com 16 spacious suites, clean, nicely furnished, well-equipped kitchens, porches, private, all with sea view, charming beach bar/restaurant, unpretentious, beach is quiet and empty, pool, dive packages available. North of town on Lighthouse Rd, **AL-A** *Island House*, PO Box 36, T9461519, F9462646. 8 different suites with kitchen and barbecue, spacious, fully equipped, TV, phone, a/c, fan, on edge of North Creek, pool, free laundry facilities, maid service, bicycles and golf carts available, diving, fishing etc can be arranged, popular with people who like to spend a month or two on the island in the winter, attentive and welcoming management, contact Colin and Lucy Brooker, or their daughter, Donna. **AL-B** *Coral Reef*, PO Box 156, T9462055, F9462911. An extensive wooden deck running all round the hotel, on the east coast away from the town, lovely colours in the sea but debris washed up frequently, rather dark studios and one-bedroom apartments with kitchenette although all sea-facing, pool, lit tennis court, fitness centre. On Front St, Angela and Douglas Gordon have a large guest suite with sea view, **A** *Beachcomber House*, also referred to as 'The Gordons', behind the government buildings, close to beach and restaurants, PO Box 110, T9462470. Includes superb breakfast, with homemade bread and muffins, and huge afternoon tea, no tax or service charges, dive packages available, open Nov-Apr only, in UK T01507-608861 for bookings during summer months when the Gordons are off the island. **A** *Guanahani Beach Hotel*, on the broad Sandy Pillory Beach on the west coast north of the town, PO Box 178, T9462135, F9461460. 16 twin-bedded rooms, 2 apartments, all with sea view, balcony, TV, a/c, fan, pool, dive packages with Sea Eye Diving.

B *Sadler's Seaview Apartments*, Duke St, PO Box 31, T9462569, F9461523. South of Cable and Wireless, 2 apartments with fan, TV, patio, fully equipped kitchens, laundry and maid service, small beach across the road, contact Marjorie Sadler.

The **Poop Deck** is a tiny bar. Set back from the road in the centre of town by the sea, local food and hamburgers at lunchtime, chicken and chips in the evenings. **Regal Begal** serves local food, on the road north of town on the west side of North Creek, a favourite lunch place. The outdoor **Salt Raker Inn** is recommended for good food and pleasant company. It is a popular meeting place and fills up on Wed and Sun barbecue nights when Mitch, from Blue Water Divers, plays the guitar and sings. For local food and lunch specials try **Touch of Class** on the road south out of town, a/c, TV, bar, filling, tasty portions. The **Turks Head Inn** is a gathering place with a friendly bar and good food. **Water's Edge**, T9461680 is run by Dave and Jan and offers a very cheerful, informal atmosphere for lunch and dinner with ample portions served and a reasonably-priced menu, lots of conch. Mitch entertains here on Saturday. Scooter rental available. **Peanut's** snack bar at the airport. Hot snacks, peanuts and drinks.

Eating
The best restaurants & bars are at the hotels

Grand Turk is not an island where you will find lots of nightlife. Most of the evening activity takes place when people get together for meals and drinks at the small inns and restaurants. Do not expect a lot of action.

Nightlife

The Shell Shack, at *Beachcomber House*, is where the artist Douglas Gordon creates jewellery from conch shell, shell and beach glass mirrors, clocks, lamps and candle covers, all different and collectable, made on the island, reasonable prices, commissions accepted. **X's Gallery**, same location as *Sadler's Sea View Apartments*. Run by Xavier Tonneau, formerly proprietor of the *Turks Head Inn*, and his partner Sue Cottle, they sell their own paintings, hand drawn and painted maps of the islands, a selection of Haitian art work and some small antiques collected in the islands.

Shopping

Local Jeeps or cars can be rented from **Tropical Auto Leasing**, US$55 per day, everything included except fuel, T9461000; **Sunshine Auto Leasing**, by airport, T9461588, recommended, **Dutchie's Car Rental**, Airport Rd, T9462244, recommended, or **C J Car Rental**, T9462744. If you rent a bicycle, jeep or car, note that the islanders completely ignore the 20 mph speed limit in town (and 40 mph outside), particularly on Pond St, recommended to stay on Front St/Duke St route through town and exercise caution elsewhere. Fatal accidents have occurred. **Boat** For those arriving by sea, there is a safe harbour and marina at Flamingo Cove, North Creek, run by Leah and Kirk, T9462227.

Transport

Turks & Caicos Islands

Salt Cay

Seven miles south of Grand Turk, Salt Cay is out of the past, with windmills, salt sheds and other remnants of the old salt industry and little else. The island was first visited by the Bermudans in 1645; they started making salt here in 1673 and maintained a thriving salt industry until its collapse in the 1960s. Production ceased all together in 1971. The main village is **Balfour Town**, divided into North Side and South Side, noted for its Bermudan buildings and pretty cottages with stone walls around the gardens. The **White House**, which dominates the skyline, was built in the 1830s of Bermudan stone brought in as ballast by the Harriott family during the height of the salt industry. The **Methodist Church** nearby, one of several churches on the island, is over 125 years old. Snorkelling is good and diving is excellent; there are 10 moored dive sites along the wall, with tunnels, caves and undercuts. In January-March you can often see the humpbacked whales migrating through the channel as they pass close to the west coast. The island has been designated a UNESCO World Heritage Site. The island can be explored on horse back, Brian Sheedy at *Mount Pleasant Guest House* will arrange this. On request dive operators on Grand Turk will take you to Salt Cay by boat, the dolphins will often accompany you on the trip.

Population: 208
Plant life was curtailed during the salt raking days to prevent rainfall. Look into some of the ruined houses & you will find salt still stored in the cellars

The most expensive and exclusive hotel is the architect-designed and owned **LL Windmills Plantation** on a 2½ mile beach, which appeals to people who want to do nothing undisturbed, 8 suites, including all food and drink, meals taken family style, local recipes, saltwater pool, no children, diving can be arranged with Salt Cay Divers, reservations (minimum 3

Sleeping

nights) *The Windmills Plantation*, 440 32nd St, West Palm Beach, FL 33407, T800-8227715, F407-8452982, on Salt Cay T9466962. Next to the hotel on 11 acres of North Beach there are plans to build *Bermuda Place*, a development of 1-2 storey units in Bermuda style. **L-AL** *Castaways*, T9466921 or 315-5360737, www.vikingresort.com 6 1-bedroom villas along the beach north of *Windmills Plantation*, available for rent Nov-Apr, self-catering, take supplies with you or you will be forced to eat all your meals at the hotels. **AL** *Pirates Hideaway*, Victoria St, T/F9466909, www.windnet.com/pirate 4 rooms for B&B, or rent whole house for self-catering, sea views, balcony, fans, meals on request, bikes and kayaks for hire, boat trips, drive packages. **AL** *Sunset Reef*, in USA T410-8893662, F410-4675744, sunsetreef @aol.com 2 bedrooms with en suite bathrooms, all amenities. At the other end of the scale is the cheerful **A** *Mount Pleasant Guest House*, T9466927, mtpleasantinfo@yahoo.com Owned by amiable host Brian Sheedy, but up for sale and in need of some renovation, a salt raker's house built in 1830, can sleep 25 in 4 very simple rooms in the main house, 2 with shared bath, and in a separate annex/guest house which has 3 basic rooms downstairs with kitchen and living room and a dormitory with 7 beds upstairs, dive package including 3 excellent meals, transfers and unlimited diving, processing facilities for dive photos, video/TV, library, bicycles, horses for riding or driving, outdoor restaurant/bar with the best food on the island. **B** *The Salt Cay Sunset House*, Victoria St, Balfour Town, T/F9466942, seaone@tciway.tc Meal packages available, special needs catered for, good food, former 1832 plantation home, high ceilings, 3 bedrooms with bath, fans, comfortable, verandah with *Blue Mermaid Sunset Café*. Mrs Irene Leggatt runs the small **C** *Halfway House* on the seashore in Balfour Town, T9466936. 4 rooms, 2 bathrooms, pleasant, clean, good homemade breakfast US$5, lunch, dinner by reservations.

Transport
There is a paved airstrip for small aircraft, around which a fence has been erected to keep out the donkeys

The island is served by *TCA*, with 2 5-min flights Mon, Wed, Fri from Grand Turk, one at 0645 and one at an indeterminate time (about 1530) in the afternoon, making a day trip possible. Alternatively, charter a flight, or get a seat on someone else's charter, which costs the same if you can fill the aircraft, or contact the District Commissioner's Office on Salt Cay (or Brian Sheedy at *Mount Pleasant Guest House*, he crosses regularly to do his shopping) for details of ferries. The only public transport on the island is the taxi van run by Nathan Smith (T9466920), airport pickup and touring; there are very few vehicles of any sort.

South Caicos

Population: 1,198
The beaches going E & N are totally deserted. You can walk for miles beachcombing along the east shore

The nearest Caicos island, 22 miles west of Grand Turk, South Caicos was once the most populous and the largest producer of salt. It is now the main fishing port having benefited from the most naturally protected harbour in the islands and is also known as East Harbour, or the 'rock'. As a result yachts frequently call here and a popular annual regatta is held at the end of May. There is excellent diving along the drop off to the south and the best snorkelling is on the windward side going east and north. Boat trips can be organized with fishermen to the island reserves of Six Hill Cays and Long Cay. Further south are the two Ambergris Cays, Big and Little, where there are caves and the diving and fishing are good.

Salt Cay

■ **Sleeping**
1 Castaways
2 Halfway House
3 Mount Pleasant Guesthouse
4 Pirates Hideaway
5 Sunset Reef
6 Windmills Plantation

Not to scale

Cockburn Harbour is the only settlement and is an attractive, if rather run down, little place with lots of old buildings, a pleasant waterfront with old salt warehouses and boats of all kinds in the harbour. The District Commissioner's house, currently unoccupied, stands atop a hill southeast of the village and can be recognized by its green roof. The School For Field Studies is in the 19th-century *Admiral's Arm Inn*, and attracts undergraduate students from abroad to the island to study reef ecology and marine resources, but otherwise there are very few visitors. Wild donkeys, cows and horses roam the island and several have made their home in an abandoned hotel construction site along the coast from the Residency. The salinas dominate the central part of the island and there is a 'boiling hole', connected to the sea by a subterranean passage, which was used to supply the salt pans. It makes an interesting walk and you may see flamingos. Call Yolanda Mills, the helpful District Commissioner, for further information, T9463211.

L-AL *South Caicos Ocean Haven*, in town, T9463444, F9463446, www.oceanhaven.tc 22 rooms, a/c, fishing can be arranged, also diving packages available, salt water pool, restaurant. **B** *Mae's Bed & Breakfast*, Forth Street, T9463207. 3 rooms, laundry service, no credit cards. A few people in the town rent out rooms. *Love's*, local dishes. *Muriel's*, Graham St, T9463535, native dishes. *Pond View*, T9463276, native dishes. *Dora's Lobster Pot* at the airport, T9463247.

Sleeping & eating

TCA and *SkyKing* connect South Caicos with Providenciales and Grand Turk. *TCA* also flies to Middle and North Caicos. There are a few taxis on the island, US$4 from the airport to *South Caicos Ocean Haven* hotel.

Transport

East Caicos

East Caicos has an area of 18 sq miles which makes it one of the largest islands. It also boasts the highest point in the Turks and Caicos, Flamingo Hill at 156 ft. A ridge runs along the north coast, but the rest of the island is swamp, creeks, mangrove and mudflats. Jacksonville, in the northwest, used to be the centre of a 50,000 acre sisal plantation and there was also a cattle farm at the beginning of the 20th century. The island is now uninhabited except for mosquitoes and wild donkeys. There is an abandoned railway left over from the plantation days and feral donkeys have worn paths through the scrub and sisal. Caves near Jacksonville, which were once mined for bat guano, contain petroglyphs carved on the walls and there is evidence of several Lucayan settlements. Splendid beaches include a 17-mile beach on the north coast. Off the north coast, opposite Jacksonville, is **Guana Cay**, home to the Caicos iguana. Yet another scheme to develop East Caicos is being proposed and hotly debated, a US$350mn cruise port and resort town, with a bridge to South Caicos. Conservationists are protesting against the potential damage to the Ramsar site and wildlife on the island, watch this space!

Originally named Guana by the Lucayans

Middle Caicos

Also known as Grand Caicos, this is the largest of the islands, with an area of 48sq miles. Its coastline is more dramatic than some of the other islands, characterized by limestone cliffs along the north coast, interspersed with long sandy beaches shaded by casuarina pines or secluded coves. The south part of the island is swamp and tidal flats. There are three settlements linked by the paved King's Road, **Conch Bar**, where there is an airstrip, a primary school and guest houses, **Bambarra** and **Lorimers**. The caves between Bambarra and Lorimers, which were used by the Lucayan Indians, were later mined for guano. Cardinal Arthur arranges cave tours and boat trips. For the caves in the national park at Conch Bar ask in Conch Bar for a guide. Archaeological excavations have uncovered a Lucayan ball court and a settlement near Armstrong Pond, due south of Bambarra, but these are not easily

Population: 272 Visit the huge caves in the national park at Conch Bar that link up with the sea. There are bats, stalactites, stalagmites & underwater salt lakes with pink shrimp

Turks & Caicos Islands

accessible. Evidence of the Lucayan civilization dates back to 750 AD. Loyalist plantation ruins can also be explored. Bambarra beach is an empty, curving sweep of white sand, fringed with casuarina trees. Middle Caicos regatta is held here and there are small thatched huts which serve as restaurants for the very popular end-August Expo (some litter remains), but otherwise there are no facilities. A sand bar stretches out to **Pelican Cay**, half a mile out, which you can walk at low tide, popular with wading birds. The view from Conch Bar beach is marred by a rusting barge in shallow water, but there is afternoon shade at the west end under a cliff where the reef meets the land. A pretty cove, popular with day trippers, is **Mudjeon Harbour**, just west of Conch Bar, protected by a sand bar and with shade under a rocky overhang. The reef again juts out from the land here before branching out westwards along the rocky coastline. This can be spectacular in the winter months with the crashing waves. South of Middle Caicos is a nature reserve comprising a frigatebird breeding colony and a marine sinkhole with turtles, bonefish and shark. The blue hole is surrounded by sandy banks and is difficult to get to, but it shows up on the satellite photo of the islands on display in the museum in Grand Turk.

In December 1998 the Crossing Place Trail was reopened. This was formerly a path worn by Lucayan Indians and later by slaves travelling between plantations, and it runs for 12 miles (seven miles can be cycled), along the north coast connecting Lorimers, Bambarra and Conch Bar. Developed by the National Trust to encourage ecotourism on the island, the trail takes in beaches, coastal cliffs, Conch Bar, Indian Caves and the Blowing Hole. It is well marked and there are plans to have shaded benches along the route. Tours from Provo and Grand Turk are available. Wear strong walking shoes.

Ask the District Commissioner's office, T9466100, for information and assistance, including boat tours and cave tours.

Sleeping **LL-L** *Blue Horizon Resort* on Mudgeon Harbour beach, T9466141, F9466139, www.bhresort.com Offers 4 small and large studio cottages and a 2-bedroomed house, screened porches, on 50 acres (land for sale), weekly rental available, bicycles, fishing, tours arranged, bring own groceries or ask for accommodation to be stocked with your requirements. **LL** *Dreamscape Villa*, www.middlecaicos.com, Bambarra beach. 3 bedrooms, 2 bathrooms, outside shower, large veranda, 80 ft from water, hammock on deck. In the USA, 185 Highland Ave, White River Junction, VT 05001, Vermont, T802-2952652. In TCI, Ernest Forbes Jr, T9466175. **L** *Seascape Villa*, www.caicosvilla.com On 2 acres of beachfront, view of reef and gardens from screened veranda, only 6 houses on this 5-mile stretch of shore, 2 miles to town, sleeps 8, 2 bedrooms, a/c on first floor, 2 queen size beds in a/c loft, well-equipped kitchen, barbecue, games, books, caretakers. In Conch Bar: **L-AL** *Eagles Rest Villas*, T9466175, in USA T215-2554640, F813-7937157. 1 studio on 5 miles of beach, sometimes for rent, amenities offered are not always available. George and Martha Volz' **AL** *Villa*, contact 1255 Carolyn Drive, Southampton, PA, 18966, T215-3220505, F215-3220593 in the USA, or the District Commissioner's office, Dolphus Arthur, T9466100. A 3-bedroom house let for 3 day minimum, week or month, Dec-Apr. Stacia and Dolphus Arthur run **C** *Arthur's Guesthouse* next to Arthur's Store, T9466122. 1 double, 1 twin-bedded room, private bath, kitchen.

Eating Canned foods and sodas are available from the few small stores in Conch Bar and fresh food arrives weekly on the ferry from Provo. However, it is advisable to bring your own food. Annie Taylor is known for her cooking and runs a restaurant on demand in her house. *Johnson's Bar* is open in Conch Bar most afternoons and evenings for cold beer, dominoes and music. *T&J Boutique* in Conch Bar has ice creams, cold drinks and fried chicken on Fri.

Transport **Air** *TCA* fly from Grand Turk, South Caicos, North Caicos and Providenciales. After clearing customs upon arrival at Provo *SkyKing* and private pilots will also stop off if flying to North Caicos, or you can charter a plane. Reliable and recommended, *Global Airways*, run by Ferrington, Lindsey and Bennet Gardiner. Do not pre-book as you may sit 2-3 hours waiting for a particular plane. *TCA* with only 1 plane, seldom flies on. **Road** Carlton Forbes runs a taxi service and fares are based on US$2 per mile for 2 people, eg Conch Bar to Bambarra US$14, to Lorimers US$20. **Bicycle** *Sports Shack* in Conch Bar sells, rents and repairs bicycles. **Ferry** A ferry service for cargo and passengers runs between Provo, Middle and North Caicos, operated by owners of *Blue Horizons Development*, contact Dale Witt, T9466141, F9466139 for times and days (probably only Saturday) the *Dale Marie* runs. Hired bicycles (eg from Whitby Plaza, US$15 per person) may be taken on board for day trips and overnight stays on Middle Caicos.

North Caicos

The lushest of the islands, North Caicos has taller trees than the other islands and attracts more rain. Like Middle and East Caicos, the south part of the island comprises swamp and mangrove. The population has declined to 1,275 inhabitants living at the settlements of Bottle Creek, Whitby, Sandy Point and Kew.

Population: 1,275

There is one Nature Reserve at **Dick Hill Creek** and **Bellefield Landing Pond**, to protect the West Indian whistling duck and flamingos, and another at **Cottage Pond**, a fresh/salt water sinkhole, about 170 ft deep, where there are grebes and West Indian whistling duck. **Pumpkin Bluff Pond** is a sanctuary for flamingos, Bahamian pintail and various waders. **Three Mary's Cays** is a sanctuary for flamingos and is an osprey nesting site. Flocks of flamingos can also be seen on **Flamingo Pond**, but take binoculars. There is a viewing point at the side of the road, which is the only place from where you can see them and at low tide they can be a long way off. There is also good snorkelling at **Three Mary's Cays** and **Sandy Point beach** to the west is lovely. There is a rough road to Three Mary's Cays suitable for jeeps. The beaches are good along the north coast where the hotels are, although the best is a seven-mile strip west of Pumpkin Bluff, where there has been no development so far. It can be reached by walking along the beach or via a dirt road past the *Club Vacanze* car park. A cargo ship foundered on the reef in the 1980s, and is still stuck fast, making it of snorkelling interest. Construction of a new deep water harbour has begun and when finished it will extend from Pine Cay to Bellefield Landing and over Dick Hill Creek.

Kew, in the centre, is a pretty, scruffy little village with neat gardens and tall trees, many of them exotic fruit trees, to provide shade. There are three churches, a primary school, a shop and two bars. **Bottle Creek**, in the east, has a high school, clinic and churches. The paved road ends here and a rough road requiring four-wheel drive continues to Toby Rock. The backstreets of Bottle Creek run alongside the creek and here you can see the importance of water conservation, with people carrying buckets to and from the municipal water tap at the rain catchment area, while donkeys, goats and dogs roam around. The area is poor, but many people are building themselves bigger and better homes. **Whitby**, on the north coast, is rather spread out along the road, but this is where the few hotels are. Several expatriates have built their homes along Whitby Beach. Sandflies can be a problem in this area, particularly if there is not enough wind, take insect repellent. **Sandy Point**, in the west, is a fishing community. North Caicos is the centre of basket making in the islands and there are several women, including Clementine Mackintosh, Eliza Swan and Cassandra Gardiner, who are expert in their craft. Prices do not vary much from those in the shops in Providenciales or locally. Eliza Swan is based in Whitby and makes beautiful bags and baskets using many colours and designs. **Wades Green Plantation**, just to the west of Kew, is the best example of a Loyalist plantation in the islands, with many ruins, including a courtyard and a prison. Archaeologists from the University of California in Los Angeles carried out excavations in 1989. The boutique section of *Papa Grunt's* restaurant in the Whitby Plaza sells crafts, potions and insect repellent cheaper than on Provo.

You are advised to bring small denomination US dollar notes as there is no bank and it is difficult to cash US$50 or US$100, travellers' cheques or money orders around the island.

Turks & Caicos Islands

Sleeping

All accommodation is in the Whitby beach area on the N coast

LL *Datai Villa*, www.datai-villa.com New in 1999, on beach, 2 separate buildings open on to patio with large deck, master bedroom in one, 2 further bedrooms in the other, sleep 2-6 people. **LL-L** *Club Vacanze* (formerly *The Prospect of Whitby*), T9467119, F9467114. A long-established hotel, nearly all guests are on an all-inclusive Italian package, luxury accommodation, very little English spoken by Italian staff, not recommended for non-Italians, pool, tennis. **LL-AL** *Ocean Beach*, T9467113, F9467386. 10 units in condominiums, room only or suites, with up to 3 bedrooms, dining room/lounge, freshwater swimming pool, diving on site and excursions with Beach Cruiser Charters. **LL-AL** *Pelican Beach Hotel*, T9467112, F9467139, www.tcim all.tc/pelicanbeach Friendly, relaxed, few facilities, 14 rooms, 2 suites, the older rooms face the beach, new packages available, run by Clifford and Susan Gardiner. **L-AL** *Bottle Creek Lodge*, T9467080, www.bottlecreeklodge.com Run by Howard and Cheryl Gibbs, members of Ecotourism Socety, lodge room or detached cabin, on top of small ridge on northeast side of Flamingo Pond, all rooms sea view, composting toilets, overhead banana leaf fans, special diets catered for, CP, kayaks, bicycles. **L-AL** *Oceanside Villa*, T/F9467301, joannesbnb@tciway.tc 3 bedrooms, 2 en suite bathrooms, large, bright, airy, comfortable, screened veranda, secluded, 300ft from beach, all rooms ocean view. Under same ownership is **AL-A** *Jo Anne's Whitby Plaza Bed & Breakfast*, T/F as for *Oceanside Villa*. Large, comfortable rooms or suites with bath, hot water, fans, king, queen or twin beds, private entrances and veranda, also 4-room housekeeping unit, short walk to Whitby beach, bicycle, kayak and canoe rental, *Papa Grunt's*, on premises. **A** *Hollywood Beach Condos*, Whitby, T9467185, F9464451. 4 1-bed units with kitchen on the beach, transportation, fishing, diving arranged, bring your own food. **A** *North Caicos Villas*, T/F9467308. One 1,200sq ft and one 800sq ft villas, all watersports, transportation arranged, bring your own food.

Eating

Simple local restaurants include *Club Titter's Restaurant and Bar*, near the airport, and *Marina View* on Kew Rd, very simple, not always open. Italian at the private *Club Vacanze*, reservations necessary. *Papa Grunt's Restaurant*, Whitby Plaza. Open 0830, credit cards accepted, indoor or screened veranda dining, native and American cuisine, fresh seafood, lots of conch, sandwiches with homemade bread US$5.75, pizza, salads, vegetarian platter, open Sun 1100-1400 for lunch. Phone, fax and email service offered in the office area. *Pelican Beach Hotel* serves good food but is only open if there are guests at the hotel.

Watersports

Diving *Beach Cruiser* at the *Ocean Beach Hotel*, T9467113, offers diving, US$50 for one-tank dive, US$80 for two-tank dive, minimum 4 people, packages and equipment hire available. Snorkelling trips also offered. **Fishing** US$200 a half day or US$375 a whole day, maximum four people, with *Beach Cruiser*. For unspoiled backwater bonefishing/flat bottom fishing, contact Whitby Plaza for trips on 27 ft launch boat. Lunch included with all day trips. **Sailing** There is a 20 ft pontoon 'flat top' boat for hire, from *Beach Cruiser*, offering trips of 1 hour, half day or full day, picnics, snorkelling etc, island hopping and visits to see iguanas on Salt Water Cay.

Transport

Air *Inter Island Airways* and *Global Airways*, run by the Gardiner family, popular private pilots, fly to North Caicos from Provo daily after your flight arrives. Cost is US$30 one way 12 mins. *TCA* has only one morning flight and one afternoon flight (never on Sun) from Provo but these are not reliable or leave to a set schedule (advise not to buy a return ticket despite what local airlines suggest as you may not return with same plane/pilot and you will have to pay again). If you wish to charter a plane the cost is US$125 (you have to pay for all the empty seats). **Road** For day trips or overnight stays you can rent a cruising bicycle at *Papa Grunts* restaurant at Whitby Plaza, island map supplied. Rates are US$15 per person per 24 hrs, for weekly rates seventh day free, credit card deposit required, T/F9467301. There are car hire facilities on North Caicos with *Saunders Rent A Car*, VHF Channel 16 'Sierra 7', or *Gardiners Auto Service*, US$35 for half day, US$70 for full day, plus US$10 tax. A taxi costs US$10 from the airport to Whitby for one person, US$12 for 2, US$15 for 3. Taxi from Sandy Point to Whitby is US$20. A tour of the island by taxi costs US$80-100, the drivers are friendly and knowledgeable but some tend to run their own errands while working.

The Turks and Caicos National Trust

The National Trust is a relatively new, non-profit, non-governmental conservation organization, working in co-operation with the Government, the World Wildlife Fund, The Nature Conservancy and local people to preserve the natural and historical heritage of the islands and develop sustainable tourism to keep the Turks and Caicos Islands 'beautiful by nature'. Projects in hand include: an exhibition on national parks, endangered animals and the islands' history in the departure terminal at Provo airport; a historically-oriented public park around the *Cheshire Hall plantation ruins near downtown Provo; public access to the 100-acre Bird Rock Point Natural Area on the northeast tip of Provo for walking and birdwatching; a fund-raising campaign and work with the Government on a financial framework for the long-term management of the national parks. For information on the National Trust, to become a member or volunteer, contact Ethlyn Gibbs-Williams, the National Trust of the Turks and Caicos Islands, Providenciales, T9415710.*

Parrot Cay

The *Parrot Cay Resort*, a luxury, 56-room hotel, was built in 1992 on this 1,300-acre private island, but it only opened in December 1998. It has already attracted the rich and famous, with a guest list that includes Paul McCartney and Bruce Willis, and it is frequently featured in glossy magazines and TV travel shows. It has beautiful landscaping, the largest freshwater pool in the TCI, two restaurants, tennis courts, gym and offers all watersports. The furniture is Indonesian, some of the staff are Asian and the food is Asian-influenced. You can have a Thai, Balinese or Swedish massage. Cotton used to be grown here and there are the remains of a plantation house. The wetlands and mangroves are to be preserved to protect wildlife. Rates start at US$460 in low season. T9467788, F9467789, www.Provo.net/ParrotCay

Dellis Cay Dellis Cay is uninhabited but frequently visited for its shells. A popular excursion is to be dropped off there for the day for shelling by a local charter boat out of Leeward Marina, no facilities.

Pine Cay

Pine Cay is an 800-acre private resort owned by a group of homeowners who also own the exclusive 12 room **LL** *Meridian Club*. Children under six years are not allowed to stay in the hotel and there are lots of restrictions on where they are allowed if brought to a villa. The homes, which are very comfortable, with spectacular views, can be rented from US$475-650 per person per day or US$2,960 per week to US$4,815 for 10 days per couple. A hurricane in 1969 left Pine Cay 5ft underwater for a while and since then the houses have been built slightly back from the beach and many of them are on stilts. There is a fairly well-stocked commissary or you can eat in the hotel; golf carts are used to get around the island. ■ *Nov-Jun. Reservations can be made through Resorts Management Inc, T800-3319154, 212-6964566, F212-6891598, locally T/F9465128.* Non-motorized watersports and tennis are available and excursions to other cays can be arranged. May is a popular time for bonefishing. Day trippers are not encouraged although visitors may come for lunch at the restaurant by prior reservation as long as they do not use the facilities; the homeowners value their privacy and put a ban on visitors if they feel there have been too many. Pine Cay benefits from a few freshwater ponds and wells, so water is no problem here and the vegetation is more lush than on Provo. On the other hand mosquito control is a constant problem. Nature trails have been laid out around the ponds and through the trees. **Water Cay** is a nature reserve and although classified as a separate island, is joined to Pine Cay by sand dunes created during the 1969

Turks & Caicos Islands

hurricane. There is an airstrip, guests usually charter a flight, and a dock if they prefer to come in with the *Meridian Club's* exclusive shuttle boat.

Little Water Cay Little Water Cay is the nearest island to Provo and inhabited by iguanas. The endangered Turks and Caicos rock iguana is now protected from threatening human presence by boardwalks which protect their burrows and nesting chambers, and there are strict rules against feeding them. A visitor's fee is charged to continue their protection. (Most tour operators have day trips, see page 328.)

Providenciales

Population:
over 10,000

'Provo' is 25 miles long and about three wide. Twelve mile Grace Bay on the north shore has many hotels and condominiums but you can walk and snorkel without feeling crowded. A surge of building work has transformed Grace Bay in the last 10 years as a string of hotels and a golf course have sprung up. Away from the smart hotels, condos and villas, however, the island is dry, scrubby and nothing like as pretty as the underwater world surrounding it. The reef is superb and attracts thousands of divers every year.

Ins & outs
See page 323 for international air services & transport for other details

Getting there Scheduled internal flights with *TCA* and *SkyKing*. Charter companies are *TCA, Inter Island Airways, Flamingo Air Services, Provo Air Charter, TCI SkyKing* and *Global Air Charters*. **Getting around** Most roads are paved, contributing to fast, erratic driving by residents; speed limits (40 mph highway, 20 mph in town) are not observed, dangerous overtaking is common. Hired cars are not generally well serviced, exchanges are common. Taxis charge US$2 per mile, a ride for one person from the airport to the *Allegro* is US$12-15, and a round trip to a restaurant or Downtown can be US$40. Tours and shopping trips about US$25 per hour. Complaints have not lowered the rates. There are usually taxis at the large hotels, otherwise phone for one.

Around the island

The **Princess Alexandra Marine Park** incorporates the reef offshore. Development of the island began in 1967 although it had been settled in the 18th century and there were three large plantations in the 19th century growing cotton and sisal. The three original settlements, **The Bight** (meaning Bay), **Five Cays** and **Blue Hills**, are fragmented and have not grown into towns as the population has increased. Instead shopping malls have been built along the Leeward Highway (Market Place, Plantation Hills, Central Square, Provo Plaza, retail stores, restaurants, lawyers and business offices). The Office of the Chief Secretary, banks, law firms, supermarkets, and travel agents are **Down Town**. **Turtle Cove** calls itself 'the heart of Provo', with a couple of hotels, a marina, dive operators, boat charters, deep sea fishing, restaurants, the tourist office, hairdressing and a few boutiques.

On the south side of the island, **South Dock** is the island's commercial port and here you will find the Customs Office and the Harbourmaster. **The Caicos Marina and Shipyard** on the south coast is many miles from shopping supplies, but it has recently changed hands and the new management is upgrading the facilities. Also on the south side is a small marina: **South Side Marina**. To the west, **Sapodilla Bay** offers good protection for yachts in all winds west through southeast. It is open to the south through southwest. **Chalk Sound**, a national park inland from Sapodilla Bay, is a shallow lagoon of marvellous turquoise colours, dotted with rocky islets.

At the northeast end, a deep channel known as **Leeward Going Through** is a natural harbour and a marina with fuel, water, ice and restaurant has been built here. There is a conch farm at the **Island Sea Centre** at Leeward. ■ *Hatchery tours 0900-1700, US$6 adults, US$3 children under 12, T9465330, F9465849, also gift shop.*

Northwest Point, a marine park offshore, has good beaches, diving and snorkelling. In 1993 a French television company shot a series of underwater game shows

Jo Jo

A bottle-nosed dolphin, known as Jo Jo, frequents the Princess Alexandra Marine Park along the north coast of Providenciales in the Grace Bay area, although he is also found occasionally in other locations. He is attracted by boats (particularly propeller noise and bubbles) and humans, apparently enjoying swimming and playing with people, while often coming in very close to the shore. If you are fortunate enough to see or swim with him, remember that he is a protected wild animal: do not touch him. He has been injured by propellers in the past, so take care if you are in a boat. Although there is a campaign for boats to fit a protective covering, very few watersports operators have agreed to do so. The Turks & Caicos Free Press of 27 March 1998 quoted one charter vessel captain as saying "We're not going to go crazy about one dolphin". The government has declared Jo Jo to be a National Treasure, but little is done to protect him. Dean Bernal, who runs public awareness campaigns on the island, has repeatedly called for special propeller guards to be fitted to Club Med waterski boats and has even offered to purchase them himself, to no avail. There is now a campaign to ban waterskiing in the marine park. For more information contact Jo Jo's warden at VHF 'Sea Base' channel 68 or 73 or T/F9415617, www.jojo.tc; the Jo Jo Dolphin Project is supported by the Bellerive Foundation. Dean Bernal can be contacted on jojo1@tciway.tc If you want to express your concern to the authorities, write to governoroffice@tciway.tc, with a copy to Dean.

here and a treacherous road was bulldozed through to the beautiful beach. They left several tiki huts which offer much needed shade for a day on the beach. Two other good places to snorkel in the Grace Bay area are just to the east of Turtle Cove, where rays and turtles can be seen on Smith's reef near the entrance to the marina, and just west of *Treasure Beach Villas*, by the White House, where there is a variety of life, including grouper, ask anybody for directions.

Inland, along Seasage Hill Road in Long Bay, is **The Hole**, a collapsed limestone, water-filled sinkhole next to a house called *By the Hole*. A tunnel to the right hand side gives access to the main pool. Do not attempt to descend. Ruins of Loyalist and Bermudian settlers' plantations and houses can be seen at **Cheshire Hall**, Richmond Hills and along the Bight road. On the hill overlooking the *Mariner Hotel* at Sapodilla Bay a pole marks the location of stones engraved with initials and dates in the 18th century possibly by shipwrecked sailors or wreckers.

Essentials

There are 3 new developments on Grace Bay Beach, all of which are hotel/condominiums with full service and restaurants: **LL** *Ocean Club West*, T9465880, F9465845, www.oceanclubresorts.com 4 buildings with 40 suites expanding to 7 buildings with 90 suites by end-2000, all resort facilities available. **LL** *Point Grace*, T9465096, F9465097, www.pointgrace.tc 31 suites in 2 condos on the beach and 4 3-plex cottages directly behind them. **LL** *The Sands Resort*, T9465199, F9465198, www.thesandsresort.com On the beach, opened end-1998, 72 units in 3 buildings, soon to have 105 suites and rooms in 5

Sleeping

When confirming rates & availability, check whether tax & service are included

Turks & Caicos Islands

buildings, 2 pools, extensive landscaping. **LL-L** *Allegro Resort & Casino* (formerly *Turquoise Reef*, soon to become an Occidental hotel), newly renovated beach front all-inclusive, 222 rooms, restaurants, pools. **LL** *Grace Bay Club*, on beach, T9465757, F9465758, www.gracebay.com Luxury accommodation, 22 elegant condos, a/c, phone, TV, watersports, tennis, pool, jacuzzi, all amenities, French restaurant, beach bar. **LL-L** *Le Deck Hotel and Beach Club*, T9465547, F9465770, ledeck@tciway.tc Same management as *Turtle Cove Inn* and also recently renovated. 26 rooms and condos, golf packages, restaurant, lovely bougainvillea in the courtyard, pool. **LL-L** *Ocean Club Beach and Golf Resort*, PO Box 240, T9465880, F9465845, oceanclb@tciway.tc Condos on the beach, comfortable, well-equipped, balconies, some with good views the length of Grace Bay, spacious deck around pool with daytime snack bar, next to Provo Golf Club, packages available, free transport to airport, bike rentals. **LL-AL** *Beaches Turks and Caicos Resort and Spa*, T9468000, F9468001. All-inclusive, luxury beachfront Sandals resort, 225 rooms and villa suites, being expanded 1999, facilities for handicapped, free form pool, 5 restaurants, 6 bars, all watersports, including scuba, land sports, fitness centre, spa, imported landscaping. **LL-AL** *Caribbean Paradise Inn*, T9465020, F9465022, www.paradise.tc 200yds from beach, by *Grace Bay Club*, 15 rooms, ocean or pool view, including breakfast buffet, snacks available, new, popular, dive gear storage, German-owned and managed. **LL-AL** *Club Méditerranée Turkoise*, Grace Bay, T9465500, F9465501. Stays on daylight savings time all year, 298 all-inclusive rooms, weekly rates, no children under 12, completely remodelled in 1999, rooms now have door locks, hairdryers, phones, TV, new bathrooms, while restaurant, bar and reception area have also been renovated, keen young organizers, lots of watersports including controversial motorized watersports in National Marine Park, communal dining, diving and golf arranged at extra cost. **LL-AL** *Platinum Resort Villas* at Leeward, T9465539, F9465421. Ask for Jean Taylor, a/c, TV, phone, 1-4

Providenciales

■ **Sleeping**

1 Allegro Resort	4 Club Mediteranée	6 Erebus Inn
2 Beaches Resort	5 Crystal Bay Resort	7 Grace Bay Club
3 Caribbean Paradise Inn	Condominiums	8 Island Princess

N
Not to scale

bedroomed villas with kitchens, sleep 2-8, including car. **LL-AL** *Turtle Cove Inn*, T9464203, F9464141, tcinn@tciway.tc 3 rate schedules, special weekly 5 packages, recently renovated with new management, 30 rooms, poolside or ocean view, smallish rooms but comfortable, suite with kitchenette available, not on beach, all watersports, at the marina, cable TV, 2 restaurants.

Along the north shore on the beach heading east are **L** *Treasure Beach Villas*, T9464325, F9464108. Run down, 18 self-catering apartments, 1-2 bedrooms, no restaurant, swimming pool. **L-A** *Erebus Inn*, on hillside overlooking Turtle Cove, T9464240, F9464704, www.erebus.tc 26 rooms, larger than those in other hotels, and a few basic chalets with wonderful views liked by divers, dive packages available, all watersports at the marina, gym and fitness centre on site, pool, tennis, 2 rooms fully equipped for ham radio operators. **B** *Airport Inn*, T9464701/9413514, F9413281, airport@tciway.tc. 2 mins to airport, close to banks, groceries, restaurants, 19 rooms, 24-hr service, shops and restaurant on site, a/c, TV, special rates for pilots, 15% discount if you book room and rental car.

In the Sapodilla area there are self-catering villas: *Casuarina Cottages*, T9464474, F9464433. 3 units, US$800-1,000 a week. *Villa Bella Casa*, 3 bed villa on Leeward Beach, T/F9465037. US$2,500 per week, guest house US$1,500 per week. *The Cottage*, Grace Bay, call Kit T9465376, F9465792, southfleetwood@tciway.tc. Guest house with pool, sleeps 4, US$150 per night, US$1,000 per week. *Villa Camilla*, on Grace Bay, T617-7312194 for rates/availability. Accommodates 2-14 people, 3 bed/3 bath villa and guest house. Tojo Properties *Caribbean Ocean View Flats*, T9413101, F9413102. Villa with 4 large 2 bed apartments, pool, all amenities. **LL** *Coral Gardens* at *White House Villa* on Grace Bay, T/F9413713, coralgardn@tciway.tc. Best snorkelling site, 12 'boutique residences' for sale or rental, 1-2 bedrooms or junior suite. **LL-L** *Crystal Bay Resort Condominiums*, T9464929, F9464825. 27 rooms, 5 miles from anywhere on the north shore, sales staff trying to sell condos.

There are plenty of self-catering condos & villas around the island

Turtle Cove *Banana Boat*, T9415706. **Eating** Dockside at Turtle Cove marina, Caribbean bar and grill, colourful, cheerful. *Sharkbite Bar and Grill*, Admiral's Club, on the water, 1100-2400, happy hour 1700-1900, nightly specials and events, T9415090. *Sunset Restaurant & Bar* , at the *Erebus* overlooking Turtle Cove, T9464240, erebus@tciway.tc. Spectacular view, serving Northwest style seafood with a Caribbean flair. *The Terrace*, T9464763. 'Creative' conch, seafood, lunch, dinner, closed Sun. *Tiki Hut*, at *Turtle Cove Inn*, T9465341. Breakfast, lunch and dinner, chicken or ribs every Wed night, US$10, extremely popular with ex-pats.

Down Town *Club Latino Bar & Grill*, open 24 hrs, slots, chicken 'n' ribs, nightclub and disco after 2000 behind Ward Construction building. *Lamont's*, T9416115. Pink building, native and absolutely-everything-American menu, to go, 0600-2300 Mon-Sat, 0900-2300 Sun. *Nyammings*, on Old Airport Rd, T9413709. New, native food with Jamaican twist. *Sweet T's Meals On Wheels*, next

Turks & Caicos Islands

9 Le Deck
10 Ocean Club
11 Point Grace
12 Treasure Beach Villas
13 Turtle Cove Inn

to Texaco service station. Native dishes, open 0600-2200, closed Sun, proprietor Mary Simmons. *Tasty Temptations*, next to the dry cleaners, T9464049. French breakfasts, sandwiches, fresh salads for lunch, good coffee, deli, open 0630-1500, closed Sat-Sun.

Airport Road   Within walking distance from the airport is *Fast Eddie's*, T9413176. Wed night buffet, open 0730-2300. Excellent native food, no alcohol on premises, reservations for groups. *Frances Place*, T9464472. Family dining 0600-2200, Jamaican touch, TV, slots, closed Sun. *Gilley's* is the only place to eat at the airport, a/c, noisy, local hangout, indifferent service and menu. 5 mins' walk from airport, *Rolling Pin Hotte Shoppe Restaurant*, T9415023. Immaculate indoor or outdoor seating, Trinidadian and native food, curry and roti, salads, 0900-2100, at Airport Plaza near *Airport Inn*. *Where Its At*, T9464185. Jamaican specialities by Yvette, curried goat and Presidente beer by the quart a must, generous portions, daily specials, 0630-2300, *Turn Table Disco* next door.

Leeward Highway   *China Restaurant*, T9465377. Mandarin cuisine, Chinese chef, a/c, open daily, no lunch Sun. In the Bight, the *Cabana Bar at Coral Gardens & White House Villas* serves conch and fish lunches 1230-1430.   *Dora's Restaurant and Bar*, near PPC power station, T9464558. Open from 0730 until very late, local recipes, filling, eat in or takeaway. *Hemingway's on the beach* is the restaurant at the *Sands Resort*, T9465199. Open daily for breakfast, lunch and dinner featuring fresh seafoods. *Hey José Cantina*, near the Tourist Shoppe, Central Square Shopping Centre, T9464812. Great food, Mexican/American, tacos, huge pizza etc, 1200-2200, closed Sunday, takeaways. At Market Place, *Mackie's Café*, T9413640. Native style breakfast and lunch daily, stewed fish and Johnny cake, Sun morning, 0800-1900, fresh seafood.   At Provo Plaza, east of WIV, TV satellite dishes, *Pizza Pizza*, T9413577, New York style pizza, 7 days a week, eat in or takeaway. Recommended.*Top O' The Cove Deli*, next to Napa auto at Suzie Turn. 'Little bit of New York-style deli', subs, bagels, order lunch by T/F9464694, beer, wine, picnic food, open 0630-1530 daily.

Grace Bay (west to east)   *Beaches Turks and Caicos Resort and Spa*, T9468000. 5 restaurants, international, continental, Tex-Mex, oriental, native style fish, visitors to property must have day/evening pass, 6 bars. *Le Deck's Le Jardin Restaurant*, T9465547. Open from 0700, European/French, Fri make your own pizza, Sun buffet US$19.95 all-you-can-eat, drinks and dessert extra, slow service, recommended in season. *Jungle Hut Café*, in newly-opened Grace Bay Plaza, native cuisine, ladies' nights, closed Tue. *Bella Luna Ristorante*, in the *Glass House* west of *Allegro*, T9465214. Dinner 1800-2130 daily, nightly specials, reservations recommended. At the Ports of Call shopping centre across the street from *Allegro*, *Lattitudes*, Tex Mex, T9465832, F9464624. Seafood and more for lunch and dinner 6 days a week, run by Jeff and Diane, formerly of *Hey José Cantina*. *Barefoot Café*, T946-JAVA. 0630-late, daily bagels, subs, cappuccino, ice cream etc. Next to Ports of Call, *Caicos Café & Grill*, T9465278. Home made pasta with French flair, grilled fish and seafood, service personal but slow, go early or late to avoid crowds, open-air, open daily 1200-2400. *Coco Bistro*, past *Caicos Café*, east of *Allegro* near *Club Med*, behind Sunshine Nursery in mature palm trees, T9465369. Indoor dining/bar, or outdoors under the palms, Mediterranean cooking, specials every night, daily for dinner, reservations advised, congenial hosts and service. East of *Allegro Resort*, *Anacaona* restaurant and bar on the beach, T9465050. Thatched roof elegance, nouvelle cuisine with Caribbean flair, exclusive and expensive, live music some evenings, guests only, reservations recommended. *Ocean Club's Cabana Bar & Grill*, T9465880, lunch, drinks, only, poolside, expensive, indifferent service. Adjacent to *Ocean Club*, *Gecko Grille*, Ocean Club Plaza, T9465885. Pretentious, opt for garden dining as indoor noise level unpleasant, bar opens 1630-2400, dining 1800-2200 daily. *Fairways Bar & Grill*, opposite *Ocean Club*, Provo Golf Course Clubhouse, T9465991. Breakfast, lunch and dinner, Wed lunch specials, Fri happy hour, popular with doctors, lawyers, business people and visiting golfers, same management as *The Terrace* in Turtle Cove.

Leeward going through   At the east end of Providenciales is *Gilley's at Leeward*, T9465094. Open from 0800-2200, by the marina, breakfast, lunch specials, good food, friendly, superb service, meet local fishermen, arrange outings, boat trips, elegant, romantic dinners.

Blue Hills settlement   *Conch House*, everything conch, 1100-late, Mon-Sat. *Caribbean Mack* (formerly *Roadrunner*). Soca, reggae, latino, nightly till late. *Pub On the Bay*, T9414453. Not to be missed, indoor or tiki hut dining on the beach, great native dishes, lobster, conch, buffets, sometimes live band. *Three Queens Bar & Restaurant*, T9415984. Excellent, reasonably-priced, local seafood lunches and dinners, by reservation only as the restaurant section is not always open.

Cinema   *Village Cinemas* is a new 2-screen movie theatre complex which will seat 370 people, T9414108.

Entertainment

Bus   *Stafford Morris' Blue Bus*, VHF16, pickup and delivery almost anywhere, including the airport, US$3 per person each way say Downtown to Grace Bay, T9413598 or flag him down. *Pelican Bus Service*, T9464092, VHF 67. **Car & bike hire**   An economy car, quoted at US$39 per day will work out to US$61.50 with taxes and insurance. Deposits are at least US$400. A 'gold' credit card qualifies for an exemption of US$11.95 per day CDW. *Provo Rent A Car*, PO Box 137, T9464404, F9464993, rentacar@Provo.net, at the airport, T9465610, a/c vehicles, jeeps, vans, recommended. *Hertz*, PO Box 66, Central Leeward Highway, T9413910, F9415213. *Budget*, Down Town, Town Centre Mall, open Mon-Sat, 0800-1700, Sun 1000-1600, T9464709, worldwide reservations 800-5270700, Suzukis, Mitsubishis, 1 day free for weekly rental. *Tropical Auto Rental*, Tropicana Plaza and *Ocean Club Condos* at Grace Bay, T9465300, F9465456, **Turks & Caicos National Car Rental**, Airport Rd, T/F9464701/ 9413514, F9413281, not always reliable vehicles delivery. *Rent-a-Buggy*, Leeward Highway, T9464158, Suzuki jeeps, VW Thing. *Provo Fun Cycles* at Ports of Call across from *Allegro*, single scooters US$25 per day, doubles US$39, packages, can take them to North Caicos on the ferry, Honda motorcycles, also bicycles and jeeps, T9465868, Provofuncycles@Provo.net; *Sunrise Auto Rental*, jeeps and scooters, Leeward Highway and *Club Med*, T9469730. *Avis* at airport and Bayview Motors, Leeward Highway, T9464705, F9464810, at *Club Med*, T9469730, Avis@provo.net, affiliated with Sunrise Auto Rental; *Scooter Bob's*, Turtle Cove Marina, T9464684, F9464283, vans, scooters and bicycles, Mon-Sat 0900-1700, Sun 0900-1200. **Taxi**: *Paradise Taxi Co*, T9413555. *Nell's Taxi*, T9413228, 9464971; *Island's Choice Taxi*, T9410409; *Provo Taxi Association* T9465481.

Transport
Be careful on the roads. Leeward Highway is especially risky

Rugged and uninhabited but worth visiting for its beautiful beach on the northwest coast and excellent diving offshore. The east shore is a marine park. Inland there is a saltwater lake, Lake Catherine, which rises and falls with the tides and is a nature reserve, home to migrant nesting flamingos, ducks and waders. The ruins of Yankee Town, its sisal press and railroad are a surface interval destination for scuba divers and sailors.

West Caicos
Once frequented by pirates, there are many wrecks between here & Provo

An old pirate lair, now uninhabited, with exceptional marine life. It has been designated a sanctuary for frigate birds, osprey and nesting seabirds.

French Cay

Turks & Caicos Islands

Background

History

The islands' first dwellers were the peaceful Tainos, who left behind ancient utensils and little else. By the middle of the 16th century not one Lucayan, as Columbus named them, remained. Like the Lucayans in the Bahamas islands, they were kidnapped for use as slaves or pearl divers, while many others died of imported diseases. The discovery of the islands, whether by Columbus in 1492 or later by Ponce de León, is hotly disputed. There is a very convincing argument that Columbus' first landfall was on Grand Turk, not Watling Island in the Bahamas, now officially named San Salvador. The infamous Caicos Banks south of the Caicos group, where in the space of 1,000yds the water depth changes from 6,000 to 30ft, claimed many of the Spanish ships lost in the central Caribbean from the 16th to the 18th century.

The Bermudan traders who settled on the islands of Grand Turk, Salt Cay, and South Caicos in the 17th century used slaves to rake salt for sale to British colonies on the American mainland, and fought pirates and buccaneers for over 200 years. During the American Revolution, British loyalists found refuge on the islands, setting up cotton and sisal plantations with the labour of imported slaves. For a while, cotton and sisal from the islands were sold in New York and London, solar salt became the staple of the economy, and the Turks and Caicos thrived, but all these products encountered overwhelming competition from elsewhere. The thin soil was an added disadvantage and a hurricane in 1813 marked the demise of cotton plantations.

Following an alternation of Spanish, French and British control, the group became part of the Bahamas colony in 1766. Attempts to integrate the Turks and Caicos failed, rule from Nassau was unpopular and inefficient and abandoned in 1848. Links with Jamaica were more developed, partly because London-Kingston boats visited frequently. The Turks and Caicos were annexed to Jamaica in 1874. After Jamaica's independence in 1962, they were loosely associated with the Bahamas for just over 10 years until the latter became independent. At that point, the Turks and Caicos became a British Crown Colony (now a Dependent Territory). The Anglican Church maintained its links with the Bahamas, which is where the Bishop resides.

The main political parties were established in 1976: the People's Democratic Movement (PDM) and the Progressive National Party (PNP). From time to time independence is raised as a political issue but does not have universal support.

The isolation of the Turks and Caicos and the benign neglect of the British government led to increasing use of the islands as refuelling posts by drug smugglers *en route* from South America to Florida. Constitutional government was suspended in 1986 after it was discovered that several Ministers were involved and direct rule from the UK was imposed while investigations continued into malpractice by other public officials. The Chief Minister and the Minister of Development were imprisoned for accepting bribes to allow drugs planes to refuel on South Caicos. The islands are still being used for trans-shipment of cocaine and other drugs.

In 1988, general elections restored constitutional government. These were won by the PDM, and Oswald Skippings took office as Chief Minister. The April 1991 elections brought the PNP, led by Washington Missick, back to power, but economic austerity measures and civil service job cuts cost the PNP its mandate and in 1995 the PDM was returned to office, holding eight seats over the PNP's four. The 13th seat was held by an independent. Continuity was assured when the PDM won the 1999 elections with a convincing mandate, taking nine seats while the PNP won four again. The Chief Minister is Derek Taylor, leader of the PDM since 1991.

Geography and people

The main islands of the Turks group, Grand Turk and Salt Cay, shelter 20% of the colony's 7,901 'belongers', as the islanders call themselves, but only 15% of the total resident population of 19,000, which includes many Haitians, Dominicans and ex-pat North Americans. The rest of the population is scattered among the larger Caicos group to the west: South Caicos, Middle (or Grand) Caicos, North Caicos, and Providenciales, the most populous, known locally as 'Provo'; Pine Cay and Parrot Cay are privately owned resort islands; East and West Caicos, inhabited from 1797 to the mid-19th century, are now the private domain of wild animals. East Caicos is home to swarms of mosquitoes and wild cattle, while West Caicos harbours land crabs, nesting pairs of ospreys and flamingos. Most of the smaller cays are uninhabited. The people of the Turks and Caicos are welcoming and friendly. The development of tourism on Provo has changed attitudes there, however, and friendliness is not universal.

Government

The Turks and Caicos are a British Dependent Territory. The British monarch is Head of State, represented by a Governor, currently John Kelly. The Executive Council chaired by the Governor is formed by six ministers, the Financial Secretary, the Attorney General and the Chief Secretary, the last two being British government appointments. Mrs Cynthia Astwood, the first Turks Islander, took over as Chief Secretary when the present British appointee left. The Legislative Council has 13 elected members and two party-appointed members.

The economy

The traditional economic activity, salt production, ceased in 1964, and for two decades there was little to generate legal income apart from fishing, government employment and some tourism. National resources are limited, even water has to be strictly conserved. Agriculture is almost non-existent. Practically all consumer goods and most foodstuffs are imported. The lack of major employment activities led in the 1960s and 1970s to thousands of local people emigrating to the nearby Bahamas or the USA to seek work. This trend has now been reversed as the economy has improved and the population is rising. Belongers have returned to work in the tourist industry and professionals trained abroad are returning to work as lawyers, accountants, etc. Poorly paid skilled and unskilled labour, much of it illegal, comes from Haiti and the Dominican Republic.

One area of growth has been that of offshore companies, over 14,000 of which were registered in the islands by 1997. There is no income tax, no company tax, no exchange control and no restriction on the nationality or residence of shareholders or directors. New legislation and the creation of the Offshore Finance Centre Unit (OFCU) were designed to regulate and promote the growth of offshore finance and encourage banking, insurance and trust companies. Five international banks have been granted offshore licences and some 2,000 offshore insurance companies have been licensed. Government revenue from offshore financial services was over US$6mn in 1997/98.

Budgetary aid from the UK for recurrent expenditure was eliminated in fiscal year 1986/87 and the islands are aiming to be self-financing. Capital aid from the UK remains, augmented by financial assistance from the European Community, the European Investment Bank and the Caribbean Development Bank.

One of the main areas of economic growth and revenue for the islands is tourism. Investment has taken place in infrastructure, particularly airfields, hotels and marinas, nearly all on Providenciales. The opening of a *Club Méditerranée* in 1984 doubled the number of visitors to the Turks and Caicos in two years. By 1991, the annual number of visitors reached 54,616, from 11,900 in 1980. The collapse of PanAm in 1992 threatened devastation of the local economy, only averted when American Airlines started flying from Miami to Provo. Numerous North American charters helped to push tourist numbers up to nearly 100,000 in 1997.

Turks & Caicos Islands

Haiti

8

Haiti

Haiti is an Indian word meaning 'high ground'. It is the Caribbean's most mountainous country. Except for a few small, mainly coastal plains and the central Artibonite River valley, the entire country is a mass of ranges. The highest peak is the 2,674m La Selle, southeast of the capital. Little remains of Haiti's once luxuriant forest cover, cut down for fuel or to make way for farming. With soil erosion and desertification far advanced, Haiti is an ecological disaster. The main regions still regularly receiving abundant rainfall are the southwest peninsula and the eastern two thirds of the northern seaboard.

The Republic of Haiti occupies the western third of the island. Haitian Créole is the only language of 85 percent of its inhabitants. It evolved from French into a distinct language. The other 15 percent speak Créole and French. About 95 percent are of virtually pure African descent. The rest are mostly mulattoes, the descendants of unions between French masters and African slaves. Haiti is famous for being the only country to have a successful slave revolt; whites have not governed for two centuries. As a result, African customs persist strongly, most noticeable in language, art, music, dance and religion, where voodoo is widely practised. Nevertheless, the influence of former French colonists and merchants is still evident, particularly in architecture, with many old buildings enhanced by the gingerbread style of elaborate fretwork, balconies and decorated gables.

Essentials

Before you travel

Documents All visitors need **passports** valid for at least six months after your departure date from Haiti. **Visas** are not needed for anyone staying 90 days or less, but everyone must have an onward ticket. All visitors, except cruise ship passengers, must complete an embarkation/disembarkation card on the plane; this is valid for 90 days, and may be extended. Keep your passport (or a copy) with you as identification to satisfy the many police controls when travelling in the interior. Baggage inspection is thorough and drug-enforcement laws are strict. There is no restriction on foreign currency. You may bring in 1 quart of spirits, and 200 cigarettes or 50 cigars. There are no export limitations.

Money
Try to break down large notes whenever possible

Currency The unit is the gourde (Cr: goud), divided into 100 centimes (Cr: kòb). Coins in circulation are for 5, 10, 20 and 50 centimes, notes for 1, 2, 5, 10, 25, 50, 100, 250 and 500 gourdes. Some 100 gourde notes are plastic, faded, smeared and look like forgeries; they are not. They have 'American Banknote Company' printed on them. Small denomination notes are in appalling condition and there is always a shortage of them. 500 gourde notes are next to useless unless you can break them down at a bank or spend them at expensive hotels: ask for smaller denominations. Coins are few and far between.

Exchange The gourde was tied at 5 to the dollar during the US occupation. In the 1980s it began to trade at a slightly lower value on a parallel market, but the official rate was kept until 1991, when the Aristide government severed the tie and let the gourde float. From 7.5 to the dollar at the time of the September 1991 coup, it fell to 15 in 1995 and 17 by mid-1997 where it stabilized. So far, so good. Now it gets complicated. Haitians routinely refer to their own money as dollars, based on the old 5 to 1 rate. Thus, 5 gourdes is called a dollar, 10 gourdes is 2 dollars, 25 gourdes is 5 dollars, etc. Prices in shops are usually in Haitian dollars, therefore multiply by five to get the price in gourdes. Visitors must constantly clarify whether the price being quoted is in Haitian or American dollars, or gourdes, now increasingly used on bills. US coins co-circulate with local coins. They are treated as if the old 5 to 1 rate was still in force. Thus, a US penny is treated as 5 kòb, a nickel is 25 kòb, and so on.

The best exchange rate is obtained from money changers, whether those on the street or those working out of offices. It is perfectly legal (see section on Port-au-Prince). The rate in banks is not far behind. It is foolish to come to Haiti with any currency other than US dollars or French francs. Currencies like sterling can be changed, but only at a massive loss. Travellers' cheques are difficult to change in some banks.

Credit cards Visa, Mastercard and American Express are widely accepted. Beware, card users will not get a good rate and are often charged a premium.

Climate
Haiti has 2 rainy seasons: Apr-May & Sep-Oct

The climate is generally very warm but the cool on- and off-shore winds of morning and evening help to make it bearable. In coastal areas temperatures vary between 20° and 35°C, being slightly hotter in April-September. The driest, coolest months are December-March. In the hill resorts the temperature is cooler.

Getting there

Air
To Port-au-Prince From Europe: *Air France* flies from Paris via Guadeloupe. **From North America**: *American Airlines* flies from New York and Miami daily. Other airlines from Miami including *ALM* and *Air France*. *Air Canada* flies from Montreal. **From Central America**: *Copa* flies from Panama City. **From the Caribbean**: *ALM* from Curaçao and Sint Maarten; *Air France* and *Air Guadeloupe* from Guadeloupe via Martinique; *Aerolíneas Santo Domingo* from Santo Domingo (see page 400); *Air Guadeloupe* from St Martin. **From South America**: *Air France* and *Air Guadeloupe* from Cayenne, French Guiane. **To Cap-Haïtien** *Turks and Caicos Airways* fly Monday-Saturday and *TCI SkyKing* five times a week from Providenciales.

Travel hints

Haiti is especially fascinating for the tourist who is avid for off-the-beaten-track experience. In order that you may make the most of your visit, we offer the following hints.

Although it is one of the poorest countries in the world, most of whose citizens suffer from one kind of oppression or another, Haiti is proud of having been the only nation to have carried out successfully a slave rebellion.

Haitians at all levels are very sensitive to how they are treated by foreigners, commonly called 'blanc'. If you treat them with warmth and consideration, they will respond with enthusiasm and friendship. There is no hostility towards 'blanc'; if you feel threatened it is probably the result of a misunderstanding. For example if someone looks at you and draws one finger across his neck, it does not mean he wants to cut your throat. Rather, it means he is hungry and is asking for a dollar.

Eye contact is very important; it is not avoided as in some other countries.

Humour plays an important role in social interactions; Haitians survive by laughing at themselves and their situation.

Haitians are physical, touching and flirting a lot.

It is important to recognize the presence of each person in a social encounter, either with a handshake or a nod. When walking in the countryside, you usually wish bon jour (before 1200) or bon soir to anyone you meet. Salud is another common greeting, at any time of day. Coffee or cola are often offered by richer peasants to visitors (Haitian coffee is among the best in the world).

Do not expect straight answers to questions about a peasant's wealth, property or income.

It is assumed that each 'blanc' is wealthy and therefore it is legitimate to try to separate you from your riches. Treat such attempts with humour, indignation or consideration as you feel appropriate.

TCA also flies Monday and Friday from Grand Turk. There are also several unscheduled or charter flights, see the Turks and Caicos chapter.

Note that flights from Miami are frequently overbooked. If you are not on a tight schedule, but have a confirmed seat, you may be asked to give your seat to a passenger with no confirmation in return for credit vouchers to be used on another flight within 12 months. Your original ticket will still be valid for the next flight, or for transfer to a different flight.

Sea Cruise ships stopped calling at Port-au-Prince years ago, partly because of passenger reaction to begging. Royal Caribbean and Crown cruise lines have leased private beaches near Cap-Haïtien for 1 day stopovers, and they have renewed their visits.

Road **Travel to the Dominican Republic** Taptaps and trucks ply the road to the border of the Dominican Republic at Malpasse/Jimaní. Repaired and improved in 1993-94 (to transport smuggled fuel), it can be done in one hour. The Ounaminthe/Dajabón crossing in the north is easily reached from Cap-Haïtien and is straightforward. You should not pay anything on leaving Haiti, but travellers have been asked for anything between US$10 and US$40 before their papers will be stamped. It is US$10 to re-enter Haiti. Visitors arriving in the Dominican Republic pay US$10. Mopeds ferry you between the Haitian and Dominican border posts for US$1. There are lots of money changers on both sides. The easiest way to get to Santo Domingo is with Terra Bus (T2237882), handled by *Chatelain Tours* (T2232400, 2225664) in Port-au-Prince, who deal with all immigration and other formalities so all you have to do is get off the bus to take care of Dominican customs, excellent service, recommended. Fare US$50 one way, US$75 return or US$80 open return, child reductions, departs Monday 0800, arrives Santo Domingo 1530, other days except Saturday departs 1400, arrives 2000, leaves from Tabarre, between Pétion-Ville and the airport, US$20 by taxi from town centre. *Tartan Tours* in Port-au-Prince; *Luz Tours*, T2231059, and *Kenya Express* (also T2231059) have weekly buses to Santo Domingo. Haitian travel agencies sometimes offer three or four day inclusive bus tours into the Dominican Republic. There are regular buses from the Dominican frontier town of Jimaní to Santo Domingo (six hours) and from Dajabón via Montecristi and Santiago de los Caballeros. Rental cars are not allowed to cross the border, but you could

See documents in Dominican Republic chapter & check with the Dominican Consulate to see if you need a visa

There is a 1-hr time difference between Haiti & the Dominican Republic

Haiti

Embassies

Canada (T2232358, F2238720), Bank of Nova Scotia Bldg, Delmas 18, BP 826
Cuba (T2576626), 18 Rue E Pierre Péguy-Ville, Pétion-Ville
Dominican Republic (T2571650, F2579215), 121 Rue Panaméricaine (50m down Rue José de San Martín), Pétion-Ville
EC Delegation (T2490141, F2490246), Delmas 60, Impasse Bravé 1, Rue Mercier Laham
France (T2220951, F2239858), 51 Place des Héros de l'Indépendance, on Rue Capois at the southwest corner of the Champs de Mars, near Hotel Palace, BP 1312
Germany (T2573128), 17 Rue Edmond Mangonès, Berthé, Pétion-Ville
Japan (T2455875, F2458834), Villa Besta Vista, Impasse Tulipe 2 Desprez, BP 2512
Spain (T2454410, F2453901), 54 Pacot, BP 386
US (T222-0200, F2231641), Boulevard Harry Truman, Bicentenaire, BP 1761 and consulate: (T2220200), 22 Rue Oswald Durand

safely leave one at the border for a few hours during a quick excursion to Jimaní. Dominican buses leave Port-au-Prince most mornings for their return trip to Santo Domingo via Malpasse, but they have no fixed time or departure point (the trip can take up to 10 hours, with two hours at the border). Ask at the *Hotel Palace* on Rue Capois, where many Dominicans stay. Buses also leave from Rue du Centre, between *Auberge Port-au-Prince* and Rue des Miracles, around 3-4 per day, mostly 25-seater a/c Mitsubishis, US$20.

Touching down

Airport information The information office at the airport is very helpful. The downstairs snackbar is cheap and friendly. Not so the upstairs restaurant at the west end of the terminal. The public area has a bookstore and a handicraft shop. Duty free goods and more crafts are on sale in the area reserved for departing passengers. Officials will allow camera film to be passed through outside the X-ray machinery.

Airlines *Air Canada* (T2460441/2): *Air France* (T2221700/1086, T2462085 at airport), 11 Rue Capois, corner Rue Ducoste, near *Le Plaza*; *ALM* (T2461090) 69 Rue Pavée, corner Rue du Peuple; *American Airlines* (T2231314, 2460100), Avenue Pie XII, near post office, always packed with people (also T2460110 at the airport); *Copa*, 35 Avenue Marie Jeanne, T2232366, or airport T2460946; *Haiti Trans Air* (T2234010/20/9258), Rue Capois near *Holiday Inn*. *Lynx Air* in Cap-Haïtien is 2621386; *TCA* T2320710.

Tourist information **Local tourist office** The Tourism Secretariat, upstairs at 8 Rue Légitime (T2232143, F2235359) and half a block from the Musée d'Art Haïtien, has poor information and no maps or brochures. Supplementary information may be sought from the Hotel and Tourism Association in Pétion-Ville, at the *Hotel Montana*, or from travel agencies. ISPAN (Institute for the Protection of the Nation's Heritage) has information on forts and plantation houses, corner of Avenue Martin Luther King and Cheriez, Pont Morin (T2453220/3118). Also at Rue 15-B, Cap-Haïtien (T2622459).

Guides expect you to buy them food if you stop to eat

Guides Young men and boys offer their services as guides. In some places it's worthwhile, it is easier to get about, you can visit places off the beaten tourist track and avoid some of the frustrations of the public transport system though generally you can get by without one. Most guides speak English or pidgin English. Max Church, a pastor who has been training English/French/Créole-speaking guides, can be called on 342622, Port-au-Prince. Guides cost about US$10-30 per day, depending where you go. Bear in mind that most guides are 'on commission' with local shop and stall-keepers. So if you ask them to bargain for you, you will not necessarily be getting a good price, nor will they necessarily go where you want to go. If you don't want a guide a firm but polite *non, merci* gets the message across. It is best to ignore altogether hustlers outside guest houses, et cetera, as any contact makes them persist.

Haiti

Touching down

Departure tax Visitors leaving by air must pay a US$25 departure tax in US currency and a 10-gourde security tax in Haitian currency. Do not buy international flight tickets in Haiti, especially not at the airport. Sales tax is very high and the application of exchange rates may be very arbitrary.

Business hours Government offices: 0700-1200, 1300-1600 (0800-1200, 1300-1800 October-April); banks: 0900-1300 Monday to Friday; shops and offices: 0700-1600 (an hour later October-April).

Official time Eastern standard time, five hours behind GMT; four hours behind early April to late October (dates vary each year).

Voltage 110 volt, 60 cycle AC. Electricity supply is unpredictable as there are insufficient funds to maintain the service. Only if sufficient rain falls to operate the hydroelectric facility will the capital have power and water. Only the best hotels have sufficiently powerful generators to make up the deficiency (see Where to stay section). As the Oloffson is on the same circuit as the Presidential Palace, it is never blacked out.

Weights & measures Metric.

Clothing As in most other countries in the Caribbean beachwear should not be worn away from the beach and poolside. Dress is casual but never sloppy. Haitians appreciate good manners and style. Above-the-knee hems for women are considered risqué but acceptable. Men always wear a shirt, but a tie is not necessary in the evening.

Tipping Budget travellers, particularly outside Port-au-Prince, are a rarity. Expect to be the subject of much friendly curiosity, and keep a pocketful of small change to conform with the local custom of tipping on every conceivable occasion. Even cigarettes and sweets are accepted. Hotels generally add 10% service charge. Baggage porters at hotels usually get US$0.50 per bag. Do not fail to reward good service since hotel and restaurant staff rely on tips to boost their meagre salaries. Nobody tips taxi, publique, camionette or tap-tap drivers, unless exceptional service has been given.

Safety Despite all the political turmoil since 1986, security is not a major problem for the foreign visitor. In fact, Haiti has much less crime than most Caribbean countries. Take normal precautions. Carry handbags securely and do not leave belongings in sight in a parked car. During any political unrest it is advisable to limit your movements in the daytime and not to go out at night. Streets are usually deserted by 2300. Foreigners are not normally targeted at such times, but seek local advice.

Travel agencies abroad In the UK, *Interchange*, 27 Stafford Road, Croydon, Surrey CR0 4NG, T020-86813612, F7600031, interchange@interchange.uk.com, organize coach tours or independent packages of accommodation, transport and excursions.

Where to stay

Hotels There are a few good hotels in Pétion-Ville, up the hillside from Port-au-Prince, mostly designed for businessmen, and a couple of international-standard beach hotels along the Côte des Arcadins, northwest of the capital. Elsewhere, however, lodgings can be idiosyncratic and variable in the quality of furnishings and service. See page 366. Details are given in the main text. The Association Hotelière et Touristique d'Haïti is at Choucoune Plaza, Pétion-Ville, T2574647. **Camping** in Haiti is an adventure. The dramatic scenery is very enticing but access to much of it is over rough terrain and there are no facilities, leaving exploring to the rugged. Campers have to take everything and create, or find their own shelter. Peasant homes dot the countryside and it is almost impossible to find a spot where you will be spared curious and suspicious onlookers. It is best to set up camp or lodging before dark. To prevent misunderstanding, it is important to explain to the locals your intentions, or better yet, talk to the local elder and ask assistance or protection. Creating a relationship with the locals will usually ensure co-operation and more privacy. Offer to pay a small amount for use of the land.

Getting around

Air   *Mission Aviation Fellowship* (T2463993) and *Caribintair* (T2460737) have flights every day except Sunday to Cap-Haïtien (US$50 round trip). They also run 2 or 3 flights a week each to Jérémie (US$70 round trip). *MAF* additionally flies Tuesday, Thursday and Saturday to Hinche (US$40 round trip). Book and pay through travel agents. Flights leave from Aviation Générale, a small domestic airport 1 km east of the international airport. *Caribintair* also operates as a charter/air taxi company. *Marien Air* (T2620527), a Cap-based air taxi service run by Paul Takeo Hodges, flies anywhere in Haiti. It also offers flights to Port-au-Prince, the Dominican Republic, Turks and Caicos, Bahamas and Jamaica.

Road   Driving in Haiti is a hazardous free-for-all with some finding it exhilarating. The streets are
See also transport   narrow, with many sharp bends and full of pedestrians in the towns. Outside the towns you
under Port-au-Prince   have to look out for animals, potholes, sleeping policemen and police roadblocks. In wet weather, city streets and main highways all get clogged with traffic and become impassable. Haitians use their horns constantly to warn pedestrians of their approach. There are few signs. Vehicles swerve unexpectedly to avoid potholes. Cars often don't stop in an accident, so, to avoid paying the high insurance excess, keep a pen and paper handy to take down a number if necessary. Fuel (leaded, unleaded or diesel) is usually available in the big provincial towns, but power cuts may prevent stations from pumping at certain times of the day. For driving to Cap-Haïtien, Les Cayes and Jacmel, an ordinary car is fine, but for Jérémie, Port-de-Paix or Hinche, a four-wheel drive is nessary. Foreigners may use a national driving licence for 3 months, then a local permit is required.

Car hire   A small Japanese saloon car such as a Nissan Sunny, with a/c, rents for about US$45 per day, US$250 per week, unlimited mileage. A basic four-wheel drive starts at US$500 per week with US$500 deposit and excess of US$1,000 for damages. *Avis* (T2464161), *Hertz*

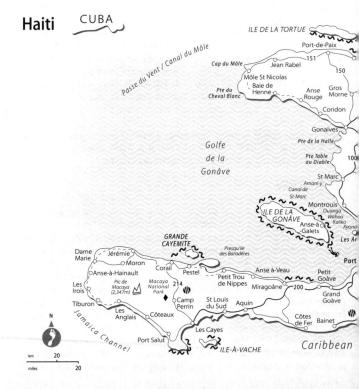

Haiti

(T2460700), *Dollar* (T2491800) and *Budget* (T2461366) all have bases near the airport; Avis is opposite the airport terminal, open 0800-1700, Hertz is in the Dynamic Entreprise Building and Dollar in the Firestone Building. Smaller companies include *Sunshine Jeep* (T2491155), *Secom* (564 Route de Delmas, T2571913) and *Sugar* (T2463413). Hertz is the only company with a base in Cap-Haïtien.

Hitchhiking Foreigners do not normally hitch. There are many young Haitian men who stick out a thumb asking for a 'roue libre', especially from foreigners. Use your discretion.

Keeping in touch

Always bad, the telephone system deteriorated even more during the 1991-94 embargo. Fewer than a third of calls get through. The Haitian international operator (dial 09) is hard to raise. However, Teleco offices in major cities are central and easy to use and the operators are helpful. Expect queues. The *Oloffson, Le Plaza, Montana* and *El Rancho* hotels have AT&T 'USA Direct' telephones for collect calls to the USA or calls anywhere in the world with an AT&T credit card, but even these connections can be problematic. Email service is very limited. The postal service is slow and poor.

Telephone
International phone code: 509

Newspapers *Le Nouvelliste* is the better of the two daily French-language newspapers. It is conservative, but tries to be impartial. Three weekly newspapers are published in French, all very one-sided, but on different sides. The pro-Aristide weekly *Libète* is the only Créole newspaper. **Radio** Radio stations use a mix of French and Créole. *Metropole* and *Tropic* are best for news. The satellite-beamed *Radio France Inter* is rebroadcast locally on FM 89.3. The *BBC World Service* can be heard on 15220 (early morning) and 7325 (evenings). *Voice of America* is on 11915 (mornings) and 9455 evenings. **Television** A commercial TV station, *Tele-Haiti*, retransmits American, French, Canadian and Latin American stations (including CNN) to cable subscribers, electricity permitting.

Media

Food and drink

Most restaurants offer Créole or French cuisine, or a mixture of both. Haiti's Créole cuisine is like its Caribbean cousins, but more peppery. Specialities include *griot* (deep-fried pieces of pork), *lambi* (conch, considered an aphrodisiac), *tassot* (jerked beef) and rice with *djon-djon* (tiny, dark mushrooms). As elsewhere in the Caribbean, lobster is widely available. Pétion-Ville has many good French restaurants. Some are French-managed or have French chefs. Haiti's wide range of micro-climates produces a large assortment of fruits and vegetables. It is popular to buy these in the regions where they grow and are freshest (prices can be bargained 40% below shop prices). The French influence is obvious in butcher shops where fine cuts of meat, cold cuts, paté and cheeses can be bought. American influence is felt in the supermarkets. Most common are US-brand foods along with smaller amounts of Haitian, French and Middle Eastern brands. Vegetarians will find Haiti extremely difficult.

Food
Bakeries sell French croissants, together with Créole bread & meat pasties

Haiti

Atlantic Ocean

nse-à-
buleur
Le Borgne
Plage Labodie
Plage Cormier
Cap-Haïtien
Caracol
Fort Liberté
Limbé
100
Limonade
0-121
Terrier Rouge
Ouanaminthe
Plaisance
Milot
Citadelle
Dajabon
Ennery
St Raphaël
St Michel de l'Attalaye
Pignon
300
Maïssade
Hinche
DOMINICAN REPUBLIC
Montagnes Noires
Thomassique
Thomonde
109
Belladère
305
Chaîne Des Matheux
Arcahaie
Mirebalais
Lascahobas
adins
Cabaret
100
300
Ibo
Etang Saumâtre
Croix-des-Bouquets
au-Prince
Pétionville
Jimani
Lago Enriquillo
ressier Thor
Malpasse
Kenscoff
Massif de la Selle
Mandàt
Jacmel
Marigot
Grand Gosier
Cayes Jacmel
Belle Anse
Sea
Anse-à-Pitres

Haitians cook nearly everything in pig fat, so even beans are to be avoided. One traveller survived on a diet of cornflakes, boiled eggs and fruit. Only the expensive restaurants and hotels will have a vegetarian option on the menu.

Drink

Haitian coffee is drunk strong & sweet, Rebo is the best brand

Haiti's Barbancourt rum is excellent. The distillery is in Damians and can be visited. Rum punch is popular but often over-sweet. The local beer, Prestige, may be too sweet for some palates but is an acceptable alternative to sweet, fizzy drinks. The Dominican beer, Presidente, is the best of the foreign beers sold in Haiti, but Beck's is more widely available. Soft drinks include Séjourne, Couronne and Sékola (banana).

Entertainment

Until the mid-1980s, Haiti used to be a very good place for nightspots. With the drop in tourism and Haitians hesitating to be out late at night in uneasy times, many places have had to close or curtail their level of entertainment. The few that survive offer a good evening's enjoyment and plenty of character. Following French custom, entertaining starts late in the evening, about 2030-2100. Nightclubbing starts around 2330 and continues into the small hours.

Flora and fauna

Haiti has no poisonous snakes or insects

Deforestation and soil erosion have destroyed habitats. Haiti is therefore poor in flora and fauna compared with its eastern neighbour. Three sites are worth visiting. One is **Lake Saumâtre**, 90 minutes east of the capital. Less brackish than Enriquillo, across the Dominican border, it is the habitat of more than 100 species of waterfowl (including migratory North American ducks), plus flamingoes and American crocodiles. The north side of the lake is better, reached via the town of Thomazeau (see page 372).

The other two are mountain parks. Relatively easy to reach is **Parc La Visite**, about five hours' hike from the hill resort of Kenscoff behind Port-au-Prince. On the high Massif de la Selle, with a mixture of pine forest and montane cloud forest, it has 80 bird species and two endemic mammals, the Hispaniolan hutia (*Plagiodontia aedium*) and the nez longue (*Solenodon paradoxus*). North American warblers winter there. It is also a nesting place for the black-capped petrel (*Pteradoma hasitata*). See page 372. Harder to reach is the **Macaya National Park**, at the tip of the southwest peninsula, site of Haiti's last virgin cloud forest. It has pines 45m high, 141 species of orchid, 102 species of fern, 99 species of moss and 49 species of liverwort. Its fauna include 11 species of butterfly, 57 species of snail, 28 species of amphibian, 34 species of reptile, 65 species of bird and 19 species of bat. In addition to the hutia, nez longue and black-capped petrel, its most exotic animals are the Grey-crowned Palm Tanager (*Phaenicophilus poliocephalus*) and the Hispaniolan trogan (*Temnotrogan roseigaster*). The endangered Peregrine falcon (*Falco pergrinus*) winters in the park. From Les Cayes, it takes half a day to get to a University of Florida base on the edge of the park which has basic camping facilities. Allow another 2 days each way for the 2,347m Pic de Macaya. See page 376. Paul Paryski (T2231400/1), a UN ecosystems expert, will give advice.

Leaf doctors, voodoo priests and sorcerers have a wealth of knowledge of natural remedies and poisons to be found in Haiti's surviving plant life. They do not share their knowledge readily. In his book *The Serpent and the Rainbow*, Harvard ethnobotanist Wade Davis gives a racy account of his attempts to discover which natural toxins sorcerers are thought to use to turn their victims into *zombis*. Almost any tree is liable to be chopped down for firewood or charcoal; a few very large species are not because they are believed to be the habitat of *loas* (spirit). Chief among them is the silkcotton tree, 'mapou' in Creole.

Shopping

The Iron Markets sell only food items, charcoal, et cetera. The Iron Market in Port-au-Prince would be a fascinating place to visit but for the hustlers who will latch on to you and make the experience hell. Try out your bargaining skills at the Iron Markets in Jacmel and Cap-Haïtien. Haitians may tell you that many of the items for sale in the few tourist shops can be bought far cheaper in markets. That may be true for them, but market vendors jack up prices for the foreigner, who will have to haggle skilfully to bring them down. People always ask for a discount in shops, except at food shops. All handicrafts can be bought at a discount. See page 367 for best buys, and under towns for individual establishments. Film processing services are the same as in the USA, but the price of film is high; transparency developing is considerably less.

Holidays and festivals

New Year and Ancestors (1-2 January), Mardi Gras (the three days before Ash Wednesday), Americas Day (14 April), Good Friday (1 May), Flag and University Day (18 May), Assumption (15 August), Deaths of Henri Christophe and Dessalines (8 and 17 October), United Nations Day (24 October), All Saints (1 November), Armed Forces Day (18 November), Discovery of Haiti (5 December), 25 December. Corpus Christi and Ascension are also public holidays.

Public holidays

The standard of the **Port-au-Prince** *Carnival* has fallen since the Duvaliers left (see page 386). Nowadays few people wear costumes and the floats are poorly decorated. There is a cacophony of music blaring out from both stands and passing floats. Excitement is provided by the walking bands (*bandes-à-pied*), cousins of the Rara bands that appear after carnival (see below). Circulating on foot, drawing a large dancing, chanting crowd in their wake, they specialize in salacious lyrics and political satire. When crowds move in different directions there is boisterous pushing. Occasional knife fights do take place. The safest place to watch is from one of the stands near the *Hôtel Le Plaza*. Carnival climaxes on the three days before Ash Wednesday, but the government lays on free open-air concerts in different parts of the city during the three or four weekends of pre-carnival.

Festivals

Many people prefer the *Carnival* a week earlier at **Jacmel**, 2-3 hours from the capital, where the tradition of elaborate, imaginative masked costumes still thrives. The music is unremarkable however.

Port-au-Prince carnival is immediately followed by *Rara*, dubbed the 'peasant carnival'. Every weekend during Lent, including Easter weekend, colourfully attired Rara bands emerge from voodoo societies and roam the countryside. They seek donations, so be ready with a few small notes. Beating drums, blowing home-made wind instruments, dancing and singing, some bands may have a thousand or more members. A good place to see it is the town of Leogane near the capital on Easter Sunday. Beware, the drinking is heavy and fights are common.

The Gede (pronounced gay-day) are *loas* who possess Voodooists on 1-2 November (*All Saints* and *Day of the Dead*). They can be seen in cemeteries or roaming the streets, dressed to look like corpses or undertakers. The lords of death and the cemetery, they mock human vanity and pretension, and remind people that sex is the source of life. They do this by dancing in a lewd fashion with strangers, causing much hilarity. For pilgrimages, see Saut d'Eau, Plaine du Nord and Limonade in the text below.

Health

Prophylaxis against malaria is essential. Tap water is not to be trusted (drink only filtered or treated water) and take care when choosing food. The local herb tea can help stomach troubles. Hepatitis is common in some areas. Good professional advice is available for the more common ailments. Ask at the hotel desk for referrals to a doctor suited to your requirements. Office hours are usually 0730-1200, 1500-1800. A consultation costs about US$10-15. Hospital care and comfort varies. See page 368 for hospital listings in Port-au-Prince. Pharmacies/chemists can fill out prescriptions and many prescription drugs may be bought over the counter. A note on prostitution: there are no laws in Haiti to suppress it. Activity seems to be evident only at night with the commonly known areas being along the main roads in Carrefour and street corners in Pétion-Ville. After hours the prostitutes move into the dive-type joints, targeting foreigners. With regard to casual sex, there is a red alert in Haiti over Aids.

Haiti

Further reading

History *The Black Jacobins*, by CLR James (about Toussaint); *Papa Doc and the Tontons Macoutes*, by Bernard Diederich and Al Burt. **Voodoo** *The Drum and the Hoe*, by Harold Courlander; *Divine Horsemen* by Maya Deren; *The Serpent and the Rainbow* by Wade Davis; *Mama Lola* by Karen McCarthy Brown. **Travelogue** *Bonjour Blanc: A Journey Through Haiti* by Ian Thomson, Hutchinson, 1992; *The Rainy Season: Haiti Since Duvalier*, by Amy Wilentz, Jonathan Cape, 1989. **Fiction** *The Comedians* by Graham Greene (set during Papa Doc's time); *The Kingdom of This World* by Alejo Carpentier (about Mackandal and Christophe); *Hadriana dans tous mes rèves*, by René Depestre, Gallimard 1988, Haiti's best known living writer who grew up in Jacmel where the story is set; *The farming of bones*, by Edwidge Danticat, Soho Press 1998, is a fictional account of the massacre of Haitians in the Dominican Republic in 1937.

Port-au-Prince

Population: 846,247
Metropolitan area:
2,000,000

What Port-au-Prince lacks in architectural grace, it makes up for with a stunning setting. Steep mountains tower over the city to the south, La Gonâve island lies in a horseshoe bay to the west, and another wall of mountains beyond a rift valley plain rise to the north. Over the years the city has spilled out of its original waterfront location, climbing further into the mountains behind. A rural exodus has swollen the population from 150,000 in 1954 to over two million now. The worst bidonvilles (shantytowns) are in a marshy waterfront area north of the centre, but most of the city is very poor. There are crowds of people everywhere, spilling off the sidewalks into the streets, moving to a cacophony of horns and engines.

Port-au-Prince Orientation

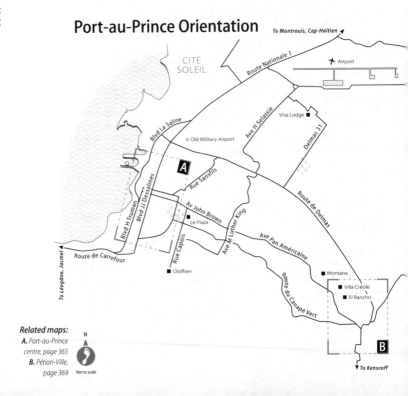

Related maps:
A. *Port-au-Prince centre, page 365*
B. *Pétion-Ville, page 369*

N
Not to scale

Ins and outs

The airport is on the northern edge of Delmas, 13 km outside Port-au-Prince, T2410516. Arrival can be pandemonium especially if more than 1 flight is being dealt with. Just get on with your affairs and try not to get distracted. Once through the squash inside you emerge into a squash outside, of taxi drivers and people awaiting friends. Knowledge of French is useful. Porters charge US$0.50 per bag. A taxi into town is US$20-25 depending on how hard you bargain, or take a seat in a taptap (open-backed truck), extra charged for large bag. To get to the airport cheaply take a shared taxi from the turning off Avenue Saint Martin (see map, formerly Avenue François Duvalier) for 3-4 km to Rue Haile Sellassie where taptaps marked 'Airport' gather; US$0.15 from here, 10 km. For those coming by bus from the Dominican Republic, see page 354.

Getting there
The so-called 'supervisors' at the airport are in fact taxi-drivers, touting for business

Shared taxis (called **publiques** or simply taxis) are flagged down. They charge a basic fare (Cr: kous) of US$0.20 that may double or treble (de kous, twa kous) depending on how far off the beaten track you go. A red ribbon tied to the inside rear-view mirror identifies them. French is needed. They stop work at about 1930. **Camionettes** (minibuses) and **Taptaps** (open-backed pickups with a brightly painted wooden superstructure) have fixed routes and fares (about US$0.15). They rarely circulate after 2030. They are difficult to manage with luggage. Camionettes to Pétion-Ville leave from Avenue John Brown, US$0.20.

Getting around
A regular taxi is hard to find. See transport for further details

Sights

The commercial quarter starts near the port and stretches inland to the east about ten blocks. It lacks charm or interest, except the area beside the port that was remodelled for the city's 1949 bicentennial. Known as the **Bicentenaire** (more formally, Cité de l'Exposition), it contains the post office, foreign ministry, parliament, American

embassy and French Institute. It is now very run down. The central reference point for visitors is the large, irregularly shaped park called the **Champs de Mars** which begins to the east of the commercial quarter. The northwest corner is dominated by the white, triple-domed, presidential palace. It was built in 1918 on the site of a predecessor that was blown up in 1912 with its president inside. In the 1991 coup, President Aristide made a stand inside the present building. Just to the northeast is the colonnaded, white and gold army high command building, where soldiers nearly lynched Aristide after dragging him out of the palace. (He was saved by the French ambassador, the American ambassador, or General Cedras, depending on whose story you believe). Immediately behind the palace, to the south, is a large, mustard-yellow army garrison that was once the fief of the ill-famed Colonel Jean-Claude Paul, indicted in Miami in 1987 for drug smuggling and poisoned the following year.

Immediately to the east of the palace, on **Place des Héros de l'Independence**, the subterranean **Musée du Panthéon National** (MUPANAH), T2228337,

Haïti

houses historical relics, including the rusted anchor of Columbus' flagship, the *Santa María*. Don't miss an 1818 oil painting of King Henri Christophe by Welshman Richard Evans, director of Christophe's Fine Arts Academy at Sans Souci. Two blocks north and two west, at the corner of Avenue Mgr Guilloux and the busy Rue Pavée, the **Sainte Trinité Episcopal Cathedral** has astounding biblical murals by the greatest naive artists, including Philomé Obin, Castera Bazile and Riguaud Benoit. Created in 1949, they are well worth seeing. The adjoining complex has a gift shop and a school whose students give excellent choral and classical music concerts (details from Sister Anne-Marie, T2225638). The pink and white stone Catholic Cathedral is four blocks to the north.

At the intersection of Rues Capois and Champ de Mars, the **Musée d'Art Haïtien** has Haiti's finest naive art collection, plus a craft shop and a small café in its garden. The collection is not large and there is no recent art, you will find that in the private galleries. ■ *T2222510. US$0.50. From 1000.* The **Maison Défly**, 7 Avenue John Paul II, built by an army commander in 1896, is in the Victorian 'gingerbread' style, characterized by steep roofs and gables, round turrets, high ceilings, balconies and rich fretwork embellishment. Not a distinguished example, it contains a museum with period furniture. ■ *T2224081. 0900-1300 Mon-Sat.* The Rue Capois has several hotels, restaurants and shops. At the southern end of Rue Capois, 1 km from the Champs de Mars, is the *Hotel Oloffson*, a much more imposing example of a gingerbread. West of Rue Capois are leafy neighbourhoods climbing into the foothills where the well-off built residences in the 19th century, and gingerbreads abound.

Watch out for pickpockets in markets, bus terminal areas & inside buses **Caution** Shantytown dwellers don't welcome obvious sightseers and people with cameras. The area between the Champs de Mars and the waterfront is deserted after dark and should be avoided. It is safe to go to most places by car or taxi at night, but don't go about on foot except in Pétion-Ville's restaurant and bar district. Remember that frequent power cuts plunge entire neighbourhoods into darkness. Drivers must always carry a licence as police blocks are common at night. Be careful of traffic when walking around town. Street vendors crowd the pavements, forcing pedestrians into the path of vehicles. Many people have been knocked down and injured.

Street names Several major Port-au-Prince thoroughfares have two names, the official one used for maps and the telephone book, and the one commonly used in speech. Often the taxi drivers only know the second. Boulevard Jean-Jacques Dessalines is also known as Grand' Rue (Créole: Gran Ri); Avenue Lamartinière is Bois Verna (Cr: Bwa Vèna); Avenue Jean Paul II is Turgeau (Cr: Tijo); Avenue John Brown is Lalue (Cr: Lali); Avenue Paul VI is Rue des Casernes (Cr: Ridekazèn); Avenue Martin Luther King is Nazon (Cr: Nazon).

Essentials

Sleeping **Hotels L-A** *Le Plaza* (formerly *Holiday Inn*), 10 Rue Capois, central location on Champs de Mars, T2239800/93. Jungly gardens, pool, tolerable restaurant, own generator, children under 18 free if sharing room, all rooms a/c, CP. **AL-B** *Oloffson* (see above), Rue Cadet Jérémie at intersection with Rue Capois, PO Box 260, T2234000. Model for Hotel Trianon in Graham Greene's *The Comedians* and eccentrically managed by Haitian-American musician Richard Morse, this is Haiti's most charming hotel. However you pay for the atmosphere and carefully cultivated faded grandeur. The smaller rooms were built as a hospital and maternity wing by the US marines. Haunt of writers, journalists and film makers, Thu buffet and live music well worth the money, pool, never lacks electricity, most rooms a/c, CP. **A** *Visa Lodge*, Rue des Nimes, Rte de l'Aéroport, T2491202/3/4, 2462662. Businessman's hotel in industrial zone near airport, pool, good restaurant, own generator, EP. **B** *Prince*, corner of Rue 3 and Ave N, Pacot, T2452764. Quiet hillside neighbourhood 15 mins' walk from taxis, own generator, all rooms a/c. **B** *Villa St-Louis*, 95 Bourdon, on the way to Pétion-Ville, T2456241, F2457949. CP, weekly rates, studio apartments. **B-C** *Park*, 25 Rue Capois, near *Le Plaza*, T2224406. Cheaper to pay in gourdes, safe, central, be prepared to wait an age for breakfast, no generator. **E-F** *Auberge Port-au-Prince*, 148 Rue du Centre. Buses from Dominican Republic disgorge their passengers amid hordes of vendors, no frills, no theft, very basic rooms with bath or inside room, fan, management surly, ground floor bar serves lunch but closes around 1900, good view from roof.

Guest houses **B** *Coconut Villa*, Rue Berthold 3, Delmas 19, T2461691. Poor location in dusty, northern suburb, own generator but turned off during day, rooms with private bath and a/c, CP. **B** *La Griffonne*, 21 Rue Jean Baptiste, Canapé Vert, T2454095/3440. Quiet neighbourhood 5 mins' walk from Ave John Brown, own generator, rooms with private bath and a/c, MAP. **B** *Sendral's*, Rue Mercier, Bourdon, near *Hotel Villa St-Louis*, T2456502. Own generator, rooms with private bath and fan, CP. **C** *May's Villa*, 28 Debussy, T2451208. Quiet neighbourhood at top of Ave John Paul II (Cr: Tijo), 10 mins' walk from nearest taxis, view, has a generator, but room lights come on with city power at about 2100, rooms with private bath and fan, CP.

Port-au-Prince Centre

NB Most of the best hotels are in Pétion-Ville, which is treated separately, although just 15 mins away. Only the most expensive hotels and guest houses have air-conditioning plus sufficiently powerful in-house generators able to cope with the long electricity blackouts in the city. Some have a generator to give partial power to the bar say but not to guest rooms. Water is also rationed, and many of the cheaper, central hotels lack both water and electricity much of the time. Check rooms in advance in the cheaper hotels, service may be deficient. Tax, service charge and energy surcharge are usually added to hotel bills. These extras have been included in the prices given here, which are very approximate because of exchange rate vagaries. While hotels are accommodating UN and NGO personnel, prices are usually quoted in US dollars and in consequence are high. Where possible, it is cheaper to pay in gourdes bought from money changers. Paying by credit card is more expensive.

Eating Almost the only decent places to eat out at night in Port-au-Prince are the *Oloffson* or *Le Plaza*, or a row of terrace cafés selling barbecued chicken at the southeast corner of the Champs de Mars (starting near Rex theatre). Bars in this area will probably try and short change you. Well-off Port-au-Princiens go up to Pétion-Ville to dine out. The following restaurants are open during the day closing at about 1600: ***Table Ronde***, 7 Rue Capois (half block from *Le Plaza*), T2234660. Good lunch, front veranda excellent for street watching, popular with politicians. ***Café Terrasse***, rear of Air France Bldg, 11 Rue Capois and Rue Ducoste, T2225468. Excellent lunch, favoured by international aid agency staffers. ***Tiffany***, Blvd Harry Truman, Bicentenaire 12, north of Tele-Haiti, T2223506/0993. Haitian, French and American food. ***Chez Yvane***, 19 Blvd Harry Truman, south of Tele-Haiti, T2220188. Créole lunch in new a/c premises. ***La Perle***, 80 Rue Pavée, between Dessalines and Rue des Miracles. Pleasant, cool, enormous sandwiches, also spaghetti, omelettes. Recommended. ***Paradis de Amis***, 43 Rue Pavée, between Centre and Dessalines. Recommended for club sandwiches, omelettes, ice cream, a/c, popular with locals, cheap, large portions, spaghetti costs US$2. The restaurant at the *Museé d'Art Haïtien*, ***Les Jardins du Musée***, T2228738, is a small oasis, but a bit pricey, popular with 'blancs', particularly French embassy staff, at lunchtime.

Drinks, such as cold beers, water, juice, rum, can be bought at the ***Supermarket de la Bonne Foie***, 52 Rue Dr Marselly Seide. Open Mon-Sat 0730-1600, small, friendly, English spoken. Recommended. Also at ***Supermarket Express*** up on the hill on John Brown. Cold beer and Guinness, UN customers.

Entertainment RAM performs Thu at the *Oloffson*, the place to be. Otherwise, the best nightlife is to be found in Pétion-Ville (see separate section). There is a red-light district on the southwest Carrefour Road that has been badly eclipsed by AIDS and political turmoil. The central part of the establishments consist of spacious, breezy, outdoor discothèques. The Dominican beer on offer is excellent and cheap, but the Dominican prostitutes and loud Dominican merengue music may have scant appeal. The city's western limits, around Mariani, have several ill-lit waterfront nightclubs, such as *Le Lambi*, where couples dance groin-to-groin to live compas bands and the men eat plate after plate of spicy, fresh-caught lambi (conch) to boost their virility.

Cinemas Cheap and interesting: the best are *Imperial* (a/c), Delmas; *Capitol* (a/c), 53, Rue Lamarre; *Paramount*, Champs de Mars. Popular foreign films (British, US, French) are shown; non-French films are dubbed into French.

Clubs ***Pétion-Ville Club***, near US ambassador's residence at the end of Rue Métreaux, a turning off Rue Panaméricaine, between Port-au-Prince and Pétion-Ville, T2577575. A social and sports club, visitors may use nine-hole golf course. For other facilities (tennis courts, racketball, gym, pool, restaurant) a 1-year temporary membership costs US$125. ***Bellevue***, near Argentine Embassy on Panaméricaine, Bourdon, a social club with tennis courts. ***Turgeau Tennis Club*** on Ave Jean-Paul II (Cr: Tijo) near corner Martin Luther King (Cr: Nazon) has a few courts. ***Jotac*** near airport has tennis courts, gym and restaurant.

Voodoo Seeing a Voodoo ceremony or dance during a short visit is not easy. They are not announced in newspapers nor on the radio. Never go unless accompanied by a Haitian, or someone already known there. Most middle and upper-class Haitians do not attend ceremonies and won't know where or when they are happening. They may even be discomforted by your interest. Tell poor, working-class Haitians about your interest. You may strike lucky. To increase your chances, time your stay to coincide with 2 November (Day of the Dead), Christmas, New Year or Epiphany (6 Jan). There are many ceremonies around these dates. If invited, take a bottle or two of rum or whisky and be ready to give generously if there is a collection. Sometimes, on the contrary, a wealthy 'oungan' (priest) or 'mambo' (priestess) will insist on lavishing drinks and food on the visitor. Don't refuse. To take pictures with a still camera or video, ask permission. You may be asked to pay for the privilege. TV crews are usually asked to pay substantial amounts. An oungan may always be consulted in his 'ounphor' (temple) even if there is no ceremony. Be ready to plead poverty if the sum requested seems exhorbitant.

Max Beauvoir (T2342818/3723), an oungan intellectual with fluent English, has initiated foreigners. Purists questioned the authenticity of the regular voodoo dances he used to lay on for tourists, but he is unquestionably an authority and talks readily to visitors. Aboudja (T2458476, or through the *Oloffson*), an English-speaking TV news cameraman, has been initiated as an oungan although he does not practice regularly. He acts as voodoo consultant for visiting journalists and TV crews.

Art and craft Some galleries have a near monopoly on certain artists, so don't expect to see a cross-section of all the major artists in any one, good gallery. The paintings hung at the *Oloffson* are for sale. *Galerie Carlos Jara* (T2457164) has a fine collection at 28 Rue Armand Holly, Pacot, 10 mins' drive uphill from the *Oloffson*. *Le Centre d'Art*, 58 Rue Roy, Pacot, T2222018. In a beautiful but crumbling old house, 2 floors of artwork with stacks of paintings, upstairs, founded 1944, open Mon-Fri 0930-1300, 1430-1600, Sat 0930-1230. The *Nader* family has two galleries: one in Pétion-Ville (see page 370); the other at 18 Rue Bouvreuil (T2450565/4524) in the leafy Croix Desprez neighbourhood is now principally a museum; *Galerie Issa* (T2223287), 17 Ave du Chili (300m from *Oloffson*) is more like a wholesale warehouse, but cheap if you know what you are looking for. *Damballa Art Gallery*, 243 Rue Magasin de l'Etat. A hole-in-the-wall gallery, wonderful. Mass produced copies of the Haitian naive masters are sold very cheaply around the Post Office, near the port. If you want to buy paintings, you are advised to take your time, look around, and be prepared for some serious bargaining. You will quickly learn which patterns are imitations or mass-produced just by seeing them repeatedly. Vendors sell 1st-class Voodoo flags outside the Musée d'Art Haïtien. Souvenir sellers also close to the *Holiday Inn*.

Comité Artisanal Haïtien, 29 Rue 3, Pacot (near *Oloffson*), T2228440. A co-operative selling handicraft from all over Haiti at good prices 0900-1600 Mon-Fri, 1000-1200 Sat. *Ambiance*, 17 Ave M, Pacot, T2452494. Haitian jewellery and pottery. *The Rainbow*, 9 Rue Pierre Wiener, Bourdon, T2456655/6039. Sells handicraft and paintings. *Fanal*, 124 Ave Christophe, corner of Rue Waag, T2451948. Antiques, handicrafts, toys, open Mon-Fri 1000-1700, Sat 1000-1400.

Shopping

Haïti

Local Taxis *Nick's Taxis* (T2577777), based at 31 Rue Panaméricaine, in Pétion-Ville, is the only radio taxi company. It charges according to the meter. A new, reliable company in Pétion-Ville is **Sunny Taxi Services**, Rue Lambert between Rue Clervaux and Rue Rebecca, T5107000. A passing Publique that is empty can be persuaded to do a private job (Cr: flete). The driver removes the red ribbon. **Chauffeurs-Guides** are cab drivers who cater to foreign visitors. Usually found outside the biggest hotels such as the *Le Plaza*, or at the airport, their cars can be used like regular taxis or hired by the hour, half day, day or for a tour. The drivers usually speak French, plus a little English. They can be booked through the Association des Chauffeurs-Guides, T2220330, 18 blvd Harry Truman. A recommended private guide/driver is Lionel Elie, Rue St Surin 20 Bis, Pétion-Ville, T2572968, also an artist, used by visiting writers and film crews, speaks English, Spanish and a little German. Price negotiable depending on the job and whether you have your own transport. Prices have been hiked to make the most of the US dollars brought in by US, UN and NGO personnel. **Air** There are flights to Jérémie,

Transport

Cap-Haïtien and Hinche. **Road** Fairly conventional-looking buses (Cr: bis) and/or colourfully converted trucks and pickups (Cr: taptap) provide inter-city transport. The place where buses and taptaps leave from is called a *station*. For example to get directions to the departure point for buses to Cap-Haïtien, ask for the *station Au Cap*. Most of the *stations* are somewhere on or between Boulevard Jean-Jacques Dessalines and the waterfront. There are no fixed departure times. Buses leave when they are packed. Roads are bad and journeys are long and uncomfortable. In trucks, it is worth paying more to sit up front with the driver.

Directory **Banks** *Promobank*, T2222461, corner of Lamarre and Ave John Brown, also a branch at Blvd du Quai and Rue Eden. *Scotiabank*, route de Delmas (beneath Canadian embassy) and branch on Rue des Miracles near corner of Blvd Dessalines. *Citibank*, T2462600, route de Delmas. Also several Haitian banks such as *Sogebank*, T2295000, and *Banque de L'Union Haïtienne*, T2230499. There are long queues in most banks for any kind of service. **Exchange:** banks offer a slightly higher rate of exchange than street changers and you are less likely to receive forged notes. Counterfeit 250-gourde notes are reported to be in circulation. Street money changers (Fr: *cambistes*) can be found on Rue Pavée, at the airport, or near the market in Pétion-Ville. It is perfectly legal but they will try and make as much as possible out of you. Check the rate on page 2 of the daily *Le Nouvelliste* newspaper. You may prefer to go in a car and do it through the window. The *cambiste* hands over the agreed sum in gourdes for you to count before you surrender the equivalent US dollar amount. They take only cash. If possible, use a *cambiste* you have seen regularly at a particular spot; never allow yourself to be steered to a *cambiste* by an informal guide. Currency dealers working out of offices give almost as good a rate. They also take TCs. Try Daniel Fouchard (T2231739) 14 Rue des Miracles, Banque de Boston Building. Many importers and big retailers give a good rate for cash, TCs and even personal cheques on US bank accounts. Try Didier Rossard (T2225163), upstairs at 115 Place Geffrard; M or Mme Handal at Express Market, Ave John Brown, 6 blocks down from *Villa St-Louis*. (See also page 354). **Communications** Internet access US$3 per hr at Centre de Formation JRC Software, Ave Magny 16, T2222632, jrcardozo@aol.com Open Mon-Sat 0800-1900, Sun 0800-1200. **Cultural Institutes** *Institut Haitiano-Americain* (T2223715) corner of Rue Capois and Rue St-Cyr, next to *Le Plaza*, 0800-1200, 1300-1700 Mon to Fri. The director is helpful to visiting travellers. *Institut Français*, corner of Blvd Harry Truman and Rue des Casernes, Bicentenaire, T2223720. 1000-1600 Tue-Fri, 0900-1700 Sat. Also has art exhibitions, concerts and plays. **Hospitals & medical services** Hospitals: recommended hospitals (all in Port-au-Prince) are *Canapé Vert*, Rue Canapé Vert, T2451052/3/0984. *Adventiste de Diquini*, Carrefour Road, T2342000/0521. *Hospital Français de Haiti*, Rue du Centre, T2222323. *St Francois de Salles*, Rue de la Révolution, T2222110/0232. **Tour companies & travel agents** *Agence Citadelle*, 17 Rue des Miracles, Place du Marron Inconnu, T2235900, F2221792. Sightseeing tours in a/c buses, travel and tours to Dominican Republic and Cuba (owner Bobby Chauvet is a leading Haitian ecologist). *Horizons Tours*, 192B Ave John Brown, T/F2458208. Tours to Cuba. *Agence Martine*, 18 angle Rues Ogé et Geffrard, Pétion-Ville, T2572740. Flights to Miami. *ABC Tours*, 156 Rue Pavée, near Sainte-Trinité, T2220335, F2231855. Courteous, helpful. *Voyage Chatelain*, Rue Geffrard, T2232400, F2235065. Handles Terra Bus to Santo Domingo including immigration formalities. *Southerland Tours*, 30 Ave Marie Jeanne, T2231600, F2220580. Because of the collapse of tourism, sightseeing tours are set up only on request. For boat trips try Bernard, T2572399, who can arrange custom made excursions on a boat sleeping 4-6, although for day trips 8 are taken, price up to US$50 per person per day, sailing to Les Cayemites and Pestel is recommended, with good beaches.

Pétion-Ville

Pétion-Ville was once the capital's hill resort lying just 15 minutes from Port-au-Prince but 450 m above sea level. Now it is considered a middle-class suburb with restaurants and boutiques. Three roads lead up from Port-au-Prince. The northern-most, the Route de Delmas, is ugly and dusty. Preferable to this is the Panaméricaine, an extension of Avenue John Brown (Cr: Lali), which is serviced by camionettes. The southernmost, Route du Canapé Vert, has the best views.

In Pétion-Ville, the main streets Lamarre and Grégoire are parallel to each other, one block apart, on the six blocks between the Panaméricaine and the Place St Pierre. Most of the shops, galleries and restaurants are on or between these two streets or within a couple of blocks of them.

Hotels **LL-AL** *El Rancho*, Rue José de San Martín, just off the Panaméricaine, T2574926, 2572080/4, F2574134, www.elrancho.inhaiti.com Elegant Resorts International, very pleasant, painted white with tiled roofs, balconies, 2 pools, fitness centre, tennis, 2 restaurants, bars, casino, nightclub, sauna, spa, EP, a/c. **L-A** *Montana*, Rue Cardozo, a turning off the Panaméricaine at the entrance to Pétion-Ville, T2574020, F2576137, htmontana@ aol.com An oasis of luxury, best views over Port-au-Prince, especially from poolside restaurant, EP, a/c, phone, TV, airport transfers, conference facilities, built on hillside with lots of stairs but elevators have been installed, non-guests can use the pool for US$3. **A** *Villa Créole*, just beyond the *El Rancho* on José de San Martín, T2571570/1, F2574935. Tennis court, pool, good view, EP all a/c. **AL-B** *Kinam* at the corner of Rue Lamarre and Rue Moise, facing Place St-Pierre, T2570462. Mock Gingerbread house, 38 rooms, 3 suites, a/c, phone, TV, restaurant, bar, small pool, handy location, under same ownership is *Le Ritz*, corner Rue Panaméricaine and Rue José San-Martin, T2576520/1, T2576508. Aparthotel, studios, good for business groups, conference facilities. **AL-B** *Ibo Lele*, at the upper side of Pétion-Ville, towards Montagne Noire, T2575668. Slightly cheaper than *Kinam*, with pool. **A-B** *Caraïbe*, central, 13 Rue Leon Nau, Nerette, PO Box 15423, T2572524. 12 rooms with large baths, a/c, restaurant, TV lounge, pool, built in 1920s, charming, friendly, helpful, family-run, French, English, Spanish spoken. Most of the larger hotels with pools will let you use their facilities for the day for a small charge.

Guest houses *Doux Séjour*, 32 Rue Magny (quiet street five blocks from Place St Pierre), T2571560, F2576518. Weekly rates, apartments or rooms with fan and bathroom. *Marabou*, 72 Rue Stephen Archer, just behind St Pierre church, T2571934. Haggle for good rate for long stay. **C** *Ife*, 30 Rue Grégoire a busy street by the market, T2570737. Some a/c, CP. **C** *Villa Kalewes*, 99 Rue Grégoire (at the upper, quiet end of the street), T2570817. CP, pool. **D** *St Joseph's Home for Boys Guest House*, Delmas 91, T/F2574237, or write to Michael Geilenfeld, Lynx Air, PO Box 407139, Fort Lauderdale, FL 33340, USA. Rates include breakfast

Pétion-Ville

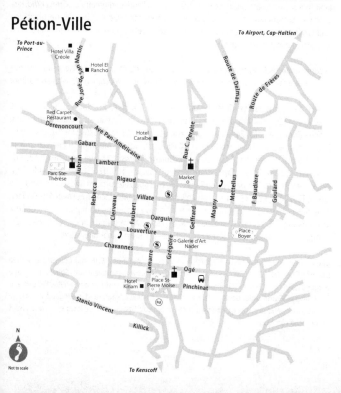

and dinner, vegetarian meals on request, laundry, bottled water, money exchange, security. For a fee the boys will escort you, give drum lessons, the home can also provide guides, translators, creole lessons, airport pickup, some of the boys perform in the Resurrection Dance Theatre, self-written dances based on their experiences when they lived on the street. Revenue from guests helps to pay for the boys, aged 8-18, who live and work as a family, running the guest house when not at classes. Founder Michael Geilenfeld was a brother with Mother Theresa before staring the home in 1985.

Eating *Plantation*, Impasse Fouchard, turning off Rue Borno, T2570979. Excellent French chef, good wine. Recommended. *Le Souvenance*, 8 Rue Gabart at the corner of Aubran, T2577688. Gourmet French cuisine. Recommended. Pricey. *Chez Gérard*, 17 Rue Pinchinat (near Place St-Pierre), T2571949. French, pricey. *Les Cascades*, 73 Rue Clerveaux, corner of Ogé, T2576704. French. *Anba Tonel Bar & Grill*, Angle Rues Clervaux et Villatte, T2577560, 2571311. *La Voile*, 32 Rue Rigaud between Lamarre and Faubert, T2574561. French, good. *1950*, 18 Rue Louverture between Grégoire and Lamarre, T2571929. Lobster, salads and pastas, lively bar scene, popular with ex-pats. *Coin Des Artistes*, 59 Rue Panaméricaine, beneath Festival Arts Gallery, T2572400. Grilled fish and lobster. *Steak Inn*, 37 Rue Magny, T2572153. Large garden, live music at weekend, bus for Santo Domingo leaves from here. *Arc-En-Ciel*, 67 Rue Grégoire, T2572055. French and German. *Le Grégoire*, 34 Rue Grégoire, T2571669. Viet and Thai, quiet. On the Kenscoff Road the *Altitude 1300*, 67 Laboule, T2559719. The place where the bourgeoisie go at weekends, with the best of créole cuisine.

Nightlife *Café Des Arts*, 19 Rue Lamarre (same house as Galerie Monnin), T2577979. Open 1900 until late, dining and live music. Upstairs is *Full Moon*. *Bash*, in the *Hotel El Rancho*, also Sat evening live jazz. *Harry's*, next to *Coin des Artistes*, see above, T2571885. Food OK, good value, 2 pool tables, often live music, latin and dance music, popular with families. *Sunset Bar*, 58 Rue Grégoire, T2576236. Run by Canadian Paul, good music, not too much compa, darts and table football, open late, relaxed atmosphere, mixed clientèle, international. *Guess Who*, Rue Gregoire. Pleasant terrace where they often have concerts. *Cheers*, 14 Rue Villatte. Great pina colada or food in a relaxed environment, ask in advance and you can rent videos and a room in which to watch them with friends.

Shopping Recommended is *La Promenade* at the intersection of Grégoire and Moïse (southeast corner of Place St-Pierre), a garden turned into small shopping promenade with an outdoor café, 1000-1800.

    Art and handicrafts *Galerie Nader*, 50 Rue Grégoire, PO Box 15410, T2575602, 2570855. Exceptional range of naïve and other modern Haitian artists, also exhibitions. *Galerie Bourbon-Lally*, 24 Rue Lamarre, corner of Rue Villate, T2576321/3397. Owned by Englishman Reynald Lally, good choice of naive art. *Galerie Monnin*, 19 Rue Lamarre, in same house as Café des Arts, T2574430. *Galerie Marasa*, 11 Rue Lamarre, T2577712. Hand-painted boxes, trays. *Expressions*, 75 Rue Clerveaux, T2570112. One of the Nader family galleries. *The Red Carpet*, 86 Rue Panaméricaine, opposite turnings for *El Rancho* and *Villa Créole*, T2572048, F2573324. Large art collection, restaurant attached. *Festival Arts Gallery*, 1 Bis, Rue Gabart, T2577956. Haitian artists who have moved on from primitivism. *Galata*, Rue Faubert, T2571114. Mainly handicrafts, especially weavings, metalwork. *Fleur De Canne*, 34 bis, Rue Gabart, T2574266. Good quality craft in a charming store.

Directory **Banks** There are several banks for foreign exchange transactions: *BUH* and *Capital* are on Rue Lamarre. Open Mon-Fri 0900-1700, Sat 0900-1300, very slow and bureaucratic. *Sogebank*, on Rue Grégoire gives faster service. *CitiBank* has an affiliate on Rue Louverture between Rue Faubert and Rue Clervaux. **Communications** *Teleco* is at the corner of Rue Magny and Rue Rigaud. All calls go through an operator, Faxes can be sent through *Speedy Fax* on Rue Louverture, between Rues Faubert and Clerveau.

Excursions near Port-au-Prince

The Gulf of La Gonâve beaches, the only ones that can be reached within an hours' drive, are not particularly good, but popular for a day trip out of the capital at weekends. Those west of the capital are poor. The best of what's available is to the north. The first beaches you get to are rather gritty, but the sand improves as you go further north. The backdrop is of arid, deforested mountainside but the calm, clear, shallow water is excellent for children. The closest is **Ibo Beach**, on an island near Km 30 of the Route Nationale 1, but it is dirty, covered in rubbish and not recommended. **The Côte Des Arcadins**, a 20-km stretch of beach hotels, begins 60 km north of the capital. The hotels all have bars and restaurants, and charge admission to day visitors. They may be crowded with wealthy Port-au-Princiens or aid agency staff at weekends. There are also public beaches with no hotels. **The Arcadins** are three uninhabited, sandy cays 3 km offshore which are surrounded by reef. The diving is excellent. **Isle La Gonâve** is also visible and dive boats visit the wall offshore.

Beaches
Haiti's best beaches are far from the capital, on the Caribbean & Atlantic coasts

Heading north along the Côte des Arcadins in geographical order: **C** *Kyona*, T257-6850/ 6863. Daily admission US$9 adults, US$$1.50 children, curved, gritty beach, loungers and tables in shade, lots of trees, locals sell paintings, turtle shells, black coral, basic rooms in bungalows or newer block, cold water, thatched open-air restaurant, volleyball, hotel dates from early 1960s. **AL** *Kaliko Beach Club*, at Km 61, PO Box 670, Port-au-Prince, T2984607/8/9, F2984610, kaliko@haitiworld.com All-inclusive, new in 1997, smart blue and white plantation style resort, popular with French Canadians, 55 rooms and growing, day pass US$30 with meals, US$15 lunch only, pleasant beach but not spectacular, pool, tennis, gardens, entertainment, créole lessons, boat cruises, conference facilities, excursions. Just along the beach is *Pegasus Diving*, PO Box 15785, T2383140. For snorkelling trips at Les Arcadins, US$20, Anse à Pirogues, US$35, and La Gonâve US$50. Diving for certified divers only to Les Arcadins, US$70 including gear, and the wall at Isle La Gonâve, US$80, 30 mins on dive boat. Fishing also available, US$200 for two people, half day, including gear, Captain, drinks and boat rental. **A-B** *Wahoo Bay*, T2229653. Includes breakfast, day pass US$6, 20 large rooms, a/c, upstairs rooms with balcony and good view of La Gonâve, good showers, pool, small but sandy beach, good swimming, loungers and tables with shade, windsurfing, horse riding, tennis, older resort but well maintained, building new rooms. **B-C** *Ouanga Bay*, at Km 65, PO Box 1605, Port-au-Prince, T2579292 ext 536, F2224422. Day pass US$3, all inclusive Sun US$18, or weekend US$45, extra for a/c, small sandy beach with man-made reef, wooden loungers, lovely new restaurant built over the water, 27 rooms and apartments right on beach, large beds, fan, TV and phones being added, bathrooms adequate, upstairs rooms reached by wobbly spiral staircases, English-speaking owner, friendly, watersports include snorkelling, windsurfing, pedalos and glass bottom boats with electric motors, diving arranged. After Montrouis, at Km 77 is **LL-L** *Moulin Sur Mer*, (Elegant Resorts International), T2221918, F2786720, moulinsm@haitiworld.com At the entrance is the **Musée Colonial Ogier-Fombrun**, in a stone 18th-century plantation building, open daily 1000-1700, adults US$2, students and children US$1, see the model of the original house and buildings, also museum pieces outside. The hotel is reached through the extensive gardens with Royal palms, peacocks, geese and ducks, beautiful setting on sandy beach, day pass US$10, 65 rooms FAP, Haitian furniture and art, a/c, hot water, tiled floors, phones, suites for families, also beach rooms for day use, two restaurants, vegetarian food available, tennis, volleyball, ping pong, pool, mini golf, playground, watersports including pedalos, kayaks, windriders, diving arranged, lots of languages spoken, golf carts for the less mobile.

Sleeping

The asphalt road to Kenscoff, in the mountains behind Port-au-Prince, starts just to the west of the Pétion-Ville police station, on the Place St-Pierre. After 10 minutes, there is a turnoff on the right at United Sculptors of Haiti, which sells good wood carvings. It skirts a huge quarry and climbs to **Boutilliers**, a peak topped by radio and television masts that dominates the city. Rewarded with a great view but promptly greeted by handicraft vendors and good-natured pestering. In about 20

Other excursions

Haiti

minutes, the main Kenscoff Road reaches **Fermathe** where the large Baptist Mission has a snack bar with fine views south, and a store selling handicraft and souvenirs (taptaps and camionettes from near the market in Pétion-Ville). There is also a museum of the 'history of this land, of this people and of serving Satan'. Voodoo is seen by the Museum as the cause of all poverty in Haiti. A turnoff near the Mission leads to Fort Jacques and Fort Alexandre (10 minutes by car or an easy 45 minutes walk), two forts on adjoining summits built after the defeat of Napoleon. The views north over the Cul de Sac plain are breathtaking. Fort Jacques is restored.

Kenscoff is a hill resort where, 30 minutes (15 km) from Pétion-Ville, but 1,500m above sea level, members of the élite retire to their country homes in July and August to escape the heat. A camionette from Pétion-Ville is US$0.30. **D** *Hotel Florville* is fairly basic and not especially friendly but provides refreshments and meals in a nice dining room. Marketday is on a Friday. The road is being worked on and you can now drive just beyond **Furcy,** from where you can hike to the summit above Kenscoff that is topped by a radio mast (about one hour), or the summit just to the west, called Morne Zombi. The ridge just to the east of the radio mast can be reached by a surfaced road in poor condition. It offers views south over a rugged, dark massif that boasts Haiti's highest peak, the 2,674m La Selle. It can get cold at the top if its cloudy.

From the ridge, a four- or five-hour hike (at a comfortable pace) along a trail heading towards the village of **Seguin** brings you to **Parc La Visite**, a nature park covering part of the massif. It has pine woods, montane cloud forest at higher altitudes, dozens of big limestone caves (one 10 km long), and strange karst-formation rocks locals call 'broken teeth' (Cr: kase dan). See further page 360. A guide is required. Camp at a disused saw mill (Cr: siri) by the trail, where water is available from a fountain. Bring thick clothes and sleeping bags; temperatures can fall to freezing at night. A waterfall is a short hike away. For longer hikes and fine views, head east with a guide and climb the 2,282m Pic Cabaio or the 2,100m Pic La Visite (another camping site). The park keeper, Jean-Claude, rents horses. Seguin lies on a sloping plateau on the massif's southern face, about one hour beyond the park. **C** pp hostal/guest house, includes breakfast and dinner. Book in advance through the restaurant *Yaquimo* in Jacmel, they will send a guide with a mule/horse to carry your luggage and show you the way to the hostal. If you are very fit the walk can be done in less than three hours. From Seguin, a five-hour hike gets you to the south-coast village of Marigot, from where you can bus back to Port-au-Prince via Jacmel in 4 hours.

Wildlife enthusiasts should visit **Lake Saumâtre** (see page 360), at the eastern end of the Cul de Sac plain near the Dominican border. The newly improved road from Croix-des-Bouquets to the border crossing at Malpasse skirts the lake's southern side. The northern side offers more chance of seeing its wildlife. On Route Nationale 3 heading northeast from Port-au-Prince towards Mirebalais, fork right at the Thomazeau turnoff to the lakeside villages of Manneville and Fond Pite. It takes 90 minutes.

South of Port-au-Prince

Set off on the RN2, the highway heading west toward Les Cayes. The lush, densely populated coastal Léogâne Plain, 45 minutes west of the capital, offers a look at rural life. East and west of the town of Léogâne, the plain is dotted with small villages and criss-crossed by bumpy lanes. After Léogâne at the Dufort junction fork left. The road climbs steeply, winding through the mountains with good views.

Jacmel

The port of Jacmel is Haiti's prettiest, but run down, city. Its name derives from an Indian word meaning 'rich land'. Quiet, Jacmel has changed little since the late 19th century when it was a booming coffee port and its wealthy merchants built New

Orleans-style mansions using cast iron pillars and balconies imported from France or the United States. The charm of its Victorian architecture is matched by a setting at the head of a 3 km wide horseshoe bay, with streets winding down three small hills to a palm-fringed, black-sand beach. A hurricane swallowed up most of Jacmel's beach and what is left is dirty with pigs rooting around in the debris.

The best views can be had from the south-facing upper veranda of the *Manoir Alexandre*, a turn-of-the-century patrician home that is now a guest house. The main square is pleasant and busy with vendors; the *Hôtel de la Place* restaurant is a good place to have lunch and watch the world go by. One block to the east opposite the church is an iron market built in 1895. Saturday is market day. The street below the *Manoir Alexandre*, Rue Seymour Pradel, has another old residence, now an art gallery called *Salubria-Brictson Galleries*. Owner Bob Brictson is in residence only a few months of the year, but if you knock you will be shown his collection of world-wide art. Closer to the beach, on Rue Commerce, more 19th-century homes have been turned into galleries or handicraft stores. The Boucard family residence at the corner of Grand' Rue and Commerce, is especially fine. At the other end of Commerce, near the wharf, note the Vital family warehouse dating from 1865. The nearby prison was built in the 18th century. Jacmel's handicraft speciality is boxes, trays, place mats and other objects covered with parrots or flowers, hand-painted in bright colours.

Sleeping **B** *La Jacmelienne*, T2883451. A modern, 2-storey hotel on the beach with pool, MAP, fans, no a/c, often no water either, all rooms with balcony and sea view, restaurant open-air and pleasant at night. **B-C** *Hotelflorida*, Rue du Commerce 29, near the Post Office, T2882805, F2883182. Breakfast available, homely, cosy living room, friendly staff, also **AL** suite with 4 beds. Next to the hotel is a French patisserie with lovely bread, pizza etc, where you can eat in the backyard. **C** *Hôtel de la Place*, 3 Rue de l'Eglise, T2882832, overlooks Place d'Armes. Good functional rooms with bathrooms, clean, pleasant restaurant, reasonable food. **D** *Manoir Alexandre*, Rue d'Orléans, T2882711. Large untended garden, faded grandeur, lots of character but shared bathroom has seen better days, lovely view from veranda, good sunset watching, breakfast included but no other meals available, appears to be run by school children. **F** *Guy's*, 52 Grand' Rue, T2883421. 10 rooms, includes breakfast, 2 with bathroom, clean, popular, good value.

Nightlife *Yaquimo Nightclub & Restaurant* is 100m west of the wharf. Fairly good food, good atmosphere, live bands. Book here for the guest house in Seguin.

Shopping There are lots of artists painting and selling their work along Portail Léogane. Most of the handicrafts are sold in the small shops by the entrance to *La Jacmelienne*.

Transport In Port-au-Prince, buses leave from the station Jacmel on Dessalines, a couple of blocks the other side of Chareron, 2½-3 hrs, US$1.50, lovely route, very crowded. In Jacmel buses leave from the gas station at the junction of Portail Léogane and Avenue de La Liberté.

Directory **Banks** Exchange: *BMH*, 60 Grand' Rue, between bus station and *Guy's Guest House*, good rates, changes TCs. You can also change money at *La Jacmelienne*, but don't expect a good rate.

Beaches
Beaches on the south coast tend to have a slight undertow

A good dirt road leads east to fine white-sand beaches. The first is Cyvadier, a tiny cove down a side-road at Km 7. The cliffs and trees surrounding the beach prevent much sunbathing, but the water is clean and pleasant. The surf can be rough at times. Fishermen cast their nets from the beach. A quiet hotel and restaurant, **L-A** *Cyvadier Plage*, T2883323, offers rooms with ceiling fans, balcony, private bath with constant water and electricity most of the time, price includes 3 meals, mostly seafood, fruit and vegetables, all fresh and local, secure, gates locked at night. At Km 15, just before Cayes Jacmel, is Raymond-les-Bains, a beach alongside the road. No facilities except showers. Beware of the slight undertow. Just after Cayes Jacmel, at Ti

Mouillage, the road runs beside two beaches. The first has a basic restaurant. From Marigot, a pretty coastal village 10 km further on, a four-wheel drive can climb a rough trail to the village of Seguin and the Parc National La Visite (see under Excurions from Port-au-Prince).

Bassin Bleu
There are excellent views over Jacmel bay on the way

A 12 km track into the hills west of Jacmel leads to Bassin Bleu, a series of natural pools and waterfalls descending a limestone gorge in tiers. The biggest, deep, blue-green pool is framed by smooth rocks and draped with creeper and maidenhair fern. Jump in for a cool swim. It takes 1½-2 hours each way on foot or horseback (horses for hire in Jacmel or in the village up the hill on the other side of the river from Jacmel, about US$6-7, depending on the quality). Take a guide, fixing a price in advance, and water to drink. If it has not rained, the road is fine for a four-wheel drive three quarters of the way. The Jacmel guide hands over to a local guide for the last kilometre which is a rough path and, at one point, requires the aid of a rope. This means an additional small fee. Guides here can be a problem, only one with the rope is needed, but you will find that you may be accompanied by others who will later demand payment. Gilbert is charming and helpful over the slippery rocks.

West of Port-au-Prince

The southwestern peninsula is the greenest and most beautiful part of Haiti, its rugged western tip has forests, rivers, waterfalls and unspoilt beaches.

The Route Nationale 2 to Les Cayes is very scenic but is frequently almost non-existent and where there is any surface it is often seriously potholed. For the first 92 km it runs along the north coast of the peninsula. At Km 68 is the town of **Petit Goave** (Cr: Ti Gwav). Visit the *Relais de l'Empereur* (T2229557), once the residence of Emperor Faustin 1 (1849-56). The hotel is no longer operating, but the caretaker will show you around.

Just 2 km down a turn-off at Km 92 is the smugglers' port of **Miragoane**, a town of narrow streets that wind around a natural harbour or climb up a hill capped by a neo-gothic church. The town is dirty, dusty, crowded and poor, bars and restaurants no longer function and the hotel is for sale. Activity has moved up to the main road where there is a large market. In the centre of the market is a good café with parking space, medium prices. A four-wheel drive is needed for the dirt road that continues along the north coast, fording rivers and passing fishing villages, as far as Petit Trou de Nippes. At Petite Rivière de Nippes, 15 km along this road, a three hour trek inland on foot or horseback (take a guide) brings you to one of Haiti's four great waterfalls, **Saut De Baril**.

After Miragoane, the main road crosses the peninsula's spine and reaches the southern, Caribbean coast at Aquin (Km 138) where you can bathe in several rivers. At **Zanglais**, 6 km farther on, there are white sand beaches near the road. (Beware of slight undertow at any beach on the south coast.) Just beyond Zanglais a ruined English fort is visible on a small offshore island, with the remains of a battery emplacement opposite, on the mainland.

Les Cayes

On a wet, coastal plain 196 km west of Port-au-Prince, Haiti's fourth city, Les Cayes (Cr: Okay) sits. It is quiet but not without charm. The Fête de Notre Dame around 15 August is recommended. Spend the day swimming, eating, drinking and watching people, and at night the crowd moves to the *musique racine* until 0200 which is irresistible. Some people sleep on the beach because hotels are usually over-booked. Advance booking is necessary at this time. In Port-au-Prince, buses, or taptaps leave in the mornings from the same area as those for Jacmel on Blvd Dessalines, for the four hour trip (US$4). Visible from the waterfront is **Ile-à-Vache** (*Population*: 5,000), a 20 km-long island that was Henry Morgan's base for a 1670 raid against Panama. It has Indian remains and good beaches on the southern side near La Hatte, the biggest village. Visit it by renting a boat with outboard (about US$25 for the day) or take the daily ferry leaving at around 1600, and pay to sleep in someone's home. Or camp, after asking permission. A more regular service goes to **Port Morgan**, a wonderful, small resort/marina run by a French couple, Didier and Françoise Boulard, T2861600, F2861603, portmorgan@globelsud.net They have their own boat service to Les Cayes, US$10, and offer tours to local villages for market and other activities. There are some beautiful hikes in the area. Accommodation **B-C** per person in immaculate bungalows includes three meals, delicious French food, restaurant open for visitors, breakfast US$5, 0730-0930, lunch from US$9, 1200-1500, dinner from US$13.50, 1700-1800, reserve before noon. Very knowledgeable and helpful hosts, willing to help with travel arrangements on the mainland.

Fortresse des Platons, a huge ruined fortress on a 600m summit overlooking the coastal plain, can be visited in a one day excursion from Les Cayes. It was built in 1804 at Dessalines' behest. Take the coast road southwest out of the city. Just after Torbeck, a rough road heads inland up a river valley via Ducis to the village of Dubreuil (trucks from Les Cayes). From Dubreuil, the fortress is a two to three hour hike up a steep trail with great views. Carry on the same trail via Formond to enter the **Macaya National Park**, which has Haiti's last virgin cloud forest surrounding the 2,347 m Pic Macaya. See page 360 for the park's vegetation and wildlife. A University of Florida base at Plaine Durand (two hours beyond the fortress) has basic camping facilities. Hire guides for hikes into the lower montane rain forest. Only the very fit should attempt the hike to the top of the Pic Macaya. It entails climbing a 2,100 m ridge and then descending to 1,000m before tackling the peak itself. Allow at least two days each way and take a guide.

Excursions

Beyond Torbeck, the coast road goes as far as **St Jean du Sud** where a small offshore cay is suitable for camping. Before St Jean du Sud, fork right at L'Acul for **Port Salut**, a 90-minute drive from Les Cayes (two buses a day, also some trucks). This

West of Port-au-Prince

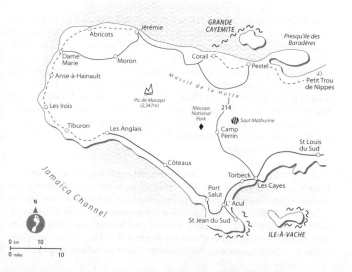

Haiti

small village (birthplace of ex-president Aristide) has a wild, 800m-long, palm-lined beach with fine, white sand that is one of the most beautiful in Haiti. The town is a haven of paved roads and laid back people who do not hassle. The beaches are beautiful and totally empty. There is a pleasant waterfall, 10 minutes' drive, 30 minutes' walk, where you can swim. Ask locals for directions.

Sleeping **C** *La Cayenne*, T2860379, by the beach, on the main street. Price depends on whether you
& eating have a/c, pool, the only restaurant in town, poor service. **C** *La Concorde*, Rue Gabions de Indigènes, T2860277. Rooms with bath, fan, EP, not always open, very comfortable. At the end of the village is a **E** *Village Touristique*, BP 118, comfortable bungalows with shower, big bed, mosquito screens, nice, quiet, right on beach, water but not always electricity, candles supplied, contact Maurice, the caretaker; or rent rooms from locals. Two other hotels are *Impérial*, in the town centre and *Meridien*, just before you enter Les Cayes, with a restaurant. In Port Salut, *Village*, booking through the *P'tit Bistro* in Pétion-Ville, T2573042. A 20 mins' walk beyond the former *Arada Inn*, now closed, leads to a good and noisy restaurant, US$3 for breakfast, US$6.25 for fish or lobster.

Transport Back to Port-au-Prince is easy until early afternoon but allow 5-6 hrs for the journey and take food and water.

West coast The adventurous can take the coastal route from Les Cayes to **Jérémie**, around the
road peninsula's tip, a remote, rugged, lush region that has changed little in 200 years. It has wild rivers, sand beaches, mountains falling steeply into the sea, and some of Haiti's last rain forest. Allow four days. Les Cayes buses or taptaps may go as far as **Les Anglais**, depending on the state of the road. A four-wheel drive may even get to **Tiburon**. Thereafter, you must hike to **Anse d'Hainault** or even **Dame Marie** before finding road good enough to be serviced by taptaps out of Jérémie. Alternatively, try getting a ride on sloops that carry merchandise and passengers along the coast. Residents in small villages all the way will cook meals and rent beds for a few dollars. 'Pripri', rafts made of bamboo lashed together and steered by a pole, ply the rivers. Anse d'Hainault and Abricots (25 km west of Jérémie) have good beaches.

The scenic, hair-raising, 97 km mountain road from Les Cayes to Jérémie, across the Massif de la Hotte, can be done in three hours, but it may be impassable after rain and must be done in daylight. One hour's drive brings you to **Camp Perrin**, a hill resort at the foot of the 2,347 m Pic de Macaya. Here there are several guest houses. Rent horses for a two-hour ride to **Saut Mathurine**, Haiti's biggest waterfall. It has good swimming in the deep, green pool at its base.

Fork right off the Jérémie Road at the Kafou Zaboka intersection for **Pestel**, a picturesque port dominated by a French fort. Worth seeing any time of the year, but especially for the Easter weekend regatta, when many Rara bands come. The town is pretty with old wooden houses, a hotel with nice rooms and a friendly owner. Five minutes from Pestel there is the *Café de la Gare* restaurant run by a Frenchman and his son (dancing in the evenings, happy hour Saturday evening), and a few bungalows for rent which are basic but OK, **C** for 2-4 people, by the sea. Charter a boat to tour nearby fishing villages such as **Les Basses** (Cr: Obas) on the Baradères peninsula and **Anse-à-Maçon** on the offshore island of **Grande Cayemite** with its splendid view of the Massif de la Hotte and distant Pic Macaya. The beaches are very beautiful and totally empty.

Jérémie With crumbling mansions overgrown by rampant vegetation, Jérémie is famed for its poets, eccentrics and isolation. The road is bad. Some buses are still running from Port-au-Prince, however, leaving from Jean-Jacques Dessalines near Rue Chareron (US$8). The 12-hour overnight ferry ride is not recommended. At least 800 (maybe as many as 1,500) Jérémie residents drowned when an overloaded ferry, the *Neptune*, sank on its way to Port-au-Prince in February 1993. MAF and Caribintair have a total of six flights a week from Port-au-Prince. They may be booked up to 10 days ahead. On a hill above the town, with a shady garden, is **D** *Hotel La Cabane* (MAP). Also out of town is **C** *Anse-du-Clerc Beach*, T2463519. Ask the owner to collect you from Jérémie airstrip. The bungalow has a thatched roof and is situated in a coconut grove by a beach of polished pebbles. The seabed is sandy. It is a very peaceful spot. Dinner and breakfast are included. Anse d'Azur, 4 km west of the town, is a white-sand beach with a rocky headland at one end home to a big cave into which you can swim.

North of Port-au-Prince

The seaboard north of the capital is arid or semi-arid most of the way to Gonaïves, and all round the northwest peninsula as far as Port-de-Paix. This area was hit by drought and famine in 1997 and severe ecological damage has occurred. From Port-de-Paix to the Dominican border, it is quite lush and green. Route Nationale 1 hugs the coast for most of the first 85 km skirting the foot of the Chaine des Matheux mountains.

Cabaret (Km 35) is the former Duvalierville. Its ugly, modernistic buildings and pretensions of becoming Haiti's Brasilia were lampooned in *The Comedians.* **L'Arcahaie** (Km 47) is where Dessalines created the blue and red Haitian flag by tearing the white out of the French tricolor. Outside L'Arcahaie, a dirt road heads east high into the Chaine des Matheux to a region where coffee and indigo was grown in colonial times. A dozen ruined plantation houses survive. The turnoff is just before the point where the highway crosses the small Mi Temps River. Sailboats leave at mid-morning from Montrouis (Km 76) for the 22 km crossing to **Anse-à-Galets** (one guest house), the main town on barren **La Gonâve Island**. In 1997 a ferry capsized just off Montrouis as it was docking. At least 172 died when passengers all crowded to one side caused the boat to turn over only 50m from the shore. At Km 96, after the Côte des Arcadins beaches, the RN1 reaches the port of **St Marc** (**F** *Hotel Belfort*, 166 Rue Louverture, clean, basic). Several fine gingerbread houses are on streets to the east of the main street. A pretty valley runs inland south-east as far as Goavier.

RN 1 is asphalted to Cap-Haïtien, but is badly potholed for 65 km between Pont Sondé & Gonaïves

The highway crosses the river Artibonite at **Pont Sondé**, entering a region of rice paddies irrigated by canals. Fork right at the Kafou Peyi intersection, 2 km north of Pont Sondé, for **Petite Rivière de L'Artibonite** (Cr: Ti Rivyè), a picturesque town built by Christophe on a steep-sided ridge overlooking the river Artibonite. Its Palace of 365 Doors was Christophe's provincial headquarters. In 1802, there was a key battle at the Crète-à-Pierrot fort (five minutes walk above the town) in which Leclerc sacrificed 2,000 men to dislodge a force of 1,200 led by Dessalines.

About 8 km after **L'Estère**, a right turnoff runs southeast 25 km to **Marchand**, a town at the foot of the Cahos mountains that was briefly Dessalines' capital. Hike into the surrounding hills to visit seven big ruined forts built by Dessalines. Near the town is a spring with a natural swimming pool. Dessalines told his soldiers that bathing here made them immune to French bullets. The house of Dessalines' wife, Claire Heureuse, still survives in the town. You can also see the foundations of his own home. After the Marchand turnoff, the RN1 crosses a semi-desert called Savane Désolée.

Amid saltpans and arid lowlands, **Gonaïves** at Km 171 is an ugly, dusty town of 70,000 (Haiti's third largest). It is called the City of Independence because Dessalines proclaimed Haiti's independence here in 1804. The unrest that toppled Jean-Claude Duvalier in February 1986 also began here. **D** *Chez Elias* is a safe, clean guest house (T2740318), Rue Egalité opposite Teleco, rooms with fan and bathroom, MAP. At *Chez Frantz* (T2740348), Avenue des Dattes, the rooms are often taken by long-term residents, but the food is Gonaïves' best. *Rex Restaurant*, Rue Louverture, half a block from the market, has Créole food and hamburgers. Buses (US$3, four hours) leave Port-au-Prince mornings from the intersection of

Haiti

Boulevard La Saline and Jean-Jacques Dessalines. In Gonaïves, mopeds operate as taxis, charging US$0.20 a ride.

After Ennery at Km 201, the RN1 climbs steeply up to the Chaine de Belance watershed and enters the green, northern region. **Limbé** at Km 245, has a museum, Musée de Guahaba, created by Dr William Hodges, a Baptist missionary doctor who runs the local hospital and supervises archaeological digs along the north coast (see La Navidad on page 382). The museum is not always open but you can ask for admission from his family who work at the Limbé hospital nearby. Fort Crète Rouge, above Limbé, is one of the many fortresses built by Christophe.

A rugged side-road from Limbé down to **Le Borgne** (Cr: Oboy) on the coast offers spectacular views. The 20 km either side of Le Borgne abound with white-sand beaches. The high, green mountains right behind add to their beauty, but the coast is densely inhabited and the beaches are often used as a public latrine. From Le Borgne to St Louis du Nord, the road is very bad but not impassable for four-wheel drive.

After Limbé, the main highway descends quickly, offering fine views over L'Acul Bay, where Columbus anchored on 23 December 1492, two days before his flagship sank.

Cap-Haïtien

Nowadays it usually referred to simply as Cap, or Okap in Créole

Cap-Haïtien, Haiti's second city, has a dramatic location on the sheltered, southeast side of an 824m high cape, from which it gets its name. It was the capital in colonial times, when it was called Cap-Français. Its wealth and sophistication earned it the title of 'Paris of the Antilles'. The colony's biggest port, it was also the commercial centre of the northern plain, the biggest sugar producing region. It was burned to the ground three times, in 1734, 1798 and 1802, the last time by Christophe to prevent it falling intact into the hands of the French. It was destroyed again by an 1842 earthquake that killed half the population. The historic centre's architecture is now Spanish influenced, with barrel-tile roofs, porches, arcades and interior courtyards.

North of Port-au-Prince

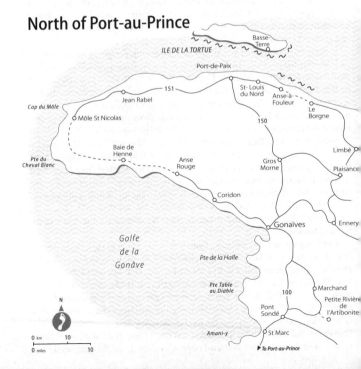

Vertières, an outlying district on the Port-au-Prince Road, is the site of the battle at which Dessalines's army definitively routed the French on 18 November 1803, forcing them to leave the island for good 12 days later. There is a roadside monument.

Cap appears to be more relaxed than Port-au-Prince and you will see people out on the streets at night. It is well worth visiting for its buildings and its surroundings but the people are not accustomed to tourists (*blancs*). The streets are filthy and streams of foul-smelling water run down them. The municipal government functions rarely and its services, such as street cleaning, are moribund. Do not drink the water, nor even use it to clean your teeth.

A-B Beck, on the mountainside, residential Bel-Air district, T2620001. Woodland setting, 2 pools, constant water, own generator, private beach at Cormier, German owner, rooms with private bath and fan, MAP. **A Mont-Joli**, on the hillside above town, T2620300/26, MontJoli@aol.com, has a pool, tennis court, good restaurant, own generator (runs 1000-1200 and 1730-0600), rooms with private bath and a/c, CP. Nearby is **C Les Jardins de l'Océan**, Boulevard de Mer, T2622277. Small hotel, nice terrace with seaview, good food à la carte, friendly atmosphere, cosy rooms all with bathroom, fan. **B Roi Christophe**, T2620414, corner of 24 and B. Central location in colonial house first built in 1724 as the French governor's palace (Pauline Bonaparte stayed here), lush gardens, pool, own generator (not big enough for a/c) runs 0600 until city power comes on, more expensive with a/c, cheaper with fan, CP. Recommended. **F Brise De Mer**, 4 Carenage (on waterfront at northern edge of town), T2620821. Friendly but reportedly not very safe, own generator (but not on all the time), rooms with private bath and fan. **F Columbia**, Rue 5, 3-K. Fan, clean, safe, very helpful owner speaks English, they do their best to make you comfortable, even when there is no water or electricity, beer, soft drinks and home cooked spaghetti on request.

Sleeping
Cap-Haïtien gets electricity only 1900-2300

Cap 2000, Rue 5 and Blvd (not far from waterfront). Sandwiches, ice cream; a popular and cheap restaurant, good food but basic, is on Ave L just past the corner with Rue 1, near *Hotel Columbia*.

Eating

Ateliers Taggart, T2621931, Rue 5 near Blvd (by *Cap 2000*). All kinds of handicrafts, especially weavings and metalwork, 1000-1700 Mon-Fri. Recommended. *Galerie Des Trois Visages*, excellent art gallery next to *Ateliers Taggart*. A tourist market by the port has handicrafts and naive paintings. Bargain hard. There is a supermarket, *Marina Market*, on the Blvd with Rue 13. Most shops close between 1700-1800.

Shopping

Local Car rental: *Hertz*, T2620369. Check price quotes very carefully. Don't leave your passport as deposit. **Air** *MAF* and *Caribintair* both have six flights a week from Port-au-Prince. A Cap-based air taxi service, *Marien Air* (T2620527) offers flights to Port-au-Prince, the Dominican Republic, Turks and Caicos, Bahamas and Jamaica. **Buses** Buses leave Port-au-Prince from the station Au Cap opposite the big Texaco garage at the junction of Delmas Road and Boulevard La Saline between 0630 and 0830, when full. The 274-km trip usually takes 6-7 hrs. Fare US$5.80. It may be necessary to change in Gonaïves, 3½ hrs, US$2. There are two principal taptap stations in Cap:

Transport

Haïti

Barrière Bouteille at southern end of town, for all destinations to Port-au-Prince, and **Port Metalique**, at A2, also south end of town, cross bridge for station for all destinations to Milot (outside *Hotel Bon Dieu Bon*), Hinche, Fort Liberté, Ounaminthe and the border.

Directory **Banks** *BNP*, good for changing TCs; also *Banque Union Haïtien* changes TCs, open until 1300. **Communications** Post Office: Ave B at Rue 17. **Tour companies & travel agents** *Cap Travel*, 84 Rue 23A, T2620517.

Excursions from Cap-Haïtien

Ruins The rich, alluvial plain to the south and east of Cap boasted a thousand plantation houses during the last years of the colonial period. ISPAN, T2622459, Rue 15 and Rue B in Cap, is a good source of information on these nearby colonial ruins, as well as Sans Souci and the Citadelle.

Beaches Excellent beaches on the north side of the cape can be reached in 20 minutes by car.
& hotels The first is **Cormier Plage**, site of the recommended **A** *Hotel Cormier Plage*
The beaches in the (T2621000). Simple chalets or rooms, including breakfast and dinner, excellent
town itself are dirty food, own generator turned on 0730-1100 and 1630-2330. Scuba diving with equip-
& lack charm ment for 10. Good wrecks and coral reefs. Run by a charming French couple, Jean-Claude and Kathy Dicqueman. If you call ahead, they will pick you up from the airport. Book ahead, because tour groups from Dominican Republic sometimes fill the place up. Take mosquito repellent.

Five minutes further west (30 minutes on foot), is **Labadie**, or **Coco beach**, a fenced-off sandy peninsula used by Royal Caribbean Lines as a private beach for its visiting cruise ships on Mondays and Tuesdays. The public may enter to use its facil-ities (pool, restaurants, watersports) for US$3.

Just beyond this beach, about 30 minutes walk, are steps down to **Belli Beach**, a small sandy cove with a hotel, **E**, nice rooms, WC, shower, fan, mosquito nets, they will cook good fish à la créole for US$4.50. Boats, some with outboards, can be rented here to visit nearby Labadie village, dramatically located at the foot of a cliff, and other beaches further along the coast, for example Paradise beach, 30 minutes, US$6, no facilities. Fix a price before boarding. Labadie village (about US$3 by boat, also reachable by scrambling over the rocks) has two guest houses, *Dessa Motel* and *Maison Amitié*, with basic rooms on the beach, both **F**. Employees will buy and cook food for a price to be negotiated. From the end of the road you can also take a boat round the cove (US$10 one way) to *Norm's Place*, an old French fortress, refur-bished by an American who is very hospitable and runs it as a guest house, **E**, with excellent food and service.

Farther still, about 10 km west of Cap, is **AL** *Club Roche Sauvage*, T2622765, an all-inclusive, 144-bed resort with its own 300m beach. Spa and diving extra. Round trip air-and-sea transfer from Port-au-Prince another US$85 per person. Beyond Roche Sauvage is Labadie Shore, Crown Cruise Line's answer to Labadie Beach.

Transport Taptaps US$0.60 to Labadie from Cap leave frequently in the morning from Champs de Mars, away from the centre and the waterfront towards the mountains. Go up Rue 22 for about 10 mins' walk, ask if you get confused, it looks a bit rural. Taptaps will drop you at the gate to Coco Beach.

La Citadelle The massive, mountain-top fortress of La Citadelle was built by King Henri
Haitians call this the Christophe between 1805 and 1820 to deter any French reinvasion (see page 386).
eighth wonder of With walls up to 40 m high and 4 m thick, and covering 10,000 sq m, 20,000 people
the world were pressed into its construction. It is dizzily perched atop the 900m high Pic La Ferrière, overlooking Cap and the entire northern plain, and controlling access to the Central Plateau. Its garrison of 5,000 soldiers (plus the royal family and its reti-nue) could have held out for a year. It is indeed impressive, and has breathtaking

Haiti

views. Restoration work has been under way for years and is well advanced. Behind the fortress, at the end of a 1.5 km level ridge with sheer drops on both sides, is the Site des Ramiers, a complex of four small forts which controlled the rear access. Worth visiting just for the views. ■ *Getting there: take the 25 km asphalt road south from Cap to the village of* Milot *in a publique (US$1) or taptap (US$0.30). Taptaps leave Cap in the morning. Hotels like the Mont Joli offer jeep tours for about US$60 per person, but don't count on the guide's information being correct. From Milot it is a steep 5 km hike through lush countryside up to the fortress (about 1½ hours, start early to avoid the heat; to find the road up to the Citadelle you need to walk through Sans Souci Palace). Wear stout shoes and be protected from the sun. Horses can be rented for about US$7 plus a tip for the man who leads the horse (dangerous in wet weather). Hire a guide even if you don't want one, just to stop others importuning and to make you feel safer (fix the fee in advance, US$10 for two, or more, for the walk). Several speak fluent French and English making the visit more interesting. Prices of refreshments at the Citadelle are higher than elsewhere (US$0.80 for a coke), but someone has had to carry them up there. Those with their own vehicle are able to drive to a carpark two thirds of the way up, reducing the walk to 1½ km. Horses available here too, US$3.50 plus tip (this last part is the hardest). Admission is US$5 to the Citadelle and Sans Souci but they will try and sell it to you for more including guide.*

Sans Souci

At Milot itself are the ruins of Christophe's royal palace, Sans Souci. More than a palace, it was an embryo administrative capital ranging over 8ha in the foothills beneath the Citadelle. Christophe sited his capital inland because of the difficulty of defending coastal cities against the overwhelming naval might of France and Britain. It included a printing shop, garment factory, distillery, schools, hospital, medical faculty, chapel and military barracks. Begun in 1810, inaugurated in 1813, ransacked after Christophe shot himself in the heart with a silver bullet in 1820, it was finally ruined by the 1842 earthquake that destroyed Cap. The admission to the Citadelle covers Sans Souci. Try not to go any day there are cruise ships at Cap or the nearby beaches. If planning to visit both sites, arrive before 1300 to have enough time, as they close at 1700. There are no buses or taptaps back to Cap after 1700.

Morne Rouge
An uprising planned in this area directly led to Haiti's independence

Morne Rouge, 8 km southwest of Cap, is the site of Habitation Le Normand de Mezy, a sugar plantation that spawned several famous rebel slaves. Leave Cap by the RN1 and take a dirt road running north from a point about 75 m west of the turnoff to the town of Plaine du Nord. Its ruins include two aqueducts and bits of walls. Voodoo ceremonies are held under a giant tree in the village. Among its rebel progeny was Mackandal, an African chief's son who ran away, became a prophetic oungan and led a maroon band. After terrorizing the entire northern plain by poisoning food and water supplies, he was captured and burned alive in January 1758. **Bois Caiman** was the wood where slaves met secretly on the night of 14 August 1791 to hold a Voodoo ceremony and plan an uprising. (It is near the Plaine du Nord Road, about 3 km south of the RN1. Ask locals to guide you once you are in the area.) Their leader was an oungan and slave foreman from Le Normand de Mezy called Boukman. The uprising a week later was the Haitian equivalent of the storming of the Bastille. Slaves put plantation houses and cane fields to the torch and massacred hundreds of French settlers. It began the only successful slave revolt in history and led to Haiti's independence. Little is left of the wood now except a giant ficus tree overgrowing a colonial well credited with mystic properties.

Plaine du Nord

The town of Plaine du Nord, 12 km southwest of Cap, is a pilgrimage centre every year on 24-25 July due to the Catholic festival of St James, who is identified with the Voodoo spirit Ogou. Voodoo societies come from all over Haiti, camp in the streets and spend the two days in non-stop drumming and dancing. Many are possessed by Ogou and wallow in a much-photographed mud pool in one of its streets. On 26 July, the feast day of St Anne, most of the Voodoo societies at Plaine du Nord

Haiti

🐟 *Where the buccaneers came from*

The French and English freebooters who began settling on Tortuga Island in 1630 were drawn by the south coast's coves, beaches and small anchorages, and a protective line of reefs with few openings. These freebooters hunted livestock left by the Spanish whom withdrew from the north and west coasts of Hispaniola in 1605 due to pirate raids. Because they smoked the meat on 'boucans', an Indian word for spit, they became known as buccaneers.

decamp to nearby **Limonade**, 15 km southeast of Cap, for another day and night of celebrations. A dirt road on the northwest side of Limonade leads to Bord De Mer De Limonade, a fishing village where Columbus' flagship, the *Santa María*, struck a reef and sank on Christmas Day, 1492. Columbus used wood from the wreck to build a settlement, **La Navidad**, which was wiped out by Taino Indians after he left. Its location was discovered by American archaeologist William Hodges while digging at the site of Puerto Real, a city founded years later on the same spot. The untrained eye will detect nothing of either settlement now, but the Hodges museum in Limbé, 20 km southwest of Cap, has relics.

Fort Liberté Fort Liberté, 56 km east of Cap, is a picturesque, French-designed town on a large bay with a narrow entrance. It is dotted with French forts that can be reached by boat. The best is Fort Dauphin, built in 1732. The bay was the site of the Caribbean's largest sisal plantation until nylon was invented. There are direct taptaps Cap-Fort Liberté, but it may be easier to return to Cap from the main road, which is 4 km from the centre of Fort Liberté. D *Bayaha*, Rue des Bourbons, by the sea, great view, terrace, quiet, good food, evening meal included in price, basic rooms, no a/c, cold water.

Frontier with Dominican Republic **Ounaminthe** is northern Haiti's chief border crossing. Accommodation is available at *Hotel Paradis* on the main street. The Dominican frontier town, Dajabón, is just 2 km from the Ounaminthe taptap station. Taptaps for US$2 from the station nordest in Cap; US$1.10 from Fort Liberté. The crossing is straightforward and the Haitain border office is very helpful. Buses leave Dajabón for many Dominican cities. The river Massacre, which forms the border, had this name long before the massacre of thousands of Haitians in the neighbouring part of the Dominican Republic under Trujillo in 1937, when the river was said to have been red with blood for days. The bridge across the river is packed with money changers and *motoconchos* (not necessary for transport to Haitian border post, which is about 1 km from Dominican side). The Dominican side of the border has been described as an armed camp, with heavy military presence controlling the flow of Haitian labour. The Haitian side, on the other hand, is more like a gypsy camp, with a thicket of tents, lean-tos and a crowd of money changers and 'guides'.

South of Cap-Haïtien For the rugged, the dirt road forking left 5 km before Milot could be an alternative route back to Port-au-Prince via Hinche and the Central Plateau (see page 384). A four-wheel drive is needed. It takes two to three hours. By public transport it takes much longer, up to two days to the capital. Vehicles tend to be old, it is very dusty and the worst stretch is from near Milot to Hinche. The first town is **Grand Rivière du Nord**, where another of Christophe's fortresses, Fort Rivière, sits atop a ridge to the east. It was used by the Cacos guerrillas who fought the US occupation from 1918 to 1920. The Americans captured the Cacos leader Charlemagne Peralte near here. **Dondon** has caves inhabited by bats. One is close to the town. The other, 90 minutes on foot or horseback up a river bed to the west of the village, has heads carved in relief on its walls, presumably by the original Indian inhabitants. In the rainy season, cars cannot ford the river near St Raphaël, but you can walk, with locals helping for a small fee.

Haiti

The Northwest

Except for Tortuga island and a coastal strip running east from Port-de-Paix, the northwest peninsula is Haiti's driest, most barren region. In recent years, especially since the 1991 coup, it has teetered on the brink of famine and toppled over in 1997 when international agencies had to bring aid.

The 86-km mountain road from Gonaïves to Port-de-Paix via Gros Morne fords several rivers and takes four hours in a four-wheel drive, needed for travel anywhere in the northwest. (Minibuses from Gonaïves, big buses from Port-au-Prince, leaving from beside the station Au Cap.) **Port-de-Paix** once made an honest living exporting coffee and bananas. Now it specializes in importing contraband goods from Miami. Vendors tout the wares on all its unpaved streets. In 1992-93, its small freighters also ferried illegal immigrants into Miami. Despite the smuggling, it is safe.

Sleeping

D *Hotel Brise Marina*, about 10 minutes from the town centre northeast along the coast. The best in the area, clean, basic rooms with bathroom, pool, restaurant OK, nice view over the sea. **C** *Le Plaza*, a few hundred metres before *Brise Marina*, looks abandoned, not well maintained, missing light bulbs, no water in pool, possible to order lunch or dinner. *Holiday Beach*, in the town centre, basic.

A coast road runs west from Port-de-Paix along the north coast of the peninsula as far as Môle St Nicolas and then returns to Gonaïves via the south coast. **Jean Rabel** is a tense town which was the site of a peasant massacre in July 1987. At least 150 died in the clash, said to have been engineered by local Duvalierist landlords seeking to crush the attempts of Catholic priests to organize landless peasants. From Jean Rabel round to Baie de Henne, the landscape is arid, windy and dusty. Old people say they can remember when it was still green and forested.

Columbus first set foot on the island of Hispaniola at **Môle St Nicolas**. It has several ruined forts built by the English and French. General Maitland's surrender of Môle to Toussaint in 1798 marked the end of a five-year British bid to gain a toehold on this end of the island. Strategically located on the Windward Passage, just 120 km from Cuba, Môle was long coveted as a naval base by the United States. The hinterland has Haiti's lowest rainfall and little grows. The main occupation is making charcoal and shipping it to Port-au-Prince. Because few trees are left, charcoal makers now dig up roots. The peninsula's south side, especially from Baie de Henne to Anse Rouge, is a mixture of barren rock and desert, but the sea is crystal clear. There are few inhabitants. With salt pans on either side, Anse Rouge ships sacks of salt instead of charcoal.

Tortuga Island

A 30-minute drive to the east of Port-de-Paix by a good, dirt road takes you to **St Louis du Nord**, a pretty coastal town from where sailing boats cross the 10 km channel to Tortuga Island, the Caribbean's biggest pirate base in the 17th century. Nearly 40 km long, 7 km wide and 464m above the sea at its highest point, its smooth rounded shape reminded seafarers of the back of a turtle. (Tortuga in Spanish and La Tortue, its Haitian name, in French.)

Its present population of 30,000 is spread all over the island. The biggest South-coast villages, **Cayonne** and **Basse-Terre**, are less than 1 km apart. A ferryboat leaves Cayonne for St Louis du Nord at 0800 and returns at about 1000, charging locals US$0.50 each way. Foreigners may have to pay up to US$10, depending on their negotiating skills. Boats crossing at other times charge more. From Cayonne there is a narrow cement road up to Palmiste serviced by a single taptap, one of the four or five cars on the island. From Palmiste, the biggest village on the rounded spine, there are spectacular views of the corniche coastline stretching from Cap to Jean Rabel, and the towering mountains behind. The best view is from the home of French Canadian priest Bruno Blondeau (T268-5138/6709), the director of a

Haiti

Catholic Church mission who has effectively governed the island since 1977. He runs 35 schools and has built all 55 km of its road. His order also operates a small, basic hotel (**F**, EP).

The best beach, 2 km long, is at **Pointe Saline**, at the western tip (34 km from Palmiste, two hours by car). This is also the driest part of the island and there is little shade. **La Grotte au Bassin**, 6 km east of Palmiste, is a large cave with a 10 m high precolumbian rock carving of a goddess. There are two other big caves: **Trou d'Enfer**, near La Rochelle ravine, and **La Grotte de la Galerie**, 1 km east of Trou d'Enfer.

The largest historic ruin on the island is a 15m high lime kiln (four à chaux), built at the end of the 18th century. Fort de la Roche, 1639, was once Tortuga's biggest fortress (70m high). Its masonry foundations can be seen at a spring where women wash clothes on the hillside above Basse-Terre. Three cannon and a bit of wall remain from Fort d'Ogeron, built in 1667.

Northeast of Port-au-Prince

Grandly called the Route National 3, the 128-km dirt road northeast from Port-au-Prince to Hinche requires a four-wheel drive and takes at least five hours (much longer by public transport). It starts by crossing the Cul de Sac plain via Croix-des-Bouquets. Here, a newly improved road branches off southeast through a parched, barren region, skirting Lake Saumâtre (see page 360 and 372) before reaching the Dominican border at Malpasse (see page 355). On the north side of the plain, the RN3 zig-zags up a steep mountainside called Morne Tapion (great views back over Port-au-Prince) to reach Mirebalais, a crossroads at the head of the Artibonite valley. It is Haiti's wettest town. The road east leads to Lascahobas and the frontier town of Belladère, the least used of Haiti's three border crossings into the Dominican Republic. The road west heads down the Artibonite valley. Before it gets too bad, a left turnoff leads up into the hills to the charming village of **Ville-Bonheur** with its church built on the spot where locals reported an appearance of the Virgin in a palm tree in 1884. Thousands of pilgrims come every 15 July. The Voodooists among them hike 4 km to visit the much-filmed **Saut d'Eau** waterfall. Overhung by creepers, descending 30 m in a series of shallow pools separated by mossy limestone shelves, the fall seems enchanted. The Voodooists bathe in its waters to purify themselves and light candles to enlist the help of the ancient spirits believed to live there.

The RN3 heads north out of Mirebalais on to the Central Plateau, where the military crackdown was especially harsh after the 1991 coup because peasant movements had been pressing for change here for years. After skirting the Peligre hydroelectric dam, now silted up and almost useless, the road passes Thomonde and reaches the region's capital, **Hinche**. The **F** *Foyer d'Accueil* is an unmarked guest house above a school that is behind the blue and white church on the east side of the main square, basic rooms with fan, rarely any power, EP. The *Hotel Prestige*, also unmarked, at 2 Rue Cité du Peuple, near the market, has not so good rooms for the same price. In Port-au-Prince, buses leave from the station Au Cap at the intersection of Boulevard La Saline and route de Delmas. MAF operates about two flights a week. East of Hinche, **Bassin Zim** is a 20 m waterfall in a lush setting 30 minutes drive from town (head east on the Thomassique Road, then fork north at Papaye). The cascade fans out over a rounded, sloping, limestone rockface. At its foot is a 60 m wide natural pool with deep, milky-blue water that is perfect for swimming.

Background

History

Columbus visited the north coast of Hispaniola, modern Haiti, on his first visit to the **Hispaniola**
West Indies, leaving a few men there to make a settlement before he moved on to
Cuba. Columbus traded with the native Tainos for trinkets such as gold nose plugs,
bracelets and other ornaments, which were to seal the Indians' fate when shown to
the Spanish monarchs. A second voyage was ordered immediately. Columbus tried
again to establish settlements, his first having been wiped out. His undisciplined
men were soon at war with the native Tainos, who were hunted, taxed and enslaved.
Hundreds were shipped to Spain, where they died. When Columbus had to return
to Spain he left his brother, Bartolomé, in charge of the fever-ridden, starving colony. The latter sensibly moved the settlement to the healthier south coast and
founded Santo Domingo, which became the capital of the Spanish Indies. The native
inhabitants were gradually eliminated by European diseases, murder, suicide and
slavery, while their crops were destroyed by newly introduced herds of cattle and
pigs. Development was hindered by the labour shortage and the island became
merely a base from which to provision further exploration, being a source of bacon,
dried beef and cassava. Even the alluvial gold dwindled and could not compete with
discoveries on the mainland. The population of some 400,000 Tainos in 1492 fell to
about 60,000 by 1508. In 1512 the Indians were declared free subjects of Spain, and
missionary zeal ensured their conversion to Christianity. A further 40,000 were
brought from the Turks and Caicos, the Bahamas and Venezuela, but by 1525 the
Indian population had practically disappeared. Sugar was introduced at the beginning
of the 16th century and the need for labour soon brought African slaves to the island.

In the 17th century the French invaded from their base on Tortuga and colonized **Birth of a**
what became known as Saint Domingue, its borders later being determined by the **colony**
Treaty of Ryswick in 1697. The area was occupied by cattle hunting buccaneers and
pirates, but Governor de Cussy, appointed in 1684, introduced legal trading and
planting. By the 18th century it was regarded as the most valuable tropical colony of
its size in the world and was the largest sugar producer in the West Indies. However,
that wealth was based on slavery and the planters were aware of the dangers of rebellion. After the French Revolution, slavery came under attack in France and the
planters defensively called for more freedom to run their colony as they wished. In
1791 France decreed that persons of colour born of free parents should be entitled to
vote; the white inhabitants of Saint Domingue refused to implement the decree and
mulattoes were up in arms demanding their rights. However, while the whites and
mulattoes were absorbed in their dispute, slave unrest erupted in the north in 1791.
Thousands of white inhabitants were slaughtered and the northern plain was put to
the torch. Soon whites, mulattoes and negroes were all fighting with shifting alli-
ances and mutual hatred.

Out of the chaos rose a new leader, an ex-slave called **François-Dominique** **Toussaint**
Toussaint, also known as Toussaint Louverture, who created his own roaming **Louverture**
army after the 1791 uprising. When France and Spain went to war, he joined the
Spanish forces as a mercenary and built up a troop of 4,000 negroes. However, when
the English captured Port-au-Prince in 1794 he defected with his men to join the
French against the English. After four years of war and disease, the English withdrew, by which time Toussaint was an unrivalled leader among the black population. He then turned against the mulattoes of the west and south, forcing their
armies to surrender. Ordered to purge the mulatto troops, Toussaint's cruel lieutenant, **Jean-Jacques Dessalines**, an African-born ex-slave, slew at least 350. Mulatto
historians later claimed that 10,000 were massacred. The same year, torrential rain
broke the irrigation dams upon which the prosperity of the area depended. They

were never repaired and the soil was gradually eroded to become a wilderness. By 1800 Toussaint was politically supreme. In 1801 he drew up a new constitution and proclaimed himself governor general for life. However, Napoleon had other plans, which included an alliance with Spain, complicated by Toussaint's successful invasion of Santo Domingo, and the reintroduction of the colonial system based on slavery. In 1802 a French army was sent to Saint Domingue which defeated Toussaint and shipped him to France where he died in prison. The news that slavery had been reintroduced in Guadeloupe, however, provoked another popular uprising which drove out the French, already weakened by fever.

19th-century revolution This new revolt was led by **Dessalines**, who had risen to power in Toussaint's entourage and was his natural successor. In 1804 he proclaimed himself Emperor of the independent Haiti, changing the country's name to the Indian word for 'high land'. Dessalines was assassinated in 1806 and the country divided between his rival successors: the negro **Christophe** in the north, and the mulatto **Pétion** in the south. The former's rule was based on forced labour and he managed to keep the estates running until his death in 1820. He called himself **Roi Henri Christophe** and built the Citadelle and Sans Souci near Milot, see below for a fictionalized account of these events, read Alejo Carpentier's *El reino de este mundo – The Kingdom of This World*, arguably the first Latin American novel to employ the technique of *lo real maravilloso*). Pétion divided the land into peasant plots, which in time became the pattern all over Haiti and led to economic ruin with virtually no sugar production and little coffee. Revolution succeeded revolution as hatred between the blacks and the ruling mulattoes intensified. Constitutional government rarely existed in the 19th century.

US intervention At the beginning of the 20th century, the USA became financially and politically involved for geopolitical and strategic reasons. Intervention in 1915 was provoked by the murder and mutilation of a president, but occupation brought order and the reorganization of public finances. Provision of health services, water supply, sewerage and education did not prevent opposition to occupation erupting in an uprising in 1918-20 which left 2,000 Haitians dead. By the 1930s the strategic need for occupation had receded and the expense was unpopular in the USA. In 1934 the USA withdrew, leaving Haiti poor and overpopulated with few natural resources. Migrants commonly sought work on the sugar estates of the neighbouring Dominican Republic, although there was hatred between the two nations. In 1937 about 10,000 Haitian immigrants were rounded up and massacred in the Dominican Republic (see Further reading).

Duvalier Dynasty In 1957 **François (Papa Doc) Duvalier**, a black nationalist, was elected president and unlike previous autocrats he succeeded in holding on to power. He managed to break the mulattoes' grip on political power, even if not on the economy. In 1964 he became President-for-Life, a title which was inherited by his 19-year-old son, **Jean-Claude (Baby Doc) Duvalier** in 1971. The Duvaliers' power rested on the use of an armed militia, the **Tontons Macoutes**, to dominate the people. Tens of thousands of Haitians were murdered and thousands more fled the country. However, repression eased under Jean-Claude though dissidence rose encouraged partly by US policies on human rights. Internecine rivalry continued and the mulatto elite began to regain power, highlighted by the President's marriage to Michèle Bennett, the daughter of a mulatto businessman, in 1980. Discontent began to grow with the May 1984 riots in Gonaïves and Cap-Haïtien, and resurfaced after the holding of a constitutional referendum on 22 July 1985 which gave the Government 99.98% of the vote. Several months of unrest and rioting gradually built up into a tide of popular insistence on the removal of Duvalier, during the course of which several hundred people were killed by his henchmen. The dictatorship of the Duvaliers (father and son) was brought to a swift and unexpected end when the President-for-Life fled to France on 7 February 1986.

The removal of the Duvaliers left Haitians hungry for radical change. The leader of
the interim military-civilian Government, **General Henri Namphy**, promised
presidential elections for November 1987, but they were called off after Duvalierists
massacred at least 34 voters early on polling day with apparent military connivance.
New, rigged elections were held in January 1988, and **Professor Leslie Manigat** was
handed the presidency only to be ousted in June when he tried to remove Namphy as
army commander. Namphy took over as military president, but four months later
he himself was ousted in a coup that brought **General Prosper Avril** to power. Dissatisfaction within the army resurfaced in April 1989, when several coup attempts
were staged within quick succession and lawlessness increased as armed gangs,
including disaffected soldiers, terrorized the population. Nevertheless, the USA
renewed aid, for the first time since 1987, on the grounds that Haiti was moving
towards democratic elections, promised for 1990, and was making efforts to combat
drug smuggling. Under General Namphy, cocaine worth US$700mn passed
through Haiti each month, with a 10% cut for senior army officers. However, Avril's
position was insecure; he moved closer to hardline Duvalierists and arrests, beatings
and murders of opposition activists increased. Foreign aid was again cut off in January 1990 when Avril imposed a state of siege and the holding of elections looked
unlikely. Finally, in March, General Avril fled the country after a week of mass demonstrations and violence. Following his resignation, Haiti was governed by an
interim President, Supreme Court judge, **Ertha Pascal-Trouillot**.

**Democracy
& the army**

Despite poor relations between Mme Pascal-Trouillot and the 19-member Council of
State appointed to assist her, successful elections were held on 16 December 1990. The
presidential winner, by a landslide margin of 67% to 15%, was **Father Jean-Bertrand
Aristide**; his nearest rival was the former finance minister Marc Bazin.

**1990 elections
& coup**

President Aristide ('Titide'), a Roman Catholic priest who was expelled from the
Salesian order in 1988 for 'incitement to hatred, violence and class struggle', was
sworn in on 7 February. His denunciations of corruption within the government,
church and army over the previous decade had won him a vast following. Among his
immediate steps on taking office were to start investigations into the conduct of
Mme Pascal Trouillot and many other officials, to seek the resignation of six gener-
als, to propose the separation of the army and police and to garner urgently-needed
financial assistance from abroad for the new administration. Aristide's refusal to
share power with other politicians, his attacks on the interests of the armed forces
and the business elite and the actions of some of his militant supporters provoked
his overthrow on 30 September 1991 by the army. Aristide fled into exile. Harsh
repression was imposed after the deposition of Aristide; at least 2,000 people were
said to have died in the first six months, almost 600 during the coup itself. People
began fleeing in small boats to the United States' Guantánamo naval base on Cuba in
an exodus that had reached 38,000 by May 1992. The USA brought it to an end by
immediately repatriating everyone without screening political asylum claims.

International condemnation of the coup was swift, with the Organization of American States, led by the USA, imposing an embargo. While the EU and other nations
did not join in the embargo, they did follow the OAS in suspending aid and freezing
Haitian government assets. The sanctions hurt, but not sufficiently to promote a for-
mula for Aristide's return; this was partly because of Washington's misgivings about
his radical populism.

**International
pressure**

The election of Bill Clinton to the US presidency in 1992 with the prospect of
more decisive US action on restoring Aristide to power prompted United Nations
involvement. Former Argentine foreign minister Dante Caputo was appointed UN
special envoy for Haiti in December 1992. With Washington making it clear it was
ready to step up sanctions, Caputo persuaded the army commander, **General
Raoul Cedras**, to agree in February 1993 to the deployment of 250 civilian UN/OAS
human rights monitors throughout Haiti. Further UN pressure was applied in June

1993 with the imposition of an oil embargo and a freeze on financial assets. As a result, an accord was reached in July whereby Aristide would return to office by 30 October, Cedras would retire and Aristide would appoint a new army chief and a prime minister.

As the 30 October deadline approached, it became clear that Aristide would not be allowed to return. In mid-October, the Haitian rulers humiliated the USA by refusing to allow a ship to dock carrying a 1,300-strong UN non-combat mission. Oil and arms sanctions were reimposed, yet Aristide supporters continued to be killed and harassed. Aristide's appointed cabinet resigned in mid-December as the régime showed no signs of weakening. In fact, as smuggled fuel from the Dominican Republic flowed in, Cedras and his collaborators set their sights on staying in power until the end of Aristide's term of office, February 1996.

Meanwhile, tensions between Aristide and the Clinton administration grew as the USA appeared unable, or unwilling, to break the impasse. Pressure from the US Black Caucus and from Florida politicians eventually persuaded Clinton to take more positive action. The policy of returning boat people was stopped. Tough worldwide sanctions, including a cessation of commercial flights, were initiated in May 1994 and the Dominican Republic was approached to control sanctions breaking. These measures led to a state of emergency in Haiti, but not an end to defiance.

Aristide's return Despite the lack of wholehearted support in the USA, an occupation of Haiti by 20,000 US troops, first proposed in June, began on 19 September 1994. Aristide returned to the presidency on 15 October to serve the remainder of his term, aided first by a 6,000 strong US force, then by 6,000 UN troops which replaced the Americans in March 1995.

General Cedras and his chief-of-staff, General Philippe Biamby, were talked into exile in Panama, while the third leader of the regime, police chief Michel François, fled to the Dominican Republic. In the months after the regime's demise, Aristide set about reducing the influence of the army and police and the USA began to train new recruits for a new police force. By April 1995, the absence of a fully-trained police force and of an adequate justice system contributed to a general breakdown of law and order. Many people suspected of robbery or murder were brutally punished by ordinary Haitians taking the law into their own hands. 'Zenglendo' thugs, often thought to be demobilized soldiers, were involved in the killing of political figures and others. The fear of violence disrupted preparations for legislative and local elections, held over two rounds in June and July 1995.

The elections gave overwhelming support to Aristide's Lavalas movement in the Senate (all but one of the seats up for election) and the Lower House (71 of the 83 seats) but the turn out was very low and the results were bitterly contested. Twenty three of the 27 competing parties denounced the election because of irregularities reported by international observers.

Economic reform under Aristide was slow and there was dissent within the Cabinet. Progress on judicial reform progressed but investigations into recent killings stalled. The US Senate consequently blocked disbursement of aid. Mob violence and extra-judicial killings continued, with the new police force unable to do anything about it.

René Préval Presidential elections were held on 17 December 1995 and for the first time power was transferred from one elected Haitian president to another. **René Préval**, a close aide of Aristide's, won a landslide victory with 87% of the vote, although only 25% of the electorate turned out and most opposition parties boycotted the event. He was inaugurated on 7 February 1996 and **Rosny Smarth** was later sworn in as Prime Minister. The new Government aimed to introduce a new privatization plan for nine state companies, based on the Bolivian system whereby companies invest in, rather than buy, a minority share of the state entity but progress was painfully slow with considerable local opposition. Agreement on a structural adjustment programme was reached with the IMF in May but was hampered by a hostile Congress and not approved until October. Haiti was treated as a political football in the US Senate, which was absorbed in its own presidential race. Aid only dribbled in, leaving civil servants and police unpaid and mounting violence in the streets. The UN Peace-keeping Force was repeatedly asked to stay for longer as the new police force was still unready to take over. Some arrests were made as the Government attempted to move against widespread corruption but nothing could be done about the nation-wide violence which claimed hundreds of lives.

Rivalries within the ruling coalition, the Lavalas Political Organization, spilled into the open at the end of 1996 when Aristide launched a new group, the Lavalas Family (Fanmi Lavalas), which became a political party in time for the senatorial and local elections held in April 1997. Less than 10% of the electorate voted in the elections for nine senators, two deputies, members of 564 local assemblies and 133 municipal representatives. The major opposition parties boycotted the poll, claiming that the electoral council was controlled by Aristide, and later called for the results to be annulled. The second round of the senatorial elections was postponed indefinitely. It was feared that if the Lavalas Family gained control of the Senate, the reform package would be blocked.

In June, Prime Minister Rosny Smarth resigned. He blamed elements of Lavalas for stirring up political unrest and the electoral council for not annulling the April elections, which were marked by fraud. His departure increased concern in Washington that the faltering political and economic recovery programme would be brought down. Smarth remained in office until October pending the appointment of a successor, but he had still not been replaced a year later. The two opposing factions of the Lavalas movement were unable to resolve their quarrel over the April 1997 elections. Local elections were completed in mid-October, allowing the formation of a permanent electoral council which was dominated by Aristide supporters. At the end of November 1997, about 1,200 UN troops began to withdraw, leaving 300 police instructors in place for another year and 400 US troops who were engaged in construction and health care. Violence and murders continued. The Organization Politique Lavalas changed its name to Organization du Peuple en Lutte (OPL) to distance itself from Fanmi Lavalas, and in February 1998 it dropped its demands to have the April 1997 elections annulled, but other parts of a political deal collapsed within a week. International donors were frustrated by the impasse, and it was claimed that millions of dollars of aid were being held up with a consequent brake on growth and poverty alleviation.

In July 1998, Education Minister Jacques Edouard Alexis was nominated as head of government. He had the support of the OPL but political infighting delayed his appointment. In January 1999, President Préval declared Alexis Prime Minister and announced he would no longer recognize parliament as its term had expired under the law governing the delayed 1995 elections. Nevertheless, amid violence and demonstrations, the Chamber of Deputies continued to meet, claiming it was entitled to sit for four years from October 1995. Confusion reigned and was intensified with the expiry of terms of office of municipal councils. A new government was finally sworn in on 26 March 1999 and a provisional electoral board two days later. The cabinet included several supporters of Aristide and five members of a group of small extra-parliamentary parties which had helped to negotiate an end to the deadlock. The OPL broke off negotiations after the murder of one of its senators. Violence continued with many deaths. The first round of much-delayed legislative and municipal elections was held on 21 May 2000, with the second round set for 25 June. The FL won a majority of the 27 Senate seats with 14 of the 19 seats being contested, and were heading for victory in the 83-seat Chamber of Deputies. Where no party won a majority a second round will settle the contest. Foreign observers described the elections as flawed but credible, but opposition parties denounced the results, claiming that supporters of the FL controlled the Conseil Electoral Provisoire (CEP), 15% of polling stations failed to open, about one million ballot papers were stolen and the FL expelled opposition observers from many polling stations. Murder and harassment of candidates and their supporters before and during the vote did not prevent the USA and the UN praising the generally peaceful voting process. Presidential elections will be held at the end of 2000 and Aristide is expected to run for elections.

The people

The Haitians are almost wholly black, with a culture that is a unique mixture of African and French influences. Haiti was a French colony until 1804 when, fired by the example of the French Revolution, the black slaves revolted, massacred the French landowners and proclaimed the world's first black republic. Throughout the 19th century the Haitians reverted to a primitive way of life, indulging in a succession of bloody, almost tribal wars. Even today African cults, particularly voodoo, play a large part in everyday life like nowhere else in the Caribbean. The country is desperately poor and the standard of living is the lowest in the Americas. According to UNICEF, the literacy rate is only 45%, while only 20% of children reach secondary school.

Government

Under the terms of the July 1993, UN-brokered agreement to restore democracy, Haiti has two legislative houses, a 27-seat Senate and an 83-seat Chamber of Deputies. The parliament in this form, with the elected president as chief of state, came into effect in October 1994.

The economy

Structure of production Haiti is the Western Hemisphere's poorest country and among the 30 poorest in the world. Seventy five percent of the people fall below the World Bank's absolute poverty level. It is overpopulated. It lacks communications, cheap power and raw materials for industry. Its mountainous terrain cannot provide a living for its rural population.

Until the embargo, the main economic problem was chronic low agricultural productivity, compounded by low world commodity prices. Just 1% of the population controls 40% of the wealth. The average farm size is less than 1ha. Only a third of the land is arable, yet most of the people live in the country, using rudimentary tools to grow maize, rice, sorghum and coffee. Deforestation has played havoc with watersheds and agriculture. Only a fraction of the land is now forested, yet charcoal continues to supply 70% of fuel needs. Agriculture generates 32% of the gdp but employs more than half the workforce. Coffee is the main cash crop, providing 8% of exports. Sugar and sisal output has slumped as population pressure has forced farmers to switch to subsistence crops. A land reform programme was begun in 1997 in the Artibonite Valley to give land to families in an area where violent land disputes have been common. Agriculture was badly hit by a drought in the northwest in 1997, causing famine in that area, and Hurricane Georges in 1998, which brought flooding. Around 100 people are believed to have perished and many thousands were left homeless. The devastation was intensified because of the lack of trees and ground cover, which allowed flooding and erosion.

Industry and commerce is limited, and heavily concentrated in Port-au-Prince. Until the embargo, assembly operations turned out baseballs, garments and electronic parts for export to the USA. After the lifting of the embargo, factories were slow to reopen because of civil unrest and electricity shortages. In addition, a 40% increase in the minimum wage, to US$2.57 per day, made Haiti's pay level marginally higher than the Dominican Republic, to which many offshore companies had relocated. Vegetable oils, footwear and metal goods are still produced for domestic consumption. Manufactured goods make up two thirds of total exports. Tourism all but disappeared in the 1980s and 1990s, at first because of a scare about AIDS, then because of the political instability. Many hotels were forced to close.

The 1987 aid cut-off by major donors hit the economy hard and gdp began to slip. **Recent trends** Aid resumed in 1990 as the prospects of elections improved. By mapping out very orthodox economic policies, the Aristide government secured pledges of more than US$400mn in international aid in July and August 1991, but it never materialized because of the coup the following month.

The three years following the coup were marked by import and export embargos, the suspension of foreign aid amounting to US$150-180mn a year and the freezing of assets abroad. There were huge job losses in the formal sector of 50,000 (35,000 in the export assembly industries alone) and of a similar amount in the informal sector. Foreign exchange earnings plummeted; the electricity and telephone systems deteriorated; prices for foodstuffs and other essential items rose sharply. The only areas to benefit were contraband and drug smuggling (56kg of cocaine passed through Haiti in 1992, 157kg in 1993 and 716kg in 1994. In 1998 a record 685kg was seized in two weeks from air passengers arriving from Panama). Remittances by the 1.5 million Haitians living abroad, put at about US$150mn a year, were not affected.

The return of Aristide and the lifting of the trade embargo led to hopes of economic recovery. The Paris Club group of lending countries cancelled US$75mn of bilateral debt and the forgiveness of debt arrears renewed access to suspended aid. International donor agencies pledged a total of US$1.2bn in various packages, but also required Haiti to follow set economic guidelines. A reform programme was drawn up, including the privatization of nine of 33 state enterprises but opposition to it delayed implementation (only a flour mill and a cement company have been sold so far). It was left to the Préval Government in 1996 to push ahead with unpopular economic reform under the aegis of the IMF in order to release aid blocked due to lack of progress. Although an IMF three-year programme was agreed in October 1996, progress in implementing it was painfully slow. Congress was seven months late in approving the 1997 budget and foreign aid donors became exasperated by the continuing strife, violence and strikes. Michel Camdessus, managing director of the IMF, criticized Congress for its tardiness, instead engaging in 'disgraceful' factionalism.

In 1999, President Préval announced a road construction programme, an agrarian reform programme for the northeast and a US$311mn short term plan to create jobs, improve living conditions and encourage participation in the elections. However, political and social disturbances did not augur well for success. The delay in congressional elections was accompanied by delays in disbursements of foreing aid; US$504 mn was suspended until the new parliament was in place.

Culture

Although Haiti wiped out slavery in its 18th-century revolution, its society still suffers from the racial, cultural and linguistic divisions inherited from slavery. Toussaint's tolerant statesmanship was unable to resist Napoleon's push to reimpose slavery. It took the tyranny and despotism of Dessalines and Christophe. Haitian despots stepped into the shoes of the French despots. The new, mulatto ruling class considered its French language and culture superior to the blacks' Créole language and Voodoo religion, which it despised. The corruption and despotism of the black political class created by Duvalier suggest that, despite its profession of *noirisme*, it internalized the mulatto contempt for its own race.

Voodoo (French: Vaudou) is a blend of religions from West Africa, above all from **Religion** Dahomey (present-day Benin) and the Congo River basin. Like Cuba's Santería and Brazil's Candomblé, it uses drumming, singing and dance to induce possession by powerful African spirits with colourful personalities. These spirits, called *loas* in Haiti (pronounced *lwa*), help with life's daily problems. In return, they must be 'served' with ceremonies, offerings of food and drink, and occasional animal sacrifice in temples known as *ounphors*.

The essence of Voodoo is keeping in harmony with the *loas*, the dead and nature. Magic may be used in self-defense, but those in perfect harmony with the universe should not need it. Magic in the pursuit of personal ambitions is frowned on. The use of black magic and sorcery, or the use of attack magic against others without just cause, is considered evil. Sorcerers, called *bokors*, exist but they are not seen as part of Voodoo. The *loas* punish *oungans* (Voodoo priests) or *mambos* (priestesses) who betray their vocation by practicing black magic. Many Haitians believe in the existence of *zombis*, the living dead victims of black magic who are supposedly disinterred by sorcerers and put to work as slaves.

Voodoo acquired an overlay of Catholicism in colonial times, when the slaves learned to disguise their *loas* as saints. Nowadays, major ceremonies coincide with Catholic celebrations such as Chistmas, Epiphany and the Day of the Dead. Lithographs of Catholic saints are used to represent the *loas*.

The role of attack and defence magic in Haiti's religious culture expanded during the slave revolts and the independence war. Many rebel leaders were *oungans*, such as Mackandal, who terrorized the northern plain with his knowledge of poisons from 1748 to 1758, and Boukman, who plotted the 1791 uprising at a clandestine Voodoo ceremony. Belief in Voodoo's protective spells inspired a fearlessness in battle that amazed the French. As a result, many Haitian rulers saw Voodoo as a threat to their own authority and tried to stamp it out. They also thought its survival weakened Haiti's claim to membership of the family of 'civilized' nations. François Duvalier enlisted enough *oungans* to neutralize Voodoo as a potential threat. He also coopted the Catholic church hierarchy. He had less success with the Catholic grass roots which, inspired by Liberation Theology, played a key role in his son's 1986 fall and Aristide's election in 1990.

After several ruthless campaigns against Voodoo, most recently in the early 1940s, the Catholic church has settled into an attitude of tolerant coexistence. Now the militant hostility to Voodoo comes from fundamentalist Protestant sects of American origin which have exploited their relative wealth and ability to provide jobs to win converts.

Language   Haitian Créole is the product of the transformation of French in Saint Domingue by African slaves who needed a common language, one the slave-owners were forced to learn in order to speak to their slaves.

More important is how Créole and French are used now. All Haitians understand Créole and speak it at least part of the time. Use of French is limited to the élite and middle class. The illiterate majority of the population understand no French at all. There is almost no teaching in Créole and no attempt is made to teach French as a foreign language to the few Créole-only speakers who enter the school system. Since mastery of French is still a condition for self-advancement, language perpetuates Haiti's deep class divisions. All those pushing for reform in Haiti are trying to change this. Radio stations have begun using Créole in the last 10 years. Musicians now increasingly sing in Créole. The 1987 constitution gave Créole equal official status alongside French. Even élite politicians have begun using Créole in speeches although some speak it poorly. Aristide's sway over the people is due in part to his poetic virtuosity in Créole. A phonetic transcription of Créole has evolved over the last 50 years, but little has been published except the Bible, some poetry and, nowadays, a weekly pro-Aristide newspaper, *Libète*. Créole is famed for its proverbs voicing popular philosophy and reflecting Haiti's enormous social divisions. The best teach yourself book is *Ann Pale Kreyòl*, published by the Créole Institute, Ballentine Hall 602, Indiana University, Bloomington IN 47405, USA. It is hard to find in Haitian bookshops. **NB** In the text above, 'Cr' means Créole version.

Haitian handicraft and naive art is the best in the Caribbean. Even such utilitarian articles as the woven straw shoulder bags and the tooled-leather scabbards of the peasant machete have great beauty. The *rada* (Voodoo drum) is an object of great aesthetic appeal. Haiti is famed for its wood carvings, but poverty has pushed crafts-men into producing art from such cheap material as papier maché and steel drums, flattened and turned into cut-out wall-hangings or sculpture. Haitian naive art on canvas emerged only in response to the demand of travellers and tourists in the 1930s and 40s, but it had always existed on the walls of Voodoo temples, where some of the best representations of the spirit world are to be found. Weddings, cock fights, market scenes or fantasy African jungles are other favoured themes. Good paintings can range from one hundred to several thousand dollars. Mass-produced but lively copies of the masters sell for as little as US$10. Negotiating with street vendors and artists can be an animated experience, offering insights into the nation's personality.

Exposure to white racism during the US occupation shook some of the mulatto intellectuals out of their complacent Francophilia. Led by Jean Price Mars and his 1919 pioneering essay *Ainsi parla l'oncle* (Thus Spoke Uncle) they began to seek their identity in Haiti's African roots. Peasant life, Créole expressions and Voodoo started to appear together with a Marxist perspective in novels such as Jacques Romain's *Gouverneurs de la rosée* (Masters of the Dew). René Depestre, now resi-dent in Paris after years in Cuba, is viewed as Haiti's greatest living novelist. Voodoo, politics and acerbic social comment are blended in the novels of Gary Victor, a dep-uty minister in the Aristide government before the coup.

Nigel Gallop writes: The poorest nation in the western hemisphere is among the richest when it comes to music. This is a people whose most popular religion wor-ships the deities through singing, drumming and dancing. The prime musical influ-ence is African, although European elements are to be found, but none that are Amerindian. The music and dance (and in Haiti music is almost inseparable from dance) can be divided into three main categories: Voodoo ritual, rural folk and urban popular. The Voodoo rituals, described above, are collective and are pro-foundly serious, even when the *loa* is humorous or mischievous. The hypnotic dance is accompanied by call-and-response singing and continuous drumming, the drums themselves (the large Manman, medium-sized Seconde and smaller Bula or Kata) being regarded as sacred.

During Mardi Gras (Carnival) and Rara (see below), bands of masked dancers and revellers can be found on the roads and in the streets almost anywhere in the country, accompanied by musicians playing the Vaccines (bamboo trumpets). Hai-tians also give rein to their love of music and dance in the so-called Bambouches, social gatherings where the dancing is *pou' plaisi'* (for pleasure) and largely directed to the opposite sex. They may be doing the Congo, the Martinique or Juba, the Crabienne or the national dance, the Méringue. The first two are of African prove-nance, the Crabienne evolved from the European Quadrille, while the Méringue is cousin to the Dominican Merengue. Haitians claim it originated in their country and was taken to the Dominican Republic during the Haitian occupation of 1822 to 1844, but this is a matter of fierce debate between the two nations. In remote villages it may still be possible to come across such European dances as the Waltz, Polka, Mazurka and Contredanse, accompanied by violin, flute or accordion.

Haitian music has not remained impervious to outside influences during the 20th century, many of them introduced by Haitian migrant workers returning from Cuba, the Dominican Republic and elsewhere in the region (as well as exporting its own music to Cuba's Oriente province in the form of the Tumba Francesa). One very important external influence was that of the Cuban Son, which gave rise to the so-called 'Troubadour Groups', with their melodious voices and soft guitar accom-paniment, still to be heard in some hotels. Jazz was another intruder, a result of the US marines' occupation between 1915 and 1934. Then in the 1950s two equally cele-brated composers and band leaders, Nemours Jean-Baptiste and Weber Sicot, introduced a new style of recreational dance music, strongly influenced by the Dominican Merengue and known as Compact Directe ('compas') or Cadence Rampa. Compas (the 's' is not pronounced) dominated the music scene until the past few years, when it has become a much more open market, with Salsa, Reggae, Soca and Zouk all making big inroads. A number of Haitian groups have achieved international recognition, notably Tabou Combo and Coupé Cloué, while female singers Martha-Jean Claude and Toto Bissainthe have also made a name for themselves abroad. One excellent troubadour-style singer who has been well-recorded is Althiery Dorival. Also highly recommended is the set of six LPs titled 'Roots of Haiti', recorded in the country, but distributed by Mini Records of Brooklyn. Finally, no comment on Haitian music would be complete without reference to the well-known lullaby 'Choucounne' which, under the title 'Yellow Bird', is crooned to tourists every night on every English-speaking Antillean island.

Mike Tarr adds: A musical revolution came with the emergence of 'voodoo beat', a fusion of Voodoo drumming and melody with an international rock guitar and keyboard sound. Its lyrics call for political change and a return to peasant values. With albums out on the Island label, and US tours behind them, Boukman Eksperyans is the most successful of these bands. People who have ignored Voodoo all their lives are possessed at Boukman concerts. Other 'voodoo beat' bands of note are Ram, Boukan Ginen, Foula, Sanba-Yo and Koudjay.

Haiti

395

Dominican Republic

9

396

Dominican Republic

The Dominican Republic, occupying the eastern two-thirds of Hispaniola, has some spectacularly beautiful scenery. The country is mountainous and has the highest peak in the Caribbean, Pico Duarte (3,175 m). It has many more forests than its neighbour, Haiti, and is green and fertile. Within a system of widespread food production are large sugar and fruit plantations and cattle ranches. The Republic has built up its tourist trade, and has much to offer in the way of natural beauty, old colonial architecture, attractive beaches, adventure sports, modern resorts and native friendliness. Public transport is good and it is easy and rewarding to explore by bus or hired car. Its population is mostly a mixture of black, white and mulatto, and is Spanish-speaking.

Essentials

Before you travel

Documents All visitors require a **passport** and most need a green **tourist card**, which costs US$10, purchased from consulates, tourist offices, airlines on departure (eg American at Miami), or at the airport on arrival before queueing for immigration. Citizens of the following countries do not need a tourist card to enter: Argentina, Ecuador, Israel, Japan, Liechtenstein, Norway, South Korea, Sweden, Uruguay. The time limit on tourist cards is 60 days, but if necessary extensions are obtainable from Immigration, Huacal Building, Santo Domingo (T6852505/2535). The easiest method of extending a tourist card is simply to pay the fine (US$2 for each month over three months) at the airport when leaving. Check all entry requirements in advance if possible. People born in the Dominican Republic but with Canadian or US citizenship report hassling from immigration officers who demand different entry forms (not tourist cards) and want to know why they threw away their Dominican citizenship. All visitors should have an outward (ticket not always asked for).

Customs The airport police are on the lookout for illegal drugs. It is also illegal to bring firearms into the country. At the land border with Haiti bags are searched and things go missing, keep a close eye on everyone, not just on customs officials. Duty-free import of 200 cigarettes or one box of cigars, plus one litre of alcoholic liquor and gift articles to the value

Dominican Republic

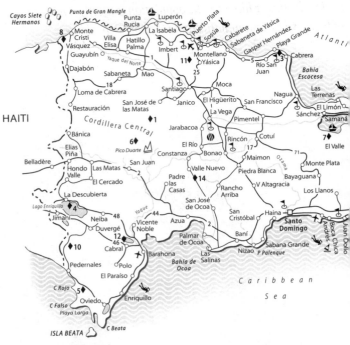

♦ **National Parks**
1 Armando Bermúdez
2 Cabo Cabrón
3 Cabo Francés Viejo
4 Isla Cabritos
5 Jaragua

6 José del Carmen Ramírez
7 Los Haitises
8 Montecristi
9 Parque Nacional del Este
10 Sierra Bahoruca

♦ **Reservas Científicas**
11 Isabel de Torres
12 Laguna de Rincón
13 Lagunas Redonda y Limón
14 Valle Nuevo

Not to scale

of US$100, is permitted. Military-type clothing and food products will be confiscated on arrival. Currency in excess of US$10,000 may not be taken out of the country without special permission.

Currency The Dominican peso (RD$) is the only legal tender. The peso is divided into 100 centavos. There are coins in circulation of 25 and 50 centavos, 1 peso and 5 pesos, and notes of 5, 10, 20, 50, 100, 500 and 1,000 pesos. In the countryside away from major centres, it can be difficult to change anything higher than a 100-peso note. **Money**

Exchange The exchange rate fluctuates against the dollar but is relatively stable. Banks and exchange houses *(casas de cambio)* are authorized to deal in foreign exchange. You will be given a receipt and, with this, you can change remaining pesos back into dollars at the end of your visit (maximum 30% of dollars changed; cash obtained against a credit card does not count). Do not rely on the airport bank being open. US dollar, Travellers' cheques or cash, is the best currency to bring. Most European currencies can be changed at the *Banco de Reservas* (and some other banks); Scandinavian currencies are very hard to change. If stuck at weekends, most hotels will offer to change money if you ask casually "Is there anywhere open to change dollars?" The rates are generally the same as in banks; cash only. ATMs are an easy way to get cash and you will get close to the market rate, plus a commission of up to 5%. They are sometimes out of action at weekends and holidays and in small places they suffer from lack of maintenance and often do not work.

Credit cards Nearly all major hotels, restaurants and stores accept most credit cards. Several banks will give cash against *Visa*, *Mastercard* or *American Express* cards, usually with 5% commission. Visa is linked with Baninter (T5085600), Asociación Popular Ahorros y Préstamos (T6890171), Asociación Dominicana de Ahorros y Préstamos (T5632171), while the Banco del Progreso (T5633233, 1-800-5282121) is linked with Visa, Mastercard and American Express. Thomas Cook Mastercard refund assistant points are Vimenca, Avenida Abraham Lincoln 306, Santo Domingo, T5327381, and the Banco del Comercio Dominicano in Puerto Plata (T5862350, Duarte y Padre Castellanos) and La Romana (T5565151, Trinitaria 59).

Banks The Central Bank determines monetary policy. Among the commercial banks in the Republic are **Scotiabank** (Santo Domingo, Santiago, and Puerto Plata), *Chase Manhattan* (Santo Domingo and Santiago), *Citibank* (Santo Domingo and Santiago), *Banco de Reservas*, *Banco Popular*, *Banco Metropolitano*, *Banco Central*, *Bancrédito*, Intercontinental, *Banco Dominicano Hispano*, *Banco Mercantil* and others. The *Banco Popular* has CASH ATMs, which take ATH (A Todo Hora), Mastercard, Cirrus, Honor, Visa, Plus and Electron. Money can be sent via *Western Union*, which operates through the local company, *Vimenca*.

Dominican Republic

Climate The climate is tropical. The rainy months are May, June, August, September and November. The temperature shows little seasonal change, and varies between 18° and 32°C. Only in December does the temperature fall, averaging about 20°C. Humidity can be high, particularly in coastal areas, making physical activity difficult.

Getting there

Air **To Santo Domingo** From North America: *American Airlines* fly from Boston, Miami and New York; *Continental*, *Queen Air*, *Tower Air* and *TWA* also from New York. *Aeromar* and *Apa International* also from Miami; *TWA* from Orlando and Boston; from other US cities, connections in Miami or San Juan, Puerto Rico. **From Europe:** *Iberia* flies from Madrid several times a week and has connecting flights from most European and Spanish cities, for example Barcelona. *Air Europa* flies from Madrid; *Lauda Air* from Milan and Rome; *Air France* from Paris daily. *Martinair* flies from Amsterdam once a week. *Condor* flies from Frankfurt, Munich and Cologne/Bonn. **From the Caribbean:** *American Eagle* from St Maarten and St Thomas. *ALM* has flights from Curaçao. *Air Guadeloupe* from Pointe-à-Pitre, Fort-de-France; *Copa*, *American Eagle*, *Air Guadeloupe*, *Aces*, *American Airlines*, *Iberia*, *Aeromar*, *TWA*, all from San Juan. *Cubana* from Havana; *Aeropostal* from Aruba and Curaçao. **From Central America:** *Copa* from Panama City, San José, Guatemala City, Managua. **From South America:** *Aserca* and *Aeropostal* from Caracas via Curaçao; *ALM* from Caracas direct; *Copa* from Lima; other capital cities are connected through Miami or Panama City.

In addition to these scheduled flights there are hundreds of charter flights from N America, Europe & S America which are usually cheaper but vary according to the season

To Puerto Plata From North America: *American Airlines* from Miami, New York. *TWA* also from New York. *Northwest Airlines* from Minneapolis. **From Europe:** *Martinair* from Amsterdam; *AOM* from Paris; *Condor* from Berlin, Cologne/Bonn, Dusseldorf, Frankfurt, Hamburg, Hanover, Leipzig, Munich and Stuttgart (some flights only in high season); *LTU* from Dusseldorf (via Gander, Newfoundland, Canada), Munich, Frankfurt and Zurich. **From the Caribbean:** *Sky King* from Providenciales; *American Eagle* from San Juan.

To Punta Cana From North America: *Lan Chile* from Miami; *TWA* and *Queen Air* from New York. *Aeromar* was also due to start a weekly service in 2000 from Miami with a stopover in Santo Domingo. **From Europe:** *Martinair* from Amsterdam; *Condor* from Berlin, Cologne/Bonn, Dusseldorf, Frankfurt, Hamburg, Hanover, Leipzig, Munich and Stuttgart. *LTU* from Dusseldorf (one flight via Gander), Frankfurt, Hamburg, Munich. *Hapag Lloyd* from Frankfurt, Hanover; *TAP* from Lisbon; *Air Europa* from Madrid; *AOM* from Paris. **From the Caribbean:** *American Eagle* and *Condor* from San Juan; *Cubana* from Havana. **From South America:** *Lan Chile* from Santiago; *Aces* from Bogotá; *Aserca* and *Aeropostal* from Caracas.

To Santiago From the Caribbean: *American Eagle* fly from San Juan, Puerto Rico.

Boat There are cargo and passenger shipping services with New York, New Orleans, Miami and South American countries. Many cruise lines from USA, Canada and Europe call at the Dominican Republic on itineraries to various ports on Caribbean islands or the mainland. Agencies which handle cruises include *Emely* (T6822744, for Festival, Holidays, Jubilee, Sur Viking). *Ferries del Caribe* has a car and passenger ferry between the Dominican Republic and Puerto Rico. The *Regal Voyager* departs Mayagüez Monday, Wednesday, Friday, 1900, 12 hours, departs Santo Domingo Tuesday, Thursday, Sunday, 2000, prices from US$131 return, including port tax, sleeper cabins available for up to 4 people, US$116, T6884400.

Travel to Haiti **Air** Air Santo Domingo from Las Américas airport to Port-au-Prince Wednesday, Thursday, Friday, 1200, one hour, return 1230, prices from US$72 before tax, T6838020. *Tropical Airways d'Haiti* fly daily from Herrera airport to Port-au-Prince at 0730, returning at 1730. **Bus** By far the easiest way is with *Terrabús*, which has a service between Santo Domingo and Pétion-Ville, US$50 one way, US$75 return, US$80 open return, T4721080, terminal at Avenida 27 de Febrero esq Anacaona, Plaza Criolla, Saturday-Monday departs 1200, arrives 0500, Wednesday-Friday departs 0600, arrives 1200, they deal with all border formalities for you

Remember there is a 1 hr time difference between Haiti (GMT-5) & the Dominican Republic (GMT-4)

Dominican Republic

Touching down

Departure tax US$10.

Hours of business Offices: 0830-1230, 1430-1830; some offices and shops work 0930-1730 Monday-Friday, 0800-1300 Saturday. **Banks**: 0830-1700 Monday-Friday. Government offices 0730-1430. **Shops**: normally 0800-1900, some open all day Saturday and mornings on Sunday and holidays. Most shops in tourist areas stay open through the siesta and on Sunday.

Official time Atlantic Standard Time, four hours behind GMT, one hour ahead of EST.

Voltage 110 volts, 60 cycles AC current. American-type, flat-pin plugs are used. There are frequent power cuts, often for several hours, so take a torch with you when you go out at night. Many establishments have their own (often noisy) generators.

Weights and measures Officially the metric system is used but business is often done on a pound per yard per US gallon basis. Land areas in cities are measured by square metres, but in the countryside by the tarea, one of which equals 624 sq m.

Clothing Light clothing, preferably cotton, is best all year round. It is recommended to take one formal outfit since some hotels and nightclubs do not permit casual dress.

Tipping In addition to the 10% service and 8% VAT charge in restaurants, it is customary to give an extra tip of about 10%, depending on service. Porters receive US$0.50 per bag; taxi drivers, público drivers and garage attendants are not usually tipped.

(except customs). *Caribe Tours* also has a service to Haiti, departing daily at 1100, arriving in Port-au-Prince at 1400, US$75 return. The return bus leaves Port-au-Prince at 0700. There are cheaper options but they take longer, are less comfortable and can be hard work to arrange. A bus goes once a day, sometimes twice, from outside the Haitian embassy, leaving when full (if it leaves in the afternoon, it stops overnight in Jimaní), *Kenya Express*, T5661045, leaves Saturday 1100, *Chuchula*, T5401151, *Luz Tours*, T5422423, leaves Tuesday at 1000 (1200 more likely). Be quick on arriving at embassy, get through gates ignoring hangers on and cries of 'passport', unless you want to wait in the street and pay someone else US$10 to take your passport in. All the passports are processed together. Payments may be required. Do not wear shorts. Another option is from *Dormitorio San Tomé*, Calle Santomé, beside Mercado Modelo, Santo Domingo (T6885100, ask for Alejandro). Alternatively, take a minibus to Jimaní from near the bridge over the Río Seco in the centre of Santo Domingo, 6-8 hours; get a lift up to the Haitian border and then get overcharged by Haitian youths on mopeds who take you across 3 km of no-man's-land for US$3. From Haitian immigration take a lorry-bus to Port-au-Prince, 3-4 hours, very dusty. You can also take Dominican public transport to Dajabón, cross to Ounaminthe and continue to Cap Haïtien. If driving to Haiti you must get a vehicle permit at the Foreign Ministry (T5331424). Hire cars are not allowed across the border. The drive from Santo Domingo to Port-au-Prince takes about six hours. Buy gourdes from money changers outside the embassy, or at the border, but no more than US$50-worth, rates are much better in Haiti. Also take US$25 for border taxes, which have to be paid in dollars cash.

Lots of travel agents do package tours to Cuba, for example *Elvira's Travel*, Avenida 27 de Febrero 279, T6878017, open 0800-1900; *Emely Tours*, Tiradentes esquina Roberto Pastoriza, Edificio Plaza JR, www.emely-tours.com offer Cubana flights for US$493 with packages of 4, 5 or 8 nights including accommodation in Havana and some sightseeing tours; *Arbaje Tours*, T5354941, 5355495, check special offers, for example two for the price of one. Details of other options can be found in the morning papers. There are also short cruises to Puerto Rico, for example with Diamond Cruises, for about US$120 per person. See above, Boat, for ferry to Mayagüez, Puerto Rico. **Ports of entry** Santo Domingo, Luperón, Puerto Plata, Samaná, Punta Cana (with 24 hours notice). **Boat documents** Customs fees US$10 per person. 30 days immigration clearance. Declare weapons and check in with Customs officials ashore at each port of entry. Do not depart from anchorage before sunrise after picking up weapons.

Travel to Cuba & Puerto Rico

Dominican Republic

Touching down

Airport information Details of airports are given in the text below. There are several: **Las Américas** (Santo Domingo, T5490450/80), **Herrera** (Santo Domingo, T5673900), **Gregorio Luperón** (Puerto Plata, T5860219), **Arroyo Barril** (Samaná), **Cibao** (Santiago, T5824894), **Punta Aguila** (La Romana, T5565565), **Punta Cana** (Higüey, T6868790) and **María Montéz** (Barahona, T5247010). In 2000 a new domestic airport was being built to replace Herrera, 40 minutes north of the centre of Santo Domingo in the Higuero sector.

Airline offices In Santo Domingo: *Air Canada, ACES, Aeroméxico, Britannia, Lufthansa, LTU* and *Finnair* all at Gustavo Mejía Ricart 54, T5415151; *Air Europa*, 27 de Febrero; *TWA*, T6899151; *Aeromar*, T5334447; *Air France*, Avenida George Washington 101, T6868419; *ALM*, L Navarro 28, T6874567; *American Airlines*, Edif IN TEMPO, W Churchill, T5425151; *American Eagle*, Juan S Ramírez esq Mahatma Gandhi, T6820077; *Carnival Air*, T5635300; *Continental*, T5626688; *Copa*, T4722223; *Iberia*, T5080188; *Martinair*, M Gómez y Juan S Ramírez, T6886661; *Cubana*, T2272040; at 27 de Febrero esq Tiradentes are *Varig*, T5659151; at George Washington 353 are *Hapag Lloyd*, T6828133 and *Condor*, T6828133. *Air Santo Domingo* information and reservations, T6838020, at Herrera airport T6836691, at Las Américas T5491110, at Punta Cana T2211170, at Puerto Plata T5860385.

Tourist information **Local tourist office** The head office of the Secretaría de Estado de Turismo is in the Edificio de Oficinas Gubernamentales, Avenida México esquina 30 de Marzo, Ala 'D', near the Palacio Nacional (PO Box 497, T2214660, F6823806, sectur@codetel.net.do); it publishes a tourism guide called *La Cotica*, which is free (some places in Santo Domingo, around the cathedral, charge US$2.45 for it). There are also offices at **Las Américas International Airport**, in Santo Domingo in the colonial city on the first floor of the Palacio Borgella near the Cathedral (T6863858), **La Unión Airport** at Puerto Plata, in Puerto Plata (Malecón 20, T5863676), in Santiago (Ayuntamiento, T5825885), Barahona (T5243650), Jimaní (T2483000), Samaná (T5382332), Boca Chica (T5235106), San Pedro de Macorís (T5293644), La Romana (T5506922), Baní (T5226018), San Cristóbal (T5283533), Pedernales (T5240409), Higüey (T5542672), El Seíbo (T5523402), Sosúa (T5712254), Cabarete (T5710962), Gaspar Hernández (T5872485), Río San Juan (T5892831), Nagua (T5843862), Las Terrenas (T2406363), Luperón (T5718303), Monte Cristi (T5792254), La Vega (T2421289), Bonao (T5253941), Constanza (T5392900). The Consejo de Promoción Turística (CPT), Avenida México 66, Santo Domingo, T6855254, F6856752, www.domrep-hotels.com.do promotes the Dominican Republic abroad (US mailing address EPS No A-355, PO Box 02-5256, Miami, FL 33102-5256). Asonahores (Asociación Nacional de Hoteles y Restaurantes), Avenida México 66, T6874676, F6874727. Useful websites are www.hispaniola.com and www.dominicana.com.do

Local tour agents El Dorado, Juan Sánchez Ramírez y Avenida Máximo Gómez, T6886661, F6866662, one block from Haitian Embassy; *Palmtours*, T6823407, 6823284, *Tanya*, MM Valencia 27, T5655691 F5426224, *Juan Perdomo Travel*, T5630744, *Emely Tours*, S F de Macorís 58, T6877114 (agent for *Cubana* and flights to Cuba), *Quality Tours*, Calle de Moya 59, T6876218 and at *Hotel Jaragua*, T6822571 and *Omni Tours*, T5656591, F5674710, or Punta Cana T6880977, F6880764, trips to Cuba, cruises and hotel special offers around the country. In Puerto Plata, Connex Caribe, Plaza Turisol, T5866879, F5866099, offers a wide variety of tours in town, to Santo Domingo and all over the Republic. *Iguana Mama* in Cabarete, T5710908, F5710734, info@iguanamama, run organized tours to climb Pico Duarte (see page 430), or hike, mountain bike or whitewater rafting in the mountains, one to eight day trips. Many other companies operate tours.

The Museo de Historia y Geografía in Santo Domingo organizes archaeological and historical tours in the Republic, visiting, for example, Cotuí, Bonao, Presa de Hatillo, Sánchez, Samaná, Pozo de Bojolo in Nagua, Lago Enriquillo and other places of interest. There is no specific programme but tours are announced in the newspapers. The co-ordinator is Vilma Benzo de Ferrer, T6886952.

· ·

Tourist offices overseas

Argentina *Arenales 1942 1-B, Buenos Aires, T541-8137704, F8140824, turismo_r.d@epsarg.com*

Belgium *Avenida Louise 271, 8th floor, 1050 Brussels, T322-6461300, F6493692, repdom.benelux.info@skynet.be*

Canada *2080 Rue Crescent, Montréal, Québec, H3G 2B8, T514-4991918, F4991393, republiquedominicaine@op-plus.net; 35 Church Street, Unit 53 Market Square, Toronto, Ontario M5E 1T3, T416-3612126, F3612130, dominicantourism@globalserve.net*

Colombia *Transversal 29 No 120-59, Barrio Santa Bárbara, Bogotá, T571-6291459, F5207061, domreptu@multphone.net.co*

France *11 Rue Boudreau, Paris 75009, T331-43129191, F44940880, otrepdom@aol.com*

Germany *Hochstrasse 17-2, D-60313 Frankfurt am Main 1, T49-69-91397879, F283430, domtur@aol.com*

Italy *Piazza Castello 25, 20121 Milan, T3902-8057781, F865861, repdom@opimaint.it*

Puerto Rico *Avenida Ashford 1452, Suite 307, Condado, San Juan, PR 00907, T787-7220881, F7247293, ofiturdr@isla.net*

Spain *Juan Hurtado de Mendoza 13, Apto 305, 28036 Madrid 1, T3491-3509483, F3506579, rep.domi@nauta.es*

UK *For information contact the embassy at 139 Inverness Terrace, London W2 6JF, T020-77276232, F020-77273693; for tourist brochures, call 0900-1600305.*

USA *136E 57 Street Suite 803, New York, NY 10022, T212-5881012/4, F5881015, dr.info@ix.netcom.com; 561 West Diversey Parkway Suite 214, Chicago, IL 60614-1643, T773-5291336/7, F5291338, domreptourism@msn.com; 2355 Salzedo Street, Suite 307, Coral Gables, Miami, Florida 33134, T305-4444592/3, F4444845, domrep@herald.infi.net*

· ·

Maps Detailed, specialized maps of the country and urban areas can be found at Gaar, on Arzobispo Nouel esq Espaillat, Santo Domingo, open Monday-Friday 0830-1900, Saturday 0930-1500. The tourist office publishes a stylized map with advertising and insets of Santo Domingo and the main tourist areas. *Berndtson & Berndtson* publish a good road map, 1:600,000, with detail on Santo Domingo, Puerto Plata and Santiago, available locally for US$5. *Scheidig* publishes the *Mapa Geográfica de la República Dominicana*, which is approved by the Instituto Geográfico Universitario and available at Gaar for US$7. There are several other good maps of the country including *Hildebrand, Nelles* and *Texaco*.

Religion Roman Catholicism is the predominant religion. There are also Episcopalian, Baptist, Seventh Day Adventist, Presbyterian and Methodist churches in the main towns. Voodoo, technically illegal, is tolerated and practised mostly in the western provinces.

Safety There are well-trained guides who speak two or more languages in Santo Domingo, who are courteous and do not push themselves on you. However, outside the historic buildings in Santo Domingo, on the beaches and at other tourist attractions, visitors will be approached by unofficial English-speaking guides, sellers of rum, women or drugs. The only value in taking an unofficial guide is to deter others from pestering you (similarly, hiring a lounger chair on the beach). Beware of drug-pushers on the Malecón in Santo Domingo and near the Cathedral in Puerto Plata. Unofficial guides often refuse to give prices in advance, saying 'pay what you want' and then at the end, if they are not happy with the tip, they make a scene and threaten to tell the police that the customer had approached them to deal in drugs etc. On no account change money on the streets. Banks and cambios offer the market rate and are safer. Be careful with 'helpers' at the airports, who speed your progress through the queues and then charge US$15-20 for their services. Single men have complained of the massive presence of pimps and prostitutes. Be prepared to say 'no' a lot.

It must be stressed that these problems do not occur in rural areas and small towns, where travellers have been impressed with the open and welcoming nature of the Dominicans. Violent crime against tourists is rare but, as anywhere, watch your money and valuables in

Dominican Republic

cities late at night and on beaches. The streets of Santo Domingo are not considered safe after 2300. Purse snatchers on motorcycles operate in cities.

Politur, the Tourist Police, has a toll-free phone 1-200-3500, or at the office in Santo Domingo T6868639.

Where to stay

Hotels are given under the towns in which they are situated. Note that five-star hotels charge an average of US$140, plus 23% tax. In aparthotels, the average price is US$130 for two. In more modest guest houses, a weekly or monthly rate, with discount, can be arranged. It is quite possible to find lodgings for US$10-15 per night away from the main resort areas, but they will be basic with erratic plumbing and electricity. All hotels charge the 23% tax; the VAT component is 13%. The better hotels have a high occupancy rate and it is best to book in advance, particularly at holiday times.

Getting around

Bus Services from Santo Domingo: *Metro Expreso*, first class (T5667126, F5419454) operate from Calle Hatuey esq Avenida Winston Churchill, near 27 de Febrero and have buses to La Vega (US$3), Santiago (US$4.70), Puerto Plata (US$6), Nagua (US$5), Moca (US$4.50), San Francisco de Macorís (US$4), Sánchez/Samaná (US$5.60) and Castillo (US$4.50) daily. In Puerto Plata, T5866063, Santiago, T5839111, Nagua, T5842259. *Caribe Tours* (T2214422) operates from Avenida 27 de Febrero at Leopoldo Navarro; the bus terminal is well organized, with ticket office, café, information desk, cash machine (Visa, Electron, Plus), cambio and waiting area with TV; most of their services are in a/c buses, with video and toilet, punctual, good service, no smoking (eg US$4 to Río San Juan or Santiago, US$3.50 to Bonao, Jarabacoa or Barahona, US$5 to La Vega, US$5.30 to Dajabón, Puerto Plata or Monte Cristi); they run to all parts except east of Santo Domingo. *Transporte del Cibao*, T6857210, opposite Parque Enriquillo, to Puerto Plata, cheaper than other companies at US$3.60, to Santiago US$3. *Terrabús*, Anacaona 15, T4721080, US$4 to Santiago, US$5.30 to Sosúa and Puerto Plata, and *Transporte Espinal* (four blocks north of Parque Enriquillo) US$4 to Santiago, US$3 to La Vega, US$3 to Bonao. *La Covacha* buses leave from Parque Enriquillo (Avenida Duarte and Ravelo) for the east: La Romana, Higüey, Nagua, San Pedro de Macorís, Hato Mayor, Miches, etc. *Astrapu* does the same routes. *Expresos Moto Saad*, Avenida Independencia near Parque Independencia runs 12 daily buses to Bonao, La Vega and Santiago. *Línea Sur* (T6827682) runs to San Juan, Barahona, Azua and Haiti. *Guaguas* for Azua, two hours US$3, depart from Avenida Bolívar near Parque Independencia; easy connections in Azua for Barahona, San Juan and Padre las Casas. For bus offices in other towns, see text.

Bus (*guagua*) services between most towns are efficient and inexpensive. In rural areas it can be easy to find a *guagua* (mini bus or pickup) but they are usually filled to the point where you can not move your legs and luggage is an uncomfortable inconvenience.

Car A valid driving licence from your country of origin or an international licence is accepted.
Local drivers can be Dominicans drive on the right. Many of them do not have licences. The Autopista Duarte is a
erratic; be on the alert. good, four-lane highway between Santo Domingo and Santiago, but dangerous. It is used by
Hand signals mean bicycles and horse drawn carts as well as motorized vehicles, while drivers switch from one
only 'I am about to do lane to the other without warning. Lots of shopping opportunities by the roadside contribute
something', nothing to the hazards, with vehicles swerving on and off the road. In 2000, the Autovía del Este was
more specific than that inaugurated, providing an excellent road from Santo Domingo out to the east, with good access roads to Higüey, Punta Cana airport, Hato Mayor and Sabana de la Mar. Also good are the main road from Santo Domingo to the west, as far as Pedernales and Jimaní, and most of the northeast coastal route from Puerto Plata to Samaná. Minor roads and many city streets are in poor condition with lots of potholes, so avoid night driving. The speed limit for city driving is 40 kph, for suburban areas 60 kph and on main roads 80 kph. Service stations generally close at 1800, although there are now some offering 24-hour service. Gasoline costs RD$32.50 (US$2) for unleaded and RD$27.90 (US$1.75) for leaded. Most police or military

posts have 'sleeping policemen', speed humps, usually unmarked, outside them. In towns there are often 'ditches' at road junctions, which need as much care as humps. The operation of traffic lights depends on electricity supply, unless they are funded by a local business. In towns the lack of a right of way makes junctions difficult; proceed with caution. Beware motorcyclists in towns. At night look out for poorly lighted, or lightless vehicles. There are tolls on all principal roads out of the capital: RD$5, exact change needed. Road signs are very poor: a detailed map is essential, plus a knowledge of Spanish for asking directions.

Drivers can expect to be stopped by the police at the entrance to and exit from towns (normally brief and courteous), at junctions in towns, or any speed-restricted area. A crackdown against policemen asking for bribes from motorists has curtailed the previous system of on-the-spot fines. **Hitchhiking** is perfectly possible.

Car hire If renting a car, avoid the cheapest companies because their vehicles are not usually trustworthy; it is better to pay more with a well-known agency. Car rental is expensive because of high import tariffs on vehicles. Prices for small vehicles start at US$40 per day but can be as much as US$90. Weekly rates are better value. Credit cards are widely accepted; the cash deposit is normally twice the sum of the contract. The minimum age for hiring a car is 25; maximum period for driving is 90 days. **Mopeds** and **motorcycles** are everywhere and are very noisy. Most beach resorts hire motorcycles for between US$20 and US$35 a day. By law, the driver of a motorcycle must wear a crash helmet, but very few do; passengers are not required to wear one.

There are usually fixed *público* rates (see under Santo Domingo) between cities, so inquire **Taxi** first. Rates are given in the text. Many drivers pack a truly incredible number of passengers in their cars, so the ride is often uncomfortable but friendly and quite an experience. If travelling by private taxi, bargaining is very important. In Santo Domingo, *Apolo Taxi* is recommended if you need to call a taxi, cheap, friendly and efficient. Motorcyclists (*motoconchos*) also offer a taxi service and take several passengers on pillion. In some towns, eg Samaná, *motoconchos* and cyclists pull four-seater covered rickshaws. Negotiate fare first.

Several companies offer air taxi or charter services within the Republic, all based at Herrera **Air** airport. *Alas Nacionales*, T5426688; *Transporte Aéreo SA*, T5674549; *Coturisca*, T5677211. *Dorado Air* (T6861067) flies between Santo Domingo and Puerto Plata several times a day on Friday and Saturday. Flights go to Santiago, Puerto Plata, Barahona, Portillo and La Romana daily. *Air Santo Domingo*, Avenida 27 de Febrero 272, esq Seminario, T6838020, has regular flights between Santo Domingo (Herrera and Las Américas) and Puerto Plata (US$44), Punta Cana (US$54), El Portillo and Arroyo Barril, Samaná (US$35); also flights from Puerto Plata to Punta Cana (US$59). Fly drive available from around US$100. Air taxis charge around US$150 per plane to Samaná and US$220 to Punta Cana.

If negotiating transport by boat, a *canuco* is a small dugout, a *yola* is a medium-sized rowing **Sea** boat taking up to 10 passengers, a *bote* takes 20 or more.

Keeping in touch

Argentina, Máximo Gómez 10, T6822977, F2212206; **Belgium**, Abraham Lincoln 504, **Embassies &** T5621661, F5623383; **Bolivia**, Federico Geraldino 58, T5658573, F5659839; **Brazil**, Winston **consulates** Churchill 32, T5320868, F5320917, brazil@mail.codetel.net.do; **Canada**, Máximo Gómez 30, T6851136, F6822691, canada@codetel.net.do; **Chile**, Avenida Anacaona 11, Mirador Sur, T5327800; **Colombia**, Abraham Lincoln y José A Soler, T5621670; **Costa Rica**, Malaquías Gil 11, Serrallés, T5656419, F5656467; **Denmark**, Abraham Lincoln 504, T5495100, F5623383; **Ecuador**, Rafael Augusto Sánchez 17, T5638363; **El Salvador**, José Brea Peña 12, T5654311; **France**, George Washington 353, T6892161; **Germany**, R Aug Sánchez, T5658811, F5675014; **Guatemala**, Santiago 359, Gazcue, T/F6895146; **Haiti**, Juan Sánchez Ramírez 33, T6865778, F6866096, Amb.haiti@codetel.net.do; **Honduras**, Salvador Sturla 12, T5655112; **Israel**, P Henríquez Ureña 80, T5421635; **Italy**, Manuel Rodríguez Objío 4, T6893684; **Jamaica**, Marginal 5, Aut 30 de Mayo, T5321079; **Japan**, Avenida Winston Churchill, Torre BHD, piso 8,

Dominican Republic

T5673365; **Mexico**, Arzobispo Meriño 265 y Mercedes, T6876444, F6877872, mbamex@codetel.net.do; **Netherlands**, Mayor Enrique Valverde, T5655240; **Panama**, Benito Monción 255, T6883789, F6853665; **Peru**, Pedro A Bobea y Avenida Anacaona, Edificio Curvo, Bella Vista, T5655851; **Spain**, Independencia 1205, T5351615, F5351595; **Sweden**, Máximo Gómez 31, T6852131; **Switzerland**, Calle Recodo 2, Edificio Monte Mirador, Bella Vista, T5333781, F5323781; **UK**, 27 de Febrero 233, Edificio Corominas Pepín, 7th floor, T4727111, F4727574; **Uruguay**, Calle Baltazar Brum 7, T6825565; **US Embassy** and Consulate, César Nicolás Penson, (embassy) T2212171, (consulate) 5412111, F6867437; **Venezuela**, Avenida Anacaona 7, Mirador Sur, T5378882, F5378780.

Post Don't use post boxes, they are unreliable. The postal system as a whole is very slow. For each 10 grams, or fraction thereof, the cost to Europe is one peso; to North America, Venezuela, Central America and the Caribbean, 50 centavos; to elsewhere in the Americas and Spain, 70 centavos; to Africa, Australia, Asia and Oceania, RD\$1.50. You can buy postal envelopes without stamps but with pictures of tourist sites, issued by the Instituto Postal Dominicano. It is recommended to use *entrega especial* (special delivery, with separate window at post offices), for two pesos extra, on overseas mail, or better still a courier service (see under Santo Domingo).

Telephone
International phone code: 809

Operated by the *Compañía Dominicana de Teléfonos* (Codetel), a subsidiary of GTE, or *Tricom*. All local calls and overseas calls and faxes to the Caribbean, European Community, US and Canada may be dialled directly from any Codetel or Tricom office (no collect calls to the UK, but they are available to many other countries). Through Codetel you call abroad either person-to-person or through an operator (more expensive, but you only pay if connected). Calls and faxes may be paid for by credit card. For phone boxes you need 25-centavo coins. Phone calls to the USA cost RD\$9.40 per minute, to Europe RD\$23.80, to Australia RD\$25.90, Puerto Rico RD\$7.80, Haiti RD\$10.90 and the rest of the Caribbean RD\$12.90. AT&T's USA-Direct is available on T1122. Canada (Telegiobe) is 1-800-3330111. Codetel publishes a bilingual Spanish/English business telephone directory for tourism (a sort of tourist's yellow pages), called the *Dominican Republic Tourist Guide/Guía Turística de la República Dominicana*, which contains a lot of information as well as telephone numbers. Emergency number: 711; information is 1411.

Internet Codetel offices in most towns have a computer for internet access, but don't expect it to work. Cybercafés are now opening in tourist areas such as Cabarete and Las Terrenas, but, again, service is often down.

Media **Newspapers** There are nine daily papers in all, six in the morning, three in the afternoon. *Listín Diario* has the widest circulation; among the other morning papers are *La Nación, El Nuevo Diario, El Caribe, Hoy, El Siglo* (has good foreign coverage). In the afternoon, *Ultima Hora* and *El Nacional* are published. *Primicias is a Sunday paper.* The English-language *Santo Domingo News*, published every Friday with listings of events, is available at hotels. *Touring* is a multilingual tourist newspaper with articles and adverts in English, German, French, Spanish and Italian. *La Información*, published in Santiago on weekdays, is a good regional paper carrying both national and international stories. **Radio and television** There are over 170 local radio stations and seven television stations. *Cable* television is available through *Telecable Nacional* and *Super Cable. Cadena de Noticias* transmits news programmes 24 hours a day and has a radio division. *Radio Mil, Radio Comercial, Radio Popular* broadcast new bulletins at 0530, 1200 and 1730. *Caribbean Travelling Network* (CTN) has news of tourist sites, good for visitors. www.dr1.com is a news and information service with daily news updates.

Food and drink

Food Local dishes include *sancocho* or *salcocho prieto* (a type of stew made of six local meats and vegetables, often including *plátanos, ñame* and *yautia*), *mondongo* (a tripe stew), *mofongo*, ground *plátano* with garlic and *chicharrón de cerdo* (pork crackling), usually served with a soup, a side dish of meat and avocado (very filling), *chicharrón de pollo* is small pieces of chicken prepared with lime and oregano, *locrio de cerdo* or *pollo* (meat and rice), *cocido* (a soup of chickpeas, meat and vegetables), *asopao de pollo* or *de camarones, chivo* (goat). Also try *pipián*, goats' offal served as a stew. Fish and seafood are good; lobster can be found for as little as US$12. Fish cooked with coconut (eg *pescado con coco*) is popular around Samaná. The salads are often good; another good side dish is *tostones* (fried and flattened *plátanos*), *fritos verdes* are the same thing. *Plátano* mashed with oil is called *mangú*, often served with rice and beans. Sweet bananas are often called *guineo*. *Moro* is rice and lentils. *Gandules* are pigeon peas, very good when cooked with coconut. *Quipes* (made of flour and meat) and *pastelitos* (fried dough with meat or cheese inside) can be bought from street vendors; can be risky. *Casabe* is a cassava bread, flat and round, best toasted. *Catibias* are cassava flour fritters with meat. The most common dish is called *bandera dominicana*, white rice, beans, meat/chicken, *plátano* or *yuca* and, in season, avocado. The traveller should be warned that Dominican food is rather on the greasy side; most of the dishes are fried. Local food can often be obtained from private houses, which act as *comedores*. Basic prices, US$3-6.

Drink Juices, or *jugos*, are good; orange is usually called *china*, papaya is *lechosa*, passion fruit is *chinola*. *Agua de coco* is coconut milk, often served cold, straight from the coconut, chilled in an ice box. Local beers are Presidente (the most popular, not more than 6% alcohol), Quisqueya and Heineken. There are many rums (the most popular brands are Barceló, Brugal, Bermúdez, Macorix and Carta Vieja). Light rum (*blanco*) is the driest and has the highest proof, usually mixed with fruit juice or other soft drink (*refresco*). Amber (*amarillo*) is aged at least a year in an oak barrel and has a lower proof and more flavour, while dark rum (*añejo*) is aged for several years and is smooth enough, like a brandy, to be drunk neat or with ice and lime. Brugal allows visitors to tour its factory in Puerto Plata, on Avenida Luis Genebra, just before the entrance to the town, and offers free daiquiris. In a discothèque, *un servicio* is a ½ litre bottle of rum with a bucket of ice and *refrescos*. In rural areas this costs US$3-4, but in cities rises to US$15. Imported drinks are very expensive. Many of the main hotels have a 'Happy Hour' from 1700-1900, on a 'two for one' basis, that is two drinks for the price of one with free snacks.

Shopping

The native amber is sold throughout the country. Do not buy amber on the street, it will as likely as not be plastic. Real amber fluoresces under ultra violet light (the shop in the Amber Museum in Puerto Plata has a UV light); it floats in saltwater; if rubbed it produces static electricity; except for the very best pieces it is not absolutely pure, streaks, bits of dirt, etc, are common. Larimar, a sea-blue stone, and red and black coral are also available (remember that coral is protected). Other items which make good souvenirs are leather goods, basketware, weavings and onyx jewellery. The ceramic *muñeca sin rostro* (faceless doll) has become a sort of symbol of the Dominican Republic, at least, as something to take home. There are excellent cigars at very reasonable prices.

Flora and fauna

The government has adopted six generic categories for environmental protection: areas for scientific research, national parks, natural monuments, sanctuaries, protected areas and wildernesses. They include many lagoons, river estuaries, islands and bays.

There are 16 national parks, nine natural monuments and six scientific reserves in the Dominican Republic. The total number of protected areas (including panoramic routes, recreational areas and ecological corridors) is 67. All are under the control of the Dirección Nacional de Parques (DNP, address below). **Armando Bermúdez** and **José del Carmen Ramírez**, both containing pine forests and mountains in the Cordillera Central are the only remaining areas of extensive forest in the Republic; it is estimated that since the arrival of Columbus, two-thirds of the virgin forest has been destroyed. The reasons for the loss are fire and the establishment of smallholdings by landless peasants. By setting up these parks the gloomy prediction of 1973, that all the Dominican Republic's forest would vanish by 1990, has been avoided. In addition, a pilot reforestation project has been started near San José de las Matas, the Plan Sierra.

The **Isla Cabritos National Park** in Lago Enriquillo is the smallest in the system; it is a unique environment, between four and 40 m below sea level. Its original vegetation has been lost either to timber collection or to the goats and cattle which once grazed it. Now covered in secondary vegetation, 106 species of plant have been identified, including 10 types of cactus. The island has a large crocodile population, an endemic species of iguana, and other reptiles. 62 species of bird have been identified, five aquatic, 16 shore and 41 land birds; 45 are native to the island. Among the birds that can be seen (or heard) are the tiny manuelito (*Myiarchus stolidus*) and the great hummingbird (*Anthracothorax dominicus*), the querebebé (*Chordeiles gundlachii*), best heard at dusk, and the cu-cú (*Athene cunicularia*), which sings at night and dawn and excavates a hole in the desert for its nest.

Los Haitises, on the south coast of Samaná Bay (Bahía de San Lorenzo), is a protected coastal region, whose land and seascape of mangrove swamps, caves and strange rock formations emerging from the sea (*mogotes*) is unmatched in the Republic. In Los Haitises you can visit the Cueva del Angel, cayes on which live many birds and humid tropical forest, as well as the mangroves.

The **Parque Nacional del Este** is on the peninsula south of San Rafael del Yuma and includes the Isla Saona. It has remote beaches, examples of precolumbian art in a system of caves and is the habitat of the now scarce paloma coronita (crowned, or white-headed dove, *Columba leucocephala*), the rhinoceros iguana and of various turtles. Management of the park has been criticized in an internationally-funded study which concluded that tours and visits by tourists were too traditional and did not pay enough attention to preserving the environment. Uncontrolled visits by hundreds of people to the caves are causing damage to their internal micro-climates and disturbing the bats. Likewise, motorboats to the beach areas affect the manatees, dolphins, turtles and iguanas while fuel and lubricants accumulate on the beach and pollute the water.

In the northwest the **Montecristi** national park, on the Haitian border, contains marine and land ecosystems, the coastal Laguna de Saladillo, dry subtropical forest and the Cayos Siete Hermanos. In the southwest, the **Sierra de Bahoruco** is a forested highland which has, among other plants, 52% of the orchids found in the Republic; it also has many species of birds. At the southernmost tip of Barahona, also in the southwest, is **Jaragua** national park, which includes the Isla Beata; on the mainland it is principally dry forest. Also designated national parks are a number of panoramic roads, botanical and zoological gardens (such as those in Santo Domingo, see page 417), aquaria and recreational parks, and sites of historic interest (La Vega Vieja and La Isabela).

The **Reservas Científicas** include lakes, patches of forest and the Banco de la Plata (Silver Banks), to which hump-backed whales migrate yearly from the Arctic for the birth of their young (see page 48 and 444).

Just before he left office in 1996, President Balaguer created new protected areas, several of which are in tourist areas and will now be off-limits for construction of hotels or housing. National parks were established in **Lago Enriquillo**; the **Bahía de Calderas** is now a national monument to protect the ecosystem in the dunes of Las Salinas, the largest sand dunes in the Caribbean; the **Bahía de Luperón** (Puerto Plata) and **Cascada del Limón** (Samaná) are also national monuments; **Laguna Rincón** in the east is now a Refugio de Fauna Silvestre; also created was the **Reserva Antropológica de las Cuevas de las Maravillas** in Boca de Soco, 15 km along the Carretera San Pedro de Macorís on the way to La Romana. Several '*vías panorámicas*' were created along scenic routes and El Puerto – Guaigui, Playa Andrés, Boca Chica and Cayo Levantado were designated Areas Nacionales de Recreo.

The National Parks Office (DNP) is at Avenida Máximo Gómez, Santo Domingo (Apartado Postal 2487, T4724204. To visit the main forest reserves you must obtain a permit from the DNP or from the authorized administration office of each park for RD$50 (US$3.95). Note that to visit Los Haitises or Isla Cabritos, prices from DNP do not include the boat fare. The DNP publishes a book, *Sistema de areas protegidas de República Dominicana*, which describes each park and details how to reach it (US$12).

The Reserva Antropológica de las Cuevas de Borbón was extended in 1996 to protect the **El Pomier** caves, in San Cristóbal, under threat from limestone quarrying. The caves are of enormous archaeological value, with over 4,000 wall paintings and 5,000 rock drawings. Cave No 1 contains 590 pictograms, making it superior to any other cave painting site in the Caribbean. The caves also house large numbers of bats. Entry is RD$5.

The **Jardín Botánico Nacional** and the **Museo de Historia Natural**, Santo Domingo, have a full classification of the Republic's flora. Of interest are the 67 types and 300 species of orchid found in this part of Hispaniola; there are a number of gardens which specialize in their cultivation. The most popular are *Oncidium henekenii*, *Polyradicium lindenii* and *Leonchilus labiatus*. The Jardín Botánico holds an orchid show each year. The national plant is the caoba (mahogany). There is a wide variety of palms, some of which grow only on Hispaniola.

The Dominican Republic is becoming a popular birdwatching destination. The national bird is the cotica parrot, which is green, very talkative and a popular pet. It is, however, protected. Among other birds that can be seen, apart from those mentioned above, are other parrots, hummingbirds, the guaraguao (a hawk), the barrancolí and the flautero. Of the island's mammals, the hutia, an endemic rodent, is endangered. Similarly in peril is the manatee, which may be seen at Estero Hondo.

Beaches and watersports

According to UNESCO, the Dominican Republic has some of the best beaches in the world: white sand, coconut palms and many with a profusion of green vegetation. The main ones are described in the text below. The beaches vary enormously in development, cleanliness, price of facilities, number of hawkers and so on. Boca Chica and Juan Dolio, for instance, are very touristy and not suitable for anyone seeking peace and quiet (except out of season); for that, Bayahibe would be a much better bet (although development is under way here). The best-known beaches are in the east of the Republic, including: Boca Chica, Juan Dolio, Playa Caribe, Guayacanes and Villas del Mar in San Pedro de Macorís; Minitas (La Romana), Bayahibe, Macao, Bávaro, Puerto Escondido (Higüey); Anadel, Cayo Levantado, Las Terrenas, Playa Rincón and Portillo in Samaná and Sánchez; Playa el Bretón at Cabrera, Playa Grande in the Province of María Trinidad Sánchez and Laguna Gri-Gri at Río San Juan, where you can also visit the beaches of Puerto Escondido, Punta Preciosa in the Bahía Escocesa and Cabo Francés Viejo. Northeast of Puerto Plata, recommended, although in many cases fully developed, beaches include Cabarete, Ermita, Magante, Playa Grande and Sosúa. At Puerto Plata itself are Playa Dorada, Costámbar, Cofresí, Long Beach, Boca de Cangrejos, Caño Grande, Bergantín, Playa de Copello and Playa Mariposa. Towards the northwest and the Haitian border there are beaches at Bahía de Luperón, Playa de El Morro, Punta Rucia, Cayos los Siete Hermanos and Estero Hondo. The Montecristi area, outside the national park, is due for development.

In the south the best beaches are Las Salinas, Monte Río, Palmar de Ocoa, Najayo, Nigua, Palenque, Nizao and those south and west of Barahona. The majority of beaches have hotels or lodgings, but those without are suitable for camping.

Watersports such as deep-sea fishing, diving and surfing can be arranged at the Náutico Clubs in Santo Domingo and at Boca Chica beach. Güibia Beach, on the Malecón, Santo Domingo, has good waves for **surfing**. All watersports can be arranged through *Actividades Acuáticas*, P O Box 1348, Santo Domingo, T6885838, F6885271 (you will be referred to their offices at Boca Chica, T5234511, or Puerto Plata, T3202567). There is excellent **scuba diving** at the underwater park at La Caleta, the small beach near the turn-off to the airport, on the Autopista de las Américas; snorkelling and diving is good all along the south coast, particularly around Bayahibe and the Parque Nacional del Este. Hotels on the north coast also offer diving and snorkelling facilities. For expert divers there are many sunken Spanish galleons on the reefs offshore. For full information on diving contact the Dirección Nacional de Parques, T2215340.

Cabarete, near Sosúa, is one of the best **windsurfing** places in the world, attracting international competitors to tournaments there. Other centres are Playa Salinas (Baní), Boca Chica and Puerto Plata; most beach hotels offer windsurfing facilities. The Cabarete Race Organization, made up of all the windsurfing operations in the area (Surf Resort, CariBic, Fanatic, Vela/Spinout, Sport Away, Happy and Surf & Sport), organizes Cabarete Race Week in

June as a non-profit event. Lots of competitions, fiestas and other events, F5713346, Mike Braden, for information.

For renting boats and **yachts**, contact the Secretaría de Turismo. There are no marinas at present but plans are being prepared. For independent yachtsmen the Dominican Republic is an excellent place to reprovision if cruising the islands. Laundry is taken in by local women.

Several international **fishing** tournaments are held each year, the catch being blue marlin, bonito and dorado. There is an annual deep-sea fishing tournament at Boca de Yuma, east of La Romana, in June. For information about fishing contact Santo Domingo Club Náutico, Lope de Vega 55, T5661682, or the Clubes Náuticos at Boca Chica and Cabeza de Toro. However, these clubs are for members only, so you will need to know someone who is a member if you want to visit.

Other sports   **Golf**   There are 22 golf courses with more planned: Santo Domingo Country Club, Cayacoa and Isabel Villas, in Santo Domingo; San Andrés Country Club and Los Marlins at Metro Country Club in Juan Dolio; La Romana Country Club, Los Links, Altos de Chavón and Dientes de Perro in Casa de Campo; Bávaro, White Sands and Cocotal Country Club in Punta Cana; Loma de Chivo at Samaná; Nagua Golf at Nagua; Playa Grande at Río San Juan; Costa Azul at Cabarete; Playa Dorada, Los Mangos and Hacienda Golf all near Puerto Plata; Los Aromas in Santiago; Bella Vista in Bonao; Jarabacoa Golf Club in Jarabacoa. For information about courses, tournaments, holidays, tours, pros, club membership etc, T2485263, F2482287. The tourist office distributes a *Golf Guide* in four languages with details and plans of each course. Several more golf courses are being built at new resorts around the country. **Tennis** can also be played at the Santo Domingo Country Club and at the tennis centre which can be found by the Autopista 30 de Mayo. **Athletics** facilities can be found at the Centro Olímpico Juan Pablo Duarte in the heart of Santo Domingo. **Target shooting** at the Polígono de Tiro on Avenida Bolívar.

The national sport is **baseball**, which is played from October to January, with national and big league players participating. The best players are recruited by US and Canadian teams; about half of the 300 professional Dominican players in the USA come from San Pedro de Macorís. Sammy Sosa, of San Pedro de Macorís, beat the world batting record in 1998 and became a figure of great national pride. There are five professional stadia, including the Quisqueya. **Basketball** is the second sport. Every town has a good outdoor court where they play every evening and anyone can join in. The talent is good, there are a lot of Dominicans in the NBA. Be careful of slippery courts and keep your elbows out! **Polo** matches are played at weekends at Sierra Prieta, 25 minutes from Santo Domingo, and at Casa de Campo (T5233333). **Boxing** matches take place frequently in Santo Domingo. **Bowling** has now become a hugely popular pastime, with the opening in late 1996 of the Sebelén Centre in Santo Domingo. It is said to be the world's most hi-tech bowling alley, with 24 lanes, computerized scoring and the usual bars, shops and video games on the periphery. Limited opening hours of 1000-1400 daily.

Mountain biking is exceptional; there are advanced off-road and single track mountain passages as well as easy-going beginner trails down to the crystal blue coast. *Iguana Mama*, founded by Patricia Suriel, from Colorado, is the only licensed biking tour operator on the North Coast, based in Cabarete, www.iguanamama.com (see page 442). **Riding** is available in several places, but like cycling, the North coast is especially rewarding. *Rancho Alcantarra*, info@dominicanadventures.com, offer day trips on quiet horses into the mountains with swimming in waterfalls, or week-long riding tours.

Holidays and festivals

Public holidays   New Year's Day (1 January), Epiphany (6 January), Our Lady of Altagracia (21 January), Duarte Day (26 January), Independence Day (27 February), Good Friday (although all Semana Santa is treated as a holiday), Labour Day (1 May), Corpus Christi (60 days after Good Friday), Restoration Day (16 August), Our Lady of Las Mercedes (24 September), Christmas (25 December).

New Year is celebrated in the capital on Avenida Francisco Alberto Caamaño Deñó (formerly Avenida del Puerto) beside the river. The major bands and orchestras of the country give a free concert which attracts thousands of people. The celebration ends with fireworks and the whole area becomes a huge disco. On *21 January* the day of the **Virgen de la Altagracia**, spiritual mother of the Dominicans is celebrated with *'velaciones'*, or night-long vigils, and African-influenced singing and music. *Velaciones* can be found in San José de Ocoa, Monte Plata, Villa Altagracia, Pedernales, Paraíso, Bajos de Haína and the province of Altagracia. In Santo Domingo, **Carnival** is at the end of *February*, notable for the parade along the Malecón on 27 February; there are other parades on *16 August*. The **Festival Presidente de Música Latina** is held in *June* in the Olympic Stadium, featuring musicians from all over Latin America. The **merengue festival** in *July* (see page 470), including festivals of gastronomy, cocktails, and exhibitions of handicrafts and fruit. Puerto Plata has a similar, annual **merengue festival** at the beginning of *October* on the Malecón La Puntilla, as does Sosúa, in the last week of *September*. In the Parque Central, there are year-end celebrations from *22 December to 2 January*. **Carnival** (www.carnaval.com.do) in Santiago de los Caballeros in *February* is very colourful; its central character is the piglet, which represents the devil. On the Sundays of *February* in Montecristi there are the festivals of the *toros* versus the *civiles*. Each town's saint's day is celebrated with several days of festivities of which one of the most popular is the **Santa Cruz de Mayo fiesta** in El Seibo in *May*. **Holy Week** is the most important holiday time for Dominicans, when there are processions and festivities such as the *guloyas* in San Pedro de Macorís, the mystical-religious *ga-ga* in sugar cane villages and the *cachúas* in Cabral in the southwest.

The fourth floor of the Museo del Hombre Dominicano, Santo Domingo (see below), has an excellent exhibition of the masks and costumes that feature in the various carnivals around the country. Generally the masks are of animals or devils, or a combination of the two, and are designed to be as hideous as possible. The costumes are very brightly coloured.

Throughout the year there are many festivals and events, cultural, agricultural, commercial and sporting. Most are held in Santo Domingo or Puerto Plata, although golf and polo tournaments are held at Casa de Campo, La Romana.

Health

It is not advisable to drink tap water. All hotels have bottled water. The supply of drinking water in Santo Domingo has been improved. The local greasy food, if served in places with dubious hygiene, may cause stomach problems. Similarly, buffet restaurants in the all-inclusive hotels have been criticized. Hepatitis is common. It is also advisable to avoid the midday sun.

Dominican Republic

Santo Domingo

Population: 4 million

Santo Domingo, the capital and chief seaport is a fine example of a Spanish colonial city. In the old part of the city, on the west bank of the Río Ozama, there are many beautiful early 16th-century buildings. Restoration of the old city has made the area very attractive, with open air cafés and pleasant squares near the waterfront Avenida Francisco Alberto Caamaño Deñó, formerly Avenida del Puerto. The modern part of the city is sprawling and haphazard in architectural styles with considerable American influence.

Ins and outs

Getting there

See page 400 for flight details

Aeropuerto La Américas, east of San Domingo, is the international airport for the capital. **Las Herreras**, on the western outskirts of town is for domestic and commercial flights, although many of these also go from Las Américas, so you should check. The 30-mins' ride from Las Américas International airport to Santo Domingo should cost no more than US$15 during the daytime but varies between companies and US$20 is usual. From the capital to the airport with the companies listed above varies from US$10 (*Alex Taxi*) to US$15 (*Apolo Taxi*). Most hotels have a taxi or limousine service with set fares throughout the city and to the airport.

Getting around

See transport page 432 for further details

Public transport is varied: there are government-run buses on the arterial routes in and out of town for commuters; shared or privately-hired taxis called *públicos*, radio taxis and motorcycle taxis. Roads in the city have been improved but traffic is still slow across the river. Another bridge is planned.

Santo Domingo

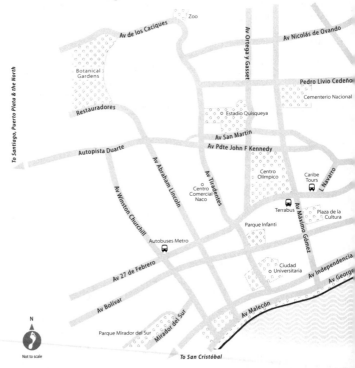

Dominican Republic

History

Santo Domingo was founded on 5 August 1498 (although the first houses were built in 1496) by Columbus' brother Bartolomé on the eastern bank of the Río Ozama and hence was the first capital in Spanish America. For years the city was the base for the Spaniards' exploration and conquest of the continent: from it Ponce de León sailed to discover Puerto Rico, Hernán Cortés launched his attack on Mexico, Balboa discovered the Pacific and Diego de Velázquez set out to settle Cuba. Hispaniola was where Europe's first social and political activities in the Americas took place. Santo Domingo itself holds the title 'first' for a variety of offices: first city, having the first Audiencia Real, cathedral, university, coinage, et cetera. In view of this, UNESCO has designated Santo Domingo a World Cultural Heritage site (Patrimonio Cultural Mundial).

Under the title of the **Quinto Centenario**, Santo Domingo played a prominent role in the celebration of the 500th anniversary of Christopher Columbus' landfall in the Caribbean (1492-1992). The Government undertook an extensive programme of public works, principally restoration work in the colonial city. A series of commemorative coins in limited editions was struck, available from the Centro de Información Numismática, Casa del Quinto Centenario, Isabel la Católica 103, T6820185, F5309164, Santo Domingo.

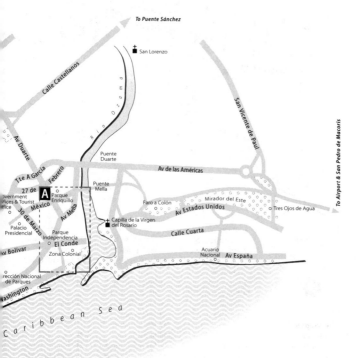

Dominican Republic

Related map:
A. Santo Domingo
old city, page 414

Santo Domingo old city

Dominican Republic

Not to scale

■ **Sleeping**
1 Hotel Aída
2 Hotel Francés
3 Hotel Ibis Conde
4 Hotel Palacio
5 Hostal Nicolás Nader
6 Hostal Nicolás de Ovando

▲ **Others**
1 Alcázar de Colón
2 Capilla de Nuestra Señora de los Remedios
3 Casa Bastidas
4 Casa de Francia / Teatro Nacional
5 Casa de Tostada / Museo de la Familia Dominicana
6 Casa del Cordón
7 Convento de los Dominicos
8 Convento San Ignacio de Loyola / Panteón Nacional
9 Fuerte de la Concepción (ruins)
10 Fuerte de San Gil (ruins)
11 Hospital-Iglesia de San Nicolás de Bari (ruins)
12 La Atarazana
13 Mercado Modelo
14 Monasterio de San Francisco (ruins)
15 Monument to Fray Antón de Montesinos
16 Museo de Duarte
17 Museo de las Casas Reales
18 Museo Mundo de Ambar
19 Palacio de Borgella
20 Parque Enriquillo
21 Parque Independencia
22 Plaza Colón
23 Puerta de la Misericordia
24 Puerta de San Diego
25 Puerta del Conde
26 Santa Bárbara (fort & church - ruins)
27 Sundial (Reloj del Sol)
28 Torre del Homenaje & Fuerte Ozama

Sights

Alcázar de Colón at the end of Las Damas and Emilio Tejera, constructed by Diego Colón in 1510-14. For six decades it was the seat of the Spanish Crown in the New World; it was sacked by Drake in 1586. Now completely restored, it houses the interesting **Museo Virreinal** (Viceregal Museum). ■ *0900-1700 daily. US$0.75.*

Capilla de La Virgen del Rosario, on the other side of the Río Ozama, near the Molinos Dominicanos at the end of Avenida Olegario Vargas. It was the first church constructed in America, restored in 1943.

Casa del Cordón, Isabel La Católica esquina Emiliano Tejera, built in 1509 by Francisco de Garay, who accompanied Columbus on his first voyage to Hispaniola. Named for the cord of the Franciscan Order, sculpted above the entrance. Now the offices of the Banco Popular; free guided tours during working hours.

Catedral Basílica Menor de Santa María, Primada de América, Isabel La Católica esquina Nouel, the first cathedral to be founded in the New World. Its first stone was laid by Diego Colón, son of Christopher Columbus, in 1514; the architect was Alonzo Rodríguez. It was finished in 1540. The alleged remains of Christopher Columbus were found in 1877 during restoration work. In 1892, the Government of Spain donated the tomb in which the remains lay, behind the high altar, until their removal to the Faro a Colón (see below). The cathedral was fully restored for 1992, with new gargoyles and sculptures at the gates showing the indigenous people when Columbus arrived. The windows, altars and roof were all returned to their colonial splendour. ■ *0900-1200, 1500-1630. No shorts allowed.*

Convento de San Ignacio de Loyola, Las Damas between Mercedes and El Conde. Finished in 1743, it is now the **National Pantheon**. It was restored in 1955 and contains memorials to many of the country's heroes and patriots. It also contains an ornate tomb built before his death for the dictator Trujillo, the 'Benefactor of the Fatherland', but his remains do not lie there. ■ *T6820185. Free. Tue-Sun 0900-1700.* **Convento de los Dominicos**, built in 1510. Here in 1538 the first university in the Americas was founded, named for St Thomas Aquinas; it now bears the title of the Universidad Autónoma de Santo Domingo. It has a unique ceiling which shows the medieval concept that identified the elements of the universe, the classical gods and the Christian icons in one system. The Sun is God, the four evangelists are the planetary symbols Mars, Mercury, Jupiter and Saturn. The University itself has moved to a site in the suburbs.

Hospital-Iglesia de San Nicolás de Bari (ruins), Hostos between Mercedes and Luperón, begun in 1509 by Nicolás de Ovando, completed 1552, the first stone-built hospital in the Americas. Also sacked by Drake, it was probably one of the best constructed buildings of the period, it survived many earthquakes and hurricanes. In 1911 some of its walls were knocked down because they posed a hazard to passers-by; also the last of its valuable wood was taken. It is now full of pigeons.

Iglesia de Santa Bárbara, off Mella to the left near Calle J Parra, near the end of Isabel La Católica. Built in 1574, sacked by Drake in 1586, destroyed by a hurricane in 1591, reconstructed at the beginning of the 17th century. Behind the church are the ruins of its fort, where there are good views. **Iglesia de la Regina Angelorum**, built 1537, contains a wall of silver near one of its altars. **Iglesia del Carmen**, built around 1615 at side of Capilla de San Andrés, contains an interesting wooden sculpture of Christ.

La Atarazana, near the Alcázar, a cluster of 16th-century buildings which served as warehouses. Now restored to contain shops, bars and restaurants. The **Museo Naval de la Atarazana** ■ *Thu-Tue, 0900-1800. Free. T6825834.*

Monasterio de San Francisco (ruins), Hostos esquina E Tejera, first monastery in America, constructed in the first decade of the 16th century. Sacked by Drake and destroyed by earthquakes in 1673 and 1751.

Dominican Republic

The mystery of Columbus' bones

After his death in 1506, Columbus was buried in Valladolid, Spain. In 1509 his body was apparently removed to Sevilla, thence together with that of his son Diego to Santo Domingo sometime in the 1540s. When France took control of Hispaniola in 1795, Cuba (still part of Spain) requested Columbus' remains. An urn bearing the name 'Colón' was disinterred from beneath the altar, sent to Havana and then back to the Cathedral in Sevilla in 1898, when Cuba became independent. In 1877, however, during alterations and repairs in Santo Domingo

cathedral, the cache of urns beneath the altar was reopened. One casket bore the inscription 'Almirante Cristóbal Colón', both outside and in. Experts confirmed that the remains were those of Columbus; the Spanish ambassador and two further experts from Spain were dismissed for concurring with the findings. A second pair of Spanish experts denied the discovery, hence the confusion over where the admiral's bones lay. The urn that was opened in 1877 is that which is now given pride of place in the Faro a Colón.

Joe Hollins

Museo de las Casas Reales, on Calle Las Damas, in a reconstructed early 16th-century building which was in colonial days the Palace of the Governors and Captains-General, and of the Real Audiencia and Chancery of the Indies. It is an excellent colonial museum (often has special exhibits). ■ *Tue-Sun 0900-1800. US$1. T6824202.* The Voluntariado de las Casas Reales has exhibitions of contemporary Dominican art.

Puerta del Conde (Baluarte de 27 de Febrero), at the end of El Conde (now a pedestrian street) in the Parque Independencia. Named for the Conde de Peñalva, who helped defend the city against William Penn in 1655. Restored in 1976, near it lie the remains of Sánchez, Mella and Duarte, the 1844 independence leaders. **Puerta de la Misericordia**, Palo Hincado and Arzobispo Portes, so named because people fled under it for protection during earthquakes and hurricanes. It forms part of the wall that used to surround the colonial city, into which are now built many of the houses and shops of Ciudad Nueva. It was here on 27 February 1844 that Mella fired the first shot in the struggle for independence from Haiti.

Reloj de Sol (sundial) built 1753, near end of Las Damas, by order of General Francisco de Rubio y Peñaranda; by its side is **Capilla de Nuestra Señora de Los Remedios**, built in the early 16th century as the private chapel of the Dávila family.

Torre del Homenaje, inside Fortaleza Ozama, reached through the mansion of Rodrigo Bastidas (later the founder of the city of Santa Marta in Colombia) on Calle Las Damas, which is now completely restored and has a museum/gallery with temporary exhibitions. It is the oldest fortress in America, constructed 1503-07 by Nicolás de Ovando, whose house in the same street is being restored and turned into a splendid hotel. ■ *US$1.*

Other old buildings are the Iglesia de las Mercedes, dating from 1555; the Puerta de San Diego, near the Alcázar; the Palacio de Borgella, Isabel la Católica, near Plaza Colón; the ruins of Fuerte de la Concepción, at the corner of Mella and Palo Hincado, built in 1543; the ruins of Fuerte de San Gil, Padre Billini, near the end of Calle Pina; and the ruins of Iglesia de San Antón, off Mella esquina Vicente Celestino Duarte.

The Ciudad Vieja and adjacent Ciudad Nueva (the area of middle-class housing of the 19th century, complete with *pulperías* – turn-of-the-century stores) are practically deserted on Sunday, a good time to stroll around and take in the architecture and atmosphere in peace.

At the mouth of the Río Ozama, the **Avenida Francisco Alberto Caamaño Deñó** (formerly Avenida del Puerto) gives access to the Antigua Ceiba, where Columbus moored his caravelles, the Plaza de Armas, the city's original drainage system and the old city wall. Steps lead up to the Alcázar de Colón where the Plaza de España has been established. The Avenida has in a short time become an open-air discothèque, more popular than the Malecón. Together with the inauguration of the

Avenida Caamaño Deñó is a boat service on the Río Ozama for sightseeing upstream (operated by Mar C por A in the vessel *Sea*). ■ *US$4, happy hour from 1800-2000, drinks two for the price of one. Mon-Fri 1800-2200, Sat 1600.* Watersports and speed-boat races can also be seen. The eastern bank of the Ozama is being restored with a new footpath, the Vereda del Almirante, an amphitheatre and a new tourist harbour. All commercial shipping will be diverted to Río Haina.

Among the attractive parks are the **Central Olímpico** (see above) in the city centre, **Parks** **Parque Independencia** (a peaceful haven amid all the traffic, with the **Altar de la Patria**, containing the remains of the country's founders, Juan Pablo Duarte, Francisco del Rosario Sánchez and Ramón Matías Mella), **Parque Colón, Parque Mirador del Este** (Autopista de las Américas, a 7 km-long *alameda*) and **Parque Mirador del Sur** (Paseo de las Indios at Mirador Sur, 7 km-long, popular for walking, jogging, cycling, picnics). **Parque Mirador del Norte** has been constructed on the banks of the Río Isabela, near Guarícano and Villa Mella. There is a boating lake, picnic areas, restaurants, jogging and cycling trails. ■ *0900-1800, Tue-Sun, US$0.40.* On Avenida José Contreras are many caves, some with lakes, in the southern cliff of Parque Mirador del Sur. Along this cliff the Avenida Cayetano Germosén has been built, giving access to a number of caves used at one time by Taino Indians. One such Lago Subterráneo has been opened as a tourist attraction. ■ *US$0.40. 0900-1730.* The road, lined with gardens, links Avenidas Luperón and Italia.

The **Jardín Botánico Nacional**, Urbanización Los Ríos. ■ *T5676211, 5652860. US$0.75, children half price. Tue-Sun 0900-1800.* **Parque Zoológico Nacional**, La Puya. ■ *T5623149. US$1, tours of the grounds US$0.75, children US$0.55. 0900-1700.* The Botanical Gardens are highly recommended (the Japanese Garden especially); horse-drawn carriages and a small train tour the grounds (US$0.75, children US$0.55), which are extensive. There is an **Acuario Nacional**, Avenida España, on the coast east of the city, a manatee is one of the exhibits, very popular; it has a café serving pizzas (there is a bus from Parque Enriquillo). ■ *T5921509. US$1. Tue-Sun 0930-1730.* **Aqua Splash**, a water fun centre is on the other side of the road. Quisqueya Park, César Nicolás Penson, is a recreational park for children. ■ *US$0.40.* The **Parque Infantil** at Avenidas Bolívar y Tiradentes is to be remodelled.

The **Faro a Colón** (Columbus Lighthouse), built at great cost (and not without controversy) in the Parque Mirador del Este, is in the shape of a cross. Where the arms of the cross intersect is the mausoleum containing the supposed remains of Columbus. The navy mounts a permanent guard over the tomb. Spotlights project a crucifix of light into the night sky, spectacular on a cloudy night, less so when it is clear. Until the lighthouse has its own solar-powered generators, the lights are lit Friday to Sunday 2000-2200 and on holidays. One of the rooms inside the lighthouse is a chapel, in others different countries have mounted exhibitions (the British exhibit concentrates on the entries for the competition to design the lighthouse: the competition was won by a British design). Many rooms are empty and the Taino museum on the second floor has yet to be mounted. The interior of the arms of the cross are open to the sky but when it rains you can shelter in the interconnecting museums. ■ *T5925217. US$1.50, US$0.30 for children. Daily 0900-1700. Photography inside permitted; guides are free, but give a tip; shorts above the knee not allowed.* East of the Lighthouse in the Parque Mirador del Este are the *cenotes* (limstone sinkholes).

Tres Ojos, a popular tourist attraction. There are actually four, not three, water-filled holes, which used to be public bathing pools going back to the times of the Taínos, but now 'Tarzan' is the only person allowed to swim. He has been doing it since 1958 and is a tourist attraction himself. You have to get a little ferry boat across the third lake to get to the fourth; it is pulled across by Antoni, who speaks some English and can tell you about the three movies made here.■ *US$1.50.Toilets. At the entrance vendors sell artesanías made from stalactites and stalagmites, an ecological horror. Bus from Parque Enriquillo US$0.20.*

Modern city   The modern city is very spread out because, until recently, there was no high-rise building. The outer city has fine avenues, especially Avenida George Washington (also known as the Malecón) which runs parallel to the sea; it often becomes an open-air discothèque, where locals and foreigners dance the merengue. The annual *merengue* festival is held here. The spectacular monument to Fray Antón de Montesinos is at the eastern end of Avenida George Washington. A new exhibition centre has been built on Avenida George Washington opposite the Parque Eugenio María de Hostos, and cultural events and shows take place here. During the 1997 *merengue* festival the Plaza Ñico Lora was inaugurated on the Malecón in front of the Parque Eugenio María de Hostos. This is to be the equivalent of Mexico City's Plaza Garibaldi, with *pericos ripiaos* from all over the country playing in the plaza.

The continuation (Prolongación) of Avenida México, which runs parallel to Avs Bolívar and 27 de Febrero, has many modern buildings, while Expreso Quinto Centenario, in the Villa Juana and Villa Francisca districts, is a new roadway which has rejuvenated these parts of the city. Other important avenues are Independencia, Bolívar, Abraham Lincoln, Winston Churchill, Núñez de Cáceres, 27 de Febrero, John F Kennedy, Juan Pablo Duarte, Ramón Matías Mella and General Gregorio Luperón. Traffic movement has been eased by the construction of a tunnel on Avenida 27 de Febrero allowing a five-minute crossing of the main commercial zone from Avenida Winston Churchill to Leopoldo Navarro. Above the tunnel, the Government has made an attractive pedestrian boulevard with small shops and bars. A huge iron clock marks the hour with chords from the merengue '*Compadre Pedro Juan*', one of the most traditional exponents of Dominican music. There are also two large screens controlling the tunnel traffic which will also be used for showing major events.

Gazcue is a quiet, attractive residential area with expensive homes built in the 1930s and 1940s, stretching west of the Zona Colonial as far as Avenida Máximo Gómez. The coral pink Palacio Presidencial with a neo-classical central portico and cupola, built by Trujillo, is at the intersection of Doctor Delgado and Manuel María Castillo. It is used by the President, but guided tours of the richly decorated interior can be arranged, T6864771 ext 340 or 360. Opposite the Palacio's grounds, at Avenida México y 30 de Marzo, are the government offices. The 1955/56 World's Fair (Feria de Confraternidad) buildings now house the Senate and Congress.

Villa Mella, a suburb to the north of the capital is famed for the traditional *Feria del Chicharrón de Villa Mella*, on 10 May, when you can eat pork crackling cooked the Dominican way. Another local attraction is the dance of the congos, a ritual of African origin.

Four bridges cross the Río Ozama: the nearest to the sea from the end of Av México is Mella (originally nicknamed La Bicicleta because it is so narrow, but now with a new bridge beside it to ease congestion), next, at the end of Av 27 de Febrero is Duarte, then a new bridge, known as Puente de la 17, which will link up with the new works and an overpass being constructed in 2000 to extend Av 27 de Febrero, and further inland Sánchez. A fourth is proposed which would link the Malécon with Avenida España, giving quicker access to the aquarium, the lighthouse, the race track, Sans Souci cruise ship terminal and restaurants.

Museums   The national museum collection, which includes a wonderful display of Taino artefacts and the ethnography section mentioned under Festivals above, is in the **Museo del Hombre Dominicano**, which forms part of the Plaza de la Cultura, founded by Joaquín Balaguer on Avenida Máximo Gómez. ■ *1000-1700, closed on Mon, US$0.75, T6873622.* It also includes the ultra-modern national theatre and national library; the **Museo de Arte Moderno** ■ *Tue-Sun 0900-1700, US$1.25, T6852153*, the **Cinemateca Nacional**, the **Museo de Historia Natural** ■ *Tue-Sun 1000-1700, café open 0700-1900, T6890106, US$0.75*, and the **Museo de Historia y Geografía** ■ *0930-1700, free, T6866668*. The **Museo de la Familia Dominicana** is housed in the Casa de Tostada (Calle Padre Billini esq Arzobispo Meriño), an early 16th-century mansion. ■ *Mon-Fri, 0900-1700. US$0.80. T6895057*. The Banco

Central has a **Museo Numismático y Filatélico**, Avenida Pedro Henríquez Ureña, opposite the main building, with stamps dating back to 1865. ■ *Mon-Fri 0900-1600. T6886512. Free.* The **Fundación García Arévalo**, in the 7 Up building, Avenida San Martín 279, near Lope de Vega, has an exhibition of pre-hispanic art and civilization. ■ *Mon-Sat 0800-1200. Free. T5407777.* For archaeologists there is the Instituto de Investigaciones Históricas, José Reyes 24. At José Reyes 6, in the Zona Colonial, is the **Instituto de la Porcelana**. ■ *T6891766.* At the entrance to the airport is La Caleta Archaeological Museum (**Museo Ceremonial La Caleta**) with a Taino burial site. However, it is closed because of hurricane damage and awaiting repairs. You can look through the gates to see the graves, but the Taíno ceramics have been removed. **Museo Mundo de Ambar**, Arzobispo Meriño 452, esq Restauración, in restored 17th century building, fascinating display of scorpions, butterflies and plants fossilized in amber, with microscopes and videos. A guided tour is recommended but not essential. Craftsmen polish and shape raw amber for sale in adjoining room. ■ *0900-1800. US$1. T6823309, F6881142.* The **Museo de Ambar**, El Conde 107 on Parque Colón, opened end-1998. Museum upstairs, shop downstairs selling amber, larimar, black coral, local gold and pearls. ■ *T2211333, F6825101. US$1.* The **Museo de la Radio y Televisión Don Lulio Moscoso** opened in 1996 in the amphitheatre of the television station on Calle Dr Tejada Florentino, collection of equipment used at the state television station and historic recordings, admission free but visit by prior arrangement. **Museo Bellapart**, Avenida John F Kennedy, showing the private art collection of Juan José Bellapart, with works from 1800 to the present day, including paintings by Julio Desangles and Jaime Colson. ■ *Mon-Sat, 0900-1800.*

Essentials

Nicolás de Ovando, Calle las Damas 53, built 1502 overlooking river and what is now the cruise ship terminal. 5-star hotel being renovated by Accor group of France, 50 rooms to be expanded to 180 when whole block restored, wonderful historical landmark, 7 patios, 3 restaurants, pool, casino, boutique when complete, opposite French embassy, very special. Away from the old city along the Malecón are the modern international-style hotels. **LL-AL** *Hotel V Centenario Intercontinental*, Av George Washington 218, T2210000, F2212020. 5 stars, very well-appointed with restaurants, pools, casino, gym, etc. A little further from the colonial centre are **LL-AL** *Renaissance Jaragua Hotel & Casino*, Av George Washington 367, T2212222, F6860528. Large spa and health club, tennis, free form pool, casino with entertainment, meetings facilities, executive floor, business centre, 5 restaurants and 300 deluxe a/c rooms and suites; and **LL-AL** *Meliá Santo Domingo*, Av George Washington 365, PO Box 8326, T2216666, F6878150. 245 rooms, a/c, pool, tennis, gym, spa, casino, completely renovated with new entrance in 1999, 3 executive floors, 2 restaurants, 2 rooms for disabled, non-smoking floor, business centre, rooms overlooking casino can be noisy, comfortable international standard. **LL-AL** *Embajador* (Occidental), Av Sarasota 65, T2212131, F5324494. 316 rooms, a/c, pool, tennis, casino, rooms larger than Meliá but despite renovation in 1998 decoration looks tired, poolside restaurant, piano bar in huge lobby, lots of shops and restaurants at entrance to hotel. **LL-AL** *Dominican Fiesta Hotel y Casino*, Av Anacaona, T5628222, F5628938. 331 rooms and suites, a/c, pool, jacuzzi, tennis, sauna, gym, 3 restaurants. **L-B** *Plaza*, T5416226, F5417251. Suites with kitchenette, very comfortable, cable TV, pool, gym, gourmet restaurant, coffee shop (if you wish to self-cater, ask hotel for utensils and tableware and buy food in nearby supermarket). Recommended. **L-AL** *Santo Domingo*, Av Independencia y Av Abraham Lincoln, T2211511, F5354050. A/c, pool, colonial style, plush and charming, main restaurant open 5 days a week for lunch, otherwise for receptions, *Café Tal*, less well-staffed. Opposite is its sister hotel **L-AL** *Hispaniola*, Av Independencia y Abraham Lincoln, T2217111, F5354050. Pleasant public areas, noisy, glitzy, casino off reception, bedrooms and corridors showing their age, bathroom adequate, very clean, good service, repairs carried out quickly, pool, disco.

Sleeping
Prices listed are high season rates & do not include taxes, normally 23%

Dominican Republic

AL *Barceló Gran Hotel Lina*, Av Máximo Gómez y 27 de Febrero, T5635000, F6865521, h.lina@codetel.net.do Good restaurant, well-equipped, casino, convenient for Caribe Tours terminal, painted orange and pink, a/c, pool. **AL-A** *Francés* (Sofitel), Calle Las Mercedes esq Arzobispo Meriño, T6859331, F6851289. Restored colonial mansion, 19 luxury rooms, lovely furnishings, restaurant in beautiful courtyard with fountain or indoors, superb French food, expensive but recommended. **A-D** *Napolitano Hotel y Casino*, Av George Washington esq Cambronal, T6871131, F6876814. 72 rooms with seaview, a/c, pool, casino.

B-C *Continental*, Av Máximo Gómez 16, T6891151, F6878397. Includes taxes and breakfast, pleasant area, pool, no discount or refund if water supply fails. **B-C** *Palacio*, Duarte 106 y Ureña, T6824730, F6875535, h.palacio@codetel.net.do Colonial mansion, standard or superior rooms with fan. **B-C** *Cervantes*, Cervantes 202, T6868161, F6865754. A/c, 171 rooms, some suites, family-run, with pool. **B-C** *Hostal Nicolás Nader*, Duarte y General Luperón, colonial mansion, in the old city, T6876674. Includes taxes, 9 rooms, best upstairs, beautifully furnished with lots of modern art for sale, main art gallery on Rafael Augusto Sánchez 22, Piantini, friendly, personal service, pleasant. **B-C** *Villa Italia*, Av Independencia 1107 casi esquina Alma Mater, T6823373, F2217461, hotel.villa@codetel.net.do 25 rooms, 3 suites, 1 apartment, a/c, phone, TV, jacuzzi on terrace, sea view, wooden furniture colour washed green, restaurant, fridge available for extra charge, attractive but service found lacking.

C-D *Comodoro*, Av Bolívar 193, T6877141, T/F5412277. A/c, pool, reasonable, with fridges in rooms. **C-D** *Naco*, Av Tiradentes 22, T5623100, F5440957. 106 rather run down rooms, a/c, pool, casino. **D** *Bellavista*, Dr F Defilló 43, Ens Bella Vista, T5320412, F5352988. Good, clean, large rooms, a/c, TV, also one tiny single room, **E**, no window, breakfast available. **D** *Royal*, Av Duarte y 27 de Febrero, T6855400. Fully a/c, small pool, good restaurant, *guaguas* leaving to north and west across the street. **E** *Aída*, El Conde and Espaillat, T6857692, 6872880, F6889350. A/c rooms have no windows, rooms with fan have balcony, some rooms sleep 3, family-run, very nice, no smoking, fairly quiet (but record shop below may be noisy in day), very central, popular, often full, Amex accepted. **E** *Alameda*, Calle Cervantes opposite *Cervantes*, T6855121. No frills but quite adequate, management amiable and helpful, English spoken, restaurant. **E** *Montesino*, José Gabriel García III, Zona Colonial, T6883346, overlooking Malecón and Montesino's statue. 4 rooms, with bath, **F** with shared bath, fan, use of kitchen, will negotiate longer stays. Next door to *Napolitano* is **E** *Palmeras del Caribe*, Cambronal 1, T6893872. Nice rooms but small, pleasant garden, use of fridge, adjoining café. **E** *Señorial*, Av Presidente Vicini Burgos 58 (Parque Eugenio María de Hostos), T6874367, F6870600. Swiss-run, a/c, good electricity and water supply, colour TV, friendly, clean and informal, good Italian food, popular with Swiss-Italian visitors, see the 1952 map on the wall.

F *Independencia*, Estrella casi esquina Arzobispo Nouel, near Parque Independencia. Price for single room, soap, towels etc provided, clean, convenient location, recommended, some rooms without windows, also has a club, bar (noisy all night), language school (across the street) and art exhibitions. **F** *Luna del Norte*, Benito González 89, T687-0124/2504. Clean, friendly, central. **F** *Radiante*, Av Duarte 7 between Av Mella and Benito González. With bath, key deposit charged. **F** *Macau*, Benito González, near Av Duarte. Dirty, very basic, Chinese-run, as is the restaurant downstairs. **F** *Ferdan*, Francisco Henríquez 107 y Carvajal, T2217710, just off Av Duarte. Buses to Boca Chica and to airport 2 blocks away, large clean rooms with bath, foreigners given rooms with windows, large discounts for long stays but you will be given room on top floors where generator does not reach and suffer power cuts. There are dozens of cheap hotels, especially around the Mercado Modelo; those on Av Duarte are usually used by prostitutes; have a good look round them before making any decision. For cheap rooms in hotels or *casas de pensión*, or for apartments for rent for longer stays in or outside the capital, look in the classified section of daily paper, *Listín Diario*. Rooms in the private house of Doña Hilkka, Abreu 7, near Iglesia San Carlos, central, cheap, charming. Business travellers can often get cheaper rates than posted by requesting '*la tarifa comercial*'.

Apart-hotels B-C *Apartahotel Delta*, Av Sarasota 53, T5350800. **B-C** *Plaza Colonial*, Julio Verne 4, T6879111, F6850054. Big, bare apartments, close to Zona Colonial, pool. *Casa de Huéspedes Sterling*, Av Bolívar 5 y Parque Independencia, T6885773, next to Codetel office. Self-catering apartments, weekly or monthly basis, fully equipped, friendly, clean, negotiate price, US$256 per month high season. **C-D** *Aladino*, H Pieter 34, T5670144. Fan and a/c. From **C** *Petit Apart-Hotel Turístico*, Aníbal de Espinosa 70, T6815454, with restaurant, terrace, disco. **C** *Plaza Florida*, Av Bolívar 203, T5670144, 5413957, F5405582.

US$20 and over for main dish: *Fellini*, Roberto Pastoriza 504, esq Winston Churchill, T5405330. Mediterranean cuisine, closed Tue. *La Bricciola*, Arzobispo Merino 152. Recommended Italian cuisine in spectacular setting in courtyard of colonial house, T6885055. *Café Coco*, Padre Billini 53, Zona Colonial, T6879624. A small restaurant owned and run by 2 Englishmen, excellent food and service, menu changes daily, highly recommended, open 1200-1500, 1830-2230, closed Sun pm and all day Mon, reservations required, dinner for 2 with wine costs about US$75. *Vesuvio I*, Av George Washington 521, T2211954. Dinner for 2 about US$90, very expensive, not worth it, touristy. In the Plaza España is *Museo de Jamón*, ceiling covered with hams, also delicious selection of *tapas*.

Eating
Many hotels have
'bufets ejecutivos' at
lunch time & gourmet
restaurants for
evening meals

US$15-20: *Mesón de la Cava*, Parque Mirador del Sur, situated in a natural cave. Good steaks, live music, dancing, great experience, very popular so reserve in advance, T5333818, open daily 1200-1500, 1800-0100. *Ché Bandoneón*, on El Conde between Damas y Parque Colón. Argentine owned, outdoor terrace, Argentine, criollo and French food, tangos, T6870023. *Lori's Steak House*, Nicolas de Bari 6, for grilled meat, T5625148. *El Rancho*, in the Feria Ganadera, T5329803. Prime imported US steaks, expensive. On Calle Padre Billini at the corner of Duarte is *Retazos*, T6886196, specializing in Dominican dishes, eg seafood such as crab stew or fish cooked in coconut milk, dinner for 2 about US$50. *Asadero los Argentinos*, Av Independencia between Av Abraham Lincoln and Máximo Gómez. Excellent Argentine food. *Cappuccino*, Av Máximo Gómez 60, T6898600. Italian owned restaurant and café, great Italian food, suave, prices to match. *David Crockett*, Gustavo Mejía Ricart 34, esq Alberto Larancuet, T2272899. Grill, excellent, around US$20-25 per person for a meal. *Les Fondues*, run by Swiss, Av Winston Churchill, Esq Paseo de los Locutores, T5620067. All types of fondue including chocolate. *Río Miño*, Jardines El Embajador, Sarasota, Centro Comercial Embajador T5345927. Creative contemporary cuisine and good Spanish food.

US$10-15: *Titanic*, in Parque Mirador, Chinese and international. *Sully's*, Av Charles Summers y Calle Caoba, T5623389. Some distance from centre, excellent, lots of seafood in Dominican, French and Italian styles, full dinner for 2 about US$50. *Restaurant Cantábrico*, Av Independencia 54, T6875101. Recommended fresh seafood. *Fonda La Atarazana*, La Atarazana 5, T6892900. Popular for créole and international cuisine. *Juan Carlos*, Av Mejía Ricart 7, T5625088. Spanish, near Olympic stadium, very good value. *El Mesón de Castilla*, Dr Báez esq Luisa O Pellerano, T6850453. *Tapas* and Spanish cuisine. *Sheherezade*, Roberto Pastoriza 226, T2272323. Arabian and Mediterranean food. *Palacio de Jade*, José María Heredia 6, Gazcue, T6863226. Cantonese cooking. *Café Berimbau*, Abraham Lincoln, esq Gustavo Mejía Ricart. Brazilian food. *Samurai*, Av Lincoln 902, T4723442. Very good Japanese. *Chino de Mariscos*, Av Sarasota 38, T5335249, 5328350. Very good Chinese seafood. *Aubergine*, Av Alma Mater y Av México. German food; *La Esquina de Tejas*, Av 27 de Febrero 343, T5606075. Offers Spanish cuisine. *Boga Boga*, Plaza Florida, Av Bolívar 203, T5414150. Spanish, US$15-20 for a meal. For good Chinese food try *Marios*, 27 de Febrero 299, T5624441. Very popular. *Seasons*, Roberto Pastoriza 14, T5652616. Spanish, hot and cold *tapas*. *Panchos Villa*, Abraham Lincoln 403, T5359429. Mexican, informal atmosphere, young crowd. *La Mezquita*, Independencia 407, T6877090. Spanish seafood, good food.

The Asociación
Nacional de Hoteles y
Restaurantes,
Asonahores, T6874676,
publishes a guide to
the best restaurants
in the capital, '
Guía de Restaurantes'

US$ 0-10: *Plaza Toledo*, Isabel la Católica 163, Plaza María de Toledo. Combination café and art gallery owned by American Betty Marshall. *Lumi's Park*, Av Abraham Lincoln 809, T5404584. The place to be, outdoor seating under cnavas, 'steak park', *churrasco*, excellent *mofongos*, full dinner for 2 with rum or beer US$30, open until dawn, also takeaway or local

Dominican Republic

delivery. **Vesuvio II**, Av Tiradentes 17, T5626060. Italian and international cuisine, better value than *Vesuvio I*. **Fogaraté**, Av George Washington 517, T6880044. Typical Dominican specialities, excellent. Recommended by Dominicans. **El Conuco**, José Joaquín Pérez, road running off behind *Jaragua*. *Comida criolla, sancocho, chivo guisado, la bandera dominicana* (meat, beans and rice, the colours of the flag) and other typical dishes. **Maniquí** in the Plaza de la Cultura is good for the local dish *mofongo* (see page 406), **Palacio del Mofongo**, Av George Washington 509, T6888121, or **Casa del Mofongo**, 27 de Febrero y Calle 7 Eva Mo, T5651778 (a long way from the centre); **Mandarín**, next to *Palacio del Mofongo*. Excellent Cantonese and Chinese food. **Spagghettíssimo**, Paseo de los Locutores 13, T5653708. Fish, seafood, meat, Italian. **El Conde**, El Conde esquina Meriño, T6326944, on Plaza Colón overlooking cathedral. Lovely spot to stop for a really cold beer when touring the old city, tables on sidewalk or cooler indoors, food average but acceptable *plato del día*, prices very reasonable considering the location. **Bariloche**, El Conde 203. Self-service food from about 1145, look at what is on offer then buy ticket at cash register, lasagne only US$1, *menú del día* US$3, huge portions. There are numerous pizzerias which are good value: **Domino's** has several delivery outlets and there is a **Pizza Hut** on the corner of Av 27 de Febrero and Av Abraham Lincoln and on El Conde and Espaillat. **Pizzarelli**, Av Tiradentes, Plaza Naco. Very tasty pizzas. Several burger bars and other Americanized fast food chains, eg **McDonalds**, **Wendy's**, **Burger King**. Many fast food places offer dishes for about US$2-3, which would cost US$8 in a hotel restaurant. There are also takeaway places where a meal costs about US$2.50. Cheapest are probably the Chinese restaurants, but in many cases the hygiene is dubious (the same applies to other basic restaurants). Several *cafeterías* serving local lunches around Mercado Modelo.

Vegetarian: Two good vegetarian restaurants are **Ananda**, Casimiro de Moya 7, T6824465, and **Vegetariano**, Calle Luperón 9 (open 0800-1500). Also **Ojas**, Calle Jonas Salk 2, T6823940 and **El Terrenal**, Malecón y Estrelleta, T6893161, some vegetarian dishes.

Cafés and snacks: *L'Avocat*, El Conde 60, café-restaurant. **Veneto Ice Cream** on Av Independencia. **La Cafetería Colonial**, El Conde 253. Good for coffee after meal at *Bariloche*, freshly ground. **The Village Pub**, in Calle Hostos 350, opposite the ruins of Hospital San Nicolás de Bari. A good place for snacks and drinks in a pub-type atmosphere, in the colonial city; and so is **La Taberna** (classical music) at Padre Billini with Las Damas. **Bachata Rosa**, Plaza de España, named after the popular album of Juan Luis Guerra, 2 huge screens with music videos. **Café del Río**, Plaza la Marina, overlooking the Ozama River. Good place for a cold beer, near the Sugar Cane Monument on eastern side of river. Try a *chimichurri* (spiced sausage), throughout the city stalls sell sandwiches, *chimichurris*, hot dogs and hamburgers. Several small restaurants specialize in roast chicken, *pollo al carbón*, with a tasty *wasa kaca* sauce. The best of these is **Pollo Caribe** on Av Winston Churchill, just below Av Sarasota. **France-Croissant**, Av Sarasota 82 y Dr Defillo, French bakery, tastiest pastries in the country, unsweetened wholemeal bread available, small café.

Nightlife **Discos** *Jubilee* in *Hotel Jaragua*, Dominican music. **Disco Piano** in *Hotel El Napolitano*. **Eclipse**, Av Venezuela 64, T5933336, dancing, good atmosphere. **Remington Palace**, Av Independencia, near the Malecón, live artists, upmarket ambience. **Shehara** and **Bella Blu** (next to *Vesuvio I*) on George Washington, American music. **Punto Final**, Av Pasteur. **El Final**. **Magic Disco**. **Jet Set**, Av Independencia, barrio El Portal. Live dance music Mon from 2200, bands include Fernando Villalona (El Mayimbe), Los Hermanos Rosario, Milly, Sergio Vargas, La Banda Gorda, you can also dance to American music. **Maunaloa Night Club** in the Centro de los Héroes also has live music and comedians, dancing every night to Dominican music. **Club 60**, Máximo Gómez 60. Rock, merengue and ballads. **Neon** in *Hotel Hispaniola*. Upmarket, occasionally has live Latin jazz. **Sentimiento**, Hostos 99. Down market with lots of merengue, very dark. For Cuban *son* music: **El Rincón Habanero**, Sánchez Valverde y Baltazar de los Reyes in Villa Consuelo. Working class enthusiasts of Cuban *son* dance between tables to old records of 1940s and 1950s. **Secreto Musical Bar**, one block away, Baltazar de los Reyes and Pimentel, similar, headquarters of Club Nacional de los Soneros, rock, merengue, salsa and ballads. *La Vieja Habana*, in Villa Mella on the northern outskirts of town, owner called Generoso. *Café Atlántico*, Av Abraham Lincoln, 1 block below Av 27 de Febrero. Popular with the 20-something crowd, also serves Mexican food. *Remos Café Música*, for dancing, Puerto Turístico Sans Souci, T5922202. *Karaoke Sea Bar*, Roberto Pastoriza 152, T5471660. The inevitable karaoke. *Hollywood Café*, Gustavo Mejía Ricart 36, T5663349. For cinema aficionados. *Fantasy*, Héroes de Luperón 29, T5332750, dancing to American music. *Schizo Dicotheque*, Plaza Andalucía, 3rd Floor, Gustavo Mejía Ricart. *Trío Café*, Plaza Cataluña, Av Lope de Vega. *Il Grappolo Café*, Plaza Catatluña, Av Lope de Vega. *Beer House*, Gustavo Mejía Ricart esq Winston Churchill. *Tierra Luna Café*, Av Winston Churchill. *Salón La Fiesta* in the *Jaragua Hotel*. *Embassy Club* in the *Hotel El Embajador*. *Napolitano*. *Hotel San Gerónimo*, Independencia. *La Azotea* in *Hotel Concorde*. *Salón Rojo*, Hotel Comodoro, Av Bolívar. *Las Vegas*, *Piano Bar Las Palmas* in *Hotel Santo Domingo*, Piano Bar Intramuros Tablao Flamenco. Hotels *El Embajador*, *Meliá Santo Domingo*, *Jaragua* have orchestras every night playing Dominican music, free.

Also *Instrumental Night Club* on Autopista Las Américas. *Exodus*, George Washington 511. *Le Petit Chateau*, Av George Washington Km 11.5, nude shows. *Félix*, Calle Félix Evaristo Mejía, good for unattached men, armed security guards, vigilant taxi drivers but beware of pickpocketing by the ladies.

Guácara Taína, Paseo de los Indios, between Avenida Cayetano Germosén and Parque Mirador, has shows of Taíno dancing in a deep natural cave with stalactites and indigenous pictographs, spectacular setting, from 1700-0200, US$4-12 (also disco, all types of music, a/c, 2 dance floors, Happy Hours and fashion shows). For daytime tours of the cave T5302662 (0900-1700), or T5331051 (1700-2100), F5304632, reserve 24 hrs in advance.

To hear *pericos ripiaos*, go on Fri or Sat night to the eating places (*colmados*) near the Malecón in Ciudad Nueva section of the city; the groups move from place to place.

Casinos Hotels *Dominican Fiesta*, *Santo Domingo*, *San Gerónimo*, *Meliá Santo Domingo*, *El Embajador*, *Naco*, *Jaragua*, *Hispaniola*, remodelled in 2000 Las Vegas style, *Lina* and *Maunaloa Night Club*, Centro de los Héroes.

Entertainment

Concerts Concerts and other cultural events are often held at the National Theatre, the Casa de Francia, corner of Las Damas and El Conde, where Cortés lived for a while (run by the French Embassy, also art gallery and library, open to non-members), and the Casa de Teatro (see below). **Theatres** *Teatro Nacional*, Plaza de la Cultura, Av Máximo Gómez, T6879131, For tickets. *Palace of Fine Arts*, Av Independencia and Máximo Gómez, T6872494. *Casa de Teatro*, small drama workshop, Arzobispo Meriño 14, T6893430. **Cinemas** In the new Diamond Plaza mall, Av de Los Próceres, there are several cinema screens.

Sports

Swimming *Agua Splash Caribe*, T5915927, open Tue-Sun, adults US$3.60, children US$2.50. **Tennis** can be played at the *Meliá Santo Domingo*, *Hotel Jaragua* and the *Centro Olímpico*, Av Juan Pablo Duarte. **Bowling** at the *Sebelén Bowling Center* (Bolera), Av Abraham Lincoln, esquina Roberto Pastoriza in a large commercial plaza. **Basketball** at the Palacio de los Deportes, a/c stadium, also matches at the Club San Lázaro and Club San Carlos. **Baseball** matches are played Oct-Jan in the Quisqueya stadium.

Shopping

The *Mercado Modelo*, on Avenida Mella esquina Santomé, includes gift shops and is the best place in the city for handicrafts; you must bargain to get a good price. Guides appointed to assist tourists in fact get a 5-10% commission from the vendor. There are also 'speciality shops' at Plaza Criolla, 27 de Febrero y Máximo Gómez. Calle El Conde, now reserved to pedestrians, is the oldest shopping sector in Santo Domingo; Avenida Mella at Duarte is a good spot for discount shopping and local colour. A flea market, *Mercado de las Pulgas*, operates on Sun in the Centro de los Héroes and at the Mercado de Oportunidades, 27 de Febrero. In contrast are the modern complexes at Plaza Naco and the new US style Unicentro shopping mall at the corner of Av 27 de Febrero and Av Abraham Lincoln; also Plaza Caribe, at 27 de Febrero y Leopoldo Navarro, the new Multicentro Churchill on Av Winston Churchill esq Gustavo Mejía Ricart (with *La Sirena*, the supermarket *Pola* and other shops) and up to 15 other Plazas Comerciales offering a variety of shops, food halls, banks and offices. Around

Duty-free at Centro de los Héroes, La Atarazana, shops in large hotels; departure lounge at airport; all purchases must be in US dollars

Dominican Republic

the corner from the Amber Museum is *Ambar Nacional*, Calle Restauración 110, T6865700, sells amber, coral and larimar, a sea-blue stone, at lower prices than the museum.

Cigars can be bought at *La Casa del Fumador*, near the Plaza Central, Fco Prats Ramírez 159, T5413390, F5414896, open Mon-Sat 1030-1400, 1500-2000, *Santo Domingo Cigar Club*, in the *Hotel Jaragua* and in the restaurant *Ambrosía*.

Bookshops *Tienda Macalé*, Calle Arzobispo Nouel 3, T6822011, near cathedral. Open daily including Sun, has a wide selection of books, especially on the Republic's history. *The Book Shop*, Plaza Cataluña Gustavo Mejía Ricart 114, casi esq W Churchill, T4122777. *Centro Cuesta del Libro*, 27 de Febrero esq Lincoln. *Thesaurus*, Av Abraham Lincoln esquina Sarasota, the newest bookshop with sofas, reading areas, a café, play area, cultural events with Dominican authors.

Music *Music Box* , Plaza Central. *Thiagos*, Calle El Conde. *Musicalia*, El Conde, T2218445, Tiradentes esquina Gustavo Mejía Ricart, T5622878. *Sonidium*, Proyecto José Contreras, Edificio 1, Local 110, Manzana 11, Av Independencia Km 10.5, T3284124. *CD Stop*, Plaza Central, T5495640. *Karen Records*, El Conde 251, T6860019.

Transport

See page 404 for long distance buses

Local Bus: The government has introduced new buses (*OMSA*) along the main corridors (*corredores*), Avs 27 de Febrero, Luperón, Bolívar, Independencia, John F Kennedy, Máximo Gómez and the west of the city, RD$3, which have improved longer journeys and transfers. Journey times have also been improved by the construction of a tunnel on Avenida 27 de Febrero, see above. Bus terminals are scattered around the city, each company has its own depot, see . **Car hire**: many places at the airport, on the road to the airport and on Malecón. There are more agencies, here are a selection: *MC Auto Rent A Car* (Avenida George Washington No 105, T6886518, F6864529), branches also at Las Americas Airport (T5490373) and Boca Chica Beach (T5234414); *Nelly* (José Contreras 139, T5358800); *Dollar* (JF Kennedy y Lincoln, T5416801); *D-Rent* (T5451366), German-run, cheap, good insurance; *Patsy*, cheap, daily rates from US$25 (T5498101); *Hertz* (T2215333); *Avis* (Sarasota y Lincoln, T5357191); *Honda* (JF Kennedy y Pepillo Salcedo, T5671015), one of the more expensive at US$55 a day. **Taxi**: *Carros públicos*, or *conchos*, are shared taxis normally operating on fixed routes, 24 hrs a day, basic fare RD$3. *Públicos* can be hired by one person, if they are empty, and are then called *carreras*. They can be expensive (US$3-4, more on longer routes); settle price before getting in. Fares are higher at Christmas time. *Públicos/conchos* also run on long-distance routes; ask around to find the cheapest. You can get to just about anywhere by bus or *público* from Parque Independencia, but you have to ask where to stand. *Conchos* running on a shared basis are becoming scarcer, being replaced by *carreras*. Radio taxis charge between US$3-5 on local journeys around Santo Domingo (US$10 per hour) and are safer than street taxis, call about 20-30 mins in advance: *Taxi Anacaona*, T5304800; *Apolo Taxi*, T5377771; *Taxi Express*, T5377777; *Taxi Oriental*, T5495555; *Alex Taxi*, T5403311; *Taxi Hogar*, T5682825; *Tecni Taxi*, T5672010; *Pronto Taxi*, T5414111. There are motorcyclists who offer a taxi service, known as *motoconchos*, RD$10, they sometimes take up to three passengers on pillion; they raise the noise level (in most towns) very considerably.

Long distance Air: Aeropuerto La Américas, 23 km out of town, T5490450/80, has been modernized, very clean and smart. Immediately on arrival there is a tourist office on your right (helpful, will make bus reservation if you want to go straight out of Santo Domingo), and just past that an office selling tourist cards, see page 398, a blackboard indicates who needs a card. Check if you need a card, or else the long queue to get through immigration will be wasted. There is a cambio next to the booth where you buy your tourist card and a bank in the customs hall for exchanging dollars; it is open Sun and at night (good rates). Pesos can be changed back into dollars, at the bank in the departure hall, but only up to 30% of what you purchased on arrival, receipt required. Car hire is to the right as you come out of the customs hall. Remember you will need a 5-peso coin for the toll if you drive in to Santo

Domingo. On departure, the queue for check-in can be long and slow for large aircraft (eg Iberia to Madrid), allow plenty of time and do not believe the young men who claim they can queue jump for you in return for payment. Check-in staff are vigilant. In the departure area are lots of duty-free shops, cafés, and limited seating. Upstairs there are good facilities with a burger restaurant which has plenty of seating and a good view of the airport.

The drive from the airport into Santo Domingo must be one of the nicest approaches to a capital city. The dual carriageway runs along the sea shore, lined with palm trees, where you can see the occasional fishing boat and the big ships coming in to port. As you go up Av España you will see the cruise ships on the river. Leaving the airport on the ground floor, the same floor as immigration and customs, you find the expensive, individual taxis. Upstairs, outside the 2nd floor, colectivo taxis cram up to 6 passengers into the vehicle; much cheaper. If arriving late at night it may be better to go to Boca Chica, about 10 km from the airport, taxi about US$15. To get to the airport cheaply take a 'Boca Chica' bus from Parque Enriquillo, either on Av Duarte or José Martí, which drops you at the main road, US$1, buses every few minutes in either direction. Alternatively take any minibus heading east to other towns from Parque Enriquillo, which will pass the turn-off to the airport; alight at the turning and walk 1½ km or take one of the many *motoconchos* waiting at the junction. This option can be done in reverse when heading into the city. Various tour agencies also run minibuses to the airport; check with your hotel.

Internal flights **Herrera airport**, west of the city (T5673900) for internal flights to Santiago, Puerto Plata, Barahona, Punta Cana and La Romana (allow plenty of time). Reserve 24 hrs before you fly, T6838020, fares vary from US$30-80.

Banks Officially possible only in banks and *cambios*, many along Isabel La Católica, but check which banks accept which TCs, see page 399. Do not change money on the street; you will undoubtedly be cheated and you also run the risk of imprisonment. *Casa de Cambio* Quisqueya, Sánchez 205, off El Conde, gives a slightly better rate than banks. **Directory**

Communications **Post Office:** *Correo Central* is in La Feria, Calle Rafael Damirón, Centro de los Héroes, T5346218, F5346318. Open 0730-1700, Mon-Fri; 0730-1200, Sat. Lista de correo (poste restante) keeps mail for 2 months. There are post offices in *Hotel Embajador*, T2212131, AILA, T5420177, Ciudad Nueva, T6856920, and Sans Souci, T5931306. To ensure the delivery of documents worldwide, use a courier service: *American Airlines* (T5425151). *DHL Dominicana*, T5417988, Servicio de Documentos y pequeños paquetes, T5412119; *Emery Worldwide*, T6881855; *Federal Express*, T5679547; *Internacional Bonded Couriers*, T5425265. **Telephone:** international and long distance, also fax: *Codetel*, Av 30 de Marzo 12, near Parque Independencia, and 11 others throughout the city (open 0800-2200); a convenient central office is at El Conde 202, open daily 0800-2200. **Internet** access also available but not always working, US$2 per hour, fax to Europe US$2 per page. Cheaper for phone calls is the *Tricom* office on Av Máximo Gómez between Bolívar and Independencia. Reserve in advance to use the internet service at the *Codetel* offices in Unicentro Plaza, T2204721, Cacique, T2207411 and Oficina Torre Cristal, T2205312. *Ciber Café*, La Lira 11, Av Roberto Pastoriza, near Abraham Lincoln, young crowd, friendly. *Dalitel*, Winston Churchill. The *Palacio de las Comunicaciones* next to the post office (at Isabel La Católica y Emiliano Tejera) does not handle phone calls.

Medical services *Clínica Abréu*, Av Independencia y Beller, and adjacent *Clínica Gómez Patiño* are recommended for foreigners needing treatment or hospitalization. Fees are high but care is good. 24-hr emergency department. Other reputable clinics are *Centro Médico UCE* and *Clínica Yunén* on Av Máximo Gómez, and *Clínica Abel González*, Av Independencia. For free consultation and prescription, *Padre Billini Hospital*, Calle Padre Billini y Santomé, Zona Colonial, efficient, friendly. **Pharmacy:** *Farmacia San Judas Tadeo*, Independencia 57 y Bernardo Pichardo, T6858165, open 24 hrs all year, home delivery, cosmetics, magazines, cafetería outside.

Language school *Escuela de Idiomas de la Universidad APEC*, Av Máximo Gómez 72, Apdo Postal 59-2, Santo Domingo, T6873181, offers Spanish courses, either 1 or 2 hrs daily, Mon to Fri, for a term. *Instituto Cultural Dominico Americano*, Av Abraham Lincoln esq Correa y Cidrón, T5350665, Spanish courses for children and adults.

Dominican Republic

Libraries *Biblioteca Nacional*, in the Plaza de la Cultura, has a fine collection and is a good place for a quiet read. *Biblioteca República Dominicana*, Dr Delgado esq Francia, T6862800, contains the *Museo del Libro*, with an exhibition of all the best works by Dominican authors. *Instituto Cultural Domínico Americano*, corner of Av Abraham Lincoln and Calle Antonio de la Maza; English and Spanish books. The *National Congress* has a good library, as do some of the universities: *Pontífica Universidad Católica Madre y Maestra*, the *Instituto Tecnológico de Santo Domingo* and the *Universidad Autónoma de Santo Domingo*.

Places of worship *Episcopal Church*, Av Independencia 253. Service in English, 0830 Sun. Also Iglesia Episcopal San Andrés, on Marcos Ruiz.

Tour companies & travel agents A tour service covers the major sites of the city, in *merenguaguas parranderas*, buses without seats with names like *La Gallera*, *La Monumental*, *La Criolla*, *La Bachatera*, T5327154. There are several tours of the city, taking in the duty-free shops, nightlife, etc. Recommended travel agents in Santo Domingo for sightseeing tours include: *Metro Tours* (T5667126), *Domitur* (T5440929), *Prieto Tours* (T6850102), *Viajes Barceló* (T6858411). *Coco Tours*, Apartado Postal 4634, T5861311, F5861237, La Bachatera, T5327154, www.cocotours.com. *Turinter*, T6864020, F6883890, www.turinter.com Also in Puerto Plata. Companies that offer tours around the Republic are given in Essentials. **NB** See warnings about unofficial guides.

North from Santo Domingo

Bonao The Autopista Duarte runs north from Santo Domingo, now a four-lane highway all the way to Santiago de los Caballeros. Around Bonao are rice paddies. To the east is the Falconbridge ferronickel mine. The town is also known as Villa de las Hortensias. There are cheap hotels near the market and on the highway are many *paradas*, *posadas* and *plazas turísticas*. The best is *Plaza Jacaranda*, 3 km north of Bonao, with shops, snackbars, a/c restaurant and **B** *Hotel Jacaranda*, T5255097. Also recommended are the two *Restaurant Típico de Bonao*, one in the town, the other 6 km north on the autopista. The area is renowned for its *queso de hoja*, fresh balls of moist white cheese. Several places along the Autopista Duarte sell this typical cheese with bread or crackers. The Museo de Arte de la Plaza de la Cultura de Bonao was opened by the artist Cándido Bido, many of whose works are exhibited here. Open Monday-Friday, it is also a painting school.

La Vega Further north is La Vega, a quiet place in the beautiful valley of la Vega Real, in the heart of the Cibao. La Vega's cathedral is a modern, concrete building. The exterior looks a little like a turreted castle while the huge bell tower slightly resembles a ship's prow surmounted by a cross. The interior is spacious, with round stained-glass windows and lights suspended from a wooden ceiling. La Vega is noted for its carnival. *Comparsas*, sponsored music groups, compete and there are competitions for the best costumes. It is a huge, noisy, rowdy affair, watch out for the local custom of hitting people with balls on ropes. They can leave nasty bruises and the police have to test them to make sure they are not solid. There is a *Codetel* office on the square. There are some basic hotels, **F**, in town and slightly better accommodation, **E**, along the highway.

Further along the road from La Vega on the right is the turn for **Santo Cerro**, an old convent where the image of Virgen de las Mercedes is venerated. From there you can get a view of the valley of La Vega Real. If you continue along the road to the other side of the hill and into the valley the ruins of La Vega Vieja can be seen. It was founded by Columbus but destroyed by an earthquake in 1564; undergoing restoration.

Jarabacoa

Continuing along the highway, on the left, is the turn for Jarabacoa. The road winds through some beautiful pine forests to the town itself, which is a popular summer hill resort in a valley in the mountains. The climate is fresh, with warm days and cool nights. On the road between La Vega and Jarabacoa are several Centros Vacacionales. It is an important agricultural area, growing coffee, flowers, strawberries, watercress and other crops, much of which is exported. The town itself is quite modern, with plenty of plots of land for sale. Everything is in walking distance and most things can be found along the main street, Calle Mario Nelson Galán. Several notable artists and sculptors live in the area and are willing to receive visitors to their studios or give classes. The best known is Roberto Flores, a professor at the Escuela de Bellas Artes in Santo Domingo, whose work can be seen in the local church, where he has painted a mural, and hanging on the walls at *Rancho Baiguate* and *Rancho Restaurant*. Much of his inspiration comes from mythology, with elongated people and angels. An up and coming artist is Eduardo Rodríguez, who paints landscapes, local mountains and rivers in bright detail. *Jarabacoa is a centre for adventure sports*

Many people come here for the rivers, to see the waterfalls or to go white water rafting or canyoning. Nearby is the *balneario* (swimming hole) of La Confluencia, at the confluence of the Río Jimenoa and Río Yaque del Norte where barbecues and dancing are held at holiday times (crowded, lots of litter). The **Jimenoa waterfalls** are worth seeing, 10 km from town, although they are often crowded with tour parties, best to go early or late and avoid Sundays. Turn off the road to La Vega past ranches breeding paso fino horses, and a 9-hole golf course. Hurricane Georges wreaked havoc in 1998, washing away the power plant and bridge by the falls. Electricity for Jarabacoa now comes from Constanza. A new walkway has been made, with wobbly suspension bridges (avoid too many people on them at any one time). The falls are very large, with a tremendous volume of water and consequent noise. There used to be a nice pool at the foot of the falls, but there is too much water now and if you want to swim you have to do it further down the river. The last wall is used for canyoning, then you swim down and come out on rocks below. Mini-rafting is on offer at weekends, US$2. Entry RD$10, which goes towards the upkeep of walkways. There is another waterfall on the Río Jimenoa, off the road to Constanza, which is more difficult to get to and unsigned, so you will have to ask for directions locally or go with a group. The falls are very steep, dropping 75 m over a cliff, and their dramatic location attracted the makers of the movie, *Jurassic Park.*Closer to town, off the Constanza road, are the **Baiguate falls** 3½-4 km, an easy walk, there is a signpost to the falls, fourth turn on the right after *Pinar Dorado*. A path leads around the hillside, hugging the side of the gorge, until you get to some steps down to a sandy river beach and the rocks beneath the falls. Hurricanes and storms have occasionally changed the geography here, but not as much as at Jimenoa.There are usually lots of tours to the falls by jeep or horse (sometimes you can ride a horse back if the previous rider has opted for the jeep return), but in 2000 Japanese engineers were working on the road and an irrigation project, so it was not open every day. *Rivers & waterfalls are spectacular features in this area*

The **Ebano Verde Scientific Reserve** is a cloud forest reserve created in 1989 to protect the tree of the same name. It is managed by the Fundación Progressio, T5651422, F5493900, a private, non-profit organization, under an agreement with the DNP. The park is very accessible, information is provided on almost every tree and paths are easy to follow. 621 species of plants have been listed so far, and 59 species of birds, of which 17 are native and 13 endangered, including *el zumbadorcito* (*Mellisuga minima*), the second smallest bird in the world, found only here and in Jamaica.

A very interesting an informative excursion is to visit the local coffee factory, **Café La Joya**, where you can see the whole process from the growing of seedlings to packing the roasted beans for export (mostly to Europe for blending). The tour usually starts with a 45-min video about the growing coffee plants, as you are not taken out onto the mountainside to visit them. Some 1 million seedlings are grown at the *Coffee factory*

Dominican Republic

factory, each of which are expected to yield 3 lbs of *café molido*. When the picked beans come back to the factory to dry, you see the whole business of drying, sorting, hulling, sorting again by size and colour with machines and then yet again by hand. There is a huge room full of women going through each bean to grade them. You see the laboratory and tasting room and there is a small shop with artesanías and coffee products which benefit the local community. Tours must be organized in advance, best done through *Rancho Baiguate*.

Sleeping **B-C** per person, FAP *Rancho Baiguate*, T5744940, F5861170, www.ranchobaiguate.com, owned and managed by Omar and Estela Rodríguez. Lovely countryside setting beside river, extensive gardens, 27 rooms from standard to luxury, or small, medium and large, hot water, good bathrooms, also 2 dormitories with 9 bunk beds in each with showers, toilets, lockers and shelves for students/groups (the hotel started out as a summer camp), unheated pool, soccer and basketball court, horse riding, helpful staff and management, friendly, English spoken, open air or indoor dining room, trestle tables and benches, rocking chairs, good place for buffet lunch if in the area or day trips from further afield, lots of tour parties come for the day, free transport into town until 2200, if there are not many guests you eat supper at the *Rancho Restaurant*. Now under same ownership is **C** *Pinar Dorado*, T5742820, F6877012, on road towards Constanza before turnoff to *Rancho Baiguate*. About 20 mins' walk from centre, 43 rooms, to be remodeled and made into an upmarket hotel for conferences and executive retreats for the US and local market. **F** *California*, on road to Constanza, Calle José Durán E 99, T5746255, F5744303, i.lupo@codetel.net.do Owned by Dutchman Jan Sheffers and his Dominican wife, new and growing slowly, 9 simple rooms, bathroom, hot water, fan, breakfast, bar, small pool, Chinese restaurant planned, popular, friendly. **F** *Hollyday*, opposite, T5742778. 23 rooms, fan, basic, hot water, bathroom has no door, dark, parking. 11 km from town on the La Vega road, *La Montaña*, T6828181. Friendly, clean, good, but need own transport to make excursions from it.

In town, **D** *Brisas del Yaque*, Luperón esq Peregrina Herrera, T5744490. New, small rooms but good bathrooms, small balcony, TV, a/c, brick and wood décor, tiled floors. **F** *Plaza Monte Rey* , Calle Mario Nelson Galán esq Sánchez, T5742672. 15 basic rooms, old unpleasant bathrooms, fan, billiards and bar on 1st floor, under new ownership so improvement planned. **F** *Hogar*, Mella 34, T5742739. Central, 5 mins' walk from Caribe Tours terminal, 8 rooms, twin beds, cold water, clean, huge old trees in patio garden, run by friendly Doña Ligia Pina, but she is retiring and the hotel is for sale.

Eating The town has several restaurants; try the *Rincón Montañés* on Calle Gaston F Deligne, near El Carmen. *Don Luis*, on square. *Rancho Restaurant*, opposite Esso station. Criollo and international, belongs to *Rancho Baiguate* and guests often eat here in the evening. The walls are lined with the work of several local artists (who you may meet dining there with the owners) and a small gallery is planned off the dining area. *El Trebol*, small outdoor bar/restaurant under leafy canopy, sandwiches, hamburgers, tacos, *plato del día* US$2.50, specials on Sun US$3, vegetarian options. Several other *comedores* and *cafeterías*. *Salto Restaurant*, on road to Salto Jimenoa, T2239759, F5744940, vmg@codetel.net.do Pleasant setting by stream, pool, sauna, bar and excellent food, specialize in goat, guinea fowl, pigeon, duck, US$6-9, or for a snack ask for a plate of mixed *longaniza*, *carne salteada* and *tostones*, great with a cold beer. Buy strawberries beside the road, locally grown, but restaurants hardly ever have them.

Sport White water rafting, canyoning, tubing, rock climbing, horse riding, mountain biking, quad bikes, jeep safaris, paragliding and hiking are all on offer here. It is one of the starting points for climbing Pico Duarte. *Rancho Baiguate's* **Aventura Máxima** is the biggest adventure sports centre and has a small army of Dominican and international specialist guides and instructors for each activity. They have also taken over **Get Wet**, still run as a separate operation, which offers river activities. A third company, **Aventuras del Caribe**, T5742669, franz.lang@codetel.net.do is run by Franz, an Austrian. He deals with small groups, is recommended for canyoning and is very safety conscious. He has rafting equipment for class 5-6 rivers which can be found on the tributaries of the Yaque del Norte, although that river is only class 3. River kayaking is in its infancy, but being developed.

Road *Conchos* in town RD$10. *Motoconcho* to *Rancho Baiguate* RD$20. To Santo Domingo, *Caribe Tours*, T5744557, from its own terminal off the main street, 0700, 1000, 1330, 1630, arrive 30 mins in advance (even earlier for the 0730 Mon bus), tickets sold only on day of departure, US$4.66, 2½ hrs. To La Vega by *guagua*, RD$20; if you want to go to the capital or Santiago, they will let you off at the right place to pick up the next *guagua*. To Constanza, you can get a 2-cabin pick-up truck via a very poor road over the mountains, but most people go back down to La Vega and up the Constanza road 10km before Bonao. All transport can be found opposite gas station.

Transport
No transport anywhere after 1800, very little after 1500

Useful services 5 banks on Mario Galán, the main street, where there is also a supermarket. *Banco de Progreso* and tourist office by the Palacio Municipal near the bus stop. *Codetel* on road to La Vega. Market on M Galán. There are a couple of travel agencies; the one next to the bus station is linked to *Rancho Baiguate*. The *Centro de Copiado y Papelería*, a stationery shop on Calle Duarte 53, T5742902, has 6 computers for internet access, US$2.33 per hour, open 0800-1300, 1400-1900.

Directory

Constanza

Beyond Jarabacoa, higher up in the mountains, is Constanza, where the scenery is even better than in Jarabacoa, with rivers, forests and waterfalls. In winter, temperatures can fall to zero and there may be frosts. The valley is famous for food production, potatoes, garlic, strawberries, mushrooms and other vegetables, and for growing ornamental flowers. The Garlic Festival is held in the middle of June, with lots of dancing.

With a four-wheel drive you can visit the **Valle Nuevo Scientific Reserve**, through which passes the very poor but spectacular road from Constanza to San José de Ocoa. Wonderful views and you pass the geographical centre of the island, marked by four small pyramids. There are also thermal springs, three Amerindian cemeteries and the Agua Blanca waterfall. During January-March the temperature can fall as low as -10°C. The reserve has a large number of plants which are unique to the island in pine and broadleaf forests. It is also good birdwatching country, look out for the stripe-headed tanager, the rufus-collared sparrow and Antillean siskin. Scientists interested in the investigative scientific work on the reserve should contact the Fundación Moscoso Puello in Santo Domingo, T5668404.

AltoCerro, T6960222, F5306193. New and highly thought of. **F** *Mi Cabaña*, clean, bath, good, T5392472. Others are *La Casa*, hotel and restaurant, *Sobeyola* and *Lorenzo*, average price in cheaper, basic hotels **F**.

Sleeping

Road There are direct buses from Santo Domingo, Santiago, La Vega and Bonao, return from Constanza at 0600 or earlier (buses will often pick you up at your hotel if you inform them in advance). The last direct bus back to Santo Domingo leaves at 1200. *Expreso Dominicano*, Avenida Independencia, 100 m west of Parque Independencia, to La Vega every hour 0700-1800, get off at junction for Constanza. You can get to/from the Santo Domingo-Santiago highway by taking a *público* or *guagua* (US$2.50) to/from Constanza. Constanza can also be reached by taking a bus to Bonao from either Santo Domingo (*guagua* US$2 from 27 de Febrero), or Santiago, then *guagua*. The last 1½ hrs of the trip to Constanza is through the finest scenery in the Republic. From Jarabacoa, see above. From Constanza you can use the *guagua* hopping system to get to Las Terrenas via San Francisco de Macorís, Nagua and Sánchez, US$1.50 for each stage. Constanza can also be reached from the south coast via San José de Ocoa (northeast of Azua, *Hotel Marien*, on the main square, without bath, clean, good value). A very basic road exists between San José de Ocoa and Constanza through the mountains, a very beautiful trip. A four-wheel drive leaves Constanza (by the

Transport

Dominican Republic

crossroads at entrance to town) Mon, Wed, Sat 1200, US$4, 5 hrs. You can sit on the roof, but beware weather changes. The front seat gets exhaust fumes.

Directory **Banks** There is an ATM (Plus, Visa). A recommended guide is Johny Tactuck, 18 Matilde Viña, T5392900.

Pico Duarte

The driest time is In the Cordillera Central near Jarabacoa and Constanza is Pico Duarte, at 3,087 m
Dec-Feb the highest peak in the Caribbean. The national park entrance is 4 km from La Ciénaga, which is reached by a road passing through some magnificent scenery from Jarabacoa. Before climbing it you must purchase a permit from the Dirección Nacional de Parques at La Ciénaga de Manabao for 50 pesos. Guagua from Jarabacoa to Manabao US$1, then walk 2½ hours to La Ciénaga or hitch (very little traffic). At La Ciénaga go to the Information hut. You can sleep here, tap in the yard for washing. It is advisable to take a guide, who will tell you that mules are necessary for the ascent, but it can be done without them. The path is clear and if you can carry your food, water and sleeping bag there is no practical reason why you need a support team, but it is difficult to negotiate entry without, particularly if you do not speak Spanish. An organized climb can be arranged with DNP, Nuevos Horizontes, Martisant, T5857887. Several agencies organize trips up Pico Duarte but they may not have anything when you want it. *Iguana Mama* in Cabarete (see page 402) charges US$350 for a three-day hike and US$425 for four days. *Rancho Baiguate* in Jarabacoa has 3- or 4-day treks to Pico Duarte (US$270-755 depending on numbers) and a 5-day trek which includes Valle del Tetero (US$450 for 4 or more people, US$930 for 1). These trips include all food, drinks, guides, equipment, mules and transport from your base to La Ciénaga. You just need to turn up with a strong pair of boots, warm clothes for night time, rain gear and a swimsuit. The climb takes two days (or more if it rains and you are stuck in a hut) and the walk from the tropical rain forest of the national park through pine woods is pleasant with great scenery. There are two huts on the path (first after one hour, second after another 5-6 hours, two hours or so more to the peak), which is clearly marked; they are lacking in 'facilities'. Take adequate clothing with you; it can be cold (below 0°C) and wet; also take torch, food and matches. The last *carro* leaves Manabao for Jarabacoa at 1600, so aim to climb the peak well before lunch on the second day.

There are also other walks in the **Armando Bermúdez National Park** and the adjoining **José del Carmen Ramírez National Park**, which do not involve such steep climbing. This is the largest protected area in the country and provides water for 12 of the country's most important rivers. It is also home to the Hispaniola parrot, Hispaniola trogon, the palm chat, hutia and wild boar. Guides are available at the park entrance. You can walk or ride a mule. Permission to enter is required and a guide is also required so you don't get lost. Guides speak Spanish and charge US$15 per day, a pack mule is US$12 and a riding mule is US$15. You can walk 3 km to Las Tablones for a swim in the pools near the guard station. From Las Tablones it is 17 km to Valle del Tetero, an open savanna area in the Ramírez National Park and relatively unvisited. A 4-5 day hike takes you along trails through La Confluencia (see above) to Valle de Bao and Las Guacanas through broadleaf forest. There are campsites but you must bring all food and other supplies.

Santiago de Los Caballeros

Santiago de Los Caballeros is the second largest city in the Republic and chief town of the Cibao valley in the north-central part of the country. The streets of the centre are busy, noisy, with lots of advertising signs; east of the centre it becomes greener, cleaner and quieter. The Río Yaque del Norte skirts the city with Avenida Circunvalación parallel to it. There are few sites of tourist interest, this is a modern, working city, although there are some old buildings. In the colonial part look out for tiles on the walls at street corners, put there in 1995 to mark the 500th anniversary of the founding of the city with the old names of the streets.

Population: 690,000 in 1994

Getting there There are good links by road from Santo Domingo (four-lane highway all the way) and Puerto Plata on the coast. Several bus companies have services to the city. **Getting around** All *carros públicos* have a letter indicating which route they are on, eg M runs on Estrella Sadhalá to the Autopista Duarte roundabout; *carros* cost RD$4, *guaguas* RD$3.50. Many congregate at El Sol y 30 de Marzo on Parque Duarte.

Ins & outs
See transport, page 432, for further details

On Parque Duarte are the **Catedral de Santiago Apóstol**, a neoclassical building (19th-century) containing the tombs of the tyrant Ulises Heureux and of heroes of the Restauración de la República; the **Museo del Tabaco**, a pink colonial building with large green rotting wooden doors ■ *Tue-Sat 0800-1200, 1500-1800*; the **Centro de Recreo** (one of the country's most exclusive private clubs) with Moorish-style arches and the **Palacio Consistorial** (1895-96). Also on Parque Duarte is the Plaza de la Cultura y Oficina Regional de Patrimonio Cultural, which is now the **Museo de la Villa de Santiago** and holds cultural and art exhibitions. ■ *Closes 1230 on Sat*. Fortaleza San Luís, overlooking the Río Yaque del Norte, is not open to the public as it is a military zone.

Sights

Other places worth visiting are the **Pontífica Universidad Católica Madre y Maestra** (founded 1962, with good 50 m swimming pool) and the **Monumento a los Héroes de la Restauración**, at the highest point in the city (panoramic views of the Cibao valley, remodelled in 1991 to include a *mirador*). Behind the monument is the newly-constructed theatre. This area is popular at weekends and fiestas and there are lots of bars and restaurants around the park. **Calle del Sol** is the main commercial street, with both vendors and the main shops. In the newer part of the town, Av Juan Pablo Duarte and Av 27 de Febrero have shopping plazas, banks and fast food restaurants.

A-C *Aloha Sol*, Calle del Sol 150, T5830090, F5830950. Rooms and suites, smart, upmarket, cool, restaurant *D'Manon* with local and international food. **B** *El Gran Almirante*, Av Estrella Sadhalá 10, Los Jardines, on road north, T5801992, F2411492. Popular with business visitors, quite good, casino. **B-C** *Hodelpa Centro Plaza*, Calle Mella 54 esq del Sol, T5817000, F5824566, Apdo 459. Smart, modern, good restaurant,disco club *Tarari* next door, no parking facilities. **B-C** *Matum Hotel & Casino*, Av Monumental, T5813107, F5818415. Being remodelled in 2000, 47 rooms, new ones with 2 beds, fridge, TV, phone, smart, old ones and public areas still a mess, pool. **C-D** *Don Diego*, Av Estrella Sadhalá, on road north, T5754186. Restaurant and nightclub. **C-E** *Ambar*, also on Av Estrella Sadhalá, T5751957. On Av Salvador Cucurullo in the centre there are four cheap hotels between 30 de Marzo and España: **F** *Dorado*, No 88, T5827563. With bath, basic, friendly. Opposite and better is **F** *Colonial*, No 115, T2473122. Small clean rooms with a/c and fan, good bathrooms, very hot water, fridge, TV, small cheap restaurant, friendly, luggage store. Also *Monterey*, No 92, T5824558 and *Lima*, on the corner, 30 de Marzo 57 esq Cucurullo, T5820620, right by where the *guaguas* depart.

Sleeping

Pez Dorado, Calle del Sol 43 (Parque Colón), T5822518. Chinese and international, fine tradition of good quality food in generous portions, very popular for Sun lunch. At the upper end of the price range is *El Café*, Av Texas esq Calle 5, Jardines Metropolitanos. The favourite of businessmen and upper class society Fresh homemade Italian food at *Ciao Ciao*, Av María R

Eating

Dominican Republic

Sánchez, Los Jardines 13, T5831092. Run by an eccentric, entertaining Italian. There are several restaurants around the monument on Av Francia and Calle del Sol, popular on Sun, including fast food outlets such as **Burger King**. **La Brasa** has barbecued chicken. **Kukara Macara** has a rustic decor, cowboy style, lots of steak including Angus, prices up to US$20 for a huge, top class piece of meat, also seafood, tacos, sandwiches and burgers, open daily 1100-0300. **Olé** JP Duarte esq Independencia, restaurant and pizzería. **Pizza Hut**, Calle del Sol 56 esq Sánchez, T5823336, and another one on Av Juan Pablo Duarte between La Salle and Constanza, T5823377. Pizzas from US$4, good, but don't expect the base to be as good as at home, the flour is not the same quality, although the kids working there are the same as anywhere, service erratic, good salad bar for vegetarians and anyone starved of veg, house wine from Chile, clean, modern, busy, popular. There is also a **Domino's** on Av 27 de Febrero, between Constanza and Este and a **McDonalds** on Calle del Sol.

For the most spectacular view across the Cibao Valley, try **Camp David Ranch**; get there by driving (or take a taxi, fare about US$10) to Km 7 on Carretera Luperón, the turn-off is on the right, unsigned, before the *El Económico* supermarket; a 10-min climb up a winding, paved road leads to the ranch. The food quality is erratic, but the view is breathtaking. Next door is **El Generalísimo**, a piano bar decorated with classic cars from the Trujillo era. Some 10 bedrooms and suites have been added, reasonably priced in our **E** range. At the foot of the hill leading up to *Camp David Ranch* is **Rancho Luna Steak House**, Carretera Luperón Km 7.5, T5813136, F5813145, definitely not recommended for vegetarians. (With thanks once again to David Beardsmore.)

Nightlife **Discothèques** *La Nuit*, in *Hotel Matum*; **El Alcázar**, in basement of *El Gran Almirante* hotel; **La Mansión**, Autopista Duarte, **La Antorcha**, 27 Febrero 58; and **Las Vegas**, Autopista Navarrete Km 9. All modern. **Champion Palace** is a huge disco for 2,000 people, open daily. **Cinema** A multiscreen cinema was being built on Av Juan Paul Duarte in 2000.

Shopping The **Mercado Modelo Turístico** is at Calle del Sol and Avenida España. Cheap amber at Calle del Sol 60, recommended. Outside town, on Autopista Duarte, are many potteries where ceramics can be bought very cheaply (how you get them home is another matter). You can do quite a lot of shopping along the Autopista, there is nothing to stop you pulling off and on the road, and you can buy fruit, vegetables, coconuts, chickens, ducks, guinea fowl, cane furniture and other items.

Transport
See page 404 for further details
Bus *Caribe Tours* (Avenida 27 de Febrero, Las Colinas, T5760790) bus to Puerto Plata US$2.66 every hour; it is easier to take *Caribe Tours* than **Metro** to Puerto Plata or the capital because *Metro* only takes passengers on standby on their Santo Domingo-Puerto Plata route. *Metro* terminal, Maimón y Duarte, T5829111, a block or so towards the centre on Duarte from the roundabout at Estrella Sadhalá (opposite direction from Codetel); 6 buses daily Santo Domingo-Santiago. **Terrabus** has its terminal at the junction of Calle del Sol and Av Francia by the Monument, shop for snacks, toilets. Service to Santo Domingo with connections for the ferry to Puerto Rico or the bus to Haiti. Other companies from the capital with good, a/c buses include Cibao (from Parque Enriquillo) and Transporte Espinal (4 blocks north of Parque Enriquillo). To Samaná, go to Puerto Plata and take **Caribe Tours** from there. *Guaguas* to San José de las Matas leave from the Puente Hermanos Patiño, by the river not far from the centre. *Guaguas* to Moca leave from Las Carreras entre Mella y San Luis, then go up Sabana Larga and 27 de Febrero picking up more passengers, RD$10 to Moca. *Guaguas* for La Vega, RD$20, go from the park at the corner of Restauración y Sabana Larga. Many other *guaguas* leave from 30 de Marzo with Salvador Cucurullo, average US$1.30, eg Puerto Plata 2 hrs, not recommended if you have lots of luggage. **Transporte del Cibao**, Restauración casi esquina J P Duarte, runs buses up to Dajabón in the northwest near the Haitian border, 2½ hrs.

Directory **Banks** *Scotiabank* on Parque Duarte, others on Calle del Sol between San Luis and Sánchez include *Banco Popular* (ATM), *Baninter*, *Citibank*, *Bancrédito* (ATM), *Banco del Progreso*, and *Banco de Reservas* (ATM). There are also a *Banco de Reservas*, *Bancrédito* and *Banco del Progreso* on Av 27 de Febrero. The only place you can change travellers' cheques is the *Banco Popular* on Calle del Sol esq

Mella, very bureaucratic, takes ages if they are busy. **Communications** Post Office: on the corner of Calle del Sol and San Luis. **Telephone:** *Codetel* is at San Luis between Restauración and Independencia, near the post office, and further out at the junction of Estrella Sadhalá and J P Duarte; take Carro A from the Parque. *Tricom* is on San Luis between Restauración and Beller, also on Av 27 de Febrero next to Bancrédito. **Tourist office** There is a tourist office in the basement of the Town Hall (Ayuntamiento), Av Juan Pablo Duarte; it has little information available, only Spanish spoken.

Excursions from Santiago de Los Caballeros

An interesting day trip is to Moca, east of Santiago, which is a coffee and cacao centre **Moca** and one of the richer regions of the country. The **Iglesia Sagrada Corazón de Jesús** belonging to the Silesian brothers dominates the town. There are some very impressive stained glass windows and mosaics, many donated by local families in the mid-1950s, some depicting local dignatories and priests. The organ is on an upper level and a spiral staircase from the musicians' gallery leads up to the clock tower, which can be climbed. The view is well worth the recommended US$1 tip to the church official. There is also a simple village church, **Iglesia de la Virgen de la Altagracia** on the square in town, white inside with paintings of Jesus' ascent to the cross. The square contains a very ancient fallen tree, fenced off, on its last legs. There is a bust of President Ramón Cáceres, 1866-1911, twice president in 1906-11. Tourist information may be found at the Town Hall at the corner of Independencia and Antonio de la Maza. It is not recommended that you stay the night, there is only one old hotel, *L'Niza*, on J P Duarte towards Santiago, which does not charge by the hour.

The road leading from Moca to Sabaneta on the coast is extremely beautiful, winding through lush green hills. At the crest of the hillside, about halfway between Moca and Sabaneta is a restaurant called *El Caffeto*, T5787058, with a magnificent view all the way down to Santiago on your right and Moca down below. Sit on the balcony if it is not too windy and have drinks or lunch (crêpes, spaghetti, meat and fish dishes up to US$10). The only drawback is that it is right above the road which can be noisy with trucks struggling up the twisty hill. A *motoconcho* from Moca will cost you about US$7 each way, negotiable. Make sure you arrange return transport. You can go from Moca to Sosúa by *guagua*, changing at the Cruce de Veragua/Sabaneta. A very recommendable trip with a magnificent view from the summit just before you cross over the mountains, of Santiago, Moca and even La Vega. The scenery is so good it is worth taking a taxi (eg US$15 to Sabaneta, rather than squashing into a *guagua*. Metrobus has buses Santo Domingo-Moca twice daily, via La Vega (Moca T5782541).

Outside Moca on the road towards the Autopista Duarte, lies El Higüerito where **El Higüerito** they make faceless dolls. Every shack is a doll factory and you can bargain for better prices than in Santo Domingo or Puerto Plata.

To the southwest of Santiago is the pleasant, mountain town of San José de las **San José de las** Matas. It has tree-lined streets, mostly modern buildings and a breezy climate. The **Matas** post office is just uphill from *Oasis*; opposite the post office is a path to a *mirador* with benches. *Codetel* at Padre Espinosa y Félix Saychuela. Nearby are the *balnearios* (bathing spots) of Amina, Las Ventanas and Aguas Calientes, all about 5-6 km away. There is fishing in the Represa del Río Bao.

Sleeping In town, on the main square, *Oasis*, with disco, pizzería and ice creams. On the dual carriageway into town, **F** *Los Samanes*, T5788316. Bath, basic, dirty, water intermittent, local food in restaurant. Nearby is *El Primitivo*. There are several restaurants and cafés.

Transport For Santiago transport congregates at the bottom end of the dual carriageway (carretera a Santiago), opposite *Texaco* (another *Texaco* in town centre), US$1.50 via Jánico. If driving from Santiago, the best road goes via Jánico: after crossing the Puente Hermanos

Dominican Republic

Patiño, turn immediately left through Bella Vista for Jánico. The road that is signed to San José de las Matas goes towards Mao. It is paved; after about 6 km an unsigned road turns left, going over the hills through Jaqui Picado, 31 km to the junction on the Jánico-San José road, 5 km before San José; lovely views, but a very rough route.

Santo Tomás   From **Jánico**, the site of Columbus' first inland fort, Santo Tomás, can be visited, although there are no remains to be seen, just a memorial stone and a flagpole in a beautiful meadow with palms, above a little river. In Jánico seek out a *motoconcho* driver who knows the way and pay about US$5 for the trip, up and down steep hills, along narrow paths and river beds. There is a small sign in Jánico on the road.

Northwest to the Haitian border

Montecristi   To the northwest of Santiago a Highway runs through the Yaque del Norte valley to the Haitian border. One route to Haiti turns south to **Mao** (Hotels: **F** *Cahoba*, T5723357, also *Céntrico*, T5722122, *San Pedro*, T5723134, *Marién*, T5253558) and continues through Sabaneta to the border town of Dajabón (see below). Instead of turning south to Mao, you can continue to Montecristi, a dusty little town at the western end of the republic's north coast. You can visit the house of Máximo Gómez, the Dominican patriot who played an important role in the struggle for Cuban independence and in the Dominican Restoration. Columbus rejected his original idea to make his first settlement here and the town was in fact founded in the 16th century, rebuilt in the 17th. In the 19th century it was a major port exporting agricultural produce. The town has an interesting old clock. (**B** *Cayo Arena*, T5793145, two bedroom apartments on the beach, great place to stay). Very near Montecristi is a peak named **El Morro** (in the national park) which has a beach (very rocky) at the foot of its east side. There are mangroves and turtles which can be seen in the clear water. The **Cayos Siete Hermanos**, a sanctuary for tropical birds, with white beaches, are a good excursion. There has been some destruction of the offshore reefs.

Sleeping and eating *Chic*, Benito Monción 44, T5792316. *Santa Clara*, Mayobanex 8, T5792307. *Cabañas Las Carabelas*, J Bolaños, T5792682. *La Taberna de Rafúa*, Duarte 84, T5792291. *Heladería y Pizzería Kendy*, Duarte 92, T5792386. *Mi Barrita*, Duarte 86, T5792487.

Haitian border   There is also a road south from Montecristi to **Dajabón** (34 km), opposite the Haitian town of Ounaminthe. This border crossing is very straightforward and informal and gives easy access to Cap Haïtien and La Citadelle. Many willing guides and *motoconcho* drivers hang around and will take travellers between the border posts, but it is not far to walk. *Caribe Tours* run buses from Santo Domingo to Dajabón, several daily, via Santiago and Montecristi. If you want to join one of these buses in Santiago it may be full. *Caribe Tours*' terminal in Dajabón is two blocks straight, then two blocks right to the border post. South of Dajabón is the *balneario* at Loma de Cabrera, recommended to visit if you are in the area. At the town of **Navarrete** on the Santiago-Montecristi Highway, a road branches north, bifurcating at **Imbert** (where there is a cheese factory and a *Codetel* office; Cristina Clare, Calle Ezekiel Gallardo A78, rents a hut (*bohío*) at the rear of her house, **F**, she will cook for you).

Luperón   The northeast fork goes to Puerto Plata (see below), the northwest road to the north coast at Luperón, which has fine beaches, suitable for watersports. It is also a good haven for yachts; the marina offers electricity and water connections for boats and there are several markets selling fish, meat and vegetables.

Sleeping and eating **A** *Hotel Luperón Beach Resort*, in Casa Marina Luperón. T5814153, F5816262 (high season price), and *Hotel Luperón*, Calle Independencia, T5718125. **F** *La Morena*, Calle Juan P Duarte 103, opposite Esso station, near *Codetel*. Bath and fan.

Restaurant La Marina, Independencia 47, T5718066. Lunch and dinner, local specialities, credit cards accepted. Frequent electricity and water cuts here.

West of Luperón by a new road is La Isabela. Here, on his second voyage (1493), **La Isabela**
Columbus founded the first European town in the Americas, with the first *ayuntamiento* and court, and here was said the first mass. Only the layout of the town is visible. The restoration and archaeological excavation of La Isabela is being undertaken by the Dirección Nacional de Parques. There is a hotel by the ruins. To get there either take a tour from Puerto Plata, or take a *carro público* from Villanueva y Kundhard, Puerto Plata, to La Isabela village, US$3.50, then a *motoconcho* to the ruins, US$7.25 return including wait at ruins, a lovely trip. Martisant, T5857887, runs group tours for US$92.

Between La Isabela and Montecristi are the beaches of **Punta Rucia** at Estero Hondo. Besides the beaches there are mangroves and interesting flora and fauna. Lodging at **LL** *Hotel Discovery Bay*, T6850151, F6866741, all-inclusive, no children under 16, watersports and other activities provided.

Puerto Plata

Puerto Plata, the chief town on the Atlantic coast (which is also known as the Amber **Sights**
Coast) was founded by Ovando in 1502. It is 235 km from the capital. There are two roads from Santiago to Puerto Plata, the older scenic road is now in poor condition. The centre of town has many old, wooden houses, many in need of repair, some new buildings and plenty of colour. A visit to the colonial **San Felipe fortress**, the oldest in the New World, at the end of the Malecón is recommended. Although renovated it is showing weather damage already. The museum contains armoury, cannon, swords, bayonets etc, and photos of the excavation and renovation of the fortress. Entry RD$10. Guided tours available. On the Malecón there is an interesting old firestation, built 1895, just down from the Parque Regalado. The Malecón is not well cared for and although there are a few bars there is nothing special. There are no decent restaurants, there is low quality housing along the seafront and the beach is dirty and smelly. Just 1,000 m past Puerto Plata, a *teleférico* (cable car) used to run to the summit of **Loma Isabel de Torres**, an elevation of 779 m, but is closed and likely to remain so for a long time. Hiking tours up the mountain can be arranged with Iguana Mama (see page 442, tour agencies). There is a statue of Christ that looks out over all of Puerto Plata; it also houses craft shops, a café and there are botanical gardens with a lovely view of the coast and mountains. You can take your chances with horses, bikes or even a car, but be prepared, the road is impassable at some points. The **Museum of Dominican Amber**, Duarte 61, houses a collection of rare amber; guided tours, Amber Museum Shop at Playa Dorada Plaza. ■ *T5862848. Foreigners US$1.25. 0900-1700.* The mountains behind Puerto Plata contain the world's richest deposits of amber. The cathedral on the Parque Central is worth a visit, under renovation in 2000 but still in use. Also on the Parque Central is the Patrimonio Cultural in a building dating from 1908 where there are interesting art exhibitions. A new **Museum of Taíno Art**, Beller y San Felipe, first floor above *artesanía* shops, only contains replicas, but is interesting. ■ *Daily, more replicas on sale in the shops below.*

If you are led into a shop by a local boy, tour guide or taxi driver, you will more than likely be paying a hidden commission on the price of your purchase, even after you bargain. If you want a guide, call the Association of Official Tour Guides, on T5862866.

To the west is the **Costambar** resort area, which has not been a success (*Bayside Hill* **Excursions**
Club, Naco group, nine-hole golf course, beach, and **Cofresí** beach, several hotels, cabins, **A-B** per person and more at weekends). At the east end of town is **Long Beach**, 2 km from the centre, US$0.15 by bus, but it is crowded at weekends, rather dirty, a sewer pipe brings effluent and litter is washed up or dropped by locals and it

Dominican Republic

is best to be on your guard. There are several small restaurants for breakfast onwards and the tourist office and Tourist Police are this end of town, but the *Hotel Montemar* is closed and the *Hotel Beach* for sale in poor condition. Just east of Puerto Plata, 4 km from the airport, is the beach resort of **Playa Dorada** with an exceptional golf course, and other sporting facilities. The *Playa Dorada Resort* is an umbrella name for a complex of large all-inclusive hotels and there are plans to build many more. **Montellano**, to the east of Playa Dorada, about half way to Sosúa, is the town in which all the processing of sugar cane is done for the north coast. It is undeveloped as a tourist town, but there are tours of the cane processing plant. For the adventurous, it has a great discothèque called *Las Brisas*, on the river, that all the locals visit, especially on Sunday afternoons. A bottle of rum, bucket of ice and two colas will cost about US$4. The town is a bit primitive, but the disco is not; guaranteed to have a great time, dancing merengue, salsa and some American music.

Sleeping

Cheap hotels can only be found in the town centre

Puerto Plata Most of the upmarket or all-inclusive hotels are along the coast except the *Ahmsa Puerto Plata Beach Resort & Casino*, at the east end on Long Beach, T5864243, F5874377. All-inclusive, 216 rooms in blocks, nice gardens, pool, well cared for, small tidy beach across the road but best to go to other beaches, lots of taxis outside, the sort of place found in package tour brochures and so difficult to get in to. **B-E** *Villas Cofresi*, T1-800-3901138, www.puerto-plata.com 3-5 bedroomed villas on Cofresi beach, good amenities. **F** *Hostal Jimessón*, John F Kennedy 41, T5865131, close to Parque Central. Old colonial building, gingerbread, painted green and white, lobby furnished with antiques and old clocks, tiled floors, the rooms are in a newer building behind, but still old style, clean, a/c, cold water, pleasant, no restaurant. **D-E** *Sunshine Hotel*, Manolo Tavárez Justo 78, T5861771, on main road. Good for public transport, 20 rooms, a/c or fan, TV, balcony, bathrooms a bit dilapidated but adequate, lumpy pillows, sheets don't fit, parking, restaurant, *Don Luís*, open 0700-2400, local, Chinese and international, good food. At Plaza Anacaona, 30 de Marzo 94-98, are **E** *Hotel/Restaurant El Indio*, T/F5861201. With breakfast and fan, clean, restaurant serves good breakfast and fish, very good value, Mexican music on Sat; a patio with native plants, palm trees and hummingbirds. **F** *Atlántico*, 12 de Julio 24, T5862503. Bath, not all rooms have hot water, fan, mosquito net, clean, simple, colonial building, friendly, back rooms quiet.

Playa Dorada The following are all-inclusive, offering similar services, eg pool, tennis, golf, best booked as part of a package from abroad. *Caribbean Village Club on the Green*, 336 rooms, T3201111, F3205386; *InterClubs Fun Royale*, 168 rooms, T3204811, F3205301; *InterClubs Fun Tropicale*, 184 rooms, same phone numbers; *Delta Dorado Club Resort*, 240 rooms, T3202019, F3203608; *Occidental Flamenco Beach*, 582 rooms, T3205084, F3206319; *Gran Ventana Beach Resort*, 510 rooms, T4122525, F4122526; *Rumba Heavens*, 192 rooms, T3205250, F3204733, a 3-star resort where many activities are limited to 1 hr a day; *Jack Tar Village Puerto Plata*, 291 rooms, T3203800, F3204161; *Ahmsa Paradise Beach Club &*

Casino, 436 rooms, T3203663, F3204858; *Occidental Playa Dorada*, 351 rooms, casino, T3203988, F3201190; *Playa Naco Golf & Tennis*, 410 rooms, T3206226, F3203329; *Puerto Plata Village*, 386 rooms, T3204012, F3205113; *Victoria Resort*, 190 rooms, T3201200, F3204862; *Villas Doradas Beach Resort*, 207 rooms, T3203000, F3204790.

The food is good at all the main hotels; there is every variety of cuisine although you may **Eating** get bored of buffet meals at the all-inclusives. In the Playa Dorada Shopping Mall is **Hemingway's Café**, T3202230. Good food and music, a/c, good service, fun at night and during the day. *Los Pinos*, international cuisine, T5863222. *Otro Mundo*, Playa Dorada Commercial Plaza. For something different, a mini-zoo with many tropical birds, offers free transport from and to your hotel, T5438019. In town: *Acuarela*, Prof Certad 3 esq Pdte Vásquez, T5865314. Open 1800-0200, garden café, in old wooden house, excellent restaurant. *Aguaceros*, Malecón 32, T5862796. Open from 1700, steaks, seafood, burgers, Mexican, tables on sidewalk, bar. *Anna's Bar and Grill*, Colón 59. Popular with ex-pats, satellite TV, dartboard.*Sam's Bar and Grill* on José del Carmen Ariza near Plaza Central. American-run, good American food, satellite TV, rooms also available. *Eddy's Pub*, Av Colón, near harbour. American burgers.

Casinos   There are 4 casinos on the north coast. *Jack Tar Village*, *Occidental Playa Dorada* **Nightlife** *Hotel*, *Ahmsa Paradise Beach Club* and *Ahmsa Puerto Plata Beach Resort*. Only the last named is in Puerto Plata, the other three are in the Playa Dorada complex. The casinos feature black jack, craps, roulette and poker. There are slot machines but these can be played only in US dollars. If you play other games in US dollars, you win in US dollars, if you play in pesos, you win in pesos. Do not change your foreign money to pesos in the casino, the rate given is very unfavourable. *Jack Tar Village Casino* offers novices a 1 hr lesson in black jack or craps at 2130 nightly, free of charge. **Discothèques** *Andromeda* in *Heavens Hotel* (the most popular), *Charlie's* in *Jack Tar Village Casino* and *Crazy Moon* in *Paradise Beach Resort*; all three are popular and offer a mix of *merengue*, *salsa* and international pop music. All have cover charges, about US$2. *Tropimal* is very popular, good mix of locals and tourists, *merengue* music.

The Playa Dorada Complex has the first real shopping mall on the north coast. Prices are slightly **Shopping** inflated, but the quality of all items, especially the locally-made ceramics, jewellery, and clothing, is superior to most sold by beach or street vendors. The mall includes a Benneton, a selection of Tiffany lamps and some very original jewellery. Souvenirs can also be bought on the beach, or in downtown Puerto Plata, where there is shop after shop to sell you trinkets.

Local   *Motoconchos*, RD$5 almost anywhere in town, negotiate a fare for longer distances. **Transport** *Guaguas*, overcrowded minibuses, leave Puerto Plata's main square or, more frequently, from the hospital on Circunvalación Sur to destinations along the north coast (*Caribe Tours* charge US$1.60 to Sosúa). *Metrobus* (T5866062, Beller y 16 de Agosto), 4 a day, and *Caribe Tours* (T5864544, at the new Caribe Centro Plaza, Camino Real, just off the Circunvalación) run a/c coaches to/from Santo Domingo, 4 hrs (for fares, see page 404). To Santiago every hour on the hour, 1000-1800, US$2.66. *Caribe Tours* run buses to Samaná via Sosúa and Cabarete, 0700, 1600 daily, 3½ hrs. Alternatively you can use the *guagua* system, changing at each town, but this will take much longer, be more uncomfortable and more costly. **Motorcycle rental**: US$20-30 a day, from any rental agency. Make sure to lock your motorcycle or scooter, as bike theft is big business in the area and there is no theft insurance on motorbikes.

Air   Gregorio Luperón international airport, T5860219 serves the entire north coast. It is 20 mins from Puerto Plata, 7 mins from Sosúa and 20 from Cabarete. Taxi from airport to Puerto Plata or Cabarete US$20, to Sosúa US$10. Small bank at airport for exchange. Do not panic at the airport when approached by Dominicans in overalls attempting to take your bag. They are baggage handlers trying to make a living. Proper tipping is about US$2 per bag.

Tourist office   *Turinter*, T6864020, F6883890, www.turinter.com Also in Santo Domingo. There is a **Directory** tourist office on the Malecón (No 20) which has plenty of useful information.

Dominican Republic

Sosúa

28 km east of Puerto Plata

Sosúa is a little town with a beautiful and lively 1-km beach, perfect for diving and watersports. Vendors' stalls and snackbars line the path along the back of the beach and you will be offered anything from sunbeds to toilets. There is a smaller public beach on the east side of town, referred to as the 'playita', where you will be less bothered by vendors. It is located by *Hotel Sosúa-by-the-Sea*. Sosúa is popular with Europeans, Americans and Canadians and is unfortunately becoming increasingly busy and scruffy. The main street (correctly named Calle Pedro Clisante, but only ever referred to as Main Street, or Calle Principal in Spanish) is lined with all variety of shops, restaurants and bars. The unusual European atmosphere stems from the fact that the El Batey side of town (the side that houses most of the hotels and restaurants) was founded by German Jewish refugees who settled here in 1941. A synagogue and memorial building are open to the public. Although many of the original settlers have moved away, services are still held, and in 1991 a 50th-anniversary party brought settlers and their relatives from all over the world for a reunion. The original houses are now lost among the modern developments. The western end of the town is referred to as Los Charamicos (the two ends are separated by the beach); this is the older side of town, where the Dominicans themselves generally live, shop and party. Pavements have been built alongside the roads to allow easier pedestrian access to the two parts.

Sosúa, although crowded with tourist spots, is a small town. Little or no attention is paid to street names or numbers. The quiet road between El Batey and Playa Chiquita should be treated with caution at night. Dress is very informal. Although it is considered impolite to wander the streets in bathing attire, dress for dinner at any location is comfortable and Caribbean.

Sleeping
LL-L *Sandcastles Beach Resort*, T5305817, F5712000, just outside Sosúa. Private beach, restaurants, self-contained, shuttle buses into Sosúa. **L** *Occidental La Esplanada*, T5713333, F5713922, ohrd.esplanada@codetel.net.do 210 rooms, all-inclusive, near casino. *Hotel Villas Carolina*, T5713626, F5711737. 61 all-inclusive units with kitchen and sitting room, 1 and 2 bedrooms, variable prices. *Coconut Palms Resort*, T5711625, F5711725. Beautiful resort, scenic hilltop view, 8 km outside Sosúa, all units with kitchen facilities, shuttle bus to town and beach, variable rates. **B** *One Ocean Place*, El Batey, T5713131, F5713144. Aparthotel, restaurant, pool, 10-min walk to beach. *Hotel Sosúa*, T5712683, F5862442, in town centre, 3 mins from main beach. Restaurant, pool, being renovated in 2000 and temporarily closed. **B** *Sosúa-by-the-Sea*, T5713222. Owned and operated by Austrian-Canadians, on Little Beach, immaculate, beautiful a/c rooms, good restaurant, pool, bar, includes breakfast and dinner (also sells timeshares). *Casa Marina Beach Club*, T5713690, F5713110,

Dominican Republic north coast

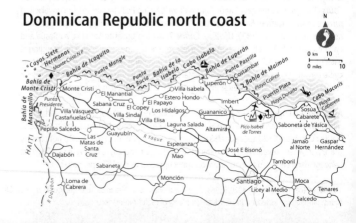

www.cmarina.com.do 300 rooms, all-inclusive, special offers may be available, located on the Little Beach, pool, restaurant, excellent value. **C** *Playa Chiquita Beach Resort*, T5712800 (**AL** full board), slightly out of the way, located on own private beach. Good restaurant, accommodation and service, and casino, has shuttle to town and beach. **C** *On the Waterfront*, Dr Rosen 1, El Batey, T5713024. 27 cabins, quiet, tropical, ocean front pool, on a cliff overlooking the sea, 5 mins to beach, special rates for groups. **C-D** *Coralillos*, unpretentious, perched on a cliff with breathtaking view of beach, T5712645. **D** per person *Paraíso de Colón*, on the road to Cabarete by the gym, T5713755, F5713235, www.paraiso. travelshop.de All-inclusive, reasonable, large bed, good rooms and suites, could do with some redecoration, damp walls, food boring, extra charge for a/c, shuttle to Cabarete, pool, OK for price, no traffic noise, just countryside behind.

Cheaper (prices **C** and under depending on season): *Jardín del Sol*, T/F5713553. Family-run, clean, pool, near town. *Margaritaville*, T/F5713553. On hilltop, clean, scenic, shuttle to town. *Tropix*, T5712291 (address: EPS-D#274, Box 02-5548, Miami, FL 33103), near centre of town. Clean, some traffic noise, beautiful pool and landscaped beautiful garden, impeccable service, good food, use of kitchen facilities. *Pensión Anneliese*, Dr Rosen, T5712208. Clean room with fridge, short walk to beach, right by *On the Waterfront* restaurant. *Koch's Guest House*, El Batey, down a dirt side street, ocean front, no beach. Use of kitchen, breakfast extra. There are many other hotels, guest houses and villas for rent, ask around locally. Try in Los Cerros for rooms to rent, **E-F**. If you are looking for a place to stay for longer than the average charter flight, or would like to get a group together to stay in a house, or have any questions regarding rentals in the Sosúa/Cabarete area, call *Sosúa Central Rental*, T/F5713648.

Eating

There fewer restaurants than there used to be, probably due to the increase in all-inclusive hotels

On the Waterfront, Calle Dr Rosen 1, El Batey, T5713024. Fish, seafood, snacks, happy hour 1600-1800, excellent food and a spectacular sunset overlooking the sea, all-you-can-eat barbecue on Fri night, pleasant entertainment nightly, on the lookout point. For an equally good view over the water go the other side of the bay to Los Charamicos to *Atlántico*, T5712878, on the cliff road from the beach. Open 1200-1500, 1900-2300, closed Thu, seafood and steak interesting menu, main dishes US$8-15, seafood platter for two US$17.50, lobster US$15/lb. There are several restaurants on Main St serving international, French, Italian food, walk around and see what takes your fancy, they change frequently. Also several eating places along the beach, some with lobster tanks, OK for lunch. For Dominican food go to Los Charamicos where there are *comedores*. *PJ's* , on corner of Main St with Duarte. Burger bar, satisfying breakfasts, chef's salad and schnitzel burger for lunch, outdoor seating for people watching. *Dundee's Burgers*, Calle Alejo Martínez, in front-of-school yard, open 1900-0700, the place to go after a night of revelling, Dundee, the American-Dominican owner, is a local fixture. *Hotel Sosúa-by-the-Sea* serves the best value buffet breakfast in town. For delicious baked products go to the *German Bakery (Panadería Alemán)*, in Villas Ana María, residential area.

Nightlife

Lots going on in Main Street

Merengue Club, huge open air club, open until 0300, no charge; next to it the *Hotel Central* has a pub, *Toff Toff*; *Tucan* disco is on the other side of the street. *La Roca*, last spot on Main St before the beach, Sosúa's oldest bar/disco/eatery,now a sports bar, big screen, serves 1lb lobster with soup or salad for US$15 (*La Bahía* opposite has lobster, soup, dessert and coffee for US$12.50!). *Moby Dick Disco*, by far the most popular disco, a/c, cover charge, beware of prostitutes/thieves hanging around. *Copacabana* also has girls working. Elsewhere, *High* disco by the casino at the east end of town, has a terrace and small indoor and outdoor swimming pool. *Eddie's Sports Bar* has 4 satellite dishes, can get anything, near *Super Super Supermarket*.

Sport

Watersports *Columbus Aqua Park* opened in 1997, 3 mins from the airport. Open 1000-1900 with water toboggans, 3 large pools, a lazy river, children's water play area, diving tower, restaurants, gift shops, bars, discos etc. **Diving** There are lots of dive operations, in town and on the beach, offering tuition and boat dives. There is no jetty and no large dive boats, so you must be prepared to wade out to a small boat, with probably no shade, and be capable of getting back into the boat without a ladder after your dive, which can be tricky if it

Dominican Republic

is rough. A recommended and long-established dive shop is Northern Coast Aquasports/ Diving, Pedro Clisante 8, T5711028, F5713883, www.northerncoastdiving.com, a US-owned company run by Mark Goldsmith, who is British. Lots of courses, multilingual staff, several boats normally taking 4-6 divers, good with novice or experienced divers, probably the most professional operation on this stretch of coast.

Transport **Local** A **taxi** to/from Puerto Plata costs US$17, a *guagua* RD$10 and a *carro público* US$7 if you take the whole car. In Sosúa, transport congregates by the *Texaco* station and the junction of Calle Dr Rosen and the Carretera. The most popular form of transport within Sosúa is the *motoconcho* (motorcycle taxi), RD$10 to anywhere in town. **Car and bike rentals** are everywhere, shop around for prices, and once again be cautioned as to theft (eg Asociación de Renta Moto Sosúa Cabarete, US$28-35 for 1-2 days, US$5-7.25 hourly, depending on type). **Bus** *Caribe Tours* from Santo Domingo, US$5.30. In Sosúa, T5713808.

Directory **Useful services** *Codetel*, Calle Dr Alejo Martínez, near corner with Dr Rosen. Next to the *Banco Popular* (ATM outside) on the small square at Calle Dr Martínez and Duarte is the *Viva Art Gallery*. Further up on Duarte is an internet café, @, also *Tricom*, on the corner before you get to *Bancrédito* (ATM outside).

Cabarete

Cabarete, famous for world class windsurfing, is 14 km east of Sosúa. Although it has grown considerably since French Canadian windsurfers first staked their claim on this small fishing village it still maintains its small town character. Besides windsurfing Cabarete offers a variety of adventure sports: mountain biking, horse riding, whitewater rafting and scuba diving. It is the windsurf capital of the world, having hosted the World Windsurf Championship. International competitions are held annually in June (see page 409), www.CabareteRaceWeek.com Conditions vary according to season: in summer there are constant trade winds but few waves, in winter there are days with no wind, but when it comes the waves are tremendous. Boards rent for US$50 per day, US$200 per week, with variations, make sure insurance is available. Highly recommended is the *Carib Bic Center*, T5710640, F5710649, www.caribwind.com It has excellent windsurfing gear for rent, with professional and experienced instructors.It also has the nicest surf shop in town and a great bar and grill. In addition to their beginner to expert equipment they also rent kayaks, boogie boards, surfboards, hobiecats and snorkelling gear. Other windsurfing schools include *Vela/Spin Out*, T5710805; *Club Nathalie Simon* (French speaking), T5710848; *Happy* (German and English speaking), T5710784; *Club Mistral*, T5710770 and *Kitesurf School*, www.flyhighandsurf.com (contact Stephan Rutter at Residencia Dominicana, T5710890). Scuba diving is popular and there are many dive schools in the area. *Northern Coast Diving* in Sosúa covers the Cabarete area (see above); also *Dolphin Dive*, T5710842 and *Caribbean Divers*, T5710218. There are many kilometres of white sand beach lined with coconut palms and a lagoon with many waterbirds. There are caves in the area, believed to be five million years old, which you can visit. They are administered by Harvey Andrews, a Canadian, entrance US$15, plus US$2 for the DNP. On the outskirts of town is El Encuentro, a surfing beach, with a consistent 'break' off the right and left. *Surf & Sport* surfing school, run by long time local surfer, Markus Bohm, offers daily lessons, US$25, for all ages and levels, T5710463. Cabarete hosts an international sand castle competition every February, when visitors construct fantastic mermaids, flowers, fruit and even the *Titanic*. A French team won in 2000.

Sleeping **L-B** *Palm Beach Condos*, T5710758, F5710752, CPBCondos@codetel,net.do Spacious, deluxe condos, 2 bedroom, 2 bathroom, hot water, fully equipped kitchens, patios with ocean views, on the beach, nanny services extra, Dominican meals delivered, perfect for families and windsurfers, central but quiet, no traffic noise, close to bakeries, restaurants and transport. **AL-B** *Home Key Management*, T5710370, F5710523, www.cabaretevillas.com Agency run

Low rise hotels, condos and guest houses line the 2 km bay

by Hans Nanny for rental beach houses and condos 10 mins' walk from Cabarete, great selection and variety of homes. Others at the upper end of the market include: **L-B** *El Magnífico*, T5710868, hotel.magnifico@codetel.net.do 10 apartments, ocean view, a/c, classic Caribbean design and amazing art deco. **LL-A** *Olas de Oro*, T5710215. **LL** *Sea Horse Ranch*, T5713880, houses. **AL-B** *Bahía de Arena*, T5710876. **A-B** *Nanny Estates*, T5710744, F5710655, ocean front. A bit out of town and therefore quieter, 2 bedroom apartments, all with seaviews, restaurant, pool, tennis.

All-inclusives: **A-B** per person *Punta Goleta*, T5710700, F5710707. 254 rooms, package tours. **A-B** per person *Amhsa Estrella del Mar*, T5710808, F5710904. 164 rooms, on beach, pool. **A-C** per person *Las Orquídeas*, T5710787, F5710853. 35 rooms, pool, tennis. **B-C** per person *Bahía Linda ARA Club*, T/F5710878. On the beach, 30 rooms. **C-D** per person *Costa Liza*, T5710920, F5710355. Small hotel, on the beach, 10 mins from town centre. **B-C** per person *Orilla del Mar*, T5710730. 95 rooms on the beach. **B-C** per person *Surf Beach Side*, T5710911.13 bungalows. **A-C** *Tropical Garden Club*, T5710715, F5710709. 226 rooms 3 km from town, 400 m from beach, set in exotic gardens, 3 restaurants, 4 pools, 8 bars. **A-C** *Tropical Goleta*, T5710940, F5710941, 3 km from town, on the beach. 104 rooms, 2 restaurants, 2 pools, jacuzzi. **A-C** *Tropical Casa Laguna*, T5710725, F5710704, across the road from the beach. 62 rooms, 48 with kitchenettes, balconies, massage, beauty salon, restaurant/bar, pool. **A-C** *Cita del Sol*, T5710720. French Canadian, restaurant, across the road from the beach. **B-C** *Windsurf Apart Hotel*, T5710718, F5710710, www.windsurfcabarete.com Studio and 2-bedroom condos, satellite TV, phone, a/c, restaurant, all watersports, central, across the street from Carib bic centre. Highly recommended. **B-C** *Coconut Palm Resort*, T5711625, moru.invest@ codetel.net.do 1, 2, and 3 bedroom apartments, quiet garden, restaurant, 20 mins from Cabarete. **B-C** per person *First Class Resort*, T5710911, all-inclusive. **B-C** *Caracol Apart Hotel*, T5710788, F5710665, only steps from the beach, 5 mins from Cabarete centre. Terrace overlooking ocean, 2 pools, fully equipped kitchenettes. **B-C** per person *Camino del Sol*, T5710894, east of the town. Package holidays, all-inclusive. **B-C** *Albatros*, T5710841, h.albatros@ codetel.net.do 11 condos which can be divided, big airy apartments, coconut palms, tropical garden, 150 m from beach and centre of Cabarete. **B-C** *La Punta*, T5710897, lapunta@codetel.net.do 12 apartments on the beach, quiet, wonderful restaurant, *Otra Cosa*. **B-D** *Caribe Surf Hotel*, T5710788, at end of beach. Owned by Swiss, Teddy Muller, new, modern, clean, reasonably priced. **B-D** *Casa Blanca*, T/F5710934. On main road, seaview, opposite Rent-a-Moto, 9 rooms, 7 apartments with kitchenette, clean, friendly.

Many more in the mid-range include: **C** *Arecoa 1*, T5710653. **C-D** *Kaoba*, T5710837, F5710879, h.kaoba@codetel.net.do Fan, hot water, reductions for over 2 weeks, rooms, apartments, studios in bungalows, good value, separate restaurant for breakfast and evening meal, across the road from the beach. **C-D** *Isla Verde Beach Hotel*, T5710807. **C** *El Carite*, T5710415. 6 bungalows, 5 mins from centre, off main road. **D-F** *Residencia Dominicana*, T/F5710890, resdom@hispaniola.com Excellent value, clean studio apartments, pool, tennis, movie screen, restaurant, manager Stephan Rutter speaks German, English and Spanish, special price for long stays. Highly recommended. **D-E** *Wilson Beach House*, T5710616. Big house with terrace, the nicest view of the bay. **E-F** *Banana Boat*, T5710630. Finnish/Canadian owned, quiet, central, kitchen facilities, laundry. Recommended. **D-E** *Condos Surfmen Mariette Lapointe*, T5713044. 9 condos, international.

Other good places in the low budget range include: **D-E** *Ali's Apartments*, T5710568. **E** *Arcoiris*, T5710751, arcoiris.cabarete@tel-call.com 10 rooms, pleasant and quiet, children's activities. **E-D** *Blue Moon Retreat*, T2230614. Good restaurant, see below. **E** *Hotel Laguna Blue*, T5710659. **D-E** *Plinsis*, T5710505. **C-E** *Pequeño Refugio*, T5710770.

Dominican Republic

Eating

Wide range of places to eat & drink, lots of beach restaurants & bars, varied cuisine. Restaurants change hands frequently

Blue Moon, T2230614. Indian food served on banana leaves, reservations required. *Blue Paradise*, T5710525. Fast food. *El Magnífico*, T5710968. Gourmet Dominican food, reservations required. *La Casa del Pescador*, T5710760. Excellent seafood. *Las Brisas*, T5710614. Buffet style dinners, affordable food. *Miros*, T5710888. Excellent dinners on the more expensive side. *New Wave*, T5710826. Serves one dish every night, Wed is popular for the excellent Indonesian satay. *Tropicoco*, T5710647. Fantastic Sat night buffet, a bit out of town. *Otra Cosa*, T5710897, at *La Punta*, see above. French Caribbean food. *Vento*, T5710977, on the beach. Italian food. *Ho La La*, T5710806. French, international food, good seafood, lobsters, good pizza. *Chez León*, on the beach. Shady terrace, speicalities of crèpes and waffles. *Le Pub*, in middle of town. French food, pleasant place, pool table. *La Dolce Vita*, T5710718. Italian food, Italian buffet Tue and Fri nights, Dominican buffet Thu night. *Bar Fly*, JT5710529. International food, fish barbecue, Mexican specialities, Chinese fondue, reservations required. *La Casita*. Sea food, best shrimp in town. *The Castle Club*, T2230601, 20 mins from Cabarete in the mountains. Unique gourmet dining experience, private dinner parties for 4-10 guests, reservations need to be made at least tow days in advance. *Pancho Villa*, Mexican restaurant in El Patio Plaza. *Onno's*, T3831448. Tapas bar in the centre of the beach, relaxed ambiance. *The Green Room*, small bar on the beach next to the Bic Centre, happy hour 1700-1900, great sangría. Cheap Dominican food is available at *Sandros*, opposite *Iguanamama*, rough and ready but nice people, good fun and good food (US$3 for 'small' portion of stew, rice, salad, beans, more than enough, beer US$1) and *Mama's* and also if you go just out of town on the same road that goes to the caves, in a small village they have recently opened 6 or 7 excellent, cheap, Dominican restaurants, *Mercedes* being one of the best. *Dick's* bakery serves you the best coffee in town.

Nightlife   Cabarete is gaining quite a reputation for its nightlife. Many of the beach restaurants double as bars and are open until after the sun comes up. You can dance the merengue or listen to rock bands. Some of the hot spots are *New Wave Café, Onno's Bar, Las Brisas* and *Tiki Bar*. Ask any local and they will point you in the direction of the party that night.

Shopping   **Supermarkets** *Albertico's*, the most complete, in town centre. *Casa Rosada*, full deli of imported meats and cheeses, beside *Iguana Mama*. *Judith*, rather limited stock but cheapest. *Producto Sosúa*, on outskirts of town, variety and affordable prices. *Colores* minimarkets, liquorstore and cigarettes.

Transport   **Taxi** Cabarete-Sosúa US$8-9, airport US$20, Puerto Plata US$20. Always check price with driver before setting off. *Guagua* to Sosúa US$0.40. *Motoconcho* US$0.40 anywhere in town, negotiate price for anywhere further, price doubles at night.

Directory   **Communications** *Codetel* is on the left as you go out of town towards Sosúa. More central is *Telecabarete*, T5710260, F5710845, also cheaper at US$1 per min to Europe, US$0.66 to USA, fax US$1.33 per page, US$0.33 to receive, internet access US$1.33 per 15 mins, US$4 per hr, open 0900-2200 for phone calls, 0730-2200 for internet. *Cocomangos*, T5710470, internet café, 13 terminals, US$2 for 15 mins, US$4.66 for 1 hr, more expensive but very fast, coffee, soft drinks, cocktails, fresh Italian ice cream. **Laundry** *Agua Azul*, T5710515, *Family Laundry* and *Banana Boat* (usually 24 hrs needed), T5710630. **Tour agencies** *Iguana Mama*, run by Patricia Suriel, T5710908, F5710734, www.iguanamama.com, is the only licensed biking tour operator on the north coast, located on the main street heading towards Sosúa, by where *Caribe Tours* stops. Guided daily tours, US$40-85, weekly adventure trips including hiking up Pico Duarte, whale watching in Samaná, bicycle rentals, specialized stump-jumpers and rock-hoppers, all equipment, maps and insurance for US$30 per day. Also contact them for whitewater rafting, canyoning and cascading, they will put you in touch with the best companies, prices from US$99 includes all equipment, transport and meals. For kids, a jungle river tour, daily educational boat rides, daily and weekly family excursions (biking and cultural). *Iguana Mama* donates 20 of its profits to local schools. *Rancho Alcantarra*, T5710816, F5710444, info@dominicanadventures.com, offers horse riding trips through the mountains with swimming in waterfalls and a Dominican lunch, daily tours, 0930-1640, US$75, week long riding tours US$900, well-cared for native horses, recommended, a great day out for beginners or experienced riders. **Useful addresses** *Servi-Med* medical centre, open 24 hrs. **Police:** T5710810.

Río San Juan

On the northeast coast, Río San Juan is a friendly town with a lagoon called Gri-Grí (*guagua* from Sosúa, 1¼ hours, may have to change in Gaspar Hernández). Boats take visitors through the mangrove forests and to see caves and rocks, and to the natural swimming pool called the Cueva de las Golondrinas (US$16 without swim, US$24 with swim, bargaining possible, US$1.60 per person if more than 10 people). Also worth visiting from the town is Puerto Escondido beach. You can walk beyond *Hotel Bahía Blanca* between mangroves and the sea to the mouth of Gri-Grí, many birds in the mangroves.

Sleeping Several large all-inclusives have been built in the area, offering lots of facilities and entertainment, including the 941-room *Bahía Príncipe San Juan*, T2261590, F2261994, on 5-km private beach, awful buffet food. Shuttle bus daily to Sosúa and Cabarete, casino, golf nearby. *Caribbean Village Playa Grande*, T5821170, F5826094. 300 rooms, on cliff above Playa Grande and golf course, an Allegro resort. *Club Costa Verde*, T2485287, F2485557. 94 rooms. Nicest hotel is **D** *Bahía Blanca*, T5892563, F5892528. Lovely location right on the sea, clean, lots of balconies, 20 rooms, near local bars. Next best is *Río San Juan*, on main street, Duarte, at brow of hill, T5892379. Many price variations from **D-E**, a/c, disco, pool, good restaurant and there is a good pizzeria, *Cachalotte*, opposite (the hotel offers boat trips on the lagoon). **E-F** *Santa Clara*, Padre Billini y Capotillo, opposite Mini Market. With or without bath and fan, electricity and water often off and then very hot. **F** *San Martín*, friendly but very dirty.

Eating *Cheo's Café Bar*, Padre Billini, casi Libertad. Pizzas, seafood, meat. *Bar/Restaurant La Casona*, fish and creole food, good value, friendly, purified drinking water, near Laguna Gri-Grí; several other eating places, mostly *pizzerías*.

Transport Transport stops at the junction of Duarte and the main road. *Caribe Tours* T5892633, to Puerto Plata US$6.30, to Samaná 0830 US$3.10, 3 hrs, to Santo Domingo 0730, 1500.

Playa Grande to Sánchez Further to the east is Playa Grande, 60 km from Puerto Plata, another beautiful new resort which is being developed, in conjunction with Playa Dorada, at a cost of many millions of dollars (lots of hawkers on the beach). The many tour companies in Sosúa offer tours to Gri-Grí and Playa Grande. Five kilometres east of Playa Grande is *Club Paradise*, T813-9499327, F813-9491008, a 'clothing optional' resort, with beautiful, secluded beaches, self-sufficient complex, watersports and entertainment.

Between Río San Juan and Samaná, the coast road runs through Cabrera to **Nagua**, a dirty fishing village on the shores of the Bahía Escocesa. Several small and medium-sized hotels: *Hotel San Carlos*; *Hotel Corazón de Jesús*; **D** *Hotel Carib Caban*, 8 km south of Nagua, studio (less in smaller room), pleasant, directly on beach, restaurant with Austrian food (hire a motorcycle to get there, US$2, T5843145). Caribe Tours T5842370, and Metro, T5842177, both pass through Nagua on their Santo Domingo-Samaná and Samaná-Puerto Plata routes.

The scenery along the north coast from Sosúa to Samaná is exceptionally beautiful. The road is paved all the way from Sosúa to Samaná. **Sánchez** is a pleasant, unspoilt little place with some basic accommodation. Much of the architecture is 19th-century, pretty, colonial. It was at one time a prosperous sea port and had a railway which ran to San Francisco de Macorís and La Vega. Bus Santo Domingo-Sánchez, *Caribe Tours* four a day, US$5. Caribe Tours daily at 1630 from Sánchez to Cabarete/Sosúa, 2½ hours, US$2.75 and on to Puerto Plata US$4.75. *Guagua* from Samaná US$2, return from Calle Duarte.

Dominican Republic

The Samaná Peninsula

Samaná

On the peninsula of Samaná is the city of the same name. Columbus arrived here on 12 January 1493, but was so fiercely repelled by the Ciguayo Indians that he called the bay the Golfo de las Flechas (the Gulf of Arrows). **Samaná Bay**, as it is now called, is very picturesque, fringed with coconut palms and studded with islets. The present town of Santa Bárbara de Samaná was founded in 1756 by families expressly brought from the Canary Islands. The city, reconstructed after being devastated by fire in 1946, shows no evidence of this past, with its modern Catholic church, broad streets, new restaurants and hotels, and noisy motorcycle taxis. In contrast to the Catholic church, and overlooking it, is a more traditional Protestant church, white with red corrugated-iron roofing, nicknamed locally 'La Churcha'. Traditional dances, such as *bambulá* and the *chivo florete* can be seen at local festivals (4 December, the patron saint's day; 24 October, San Rafael). A causeway links three islands in the bay, which can be reached by taking the road to the *Hotel Cayacoa*. Steps to the bridge are found by walking through the car park and keeping the hotel on your right.

Humpback whales return to Samaná Bay every year between December and March to mate and calve. Various tours go whale-watching, certainly worthwhile if you are in the area at that time of year. This is recognized as one of the ten best places in the world to see whales and very convenient for the average tourist as they are so close to the shore. See also page 48. Tour companies and boat owners organize whale-watching trips from mid-January to mid-March, from about US$35 per person, an incredible experience. For reputable tour guides and people who care about conservation, phone Kim Beddall, T5382494, owner of *Victoria II*, concise, interesting, friendly tours at 0900 and 1330. She distributes an informative guide, *Whales of Samaná* by Ken de Pree, which explains the behaviour and life cycle of the humpbacks. There are about 40 registered boats, monitored by the DNP, who have a whale watch coordinator based at CEBSE (see below). Standards improve each year, strict regulations are in place to protect the whales and the captains hold weekly meetings. Reservations are essential with all captains as they are often booked up with bus loads of tourists brought from all over the country. In 1999, 32,000 people visited in the season.

Since March 1999, Samaná Bay has been part of a 20,000 sq km **marine sanctuary**. CEBSE, an NGO for the conservation of Samaná Bay, is campaigning for the bay to be made a biosphere reserve. CEBSE has built a new nature centre at Tiro Blanco, the green zone in the town of Samaná, and is involved in community projects. There is a small museum, entrance US$1, T5382042, with exhibits of the fauna,

Samaná Peninsula

flora, history and culture of the area, including a 45 ft skeleton of a humpback whale and a dolphin. Displays are in Spanish and English and there are temporary exhibitions, for example whales in season. The museum is still in its infancy but more exhibits are planned, including Taíno objects. The NDP is also based here.

An airport for the peninsula is at Arroyo Barril (8 km from town, good road, but only 25 minutes flying time from Santo Domingo), which is being upgraded to take international traffic. Delays in construction works while the new government undertook new technical studies in 1996-97 provoked local people to form the Comité Samaná Se Cansó de Esperar (Samaná-got-tired-of-waiting-committee) to push for the recommencing of the works. The first phase was completed and opened in 1999; the second phase will allow larger aircraft to land. Many Caribbean-cruising yachts anchor at Samaná, taking advantage of the calm waters.

L *Occidental Gran Bahía*, T5383111, F5382764, h.granb@codetel.net.do 110-room, **Sleeping** charming luxury resort on coast road, 10 mins, 8 km east of town, also 8 villas with pool, all facilities available, less in low season, small beach, good food and service, compact 9-hole golf course, watersports, tennis, horseriding, heliport, shuttle service to Cayo Levantado. **L** *Cayacoa Beach*, T5383131, F5382985. On a hill overlooking the town, view of the bay, beautiful gardens, watersports. **LL-L** *Hotel Occidental Cayo Levantado*, on the island, 10 mins by boat from Samaná, T5383141, F5382998. White beaches, all-inclusive, 44 rooms in main building or bungalows, restaurant, beach bar. **C-D** *Tropical Lodge*, on Malecón, T5382480. 12 rooms, own generator, continuous hot and cold water, basic but clean and good restaurant. **E-F** *Nilka*, Santa Bárbara y Colón, T5382244. 11 rooms, with a/c (cheaper with fan), all with bath, hot water, popular. *Guest House Alcide*, T5382512. **E** *Cotubanamá*, T5382557, go west along the Malecón to the roundabout and turn right, the hotel is one block up on the left. Clean, adequate, fan, bedside light, make sure you get a room with a door which locks properly, hot water sometimes, doesn't last long, no food, repairs take ages, if ever. **F** *Paraíso*, near *rotunda*, central but quiet, modern, good and clean, good cold shower. There are other hotels, eg *King*, T5382404, *Casa de Huéspedes*, T5382475 and *Ursula*, T5382402.

Going east along the Malecón: *L'Hacienda*, T5382383. Grill and bar open from 1200, the best **Eating** in town, excellent specials, main dishes US$8-10, about US$22 per person for two courses, *The local cuisine is* drinks, tax and service. *Bar Le France*, T5382257. Café style. *Le Café de Paris*, brightly *highly regarded,* painted, pizzeria, good crêperie, ice cream, breakfast, cocktails, loud rock music, very slow *especially the fish &* service when busy, can take 45 mins to get the bill. *Café del Mar*, T5382021. Open for break- *coconut dishes* fast from 0800, then spaghettis, hamburgers and Dominican food, cocktails, good. *La Mata Rosada*, T5382388, opposite the harbour. French-run but lots of languages spoken, popular with ex-pats, not always open, seafood, about US$10 per person. *Camilo's*, T5382781. Local and not-so-local food, reasonable (takes credit cards).

Road *Concho* or *guagua* in town RD$3/US$0.20; *carreras* US$3.50-4. *Guagua* to Sánchez **Transport** from market place US$2, recommended excursion. From the capital either via San Francisco de Macorís (where *Caribe Tours* has a terminal, 5 hrs with ½ hr stop), Nagua and Sánchez, or via Cotui, Nagua and Sánchez (*Caribe Tours* and *Metro*, 4 hrs). Alternatively from the capital by bus or *público* to San Pedro de Macorís, then another to **Sabana de la Mar** (see page 459) and take the ferry across the bay. Return to Santo Domingo, *Caribe Tours*, T5382229, at 0700, 0900, 1400, 1530, 1630, US$5.50. *Metro*, T5382851, at 0800, 1500, via Sánchez US$3, Nagua US$3, San Francisco de Macorís US$4.40, to Santo Domingo US$6. *Caribe Tours* from Samaná to Puerto Plata (US$5.50) via Sánchez, Nagua, Cabrera, Río San Juan, Gáspar Hernández, Cabarete (US$4) and Sosúa daily 1600, 4 hrs. If you want to get off at any of these intermediate stops, check that you will be allowed to retrieve your luggage from the hold or take it on board with you, the driver is not supposed to open the luggage hold mid-journey. *Línea Gladys* to Santiago, US$4.50, from traffic lights west of town.

Dominican Republic

Directory **Useful services** Petrol station at the dock, open 0700-2200. *Banco del Cambio*, behind *Samaná Tours*, changes cheques. *Baninter* has ATM inside, gives cash against Visa, 6% commission, open 0830-1500 Mon-Fri. Also *Banco Reserva*, but no ATMs.*The Clínica Vicente*, T5382535, is the most advanced in Samaná, with ultrasound and X-rays. Dr Vicente and Farmacia Bahía are opposite *Hotel Cotubanamá*. There is a new ambulance and health services are improving. Post office behind *Camilo's*, just off Parque; *Codetel*, Calle Santa Bárbara, 0800-2200 daily for phone, fax and email. *Compucentro* in the same building but round the corner on Calle Lavandier, also has email facilities, T5383146, compucentro@hotmail.com, open 0900-1230, 1500-1800 Mon-Fri, US$2.75 per hour, minimum charge US$1. Tourist information at Samaná Information Service, T5382451, on Malecón; alternatively, T5382206 (Ayuntamiento), or 5382210 (Governor's office).

Excursions from Samaná

Parque Nacional de Haitises
Across the bay, is a fascinating area of mangroves, *mogotes* and caves, which were used by the Taínos and later by pirates. There are anthropomorphic cave drawings and other pictures, best seen with a torch, and some carvings. The park is rich in wildlife and you can see lots of birds, such as frigate birds, rey congo, ibis and pelicans. Some of the caves have bats, there are manatee in the mangroves and inland the solenodonte (*Solenodon pardoxus*), a mammal and insectivore found only on Hispaniola. Visits can be arranged by launch for US$45 including lunch with departures from Sánchez and Samaná; various companies organize tours to Los Haitises and to caves in the area (eg Amilka Tours, T5527664, daily from Sánchez, takes large tour parties and is the most regular but does not always have the best guides). It takes longer to get there by boat from Samaná, so it is better to start from Sánchez. Do not choose a small boat in windy weather, it will get rough and you will get wet. You may get wet anyway, it rains frequently, but some boats provide waterproof capes. The DNP, from whom permits must be obtained, also organizes tours, US$35 for 12 passengers (in Sabana de la Mar, T5567333); see page 408.

Cayo Levantado
There are several beautiful offshore islands. Cayo Levantado is a popular picnic place, especially at weekends when the beach is packed. The white sand beach is nice, though, and there are good views of the bay and the peninsulas on either side. There is a hotel on the island (see above); good drinks and fish lunches are for sale. Public boats go there from the dock in Samaná (US$6-8 return, buy ticket at Malecón No 3, not from the hustlers on the pier, lots of boats daily outward 0900-1100, return 1500-1700); alternatively, take a *público* or *motoconcho* 8 km out of town to Los Cacaos (US$3) to where two companies, *Transportes José* and *Simi Báez*, run boats to the island but the price is about the same (the latter company also does fishing and whale-spotting trips). Cayo Levantado is often included as a lunch and swim stop after a whale watching tour (in season, see page 48).

A lovely drive is to go east of Samaná around the tip of the peninsula to Las Galeras, through beautiful scenery past lots of bays and several small beaches where you can stop and swim. **Anacaona** is a good beach about 8 km away, kept spotless, showers, loungers, beach bar run by Hervé. Then you pass *Simi Báez* (whale watching, boat trips) before you get to the *Hotel Gran Bahía*, approached through a tunnel/avenue of trees, most spectacular. The hotel has a lovely view of Cayo Levantado and other islets.

Las Galeras

At the eastern end of the peninsula is **Playa Galeras**, 26 km (one hour, US$1.75 by *guagua*, from market and dock in Samaná, US$4.50 by *motoconcho*), worth a visit. The 1 km beach is framed by the dark rock cliffs and forested mountains of Cape Samaná and Cape Cabrón, under discussion to become a national park. The village is popular with Europeans, several of whom have set up small hotels and restaurants, but it is still unspoilt. Diving is good with several sites around the bay and the headland. There is a fair amount of weed on the beach but it is unspoilt and 'unimproved', with trees for shade.

Twenty minutes away by boat, or 40 minutes by jeep along a very rough track is the deserted **Playa Rincón**, dominated by the cliffs of 600 m high Cape Cabrón. The whole peninsula is beautiful and the diving is superb, but many beaches are accessible only by boat (and the Samaná boatmen charge the earth). Others are reached by a dirt road, negotiable by ordinary cars. Check locally before swimming at deserted beaches where there can be strong surf and an undertow. Drownings have occurred frequently near El Valle.

A-B *Villa Serena*, next to the shore, T5830203, F5382545. Canadian-owned, painted turquoise, pink and white, cool, plantation-style, undergoing expansion works in 2000, huge, stylish rooms, private terrace overlooking sea and little islet, rocky coast but small, sandy beach, a/c and fans, gourmet restaurant, tours organized. **A** *Club Bonito*, T5380203, F6960082, club.bonito@codetel.net.do, the first hotel on the right along the beach track, orange building.Very central, Italian restaurant *Il Pirata*, with seafood specialities, bar, boutique, pool, high class but still unfinished in 2000, beach volleyball. Next along the beach is **A** *Todo Blanco*. As the name suggests, it is all white, gingerbread style, pretty, balconies, restaurant, tour desk, horses to rent. **C** *Moorea Beach*, T5380007, T5380202. 12 rooms, seaview, 200 m from beach, in palm trees, painted white, in good order, pool, quiet but close to village centre, bar, restaurant, Dominican specialities, run by Bernard (German) and Eleni (Greek), who speak lots of languages, breakfast included in price. **C-D** *¿Casa Por Qué No?*, T/F5382545, between the Plaza Lusitania shopping arcade and *Club Bonito*. French Canadian owned bed and breakfast. **E** *El Paradiso*, owned by Peter Traubel of Dive Samaná, T5380210. Cabins. **F** *Villa Marina*, 800 m north of beach on road to Samaná. Italian-owned, 11 basic rooms with fan and bathroom, includes breakfast, excellent meals (fish platters or Italian food), served at reasonable prices under supervision of Vittorio Grillo, T/F5382545. At the end of the beach track is the 250-room *Casa Marina Bay* resort development, all-inclusive, T5380020, with plans for time share apartments and golf courses, sports centres etc. Lovely location on its own reef-protected bay surrounded by palm trees, quiet, peaceful, kayaks, calm water, shallow for kids.

Sleeping

Behind the dive shop is *Jardín Tropical*, restaurant and bar, daily specials US$5.*L' Aventura*, good pizza for US$4.50. *Chez Denise*, T5380219. French food, crêpes, salads, from US$3.50. *El Marinique*, restaurant and *cabañas* west along the beach under palm trees, sea view from the restaurant, no beach, simple accommodation. Locals eat at the mini-*comedores* on the beach at the end of the road where the *guaguas* stop, not recommended for hygiene but plenty of local colour. You can find boatmen here for trips to other beaches.

Eating
Good food at the hotels

Diving *Dive Samaná*, T/F5380001, at the end of the road on your left by the beach, run by Peter Traubel, boat *Highlander* takes 24 passengers or 12 divers, great diving, CMAS, no jetty, no service so load your own gear, no shade on board, good new rental equipment. Also **coastal excursions**, **snorkelling trips**, boat transfers to Rincón and **whale watching** US$40 in season with underwater microphone.

Sport

Codetel is next to a small supermarket, *De Todo Un Poco*, which stocks the basics including lots of rum. Further up the road there is a Supermercado. An *artesanía* sells lots of Haitian-style art and stylized beach pictures by 'Adolfo'. *Tricom*, *Caribe Tours* and *Western Union Cambio* are by the Spanish restaurant *El Pescador*. At the entrance to the village on the right as you come in is Rancho Galeras (horse hire) and a disco.

Directory

Dominican Republic

Las Terrenas

On the north coast of the peninsula is Las Terrenas, with some of the finest beaches in the country, from which, at low tide, you can walk out to coral reefs to see abundant sea life. The region is frequently visited by divers, drawn by its excellent reefs, sponges and underwater caves. Insect repellent is necessary at dawn and dusk to combat the sandflies. Many people go there by private plane, but it is reachable by a paved 17-km road from Sánchez which zig-zags steeply up to a height of 450 m with wonderful views before dropping down to the north coast. The road Samaná-Las Terrenas via Limón was being paved in 2000. Las Terrenas village is developing rapidly to cope with the influx of tourists: the wooden houses are being replaced by concrete ones; in high season (December-April, July-August) there is a lot of traffic noise; the beaches, except Playa Bonita, are sometimes crowded, but they are mostly clean and remain beautiful. Out of season it is very pleasant. Horseriding can be arranged through *El Portillo* or *Tropic Banana* (stables run by Luc, who is Swiss) on healthy, well-schooled animals, for beach or mountain rides.

Around Las Terrenas Where the road reaches the shore, at the cemetery in Las Terrenas village, a left turn takes you along a sandy track that winds between coconut palms alongside the white sand beach for about 5 km, past many French and Italian-run guest-houses and restaurants. At the end of the beach, walk behind a rocky promontory to reach Playa Bonita, with hotels, guest houses and restaurants; there are apartments beside *Hotel Atlantis*. Beyond the western tip of this beach is the deserted Playa Cosón, a magnificent 6-km arc of white sand and coconut groves ending in steep wooded cliffs (1½ hour walk or US$1 on *motoconcho*), an Italian development is planned here. A right turn at Las Terrenas takes you along a potholed road about 4 km to the largest hotel in the area, *El Portillo* (see above), which looks rather out of place, being a large multistorey building. The airstrip is behind it on the other side of the road. 10 km further on is **El Limón**, a farming village on the road across the peninsula to Samaná. This is a very pretty route and lots of places offer horses for hire along the roadside. From El Limón you can ride or hike for an hour into the hills to a 50 m high waterfall and swim in a pool of green water at its foot. The **Cascada del Limón** was made a National Monument in 1996. Behind the falls is a small cave. The landscape between the village and the falls is beautiful, with many different fruits growing in the woods. If taking a guide to the falls, fix the price in advance (the falls can be deserted, do not take valuables there). In 1998 access to the falls was regulated to prevent erosion and other ecological damage; it is now prohibited to visit other than on foot or on horseback. Guides are now regulated and work on a cooperative basis. *Motoconcho* Las Terrenas – El Limón US$2.50, but they will try to charge US$5-10.

Sleeping
Most hotels are small; those on beach have prices ranging up to 'B', but those in town or behind those on the beach can be very cheap

Cacao Beach, T2406000, F2406020, east of *Tropic Banana*. All-inclusive, 181 rooms, biggest hotel, sailing boats for rent. **A-B** per person, *Aligio*, T2406255, F2406169. Italian, all-inclusive, pool, dive centre, good beach, attractive, pretty, leafy gardens, nice pool, peaceful, good. **C** *Tropic Banana*, T2406110. 25 rooms, breakfast included, tennis, coaching available, pool, fans, screened windows, balconies, one of the larger guest houses, good value food, popular bar with live merengue nightly. **B-C** *Las Cayenas*, T2406080, west end of Las Terrenas, beach front. Nice hotel run by Swiss-French lady, Marie Antoinette Piguet, rooms with or without balcony including breakfast and taxes, also large room for 4, good value. On Playa Bonita (see below) are **B-C** *Atlantis*, T2406111, F2406205. Breakfast included, French-run with excellent French cuisine, chef used to work for President Mittérand. **C-D** *Acaya*, Playa Bonita, T2406161, F2406166. Two buildings on the beach, 16 rooms, hot water, fan, terrace, dive shop, nice atmosphere, good breakfast and thatched restaurant, international menu with specialities like meat and fish fondue. **C-D** *Palo Coco*, on main road at entrance to Las Terrenas. Good. **E** *Casa Grande*, right on beach. Friendly, run by 2 German women, good kitchen, nice location. **C-D** *Kanesh*, at end of west track to beach, T2406187, F2406233. Run by Tamil/Swiss, some rooms cheaper. **B** *El Portillo*, 5 km east of cemetery, T2406100, F2406104. 171 rooms and cabins, no a/c, secluded, used by Spanish package holidays, own airstrip, good snorkelling, watersports, tennis, horseriding, bicycles, entertainment, large grounds on huge beach, uncrowded, all-inclusive; all 3 are on beach and have swimming pools. **D** *Castello Beach*, run by Dominicans, service criticized, includes breakfast, beachfront, pool, diving school. **E** *Aloha*, run by Spanish, includes breakfast, T2406287. **E** *Casas del Mar*, run by French, includes breakfast. **E-F** *L'Aubergine*, T2406167, F2406070. Price depends on room and number of people, run by French Canadians, near *Cacao* and beach, quieter than hotels on beach, very good, restaurant closed Sun. **C-E** *Villa Caracol*, along from *L'Aubergine*. Clean, friendly, quiet. **E** *Papagayo*, T2406131, on beach road. Rather noisy beside disco, good, bath, clean, fans, screened windows, breakfast included, small bar and restaurant, dive shop on site. **E** *Casa Robinson*, set back from beach, 200m from village centre,T2406070. Also rather noisy, double rooms with shower and terrace or small suites with kitchenettes and balconies. **E** *Los Pinos*, Swiss-run, family atmosphere, clean, excellent, large rooms with mosquito nets, shared bath, nice balcony, new restaurant, a steakhouse also serving meat fondues, helpful, transport to Sánchez can be arranged. **E** *La Louisiane*, T2406223, F2406070. French-run, 5 rooms, some with kitchen, good value, reduced rates for long stays. **F** *Dinny*, on the beach, clean, central, noisy all night, near the main junction, ask for quieter room away from road. **E** *Casa Nina*, turn right for 800 m along the beach in Las Terrenas. French-run, renovated, cosy cabins. **F** *Casa de los Tres Locos*, on the way to Playa Bonita. Nice bungalows in huge garden, Austrian-run. *Coyamar*, 1st hotel at Playa Bonita, German-run, 12 rooms, nice, cosy, beachfront, friendly, helpful. Each hotel has its own electricity generator and water supply.

Eating

Paco Cabana, French, very good, nice bar. The restaurant in *Hotel Palo Coco* is Spanish-run with daily menu for US$5.50 with glass of wine and dessert. *Pizzería al Coco*, Playa Bonito, next to *Mambo* disco. Good pizzas, Swiss-run, excellent Swiss food, nice atmosphere, also **C** bungalows to rent for 1-3 people. By the beach in the grounds of *Hotel Las Cayenas*, but independent, is *La Parrilla*, friendly, good food, open air or under thatched roof, also bar; *La Campanina*, next to *Hotel Aligio*. Good Italian food. *Aubergine*, next to *Hotel Cacao Beach*. Canadian-run, excellent seafood, fine French cuisine, also pizzas and some Chinese dishes. *Iñaki & Isabel*, between *Salsa* and *Casa Papón*. Pueblo de los Pescadores, best seafood in town, fresh daily, nice little restaurant right by the sea, friendly, owners are Basque. *Dinny*, beach front. Good Dominican food, serves excellent breakfast with *jugos* and lots of fresh fruit. *Bar Janine*, German-run, good food, good prices. *Indiana Café*, next to *Iñaki & Isabel*. Meeting point, nice seafront spot with good atmosphere, serves Mexican food. *Casa Azul*, Swiss/Dominican-run, sandwiches, salads, Spanish tortilla, hamburgers, good for breakfast, lunch or dinner, on beach by main junction. *Casa Papón*, right by the sea. Good food. *La Salsa*, thatched roof restaurant on the beach near *Trópico Banana*. French-owned, expensive. *Sin Fronteras*, on the main road. Sandwich place. Recommended. *Louisiana*, small bar, French-run, lovely spot. *Suni*, Dominican food, cheap and good on Calle Principal. Small places along main street may have only 1-2 items on menu but food is usually good and much cheaper than a restaurant. *La Crêperie*, esq Pacot. *Hemingway Café*, Centro Paseo. French-run, good food. *Sucresale*, at the main road. French bakery, breakfast and pastries. *Le Saigon*, next to the Police station. Vietnamese-run, Vietnamese and Chinese food, very good.*Havana Café*, in the new Centro Casa Linda in front of the cemetery. Nice food. *Le Piaf*, a bar at the *pueblo de los pescadores* on the beach. Also at the *pueblo de los pescadores*, *Pizza Playa*, very good pizzas, fish and other dishes.

Nightlife

Popular disco is *Mambo Bar*, next to *Papagayo*, open weekends only, also *Tibidabo* and *Nuevo Mundo*.

Sport

The *Cacao Beach* rents sailboats. There are several dive shops, including one at *Tropic Banana*, T5899410, courses available, one of the best for watersports. Windsurfing and sailing are mostly only available at the all-inclusive resorts but equipment can be rented at the Pura Vida office, between the cemetery and Paco Cabana. Diving schools at the *Kanesh Hotel*, the *Castello Beach* (Alex Abbas) and the *Bahía Las Ballenas* hotel, Playa Bonita. Tennis lessons at *Tropic Banana*, 0900-1100, US$13.50 1 hr, US$20 2 hrs, sparring partner US$6.50 per hour.

Dominican Republic

Transport **Road** *Caribe Tours* stops in Sánchez on the way to Samaná, from Santo Domingo or Puerto Plata, in Sánchez T5382229. You will be met by *moto conchos* who will take you and your luggage over the hill to Las Terrenas, spectacular if it is not raining, the less luggage the better, US$3 to the *guagua* stop, up to US$4.50 to a hotel further along the beach. A taxi (minibus) Sánchez-Las Terrenas costs US$20, Samaná-Las Terrenas US$47. Note that *guaguas* which meet arriving **Caribe Tours** buses in Sánchez overcharge for the journey to Las Terrenas (US$4.75-9.50). You can get along the coast by *guagua* from Cabarete to Las Terrenas via Río San Juan, Nagua and Sánchez, US$1.50 for each stage, but **Caribe Tours** is more comfortable. *Motoconchos* wizz up and down the road through the village and weave their way along the beach track, RD$10-15 depending on how far you go. They are twice the price of what you pay in Samaná for local journeys and 50% more expensive for longer trips, eg Samaná-Las Terrenas RD$100, Las Terrenas-Samaná RD$150 after much negotiation.

Directory **Banks** *Baninter* in centro comercial in the middle of the village. *Banco del Progreso* has an ATM but it is not always working. *Crediprogreso* in the centre Paseo down by the cemetery. *Agencia de Viajes Vimenca*, Remeses Vimenca, on the main road. *Western Union* for fast money transfers, exchanges money at the best rates in town. Another *casa de cambio* near *Tropic Banana*. **Useful addresses** For tourist information and hotel booking service go to *Sunshine Services*, Calle del Carmen, T/F2406164, run by Swiss; Spanish, English, German, French and Italian spoken. Lots of information and help, also car and motorbike rental, excursions (about 25), fishing and boat trips. *La Casa de las Terrenas*, Calle Principal, T/F2406251, casater.resa@codetel.net.do, can also help with information, tours, bookings etc. **Communications** *Codetel* has a phone and fax office, open daily 0800-2200, credit cards accepted. There is now an internet café, *CCL Comuni-Centro Las Terrenas*, at the junction where the road forks take the left fork heading for the beach, it is on your right, upstairs, RD$10/5 mins, printout RD$2, phone Europe RD$15/1 min, post cards, cambio downstairs. In many shops they sell 'express' stamps which are more expensive but the delivery time is not much shorter. Large new supermarket, *Tío Billy*, in the centro comercial. There is a petrol/gasoline station. Motorbikes (US$15-25) and mountain bikes (no brakes) can be hired. Jeep rental US$60.

East from Santo Domingo

The eastern end of the island is generally flatter than the rest of the island, although the hills of the Cordillera Oriental are attractive and provide some great views. Cattle and sugar cane are the predominant agricultural products and this is definitely cowboy country. However, much of the sugar land has been turned over to more prosperous activities such as tourism, the *Casa de Campo* development being a prime example. There are fewer forests here and the climate is drier. Palm trees have been planted along the coast, which is fringed with white sand beaches, making it very attractive for mass tourism. A new *autopista* has been built all along the coast from Santo Domingo to La Romana. Most of it is already open, cutting journey times considerably. However, avoid driving at night, traffic is fast and many drivers do not dip their headlights.

Boca Chica

Do not visit at the weekend About 25 km east of Santo Domingo is the beach of Boca Chica, the principal resort for the capital. It is a reef-protected shallow lagoon, with many kilometres of white sand. Offshore are the islands of La Matica and Pinos. Tourist development has been intensive and, at weekends, the place is invaded by the citizens of Santo Domingo (and by attendant hawkers, disreputables and prostitutes – locals refer to it as Boca SIDA, AIDS in Spanish). There are a great many hotels, aparthotels and restaurants of different standards with lots of bars and nightlife. Vendors line the main road, selling mostly Haitian paintings of poor quality but they are colourful. Efforts have been made to clean up the town, with residents being encouraged to paint their houses, streets have been paved and pavements restored. The main street is closed to traffic at night and the restaurants move their tables on to the road. It is worth considering staying here if arriving at the airport late at night, rather than looking for a hotel in the capital. Prices are generally higher here than at the north coast resorts.

LL-AL *Coral Hamaca Beach Hotel & Casino*, T5234611, F5236767, PO Box 2973, Santo Domingo. Vast pink resort hotel, *Hamaca Garden* with 383 rooms and *Hamaca Beach* with 240 rooms, all-inclusive. **L** *Boca Chica Resort Beach Club*, T5632000, F5635236. All-inclusive, 437 rooms, bright orange and white, memorable. On same road as *Sun Set* and *Hamaca* (Calle Duarte at eastern end of town) is **C-D** *Mesón Isabela*, T5234224, F5234136, in room, more in apartment without tax. French-Canadian and Dominican owned, bar, pool, family atmosphere, quiet, personal service, breakfast, light lunches on request, across road to beach, cookers in some rooms. Next door is **C-D** *Neptuno's Club Guest House* (for restaurant, see below), with bath, free coffee, very satisfactory. **C** *Calypso Beach Hotel*, Calle Caracol esquina 20 de Diciembre, T5234666, F5234829. Not on beach, but close, some rooms overlook small pool, new, well kept, pleasant, lots of plants, small bar, restaurant, billiards. **C-D** *Villa Sans Souci*, Juan Batista Vicini 48, T5234461, F5234136. Includes tax, clean, beautiful, pool, restaurant, bar. **A-B** *Sun Set*, T5234580, F5234975. Opposite is **E** *Mozart*, bargaining possible, rooms remodelled but airless, friendly, nice hot tub. **C-D** and up *Las Kasistas del Sol*, Primera y 2 de Junio, away from beach, T5234386, F5236056. Pool, restaurant, clean, beautiful setting, good service, friendly. **D-E** *La Belle*, Calle Juan Bautista Vicini 9, T5235959, F5235077, on corner of highway. Very nice, a/c, pool, colour TV, permanent water and electricity (but may be turned off in low season when quiet). **C-D** *Mango*, near Calle Juan Bautista Vicini, T5235333. Fan, TV, pool, nice garden. **C-F** *Villa Don*, Calle Juan Bautista Vicini 11, T/F5234679. Variety of rooms, private or shared bathroom, apartment with kitchen, discounts for long stays, some with TV, a/c, fridge, one or two beds, clean, cheap rooms are basic but adequate, small pool, right by road, bar, credit cards accepted. **F** *Don Paco*, Duarte 6, T5234816. Central, clean, friendly, own generator but not always on if few guests, ask for it to be turned on. The cheapest guest houses are on Avenida Las Américas heading towards the airport, about 1½ km from beach.

Sleeping

L'Horizon is excellent and *Buxeda* is recommended for seafood, especially *centolla* (crab). Also recommended is *Neptuno's Club*, T5234703, F5234251, east of *El Hamaca*. Built over water, with pier, good fish watching, swimming rafts, seafood, German-owned, menu is German and English, 0900-2230, closed Mon, reservations essential, now has replica of the *Santa María* for trips along the beach. Other good restaurants are *Casa Marina*, *Porto Fino*, *Pequeña Suiza*. On the beach *fritureras* sell typical dishes, among them the famous *yaniqueques* – Johnny cakes. There is a good all-night, palm-covered burger hut where people gather for late-night satellite TV entertainment.

Eating

Dominican Republic southeast coast

Dominican Republic

Nightlife There are numerous quaint bars for couples on Calle Duarte. In the same area is plenty of variety for unattached males, but beware of pickpockets; otherwise safe.

Transport **Road** **Taxi**: Santo Domingo-Boca Chica US$25, US$15 from the airport, *guagua* US$1 from either Parque Enriquillo or Parque Independencia, or the corner of San Martín and Avenida París but not after dark. If driving from the capital, look carefully for signposts to whichever part of Boca Chica you wish to go.

Directory **Banks** *Banco Popular* will change TCs at good rates. There are several exchange houses.

Juan Dolio

The Guayacanes, Embassy and Juan Dolio beaches, east of Boca Chica, are also popular, especially at weekends when they can be littered and plagued with hawkers (much cleaner and very quiet out of season). The whole area is being developed in a long ribbon of holiday homes, hotels and resorts, and a new highway is improving access. **Los Guayacanes** has a nice little beach and the village is less overcrowded than Boca Chica. Buses going along the south coast will drop you, and pick you up again, at the various turn-offs to the beaches. **Juan Dolio** village is low key, with hotels, apartments, a few small bars, a tour agency and dive shop. Tourist taxis from the Juan Dolio hotels charge US$44 for a return trip to Santo Domingo with a three-hour wait. Taxi to the airport US$20 one-way (T5262006).

Inland from this stretch of coast, if you want a change from sea bathing, there is the recommended *balneario* at **Santo Cristo de Bayaguana**, some 45 km from the capital. New Year's Day is the start of religious and folkloric festivities in honour of Santo Cristo, kept in the church of Bayaguana, including bull fights.

Sleeping **Los Guayacanes** **C** per person *Playa Esmeralda*, Paseo Vicini, T5263434, F5261744,
& eating www.playa-esmeralda.com All-inclusive, thatched stone hotel on nice beach, shallow like Boca Chica and protected by reef, nice gardens, pool, quiet, low key, but beach can get busy at weekends with Dominicans from the capital, diving. **C-D** *Sol-y-Mar*, Calle Central 23, T5262514. Includes breakfast, very clean big rooms, own beach, helpful, French/Canadian-run, overpriced restaurant. **C-D** *Woody's Guesthouse & Deli*, Calle Central. Small beach, restaurant, Swiss owner, T5261226. Cheaper is *Las Brisas*, family-run, also on Calle Central. A recommended restaurant is *El Refugio de los Desperados*, near Auberge Sol-y-Mar. Basic but excellent cooking, try fresh lobster with pasta for US$4.50.

Juan Dolio All the large hotels are all-inclusive and offer pools, tennis, sports facilities, restaurants, bars and entertainment: *Meliá Juan Dolio*, T5261521, F5262184. 270 rooms, spa fitness centre. *Caribbean Village Decameron*, T5262009, F5261430. 300 rooms, casino. *Caribbean Village Tropics*, same phones, 139 rooms. *Coral Costa Caribe*, T5262244, F5263141. 492 big rooms, good bathrooms, gardens full of palm trees, pretty pool, 4 restaurants, bars, nice beach with shade, artificial reef. Roped off swimming area, tennis, watersports, many limited to 1 hr daily, diving, casino, variable nightly entertainment, excursions, a popular resort. *Metro Hotel & Marina*, T5262811, F5261808. 223 rooms, golf, not on the beach, other side of autopista. *Talanquera Country & Beach Resort*, T5261510, F5262408. 508 rooms, suites and villas, 5 pools, 150 m of beach, PADI 5-star dive facility, shuttle to country club with riding, caves, archery, golf course. Near *Metro* is La Llave Plaza with Italian, German, Spanish restaurants, a minimarket, gift shop and travel agent. The road between the beach and the highway is in poor condition; on it are **C-D** *Ramada Guesthouse*, T5263310, F5262512. Meals US$18.50 FAP, pool, disco bar, watersports; opposite is *Marco's* restaurant and bar, German. There is a good selection of modern, modestly-priced apartments for rent, by day, week, month or year, eg *Yamina*, T5261123 (operated by Villas del Mar Realty, reliable).

East of Juan Dolio is the resort of Villas del Mar, with *Barceló Capella Beach Resort*, T5261080, F5261088. 283 rooms, all-inclusive, pools, lots of watersports, including scuba

Discovery of a long-lost city

In 1997 archaeologists working in the Parque Nacional del Este revealed they had found the remains of a substantial Taino settlement with three large ceremonial plazas, which could have supported thousands of people in pre-Columbian times.

The missionary Bartolomé de las Casas described the destruction of a city in 1503 and it is believed it could be the same one.

The attack had been provoked by the killing of a few Spaniards, provoked in turn by the death of an Indian chief when a Spaniard's hunting dog was unleashed on him as his people were loading bread onto a Spanish ship.

The site, known as La Aleta, surrounds a cenote, or limestone sinkhole, where divers have recovered carved wooden axes, baskets, ornate pottery and other artifacts thrown in the water. It is believed to be a ceremonial site. The plazas, or ball courts are 68 m long, 14 m wide and lined by 1½ m tall limestone blocks. Kitchen areas have also been found, complete with stones used to grind oyster shells embedded with fragments of shell.

diving and fishing, tennis, bikes, games room, restaurants, golf packages. At Km 11 on the road to San Pedro de Macorís, Villas del Mar, is **L** *Occidental Playa Real*, T5261114, F5261623, h.preal@codetel.net.do All-inclusive, 390 rooms and suites. There are also several apartment developments.

San Pedro de Macorís
Population: 86,950

On the Río Higuamo, this is an industrial sea port whose economy is heavily dependent on the sugar estates which surround it. It is the third largest city. Tourist development is also under way here. Facing the river is the neo-classical cathedral, San Pablo Apostolo, with a tower which can be seen all over town. In the city is the Universidad Central del Este and a baseball stadium. Many baseball players have gone on from here to play in the US Major Leagues. There is a marked cultural influence from immigrants from the Leeward and Windward Islands, known as *cocolos*, especially in the dances called *guloyas*. Another name is *momise*, which derives from the English mummer tradition; dance-dramas known as *la danza salvaje* (the wild dance), *la danza del padre invierno* (the dance of Father Winter, which imitates the St George and the Dragon legend) and *la danza de El Codril* take place on 29 June, St Peter, and other festivals. For further information T5293600 (Ayuntamiento) or 5293309 (provincial government).

Sleeping and eating **B** *Howard Johnson Hotel Macorix*, Calle Gastón F Deligne, T5292100, F5299239. All-inclusive, 170 rooms, pool, tennis, 3 restaurants, executive floor, well-kept gardens. Outside town, on the way to La Romana, 2km down a side road through sugar cane, is *Santana Beach*, all-inclusive, new in 1999. 400 rooms, 600 more planned, low-rise buildings painted yellow and white, around large pool. Mock Dominican village also being built with a disco, shops, chapel and tennis courts nearby. Lots of activities, horse riding, quad bikes, bicycles, wave runners, windsurfing, diving, water skiing, beach being improved with imported sand, lots of palm trees and shade, shallow sea, good for children, buffet or three à la carte restaurants. *Robby Mar*, Calle Domínguez Charro 35, T5294926, turn right at roundabout at entrance to San Pedro when coming from Santo Domingo, continue to bridge, restaurant signed just before bridge. Recommended fresh seafood.

Transport Several bus terminals with scheduled services to Santo Domingo, La Romana and other eastern towns. *Guaguas* for Sabana de la Mar (ferry to Samaná) leave from near the baseball stadium and are very full, you may have to share a seat. It is not possible to go directly to Sabana de la Mar, you have to change in Hato Mayor, from where the scenery is wonderful but the road badly potholed.

Dominican Republic

La Romana
Population: 101,350

East of San Pedro is La Romana. The city has a large Parque Central which is being remodelled, a job which looks like taking some time. The church of Santa Rosa de Lima is on a little rise, fronted by a small park, close to Parque Central. One block behind the church is the Mercado Modelo and most buses leave from here. The central commercial area is large, the town spread out. It is a sugar town, with railways to carry the harvest to the docks. La Romana can be reached by air (international airport) and by bus or *público* from Santo Domingo (US$2). If driving from the capital, at the western edge of La Romana, by a large stadium, the road forks three ways: sharp right for Higüey and Parque Nacional del Este; the middle road, bearing right, for the town centre; straight on for Guaymate.

Sleeping C *Aby's*, Calle Amatista 6, T5565887, F5665047. Rooms or suites with kitchens, best rooms upstairs, good view over town to river and sea, too much furniture makes rooms feel small, but comfortable, tiny shower, all rooms different, tiny pool, bar, restaurant, small breakfast and taxes included in price, quiet suburban area but dogs bark all night. **D-E** *Olimpo*, Av Padre Abreu esq Pedro A Lluberes, T5507646, F5507647. 56 large rooms, 1 suite, very spacious, breakfast included, price negotiable for longer stays, simple but clean, hot water, safes in room, fridge, bottled water, phone, TV, laundry services, parking, security, can be noisy at night depending on where your room faces, train horns, *motoconchos*, mock-Greek décor in public areas, restaurant serving Dominican and international food, 0600-1500, 1800-2300. **F** *Frano*, Av Padre Abreu. 21 rooms, with a/c, less without, inconveniently located away from main plaza and restaurants. 500 m away is **F** *Bolívar*, as good. *Hotel y Cabañas Tío Tom*, 4½ km before town on road from capital, T5566212, F5566201. 2 standards of cabin, **E** with fan and **D** with a/c, bar, good but restaurant below average, separate pizzería, pool, hot water, disco, taxi from La Romana US$8.45. About 2 km closer to town is **F** *Andanamay*, T5566102, with bath and fan. **F** *San Santiago*, Calle Hernández, with bath.

Eating *Pizza Alondra*, T5504115, 1 block from square towards the river. Outdoor seating, pleasant at night, pizzas US$3.50-14.50, and a few other dishes, *empanadas, tostones*, open Mon 1600-2400, Tue-Sun 1000-2400.

Directory **Communications:** *Codetel* is on the main square, internet access US$2 per hour, but not always working. *Tricom* one block southwest of square.

Casa de Campo

This is the premier tourist centre in the Republic. The resort was built in 1974 by Charles Bluhdorn, the founder of Gulf & Western, which originally grew sugar cane on the land. After he died the Cuban-American family Fanjul bought it and opened it to paying guests. It is currently operated by Premier Resorts and is kept isolated from the rest of the country behind strict security. It is vast, exclusive, with miles of luxury villas surrounded by beautifully tended gardens full of bougainvillea and coleus of all colours. A new marina is being built at the mouth of the Río Chavón, known as Boca Chavón, from where you can take boat trips up the river. **LL** *Casa de Campo*, 10 km to the east of La Romana, PO Box 140, La Romana, T5233333, F5238548, www.casadecampo.cc: Hotel, villas, bars, restaurants and country club with private airport, many sporting facilities (on land and sea), including golf courses, 13 tennis courts and polo fields (150 horses for all types of riding activity), in 7,000 acres. The Playa Minitas beach is within the complex, but this is surprisingly small and can get crowded.

Altos de Chavón

Altos de Chavón is an international artists' village in mock-Italian style built by an Italian cinematographer near La Romana, in a spectacular hilltop setting above the gorge through which flows the Río Chavón. Students from all over the world come to the art school, but the village is now a major tourist attraction and is linked to *Casa de Campo*. There are several restaurants of a variety of nationalities, expensive shops, art gallery, disco, and the Church of St Stanislaus, finished in 1979 and consecrated by Pope John Paul II, which contains the ashes of Poland's patron saint and statue from Krakow. There is also an excellent little **Museo Arqueológico Regional**, with explanations in Spanish and English and lots of information about the Taínos, open 0900-1700 (free) and an amphitheatre for open air concerts which was inaugurated with a show by Frank Sinatra (many international stars perform there, eg Julio Iglesias, Gloria Estefan, as well as the best Dominican performers). There is a free bus every 15 minutes from *Casa de Campo*. Carros públicos from La Romana to *Casa de Campo* US$0.20. Taxi from La Romana US$15-20.

Off La Romana is the Isla Catalina. Although inland the southeast part of the island is dry, flat and monotonous, the beaches have fine, white sand with some of the best bathing in waters protected by reefs and excellent diving. *Costa Lines* run excursions for the day (they call it Serena Cay), travel agents also run tours for US$30-68 including lunch, supper and drinks; T5857887, Martisant, cheapest, or Turinter, Insular, Prieto (T6850102), most expensive. Cruise ships also call at the island, disgorging some 98,000 passengers in a winter season. New rules were announced in 1996 to protect the ecology of the island, which is under the permanent supervision of the Dominican Navy and the Ministry of Tourism. All works that may affect the vegetation have been prohibited and work on building sun shades for tourists has been suspended, although *Costa Cruise Line* is still permitted to expand the beach area for its passengers' use. The island's flora and fauna is to be catalogued with a view to incorporating it into the Sistema Natural de Areas Protegidas. The Río Chavón area east of La Romana and Casa de Campo was declared a protected zone at the end of 1995 to safeguard a large area of red and black mangroves.

Isla Catalina

Bayahibe is a fishing village on a small bay in a region of dry tropical forest and cactus. It is reached by a road which turns off the highway to Higüey (*carro público* La Romana-Bayahibe US$2.50, or take a Higüey bus to the turnoff and take a *motoconcho*, US$1). The fishing village is a great place to stay, with excursions, diving, budget lodgings and cafés. Small wooden houses and the green wooden church of the village are on a point between the little bay and an excellent, 1½ km curving white sand beach fringed with palms. Plenty of fishing and pleasure boats are moored in the bay and it is from here that boats depart for Isla Saona. At the end of the bay, however, is one of the all-inclusive resorts which have been built along the coast, east and west of the village, pushing at the boundaries of the national park to the east. **Isla Saona** is a picture book tropical island with palm trees and white sandy beaches, set in a protected national park. However it is also an example of mass tourism, which conflicts with its protected status. Every day 1,000 tourists are brought on catamarans, speed boats or smaller *lanchas*, for a swim, a buffet lunch on the beach and departure around 1500 with a stop off at the 'swimming pool' a patch of waist-deep water on a sand bank. The trip is very popular and large quantities of rum are consumed, but the sea looks like rush hour when the boats come and go. If you arrange a trip independently on a smaller boat, the local association of boat owners assures uniform prices. The all-inclusive resorts have their own dive operations, but there is an independent dive shop in Bayahibe, *Scubafun*, run by Germans, Werner and Martina Marzilius, T3016999. Their clients range from *Casa de Campo* guests to backpackers, beginners to experienced divers. They are very flexible and will do almost anything on request. It is a short walk from their shop to the boat and there is no jetty, but they take all your equipment on board. Wear shoes when you go in the water as there is broken glass. Some of the best diving in the country is in this area, in the National Park, and although local fishermen are still spearfishing, the reef is in good condition and there are plenty of fish, more in some areas than others. Dolphins are often seen from the boat, while underwater you find sharks and rays off Catalinita Island, east of Saona, reef sharks at La Parguera, west of Saona, the wreck of *St George* close to the *Dominicus* and fresh water caves inland for experienced divers. Two-tank dives with a beach stop cost US$56-75, depending on the distance, a trip to Saona, Catalina or Catalinita, including national park fees, drinks and

Bayahibe
About 25 km east of La Romana

Dominican Republic

snacks, costs US$75-100. Rental equipment includes underwater cameras and scooters. A day trip to Saona Island costs US$44.

Sleeping *Amhsa Casa del Mar*, T2218880, F2218881, amhsa@codetel.net.do, west of the village, landmark blue roofs. 568 rooms, all-inclusive, 4 restaurants, watersports, gym, children's activities, lots of sports. East of Bayahibe are: *Club Viva Dominicus*, T6865658, F6878583. 500 rooms, all-inclusive, loads of facilities and entertainment, some rooms in thatched bungalows like *bohíos*. *Coral Canoa Beach Hotel*, T5626725, F5620660. 558 rooms, all-inclusive, 800 m from Parque Nacional del Este, lots of activities but some rationed to 1 hr a day, seminars on Taíno culture, excursions into the park. Cheaper lodgings are in the village itself. **E** *Hotel Bayahibe*, T7073684, F5564513. New, best in village, rooms have 2 beds, bathroom, hot water, fan, balcony, restaurant, cafetería, right by the water and dive boats. *Cabañas* for rent, for as little as US$10, ask around, don't expect hot water; **E-F** Doña Olga's are good. Also **F** *Cabañas Trip Town*, T7073640. Clean, private bathroom, on main street, near beach.

Eating *Big Sur*, on the beach, Italian-owned, great food. *Restaurante La Punta*, seafood. *Café Caribe*, breakfasts and other meals. *Adrian café* and restaurant. *La Bahía*, fish dishes, international calls, main street, on the beach. *Cafetería Yulissa*, good breakfast, recommended. *El Oasis*, also recommended for breakfast.

San Rafael de Yuma East of Bayahibe on the road from Higüey to the coast, is San Rafael de Yuma, an unremarkable town but the location of one of the oldest fortified houses (*casa fortaleza*) built in 1505-1508 by Indian slaves for Ponce de León. The **Casa de Ponce de León** is known locally as **Las Ruinas**, but in fact it has been restored and is in excellent health. The building is tall, with two floors, square, stone with a tiled roof. Large wooden doors face away from the approach to the house, which is set in pleasant gardens. Inside there is some mahogany furniture, a bed, a desk and some items supposedly belonging to Ponce de León. The guardian will give you a tour (for a tip) if you want. A tunnel used to run a long way underground into what is now a sugar cane field. To get there, turn left in the town, take the unpaved road past the primary school and drive for 1km to the entrance, which is on the right by an electricity pole. There is no sign.

Boca de Yuma On the coast at the mouth of the Río Yuma, is Boca de Yuma, a fishing village which has seen better days. Hurricane damage has left it a very sad place and there is no evidence of improvement. Everything is for sale. The coastline is rocky and there are islets offshore, with tunnels made by the waves. From the cove at the east end of the village you can get a rowing boat ferry across the Río Yuma for RD$10, and walk along a stony path (quite hard work) to a nice beach. Alternatively you can hire a motor boat to take you straight there, but make sure you arrange a collection time. It used to be possible to take trips a long way up river, but since the hurricane you can only go about 1 ½ km. West of the village the road passes the cemetery and then turns right for the Cueva de Verna, a cave with a big chamber, but you are not allowed far in. It is believed that the cave system goes as far as Bayahibe, you can hear an underground river and there are lots of bats. If you go in the mornings you have to pay at the DNP hut, but in the afternoons it is often free. The track is very rough, better to walk.

Sleeping **E-F** *Club El 28*, T2230503, on the right as you come into the village, on the hill with view of sea. Nine cabañas with bath, but full with long-term rentals in 2000, very murky pool, Italian restaurant, quiet, run down, the only public telephone, fax and satellite TV. **F** *dormitorio Justina* in town, on road parallel to the sea, one block inland, very cheap, very basic and not secure. Some *cabañas* on the waterfront have been blown away and there are lots of empty houses which used to be holiday homes. Better to stay elsewhere and come on a day trip. There are a couple of small restaurants in shacks on the seafront, nothing special, snack bars, *comedores*.

The main town in the far east of the island is the modern, dust and concrete Higüey. **Higüey**
The focal point of interest is the **Basílica de Nuestra Señora de la Altagracia**
(patroness of the Republic), which can be seen for miles away. It is a very impressive
modern building in a huge park surrounded by a wall, to which every year there is a
pilgrimage on 21 January; the statue of the virgin and a silver crown are in a glass case
on the altar and are paraded through the streets at the end of the fiesta. According to
legend, the Virgin appeared in 1691 in an orange tree to a sick girl. Oranges are conveniently in season in January and huge piles of them are sold on the streets, while
statues made of orange wood are also in demand. The Basilica was started by Trujillo
in 1954, but finished by Balaguer in 1972. The architects were French, the stained
glass is French, the bronze doors (1988) are Italian, portraying the history of the
Dominican Republic. The theme throughout is of the orange tree, with wood of the
orange tree used extensively. People wearing shorts are not allowed to enter. The old
17th-century church, which used to be the site of the pilgrimage is still standing,
having been restored at the beginning of the 20th century after earthquake damage.
On the square outside are a cinema, a *casa de cambio*, banks and a restaurant. *Codetel*
is on the Av de la Libertad near the new Basilica. The post office is on Agustín
Guerrero, the street running up to the entrance to the new Basilica.

Sleeping If you come during the fiesta all the best places will be fully booked. The cheap
places will double their prices. At any other time it is hardly worth staying. **C-D** *Hotel Barceló
El Naranjo*, T5543400, F5545455, one block from Basilica on road to El Seibo. A/c café, restaurant, disco, conference centre. *El Topacio*, T5545910. **F** *Brisas del Este* and **F** *Casa Blanca*
are opposite each other by the entrance to the Basilica, prices rise to **D** for the fiesta, when it
is incredibly noisy and you can't sleep anyway, very basic, uncomfortable beds, intermittent
plumbing. On the outskirts of town there are several *cabañas*, available by the hour or **E-F**
overnight (prices rise at weekends), where you pay at a window, its all anonymous, and get a
cabaña, often with garage, with a/c, TV and condoms, eg *Mi Casa*, 3km on the road to La
Romana, others on the road to El Seibo, clean and pleasant.

Eating No good restaurants here, just a few *comedores* near the old basilica, or *Pollos
Victorina* for chicken and chips or *tostones* beside *Hotel El Naranjo*.

Transport Buses from Santo Domingo cost US$4; bus from La Romana US$2.

Due east from Higüey, on the coast again, is Punta Cana which has some beautiful **Punta Cana**
beaches, good diving and an international airport. The Grupo Punta Cana owns most
of the land which is behind a substantial wire fence, awaiting future development.
There are only two resorts and no small hotels. Julio Iglesias and Oscar de la Renta
have built villas in the exclusive Los Corales, but it is all very private. Independent visitors find it difficult to find a public beach as the hotels will not allow non-residents
through their property. The **Marina Punta Cana** has a capacity for 22 yachts and eight
other sailing boats, immigration and customs services provided by officers at the
Punta Cana airport (24 hours' notice required if arriving by sea), guard and watch-
man. International sailing competitions are held here. A golf course was being built in
2000 between the *Club Med* and the *Punta Cana Beach Resort*. Horse riding is also
available at the Rancho Punta Cana, US$24 for a two-hour ride along the beach.

Sleeping There is a *Club Méditerranée*, T5675228, F5652558, PO Box 106, Higüey. 334
rooms, children's clubs, circus school, 10 tennis courts, pool, windsurfing and lots of other
land and watersports. **LL-AL** *Punta Cana Beach Resort*, PO Box 1083, T6870752, F6878745.
400 rooms, beautiful beach, good diving, marina, but sparse public transport. The *Punta
Cana Yacht Club* has villas and one-bedroom apartments, T5653077.

Transport Most people staying at the resorts arrive by plane and only leave the resort on a
tour bus; taxis are very expensive, *Club Med* to airport, US$10, *Club Med* to Bávaro, US$20, if

Dominican Republic

they wait for you the price doubles. There is lots of car rental in the area. Many hotel employees live in Higüey, so there are buses, minibuses and pick-up trucks for US$1.25, but they go to the village rather than the hotels, which are much further along the coast.

Bávaro   Continuing round the coast, there are many other beaches to be visited, with white sand and reef-sheltered water. The area now known as Bávaro was once a series of fishing villages, but they have disappeared under the weight of hotels which contrast with the shacks still hanging on in places. At **Cabeza de Toro**, the most easterly point of the island the local people are trying to benefit from tourism by selling arts and crafts from their huts and there is a Plaza Artesanal where a lot of Haitian art is for sale. In this area are the *Catalonia Bávaro, Allegro Resort Bávaro Grand* and the *Natura Park* hotels. The *Natura Park* (Blau Hotels) is set in protected wetland and mangroves. The hotel beaches have been 'improved' with imported sand, but there is a public beach near the Plaza where there is an outpost of the *Club Náutico de Santo Domingo* (fishing tournaments) and Italian investors are building the *Residencial Guadeloupe*, T5520827, F2210754, as an alternative to the large resorts, with villas, a restaurant and a commercial centre, set back from the beach. Further north is the *Bávaro Beach Resort*, where the Barceló hotel chain has a huge complex with the *Bávaro Garden, Bávaro Golf, Bávaro Casino, Bávaro Beach* and *Bávaro Palace*. It is so big that a little train runs around the complex, which includes a casino, church, golf, tennis, baseball and football pitches. There is a good Mercado Artesanal on the beach, known as Bibijagua, cleverly signed as BI_2JH_2O. You can buy handicrafts, rum, cigars, T-shirts, art etc and there are restaurants and bars to make a change from the all-inclusive lifestyle. Do not buy the shells, turtles and stuffed sharks. You can hire microlites and quad bikes or take a glass bottom boat trip.

At a roundabout further north you have access to the new *Costa Bávaro*, being built in 2000, *Villas Bávaro*, and the Meliá hotels, *Tropical* and *Caribe*. The *Cocotal Golf and Country Club* with lots of villas was also under construction in 2000. Apartments and villas are for rent in this area, there is the new *H10 Bávaro Resort* and the *Hotel Carabella Bávaro* and at the end of the road is **Playa El Cortecito**, where you find bars, restaurants, hostals, *Tricom*, a pharmacy, medical centre and minimarket. *Captain Cook* is a great restaurant on the beach with lots of tables in the shade, they specialize in lobster and shrimp (US$14/lb), but a mixed plate of seafood with fried potatoes and salad washed down with a jug of sangría is recommended, under US$20 for a full meal. Free boat transport from the hotels. Further along the coast are the *Fiesta Bávaro, Fiesta Beach* and *Fiesta Palace*, the *Occidental Flamenco* and the Plaza Bávaro, where there are shops, a disco, Banco Popular, artesanías, Harrison's jewellers and the offices of Manatí Park. Also in this area, the *Meliá Bávaro* and *Paradisus Punta Cana*, one of the most expensive, with peacocks, lagoons and pools. Finally there are three Iberostar hotels and six Ríu hotels, of which the most elegant is the last one, the *Ríu Palace Macao*, designed for families or older couples on a large beach, Playa Arena Gorda, with masses of palm trees for shade. All these hotels are usually booked from abroad as package holidays and most of them are all-inclusive.

The **Manatí Park Bávaro** is a controversial tourist attraction with dolphins (caught and sold by Cuba), sea lions, birds, turtles and dancing horses (Wednesday, Saturday 2145) as well as a replica Taíno village. ■ *0930-1800. US$21 adults, US$10 children. T5520807, F5520810. To swim with the dolphins costs US$65 and must be booked in advance. Tours are available from agencies in Santo Domingo, see newspapers for offers.*

Higüey to Hato Mayor   A road runs west from Higüey to Hato Mayor, via El Seibo, passing through hilly cattle and agricultural land. The 'living fences' are covered in pink blossom in January. After **El Pavón** there are huge sugar cane fields with oxen, trains, *bateyes* where the cutters live and much poverty. There are lots of little villages where you can stop for snacks and fruit and lots of buses. The road is rough either side of **El Seibo** (also spelt El Seybo) and the bridge is down at the entrance to the town. El Seibo is a quiet little town with painted houses, like many others in the region. It is the centre of the cattle business and festivals involve cattle, with bullfighting in May and rodeos occasionally, while cockfighting is popular on Sundays. It has a 16th-century church, the first to be built in the east, with a beautiful brick dome and ceiling. The mother of Juan Pablo Duarte was born here and there is a statue to her outside the church. It is a dusty town, not worth stopping in, but it has two gas stations, Baninter and food shops if you need them. (**F** *Hotel Santa Cruz*, T5523962, on hill above road to Hato Mayor; **F** *Las Mercedes*, clean, quiet, pleasant, no generator; the town's water supply depends on the electricity supply.)

North of El Seibo is **Miches** on the coast, reached by a pretty, twisty road over the mountains. After Pedro Sánchez the road deteriorates and the paving peters out. From the top you can see across to Samaná, lovely views down to the coast with the changing colours of the sea. Miches is a scruffy, muddy village which has not been developed for tourism and the huge beach here is wild, unimproved and goes on for miles. At Miches is **C-D** *Coco Loco Beach Club*, small hotel with 10 bungalows, T5535920, F5535839, www. abatrev.com/cocoloco, seaview, Swiss management, large tropical garden, own fruit and vegetables, restaurant, bar, criollo food. However, it was very run down in 2000 and probably for sale, so phone beforehand. **F** *Hotel Comedor Orfelina* in the village, is one block from the sea on the road running northeast of the parque, basic. *Hotel La Loma* was being built in 2000, expected to open in 2001, up on the hillside with a fabulous view of the coast, will be the most comfortable place to stay. There is a dirt road along the coast from Miches to Sabana de la Mar, which is poor, four wheel drive is recommended, particularly in wet weather. Although some locals race along it, it will take you over an hour if you care for your vehicle.

Hato Mayor is a junction for routes north-south between Sabana de la Mar and San Pedro de Macorís and east to Higüey, with connections for Santo Domingo. It is another dusty town and not much to recommend it other than its transport links. On the square are the church and *Codetel*. *Banco Popular* and *Banco de Reservas* are on Calle Mercedes, the main street, while *Baninter* is on Duarte, the road to Sabana de la Mar. There are a few basic *pensiones* including **F** *Hotel El Centenario* on Calle Las Mercedes, no phone, no keys, girl opens the door for you when necessary, cold water, adequate. The place to be at night is *El Corral*, Calle Mercedes 28, T5532225, thatched wooden and bamboo ranch-type bar and restaurant which plays American-Latin music. Small beer US$1, hamburger US$2, meat dishes up to US$5, quick service for drinks, slow for food because the meat is frozen so you have to wait for it to thaw. Two blocks from the square is a Shell station at Duarte y San Antonio. By the station, on Duarte, *guaguas* leave for Santo Domingo, US$2, and San Pedro de Macorís, US$0.90; on San Antonio they leave for Sabana de la Mar, US$1.55. Driving to Santo Domingo, either take the road to San Pedro de Macorís and turn west along the coast, or take the inland route, Ruta 4, which turns west before San Pedro. This again is sugar country; note the large steam engine in the open space at Ingenio Consuela. Ruta 4 crosses the Río Higuamo by a big bridge with traffic lights by the national cement works. The road continues through sugar cane fields to the capital.

At Km 20 on the road from Hato Mayor to Sabana de la Mar, down a poor track, is *Tropical Plantation*, a flower farm that welcomes visitors. ∎ *Entry US$6.50 with a three-hour tour, US$13.50 including lunch, children half price, restaurant open 0900-1800. T4709673.* **Sabana de la Mar** lies at the east of Parque Nacional Los Haitises and is the ferry port for boats to Samaná across the Bahía de Samaná. A new museum is opening on the waterfront in the same building as the DNP office, which will showcase local flora and fauna. Boatmen will offer to take you on a tour of Los Haitises, anything is negotiable. There are no organized tours of the park from here as there are the other side of the bay. Also along the waterfront are several fish restaurants, a good place to wait for the ferry as you have a view of the boats. The ferry departs at 1100 (sometimes also 1500) and 1700 for Samaná, returning 0900 (1100)

Hato Mayor

Dominican Republic

and 1500 from Samaná, RD$40 one way, which you pay on the boat, but you also have to pay RD$10 to the men who load you. The pier no longer reaches deep water and at low tide you have to clamber aboard a yola, which is pushed out by strong young men to the ferry. The process is uncomfortable, wet and involves a lot of pushing and shouting. The crossing is also uncomfortable, wet and rough, not easy with a lot of luggage.

Sleeping There are several hotels near the pier, all **F**, and lots of *comedores* and restaurants. *Don Quixote*, T5567911, 6 rooms with 2 beds. *Sabana de la Mar*, nicely painted outside, cheap. *La Tía*, T5567318, along the shore, also known as *Brisas de la Bahía*, bath, fan, restaurant. Inland, about 2km on the road towards Hato Mayor, is **Hotel Bella Montana**, T2485982

West from Santo Domingo

The far southwest of the Republic is a dry zone with typical dry-forest vegetation. It also contains some of the country's most spectacular coastline and several national parks. A good highway runs from the capital, toll DR$5. Despite the construction of an international airport at Barahona, tourist development has been slow in comparison with other regions, with only a handful of resorts and large hotels operating. For the time being, exploring by car is the best way to enjoy this relatively untouched area. The Carretera Sánchez begins at the western end of Av Independencia and Av George Washington in Santo Domingo and is clearly signposted. To the west of Santo Domingo is **Haina**, the country's main port and an industrial zone. It has a teachers' vacation centre and a country club with swimming pool (members only).

San Cristóbal San Cristóbal in the interior, 25 km from the capital, was the birthplace of the dictator **Rafael Leonidas Trujillo**. Trujillo's home, the Casa de Caoba (now rapidly disintegrating, but open 0900-1700, caretaker will show you around, tip US$2.50) may be reached by *público* from behind the market, or by motorcycle taxi (US$0.35), though you may have to walk the last kilometre, uphill. You can also visit El Palacio del Cerro, the luxury residence which he built but never lived in. The Iglesia Parroquial (built in the 1940s as the planned last resting place of Trujillo) is four blocks from the recently restored and handsome Parque Central. Other attractions are the Palacio del Ayuntamiento in which the Republic's first constitution was signed, the Iglesia de Piedras Vivas, the caves at El Pomier (with Taino petroglyphs, see Flora and fauna) and the Santa María caves, where African-influenced stick and drum festivals are held. The local saint's day festival is from 6-10 June. Nearby are La Toma natural pools, for scenery and swimming (open 0900-1800 Mon-Fri, 0700-1930 Sat-Sun, US$1.25), and the beaches at **Palenque**, **Nigua** and **Najayo** (públicos leave regularly from the Parque Central). At the last named are the ruins of Trujillo's beach house on the hill overlooking the beach. These beaches are popular as excursions from Santo Domingo; development has been planned for some time but so far they remain unspoilt. There are lots of beach bars serving fried fish and local food but no hotels. The music can be overbearing at times but at Palenque the dark sand beach is deserted at the far end and you don't have to walk far to get away from the crowds. Good swimming at Palenque, rougher at Najayo but there is an artificial wave breaker. Nigua is a quiet town south of San Cristóbal. The 16th century Ingenio Diego Caballero, and the 18th century Boca de Nigua sugar mills can be visited.

Sleeping and eating **F** *Las Terrazas*, a government-owned hotel in the centre. Is best avoided, nothing works. **F** *Constitución*, Av Constitución, T5283309. Central, basic. On the road to Santo Domingo are a couple of small hotels, **F** *La Ruta*, with small breakfast, has a helpful owner. Several basic restaurants around Av Constitución. A famous local dish is *pasteles en hojas*, made from plátano, minced meat and other ingredients.

Dominican Republic

Transport Minibus Santo Domingo-San Cristóbal from the Malecón, US$0.85, *público* US$1.30; radio taxi US$14-20; La Covancha company organizes group transport (27 passengers) to San Cristóbal, La Toma and Palenque Beach.

From San Cristóbal the road runs west to Baní, birthplace of Máximo Gómez, **Baní** 19th-century fighter for the liberation of Cuba. The town is a major producer of sugar cane, coffee, vegetables, bananas and salt. The parish church is Nuestra Señora de Regla (festival, 21 November). The local goats' milk sweets from **Paya**, 5 km east of the town centre on main road, are renowned throughout the country, for example from *Las Marías*. **Las Tablas**, a village nearby, was one of the last places to conserve indigenous ways of life.

Sleeping and eating E *Hotel Caribani*, Calle Sánchez, T5225281. *Hotel Brisas del Sur*, T5223548. Cheaper hotels to be found near the market on Máximo Gómez. *Disco Sur*, on three floors, in the centre. *Pizzería Mi Estancia* on Padre Billini. Huge pizzas, good value. *Imogen Café*, Duarte esq Uladislao Guerrero. Fresh food in open air setting. *Restaurant Rancho Escondido*, Km 2.5 on Carretera Sánchez highway to Santo Domingo.

Transport Minibus from Santo Domingo, US$2.

The beach closest to Baní, 5 km south at Los Almendros, is mostly pebbly and usu- **West of Baní** ally dirty, especially at weekends. Better to carry on southwest to **Las Salinas**. Of the two roads west out of Baní, take the one to **Las Calderas** naval base for Las Salinas. There is no problem in going through the base (photography is not allowed); after it, turn left onto an unmade road for 3 km to the fishing village of Las Salinas, passing the unique sand dunes of the Bahía de Calderas, now a national monument, see page 408. The bay is an inlet on the **Bahía de Ocoa**, shallow, with some mangroves and good windsurfing and fishing. In the village is C-D *Las Salinas High Wind Center*, hotel, restaurant, windsurf centre, price per room. Beyond the village are the salt-pans which give it its name and then the point surrounded by a grey sand beach (one bar, calm waters, no facilities). Across the inlet are the undeveloped white sand beaches of Corbanito; fishermen will go across for US$2, apparently.

The fishing village of **Palmar de Ocoa** (99 km from Santo Domingo) hosts a fishing tournament each year; it is reached by a pot-holed road branching off the Baní-Las Salinas road, going along the northern shore of the Bahía de Calderas. Poor roads go to Corbanito, no development whatsoever. Palmar has lots of summer houses, a grey sand, pebbly beach, calm waters and a newly-built, poor village behind the summer houses. There is no large-scale tourist development. The setting is beautiful, looking across the bay to the mountains inland.

The main road west, in excellent condition, carries on from Baní through Azua to Barahona. **Azua de Compostela** was founded in 1504 on the orders of Fray Nicolás de Ovando; at one time Puerto Viejo (now the site of an industrial complex) was an alternative port to Santo Domingo. An important victory by Dominican troops against the Haitian army took place here on 19 March 1844 and an annual celebration commemorates the event. It is an isolated town in one of the hottest and most unwelcoming parts of the Republic. Some 19th-century buildings have survived and there are some pretty, brightly painted wooden houses off the main thoroughfares. The Playa Monte Río to the east of town is rough and stony; the smaller Playa Blanca is better. Both are hard to reach without four-wheel drive. Hotels: *Altagracia*, T5213813; *Brisas del Mar*, T5213813; also F *La Familiar*, T5213656, with shower and fan; *Hotel Restaurant San Ramón*, T5213529 (none is of high quality). Restaurants: *El Gran Segovia, José Segundo, Mi Bosquecito Bar, Patio Español*. Santo Domingo-Azua is two hours by *guagua*, US$4.15, *público* US$3.55, and Azua has good bus connections for Barahona, under two hours, US$4.15, San Juan and Padre Las Casas.

Dominican Republic

Barahona

Barahona was founded in 1802 by the Haitian leader, Toussaint Louverture, when he was briefly in control of the whole of Hispaniola. Its economy initially rested on the export of precious wood (eg mahogany) to Europe. In the 20th century the sugar industry was developed but the large sugar mill to the north of town is now closed pending privatization. Most hotels and restaurants are found on the sea-front Malecón. The Parque Central, five blocks up, is the commercial hub of the town and a pleasant spot to sit (although you may be pestered) The province of Barahona produces coffee (excursions can be made to Platón or Santa Elena), sugar, grapes, salt, bananas and other fruits, also gypsum and seafood. Barahona's old domestic airport has been replaced by the international Aeropuerto María Montés and the area is scheduled for tourist development.

Sleeping **LL-L** *Amsha Riviera Beach*, Av Enriquillo 56, T5245111, F5245798, www.amhsa.com Newly-built all-inclusive outside town with own beach. 108 good comfortable rooms, many with balconies, buffet meals, pool and poolside bar. It is possible to negotiate a cheaper, room-only rate, especially out of season. *Coral Sea Divers* on site, excellent diving at nearby reefs and in the Bahía de Neiba, where experienced divers can see manatees. Run by German Michael Schroeder, US$35-45 per boat dive, depending on equipment rented. **E** *Hotel Caribe* on same road, but closer to town, T5242185. Excellent open-air restaurant (*La Rocca*) next door. **E** *Hotel Guaracuyá*, T2330748, on its own beach closer to town than the Amhsa. Rather gloomy and dilapidated, but good value, with a/c. In town, **F** *Gran Hotel Barahona*, Calle Jaime Mota 5, T5423442. Fan, restaurant, simple. **E** *Micheluz*, Av 30 de Mayo 28, T5242358. A/c, cheaper with fan, cold water, restaurant. **F** *Hotel Cacique*, Av Uruguay (behind Parque Infantil), T5244620. Basic, clean. In **Baoruco**, 16 km from Barahona, **L-AL** *Clarion Resort*, T5421111, F5426060, www.clarion-resort.com New all-inclusive opened in 2000, 105 rooms, all facilities, private beach. **B-C** *Casa Bonita*, T6960215, F2230548, in hills. 12 rooms in bungalows with nice gardens, pool, spectacular view over forest and beaches, very clean rooms, excellent service, a/c available, expensive restaurant.

Eating *Brisas del Caribe* seafood restaurant at northern end of Malecón, T5242794. Excellent food and service, reasonable prices, pleasant setting, popular at lunchtime. *El Curro Steak House*, Calle Luperón, opposite cinema, T5243645. Meat and fish specialities, good value, outside sitting area, owner speaks English. *La Rocca*, next to *Caribe Hotel* on Malecón. Great breakfast menu, inexpensive, but not as good as it was. *D'Lina Pizza* , Av 30 de Mayo. Cheap and very large portions. *Panadería del Sur*, Uruguay y Luperón. Recommended for fresh bread, breakfasts and snacks. *José*, comida criolla and video, on Jaime Mota. 3 discos, *Imperio* next to *Riviera Beach*. *Costa Sur* with restaurant almost opposite *Riviera Beach*. *Mega Plus*, one block north of *Riviera Beach*.

Transport **Air** The **María Montés airport**, named after a Dominican Hollywood actress of the 1940s and 1950s, opened in 1996, is designed to promote tourism development in the area. In theory there are daily connections with Santo Domingo and Port-au-Prince with *Caribair*, T5472767, but don't rely on it. **Bus** Journey time from the capital is 3 hrs. Minibus fare is US$3, *público* US$4, *Caribe Tours* runs 2 buses a day (group transport also available with *Metro Tours*, *La Covacha* and *Taxi Raffi*). To Jimaní 2½ hrs, US$3.30. *Concho* or *guagua* in town RD$3/US$0.25; *carrera* US$3-4.

Directory **Banks** *Banco Popular* on Parque Central has an ATM (Plus, Visa). *Codetel* across the square, open daily 0800-2200.

Barahona &
beaches
further south
Be careful when swimming at the small, public beach at Barahona, as there are frequently stinging jelly fish, it is also filthy, as is the sea, and theft is common. About 70% of the coral reef off Barahona is reported to be dead. Those with a car can visit other, more remote beaches from Barahona (public transport is limited to *públicos*).

A new road has been built south of Barahona, running down the coast through some of the most beautiful scenery in the Republic, mountains on one side, the sea on the other, leading to Pedernales on the Haitian border (146 km). All along the southern coast are many white sand beaches which offer the best snorkelling and scuba diving in the Republic. The first place is the pebble beach of **El Quemaito**, where the river comes out of the beach, the cold freshwater mixing with the warm sea; offshore is a reef.**B** *Hotel El Quemaito,* T/F2230999. Small Swiss-run beach resort, pleasant gardens, good restaurant. After Quemaito is the village of **El Arroyo**. Inland about 15km along a dirt track are the open-cast mines where the semi-precious mineral, larimar, is dug. Larimar is mined only in the Dominican Republic. Miners will sell you fragments of stone, usually in jars of water to enhance the colour, for US$5-10, depending on size and colour. Back on the main road, you pass through Baoruco and La Ciénaga (small stony beaches and rough tides) before the road comes right down to the sea before **San Rafael** (about 40 minutes from Barahona) where a river runs out onto a stony beach. The forest grows to the edge of the beach. Where the road crosses the river is a *pensión* with a cold water swimming hole behind it (the swimming hole is safer than the sea as enormous waves surge onto the beach). Construction is under way here. At weekends it gets very crowded. Between San Rafael and **El Paraíso** rooms are available for rent. As the road approaches El Paraíso, see the changing colours where underground rivers flow into the sea. At El Paraíso, 31 km from Barahona, are a Texaco station and **F** *Hotel Paraíso* (T2431080, big rooms with bath, clean, TV). *Paola* restaurant, on the main road, is recommended and cheap. At **Los Patos** another river flows into the sea to form a cool bathing place; *comedores*, disco, very basic *Dormitorio Virginia.*A great place to spend the day at a weekend to watch Dominicans at play, excellent swimming. Note that most of these beaches have domestic animals, so there are droppings on the sand. There are cool, freshwater lagoons behind several of the other beaches on this stretch of coast. Limón lagoon is a flamingo reserve.

The road south of Los Patos was very badly damaged by Hurricane Georges in 1998 and there are still many unrepaired (*derrumbes*) landslides. It is very dangerous to drive at night. At Caletón traffic is forced to divert onto unmade tracks, virtually impassable without 4WD after rain, long delays if a lorry gets stuck.

At the village of **Enriquillo**, 54 km south of Barahona, a new dock has been constructed (**F** *Hotel Dayira*, on main road, no phone, basic; **F** *Dormitorio Juan José*, even more primitive, no phone). Last place for fuel until Pedernales, 80 km away, but no unleaded. You must explore for yourself: the area is not developed for tourism, yet. It is scheduled for development. Between Enriquillo and Pedernales the beaches are all sandy, but few are accessible and there are no facilities. After Enriquillo the road turns inland up to Oviedo and then skirts the Parque Nacional Jaragua as it runs a further 60 km to Pedernales. **Oviedo**, with the atmosphere of a desert settlement, has no hotels or decent restaurants and is one of the hottest places in the country.

Pedernales is the most westerly town of the Republic, on the Haitian border. This is a major crossing point for migrant Haitian sugar and construction workers. There is no immigration office so in theory only Haitians may enter Haiti here. Every Friday there is an informal market in the no-man's-land at the border, where Haitians sell cheap counterfeit clothing brands, smuggled spirits and a vast array of plastic kitchenware. There are few decent hotels in Pedernales. The best is **C** *Caribe Sur*, on nearby Playa Pedernales, a/c, hot water. **F** *Rossy*, no phone, is extremely basic. Rudimentary *comedores* in town. Beautiful beaches include **Playa Pedernales**, the local beach and centre of fishing activity, **Cabo Rojo** (four wheel drive required, usually deserted, little shade, overshadowed by ex-Alcoa bauxite plant) and **Bahía de las Aguilas**, where there is abundant fishing. The last two are within the **Parque Nacional Jaragua** which includes the islands **Beata** and **Alto Velo**. The vegetation is largely cactus and other desert plants, but there are also mahogany, frangipani and

Pedernales

extensive mangroves. There is a tourism proposal to develop the southwest coastal area around Pedernales and provide 5,000 jobs for the local people, who currently live off the exploitation of clay. Development plans call for the construction of 1,500 rooms in the beach areas, the renovation of the port and of the airport of Cabo Rojo, less than 30 km from Pedernales.

North of Pedernales a terrible road runs through lush and hilly countryside along the Haitian border via Aguacate and Puerto Escondido to Duvergé, where it joins the road to Jimaní (see below). This road, which effectively marks the border, cuts through the 800 sq km **Parque Nacional Sierra de Baoruco**, one of the country's wildest regions, densely covered in pine forests and subtropical rainforest. There are frequent and friendly military checkpoints but hardly any traffic and impassable without a four-wheel drive. The views are magnificent, particularly of Lago Enriquillo to the north.

Inland from Barahona

There is no accommodation on the lake shore

Near the Haitian border, is **Lago Enriquillo**, whose waters, 30 m below sea level, are three times saltier than the sea. The whole area was made a national park in 1996 (see page 408). It has a wealth of wildlife including some 500 American crocodiles (best seen in the morning), iguanas and flamingoes. The crocodiles and iguanas can best be seen on the largest of the three islands in the lake, which make up the **Cabritos National Park**, which is also where the crocodiles lay their eggs and spend their nights. A large colony of flamingoes overwinters at the lake. The rhinoceros iguana and the ricord iguana have become quite tame and approach people in search of treats. You need to purchase a Dirección Nacional de Parques (DNP) permit (RD$50 for boatloads of up to 6 people) at the ranger station east of La Descubierta (0700-1630) to visit the island and only groups with a guide are permitted to go there. The 30-minute boat trip to the island must be booked at the DNP office in La Descubierta; only groups with a guide are permitted. Several boatmen are recommended by the DNP. It costs US$6 per person (maximum 18 people) to go with Elena Nunciatini, T5375831, cellular 2249525, F5668809. The two smaller islands are Barbarita and La Islita. To visit the lake it is best to have one's own transport if short of time because, even though public transport runs both on the north and south shores, there is no guarantee of travelling on (or returning) the same day. Note that there is a filling station in Duvergé but no fuel elsewhere in this area. Take plenty of suntan lotion and go as early as possible as the temperature has been known to rise to 50°C.

If not in your own car, you can either take a tour from the capital, or contact the DNP, or take a *guagua* from Avenida Duarte y Avenida 27 de Febrero to Neiba, US$2.60 (also reached by *guagua* from Barahona, US$2), and then make a connection for La Descubierta, US$1.30. Alternatively take a bus from Santo Domingo to Jimaní (US$6.50, *La Experiencia* and *Riviera* companies; the journey takes eight hours) and get off at La Descubierta. Before Neiba is Galván, in a banana-growing area; the landscape is very flat. Between Galván and Neiba is Balneario Las Marías, a sulphur spring surrounded by oak trees.**Neiba** is known for its grapes (allegedly very sour), sold on the main square in season; F *Hotel Comedor Babei* on square, *Hotel Comedor Dania* on a street off the road going east out of town.

The road around the lake is fully paved and there are many good views. A portion of the Parque Nacional Isla Cabritas is on the north shore at La Azufrada, before La Descubierta. At **La Azufrada** is a swimming pool of sulphurous water, good for the skin. The pool is clean but the surroundings are littered. A path along the beach gives views of the lake and of Las Caritas, a line of rocks with precolumbian petroglyphs (an even better place to see them is signposted on the road). **La Descubierta**, at the northwest end, is a pleasant village with a celebrated *balneario*, Las Barías. The water is very cold; it is surprising how such an arid area can produce so much water to feed the lake. After La Descubierta are the springs and *balneario* of Boca del Chacón. La Descubierta is a nice town to relax for a day or two. F*Hotel Padre Bellini*, double bed, fan, private bath, very clean, secure, water 24 hours; F *Dormitorio Leo* is opposite. F *Hotel del Lago is also nearby.*

Jimaní, at the western end of the lake (not on the shore), is about 2 km from the Haitian border. There is a constant coming and going of *guaguas* and *motoconchos*
across the no man's land between the two borders and, unlike Pedernales, this is an
authorized crossing point. You have to pay a US$10 departure tax, a US$10 entry tax
and a further US$10 if you wish to return. You are not allowed to take a hired car
across the border. Customs officers in Jimaní are not above taking items from your
luggage. If you go to the border you will see queues of trucks waiting to cross; Haitians sell Barbancourt rum and perfumes. Jimaní is a spread out town of single-storey housing; **E** *Hotel Jimaní*, T2483139, onroad east out of town, appears to
be converted military accommodation, no hot water, little service but nice pool,
decent restaurant and ice cold beer. *Restaurant Los Lagos*, Duarte y Restauración,
excellent *chivo y gandules* (goat and beans), stays open late as town's main meeting
place, also has disco *Krystal*. Cabins are being built on the road into town from the
lake's north shore. The road around the south side of the lake goes through El Limón
and La Zurza, another sulphurous *balneario*. From the lake to Barahona, the road
goes through Duvergé, La Colonia (with a statue of Enriquillo, "the first fighter for
independence in the New World") and Cabral. At **Cabral** is a turning marked Polo;
the road climbs to a spot, with good views of Lago Rincón, where the road appears to
slope upwards, but if you put your car in neutral, or place a ball or can on the road it
seems to run uphill. The place is called the **Polo Magnético**; university studies have
shown it to be an optical illusion, but it is a source of great discussion. Get a local to
show you the best spots. From Cabral the road runs through very dry, low-lying land
(there is a project to protect the dry forest, also experimental agricultural projects).

Background

History

Although the Spanish launched much of their westward expansion from Santo **The colony**
Domingo, their efforts at colonizing the rest of the island were desultory. Drake *See also the history*
sacked Santo Domingo in 1586, the French gained control of the western part of the *section in the Haiti*
island in 1697 and, by the mid-18th century, the number of Spaniards in the eastern *chapter for more on*
part of the island was about one-third of a total of 6,000. Since there was little com- *Columbus' early*
mercial activity or population of the interior, it was easy prey for Haitian invaders *colonization of*
fired with the fervour of their rebellion at the turn of the 19th century. Between 1801 *Hispaniola*
and 1805, followers of Toussaint L'Ouverture and Dessalines plundered the territory. Sovereignty was disputed for the next 17 years, then, in 1822, Haiti took control for a further 22 years.

After the declaration of the Dominican Republic's independence in 1844, by the **Independence**
writer Duarte, the lawyer Sánchez and the soldier Mella, the country underwent yet
another period of instability, including more Haitian incursions and, in 1861, a
four-year re-annexion with Spain. Independence was regained in the War of Restoration (la Restauración), but with no respite in factional fighting or economic disorder. Apart from the dictatorship of Ulises Heureaux (1882-84, 1887-99),
governments were short-lived. The country must be one of the very few where a
Roman Catholic archbishop has served as head of state: Archbishop Meriño was
President from 1880 to 1882.

In 1916, the USA occupied the Dominican Republic, having managed the country's **The Trujillo**
customs affairs (on behalf of US and European creditors) since 1905. When the USA **dictatorship**
left in 1924, the Republic had a fully organized army, whose commander, Rafael
Leonidas Trujillo Molina, became President in 1930. Thus began one of the most
ruthless dictatorships ever seen in the Dominican Republic. With either himself or
his surrogates at the helm (Héctor Trujillo, 1947-60, and Joaquín Balaguer,

1960-62), Trujillo embarked on the expansion of industry and public works, the introduction of the national currency and the liquidation of the country's debts. Nevertheless, his methods of government denied any form of representation and included murder, torture, blackmail and corruption. During his reign, in 1937, an estimated 10,000 Haitian immigrants were slaughtered, prolonging the hatred between the two republics which had begun in the early 19th century.

The Balaguer Trujillo was assassinated in 1961. President Balaguer immediately set about eradi-
presidencies cating his family's influence, but in 1962 Balaguer was defeated in elections by Dr Juan Bosch of the Partido Revolucionario Dominicano (PRD). After seven months he was ousted by a miltary coup led by Colonel Elías Wessin y Wessin. The PRD, with the support of a group of young colonels, tried to win back constitutional government in 1965, but were prevented from doing so by the army, backed by the USA and the Organization of American States. New elections were held in 1966; they were won by Balaguer, at the head of the Partido Reformista Social Cristiano (PRSC). He remained in office until 1978, forging closer links with the USA, but not without facing coup attempts, right-wing terrorism and left-wing guerrilla incursions.

A PRD President was returned in 1978, Antonio Guzmán, whose chief aims were to reduce army power and eliminate corruption. A month before leaving office in 1982, he committed suicide. It is alleged that he had discovered that members of his family, who had held office under him, had been involved in corruption, but this has never been proved. His successor, Dr Salvador Jorge Blanco, also of the PRD, presided over severe economic difficulties which led to rioting in 1984 in which 60 people died. The party split over the handling of the economy, helping Joaquín Balaguer to win a narrow majority in the 1986 elections giving him a fifth presidential term. The 1990 elections were contested by two octogenarians, Dr Balaguer (83) and Dr Juan Bosch (80), now of the Partido de la Liberación Dominicana (PLD). Dr Balaguer won a sixth term of office by a very narrow majority, which was subjected to a verification process after Dr Bosch alleged fraud had taken place in the capital. The May 1994 elections had the same outcome, after Balaguer had decided very late in the campaign to stand for re-election. His chief opponent was José Francisco Peña Gómez of the PRD. First results gave Balaguer the narrowest of victories. Peña Gómez, supported by many outside observers, claimed that fraud had taken place and the election was reviewed by a revision committee appointed by the Central Electoral Junta. The committee found numerous irregularities, but its findings were ignored by the Junta which awarded victory to Balaguer, once again by the narrowest of margins. To defuse the crisis, Balaguer signed a pact with Peña Gómez allowing for new elections in November 1995; Congress rejected this date, putting the new election back six months to 16 May 1996. Peña Gómez and the PRD, angry at Congress' decision, boycotted Balaguer's inauguration.

1996 election Almost at once campaigning began for the 1996 presidential election. The PRD
campaign selected Peña Gómez again while the PLD chose Leonel Fernández as its candidate, to replace Juan Bosch who had retired. Within the PRSC, jockeying for the candidacy was beset by scandals and power struggles, exacerbated by the absence of an appointment by Balaguer himself.

Violent demonstrations and general strikes against economic hardship occurred in 1987, 1990 and 1991, in the last instance following the signing of an IMF accord. As a result of the government's structural adjustment programme, however, improvement was recorded in most productive sectors, the level of reserves and the rate of inflation. Positive economic results did not prevent spending on health and education lagging behind other public sectors. Unemployment remained high and many Dominicans were tempted by better opportunities in the USA and Puerto Rico. In 1995 there was speculation over whether the government would seek a new structural adjustment programme from the IMF. Renewed economic problems, compounded by the continuing failure of the electricity industry (see Economy below), forced the government to raise taxes and support the peso. At the same time, unauthorized increases in public transport fares led to riots in March and June 1995. With the PRD accusing the PRSC of fuelling the protests in order to create instability and thus undermine the 1996 elections, with growing revelations of corruption in government departments and with infighting unabated in the PRSC, the political climate was tense.

Relations between the Dominican Republic and Haiti became very strained in 1991 after President Balaguer ordered the deportation of all illegal Haitian immigrants under the age of 16 and over 60. Many from outside these age groups left, putting pressure on the resources of President Aristide's government. Attitudes to the overthrow of Aristide were ambivalent because the Dominican Republic officially supported the Organization of American States' trade embargo while politicians vocally and traders in practice defied it. Soon after Aristide's return to power, legitimate trade with Haiti resumed and various meetings at ministerial level took place. Balaguer and Aristide also met briefly. In 1996, Haiti's new president, René Préval, paid his first official visit abroad to the Dominican Republic. Agreements were signed for joint projects in the border region.

In the first round of the 1996 elections, Peña Gómez received 46% of the vote, compared with 39% for Leonel Fernández. However, in the second round, Balaguer gave his support to Fernández, in an effort to keep Peña Gómez (who suffered racial abuse because of his Haitian ancestry) from the presidency, and he won 51% of the vote. Balaguer was expected to continue to influence the new government's policies through Congress, at least until the 1998 congressional elections. The PLD was in a minority in both houses, holding only one Senate seat, compared with 15 for the PRSC and 14 for the PRD, and 13 congressional seats, compared with 58 for the PRD and 48 for the PRSC, with one independent.

President Leonel Fernández was sworn in on 16 August 1996 and appointed a cabinet largely from his own party, after a cooling of relations with Dr Balaguer. In his inauguration speech he pledged to fight poverty, while earlier promising to modernize the economy and fight corruption. The new Attorney General, Abel Rodríguez del Orbe, was put in charge of an anti-corruption programme. There was criticism when the President increased his own salary from RD$3,500 to RD$90,000 a month, with similar increases for ministers and other top officials. The Chamber of Deputies then voted itself an increase of 100% to RD$60,000 a month, but delayed approving the 1997 budget, so the President raised public sector wages by decree with a minimum public sector wage of RD$1,400 a month. In 1997 relations with the PRSC deteriorated rapidly because of investigations into land purchase scandals involving members of the previous administration. Land which was in national parks or in protected areas of special scientific interest, or expropriated under the agrarian reform programme for distribution to small farmers, was found to have been allocated to PRSC officials and sold on for profit, mostly for tourism development. There was also a shake up in the top ranks of the military and police, with some linked to drugs offences, others to unsolved murders and disappearances.

The Fernández administration

José Francisco Peña Gómez lost his fight with cancer and died in May 1998. Six days later, his party, the PRD, won a landslide victory in the congressional and municipal elections, winning 85 of the 149 seats in an expanded (from 120 seats) Chamber of Deputies and 24 of the 30 Senate seats. The governing PLD came second with 49 and four seats respectively, while the PRSC managed only 15 and two seats.

At the beginning of 1999 tension was eased among the three main political parties with the holding of talks to resolve issues concerning the Junta Central Electoral (JCE), which supervises elections, and the Liga Municipal Dominicana (LMD), which allocates finance to local authorities. Presidential elections in 2000 were keenly fought between Balaguer for the PRSC, Danilo Medina for the ruling PLD and Hipólito Mejía for the PRD. The government was credited with achieving

2000 elections

Dominican Republic

economic growth, but it was perceived that the benefits had not been widely enough distributed and corruption within the administration was alleged. Despite his age and infirmities, Balaguer (93) was seen as an influential power broker and a force to be reckoned with. Mejía won 49.87% of the vote, Balaguer 24.6% and Medina 24.9%. As no one achieved the 50% required for an outright win, a second round was technically necessary, but after both other candidates visited Balaguer, both he and Medina pulled out of the race, leaving Mejía the victor. The PRD now controls the presidency, the legislature and the majority of the municipalities.

Government

The Dominican Republic is a representative democracy, with legislative power resting in a bicameral Congress: a 30-seat Senate and a 149-seat Chamber of Deputies. Senators and deputies are elected for a four-year term, as is the President, in whom is vested executive power.

The economy

Structure of production
There are six main agricultural regions: the north, the Cibao valley in the north central area, Constanza and Tiero, the east, the San Juan valley, and the south. Cibao is the most fertile and largest region, while the eastern region is the main sugar-producing area. Sugar was traditionally the main crop, but diversification out of sugar cane, the conversion of some cane lands into tourist resorts, the expulsion of Haitian cutters and a slump in productivity led to lower volume and value of sugar production. Non-traditional products have been gaining in importance. These include fruit and vegetables, plants and cut flowers, marine products, processed foods, cigars and other agroindustrial products. Growth of the cigar industry has put the Dominican Republic in top place among the region's exporters, exceeding both Honduras and Cuba, with sales of around US$400 mn a year.

Since 1975 gold and silver mining has been of considerable importance. Large gold, silver and zinc deposits have been found near the Pueblo Viejo mine, where the oxide ores were running out, and a major gold and silver deposit has been discovered in the Haitian border area, which could mean a joint operation to establish an open cast mine. The country also produces ferronickel, which has overtaken sugar as the major commodity export earner. Reserves are estimated at 10% of total world deposits.

Other sources of income are the 52 industrial free zones, with some 500 companies, where manufactured goods are assembled for the North American market (generating exports of US$3 bn in 1998), and remittances from Dominicans resident abroad of about US$1.4 bn a year.

The largest foreign exchange earner nowadays is, however, tourism, with annual receipts exceeding US$2 bn. The industry generates 20% of gdp and employs about 5% of the labour force, 50,000 in direct jobs and 110,000 indirectly. New hotel projects brought the number of hotel rooms to 49,623 at end-1999, compared with 11,400 in 1987. These are mainly concentrated in the Puerto Plata area, the Samaná peninsula, on the east coast (Punta Cana-Higuey-Bávaro-El Cortecito), Santo Domingo and San Pedro or Juan Dolio-Guayacanes. More are being built and plans are to increase capacity by 50%. Nearly half of hotel rooms are sold on an all-inclusive basis. Tourist arrivals in 1998 were affected by Hurricane Georges and bad publicity in the UK over food hygiene, but the 1999 figure was 2.1 mn, not including returning Dominicans.

Recent trends
In the first half of the 1980s, a combination of fiscal and external account problems brought about a sharp decline in the rate of gdp growth and led the Government to turn to the IMF for financial assistance. The Government agreed to reduce its fiscal deficit and take a number of other austerity measures, including a gradual devaluation of the peso. It failed to meet targets, so the programme was suspended in early

1984. Government measures to remove subsidies, as part of the austerity package agreed with the IMF, led to riots in Santo Domingo in April 1984. A one-year standby loan facility worth RD$78.5 mn was eventually approved in April 1985 but not renewed because of political opposition. Despite the widespread unpopularity of policies designed to satisfy IMF demands, President Balaguer in 1990-91 negotiated a new IMF agreement. Having repaid debts worth US$81.6 mn to the IMF, World Bank and other multilateral agencies, an IMF standby agreement was approved in August 1991. The terms of the accord, which included the unification of the exchange rates, an end to price controls, balancing state corporation budgets and a commitment to pay outstanding foreign debt arrears, were greeted by a series of general strikes. Agreement with the IMF did, however, permit the rescheduling of US$905 mn of debt with the Paris Club group of foreign governments in November 1991, with further successful renegotiations of official debt in 1992. The IMF signed a new US$44 mn standby facility in July 1993. In February 1994, commercial bank creditors signed an agreement to reschedule US$1.04 bn of debt.

The major problems confronting the Government in 1990 were the high rate of inflation, unofficially estimated at 100% a year, and the disruptive electricity crisis, which had got steadily worse for several years. Inflation, pushed by heavy government spending on public works and increasing subsidies, was reduced to 4.6% in 1992 and 2.7% in 1993 as a result of a curtailment of spending, both in a refusal to increase public sector wages and after the completion of major public works. Increased government expenditure in 1994 contributed to inflation of 14.3%. In September 1994 the Central Bank introduced a series of measures to stabilize the peso against the dollar and reduce a 691 million peso government deficit. A fiscal surplus of 1,720mn pesos was achieved in 1995, helping inflation to come down to 9.2%. Gdp has grown strongly since then, helped by an expanding tourist industry and other services. Inflation has remained in single figures since 1995. In 1999 the Dominican Republic recorded the highest gdp growth rate in the Americas, with a rate of 8.3%.

The new government which took office in 1996 pledged to modernize the economy and privatizations and tax reform were on the agenda. However, its minority position in the Legislature made it difficult for its bills to become law. A privatization bill allowing a maximum of 50% of a state enterprise to be sold was introduced in September 1996, with the aim of pulling companies such as the sugar and electricity enterprises out of bankruptcy. Progress was painfully slow. The 1997 budget was also deadlocked in Congress, with conflict over higher value added tax (ITBIS), duties on alcohol and tobacco, reduced import tariffs, a new Monetary and Financial Code and privatization. The 1998 budget, passed after heated debate, was the first to be approved by Congress since the Government took office in 1996. An improved political climate in 1999 led to the approval of several bills by the Senate, including the Monetary and Financial Code. The Corporación Dominicana de Electricidad (CDE) was finally put up for sale, with 19 out of 43 companies selected for a final round of bidding.

Culture

The Dominicans are a mixture of African black and white, with a strong European **The people** strain. Although Dominicans often call themselves Indians, the Taínos were in fact wiped out within a few generations of the arrival of the Spanish. These English terms should, however, be qualified: 'blanco' (white) refers to anybody who is white, light-skinned mulatto, or substantially white with either or both Indian (appearance) or African admixture; 'indio claro' (tan) is anyone who is white/black mixed; 'indio oscuro' (dark Indian) is anyone who is not 100% black (ie with some white admixture); 'negro' is 100% African. Negro is not a derogatory term. There is a certain aspiration towards the Indian; this can be seen not only in the use of the original name for the island, Quisqueya (and Quisqueyanos), but in place names (San Pedro

Dominican Republic

de Macorís, from the Macorix tribe, the other Indian inhabitants being the Taino and the Ciguayo) and in given family names (Guainorex, Anacaona, etc). Unlike in Haiti, the Dominicans' culture and language are hispanic and their religion Roman Catholic. Economically, the country is much more developed, despite a stormy political past and unsavoury periods of dictatorship, particularly under Generalísimo Trujillo (1930-61). Nevertheless, in a material sense the country prospered during the Trujillo era and the standard of living is much higher than it is in Haiti. Many people seek a better life elsewhere, however, and Dominicans make up the largest group of Hispanics in New York, while those left behind rely on their relatives' remittances of dollars to make ends meet.

Music & dance The most popular dance is the merengue, which dominates the musical life of the Dominican Republic; a great many orchestras have recorded merengue rhythms and are now world-famous. The traditional merengue is played by a three-man group called a *perico ripiao*, or *pri-prí*, which consists of a *tambora* (small drum), an accordion and a *güira* (a percussion instrument scraped by a metal rod, or, as originally used by Indians, a gourd scraped with a forked stick). Since the 1970s the merengue has got much faster, with less formal steps. There is a merengue festival in the last week of July and the first week of August, held on the Malecón in Santo Domingo. Puerto Plata holds its merengue festival in the first week of October and Sosúa has one the last week of September. Juan Luís Guerra is considered the greatest exponent of Dominican merengue in recent years. He won a Grammy award for *Burbujas de Amor* and has travelled the world with his music. Other outstanding merengueros are Fernandito Villalona, Sergio Vargas, Eddy Herrera, Los Toros Band, la Banda Gorda and Joseíto Mateo, considered for decades the 'King' of merengue. The group *Los Ilegales* have also gained international fame with their musical form called 'merenhouse'.

Other popular dances are the *mangulina*, the *salve*, the *bambulá* (from Samaná), the *ritmo guloya* (especially in San Pedro de Macorís, see also that section), the *carabiné* (typical of the region around Barahona), and the *chenche matriculado*. Salsa is very popular in dance halls and discos (every town, however small, has a discothèque). *Bachata* is Dominican 'country music', usually songs of unrequited love, to the accompaniment of virtuoso guitar, percussion, *güira* and bass.

Literature In the colonial period, Santo Domingo encouraged the development of literature within the framework of the first seats of learning in Spanish America. The early colonists expressed their inspiration most readily in poetry and the verses of Elvira de Mendoza and Leonor de Ovando are frequently cited as examples of that time. Among the many Dominican poets famed within the country in subsequent years are Gastón Fernando Deligne, Fabio Fiallo and the national poet, Pedro Mir, author of *Hay un país en el mundo*. The two dominant political figures of the latter half of the 20th century, Joaquín Balaguer and Juan Bosch, are also well known for their literary output, Balaguer in many styles, especially poetry, Bosch in short stories. Of the present generation of writers, Frank Moya Pons and Bernardo Vega stand out as writers of mainly historical works. Julia Alvarez, who now lives in the USA, has written very readable and interesting novels about the Trujillo era, fear and exile, a good introduction to the Dominican Republic. They include *How the García girls lost their accents*, *In the time of the butterflies* and *Yo*.

Painting The first major representations of the country in painting came after 1870 with the establishment of a national identity through the Restauración movement and the consolidation of independence from Haiti. The first important painter was Alejandro Bonilla while the Spaniard José Fernández Corredor is credited with the foundation of the first painting school in the country. From this period the artists Arturo Grullón, Luis Desangles (Sisito), Leopoldo Navarro and Abelardo Rodríguez Urdaneta stand out. The last named is famous as painter, sculptor and photographer. In the 1930s, Jaime Colson, Yoryi Morel and Darío Suro were precursors of *costumbrismo* (art of customs and manners). Contemporary painters have followed the various styles which have prevailed throughout the art world. Those who have gained an international reputation are Iván Tovar, Ramón Oviedo, Cándido Bidó, José Rincón Mora, José Ramírez Conde and Paul Giudicelli. Exhibitions of Dominican art are held frequently in Santo Domingo galleries, for example the Voluntariado de las Casas Reales, Galería Nader, Museo de Arte Moderno, El Pincel, La Galería, and others. For additional details on Dominican painters, consult *Arte contemporáneo dominicano*, by Gary Nicolás Nader, and *Antología de la pintura dominicana*, by Cándido Gerón.

El Consejo Presidencial de Cultura and UNESCO have made an evaluation of murals painted in Santo Domingo, counting 187 as part of the national heritage. They can be found in the Centro de los Héroes, Universidad Autónoma de Santo Domingo, Palacio de Bellas Artes, buildings in the Plaza de la Cultura, the Ayuntamiento, Banco de Reservas and Instituto del Seguro Social. Murals have been painted by Jaime Colson, Jamie Vela Zanetti, Eligio Pichardo, José Ramírez Conde, Paul Giudicelli, Clara Ledesma and Amable Sterling.

Dominican Republic

Puerto Rico

10

Puerto Rico

Puerto Rico may be part of the USA but its music and dance is a mixture of both Spanish and African rhythms. The country, as a result, is a mixture of very new and very old. It exhibits the open American way of life yet retains the more formal Spanish influences. This is reflected in the architecture, not just the contrast between the colonial and the modern in urban areas but also in the countryside, where older buildings sit side by side with concrete schools and dwellings. It is found in the cuisine, a plethora of fast food restaurants together with local cooking which has its roots in the hybrid culture of all the Caribbean and in the music, where rock music and salsa are played in beach resorts but in the hilly interior, Puerto Rican music can be heard. However, if you do not stray beyond the tourist areas on the coast, you will not experience the real Puerto Rico.

Old volcanic mountains, long inactive, occupy a large part of the interior, with the highest peak, Cerro de Punta, at 1,338 m in the Cordillera Central. North of the Cordillera is the karst country where the limestone has been acted upon by water to produce a series of small steep hills (mogotes) and deep holes, both conical in shape. The mountains are surrounded by a coastal plain with the Atlantic shore beaches cooled all the year round by trade winds.

Essentials

Before you travel

Documents All non-US residents need a US visa, or a US visa waiver for participating countries. All requirements are the same as for the USA.

Money **Currency** United States dollar. Locally, a dollar may be called a *peso*, 25 cents a *peseta*, 5 cents a *bellón* (but in Ponce a *bellón* is 10 cents and a *ficha* is 5 cents). Most international and US credit cards are accepted. **Exchange** Currency exchange at *Banco Popular*; *Caribbean Foreign Exchange*, 201B Tetuán, Old San Juan, T7228222, and at the airport; *Deak international* at the airport; *Scotia Bank* exchange only Canadian currency; *Western Union* for cable money transfer, *Pueblo Supermarket*, Old San Juan. **Banks** *Banco Popular; Banco de San Juan; Banco Mercantil de Puerto Rico*; and branches of US and foreign banks. *Banco de Santander*, of Spain, is the second largest bank in Puerto Rico.

Climate Tradewinds make the temperatures of 28-30°C bearable in the summer. Temperatures in the winter drop to the range 21-26°C and the climate all the year round is very agreeable. Rain falls mainly from May to October, with most precipitation from July to October.

Getting there

Air **From Europe** *Martinair* from Amsterdam; *Condor* from Frankfurt; *Iberia* from Barcelona and Madrid; *British Airways* from London Gatwick. Lots of other flights with connections in JFK New York or Miami. **From Latin America** Most South and Central American countries are connected via Miami or Panama City but there are also direct flights from Caracas (*Lacsa*, *AA*), Bogotá (*Aces*), Maracaibo and Valencia (*ALM*), Lima, Panama City, Guatemala City, San

Puerto Rico

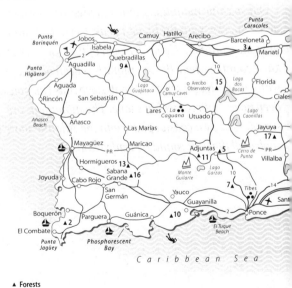

N

Not to scale

▲ **Forests**

1 Aguirre	6 Ceiba	11 Guilarte
2 Boquerón	7 Cerrillos	12 Jobos
3 Cambalache	8 El Yunque	13 Maricao
4 Carite / Guavate	9 Guajataca	14 Piñones
5 Casa Pueblo	10 Guánica	15 Río Abajo

Tourist offices overseas

Argentina, *T54-11-43144525*.

Brazil, *T55-11-8220533*.

Canada 2 *Bloor Street West, Suite 700,*
Toronto, Ontario, M4W 3R1, T416-9699025,
F9699478.

France Express Conseil, 5 bis, rue du Louvre,
75001 Paris, T331-44778806, F42600545.

Germany T49-69-350047.

Italy T39-0266-714403.

Mexico, T525-2021844 ext 13.

Netherlands, *T312-06427909*.

Paraguay, *T5952-1497264*.

Spain Calle Serrano, 1-2° izda, 28001, Madrid,
T3491-4312128, 800-898920, F5775260.

UK, T0800-898920.

Uruguay, T5982-7104430.

USA **New York** T800-2236530,
F212-8181866, **Los Angeles** T213-8745991,
F8747257, **Miami** T305-3818915, F3818917.

Venezuela, T582-7619930.

Pedro Sula (all *Copa*) and San José (*Lacsa*). **From the Caribbean** Anguilla, Antigua, Aruba, Barbados, Casa de Campo (Dominican Republic), Curaçao, Dominica, Fort-de-France, Grand Cayman, Grenada, Pointe-à-Pitre, Port-au-Prince, Port of Spain, Puerto Plata, Punta Cana, St Barts, St Croix, St Kitts, St Lucia, St Maarten, St Thomas, St Vincent, Santiago and Santo Domingo (Dominican Republic), Tobago, Tortola and Virgin Gorda, with *LIAT, American Airlines, American Eagle, Air Guadeloupe, ALM, British Airways, Dominair* and others. **From the USA** A great many US cities are served by *American Airlines, Delta, American Trans Air, Northwest Airlines, Continental, Tower Air, TWA, US Air* and *United Airlines*.

Cruise ships call at San Juan and Ponce. *Ferries del Caribe* run a passenger and car (no hire cars) ferry service to/from the Dominican Republic from Santo Domingo to Mayagüez (Tue, Thu, Sun, 2000, arrives 0800, returns Mon, Wed, Fri, same times) with a bus link across the island to San Juan (T8324800, see page 400 for further details). There is a weekend passenger

Boat

Puerto Rico

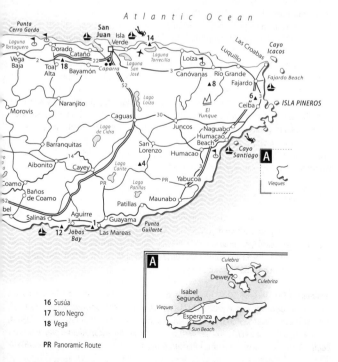

16 Susúa
17 Toro Negro
18 Vega

PR Panoramic Route

Touching down

Departure tax None is payable, although *LIAT* demands a 'security tax' of US$5.

Tourist Zone Police The Puerto Rico Tourist Zone Police are at Vieques Street, Condado (T7220738 and 7245210). They can help you settle problems with taxis. Emergency T911.

Tipping Service is usually included in the bill, but where no fixed service charge is included, it is recommended that 15-20% is given to waiters, taxi drivers, etc.

Communications Spanish is the first language with less than 30% of the population speaking English fluently.

Safety We have received several warnings from travellers. Of all crimes 65% are related to drugs trafficking. La Perla is known as San Juan's most dangerous slum and the end of Calle Tanca should be avoided as it is a favourite drinking and drug dealing area for residents. Female tourists should avoid the Condado beach areas at night and all areas of San Juan can be dangerous after dark. Take precautions against theft from your person and your car, wherever you are on the island. Hiking on mainland beaches is not a good idea; never stay on a beach if you are alone, beautiful areas such as Carite or Route 186 above El Verde look like great hiking spots but do not always attract people with good intentions. Safety in numbers. Take advice locally.

Water Drought has frequently forced the imposition of water rationing in greater San Juan and 10 other towns. Water remains in short supply despite emergency dredging of the Carraizo reservoir, which had lost 65% of its capacity because of silt.

launch on the *Caribe Cay* between Fajardo and St Thomas, 1¾ hours, Saturday 0830, US$70 return, T8608809. **Ports of entry** Mayagüez, Ponce, Fajardo, San Juan (not Boquerón). **Boat documents** Clearance required from Customs, Immigration and Agriculture. Foreigners must meet same entry requirements as into USA (US$90 if you arrive without a visa) US vessels must pay a US$25 annual customs fee (a sticker). US citizens must clear into Puerto Rico when coming from USVI. Do not bring in fruit, vegetables or garbage into the USA/Puerto Rico. Boats and firearms must be registered after 60 days. **Marinas** There is a liveaboard community at Boquerón. Ponce is a good place to provision, with wholesale houses, Sears, Walmart, nearby. Fajardo is headquarters for marinas, boat supplies and haul-out. Puerto del Rey marina has 750 slips, transient rate US$1 per foot per day (includes water, electricity, cable TV); Palmas del Mar, 40 slips, also many houses on the water have space to rent with water and electricity. Small anchorage area has cleaner water than stagnant marina. Nothing nearby, car rental needed, US$24 per day at Thrifty. **Anchorages**: Boquerón, La Parguera, Guánica, Ponce, Fajardo, Vieques, Culebra has many (see Bruce Van Sant's *Guide to the Spanish Virgin Islands*). Ponce Yacht Club (members) allows one night free to other Yacht Club members. Haul out: Isleta, Puerto del Rey, Palmas del Mar, Villa Marina. Get **weather** from VHF weather, VI Radio or local AM station.

Touching down

Airport information There are airport limousines to a number of hotels. Set rates for Taxi Turístico: Zone 1, Luis Muñoz Marín airport to Isla Verde, US$8; Zone 2, airport to Condado/Miramar, US$12; Zone 3, airport to Pier area in Old San Juan, US$16. Between and beyond the zones rates are metered (make sure the taxi meter is used; note that drivers prefer not to go to old San Juan, the beach areas are much more popular with them).

Airlines *ACES*, T800-8462237, www.acescolombia.com; *Air Canada*, T800-7763000, www.aircanada.ca; *Air France*, T800-2372747, www.airfrance.com; *Air Guadeloupe*, T2530933; *Air Jamaica*, T800-5235585, www.airjamaica.com; *Air St Thomas*, T800-5223084, www.airstthomas.com; *ALM*, T800-3277230, www.alm.com; *American Airlines and American Eagle*, T800-4337300, www.aa.com; *American Trans Air*, T800-2252995, www.ata.com; *BWIA*,

T800-5382942, www.bwia.com; *COPA*, T800-3592672, www.copaair.com; *Continental*, T800-5250280, www.continental.com; *Delta*, T800-2211212, www.delta-air.com; *Iberia*, T800-7724642, www.iberia.com; *Isla Nena*, T7416362; *Lacsa-Grupo Taca*, T800-2252272, www.grupotaca.com; *LIAT*, T7913838, www.flyliat.com; *Northwest Airlines*, T800-3747747, www.nwa.com; *United Airlines*, T800-2416522, www.ual.com; *Vieques Air Link*, T2533644, www.vieques-island.com/val

Local tourist offices The Puerto Rico Tourism Company, PO Box 902-3960, San Juan **Tourist**
00902-3960, www.prtourism.com, publishes lots of brochures and booklets including *Travel* **information**
and Sports Planner, www.travelandsports.com, and *Qué Pasa!* Which comes out every two
months and has a useful Tourist directory. Information centres also at the international
airport (T7911014, F7918033; next to the *Condado Plaza Hotel*, T7212400 (ext 2280); La Casita,
near Pier One, Old San Juan, T7221709, F7225208; Rafael Hernández Airport, Aguadilla,
T8903315, T8900220; Citibank Building, 53 McKinley East, facing plaza, Mayagüez, T8315220,
F8313210; Casa Armstrong-Proventud, Plaza Las Delicias, Ponce, T8405695, F8435958.

Regional tourist offices Adjuntas, T8292590; Añasco, T8263100 ext 272; Bayamón,
T7988191; Cabo Rojo, T8511025; Camuy, T8982240; Culebra, T7423291; Dorado,
T796-5740/1030; Fajardo, T8634013; Guanica, T8212777; Jayuya, T8285010; Luquillo,
T8892851; Naguabo, T8740389; Rincón, T8235024; Vieques, T7415000. For details on
museums, contact the Puerto Rico Institute of Culture, Museums and Parks Programs,
T7245477. Out in the country, tourist information can be obtained from the town halls,
usually found on the main plaza. Hours are usually Monday-Friday, 0800-1200, 1300-1430.

Local tour operators *Colonial Adventure*, T7290114, walking tour of San Juan's cultural
and historical highlights Mon-Sat 0930 and 1400, US$20 including museum entry fees.
Countryside Tours, T7239691, Víctor Valvín takes you to the University of Puerto Rico, the first
Governor's house in Trujillo Alto and a (hard to find) typical lunch, pointing out typical plants
and trees along the way, US$30, delightful cultural experience, recommended to get to know
Puerto Rico. *Hillbilly Tours*, day trips from San Juan into the hills, run by Edwin Betancourt,
T7605618, helpful with information. *Tropix Wellness Outings*, Víctor López specializes in
tailor-made tours, one day or many days, for example caves (vigorous, hiking, body rafting),
kayaks (Culebra), hiking (rain forest), Guanica (dry forest), you stay in nice hotels and
paradores, T2682173, F2681722, tropix@msn.com *Northwestern Land Tours*, Andrés Alicea
offers day trips to the Indian ceremonial centre, Guanica Forest, El Yunque, Ponce, Río Camuy
Caves etc, T3740783. *Copladet Nature & Adventure*, T7658595, transport, custom day tours
or longer. *Rico Suntours*, T7222080, riding, horseracing, nightlife. For caving (see page 484),
Aventuras Tierra Adentro, expert guides Rosario Boscarino and Francis Reyes will lead you
through an exciting adventure, T7660470, F7547543, 272B Avenida Pinero, University Gardens,
Río Piedras, PR 00927. *Encantos Ecotours*, also known as *Piñones Ecotours*, T2720005,
www.ecotourspuertorico.com, bikes and kayaks, tours and rentals, also surf rafting in Piñones.

Roman Catholic, Episcopal, Baptist, Seventh Day Adventist, Presbyterian, Lutheran, Christian **Religion**
Science and Union Church. There is also a Jewish community. At the Anglican-Episcopal
cathedral in San Juan there are services in both Spanish and English.

Where to stay

The summer season runs from 16 April to 14 December and is somewhat cheaper than the
winter season, for which we give rates where possible. An 11% tax is charged on the room
rate in hotels with casinos, 9% in those without casinos.

There are 18 *Paradores Puertorriqueños* to put you up while touring, some old, most
new, some quiet and peaceful (for example *Coamo, Gripinas, Juanita, Casa Grande*), some used
by local families for boisterous entertainment, with prices at US$55-100d: the majority are to
the west of San Juan; for reservations T7212884 or from the USA T1-800-4430266. Many
paradores are not what the average traveller wants, so do some research first. They are based

Puerto Rico

on the Spanish *parador*, convenient places to stay when on the road, but lack the old charm of their Spanish counterparts. *Tourism Marketing Group*, T7218793, arranges Fly-Drive packages, with car hire and accommodation at *paradores*; rates depend on which *paradores* you choose, but three days, two nights, starts at US$165 per person in a double room, six days, five nights US$350 per person.

Camping
Camping is permitted in the forest reserves; you have to get a permit in advance see below. Camping is also allowed on some of the public beaches. Beach campsites are generally not as safe except for large parties although Culebra, Mona Island and the private campgrounds of Cabo Rojo and Hatillo are all right. El Yunque rainforest, north side, is also not safe but the US Federal Forest Service is working on the problem and now lock the gates at 1800. The private campsite near the south entrance to the rainforest is much safer. Government agencies expect everyone to arrive or call before 1500. You can take públicos to some of the camping places, but with difficulty, car rental is advised.

The Government agency *Fomento Recreativo* (T722-1551 for reservations, PO Box 9022089, San Juan, PR 00904-2089) administers the following campgrounds and cabins: Luquillo Beach, Seven Seas (Fajardo), Punta Guilarte (Arroyo), Monte del Estado (Maricao), Boquerón, Tres Hermanos (Anasco), Rincón. Only Seven Seas is safe enough to recommend. Luquillo is a terrific campsite but you need to be in a large party to be safe. Two-bedroom cabins and villas are offered on five of their beaches, villas are newer and nicer.

The *Negociado del Servicio Forestal* (part of the Departamento de Recursos Naturales y Ambientales – DRNA) administers seven campgrounds and cabins and Mona Island, PO Box 9066600, Puerta de Tierra, San Juan, Puerto Rico 00906-6600, T7243724, F7215984. You need a permit and reservation, fee US$4 per person a night (cabins in Guilarte US$20), easiest to go to their office at Club Náutico by the marina at the Dos Hermanos bridges on the way to Old San Juan. They will also help you plan an itinerary. Permits and changes to reservations can be made at regional offices. Open reservations allowing flexibility within a certain time period can be made in advance by writing to Department of Natural Resources, Division of Forest Land Use Permits, PO Box 5887, Puerta de Tierra, San Juan, PR 00906. Their camp grounds are: Carite Forest, Toro Negro Forest Reserve, Guilarte Route 131 and 518, Coamo Hot Springs, Susua Dry Forest, Guanica Forest, Guajataca Forest, Rió Abajo Forest, Cambalache Beach. El Yunque rain forest is administered by the US Forest Service, T8881880 and ask for camping information, or get free permit at El Portal, Route 191, north side, before 1600. The Autoridad de Conservación y Desarrollo de Culebra (ACC) administers the Flamenco Beach campgrounds on Culebra, PO Box 217, Culebra, PR 00775, T7420700, US$10 per tent per night, they often accept walk-in reservations in winter but in summer, especially at weekends, it is like a zoo.

Getting around

Air
Several local airlines operate services within Puerto Rico, including **American Eagle** and **Vieques Air Link**, and they have offices either at the **Luis Muñoz Marín International Airport**, or the Isla Grande Airport. There are three daily **American Eagle** flights between San Juan and Ponce and several to Mayagüez. Some charter or inter-island flights leave from the Isla Grande airport.

Bus
City buses run to a 30 or 45 min schedule. Many don't operate after 2200

Bus stops are marked *Parada*, or *Parada de guaguas*. From the terminal near Plazoleta del Puerto in Old San Juan, **B21** goes along the upper road along the ocean (near *Caribe Hilton*) to Condado (Condado Plaza, El Canario) then up Avenida de Diego to stop 18 on Ponce de León, and then out to Plaza las Américas Shopping Mall. **A5** goes along the lower road to Ponce de León and then down Avenida de Diego to Isla Verde (*El San Juan, Ritz Carlton* etc) and to Iturregui terminal. To get to the airport by bus from Old San Juan is complicated. Take **A5** bus to Isla Verde terminal, then **C45** or **B40** to the airport. From Condado take **B21** to Avenida de Diego, then **A5**, then as above. **Metrobus 1** (US$0.50) goes from Old San Juan along the upper road along the ocean to Avenida Ponce de León and then to Rio Piedras. **Metrobus E** goes to Rio Piedras via the express way to Hato Rey.

The best and easiest form of transport if you want to see the island; public transport is not **Car**
always easy and finishes early. There are many car rental agencies, including at the airport,
Hertz (T7910840, www.hertz.com), *Budget* (T7913685, www.budget.com), *AAA* (T7911465),
Leaseway (T7915900, www.leaswaypr.com). *Target* (T7281447, www.targetrentacar.com),
not at airport, among the cheapest, will negotiate rates. *Charlie's Rental* (T7282418,
www.charliecars.com) in Condado and Isla Verde among the cheapest, 24-hour service. *L &
M*, *Condado* (T7911160, www.imcarrental.com), free pick-up, make sure you get it even for
day hire. For the less mobile, *Wheelchair Getaway Rent a Car* (T7264023, 800-8688028) has
vehicles which can accommodate a wheelchair. A small car may be hired for as little as US$25
(not including collision damage waiver, US$12.50, insurance is sometimes covered by your
credit card) for 24 hours, unlimited mileage (national driving licence preferred to international
licence), but rates vary according to company and demand.

Maps The *Rand McNally* road map is recommended (US$1.85); the *Gousha* road map
costs US$2.95 at Texaco stations. The tourist office distributes an *Official Transportation Map*
with town maps of San Juan, Caguas, Ponce, Mayagüez, Aguadilla and Arecibo, but a better
road map of the whole island is the *ITM Traveller's Reference Map*, Scale 1:190,000, published
by ITMB, 345 West Broadway, Vancouver BC Canada V5Y 1P8. A good map is essential because
there are few signs to places, but frequent indications of Route numbers and intersections.
Avoid driving in the San Juan metropolitan area as traffic can be very heavy. Car theft and
burglar damage is a major problem in the San Juan area. Make sure you use all the security
devices given you by the rental company. Many people actually recommended you do not
stop at red lights after 2200, because of hold-ups, just pause, look and go. Best not to drive at
night; lock car doors.

All taxis are metered, charge US$1 for initial charge and US$0.10 for every additional half mile; **Taxi**
US$0.50 for each suitcase; US$1 is charged for a taxi called from home or business. Minimum
fee US$3. Taxi drivers sometimes try to ask more from tourists, so beware, insist that the meter
is used, and avoid picking up a taxi anywhere near a cruise ship. If they refuse, tell them you
will call Puerto Rico Tourist Zone Police, T7220738, or the Public Service Commission,
T7515050, ext 253. They can revoke a taxi license. White tourist taxis with a logo on the side
offer fixed rates to and from tourist sites, for example airport, San Juan Pier, but outside those
areas they are metered. **Zone 4**, Piers to Old San Juan, US$6; **Zone 5**, Piers to Puerta de Tierra,
US$6; **Zone 6**, Piers to Condado/Miramar, US$10; **Zone 7**, Piers to Isla Verde, US$16. When
metered, tourist taxis charge US$1.30 per mile, ask for final price.

There are also shared taxis, usually Ford minibuses (*carros públicos*) which have yellow
number plates with the letters P or PD at the end and run to most parts of the island from one
main plaza to the next. They usually carry about 10 people and are not particularly
comfortable. The Río Piedras *terminal de públicos* handles all departures to the east. Many
públicos for the west leave from *puntos* near parada 18 in Santurce. Also some leave from the
main post office and others collect at the airport; elsewhere, ask around for the terminal. They
do not usually operate after about 1600 and some connections do not operate after 1500, for
example Río Piedras-Fajardo. They are also very scarce on Sunday and public holidays. *Público*
to Caguas costs US$1.25; Río Piedras-Fajardo 1½ hours (US$3); to Ponce takes two hours
(US$6-7). A service referred to as *línea* will pick up and drop off passengers where they wish.
They operate between San Juan, and most towns and cities at a fixed rate. They can be found
in the phone book under Líneas de Carros. *Públicos* are a good way of getting around,
provided you are prepared to wait up to a couple of hours for the car to fill up. It is not
recommended, however, if you want to get to out of the way places, such as the Arecibo
Observatory, the Camuy Caves, or the Tibes Indian Ceremonial Centre, when a hired car is
essential. If you hire a *público* for yourself it works out expensive, for example San Juan airport
to Ponce US$75.

Train An urban rail service is under construction in San Juan and trains are supposed to start
running in 2001.

Puerto Rico

Keeping in touch

Post Inside the new post office building in Hato Rey, on Avenida Roosevelt, there is a separate counter for sales of special tourist stamps. In Old San Juan, the post office is in an attractive old rococo-style building, at the corner of San Justo and Recinto Sur. Stamps may be bought at hotels and the airport. *Poste restante* is called General Delivery, letters are held for nine days.

Telephone
International phone code: 787

Operated by *Puerto Rico Telephone Co*, state-owned. Local calls from coin-operated booths cost US$0.10, or US$0.25 from a private pay phone, but from one city to another on the island costs more (for example US$1.25 Ponce-San Juan). Local calls from hotel rooms cost US$2.60 and often a charge is made even if there is no connection. Payphones now charge a fee of US$0.25, either deducted from your prepaid card or with a coin. The cheapest way to phone abroad is from *Phone Home*, 257 Recinto Sur, Old San Juan, T7215431, F7215497, opposite the post office by Pier 1, US$0.36 per minute to the USA, discounts on all other calls abroad, no three-minute minimum charge, faxes also sent and received. Overseas calls can be made from the AT&T office at Parada 11, Avenida Ponce de León 850, Miramar (opposite *Hotel Excelsior*, bus T1 passes outside, a chaotic place), from an office next to the Museo del Mar on Pier One, and from the airport. Three minutes to New York, US$1.50 and to the UK, US$3. For Canada Direct, dial 1-800-4967123 to get through to a Canadian operator. The blue pages in the telephone book are a tourist section in English, divided by subject.

Media **Newspapers** *San Juan Star* is the only daily English paper. There are three Spanish daily papers of note, *El Mundo*, *El Vocero* and *El Nuevo Día*. **Radio** There are seven radio stations: WDAC-FM, 105.7FM Alfa Rock 106; WKAQ-FM, 104.7FM KQ105; WIOA-FM 99.9FM Cadena Estereotempo; WMEG-FM, 106.9FM La Mega Estación; WDOY-FM, 96.5FM Y-96; WOYE-FM, 94.7FM Cosmos 94; WOSO-AM, 1030AM Radio Woso.

Food and drink

Local food Good local dishes are the mixed stew *asopao*, (chicken, seafood, etc). *Mofongo*, mashed plantain with garlic served instead of rice, is very filling. *Mofongo relleno* is the *mofongo* used as a crust around a seafood stew. *Sancocho* is a beef stew with various root vegetables, starchy but tasty. *Empanadillas* are similar to South American *empanadas* but with a thinner dough and filled with fish or meat. *Pasteles* are yucca, peas, meat, usually pork, wrapped in a banana leaf and boiled. *Tostones* are fried banana slices. Rice is served with many dishes; *arroz con habichuelas* (rice with red kidney beans) is a standard side dish. Sometimes a local restaurant will ask if you want *provisiones*; these are root vegetables and are worth trying. *Comida criolla* means 'food of the island', *criollo* refers to anything 'native'. Some local fruit names: *china* is orange, *parcha* passionfruit, *guanábana* soursop, *toronja* grapefruit; juices are made of all these, as well as guava, tamarind and mixtures. *Papaya* in a restaurant may not be fresh fruit, but *dulce de papaya* (candied), served with cheese, a good combination. Guava is served in a similar manner.

Puerto Rico

As most food is imported, the tourist, picknicker, or anyone economizing can eat as cheaply in **Restaurants**
a restaurant as by buying food in a grocery store. Outside San Juan a network of 42
restaurants, called **Mesones Gastronómicos**, has been set up. These places serve Puerto
Rican dishes at reasonable prices. Most of the *Parador* restaurants are included; a full list is
available from tourist offices.

Local beers are *Medalla* (a light beer), *Gold Label* (a premium beer, very good but hard to find) **Drink**
and *Indio* (a dark beer); a number of US brands and *Heineken* are brewed under licence. Rums
include *Don Q*, the local favourite, *Palo Viejo*, *Ron Llave* and the world-famous *Bacardi* (not so
highly regarded by puertorriqueños). *Ron Barrilito*, a small distillery, has a very good reputation.
Many restaurants pride themselves on their *piñas coladas*. *Maví* is a drink fermented from the
bark of a tree and sold in many snack-bars. Home-grown Puerto Rican coffee is very good.

Shopping

Puerto Rico is a large producer of rum, with many different types ranging from light rums for *Many of the tourist*
mixing with soft drinks to dark brandy-type rums (see above). Hand made cigars can be *shops in the old city sell*
found in Old San Juan and Puerta de Tierra. There is a place in the bus station complex in San *Andean goods*
Juan where cigars are rolled using Dominican leaf, which is better than local leaf. Shopping
malls inlcude *Plaza las Américas* in Hato Rey, others include *Plaza Carolina* in Carolina, *Río
Hondo* in Levittown, *Plaza del Carmen* in Caguas and *Mayagüez Mall* in Mayagüez. There are
more traditional shops, but also many souvenir shops in Old San Juan. Imported goods from
all over the world are available. Local artesanías include wooden carvings, musical
instruments, lace, ceramics (especially model house fronts, for example from La Casa de Las
Casitas, Cristo 250), hammocks, masks and basketwork. There are several shops in San Juan, but
it is more interesting to visit the workshops around Puerto Rico. Contact the Centro de Artes
Populares (T7246250) or the Tourism Company Artisan Office (T7212400 ext 2201) for details.
    There are a number of bookshops in the metropolitan area: *The Bookstore*, in Old San
Juan, 257 San José, T7241815, has an excellent selection of English and Spanish titles. *The
Instituto de Cultura Puertorriqueña*, Plaza de San José, has a good book and record shop with
stock of all the best known Puerto Rican writers (all in Spanish). Another record shop near
here is *Saravá*, Cristo at the corner of Sol 101, local, Caribbean, jazz and 'world music'.

Flora and fauna

Although less than 1% of the island is virgin forest, there are several forest reserves designed
to protect plants and wildlife. At the highest altitude you find dwarf cloud forest, with palms,
ferns and epiphytes. On exposed ridges it has a windswept appearance. Below the dwarf
forest is the rainforest and below that the subtropical wet forest, with open-crowned trees
and canopy trees such as *Cyrilla racemiflora*, which is large with reddish bark. Classifications
below this include the lower wet forest (Tabanuco) and the subtropical moist forest zone,
which covers most of Puerto Rico, and dry forest, found along the south coast and the eastern
tip of the island. One of the most notable creatures on Puerto Rico is the inch-long tree frog
called a *coquí*, after the two-tone noise it makes.
    In **El Yunque Tropical Rain Forest** (called The Caribbean National Forest) there are an
estimated 240 types of tree (26 indigenous), and many other plants, such as tiny wild orchids,
bamboo trees and giant ferns. The total area is 11,270 ha and 75% of Puerto Rico's virgin
forest is here. Several marked paths (quite easy, you could walk two to three in a day, no guide
needed), recreational areas and information areas have been set up. It is also home to the
Puerto Rican parrot, which has been saved from extinction but there are only 30 left. The
whole forest is a bird sanctuary.
    Mangroves are protected in **Aguirre Forest**, on the south coast near Salinas, at the Jobos
Bay National Estuarine Research Reserve, at the west end of Jobos Bay from Aguirre, and at
Piñones Forest, east of San Juan. Unlike the north coast mangroves, those on the south coast
tend to die behind the outer fringe because not enough water is received to wash away the
salt. This leaves areas of mud and skeletal trees which, at times of spring tide, flood and are

Puerto Rico

home to many birds. In winter, many ducks stop on their migration routes at Jobos. Also at **Jobos Bay**, manatees and turtles can be seen. A short boardwalk runs into the mangroves at Jobos, while at Aguirre a man runs catamaran trips to the offshore cays, and there are some good fish restaurants; take Route 7710. For Jobos Bay take Route 703, to Las Mareas de Salinas (marked Mar Negro on some maps). Before going to Jobos, contact the office at Jobos, Box 1170, Guayama, Puerto Rico 00655, T8640105, or 7248774 in San Juan.

The largest number of bird species can be found at the 655-ha **Guánica Forest**, west of Ponce, which is home to 700 plant species of which 48 are endangered and 16 exist nowhere else. (*Las aves de Puerto Rico*, by Virgilio Biaggi, University of Puerto Rico, 1983, US$12.95, is available in San Juan, for example the bookshop in Fort San Cristóbal; Herbert Raffaele's *Guide to the Birds of Puerto Rico and the Virgin Islands* is also recommended.) Guánica's dry forest vegetation is unique and the forest has been declared an International Biosphere Reserve by UNESCO. There are 10 marked trails through the forest, but it may be advisable to contact the wardens for directions before wandering off. It can be hot in the middle of the day so don't be too ambitious in which trail you choose. The Ballena Trail is quite short and you will see lizards, snakes, birds and a 700-year old guayacán tree, very gnarled and not as big as you might expect. If you want to head for the beach, Playa de Ventanas is within the Reserve. ■ *T7231770. Daily 0900-1700, no admission charge; wear protective clothing and take drinking water.* The **Punta Ballena Reserve** is next to the Guánica Forest and included in the Biosphere Reserve because of its coastal ecosystem. It contains mangrove forest, manatees, nesting sites for Hawksbill turtles, and crested toads. Beach access off Route 333.

Puerto Rico also has some of the most important caves in the western hemisphere

The Río Camuy runs underground for part of its course, forming the third largest subterranean river in the world. Near Lares, on Route 129, Km 9.8, the **Río Camuy Cave Park** has been established by the Administración de Terrenos (PO Box 3767, San Juan, T8983100), where visitors are guided through one cave and two sinkholes, open Tuesday to Sunday, and holidays 0800-1600, last trip 1545, US$10 for adults, US$7 for children, highly recommended, very easy, but entry is limited. There are fine examples of stalactites, stalagmites and, of course, plenty of bats. Keen photographers should bring a tripod for excellent photo opportunities. Several caving tour specialists can take you to a different and undeveloped part of the cave system. Offered in three degrees of difficulty, they explore underground caves, pre-Columbian petroglyphs, rivers and sinkholes. No prior knowledge needed but you need to be in good physical shape as you will have to travel on a hot-line, rappel and body raft, about US$85 for a day's adventure starting at dawn, returning to San Juan by 1800. See page 479 for tour agents. Also close is the privately-owned **Cueva de Camuy**, Route 486, Km 1.1; much smaller and less interesting, with guided tours, the area also has a swimming pool and waterslide, amusements, café, ponies, go-karts, entertainments. ■ *US$1, children US$0.50, daily 0900-1700 (till 2000 Sun).* Nearby is **Cueva del Infierno**, to which 2-3 hour tours can be arranged by phoning 8982723. About 2,000 caves have been discovered; in them live 13 species of bat (but not in every cave), the *coquí*, crickets, an arachnid called the *guavá*, and other species. Contact the Speleological Society of Puerto Rico (Sepri) for further details.

Other forest reserves, some of which are mentioned in the text below are Aguirre (T8640105), Boquerón (T8517260), Cambalache (T8811004), Carite (T7474545), Casa Pueblo Forest (T8524440), Ceiba (T8524440), Cerrillos (T7243724), Guánica (T8215706), Guajataca in the northeast (T8721045), Guilarte (T8295767), Maricao (T7243724), Mona Island (T7243724), Piñones (T7917750), Río Abajo (T8806557), Susúa (T7243724), Toro Negro (T8673040), Vega (T8332240), all of which can also be contacted through the Central Office in San Juan, T7243724, or at prforests@hotmail.com

Diving and marine life

The shallow waters are good for snorkelling and while a boat is needed to reach deeper water for most scuba diving, divers can walk in at Isabela. Visibility is not quite as good as in some other islands because of the large number of rivers flowing out to the sea, but is generally around 70 ft. However, an advantage is that the freshwater attracts a large number of fish. Manatees can occasionally be seen and humpback whales migrate through Puerto Rican waters in the autumn.

There are many companies all round the island offering boat dives, equipment rental and diving instruction, including *Caribbean School of Aquatics*, in Fajardo, T7286606, NAUI, PADI, sailing, Greg Korwek has 30 years' experience here, leader in safety standards, knows every reef; *Diving Center*, T8600183, Las Croabas, Edgar Espinosa, SSI, very knowledgeable, dives to suit your level of experience; *Coral Head Divers*, Marina de Palmas, Palmas del Mar Resort, Humacao (T8507208, F8504445, coralheaddivers@hotmail.com, US$50-75); *Caribe Aquatic Adventures*, San Juan Bay Marina, Miramar (T2818858, www.caribeaquaticadventure.com, US$90-110). Diving also at some of the larger hotels. Companies in San Juan and to the east also dive Culebra and Vieques, but there are dive shops on those islands if you want to avoid long boat rides. Check how many divers are taken on the boats, some companies cater for small groups of 6-7 divers, but several of the larger operations take out parties of 40 or 80. Look for instructor's certificate, motor boat operator's licence and coast guard inspection sticker on the boat. If any are missing you will not be insured. The inspection sticker on the boat specifies how many paying passengers are allowed.

Luquillo Beach has two snorkelling spots: in town, off the point between the surfers' beach, **La Pared** and **Blue Beach** (the beach in front of the tallest condos), and at the point of the Balneario Luquillo, past the 'no swimming' signs (beware of current, and jet skis at weekends). **Seven Seas Beach** has some good snorkelling right off the beach and there are reefs to the east. *Caribe Kayak Tours & More*, near Fajardo, specialize in small groups for snorkelling and kayaking (ocean and Lagoon) starting from Seven Seas Beach, US$40, 4½ hours, includes lunch and equipment, T8897734. Many dive shops will also take you snorkelling.

Dive centres

Snorkelling
Always be aware of jet skis & other motorized craft: they will be oblivious to you

Beaches and watersports

Swimming from most beaches is safe; the best beaches near San Juan are those at **Isla Verde** in front of the main hotels; **Luquillo** to the east of San Juan is less crowded and has a fine-sand beach from where there are good views of El Yunque (controlled car parking, US$2 per car all day, if arriving by público from San Juan, ask to get off at Balneario Luquillo, which is 1 km west of the town). There are showers, toilets and lifeguards, food kiosks and souvenir shops, it is peaceful during the week but noisy at weekends. The north coast Atlantic sea is rougher than the east and south waters, particularly in winter; some beaches are semi-deserted. There are 13 *balneario* beaches round the island where lockers, showers and parking places are provided for a small fee. Some have cabins, tent sites or trailer sites. *Balnearios* are open Tuesday-Sunday 0900-1700 in winter and 0800-1700 in summer. Never leave anything unattended on the beaches in Puerto Rico. If you are alone it is probably best to leave.

Swimming

The most popular beaches for surfing are the **Pine Beach Grove** in Isla Verde (San Juan), **Jobos** (near Isabela in the northeast, not the south coast bay), **La Pared** in Luquillo, officially listed as dangerous for swimming but used for surfing tournaments, **Surfer** and **Wilderness** beaches in the former Ramey Field air base at Punta Borinquén, north of Aguadilla and **Punta Higuero**, Route 413 between Aguadilla and Rincón on the west coast. Several international surfing competitions have been held at Surfer and Wilderness.

Surfing & windsurfing

The **Condado lagoon** is calm with steady winds and is popular for windsurfing, as is **Boquerón Bay**, off Isla Verde beach, and **Ocean Park beach**. Only experts can cope with conditions on the northeast shore near Aguadilla: **Jobos**, **Wilderness** and **Surfer** beaches, where the winds are good and the waves break with excellent shape. **Rincón** is the same. **La Parguera** is great for slalom conditions, a great sail to Cayo Enrique on protected waters with lots of wind.

Puerto Rico's coastline is protected in many places by coral reefs and cays which are fun to visit and explore. **La Cordillera** is a nature reserve of cays and rocks off the northeast tip of Puerto Rico, including Icacos, Diablo, Ratones and Las Cucarachas, which have a rich coral reef, clear water and sandy beaches. There is an abandoned limestone quarry on the south side of Icacos. The cays are easily accessible by boat from Las Croabas or Fajardo. You can also snorkel

Day sails

or scuba around the cays by seaplane from San Juan, Zoltan at *Seaplanes in Paradise*, knows all the best spots, US$150 per person for four people, T7250243, www.spiderlink.net/seaplanes. There are many sailboat excursions from Fajardo with snorkelling, lunch and drinks, usually US$55 per person on catamarans (also known as cattlemarans taking 49 people), more on the monohulls. Also sailboats from Marina del Rey, San Juan and **La Parguera**.

Sailing   There are four marinas at **Fajardo, Puerto del Rey**, the **Club Náutico** at Miramar and another at **Boca de Cangrejos** in Isla Verde (both in San Juan) and one at the *Palmas del Mar Resort* near Humacao. There is a marina for fishing motor launches at **Arecibo**. Sailing is popular, with winds of about 10-15 knots all year round. Craft of all sizes are available for hire. There are several racing tournaments; a major international regatta is the **Discover the Caribbean** series in September and October. Power boats appeal to the Puerto Rican spirit and there are a lot of races, held mostly off the west coast from Mayagüez Bay to Boquerón Bay. A huge crowd collects for the Caribbean Offshore Race, with professionals and celebrities participating.

Fishing   Deep-sea fishing is popular and more than 30 world records have been broken in Puerto Rican waters, where blue and white marlin, sailfish, wahoo, dolphin, mackerel and tarpon, to mention a few, are a challenge to the angler. An international bill fish competition is held in September at the Club Náutico de San Juan (T7220177), one of the biggest tournaments in the Caribbean. Fishing boat charters are available: for example *Mike Benítez Fishing Charters Inc*, at the Club Náutico de San Juan, PO Box 5141, Puerta de Tierra, San Juan, PR 00906, T7232292 (till 2100), 7246265 (till 1700), F7251336, www.mikebenitezfishing.com, prices from US$125-1,200. Others in San Juan include *Captain Mike's Sportfishing*, T7217335 and *Caribbean Outfitters*, T3968346, www.fishinginpuertorico.com Others around the island are mentioned in the text below. You can also fish in the many lakes inland where there are large-mouthed bass and peacock bass. Contact the Department of Natural Resources, T7248774, ext 445 for details. Marcos Hanke, T7631929, will take you fly fishing, US$200 half day, catch and release, knowledgeable about freshwater lakes.

Other sports   There are 18 **golf** courses around the island, many of which are professionally designed championship courses. The *Hyatt Cerromar* and *Hyatt Dorado* hotels in Dorado have four excellent 36-hole championship golf courses, T7961234, www.hyatt.com; among the 18-hole courses, *Berwind Country Club* (T8763056) accepts non-members on Tuesday, Thursday and Friday, *Palmas del Mar* (Humacao, T2852221, www.palmasdelmar.com), Westin Riomar (Río Grande, T8886000), and Punta Borinquén (Aguadilla, nine holes, T8902987) all have golf pros and are open to the public. Over 100 **tennis** courts are available, mostly in the larger hotels. There are also 17 lit public courts in San Juan's Central Park, open daily, with tennis pro, T7221646. The *Palmas del Mar* resort, at Humacao, has 20 courts. **Cockfighting** season is from 1 November to 31 August and is held at the new, air-conditioned Coliseo Gallístico in Isla Verde, near the *Holiday Inn* (Route 37, Km 1.5) on Saturdays, 1300-1900, T7911557. Admission from US$4 to US$10. **Horse racing** at El Comandante, Route 3, Km 15.3, T8762450, www.elcomandante.com Canóvanas is one of the hemisphere's most beautiful race courses. Races are held all the year round (Wednesday, Friday, Sunday and holidays, 1415-1730). Wednesday is ladies' day. Children under 12 not admitted at any time. On mountain trails or beaches, **riding** is a good way to see the island. Puerto Rico also prides itself on its paso fino horses. There are over 7,000 registered paso fino horses on the island and several horse shows are held throughout the year which are well worth attending. The two best known are the **Dulce Sueño Fair**, Guayama, the first weekend in March, and the **Fiesta La Candelaria**, Manatí, the first weekend in February. At Palmas del Mar, Humacao, there is an equestrian centre T8526000, ext 12721 which offers beach rides and riding and jumping lessons. Hacienda Carabalí, T8895820, reservations required, Luquillo, Route 992, Km 4, offers beach or hill riding and has paso fino horses, groups of up to 40 for trail rides. *Tropical Trails Rides*, Route 4466, Km 1.8, Isabela, beach, forest and cliff trails, Craig Barker has 20 beautiful paso fino horses, about 1½ hours west of San Juan, US$35 per two hours, T8729256. At the *El Conquistador Resort* complex, T8631000, ask for Richard and the ferry to the horses on Isla Palominos. **Polo** is becoming popular and the *Ingenio Polo Club* hosts the Rolex Polo Cup on its 25-acre grounds by the Loiza River in March.

Popular **spectator sports** are boxing and baseball (at professional level, also a winter league at San Juan stadium, US$4 for a general seat, US$5 box seat, Tuesday is Ladies' Night), basketball, volleyball and beach volleyball. Running is also popular. Puerto Rico is a member of the Olympic Committee. The island made a bid to host the 2004 Olympic Games.

Holidays and festivals

New Year's Day, Three Kings' Day (6 January), De Hostos' Birthday (11 January), Washington's Birthday (22 February), Emancipation Day (22 March), Good Friday, José de Diego's Birthday (16 April), Memorial Day (30 May), St John the Baptist (24 June), Independence Day (4 July), Muñoz Rivera's Birthday (17 July), Constitution Day (25 July), Dr José Celso Barbosa's Birthday (27 July), Labour Day (1 September), Columbus Day (12 October), Veterans' Day (11 November), Discovery of Puerto Rico (19 November), Thanksgiving Day (25 November), Christmas Day.

Public holidays

Everything is closed on **public holidays**. One of the most important is *24 June*, though in fact the capital grinds to a halt the previous afternoon and everyone heads for the beach. Here there is loud *salsa* music and barbecues until midnight when everyone walks backwards into the sea to greet the Baptist and ensure good fortune. **Día de la Constitución**, *25 July*, takes place at a weekend and it is almost impossible to get a hotel room. Reservations should be made in advance. Every town/city has local holidays for **crop-over festivals** (pineapple, tobacco, sugar cane, etc) and for celebration of the town's saint. These festivals can be great fun, especially the Carnival in Mayagüez late May.

Festivals
There is a festival somewhere every week

Health

'La monga' is a common, flu-like illness, nothing serious, it goes away after a few days. Avoid swimming in rivers: bilharzia may be present. There has been dengue fever, take care not to get bitten by mosquitoes. The northeast coast is particularly risky. Government and private hospitals. Ambulance, T3432500. Emergency T911.

San Juan

Founded in 1510, San Juan, the capital spreads several kilometres along the north coast and also inland. The nucleus is Old San Juan, the old walled city on a tongue of land between the Atlantic and San Juan bay. It has a great deal of charm and character, a living museum; the Institute of Culture restores and renovates old buildings, museums and places of particular beauty. The narrow streets of Old San Juan, some paved with small grey-blue cobblestones which were brought over as ships' ballast, are lined with colonial churches, houses and mansions, in a very good state of repair and all painted different pastel colours.

Population: about 1 mn

Ins and outs

Getting a taxi from the airport is your best bet, buses from the airport to San Juan and back are complicated. There is a despatch desk for *públicos* at the airport. See further page 478.

Getting there

Small yellow buses, or trolleys, run around the old city all day 0600-2200, free, *paradas* (stops) are marked. They start from La Puntilla and Covadonga public car parks. There is also a trolley service in the Isla Verde beach area from Punta Las Marías. There is a city bus (*guagua*) service with a fixed charge of US$0.25 for standard route, US$0.50 for longer. (No change given; make sure you have right money.) They have special routes, sometimes against the normal direction of traffic, in which case the bus lanes are marked by yellow and white lines.

Getting around

Puerto Rico

Bus stops are marked by white and orange signs or yellow and black notices on lampposts marked 'Parada'. Up until the 1950s tramcars ran between Río Piedras and Old San Juan along Avs Ponce de León and Fernández Juncos. To this day directions are given by *Paradas*, or tram stops, so you have to find out where each one is.

Sights

Some of the restored and interesting buildings to visit include **La Fortaleza**, the Governor's Palace, built between 1533 and 1540 as a fortress against Carib attacks but greatly expanded in the 19th century. It is believed to be the oldest executive residence in continuous use in the Western Hemisphere. Access to the official areas is not permitted. ■ *0900-1600 Mon-Fri, T7217000 ext 2211; guided tours in English on the hour, in Spanish every 30 mins.* The **Cathedral** was built in the 16th century but extensively restored in the 19th and 20th. The body of Juan Ponce de León rests in a marble tomb. ■ *Daily 0630-1700.* The tiny **Cristo Chapel** with its silver altar, was built after a young man competing in 1753 in a horse-race during the San Juan festival celebrations plunged with his horse over the precipice at that very spot. ■ *Tue 1000-1600.* Next to it is the aptly-named **Parque de las Palomas**, where the birds perch on your hand to be fed. This practice is best avoided, however, as we have heard of people contracting a lung virus and ending up in hospital. **San Felipe del Morro** was built in 1591 to defend the entrance to the harbour, and the 11ha **Fort San Cristóbal** was completed in 1772 to support El Morro and to defend the landward side of the city, with its five independent units connected by tunnels and dry moats, rising 46m above the ocean. Good views of the city. ■ *Both open daily 0900-1700. Free. T7296777, www.nps.gov/saju Tours of El Morro in English at 1100 and 1500, tours of San Cristóbal in English at 1000 and 1400.* The **Plaza del Quinto Centenario**, inaugurated on 12 October 1992 to commemorate the 500th anniversary of Columbus' landing, is a modernistic square on several levels with steps leading to a central fountain with hundreds of jets (good view of El Morro, the cemetery

San Juan Orientation

N

Not to Scale

Related maps:
A. Old San Juan,
page 490-491

■ **Sleeping**
1 Beach Buoy Inn
2 Best Western Pierre
3 Caribe Hilton

4 Casa Mathiesen
5 Condado Plaza
6 El Canario Inn

7 Excelsior
8 Green Isle Inn
9 Hostería del Mar

and sunsets). The restored **Cuartel de Ballajá**, once the barracks for Spanish troops and their families, was also inaugurated 12 October 1992 with the **Museum of the Americas** on the second floor tracing the cultural development of the history of the New World. ■ *Mon-Fri 1000-1600, Sat-Sun 1100-1700. Free. T7245052. Guided tours available weekdays 1030, 1130, 1230 and 1400.* The **Dominican Convent** built in the early 16th century, later used as a headquarters by the US Army, is now the office of the Institute of Culture, with a good art gallery. Cultural events are sometimes held in the patio, art exhibitions in the galleries. ■ *Open Wed-Sun, 0900-1200, 1300-1630. T7240700.* The 16th-century **San José** church, originally a Dominican chapel, is the second oldest church in the Western Hemisphere and once the family church of Ponce de León's descendants. Ponce was buried here until moved to the Cathedral in the 20th century. ■ *Mon-Sat 0830-1600, Sun mass at 1200.* The early 18th century **Casa de los Contrafuertes** believed to be the oldest private residence in the old city, now has periodic art exhibitions on the second floor and a small pharmacy museum with 19th-century exhibits on the ground floor. ■ *Wed-Sun, 0900-1630. T7245949.* The **Casa Blanca**, 1 Calle San Sebastián, was built in 1523 by the family of Ponce de León, who lived in it for 250 years until it became the residence of the Spanish and then the US military commander-in-chief. It is now a historical museum which is well worth a visit. ■ *Tue-Sun 0900-1200, 1300-1630. US$2 adults, US$1 children. T7244102. Guided tours Tue-Fri by appointment.* The **Alcaldía**, or City Hall, was built 1604-1789. ■ *Mon-Fri 0800-1600 except holidays. T7247171, ext 2391.* The **Intendencia**, formerly the Spanish colonial exchequer, a fine example of 19th-century Puerto Rican architecture, now houses Puerto Rico's State Department. ■ *Mon-Fri 0800-1200, 1300-1630. T7222121.* The **naval arsenal** was the last place in Puerto Rico to be evacuated by the Spanish in 1898, exhibitions are held in three galleries. ■ *Wed-Sun, 0900-1200, 1300-1630. T7245949.* The **Casa del Callejón** is a restored 18th-century house containing two colonial museums, the architectural and the Puerto Rican Family. ■ *T7255250. Both closed for restoration.*

Puerto Rico

Museums Apart from those in historic buildings listed above, there are the **Pablo Casals Museum** in an 18th-century house beside San José church, with Casals' cello and other memorabilia. ■ *T7239185. US$1 adults, US$0.50 children. Tue-Sat 0930-1730.* The **San Juan Museum of Art and History**, Norzagaray y MacArthur, built in 1855 as a marketplace, now a cultural centre with exhibition galleries. ■ *Tue-Sun, 1000-1600. T7241875.* The **Casa del Libro** is an 18th-century house on Calle Cristo, has a collection of rare books, including some over 400 years old. ■ *Tue-Sat, except holidays, 1100-1630. T7230354.* And the **Museum of the Sea** on Pier One, with a collection of maritime instruments and models. ■ *Open when the pier is open for cruise ships. T7252532.* The **Indian Museum** at Calle San José 109 on the corner of Luna concentrates on Puerto Rican indigenous cultures, with exhibits, ceramics and archaeological digs. ■ *Tue-Sat 0900-1600. No admission charge. T7245477.* Another museum in the old city is a military museum at **Fort San Jerónimo**. ■ *Wed-Sun, 0930-1200, 1300-1630. T7245949.*

Metropolitan San Juan The metropolitan area of San Juan includes the more modern areas of Santurce, Hato Rey, and Río Piedras. **Río Piedras** was founded in 1714 but became incorporated into San Juan in 1951. On the edge of Río Piedras, the gardens and library of the former governor, Luis Muñoz Marín, are open to the public, with a museum showing his letters, photos and speeches. ■ *T7557979. Tue-Sat 0900-1300.*

The **University of Puerto Rico** at Río Piedras is in a lovely area. The **University Museum** has archaeological and historical exhibitions, and also monthly art exhibitions. ■ *T7640000, ext 2452. Open Mon-Fri, 0900-2100, weekends 0900-1500.* The

Old San Juan

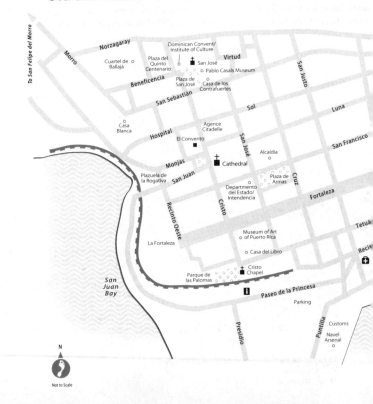

Botanical Garden at the Agricultural Experiment Station has over 200 species of tropical and subtropical plants, a bamboo promenade (one variety can grow four feet in a day), an orchid garden (over 30,000 orchids), and an aquatic garden. ■ *T7634408, www.upr.clu.edu Daily 0800-1630.*

Hato Rey is the financial district of San Juan nicknamed 'the Golden Mile'. The **Luís Muñoz Marín Park** on Avenida Jesús T Piñero covers 35ha, which can be toured by a 1 km cable car. ■ *Open Tue-Sun 0900-1700.* The **Sacred Heart University** with the **Museum of Contemporary Puerto Rican Art** is in Santurce. ■ *T2680049, Tue-Sat 0900-1600, Sun 1100-1700.* The modern **Fine Arts Center**, opened in 1981, with theatres and halls at the corner of De Diego and Ponce de León. ■ *T7244751.* The residential area **Miramar** has several moderately priced hotels as well as some expensive ones. Miramar is separated from the Atlantic coast by the **Condado lagoon** and the Condado beach area, where the luxury hotels, casinos, nightclubs and restaurants are concentrated. From Condado the beach front is built up eastwards through Ocean Park, Santa Teresita, Punta Las Marías and Isla Verde. Building is expanding along the narrow strip beyond Isla Verde, between the sea and the airport. Along this road, Avenida Boca de Cangrejos, there are lots of food trucks selling barbecued specialities.

Excursions

A ferry, Old San Juan (Pier Two) – Hato Rey, Cataño, crosses every 30 minutes, 0600-2200, weather permitting, T7881155, US$0.50, to Cataño. In October 1999 an enormous statue of Columbus made by a Georgian, Zurab Tsereteli, is to be assembled in sections here as a major tourist attraction. From Cataño waterfront. you can catch a *público* (US$1 per person), or bus C37 to about five blocks from the **Bacardí rum distillery.** ■ *Route 888, Km 2.6, T7881500, www.bacardi.com There are free conducted tours around the plant Mon-Sat, every 30 mins 0830-1630, travelling from one building to the next by a little open motor train. Closed for Christmas holidays.*

On Route 2, shortly before Bayamón, is the island's earliest settlement, **Caparra**, established by Ponce de León in 1508. Ruins of the fort can still be seen and there is a **Museum of the Conquest and Colonization of Puerto Rico**. ■ *T7814795. Open daily 0900-1600.*

Puerto Rico

Essentials

Sleeping

Most of the large San Juan hotels are in **Condado** or **Isla Verde** and overlook the sea, with swimming pools, nightclubs, restaurants, shops and bars. To get value for money, it may be advisable to avoid the luxury hotels on the sea front. There is plenty of cheaper accommodation within walking distance of the beaches and lots of beachfront apartments at very reasonable prices for stays of a week or more, look in the local newspaper, *El Nuevo Día* for notices, usually quote monthly rates but available for shorter stays.

Acosta
Toro
O'Donnel
Fort San Cristóbal
Muñoz Rivera
To Condado
Plaza Colón
La Capilla
Casa del Callejón
Ponce de Léon
Tapiá Theatre
Adolfo de Hostos Archaeological Museum
Paseo la Covadonga
Sur
Plazoleta del Puerto
Comercio
Wyndham Old San Juan & Casino
La Marina
Museum of the Sea
Pier 1
Pier 2
Pier 3
Ferry to Cataño

▶ *Defeat of the great unwashed*

1997 was the 200th anniversary of the attack on San Juan by General Abercrombie in the last and largest attempt by the British to take the Island. On 17 April 1797, 68 ships and over 3,000 troops anchored off Punta de Cangrejos. The next day they landed, occupied the town of San Mateo de Cangrejos, and Abercrombie set up command in the summer residence of Bishop La Cuerda. They marched on San Juan but were unable to penetrate its defences despite continuous bombardment. The seige

was raised when local reinforcements arrived with 800 infantry and two cavalry divisions from Guaynabo and Bayamón. Fighting was fierce in the counterattack and continued until 30 April, when Abercrombie decided to retreat and re-embark his troops. According to the report in The Times on 9 June the expeditions difficulties were so severe that "officers and men under Sir Ralph Abercrombie laboured for 15 days without even being able to change their clothes."

Condado LL *Radisson Ambassador*, 1369 Ashford, T7217300, F7236151, www.radisson.com 233 rooms, suites, casino. **LL** *San Juan Marriott Resort & Casino*, 1309 Ashford Av, T7227000, F2896182, www.marriottpr.com 525 rooms, 2 pools, health club and spa. **LL** *Caribe Hilton*, on the old city side of Condado bridge, T7210303, F7258849, www.caribehilton.com Luxury, expensive suites, being expanded to 970 rooms by 2001, first stage of exansion completed with public areas redesigned, new conference centre, new swimming complex, casino, set in 17 acres of gardens, many sporting facilities, good swimming, breakwater. On the Condado side of the bridge is the **LL** *Condado Plaza Hotel & Casino*, 999 Ashford Av, T7211000, F7214613. Also expensive, 570 rooms, suites, casino, with 7 restaurants including *Tony Roma's*, small beach, protected swimming. **LL-AL** *Days Inn Condado Lagoon*, 6 Clemenceau, T7210170, F7244356, www.daysinn.com 48 rooms, good, with good restaurant. **L** *Best Western Pierre*, 105 De Diego, T7211200, F7213118. Designed for business travellers or families. Good value are the three Canario hotels, B&B, www.canariohotels.com: **AL** *El Canario by the Sea*, 4 Condado Av, T7228640, F7254921. 25 rooms, close to beach, comfortable. **AL** *El Canario Inn*, 1317 Ashford, T7223861, F7220391. 1 block from the beach, good, clean, safe. **AL** *El Canario by the Lagoon*, 4 Clemenceau, T7228640, F7238590, 40 rooms with balcony, 1 block from beach. **AL-C** *Embassy*, 1125 Sea View, T7258284, F7252400, home.att.net/~embassyguesthouse 20 rooms, good bathroom, TV, a/c, pool on the beach. **A-B** *Aleli By The Sea*, 1125 Sea View St, T7255313, F7214744, on seafront. Kitchen facilities, good, no pool, parking.

Ocean Park L-B *Hostería del Mar*, 1 Tapia St, T7273302, F2680772, prhtasmallhotels.com, on the beach. 17 rooms, nice restaurant, nice place to stay. **AL** *Numero Uno on the Beach*, 1 Santa Ana, T7265010, F7275482. 12 rooms, safe behind barred doors and high walls, good beach but not safe after dark, with pool, gay friendly. **B-C** *Beach Buoy Inn*, 1853 McLeary, T7288119, F2680037. Also safe behind barred doors and high walls, but on busy road so some traffic noise, windows sealed in some rooms, no view but pleasant, complimentary breakfast with lots of coffee, Danish pastries and newspapers, no restaurant, helpful, parking, shopping close by, beach towels.

Isla Verde LL *Ritz Carlton San Juan Hotel & Casino*, T2531700, F2531777. 414 rooms, most expensive, on the beach. **LL** *San Juan Grand Beach Resort and Casino*, on Route 37 (the main road through Isla Verde), T7916100, F7918525, www.sjgrand.com. 400 rooms, deluxe, lots of restaurants. **LL** *Wyndham El San Juan Hotel and Casino*, Ocean Front, T7911000, F7910390, www.wyndham.com. 389 rooms, look at the lobby even if you do not stay, red marble and mahogany. **A-C** *La Casa Mathieson*, Uno 14, T7268662, and *Green Isle*, Uno 36, T7264330, are jointly owned, greeninn@prt.net Both charge the same, both near airport, and have swimming pools, cooking facilities, friendly, free transport to and from airport. **B** *El Patio*, Tres Oeste 87, Bloque D-8, Villamar, T7266298. 14 rooms, swimming pool, use of kitchen, laundry.

Old San Juan LL *El Convento Hotel & Casino*, a converted Carmelite nunnery at Cristo 100, T7239020, F7212877, www.elconvento.com A charming hotel with a Spanish atmosphere and the dining room is in the former chapel, exclusive, very good service, 58 rooms, swimming pool, nice garden in which to have a drink, unfortunately the plaza opposite is a nocturnal campsite for junkies/alcoholics and stray cats. **LL-A** *Galería San Juan*, Norzagaray 204, T7236515. 300-year-old rambling house with inner courtyards, artist's residence and studio, art, antiques, views everywhere, labyrinth, rooms and suites, breakfast included. **LL** *Wyndham Old San Juan Hotel & Casino*, T7215000, F2891950, www.wyndham.com New 240-room hotel by cruise ship dock, near the square, great view of bay from rooftop pool. Guest houses on Calle San Francisco, information from Joyería Sol, Tanca 207, fan, cooking and washing facilities, friendly and helpful, but absolutely filthy and like cells. Also in Old San Juan are **A-D** *Central*, San José 202, T7222751. Good location on main plaza, but reportedly used by short stay visitors and drug dealers, very basic, no charm, ask for a room with fan away from a/c units, also ask for towels when checking in so you do not have to run up and downstairs again. **C-F** *Enrique Castro Guest House*, Tanca 205, T7225436, at Relojería Suiza Mecánico Cuarzo, 2nd Floor (Box 947). Welcoming but rather old and dirty, run by Enrique and his son, Vincente, communual showers, some with hot water, rooms a/c, washbasin, fridge, kitchen available, rooms without a/c can be uncomfortably hot. **AL-C** *The Caleta*, 11 Caleta de las Monjas, T7255347, www.thecaleta.com Furnished apartments run by Michael Giessler, weekly rates from US$350, occasional nightly rental, coin laundry.

Picturesque area, hilly cobbled streets, ocean views but no beach swimming

Miramar *L-AL* *Excelsior*, 801 Ponce de León, T7217400, F7230068, hotelexcelsior@compuserve.com 140 rooms, studios and 2-room suites, popular gourmet restaurant, bar, pool, rooms overlooking freeway are noisy, business type hotel. Under same management is **B** *Olimpo Court*, 603 Av Miramar, T7240600. 45 rooms and studios with kitchenettes, restaurant, parking. **B** *Miramar*, 606 Av Ponce de León, T7226239, F7231180. 'Not chic', but OK, business travellers on a budget, sea view from 5th floor front, dirty carpets, ask for room without carpet, longer stays possible.

Residential area, easy bus to old San Juan, not great at night

Old San Juan *Fortaleza*, Fortaleza 252. For Puerto Rican cuisine. *Bistro*, Cruz 152. A pleasant, small restaurant and bar with tasty local food at reasonable prices. *Chef Marisol*, Cristo. California cuisine with imported ingredients, including imported fish. *La Mallorquina*, San Justo 207, T7223261. The oldest restaurant in the Caribbean. Recommended. Also on San Justo: *Café de Paris*, No 256; *Szechuan*, Chinese, No 257, and other cafés and *Taco Maker*, No 255. There are several Mexican places in the city, eg *Parián* on Fortaleza; *Taza de Oro*, Luna 254, near San Justo. *Bodegón de La Fortaleza*, Fortaleza 312; *El Siglo XX*, Fortaleza 355, T7241849. Consistently good, great breakfast, lunch and dinner, not expensive, excellent service, spectacular paella. *La Danza*, corner of Cristo and Fortaleza, T7231642; *La Bombonera*, San Francisco 259. Restaurant and pastry shop, good value breakfast, 1960s atmosphere, antique coffee machine; *4 Seasons Café*, in *Hotel Central*, Plaza de Armas. For good value local lunches; *Tropical Blend*, juice bar in La Calle alley on Fortaleza; *El Batey* bar, Cristo 101, just behind El Convento. Recommended; *Cafetería Manolin*, San Justo 258. A/c, packed with locals at breakfast, Puerto Rican food, lunch specials daily. *Nono's*, San Sebastián y Cristo. Bar, burgers, salads, steaks, sandwiches, and nearby on San Sebastián (all on Plaza San José), *Patio de Sam* very good for local drinks (happy hour 1600-1900), and *Tasca El Boquerón*. On Av Ponce de León, *El Miramar*. Good, but not cheap. *La Buena Mesa*, 605 Ponce de León. Good, small, middle price range. Several bars and cafés on Plaza Colón in Old San Juan.

Eating

Condado There is a huge selection of restaurants in Condado, from the posh to all the fast food chain restaurants. Similarly, Isla Verde is well-served by the fast food fraternity; on the beach at Isla Verde is *The Hungry Sailor* bar and grill. Sandwiches, tapas, burgers, with a snack bar next door. *Cecilia's Place*, Rosa St, Isla Verde. *Frida's*, Av Domenech 128, Hato Rey, T7634827, www.letsdine.com/fridas. Mexican, around US$12, quite upscale, good.

Fondas For breakfast or lunch seek out the *fondas*, not advertised as restaurants but usually part of a private home, or a family-run eating place serving *criollo* meals which are filling and

Puerto Rico

good value. Recommended in San Juan are: *Macumba*, 2000 Loíza. *Casa Juanita*, 242 Av Roosevelt, Hato Rey. Try chicken asopao or pork chops con mangu. *Cafetería del Parking*, 757 José de Diego. Interior, Cayey (specialities include *mondongo*, and *boronia de apio y bacalao* – cod and celery root). *D'Arcos*, 605 Miramar, Santurce. Speciality is roast veal with stuffed peppers and white bean sauce, also try *pega'o* (crunchy rice).

Nightlife *Jazz at The Place*, Fortaleza 154 in old San Juan. No admission charge, drinks about US$2. *Shannons Irish Pub*, Condado. Bus from airport passes it, live music (rock and roll), beer US$2.50. Recommended. *Caribe Hilton* is a favourite nightspot, also the other 4-5 star hotels.

Directory See page 476 to 482 for listings of airline offices, bank, post, telephone services, hospitals, medical facilities and local tour agents.

The interior

Out of the metropolitan area, 'on the island' are a variety of excursions; as it is a small island it is possible to see forested mountains and desert-like areas in only a short time. However, because the public transport system is rather limited, it is difficult if not impossible to visit some places without a rented car. The cool climate in the mountains has caused resort hotels to be built in several towns inland.

El Yunque

El Yunque (see also page 483), or **Caribbean National Forest**, is a tropical forest and bird sanctuary, the largest rain forest in the US forest service system. The forest is divided into north side and south side, with no road connection. After a series of landslides everyone has given up and Route 191 is permanently closed in the middle; you have to drive all the way around to get to the south side or hike (a bit tricky to get past the landslides). Concrete trails to the various peaks: El Yunque (The Anvil) itself, Mount Britton, Los Picachos, as well as to waterfalls and look out towers giving excellent views. There are 13 trails in all, covering 37 km. The Baño Grande is the shortest, taking about 45 minutes and passing a large man-made pool built by the Civilian Conservation Corp in the 1930s. The Big Tree Trail is about the most strenuous, taking 1¾ hours and ending at La Mina waterfall. In view of the heavy rainfall, another name for the forest is Rain Forest. Visitors need not worry unduly, as storms are usually brief and plenty of shelter is provided. If you have worked up an appetite walking, on your way out, heading south on Route 191, there is a collection of food stalls on your left selling fish, plantain, yuca and fruit licuados, delicious. *The Palma de Sierra Centre* is open daily 0815-1600, 1 Nov-1 Mar, 0915-1700 2 Mar-31 Oct, T8872875, groups should contact El Yunque Ranger District, PO Box B, Palmer PR00721. In 1996 *El Portal, Centro Forestal Tropical*, opened, with exhibitions, educational and conservation material, patios where you can relax and admire the view, 100-seat theatre showing a 30-min documentary film on El Yunque, in Spanish followed by an English version. US$3 adults, US$1.50 children and older people. Daily 0900-1700. ■ *Getting there: El Yunque is reached via Route 3 from San Juan towards Fajardo, and then right on Route 191. El Portal is at the entrance on Route 191. The Park Service publishes a good map. Camping is allowed with a free permit from El Portal, but there are no facilities and it is not recommended for security reasons. T8881810 for information or go to El Portal before 1600. www.r8web.com/caribbean*

The south side of the forest is approached from Naguabo up Route 191. No facilities have yet been developed but there are plans. The soil and weather here is different from the north. The north is red clay (and soggy) and the south is almost sandy (fine granite), while it is less humid and cooler. It is also quieter, with no tour buses or parking lots.

Puerto Rico

South side *Robin Phillips* has several rustic cabins, **D**, and tent sites on his fruit farm. Robin **Sleeping**
and Sita will guide you through the forest or to the petroglyphs. Terrific views to the sea.
Robin is full of information. T8742138 or write to Adventures with Nature, HC1, Box 4449,
Naguabo, PR 00718, www.rainforestinn.net Also 2 excellent B&Bs on Route 191 through
Naguabo, wonderful views of forest, rivers, waterfalls: *Casa Cabuy*, T8746221. *Casa
Flamboyan*, T8746074. Pool, luxury.

Eastern tour

An interesting round trip through the east half of the island can be done by a series of
públicos from San Juan – Río Grande – Luquillo – Fajardo – Humacao – Yabucoa –
Guayama – Cayey – Aibonito – Barranquitas – Bayamón – San Juan. If travelling by
car, a variant between San Juan and El Yunque takes you on Route 187 from Isla
Verde, outside San Juan, to Loíza along a stretch of the north coast, which includes
the **Piñones State Forest**, sand blown and palm-lined road. Some parts are
unspoilt, some parts pass through apartment blocks on the outskirts of towns, and
the road is a popular rush-hour route. The bay at Vacía Talega is beautifully calm.
The section which joins the coast to Route 3 at Río Grande is also tree-lined and
attractive. There is a big Westin resort and several golf clubs in the Río Grande area.
In the hills above Rio Grande is *La Casa De Vida Natural Health Spa*, a holistic health
retreat and vegetarian bed and breakfast, lots of therapies available, steam baths,
jacuzzi, T8874359, www.lacasaspa.com

Luquillo was founded in 1797 when a group of colonizers led by Cristóbal de **Luquillo**
Guzmán moved from San Juan to escape frequent British naval attacks. The town
was named after the Indian cacique Loquillo, who died a few years after the last
Indian rebellion of Boriquén that took place following the seizure of the Spanish settlement of Santiago by the shores of the Río Daguao in 1513. In honour of the anniversary of its founding, in 1997 a new landscaped plaza municipal was inaugurated
with a huge statue of the cacique Loquillo. There is a beach in town and a *balneario*
west of town (see page 485); just by the latter is a row of restaurants on the slip road
off the dual carriageway (Route 3). *Públicos* from San Juan to Luquillo are marked
Fajardo, US$3, no return *públicos* after 1500.

Fajardo is a boating centre with several marinas and a public beach at Seven Seas; **Fajardo**
beyond Seven Seas is Las Croabas beach. Offshore is an uninhabited, but much visited, coral island, Icacos. **Las Cabezas de San Juan** is a nature reserve on the headlands (three promontories) north of Fajardo on Route 987, Km 6. A 19th-century
lighthouse contains a nature centre and its observation deck has a great view of El
Yunque and surrounding islands. There are trails and boardwalks, guides and
explanatory signs of the different ecological habitats. ■ *T7225882, or T8602560 at
weekends, www.fideicomiso.org US$5 adults, US$2 children. Fri-Sun, tours, reservations required.* Off Humacao Beach/*Balneario* is a tiny cay called **Cayo Santiago**,
also known as **Monkey Island**. It is inhabited by over 500 tiny monkeys, which are
protected. The island is closed to the public although there are sightseeing tours
which get you close enough to see the monkeys through binoculars.

Sleeping West of Fajardo on the hill is **LL** *Wyndham El Conquistador Resort & Country
Club*, 1000 Conquistador Av, T8631000, F8636500, www.wyndham.com A large complex
with 918 rooms, 16 restaurants, casino, golf course for hotel guests only, lots of facilities, private ferry to nearby sandy cay, white beach. Further south is **LL-L** *Doral Resort at Palmas
del Mar*, 170 Candelero Drive, near Humacao, T8526000, F8526320, www.palmas
delmar.com, on long stretch of beach. Can be rough seas, condos, marina, 2 top golf courses,
20 tennis courts, horse riding, diving, marina, mega resort complex, many restaurants, pools
etc. The only paradores on the east side are **B** *Martorell* at Luquillo, 6A Ocean Drive,
T8892710, F8894520. Close to beach, includes breakfast, kitchen, shared bath. You pay for

Puerto Rico

the location, advisable to reserve in advance here at any time. **AL-B** *La Familia*, on Route 987, Km 4, Las Croabas, Fajardo, T8631193, F8605345, www.hotellafamilia.com 35 rooms, rather small, a/c, bath, TV, breakfast included, pool. **A-B** *Las Delicias*, Fajardo Playa, T8631818. On the dock, across street from post office and customs building, convenient for ferry to Vieques and Culebra. Very good, nice staff, 21 rooms, a/c, restaurant, bar. **B** *Anchor's Inn*, Route 987 Km 27, Fajardo, T8637200. Nice rooms, a/c, TV, good facilities but no breakfast, bar/restaurant expensive, part of Mesones Gastronómicos programme. In Fajardo try **D** *Guez House de Express*, near ferry dock, 388 Union, T8631362, small.

Campground on the beach, Seven Seas, Fajardo, T8638180. US$10 per tent, safer than some because of nearby trailer park but safety depends on numbers. Also on the beach (*balneario*) at Luquillo, T8895871. US$17 with electricity, US$13 without, take own tent, occasional security but best to pick a time when other campers are around, eg weekends and holidays, safety in numbers, not safe if less than 12 campers, shower, toilets, barbecue.

Eating *Rosa's Seafood* in Fajardo, Route 195, Tablazo 536, T8630213. Puerto Rican food and steak. *Lighthouse*, near Roosevelt Roads. Inexpensive meals. *Plaza Caliente Seafood*, on the beach at Puerto del Rey Marina, T8609162.

Watersports **Marinas** Isleta Marina, Playa Puerto Real, T6432180 (Ventajero Sailing Charters, T8631871, domingoj@coqui.net, day sails and overnight charters); Marina Puerto Chico, Route 987, Km 2.4, T8630834; Marina Puerto Real, Playa Puerto Real, T8632188; Puerto del Rey Marina, Route 33, Km 51.4, T8601000, www.puertodelrey.com (Sea Ventures Pro Dive Center, PADI 5-star, T800-7393483, www.divepuertorico.com, *East Wind* catamaran with underwater windows, 1000 departure to islands for beaches and snorkelling, T8603434, sailcats@ hotmail.com); Sea Lovers Marina, Route 987, Km 2.3, T8633762; Villa Marina Yacht Harbour, Route 987, Km 1.3, T8635131 (Club Nautico Powerboat Rentals, T8602400, boatrent @coqui.net, Caribbean School of Aquatics, T7286606, catamaran for cruises and day sails, dive boat for snorkelling and diving); Wyndham El Conquistador Marina, 1000 El Conquistador Av, T8636594 (Palomino Island Divers, T8631000, Tropical Fishing & Tournaments, T2664524, deep sea sport fishing). Lots of other companies offering day sails, snorkelling, diving and fishing.

The southeast

One of the prettiest parts of Puerto Rico, which should be visited, lies south of Humacao, between Yabucoa and Guayama. Here are the villages of **Patillas** (*público* from Guayama) and **Maunabo** (*público* from Patillas, and from Yabucoa). There are a number of restaurants in this area, especially on the coast, which sell good, cheap food. **Yabucoa** is the east starting point of the Panoramic Route which runs the length of the island. There is an extension to the Route around the Cerro La Pandura and the Puntas Quebrada Honda, Yaguas and Toro; this affords lovely views of the Caribbean coast and Vieques island. **Guayama**, the cleanest town in Puerto Rico, it claims, has a delightful square, on which are the church and the **Casa Cautiño**, built in 1887, now a museum and cultural centre. Route 3, the coastal road around the east part continues from Guayama to Salinas (see below), where it joins Route 1 for Ponce.

Sleeping Near Patillas is **AL-B** *Caribe Playa*, Route 3, Km 112, right on the Caribbean, T8396339, F8391817, www.caribeplaya.com 32 beachfront rooms, sleep 4, a/c, fan, TV, patio or balcony, comfortable, pool and whirlpool, children's pool, open air restaurant (order dinner in advance), library, sea bathing and snorkelling in a small, safe area, barbecue, hammocks, boat trips for fishing, diving, snorkelling, very friendly and helpful. Near Maunabo, is **C** *Playa Emajaguas Guest House*, off the Ruta Panorámica, Route 901, Km 2.5, T8616023. Lovely view, short walk down private path to empty beach (rough sea, currents), owned by Victor Morales and Edna Huertos, 7 apartments with kitchens, friendly, helpful, tennis court, pool table, horses. Good seafood restaurants nearby. At Yabucoa, **A-B** *Palmas de Lucía*, Route

£4000 worth of holiday vouchers to be won!

... that can be claimed against any exodus, Peregrine or Gecko's holiday, a choice of around 570 holidays that set industry standards for responsible tourism in 90 countries across seven continents.

exodus

The UK's leading adventurous travel company, with over 25 years' experience in running the most exciting holidays in 80 different countries. We have an unrivalled choice of trips, from a week exploring the hidden corners of Tuscany to a high altitude trek to Everest Base Camp or 3 months travelling across South America. If you want to do something a little different, chances are you'll find it in one of our brochures.

Peregrine

Australia's leading quality adventure travel company, Peregrine aims to explore some of the world's most interesting and inaccessible places. Providing exciting and enjoyable holidays that focus in some depth on the lifestyle, culture, history, wildlife, wilderness and landscapes of areas that are usually quite different to our own. There is an emphasis on the outdoors, using a variety of transport and staying in a range of accommodation, from comfortable hotels to tribal huts.

Gecko's

Gecko's holidays will get you to the best places with the minimum of hassle. They are designed for younger people who like independent travel but don't have the time to organise everything themselves. Be prepared to take the rough with the smooth, these holidays are for active people with a flexible approach to travel.

To enter the competition, simply tear out the postcard and return it to Exodus Travels, 9 Weir Road, London SW12 OLT. Or go to the competition page on www.exodus.co.uk and register online. Two draws will be made, Easter 2001 and Easter 2002, and the winner of each draw will receive £2000 in travel vouchers. If you do not wish to receive further information about these holidays, please tick here. ☐
To receive a brochure, please tick the relevant boxes below
(maximum number of brochures 2)

exodus	Peregrine	Gecko's
☐ Walking & Trekking	☐ Himalaya	☐ Egypt, Jordan & Israel
☐ Discovery & Adventure	☐ China	☐ South America
☐ European Destinations	☐ South East Asia	☐ Africa
☐ Overland Journeys	☐ Antarctica	☐ Thailand & Laos
☐ Biking Adventures	☐ Africa	☐ India

Please give us your details:

Name: --

Address: --

Postcode: --

e-mail: ---

Which footprint guide did you take this from?

----

getaway tonight on www.exodus.co.uk

exodus
The Different Holiday

getaway tonight on

www.exodus.co.uk

exodus
The Different Holiday

1

2

exodus
9 Weir Road
LONDON
SW12 0BR

BUSINESS REPLY SERVICE
Licence No SW4909

901 at Route 9911, T8934423, F8930291, www.palmas delucia.com New parador, 27 rooms, clean, pool, restaurant, waves can be rough at nearby beach. At Punta Guilarte, near Arroyo, there are cabins, **B**, on the beach, no camping, T8393565. Inland, north of Barranquitas is **C** *Residencia Margarita*, restaurant, useful for people following the Panoramic route.

The Carite Forest lies west of Yabucoa on the Panoramic Route. Covering an area of 2,428 ha, its highest peak is Cerro La Santa at 903 m. The Forest Supervisor, Thomas Espinar (Km 20 Route 184), is very helpful and can tell you what there is to do including getting someone to bring you kayaks to rent on the lake. Bring permit from San Juan or Servicio Forestal regional office in Guayama, T8643262. Two camping areas: Charco Azul and Guavate (the latter closer to the forestry office, phone and supplies) with bathrooms. If you have a car you will be given a key to get it into the campsite. By *público*, from Rio Piedras terminal, San Juan, occasionally direct to Barrio Guavate, Carite, otherwise to Caguas and change. The *público* will drop you quite close to the office where you check in. **Carite Forest**

The south and west

A round trip through the west half of the island would take in Ponce, the second city (reached by motorway from San Juan via Caguas), Guánica, Parguera, San Germán, Boquerón, Mayagüez (the third city), Aguadilla, Quebradillas and Arecibo, with side trips to the Maricao State Forest and fish hatchery, the Río Abajo State Forest and Lake Dos Bocas, the precolumbian ceremonial ball-park near Utuado, and the **Arecibo observatory**, with the world's largest radio telescope. ■ *Route 625, T8782612, www.naic.edu, the Fundación Angel Ramos Visitor Center, open Wed-Fri 1200-1600, Sat and Sun 0900-1600.*

Off the motorway which runs from San Juan to Ponce is Baños de Coamo, which was the island's most fashionable resort from 1847 to 1958; legend has it that the spring was the fountain of youth which Juan Ponce de León was seeking. Take Route 153 from the motorway and then 546. It has been redeveloped by Paradores Puertorriqueños and still has a thermal bath (see under Sleeping). About 45 minutes southeast of Coamo is **Salinas**, a fishing and farming centre. There are several good seafood restaurants on the waterfront. The Marina de Salinas offers moorings and other services to yachties as well as boat transport to islands and accommodation, T7528484, F7687676, jarce@coqui.net **Baños de Coamo**

Sleeping B *Baños de Coamo* at the end of Route 546, Coamo, Puerto Rico 00640, T8252186, F8254739, www.banoscoamo.com Thermal water springs (maximum 15 mins) and an ordinary pool (spend as long as you like), 48 rooms, bar, restaurant with limited hours.

Ponce

The city is now very pleasant to walk around. Much renovation has taken place in the heart of the city; the Casas Villaronga and Salazar-Zapater have been restored (the latter to accommodate the Museo de Historia de Ponce), other houses are being repainted in pastel shades, streets have been made into pedestrian areas, and the large, air-conditioned market on Vives and Atocho (north of the plaza) has been remodelled.

The cathedral is worth a look, and so is the black and red fire-station, built for a fair in 1883. Both buildings stand back to back in the main square, **Plaza Las Delicias**, which has fountains and many neatly-trimmed trees. Also on the plaza is the **Casa Armstrong-Poventud** (or Casa de las Cariatides), facing the Cathedral, with the Instituto de Cultura Puertorriqueño (Región Sur) and tourist information centre. ■ *Mon-Fri 0800-1200, 1300-1630; the Instituto is open 0900-1200, 1300-1600* **Sights**

Puerto Rico

Tue-Sun. East of the plaza is the **Teatro La Perla**, painted cream, white and gold, the city's cultural centre (19th century), restored in 1990, as was the Alcaldía on the Plaza.

There are 3 gardens here, 1 Spanish, 1 American & 1 Puerto Rican

Ponce has a very fine **Museum of Art**, donated by a foundation established by Luis A Ferré (industrialist, art historian and Governor 1968-72) in a modern building designed by Edward Durrel Stone, with a beautiful staircase, now famous. It contains a representative collection of European and American art from the third century BC to the present day. As well as an extensive Baroque collection and fine examples of pre-Raphaelite painting, there is a small collection of precolumbian ceramics and two cases of beautiful Art Nouveau glass. Most of the best Latin American painters are exhibited and there are often special displays. ■ *Open daily 1000-1700. US$3 for adults, US$2 for children under 12. T8480511.*

The **Ponce History Museum** on Calle Isabela 51-53, near La Perla, opened in 1992 and has 10 exhibition halls with photographs, documents and memorabilia provided by locals, as well as models and other exhibits chronicling the city's history. Guided tours in English, Spanish or French. ■ *Weekdays 1000-1700, weekends 1000-1800, closed Tue. US$3 adults, US$1 children. T8447071.* The **Museo de la Música Puertorriqueña**, Calle Cristina 70, T8449722. ■ *Tue-Sun 0900-1200 and 1300-1730, catalogue US$3.*

On **El Vigía** hill is the **Observation Tower**. ■ *Tue-Wed, 0900-1730, Thu-Sun 1000-2200. US$0.50.* The **Museo Castillo Serrallés** is also on El Vigía hill. This fine, 1930s mansion has been restored by the Municipio. ■ *US$3, children US$1.50, groups must reserve in advance. Tue-Sun 0900-1700. T2591774.*

Outside the town by the **Yacht and Fishing Club** is a good place to be at the weekend having a vibrant atmosphere. A wooden broadwalk, La Guancha, has been built along the edge of the harbour. There are kiosks selling *pinchos* and other local treats, simple meals, cold beer and drinks. At one end is an open-air stage for live music or DJs with big sound systems. The music is ear-splittingly loud, especially at weekends. A two-storey building houses a restaurant, small theatre, tourist office and police substation. There is also an observation tower you can climb up. The beach is being developed, with a large recreation area (tennis, basketball courts). ■ *Getting there: taxi or own car needed. Ponce Yacht & Fishing Club, T8429003, www.nautico.com*

Excursions

All the ball courts & plazas are said to line up with solstices or equinoxes

A short drive away on Route 503, Km 2.1, in the outskirts of the city, is the **Tibes Indian Ceremonial Center**. This is an Igneri (300 AD) and pre-Taino (700 AD) burial ground, with seven ball courts (*bateyes*) and two plazas, one in the form of a star, a replica of a Taino village and a good museum. The site was discovered in 1975 after heavy rain uncovered some of the stone margins of the ball courts. Under the Zemi Batey, the longest in the Caribbean (approximately 100 by 20 m), evidence of human sacrifice has been found. Underneath a stone in the Main Plaza, which is almost square (55 by 50 m), the bodies of children were found, buried ceremonially in earthenware pots. In all, 130 skeletons have been uncovered near the Main Plaza, out of a total on site of 187. The park is filled with trees (all named), the most predominant being the higuera, whose fruit is used, among other things, for making maracas (it's forbidden to pick them up though). ■ *Tue-Sun (and Mon holidays, when closed Tue), 0900-1600. T8402255, US$2; bilingual guides give an informative description of the site and a documentary is shown.*

Hacienda Buena Vista, at Km 16.8 on Route 123, north of the city, is another recommended excursion. Built in 1833, converted into a coffee plantation and corn mill in 1845 and in operation till 1937, this estate has been restored by Fideicomiso de Conservación de Puerto Rico. All the machinery works (the metal parts are original), operated by water channelled from the 360 m Vives waterfall; the hydraulic turbine which turns the corn mill is unique. ■ *Fri-Sun, tours at 0830, 1030, 1330 and 1530; groups of 20 or more admitted Wed and Thur. US$5 adults, US$1 children under 12. T7225882 (at weekends 8487020), www.fideicomiso.org. Reservations are necessary for the 2 hr tour (in Spanish or English).*

Puerto Rico

At weekends trips can be made to the beach at **Caja de Muerto**, Coffin Island, the ferry (if still running) leaves from La Guancha at 0900, returns 1600. There is a fishing pier, barbecue area, information office and beautiful beach with clear water. A trail to the 1880 lighthouse leads from White Beach where the dock is. Very good snorkelling. ■ *T8484575. US$5.50 return, children US$3.50.*

LL *Ponce Hilton & Casino*, 1150 Caribe Av, on the beach, T2597676, F2597674, www.ponce-hilton.com 153 rooms, convention centre for 1,500, all the business and sporting facilities you expect of a Hilton. **L-AL** *Ponce Holiday Inn & Tropical Casino*, Route 2, Km 221.2, west of the city on the bypass, T8441200, F8418683, www.holidayinn.com 116 refurbished rooms, tennis, pools, and golf arrangements made. **A-B** *Meliá*, 2 Cristina, just off main plaza, T8420260, F8413602, home.coqui.net/melia 77 rooms, a/c, TV, bath and breakfast, small stuffy rooms, not nice, roof top and garden terraces. **B** *Bélgica*, 122 Villa, in old centre, next to Plaza Delicias, on free trolley route for touring city, T8443255, F8446149. Refurbished, tasteful, clean, huge rooms with balcony overlooking city hall, some with 2 double beds, friendly. There are about 5 other guest houses. West of Ponce at **Guayanilla**, is **AL-B** *Pichi's*, Route 132, Km 204, T8353335, www.pichis.com, next to *McDonalds*. 58 big rooms, a/c, TV, phone, excellent service, pool, restaurant, bar, meeting rooms and banqueting facilities.

Sleeping

The restaurant of the *Meliá* hotel is good (look out for the 'Breaded Lion' on the menu), there is a vegetarian restaurant in the Plaza del Mercado shopping centre, Calle Mayor, 4 blocks northeast from main plaza. Fast food places on main plaza.

Eating

There are several flights daily from San Juan. The *público* from San Juan takes 2 hrs. Públicos serve outlying districts if you have not got a car. Most *carros públicos* leave from the intersection of Victoria and Unión, three blocks north of the plaza (fare to San Juan US$6-7; to Guayama, either direct or via Santa Isabel, US$3).

Transport

Tourist information The Puerto Rico Tourism Co is on Route 1 west of Route 52 on the south side, open Mon-Fri 0800-1700, T8430465, www.prtourism.com

Directory

Guánica

Going west from Ponce is Guánica, the place where American troops first landed in the Spanish-American war. It has an old fort from which there are excellent views. Although Guánica has a history stretching back to Ponce de León's landing in 1508, the first of many colonist landings in the bay, the town was not actually founded here until 1914. For details on the Guánica Forest see page 499. A cabin site is being developed, rather primitive, with a visitor centre. The on-site forest supervisor is Miguel Canals. Outside Guánica is a *balneario* with a large hotel alongside, *Copamarina*. Scuba diving and other watersports are possible here with Dive Copamarina, T8210505, www.copamarina.com; the wall is close to the shore and there are drop-offs and canyons. You can get to **Gilligans Island** by 15-minute water taxi. Go past Balneario Caña Gorda on route 333, turn right towards Punta Jacinto and the pier. There is a fishing pier, barbecue area, information office and beautiful beach. ■ *0900-1700, closed Mon (or Tue if Mon is a holiday).*

Puerto Rico

LL-L *Copamarina Beach Resort*, Route 333, Km 6.5, T8210505, F8210070, www.copamarina.com. Set in 6.5 ha tropical estate, 106 rooms, a/c, TV, balcony, 2 pools, tennis, watersports, PADI dive centre, tour desk, restaurants, on eelgrass beach but good swimming on nearby Gilligans Island.

Sleeping

Further west is La Parguera, originally a fishing village and now a popular resort with *paradores*, guest houses, fish restaurants, fast food outlets. Noisy on holiday weekends. Fishing, kayaking, mountain biking and other activities are offered. Parguera Divers are at *Posada Porlamar*, T8994171, for wall diving. *Parguera Fishing Charters*,

La Parguera

T8994698, hometown.aol.com/mareja, will take you reef fishing or out to catch marlin, dorado, wahoo and tuna. Nearby is **Phosphorescent Bay**, an area of phosphorescent water, occurring through a permanent population of minescent dinoflagellates, a tiny form of marine life, which produce sparks of chemical light when disturbed. One hour boat trips round the bay depart between 1930 and 2230, every 30 minutes, US$12 per person, the experience is said to be rather disappointing, however, and it is best to go on a very dark night or even when it is raining. Mosquito Bay on Vieques is much better.

Sleeping **A-B** *Villa Parguera*, Route 304, T8997777, F8996040, www.villaparguera.com 70 rooms, sea view, by docks, rent boat to get to mangrove canals and cays for good swimming and snorkelling, restaurant, live music and dancing at weekends. **A-B** *Posada Porlamar*, Route 304, Km 303, T8994015, F8995558, netdial.caribe.net/~posada/. 24 rooms, TV, phone, on the canals, dock, watersports arranged, dive shop on site, dive packages available. **A-B** *Estancia La Jamaca* , Route 304, T/F8996162, inland. 8 rooms, quiet, country noises at night.

San Germán Inland from La Parguera, off the main Route 2, San Germán has much traditional charm; it was the second town to be founded on the island and has preserved its colonial atmosphere. It is an excellent base from which to explore the mountains and villages of southwest Puerto Rico. The beautiful little Porta Coeli chapel on the plaza contains a small, rather sparse museum of religious art. ■ *Wed-Sun, 0830-1200, 1300-1630.* A university town: it can be difficult to get cheap accommodation in term time. **B** *Oasis*, 72 Luna, T8921175, F8924546, has 52 rooms, not as close to the beach as it claims, but is ideal for the hills, getting old and shabby, water intermittent, restaurant, pool.

Boquerón

On the south side of the west coast is Boquerón, in Cabo Rojo district, which has an excellent beach for swimming. It is very wide and long, admission US$1, camping, changing rooms, beach and first 30 m of sea packed with bodies on holiday weekends. About 1½ km away across the bay is a beautiful, deserted beach, but there is no road to it. The small village is pleasant, with typical bars, restaurants and street vendors serving the local speciality, oysters. This is one of the cheapest spots on the island because it is a centre for the Compānia de Fomento Recreativo to provide holiday accommodation for Puerto Rican families.

South of the town is **Boquerón Lagoon**, a wildfowl sanctuary; also the **Cabo Rojo Wildlife Refuge**, with a visitors' centre and birdwatching trails. The **Cabo Rojo lighthouse** (Faro), at the island's southwest tip is the most southerly point on the island with a breathtaking view; the exposed coral rocks have marine fossils and, closer inshore, shallow salt pools where crystals collect. The vegetation is dry scrub and you can find the slow growing hard wood, lignum vitae. Popular beaches in this area are **El Combate** (miles of white sand, undeveloped, but now a favourite with university students), south of Boquerón, and **Joyuda** (small island just offshore offers good snorkelling and swimming, but beach itself not spectacular) and **Buyé** (camping US$8 a night) to the north. At Joyuda you can go fishing, snorkelling or take a trip to Mona Island with Tour Marine Adventures, on the beach near *Perichi's*, T8519259, tourmarine@yahoo.com

Sleeping **C-D** *Canadian Jack's Guest House*, PO Box 990, Boquerón, PR 00622, T8512410. Private bath-
Jack also rents room, colour TV, clean and comfortable but noisy on Fri, Sat nights when the streets are
hammocks crowded with people partying, fantastic spot. **A-B** *Boquemar*, end of Route 100, Int 101, Gil
overlooking Bouye St, T8512158, F8517600. 75 rooms, a/c, bar, restaurant, pool, facilities for disabled, park-
the water ing. At Cabo Rojo, **B** *Punta Aguila Villas*, T7254659, past the salt flats and *Agua El Cuello* restaurant. On shallow eelgrass beach but near 2 good swimming beaches, good hiking area,
gazebos, jacuzzi, pool, 2 bedrooms. Next door is **AL-A** *Parador Bahía Salinas*, Route 301,

Km 11.5, T2541212, F2541215, www.bahiasalinas.com Lovely setting, 24 rooms, most with porch for sunset watching, pool, kayaking, sailing, fishing, Caribbean Reef Divers on beach, T2544006, divingjm@coqui.net **AL-B** *Perichi's*, Route 102, Km 14.3, Playa Joyuda, T8513131, F8510560, perichi@tropicweb.net 41 rooms, well-run, with good award-winning restaurant. **B** *Centro Vacacional de Boquerón*, run by Fomento Recreativo, fully self-contained, with barbecues, beach cabins. Foreigners are welcomed, but it is so popular with Puerto Ricans that you may have to make an application up to 3 months in advance. There are other hotels and a *parador*, **A-B** *Joyuda Beach*, Route 102, Km 11.7, T8515650, F2553750, www.guiapr.com/joyudabeach 41 rooms, restaurant. **Camping** *Villa Plaza* (Denigno Ojeda Plaza) on the road to Cabo Rojo lighthouse, Route 301, Km 6.6, T8511340. Cabins, pool, electricity, security, US$25 per tent per night, US$20 for more than one day, take insect repellent.

Joyuda is famous for seafood restaurants on the beach; inexpensive food, good quality, nice atmosphere, whole, grilled fish is a must, especially snapper (*chillo*). **Eating**

Mayagüez is a crowded city with little of interest to the tourist. There are botanical **Mayagüez** gardens, at the Tropical Agricultural Research Station, near the University of Puerto Rico. ■ *Mon-Fri, 0730-1630. Free.* The city also has a zoo. ■ *Tue-Sun, 0900-1630. Adults US$1, children US$0.50.* The tourist office is in the Municipalidad on Plaza Colón but has no tourist information available.

Sleeping L-AL *Mayagüez Resort & Casino*, Route 104, Km 3, T8317575, F2653020. 141 rooms in 20 acres, view of harbour, business hotel and resort of international standard. **A-C** *Embajador*, 111 Ramos Antonini, Este, T8333340, F8347664. 29 rooms, central, phones, TV, restaurant, facilities for wheelchair visitors, laundry room. **B** *El Sol*, 9 Santiago Riera Palmer St, East Mayagüez, T8340303, T/F2657567, home.coqui.net/bechara/hotel_e.htm 52 rooms, breakfast included, TV, fridge, phone, hair dryer, bar, restaurant, pool, in city centre. **E** *RUM Hotel*, hotel of the Recinto University of Mayagüez, T8324040. Safe, pool, library, similar prices at other branches of the University. North of Mayagüez at Tres Hermanos, Bahía de Añasco, at Route 115 Km 5, is a **campground** with beach and pool, **B** cabins sleep 6, camping with water and electricity US$10 per tent per night.

Eating *Vegetarian Restaurant*, José de Diego. Open 1100-1400. *Fuente Tropical*, same street. Run by Colombians, good fruit shakes and hamburgers. *Recomeni*, Vigo. Good inexpensive food, open all hours, eat in or takeaway.

Transport *Públicos* leave from a modern terminal in Calle Peral. Bus to San Juan US$10.

Mona Island, 80 km west of Mayagüez, is fascinating for historians and nature lov- **Mona Island** ers, with turquoise sea and white sand. Originally inhabited by Taino Indians and then by pirates and privateers, it is now deserted except for its wildlife. Here you can see 1m-long iguanas, colonies of sea birds and bats in the caves (possibly pirates too). Sixty-metre high cliffs are dotted with caves, ascending to a flat table top covered with dry forest. The island is managed by the Department of National Resources (T7221726), who have cabins to rent with prior permission. Camping is allowed at Sardinera Beach, where there are bathrooms. There are no restaurants or facilities. Take all your food and water with you and bring back all your rubbish.

Transport Boats from Boquerón or Cabo Rojo 4 hrs, US$1,200 for 20-person boat, less for 14-person boat, leave before dawn. Contact Captains Porfirio Andujar, T8517359, Ramón Peña, T2552031; Catalino Lallave, T2855129; David Rodríguez, T8511885; Luís Ortiz, T8516276. Planes to Mona are planned following work on the runway. Check with the PR Forestry Service or Vieques Air Link (Coptco Aviation T7290000 for private charter).

Directory Tour agencies *Eco Aventuras*, PO Box 22768, San Juan, PR 00931-2768, T8865309. Karina Zuñiga has specialized trips about 5 times a year, providing meals, transport, tents, permits,

Puerto Rico

information and planning, US$175 per person for 7 days with 20 people, US$135 per person for 4 days with 4 people. *Aventurisla*, PO Box 22242, San Juan PR 00931-22242, T7907816. Ricardo Otero offers much the same trip only you bring your own tent. *Tour Marine*, HC 1 Box 16346, Cabo Rojo, PR 00623-9719, T8519259, 3752625. Offers Mona Island charters for parties of 6-12, take your own tents.

Rincón

Humpback whales visit in winter & can be seen playing in the surf. Divers sometimes see them

Going north from Mayagüez, you come to Rincón, on the westernmost point of the island. Here the mountains run down to the sea, and the scenery is spectacular. For a great panoramic view visit the Punta Higuera Lighthouse, built on a cliff overlooking the surf where the Atlantic and Caribbean meet. The town itself is unremarkable, but the nearby beaches are beautiful and the surfing is a major attraction. The beaches are called Steps, Domes (named after the nearby nuclear storage dome) and the Public Beach, with lifeguard. Pools, Sandy Beach and Antonio's are north of Punta Higuera and popular with winter surfers. Domes and María's are further south and offer good, clean waves. *West Coast Surf Shop* (and tours) in Rincón, T8233935. PADI dive school, *Tanks-a-lot*, T8236301, also arrange excursions to the island of **Desecheo**, 19 km off the coast of Rincón. Desecheo is near Mona Island, but smaller, deserted, and has terrific diving offshore.

Sleeping and eating LL *Horned Dorset Primavera*, Route 429, Km 3, T8234030, F8235580, www.horneddorset.com No children under 12, no TV, no organized activities, 30 suites, Spanish colonial style, mahogany furniture, prides itself on offering privacy, good restaurant, beach not good for swimming, seafront rooms can be noisy if sea is rough with waves pounding on wall below, pool, nothing much to do. **AL-A** *Villa Cofresí*, Route 115, Km 12.3, T8232450, F8231770, www.villacofresi.com 51 rooms, on the beach, TV, kitchens, restaurant, bar, outdoor restaurant, watersports. **AL-A** *Villa Antonio*, alongside it, also at Route 115, Km 12.3, T8232645, www.villa-antonio.com. 55 rooms (1 or 2 bedrooms) on a good beach for swimming and near good surfing beaches, a/c, volleyball, tennis, pool, kitchen, TV, parking, bar and restaurant close by. **AL-A** *The Lazy Parrot Inn and Restaurant*, Route 413, Km 4.1, Barrio Puntas, T8235654, F8230224, www.lazyparrot.com In La Cadena hills overlooking coast, rooms sleep 4 in family room, also honeymoon suite, a/c, cable TV, fridge, restaurant closed Mon. At **Puntas**, Carmen's grocery store has rooms, basic, cooking facilities.

Transport Rincón can be reached by *público* from Mayagüez or (less frequent) from Aguadilla. Public transport is scarce at weekends.

Aguadilla

North of Rincón the road leads to **Aguadilla**, another good spot for sunset watching. Crash Boat Beach is a popular surfing beach just to the north and lots of watersports are on offer. *Aquatica Underwater Adventures*, Route 110, Km 10, T8906071, www.aquatica.cjb.net, offers diving and fishing and trips to Desecheo. There is a golf course at the old Ramey base, originally designed for Eisenhower, Punta Borinquén Golf, Route 107, T8902987, with tuition, pro-shop and practice range.

Sleeping and eating L-B *La Cima*, Route 110, Km 9.2, Barrio Maleza Alta, T8902016, F8902017, www.lacima.com 40 rooms, a/c, TV, phone, pool, exercise room, within reach of 6 beaches and golf. **A-B** *Parador El Faro* , Route 107, Km 2.1, T8828000, F8913110, www.ihppr.com 50 rooms, built 1990, TV, phone, *Tres Amigos* restaurant for Puerto Rican and international food. Under same ownership is the 33-room **B-C** *Parador Borinquén* , Route 467, Km 2.1, T8910451, F8828008. **A-B** *Hacienda El Pedregal*, Route 111, Km 0.1, T8822865, F8822885, www.haciendaelpedregal.com 27 rooms, view of ocean and sunsets, attractive rooms, TV, phone, parking, restaurant, bar, pools.

North coast road

Route 2, the main road in the north, runs from Aguadilla through Quebradillas to Arecibo, then through urban areas to some extent from Arecibo and completely from Manatí to San Juan. South of Quebradillas in the Montañas Aymamón is the

Bosque Estatal de Guajataca, a dry forest with a large number of bird species, on Route 446. There are over 40 walking trails with 40 km of maintained footpaths through the Karst region, three picnic areas and two camping areas with tent sites. The on-site supervisor is Edwin Avila. Get your permit in San Juan or the regional office in Aguadilla, T8904050 (see page 480). South of Arecibo in the Karst country is the **Bosque Río Abajo**, a 2,023-ha reserve off Route 10. It contains 70 trails and dirt roads, ideal for viewing plant and birdlife, 15 commercial plantations (teak, mahogany, maga trees), two new campsites, two natural springwater swimming pools and some amazing bamboo near the end of the road. The on-site forest supervisor is José Casanovas. There is also a private campsite at Dos Bocas: *T J Ranch*, a coffee farm run by Tony and Juanita, pool, toilets, no electricity, US$5 per person, breakfast on request, go over the dam on Route 146, first left straight up to the top, past phone booth, then at intersection turn left (small sign for T J Ranch), T8801217, HC02 Box 14926, Arecibo, PR 00612.

If you have the time it is much nicer to drive along the coast then along Route 2. Take Route 681 out of Arecibo, with an immediate detour to the Poza del Obispo beach, by Arecibo lighthouse. Here a pool has been formed inside some rocks, but the breakers on the rocks themselves send up magnificent jets of spray. The bay, with fine surf, stretches round to another headland, **Punta Caracoles**, on which is the **Cueva del Indio** (small car park on Route 681, US$1 charge if anyone is around). A short walk through private land leads to the cave, a sea-eroded hole and funnel in the cliff; watch out for holes in the ground when walking around. There are Taino/Arawak drawings in the cave. *Públicos* run along Route 681 from Arecibo. Rejoin Route 2 through Barceloneta. The State Forest of Cambalache is between Arecibo and Barceloneta. Cambalache Beach has two camping areas, La Boba and La Rusa, with water and showers. **Warning** Safety depends on numbers. There are eight trails and the beach. The on-site supervisor is Jorge Carnaval, T8787279.

The coast road is not continuous; where it does go beside the sea, there are beaches, seafood restaurants and some good views. Route 165, another coastal stretch which can be reached either through **Dorado** on the 693 (where there are three large Hyatt hotels and several golf courses, www.hyatt.com), or through Toa Baja, enters metropolitan San Juan at Cataño.

Sleeping & eating

Near **Isabela** on the coast is LL *Villa Montana*, Route 4466, Km 1.2, T8729554, F8729553, www.villamontana.com Nice resort, tranquil spot, miles of sand dunes and surf, protected area for swimming, tennis, restaurant by pool bar, villas with kitchens, not much else, lots to do during the day but nothing at night. **AL-A** *Villas del Mar Hau*, T8722627, F8722045, www.indio.net/villashau Beachfront cabins, some with a/c, some with fans, a few tent sites, US$10, private farm on beach, horse riding nearby. At **Arecibo** there are several hotels and guest houses around the main square, **D** *Hotel Plaza*. Near **Quebradillas**, Route 2, Km 103.8, are **A** *El Guajataca*, T8953070, F8952204, gymguaja@caribe.net Beautifully located on a beach (dangerous swimming). 38 rooms, pool, entertainment, restaurant, bars. On the other side of the road, and higher up the hill at Km 7.9, Route 113, is **AL-A** *Vistamar*, T8952065, F8952294, www.paradorvistamar.com 55 rooms, also with pool, restaurant and bar with view down to ocean, live music Sat.

Camping *Punta Maracayo Camping*, next to Sardinera beach, Km 84.6 on Ruta 2, T8200274. Owned by Hatillo Municipality, surreal with concrete dinosaurs, elephant etc next to campsite, small sheltered cove, calm water, good swimming, sand average, pool, cabins US$135 for 2 nights, US$25 additional nights, tent sites US$50 for 2 nights, US$20 additional nights, guard, fenced in, busy at weekends and in summer.

Panoramic Route

Heading east from Mayagüez is the Panoramic Route which runs the whole length of Puerto Rico, through some of the island's most stunning scenery. It passes through the Cordillera Central, with large areas of forest, and there are several excursions to various countryside resorts. Despite the fact that you are never far from buildings,

Puerto Rico

schools or farms, the landscape is always fascinating. In the evening the panoramas are lovely and you can hear the song of the *coquí*. No trip to the interior should miss at least some part of the Panoramic Route, but if you want to travel all of it, allow three days. The roads which are used are narrow, with many bends, so take care at corners. The **Maricao State Forest** (Monte del Estado) is the most westerly forest on the Route; its visitors' areas are open from 0600 to 1800, T7243724. It is a beautiful forest with magnificent views, an observation tower and a fish hatchery.

Sleeping and eating AL *Parador Hacienda Juanita*, Route 105, Km 23.5, Maricao, T8382550, F8382551, www.haciendajuanita.com 21 modest rooms, breakfast and dinner included in price, part of an old coffee plantation, bar, restaurant, pool, volleyball, tennis, basketball, gardens, walking trails, parking, facilities for disabled, cool at night. **B** *Fomento Recreativo* cabins at Km 13.1, Maricao Rd 120, T8735632. Not a natural setting but cabins have a fireplace, sleep 6 and have cool mountain air up Monte del Estado. *Ginger Hill Vegetarian Guest House*, Las Marías, T8724079, gngrhill@prtc.net Remote, coffee plantation, paths, bed and breakfast meal plan in season. *The Yellow House*, east of Las Marías, T8272758, Mr Birdsell. Very rustic guest house in the middle of nowhere. Recommended for budget travellers.

Susua & Guilarte South of the Panoramic Route between Sabana Grande and Yauco on Route 371 is the **Bosque Estatal de Susua**, a dry forest with recreational areas, a river, 40 tent sites and showers. Acquire permits in San Juan or the Ponce regional office, T8444051 (see page 480). As it approaches **Adjuntas** and the transinsular Route 10, the Panoramic Route goes through the **Bosque de Guilarte**, again with fine views, flowering trees, bougainvillaea, banks of impatiens (busy lizzie, *miramelinda* in Spanish), and bird song (if you stop to listen). Off Routes 131 and 518, south of Adjuntas, there is a trail through eucalyptus trees up to the peak with a nice view. It is cool, you are in the clouds. There are five basic cabins, **F**, with two sets of bunk beds, musty smell, bring permit, bedding, cooking things etc, shared bathroom, no electricity, barbecues, picnic tables. On site forest supervisor Rubén Padrón, get permit from San Juan or Ponce regional office, T8444051 (see Camping, page 480).

Sleeping and eating C *Hotel Monte Río*, 2 blocks from Plaza in Adjuntas, Calle H, T/F8293705. Pool, economical, convenient, restaurant and bar.

Toro Negro After Adjuntas, the road enters the **Toro Negro Forest Reserve**, which includes the highest point on the island, **Cerro de Punta** (1,338 m). This is a smaller area than El Yunque, with fewer rivers. There are many very tall eucalyptus trees along the road. Lago El Guineo and Lago de Matrullas are Puerto Rico's highest lakes. The reserve has five trails, one to an observation tower with views of the mountains and lakes. A camping area (14 tent sites), has showers and toilets. There is a natural springwater swimming pool further down the road open May-September. Permit needed from Servicio Forestal in San Juan or regional office in Ponce, T8444051. The on-site forest supervisor is René Román. The Recreation Areas in Toro Negro are open from 0800-1700.

Jayuya Just north of the Panoramic Route is Jayuya, overlooked by Cerro de Punta and Tres Picachos in a beautiful mountain setting. It is known as the indigenous capital of Puerto Rico and is named after the Indian cacique Hayuya, the last to submit to the Spaniards. Two monuments commemorate the Taino heritage: a statue of Hayuya sculpted by Tomás Batista in 1969, and the Tumba del Indio Puertorriqueño, containing a Taino skeleton buried in the traditional foetal position. In November Jayuya celebrates an indigenous festival in honour of Hayuya. Sleep can be had at **AL-A** *Parador Hacienda Gripiñas*, Route 527 Km 2.7, T8281717, F8281719. 19 rooms in a coffee plantation house built in 1858, set in lovely gardens, bar, restaurant, pool, parking, facilities for disabled.

Puerto Rico

After this high, lush forest with its marvellous vistas, the Panoramic Route continues to Aibonito, around which the views and scenery are more open, mainly as a result of deforestation(**C-E** *Swiss Inn Guest House*, Route 14 Km 49.3, T7358500, run by Gregory Muñoz, 8 rooms with shower, fans, balcony, TV, microwave, fridge, price negotiable for longer stays, very friendly and helpful, up in the mountains). Thence to Cayey and, beyond, another forest, Carite (also known as Guavate, see page 497). Finally the road descends into the rich, green valley which leads to Yabucoa. Between Aibonito and Barranquitas is the Cañón San Cristóbal, where you can climb down a mountain trail between steep walls to the bottom, where the temperature is considerably warmer, four-hour trip. Call Félix Rivera, T7355188, for a guide, you will need one to find the way. He usually meets people at *La Piedra* restaurant, on Route 7718, one of Puerto Rico's gastronomic delights. You can see the canyon from the top from a dirt road off Route 162, very impressive.

*(margin: **Cañon San Cristóbal**)*

From various points on the Panoramic Route you can head north or south; for example Route 10 goes south from Adjuntas to Ponce, or north to Utuado and then on to **Río Abajo State Forest** where there are a swimming pool and various picnic spots. ■ *0600-1800*. It is approached through splendid views of the karst hills and the **Dos Bocas Lake**. Free launch trips are offered on this lake at 0700, 1000, 1400 and 1700; they last two hours and are provided by the Public Works Department. Route 10 reaches the north coast at Arecibo.

The Caguana Indian Ceremonial Park, west of Utuado, dates from about 1100 AD, and contains 10 Taino ball courts, each named after a Taino *cacique* (chieftain). The courts vary in size, the longest being about 85 m by 20 (Guarionex), the largest 65 by 50 (Agueybana). These two have monoliths in the stones that line the level 'pitch', and on those of Agueybana there are petroglyphs, some quite faint. None of the monoliths is taller than a man. A path leads down to the Río Tanamá. The setting, amid limestone hills, is very impressive. It is believed to be a site of some religious significance and has been restored with a small museum in the 13-acre landscaped botanical park containing royal palm, guava, cedar and ceiba. ■ *It is on Route 111 to Lares*, Km 12.3. 0900-1700 (gate to the river closes at 1630). Free.

*(margin: **Caguana Indian Ceremonial Park**)*

Further west of Utuado, **Lares** is a hilltop town (*públicos* go from one block from church) from where you can either carry on to the west coast at Aguadilla, or head north on one of the many routes to the Atlantic coast. Route 453 passes **Lago de Guajataca**, continuing as Route 113 to Quebradillas. Route 455 branches west off the 453, leading via a short stretch of the 119 to the 457 and 446 (good view at the junction of these two). Route 446 traverses, as a single track, the **Bosque Estatal de Guajataca**. Route 129 goes to Arecibo, passing the **Río Camuy Cave Park**, with side trips to the Cueva de Camuy and the Arecibo Observatory (see page 484). Driving on the country roads in the area between the Panoramic Route and the north coast is twisty but pleasant, passing conical limestone hills (*mogotes*) and farms set among patches of lush forest.

(margin: Puerto Rico)

Sleeping **AL-C** *Parador J B Hidden Village*, Route 416, Barrio Piedras Blancas, Aguada, T8688686, F8688701. 33 rooms built in 1990, a/c, bar, restaurant, pool, parking, facilities for disabled. **A-B** *Casa Grande*, Barrio Caonillas, Utuado, Route 612, Km 0.3, T8943939, F8943900, www.hotelcasagrande.com. 20 rooms in attractive mountain setting, former coffee plantation, balconies, hammocks, yoga, kayaking, bar, *Jungle Jane's* restaurant, pool.

Vieques

Population: 9,400

Vieques, a peaceful, relaxing, low-key island of rolling hills, is located 11 km across the sea from Puerto Rico. It was catapulted into the limelight in 1999-2000 when locals campaigned for the removal of the US military from their bases at the east and west ends of the island. The island is about 34 km long by 6 km wide, the inhabitants mostly concentrated in the main town of Isabel Segunda. The island was named Graciosa by Columbus, after a friend's mother, but was better known as Crab Island by pirates who frequented its waters.

Ins and outs

Getting there
See transport, page 508, for further details

Fajardo is the closest sea and air port. Take the ferry from Fajardo or catch a plane from San Juan or Fajardo. *Vieques Air Link* (T7413266) have flights from Fajardo (10 mins, T8633020), San Juan International (30 mins, T7223736), as well as Isla Grande and St Croix (30 mins, T7789858) many times a day. *Isla Nena*, T7411577, and the charter airline, *Air Culebra*, T2686951, also fly to Vieques.

Getting around

Públicos meet you at the airport and ferry dock, posted rates (none higher than US$3.00), but some drivers will try to overcharge you, ask the price first, or let your hotel/guest house arrange transport for you. Car hire is widely available.

Sights

The biggest 'action' is on Sat night in Esperanza. Everyone promenades along the sea front dressed in their finest, talking & flirting, before going to a nightclub or bar

There is an excellent historical museum at the beautifully restored fort, **El Fortin Conde de Mirasol** which was the last fort begun by the Spanish in the Western Hemisphere. ■ *Week days by appointment, T7411717, 7418651 evenings. Wed-Sun 1000-1600.* There is another interesting exhibit at the **Punta Mulas Lighthouse**. ■ *T7415000. Daily 0800-1630.*

The US Military owns two thirds of the island, the east third and west third, with the civilian population living on the middle strip. Both bases are theoretically open to the public upon presentation of any photo identification except on days when the red flag is up: when manoeuvers and/or bombing practice are underway. However, since December 1999 Naval security guards have prevented tourists gaining access to beaches even when no exercises have been taking place. The beaches can still be

Vieques

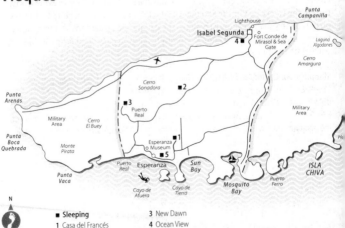

■ **Sleeping**
1 Casa del Francés
2 Crow's Nest

3 New Dawn
4 Ocean View
5 Posada Vistamar

reached by boat. The Navy's reaction was as a result of the establishment of a protest camp at the gates. The US Navy is under pressure to leave and return the land to the people. In 1999 the Governor requested an immediate end of US weapons training on the island after a civilian was killed in a bombing error, see page 512. The military is heard but not much seen, planes and helicopters fly low but since only a handful of personnel are permanently stationed on the island, it is not a base town atmosphere. The land owned by the military is mostly untouched, creating a bird sanctuary and nature preserve.

Vieques has over 52 beaches in secluded coves, the few developed beaches have peo- **Beaches &** ple and exuberant groups of picnickers, the rest are deserted. Public **Sun Bay** has **resorts** picnic and camping areas (no shade in camping area, but there is lots of petty theft so not many people camp there).

Tourism is an infant industry on this island, but is rapidly being promoted to provide employment and reduce poverty. Hotel construction includes the US$30 mn *Casa de Playa Beach Villages* a condo-hotel with 210 rooms and 70 villas. The port and airport are also being expanded and modernized. The small beach town of **Esperanza** is the main area of guest houses and tourist related restaurants, bars, dive companies (Blue Caribe Dive Center, SSI facility, full service, T7412522, PO Box 1574), et cetera. The **museum** in Esperanza has archaeological and natural history exhibits. ■ *Tue-Sun, 1100-1500, T7418850.*

Small, hardy, island horses, most with paso fino blood lines (that means smooth gaits with no bouncing) are still used as transport, and wild horses roam the island. Renting a horse is an exciting way to explore the beaches and coves.

Mosquito Bay, also known as **Phosphorescent Bay** (the BBC broadcast a documentary about this in 1994), is a large, but very shallow bay, surrounded by mangrove trees and full of bioluminescent organisms. Sightseeing trips go at night (recommended are the tours that use non polluting electric boats or kayaks), US$15-18. The organisms glow when disturbed. The glow generated by a 13 cm fish is about a 39 cm circle of light brighter than a light bulb. Swimming in this glow is a wonderful experience. Clark, T7417600, has a small boat; Sharon Grasso at *Island Adventures*, T741-0717/0720, www.biobay.com, has an electric boat, naturalist; *Blue Caribe Divers*, T7412522, SSI, PADI, for kayak tours and night scuba dives.

Essentials

Esperanza **LL-L** *Inn on the Blue Horizon*, **Sleeping**
Route 996, Km 4.2, T7413318, F7410522,
www.enchanted-isle.com/bluehorizon, on
the beach west of Esperanza. Former pineapple plantation, run by Billy Knight and
James Weis, from New York, 9 rooms with
antique furniture, pool, popular bar and restaurant. **AL** *La Casa del Francés*, T7413751,
F7412330, www.enchanted-isle.com/
lacasa, Route 996. 18 rooms, classical sugar
plantation Great House, designated historical landmark, bar, restaurant, pool, 5-min
walk out of Esperanza. **B** *Amapola*,
Flamboyan 144, T7411382, F7413704,
www.enchanted-isle.com/amapola A/c
rooms with private baths. **C-D** *Bananas
Guest House*, T7418700, facing the ocean.
Popular, pleasant American restaurant,
some rooms a/c. **D** *Tradewinds*, owned by

[map showing: Puerto Negro, Puerto Diablo, Laguna Monte Largo, Laguna Diablo, Bahía Icacos, Punta Este, Cerro Matías, Bahía Salina del Sur, Bahía ...enada..., ...unta ...onejo]

Puerto Rico

Janet and Harry Washburn, PO Box 1012, T7418666. Bar, restaurant. Smaller and cheaper guest houses include: *La Central* (T7410106), *Posada Vistamar* (T741 8716); *La Concha* (T7412733). For apartments in Esperanza try *Acacia Apts*, 236 Acacia St, T/F7411856. Owned by Jürgen Meuser and Manfred Kissel, clean, cosy, friendly. Or *La Piña*, 222 Acacia St, T/F7412953. Owned by Elswith Petrakovic.

Isabel Segunda A-B *Ocean View*, Box 124, 751 Calle Plinio Peterson, T7413696, F7411793. Concrete block hotel right on water's edge next to ferry dock, 35 rooms with balconies, Chinese restaurant next door under same ownership, car rental for guests. **B-C** *Sea Gate Hotel*, near the fort, T7414661, F7412978. 16 rooms high up on hill, good views, pool, tennis. *Casa La Lanchita*, ocean front, T7410023. *Vieques Inn*, downtown, T7411500. Inland is **L-AL** *Hacienda Tamarindo*, Box 1569, Vieques, PR 00765, Route 996, Km 4.5, T7418525, F7413215, www.enchanted- isle.com/tamarindo 16 rooms and suites, breakfast included, no children under 15, hotel built around a large tamarind tree, each room different, on hill with sea views, pool down the hill, run by Burr and Linda Vail. **L-B** *Crow's Nest*, Box 1521, Route 201, Km 1.6, T7410033, F7411294, www.enchanted-isle/crowsnest 15 rooms with kitchenettes or 2-bedroom suites with living areas, set in rolling hillside, pool, restaurant. Or **D** *New Dawn*, PO Box 1512, T7410495. An unusual guest house built on 2ha of land with horses grazing off the huge veranda, is 5 km from the beach, frequently booked by women's groups for retreats, 2-storey wooden house, large deck and hammocks, rooms, dorms **F** per person, and tentsites, all with shared bath and outdoor showers or you can rent the entire place (sleeps 20+) with or without a cook, for US$250 per day, US$3,000 per month. For villa rentals contact Connections (T7410023).

Eating Almost all of the island's restaurants are part of a hotel or guest house listed above. There are numerous small places offering take out or eat in sandwiches, hamburgers, barbecue chicken, etc. **Esperanza** *Inn on the Blue Horizon* has *Café Blu* for fine dining, open Wed-Sun 1800-2200, lunchtimes Sat, Sun, reservations recommended, T7413318, and *Blu Bar* with happy hour 1600-1800 every day and lighter food 1200-2145, bar until 0030. *Bananas*, T7418700, Flamboyán St. Pub food and pizzas, beachfront, food until 2200-2300, bar open late, especially at weekends. *Crabwalk Café*, next to *Tradewinds*. Sandwiches, salads, open from 0800. *Trapper John's*, T7411325. Food until 2400, frozen drinks US$5. *La Central*, T7410106. For Puerto Rican food, *empanadas*. *Eddie's* for dancing, rum and beer, live music last weekend every month. **Isabel Segunda** *Café Mar Azul*, bar on ocean front, T7413400. Open 0900-0100, later at weekends, happy hour 1700-1800. *Taverna Española*, T7411175. Spanish food.

Transport **Ferry** From Fajardo, the car, cargo and passenger ferries leave Mon-Fri 0400 (cars), 0930 (passengers), 0930 (cars), 1300 (passengers), 1630 (passengers and cars), Sat, Sun 0930, 1500, 1800, no car ferries. Vieques-Fajardo Mon-Fri at 0600 (cars), 0700 (passengers), 1100 (passengers), 1330 (cars), 1500 (passengers), 1830 (cars), Sat, Sun 0700, 1300, 1630, in Fajardo call the Port Authority office to transport a car, T8630852, 900-4622005, in Vieques T7414761, open for reservations 0800-1100, 1300-1500, reservations needed for cars only, book 2-3 weeks in advance, US$26 average return, passenger fare is US$2.25 one way, crossing takes 1½ hrs. At weekends the ferries are often full and advance reservations are recommended. **Road** Car rentals available at *Maritzas Car Rental* (T7410078), *Island Car Rentals* (T7411666), *Steve's* (T7418135), *Fonsin* (T7418163) or *Vieques Cars* (T7411212). Bicycle rental through *DYMC* (T3162617). Horse rentals can be arranged by your guest house.

Directory **Tourist information** Useful websites include www.vieques-island.com, www.enchanted-isle.com, www.viequespr.net and www.goto.com. **Useful numbers** Police: T2020, Fire: T2111, Hospital: T2151.

Puerto Rico

Culebra

Culebra has a climate and landscape similar to that of the Virgin Islands, with tropical for- est on the hills and palm groves near the beaches. It is even better than Vieques, with less petty theft, less heavy drinking, better accommodation, more peace and more beautiful beaches though the island is poor, with very high unemployment; most people who have jobs work for the municipality or in construction. It is about 11 km long and 5 km wide.

Population: 3,500

Ins and outs

Air Flights from San Juan International airport take 30 mins, from Isla Grande airport 30 mins and from Fajardo 15 mins. The ferry from Fajardo to Culebra takes about 1½ hrs, and costs US$2.25 per person each way, cars about US$26 return. **Sea** Ferries which take cars are slower and rougher and passengers tend to get seasick.

Getting there
See transport, page 511, for further details

There are only two *guaguas*, carrying 28 people. If they don't turn up at the airport you will have to walk into town. Cars and bicycles can be hired and there is also a taxi service.

Getting around

Sights

The main village, **Dewey** (called Pueblo by the locals) is attractively set between two lagoons. A visitor's information centre is in the City Hall. About 40% of the land is park or national reserve, including many beaches. The **Culebra National Wildlife Refuge** (T7420115), 600 ha, comprising 23 offshore islands and four parcels of land on Culebra, protects large colonies of sea birds, particularly terns, red-billed tropic birds and boobies, and nesting sea turtles: hawksbill, leatherback, loggerhead and green. Volunteers are welcomed to help Wildlife Refuge rangers count and protect nests and hatchlings. Contact Culebra Leatherback Project, PO Box 617, Culebra, PR 00775, T7420050, volunteers needed April-August.

There are good, sandy beaches, clear water and a coral reef. Flamenco Beach is 1½ km long with white sand and exquisitely beautiful clear turquoise water, a reef at one end and waves at the other. It is almost deserted except for a few guest houses at the far end selling a limited amount of drinks, but it becomes a zoo at summer week- ends. **Culebrita** and **Luís Peña** are two small cays offshore with beaches. Both are wildlife sanctuaries.

Scuba diving with *Culebra Divers*, opposite ferry dock, Walter Frei (Swiss) and Monica (both instructors) run a guest house in the hills and you can get a week's dive package or just go out for the day, T7420803, PO Box 474, Culebra, PR 00775. *Culebra Dive Shop*, T7420566 and Dinghy Dock, *Reef Link Divers Scuba*, T7420581, reeflink@aol.com Kayak rental from *Reef Link Divers* and from *Ocean Safari*, Jim and Barbara Peterson (T3791973), US$25 half day, guided expeditions US$45 half day, US$70 full day, Jim will deliver to various places so you can kayak to nearby islands. Several people offer boat trips or water taxi, some of whom can also do fish- ing. *Lanas Water Taxi* and glass bottom boat trips, from the dock behind *Mamacitas*, T4130325, to Culebrita US$40, Luis Peña US$20, glass bottom tours US$15, snorkelling tours US$20-40. *Culebra Boat Rental*, T7873559, hires 6-person skiffs for exploring and transport.

Watersports

Essentials

LL-A *Villa Flamenco Beach*, on the beach, 2 miles from town, problems with reservations, get confirmation that you will get the villa you want, call Isabel at the villas T2420319 or the booking agent, Marta Canovanas, T7423144. Range of studios, 3-bedroom villas, nice place to stay, some with ocean view. **AL** *Rustic Eco-Cottages*, on the hill at Mosquito Bay, T7423136, PO Box 239, Culebra, PR 00775. One cottage sleeps 2, the other 4, includes

Sleeping

Puerto Rico

☞ **The flag**

22 December 1995 was the 100th anniversary of the lone star flag of Puerto Rico, marked by hoisting it alone at the Ateneo Puertorriqueño, in clear violation of US law which states that the US flag should always be flown alongside state or other territorial flags. All over the island the flag was flown as a gesture of pride in Puerto Rican nationality. The flag was first used on 22 December 1895 and adopted as a national symbol. In 1898 the flag became the mark of resistance to the US invasion; the lone star was the 'guide of the patriots', and in the 1930s it was adopted by the Nationalist Party. When Puerto Rico became a Commonwealth in 1952 it was officially adopted as the national flag but after the Cuban revolution the US administration became suspicious of nationalists and people who displayed the flag were considered subversives.

breakfast, minimum 1 week rental, open Dec-Apr, solar power, composting toilets, no kitchens, no hot water, jeep rental needed, 2 mins down lovely trail to beach, good swimming and snorkelling, kayaks to rent, have to eat lunch and dinner out. **L-AL** *Club Seabourne Mini Resort*, Fulladoza Bay, T7423169, seabourne@gobeach.com Villas and rooms, breakfast included, good restaurant, bar, pool, view, 1 mile from town, car hire needed. **A** *Culebra Beach Resort*, T7420319. Run by Max and Esmeralda, next to *Villa Flamenco*, on the beach, nice, simple, clean rooms with kitchen, pleasant, helpful, lots of repeat business. **AL-A** *Villa Boheme*, Ensenada Honda, T/F7423508, on edge of town, harbour front. Family place, well-managed, clean, a/c, fans, 8 rooms with communal kitchen, 4 apartments with private kitchens, patio on the bay, lovely breeze. **B** *Arynar Villa*, T7423145. 2 rooms in lovely house on hill, less than a mile to town, Bernie does boat trips to Culebrita, car hire available. **AL-B** *Posada La Hamaca*, 68 Castelar, T7423516, F7420181, www.posada.com Well kept, only 10 rooms, private bath, beach towels, book in advance, next to *Mamacitas* on the canal, can be smelly. **B-C** *Mamacitas Guest House*, T7420090. With or without kitchens, popular place to stay with popular restaurant, the most activity in Culebra, can be noisy at night. **A-C** *Casa Ensenada*, T7423559. 3 rooms, private access, patio, on bay, nice breeze. **B-C** *Villa Fulladoza Guest House*, T7423576, on the bay. Best value, kitchens, short walk to town, usually booked up. **C-D** *Kokomo*, PO Box 786, T7420719, opposite ferry dock. Warm side of town, some rooms a/c. **D** *Coral Island Guest House*, PO Box 396, T7423177, on waterfront near ferry terminal. 5 bedrooms, sleeps 12, living room, kitchen, fans, US$240 weekly, group rates available, credit cards accepted, in the USA contact John Dinga, 17 Riverbank Rd, Quincy, MA02169, T617-7730565. *Casa Katrina*, T7423565, in town, view of bay. Weekly rates. *Bay View Villas*, PO Box 775, T7423392. Two 2-bedroomed villas, US$1,300 per week or US$1,000 per week, well-equipped, on the way to Punta Soldado, good views overlooking Ensenada Honda, walking distance of Dewey. **L-AL** *Tamarindo Estates*, T7423343. Pool, dock, private bay, snorkelling, dirt access road with potholes, 2 miles to town, car hire needed, restaurant open occasionally, warm side of island. *Pelican Enterprise & Culebra Island Realty*, T7420052, do house rentals, island-wide.

Camping *Culebra Campgrounds* are government-run, US$10 per site, up to 6 people per tent, 2-night minimum, 140 tent sites, bathrooms and water provided but that's all. Not crowded during winter months, just turn up, office open 0700-1800, T7420700. To make a reservation (essential Jun-Sep) send US$20 cheque to Autoridad de Conservación y Desarrollo de Culebra, attn Playa Flamenco, Apartado 217, Culebra, PR 00775 USA.

Eating There are several small restaurants in Dewey, offering local dishes and seafood. Takeaways available. Prices range from US$3-20. *Dinghy Dock Restaurant* on the water in the lagoon, breakfast, lunch and dinner, American and Caribbean food, kayak rental from their dock in town. *El Pesquerito*, breakfast and lunch, Puerto Rican and seafood, US$3-8. *Wai-Nam*, Chinese, lunch and dinner, US$3-8. Also restaurants at the hotels, *Mamacitas*, *Seabourne*, *Tamarindo*. For those who are self catering, there are 7 grocery stores, *Culebra Deli*, a fish market and a liquor store. Everything is imported so prices are high.

Local Road Bicycle hire is US$12 per day from *Culebra Bike and Beach* (T7420434), Richard (T7420062) or Wille (T7420563); cars and jeeps from *Prestige* (7423242), *Richard and Kathy's Rentals* (T7420062), *Willy Solis* (T7423537), *R & W* (T7420563) and *Jerry's Jeeps* (T7420587). Taxi service with Marcelino (T7420292) or Cito (T7422787).

Air *Isla Nena*, at San Juan International airport, T(888)2636213, 7420972, flies 4 times a day San Juan-Culebra, US$60 one way, US$115 return, also 3 times a day Culebra-Fajardo, US$25 one way, and Culebra-St Thomas US$50 on the mail flight Tue and Thur. *Vieques Air Link*, T7420254 in Culebra, T8633020 in Fajardo, San Juan-Culebra twice a day, US$50, from Isla Grande, and 3 times a day Fajardo-Culebra, US$25. *Air Culebra* is a charter company, T2686951, 7420446, US$300 one way for up to 5 people.

Ferry Fajardo-Culebra, Mon-Fri 0930, 1500, 1600 (cars), Wed, Fri 1000 (cars), Sat, Sun 0430 (cars, every other Sat), 0900, 1600. Return Culebra-Fajardo Mon-Fri 0700 (cars), 1100, 1630, Wed, Fri 1300 (cars), Sat, Sun 0700, 1400, 1730, 1800 (cars, every other Sat). Reservations 2-3 weeks in advance needed for cars. Fajardo ticket and information office is open 0800-1100, 1300-1500, T8630705, 1-800-9812005 (Culebra T7423161). (It is best to arrive in Fajardo in time for the last ferry if you are going to the islands; there is little to do in the town and it is not a cheap place). *At weekends the ferries are usually full, best to reserve a ticket*

Tourist Office Dolly Camareno is the director of the municipal tourist office, T7423291, F7420111, www.culebra.org

Background

History

Columbus, accompanied by a young nobleman, Juan Ponce de León, arrived in Puerto Rico on 19 November 1493. Attracted by tales of gold, Ponce obtained permission to colonize Boriquén (or Boriken), as it was called by the natives. Boriquén (later altered to Borinquén in poetry) meant 'land of the great lord' and was called that because of the belief that the god, Juracan, lived on the highest peak of the island and controlled the weather from there. The word 'hurricane' is derived from this god's name. In 1508 Ponce de León established the first settlement at Caparra, a small village not far from the harbour of San Juan. A year later the Spanish Crown appointed him the first Governor. In 1521, however, the settlement was moved to the present site of Old San Juan as the former site was declared unhealthy. In that year Ponce de León was mortally wounded in the conquest of Florida.

Because of Puerto Rico's excellent location at the gateway to Latin America, it played an important part in defending the Spanish Empire against attacks from French, English and Dutch invaders. After the Spanish-American war, Spain ceded the island to the United States in 1898. The inhabitants became US citizens in 1917, with their own Senate and House of Delegates, and in 1948, for the first time, they elected their own Governor, who is authorized to appoint his Cabinet and members of the island's Supreme Court. In 1952 Puerto Rico became a Commonwealth voluntarily associated with the United States.

The island's status is a matter of constant debate for both political and economic reasons as Puerto Rico is heavily dependent on US funding. The New Progressive Party (NPP) favours Puerto Rico's full accession to the USA as the 51st state. The Popular Democratic Party (PDP) favours enhancement of the existing Commonwealth status. Pro-independence groups receive less support, the Puerto Rican Independence Party (PIP) struggles to gain seats in Congress. A referendum on Puerto Rico's future status was held in 1991, but voters rejected the PDP administration's proposals to guarantee that they remain citizens of the USA regardless of any change in Puerto Rico's political status. The 1991 vote was seen as a rejection of the

Puerto Rico

policies of the governing party and Governor Rafael Hernández Colón subsequently decided not to seek re-election in the 1992 elections. The elections were convincingly won by the pro-statehood NPP, who secured 36 seats in the House of Representatives and 20 in the Senate. The new Governor, Pedro Rosselló, took office in January 1993.

In November 1993 another referendum was held on the future political status of the island. Voter turnout was high, at 73.6%, of whom 48.4% voted for Commonwealth Status, 46.2% for statehood and 4.4% for independence. Although the result was close, it was seen as a set-back for the pro-statehood government.

Governor Rosselló was re-elected and sworn in on 2 January 1997. The NPP won 19 seats in the Senate against seven for the PDP and one for the PIP. In the Lower House the NPP won 38, PDP 12 and PIP one. In both houses, extra seats were allocated to opposition parties as required by the constitution.

In September 1998 the island was ravaged by Hurricane Georges on its way through several Caribbean islands. Twelve people were killed and damages were estimated at US$2 bn. 28,000 people sought refuge in shelters and 800,000 were without electricity as President Clinton declared Puerto Rico a disaster area. Banana, coffee and plantain crops were destroyed, 40% of hotel rooms needed repairs and there was considerable damage to El Yunque rainforest, which received the brunt of the storm as it travelled westwards.

In December 1998 Puerto Ricans voted yet again in a referendum on the island's status. 46.5% of the vote was in favour of statehood, but 50.2% voted for 'none of the above' options, which were to continue the present Commonwealth status, enter the USA as a state of the union, free association, or become independent, with a 10-year transitional period for any change in status. 'None of the above' was included at the request of the opposition PDP, which supports the present Commonwealth status but objected to the wording on the ballot paper. Seventy-one percent of the electorate turned out to vote. Governor Rosselló was criticized for using US hurricane relief (US$1.5 bn) as an argument in favour of statehood and was widely accused of exploiting the emergency for political purposes. After the vote he argued that the statehood option had won, but with the majority against him it appeared unlikely that the US Congress would agree. In September 1999, 11 Puerto Ricans jailed for participation in Fuerzas Armadas de la Liberación Nacional (FALN) activities in 1974-83, were released early on the authority of President Clinton, on condition that they not take part in any armed operations nor associate with ex-prisoners. They were, however, allowed to participate in a pro-Independence rally.

The presence of the US Navy on Vieques became a source of much contention after a civilian was killed in April 1999 during bombing practice. Local people on Vieques and Puerto Rico protested and called for an end to the use of live ammunition and the return of military occupied land to the people of Vieques. Exercises using live ammunition were suspended in May 1999 but demonstrators set up a protest camp at the base. Governor Rosselló rejected a US presidential panel's recommendation that exercises should continue for another five years. President Clinton offered to limit operations to 90 days a year instead of the previous 180, and then conceded that live ammunition would no longer be used, while offering US$40 mn in development aid for the island if residents accepted the five-year continuation. His proposals were rejected. A revised proposal from the Pentagon was also rejected and civil disobedience intensified during 2000. In May 2000 US Navy aircraft resumed bombing practice after removing and arresting 224 people from the military base. Dummy ammunition was used and those arrested were released without charge. A referendum has been proposed to gauge local opinion, to be held sometime between August 2000 and February 2002.

The people

The population is 3.8 million, of which about 1.5 million live in San Juan, although about another two million Puerto Ricans live in the USA. Average life expectancy is 73.8 years and gdp per capita is US$12,212, the highest in Latin America, although not up to the level of mainland USA. The people are largely an amalgam of Amerindian, Taino-Arawak, Spanish and African. Most Puerto Ricans do not speak English and less than 30% speak it fluently. Puerto Ricans are sometimes referred to as Boricuas after the Indian name of the island. Second generation Puerto Ricans who were born in New York, but who have returned to the island, are called Nuyoricans. The people are very friendly and hospitable but there is crime, linked to drugs and unemployment.

Government

Puerto Rico is a self-governing Commonwealth in association with the USA (Estado Libre Asociado de Puerto Rico). The chief of state is the President of the United States of America. The head of government is an elected Governor. There are two legislative chambers: the House of Representatives, 51 seats, and the Senate, 27 seats. Two extra seats are granted in each house to the opposition if necessary to limit any party's control to two thirds. Puerto Ricans do not vote in US federal elections, nor do they pay federal taxes, when resident on the island.

The economy

Great social and economic progress has been made in the past 30 years, as a result of the 'Operation Bootstrap' industrialization programme supported by the US and Puerto Rican governments, which was begun in 1948. Accordingly manufacturing for export has become the most important sector of the economy, in place of agriculture. Until 1976, US Corporations were given tax incentives to set up in Puerto Rico and their profits were taxed only if repatriated. Industrial parks were built based on labour intensive industries to take advantage of Puerto Rico's low wages. In the mid-1970s, however, the strategy changed to attract capital intensive companies with the aim of avoiding the low wage trap. Nowadays about 70% of manufacturing income is repatriated; manufacturing produces about 40% of total output, but only 20% if remittances are excluded, about the same as in the 1950s. Investment has also fallen recently to 17% of gdp, having risen from 15% in 1950 to 30% in 1970.

Structure of production

The principal manufactures are textiles, clothing, electrical and electronic equipment, chemicals and pharmaceuticals. Dairy and livestock production is one of the leading agricultural activities; others are the cultivation of sugar, tobacco, coffee, pineapples and coconut. Rum has been a major export since the 19th century and the island supplies 83% of all the rum drunk in mainland USA. Tourism is another key element in the economy although it contributes only about 7% to gdp. The industry is profitable and a large employer. Over four million people visit Puerto Rico each year (about one million are cruise ship passengers) and spend about US$1.9 bn.

Despite the progress made to industrialize the country, the economy has suffered from US budget cuts. Some 30% of all spending on gnp originates in Washington and high unemployment is possible because of food stamps and other US transfers. Migration is a safety valve, and there are more Puerto Ricans living in New York than San Juan. The economy depends heavily on the tax incentives (known as Section 936) given to US mainland companies and on federal transfers. Puerto Rico is also used to channel loans to other Caribbean and Central American countries under the Caribbean Basin Initiative (CBI). President Clinton cut the Section 936 tax exemption for US companies and introduced legislation to Congress in 1993 to replace it with a more modest tax credit linked to wages paid by those companies in Puerto

Recent trends

Puerto Rico

Rico rather than to profits. This was also likely to reduce sharply the amount of finance available to other CBI countries. It is estimated that 100,000 Puerto Ricans are employed by companies operating under Section 936 (of which 23,000 are in pharmaceuticals) and another 200,000 are indirectly employed. Clinton's proposals were modified by the US Senate Finance Committee after much lobbying by Caribbean and Central American governments and companies, although the outcome represented a reduction in US budgetary spending. In his 1998 budget submission to Congress, President Clinton proposed that existing Section 30A of the tax code be made permanent to provide an estimated US$417mn a year in tax incentives to compensate for the phasing out of Section 936. Section 30A allows companies to claim 60 of wages and capital investment as allowances against tax.

The agreement between the USA, Canada and Mexico for the North American Free Trade Agreement (NAFTA) also has implications for Puerto Rico because of competition for jobs and investment. Although wage levels are lower in Mexico, Section 936 gives companies in Puerto Rico an advantage in pharmaceuticals and hi-tec industries. In low-skill labour-intensive manufacturing, such as clothing and footwear, Mexico has the advantage. Puerto Rico currently employs 30,000 in the clothing industry.

Culture

Music & dance
There are several music festivals each year, celebrating different styles & forms, including a Jazzfest in May & the Casals Music Festival in Jun

The island was Spanish until 1898 and one of the oldest musical traditions is that of the 19th-century Danza, associated particularly with the name of Juan Morel Campos and his phenomenal output of 549 compositions. This is European-derived salon music for ballroom dancing, slow, romantic and sentimental. The Institute of Puerto Rican Culture sponsors an annual competition for writers of danzas for the piano during the Puerto Rican Danza Week in May. The peasants of the interior, the Jíbaros, sing and dance the Seis, of Spanish origin, in its many varied forms, such as the Seis Chorreao, Seis Zapateao, Seis Corrido and Seis Bombeao. Other variants are named after places, like the Seis Cagueño and Seis Fajardeño. Favoured instruments are the *cuatro* and other varieties of the guitar, the *bordonúa*, *tiple*, *tres* and *quintillo*, backed by *güiro* (scraper), *maracas*, *pandereta* (tambourine) and *bomba* (drum) to provide rhythm. One uniquely Puerto Rican phenomenon is the singer's 'La-Le-Lo-Lai' introduction to the verses, which are in Spanish 10-line *décimas*. The beautiful Aguinaldos are sung at Christmastime, while the words of the Mapeyé express the Jíbaro's somewhat tragic view of life. Many artists have recorded the mountain music, notably El Gallito de Manatí, Ramito, Chuito el de Bayamón, Baltazar Carrero and El Jibarito de Lares. A popular singer is Andrés Jiménez, 'El Jíbaro', whose rustic songs of Puerto Rican folklore were honoured at Christmas 1993 by a concert with the Symphonic Orchestra of Puerto Rico and the Choir of the Conservatorio de Música de Puerto Rico, in which many traditional instruments were used.

Puerto Rico's best-known musical genre is the Plena, ironically developed by a black couple from Barbados, John Clark and Catherine George, known as 'Los Ingleses', who lived in the La Joya del Castillo neighbourhood of Ponce during the years of the First World War. With a four-line stanza and refrain in call-and-response between the 'Inspirador' (soloist) and chorus, the rhythm is distinctly African and the words embody calypso-style commentaries on social affairs and true-life incidents. Accompanying instruments were originally tambourines, then accordions and *güiros*, but nowadays include guitars, trumpets and clarinets. The Plena's most celebrated composer and performer was Manuel A Jiménez, known as 'Canario'.

There are relatively few pure black people in Puerto Rico, although the majority have some African blood, and the only specifically black music is the Bomba, sung by the 'Cantaor' and chorus, accompanied by the drums called *buleadores* and *subidores* and naturally also danced. The Bomba can be seen and heard at its best in the island's only black town of Loiza Aldea at the Feast of Santiago in late July. Rafael Cepeda and his family are the best known exponents.

For a modern interpretation of traditional music, recordings by the singer/composer Tony Croatto are highly recommended, while Rafael Cortijo and his Combo have taken the Plena beyond the confines of the island into the wider world of Caribbean salsa.

The Jíbaro, mentioned above, is a common figure in Puerto Rican literature. The **Literature** origin of the name is unknown, but it refers to the *campesino del interior*, a sort of Puerto Rican equivalent to the gaucho, native, but with predominantly hispanic features. The Jíbaro, as a literary figure, first appeared in the 19th century, with Manuel Alonso Pacheco's *El gíbaro* emerging as a cornerstone of the island's literature. In 29 'scenes', Alonso attempted both to describe and to interpret Puerto Rican life; he showed a form of rural life about to disappear in the face of bourgeois progress. The book also appeared at a time (1849) when romanticism was gaining popularity. Prior to this period, there had been a definite gulf between the educated letters, chronicles and memoires of the 16th to 18th centuries and the oral traditions of the people. These included *coplas*, *décimas*, *aguinaldas* (see above) and folk tales. The Jíbaro has survived the various literary fashions, from 19th-century romanticism and *realismo costumbrista* (writing about manners and customs), through the change from Spanish to US influence, well into the 20th century.

One reason for this tenacity is the continual search for a Puerto Rican identity. When, in 1898, Spain relinquished power to the USA, many Puerto Ricans sought full independence. Among the writers of this time were José de Diego and Manuel Zeno Gandía. The latter's series of four novels, *Crónicas de un mundo enfermo* (*Garduña* – 1896, *La charca* – 1898, *El negocio* – 1922, *Redentores* – 1925), contain a strong element of social protest. As the series progresses, a new theme is added to that of local economic misery, emigration to New York, which booms after 1945. For a variety of domestic reasons, many fled the island to seek adventures, happiness, material wealth in the United States. While some writers and artists in the 1930s and 1940s, for example Luis Lloréns Torres, tried to build a kind of nationalism around a mythical, rural past, others still favoured a complete separation from the colonialism which had characterized Puerto Rico's history. For a while, the former trend dominated, but by the 1960s the emigré culture had created a different set of themes to set against the search for the Puerto Rican secure in his/her national identity. These included, on the one hand, the social problems of the islander in New York, shown, for example, in some of the novels of Enrique A Laguerre, *Trópico en Manhattan* by Guillermo Cotto Thorner, stories such as *Spiks* by Pedro Juan Soto, or plays like René Marqués' *La carreta*. On the other there is the Americanization of the island, the figure of the 'piti-yanqui' (the native Puerto Rican who admires and flatters his North American neighbour) and the subordination of the agricultural to a US-based, industrial economy. Writers after 1965 who have documented this change include Rosario Ferré and the novelist and playwright, Luis Rafael Sánchez. The latter's *La guaracha del Macho Camacho* (1976), an alliterative, humorous novel, revolves around a traffic jam in a San Juan taken over by a vastly popular song, *La vida es una cosa fenomenal*, a far cry from the Jíbaro's world.

Puerto Rico

US Virgin Islands

11

US VirginIslands

The US Virgin Islands, in which the legacies of Danish ownership are very apparent, contain three main islands: St Thomas, St John and St Croix. There are 68 islands in all, that lie about 40 miles east of Puerto Rico, although most of them are uninhabited. They have long been developed as holiday centres for US citizens and because of that are distinct from the British Virgin Islands, which have only recently started to develop their tourist potential. The population, mainly black, has always been English-speaking, despite the long period of Danish control. Some Spanish is in use, particularly on St Croix. The West Indian dialect is mostly English, with inflections from Dutch, Danish, French, Spanish, African languages and Créole.

Essentials

Before you travel

Documents US citizens do not, of course, require passports for visits to the US Virgin Islands but they do need proof of citizenship to return to the USA. Visitors of other nationalities will need passports, visas (or waiver for participating countries) and return/onward tickets, as they would for the mainland USA.

Money The US dollar is the currency. Credit cards are widely accepted in major tourist resorts and duty free shops, less so by local businesses.

Climate The climate in the Virgin Islands is very pleasant, with the trade winds keeping the humidity down. The average temperature varies little between winter (25°C or 77°F) and summer (28°C or 82°F). Average annual rainfall is 40ins. On 17 September 1989, Hurricane Hugo ripped across St Croix causing damage or destruction to 90% of the buildings and leaving 22,500 people homeless. In September 1995 the islands escaped the worst of Hurricane Luis but were hit by Hurricane Marilyn, causing damage estimated at US$3.5bn. St Thomas was the worst hit, with five deaths and a quarter of all homes destroyed. In July 1996 the hurricane season came early with the arrival of Bertha, but the 80 mph winds caused only relatively minor damage.

Getting there

Air **From the USA**: there are scheduled flights to St Croix and/or St Thomas with *American Airlines* (Baltimore, Boston, Miami, New York), *Delta* (Atlanta, Detroit, New York), *United Airlines* (Chicago, Washington DC), *Continental* (New York), *US Air* (Philadelphia). **From Europe**: there are no direct flights, connections can be made via Miami or Puerto Rico, St Maarten and Antigua. Regional airlines link the USVI with **other Caribbean islands** and there are flights to Anguilla, Antigua, the Dominican Republic, St Barthélémy, Puerto Rico (San Juan, Vieques and Fajardo), St Kitts, Nevis, St Maarten and the BVI. *Air Sunshine*, a charter air line has flights to San Juan, St Thomas, St Croix, Tortola and Virgin Gorda, T888-8798900, 800-3278900. *Bohlke International Airways*, T7789177 has a charter service between St Thomas and St Croix and day trips to Virgin Gorda and Anegada in the BVI with lunch, swimming, sightseeing. *American Eagle, Gulfstream International, Cape Air* and *Seaborne Aviation* all run services several times daily between Puerto Rico, St Thomas and St Croix.

During the winter season there are many charter flights from the USA (Midwest, Northeast), Canada, UK & Denmark

Boat Ocean going ships can be accommodated at **Charlotte Amalie** in St Thomas and **Frederiksted** and the **South Shore** cargo port in St Croix. There are regular services between the USVI and the BVI. *Native Son* (T7748685) and *Smith's Ferry* (T775292) alternate services from Charlotte Amalie to West End, Tortola (45 mins, US$35 return) and on to Road Town, Tortola (90 mins, US$35 return), several daily, some stop in Red Hook. *Smith's Ferry* also to Virgin Gorda. *Inter Island Boat Services* (T7766597) several daily between Cruz Bay, St John and West End, Tortola; three times a week, Red Hook and Cruz Bay to Jost Van Dyke, BVI; twice a week Red Hook-Cruz-Virgin Gorda. *Nubian Express*, T284-4954999 between West End, Tortola, and St John and Red Hook, St Thomas, Sunday-Friday, three daily. *Caribe Cay* sails between St Thomas and Fajardo, Puerto Rico at weekends, US$70 return, T8608809 in Puerto Rico. **Ports of entry** Charlotte Amalie, St Thomas; Christiansted and Frederiksted, St Croix; Cruz Bay, St John. **Documents** The USVI are a territory of the USA but constitute a separate Customs district. US boats with US citizens have to clear in here when coming from Puerto Rico (can be done by phone on St Croix) and all other islands. To find out more about custom fees, call Mr Harrigan on T7742510, ext 223. St Croix customs T7731011. When arriving by boat it is essential to ensure that you have the correct visas for immigration purposes. All vessels must clear in upon arrival from a foreign port and all crew members aboard must go ashore with the captain to obtain entry into the USVI. Clearing customs and immigration on St John is a pain due to the crowded harbour. Anchor if you can find room, try northwest end of island or just outside harbour, you can walk from beaches at Hawksnest. On St Croix, foreign boats or boats with foreign passengers clear customs at Gallows Bay Dock.

Touching down

Local tourist office On St Thomas, the Tourist Information Centre at the airport is open daily 0900-1900. Offices at the town waterfront and at the West Indian Company dock are open 0800-1700 Monday-Friday (PO Box 6400, Charlotte Amalie, USVI 00804, T7748784, 800-3728784, F7744390). On St Croix, there is a Tourism Booth at the airport in the baggage claim area and next to it the First Stop Information Booth. In Christiansted there is a Visitor's Bureau on Queens Cross Street near Company Street (open Monday-Friday 0800-1700, PO Box 4538, Christiansted, USVI 00822-4538, T7730495, F7735074), and in Frederiksted the Visitors' Centre is opposite the pier in the Custom House Building, Strand Street, USVI 00840 (T7720357). There is also an office next to the post office in Cruz Bay, St John (PO Box 200, Cruz Bay, USVI 00831, T7766450). www.usvi.net has a lot of tourist information.

Tourist information
See individual islands for airport information

Maps The Government offers a free road map (available at Tourist Information Offices) but considerable optimism was used in showing road classifications, especially on the St John map. Some of the 'paved highways' are really bad, unpaved roads which require hard, four-wheel drive. Texaco issues a map of the US islands, as does Phillip A Schneider, Dept of Geography, University of Illinois at Urbana-Champaign, price US$3.95.

Finding out more The publications, *St Croix This Week*, *St John's Times*, *Virgin Island Playground*, *What To Do St Thomas and St John* and *St Thomas This Week* have regularly updated tourist information, including shopping news, ferry schedules, taxi fares, restaurants, nightlife and other tourist news. *Island Trader* is published weekly, free, good source of events and activities. Also specialist pamphlets on honeymoons, diving etc.

Where to stay

There is an 18% tax on all forms of accommodation in the US Virgin Islands. Hotels may also charge a US$1 per night Hotel Association charge and/or a 2½-3% energy tax. High season is mid-December to mid-April, but higher prices are sometimes into May despite lower hotel occupancy.

See individual towns for further information

Getting around

Driving in Charlotte Amalie during business hours is a slow business. It is best to park and walk (municipal car park beside Fort Christian). Country speed limits are 35 mph, in towns they are 20 mph, although the traffic is so heavy you will be lucky if you can go that fast. On St John the speed limit is 20 mph everywhere. Driving is on the left, even though the cars are lefthand drive. There is a seatbelt law for the driver and front seat passenger that the police enforce with a vengeance (US$50 fine).

Car
Donkeys, goats, chickens & cows have the right of way

There are lots of flights between St Croix and St Thomas. Seaborne Aviation (T7736442) has a daily service between Christiansted Harbour and Charlotte Amalie, nine times a day, arriving at the dock in 18 minutes, US$55 one way for non-VI residents.

Air

A hydrofoil goes from Yacht Haven Marina, St Thomas, to Gallows Bay Dock, St Croix at 0715, 1445, return 0915, 1630, in winter (in summer 0715, 1515, return 0915, 1700) US$37 one way, US$70 return, T7767417. Ferry St Thomas-St John, 20 minutes from Red Hook (US$3 adult, US$1 child), 45 minutes from Charlotte Amalie (US$7 adult, US$3 child), Cruz Bay-Red Hook hourly, Cruz Bay-Charlotte Amalie seven a day.

Sea

US Virgin Islands

Touching down

Departure tax No departure tax at the airport (price of US$5 is included in the ticket).

Hours of business Banks open Monday-Friday, 0830-1500. Government offices open Monday-Thursday, 0900-1700. Banks, filling stations and government offices close for local holidays.

Official time Atlantic Standard Time, 4 hrs behind GMT, 1 hr ahead of EST.

Useful addresses Air Ambulance: Bohlke International Airways, T7789177 (day), 7721629 (night); recompression chamber 7762686. **Ambulance:** 911. **Fire:** 911. **Police:** 911.

Voltage 120 volts 60 cycles.

Clothing Bathing suits are considered offensive when worn away from the beach, so cover up. There is even a law against it, you can get a fine for having your belly showing. It is illegal to go topless on Magens Beach.

Tipping As in mainland USA, tipping is 15%; hotels often add 10-15%.

Safety Take the usual precautions against crime: lock your car, leave valuable jewellery at home and be careful walking around at night. The tourist office recommends that you do not go to deserted beaches on your own but in a group. Couples have been held up at gunpoint and robbed and/or raped on the beach after dark. In 1996 the shooting on St Thomas of three tourists prompted the reinstatement of a 2200 curfew for youths under 16 and increased police patrols. However, eight tourists were later shot at in a restaurant car park. Other security problems, probably drugs related, have arisen on St John and St Croix. Youth unemployment is a problem.

Keeping in touch

Telephone
International phone code: 340

Local telephone calls within the USVI from coin-operated phones are US$0.25 for each five minutes. Privately owned payphones charge for local calls, even 800 numbers. Vitelco does not make extra charges. Radio Shack offers pre-paid cellular service, T7775644, 7741314, so does Cellular One, bring your own phone or buy one of theirs, US$0.52 per minute in USVI and Puerto Rico.

Media

The Daily News is published daily, US$0.50, and on Friday it includes the weekend section, a complete listing of restaurants, nightclubs, music and special events for the week, for all three islands.

Shopping

See individual towns for further information

The USVI are a free port and tourist related items are duty-free. Shops are usually shut on Sunday unless there is a cruise ship in harbour. There are several local rums in white or gold: Cruzan (guided tours of the distillery, on St Croix, Monday-Friday 0900-1130, 1300-1615, but phone in advance, T6922280; US$3 adults, US$1 children), Old St Croix and Brugal.

Flora and fauna

The Virgin Islands' national bird is the yellow breast (Coereba flaveola); the national flower is the yellow cedar (Tecoma Stans). The mongoose was brought to the islands during the plantation days to kill rats that ate the crops. Unfortunately rats are nocturnal and mongooses are not and they succeeded only in eliminating most of the parrots. Now you see them all over the islands, especially near the rubbish dumps. There are many small lizards and some iguanas of up to 4ft long. The iguanas sleep in the trees and you can see them and feed them (favourite food hibiscus flowers) at the Limetree beach and the Red Hook *Tickles* 'iguana garden'. St John has a large population of wild donkeys which are pests; they bite, steal picnic lunches and ruin gardens. On all three islands, chickens, pigs, goats and cows have the right of way on the roads.

US Virgin Islands

Tourist offices overseas

Canada 3300 Bloor Street W, Suite 3120, Centre Tower, Toronto, Ontario, M8X 2X3, T416-2331414, F416-2339367.

Denmark Park Allé 5, DK-8000, Aarhus Center, T86-181933, F86-181934.

Italy Via Gherardini 2, 20145, Milan, T02-33105841, F33105827.

Puerto Rico 60 Washington St, Suite 1102, San Juan 00907, T787-7228023, F7246659, ncumpiano@usa.net

UK Molasses House, Clove Hitch Quay, Plantation Wharf, York Place, London SW11 3TN, T020-79785262, F020-79243171.

USA There are offices of the USVI Department of Tourism in the USA at: 500 North Michigan Av, Suite 2030, Chicago, IL 60611, T312-6708784, F6708788/9; 2655 Le Jeune Rd, Suite 907, Coral Gables, FL 33134, T305-4427200, F4459044; 1270 Av of the Americas, Suite 2108, New York, NY 10020, T212-3322222, F3322223; The Hall of States, 444 North Capital St, NW Suite 298, Washington DC, 20001, T202-6243590, F6243594; 245 Peachtree Center Av, Marquis One Tower, Suite MB-05 Atlanta, GA 30303, T404-6880906, F5251102; 3460 Wilshire Boulevard, Suite 412, Los Angeles, CA 90010, T213-7390138, F7392005, usvi_la@msn.com

Most of St John is a national park. Hassel Island, off Charlotte Amalie, is also a park. The National Parks Service headquarters is at Red Hook, St Thomas. Also in Red Hook is the Island Resources Foundation (T7756225; US office, 1718 P Street NW, Suite T4, Washington DC 20036, T2659712). This non-governmental office is also a non-profit-making consulting firm open to serious researchers and investigators seeking information on wildlife, tourism and the environment who may use the extensive library. It may also be used as a contact base for those seeking specialist information on other islands. The Audubon Society is represented on St John by Peg Fisher at the At Your Service Travel Agency. *Virgin Islands Birdlife*, published by the USVI Co-operative Extension Service, with the US National Park Service, is available for birdwatchers. The National Park Headquarters has an excellent, reasonably priced selection of reference books for marine life, flora, fauna and island history.

On St Croix, the National Parks Service office is in the old customs building on the waterfront. Buck Island is a national marine park. In Christiansted, contact the Environmental Association, PO Box 3839, T7731989, office in Apothecary Hall Courtyard, Company Street. The Association runs hikes, boat trips and walks, and in March-May, in conjunction with Earthwatch and the US Fish and Wildlife Department, takes visitors to see the leatherback turtles at Sandy Point (T7737545 for information). The association has made Salt River (see page 538) a natural park for wildlife, reef and mangroves. There are books, leaflets, etc, available at the association's office.

Holidays

New Year's Day, Three Kings Day (6 January), Martin Luther King Day (15 January), Presidents' Day (19 February), Holy Thursday, Good Friday, Easter Monday, Transfer Day (31 March), Memorial Day (28 May), Organic Act Day (18 June), Emancipation Day (3 July), Independence Day (4 July), Hurricane Supplication Day (27 July), Labour Day (beginning of September), Puerto Rico/Virgin Islands Friendship Day (mid-October), Hurricane Thanksgiving Day (mid-October), Liberty Day (1 November), Veterans' Day (11 November), Thanksgiving Day (mid-November), Christmas Day (25 December).

Public holidays
For information on local festivals see individual island Essentials sections

Health

St Thomas has a 250-bed hospital, T7768311, St John has a seven-bed clinic, T7766400, and St Croix has a 250-bed hospital, T7786311. All three have 24-hour emergency services. Mobile medical units provide health services to outlying areas. **Red Hook Family Practice** is open Monday-Friday 1000-1600, walk in.

US Virgin Islands

St Thomas

Population: 51,000

St Thomas rises out of the sea to a range of hills that runs down its spine. The highest peak, Crown Mountain, is 1,550ft. On St Peter Mountain, 1,500ft, is a viewpoint at Mountain Top. Various scenic roads can be driven such as Skyline Drive (Route 40), from which both sides of the island can be seen simultaneously, and Mafolie Road (Route 35) that leaves the capital, Charlotte Amalie, heading north to cross the Skyline Drive becoming Magens Bay Road, and descends to the beautiful bay. Much of the island has been built upon, especially on its east half. St Thomas is 13 miles long and less than three miles wide, with an area of 32 square miles.

Ins & outs

See transport, page 533, for further details

Getting there The **Cyril E King** (STT) airport; the taxi stand is at the far left end of the new terminal, a long way from the commuter flights from Puerto Rico and other islands. Taxi to town US$5 per person (US$5 for each additional passenger). There are public buses every 20 mins 0600-1900 from the terminal to the town, US$1. Boats come in to Charlotte Amalie or Red Hook in the east. **Getting around** Vitran bus services (US$0.75 city fare, US$1 country fare, exact change) have 34 a/c buses that run from town to the university (passing near Yacht Haven Marina), to Four Winds Plaza and to Red Hook (past the hospital, K-Mart, Kost U Less), every hour. Hourly open-air taxi-buses charge US$3 for the trip from Red Hook to Market Square. All types of wheels are available and rental firms are plentiful.

US Virgin Islands

St Thomas

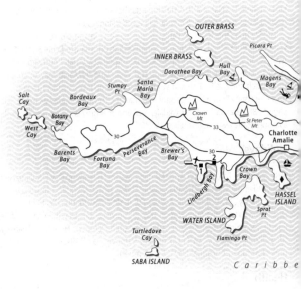

N

Not to scale

■ **Sleeping**
1 Best Western Carib Beach
2 Best Western Emerald Beach
3 Blue Beard's Beach Club & Villas
4 Blue Beard's Castle

5 Bolongo Beach Resort
6 Colony Point Pleasant
7 Elysian Beach Resort
8 Marriott Frenchman's Reef Resort

Diving and marine life

For divers, there are over 200 dive sites, caves, coral reefs, drop offs and lots of colourful fish to see, although be careful of short sighted barracuda if you swim into murky water. There are several wrecks of ships and even a wrecked plane to explore. *At-a-glance snorkeller's Guide to St Thomas* by Nick Aquilar describes 15 snorkel spots in detail. Spearfishing is not allowed and you may not remove any living things from underwater such as coral, live shells or sea fans.

Many of the resorts offer diving packages or courses and there are at least 15 dive companies. Equipment and instruction for underwater photography are available. A one-tank dive costs around US$50 while a two-tank dive starts from US$70. *Coki Beach Dive Centre*, T7754220 offers an introductory dive for US$40, cruise ships bring their guests here. *Chris Sawyer Diving Centre*, Red Hook, T7757804, www.sawyerdive.vi, specializes in quality service to small groups, great all day, wreck of the *Rhone* trip once a week (dives for locals on Sunday), certification classes every two weeks. There are many other operators around the island and at major hotels, also several liveaboard sail/dive charters, worth contacting if you want to spend more time on and under the water: *Regency Yacht Vacations* (T800-5247676), *VIP Yacht Charters* (T800-5242015), *Island Yachts* (T800-5242019), *Red Hook Charters* (T800-2334938). Some dive moorings have been placed around St Thomas but they are not particularly well maintained (check before using). There are plans to install more moorings to protect the reef from anchor damage.

Divesites
The waters around the islands are so clear that snorkelling is extremely popular

Dive centres

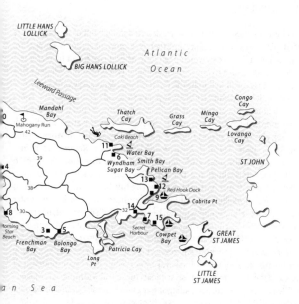

US Virgin Islands

The Atlantis **Submarine** dives to 150ft for those who can not scuba dive but want to see the exotic fish, coral, sponges and other underwater life. Located at Building VI, Bay L, Havensight Mall, St Thomas, T7765650 for reservations, or 7760288 for information (also kiosk on waterfront, usually six dives daily). You have to take a four-mile launch ride on the *Yukon III* to join the submarine at Buck Island. One hour day dives US$72, children 4-14 US$27, 15-17 US$36.

VI Ecotours, T7792155, offer **kayaking** and **snorkelling** in the marine sanctuary in the last mangrove lagoon left on the south side of St Thomas. No experience necessary. If there is enough demand they run a night trip, recommended.

Whale watching *The Environmental Association of St Thomas-St John (EAST)* organizes whale watching during the migration season at the beginning of the year. Humpbacks are the most commonly sighted. Trips leave from the St Thomas' VI National Park dock in Red Hook on a 77 ft catamaran, US$55 for non-members, US$45 for EAST members, for information T7761976, 775012.

Fishing There is deep sea fishing with the next world record in every class lurking just under the boat. The USVI Fishing Club Tournament is in June, contact the American Yacht Harbour for details, F7765970. The Bastille Day Kingfish Tournament is in July and the USVI Open Atlantic Blue Marlin tournament is held in August every year (T7742752); other game fish include white marlin, kingfish, sailfish, tarpon, Alison tuna and wahoo. No fishing licence is required for shoreline fishing; government pamphlets list 100 good spots (T7756762). For sportfishing charters and information contact Charterboat Centre (T800-8665714), also known as St Thomas Sports Fishing, T7757990. They are a central agency for booking sports fishing charters in the Virgin Islands.

Beaches and watersports

There are 44 beaches on St Thomas. Few are deserted though out of season they are less crowded. The most inaccessible, and therefore more likely to be empty, are those along the northwest coast, which need four-wheel drive to get there. Otherwise, for solitude, take a boat to one of the uninhabited islets offshore. **Magens Bay** on the north coast is considered to be the finest on the island and wonderfully safe for small children. It has an entry fee of US$1 per person and a charge for cars. There are changing facilities and you can rent snorkelling equipment (but the snorkelling is not the best on the island) and loungers. Other good beaches are at **Lindbergh Bay** (southwest, close to the airport runway, good for plane spotters), **Morningstar Bay** (south coast near *Marriott Frenchman's Reef Beach Resort*, beach and watersports equipment for hire), **Bolongo Bay**, **Sapphire Bay** (east coast, beach gear for rent, good snorkelling) and **Brewer's Bay** (can be reached by bus from Charlotte Amalie, get off just beyond the airport). **Hull Bay** on the north coast is good for surfing and snorkelling. At **Coki Beach** (northeast, showers, lockers, water skiing, jet skiing) snorkelling equipment can be rented for US$6, snorkelling is good just off the beach. Windsurfing lessons and rentals at Morningstar, Magens Bay, Sapphire Beach, Secret Harbour and the *Renaissance Grand*. *West Indies Windsurfing* will deliver rental equipment to wherever you are staying, T7756530, not only windsurfing boards but also sunfish and kayaks. Snorkelling gear can be rented at all major hotels and the dive shops. Sunfish sailboats for rent at Morningstar, Magens Bay and the *Renaissance Grand*. Parasailing at some hotels or call *Caribbean Parasail and Watersports*, T7759360, who have a variety of jet skis etc to go fast and make a noise, or pedalos to go slowly and peacefully.

Day sails Day sailing of all types and cruises are available. Half day sails from US$50, full day from US$100 and sunset cruises from US$40 are offered by many boats. Prices depend on how your trip is booked. Most expensive are those booked on a cruise ship, as lots of commissions have to be paid. Before taking a day trip on any boat, ask about size, any shade awning and the number of passengers. Many day sail boats limit their guests to six passengers, take a stop for snorkelling and provide drinks; however, it is often cheaper to take one that crowds the tourists on. You can explore on your own by renting a small power boat from *Nauti Nymph* (T7755066), 23-29ft Fountain Power Boats; *See An Ski* (T7756265), 22/24/28-ft makos single/double engines. *Virgin Islands Power* (VIP) Yacht Charters (bought end-1998 by the Winfair Group), T7761510, 800-5242015, F7763801, 6118 Frydenhoj, No 58, St Thomas, VI 00802-1402, has the largest power yacht charter fleet and sport fishing fleet in the Caribbean, bareboat or crewed, US$3,000-6,000 a week in summer, US$4,200-6,700 in winter. Charter yachts available in a wide variety of luxury and size, with or without crew, cost about the same as a good hotel.

The annual Rolex Cup Regatta is held at St Thomas Yacht Club at Easter (T7756320). Pigs in Winter is a two-day autumn regatta, with races from STYC to Coral Bay and back. Other events include Caribbean Ocean Racing Triangle tune up race in mid-February, Optimist regatta in mid-June, women's laser regatta in November. **Regattas**

There are a few public **tennis** courts (two at Long Bay and two at Sub Base), which operate on a first come first served basis, but the hotel courts at the major resorts are mostly lit for night time play and open for non-residents if you phone in advance to book. There is an 18-hole, 6,022 yd **golf** course with lovely views at Mahogany Run, green fee US$90 per person, cheaper after 1400 (T800-2537103). **Horse racing** is a popular spectator sport. Bayside Spa and Fitness Centre, across from *Bolongo Bay Resort*, charges US$50 per month, no enrolment fee. Half Moon Stables offer trail rides and lessons, T7776088. **Other sports**

Charlotte Amalie

The harbour at Charlotte Amalie, capital of St Thomas and also of the entire USVI, still bustles with colour and excitement, although the harbour area can be a startling contrast for the visitor arriving by sea from the British Virgin Islands. As the Fort Christian Museum puts it, "Oversized, architecturally inappropriate buildings have marred the scenic beauty of the harbour. Harbour congestion has become a major problem." One could add that by day the streets are congested too. At night visitors tend to stay within their resorts. But as the museum also says, there are still a number of historical buildings. **Harbour**
Population: 12,331

The town was built by the Danes, who named it after their King's consort, but to most visitors it remains 'St Thomas'. Beautiful old Danish houses painted in a variety of pastel colours are a reminder of the island's history. One recently opened to the public is **Haagensen House**, the home of a former Danish banker, with a courtyard, gardens and antique furniture. ■ *T7749605. US$6, free shuttle service from Emancipation Garden. Daily 0900-1600.* For a good view of the town and the surrounding area, take the **Paradise Point Tramway**, across the street from the cruise ship dock and Havensight Mall, actually a cable car which takes you on a seven-minute ride up 700ft to Paradise Point where there is an observation deck and a bar. You can see the harbour, cruise ships and other boats and lots of neighbouring islands. ■ *T7749809, F7749955. Daily 0900-1700. US$12 round trip.* **Danish influence**

There are also some picturesque churches and one of the oldest synagogues in the Western Hemisphere (1833). Situated on Crystal Gade the synagogue is an airy, domed building, with a sand floor and hurricane-proof walls; it has books for sale in the office, iced springwater and visitors are given a 10 minute introduction for free. It is worth a visit. In 1996 the Hebrew Congregation of St Thomas celebrated the 200th anniversary of its founding with lots of services and commemorative events. **Churches**

US Virgin Islands

The Dutch Reformed Church is the oldest established church, having had a congregation since 1660 although the present building dates from 1846. The Frederick Lutheran Church dates from 1820 and its parish hall was once the residence of Jacob H S Lind (1806-27).

Fortifications There are several old fortifications within the town. **Bluebeard's Castle Tower** and **Blackbeard's Castle**, the latter allegedly built in 1679 and lived in by the pirate and his 14 wives (there is no proof of this), is now an inn and restaurant. The **Virgin Islands Museum** is in the former dungeon at Fort Christian (1666-80). There are historical and natural history sections and an art gallery. ■ *T7764566 to check times. Free, but donations welcome as much restoration work remains to be done. Mon-Fri, 0830-1630.* In contrast to the red-painted fort is the green **Legislative Building**, originally the Danish police barracks (1874), open Monday-Friday.

Other town Government House, off Kongens Gade, was built in 1865-87. The Enid M Baa
sights Library and Archive is on Main Street, it is another early 19th-century edifice. Two historical buildings which cannot be visited are the former Danish Consulate, on Denmark Hill and the house of the French painter, Camille Pissaro, on Main Street. The Dockside Bookshop in Havensight Mall (at the Cruise Ship Dock) has books and other publications on the Virgin Islands and the Caribbean in general. The Old

Charlotte Amalie

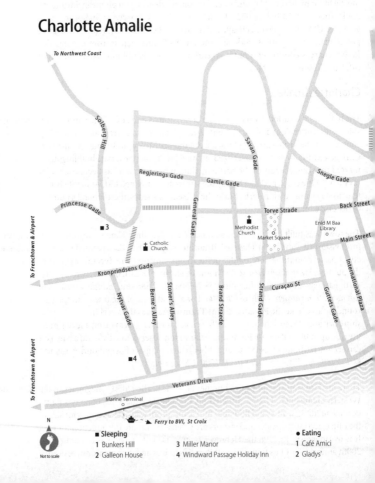

To Northwest Coast

Solberg Hill

Regjerings Gade

Savan Gade

Gamle Gade

Snegle Gade

Princesse Gade

Back Street

To Frenchtown & Airport

■ 3

General Gade

Torve Strade

Methodist Church

Enid M Baa Library

Market Square

Main Street

✝ Catholic Church

Kronprindsens Gade

Nytvar Gade

Berne's Alley

Stoner's Alley

Brand Straede

Strand Gade

Curaçao St

International Plaza

Guttets Gade

To Frenchtown & Airport

■ 4

Veterans Drive

Marine Terminal

N

Ferry to BVI, St Croix

Not to scale

■ Sleeping		● Eating
1 Bunkers Hill	3 Miller Manor	1 Café Amici
2 Galleon House	4 Windward Passage Holiday Inn	2 Gladys'

Mill, up Crown Mountain Road from Sub Base traffic light is an old sugar mill open to the public. **Estate St Peter Greathouse and Botanical Gardens** has 500 varieties of plants, a stunning view and an art gallery for local artists.

Water Island, at the west end of St Thomas' main harbour, is the smallest inhabited island. It was purchased from Denmark by the USA in 1944 to use as a military base during the Second World War. Fort Segarra was built as an underground fort and later the island was used to test weapons. It was transferred to the Department of the Interior from Defense in 1952. A year later a 40-year lease of the entire island was given to a developer for construction of a hotel and homes. The hotel closed after Hurricane Hugo in 1989. The island's ownership was turned over to the VI Government and private island homeowners in December 1996. While the marina and hotel property is to be torn down, the local government has constructed open-air buildings on the beach available for public use. Its name comes from the freshwater ponds, now salt ponds, once plentiful on the island. At weekends the beach is busy with local residents, charterboat guests and the anchorage is filled. During the week, the *Kontiki* floating booze cruise makes daily stops; other day-charter boats may also stop when weather is rough. Larry's Ferry operates from Water Island to Crown Bay Marina, US$3 one way and special rates for islanders; moorings have been placed at the dock for use by people living on boats.

Water Island

US Virgin Islands

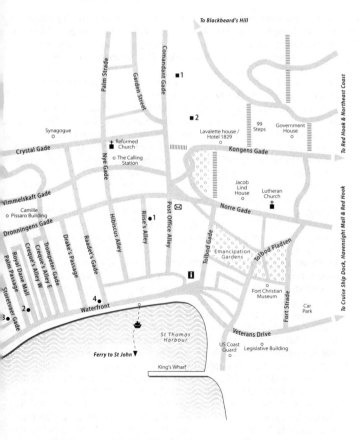

3 The Green House
4 Planet Hollywood

Hassel Island   Hassel Island is part of US National Parks. There are ruins on the shore but no development has yet been carried out. Hire a boat or take your dinghy to the dilapidated
dock; walk towards the ocean for a picnic and a great view of Frenchman's Reef and
watch the ships entering the harbour; then hike on a trail to an old building; climb
the wall at the back of the building to get an outstanding view of the area from
Frenchman's Reef to Green Cay where you can see the surf breaking on three sets of
rocks that are difficult to see from the water. Around the other end of the island is a
small liveaboard boating community.

Essentials

There are many hotels, guest houses, apartments, villas and cottages on St Thomas, the
cheaper places to stay are in town or up in the hills, while the newer, chain hotels on the
beach are at the top of the range. Summer rates are about 20% cheaper than winter. There is
a Hotel Association counter at the airport which can help you with reservations. Please note
that non-inclusion does not imply non-recommendation. Unfortunately, because of the
increase in crime, you are not advised to walk around downtown Charlotte Amalie at night,
take a taxi. Between downtown and Havensight the police have put up signs advising you
not to walk along the waterfront path. Also be careful if walking to the Crystal Gade Synagogue and never walk there at night.

Sleeping   **Resorts, apartments and condominiums** are clustered around the east end, such as the
The Department of   **LL** *Elysian Beach Resort* on Cowpet Bay, T7751000, F7760910. 180 rooms and suites, fitness
Tourism website for   centre, tennis, pool, jacuzzi, watersports centre offering diving, kayaking, parasailing, use of
hotel rates is   facilities at *Bluebeard's* (see below) and **LL-L** *Point Pleasant Resort*, 6600 Estate Smith Bay,
http://st-thomas.   T7757200, F7765694, www.pointpleasantresort.com Children sharing parents' room free
com/rates   under 21, 95 suites in 15 acres of tropical gardens, pool, tennis, watersports. Next door is
LL *Renaissance Grand Beach Resort* on Water Bay, PO Box 8267, T7751510, F7752185,
www.renaissance hotels.com 290 hill or beachside rooms and 36 suites, well-appointed, 2
pools, 6 lit tennis courts, fitness centre, restaurants, bars, children's programmes, complimentary watersports, sailing, fishing and diving can be arranged, conference facilities, lovely
views over the resort's own beach to St John and the British Virgins. **LL** *Sapphire Beach
Resort & Marina*, T7756100, F7772403, www.usvi.net/hotel/sapphire 171 rooms, pool,
suites, villas, watersports, tennis, kitchens, restaurant, children under 19 free when sharing,
children's activities. **LL** *Secret Harbour Beach Resort*, T7756550, F7751501,
www.st-thomas. com/shb.vi. 64 suites, popular with honeymooners, watersports, tennis,
kitchens, restaurant. On the south coast is **LL-L** *Bolongo Bay Beach Club & Villas*, 7150
Bolongo, T7751800, F7753208, www.bolongo.com. EP, CP or all-inclusive family resort, kids'
offers, pool, beach, tennis, kitchen facilities, 2 restaurants. Among others, and overlooking
the entrance to Charlotte Amalie harbour and above Morningstar Beach, the huge
LL *Marriott Frenchman's Reef Beach Resort*, PO Box 7100, T7768500, F7156191,
www.marriott-fr.vi 408 rooms and suites, all facilities, and its 96-room sister property
LL *Marriott Morning Star Beach Resort* alongside, www.marriott-ms.vi Lots of restaurants
and bars, fitness centre, water ferry to town, watersports, pools, tennis, excursions, access for
the disabled. West of Charlotte Amalie are **LL** *Best Western Emerald Beach Resort*, 8070
Lindbergh Bay, T7778800, F7763426, www.emeraldbeach.com 90 rooms, pool, bar, restaurant, 'The Palms' rooms have ocean and airport view, tennis, watersports. Its sister resort
L-AL *Best Western Carib Beach Resort*, T7742525, F7744131, same website. Smaller at 60
rooms, pool, casual, both on Lindbergh Bay, sheltered beach at end of airport runway, only
drawback is aircraft noise. On the same bay, **AL** *Island Beachcomber*, PO Box 302579,
T7745250, F7745615, www.st-thomas.com/islandbeachcomber. 47 rooms, on beach, by airport, free shuttle to town. **LL** *Pavilions and Pools*, 6400 Estate Smith Bay, T/F7756110,
www.pavilionsandpools.com. 25 rooms with salt pools, kitchens, restaurant, newly renovated, private. **LL** *The Ritz Carlton*, 6900 Great Bay, T7753333, F7754444. 152 rooms, very
expensive and luxurious. **LL** all inclusive *Wyndham Sugar Bay Resort*, near the *Renaissance
Grand*, T7777100, F7777200, www.wyndham.com/resorts 300 rooms, also very expensive,

3 pools, watersports, tennis, fitness centre, scuba, beach volleyball, non-residents can get an all-inclusive day pass for US$50.

Small hotels and guest houses L-AL *Admiral's Inn*, T7741376, F7748010, www.admirals-inn.com 12 rooms, seaside on Frenchtown Point. **L-AL** *Limestone Reef Terraces*, on Water Island, T7742148, pmurray@nerc.com Studio apartments and 3-bedroom villa with car, overlooking Honeymoon Beach. **AL-A** *Danish Chalet Inn*, T7745764, F7774886, www.wininn.com Good value, 10 rooms, friendly owners. **A-B** *Island View Guest House*, T7744270, F7746167, www.st-thomas.com/islandviewguest house Great place to stay before or after a charter, near airport, great view. In Charlotte Amalie: **LL** *Bluebeard's Castle*, on hillside overlooking town, T7741600, F7745134. 183 rooms, sports, pool, free shuttle to Magens Bay Beach and to Veterans' Drive. Heading towards the airport, is **LL-L** *Windward Passage Holiday Inn*, PO Box 640, T7745200, F7741231. Pool, restaurant, 151 rooms, walking distance of shops and ferries, shuttle to beach. **AL** *Villa Blanca*, T7760749, F7792661, www.st-thomas.com/villablanca 14 rooms, large gardens, on hillside, view of town and harbour, pool, quiet, family run. **AL-A** *Bunker Hill Hotel*, 7A Commandant Gade, T7748056, F7743172, www.bunkerhillhotel.com 15 rooms, a/c, TV, pool, airport transfers. **AL-B** *Galleon House*, PO Box 6577, T/F7746952, www.st-thomas.com/galleonhouse Swimming pool, veranda, gourmet breakfast, snorkel gear provided, discounts for senior citizens. **B-C** *Miller Manor*, PO Box 1570, on the hill behind the Catholic Cathedral, T7741535, F7745988, millermanor-aida-leo@worldnet.attnet Clean, very friendly, a/c, 5 mins' walk to town, microwave and fridge in each room.

Little St James, a 72-acre island, off the southeast of St Thomas, has an antique-furnished villa, sleeps 8 and comes with 2 boats, captain and staff, all-inclusive. Contact *Caribbean Chapters* in the UK for rental information, T44-1244-341131, popular with the rich and famous, eg Kevin Costner.

For luxury & peace rent your own island

There are many very good restaurants on the island, most of which are listed in *Here's How* and *St Thomas This Week*, or you can get details in your hotel. The large hotels all have their own restaurants so you will not be short of places to eat.

Eating

Award-winning ribs from *Bill's Texas Pit BBQ*, a mobile truck which shows up Tue-Sat in the Waterfront and Red Hook, also for lunch at Sub Base, the best on the island. The area west of the Market Square is more local, with restaurants and bars. *Bumpa's*, waterfront, T7765674. Upstairs, outdoors, small breakfast and lunch spot overlooking harbour, locally popular and inexpensive, no credit cards. *Café Amici*, in A H Riise's Mall, T7765670. Open Mon-Sat 1030-1530, Sun 1030-1500, Italian and Mediterranean food, moderate prices. *Cuzzins Caribbean Restaurant & Bar*, Back Street, T7774711. Open for lunch Mon-Sat, dinner Tue-Sat, good, large, local meals, lunch can be dinner! West Indian cuisine, conch, fish, also drinks such as sea moss and maubi, vegetarian plates available. *Glady's Café*, in Historic Royal Dane Mall, T7746604. Open 0700-1530, Mon-Sat, local dishes such as salt fish and dumplings, mutton stew. *Hard Rock Café*, T7775555, on waterfront at International Plaza, usual burgers and sandwiches, also vegetarian. *Hotel 1829*, on Government Hill, T7761829. Superb food and service, expensive, if you can't afford it go and have a look anyway, lovely old building and great view, happy hour 1700-2000, dinner daily. For great French cuisine, *The Banana Tree Grill* at Bluebeard's Castle, T7764050. Expensive, open for dinner Wed-Mon. *The Green House*, on harbour front, Veterans Drive, T7747998. Excellent restaurant at reasonable prices, attracts younger crowd, steak, ribs, burgers, open 0800-2200, serves drinks, bar open until 0200, happy hour 1630-1900. *Virgilio's*, between Main and Back Streets, up from Storetvaer Gade, T7764920. Italian, good food and service, not cheap, lunch 1130-1500, dinner 1700-2200 Mon-Sat. There are several places on Back Street, bars and bistros for breakfast, lunch or dinner. *West Indian Coffee Company* , T7749763. An excellent coffee shop with sandwiches, muffins, light lunches etc, speciality coffees, beans or ground, open 0630-1700 Mon-Sat, Sun from 0700.

Frenchtown *Alexander's Café*, T7744349. Grills, ribs, chilli and Italian, open Mon-Sat for lunch and dinner. *Craig and Sally's*, T7779949. International influences, new wave of

American cuisine, very popular, open for lunch Tue-Sat, dinner Tue-Sun. *Eunice's Terrace* , Smith Bay, T7753975. West Indian food, callaloo, seafood, another local place famous for having fed Bill Clinton. *Hook, Line and Sinker*, T7769708. American, steak and seafood, vegetarian options, daily specials, open breakfast, lunch and dinner Mon-Sat. *The Point at Villa Olga*, at Villa Olga, T7744262. Not cheap, but excellent food.

Sub Base/Crown Bay *Tickle's Dockside Pub*, T7761595 at Crown Bay Marina, T7759425 at American Yacht Harbour. American, burgers, chicken and ribs, open daily for breakfast, lunch and dinner. *L'Escargot*, Sub Base, T7746565. Continental, inevitable snails in garlic butter, open Mon-Sat for lunch and dinner. *Molly Malone's*, above *Tickle's*, overlooking water, open Tue-Sun.

East End/Red Hook *Duffy's Love Shack*, Red Hook Plaza, T7792080. Good lunches, some unusual meals plus burgers, American, hotspot, very busy weekends, open daily. *Sopchoppy's*, waterfront, on upper level of American Yacht Harbour. *Latitude 18*, across the water from Red Hook Harbour, T7792495. Dinghy dock. Live entertainment occasionally, good food, varied, steak, seafood and pasta. *Romano's*, Smith Bay, T7750045. Italian and continental, lamb, seafood and pasta, open from 1800 Mon-Sat.

Nightlife

St Thomas offers the greatest variety of nightlife found in the Virgin Islands although many clubs have closed since the hurricanes

Bands and combos play nightly at most hotels. Several of the hotels offer limbo dancing three or four nights a week and the ubiquitous steel bands remain a great favourite with both visitors and inhabitants. At any time you will hear plenty of bass booming from the smart cars cruising the town's streets. *Bakkeroe's Night Club*, at the *Marriott Beach Resorts*, T7768500, live entertainment and dancing, Crucian rum special 2000-2200, any rum-based drink US$2. *SIBS* on the mountain, Charlotte Amalie offers happy hour, bar, late night crowds, pool tables. *Room With A View* at *Bluebeard's Castle* offers free champagne to ladies 2200-0100. *Fat Tuesday*, downtown Charlotte Amalie, has happy hour all night and the famous Daiquiris. *Club Ryno*, Palm Passage, T7771059, has live jazz Fri nights. Frenchtown offers some entertainment as some restaurants have live music. The Reichhold Centre for the Arts, part of the University of the Virgin Islands, has programmes with local or international performers. Concerts and other live music are held in Tillett Gardens, T7751929.

Festivals

The carnival in **April** (T7763112 for precise date and events) is most spectacular. Dating back to the arrival of African slaves who danced bamboulas it was originally based on ritual worship of the gods of Dahomey. The festivities have since been redirected towards Christianity with a marked US influence. Parades with costumed bands include the J'Ouvert Morning Tramp, the Children's Parade, Mocko Jumbis on stilts and steel bands. There are beauty queens and at least four groups of baton twirling majorettes.

Shopping

Charlotte Amalie is packed with duty free shops & shoppers of all description

If you want to shop seriously, then this is the cheapest island of the three and has the largest selection. Nevertheless it is a good idea to have done your research at home and know what you want to buy. **NB** The prices you see on the shelves of supermarkets and what you are charged are not always identical. *Havensight Shopping Mall* is recommended for people who want to get away from crowds and parking problems, smaller selection than in town, but same shops. For food: *Gourmet Gallery* at Crown Bay Marina and *Havensight Deli* in Havensight Mall. Local produce can be bought in the Market Square (most produce brought in by farmers on Sat 0530) and there are some small supermarkets and grocery stores. *Solberg Supermart* on Solberg Hill has a launderette (US$2 a load). *Marina Market*, in Red Hook is a good gourmet-type deli, opposite St John Ferry Dock. *K-Mart* near Four Winds sells inexpensive clothes, sporting goods, camping equipment and household goods. *Pueblo Supermarket*, near Safe Haven Marina, Crown Bay Marina, K-Mart and Kost U Less. Good arts and crafts centre at *Tillet Gardens*, opposite Four Winds Plaza. You can watch the craftsmen at work.

Tour operators

There are group tours by surrey, bus or taxi. Island tours in an open bus cost US$12 per person, many leave from Main Street at about 1200; complete tours only are sold. **Helicopter**: to tour the islands by air, contact *Air Center Helicopters*, T7757335; or *Seaborne Seaplane Adventures*, T7774491. US$79 per person.

Air Cyril E King international airport is 2 miles, 12 mins, from Charlotte Amalie. Seaplanes **Transport** come in at the Seaplane base (SPB) in the capital's harbour.

Road **Taxis**: cabs are not metered but a list of fares is published in *St Thomas This Week* and *What To Do*; a fares list must be carried by each driver. Rates quoted are for one passenger and additional passengers are charged extra; drivers are notorious for trying to charge each passenger the single passenger rate. Airport to Red Hook is US$10 for one, US$6 each additional passenger, town to Magens Bay is US$6.50 for one, US$4 for extra person. When travelling on routes not covered by the official list, it is advisable to agree the fare in advance. There are extra charges between 2400 and 0600 and charges for luggage. A 2 hr taxi tour for 2 people costs US$30, additional passengers US$12 each. VI Taxi Association T7747457, Wheatley Taxi Service and Tours, T7751959. Gypsy cabs, unlicenced taxis, operate outside Charlotte Amalie; they are cheaper but if you use one make sure you agree fare and route before you get in. **Car park**: US$0.50 per hour, US$4 per day, east of Fort, access from Hospital Gade behind Zora Sandal Shop, facing Public Safety Building. **Car hire**: Rental agencies include *Budget* (T7765774), *Cowpet* (7757376), *Avis* (7741468), *Sun Island* (7743333), *Discount* (7764858), *VI Auto Rental* (7763616, Sub Base); most have an office by the airport. Rates range from US$40 to US$80 per day, unlimited mileage, vehicles from small cars to jeeps. Honda scooters, from A1's, T7742010, for example, range from US$25 to US$40 per day. *Budget* US$45 with 2nd day free and coupons for entry into local attractions.

Ferry There are a number of ferry boats to various destinations, including one from Red Hook to nearby St John (every hour from 0800 to 2400 plus 0630 and 0730 Mon-Fri, takes 20 mins, US$3 each way). Charlotte Amalie to St John, US$7, 45 mins; there is also a ferry from downtown to *Marriott Frenchman's Reef Hotel* and Morningstar beach, this ferry is free for hotel guests, US$3 each way, leaving every hour 0900-1700, 15 mins, a nice way to go to the beach. *Dohm's Water Taxi* can meet you in the USVI and take you to the BVI, clearing customs as well, T7756501.

Anchorages Most moorings in St Thomas are privately owned. It is illegal to use a private mooring without permission from the DPNR. Charter companies own a few for their fleets. The dive companies of St Thomas have placed some moorings near some dive locations on Buck Island, Saba Island, Little St James Island and a few others. No directions or restrictions on their use. There are dinghy docks at Yacht Haven Marina, along the waterfront near Coast Guard dock, Frenchtown Marina, Crown Bay Marina, Water Island Ferry Dock (privately owned).

Banks US banking legislation applies. *Banco Popular de Puerto Rico*, T7767800. *Bank of Nova* **Directory** *Scotia*, T7740037. *Chase Manhattan*, T7762222. *Citibank*, T7744800. *First VI Federal Savings Bank*, T7742022. **Communications** There is an AT&T calling centre at Havensight and a calling service centre at Sub Base, located in Crown Bay Marina, called St Thomas Communications. You can make local and overseas calls, send faxes, check email, access internet for US$3 per 15 mins and send mail etc. The postal system is the same as in the USA. They will also hold mail for tenants at the marina. *Jascom*, Havensight Mall, building III, upper level, internet access and other services. **Embassies and consulates** On St Thomas: *Danish*, T7741780. *Dominican Republic*, T7752640. *Dutch*, T7760656. *Finnish*, T7766666. *French*, T7744663. *Norwegian*, T7761780. *Swedish*, T7761900. **Security** Be careful of your possessions on the beach, particularly Coki Beach, and never leave anything unattended. Also be careful if walking to the Crystal Gade Synagogue and never walk there at night. **Tourist office** Very good tourism information centre and hospitality centre (to hold packages etc) behind the Post Office on Main Street, across from the Vendors Plaza, for maps, hotel information, brochures, posters. PO Box 6400, T7748784, F7744390.

US Virgin Islands

St John

Population: 3,500 *The island is covered with steep hills and is hot. The roads are steep and rocky and require four-wheel drive to get to many places. A drive from Cruz Bay across to Coral Bay is a worthwhile experience and allows you to appreciate how much land is owned by the park, though there is not much in Coral Bay. Skinny Legs is where the old hippies and liveaboard cruisers hang out. The population is mainly concentrated in the little town of Cruz Bay and the village of Coral Bay. Only 16 miles square, St John is about five miles east of St Thomas and 35 miles north of St Croix.*

Ins & outs
See transport, page 537, for further details

Getting there There is no airport on St John. Visitors arrive by ferry, see page 520 (boat) or by private yacht, see page 537 (anchorage). **Getting around** There are three main roads though government maps show more roads that are barely passable 4-wheel drive dirt tracks. The road from Cruz Bay to Coral Bay is only 7 miles but it takes about 40 mins to drive it. Long distance backpacking is not recommended as a way of getting around as the island is hot and hilly. You can always start walking and then catch a taxibus. Hitchhiking is easy.

Beaches and watersports

North shore beaches can go from calm to a surfer's delight in winter when northerly swells roll in from the Atlantic, making the sea rough and dangerous. Go to the south for calm beaches and anchorages. In the national park there are snack bars at Cinnamon Bay and Trunk Bay only. Bring water and lunch if you are hiking or going to other beaches which will not be so crowded.

Off **Trunk Bay**, the island's best beach, is an underwater snorkelling trail maintained by the National Parks Service. Not surprisingly, the beach tends to get rather crowded (especially when tour groups come in); lockers for hire, US$2 (deposit US$5), snorkelling equipment US$6 (deposit US$40) return by 1600. Other good beaches include **Hawk's Nest Bay**, **Caneel Bay**, **Cinnamon Bay** (there is a small museum of historical photographs and pictures here), **Salt Pond** (excellent beach with good snorkelling and a spectacular hike to Ram's Head), **Lameshur Bay** (difficult road but worth it), **Maho Bay** (beach is 5 ft from the road, lots of turtles, sometimes tarpon, nice and calm) and **Solomon Bay** (unofficial nudist beach about 30 minutes' walk from the road). **Reef Bay** has excellent snorkelling.

Windsurfers can be rented at Cinnamon Bay and Maho Camps, sunfishes at Maho Camp. *Coral Bay Watersports*, T7766850, next to *Serafina*, rents power boats, sport fishing and tackle, they also offer diving, snorkelling, kayaking and windsurfing. Half and full day sails and fishing trips can be arranged by *Connections*, T7766922, *Noah's Little Arks (Zodiacs)*, T6939030, *Proper Yachts*, T7766256. You can rent a power boat with *Ocean Runner Powerboats*, T6938809. For one and two-tank **scuba dives**, wreck dives and night dives: *Low Key Watersports* at Wharfside Village, specializes in personal attention, also **kayaking**, T800-8357718, 6938999; *Cruz Bay Watersports*, three locations, T7766234, offers a free snorkel map. Other dive operators are *Cinnamon Bay Watersports*, T7766330 (also kayaking and windsurfing), *East End Divers*, T7794994 or 6937519, Coral Bay. You can **snuba** (air in the boat, not on your back) at Trunk Bay, T6938063. *St John Snorkel Tours* have day and night tours, guided Reef Bay hikes, T7766922.

Regattas
Yacht races include St John Yacht Club Island Hopper Race (January); Coral Bay Yacht Club (meets at *Skinny Legs*) CATS (programme for children), ANTS (adults) and Thanksgiving Day Regatta.

Other sports
There is **tennis** at the large resorts and also two public courts available on a first come first served basis. You can go **rock climbing** with Adventures Unlimited, T6935763. **Horse riding**, Carolina Corral, T6935778, beach rides, sunset and full moon rides.

The population of St John fell to less than a thousand people in 1950 when 85% of the land had reverted to bush and second growth tropical forest. In the 1950s Laurance Rockefeller bought about half of the island but later donated his holdings to establish a national park which was to take up about two-thirds of the predominantly mountainous island. The **Virgin Islands National Park** was opened in 1956 and is covered by an extensive network of trails (some land in the park is still privately owned and not open to visitors). Several times a week a park ranger leads the Reef Bay hike, which passes through a variety of vegetation zones, visits an old sugar mill (Annabel) and some unexplained petroglyphs and ends with a ferry ride back to Cruz Bay. The trail can be hiked without the ranger, but the national park trip provides a boat at the bottom of the trail so you do not need to walk back up the three-mile hill. You should reserve a place on the guided hike at the Park Service Visitors' Centre, Cruz Bay (on north side of harbour) open daily 0800-1630, T7766201; information on all aspects of the park can be obtained here, there are informative displays, topographical and hiking trail maps, books on shells, birds, fish, plants, flowers and local history, sign up here for activities. The trails are well-maintained and clearly signed with interpretive information along the way. Insect repellent is essential. A seashore walk in shallow water, using a glass bottomed bucket to discover sea life, is recommended. There is a snorkel trip around St John in which the boat takes you to 5-6 reefs not accessible by land (and therefore less damaged), which is a good way to see the island even if you do not snorkel. An informative, historical bus tour goes to the remote East End. There are evening programmes at Cinnamon Bay and Maho Bay camps, where rangers show slides and movies and hold informal talks. For detailed information on what to do and where to find it, *Exploring St John* covers hiking trails, 39 beaches and snorkel spots, historic sites and jeep adventures. A fee of US$4 is charged to enter the park at Trunk Bay and to view the Annabel ruins.

National park
There are 22 hikes in all, 14 on the north shore, 8 on the south shore

Essentials

LL *Caneel Bay Resort*, PO Box 720, T7766111, F6938280, www.caneel bay.com Lots of packages available in a variety of rooms or cottages, 166-room resort built in the late 1950's by Laurance Rockefeller, since 1993 managed by Rosewood Hotels and Resorts, several restaurants, bars, dress smartly after sunset, 11 all-weather tennis courts, complimentary watersports for guests including sunfish, windsurfers, also boat rentals, fishing and diving available, kids club and exercise club, ferry service between Caneel Bay and downtown St Thomas, also to sister

Sleeping
Rates are published by the Department of Tourism, http://st-john.com /rates

St John

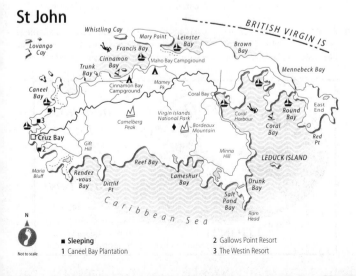

■ **Sleeping**
1 Caneel Bay Plantation

2 Gallows Point Resort
3 The Westin Resort

US Virgin Islands

resort of *Little Dix Bay* on Virgin Gorda, BVI. **LL** *Westin Resort*, PO Box 8310, T6938000, F6934500, www.westin.com 285 rooms and suites in 47 acres, huge pool, conference facilities, watersports, tennis etc. **LL-L** *Gallows Point Resort*, PO Box 58, T7766434, F 7766520, www.gallowspointresort.com 52 suites, fans, pool, watersports, kitchen facilities. **LL** *Suite St John* at Gallows Point, PO Box 567, T7766969, www.gallowspoint.com 8 1-bedroom condos, sleep 4, luxury, full kitchens, every convenience, pool, beach. Within walking distance of town are **LL** *Caribbean Villas*, PO Box 458, T7766152, www.caribbeanvilla.com 2-bedroom villas, pool, personal service, attentive management; and *Caribe Havens*, PO Box 455, T/F7766518, www.caribehavens.com Lovely views, 10 homes. **AL-C** *The Inn at Tamarind Court*, in Cruz Bay, PO Box 350, T7766378, F7766722, www.tamarindcourt.com Inexpensive breakfast and dinner, bar, music and movies some nights.

At Cinnamon Bay (frequent taxibuses from Cruz Bay) there is a **AL-A** campground and chalet site run by the National Park Service, usually full so book in advance, maximum stay 2 weeks; bare site **E**, a few shared showers, food reasonably priced in both the cafetería and grocery store. Write to *Cinnamon Bay Campgrounds*, PO Box 720, St John, USVI, 00831, T776 6330, F7766458. At Maho Bay (8 miles from Cruz Bay, regular bus service) there is a privately run campground, write to **AL** *Maho Bay Camps Inc*, Box 310, Cruz Bay, St John, USVI 00831, T7766240, F7766504, www.maho.org **AL** 'tent cottages' are connected by a raised boardwalk to protect the environment, lots of steps, magnificent view from restaurant, lots of planned activities, attracts socially conscious, environmentally aware guests and staff, guests come back year after year, possible to work in return for your board. They also own **L** *Harmony Studios* (same address, phones, www.harmony-studios.com). Largely built from recycled materials, solar energy, 12 rooms, handicap access and **L-AL** *Estate Concordia Studios*, T6935855, F6935960, www.concordia-studios.com 9 luxury condos overlooking Salt Pond Bay and **AL** 5 eco-tents, multi-level tent cottages with kitchen and bathroom. **L-AL** *Serendip Vacation Condos*, PO Box 273, T/F7766646, www.st-john.com/ serendip Fully equipped apartments. Other apartments/condos include **LL-L** *Battery Hill*, T/F6938261, www.batteryhill.com 9 units, good view, breezy, walk to beach or town. **LL** *Coconut Coast Villas*, T6939100, F7794157, www.coconutcoast.com 10 studios, 6m from water, kitchens, snorkelling. **LL** *Suite St John at Lavender Hill Estates*, T7766969, F7794486, www.lavenderhill.com 11 waterfront condos, private balconies, some have computers, pool. **LL-L** *Villa Bougainvilla*, T7766420, F7766920, www.DonaldSchnell.com Artist owned and maintained. To rent a villa contact *Vacation Vistas*, PO Box 476, T7766462, www.vacationvistas.com 9 houses to rent all round the island, some with pools. *Catered to* has rental homes and luxury villas, PO Box 704, Cruz Bay, St John, USVI 00831, T7766641, F6938191, www.cateredto.com Others include *Vacation Homes*, PO Box 272, Cruz Bay, T7766094, F6938455 and *Windspree Vacation Homes*, T6935423, F6935623, www.windspree.com who have homes and villas in Coral Bay.

Eating At the highest viewpoint on the island on Centerline Road, Bordeaux Mountain, is *Chateau Bordeaux*, T7766611. Fine dining, expensive, dinner only, reservations advised. **In Cruz Bay** *Asolare*, Northshore Rd, T7794747. Expensive, Euro-Asian cuisine, lovely setting,

dinner only, reservations recommended. *Café Roma*, T7766524. Italian food and good pizza, open evenings, also vegetarian dishes. *Chilly Billy's* upstairs at the Lumber Yard, T6938708. Serves great Bloody Marys for breakfast or any time, open 0800-1400 daily, breakfast all day on Sat and Sun. *Ellington's* at Gallow's Point, T6938490. Continental and seafood, lunch and dinner, closed Mon. *Global Village Cuisine on Latitude 18*, in the middle of Mongoose Junction, T6938677. Open air garden restaurant, open 0830-2200, American and fish. *Morgan's Mango*, T6938141. Excellent seafood and steak, also vegetarian, open air dining, great sauces, open evenings only, 1730-2200, reservations recommended. *Paradiso*, at Mongoose Junction, T6938899. American food, has children's menu, eat indoors or on balcony, open Mon-Sat 1100-1500, quite expensive. *Pusser's*, overlooking Cruz Bay, T6938489. On three floors, Crow's Nest, Oyster Bar and Beach Bar, American influenced West Indian food, seafood, open 1100-2200. *Panini Beach*, T6937030. Pricey, seafood/Caribbean, dinner from 1800.*The Lime Inn*, T7766425. Seafood, steak, excellent lobster and pasta, all you can eat night on Wed, very popular with locals and visitors. **At Coral Bay** *Skinny Legs* (named for owners), T7794982. Local hangout, soup, sandwiches, grills and fish, open daily 1100-2100. *Shipwreck Landing*, T6935640. American cuisine, conch fritters, frozen drinks, nightly specials, open air dining, live music every weekend.

Nightlife Up to date information on events is posted on the trees around town or on the bulletin board in front of *Connections*. In Cruz Bay, the place to go and dance is *Fred's*, calypso and reggae Wed and Fri; guitar and vocals at *Pusser's*. Popular places to 'lime' (relax) are *JJ's*, and sitting in Cruz Bay Park, watching the world go by.

Festivals *Carnival*, St John's carnival is in the week of **4 July**, but there are lots of events in the two preceding weeks.

Shopping Scattered around Cruz Bay and concentrated in Wharfside Village and Mongoose Junction are shops selling souvenirs, arts and crafts and jewellery. Right in the Park is Sparkey's, selling newspapers, paperbacks, film, cold drinks, gifts. The *St John Drug Center Inc*, open 7 days a week. For groceries: *Starfish Market* and *Marina Market* in Cruz Bay, *Joe's Discount* near *Shipwreck Landing* in Coral Bay. *Maiden Apple*, health food store, 1st floor of Boulton Centre, T6938781. Liquor and drinks at *Cases by the Sea* near Coral Bay Watersports, grocery near *Shipwreck Tavern*, *Joe's Discount* and *Pickles Deli*. Food is expensive (rum is cheaper than water) and the selection is limited. If you are camping for a week, shopping at the big supermarkets on St Thomas is a good idea. Fish and produce is sold from boats a couple of times a week at the freight dock. *Love City Videos* at the Boulton Centre, rents videos. *Laundromat* next to *Raintree Inn*, Cruz Bay, Mon-Fri 0830-1730, Sat 0830-1200.

Transport **Bus** There are 2 Vitran buses, US$1 exact change only, from Cruz Bay to Coral Bay and Salt Pond about every hour. If one breaks down you have to wait for the next, a/c turned-off going up hill, turned on for descent. **Car** Vehicles may be rented, but parking is very difficult and you may have to walk a long way from where you can leave your car. There are 3 service stations, open 0800-1900, in Cruz Bay and Coral Bay, may be closed on holidays. Rental agencies include: *Hertz*, T7766695; *Delbert Hill's Jeep Rental*, T7766637; *Budget*, T7767575; *Avis*, T7766374; *Cool Breeze*, T7766588, *St John Car Rental*, T7766103; rates start from US$50 per day. **Taxi** Official taxi rates can be obtained from St John Police Department or by asking the taxi driver to show the official rate card (see page 533 for details). A 2-hr island tour costs US$30 for 1 or 2 passengers, or US$12 per person if there are 3 or more. Taxi from Cruz Bay to Trunk Bay, US$5; to Cinnamon Bay US$5.50. It is almost impossible to persuade a taxi to take you to Coral Bay, so hitchhike by waiting with everyone else at the intersection by the supermarket deli.

Ferry Ferry to St Thomas: hourly 0700 to 2200 and 2315 to Red Hook, every 2 hrs 0715 to 1315, 1545 and 1715 to Charlotte Amalie (see page 533).

Anchorages On St John, the US Park Service has placed moorings to protect the reefs and seagrass areas. A yacht is limited to anchoring in the US Park for no more than 14 days a year.

US Virgin Islands

Park moorings on north shore: Caneel Bay, Hawksnest, Cinnamon Bay, Maho, Francis Bay; on south shore: Salt Pond, Little Lameshur and Great Lameshur. Forbidden to anchor on south shore, moorings must be used. There are some private moorings for day charter boats in Maho Bay, Cruz Bay. Great Cruz Bay and Coral Bay are not within the park territory and have privately owned moorings.

Directory **Banks** *Chase Manhattan* in Cruz Bay, T7757777. *Banco Popular de Puerto Rico*, T6932777. *Bank of Novia Scotia*, T6939932. St John's banking hours are 0830-1500 Mon-Fri. **Communications** *Connections West* (Cruz Bay, T7766922), as well as arranging sailing trips and villa rentals, is the place for business services, local and international telephone calls, faxes, Western Union money transfers, photocopying, word-processing, notary, VHF radio calls and tourist information (they know everything that is happening). *Connections East*, T7794994. Does the same thing in Coral Bay. *Coral Bay Marine Services* for mail drop, message centre, if you have your own computer you can use their phone to access email. **Security** St John is not free of crime. There have been reports of attacks on Cinnamon Bay Beach, while crack cocaine is sold fairly openly on the streets in Cruz Bay. The island is generally safer than St Thomas, but do not be lulled into a sense of false security. Take the usual precautions. **Tour agencies** As well as the National Parks service in the text above, *Thunderhawk Trail Guides*, T7741112. Offer hikes through the national park. **Tourist information** The St John newspaper, *Tradewinds*, is published bi-weekly, US$0.50. The funny, informative, free, *St John Guidebook* and map is available in shops and also at the ticket booth at the ferry dock. **Tourist office** PO Box 200, Cruz Bay, T7766450.

St Croix

Population: 55,000

St Croix has it all : swimming, sailing, fishing, & above all, diving

The east of the island is rocky and arid terrain, the west is higher, wetter and forested. Columbus thought that St Croix looked like a lush garden when he first saw it during his second voyage in 1493. He landed at Salt River on the north coast, which has now been approved as a national park encompassing the landing site as well as the rich underwater Salt River drop off and canyon. It had been cultivated by the Carib Indians, who called it Ay-Ay, and the land still lies green and fertile between the rolling hills. St Croix is the largest of the group with 84 square miles, lying 40 miles south of St Thomas. The name is pronounced to rhyme with 'boy'. People born on the island are called Crucians, while North Americans who move there are known as Continentals.

St Croix

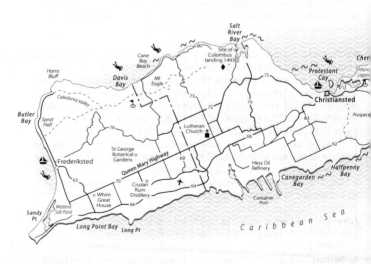

US Virgin Islands

Getting there See page 520 for details of flights to **Alexander Hamilton** international airport. Taxis from the airport to Christiansted are US$5, to Frederiksted, US$4. A taxi dispatcher's booth is at the airport exit. A bus service runs between the airport and Christiansted every 1½ hrs, change buses at La Reine terminal. **Getting around** A bus service runs between Christiansted and Frederiksted. The major car rental agencies are represented at the airport, hotels and both cities. A four-wheel drive car (US$40-50 a day) is ideal to drive along the scenic roads, for example to Ham's Bay or Point Udall. There is a distinct lack of road signs on St Croix, so if you use a car, take a good map.

Ins & outs
See transport section for further details

Diving and marine life

Scuba diving is good around St Croix, with forests of elkhorn coral, black coral, brain coral, sea fans, a multitude of tropical fish, sea horses under the Frederiksted pier (great day or night dive for novices, an easy shore dive and one of the best in the USVI), walls and drop offs, reefs and wrecks. The wrecks are varied, some 40 years old and some recent, with marine life slowly growing on the structures and schools of fish taking up residence. They range from 75-300 ft in length and 15-110 ft deep, providing something for everyone, from the beginner to the experienced, and should not be missed. Butler Bay off Frederiksted is home for six shipwrecks. Nearby in Truck Lagoon there are the remains of around 25 old truck chassis that were sunk by Hess Oil to promote marine growth and create an artificial reef. The wrecks of the *North Wind*, *The Virgin Islander Barge* and *Suffolk Maid* are close together, but usually done as two separate leisurely dives otherwise you have to swim rather briskly to get round them all. There are also the *Rosaomaira*, the deepest of the wrecks, and the *Coakly Bay*, the newest, while in between them is the *Sondra*, a shallow dive which can even be snorkelled, although there is not a great deal remaining on the site. Just behind the *Sondra* is the wreck of a small sailing boat.

Dive sites

At **Buck Island** there are underwater snorkelling trails, the two main ones being Turtle Bay Trail and East End Trail, but the markers are in disrepair. The fish are superb, but much of the coral is dead because of hurricane damage; it is hoped that it will come back and some regrowth has been noted. The reef is an underwater national park covering over 850 acres, including the island. Hawksbill turtles nest on Buck Island and, during a 1993 Buck Island National Monument Sea Turtle Research Programme, Sandy Point Leatherbacks were also observed nesting there. Half day tours to Buck Island, including 1¼ hours snorkelling and 30 minutes at the beach can be arranged through hotels or boat owners on the waterfront at Christiansted. Anchorage is crowded 1000-1600 with day charters; watch the charter boat race for the best spots at 1000 and 1600. Only six operators are licensed to take day charters to the island, which means that they are often crowded, particularly when cruise ships are in town. Another attraction is the **Salt River coral canyon**.

BUCK ISLAND

US Virgin Islands

Dive centres

During Feb, Mar & Apr you are likely to see humpbacked whales near the islands

Diving trips are arranged by several companies all round the island, many of which also charter boats out and offer sailing lessons. Dive companies include: *Dive Experience*, Christiansted, T7733307, 800-2359047, www.st-croix.com/diveexperience, who will dive even if only 2 people sign up, good offers on prices and good equipment, including masks with prescription lenses; *Anchor Dive Centre*, Salt River National Park, T/F7781522; *Cane Bay Dive Shop*, T7739913, F7785442, www.canebayscuba.com, great bay for snorkelling and wall diving, beach or boat dive; *Scubawest*, Frederiksted, T7723701, F7721852, www.divescubawest.com, specializes in pier night dives and wrecks; *St Croix Ultimate Blue Water Adventures (SCUBA)*, T7735994, www.stcroixscuba.com. Dive packages can be arranged through your hotel. Boats sometimes go out to watch humpbacked whales during the months when they are often sighted around the islands.

For those who don't want to get wet, there is the semi-submersible *Oceanique*, T7737060, with day and night excursions in Christiansted harbour and around Protestant Cay.

Beaches and watersports

Good beaches can be found at **Davis Bay**, **Protestant Cay**, **Buccaneer**, **the Reef**, **Cane Bay** (good snorkelling), **Grapetree Beach** and **Cormorant Beach**. Cramer Park on the east shore and Frederiksted beach to the north of the town, both have changing facilities and showers. Rainbow Beach Club, 1½ km north of Frederiksted, has a spectacular sandy beach, restaurant and beach bar. All beaches are open to the public, but on those where there is a hotel (*Buccaneer* – good snorkelling) which maintains the beach, you may have to pay for the use of facilities. Generally the north coast is best for surfing because there are no reefs to protect the beaches. On the northwest coast, the stretch from Northside Beach to Ham's Bay is easily accessible for shell collecting (but watch out for sea urchins at Ham's Bay beach); the road is alongside the beach. The road ends at the General Offshore Sonorbuoy Area (a naval installation at Ham's Bluff), which is a good place to see booby birds and frigate birds leaving at dawn and coming home to roost at dusk. Shells can also be found on Sprat Hall beach (ask at *Sprat Hall Plantation* for details). There is an annual Coral Reef Swim towards the end of October, T7732100.

Water skiing, jet skiing, windsurfing and parasailing are all on offer (St Croix Watersports, T7737060). There are several companies offering day sails on crewed yachts. Annapolis International Sailing School has a dock with a few moorings, teaches sailing and may rent boats for day sailing to qualified individuals.

The Mumm's Cup Regatta is held in November, with three days of ocean racing off the east coast. Other races include the Hookanson Memorial Race in January and the John Stuart Jervis Memorial in December. Contact the St Croix Yacht Club for details, T7739531.

Other sports

Most of the large hotels have **tennis** courts for residents, but you can also play at the *Buccaneer Hotel* (eight courts, US$5 per person for non-guests), the *Carambola* (four grass courts, two lit for night play and another five clay courts at the golf club, pro US$50 per hour, guests offered free 30 minute clinics Tuesday-Friday morning), Chenay Bay, Club St Croix, The Reef Club (two courts, US$5 per person, per hour), the *Tamarind Reef Hotel* (two cal grass courts, non-guests US$8 per person per hour, US$5 evenings) and others. There are four public courts at Canegata Park in Christiansted and 2 public courts near the fort in Frederiksted which can be used free of charge on a first come first served basis. Two 18-hole **golf** courses, one at the *Carambola* (T7785638), with pro shop, putting green and driving range, and the other at the *Buccaneer Hotel* (T7732100), also with putting green and pro shop. There is also a nine-hole course at The Reef (T7738844), green fee US$12.50. **Horse riding**: Paul and Jill's Equestrian Stables (T7722880 or 7722627), at Sprat Hall Plantation, one and a half miles north of Frederiksted, on Route 58, reserve three days in advance if possible for rides through the rain forest, past Danish ruins, for all levels of ability, English or Western styles, US$50 for two hours, no credit cards. You can play **croquet** at the *Tamarind Reef Hotel*. Rent a **mountain bike** and join St Croix Bikes & Tours for a tour of the rain forest or beach areas of west end of island, T7722343, www.stcroixbike.com. VI Cycling organize regular weekly rides and races for which there is a US$5 fee per participant, Mike Mcqueston T7730079.

In February/March a week of sports-related events culminate in the St Croix International Triathlon which attracts over 600 participants. Phone Tom Guthrie or Miles Sperber, T7734470, for details of running courses and tours. For the Virgin Islands Track and Field Federation, contact Wallace Williams (secretary), PO Box 2720, Christiansted, T7735715.

Christiansted

The old town square and waterfront area of Christiansted, the old Danish capital, still retain the colourful character of the early days. Overhanging second-floor balconies designed by the Danes to shade the streets serve as cool arcades for shoppers. Red-roofed pastel houses built by early settlers climb the hills overlooking Kings Wharf and there is an old outdoor market. Many of the buildings are being restored and the dock is being improved to take small cruise ships (the reef prevents large ships entering the harbour), but it is unlikely to be overrun with cruise ship tourism like St Thomas. Old Christiansted is compact and easy to stroll. The best place to start is the Visitors' Bureau on 5A Company Street. Here you can pick up brochures. Starting in February for six weeks the St Croix Landmarks Society runs house tours every Wednesday, T7720598.

Across the way is **Fort Christiansvaern**, which the Danes built in 1774 on the foundations of a French fort dating from 1645. ■ *US$2. 0800-1645*. See the punishment cells, dungeons, barracks room, officers' kitchen, powder magazine, an exhibit of how to fire a cannon, and the battery, the best vantage point for photographing the old town and harbour. The fort and the surrounding historic buildings are run by the National Parks Service. In front of the fort is the old customs house, now the National Parks Service office.

The **Steeple Building** is a minute's walk away. Built as a church by the Danes in 1734, then converted into a military bakery, storehouse and later a hospital, it is now a museum of the island's early history. ■ *US$2. 0930-1200, 1300-1500*.

The area here is a treasury of old Danish architecture, and many of the original buildings are still in use. The West India and Guinea Co, which bought St Croix from the French and settled the island, built a warehouse on the corner of Church and Company Streets in 1749 which now serves as a post office, Customs House and public toilets.

Across the way from Government House on King Street is the building where the young Alexander Hamilton, who was to become one of the founding fathers of the USA, worked as a clerk in Nicolas Cruger's counting-house. Today the building houses the Little Switzerland shop.

Government House has all the hallmarks of the elegant and luxurious life of the merchants and planters in the days when 'sugar was king'. The centre section, built in 1747 as a merchant's residence, was bought by the Secret Council of St Croix in 1771 to serve as a government office. It was later joined to another merchant's town house on the corner of Queen Cross Street and a handsome ballroom was added. It has been extensively renovated and was expected to reopen at the end of 2000. Across Queen Cross Street from Government House is the Dutch Reformed Church.

Queen Cross Street leads into Strand and the fascinating maze of arcades and alleys lined with boutiques, handicrafts and jewellery shops. Along the waterfront there are bars, restaurant pavilions, a boardwalk and an aquarium. ■ *US$3. Wed-Sun, 1100-1600*. Just offshore is **Protestant Cay** (just called The Cay), reached by ferry for US$3 return for the pleasant beach, and the *Hotel on the Cay* with restaurants, pool, tennis, watersports.

US Virgin Islands

Around the island

Agriculture was long the staple of the economy, cattle and sugar the main activities, and today there are the ruins of numerous sugar plantations with their Great Houses and windmills. **Estate Whim** is restored to the way it was under Danish rule in the 1700s and is well worth a visit; it is a beautiful oblong building housing a museum of the period, and in the grounds are many of the factory buildings and implements. ■ *T7720598. Adults US$5, children under 12 US$1. Mon-Sat 1000-1600.* There is a gift shop. Candlelight concerts and other parties and functions are held here. **St George Botanical Garden**, just off Centreline Road (Queen Mary Highway), in an old estate, has a theatre as well as gardens amid the ruined buildings. The 17-acre site was built on a Precolumbian settlement. ■ *US$5 for non-members. Mon-Sat 0800-1600.* Judith's Fancy, from the time of the French, is now surrounded by building developments and has less to see than the other two.

Today agriculture has been surpassed by tourism and industry, including the huge Hess oil refinery on the south coast. However, youth unemployment is a problem and the economy of St Croix is not as healthy as that of the other islands. Many businesses are shuttered in Christiansted and Frederiksted and the island is in need of some revitalization.

In 1999, President Bill Clinton declared the island a disaster area after it was hit by Hurricane Lenny, which killed three people and caused damage estimated at over US$32mn. The destruction caused is no longer evident.

Frederiksted Frederiksted, 17 miles from Christiansted, is the only other town on St Croix and although quiet, its gingerbread architecture has its own charm. Public taxis link the two towns and there are taxis from the airport to Frederiksted. Historic buildings

Christiansted

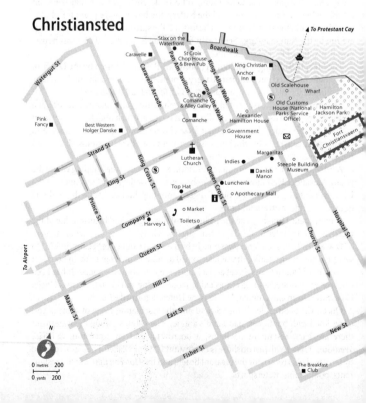

such as **Victoria House**, 7-8 Strand Street, and the Customs House, have been repaired following hurricane damage. **Fort Frederik** (1752) is a museum; it was here that the first official foreign salute to the 13 US States was made in 1776 (see also **Sint Eustatius**). Also here was read the proclamation freeing all Danish slaves in 1848. An exhibition of old photos and newspaper articles and other display items show the destruction caused by hurricanes, including the one which hit Charlotte Amalie harbour. ■ *Free. Mon-Fri, 0830-1600.* A new pier, to accommodate at least two cruise ships, was built in 1993. On a non-cruise ship day Frederiksted seems like a ghost town, but every other Wednesday is Harbour Night, when cruise ships stay late and the town stays open with special entertainments.

The rain forest to the north of town is worth a visit. Two roads, the paved Mahogany Road (Route 76) and the unpaved Creque Dam Road (Road 58) traverse it.

Essentials

Best resorts: **LL** *Buccaneer*, PO Box 25200, on Gallows Bay, north coast, T7732100, F7788215, www.thebuccaneer.com 132 luxury rooms, 340 acres, 3 beaches, sports including golf (see above), tennis, fitness centre, health spa, watersports centre, several restaurants, lots of packages available, and **LL-L** *Sunterra Resorts Carambola Beach*, on Davis Bay, PO Box 3031, north coast, T7783800, F7781682, www.sunterra.com 146 rooms in 25 2-storey villas, tennis with pro, golf packages available, pool, jacuzzis, snorkelling, scuba.

Christiansted: **LL-B** *Club Comanche*, Comanche Walk, 1 Strand St, T7730210, F7139145, www.usvi.net/hotel/comanche Older style, no 2 rooms alike, cable TV, a/c, on waterfront, pool, shop, dive packages, family run, staff helpful. Also restaurant. **L** *Hotel on the Cay*, on Protestant Cay, see above, in Christiansted harbour, PO Box 4020, T7732035, F7737046. Free ferry service, 55 rooms, also timeshare with kitchenettes, excellent

Sleeping
For hotel rates consult
http://st-croix.com
/rates

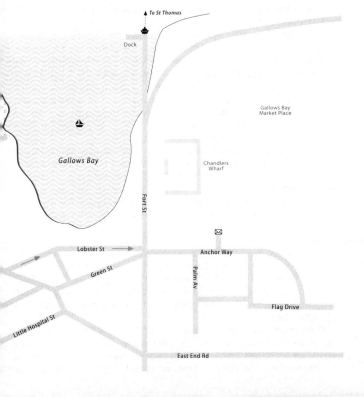

US Virgin Islands

snorkelling, pool, beach, the only one in town, watersports, tennis, restaurants. **L-AL** *King's Alley*, 57 King St, on waterfront, T7730103, F7734431. 35 rooms, a/c and fans, pool. **AL** *Caravelle*, 44A Queen Cross St, T7730687, F7787004, www.hotelcaravelle.com. 44 rooms, also good, pool, diving, transport to other sports facilities, diving packages available. **AL** *Danish Manor*, 2 Company St, T7731377, F7731913, www.danishmanor.com. Pool in old courtyard, renovated rooms. **AL** *King Christian*, 59 King's Wharf, PO Box 24467, T7736330, F7739411, www.kingchristian.com Basic, noisy with late night bands, a/c, fan, watersports, pool, convenient. **AL-B** *Pink Fancy*, 27 Prince St, 5 mins from shopping centre and water-front, T7738460, F7736448. Bar, pool, in 18th-century townhouse, completely renovated. Near town is **AL** *Hilty House Inn*, T/F7732594 hiltyhouse@worldnet.att.net In a historic plantation house, house or cottage, breakfast included, pool. **C** *The Breakfast Club*, 18 Queen Cross St, T7737383, F7738642, www.the-breakfast-club.christiansted.vi.us 9 rooms with bath and kitchenette, gourmet breakfasts, hot tub on deck, nice view, manager is skilful golf player. **Near Christiansted:** **LL** *Chenay Bay*, PO Box 24600, T7732918, F7736665, www.chenaybay.com Secluded, private 1 room cottages with kitchenettes on nice north coast beach, windsurfing, honeymoon, family packages available, tennis, pool, snorkelling, kayaks, windsurfing school and board rental; and **LL-L** *Cormorant Beach Club and Hotel*, T7788920, F7789218, www.cormorant-stcroix.com 1st class, beach, tennis, pool, deluxe, gay friendly. **West of Christiansted**, **L** *Hibiscus Beach Hotel*, T7734042, F7737668, www.1 hibiscus.com 37 beach front rooms, hammocks on the beach, access for handicapped to beach, pool, restaurant, watersports in all-inclusive packages, lots of special deals offered.

Northeast coast: **L** *Tamarind Reef Hotel*, T7734455, F7733989, www.usvi.net/hotel /tamarind 46 rooms, half have kitchenettes, a/c, fan, TV, balcony, all with seaview, two beaches, pool, snorkelling, boardsailing, kayaking at hotel, or diving, fishing, sailing from adjacent Green Cay Marina, croquet and tennis lawn, packages available. **LL** *Divi Carina Bay Resort and Casino*, T7739700, F7736802, www.diviresorts.com The most eastern resort, 146 rooms, lots of facilities and gambling.

Frederiksted: Half a mile from town, **LL-AL** *Sandcastle On The Beach*, T7721205, F7721757, www.gaytraveling.com/onthebeach Pool, 23 rooms, kitchenettes, restaurants, serves gay community. **A** *The Frederiksted*, 442 Strand St, T7720500, F ext 151. Modern, fridge, TV, phones, pool, restaurant, bar, good. **North of Frederiksted** **LL-L** *Cane Bay Reef Club*, PO Box 1407, Kingshill, T/F7782966, www.canebay.com 8 suites with balconies over the sea, pool, restaurant, bar, rough sea but short walk to beach, weekly rates cheaper. **LL-L** *Waves At Cane Bay*, PO Box 1749, Kingshill, T7781805, F7784945, www.thewaves atcanebay.com 12 oceanfront studios with balconies and cable TV, natural grotto pool, beach, good snorkelling and scuba from property. **South of Frederiksted** **AL-A** *Cottages by the Sea*, PO Box 1697, T7720495, F7721753, www.travelfacts.com/ Good beach, watersports, 6 day maid service, good.

There are several rental agents for villas and condominiums: *American Rentals*, 2001 Old Hospital St, Christiansted, T7738470, F7738472; *Island Villas*, 6 Company St, Christiansted, T7738821, F7738823, www.ecani.com/island.villas All with a wide price range; *Richards and Ayer Associates Realtors*, 340 Strand St, Frederiksted, T7720420, F7722958, www.ayervirgin islands.com **LL** *Villa Madeleine*, T7788782, F7732150, www.enjoystcroix.com On hillside, luxury villas, private pools, ocean view, seasonal restaurant.

Eating *St Croix This Week* has a full listing of the very many places to eat, from low budget to elegant dining. Restaurant life on St Croix includes charcoal-broiled steaks and lobsters, West Indian Créole dishes and Danish and French specialities. Do not miss the open-air Crucian picnics. Local dishes include stewed or roast goat, red pea soup (a sweet soup of kidney beans and pork), callalou (dasheen soup); snacks, Johnny cakes (unleavened fried bread) and pate (pastry filled with spiced beef, chicken or salt fish); drinks, ginger beer, *mavi* (from the bark of a tree).

Christiansted: *Club Comanche*, Strand St, T7730210. Popular and good for lunches and dinners, one of the oldest places in town. *Top Hat*, Company St, between King Cross St and Queen Cross St, T7732346. Excellent and spotlessly clean but pricey at US$20-28 for entrées, Scandinavian food, Smorgaasbord, steaks and seafood, open Mon-Sat dinner only.

Lunchería, on Company St, in the courtyard of Apothecary Hall, T7734247. Mexican food, cheap margaritas, live music, open Mon-Sat lunch and dinner. Also on Company St are *Harvey's Bar and Restaurant*, T7733433. Local cuisine, conch, callaloo, goat stew. *Margaritas*, Company St. Inexpensive Tex-Mex food, open Mon-Sat for lunch and dinner. *Tommy T's Paradise Café*, Queen Cross St, T7732985. Small local bar/restaurant, breakfast, lunch and dinner, sandwiches and daily specials, claustrophobic, no credit cards. *Indies*, Company St, T6929440. Seafood and West Indian restaurant, also Sushi on Wed and Fri nights at the bar. *Stixx on the Waterfront*, Pan Am Pavilion, T7735157. Informal, breakfast, lunch and dinner, pasta, pizza, seafood, daily specials, Sun brunch 1000-1400 includes champagne and mimosas, popular bar; watch the seaplanes from Kings Alley Yacht Club.

Frederiksted: the *Blue Moon*, 17 Strand St, T7722222. Seafood and native dishes plus music, dinner Tue-Sat, daily specials, great Sun brunch with jazz. *Motown Bar and Restaurant*, T7729882, Strand St. Goat stew, conch, shrimp, open for breakfast, lunch and dinner daily, not expensive.

Out of town: the restaurant at *Paradise Sunset Beach Hotel*, Ham's Bluff, has been recommended, great sunset too, seafood and local food, open Mon-Thur for lunch and dinner. *Baggy's Wrinkle* and *Baggy's Too* at St Croix Marina, Gallows Bay. Inexpensive daily specials, American food and barbecue, open Tue-Sun all day, no credit cards. *Columbus Cove*, Salt River National Park, near Columbus Landing. Open daily for breakfast, lunch and dinner, meat, fish and chicken platters, large portions, most dinners under US$15. *The Waves at Cane Bay*, T7781805. Romantic dining, expensive, good food and service, open for dinner Tue-Sat.

Nightlife Most hotels provide evening entertainment on a rotating basis, the custom of many of the Caribbean islands, so it is sometimes best to stay put and let the world of West Indian music and dance come to you. The *Hibiscus Beach Hotel* hosts the Caribbean Dance Company on Fri at 2030, evocative, and a steel pan band on Wed at 1830, also electric mandolin on Thur and a jazz trio on Sat at 2000. Some restaurants also provide entertainment, eg *Tivoli Gardens* (Queen Cross and Strand Streets), *Lizards* (Strand St) and *The Galleon* (Green Cay Marina, piano bar). *The New Wreck Bar*, Hospital St. Crab races on Fri, folk guitar on Wed, Green Flash rock Thur-Sat. *The Blue Moon*, 17 Strand St. Live jazz every Fri and on full moons. *Kings Alley Yacht Club* has open-air bandstand with music afternoons and evenings. *Parrot's Perch* serves dinner, happy hour and evening entertainment. Every other Wed night in Frederiksted, Harbour Night, with arts, crafts, dancing, T7724242. Live music at *Deep End Bar* at Green Cay Marina. *Two plus Two Disco*, Northside Rd, west of Christiansted (closed Mon). Live entertainment Fri and Sat, US$5 cover charge; snack bar from 1200 till 1800. Most cultural events take place at the Island Centre, a 600-seat theatre with an open air amphitheatre seating another 1,600, where drama, dance and music are performed.

Festivals St Croix's Festival lasts from early **December**, through Christmas to 6 January. There is another festival on the Saturday nearest to **17 March**, St Patrick's Day, when there is a

US Virgin Islands

splendid parade with floats and music (T7731139). *Mocko Jumbi* dancing (on stilts) takes place at festivals and on other occasions; for information on Mocko Jumbi, contact Willard S John, PO Box 3162, Frederiksted, St Croix, USVI 00840, T7738909 (day), 7720225 (evening). In **November** there is a Thanksgiving Jump-Up, T7138012.

Shopping *St Croix Leap* (Life and Environmental Arts Project, PO Box 245, Frederiksted, T7720421), on Route 76, the Paved Rain Forest Rd, is a non-profit woodworking centre, from which the artefacts may be bought direct. They take orders for custom made work and will ship finished work, anything from totem poles to salad servers in a variety of woods. *Many Hands*, Pan Am Pavilion, sells only arts and crafts from the Virgin Islands. For special jewellery go to *Sonya's*, in Christiansted, and see her hand-wrought gold and silver things. *The Natural Jewel*, King St, for pearl and larimar. St Croix Landmarks, museum store, teak, antique furniture, works by island artists, books and cards. The market in Christiansted is on Company Street, and has been on the site since 1735. *The Newstand* on Company St has US papers, magazines, other reading matter. *Quin House* on Company St has galleries, Caribbean maps and prints, museum replica jewellery, mahogany furniture. For groceries, *K-Mart*, *Cost U Less* at Sunshine Mall and *Extras*, and several *Pueblo* stores on the bus route. Gallows Bay has *Gallows Bay Market* (small, upscale, also US papers), PO, bank, bookstore, hardware store, marine store (another one at St Croix Marine). Laundry at Jonah's drop off at St Croix Marine.

Transport **Bus** The bus service runs between Christiansted and Frederiksted, 0530-2130 every 30 mins (every hour on Sun), US$1, timetable from airport or bus driver. **Taxi** A taxi tour costs US$25 per person, less for groups; contact St Croix Taxi and Tours Association, Henry E Rholsen Airport, T7781088, PO Box 1106, Christiansted, F7786887; Combined Tours, T7722888. Taxi vans run between Christiansted and Frederiksted, US$1.50. **Car hire** Rental agencies include *Avis*, at the airport, T7789355/9365. *Budget* at the airport, T7789636, or Christiansted (*King Christian Hotel* T7732285), also *Hertz*, T7781402, or *Buccaneer Hotel*, T7732100 Ext 737; *Caribbean Jeep and Car Rental*, 6 Hospital Street, Christiansted, T7734399; *Green Cay Jeep and Car Rental*, T7737227; *Berton*, one mile west of Christiansted, T7731516.

Anchorages St Croix divers have placed mooring buoys at wall dive locations to prevent damage to the reefs while anchoring. There are no restrictions to their use; they only ask that stays be limited to 4 hrs so that another boat might use reef for second dive of the day. In anchorages, all moorings are privately owned. Buck island has moorings placed within the snorkelling area for day use only. Overnight anchoring is not allowed and boats must anchor in sand at southwest end of island. Marinas at St Croix Marine, Anapolis Sailing School, St Croix Yachting Club, Green Cay Marina, Salt River Marina. Anchorages at Christiansted, Frederiskted (deep so very difficult), Green Cay, Teague Bay by St Croix Yacht Club (reciprocates with members of other yacht clubs).

Directory **Embassies & consulates** *Dutch*, T7737100. *Norwegian*, T7737100. **Tourist Office** PO Box 4538, Christiansted, T7730495, F7735074. **Useful addresses** **People to people programme:** if you wish to contact someone in a similar profession to your own, contact Geri Simpson, PO Box 943, Kingshill, St Croix, USVI 00851, T7788007.

US Virgin Islands

Background

History

The islands were 'discovered' by Columbus on his second voyage in 1493 and, partly because of their number, he named them 'Las Once Mil Vírgenes' (the 11,000 virgins) in honour of the legend of St Ursula and her 11,000 martyred virgins. There were Indian settlements in all the major islands of the group and the first hostile action with the Caribs took place during Columbus' visit. Spain asserted its exclusive right to settle the islands but did not colonize them, being more interested in the larger and more lucrative Greater Antilles. European settlement did not begin until the 17th century, when few Indians were to be found. St Croix (Santa Cruz) was settled by the Dutch and the English around 1625, and later by the French. In 1645 the Dutch abandoned the island and went to St Eustatius and St Maarten. In 1650 the Spanish repossessed the island and drove off the English, but the French, under Philippe de Loinvilliers de Poincy of the Knights of Malta, persuaded the Spanish to sail for Puerto Rico. Three years later de Poincy formally deeded his islands to the Knights of Malta although the King of France retained sovereignty. St Croix prospered and planters gradually converted their coffee, ginger, indigo and tobacco plantations to the more profitable sugar, and African slavery was introduced. Wars, illegal trading, privateering, piracy and religious conflicts finally persuaded the French Crown that a colony on St Croix was not militarily or economically feasible and in 1695/96 the colony was evacuated to St Domingue.

A plan for colonizing St Thomas was approved by Frederik III of Denmark in 1665 but the first settlement failed. The Danes asserted authority over uninhabited St John in 1684, but the hostility of the English in Tortola prevented them from settling until 1717. In 1733 France sold St Croix to the Danish West India & Guinea Company and in 1754 the Danish West Indies became a royal colony. This was the most prosperous period for the Danish islands. After the end of Company rule and its trading monopoly, St Thomas turned increasingly toward commerce while in St Croix plantation agriculture flourished. St Thomas became an important shipping centre with heavy reliance on the slave trade. Denmark was the first European nation to end its participation in the slave trade in 1802. Illegal trade continued, however, and British occupation of the Virgin Islands between 1801 and 1802 and again between 1807 and 1815 prevented enforcement of the ban.

The Danish Virgin Islands reached a peak population of 43,178 in 1835, but thereafter fell to 27,086 by 1911. Sailing ships were replaced by steamships which found it less necessary to transship in St Thomas. Prosperity declined with a fall in sugar prices, a heavy debt burden, soil exhaustion, development of sugar beet in Europe, hurricanes and droughts and the abolition of slavery. In 1847 a Royal decree provided that all slaves would be free after 1859 but the slaves of St Croix were unwilling to wait and rebelled in July 1848. By the late 19th century economic decline became pronounced. The sugar factory on St Croix was inefficient and in the 20th century the First World War meant less shipping for St Thomas, more inflation, unemployment and labour unrest. The Virgin Islands became a liability for Denmark and the economic benefits of colonialism no longer existed. Negotiations with the USA had taken place intermittently ever since the 1860s for cession of the Virgin Islands to the USA. The USA wanted a Caribbean naval base for security reasons and after the 1914 opening of the Panama Canal was particularly concerned to guard against German acquisition of Caribbean territory. In 1917, the islands were sold for US$25mn but no political, social or economic progress was made for several years. The islands were under naval rule during and after the War and it was not until 1932 that US citizenship was granted to all natives of the Virgin Islands.

A devastating hurricane in 1928, followed by the stock market crash of 1929, brought US awareness of the need for economic and political modernization. Several years of drought, the financial collapse of the sugar refineries, high

US Virgin Islands

unemployment, low wages and very high infant mortality characterized these years. In 1931 naval rule was replaced by a civil government. In 1934, the Virgin Islands Company (VICO) was set up as a long term development 'partnership programme'. The sugar and rum industry benefited from increased demand in the Second World War. VICO improved housing, land and social conditions, particularly in rural areas, but the end of the wartime construction boom, wartime demand for rum and the closing of the submarine base, brought further economic recession. However, the severance of diplomatic relations between the USA and Cuba shifted tourism towards the islands. Construction boomed and there was even a labour shortage. With immigrant labour, the population increased and by 1970 per capita income reached US$2,400, five times that of the Caribbean region as a whole, with about half of the labour force engaged in tourist activities and tourism providing about 60% of the islands' revenues. With the shift from agriculture to tourism, VICO was officially disbanded in 1966, along with the production of sugarcane. Various tax incentives, however, promoted the arrival of heavy industry, and during the 1960s the Harvey Alumina Company and the Hess Oil Company began operating on St Croix. By 1970, the economy was dominated by mainland investment and marked by white-owned and managed enterprises based on cheap imported labour from other Caribbean islands.

In September 1989, St Croix was hit by Hurricane Hugo, which tore through 90% of all buildings and left 22,500 people homeless. The disaster was followed by civil unrest, with rioting and looting, and US army troops were sent in to restore order, The territorial government, located on St Thomas had been slow to react to the disaster on St Croix and was strongly criticized. After the hurricane, a referendum endorsed the establishment of some sort of municipal government on each island which would be more responsive to that island's needs and legislation to that effect was introduced into the Legislature in July 1993. St Croix's feeling of neglect led to attempts to balance the division of power between the islands, but calls for greater autonomy grew. After some delay, a referendum was held in October 1993, which presented voters with seven options on the island's status, grouped into three choices: continued or enhanced status, integration into the USA, or independence. However, the vote was inconclusive, with only 27% of the registered voters turning out, whereas 50% were needed for a binding decision. Of those who did, 90% preferred the first option, leaving the process of constitutional change in some disarray.

In 1993 the government of the USVI reached agreement with the Danish company, the East Asiatic Company Ltd, to buy the West Indian Company Ltd (WICO), whose major holdings on St Thomas included a cruise ship dock, the Havensight Shopping Mall, a 7.2-acre landfill, the former Danish consulate, Denmark Hill, and some undeveloped land. WICO had remained in Danish hands after the 1917 purchase of the islands by the USA and had retained the right to dredge, fill and develop submerged lands in the east part of St Thomas harbour, despite local opposition. The US$54mn sale was described locally as wiping out the last vestiges of Danish colonialism.

In 1998 gubernatorial elections were won by Charles Turnbull, a retired university professor representing the Democratic Party. He defeated the independent incumbent, Roy Schneider, by 19,138 votes to 13,334.

Government

In 1936 the Organic Act of the Virgin Islands of the United States provided for two municipal councils and a Legislative Assembly in the islands. Suffrage was extended to all residents of twenty one and over who could read and write English. Discrimination on the grounds of race, colour, sex or religious belief was forbidden and a bill of rights was included. Real political parties now emerged, based on popular support. In 1946, the first black governor was appointed to the Virgin Islands and in 1950 the first native governor was appointed. In 1968 the Elective Governor Act was passed, to become effective in 1970 when, for the first time, Virgin Islanders would elect their own governor and lieutenant governor. The Act also abolished the presidential veto of territorial legislation and authorized the legislature to override the governor's veto by a two-thirds majority vote. The USVI is an unincorporated Territory under the US Department of Interior with a Delegate in the House of Representatives who (since January 1993) has a vote in sittings of the whole House. A Democrat, Donna Christian-Green, was elected in 1998. The Governor is elected every four years; there are 15 Senators; judicial power is vested in local courts. All persons born in the USVI are citizens of the United States, but do not vote in presidential elections while resident on the islands.

The economy

USVI residents enjoy a comparatively high standard of living (the cost of living is the highest in the USA), unemployment is low, at around 4% (mostly on St Croix), but the working population is young and there is constant pressure for new jobs. The islands used to rely on the alumina plant, and the Hess oil refinery, operating well below capacity, for employment and income, but nowadays the major economic activity is tourism. Over two million visitors come every year. The number of hotel rooms is now over 5,000, generating jobs for two-thirds of the labour force. There is a perennial conflict between the hotel industry, which provides employment, fixed investment and pays taxes, and the cruise ship industry, which contributes comparatively little to the islands. The number of stayover visitors fell to around 500,000 from over 700,000 at the beginning of the 1990s with hotel occupancy rates averaging little more than 50%. Cruise ship passengers, however, reached a record 1.6 mn in 1998, but landing mostly in St Thomas, with St Croix receiving only about 150,000.

Industry is better developed than in many Caribbean islands and exports of manufactured goods include watches, textiles, electronics, pharmaceuticals and rum. In 1998 Hess Oil Co and Petróleos de Venezuela signed a joint venture agreement to create a US$625mn company called Hovensa to operate the refinery on St Croix. Industrial incentives and tax concessions equivalent to those enjoyed by Puerto Rico, are designed to attract new investors with US markets to the islands. Over 30 large US corporations have set up manufacturing operations in the USVI and industrial parks are being built.

Agriculture has declined in importance since sugar production ended, and the poor soil prevents much commercial farming. Emphasis is placed on growing food crops for the domestic market and fruit, vegetables and sorghum for animal feed have been introduced. Fishing in the USVI waters is mostly for game rather than for commercial purposes. The islands' lack of natural resources makes them heavily dependent on imports, both for domestic consumption and for later re-exports, such as oil and manufactured goods.

US Virgin Islands

British Virgin Islands

12

British Virgin Islands

The British Virgin Islands (BVI), grouped around Sir Francis Drake Channel, are less developed than the US group, and number some 60 islands, islets, rocks, and cays, of which only 16 or so are inhabited. They are all of volcanic origin except one, Anegada, which is coral and limestone. Most of the land was cleared years ago for its timber or to grow crops, and it is now largely covered by secondary forest and scrub. In the areas with greatest rainfall there are mangoes and palm trees, but generally the islands can look brown and parched, green and lush only just after rain. Mangrove and sea grape can be found in some areas along the shore.

While there are some large resorts in the BVI, there are no high-rise hotels, casinos and very few nightclubs, as found in some of the other islands which depend heavily on tourism. In fact, there is very little to do at all on land and nearly everything happens in the beautiful water which surrounds the islands. If you are keen on watersports and sailing and have adequate finance (the Virgin Islands are not cheap), you will enjoy island hopping.

Essentials

Before you travel

Documents An authenticated birth or citizenship certificate or voter's registration may suffice for US or Canadian citizens. All other nationalities need a valid **passport** and a return or **onward ticket**. Visitors from some countries, such as Guyana, require a visa. The Chief Immigration Officer is in Road Town, T4943701.

Money **Currency** The US dollar is the legal tender. There are no exchange control restrictions. Try to avoid large denominated travellers' cheques. Cheques accepted rarely, cash is king. There is a 10% stamp duty on all cheques and travellers' cheques. **Credit cards** Credit cards are all right for most hotels and the larger restaurants, but not for the majority of the bar/restaurants. Credit cards are not accepted on Anegada except at the *Anegada Reef Hotel*. **Banks** *Bank of Nova Scotia*, Road Town, T4942526. *Barclays Bank*, Road Town, T4942173, F4944315, with agencies in The Valley, Virgin Gorda, T4955217, F4955163. *Chase Manhattan Bank*, Road Town, T4942662, F4945106. *Development Bank of the Virgin Islands*, T4943737. *Banco Popular de Puerto Rico*, Road Town, T4942117, F4945294. *VP Bank (BVI) Ltd*, 65 Main Street, Road Town, T4941100, F4941199.

Climate The temperature averages 84°F in summer and 80°F in winter. At night temperatures may drop about 50°F. Average annual rainfall is 40 ins.

Getting there

Air There are international airports on Beef Island for Tortola, on Virgin Gorda and on Anegada, but no direct flights from Europe or from the USA. **From Europe** Same day connections can be made through Puerto Rico (*British Airways* from London, *Iberia* from Madrid) or Antigua (*BWIA* or *British Airways* from London). **From the USA** Connecting flights can be arranged through Puerto Rico or the USVI. *American Eagle* (T4952559), *Air Sunshine, Cape Air* and *LIAT* fly several times a day from San Juan. **From the Caribbean** *LIAT* (T4951187) flies to Tortola from Anguilla, Antigua, Barbados, Grenada, St Kitts, St Lucia, St Maarten, St Vincent, Trinidad, Puerto Rico. *Winair* (T4942347) flies from St Maarten to Tortola. *Air Sunshine* and *Cape Air* fly from St Thomas and San Juan. Virgin Gorda's air links are not especially good. *Air St Thomas* and *Air Sunshine* fly from St Thomas and San Juan, while *M & N Aviation* (T4955553) and *Vieques Air Link* also fly from San Juan. *Seaborne Aviation* (T340-7736442) fly to West End, Tortola, from St Thomas with a seaplane three times a week. Charter flights with *Fly BVI* (T4951747), *Clair Aero Services* (T4952271), *Air St Thomas* (T4955935), *Caribbean Wings* (T4952309), *M & N Aviation* (T4955553) and *Air Sunshine* (T4958900).

Boat There are frequent connections with the USVI and within the BVI, see the USVI chapter. *Inter-Island Boat Services*, T4954166; also water taxi available, T7766501. *Native Son Inc*, T4954617, *Smiths Ferry Services*, T4942355, *Speedy's*, T4955240, *Nubian Princess*, T4954999. Fares between Tortola and St John are about US$40 round trip (US$28 children aged 3-11).

Ports of entry (British flag) Port Purcell at Road Town is the principal port of entry with an 800 ft, deep water berth for cruise ships; a second 550 ft pier was built in 1994; Government Jetty, Road Town, is also used. There are others at West End (Soper's Hole), Tortola; St Thomas Bay, Virgin Gorda; and Great Harbour, Jost Van Dyke. Small cruise ships can be seen off many of the islands. Anegada is a port of entry, customs and immigration can be cleared 0715-1715 Monday-Friday, 0800-1530 Saturday-Sunday.

Jetskis must be declared on entry to the BVIs **Boat documents** Customs clearance fee US$0.75, harbour dues US$7, US$10.50 for a boat registered under the name of a corporation. The captain may clear the crew, taking passports and boat documentation ashore. You may clear in and out at the same time if staying less than 72 hours. Weekends incur overtime charges.

Touching down

Departure tax US$10, if you leave by air, and US$5 departure tax by sea. There is a cruise ship passenger tax of US$7.

Emergency Police, Fire or Ambulance, T999. The Virgin Islands Search and Rescue (VISAR) is a voluntary 24-hour marine service, T999 or Ch 16.

Hours of business Banks open Monday-Friday, 0900-1400, **Barclays** is open until 1500, **Chase Manhattan** until 1600, also Chase opens on Saturday 0900-1200. Shops open Monday-Friday, 0900-1700.

Government offices open Monday-Friday, 0830-1630.

Official time Atlantic Standard Time, four hours behind GMT, one ahead of EST.

Voltage 110 volts, 60 cycles.

Clothing Island dress is casual and only the most exclusive restaurants require formal clothes. However, bathing suits are for the beach only, it is very offensive to locals to see bare chests and bellies, so cover up.

Anchorages The BVI National Parks Trust (T4943904) has placed moorings at many dive sites, available on a first come, first served basis. Purchase mooring use sticker from customs, fee US$2 per person per day or US$25 per week. Buoys are colour coded: yellow for commercial dive boats, white for a boat with divers, orange for snorkelling and day use, and blue for dinghy docks. Moorings have been placed and are maintained by Moor Seacure at *Cooper Island Beach Club*, Marina Cay, *Drake's Anchorage*, *Abe's* (Jost Van Dyke), Penn's Landing, Leverick Bay, *Rhymer's*, Cane Garden Bay, *Anegada Reef Hotel*, Soper's Hole Marina, *Harris' Place*, Vixen Point (Prickly Pear Island, Gorda Sound), *Last Resort* (Trellis Bay), at US$20 per night. In winter months, northerly swells and high surf can make northern anchorages (and landing at the Baths) untenable. Listen to ZBVI 780AM for weather reports. There are 12 marinas on Tortola, three on Virgin Gorda, one on Peter Island and one on Marina Cay.

Touching down

Local tourist office The BVI Tourist Board, 2nd floor, AKARA Building, Wickhams Cay 1, PO Box 134, Road Town, T4943134, F4943866, bvitourb@caribsurf.com; there is also an office at Virgin Gorda Yacht Harbour, T4955181, F4943866; some offices overseas can help with reservations. *The BVI Welcome* is a bimonthly colour tourist guide now on line as well, www.bviwelcome.com *The Tourism Directory* is published annually and is a detailed listing of services. The tourist board has these and many other brochures.

Tourist information

Maps The Ordnance Survey publishes a map of the BVI in its World Maps series, with inset maps of Road Town and East End, Tortola, tourist information and some text; Ordnance Survey, Romsey Road, Southampton, SO9 4DH, T01703-792792. The tourist office distributes a road map, updated annually with some tourist information on resorts, restaurants and what to do.

Where to stay

Hotels There is a 7% hotel tax and a 10% service charge in the BVI. Rates apply to double rooms, EP, winter-summer. **Camping** Allowed only on authorized sites. **Villas** There are some truly luxurious houses for rent if you can afford them, with the most famous, or infamous, being Richard Branson's house on Necker Island. A wide choice of stylish properties is on offer.

Getting around

Clair Aero flies from Tortola to Anegada Monday, Wednesday, Friday and Sunday, US$27 one-way, or hire the whole plane, US$300, seats eight people, T4952271. *Fly BVI* is a small charter airline with 7 aircraft which is often cheaper and more convenient than a scheduled flight if there are a few of you, to Anegada US$125 one-way T4951747, 800-1-FLY BVI,

Air

British Virgin Islands

F4951973,www.fly-bvi.com. Pack light, there is limited luggage space on the small aircraft. Alternatively take a day trip to Anegada, US$110 per person including taxi, air fare, lobster lunch at the *Big Bamboo*, contact Nikki and Barry Abrams, owners of Fly BVI.

Road **Bicycle** All bicycles must be registered at the Traffic Licensing Office in Road Town and the licence plate must be fixed to the bicycle, cost US$5. *Last Stop Sports* in Nanny Cay rents and repairs quality mountain bikes, rental US$20 per day, T4940564, F4940593, lssbikes@surfbvi.com

Bus There is a local bus service on Tortola with cheap fares (US$2-4) but erratic timetable. Scheduled (but nowhere near actual) times are: Road Town to West End, 0700, 0835, 1000; West End to Carrot Bay, 0730, 0900, 1030. From Carrot Bay it goes to Road Town, East End and

British Virgin Islands & national parks

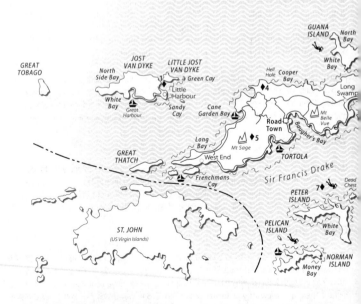

back to Road Town. In the afternoon it leaves West End at 1515 and 1645. Call **Scatos Bus Service** for information, T4945873.

Car There are only about 50 miles of roads suitable for cars. Drive on the left. Maximum speed limit 40 mph, in residential areas 20 mph. Minimokes and jeeps can be hired on Tortola, Virgin Gorda and Anegada. Car rental offices (or Police Headquarters) provide the necessary temporary BVI driving licence (US$10) but you must also have a valid licence from your home country. **Car hire** It is advisable to book in advance in the peak season. Rates range from US$40-45 per day in winter for a small car, US$45-70 per day for jeeps, usually about US$10 less in summer. Credit card needed with US$500 deposit. **Tortola**: *Alphonso Car Rentals*, Fish Bay, T4948746, F4948735, cars US$40-45 per day, jeeps US$50-70 per day, 20% less in summer; *Avis Rent-a-Car*, opposite Botanic Gardens, Road Town, T4942193, or West End,

Jeeps may be more useful for exploring secluded beach areas

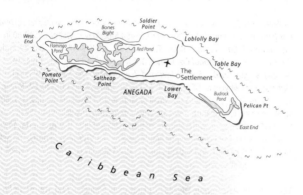

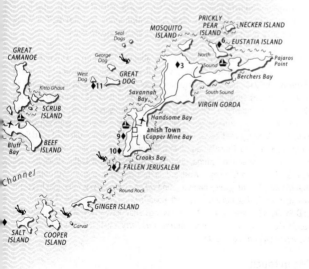

◆ National Parks	6 Prickly Pear
1 Diamond Cay	7 Rhone's Anchor
2 Fallen Jerusalem	8 Rhone Marine Park
3 Gorda Peak Park	9 Spring Bay & The Crawl
4 Mt Healthy & Windmill Ruin	10 The Baths & Devil's Bay
5 Mt Sage	11 West Dog

N

Not to scale

British Virgin Islands

👉 *Tourist offices overseas*

Germany *Wallstrasse 56, D-40878, Dusseldorf/Ratingin, T49-2102-711183, F49-2102-21177, rombergg@tonline.de*

Italy *Piazza Castello 11, 2021 Milan, T392-72022329, F392-72022306, aigo@internetforce.com*

UK *110 St Martin's Lane, London WC2N 4DY, T020-72404259, F020-72404270, christine.oliver@fcb.co.uk*

USA *370 Lexington Avenue, Suite 1605, New York, NY 10017, T212-6960400, F212-9498254, bvitouristboard@ worldnet.att.net; 1804 Union Street, San Francisco, CA 94123, T415-7750344, F415-7752554, bvitbsfo@pacbell.net; 3390 Peachtree Road NE, Suite 1000, Lenox Towers, Atlanta, GA 30326, T404-2408018, F404-2332318; 3450 Wilshire Boulevard, Suite 108-17, Los Angeles, CA 90010, T310-2872200, F310-2872753.*

T4954973, US$35-50 per day winter, US$25-40 summer, cheaper weekly rates; *Denzil Clyne Car Rentals*, West End, T4954900, jeeps US$45-85 per day in winter, US$40-60 in summer; *International Car Rentals*, Road Town, T4942516, F4944715, intercar@candwbvi.net, US$30-70 per day; *National Car Rental*, Duff's Bottom and Long Bay, T4943197, US$45-75 per day. **Virgin Gorda**: *Andy's Taxi and Jeep Rental*, The Valley, T4955511, F4955820, fischers@ candwbvi.net, VHF16, US$50-55 per day, guided tours US$30; *L & S Jeep Rentals*, South Valley, T4955297, F4955342, small or large jeeps, US$45-70 per day, US$280-455 per week, free pick up in Spanish Town; *Speedy's Car Rentals*, The Valley, T4955235 and Leverick Bay, T4955240 discount with return ferry ticket, US$40-80 per day. **Anegada**: *Anegada Reef Hotel*, T4958002, F4959362, minibus and bicycle rentals; *DW Jeep Rentals*, The Settlement, T4959677, 2-door jeeps and Subaru vans, US$40-55 per day, US$240-300 per week, free drop off and pick up at airport.

Taxi *BVI Taxi Association*, T4942875, island tours arranged. **Taxi stands**: in Road Town, T4942322; on Beef Island, T4952378. Taxis are easy to come by on Tortola and fares are fixed, ask for a list or get one from the tourist office. The fare from Beef Island Airport to Road Town, Tortola is US$15 or US$8 if shared. On Virgin Gorda, *Mahogany Taxi Service*, The Valley, T4955469, F4955072, offers tours and day trips, as well as car and jeep rental.

Sea The ferry fares between Tortola and Virgin Gorda are about US$20 return and from Tortola to Jost Van Dyke US$15. Always check availability and departure times in advance. The *North Sound Express*, T4952138 has six daily crossings Beef Island-Spanish Town-Bitter End, 30 minutes, reservations essential. To Leverick Bay (for Mosquito Island), 25 minutes, US$20 one way, 1300, 1545, 1730. Return 0645, 0845, 1145, 1445, 1615. Bus service (not included in fare) to and from Road Town waterfront (Pussers) and Beef Island ferry dock. *Speedy's*, T4955240, has four crossings Monday, Wednesday, Friday and Saturday between Virgin Gorda and Road Town, six on Tuesday and Thursday, and two on Sunday, also a service continuing to St Thomas, Tuesday, Thursday and Saturday. *Smiths Ferry Services*, T4942355, 4954495, cross from Virgin Gorda to Road Town then West End on their way to St John and St Thomas four times a day Monday-Saturday, three times on Sunday. *Peter Island Ferry*, T4952000, has eight daily crossings from the Peter Island Ferry Dock, Road Town, to Peter Island, US$15 round trip. *Jost Van Dyke Ferry Service*, T4942997, four crossings a day between West End and Jost Van Dyke Monday-Saturday, three on Sunday. *Marina Cay Ferry*, T4942174, runs between Beef Island and *Pusser's Marina Cay* eight times a day.

Keeping in touch

Post There is a post office in Road Town, branches in Tortola and Virgin Gorda and sub-branches in other islands. Postal rates for postcards are US$0.30 to the USA, US$0.35 to Europe and US$0,45 to the rest of the world; for aerogrammes US$0.35; for letters to the USA US$0.45, to Europe US$0.50, to the rest of the world US$0.75.

British Virgin Islands

Direct dialling is available locally and worldwide. All telecommunications are operated by Cable & Wireless. Telephone, facsimile transmission, data transmission, internet access and telegraph facilities are all available. Phone cards are available, US$5, US$10, US$15 and US$20, discount rates in evenings at weekends. To make a credit card call, dial 111 and quote your Amex, Discover, Visa or Mastercard number. Dial 119 for the operator or 110 for the international operator. Cable & Wireless is at the centre of Road Town at Wickhams Cay I, open 0700-1900 Monday-Friday, 0700-1600 Saturday, 0900-1400 Sunday and public holidays, T4944444, F4942506; also in The Valley, Virgin Gorda, T4955444, F4955702. They also operate Tortola Marine Radio, call on VHF Ch 16, talk on 27 or 84. The CCT Boatphone company in Road Town offers cellular telephone services throughout the Virgin Islands for yachts, US$5 per day for service, US$4 per minute; there is also a prepaid cellular service, CCT Flexphone, T4943825. To call VHF stations from a land phone, call Tortola Radio, T116. Caribbean Connections at Village Cay Marina, T4943623, has phone, fax, email, courier service. Moorings allows use of phone for collecting email. Village Cay Marina has a computer room.

Telephone
International phone code: 284

Newspapers The Island Sun is published on Friday, while the BVI Beacon comes out on Thursday. The Limin' Times, printed weekly, is a free magazine giving entertainment news: nightlife, sports, music etc. **Radio** Radio ZBVI broadcasts on 780AM. Weather reports for sailors are broadcast hourly from 0730 to 1830 every day. There are four FM stations: Reggae at 97.3, Country at 94.3, Z Gold at 91.7 and ZROD at 103.7.

Media

Food and drink

Most things are imported and will cost at least the same as in Florida. Try local produce which is cheaper, yams and sweet potatoes rather than potatoes, for example. Fish dishes are often excellent, try snapper, dolphin (fish, not the mammal), grouper, tuna and swordfish, and don't miss the lobster. Once the centre of rum production for the Royal Navy 'Pussers' (Pursers), rum is still available from Pusser's or supermarkets. Local rums of varying quality are also sold by hotels and restaurants.

There are lots of good restaurants across the islands

Shopping

The BVI is not duty-free. There are gift shops and boutiques in Road Town, Tortola and in Spanish Town, Virgin Gorda. The BVI Philatelic Bureau or Post Offices sell stamps for collectors. You can also buy BVI coins, but they are not used as a currency. *Samarkand*, on Main Street, Tortola, sells gold and silver jewellery created by the local Bibby family with nautical themes; you can buy earings of yachts, pelicans, etc and they will make anything to order, samarkand @caribwave.com, also a branch at Soper's Hole Wharf, West End: *Caribbean Jewellers*. *Sunny Caribbee Herb and Spice Co* (PO Box 286), is on Main Street with *Sunny Caribbee Gallery* next door, also at *Skyworld Restaurant* and *Long Bay Hotel*, selling spices, herbs, preserves and handicrafts, mail order and shipping services available. *Pusser's Co Store* in Road Town and West End, Tortola, and Leverick Bay, Virgin Gorda, sells nautical clothing, luggage and accessories as well as Pusser's Rum. *Turtle Dove Boutique*, in Road Town, has a good selection of gifts and home furnishings and is the only place selling a reasonable selection of books (other than romances and thrillers stocked by hotels). *Caribbean Handprints*, Main Street, has a silkscreen studio and shop with local designs and clothing made on site. An open air market close to the Tourist Office offers a selection of T-shirts and other souvenirs.

Diving and marine life

There is much to see around the Virgin Islands and considerable work is being done to establish marine parks and conserve the reefs. The Department of Conservation and Fisheries is in charge of the BVI's natural resources and a fisheries management plan aims to avoid over-fishing and help conserve the reefs. The 17½ km **Horseshoe Reef** off the south shore of Anegada is the third largest reef in the world (after the Great Barrier Reef and Belize) and now a Protected Area, with an anchor and fishing ban in force. The anchor ban is expected to remain indefinitely although permanent moorings will be put at popular dive sites. There are 80 visible wrecks around Anegada and many more covered by coral; about 300 ships are believed to have foundered on the reef.

Humpback whales migrate to the islands every year and the Department of Conservation and Fisheries is trying to estimate their numbers with the aim of designating the BVI waters as a marine mammal sanctuary. If you see any (mostly north of Tortola), let them know. Similarly, turtles are being counted with the help of volunteers in order to draw up environmental legislation to protect them. Leatherback turtles travel to north shore beaches to nest, but their numbers have been declining fast. Hawksbill and Green turtles are more common but still endangered. For several months of the year the killing of turtles or taking their eggs is prohibited and the export of turtle products is illegal. If you see turtle on the menu, or a turtle shell product, please do not buy it; even the legal killing damages the population.

There are over 60 charted dive sites, many of which are in underwater national parks. They include walls, pinnacles, coral reefs, caverns and wrecks. The most visited wreck is that of the *Rhone*, sunk in 1867 in a storm and broken in two. The bow section is in about 80 ft of water and you can swim through the hull. The stern is shallower and you can see the prop shaft and the propeller (and an octopus). Another wreck is the 246-ft *Chikuzen* sunk in 1981 about six miles north of Tortola, where you will see bigger fish such as barracuda and rays. Most Caribbean and Atlantic species of tropical fish and marine invertebrates can be found in BVI waters, with hard and soft corals, gorgonians and sea fans. Watch out for fire coral, sea urchins and the occasional bristle worm. Visibility ranges from 60-200 ft and the water temperature varies from 76°F in winter to 86°F in summer. Wet suits are not essential but most people wear them.

A moorings system has been set up to eliminate anchor damage to the coral and all users of the moorings must have a national parks permit. These are available through dive operators, charter companies, government offices and the National Parks Trust, T4943904. The revenue goes towards maintenance and new moorings. As yet, there is no legislation to prohibit anchoring in areas other than in the marine parks, but it is actively discouraged. National Parks Trust moorings (of which there are currently 180 with another 70 planned) are located at The Caves, The Indians, The Baths, Pelican Island, Carrot Shoal, dive sites at Peter Island, Cooper Island, Ginger Island and Norman Island, the *Rhone's* anchor, the wreck of the *Rhone*, the wreck of the *Fearless*, Deadchest Island, Blonde Rock, Guana Island, The Dogs and other popular diving and recreational sites.

Dive centres There are several dive shops around the islands which offer individual tours, package deals with hotels or rendezvous with charter boats. Rates depend on the distance to the dive site but are generally US$80-90 for two tanks, including equipment hire. A day's resort course and shallow dive costs about US$95. *Baskin in the Sun*, established in 1969 and a PADI five-star dive centre, is at Prospect Reef, Peter Island and Soper's Hole. Packages can be arranged with all the major hotels and in fact they are often full with package business so book individual diving in good time. They win awards for excellence and readership surveys, T4942858, 800-6502084, F4944304, www.dive-baskin.com *Dive BVI*, another PADI five-star operation (also NAUI courses) is at Virgin Gorda Yacht Harbour, Leverick Bay and Marina Cay, Box 1040, Virgin Gorda, T4955513, 800-8487078, F4955347, www.divebvi.com *Blue Water Divers* has been at Nanny Cay since 1980 and is also at Hodges Creek Marina/Maya Cove, Box 846, Road Town, T4942847, F4940198, bwdbvi@surfbvi.com *Kilbride's Sunchaser Scuba* is at the *Bitter End Yacht Club*, North Sound, Box 46, Virgin Gorda, T4959638, 800-9324286, F4957549. *Underwater Safaris*, a PADI five-star, NAUI and SSI facility, is at *The Moorings*, Road Town (PO Box 139, T4943965, 800-5377032, F4945322), and has a small shop on Cooper Island which is used as a surface interval between dives in the area, for example the *Rhone*. Air refills are available here. *Underwater Safaris* (and most other companies) will take you anywhere you want to dive, even if there is only one passenger on the boat, and each dive tour location is determined by the first people to book, although they normally only go to sites within 30 minutes of Road Town. If you want your own dive boat for the day with your own instructor, contact *Underwater Boat Services*, T4940024, F4940623, www.scubabvi.com, VHF 16, minimum fee per boat US$250 or US$90 per person. Diving and watersports cruises can be booked with *Promenade Cruises* at *Village Cay Marina*, T4946020, F4960999, www.yacht promenade.com They take a maximum of 10 guests on a 65-ft trimaran with five crew including two dive instructors, with windsurfers, waterskiing and tubing for when you are not underwater. Another trimaran is the 105-ft *Cuan Law*, the world's largest, which has 10 state rooms, seven crew including dive instructors, kayaks, waterskis, hobie cats and underwater photography, T4942490, F4945774, www.diveguideint.com/cuanlaw Underwater photography, camera rental, and film processing is offered by *Rainbow Visions Photo Center*, Prospect Reef, Box 680, Road Town, T4942749. They often join dive boats and take video film of you underwater. Great fun and excellent quality but expensive.

Beaches and watersports

There are lovely sandy beaches on all the islands and many of them are remote, empty and accessible only from the sea. The clean, crystal-clear waters around the islands provide excellent snorkelling, diving, cruising and fishing. Most of the hotels offer a wide variety of watersports, including windsurfing, sunfish, scuba, snorkelling and small boats. *Jet skis are banned*

'Bareboating' (self-crew yacht chartering) is extremely popular and the way most visitors see the islands. The BVI are one of the most popular destinations in the world for bareboaters. If you do not feel confident in handling a yacht, there are various options from fully-crewed luxury yachts to hiring a skipper to take you and your bareboat out for as long as you need. You can also rent a cabin on a private charter yacht, several charter companies find this a useful way of filling a boat. Navigation is not difficult, the water and weather are generally clear and there are many excellent cruising guides and charts for reference. Most of the islands offer at least one beautiful bay and it is possible even at the height of the season to find deserted beaches and calm anchorages. Bareboaters are not supposed to sail to Anegada because of the hazardous, unmarked route through the reef and generally only crewed yachts go there. The exception is the fleet of Moorings, which organizes a special flotilla once a week from the *Bitter End Resort & Yacht Club* for its clients. If you are sailing independently, however, check the charts, ensure you approach in clear daylight when the sun is high, or call the *Anegada Reef Hotel* at Setting Point when you are within sight and they will direct you over the radio. Charter companies are too numerous to list here, there are many on Tortola and several more on Virgin Gorda. Contact the tourist office for a list of bareboats with prices. For crewed yachts, *The Moorings*, T4942332, F4942226; *Yacht Connections*, T4945273, F4944250, www.yacht-connections.com; *Sail Vacations* (operates the 72-ft luxury ketch *Endless Summer II*), T4943656, 800-3689905, F4944731, www.EndlessSummer.com; *Regency Yacht Vacations*, at the Inner Harbour Marina, Wickham's Cay I, T4951970, F4951415, www.regencyvacations.com (luxury 45-200 ft yachts for 2-20 people, gourmet cuisine, watersports); *BVI Yacht Charters*, T4944289, F4946552; *Catamaran Charters*, T4946661; *Wanderlust Yacht Vacations*, T/F4942405, www.wanderlustcharters.com, and several others, will be able to match your needs with the hundreds of charter yachts available. Marinas are plentiful with yard services, haul out, fuel docks, water and showers. **Sailing**

Sailing and boardsailing schools offer three-hour to one week courses. The *Nick Trotter Sailing School* at the *Bitter End Resort & Yacht Club*, North Sound, T4942745, F4944756, has sailing and windsurfing courses for all ages with a wide variety of craft, very popular, principally for guests because of its isolated location. *Offshore Sailing School Ltd*, at *Prospect Reef*, T800-2214326, www.offshore-sailing.com, has courses on live-aboard cruising as well as learn-to-sail on dinghies. *Full Sail Sailing School* offers day sail and liveaboard courses with ASA certification at Seabreeze Marina, East End, T4940512, F4940588, fullsail@surfbvi.com For private instruction with ASA certification, call Linda Hall, Tortola Marine Management Bareboat Vacations, T800-6330155.

The annual spring Regatta is held in Sir Francis Drake's Channel, considered one of the best sailing venues in the world. It is one third of the Caribbean Ocean Racing Triangle (CORT) series of regattas, with the exact date each year revolving around the St Thomas Rolex Cup which is held over Easter. The Regatta may be held before or after Easter depending on whether Easter is early or late. International yachtsmen and women compete alongside local islanders from Puerto Rico, the USVI and BVI as crew or hiring their own bareboats. The Regatta Village (and parties) is at the *Moorings Marina*, with several local restaurants serving low-priced meals. Contact the *Royal BVI Yacht Club*, T4943286. Ask for regatta discounts on rooms or slips. March 1988 was the first annual Dark and Stormy Race from Tortola to Anegada, started to celebrate the 25th anniversary that year of *Neptune's Treasure* restaurant run by Vernon Soares and family. Fireworks, dancing, food, drink and entertainment greet sailors on arrival in Anegada, where they take a day off before racing back to the West End Yacht Club (sponsored by the Royal BVI Yacht Club, T4943286 for information). The Annual Anegada Yacht Race is in August, with a route from Road Town to Anegada, and in November *Pusser's* sponsor a round-Tortola race. There are races of one sort or another going on all year round, check *The Welcome*, or www.bviwelcome.com, for what is coming up, or contact the Royal BVI Yacht Club.

A cruising permit is required by everyone cruising in the BVI: 1 December-30 April, all recorded charter boats US$2 per person per day, all non-recorded charter boats US$4 per person per day; 1 May-30 November, US$0.75 and US$4 respectively. All privately-owned yachts cruising in the BVI are charged nominal cruising fees. Dive boats, sport fishing boats etc should contact the Customs Department for cruising permit regulations. Permits are required if you want to use any National Parks Trust moorings, call The Trust office at T4943904.

Several companies offer snorkelling tours and there are lots of yachts offering day-sails to all the little islands at around US$70-90 with snorkelling, beverages and sometimes lunch, but avoid them when the cruise ships are in town as they are often packed out. An interesting addition to day sail craft is the *Gli Gli* Carib canoe, which has been brought to the BVI following its original journey in 1997 from Dominica to Guyana as part of a celebration of Carib culture. Reservations with Aragorn Dick-Read, T4951849, dreadeye@surfbvi.com, tours include a BBC video of the canoe's construction, US$65 for a full day sail including traditional Carib lunch. All day sail boats should carry the symbol of the Daycharter Association of the British Virgin Islands (a circular badge with the name of the association surrounding an anchor and the flag) to prove they are properly licensed and have had safety checks.

Windsurfing Windsurfing is popular in the islands and there is an annual Bacardi Hi-Ho (hook in and hold on) race which attracts windsurfers from all over the world. The week long event involves inter-island racing with accommodation on sailing yachts and lots of watersports, fun and parties. Boardsailing BVI is at Trellis Bay, Beef Island, T4952447, F4951626, and at Nanny Cay (a BIC Centre), T4940422, www.windsurfing.vi, with schools and shops. As well as windsurfing they offer kayaks, surf boards and sail dinghies. Hi Ho at *Prospect Reef*, T4948304, F4940003, has sales, rentals and instruction, also with kayaks and surfboards. Both schools have good equipment for beginners and advanced sailors. Last Stop Sports, at Nanny Cay, T4940564, F4940593, lssbikes@surfbvi.com, has rental windsurfers, single and double kayaks, surfboards and bodyboards, lessons available. Many of the larger hotels have watersports equipment for their guests.

Fishing Sport fishing is becoming more popular with many companies offering day trips aboard sport fishing boats: *Anegada Reef Hotel*, Anegada, US$500-900, T4958002, F4959362, offers sport fishing on a 46-ft Hatteras, inshore and bonefishing and has a tackle shop; *Pelican Charters*, Prospect Reef, T4967386, has a 46-ft Chris craft sportfisherman, US$600-950 for sportfishing, US$1,200 for marlin, full facilities. *Persistent Charters*, West End, T4954122, charge US$350 half day, US$650 full day on a 31-ft Tiara, everything included. A local permit is required for fishing, call the Fisheries Division for information, T4945682; spearfishing is not allowed, hunting on land is also banned and no firearms are allowed. There are areas known to house ciguatera (fish poisoning) around the reefs, so it is important to contact the Fisheries Division before fishing of any kind is undertaken.

Other sports There is a **tennis** club on Tortola and many hotels have their own courts. **Golf** has not been developed although a couple of the hotels have small practice courses. **Horse riding** can be arranged through the hotels, or T4942262, Shadow's Stables, or T4940704, Ellis Thomas, for riding through Mount Sage National Park or down to Cane Garden Bay, Tortola. Alex Parillon has horses on Virgin Gorda. **Walking** and **birdwatching** are quite popular and trails have been laid out in some places. Sage Mountain on Tortola and Gorda Peak on Virgin Gorda are popular hikes. Spectator sports include cricket and soft ball. **Gyms** include *Bodyworks*, T4942705, and *Cutting Edge*, T4959570. *Prospect Reef* has a healthclub called *Healthy Prospects* where you can do aerobics (called *Body Images*, T4944713), yoga, tennis and nine-hole pitch and putt, T4943311 ext 245.

Holidays and festivals

New Year's Day, Commonwealth Day (2nd Monday in March), Good Friday, Easter Monday, Whit Monday in May, Queen's Birthday (2nd Monday in June), Territory Day (1 July), Festival beginning of August, St Ursula's Day (21 October), Prince Charles' Birthday (14 November), Christmas Day, Boxing Day.

Public holidays

The **BVI Summer Festival** is held over two weeks at the end of *July* and beginning of *August*. There is entertainment every night with steel bands, fungi and calypso music, a Prince and Princess show and a calypso show. During the year there are many regattas, such as the annual **BVI Spring Regatta** in *April*, **Foxy's Wooden Boat Regatta** in *September* and windsurfing events, which attract many extracurricular activities and lots of parties.

Festivals

Health

Peebles Hospital is a public hospital with X-ray and surgical facilities. Private X-ray and laboratory facilities are offered by B&F Medical Complex and Medicure Ltd. There are 12 doctors on Tortola and one on Virgin Gorda, two dentists and a small private hospital, the Bougainvillea Clinic which specializes in plastic surgery. Be careful in the sun, always use a sunscreen.

Tortola

Tortola, the main island, is where 81% of the total population live. Mount Sage, the highest point in the archipelago, rises to 1,780 ft, and traces of a primeval rain forest can still be found on its slopes. Walking trails have been marked through Mount Sage National Park. The south part of the island is mountainous and rocky, covered with scrub, frangipani and ginger thomas. The north has groves of bananas, mangoes and palm trees, and long sandy beaches.

Population: 16,000

Road Town

On the south shore, is the capital and business centre of the territory, dominated by marinas and financial companies, many of which line the harbour. Main Street houses many of the oldest buildings, churches and the colonial prison (replaced by a modern prison in 1997 for 120 inmates), and is the most picturesque street. Until the 1960s, Main Street was the waterfront road, but land infill has allowed another road, Waterfront Drive, to be built between it and the sea. A dual carriageway runs from Port Purcell to Wickhams Cay, which will later be extended to Fort Burt, so expect disruption in Road Town. Cruise ships call frequently at a dock in the Wickhams Cay area opened late-1994. There are many gift shops, hotels and restaurants catering for the tourist market. In 1992-93, very grand and imposing government offices were built on the waterfront overlooking the harbour entrance. Banks, offices, Cable and Wireless, the tourist office and a small craft village are also in this area. All these buildings are built on infilled land, called Wickhams Cay; the restaurant *Spaghetti Junction* was once a bar overlooking the water but is now some way back, divided from the sea by roads and office buildings. There are plans to develop the cruise

British Virgin Islands

landing site in Road Harbour, with an expansion of the pier, facilities to accommodate two vessels at a time, a terminal building, tourist information office and a marine tour dispatch area for boat trips, all linked by a boardwalk to connect Old Road Town with the new development.

The Governor resides in **Government House** above Waterfront Drive overlooking the harbour (T4942345). The house is in a classical style, painted white with green shutters and surrounded by beautifully tended gardens with a fine display of flamboyant trees in the front.

The four acre **Joseph Reynold O'Neal Botanic Gardens** near the Police Station in Road Town (free admission, donations welcomed) has a good selection of tropical and subtropical plants such as palm trees, succulents, ferns and orchids. There is a good booklet which gives a suggested route round the garden, pond, orchid house, fern house and medicinal herb garden. It is a peaceful place, luxuriant, with magnificent pergolas, recommended. The small BVI Folk Museum in a lovely old wooden building on Main Street behind *Pusser's Bar* is opened on request.

Around the island

There are also communities at East End and West End. **West End** has more facilities for visitors. *Sopers Hole* is a port of entry (ferries to St Thomas, St John and Jost Van Dyke leave from here) and popular meeting place for people on yachts. *Pussers* is alongside the moorings and there are several shops, including a dive shop and some boutiques. All the buildings are painted in bright pinks and blues. It is very relaxing to sip cocktails on the dock and watch the yachts come and go. The *Jolly Roger*, on the opposite side of the bay is a popular yachtie hangout. The area is famous for being the former home of Edward Teach (Blackbeard the pirate).

Tortola

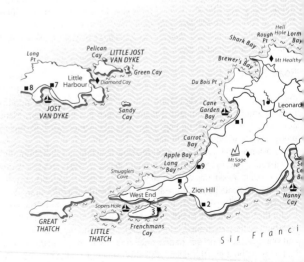

N

Not to scale

The best beaches are along the northwest and north coasts. **Smugglers Cove**, **Long Bay** and **Apple Bay**, West End, have fine sandy beaches. If you have no transport, Smugglers Cove is an hour's walk on a dirt road over a steep hill from West End. The beach is usually deserted. **Cane Garden Bay** is the best beach and yachts can anchor there. There are two reefs with a marked gap in between. The Callwood Rum Distillery at Cane Garden Bay still produces rum with copper boiling vats and an old still and cane crusher in much the same way as it did in the 18th century. Apple Bay is popular with surfers from November for a few months, as is the east end of Cane Garden Bay and **Josiah's Bay**. **Brewers Bay** is a long curving bay with plenty of shade and a small campsite in the trees by the beach. Elizabeth Bay and Long Bay, East End, are also pleasant beaches. **Carrot Bay** is stony, there is no sand, but there are lots of pelicans and the village is pleasant, having a very Caribbean feel with several bars, palm trees and banana plants. Watch out for strong rip currents at some of the north shore beaches, and seek local advice before swimming, especially if the surfers are out.

Tortola is superb, but the full flavour of the BVI can only be discovered by cruising round the other islands. You can also take day trips on the regular ferry to Virgin Gorda, with lunch and a visit to The Baths included if you wish.

Essentials

Road Town LL-AL *Treasure Isle*, on hillside overlooking the marina and Sir Francis Drake **Sleeping**
Channel, PO Box 68, T4942501, F4942507. 40 rooms and 3 suites, pool, tennis, restaurant, a/c, TV, convenient for business travellers, used by people on crewed yacht charters for first and last night, helpful staff at front desk. Under same ownership and used by *Treasure Isle* for all watersports is the **LL-A** *Moorings/Mariner Inn*, at the dockside for bareboat charters, PO

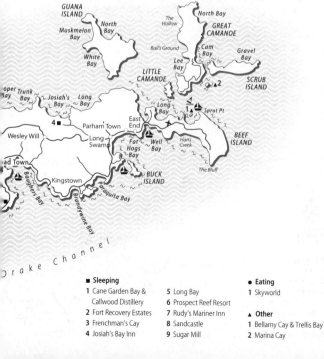

■ Sleeping		● Eating
1 Cane Garden Bay & Callwood Distillery	5 Long Bay	1 Skyworld
2 Fort Recovery Estates	6 Prospect Reef Resort	▲ Other
3 Frenchman's Cay	7 Rudy's Mariner Inn	1 Bellamy Cay & Trellis Bay
4 Josiah's Bay Inn	8 Sandcastle	2 Marina Cay
	9 Sugar Mill	

British Virgin Islands

Box 139, T4942332, F4942226. 36 standard rooms with kitchenette, 4 suites, fan, tennis, small pool by bar, briefing room for those setting out on yachts, informal and relaxed but well organized, *Underwater Safaris* dive shop on site. **L-AL** *Village Cay Resort and Marina*, PO Box 145, directly opposite on the other side of the harbour, T4942771, F4942773, www.villagecay.com. 18 clean, bright rooms, well-furnished although a bit sterile, TV, phone, cheaper rooms face inland, restaurant and bar overlooking yachts, good food, buffet with entertainment Fri 1800-2300, also showers, toilets and launderette for sailors. **LL-A** *Maria's By The Sea*, PO Box 206, T4942595, F4942420. By new government buildings, overlooks sea but no beach, older part is simple, all have kitchenette, a/c, TV, phone, double beds, new wing has bigger rooms, balconies, conference room, friendly, Maria's cooking recommended, specials include lobster, conch, steak, light and airy entrance with bar, pool. **L-C** *Sea View Hotel*, PO Box 59, T4942483, F4944952, jumukhal@surfbvi.com 22 rooms, 1

Road Town

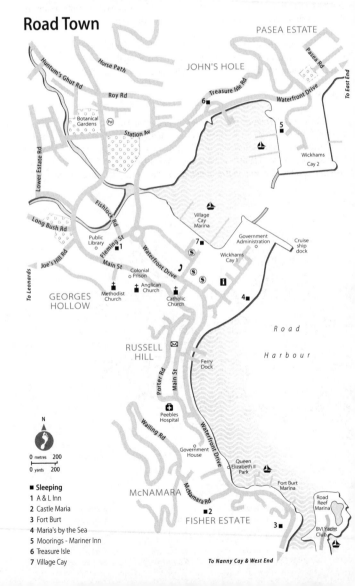

■ Sleeping
1 A & L Inn
2 Castle Maria
3 Fort Burt
4 Maria's by the Sea
5 Moorings - Mariner Inn
6 Treasure Isle
7 Village Cay

British Virgin Islands

efficiency apartment, pool, quite noisy because of traffic but good value, 200 m further on is **LL-A** *Fort Burt*, on hillside opposite Marina, PO Box 3380, T4942587, F4942002, fortburt @surfbvi.com Fort built by Dutch, first hotel on island built 1953, renovated 1998, 12 rooms, 6 suites, 2 of which have plunge pool, restaurant and bar, convenient location, good views. **AL-B** *Hotel Castle Maria*, up the hill overlooking Road Town, PO Box 206, T4942553, F4942111, hotelcastlemaria@surfbvi.com 30 rooms, some triple and quads, kitchenette, a/c, cable TV, pool, restaurant, bar, car rentals, popular with local business travellers. **B** *A & L Inn*, 3 Fleming St, PO Box 403, T4946343, F4946656. 14 rooms with 2 double beds, a/c, TV, phone, café. About the cheapest on the island is **C-D** *Wayside Inn Guest House*, Road Town, near library, PO Box 258, T4943606. 20 rooms, with fan, adequate but basic, shared bathrooms but not very clean.

South coast Heading west from Road Town you come to **LL-A** *Prospect Reef Resort*, PO Box 104, T4943311, F4945595, www.prospectreef.com A 15-acre resort specializing in package holidays, wide variety of rooms, studios, town houses and villas, some with sea view, some without, comfortable, welcoming, tennis, pitch and put, sea water pool, freshwater swimming lane pool, diving pool, health and fitness centre, *Baskin in the Sun* dive shop, marina, sailing, fishing, café and restaurant, conference centre for 150, car rental, complimentary sports equipment, boutiques, shuttle service. **LL-B** *Nanny Cay Resort and Marina*, PO Box 281, T4942512, F4943288. 42 rooms, a/c, TV, VCRs, kitchenette, phone, deluxe rooms have 2 queen-size beds, standard rooms are darker, smaller, restaurants, bars, boutiques, tennis, *Blue Water Divers* dive shop, car rental, windsurfing and sailing, used by short stay people going out on bareboat charters. **LL-L** *Villas at Fort Recovery Estate*, PO Box 239, T4954354, F4954036, www.fortrecovery.com 17 spacious and nicely furnished a/c villas of different sizes on small beach. Breakfast included, built around 17th-century Dutch fort, commissary, no restaurant, but à la carte room service available including complimentary dinner and snorkel trip for stays of over 7 nights, yoga, massage, good snorkelling offshore, pool, car essential. **LL-AL** *Frenchman's Cay Hotel*, PO Box 1054, West End, T4954844, F4954056, www.frenchmans.com Beautiful hillside location on the cay overlooking the south coast of Tortola, 9 villas, all with view, fans, phone, a quiet resort with lots of repeat business, small sandy beach with reef for snorkelling, hammocks, tennis (fee for non-guests), pool, library, games, short trail out to point, Sun beach barbecue, bar, restaurant, TV in clubhouse. **A-C** *Jolly Roger Inn*, T4954559, F4954184, www.jollyrogerbvi.com A small inn and bar on waterfront at Sopers Hole. Run by New Yorkers, live music at weekends so do not stay here if you want peace and quiet, convenient for ferries (see above), 6 brightly decorated, clean rooms, some with shared bathroom, fans, screens, singles, doubles, triples available, good breakfasts, busy restaurant and bar, meeting place. *Little Thatch*, PO Box 8309, St John, USVI 00831, T4959227, F4959212, thatch@surfbvi.com A 54-acre private island off West End and Soper's Hole. Has been developed with a main house sleeping 10 and 5 cottages, pool, beach bar, watersports, volleyball, table tennis, badminton, US$9,250-10,550 all-inclusive island rental, 3 nights minimum.

West coast Heading northeast, **LL-L** *Long Bay Beach Resort*, PO Box 433, T4954252, www.longbay.com 80rooms, studios and villas spread along the beach and up the hillside, a/c, TV, phone, fridge, 130-ft pool, the biggest in the BVI, tennis, pitch and put, spa and gym, car rental, 2 restaurants with vegetarian options, bars, surfboards, snorkelling equipment, nice beach, sandy with some rocks, level of sand can shift depending on season. **LL-B** *Sebastian's On The Beach*, PO Box 441, Apple Bay, T4954212, F4954466, www.sebastiansbvi.com Located either side of road, informal and popular surfers' hangout, 8 comfortable beachfront rooms with balcony, 4 rear rooms which connect, 12 more rooms across the road at rear of office around patio, 2 rooms above office, 10% service, fans, fridge, payphones, grocery 0800-2200, restaurant/bar overlooking sandy beach, happy hour 1600-1800, blend own rum, surfboards and boogieboards for rent. Expanding in 2000 with the construction of *Sebastian's Cliffhouse Villas*, 9 luxury 2-bedroomed suites with huge balconies and views to Jost Van Dyke, fully equipped and every comfort. **LL-AL** *Sugar Mill Hotel*, PO Box 425, Little Apple Bay, T4954355, F4954696, www.sugarmillhotel.com 21

British Virgin Islands

rooms, most with kitchenettes, prestigious restaurant, beach bar, pool, no children in season. Along this stretch of coast there are lots of rental villas, many of which are advertised simply with a notice outside, usually about US$90 per day. At the upper end of the scale, **Areana Villas**, PO Box 263, T4945864, F4947626, www.areanavillas.com Several villas for rent, the cheapest in winter at US$1,400 per week and the most expensive at US$10,500 per week, most have daily maid service, **Sunset House** has a cook as well. **B-C** *Cane Garden Bay (Rhymer's) Beach Hotel*, Cane Garden Bay, PO Box 570, T4954639, F4954820. 27 basic but clean rooms, most with double bed and single bed, right on sandy beach, beach towels provided, store and shop, laundromat, restaurant/bar on beach, watersports companies on either side of hotel. **LL-B** *Ole Works Inn*, Cane Garden Bay, T4954837, F4959618, oleworks@candwbvi.net Built around 300-year-old sugar factory, on beach, 18 rooms, honeymoon tower, bar, restaurant, gift shop. **AL-B** *Sunset Vacation Apartments*, T4954751, F4959114. 8 1-bedroom and 2 2-bedroom apartments, close to beach, maid service. **AL-A** *ELM Beach Suites*, PO Box 96, T4942888, F4946455, elm@surfbvi.com 5 1-bedroom apartments, on the beach, beach bar serves lunch, cable TV, gift shop.

North coast **LL-B** *Lambert Beach Resort*, PO Box 534, East End, T4952877, F4952876, lambert@caribsurf.com On a beautiful cove, 38 rooms and suites in villas which can sleep 8, beach-front dining, pool, tennis, watersports, boat trips, diving and other excursions can be arranged, library, videos, Italian-owned, Italian décor. **LL** *Elizabeth Beach Resort*, now managed by *Lambert Beach Resort*. 2 and 3-bedroom villas, jeep included, on hillside with spectacular views from huge verandas across bay and down to sandy beach below. **LL** *Elizabeth Beach Villa*, Box 46, Virgin Gorda, T4959458, F4957034, trotter@surfbvi.com Run by Nick and Jenny Trotter, great view, huge doors onto 200 sq ft veranda with covered eating area, 3 bedrooms, a/c, beach, use of nearby resort's facilities. **A-B** *Josiah's Bay Inn*, PO Box 925, Josiah's Bay, T/F4951488, jbibvi@yahoo.com Short walk to beach, 1-4 bedroom apartments, kitchens, TV, balconies with sea view, weekly rates, maid service twice a week, popular with surfers, take insect repellent, close to 4 beaches. **LL-AL** *Josiah's Bay Cottages*, run by Best Vacations, Box 306, Road Town, T4946186, F4942000, bestvac @surfbvi.com 9 1-bedroom cottages in garden, 5-min walk to beach, pool.

East End **A-C** *Seabreeze Yacht Charters & Hotel*, PO Box 528, East End, T4951560, F4951561. 8 rooms for sailors, marina, yacht charters, pool, commissary. **LL-A** *Tropic Island Villas*, PO Box 3012, Road Town, Maya Cove, T4952002, F4952155, www.tropicisland.com Studios and 2 bedroom apartments.

Camping At *Brewer's Bay Campground* on north coast, PO Box 185, T4943463. Bare site US$10, tent hire US$35 for 2 people, babysitters available, beach bar and simple restaurant.

Self catering There is lots of self-catering accommodation in what are variously known as houses, villas, apartments, guest houses, 'efficiencies' or 'housekeeping units'. Prices are usually set on a weekly basis according to size and standard of luxury, and there is often a 30-40% discount in the summer. Contact the tourist office for a full list and individual brochures.

Eating **Road Town** Restaurants serving West Indian specialities include *C & F Restaurant*, Purcell Estate, T4944941. Very popular with visitors and locals, excellent local food, slow but friendly service, dinner 1830-2300. *Mario's*, Palm Grove Shopping Centre, T4943883. West Indian specialities, clean, a/c, good service, generous portions, open daily 0700-2300, happy hour 1700-1900. *New Happy Lion*, next to Botanic Gardens, T4942574. Mon-Sat from 0700, noted for fresh fish and local dishes, also apartments to rent. *Beach Club Terrace*, at Baughers Bay, T4942272. Open 0800-2200, fish, mutton, conch and other West Indian food. *Aries Club*, Baughers Bay, T4941537. 0700-2200, Mon-Sat, West Indian, seafood specialities. *Roti Palace*, Russel Hill, T4944196. East Indian specialities from Trinidad and Guyana, huge rotis. *The Fish Trap*, at the Columbus Centre, behind Village Cay Marina, T4943626. Open for lunch 1130-1500 Mon-Fri, 1130-1400 Sat and dinner daily 1830-2300, open-air, reservations recommended, good seafood, inside is a popular yachtie bar open 1630-late serving good lower-priced bar meals. *The Captain's Table*, on the waterfront by Village Cay Marina, T4943885. A French restaurant serving escargots, lobster, fish, lunch Mon-Fri, dinner daily from 1800. *Pusser's Co Store & Pub* on Main St, Road Town, T4943897. Yachties' meeting place, good pub atmosphere, open 1100-2200, on ground floor bar, store and restaurant for simple dishes such as English pies and New York deli sandwiches, nickel beer on Thu, really is US$0.05 but not recommended, Tue 'ladies night', 'pain killer' cocktails recommended, strongest is 'brain killer', *Pusser's* also at Sopers Hole, Marina Cay and Leverick Bay. Visit 3 and get *Pusser's* banner. *Tavern in the Town*, Road Town, next to *Pusser's*, T4942790. Traditional English pub food and atmosphere, sells Newcastle Brown Ale, garden looks out across harbour, open 1100-2300, closed Sat. *Mac's*, in the Clarence M Christian Building, T4946364. Local dishes, salads, pizza and pastries, open 0700-2000. *Midtown Restaurant*, Main St, T4942764. Curried conch, baked chicken, beef, whelk, saltfish, Mon-Sat 0700-2300. *Mr Fritz Oriental Restaurant*, in the Little Denmark building, T4945592. Classic Chinese dishes, lunch 1130-1530, dinner 1730 onwards. *Capriccio di Mare*, Waterfront Drive by ferry dock, over-looking water, T4945369. Italian café serving excellent coffee and delicious, if overpriced, snacks and continental lunches, open 0800-2100, Mon-Sat. *Spaghetti Junction*, Waterfront Drive opposite Palm Grove shopping centre upstairs in small blue building, T4944880. Italian, seafood and Caribbean dishes, open 1800-2200. *Cafésito*, in Romasco building, T4947412. West Indian and international food, daily specials, 1100-2300. *BVI Steak, Chop and Pasta House*, in *Hotel Castle Maria*, T4945433. Overlooking harbour, good food, congenial hosts Tom and Fran, open daily 0730-1000, 1130-1400, 1800-2200. *Virgin Queen*, Road Town, T4942310. Homemade pizza plus West Indian and European food, a popular watering hole for English and American residents, open 1100-2400, Sun-Fri, last orders for food 2200, 1800 until late on Sat. *Crandall's Pastry Plus*, T4945156. West Indian bakery across from Road Reef Marina, also rotis and main meals, 0800-1700. *Scato's Snack Bar*, T4942230. Above Sylvia's laundromat on Flemming Street, open daily 1200-2200, local dishes.

Nanny Cay *The Struggling Man*, Sea Cows Bay, between Road Town and Nanny Cay, T4944163. West Indian, breakfast, lunch and dinner. *Marina Plaza Café*, Nanny Cay Marina, T4944895. 0700-2100, Caribbean specials and international dishes. *Peg Leg Landing*, water's edge at Nanny Cay. Open from 1600, happy hour 1630-1830, bar meals from 1630, dinners from 1900.

West End *Pusser's Landing*, T4954554 and *Jolly Roger*, T4954559, fun, yachtie hangout, good pizza and burgers, good cheap breakfast, open 0700-2300, and many more excellent restaurants in the hotels and yacht clubs. *Frenchman's Cay Hotel*, T4954844. Breakfast 0800-1030, lunch 1130-1430, dinner 1830-2100, closed Mon, West Indian and continental cuisine, pool and tennis court available for diners.

Apple Bay *The Sugar Mill*, in an old mill in Apple Bay, T4954355, run by Californians, Jinx and Jefferson Morgan. Gourmet and elegant, 4-course dinner 1900, reservations, their cookbook is on-line, with some 250 recipes, hotel attached, breakfast and lunch at beach bar. *The Apple*, Little Apple Bay, T4954437. Specializes in local seafood dishes, happy hour 1700-1900 with coconut chips and conch fritters. *Sebastian's On The Beach*, T4954212. Breakfast, lunch, dinner, international, happy hour 1600-1800.

Carrot Bay *Mrs Scatliffe's*, T4954556. Upstairs in a yellow and white building opposite the Primary School, local cuisine, home grown fruit and vegetables, family fungi performance some evenings after dinner, lunch Mon-Fri 1200-1400, dinner daily 1900-2100, reservations essential. *Palm's Delight*, on the water, T4954863. Restaurant and snack bar, delicious barbecue and local cuisine, rotis and shrimp creole, open 1800-2200. *North Shore Shell Museum*, T4954714. Cracked conch, lobster, West Indian cooking, breakfast, lunch and dinner, happy hour 1600-1800. *Clem's By The Sea*, T4954350. West Indian specialities, goat stew, boiled fish and fungi, steel band, Mon, Sat, open 0900 until late.

British Virgin Islands

Cane Garden Bay You can 'Jump Up' (Caribbean music), almost every night at *Rhymers*, T4954639. Serves breakfast, lunch and dinner, lobster special Thu night. Folk music at *Quito's Gazebo*, T4954837. Restaurant and beach bar at north end of Cane Garden Bay, lunch 1130-1500, rotis and burgers, dinner 1830-2130, fish fry Fri, closed Mon, local art work for sale. *Round Hill Catering*, T4959353. Open Mon, Tue, Thu, Fri, Sat, 1830-2130, reservations needed, home cooked local dishes served on balcony. There are a number of small restaurants serving excellent food along the road going towards the rum distillery ruins; check in the late afternoon to make reservations and find out what the menu will be.

Inland 10 mins' drive from Road Town or Cane Garden Bay is the *Skyworld Restaurant*, T4943567. With a panoramic view of all the Virgin Islands, food and prices reasonable, open from 1000, lunch 1130-1430, dinner 1700-1945, recommended for view. *Mario's Mountain View*, at the foot of Sage Mountain National Park, T4959536. Continental and local dishes, lunch 1100-1500, dinner 1830-2200.

East End *Brandywine Bay Restaurant*, run by Cele and Davide Pugliese, T4952301, F4951203. 10 mins' drive from Road Town, one of the most exclusive restaurants on Tortola, indoor and outdoor dining, grills and Florentine food, cocktails 1730, dinner 1830-2100, closed Sun, reservations, Channel 16, anchorage 15-ft draft. *De Cal*, T4951429, on Blackburn Highway at Fat Hog's Bay. Local style, rotis, pizza, breakfast, lunch, dinner, 0700-2200. *Pelican Roost*, at Tropic Island Yachts overlooking Maya Cove, T4951515. 0800-2200, conch, fritters, fresh fish. *Bing's Drop Inn Bar and Restaurant*, at Fat Hog's Bay, T4952627. Home cooked dinners, excellent conch fritters, also after hours dance spot.

If you are self-catering, you can get reasonably priced food from *K Mart's* and other supermarkets at Port Purcell or at the *Rite Way* supermarkets a little closer to town. At the entrance to the *Moorings*, Wickhams Cay II, is the *Bon Appetit Deli*, T4945199. Where you can get cheese and wine as well as regular provisions; they also do sandwiches and lunch specials and party services. In Road Town is *Fort Wines Gourmet Shop*, T4942388, a wine shop with a high class image but reasonable prices, you can also eat there, excellent light snacks (eg quiche) and wine by the glass.

Nightlife In Road Town, *The Pub*, at Fort Burt Marina, T4942608. Dancing Fri-Sat, they also serve lunches and dinners, happy hour 1700-1900 daily and all day Fri with free hot wings 1700-1900 and music 1800-2200. *Stone's Nest* is a weekend disco in Road Town, T4945182. The hotels organize live bands and movie nights. At East End is *Bing's Drop Inn Bar*, see above. *Pusser's Landing*, at Frenchman's Cay, T4954554. Bands on Fri and Sat. *Jolly Roger*, at West End, T4954559. Live music most weekends and often has visiting bands, call for details. *Bomba's Shack*, on the beach in Apple Bay, T4954148. Music Wed and Sun, famous full moon party every month, sleep before you go, the party goes on all night. *Romeo's*, Apple Bay, T4954307. Thu barbecue and music, Sat fish fry and music. *Quito's Gazebo*, Cane Garden Bay, T4954837. Live music nightly and the beat is quickened at weekends and holidays, making it a popular beach front dance spot. *Calamaya*, Maya Cove, on the dock side at Hodge's Creek Marina, T4952126. Breakfast, lunch, dinner, Fri live music, happy hour with tapas 1600-1800, bar menu.

Directory **Laundry** *Sylvia's Laundromat*, next to Public Library on Flemming St, Road Town, T4942230. *Freeman's Laundromat*, beside Barclays Bank, Wickham's Cay, T4942285. Marinas usually have laundromats. See telephone listings for out of town laundries.

Beef Island This island was famed as a hunting ground for beef cattle during the buccaneer days. The island is linked to Tortola by the Queen Elizabeth bridge. The main airport of the BVI is here. (Taxi to Road Town, US$15.) Long Bay beach is on the north shore. Also Trellis Bay which has an excellent harbour and bars. *The Last Resort*, run by Englishman Tony Snell, based on Bellamy Cay, provides a lavish buffet menu plus one-man show cabaret, bar open all day, happy hour 1700-1900, dinner 1930, cabaret 2130, ferry service available, reservations required, T4952520 or channel 16. Also *Boardsailing* BVI, the *Conch Shell Point Restaurant* (T4952285, VHF Ch 16) and a painting and jewellery shop. **LL-A** *Beef Island Guest House* has four rooms on the beach, PO Box 494, East End, T4952303, F4951611, food available at its *De Loose Mongoose Bar*, VHF Ch 16, 0800-1600, 1800-2100, mostly burgers and sandwiches. *Airport Restaurant*, T4952323, West Indian, open from 0730, dinner by reservation. Villas include **LL** *Allamanda Estate*, Box 848, Road Town, T4951473. **LL** *Well Bay Villas and Beach*, Box 149, Road Town, T4952328. T/F4952206.

Marina Cay

This tiny private island of six acres just north of Beef Island was where Robb White wrote his book *Our Virgin Isle*, which was made into a film starring Sidney Poitier and John Cassavetes. A charming cottage hotel, **LL-AL** *Pusser's Marina Cay*, comprises most of the island, which is encircled by a reef, offering some of the best snorkelling in the BVI. Marina facilities (boats use mooring buoys and a dinghy dock), laundry, showers, diving, kayaking, sailing, snorkelling et cetera, there are four rooms and two villas available, MAP, T4942174, F4944775, marinacy@surfbvi.com, or VHF ch 16, PO Box 626, Road Town. Bar, restaurant, beach barbecue on Friday, Pussers Co Store, selling clothes and travel accessories. Ferry service from Trellis Bay jetty, eight daily, ferries after 1900 on request for restaurant guests only. If sailing, enter from the north.

Guana Island

North of Tortola, Guana Island is an 850-acre private island and wildlife sanctuary as well as having a very expensive hotel. **LL** *Guana Island*, PO Box 32, Road Town, T4942354, F4952900, www.guana.com 15 rooms in stone cottages, 1 secluded beach house, tennis, restaurant, watersports, US$35 for airport transfers, no credit cards. The island is available for rent for up to 30 guests. The owners discourage visitors apart from guests, in order to keep the island a sanctuary for wildlife. A few flamingos have been introduced to the island. They live in a small pond where the salinity fluctuates widely so their diets are supplemented with food and water if they need it. The birds used to live in a zoo, so they are fairly tame.

The Dogs

Northeast of Tortola are The Dogs, small uninhabited islands. West Dog is a national park. On Great Dog you can see frigate birds nesting. The islands are often used as a stopping off point when sailing from North Sound to Jost Van Dyke, and are popular with divers coming from North Sound. The dive sites are not spectacular but there are some interesting rock formations, with canyons and bridges. The best anchorages are on George Dog to the west of Kitchen Point and on the south side of Great Dog.

Virgin Gorda

British Virgin Islands

Over a century ago, Virgin Gorda was the centre of population and commerce. It is now better known as the site of the geological curiosity called The Baths, where enormous boulders form a natural swimming pool and underwater caves. The island is seven miles long and the north half is mountainous, with a peak 1,370 ft high, while the south half is relatively flat.

Population: 5,000

Around the island

There are some 20 secluded beaches; the most frequented are **Devil's Bay**, **Spring Bay**, and **Trunk Bay** on the west coast. Between Devil's Bay and Spring Bay are **The Baths**. The snorkelling here is good, especially going left from the beach. Climbing over and around the boulders is fun for the adventurous and there is an easy trail with ladders and bridges for those who are not so agile. However, exploring in the water with a mask and snorkel is the recommended way to do it. Unfortunately the popularity of The Baths with tour companies and cruise ships has led to overcrowding. There are many day trips from Tortola and when a cruise ship is in port you can not move on the beach. Choose carefully which day you visit. North of the island is **North Sound**, formed to the south and east by Virgin Gorda, to the north by Prickly Pear Island, and to the west by Mosquito Island. On the southeast tip is **Copper Mine Point**, where the Spaniards mined copper, gold and silver some 400 years ago; the remains of a mine built by Cornish miners in 1838 can be seen and work is being done, as funds permit, to stabilize the Engine House and other ruins. The rocky façade here is reminiscent of the Cornish coast of England. The amateur geologist will find stones such as malachite and crystals embedded in quartz. All land on Virgin Gorda over 1,000 ft high is now a national park, where trails have been blazed for walking. Just off the southwest tip of the island is **Fallen Jerusalem**, an islet which is now a National Park. There is a 3,000-ft airstrip near the main settlement, **Spanish Town**. The Virgin Gorda Yacht Harbour is here and besides the marina facilities with full yachting chandlery, there is a good supermarket, dive centre, bar/restaurant, a craft shop selling stamps, souvenir and clothes shops and phones, post box and taxis. **Bitter End** and **Biras Creek** are good anchorages and both have a hotel and restaurant. *Biras Creek* charges US$15 for moorings; yachtsmen may use Deep Bay beach but others are reserved for hotel guests. *Bitter End* charges US$20 including water taxi to shore in the evenings. There is no road to either resort, you have to get a hotel launch from Gun Creek or the North Sound Express from Beef Island to *Bitter End Resort & Yacht Club*. Saba Rock is just off *Bitter End*; formerly the home of the *Pirate's Pub and Grill*, now the *Saba Rock Resort*.

Essentials

Sleeping **South LL** *Little Dix Bay*, PO Box 70, Virgin Gorda, T4955555, F4955661, Rosewood@ GTE.net Luxury 98-roomed chalet hotel, with four 1-bedroom suites, on ½-mile beach, watersports arranged, tennis, health and fitness centre, hiking trails in surrounding hills, quiet, lovely gardens in extensive grounds, no TV or pool, strict dress code after sunset, 70% repeat guests in winter, honeymooners in summer, children's programme isolated from rest

Virgin Gorda

■ **Sleeping**
1 Biras Creek Estate
2 Bitter End Yacht Club
3 Drake's Anchorage
4 Fischer's Cove
5 Guavaberry Spring Bay
6 Leverick Bay
7 Little Dix Bay
8 Mango Bay Resort
9 Nail Bay Estate Villas
10 Ocean View
11 Olde Yard Inn
12 Paradise Beach Resort

British Virgin Islands

of resort, lots of packages available, in USA T800-9283000, also owns and operates the airport and the Virgin Gorda Yacht Harbour, a large marina in St Thomas Bay offering most facilities. **LL-C** *Ocean View/The Wheelhouse*, PO Box 66, T4955230. 12 rooms, close to ferry and harbour, pink building, small rooms but adequately furnished, TV, fan, a/c, restaurant, bar. **AL-B** *Bay View Vacation Apartments*, The Valley, Box 1018, T4955224, F4955329. 2-bedroom apartments, kitchen, near town and beach, contact Nora Potter. **LL-AL** *Fischer's Cove Beach Hotel*, St Thomas Bay, PO Box 60, T4955252, F4955820, www.islandsonline.com/fischerscove 12 studio rooms, some with fan, some a/c, or 8 cottages with kitchenette, less space, some beachfront, balcony restaurant overlooking sea open 0730-2200, beach barbecue when calm. **LL-A** *Guavaberry Spring Bay*, run by Tina and Ludwig Goschler, PO Box 20, T4955252, F4955283, www.guavaberryspringbay.com Well-equipped wooden cottages, beautiful location, friendly, sandy beach with shade 5 mins' walk through grounds, to the south are The Baths, to the north The Crawl, a National Park enclosing a natural swimming pool and more boulders. They also manage **LL** *Island Time*, Little Trunk Bay, 5 bedrooms and bathrooms in separate units, tennis, pool, **LL** *On-The-Rocks*, Little Trunk Bay, 2 bedrooms, covered terrace, large garden, beach, **LL** *Las Brisas*, Top of the Baths, 2 bedrooms and **LL** *Casa Rocalta*, Spring Bay, 3 bedrooms. *Toad Hall*, contact Stephen and Marie Green, PO Box 7, T4955397, F4955708, www.toadhallvg.com Luxury rental home, 3 bedrooms with garden showers, private access to The Baths beach along spectacular wooden walkway, pool among the boulders, caves to explore, great for agile children, US$3,500-4,500 per week. **LL-A** *Olde Yard Inn*, owned by Carol Kaufman, PO Box 26, T4955544, 800-6539273, F4955986, oldeyard@surfbvi.com Convenient for airport, 14 rooms, 1 suite, a/c available, downstairs rooms rather dark, pool, jacuzzi, health spa, poolside restaurant, St Lucian chef, good food, pleasant gardens, library with piano, games room, croquet, hammocks, small shop, complimentary shuttle or 10-15 mins on trail to beach, family-run. There are several villas to rent around The Valley and Spring Bay and a few agencies, eg Virgin Gorda Villa Rentals, Box 63, T800-8487081, 4957421, leverick@surfbvi.com

North Up the west coast, north of the Valley are two resorts which were built as one, so the villas are the same, **LL-A** *Mango Bay*, PO Box 1062, T4955672, F4955674, mangobay@surfbvi.com 5 villas which can make 1-bedroomed units or the apartments can be connected to provide 2 or 3 bedrooms, very clean, light and airy, tiled floors, light colours, a/c, phone, also 5-bedroomed villa, *Katiche Point*, with its own horizon swimming pool, sunken bath made out of Virgin Gorda boulders in the master bedroom and hammocks in the Crow's Nest for great views, pretty shrubbery, narrow sandy beach, lovely sea view, jetty, kayaks, Italian management. **LL-AL** *Paradise Beach*, PO Box 1105, T4955871, F4955872, www.islandsonline.com/paradisebeach 7 units in 3 houses, snorkelling and fishing gear available, dinghy, quiet, rental car included. Further north at Nail Bay is a new development of villas, apartments and hotel, **LL-L** *Nail Bay Estate Villas*, T4948000, F4955875, www.nailbay.com They now manage *Diamond Beach Villas*, *Flame Trees*, *Sunset Watch* and *Turtle Bay Villa*, summer packages include car hire and you can also book dive packages. On the north coast is **L-AL** *Leverick Bay Hotel and Vacation Villas*, PO Box 63, T4957421, F4957367, leverick@surfbvi.com Offering a wide variety of spacious accommodation from hotel rooms to villas and condominiums built up a hillside with a great view of the jetty and the bay, *Pussers* is on site and all the buildings are painted the bright multi-colours which are *Pussers'* emblem, use *Pussers'* restaurant or cross the water to *Drake's Anchorage* on Mosquito Island opposite, tennis, pool, watersports, *Dive BVI* operates from here, food store, laundry, shops, beauty therapy and massage at *The Spa*, T4957375. Perhaps the most exclusive resort on the island is **LL** *Biras Creek*, PO Box 54, T4943555, F4943557, biras@surfbvi.com Member of the Relais et Chateaux group, reached by launch from Gun Creek, or on the North Sound Express from Beef Island, on a spit of land overlooking both North Sound and Berchers Bay. Luxury, beautifully decorated cottages and grand suites spread along the Atlantic coast, no children under 6, those under 8 are not allowed in the dining room but have early dinner and babysitter, no phones or a/c, 2 floodlit tennis courts with pro, sailing trips and other watersports arranged, free watersports instruction, small pool overlooking ocean, nice little beach in sheltered bay with mangroves, very private, beach barbecues, good menu and

British Virgin Islands

wonderful view from the split level restaurant, popular with honeymooners, sailing packages with some nights on board available. **LL** *The Bitter End Yacht Club and Resort*, North Sound, PO Box 46, T4942746, 800-8722392. Reached by launch from Gun Creek or the North Sound Express from Beef Island (US$18 one-way) or by yacht. Refurbished in 1999 in multi-million dollar project. Lively, popular, action-packed for water lovers with a marina, sailing in all sizes of boats for all ages, yacht charters, facilities for visiting yachts, fishing (reef and bone), windsurfing, diving, anything any water lover would want, plus instruction, stay on your boat, charter one of the 8 liveaboard yachts, or use the 100 rooms and chalets, comfortable big beds, very spread out along coastal hillside (used to be 2 resorts), can be a long walk from your room to the clubhouse but taxi service available, the older, cheaper rooms are closest, 3 restaurants, the *Clubhouse and Seafood Grill, the Carvery* and *the Emporium Pub*, shops, food stores, conference room, new telecommunications system, free room for children in summer, lots of packages or room only rates.

Eating   For upmarket, elegant dining try *Biras Creek*, T4943555. 5-course fixed price dinner plus 15% service, 1930-2100, dress smartly. *Little Dix Bay*, T4955555 ext 174. 3 full service restaurants open 0700-2100. *Bitter End Yacht Club*, T4942746. For the sailing fraternity, champagne breakfast US$15, buffet lunch US$20, dinner US$30. *Giorgio's Table*, Mahoe Bay, T4955684. Next to *Mango Bay* resort, authentic Italian food, 80% of ingredients imported from Italy, open 0900-2200. *Olde Yard Inn*, international food in a garden setting, small, intimate, classical music, lunch and dinner. Restaurants serving West Indian recipes include *Anything Goes*, The Valley, T4955062, VHF Ch16. Curries and seafood, 1100-2200, takeaway and delivery locally; *The Wheelhouse*, at *Ocean View Hotel* by Yacht Harbour, T4955230. Chicken or fresh fish served curried or with native sauce; *Spanish Town Café*, T4955555 ext 201. Gourmet food from the chefs at *Little Dix Bay Resort* at the commissary at the Yacht Harbour; *Fischers Cove*, T4955252. International and local food and beach barbecues. Also *Crab Hole*, South Valley, T4955307. Locals eat here, inexpensive West Indian food, curries, roti, callalou, conch, entertainment on Fri 0930-2400. *Lobster Pot*, at *Andy's Chateau de Pirate*, T4955252, VHF 16. Beach pig roast on Mon, seafood buffet on Thu, barbecue on Sat, all boat captains receive 'bliss pirate' cocktail and 30% off main course with ID. *The Bath and Turtle*, Virgin Gorda Yacht Harbour, T4955239. Standard pub fare, open 0730-2200 daily, live entertainment Wed, good place to wait for the ferry. *Pusser's* Leverick Bay, T4957369. Breakfast and lunch 0800-1800 at beach bar, dinner 1800-2200 on the veranda, steaks, seafood, pies. *Rock Café & Sports Bar*, T4945482. Open daily, mix of Italian and Caribbean dishes, moonlight parties and round the world sports. *Mad Dog*, next to the parking lot at The Baths, T4955830. Drinks, sandwiches, T-shirts and friendly conversation, open 1000-1900. *Poor Man's Bar*, on the beach at The Baths. Also selling T-shirts, open 0930-1800, be sure to bring a bottle of water just in case it is shut, toilets round the back. *Top of the Baths*, T4955497. Indoor and outdoor dining, breakfast, lunch and dinner. In the north, *Fat Virgin's Café*, at *Biras Creek*, T4957052. Waterside café by the dock, burgers, sandwiches, soups and coffee. *Saba Rock Resort*, opposite *Bitter End Yacht Club*, T4957711. Bar with deck over the water, pub grub at lunch time, buffet carvery and salad bar for dinner, also 5 rooms, water taxi service around North Sound. *Drake's Anchorage* , see below. *Sand Box*, on Prickly Pear Island, T4959122, channel 16. Beach bar, open 1100-2200, happy hour 1600-1800, Mon Ladies night, Wed lobster night, complimentary pickup from Leverick Bay, moorings, volleyball.

Nightlife   Live music at *The Bath and Turtle* and *Little Dix Bay*, live music and/or DJ at *Pirate's Pub*, *Pussers*, *Bitter End*, *Andy's Chateau*, *Mine Shaft* (also a fun place to eat), *Chez Bamboo* and *Copper Mine*. Check the bulletin board at the Virgin Gorda Yacht Harbour for special events and concerts.

Mosquito Island   Mosquito Island is privately owned by **LL** *Drake's Anchorage Resort* and enjoys beautiful views over North Sound to Virgin Gorda and Prickly Pear Island. This 125-acre island is just northwest of Leverick Bay and can only be reached by boat (complimentary 5-min boat trip to hotel from Leverick Bay). There is a lovely beach at South Bay, sandy with boulders, and there are trails leading from the hotel to this and other quiet, sandy coves but they are for hotel guests only. The island can be rented in its entirety, or you can just use the hotel, which has three villas, four suites and four rooms, all ocean front, only 24 guests, very expensive, rates include three meals and watersports, bars, restaurant open to outside diners, moorings, windsurfing, very quiet and relaxed atmosphere, PO Box 2510, Virgin Gorda, T4942254, 800-6246651, in the USA T617-9699913, F617-9691673, www.drakesanchorage.com, restaurant open 0730-1000, 1200-1400, candlelit dinner seating time 1900, French-style menu, reservations essential for dinner before 1500. Closed July, August and September.

Prickly Pear Island forms the northeast edge of North Sound. It has a lovely beach at Vixen Point with a small beach bar and a watersports centre. This is a great spot for volley ball, with a net permanently on the beach. Moorings near the *Sand Box* beach bar, with showers and ice, T4858122, VHF 16. The only legal jetski rental operation in the BVI is here. The island gets crowded when cruise ships come in.

Prickly Pear Island

This 74-acre, private island northeast of Virgin Gorda is owned by Richard Branson, who wanted a Virgin island to add to his Virgin enterprise. It is available for rent, contact Necker Island (BVI) Ltd, 1 Uxbridge Street, London W8 7TQ, T020-73136109, F77278343, toll free in USA 800-5574255, www.neckerisland.com The house and two cottages, all in Balinese style, sleep 26, fully staffed and cost an arm and a leg. New in 1999 was the Bali Cliff open-sided bedroom and bathroom, made in Indonesia and re-assembled on the island. In 2000 a Balinese beach pool and dining pavilion were constructed. Lovely beaches, protected by a coral reef, tennis and watersports provided, private. Powerboat from Beef Island, 40 minutes, expect to get soaked, or go by helicopter, or boat from Virgin Gorda, much quicker.

Necker Island

In the chain of islands running southwest from Virgin Gorda is Cooper Island, which has a beautiful beach and harbour at Manchioneel Bay with palm trees, coral reefs and **L-A** *Cooper Island Beach Club* (PO Box 859, Road Town, T4943721, F4943721, in USA Parlmes Enterprises Inc, Box 512, Turners Falls, MA 01376, T413-8633162, 800-5424624, F413-8633662, info@Cooper-Island.com). British owned and managed, there are 12 guest rooms with kitchen and bathroom, breakfast on request, lunch 1130-1430, dinner from 1830, reservations preferred, bar all day from 1000, do your grocery shopping on Tortola, electricity generator evenings only. **LL-AL** *Cooper Island Hideaways*, two beach front cottages, contact Ginny Evans, 1920 Barg Lane, Cincinnati, OH 45230-1702, T513-2324126, ginnyevans@aol.com The supply boat leaves Road Town Monday, Wednesday, Saturday, other days use *Underwater Safaris*' dive boat from *The Moorings*, Road Town; they have a small dive shop on the island and use the beach club for surface intervals or to pick up divers from yachts anchored in the bay, dive equipment for sale or rent, airfill station, photographic services.

Cooper Island
Population: 9

Very few people visit this lovely island, there are no ferries and access is only by private boat. There are two salt ponds from which salt is gathered by two ageing residents. A bag of salt is still sent to the British monarch every year as rent for the island, the remainder is sold to visitors and local restaurants. The two old men who live there welcome visitors and will show you the salt forming and packing process. They have a hut from which they sell conch shells and shell necklaces. There is a small settlement on the north side as well as a reef-protected lagoon on the east shore. The main reason people come here is for a rest stop between dives. The British mail ship *Rhone*, a 310-ft steamer, sank off Salt Island in a hurricane in 1867 and the site was used in the film *The Deep*. Those who perished were buried on Salt Island. The wreck is still almost intact in 20-80 ft of water and is very impressive. There are moorings provided at Lee Bay, just north of the *Rhone*, for those diving the wreck, to minimize anchor damage. The dive is usually divided between the bow section and the stern section; in the former you can swim through the hull at a depth of about 70 ft, be prepared for darkness. In calm weather it is possible to snorkel part of it.

Salt Island
Population: 20

British Virgin Islands

Dead Chest A tiny island in Salt Island Passage, between Salt Island and Peter Island, this is reputedly the island where the pirate Blackbeard abandoned sailors: "15 men on a Dead Man's Chest – Yo Ho Ho and a bottle of rum!".

Peter Island This 1,000-acre island has a tiny population and offers isolated, palm-fringed beaches, good anchorage and picnic spots. The exclusive, luxury, **LL** *Peter Island Resort and Yacht Harbour* reopened 1999 after a complete facelift and hurricane repairs. It is built on reclaimed land jutting out into Sir Francis Drake Channel, forming a sheltered harbour with marine facilities. Built by Norwegians, there are chalet-type cottages, harbour rooms, or beach rooms, a pool, tennis, horseriding, watersports, fitness centre, massage room, dress formally in evening, T4952000, in USA 800-3464451, F4952500, www.peterisland.com, PO Box 211, Road Town. Eight daily ferry departures from Tortola, private guest launch from Tortola or St Thomas, helicopter from St Thomas or San Juan. The marina by the dive shop has a commissary selling basic foods, snacks and ice creams, and there are shower facilities for visiting sailors.

Norman Island The island is reputed to be the 'Treasure Island' of Robert Louis Stevenson fame.
Be careful with the wild The floating bar/restaurant *William Thornton II*, T4940183 or VHF Ch 16 is
cattle: their tempers anchored in the Bight of Norman to the north of the island. The first *William Thorn-*
are unpredictable *ton*, a converted 1910 Baltic Trader sank in 1995. There is also the *Billy Bones* beach bar, open for lunch and dinner, but otherwise the island is uninhabited. Launch service from Fort Burt Marina, Road Town, daily at 1715. On its rocky west coast are caves where treasure is said to have been discovered many years ago. These can be reached by small boats and there are several day trips on offer. There is excellent snorkelling around the caves and the reef in front slopes downward to a depth of 40 ft. **The Indians** off the northwest of Norman Island are pinnacles of rock sticking out of the sea with their neighbour, the gently rounded **Pelican Island**. Together they offer the diver and snorkeller a labyrinth of underwater reefs and caves. There are moorings, US$20, and tie-up for dinghies.

Jost Van Dyke

Population: 300 Lying to the west of Tortola, the island was named after a Dutch pirate. It is mountainous, with beaches at White Bay and Great Harbour Bay on the south coast. Great Harbour looks like the fantasy tropical island, a long horseshoe shaped, white sandy beach, fringed with palm trees and dotted with beach bar/restaurants. The local people are very friendly with lots of stories to tell. Jost Van Dyke is a point of entry and has a Customs House at the end of the dock at Great Harbour. In January 1991, the island was provided with electricity for the first time and a paved road. There are moorings in Little Harbour where a marina is slowly being built and anchorages at Great Harbour, Sandy Cay and Green Cay. It is surrounded by some smaller islands, one of which is **Little Jost Van Dyke**, the birthplace of Dr John Lettsome, the founder of the British Medical Society.

Sleeping **LL-AL** *Sandcastle*, at White Bay, T4959888, F4959999, www.sandcastle-bvi.com Owned by Debby Pearse and Bruce Donath, 4 wooden cottages, basic amenities but great for total relaxation, hammocks between palm trees on the beach, snorkelling, windsurfing. *The Soggy Dollar Bar* is popular at weekends, most people arrive by boat and swim or wade ashore, aspires to be the birthplace of the infamous 'painkiller'. **LL-B** *Rudy's Mariner Inn*, Great Harbour. T4959282. 5 rooms, beach bar and restaurant, kitchenettes, grocery, water taxi. Also *Rudy's Villa*, 2 rooms, bathroom. **LL-AL** *Sandy Ground Estates*, PO Box 594, West End, Tortola, T4943391, F4959379, sandygroundjvd@candwbvi.net 8 luxury villas, provisioning, free water taxi from/to Tortola. **LL** *White Bay Villas*, T410-6267722, F6267222, jkwhitebay@aol.com 1, 2 and 3 bedroomed villas, luxury, cheaper in summer. *White Bay Campground*, T4959312. Nice site, right on beautiful, sandy, White Bay, tents US$35, or bare sites US$15 (3 people).

Little Harbour *Harris' Place*, T4959302. Open daily, bar, restaurant, grocery, water taxi, live **Eating**
music, Harris calls his place the friendliest spot in the BVIs, breakfast, lunch and dinner, happy
hour 1100-1500, live music, all you can eat lobster night on Mon, ferries from Tortola and St
Thomas/St John arranged for these feasts. *Sidney's Peace and Love*, T4959271 or VHF Ch 16.
Open from 0900, happy hour 1700-1830, pig roast Mon and Sat 1900, US$20, or all you can
eat pig and ribs, US$20, barbecue rib and chicken Sun, Tue and Thu, US$15, otherwise lunch
and dinner usual steak, fish, shrimp or lobster. *Abe's By The Sea*, T4959329, F4959529,
abes@bvimail.com Breakfast, lunch and dinner, grocery store, happy hour 1700-1800, pig
roast on Wed, US$18, call VHF Ch 16 for reservations, also has 3 rooms overlooking harbour,
can be 1 apartment, **B**, friendly family.

Great Harbour *Sandcastle* (see above), White Bay. For breakfast, lunch and gourmet, can-
dle-lit dinner (must reserve dinner and order in advance to your specifications). *Ali Baba's*,
T4959280. Run by Baba Hatchett, west of the Customs House. Breakfast, lunch and dinner,
happy hour 1600-1800. *Rudy's Mariner's Rendezvous*, reservations T4959282 or VHF Ch 16.
Open for dinner until 0100, US$12.50-22.50. *Club Paradise*, T4959267, F4959633 or VHF Ch
16. Open daily, Mon lobster special US$20, Wed pig roast US$15, live entertainment regularly, lunch 1030-1600, dinner 1800-2100. *Foxy's Bar*, T4959258. Friendly and cheap, lunch
Mon-Fri rotis and burgers, dinner daily, reservations by 1700, spontaneous calypso by Foxy,
master story-teller and musician, in afternoon until end of happy hour, big parties on New
Year's Eve and other holidays, hundreds of yachts arrive, wooden boat regatta on Labour Day
draws hundreds of boats from all over the Caribbean for a 3-day beach party, very easy to get
invited on board to watch or race, special ferry service to USVI and Tortola. *Happy Laury*,
T4959259. Very good value for breakfast, happy hour is 1500-1700, try the Happy Laury Pain
Killer. Restaurants take turns in sponsoring a pig roast nightly in season.

This small uninhabited islet just east of Jost Van Dyke is owned by Laurance **Sandy Cay**
Rockefeller. It is covered with scrub but there is a pleasant trail set out around the
whole island, which makes a good walk. Bright white beaches surround the island
and provide excellent swimming. Offshore is a coral reef.

Anegada

Unique among this group of islands because of its coral and limestone formation, *Population: 153*
the highest point is only 28 ft above sea level. There are still a few large iguanas,
which are indigenous to the island. The Anegada Rock Iguana is part of a national
parks trust breeding programme after numbers declined to only 100, largely
because juveniles fell prey to wild cats. Contact Rondel Smith, the national parks
trust warden on Anegada (also a taxi driver), who can take you to see their burrows
in the wild and the hatchlings in pens outside the Administration Building in the
Settlement. Flamingos also used to be numerous on the island but were decimated
by hunters. Twenty flamingos were released in 1992 in the ponds and four wild
ones joined them two years later. In 1995 they bred five chicks, something of a
record with flamingos reintroduced into the wild and now there are 41 birds. They
are best seen from the little bridge over The Creek on the road from the *Anegada
Reef Hotel* to the airport turn off. Hawksbill and Green Turtles nest all along the
north shore; the Government has drawn up a conservation policy and the waters
around the island are protected. The waters abound with fish and lobster, and the
extensive reefs are popular with snorkellers and scuba divers who also explore
wrecks of ships which foundered in years past. Some were said to hold treasure,
but to date only a few doubloons have been discovered. Anegada has excellent
fishing and is one of the top bone fishing spots in the world. From the wharf on the
south shore, all the way round to the west end, across the entire north shore (about
11 miles) is perfect, uninterrupted, white sandy beach. Any fences on the beach are
to keep out cattle, not people. Loblolly Bay is popular with day trippers, partly
because it has a beach bar at either end (*The Big Bamboo* at the west end is busier

British Virgin Islands

and more accessible than *Flash of Beauty* at the east end), the only places where there is shade, but also for the reef just off shore where snorkellers can explore caverns and ledges and see coral, nurse sharks, rays, turtles, barracuda and shoals of colourful fish. The beach is generally deserted. Bring water and sun screen.

The Settlement is a collection of wooden homes and some newer houses, a smart new government building, a few bars, little shops, a bakery, jeep hire and church. A short stretch of concrete road leads from The Settlement to the airport turn off; all other roads on the island are sand. There is no public transport except taxis and the best way to get around is to hire a jeep, bicycle or walk (take an umbrella for the sun or walk in the early evening). The island is very quiet and relaxed. There is an airstrip 2,500 ft long and 60 ft wide, which can handle light aircraft. Day trips by boat from Tortola are available. There is no regular ferry service.

Sleeping **LL-L** *Anegada Reef Hotel*, T4958002, F4959362 or by VHF Ch 16. 18 rooms, where there is an anchorage, fishing packages, dive equipment, beach bar, restaurant, great service, famous lobster barbecue, if arriving by yacht radio in advance for directions through the reef, minibus and bicycle hire, taxi service, boutique, closed Sep-Oct. Also under same management, **AL-B** *Anegada Reef Cottages & Villa*, at Setting Point. 2-bedrooms, 2 bathrooms. **A-B** *Ocean Range*, in the Settlement, T4959023. Single and adjoining rooms, kitchenettes available, sea view. *Anegada Beach Cottages*, Box 2710, Anegada, Pomato Point, T4959466, F916-6833304, www.anegadabeachcottages.com Rates on request, snorkelling, fishing. **L** *Bonefish Villa*, Nutmeg Point on beach, close to restaurant, T4958045, smgeorge@worldnet.att.net Includes service and taxes.

Camping *Anegada Beach Campground*, T4959466. US$20-36 prepared site, bare site US$7 per day, plus 10% service, no credit cards, beach bar, restaurant, snorkelling. *Neptune's Treasure*, T4959439. Campsite and tents available US$15-25 per night, US$90-150 per week, US$7 bare site, no cooking, restaurant on site. *Mac's Place* campsite, T4958020. 8 ft by 10 ft tent US$38, prepared sites US$15-35, showers, toilets, grills, eating area.

Eating *Pomato Point Beach Restaurant*, T4959466, VHF Ch 16, barbecue dinners, reserve by 1600. *Neptune's Treasure*, T4959439. Breakfast, lunch, dinner, camping available, delicious breads and chutneys, make sure you take some home. *Big Bamboo*, T4952019. See above, Aubrey and his wife serve delicious lobster and conch on the beach at Loblolly Bay, VHF Ch 16. *Anegada Beach Club*, T4959466, Channel 16. Garden setting, on waterfront, breakfast, lunch and dinner (reservations required for dinner), barbecue lobster. *Anegada Reef Hotel*, T4958002. Breakfast, lunch and dinner but reserve by 1600 for dinner. *Cow Wreck Bar and Grill*, T4959461, on the beach. Open for lunch and dinner, lobster, conch and ribs. *Dotsy's Bakery and Sandwich Shop*, in The Settlement, T4959667. Open 0900-1900 for breakfast, lunch and dinner, fish and chips, burgers, pizza as well as breads and desserts. *Flash of*

Anegada

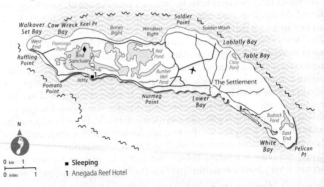

■ Sleeping
1 Anegada Reef Hotel

Beauty, at east end of Loblolly Bay, T4958104, Channel 16. Drinks, snacks and seafood, including lobster, open 1000-2100. Ask around in The Settlement for restaurants serving native dishes. Recommended to make dinner reservations before 1600 at all restaurants.

Background

History

Although discovered by the Spanish in 1493, the islands were first settled by Dutch planters before falling into British hands in 1666. In 1672 the Governor of the Leeward Islands annexed Tortola and in 1680 planters from Anguilla moved into Anegada and Virgin Gorda. Civil government was introduced in 1773 with an elected House of Assembly and a part-elected and part-nominated Legislative Council. Between 1872 and 1956 the islands were part of the Leeward Islands Federation (a British Colony), but then became a separately administered entity, building up economic links with the US Virgin Islands rather than joining the West Indies Federation of British territories. In 1960 direct responsibility was assumed by an appointed Administrator, later to become Governor. The Constitution became effective in 1967 but was later amended in 1977 to allow the islands greater autonomy in domestic affairs. In 1994, the British Government accepted a proposal from a constitutional review commission for the Legislative Council to be enlarged from nine to 13 seats. The four new members represent the territory as a single constituency. This plan created the first mixed electoral system in the UK, in which voters have one vote for their constituency member as usual, plus four votes for the new territory-wide representatives. The British government pushed it into effect before 6 December 1994, the last date for the dissolution of the legislature. There was considerable disquiet in the BVI and in the UK at the way in which it was rushed through without prior consultation and without the support of Mr Stoutt's government.

Mr H Lavity Stoutt, of the Virgin Islands Party (VIP), became Chief Minister in 1967-71 and again in 1979-83 and in 1986. At the elections in February 1995 the Virgin Islands Party, still led by Mr Lavity Stoutt, won a third consecutive term in office with six seats. The Concerned Citizens' Movement (CCM) and the United Party (UP) each won two seats. Three independents were elected and one formed an alliance with the VIP. However, Mr Stoutt died in May 1995 and the Deputy Chief Minister Ralph O'Neal took over as Chief Minister. The VIP won the by-election after Mr Stoutt's death.

In the May 1999 elections the VIP retained power, winning seven seats, but it faced a less divided opposition. The newly-formed National Democratic Party (NDP), led by Orlando Smith, attracted support from young professionals, winning five seats, while the CCM won one and the UP failed to win any.

The people The two major islands, Tortola and Virgin Gorda, along with the groups of Anegada and Jost Van Dyke, contain most of the total population of about 20,000, which is mainly of African descent. The resident population was only 10,985 in 1980 and most of the increase has come from inward migration of workers for the construction and tourist industries. About half the present population is of foreign origin. There has recently been a return flow of people from the Dominican Republic, whose parents and grandparents were originally from Tortola, seeking a higher standard of living. Everyone speaks English.

Government A nearly self-contained community, the islands are a Crown Colony with a Governor appointed by London, although to a large extent they are internally self-governing. The Governor (Frank Savage, appointed 1998) presides over the Executive Council, made up of the Chief Minister, the Attorney-General and three other ministers. A Legislative Council comprises 13 members elected by universal adult suffrage (of which nine represent district constituencies and four represent the whole

British Virgin Islands

territory), one member appointed by the Governor, a Speaker elected from outside by members of the Council, and the Attorney-General as an ex-officio member.

The economy

The economy is based predominantly on tourism; the islands offer up-market tourism in quiet, unspoiled surroundings and earnings are around US$150 mn a year. There are approximately 1,300 hotel rooms, half of which are on Tortola and a third on Virgin Gorda, the rest being scattered around the other islands, but nearly half of those visitors who stay on the islands charter yachts and only sleep on land for their arrival and departure nights.

Tourism in the BVI was hit badly by the recession in 1991. A new charter yacht strategy was announced in 1992, removing import duty and introducing licences to encourage more business. The Government aimed to attract quality operators in a more highly structured environment with streamlined entry regulations. Crewed yachts have been pushed rather than increasing bare boat charters. In another development to promote the islands, the British Virgin Islands Film Commission was set up to encourage film production in the islands and the previous permit fee was lifted. In 1996 commissions on shoots rose to US$1 mn from US$0.4 mn in 1995. Film crews were expected to bring considerable economic benefit through their use of local services and labour.

Since 1991 the tourism industry has shown improvement, particularly in the numbers of cruise ships calling. A new US$6.9 mn, 550-ft cruise ship pier was inaugurated at Road Town, Tortola, which can accommodate two medium-size cruise liners. The Government is aiming to attract the upper end of the cruise market and not to encourage the very large ships. Tourist arrivals and earnings are now growing steadily at about 4-5% a year.

A growth industry of the last few years is the offshore company business and shipping, which have benefited from uncertainty in Hong Kong and Panama. International Business Company legislation passed in 1984 allows locally registered foreign companies tax exemptions with little currency risk as the US dollar is the national currency. By the end of 1997 over 250,000 companies had been registered as IBCs (of which about 35,000 had transferred from Hong Kong when it was returned to China) and fees from new licences generated substantial revenues. In 1997 licence fees for banks and trust companies were doubled to US$20,000 a year. Diversification of the offshore financial centre is being sought; currently over one third of government revenue comes from this sector. In 1994 the Legislative Council passed an insurance law, designed to regulate all insurance business in the BVI including captive insurance and reinsurance. New legislation to cover mutual funds was approved in 1996. The Act came into force at the beginning of 1998 and during its first year 1,700 licence applications were processed. In 1996 the number of registered ships and yachts increased from 596 to 693. A register for mega yachts is planned.

Industry on the islands is limited to small scale operations such as rum, sand or gravel, and desalination plants are being built. Farming is limited to fruit, vegetables and some livestock, some of which are shipped to the USVI. Fishing is expanding both for export, sport and domestic consumption. However, nearly all the islands' needs are imported.

Although the budget is in surplus, the Government is still receiving British capital assistance, as well as funding from the EC, the Caribbean Development Bank and the Commonwealth Development Corporation. Loans have also been raised from commercial banks. The British government is now curtailing its capital funding and other sources of foreign finance are being explored.

Leeward Islands

13

Leeward Islands

The Leeward Islands are a geographical grouping of small, mostly volcanic islands in the northeastern Caribbean. The islands are a mixture of French, Dutch and British colonies and ex-colonies and combine within a small area very varied and rich cultures. Whereas in colonial times they were nearly all sugar producers, today they rely on tourism for a large part of their foreign exchange earnings and jobs. From luxury resorts to intimate guesthouses, gourmet restaurants to barefoot beach bars, there is a wide range of attractions on offer. Sailing, diving and other watersports are well developed and highly rewarding.

Antigua

Population: 65,000 *Antigua, with about 108 square miles, is the largest of the Leewards, and also the most popular and the most developed. Its dependencies are nearby Barbuda and Redonda. The island is low-lying and composed of volcanic rock, coral and limestone. Boggy Peak, its highest elevation, rises to 1,330 ft. There is nothing spectacular about its landscape, although its rolling hills and flowering trees are picturesque. Its coastline however, curving into coves and graceful harbours with 365 soft white sand beaches fringed with palm trees, is among the most attractive in the West Indies.*

Ins and outs

Getting there
See transport page 599, for further information

Air *British Airways* (T4620876, 3 direct flights a week from London Gatwick, connections with Barbados, Port of Spain and St Lucia), *BWIA* (2 flights a week from London Heathrow) and *Virgin Atlantic* (2 flights a week from Gatwick), *Condor* (1 flight a week direct from Frankfurt), *Air France* (twice a week from Paris). *American Airlines* (from Orlando, Miami), *Continental* (from Newark, NJ), *BWIA* (from New York, Miami), *BWIA* and *Air Canada*, T4621147 (from Toronto). There are frequent air services to neighbouring islands (Anguilla, Barbados, Barbuda, Dominica, Martinique, Grenada, Guyana, Jamaica, Nevis, Guadeloupe, Trinidad, St Barts, St Croix, St Kitts, St Lucia, St Maarten, St Thomas, St Vincent, Puerto Rico, Tortola) operated by *LIAT* (T4620700), *BWIA* (T4620260), *Continental*, *American Eagle*, *Air Guadeloupe*, *Cardinal Airlines*. *Carib Aviation* arranges charters to neighbouring islands in

Antigua

planes carrying 5, 6 or 9 passengers and can often work out cheaper and more convenient than using *LIAT*. The office is at the airport, T4623147, 0800-1700, after office hours T4611650. They will meet incoming flights if you are transferring to another island, and make sure you make your return connection. Also day tours. **Ferry** to Montserrat leaves Heritage Quay 0630, 1600, returning from Little Bay 0800, 1730, US$55.50/EC$150 return weekdays, US$27.75/EC$75 weekends. Be at the dock at least an hour beforehand to clear immigration, which stops 30 mins before departure (time limit strictly enforced). At holiday times get there even earlier. French boat, previously used between French Antilles, good condition, efficient. There are occasional boat services to St Kitts and Dominica; see boat captains at Fisherman's Wharf. There is a cargo boat to Dominica once a week and you can arrange a passage through Vernon Edwards Shipping Company on Thames Street; very basic facilities.

Renting a **car** or **motorcycle** is probably the best way to see the islands' sights if you have only a short time to spend, as the bus service is inadequate. **Cycling** is not very interesting, the roads are generally flat and traffic is moderate. There are car hire rental companies are in St John's and some at airport, most will pick you up. A local driving licence, US$20, valid for three months, must be purchased on presentation of a foreign licence. There is a 24-hr petrol station on Old Parham Road outside St John's. Petrol costs US$2.25 per gallon everywhere. Be careful with one way streets in St John's. At night people do not always dim their headlights. **Minivan** (shared taxis) go to some parts of the island (for example Old Road) from the West End bus terminal by the market in St John's. **Bus**, which are banned from the tourist area (north of the line from the airport to St John's), run frequently between St John's and English Harbour, EC$2.50. There are also buses from the east terminal by the war memorial to Willikies, whence a 20-min walk to Long Bay beach and to Parham. There are no buses to the airport and very few to beaches though two good swimming beaches on the way to Old

Getting around
Drive on the left, watch out for pot holes, narrow streets & animals straying across the street in the dark

Barbuda

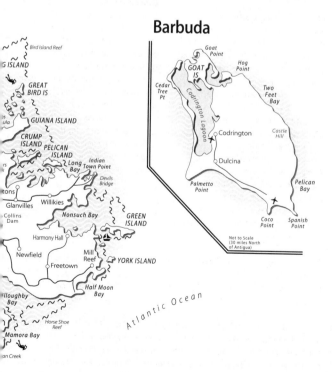

Essentials

Documents *A valid onward ticket is* necessary. American, Canadian and British nationals need only photo ID and proof of citizenship. **Passports** but not **visas** are required by nationals of other Commonwealth countries and British Dependent Territories, if their stay does not exceed six months. The following countries need valid passports but not visas: Argentina, Austria, Belgium, Brazil, Chile, Denmark, Finland, France, Germany, Greece, Ireland, Italy, Japan, Liechtenstein, Luxembourg, Malta, Mexico, Monaco, Netherlands, Norway, Peru, Portugal, Spain, Suriname, Sweden, Switzerland, Turkey and Venezuela. Nationals of all other countries require visas, unless they are in transit for less than 24 hours. Visitors must satisfy immigration officials that they have enough money for their stay. You will not be allowed through Immigration without somewhere to stay. The Tourist Office can help you and you can always change your mind later.

Money Currency *Eastern Caribbean dollars are used, at a rate of EC$2.65 = US$1.* It is advisable to change some currency at the airport on arrival. **Exchange** US dollars are accepted in most places, but no one will know the exchange rate of other currencies. The conventional rate of exchange if you want to pay in US dollars is EC$2.50=US$1, so it is worth changing money in a bank. **Credit cards** are accepted, especially Visa and American Express, but small restaurants will take only cash or Travellers' cheques. Always verify whether hotels, taxis et cetera are quoting you US or EC dollars, you can be cheated. Take care not to get left with excess EC$ on departure, you will not be able to exchange them for another currency except at

a very poor rate with a taxi driver. The airport **bank** is open 0900-1500, Monday-Thursday, closes at 1330 on Friday just as American Airlines come in from New York, closed when BWIA flight comes in from Europe.

Departure tax *There is an airport departure tax of EC$50, US$20 per person. Children under 12 pay half. Cash only.*

Communications *The international telephone code for Antigua and Barbuda is 268. See page 627 for further details.*

Ports of entry *(Own flag). All yachts must clear in and obtain a cruising permit in Antigua but may clear out of either Antigua or at the C & I office in Barbuda. Customs and Immigration offices are at English Harbour (no overtime charges), Crabbs Marina, St John's and Jolly Harbour (boats must be brought inside the marina for exit clearance).*

Boat documents *Entry fees are US$2 for boats up to 20ft, US$4 for 21-40ft, US$6 for 41-80 ft. Monthly cruising permits are US$8 for boats up to 40 ft, US$10 for 41-80 ft. There are additional fees for anchoring or stern to dockage in English Harbour and Falmouth, an EC$5 charge per person plus electricity and water used. Dinghies must show lights at night and barbecues are prohibited in the harbour. The Antigua and Barbuda Marine Guide is distributed free by the Department of Tourism and contains lots of information on anchorages and marine supplies, www.antiguamarineguide.com*

Road can be reached by bus. **Taxi** have H registration plates. In St John's there is a taxi rank on St Mary Street, or outside Bryson's supermarket. They are not metered and frequently try to overcharge, or else have no change, so agree a price first, they should have a EC$ price lis so ask to see it.

Climate Antigua is a dry island with average rainfall of about 45ins a year and although September-November is considered the rainy season, the showers are usually short. Temperatures range from 73°F to 85°F between winter and summer and the trade winds blov constantly. Antigua has been in the path of several hurricanes since 1995, which was a par ticularly devastating year. In 1999 Hurricane Lenny brought floods and mud slides and caused damage estimated at EC$136 mn.

Marinas There are marinas at English Harbour, Falmouth Harbour (Antigua Slipway, Falmouth Harbour Marina, Catamaran Marina, Antigua Yacht Club), Parham Harbour (Crabbs Slipway), Jolly Harbour, St James's Club, and anchorages at Cades Reef, Carlisle Bay, Morris Bay (Curtain Bluff), Ffryes Bay, Crab Hill Bay, Five Islands Bay, Deep Bay, Morris Bay (Jolly Beach), Dickenson Bay, Parham Harbour and at several of the small islands if you can negotiate the reefs, for example Long Island, Guiana Bay, Green Island and Nonsuch Bay.

Business hours Banks: 0800-1400 Monday-Thursday; 0800-1200 and 1400-1600 Friday. Bank of Antigua opens Saturday 0800-1200. **Shops:** 0800-1200, 1300-1600 Monday-Friday. Thursday and Saturday are early closing day for most non-tourist shops. On Sunday everything closes except churches and Kings Casino, although Kentucky Fried Chicken and Epicurean opens in the afternoon.

Official time Atlantic standard time, four hours behind GMT, one ahead of EST.

Voltage 220 volts usually, but 110v in some areas, check before using your own appliances. Many hotels have transformers.

Tourist offices overseas Canada: 60 St Clair Avenue East, Suite 304, Toronto, Ontario, M4T IN5, T416-9613085, F9617218. **France:** 43 Avenue de Friedland, 75008 Paris, T33-1-53751571, F33-1-53751569. **Germany:** Thomas Str 11, D-61348, Bad Homburg, T49-617221504, F49-617221513. **Italy:** Via Santa Maria alla Porta 9, I-20123 Milan, T/F39-2877983. **UK:** Antigua House, 15 Thayer Street, London W1M 5LD, T020-74867073/5, F020-74869970, antbar@msn.com **USA:** 610 Fifth Avenue, Suite 311, New York, NY 10020, T212-5414117, F5414789; 25 SE 2nd Avenue, Suite 300, Miami, FL 33131, T305-3816762, F305-3817908.

Safety Normal precautions against theft should be taken. Vendors on the beach can be a problem but in 1995 joint army and police patrols were deployed on beaches to remove 'unlicenced vendors, vagrants and loiterers' after a fatal shooting of a holiday maker during a beach robbery. There have been some serious incidents on isolated beaches, so caution should be taken in these areas. Generally, however, despite the poverty, Antigua is free from hassle for the traveller.

Health Tiny sandflies, known locally as 'Noseeums' often appear on the beaches in the late afternoon and can give nasty stings. Keep a good supply of repellent and make sure you wash off all sand to avoid taking them with you from the beach. Do not eat the little green apples of the manchineel tree, as they are poisonous, and don't sit under the tree in the rain as the dripping oil from the leaves causes blisters. Some beaches, particularly those on the west coast, get jelly fish at certain times of the year, for example July/August.

Public holidays New Year's Day, Good Friday, Easter Monday, Labour Day (first Monday in May), Whit Monday (end-May), Queen's Birthday (second Saturday in June), Caricom Day, beginning of July (whole island closes down), Carnival (first Monday and Tuesday in August), Independence Day (1 November), Christmas Day and Boxing Day.

Leeward Islands

Flora and fauna

Around 150 different birds have been observed in Antigua and Barbuda, of which a third are year-round residents and the rest seasonal or migrants. Good spots for birdwatching include **McKinnons salt pond**, north of St John's, where thousands of sandpipers and other water birds can be seen and where yellow crowned night-herons breed. **Potworks Dam** is noted for the great blue heron in spring and many water fowl. **Great Bird Island** is home to the red-billed tropic bird and on **Man of War Island**, Barbuda, frigate birds breed. At **Pasture Bay**, on Long Island, the hawksbill turtle lays its eggs from late May to December. The Wide Caribbean Sea Turtle Conservation Network (Widecast) organizes turtle watches.

Diving and marine life

Dive sites There are barrier reefs around most of Antigua which are host to lots of colourful fish and underwater plant life. Diving is mostly shallow, up to 60 ft, except below **Shirley Heights**, where dives are up to 110 ft, or **Sunken Rock**, with a depth of 122 ft where the cleft rock formation gives the impression of a cave dive. Popular sites are **Cades Reef**, which runs for 2½ miles along the leeward side of the island and is an underwater park; **Sandy Island Reef**, covered with several types of coral and only 30-50 ft deep; **Horseshoe Reef**, **Barracuda Alley** and **Little Bird Island**. There are also some wrecks to explore, including the *Andes*, in 20 ft of water in Deep Bay, but others have disappeared in the recent hurricanes. Diving off Barbuda is more difficult unless you are on a boat with full gear and a compressor, as no one offers diving there. The water is fairly shallow, so snorkelling can be enjoyable. There is little information on the island about conservation and few warnings on the dangers of touching living coral.

Dive centres Dive shops are located nearly all round the island and include: Aquanaut Diving Centre, at *St James's Club*, T4605000; Dive Antigua, *Halcyon Cove Hotel*, T4623483, F4627787, birkj@candw.ag; Curtain Bluff Dive Shop, *Curtain Bluff Hotel*, T4628400 (certified hotel guests only); *Deep Bay Divers* in St John's, T4638000; *Dockyard Divers* at Nelson's Dockyard, T4601178, F4601179; *Octopus Divers* at English Harbour, T4606286, F4638528, octopusdivers@candw.ag; *Long Bay Hotel*, T4602005 (certified hotel guests only).

Beaches and watersports

Tourist brochures will never tire of telling you that there are 365 beaches on Antigua, one for every day of the year, some of which are deserted. The nearest beach to St John's is **Fort James** which can be pleasant, with its palm trees and a few boulders. However it gets crowded at weekends and at times it becomes rough and so has a milky appearance, lots of weed and is not good for swimming. It is also rather secluded and confrontations with drug-users have been recorded there, so do not go alone. Further but better is **Dickenson Bay** but there are hotels all along the beach which fence off their property and some pump sewage into the sea which can be smelly. **Soldier's Bay**, next to the *Blue Waters Hotel*, is shallow and picturesque. Instead of following the sign, park your car in the hotel car park, which has shade, walk left across the property, climb through the hole in the fence and in about three minutes you are there. Also good is **Deep Bay** which, like most beaches, can only be reached by taxi or car. There are several nice beaches on the peninsula west of St John's, past the *Royal Antiguan Hotel*. On **Trafalgar Beach** condominiums have been built on the rocks overlooking the small, sheltered bay. If you go through Five Islands village you come to **Galley Bay**, a secluded and unspoilt hotel beach which is popular with locals and joggers at sunset. The four **Hawksbill** beaches at the end of the peninsula, one of which is a nudist beach (free public entry, very secluded, security guard on duty, pleasant atmosphere), are crescent shaped, very scenic and unspoilt. Take drinks to the furthest one as there are no facilities and you may have the place to yourself. At **Half Moon Bay**, in the east there is plenty of room; the waves can be rough in the centre of the bay, but the water is calm at the north end. Near English Harbour is **Galleon Beach**, which is splendid, but again can only be reached by taxi or car or water taxi from English Harbour, EC$2. It has an excellent restaurant. Also excellent is **Pigeon Point**, reached by turning left at the *Last Lemming* restaurant and following the path up and over the hill. **Dark Wood Beach**, on the road from St John's to Old Road round the southwest coast, is very nice, quiet, with a bar and restaurant at the south end.

Antigua offers sailing, waterskiing, windsurfing, parasailing, snorkelling and deep-sea **Day sails** fishing. Cocktail and barbecue cruises are reasonably priced. *Shorty's Glass Bottom Boat* at Dickenson Bay, takes people out to the coral reefs; there are also excursions to Bird Island, food and drink provided. Trips round the island with stops at smaller islands such as Bird Island, Prickly Pear Island, or even Barbuda or Montserrat, can be arranged for US$60-90 on the catamarans run by *Kokomo Cat* (T4627245, www.kokomocat.com) and *Wadadli Cats* (T4624792, www.wadadlicats.com). *Sentio* is a luxury 50ft sailing yacht for small groups, honeymooners, families, for special trips, beach exploring, overnight to Barbuda or sailing instruction (T4647127). The *Caribbean Queen* is a 69 ft catamaran which sails the Antiguan waters with a live steel band, barbecue, snorkelling and more (T4618675, www.ticruises.com). There is also, of course, the *Jolly Roger* (T4622064), a wooden sailing ship used for entertaining would-be pirates, with Wednesday and Friday lunchtime cruises from Jolly Beach, Thursday cocktail cruises from the *Royal Antiguan*, and Saturday night barbecue and dancing cruise, helped along with rum punch.

Races are held throughout the year. The *Antigua Yacht Club* holds races every Thurs- **Sailing** day and anyone wishing to crew should listen to English Harbour Radio at 0900 on VHF 68/06 that morning. *Jolly Harbour Yacht Club* holds Saturday races as well as the Red Stripe Regatta in February and Jolly Harbour Regatta in September. The Classic Regatta in mid-April is spectacular, with yawls, ketches, schooners and square-masted vessels displaying their sails. Antigua Sailing Week begins at the end of April with five days of races and noisy parties, attracting hundreds of boats. The first Carib Cup Regatta was held in July 1995 with five teams of three boats competing.

A marina was built at Jolly Harbour in 1992, just south of Ffryes Point. Several day charter boats have moved there. For cruisers or bareboat charters Antigua offers good provisioning and marine supplies abound, with facilities to haul out boats as well. Haulout can be done at Antigua Slipway, Crabbs Marina or Jolly Harbour; there are several other marinas as well. Charter fleets include Sunday Yachts and Nicholson's Yacht Charters. There are too many anchorages to list.

For fishing charters, *Overdraft*, a 40ft fibreglass deep-sea fishing boat leaves from **Fishing** Falmouth Harbour, US$350 per four hours, US$550 per eight hours, T4620649, 4633112, F4623119, nunesb@candw.ag; *M/Y Nimrod*, US$1,300 per full day, also scuba diving, based at Falmouth Harbour, T4638744; *Obsession* is a 45ft Hatteras which leaves from Falmouth Harbour, T4623174. There is a sport fishing tourna- ment over the Whit weekend at the end of May.

Dickenson Bay is the only beach with public hire of watersports equipment but **Watersports** some hotels will hire to the public especially out of season, for example the *Jolly Beach Resort* near Bolan's Village (bus from West End bus station). Halcyon Cove Watersports at the *Rex Halcyon Cove* has waterskiing, windsurfing (lessons for beginners) and small sailing craft for rent, T4620256. The *Sandals* all-inclusive resort on Dickenson Bay will admit outsiders, at US$150 per couple 1000-1800 or US$130 for the evening, giving you the use of all sports facilities, meals, bar etc. Pat- rick's Windsurfing School at the *Lord Nelson Beach Club* at Dutchman's Bay north of the airport (no frills accommodation and food), offers instruction to intermediate and advanced windsurfers. *Pineapple Beach Allegro Resorts* has a variety of watersports (T4632006). *Destination Antigua* offers kayaking, T5603982.

There are two **golf** courses: a professional (but rather dried out) 18-hole one at **Other sports** Cedar Valley, near St John's, T4620161 and an 18-hole course at Jolly Beach. The Antigua Open is played at Cedar Valley in November. Rental equipment available at both courses, but not very good at Cedar Valley. Miniature golf can be played at *Put- ters Bar & Grill*, Dickenson Bay, T4634653, where there is a challenging, 18-hole, floodlit course.

Leeward Islands

Many of the large hotels have **tennis** courts: *Royal Antiguan Hotel*, T4623733, Deep Bay; *Hodges Bay Club*, T4622300; Temo Sports, English Harbour (sports complex with floodlit tennis courts, glass-backed squash courts, bar/bistro, equipment rental, open Monday-Saturday 0700-2200, no credit cards, T4601781, VHF 68). There is a tennis and squash club open to the public next to the *Falmouth Harbour Beach Apartments*. The Jolly Harbour development includes BBR Sportive, with lit tennis and squash courts (US$20 per 30 minutes) and a 25 m swimming pool, open 0800-2100, food and drink available, T4626260, VHF Channel 68.

Riding is available for beginners through the hotels. *St James's Club* arranges horseriding, T4605000. *Spring Hill Riding Club*, on the road to Rendezvous Bay, offers tuition from BHS qualified instructors, English style, show jumping, cross country course, horses and ponies, beach rides, forest rides, open daily from 0730, contact Sarah Scott, T4638041.

Cricket is the national sport and test matches are played at the Recreation Ground. There are matches between Antiguan teams and against teams from neighbouring islands. The cricket season runs from January to July. Seasons for other spectator sports are: netball January-July, basketball September-December, volleyball December-July, football August-February.

Horse racing takes place on public holidays at Cassada Garden Race Track.

For **work outs**: *Get Physical* at Woods Centre, state of the art fitness centre open 0600-2200, T4629539; Equilibrium at Gambles Medical Centre has toning tables with personal trainers, T4627919. The *National Fitness Centre*, off Old Parham Road behind the Price Waterhouse building, has a good gym, with weight and exercise machines, price negotiable for multiple visits. Open Monday-Friday 0600-2100, Saturday 0900-1600, aerobics classes in the evenings, T4623681.

Organized **hikes** are arranged frequently to historical and natural attractions and can be a good way of seeing the island. Once a month the Historical and Archaeological Society organize hikes free of charge, PO Box 103, St John's, T4621469. Hash House Harriers arrange hikes off the beaten track every other Saturday at 1600, free of charge, contact Hash Master, c/o *O'Grady's Pub*, Nevis Street. For other walking and exploring, see Tour operators in Essentials.

St John's

Population: 30,000

Most activity now takes place around the 2 quay developments

Built around the largest of the natural harbours is St John's, the capital. It is rather quiet and run-down and are rather tatty but parts have been developed for tourism and the town is a mixture of the old and the new. New boutiques, duty-free shops and restaurants are vying for custom. **Redcliffe Quay** is a picturesque area of restored historical buildings now full of souvenir shops and the only toy shop in town. **Heritage Quay**, opened in 1988, is a duty free shopping complex strategically placed to catch cruise ship visitors. It has a casino and a big screen satellite TV and is a cool, pleasant place to have a drink. When a cruise ship is in dock hundreds of passengers come ashore and it becomes very crowded.

However, St John's does have interesting historical associations. Nelson served in Antigua as a young man for almost three years, and visited it again in 1805, during his long chase of Villeneuve which was to end with the Battle of Trafalgar. Some of the old buildings in St John's, including the Anglican Cathedral, have been damaged several times by earthquakes, the last one in 1974. A cathedral in St John's was first built in 1683, but replaced in 1745 and then again in 1843 after an earthquake, at which time it was built of stone. Its twin towers can be seen from all over St John's. It has a wonderfully cool interior lined with pitchpine timber. Donations requested.

Museums The **Museum of Antigua and Barbuda** at the former Court House in Long Street is worth a visit, both to see the exhibition of precolumbian and colonial archaeology and anthropology of Antigua and for the Court House building itself, first built in 1747, damaged by earthquakes in 1843 and 1974 but now restored. There is also Viv

Richards' cricket bat, with which he scored the fastest century, various 'hands on' items and games. The Historical and Archaeological Society (HAS) based at the museum publishes a useful and interesting newsletter, full of stories about the islands and research developments. They also organize field trips. You can also visit Viv Richards' childhood home on Viv Richards' Street. ■ *T/F4624930/1469, museum@candw.ag Free, although donations requested; gift shop. Mon-Fri 1000-1500, Sat 1000-1300. A 20-min video is available on order from the Museum Gift Shop, US$20, which details St John's historical buildings, the Dockyard, archaeological sites, Barbuda's caves and landscapes.* The **Museum of Marine and Living Art**, Gambles Terrace, opposite Princess Margaret School, T4621228, F4621187, exhibits of seashells, shipwrecks and precolumbian history. Recommended weekly lectures by appointment, Thursday 1000, on the evolution of the earth and the formation of the continents and civilizations.

A short drive west of St John's are the ruins of **Fort Barrington** on a promontory at **Fortifications**
Goat Hill overlooking Deep Bay and the entrance to St John's Harbour. These fortifications were erected by Governor Burt, who gave up active duty in 1780 suffering from psychiatric disorders; a stone he placed in one of the walls at the Fort describes him grandly as 'Imperator and Gubernator' of the Carib Islands. The previous fortifications saw the most action in Antigua's history with the French and English battling for possession in the 17th century. At the other side of the harbour are the ruins of **Fort James**, from where you can get a good view of St John's. There was originally

St John's

To Fort Road, Dickenson Bay & NW Coast

St John's St

Warping Lane

Popeshead St

Bishopgate St

North St

Newgate St

Thames St

Bryson's Supermarket

Church St

Old Pier

Museum

Long St

High St

Heritage Quay

St Mary's St

Redcliffe Quay

Market St

Corn St

Temple St

Cross St

Redcliffe St

Methodist Church

Deep Water Harbour

Nevis St

Tanner St

Country Pond

Anglican Cathedral

Church Lane

Government House

Catholic Cathedral

Recreation Ground

War Memorial

1

Independence Av

To Airport

To East Coast

Green Bay

Valley Rd

2

Market

All Saints Rd

South St

New St

Rodney St

Nelson St

Hawkins St

Handicraft Centre

Drake St

Camacho Av

To Parliament & East Coast

To East Coast

N

metres 100
yards 100

To Five Islands & SW Coast

🚌 **Buses**
1 East Bus Stand
2 West Bus Stand

To All Saints English Harbour

To All Saints English Harbour & SE Coast

Leeward Islands

a fort on this site dating from 1675, but most of what can now be seen dates from 1749. To get there, head north out of St John's, turn west by *Barrymore Hotel* to the sea, then follow the road parallel to the beach to the end.

Around the island

Finding your way around is not easy and street names are rarely in evidence. The Ordnance Survey map, US$7.50, is recommended if you are exploring the island. It is a little dated, but there is nothing better. A map hand drawn by Brian Dyde is available from several locations and is adequate for driving around.

On the other side of the island is **English Harbour**, which has become one of the world's most attractive yachting centres and is now a 'Hot Spot' at night for tourists. Here 'Nelson's Dockyard' has been restored and is one of the most interesting historical monuments in the West Indies. It was designated a national park in 1985 (Parks Commissioner, T4601379). ■ *US$1.60, children under 12 free. Souvenirs and T-shirts are on sale at the entrance.* The **Nelson's Dockyard Museum** has recently been renovated to give the complete history of this famous Georgian Naval Yard and the story of famous English Harbour. See *Admiral's Inn*, with its boat and mast yard, slipway and pillars still standing but which suffered earthquake damage in the 19th century. The *Copper and Lumber Store* is now a hotel, bar and restaurant. *Limey's Bar* has a good view of the harbour and is a nice place for a drink. Next to it is an art centre with work by local artists including Katie Shears, who specializes in flora and fauna. The Ralph A Aldridge shell collection in a wall case is fascinating, all the shells were found in Antiguan waters. On the quay are three large capstans, showing signs of wear and tear. Boat charters can be arranged from here; also a 20-30 minute cruise round the historic Dockyard for US$6 on *Horatio*, from outside the *Copper and Lumber Store*, depending on seasonal demand. A footpath leads round the bay to **Fort Berkeley** at the harbour mouth, well grazed by goats, wonderful views. Near the Dockyard, Clarence House still stands where the future King, William IV stayed when he served as a midshipman in the 1780s.

On the left of the road from English Harbour to Shirley Heights are the remains of the British Navy's magazines and a small branch road to the Dow Hill Interpretation Centre. There is a gift shop, restaurant, small museum with shell display and an

English Harbour & Shirley Heights

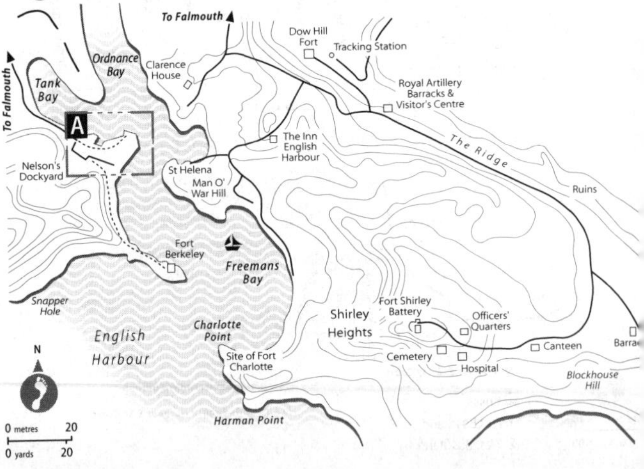

Related map:
A. Nelson's Dockyard,
page 293

0 metres 20
0 yards 20

audio visual room which puts on a display about every 30 minutes on Antigua's history, highly recommended. Local guides also available.

At **Shirley Heights**, overlooking English Harbour, are the ruins of fortifications built in the 18th century with a wonderful view. Some buildings, like officers' quarters, are still standing, restored but roofless, which give an idea of their former grandeur. At the lookout point, or Battery, at the south end is a bar and restaurant. On Sunday a steel band plays 1500-1800, followed by reggae 1800-2200, very loud and popular, can be heard at the dockyard below. Barbecued burgers, chicken, ribs and salad. There is often some activity on Thursday too. It is rather touristy and very crowded, the crowd is often drunk and drugs are sold.

Great George Fort, on Monk's Hill, above Falmouth Harbour (a 30 minute walk from the village of Liberta, and from Cobb's Cross near English Harbour) has been less well preserved. There is a museum of precolumbian artefacts in the Dow Hill tracking station building (formerly used in connection with the US Apollo space programme). It can be visited by prior arrangement, or on Thursday afternoons there are tours, starting from Nelson's Dockyard and taking in Dow Hill (check the details at Nicholson's travel agency). If advance notice is given, the Antigua Rum Distillery welcomes visitors.

Fig Tree Drive between Old Road and the Catholic church on the road going north from Liberta, is a steep, winding, bumpy road, through mountainous rainforest. It is greener and more scenic than most of the island, but the rainforest is scanty and incomparable with islands like Dominica. There was lots of road construction work in 2000. If travelling by bicycle make sure you go *down* Fig Tree Drive from the All Saints to Liberta road, heading towards Old Road, the hill is very steep.

Boggy Peak, in the southwest, is the highest point on the island and from the top you can get wonderful views over to Guadelupe, St Kitts, Nevis and Montserrat. It is a good walk up, or you can take a car. From Urlings walk (or take minibus) about ½-¾ mile in the direction of Old Town. There is a clear track on the left (ask the bus driver to drop you off there) which is very straight then ascends quite steeply. When you get to the top, walk round the fence surrounding the Cable and Wireless buildings to get a good view in all directions. It takes over an hour to walk up (signs say it is a private road) and you are advised not to wander around alone.

A recommended excursion to the east coast, if you have a car, is to take the road out to the airport from St John's. Do not enter the airport but take the right fork

Nelson's Dockyard

Leeward Islands

1 Admiral's Inn, with Pitch & Tar Store, Provision Store
2 Boat House & Sail Loft
3 Copper & Lumber Store (Hotel)
4 Market building; (Cable & Wireless, Bank & shops)
5 Naval Officers' House museum & shops
6 Officers' Quarters (Art studios, shops & toilets)

N
Not to scale

which runs alongside it. After about 1½ miles take a right turn down a small road to St George's Church, on Fitches Creek Bay, built in 1687 in a beautiful location, interesting gravestones. From there, follow the rough road round the coast to **Parham**, which is interesting for being the first British settlement on the island and having an unusual octagonal church, St Peter's, which dates from the 1840s, is lovely and flamboyant, trees surround the church and enhance its attractiveness. From Parham take the road due south and then east at the petrol station through Pares to Willikies. On this road, just past Pares Village, is a sign to **Betty's Hope**, a ruined sugar estate built in 1650 and owned by the Codrington family from 1674-1944. Restoration was carried out by the Antigua Museum in St John's and it was officially opened in 1995. One of the twin windmills can actually be seen working, making it the only operational 18th-century windmill in the Caribbean. There is a visitors' centre (open Tuesday-Saturday 1000-1600) which tells the story of life on a sugar plantation. Well worth a visit. For a guided tour contact the Antigua Museum, T4624930.

After Willikies the road is signed to the *Pineapple Beach Club* at Long Bay, but before you get there, take a right turn down a small road, which deteriorates to a bumpy track, to **Devil's Bridge** at Indian Town Point. The area on the Atlantic coast is a national park where rough waves have carved out the bridge and made blowholes, not easily visible at first, but quite impressive when the spray breaks through. Good view of Long Bay and the headland.

Returning through Willikies to Glanvilles, take a left turn shortly after St Stephen's Church down a small road south past Collins Dam. When you meet up with the main road (petrol station) turn left and then right towards St Phillips. The scenery after this village is quite attractive, there are several ruined sugar mills dotting the landscape. The road continues on to Half Moon Bay and tracks lead up the coast to Mill Reef and many small beaches and jetties.

Essentials

Sleeping
There is a 10% service charge & 8.5% government tax at all hotels. Porters expect a tip of EC$1 per bag

There are hotels, resorts and apartments all round the island and more are being built all the time. We have not space to mention them all, this is a selection. The greatest concentration of developments is in the area around St John's, along the coast to the west and also to the north in a clockwise direction to the airport. A second cluster of places to stay is around English Harbour and Falmouth Harbour in the southeast of the island. Many may be closed Sep-Oct in preparation for the winter season. Full lists of hotels, apartments, villas and guesthouses should be available from the tourist office at the airport, although it is not always easy to get hold of. The tourist office will book you a hotel room on arrival if you have not already done so. There are lots of self-catering apartments available all round the island but a common complaint is that sufficient provisions are not available locally and you have to go into St John's for shopping. **Camping** is illegal.

St John's L-A *Heritage Hotel*, Heritage Quay, PO Box 1532, St John's, T4621247/8, F4621179, heritagehotel@candw.ag, right by cruise ships. Caters for business travellers, discounts available. In same management group is **AL** *City View*, Newgate Street, PO Box 2692, T5620256-9, F5620242, cityviewhotel@candw.ag. 38 rooms with patios, a/c, kitchen, fridge, cable TV, phone, restaurant and room service, conference room. **A-B** *Courtsland*, Upper Gambles, PO Box 403, T4621395, F4621699. **C** *Joe Mike's Hotel*, in Corn Alley and Nevis St, PO Box 136, T4621142, F4626056, joemikes@candw.ag Special rates can be negotiated but not by phone, rooms OK, no balconies, weak a/c, no food but downstairs are fast food, restaurant and bar, casino, ice cream parlour, cocktail lounge, beauty salon and mini-mart. **C** *Roslyn's Guest House*, Upper Gambles, very near cricket ground, PO Box 161, T4620762. 2 double rooms, friendly lady owner. **C** *Murphy's Apartments*, PO Box 491, All Saints Road, T4611183. Run by Elaine Murphy, apartments modernized, every amenity, breakfast US$5, also longer term lets, lovely garden. **E** *Pigottsville Guest House*, at Clare Hall, PO Box 521, T4620592. No signs, about 2 miles from the airport and within easy walking distance of St John's, 20 rooms. **E-F** *Montgomery Hotel*, Tindale Road, T4621164. Usually plenty of room except during carnival and cricket matches, central but not a very nice part of town, noisy roosters across the street, scruffy and basic, 24 small rooms, 8 with private bath, rest with shared bath, rats in downstairs rooms, no water after midnight, cable TV, the owner also has some apartments north of St John's.

West of St John's The **LL-L** *Royal Antiguan*, 3 miles from St John's, PO Box 1322, T4623733, F4623732, www.antigua-resorts.com Depressing drive through tatty suburbs, 278 rooms, high rise, comfortable, good facilities but run down, quiet in summer, casino (only slot machines), pool, tennis etc. Further round the coast **LL** *Hawksbill Beach Resort*, 4 miles from St John's (a US$12 taxi ride), PO Box 108, T4620301, F4621515, www.hawks bill.com. 39 acres and four lovely beaches, good food, pleasant rooms with ceiling fans, friendly staff, tennis, table tennis, pool, watersports, rooms in two-storey blocks or cottages.

Runaway Bay LL-AL *Barrymore Beach Club*, PO Box 1774, on Runaway Bay, 2 miles from St John's, T4624101, F4624140. Rooms and apartments, clean, comfortable, on 1½ miles of white sand beach. Recommended. **LL-B** *Runaway Beach Club*, on Runaway Bay, PO Box 874, T4621318, F4624172. Friendly, beachfront cabins, 24 rooms or villas, 110V electricity, excellent beach restaurant, *The Lobster Pot*. **AL-A** *Sand Haven Hotel*, PO Box 246, T4624491. On clean, sandy beach with shade from palm trees and sea grape, 16 double or family rooms includes breakfast, special deals for visiting cricket teams, 5-10 min beach walk from *Barrymore Beach Apartments*, vehicle hire needed.

Dickenson Bay LL-A *Antigua Village*, PO Box 649, St John's, T4622930, F4620375. Studio or beach front 1-2 bedroomed villa, there is a small store for provisions, nothing exciting, watersports. **LL** *Sandals Antigua*, PO Box 147, T4620267, F4624135, sandals@candw.ag. Couples only, all-inclusive, 191 comfortable rooms, 100 more to be built on land next door, several restaurants, diving, waterskiing, other watersports, tennis, 5 jacuzzis, 5 pools. **LL-AL** *Rex Halcyon Cove Beach Resort*, PO Box 251, T46202568, F4620271. 210 rooms, on the beach with full watersports facilities includes diving and fishing, pool and tennis. **LL-AL** *Siboney Beach Club*, PO Box 222, T4620806, F4623356, siboney@ candw.ag. 12 a/c suites in gardens by beach, restaurant, watersports available nearby, good except that the condos on one side are an eyesore and whatever was on the other side is now abandoned and crumbling into the sea.

North coast LL-AL *Blue Waters*, PO Box 256, T4620290, F4620293, www.blue waters.net 77 rooms and villas on beach, room only or all inclusive, pool, watersports.

Southwest AL *Jolly Harbour Beach Resort, Marina and Golf Club*, PO Box 1793, T4626166, F4626167, www.jollyharbour-marina.com A/c, rooms, suites, villas on waterfront, plenty of activities, watersports, pool, tennis, squash, golf, shopping centre and restaurants. **AL** *Jolly Beach Resort*, Jolly Beach, PO Box 744, T4620061, F4629000 (formerly *Club Antigua*). All-inclusive including watersports, adjacent to marina. Closing in Sep for refurbishment, due to reopen in Dec. **LL-AL** *Coco's Antigua*, PO Box 2024, T4602626, F4629423, cocos@candw.ag 20 rooms in chattel style cottages, view of Jolly Beach, built on a bluff, fan, fridge, restaurant. **LL** *Curtain Bluff*, PO Box 288, T4628400, F4628409, www.curtainbluff.com On small peninsula, beaches either side, 63 rooms with seaview, suites, restaurant, tennis with shop, croquet, putting green, all-inclusive.

Falmouth Harbour AL-A *Falmouth Beach Apartments* (same management as *Admiral's Inn*), PO Box 713, St John's, T460-1027/1094, F4601534. Good value, 23 hillside or beach front studio apartments on or near private beach, very clean, friendly staff, boats and other watersports equipment, all apartments have lovely view of harbour. **AL-B** *Catamaran Hotel and Marina*, on narrow beach, friendly, PO Box 958, T4601036, F4601506.

English Harbour AL-A *Admiral's Inn*, PO Box 713, T4601027, F4601534. 14 rooms of varying sizes in restored 17th-century building, very pleasant, transport to the beach, complimentary sunfish and snorkelling equipment, excellent location, good food. **LL-A** *Copper*

Leeward Islands

and Lumber Store (restored dockyard building), PO Box 184, T4601058, F4629215. Studios and suites available, boat transport to nearby beaches. **LL-AL** *Galleon Beach*, PO Box 1003, T4601024, F4601450, galleonbeach@candw.ag. 1 or 2 bedroom villas with additional sofa bed, on beach at Freemans Bay, *Colombo's* Italian Restaurant on site, fully equipped, tennis, sunfish, windsurfing, ferry to Nelson's Dockyard. Recommended. **LL-AL** *The Inn at English Harbour*, PO Box 187, St John's, T4601014, F4601603. Set in 10 acres with lovely white sand beach, 6 hillside rooms with view of bay, 22 beach front rooms, beach bar or terrace restaurant, watersports provided, tennis and golf nearby.

Southeast **LL** *St James's Club*, PO Box 63, T4605000, F4603015, reservations@antigua -resorts.com, on peninsula in Momora Bay. All-inclusive, 178 rooms and villas, lots of facilities, casino, marina, 3 restaurants, three pools, championship tennis.

East **LL** *Long Bay Hotel*, PO Box 442, T4632005, F4632439, www.longbay-anti gua.com Open Oct-May, MAP, 18 rooms, 5 cottages, 1 villa, sandy beach, tennis, diving, watersports, family-run. **LL** *Mango Bay*, PO Box W1400, on the water in St Phillips parish, T4606646, F4608400, www.u-c.com/MangoBay-Antigua. Sister hotel in Barbados, all-inclusive, 64 rooms, all watersports and nightly entertainment provided, French chef. **AL** *Harmony Hall*, T4604120, F4604406, www.harmonyhall.com Includes breakfast and use of boat, meal plans available, excellent restaurant, pool, dock for visiting yachts, beach, very popular.

Long Island **LL** *Jumby Bay*, was purchased by Halfmoon Jamaica and reopened Dec 1999 but refurbishment and expansion continue at the 300-acre property, which will have 68 rooms, 12 2-3 bedroom villas and private cottage, with an infinity swimming pool, spa and tennis.

Near airport If you are changing planes and have to stop over, **A-D** *Amarylis*, on Airport Road, PO Box 2624, T4628690, F5620375. New in 1998, 22 rooms, comfortable, with *Calypso Café* formerly in St John's, good West Indian and seafood in a nice atmosphere. **B** *The Airport Hotel*, T4621191, F4621534. Where some airlines dump you if a missed connection is their fault, is being renovated and is generally quite nice now, friendly staff, good restaurant and bar with outdoor patio, reasonably priced food, happy hour drinks Mon-Fri.

Eating

Oranges are green, while the native pineapple is black

In addition to a wide selection of imported delicacies served in the larger hotels, local specialities, found in smaller restaurants in St John's, often very reasonable, should never be missed: saltfish (traditionally eaten at breakfast in a tomato and onion sauce), pepper-pot with fungi (a kind of cornmeal dumpling), goat water (hot goat stew), shellfish (in reality the local name for trunk fish), conch stew and the local staple, chicken and rice. Ducana is made from grated sweet potato and coconut, mixed with pumpkin, sugar and spices and boiled in a banana leaf. Tropical fruits and vegetables found on other Caribbean islands are also found here: breadfruit, cristophine, dasheen, eddo, mango, guava and pawpaw (papaya). Locally made Sunshine ice cream, American style, is available in most supermarkets. Imported wines and spirits are reasonably priced but local drinks (fruit and sugar cane juice, coconut milk, and Antiguan rum punches and swizzles, ice cold) must be experienced. The local Cavalier rum is a light golden colour, usually used for mixes. Beer costs US$2-2.50 in bars, although street bars in the market are cheaper. cases of beer can be bought at good prices from Wadadli Brewery on Crabbs peninsula. There are no licensing restrictions. Tap water is safe all over the island. Most luxury hotels provide rainwater. If you are planning to eat out in hotels, you need to allow at least US$300 per person per week, but it is possible to eat much more cheaply in the local restaurants in St John's. A 7¾% tax on all meals and drinks is added to your bill. Restaurants tend to move, close down or change names frequently.

St John's *Chutneys* on Fort Rd, T4622977. Serves good Indian food (Indian chef). *Hemingway's*, T4622763. Drink, lunch or dinner West Indian style upstairs on cool veranda overlooking Lower Mary Street at entrance to Heritage Quay, open Mon-Sat from 0830, main course EC$24-60. *Home*, Gambles Terrace, T4617651, 20-min walk from tourist area but worth it. Caribbean haute cuisine, Italian pasta dishes, exotic desserts, about EC$80-100 per person, very elegant but no stiff formality, friendly atmosphere, service excellent, welcoming to families, run by Antiguan Carl Thomas and his German wife Rita, open from 1800-2300. *Julian's* on Church and Corn Alley, T4624766, closed Mon. Lovely courtyard setting of an old home, English chef provides delicious lunch and dinner, winner of AAA Diamond Award 1998. *O'Grady's*, Nevis St. Good for pub grub, darts and pool, packed on Wed when Laurie Stevens sings. *Mama Lolly's*, best vegetarian food in Redcliffe Quay, T5621552, mamalol@candw.ag *Peach Tree Restaurant & Bar*, All Saints Road, T5622067. Run by Glen Gittens, vegetarian options. *Pizzas in Paradise*, at Redcliffe Quay, T4622621. Very popular at lunch time, salads and sandwiches as well as pizzas, open Mon-Sat 0830-2300. *The Redcliffe Tavern*, T4614557. Good lunch, EC$17-35, evening main course EC$25-40, open Mon-Sat 0800-2330. *Smoking Joe's*, opposite the cricket ground. For barbecued ribs, chicken, etc, Joe is a local calypsonian. *The Hub*, Long St and Soul Alley, opposite the Museum, T4620616. Open daily from 0730 until 2200 (or later for drinks), good meals, live jazz on Sat night, local cuisine, friendly, pleasant atmosphere. For fast food lovers there is *Kentucky Fried Chicken* on High and Thames Sts, and a 2nd branch on Fort Rd, T4621973.

In Hodges Bay area, near the airport, *Le Bistro*, T4623881. Excellent French food, dinner only, closed Mon. At airport, *Big Banana*, is surprisingly good, clean and efficient, closed Sun.

Runaway Bay Cricketing friends Richie Richardson and David Folb (Chairman of Lashings Cricket Club in Maidstone, Kent), took over *Lashings Beach Café* at *Sandhaven* in 1999, bar and restaurant, from chilli to lobster, special deals at hotel for visiting cricket teams, if you beat the Lashings team you get free food and drinks. On Wed and Fri nights, an English family serves fish and chips (and shrimp and Pot Pies) from a truck on the road just past the *Siboney* driveway, very busy, lots of locals, not to be missed.

Galley Bay *Chez Pascal*, overlooking Galley Bay, T4623232. Gourmet, authentic French food from French chef Pascal.

Jolly Harbour At Jolly Harbour marine complex there is an Italian *trattoria*, *Al Porto*, T4627695. Pasta, pizzas, seafood in al fresco setting, poor service, meals from US$10, open daily lunch and dinner, closed 1500-1900. *Peter's* next door. Excellent, barbecued fresh fish and lobster, prices from EC$15. Recommended. *OJ's Beach Bar & Restaurant*, Crab Hill, T4600184, on beach. Excellent setting, simple menu but good food and service, economical prices, no credit cards.

English Harbour There is a restaurant and bar on Shirley Heights, steel band and barbecue every Sun afternoon (see page 593). *Abracadabra* just outside Nelson's Dockyard, T4602701. Lively video bar, live music some evenings, Italian and Continental dishes, open every evening, closed Sep-Oct. *Admiral's Inn*, Nelson's Dockyard, T4601027. Breakfast (slow but good value, recommended), lunch and dinner (limited selection but good, slightly overpriced), yachtsman's dinner EC$40, closed Sep. Near St James' Club, *Alberto's*, T4603007. Choice dining spot frequented by ex-pat 'locals' plus celebrities like Eric Clapton, Timothy Dalton, Italian run, open air tropical setting, fresh seafood and pasta always available, reservations essential. Recommended. *Catherine's Café* at the Antigua Slipway in Nelson's Dockyard, T4605050. French chef, divine crêpes, quiches, assorted salads, lovely setting right on water, open daily, breakfast and lunch only. Highly recommended. At *Galleon Beach Club*, English Harbour, *Colombo's* T4601452. Italian restaurant, recommended for good food but expensive, open 1200-1500, 1900-2230, reggae band Wed. *Grace Before Meals*, between English Harbour and Falmouth Harbour. A cheaper alternative to the many expensive restaurants, rotis, pizzas and other good value meals to eat in or take away. Between English and Falmouth Harbours, *Le Cap Horn*, T4601194. Pizzeria, Argentine Churrasco steak, lobster, some French dishes, great food, open 1830-2300. *Mario's Pizzeria*, T4601318. Delicious pizza baked in stone ovens, also famous for fresh bread. *Southern Cross*, expensive Italian restaurant upstairs on newly constructed jetty off Antigua Yacht Club, delicious food, wonderful setting, closed in summer. *The Copper and Lumber Store* is overpriced, you pay for the 'atmosphere', which is not to everybody's taste and the portions are small, but excellent.

Leeward Islands

East *Eastern Parkway*, also known as *Harry's Bar* is at Half Moon Bay Beach, T4604402. Open-air covered beach bar, snacks, cold drinks, burgers and local specialities like bread and saltfish, goat curry, very casual dining on premises or takeaway, open daily, local entertainment Sun afternoon.

Festivals   **Antigua** Carnival is at the end of *July* and lasts until the 1st Tuesday in *August*. The main event is 'J'ouvert', or 'Juvé' morning when from 0400 people come into town dancing behind steel and brass bands. Hotels and airlines tend to be booked up well in advance. For information contact the Carnival Committee, High St, St John's, T4620194. **Barbuda** has a smaller carnival in *May*, known as '**Caribana**'. An annual **jazz festival** is held, usually in late *May*, with concerts at Fort James, the *Sandpiper Reef Hotel*, King's Casino and on the *Jolly Roger*. Contact the Tourist Office for a programme. A **hot air balloon festival** is held at the end of *October*.

Nightlife   The largest hotels provide dancing, calypso, steel bands, limbo dancers and moonlight bar-
English Harbour area   becues. There are cinemas, nightclubs, discothèques and casinos. English Harbour is safer for
has become the 'hot   evenings out, especially for women alone. In the Dockyard, Fri night *Copper and Lumber*
spot' for tourists   have 2 for the price of 1, Wed Jazz, Thur karaoke. *Julian's*, upstairs bar has jazz nights, *Galley Bar* is also popular with occasional entertainment. *Mad Mongoose* and *Abracadabra* nearly always lively, with dancing at *Abracadabra*. *Ribbit Club*, near Deep Water Harbour. *The House*, on the airport road, both very local; *Putters*, Dickenson Bay, has mini golf course . The *Kings Casino* in Heritage Quay awaits cruise ship passengers. Be warned that casino employees entice you off the street with the lure of winning easy money. After an initial spell of amazing luck, one reader (not a gambler) lost US$3,500 in 20 mins. Casinos at *Royal Antiguan* (only slot machines) and *St James's Club*. The newest is *Casino Riviera*, Runaway Bay, opened 1999 with gaming tables, bar, restaurant serving lunch and dinner and live evening entertainment. At *Dubarry's* bar there is jazz on Sun night, rum punch party on Tue, barbecue on Thur, take swimsuit, parties tend to end up in, not just by, the pool. *Miller's*, at Fort James. Serves lunch, dinner, or just drinks, often has live music, for example reggae bands, especially on Sun after Shirley Heights, owned by a local jazz hero. Laurie Stevens, British, provides nightly, musical entertainment around the island: Mon, *Tradewinds*; Tue *Halcyon Hotel*; Wed, *O'Grady's Irish Pub* on Nevis Street; Fri, *Columbos* in English Harbour; enquire about other evenings. His wife, Lisette, is a palmist, so ask about a reading if you want to see into the future. A free newspaper, *It's Happening, You're Welcome*, contains lots of information on forthcoming events.

Shopping   The market building is at the south end of Market Street but there are goods on sale all
Market day in   around. In season, there is a good supply of fruit and vegetables, which are easy to obtain on
St John's is Sat   the island. The main supermarket in St John's is *Bryson's*, on Long Street. *Woods Center* is a new, modern shopping mall with a wide variety of shops including *The Epicurean Supermarket*, the most modern, well stocked supermarket on the island, a drugstore, post office, dental clinic, dry cleaners and numerous other shops. Most grocery stores open 0800-2200, although many close at 1300 on Thu. You can buy fish from the fishing boats at the back of the Casino or from *Caribbean Seafoods* in Cassada Gardens near the horse racetrack (T4626113), large selection of cleaned and ready to cook seafood, freshly caught (by their own fishing boat), vacuum packed and quick frozen. Heritage Quay (has public toilets) and Redcliffe Quay are shopping complexes with expensive duty-free shops in the former, and boutiques. The latter has bars and restaurants. There are several shops on St Mary Street and others nearby, which stock clothing, crafts and other items from neighbouring islands, for example *Caribelle Batik*, T4622972. There are two grocery and liquor stores at *Antigua Yacht Club* dock. Some tourist shops offer 10% reductions to locals: they compensate by overcharging tourists. Duty free shops at the airport are more expensive than normal shops in town. *The Map Shop* (St Mary Street) carries a good selection of Caribbean literature plus reference books and guides to history, culture, fauna and flora of the Caribbean. *PC Book Revue*, further up the road has lots of old issues of magazines. The public library on Market St has a good Caribbean section, particularly non-fiction, for those who want to read but not buy. *Harmony Hall*, Brown's Bay Mill, near Freetown, T4604120. An art gallery and gift shop,

open daily 1000-1800, exhibiting and selling paintings, sculpture and crafts from leading Caribbean artists, popular for a lunch stop at the restaurant while touring by car or yacht.

Local Bicycle At English Harbour, *Yati Bike rentals*, T4627955. Bicycle hire from *Cycle Krazy* on St Mary's St, T4629253. *Bikes Plus*, T4622453. **Bus** Bus frequency can be variable, and there are very few after dark or on Sun. Buses usually go when they are full, ask the driver where he is going. They are numbered and destinations are on display boards at the West Bus Station.Buses to Old Rd are half hourly on average, though more frequent around 0800 and 1600. **Car hire** *Hertz*, T4624114/5; *Avis*, T4622840, *Dollar Rental*, T4620362 (Factory Road); *National*, T4622113; at *Oakland Rent-A-Car* you can negotiate good rates, contact Ann Edwards, T4623021. Rates are from US$58 per day, US$225 a week (no mileage charge), including insurance charges, in summer, more in winter. **Helicopter** *Caribbean Helicopters*, helitours, custom charters and day trips from US$69 per person, daily, 0900-1700, T4605900. **Hitchhiking** is easy in daylight but at night you might fall prey to a taxi driver. **Taxi** There is a list of government approved taxi rates posted in EC$ and US$ at the airport just after customs. From St John's to Runaway Bay, 10 mins, is US$6. A day tour normally costs about US$70 for 1-4 people, US$76 for 5-7 people. Taxi excursions advertised in the hotels are generally overpriced.Tips for taxi drivers are usually 10% of the fare.

Transport

Air From the airport to *Admiral's Inn, St James's Club, Falmouth Beach Apartments, Curtain Bluff, Harmony Hall*, Darkwood Beach et cetera is US$24/EC$64; to *Sandals, Antigua Village* and Dickenson Bay area US$13/EC$34; to *Blue Waters* US$10/EC$27; *Hawksbill* and Five Islands US$16/EC$42. From the airport to town EC$21 per person. If going to the airport early in the morning, book a taxi the night before as there are not many around. A day tour normally costs about US$70 for 1-4 people, US$76 for 5-7 people. Taxi excursions advertised in the hotels are generally overpriced.Tips for taxi drivers are usually 10% of the fare. **V C Bird airport**, some 4½ miles from St John's, is the centre for air traffic in the area. There are direct flights from the UK, Germany, France, North America and frequent services from neighbouring islands.

Banks *Scotia Bank, Barclays Bank, Royal Bank of Canada, Bank of Antigua, Antigua and Barbuda Investment Bank, Antigua Commercial Bank*. Mosts banks take Mastercard and Visa. The *Swiss American Bank of Antigua* is open on Sat morning (also a branch in St John's). A tax of 1% is levied on all foreign exchange transactions but there may be additional charges on TCs. Casinos will change TCs without a fee. *American Express* is at Antours near Heritage Quay, staff helpful and friendly. **Communications** Post: Post office at the end of Long Street, St John's, opposite the supermarket. Open Mon-Thu, 0815-1200, 1300-1600, until 1700 on Fri; also a Post office at the airport, Woods Centre (easier parking) and at English Harbour. A postcard to the USA costs EC$0.45. *Federal Express* is on Church Street. *DHL* is in the Vernon Edwards building on Thames Street. **Telephone:** *Cable and Wireless Ltd*, 42-44 St Mary's Street, St John's, and at English Harbour. **Internet** Cable and Wireless Cybercafé at Antigua Yacht Club (bring your own computer, or use theirs). Also email, messages, etc, at *International Connections* at AYC dock. Antigua's international phone code is 268. **Embassies and consulates** The *British High Commission* is at the Price Waterhouse Centre (PO Box 483), 11 Old Parham Road, St Johns, T4620008/9, F4622806. **Tourist information** Local tourist office: *Antigua Tourist Office*, corner of Nevis St and Friendly Alley. Postal address: PO Box 363, St John's, Antigua, West Indies. T4620480, F4622483, info@ antigua-barbuda-ca.com. Open 0830-1600 (Mon-Fri) and 0830-1200 (Sat). Gives list of official taxi charges and hotel information. Also has an office at airport, will help book accommodation principally at the more expensive resorts. The Antigua Hotels and Tourist Association, PO Box 454, Island House, New Gates St, St John's, T4620374, F4623702. **Tour operators:** *Mac's Tracks*, run by Brian MacMillan, PO Box 107, St John's (home T4627376), F4611187, 2-4 hr hikes at weekends or on special request, from US$10 per person, exploring the countryside, lunch and transport to start of hike can be arranged, to Boggy Peak, Mt McNish, Monterose Hill, Signal Hill and Green Castle Hill. *Tropikelly Trails*, PO Box W1920, St John's, T4610382, US$65 per person, Mon-Fri tours includes drinks, lunch, hotel pick-up, 5-6 hrs to Body Pond, Monks Hill, the pineapple farm at Claremont Estate, Boggy Peak and the silk cotton tree at Cades Bay, where 10 people can stand inside the hollow trunk.

Directory

Leeward Islands

Barbuda

Population: 1,100

Some 30 miles to the north is Barbuda, a flat coral island some 68 miles square, one of the two island dependencies of Antigua. Most of the population live in the only village on the island, **Codrington**, which stands on the edge of the lagoon.

The people of Barbuda are unusually tall, descendents of the Corramante tribe in Africa and used by Codrington in his experiments in slave breeding. Barbuda has some excellent beaches and its seas are rich with all types of crustaceans and tropical fish. **Palaster Reef** is a marine reserve to protect the reef and the shipwrecks (there are around 60 ships documented). You can swim from the beach to the reef. This is one of the few islands in the area where there is still much wildlife, although much of it introduced by man: duck, guinea fowl, plover, pigeon, wild deer, pigs, horses and donkeys.

There is an impressive **frigate bird colony** in the mangroves in Codrington Lagoon, particularly on Man of War Island where hundreds of birds mate and breed in August-December. Local fishermen will take you out there; you can get quite close for photography or just to watch. Popular with ornithologists working nine months of the year in Antarctica, who spend their holidays coming to see 'their' frigate birds in Codrington Lagoon. Ask the guide to drop you at Palm Bay on the west side of the lagoon and pick you up 4-5 hours later.

Meanwhile walk the 17 miles of beaches, up north or down south, but bring a hat and sunscreen. There are no beach bars or vendors, you will probably be the only person for miles. There is no shade except around Palm Beach where there is a lot of litter. The island has a Martello Tower and fort. The tower is 56ft high and once had nine guns to defend the southwest approach. It now has a swarm of killer bees in the cellar – take care. From Codrington, River Road runs three miles to **Palmetto Point** (with beautiful pink sand beaches), past Cocoa Point and on to Spanish Point, a half-mile finger of land that divides the Atlantic from the Caribbean Sea. There is a small ruin of a lookout post here and the most important Arawak settlements found in Barbuda.

One of Barbuda's main sources of income is the mining of sand. In 1993 a High Court injunction against the mining led to a severe cash crisis and public employees were not paid for several months. The injunction was imposed pending the resolution of a dispute between the Government and the island council over who has authority for sand mining. Mining of sand at Palmetto Point allegedly damaged a pure water supply. The Minister of Agriculture and two businessmen were convicted of breaching the injunction, but the Minister was subsequently pardoned by the Governor General.

Barbuda is being developed as a tourist resort with attractions for **snorkellers** and **skin-divers** such as exploring old wrecks. The elkhorn coral and staghorn coral formations are very impressive. Take your own scuba equipment or hire it from Byron Askie (tanks US$20, regulator US$20, BC US$15, weights US$5, wetsuit US$10). Snorkelling equipment is available but is more expensive than on Antigua.

Sleeping

There are 3 hotels, 2 villas & a few guesthouses, although more are planned

A *Nedd's Guest House* in Codrington, T4600059. Clean and airy rooms upstairs, call prior to arrival and fix room rate with Mr McArthur Nedd, use of kitchen, mini-mart downstairs, bakery just behind the guesthouse in the next street, no road name signs. Houses are also available for rent at about US$35-70, phone Evans at the car rental for help. *Bus Stop Guest House*, T4600081. Bed and breakfast. **A-C** *Byron Askie's Guest House*, T4600065, VHF 16 Red Fox. Rooms and houses, also day trips, picnics, fishing, birdwatching, boat hire, waterski, windsurfing, nearly anything can be arranged. *Coco Point Lodge*, T4623816, F4625340, in the USA T212-9861416. Charges US$750 double per night including all meals and drinks and airfare from Antigua, is quiet and exclusive, islanders and non-guests are not admitted. *K-Club*, T4600300, F4600305, in the UK T020-79365000, or through Elegant Resorts or Unique Hotels, T01453-835801, F01453-835525. Owned and designed by Italians, opened in 1991, 34 rooms, from US$1,200 a night (US$950 off season) plus US$200 air fare, with its own 9-hole golf course (the grass was laid on soil cleared from the mangrove swamp so there are problems now with salt) as well as watersports, welcomes islanders and non-residents, open mid-Nov to end-Aug, no children under 12. *Palmetto Beach Hotel*, T4600440, www.palmetto hotel.com, beach front on 11-mile beach. 24 rooms and suites.

The Lime, at the jetty where you embark for boat trips is a nightspot. If you prefer to have lobster or fish with a family, ask Mr Nedd to call George for you. Fix the price beforehand and George will cook. Do not expect many 'mod cons' on Barbuda. Several small snack bars, ask locally. The *Palm Tree* and *Park Terrace* restaurants for local food.

Eating

Excellent 1:25,000 **maps** should be available from the Codrington post office or the map shop in Jardine Court, St Mary's, St John's (also good 1:50,000 maps of Antigua). It is safer to get one before you arrive in Barbuda, you can not rely on anything being in stock.

Shopping

Easily reached by air (taking 10 mins, US$45 return), or (with some difficulty and at a high price, US$150) by boat from St John's. **Air** There are two airports. The main one is just south of Codrington. *Carib Aviation* will arrange charters and day trips. Return ticket costs US$63, or US$67 if you buy it less than 3 days before departure. The 2nd airport is near Cocoa Point and only serves *Coco Point*. Day tours from Antigua include the Bird Sanctuary, Highland House, the Caves and the Martello Tower, contact Barbara Japal, Caribrep, T4632070, F5601824. **Boat** Charter boats do day trips but you will not see much of Barbuda. **Road** It is possible to hire jeeps (US$50 per day including insurance, from Junie Walker, T4600159, or Oliver, T4600146) or **horses** in Codrington, otherwise everywhere is a long hot walk, so take drinks with you. The *Barbuda Taxi Association* will do tours, T4600081.

Transport

Redonda

Antigua's second dependency, 35 miles to the southwest and at half a mile square, is little more than a rocky volcanic islet and is uninhabited. Columbus sighted the island on 12 November 1493 and named it after a church in Cadiz called Santa María la Redonda. He did not land, however, and thus did not formally claim the island. Neither did anyone else until 1865 when Matthew Dowdy Shiell, an Irish sea-trader from Montserrat, celebrated the birth of a long-awaited son by leading an expedition of friends to Redonda and claiming it as his kingdom. In 1872, the island was annexed by Britain and came under the jurisdiction of the colony of Antigua, despite protests from the Shiells. The Title of King was not disputed, however, and has survived to this day. The island was never inhabited although for some years guano was extracted by the Redonda Phosphate Company until the works were blown away by a hurricane.

In 1880 MD Shiell abdicated in favour of his son, Matthew Phipps Shiell, who became King Felipe of Redonda but emigrated to the UK where he was educated and became a prolific and popular novelist. His most well-known novel was *The Purple Cloud* (1901), which was later made into a film, *The World, the Flesh and the Devil*, starring Harry Belafonte. On his death in 1947 he appointed as his literary executor and successor to the throne, his friend John Gawsworth, the poet, who became Juan, the third King of Redonda, but continued to live in London. His reign was notable for his idea of an 'intellectual aristocracy' of the realm of Redonda and he conferred titles on his literary friends, including Victor Gollancz, the publisher, JB Priestley, Dorothy L Sayers and Lawrence Durrell. This eccentric pastime hit a crisis when declining fortunes and increasing time spent in the pub sparked a rash of new titles to all and sundry, a number of abdications in different pubs, and the succession was, and still is, disputed.

The Redondan Cultural Foundation is an independent association of people interested in Redonda, its history and its monarchs, which tries to steer through the minefield of Redondan politics. It was established in 1988 by the late Reverend Paul de Fortis and exists to promote the writings of MP Shiell, John Gawsworth and other authors of the realm's 'intellectual aristocracy'. It celebrates Redonda as 'the last outpost of Bohemia'. The foundation published *The Kingdom of Redonda*

1865-1990 in association with the Aylesford Press (1991), and also publishes a regular newsletter. A range of titles by and about Sheill and Redonda is published by John D Squires, JDS Books, The Vainglory Press, PO Box 292333, Kettering, Ohio 43526, USA, jdsbooks@ameritech.net

Meanwhile, on Redonda, all is much the same for the goats, lizards and sea birds, who live an undisturbed life apart from the occasional bird watcher who might come to find the burrowing owl, now extinct on Antigua.

Background

History

Antigua (pronounced Ant*ee*ga) was first inhabited by the Siboney (stone people), whose settlements date back to at least 2400 BC. The Arawaks lived on the island between about AD 35 and 1100. Columbus landed on his second voyage in 1493 and named the island Santa María de la Antigua. Spanish and French colonists attempted to settle there but were discouraged by the absence of freshwater springs and attacks by the Caribs. In 1632 the English successfully colonized the island and, apart from a brief interlude in 1666 when held by the French, the island and its dependencies, Barbuda and uninhabited Redonda, remained British. Sir Christopher Codrington established the first large sugar estate in Antigua in 1674 and leased Barbuda to raise provisions for his plantations. Barbuda's only village is named after him. Forests were cleared for sugarcane production and African slave labour was imported. Today, many Antiguans blame frequent droughts on the island's lack of trees to attract rainfall, and ruined towers of sugar plantations stand as testament to the destruction and consequent barrenness of the landscape. In the 17th and 18th centuries, Antigua was important for its natural harbours where British ships could be refitted safe from hurricanes and from attack. The Dockyard and the many fortifications date from this period. *Shirley Heights, The Story of the Red Coats in Antigua*, by Charles W E Jane, published by the Reference Library of Nelson's Dockyard National Park Foundation at English Harbour, Antigua, in 1982, gives a detailed account of the military history of the island and the building of the fortifications, price US$4.

The slaves were emancipated in 1834 but economic opportunities for the freed labourers were limited by a lack of surplus farming land, no access to credit, and an economy built on agriculture rather than manufacturing. Conditions for black people were little better than under slavery and in many cases the planters treated them worse. Poor labour conditions persisted and violence erupted in the first part of the 20th century as workers protested against low wages, food shortages and poor living conditions. In 1939, to alleviate the seething discontent, the first labour movement was formed: the Antigua Trades and Labour Union. Vere Cornwall Bird became the union's president in 1943 and with other trade unionists formed the Antigua Labour Party (ALP). In 1946 the ALP won the first of a long series of electoral victories, being voted out of office only in 1971-76 when the Progressive Labour Movement won the general election. For a graphic account of the terrible conditions in which black people lived and worked during slavery and its aftermath, read *To Shoot Hard Labour (The Life and Times of Samuel Smith, an Antiguan Workingman 1877-1982)*, by Keithlyn B Smith and Fernando C Smith, published by Karia Press, London, and Edan's Publishers, Toronto.

Antigua was administered as part of the Leeward Islands until 1959 and attained associated status, with full internal self-government in 1967. Antigua and Barbuda, as a single territory, became independent in November 1981, despite a strong campaign for separate independence by Barbuda. Vere C Bird became the first Prime Minister and in 1989, at the age of 79, he took office for the fourth consecutive time. The general elections were marked by some irregularities and allegations of bribery, but the ALP won 15 of the 16 seats for Antigua in the 17 seat House of

Behind the façade

Many visitors regard Antigua as the ideal Caribbean holiday destination. The role of tourism in Antigua today is, however, one of the objects of a vehement attack in Jamaica Kincaid's book A Small Place *(1988). Addressed to the foreign visitor, the essay proposes to reveal the realities underneath the island's surface. What follows is a passionate indictment of much of Antiguan government, society, the colonists who laid its foundations and the modern tourist. It is a profoundly negative book, designed to inspire the visitor to think beyond the beach and the*

hotel on this, or any other, island. Jamaica Kincaid was brought up on Antigua (she now lives in the USA), and memories and images from her childhood figure strongly in her other books to date.

Her novel, The Autobiography of My Mother *(Vintage, 1996), is dedicated to the Nobel poet laureate, Derek Walcott, of St Lucia. It is again semi-autobiographical, set in the Caribbean, exploring the love-hate relationship of mother and daughter, suitability for motherhood, power and control.*

Representatives, the remaining seats being taken by the United National Democratic Party and the Barbuda People's Movement, for Barbuda. Mr Bird appointed a largely unchanged cabinet which included several members of his family.

In 1990 the Government was rocked by an arms smuggling scandal which exposed corruption at an international level when allegations were made that Antigua had been used as a transit point for shipments of arms from Israel to the Medellín cocaine cartel in Colombia. Communications and Works Minister, Vere Bird Jr, the Prime Minister's son, became the subject of a judicial inquiry, following a complaint from the Colombian Government, for having signed authorization documents. His Cabinet appointment was revoked although he remained an MP. The Blom-Cooper report recommended no prosecutions although it undermined the credibility of the Government and highlighted the rivalry between the two sons, Vere Jr and Lester Bird. The report also recommended that Vere Bird Jr be banned for life from holding public office.

Repeated calls for the resignation of Prime Minister Vere Bird were ignored although several ministers resigned from his Government. Demonstrations were organized in 1992 by the newly-formed three-party United Opposition Front, seeking the resignation of the Prime Minister amid allegations of his theft and corruption. Fresh allegations of corruption were published in 1993 by the weekly opposition newspaper, *Outlet*, concerning property development contracts and misuse of public funds, resulting in a libel action issued by Lester Bird. *Outlet*, edited by Tim Hector, has for many years been the most outspoken critic of the Bird administration, frequently exposing corruption and fraud.

Vere Bird finally retired as Prime Minister in February 1994 at the age of 84. He was succeeded by his son, Lester, who led the ALP into the general elections held in March, winning its ninth out of 10 elections held since 1951. The Government's unpopularity was reflected in the vote and the ALP saw its representation cut from 15 to 11 seats in the House of Representatives. The Barbuda People's Movement retained its seat, while the United Progressive Party (formerly the United Opposition Front), led by Baldwin Spencer, won five seats, the largest number for any opposition party in the country's history. Tim Hector was appointed an opposition senator, having stood against Vere Jr in the election and lost. Vere Bird Jr, who is the chairman of the ALP, was not appointed to the new cabinet.

In 1995, Hugh Marshall, a former trade minister launched a new party, the People's Democratic Movement.

The new government was not free of allegations of corruption scandals (Ivor Bird, a younger Bird brother and general manager of the ZDK radio station was arrested and fined for taking possession of 12kg of cocaine at the airport) although Prime Minister Bird made efforts to portray a more professional administration.

☞ Tourism versus conservation – more controversy

In 1997 the government signed an agreement with Johan Holdings Berhad, of Malaysia, for the construction by Asian Village Holdings of a tourist resort on **Guiana Island** off the northeast coast of Antigua, together with Crump Island, Hawes Island and the mainland area of Coconut Hall. This massive development will cover 1,500 acres and comprise 2,000 hotel rooms (6 hotels), villas and condominiums, two golf courses and a casino. Guiana Island is an ecologically sensitive area and the Antiguan government has been criticized for not demanding a full environmental impact study. A debate in the House of Representatives on the development was boycotted by the opposition UPP, resulting in the approval of a government motion to authorize the project. The UPP complained that there had been no public discussion of the issue, while Prime Minister Bird promised 4,000 jobs, US$100mn in foreign exchange earnings, tax income, business opportunities and more besides. The group of islands is surrounded by reefs, with mangroves providing important nesting sites and nursery grounds. Guiana Island, 352 acres, is home to the fallow deer (Dama dama), the endangered West Indian tree duck (Dendrocygna arborea) and the tropical mocking bird (Mimus gilvus). Most of the islands are covered with xerophytic trees and scrub. Remains of Indian habitation have been found on Guiana Island, dating from around 3,000 BC. In the mid 18th century it was owned by Charles Tudway of Parham Hill estate. In 1812, Sir William Codrington III bought the island and farmed it until it was sold out of the family in 1929. A British couple who lived on the island for 30 years and cared for the deer, were removed in 1997 and their house demolished; 300 fallow deer are also to be removed. The old Great House is uninhabited but there was a proposal to restore it, creating a lodge and interpretation centre for a nature reserve. Archaeologists appealed for the chance to study the island before it went under the bulldozer. Development began in 1998.

Economic adjustment was given priority and new tax policies sparked protest demonstrations and strikes. Efforts were made to clean up Antigua's poor reputation with the appointment in 1996 of a special advisor on control of illicit drugs and money laundering. Eleven offshore banks were closed by end 1997 and new legislation was approved in 1998 to close loopholes taken advantage of by international criminal organizations. However, this did not go far enough to satisfy US and UK regulators, who believed money laundering was still taking place. The Government bowed to the criticism and set up a committee in 1999 to study the areas of concern in its offshore financial services legislation.

In March 1999 the ALP won its sixth successive general election, increasing its representation in parliament to 12 seats, while the UPP won four and the BPM retained the Barbuda seat. The new cabinet was notable for the appointment of Vere Bird Jr as Minister of Agriculture, Lands and Fisheries.

Government

Antigua and Barbuda is a constitutional monarchy within the Commonwealth and the British Crown is represented by a Governor General. The head of government is the Prime Minister. There are two legislative houses: a directly elected 17-member House of Representatives and a 17-member Upper House, or Senate, appointed by the Governor General, mainly on the advice of the Prime Minister and the Leader of the Opposition. Antigua is divided into six parishes: St George, St John's, St Mary, St Paul, St Peter and St Phillip. Community councils on Antigua and the local government council on Barbuda are the organs of local government. The Barbuda Council has nine seats, with partial elections held every two years. In the 1997 elections, the Barbuda People's Movement (BPM) defeated the New Barbuda Development Movement, an offshoot of the governing Antigua Labour Party, winning all five seats up for election, The BPM now controls all nine seats.

The economy

The economy was long dominated by the cultivation of sugar, the major export earner until 1960 when prices fell dramatically and crippled the industry. By 1972 sugar had largely disappeared and farming had shifted towards fruit, vegetables, cotton and live-stock. The economy is now based on services, principally tourism and offshore banking where improvements in legislation were made in 1999-2000 to prevent money laundering. Hotels and restaurants contribute about 25% of gross domestic product and employ about one third of the work force. Tourism receipts make up about 60% of total foreign exchange earnings and there are about 5,000 hotel rooms. Tourist numbers were hit by the hurricane damage of 1995 which carried over into 1996. However, in 1997 stopover arrivals and cruise passenger arrivals increased. 1998 was another hurricane year, but the effects of Georges were not so severe as Luis in 1995 and hotels soon completed repairs. The start of Virgin Atlantic air services from London helped tourist arrival statistics. In 1999, stayover arrivals rose by 1.9% to 207,862, while cruise ship passengers were down by 3.3% to 325,195. However, the winter season 1999/2000 brought a sharp drop of 11.9% in stayover arrivals, with a 22% fall in visitors from the USA 18% from Germany and 13% from Canada.

There is some light industry which has been encouraged by tax and other incentives, but manufacturing for export is hampered by high wages and energy costs. A major expansion of tourist infrastructure has taken place, with development of harbour, airport, road and hotel facilities. This investment has not yet touched the bulk of the population and in rural areas small wooden shacks still constitute the most common form of dwelling, often alongside resorts and villa developments. Economic growth slowed in the early 1990s; political instability and corruption discouraged private sector investment, while government finances were weakened by high levels of debt, wages and tax evasion. Since the 1995 hurricane, however, gdp has picked up and strong growth rates recorded.

The hurricane disaster of 1995 and its effect on the tourist industry had a knock-on impact on the fiscal accounts because of a sharp fall in tax revenues and increased spending demands. The Government turned to the IMF and World Bank for advice, and subsequently introduced an austerity plan which was reinforced by the 1996/97 budget. Spending cuts were announced for the public sector with a two year wage freeze although the Government rejected the IMF proposal for redundancies, abolition of price controls and privatizations. By 1998 most of Antigua's public external debt had been rescheduled, following agreements with Japan and Italy at the beginning of the year. Nevertheless, by 1999 the fiscal deficit was 7% of gdp because of increased public sector wages, import tax waivers and reduced earnings by public utilities.

St Kitts and Nevis

The islands of St Kitts (officially named St Christopher) and Nevis are in the north part of the Leeward Islands in the Eastern Caribbean. Wherever you go on these two small islands there are breathtaking, panoramic views of the sea, mountains, cultivated fields and small villages. Both islands are fully aware of their heritage and care for their historical buildings. Owing to the early colonization, many are of stone and are in interesting contrast with those of wood. While one federation, the sister islands are quite different. St Kitts, the larger, is more cosmopolitan and livelier, while Nevis is quieter and more sedate.

Ins and outs

Getting there
See transport, page 626, for further details

Air *JMC Airways* offers a weekly charter flight directly into St Kitts from London and is the most convenient way to get there from the UK. Connections to North America and Europe can be made through San Juan (*American Eagle* and *LIAT*), St Maarten (*LIAT* and *Winair*), Barbados (*LIAT*) and Antigua (*LIAT*). There are good connections with other Caribbean Islands (Anguilla, Grenada, St Croix, St Eustatius, St Lucia, St Thomas and Tortola) with *LIAT* and Windward Islands Airways (*Winair*). Weekly charters include *Royal* from Toronto throughout the year and seasonal weekly charters from Detroit, Chicago, Dallas and Boston. **RL Bradshaw International**, St Kitts' main airport, is two miles from Basseterre (a 2 min walk

St Kitts

to the bus stop at the roundabout northeast of Independence Square, EC$1.25 return the Basseterre). There is also an airport on Nevis, at Newcastle airfield, seven miles from Charlestown (on the main road, bus to Charlestown EC$3.50), served by *LIAT*, *Winair*, *Coastal Air Transport* and light charter aircraft from St Kitts, Anguilla, Antigua, St-Barthélémy, St Croix and St Maarten. Expect to have your baggage searched on your way in to the island. Departure delays have been minimized by improved facilities on both islands. *Nevis Express* has up to 10 daily flights between St Kitts and Nevis. The grander hotels on Nevis will arrange chartered air transfers from Antigua or St Kitts for their guests (for instance, Carib Aviation from Antigua), highly recommended to avoid the crush. **Boat** The new port in Basseterre is Port Zante, which can accommodate two of the largest cruise ships (an increasingly popular way to visit the island) and will eventually boast a huge hotel, casino and many shops, although at present it is landscaped with flowers, grass and bushes and a smattering of buildings under construction.

Getting around
Driving is on the left

Buses on both islands are cheap and speedy. Drivers are generally very obliging and, if asked, may even divert their route to accommodate you. They run from very early in the morning until 2300 on St Kitts, but on Nevis there is a reduced service after 1600 and very few after 1800. Buses are identified by their green H registration plate, flag them down with a wave. **Cars**, jeeps, mini mokes can be hired from US$30-35 per day from a variety of agencies on both islands. The main road on St Kitts is, for the most part, very good and motorists, especially bus drivers, can be very fast. Watch out for corners and be alert at all times. The main road is not as good on Nevis, where storm ditches frequently cross the paved road; drive slowly and carefully. Traffic has increased and parking in Charlestown is difficult. Fuel is US$2 per gallon. Most rental companies will help you obtain the obligatory temporary driving licence, EC$100, valid for a year, from the Fire Station, Ponds Road, Police Station, Cayon Street, or Inland Revenue Dept, Bay Road, above Post Office. Several passenger **ferries** including the *Caribe Queen*, *Carib Breeze* and *MV Sea Hustler* operate on a regular schedule between St Kitts (departing from the Bayfront jetty close to the bus terminal down town) and Nevis.

Climate

The weather is pleasant all year round but the best time to visit is during the dry months from Nov-May. The temperature varies between 17°C and 33°C, tempered by sea winds and with an average annual rainfall of 55 ins on St Kitts and 48 ins on Nevis. St Kitts received severe damage from the flooding associated with Hurricane Lenny in November 1999. Coastal roads were cut, buildings damaged and the Fort Zante tourist project was so badly hit that its future was in the balance.

Flora and fauna

Both islands are home to the green vervet monkey, introduced by the French some 300 years ago, now dwelling on the forested areas in the mountains. They can be seen in many areas including Brimstone Hill. Scientists have been studying these attractive little creatures and many have been exported; being relatively free of disease they are used for medical research. The monkey is the same animal as on Barbados but the Kittitians used to eat them. Another animal, the mongoose, imported by colonists to kill rats in the sugar estates and snakes never achieved its original purpose (rats being nocturnal whereas the mongoose is active by day) and survives in considerable numbers. It has contributed to the extinction of many species of lizard, ground nesting birds, green iguanas, brown snakes and red-legged tortoises. There are also some wild deer on the southeast peninsula, imported originally from Puerto Rico by Philip Todd in the 1930s. In common with other West Indian islands, there are highly vocal frogs, lots of lizards (the anole is the most common), fruit bats, insect bats and butterflies, although nothing particularly rare. Birds are typical of the region, with lots of sea fowl like brown pelicans and frigate birds to be seen, as well as three species of hummingbirds. Fish abound in local waters (rays, barracuda, king fish and brilliantly coloured smaller species) and the increasingly rare black coral tree can be sighted in the reef of the same name.

St Kitts & Nevis have the earliest documented evidence of honey bees in the Caribbean

Leeward Islands

Essentials

Documents US and Canadian visitors do not require passports but need only produce proof of citizenship to stay up to six months. Other nationalities need passports and a return ticket but for up to six months visas are not required for Commonwealth and EU countries, Finland, Iceland, Liechtenstein, Norway, San Marino, Sweden, Switzerland, Turkey, Uruguay, Venezuela and nationals of other member countries of the OAS, with the exception of the Dominican Republic and Haiti who do require visas. Visas can be extended for US$20 per month for the first three months and then US$30 for the following three months up to a maximum of six months.

Currency East Caribbean dollar: EC2.70=US$1. US dollars accepted. When prices are quoted in both currencies, for example for departure tax, taxi fares, a notional rate of EC$2.50 = US$1 is used. There are no restrictions on the amount of foreign currency that can be imported or exported, but the amount of local currency exported is limited to the amount you imported and declared. Visa is the most widely used, Access/Mastercard and Diners Club are not so popular.

Departure tax There is an airport departure tax of US$17 per person, not payable for stays of less than 24 hours (or when you leave on the same flight number as you arrived the previous day, that is slightly more than 24 hours), and an environmental levy of US$1.50.

Ports of entry (Own flag). List all anchorage stops on cruising permit at the Port Authority in Basseterre and clear with immigration in Nevis. Charges are EC$20 up to 20 tons, EC$35 up to 30 tons, EC$38 up to 50 tons. Port dues EC$6-25 based on size. There is no additional charge in Nevis once you have cleared in St Kitts.

Anchorages Port Zante Marina in Basseterre, White House and Ballast Bay are the best on St Kitts, Oualie Beach on Nevis is beautiful. Good groceries, alcoholic drinks, laundry, propane. Can have fuel delivered to dock and buy water by the cubic ton. Marina charges including water: under 40ft, US$0.40 per foot; 40-70ft, US$0.60; over 70ft, US$1.20. For information, Port Authority, T4658121, Port Zante, T4665021.

Official time Atlantic Standard Time, four hours behind GMT, one ahead of EST.

Voltage 230 volts AC/60 cycles (some hotels have 110V).

St Kitts and Nevis are small islands, yet have a wide variety of habitats, with rainforest, dry woodland, wetland, grassland and salt ponds. The forests (of which a small percentage are rain forests) on the sister islands are restricted in scale but St Kitts is one of the few areas of the world where the forest is expanding. It provides a habitat for wild orchids, candlewoods and exotic vines. Fruits and flowers, both wild and cultivated, are in abundance, particularly in the gorgeous gardens of Nevis. Trees include several varieties of the stately royal palm, the spiny-trunked sandbox tree, silk cotton, and the turpentine or gum tree. Visitors can explore the rainforests on foot with guides and gentle hikes through trails and estates also reap many rewards in terms of plant-gazing. Several trails are clear and do not need a guide, although it should be noted that there are no marked trails; care should be taken and advice sought. Comparatively clear trails include Old Road to Philips, the old British military road, which connected the British settlements on the northeast and southwest coasts of St Kitts without going through French territory when the island was partitioned. It should be noted, however, that with the passage of Hurricane Luis in 1995 this trail was badly damaged. Efforts have been made to clear the trail but excessive rainfall subsequently made the road difficult to traverse. There are also trails from Belmont to the crater of Mount Liamuiga, from Saddlers to the Peak, from Lamberts or the top of Wingfield Heights to Dos d'Ane lake (known locally as Dos d'Ane pond).

Media *Newspapers* The Observer, The Democrat, *the* Leeward Times (weekly) or The Labour Spokesman *(twice weekly). Other useful publications are* The St Kitts and Nevis Visitor *(annual), the official publication of the Hotel and Tourism Association, available at hotels and the tourist offices. Check the range of* **books** *at St Christopher Heritage Society, Basseterre, and Museum of Nevis History, Charlestown.* St Kitts, Cradle of the Caribbean *by Brian Dyde and* Nevis, Queen of the Caribees *by Joyce Gordon are both published by MacMillan.* **Radio and TV** *AM/FM ZIZ Radio medium wave 555 kHz and 96 FM; Choice 105 FM. VON Radio in Nevis 895 kHz medium wave and Radio Paradise 825 kHz. Two TV stations: the state run ZIZ and Nevis-based Christian station Trinity Broadcasting.*

Tourist offices overseas *Canada 365 Bay St, Suite 806, Toronto, T416-3686707, F3683934, skbnevcan@sympatico.ca* **Germany**: *Walter Kolbstrasse 9-11, 60594 Frankfurt, T49-699621640, F49-69610637.* **UK**: *10 Kensington Court, London W8 5DL, T020-73760881, F020-79376742, StKitts.Nevis@btinternet.com* **USA** *414 East 75th St, New York NY 10021, T212-5351234, F212-7346511 and Benford Assoc, 1464 Whippoorwill Way, Mountainside, NJ 07092, T908-2326701, F908-2330485.*

Laundry *Warners, Bird Rock Road, Basseterre, T4658630, including dry cleaning (allow a week). Others include Dr Cleaners, T4668075/6; the People's Store, T4652056; Elite Laundry Enterprise, T4656508. In Nevis, Clean Wash Laundrette, T469-0681/1188.*

Safety *Note that the penalties for possession of narcotics are very severe and no mercy is shown towards tourists. Theft has increased, do not leave your things unattended in a car or on the beach.*
Health *Mains water is chlorinated, but bottled water is available if preferred for drinking, particularly outside the main towns. Dairy produce, meat, poultry, seafood, fruit and vegetables are generally considered safe. A yellow fever or cholera vaccination certificate is required if you are arriving from an infected area.*

Public holidays *New Year's Day (1 Jan), Carnival Day/Las' Lap (2 Jan), Good Friday, Easter Monday, May Day (1st Mon in May), Whit Monday (end of May), the Queen's birthday (June), Aug Mon/Emancipation Day (beginning of the month), National Heroes Day (16 Sep), Independence Day (19 Sep), Christmas Day (25 Dec), Boxing Day (26 Dec).*

Diving and marine life

There is very good snorkelling and scuba diving. Most dive sites are on the Caribbean side of the islands, where the reef starts in shallow water and falls off to 100 ft or more. Between the two islands there is a shelf in only 25 ft of water which attracts lots of fish, including angelfish, to the corals, sea fans and sponges. There is black coral off the southeast peninsula, coral caves, reefs and wrecks with abundant fish and other sea creatures of all sizes and colours. Off St Kitts good reefs to dive include **Turtle Reef** (off Shitten Bay) which is good for beginners and snorkelling, **Coconut Reef** in Basseterre Bay and **Pump Bay** by Sandy Point. Much of the diving is suitable for novices and few of the major sites are deeper than 70 ft. Several wrecks and some other sites are actually shallow enough for very rewarding snorkelling although the very best snorkelling around St Kitts is only accessible by boat.

Dive sites

Kenneth's Dive Centre based in Basseterre (Bay Road, and also at Timothy Beach, T4657043, F4656472); Kenneth Samuel (friendly, helpful) is a PADI-certified Dive Master offering courses, dive packages (single tank dive US$50, US$75 two-tank dive, four day package US$245) and all equipment. There are facilities for people with disabilities. He uses catamarans, *Lady Peggy* and *Lady Madonna,* or a 32ft motor launch, *Lady Majesta. Pro-Divers* gives PADI instruction, T4653223, F4650265, prodiver@caribsurf.com, dive gear available for rent, dive packages

Dive centres

Leeward Islands

available, single-tank dive US$45, two-tank dive US$70, resort course US$75, three-day PADI Open Water certification US$300, three-hour snorkelling US$35. Ocean kayaks available for hire. *St Kitts Scuba* is at Birdrock Beach Hotel, offering PADI instruction, T4651189, F4653696, two-tank dive US$65, resort course US$65, PADI Open Water certification US$350.

Snorkelling off **Oualie Beach**, Nevis, is excellent and also good at Nisbett Beach and Tamarind Bay. *Scuba Safaris*, run by Ellis Chaderton, is based at Oualie Beach, T4699518, F4699619: diving (US$45 for a single-tank dive, US$80 for two tanks), PADI and NAUI instruction and equipment rental.

Beaches and watersports

St Kitts Most of the beaches are of black, volcanic sand but the beaches known as **Frigate Bay** and **Salt Pond** fringing the southeast peninsula have white sand. Swimming is very good in the Frigate Bay area where all watersports are available. The southeast peninsula itself also has white sand beaches.**Banana Bay,Cockleshell Bay** and **Mosquito Bay** all have sandy beaches, calm water and picturesque views of Nevis just across the straits. There has been little development here so far, but there is the *Turtle Beach Bar and Grill* at Mosquito Bay with a complete range of watersports on offer. Villas are planned here and hotels on other peninsular beaches. Swimming is not safe on the Atlantic side of the island because of strong currents.

Leeward Island Charters' Caona II, a 47-ft catamaran, 67-ft *Eagle*, or *Spirit of St Kitts*, a 70ft catamaran, T4657474, F4657070, office next to the *Ballahoo* restaurant above the Circus for bookings and private charters, take visitors on a sail, snorkel and beach barbecue. Sailing is becoming increasingly popular. The *St Kitts-Nevis Boating Club* (T4658766) organizes sunfish races which are fun, check the bulletin board for details at *PJ's Pizza Bar* (T4658373), Frigate Bay, the *Ballahoo* (T4654197) in Basseterre, or Dougie Brookes who manages the boatyard *Caribee Yachts*, T4658411. *Blue Water Safaris* has one boat, *Caretaker* (38 ft) and two catamarans, *Falcon*(55 ft) and *Irie Lime* (65 ft), offering fishing (US$60 per person), moonlight cruises (US$25), party cruises (US$25), Nevis day tours (US$60), sunset cruises (US$35) and snorkelling trips (US$35), private snorkelling, sailing and fishing charters (US$360 half day), T4664933, F4666740, waterfun@caribsurf.com *Mr X Watersports*, located next to *Monkey Bar* in Frigate Bay, T4654995, rents windsurfing and snorkelling equipment, fishing trips and weekly all-inclusive packages.

There is a wide range of other water-based activities, such as jet-skis, waterskiing, windsurfing et cetera. *Fantasy Parasailing* takes up to six up in the air with optional dips in the sea, T4668930, F4651802, bentels@caribsurf.com Deep sea fishing can be arranged; Oliver Spencer, a fisherman based in Old Road is happy to take visitors, T4656314. In summer there is a race for windsurfers and sunfish to Nevis.

Nevis Nevis had superb white sandy beaches, particularly on the leeward and north coasts although these were struck by Hurricane Lenny in 1999 and much of the sand was washed away. The beautiful four mile **Pinney's Beach** is only a few minutes' walk from Charlestown and is never crowded. The entire middle stretch of Pinney's Beach has been given over to a 196-room *Four Seasons Hotel*. The sun loungers are for guests only but the public has access to the beach. Huge amounts of sand were imported after Lenny and breakwaters were built to protect the beach by the hotel. Watersports facilities are available at *Oualie Beach Club*. *Nevis Watersports*, at Oualie Beach, T4699060, offers waterskiing, US$20 per person per pull, US$60 for 30 minutes; deep sea fishing US$80 per hour (minimum three hours); snorkelling US$30 per half day. Watersports also at *Newcastle Bay Marina*, T4699395 or information from *Mount Nevis Hotel and Beach Club*, T4699373, F4699375. On the Atlantic side of Nevis, the beaches tend to be rocky and the swimming treacherous; there is, though, an excellent beach at White Bay in the southwest.

Horse riding, mountain climbing, cycling, tennis and golf are available. On St **Other sports**
Kitts there are *Trinity Stables* (beach tours US$25 per hour, rainforest tour US$40),
T465-3226/9603, and *Royal Stables* at West Farm, T4652222, F4654444, on Nevis at
the *Hermitage Plantation*, T4693477, F4692481, where they also have horse-drawn
carriage tours, US$50 per 30 minutes and horse riding US$45 for 1½ hours. Nevis
horses are Thoroughbred/Creole crosses, mostly retired from racing on Nevis. *Blue
Water Safaris* (see above) now offer mountain biking tours (US$15), island biking
tours and beach outings. Royal St Kitts Golf Course is an 18-hole international
championship golf course at Frigate Bay (T4658339, 4654463 – use and hire of buggies compulsory) and there is a nine-hole golf course at Golden Rock, St Kitts
(T4658103), where a fun day is held on the last Sunday of the month. On Nevis, the
Four Seasons has an 18-hole golf course (T4691111, F4691112). The St Kitts Triathlon is held on the second Sunday in May. Professional triathletes compete to gain
official points to qualify for the Olympic games; this is preceded by an amateur race.
The grandstand is at *Timothy Beach Hotel*. On Nevis **horse racing** is the second
most popular sport after cricket. The *Nevis Turf and Jockey Club* meets six times a
year to race island thoroughbreds: New Year's Day, Tourism Week (February),
Easter, August during Culturama, Independence Day and Boxing Day. Facilities
past Market Shop and down Hanley's Road include a new grandstand seating 200,
washrooms, a parimutual booth, good food and dancing well into the night,
T4698442. There is a minimum of five races and horses sometimes come from
neighbouring islands. Contact Richard Lupinacci at the *Hermitage Inn* for details,
T4693477, F4692481. Look out for the more amusing donkey races.

St Kitts

St Kitts has an area of 68 square miles, made up of three groups of rugged volcano peaks   Population: 35,340
*split by deep ravines and a low lying peninsula in the southeast where there are salt
ponds and fine beaches. The dormant volcano, Mount Liamuiga (3,792ft, pronounced
Lie-a-mee-ga) occupies the central part of the island. The mountain was previously
named Mount Misery by the British, but has now reverted to its Carib name, meaning
'fertile land'. The foothills of the mountains, particularly in the north, are covered with
sugar cane plantations and grassland, while the uncultivated lowland slopes are covered with forest and fruit trees.*

Basseterre

The small port of Basseterre is the capital and largest town. By West Indian standards,   Population: 15,000
it is quite big and as such has a quite different feel from its close neighbour, Charlestown. It was founded some 70 years later in 1727. Earthquakes, hurricanes and finally
a disastrous fire destroyed the town in 1867 and consequently its buildings are comparatively modern. There is a complete mishmash of architectural styles from elegant
Georgian buildings with arcades, verandas and jalousies, mostly in good condition, to
hideous 20th-century concrete block houses. In recent years, the development of
tourism has meant a certain amount of redevelopment in the centre. An old warehouse on the waterfront has been converted into the Pelican Mall, a duty-free shopping and recreational complex. It also houses the tourist office and a lounge for guests
of the *Four Seasons Hotel* in Nevis awaiting transport. A new deep water cruise ship
berth has been built on the waterfront on 25 acres of reclaimed land between Bramble
Street and College Street in the heart of Basseterre, capable of accommodating the
largest ships afloat, together with a sailing and power boat marina, and berthing facilities for the inter-island ferry, the *Caribe Queen*. An expanded shopping area with
space for craft vendors and small shops is under construction.
  The Circus, styled after London's Piccadilly Circus (but looking nothing like it),
is the centre of the town. It is busiest on Friday afternoon and comes alive with locals

'liming' (relaxing). The clock tower is a memorial to Thomas Berkely, former president of the General Legislative Council. South down Fort Street is the imposing façade of the Treasury Building, to be converted into a museum of national culture and arts by 2000, with its dome covering an arched gateway (it is equally impressive from the bay). Next door is the post office ■ *Weekdays 0800-1500, 0800-1100 on Thu, 0800-1200 on Sat.* Head north up Fort Street, turn left at the main thoroughfare (Cayon Street) and you will come to **St George's church**, set in its own large garden, with a massive, square buttressed tower. The site was originally a Jesuit church, Notre Dame, which was raised to the ground by the English in 1706. Rebuilt four years later and renamed St George's, it suffered damage from hurricanes and earthquakes on several occasions. It too was a victim of the 1867 fire. It was rebuilt in 1856-69 and contains some nice stained glass windows. There is a fine view of the town from the tower.

Independence Square was built in 1790 and is surrounded now by a low white fence; eight gates let paths converge on a fountain in the middle of the square (it looks like the Union Jack when seen from the air). There are gaily painted muses on top of the fountain. Originally designed for slave auctions and council meetings, it now contains many plants, spacious lawns and lovely old trees. It is surrounded by 18th-century houses and at its east end, the Roman Catholic cathedral with its twin towers. Built in 1927, the Immaculate Conception is surprisingly plain inside. At 10 North Square Street you can visit the very attractive building housing The **Spencer Cameron Art Gallery**. See Rosey Cameron-Smith's paintings and prints of local views and customs as well as an impressive selection of the work of other artists too, T/F4651617. On West Independence Square, the courthouse reflects the old one which burnt down in 1867. It is an impressive building in the colonial style. The Bank of Nova Scotia houses some interesting paintings of Brimstone Hill by Lt Lees

Basseterre

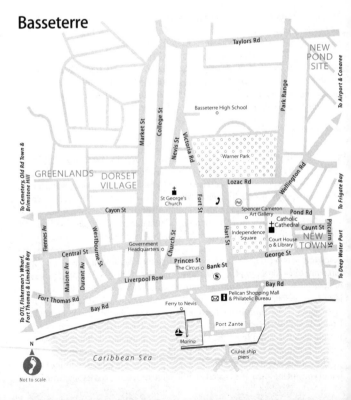

of the Royal Engineers, circa 1783. **St Christopher Heritage Society**, Bank Street has a small, interesting display of old photographs and artefacts. They work on conservation projects and are grateful for donations. ■ *Off West Independence Square, PO Box 338, Basseterre, T4655584. Mon-Tue, Thu-Fri 0830-1300, 1400-1600, Wed, Sat, 0830-1300*. Basseterre is very quiet on Sunday and most of the restaurants are closed, but with the increase in tourism, more places are opening on Sundays, especially if a cruise ship is in.

Around the island

A clockwise route around the island will enable you to see most of the historical sites. A cheap way of touring the island is to take a minibus from Basseterre (Bay Road) to Dieppe Bay Town, then walk to Saddlers (there might be a minibus if you are lucky) where you can get another minibus back to Basseterre along the Atlantic coast. There are several good island tours, including excellent hiking tours to the volcano and through the rain forest with *Kriss Tours* (US$50 per full day, overnight camping US$90, T4654042) and *Greg's Safaris*, recommended, pleasant and informative, (US$40-80, T4654121, F4650707, www.skbee.com/safaris, PO Box 1063). Periwinkle Tours offers guided walks (US$30-35, T4656314, F4657210).

Evidence of sugar cane is everywhere on the comparatively flat, fertile coastal plain. You will drive through large fields of cane and glimpse the narrow gauge railway which is now used to transport it from the fields. Disused sugar mills are also often seen. Around the island are the **Great Houses**: Fairview, Romney Manor (destroyed by fire in 1995), Golden Lemon, the White House, Rawlins and perhaps most famous for its colonial splendour, Ottley's. They have nearly all been converted into hotels and have excellent restaurants.

The island is dominated by the southeast range of mountains (1,159ft) and the higher northwest range which contains **Mount Verchilds** (2,931 ft) and the crater of **Mount Liamuiga** (3,792ft). To climb **Mount Liamuiga** independently, get a bus to St Paul's. Just after the village entrance sign there is a track leading through farm buildings which you follow through the canefields. After 20 minutes take a left fork, ask people working in the fields if you are unsure. At the edge of the forest, the track becomes a path, which is easy to follow and leads through wonderful trees. If you hear something crashing through the upper branches, look up quickly before the monkeys disappear. At 2,600ft is the crater into which you can climb, holding on to vines and roots; on the steady climb from the end of the road note the wild orchids in the forest. A full day is required for this climb which is really only for experienced hikers. To get beyond the crater to the summit you need a guide. You can reach the attractive, but secluded, Dos D'Ane pond near **Mount Verchilds** from the Wingfield estate, a guide is recommended. **Mountain treks**

The west coast particularly is historically important. It is guarded by no less than nine **forts** and the magnificent Brimstone Hill Fortress. Taking the road out of Basseterre, you will pass the sites of seven of them: Fort Thomas, Palmetto Point Fort, Stone Fort, Fort Charles, Charles Fort, Sandy Point Fort and Fig Tree Fort. The remaining two are to the south of Basseterre: Fort Smith and Fort Tyson. Little remains of any of them. A peaceful spot to admire some of Stone Fort's ruins is a swing for two built by local Rastaman, Jahbalo. At Trinity Church, turn right, up the dirt path. At the well-preserved sugar mill there are some ruins to your right. Climb the small mound to find the swing with a view towards cane fields and the Caribbean (sunset recommended). **The west coast**

The the first point of historic interest is situated just before Old Road Town. Sir Thomas Warner landed at Old Road Bay in 1623 and was joined in 1625 by the crew of a French ship badly mauled by the Spanish. Initially befriended by the local Carib chief Tegreman, as many as 3,000 Caribs, alarmed at the rapid colonization of the

Leeward Islands

island, tried to mount an attack in 1626. 2,000 of them were massacred by the combined French and English forces in the deep ravine at **Bloody Point** (the site of Stone Fort). An amicable settlement meant that the English held the central portion of the island roughly in line from Sandy Point to Saddlers in the north to Bloody Point across to Cayon in the south. French names can be traced in both of their areas of influence (Dieppe Bay Town in the north, the Parishes are called Capisterre and Basseterre in the south). The southeast peninsula was neutral. This rapprochement did not last many years as following the colonization of Martinique and Guadeloupe, the French wished to increase their sphere of influence. St Kitts became an obvious target and in 1664 they squeezed the English from the island. For nearly 200 years the coast was defended by troops from one nation or another.

At Old Road Town you turn right to visit **Wingfield Estate**. You drive through a deserted sugar mill and the edge of rain forest. Unfortunately Romney Manor was destroyed by fire in 1995 but the beautiful gardens remain with pleasant views over the coast and a giant 350-year old saman tree. ■ *The estate is home to Caribelle Batik, open Mon-Fri, 0830-1600, T4656253, F4653629.* Apart from a well-stocked shop you can watch the artists producing the highly colourful and attractive material. A guide will explain the process. Also near here the remains of the island's Amerindian civilization can be seen on large stones with drawings and petroglyphs. If you keep driving to the left of Romney Manor and Caribelle Batik, you will find one of the highest paved roads on the island. It is a tough climb so be sure to have a sturdy car or legs. Follow the road up until it ends. A large flat rock at the top is perfect to admire the spectacular view of the mountains in solitude. To the right hand side is a smaller path that leads to an incredible overview of Bat Hole Ghaut. Magnificent views of tropical rainforest in myriad greens. A very secluded spot.

At the village of **Middle Island**, you will see on your right and slightly up the hill, the church of St Thomas at the head of an avenue of dead or dying royal palms. Here is buried Sir Thomas Warner who died on 10 March 1648. The raised tomb under a canopy is inscribed "General of y Caribee". There is also a bronze plaque with a copy of the inscription inside the church. Other early tombs are of Captain John Pogson (1656) and Sir Charles Payne, "Major General of Leeward Carribee Islands" who was buried in 1744. The tower, built in 1880, fell during earth tremors in 1974.

Brimstone Hill   Turn right off the coastal road just before *J's Place* (drink and local food, open from 1100, T4656264, watch the caged green vervet monkeys, they are very aggressive) for the **Fortress of Brimstone Hill**, one of the 'Gibraltars of the West Indies' (a title it shares with Les Saintes, off Guadeloupe). Sprawled over 38 acres on the slopes of a hill 800ft above the sea, it commands an incredible view of St Kitts and Nevis and on clear days, Anguilla (67 miles), Montserrat (40 miles), Saba (20 miles), St Eustatius (5 miles), St-Barts (40 miles) and St-Martin (45 miles) can be seen. The English mounted the first cannon on Brimstone Hill in 1690 in an attempt to force the French from Fort Charles below. It has been constructed mainly out of local volcanic stones and was designed along classic defensive lines. The five bastions overlook each other and also guard the only road as it zig zags up to the parade ground. The entrance is at the Barrier Redan where payment is made. Pass the Magazine Bastion but stop at the Orillon Bastion which contains the massive ordnance store (165ft long with walls at least 6ft thick). The hospital was located here and under the south wall is a small cemetery. You then arrive at the Prince of Wales Bastion (note the name of J Sutherland, 93rd Highlanders 24 October 1822 carved in the wall next to one of the cannons) from where there are good views over to the parade ground. Park at the parade ground, there is a small snack bar and good gift shop near the warrant officer's quarters with barrels of pork outside it. Stop for a good video introduction at the DL Matheson Visitor Centre. A narrow and quite steep path leads to Fort George, the Citadel and the highest defensive position. Restoration is continuing and several areas have been converted to form a most interesting museum. Barrack rooms now hold well-presented and informative displays (pre-columbian,

American, English, French and Garrison). Guides are on hand to give more detailed explanations of the fortifications. The fortress was eventually abandoned in 1852 but was inaugurated as a national park by the Queen in October 1985. ■ *0930-1730 daily, entrance EC$13 or US$5 for foreigners, EC$2 for nationals, it is highly recommended both for adults and children (half price). Allow up to two hours. The local minibus to Brimstone Hill is EC$2.25, then walk up to the fortress, less than 30 minutes but extremely steep. For fit climbers only.*

To continue the island tour, drive on, looking out for the **Plantation Picture House** at *Rawlins Plantation Inn* on the right, up a long drive through canefields. Here there is a lovely art gallery with stunning views, housing paintings and prints by Kate Spencer. ■ *T4657740. 1100-1700.* Keep driving up the road to Rawlins Plantation. Tour the magnificent gardens full of tropical plants and flowers. Back on the main road, continue north. There is a a black sand beach at **Dieppe Bay** which is a good place to stop for lunch, at the upmarket and excellent *Golden Lemon*. Pass through Saddlers and stop at the **Black Rocks**. Here lava has flowed into the sea providing interesting rock formations. Continue on to **Ottley's Plantation** which is also worth a visit. The grounds are not as magnificent as at Rawlins but there are easy, well-marked short walks through the rainforest. Continue on the main road through Cayon (turn right uphill to Spooners for a look at the abandoned cotton ginnery) back to Basseterre via the RL Bradshaw Airport. With advance notice, you can tour the sugar factory near the airport, very interesting and informative. ■ *Tours are only during harvest season, Feb-Aug, T4658157.*

In the hills of St Peter's, just north of Basseterre, is **Nature's Kingdom**, a miniature, island-style wildlife observatory which features animals, fruit trees and plants from around the world. Meet Tom and Jerry, the friendly monkeys. ■ *T4657038. Tours are available. Bar and barbecue.*

The north coast

To visit the southeast peninsula, turn off the roundabout at the end of Wellington Road (opposite turning to the airport) and at the end of this new road turn left. This leads to the narrow spit of land sandwiched between North and South Frigate Bays. This area is being heavily developed, the natural lagoons providing an additional attraction. A number of establishments have been built, including the *Royal St Kitts Beach Resort and Casino*, with tennis courts and an 18-hole golf course. A Hyatt hotel is planned for Friars Bay, with 200 rooms and 75 villas, and the Golf View Estates development at Frigate Bay adds another 37 condominiums. Other hotels are expanding or renovating. The six-mile Dr Kennedy A Simmonds Highway runs from Frigate Bay to Major's Bay. After Frigate Bay the peninsula is almost deserted and quite different from the rest of the island. The road climbs along the backbone of the peninsula and overlooks North and South Friars Bays where you may see green vervet monkeys before descending to White House Bay. Skirt the Great Salt Pond. Half way round turn left to reach Sandbank Bay, a lovely secluded bay (unmarked left turn down dirt road opposite Great Salt Pond). Continue on the main highway and turn left for Cockleshell Bay and Turtle Beach (good for watersports and stunning views across

The southeast peninsula

Southeast Peninsula

North Frigate Bay
North Friar's Bay
Frigate Bay
South Friar's Bay
White House Bay
Sand Bank Bay
Ballast Bay
Great Salt Pond
Green Point
Turtle Beach
Shitten Bay
Mosquito Bay
Major's Bay
Banana Bay
Cockleshell Bay
Nag's Head

N

0 km   1
0 miles   1

Leeward Islands

to Nevis). The main road leads to Major's Bay. At the moment most of the peninsula is isolated and extremely attractive, although tourist development is planned. Despite the road the majority of beaches are difficult to reach. Try to obtain local knowledge if you want to visit them.

Nevis

Population: 9,000

Across the two-mile Narrows Channel from St Kitts is the beautiful little island of Nevis. The islands covers an area of 36 square miles and the central peak, 3,232 ft, is usually shrouded in white clouds and mist. It reminded Columbus of Spanish snow-capped mountains and so he called the island "Las Nieves". (It reminds others, in the wet, of the English Lake District, as does St Kitts.) For the Caribs, it was Oualie, the land of beautiful water. Smaller than St Kitts it is also quieter. The atmosphere is civilized, but low-key and easy-going; all the same, it is an expensive island. Less fertile than St Kitts, the principal crop used to be cotton but only 32 acres were planted in 1995. Agricultural workers have left their smallholdings for jobs in hotels or driving taxis as numbers of tourists, particularly from North America, have risen.

Charlestown

The main town is Charlestown, one of the best preserved old towns in the Caribbean. Situated on Gallows Bay and guarded by Fort Charles to the south and the long sweep of Pinney's Beach to the north, it is a small town with a compact centre. At first sight it would be easy to be disappointed. However there are several interesting buildings dating from the 18th century and the excellent Museum of Nevis History.

D R Walwyn's Plaza is dominated by the balconied Customs House built in 1837 on a much older site and housing the Customs and Agricultural Ministry. Immediately to the north is the post office. Opposite it on the other side of the square is the tourist office. **Memorial Square** is larger and more impressive than D R Walwyn's Plaza, the War Memorial is in a small garden. Explore the courthouse and library. It was built in 1825 and used as the Nevis Government Headquarters but largely destroyed by fire in 1873. The curious little square tower was erected in 1909-10. It contains a clock which keeps accurate time with an elaborate pulley and chain system. Visit the library and you can see them together with the weights among the elaborate roof trusses. ■ *Mon-Fri 0900-1800, Sat 0900-1700. The courthouse is not open to the public, look in through the open windows.*

Charlestown

To Pinney's Beach & Newcastle

Low St
Craddock Rd
Museum of Nevis
St Paul's
Wesleyan Holiness Manse
Methodist Manse
Methodist Church
Chapel St
Ferry to St Kitts
Main St
Prince Charles St
Pier
Cotton Ginnery
D R Walwyn's Plaza
Customs
Happy Hill Alley
Market Place
Philatelic Bureau
Memorial Square
Prince William St
Jewish Cemetery
Market St
Court House & Library
Government Rd
Pol
Island Rd
Grove Park Cricket Ground
N
Not to scale
To Bath & Fig Tree

Along Government Road is the well-preserved **Jewish Cemetery** dating back to 1679, it is locked although entrance is allowed. The key is just above the cemetery at Hunkins shop. At the small market a wide range of island produce, including avocados, ginger root, yams and sweet potatoes, is on sale but go early if you want to catch the bustle. **Markets** are held on Tuesday, Thursday and Saturday mornings, best on Saturday. Market Street to the right houses the philatelic bureau. ■ *0800-1600 Mon-Fri, air conditioned.* The **Cotton Ginnery** was, until 1994, in use during the cotton picking season (February-July). In 1995 it was moved out to the New River Estate, Gingerland, where it is in a renovated building next to the sugar mill ruins there. As part of the Nevis Port upgrade, another Cotton Ginnery building now houses 10 gift shops and a restaurant. On Chapel Street the **Wesleyan Holiness Manse** built in 1812 is one of the oldest stone buildings surviving on the island while the Methodist Manse (next to the prominent Church) has the oldest wooden structure, the second floor being built in 1802.

The **Museum of Nevis History** at the Birthplace of Alexander Hamilton is next to the sea and set in an attractive garden which contains a representative collection of Nevis plants and trees. The original house was built around 1680 but destroyed in the 1840s probably by an earthquake. This attractive two storey house was rebuilt in 1983 and dedicated during the Islands' Independence celebration in September of that year. The Nevis House of Assembly meets in the rooms upstairs (again restored after being damaged by Hurricane Hugo), while the museum occupies the ground floor. Alexander Hamilton, Nevis' most famous son, was born in Charlestown on 11 January 1757. He lived on Nevis for only five years before leaving for St Croix with his family. About half of the display is given over to various memorabilia and pictures of his life. The Museum of Nevis History contains examples of Amerindian pottery, African culture imported by the slaves, cooking implements and recipes, a rum still, and a model of a Nevis lighter. There are also the ceremonial clothes of the Warden which were worn on the Queen's birthday and Remembrance Day. A section is devoted to the conservation of reefs, conch and the rain forest. There is a small shop which sells local produce and some interesting books. All proceeds go to the upkeep of the museum. ■ *T4695786, Mon-Fri 0900-1600, Sat 0900-1200, US$2.*

Around the island

Taking the road south out of Charlestown, you can visit the rather unkempt **Fort Charles**. Fork right at the Shell station and again at the mini roundabout, keep right along the sea shore (rough track), past the wine company building and through gates at the end of the track. The fort was built before 1690 and altered many times before being completed in 1783-90. Nothing much remains apart from the circular well and a small building (possibly the magazine). The gun emplacements looking across to St Kitts are being badly eroded by the sea, eight cannon point haphazardly to sea. The Nevis Council surrendered to the French here in 1782 during the seige of Brimstone Hill on St Kitts.

Back on the main road and only about half a mile outside Charlestown lies the largely ruined **Bath Hotel** and **Spring House**. Built by the Huggins family in 1778, it is reputed to be one of the oldest hotels in the Caribbean. The Spring House lies over a fault which supplies constant hot water at 108°F. ■ *Mon-Fri 0800-1700, Sat 0800-1200, EC$5 to bathe, EC$1.50 towel rental. Most locals bathe further downstream for free.* A new building has been erected here to house the **Horatio Nelson Museum** dedicated in 1992 to commemorate the 205th anniversary of the wedding of Admiral Nelson to Fanny Nisbet. Based on a collection donated by Mr Robert Abrahams, an American, the collection contains memorabilia including letters, china, pictures, furniture and books (request to see the excellent collection of historical documents and display of 17th century clay pipes). It is well worth a visit as it contains an interesting insight into the life of Nelson and his connection with Nevis. He was not always popular having come to the island to enforce the Navigation Acts which forbade the newly independent American states trading with British Colonies. Nelson in his ship *HMS Boreas* impounded four American ships and their cargoes. The Nevis merchants immediately claimed £40,000 losses against Nelson who had to remain on board his ship for eight weeks to escape being put into gaol. It was only after Prince William, captain of *HMS Pegasus*, arrived in Antigua that Nelson gained social acceptability and married the widow Fanny Woodward Nisbet (reputedly for her uncle's money: this proved a disappointment as her uncle left the island and spent his wealth in London). ■ *Mon-Fri, 0900-1600, Sat 0900-1200, US$2, gift shop.*

At Stoney Grove is the new **Caribbean Cove** amusement park, with Disneyland-style miniature golf, bumper boats, video arcade and a restaurant. ■ *T4691286, F4691354. Sun-Thur 1000-2200, Fri-Sat 1000-2400, adults EC$17.50, children EC$7.50.*

More evidence of the Nelson connection is found at the **St John's Fig Tree Anglican Church** about two miles on from the Bath House. Originally built in 1680, the church was rebuilt in 1838 and again in 1895. The marriage certificate of Nelson and Fanny Nisbet is displayed here. There are interesting memorials to Fanny's father William Woodward and also to her first husband Dr Josiah Nisbet. Many died of the fever during this period and taxi drivers will delight in lifting the red carpet in the central aisles for you to see old tomb stones, many connected with the then leading family, the Herberts. The graveyard has many examples of tombstones in family groups dating from the 1780s.

Slightly off the main road to the south lies **Montpelier Great House** where the marriage of Nelson and Nesbit actually took place; a plaque is set in the gatepost. The

Nevis

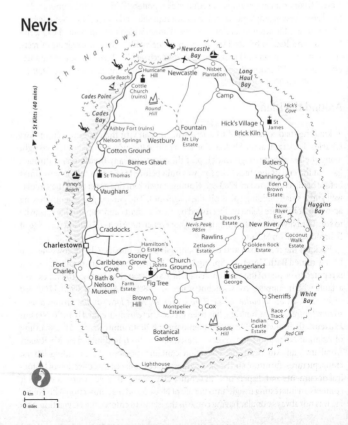

plantation is now a hotel with pleasant gardens. Enormous toads live in the lily ponds formed out of old sugar pans. A very pleasant place for lunch or a drink. Beyond the house lies **Saddle Hill** (1,250 ft). It has the remains of a small fort and it is reputedly where Nelson would look out for illegal shipping. You can follow several goat trails on the hill, giant aloes abound, a track starts at Clay Ghaut, but most trails beyond the fort are dense and overgrown. The *Hermitage* (another of the Great Houses) is signposted left just after the sign for the Montpelier. Near Montpelier is the **Botanical Garden**, seven acres of cactus, bamboo, orchids, flowering trees and shrubs, heliconias and rose gardens, a mermaid fountain, a greenhouse with bridges, ponds, waterfall and tea house with English high tea and gift shop. ■ *Gardens open 0800-1700, EC$20, children half price, tea house 1000-1700, T4693399, F4692875.*

The small parish of **Gingerland** is reached after about three miles. Its rich soils made it the centre of the island's ginger root production (also cinnamon and nutmeg) but it is noteworthy for the very unusual octagon Methodist Church built in 1830. You turn right here along Hanleys Road to reach **White Bay Beach**. Go all the way down to the bottom and turn left at the Indian Castle experimental farm, past the race course (on Black Bay) and Red Cliff. There is a small shelter but no general shade. Beware, this is the Atlantic coast, the sea can be very rough and dangerous. On quieter days, the surf is fun and provides a welcome change from the quiet Leeward coast at Pinney's. There is a reef further out which is good for fishing (several fishing boats in the bay, one may take you out). There are good views across to Montserrat. On the way back beware of the deep (and hidden) storm drain crossing the road near the church. At Clay Gaut, Gingerland, is the **Eva Wilkin Gallery** in an old windmill. Started by Howard and Marlene Paine, it has a permanent exhibition of paintings and drawings by Nevisian Eva Wilkin (whose studio it was until her death), prints of which are available, also antique maps, et cetera.

After Gingerland the land becomes more barren. Several sugar mills were built here because of the wind, notably **Coconut Walk Estate**, **New River Estate** (fairly intact) and the **Eden Brown Estate**, built around 1740. A duel took place between the groom and best man at the wedding of Julia Huggins. Both men were killed, Julia became a recluse and the great house was abandoned. It has the reputation of being haunted. Although government owned and open to the public, the ruins are in a poor condition and care should be taken.

The island road continues north through Butlers and Brick Kiln (known locally as Brick Lyn), past St James church (Hick's village), Long Haul and Newcastle Bays (with the *Nisbet Plantation Inn*) to the small fishing community of **Newcastle**. You can visit the Newcastle Pottery where distinctive red clay is used to make among other things the traditional Nevis cooking pot. The Newcastle **Redoubt** can be seen from the road. Built in the early 17th century, it was used as a refuge from Carib attack and may have been the site of a Carib attack in 1656. The airport is situated here.

The road continues through an increasingly fertile landscape and there are fine views across the Narrows to the southeast peninsula of St Kitts, looking for all the world like the west coast of Scotland. Note **Booby Island** in the middle of the channel, it is mostly inhabited by pelicans (all birds are referred to as boobies by the local population). It offers good diving. The road between here and Charlestown often passes gardens which are a riot of colour. The small hill on your left is **Round Hill** (1,014ft). It can be reached on the road between Cades Bay and Camps Village (there is supposed to be a soufrière along this road). Turn off the road at Fountain Village by the methodist church. There are good views from the radio station at the top over Charlestown, across to St Kitts and beyond to Antigua. Do not expect to see much wildlife however. There is a small beach at **Mosquito Bay** and some good snorkelling can be had under the cliffs of Hurricane Hill. The *Oualie Beach Hotel* offers a range of watersport facilities including scuba diving and snorkelling equipment. On Sunday afternoons there is often live music and a barbecue at Mosquito Bay. Sailing trips can be negotiated with locals.

Leeward Islands

Under Round Hill lies **Cottle Chapel** (1824). It was the first Anglican place on Nevis where slaves could be taught and worship with their master. Ruined now, its beautiful little font can be seen in the Museum of Nevis History. Nearby, just off the island road, lies **Fort Ashby**. Nothing remains of the Fort (it is now a restaurant on Cades Bay although the cannons are in their original positions). It protected Jamestown, the original settlement and former capital, which was supposedly destroyed by an earthquake and tidal wave in 1690, and was originally called St James' Fort. Drive past the Nelson springs (where the barrels from *HMS Boreas* were filled) and **St Thomas' Church** (built in 1643, one of the oldest surviving in the Caribbean) to Pinney's Beach. There are many tracks leading down to the beach often with a small hut or beach bar at the end of them. The *Four Seasons Hotel* lies in the middle of the beach. The sun loungers are reserved for guests only but the beach is public. Behind the resort is the Robert Trent Jones II golf course which straddles the island road. The manicured fairways and greens are in marked contrast with the quiet beauty of the rest of the island but the hotel's considerable efforts at landscaping have lessened its impact.

There are many interesting walks over old sugar plantations and through the rain forest on **Mount Nevis**. *Sunrise Tours* (T4692758) arranges trips to Nevis Peak (four hours round trip, US$35 per person), Saddle Hill (1½ hours, US$30) or the Water Source (3 hours, US$40). *Heb's Nature Tours* is run by Michael Herbert, Rawlins Village, Gingerland, T4692501, offering similar tours: Mount Nevis (5 hours, US$35-40), Rainforest hike (4 hours, US$25-30), Saddle Hill hike (3 hours, US$20-25), medicinal plants (2 hours, US$15) and Camp Spring (2½ hours, US$15-20), price depends on numbers. *Top to Bottom* is run by biologists Jim and Nikki Johnson, who are very flexible and organize walks to suit you, also a night-time, star-gazing walk, mostly 2-3 hours, US$20 per person, children half price, snacks of fruit and coconut included (T4699080). David Rollinson of *Eco-Tours* (T4692091, droll@caribsurf.com) is very knowledgeable; he offers 'eco rambles' over the 18th century Coconut Walk and New River Estates and a 'Sugar trail' Mountravers hike over the old Pinney Estate (US$20 per person) as well as Sunday morning strolls round historic Charlestown (US$10 per person). *All Seasons Streamline Tours*, T4691138, F4691139, at Bath Estate, offer a/c mini-bus tours around the island.

Essentials

Sleeping:
St Kitts
There is a wide variety of accommodation ranging from first class hotels to rented cottages, but it is advisable to book well in advance. Large reductions are available in summer. There is a 7% occupancy tax and 10% service charge. In restaurants about 10-15% is expected. The St Kitts/Nevis Hotel Association can be reached at PO Box 438, Basseterre, St Kitts, T4655304, F4657746.

Basseterre LL-AL *Ocean Terrace Inn (OTI)*, Box 65, T4652754, F4651057, tdcoti@ caribsurf.com A/c, TV, apartments and suites, 3 pools, wedding gazebo, fitness centre, beach shuttle, *OTI* also organizes tours and other activities such as scuba diving, evening shows and has a fairly expensive but nice restaurant with views over Basseterre harbour, good service throughout. **L-A** *Palms Hotel*, PO Box 64, T4650800, F4655889, www.palms hotel.com, central, on the Circus. 12 pleasant junior, 1 and 2-bedroom suites, a/c, phones, cable TV, mini bar, tea and coffee machine. **C-E** *Central Guest House and Apartments*, T465-2278/4062, ideally located in the heart of town. Rooms with or without kitchenette. **C-E** *Glimbaro Guest House*, Cayon St and Market St, T4651786, F4659832. Signed 'Guest House, Pest Control, Fumigation...', new rooms, a/c, cable TV, some with bath and patio, cheaper rooms with shared bathrooms, 10% off weekly rates, fans, phone, *Pisces* restaurant with good local food, especially fish. **C-E** *Parkview Inn*, Victoria Rd, next to Parkview Amusements, Box 64, T4652100. Very basic. **C-E** *Sea View Inn*, Bay Rd, T4652278/4654062, opposite buses. Newly renovated 10 double rooms, 6 suites, a/c, good restaurant, convenient for central Basseterre.

Outside Basseterre The highly recommended **LL** *Rawlins Plantation*, 16 miles from Basseterre in the northwest of the island. Box 340, T4656221, F4654954, Rawplant@caribsurf.com Pricey, but beautiful, tranquil and offers grass tennis, swimming pool, horse riding and croquet, no credit cards accepted, 10 cottages, laundry service and afternoon tea included. **LL-L** *The Golden Lemon Hotel and Villas*, Dieppe Bay, T4657260, F4654019, in the USA T1-800-6337411, www.goldenlemon.com, on black sand beach about 15 miles from Basseterre. 34 rooms, having built some 1-2 bedroom beachfront cottages with pools next to the original great house building dating from 1610, pool, tennis, watersports, restaurant, each room is tastefully furnished with West Indian antiques, lovely atmosphere, no children under 18. Highly recommended. 520ft above sea level in 35 acres, is the **LL** *Ottleys Plantation Inn*, PO Box 345, T4657234, F4654760, www.ottleys.com Rooms in the 1832 great house or cottages, a/c, fans, restaurant, pool, nice walks, beach shuttle, tennis/golf shuttle, packages including some meals available. **LL-A** *Bird Rock Beach Hotel*, owned/managed by former Director of Tourism, Larkland Richards, PO Box 227, T4658914, F4651675, brbh@caribsurf.com Renovated 1998, 38 rooms/suites, a/c, TV, up on the cliffs overlooking the tiny black sand beach and industrial estate, inconvenient suburban location, taxi to Basseterre US$8, pool, tennis, volleyball, watersports, 2 restaurants, 3 bars. **L-B** *Rock Haven Bed and Breakfast*, PO Box 821, T/F4655503. Good views, close to beaches and golf, great breakfast. **AL-B** *Morgan Heights Condominiums*, PO Box 735, T4658633, F4659272. Beautiful views of Atlantic Coast and southeast peninsula, breezy, friendly management, excellent restaurant. The **AL-B** *Fairview Inn*, close to Basseterre is a cottage complex situated around an 18th century great house, Box 212, T4652472, F4657050, wall@caribsurf.com **B-C** *Earle's Vacation Home*, PO Box 604, T4657546, F4667868. Family-style furnished, self-contained 1-2 bedroom apartments. **B-D** *Vacation Inn*, corner of Cayon and College St, T465-4628/0363. Convenient for town, noisy but clean. Reductions for children under 8, a/c, fans, restaurant, pool. West of Basseterre, **C** *Trinity Inn Apartments*, Palmetto Point, T4653226, F4659460, www.islandimages.com-trinity A/c, pool, restaurant, riding stables, very friendly, excellent value. **D** *Llewelyn's Haven Guest House*, T4652941. Basic, clean, good views of Basseterre and bay. *Glasford Apartments*, PO Box 486, T4657974, F4659413. Self-contained units with ocean view just outside Basseterre. *Vientomarsol*, PO Box 323, T4658514. 2 comfortable cottages for 4 people, on Conaree Beach.

Frigate Bay area **LL-L** *Island Paradise Beach Village*, PO Box 444, T4658035, F4658236, Islandparadise@caribsurf.com 62 condominiums set in 5 acres of woodland on the Atlantic beach, laundry, barbecue, pool, *PJ's Pizza*, store, 1-3 bedrooms, US$895-1,835 per week. Dominating Frigate Bay with its golf course and casino is the all-inclusive **LL-L** *Royal St Kitts Beach Resort & Casino*, T4651290, F4651031, on 26 acres, 15 min walk or take shuttle bus to beaches on Atlantic and Caribbean. 236 a/c rooms, some quieter than others, all have balcony or patio, 221 condos overlooking the ocean with convention and banqueting centre, casino, nightclub and other entertainment, disco, restaurants, watersports, 18-hole championship golf course, tennis, table tennis, bicycles, lagoon fishing, pedaloes, spa, beauty treatment, fitness centre, medical centre. **LL-L** *Sun 'N' Sand Beach Resort*, PO Box 341, T4658037/8, F4656745. Studios or bedroomed cottages on Atlantic beach, a/c, fans, pool, TV, some deluxe honeymoon rooms, well run, lovely gardens, good food. Recommended. **LL-AL** *Coconut Beach Club (Timothy Beach Resort)*, PO Box 81, T4658597, F4657723, on Caribbean beach. Little shade, studios and suites, watersports, sailing, pool, a/c, TV, café. **LL-AL** *Frigate Bay Resort*, PO Box 137, T4658935, F4657050, www.frigatebay.com Rooms and suites, a/c, Olympic size pool, restaurant. **LL-AL** *Leeward Cove Condominium*, PO Box 123, T4658030, F4653476, on Atlantic Beach. 1-2 bedroom self-catering apartments, a/c, free green fees at Golf Club, mini-mart, laundry service, free car per week's stay. **LL-AL** *Paradise Beach Resort & Casino*, T4668063. 2 and 3-storey villas, a/c, on the beach, Olympic sized swimming pool, health spa, tennis courts, watersports, riding, excursions. **LL-AL** *Sea Lofts on the Beach*, PO Box 813, T/F4651075. Condominiums in 3 acre gardens on Atlantic Beach, 2 bedrooms, US$825-1200 per week, pool, 2 tennis courts, barbecue, stores, free green fees. **B** *Gateway Inn*, PO Box 64, T4657155, F4659322, gateway@caribsurf.com 10 self-catering apartments, a/c, phone, TV, laundry, 10 mins from beach or golf course, US$480 per week.

C *Rock Haven Bed & Breakfast*, PO Box 821, T/F4655503. Suite with kitchen facilities, TV, laundry facilities, views of both coasts. *Palms Bay Condominiums*, PO Box 393, T465-5555, F4656400. New condos with spectacular views.

Sleeping: Nevis Accommodation on Nevis tends to be up-market, in reconstructions of old plantation Great Houses, tastefully decorated in an English style (collectively called *The Inns of Nevis*). Some have reciprocal arrangements whereby you can stay at one and use the facilities of the others. They are well worth a visit. After the 1998 hurricane season the hotels made a tremendous effort to repair damage in time for the winter season. *The Four Seasons* employed 700 workers to restore the gardens and buildings, and planted 7.5 acres of grass turf and hundreds of mature palms. The other plantation inns suffered less damage and lost only a few of their trees. *The Four Seasons* was badly hit again by Hurricane Lenny in 1999 and remained closed for a year until the winter season 2000/2001.

LL *Four Seasons Resort*, 196 rooms, on Pinney's Beach, PO Box 565, T4691111, F4691040, in North America 800-3223442, www.fourseasons.com Expected to reopen end-Nov 2000, Robert Trent Jones II 18-hole championship golf course, pro-shop, Peter Burwash tennis complex, pools, watersports including diving, sailboats, windsurfing, fitness centre, conference centre, poolside restaurant and all entertainment including children's activity programme and live music, particularly in high season, transport by boat from St Kitts US$65 per person return.The **LL** *Nisbet Plantation Beach Club*, St James, built on site of 18th-century plantation on ½ mile beach unfortunately close to airport, T4699325, F4699864, www.nisbetplantation.com 38 comfortable rooms in cottages/suites with ceiling fans, tennis, swimming pool, croquet, a beach bar and pavilion, huge breakfasts, delicious afternoon tea and excellent dinner, all included in rates, laundry, local phone calls and postage complimentary. Highly recommended. **LL** *Tamarind Bay Cliffdwellers Villas*, PO Box 311, T4698262. A distinctive new villa resort with private home atmosphere and luxury hotel facilities offering beachfront and hillside locations.

LL-L *Hermitage Plantation*, St John's Parish, T4693477, F4692481, www.hermitage nevis.com Run by Richard and Maureen Lupinacci, very friendly, beautiful cottages, 4-poster beds, tennis, pool, massage, reflexology etc, stunning setting, many guests extend their stay, romance/equestrian/adventure/diving packages offered. Highly recommended. **LL-L** *Montpelier Plantation Inn and Beach Club*, also St John's, PO Box 474, T4693462, F4692932, www.montpeliernevis.com 750ft above sea level but with private landscaped beach as well, a favourite with British tourists, delightful, friendly and helpful, pool, tennis, beach shuttle, child reductions, 17 rooms.The **LL-L** *Mount Nevis Hotel and Beach Club*, PO Box 494, T4699373, F4699375, www.mountnevishotel.com Built 1989, family-owned, 32 rooms and studios, a/c, TV, VCR, phone, breakfast included, pool, fitness centre, massage.

LL-AL *Golden Rock Plantation Inn*, St George's Parish, T4693346, F4692113, www.golden-rock.com 7 cottages, 15 rooms in 18th-century plantation house, 2-storey suite in old windmill for honeymooners/families, antique furniture, 4-poster beds, ocean view all the way to Montserrat, family plan available, pool, tennis, beach shuttle, specialist interest tours, principally of ecological content, excellent hiking excursions, enjoy afternoon tea and watch the monkeys. **LL-AL** *Hurricane Cove Bungalows*, T/F4699462, www.hurricanecove.com, on hillside with wonderful seaview. 11 1-3 bedroomed, well-equipped wooden bungalows of Finnish design, some with private pools, swimming pool, above Oualie beach, path down to beach, good snorkelling. Sports facilities nearby, 3 night minimum stay in winter, long term discounts. Highly recommended. **LL-AL** *Old Manor Estate and Hotel*, PO Box 70, T4693445, F4693388, reservations 0800-8927093, www.cpscaribnet.com/oldmanor In restored 1690 sugar plantation has 14 rooms including a cottage 800ft above sea level, tropical gardens, beach shuttle, pool, beach restaurant. **LL-AL** *Oualie Beach Hotel*, on the beach, T4699735, F4699176, www.oualie.com Safe for children, friendly, informal, comfortable, mountain bikes, diving and other watersports, 32 well equipped rooms, studios, all with view of bay, deluxe rooms on beach, email access for guests. **LL-AL** *Pinney's Beach Hotel*, in Charlestown, PO Box 61, T4695207, F4691088. 48 rooms, 7 cottages, pool, watersports, horse riding, on the beach, dining room has no view, food and service reported poor off season, rooms in need of redecoration.

There are also many guesthouses, apartments and cottages including **A** *Yamseed Inn*, T4699361. 4 rooms including delicious breakfast, lovely view of St Kitts, beautiful gardens, excellent value. Friendly, helpful owner Sybil Siegfried can arrange crossings from St Kitts and car hire. **C-E** *Sunset View*, PO Box 503, T4693464. **C** *Sea Spawn Guest House*, PO Box 233, T4695239, 5 min walk north of Charlestown, 2 from Pinney's Beach. 6 fishing boats, car rental and kitchen and dining facilities, quiet. **B-D** *Al's Guest House, Apartments and Cottages*, PO Box 447, T469-0378/5256, in central Gingerland.

Food on the whole is good. Apart from almost every kind of imported food and drink, there is a wide variety of fresh seafood (red snapper, lobster, king fish, blue parrot), and local vegetables. The excellent local spirit is CSR – Cane Spirit Rothschild – produced in St Kitts by Baron de Rothschild (now in a joint venture with Demerara Distillers Ltd of Guyana). It is drunk neat, with ice or water, or with 'Ting', the local grapefruit soft drink (also highly recommended). Tours of the CSR factory are possible. The hotels have restaurants, usually serving local specialities. Most of the Plantation Inns on both islands offer Sunday brunch, usually a three course meal and excellent value at around US$25 per person.

Eating: St Kitts

For elegant dining in a cool, natural environment, try the *Royal Palm* at *Ottley's Plantation Inn*, away from the hustle and bustle. There are also many places offering snacks, light meals, ice creams and drinks in Basseterre and in the Frigate Bay area. Look out for places selling excellent local patties and fruit juices. On Church St, *Cisco's Place*, T4659009. For inexpensive lunches and delicious Chinese food on weekend nights. For great local snacks and baked goods, try *Jakki's*, T4656043, on Cayon St across from *Uncle T's* (for fast food, greasy). Relax on Jakki's open air balcony. The only international fast food chain is *Kentucky Fried Chicken* on Bay Rd, T4667751, the popular local equivalent is *Redi-Fried Chicken*, T4651301. Tasty chicken and chips, cheaper, on Adlam St, around the corner from the cinema. *Fisherman's Wharf*, T4652754, beside *OTI* offers tasty fresh fish, barbecue chicken etc and help yourself to vegetables for US$25-35, conch chowder recommended. *Ballahoo* in town, T4654197, F4657070. Great central meeting place, lovely view of the Circus, excellent local food at reasonable prices, open Mon-Sat 0800-2200. Also in Basseterre *Circus Grill*, T4650143. Good well-presented food, a bit more expensive than *Ballahoo*, open Mon-Sat 1130-2200. *Chef's Place*, Church St, T465176. Good breakfasts and West Indian food at reasonable price, 0900-2100 Mon-Sat, no credit cards. *Star of India*, Victoria Rd, T4661537. Chef from Bombay, authentic Indian food. *Georgian House*, South Independence Square, T4654049. Open Wed-Sat 1830-2130, reservations only, in the house's walled garden is *Mango's Bar and Bistro*, complete with mango and banana trees, good food and a favourite hangout for visitors and locals alike, open Mon-Sat 1130-1600, dinner 1830-2130, Fri dancing until late, T4654049. Good, predictable Chinese food is at *Kim Sha*, Bay Rd, T4660022, and *Kim Xing*, Cayon St, T4666692. Generous portions, fast service, reasonable prices. *Arlecchino*, Amory Mall, Cayon St. Italian restaurant, friendly owner, Jasmine makes a delicious coffee shake, T4659927, open 0900-1500, 1800-2230. *Royal Ethiopian*, Cayon St, T4657741, vegetarian. *Stone Walls*, Princess St, T4655248. Expensive but excellent food, special theme nights, open Mon-Sat 1700-2300, in pleasant garden. *Vegetarian Plus* in TDC Mall. Open Mon-Sat 0800-2300, one of the few places open on Sun 1000-2200, T4650709. *Bayembi Cultural Café*, Bank St, T466280. Good snacks, occasional Fri night street parties. *Rank's Eat Rite Specialities*, corner St Johnson Av and Union St, T4658190. Fresh, low fat meals, quaint, clean, friendly, veggie/fish burgers, tuna melt, fish meals, local drinks. *Victor's Hideaway*, Stainforth St, New Town, Basseterre, T4652518. Open 0900-1500, 1830-late. *Pizza Lovers*, George St, New Town. Filling, tasty, cheap, T4656870. For a very local experience try *Razba's Veggie Pizza Parlour*, T4656738, on St Johnston's Av. Most of the clientele is Rastafarian vegetarians who come for a good 'lime' and are friendly to new faces. Similar atmosphere 2 blocks away at *Rasco-Tec*, look for the Bob Marley mural, T4668843. *Central Delight*

Refreshment Bar, Central St, T4651142. A place to relax, ice cream, hamburgers, hot dogs, sandwiches. *The Family Snackette*, Liverpool Ros, T4652601. Quaint setting, local food and drinks. *Cranstoun*, T4668993. Kittitian cooking and fast food. *Ribs and Rolls*, Princess St, T4663474. Ribs and pastries.

Sunset Café in Frigate Bay, *Timothy Beach Resort*, T4653020. Serves local seafood, burgers, open daily, 0700-2300, good. *The Patio*, Frigate Bay, T4658666. Open Dec-May, local and international cuisine, complimentary white wine and open bar with dinner, run by Peter and Joan Mallalieu like a private dinner party so reservations essential, entrées US$25-30, dress smartly. *PJ's Pizza*, Frigate Bay, T4658373. Open from 1000 Tue-Sat. *Doo Wop Days*, an Italian Café and Bar in Frigate Bay, T4651960, F4658506. Owned by Joe and Linda Pozzolo who have 50's, 60's and 70's entertainment and karaoki on weekends. *Marshall's*, at *Horizons Villa Resort*, Frigate Bay, T4668245. Romantic poolside dining with ocean view, exquisite food, not to be missed. The *New Anchorage Bar and Restaurant*, T4658235, on the beach. *Breezes*, at *Sun and Sand Condominiums*, T4658037. Breezy with excellent ocean view, pricey menu with tasty, but small, portions. At the end of the peninsula, out at *Turtle Beach Bar and Grill*, T4699086, F4667771. Excellent barbecue, vegetarian options, friendly, open daily 0945-1800 and Thur-Sat 1900-2100, live steel band on Sun and lunch time. Small restaurants around the island serving West Indian food, include *Manhattan Gardens*, Old Rd, T4659121. Across the street, try *Sprat Net*, by the sea, T4656314. Run by Spencer family, serves fresh fish and goat water, busy at weekends. Highly recommended for good atmosphere and reasonably priced food, one of the places to be at weekends, open Thur-Sun. In Cayon in the east, *Penny's*, and *Off Limit Bar*, T4669821. Cater mostly for locals, local food, burgers, drinks, spacious and clean in village setting. Local bakeries have a variety of savoury and sweet baked goods at affordable prices. Most now have small dining sections as the competitive bakery business heats up. The main bakeries are *Fancy Loaf*, T4655415, *American Bakery*, T4652136, *Island Bakeries Ltd*, T4658034, *Browne & Sons*, T4652776, *Fraites & Sons*, T4654629 and *Fulton's*, T4659538.

Eating: Nevis   The best restaurants are in the hotels and it is usually necessary to reserve a table. The above hotels provide exceptional cuisine as well as barbecues and entertainment on certain nights of the week, eg *Oualie Beach* has a Caribbean buffet on Sat with live music and masquerade dance, and surf and turf beach barbecue on Tue. There are very few eating places in Charlestown: *The Rainbow Café*, behind Barclays Bank. Open daily 0700 until late, warm smiles, great service, soothing music, cold drinks, expresso cappuccino, bagels, sandwiches, roti, croissants. *Callaloo* on Main St, T4695389. Serves lunch from US$4 and dinner from US$6, local food, hamburgers, sandwiches, pizzas from 1800, open Mon-Thur 0700-2200, Fri, Sat 0700-2400, no smoking, bring your own wine, friendly service. *Eddy's* on same street is a tourist favourite for local food, T4695958. Drinks and music with string bands, bush bands or steel bands Sat 2000-2300, Happy Hour Wed 1700-2000. *Cotton House*, T4690305, at the Cotton Ginnery Mall. Local food with sea view, specializes in goat water and souse. *Calypso Bistro*, Heritage Plaza, T4695110. Courtyard garden bar and grill. *Saints and Sinners*, T4690445, Lower Craddock Rd. Local dishes and seafood. *Miss June's*, Jones Bay, T4695330. Open three times a week, Caribbean dinner party, preceded by cocktails and *hors d'oeuvres*, wine, dessert, coffee and liqueurs included in price, numbers strictly limited so reservations essential. The *Oualie Beach Club* does local lunches and dinners, T4699735, 0700-2100. *Sunshines by the Sea*, T4695817. Seafood and Sun bonfire on Pinney's Beach. Most restaurants only open in the evenings in the off season or even shut completely. *Prinderella's*, on the beach at Tamarind Bay, T4691291. Lunch 1100-1500, dinner 1800-1930, closed Tue, good for Happy Hour and dancing until 0300 on Fri night, brunch on Sun. *Jamestown Beach Café*, T4699224. Open daily from 1000. *Mem's Pizzería*, Prospect Garden, T4691390. Excellent lobster pizza, seafood recommended. *Sand Dollar Bar and Grill*, T4695319, F4690614, next to the *Four Seasons Hotel*. Offers entertainment and happy hour Tue-Fri, closed Mon, party night is Fri, very popular. For excellent local food try *Cla Cha Del Restaurant and Bar*, T4691841, completely out of the way in Newcastle (close to the airport) with good atmosphere at weekends. *Jade Garden*, T4699762, Newcastle. Healthy cuisine, salads, pizza, deli. *Newcastle Bay Marina*, T4699395. Italian and Spanish dinners. *Beachcomber Bar and Grill*, T4691192, F4693388, on Pinney's Beach. A great place to meet people. *Unella's By the Sea*,

T4695574, on the Waterfront offers great views although the service is slow. *Cliffdweller's Sunset Terrace*, T4698262, F4655195, on Tamarind Bay offers spectacular views of St Kitts. *Tequila Sheilas*, T4698633, F4690129, on Cades Bay. *The* place to be at weekends with dancing until late. For a more local, relaxed atmosphere try *Muriel's Cuisine*, T4695920 on Happy Hill. *Seafood Madness*, T4690558. Great for takeaway orders, at the *Sea Spawn Guest House*. **Hill Top Bar and Restaurant**, T4693635, on Pond Hill. At *Caribbean Cove*, there is an American-style restaurant, T4691286. At the Botanical Gardens *Martha's Tea House* serves sandwiches, scones with Devonshire cream and tapas, panoramic views, T4693680. *Culturama Bar*, Jessups, T4695206. Seafood specialities.

Nightlife

Steel pan on Fri nights at *OTI*. A good place for a drink in Basseterre is *TOTTs*, opposite Post Office on the Bay Rd. *Malloy's Irish Pub*, next to Bird Rock Beach. One-of-a-kind alternative to other forms of nightlife on St Kitts, friendly Irish atmosphere with reasonably priced Irish snacks. *Flamingo Restaurant and Bar*, T4650898, on Monkey Hill. Pool tables and a small dance floor. On Fri night the place to be is *Monkey Bar* at Frigate Bay. Open for dancing on the beach, everyone goes but only gets going after midnight. In Basseterre, dance floors are at *Mango's*, T4654049. For Fri dancing. In the country, *BCA*, T4657606/7, at Saddlers; *Manhattan Gardens*, T4659121, in Old Road Town, and *Off Limit*, in Cayon, T4669821. Nightclubs include *Lions Den Club*, T4652582, in Bird Rock, and *Eclipse* at Canada Estate, T4668188. Fairly smart, open Fri and Sat 2200-0530. On Sun almost everything closes down in Basseterre, but occasionally *Monkey Bar* will be 'happening' and *Turtle Beach* at the end of the southeast peninsula usually has sunset dancing until midnight. Dance spots on **Nevis** include *Prinderella's* at Tamarind Bay, T4691291, where anything goes; *Tequila Sheilas* at the end of Pinney's Beach, T4698633; *Sand Dollar Bar & Grill*, next to *Four Seasons*, T4695319.

Festivals

St Kitts & Nevis are very proud of their masquerade traditions

The liveliest time to visit **St Kitts** is for the carnival held over *Christmas* and the *New Year*. It gets bigger and better every year with parades, calypso competitions and street dancing. For details, contact the Department of Tourism. St Kitts also holds a music festival at the end of **June**; four nights of calypso, reggae, R&B, jazz, street style, gospel, country and western and rap, with local and famous overseas artists. On **Nevis**, the annual equivalent of carnival is *Culturama*, held in end-**July** and **August**, finishing on the first Monday in August. There is a Queen show, calypso competition, local bands and guest bands and many 'street jams'. The Nevis Tourist Office has full details or contact the Department of Culture, T4695521, Mon-Fri 0800-1600.

Shopping

Shop opening hours 0800-1600, Mon-Sat. Early closing on Thu & also Sat for some shops

The shopper has plenty of choice and is not swamped by US or British merchandise. Shops are well stocked. Local Sea Island cotton wear and cane and basketwork are attractive and reasonable. *Walls Deluxe Record and Bookshop* on Fort Street has a good selection of music and Caribbean books, open Mon-Thur 0800-1700, Fri 0800-1800, Sat 0800-1630. *The Island Hopper Boutique* at the Circus, underneath the *Ballahoo* restaurant, stocks the Caribelle Batik range of cotton fashions and also carries clothes from Trinidad, St Lucia, Barbados and Haiti; open 0800-1600 Mon-Fri, 0800-1300 Sat, T4652905; also at The Arcade, Charlestown, Nevis, T469-1491/5426. The Stonewall Boutique on Princes Street sells quality local crafts and imports. *The Plantation Picture House*, at Rawlins Plantation is Kate Spencer's studio and gallery of portraits, still life and landscapes in oils and watercolours, her designs are also on silk, open 1100-1700. She also has a shop in Basseterre, on Bank Street, just off the Circus, called Kate, with paintings, prints, silk sarongs, hats by Dale Isaac, and another shop in Main Street, Charlestown. *Glass Island*, 4 Princes St, T/F4666771, www.glassisland.com, is a working glass shop which produces glass tiles, platters, jewellery and gifts. There are several local craft shops in Charlestown. Next to the tourist office is *Nevis Handicraft Co-operative*. On the road to the *Four Seasons Hotel* is an industrial estate with shops selling crafts and a toy shop. In Newcastle there is a pottery with red clay artefacts including bowls and candleholders. You can watch potters at work. The kilns are fired by burning coconut husks.

The public markets in Basseterre and Charleston are busiest Sat morning, good for fruit and vegetables, also fish stalls and butchers. Supermarkets in Basseterre include *B & K Superfood*

Leeward Islands

on the south side of Independence Square and George Street, *Horsfords Valumart* on Wellington Road, and *Rams* on Bay Road and at Bird Rock. On Nevis, there are well-stocked supermarkets: *Nisbets* in Newcastle and Superfood, Parkville Plaza, Charlestown

There are philatelic bureaux on both St Kitts and Nevis which are famous (the latter more so) for their first day covers of the islands' fauna and flora, undersea life, history and carnival. The St Kitts bureau is in *Pelican Shopping Mall*, open Mon-Wed, Fri-Sat 0800-1200, 1300-1500, Thur, 0800-1100. The Nevis bureau is open Mon-Fri, 0800-1600.

Transport **Air** It is possible to get a bus from Basseterre to the airport and walk the last 5 mins from the main road; some buses might go up to the terminal. If you have not much luggage, it is easy to walk from Basseterre to the airport. There is no currency exchange at the airport. There are duty free and gift shops and a café. On Nevis the airport is a bus ride from Charlestown, EC$3.50. A runway extension is being built to enable jets to land. There is a small snack shop at the airport. Minibuses do not run on a scheduled basis but follow a set route (more or less), EC$1-3 on most routes, EC$3 from Basseterre to the north of the island, frequent service from the bus terminal close to the market area on the Bay Road from where buses go west to Sandy Point. To catch a bus east, wait off Bakers Corner at the east end of Cayon Street, not obvious, ask someone. There are no minibuses to Frigate Bay and the southeast peninsula. On Nevis buses start outside Foodworld Cash & Carry supermarket and go to all points, but not on a regular basis, EC$1-3, an island tour is possible, if time consuming. There are direct charter flights from London and connections can be organized from North America, Europe and other Caribbean Islands.

If visiting at carnival time you should book car hire a long time in advance **Car hire** If you rent for three day minimum you can arrange for a car on the sister island if you do a day trip to St Kitts or Nevis. Hire companies include: *TDC Rentals*, West Independence Square, Basseterre, T4652991, F4651099, or Bay Road, Charlestown, T4695960, F4691329, also at *Four Seasons*, T4691111; *Caines Rent-A-Car*, Princes Street, Basseterre, T4652366, F4656172; *Sunshine Car Rental*, Cayon Street, Basseterre, T4652193, Hondas and Korando jeeps. Others include *A & T Car*, T4654030; *Delisle Walwyn*, T4658449; *Huggins*, T4658080; *Courtesy Car Rentals*, T4657804; *G & L*, T4668040/1. If you are arriving in St Kitts from Nevis, there are several car hire companies on Independence Square, some 3 mins' walk from the ferry pier. One of the most convenient is *Avis Car Rental*, South Independence Square Street, T4656507, F4666846 (Suzuki jeeps, Nissan automatics, efficient). *Nisbett Rentals Ltd*, 100yds from Newcastle airport, Minimoke US$40 per day, collision damage waiver US$8 per day, recommended, particularly if you are flying in/out of Nevis, T4699211, open 0700-1900. *Avis*, T4691240, and *Discount*, T4690343. Also on Nevis through Striker's (Hermitage), T4692654, Carlton Meade; **bicycle rental** on Craddock Road, T4695235. Companies insist on you having collision damage waiver, which adds another US$5-10 to quoted rates. There is a 5% tax on car rentals.

The Visitor magazine & airports have a list of recommended fares. There is no need to tip **Taxi** Taxis have a yellow T registration plate. Maximum taxi fares are set, for example: **On St Kitts**, from Airport to Basseterre EC$18, to Frigate Bay, EC$29, to Sandy Point EC$40. From Basseterre to Old Road, EC$27, to Frigate Bay, EC$20, to Middle Island, EC$27 to Sandy Point EC$32, to Romney Manor (return) EC$68, to Brimstone Hill (return) EC$86.40. Taxis within Basseterre cost EC$10, with additional charges for waiting or for more than two pieces of luggage. Between 2300-0600 prices rise by 25%. A southeast peninsula tour is EC$106, an island tour EC$159. **On Nevis** a taxi from the airport to Charlestown costs EC$37, to *Oualie Beach*, EC$24, to the *Montpelier Inn*, EC$55, to *Hermitage Inn*, EC$45 and to *Nisbet Plantation Inn*, EC$21. Fares from Charlestown to *Pinneys Beach Hotel*, EC$13, to *Four Seasons* EC$18, to *Cliffdwellers* EC$26.50, to *Oualie Beach* EC$29, to *Mount Nevis Hotel* EC$42. A 50% extra charge is made on Nevis between 2200 and 0600. An island tour of Nevis costs US$50 for about 3 hrs, but you can bargain it down if no cruise ship is in port. The number of taxis on Nevis quadrupled to some 130 in the five years to 1999 to meet the greater demand from tourists.

Leeward Islands

Boat The crossing between St Kitts and Nevis takes about 45 mins and costs EC$20 round trip. Departs Basseterre, Mon 0800, 1600; Tue 1300; Wed 0700, 1600, 1900 (good day for day trip); Fri 0830, 1600; Sat 0830, 1600. Departs Charlestown, Mon 0700, 1500; Tue 0730, 1800; Wed 0800, 1800; Fri 0730, 1500; Sat 0730, 1500. Confirm sailing times with Ministry of Communications, T4652521, Mon-Fri 0800-1600. Tickets can only be purchased from the quay just prior to departure, so turn up about 1 hr in advance to avoid disappointment. Island tours operate from St Kitts and there is also a water taxi service between the 2 islands: US$25 return, minimum 4 passengers, 20 mins, operated by Kenneth's Dive Centre, T4652670 in advance, or ProDivers, US$20, 10 mins, T4653223, 4699086. The *Four Seasons Hotel* has ferry boats running exclusively for guests' flights. Nevis Express runs a shuttle air service between St Kitts and Nevis, US$20, 6 mins, also charter service.

Airlines *LIAT*, *TDC Airline Services*, PO Box 142, Basseterre, T465-2511/2286, and *Evelyn's Travel*, on Main Street, Charlestown, general sales agent for *BWIA*, *LIAT*, *American Airlines* and *British Airways*, PO Box 211, Charlestown, T469-5302/5238; *BWIA*, T4652286 on St Kitts, 4695238 on Nevis; *American Eagle*, T4658490 (St Kitts); Winair, Sprott Street, Basseterre, T4652186 on St Kitts, 4695583 on Nevis; *Carib Aviation*, T4653055 (the Circus, Basseterre and R L Bradshaw airport, St Kitts), F4653168, T4699295 (Newcastle Airport, Nevis). *Nevis Express*, T4699755/6, F4699751, www.nevisexpress.com *Air St Kitts Nevis*, PO Box 529, Basseterre, T4658571, F4699018, a charter company specializing in day excursions and other services to neighbouring islands for example Saba, St Maarten, Antigua, Guadeloupe, Barbados, USVI. Also air ambulance with medical staff. **Banks** *The Eastern Caribbean Central Bank (ECCB)* is based in Basseterre, and is responsible for the issue of currency in Antigua and Barbuda, Dominica, Grenada, Montserrat, St Kitts and Nevis, St Lucia and St Vincent and the Grenadines. There is a local bank on St Kitts: *St Kitts-Nevis-Anguilla National Bank* (5 branches: on the corner of Central Street and West Independence Square Street; Pelican Mall; Sandy Point, T465-2204/6331/2701 open 0830-1500 except Thur 0830-1200, Sat 0830-1100, a branch at Saddlers Village, T4657362, opens 0830-1300 except Thur 0830-1200 and Sat 0830-1100) and on Nevis, West Square St, Charlestown, T4695244, same hours. In addition, on Nevis, there is the *Nevis Co-operative Banking Co Ltd* and the *Bank of Nevis*. Foreign banks on St Kitts: *Barclays Bank Plc* (on the Circus, Basseterre, T4652519, open Mon-Thur 0800-1500, Fri 0800-1700, the other at Frigate Bay, open Mon-Thur 0800-1300, Fri 0800-1300, 1500-1700, T465-2264/2510), *Royal Bank of Canada* (on the Circus, Basseterre, T4652519, open Mon-Thur 0800-1500, Fri 0800-1700, T465-2259/2389), *Bank of Nova Scotia* (Fort Street, open Mon-Thur 0800-1500, Fri 0800-1700, T4654141); on Nevis, *Barclays* (T469-5467/5309) and *Bank of Nova Scotia* (T4695411). Open 0800-1500 Mon-Thur, Fri until 1700. Avoid lunchtimes (1200-1300) and after 1500 on Fri as banks are busy with local workers. If you are in a hurry, choose a foreign bank as their queues are often shorter. Visa and MasterCard accepted by all 3. ATMs are available at all banks but dispense local currency only. **Communications** Post: Post office in Basseterre is on Bay Road, open Mon-Sat 0800-1500 except Thu when it closes at 1100 and Sat at 1200; in Charlestown on Main St, open from 0800-1500 except Thu, closes at 1100, and Sat at 1130. Airmail letters to the UK take up to 2 weeks. Courier services including *DHL*, *Fed Ex*, on both islands. **Telephone:** the telephone company, *Cable & Wireless*, has digital telecommunications systems for the two islands and international direct dialling is available. Telemessages and faxes can be sent from the main office on Cayon Street, Basseterre. Credit card calls T1-800-8778000. USA direct public phones available at C & W office. Phone cards are sold in denominations of EC$10, 20 and 40. Coin boxes take EC quarters minimum and EC dollars. Codes: 869-465/6 (St Kitts), 869-469 (Nevis). Call charges are from US$5 for 3 mins to the USA, Canada or the UK. *The Boat Phone Company* on the Victoria Road, T/F4663003, F4653033, offers cellular phone service for yachts. **Embassies and consulates** There is a Venezuelan Embassy on St Kitts and an Embassy of the **Republic of China on Taiwan**. There are also Honorary Consuls of **Spain**, **Germany**, **Trinidad and Tobago**, **France** and the **Netherlands**. The acting **British High Commissioner** is in Antigua. **Tourist information** Local tourist office: The St Kitts Department of Tourism (Pelican Mall, PO Box 132, Basseterre, T465-2620/4040, F4658794, mintc&e@caribsurf.com) and the Nevis Tourist Office (Main Street, Charlestown, T4691042, F4691066, nevtour@caribsurf.com) are both extremely helpful, with plenty of information available, open Mon-Fri 0800-1600, with the Nevis office also open Sat 0900-1200.

Directory

Leeward Islands

Background

History

Before Columbus's arrival in 1493, there were Amerindians living on both islands, whose relics can still be seen in some areas. As in most of the other islands, however, they were slaughtered by European immigrants, although the Caribs fought off the British and the French for many years and their battle scenes are celebrated locally. St Kitts became the first British settlement in the West Indies in 1623 and soon became an important colony for its sugar industry, with the importation of large numbers of African slaves. In April 1690 a severe earthquake struck, causing heavy damage to St Kitts, Nevis and Redonda. It was followed by a tidal wave which compounded the damage and, it is believed, destroyed Nevis' first capital, Jamestown.

For a time St Kitts was shared by France and England; partition was ended by the Peace of Utrecht in 1713 and it finally became a British colony in 1783. From 1816, St Christopher, Nevis, Anguilla and the British Virgin Islands were administered as a single colony until the Leeward Islands Federation was formed in 1871. (For a detailed history of Nevis during this period, read *Swords, Ships and Sugar–A History of Nevis to 1900*, by Vincent Hubbard, available in St Kitts and Nevis bookshops.)

From 1958, St Kitts-Nevis and Anguilla belonged to the West Indies Federation until its dissolution in 1962. In 1967 their constitutional status was changed from Crown Colony to a state in voluntary association with Britain, in a first step towards self-government. Robert L Bradshaw was the first Premier of the Associated States. Local councils were set up in Anguilla and Nevis to give those islands more authority over local affairs. Anguilla broke away from the group and was re-established as a Crown Colony in 1971. During the 1970s independence was a burning issue but Nevis' local council was keen to follow Anguilla's lead rather than become independent with St Kitts. Negotiations were stalled because of British opposition to Nevis becoming a Crown Colony. Eventually, on 19 September 1983, St Kitts and Nevis became independent as a single nation.

The main political parties are the People's Action Movement (PAM), the St Kitts and Nevis Labour Party (SKNLP), the Nevis Reformation Party (NRP) and the Concerned Citizens Movement (CCM). Dr Kennedy Simmonds (PAM) was elected Prime Minister in 1980 and held office until July 1995.

Elections in November 1993 were highly controversial when the PAM and the SKNLP each won four seats, the CCM two and the NRP one. The CCM declined to join in a coalition government to form a majority with either major party. The Governor then asked Dr Kennedy Simmonds to form a minority government with the support of the NRP, the PAM's previous coalition partner. This move was highly unpopular, given that the Labour Party had won 54.4 percent of votes cast in St Kitts compared with 41.7 percent for the PAM. A state of emergency was declared for 10 days in December because of rioting and other disturbances, a curfew was imposed for five days and a detachment of soldiers from the Regional Security System joined the local police force for a week. Negotiations between Dr Denzil Douglas, the SKNLP leader, and Dr Simmonds, for a caretaker government for six months followed by fresh elections, failed. More clashes greeted the budget presentation in February 1994 with the SKNLP boycotting parliament (except to take the oath of allegiance in May) in support of fresh elections.

Also during 1994, St Kitts was rocked by a corruption scandal linked to senior political officials involving drugs trafficking, murder and prison riots. It was alleged that traffickers were exploiting St Kitts and Nevis and avoiding the better monitored, traditional routes. The crisis pushed the Government into calling a forum for national unity, at which it was decided that a general election should be held, three years ahead of schedule. In the meantime, all parties in the National Assembly participated in decisions on matters such as foreign investment and a code of conduct to regulate political activity. A Commonwealth observer team monitored the elections to prevent a recurrence of the 1993 disturbances.

In the months leading up to the 3 July elections, British police officers were brought in to assist the local police force. The campaign itself was marred by political party rivalry which was often violent, but the result was an overwhelming victory for the SKNLP, which won seven seats. The PAM was reduced to one, while the CCM and the NRP continue to hold two seats and one seat respectively. Dr Denzil Douglas became Prime Minister. In 1998 the police force was returned to local command.

In 1992 Mr Simeon Daniel, the Premier of Nevis for 21 years, lost his assembly seat in elections which saw Mr Vance Amory (CCM) become the new leader. Mr Amory is in favour of the secession of Nevis from the federal state and legislation was prepared in 1996. However he failed to get it debated in the House of Assembly in November because of a boycott of the session by the NRP. Caricom proposed the establishment of a commission to examine the future relations of St Kitts and Nevis in an attempt to avoid a hasty and messy secession. A three-member commission was sworn in at end-1997 to review the constitution.

Elections for the Nevis Island Assembly were held in February 1997 and Mr Amory was returned to power. The CCM retained its three seats and the NRP held its two seats. Nevis' assembly voted unanimously for secession in 1997. However, a referendum on succession in July 1998 was unsuccessful when it failed to gain the approval of two-thirds of the electorate. Talks on constitutional reform were held in 1999 between the Federal Government and the Nevis Island Administration.

In September 1998 Hurricane Georges devastated the island of St Kitts. About 75 percent of homes were extensively damaged. A record clean up brought the island back to normal by the end of the year and most tourist facilities were open for business by the winter high season. In November 1999 the leeward side of both islands was hit by Hurricane Lenny, which brought high seas and flooding, wiping out many beaches and damaging hotels. *The Four Seasons Hotel* in Nevis remained closed for a year for repairs which included importing sand and constructing a breakwater to protect the beach by the hotel.

General elections were held in March 2000 and the SKNLP was returned to power, winning all eight seats in St Kitts. There was no change in Nevis, the CCM winning two seats and the NRP one. Kennedy Simmonds, leader of the PAM since 1976, announced his resignation in 2000. The PAM had claimed massive fraud in the elections, in which it lost its single seat although the party won 35.5% of the vote in St Kitts.

Government

St Christopher and Nevis is a constitutional monarchy within the Commonwealth. The British monarch is Head of State and is represented locally by a Governor General. The National Assembly has 11 seats, of which three are from Nevis constituencies and eight from St Kitts. There are also four nominated Senators. Under the Federal system, Nevis also has a separate legislature and may secede from the Government of the Federation.

The economy

Sugar, the traditional base of economic production, nowadays accounts for only about 2% of gdp, although it still occupies a dominant role within the agricultural sector and generates about a third of export revenues. Production has been in the hands of the Government since 1975, but with low prices for sugar in the world markets, hurricane damage, droughts and the falling value of the euro, the industry runs at a loss. World Bank consultants recommended policy changes, which included allowing private investment in the industry and production incentives for cane cutters. Initially, management of the state-owned Sugar Manufacturing Company was contracted to Booker Tate, of the UK, for 1991-93, with financial assistance from the World Bank. Sugar production in 1991-96 was around 19,000-20,000 tonnes, with fluctuations resulting from drought, hurricanes and cane fires. In 1997, however, the crop was estimated at 31,374 tonnes with higher yields, but it fell back again in 1998 to 24,331 tonnes. In 1994 it was announced that the company was to be divested, with the Government having a minority shareholding.

The Government has been encouraged to diversify away from sugar dependence and reduce food imports. More vegetables, sweet potatoes and yams are now being grown, while on Nevis, Sea Island cotton and coconuts are more common on smallholdings. Livestock farming and manufacturing are developing industries. There are enclave industries, such as electronic assembly, data processing and garment manufacturing (now over a quarter of total exports), which export to the USA and Caricom trading partners, while sales of sugar-based products such as pure cane spirit go mainly outside the region.

Tourism has become an important foreign exchange earner, and now contributes about 10% of gdp. The construction industry has benefited from the expansion of tourist infrastructure. The Government is increasing cruise ship arrivals with a port improvement project to enable two cruise liners to berth at the same time, while stopover arrivals will be encouraged by the large resort development projects on the southeast peninsula of St Kitts, and airport improvements.

Growth rates in the 1990s fluctuated according to hurricane damage and construction demands, averaging 4.5% in 1993-97. Hurricane Georges in 1998 and Lenny in 1999 were particularly costly. The IMF approved emergency financial assistance of US$2.3mn after Georges to support a recovery programme, while noting that damage of US$400mn was considerably more than annual gdp. A five-year economic programme announced in 2000 was designed to overhaul the tax system to achieve a fiscal surplus after three years of deficit and a rising level of debt. Tax revenues were hit by the closure of *The Four Seasons Hotel*, which contributes half of all hotel taxes in Nevis.

Anguilla

Population: 8,960
1992 census

Anguilla is a small island, about 35 miles square, and the most northerly of the Leeward Islands. The island is low lying and, unlike its larger sisters, it is not volcanic but of coral formation. It is arid, covered with low scrub and has few natural resources. However, it has excellent beaches and superb diving and snorkelling, protected by the coral reefs. The island's name is the Spanish word for 'eel', a reference to its long, narrow shape. Its Carib name was Malliouhana. The people of Anguilla, predominantly of African descent but with some traces of Irish blood, are very friendly and helpful and it is one of the safest islands in the Caribbean.

Ins and outs

Getting there
See transport, page 639, for further details

Air *LIAT* has daily flights from Antigua; (T268-4620700), or *Caribaviation* (T268-4623147) charter flights will meet any incoming flight and fly you to Anguilla without you having to clear customs in Antigua. *LIAT* also connects Anguilla with St Kitts and Nevis, St Maarten and St Thomas (the LIAT office is at Gumbs Travel Agency, T2238 and also at T2748). *American Eagle* (T3131/3500) has a daily air link with Puerto Rico which connects with their other US flights. *Winair* (T2238/2748, F3351) provides several daily flights from St Maarten (10 mins) and has a service to St Barts. *Coastal Air Transport* (T2431) flies from St Croix, USVI. *Tyden Air* (T2719, F3079, The Valley) operate charters and air taxi services to the British and US Virgin Islands, St Maarten and St Kitts. In St Maarten, you can get bookings for Anguilla on the spot. *Transanguilla*, another air taxi service, offers the 5 min flight for US$35 each way.

Boat The principal port is **Sandy Ground**, T6403. The service for the ferry between Blowing Point and Marigot starts at about 0730 and continues every 30-40 mins until 1900. You pay the US$2 departure tax after putting your name and passport number on the manifest (at booth at head of pier in Marigot or find the ferry clerk in the waiting area near Immigration Office) and before boarding at Marigot but you pay the fare on the boat. The same applies when leaving from Anguilla. Have your passport and tax receipt handy when boarding. *Link Ferries* run a high speed catamaran service from Blowing Point to Marigot, 0840, 1240, 1730, return 1120, 1430, 1800 and from Blowing Point to Juliana airport 1210, return 1400, complimentary drinks on board, help with luggage at airport, also private charters anytime, T2231/3290, F3290, www.ai/link/. On Tue, the *MV Deluxe* does a day trip to St Barths, T6289, F6322, leaves 0915, returns 1700, US$65 return.

Getting around
Driving is on the left.
Speed limit 30 mph

There are several **car hire** companies on the island. Hired cars can not be picked up from the airport because of local regulations, they have to be delivered to your hotel, but they can be dropped off at the airport. Fuel costs US$1.84 per gallon for regular, US$1.86 unleaded. Watch out for loose goats on the roads. A local driving permit is issued on presentation of a valid driver's licence from your home country and can be bought at car rental offices; US$10 for three months. **Hitchhiking** is very easy and it is also possible to hire **bicycles**.

Climate

The climate is subtropical with an average temperature of 80°F and a mean annual rainfall of 36 ins, falling mostly between September and December. Any cloud and rain early in the day has usually cleared by mid-morning.

Flora and fauna

Although you will see colourful gardens with flowering hibiscus, bougainvillea and other tropical plants, the island is mostly covered with scrub. The north coast has the most unspoilt open areas which have not been cultivated or built on. There are steep cliffs of over 100ft high, with caves and sink holes, and inland are areas of dense vegetation. The most common plants are the white cedar, pigeonwood, manchineel, frangipani, five-finger trees, bromeliads and cacti. In this area you can find lizards, iguanas, snakes, bats and birds. Katouche Valley has a beach, a mangrove pond and a forest where you can find orchids and bromeliads and some patches of bamboo

Anguilla

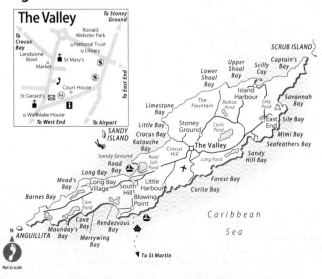

Leeward Islands

Essentials

Documents *All visitors need an onward ticket. All must also have a valid* **passport***, except US citizens who need only show proof of identity with a photograph.* **Visas** *are not required by anyone. Proof of adequate funds is required if the Immigration Officer feels so inclined.*

Currency *The East Caribbean dollar. US dollars always accepted.*

Departure tax *There is a departure tax of US$10 at the airport and US$2 at the ferry.*

Boat documents *(Own flag). In Road Bay get a cruising permit for other anchorages. Customs and Immigration at Blowing Point ferry port and Road Bay at Sandy Ground (at Police Station next to Johnno's on north side, near small pier). Free* **anchorage** *in Road Bay and Blowing Point. Fees are based on official tonnage. Charter boats pay additional anchoring fees. Bring your crew lists. There is a* **departure tax** *of EC$5 per person. Little Bay, Sandy Island and Prickly Pear have permanent moorings, other places have designated anchoring sites. Boats may not anchor in Rendezvous Bay or Little Bay. Every boat visiting a marine park must get a permit to tie up or anchor, fee US$15 for private vessels, US$23 for charter boats. If you want to scuba dive you pay a fee of US$4 per tank.*

Business hours *Government offices 0800-1600 Monday-Friday;* **banks** *0800-1500 Monday-Thursday, 0800-1700 Friday.* **Shops** *open 0800-1700 or 1800, some grocery stores are open until 2100, a few on Sunday.* **Gas stations** *are open in The Valley, Monday to Saturday 0700-2100, Sunday 0900-1300, and at Blowing Point, Monday to Sunday 0700-2400.*

Official time *GMT minus four hours; EST plus one hour.*

Voltage *110 volts AC, 60 cycles.*

Weights and measures *Metric, but some imperial weights and measures are still used.*

Communications *The international code is 264-497, followed by a four-digit number. See page 640 for further details.*

Media *Newspapers* Chronicle *daily,* The Daily Herald, The Light, *a local weekly.* What We Do In Anguilla *is an annual tourist magazine and a monthly tourism newspaper updates it, www.anguillatourguide.com* Anguilla Life *is a quarterly magazine.*
Radio *Radio Anguilla (T2218) is on medium wave 1505 kHz and ZJF on FM 105 MHz.*

Tourist offices overseas *Germany, c/o Sergat Deutschland, IM Guldenen Wingert 8-C, D-64342, Seeheim, T49-6257-962920, F49-6257-962919, r.morozow@t-online-de* **Italy**, *Piazza Bertarelli 1, 20122 Milan, T39-02-72022466, F39-02-72020162, Bdp-comunicazione@iol.it* **UK**, *3 Epirus Road, London, SW6 7UJ, T020-79377725, F020-79384793, windotel@BTInternet.com* **USA**, *c/o Westcott Group, 39 Monaton Drive, Huntington Station, NY 11746, T516-4250900, F516-4250903, info@westcott-group.com* **Puerto Rico**, *Amarylis Davila, RSVP Travel Service, PO Box 16328, San Juan, T/F787-7250882, atbpr@hotmail.com*

Clothing *Bathing costumes are not worn in public places. Nude bathing or nude sunbathing is not allowed.*

Public holidays *New Year's Day, Good Friday, Easter Monday, Labour Day, Whit Monday, end of May (Anguilla Day, commemorates the Anguilla Revolution which began 30 May 1977), the Queen's official birthday in June, the first Monday (August Monday) and the first Thursday (August Thursday) and Friday (Constitution Day) in August, 19 December (Separation Day), Christmas Day, Boxing Day.*

among the pepper cinnamon, mawby, sherry and turpentine trees. The valley ends at Cavannagh Cave, which was mined for phosphorous in the 19th century, but now is home to bats, birds, crabs and lizards. Birdwatching is good at Little Bay, Crocus Bay's north point and at the many ponds and coves, T2759 for information. It is intended that the wetlands will eventually become sanctuaries. Ninety three species

Leeward Islands

of birds have been recorded on Anguilla, including the blue faced booby, kingfisher and the great blue heron. The national bird is the turtle dove, which is protected. The National Trust publishes *A Field Guide to Anguilla's Wetlands*, listing all the birds, flora and history of the ponds, US$15. A tree planting programme has been organized by the Anguilla Beautification Club (ABC); donations are welcome and you can 'adopt a tree'. Contact *ABC Trees*, PO Box 274, Anguilla.

Diving and marine life

Dive sites

The Government is introducing a marine parks system, installing permanent moorings in certain areas to eliminate anchor damage. Designated marine parks include Dog Island, Island Harbour, Little Bay, Prickly Pear, Sandy Island, Seal Island and Shoal Bay. Mooring permits are required. Do not remove any marine life such as coral or shells from underwater. Spear fishing is prohibited. Stoney Bay Marine Park Underwater Archaeological Preserve was opened in March 1999 for limited public diving, although surveying, mapping and historical research was not complete. The park is protecting the wreck of a Spanish ship, *El Buen Consejo*, which ran aground on 8 July 1772 off the northern tip of Anguilla while on its way to Mexico with 50 Franciscan missionaries bound for the Philippines. It now lies about 100 yd offshore at a depth of 30 ft, with cannons, anchors and historical artefacts. Dives are fully guided and can only be done with *Shoal Bay Scuba and Watersports*. You are shown a video and given an overview of the ship's history before you go down. Eventually dive trails with plaques will be installed.

There are good dives just off the coast, particularly for novices or for night dives, while the others are generally in a line due west of Sandy Island, northwest of Sandy Ground, and along the reef formed by **Prickly Pear Cays** and Sail Island. Off **Sandy Island**, there are lots of soft corals and sea-fans, while at Sandy Deep there is a wall which falls from 15-60ft. There are also several wrecks, nine of which have been deliberately sunk as dive sites around the island, the most recent in 1993.

Further west, **Paintcan Reef** at a depth of 80ft contains several acres of coral and you can sometimes find large turtles there. Nearby, **Authors Deep**, at 110 ft has black coral, turtles and a host of small fish, but this dive is more for the experienced diver. On the north side of the Prickly Pear Cays you can find a beautiful underwater canyon with ledges and caves where nurse sharks often go to rest. Most of the reefs around Anguilla have some red coral; be careful not to touch it as it burns.

Dive centres

Scuba diving can be arranged through *The Dive Shop*, PO Box 247, Sandy Ground, T2020, F5125, excellent courses are available at this five-star PADI training centre, recommended. Retail shop open daily 0800-1600, snorkelling and diving equipment for sale or rent. All dives are guided boat dives; a single-tank dive costs US$40, a two-tank dive US$70, night dives US$50. *Anguilla Divers*, based at *La Sirena*, Meads Bay and Island Harbour, dive the east end of the island and offer PADI courses, in English, French, German or Spanish, T4750, F4632, axadiver@anguillanet.com *Shoal Bay Scuba & Watersports*, T4371.

Beaches and watersports

There are 12 miles, 45 beaches, of fine white coral sand and crystal clear water. Most of them are protected by a ring of coral reefs and offshore islands. The beaches are clean, and many of them are relatively unpopulated, but nude (or topless for women) swimming or sunbathing is not allowed. **Shoal Bay** is the most popular beach and claims to be one of the most beautiful in the Eastern Caribbean. There are hotels, snack bars for lunch, although only one has a toilet. The snorkelling is good, with the closest of two reefs only 10 yd from the shore and you can rent snorkelling equipment. You can also rent lockers, beach umbrellas, loungers, rafts and towels. **Mead's Bay** is also popular with more expensive bars, hotels and watersports. **Road**

Leeward Islands

Bay/Sandy Ground has most nightlife and restaurants and is the starting point for most day trips, dive tours and a popular anchorage for visiting yachts. Watersports equipment rentals can be organized here. **Scilly Cay** is a small cay off Island Harbour with good snorkelling. A free ferry takes you to the bar on a palm-clad beach where walls are made from conch shells. Live music on Wednesday, Friday and Sunday. *Smitty's Bar*, across the water at *Island Harbour* is less sophisticated, tables made from old cable barrels, TV, pool room, popular with the locals. The restaurant was rebuilt after Hurricane Luis flattened the first one in 1995. Smitty gets his fish, crayfish (US$20) and lobster (US$25) straight off the boats. Beach chairs and umbrellas are complimentary and snorkelling is good just off the beach. **Captain's Bay** is rougher but the scenery is dramatic and not many people go there. The dirt road is full of potholes and goats and may be impassable with a low car. At **Crocus Bay** the rocks on both sides have nice coral and underwater scenery. There is a bar/restaurant and toilets. At the end of **Limestone Bay** is a small beach with excellent snorkelling, but be careful, the sea can be rough here. **Little Bay** is more difficult to reach but eagle rays and turtles can be seen and as well as excellent snorkelling it is a birdwatcher's and photographer's dream; turn right in front of the old cottage hospital in the Valley, after about half a mile there are some trails leading down to the water, fishermen have put up a net for the last bit. Glass bottom boats and cruise boats also come here or you can get a boat ride from Crocus Bay.

   Windsurfing and **sailing** are readily available and some of the hotels offer water skiing, paddle boats, snorkelling, fishing and sunfish sailing. Parasailing can be arranged at Shoal Bay. Anguilla Watersports offer waterskiing, T5821. Jet skiing is prohibited. There are glass bottom boats which can be hired for one or two people to operate themselves or crewed for groups. Sport fishing is available, contact *Gotcha*, T2956; *Johnno's*, T2728; *Rampoosin*, T8868; *Sandy Island Enterprises*, T5643; *No Mercy*, T6383. Yacht or motorboat charters are offered with beach and snorkelling cruises around the island or trips to St Phillipsburg, St Maarten, charters to Saba, Statia, St Barts on request. Operators change frequently but in 2000 the following were in Anguillian waters: Captain Kasha Brooks of Island Yacht Charter Co, T3743, F3738, has *Pyrat*, a 35-ft power boat and a 30-ft Beneteau sailboat, *Eros; Adventure Star*, a 32-ft motorboat, T4750; *El Tigre*, Sail Anguilla catamaran, T3304; *Chocolate* catamaran, T3394; Sandy Island Enterprises has a motorboat, T5643; *Gotcha*, 30-ft motorboat, T2956; *Sail My Way*, 30-ft sailboat, T6655; *No Mercy*, motorboat, T6383; *Its Fun Time*, 32-ft power boat for day trips and fishing, T/F6511, funtimecharters@yahoo.com **Boat racing** is the national sport, the boats being a special class of wooden sloop made in Anguilla. There are frequent races, but the most important are on Anguilla Day (30 May) and during Carnival Week in August.

Other sports There are public **tennis** courts at Ronald Webster Park. Several hotels have tennis courts. The *Malliouhana* has four championship courts for guests only; *Cinnamon Reef* has two at a cost of US$25 per hour for non-residents, free for guests; *Cap Juluca*, *Sonesta* and *Cove Castles* all have courts for guests' use only, others make a charge for non-guests: *Carimar Beach Club*, US$20 per hour; *The Mariners*, US$20 per hour; *Masara Resort*, US$10 per hour; *Rendezvous Bay*, US$5 per hour; *Spindrift Apartments*, US$5-10 per hour. For spectator sports, call the Sports Officer, T2317, for information on fixtures. There is **cricket**, **basketball**, **soccer**, **volley ball**, **soft ball**, **cycling** and **track and field**. **Horse riding**, with trail rides or riding lessons, is offered by El Rancho del Blues, T6164. *Body & Soul Health and Fitness Club*, Sandy Ground, T/F8364, offers aerobics, reebok step and soca dance classes.

Around the island

Near **The Valley**, the island's administrative centre, with a population of 500, **Wallblake House** is a restored, 18th-century plantation house where the priest from **St Gerard's Roman Catholic Church** lives. The Church itself is worth a visit to see the unusual ventilation. Several resident artists exhibit their work on Saturday mornings during the winter season in the grounds of Wallblake House. The Archaeological and Historical Society has tours in season on Tuesday from 1000, T2759. **Anguilla National Museum** is in a restored Anguillian cottage just west of the Public Library, T5297. It holds cultural and environmental exhibitions and there is information on hiking trails and historical sites. At Sandy Ground Village, you can see the salt pond, around Great Road Pond, although it is not currently in operation.

Northeast of The Valley, by Shoal Village, is **The Fountain** national park. Its focus is in fact a cave which has a source of constant fresh water and a series of Amerindian petroglyphs. Artefacts have been found and it is hoped they will be housed in a museum at the site, but the national park is still closed. Anguilla awaits detailed archaeological investigation, but it is thought that the island had several settlements and a social structure of some importance, judging by the ceremonial items which have been found. Contact the National Trust at the Museum Building in The Valley, or the Anguilla Archaeological and Historical Society for more information both of which are involved in several publications including a Review (PO Box 252). There is a very small museum of artefacts found on site at the *Arawak Beach Resort*, together with replicas of furnishings, pottery and baskets, T4888, F4498. There is also a mini museum at the *Pumphouse* bar, Sandy Ground. The building was once part of the salt factory and equipment used in the salt making process is on display, T5154. A local historian, Mr Colville Petty OBE, collects traditional household artefacts, known as the Heritage Collection, which he has on display at his home at Pond Ground, East End. ■ *T4440, F4067. US$5, children under 12 US$2. Mon-Sat 0900-1700, Sun by appointment.*

Big Spring Cave is an old Amerindian ceremonial centre where you can see petroglyphs. It is near **Island Harbour**, a fishing village with Irish ancestory. The National Trust has a map of archaeological and historical sites of Anguilla, worth getting if you want to explore caves, Amerindian sites or sugar mill rounds, T3041, PO Box 1234.

Local deposits of clay have been found and pottery is now made on the island. The work of Barbadian potter and sculptor, Courtney Devonish, and his students, is on display at the **Devonish Cotton Gin Art Gallery** in the Old Factory Plaza opposite the Catholic Church, T2949. There are sometimes pottery demonstrations on Saturday.

Day trips can be arranged to some of the neighbouring islands or to the offshore islands and cays. **Sandy Island** is only 15 minutes from Sandy Ground harbour and is a pleasant desert island-type place to swim, snorkel and spend half a day or so. ■ *Motorboats or sailboats cross over hourly 1000-1500, US$8 per person. Lunch or drinks available from a beach bar under coconut palms, T6395/5643.*

There are trips to **Prickly Pear**, six miles from Road Bay, which is well worth a visit, where you can snorkel if you are not a scuba diver, or to some of the other cays where you can fish or just have a picnic.

Scrub Island, two miles long and one mile wide, off the northeast tip of Anguilla, is an interesting mix of coral, scrub and other vegetation and is worth a visit. It is uninhabited, except by goats, and can only be reached by boat. There is a lovely sandy beach on the west side and ruins of an abandoned tourist resort and airstrip. There can be quite a swell in the anchorage, so anchor well. Boats go from Road Bay, Shoal Bay or Island Harbour.

Chartered yachts and motorboats leave from Road Bay or from Island Harbour for Scilly Cay, privately owned by Eudoxie and Sandra Wallace and also named **Gorgeous Scilly Cay**. They also have their own boat with a free ferry service. ■ *1000-1700, lunch only, live music Wed, Fri, Sun, closed.*

Essentials

Sleeping
An 8% tax & 10-15% service charge will be added to the bill

Anguilla has the reputation of catering for upmarket, independent travellers. This is reflected in the number of relatively small, but expensive hotels and beach clubs. Bargains can be found in the summer months, with discounts of up to 50%. The Anguilla Department of Tourism has a list of all types of accommodation. Inns of Anguilla is an association of over 20 villas or small hotels at moderate prices.

The following have flexible accommodation in rooms, suites, studios or villas, winter- summer prices quoted. **Anti-clockwise from Road Bay LL-L** *The Mariners Cliffside Beach Resort*, Sandy Ground, T2671, F2901, www.offshore.com.ai/mariners/ 66 rooms, suites and cottages, gingerbread style, 8½ acres, on beach, watersports, pool, tennis. **LL** *Malliouhana Hotel*, Mead's Bay, PO Box 173, T6011, F6011, UK T0117-9241003. 55 rooms, no credit cards, suites up to US$2,175, every luxury, 'sprawlingly sybaritic public areas', very posh, attentive service, award-winning restaurant on beach, watersports (most complimentary), tennis, two pools, children welcome, playground and pool by the beach (hotel is closed Sep and Oct each year for refurbishment). **LL-AL** *Carimar Beach Club*, Mead's Bay, PO Box 327, T6881, F6071, www.carimar.com 24 comfortable 1-3 bedroom apartments, beach, tennis, dive package available. **LL** *Frangipani Beach Club*, luxury resort on Mead's Bay beach, T6442, F6440. 15 units, Spanish style tiled roofs, multilevel, tiled floors, fans, cool, comfortable. **LL-AL** *La Sirena*, Meads Bay, T6827, F6829, www.la-sirena.com 20 individually designed rooms, 5 villas, short walk to beach through gardens, 2 pools, restaurant, dive centre, 10% discount for repeat visitors. **LL-L** *Coccoloba Valtur*, Barnes Bay, T8800, F8126. 100 rooms, suites, villas all-inclusive, Italian-run, emphasis on health with fitness centre and cardio-aerobics instruction, day pass available for spa, beautiful beach, 2 pools, colourful gardens, gingerbread verandahs round the villas. **LL** *Cove Castles Villa Resort*, Shoal Bay West, T6801, F6051, T800-3484716, PO Box 248, futuristic architecture, 4 3-bedroom villas, 8 2-bedroom beach houses, very expensive, housekeeper, phone, TV, beach, tennis, sunfish, bicycles included, watersports available. **LL** *Cap Juluca* at Maundays Bay, T6666, F6617, www.capjuluca.com Moorish design, bright white, luxury resort, 98 rooms, every facility here, with 2 beaches, pool, watersports, tennis, also suites and 3-5 bedroom villas, CP, full children's activity programmes with watersports and tennis, 179-acre estate. **LL** *Sonesta Beach Resort Anguilla*, on Merrywing Bay, T6999, F6899, sonesta@anguillanet.com Opulent Moorish style, 100 rooms and suites, large pool, 2 tennis courts, fitness centre, conference centre, 2 restaurants, complimentary afternoon tea. **LL** *Anguilla Great House*, Rendezvous Bay, T6061, F6019. 27 simple rooms, open-air restaurant and bar on beach, pool, kayaks, windsurfers, sunfish, snorkelling and fishing gear. **LL-AL** *Rendezvous Bay Hotel*, PO Box 31, T6549, F6026, www.rendezvousbay.com 30 rooms, villas up to US$425, beach, tennis, family run, helpful, rooms with veranda only a few metres from the sea, moderately good snorkelling, lovely beach, run by the Gumbs family. **LL-L** *Cinnamon Reef*, Little Harbour, T2727, F3727, in the USA and Canada T800-3467084, F914-7635362, in the UK, T01453-835801, F01453-835525. 22 villa rooms, beach sheltered, no surf but good snorkelling and sunfish sailing, pool, tennis, library, spectacular dining room, good food, friendly service, no children under 12 in winter. **LL-L** *Arawak Beach Resort*, PO Box 433, T4888, F4898. Octagonal villas on the northeast coast near Big Spring ceremonial centre, overlooking Scilly Cay, mini museum, health bar and restaurant. **LL-AL** *Fountain Beach*, Shoal Bay, T3491, F3493. 14 rooms, studio, or 2 bedroom suite, a/c, fans, kitchen facilities, restaurant, pool, beach. **LL-A** *Masara Resort*, Katouche Bay, T3200, F3223. 10 units, 1 or 2 bedrooms, beach nearby.

For something a bit different, *Hotel de Health* near Sandy Hill Bay, T4199, F4194. Combines medical services with your holiday, 17 self-contained units, wheelchair access, cardiopulmonary clinic, caters for guests with special medical needs including renal dialysis, team of Canadian doctors may perform minor elective surgery.

Villas and apartments Among the cheapest to rent are **A-B** *Syd Ans Apartments*, Sandy Ground, T3180, F5381, www.inns.ai/sydans 1 bedroom apartments, Mexican restaurant, close to Tamariain Watersports. **A-C** *Sea View*, Sandy Ground, T2427. 1-3 bedrooms, ceiling fans, kitchen facilities, beach nearby, clean, comfortable, enquire at the house next door for a room. **B-C** *La Palma*, Sandy Ground, T3260, F5381. 3 studios, on beach, restaurant, ceiling fans.

At Lower South Hill, **AL** *Inter Island*, T6259, F8207. 14 rooms, apartments, fans, kitchen facilities, restaurant. **LL-L** *Paradise Cove*, T6603, F6927, para-cove@anguillanet.com 14 1-2 bedroomed units with kitchen, jacuzzis, Olympic size pool, children's pool, café, a/c, fans, maid service, near beach. **LL-AL** *Blue Waters Beach Apartments*, Shoal Bay West, T6292, F6982. 9 1-2 bedroomed, self-catering apartments on the beach, fans, restaurant, baby sitting and maid service. **LL-A** *Ferry Boat Inn*, Blowing Point, T6613, F6713. 8 1-2 bedroomed apartments with view of sea and St Martin, a/c, fans, restaurant, daily maid service. **LL-L** *Shoal Bay Villas*, T2051, F3631, sbvillas@anguillanet.com 13 spacious 1-2 bedroomed suites and studios with kitchen, near *Le Beach* restaurant, open 0700-2200, pool, watersports. **LL-A** *Harbour Villas*, T4393, F4196, hvillas@anguillanet.com. Overlooking Gorgeous Scilly Cay, 7 apartments, 1-3 bedrooms, kitchens, laundry facilities, balcony, gardens lead down to beach.

Anguilla Connection Ltd at Island Harbour, T4403, F4402, www.luxuryvillas.com. Selection of 1-4 bedroom villas and apartments for rent, with several services on offer, US$170-500. *Select Villas of Anguilla*, Innovation Center, George Hill Road, T5810, F5811. 10 villas of different sizes around the island, cheapest US$650 per week in summer, most expensive US$1,100 per week in winter, daily rates available.

Guest houses Travellers on a lower budget or those wanting to avoid hotels can find accommodation in one of about 10 guest houses. These include **C-E** *Casa Nadine*, The Valley, T2358. 11 rooms, EP, with shower, kitchen facilities, basic, but very friendly and helpful, price reductions for longer stays, good views over The Valley from the roof. **C** *Lloyd's Guesthouse*, Crocus Hill. 12 rooms, all with bathroom, bed and breakfast, some refurbished and spotless, public rooms show signs of wear, meals taken with the family US$10 for dinner, local dishes, drinks served but no bar.

Anguilla under US$100 is an all-inclusive package with some meals, accommodation, ground transfers, car rental, tax and gratuities, for details contact Innovative Marketing Consultants, same company as *Select Villas of Anguilla*, above.

There are many excellent places to eat on the island for all palates and all budgets, from the elegant to beach barbecues. Beach bars and casual waterfront places provide a good lunch, for example *Smitty's*, see page 634. The tourist guide *What We Do In Anguilla* has a listing. Most of the restaurants are small and reservations are needed, particularly in high season.

Eating
Gourmet restaurants in hotels are expensive

Ship's Galley, Sandy Ground, T2040. Breakfast, lunch and dinner, West Indian cooking, closed Wed. *Barrel Stay*, Sandy Ground, T2831. Overpriced because of all the charter boat tourists, French/Creole, fish soup, lobster, steak, open for lunch and dinner. *Arlo's Place*, South Hill, T6810. Italian American, homemade pasta, open 1900-2200, closed Sun. *KoalKeel*, The Valley, T2930, F5379. Also expensive, in a restored 18th-century home of the island's administrator, known as Warden's Place, with 100-year-old rock oven, Euro-Caribbean style, chef Leonard 'Smoke' Sharplis prepares 5 or 7 course menus, open Tue-Sat dinner only, pastry shop open daily. *Old House*, George Hill, T2228. Overlooking airport, watch flights from an old concrete tower, happy hour 1700-1900, hot appetizers, open daily for breakfast, lunch and dinner, local food, seafood and grills. *The Ferry Boat Inn*, Blowing Point, on beach near ferry terminal, T6613, www.ai/ferryboatinn View of St Maarten, European and West Indian food, lunch and dinner except Sun, also rental apartments, well-equipped, airy, maid service. *Le Saint Clair*, T2833, F3663, VHF 16. French/Caribbean restaurant on beach front in Sandy Ground, some Japanese dishes, open lunch and dinner, Sun brunch with live music 1000-1600, US$15, live jazz Mon, Thur, Sat, closed Sun night. *Ripples*, Sandy Ground, T3380. Award-winning chef, try his lobster fritters, varied menu including vegetarian, open daily 1830-2300. *Leduc's*, Barne's Bay, near *Coccoloba*, T6393. In an old Anguillian house, French cuisine, lunch and dinner, 3-course prix-fixe 1830-1930. *Blanchard's*, Meads Bay, run by Bob and Melinda Blanchard, elegant wine list

Leeward Islands

and fine dining with Oriental influences. *Roy's Place*, Crocus Bay, beach front, T2470. Draught beer, fresh seafood, happy hour 1700-1900, Sun brunch of roast beef and Yorkshire pudding, open 1200-1400, 1800-2100, closed Mon. For Chinese breakfast, lunch and dinner, *The Landing Strip*, T2268. View of airport, eat in or takeaway, Clarita Mason Mall on George Hill Road, open daily. *Zara's Seafood Restaurant*, Shoal Bay, in gardens of *Alamanda Beach Club*, T3229. Local chef, Rotary Club meets here Thur 1800 for dinner. *Le Beach Bar & Restaurant*, oldest restaurant on Shoal Bay East, T5598. Steakhouse, surf'n'turf, salad bar, pizza, open daily for breakfast, lunch and dinner, happy hour 1700-1830, near *Shoal Bay Villas*. *Trattoria Tramonto & Oasis Beach Bar*, Shoal Bay West, next to *Blue Waters*, T8819, northern Italian chef, serious Italian cuisine, lunch casual 1200-1500, sunset champagne cocktails 1700-1800, dinner 1900-2130, only 10 tables so reservations essential, closed Mon. *Madeiriman Reef*, Shoal Bay, T3833, breakfast, lunch and dinner, barefoot or elegant. *Hibernia*, Island Harbour, T4290. Run by French and Irish couple, international menu with influences from their travelling experiences, closed low season. *Pepperpot*, The Valley, opposite high school, T2328. Open 0700-2200, local food, local customers, especially after work, rotis, salt fish, curried goat, patties, takeaway available.

For those who are self-catering, *Fat Cat*, Main Road, George Hill, T2307. Meals to go from the freezer, picnic meals, pies and cakes, open 1000-1800, closed Sun. *Gee Wee's Bakery & Catering*, on West End main road, T6462. Breads, cakes, pastries, sandwiches, Jamaican jerk chicken and pork, parties catered for, eat in, takeaway or delivery service. *Shalack's Café*, opposite *Albert's Supermarket*, T3272. Cafeteria-style restaurant has variety of ready prepared meals, come in or order. *Vista Food Market*, South Hill Roundabout, T2804. Good selection, cheeses, meats, pâtés, wines, beer, Cuban cigars etc, open Mon-Sat 0800-1800. *Ashleys Supermarket*, South Valley. Open Mon-Fri 0700-2030, Sat 0700-2200, has a good range including produce from other islands.

There is now a smooth Anguillian Rum, a blend from other islands matured in oak barrels designed to be drunk on the rocks rather than in a punch. Visit the rum tasting room at PYRAT Rums' factory on Sandy Ground road, open Mon-Fri 0800-1700, T5003.

Nightlife Out of season there is not much to do during the week. On Fri the whole island changes, several bars have live music, check the local papers, try *Lucy's Palm Palm*, Sandy Ground, or *Round Rock*, Shoal Bay. On Fri go to *Johnno's Place*, Sandy Ground; on Sun to brunch at *Roy's Place*, Crocus Bay, then around 1500 at *Johnno's Place* for a beach party. When the music dies people go to the neighbouring bar, *Ship's Galley* for the night shift. *Uncle Ernie* beach bar on Shoal Bay has a live band playing all day on Sun. *Madeariman Reef Restaurant*, Shoal Bay, soca, calypso, reggae on Fri, Sat, Caribbean night with Spraka Wed. *Gorgeous Scilly Cay* has live daytime music on Wed, Fri and Sun, T5123. At the weekend the *Dragon Disco* opens around midnight. *Mirrors Night Club and Bar*, at Swing High, above Vista Food Market, juke box with music from 1960s to now, happy hour nightly at 1900-2000, live entertainment at weekends. *The Dunes*, reggae and folk music from the Caribbean during March at the full moon at Rendezvous Bay. *The Pumphouse*, in the historic Anguilla road Salt Co Factory, Mon-Sat 1900-0200, eat, drink, dance or relax, T5154.

In high season the resort hotels have live music, steel bands etc, check in the tourist *What We Do in Anguilla* monthly magazine. Look for shows with North Sound, Missington Brothers the most popular bands. Dumpa and the Anvibes is led by Pan Man Michael (Dumpa) Martin, who has recorded a CD/cassette of a blend of local music. There is no theatre but plays are sometimes put on at the Ruthwill Auditorium. The Anguilla National Creative Arts Association (ANCAA) has a performing arts section, the National Theatre Group, which has training workshops and performs at hotels during high season. Visitors with theatre expertise are welcome to participate. Contact the theatre co-ordinator, Ray Tabor, T6685, rbtabor@anguillanet.com. The Mayoumba Folkloric Theatre puts on a song, dance and drama show at *La Sirena*, Meads Bay, on Thur nights, T6827.

Carnival is at the beginning of **Aug** (the Fri before the first Mon), when the island comes to **Festivals**
life with street dancing, Calypso competitions, the *Carnival Queen Coronation*, the *Prince and Princess Show*, nightly entertainment in The Valley and beach barbecues. *The Anguilla International Arts Festival* is held every other year (next in 2001, dates to be announced) and includes workshops and an arts contest. For details T2949, F2735, www.artfestival.ai

General *Ellie's Record Shop* sells Caribbean and international music, T5073, F5317 .Open **Shopping**
1000-1800 at Fairplay Commercial Complex. There are lots of places selling T-shirts, beachwear and gifts. *Caribbean Fancy* boutique and gift shop is at George Hill at the traffic light, T3133, F3513.

Art galleries *Devonish Art Gallery*, George Hill Landing, T2949, F2735, http://devonish.ai, with works by Courtney Devonish and other local and international sculptors, painters, potters et cetera. *Loblolly Gallery*, South Hill Plaza, West End, T2263. Open Tue-Sat 0900-1700, features 4 local artists working in oil and acrylic. *L'Atelier* , Michèle Lavalette, a French artist and photographer who specializes in flowers, in oil, acrylic and pastels, has her studio in North Hill, T5668. Open daily 1000-1730, she has designed postage stamps. Mother Weme (Weme Caster) sells originals and limited edition prints of her paintings of local scenes from her home on the Sea Rocks, near Island Harbour, T4504 for an appointment, prices for prints start from US$75 and for her acrylic and oil paintings from US$300. *Savannah Gallery*, on the road to Crocus Bay, The Valley, T2263, F4017. Paintings, prints and crafts from all over the Caribbean, a lot of Haitian art, several local artists too. *The Arts and Craft Centre*, next to the Public Library, T2949. Pottery, lace, locally made dolls, shell art, paintings and prints. *Cheddie's Carving Studio* , on the main road west, T6027. Cheddie Richardson is a wood sculptor who uses the rose berry roots found among the rocks on the shore, some of his pieces have been cast in bronze.

Bookshop *National Bookstore*, in the Social Security Complex next to Cable and Wireless, The Valley. Open Mon-Sat 0800-1700, wide selection of novels, magazines, non-fiction, children's books, tourist guides, Caribbean history and literature, managed by Mrs Kelly. A *Dictionary of Anguillian Language* has been published in a 34 page booklet, edited by Ijahnia Christian of the Adult and Continuing Education Unit following the Cultural Educational Fest.

Malliouhana Travel and Tours, The Quarter, T2431/2348, F3166, mtt@anguillanet.com **Tour operators**
Bennie's Travel and Tours, Caribbean Commercial Centre, transfers, car rental, island tours, day trips, T2788/2360, F5052, bennies@anguillanet.com *J N Gumbs' Travel Agency* is the local LIAT and Winair agent, T2238/9, F3351.

Air Wallblake airport is just outside The Valley, T2514. International access points for **Transport**
Anguilla are Antigua, St Maarten or San Juan, Puerto Rico. Hotel transfers are not allowed, so you have to take a taxi on arrival. Fares are expensive and usually quotes in US dollars, not EC dollars: from Wallblake airport to The Valley costs about US$6; from The Valley to Blowing Point (ferry) US$12. Fares are fixed by the Government but drivers try to overcharge. Dispatchers are at the airport (T5054) and ferry (T6089), there is no central office.

Boat There is a ferry between Blowing Point (departure tax EC$5/US$2) and Marigot and St Martin which takes at least 20 mins and costs US$10 daytime, US$12 night-time, one way (pay on board). Taxis are available at the airport, the ferry terminal; rates are set by the government.

Car hire There are several car hire companies, including *Apex (Avis)*, *The Quarter*, T2642, F5032; *H and R*, The Valley, T2656/2606; *Island Car Rentals*, T2723, F3723, islandcar@ anguillanet.com *Summer Set Car Rental*, T5278/5778, F5444, summerset@anguilla net.com *Highway Rent-a-Car*, George Hill, by the traffic lights, T2183, F2306, www.rental cars.ai, *Rodco*, www.mrat.com/rodco. Rates are from US$25 per day off season, US$40 per day high season, plus insurance, jeeps from US$45. You can normally bargain for a good rate if you rent for more than 3 days, seventh day is usually free, some offer discounts on internet

Leeward Islands

bookings. **Bicycle hire** Rented from *Happy Trails Mountain Bike Rentals*, PO Box 354, George Hill Rd, T5810, F5811.

Taxi Expensive and the driver usually quotes in US dollars, not EC dollars. To hire a taxi for a tour of the island works out at about US$40 for two people, US$5 for additional passengers. Dispatchers are at the airport (T5054) and ferry (T6089), there is no central office.

Directory **Banks** In The Valley, *Barclays Bank International*, T2301/2304, F2980, Box 140. *National Bank of Anguilla*, T2101, F3310, www.nba.ai *Scotiabank*, Fairplay Commercial Centre, The Valley, T3333, F3344. **Communications** **Post:** The main post office is in The Valley, T2528, F5455. Open Mon-Fri 0800-1530. Commemorative stamps and other collections sold. **Telephone:** *Cable and Wireless*, T3100. Operates internal and external telephone links (IDD available), cellular, internet and fax services, open Mon-Fri 0800-1700, Sat, Sun, holidays 0900-1300. Caribbean phone cards are available throughout the islands. There are 2 AT&T USA direct telephones by Cable and Wireless office in The Valley and by the airport. For credit card calls overseas T1800-8778000. **Medical facilities** The *Princess Alexandra Hospital*, T2551/2. **Emergency:** T911/999. **Doctor:** T3792/6522/2882 and T2632/3233. **Pharmacy:** T2366/2738. **Optometrist:** T3700. Most people drink bottled water but there is also rainwater or desalinated water for household use. **Tourist offices** *Anguilla Department of Tourism*, PO Box 1388, Old Factory Plaza, The Valley, T2759, F2710, www.anguilla-vacation.com,net.ai Open weekdays 0800-1700. The office at the airport is also closed at lunchtime, but the customs officers will often phone for a hotel reservation for you. No one is keen to give you the numbers of cheaper guesthouses. TV Cable Channel 32 shows a 30-min programme called Touring Anguilla, which goes out continuously, giving information on the island. The *Anguilla National Trust* welcomes members, office in the Museum Building, The Valley, T5297, F5571, axanat@anguillanet.com

Background

History

The earliest known Amerindian site on Anguilla is at the northeast tip of the island, where tools and artefacts made from conch shells have been recovered and dated at around 1300 BC. Saladoid Amerindians settled on the island in the fourth century AD and brought their knowledge of agriculture, ceramics and their religious culture based on the god of cassava. By the sixth century large villages had been built at Rendezvous Bay and Sandy Ground, with smaller ones at Shoal Bay and Island Harbour. Post Saladoid Amerindians from the Greater Antilles arrived in the tenth century, building villages and setting up a chiefdom with a religious hierarchy. Several ceremonial items have been found and debris related to the manufacture of the three-pointed zemis, or spirit stones, associated with fertility rites. By the 17th century, Amerindians had disappeared from Anguilla: wiped out by enslavement and European diseases.

Anguilla was first mentioned in 1564 when a French expedition passed en route from Dominica to Florida, but it was not until 1650 that it was first colonized by the British. Despite several attempted invasions, by Caribs in 1656 and by the French in 1745 and 1796, it remained a British colony. From 1825 it became more closely associated with St Kitts for administrative purposes and ultimately incorporated in the colony. In 1967 St Kitts-Nevis-Anguilla became a State in Association with the UK and gained internal independence. However, Anguilla opposed this development and almost immediately repudiated government from St Kitts. A breakaway movement was led by Ronald Webster of the People's Progressive Party (PPP). In 1969 British forces invaded the island to install a British Commissioner after negotiations had broken down. The episode is remembered locally for the unusual presence of the London Metropolitan Police, who remained on the island until 1972 when the Anguilla Police Force was established.

The post of Chief Minister alternated for two decades between the rival politicians, Ronald Webster and Emile Gumbs, leader of the Anguilla National Alliance

(ANA), the latter holding office in 1977-80 and 1984-94. Mr Gumbs (now Sir Emile) retired from politics at the general elections held in March 1994. These elections proved inconclusive, with the ANA, the Anguilla United Party (AUP) and the Anguilla Democratic Party (ADP) each winning two seats and an Independent, Osbourne Fleming (who was Finance Minister in the ANA government) winning the seventh. A coalition was formed by Hubert Hughes, leader of the AUP, and Victor Banks, ADP, and the former was sworn in as Chief Minister. Mr Hughes had been a Minister in the 1984 ANA government, but had been dismissed in 1985, subsequently joining the opposition AUP, then led by Ronald Webster.

The March 1999 general elections were won by the governing coalition: the AUP and the ADP won two seats each while the ANA won three. Hubert Hughes (AUM) was sworn in as Chief Minister. His period of office was short-lived, however. The House of Assembly was paralysed after Mr Hughes lost a legal case against the Speaker and the ruling coalition fell apart when the ADP leader, Victor Banks, resigned from the administration and allied his party with the ANA. New elections were held in March 2000. The ANA again won three seats, the AUP two, ADP one and an independent one. Osbourne Fleming, leader of the ANA, became Chief Minister on 6 March, in coalition with the ADP.

Anguilla was another island to be badly hit by Hurricane Lenny in November 1999. Flooding reached depths of 14 ft and livestock perished. Most hotels managed to clean up for the winter season, only one remaining closed until well into 2000.

Government

In 1980, Anguilla formally separated from the State and became a British Dependent Territory with a Governor to represent the Crown. A new constitution was introduced in 1982, providing for a Governor, an Executive Council comprising four elected Ministers and two ex-officio members, and an 11-member legislative House of Assembly presided over by a Speaker. In 1990 the constitution was amended to give the Governor responsibility for international financial affairs. A new post of Deputy Governor was created, to replace the Permanent Secretary for Finance as a member of the Executive Council and House of Assembly.

The economy

The main economic activities used to be livestock raising, lobster fishing, salt production and boat building, but tourism is now the major generator of foreign exchange and employment. There are some 800 rooms available in guest houses, villas and apartments and hotels, although the number is steadily rising. The hurricane season in 1995 caused havoc to the industry. Total visitor arrivals fell by 15%, with stopover visitors falling by 16.5% from 1994. Gdp declined in 1995 after a growth rate of 8.1% in 1994. Since then, however, growth has picked up to 3.4% in 1996 and 6.5% in 1997 as the number of visitors has recovered. Growth has been led by tourism, construction, communications and financial services. 1999 was another year of healthy gdp growth of 8.2%, but Hurricane Lenny at the end of the year meant that growth would be slower in 2000 at around 5.6%.

There is some offshore banking and the Government aims to establish a reputable offshore financial services industry. Thirty out of the 43 offshore banks, who pay an annual licence fee to the Government, had their licences cancelled in 1990 following a review of the sector. At end-1991 the House of Assembly approved legislation to tighten control of offshore finance, giving the Governor complete and final authority over the granting of licences. New financial services legislation enacted in late 1994 and a new marketing strategy led to an increase of 23 in the number of registered offshore financial companies that year.

Previously, high levels of unemployment led to migration to other Caribbean islands and further afield, but the unemployment rate has fallen from 26% in 1985 to

Leeward Islands

almost nil and shortages of labour have delayed expansion programmes, as well as putting pressure on prices and wages. Work permits have been granted to more than 1,000 non-Anguillans, but many people have two jobs. Workers' remittances are crucial, particularly since the 1984 suspension of budgetary support in the form of UK grants-in-aid, although the British Government does still provide aid for the development programme, along with other donors such as the EU and the Caribbean Development Bank. There is no income tax and the Government gets its revenues from customs duties, bank licences, property and stamps.

Montserrat

Montserrat, known as 'the Emerald Isle', is dominated by three mountain ranges. Mount Chance, in the Soufrière Hills, rises to 3,000 ft above sea level. This active volcano had been erupting for two years before it exploded in August 1997 destroying some villages and the capital, Plymouth. As a result, the south, which like the rest of the island used to be all lushly green, is now grey with ash. Montserrat has been off-limits for tourism for a few years but the still-active volcano is now attracting visitors and facilities are being restored. About 11 miles long and seven miles wide, although the volcano's eruptions have increased the land surface in the south. Its nearest neighbours are Nevis, Guadeloupe and Antigua.

Ins and outs

Getting there
See transport, page 647, for further details

William H Bramble Airport, on the east coast is closed because of falling ash or other volcanic activity. Air service is now provided by helicopter to **Gerald's Heliport** from Antigua or St Kitts, charter or scheduled. You get a good view of the island and the volcano on the 20-min flight from Antigua. Alternatively there is a **ferry** from Antigua which takes an hour.

Getting around
Driving is on the left

Roads are paved and fairly good, but narrow and twisty. Drivers travel fast, passing on blind corners with much use of their horns. With a valid driving licence, you can obtain a local 3 month licence (EC$30/US$12) at the Police Station in Salem, open 24 hrs Mon-Fri, T4912555. There are several **car hire** companies (the cars are mostly Japanese). **Hitching** is safe and easy because the local people are so friendly. Similarly, don't be afraid to pick them up when you are driving. The standard fare in mini-buses is EC$2-3. Outside the fixed times and routes they operate as taxis and journeys can be arranged with drivers for an extra fee. **Taxis** are usually small buses, which can be shared. Fares are set and listed by the Tourist Board.

Climate

Although tropical, the humidity in Montserrat is low and there is often rain overnight which clears the atmosphere. The average temperature is 26-27°C with little variation from one season to another. The wettest months, according to official statistics, are April and May plus July through to September, although weather patterns are changing here, as elsewhere.

Flora and fauna

Studies of the effect of the volcanic eruptions on flora and fauna have not yet, to our knowledge, been undertaken. Natural vegetation is confined mostly to the summits of hills, where elfin woodlands occur. At lower levels, fern groves are plentiful and lower still, cacti, sage bush and acacias. Flowers and fruit are typical of the Caribbean with many bay trees, from which bay oil (or rum) is distilled, the national tree, the mango and the national flower, *Heliconia caribaea* (a wild banana known locally as 'lobster claw'). There are 34 species of birds resident on the island and many more migrants. Unique to Montserrat is the Montserrat oriole, *Icterus oberi*, a black and gold oriole named the national bird. There are also the rare forest thrush, the bridled quail dove, mangrove cuckoo, trembler and purple throated carib. Many of these can be seen along the Centre Hills trail in the middle of the island between the ash-covered Soufriere Hills and the Silver Hills. The vegetation here is biologically diverse and supports a variety of wildlife. Montserrat cannot boast many wild animals, although it shares the terrestrial frog, known as the mountain chicken, only with Dominica. Agoutis, bats and lizards, including iguanas which can grow to over 4 ft in length (they used to take the balls on the golf course, mistaking them for eggs), can all be found and tree frogs contribute to the island's 'night-music'. A walk around the Silver Hills in the extreme north reveals a dramatic coastline where you can find lots of seabirds. At Pelican Point on the east coast is the only breeding colony on the island of magnificent frigate birds, while elsewhere you can see the red-billed tropic bird, the mangrove cuckoo and the pearly-eyed thrasher. Contact the Montserrat Forest Rangers for trail hikes across the island to see the variety of fauna and flora.

Montserrat

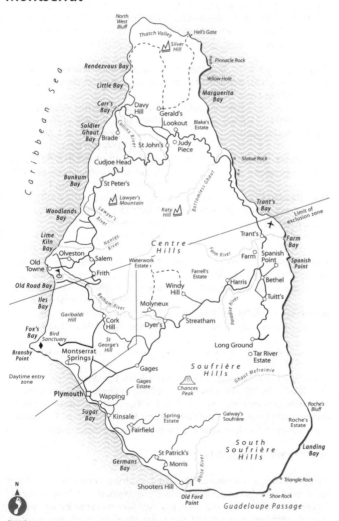

Essentials

Documents A valid **passport** is required except for US, Canadian and British visitors, who must only show proof of citizenship for stays of up to six months. Citizens of Caricom countries may travel with their official ID card. **Visas** may be required for visitors from Haiti, Cuba and Eastern bloc countries, which can be obtained from British consulate offices. An onward or return ticket is required.

Currency The currency is the East Caribbean dollar (EC$). The exchange rate is fixed at EC$2.67 = US$1, but there are variations depending on where you change your money. US and Canadian dollars are widely accepted. All major credit cards are accepted, as are traveller's cheques.

Customs 200 cigarettes, 50 cigars, 40 ozs of alcoholic beverages, six ozs perfume. Little Bay (Main Office, Bredes), open 0800-1600 Monday-Friday, for yachts and small craft, T4913816, 4912456, F4916909, customms@candw.ag

Departure tax US$8 for Caricom residents and US$13 for visitors.

Hours of business Government offices: 0800-1600, Monday-Friday. **Shops**: the same as government but early closing Wednesday and Saturday afternoons.

Communications The international code for Montserrat is 664, followed by a seven-digit number. See page 648 for further details.

Official time Atlantic Standard Time, four hours behind GMT, one ahead of EST.

Port of entry Little Bay, 55m jetty with a depth of 1.7m-4.6m. Contact the Montserrat Port Authority, channel 16, for mooring details.

Voltage Electric current is 220/110 volts, 60 cycles.

Media Newspapers There are two weekly newspapers, the Montserrat News and the Montserrat Reporter. **Radio** Radio Montserrat ZJB relays the BBC World Service news at 0700 daily and the Voice of America news at 0800. Gem Radio is an exclusive outlet for the Associated Press.
Television Satellite TV Cable is operational in most areas, and stations broadcasting from nearby islands can be received.

Diplomatic representation All embassies and consulates are based in Antigua.

Tourist offices overseas Germany, Montserrat Tourist Board/West India Committee, Lomer Strasse 28, D-22047 Hamburg 70, T4940-6958846, F4940-3800051. **UK**, c/o CTO, 42 Westminster Palace Gardens, Artillery Row, London SW1P 1RR, T020-72224325, F020-72224325, cto@carib-tourism.com **USA**, c/o CTO, 80 Broad St, 32nd floor, New York, NY 10004, T212-6359530, F212-6359511, get2cto@dorsai.org

Public holidays New Year's Day, St Patrick's Day (17 March), Good Friday, Easter Monday, Labour Day (first Monday in May), Whit Monday (7th Monday after Easter), first Monday in August, Christmas Day, Boxing Day (26 December) and Festival Day (31 December).

The Montserrat National Trust has been relocated to Olveston, on the North Main Road, T4913086, F4913046. It is rebuilding its museum and constructing a Natural History Centre and a Botanical Garden. There will be a volcanic interpretative centre created with the help of the Montserrat Volcanic Observatory and the reference library on the island's fauna and flora will be accessible for visitors.

Beaches and watersports

Montserrat's beaches are volcanic 'black' sand, which in reality means the sand may be a silvery grey or dark golden brown colour. The single white coral beach is at Rendezvous Bay in the north of the island. It is a stiff hike from Little Bay along a very steep mountainous trail (not suitable for small children). Take food and water, it is a long hot walk until you reach your refreshing swim. There is no shade on the beach, avoid the poisonous manchineel trees and the spiney sea urchins among the rocks at the north end. You can also take a boat and it is quite a good idea to walk there and arrange for a boat to come and pick you up at an agreed time. The best of the rest of the beaches, all on the west of the island and black sand, are Woodlands (National Trust, beach house, washrooms), where you can safely swim through caves, Lime Kiln Bay, tiny Bunkum Bay, Fox's Bay (nice beach but pebbly and rocky just off-shore, snorkelling worthwhile at north end, Emerald Isle (near Montserrat Springs), Old Road (by the *Vue Pointe Hotel*) and Little Bay in the north. Sports fishing, or just boat rides around the island to see ruined Plymouth and other villages, can be arranged with Bruce Farara, Brades, T4918802, farara@hotmail.com and Danny Sweeney, Olveston, T4915645, mwilson@candw.ag

Diving and marine life

Before the volcano disrupted normal life, Montserrat was gaining a modest reputation as an undiscovered destination with much virgin diving. The National Trust is planning to set up a National Marine Park which will include a reef building project. The best sites are along the northwest coast and have not been harmed at all by the volcano. Shore diving is good from Lime Kiln Bay, where there are ledges with coral, sponges and lots of fish; Woodlands Bay, where there is a shallow reef at 25 to 30 ft; and at Little Bay. There are some shallow dives from boats, suitable for novices or a second dive, but also deep dives for experienced divers. Pinnacle is a deep dive, dropping from 65 to 300 ft, where you can see brain coral, sponges and lots of fish. Diving and kayaking are offered by Sea Wolf Diving School, Woodlands, T4917807, F4913599, krebs@candw.ag A shore dive costs US$40, a single tank boat dive US$50, two tanks US$70, scuba equipment hire US$30, snorkel gear rental US$10, PADI Open Water certification course US$375. Wolf and Inge Krebs started the dive operation in the early 1990s and there is little they don't know about Montserrat underwater, www.swiftsite.com/seawolfdivingschool

Around the island

The volcano is now a tourist attraction and when it is not active it is possible to get fairly close to see the grey, ash-covered flanks of what was Chances Peak, in stark contrast with the Centre Hills, which are still green, forested and fertile. There is a viewing point on St George's Hill, from where you can see Plymouth, the former capital, which has been flooded with ash up to the first floor of the colonial buildings and completely destroyed. Even if you don't see the volcano in action, you can watch videos at the Montserrat Volcano Visitor's Centre and the Montserrat Volcano Observatory, Mongo Hill, T4915647, F4912423, www.mvomrat.com The scientists at the Observatory monitor eruptions and issue warnings when necessary. An expert guide will give you a tour of the Observatory and explain the work of the scientists, showing the seismographs and explaining the chronology of events. If the volcano is dangerously active visitors are excluded, of course. Staff at the Observatory are to move in mid-2001 from the existing premises, five miles north of the volcano, to a new building three miles northwest of the volcano.

Essentials

With the re-occupation of the area on the west coast, south to the Belham River Valley, work is now going ahead to renovate the hotels. There are a few guest houses open in the north. Prices start from around US$50 for a double room, bed and breakfast.

Sleeping

Hotels *Tropical Mansions*, PO Box 404, Sweeneys, T4918273, F4918275. Opened at the end of 1999, 18 rooms, a/c, fan, cable TV, phone, pool, restaurant. The *Vue Pointe*, having been closed for several years was due to reopen in 2000 after extensive renovations, PO Box 65, T4915210, F4914813. This family-run hotel by Old Road Bay used to be the premier hotel on the island, with its hexagonal rondavels, or cottages, hotel rooms, pool, tennis and entertainment.

Guest houses (offering B&B) **B** *Grand View*, PO Box 350, Baker Hill, T4912284, F4916876, grand@candw.ag Twin beds, private or shared bathroom, or double bed, kitchenette and private bathroom, TV, parking, dinner by reservation only, transfers on request. **B-C** *Rita's*, Mahogany Drive, Woodlands, T4914006. Large or small double room with private bathroom. **C** *Erindell*, Woodlands, T4913655, erindell@candw.ag Run by Shirley and Lou Spycalla, private entrance, twin beds, private bathroom, TV, phone, fans, cooking facilities, pool, free laundry, discounts for Caricom residents. *Barbara Gough*, Woodlands, T/F4915922.

Rooms and apartments C *Egret House*, Woodlands, T/F4915316. Owned by Gloria Boekbinder, apartment overlooks Woodlands Beach, sleeps two, no children, bedroom with large bed, sitting room, kitchen, bathroom, shower, stairs to sundeck and pool, daily maid service and towel change, TV, phones, fans. **A** *David and Maureen Hood*, PO Box 64, Olveston, T4915248, F4915016. Weekly and monthly rates, discounts for Caricom residents, apartment sleeps 2, views of sea and mountains, quiet, TV, phone, washing machine, kitchen, meals can be arranged. *David and Clover Lea*, St Peter's, T4915812, www.volcano-island.com 2-bedroom guest house with 2 bathrooms, veranda, or 1 bedroom with bath and veranda, or room adjoining main house with 2 beds which can be pushed together or bunked, bathroom, deck, fridge, TV, phone, email, tent and camping equipment available, family atmosphere, the Leas have 3 sons to enliven your stay. *Richard Aspin*, Olveston, T4916346, F4918867, monmedia@candw.ag. In residential area, 2-bedroom, 1 bathroom apartment, large kitchen, sitting room with veranda, bedroom patio opens onto gardens.

Villa rental Montserrat has a large number of comfortable villas built by ex-pats, many of them Canadians, as holiday or retirement homes. Although a lot of them were built close to Plymouth and are now in the exclusion zone, many were around Old Towne, Olveston and Woodlands, and apart from a coating of ash from time to time, escaped any damage. Most have their own pools, terraces with lovely views, gardens and maid service. Rental agencies include: *Kirwan's Secluded Hideaway*, Olveston, T4913405, F4912546; *Montserrat Company Ltd*, PO Box 221, Olveston, T4912431, F4914660; *Montserrat Enterprises Ltd*, PO Box 58, Old Towne, T4912431, F4914660; *Neville Bradshaw Agencies*, PO Box 270, Old Towne, T4915270, F4915069; *Jacquie Ryan Enterprises Ltd*, PO Box 425, Olveston, T4912055, F4913257; *Tradewinds Real Estate*, PO Box 365, Old Towne, T4912004, F4916229, www.tradewindsmontserrat.com; *West Indies Real Estate*, PO Box 355, Olveston, T4918666, F4918668, www.wirealest.com

Eating

Several places do takeaway meals

A large frog called mountain chicken, indigenous here and in Dominica, is the local delicacy. Goat water stew is another local dish commonly found on the menu. Most other foods, like steak and fish, are imported. For self-catering visitors there are supermarkets with imported and local produce and grocery stores and bakeries. A lot of the eating places are not open all the time, others only open if you make a reservation in advance, so it is best to check.

Ziggy's Restaurant, T4918282, Mahogany Loop, second turning on the right from the main road. Dinner by reservation only, Ziggy has been serving great food since the early 1990s, lobster quadrille, jerk pork, chocolate sludge. *Gourmet Gardens*, T4912000, Olveston. Reservations preferred, takeaway available. *La Colage Bar & Restaurant*, St John's, T4914136. Creole cuisine, boutique for clothes and accessories attached. *Tina's Restaurant*, Brades Main Road, T4913538. Local food, chicken and fish and local vegetables. *Morgan's Spotlight Bar & Restaurant*, St John's, T4915419. Local food, large portions, goat water. *Sub's Bar & Restaurant*, Brades Main Road, T4915158. Local and creole menu. *The People's Place*, Forgarthy Hill, T4917528. Lunches and takeaway meals, local food, great roti. *Monica's Bar*, Salem, T4914182, Takeaway lunches. *Di's Snackette*, Davy Hill Main Road, T4915450.

Lunches and snacks. *Annie's Snackette*, Davy Hill Main Road, T4915380. Snacks and takeaway. *Burger Deluxe*, Brades Main Road, T4917316. Open Mon-Sat for burgers. *Margaret & Danny's Barbecue*, Woodlands Beach, T4915645. As well as sport fishing and boat rental, Danny offers a beach barbecue on Sun and Thur, fish, chicken and side dishes. *Bitter End Beach Bar*, Little Bay, T4913146. Seafood and snacks on the beach. *Tuitt's Pizzeria*, Brades Main Road, T4914606. Open Mon-Sat for pizza. *Wilson's Place*, Salem, T4913048. Open Mon-Sat, the place for chicken. *Venelle's Cook Shop*, St John's, T4915940. Open Fri and Sat for fish, chicken and snacks. *Richard Samuel's*, Sweeneys, T4912475. Fresh bread and snacks. *Cockpit Bar & Restaurant*, at Gerald's Heliport, T4914478. Montserrat version of the airport café, serves breakfast and lunch, popular for 'liming'. *Root's Man Beach Bar*, Carrs Bay, T4915957. Vegetarian meal in rustic setting, orders only. *Howe's Flamboyant Bar*, St John's, T4913008. Pool table for entertainment after a meal. *Fins & Wings*, Cudjoe Head, T4918219. Lunch or takeaway, fish, chicken, local drinks. *The Attic*, Olveston, T4912008. Open for breakfast and lunch. *Etcetera Shoppe*, 540 Runaway Point Circle, Olveston, T4915146. Call for reservations, only open for Wed lunch, Fri night dinner and Sun brunch. *Val's Takeaway*, St John's, T4916854. Lunches Mon-Fri. *Economy Bakery*, Brades Main Road, T4916678. Fresh bread, sandwiches and snacks. *Bessie's Tasty Pastry*, St John's, T4917089. Pastries and cakes, orders taken.

Not surprisingly in the 'Emerald Isle', **St Patrick's Day** (a national holiday) is celebrated on *17 March* with concerts, masquerades and other festivities. The **Queen's Birthday** is celebrated on the 2nd Saturday in *June* with parades, salutes and the raising of flags. Another national knees-up is **August Monday Weekend**, connected to **Emancipation Day** on 1 August, commemorating the abolition of slavery in 1834. There are beach barbecues and picnics all weekend. Cudjoe Head Day on the Saturday starts with a big breakfast and carries on late into the night, while St Peter's Anglican Fete is held in the village rectory grounds on the Mon. The island's main festival is the **Christmas** season, which starts around *12 December* and continues through New Year's Day. There are shows, concerts, calypso competitions, jump ups and masquerades and of course lots of festivities and parties on **New Year's Eve**, helped down with lots of goat water. **Festivals**

Montserrat is not the place to come for shopping, but there are places where you can find locally printed T-shirts, local Sea Island goods, crafts, jams, jellies and tropical drinks. For music, T-shirts and other clothing go to *Arrow Manshop*, Salem, T4913852, or *Sweeneys*, T4916355. Photos of Montserrat and the volcano are sold at *Kevin's Photo Shop*, Cudjoe Head, T4916177, and at *Woolcock's Craft & Photo Gallery*, Davy Hill, T4912025, while *Sea Wolf*, Woodlands, T4917807, have postcards of underwater Montserrat and other crafts and gifts. Art and crafts and other souvenirs at *Oriole Gift Shop*, Salem, T4913086, next to the National Trust. *Kiernon's Products*, Cudjoe Head, T4916385, sells local pepper sauce, guava cheese, jellies, liqueurs and other local goodies. Leslie and Cynthia Williams sell honey in Brades, T4914014. **Shopping**

Sightseeing tours can be arranged with *Carib World Travel*, Sweeneys, T4912714, F4912713; *Double X Tours*, Olveston, T4915470, meader@candw.ag; *Grant Enterprises & Trading*, Olveston, T4919654, casselj@candw.ag; *Jenny's Tours*, PO Box W471, St John's, Antigua, T268-4619361, burkeb@candw.ag; *Runaway Travel*, Sweeneys, T4912776, runaway@candw.ag **Tour operators**

Air Helicopter service daily except Wed from Antigua, US$66 return. Mon and Fri at 0730, 1300, 1720, Tue, Thur and Sat at 0730, 1720, Sun at 0730, 1450, 1720. Agents in Antigua are *Carib Aviation*, VC Bird International Airport, PO Box 318, T268-4623147, F268-4623125, caribav@candw.ag Agents in Montserrat are *Montserrat Aviation Services*, Nixons, PO Box 257, T4912533, F4917186. Charter helicopter service is offered by *Caribbean Helicopters*, PO Box 170, Jolly Harbour, Antigua, T268-4605900, F268-4605901, helicopters@candw.ag *Island Aviation Ltd*, PO Box 1479, Basseterre, St Kitts, T869-4661325, F869-4661363, helico@caribsurf.com, operates a charter helicopter service from St Kitts to Montserrat. You can take only one piece of luggage on the helicopter, but unlimited **Transport**

amounts on the boat. **Boat** *Opale Express* ferry from Heritage Quay, St John's, Antigua, to Little Bay, Montserrat, seats 300, a/c, leaves Antigua 0630, 1600, returns from Little Bay 0800, 1730, 1 hr, EC$150 return Mon afternoon to Fri morning, EC$75 return at weekends. Agents in Antigua, *Carib World Travel*, Lower Redcliffe St, St John's, PO Box W122, T268-4802980, F268-4802985; in Montserrat, *Montserrat Aviation Services* (see above). **Car hire** *Be-Peep's Car Rentals*, Olveston, T4913787, for cars and jeeps; *Equipment & Supplies Ltd*, Olveston, T4912402, for cars and vans; *Ethelyne's Car Rental*, Olveston, T4912855; *Grant Enterprises & Trading*, Olveston, T4919654; *KC's Car Rentals*, Olveston, T4915756; *Montserrat Company Ltd*, Old Towne, T4912431; *Neville Bradshaw Agencies*, Olveston, T4915270; *Joe Oliver*, Barzey's, T4914276, for jeeps; *MS Osbourne Ltd*, Brades, T4912494; *Pickett Van Rentals*, Salem, T4915470, for vans; *Zeekies Rentals*, Baker Hill, T4914515.

Directory **Banks** *Bank of Montserrat*, St Peters, PO Box 10, T4913843, F4913163, open Mon, Tue Thur 0800-1400, Wed 0800-1300, Fri 0800-1500; *Royal Bank of Canada*, Olveston, PO Box 222, T4912426-8, F4913391, open Mon-Thu 0800-1400, Fri 0800-1500. The American Express agent is *Carib World Travel*, at Sweeneys, T4912714, F4912713. **Communications** Post: Post Office open Mon-Fri 0815-1555, T4912457. The Philatelic Bureau is in Sweeneys, T4912996, F4912042. It has 6 issues a year and a definitive issue every 4-5 years, having issued its own stamps since 1876. The volcanic eruption is featured, as is the eclipse of the sun. **Telephone**: *Cable and Wireless* (West Indies) Ltd, at Sweeneys, T4912112, F4913599 (open Mon-Fri 0800-1600), operates the telecommunications system with a digital telephone system, international dialling, telegraph, facsimile and data facilities. Phone cards are available, as are credit card service, toll free 800 service and cellular phones. **Medical facilities** There is a government health service. The hospital is in St John's, for most routine and surgical emergencies, T4912802. Private doctors and a dentist are also available. Serious medical cases are taken by helicopter to Antigua or Guadeloupe. During the rainy season there are mosquitoes and 'no-see-ums', but a good anti-bug repellent should suffice. Rooms that lack a/c often provide mosquito nets for beds. No poisonous snakes or insects. **Tourist Information** Local tourist office: *Miss Ernestine Cassell*, Director of Tourism, Salem, T4912230, F4917430, www.visitmontserrat.com

Background

History

Columbus sighted Montserrat on 11 November 1493, naming it after an abbey of the same name in Spain, where the founder of the Jesuits, Ignacio de Loyola, experienced the vision which led to his forming that famous order of monks. At that time, a few Carib Indians lived on the island but by the middle of the 17th century they had disappeared. The Caribs named the island Alliouagana, which means "land of the prickly bush". Montserrat was eventually settled by the British Thomas Warner, who brought English and Irish Catholics from their uneasy base in the Protestant island of St Kitts. Once established as an Irish-Catholic colony, the only one in the Caribbean, Catholic refugees fled there from persecution in Virginia and, following his victory at Drogheda in 1649, Cromwell sent some of his Irish political prisoners to Montserrat. By 1648 there were 1,000 Irish families on the island. An Irishman brought some of the first slaves to the island in 1651 and the economy became based on sugar. Slaves quickly outnumbered the original British indentured servants. A slave rebellion in 1768, appropriately enough on St Patrick's Day, led to all the rebels being executed and today they are celebrated as freedom fighters. Montserrat was invaded several times by the French during the 17th and 18th centuries, sometimes with assistance from the resident Irish, but the island returned to British control under the Treaty of Versailles (1783) and has remained a colony to this day.

There are several small political parties, including the People's Liberation Movement (PLM), the National Development Party (NDP), the National Progressive Party (NPP), the Movement for National Reconstruction (MNR) and the People's Progressive Alliance (PPA), although the current Chief Minister, David Brandt, is

Hurricanes and volcanoes

In 1989, Montserrat was devastated by Hurricane Hugo, the first hurricane to strike the island for 61 years. No part of the island was untouched by the 150mph winds as 400-year-old trees were uprooted, 95% of the housing stock was damaged or destroyed, agriculture was reduced to below subsistence level and even the 180 ft jetty at Plymouth harbour completely disappeared, causing problems for relief supplies. However, within a few months, all public utilities were restored and the remaining standing or injured trees were in leaf again.

In 1995 the lives of Montserratians were again disrupted, this time by volcanic activity. The residents of Plymouth and villages in the south were evacuated to the north as lava, rocks and ash belched from the Soufrière Hills for the first time since the 1930s. Activity increased in 1997; during March and April pyroclastic flows reached two miles down the south side of the volcano, the former tourist attractions of the Great Alps Waterfall and Galways Soufrière were covered, there was a partial collapse of Galways Wall and lava flowed down the Tar River Valley. In May the volcanic dome was growing at 3.7 cubic metres per second and in June a huge explosion occurred when a sudden pyroclastic flow of hot rock, gas and ash poured down the volcano at 200mph. It engulfed 19 people, destroyed seven villages and some 200 homes including Farm's and Trants to the north of the volcano. The dead and missing people were reported to have gone back to their homes in the evacuated zone to feed their animals and tend to their property. The flow, which resulted from a partial collapse of the lava dome, came to within 50 yds of the sea, close to the airport runway, which had to be closed. The eruption sent an ash cloud six miles into the air and people were forced to wear ash masks. In August another bout of activity destroyed Plymouth, which caught fire under a shower of red hot lava. It now looks like a lunar landscape, completely covered by grey ash. In December 1997 there was a huge dome collapse which created a 600 m amphitheatre around Galways Soufriére. The lava flows destroyed the deserted communities of St Patrick's, Gingoes and Morris and severely damaged Trials, Fairfield and Kinsale, south of Plymouth. The White River delta was increased to about 1½ km and the water level rose by about 1 m. During 1998-99 dome collapses continued, with ash clouds at times up to eight miles high, but scientists reported that the dome, while still hot, was gradually cooling and entering a quieter phase. In 2000, however, there was further activity. For daily scientific updates about the volcanic activity try the Internet at www.geo.mtu.edu/volcanoes /west.indies/soufriere/govt

an independent. At the last elections, in 1996, there were 4,206 votes cast, out of 7,238 registered electors, many of whom had left the island. Four of the constituencies are in areas fully or partially evacuated.

The main concern of the government since 1995 has been the relocation of the remaining population to the north of the island out of reach of the volcano. In August 1997, after the main explosion and the destruction of Plymouth there were still 1,400 people in shelters, of whom 800 were in churches and 600 in factory shells. There were controversial proposals from British authorities for a complete evacuation of the island, but Chief Minister Brandt campaigned for the release of funds already allocated by the UK for developing the north.

In June 1998, it was announced that Britain would allocate £75mn to Montserrat in the two financial years to April 2001, compared with £59.3mn in the previous three. The amount would comprise budgetary aid, development spending and emergency assistance. A plan for sustainable development of the north of the island was circulated for public consultation and signed in January 1999. Objectives of the plan included job creation, population growth and a greater role for the private sector. Houses were built at Judy Piece for the evacuated villagers of Long Ground and more were under construction at Lookout, Shinn and at Davy Hill, with the aim of reuniting communities. In August, residents and businesses were authorized to return to the central zone, between Lawyers River and Nantes River. South of Nantes

River to the Belham River Valley (including Salem, Friths and Old Towne) was considered less dangerous than previously and a programme to clean the area of ash was started. Reoccupation of this area began on a limited basis at end-September.

By the end of 1999, the crisis appeared to have receded, Montserratians were beginning to trickle back to the island from the UK, Antigua or other Caribbean islands, and tourism was actively encouraged again to kick start the economy. It was estimated at the beginning of 2000 that the population had risen to 5,000, compared with a low of 3,400 two years previously, with 120 people remaining in shelters. Although many Caricom workers had been employed in the construction business, in April 2000 the Government announced that they would henceforth have to seek work permits, in order to give priority to returning Montserratians seeking employment. The Soufriere Hills volcano continues to be active, but it is hoped that the safe zone will remain safe and that the line of the exclusion will not have to be adjusted.

Government

A British dependent territory, Montserrat has a representative government with a ministerial system. Queen Elizabeth II is Head of State and is represented by a resident Governor (Mr Tony Abbott was appointed Governor in 1997). The Government consists of a Legislative and an Executive Council, with elections being held every five years for membership in the former. The head of Government is called the Chief Minister; a Speaker presides over the seven-member Council of Representatives. As executive authority and head of the civil service, the Governor is responsible for defence, internal security and external affairs. A constitutional reform in 1989 added financial services to the Governor's powers and recognized Montserrat's right to self-determination. Montserratians have frequently discussed the pros and cons of opting for independence, but the official position is that economic independence must precede political independence, so with the current volcanic uncertainties colonial status may remain for many years to come.

The economy

Tourism used to contribute about 30% of gdp, it was the largest supplier of foreign exchange and the Government actively encouraged investment in tourism projects. The influx of foreign residents in the 1980s saw a sharp rise in real estate deals and building construction with a parallel dependence on imports of capital and consumer goods. Gross domestic product grew rapidly at the end of the 1980s, expanding by 12.8% in 1988, although a slower rate was recorded in 1989 because of the devastation wreaked by Hurricane Hugo. Ninety-five percent of the housing stock was totally or partially destroyed; production and exports were disrupted, infrastructure was severely damaged; public sector finances were hit by reduced income and greater expenditure demands; tourism slumped. Similar economic disruption occurred as a result of the volcanic eruption in 1995-1997 (see box) when the south had to be evacuated to the north. Most ex-pats left the island and tourists stayed away. The island now depends on aid from the UK but is beginning to recover, with new construction and hotels opening up again.

The people

The vast majority of the people are of African descent. Before the volcano erupted there was an influx of white Americans, Canadians and Britons who purchased retirement homes on the island. Montserratians are notable for their easy friendliness to visitors, speaking English flavoured by dialect and the odd Irish expression. There is virtually no crime and everyone leaves their doors unlocked. The population used to hover around 11,000, but emigration since the volcano started erupting in 1995 has reduced numbers. Many Montserratians are living in temporary accommodation in Antigua and others have relocated elsewhere in the Caribbean or in the UK. Evacuees are returning, however, with the British government paying their travel costs (subject to certain restrictions).

Culture

The Irish influence can still be seen in national emblems. On arrival your passport is stamped with a green shamrock, the island's flag and crest show a woman, Erin of Irish legend, complete with her harp, and a carved shamrock adorns the gable of Government House. There are many Irish names, of both people and places, and the national dish, goat water stew, is supposedly based on a traditional Irish recipe, although some historians claim it is of African origin. A popular local folk dance, the Bam-chick-lay resembles Irish step dances and musical bands may include a fife and a drum similar to the Irish bodhran.

The African heritage dominates, however, whether it be in Caribbean musical forms like calypso (the veteran Arrow is now an international superstar and can still be found on the island, having moved his operation north out of the volcano evacuation zone), steel bands or the costumed masqueraders who parade during the Christmas season. Another element in the African cultural heritage are the Jumbie Dancers, who combine dancing and healing. Only those who are intimate with the island and its inhabitants will be able to witness their ceremonies, though. Local choirs, like the long-established Emerald Isle Community Singers, mix calypso with traditional folk songs and spirituals in their repertoire, and the String Bands of the island play the African shak-shak, made from a calabash gourd, as well as the imported Hawaiian ukelele.

There are drama and dance groups in Montserrat, which perform occasionally. Sir George Martin's famed recording studios, the Air Studios, on the edge of Belham Valley, used to attract rock megastars such as Elton John, the Rolling Stones and Sting to the island, but the studios were closed after Hurricane Hugo. Natural disasters, such as the volcanic eruption, have left a legacy on the cultural output of the island, generating art, songs, poems, photography, stories, etc. In 1997, Sir George Martin organized a gala fundraising concert for Montserrat at the Royal Albert Hall in London, which included Paul McCartney, Elton John, Eric Clapton, Sting, Mark Knopfler, Jimmy Buffet and Arrow, who had used Air Studios in the past. At the same time a show was put on at Gerald's Bottom on Montserrat by other musicians who had used the recording studios. *The Climax Blues Band* reformed for the occasion and Bankie Banks appeared, along with 18 local acts in what was optimistically called 'Many Happy Returns'. A second 'Many Happy Returns' concert was held in 1999 to coincide with St Patrick's Day festivities, after a previous attempt in 1998 was postponed because of Hurricane Georges. Local and London-based bands, choirs and acts attracted a crowd of 3,000, or 75% of the population at that time, and the finale was provided by the king of soca, Arrow and his band.

NB On Montserrat a Maroon is not a runaway slave but the local equivalent of 'barn-raising', when everyone helps to build a house, lay a garden, etc.

In the Macmillan series, *Montserrat: Emerald Isle of the Caribbean*, by **Howard A Fergus**, has been recommended, his *History of Montserrat* was published by Macmillan in 1994 and is an interesting and informative work; also *Alliouagana Folk*, by **J A George Irish** (Jagpi 1985), as an introduction to Montserratian language, proverbs and traditions. *Fire from the Mountain*, by **Polly Pattullo** (Constable 2000) is an account of the explosion in 1997 of the Soufrière Hills volcano.

Further reading

Leeward Islands

14

Netherland Antilles, the 3 S's

The '3 S's', Saba, Sint Eustatius (Statia) and Sint Maarten are 880 km north of the rest of the Netherlands Antilles group, the ABC islands (Aruba, Bonaire and Curaçao), which lie off the coast of Venezuela. Each has a distinct character and flavour, St Eustatius being the poorest, Saba the smallest and despite some development still deserving of its official title, 'the unspoiled Queen', and Sint Maarten the most developed and wealthy.

Lacking in natural resources, they all depend to a greater or lesser degree on tourism for their foreign exchange revenues, but are developing their potential in different ways. Saba's strength is the richness of the underwater world surrounding the island and is noted for its pristine diving locations. Sint Maarten has the best beaches and resorts, while St Eustatius promotes its historical associations.

Saba

Population: 1,200 *The island is an extinct volcano which shoots out of the sea, green with lush vegetation but without beaches. In fact there is only one inlet amidst the sheer cliffs where boats can come in to dock. The highest peak of this rugged island is Mount Scenery (887 m), also known as 'the Mountain', and the highest point in all the Netherlands. Because of the difficult terrain there were no roads on Saba until 1943, only hand-carved steps in the volcanic rock. Saba, pronounced 'Say-bah', only 13 sq km, lays claim to the world's shortest runway (400 m). It lies 45 km south of St Maarten and 27 km northwest of Sint Eustatius.*

Ins and outs

Getting there **Air** Large aircraft cannot be accommodated although there are plans to build a longer runway. Planes do not land in bad weather in case they skid off the end. *Winair* (T54237 in St Maarten), the only scheduled airline, has 4-5 daily 20-seater flights from St Maarten (15 mins, US$88 return) some of which come via St Eustatius or St Barts. It is essential to reconfirm your return flight. **Sea** *The Voyager*, a monohull boat carrying 150 passengers, leaves Marigot, St-Martin, Tue 0830, returns 1615, leaves **Bobby's Marina**, Philipsburg, Sint Maarten, Thur 0830, returns 1615, one way US$40 (children half price), return US$60. Island tour of Saba with lunch, US$30, reservations recommended. Dockside Management, Sint Maarten,

Saba

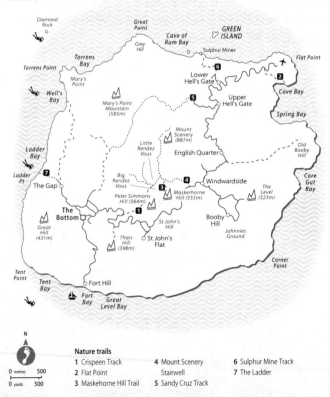

Nature trails
1 Crispeen Track
2 Flat Point
3 Maskerhorne Hill Trail
4 Mount Scenery Stairwell
5 Sandy Cruz Track
6 Sulphur Mine Track
7 The Ladder

Essentials

Documents See page 1002. Saba is a free port so there are no customs formalities.

Currency The florin or guilder is the local currency, but US dollars are accepted everywhere. Visa and Mastercard are the only widely accepted credit cards. Hotels and dive shops accept credit cards, but no one else does. You may be charged extra for using credit cards because of the slow processing arrangements.

Departure tax Airport departure tax is US$5 to Netherlands Antilles, US$10 elsewhere.

Ports of entry (Dutch flag). Go ashore to clear immigration with the Harbourmaster at Fort Bay or with the Police in The Bottom.

Anchorages Fort Bay has three free moorings but it is rolly with southeast winds. The Ladder and Well's Bay moorings (yellow buoys) are available for use by yachts for US$2 per person for anchoring and snorkelling, and US$2 per person for each dive you take on your own. Use a strong line and plenty of scope. Marine patrol will collect fees and explain the rules and regulations. The

Marine Park has a leaflet with map of anchorages and dive sites.

Tourist office overseas Antillenhius, Badhiusweg 173-175, 2597JP Den Haag, The Netherlands, T31-70-3066111, F31-70-3066110. Dutch Caribbean Travel Center, Karlstrasse 12, 60329 Frankfurt/Main, Germany, T49-69-24001830, F49-69-24271521. The Tourist Board's website is: www.turq.com/saba

Official time Atlantic Standard Time, four hours behind GMT, one ahead of EST.

Police T63237.

Voltage 110 volts AC, 60 cycles.

Communications The international phone code is 599-1 followed by 5 digits.

Public holidays New Year's Day, Good Friday, Easter Sunday and Monday, Queen's Coronation Day (30 April), Labour Day (1 May), Ascension Day (Thursday), Saba Days (beginning of December), Christmas Day, Boxing Day.

T24096, F22888, dockside2@megatropic.com *The Edge* is supposed to sail Wed, Fri, Sun at 0900, 1 hr, from Simpson Bay/Pelican Marina, St Maarten, T42640, US$40 one way, US$60 return, but be sure to check, often not running. On windy days crossing can be very rough. Travellers prone to sea sickness may be advised to travel by air instead. A deep water pier at Fort Bay allows cruise ships to call.

Getting around There are no buses on the island but you can hire a jeep or car. Drive on the right. *Johnson's Rent A Car*, at Juliana's Guest House, Windwardside, T62469, F62389; *Scout's Place Car Rental*, Windwardside, T62205, F62388; *Caralfan Rent A Car* Saba, T/F62575, caralfan-rent-a-car@ mailcity.com Doing it through a hotel can cost you US$10 more. Hitchhiking is safe, very easy and a common means of getting about. Alternatively you can walk. It is about 1½ hrs hike from the airport to Windwardside, through different scenery, vegetation and climate. There are taxis at the airport and a few others around the island: *Wilfred*, T62238; *Garvis*, T62358; *Billy*, T62262; *Evelyn*, T63292; *Anthony*, T62378; *Manny*, T63328; *Wayne*, T62277. They can be hired for tours round the island (US$40) and the drivers are knowledgeable guides. Some are also fishermen or hotel owners, so they can be valuable contacts.

Climate The average temperature is 25-28°C, 78-82°F during the day but at night it can fall to 16-18°C, the low 60°Fs. The higher up you get, the cooler it will be; so take a jersey, if hiking up the mountain. Average annual rainfall is 42 insurance

Flora and fauna

In September 1998, Hurricane Georges passed just a few kilometres south of Saba, with wind speeds of 180 miles per hour high up in the hills. Many of the bigger trees were blown down, but the island quickly recovered and the lower mountain slopes became green and lush after the rain. The Elfin Forest took longer to recover. Underwater, there was some damage to shallow reefs, but deeper sites were untouched. However, in 1999 Hurricane Lenny attacked from the west, the Caribbean side of the island, and almost totally destroyed the rainforest. Most of the trees were blown down or snapped off so now the mosses and rainforest undergrowth do not grow. Other plants grow very fast but do not renew the forest. Since the hurricane there has not been so much rain, probably because of the lack of trees. A great deal of time, money and political will is needed to reverse the damage, but repairs to infrastructure such as the airport buildings and the port will probably take priority.

Vegetation on Saba changes according to altitude and a walk up Mount Scenery used to be a sightseeing highlight for the many different types of tropical vegetation. At an altitude of 490-610 m there is secondary rain forest with trees of between 5 and 10 m high. Further up there are tree ferns of 4-5 m, then palm trees, then at 825 m the cloud forest begins (known as Elfin Forest), where you find the mountain mahogany tree (*freziera undulata*). Since Hurricane Lenny, however, the forest remains only in protected pockets. Wildlife on the island is limited to the endemic anole lizard (*anolis sabanus,* widespread), iguanas (the green iguana, *iguana iguana,* the island's largest, can be seen on Old Booby Hill in the afternoon, sunning themselves), a harmless red-bellied racer snake (*alsophis rufiventris,* can be seen on the Sandy Cruz and Mary's Point trails if you are quiet), and over 60 species of birds have been recorded, with many migratory birds coming to nest here. The trembler and the purple-throated hummingbird can be seen in the Elfin forest and the Sandy Cruz rain forest, where you can also find the wood hen (bridled quail dove).

The Saba Conservation Foundation preserves the environment on land and underwater, developing protected areas, maintaining trails and promoting nature conservation. The Foundation can be contacted through the tourist office or write to Saba Conservation Foundation, The Bottom, Saba. In the USA the Friends of the Saba Conservation Foundation (FSCF) raises money for conservation, 506 Tiffany Trails, Richardson, Texas 75081.

Diving and marine life

Diving tourism is popular in the marine park, which is noted for its 'virginity'

There are many dive sites of 27-30 m and if you are doing three dives a day you must follow your dive tables and stay within your limit. It is recommended that you take every fourth day off and rest or go hiking. All three dive operations offer à la carte diving and arrange taxi pick-ups from hotels.

The waters around Saba became a marine park in 1987 and 36 permanent mooring buoys have been provided for dive boats (less than half of which are for big boats). The park includes waters from the highwater mark down to 60 m all the way around the island. Spearfishing is prohibited (except by Sabans, free diving in certain areas), as is the removal of coral or shells (Sabans are limited to 20 conch per person a year without the use of scuba). Saba has no permanent beaches so diving and snorkelling is from boats, mostly along the calmer south and west coasts.

The west coast from **Tent Bay** to **Ladder Bay**, together with **Man of War shoals**, **Diamond Rock** and the sea offshore comprise the main dive sites, where anchoring and fishing are prohibited. From Ladder Bay to Torrens Point is an all-purpose recreational zone which includes Saba's only beach at **Well's Bay**, a pebbly stretch of coast with shallow water for swimming and areas for diving, fishing, and boat anchorage. The beach comes and goes with the seasons and ocean currents but when it is there it is scenic and good for snorkelling. The concrete road ends here but there are no facilities so take your own refreshments and arrange for a taxi to pick you up later. Another anchorage is west of Fort Bay. East of Fort Bay along the south, east and north coast to Torrens Point is a multiple use zone where fishing and diving are permitted. Some of the most visited dive sites are **Third Encounter**, **Outer Limits**,

Diamond Rock and Man of War. **Tent Reef** is also a favourite. **Ladder Labyrinth** is a dive site which is good for snorkelling.

Dive operators have been granted permits and they collect the mandatory visitor fees (US$3 per person per dive) to help maintain the park which is now self-financing. The marine park office is at Fort Bay, PO Box 18, The Bottom, T/F63295, www.sabapark.com It is managed by a Dutchman, David Kooistra, and a Saban, Percy Tenhott, who are very helpful and keen to talk about conservation. Percy gives an illustrated lecture at 1830 on Tuesday at *Juliana's*, or on demand for groups. The guide to the dive sites, *Guide to the Saba Marine Park*, by Tom Van't Hof, published by the Saba Conservation Foundation, is highly recommended, available at dive shops, the museum and souvenir shops, US$15. Saba now has a four person recompression chamber at Fort Bay, donated by the Royal Netherlands Navy, which is administered through the Marine Park but operated by medical school people. Summer visibility is 23-30 m with water temperatures of about 30°C, while winter visibility increases to 38 m and water temperatures fall to 24°C. Saba's rugged, volcanic terrain is replicated underwater where there are mountains, caves, lava flows, overhangs, reefs, walls, pinnacles and elkhorn coral forests.

Not much fishing is done in these waters, so there is a wide range of sizes and varieties of fish to be seen. Tarpon and barracuda of up to 2½ m are common, as are giant sea turtles. From January to April humpback whales pass by on their migration south and can be encountered by divers, while in the winter dive boats are often accompanied by schools of porpoises. Smaller, tropical fish are not in short supply and together with bright red, orange, yellow and purple giant tube sponges and different coloured coral, are a photographer's delight. Divers are not allowed to feed the fish as it has been proved to alter fish behaviour and encourage the aggressive species.

There are three dive shops on Saba. *Saba Deep* at Fort Bay, near the pier, T63347, F63397, www.sabadeep.com, PO Box 22, has NAUI and PADI instructors. They have two 25-ft inflatable boats. Boats return to shore between dives so you can spend your surface interval in the air conditioned bar *In Two Deep*, rather than being tossed about at sea. All your gear is taken care of during your stay or there is well-maintained rental equipment. A two-tank dive costs US$90, including equipment (US$10 for wet suit), park fees (five percent surcharge for credit cards). **Dive centres**

Sea Saba Advanced Dive Centre at Lambee's Place, Windwardside, T62246, F62362, www.seasaba.com, PADI and NAUI, have two large boats, with shade and sun deck, but limit groups to 10 people. Their trips are more of a cruise and recommended if there is a non-diving partner, the surface interval is spent at Well's Bay for sunbathing and snorkelling. Drinks are available on board, some people take snacks for the 60-90 minute interval. The atmosphere is relaxed and unrushed, you return to dock after the second dive at about 1430. A two-tank dive costs US$90 including park fee and tax plus US$10 for equipment.

Saba Divers at *Scout's Place*, Windwardside, T62740, F62741, www.saba divers.com The most recent addition to the diving scene, run by Wolfgang Tooten and Barbara Schäfer, of Germany. PADI, SSI, DAN, CMAS courses offered in several languages, diving and accommodation packages available. The dive shop is at *Scout's Place* and is under the same management, but you don't have to stay there to dive with them. Similar diving prices to the other companies, all new equipment in 2000.

Walking

Before the road was built people got about Saba by donkey or on foot and there are still numerous steep trails and stone steps linking villages which make strenuous, yet satisfying, walking. The Saba Conservation Foundation preserves and marks trails for those who like a challenge and for those who prefer a gentle stroll. All of them are accessible from the road and many can be done without a guide. However they are all on private land and you are requested not to stray off the tracks. Named trails

Netherland Antilles

include: The Ladder, Crispeen Track, Maskehorne Hill Trail, Mt Scenery Stairwell, Sandy Cruz Track, Sulphur Mine Track and Flat Point.

The most spectacular hike is probably the one from Windwardside up 1,064 steps of varying sizes and intervals to the crest of **Mount Scenery**, best done on a clear day otherwise you end up in the clouds. It is a hard slog, 1½ hours each way, but a road goes part of the way up. The summit has now been cleared (Cable & Wireless have built a telecommunications tower there by helicopter drops) and there is a spectacular view down to Windwardside and the surrounding isles if it is not cloudy. The view is not panoramic, however, and the greater pleasure is in the ascent through what is left of the rainforest. Take a sweater and waterproof jacket, it can be very rough and slippery after rain, although there has not been so much rain since the hurricane wiped out most of the forest. There are lots of birds, lizards, snakes and land crabs, and the botanical changes are noticeable as you climb. There is also a five-hour walk through a variety of ecosystems circling Mount Scenery. Starting from Windwardside, walk up the road to Upper Hell's Gate, then take the Sandy Cruz trail to the banana plantation. Proceed on the Sandy Cruz trail extension to Troy Hill, where you meet the road which takes you to The Bottom. A short walk up the road out of The Bottom towards Windwardside brings you to the start of the Crispeen trail, which is followed back to Windwardside.

The Ladder is a long path of stone steps from the shore up to The Bottom, up which all provisions used to be hauled from boats before the road was built. There is a picnic place overlooking Ladder Bay. For the **Sulphur Mine** take the turning at **Hell's Gate** (church has a big sign saying Hell's Gate outside it!), past the *Gate House Hotel* and keep on to the end of the houses. After some steps the trail begins. Walk for about 20 minutes until you get to a sign for a turning to the right leading down to the remains of the old mines and the cliffs of the north coast, with splendid scenery. It is also possible to carry on along the island, through forests less damaged by the hurricanes, towards **Mary's Point**. However, the Conservation Foundation does not recommend you go far along this old path as several people have got lost. Best to take a guide. There are magnificent views of the northern coastal cliffs but there is a danger of rock falls set off by feral goats which may be above you. A very nice lookout point is from **Booby Hill**, up the 66 terraced steps to the Booby Hill Peak.

The tourist office has leaflets on the nature trails and hiking on Saba, but in many places a guide is recommended. Interpretative and directional signs are variable because of weather damage. *Saban Trails… A Walking & Hiking Guide* published by the Saba Conservation Foundation, gives information on 11 trails and the flora, fauna and historical remains. However it was published in 1998 before Hurricane Lenny. James Johnson (T63281 work, T63307 home), a local man and the trails manager, does guided tours after 1500 weekdays and all day at weekends, US$40-50 per group, maximum eight people. He knows the island intimately and carries a bush knife to hack away obstacles. Although he only knows local plant and animal names, he makes up for his lack of scientific knowledge in stories about past inhabitants (his relatives). Tom Van't Hof (author of the Marine Park guide and Chairman of the Saba Conservation Foundation) is a biologist and also guides walks, so would appeal to more scientific walkers. He lives in The Bottom, by the Art Gallery.

Other sports There is a **tennis** court (concrete) at the Sunny Valley Youth Centre in The Bottom which is open to the public. **Basket ball** and **volley ball** matches are held, contact the tourist office for a schedule.

Around the island

There are four picture book villages on Saba, connected by a single spectacular 10½ km road which begins at the airport and ends at the pier. The road itself is a feat of engineering, designed and built by Josephus Lambert Hassell (1906-83) in the 1940s, who studied road construction by correspondence course after Dutch engineers said it was impossible to build a road on Saba. From the airport, the road rises to **Hell's Gate** and then on through banana plantations to **Windwardside**, a walk of 20-30 minutes, where most of the hotels and shops are situated. There is a small museum, a bank and post office. **Lambee's Place**, originally the home of Josephus Lambert Hassell, now houses the tourist office, Sea Saba Dive Shop, Breadfruit Gallery, El Momo Folk Art, The Carmel Shop (gifts) and *Y2K Café* (bakery, bar and grill). On the first Sunday in each month, a 'happening' is held in the grounds of the **Harry L Johnson Museum**. Everyone dresses in white (including visitors), plays croquet and drinks mimosas. The museum was a sea captain's house, built in 1840 and is a typical, tiny, four-room Saban house on one floor. It is filled with antique furniture and family memorabilia. The kitchen is in its original state. ■ *US$2, 1000-1200, 1300-1530, Mon-Fri.*

The road goes on past Kate's Hill, Peter Simon's Hill and Big Rendezvous to **St John's**, where the schools are, and which has a wonderful view of St Eustatius, then climbs over the mountain and drops sharply down to **The Bottom**, the island's seat of government, with a population of 350. The Bottom is on a plateau, 245 m above the sea, and gets its name from the Dutch words *de botte*, meaning 'the bowl'. It can be hot, as there is little breeze. Leaving The Bottom, the road makes its final descent to Fort Bay, where small cruise ships, yachts and the ferry from St Maarten arrive at the 85 m pier. Most of the houses on the island are painted white with red roofs and some have green shutters. Heleen Cornet's book, *Saban Cottages*, gives background information on some interesting houses. There are watercolour workshops.

Windwardside

To Hell's Gate

Saba Chinese

Brigadoon

Roman Catholic
Church of St Paul's
Conversion

Y2K Grill   Carmel
& Bakery   Shop
Breadfruit
Gallery   El Momo
Folk Art
Sea Saba   Lambee's Place
Dive Shop   Barclays

To St John's

Holy Trinity
Anglican Church

The Level

The Cottage Club

Antilles

Harry L Johnson Museum   Scout's Place &   Library
Saba Divers

Guido's   El Momo Cottages

Juliana's/Tropics Café/
Johnson's Rent a Car   Booby Hill

N

0 metres   50   Captain's Quarters
(temporarily closed)
0 yards   50

Essentials

Sleeping
It is an expensive island, difficult for budget travellers

There are no resort hotels yet on Saba and even the most expensive are small and friendly. December to April is the busiest season, although divers come throughout the year. July is also busy because of Carnival and students return from foreign universities. Hotels do not usually give you a room key; there is no crime. The four policemen on the island boast that the cells are only used as overspill when the hotels are full! All the hotels offer dive packages with the three dive shops. There is a 5% room tax, sometimes a 3% turnover tax (TOT) and usually a 10-15% service charge.

Windwardside AL-A *Captain's Quarters*, T62201, F62377. Temporarily closed in 2000 for renovation. Best known, sea captain's house, sea view, restaurant, bar, pool. **AL-A** *Juliana's*, further up the hill, T62269, F62389, www.julianas-hotel.com Owned by Juliana and Franklin Johnson, descendants of original settlers, smaller rooms than *Captain's Quarters* but each has kitchenette, cable TV, some have balcony or patio, also apartment and 2 cottages, good views, pool, café, bar. **A-B** *Scout's Place*, PO Box 543, T62205, F62388, sabadivers@unspoiled queen.com Being redeveloped by Germans in 2000 as a dive resort, packages available, beautiful views, 3 basic but comfortable rooms in former government guesthouse, 10 rooms in new wing, most with cable TV, fan and fridge, simple, relaxed, slow service, pool, restaurant. **AL** *The Cottage Club*, outside Windwardside, on hill with wonderful views east, T62486, F62476, cottageclub@unspoiledqueen.com Owned by Jansen family who also own supermarket, 10 white cottages with red roofs in local style, kitchen, TV, phone, natural stone swimming pool.

On Booby Hill LL *Willard's of Saba*, PO Box 515, T62498, F62482, willard@sint maarten.net Luxury or VIP suites in main building or bungalows further up the hill, all with incredible views, tennis, jacuzzi, pool, restaurant, bar/TV, long walk out of town up a slope so steep some taxi drivers refuse to go up it, jeep therefore recommended, good for those who want peace and quiet and are prepared to pay for it, no children under 14. **C** *El Momo Cottages*, half way up Jimmy's Hill, 5 mins from Windwardside, PO Box 519, T/F62265, www.elmomo.com Up 60 steps, superb view, beautiful garden, 5 rooms, built in gingerbread style, separate bathroom building, simple but clean, friendly, great breakfast US$5.95, snacks available, pool, the only place for budget travellers, so essential to book, owned and managed by Oliver and Angelika Hartleib.

The Bottom AL *Cranston's Antique Inn*, T63203, F63469. 130-year old inn, 5 rooms, 4-poster beds, pool. **B** *Caribe Guesthouse*, T/F63259. Clean comfortable, no frills, 6 rooms, kitchen available. **LL-L** *Queen's Gardens Resort*, PO Box 2, T63494, F63495, www.queen saba.com Troy Hill, overlooking The Bottom. 12 1-2 bedroom apartments, fully equipped, TV, phone, fans, spectacular view, garden, discounts for weekly rates, *Mango Royale* restaurant.

Hell's Gate AL-A *The Gate House*, T62416, F62550, sabagate@aol.com 6 rooms, all with bath, 2 have kitchens, café for breakfast and dinner, artwork by owner Jim Siegel, pool.

The tourist office has a list of 1-3 bedroom **cottages** and **apartments** for rent from US$50 a night, which can be let on a weekly or monthly basis, and can also provide hotel rates. They will also make reservations. **Windwardside** contact David Johnson, T62254, for **B** *Effie's Cottage*, 1 bedroom, **B** *The Look Out*, 2 bedrooms, and **A** *Rainbow Cottage*, 2 bedrooms. 5-min walk from Windwardside at the Level are: **C** *Renz Apartment*, T62316 (Mr and Mrs Renz), sleeps 2, pool; **C** *Welgelegen Cottage*, T62244 (Mrs Johnson), 1 bedroom, and **C** *Ocean View*, T/F62297 (Mrs Peterson), studio. **B** *Carpenter's Cottage*, T62224 (Mrs Pape), toddpape@wwa.com 1 bedroom. **AL** *Daphne Cottage*, T63361 (Chuck and Ed Vaughn). 2 bedrooms. **Hell's Gate AL** *Susanna's Cottage*, T62427 (Julie and Andrew Hassell), 2 bedrooms. **The Bottom AL-B** *Midtown Apartments*, T63394, F63263. 9 1-2 bedroom apartments, fully equipped, a/c, TV.

Windwardside At *Scout's Place*, T62205. Breakfast 0700-1000, lunch, sandwiches and salads. *Saba Chinese Restaurant*, T62353. Cantonese food, salads, steaks, good food, great view, open Tue-Sun 1730-2300, also lunch on Sun 1100-1500, from US$8, best bet for a late meal, no reservations. *Tropics Café* at *Juliana's*, Windwardside, T62469. Does daily breakfast, burgers and snacks at lunchtime, sandwiches with homemade bread, full dinner daily except Mon US$9-16, go early, poolside with sea view, takeaway available. *Brigadoon*, T62380. In old Saban house close to centre, good reputation with locals, open daily 1800-2100, dinner from US$10, lunch for groups by reservation only, international, creole and Caribbean food, fresh seafood, lobster tank. *Y2K Café*, Lambee's Place. Bakery, bar and grill, pastries and pizzas, kids' menu, great new restaurant, breakfast, lunch and dinner 0630-2130, closed Sun.

Eating
Many restaurants close by 2130. Eat early

Rest of the island Native specialities and other West Indian food at *Queenie's Serving Spoon*, The Bottom. Open 0900 but not for breakfast, dinner served family style, no credit cards, call for reservations T63225. *Lollipop*, T63330. A small restaurant on the mountainside overlooking The Bottom on the way to St John's, free taxi pick-up (waiter is also the driver), excellent 3-course meal for about US$20, fresh lobster, conch melts in the mouth, local cuisine including goat and land crab, open breakfast, lunch or dinner, recommended for lunch, walk it off afterwards. *Midway Bar & Restaurant*, St John's, T63367. Local food, goat, chicken, special barbecues, good view, dinner only, reservations required, no credit cards, free transport offered. *In Two Deep*, Fort Bay, T63438. Used by divers, open 0800-1600, New England style food, overlooks water, lunch US$10-12. *Sunset Bar*, near Ladder Bay, T63472. Breakfast 0800-1000, lunch 1100-1330, dinner 1900-2230, free transport for dinner, local dishes and seafood, reservations necessary, no credit cards. *The Gate House*, Hell's Gate, T62416. Dinner 1830-2100, free transport, closed Wed, Caribbean cuisine, seafood, poultry, meat, locally grown vegetables, and herbs, open all day for drinks on the terrace, good view. *Half Way*, a bar/restaurant on the roadside between The Bottom and Windwardside, serves local food and is a good place to meet local drinkers.

Most of the nightlife takes place at the restaurants. At weekends there are sometimes barbecues, steel bands and dances. Generally, though, the island is quiet at night. In Windwardside, *Guido's* on Fri, Sat, pool room makes way to a disco, popular with all sections of the community, soca, reggae, rap and disco, loud. In The Bottom, there is life in the bar of *Antique Inn*, until about 2300, run by Francesca from the Dominican Republic. Later on go to her sister's bar opposite *The Inner Circle*, which has merengue music, popular with locals for dancing. The *Mango Royale* restaurant at the *Queen's Garden Resort* has a Fri barbecue with live music 1800-2100 and Sunday steel pan brunch 1200-1500.

Nightlife

Coronation Day & Queen's Birthday is *30 April*, when there are ceremonies commemorating the coronation of Queen Beatrix and the Queen's birthday. **Carnival** (Saba Summer Festival) is a week near the end of *July* and is celebrated with jump-ups, music and costumed dancing, shows, food, games and contests including the Saba Hill Climb. There are parades

Festivals

Netherland Antilles

on the last weekend and Carnival Monday at the end is a public holiday. **Saba Days** are a mini-carnival at the first weekend in *December*, when donkey races are held, with dancing, steel bands, barbecues and other festivities.

Shopping

Shops open 0900-1200, 1400-1800

Local crafts have been developed by the Saba Artisan Foundation in The Bottom and include dolls, books and silk-screened textiles and clothing. The typical local, drawn-thread work 'Saba Lace' (also known as 'Spanish Work' because it was learned by a Saban woman in a Spanish convent in Venezuela at the end of the last century) is sold at several shops on the island. Each artisan has his or her own style. Taxi drivers may make unofficial stops at the houses where Saba lace, dolls, pillows etc are made. Boutiques in Windwardside sell a variety of gifts. There are several **art galleries** in Windwardside where local artists have their studios and sell their watercolours, oil paintings, prints and sculptures. Ask the tourist office for a leaflet. **Saba Spice** is the local rum, very strong (150° proof) and mixed with spices, sugar and orange peel.

Directory

Banks *Barclays Bank*, Windwardside, T62216. Open 0830-1530, Mon-Fri, currency exchange, advances, transfers, TCs. *Antilles Banking*, Windwardside. Open Mon-Wed 0830-1500, Thu-Fri 0830-1600. **Communications** Post: airmail takes about 2 weeks to the USA or Europe. Federal Express is available. The post office in Windwardside is open 0800-1200, 1300-1700. **Telephones:** most hotels have direct dialling worldwide, otherwise overseas calls can be made from Landsradio phone booths in Windwardside or The Bottom. **Medical services** Hospital: T63288. **Places of worship** There are 4 churches: Anglican, Roman Catholic, Wesleyan Holiness and Seventh Day Adventist. **Tourist office** *The Saba Tourist Board* (Glenn Holm, Zuleyka and Angelique) is at Lambee's Place in Windwardside, open Mon-Fri, 0800-1200, 1300-1700, PO Box 527, T62231, F62350, www.turq.com/saba Plenty of leaflets and maps and the staff are friendly and helpful.

Background

History

See also background to the Netherlands Antilles, the ABC chapter, page 1037

Saba was first discovered by Columbus on his second voyage in 1493 but not colonized. Sir Francis Drake sighted it in 1595, as did the Dutchmen Pieter Schouten in 1624 and Piet Heyn in 1626. Some shipwrecked Englishmen landed in 1632, finding it uninhabited. In 1635 the French claimed it but in the 1640s the Dutch settled it, building communities at Tent Bay and The Bottom. However, it was not until 1816 that the island became definitively Dutch, the interregnum being marked by 12 changes in sovereignty, with the English, Dutch, French and Spanish all claiming possession.

The people

Although the island was once inhabited by Caribs, relics of whom have been found, there is no trace of their ancestry in the local inhabitants. The population is half white (descendants of Dutch, English and Scots settlers) and half black. Their physical isolation and the difficult terrain has enabled them to develop their ingenuity for self sufficiency and to live in harmony with their environment. Originally farmers and seafarers, the construction in 1963 of the Juancho E Yrausquin Airport on the only flat part of the island, and the serpentine road which connects it tenuously to the rest of the island, brought a new and more lucrative source of income: tourism.

The island's geographical limitations have meant that tourism has evolved in a small, intimate way. About 24,000 tourists visit each year, most of whom are day trippers. There are only 100 beds available in the hotels and guest houses, as well as a few cottages to rent. Those who stay are few enough to get to know the friendliness and hospitality of their hosts, who all speak English, even though Dutch is the official language. In 1993 the Dutch Government stopped 'driver licence tourism'.

Previously, driving tests taken in Saba were valid in Holland, where it is more difficult to secure a licence. The system brought Saba an income of about US$300,000 a year. Currently, the major source of income is the US Medical School, opened in 1993, which attracts over 250 (mainly US) students from overseas, who spend about US$1,000 a month. Development is small scale; the island still merits its unofficial title, 'the Unspoiled Queen'. There is no unemployment among the workforce of 600. The island is spotlessly clean; the streets are swept by hand every day. The main road has concrete barriers, partly to prevent cars driving over the edge and partly because of landslides, which can be frequent after rain.

Sint Eustatius

The island is dominated by the long-extinct volcano called 'The Quill' at the south end, inside which is a lush rainforest where the locals hunt land crabs at night. Visitors are advised, however, to go there only during the day. The north part of the island is hilly and uninhabited except for Statia Terminals, a fuel depot; most people live in the central plain which surrounds the airport. Statia is a very poor island and has a run down appearance. If you are coming from Saba, you will be struck by the contrast in cleanliness and the state of repair of people's houses. The name 'Statia' comes from St Anastasia, as it was named by Columbus, but the Dutch later changed it to Sint Eustatius.

Ins and outs

Air *Winair* has several daily 20-min flights from St Maarten (US$80 return) connecting with flights from the USA, Europe and other islands. It is possible to get to Statia in a day from many US cities. There are other connecting Winair flights from St Kitts (15 mins) and Saba (10 mins). *Golden Rock Airways* can arrange charters. All flights are in small planes, although the airport has been extended to 1,600m to allow larger jets to land.

Getting there
You get an impressive view of The Quill when you come in to land

There is no public transport on the island but cars and taxis can be hired. Driving is on the right, but some roads are so narrow you have to pass where you can. To hire a **car** you need a driving licence from your own country or an international driver's licence. Watch out for cows, donkeys, goats and sheep roaming around freely. They are a traffic hazard. The speed limit is 50 km (31 miles) per hour and in residential areas it is 30 km (19 miles) per hour. **Mopeds** are also available for hire. **Taxi** drivers are well-informed guides and can arrange excursions, although most places are within walking distance if you are energetic (less than 30 mins' walk airport to town). Airport to town is US$4, most other trips US$2-4 per person. An island tour costs US$40 for 4 people, US$7 for every additional passenger.

Getting around
See transport, page 673, for further details

Average temperature is around 27°C in the daytime and 23°C at night. Average rainfall is 45in a year. Average water temperature in the sea is 26°C.

Climate

Flora and fauna

Despite the small size of the island, in the 17th and 18th centuries there were more than 70 plantations, worked intensively by slaves. As a result, most of the original forest has disappeared except in the most inhospitable parts of the volcano. Nevertheless there are 17 different kinds of orchid and 58 species of birds, of which 25 are resident and breeding, 21 migrants from North America and 12 seabirds. The harmless racer snake is found here, as on Saba, and there are iguanas, land crabs, tree frogs and lots of butterflies. Unfortunately there are lots of goats too, which eat everything in sight.

STENAPA, the St Eustatius National Parks Foundation, was founded in 1996. This organization is responsible for the marine park, The Quill, Boven, Gilboa Hill,

Netherland Antilles

Signal Hill and Little Mountain. These areas and portions of The Quill, above 250 m, are now protected. In 1998 The Quill was declared a national park, consisting of the volcano and the limestone White Wall to its south. The Quill is protected from the 250 m line, but the White Wall is protected down to the high water line. STENAPA has developed the 14-acre Miriam C Schmidt Botanical Garden on the southeast side of The Quill in the area called 'Behind the Mountain'. There is a picnic pavilion, barbecue areas, marked trails, a bee yard and orchid gardens.

At the crater of **The Quill** there are many species usually found in tropical rain forest: huge tree ferns; mahogany; giant elephant ears; begonias; figs; plantains; bromeliads; the balsam tree and many more. The southern slope of the mountain has not been fully explored by botanists. In the future STENAPA hopes to attract scientists to study plants, animals and marine life. Recently experts have been on the island to study the endangered iguanas and the rare racer snake. The Antilles Iguana (*Iguana delicatissima*) is rare and threatened. The young and females vary from bright green to dull grey, while the large males can be nearly black. The population is

Sint Eustatius

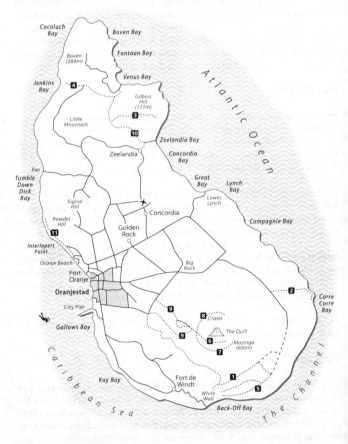

Not to scale

Nature trails

1 Around the mountain	5 Soldier Gut	9 The Quill
2 Corre Corre Bay	6 The Crater	10 Venus Bay
3 Gilboa Hill	7 The Mazinga	11 White Bird
4 Jenkins Bay	8 The Panorama	

Essentials

Documents See page 1002. There are no customs regulations as Statia is a free port.

Currency The currency is the Netherlands Antilles florin or guilder, but US dollars are accepted everywhere. **Credit cards** are not widely used (Amex hardly ever accepted, Visa and Mastercard better). Check at hotels and restaurants. US$100 bills often not accepted.

Departure tax Airport departure tax is US$5 for Antilles, US$10 international. If you visit for the day and pay departure tax on St Maarten, you do not have to pay the tax when you leave Statia. If you pay the tax on Statia and are in-transit on St Maarten you do not have to pay tax on St Maarten. You will need to show your tickets and boarding pass for your next flight at the tax window.

Airlines Windward Islands Airways (Winair) T82362/82381, F82485.

Ports of entry The Harbour Office is open 0800-1700, after hours sailors should see guard at the gate who will give directions to the local police station. If not leaving before 0800 clear customs in the morning, T82205, F82888, VHF Channel 14. The Harbour Master, Murvin Gittens, works Monday-Friday, 0800-1600. Fly an Antillean flag.

Anchorages Oranje Baii is the only anchorage, prices are based on tonnage, 0-5 tons US$5; 6-15 tons US$10; +16 tons US$15. These rates are valid for three days. After three days, sailors pay an extra fee of US$5 per day. The long pier accommodates ships with draft not exceeding 14ft, the short pier has vessels with draft of up to 10ft. Marine weather is on VHF 1 or 162.550 MHz continual broadcast. Blue Bead Restaurant sells ice.

Official time Atlantic Standard Time, four hours behind GMT, one ahead of EST, all year.

Voltage 110 volts A/C 60 cycles.

Tourist office overseas In **USA/Canada**: Gail Knopfler, Classic Communications International, PO Box 6322, Boca Raton, FL33427, T561-3948580, F4884294, statiatourism@juno.com In **Europe**: Antillen Huis, Badhuisweg 173-175 Postbus 90706, 2509 LS's-Gravenhage, **Holland**, T70-3066111, F3066110; **Germany**, T0692400 183, F069-24271521, Dutch.Caribbean-TC@t-online.de

Communications The international phone code is 599-1, followed by 5 digits.

Clothing No topless bathing anywhere on the island and men are not allowed to walk without shirts on in public streets.

Public holidays New Year's Day (fireworks at midnight), Good Friday, Easter Sunday, Easter Monday, Queensday (30 April), Labour Day (1 May), Ascension Day, Statia Day (16 November), Christmas Day, Boxing Day.

---

stronger here than on neighbouring islands because the mongoose was never introduced here. Neither was the Green Iguana, with which it has interbred on some islands. They are now protected by law and human consumption is no longer allowed. The Red-bellied Racer (Alsophis rufiventris) is a small snake found only on Statia and Saba. It is brown with black markings on its back and a pink belly. It is not poisonous and kills its prey (small reptiles, baby rats) by strangulation.

Diving and marine life

Statia's waters offer a wonderful combination of coral reefs, marine life and historic shipwrecks. Water visibility can be over 30 m and snorkelling is also very good. Diving is excellent, with plenty of corals, sea fans, hydroids and big fish such as groupers and barracudas, as well as rays, turtles and the occasional dolphin but unlike some other Caribbean diving destinations, you will not bump into any other divers underwater. St Eustatius Marine Park was established in 1996 and became operational in 1998. STENAPA has identified four protected areas: the southern

👉 *Morning glory*

part from Crooks Castle to White Wall is a restricted fishing zone; the wreck sites in Oranje Bay, STENAPA Reef (a modern wreck site) and the northern marine park are open for fishing and diving. Marine park fees are US$3 per dive, US$3 per snorkelling trip when using the park buoys, US$35 for a non-resident annual pass. You may not anchor anywhere in the park, spear guns and spear fishing are prohibited in all waters around Statia, nothing may be removed, whether animals, plants or historical artefacts, you may not touch or feed marine life. The marine park office is at Lower Town, close to the harbour.

The Supermarket, 1 km off the coast from Lower Town at a depth of 18 m, has two shipwrecks 15m apart with beautiful coral, red and purple sponges, shoals of fish, sea turtles and the rare flying gurnard. **The Garden** is another very beautiful reef with hundreds of fish of all kinds from the smallest wrass to large barracudas and extremely tame angel fish. As yet there are few divers on Statia so fish are generally tame and do not swim away.

Dive centres *Dive Statia* is run by Rudi and Rinda Hees T82435, F82539, divestatia@megatropic.com, Lower Town, PO Box 158, in USA: 8521 N Georgia, Oklahoma City, OK 73114, F405-8437846. They have a small, rigid inflatable boat for up to 10 divers but six is comfortable. The boat is moored off the beach in front of the dive shop and you have to carry all your equipment down to the sea, wade out and pass it to the guide on the boat. They only take certified divers, although a full range of courses is offered, and do three dives a day with night dives on request. Once in the water the dives are not strictly guided, buddies may go off and explore. Some dives are deep (take care not to get lost) and the operation does not really cater for inexperienced or nervous divers. A two-tank dive is US$75, equipment rental is available, PADI Open Water four-day course US$350, snorkel trips US$25 with equipment, photographic and video equipment rental, 3-7 day accommodation and diving packages available with most hotels.

Another dive shop, *Golden Rock Dive Centre*, is opposite the *Blue Bead Restaurant*. Owned by Glen Fairs, T/F82964, www.goldenrockdive.com One dive US$45, hotel/dive packages, PADI open water course US$350. *Golden Rock* also offers charter fishing and boat trips to Saba and operates the underwater snorkel museum for the St Eustatius Historical Foundation. *Scubaqua* (PADI, SSI, CMAS) is at the *Golden Era Hotel*, T/F82160/82345, scubaqua@megatropic.com with their own pier. They have two boats, taking 6 or 12 divers, and an inflatable for dive courses. Groups per instructor are no more than six and the captain stays on board the boat. Drift diving for whale watching is organized between end-January and April and they also offer waterskiing, wakeboards and fishing trips. A single dive costs US$29, equipment rental US$20, snorkelling trips with lunch on the beach US$25, full Open Water certification course with equipment is US$350. You must dive with a local company as it is not possible to fill tanks. On leaving Statia Customs officials may give you and your luggage a rigorous search if they discover you are a diver. They are looking for treasure, or artefacts, beware. The *MV Caribbean Explorer*, 16-passenger, 100ft liveaboard, includes Statia in its week-long tour of the northeast Caribbean, with five dives in the Marine park. Contact Explorer Ventures Ltd, www.caribexplorer.com, see page 683.

Beaches and watersports

Oranje Beach stretches for 1½ km along the coast away from Lower Town. The length and width of the beach varies according to the season and the weather, but being on the Leeward side it is safe for swimming and other watersports. On the Windward side are two fine beaches but there is a strong undertow and they are not considered safe for swimming. **Zeelandia Beach** is 3 km of off-white sand with heavy surf and interesting beachcombing, particularly after a storm. It is safe to wade and splash about in the surf but not to swim. There is a short dirt road down to the beach; do not drive too close to the beach or you will get stuck in the sand. Avoid the rocks at the end of the beach as they are very dangerous. **Lynch Beach**, also on the Atlantic side, is small and safer for children in parts, but ask local advice. Stay near the shore. There is no lifeguard at any of the beaches.

There is little to offer on Statia for the sporting enthusiast. At the Community Centre on Rosemary Laan: **tennis** (US$5), **basketball**, **softball** and **volleyball**; changing rooms are available. Tennis, volleyball and basketball also at Gene's Sports Complex, T82711, as well as **table tennis**, **dominoes**, **checkers**, open Monday-Saturday 1430-2230, Sunday 0800-1800. There is also a children's playground. **Other sports**

Walking

The tourist office has a guide leaflet describing 11 trails. **Quill** hikes with local guides are available with a voucher system from the tourist office or participating hotels. Hikers should be aware that some of these trails are in bad condition, overgrown and sometimes difficult to follow. STENAPA is in the process of restoring and extending Statia's trail system. They plan to make a trail from town to the botanical garden which will wind around the south side of The Quill. STENAPA also plans to restore the path around the rim of The Quill (damaged in 1989 by Hurricane Hugo). The foundation has built a new, clearly marked, trail from Rosemary Lane to the rainforest crater at the top of The Quill, which is remarkable for its contrast with the dry scrub of the rest of the island. After about 20 minutes' walk there is a left turn to The Quill. Carry on if you want to overlook the White Wall. The walk up to the lip of the crater is easy. You will see butterflies, all sizes of lizards, hundreds of land crabs and, if you go quietly, some snakes (for example the red-bellied racer snake). At the top in one direction is the panorama trail. The other direction leads to the highest point, called **Mazinga**, which affords a magnificent view. The first 10 minutes of the walk to the Mazinga is easy, then there is a turn to the left marked. From here it becomes a scramble because of hurricane damage. The last 20 m up to the summit itself is for the very experienced only. The plant life includes mahogany and bread fruit trees, arums, bromeliads, lianas and orchids. Although it is still quite a hike (approximately 45 minutes), the new path is in much better shape and it is not nearly as steep as the old trail. From the rim, hikers can walk down a path to the centre. The vegetation in the crater is very dense and a local guide is recommended. The crater is the breeding ground for land crabs, which Statians catch at night by blinding them with a flashlight. Charley (brother of Roland Lopes at the tourist office) works as a professional hiking guide. He arrives at dawn in full combat uniform and beret like Rambo and tends to go quickly without much explanation, fine for the walk round The Quill crater but better to go alone if birdwatching.

Netherland Antilles

A road, and then a track, leads round the lower slopes of The Quill to the **White Wall**, a massive slab of limestone which was once pushed out of the sea by volcanic forces and is now clearly visible from miles away across the sea. You can also see it from **Fort de Windt**, built in 1753, the ruins of which are open to the public, at the end of the road south from Lower Town. St Kitts can also be seen clearly from here. About 14 forts or batteries were built around the island by the end of the 18th century but the ruins of few of them are accessible or even visible nowadays. STENAPA has made a new trail to the **Boven**, the highest peak on the north side of the island. This is a strenuous hike (four hour round trip and steep at times) but well worth it for the view, for dedicated hikers.

Oranjestad

Oranjestad is the capital, situated on a cliff overlooking the long beach below and divided between Upper Town and Lower Town. The town used to be defended by **Fort Oranje** (pronounced Orahn'ya) perched on a rocky bluff. Built in 1636 on the site of a 1629 French fortification, the ruins of the fort have been preserved and large black cannons still point out to sea. The administrative buildings of the island's Government are here. The fort was partly destroyed by a fire in 1990, but has been restored since then. Other places of historical interest include the ruins of the **Honen Dalim Synagogue** built in 1739 and the nearby cemetery. Statia once had a flourishing Jewish community and was a refuge for Sephardic and Ashkenazic Jews, but with the economic decline after the sacking of Oranjestad by Admiral Rodney, most of the Jewish congregation left. The **Dutch Reformed Church**, consecrated in 1755, suffered a similar fate when its congregation joined the exodus. The square tower

Oranjestad (St Eustatius)

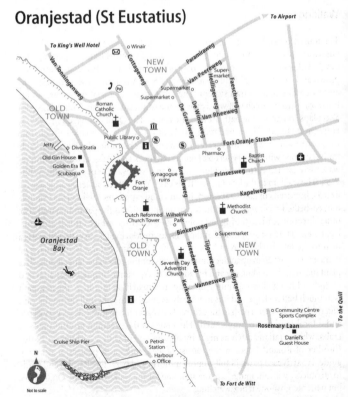

has been restored but the walls are open to the elements. The surrounding graveyard has some interesting tombs. Legend has it that it was here that Admiral Rodney found most of his booty after noticing that there were a surprising number of funerals for such a small population. A coffin, which he ordered to be opened, was found to be full of valuables and further digging revealed much more.

On Wilhelminaweg in the centre, the 18th-century Doncker/De Graaff House, once a private merchant's house and also where Admiral Rodney lived, has been restored and is now the **Museum of the St Eustatius Historical Foundation**. There is a pre-columbian section which includes an Amerindian skeleton and a reconstruction of 18th-century rooms at the height of Statia's posperity. It is worth a visit for the graphic descriptions of the slave trade. Archaeological excavations at Golden Rock near the airport have uncovered a large Amerindian village with the only complete floor plan of Indian houses found in the Caribbean. All the houses are round or slightly oval, ranging in size and accommodating anything up to 30 people. Large timbers up to 8 m high were set in deep holes for the framework of the biggest houses. The museum contains some pottery buried in the ceremonial area of the village next to a grave. ■ *T82288, US$2 or US$1 for children, 0900-1700 Mon-Fri, 0900-1200 Sat, Sun and holidays, the curator normally shows you around, explaining the history of the exhibits.*

It is possible to walk round the village and see the sights in a morning. The museum or tourist office will provide you with a Walking Tour brochure listing the historical sites and other walking tours. In its heyday Lower Town stretched for 3 km along the bay, with warehouses, taverns and slave markets attracting commercial traffic. Parts are now being restored as hotels or restaurants. Seven privately-owned houses are being renovated as part of the Historic Core Development Plan, of which four had been completed by the end of 1999. If you like beach combing, blue, five-sided slave beads over 200 years old can be found along the shore at Oranjestad.

Berkels family museum is on the Lynch Plantation, a domestic museum with a collection of household utensils and antiques on the northeast side of the island, T82338.

Essentials

The *Talk of the Town*, one of the longest established hotels, has been leased to the new medical school on Statia and is not seeking other guests for a few years. **AL** *Old Gin House*, T82319, F82135, www.oldginhouse.com Re-opened 1999 after renovation, built with old bricks of 18th-century cotton gin house, 14 rooms, large beds, a/c, TV, phones, breakfast included. **AL-B** *Kings Well*, between Upper and Lower Town, north end of beach by Smoke Alley, T/F82538. Run by Win and Laura, about the nicest place to stay, popular with divers and sailors, rooms sparsely furnished but large, includes breakfast, ceiling fans, not always very clean, some rooms overlook bar, more expensive have spectacular sea view, accepts Visa/Mastercard. **A** *Golden Era Hotel*, Lower Town, PO Box 109, T82345, F82445, goldera@sintmaarten.net On the beach, modern, 20 rooms, not much charm but convenient and dive shop on premises, manager Roy Hooker is also the cook, friendly but extremely slow service, snack bar/restaurant good, credit cards. **C** *Country Inn*, at Concordia near airport, Biesheuvelweg, owned by Mrs Iris Pompier, T/F82484. 6 guest house rooms, noisy a/c but essential, TV, fridge, includes breakfast, other meals on request, hot and cold water, travellers' cheques but no credit cards. **C** *Henriquez Apartments*, Golden Rock, T82299, F82517. On road to airport, 3 mins' walk, 9 apartments, 1 or 2 bedrooms, a/c, TV, mini-fridge, bar and restaurant, barbecue, weekly and monthly rates negotiable. Off the road towards The Quill, **D** *Daniel's Guest House*, on Rosemary Laan, T82358. Unmarked, ask in Brown's supermarket at bottom of road, Miz Brown is very helpful, no hot water but use of kitchen, taxi available.

Sleeping

Expect a 7% government tax, 15% service charge on top of quoted rates & sometimes a 5% surcharge.

The tourist office has a list of home rentals

Netherland Antilles

Eating

Tap water is usually rainwater & not for drinking

The Old Gin House, recently renovated, gourmet dining. Good creole and international food at the *Golden Era Hotel*, service can be slow, order well in advance. *The King's Well*, good lobster, steak, German food, Jaeger and Wiener Schnitzels, cocktails, friendly atmosphere, owners like to chat and play cards with guests, lunch is served 1200-1400, dinner from 1800-2100, reservations requested. Cheaper meals at *Chinese Restaurant*, Prinsesweg 9, T82389. Shut Sun, tell cook not to put in monosodium glutamate, no credit cards. *Happy City Chinese Restaurant*, around the corner from Duggins Supermarket, T82540. Open 1130-2300, a/c, no smoking, closed Wed. *Ocean View Terrace*, just by tourist office and Governor's House, T82733. A nice place to take a break while touring town or to have a drink and watch the sunset, Chef Percyvan Putten has improved the menu considerably, seafood specials and shrimp creole highly recommended, daily specials are reasonably priced and good, sometimes have live music, happy hour and BBQ on Fri, good place to meet locals, closed Tue. *Blue Bead Bar and Restaurant*, right on beach, T82873. West Indian, American, Indonesian and international food, reasonably priced daily specials, lunch Mon-Sat 1130-1430, Sun brunch 1100-1430, dinner 1800-2100, bar hours 1000-2200, occasionally stays open later. *Cool Corner*, on the square opposite museum, T82523. Currently the most popular bar on the island, run by Chucky, a friendly Chinese who manages to serve drinks, talk to customers and prepare decent Chinese food. *Sonny's Place*, next to *Mazinga Gift Shop*, T82609. Popular hangout for locals and terminal employees, pool and football tables, music is good, if sometimes too loud, Sonny serves good creole and Chinese food at reasonable prices, lunch and dinner, chicken, fish and daily specials recommended, service can be slow.

Self-catering For fresh **fish**, go to the fish processing plant (Statia Fish Handling) at Lower Town opposite short pier, Mon-Fri, usually 0800-1300 depending on the catch, they will clean the fish for you. If it is not available at the fish plant approach the local fishermen at the harbour. Grocers sell frozen fish. Lobster is available fresh Nov-Mar. Fresh **bread** is baked daily in outdoor charcoal-fired stone ovens and best bought straight from the oven at "fresh bread time", which varies according to who makes it. Bake sales are announced by the town crier: open air **takeaway** meals of local dishes some Fri and Sat, from 1100, usually at *Charlie's Place* just below *Mazinga Gift Shop* and Africa Crossroads Park opposite museum. Hotels serve purified water. Bottled water is sold at groceries.

Nightlife Statians like partying and every weekend something is always going on. Quite often you will hear a 'road block' from far away: cars stopped with huge stereos blaring and everyone jumping up in the street. Ask anybody what is going on next weekend, or just wait for the music to start in the evening. The only nightclub is *Largo Height Disco* by the cable TV station at Chapel Piece, closed Wed, busy mainly Fri and Sat, run by Pamela Hook, good zouk music and local food. *Smoke Alley Bar* is a rustic place with a pool table and occasional live music. Open most days from 1400, open-air bar overlooks the water and is a lovely place to watch the sunset.

Shopping Lots of shops or businesses are in people's homes with no visible sign of the trade from the outside, but if you ask for help it will be willingly given and you will find the right place. Offices and stores are usually open 0800-1800, although supermarkets stay open until 1900. *Mazinga Gift Shop* sells local books and a wide range of gifts and duty free liquor, T82245, F82230. Some local crafts, mostly woodworking, are sold at *Paper Corner*, *Dive Statia* and *Under the Tree* next to *Allrun Supermarket*. Arts and crafts also sold at the *Little House on the Bay*, run by the St Eustatius Historical Foundation.

Festivals There are several occasions for celebrations during the year. On **Easter Monday** there are beach picnics with music and drinking. Former **Queen Juliana's birthday** is celebrated on *30 April* with cultural events, sports, food and music. **Emancipation Day** on *1 July* has ceremonies and celebrations of the abolition of slavery. The **Antillian Games** are held in the 2nd week of *July* with sporting competitions between all the islands of the Netherlands Antilles. **Carnival**, last 2 weeks in *July*, is celebrated with steel bands, picnics, sports and contests and also including a Grand Parade on the last Sunday of the month. Just about everybody who can walk on the island shows up in costume and marches through town. **Antillian Day** is on *21 October*, with flag ceremonies, games and fetes. **Statia/America Day** is on *16 November*, with lots of cultural festivities and activities commemorating the First Salute to the American Flag by a foreign government in 1776. On **Boxing Day** actors parade through the streets depicting the social, cultural or political group of the year, stopping at various homes for food and drink.

Car hire Companies include *Brown's*, T82266, F82454, US$45 per day including tax and insurance, weekend deals; *Rainbow*, T82811, F82586, US$35 plus US$5 CDW; *Walkers*, T82719, US$35 plus tax and insurance; *ARC*, T82595, F82594, US$35 plus tax and insurance, near airport; *Lady Ama's Services*, T82451, F82572, US$30-45, 5% surcharge on day rates; *Avis*, T82421/82303, F82285, US$40 per day, US$35 second day (CDW is US$7.50 per day, US$50 per week); *Co-Rentals*, T82941, F82940, US$35 per day, 5% surcharge insurance and gasoline; *R/DSON Jeep Rental*, T82149, US$30 per day, US$180 per week. Try *Lopes Car Rental*, T82291, for **cars**, **motor bikes**, **scooters** and **donkey carts**. Scooters also from *Dive Statia*, T82435, F82539.

Transport

Banks *Barclays Bank*, Wilhelminaweg, T82392. Open Thur, Fri 0830-1530. The Post Office Bank, *Post Spaarbank*, is open Mon-Fri 0730-1200, 1300-1630 except Fri when it closes at 1645. The *Windward Islands Bank* is by *Mazinga Gift Shop*, open Mon-Fri 0830-1200, 1300-1530, T82846, F82850. **Communications** Post: the post office is at Fiscal Rd, T82207, F82457. Open Mon-Fri 0730-1200, 1300-1630 except Fri when it closes at 1645. Airmail letters to the USA, Canada, Holland, US$1.25 1st 10 gm, to the Caribbean US$1, postcards US$0.62 and US$0.51, aerograms US$0.71. Express mail is available. Limited banking services also available. There are special stamp issues and First Day Covers for collectors. *DHL* agent is Peggy van der Horde-Jacobson, Lampeweg 33, T/F82401, packages to the USA US$22-30 1st 90 gm. Lady Ama's Services is agent for *Federal Express*. **Telephone:** Fax and cablegrams at Landsradio, Van Tonningenweg. Open Mon-Fri, 0730-1930, Sat, Sun 1200-1800, pay phone on the wall for local calls, accepts only US quarters (US$0.25). For operator assisted overseas prepaid and collect calls, telegrams, telex and fax pay at counter when you place your call. Telephone cards of US$10 and US$17 can be used at phone booth outside near Police Station and at the corner of Korthalsweg, at the airport, at the harbour and the road to the airport, for local or international calls. **Medical facilities** The *Queen Beatrix Medical Centre* is on Prinsesweg, T82371 for an ambulance, or T82211 for a doctor. 2 doctors are on 24-hr call. Outpatient hours are 0800-1200, Mon-Fri, or by appointment, from 1400, Sat-Sun from 1000 for emergencies only. The resident dentist is Dr JM Tjien A Fat, at the Medical Centre Mon-Fri 0800-1700, T82371/82211 or at home T/F82750. **Places of worship** Anglican, Apostolic Faith, Methodist, Roman Catholic, Bahai, Baptist, Pentecostal and Seventh Day Adventist. **Tourist offices** The *St Eustatius Tourism Development Foundation*, Fort Oranjestraat, Mon-Fri 0800-1700, T/F82433, www.turq.com/statia Tourism Information booth at the airport, T82620; at the Harbour Office, T82205. *The St Eustatius Historical Foundation*, Wilhelminaweg 3, PO Box 71, Oranjestad A255, T82288, F82202 c/o Eutel. The Foundation publishes a newsletter 4 times a year and runs the Museum (see above) and the Tourist Information Center and Gallery, 'Little House on the Bay', a replica gingerbread house, open Mon-Sat 0930-1200, Sun 1500-1700, but staffed seasonally by volunteers so opening times are approximate. Local artists and artisans sell their work here. The town crier (Mr Cyril Lopes) announces events with loudspeakers on his car as he drives around town. Listen for news of jump-ups, sports events, food sales or community events. *STENAPA*, Jan Faber, President, White Wall Road, St Eustatius, Netherlands Antilles, T/F82661. Good information on walks, trails and conservation at the office by the dock.

Directory

Netherland Antilles

Background

History

See also background to the Netherlands Antilles, the ABC chapter, page 1037

Sint Eustatius, or Statia, 56 km south of St Maarten and 27 km southeast of Saba, was originally settled by Caribs and evidence of their occupation dates back to AD 300. The island was sighted by Columbus on his second voyage but never settled by the Spanish. The Dutch first colonized it in 1636 and built Fort Oranje, but the island changed flag 22 times before finally remaining Dutch in 1816. The island reached a peak of prosperity in the 18th century, when the development of commerce brought about 8,000 people to the tiny island, over half of whom were slaves, and the number of ships visiting the port was around 3,500 a year. Trading in sugar, tobacco and cotton proved more profitable than trying to grow them and the slave trade was particularly lucrative, gaining the island the nickname of 'The Golden Rock'.

The island still celebrates 16 November 1776 when the cannons of Fort Oranje unknowingly fired the first official salute by a foreign nation to the American colours. At that time, Statia was a major trans-shipment point for arms and supplies to George Washington's troops, which were stored in the yellow ballast brick warehouses built all along the Bay and then taken by blockade runners to Boston, New York and Charleston. However, the salute brought retaliatory action from the English and in 1781 the port was taken without a shot being fired by troops under Admiral George Brydges Rodney, who captured 150 merchant ships and £5mn of booty before being expelled by the French the following year.

With continuing transfers of power, the economy never recovered, many merchants were banished and the population began a steady decline. The emancipation of slaves in 1863 brought an end to any surviving plantation agriculture and the remaining inhabitants were reduced to subsistence farming and dependency upon remittances from relatives abroad. Prosperity has returned only recently with the advent of tourism and the island is still relatively underdeveloped.

The people

Statia is quiet and friendly and the poorest of the three Windward Islands, with only 2,100 people living on the 30.6 sq km island. A variety of nationalities are represented, the island having changed hands 22 times in the past, but the majority are of black African descent. Everybody speaks English, although Dutch is the official language and is taught in schools.

The economy

The traditional economic activities of fishing, farming and trading have been augmented by an oil storage and refuelling facility, but the major hope for prosperity, tourism, has not fulfilled its promise. Stayover visitors fell from 10,000 in 1994 to an average of 8,500 in 1995-97. Hotel capacity fell and the general quality also declined. However, in 1998-99 there was a small resurgence in the hotel business, with the opening of the renovated 14-room *Old Gin House* in town. It remains the sort of place where you will be greeted by passers by and there is no crime.

Sint Maarten

The island is shared amicably by the Dutch, who have the southern 37 sq km of the island, and the French, calling their half Saint-Martin, who own the northern 52 sq km, an arrangement settled by the 1648 Treaty of Mount Concordia. The salt ponds in the south of the island attracted the Dutch and during the early 19th century the island enjoyed modest prosperity. With the abolition of slavery however, the population declined, as did the salt exporting industry. In the last 20 or so years the island has flourished once again, this time as a beach holiday destination. The Dutch side of the island has the main airport and seaport and the majority of tourists. There are no border formalities, only a modest monument erected in 1948, which commemorates the division of the island three centuries earlier. The west part of the island is low-lying and mostly taken up by the Simpson Bay Lagoon, which provides a safe anchorage for small craft. The lagoon is separated from the sea by a narrow strip of land on which the airport has been built. The rest of the Dutch part is hilly and dry and covered with scrub, although it can quickly turn green after rain. The French side is noticeably Gallic and few speak English.

Ins and outs

Air From Europe *Air France*, 6 times a week and *AOM French Airlines*, 4 times a week from Paris, *KLM*, twice a week from Amsterdam in a joint operation with ALM. **From North America** New York (*American Airlines*, *Continental*, *TWA*), Charlotte (*US Air*), Miami (*American Airlines*), Orlando (*American Airlines*), Philadelphia (*US Air*, *American Airlines*). **From the**

Getting there
See transport, page 683, for further information

Sint Maartin

- ■ **Sleeping**
- 1 Club Orient
- 2 Le Samanna
- 3 Pavillon Beach
- 4 Royal Beach
- 5 Bel Air Beach
- 6 Cupecoy
- 7 Maho Beach
- 8 Oyster Pond & Dawn Beach

N

Not to scale

Netherland Antilles

Essentials

Documents See page 1002. In addition, under a 1994 Franco-Dutch immigration accord, visitors to Dutch Sint Maarten have to meet French immigration criteria, even if not visiting the French side. Therefore, many nationalities now have to obtain a French visa before embarking on a shopping trip to Philipsburg. The local immigration officials are particularly concerned that you fill in your tourist card with a hotel address, even if you do not know whether you'll be staying there.

Currency Netherlands Antilles guilders or florins are the official currency, but the most common currency is the US dollar, which you need never change at all. You will get a poor exchange rate for French francs. It is often difficult to get change from payments in any currency other than US dollars. **Credit cards** widely accepted.

Departure tax US$6 when leaving for the Netherlands Antilles, US$20 for other destinations at Juliana Airport except for French visitors returning to Guadeloupe or France. Passengers staying less than 24 hours are exempt. Travel agents ask for US$3 to confirm flights. Airport flight information T52161.

Boat documents Yacht clearance is done at the port, both in and out. Off season hours 0900-1200, 1300-1600 Monday-Friday, 0900-1200 Saturday, longer hours in season, page port Authority for Sunday clearance.

Ports of entry (Dutch/French flag) Philipsburg and Marigot.

Anchorages Great Bay, Orient Beach, Oyster Bay, Marigot, Simpson Bay, Simpson Bay Lagoon Marinas: Great Bay Marina, Bobby's Marina, in Simpson Bay Lagoon: Simpson Bay Yacht Club, Island Water World, Port de Plaisance Marina, Palapa Marina. Mail/fax/phone: Dockside Management and The Mailbox. Charter fleets include Jet Sea, Moorings, Nautor Swan, Sunsail, Stardust ATM, Sun Yachts.

Marinas No fee yet for Simpson Lagoon bridge. Dutch bridge openings 0600, 1100, and 1730, outbound boats first. The French side opens Monday-Saturday 0900, 1400, 1730, Sunday 0900, 1730. Good groceries and laundry in Lagoon. Radio net VHF 78 at 0730. Send mail with someone flying out or Federal Express. Duty free Caribbean headquarters for boat parts, outboard motors, beer.

Tourist offices overseas **Holland** Minister Plenipotentiary of the Netherlands Antilles, Antillenhuis, Badhuisweg 173-175, Postbus 90706, 2509 LS's-Gravenhage, T070-3066111, F070-3066110. **Canada** 3300 Bloor Street West, Suite 3120-Centre Tower, Toronto, Ontario M8X 2X3, T416-2334348, F416-2339376. **USA** St Maarten Tourist Bureau, 675 Third Avenue, Suite 1806, New York, NY 10017, T1-800-7862278, 212-9532084, F212-9532145; Yesawich, Pepperdine and Brown, Public Relations Division, 1900 Summit Tower Boulevard, Suite 600, Orlando, FL32810, T407-8751111, F407-8751115. **Brazil**: Av Ipiranga 318, Bloco A, CEP 01046-010, São Paulo, T55-11-2145588, F55-11-2583575; Av Rio Branco 181-c, 3303, CEP 20040-007, Rio de Janeiro, T55-21-2201484, F55-21-2203212.

Communications The international phone code is 599-54 followed by 5 digits.

Official time Atlantic Standard Time, four hours behind GMT, one ahead of EST.

Voltage 110 volts AC. Note that it is 220 volts on the French side.

Public holidays New Year's Day, Carnival Monday (April), Good Friday, Easter Monday, 30 April, Labour Day (1 May), Ascension Day, St Maarten Day (11 November), Christmas Day, Boxing Day.

Caribbean There are many from: Anguilla, Antigua, Barbados, Cuba, Curaçao, Dominica, Dominican Republic, Martinique, Grenada, Guyana, Nevis, Guadeloupe, Trinidad and Tobago, Saba, St Barthélémy, USVI (St Croix and St Thomas), St Eustatius, St Kitts, St Vincent, Puerto Rico, St Lucia, Jamaica, and the British Virgin Islands (Tortola), with a variety of regional and international carriers. **From South America** ALM also flies from Caracas and Valencia via Curaçao.

Sea There are no long distance sea communications except cruise ships which usually stay 5-9 hrs.

There can be a shortage of **cars** or jeeps for hire in high season. It is advisable to request one from your hotel when you book the room. Out of season car rental is inexpensive. Foreign and international driver's licences are accepted. Drive on the right. The speed limit is 40 km per hour in urban areas, 60 km per hour outside town, unless there are other signs. The roads on both sides of the island are very busy and full of pot holes, making them rather unsafe for mopeds or walking, particularly at night. There is a fairly regular **bus** service during the day between Philipsburg and Marigot but no regular bus service between Philipsburg and the airport. Mini-vans or tour buses offer **tours** and are generally cheaper than **taxis**. Island tours from US$15; for more information ask at the tourist office on the square. **Hitchhiking** is possible but allow 30 mins waiting time; it is not recommended for women.

Average temperature is 26.5° C, 80° F and average annual rainfall is 45in.

Flora and fauna

In 1997 the *Nature Foundation Sint Maarten* (T20267, F20268) was set up, with assistance from the WWF, to protect and manage natural parks and educate the general population and students on their significance. Two parks form the initial programme, a marine park covering the coastal waters and some adjacent coastline from Oyster Bay to Cupecoy Beach, and a hillside park in the Cul-De-Sac area. A nature conservation newsletter is published, which will give details of progress.

Diving and marine life

Water visibility is usually 23-38m and the water temperature averages over 21° C, which makes good snorkelling and scuba diving, from beaches or boats. **Wreck Alley** on Proselyte Reef, has several wrecks which can be explored on one dive. *HMS Proselyte* is a 200 year-old British frigate (mostly broken up and covered in coral, although cannons and anchors are visible), while *The Minnow* and *SS Lucy* are modern ships deliberately sunk as dive sites. Diving the east side of the island is recommended in good weather, either from the shore or drift diving from a boat. The coral barrier reef is undamaged by silt run off and there are lots of fish, fed by Atlantic currents.

Training with NAUI instructors or just equipment rental is offered by *Leeward Island Divers* (T43320), *Ocean Explorers* at Simpson Bay (T45252), *Trade Winds Dive Center* at Great Bay Marina (T75176, PADI and SSI certification also offered, US$45 single tank 15m dives 0900, 1100, 1300 Monday-Friday, 1000, 1300 Saturday, Sunday).

Beaches and watersports

The bays on the south and west shores are excellent for swimming, diving and fishing, and the beaches are of fine white sand. The most popular beach is **Mullet Bay**, where you can rent umbrellas, beach chairs et cetera. It can get crowded in season and all weekends. On the east side is **Oyster Pond**, a land-locked harbour which is difficult to enter because of the outlying reefs, but which is now home to a yacht club and is a centre for bare boat charter. **Dawn Beach** nearby is popular with body surfers and snorkelling is good because of the reefs just offshore; **Guana Bay**, next to Dawn Beach, is the bodysurfers' best beach. **Maho Beach**, by the airport, has regular Sunday beach parties with live music competitions; don't forget to duck when planes arrive. The most westerly beach on the Dutch side of the island is **Cupecoy**, where rugged sandstone cliffs lead down to a narrow sandy beach, providing morning shade and a natural windbreak.

Every conceivable form of watersport is usually available. Surfing is possible all year round from different beaches depending on the time of the year

Netherland Antilles

Hurricanes Luis and Lenny

St Maarten was one of the islands worst hit by Hurricane Luis in September 1995. Six people were killed, damage of US$1bn was reported and at least 2,000 people lost their jobs in the tourist industry when hotels and about 300 yachts were smashed. The shanty towns housing Haitians and Dominicans (many of them illegal immigrants) were flattened and the Government moved quickly to bulldoze the remains, offering jobs and a tent camp for those with papers and deportation for those without. Rebuilding of public buildings, including the hospital, started quickly; cruise ships returned in October but the airport was closed to commercial traffic until November. Only a third of all the private homes were insured, while others (including the Dawn Beach Resort) were victims of a crooked insurance broker who disappeared with their premiums. Only half the island's hotel rooms were open for the winter season and several resorts remained closed. The hurricane highlighted low building standards and dodgy construction practices, particularly with newer houses. As soon as Phillipsburg got back to normal, it was hit by another hurricane, and then another, until it had been hit by a total of six in 1996-99. In November 1999, Lenny struck from the Caribbean side, bringing winds and floods and more death and damage. Most hotels closed for repairs, flights were cancelled and cruise ships stayed away until December. Many insurance companies have decided to cease providing cover for Sint Maarten.

There are **boat charter companies** with sailing boats and motor boats, with or without a crew. You find most of them around Bobby's Marina, Philipsburg, from US$200 a day for bare boat. There are around 40 boats offering different trips around the islands, some just going out for snorkelling on the reefs or taking cruise ship passengers around. The *Swaliga*, a motor catamaran (US$50 per person plus US$7 port charge) sails daily to St Barts from Philipsburg. Also the 70-ft motor cata-maran, *Quicksilver*. There are several other sailings from Philipsburg which can be booked through Dockside Management (T2024096) or hotels. On certain days there are sailings from Pelican Marina at Simpson Bay, or from Marigot. The trip to St Barts is normally quite rough and unpleasant on the way there but more pleasant on the return journey. Check the weather, the swell and the waves can be up to 3½ m even on a nice day. The *Golden Eagle*, a new wing mast 76-ft catamaran sails to Tintamarre from Great Bay Marina, four hours, US$45 per person, breakfast on board, snorkelling gear, T75828/30068. Most boats offer some snacks, sodas and rum punch. Trips cost from US$50-75, plus departure tax. Check what is available from Marigot too. Some of the time share resorts offer free boat trips with snorkelling, lunch, taxis, (you pay departure tax), if you participate in a sales drives. For **fishing** there are numerous boats available for a whole (US$500-750) or half (US$280-375) day from Bobby's Marina, Pelican Marina or Great Bay Marina. Arrangements can be made through the hotels or contact *Leeward Islands Divers*, see above, or *Rudy's Fishing*, Beacon Hill, T52177. Marlin, barracuda, dolphin (not the mammal) and tuna are the best catches. Game fishing tournaments are held all year round.

The largest annual regatta, the **Heineken Regatta**, takes place each February or March and lasts for three days with a round the island race on the Sunday. It is well attended with nearly 300 boats in nine classes. A race to Nevis and back is held in mid-June with a day for resting/parties. Other regattas held are for catamarans, match racing with charter boats, windsurfing et cetera. For more information check with St Martin Yacht Club, Simpson Bay (La Palapa Marina) or ask Robbie Ferron at Budget Marina in Philipsburg. A popular half day excursion is match racing on *Canada II*, *True North*, *True North IV* or *Stars and Stripes*, boats from the Americas Cup, US$60, races Wednesday 1315, three hours (T43354, Bobby's Marina).

Other sports All the large hotels have **tennis** courts, many of which are lit for night play, but check availability. There is an 18-hole championship **golf** course at *Mullet Bay Resort*, which stretches along the shores of Mullet Pond and Simpson Bay Lagoon. Running is organized by the *Road Runners Club*, St Maarten, with a fun run of 5-10 km every Wednesday at 1730 and Sunday at 1830, starting from the *Pelican Resort & Casino* car park. On Sunday at 0700 there are two 20 km runs. There are monthly races with prizes and an annual relay race around the island to relive the legendary race between the Dutch and the French when they divided the island. Contact Dr Fritz Bus at the *Back Street Clinic* or Malcolm Maidwell of *El Tigre*, T44309/22167. *Crazy Acres* Riding Centre takes groups **horseriding** every weekday morning at 0900 from the Wathey Estate, Cole Bay, to Cay Bay, where horses and riders can swim, T42793. Make reservations two days in advance.

Philipsburg

Philipsburg, the capital of Dutch St Maarten, is built on a narrow strip of sandy land between the sea and a shallow lake which was once a salt pond. It has two main streets, Front and Back, and a ringroad built on land reclaimed from the salt pond, which all run parallel to Great Bay Beach, perhaps the safest and cleanest city beach anywhere. Front Street is full of shops offering duty-free goods. Back Street contains low cost clothes shops and low budget Chinese restaurants.

The **St Maarten Museum** at Museum Arcade on 7 Front Street, is a restored 19th-century house, exhibiting the history and culture of the island. There is a museum shop. ■ *1000-1600 Mon-Fri, 0900-1200 Sat, closed Sun.* The historic **Courthouse** dating from 1793, on De Ruyterplein, better known as Wathey Square, faces the pier. In the past it has been used as a Council Hall, a weigh station, jail and until 1992, a Post Office. Now renovated, it is used exclusively as a courthouse.

The **harbour** is frequented by cruise ships and a host of smaller craft and the town gets very crowded when up to eight cruise ships are in port. Captain Hodge's Wharf can handle 1,800 passengers per hour and has a tourist information desk, telephones, toilets, taxis and live entertainment. A huge harbour extension is planned. For information on outdoor concerts, choirs, theatre and art exhibitions, ask at the Cultural Center of Philipsburg on Back Street (T22056).

There is a **zoo** on Arch Road in Madam Estate, close to New Amsterdam shopping centre (difficult to find, ask for directions), with a small exhibition of the fauna and flora from the islands. ■ *T32030, US$4, children US$2, weekdays 0900-1700, weekends 1000-1800.*

There are several ruined fortresses, but not a lot remains of them. **Fort Amsterdam** was the first Dutch fort in the Caribbean, built in 1631 but captured by the Spanish in 1633 and partly pulled down before they left the island in 1648. It was still used for military purposes until the 19th century and as a signalling and communications station until the 1950s. Fort Amsterdam can be reached through the grounds of a private timeshare development. The guard allows visitors to park outside and walk to the fort. **Fort Willem** has a television transmitting tower and there is a good view from the top. Construction was started by the British, who called it Fort Trigge, at the beginning of the 19th century, but the Dutch renamed it in 1816. Fort Bel-Air and Sint Peter's Battery gave way to modern development although a few ruins are still visible near Great Bay Marina.

You can take a day trip round the island, visiting the ruined Fort Amsterdam overlooking Philipsburg and the French part of the island. It is well worth having lunch in one of the many French restaurants in Grand Case or the other French villages. Generally, however, there is not much of either historical or natural interest to see on the island, and most excursions are day trips to neighbouring islands: Anguilla, St Barthélémy, Saba, St Eustatius, St Kitts or Nevis, either by boat (see Beaches and watersports) or by plane. Timeshare resorts such as *Pelican* and *Divi Little Bay* offer trips to other islands and excursions in return for listening to their sales pitch.

Around the island

Netherland Antilles

Essentials

There is a 5-8% Government tax on all hotel bills and a 10-15% service charge. Some add an energy surcharge. Prices are high but package deals in summer can be good value if you are prepared to shop around. In 2000 several hotels were still closed or partly open after hurricane repairs. Check for availability of sports and other facilities.

Large resort hotels LL-L *Mullet Bay Resort & Casino*, T52801, F54281. 600 rooms-suites, temporarily closed 1999-2000 for renovations, golf course still open, so is **LL-L** *The Towers At Mullet Bay*, casino, watersports, golf, tennis, pool, close to airport, 8 km from Philipsburg, T53069, F52147. 81 units, a/c, kitchenettes, TV, VCR etc. **LL-L** *Cupecoy* perched on a cliff above Cupecoy beach, T52086 F52243. Condo/villa resort, pool, tennis, casino. **LL-L** *Maho Bay*, T52115, F53180, 615 rooms/suites, casino, pool, tennis, 20% service charge, right by airport. **LL-A** *Pelican Resort & Casino*, on Simpson Bay, T/F42503, F42133. 5 pools, tennis etc, 342 1-2 bedroom suites, lots of facilities. **LL-AL** *Divi Little Bay Beach Resort*, T22333, F25410. 159 rooms, tennis, 2 pools, watersports. **LL-AL** *Great Bay Beach Hotel & Casino*, T22446, F23008. Convenient for Philipsburg, all resort facilities, all-inclusive packages available, activities organized, games around the pool, barbecue buffet Mon, 285 rooms-suites.

Mid-sized hotels and resorts LL *Bel Air Beach Hotel*, at Little Bay, T23362, F25295. 67 1-2 bedroomed suites, tennis, pool, open air restaurant. **LL-AL** *Holland House Beach Hotel*, PO Box 393, T22572, F24673. 54 rooms downtown, most with kitchenettes, open air restaurant, on the beach, convenient. **LL-AL** *La Vista*, near *Pelican*. 24 suites and cottages, tennis, pool, horse riding, T43005, F43010. **A-C** *Seaview Hotel*, 45 rooms, some with showers, on Great Bay Beach, Philipsburg, casino, a/c, TV, children under 12 free, T22323, F24356. **LL-L** *Atrium Resort*, PO Box 115, Simpson Bay T42125, F42128. 87 1-2 bedroom suites, beach front restaurant, wheelchair facilities, watersports etc at the *Pelican*. **LL-L** *Caravanserai*, Beacon Hill

Philipsburg

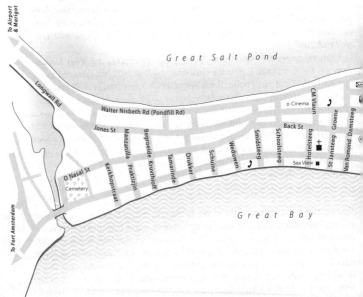

Road 2, on Burgeux Bay, close to airport, T54000, F54001. Shopping mall, casino etc, 118 deluxe suites and bungalows, coffee shop, pool, tennis, whirlpool. Also on Simpson Bay, **LL-C** *White Sands Beach Club*, PO Box 3034, T54370, F52245. 11 rooms, private retreat, couples only, special deals for cash customers, all beach front units, no restaurant but several nearby. Airport runway runs parallel to this part of Simpson Bay. **LL-AL** *Oyster Bay Beach Resort*, on peninsula, T36040, F36695. 40 rooms, next to Dawn Beach in large grounds, pool, watersports, boat rental. **LL-L** *Princess Heights*, Dawn Beach, T36905, F36007. 15 luxury villas with full kitchens, pool.

Small hotels **L-A** *Pasanggrahan Royal Inn*, in Philipsburg, PO Box 151, T23588, F22885. Formerly the Governor's home, the oldest inn, 30 rooms, pool, no children under 12, nice atmosphere. **LL-A** *Summit Resort Hotel*, PO Box 456, on hill overlooking lagoon with view of Marigot, T53702, F52615. A/c suites with king size bed and queen size sofa bed, balconies, kitchenettes, pool with view from sundeck, tennis, beach shuttle, outdoor café. **LL-A** *Mary's Boon*, on Simpson Bay beach, T54235, F53403, marysboon@megatropic.com 14 studios with kitchenettes, pets welcome but no children under 14. **B-C** *Sea Breeze*, 8 Welgelegen Rd, Cay Hill, T26054, F26057. 5 mins from Little Bay Beach, 30 rooms, most with kitchenette, pool, quaint residential area. **B** *Midtown Motel*, 42 Back St, T26838. Built end 1995, clean, modern, very friendly, near shops, casinos etc.

Apartments The Tourist Office has a list of apartments, villas and houses to rent weekly or monthly. The best way of finding an apartment is to look in the newspaper. There are several apartments for rent on Back St, look for signs on the houses. A studio will cost about US$400-500 per week in a good location. Apartments at Simpson Bay Beach cost US$350-500 per week.

Front Street (guest houses) **C-E** *Marcus*, 7 rooms, T22419, **E** *Seaside*, 5 rooms, PO Box 72. On **Back St**: **B-C** *Lucy's*, PO Box 171, T22995. 9 rooms, clean and adequate, friendly and helpful, but overpriced, no children under 6; **C-E** *Jose's*, T22231. Prepay for 6 nights, get 7th free, 11 rooms, very basic, mosquitoes. **AL-C** *Joshua Rose*, 17 Back St, T24317, F30080. Slightly better, a/c but still mosquitoes, 14 rooms, walk to beach, Chinese Restaurant.

Simpson Bay **AL-B** *Morning Glory*, 6 Roberts Drive, T/F55288. 14 apartments on beach, no credit cards. **L-AL** *The Horny Toad*, 2 Vlaun Drive, T54323, F53316, hornytoad@ sintmaarten.net 8 studios, no children under 7, right on beach, not seriously troubled by aircraft noise, well cared for, pretty patio gardens. **A-B** *Calypso*, PO Box 65, Simpson Bay, T54233. 8 efficiency apartments.

Pointe Blanche **A-B** *Great Bay Marina*, PO Box 277, T22167. 10 rooms, fridge, a/c, TV, grocery, pier facilities. **AL-B** *Tamarind*, T24359, F25391, tamarind@sintmaarten.net 48 apartments with kitchenettes, swimming pool, deli.

Cole Bay **A-B** *Carl's Unique Inn*, Orange Grove, PO Box 175, T42812, F45376. 16 a/c studios and rooms including breakfast, meeting facilities, bakery and grocery downstairs. **C** *Ernest*, Bush Road 36, T22003.

Not to scale

Walter Nisbeth Rd

Government Building

Taxis   Parking

E Camille Richardson St

Pharmacy   CA Cannegieter St

Cultural Centre

Catholic Church

Front St   Old St   DC Steeg

they uare

Pasanggrahan
St Maarten Museum

Library

Joshua Rose Guesthouse

Bobby's Marina

Great Bay Marina

To Point Blanche

To North Shore

Vogesstreet

Terpentin

Secretarissteeg

Pastorissteeg

Hendrik

Netherland Antilles

Swimming pool, 16 rooms, a/c, TV. **B-C** *George's*, T45363. 10 rooms in Cole Bay, 10 rooms in Philipsburg, a/c, kitchen.

Eating   All the major hotels have restaurants with international cuisine. Pick up a free tourist guide to choose from the myriad restaurants now open on St Maarten with food from all over the world. The traditional local liqueur is *guavaberry*, made from rum and the local berries, whose botanical name is *Eugenia Floribunda*. They are not related to guavas. The berries are found on the hills and ripen just before Christmas. Used nowadays mostly in cocktails.

Philipsburg *Le Bec Fin*, Front St 119, French, elegant, favoured by the Dutch Royal Family and winner of awards, T22976 for reservations. Highly recommended. *Le Bec Fin Café* serves American and seafood. Front St is full of good restaurants and even a *Burger King*. Americanized French at *L'Escargot*, Front St 84, T22483. *Da Livio*, west end, T22690. High class Italian restaurant on waterfront, run by Livio Bergamasco and his British wife, excellent seafood and pasta, not cheap, pastas from US$9, main courses from US$24. *San Marco*, Front St, is an Italian restaurant, nice location overlooking sea, good for a break from shopping, T22166. *Shiv Sagar*, Front St 3, T22299. Indian food, large portions, Tandoori specialities. Indonesian rijsttafel at the hotels. For the budget minded try Back St where you mostly find Chinese and *roti* places. *Grill and Ribs*, Simpson Bay Rd, T54498. The best ribs on the island, all you can eat for US$12.95, reservations essential.

Simpson Bay area   *Turtle Pier Bar and Restaurant*, Airport Rd 80, T52230. Reasonably priced at US$10 maximum per dish with an interesting setting in a mini zoo with parrots, monkeys, turtles etc, live music 2 or 3 times a week; *Lynette's*, Airport Rd, T52865. Local restaurant with good seafood and steak quite close to airport US$40 per person including wine and tip, weekly calypso revue with *King Beau Beau*, and upstairs is *Clayton's* sport bar, where you can see most major sporting events on a big screen TV. *Don Carlos*, T53112. Tasty Mexican food, US$10-15 per person for dinner, open daily 0730-2230, Mexican buffet Thur, US$12.95, all you can eat. *Boat House*, T45409. For drinks and food, live music several times a week, reservations essential. *Tokyo* Atlantis Casino. Cupecoy, sushi bar and restaurant. *The Greenhouse Bar and Restaurant*, next to Bobby's Marina at Great Bay, T22941. View over yachts, menu includes hamburgers, steak and local fish, disc jockey, dancing, Tue night 2 drinks for the price of 1. *Rembrandt Café* at New Amsterdam shopping centre. A Dutch coffee shop/café, very popular for late drinks, best after 2100-2200. The most popular bars with nice sunsets are *Greenhouse* and *Chesterfield*, Great Bay, T23484. Where you can find yachtsmen if you want to hitchhike by boat.

Nightlife   There are nine casinos and they are a major attraction, most opening from noon to 0200. The largest is *Casino Royale* at the *Maho Beach Hotel*, open 1300-0400 daily. *Lightning* is across from Simpson Bay Yacht Club Marina on Airport road, also sport via satellite. The *Studio 7* discothèque at Grand Casino, Mullet Bay, is the most visited, entrance US$10 including one drink, can be higher if they have a special show, all drinks US$6, the disco starts late, recommended to pass the time in *Cheri's* bar, a 5-min walk away, when people leave there most head for the disco. *Comedy Club* (Maho) have stand up comedians Tue-Sun, 2130 and 2330, US$10 cover charge, most comedians from HBO or Carsons, well worth the price. Most resorts have live entertainment, such as limbo dancing, fire eating or live music, both local and international. In Philipsburg, *The Movies*, on Pondfill, has newly released films, US$5. *The News* is good for dancing, with live music every other night, extremely popular. Look out for *Jack* (Irish folk songs etc), *G-Strings* (pop-rock 1950s-70s), *King Beau Beau*, the most popular bands of the last few years, whose music fills all the bars.

Festivals   **Carnival** starts in *mid-April* and lasts for 3 weeks, culminating in the burning of King Mouí-Mouí. It is one of the biggest in the area, with up to 100,000 people taking part. Most events are held at the Carnival Village, next to the University.

Duty-free shopping is a tourist attraction, but it helps if you have an idea of prices at home **Shopping** to compare, and shop around as prices vary. In the electronics and camera shops many outdated models are on display. European visitors planning to take home hi-fi or domestic appliances should make sure that they can be switched to 220 volts. Check your duty-free allowance when returning home. Most of the shops are along Front St. Open 0800-1200, 1400-1800. The large **food** stores have imported foods from Holland, France and the USA (good wine, beer and spirits prices). *Barrel Liquor*, 114 Old St (a mini mall), sells the cheapest **liquor** in town. Many liquor stores will deliver to your hotel or boat.

Air The international airport is **Juliana**, at Simpson Bay. A taxi into Philipsburg costs **Transport** US$10-12. If you need to eat while waiting for a plane, the best place is a bar/restaurant across the street with a supermarket.

Bicycle 2-wheeled transport hire from *Super Honda*, Bush Rd Cul-de-Sac, T25712; *Moped Cruising*, Front St, T22330; *OK Scooter Rental*, at *Maho Beach Hotel* and *Cupecoy Resort*, T42115, 44334. Mountain bike hire from *Tri-Sport Rent a Bike*, Airport Rd, T54384, US$15 per day, delivery and pickup available, guided tours.

Boat *The Voyager*, a high speed motorboat leaves 0830 Thur from **Bobby's Marina** for Saba, return same day 1615, US$40 one way, US$60 return; *Voyager* also to St Barths, Mon, Tue, Wed, Fri, US$50 return, plus US$7 port surcharge, T24096. Boats to Anguilla leave from the French side. See page 678 for boats to St Barths. The *MV Caribbean Explorer*, a 100ft, 16 passenger liveaboard dive boat leaves Philipsburg every Sat for a week-long tour of the northeast Caribbean including Saba, Statia, St Kitts. Contact Explorer Ventures Ltd, PO Box 488, Mabank, Texas 75147-0488, T903-8878521, F903-8878526, www.caribexplorer.com

Bus There is a fairly regular bus service from 0700 until 2400 to Marigot (US$1.50 Philipsburg-Marigot), French Quarters and St Peters, and from Marigot to Grand Case on the French side. After 2000 there are few buses. The best place to catch a bus is on Back Street. Buses run along Back St and Pondfill and only stop at bus stops. Outside towns, however, just wave to stop a bus. Fare is usually US$0.85 in town, US$1 for short trips, US$2 for long trips. There is no regular bus service between Philipsburg and the airport although the route to *Mullet Bay Resort* passes the airport. Buses on this route run mostly at the beginning and the end of the working day (although there are a few during the day) and drivers may refuse to take you, or charge extra, if you have a lot of luggage.

Car hire Many car hire companies have offices at the airport or in the hotels; free pick up and delivery are standard and you can leave the car at the airport on departure. Prices range from US$25-55 per day. Car hire companies include: *Risdon's Car Rentals*, Front St, T23578; *Avis*, Cole Bay, T42316; *Hertz*, Juliana Airport, T54541; *Budget*, Philipsburg, T44038, *Cannegie Car Rental*, Front St, T22397; *Empress Rent-a-Car* T463638 and at hotels; *Opel Car Rental*, Airport, T44324; *Speedy Car Rental*, Airport, T23893; *Roy Roger's*, Airport, T52701, US$30 plus US$10 CDW.

Taxi There are plenty of taxis, which are not metered so check the fare first, which is fixed according to your destination. Trips to other beaches or tours of the island can be arranged with taxi drivers: island tour US$35 plus US$2 for each additional passenger; hourly rate US$10 plus US$2.50 each additional 15 mins. From Philipsburg to Juliana airport US$10-12, Dawn Beach US$18, Marigot US$10, Mullet Bay US$5, Pelican Resort US$8, all for 2 passengers, additional passengers US$2 each. Night tariffs are an extra 25% 2200-2400, an extra 50% 0001-0600. Pick up taxi at the square in Philipsburg (T22359) or Juliana airport (T54317).

Airlines Airline offices at the airport: *ALM*, T54240/54210. *Air Guadeloupe*, T54212. *KLM*, T52120. **Directory** *LIAT*, T54203. *American Airlines*, T52040. *Air France*, T54212. *Air St Barthélemy*, T53151. *BWIA*, T54646. *Ogden Aviation*, T54234. *Continental*, Northwest and USAir, T54344. *Lufthansa*, T52040. *Winair* T54230/54237, F54229/52002. **Banks** *Scotiabank*, Back St, T22262, 1% commission on TCs.

Netherland Antilles

Windward Islands Bank, T23485. Charges US$5 per TCs cashed. *Barclays Bank*, 19 Front St, T22491. *Chase Manhattan Bank*, Mullet Bay, T44204. *Algemene Bank Nederland*, main office at Front St, T23505. *Citco Bank Antilles*, 16 Front St, T23471, 3 other offices on the island as well. *Nederlandse Credietbank*, T22933. Open 0830-1530, Mon-Fri (some open Sat morning). **Communications** Post: 2 safe places for holding mail are *Bobby's Marina*, PO Box 383, Philipsburg and *Island Water World*, PO Box 234, Cole Bay. It is not possible to send a parcel by sea, only airmail which is expensive. **Telephone:** telephone codes for the Dutch side of the island can be bought at *Landsradio* telecommunications office in Cannegieter St, open 0700 until midnight, or at Landsradio's offices at Simpson Bay, Cole Bay and St Peter's. Note that card phones at Juliana airport, although marked as 'téléphone' and displaying instructions in French, do not work with French phone cards. **Internet:** *Notions*, cybercafé on the airport road near Simpson Bay. *St Maarten Yacht Club Marina Business Centre* and *Simpson Bay Marina Business Centre* have computers and email service. **Medical facilities** There is a new hospital on Cay Hill with 60 beds, all basic specialism, a haemodialyse department and 24-hr emergency services, T31111. **Ambulance:** T22111. A helicopter airlift to Puerto Rico is available for extreme medical emergencies. **Media** Newspapers: free weekly newspaper, *Today*, published in English and distributed in hotels, retail stores and other outlets on Sint Maarten, Anguilla and St Barthélémy as well as on regional airlines. *The Chronicle, The Herald Caribbean* and *The Guardian* come out six times a week and *Newsday* twice a week. After 1500 in the shops on Front Street or at the airport you can find US newspapers (*New York Times, Miami Herald* and *San Juan Star*). American magazines (30-40% more expensive than the USA) are especially good at Paiper Garden, Front Street. **Radio:** PJD2 Radio is on medium wave 1300 kHz and FM 102.7 mHz. **Places of worship** Many denominations are represented. Seventh Day Adventist, Anglican, Baptist, Jehovah's Witness, Methodist, Roman Catholic, Church of Christ, Baha'i, The New Testament Church of God. Look in *Today* (see below) for details of services. **Tourist offices** Imperial building, 23 Walter Nisbeth Rd, 3rd Flr, T22337, F22734, www.st-maarten.com. Well supplied with brochures and guides to St Maarten, and the monthly *St Maarten Holiday*. Sightseeing tours available by bus or by car. **Useful numbers** Police: T22222. **Fire:** T54222. **Ambulance:** T22111. **Hospital 24-hr emergency services**, T31111.

Background

History

See also background to the Netherlands Antilles, the ABC chapter, page 1037

The Amerindians who originally settled on the island named it Sualouiga, meaning land of salt. The belief that Columbus discovered the island on his second voyage in 1493 is disputed, with historians now claiming it was Nevis he named St Martin of Tours, and that later Spanish explorers misinterpreted his maps. Nevertheless, the Spanish were not interested in settling the island and it was not until 1629 that some French colonists arrived in the north, and then in 1631 the Dutch were attracted to the south part by the salt ponds. By this time, there were no Caribs left on the island and the two nationalities lived amicably enough together. Spain then reconsidered and occupied Sint Maarten from 1633 to 1648, fending off an attack by Peter Stuyvesant in 1644 which cost him his leg.

When the Spanish left, the Dutch and French settlers returned and after a few territorial skirmishes, they divided the island between them with the signing of the 23 March 1648 Treaty of Mount Concordia. Popular legend has it that the division was settled with a race starting from Oyster Pond. The Frenchman went north and the Dutchman went south, but the Frenchman walked faster because he drank only wine while the Dutchman's penchant for Genever (a drink similar to gin) slowed him down. Since 1648, however, St Maarten has changed hands 16 times, including brief occupations by the British, but the Dutch-French accord has been peaceably honoured at least since it was last revised in 1839.

At the height of its colonial period, sugar cane and livestock were the main agricultural activities, although the poor soil and lack of rain meant they were not very profitable. The abolition of slavery in 1863 broke up the plantation system and the population began to decline as ex-slaves left to look for work elsewhere. Most of the salt produced from the Great Salt Pond behind Philipsburg was exported to the USA and neighbouring islands, but by 1949 this industry had also ended and a further exodus to other islands took place. The remaining population survived on subsistence farming, fishing and remittances from relatives abroad.

However, in 50 years the island has become unrecognizable, hotels and resorts, villas and guest houses now line the shore and there is no bay untouched by tourism. In 1997, 885,956 cruise ship passengers spent a day in St Maarten (not including yachties), while 647,721 people landed at Princess Juliana International Airport to visit St Maarten (and French St-Martin), attracted by the duty-free shopping, casinos and a wide range of accommodation, as well as the beaches and watersports. Little of historical interest remains, except the walls of Fort Amsterdam overlooking Philipsburg, and a few other ruined fortifications, but this has not hindered the tourist industry, which is among the most successful in the region. For those who want more than sun, sand and sea, St Maarten's well-developed transport links make it an excellent jumping-off place for visiting other islands. Nearly 250,000 people are usually classified as in transit, making their way to other destinations with only a brief stop over in St Maarten.

Controversy arose in 1992 over the Dutch Government's decision in July to introduce 'higher supervision' of the St Maarten Island Council following an inquiry into its administration. The change meant that expenditure decisions by the island government had to be approved by the Lieutenant-Governor. In February 1993 supervision was tightened further with all major decisions requiring approval. There had been many reports of crime, corruption and financial maladministration and the USA was particularly concerned about suspected widespread drug smuggling through Juliana airport, where there were no customs controls. During 1993 several prominent members of government, including the hugely influential Dr Claude Wathey, leader of the St Maarten Democratic Party and former Prime Minister, his son Al Wathey, formerly the airport board chairman, Ralph Richardson, the former Lieutenant Governor, and Frank Arnell, the airport manager as well as other influential colleagues, came under judicial investigation in connection with irregularities in the airport and Great Bay harbour expansion projects. Investigations were also carried out in France, Italy and other countries. In 1994, the four men were jailed for forgery and perjury, while two Italians were jailed for drugs trafficking (Dr Wathey died in January 1998). The St Maarten executive council agreed to introduce customs checks at seaports and Juliana airport from January 1994 in an effort to control trafficking in arms, drugs and illegal immigration. The higher supervision order was extended until 1 June 1994 and France and the Netherlands agreed jointly to monitor air and sea traffic around the island.

In 1994 the electorate were asked whether they wished to remain part of the Netherlands Antilles, have separate status within the kingdom (like Aruba), have complete integration with the Netherlands, or be independent. At the referendum in October, 59.8% voted for the status quo, while about 30% wanted separate status. This was the lowest vote in favour of remaining in the Federation, compared with 90.6% in St Eustatius, 86.3% in Saba, 88% in Bonaire and 73.6% (in 1993) in Curaçao.

The island's council election in April 1995 gave five seats each to the Democratic Party (DP) and the St Maarten Patriotic Alliance (SPA). The latter had governed since June 1994 in alliance with the Progressive Democratic Party. The Serious Alternative People's Party (SAPP) won the remaining seat on the 11-member council and agreed with the DP to form an alliance which took office in July. The DP won 4,323 of the 9,536 votes cast against 4,177 for the SPA, while the DP's leader, Sarah Westcott-Williams won the highest individual vote with 2,204. However, the coalition government collapsed in October 1995 following the resignation of one DP commissioner and two from the SAPP.

In May 1999 new island council elections were held which produced a majority government and marked the end of unstable coalitions. The DP won seven seats, the SPA three and the National Progressive Party (NPP) one.

Netherland Antilles

The people The population of at least 62,000 (33,459 in St-Maarten and 28,518 in St Martin) has mushroomed with the tourist boom: the 1950 St Maarten census gave the total population at 1,484. While many of the residents were formerly ex-patriates who returned to their island, there is a large proportion who have come from other Caribbean islands to seek work. Few people speak Dutch, the official language, although Papiamento has increased with the migration of people from the ABC Dutch islands. Nearly everybody speaks English and there is a large Spanish-speaking contingent of guest workers from the Dominican Republic.

French Antilles

15

French Antilles

The French Caribbean Islands form two Départements d'Outremer: one comprises Martinique, and the other Guadeloupe with its offshore group, Marie-Galante, Les Saintes, La Désirade, and two more distant islands, Saint-Barthélémy and the French part of Saint-Martin (shared with the Dutch). Geographically, the main islands form the north group of the Windward Islands, with the ex-British island of Dominica in the centre of them. Saint-Barthélémy and Saint-Martin are in the Leeward group.

The larger islands of Guadeloupe and Martinique both have an area of mountains and forests where you can find rushing streams, waterfalls and pools for bathing in. The best beaches, however, are in the more arid parts, which are flatter. The smaller islands are fairly hilly but dry, particularly those in the Leewrd group. Some beautiful French colonial architecture remains, with intricate fretwork in the gingerbread style, but the modern buildings are concrete blocks and lack charm, looking as though they have been picked up in France and dropped on the islands by mistake.

The islands have the same status as any Département in European France. The inhabitants are French citizens. The currency is the French franc (F). The people speak French. Visitors are often surprised by how French the islands are. The connection with France confers many benefits on the islands, which enjoy French standards of social legislation etc, but it also drives up the cost of living, which is rather higher than elsewhere in the Caribbean.

Essentials

Before you travel

Documents The regulations are the same as for France. In most cases the only document required for entry is a **passport**, the exceptions being citizens of Australia, South Africa, Bolivia, Dominica, St Lucia, Barbados, Jamaica, Trinidad, Haiti, Honduras, El Salvador, Dominican Republic, Turkey, when a **visa** is required. In 2000, for a trial period of three months, St Lucians were allowed to enter without visas for visits of up to 15 days. If successful, the scheme may be extended to other countires in the Organization of Eastern Caribbean States (OECS). Any non-EU citizen staying longer than three months needs an extended visa. Citizens of the United States and Canada staying less than three weeks do not need a passport, although some form of identification with a photo is required. A valid passport is recommended to avoid unnecessary problems and delays and is required for everybody staying more than three weeks. An onward ticket is necessary but not always asked for.

Customs With the abolition of EU frontiers, Europeans are able to bring back the same entitlements as from mainland France. However you could run into problems if returning via Antigua, with a long, uncomfortable wait in transit. Take a direct flight to France if buying in bulk.

Money Banking hours are given under the various islands, as are the names of banks. There are money-changing offices in the big hotels and at airports. The French franc is the legal tender, but US$ are preferred in Saint-Martin and are widely accepted elsewhere. There is no limit to travellers' cheques and letters of credit being imported, but a declaration of foreign bank notes in excess of 3,500F must be made.

Vaccination Vaccination certificates are not required if you are French, American or Canadian, but if you come from South America or some of the Caribbean Islands an international certificate for small pox and yellow fever vaccinations is compulsory.

Food and drink

Restaurants Restaurants divide fairly neatly into generally very expensive French cuisine or the more moderate créole. There is not much evidence of the *plat du jour* as there would be in France. Children may find créole food rather spicy. Fast food hamburger bars are not common.

Local cuisine A delightful blend of French, African, and Indian influences is found in Créole dishes, and the cuisine is quite distinctive. Basic traditional French and African recipes using fresh local ingredients; seafood, tropical fruits and vegetables are combined with exotic seasonings to give original results rich in colour and flavour. Here are local specialities not to be missed.

   Ti-boudin, a soft well-seasoned sausage; *court bouillon de poisson* or *blaff* is *lambis* (conch), red snapper or sea urchin cooked with lime, white wine and onions; *ragout*, a spicy stew often made with *chatrous* (squid), or conch, with meat; *colombo*, a recipe introduced by Hindu immigrants in the last century, is goat, chicken, pork or lamb in a thick curry sauce; *poulet au coco*, chicken prepared with onions, *piment* (hot peppers) and coconut; chunks of steakfish (usually tuna, salmon, or red snapper) marinaded and grilled; *morue* (salt cod) made into sauces and *accras* (hot fishy fritters from Africa) or *chiquetaille* (grilled), or used in *feroce d'avocat*, a pulp of avocados, peppers and manioc flour; *langouste* (lobster), *Crabe* (crab), *écrevisses, ouassous, z'habitants* (crayfish), *gambas* (prawns) and *vivaneau* (snapper) are often fricaséed, grilled or barbecued with hot pepper sauce. Also popular are *crabe farci* (stuffed crab) and *oursin farci* (stuffed urchin).

   Main dishes are usually accompanied by white rice, breadfruit, yams or *patate douce* (sweet potatoes) with plantains and red beans or lentils. *Christophine au gratin*; a large knobbly pear-shaped vegetable grilled with grated cheese and breadcrumbs, or a plate of fresh *crudités* are delicious, lighter side dishes.

Tourist offices overseas

Belgium Service Official Français du
Tourisme: 21 Avenue de la Toison d'Or, 1060
Brussels, T25130762, F25143375.

Canada French Government Tourist Office,
1981 Avenue MacGill College, Suite 490,
Montréal, Quebec, H 3A 2W9, T514-2884264,
F8448901; 30 St Patrick Street, Suite 700,
Toronto, T416-5934723, F9797587; Office du
Tourisme de la Martinique au Canada, 2159
Rue Mackay, Montréal PQH 3G 2JZ,
T514-8448566, F8448901.

France Office Inter-Régional du Tourisme
des Antilles Françaises, 2 Rue des Moulins,
75001 Paris, T44778600, F49260363; Gîtes de
France, 35 Rue Godot de Mauroy, 75009 Paris,
T47422543. Guadeloupe Tourist Office, 43 rue
des Tilleuls, 92100 Boulogne,
T33-01-46040088, F46047403. Saint-Martin
Tourist Office, 12, rue de Madrid, 75008 Paris,
T3301-53424100, F43873285.

Germany Bureau du Tourisme de la
Guadeloupe, Bethmannstrasse 58, 6000
Frankfurt AM Main 1, T0049-69283293,
F69287544, guadeloupe@karibik.org;
Fremdenverkehsamt Martinique,
Westendstrasse 47-D, 60325 Frankfurt am
Main, T49-6997-590497, F6997-590499.

Italy Via Larga, 7, 20122 Milan,
T392-58486655, F58486222.

Spain Administration: Gran Via, 59-28013
Madrid, T5418808, F5412412.

Sweden/Denmark Ny Ostergade 33, DK
1101 Copenhagen, T45-33114912,
F45-33142048; The Commercial
Representative Office Nordic Countries, PO
Box 4031 Fregativägen 14, South 181 04
Lidingo, T468-7655865, F7659360.

Switzerland Löwenstrasse 59, Postfach
7226, 8023 Zurich, T12213578, F12121644.

UK 178 Piccadilly, London, T020-76292869,
F020-74936594.

USA French West Indies Tourist Office, 444
Madison Av, 16th floor, New York, NY 10020,
T212-7571125, F212-8387855; The Martinique
Promotion Bureau, 444 Madison Av, 16th floor,
New York, NY10022, T212-8387800, F8387855,
Martinique@nyo.com; French Government
Tourist Office, 645 North Michigan Avenue,
Suite 3360, Chicago, Illinois 60611,
T312-7517800; French Government Tourist
Office, 9454 Wilshire Blvd, Beverley Hills, CA
90212, T310-2716665; Guadeloupe Tourist
Office, 161 Washington Valley Road, Warren,
NJ 07059, T88-4-GUADELOUPE,
F732-3020809. French Government Tourist
Office, Suite 205, 2305 Cedar Spring Road,
Dallas, TX 75201, F214-7204010.

Les Antilles, produced by Nouvelles Frontières
(Les Éditions JA, Second edition, Paris, 1987),
contains both practical information and very
interesting background information on
geography, local customs and architecture,
and the French Antilles' place in the
Caribbean and in relation to France.

French Antilles

Exotic fresh fruit often ends the meal; pineapples, papayas, soursops and bananas can be found all year round and mangoes, mandarin oranges, guavas and sugar apples in season. Ice cream (*glace*) is also a favourite dessert.

As in other Caribbean islands the main alcoholic drink is rum. Martiniquan rum has a distinctive flavour and is famous for its strength. There are two main types: white rum (*blanc*) and dark rum (*vieux*) which has been aged in oak vats and is usually more expensive. *Ti punch* is rum mixed with cane syrup or sugar and a slice of lime and is a popular drink at any time of the day. *Shrub* is a delicious Christmas liqueur made from rum and orange peel. *Planteur* is a rum and fruit juice punch. There is a huge choice of Martiniquan rum, recommended brands being Trois Rivières, Mauny, Neisson and St Clément. There are different brands on Guadeloupe. French wines are available, although even red wine is usually served as a cool drink with ice. The local beer is *Lorraine*, a clean-tasting beer which claims to be 'brewed for the tropics'. *Corsaire*, made in Guadeloupe, is bitter tasting and insipid. Locally-brewed

Drink
Tap water is drinkable

Guinness, at 7% alcohol by volume, stronger than its Irish counterpart, is thick and rich. *Malta*, a non-alcoholic beverage similar to malt beer, is produced by most breweries and said to be full of minerals and vitamins. Thirst quenching non-alcoholic drinks to look out for are the fresh fruit juices served in most snackbars and cafés. Guava, soursop, passion fruit, mandarin, and sugar cane juice are commonly seen.

Guadeloupe

Population: 422,000

Guadeloupe is really two islands, Basse-Terre and Grande-Terre, separated by the narrow bridged strait of the Rivière Salée. To the west is mountainous Basse-Terre, with the volcano Grande Soufrière (1,484 m) at its centre. It has an area of 848 sq km, a total of 150,000 inhabitants, and the administrative capital of the same name on its southwest coast. The commercial capital is Pointe-à-Pitre, situated in the flat half of the island, Grande-Terre. The names of the two parts shows a most un-Gallic disregard of logic as Basse-Terre is the higher and Grande-Terre is the smaller; possibly they were named by sailors, who found the winds lower on the Basse-Terre and greater on the Grande-Terre side.

Ins and outs

Getting there

See transport, page 708, for further details

Air From Europe Like Martinique, Guadeloupe is on *Air France*'s direct route from Paris (about eight hours). Other French airlines with services to Guadeloupe include *AOM French Airlines* (from Paris), *Air Liberté* (Paris), *Aerolyon* (Lyon, Marseille, Nantes, Toulouse). *Condor* flies from Frankfurt. **From North America** *Air Canada* has direct flights from Montréal. *Air France* and *Air Guadeloupe* fly from Miami. *American Eagle* has flights from San Juan, with connections from the USA. **From the Caribbean** *LIAT* offers inter-Caribbean connections to Antigua, Barbados, Dominica, Fort-de-France and St Lucia. *Air Guadeloupe* connects Pointe-à-Pitre with Antigua, Dominica, Fort-de-France (lots of flights every day), La Désirade, Marie-Galante, Port-au-Prince, St Barts, Sint-Maarten, St Martin, San Juan, Santo Domingo and Terre-de-Haut. Other services include *Air France* from Antigua, Caracas, Cayenne, Fort-de-France and Port-au-Prince; Cubana from Havana. **Sea** Numerous cruise lines sail from US and French ports. Pointe-à-Pitre has berths for four cruise ships and marinas for yachts. There are fast, scheduled ferry services between Pointe-à-Pitre, Marie-Galante, Les Saintes, Dominica and Martinique (see page 773 for details). *ATE/Trans Antilles Express* (*L'Express des Iles*) offers excursions with accommodation, day trips with lunch, or transport only, T831245, F911105, La Darse, Pointe-à-Pitre. Agents include T-Maritimes Brudey Frères, Centre St-John Perse, 97110 Pointe-à-Pitre, T916087. You can get a small motor-sail vessel to Dominica from Pointe-à-Pitre for not much less than the flight. The boat leaves at 1300, three days a week, takes two hours, is not very comfortable and sea sickness is a distinct possibility.

Getting around

Bicycles can be rented. Hitchhiking is no problem & if you speak French it is a great way to meet local people, who are very friendly

Bus There are three main bus terminals in Pointe-à-Pitre, see page 708 for specific running times. It is possible to cover the whole island by bus in a day – cheap, interesting and easy, but exhausting. You can just stop the bus at the side of the road or wait at the bus stations in the villages. Buses are crowded and play zouk music at top volume (exhilarating or deafening, depending on your mood); have your money ready when you get off.

Car Car hire is available mainly at the airport. A small, old Peugeot will cost about 350F per day. In Pointe-à-Pitre, there is a small office above an ice cream parlour on Avenida V Hugues, just off Place de la Victoire, which has a small selection. Rental can also be arranged through the major hotels. International and local agencies are represented. Pointe-à-Pitre has a dual carriage ring road which runs from Gosier across the Rivière Salée to the industrial centre at Baie-Mahault and south towards Petit-Bourg. It is well used and the driving is very French with dead animals on the road quickly covered with lime. **Taxis** are rather expensive; they are metered and some now accept credit cards. All fares increase at night. They are mainly found at the airports and outside the main hotels, although you can also phone for one.

Essentials

Exchange Hotels give the worst rates, then banks, but their rates vary so shop around. Post offices change dollars but not all makes of travellers' cheque, slow service. The best rates can be found in Edouard Saingolet, Bureau de Change, rues Nozières et Barbès, Pointe-à-Pitre (T903463), open daily (morning only Saturday and Sunday). There is one exchange facility at the airport and it is closed all day Monday. There is a 24-hour automatic teller at Bas-du-Fort marina which accepts most European currencies, US, EC and Canadian dollars and yen. It can be difficult to change EC dollars.

Departure tax No departure tax. It is included in fares.

Ports of entry (French flag) Deshaies, Basse-Terre and Pointe-à-Pitre are ports of entry but Iles des Saintes is not. No charge for EU or US citizens. French forms to fill in.

Anchorages Pointe-à-Pitre has good groceries, marine supplies, fuel, water, free 220 electricity, bus to town from marina. Free

dinghy dock in marina. Duty free fuel when you clear out of the country. Charter companies include Moorings, Jet Sea, Stardust ATM.

Voltage 220 volts AC, 50 cycles.

Hours of business Shops: 0800-1200, 1430-1700 weekdays, morning only on Saturday; **government offices**: open 0730-1300, 1500-1630 Monday and Friday, 0730-1300 Tuesday-Thursday. **Banks**: 0800-1200, 1400-1600 Monday to Friday.

Useful addresses Gendarmerie: T820059, **Police**: T821317 in Pointe-à-Pitre, 811155 in Basse-Terre; **Nautical assistance**: T829108.

Public holidays New Year's Day; Easter Sunday and Easter Monday; Labour Day on 1 May; Ascension Day; Whit Monday; 8 May VE Day; 27 May Slavery Abolition Day; National/Bastille Day on 14 July; Schoelcher Day on 21 July; Assumption Day in August; All Saints Day on 1 November; All Souls Day on 2 November Armistice Day on 11 November and Christmas Day.

French Antilles

The temperature on the coasts varies between 22°C and 30°C, but is about 3°C lower in the **Climate** interior. January to April is the dry season (called *carême*), July to November the wet season (*l'hivernage*), with most rain falling from September to November. Trade winds moderate temperatures the year round.

Flora and fauna

Guadeloupe is in some ways reminiscent of Normandy or Poitou, especially the farms, built in those regional styles. The comparatively low-lying Grande-Terre is mainly given over to sugar cane and livestock-raising. Mostly a limestone plateau, it does have a hilly region, Les Grands-Fonds, and a marshy, mangrove coast extending as far north as Port-Louis on its west flank.

The island's national park (**Seventh French National Park**, Habitation Beausoleil, BP 13 Montéran, 97120 Saint-Claude, T802425, F800546) includes 30,000 ha of forest land in the centre of Basse-Terre (known as the **Parc Naturel**), which is by far the more scenic part. As the island is volcanic there are a number of related places to visit. The park has no gates, no opening hours and no admission fee. Do not pick flowers, fish, hunt, drop litter, play music or wash anything in the rivers. Trails have been marked out all over the park, including to the dome of Soufrière volcano with its fumaroles, cauldrons and sulphur fields (see below). The national park includes three protected land and sea reserves, open to the public: **Les Réserves Naturelles des Pitons du Nord et de Beaugendre, La Réserve Naturelle du Grand Cul-de-Sac Marin** and **La Réserve Naturelle de Pigeon**, or **Réserve Cousteau** (see below). The waters after which the Caribs named the island come hot (as at the Ravine Chaude springs on the Rivière à Goyaves), tumbling (the waterfalls of the Carbet River and the Cascade aux Écrevisses on the Corossol), and tranquil (the lakes of Grand Étang, As de Pique and Étang Zombi).

A **Maison du Volcan** at Saint-Claude (open 1000-1800) and a **Maison de la Fôret** (1000-1700) on the Route de la Traversée give information on the volcano and its surrounding forest. From the Maison de la Forêt there are 10, 20 and 60-minute forest walks which will take you deep among the towering trees. The **Cascade**

Guadeloupe & outer islands

aux Ecrevisses, a waterfall and small pool, is about 2 km from the Maison (clearly marked) and is a good place to swim and spend the day; popular with the locals. Also on the Route de la Traversée is the **Parc Zoologique et Botanique** above Mahaut, which allows you to see many of the species which exist in the Natural Park, such as mongoose, racoon, iguana and land turtle, unfortunately in very small cages.
■ *Open 0900-1700. Entrance 25F, children 15F. T988352. It is worth a visit for the fine*

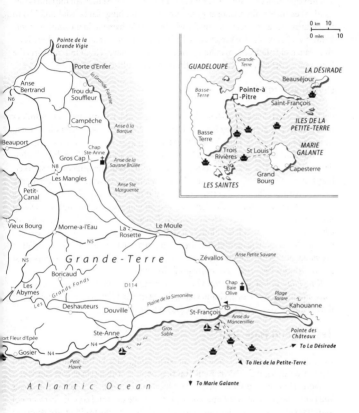

● *Les Saintes & Marie Galante*

panoramic views from the café (free drink included in entrance ticket) and the Ti-Racoon *restaurant is simple but excellent, serves lunch daily except Mon.*

The national park's emblem is the *raton laveur* (racoon) which, although protected, is very rare. You are much more likely to see birds and insects in the park. On La Désirade a few agoutis survive, as well as iguana, which can also be found on Les Saintes. Much of the island's indigenous wildlife has vanished.

The vegetation of Basse-Terre ranges from tropical forest (40% of the land is forested: trees such as the mahogany and gommier, climbing plants, wild orchids) to the cultivated coasts: sugar cane on the windward side, bananas in the south and coffee and vanilla on the leeward. As well as sugar cane on Grande-Terre, there is an abundance of fruit trees (mango, coconut, papaya, guava, etc). On both parts the flowers are a delight, especially the anthuriums and hibiscus.

Diving and marine life

On the Leeward Coast (Côte-Sous-le-Vent, or the Golden Corniche), is the **Underwater Reserve** developed by Jacques Cousteau. *Nautilus*, from Malendure beach, south of Mahaut, black sand, T988908, F988566, is a glass-bottom boat which takes you round the marine park, departs 1030, 1200, 1430 and 1600, 80F adults, 40F children 5-12 years. The boat anchors for about 15 minutes off **Ilet Pigeon** for snorkelling, but it is rather deep to see much. In wet weather the water becomes too murky to see anything. The boat is often booked solid by cruise ship visitors. There is a créole restaurant on the beach where you can eat while waiting for the boat. Diving trips can be arranged at *Les Heures Saines*, T988663, at Rocher de Malendure, or *Chez Guy et Christian*, Plaisir Plongée Caraïbe, T988243, F988284, friendly, recommended for beginners' confidence, well-equipped, packages with accommodation provided, at Pigeon, Bouillante. There are lots of other companies along this coast and on Grand-Terre, with no shortage of dive sites.

King Papyrus is a glass-bottom boat which runs excursions through the Rivière Salée and the mangroves of Grand Cul de Sac Marin, to l'Îlet Caret and coral reef off the northeast coast of Basse-Terre, see Daysails below.

Beaches and watersports

Guadeloupe has excellent beaches for swimming, mostly between Gosier and St-François on Grande-Terre. **Petit Havre** is popular with its small coves and reefs offshore. Here are mostly fishermen and locals and a small shed selling fish meals and beer. The best is at **Ste-Anne** where the fine white sand and crystal clear water of a constant depth of 1.5 m far from shore make idyllic bathing; the **Plage du Bourg** in town is ideal for young children, the **Plage de la Caravelle** is excellent with access only through the *Club Med*. About 2 km from the town is the **Plage de Bois Jolan**, reached down a track, where the water is shallow enough to walk to the protecting reef. Further east are good beaches at St-François and the 11-km road to Pointe des Colibris skirts the Anse Kahouanne with lots of tracks going down to the sea; sand is limited but there are snorkelling possibilities.

On the north coast of the peninsula is **Plage Tarare**, the island's only nude bathing beach where there is a good restaurant by the car park. It is not a good place for women to arrive unaccompanied. **Plage de l'Anse à la Gourde** has good sand and is popular with campers at weekends. More deserted beaches can be found on the northeast of Grande-Terre.

On the leeward coast of Basse-Terre are some good beaches. South of Pointe Noire on the west coast is **Plage Caraïbe**, which is clean, calm and beautiful, with restaurant *Le Reflet* (helpful owners), picnic facilities, toilets and a shower. A small, black sand beach, **La Grand Anse**, just west of Trois Rivières, has a barbecue and drinks (expensive) on the beach and a shower and toilets (which do not always work). In the northwest, La Grande Anse, 30 minutes' walk north of Deshaies, is superb and undeveloped with no hotels, golden sand but no snorkelling except round a large rock where the current is quite strong. Body surfing is good when the waves are big. Camping sites in the area and a beach restaurant at the south end with charcoal-grilled chicken and rice. There are several snack bars half way along the beach, serving sandwiches and drinks. On Sunday local people sell hot créole food quite cheaply. The beaches on the north coast of Basse-Terre can be very dangerous and at **Plage de Clugny** there are warning signs not to swim as there have been several drownings.

Most of the hotels on the seaboard offer windsurfing for guests and visitors, and some arrange waterskiing and diving courses. Windsurfers gather at the *UCPA Hotel Club* in Saint François. The tradewinds are best December-May and the best places are St-François, Ste-Anne and Gosier. Courses and board rental are available at *Sport Away Ecole Nathalie Simon*, St-François, T/F887204, *LCS*, Ste-Anne, T881517, F881521, and *UCPA*, St-François, T886480, F884350. Surfing is also now popular at Le Moule, Port-Louis, La Pointe des Châteaux, Sainte-Anne and St-François. The *Comité Guadeloupéen de Surf* is at the *Karukera Surf Club*, Le Moule, T231093. There is also the *Arawak Surf Club*, T236068, F237589.

Sailing boats can be chartered for any length of time from Captain Lemaire, Carénage A, Route du Gosier, 97110 Pointe-à-Pitre. With a crew of three the cost works out at about US$75-100 per person per day, excluding food, or US$250-300 per boat. There are two marinas between Pointe-à-Pitre and Gosier, and good, shallow-draught anchorage at Gosier. The Route du Rhum boat race is held every four years, with multi-hull boats racing between Saint-Malo and Pointe-à-Pitre. The record is 14 days, 10 hours and 8 minutes.

Sailing

There are several excursions offered, ranging from the booze cruise or sunset cruise variety to more scientific and educational trips. *King Papyrus* at Marina Bas du Fort, Gosier, T909298, F907171, takes you on an all day cruise to Ilet Caret with a visit to the mangroves. The mangroves can also be visited on water scooters, T887193 in St-François, or T850277 for excursions starting from Morne-à-l'Eau. *La Compagnie des Bateaux Verts, the Green Boat Company*, Marina Bas-du-Fort, T907717, F907920, starts with the Aquarium and then takes you to the marine park on the 48-passenger glass-bottomed *Kio*, with scientists on board to explain the oceanographic ecosystems. *Falling Star*, a 46-ft catamaran, offers all-day sails to the island of Petite-Terre, T885396, F887794. *Awak*, a 46-ft vedette with a glass bottom, also goes to Petite-Terre, T885353, F886043. From Pigeon Buillante there are several glass bottomed boat excursions: *Aquarius* has three 2-hour trips, at 1000, 1230 and 1500, T988730, F901185. *Nautilus* has two glass-bottomed boats and a submarine for visits to the ocean floor, see above.

Day sails

Deep sea fishing is best off the Côte-sous-le-vent, where the fishing area is about 20 minutes from Ilet Pigeon. Blue marlin, kingfish, barracuda, bonita can be fished all year round, but there are seasons for other species. There are lots of fishing contests organized throughout the year. Well-equipped boats go out for full or half day excursions from Bouillante: *Fishing Club Antilles*, T987010, Francis Ricard, T987377; and from Le Rocher de Malendure: Franck Nouy, T987084, who also offers 5 and 8-day trips. Fishing boats also go out from Marina Bas du Fort and Gosier.

Fishing

Hiking in the Parc Naturel, contact the Organisation des Guides de Montagne de la Caraïbe (OGMC), Maison Forestière, 97120 Matouba, T800579, a guided hike to La Soufrière will cost around 300 F, make sure the guide speaks a language you understand. Approximate hiking times, mileage and description of terrain and flora are included in the booklet *Promenades et Randonnées*. **Horseriding** at *Le Criolo*, Saint-Félix, T97190 Gosier, T840486, La Martingale, La Jaille, T262839 and *Ranch Caraïbes*, T821154. Also *Horse Farm*, St-Claude, T815221, F819073, for groups of

Other sports

French Antilles

6-12 people riding in the forest. **Tennis**, with lighting for night games, at several hotels, including *Auberge de la Vieille Tour*, *PLM Arawak*, *Salako*, *Creole Beach*, *Novotel*, and *Village Viva* (also squash, T908766), all at Gosier, *Méridien*, *Hamak*, *Trois-Mâts* at Saint-François. For tennis clubs, contact *Ligue de Tennis*, T909097, Centre Lamby Lambert, same phone, *Marina Tennis Club*, T908291, *Amical Tennis Club*, same phone, all at Gosier. In August a keenly watched **cycling** race takes place over 10 days, going to all parts of the island. Le Tour Cycliste de la Guadeloupe draws competitors from Guadeloupe and internationally and is an excuse for festivities and parties. The Association Guadeloupéenne de VTT (mountain biking association) can be contacted at Pointe-à-Pitre, T828267. For cycling tours of Guadeloupe, *Karucyclo*, T822139, 284659. There is one 18-hole, international **golf course** at Saint-François (T884187, F884220), designed by Robert Trent Jones on the edge of the lagoon.

Bullock cart racing is popular on the west coast of Grande-Terre and draws large crowds. They race along the flat, then turn sharply and charge up a steep hill. The wheels are then chocked and they have to see how far they can get, zig-zag fashion, with about 10 minutes of very hard work. Much shouting, plenty of beer, food tents and an overloud PA system. **Cockfighting** is very popular and there are pits all over the place. The season runs from November to July and involves serious gambling. The only pit open all year is Bélair, Morne-à-l'Eau, Tuesday, Thursday, Friday and Sunday, T242370. Visitors are welcome.

Pointe-à-Pitre

Population: 141,000 *On Grande-Terre at the south end of the Rivière Salée, Pointe-à-Pitre is the chief commercial centre of Guadeloupe near both the airport shipping port. The city lies to the south of the Route Nacional N1 and any of the intercepts will take you to the city centre. It is quite compact, a functional city, variously described as characterless, or colourful and bustling. Its early colonial buildings were largely destroyed by an earthquake in 1843; nowadays it is an odd mixture of parts which could have been transplanted from provincial France and parts which are Caribbean, surrounded by low-cost housing blocks.*

Sights The central **Place de la Victoire** was once the site of a guillotine, and the streets adjacent to it contain the oldest buildings. Having been refurbished in 1989 it lost several of its large trees in Hurricane Hugo but there are still some flame trees at the north end and pleasant gardens. In the middle is a statue to Félix Eboue (1884-1944), a Governor General. There is a bandstand and lots of cafés surrounding the park with tables outside, very pleasant but crowded with office workers at lunch time. The buildings around the park are a mixture of coloured tin roofs and concrete. At its south end is **La Darse**, where the inter-island ferries tie up. When the boats arrive/depart there is plenty of activity and chaotic scenes with buses and taxis fighting for space. At the southwest corner of the Place is a war memorial dedicated to *La Guadeloupe et ses enfants, morts pour La France 1914-18*, flanked by two First World War guns. Behind it is the tourist office (quite helpful, some English spoken). On the east side of the Square is the Renaissance Cinema.

The **Place de l'Eglise** lies northwest of the Place de la Victoire behind the *Hotel Normandie* and contains the ochre-coloured **Basilique de St Pierre et St Paul**, an 1830s structure held up by unusual metal columns supporting a gallery running around the top of the church with some elaborate gingerbread-style metal work. Outside there is a bubbling fountain and a statue of Admiral Gourbeyre who helped the people of Pointe-à-Pitre after the huge 1843 earthquake (see Fort Louis Delgrès, Basse-Terre). The square is flanked by the 1930s art deco Palais de Justice and looks quite attractive with florists on the street.

The colourful red-roofed central **market** place (between rues Peynier, Fréboult, St-John Perse and Schoelcher) is indeed bustling, with the nearest thing to local

French Antilles

hustlers, women (some wearing the traditional Madras cotton hats) who try to sell you spices, fruit, vegetables or hats. There are other markets on the dockside in Place de la Victoire, between Boulevard Chanzy and the docks and between Boulevard Légitimus and the cemetery. Local handicrafts, particularly Madras cotton (from which the traditional costumes of the *doudous*, or local women, are made), are good buys. Such items are in great contrast to the French fashions, wines and perfumes available at normal French domestic prices in the shops.

Musée Schoelcher celebrates the liberator of the slaves and has exhibits on the slave trade. ■ *0900-1230, 1400-1730, closed Wed, Sat afternoon and Sun, entry 10 F. 24 rue Peynier, T821804.* **Musée Saint-John Perse**, in a lovely colonial-style house,

Pointe-à-Pitre

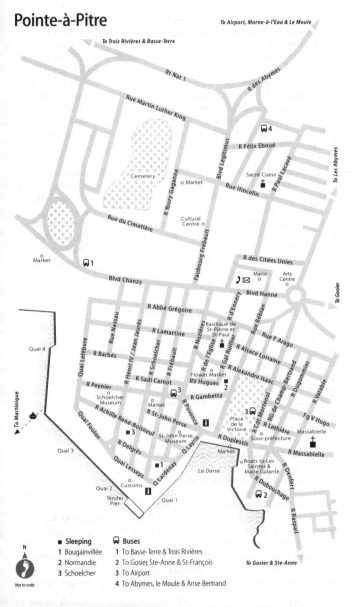

To Airport, Morne-à-l'Eau & Le Moule

To Trois Rivières & Basse-Terre

Rt Nat 1

R des Abymes

Rue Martin Luther King

🚌4

R Félix Eboué

To Les Abymes

Cemetery

Blvd Légitimus

R Youry Gagamne

Market

Sacré Coeur

R Paul Lacavé

Rue Hincelin

Rue du Cimetière

Cultural Centre

Faubourg Frébault

R des Cités Unies

Market

🚌1

Mairie

Arts Centre

Blvd Chanzy

✆ ✉

Blvd Hanne

To Gosier

R Abbé Grégoire

R d'Ennery

Rue Bébian

R Nassau

R Lamartine

R Nozières

Basilique de St-Pierre et St-Paul

R Gal Ruillier

Rue F Arago

Quai 4

Quai Lefabvre

R Barbès

R Henri IV / Jean Jaurès

R Schoelcher

R Frébault

R de l'Église

R Alsace Lorraine

R Alexandre Isaac

R Dugommier

R Variable

R Peynier

R Sadi Carnot

Flower Market

RV Hugues

🚌3

2

To Martinique

Schoelcher Museum

Market

R Poyence

R Gambetta

3

R Cdt Mortenol

R de Champ-Bertrand

Fg V Hugo

Quai Foulon

R Achille René-Boisneuf

R St-John Perse

ℹ

Place de la Victoire

R Lethière

Massabielle

■3

St-John Perse Museum

Q Layrie

Sous-préfecture

R Massabielle

Quai 3

R Delgrès

R Duplessis

Market

Quai Lesseps

Q Lardenay

①1

La Darse

Boats to Les Saintes & Marie Galante

R Denfert

Customs

ℹ

R Dubouchage

🚌2

Quai 2

Q Lardenay

Quai 1

Tender Pier

R Raspail

To Gosier & Ste-Anne

N

👣

Not to scale

■ Sleeping	🚌 Buses
1 Bougainvillée	1 To Basse-Terre & Trois Rivières
2 Normandie	2 To Gosier, Ste-Anne & St-François
3 Schoelcher	3 To Airport
	4 To Abymes, le Moule & Anse Bertrand

is dedicated to the poet and diplomat who was awarded the Nobel Prize for literature in 1960. The upper floors house items relating to the poet, with photographs, personal effects, a library and videothèque, while downstairs has been recreated as a typical 19th-century creole home. ■ *0830-1230, 1430-1730, closed Sat afternoon and Sun, entry 10F, children half price. 9 rue Nozières et A R Boisneuf, T900192.* On AR Boisneuf is the old town hall, being restored. It has a stone/brick ground floor and a fine wooden first floor with an intricately carved gutter.

Grande-Terre

Just outside Pointe-à-Pitre on the N4 towards Gosier is **Bas du Fort**, the site of the large new marina, said to be the biggest in the Caribbean. The aquarium is also here, at Place Créole. It has about 30 ponds with species only from the Caribbean Sea, including fish, turtles and nurse sharks. ■ *Daily 0900-1900, 35F, children under 12, 20F. T909238.* At the next turning off the main road to Gosier (follow the signs to the CORA hypermarket) are the ruins of the 18th-century fortress, **Fort Fleur d'Epée** which once guarded the east approaches to Pointe-à-Pitre. There are now pleasant, shady gardens within the ramparts. Art exhibitions are regularly held either in the officers' quarters or in the underground rooms. Also note the pre-war graffiti with pictures of old sailing ships. Excellent views of Pointe-à-Pitre and across Petit Cul-de-Sac Marin towards the mountains of Basse-Terre. ■ *Daily 0800-1800, free.*

Gosier Gosier itself is the holiday centre of Guadeloupe, with hotels, restaurants, nightclubs. There has been lots of building in this area, even up into the hills above the coast road. Nevertheless, Gosier is a pleasant place with a marvellous picnic spot overlooking a small beach (Plage de l'Anse Canot), a little island about 100 m offshore (Ilet du Gosier) and lighthouse. You could swim to it, there is a channel marked by buoys, but watch out for speed boats. There are a few old wooden houses up the hill from the church, where one or two are restaurants. The modern resort with the large hotels has been built on reclaimed mangrove marshes but the beach is nice with the usual watersports facilities. Gosier is quite sleepy but wakes up at night when the restaurants open.

South coast east of Gosier The south coast between Gosier and **Sainte-Anne** is hilly with cliffs, making it particularly suited to development and on most headlands there are huge condominium developments looking across the sea to Marie-Galante as well as to the south tip of Basse-Terre. Sainte-Anne is a small, pleasant town and has a small church with a slightly crooked spire overlooking the square. Here you will find the **Plage de la Caravelle**, rated by some as the best on the island. The land gradually subsides towards **St-François**, originally a fishing village but now home to *Méridien*, *Hamak*, *La Cocoteraie* and *Plantation Ste-Marthe* which are all luxury hotels. There is a light aircraft landing strip and 18-hole par 71 golf course designed by Robert Trent Jones. You can catch the ferry to La Désirade from here. Watersports equipment can be hired from several companies at the marina.

The rugged **Pointe des Châteaux** at the easternmost tip of the island is part of the national park. From the car park, there is a small, self-guided walk to the cross (**Pointe des Colibris**) erected in 1951, on the point where there are two 'compass' tables showing distances to various landmarks. The limestone outcrop is quite steep in places but the view over the inshore island of **La Roche** (housing a colony of sooty terns, *sterna fuscata*) to La Désirade in the distance, is spectacular especially on a windy day when the sea whips over the rocks. It is worth taking the slightly longer return path around the headland as you get good views of the completely flat **Petite Terre** with its lighthouse and on clear days Marie-Galante (30 km), Les Saintes (60 km) and Dominica (75 km). Note the **Grandes Salines** (salt lagoons) where flamingoes were once common. There are signs on the walk pointing out particular plants and describing features. There is a restaurant selling welcome cold drinks and exotic ice cream. **NB** the beach between the two points is dangerous.

Between Saint-François and **Le Moule**, a colonial mansion at **Zévallos** can be visited. Le Moule was the original capital of Guadeloupe and there are still some cannon from the fortifications against English attack. A precolumbian Arawak village, called Morel, has recently been uncovered on the beautiful sandy beaches north of the town. The **Musée d'Archéologie Précolombienne Edgar Clerc** is at La Rosette. It houses the collection of the researcher, Edgar Clerc, of artefacts found on Guadeloupe and also puts on temporary exhibitions. ■ *0900-1230, 1400-1730, free.* On the Abymes road (D101) from Le Moule is the **Distillerie Bellevue**, makers of Rhum Damoiseau. ■ *Tours Mon-Fri 0800-1400.* From Le Moule you can either return to Point-à-Pitre through **Les Grands Fonds**, or continue up the rugged, rough Atlantic coast to **Pointe de la Grande Vigie** in the extreme north. Take a good map as it is easy to get lost on the little roads in the sugar cane fields. After travelling through the small towns of La Rosette, Gros Cap and Campèche (small restaurant/bar), the countryside becomes more barren. At **Porte d'Enfer** (Hell's Gate) there are a number of barbecue places and little huts at the mouth of an inlet. You can camp here. There is not much sand and the sea can be dangerous, do not go too far out. The coastline from here is very rocky with cliffs and spectacular views.

East coast

French Antilles

Grande-Terre's leeward coast has beaches at Port-Louis and Petit-Canal which are the usual concrete towns with restaurant and filling station. North of Anse Bertrand there is a fine clean, sandy beach, Anse Laborde, which has plenty of shade, a restaurant, and a reef close to the beach, good for snorkelling. Inland, at **Morne-à-l'Eau**, there is a remarkable terraced cemetery built around a natural amphitheatre, very attractive on All Saints Day when lit by thousands of candles. Beware of large crowds.

Leeward coast

Basse-Terre

On the other wing of the island, Basse-Terre is the administrative capital of Guadeloupe and the entire Department. There are some very pretty and authentic old buildings of the colonial period in the city. It is a charming port town of narrow streets and well-laid-out squares with palm and tamarind trees, in a lovely setting between the sea and the great volcano La Soufrière.

There is an interesting 17th-century cathedral and the ruins of **Fort Louis Delgrès**, well-preserved and full of interesting ramparts and bastions (original building 1667, considerably enlarged in the 18th century. The British occupied the fort in 1759-1763 and again in 1810-1816 when it was known as Fort Mathilde. It was fought over and renamed many times, being given its present name in 1989 in memory of the man who escaped the forces of Bonaparte after the reimposition of slavery in 1802. ■ *T813748, daily 0700-1700, free.* The **Grande Caverne**, formerly the billet of the non-commissioned officers, is now a cultural museum, with an exhibition of clothes and photographs of the area. In the cemetery is the tomb of Admiral Gourbeyre. The date of his tomb is not that of his death (he disappeared in 1845) but of 8 February 1843 when there was a huge earthquake; the Admiral was instrumental in disaster relief.

Saint-Claude, a wealthy suburb and summer resort 6 km into the hills, is surrounded by coffee trees and tropical gardens. **Matouba**, above Saint-Claude, is an East Indian village in lovely surroundings (waterfall and springs) with a good restaurant. On the outskirts of the village is a monument to Louis Delgrès on the spot where he and his companions were caught and killed by Napoléon's troops. There are hot springs a good walk above the village (1,281 m) and the bottling plant for the local mineral water.

Sights
Market day is Sat

La Soufrière On Basse-Terre island one of the main sights is the volcano La Soufrière, reached through a primeval rain forest. A narrow, twisty road leads up from Basse-Terre town to a car park at **Savane à Mulets** (1,142 m) from where the crater, 300 m higher, is a 1½ hour climb up the Chemin des Dames, a fascinating trail with changing flora, but becoming eroded through overuse. Buses go to Saint-Claude from where it is a 6-km walk to Savane à Mulets. (The best clothing for the climb is the least; jackets worn against the dampness merely compound the problem; but take a sweater, it can get quite chilly. Leave some spare clothes in the car.) From the top there is a spectacular view, if you are not enveloped in clouds, which is usually the case, observe the mountain for a few days to see whether early morning or midday is clearest, above the lush jungle foliage on the east slopes and sulphurous fumes spurting over yellow and orange rock. The summit is quite flat; the main vent is to the south (the view is more interesting than the Soufrière) and there are discs in the ground to help you find it in the fog.

Basse-Terre

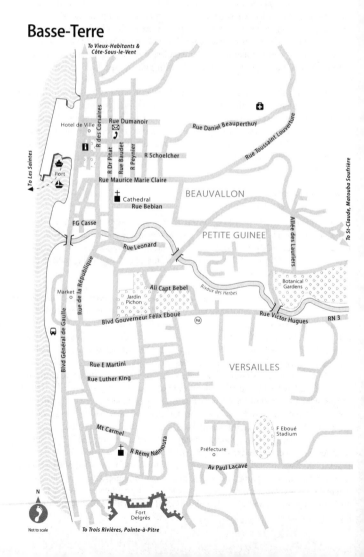

It is possible to come down on the Trace Micael, along a forest path, to the **Chutes de Carbet** waterfalls where the water becomes cool and clear. Carry on down, past more waterfalls, until you get to a car park (often full, parking can be a problem).

If starting from the bottom, take a bus from Capesterre to Routhiers, 10F, then walk along the D3 road until it ends. Follow a trail and within 50 minutes you will reach the third waterfall of 20 m. Go back 100 m and follow the trail upwards again until you reach the 110 m, second waterfall, 711 m above sea level. The path is stony and you have to cross the Carbet on a rope bridge. You can swim in the warm, sulphuric pool below the fall but if you visit when there is rain higher up, beware of flash floods. From here you can continue climbing to the first waterfall, at 125 m, or turn southeast to the picnic place, Aire d'Arrivée, 15 minutes, where there are barbecue stalls (good chicken). The D4 road starts here and descends to St-Sauveur. Along the road to the Chutes du Carbet are **Les Jardins de Saint-Eloi**, flower gardens open to the public. You can buy flowers here or have them packed for export. T863922, F868581.

La Citerne, a neighbouring volcano, has a completely round crater. There is a trail but part requires climbing ladders straight up the wall. There are more leisurely trails to other craters, fumaroles and lakes.

Also on this side are **Grand Etang** and **Etang Zombi**. You can drive, hitchhike or walk down the D4 road from the Chutes de Carbet to the edge of Grand Etang and walk around it, about one hour through lush vegetation. Do not swim in the lake because of bilharzia. There are also marked trails to **Etang de l'As de Pique**, high above Grand Etang to the south on the slope of la Madeleine (two hours) and the Trace de Moscou which leads southwest to the Plateau du Palmiste (2½ hours), from where a road leads down to Gourbeyre. Walk down to St-Sauveur for fine views over banana plantations, the coast and Les Saintes. Allow at least five hours to walk from Capesterre to St-Sauveur via the waterfalls and Grand Etang and wear good hiking shoes.

Parc Naturel You can walk the Trace Victor Hugues, along the main ridge of Basse-Terre (a 29-km hike), and a number of other Traces. A parallel route follows the River Moreau from Goyave up to the Chutes du Moreau, a hike which has been described as "fulfilling all hike lovers' expectations" by one reader. Turn off the N1 opposite the turning to Goyave and signposted to the falls. The made up road turns to gravel and then ends. From here the trail will take you about two hours with five river crossings, so take appropriate footwear. After the fifth crossing the trail rises steeply and there are steel ropes to help you up the slope. From here it is another 10 minutes to the falls. Also recommended is the River Quiock trail, but take the Serie Bleu map; despite being well-marked originally, storm damage has made it difficult to find all the markers. It can be very muddy, wear good boots. You can start from the car park at the Cascade aux Ecrevisses (see above) on the D23. Walk 300 m along the road and take a path to the right (follow the sign to the Pathfinders camp) to Piolet, near the entrance to the Bras-David-Tropical-Parc on the other side of the road. The trail leads down to where the River Quiock meets the larger river Bras-David, carefully cross the river, then the trail heads west along the Quiock until returning to the D23. Hitchhike back to your car (if you have one). The walk will take you 3-4 hours depending on the state of the trail. Other features of the Natural Park are described under Flora and fauna, above. For hiking guides, contact the Bureau des Guides, Basse-Terre, T991873. The Association of Mountain Climbing Guides is at St-Claude, T802425.

East coast With a population of 18,000, **Capesterre-Belle-Eau** is the third largest town and is an important agricultural centre with lots of shops, restaurants and a market. Above the town is the garden of Paul Lacavé, which can be visited. North of the town is the **Allée de Flamboyants**, a spectacular avenue of flame trees which flower May-September. South of the town is the **Allée Dumanoir**, a magnificent 1 km avenue of royal palms.

At **Sainte-Marie**, a statue erected in 1916 commemorates the site of Columbus' landing in 1493. It has now been defaced by nationalists. South of Sainte-Marie, near Carangaise, there is a Hindu temple, built in 1974 by René Komla, richly decorated with statues of Vishnu and Ganesh outside.

The most northern town on this side of Basse-Terre is Petit-Bourg, on the opposite side of the bay from Pointe-à-Pitre and overlooking the little islands in the Petit Cul-de-Sac Marin. Inland from here, at Cabout, is **Le Domaine de Valombreuse, Parc Floral,** where over 1,000 species of flowers can be found and masses of birds enjoying the plant life. Flowers are for sale and can be packed for export and collected at the airport. ■ *0900-1700, T955050, F955090, valomb@outremer.com Guided tours available for groups, restaurant by a river in the forest open for lunch, and for dinner for groups of 10 or more by reservation.*

Southern Basse-Terre Besides the Maisons du Volcan and de la Fôret (see above), there are **Maisons du Café** at La Grivelière, Vieux Habitants (T984842) and a **Centre de Broderie**, Fort l'Olive, Vieux-Fort (daily 0830-1800, T920414), showcasing the work of some 40 lacemakers and embroiderers. Lots of shopping opportunities for tablecloths, bedlinen, clothing or handkerchiefs. Vieux-Fort is on the island's southwest tip, the other side of the Monts Caraïbes from the main Basse-Terre to Pointe-à-Pitre road. There are nice gardens surrounding the lighthouse, with good views. One or two cannon can be seen from the old battery. Good créole restaurant with dance hall attached.

Also visit the ancient Amerindian rock carvings dating from around 300-400 AD, at the **Parc Archéologique des Roches Gravées**, near Trois Rivières, on Basse-Terre's south coast; the most important is a drawing of the head of a Carib chief inside a cave where he is presumably buried. The archipelago of Guadeloupe apparently has the largest concentration of inscribed stones in the world. The site is now in a garden setting, with wardens (it's a good idea to consult the leaflet because some of the engravings on the stones are hard to decipher; many are badly eroded; the pamphlet also explains the garden's trees). ■ *T929188, 0830-1700, 4F entry, children free, The park is a 10-min walk down from the church in Trois Rivières where the buses stop.* Five minutes further down the hill is the boat dock for Les Saintes (paying car park).

West coast Between Basse-Terre town and the Route de la Traversée on the west coast are **Vieux-Habitants**, with a restored 17th-century church, and the underwater reserve (see page 696). Contact the Syndicat d'Initiative de Bouillante, T987348, for information on the Bouillante area, which considers itself the capital of diving, including gîtes, restaurants and dive operators.

A good hike is the Trace des Contrebandiers, three hours, from the Maison du Bois, Pointe Noire. A long but beautiful road takes you to the Trace. When you leave the trail on the other side you need to hitchhike because there are no buses.

North of the Traversée, on the N2, is **Pointe Noire**, a small fishing town. Just south of the town is the **Maison du Bois** at Bourg, a cabinet-making and woodworking centre with a permanent exhibition of household implements, furniture and other things made of wood. ■ *Daily, 0915-1700, 5F.* Also near here at Grand Plaine is the **Maison du Cacao**, with displays on the origin of cocoa, its cultivation and processing and you can taste it. ■ *Daily 0900-1700 except Sun 0900-1300, T982523, F982123.* On the Côte-Sous-Le-Vent are the calm, clean beaches at Ferry and Grand-Anse and the rougher ones at Deshaies. **Deshaies** is attractive, strung out along the beach with cliffs at each end; there are hotels, restaurants (*Le Madras* and the more expensive *Le Mouillage*, offering local food such as fish, créole chicken), basketball and tennis courts. There is an information (unmanned) centre at **Batterie de Deshaies** overlooking the town, with information on the vegetation of the area. All that remains of the old fort are some rusty cannons and the outline of various buildings but it is a popular, shady picnic spot and there are barbecue places.

Round the north of Basse-Terre is the town of **Sainte-Rose** where you can visit the rum museum, **Musée du Rhum**, at the **Distillerie Reimonencq**, Bellevue Ste-Rose. In addition to the exhibitions on sugar and rum making, there is a display of butterflies and other insects in the **Galerie des Plus Beaux Insectes du Monde** and 30 model sailing ships from the earliest to the present day. ■ *T287004, F288255, open 0900-1700 Mon-Sat, adults 40F, children 20-25F.* The road continues south to Lamentin and the hot springs at Ravine Chaude (Thermal Station T257829). Near Lamentin you can visit the **Domaine de Séverin** distillery at La Boucan, still using a paddle wheel. Guided tours are available twice a day on a miniature train. You can taste and buy both white and aged rums and fruit punches and special air packages can be ordered. ■ *Open 0800-1300, 1400-1800, Sun 0900-1200, tours in the morning except Sun. T289196, F283666. Restaurant open for lunch Tue-Sun, and dinner Thu, Fri, Sat, local specialities, accommodation available, recommended.* There is also the **Grosse-Montagne** distillery for guided tours and tastings.

Northern Basse-Terre

French Antilles

Essentials

Pointe-à-Pitre Top of the range is **A-B** *La Bougainvillée*, 9 rue Frébault, T901414, F913682. Comfortable, a/c, plumbing could be better, good expensive restaurant. **A** *Anchorage Hôtel Saint John*, rue Quai Lesseps, T825157, F825261. A/c, TV, balcony, comfortable, very good. **B-C** *Normandie*, 14 Place de la Victoire, T823715. With shower and a/c, cheaper without bath, popular, best to book in advance, restaurant is good. **C-D** *Schoelcher*, rue Schoelcher. not very clean, reasonably-priced restaurant. **C-D** *Relais des Antilles*, corner of rue Massabielle and rue Vatable, just off the Place de la Victoire. Basic, noisy but friendly and cheap, with toilet. **C-D** *Karukera*, 15 rue Alsace-Lorraine. With bath, no fan, not good. **C-D** *Pension Mme Rilsy*, T918171, 34 Bis Rue Pegnier. Includes breakfast, very friendly. Reported to take students only.

Sleeping: Grande-Terre
The tourist board has current hotel price lists (they run an information desk at Raizet airport but do not make reservations)

Bas du Fort Bay/Gosier (tourist area). **LL** *Auberge de la Vieille Tour*, Montauban, 97190 Gosier, T842323, F843343. Named after an 18th-century sugar tower incorporated into the main building, is on a bluff over the sea, beach, pool, tennis, 182 rooms, three two-room bungalows and eight rooms in French colonial style, gourmet restaurant, like a number of others this is a member of PLM-Azur group. Another is **LL-L** *Marissol Bas-du-Fort*, 15 mins from Pointe-à-Pitre, 195 rooms and bungalows, restaurants, discothèque, tennis, beach with watersports and a spa/gym with instructors and physiotherapist, T908444, F908332. **LL-A** *Canella Beach*, Pointe de la Verdure, BP 73, 97190 Gosier, T904400, F904444. 146 studios and suites on waterfront, a/c, TV, phone, showers, kitchens, balconies, pool, children's pool, tennis, beach, multilingual staff, excursions and watersports arranged, 11 km from airport, beachside restaurant. **LL-AL** *La Créole Beach*, Pointe de la Verdure, BP 61, 97190 Gosier, T904646, F904666. 156 rooms, a/c, showers, TV, phone, minibar, good sized rooms, pool, bar and restaurant, watersports arranged, tennis, volley ball and putting green available. Also under same management are **LL-A** *Les Résidences Yucca*, 100 studios and **LL-AL** *Hôtel Mahogany*, 64 rooms and suites, which share facilities of *La Créole Beach*. **AL** *Arawak*, T842424, F843845. Nice beach, pool, a/c, buses 400 m away, modern, used by tour groups, comfortable rooms but poor food, not very friendly service. **LL-AL** *Callinago*, T842525, F842490. 107 rooms, beach, pool. Also apartments at *Callinago Village*. **C** *Serge's Guest House*, on seafront, T841025, F843949. Very basic, not very clean, convenient for buses and beach, has nice garden and swimming pool. In the same area, **B** *Les Flamboyants*, T841411, F845356. Pool, seaview, some kitchenettes, friendly, is clean, a/c. A smaller establishment is the **E-F** *Hotel Corossol*, Mathurin, 97190 Gosier, T843989. Eight rooms, friendly, good meals, 20 minutes' walk to Gosier. Many places advertise rooms to let.

Sainte-Anne *Club Méditerranée* has a hotel-village: *La Caravelle*, on a spectacular white sand beach, perhaps the best on Guadeloupe, surrounded by a 13 ha reserve; atmosphere strictly informal (nude bathing), all sports equipment available, deep sea fishing and golf at extra cost, children's clubs, circus school, 324 rooms, some with three beds, some singles, T854950, F854970. Near Sainte-Anne: **AL** *Relais du Moulin* , T882396, F880392. 40 a/c bungalows, recommended restaurant, pool. **AL** *Motel Sainte-Anne*, T882240. 10 rooms, a/c. **AL** *Auberge le Grand Large*, T854828, F881669. Neither grand nor large, but friendly and with good restaurant on the beach. **AL** *Mini Beach*, T882113, F881929. 1 km from town, also on the beach, relaxed, good location, many restaurants nearby, can fall to half price in summer, good restaurant, excellent fish soup, a meal in itself. Between Gosier and Sainte-Anne, at La Marie-Gaillarde, is **B-C** *La Marie-Gaillarde*, T858429, overlooking Les Grands Fonds, 2 km from Petit Havre beach. Nine rooms can fit 3-4 people, with restaurant and bar. **LL-AL** *La Toubana*, BP 63, 97180 Ste-Anne, T882578, F883890, toubana@ leaderhotels.gp 32 cottages, a/c, kitchenettes, phones, terraces, pool, private beach, tennis, pocket billiards, views of nearby Caravelle beach, *Club Med* and islands, *Toubana* is Arawak for little house, restaurant serves French and Créole cuisine.

Saint-François **LL** *Méridien*, T885100, F884071. Modern and conventional seaside complex, 265 rooms, beach, lots of watersports, pool, golf, tennis, flying school, dock, discothèque, and casino. **LL** *La Cocoteraie*, Avenida de l'Europe, T887981, F887833, cocoteraie@wanadoo.fr 50 deluxe suites, beach front, pool side, garden view or marina view, between lagoon and golf course, spectacular pool, tennis, beautiful architecture. **LL-L** *Plantation Ste-Marthe* (Euro Dom Hotels), T931111, F887247, psm@ netguacom.fr Former sugar plantation on hill away from sea, new colonial-style buildings, 120 magnificent rooms of 42 or 65 sq m with large terrace, a/c, restaurant, bars, 900 sq m swimming pool, close to golf course, seven-acre property, fully equipped conference centre. **LL-AL** *Anse des Rochers Anchorage*, BP 215, 97118 St François, T939000, F939100, www.hôtels-anchorage.com 228 spacious rooms in three buildings plus 32 villas with four rooms each, a/c, kitchenettes, beautiful seaside resort, Créole architecture, in 25 acres of gardens, fine restaurants, huge pool, tennis, volleyball, excursions, watersports, golf nearby. **LL** *Hamak*, T885999, F884192, hotel.hamak@wanadoo.fr 54 bungalows, private beach, marina, landing strip, sports. **AL-A** *Hôtel Kaye'la*, T887777, F887467, on the marina. Built 1990, 75 rooms for up to four people, a/c, pool, bar, restaurant, walking distance to Saint-François restaurants, convenient for boat trips from marina. **C** *Chez Honoré*, Place du Marché, T884061, F886073. Clean, simple, friendly, noisy because of the disco next door but still one of the cheapest in the French West Indies. Good seafood restaurant.

Pointe des Châteaux **LL** *Iguana Bay Villas*, T884880, F886719. 17 villas, 2-3 bedrooms, private pools, overlooking La Désirade, pretty beach, private. **Le Moule** **LL-AL** *Tropical Club Hotel*, BP 121, 97160 Le Moule, T939797, F939700, Plage des Alizés. 100 rooms, 1-4 people, a/c, TV, kitchenette, phone, terrace, fan, pool, volley ball, ping-pong, restaurant, snack bar, in coconut grove on beach, watersports, tennis and golf available nearby.

Sleeping:
Basse-Terre
Accommodation is neither plentiful nor high class in Basse-Terre city

Basse-Terre **E** *Hotel Basse-Terre-Charlery*, 56 rue Maurice Marie Claire, T811978. Central, basic, clean and cheap, good oriental restaurant next door. Also central is **D** *Le Drouant*, 26 rue Dr Cabre. At **Saint-Claude** **AL-A** *St Georges*, Rue Gratien Parize, T801010, F803050. 40 rooms including two suites, fitness room, squash, pool, billiards, meeting rooms, bar, restaurant *Le Lamasure*, snack bar, new in 1996. **A-B** *Relais de la Grand Soufrière*, an elegant but rather poorly-converted old plantation mansion, a/c, attractive surroundings, old wooden furniture, friendly staff, T800127, F801840, regular bus service to Basse-Terre, including Sun. **Bouillante** **LL-A** *Domaine de Malendure*, T989212, F989210. 50 loft suites with views of Ilet Pigeon, on hillside, 400 m from sea, a/c, TV, phone, mini-bar, good location for diving or walking, pool, restaurant, car rental, shuttle to Malendure beach or Grand Anse beach, car rental in advance recommended. **Deshaies** **L** *Fort Royal*, T255000, F255001. Used to belong to *Club Med*, now Touring Hotel Club, dramatically situated on a promontory between two beautiful but rather rough beaches. **LL-AL** *Pointe Batterie Villas*, T285703, F285728. 24 1-2 bedroom villas, a/c, decks, pool, new, on the water, charming, some have private pools, excellent restaurant, full hotel services. **B** *La Vigie*, overlooking Deshaies bay. Small studios with kitchenette, bathroom, terrace, fan, cleaned daily, T284252. **D** *Chez M Eric Bernier*, T284004 or 284270. Rooms on waterfront, opposite *Le Mouillage* restaurant more rooms are available. An apartment **E** *Chez Jean Memorin*, T284090, just outside town on hill in direction of Grand Anse beach. 1 bedroom, TV. **AL-B** *Auberge de la Distillerie*, Route de Versailles, Tabanon, 97170 Petit Bourg, T942591, F941191. 16 rooms, a/c, TV, phone, mini-bar, pool, jacuzzi, pocket billiards, country inn at entrance to Parc Naturel surrounded by pineapple fields, créole restaurant, *Le Bitaco* and small pizza café, the owner also designed **AL-A** *Créol'Inn*, Bel'Air Desrozières, T942256, F941928. 20 cabins in wooded area, a/c, TV, fans, phone, kitchenette, hammocks, pool, barbecue, snack bar. **Trois Rivières C** *Le Joyeux*, a 3F bus ride from the centre of the town (bus stop right outside) or short walk, in Le Faubourg, 100 m above the sea, T927478, F927707. Six simple rooms, kitchenettes, Créole restaurant, bar, disco, closed Mon except for reservations, good views to Les Saintes, very friendly, Monsieur will drive you to the boat dock for nothing, the family also run a small supermarket and the Serie Bleu maps are sold there. **LL-AL** *Le Jardin Malanga*, T926757, F926758. Beautifully renovated 1927 Créole house and bungalows, hillside setting in banana plantation, lovely views, a/c, TV, terraces, mini-bar, bath tubs, huge beds, pool, car rental in advance recommended. **AL** *Grand'Anse*, T929047, F929369. Bungalows, also has Créole restaurant and views. *Les Gîtes de l'Habitation Cardonnet*, T927055. Five self-contained cottages.

Throughout the island there are a large number of gîtes for rent on a daily, weekly or monthly basis. Weekly rates range from 700F to 3,000F, but most are in the 1,000-1,500F bracket. The tourist offices in both Pointe-à-Pitre and Basse-Terre have lists of the properties available and should be consulted in the first instance, or you can contact the Association Guadeloupéenne des Gîtes Ruraux et du Tourisme Vert (Relais Guadeloupe des Gîtes de France), BP 759, 97171 Point-à-Pitre, Cedex, T916433, F914540, www.gites-2-france.fr, who have an office next to the Tourist Office on rue Provence. Gîtes are arranged by the local Syndicats d'Initiative. For example, the Syndicat d'Initiative de Deshaies, T284970, lists 14 local people who let gîtes. Some gîtes are quite isolated, so choose one that is conveniently located. The Syndicats charge a 5% rental fee. One recommended gîte in Trois Rivières is **E** *Chez Dampierre*, T989869, a bungalow for two in a beautiful garden, convenient location.

The tourist offices also have lists of villas for rent (there are a number in Saint-François, for instance); prices vary between 1,500F and 4,500F depending on number of occupants, size of villa and season.

Gîtes

Compared with metropolitan France, camping is not well organized and the tourist office does not have much information. 7 km east of Ste-Anne is *Camping du Voyageur*, T/F883674, Chateaubrun 97180 Ste-Anne, cooking facilities but no washing machine, **F** for two people, tent rental, gîtes, clean, beach 10 mins' walk. A small campsite is *Sable d'Or*, near Deshaies, Basse-Terre, T813910. **F** per tent for two people. Also small bungalows, **D-E**, cooking facilities, pool. There are buses from Pointe-à-Pitre. *Camping Traversée* is near Mahaut on Basse-Terre, not suitable for tents after heavy rain, they float away. Otherwise ask mayors if you may camp on municipal land, or owners on private property. Camper vans can be arranged through Découverts et Loisirs Créoles in Abymes, T205565.

Camping

Pointe-à-Pitre *Oasis*, rues Nozières et A R Boisneuf (French), T820270. *Relais des Antilles* (cheaper, but good Créole cooking), near the *Auberge Henri IV*, in a private house, good, cheap meals (ask Valentin at the *Auberge* for directions). *Krishna*, 47 rue A R Boisneuf, Indian. *Le Moundélé*, rue Juan Jaurès, T910430, African. **Grande-Terre holiday coast** *La Case Créole*, Route de la Rivière. *Chez Rosette*, Av Général de Gaulle, both Créole at Gosier. *Le Boukarou*, rue Montauban, T841037. Good Italian, pizza made on charcoal grill, moderately priced. Lots of small restaurants in **Gosier**: pizzas, Vietnamese, Chinese and of course French. The local pizza house is near the park, good for takeaways. The *pâtisserie* is good for an early morning coffee while collecting the *baguettes*; *La Mandarine*, funny staff, worth a stop; *Chez Gina*, in a little village cafétière, 2½ km inland from Les Sables d'Or campsite, up the hill, excellent food, order in advance in the morning for an evening meal, four courses and apéritif, served in a sort of garage with flowers, friendly, don't be put off by the untidy surroundings. *Côté Jardin*, at Bas du Fort marina. French. *La Plantation*, same location, same cuisine. **Sainte-Anne** *Chez Yvette* is budget-priced. *La Toubana*, T882557, perched high

Eating: Grande-Terre
Apart from the hotel restaurants, there are a large number of restaurants, cafés & patisseries on Guadeloupe. Many are closed in the evening

French Antilles

above village overlooking *Club Med*. Nice but expensive French cuisine, lobster specialities, pool and sun deck, take swimming gear. The *Relais du Moulin*, T882396, has an excellent French-Créole menu. **Saint-François** *Madame Jerco* has good food in a small creaking house. Close to the old harbour of St-François, *Kotesit*, T884084, fresh langouste and other seafood, don't miss the 'marquise au chocolat'. On the way to Pointe des Chateaux, *Iguane Café* uses local fresh ingredients, good service. At **Campêche** there is a small restaurant in the middle of the village, cheap and welcome relief if travelling in this area.

Eating: **Basse-Terre**	*Chez Paul* in Matouba, T802920, has been recommended for Créole and East Indian cuisine. At Bouillante, *Chez Loulouse*, Plage de Malendure, T987034, beach restaurant, créole fair. *Restaurant de la Phare*, Vieux Fort, good créole cooking, excellent fresh fish, reasonable prices, dance hall attached. **Deshaies** several reasonably priced restaurants including *Le Madras* and *Le Mouillage*, serving créole food. For breakfast try the *boulangerie* opposite *Le Mouillage* for croissants, pain au chocolat, coffee, juice. The *Relais de la Grande Soufrière*, at Saint-Claude. Very good créole meals at reasonable prices, T800127. For a description of local cuisine, see page 690.

Nightlife	Around the Marina Bas-du-Fort there are several bars with live music, such as *Velvet, Le Jardin Brésilien, Zoo Rock* and *La Mexicana*. There is also a disco, *La Citée Perdue*. Other discos can be found in Gosier: *Le 116, Le Caraïbe II, New Land, Le Zenith*. At Le Moule, there is *Shiva*. There is a casino in Gosier, open from 2100, closed Sun, bring identification, at Pointe de la Verdure, T841833, and another at St-François, open from 2100, closed Mon, bring identification, Av de l'Europe, T884131. Two cinemas in Pointe-à-Pitre, Renaissance, with 2 screens, T820194, and Rex, with 4 screens, T822020. Basse-Terre also has the D'Arbaud cinema, 2 screens, T811835.

Festivals	**Carnival** starts on Epiphany and runs through Ash Wednesday with different events each Sunday, the main ones on the last weekend. The **Fish and Sea Festival** is in *mid-April* with beach parties, boat races, crab races, etc. **La Fête des Cuisinières** (Cooks' Festival) in the middle of *August* is a lot of fun with parades in créole costumes and music as well as food and cooking. It is held on the feast of St Lawrence, the patron saint of women cooks, and the event starts with a Mass. Some 250 cordon bleu cooks from the Women's Cooking Association wear their typical colourful dresses with madras scarves and lots of jewellery for the parade through Pointe-à-Pitre. Other festivals include the **Fête du Gwo Ka** (Festival of the Big Drums) in *July*, the **Old Creole Songs Festival** in *October*, St Cecilia's Day in *November*.

Shopping	An unusual fruit, the *carambole*, can be bought in Pointe-à-Pitre. The location of the markets is given above. *Good Mamouth Supermarket* near Le Raizet airport 3.50F by bus from Pointe-à-Pitre. There are lots of hypermarkets just like in France, stocked with excellent cheese counters and massive wine departments (both French only of course). They also sell chemist sundries, toys, electrical equipment, film, cameras etc. Most have film processing facilities where prints will be ready in 24 hours or less. Generally open Monday to Saturday 0800-2030. Expensive, everything imported from France. In Gosier there is a supermarket on the road to Plage de l'Anse Canot, open on Sunday, otherwise hypermarkets are better value and cleaner.

Tour operators	The *Organization des Guides de Montagne de la Caraïbe* has its Guadeloupe branch at St-Claude, T802425. Guides certified by the French government are available for hikes of 1-5 days. *Emeraude Guadeloupe*, St-Claude, T819828, F819812, also offers hiking in forests and mountains, with cultural visits and contact with local families, also lodging in small hotels, mountain bike excursions and other activities. *Parfum d'Aventures*, St-François, T884762, F884791, has canoes and kayaks, 4-wheel drive excursions, hiking and water scooters. *Guadeloupe Découverte*, Jarry, T252087, F266665, similar trips with canoes and kayaks, hiking, mountain biking and 4-wheel drive excursions. Also *Sports d'Av*, Jarry, T325841, F266665.

Transport	**Air** Le Raizet airport was replaced in 1996 by the new, modern **Pole Caraïbes airport**. The former is still used for regional flights, while the latter is for international arrivals and

departures. Information, T211472, arrivals, T903232, departures, T903434. They are quite far apart, a taxi ride, and if you have a rental car (kept on the old airport side of the airfield) you will have to get the shuttle to the new terminal. There is no bus service to the new airport, but take the shuttle bus to Le Raizet and then bus into town from the other side of the car park, over roundabout and outside Cora (Mamouth) supermarket, 5.70F to Place de la Victoire. No buses Saturday afternoon or Sunday. Taxi fares from the airport are approximately US$20 to Gosier, US$40 to Sainte-Anne, US$60 to Saint-François and US$16 to Bas-du-Fort. Prices go up by 40% 2100-0700, all day Sunday and on holidays. To call a taxi, T207474.

Road Bus: In Pointe-à-Pitre there are three main bus terminals: from rue Dubouchage, La Darse (by Place de la Victoire), buses run to Gosier (5F), Sainte-Anne (15F), Saint-François (15F); for north Grande-Terre destinations, buses leave from the Morne Ferret and Mortenol station, off Blvd Légitimus. From Bergevin station, Blvd Chanzy (near the cemetery) they go to Trois Rivières (27F) and Basse-Terre (30F, 2 hrs). Pointe-à-Pitre to La Grande Anse, 20F, 1¾ hrs. Buses from Pointe-à-Pitre to Deshaies leave from Gare Routière, 1¼ hrs, 25F. Basse-Terre to Trois Rivières, 20 mins. The terminal in Basse-Terre is on Boulevard Général de Gaulle, between the market and the sea. Buses run between 0530 and 1800, leaving for the main destinations every 15 mins or so, or when full. After 1800 and after 1300 on Sat and Sun it is often impossible to get anywhere. The airport bus leaves from 0800 from outside Renaissance Cinema, Place de la Victoire, Pointe-à-Pitre, 5.70F.

   Organized bus tours and boat excursions are available but expensive, about 330-400F in a bus for about 40 people. Check with tourist office, Petrelluzzi Travel Agency (American Express Agents), 2 rue Henri IV, Pointe-à-Pitre, and other agencies.

Car There can be major traffic holdups in the rush hour in and around Pointe-à-Pitre; expect to find slow moving traffic on the major routes for up to 20 km out of the capital. Bottlenecks include the roundabout at the university at Bas-du-Fort, the turning to Le Raizet and beyond to Abymes and the turnoff to Baie-Mahault. In the city, parking is a nightmare in the daytime. There are no car parks, just meters. There are two zones, green (about 5F for maximum eight hours) and orange (cheaper). The system does not operate 1230-1400. Most traffic is one way.

Car hire All the usual international car hire firms are represented: *Avis*, T211354, F211355; *Budget*, T827250, F917208; *Europcar*, T266064, F268373; *Hertz*, T938945, F916959, and there are offices at the airport. At Trois Rivières, Rosan Martin, *Location de Voitures*, is close to the dock, T929424, 262F per day, unlimited mileage, for a Renault B571, deposit 3,000F or credit card. *Tropic-Car*, 25 rue Schoelcher, 97110 Pointe-á-Pitre, T918437, F913194, evenings and weekends T840725, has a variety of models for hire. Fully equipped camper vans can be hired from several agencies: *Antilles Local Soleil*, Gosier, T957200; *Vert'Bleu Location*, T285125, F285295. There are also **mopeds** for hire in Pointe-à-Pitre, Gosier, Saint-François, or through hotels. **Motorbikes** from *Equateur Motos*, T845994, F845977. *Dom Location*, Rue Saint-Aude Ferly, Saint-François, T/F888481, hires scooters, motorbikes and cars half day to one week, scooters 170F per day. Mokes and scooters can be rented at Sainte-Anne. If you don't have a credit card you normally have to deposit up to 5,000F for a car; 3,000F for a scooter; and 1,000F for moped or bicycle. **Bicycle** rental from *Velo-Vert*, Pointe-à-Pitre, T831574, *Le Relais du Moulin*, near Sainte-Anne, T882396, *Rent-a-Bike*, *Meridien Hotel*, Saint-François, T845100, *Atlantic*, Saint-François, around 70F per day.

Airline offices *Air France*, Boulevard Légitimus, Pointe-à-Pitre, T825000/823000/826161; *Air Canada*, T836249/211277/211334; *LIAT*, T211393; *Air Liberté*, T930858/211468/266131; *AOM*, T211484; *American Airlines*, T211366; *Nouvelles Frontières* for charter flights, T903636, Pointe-à-Pitre. *Air Guadeloupe*, T211290/824700, 10 rue Sadi Carnot, Pointe-à-Pitre, T901225. **Banks** *Banque Nationale de Paris* (good for Visa cash advances), *Banque Populaire, Banque des Antilles Françaises*, *Crédit Maritime , Crédit Agricole* and *Société Générale de Banque aux Antilles*, all have branches throughout the island. Banks charge 1% commission and 4% *dessier* (filing fee). No commission charged on French traveller's cheques. Exchange is handled up to midday so go early to avoid the late morning pandemonium. *American Express* is at Petreluzzi Travel, 2 rue Henri IV, English spoken,

Directory

French Antilles

helpful. Credit cards are widely accepted, including at the hypermarkets. **Communications** Post : Post office and telephone building in Pointe-à-Pitre is on Boulevard Hanne, crowded, sweltering. Post and phones in Basse-Terre is on rue Dr Pitat, between Dumanoir and Ciceron, smaller but a bit more comfortable than the Pointe-à-Pitre office. Parcel post is a problem and you can usually send parcels of up to 2 kg only. In Pointe-à-Pitre there is an office near the stadium where you can mail parcels of up to 7 kg by air but it is unreliable; one correspondent sent a tent but received a cake wrapped in the same paper. Unlike in France, stamps are not sold in bars and tobacconists, go to post offices in small towns to avoid the crush of the main offices. **Telephone:** For local calls you must buy phone cards (*télécartes*, 40F or 96F, from a *tabac*), fairly essential when phoning ahead to book accommodation; to call abroad, you must hand over identification at the desk (calls to the USA 12.85F per minute, Europe 18.50F per minute, Australia 23.10F per minute; hotels charge twice as much). You can not make a credit card or collect call abroad from a pay phone. You can not have a call returned to a pay phone either. **Embassies & consulates** Belgium, T268477, F268612. **Denmark**, Blvd Pte Jarry, 97122 Baie Mahault, T266610, F266618. **Ecuador**, T942172, F820813. **Germany**, T823737, F830429. **Netherlands**, 5 rue de Nozières, Pointe-à-Pitre, T820116, F913508. **Sweden**, Impasses Georges Claude, 97122 Jarry, T952957, F950199. Diplomatic representation also in Martinique. **Hospital** T891010/891120 in Pointe-à-Pitre. There are nine hospitals and 15 clinics.There are also 3 health spas for alternative treatments: René Toribio-Ravine Chaude, T257592, F257628, with water coming directly from the Soufrière volcano; Manioukani Spa, Marina de Rivière-Sens, T990202, F816523, for thalassotherapy; the Harry Hamousin Centre, T805353, F800608, with hot sulphurous water coming from the Matouba springs at a temperature of 49.6°C. **Tourist information** Local tourist offices: Tourist offices in Guadeloupe, www.antilles-info-tourism.com/guadeloupe: 5 Square de la Banque, BP 422-97163, Pointe-à-Pitre, T820930, F838922 (the Gîtes office next door is helpful); Maison du Port, Cours Nolivos, Basse-Terre, T812483; Avenida de l'Europe, Saint-François, T884874, and at airport. **Maps** The Serie Bleu maps (1:25,000, seven maps of Guadeloupe, No 4601G-4607G) issued by the Institut Geógraphique National, Paris, which include all hiking trails, are available at the bigger book stores in the rue Frébault in Pointe-à-Pitre, and at *Le Joyeux* hotel in Trois Rivières/Le Faubourg for 52F. Also available from MapLink in the USA, T805-6926777. National Park: Parc Naturel de la Guadeloupe, Habitation Beausoleil, Montéran, BP 13-97120, Saint-Claude, T802425, F800546.

Outer islands of Guadeloupe

The outer islands of Guadeloupe are among the least visited of the West Indian islands; they can easily be reached by air or boat from Guadeloupe. One can still get on a trading schooner between the islands if patient.

Les Saintes

Population: 2,036

On Les Saintes, a string of small islands named Los Santos by Columbus, only Terre-de-Haut and Terre-de-Bas are inhabited. The people are descendants of Breton fisherfolk who have survived among themselves with little intermarriage with the dominant West Indian races. Sugar cane was never introduced here as a plantation crop and so large numbers of black slaves never came either. The population is predominantly light-skinned and many people have blue eyes. Some still wear the same round hats, the salako, that Breton fisherfolk used to wear, and fishing is still the main occupation on the islands. They are a popular excursion from Guadeloupe now, but are not too spoilt, and with a good, natural harbour, many small cruise ships spend the day here. Nevertheless, to get a better idea of the islanders' traditional way of life, staying overnight is recommended so that you can appreciate it once the day trippers leave at 1600. Public holidays are particularly heavy days with hundreds of day trippers.

Terre-de-Haut

Terre-de-Haut is the main island visited by tourists. Irregularly shaped and surprisingly barren, it is about 6 km long and 2 km wide at its widest point. Most of the 1,500 inhabitants live around the Anse Mire, looking across the **Ilet à Cabrit**. There are some excellent beaches including that of Pont Pierre, also known as Pompierre, where snorkelling is good and camping is possible, Marigot, L'Anse du Figuier (good diving, no shade), L'Anse Crawen (nudist) and Grand'Anse (white sand, rougher waters, swimming not allowed). The UCPA sailing school at Petit Anse offers half or full day sailing or windsurfing courses. Walking on the islands is good, either from the town to the beaches, or to the top of Le Chameau (TV mast on top) on Terre-de-Haut's west end (spectacular views of Les Saintes, Marie-Galante, Guadeloupe and Dominica).

An easy trail, Trace des Crétes, starts at Terre-de-Haut. Turn right at the pier, follow the main street about 100 m, turn left at the chapel and follow the road up to Le Marigot (look out for the *sentier du morne morel* sign behind the restaurant on the south side of the bay) and on to the beach of Baie de Pont Pierre, a lovely golden beach with rocks, Roches Percées, in the bay. Boats and diving equipment can be rented at the landing stage. Goats can be a nuisance if you decide to picnic here. At the end of the beach the trail leads up the hill where you have a good view of the islands, if you keep left, one branch of the trail leads to Grand'Anse beach. The 'white' cemetery, **La Cimétière Rose**, worth visiting, pretty, with paths bordered by shells, is close to the beach and from here you can walk back to Terre-de-Haut, about 1½ hours in total. Alternatively, you can walk along Grand'Anse and on to Pointe Rodriguez and the small cove Anse Rodriguez below it.

There are beautiful views also from **Fort Napoléon**, high up above the town on Pointe à l'Eau. The views demonstrate the strategic importance of Les Saintes (the Gibraltar of the Caribbean), and the museum in Fort Napoléon gives the French view of the decisive sea battle of Les Saintes (1782 – the English Admiral Rodney defeated and scattered the fleet of France's Commander de Grasse, who was preparing to attack Jamaica). The fort itself is rather disappointing but the exhibitions are good with interesting models of the ships and battles. A guide will give you a 30-minute tour (in French) of the main building. If not historically-minded, just sit and watch the weather. There are exhibits also of local fishing (including a *saintois*, a local fishing boat, originally with blue and white striped sail, but now diesel-powered) and crafts, a bookshop and drinks on sale. Around the ramparts is the **Jardin Exotique** which specializes in growing succulents and includes a wild area where plants native to Les Saintes are grown. ■ *0900-1230 except 1 Jan, 1 May, 15-16 Aug and 25 Dec. 20F to enter, children 6-12 half price.* On the Ilet à Cabrit are the ruins of **Fort Joséphine**.

Terre-de-Bas is home to about 1,500 people, mostly fishermen. There is a pottery which also gives some employment, but many have left for work in France. Boats land at **Grande Baie** which is a small inlet guarded by a fort and two small statues. You get good views of La Coche and Grand Ilet (two of the uninhabited islands) on the way across. There is a good little information centre at the dock. Buses will meet the ferry and you can go to the main settlement at Petite Anse where there is a new fishing port as well as the secondary school for the islands and a pretty little church with a red roof (tour approximately 40 minutes 30F). The beach at Grand Anse is very pleasant and there are a few bars and restaurants nearby (*A La Belle Etoile* is actually on the beach). There is a track which runs from Petite Anse to Grand Anse which is a good walk. It is very quiet compared with Terre-de-Haut. Salakos and wood carvings are made by local inhabitants. **Terre-de-Bas**

Terre-de-Haut LL-A *Bois Joli*, reached by 10-min boat ride or 5-min scooter ride from **Sleeping** town, at the west end of the island on hillside, T995038, F995505, gorgeous setting, hotel van transport to town or airport, 22 rooms, 8 bungalows, MAP, most have a/c, phones, pool, bar, restaurant, 2 beaches, watersports. **AL** *Kanaoa*, Anse Mire, T995136, F995194. 8 rooms, 2 studios, 6 bungalows, a/c, but rather basic, fair restaurant used by tour groups, evening entertainment in season, English spoken, beautiful waterfront setting 10 mins' walk from landing jetty, very quiet. **B** *La Saintoise*, T995250, in town. 10 rooms, a/c, restaurant, breakfast included. *Auberge Les Petits Saints aux Anacardiers*, La Savane, T995099, F995451. Former mayor's house overlooking town and bay, furnished with French antiques, attractive,

French Antilles

intimate, 10 rooms, 2 bungalows, 1 suite, a/c, clean, pool, sauna, art gallery, good restaurant. **B** *Jeanne d'Arc*, T995041, at Fond de Curé village on south coast, good, 10 rooms.

Terre-de-Bas There is one hotel, *Le Poisson Volant*, 9 rooms, T998147.

On both Terre-de-Haut and Terre-de-Bas there are rooms and houses to rent; tourist office has list of phone numbers. Recommended are Mme Bonbon, T905052, on the road to the airfield, who has several rooms; Mme Bernadette Cassin, T995422, clean studio under her house on road to cemetery, cheaper without kitchen facilities, if she is full she has family and friends who offer rooms; and Mme Maisonneuve, T995338, on the same road as the *Mairie*. Reservations are generally recommended in peak season, especially Christmas and New Year. The telephone at the jetty only takes phone cards. Not good for first impressions but otherwise idyllic. There is a shortage of water on the island.

Eating   **Terre-de-Haut** Plenty of restaurants, specialize in seafood and offer *menus* for about 60F, but try the *tourment d'amour* coconut sweet. Home made coconut rum punches are also recommended, particularly in the little bar on the right hand side of the *gendarmerie* in front of the jetty. Check beer prices before ordering, cheapest 15F. *Le Mouillage* restaurant, T995057, recommended. *Le Genois*, T995301, excellent and cheap pizza house on water's edge by harbour square, also does takeaways. *La Saladerie*, at top of steps on road to Fort Napoléon, T995343, popular, not always open out of season. *Galerie de la Baie*, first floor overlooking harbour, snacks and very expensive ice cream. The *boulangerie* next to the *Mairie* is open from 0530, good. The supermarkets are expensive, double French prices. There are a couple of markets every morning on the road towards the post office, good for fresh produce. **Terre-de-Bas** There are two or three restaurants serving creole food and snacks.

Terre-de-Haut & Les Saintes

Air Three daily flights from Pointe-à-Pitre, some via Marie-Galante, 15 mins, *Air* **Transport**
Guadeloupe, 180F one way, 360F return, children 270 return. **Ferry** Deher CTM (T995068,
F995683) have six daily boats from Trois Rivières (Guadeloupe) to Terre-de-Haut, 95F round
trip. *Trans Antilles Express* from Pointe-à-Pitre to Terre-de-Haut daily 0800 all year, return-
ing 1600; also from Marina Saint-François, Tue, Wed, Thu, 0800, Dec-May, returning 1600
same days, all 160F round trip, children 85F. *Transport Maritimes Brudey Frères*, T900448,
from Marina Saint-François to Les Saintes Mon, Fri, 0800 Dec-May, and from Darse,
Pointe-à-Pitre to Les Saintes and Marie Galante daily 0800, returning 1545, same prices as
Trans Antilles Express. There are also day charters from Pointe-à-Pitre and Saint-François
Marina in high season. The crossing takes about 45 mins, but it can be rough, not suitable for
those prone to seasickness. The ferry between Terre-de-Haut and Terre-de-Bas runs about 5
times a day (0800, 0930, 1330, 1500 and 1600, 25F, 15F for children, return) passing the Pain
de Sucre and stopping briefly at the *Bois Joli* (except 0800 and 1500 boats). **Road Bus**:
mini-buses take day trippers all over Terre-de-Haut; tour of the island 52F, bus up to Fort
Napoléon, 10F (or 25 mins' walk). No transport after dark. **Bike**: there are few cars, unlike on
Guadeloupe. Scooter rental, 200F per day, also bicycles, several central locations, 80F per
day. It is not necessary to hire a scooter for the whole day, as you can walk to most places, but
it may be nice to have one in the afternoon to go to the beach at Pompierre or Figuier.
Scooters are banned from the town 0900-1200, 1400-1600 and have to be pushed. At the
Mairie you can get some very basic information and a poor map.

Marie-Galante

Marie-Galante, a small round island of 158 sq km, is simple and old-fashioned but *Population: 13,463*
surprisingly sophisticated when it comes to food and drink. It was named by Christopher Columbus after his own ship, the *Santa María La Galante*, and has three settlements. The largest is **Grand-Bourg** (rather run down) in the southwest with a
population of around 8,000; **Capesterre**
is in the southeast and **Saint-Louis**
(sugar factory, see the bullock carts
delivering cane during the cutting season) in the northwest. By Grand-Bourg
plage try the *batterie de sirop*, selling a
treacle-like sugar cane syrup mixed with
rum and lime or with water.

The beaches, so far almost completely
untouched by the tourist flood, are
superb. By Capesterre, the Plage de la
Feuillère has fine sand beaches and is protected by the coral reef offshore. Follow the
path north to Les Galeries, which are large
cliffs eroded by the sea to make a covered
walkway over 15 m above sea level. There
is a pleasant beach at **Anse de Vieux Fort**,
the site of the first settlement on the island
in 1648 and of a series of fierce skirmishes
between the French and the Amerindians.

The **Trou à Diable** (off the D202) is a
massive cave which runs deep into the
earth. To visit it, it is essential to have
strong shoes, a torch with extra batteries, and a guide. It is a very remote spot
and there is no organized tourism. The
descent requires ropes and should not
be attempted unassisted. The walk from
the road is striking.

Les Saintes

The D202 road meets the D201 at La Grande Barre, from where there are good views of the north end of the island and to Guadeloupe. On the coast there are limestone cliffs over 30 m high which have been eroded in places to form spectacular arches with the sea splashing through them. One is at Gueule Grand Gouffre (cold drinks on sale) and another, less good example, further east at Caye Plate.

In the 19th century the island boasted over 100 sugar mills; a few have been restored and may be visited: Basses, Grand-Pierre, Agapy and Murat. Some are still operating. The former plantation houses of **Château Murat** (museum open Monday-Thursday 0900-1300, 1500-1800, Saturday and Sunday 0900-1200, free) and **Brille** are interesting. Murat gives a good impression of the great 18th century sugar plantations; below the sweeping lawn lies the old sugar mill with cane crushing machinery still intact. Behind the house is a walled herb garden.

The **Bellevue** rum distillery on the D202 is a cottage industry. The rum (clear and branded as '*agricole*') is very powerful and you will be invited to taste and buy. You may also be offered bags of brown sugar and dessicated coconut, a surprisingly nice combination. At the **Distillerie Bielle** you can taste and buy rum as well as ceramic rum flasks made at the pottery *atelier*, open 1000-1200, Monday-Saturday, T979362. The **Distillerie Poisson** in the west on the N9 makes the Père Labat rum and is open for visits (also small museum) with tastings of rum and liqueurs, 0700-1100, Monday-Saturday, T970379. There is a cinema in Grand-Bourg, El Rancho, which has movies dubbed into French.

Sleeping **St-Louis** *Le Salut* is in the town centre south of the pier, T970267. 15 rooms, a/c, restaurant and bar. North of St-Louis, 2km from Vieux-Fort beach on a cliff, is *Au Village de Menard*,

Marie Galante

T970945. 7 bungalows, pool, mountain bikes, English spoken. Near St Louis is **L-AL** *Cohoba*, at Folle Anse, T805-9679850 in Europe. 100 rooms in Créole-style bungalows, 30 with kitchenettes, a/c, TV, well-equipped, 2 restaurants, dramatic pool, large conference room, bar, superb white sand beach. Other hotels are in **C-D** range. **Grand-Bourg** *L'Auberge de l'Arbre à Pain*, Rue Jeanne d'Arc, T977369. 7 rooms with breakfast, a/c, restaurant and bar. **Capesterre**, *Hotel Hajo*, Beaurenom, T973276. 6 rooms, fan, restaurant and bar. *Le Soleil Levant*, 42 rue de la Marine, on hill overlooking Capesterre and sea, T973155, F974165. 10 rooms and studios, tiny pool, kitchenettes, restaurant for breakfast and dinner, evening entertainment, car rental. *Le Touloulou*, T973263, F973359. On the Grand Bourg road, 2 km from Capesterre . Clean, well-equipped bungalows backing directly on to the sea, discothèque and restaurant nearby. *Le Belvedere* , 4 km from Capesterre, 5km from Grand-Bourg, 2 mins from the beach, T/F973295. 7 rooms, 12 beds, terrace restaurant in the trees open for lunch and dinner, creole seafood, crayfish, bouillabaisse, evening entertainment, welcome cocktail. There are rooms to let (enquire at the tourist board), and gîtes, contact Gîtes de France Guadeloupe, BP 759, 97110 Pointe-à-Pitre, T916433, F914540. For accommodation, 24-hr advance booking is necessary.

Air To get to the island there are regular flights (20 mins) from Pointe-à-Pitre, which is only 43 km away (*Air Guadeloupe*, as above, 360F round trip, children 270F). *Marie-Galante Aviation*, T977702, offers charters and air taxi service. **Sea** There are ferries between Pointe-à-Pitre and Grand-Bourg and it is possible to do a day trip (85F one way, 160F return, children 85F, 1-1½ hrs, times are posted on the booth at the dockside): The *Maria* and *Trident* (Brudy Frères, Centre St-John Perse, Point-à-Pitre, T916087) have daily crossings to Grand Bourg via Saint-Louis, 0545, 0800, 1500 Mon-Fri, 0800, 1300 Sat, 0800, 1645 Sun, returning 1300, 1630 Mon-Fri, 0930, 1630 Sat, 1530, 1800, 1900 Sun. *Trans Antilles Express*, T831245, Quai Gatine Gare Maritime, Pointe-à-Pitre, has fast catamarans taking 300-450 passengers. To Grand-Bourg departing 0800, 1230, 1700 Mon-Sat, 0800, 1700, 1900 Sun, returning from Grand-Bourg 0600, 0900, 1545 Mon-Sat, 0600, 1545 1800 Sun. To Saint-Louis 1230 Mon, Sat, returning 0700 Mon and 1800 Fri. Saint-François to Saint-Louis departing Tue and Thu 0800, returning same days 1645. *Amanda Galante*, a car ferry, T831989, crosses from Pointe-à-Pitre to Saint-Louis in 1½ hrs, 560F car and driver return, 50F for each passenger, takes 22 cars and 156 passengers. *Trans Antilles Express* offer full and half-day tours to Marie-Galante from Pointe-à-Pitre, includes boat trip, visits to beaches, the towns, sugar factories, rum distillery (plus tasting) and other sites (0800-1630 daily, except 0730 weekends, 230F, or 180F for half day, meals 75F extra). Generally you are better off hiring a car or scooter and doing it independently. You can also get a ferry Les Saintes-Marie Galante-Saint-Louis on Tue and Thu in high season. **Road Bus**: on the island there are buses and taxis. **Car hire**: self-drive cars can be hired from the airport or in the towns. Rates for a full day 250F, for part of a day 190F (2,000F deposit); scooters 150F (1,000F deposit).

Transport

Tourist information Passage des Braves, 97112 Grand-Bourg, T978197, F978190. The Marie-Galante Bureau du Tourisme is at Rue du Fort, BP15, 97112 Grand-Bourg, T975652, F975654.

Directory

La Désirade

La Désirade is an attractive but rather arid island whose inhabitants make a living in fishing, sheep-rearing and cultivating cotton and maize. A road 10 km long runs from the airport along the south coast to the east end of the island, where a giant cactus plantation can be seen. Also at the east end of the island is Pointe du Mombin where there is an outstanding view of the coastline. There are excellent beaches, such as at Grande Anse and Souffleur. Perhaps the nicest is in the east at a village called Baie-Mahault, enhanced by a good restaurant/bar, *Chez Céce*, where you can sample dozens of different rum punches. The northern part of the island is rugged, with cliffs and ravines, beautiful but inhospitable.

Population: 1,700

Columbus named the island La Desiderada as it was the first land he saw on his second voyage in 1493. Archaeological research has shown evidence of Amerindian

French Antilles

settlement but it was uninhabited when Columbus passed by. La Désirade was occupied by the French for the first time in 1725, when all the lepers on Guadeloupe were deported there during an epidemic. In 1930 a leper hospital was built, but it was closed in 1954.

Rainfall is very low here and the dry season lasts from January to August. The lack of freshwater has always hampered economic activity. In 1991, however, La Désirade was linked to Grande-Terre underwater with a freshwater supply.

Sleeping & eating D *L'Oasis du Désert*, Quartier Désert Saline, T200212, 8 rooms, restaurant, reservations advisable. *Le Mirage*, T200108, F200745, 7 rooms, restaurant. *Le Kilibibi*, T200097, local specialities. *La Payotte*, seafood, T200194. *Chez Marraine*, T200093, créole.

Transport **Air** There are daily 10-min air services from Guadeloupe 0700, 1545 Mon, Thu, Fri, return 0730, 1615 (*Air Guadeloupe*), 360F round trip, children 270F. **Sea** Boat services from St-François, Guadeloupe, by Vedette Impériale, a rapid motorboat, T885806, journey time 45 mins. Departs Mon-Fri and Sun 0800 and 1700, Sat 0800, 1400, 1700, return Mon-Fri 0615 and 1600, Sat 0615, 1100, 1600, Sun 0600, 1600, 120F return, children 60F. Some companies offer day trips with tours and meals for 300F. **Road** Taxi/minibuses normally meet incoming flights and boats. There are bicycles and scooters for hire.

Background

History

Christopher Columbus discovered Guadeloupe in 1493 and named it after the Virgin of Guadalupe, of Extremadura, Spain. The Caribs, who had inhabited the island, called it Karukera, meaning 'island of beautiful waters'. As in most of the Caribbean, the Spanish never settled, and Guadeloupe's history closely resembles that of Martinique, beginning with French colonization in 1635. The first slaves had been brought to the island by 1650. In the first half of the 17th century, Guadeloupe did not enjoy the same levels of prosperity, defence or peace as Martinique. After four years of English occupation, Louis XV in 1763 handed over Canada to Britain to secure his hold on these West Indian islands with the Treaty of Paris. The French Revolution brought a period of uncertainty, including a brief reign of terror under Victor Hugues. Those landowners who were not guillotined fled; slavery was abolished, only to be restored in 1802. Up to 1848, when the slaves were finally freed by Victor Schoelcher, the island's economy was inhibited by sugar crises and imperial wars (French and English). After 1848, the sugar plantations suffered from a lack of manpower, although indentured labour was brought in from East India.

Despite having equal status with Martinique, first as a Department then as a Region, Guadeloupe's image as the less-sophisticated, poor relation persists. In common with Martinique, though, its main political voice is radical (unlike the more conservative Saint-Barthélémy and Saint-Martin), often marked by a more violent pro-independence movement.

In the presidential elections of 1995, Guadeloupe gave 38.2% of the vote in the first round to Jacques Chirac and 35.1% to the Socialist candidate, Lionel Jospin. However, in the second round, M Jospin won 55.1% compared with 44.9% for M Chirac, although the turnout was even lower than in 1988, with an abstention rate of over 50%. In the National Assembly elections in 1997 the RPR, PPDG, the Socialist Party and a non-aligned left winger each won a seat, the last one defeating a sitting PPDG candidate. Abstention was high again, at 52.7% of the electorate.

Government

Guadeloupe is administered by a prefect, appointed by the French Ministry of the Interior. The local legislature consists of a 43-seat general council, elected by popular vote, which sits for six years, and a 41-seat regional council made up of the locally-elected councillors and the two senators and four deputies elected to the French parliament. Guadeloupe also sends two councillors to the Economic and Social Council in Paris. Political parties include the Socialist Party, the Communist Party, Union for French Democracy, Union for the Liberation of Guadeloupe and Rally for the Republic.

The economy

Agriculture and, increasingly since the 1970s, tourism are the principal activities. Bananas have displaced sugar as the single most important export earner accounting for a quarter of all exports. Sugar and its by-products (rum and molasses) generate about 15% of exports. Melons and tropical flowers have been promoted for sale abroad, while many other fruits, vegetables and coffee are grown mainly for the domestic market.

Wages and conditions similar to those in metropolitan France force the price of local products to levels viable only on the parent market; 66% of all exports go to France and 11% to Martinique (most exports are agricultural products). At the same time, the high rate of imports raises local prices above those of the island's non-French neighbours. Consequently there has been little move towards industrialization to satisfy a wider market and unemployment is high.

Investment in the tourism industry has raised the number of hotel rooms on Guadeloupe to an estimated 8,000. Nearly 90% of stopover visitors come from Europe, mostly from France. Although the North American market has been growing strongly it is only about 8% of the total of about 180,000 a year. Cruise ship passengers have shown spectacular growth in the 1990s, reaching over 75,000 a year.

Saint-Martin

Saint-Martin, the largest of Guadeloupe's outer islands, at 52 sq km, is divided between France and the Netherlands. See Netherlands Antilles section for general description and information. The French part used to be a sleepy place, but has become very Americanized since the building of the yacht marina and lots of luxury hotels. There is no restriction on travel between the two halves of the island. The French side is a sub-prefecture of Guadeloupe, with the sub-prefect appointed in Paris. There is an elected town council, led by a mayor. The economy is entirely dependent upon tourism, with the twin attractions of duty-free shopping and the sea.

Population: 28,518

Ins and outs

Air International flights arrive at the Juliana airport on the Dutch side. On the French side is the **Espèrance airport** which can only take light planes. Airport information, T875303. *Air Guadeloupe* (address under Guadeloupe above) has scheduled services to Espérance from Fort-de-France, Pointe-à-Pitre, Port-au-Prince and Saint-Barthélémy. *Air St Barthélémy* flies from Basse-Terre and St-Barts. *Air St Martin* fly to Espérance from Pointe-à-Pitre. A five-seater helicopter run by *Héli-inter Caraïbes*, T873588, runs day tours to St-Barts, US$700, and Anguilla, US$645, from Anse Marcel every day. Charters also available. *Trans Helico Caraïbes* offers helicopter tours of St-Martin; US$170 for 10 mins for four people, US$370 for 25 mins, T290541, 872187. **Ferry** Besides the ferry to Anguilla (see page 631), connections can be made with Saint-Barthélémy; St Barts Express, T879903, twice daily except Sun and holidays, departs Gustavia 0715, 1530, departs Marigot market place 0900,

Getting there
See also Sint Maarten, for connections with neighbouring islands

1715 (see page 726 for further details). *Voyager* high speed ferries linking St-Martin with St-Barts (and Saba) depart Marigot waterfront 0845 Mon-Sat, 1½ hrs, depart Gustavia 1600, US$50 return plus US$6 port fees, T871068. Can be an unpleasant trip. If rough, take the plane. Try putting a notice up at the Capiteneri Marina Port La Royale for hitching a lift to other islands.

Getting around
It is easy to hitchhike

Buses run from Marigot to Grand Case (terminal at Star Market gas station) (US$1) and from Marigot, French Quarters and St Peters to Philipsburg, normally from 0600-2200, every 15 mins approximately, US$1.50. Traffic jams on Sat evening cause serious delays. **Car hire** from several agencies, for example *L C Fleming*, Les Portes de St Martin, Bellevue, T875001 (also travel agency). *Avis Bellevue*, T875060. Many others. Scooter rental from US$20 per day including helmets and insurance from *Concordia*, T871424, and *Eugene Moto*, T871397. Plenty of **taxis**, with controlled fares depending on the distance and number of people, no meters. You find them next to the tourist office in Marigot, T875654, in Grand-Case, T877579. From Juliana airport to Marigot about US$10, Marigot to Grand Case US$10, Marigot to Oyster Pond, US$26, 2½-hr island tour US$50, add 25% 2200-2400 and 50% 2400-0600.

Marigot

The capital of French Saint-Martin, lies between Simpson Bay Lagoon and the Caribbean sea. ('Marigot' is a French West Indian word meaning a spot from which rain water does not drain off, and forms marshy pools.) Shopping is good. Boutiques offer French prêt-à-porter fashions and St-Barts batiks, and gift shops sell liqueurs, perfumes, and cosmetics at better duty-free prices than the Dutch side.

At the *Marina Port La Royale* complex there are chic shops, cafés and bistros where

Saint-Martin

■ **Sleeping**
1 Club Orient
2 Le Samanna
3 Pavillon Beach
4 Royal Beach
5 Bel Air Beach
6 Cupecoy
7 Maho Beach
8 Oyster Pond & Dawn Beach

N
Not to scale

Essentials

Exchange *The US dollar is as widely used as the franc, but watch the rate.* **Credit card** *transactions are usually in US$. It is sometimes difficult to get change from payments in francs. Dollars are preferred. The best place for exchange is the post office in Marigot where they will change all currencies and travellers' cheques, but normally only into francs. There are several exchange houses for changing from francs to dollars, one in rue du Kennedy and one in the Marina Royale complex. Two* **banks***, both on rue de la République, Marigot, Banque des Antilles Françaises and Banque Française Commerciale.*

Departure tax *See page 676 for departure tax from Juliana airport.*

Ports of entry *(French flag) Marigot. See page 676 for further details.*

Marinas *Captain Oliver's Marina, Oyster Pond, T873347; Marina Port La Royale, Marigot, T872043; Port de Lonvilliers, Anse Marcel, T873194; Régie du Port de Marigot, T875906.*

Hours of business *Shops open around 0900 and close between 1800-1900 with normally a 2-hour lunch break between 1200-1500, depending on the shop.* **Banks** *open 0830-1530 Monday-Thursday, till 1630 on Friday; both slightly different from the Dutch side.*

Voltage *220 volts, 60 cycles (compared with 110 volts on the Dutch side).*

Useful addresses *Gendarmerie: T875010.* **Police***: T878833.* **Fire***: T875008.*

Communications *The international code for St-Martin is 590. See page 723 for further details.*

Media *Newspapers* *Le Monde, France Soir and Le Figaro from France are available 1-3 days after publication. France Antilles, same day. A few German and Italian magazines are sold at Maison de la Presse (opposite post office) and other locations.*

Public holidays *See page 693.*

See also Essentials, page 690

French Antilles

you can sit and watch the boats. Rue de la République and rue de la Liberté also have good shopping with fashion names at prices below those of Europe or the USA. Marigot has a large crop of art galleries, including *Camaïeu* on rue Kennedy, Espace Expo Marina Royale, *Galerie Valentin* at 117 Les Amandiers, *Galeries Gingerbread* and *Mahogany* at the Marina Royale, *Graffiti's* at Les Amandiers and *Roland Richardson* at Front de Mer. A fruit market is held every morning in the market place next to Marigot harbour. It is best on Wednesday and Saturday. On the right hand side of the market place is the tourist office and taxi rank; also the only public toilet on the French side. From here it is a 10-minute walk to **Fort St Louis** (restored 1994) overlooking Marigot Bay and Marigot. Follow the signs from the tourist office.

On the waterfront the historical and archaeological **Museum** 'On the trail of the Arawaks', has a well-presented exhibition from the first settlers of Saint-Martin around 3500 BC to 1960. ■ *0900-1300, 1500-1830, Mon-Sat, T292284, may open longer during high season. US$5 (US$2 children).*

Around the island

Grand Case, 13 km from the capital, is anything but grand. It is a quaint town between an old salt pond (which has been partially filled in to provide the Espérance airstrip) with a long sandy and secluded beach. At the far northeast end is another beach, Petite Plage, delightfully *petite* in a calm bay. Every other Saturday all year round there are sailing races of old fishing boats between Anguilla and St-Martin, mostly to Grand Case. Ask for information at the *Ranch Bar* at the beach (live music every Sunday).

Anse Marcel, north of Grand Case, is a shallow beach, ideal for small children. South of Grand Case is **Friar's Bay**, a sheltered bay with a couple of restaurants, from where you can walk along a path to **Happy Bay**. Inland, **Pic Paradise** (424 m) is a good lookout point from where, on a fine day, you can see Anguilla, Saba, St Eustatius, St Kitts, Nevis and St-Barts. However, the 20-minute trail is poorly marked and the view becoming obscured by thick vegetation at the summit. By four-wheel drive you can reach the top on the track used for access to the radio-television transmitting tower at the top, take a turn off at Rambaud on the Marigot-Grand Case road. There are also footpaths from **Colombier** (1½ km) and **Orléans** (1 km). Colombier is a small, sleepy village with some wonderful gardens, well worth a visit. In Orléans you can visit Roland Richardson, the only well-known native artist on St-Martin, whose home is open 1000-1800 on Thursday, T873224.

On the Atlantic, **Cul-de-Sac**, is a traditional village, and departure point for boats to the **Île de Tintamarre** and **Pinel Island** just offshore. The sea is calm and fishing boats come in here. **Baie Orientale** (Orient Bay) is beautiful but rough (beware of its undertow); it has a nudist section which is considerably less crowded than the rest. There are several new developments along the beach and the naturist area is often overrun with day visitors and shrinking. Windsurfers and catamarans can be hired from the south end of the beach, friendly staff, good protected area for beginners and more open waters. For the intrepid, or foolhardy, depending on your point of view and courage, there is bungee jumping from a parasail at 100 m, US$85, not done on very windy days. From here you can find boats to Caye Verte, just offshore.

There is a butterfly farm on Le Galion Beach Road next to the Bayside Riding Stables, Baie L'Embouchure, run by John Coward (claims family ties to the more famous Noel). Lovely collection of butterflies, very beautiful, most active in the morning, small gift shop, refreshments, admission US$2-5 per person, depending on the owner's mood, open 0900-1630, daily, T873121.

Further south, snorkelling is good at Coconut Grove. Topless bathing is accepted at all beaches on the French side, but not on the Dutch.

From Marigot to Anguilla by ferry boat (20 minutes), see page 631. Sailing trips with lunch and snorkelling to beaches on St-Martin or smaller islands such as Tintamarre, Sandy Island or Prickly Pear (see Anguilla), cost about US$70 per person. Boat charter companies, with or without crew, are around *Marina Port La Royale*, about US$360 per day for four people on a yacht with crew, or US$200-1,500 for a motor boat. A full range of diving services is offered by several companies: *Blue Ocean* at Baie Nettlé, T878973, *Octoplus* at Grand-Case, T872062, *Scuba Fun* at Anse Marcel, T873613, *Sea Dolphin* at the *Flamboyant*, Baie Nettlé, T876072, and Sea Horse Diving at the *Marine Hotel*, T878415. Sport fishing can be arranged at the Marina Port Royale, Marina Anse Marcel or Marina Oyster Pond.

There are two squash courts at *Le Privilège* (T873838). Horse riding at *Caïd* and *Isa*, Anse Marcel, T874570, daily rides at 0900 and 1500 if there is enough demand, US$45, 2½ hours, reservations one day in advance. Beach rides also with *OK-Corral*, Oyster Pond, up to Orient Bay, US$50 per person, 2½ hours, T874072.

For nature hikes, contact Serge L'homme if you can get hold of him. He runs a spice stall in Marigot market (he wraps the spices in red gingham) and on hikes he makes fruit punch while his wife cooks lunch. You can also contact the Association of Hiking Guides, T292020.

Essentials

Sleeping There are a number of luxury resorts dotted around the coast, lesser establishments and guest houses and a building boom has raised the total number of hotel rooms to 3,758. Deep discounts are available at the larger resorts. We list here only a very small selection; non-inclusion does not mean non-recommendation. The tourist office lists only those in the upper range, guest houses in Grand Case are rented from US$350-450 per week, but for low budget accommodation you would be better in the Dutch half.

Hotels LL *La Samanna*, Baie Longue, T876400, F878786. One of the most exclusive resorts in the Caribbean, 80 rooms, suites and villas, mediterranean-style hotel overlooks spectacular beaches, set in 55 acres with lush gardens, excellent dining, fitness centre, pool, all watersports, tennis. **Baie Nettlé**: **LL-L** *Anse Margot*, T879201, F879213, on beach in gardens between lagoon and sea. 96 rooms and suites in eight buildings, Créole-inspired architecture, spacious rooms, a/c, satellite TV, lots of luxuries, two pools, two jacuzzis, good restaurant. **LL-AL** *Marine Hotel Simson Beach*, T875454, F879211, a Mercure Coralia hotel. 175 rooms and loft suites, lagoon, pool or garden views, a/c, fans, kitchenettes, on beach, popular, pool, children's pool, tennis, beach volleyball, indoor games, aquagym,

Marigot

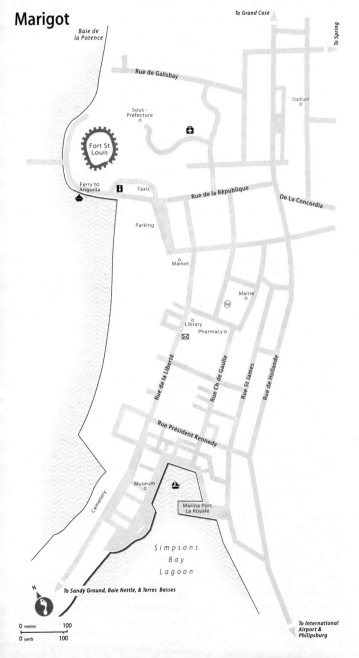

Baie de la Potence

Rue de Galisbay

To Grand Case

To Spring

Stadium

Sous-Préfecture

Fort St Louis

Ferry to Anguilla

Taxis

Rue de la République

De La Concordia

Parking

Market

Mairie

Library

Pharmacy

Rue de la Liberté

Rue Ch de Gaulle

Rue St James

Rue de Hollande

Rue Président Kennedy

Museum

Marina Port La Royale

Cemetery

Simpsons Bay Lagoon

N

To Sandy Ground, Baie Nettlé, & Terres Basses

0 metres 100
0 yards 100

To International Airport & Philipsburg

windsurfing, restaurant, bar, evening entertainment. **AL-A** *Royal Beach*, T/F878989. Modern, a/c, beachfront but not all rooms have seaview, pool, bar, restaurant, watersports nearby. **Grand Case: AL-B** *Hévèa*, 163 Boulevard de Grand Case, T875685, F878388. Small colonial-style hotel, 4 rooms, 3 studios, 3 apartments with kitchenettes, gourmet restaurant, beach across the street. **AL-A** *Grand Case Beach Club*, 23 Route de Petite Plage, T875187, F875993. 76 rooms and apartments, watersports, on the beach, orchestra plays in the evening in high season. **AL** *Chez Martine*, T875159, F878730. Five rooms, one suite, excellent restaurant, overlooks Grand Case Bay. **LL-A** *Le Pavillon Beach*, Plage de Grand Case, T879646, F877104. New, elegant hotel on lagoon, walking distance from Grand Case, six studios, 17 suites and one honeymoon suite, a/c, fans, TV, kitchenettes, phones, beach, watersports and land sports can be arranged. **Anse Marcel: LL-AL** *Le Meridien*, BP 581, T876700, F873038. In two parts: *L'Habitation*, 266 rooms and *Le Domaine*, 145 rooms, the latter more expensive but both 4-star, marina alongside for boat trips, surrounded by 150-acre nature reserve, two pools, jacuzzis, health club, tennis, squash, racquet ball courts, archery, shuttle to towns and casino, four restaurants, bars. **Baie Orientale: LL** *Club Orient* (naturist), T873385, F873376. Tennis, volleyball, watersports, massage, 80 rooms or chalets for 3-4 people, restaurant. **L-AL** *Mont Vernon*, T876200, F873727, MontVernon @aol.com 370 suites, large swimming pool, facilities for children, land sports and watersports. **Oyster Pond: LL** *Captain Oliver's*, T874026, F874084. Right on the border, 50 bungalows with kitchenette and balcony, pool, boat shuttle to Dawn Beach, 2 restaurants, evening entertainment, lots going on here at Captain Oliver's Marina, Moorings-Sun Yacht on site for yacht charters and other watersports on offer. **Marigot: B** *Rosely's*, T877017, F877020, 39 studios, 7 duplex, Concordia. Pool and jacuzzi in garden, kitchenette, a/c, restaurant, English spoken, very nice. **C** *Malibu*, also in Concordia, a few blocks from the centre of Marigot, T879898, F879234. 43 rooms, modern, kitchens, fridge.

Guest houses **Grand Case, A-B** *Les Alizés*, T877109, F877351. 8 rooms, kitchenette, TV, beach. **A-B** *Morning Star*, T879385, F877208. 12 rooms, a/c. **C** *Grand Case Beach Motel*, T878775, F872655. 7 rooms, kitchenette, garden, a/c, beach. **Galisbay, C** *Le Cigalon*, Rue Fichot, T870819, F877984. 10 rooms, garden, a/c. **St James, C** *Fantastic*, Rue Low Town, T877109, F877351. 20 rooms, kitchenette, TV, a/c. **Orléans, B-C** *Rising Sun Inn*, T873352. 12 rooms, a/c. **Baie Orientale, AL** *Maison de Récréation*, T874398, F874397. Two rooms, a/c, garden, TV, breakfast, pool, beach.

Apartments and villas There are several agencies listed by the tourist office which can arrange short or long term lets: *Carimo*, T875758. *C Coudart*, T872013. *IMAGE*, T877804. *IMMO-DOM*, T870038. *Immobilier St-Martin Caraïbe*, T878761. *Immobilière Antillaise*, T870095. *Impact*, T872061. *Investimmo*, T877520. *Sprimbarth*, T875865. For luxury villas contact *French Caribbean International in the USA*, T800-3222223, www.frenchcaribbean.com

Eating French cuisine in all hotel restaurants on the French side is quite good but expensive. Picturesque gourmet dining places on the seashore are the islanders' favourites. The likelihood of finding a cheap meal is rare but the absence of tax on alcohol makes retail purchases inexpensive. Many restaurants close in Sep-Oct. A useful restaurant guide is *Ti-Gourmet*, published annually in French and English, free and widely available.

Marigot The *Mini-Club*, T875069, with its bar and dining arbour, French and créole, serves a Caribbean buffet Wed and Sat, closed Aug and Sep. *La Maison sur le Port* (T875638), and *Le Poisson d'Or* (on the harbour, part art gallery, closed Sep-Oct, T877245) offer excellent French cuisine and seafood. *Le Bar de la Mer*, Boulevard de France (T878179), serves lunch and dinner, good place to go before a disco. Many bars on the water front next to the tourist office serving barbecue lunch and dinner. For travellers on a small budget try the snackbars and cafés on Rue de Hollande. There are also lots of restaurants overlooking the boats at Marina Port la Royale, many with open air dining. *Brasserie de la Gare*, a brasserie and pizzeria, open daily 1130-2230, T872064. More upmarket and expensive is *Jean Dupont*, T877113. French gourmet with some Vietnamese and Thai specialities, open 1130-1530 (except Sun in low season), 1730-2300. Browse around, see what takes your fancy.

Grand Case has a reputation of having more restaurants than inhabitants. Most are on the street next to the beach but these are generally more expensive than those on the other side of the boulevard and not recommendable on a windy night. *Fish Pot*, 82 Boulevard de Grand Case. Overlooking the sea, sea food, excellent food and formal service but at a price, T875088, F872037, open 1130-1500 in high season, dinner 1800-2230. *Rainbow* 176 Boulevard de Grand Case, T875580. Traditional French cuisine, good service. *L'Alabama*, 93 Boulevard de Grand Case, T878166. Owners Pascal and Kristin are most welcoming, traditional French food in garden away from traffic noise. At the small snackbars near the little pier you can find barbecue fish, ribs and lobster as well as other local snacks, very popular at weekends and holidays, recommended. At weekends there is usually live music in one of the bars/restaurants along the beach. *Chez Yvette*, Quartier d'Orléans, T873203. No sign, simple interior, authentic créole cooking.

Baie Orientale *Bikini Beach* for Spanish *tapas*, *paella* and *sangria*, helped along with Brazilian music some nights, T874325.

Carnival is held pre-Lent and most of the events are on the waterfront in Marigot. It is not as big and grandiose as on the Dutch side, where carnival is held a few weeks later, but there are calypso and beauty contests and a Grand Parade. **Bastille Day** (*14 July*) has live music, jump-ups and boat races; the celebrations move to Grand Case the weekend after (more fun) for **Schoelcher Day** on *21 July*. In Grand Case on **New Year's Day** there is a small parade with live music, while at **Easter** another parade is held with a lot of dancing. **Festivals**

L'Atmosphere is a disco for 'chic' French people, at Marina Port La Royale, very little English spoken, drinks US$6. *Le Bar de la Mer*, T878179, at the waterfront is a popular meeting place for French-speaking young travellers, with live music once a week. *La Fiesta*, Marigot waterfront. South American music, Brazilian house band, popular bar for locals. Grand Case normally has live music Fri-Sun in high season with beach party style entertainment in one of the many bars. *Surf Club South*, Cul-de-Sac, T295040. Run by Andy Susko, a New Jersey-type bar, has beach parties every other Sun, all food and drinks US$1, with mainly 60s and 70s music, great fun. *Circus* bar, T877864, in Baie Nettlé in the newly built resort area, a popular night bar, live music once in a while. *Le Privilège Disco* at Anse Marcel, T874617. US$10 entrance, one drink included, one of the best but taxis expensive to get there, open from 2300, closed Mon, in Sep only opens Thu, Fri, Sat. Every full moon there is a beach party at Friar's Bay starting around 2100-2200, barbecues on the beach every Fri and Sat. **Nightlife**

Airline offices Marigot: *Air Caraïbes*, T292525. *Air France*, T290202. *Air Guadeloupe*, T875374. *Nouvelle Frontières*, T872779. *Tropical Helicopter Services*, T879481. Grand Case: *Air Caraïbes*, T878480. *Air Guadeloupe*, T877659. *Air St-Barthélémy*, T871036. *Air Saint-Martin*, T871036. *Trans-Helico-Caraïbes*, T290541/872187. Bellevue: *AOM*, T292525. Anse Marcel: *Heli-Inter Caraïbes*, T873588. Many others at Juliana airport on the Dutch side. **Banks** Banks with ATMs include *Banque des Antilles Françaises (BDAF)*, Rue de la République, Marigot, T875331. *Banque Française Commerciale (BFC)*, Bellevue, T875380. *Banque Inchauspe & Cie*, Rue Général de Gaulle, T872121. **Communications** Post: The post office will hold mail, but only for two weeks. Letters sent c/o Capiteneri Marina Port La Royale, Marigot, will be kept 4-6 weeks. Telephone: There are several telephone booths on the French side but they only take telephone cards. 120 units for 90F, sold at the post office and at the bookshop opposite. There are 8 telephones on the square in Marigot and 2 in Grand Case in front of the little pier. To call the Dutch side use the code 00-599-54. To call the French side from the Dutch side use the code 00-590. All Dutch side numbers have 5 digits while French side numbers have 6. Calls from one side of the island to the other are expensive. **Cultural Associations** *L'Association Archéologique Hope Estate*, Rtd de Fort St-Louis, BP 38, T873941, set up in 1989 to protect the island's heritage, Docteur François Petit, T292284. *La Fondation Historique et Culturelle de Saint Martin*, an umbrella organization for all the artistic movements on the island, under the leadership of Roland Richardson, T873224. **Medical facilities** Hospital: T875007 Ambulance: T878625 (day), 877200 (night). **Tourist information** Local tourist office: Port de Marigot, 97150 Saint-Martin, T875721, F875643, www.st-martin.org **Directory**

French Antilles

Saint-Barthélémy

Population: 5,038   *Saint-Barthélémy (also known as St-Barts or St-Barth's), in the Leewards, has lush volcanic hillsides and 32 splendid white sandy beaches, most of which are protected by both cliff and reef. The people are generally known for their courtesy and honesty. It is inhabited mostly by people of Breton, Norman, and Poitevin descent who live in quiet harmony with the small percentage of blacks. Immigrants from mainland France have taken the best jobs in hotels and restaurants though and relations there are sometimes strained. St-Barts has become a very 'chic' and expensive holiday destination; the Rockefellers, Fords, and Rothschilds own property on the island, while the rich, royal and famous stay in the luxury villas dotted around the island. It is 21 sq km, 230 km north of Guadeloupe, 240 km east of the Virgin Islands, and 35 km southeast of Saint-Martin.*

Ins and outs

Getting there   **Air**   Scheduled flights from Anguilla (*Winair, Coastal Air Transport*), Pointe-à-Pitre (*Air*
Only small planes   *Guadeloupe*), Saba (*Winair*), St Croix (*Coastal Air Transport*), Sint Maarten (*Winair, Air*
carrying a maximum   *Guadeloupe*), St Martin (*Saint Barth Commuter, Air Guadeloupe*), St Thomas (*Air St*
of 20 passengers can   *Thomas*), San Juan (*Air St Thomas, Air Guadeloupe*). Charters available locally with *St*
land on the short   *Barth Commuter*, T275454, *Air St Martin*, T276190 and *Air Caraïbes*, T279941. *Air*
runway   *Guadeloupe* T276190, *Winair* T276101, *Air St-Barthélémy* T277190, *Air St Thomas*
T277176. **Sea**   *Gustavia Express* goes to St Martin, Mon-Sat, departs Gustavia 0715, 1530,
departs Marigot market place 0900, 1715, adults one way US$36 including US$6 tax, round
trip US$56, children up to 12 US$26 and US$31, cheaper for residents, ID required, T275410,
277724, F277723 in Gustavia, T879903, F877303 in St-Martin. *Voyager* have scheduled services between St Maarten/St Martin, St-Barts and Saba, contact St-Barth Ship Service for
details, Quai de la République, T277738, F276795. Several catamarans go to St-Barts from
Sint Maarten, leaving in the morning and returning in the afternoon so you can do a day trip.
There are no other regular boats to other islands.

Getting around   There is a **taxi** stand at the airport T277581, and in Gustavia T276631. **Minibuses** (and ordi-
See page 729 for   nary taxis) do island tours, 2½-3 hrs, US$45 for two people, dropping you off at Baie de
further details   Saint-Jean and collecting you later for the boat if you are on a day trip. It is not easy to hire a
car for only one day, except out of season, mini mokes from 210F per day: ask your hotel to
obtain a car if required.

Diving and marine life

There is excellent diving all round St Barts, especially out round the offshore rocks,
like the Groupers, and islands like Ile Fourche. Sometimes in May the migrating
sperm whales pass close by. From April to August female sea turtles come to
Colombier, Flamands and Corossol to lay their eggs.

There are four **dive shops** in Gustavia: *La Bulle*, T276225; *St Barth Plongée*,
T275444; *Marine Service*, T277034, *West Indies Dive*, T279179 and *Odysée Caraïbe*,
T275594. A single dive costs about US$50, or there are packages of five or 10 dives
for US$220 or US$400. PADI open water certification costs US$480.

Deep sea fishing for marlin, tuna, wahoo and dolphin can be arranged with
Océan Must Marina at La Pointe, Gustavia, T276225, F279517, VHF 10, who also
charter boats for cruising, diving, waterskiing and offer a full service marina. *Marine
Service* at Quai du Yacht Club, Gustavia, T277034, F277036, VHF 74, also do deep
sea fishing trips and the same watersports and boat rentals. The price depends on the

type of boat (4-8 people) and ranges from US$470-640 for a half day to US$780-1,100 for a full day with open bar and picnic lunch. The catch is the property of the boat.

Beaches and watersports

Some beaches are more accessible than others, most uncrowded. The main resort area is **Baie de Saint-Jean**, which is two beaches divided by Eden Rock, the most visited beach with several bars and restaurants open for lunch or a snack, watersports, but no waterskiing, small boats, snorkelling rentals, ideal for families, good windsurfing, safe swimming, some snorkelling. Motorized watersports are only allowed 150 m off the beach. Others are **Lorient**, **Marigot**, **Grand Cul de Sac** on the north coast, **Grande Saline**, **Gouverneur** on the south, and **Colombier** and **Flamands** at the northwest tip, to name but a few.

To get to **Gouverneur** from Gustavia take the road to Lurin. A sign will direct you to the dirt road leading down to the beach, lovely panoramic view over to the neighbouring islands, where there is white sand with palm trees for shade. A legend says that the 17th century pirate, Montbars the Exterminator, hid his treasures in a cove here and they have never been found. Also a very good spot for snorkelling.

Colombier beach is the most beautiful on St Barts. It can not be reached by car but is well worth the 20-30 minutes' walk during which you have majestic views of the island. Park the car at Colombier, there are several trails going down to the beach. There are also several day tours by boat from Gustavia. **Flamands** beach is of very clean white sand, bordered with Latania palm trees. The surf can be rough, watersports available. In **Corossol** is the **Inter Oceans Museum**, a private collection of 9,000 seashells, corals and stuffed fish from all around the world. ■ *T276297. Tue-Sun 0900-1230, 1400-1700 (Mon groups only). 20F.* Petite Anse de Galet, in

French Antilles

Saint-Barthélemy

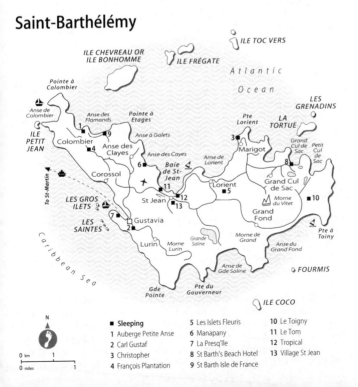

■ Sleeping	5 Les Islets Fleuris	10 Le Toigny
1 Auberge Petite Anse	6 Manapany	11 Le Tom
2 Carl Gustaf	7 La Presqu'île	12 Tropical
3 Christopher	8 St Barth's Beach Hotel	13 Village St Jean
4 François Plantation	9 St Barth Isle de France	

French Antilles

Essentials

See also page 690

Currency As on Saint-Martin, dollars are widely accepted but shops and restaurants will give a bad rate of exchange.

Anchorages (French flag) Outside the inner harbour of Gustavia, daily anchorage fee of US$2.50-5, depending on location. Inside the main harbour, stern to or on double moorings, fees are based on length of boat. Water, waste disposal, showers and toilets are available at the dock. Other anchorages around the island are free.

Provisioning and some marine supplies.

Hours of business 0800-1200, 1430-1700, morning only on Wednesday and Saturday.

Useful addresses Gendarmerie:T276012. **Police:** T276666. **Fire:** T276231. **Sub Prefect:** T276328. **Radio** St Barts: T277474, broadcasting on FM 98 mHz.

Public holidays See Guadeloupe, page 693. See below for festivals.

Gustavia, 3-5 minutes' walk from Fort Karl, is also known as Shell beach because it is covered in shells, not sand. Trees give shade and swimming is safe, shelling is of course extremely good.

St Barts is a popular mid-way staging post on the yachting route between Antigua and the Virgin Islands. Boat charters are available, also courses in, or facilities for, windsurfing (Toiny is the windsurfers' favourite beach), snorkelling (very good, particularly at Marigot), waterskiing and sailing. *Windsurfing Paradise*, Baie de Saint-Jean, T277122, is a Bic Centre, offering lessons and equipment rental. *Eden Rock Beach Club Gleveau Henri*, also at Baie de Saint-Jean, T277477, has Fanatic equipment for rent, while at the *Saint-Barth Beach Hotel*, Grand Cul-de-Sac, *Wind Wave Power* has Mistral gear at their windsurf school. Surfboard rental (not windsurfing) at Hookipa, T277131. Sailing and snorkelling cruises are offered by several catamarans. They go to Colombier beach, Fourchue Island, Tintamarre, Anguilla or St-Martin. Half day cruises cost US$55-60, whole day with lunch US$90-95, sunset cruises US$46, or with dinner, US$70-80.

Other sports **Tennis** at several hotels, guests take priority: *St-Barth Beach Hotel, Manapany, Flamboyant Restaurant, Isle de France, Guanahani*. Also at ASCCO in Colombier, 2 lit courts, T276107, AJOE in Lorient, two courts, one lit court, T276763. Some opportunities for **hiking. Horse riding** at Flamands, Laure Nicolas, T278072. **Body building** at *St Barth Beach Hotel*, open 0730-2130, 100F, instructor on duty all the time. At the end of November or beginning of December the Swedish Marathon Race (Gustavialoppet) is held, a traditional annual race of 3, 10 and 15 km for men, women and children from anywhere.

Gustavia

In Gustavia, the capital, there are branches of several well-known French shops (such as Cartier). The small crowd of habitués *is mostly young, chic, and French. The food, wine, and aromas are equally Gallic. The harbour or Carénage was renamed Gustavia after the 18th-century Swedish king, Gustavus III, and became a free port, marking the beginning of the island's greatest prosperity.*

In 1852 a fire severely damaged the capital, although the Swedish influence is still evidenced in the city hall, the belfries, the Forts (Karl, Oscar and Gustave), the street names and the trim stone houses which line the harbour. In the southeast inner corner in front of the Anglican church, is a truly massive anchor. Probably from a British Royal Navy Frigate, and dating from the late 18th Century, it weighs 10 tons. Marked "Liverpool...Wood...London", it came to Gustavia by curious means in

French Antilles

1981. The cable of a tug towing a barge across from St Thomas fouled on something at the entrance of the harbour. A local man dived down to have a look and found the anchor. It is thought that the cable dragged it up as the tug left St Thomas. Suspended below water, unseen, it got carried across. **St Barts Municipal Museum** with an exhibition of the history, traditions and local crafts of the island, is at La Pointe, near the *Wall House*. ■ *Mon-Thu 0830-1230, 1430-1800, Fri 1500-1800, Sat 0830-1200, entrance 10F, T278907.*

From Gustavia, you can head north to the fishing village of **Corossol** (see above), continuing to Colombier and the northwest beaches; south over Les Castelets and the hills of Morne Lurin to Anse du Gouverneur; or to Saint-Jean and beaches and settlements on the east end. A hired car can manage all the roads.

Essentials

Gustavia C *La Presqu'île*, T276460, F277230. 10 rooms. Restaurant specializes in French and Créole cooking. **LL** *Carl Gustaf*, rue des Normands, Gustavia 97133, T278283, F278237, www.st-barths.com/hotel-carl-gustaf/index.html, overlooking harbour, 14 one or

Sleeping

Gustavia

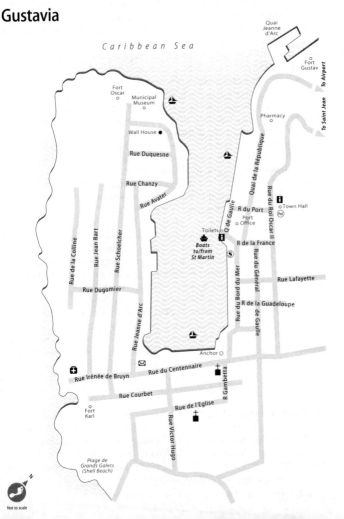

two-bedroom suites, luxury, with high prices to match, breakfast and airport transfers, a/c, TV, kitchenette, private mini pool and sun deck, fax, stereos, gym-sauna, pool side restaurant, short walk to beach.

North coast **L-AL** *Auberge de la Petite Anse*, T276489, F278309. 16 bungalows, pool, no restaurant, only Amex credit card accepted, receptionist only there when you check in or out, picturesque but difficult path to Colombiers Beach starts here. At Colombier, overlooking Flamands beach is **LL** *François Plantation*, T276825, F276126. Elegant plantation style hotel with 12 bungalows, pool, good restaurant, breakfast in room, a/c, fan, telephone, satellite TV. **LL** *St Barth Isle de France*, BP 612, Baie de Flamands 97098, T276181, F278683, isledefr@saint-barths.com Luxury hotel, 31 rooms, bungalows and suites, tennis, two pools, squash, fitness centre, open air restaurant, marble bathrooms, can arrange watersports and horse riding, closed Sep-Oct. The luxury, four-star **LL** *Manapany Cottages*, T276655, F277528. Cottages, suites, apartments and rooms on hillside, descending to beach, 56 beds in all, largest pool on the island, tennis, jacuzzi, some villas have private pools, two gourmet restaurants. **LL-L** *Emeraude Plage*, T276478, F278308. 24 bungalows, 3 suites, 1 villa, a/c, fans, terrace, kitchen, beach. **LL** *Relais & Chateaux Filao Beach*, T276484, F276224, www.integra.fr/relaischateaux 30 rooms on beach, 3-star hotel, poolside bar and restaurant. **LL** *Le Tom Beach Hotel*, Plage de St-Jean, T275313, F275315. 12 rooms on beach, luxury four-poster beds, a/c, fans, private terraces, popular restaurant with good view and fresh lobster specialities, multilingual staff. **LL-AL** *Village St-Jean*, T276139, F277796, on hillside overlooking Baie de Saint-Jean. 20 1-2 bedroom cottages with kitchenettes, four rooms with mini-fridge, special packages available, a/c, fans, phones, pool, jacuzzi, Italian restaurant, short walk to beach, managed by Charneau family, watersports facilities. **LL** *Eden Rock*, T277294, F278837, edenrock@saintbarts.com On a promontory in St-Jean bay. Clear waters all around you, two beaches, watersports centre and 27-ft boat for fishing, short walk along beach to airstrip, two fine restaurants, lobster tank, exceptional wine cellar, 12 rooms, a/c, all luxuries, multilingual staff. **LL-AL** *Le Tropical*, St-Jean beach, T276487, F278174. 20 seaview and gardenview rooms with cool white bedlinen and drapes, overlooking beach, a/c, fans, phones, TV, in lush garden, pool with panoramic sea view, short walk to beach, excursions arranged, closed 1 Jun-15 Jul. A few hundred yards from Lorient beach is **LL** *La Banane*, T276825, F276844. Owned by Jean-Marie Rivière, who owns two nightclubs in Paris. Pastel painted bungalows, all different, 9 rooms, beautifully furnished and decorated, two pools, lots of bananas, fine dining, cabaret show every evening. In the hills above Lorient, **LL-L** *Les Islets Fleuris*, Hauts de Lorient 97133, T276422, F276972. Seven studios, pool, kitchenettes, lovely views over coastline, maid service, car rental available with room package. **LL** *The Christopher Hotel*, Pointe Milou, T276363, F279292, a Sofitel Coralia hotel with 4 stars. 41 rooms, a/c with sitting room and bathroom, terrace, balcony or patio, three rooms with facilities for the disabled, shuttle service to beaches, large pool, Total Fitness Club, watersports arranged, closed in Sep. **LL-L** *El Sereno*, T276480, F277547. 18 rooms, 9 villas, 14 suites, a/c, TV, telephone, fridge, large pool, superb restaurant, gardens, hammocks, private beach, the hotel also manages **LL-L** *El Sereno Beach Villas*, nine villas on hillside, a/c, TV, phones, fans, kitchen, use of hotel facilities. **LL** *St Bart's Beach Hotel*, T276070, F277557, www.saintbarthbeachhotel.com 36 rooms and 8 luxury villas, pool, gym, tennis, windsurfing school, built on strip of land between sea and lagoon, conference facilities. In the east, at Anse de Toiny, **LL** *Le Toiny*, T278888, F278930, www.letoiny.com 4-star hotel, includes breakfast, service, tax and airport transfers, 13 villa suites with a/c, fans, TV, phone, fax, plunge pools, restaurant, bar, room service, high luxury, closed Sep-Oct.

Apartments and villas In the USA contact *French Caribbean International*, T800-3222223, www.frenchcaribbean.com On St-Barts contact the following agencies: *Sibarth Real Estate*, BP 55, Gustavia, 97133 St-Barts, T276238, F276052, 105062.1516@compuserve.com *New Agency*, Quai de la République, Gustavia, T278114, F278767. *Claudine Mora Immobilier* (CMI), Galeries du Commerce, Saint-Jean, T278088, F278085. *Immo-Antilles*, Gustavia, T279046, F276795. *Ici et Là*, Quai de la République, T277878, F277828.

Food in St-Barts is expensive. Expect to pay minimum US$25 for dinner per person. There are **Eating** many excellent restaurants all over the island, mostly French but some Créole and Italian. Very few vegetarian options but nearly all restaurants serve seafood. Several good ones on Saint-Jean beach; the hotel restaurants are generally good.

Gustavia *Wall House*, T277183 for reservations, for good French cuisine on the waterfront with harbour view but overpriced wine; *Au Port* also offers fine dining overlooking the harbour, better value for money. T276236 for reservations, one of the most expensive restaurants on the island; *Le Repaire* is a good restaurant at the *Yacht Club*, overlooking the harbour open 0600-0100, closed Sun, on rue de la République, offers few but well-prepared French dishes (also has a few rooms to let, T277248); *Bar Le Select* is a central meeting spot, an informal bar for lunch with hamburger menu, but also one of the most popular night-time bars and sort of general store, with a few tables in a small garden. *L'Escale*, across the harbour, a pizza, pasta place with low prices for St Bart's but still expensive, closed Oct, T278106. A local place serving Créole food is *Eddy's*, T275417, closed Sun. For early starters try the bakery on rue du Roi Oscar II, they open 0600, closed Mon. *La Crêperie* on the same street is open 0700-2300, closed Sun, and does American and Continental breakfast as well as sweet and savoury *crêpes*, salads and ice creams. Not to be missed is *La Gloriette*, on the beach at Grand Cul de Sac, T277566, serving superb, authentic Créole cuisine.

Carnival is held before Lent, on Mardi Gras and Ash Wed. The **Festival of Gustavia** is *20* **Festivals** *August*, with dragnet fishing contests, dances and parties, while *24 August* is the day of the island's patron saint, St-Barthélémy, when the church bells ring, boats are blessed and there are regattas, fireworks and a public ball. On *25 August* the **Feast of St Louis** is celebrated in the village of Corossol, with a fishing festival, *petanque, belote*, dancing and fireworks. In the last week of *July* the northern villages hold special events. **Fête du Vent** is held in Lorient on *26-27 August* with dragnet fishing contests, dancing, lottery and fireworks.

The **St Barts regatta** in *February* is the main event for sailors. Other regattas should be checked at *Lou Lou's Marine Shop*, Gustavia, because none is fixed annually. Every other year in *May* there is a transatlantic sailboat race from Brittany in France to St-Barts. The local traditional sailboats participate on all public events with their own regattas like **Bastille Day**, **Gustavia Day** and one regatta a month.

A **music festival** is held annually in *January* with 2 weeks of classical, folk, jazz music and ballet performed by both local school children and guest artistes and musicians from abroad in Gustavia and Lorient churches. A **gourmet festival** is held in *April*, and an **International Art exhibition** in *December*. On the last weekend in *April* is the **St-Barth Festival of Caribbean Cinema**, a small, informal festival for filmmakers throughout the Caribbean. All films are shown in their original language (with French subtitles).

In Gustavia at *Bar Le Select* (closed Sun). In Lurin try *Why Not?* (open from 2100, disco, bil- **Nightlife** liards, T278867), *La Banane* Cabaret Show now plays at *El Sereno Beach Hotel*. There are dis- *Most of the nightlife* cos at *Le Petit Club* in Gustavia, T276633, and *Le Feeling*, Lurin, T278867. Contact the tourist *starts around the bars* office for details of concerts and ballets held in the Jan music festival, see below. *at Bay Saint Jean*

Wide range of goods available from T-shirts to duty-free luxury goods and fine wines. There **Shopping** are five small shopping centres in Saint-Jean: La Savane, Les Galeries du Commerce, La Villa Créole, Centre Commercial de Sain-Jean and Centre Commercial de Neptune. Gustavia also has lots of shops. St-Barths is the place to find designer labels such as Gianni Versace, Hermès and Ralph Lauren.

Car hire Many agencies at the airport. *Hertz* T277114, *Avis* T277143, *Budget* T276630, **Transport** *Turbe* T277142, *Gumbs Rental* T277532, *Questel* T277322, *Aubin* T277303, *Europcar* T277333, *Soleil Caraïbes* T276718, *Island Car Rental* T277001. Scooters can be rented from *Rent Some Fun* T277059, *Chez Beranger* T278900, *Saint Barth Moto Bike* T276789. *Denis Dufau*, Saint-Jean, T275483, is a Harley Davidson shop. There are two gas stations, one near the airport terminal, open Mon-Sat 0730-1700, the other in Lorient open Mon-Wed, Fri

French Antilles

0730-1700, Sat morning. There is self-service with payment to the cashier, or automatic service machine open 24 hrs using Visa card, maximum allowance F600.

Directory **Banks** *Banque Nationale de Paris* (0745-1200, 1405-1530) with an ATM that is supposed to work 24 hrs with US and European credit cards, Visa, Mastercard and Eurocard, but is reported to work only with the French 'carte bleue', T276370, F278570. *Banque Française Commerciale* (0745-1215, 1400-1630, Mon, Tue, Thu, Fri), withdrawals at counter with Visa, Mastercard and Eurocard, T276262, F278775, both in Gustavia. BFC head office is at Saint-Jean, Galeries du Commerce (open Tue-Fri 0815-1215, 1400-1700, Sat 0800-1300) where there is an ATM open 24 hrs for withdrawals in US$ or F, T276588, F278148. Crédit Martiniquais, at Le Carré d'Or in the centre of Gustavia (open Mon-Fri 0815-1215, 1400-1615), T278657, F278279. *Crédit Agricole*, rue Bord de Mer, Gustavia, ATM accepts nearly all cards including eurocheque cards (cheaper than cash advance with credit card), also automatic bank note exchange machine (open Tue-Fri 0800-1300, 1430-1700, Sat 0800-1300), T278990, F276461. *Crédit Lyonnais West Indies*, rue Auguste Nyman, Gustavia (open Mon-Fri 0900-1200, 1400-1700), T279200, F279191. **Communications** **Post**: In Gustavia there are 3: open 0800-1500 Mon, Tue, Thu, Fri, 0800-1200 Wed, Sat, T276200, F278203; in Saint-Jean: open 0800-1400 Mon, Tue, Thu, Fri, 0730-1100 Wed, Sat, T276402. In Lorient: open 0700-1100 Mon-Fri, 0800-1000 Sat, T276135. **Telephone**: The SiBarth agency on General de Gaulle in Gustavia, T276238, F276052, has a fax service and a mail holding service. There are phone booths on the Quai de Gaulle, at the airport, Galeries du Commerce and Flamands, among other places. There are some phones which take coins but most take phone cards. There is a USA Direct phone at the airport; you can phone the USA using a phone card and have the recipient return the call to the payphone. **Medical facilities** T276035. **Doctor** on call: T277304. **Tourist information** Local office Quai de Gaulle, Gustavia, T278727, F277447. Open Mon-Thu 0830-1230, 1430-1800, Fri 0930-1230, 1430-1600. St Barths Online: www.st.barths.com

Background

History

Although called Ouanalao by the Caribs, the island was renamed after Christopher Columbus' brother, Saint-Barthélémy when discovered in November 1496. It was first settled by French colonists from Dieppe in 1645. After a brief possession by the Order of the Knights of Malta, and ravaging by the Caribs, it was bought by the Compagnie des Iles and added to the French royal domain in 1672. In 1784, France ceded the island to Sweden in exchange for trading rights in the port of Göteborg. In 1801, St Barts was attacked by the British, but for most of this period it was peaceful and commercially successful. The island was handed back to France after a referendum in 1878.

Government and economy

St Barts is administered by the sub-prefect in Saint-Martin and is a dependency of Guadeloupe. The island has its own elected mayor, who holds office for seven years. Much the same as Saint-Martin, St Barts relies on its free port status and its anchorages and beaches for the bulk of its revenue. It is popular with both French and North American visitors and, despite the limitations of its airstrip, it is claimed that twice as many tourists as the island's population pass through each month.

Norman dialect is still widely spoken while many islanders also speak English, but French is the dominant language. A few elderly women still wear traditional costumes (with their characteristic starched white bonnets called *kichnottes*); they cultivate sweet potato patches and weave palm fronds into hats and purses which they sell in the village of Corossol. The men traditionally smuggled rum among neighbouring islands and now import liqueurs and perfumes, raise cattle, and fish for lobsters offshore.

Martinique

Throughout the island of Martinique the scenery is dramatic and very beautiful, with   Population: 399,000
*lush rainforest coating the slopes of the mountains and swathes of sugar cane grown on
the plain. The island is 65 km long and 31 km wide with mountains in the north and
south and a low-lying 'waist' where most people live. The coastline is irregular in the
southern half, with peninsulas and promontories protecting islets and sandy bays. The
Caribbean Sea is to the west, the Atlantic Ocean to the east. Martinique's neighbouring
islands are Dominica to the north and St Lucia to the south.*

French Antilles

Ins and outs

Air Scheduled direct flights from Europe, from France only, are with *Air France*, which has   **Getting there**
flights from Paris; *Air Liberté* flies from Paris; *AOM French Airlines* from Paris. *Aerolyon* from   *See page 745 for*
Lyon, Marseille, Nantes, Toulouse. *Air France* also has direct flights from Cayenne, Caracas,   *further details*
Miami, Pointe-à-Pitre, Port-au-Prince. Ask *Air France* for youth fares if under 26, or for sea-
sonal prices. *Nouvelles Frontières* has charter flights from France. *Air Guadeloupe* has afternoon flights from San Juan, so same-day connections are possible from the USA. *Air
Guadeloupe* flies from Miami. Local airlines include *Air Guadeloupe* which flies from Barbados, Canouan, Dominica, Guadeloupe, St Lucia, St Maarten, St-Martin, St Vincent and Union
Island, Port-au-Prince, San Juan, Santo Domingo. *Cubana* from Havana, while *LIAT* flies from
Antigua, Barbados, Dominica, Guadeloupe, St Lucia and St Vincent. **Sea** *L'Express des Iles*
hydrofoil ferry service to St Lucia, Dominica and Pointe-à-Pitre, Guadeloupe. Fares and
schedules are published in the daily newspaper, *France-Antilles* or contact Terminal Inter Iles
97200 Fort-de-France, T631211, F633447. Overnight packages available with several hotels,
also car hire.

There are plenty of **buses** running between Fort-de-France and the suburbs which can be   **Getting around**
caught at Boulevard Général-de-Gaulle. The buses are all privately owned and leave when   *There are no buses to*
they're full and not before. Short journeys cost around 6F if paid for in advance more if paid   *the airport (though the*
on the bus, and the buses run from 0500-2000 approximately. To request a stop shout   *Ste-Anne buses go*
"arrêt"! To go further afield the *taxi collectif* (estate cars or minibuses) are the best bet.   *close), a metered taxi is*
'Taxicos', or TCs, run until about 1800 and leave Pointe Simon for all the communes;   *the only way of getting*
Ste-Anne 39F, Diamant 19F, St-Pierre 18F. There are numerous car hire firms at the airport   *into town, costing*
and around town, see page 745 for details.   *70-120F*

The lushness of Martinique's vegetation is evidence that it has a far higher rainfall than many   **Climate**
of the islands, due to its mountainous relief. The wet season lasts from June to late November
and the frequency of sudden heavy showers make an umbrella or raincoat an essential piece
of equipment. The cooler dry season lasts from December to May and the year round average temperature is 26°C although the highlands and Montagne Pelée are quite cool.

Watersports

Sailing and **windsurfing** at *Club de la Voile de Fort-de-France*, Pointe de la Vièrge,
T614969, and Pointe des Carrières, T633137; *Club Nautique de Marin*, Bassin la
Tortue, Pointe du Marin, T749248; *Club Nautique du François*, Route de la Jetée,
T543100; *Club Nautique du Vauclin*, Pointe Faula, T745058; *Yacht Club de la
Martinique*, Fort de France, T702360; *Base de Plein Air et de Loisirs*, Anse
Spoutourne, Tartane, T582432. There are glass bottom boats, motor boats, sailing
boats for excursions and lots of craft for hire. Windsurfing is available on hotel
beaches where there are board rentals. Jet skiing, sea scooters and waterskiing at

Pointe du Bout hotel beaches, *Marouba Club* (Carbet) and Pointe Marin beach in Ste-Anne. Many hotels like Bambou, La Dunette, Diamant-les-Bains organize **fishing** trips with local fishermen for their guests. Deep sea fishing can be arranged at *Bathy's Club* (*Meridien*), T660000 or *Rayon Vert*, T788056, around 4,000F per boat.

Yole (yawl) races (large sailing boats with coloured sails and teams of oarsmen) are an amazing sight at festivals all over the island from July to January. In Fort-de-France races take place in November and December from the little beach next to Desnambuc quay. Other major sailing occasions include the Schoelcher International Nautical Week in February, with sailing and windsurfing competitions; International Sailing Week in March (Yacht Club of Fort-de-France); the Aqua Festival, the Great Nautical Celebration at Robert in April; the Yawl Regatta

Martinique

Essentials

Documents See page 690.

Customs In Fort-de-France open 0800-1100, 1300-1700 daily, including holidays, no overtime fees charged; at Le Marin from 0730 until lunchtime, at St Pierre on Wednesday morning.

Money *Cost of living* Remember that the standard of living is high and expect to pay French prices or higher, which means expensive. Small beers or cokes cost around 15F in a tourist bar, 10F in a local bar, 6F in a supermarket, petrol 5F per litre, a nice meal at a good restaurant including wine will be at least 350F for two. A 2-3 course set lunch will cost 60-70F per person, with house wine at around 7F a glass.

Ports of entry (French Flag) Fort-de-France, St-Pierre, Le Marin. No fees or visas for EU or US citizens. French forms to clear in and out.

Anchorages The facilities are among the best in the Caribbean. Anchorages at St-Pierre, Fort-de-France, Anse Mitan, Les Trois-Ilets, Anse Noir, Grand and Petit Anse d'Arlets, Ste-Anne, Cul-de-Sac Marin. Marinas at Fort-de-France, Les Trois-Ilets, Le Marin. The marina at Pointe du Bout is reported safe, but congested and hot. Major charter companies include Moorings Antilles at Club Nautique du Marin (T747539, F747644), Sun Sail (Soleil et Voile, Capitainerie Marina Pointo du Bout, T660914), and Stardust (Port de Plaisance du Marin, T749817, F749812). Many other smaller companies. Excellent provisioning, stock up on French wines.
For those looking to hitch on a boat, consult the noticeboards at the Yacht Clubs, especially the bar at the Public Jetty and refuelling at the west end of Boulevard Alfassa on the Baie des Flamands.

Hours of business *Shops* are open from 0900-1800 (**banks** from around 0730) and until 1300 on Saturday. Nearly everything closes from 1200-1500 and on Sunday.

Laundry There are several launderettes in Fort-de-France; Lavexpress, 61 rue Jules-Monnerot; Laverie Self-Service, Lavematic, 85 rue Jules-Monnerot, Terres Sainville, T637043. Laundry service behind Pointe du Bout marina, also at Bakoua Marina dock.

Useful addresses *Fire department*: T18. *Police*: T17. Gendarmerie, rue Victor Sévère, 97200 Fort-de-France, T635151. **Hôtel de Police**: T553000. **Sea rescue**: T639205, 632088. radio phone (international), T10. **Radio taxi**: T636362.

Voltage The electric current is 220 volts AC.

Weights and measures The metric system.

Public holidays See page 693.

See also page 690

French Antilles

Tour of Martinique in July or August, when over a period of eight days about 20 yawls set off for a colourful race.

Diving is especially good along the coral reef between St-Pierre and Le Prêcheur, over the wrecks off St-Pierre and along the south coast. A medical certificate is required unless you are a qualified diver, in which case you need your certification card. There are lots of dive operators, most of which are based at the large hotels.

For those who do not dive, there are the *Kelennea* glass-bottomed boat at Marina Pointe du Bout, Trois Ilets, T660550, F660552 and the *Aquabulle* at Marin, T746969, which has a glass hull. To get even further under the water, there are two semi-submersibles: *Aquascope Seadom Explorer*, Marina Pointe du Bout, T683609 and *Zemis Aquascope*, Rue de Caritan, Ponton de la Mairie, T748741.

Tennis courts are at many large hotels; *Bakoua*; *Club Méditerranée*; *Plantation Leyritz*; *PLM Azur Carayou*; *Novotel*; *Meridien, Framissima, Hôtel Casino la Batelière* and others where visitors can play at night as well as during the day. There are also about 40 clubs round the island where you can play by obtaining temporary

Other sports

membership. For more information contact *La Ligue Regional de Tennis*, Petit Manoir, Lamentin, T510800.

Golf At Trois-Ilets is a magnificent, 18-hole championship golf course designed by Henry Trent Jones, with various facilities including two tennis courts, shops, snackbar, lessons and equipment hire. Green fees in high season are US$46 and in low season US$39, or you can book for a week (US$285, US$227) or a month (US$960, US$900). Electric carts and other equipment are available for rent. Contact *Golf Country Club de la Martinique*, 97229 Trois-Ilets, T683281, F683897. Two mini-golf courses are at Madiana Plage à Schoelcher and Anse l'Etang à Tartane.

Riding is a good way to see Martinique's superb countryside; Ranch Jack, Morne Habitue-Quartier Espérance, T683769; Black Horse, La Pagerie, Trois-Ilets, T683780; La Cavale, Diamant, T762294; and others offering schooling, hacking and other facilities. At *Plantation Leyritz* there are two horses for guests' use.

Cycling Touring the island by bike is one of the activities offered by the Parc Naturel Régional. For information T731930. VT Tilt, Anse Mitan, Trois-Ilets, offers excursions by bike and cycle groups, T660101, F511400.

Spectator sports Mongoose and snake fights and cockfights are widespread from December to the beginning of August at Pitt Quartier Bac, Ducos, T560560; Pitt Marceny (the most popular), Le Lamentin, T512847, Pitt Cléry, Rivière-Pilote, T626169 and many others. Horse racing is at the Carrère racetrack at Lamentin, T512509.

Fort-de-France

Fort-de-France was originally built around the Fort St-Louis in the 17th century. The settlement's first name was Fort-Royal and its inhabitants are still called *Foyalais*. From 1681 it was the headquarters of the Royal Governor although St-Pierre was the commercial capital and seat of the bishop. It became the capital of the island in 1902 when St-Pierre was completely obliterated by the eruption of Montagne Pelée. Fort-de-France was entirely destroyed by fire 11 years previously and there are no buildings left that existed before then. The city of today consists of a bustling, crowded centre bordered by the waterfront and the sprawling suburbs which extend into the surrounding hills and plateaux. The bars, restaurants, and shops give a French atmosphere quite unlike that of other Caribbean cities. Traffic is very dense and street parking is almost impossible. Park near la Savane (3F per hour). Most people live in the suburbs and even the discos are out of the old town centre, which is deserted at weekends after Saturday midday. The port of Fort-de-France is situated to the east of the town centre, where the Baie du Carenage houses the naval base, yacht club, cargo ships and sometimes luxury cruise liners.

Sights The impressive **Fort St-Louis** still functions as a military base. Built in Vauban style, it dominates the waterfront. Once inside beware the low ceiling arches said to have been designed to foil the invading English who were generally taller than the French at that time. Wonderful views from the top. At the Gate there is a visual display and gift shop. Identification is required when you buy the ticket. Parts of the fort are off-limits. ■ *Excellent, informative guided tours (English, Spanish, French), every half hour, 0900-1530 Mon-Fri, 1000-1500 Sat, 1 hr, 25F, by Les Amis du Fort-St-Louis. T605459.* Adjacent to the fort is **La Savane**, the old parade ground, now a park of 5 ha planted with palms, tamarinds, and other tropical trees and shrubs. The park contains statues of two famous figures from the island's past: Pierre Belain d'Esnambuc, the leader of the first French settlers on Martinique; and Empress Josephine (now beheaded), first wife of Napoléon Bonaparte, who was born on the island.

The **Bibliothèque Schoelcher** is situated on the corner of Rue Victor Sévère and Rue de la Liberté, just across the road from the Savane. Schoelcher (1804-1893) devoted his life to the abolition of slavery. He gave his library to Martinique but most was burned in the fire. The building to house the collection was commissioned, but not built, before the fire. It was designed by Henry Picq, a French architect married to a woman from Martinique. The Eiffel engineering company constructed it in iron, shipped it to the island and it opened in 1893. On the exterior you can see the names of freedom campaigners, including John Brown, of the USA, William Wilberforce, of the UK and Toussaint Louverture, of Haiti. Today it still functions as a library and regularly holds exhibitions. ■ *0830-1730, Mon-Thu, 0830-1200, Fri-Sat. T702667.*

Just along the Rue de la Liberté towards the seafront is the **Musée Départemental d'Archéologie Précolombienne**. It contains relics of the Arawak and Carib Indians: pottery, statuettes, bones, reconstructions of villages, maps, et cetera. Worth a visit. ■ *0900-1300, 1430-1700 Mon-Fri, 0900-1200 Sat. 5F, children 10F. T715705.*

In the centre of town, in the Square of Père Labat, Rue Schoelcher, there is a second chance to see the architecture of Henri Picq with the **Cathedral of St-Louis** which towers above the Fort-de-France skyline. This, too, is mainly of iron, in a romanesque-byzantine style. The arms of past bishops, in stained glass, give colour to the choir.

French Antilles

Fort-de-France

N
Not to scale

🚌 **Bus Stations**
1 Bus Terminal
2 Taxi Collectif Terminal

Newly opened in 1999, but in a beautiful creole villa dating back to 1887, was the **Musée Régional d'Histoire et d'Ethnographie de la Martinique** on Boulevard Générale de Gaulle, opposite the Atrium Theatre. It is strong on the origins, customs and traditions of the people of Martinique. ■ *20F, children 5F, T728187, F637411.*

The **Parc Floral et Culturel** (also called **Galerie de Géologie et de Botanie** or **Exotarium**) is a shady park containing two galleries, one of which concentrates on the geology of the island, the other on the flora, and mid-19th century wooden barracks now housing 11 workshops for local artisans. Almost 2,800 species of plants have been identified in Martinique and the Parc Floral has a very good selection. ■ *0900-1230 Mon-Fri, 1430-1730, closed Sat, Sun. 12F adults, 3F children. T706841.*

Next to the Parc Floral are a feature of Fort-de-France not to be missed, the **markets**. The fishmarket is by the Madame River, facing the Place José Martí, where fishermen unload from their small boats or *gommiers*. Close by is one of several markets selling fruit, vegetables and flowers as well as exotic spices. The markets hum with activity from 0500 to sunset, but are best on Friday and Saturday. A fresh green coconut hacked open with a machete, makes a refreshing drink for about 7F.

Around the island

The northwest coast

The coastal road heading north through Schoelcher from Fort-de-France hugs the coast, zigzagging north through **Case-Pilote** (named after a friendly Carib chief) where there is a 17th-century church. It then passes through several fishing villages and is flanked by beaches that gradually become blacker with volcanic sand. **Le Carbet** is where Columbus is presumed to have landed (monument). A *carbet* was the great meeting house of the Caribs. There are several good restaurants, mostly fish, on the beach. **Habitation Anse Latouche** is at the end of Carbet village on the coast. The ruins of a 17th-century sugar plantation are surrounded by a beautiful garden focusing on local flowers and shrubs. ■ *Mon-Sat 1000-1600. Entry 15F, children 7-12 10F, or 40F and 15F for joint entry to Balata Gardens. T781919.* At the popular beach of **Anse Turin** just north of Le Carbet, is the small **Gauguin Museum**. The artist stayed at Anse Turin during 1887 before he went to Tahiti. The museum has letters, sketches and some reproductions of his work. Local artists' paintings and ceramics are sometimes on sale. There is an interesting section on the local traditional women's costume and its elements, *la grande robe, le madras, le foulard.* ■ *0900-1730 daily. 20F. T782266.*

St-Pierre To the north of Carbet is the famous **St-Pierre**. The town is well worth a visit and is an eerie reminder of destructive natural forces that dominate life in the Caribbean. The modern village is built on the ruins of the former capital of Martinique, which was destroyed by a cloud of molten volcanic ash when Montagne Pelée erupted on 8 May 1902. As the cultural and economic capital, the town was known as the 'Petit Paris' of the West Indies. Out of 30,000 inhabitants there was only one survivor, named Auguste Cyparis, an illiterate casual labourer who had been thrown drunk into a cell for the night. Today his small cell is one of the ruins that visitors can still see. The prison is beside the remains of the once splendid and celebrated theatre of St-Pierre on Rue Victor Hugo. You can see the broad sweep of steps up to the entrance, the huge stage area, the first floor boxes and the rusting remains of the electric stage lighting. In the **Musée Volcanologique Franck-Perret, Museum of Vulcanology** is an interesting collection of objects (mostly by Perret, an American) and documents evoking life before 1902 and remains from the disaster: household metal and glass objects charred and deformed by the extreme heat, photographs and volcanology displays. ■ *0900-1700 daily. 10F. T781516.* The bridge over the Rivière Roxelane, built in 1766, leads to the oldest part of the town, the **Quartier du Fort**.

The ruins of the church are among the most moving. The Rue Levassor leads to the **Maison Coloniale de Santé**, beside the river, with interesting insights into treatment for the mentally ill at the time. All sites free admission, information in French and English. Visit early before the cruise ship parties, or after they leave for lunch.

The next village on the coastal road is the picturesque fishing village of **Le Prêcheur**. Madame de Maintenon, who married Louis XIV lived here. The three bells outside the church date from that time. The road then continues towards the spectacular beach of **Anse Céron** where the sand seems to be at its blackest. A rock called the Pearl juts out from the sea which is roughish but swimming is possible. It is a wild and beautiful beach, a pleasant change from the calm, white sand tourist beaches in the south. Turn inland to **Habitation Céron**, a plantation where the early sugar buildings are largely intact and there is an attractive botanic walk. There are huge ponds where succulent crayfish are raised. These, with homegrown fruit and vegetables make an excellent three-course lunch for 170F including a rum punch. ■ *0930-1700 daily. T529453*. The coastal road ends a mile or two further on at another beach, Anse Couleuvre.

It is possible to follow a track 18 km through the rainforest around the northern coast, but a guide is essential (see directory, page 747). The first 20 minutes on a concrete road are discouraging, but once in the forest the path is cooler and the views beautiful. At the extreme north of the island is another small fishing village, **Grande Rivière** set in breathtaking scenery characteristic of this part of the island; plunging cliffs covered with the lush vegetation of the rainforest. The island of Dominica faces the village from across the sea. Winding roads lead through the mountains to the next village, Macouba, perched on top of a cliff.

Care must be taken to avoid the fer-de-lance snake & bilharzia in the streams

The tropical rainforest and Montagne Pelée

La Route de la Trace winds through the tropical rainforest on the slopes of the Pitons du Carbet from Fort-de-France to **Morne Rouge** on the southern slope of Montagne Pelée. The town was hit by a second eruption of Pelée on 20 August 1902. A new park has been opened, called **Le Jardin de la Pelée**, on the hill above the town, where there is a fine display of local flora, well labelled, and information on the volcano (T524251). From Morne Rouge there is a road to St-Pierre on the coast, so a circuit is possible. The forest itself is truly magnificent, covering the sides of the steep, inland mountains (Les Pitons de Carbet and Pelée) with a bewildering array of lush, green vegetation that stretches for miles. Giant bamboo, mountain palms, chestnut and mahogany trees, over a thousand species of fern and many climbing and hanging parasitic plants and orchids are examples of rainforest vegetation. The forest is protected as part of Martinique's Parc Naturel and makes interesting walking country (see directory, page 747).

Route de la Trace

At **Balata**, not far from the capital along the Route de la Trace is the bizarre building of **Sacré Coeur**, a smaller version of Paris's votive Sacré-Coeur de Montmartre, perched high up in the forest. A little further along the road is the **Le Jardin de Balata** with superb views across the Baie de Fort-de-France to Trois-Ilets. The gardens feature a collection of 3,000 species with magnificent anthuriums, ranging from dark maroon, crimson and pink to white. Look out for the numerous hummingbirds and brilliant green lizards. Umbrellas are provided if it is raining and the foliage gleams impressively when wet. ■ *0900-1700 daily. 40F, children aged 7-12, 15F, includes entry to Habitation Anse Latouche. T644873, F647340. Signs are in French.*

As the Route de la Trace winds its way through the rainforest, the flanks of the surrounding mountains are clearly visible, covered with cultivated tropical flowers such as anthuriums and ginger lilies. **Montagne Pelée** is reached via a track branching off the Route de la Trace, between Morne Rouge and **Ajoupa-Bouillon**, where there is a delightful garden-park, **Les Ombrages Botaniques**. ■ *0900-1700. 20F, children 10F*. From the car park at the foot of the volcano there is a view of the Atlantic Coast, Morne Rouge and the bay of St-Pierre. The mountain air is deliciously

French Antilles

fresh and cool even at the foot of the volcano. Not far away are **Les Gorges de la Falaise**, a series of small gorges along 3 km of the Falaise River, wonderful for swimming in, accessible only by following the course of the river on foot. Much of the walk is actually wading in the water and you clamber over waterfalls, making the carrying of cameras impractical. ■ *The local Syndicat d'Initiative in Ajoupa-Bouillon organizes guided tours up the river, T533287. 45F including waterproof pack and fruit juice.*

North coast

The area of **Basse-Pointe** is the pineapple cultivation area of the island, where huge fields of spikey pineapple tops can be seen. Basse-Pointe is an old settlement with a late 17th-century church and a good view of the cliffs from the cemetery. Inland from here is **Plantation Leyritz**, a former plantation complex, complete with slave houses and machinery. The restored 18th-century owner's house is now an elegant hotel where the French government has entertained the presidents of the USA and Senegal. You can walk round the gardens and eat in what was once the sugar boiling house. There is an exhibition of tiny tableaux featuring dolls made from plants and vegetables, exploiting the colours and textures of tropical leaves. ■ *1000-1830 daily, T785392.* The coast road continues from Basse-Pointe to Macouba (see above) and Père Labat's church. Bananas grow all the way from here to Grand Rivière, where the road ends.

From the N1 road along the northeast coast of the island tempting beaches with crashing waves are visible, but the Atlantic Coast is too dangerous for swimming. However, there is a safe beach at Anse Azérot, just south of **Ste-Marie**. To the north is **Fond St-Jacques**, a cultural centre which used to be a Dominican monastery and sugar plantation. Buildings date from 1689 and at its height the Dominicans utilized 1,000 slaves. It was here that Père Labat perfected the distilling of rum. His memoirs are a prime source of information on plantation life. Modern exhibitions are also held at the centre. ■ *Mon-Fri 0800-1700, adults 15F, children 5F. T691012.* Nearby, **Musée du Rhum Saint-James** in the St James Distillery, includes an explanation of the process of rum production and its history, and rum tasting. ■ *Mon-Fri, 0900-1700 and Sat, Sun 0900-1200, admission and tour free. T693002.*

The seafront at **La Trinité** is a grand promenade with modern and 19th-century buildings and monuments, which looks out onto the Presqu'île de la Caravelle, where the vegetation is scrubby but the scenery is gently interesting. The peninsula has beaches at Tartane (the only village on the Caravelle), Anse l'Etang (the best, surfing possible) and Anse du Bout. It is an area protected by the **Parc Naturel** of Martinique; several well-marked paths criss-cross the peninsula so that visitors can enjoy the varied flora and fauna. It is also possible to visit the historic ruins of the **Château Dubuc** and various buildings that belonged to the Dubuc family, including slave smugglers and privateers. ■ *0830-1730 daily. 15F, children 6F. T474548.*

Southeast coast From the Caravelle peninsula the Atlantic coast is characterized by deep, protected, shallow, sandy bays, good for swimming, surfing and sailing. The road runs southeast through Le Robert and Le François to the more mountainous area around **Le Vauclin** where the main activity is fishing. There are some interesting art-deco buildings from the 1920s on its steep streets. There are innumerable islets offshore. The Baignoire de Josephine has sand-banks and is featured on local boat trips. Pointe Faula is a very safe beach here, with dazzling white sand and shallow water. To the south of Vauclin a road leads to Anse Macabou, a group of impressive white sand beaches.

South Martinique

The small village of **Les Trois-Ilets**, across the bay from Fort-de-France, has a charming main square and is surrounded by tourist attractions. Empress Josephine, born Marie Josèph Rose Tascher de la Pagerie, was baptized in the church on the square. Her mother is buried here and the church, restored with money from Napoléon III, is rather a shrine to the Napoleonic legend. Even more so is **Le domaine de la Pagerie**, the family's sugar plantation, about 4 km from the village. Josephine was probably born here in 1763, and lived here until she was 16. In 1766 a hurricane blew away the graceful plantation house and the family lived above the sugar boiling house. Now an attractive evocation of that time, the ruins can be seen and, in the renovated kitchen, a stone building, there is an excellent collection of furniture, documents and portraits. ■ *Tue-Fri 0900-1730, Sat-Sun 0900-1300, 1430-1730, 20F, children 5F. T683455, F683841.* At Pointe Vatable, 2 km east of Trois-Ilets, is the sugar cane museum (**La Maison de la Canne**) which uses documents, machinery and superb models of sugar processing plant to illustrate the history of the Martiniquan sugar industry. Recommended. Guided tours are available. ■ *0900-1700 daily except Mon, 15F, children 5F. T683204.*

A short bus ride from Trois-Ilets is the tourist complex of **Pointe du Bout**, directly opposite Fort-de-France, and linked by *vedettes* (regular ferries) every 15 minutes. Three companies operate the service. Return tickets cost 32F and are valid on all ferries (bicycles at no extra charge). There is a marina, a créole village, where some of the shops, cafés, bars, restaurants and souvenir stands can be found, discothèques, sport facilities and a conglomeration of luxury hotels. There is plenty of evening entertainment. The first beach after stepping off the ferry is a crowded strip of sand in front of the *Hotel Meridien*, almost completely covered with deckchairs for hire. Perhaps preferable is the beach at **Anse Mitan**, a five-minute walk away, where there are numerous reasonably priced restaurants and bars. There is a direct ferry from the capital every 15 minutes. **Anse à l'Ane**, a little way along the coast to the west is quieter than Anse Mitan and Pointe du Bout and has a pleasant atmosphere.

At **Grande Anse** is a magnificent beach, less frequented by tourists than the beaches at Pointe du Bout, although it does get more crowded at weekends. The pretty village of **Anse d'Arlets** is nearby. Direct ferry from Fort-de-France.

Just south of Anse d'Arlets and around the **Pointe du Diamant** is **Le Diamant**. This is an idyllic golden sand beach stretching for 4 km along the south coast and dominated by the famous **Rocher du Diamant** (Diamond Rock). This huge 176 m rock, of volcanic origin, is about 4 km out to sea and was occupied by the English during the Napoleonic Wars. They stationed four cannons and about 20 sailors there in 1804 before the French reconquered it a year and a half later. British ships passing it still salute "Her Majesty's Ship Diamond Rock". Negotiate with a fisherman if you want to visit.

Inland and to the east of Diamant is the town of **Rivière-Pilote**, the largest settlement in the south of the island. The **Mauny Rum distillery** is located here, where free guided tours are available. ■ *Mon-Fri 0930-1730, Sat 0900-1300. T626208.* The famous **Cléry cock-fighting pit** stages regular mongoose-snake fights. ■ *Sun afternoon, T626169.* From the town of **Le Marin**, southwards are long white sand beaches lined with palm groves, and calm clear sea which epitomize the classic image of the Caribbean. Marin itself boasts a very fine 18th-century Jesuit church. The largest marina on the island is here.

At **Ste-Anne** is the extensive *Club Méditerranée* complex. It has its own section of beach adjacent to the long public beach, which has a spectacular view along the southwest coast, including Rocher du Diamant. Ste-Anne beach is picturesque and shady with trees that overhang the sea in some places. The water is calm, ideal for toddlers. There is a wide selection of lively bars and restaurants, some selling snacks or *menu du jour*, others more expensive. You can rent all types of watersports

French Antilles

equipment: windsurfers, catamarans, seedoos, kayaks, sunfish, or take a sea plane ride. The swimming area is marked off with yellow buoys. Irregular ferries sail from Fort-de-France, 2½-3½ hours. There is a fine Jesuit church of 1766 opposite the jetty. ■ *T767272 for an all-inclusive day pass.*

The road heading east from Marin leads to the beach at **Cap Chevalier**, a popular family beach at weekends, but choppy, as it faces the Atlantic. Among others along the barrier reef, the **Ilet Chevalier**, a bird sanctuary, is visible from here.

At the southernmost tip of the island is the famous Grande Anse des Salines and the beaches of Dunkerque, Baham and Anse Trabaud, all of which are remarkably attractive. Inland from Anse Trabaud lies the salt marsh and the forest petrified by former lava flow. The forest is now sadly diminished thanks to the efforts of museums and souvenir hunters. Birdwatching is good at the Etang des Salines and in the sandy marshes around the Baie des Anglais.

Essentials

Sleeping
Two useful websites are www.club-hoteliers-martinique.asso.fr & www.martinique-hotel.com

Martinique offers a wide range of accommodation from the modest family-run *auberges* scattered over the remote and spectacular north, to the huge five-star complexes of Pointe du Bout and Trois Ilets, the main tourist area, in the south. 20 hotels with over 60 rooms are classed as *Grand Hôtellerie*. About 100 smaller places are grouped as *Relais Créoles*. The *Sucrier Créole* is awarded to hotels with a high quality of service and hospitality. *Gîtes*, furnished holiday apartments and bungalows are widely available, some connected to hotels. Information and reservations can be made through Centrale de Réservation, BP 823-97200 Fort-de-France Cédex, T715611, F736693. The tourist office at the airport is helpful and will telephone round the hotels to get you a room for your first night if you have not booked beforehand. Alternatively, for *gîtes* and country guest houses, contact the Fédération Martiniquaise des Offices de Tourisme et Syndicat D'Initiative, Maison du Tourisme Vert, 9 Boulevard du Géneral de Gaulle, BP 1122, 97248 Fort-de-France Cédex, T631854, F701716. Generally, prices are high. Some hotels add 10% service charge and/or 5% government tax to the bill.

Pointe du Bout and **Les Trois-Ilets** These are the main tourist centres, and are well equipped with shops, nightclubs, casinos, a marina, facilities for golf, watersports and tennis as well as several beaches. Trois-Ilets benefits from the facilities of Pointe du Bout and the pleasant beaches of Anse Mitan and Anse à l'Ane, a 20-min ferry ride from Fort-de-France. The main hotels are **LL-AL** *Meridien*, 97229 Trois-Ilets, T660000, F660074. Recently renovated huge modern complex with 295 rooms and traditional bungalows dating from the 1960s in splendid, mature landscaped grounds. The marina village is fun to walk through (you could take a picnic lunch, food and drink is expensive). Excellent evening entertainment, sometimes the national ballet company. **LL** *Bakoua* (named after traditional Martiniquan straw hats), T660202, F660041, a *Coralia* hotel. Créole ambience with touch of sophistication, a/c, TV, phone, minibar, 139 apartments and rooms, two restaurants, excellent buffet of local dishes, tennis, fitness centre, pool, on beach, evening entertainment includes the ballet, Martinique-style cabaret in English and French. **LL-L** *Novotel Coralia Carayou*, Pointe du Bout, 97229 Trois Ilets, T660404, F660057. 201 spacious rooms in seven acres of gardens overlooking Fort de France bay, right on beach, walking distance to shops, restaurants at marina, two restaurants, watersports. **L-B** *Hôtel la Pagerie*, pool, T660530, F660099. **A-B** *Auberge de l'Anse Mitan*, T660112, F660105. A friendly, family-run hotel with apartments and rooms. **B-C** *Le Nid Tropical*, rents studios and has a lively beach bar and restaurant, T683130, F684743. Also camping, see below. **B** *La Bonne Auberge*, T660155, F660450. Again basic but clean, offering underwater fishing and watersports.

Fort-de-France **AL-B** *Squash Hotel*, 3 Boulevard de Verdun, T630001, F630074. 108 modern rooms, TV, minibar, pool, three squash courts, gym, dancing room, saunas, jacuzzi, billards, conference facilities. **A-B** *Impératrice*, T630682, F726630, rue de la Liberté. 1950s décor and architecture, apparently unchanged since it was built in 1957. **B** *La Malmaison*, rue de la Liberté, opposite the Savane, T639085, F600393. Good and clean, spacious, recommended for price range but some rooms smell of cigarettes, higher prices during Carnival. Both these hotels have lively bars and restaurants frequented by a young crowd. **B-C** *Le Gommier*, 3 rue Jacques Cazotte, T718855, F730696. One of the oldest buildings in town. Has clean spacious rooms and good continental breakfasts, friendly management. In the elegant suburbs of Didier is the **B-C** *Victoria*, Route de Didier, 97200 Fort-de-France, T605678, F600024, on hillside overlooking bay. Popular with businessmen as well as holiday makers, 37 rooms, good restaurant, a/c, TV, phone, fridge, buses into town every few minutes, pool. The **C** *Balisier* on 21 rue Victor Hugo is also very centrally located with a view over the port, T/F714654. Good value. **C** *Carib*, 9 rue du Matouba, T601985. Newly renovated, a/c, wrought iron beds, hardwood floors, very clean and appealing, good location. Recommended. On rue Lazare Carnot is **C** *Un Coin de Paris*, T700852, F630951. Small, friendly and cheap. **Schoelcher**, on the outskirts of Fort-de-France, is **LL-L** *Framissima* , T614949, F617057. Pool, tennis courts, gym, disco, conference facilities, restaurant, bars, casino, very fine hotel. Recommended.

Diamant   Miles of superb, uncrowded beach with magnificent views of coastal mountains and, of course, Diamant Rock. **LL-L** *Novotel Diamant Le Coralia*, at Pointe de la Chery Diamant, T764242, F762287, H046@accor-hotels.com Recently extended, in garden setting, 181 a/c rooms, 4 rooms for wheelchair guests, beach or pool views, 4 restaurants, including creole, tennis, archery, pedal boats etc, **AL** *Mercure Inn Coralia Diamant* , at Pointe de la Chery Diamant, T764600, F762599. On hillside in tropical garden, 149 a/c rooms with kitchenette, 2 rooms for wheelchair guests, panoramic views of Rocher du Diamant, 3 restaurants, creole, Italian and international. **AL** *Calypso*, Les Hauts du Diamant, 97223 Diamant, T764081, F764084, 500 m from beach, walking distance to village. 60 rooms and suites in 11 buildings, superb views of Diamant Rock, pool, bar, restaurant, car rental. **AL-B** *Diamant les Bains*, T764014, F762700. Fine views over swimming pool and sea. **AL** *Le Village du Diamant*, T764189, F635332. 59 basic, beachside bungalows, rooms or apartments for rent.

Ste-Luce **AL-B** *Pierre et Vacances*, at Pointe Philippeaux, T621262, villagesteluce@martinique-hotels.com Holiday village familiarly called *Village de Sainte-Luce*, with 334 nicely decorated apartments, ranging from studios for 2-3 people to apartments with 3 rooms for 6 people, 10 apartments for wheelchair guests, near the beach, views to Rocher du Diamant and on clear days to St Lucia, diving and watersports. **AL** *Mercure Inn Coralia Les Amandiers*, by Fonds Larion beach at Désert, a district of Ste-Luce village, T623232, F623340, les.amandiers@martinique-hotels.com Along the beach, close to the fishing village, nice 3-star hotel, 117 rooms, all with terrace or loggia, 4 rooms for wheelchair guests. **A** *Amyris*, by the beach of Pointe Philippeau, T621200, F621210, amyris@cgit.com Three-star, in Karibéa chain, 110 rooms of which are wheelchair-accessible, all amenities, very nice. In the same hotel chain, 2km from Ste-Luce and 300 m from the beach is *Caribia* aparthotel, T622062, F625952, in the Désert area. 76 apartments. **B** *Aux Délices de la Mer*, T625012. Offers fishing amongst other activities, only five rooms, créole restaurant.

Outside Ste-Anne To the north, is the *Club Med Village Les Boucaniers*, T767452, F767202. Lots of tennis and land based sports, waterskiing, windsurfing, sailing, diving and golf at extra cost, no children under 12, 313 rooms, a/c. Just south of Ste-Anne on sandy beach is **LL-AL** *Hôtel Anse Caritan*, BP 24, 97227 Sainte-Anne, T767412, F767259. 96 rooms with views across to Diamond Rock, a/c, terraces, kitchenettes, phone, pool, restaurant, watersports and excursions arranged. **L-AL** *Domaine de Belleford*, 97227 Sainte-Anne, T769232, F769140. Recently renovated, 186 rooms and suites in five sections, 500 m from beach, popular with Europeans, a/c, terraces, kitchenettes, four pools, two restaurants, bar, boutiques, car rental.

Atlantic coast **LL-B** *La Frégate Bleu*, T545466, F547848. Seven spacious, elegant seaview rooms, a/c, fans, kitchenettes, terraces, charming hilltop site, gingerbread trimmings, rooms decorated with antiques, Persian rugs, four-poster beds, helpful, English-speaking staff.

B-C *Chez Julot*, rue Gabriel Perí, **Vauclin**, T744093. A modest but pleasant hotel, one street back from foreshore road, a/c. Restaurant, bar. **A-B** *Les Brisants*, T543257, F546913, at **François** provides good Créole cuisine. On the old N1, near **Trinité**, within easy reach of the Caravelle peninsula, **A-B** *St Aubin*, T693477, F694114. A magnificent colonial-style hotel, once a plantation house, splendid location, views and exterior, but interior badly damaged by 1960s refurbishment, 15 a/c rooms. **AL** *Le Village de Tartane* is near the pretty fishing village of **Tartane**, T580633, F635332. A/c bungalows with kitchenette around pool. In Tartane, **B-C** *Madras*, hotel and restaurant, on the beach, spotless rooms, seaview or road view, T583395, F583363. **A-C** *Hôtel Primerêve*, Anse Azérot, just south of Sainte Marie, T694040, F690937. 20 rooms, 80 suites, new hotel on hillside, elegant, 5-min walk to superb beach, secluded cove, pool, good restaurant, tennis, snorkelling, easy access to rainforest. **LL** *Habitation Lagrange*, Le Marigot, T536060, F535058. 16 rooms, one suite, a/c, four poster beds, terraces, luxury, in tropical gardens, 18th century buildings, decorated in colonial style, private, romantic, beautiful pool, tennis, superb restaurant, in the rainforest, 20 mins from beach.

Basse Pointe AL-A *Plantation de Leyritz*, T785392, F789244. A former plantation house set in beautiful grounds with a lot of insects because of all the fruit trees and water, glamorous accommodation, excellent restaurant serving local specialities, efficient and friendly service, pool, tennis courts, health spa, discothèque. In the remote, northern-most commune, **Grand-Rivière**, a small fishing village surrounded by rainforest and close to several idyllic black sand coves, **D** *Chanteur Vacances* is a simple, clean hotel with only seven rooms, shared facilities, restaurant, T557373.

West coast One of the few hotels within easy reach of the ruined town of **St-Pierre**: is **C** *La Nouvelle Vague*, T781434. Five rooms only (doubles), rooms over bar, overlooks beach. On **Carbet's** enormous black sand beach are **C** *Le Cristophe Colomb*, T780538, F780642, good value, and the more upmarket **LL-AL** *Marouba Club*, T780021, F780565, which has apartments and bungalows, pool, disco, CP or MAP rates.

Finally, convenient for the airport, at **Ducos**: in the plain of Lamentin, **C** *Airport*, six rooms, basic a/c, hot water, no restaurant, T560183.

Youth hostels Fédération des Oeuvres Laiques (FOL) has a hostel, along the Route de Didier, Rue de Prof Raymond Garcia, T640410, 640017, head office at 31 Rue Perrinon, Fort de France, T635022, F638367. The hostel is several miles from the town centre and difficult to find, only one small FOL sign. No public transport in evenings, taxis can make staying here expensive. Rooms, **C**, sleep two or four with shower and toilet, basic, renovated 1994.

Camping The most convenient campsite for Fort-de-France is at Anse à l'Ane, *Le Nid Tropical* campsite, 70F for two people if you have your own tent, 100F, if you rent one, also cabins and apartments with kitchenette, T683130, F684743. A small bakery/restaurant on the beach serves cheap meals, bread and pastries. On the south coast, Ste-Luce has a good campsite with adequate facilities in the *VVF Hotel*, but the beach is not nice. There are no tents for hire. T625284. *Camping Municipal* at Ste-Anne is a popular campsite with a pleasant situation in a shady grove right on the beach, 50F, cheap food available. Next to the *Club Med*, it is on the cleanest and nicest beach. You can rent tents from Chanteur Vacances, 65 Rue Perrinon, Fort-de-France, T716619, around 35F per day.

Eating Sampling the French and Créole cuisine is one of the great pleasures of visiting Martinique. There is an abundance of restaurants, cafés, and snack bars to be found everywhere. The quality is generally very high so it is worth being adventurous and trying the various dishes and eating places. The main meal of the day is at midday and many restaurants and cafés offer very reasonable fixed price *menus du jour* ranging from 30-60F. Here are some worth seeking out. For a description of local food, see page 690.

Fort-de-France *Le Blenac*, 3 rue Blenac, T701841. Closed Sun evening. *King Creole*, 56 Av des Caraïbes, T701917. Closed Sat midday and Sun. For crêpes and salads try *La Crêperie*, 4 rue Garnier Pagès, T606209. Closed Sat midday, Sun. *Espace Créole*, 8 rue Voltaire, T700595. Open Mon-Sat 1100-2200. *Le Victor Hugo*, 69 rue V Hugo, T636108. Closed Sun midday. *Marie Sainte*, 160 rue V Hugo, T700030. Open daily except Sun. In the market at Fort-de-France are small kiosks selling créole *menu du jour* for 50F including dessert and drink, other meals also served, with tablecloths and flowers on table, Miriam enthusiastically greets customers at *Chez Louise* and explains menu in English. For an Italian atmosphere try *Le Vieux Milan*, 60 Av des Caraïbes, T603531. Excellent pizza for US$7-11, closed Sat, Sun. There are several restaurants serving Vietnamese and Chinese food, including *Le Cantonnais*, Marina Pointe du Bout, T660233. Open daily. *Le Chinatown*, 20 rue Victor Hugo, T718262. Mon-Fri lunch. *Indo*, 105 route de la Folie, T716325. Vietnamese, closed Sun evening and Mon. *Le Jardin de Jade*, Anse Colas, T611550. Closed Sun evening. *Le Kiwany's*, 2 rue Kernay, Trinité, T584244. Closed Sun evening, Mon. *Le Xuandre*, Vietnamese, Voie No 2 Pointe des Nègres, T615470. Evenings only, closed Mon. Other nationalities are also well represented: *Le Couscousser*, 1 rue Perrinon, looking out on to Bibliothèque Schoelcher. Excellent with choice of sauces and meats to accompany *couscous*, reasonably priced, interesting, rather young Algerian red wine goes well with the food, open Mon-Fri 1200-1500, 1900-2300, Sat 1900-2300, T600642. *Les Cèdres*, Lebanese, in rue Redoute de Matouba. Excellent humous, kebabs and other Lebanese meze, owner speaks English, all major credit cards accepted. *Le Salambo*, Tunisian, Patio de Cluny, T704778. Closed Sun, Mon, Tue. *Le Beyrouth*, Lebanese, 9 rue Redoute de Matouba, T606745. Lunch menu from 80F. *Le Méchoui*, Moroccan, Pte Simon, behind Bricogite. Reservations preferred, takeaway service, T715812, open 1200-1600, 1900-2400, closed Sun. *Las Tapas de Sevillas*, Spanish, 7 rue Garnier Pagès, T637123.

For travellers on a smaller budget wishing to eat out in the capital there are plenty of good snackbars and cafés serving various substantial sandwiches and *menus du jour*. The area around Place Clemenceau has lots of scope; *Le Clemenceau* is very good value and extremely friendly – try the *accras* or a fresh *crudité* salad. *Le Lem* on Boulevard Général-de-Gaulle has superior fast food at low prices and a young crowd. It also stays open later than many restaurants that close in the evenings and on Sun. Behind the Parc Floral on rue de Royan is the *Kowossol*, a tiny vegetarian café which serves a cheap and healthy *menu du jour*. The pizzas are recommended and the fruit juice is especially delicious – try *gingembre* (ginger) or *ananas* (pineapple). On François Arago *Los Amigos* and *Le Coq d'Or* are particularly good for substantial sandwiches for around 12F. Try *poisson* (steak fish) or *poulet* (chicken). *Le Renouveau* on Boulevard Allègre offers delicious, filling *menus du jour* for 40F, again with a warm welcome. As in France, there are *Traiteurs* opening up, offering stylish takeaway meals which you select at the shop, helpful to vegetarians. Ask for the latest list at the tourist office.

The place to head for in the evening when these eateries close (except *Le Lem* which stays open until 2100), is the Boulevard Chevalier de Ste-Marthe next to the Savane. Here, every evening until late, vans and caravans serve delicious meals to take away, or to eat at tables under canvas awnings accompanied by loud Zouk music. The scene is bustling and lively, in contrast to the rest of the city at night-time and the air is filled with wonderful aromas. Try *lambis* (conch) in a sandwich (15F) or on a *brochette* (like a kebab) with rice and salad (30F). Paella and *Colombo* are good buys (40F) and the crêpes whether sweet or savoury are delicious.

Anse Mitan Amongst the many restaurants across the Baie des Flamands is the charming *L'Amphore* where the fresh lobster is delicious, T660309, closed Mon-Tue, lunchtime, open every evening 1900-0300. *Bambou* is a little further along the beach, specializes in fresh fish and offers an excellent *menu du jour*. *Chez Jojo* on the beach at Anse à l'Ane, T683743, has a varied seafood menu. Two-star restaurants include *Auberge de l'Anse Mitan*, T660112. Open every evening, reservations required. *Hemingway's* off Anse Mitan beach. Flat fee for créole buffet, small or large plate, opens 1900, arrive early for first sitting, soon fills up. *La Bonne Auberge*, Chez André, T660155. *La Langouste*, T660499. Open daily. *La Villa Créole*, T660553. Closed Sun-Mon lunch. At Diamant, *La Case Créole*, Place de l'Église, T660000.

French and Créole, seafood and other specialities, open daily 1100-1600, 1900-2330. *Hôtel Diamant Les Bains* has a reasonable and well-situated restaurant specializing in seafood, T764014. Shut Wed. There are several other restaurants in the town which front directly on to the beach, mostly offering créole cooking and seafood. In Pointe du Bout marina, *La Marine Bar and Restaurant*, good pizza, drink wine, not beer, good seafood platter. *l'Embarquerie* snack bar by ferry dock has happy hour 3 times a day, 1030-1130, 1430-1530, 1700-1800, buy a local Corsaire beer, get one free. *Pizzeria* and snack bar at innermost corner of Pointe du Bout marina sells beer for 10F. Reasonably priced salads and *menu du jour* at *Hibiscus Restaurant* with use of hotel pool for the afternoon. *Bakou Hotel* dock bar is a great place to meet yachties and watch the sunset.

West coast At Carbet the *Grain d'Or*, a spacious airy restaurant, is another good spot to sample Martinique's seafood specialities, T780691, open daily. *Le Trou Crabe*, at Le Coin, at beginning of village, T780434, F780514. Open daily except Sun evenings, beach restaurant, rather smart, French and créole cuisine, offers Lyonnais specialities. Directly on the beach, *L'Imprévu*, T780102, F780866. Open daily except Sun and Mon evenings, créole musical entertainment Fri evening except during Lent, very local, créole specialities including shark, lobster, three courses and house wine from US$22. On the coast, north of St-Pierre is *Chez Ginette*, good food but overpriced, T529028, closed Thu.

North coast The restaurant at *Plantation Leyritz* near Basse Pointe is in the restored plantation house and has waterfalls trickling down the walls giving a cool, peaceful feel to the place, elegant dining, good food and service, open daily, T785392. At Grand' Rivière, *Chez Tante Arlette* serves excellent créole food in cool, pleasant surroundings, finished off with home made liqueurs, rue Louis de Lucy de Fossarieu, T557575.

South coast At Ste-Anne, dine in style at the *Manoir de Beauregard* or at *Les Filets Bleus*, on the beach and lighter on the pocket, T767342, closed Sun evening, Mon. *Anthor* on front street and *L'Ouire Mer* serve reasonable créole meals and pizza. *Les Tamariniers* chef decorates expensive dishes with flowers, closed Tue evenings, Wed. *Poi et Virginie*, overlooks bay with good seafood, closed Mon. At Cap Chevalier, *Chez Gracieuse* is a good, moderate-price créole restaurant, choose the terrace and order the catch of the day, T767231, open daily.

Entertainment

For those whose visit does not coincide with any festivals, there is plenty of other entertainment

The *Ballet Martiniquais* (T634388) is one of the world's most prestigious traditional ballet companies. Representing everyday scenes in their dance, they wear colourful local costume and are accompanied by traditional rhythms. Information about performances and venues, usually one of the large hotels (*Novotel, Caritan, Carayou, Méridien, Bakoua*) can be obtained from the tourist office. Every year in July, SERMAC (Parc Floral et Culturel and at the Théâtre Municipal) organizes a two-week arts festival in Fort-de-France with local and foreign artistes performing plays and dance, T716625. CMAC (Centre Martiniquais d'Action Culturelle, Av Franz Fanon, Fort-de-France, T617676) organizes plays, concerts, the showing of films and documentaries all year round and an annual festival in December.

Cinemas There are several comfortable, a/c cinemas in Fort-de-France and the various communes. No film is in English; tickets cost 30F. A state-of-the-art multiscreen complex is in the Palais de Congres de Madiana, T721515, northwest of the centre of Fort-de-France at Schoelcher. Turn off the main highway just before Anse Madame, taking the road right, leading to the university. The road to the Palais is the first on the right.

Theatres The main theatres are the *Théâtre Municipal* in the lovely old Hôtel de Ville building and *Théâtre de la Soif Nouvelle* in the Place Clemenceau. The *Théâtre Atrium*, on the corner of rue de la Redoute du Marouba, opened in 1998, state of the art hall, shows every evening, operas, plays, concerts, dance etc, T607878, F608820, atrium-info@cgste.mq

Festivals Martinique has more than its fair share of festivals. The main pre-lenten carnival, **Mardi Gras**, takes place in *February or March* when the whole of Martinique takes to the streets in fantastic costume. On **Ash Wednesday**, black and white clad 'devils' parade the streets lamenting loudly over the death of Vaval. At **Eastertime**, the children fly coloured kites which once had razors attached to their tails for kite fights in the wind. At **Toussaint** in *November*, the towns are lit by candlelight processions making their way to the cemeteries to sit with the dead.

Every village celebrates its **Saint's Day** with games, shows and folk dancing, usually over the nearest weekend. The town of Saint-Marie holds a **cultural festival** in *July*, and Ajoupa-Bouillon has a **festival of the crayfish**, while in *August* the town of Marin holds its **cultural festival**.

Among the many other festivities there is the **Martinique Food Show**, in *April*, a culinary fair with lots of competitions; **the May of St-Pierre**, in *May*, which commemorates the eruption of the volcano Montagne Pelée; the biennial International **Jazz Festival**, or **World Crossroads** of the Guitar, in *December*.

Nightlife

Nightclubs abound and tend to be very expensive (70F to get in and the same price for a drink, whether orange juice or a large whisky). Nightclubs include *Le New Hippo*, 24 Boulevard Allègre, Fort-de-France, T602022; *Le Cheyenne*, 4 rue Garnier Pagès; *Le West Indies*, rue Ernest Deproge; *Zipp's Club*, Dumaine, François, T546545. Casinos charge 60F entrance fee if you are not staying at the hotel, take passport or identification card. There are several bars (*piano bar* or *café théâtre*) where you can listen to various types of music. At *Coco Loco*, rue Ernest Deproge in Fort-de-France, regular jazz sessions are held, T636377. Others include Manikou Night, Jazz Club St-James, rue Pietonne des Villages de Rivière Roche, Fort-de-France, *Le Papagayno*, Rond Point du Vietnam Héroïque, in Fort-de-France. Out of town, *Crazy Night*, on the road to Diamant, recommended. Most large hotels lay on Caribbean-style evening entertainment for tourists; limbo dancers, steelbands, etc. The new, main casino is at Schoelcher, the *Casino Plaza*, with tables and slot machines, near the *Hôtel Framissima*. Hôtel Meridien has a casino 2300-0300, proof of identity is required for entry. *Choubouloute*, the local entertainments guide, is found in most bars and hotels.

Shopping

Fort-de-France has ample scope for shoppers, with an abundance of boutiques selling the latest Paris fashions, as well as items by local designers, and numerous street markets where local handicrafts are on sale. Seekers of clothing and perfume should head for rue Victor Hugo and its two *galleries* (malls). Jewellery shops are mostly in rue Isambert and rue Lamartine, selling crystal, china and silverware, and unique gold jewellery. At markets in the Savane and near the cathedral bamboo goods, wickerwork, shells, leather goods, T-shirts, silk scarves and the like are sold. Wines and spirits imported from France and local liqueurs made from exotic fruits are readily available, and Martiniquan rum is an excellent buy. There are large shopping centres at Cluny, Dillon, and Bellevue and the big La Galléria on the airport road. Annette supermarket at Le Marin has a free shuttle service from the Marina. St Anne has several small groceries open daily, catering to the tourist trade. American and Canadian dollars are accepted nearly everywhere and many tourist shops offer a 20% discount on goods bought with a credit card or foreign travellers' cheques.

Transport

Air Lamentin Airport, T421600. A new, modern airport. There is a tourist office for hotel reservations and information, T421805, *Crédit Agricole* and *Change Caraïbes* for foreign currency exchange (see below), car rental offices and ground tour operators. To get to the airport at Lamentin, either take a taxi, or take a bus marked 'Ducos' and ask to be set down on the highway near the airport. The fare is 8.70F and the buses take reasonable-sized luggage. Do not attempt to cycle to or from the airport, and Fort-de-France or Trois-Ilets, as the highway is 4 lanes each way, traffic is heavy and fast, and the shoulder is almost non-existent.

Road **Car hire**: *Europcar Interent*, Aéroport Lamentin, T421688, F518115, Fort-de-France T733313 and several hotels; *Hertz*, kiosk at the airport, T421690, F514626; *Avis* at the airport, T421692. Prices start from 200F a day for a Citroën AX or Renault 5. It will normally be cheaper to have unlimited mileage. You can get a discount if you book your car from abroad at least 48 hrs in advance. An international driver's licence is required for those staying over 20 days. Car hire companies in Fort de France close at weekends. If you want to return a car you have

French Antilles

to go to the airport, you can't even drop off the key in town. One look at Fort-de-France's congested streets will tell you it's well worth avoiding driving in the city centre. Parking in central Fort-de-France is only legal with a season ticket and the capital's traffic wardens are very efficient; cars may be towed away. **Motorcycle**: Mopeds can be hired at *Funny*, in Fort-de-France, T633305; *Discount*, Trois-Ilets, T660534; and *Grabin's Car Rental*, Morne Calebasse, T715161. Motorcycles of 125cc and over need a licence, those of 50cc do not. Rental for all is about 170F per day. A bicycle can be hired for 50F per day, 250F per week, 350F per fortnight, from *Funny*, T633305; *Discount*, T660437; *TS Location Sarl*, T634282, all in Fort-de-France. **Taxi**: There is a 40% surcharge on taxi fares between 1900 and 0600 and on Sun. Taxi stands are at the Savane, along Boulevard Général-de-Gaulle and Place Clemenceau.

Sea Boat: Agents for the *Atlantica* ferry to Dominica and Guadeloupe are Brudey Frères, 108 rue Victor Hugo, 97200 Fort-de-France, T700850 for timetable information. Martinique is on the route of most Caribbean cruises. Information on travelling by cargo boat can be obtained from the travel agency next door to the CGM office at the harbour, but if going to South America it is cheaper to fly. **Ferry**: There are ferries running between Desnambuc quay on the seafront and Pointe du Bout, Anse Mitan and Anse à l'Ane. These run until about 2300 to Pointe du Bout and 1830 to Anse Mitan and Anse à l'Ane and apart from a few taxis are about the only form of transport on a Sun or after 2000. Make sure you get on the right one. The 20-min ferry from Fort de France to Trois-Ilets costs 30F return, is punctual, pleasurable and saves a 45-min drive by road. To the *Méridien* there is only 1 boat each hour (don't believe boatmen who say they go near, they drop you at Anse à l'Ane which is a long hot walk away). For information about ferry timetables call 730553 for Somatour and 630646 for Madinina.

Directory **Airline offices** *Air France*, T553300; *Air Liberté*, T425051, 421837; *AOM French Airlines*, T700916, 590560; *Air Martinique*, T421660, 511111; *Nouvelles Frontières-Corsair*, T705970; *American Airlines*, T421919, 511229; *LIAT*, T421602, 512111. Charter companies include *Air Foyal*, T511154; *Air Caraïbe*, T511727; *Air St-Martin*, T515703; *Jet Aviation Service*, T515703; *Antilles Aero Service*, T516688; *Envol*, T684549 (sight seeing trips round the island). **Banks** *Change Caraïbes*, Airport, open 0730-2130 Mon-Sat, 0800-1200, 1400-2100 Sun, T421711, rue Ernest Deproge, 97200, Fort-de-France, open 0730-1800 Mon-Fri, 0800-1300 Sat, T602840; *Crédit Agricole* also has an office at the airport for currency exchange, open 0730-1230, 1430-1800 Tue-Fri, 0800-1130 Sat, T531259, also at rue Ernest Deproge, T731706, closed Mon, open Sat morning. *Banque Française Commerciale*, 6/10 rue Ernest Deproge, T638257. *Banque des Antilles Françaises*, 34 rue Lamartine, T607272, *Société Générale de Banque aux Antilles*, 19 rue de la Liberté, T597070. *Crédit Martiniquais*, 17 rue de la Liberté, T599300. *BRED*, Place Monseigneur Romero, T632267. *Martinique Change*, 137 rue Victor Hugo, T638033 and in Trois-Ilets T660444. *Banque National de Paris*, 72 Av des Caraïbes, T594600 (the best for cash advances on Visa, no commission). Banks and exchange houses charge 5% commission on travellers' cheques. Not all banks accept US dollar travellers' cheques. Some banks charge 15-30F for any size transaction, so change as much as you think you're going to need. Always go to the bank early; by mid-morning they are very crowded. Do not change US dollars at the Post Office in Fort-de-France, you lose about 15% because of the poor exchange rate and commission. *American Express* at Roger Albert Voyages, 10 rue Victor Hugo, upstairs, efficient. **Communications** **Post**: Post offices are open from 0700-1800 and Sat mornings. The main post office is on rue de la Liberté and always has long queues. Post card to USA 3.70F. **Telephone**: Nearly all public telephones are cardphones except a few in bars and hotels which take coins. At the PTT office in rue Antoine Siger, just off the Savane, there are numerous card and coin phones and *Télécartes* (phone cards) are sold. These can also be bought in most newsagents, cafés, and some shops for 36.50F upwards. A 50-unit card (about US$8) lasts nearly 4 mins when phoning North America; a 120-unit card costs about US$16. Don't get caught out on arrival at the airport where there are only cardphones. Try the tourist office where they are very helpful and will phone round endless hotels to find the unprepared new arrival a room. You can not have a call returned to a payphone. Directory enquiries, T12. To make a long distance credit card or collect phone call from a pay phone: buy the smallest card possible and insert in phone, dial 0800-990011 to get USA direct English speaking operator for credit card or collect or dial USA DIRECT calls. Other lines available for Sprint and MCI. Check in the phone book for other numbers. To dial non-French islands in Caribbean dial 00 plus three-figure code and local number. **Embassies & consulates** See also Guadeloupe directory. **Germany** Acajou, BP 423, 97292, Le Lamentin, T503839. **Mexico** 31 Rue Moreau de Jonnes, 97200, Fort-de-France, T605024. **Spain** Route de Chateauboeuf, 97200, Fort-de-France, T750312.

Switzerland CA Californie, 97232, Le Lamentin. **UK** Honorary Consul Mme Jane-Alison Ernoult, T615630. **Hospitals** There are 18 hospitals and clinics which are well-equipped and well-staffed. EU citizens have reciprocal state health rights and hospitals are up to metropolitan France standards. In an emergency: *SAMU*, Pierre Zobda Quitman Hospital, 97232 Le Lamentin, T751515. Ambulance service T715948. *The Sea Water Therapy Centre* is at Grand Anse, 97221 Carbet, T780878. **Places of worship** Although the majority of the population is Catholic there are other churches represented include the Seventh Day Adventists, Baptists, the Evangelical Awakening Assembly, the Full Evangelical Mission and the Evangelical Christian Mission. There is a synagogue, Anse Gouraud, Schoelcher. **Tourist information** Local tourist office Lamentin Airport, T421805; Bord de la Mer, Fort-de-France, T637960, F736693, http://martinique.org Office Départemental du Tourisme de la Martinique, BP 520, 97206 Fort-de-France Cédex. There are local information bureaux (Syndicat d'initiative) all round the island, many of which can be found through the town hall (mairie). **Local travel agents:** Guided tour: of the island by bus, trips on sailing boats and cruise ships around Martinique and to neighbouring islands, and excursions on glass-bottom boats are organized by the following companies: *STT Voyages*, 23 rue Blénac, Fort-de-France, T716812; *Carib Jet*, Lamentin Airport, T519000; *Madinina Tours*, 89 rue Blénac, 97200 Fort-de-France, T706525, F730953; *Caribtours*, Marina Pointe du Bout, 97229 Trois-Ilets, T660448, F660706; *Colibri Tours*, Immeuble Laouchez-ZI, Cocotte 97224, Ducos, T771300, F771289; *AVS* Angle des rues F Arago et E Deproge, Fort-de-France, T635555; *M Vacances*, 97290 Marin, T748561, F747107; *Biguine Voyages*, 51 rue Victor Hugo, Fort-de-France, T718787, F605596. Ms Mylene Richard, *Caribbean Spirit*, 23 rue Simón Bolívar, 97200 Fort-de-France, T274651, F724651, arranges tours and accommodation for the physically disadvantaged. Touring on foot: contact the *Parc Naturel Régional*, Boulevard Général-de-Gaulle, T731930, for well-organized walks in the island's beauty spots such as the rainforest and the Caravelle Peninsula. The charge is 60-80F per person and includes the coach fare to the walk's starting point. Guides can be found through the tourist office, or at Morne Rouge for climbing Montagne Pelée and at Ajoupa-Bouillon for the Gorge de la Falaise walk.

Background

History

When Christopher Columbus sighted Martinique in 1493, it was inhabited by the Carib Indians who had killed or absorbed the Arawaks, the previous settlers of the Lesser Antilles some 200-300 years previously. He did not land until 15 June 1502, when he put in at Le Carbet. Columbus named the island Martinica in honour of St Martin; the Caribs called it Madinina, or island of flowers.

The Spanish never settled. In 1635 Martinique was colonized by the French under the leadership of Pierre Belain d'Esnambuc. His nephew, Jacques du Parquet, governed in 1637-58 and started to develop the island; when he died, his widow took over. The cultivation of sugar cane and the importation of slaves from West Africa commenced. Fierce battles took place between the Caribs and the French until 1660 when a treaty was signed under which the Caribs agreed to occupy only the Atlantic side of the island. Peace was shortlived, however, and the Indians were soon completely exterminated. Louis XIV bought many of the du Parquet land rights and appointed an administrating company, making Martinique the capital of France's Caribbean possessions.

During the 17th and 18th centuries England and France fought over their colonial possessions and in 1762 England occupied Martinique for nine months, only to return it with Guadeloupe to the French in exchange for Canada, Senegal, the Grenadines, St Vincent, and Tobago. France was content to retain Martinique and Guadeloupe because of the importance of the sugar cane trade at the time.

More unrest followed in the French Caribbean colonies when in 1789 the French Revolution inspired slaves to fight for their emancipation. White artisans, soldiers, small merchants and free people of mixed race also embraced its principles. In 1792 a royalist governor re-established control but he was expelled by a revolutionary force sent from France. The capital, Fort-Royal became

République-Ville and Paris abolished slavery. Martinique was occupied by the English again from 1794 to 1815 (with one interruption), at the request of the plantation owners of the island who wanted to preserve the status quo and put down slave revolts.

Slavery was finally abolished in 1848 by the French and in the late 19th century 25,000 immigrant workers from India and a few from Indo-China came to Martinique to supplement the remaining workforce on the plantations.

In 1946 Martinique became an overseas Département (DOM), with all the rights of any department in metropolitan France. The bill was steered through the National Assembly by Martinique's Deputy, Aimé Césaire (1913-), poet, mayor of Fort-de-France and a pioneer of *négritude* (see page 750). In 1974 Martinique became a Région, giving it more economic advantages and investment and funding opportunities.

Political parties include the Progressive Party of Martinique, Socialists, Communists, Union for French Democracy, Rally for the Republic and several small left-wing parties. A small independence movement exists but most people prefer greater autonomy without total independence from France.

In 1988 Martinique voted for the Socialist François Mittérand for president and in the 1995 elections the island remained socialist. In the second round the socialist candidate, Lionel Jospin received 58.9% of the vote compared with 41.1% for the present incumbent, Jacques Chirac. However, the turnout was low at only 48.9% of the electorate, lower than the 79.2% turnout in France as a whole. In the National Assembly elections in 1997 the right wing Rassemblement pour la République (RPR) held two seats in Martinique but lost a third to a supporter of independence from France. The fourth Martinique seat was retained by the left wing Parti Progressiste Martiniquais.

Geography

Martinique is volcanic in origin and one active volcano still exists, Montagne Pelée (1,397 m), situated to the northwest, which had its last major eruption in 1902. The rest of the island is also very mountainous; the Pitons de Carbet (maximum 1,196 m) are in the centre of the island and Montagne du Vauclin (504 m) is in the south. Small hills or *mornes* link these mountains and there is a central plain, Le Lamentin, where sugar cane is planted. An extensive tropical rainforest covers parts of the north of the island, as well as pineapple and banana plantations. The coastline is varied: steep cliffs and volcanic, black and grey sand coves in the north and on the rugged Atlantic coast, and calmer seas with large white or gold sand beaches in the south and on the Caribbean coast. The Baie de Fort-de-France bites into the western coastline creating a sheltered bay where there are mangroves and wetlands. The Atlantic coast south of the Caravelle peninsula is good for windsurfing and scuba diving, due to the shelter afforded by headlands and islands for its shallow bays.

The population of the island is over 400,000 of which half live in Fort-de-France, the capital, and neighbouring *communes*, including Schoelcher to the west and the industrial zones to the east. The industrial town of Le Lamentin, slightly inland and nar the international airport, is the second largest town. The rest of Martinique is fairly evenly scattered with the small towns or *communes*.

Government

Martiniquans are French citizens and Martinique, a Department, is officially and administratively part of France. The President of the French Republic is Head of State. Local government is headed by a Prefect (for France), the President of the General Council (for Martinique) and the President of the Regional Council (for Martinique). There are two legislative bodies: the General Council (45 seats, elected for six years) and the Regional Council (41 seats). It is represented by four directly elected Deputies to the National Assembly in Paris, by two indirectly elected Senators in the Senate and by one representative on the Economic and Social Council. The General Council votes on matters of interest to the department, administers and manages local services and allocates funds to the local councils: *communes*. Martinique has 34 *communes*, each with a mayor and elected municipal council.

The economy

Martinique is dependent upon France for government spending equivalent to about 70% of gnp, without which there would be no public services or social welfare. Even so, unemployment is high at over a quarter of the labour force, the economy is stagnant and the balance of payments deficit expands continuously. The economy is primarily agricultural, about 5% of the economically active population is engaged in farming and fishing, and the main export crops are bananas, rum and melons, while aubergines and flowers are being developed. Crops grown mainly for domestic consumption include yams, sweet potatoes, Caribbean cabbages, manioc, breadfruit, plantains, tomatoes and green beans. Fishing contributes to the local food supply but much of the domestic market is met by imports. Most manufactured goods are imported, adding to the cost of living. There is some light industry and the major industrial plants are an oil refinery, rum distilleries and a cement works, while there is also fruit canning, soft drinks manufacturing and polyethylene and fertilizer plants.

Tourism is the greatest area of economic expansion. Of the total stopover visitors, 80% come from France and 3% from the USA, while of the total cruise ship visitors, 72% come from the USA, 14% from the whole of Europe and 9% from Canada. Tourism income is now around US$300 mn a year; cruise ship passengers spend an average of US$22 per person.

Background to the French Antilles

History

Both the main islands were sighted by Columbus on his second voyage in 1493, but no colonies were established by the Spanish because the islands were inhabited by the Caribs (who are now virtually extinct); it was not until 1635 that French settlers arrived. Because of their wealth from sugar, the islands became a bone of contention between Britain and France; other French islands, Dominica, St Lucia, Tobago, were lost by France in the Napoleonic wars. The important dates in the later history of the islands are 1848, when the slaves were freed under the influence of the French 'Wilberforce', Victor Schoelcher; 1946, when the islands ceased to be colonies and became Departments; and 1974, when they also became Regions.

Culture

The cultural, social and educational systems of France are used and the official language is French. However, Créole is widely spoken on Guadeloupe and Martinique; it has West African grammatical structures and uses a mainly French-derived vocabulary. Although still not officially recognized, it is the everyday language of the Guadeloupean and Martiniquan people and can be heard on the radio, where some stations use it almost exclusively. English is not widely spoken, although it is becoming more common in hotels and particularly on St-Barts, where it is understood nearly everywhere and on St-Martin, where it is the common language. A knowledge of French is therefore a great advantage. **Language**

Another feature common to the two main islands is the pre-Lenten Carnival, said to be more spontaneous and less touristy than most. There are also picturesque Ash **Carnival**

Wednesday ceremonies (especially in Martinique), when the population dresses in black and white, and processions take place that combine the seriousness of the first day of the Christian Lent with the funeral of the Carnival King (Vaval).

Music & dance Also shared are the African dances: the *calinda, laghia, bel-air, haut-taille, gragé* and others, still performed in remote villages. The famous biguine is a more sophisticated dance from these islands, and the mazurka can also be heard. French Antillean music is, like most other Caribbean styles, hybrid, a mixture of African (particularly percussion), European, Latin and, latterly, US and other Caribbean musical forms. Currently very popular, on the islands and in mainland France, is zouk, a hi-tech music which overlays electronics on more traditional rhythms.

Customs Traditional costume is commonly seen in the form of brightly-coloured, chequered Madras cotton made into elegant Parisian-style outfits. It is the mixture of French and Créole language and culture that gives Martinique and Guadeloupe an ambience quite different from that of the rest of the Caribbean. An extra dimension is added by the Hindu traditions and festivals celebrated by the descendants of the 19th century indentured labourers.

Sports The spectacles of cockfighting and mongoose versus snake are popular throughout the French Islands. Betting shops are full of atmosphere (they are usually attached to a bar). Horseracing is held on Martinique, but not Guadeloupe, but on both islands gambling on all types of mainland France track events is very keen.

Literature The dominance of French educational and social regimes on its colonial possessions led, in the 1930s and 1940s, to a literary movement which had a profound influence on black writing the world over. This was *négritude*, which grew up in Paris among black students from the Caribbean and Africa. Drawing particularly on Haitian nationalism (1915-30), the *négritude* writers sought to restore black pride which had been completely denied by French education. The leaders in the field were Aimé Césaire of Martinique, Léopold Senghor of Senegal and Léon Damas of Guyane. Césaire's first affirmation of this ideology was *Cahier d'un retour au pays natal* (1939); in subsequent works and in political life (he was mayor of Fort-de-France) he maintained his attack on the "white man's superiority complex" and worked, in common with another Martiniquan writer, Frantz Fanon, towards "the creation of a new system of essentially humane values" (Mazisi Kunene in his introduction to the Penguin edition of *Return to My Native Land*, 1969).

Windward Islands

16

Windward Islands

The Windward Islands include four independent nations: Dominica, St Lucia, St Vincent and the Grenadines and Grenada as well as the French Antilles which are departments of France. They form a series of volcanic peaks jutting out and forming a barrier between the Atlantic Ocean and the Caribbean Sea. Sulphur fumaroles and hot springs can be found on some islands where the volcanoes are dormant but not dead. There are large areas of rainforest with national parks protecting places of biodiversity or natural beauty, and the islands are a haven for birds and other wildlife. Hikers and birdwatchers are spoilt for choice in the larger islands of the Windwards, while yachtsmen are similarly blessed when navigating among the smaller Grenadines, one of the world's most popular sailing destinations. Bananas are still an important source of income on the Windward Islands, but agriculture is diversifying with other tropical fruits now being exported. Tourism is the leading foreign exchange earner, providing the jobs which have been lost in traditional activities.

Dominica

Dominica (pronounced Domineeca) is one of the largest and most mountainous of the anglophone Windward Islands. The highest peak, Morne Diablotin, rises to 4,747 ft and is often shrouded in mist. It is known as the Nature Island of the Caribbean with parks and reserves protecting vast areas of forest that cover most of the interior. In addition, the frequent rainfall and many rivers have led to some very dramatic seascapes with beautiful hard and soft coral. It is 29 miles long and 16 miles wide, with an area of 290 square miles.

Ins and outs

Getting there
See transport, page 772, for further details

Air There are no direct flights **from Europe** or **North America** to Dominica. Connections must be made in Puerto Rico, St Maarten, Antigua, St Lucia, Martinique or Guadeloupe. *LIAT* flies from Antigua, Barbados, Martinique, Guadeloupe, St Lucia; *Air Guadeloupe* from Guadeloupe, Barbados, Martinique (all into Canefield). *Cardinal Airlines* flies from Antigua, St Maarten, Barbados, and between Canefield and Melville Hall airports. *American Eagle* flies daily from San Juan; *Helenair* has a daily flight from St Lucia into Canefield.

Getting around
There are few road signs, but with a good map finding your way is not difficult

Road Car hire rates are about US$60 per day for a small Hyundai, including collision damage waiver and US$70 for a jeep; unlimited mileage for hiring for three days or more. A car rental phone can be found at the airport and several of the companies will pick you up from there and help to arrange the licence. It may be preferable to rent a car or jeep as the **taxi** service is expensive and buses take a lot of planning. Dominicans drive fast in the middle of the road and many visitors prefer to take a taxi so that they can enjoy the views. Main roads are fairly good; the Portsmouth-Marigot road built in 1987 is excellent, but in towns and south of Roseau, roads are very narrow and in poor condition. The tourism office in the Old Market, Roseau, sells Ordnance Survey maps. **Hitching** rides in the back of the ubiquitous pick-up trucks is possible although often difficult at weekends. You have nothing to fear if you offer local people a lift, all are unfailingly courteous; the carrying of machetes is not an indication of likely violence, the bearer is probably just on his way home from his banana field! Apart from the Soufrière/Scotts Head route, it is difficult to get anywhere on the island by **public transport**, and return to Roseau, in one day because buses leave Marigot, or wherever, to arrive in Roseau around 0700, then return at about 1300. It is just possible to get to Portsmouth and return in one day, the first bus is at 1000, returning at 1600.

Climate
Daytime temperatures average between 70° F and 85° F, though the nights are much cooler, especially in the mountains. The rainy season is from July to October though showers occur all through the year. Note that the mountains are much wetter and cooler than the coast, Roseau receives about 85 in of rain a year, while the mountains get over 340 in.

Flora and fauna

There are several national parks, including the **Morne Trois Pitons** (17,000 acres) in the south, the **Central Forest Reserve** and the **Northern Forest Reserve**, which together protect rainforest covering much of the island's mountainous interior. At the highest levels on the island is elfin woodland, characterized by dense vegetation and low-growing plants. Elfin woodland and high montane thicket give way to rainforest at altitudes between 1,000 and 2,500 ft, extending over about 60% of the island. Despite the large area of forest, protection is essential against cutting for farmland and other economic pressures, as a water source and as a unique facility for scientific research. It is hoped that tourism can coexist with conservation, since any losses, for whatever reason, would be irreversible.

The **Cabrits Peninsula** in the northwest was declared a national park in 1986. Covering 1,313 acres, its twin hills covered by dry forest, is separated from the island by marshland (a pier and cruise ship reception centre have been built) which is a nesting place for herons and doves and hosts a variety of migrant bird species. A walk through the woods and around the buildings of **Fort Shirley** (abandoned in 1854) will reveal much flora and wildlife. The scuttling hermit (or soldier) and black crabs, ground lizard (abòlò) and tree lizard are most visible.

Dominica

Essentials

Documents All visitors entering Dominica must be in possession of an **outward ticket** and a valid **passport**. Proof of citizenship with photo only is acceptable for US and Canadian citizens. A Carte identité allows French nationals to visit for up to two weeks. Visas are required by nationals of communist countries: they can be obtained from the Ministry of Home Affairs, Government Headquarters, Roseau. Immigration will normally grant you a stay of 21 days on arrival; extensions can be applied for but you will need a return or onward ticket.

Warning The police are strict in their enforcement of anti-narcotic laws. The present Government takes a strong stand on "moral" issues.

Currency East Caribbean dollar.

Departure tax EC$30 and a security service charge of EC$5, or US$12 if you pay in dollars. Day trippers pay EC$5; under 12s are free.

Ports of entry (Own flag) Roseau, Portsmouth and Anse du Mai in the east. Obtain coast-wide permit. EC$1 to clear in. Customs main office is at the deep water harbour at Woodbridge Bay where all the large ships come in (T4484462) but you can also clear at the Bayfront. Other offices are at Roseau, Anse de Mai, Portsmouth and at both airports.

Anchorages Salisbury, Castaways Beach Hotel, Layou River. A marina is being built at the Coconut Beach Hotel near Portsmouth,

with slips for 40 boats, full service. Do not anchor in Scotts Head/Soufrière Bay (marine reserve) or Douglas Bay or where fishing activities are underway. Waste disposal at the commercial docks in Portsmouth and Roseau.

Hours of business Government offices: Monday, 0800-1300, 1400-1700, Tuesday to Friday, close one hour earlier in the afternoon; the only government offices open on Saturday are the tourist kiosk in Old Market Plaza, and the tourist office at Canefield airport (open daily 0615-1115, 1415-1730 – or last flight); the Melville Hall tourist office is only open at flight arrival times. **Shops**: 0800-1300, 1400-1600, Monday-Friday, 0800-1300 Saturday. Some of the larger supermarkets in Roseau stay open until 2000 and tiny, local shops may still be open at 2200 even on Sunday. **Banks**: 0800-1500 Monday-Thursday, 0800-1700 Friday.

Communications The official title, **Commonwealth of Dominica**, should always be used in addresses to avoid confusion with the Dominican Republic. The International phone code is 767. See page 773 for further details.

Official time Atlantic Standard Time, four hours behind GMT, one ahead of EST.

Useful numbers T999 for Police, Fire and Ambulance.

Voltage 220/240 volts AC, 50 cycles. There is electricity throughout the island, but many places lack running water, especially in the

Dominica is a botanist's & a birdwatcher's paradise

In addition to the huge variety of trees, many of which flower in March and April, there are orchids and wild gardens of strange plant life in the valleys. Bwa Kwaib or Carib wood (*Sabinea carinalis*) was declared the national flower in 1978 which can be found mostly growing along parts of the west coast.

Indigenous birds to the island are the Imperial parrot, or Sisserou (*amazona imperialis*), which is critically endangered, and its marginally less threatened relative, the Red-necked parrot, or Jacquot (*amazona arausiaca*). The Sisserou has been declared the national bird. They can be seen in the Syndicate area in the northwest which is now a protected reserve and the site of a future information and research centre for visitors and scientists (accessible by four-wheel drive only). There is a nature trail but signs are difficult to spot. The parrots are most evident during their courting season, in April and early May. To get the best from a parrot-watching trip, it is worth taking a guide. Bertrand Jno Baptiste, of the Forestry Division (T4482401) is highly recommended and charges EC$80 a group. While there are other rare species, such as villages between Marigot and La Plaine.

Language English is the official language but **patois** is spoken widely. It is very similar to that spoken on St Lucia and to the créole of Martinique and Haiti but people tend to speak more slowly (see page 777).

Radio DBS broadcasts on AM 595 kHz and FM 88.1, 88.6. 89.5, 103.2 and 103.6 MHz. Kairi Fm is the most listened to radio station with a more lively presentation style than the state-owned DBS. It is on FM 93.1, 107.9 MHz. Vol is on AM 1060 KHz, FM 102.1, 90.6 MHz. There are two religious radio stations (one Protestant and one Catholic) as well as a repeater for St Lucian Radio Caribbean International on FM 98.1 Mhz.

Tourist offices overseas France KPMG Axe Consultants, 12 Rue de Madrid, 75008 Paris, France, T53-424100, F43-873285. **UK** Dominica High Commission, 1 Collingham Gardens, Earls Court, London SW5 0HW, T020-78351937, F020-73738743, or the Caribbean Tourism Organization, Suite 3.15, Vigilant House, 120 Wilton Road, Victoria, London SW1V 1JZ, T020-72338382, F020-78738551. **USA** Dominica Tourist Office, 10 East 21st Street, New York, NY10010, T212-4757542, F4759728, Dominicany@msn.com

Travel agents abroad Trips Worldwide, 9 Byron Place, Clifton, Bristol BS8 1JT, T0117-9872626, F0117-9872627, www.tripsworldwide.co.uk, ATOL, member of LATA, specialists in holidays to help you get off the beaten track.

Clothing informal, though swimsuits are not worn on the streets. A sweater is recommended for the evenings. When hiking take a raincoat and/or a pullover; a dry T-shirt is also a good idea. Take good walking shoes.

Laundry Mr Clean Laundry, Federation Drive, Roseau, EC$16 for big load, they wash it for you. Island Wash Launderettes in Newtown and Pottersville (both Roseau).

Safety Crime is rising and there have been mugging cases on beaches at Castle Bruce in the east and Hampstead on the northeast coast. There are often robberies around Calibishie and you must never leave valuables unattended on the beaches in that area, even if you can see them. Lock them, hidden, in your car. Grand Bay is an area to avoid at carnival time, which is celebrated with much 'enthusiasm', including guns and machetes. Theft is normally non violent and is of cash and easily saleable items (for example jewellery) rather than credit cards. Always report theft to the police, they generally have a shrewd idea of where to look for stolen goods and jewellery is often recovered.

Public holidays 1 January; Carnival; Good Friday and Easter Monday; first Monday in May; Whit Monday; first Monday in August; 3/4 November (Independence); Christmas Day and Boxing Day. 2 January is a merchant's holiday, when all shops and restaurants are closed, although banks and hotels remain open; Government offices will in most cases not be open.

the Forest Thrush and the Blue-headed hummingbird, there are a great many others which are easily spotted (the Purple-throated Carib and Antillean-crested humming-birds, for instance), or heard (the Siffleur Montagne). Waterfowl can be seen on the lakes, waders on the coastal wetlands (many are migrants). There are various bat caves, most particularly at Thiband on the northeast coast.

There are fewer species of mammal (agouti, manicou-opossum, wild pig and bats), but there is a wealth of insect life (for example, over 55 species of butterfly) and reptiles. Besides those mentioned above, there is the rare iguana, the crapaud (a large frog, eaten under the name of mountain chicken) and five snakes, none poisonous (includes the boa constrictor, or tête-chien). Certain parts of the coast are used as nesting grounds by sea turtles (hawksbill, leatherback and green). As a result of over-hunting, the Forestry Division has extended the close season for hunting wildlife like crapaud. Visitors should be mindful of this when thinking about ordering such foods in restaurants.

The Forestry Division in the Botanical Gardens, Roseau, has a wide range of publications, trail maps, park guides, posters and leaflets (some free) on Dominica's wildlife and National Parks, T4482401, F4487999.

Diving and marine life

Many drop-offs are close to the beaches but access is poor & boats are essential

Dominica is highly regarded as a diving destination and has been featured in most diving magazines as 'undiscovered'. Features include wall dives, drop-offs, reefs, hot, freshwater springs under the sea, sponges, black coral, pinnacles and wrecks, all in unpolluted water. Due to steep drops the sediment falls away and visibility is excellent, at up to 30 m depending on the weather.

Dive sites There is a marine park conservation area in **Toucari Bay** and part of **Douglas Bay**, north of the Cabrits, but the most popular scuba sites are south of Roseau, at **Pointe Guignard**, **Soufrière Bay** and **Scotts Head**. An unusual site is **Champagne**, with underwater hot springs where you swim through bubbles, fascinating for a night dive, also good for snorkelling, lots of life here. This area in the southeast, **Soufrière-Scotts Head**, is now a marine park without moorings so that all diving is drift diving and boats pick up divers where they surface. Areas may be designated for diving and other areas for fishing. Along the south and southeast coast there are more dive sites but because of the Atlantic currents these are for experienced, adventurous divers only. Note that the taking of conch, coral, lobster, sponge, turtle eggs et cetera is forbidden and you may not put down anchor in coral and on reefs; use the designated moorings. Snorkelling is good in the same general areas as diving, including Douglas Bay and the Scott's Head/Soufrière Bay Marine Reserve.

Whale watching is extremely popular, although the success rate is relatively low. The World Wildlife Fund and many marine conservation groups have used Dominica as a base for documentaries and conferences, so much is known about the local population. It appears that female whales and their calves are in the Caribbean waters for much of the year, with only the mature males leaving the area to feed for any length of time. If your trip is successful, you could be treated to the sight of mothers and their young swimming close to the boat, or young males making enormous jumps before diving below the waves. Dolphin are abundant too, particularly in the Soufrière Bay area and even if you miss the whales your boat is accompanied by a school of playful dolphin. Several different types of whales have been spotted not far from the west shore where the deep, calm waters are ideal for these mammals. Sperm whales are regularly seen, especially during the winter months, as are large numbers of spinner and spotted dolphins. You can also sometimes see pilot whales, pseudorcas, pygmy sperm whales, bottlenose dolphins, Risso's dolphins and melon-headed whales. Whale watching trips can be arranged with the *Anchorage Hotel* (Thursday, Sunday 1400-1800), *Dive Dominica* (Wednesday, Sunday 1400), *Rainbow Sportfishing* or *Game Fishing Dominica* and cost US$40-50 per person.

Dive centres Scuba diving is permitted only through one of the island's registered dive operators or with written permission from the Fisheries Division. Single-tank dives are from US$42 and two-tank dives are from US$63. Snorkelling trips are around US$26, particularly recommended for the Champagne area. *Dive Dominica Ltd*, at the *Castle Comfort Lodge* (PO Box 2253, Roseau, T4482188, F4486088, www.divedominica.com), offers full diving and accommodation packages, courses, single or multiple day dives, night dives and equipment rental. Owned by Derek Perryman, this company is one of the most friendly and experienced operations, recommended for its professional service. *Anchorage Dive Centre* (T4482638, F4485680, anchorage@cwdom.dm, US$65 two-tank dive includes weights and belt) is based at the *Anchorage Hotel*, Castle Comfort, with a sister operation at the *Portsmouth Beach Hotel*. This is another long established operation with a good reputation, owned by Andrew Armour. Other dive companies are *Dive*

Castaways at the *Castaways Beach Hotel* (T4496244, F4496246, www. cast-aways.dm), US$40 one dive, US$65 for two-tank dive, which covers the northern dive sites; *Cabrits Dive Centre*, who operate from Picard Estate, Portsmouth, T4453010, F4453011, cabritsdive@cwdom.dm A PADI five-star dive centre diving and snorkelling in the less-visited north of the island; *East Carib Dive* at Salisbury (T4996575, F4496603, www.eastcaribdive.dm) is based at the *Lauro Club*, contact Gunther Glatz; and *Nature Island Dive* at Soufrière (T4498181, F4498182, www.natureislanddive.dm, also kayaking and mountain biking), run by a team of divers from around the world, courses on the bayside recommended. A two-tank dive is US$70, snorkelling trip US$26, equipment rental US$16. Ask them about accommodation and dive packages, they have a bayside wooden cottage on stilts with porch for up to four divers, *Gallette*. Due to open soon is *Anse-à-Liane Lodge & Dive Centre* at Colihaut, T4466652, F4466651, www.ansealianedive.com, offering PADI and BSAC courses, accommodation, restaurant and excursions.

Beaches and watersports

Compared with other Caribbean islands, Dominica has few good beaches, but does have excellent river bathing. The Caribbean side of Dominica gains or loses sand according to swells and storms but the black coral sandy areas are few and far between. A small one exists just off Scotts Head (favoured as a teaching ground for divers, snorkellers and canoeists, so sometimes crowded), but further north you must travel to Mero beach or *Castaways Beach Hotel*. **Macousheri Bay** and **Coconut Beach** near Portsmouth are probably the best areas for Caribbean bathing. Don't be tempted to swim anywhere near Roseau or the larger villages because of effluent. For some really beautiful, unspoilt, white sandy beaches, hire a four-wheel drive and investigate the bays of the northeast coast. **Turtle Beach**, **Pointe Baptiste**, **Hampstead** and **Woodford Hill** are all beautiful but on the Atlantic coast terrific underswells and freak waves make swimming dangerous. Look at the sea and swim in the rivers is the safest advice. Very strong swimmers may be exhilarated by **Titou Gorge**, near Laudat, where the water flows powerfully through a narrow canyon and emerges by a hot mineral cascade.

Gusty winds coming down from the hills make sailing difficult and unreliable; conditions are rarely suitable for the beginner. *Carib Cruises* has various cruises on a 70-ft catamaran taking 80 people or a 24-ft boat for smaller parties, T4482489, F4483500. *Game Fishing Dominica* is a new operation at the *Castaways Beach Hotel* (T4496638) with charters at US$400 half day or US$600 full day. *Rainbow Sportfishing/Charters* can take you fishing in the Martinique channel, which is a migratory route, or take you on a cruise to Martinique or Les Saintes, T/F4488650, rollei@cwdom.dm The first Dominica International Sportfishing Tournament was held in 1996 and annually since then in May. Sea kayaks can be hired from Nature Island Dive, rates are US$11 per hour, US$26 per half day and US$42 per full day, lifejackets and instruction in Soufrière Bay provided. Guided tours are available.

> *Very few watersports are on offer*

The best harbour for yachts is Portsmouth (Prince Rupert Bay), but you should guard your possessions. Stealing from yachts is quite common. The new jetty in Roseau (see below) is designed for small craft, such as yachts, clearing for port entry. Both the *Reigate Waterfront* and *Anchorage Hotels* have moorings and a pier, and yachtsmen and women are invited to use the hotels' facilities.

Football and **cricket** are among the most popular national sports; watch cricket in the beautiful setting of the Botanical Gardens or at the dramatic pitch at Petit Savanne where two sides of the boundary line run along a cliff overlooking the Atlantic. Hitting a six will mean the loss of a ball into the ocean. **Basketball** and **netball** are also enthusiastically played. There are hard **tennis** courts at the privately-owned Dominica Club (T4482995), *Reigate Hall* and *Castaways*, rental for

> **Other sports**

minimal fee, bring your own racket. *Anchorage Hotel* and Dominica Club have **squash** courts. **Cycling** is growing in popularity and the island's roads, although twisty, are good. Mountain bikes can be hired from *Nature Island Dive* at Soufrière (T4498181), US$11 per hour, US$21 per half day, US$32 per full day, where there are marked off-road trails. Full day guided biking trips cost US$84 per person. **Hiking** in the mountains is excellent, and hotels and tour companies arrange this type of excursion. **Mountain climbing** can be organized through the Forestry Division in the Botanical Gardens, Roseau, T4482401. Guides are necessary for any forays into the mountains or forests, some areas of which are still uncharted. **Horse riding** can be arranged through *Evergreen Hotel*, T4483288.

Roseau

The town is in chaos on the days cruise ships come in

Roseau (pronounced *Rose-oh*), the main town, is small, ramshackle and friendly, with a surprising number of pretty old buildings still intact. The houses look a bit tatty with rusting tin roofs and a general lack of paint, but there is still some attractive gingerbread fretwork in the traditional style on streets like Castle Street. Quite a lot of redevelopment has taken place over the last few years, improving access and making the waterfront more attractive. The Old Market Plaza has been made into a pedestrian area, with shops in the middle. The old, red market cross has been retained, with 'keep the pavement dry' picked out in white paint. Between the Plaza and the sea is the old post office, now housing the **Dominican Museum**, which is well worth a visit. The post office is on the Bay Front at the bottom of Hillsborough Street. It has a colourful mural depicting the development of Dominica's postal service, and a Philately Counter. The **market**, at the north end of Bay Street, is a fascinating sight on Saturday mornings from about 0600-1000; it is also lively on Friday morning, closed Sunday. The sea wall was completed in late 1993, which has greatly improved the waterfront area of town, known as the **Bay Front** or **Dame Eugenia Charles Boulevard**, after the Prime Minister who promoted the development. The Roseau jetty, destroyed by Hurricane David in 1979, was rebuilt in the Seawall and Bay Front Development Project for the use of yachts and other small craft. A promenade with trees and benches, a road from the Old Jetty to Victoria Street, and parking bays take up most of the space. A new T-shaped cruise ship jetty was completed in 1995 and for several weeks in the winter season ships tower above the town pouring forth tourists into 16-seater taxis for tours around the island. Although small, you may need to ask for directions around Roseau. Streets have been given signs but it is still tricky to find your way around. There is a one way traffic system: vehicles going west go along Great George Street, those going east use Queen Mary Street.

The 40-acre **Botanical Gardens** dating from 1890 are principally an arboretum; they have a collection of plant species, including an orchid house. Several Jacquot and Sisserou parrots can be seen in the bird sanctuary in the park, thanks in part to the Jersey Wildlife Preservation Trust. Breeding programmes are underway and it is hoped that some of the offspring will be released to the wild.

The town has no deep-water harbour; this is at **Woodbridge Bay** over a mile away, where most of the island's commercial shipping is handled, and some tourist vessels are accommodated.

Around the island

Trafalgar waterfalls

Bathing is possible in pools in the river beneath the falls

The Trafalgar waterfalls in the Roseau Valley, five miles from the capital, have been the most popular tourist site for many years. Hot and cold water flowed in two spectacular cascades in the forest, but unfortunately the volume of the hot fall was sharply diminished by a hydroelectric scheme higher up and a landslide after the September 1995 hurricanes covered both the hot and cold water pools. Entrance to this and other 'ecological' sites in Dominica is US$2; tickets should be bought in advance from agencies. The path to the falls is easy to follow, but if you want to go further than the viewing point, take a guide because there is a lot of scrambling over rocks and it can be difficult at times. Trying to cross over the falls at the top is very hazardous. There are always lots of guides, you will probably be approached well before reaching the start of the trail. Some guides can be abusive if you insist on going alone. Agree the price before setting out, around EC$10 for two or more people in a group. Some guides are official and wear badges. The Trafalgar Falls are crowded because they are close to the road (bus EC$5 from outside the Astaphan supermarket in Roseau or two-hour walk). A natural sulphur pool has been set up at *Papillote* restaurant by the falls, in lovely gardens. Its a great place to relax by moonlight with a rum punch. There is also a one hour trail from the sulphur springs of the tiny settlement of Wotten Waven through forest and banana plantations across the Trois Pitons River up to the Trafalgar Falls.

D'Auchamps Gardens are about a mile out of Trafalgar Village on the way back to Roseau. The designer, Sara Honychurch, has laid out the family estate with a huge **D'Auchamps Gardens**

Roseau

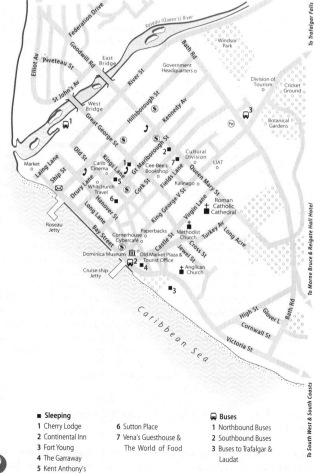

■ Sleeping
1 Cherry Lodge
2 Continental Inn
3 Fort Young
4 The Garraway
5 Kent Anthony's Guesthouse
6 Sutton Place
7 Vena's Guesthouse & The World of Food

🚌 Buses
1 Northbound Buses
2 Southbound Buses
3 Buses to Trafalgar & Laudat

Not to scale

variety of wild and cultivated plants with a citrus orchard and a traditional Caribbean garden. More species are being added weekly and plants are well labelled. Emphasis is on the origin and uses of plants, whether medicinal or agricultural. ■ *Daily 0900-1600. T4483346, www.delphis.dm/dauchamps You can walk round on your own or have a guided tour.*

Morne Trois Pitons National Park

Much of the south part of the island (17,000 acres) has since 1975 been designated the Morne Trois Pitons National Park and in 1998 it became a World Heritage Site. Evidence of volcanic activity is manifested in hot springs, sulphur emissions and the occasional small eruption. Its attractions include the **Boiling Lake** (92°C), which may be the largest of its kind in the world (the other contender is in New Zealand) and reached after a six-mile climb from Laudat. You have to return on the same path as an alternative trail is no longer maintained. An experienced guide is recommended as the trail can be treacherous, particularly if the mist descends, but it is easy to follow once you are on it (guides charge about EC$100 per couple, EC$180 for two couples; Lambert Charles, T4483365, strong and knowledgeable; Kenrich Johnson, friendly, informative; Edison and Loftus Joseph, Wotten Waven, T4489192 at a telephone box, cheaper than organized tours, the brothers are shoe makers).

In the valley below the Boiling Lake is a spectacular region known as the **Valley of Desolation**, where the forest has been destroyed by sulphuric emissions. A small volcanic eruption in 1997, not considered cause for alarm, caused ash to scatter over an area of about 50 ft sq. At the beginning of the trail to the Boiling Lake is the Titou Gorge, now considerably damaged by rock fall from the hydroelectric development in the area, where a hot and a cold stream mingle. A new track, the Kent Gilbert Trail, has been cut; it starts in La Plaine and is about 4½ miles long. It affords views of the Sari Sari and Bolive Falls, but avoids the Valley of Desolation. While this makes it a less strenuous route, it also renders it less impressive.

Also in the park is the **Freshwater Lake**; it is to the east of **Morne Macaque** at 2,500 ft above sea level, and can be reached by road (two miles from Laudat). Do not swim here, it is the drinking water reservoir for Roseau. A trail leads in 45 minutes on foot (follow the road where the river joins the lake about half a mile to the pipeline, take the path to the left through the dense forest) to the highest lake in the island, Boeri, situated between Morne Macaque and **Morne Trois Pitons**. Work on a hydroelectric project in this area was completed in 1991. There have been lasting consequences for both the Trafalgar Falls (a diminished flow of water) and the Freshwater Lake (a lower water level).

The National Park Service has built a series of paths, the Middleham Trails, through the rain forest on the northwest border of the park. The trails are accessible from Sylvania on the Transinsular Road, or Cochrane, although the signs from Sylvania are not very clear. The road to Cochrane is by the Old Mill Cultural Centre in Canefield, once through the village the trail is marked. About 1½-2 hours walk from Cochrane are the **Middleham Falls**, about 250 ft high, falling into a beautiful blue pool in the middle of the forest. Once past the Middleham Falls the trail emerges on the Laudat road. Turn inland at *Sisserou Hotel* and then immediately right behind the Texaco garage (30 minutes' walk from Roseau) a steep road leads 2½ miles up to Giraudel (50 minutes' walk). From behind the school here a trail goes up through a succession of smallholdings to **Morne Anglais** (3,683 ft) (2 hours' walk from Giraudel). This is the easiest of the high mountains to climb and you get some lovely views of the whole island. The trail is fairly easy to follow but someone will need to show you the first part through the smallholdings. Ask in the village or go with *Dominica Tours*.

South of Roseau

In the far south are the villages of **Soufrière** and **Scotts Head**. Both are worth visiting for their stunning setting on the sea with the mountain backdrop and brightly painted fishing boats pulled up on the shore. There are plenty of buses (EC$3) to

Scotts Head, over the mountain with excellent views all the way to Martinique. Ask around the fishing huts if you are hungry, and you will be directed to various buildings without signs where you can eat chicken pilau for EC$6 and watch dominoes being played. There is a friendly café, *Sundowner*, on the main road just across from the most active fishing area (this boasts the only lavatories for the use of visitors).

On the south coast is **Grand Bay**, where there is a large beach (dangerous for swimming), the 10 ft high Belle Croix and the **Geneva Estate**, founded in the 18th century by the Martinican Jesuit, Father Antoine La Valette, and at one time the home of the novelist Jean Rhys. From Grand Bay, it is a two hour walk over the hill, past Sulphur Spring to Soufrière. Grand Bay should be avoided during Carnival, which is celebrated over-enthusiastically and aggressively. Tourists were attacked in 1997 with guns and machetes wielded by a group of men in costumes. The area has a reputation for violence related to the growing of marijuana which is smuggled to Martinique.

The Leeward coastal road, north from Roseau, comes first to **Canefield**, passing the turning for the twisting Imperial Road to the centre of the island, and then the small airport. The coast road passes through **Massacre**, reputed to be the settlement where 80 Caribs were killed by British troops in 1674. Among those who died was Indian Warner, Deputy Governor of Dominica, illegitimate son of Sir Thomas Warner (Governor of St Kitts) and half-brother of the commander of the British troops, Colonel Philip Warner. From the church perched above the village there are good views of the coast. The next village is **Mahaut** and just north of here near DCP a newly paved road, called Warner Road, climbs steeply up towards Morne Couroune. It then levels out and joins the main Layou Valley road at the Layou Valley Plaza, a few kilometres west of the Pont Cassé roundabout. The views are stunning and are best when coming down hill.

North of the Transinsular road are the **Central Forest Reserve** and **Northern Forest Reserve**. In the latter is **Morne Diablotin**. Take a bus from Roseau to Dublanc, walk 1½ hours on a minor road and you will see a sign. The trail to the summit is very rough, about three hours steep walking and climbing up and 2½ hours down, not for the faint hearted, you are advised to take a guide.

Leeward coast

Portsmouth

The coastal road continues to Portsmouth, the second town. An excellent market is held here twice a week with all local fruits, vegetables and spices for sale. Nearby are the ruins of the 18th-century **Fort Shirley** on the Cabrits, which has a museum in one of the restored buildings (entry free). It is very run down but there is an excellent plan of how the fort once was. Clearly marked paths lead to the Commander's Quarters, Douglas Battery and other outlying areas. The colonial fortifications, apart from the main buildings which have been cleared, are strangled by ficus roots, and cannon which used to point out to sea now aim at the forest. A new visitors' centre has been built at the cruise ship jetty (small ships only); interesting, puts the whole fortification into perspective. Prince Rupert Bay has been much visited: Columbus landed

Portsmouth

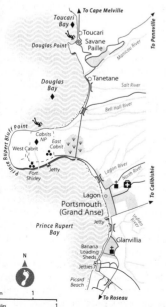

Windward Islands

here in 1504 and in 1535 the Spanish Council of the Indies declared the bay a station for its treasure ships. Sir Francis Drake, Prince Rupert and John Hawkins all visited the bay to trade with the Caribs. Construction of Fort Shirley began in 1774. It was abandoned by the army in 1854. Restoration of the fort began in 1982. There are excellent views across the Guadeloupe Channel on the road to Clifton which also goes through some lush forest. The beach at Douglas Bay is of yellow sand but is quite stony.

Indian River From the bridge just south of Portsmouth, boats make regular, one-hourly trips up the **Indian River** (EC$25 per person), a peaceful trip (40 minutes) through a tunnel of vegetation as long as you are not accompanied by boatloads of other tourists. Competition for passengers is keen. Negotiate with the local boatmen about price and insist they use oars rather than a motor, so as not to disturb the birds and crabs. There is a bar open at the final landing place on this lovely river which accommodates large numbers of cruise ship passengers and serves them the very potent spiced rum, aptly named *Dynamite*. You can then continue on foot through fields and forest to the edge of a marsh where migrating birds come in the winter months. The river and the swamps and marshes are being considered for inclusion in the national parks system.

The north From Portsmouth, one road carries on to the **Cabrits National Park** and the island's north tip at **Cape Melville**. An unpaved road leads off this at Savanne Paille; impassable except on foot, it is a beautiful route over the mountain, through a valley with sulphur springs, to Penville on the north coast, from where you can pick up the road heading south. Allow several hours.

Another road from Portsmouth heads east, following the Indian River for much of the way, winding up and down to the bays and extensive coconut palm plantations of the northwest coast, Calibishie, Melville Hall airport and Marigot. There are some beautiful sandy beaches at Hampstead and Larieu. **Calibishie** is a charming fishing village looking out towards Guadeloupe. There are hiking trails to the forest and wide, sandy beaches nearby; local guides are available. Transport to most areas in the northern part of the island is good, as is accommodation in and around the village. There are some small grocery stores, restaurants, post office, petrol station and a health clinic. Fishing boats come in at around 1630 and sell their catch at the bayside.

Transinsular road The shortest route from Roseau to Marigot and Melville Hall is via the Transinsular Road. It climbs steeply with many bends from Canefield. Along this road you will see coconut and cocoa groves; look out for the land crabs' holes, the orange juveniles come out in the daytime, the white adults at night. There are banana plants all along the gorge, together with dasheen, tannia, oranges and grapefruit. At Pont Cassé, the road divides three ways at one of the island's few roundabouts. One branch turns left, down the Layou Valley, to join the Leeward coast at Layou; the Transinsular Road goes straight on, through Bells, to Marigot; the third branch goes east (the path up the Trois Pitons is signed on the right just after the roundabout, three hours to the summit), either to Rosalie and La Plaine on the southeast Windward coast, or to Castle Bruce and the Carib Territory. The northern road, to Marigot, follows the Pagua River as it descends from the Central Forest Reserve to Pagua Bay on the Atlantic Ocean. At Hatton Garden, on the Bay, just south of Marigot, is **Habitation Chabert**, a restored 19th-century lime and sugar factory, now a museum of French and Créole furniture, artefacts, weapons and maps. ■ *US$4. Daily 0900-1600.*

Heading west from Pont Cassé the road affords some spectacular views. Layou River has some good spots for bathing, two of which are particularly good. Just over four miles from the roundabout there is a track to the right signposted suspension bridge, which descends to the river; bathe by the bridge. A mile further on along the road look for a narrow foot path on the right, immediately before a sizeable road bridge. It passes through a banana field to the riverside. On the opposite bank a concrete bath has been built around a hot spring to create an open-air hot tub with room for four or five good friends.

A 20-minute walk from *Spanny's Bar* on the main road leads you to Penrice Falls, two small waterfalls. There is great, but cold, swimming in the pool at the second fall.

At Bells there is a fascinating and beautiful walk to **Jacko Flats**. Here a group of maroons (escaped slaves) led by Jacko had their encampment in the late 17th and early 18th centuries. Carved into the cliffs of the Layou River gorge, a flight of giant steps rises 300 ft up to a plateau on which the maroons had their camp. Ask at the *Paradise Bar* in Bells for a guide and dress for river walking since much of the trail is in the river itself.

The **Emerald Pool** is a small, but pretty waterfall in a grotto in the forest, 15 minutes by path from the Pont Cassé-Castle Bruce road. Avoid the area on days when cruise ships have docked, as hundreds of passengers are taken to visit the Pool, with resulting damage to its delicate ecology. There is a picnic area, and toilet facilities are being built. There are no buses from Roseau but you can catch a minibus to Canefield and wait at the junction for a bus going to Castle Bruce.

The Atlantic coast

This coast is much more rugged than the Caribbean, with smaller trees, sandy or pebbly bays, palms and dramatic cliffs. Castle Bruce is a lovely bay and there are good views all around. After Castle Bruce the road enters the **Carib Territory**, although there is only a very small sign to indicate this. At the north end there is another sign, but it would still be easy to drive through the territory without seeing anything of note except a few small souvenir shops selling basket work. In fact, there is much to see; to appreciate it fully, a guide is essential. **Horseback Ridge** affords views of the sea, mountains, the Concord Valley and Bataka village. At **Crayfish River**, a waterfall tumbles directly into the sea by a beach of large stones.

The Save the Children Fund has assisted the Waitikubuli Karifuna Development Committee to construct two traditional buildings near **Salybia**: a large oval *carbet* (the nucleus of the extended Carib family group), and an A-frame *mouina*. The former is a community centre, the latter a library and office of the elected chief. The Carib chief is elected for five years and his main tasks are to organize the distribution of land and the preservation of Carib culture. In 1999, Garnet Joseph was elected chief of the Carib community and chairman of the Carib Council, replacing Hilary Frederick (1979-84, 1994-99). The dilapidated Church of the Immaculate Conception at Salybia is being restored as a Carib Museum (opening date uncertain; it has been replaced by the new church of St Marie of the Caribs, which opened in May 1991), its design is based on the traditional *mouina* and has a canoe for its altar, murals about Carib history both inside and out. Outside is a cemetery and a three-stone monument to the first three Carib chiefs after colonization: Jolly John, Auguiste and Corriett.

Traditional methods of making canoes from tree trunks can be seen in the Carib Territory. In May 1997 a group of 11 Caribs paddled a 35 ft canoe, carved from a gommier tree, to Guyana via Martinique, St Lucia, St Vincent, Grenada and Trinidad and Tobago, reversing the migratory journey of their ancestors.

L'Escalier Tête-Chien, at Jenny Point in Sineku is a line of rock climbing out of the sea and up the headland. It is most obvious in the sea and shore, but on the point each rock bears the imprint of a scale, circle or line, like the markings on a snake. It is said that the Caribs used to follow the snake staircase (which was made by the Master Tête-Chien) up to its head in the mountains, thus gaining special powers. There are more prosaic, geological explanations.

Taking the road from Pont Cassé to the southeast part of the island, you come to Rosalie. Cross the River Rosalie and go south to Pointe Daniel and Délices, passing through La Plaine. At La Plaine a fairly easy trail can be followed to the **Sari Sari Falls** (about 150 ft high). At Délices, you can see the **Victoria Falls** from the road. The Forestry Division plans to improve the rugged trail to the Falls. Be sure to take an experienced guide if you attempt the steep hike to these Falls (or the Sari Sari Falls) and avoid it in the rainy season. The White River falls in to the Atlantic at **Savane Mahaut**, reached by a steep road from Victoria Laroche down to the sea. There are delightful places to picnic, rest or swim in the river. At the weekend local families picnic and wash their cars here. If it has not rained much the previous day you can follow the river up, jumping from one to another of the big stones in the river bed. Be wary of flash floods and do not attempt to cross the river if there has been heavy rainfall as you might not be able to get back. Sea bathing here is very dangerous.

A road has been cut between the village of **Petite Savanne** and the **White River** linking the south and east coasts. It is extremely steep but offers spectacular views.

Essentials

Sleeping

Roseau

There are some small, informal hotels, guest houses & apartment facilities here.

Do verify whether tax (5%) is included in the quoted rate

Hotels **LL-A** *Fort Young Hotel*, within the old fort, PO Box 519, T4485000, F4488065, www.fortyounghotel.com Ocean front rooms and suites of an excellent standard and full conference facilities for the business traveller, lots of facilities, service brusque, food adequate, pool, exercise room, jetty, waterfront restaurant, the atmosphere is more relaxed on weekends, special events like concerts and barbecues and a popular Happy Hour every Friday, 1800-1900. Also the **L-AL** *Garraway*, Place Heritage, 1 Bay Front (Dame Eugenia Charles Boulevard), PO Box 789, T4498800, F4498807, www.delphis.dm/garraway.htm 31 rooms and suites, again of a good standard, conference facilities, restaurant, cocktail bar, senior citizen discounts and weekend deals available to encourage tourists. **AL-B** *Sutton Place Hotel*, 25 Old St, PO Box 2333, T4498700, F4483045, www.delphis.dm/sutton.htm One of the newest hotels on the island, 8 rooms, beautiful decor, excellent service, self-catering suites available.

Apartments are available to rent in & around Roseau, check at the Tourist Office, look in the New Chronicle, Tropical Star or ask a taxi driver

Guest houses **A-C** *Itassi Cottages*, on Morne Bruce, contact Mrs U Harris, PO Box 2333, T4484313, F4483045, sutton2@tod.dm Self-catering, spectacular view of south coast, 1 studio, 2 cottages, attractively furnished, phone, TV. **C** *Honychurch Apartment*, 5 Cross St, T4483346, PO Box 1889. Very central, discounts for a week, even nicer to stay at their *D'Auchamps Apartments* up in the Trafalgar Valley and hire a car, see below. **D** *Cherry Lodge*, 20 Kennedy Av, T4482366. Historic and quaint, some rooms with bath, rooms can be noisy and mosquitoes abundant, coils provided but no fans, good value meals available to order. **D-E** *Bon Marché Guest House*, 11 Old Street, PO Box 449, T4482083. 6 rooms, fans, bar, souvenir shop and boutique on site. **D-E** *Continental Inn*, 37 Queen Mary St, T4482214, F4487022, continental@cwdom.dm 11 rooms, a/c, fans, TV, bar, pizza restaurant, entertainment, used by travelling salesmen and visiting sailors. **D-E** *Ma Bass Central Guest House*, 44 Fields Lane, T4482999. 7 rooms, fans, food available. **E** *Kent Anthony Guesthouse*, 3 Great Marlborough Street, T4482730. 18 rooms, with fan and bath, cheaper rooms without, breakfast on request, rooms of varying standard, has gone downhill, lack of maintenance, brusque landlady. **E** *Vena's Guesthouse*, 48 Cork St, T4483286. 15 rooms, prices higher during carnival, Jean Rhys' birth place, interesting, rather inefficient, rooms small and grim, rooms without bath more spacious and comfortable but noisy as on the corner of the 2 main streets, *The World of Food* restaurant is next door.

South of Roseau

Outside Roseau, up a steep and windy hill (King's Hill), is **L-C** *Reigate Hall*, T4484031, F4484034. A splendid location but laid back management, recommended for sunset rum punch to watch the Green Flash. 15 rooms and suites, a/c, service in restaurant sloppy and slow, pricey, bar, swimming pool, tennis courts, dive packages with Dive Dominica. Further up the Roseau Valley are **A-E** *Chez Ophelia Cottage Apartments*, PO Box 152, T4483438, F4483433, mariem@mail.tod.dm Your host is the famous singer Ophelia, Dominica's 'First Lady of Song', close to Trafalgar Falls. **C** *Cocoa Cottage*, PO Box 1641, T4480412. A neat, clean and homely B&B in the middle of Trafalgar Valley. **C** *Roseau Valley Hotel*, T4498176, F4498722. 11 rooms and suites, also cottages for longer term rental.

L-A *Evergreen*, PO Box 309, T4483288, F4486800, www.delphis.dm/evergreen.htm 16 **Castle Comfort**
rooms, with breakfast, a/c, TV, bar. **AL** *Exotica*, PO Box 109, T4488839, F4488829, www.exot-
ica-cottages.com Nestled under the peaks of Morne Anglais close to Giraudel, new
ecotourism centre, run by Athie Martin, president of the Dominica Conservation Society, 8
wooden cottages, sympathetic design, good base for hiking, self-catering, with advance the
Sugar Apple Café will prepare meals. **AL-A** *Castle Comfort Lodge*, PO Box 2253, T4482188,
F4486088, www.castlecomfortdivelodge.com Very friendly, professional, 15 rooms, excellent local food, good service. A 7-night 10-dive package available includes transfers, 1-night
dive, unlimited shore diving, tax and service, US$990 (see page 758). **AL-B** *Anchorage*, on
seafront, T4482638, F4485680, www.anchoragehotel.dm Waterfront restaurant, rooms
rather tatty and run down, bar, friendly but slow service, food nothing special although
Thursday buffet very good and popular with locals, swimming pool and diving facilities, a
7-night, 10-dive package available, squash court with rather low ceiling. A friendly and
delightful place to stay, family-run, with good restaurant and excellent service is
AL-C *Reigate Waterfront*, PO Box 134, T4483111, F4484034. Restaurant with well-known
barbecue Wednesday night, 24 rooms, recently refurbished.

LL-A *The Wesleeann Hotel and Suites*, PO Box 1764, T4490419, F4492473, towers over 8th **Near Canefield**
Street in Canefield. Tastefully decorated apartments with kitchen, bathroom, balcony and
daily maid service, for daily or longer rental. **AL-B** *Ambassador*, within walking distance of
Canefield airport, PO Box 2413, T4491501, F4492304. Reasonable restaurant, comfortable,
but can be noisy, good for business visitors. **AL-C** *The Hummingbird Inn*, Morne Daniel, PO
Box 1901, Roseau, T/F4491042. Rooms (small, luggage a problem) or a suite, run by Mrs
Finucane who is knowledgeable on Dominica, peaceful, simple, comfortable, good food,
slow service, stunning views down the hill over the sea, 5 minutes north of Roseau, on bus
route. **A** *Crescent Moon Cabins*, PO Box 2400, Roseau, T/F4493449, www.delphis.dm/
crescentmooncabins/, high above Mahaut but reached from the main Transinsular Road,
about 30 mins from Roseau. Well-furnished wooden cabins in a delightful, secluded setting,
double and single bed, run by Ron and Jean Viveralli, good home cooking, local style, fresh
fruit and vegetables from on-site greenhouse and gardens, own roasted coffee, fresh spring
water, breakfast US$8, lunch US$10, can be packed for picnic, dinner US$15, car hire recom-
mended, *Island Car Rentals* will give a discount for guests. **B-C** *Sunset Guest House*,
T4491339, near Canefield airport. Friendly, clean, near bus route to Roseau.

AL-A *Papillote Wilderness Retreat*, PO Box 2287, T4482287, F4482285, www.papillote.dm **Near Trafalgar**
10 suites or cottage in beautiful botanical gardens landscaped by owner Anne Jean Baptiste, **Falls**
with hot mineral pool and geese, birdwatching house, food good but slightly limited for long
stay; restaurant for non-residents near road, lunch and dinner, food well prepared and nicely
presented, closed Sunday (avoid days when cruise ship passengers invade, reservations
required), arts and crafts boutique, take torch and umbrella, good road from the nearby village of Trafalgar all the way to the falls car park, spectacular setting. On the road to Trafalgar
and Papillote, the Honychurch family rents self-contained cottages on their lovely estate,
C *D'Auchamps*, PO Box 1889, T4483346, bienerb@cwdom.dm **B-C** *Roxy's Mountain Lodge*
in Laudat, PO Box 265, T/F4484845, bruneyr@cwdom.dm 2,000 ft above sea level, established 1960, good breakfast and hearty supper, friendly owners, 17 basic rooms, good beds,
hot showers, also apartment, 4-6 people, convenient for visiting Boiling Lake, Boeri Lake,
Middleham Falls, Trafalgar Falls and Freshwater Lake, all within walking distance, guides
arranged if required, transport into Roseau 0700 except Sunday, returning 1615, EC$3. Also
in Laudat, **C** *Symes-zee Villa*, PO Box 1728, T448-2494/3337, F4484476. 16 rooms. **C-D** *Falls
View Guest House*, within sight of the falls, T/F4480064. 10 rooms, good walking, Dominican
cuisine, bar.

On the extreme south coast, east of Scotts Head, reached from Soufrière, are *Petit Coulibri* **South coast**
Guest Cottages, on the Petit Coulibri Estate which used to grow sugar, cacao, and until
recently aloe vera, but still grows citrus. The main house and guest cottages were sold in
1999 and are not expected to reopen until February 2001, built 1,000 ft above sea,

overlooking Martinique, isolated setting, described by some as one of the most beautiful places in the world. In Scotts Head is **B-D** *Herche's Place*, Bay Street, T4487749, F4498000, herches @cwdom.dm 10 rooms, fans, a/c, TV, *Sundowner Café*, watersports, diving, fishing arranged. Other self-catering apartments include **C** *Castille Apartment*, Scotts Head, T4482926. *Ocean View Apartments*, T4498266. Owned by the very hospitable Frank and Caroline Charles, 1 or 2-bedroom apartment, nicely furnished, large secluded garden with fruit trees, mosquito nets, also 2 rooms in main house, maid and laundry service offered and transport to airport. **AL** *Zandoli Inn*, PO Box 2099, T4463161, F4463344, www.zandoli.com, south coast at Roche Cassee near fishing village of Stowe. New, well laid out, secluded, superb mountain and seaviews to Martinique, 5 rooms with balconies, includes continental breakfast, plunge pool, 6 acres of seaside tropical forest.

Leeward coast **L-AL** *Lauro Club*, Grand Savanne, PO Box 483, Roseau, T4496602, F4496603. Self-contained bungalows sleep 1-4, half-way between Roseau and Portsmouth, multi-lingual Swiss owners, pool, bowls, small shops and snack bar in central building, built on cliff top overlooking sea, access to sea but no beach, own transport essential, isolated, in a dry area, little shade, mostly used by French package tourists, surprisingly poor food. **AL-A** *Castaways*, Mero, PO Box 5, T4496244, F4496246, just north of St Joseph. Convenient with hired car for visiting all parts of the island, on black sand beach, restaurant, beach barbecue on Sunday, popular, watch out for beach cricket balls, staff slow but friendly, reasonable rooms all with balcony and seaview but in need of redecoration, ask for fan and mosquito net, good tennis court, sailing sometimes available, dive shop attached, German spoken, dive package available. **AL-A** *Sunset Bay Club*, Batalie Beach in the middle of the west coast, T4466522. Run by Belgian family, all-inclusive or room only, bungalows, suites, pool, sauna. *Anse-à-Liane Lodge*, north of Colihaut, T4466652, F4466651, www.ansealianedive.com Due to open late-2000, 10 rooms, 5 mins from sea with diving on beach below, a/c, restaurant, pool, tours planned.

Portsmouth **AL-B** *Picard Beach Cottage Resort*, T4455131, F4455599, pbh@cwdom.dm An attractive open-sided restaurant and bar, self-catering cottages which, at a pinch, can sleep 4, good sea bathing with coral reef, 7-night, 10-dive, package available. Further apartments are being built on the beach. On Picard Beach, **B** *Coconut Beach*, T4455393, F4455693. Beachfront bungalows, apartments, snorkelling, diving, windsurfing, volleyball, excursions, restaurant, marina planned. **C** *Mango Bay Hotel*, Prince Rupert's Bay, T/F4453099/4624. Pleasant, modern rooms, fans, bathroom, no mosquito screens, adjoining *Chez Darny* restaurant. Ask around for low budget rooms/huts to let. **C** *Sister Sea Lodge*, Prince Rupert's Bay. Beach bar, T/F4455211, sangow@cwdom.dm Fresh fish and 6 apartments set in lovely gardens, spacious, self-contained, insect nets, 2 double beds, bathroom, run by Elka and Harta (German) Sango, yachts can moor in the bay, sandy outside beach bar. **D** *Casa Ropa*, on Bay Street, T4455492, F4455277. Rooms or apartments with bath, single downstairs, friendly, clean. **E** *Douglas Guest House*, Bay Street, T4455253. Single, double or triple rooms, ask for fan, clean, next to noisy disco and cinema.

North coast **Calibishie** **LL-B** *Pointe Baptiste* estate rents out the Main House, sleeping 8, includes cook and maid, weekly rates available, spectacular view from the airy verandah, house built in 1932, wooden, perfect for children, cot, also smaller house sleeping 2, self-catering, book locally through the housekeeper Geraldine Edwards, T4457322. **L-A** *Eden Estate House* is also available for rent, T4482638, F4485680. 3 bedrooms, in middle of coconut and fruit plantation, only 3 miles from Melville Hall airport, maid service can be provided. **L-B** *Oceanview Cottage*, T4457614, near Calibishie and Melville Hall airport. Beautifully situated self-catering apartment on wooded ridge overlooking Hodges Bay. **AL** *Wind Blow Estate*, Calibishie, www.delphis.dm/windblow/ or in the USA Lewis Watkins, 18875 Cortez Blvd, Brooksville, Florida, T352-7997353. Apartments, 1 or 2 bedrooms, fans, sun deck, great view of Guadeloupe and Marie Galante, parking, security guard, sisserou parrot nests on the estate. In Calibishie, **AL-C** *Veranda View*, T4458900, lawrence@cwdom.dm Run by Mrs Teddy Lawrence, facing beach, beautiful view of Guadeloupe, clean, 3 bright and large rooms, includes breakfast, light cooking facilities, hot showers. **A-B** *Sea Cliff Cottages*, 15 mins walk from Calibishie, T/F4458998 December-May, T/F6137563116 May to December, sherwood@mv.igs.net 3 cottages, 1-3 bedrooms, kitchens, veranda, fruit trees in the garden for seasonal use, path to beach, snorkelling good, river good for children to play in, small island within swimming distance. **C** *Windswept Guest House*, T4458982/7236, between Calibishie and airport. Quiet, secluded, clean, close to excellent beach. In **Marigot D** *Thomas Guest House*, west end of main street, T4455591. Clean, basic, near Melville Hall airport (check in advance if it is open). **D** *Paul Carlton's Guest House*, east end of main street. 6 clean, basic rooms, but reported unhelpful and unfriendly.

A *Layou Valley Inn*, PO Box 196, T4496203, F4485212. 5 rooms, very comfortable, excellent cuisine, high in the hills with superb views, need a car to get there. **B** *Floral Gardens*, Concord Village, at the edge of the Carib Territory, T/F4457636. Comfortable rooms, with breakfast, apartments, **A**, 10% discount for stays of 5 days and over, dinner, excellent food but expensive and service very slow, lovely gardens by the Pagua River where you can swim, 15 mins away from beaches of Woodford Hill, electrics basic, ask for a mosquito coil for your room, many minibuses in the morning, easy to get a pick-up, bus to Roseau EC$9, 1 hr, bus to airport and Woodford Hill Beach, lovely walks in the area, either into the Carib territory or around Atkinson further north. Charles Williams and his wife, Margaret, run the **C-E** *Carib Territory Guest House*, Crayfish River, on the main road, T4457256, www.delphis.dm/ctgh.htm She cooks if meals are ordered in advance but there are no restaurants nearby as an alternative and you may go hungry, water intermittent, good base for exploring, he also does island-wide tours but is better on his own patch. About a mile away, **F** *Olive's Guest House* at Atkinson, T4457521. Slightly set back off the road, bamboo huts, comfortable, friendly, meals extra.

Inland

Camping is not encouraged and, in the national parks, it is forbidden. Designated sites may be introduced in the future.

Eating

On weekdays in the capital the lunch hour begins at 1300 and places fill up quickly. Dominicans eat their main meal at lunch time and it is often hard to get anything other than takeaways after 1600 or on Sun except at hotels. If you have a car, try different hotel restaurants on different nights and check when the barbecue specials etc are being held. Generally, Dominicans eating out do so in restaurants at lunchtime and in hotels at night.

Roseau
At hotels 3% sales tax may be added to meal charges

La Robe Créole, 3 Victoria St, T4482896. Créole and European, vegetarian available, good but expensive, service inattentive, open Mon-Sat 1100-1500, 1830-2130. Under the same ownership is the *Mousehole Café*, underneath. Excellent for little pies and local pasties. *Mousehole Too*, 10 Kennedy Av, near Whitchurch Centre, T4482896. Has seating, open 0800-1500. *Pearl's Cuisine*, 50 King George V St. Good local food and service, reasonable prices, also mobile wagon in town centre catering for lunchtime takeaway trade. *Restaurant Paiho*, 10 Church St, T4488999. Good Chinese food, delicious fruit punch, uncrowded, slightly pricey, open Mon-Sat 1100-1500, 1730-2230, Sun 1800-2200. *Coco-Rico*, Bayfront. French restaurant, bar, wine store and grocery, excellent range, good service, pleasant environment, sidewalk café. *Torino's*, above Prevo Cinemall on corner of Old St, Kennedy Av. Excellent home made pasta, evenings only, and the best cappuccino on the island, open 0800-2200 Mon-Sat. *The World of Food*, next to *Vena's Guesthouse*. Local dishes but unexciting, good breakfast about EC$10, lunch and dinners EC$20-30, drink your beer under a huge mango tree which belonged to writer Jean Rhys's family garden. *Guiyave*, 15 Cork St. For midday snacks and juices, patisserie and salad bar, popular, crowded after 1300. *Cartwheel Café*, Bay St (next to Royal Bank of Canada). Clean, on waterfront, good place to stop for a coffee; *Continental Inn*, 37 Queen Mary St, Roseau, T4482214/5. Open 0700-2130, créole cuisine, mountain chicken, seafood, rotis, delivery in Roseau area, credit cards accepted. *Cornerhouse*, 6 King George V St, T4499000. Opposite Old Market, open Mon-Thu 0730-2200, Fri-Sat 0730-2400, soups, salads, sandwiches, excellent bagels, music, books,

Windward Islands

magazines, newspapers, internet access, popular pub quiz night Wed 2000. *Port of Call*, 3 Kennedy Av near Bay Front, T4482910. Bar and restaurant, open 0830-2300 or until 2200 on Sun, snacks or à la carte, créole, seafood, takeaway available. *Creole Kitchen Ltd*, in Woodstone Shopping Mall on corner of George St and Cork St. Fried or barbecued chicken, sandwiches, burgers, cold drinks, open Mon-Thu 0800-2300, Fri-Sat 0800-1200, Sun 1500-2300. *Cottage Restaurant*, Hillsborough St. Friendly, fish, rice, salad and provisions for EC$10. *Orchard*, corner of Great George and King George V Sts. Friendly yet slow service, but food OK, good *callaloo*. For vegetarian food try *Back-A-Yard*, on Castle St, just up the hill from the *Garraway Hotel*. Lots of 'snackettes', for example *Hope Café*, 17 Steber Street. Good local dishes and snacks, lively, open till late; *Celia's Snack*, on Great Marlborough St, EC$1.50 for delicious bread and codfish, good local ice cream, fruit juice. *Erick's Bakery* has a small patisserie on Old St for 'tasty island treats'. On Thursday night the *Ocean Terrace Restaurant* at the *Anchorage* has a good value barbecue buffet and reggae band. If staying in town there are 2 places worth taking a taxi to eat: *Papillote* (see page 767), T4482287. Book before 1600, take swimming costume and towel for bathe in sulphur pool under the stars; *Reigate Hall Hotel* (also see above), book ahead, slow service but ask to eat out on balcony overlooking valley of Roseau, catch the sunset for spectacular view.

Around the island *George Chicken Shack*, on roadside between Emerald Pool and Pont Cassé. Small bar, cold beer and great fried chicken. *La Flambeau Restaurant* at Picard Cottage, near Portsmouth. Comfortable, has an attractive beachside setting and a varied menu. *Purple Turtle*, Lagoon, Portsmouth, T4455296. On beach, open Mon-Fri 1000-2300, Sat-Sun 1000-0200, snacks and full meals, local and international food, karaoke at weekends. *Mango's Bar & Restaurant*, Bay Street, Portsmouth, T4453099. Yellow and white house with tin roof, mural inside of island life, varied menu, open daily 0800-2300, credit cards accepted. *The Almond Beach Bar and Restaurant* at Calibishie on the north coast has very good food and fresh fish. *La Guingette de Calibishie*, Main Road, T4457783. French chef, French wines, seafood, steak, chicken, barbecue and entertainment Friday, open daily 0800-2300, view of Les Saintes from terrace. The *DomCan's Café* is pleasantly located right on the beach at Calibishie, T4458769. Good service, open 0900-2200, lunch of sandwiches and burgers, dinner fish, chicken, mountain chicken. *New Stop Café and Bar*, close to Trafalgar Falls. Overlooking river, just down the road from *Papillote*, tiny, outdoors, seats 10-15 people, delicious food, contact the proprietors in the morning (c/o Mayfield Denis) to arrange menu, also good for beer, conversation and reggae. *Forest Bistro*, T4487105. Near school, Soufrière, run by André and Joyce Charles, reserve in advance for lunch or dinner, generous portions of home cooked fresh fish, home grown vegetables, licensed. *The Sundowner Café*, *Herche's Place Hotel*, T4487749. Open Tue-Sun, jazz nightly, extensive menu, specializes in fish and seafood, great view of Scott's Head. *Roger's Fish Shack and Bar*, Scotts Head, good food and service. *Chez Wen*, Scott's Head, T4486668. Overlooking the bay serving shellfish and drinks, popular with divers. *Marilyn's*, by the Rosalie River in the east, about 1 mile from boxing plant, run by Americans Marilyn and Tony, lovely setting on covered patio with river gushing over large rocks amid lush foliage, limited menu of local and American food, rooms to rent planned.

Local food Fried chicken, bakes (a fried dough patty filled with tuna, codfish or corned beef) and rotis (pancake-like parcel of curried chicken and veg) are the most popular snacks available in most bakeries. There is plenty of local fruit and vegetables, fish and 'mountain chicken' (crapaud, or frog) in season. Try the seedless golden grapefruit, US$1 for 6 in the market. The term 'provisions' on a menu refers to root vegetables: dasheen, yams, sweet potatoes, tannia, pumpkins, etc. To buy fresh fish listen for the fishermen blowing their conch shells in the street; there is no fish shop but fish can be bought in the market on Fri and Sat, get there early, usually EC$7 per pound. Try the sea-moss drink, rather like a vanilla milk shake (with a reputation as an aphrodisiac), also drunk on Grenada, see page 858. There is little in the way of international or fast food on the island except, *Kentucky Fried Chicken*, corner of Great George Street and Great Marlborough Street and *Perky's Pizza*, corner of Queen Mary Street and Cork Street. Good range, tasty, not too expensive.

The Arawak House of Culture, Hillsborough Street in Roseau, next to Government Headquarters, can seat 540 for plays, concerts, dance shows and recitals. Performances are also held at the Old Mill Cultural Centre in Canefield. Mid-week entertainment at *Anchorage* and *Reigate Waterfront* hotels. Weekends at *Fort Young Hotel*, Friday night happy hour 1800-1900, live music, popular with ex-pats, tourists and locals alike, nightclub open Friday and Saturday. *Symes-Zee* on King George V Street is the spot to be on Thursday night with live jazz and friendly atmosphere. Discos at Canefield: *Warehouse* on Saturday, in converted sugar mill by the airport, gets going after 2400. Recommended. For lovers of zouk music, try *WCK*, *Midnight Grooves* or *First Serenade*; the disco at the *Q-Club* on Friday gets going after 2400. *Scorpio's Disco*, Morne Daniel, upmarket, a/c, gets going after 2400. *Cellars Bar*, downstairs at *Sutton Place Hotel*, Old Street. Lively after-work bar, big screen TV, karaoke, jazz, a/c. *Carib Cinema*, Old Street and Kennedy Avenue. A/c, 2 bars, 4 shows at weekends, 1 nightly on weekdays, T4481819, F4499523. In Portsmouth, *Rivers International Nightclub and Bar*, opposite Ross University. Open Friday–Sunday from 2200, a/c, local and international music T4454777.

Nightlife

The main one is **Carnival**, on the Monday and Tuesday before *Ash Wednesday*; it is not as commercialized as many in the Americas as it lacks the sponsorship of a carnival like Trinidad's, but it is one of the most spontaneous and friendly. Sensay costume has returned to the streets: layer upon layer of banana or cloth is used for the costume, a scary mask is worn over the face, usually with horns, and large platform clog boots finish the effect. Large quantities of beer are required for anyone who can wear this costume and dance the streets for several hours in the midday sun. The **Independence Folk Festival** starts in late *September* running up to **Independence Day** in *November*. Independence celebrations (3/4 November) feature local folk dances, competitions, storytelling, music and crafts. On **Créole Day**, the last Friday in *October*, the vast majority of girls and women wear the national dress, 'la wobe douillete', to work and school and most shop, bank clerks etc speak only Créole to the public. **Domfesta**, The Festival of the Arts, takes place during *June* and includes exhibitions by local artists (notably Kelo Royer, Earl Etienne, Arnold Toulon), concerts and theatre performances (see local papers, *The Chronicle*, *The Independent* or *The Tropical Star*, for details or ask at hotel.) In *October* Dominica hosts the **World Creole Music Festival**, with Cadence, Zouk, Campa and Soukous. For information about any festivals contact the Dominica Festivals Commission, 23 Great Marlborough St, Roseau, T4484833, F4480229, dfc@cwdom.dm An annual **Divefest** is held in *July*, with lots of activities, races, underwater treasure hunts, cruises etc. Funds are being raised for a recompression chamber, contact the Watersports Association, T4482188, F4486088, dive@cwdom.dm

   Around the island villages hold their own festivals: Isidore in Grand Bay at Pentecost; Fête Marin (St Peter's) in Portsmouth in June-July, as well as in Soufrière/Scott's Head, Colihaut/Dublanc and Anse de Mai; St Theresa in Salisbury in October; St Anne in Mahaut on 26 July; St Géraud in St Joseph in October and Feast of La Salette in Point Michel in September.

Festivals
During Carnival, laws of libel & slander are suspended

The *Craft Market*, at the Old Market, is a good place to start and get an idea of what is available. Best shops for crafts in Roseau are the *Caribana*, 31 Cork St, T/F4487340, which also has an art gallery for Dominican artists and, for the famous vetiver-grass mats, *Tropicrafts*, Queen Mary St, where you can see the women making the mats. It takes 4 weeks to complete a 10 ft mat. Note 4% extra charged on VISA. *Rainforest*, 17 Old St, T4488834, well produced local and other Caribbean goods, US$1 given towards protection of Dominica's eco-system, owner Helen Rolle runs *Rainbow Art School*, which was responsible for the mural in Bay Street. Portsmouth has a sizeable craft shop at the Cruise Ship Berth on the Cabrits but prices are much higher than in Roseau, for example a bar of coconut soap was 4 times the price. Other good buys are local Bay Rum (aftershave and body rub), soap, tea, coffee, marmalade, hand cream, shampoo, spices, chocolate and candles. Bello 'Special' or 'Classic' pepper sauce is a good souvenir. The public market is lively and friendly. Try a jelly coconut. *Cee-Bee's Bookshop*, 20 Cork St and *Paperbacks* at 6 King George V St. For Caribbean and other English books and magazines. *Front Line Co-operative Services Ltd*, 78 Queen Mary St, T4488664. Books, CDs, cassettes, stationery, photography etc. *Dominica*

Shopping
Straw goods are among the best & cheapest in the Caribbean; they can be bought in the Carib Territory & Roseau

Pottery has a showroom on corner of Bayfront and Kennedy Ave with plenty of original pieces made by inmates of the prison. Batiks are made locally and available from *Cotton House Batik*, 8 Kings Lane. Many local crafts available at the *NDFD Small Business Complex*, 9 Great Marlborough St. *Whitchurch Supermarket*, Old St. A good range at reasonable prices, open Mon-Thu 0800-1900, Fri-Sat 0800-2000. The largest supermarket is *Brizee's Mart*, 5 mins from Roseau centre, T4482087, Canefield. Open Mon-Thu 0900-2000, Fri-Sat 0900-2100.

If you are in a self-catering cottage anywhere on the island, local farmers may visit with their fresh produce for sale. At Portsmouth there is an excellent market twice a week where you can find fresh fruit, vegetables and spices locally grown. Fishing villages such as Calibishie are good sources of fresh fish; go down to the bay side around 1630 when the boats come in and get some kingfish or snapper for your evening meal.

Transport **Air** Dominica has 2 airports, the older **Melville Hall** (DOM) in the northeast, which handles most planes (including *Liat*), and **Canefield** (DCF) near Roseau, which takes only very small aircraft. Check which your flight will be using. Variable winds and short landing strips mean that planes do not land before 0600 or after 1800 in the dark. Melville Hall has no currency exchange facilities, so if you are arriving from Europe it is best to have US dollars to hand. Melville Hall is 36 miles from Roseau; shuttle taxis cost US$18 per person, whichever route the driver takes. From Melville Hall to Portsmouth by taxi is EC$30. These rates are per seat; find someone to share with, or it will be assumed you want the vehicle to yourself, which is much more expensive. Canefield is only a 10 mins drive from Roseau; taxi fare to town is US$8 per person for up to 4 passengers. Minibus (public transport) fare from Canefield to Roseau is EC$1.50. (You must flag one down on the highway passing the airport, frequent service weekdays, very few on Sunday.)

Road Bicycle: Mountain bikes can be rented from *Nature Island Dive*, T4498181, F4498182, US$11 per hour, US$21 half day, US$32 per day. Biking excursions also arranged, US$84 per person with guide. Roads are good for cycling, traffic is generally light with the exception of the stretch from Roseau to Layou. Between Canefield and Pont Casse it is very steep, twisty and challenging.

Bus Minibuses run from point to point. Those from Roseau to the northwest and northeast leave from between the east and west bridges near the modern market; to Trafalgar and Laudat from Valley Road, near the Police Headquarters; for the south and Petite Savane from Old Market Plaza. They are difficult to get on in the early morning unless you can get on a 0630 bus out to the villages to pick up schoolchildren and return in similar fashion. Many buses pass the hotels south of Roseau (for example *Anchorage*). Fares are fixed by the Government. Roseau to Salisbury is EC$3.50, to Portsmouth EC$7.50, to Woodford Hill EC$9, to Marigot EC$9, to Castle Bruce EC$7, Canefield EC$1.50, Laudat EC$3, Trafalgar EC$2.25, Soufrière/ScottsHead EC$3.

Driving is on the left. The steering wheel may be on either side. The speed limit is 10 mph near schools, 20 mph in Roseau & villages. No limit elsewhere

Car You must purchase a local driving permit, valid for 1 month, for EC$30, for which a valid international or home driving licence is required. The permit may be bought from the police at airports, rental agencies, or at the Traffic Dept, High Street, Roseau or Bay Street, Portsmouth (Mon to Fri). **Car hire** *Island Car Rentals*, PO Box 40, Goodwill Road, Roseau, T448-2886/3425, F4480737, www.delphis.dm/flydrive.htm Offers packages with choice of accommodation at 23 hotels island-wide, for example 7 nights US$499 per person, 2 nights US$245, free delivery and pick up anywhere, 24-hr emergency service. *Garraway Rent-a-Car*, 17 Old St, Roseau, T4482891, a/c car US$50 per day; *Best Deal*, T4499204, www.delphis.dm/bestdeal/index.htm Popular and reliable; *Anselm's*, 3 Great Marlborough St, T4482730, F4487559. *Budget*, Canefield Industrial Estate, opposite airport, T4492080, F4492694, recommended as cheaper, more reliable and informative than some other companies, courteous and efficient, cars in good condition. *Wide Range Car Rentals*, 79 Bath Rd, T4483181, F4483600. Rents out old Lada cars for US$30 per day, not recommended for smaller roads, also Suzuki jeeps, US$60 per day including 80 miles and collision protection free; Valley, PO Box 3, T4483233, F4486009, www.valleycarrentals.com On Goodwill Road, next to Dominican Banana Marketing Corporation, or in Portsmouth, T4455252, free delivery to Canefield and within 5 miles of Roseau or Portsmouth offices, cars in need of maintenance but in the cheaper category; also on Goodwill Road, S T L, US$387 per 10 days including EC$20 licence and insurance, PO Box 21, T4482340, free deliveries as for Valley, but only in Roseau area. It is extremely difficult to hire a vehicle between Christmas and New Year without prior reservation.

Taxi Taxis and minivans have HA or H on the license plate. A sightseeing tour by taxi will cost US$18 per hour per car (4 people), but it is wise to use experienced local tour operators for sightseeing, particularly if hiking is involved. Fares on set routes are fixed by the Government. Ask at your hotel for a taxi and if you want one after 1800 you should arrange it in advance. In Roseau, *Mally's Tour & Taxi Service*, 64 Cork St, T448-3360/3114, F4483689 (if planning a day trip out of town on public transport, you can sometimes arrange to be picked up and returned to Roseau by their airport taxi service), *Eddie*, 8 Hillsborough St, T4486003, and others.

Sea A daily ferry service operates between Dominica and the French islands. The L'Express des Iles agency office is upstairs in the Whitchurch Centre, T4482181, F4485787. The channel where the Atlantic meets the Caribbean can be very rough sometimes so this crossing is not for the faint-hearted.

Airline offices *LIAT*, King George V St, Roseau, T4482421/2, Canefield airport T4491421, Melville Hall T4457242. Agent for *Air Guadeloupe* and *Helenair* is *Whitchurch Travel*, Old St, Roseau, T4482181, or Canefield Airport, T4491060. *Cardinal Airlines*, T4487432, F4498923. *American Eagle*, T4457204. *Mussons Travel*, also for flight bookings, T4482550.

Directory

Banks *Royal Bank of Canada*, Bay St, Roseau, T4482771. *Barclays Bank Plc*, 2 Old St, T4482571 (branch in Portsmouth, T4455271). *National Commercial Bank of Dominica*, 64 Hillsborough St, T4484401. Opens lunchtime, branch at Portsmouth, T4455430. *Banque Française Commerciale*, Queen Mary St, T4484040. *Scotia Bank*, 28 Hillsborough St, T4485800. American Express agent is Whitchurch Travel, T4482181, efficient and helpful for emergency cheque cashing. Visa and Mastercard well accepted with cash advances from all banks.

Communications Post: Hillsborough St and Bay St, Roseau, 0800-1600 Mon-Fri. A mural depicts the development of the postal service in Dominica. It has a list of other stamp sellers around the island. Paperbacks on Cork St and other stationers or gift shops. A postcard to the USA or Europe costs EC$0.55, letters EC$0.90. Parcels go airmail only. Post your mail at the main post office if possible, post boxes around the country are not all in operation and there is no indication of which ones have been taken out of service. DHL is in the Whitchurch Centre, represented by Whitchurch Travel Agency, T4482181, F4485787. **Telephone:** telephone and fax services at *Telecommunications of Dominica (TOD)*, Mercury House, Hanover St, Roseau. Open 0700-2000, Mon-Sat. Phone cards are available for EC$10, 20 and 40 from Telecommunications of Dominica and some shops. *Cable & Wireless* has pre-paid phone cards, cellular service, credit card calling and a cybercafé on Kennedy Av, Roseau, T4481000, F4481111, www.cwdom.dm *Cornerhouse*, 6 King George St, T4499000. 3 computers for internet access, cornerhoused@hotmail.com, with salads, snacks and juices.

Embassies and Consulates *Venezuelan Embassy*, T4483348. *Embassy of the Republic of China*, T4491385. Honorary Consuls include *Belgium*, T4482168. *France*, T4482033. *Guyana*, T4482594. *Netherlands*, T4483841. *Spain*, T4482063. *Sweden*, T4482181. *UK*, T4481000.

Medical services Hillborough St clinic is quite large with 8-10 doctors practising and at least 1-2 present all the time, pharmacy attached. *Princess Margaret Hospital*, T4482231. New casualty department built with French money, good and efficient, but note that you have to pay in advance for everything (for example EC$80 for consultation, EC$160 for X-ray). Outside Roseau there are also hospitals in Grand Bay, T4463706; Marigot, T4457091 and Portsmouth, T4455237. *The New Charles Pharmacy*, T4483198, F4485285. Open 0830-1630, offers free prescription delivery in Roseau.

Tourist information Local tourist offices: the Dominica Division of Tourism has its headquarters in the National Development Corporation, in a converted Rose's Lime Juice factory, Valley Road, Roseau (T4482045, F4485840, www.dominica.dm). There is a Dominica Information Desk in the arrival section of VC Bird International Airport, Antigua, open daily. A useful brochure is *Discover Dominica* available free from the tourist offices at both airports or in the Old Market Square (open Mon-Fri 0800-1600, Sat 0900-1300). Other useful guides and booklets are produced by the Forestry Division and are available from their offices in the Botanical Gardens, priced from EC$0.25-EC$15. **Tour operators**: island tours can be arranged through many of the hotels, for instance *Dominica Tours* at the *Anchorage Hotel*, T4482638, F4485680, PO Box 34 (an 8-day, 7 night package includes accommodation, all meals, transfers, plus a photo safari, hiking, birdwatching, boating and sailing, costs about US$1,000 per person). The most knowledgeable operators are *Antours* (Anison's Tour and Taxi Service), 10 Woodstone Shopping Mall, Roseau, T4486460, F4486780. *Ken's Hinterland Adventure Tours and Taxi Service (Khatts Ltd)*, Ken and Clem recommended, lots of languages spoken, 62 Hillsborough Street, Roseau, T4484850, F4488486, khatts@cwdom.dm *Lambert Charles*, strong on conservation and hiking, no office but T4483365. Other operators include: *Rainbow Rover Tours*, PO Box 448, T4488650, run by Ivor Rolle; *Paradise Tours*, 4 Steber Street, Pottersville, Roseau, T4485999, F4484134; Bobby Frederick of *Ras Tours*, T4480412 is featured in *National Geographic Traveller Magazine*, tours can be tailored to visitors needs and a half day tour costs US$40; *Alfred Rolle's Unique Tour Services*, Trafalgar Village, T448-7198, or through *Papillote*, Alfred is recommended. *Escape*, T4485240, www.delphis.dm/escape, open Nov-Apr, offers river rafting, river hiking, tubing and other adventure activities, from US$70 per person (minimum US$140), includes equipment, transport, guide, insurance, canyoning and cascading offered. Check beforehand which tours are offered on a daily basis or once or twice a week. You may have to wait for the tour you want or be offered an alternative. German, French, Spanish and English are offered at different agencies. The *Whitchurch Travel Agency*, PO Box 771, Old Street, Roseau, T4482181, F4485787, www.whitchurch.com, handles local tours as well as foreign travel and represents American Express Travel Related Services, several airlines and L'Express des Iles. Fun, Sun Inc at 21 Hanver St, T4486371, F4481606. *Mussons Travel*, Old Street, T4482550, F4482560, helpful reconfirming flights. **Maps**: The Ordnance Survey, Romsey Road, Southampton, SO9 49H, UK, T01703-792792, publishes a 1:50,000 colourful map of Dominica, with a 1:10,000 street map insert of Roseau, includes roads, footpaths, contours, forests, reserves and National Parks. This can be bought at the Old Market tourist office in Roseau.

Background

History

The Caribs, who supplanted the Arawaks on Dominica, called the island Waitikubuli ("tall is her body"). Columbus sighted it on 3 November 1493, a Sunday (hence the modern name), but the Spanish took no interest in the island. It was not until 1805 that possession was finally settled. Until then it had been fought over by the French, British and Caribs. In 1660, the two European powers agreed to leave Dominica to the Caribs, but the arrangement lasted very few years; in 1686, the island was declared neutral, again with little success. As France and England renewed hostilities, the Caribs were divided between the opposed forces and suffered the heaviest losses in consequence. In 1763, Dominica was ceded to Britain, and between then and 1805, it remained British. Nevertheless, its position between the French colonies of Guadeloupe and Martinique, and the strong French presence over the years, ensured that despite English institutions and language the French influence was never eliminated.

During the 19th century, Dominica was largely neglected and underdevelopment provoked social unrest. Henry Hesketh Bell, the colonial administrator from 1899 to 1905, made great improvements to infrastructure and the economy, but by the late 1930s the British Government's Moyne Commission discovered a return to a high level of poverty on the island. Assistance to the island was increased with some emphasis put on road building to open up the interior. This, together with agricultural expansion, house building and use of the abundant hydro resources for power, contributed to development in the 1950s and 1960s.

Dominica devastated

In 1979 the island was devastated by Hurricane David, 37 people were killed and 60,000 were left homeless. Much of what David left standing was felled by Hurricane Allen the next year. In 1995 Dominica was hit by three storms in August and September. Storm Iris damaged roads and spoilt some crops and Hurricane Luis destroyed many roads, seafronts and coastal properties and devastated the banana crop. Finally Hurricane Marilyn finished off the job that Luis started, causing great damage in the northeast where the eye passed over. One person was killed and another seriously injured, but the biggest problem was the loss of banana income.

In 1939, Dominica was transferred from the Leeward to the Windward Islands Federation; it gained separate status and a new constitution in 1960, and full internal autonomy in 1967. The Commonwealth of Dominica became an independent republic within the Commonwealth in 1978. The Dominica Labour Party dominated island politics after 1961, ushering in all the constitutional changes. Following independence, however, internal divisions and public dissatisfaction with the administration led to its defeat by the Dominica Freedom Party in the 1980 elections. The DFP Prime Minister, Miss (now Dame) Mary Eugenia Charles, adopted a pro-business, pro-United States line to lessen the island's dependence on limited crops and markets. She was re-elected in 1985 and again in 1990, having survived an earlier attempted invasion by supporters of former DLP premier, Patrick John. (For a thorough history of the island, see *The Dominica Story*, by Lennox Honychurch, The Dominica Institute, 1984, revised and republished 1995, ISBN 0-333-62776-8.)

In the general election of 1990 the Dominica Freedom Party (DFP) retained its majority by a single seat, winning 11 of the 21 seats. The official opposition was the recently-formed (1988) United Workers Party (UWP) led by Edison James with six seats, while the former official opposition party, the Dominica Labour Party (DLP) won four seats. A by-election in 1993 increased the UWP's representation to seven seats while the DLP lost one.

In 1995 Dame Eugenia retired at age 76, having led her party since 1968, and the DFP campaigned for the June general elections under the leadership of Brian Alleyne, External Affairs minister in her government. However, the contest was won by the UWP, with 11 seats, while the DFP and the DLP won five each. Mr Edison James was sworn in as Prime Minister. Mr Alleyne and Mr Rosie Douglas, leader of the DLP, were to share the position of Leader of the Opposition, taking the post a year at a time. In 1996, Mr Alleyne resigned and was replaced as leader of the DFP by Charles Savarin, who was elected unopposed.

General elections were held in January 2000, at which the DLP won 42.9%, the UWP 43.4% and the DFP 13.6% of the vote, while the turnout was 60.2% of the electorate. The DLP and DFP formed a coalition and on 3 February Rosie Douglas was sworn in as Prime Minister. One of the new government's first decisions was to shelve plans for a new airport and related hotel development in the northeast, a project which the DFP and DLP had criticized when in opposition on the grounds of cost and inappropriate location.

The people

Materially, it is one of the poorest islands in the Caribbean, but the people are some of the friendliest. Many of them are small farmers, the island's mountainous terrain discourages the creation of large estates. In Dominica, over 2,000 descendants of the original inhabitants of the Caribbean, the once warlike Caribs, live in the Carib Territory, a 3,700-acre 'reservation' established in 1903 in the northeast, near Melville Hall airport. There are no surviving speakers of the Carib language on the island. The total population, which is otherwise almost entirely of African descent, is

Windward Islands

around 74,400, of whom about 29% live in the parish of St George, around Roseau, the capital, on the Caribbean coast. Other parishes are much more sparsely populated. The parish of St John, in which Portsmouth (the second largest town) is situated contains only about 5,000 people, or seven percent of the population.

Like St Lucia, Dominica was once a French possession and although English is the official tongue, most of the inhabitants also speak créole French (French-based patois). In the Marigot/Wesley area a type of English called 'cocoy' is used; the original settlers of the area, freed slaves, came from Antigua and are mostly Methodists. Catholicism predominates, though there are some Protestant denominations and an increasing number of fundamentalist sects, imported from the USA.

Government

Dominica is a fully independent member of the British Commonwealth. The single chamber House of Assembly has 31 members: 21 elected by the constituencies, nine Senators appointed by the President on the advice of the Prime Minister and Leader of the Opposition, and the Attorney-General. The Prime Minister and Leader of the Opposition also nominate the President, currently Vernon Shaw, who holds office for five years.

The economy

Owing to the difficulty of the terrain, only about a quarter of the island is cultivated. Nevertheless, it is self-sufficient in fruit and vegetables and agriculture contributes about 20% to gross domestic product. The main products are bananas (the principal export), coconuts (most of which are used in soap and cooking oil production), grapefruit, limes and other citrus fruits. Bananas were badly hit by Hurricane Hugo in 1989 when over 70% of the crop was damaged and by Hurricane Luis in 1995 when 95% of the crop was lost. The opening up of the European market in 1992 affected Dominica's banana industry. Together with the other Windward Islands producers it has to compete with the large exporters from the US dollar areas, mainly in Latin America. Prices paid to local farmers have fallen because they are unable to match the economies of scale found in Latin America. The number of banana farmers has fallen from 4,366 in 1995 to 2,534 in 1999 while banana exports declined from 28,602 tonnes in 1998 to 27,264 tonnes in 1999. Other crops are under development, such as coffee, cocoa, mango, citrus and root crops such as dasheen, which are being promoted to diversify away from bananas. There is a very successful aqua culture project, prawn farming.

Manufacturing industry is small but takes advantage of locally-generated hydroelectricity. Under pressure to purchase Caribbean products for their cruise ships, Royal Caribbean Cruise Lines buys 3 mn bars of soap a year from Dominica Coconut Products (DCP), Dominica's largest business. In 1995, Colgate Palmolive, the US transnational company, acquired a controlling interest in DCP. Labour intensive electronic assembly plants and clothing manufacturing are being encouraged for their foreign exchange earnings potential, while data processing is also growing. There is a large pool of labour for garment production which attracts manufacturers, but they often move on to other areas when their duty-free concessions expire, usually after 10 years.

Tourism is being promoted with the emphasis officially on nature tourism. After a sluggish start in the early 1990s because of the world slowdown, arrivals jumped by 7.3% in 1993, 11.3% in 1994 and 5.4% in 1995 to reach a total of 68,838 in that year. Since then total stayover visitor arrivals have remained steady at around 74,000. The authorities claim they do not wish to jeopardize the 'Nature Island' image, but concern has been expressed by conservationists over damage to the environment. In 1997 the government entered an agreement with Green Globe, the environmental division of the World Travel and Tourism Council, to develop Dominica as a 'model ecotourism destination'. The three-year programme will provide technical expertise in environmental management and promote Dominica through an international network of environmentally responsive travel companies. The aim is for the development of sustainable long-term tourism projects. Meanwhile, the island's hotel capacity continues to expand. Several new hotels and expansions of existing facilities are planned, to raise visitor numbers to 148,000 by 2004, with investments from Canada, Sweden and other foreign sources. A jetty for cruise ships, with related facilities, has been built at Prince Rupert Bay and in 1995, 267 cruise ship calls were made, compared with 40 in 1990, having shown steady growth each year. In Phase Two of the Roseau Seawall and Bay Front Development Project, a dedicated cruise ship berth was finished in 1995, which has further increased passenger numbers. A jetty for the high speed ferries between Dominica, Martinique and Guadeloupe (French funding) was built in 1995, damaged by the hurricane and since repaired. Also completed in 1996 on the bayfront is a fish landing and processing plant (Japanese funding). Construction is also under way to strengthen sea defences north and south of Roseau.

There is controversy over the Government's decision in 1992 to grant economic citizenship to investors; the first to be granted passports all came from Taiwan. By the end of 1994 615 people had been granted economic citizenship; they paid US$7.1 mn into an escrow account, of which US$5.4 mn was withdrawn to buy shares in a linked hotel company. Since then there has been a surge of interest from Eastern Europe, and in 1999 it was reported that 300 Russians had bought passports, for US$50,000 each. The US State Department expressed concern about money laundering and Canada arrested a group of Chinese-Dominicans on suspicion of running a smuggling operation.

The mining industry also became a controversial issue in 1996, when the House of Assembly passed a bill vesting all mineral rights in the government, whether on public or privately owned land. Soon afterwards, BHP Minerals International of Australia, began drilling in northeast Dominica to establish the extent of copper deposits there. The Dominica Conservation Association demanded an environmental impact study before any commercial mining took place and effectively halted proceedings.

In 1997 the first offshore banks were registered in a bid to increase fee income from abroad. Legislation was prepared for international shipping registration, offshore trust companies and exempt insurance companies. Six internet gambling companies were also granted operating licences. International Business Companies (IBC) can be formed over the internet and the Government has chosen to follow the British Virgin Islands model for registration because it does not require such demanding regulatory work or supervision as the Barbados model, which needs a double taxation treaty.

Culture

Popular culture reflects the mixture of native and immigrant peoples. While most places on Dominica have a Carib, a French or an English name, the indigenous Carib traditions and way of life have been localized in the northeast, giving way to a dominant amalgam of Créole (French and African) tradition. Dominicans are proud of their local language, which is increasingly being used in print. A dictionary was published in 1991 by the Konmité pou Etid Kwéyòl (Committee for Créole Studies). You can get hold of this at the Cultural Division, 30 Queen Mary Street on the corner of King George V Street in Roseau. Opposite is the cultural centre for the Carib community, Kalinago, which contains lots of general information about the Carib Reserve and its people and has a selection of Carib goods for sale. There has recently been a great increase in the awareness of the arts and crafts. Both at Caribana, the craft and art gallery (see page 771), the Alliance Française French cultural centre, and in the media, the poets, writers and artists of Dominica have been reading or exhibiting their work. Ask at Caribana, T4487340, when the next poetry workshop or exhibition, is to be held, or wander the side streets of Roseau to find small shops and galleries. Dance and choral artists are active mostly around Christmas, when there are diverse concerts given by church choirs and Dominica's National Chorale.

Literature The best known of Dominica's writers are the novelists Jean Rhys and Phyllis Shand Allfrey. Rhys (1894-1979), who spent much of her life in Europe, wrote mainly about that continent; only flashback scenes in *Voyage in the Dark* (1934), her superb last novel, *Wide Sargasso Sea* (1966), which was made into a film in 1991, her uncompleted autobiography, *Smile Please* and resonances in some of her short stories draw on her West Indian experiences. Allfrey published only one novel, *The Orchid House* (1953); *In the Cabinet* was left unfinished at her death in 1986. Allfrey was one of the founder members of the Dominica Labour Party, became a cabinet minister in the short-lived West Indian Federation, and was later editor of the *Dominica Herald* and *Dominica Star* newspapers. *The Orchid House* was filmed by Channel 4 (UK) in 1990 for international transmission as a four-part series.

St Lucia

St Lucia (pronounced 'Loosha') is the second largest of the Windwards, lying between St Vincent and Martinique with an area of 238 square miles. The scenery is of outstanding beauty, and in the neighbourhood of the Pitons, it has an element of grandeur. The highest peak is Morne Gimie, 3,118 ft, but the most spectacular are Gros Piton, 2,619 ft, and Petit Piton, 2,461 ft, which are old volcanic forest-clad plugs rising sheer out of the sea near the town of Soufrière on the west coast. A few miles away is one of the world's most accessible volcanoes. Here you can see soufrières: vents in the volcano which exude hydrogen sulphide, steam and other gases and deposit sulphur and other compounds in pools of boiling water. The mountains are intersected by numerous short rivers which in places debouch into broad, fertile and well-cultivated valleys. The island has become a popular tourist destination, with sporting facilities, splendid beaches, clear, warm sea and sunshine. The films Dr Doolittle, Water and Superman II were shot here.

Ins and outs

Getting there
See transport, page 806, for more details

Air **From Europe** The only direct scheduled services are with *BWIA*, *Virgin Atlantic* or *British Airways* from London, *Condor* from Frankfurt and *Air Liberté* from Paris. Flights from Europe usually come via Antigua or Barbados. **From North America** *BWIA* has flights, via Barbados from New York, and Miami. *Air Jamaica* from New York, other cities planned. **From Canada** *Air Canada* flies from Toronto. **From the Caribbean** There are also excellent connections from Antigua (*LIAT*), Barbados (*LIAT*, *Helenair*, *Air Jamaica* and *British Airways*), Dominica (*LIAT*, *Helenair*), Grenada (*LIAT*, *Helenair*), Guadeloupe (*LIAT*), Montego Bay and Kingston (*Air Jamaica*), Martinique (*LIAT*, *Air Guadeloupe*), San Juan (*LIAT*, *American Eagle*), Tortola, BVI (*LIAT*); St Maarten (*LIAT*), St Vincent (*LIAT*, *Helenair*), Trinidad and Tobago (*BWIA*, *Helenair*, *LIAT*).

Boat *Windward Lines Ltd* operate a weekly passenger and cargo ferry service linking Venezuela (Güiria or Pampatar, Margarita), Trinidad, St Vincent, Barbados and St Lucia, arriving St Lucia 0800 Saturday, departing Sunday around 1900, see page 25. *Express Des Iles*, does a day-trip (shopping trip) to Martinique on Saturday, EC$172 round trip, leaving 0700, arriving Fort-de-France 0820, return 1700 arrive 1820, tax included, reservations Cox & Co Ltd, William Peter Boulevard, T4522211/3, F4531868, or travel agents. Continues to Guadeloupe, Les Saintes and Dominica. Many cruise lines call. There is a US$10 per person tax on cruise ship passengers.

Bus is the cheapest means of getting around St Lucia. The service has been described as tiresome by some, but as reliable by others. St Lucia's buses are usually privately-owned minibuses and have no fixed timetable. The north is better served than the south and buses around Castries and Gros Islet run until 2200, or later for the Friday night Jump-up at Gros Islet. There are several **car hire** companies on the island, but it is cheaper and more reliable to hire in advance. Signposting has been greatly improved so that renting a car and exploring by yourself is now much easier. Although there are about 500 miles of roads on the island only 281 are paved so be prepared for some rough driving. Local drivers are fairly rough too, steer clear of them if possible. If **cycling**, the best way to get round the island is anti-clockwise, thus ensuring long but gradual uphills and steep, fast downhills.

Getting around
Driving on the left

Windward Islands

St Lucia

Essentials

Documents *Citizens of the UK, USA and Canada may enter with adequate proof of identity, as long as they do not intend to stay longer than six months. Citizens of the Organization of Eastern Caribbean States (OECS) may enter with only a driving licence or identity card. **Visas** are not required by nationals of all Commonwealth countries, all EC countries except Eire and Portugal, all Scandinavian countries, Switzerland, Liechtenstein, Turkey, Tunisia, Uruguay and Venezuela. Anyone else needs a visa, check requirements etc at an embassy or high commission. Without exception, visitors need a **return ticket**. You also need an **address** for where you are staying.*

On arrival you will be given a 42-day stamp in your passport. The immigration office at the central police station in Castries is very bureaucratic about extensions; they cost EC$40 per period and it is worth getting one up to the date of your return ticket.

Work permits are very difficult to get and cost EC$5,000, plus EC$100 for the application form. If you work for a volunteer, educational or international organization you can obtain an exemption of work permit which is free. This is the responsibility of your employer.

Currency *East Caribbean dollar. Change currency at a bank where you can get 5-10% less on the exchange than at hotels. There is no rate quoted for many currencies, such as Deutsch Marks; if you insist, Canadian banks will convert them first into Canadian dollars and then into EC dollars, but you get a poor rate. The Thomas Cook representative is on Brazil Street.*

Departure tax *At both airports there is a departure tax of EC$54, US$20, except for St Lucian nationals going anywhere and Caricom nationals travelling within Caricom, for whom it is EC$35, US$13.*

Ports of entry *(Own flag) Rodney Bay (Customs open 0800-1800 but overtime charges from 1600), Marigot, Castries, Soufrière (clear in at police station) and Vieux Fort. Pratique EC$10 up to 100 tons. Clearance EC$5 for under 40 ft, EC$15 for over 40 ft. Navigational aids EC$15. EC$25 for a 24-hour permit to visit the Pitons at Soufrière. Charter boats pay additional fees. Permission is granted to stay up to two months, extensions cost extra.*

Anchorages *There are anchorages at Rodney Bay, Castries, Marigot Bay (managed by Moorings), Soufrière (see page 784) and Vieux Fort. Marinas at Rodney Bay, Marigot and Castries Yacht Centre.*

Hours of business *Shops: 0800-1230, 1330-1700 Monday-Friday (shops close at 1200 on Saturday); **Banks**: 0800-1300 Monday-Thursday, although some are open until 1400-1500, plus 1500-1700 on Friday; **Government offices**: 0830-1230, 1330-1600 Monday-Friday.*

Official time *Atlantic Standard Time, four hours behind GMT, one ahead of EST.*

Voltage *220v, 50 cycles.*

Weights and measures *Imperial, though metric measurements are gradually being introduced.*

Climate
The mean annual temperature is about 26°C

The dry season is roughly from Jan-Apr. The rainy season starts in May lasting almost to the end of the year. The island lies in lattitudes where the northeast trade winds are an almost constant, cooling influence. Rainfall varies (according to altitude) in different parts of the island from 60 to 138 in. Tropical storms in the 1990s caused flooding and mudslides as the rain poured off the hills, taking banana plantations in its path. In November 1999 Hurricane Lenny hit from the west, unusual because most hurricanes come from the east out in the Atlantic. High waves caused severe damage to beaches and property on the west coast, many small houses and the new craft market, among other businesses, were washed away at Soufrière. Relentless six-metre waves and strong winds smashed the coast from one end to the other during a four-day siege, washing away the sand.

Communications *The International code for St Lucia is 758. See page 807 for further details.*
Media Newspapers *The Voice comes out three times a week, and* The Mirror, The Weekend Voice, One Caribbean, The Crusader *and* The Star *appear weekly.*
Radio *There is a commercial radio station, Radio Caribbean International (RCI), which broadcasts daily in Kweyol and English, and a government- owned station, Radio St Lucia (RSL), which also broadcasts in Kweyol and English. It has some fine programmes such as Sports Zone and if you want to hear the concerns of St Lucians listen to Constitution Park at 1400 (only the Thursday broadcast is in Kweyol). RCI and RSL have 2 FM and an AM station each. A third station, the Wave (formerly GEM), has 2 FM, and broadcasts rhythm and soul.*
Television *Two local stations: HTS on Channel 4 and DBS on Channel 10. HTS has an occasional programme in Kweyol and speeches by government officials. There is much cable TV.*

Tourist offices overseas
France *ANI, 53 Rue François Ler, 7th floor, Paris 75008, T47-203966, F47-230965.*
Germany *Postfach 2304, D-61293 Bad Homberg 1, T06172-304431, F06172-305072.*
UK *421a Finchley Road, London NW3 6HJ, T0171-4313675, F0171-4317920, stlucia@pwaxis.co.uk* **USA and Canada** *9th Floor, 820 2nd Avenue, New York, NY 10017, T800-4563984.*

Clothing *Lightweight clothing all year; a summer sweater may be needed on cooler evenings. Short shorts and swimming costumes are not worn in town. An umbrella or light mac may be handy in the wet season.*

Laundry *There are no self-service launderettes on St Lucia, but there are dry cleaners at Rodney Bay, Gros Islet and Gablewoods Mall in the north of the island. Sparkle, in Gros Islet, will collect and deliver laundry to a boat or marina.*

Safety *When visiting the waterfalls and sulphur springs on Soufrière note that 'guides' might expect large payments for their services. Be prepared to say no firmly, they are persistent and bothersome. Children may try to squeeze money out of tourists offering to dive for a dollar in the harbour. Visiting with a hired car (H reg) can be a hassle and beach bums will even follow you into the church. The signs to Sulphur Springs are sometimes removed so you have to ask the way and are expected to give a tip. Readers' letters have spoken of harassment and hostility towards tourists and there is drug abuse and crime. However, the problem is not on the scale of Jamaica. People staying at well-protected resorts and using organized tours generally have no problem. Be careful taking photographs, although everybody seems to be accustomed to cameras in the market. The use and sale of narcotics is illegal and penalties are severe. Most readily available is marijuana, which is frequently offered to tourists, but hard drugs can also be a problem.*

Public holidays *New Year's Day, Independence Day on 22 Feb, Good Friday, Easter Monday, Labour Day on 1 May, Whit Monday, Corpus Christi, Carnival, Emancipation Day in Aug, Thanksgiving Day, National Day on 13 Dec, Christmas Day and Boxing Day.*

Flora and fauna

The fauna and flora of St Lucia is very similar to that of Dominica, the Windwards chain of islands having been colonized by plants and animals originally from South and Central America, with some endemic species such as sisserou and jacquot. Rainforest would have covered most of the island prior to European colonization but the most dramatic loss has been in the last 20 years. Much of the remaining forest is protected, mainly for water supply, but also specifically for wildlife in places. There are many orchids and anthurium growing wild in the rain forests, while tropical flowers and flowering trees are found everywhere. To date, 1,179 different species of flowering plants have been documented. There are several endemic reptile species including St Lucia tree lizard, pygmy gecko, Maria Island ground lizard and

Turtles at Grand Anse

A 1,000-pound amphibian slips from the ocean waves and pauses on the edge of the surf. All is quiet. In the light of the moon, rain or not, she hauls her heavy body further up the beach. A cluster of people stand motionless and nearly breathless, fearful that the giant sea turtle will sense them and return to the ocean without laying her eggs. The leatherback turtle (Demochelys coricea) roams the open oceans, feeding on a diet of giant jellyfish. Only a mature female comes ashore and then only to make a nest and lay 60-120 eggs, perhaps several times in one season but only every two to three years.

All sea turtles are endangered. Sand mining, construction close to the water, human and other animal and bird predators, destroy habitats. The eggs are a popular aphrodisiac, considered particularly effective if taken from the female before they are laid, killing the proverbial goose that laid the golden egg. Grand Anse beach in St Lucia is one of the most important beaches in the Caribbean for the nesting leatherbacks. From honeymooners to retirees, tourists and St Lucians, all hope for a memorable experience when the sea turtle comes ashore, counting the leathery eggs as they drop, perhaps being able to touch her as she lays, oblivious to all.

This wild and beautiful beach is disappearing as more and more sand is removed by truck after truck, busily making a buck selling sand for concrete blocks. If she lays, she will lay the eggs in the water she finds just below the shallow sand and the eggs won't hatch.

Annette Blackburn

Maria Island grass snake. The only snake which is dangerous is the fer de lance which is restricted to dry scrub woodland on the east coast near Grande Anse and Louvet and also near Anse La Raye and Canaries in the west. The agouti and the manicou are present throughout the island, but rarely seen.

The national bird is the colourful St Lucian parrot (*Amazona versicolor*), which can be seen in the dense rain forest around Quillesse and Barre de l'Isle. A successful conservation programme established in 1978 probably saved the species from extinction and allowed numbers to rise from 150 birds in 1978 to over 400 by 1994. However, Tropical Storm Debbie blew over the hollow trees they nest in and most St Lucian parrots moved north, although they are increasing again in the Des Cartier Quillesse/Edmond region. Other endemic birds are the St Lucia oriole (endangered), Semper's warbler (believed extinct) and the St Lucia black finch (endangered). Several other species such as the white breasted thrasher are also rare and endangered. Measures are being taken to protect these birds and their habitats. In the north of the island birdwatching is good at Bois d'Orange swamp, Piton Flor Reserve and Grand Anse; in the west at Edmond Forest Reserve and in the south Eau Piquant Pond, also called Boriel's.

The transinsular rainforest walk from Mahaut to Soufrière via Fond St Jacques (about two to 2½ hours Mahaut to Fond St Jacques) is good for birdwatching. You need a permit from the Forestry Department. Tours are franchised to tour operators and a guide is certainly useful but organized tours are often noisy and scare the parrots higher into the mountains. Get your own permit from Forestry at Union if you feel confident about finding your own way. There is a good chance of seeing the St Lucian parrot on the Barre de l'Isle rainforest walk, for which a permit is also needed. Only the lower half of the trail is visited by groups, because the upper part has not yet been protected against human erosion. However, it is possible to climb all the way up to Mount La Combe (about two hours from the road) on a path which is not too difficult for hikers. The bird enthusiast is advised to get a permit (EC$25) and organize a private trip in a small party.

In the north of the island, Pigeon Island, Pointe du Cap and Cap Hardy are worth visiting for their landscapes, seabird colonies and interesting xerophytic vegetation, including cactus, thorn scrub et cetera. Cap Hardy is being developed, called the Mt Hardy peninsula, at the northern most tip of Cap Estates. Union is the site of the Forestry Department headquarters, where there is a nature trail, open to the public, a medicinal garden and a small, well-organized zoo. The Forestry Department also organizes hiking across the island (franchized to several local tour operators, twice a week, with pickup from your hotel) through rainforest and mature mahogany, Caribbean pine and blue mahoe plantations which will give you the best chance of seeing the St Lucia parrot, as well as other rainforest birds: thrashers, vireos, hummingbirds, flycatchers et cetera. Contact Adams Toussaint, T4502231 ext 306 or 4502078, who is in charge of all Forestry Department tours. Wear good shoes and expect to get wet and muddy. Camping in the rainforest is now possible. Hike the nearly 10-mile forest trail from Barre de l'Isle to Quillesse; overnight in a forest house or camp in a tent. Recommended for the physically fit and experienced hikers. A new trail has been opened up in the Edmond Forest Reserve: the Enbas Saut Falls trail (below the Falls), moderate to strenuous, at the foot of Mount Gimie, with a combination of rainforest, cloud forest and elfin woodlands.

The isolated east coast beaches are rarely visited and have exceptional wildlife. Leatherbacks and other turtles nest at Grand Anse and Anse Louvet and the Fisheries Department/Naturalists Society organize nocturnal vigils to count nesting females and discourage poachers. Sadly, in 2000, St Lucia resumed the legal slaughter of hawksbill and leatherback turtles, despite an outcry from conservationists. This area is also the main stronghold of the white-breasted thrasher and St Lucia wren; there are also iguanas (although you will be lucky to see one) and unfortunately the fer de lance snake, although attacks are extremely rare. The bite is not always fatal but requires hospitalization (it is extremely painful). Avoid walking through the bush, especially at night, and wear shoes or boots and long trousers.

La Sorcière and Piton Flor are densely forested mountains in the north with excellent rainforest vegetation. Piton Flor can be walked up in 40 minutes although it is a strenuous climb and you will need to ask how to get to the top, from where there are spectacular views. It is the last recorded location of Semper's warbler, an endemic bird now probably extinct.

In the south, Cap Moule à Chique has spectacular views and good bird populations. The **Maria Islands**, just offshore, are home to two endemic reptiles, a colourful lizard and small, rare, harmless snake, the Kouwes snake (see page 45). The National Trust (T4525005) and Eastern Caribbean Natural Areas Management Programme (ECNAMP) run day trips with a licensed guide. All participants must be capable swimmers. Interpretive facilities are on the mainland at Anse de Sables, where you can arrange boat transport. Unauthorized access is not allowed. Good beach, excellent snorkelling. From 15 May to 31 July public access is not permitted while the birds are nesting. However, you can visit the **Fregate Islands Nature Reserve**, handed over to the National Trust by the Government in 1989. Frigate birds nest here and the dry forest also harbours the trembler, the St Lucian oriole and the ramier. The reserve includes a section of mangrove and is the natural habitat of the boa constrictor (tête chien). **Praslin Island** is one of the two islands where the St Lucian whiptail lives. The males, about 18 cm long, sport the colours of the national flag. They used to live only on Maria Major Island until being successfully introduced here to prevent annihilation by hurricanes or any other natural disaster. A National Trust day trip with guide, lunch and boat will cost about EC$90.

Some of these areas are very isolated and you are recommended to get in touch with the relevant organizations before attempting to visit them. In 1997 the Tourist Board announced the development of a series of nature trails as part of a nature/heritage tourism programme, after a survey showed nature and the environment was a major reason for holiday makers to visit St Lucia. There will be gentle hikes and strenuous climbs, including a two and a half mile Morne Tabac climb, a ridge hike beginning at Malmaison; the Anse Galet Nature Walk and the eight mile Morne Gimie Climb over four mountain peaks. New nature interpretation centres and national parks are being developed.

Windward Islands

The St Lucia Naturalists' Society meets irregularly. Check the meeting schedule with the Castries Central Library, Derek Walcott Square, T4522875. The St Lucia National Trust has field trips, usually the last Sunday of the month, popular with locals and tourists of all ages. The National Trust (T4525005) and the Naturalists' Society (T4522611) offer excursions involving participation in conservation. The (irregular) trips start on weekends around 0700 in front of the Library and cost EC$10. They include visits to waterfalls, beaches, rain and mangrove forests, where you are not allowed entry without a guide or permission from the National Trust or relevant Ministry. Bird watching trips start at 0500. Turtle watching is organized during March to July when Green, Hawksbill and Leatherback turtles come ashore to lay eggs (Saturday, 1600, at the Library, EC$10, return around 0700, take food, drink, torch, insect repellent, good walking shoes, warm clothing, tents supplied, be prepared for wind, rain or perfect nights, children welcome, contact Lenita Joseph for information, T4523622). Turtle watches are expected to continue, even though the area is being developed. It is guarded and closed to sand mining (see page 782) so the beach is coming back.

Diving and marine life

Dive sites
Visitors must dive with a local company

There is some very good diving off the west coast, although this is somewhat dependent on the weather, as heavy rain tends to create high sediment loads in the rivers and sea. Diving on the east coast is not so good and can be risky unless you are a competent diver. Several companies offer scuba diving with professional instructors, catering for the experienced or the novice diver. One of the best beach entry dives in the Caribbean is directly off **Anse Chastanet**, where an underwater shelf drops off from about 10 ft down to about 60 ft and there is a good dive over **Turtle Reef** in the bay, where there are over 25 different types of coral. Below the **Petit Piton** are impressive sponge and coral communities on a drop to 200 ft of spectacular wall. There are gorgonians, black coral trees, huge barrel sponges and plenty of other beautiful reef life. The area in front of the *Anse Chastanet Hotel* is a Marine Reserve, stretching from the west point at **Grand Caille North** to **Chamin Cove**. The area is buoyed off and only the hotel boats and local fishermen's canoes are allowed in. Just by the jetty, a roped-off area is used by snorkellers and beginner divers and is an exceptionally rewarding spot. Other popular dive sites include **Anse L'Ivrogne**, **Anse La Raye Point** (good snorkelling also at **Anse La Raye**) and the **Pinnacles** (an impressive site where four pinnacles rise to within 10 ft of the surface), not forgetting the **wrecks**, such as the *Volga* (in 20 ft of water north of Castries harbour, well broken up, subject to swell, requires caution), the *Waiwinette* (several miles south of Vieux Fort, strong currents, competent divers only), and the 165-ft *Lesleen M* (deliberately sunk in 1986 off Anse Cochon Bay in 60 ft of water).

The Fisheries Department is pursuing an active marine protection programme

Divers should avoid taking any coral or undersized shellfish. Corals and sponges should not even be touched. It is also illegal to buy or sell coral products on St Lucia. The Soufrière Marine Management Association coordinates problems between local fishing boats, divers and yachts and preserves the environment between Anse Chastanet and Anse L'Ivrogne to the south. They have placed moorings from Anse Chastanet along the coast just past The Pitons. Yachts are required to take moorings. Collection of marine mammals (dead or alive) is prohibited, spearguns are illegal and anchoring is prohibited. Yacht moorings are EC$40 for 1-2 nights and EC$57 for up to a week. Rangers come by at night to collect the fee and explain the programme. Dive moorings have been installed and are being financed with Marine Reserve Fees, EC$8 daily, EC$27 a year.

Dive centres
Scuba St Lucia (PADI five-star, BSAC, SSI and DAN) operates from Anse Chastanet, PO Box 7000, Soufrière, T4597355, F4597700, three dive boats with oxygen on each one, photographic hire and film processing, video filming and courses, day and night dives, resort courses and full PADI certification, multilingual staff,

pick up service Tuesday to Saturday from hotels north of Castries, day packages for divers, snorkellers, beginners and others include lunch and equipment. *Buddies Scuba* at Vigie Marina, T4525288, two-tank day dives, one-tank night dives, camera rental, open water certification or resort course, dive packages available. *Moorings Scuba Centre* at Marigot Bay, T4514357, and *Windjammer Diving* at the resort on Labrellotte Bay, T4520913, both offer PADI courses. The St Lucia Tourist Board can give help and advice on sites and the dive companies. A single-tank dive costs around US$45-55, introductory resort courses are about US$70, a 10-dive package US$265 and open water certification courses US$390-400.

Whale and dolphin watching is now becoming popular. *Douglas Sailing Tours*, run by Douglas Rapier, T4577777, charges US$95 for a full day sailing tour to Martinique with whale watching on the way.

Beaches and watersports

All the west coast beaches have good swimming but many are dominated by resort hotels. Many lost sand during Hurricane Lenny in 1999 (see page 780). The Atlantic east coast has heavy surf and is dangerous but with very spectacular and isolated beaches and is difficult to get to without local knowledge or the Ordnance Survey map and four-wheel drive) which make a pleasant change from the west coast. Many are important habitats and nesting places for the island's wildlife. **Cas en Bas** Beach can be reached from Gros Islet (45 minutes' walk, or arrange taxi), it is sheltered, shady and a bit dirty but challenging for experienced windsurfers. **Donkey Beach** can be reached from there by taking a track to the north (20 minutes' walk), the scenery is wild and open and it is windy. To the south of Cas en Bas Beach are **Anse Louvet**, **Anse Comerette** and **Anse Lapins**, follow the rocks, it is a 30-minute walk to the first and an hour to the last. Access is also possible from Monchy. They are deserted, wind-swept beaches and headlands. There are Indian stone carvings on **Dauphin Beach**, which can be reached from Monchy (reasonable with jeep). Once on the beach, wade across the river and walk back in the flat, clear area below the bush land, after about 50 m you'll find long stones with regular depressions. Another 20 m and you'll find a stone pillar about which Robert Devaux wrote: "The carving appears to be a family of three – male, female and child. It is finely executed and must have taken some prehistoric 'Michelangelo' a considerable time to complete the carving" (*St Lucia Historic Sites*, St Lucia National Trust, 1975, highly recommended, in the library at the Folk Research Centre). Unfortunately the stone pillar has been badly tampered with. A few metres further inland is the ruin of a colonial church tower, destroyed in 1795 during the French Revolution of St Lucia together with the rest of the settlement. **Grande Anse**, further south, is a long windy beach, currently not open to the general public although turtle watching is organized. Sand miners were destroying the beach but they have now been banned. Development is rumoured, with two hotels and 1,000 houses.

Anse Louvet is a sheltered beach in a stunning setting, reached from Desbarra (three hours walk but no longer drivable) or Aux Leon (two hours walk or drive if possible, but track is steep, washed out and impassable on a wet day). Ask locally about the state of the roads, which change frequently. Walking takes as long as driving; if you walk take lots of water. La Sorcière mountain forms a long wall which seems to separate Louvet from the rest of the world. Rugged cliffs are beaten by waves and there is a blow hole. A high waterfall in the forest can be reached by following the river from the ford in the main valley (little water flow). Vanilla grows wild in the sheltered valley.

Louvet has a special, spooky atmosphere

The beaches on the west coast north of Castries can be reached by bus with a short walk down to the sea. **Vigie** (1½ miles from Castries) is a lovely strip of sand with plenty of shade, popular and cleaned regularly. Its only drawback is that it runs parallel to the airport runway but that is compensated by the lack of hotels (except *Rendezvous* at one end) and low levels of pollution. Used by locals and no hassling. **Choc**

Health

Sun Despite the breeze, the sun is strong. Take precautions, wear a hat and use high factor sun tan lotion (Banana Boat is a local range) or sun screens. Take particular care with children, who are often seen terribly burned, keep them in T-shirts.

Water Drinking water is safe in most towns and villages. Many rivers, however, cannot be described as clean and it is not recommended that you swim or paddle in them unless you are far upstream. There is bilharzia. If there has been very heavy rain there is often no water supply. This is because the intake pumps at the rivers clog up with silt and the water authority has to shut off all the pumps and clean them out before they can start pumping again. Hotels usually provide bottled water for drinking when this happens.

Facilities Most villages have health centres. The new Tapion hospital has 12-14 doctors' offices, laboratory, but no casualty department. For emergency T999; Aerojet Ambulance for air evacuation, T4521600, F4532229; Victoria Hospital, Castries, T4522421/4537059; St Jude's, Vieux Fort, T4546041, Soufrière Casualty, T4597258, Dennery, T4533310. Larger hotels have resident doctors or doctors 'on call', visits cost about EC$50. If given a prescription, ask at the Pharmacy whether the medication is available 'over the counter', as this may be cheaper. The AIDS hotline is T4527170. As on most Caribbean islands, there is dengue fever (see page 58), carried by the mosquito, Aedes egyptii so take anti-mosquito repellent.

Bay has good sand, shade and chairs next to the restaurant, *Waves* (get off the bus after *Sandals Halcyon*). **Marisule** is a small beach, but popular with the locals. **Labrellotte Bay** is also popular and you can get lunch at *East Winds* or *Windjammer Landing*. **Bois d' Orange** is a deserted bay (except on public holidays), best reached on foot or four-wheel drive. **Rodney Bay** has another excellent beach at Reduit, dominated by the *Rex St Lucian* (parasailing) and *Royal St Lucian* hotels, where you can use their bars and sports hire facilities but it is crowded with their guests. The northern part of the bay is cut off by the marina and it is now a 45-minute walk or five to 10 minute bus ride into Gros Islet. There are more beaches on the way to **Pigeon Island**, with ample shade and two small beaches on Pigeon Island itself. Further north by *Odyssey St Lucia* **Smugglers' Cove** is another good snorkelling spot.

Heading south from Castries there are beaches at all the small towns but they are not generally used by tourists and you may feel an oddity. **Marigot Bay** is a popular tourist spot. **Anse Chastanet** is well used and claims to have the best snorkelling on the island (see page 784). **Anse Cochon** is also popular, visited by boats doing day trips, being accessible only by sea with no facilities. The smell of motor boats can be unpleasant. The trade winds blow in to the south shore and the sandy beach of **Anse de Sables** near Vieux Fort offers ideal **windsurfing**. Many hotels hire out hobbycats, dinghies, windsurfing equipment, jet bikes and small speedboats.

Sailing At **Marigot Bay** and **Rodney Bay** you can hire any size of craft, the larger ones coming complete with crew if you want. Many of these yachts sail down to the Grenadines. Rodney Bay has been developed to accommodate 1,000 yachts (with 232 berths in a full-service boatyard) and hosts the annual Atlantic Rally for Cruisers race, with over 150 yachts arriving there each December. Charters can be arranged to sail to neighbouring islands. At Rodney Bay Marina is: *Trade Winds Yachts*, T4528424, F4528442, an extensive range of services on offer, bareboat or crewed charters, liveaboard sailing school, trips to Martinique or St Vincent (one-way available); *Sunsail Stevens Yachts*, T4528648, bareboat or crewed charters, one-way cruises to the Grenadines, and *Destination St Lucia*, T4528531, yachts from 38-51 ft, multilingual staff. At Marigot Bay: *The Moorings*, T4514357, bareboat fleet of 38-50 ft Beneteaus and crewed fleet of 50-60 ft yachts, 45-room hotel for accommodation prior to departure or on return, watersports, diving, windsurfing. Soufrière has a good anchorage, but as the water is deep it is necessary to anchor close in. There is a pier for short term tie-ups. **Fishing** trips for barracuda, mackerel, king fish and other varieties can also be arranged. Several sport fishing boats sail from Rodney Bay Marina. There is an annual billfish tournament, at which in 1993 a 549-lb blue marlin was landed, breaking the record. Charter fleets include *Sunsail Stevens* (T4528648), *Tradewinds* (T4528424), *Moorings* (T4514357), *Destination St Lucia* (T4528531).

Day sails

As some of the best views are from the sea, it is recommended to take at least one boat trip. There are several boats which sail down the west coast to Soufrière, where you stop to visit the volcano, Diamond Falls and the Botanical Gardens, followed by lunch and return sail with a stop somewhere for swimming and snorkelling. The price usually includes all transport, lunch, drinks and snorkelling gear; the *Unicorn*, a 140-ft replica of a 19th-century brig which started life in 1947 as a Baltic trader (used in the filming of *Roots*) sails 0930 Monday to Friday in high season, and has been recommended, US$80 per person, children under 12 years half price except on Friday, when they only have to pay US$15, including lunch and the inevitable rum punch. Champagne and sunset cruises on Wednesday, Thursday and Friday, 1700-1900, US$40. Can be booked through hotel tour desks (*Unicorn* is based at Vigie Marina, T4526811). Other excursions on catamarans (*Endless Summer*, recommended) and private yachts can be booked with tour operators in Castries or through the hotels. At the swimming stop on the return journey local divers may try to sell you coral. It is illegal and if you buy it a reef dies as a result. The catamarans are usually very overcrowded and devoid of character but cost the same as the *Unicorn*. An alternative to the brig is to charter a yacht with skipper and mate; a 40-ft Beneteau for up to six people (eight if some children) costs around US$350 per day and will take you wherever you want including drinks and meals. Motor boats can also be chartered for customized trips including fishing and snorkelling. Only local companies are allowed to operate day charters. Recommended is *Dinask*, a 40-ft sailing boat at Rodney Bay, contact Capt Christian Bonnaudeau (Capt Moustache), T4847060, F4520183. A week's trip to the Grenadines costs around US$2,700, low season, for up to four passengers, skippered by Christian (who bakes bread) and Lysiane (who does most of the cooking), both are licensed with many years' experience in the area.

Other sports

There is a **golf** course at Cap Estate, the St Lucia Golf & Country Club, with nine holes which can be played as 18 (green fee US$30-40, T4508523) and a private course for guests at La Toc. The former will be expanding to be a championship 18-hole course, with associated villas, condos et cetera. The larger hotels usually have **tennis** courts, or there is the St Lucia Tennis Club. The Roscoe Tanner Tennis Village, at *Odyssey St Lucia* (formerly *Club St Lucia*), has lots of tennis courts and holds international tournaments, for example Davis Cup, Legends Tournament, T4500551 for bookings. Several other hotels have tennis courts for public use and lessons can be arranged. **Squash** is available at St Lucia golf clubhouse at Cap Estate and the St Lucia Yacht Club (two courts, a/c, wooden floored, glass backed, open 0800-1600, racquets for hire, balls for sale, T4528350). The St Lucia Racquet Club at *Odyssey St Lucia* also has a court and optional instruction, T4500551. **Cycling** can be arranged through *Carib Travel*, T4522151, who have 15 Rockhoppers and offer a trip starting at Paix Bouche through mountain villages down to Gros Islet.

Horses for hire at *Trim's Stables*, Cas-en-Bas (PO Box 1159, Castries, T4508273), riding for beginners or advanced; also offers lessons, one-hour rides US$35, 2hrs US$45 and picnic trips to the Atlantic, US$55. *Country Saddles*, T4500197, highly recommended for a ride through the countryside and the seashore, good horses, guides are encouraging with beginners but still manage to give the more experienced lots of fun. Ask at Trim's Stables for information on horse racing, which is just beginning. Races are at Cas-en-Bas and in Vieux Fort. The *International Riding Stables* in Gros Ilet also does trail rides and caters for all levels of rides, T4528139, choice of English or Western style. *North Point Riding Stables*, Cap Estate, takes groups to Cas-en-Bas Beach, Donkey Beach, Pigeon Point or Gros Islet, one and a half hours, minimum age 12, T4508853.

Laborde's Gym, Old La Toc Road, **exercise equipment** and body building, open Monday to Friday 0600-2000, T4522788, no credit cards. *Body Inc* at Gablewoods Mall has weight training, aerobics and a cardio centre, T4519744. *Hotel Le Sport* specializes in health and fitness, with tennis, cycling, weight training, volley ball et cetera, all inclusive packages. St Lucia Racquet Club offers fitness classes and a Nautilus gym, T4500551. Jogging is organized by The Roadbusters, who meet outside JQ's Supermarket, La Clery, on Tuesday and Thursday at 1700 and on Sunday at 0800, call Jimmie James for details, T4524790 evenings. Cricket and football are the main spectator sports, also basketball, netball and volleyball are increasingly popular. Every village has a **cricket** game at weekends or after work in the season, using makeshift equipment such as sticks or palm frond bases as bats. **Combat** is a new game played 0900-1200 at weekends, T4529634, you are provided with fatigues and compressed gas cylinder guns which fire orange paint balls. Two teams battle to capture the flag.

Castries

Population: 60,000 *The capital, Castries, is splendidly set on a natural harbour against a background of mountains. It used to be guarded by the great fortress of Morne Fortune (Fort Charlotte and Derrière Fort). There is a spectacular view from the road just below Morne Fortune where the town appears as a kaleidoscope of red, blues, white and green and it promises much. However, it can be a disappointment as close to the town is thoroughly modern but the bustle of its safe streets more than compensates. The city centre is very crowded when cruise ships come in.*

Background The town was originally situated by Vigie and known as Carenage (the dock to the west of Pointe Seraphine is still referred to as Petit Carenage). An area of disease and defensively vulnerable, it was moved in 1768 and renamed Castries after the Minister of the French Navy and the Colonies, Marechal de Castries.

Largely rebuilt after being destroyed by four major fires, the last in 1948, the commercial centre and government offices are built of concrete. Only the buildings to the south of Derek Walcott Square and behind Brazil Street were saved. Here you will see late 19th and early 20th century wooden buildings built in French style with three storeys, their gingerbread fretwork balconies overhanging the pavement. *Rain* restaurant (now closed), 1885, is a fine example. The other area which survived was the market on the north side of Jeremie Street. Built entirely of iron in 1894, it was conceived by Mr Augier, member of the Town Board, to enhance the appearance of the town and also provide a sheltered place where fruit and produce could be sold hygienically. A new market has been built next door to house the many fruit sellers and their huge selection on the ground floor, while on the first floor and in an arcade opposite are vendors of T-shirts, crafts, spices, basket work, leeches and hot pepper sauce who have been relocated from the streets outside. Further along Jeremie Street on the waterfront is a new shopping centre with duty-free shops: La Place Carenage, almost opposite Pointe Seraphine. For a small fee a water taxi can enable you to shop at both. Good restaurant upstairs at Carenage. The tallest building in the city is the seven-storey Financial Centre at the corner of Jeremie and Bridge Streets, with a joyous sculpture by Ricky George.

Castries used to be twinned with Taipei but now it has close relations with mainland China and there are plans to build a sports stadium, a four-lane highway from Vieux Fort to Castries and other projects with Chinese investment. Work has started on a carpark by the market and government buildings for 362 cars, with a cinema, day care centre, etc.

Derek Walcott Square was the site of the Place D'Armes in 1768 when the town transferred from Vigie. Renamed Promenade Square, it then became Columbus Square in 1893. In 1993 it was renamed in honour of Derek Walcott, the poet (see page 811). It was the original site of the courthouse and the market. The library is on its west side. The giant Saman tree is about 400 years old. On its east side lies the **Cathedral** which bursts into colour inside. Suffused with yellow light, the side altars are often covered with flowers while votive candles placed in red, green and yellow jars give a fairy tale effect. The ceiling, supported by delicate iron arches and braces is decorated with large panelled portraits of the apostles. Above the central altar with its four carved screens, the apse ceiling has paintings of five female saints with St Lucy in the centre. The walls have murals by Dunstan St Omer, probably the most famous of St Lucia's artists (see page 811). They are of the stations of the cross and are unusual in that the people in the paintings are black. The figures in his murals in rural churches are of local people.

As you wander around the town, note the **Place Jean Bapiste Bideau** (a sea captain who dedicated his life to freedom and heroically saved the life of Simón Bolívar)

Castries

and the mural on Manoel Street by the St Lucia Banana Growers Association building. It was painted in 1991 by Dunstan St Omer and two of his sons and depicts scenes of St Lucian life: banana boats, tourism, 18th-century sea battles, the king and queen of the flower festivals and Carib Indians.

Most Ministries have moved into new Government Buildings on John Compton Highway on the waterfront. Some offices are still scattered all over town, but a fourth building is under construction for them.

On the outskirts of Castries is **Pointe Seraphine**, a duty-free complex, near the port. From Castries take the John Compton Highway north towards Vigie airport and branch off just past the new fish market. All of the goods are priced in US dollars and it consists largely of chic boutiques. The tourist board head office is here, and there is an information desk serving the cruise ship passengers. ■ *0800-1630 Mon-Fri. There are plenty of people who will 'mind your car' here. Ignore them.* The rather curious pyramid-shaped building is the Alliance Française, the French cultural centre built in conjunction with the St Lucia Ministry of Education.

Excursions If you continue on the John Compton Highway past the sports complex, turn left at the roundabout to go to the airport, you are sandwiched between the runway on your left and the beautiful Vigie beach on your right. There is a small war cemetery here commemorating those from the British West Indies regiment who lost their lives and a new monument and resting place dedicated to the St Lucian women who also served. You can drive around Vigie point. After the airport, go straight ahead past the French Embassy. The Archaeological and Historical Society and St Lucia National Trust are located here. Continue around the peninsula and on the descent, there is a turn to the lighthouse for lovely views. There is much evidence of the military past with some of the decrepit buildings still in use at the highly rated secondary school for boys, St Mary's College.

Just south of Castries you can walk (unfortunately only on the main road, allow about one hour each way) or drive to the Governor's Mansion with its curious metalwork crown, at the top of Mount Morne. From here carry on to **Fort Charlotte**, the old Morne Fortune fortress (now Sir Arthur Lewis Community College). You will pass the Apostles' battery (1888) and Provost's redoubt (1782). Each has spectacular views, but the best is from the Inniskilling Monument at the far side of the college (just beyond the old Combermere barracks) where you get an excellent view of the town, coast, mountains and Martinique. It was here in 1796 that General Moore launched an attack on the French. The steep slopes give some idea of how fierce the two days of fighting must have been. As a rare honour, the 27th Inniskillings Regiment were allowed to fly their regimental flag for one hour after they took the fortress before the Union Jack was raised. The college is in good condition having been carefully restored in 1968. Sir Arthur Lewis, Nobel Laureate in Economics, is buried in the grounds of the Community College which bears his name. The site is just in front of the steps leading to the Inniskilling Monument.

On returning to Castries, branch left at the Governor's mansion to visit **La Toc** point with its luxury *Sandals* hotel. Take the road to the hotel through its beautiful gardens and take the path to the right of the security gate if you want to visit the beach. Further on is the road leading to Bagshaws studio. Down a long leafy drive, you can buy attractive silkscreen clothes and household linens and visit the printshop to watch the screen printing process. ■ *Mon-Fri 0830-1600, Sat 0830-1200. Carry your return ticket for a discount.* Close to Bagshaws is La Toc Battery, the best restored military fort, visited mostly by cruise ship visitors. For information call Alice Bagshaw, T4526039, or inquire at the shop.

North to Pointe Du Cap

The part of the island to the north of Castries is the principal resort area, it contains the best beaches and the hotels are largely self contained. It is the driest part of the island with little evidence of the banana plantations or rain forest. The John Compton highway leaves Castries past Vigie airport and follows the curves of Vigie Beach and Choc Bay. Where the road leaves the bay and just before it crosses the Choc River, a right turn to Babonneau will take you past the Union Agricultural station (about one mile) where there is a nature trail and interpretive centre. A mini zoo boasts a pair of St Lucian parrots. The trail goes through a nursery and herbal garden before going through Caribbean pine trees, latanier palms and cinnamon and bay trees. It takes about 20 minutes.

Back on the main highway, the road passes the turning to Labrellotte Bay (dominated **Rodney Bay** by the *Windjammer Hotel*) before reaching Rodney Bay and the town of Gros Islet. Here is the site of the **US Naval Air Station of Reduit**. Built in February 1941, the swamps were reclaimed and the bay dredged. It was the first of a chain of bases established to protect the Panama Canal. Acting as a communications centre (code name 'Peter Item'), it supported a squadron of sea planes. The base was eventually closed in 1947. The whole area now supports a mass of tourist facilities including the *Rex St*

Windward Islands

Rodney Bay

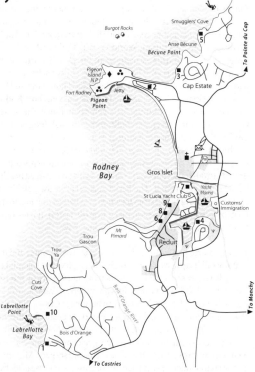

■ **Sleeping**	4 Marlin Quay	8 Rex St Lucian
1 Eastwinds Inn	5 Odyssey St Lucia	9 Royal St Lucian
2 Hyatt Regency	6 Papillon	10 Windjammer Landing
3 Le Sport	7 Rainbow	

Lucian and *Royal St Lucian* hotels, restaurants and sport facilities. You can pass through the entrance gates of the old Naval Air Station or take the next left turn off the main road to reach the hotels and restaurants. If you drive past them all to the end of the road there is good access to the beach. Rodney Bay is an excellent base for watersports; it is ideal for windsurfing. At the back of the development is a 1,000-boat marina. Development is still taking place and at Rodney Heights a huge area has been set aside for condominiums. The normally sleepy fishing village of **Gros Islet** holds a popular jump-up in the street each Friday night, from 2200, music, dancing, bars, cheap food, rather touristy but enjoyed by night owls. Try the grilled conch from one of the booths selling local dishes but stay away from anyone offering drugs.

Pigeon Island About three quarters of a mile after Elliot's Shell filling station on the outskirts of Gros Islet, turn left to Pigeon Island National Landmark (see page 782), once an island, now joined to the mainland by a causeway on which a 300-room *Hyatt Regency* hotel has been built with a bright blue roof, opening in 2000. The park was opened by Princess Alexandra on 23 February 1979 as part of St Lucia's Independence celebrations (entrance EC$5). It has two peaks which are joined by a saddle. The higher rises to a height of about 360 ft. Owned and managed by the National Trust, the island is of considerable archaeological and historical interest. Amerindian remains have been found, the French pirate François Leclerc (known as Jamb de Bois for his wooden leg) used the large cave on the north shore and the Duke of Montagu tried to colonize it in 1722 (but abandoned it after one afternoon). From here, Admiral Rodney set sail in 1782 to meet the French navy at the Battle of Les Saintes (see under Guadeloupe). It was captured by the Brigands (French slaves freed by the leaders of the French revolution) in 1795 but retaken in 1798 by the English. Used as a quarantine centre from 1842 it was abandoned in 1904 but became an US observation post during World War II. The island finally became the home of Josset Agnes Huchinson, a member of the D'Oyly Carte Theatre who leased the island from 1937 to 1976. The bay became a busy yacht haven and 'Joss' held large parties to entertain the crews. Her abandoned house can still be seen on the south shore of the island. On the lower of the two peaks lies **Fort Rodney**. There is a steep climb but well worth it for the 360 degree panorama. The museum (located in the Officers' Mess and recently rebuilt to the original design) contains an interesting display of the work of the National Trust as well as a comprehensive interpretive exhibition. ■ *EC$10, open every day 0900-1800; museum closed Sun.* The park also contains *Jambe de Bois* restaurant which is recommended for snacks and a cool drink ■ *0900-1600, closed Sat.* You can swim off the small beach, although sandy, it has a lot of broken coral. The park is a good place for watching sea birds. Offshore are the remains of the Castries telephone exchange, donated to the Fisheries Department by Cable and Wireless to make an artificial reef. It is also accessible by boat and there is a regular ferry service from Rodney Bay.

North coast The road north passes through the Cap estate (golf course and the *Odyssey St Lucia*) to **Pointe du Cap**, a viewpoint some 470 ft high with a splendid panorama along the coast. If you wish to explore further the north part of the island contact Safari Adventures Ltd (T4528778) who run all terrain vehicles to Cas-en-Bas beach. A good circular walk from Gros Islet can be done to Cas-en-Bas taking the road past *La Panache Guesthouse* (ask the owner, Henry Augustin for directions if necessary, he is always willing to help) down to the beach (sheltered, shady, a bit dirty), then following tracks north until you reach the golf course, from where you return along the west coast to Gros Islet. You will see cacti, wild scenery, Martinique and no tourists. The sea is too rough to swim. If exploring the Atlantic beaches by vehicle, make sure it is four-wheel drive, check your spare tyre and tools, take OS map and water, be prepared to park and walk, and if possible take a local person with you. Always take local advice on the state of the roads, which change quickly. For more details, see above, Beaches and watersports.

The road to Monchy from Gros Islet is a pleasant drive inland through several small villages. You gradually leave the dry north part of the island and climb into forest. The ridge between Mount Monier and Mount Chaubourg gives particularly impressive views over the east coast. You will also pass through Paix Bouche where it is thought that Napoleon's empress Josephine was born. There are no road signs. Watch out for the names on schools and if in doubt at junctions bear west. At the larger village of Babonneau, you can turn right to follow the river down to the coast at Choc Bay or go straight on to Fond Cacao where a west turn will take you back to Castries. The road to Forestière is the access point for the climb to Piton Flor (1,871 ft).

East coast to Vieux Fort

The road from Castries to Cul de Sac opened in 1999 and was immediately popular with cars and trucks. It is quite a straight road running along the sea and is a welcome relief from the hairpin curves of the old Morne Road. The Castries end starts at the roundabout on La Toc Road, goes through two short tunnels and comes out in the Cul de Sac valley, where a right turn takes you towards the beautiful Marigot Bay and the West Coast Road to Vieux Fort. A jog to the left and then a quick right takes the East Coast Road to the southern end of the island. The West Coast Road is full of mountain curves but has less traffic than the East Coast. Together they present a very scenic drive round the island.

The transinsular road goes through extensive banana plantations with the occasional packaging plant, through the village of Ravine Poisson before climbing steeply over the **Barre de l'Isle**, the mountain barrier that divides the island. There is a short, self-guided trail at the high point on the road between Castries and Dennery, which takes about 10 minutes and affords good views of the rainforest and down the Roseau valley. There is a small picnic shelter. It can be slippery after rain. The experience is rather spoilt by the noise of traffic. A longer walk to **Mount La Combe** can also be undertaken from this point (see page 782). Be careful in this area as it is known as the drug growing region. Cyclists and hikers have reported that the locals are not particularly friendly and their stares can make you feel uncomfortable.

Dennery The road descends through Grande Rivière to Dennery where the vegetation is mostly xerophytic scrub. Dennery is set in a sheltered bay with Dennery Island guarding its entrance and dominated by the Roman Catholic church. Here you can see the distinctive St Lucia fishing boats pulled up on the beach. Carved out of single tree trunks, the bows are straight and pointed rather than curved and are all named with phrases such as 'God help me'. A US$6 mn fishing port has been built with improved moorings, cold storage and other facilities, with Japanese assistance. There are lots of small bars but no other facilities. You can follow the Dennery River inland towards Mount Beaujolais. At Errard there is a photogenic waterfall. Permission should be obtained from the estate office before attempting this trip. ■ *Plantation tour with lunch and hotel transfers costs US$50. Book through tour company.*

Fregate Island **Fregate Island Nature Reserve**, on the north side of Praslin Bay has a small but interesting visitor centre. The two small islands provide nesting sites for the frigate bird and the north promontory of Praslin bay gives a good vantage point. The reserve is closed from May to July during the breeding season. At other times call the National Trust, T4525005 for a guide. The area is also of some historical interest as there was an Amerindian lookout point in the reserve. It was also the site of a battle between the English and the Brigands. It used to be known as Trois Islet and the nearby Praslin River is still marked as Trois Islet River on maps today.

Praslin is noted as a fishing community with traditional boat building. The road leaves the coast here and goes through banana plantations and the villages of **Mon Repos** and Patience. Mon Repos is a good area to witness the flower festivals of La Rose and La Marguerite. Between Praslin and Mon Repos are the **Mamiku Gardens**:

Botanical Gardens and Woodland Walks on an estate owned by Baron de Micoud in 1766 but later a military post and site of a battle with brigands. ■ *T4528236, www.mamiku.com Daily 0900-1700, EC$15 for foreigners, EC$10 for locals, there is a snack bar and souvenir shop*. The coast is regained at **Micoud**. There are one or two restaurants (including *Palm*, simple and clean), a department store, post office and a branch of Barclays bank. It is also the centre of St Lucia's wine industry: banana, guava, pineapple and sugar cane brewed and bottled under 'Helen Brand'. One mile west of Micoud is Latille Gardens with fruit, flowers, trees and waterfalls. From Mahaut Road follow signs to the south. Tours can also be arranged through hotels and include a walk through the Descartes Rainforest Trail, T4540202.

Mangrove swamps can be seen at **Savannes Bay Nature Reserve**. The bay is protected by a living reef and is a very active fishing area. The shallow bay is excellent for the cultivation of sea moss, an ideal breeding ground for conch and sea eggs. Scorpion island lies in the bay and to the north are more archaeological sites on Saltibus Point and Pointe de Caille (the latter excavated by the University of Vienna in 1983 and 1988).

Vieux Fort
Population: 14,000

After about three miles you reach Vieux Fort, the island's industrial centre, where the Hewanorra international airport is situated. It is an active town with a good Saturday market, a lot of traditional housing and gaily-painted trucks for transport, although they are gradually being replaced by the ubiquitous Toyota vans. The area is markedly less sophisticated than the north of the island. The town boasts two new supermarkets in malls, *JQs* and *Julian's*. The latter has a cinema. The post office is on Theodore Street which with the police station is right in the middle of the town. Fishing boats are pulled up on the small beach but there is no proper beach here. On Clarke Street you will pass the square with a war memorial and band stand. The bus terminal is at the end of Clarke Street near the airport. Vieux Fort makes a good base for exploring the south of the island. Helen Brand, the local wine producer, is just outside Vieux Fort. You can try the different wines (rather like a heavy port) and take an unusual souvenir home. Ask your taxi driver to stop there on the way to the airport.

The perimeter road skirts Anse de Sables beach (no shade), the base for *Club Med* watersports and looks across to the **Maria Islands** (see further page 783). The interpretive centre on the beach is not always open. If you want to visit **Cap Moule à Chique**, turn left at the T junction and follow the road to the banana loading jetty (on Wednesday you will pass truck after truck waiting to be weighed). Bear left and go up a badly maintained track. Finally go left again through the Cable and Wireless site up to the lighthouse. The duty officer will be glad to point out the views including the Pitons, Morne Gomier (1,028 ft) with Morne Grand Magazin (2,022 ft) behind it. Unfortunately Morne Gimie (3,118 ft) is largely obscured. Further to the east is Piton St Esprit (1,919 ft) and Morne Durocher (1,055 ft) near Praslin. The lighthouse itself is 730 ft above sea level and also has good views over the Maria islands and southwest to St Vincent.

West coast to Soufrière and the Pitons

The West Coast Road was opened in 1995 and is in excellent condition with good signposting and many viewpoints. It is a very curvy, but spectacular, drive down to Soufrière. Take the transinsular highway out of Castries and instead of branching left at Cul de Sac bay carry straight on. The road quickly rises to La Croix Maingot where you get good views of the Roseau banana plantation.

Marigot Bay

On reaching the Roseau valley, one of the main banana growing areas, take the signposted road to Marigot Bay (plenty of 'guides' waiting to pounce). A good place to stop for a drink, the *Marigot Bay Resort* dominates both sides of the valley. In between is a beautiful inlet which is a natural harbour and provided the setting for *Dr Doolittle*. It supports a large marina and not surprisingly a large number of yachts in transit berth here to restock with supplies from the supermarket and chandler. You will notice a small strip of land jutting out into the bay. This has a small beach (not particularly good for swimming) and can be reached by the *gingerbread express* (a small water taxi, EC$2 return, refundable at *Doolittle's* if you eat or drink there) either from the hotel or the customs post. It is a good place for arranging watersports and the staff of the resort are most helpful. There is a police station and immigration post here. High above the bay are *JJ's* and *Albert's* bars, popular alternatives to Gros Islet on Friday nights. You can also eat well at *JJ's*, a much cheaper alternative to the expensive restaurants at Marigot Bay.

At the bottom of the Roseau Valley, the road to Vanard and Millet branches off to the left (signposted). Millet is high up in the mountains and offers a good view of the rainforest. The road ends there. An interesting detour is **Jacmel** (take first right hand turn off Vanard road). If you take the first left turn in the village you reach the church, the altarpiece of which was painted by Dunstan St Omer (see page 811). Father Cecil Goodman can be asked to open the church if it is not already open. Donations welcome to maintain the church.

The main road continues to Soufrière and passes through the fishing villages of **Anse La Raye** and Canaries (no facilities). South of Anse La Raye, a well-restored sugar mill, La Sikwi, can be visited, EC$5 or EC$15 with guide. It is near the river on the way to a waterfall, in a garden containing many regional crop species. Boa constrictor come here to be fed and with luck you will see one. The bar and restaurant open on demand. A narrow, steep, bad road branches off to the right just before Canaries and leads to a restaurant run by Chef Harry from the *Green Parrot* (no regular service, used for private functions). Half way along this road, before it gets really steep, you can park and climb down the hill towards Canaries. There is a man-made cave and oven used by escaped slaves. Difficult to find (as intended), you need a knowledgeable local to show you where it is. There are also many waterfalls in the vacinity of Canaries, some of which are visited by organized tours. If you go independently you need a four-wheel drive and a guide. The closest is right at the end of the road into the rainforest, others are 30 minutes to two and a half hours walk away. It is safe to swim. South of Canaries is Anse La Liberté (pronounced La Betty). It can be reached by water taxi from Canaries, EC$2, or on foot from Belvedere along a trail (10 minutes down, 15 minutes up) which will become a nature trail. There are many brigand holes in the area.

Canaries

After Canaries the road goes inland and skirts Mount Tabac (2,224 ft) before descending into Soufrière. This is the most picturesque and interesting part of the island, with marvellous old wooden buildings at the foot of the spectacular Pitons, surrounded by thick vegetation and towering rock formations looming out of the sea. Note that Petit Piton is dangerous to climb (several people have fallen off in recent years) and also that it is restricted Crown Lands. This does not stop local guides offering to show visitors up, though, for about EC$80. Because of its location, the town is a must for tourists although it is not geared for people wanting to stay there and nobody seems bothered about visitors. It can help to have a hotel guide or dayboat skipper with you. In any event it is not cheap, expect to be charged for everything. Indeed, it is essential if you have no transport of your own and want to see the volcano and the Pitons, as there are no buses back to Castries after midday unless you make a roundabout journey via Vieux Fort. To do this, leave Castries at 0800, the ride can take two hours. After visiting Soufrière, wait at the corner opposite the church and ask as many people as possible if they know of anyone going to Vieux Fort; you will get a lift before you get a bus. It is important to get off at Vieux Fort 'crossroads', where there are many buses returning to Castries by another route, one and a quarter hours. Buses to Castries leave from the market area. If you arrive by boat head for the north end of the bay, you will find plenty of help to tie up your yacht (EC$5) and taxis will appear from nowhere. It is a much cheaper alternative to tying up at the jetty. ■ *Organized tours are available from the hotels further north, by sea or road, from around US$65-80 including lunch, drinks, transfers and a trip to Soufrière, Diamond Gardens and the Sulphur Springs (see below).*

Soufrière
Population: 9,000

Soufrière was severely damaged in Nov 1999 by Hurricane Lenny, which brought 20-ft waves & destroyed about 70 houses & infrastructure

Windward Islands

Soufrière is a charming old West Indian town dating back to 1713 when Louis XIV of France granted the lands around Soufrière to the Devaux family. The estate subsequently produced cotton, tobacco, coffee and cocoa. During the French Revolution, the guillotine was raised in the square by the Brigands but the Devaux family were protected by loyal slaves and escaped. It is situated on a very picturesque bay totally dominated by the Pitons. The water here is extremely deep and reaches 200 ft only a few yards from the shore, which is why boats moor close in. To reach Anse Chastanet from here take the rough track at the north end of the beach (past the yacht club) about one mile. This is an absolute must if you enjoy snorkelling (the south end near the jetty is superb but keep within the roped off area, the north end is also good with some rocks to explore, but avoid the middle where boats come in). The hotel has a good and inexpensive restaurant (although if you are on a budget you may prefer to take a picnic) and the dive shop is extremely helpful, they will hire out equipment by the hour. The *Unicorn, Endless Summer* and day boats stop here for snorkelling and a swim in the afternoon on their return to Castries.

Diamond Gardens Most visitors come to the town to see the Diamond Gardens and Waterfall and the Sulphur Springs. There are no road signs in Soufrière and locating these two places can be difficult (or expensive if forced to ask). From the square take the road east past the church (Sir Arthur Lewis Street) and look for a right hand turning to reach the Diamond Gardens. These were developed in 1784 after Baron de Laborie sent samples taken from sulphur springs near the Diamond River to Paris for analysis. They found minerals present which were equivalent to those found in the spa town of Aix-la-Chapelle and were said to be effective against rheumatism and other complaints. The French King ordered baths to be built. Despite being destroyed in the French Revolution, they were eventually rebuilt and can be used by members of the public for about EC$6.50. The gardens are well maintained and many native plants can be seen. ■ *T4524759. EC$6 (children EC$3), daily 1000-1700. Only official guides are allowed in, do not accept offers from those at the gates. All the carparks are free, no matter what some people may tell you.*

Sulphur Springs To get to the Sulphur Springs take the Vieux Fort road between wooden houses about half way along the south side of Soufrière square. Follow the road for about two miles (you can stop off on the way to visit the **Morne Coubaril Estate**, an open-air farm museum, guided tour EC$15, working family plantation, processes cocoa, copra, cassava, T4597340) and you will see a sign on the left. You will also be able to smell the springs. Originally a huge volcano about 5 km in diameter, it collapsed some 40,000 years ago leaving the west part of the rim empty (where you drive in). The sign welcomes you to the world's only drive-in volcano, although actually you have to stop at a car park. The sulphur spring is the only one still active, although there are seven cones within the old crater as well as the pitons which are thought to be volcanic plugs. Tradition has it that the Arawak deity *Yokahu* slept here and it was therefore the site of human sacrifices. The Caribs were less superstitious but still named it *Qualibou*, the place of death. There is a small village of about 40 inhabitants located inside the rim of the volcano. Water is heated to 180°F and in some springs to 275°F. It quickly cools to about 87°F below the bridge at the entrance. There has been much geothermal research here since 1974. From the main viewing platform, you can see over a moonscape of bubbling, mineral rich, grey mud. It is extremely dangerous to stray onto the grey area. The most famous 'crater' was formed a few years ago when a local person fell into a mud pocket. He received third degree burns. ■ *EC$3, every day 0900-1700. There are good, informative guides (apparently compulsory) on the site but you must be prepared to walk over uneven ground. Allow approximately 30 mins.*

South of Soufrière In the valley between Petit Piton and Gros Piton, a luxury all-inclusive resort, *Jalousie Plantation*, has been built despite complaints from ecological groups and evidence from archaeologists that it is located on a major Amerindian site. An important burial ground is believed to be under the tennis courts and there have been many finds of petroglyphs and pottery. Take the turning opposite the Morne Coubaril Estate on the unsigned concrete road. Half way along the drive to *Jalousie* you will see a little sign to a small, warm waterfall on your left. A Rastaman will collect about US$2 for access. You can relax in the warm waters after the hassle of visiting Soufrière.

South of Soufrière, near Union Vale estate, is the new two-hour Gros Piton trail. The village of Fond Gens Libre is at the base of the mountain, accessible by jeep or high-clearance car although you will have to ford a couple of streams. Enquire at Forestry, T4502231. Call Charmaine Desir, Fond Gens Libre Tour Guides Association, T4593833, to arrange a guide. The trip up and back is about six hours. A guide costs about EC$20, but if you have your own transport you can do it on your own. It is strenuous, so you must be in good physical condition. It should not be attempted in wet weather.

The road from Soufrière to Vieux Fort takes about 40 minutes by car. The branch of the road through **Fond St Jacques** (another church painted by Dunstan St Omer) runs through lush rain forest and a track takes you to the west end of the rain forest trail. In a few miles the road rapidly descends from Victoria Junction (1,200 ft) to the coastal plain at **Choiseul**. Choiseul is a quaint old West Indian village, there is a fish market and church on the beach. Caraibe Point is the last place on St Lucia where Caribs still survive, a small community of potters living in simple thatched houses. North of Choiseul is a petroglyph, visible from the road, although you must park and then walk a little way. Outlined in white, under a protective roof, it is just down the cliff toward the sea. On the south side of Choiseul is the Art and Craft development centre teaching skills in bamboo handicrafts and you can buy pottery and carvings, as well as baskets. Bigger pieces of furniture are made from mahogany in the workshops at the back of the complex. The centre has an outlet in the market in Castries. There is a snack bar.

Southeast of Choiseul, there are Arawak petroglyphs on rocks in the Balenbouche River. You will probably need somebody to show you the way from Balenbouche or Saltibus. Balenbouche Estate is an old sugar plantation where you can stay in the estate home or in a cottage, good local food, contact Uta Lawaetz, T4551244. Stonefield Estate also has very fine petroglyphs, but you will need to ask if someone will show you them in the bush. This is a working cocoa plantation, also with luxurious accommodation, T4530777. The village of Labourie also has accommodation available if you ask around. It is a very picturesque and friendly spot.

Essentials

Sleeping

Many of the hotels are resorts, providing everything their guests need. Apart from those around Rodney Bay, they are remote and you will have to arrange car hire or expensive taxis to get around the island or go to restaurants. All-inclusive resorts are usually, but not always booked from abroad. Many smaller hotels have grouped themselves as The Inns of St Lucia, representing a third of the total number of rooms on the island.

There is a 10-15% service charge & a 8% government tax on all hotel bills

Working roughly north to south down the west coast: **Far north LL** *Club St Lucia*, in receivership in 2000, but still open, T4500551, F4500281. 372 rooms, making it the island's largest hotel, organized into five villages, each with its own mayor and staff, brightly painted cottages, rooms and suites, an all-inclusive family resort including free membership of the Roscoe Tanner Tennis Village on site, seven tennis courts, gymnasium, squash court and four swimming pools, waterslide, floating trampoline, two beaches, lots of watersports, teen and mini club, fun park, food served buffet style, eat and drink as much as you like, golf costs about US$60 per week, diving US$60 per day, entertainment for families with theme

Larger hotels
Service isn't always added to the bill, check. Tipping of 10-15% is customary: porters (US$1 a bag); taxi drivers & others in service expect tips

evenings, stay at home if you don't like steel bands, all-inclusive day passes for visitors EC$175, half-day EC$115. **LL** *Le SPORT*, in the north at Cap Estate, T4508551, F4500368, www.lesport.com.lc For health and fitness lovers, lots of sporting facilities, massage, beauty salon, all-inclusive, extra charge for specialist treatments such as reflexology, Reike, irdology, acupuncture. Nesting turtles on the beach, security guards protect them.

Rodney Bay LL-L *Rex St Lucian*, Reduit Beach, T4528351, F4528331, rexstlucian@ candw.lc Right on the beach, took a battering from Hurricane Lenny but beachfront rooms now restored. 120 a/c rooms, restaurants, pool, entertainment, good facilities, conveniently located, with *Papillon* all-inclusive section, 140 rooms and butterfly-shaped pool, watersports, tennis, discotheque, restaurants and the **LL** *Royal St Lucian*, its sister property, next door, T4529999, F4529639. 98 luxury suites, interconnecting pools, swim up bar and waterfalls, restaurants, use of sports facilities at *Rex*, bit inconvenient. Facilities for wheelchair users at both hotels. **LL-A** *Islander Hotel*, T4528757, F4520958, short walk to Reduit beach, or complimentary bus. 60 rooms or 20 apartments, no watersports offered, but close to all Rodney Bay facilities, friendly and efficient staff. **AL-B** *Rainbow*, Rodney Bay, T4520148. F4520158, rainbow@candw.lc Further down same road as *Rex* and *Royal*, across the road from the beach, next to *Gazebo* restaurant where local bands play at weekends, tennis, fitness centre, pool, snack bar, very colourful, pleasant. **AL** *Harmony Marina Suites*, on Rodney Bay lagoon, close to beach, T4528756, F4528677. Recently modernized studios and apartments, restaurant, bar, pool, mini-mart, watersports including canoeing. **A-B** *Candyo Inn*, Box 386 Rodney Bay, T4520712, F4520774. 8 suites, 4 rooms, a/c, pool, snack bar, good value, lovely inner patio, has won awards, used as overflow by overbooked hotels. **AL-A** *Bay Gardens Hotel*, Rodney Bay, T4528060, F4528059, baygardens@candw.lc 71 rooms, 2 pools, restaurant, a/c, TV, conference facilities. **AL-A** *Palm Tree*, next to *Bay Gardens* on main highway, T4528200, F4528094, www.caribtrade.com/palmtree Rectangular pool. The *Hyatt Regency* opened in 2000 on Pigeon Point, a landmark because of its bright blue roof and offering the first casino on St Lucia. Just up the road a bit is **A-C** *Sunny Isles Hotel*, T4580800. 18 rooms, a/c, cable TV, pool, some rooms have kitchenette and veranda.

Labrellotte Bay LL *East Winds Inn*, T4528212, F4529941, eastwinds@candw.lc 26 hexagonal bungalow rooms, in tropical gardens close to the beach, all-inclusive. **LL-L** *Windjammer Landing*, PO Box 1504, T4520913, F4520907, www.wlv-resort.com A beautiful resort in a lovely hillside setting, but isolated, probably the best villa complex with hotel facilities, 1-bedroomed suites clustered together, 2/4-bedroomed villas more spread out with own plunge pool, luxury resort, tennis and all watersports available, on a rather small beach, honeymoon, family, diving packages available, 30 min walk to a bus route or EC$20 taxi to Rodney Bay. Recommended.

Choc Bay LL *Wyndham Morgan Bay Hotel*, T4502511, F4501050. All-inclusive, 240 rooms north of Castries on the beach, pool, watersports, tennis. **LL** *Sandals Halcyon Beach*, Choc Beach, T4530222, F4518435. All-inclusive, about 300 rooms after expansion, couples only, all facilities interchangeable with *Sandals St Lucia*, transport between 2 sites.

Castries LL *Rendezvous*, Vigie Beach, T4524211, F4527419, www.rendezvous.com.lc Couples only, all inclusive, has some self-catering cottages, many facilities, tennis, gym, jacuzzi, sauna, scuba, yacht cruises, lots of sports equipment, noise of aircraft landing and taking off. **LL** *Sandals St Lucia Golf Resort & Spa*, T4523081, F4521012. 329 rooms and suites, luxuriously appointed, couples only, all-inclusive, tennis courts, golf course, watersports, facilities for wheelchair users. **AL-A** *Top of the Morne Apartments*, Morne Fortune, T4523603, F4590936. 1-2 bedrooms for 1-5 people, very friendly, spectacular view, car rental, pool. **AL-B** *Auberge Seraphine*, Vigie Marina, T4532073, F4517001. 22 rooms, pool, restaurant, a/c, TV. **B** *Caribees*, La Pansée, overlooking Castries, PO Box 1720, T4524767, F4531999, Caribbees@candw.lc New, 60 rooms, pool, tennis, a/c, TV, good restaurant, courtesy bus to town.

Marigot Bay LL-AL *Marigot Bay*, T4514357, F4514353. A Club Mariner resort, dive shop, sailing, yacht chartering and watersports, there is a pleasant beach 300 yds away by ferry. Across the bay is **LL-A** *Marigot Beach Club*, PO Box 101 Castries, T4514974, F4514973, www.marigotbeach.com Waterfront restaurant and bar, *Café Paradis* open from 0800, sailing, kayaking, PADI dive shop run by Rosemond Clery, pool, sundeck, beach, studios with kitchenette, fans, bathrooms and patio or villas with 1-3 bedrooms on hillside. **AL** *Seahorse Inn*, PO Box 1825 Main Post Office, north side of Marigot Bay, Castries, T4514436, F4514872, www.seahorse-inn.com 8 bedrooms, more planned, waterside cottage with own dock US$600-950 per week, beach short walk, pool, restaurants including *Doolittle's* within walking distance, watersports arranged.

Around Soufrière LL *Jalousie Hilton Resort and Spa*, Soufrière, PO Box 251, T4597666, F4597667, www.hilton.com 115-room luxury resort built amid much controversy over its location at the foot of the Pitons, Sunday brunch at the beach restaurant EC$90, Friday night buffet, traditional Caribbean EC$85, reservations required, space limited, luxury yacht transfers available from Castries, interesting snorkelling further along the shore, but swimming and snorkelling at the resort disappointing. **LL** *Ladera Resort*, PO Box 225, Soufrière, T4597323, F4595156, www.ladera-stlucia.com Spectacular setting between Gros Piton and Petit Piton, 1,000 ft up, 1-3 bedroomed luxury villas and suites, every luxury, very cold plunge pools, sixties style swimming pools, used to film *Superman II*, good restaurant, lots of birds and mosquitoes. **LL-L** *Anse Chastanet*, PO Box 7000, Soufrière, T4597000, F4597700, www.anse chastenet.com Hillside and beachside suites, really special, romantic, luxurious, stunning views in all directions, open balconies, airy, only drawback is the walk uphill after overindulging at dinner, the best scuba diving on the island, consistently highly rated dive operation, diving packages available, watersports, tennis, spa, lovely beach setting, restaurant on the beach and halfway up the hill, live music in the evenings, walks and excursions available, isolated. Highly recommended. **LL-L** *Stonefield Estate*, PO Box 228, Soufrière, T4597037, F4595550, www.stonefieldvillas.com 15 villas sleeping 1-8 on 26-acre estate, 2 pools, Japanese garden, petroglyphs, cook and staff, beach shuttle, view of Pitons, beautifully furnished.   **AL-B** *Humming Bird Beach Resort*, T4597232, F4597033, hbr@candw.lc Only 10 rooms and a hillside cottage, nice gardens, pool, beach, near Soufrière. **AL-B** *The Still Plantation and Beach Resort*, PO Box 246, T4597261, F4597301, duboulayd@candw.lc 400-acre plantation, apartments, studios on the plantation or beachfront rooms, popular, pool, beach restaurant, spectacular view of Pitons. There is also a *Club Méditerranée* at Vieux Fort, reservations through Paris Office, T331-55262627, or locally T4546546, F4549641, pool, lots of windsurfing, sailing, tennis.

The Ladera Resort has 24 rooms, each lacking a west wall providing an uninterrupted view of the Pitons & a close encounter with the animal kingdom

Castries C *Chesterfield*, southern end of Bridge Street, T/F4521295. Central, 16 rooms, tropical garden, some rooms with balcony, great view, a/c, kitchen, excellent value. **E** *Chateau Blanc*, on Morne du Don Road 300 m away, 7 rooms with fan and bathroom, basic but good central location, food available, T4521851, F4527967; **E** *Thelma's Guesthouse*, Waterworks Rd, T4527313. No sign, white building, green awnings, above (closed) *Rising Sun* restaurant, shared bathroom, lounge, kitchen, clean, central, owner Theresa Debique is warm and caring.

Small hotels & guesthouses

Morne Fortune (above Castries) **AL-A** *Green Parrot*, PO Box 648, Castries, T4523399, F4532272. 62 rooms, a/c, balconies, adjacent to excellent restaurant of same name, MAP supplement US$45. **C** *Bon Appetit*, near *Dubois Guesthouse*, T4522757, F4527967. Beautiful view, clean, friendly, cable TV, restaurant, 3 rooms with bathroom includes breakfast, book early for evening meal, popular. Recommended. **C** *Harbour Light Inn*, City Gate, T4523506, F4519455. 3 min walk to Vigie Beach, parking, 16 rooms, a/c or fan, private bath, hot water, cable TV, balcony all round building, panoramic view, restaurant, bar. **C** *Tropical Haven*, La Toc, 10 min by car from town, T4523505, F4525476. 10 rooms and 2 apartments (negotiable), popular with doctors visiting Victoria hospital, no credit cards, more than adequate, excellent food. **D** *Dubois Guesthouse*, T/F4522201. 4 rooms, a long way from anything but on bus route. **D-C** *Sunset Lodge Guesthouse*, near Vigie Airport John Compton Highway, T4522639, F4536736. Convenient, a/c, TV, restaurant, bar, nothing special, ask for a room

Windward Islands

away from the road. **E** *Morne Fortune Guest House*, T4521742. Single rooms are big enough for two, shared bathrooms, spacious, well-equipped kitchen for self-catering, very clean, restaurant, bakery close by, when coming from town turn left at Shell station on the Morne and right at the T-junction, guest house on right after 100 m, across the road from the Sir Arthur Lewis Community College campus, where there are two restaurants. Run by Mrs Regina Willie, helpful, informative, monthly rates available, good access to public transport. **E** *Summersdale Hideaway*, T4521142 for directions. 20 min walk north of Vigie airport, off the main road and bus route, cheap restaurant.

Vide Bouteille (just outside Castries)   **AL** *Top of the World Apartments* in the hills at Marisule, T450-1520/2015, F4501188. A 15-min walk from Labrellotte Bay. The Zephirin family has cottages to let, self-catering. **B-D** *Serenity Lodge*, 5 km from Castries overlooking Choc Bay, T4521987, F4516019. 12 rooms, few facilities but good. **D-E** *Modern Inn*, on the main road north of Castries, 3 km from Vide Bouteille, T4524001, F4537313. Friendly, good rooms, very clean and pleasant, breakfast available.

Gablewoods Mall   A-B *Orange Grove Hotel*, T4528213, F4528094, is set in the hills of Bois d'Orange, where a new shopping centre is being built. 51 rooms, 11 suites, patio or balcony, cable TV, hairdryers, restaurant, pleasant staff, very comfortable, rectangular pool, complimentary bus to beach. **B** *Friendship Inn*, T4524201, F4532635. Rooms with kitchenette and baby sitting services, small pool, restaurant. Nearby the **D-E** *Sundale Guest House*, T4524120. Very popular, includes breakfast, own bathroom, fan, TV in lobby, check availability. Further north, on highway to Gros Islet, **D-E** *The Golden Arrow*, T4501832, F4502329. 15 clean, pleasant rooms, all with private bathroom, no single rooms, walking distance from beach and bus, friendly host, breakfast and dinner available. **D** *Parrots Hideaway*, T/F4520726. 7 rooms, 3 suites, one apartment, discounts for long stays, bar, restaurant, creole menu, charming hostess.

Gros Islet   L-C *Tropical Breeze*, 38 Massie St, Massade, Gros Islet, T/F4500589. Guesthouse and 1-4 bedroomed apartments, fully equipped, TV, phone, kitchens, group rates on request, backs on to police station. **L-A** *Tuxedo Villas*, popular location, T4528553, F4528577. **B** *Blue Lagoon*, PO Box 637, T4508453. Rooms and cottages, restaurant and bar, lovely gardens. **B** *Glencastle Resort*, Massade, on hillside overlooking Rodney Bay, PO Box 143 Castries, T4500833, F4500857. New, luxurious, good value for money, a/c, pool, 17 rooms, restaurant. Only snag is that it is opposite small, detention centre, but does not matter really, complimentary daily shuttle to Reduit or Pigeon Island beach. **B-D** *B&B Hotel*, on Gros Islet highway, Massade, PO Box 497, T4508689, F4508134, within walking distance of Marina, beaches and Pigeon Island causeway. A/c, fans, kitchenettes in some rooms, noisy at night with loud music. **C-E** *Alexander's Guesthouse*, T4508610, F4508014, a new building on Mary Thérèse St, one min from beach. Clean, safe, friendly, helpful, kitchen, credit cards accepted. **D** *Bay Mini Guest House*, Bay St, painted bright orange, the only guesthouse on village beach, T4508956. Minimum stay 2 nights, spacious rooms, fan, bathroom, two studios with kitchenettes, run by Klaus Kretz, speaks German and English. **D** *La Panache*, PO Box 2074, T4500765, F4500453, augustinh@candw.lc, on Cas-en-Bas Rd. Run by Henry Augustin, helpful and friendly, also Roger, who can give information on Atlantic beaches and coastal walking, bird watching tours (whether staying there or not), includes tax and service, 7 rooms, 2-bedroom apartment, own bathroom, fridge, some with cooking facilities, hot water, insect screens, clean, fans, pleasant hillside gardens with plants labelled, good meals, breakfast daily US$3-8, tasty créole dinners some evenings US$11 or dinners can be ordered from outside, snacks during day, bar with excellent alcoholic and non-alcoholic cocktails, laundry EC$10 per load, no food Friday nights when everyone goes to *Jump-up*. Highly recommended. **D-E** *Nelson's Furnished Apartments* on Cas-en-Bas Rd, T4508275. **D-E** *Daphil's*, Marie Thérèse St, T4509318, F4524387. Basic, fan, very noisy Fri nights, close to 'jump-up'.

Coubaril   B-C (per person) The Benedictine nuns have 22 rooms with private bathrooms, a/c, fans, dinner and breakfast included, in a lovely wooded setting, tranquil, secluded, 15 min easy walk along wooded road to frequent public transport. To get there, head south to the Morne junction at the Shell station, then right turn down hill, take second right to the nunnery, T4521282, the chapel is packed for Christmas Eve mass, the nuns serve refreshments afterwards.

Marigot Bay AL *The Inn On the Bay*, PO Box 387, Castries, T4514260, F4514264, www.saint-lucia.com Only 4 rooms, spacious, overlooking Marigot Bay, great view from pool and balcony, breakfast included, tours and car hire arranged, run by friendly Normand Viau and Louise Boucher. Next door and just before you fall off the cliff, is **AL-C** *Cliff House*, T4514241, www.cliff-house.com Owned by Alice Bagshaw of silk screen factory, 2 rooms, bed and breakfast, spectacular view, can rent whole house, car hire and airport transfers arranged, both properties along half mile unpaved road, away from Marigot Bay activities, secluded, beautiful views.

Soufrière A-C *Khayere Pann*, T4597441. Walking distance from shops and beach, MAP, airport transfers, quiet, friendly, great views, wonderful atmosphere, library, cheaper in loft without bath. **B** *Chez Camille*, 7 Bridge St, T4595379, clean and friendly, family room available, kitchen, good restaurant attached (does takeaways). **D** *Soufrière Sailing Club Guest House*, T4597194. 4 rooms, meals available, no credit cards. **D-E** *Home Guesthouse*, T4597318, on the main square. Clean, pay cash, TC's not accepted. **E** Peter Jackson rents a double room in his house on the edge of Soufrière, PO Box 274, T4597269. Basic but good, full cooking facilities, Peter is friendly and helpful.

Lack of good, cheap accommodation, most appear to charge about US$30 for a basic room without private facilities

East coast B-C *Foxgrove Inn*, T4553271, F4553271. 12-bedroomed hotel, on hillside with view of Praslin Bay and Fregate Islands, beach 2 km, pool, nature trails, riding stables, good food, breakfast included, half board available, discounts for long stay, owned by Mr and Mrs Louis-Fernand, new conference room for 100 has view to Atlantic. **C** *Manje Domí*, 5 km south of Micoud, T4550729. Guesthouse with restaurant and bar, turn at Anse Ger junction, 1½ km to guesthouse on top of hill. 4 rooms, each with patio, screens, fans, very low-key, countryside setting, excellent breakfast included, meals are seafood, fresh local vegetables, fruits, pleasant, the name means 'good eating, good sleeping' in Kweyol, and it lives up to its name.

Vieux Fort A-B *Sky Way Inn*, T4547111, F4547116. Restaurant, nightclub, pool, shuttle service to airport and beach. **B** *Juliette's Lodge*, Beanfield, PO Box 482, Vieux Fort, T4545300, F4545305. 16 rooms, a/c, TV, bathroom, all with ocean view, restaurant, bar, 10 min to beach, close to airport, run by Juliette and Andrew Paul, friendly, helpful. **D** *Kimatrai Hotel*, Vieux Fort, 5 min from Hewanorra, T4546328. Restaurant, also has self-catering apartments with good view of sea but little else of note. **D-F** *St Martin*, T/F4546674, on main street. Clean, friendly, cooking and washing facilities.

B *Cloud's Nest Apartments*, Vieux Fort, T4546711. 1-3 bedroom apartments. **L-B** *Villa Beach Cottages*, Choc Beach, T4522691, F4525416. No credit cards. **C** *Dornelly's Inn*, Box 1733, Balata PO, T4525561, F4519261. 2 miles from Castries at Balata on Allen Bousquet Highway to Babonneau, 12 fully furnished 2-bedroom apartments with kitchenettes, balconies, cable TV, phone, fan, minibus to town stops outside, long-term rates negotiable. Villa rentals for short or long terms can be arranged, usually with maid service and car hire: *Barnard Sons & Co*, Bridge St, PO Box 169, Castries, T4522216, F4531394. *Property Shop*, Rodney Bay, T4508288, F4500318. *Tropical Villas*, Cap Estate, Box 189, Castries, T4508240, F4508089. *Marlin Quay*, PO Box 2204, Gros Islet, T4520393, F4520383. On the waterfront in Rodney Bay, a villa resort offering a variety of rooms, studios and 1-2 bedroomed terraced villas, very comfortable and spacious, well equipped, views over lagoon, some with jacuzzi on roof, decks, verandas. Highly recommended for families or couples, restaurants attached, 2 pools, one small, one 40 ft long for exercise swimming.

Apartment hotels & villas
There are several apartment hotels & villas for rent. Full details from tourist offices

Not recommended, not encouraged, particularly on beaches, no facilities, lots of sandflies and very strong land crabs which could break into your tent!

Camping

Eating

All the large hotels have a selection of restaurants and there are snack bars and restaurants all along the west coast. Most places add on a 10% service charge, the menu usually specifies and it is rarely left to your discretion. Street vendors: Mr Emilio by the bus stop on Peynier St, across from the Courthouse, Castries, for ice cream, EC$2.50 for a cup. Snokone ice cream vendors roam the beach and streets, a cup of ice cream should cost EC$2.50. In Castries cold drinks are sold on street corners, EC$1 for a coke, drink it and return the bottle. Coconut water sold by vendors is always refreshingly cool and sterile. Drink from the coconut. For other foods such as bakes, floats, fish, chicken, dal rotis (split pea), be sure that they are freshly cooked for the best flavour.

Castries *Kimlans*, Derek Walcott Square, T4521136. Upstairs café and bar with verandah, cheap, serves local food, open 0700-2300 Mon-Sat. *Café Panache*, on Derek Walcott Square, next door to the Central Library on Bourbon St, in the 100-year old former home of Nobel Laureate Sir Arthur Lewis. Downstairs is the cocktail lounge and buffet breakfast and lunch, popular with locals, upstairs is the high class dining room, more expensive, for evening meals, looking out over the square, good food, amiable service, moderate prices. *Chung's*, on the corner of Coral and Brazil Street, upstairs above Starlite, T4521499. Open 1100-2000 or so, pleasant and airy, good food, inexpensive, for EC$16.50 you get soup, 3 choices from the menu and coffee, MSG used in a few dishes, if you don't want it, say so, will also cater for allergies, such as wheat, just ask, everything delicious. Recommended. *Aft Deck*, La Place Carenage, T4521902. Harbour view, top floor, popular for lunch. *Royal Castle*, Bridge St, near Barclays Bank and the Post Office. New fast food outlet, joint venture from Trinidad and competition for *KFC*, good chicken and fries, not such heavy breading as *KFC*. *Flamingo*, William Peter Blvd. Favourite local place for a cheeseburger (EC$6.50) or roti, open until about 1600, closes about 1200 on Sat, not pretty but that's OK, for a chicken roti specify you want it without skin and bones, which the St Lucians eat. *Quick Bite*, on Mongiraud, adjacent to the S&S building, T4523063. Vegetarian salad bar and takeaway, specializes in soya meals. There are about 10 good value local eateries in the street adjoining the central market, tables outside, heaped plates of local food, lunchtime only.

South of Castries On the Top of the Morne, *Bon Appetit* is recommended for its daily specials and spectacular views, but is not cheap, meals from EC$35, T4522757. Also on the Morne, *San Antoine*, T4524660. A plantation great house, lovely gardens, elegant dining room, closed until mid-2001. In the same area *The Green Parrot*, T4523399. 4-course dinner EC$95, serves excellent lunches daily, lots of Caribbean specialities and good selection of tropical vegetables, have a cocktail in the lounge before dinner, the chairs are worth it alone, shows Wednesday, Saturday, ladies' night Monday.

North of Castries *D's Restaurant*, Edgewater Beach Hotel, T4537931. Indoor or on patio, relaxing setting on beach, good selection on menu, mainly lunch time, creole special EC$20. Recommended. *Froggie Jack's*, tucked away at Vigie Cove, T4525142, riouxj@candw.lc Great views of harbour at sunset, open for lunch and dinner, run by former executives at *Anse Chastenet* and *Jalousie*. *Coal Pot*, outstanding, at Vigie Marina, T4525566. French chef, the place to eat at the moment, reservations essential, lunch and dinner except Saturday when dinner only, closed Sunday. Next to it is the little *Café au Lait*, which does takeaway, T4530959. *Vigie Beach Bar*, beside *Rendezvous Hotel* serves good rotis and inexpensive cold beers; in Gablewoods Mall there are a selection of fast food outlets open from 0800-2100 daily: Southeast Asian, pizza, ice cream. *Tiggis*, T4524815, a/c, very good food and service, popular for lunch but dinner looks like leftovers, open Mon-Sat 0830-2200, soups, meals, baguettes, sandwiches, desserts, free salad bar with all dinners, choose your own fresh sauce. *Miss Saigon* next door, T4517309. Serves full English breakfast, EC$18, Chinese and Oriental lunch and dinner, open daily. *Friends* at Casa Vigie, first floor, just below the Venezuelan embassy. Patisserie and café, very good sandwiches, attractive, open Mon-Thu, Fri 1000-2400, Sat 1000-1800, lovely walk from here to the Vigie lighthouse. *Waves* restaurant, bar and dancing at Choc Bay, short distance past Gablewoods Mall. Beach setting, very pleasant. *En Bas Bwapen Creole Kitchen*, behind a galvanized fence at the bend in the Castries to Gros Islet road as it runs by the airport runway, T4521971. Breakfast and lunch, very local, most expensive meal EC$10 with local juice. *BJ's Pepper Pot*, along the main road in Marisule, about halfway between Castries and Rodney Bay, T4501030. Speciality is Jamaican cooking, prices up to EC$18, open Tue-Sat, from 1100.

Memories of Hong Kong, opposite *Royal St Lucian* hotel, T/F4528218. Chinese chef from Hong Kong, expensive but excellent, you can inspect the kitchens, open Mon-Sat 1700-2230. Same owners also run *Thai Royal*, opposite Scotia Bank, T4529249. Open Mon-Sat 1700-2230, private dining room available. *The Lime* serves good meals and snacks at moderate prices, T4520761. Friendly, open from 1100 till late, closed Tue. *Triangle Pub*, across from *the Lime*, T4520334. Open daily 1100-late, local food and barbecue, eat in or take out, live bands, pan, jazz. *Buzz* opposite *Royal St Lucian*, T4580450. Open for lunch, dinner, Sunday brunch, closed Mon. *Razmataz*, opposite *Royal St Lucian*, T/F4529800. Indian, good, friendly, open from 1600, closed Thu. *Pizza Pizza*, T4528282. Waterside garden dining, not very good pizzas. *Shamrock's Pub*, T4528725. 6 TVs, pool tables, darts, pub grub, open daily. *Capone's*, is a restaurant in the speakeasy style of the 1920s, open for dinner only and quite expensive, but attached to a *pizzeria*, open from 1100, both closed Sun-Mon, with prices starting at EC$12, T4520284. *Charthouse*, T4528115. Closed Sun, known for its steak, seafood and spare ribs, excellent rib steak. *Miss Saigon*, T4517309. Southeast Asian cuisine, good, open daily. *Snooty Agouti*, night place with jazz/blues, gourmet coffee, cocktails, food, gooey desserts, breakfast waffles, art gallery, boutique, book swap, backgammon, Internet, open until midnight. Further along the road and directly on the beach at Reduit is *Spinnakers*, T4528491. Breakfast, lunch and dinner daily, with full English breakfast EC$26, happy hour 1800-1900, excellent location, though food and service suffer when it is busy, good too for coffee and desserts, they also hire out loungers for EC$5 per day. *Key Largo*, on the highway, T4520283. New building, wide patio, not interested in serving between lunch and dinner, delicious, authentic, huge Italian pizzas, reasonably priced, if you like hot food ask for the hot sauce, but be careful! *Mel's & HH's*, between *Islander* and *Pepper's*, T4520363. Traditional English pub food, Sunday roast beef and Yorkshire pudding, steak and kidney pie, Cornish pasties, etc, closed Mon, open from 1230. In the marina complex is *The Bread Basket* for breakfast or lunch, open Mon-Sat 0730-1700, Sun 0730-1200. *The French Restaurant*, at the marina, waterfront, T4500022. French Créole cuisine, seafood a speciality, open daily 1600-2400, reservations advisable, free entrance to *Le Chalet* night club with dinner receipt. *Three Amigos*, also at the marina, T4520351. Mexican restaurant and bar, daily poolside Mexican barbecues, open from 0700. *The Bistro*, close to marina, seafood a speciality, also English pub grub and daily specials, happy hour drinks, nice setting on waterfront, open daily except Thu from 1700, T4529494. Opposite is *Burger Park and Miniature Golf*, T4520811, open 1100-2200, closed Thu, eat in or take out, good selection including vegetarian, playground, 18-hole miniature golf. *Mortar and Pestle*, T4528711. Waterfront bar and restaurant, mini-mart, dinghy dock, at *Harmony Marina Suites*, open daily 0700-2300, live entertainment Tue, Thu, Sat. About 1km past the Gros Islet turnoff is *T's Place*, bright little red and white Coca Cola signs cover most of the building. Open Mon-Fri 0600-1800, full meals EC$10-12, Fri barbecues.

Rodney Bay

The Great House Restaurant, T4500450. Traditional tea from 1630-1730 is worthwhile for watching the sunset, and affordable, happy hour 1730-1830, dinner expensive, 1900-2200, closed Mon.

Cap Estate

Several hotels for lunch and dinner, but *JJ's Restaurant and Bar* on the road down to the bay is a cheaper alternative, T4514076. Specializes in fresh local dishes and seafood, open from 1000 till late, Wed night recommended, reasonably priced crayfish, crab and lobster (in season), Fri night jam session. *Chateau Mygo*, T4524772. St Lucian-Indian cuisine, open daily 0700-1100, serves traditional hot bakes and cocoa tea for breakfast, credit cards accepted, reservations advised. *Shack Bar & Grill*, open daily from 1500, dinner 1830-2200.

Marigot Bay

Windward Islands

Soufrière *The Still* specializes in authentic St Lucian dishes, T4597224. Open daily 0800-1700 it is not cheap but serves local vegetables grown on site. *Spotlight* near *Home Guesthouse* and Barclays Bank. Good local food, tuna and kingfish recommended, lunches and dinners EC$16-25. *Jacquot*, on Church Street, try the Jacquot Special cocktail. *The Humming Bird* is a good place to eat and take a swim, T4597232. French, Créole and seafood, daily specials, disappointing food, good views, open from 0700. *Dasheene*, at *Ladera Resort*, T4597323. Good food, award-winning Austrian chef cooks with local produce, wonderful views, worth coming here even if only for a drink just for the views. Recommended. The *Purity Bakery* near the church in the main square serves breakfast with good coffee, rolls and cakes. *Le Haut Plantation* on the west coast road 1 km north of Soufrière. Huge TV in sports bar, open 1000-2100, also 6 rooms, small. At Étangs Soufrière, on the road to Vieux Fort, is *The Barbican* restaurant and bar, T4597888. Run by the very welcoming Mr and Mrs Smith, local food at local prices, good home cooking, not sophisticated, but clean, popular. *The Old Courthouse*, T4595002. Bar, restaurant, batik gallery, French Créole and Southeast Asian dishes, waterfront dining, open daily, credit cards.

Vieux Fort *Il Pirata*, T4546610, Italian restaurant on the beach, prices from EC$25, attached to a motel, open Tue-Sun 0700-2130. Close to Hewanorra airport and near *Club Aquarius* by sign for beach cottages to rent is the *Annex*, T4546200. Open from 0900 to midnight weekdays, 1000-0200 weekends, good food. *Sandy Beach* restaurant and bar on the beach and on the highway .Excellent location, delightful stopping place, good food, a bit overpriced but not dreadful, have a swim and lunch. *Sapphire*, near bus station, opposite football pitch. Good local food at low prices, run by Frenchman who brought his mother from France to cook, she speaks no English or Patois.

Festivals *Carnival* is a high point in the island's cultural activities, when colourful bands and costumed revellers make up processions through the streets. After some debate it was decided to move Carnival in 1999 from Febuary to **July**, partly so as not to conflict with Trinidad's Carnival. On the Saturday are the calypso finals, on Sunday the King and Queen of the band followed by J'ouvert at 0400 until 0800 or 0900. On Monday and Tuesday the official parades of the bands take place. Most official activities take place at Marchand Ground but warming-up parties and concerts are held all over the place. Tuesday night there is another street party.

There is lots of music, dancing & drinking. Everything goes on for hours, great stamina is required to keep going

    Independence Day is **22 February** and is celebrated quite extensively. There is a large exhibition lasting several days from the various ministries, business and industry, and NGOs, such as the National Trust, and various sporting events, serious discussions and musical programmes. On the Sunday preceeding 1 **May**, the *Festival of Comedy* is held at Pigeon Point (Cultural Centre if it is raining), organized by the National Trust. The annual *St Lucia Jazz Festival* in **May** is now an internationally recognized event, drawing large crowds every year. Most concerts are open-air and take place in the evening, although fringe events are held anywhere, anytime, with local bands playing in Castries at lunchtime. As well as jazz, played by international stars, you can hear Latin, salsa, soca and zouk, steel drums or Bob Marley. For more details www.stluciajazz.com Tickets from US$35 or a season pass US$230. On 29 June St Peter's Day is celebrated as the Fisherman's Feast, in which all the fishing boats are decorated. The *Feast of the Rose of Lima* (Fét La Wòz), on **30 August**, and the *Feast of St Margaret Mary Alacoque* (La Marguerite), on **17 October**, are big rival flower festivals. Members of the societies gather in various public places around the island to dance and sing in costume. The first Monday in **October** is *Thanksgiving*, held either to give thanks for no hurricane or for survival of a hurricane.

    Another very interesting festival is *Jounen Kweyol* (Creole Day), on the last Sunday in **October**, although activities are held throughout the month. Four or five rural communities are selected for the celebration. There is local food, craft, music and different cultural shows. Expect traffic jams everywhere that day because people like to visit all the venues across the island. A lot is in kweyol/patois, but even without basic language skills you will have a good time and a chance to sample mouth-watering local food.

    St Cecilia's Day, held on **22 November**, is also known as *Musician's Day* (St Cecilia is the patron saint of music). *St Lucy's Day*, 13 December, used to be called Discovery Day, but as Columbus' log shows he was not in the area at that time, it was renamed (see page

809). It is now known as the National Festival of Lights and Renewal. St Lucy, the patron saint of light, is honoured by a procession of lanterns. For details contact Castries City Council, T4522611 ext 7071.

Most of St Lucia's nightlife revolves around the hotels, while some restaurants host live bands. The choice varies from steel bands, jazz groups, folk dancing, crab racing, fire eating and limbo dancers. The hotels welcome guests from outside. In May, nightlife is dominated by the annual jazz festival with lots of outdoor concerts. **Nightlife**

Around Rodney Bay, venues like *The Lime* are popular places for those who just want to hang out. *Indies* is a nightclub and disco (over 21s) next to the *Bay Gardens Hotel*, Rodney Bay, and *Le Chalet*, near the Rodney Bay Marina are the hot spots. *Back Door@Indies* is also good, a good selection of Caribbean and international music can be heard, depending on the night, look out for specials, Wed package for US$15 includes admission, free drinks and round trip taxi to nearby hotels, EC$20 cover charge Fri and Sat, free shuttle bus from major hotels, late night happy hour 2200-2400. *Café Panache*, on the square in Castries and *Annex* in Vieux Fort have live music regularly, the former also encourages local poets. *JJ's*, Marigot, casual, good mixture of locals and tourists, Caribbean music in simple disco, Fri can be very busy, Sat pleasantly so, frequent shows, live bands, karaoke, taxi service can be arranged, T4514076. The highlight of the week, for locals and visitors however, is Fri night's jump up at Gros Islet, where it is hard to resist getting involved. For a more cultural evening, tours are available to La Sikwi, patois for sugar mill, at Anse La Raye. There is a visit to the 150 year-old mill, followed by a full costume play reliving life in the village on a stage set into the hills with jazz bands and local acts.

There are (irregular) **shows**: concerts, drama, dance, comedy, at the National Cultural Centre (Castries), the *Light House Theatre* (Tapion) and the *Great House Theatre* (Cap Estate). They can give you a better taste of St Lucian culture than hotel shows which are adapted to international taste. Contact the Department of Culture for programmes as shows are often poorly advertised. Tickets available at the Department of Culture and Sunshine Bookstore (Gablewoods Mall). International stars also give performances, eg Seamus Heaney, Vladimir Ashkenazy and Lesley Garrett gave readings/concerts in 1999-2000.

There are now **cinemas**: at the Julian's supermarket building in the Rodney Bay area, and at Julian's supermarket, Vieux Fort, usual showings 2000 and 2200, some highly rated films.

Pointe Seraphine, next to the main port in Castries, is a designer-built, **duty-free** shopping centre (same opening hours as other shops, so closed Sat afternoon), with many tourist-oriented outlets, restaurants, entertainment and tour operators. **Shopping**

In the centre Llewellyn Xavier has an art gallery selling his own work as well as an interesting range by other artists including Derek Walcott and Canute Caliste (see page 811). Goods bought here can be delivered directly to the airport. Cruise ships can tie up at the complex's own berths.

Batik fabrics and cotton clothing from *Caribelle Batik* on Old Victoria Road, The Morne and Bridge Street; Bagshaw's silk screening workshops at La Toc, T4522139, are very popular, studio open Mon-Fri 0830-1630, Sat 0830-1200, also shops at *Marigot* and *Windjammer*; souvenirs from Pointe Seraphine, Hewanorra duty-free and Soufrière; high quality local crafts and paintings from *Artsibit*, corner of Brazil and Mongiraud Streets, open Mon-Fri 0900-1700, Sat 0930-1300. *Eudovics Art Studio*, T4522747, in Goodlands, coming down from the Morne heading south, sells local handicraft and beautiful large wood carvings. Daniel Jean-Baptiste makes hand-painted, limited edition, silk artwork, call T4508000 for a private studio visit. Perfume from *Caribbean Perfumes*, by *Green Parrot*, T4537249. *Peppers*, large store in Rodney Bay, next to *Mel's* opposite new JQ Mall, toys, souvenirs, T-shirt printing, custom designs, US$3.40.

Sunshine Bookshop, Gablewoods Mall, books, foreign newspapers and magazines, open Mon-Fri 0830-1630, Sat half day; *Book Salon*, Jeremie Street on corner of Laborie Street, good selection of paperbacks, several books on St Lucia, also stationery. *Rodney Bay Shipping Services* runs a book exchange, 2 for 1, mostly spy thrillers and light novels, not a huge selection, but useful. *Garden Gate Flowers* has takeaway boxes (cargo transport) and bouquets (hand luggage) of pink and red ginger, heliconia, anthuriums, 48 hrs notice required for export, US$12-30, at *Bois D'Orange* T4529176, at *Hewannora* T4547651, F4529023.

Windward Islands

Market day in Castries is Sat, very picturesque (much quieter on other days, speakers of Patois pay less than those who do not). A new public market has been built on the Castries waterfront, with the old market building renovated and turned into a craft market. *Wire World*, booth 3, charming figures by the award-winning Paulinus Clifford, T4538727, also at Pointe Seraphine, he and the next artisan, Augustus Simon, a potter, T4521507, will craft to order. Buy a coal-pot (native barbecue) for EC$12 and bring it home on your lap. Buy a cocoa stick or 10 for US$5. To make hot chocolate, put two tablespoons of grated cocoa in a pan with half a pint of water and boil for 15 min, strain, then add dry milk, sugar, cinnamon and nutmeg to taste. There is a new *Fisherman's Co-operative Market* on the John Compton Highway at the entrance to Pointe Seraphine. Many fishermen still sell their catch wherever they can. Fish is cheap and fresh. *JQ's* supermarket at the traffic lights at the end of the Vigie runway, open Mon-Fri 0800-1900, Sat 0800-1600, bank next door, fair range of goods, also supermarket on the William Peter Boulevard. Wholesale meat from *Chicken Galore* behind Shell station on Manoel Street. *Gablewoods shopping Mall*, between Rodney Bay and Castries, has a selection of boutiques, gift shops, book shop, post office, pharmacy, deli, open air eating places and *Julian's Supermarket*, open Mon-Thu until 2000, Fri, Sat until 2100. Next door is a delicatessen with a choice of frozen and defrosted foods. A few doors away is the *Sea Island Cotton Shop*, the outlet for Caribelle Batik clothes. On the way to Gros Islet from Castries turn left just after the Texaco station for the studio *Zaka's*, where masks and totems are carved from driftwood collected along the Atlantic coast or discarded lumber off-cuts found in the forest. Prices from EC$140, open Mon-Fri 1000-1500, T4520946, also available from *Snooti Agouti* in Rodney Bay. Rodney Bay Marina has a variety of shops: *Pieces of Eight* has a good choice of gifts, although few are made in St Lucia; *Le Marché de France* Supermarket is one of the few to open on Sunday morning; the *Bread Basket* sells excellent fresh loaves, sandwiches and cakes. Soufrière has a market on the waterfront. At Choiseul, on the southwest coast, there is an art and craft centre, T4593226, but it is rather dated.

Transcript *If leaving the country temporarily with electronic equipment such as computers, register the goods at the airport to avoid problems on return*

Air St Lucia has two airports: **George F Charles Airport** (formerly Vigie) (T4521156), for inter-island flights only (two miles from Castries, taxi for EC$20, no exchange facilities), and **Hewanorra International Airport** (T4546355) in the Vieux Fort district, where international flights land; there is an air shuttle to Vigie by helicopter, 12 mins, US$90. Alternatively a taxi to Castries costs EC$150 (though, out of season, you can negotiate a cheaper rate) and it will take you 1½-2 hrs to reach the resorts north of Castries. A new service is the St Lucia Air Shuttle, run by *Paradise Tourist Services*, Rodney Bay, behind *Julian's supermarket*, by reservation only, US$17.50 one way, US$33 round trip, per person, credit cards accepted, T4529329, F4580979, www.stluciatip.com If you are travelling light you can walk to the main road and catch the minibus or route taxi to Castries, or if you are staying in Vieux Fort you can walk there, but be careful of the fast traffic. No baggage storage yet available at Hewanorra. Try to arrange it with one of the Vieux Fort hotels.

Boat Captain Artes of the S/H *Krios*, Rodney Bay Harbour, runs a boat taxi (sailing) service: to Martinique, three days, US$220 plus customs charges, Customs officers will contact his boat for you. Highly recommended, even for the seasick. Ferries around the island include: *Rodney Bay Ferry* shuttles between the marina shops, *Marlin Quay, St Lucian Hotel, Mortar and Pestle* and *Pigeon Island*, fares within the marina US$4 return, children under 12 half price, T4520087, F4528816, also half day trips to Pigeon Island including lunch, US$40, bookings at the Yellow Hut by the entrance to the *Lime Restaurant's* car park. The *Gingerbread* express in Marigot Bay costs EC$2 return, but is refunded by *Doolittle's Restaurant* if you eat or drink there and present your tickets.

Bus There are several bus stands in Castries: those going to Gros Islet and Rodney Bay leave from behind the market on Darling Road; to Dennery from the Customs shed on Jeremie Street; to Jacmel, Marigot (be prepared to walk over steep hill as few buses turn off into the bay), Bois D'Inde and Roseau Valley from Victoria Street; to Vieux Fort from Jno Baptiste Street off Darling Road. From Castries to Vieux Fort, EC$7; to Choc Beach, EC$1; to Soufrière, EC$7; to Dennery EC$3; to Gros Islet EC$2; to Morne Fortune EC$1.25; from Gros Islet to

Rodney Bay EC$1; from Soufrière to Vieux Fort EC$4; children half price. Ask the driver to tell you when your stop comes up, they are usually co-operative.

Car Car hire starts at about US$50-60 per day, jeep rental is US$70 per day, US$295-390 a week; if you hire for eight days you will be charged for one week and one day. Insurance is another US$15-20 per day. A 5% tax is added to everything. A temporary licence costs EC$30. If arriving at George F L Charles (formerly Vigie) airport, get your international licence endorsed at the immigration desk (closed 1300-1500) after going through Customs. Car hire companies can usually arrange a licence. Car rental agencies include *Avis*, Vide Bouteille (T4522700, F4531536) and lots of other locations; *Hertz* headquarters at Rodney Bay (T4520680, F4528980), rates from US$55; *Budget*, in Castries, airport and Marisule T4520233, F4529362; *Gibin* at Rodney Bay Marina, T4529528, has Suzuki jeeps US$70 and cars US$45-70, manual or automatic, a/c or not. Most have offices at the hotels, airports and in Castries. Check for charges for pick-up and delivery. If dropping off a car at George F L Charles airport you can sometimes leave the keys with the tourist desk if there is no office for your car hire company. Filling stations are open Mon-Sat 0630-2000, selected garages open Sun and holidays 1400-1800. Leaded fuel costs EC$6, unleaded EC$6.50.

It is often cheaper to organize car hire from abroad. You can only hire a car if aged 25 or over

Water taxis and **speedboats** can be rented. Wayne's Motorcycle Centre, Vide Bouteille, T4520680. Rents **bikes**; make sure you wear a helmet and have adequate insurance, potholes are everywhere.

Taxi Fares are supposedly set by the Government, but the EC$160 Castries-Soufrière fare doubles as unlucky tourists discover that there are no buses for the return journey. *Club St Lucia*, in the extreme north, to Castries, about 10 miles away, costs EC$40-50 one way for 1-4 people, EC$10 per additional passenger. Fare from Castries to Gros Islet (for Friday evening street party), EC$32; to Pigeon Island National Park, EC$42 one way; to Vigie airport, EC$13; to Hewannora airport, EC$150; Vigie airport to Rodney Bay EC$43; Marigot Bay to Hewanorra airport EC$120; to Vigie airport EC$60, to Castries EC$53 (30 mins). If in doubt about the amount charged, check with the tourist office or hotel reception. You can see a copy of the fixed fares at the airport. At rush hour it is almost impossible to get a taxi so allow plenty of time, the traffic jams are amazing for such a small place. A trip round the island by taxi, about US$20 per hour for 1-4 people, can be arranged with an additional US$5 per hour for a/c. Recommended taxi drivers are Kenneth James, T4536844, 4519778 and Raymond Cepal, pager T4843583.

Always agree the fare before you get in

Airlines The following airlines have offices on Brazil St, Castries: *LIAT* (T4523051, or at Hewanorra airport T4546341, or George F Charles (Vigie) airport T4522348, F4536584); *Air Canada* (T4523051, at Hewanorra T4546249); *Air Jamaica* at Hewanorra, T4548869, reconfirmations only; *British Airways* is at Cox and Co Building, William Peter Boulevard (T4523951, F4522900 and at Hewanorra T4546172); *Air Martinique*, George F Charles Airport (T4522463); *American Eagle* at George F Charles airport, T4521820/1840; *American Airlines* ticket office on Micoud near Bridge St, no phone; *Helenair*, at George F Charles airport, T4527196, F4527112. *St Lucia Helicopters* at Pointe Seraphine, T4536950.

Directory

Banks *Bank of Nova Scotia* (T4522292), *Royal Bank of Canada* (T4522245), *Canadian Imperial Bank of Commerce* (T4523751), all on William Peter Blvd, Castries; *Barclays Bank* (T4523306), and the *St Lucia Co-operative Bank* (T4522881), on Bridge St, *National Commercial Bank*, Waterfront (T4522103), Castries. *Barclays*, *CIBC*, *National Commercial Bank* and *St Lucia Co-operative Bank* have branches in Vieux Fort, and Barclays and National Commercial Bank in Soufrière; *Barclays* and *Royal Bank of Canada* (T4529921) at Rodney Bay marina. **NB** Banks opening hours vary, but most are open 0800-1500 Mon-Thu, 0800-1700 Fri. Barclays Bank and Royal Bank of Canada at Rodney Bay open Sat until 1200, as does the National Commercial Bank in Castries.

Communications Post: Main post office is on Bridge St, Castries, open Mon-Fri, 0830-1630, Sat, 0800-1200, poste restante at the rear. Fax and photocopying facilities upstairs. Postcards to Europe EC$0.50, to the USA EC$0.40; letters to Europe EC$1.10, to the USA and UK EC$0.95. The DHL office is on Bridge St. **Telephone:** the island has an adequate telephone system, with international direct dialling, operated by Cable and Wireless, Bridge St, Castries. There is a sub-office on New Dock Rd, Vieux Fort.

Windward Islands

Fax facilities at both offices. Hotels do not generally allow direct dialling, you will have to go through the operator, which can be slow and costly. Intra-island calls are EC$0.27 in the Castries zone, EC$0.45-0.75 to other zones, depending on time of day and day of week. Pay phones use EC$0.25 and EC$1 coins. Cable and Wireless phone cards are sold for EC$10, EC$20, EC$40 or EC$53; with these you can phone abroad. There is a credit card phone at Vigie airport operated via the boat phone network, open daily 0800-2200. The International code for St Lucia is 758. Call USA T1-800-6747000; Sprint Express T1-800-2777468; BT Direct T1-800-3425284; Canada Direct T1-800-7442580; USA Direct phone at Rodney Bay Marina, or T1-800-8722881. If you want to dial a toll-free US number, replace the 800 with 400. You will be charged a local call. **Internet** *Snooty Agouti* (Rodney Bay) is the first 'cyber café' with one terminal (EC$20 per 30 mins). There are also internet services at the *Gablewoods Mall* office of Cable & Wireless, where there are several terminals, EC$7.50 for 30 mins and also in the University Centre.

Cultural centres *Alliance Française de Sainte Lucie*, in the pyramid at Pointe Seraphine, T4526602, courses and cultural events, library etc. *Bonsai Society* meets every 2nd Thu of the month, 1700, contact Mary Charles, T4501258.

Embassies & consulates *Danish* Consulate, Cap Estate Golf Club, PO Box 328, Castries, T4508522/3, F4508317. Embassy of the *Republic of China*, Cap Estate, Gros Islet, PO Box GM 999, T4520903, F4529495. *French* Embassy, Clarke Avenue, Vigie, T452-2462/5877, F4527899. *Italian* Vice Consul, Reduit, PO Box GM 848, T4520865, F4520869. *Netherlands* Consulate, M & C Building, Bridge St, PO Box 1020, Castries, T4522811, F4523592. *Organization of American States*, Vigie, T4524330. *Organization of Eastern Caribbean States*, Morne Fortune, T4522537. *UK*, British High Commission, NIS Building, Waterfront, PO Box 227, Castries, T4522484, F4531543, open Mon-Fri 0830-1230. *Venezuelan* Embassy, Casa Vigie, PO Box 494, Castries, T4524033, F4536747, open Mon-Fri 0900-1430.

Language schools Spanish lessons at all levels at the *Venezuelan Institute*, Sans Souci, T4522555. Patois lessons at the Folk Research Centre, T4522279.

Tour companies & travel agents Most hotels will arrange tours (US$40-80) to the island's principal attractions around Soufrière either by road, boat or helicopter. Coach tours are cheaper and are usually daily in high season, falling to once or twice a week off season. Alternatives are to go by boat (easy between Castries and Soufrière, some hotels have their own boats: *Anse Chastanet, Jalousie Plantation, Windjammer Landing* and *Sandals*) or by helicopter (recommended for a spectacular view of the sulphur springs). From Pointe Seraphine a north island helicopter tour costs US$40, 10 mins; south island US$80, 20 mins; a heli-hike with tour of Atlantic beaches and Cactus Valley US$65, T4500806; helicopters can also be hired for airport transfers, US$85 from Pointe Seraphine to Hewanorra, also pick-up from some hotels, St Lucia Helicopters, PO Box 2047, Gros Islet, T4536950 and Eastern Caribbean Helicopters, PO Box 1742, Castries, T4536952 at Vigie airport. Local tour operators offer highly recommended plantation tours; Errard, Marquis and Balenbouche offer fascinating insights into colonial history and local environments. A tour of a working banana plantation, US$50, is recommended, you see a lot of the country and see and taste a lot of native fruit and vegetables. There are now ten sites which comprise the St Lucia Heritage Tourism Programme, T4516220, including La Tille Falls, Fond d'Or Nature and Historical Park, Fond Lattisab Creole Park and the Folk Research Centre. Costs vary from EC$5-30, depending on the activities offered. More are being developed. St Lucia Distillers has an excellent rum factory tour with tasting, shop for purchases, south towards Marigot, T4514258. You can take a carriage ride through the north of the island, or spend an evening cruising into the sunset with as much champagne as you can drink. There are also day trips to neighbouring islands: Dominica US$215, Grenadines including sail, US$199, Barbados US$225 and others. The National Trust runs excursions to Maria Island and Fregate Island Reserve, see Fauna and flora, above. The main tour agencies are *St Lucia Reps/Sunlink Tours*, T4528232, F4520459, www.stluciareps.com. *Spice Travel*, T4520866, www.casalucia.com; *Solar Tours*, T4519041; *Barnards Travel*, T4522214. In Vieux Fort *is Rainbow Option Tours & Services*, run by Nadine Edwards (T4548202), Paula Edwards (T4549156) and Julius James (T4545014). *ATV Adventures* have guided ATV rides, T4526441, F4522810, mctours@candw.lc, PO Box 99, Castries. **Maps** of the island may be obtained from the Land Survey in the last government building. At 1:50,000 they are the best but not 100% accurate. Ordnance Survey, Romsey Rd, Southampton, UK (T01703-792792), produce a map of St Lucia in their World Maps series which includes tourist information such as hotels, beaches, climbing and climate. The Tourist Board map is free.

Tourist offices *St Lucia Tourist Board*, Pointe Seraphine, PO Box 221, Castries, St Lucia, T4525968, F809-4531121, www.stlucia.org. There are Tourist Board information centres at the Pointe Seraphine Duty-Free Complex; George F Charles Airport (most helpful but closed for lunch 1300-1500), T4522596; Hewanorra Airport (very helpful, particularly with hotel reservations, only open when flights are due or leave), T4546644 and Soufrière (very helpful, local phone calls free), T4597419. *The Tropical Traveller* is distributed free to hotels, shops, restaurants etc every month and contains some extremely useful information. The St Lucia Hotel and Tourism Association publishes a tourist guide, *Visions of St Lucia*, PO Box 545, Castries, T4525978, F4527967, also of a high standard and widely available.

Background

History

Even though some St Lucians have claimed that their island was discovered by Columbus on St Lucy's day (13 December, the national holiday) in 1502, neither the date of discovery nor the discoverer are in fact known, for according to the evidence of Columbus' log, he appears to have missed the island and was not even in the area on St Lucy's Day. A Vatican globe of 1520 marks the island as Santa Lucía, suggesting that it was at least claimed by Spain. In 1605, 67 Englishmen en route to Guiana made an unsuccessful effort to settle though a Dutch expedition may have discovered the island first.

At this time the island was inhabited by Caribs. There are Amerindian sites and artefacts on the island, some of which are of Arawak origin, suggesting that the Caribs had already driven them out or absorbed them by the time the Europeans arrived, as no trace of the Arawaks was found by them. The Indians called their island Iouanalao, which may have meant: where the iguana is found. The name was later changed to Hiwanarau and then evolved to Hewanorra. In 1638 the first recorded settlement was made by English from Bermuda and St Kitts, but the colonists were killed by the Caribs about three years later.

In 1642 the King of France, claiming sovereignty over the island, ceded it to the French West India Company, who in 1650 sold it to MM Houel and Du Parquet. There were repeated attempts by the Caribs to expel the French, several governors were murdered. From 1660, the British began to renew their claim to the island and fighting for possession began in earnest. The settlers were mostly French, who developed a plantation economy based on slave labour. In all, St Lucia changed hands 14 times before it became a British Crown Colony in 1814 by the Treaty of Paris.

From 1838, the island was included in a Windward Islands Government, with a Governor resident first in Barbados and then Grenada. Universal adult suffrage was introduced in 1951. The St Lucia Labour Party (SLP) won the elections in that year and retained power until 1964. The United Workers' Party (UWP) then governed from 1964-79 and from 1982 onwards. In 1958 St Lucia joined the West Indies Federation, but it was short-lived following the withdrawal of Jamaica in 1961-62 (see page 312). In 1967, St Lucia gained full internal self-government, becoming a State in voluntary association with Britain, and in 1979 it gained full independence.

From 1964 until 1996 the UWP was led by Mr John Compton, who held power in 1964-79 and subsequently won elections in 1982, 1987 and 1992. In 1996 Mr Compton retired as leader of the UWP (subsequently receiving a knighthood in the 1997 UK's New Year's Honours List) and was replaced as Prime Minister and leader of the party by Dr Vaughan Lewis, former Director General of the Organization of Eastern Caribbean States (OECS), who led the party into the 1997 elections. The leader of the SLP, Julian Hunte, resigned after his party's poor performance in the by-election which brought Dr Lewis into parliament. He later announced his intention of standing as an independent in the 1997 general elections. He was replaced by Dr Kenny Anthony.

The May 1997 elections were a triumph for the SLP, who had been in opposition for 25 years apart from a brief period in 1979-82. They won 16 of the 17 seats, with the UWP gaining the single remaining seat, a result which took even the SLP by surprise. The new government's priorities were to diversify the economy, create employment, conduct an audit of public spending and investigate corruption claims.

In 1998, the UWP unanimously elected Sir John Compton (73) as its leader again after Dr Vaughan Lewis declined the nomination, but Sir John later resigned and Dr Vaughan Lewis is now the leader.

Government

St Lucia is an independent member of the Commonwealth and the British monarch is the Head of State, represented by a Governor General (Dame Pearlette Louisy, the first woman to hold the post). The 17-member House of Assembly is elected every five years, while the 11 members of the Senate are appointed by the Governor General, six on the advice of the Prime Minister, three on the advice of the Leader of the Opposition and two of his own choice. The Constituency Boundaries Commission has recommended that the number of constituencies is increased from 17 to 19 in time for the general elections to be held by 2002.

The economy

St Lucia's economy has historically been based on agriculture, originally sugar, but since the 1920s particularly on bananas and also cocoa and coconuts. It has the largest banana crop in the Windward Islands. Banana exports rose from 99,000 tonnes in 1991 to 135,000 tonnes in 1992 but fell back to 108,830 tonnes in 1993, were drastically cut by storm damage in 1994 and after recovery in 1995-96, slumped to 65,197 tonnes in 1999. The industry has suffered because of low prices; strikes by farmers have caused further damage, and in 1994 the St Lucia Banana Growers Association (SLBGA) was put into receivership with debts of EC$44 mn. The SLBGA was returned to the control of growers in 1996 with changes in the composition and accountability of its board. The association sought assistance from several financial institutions and aid agencies but the SLP government elected in 1997 pledged to pay off its debts and transform the SLBGA into a company, owned and managed by farmers. Privatization of the SLBGA was completed in 1998 and it is now known as the St Lucia Banana Corporation. Greater competition in the European banana market, particularly after EC unification in 1992, is leading to diversification away from bananas; dairy farming, flowers and fisheries are being encouraged. A five-year Social Recovery and Poverty Alleviation Programme, financed mostly by the EU will support improvements in housing sanitation, health care, adult education and community development for groups like banana farmers who are affected by changes in the economy.

There is also some industry, with data processing and a diversified manufacturing sector producing clothing, toys, sportswear and diving gear, and 14% of the workforce is now engaged in manufacturing. However, unemployment in the manufacturing sector rose sharply in 1996 with the closure of three foreign-owned garment factories, which had been operating for nearly 10 years, the period during which tax-free concessions are granted. Since then, more companies have closed (garments, informatics) and jobs lost. The island is promoted as a location for industrial development within the US Caribbean Basin Initiative. An oil transshipment terminal has been built and the Government has set up several industrial estates. There are plans to establish a free zone at Vieux Fort, where a new deep water container port was opened in 1993. Public sector investment in large scale infrastructure projects includes electricity expansion and road construction.

Tourism is now a major foreign exchange earner, and some 250,000 visitors stay on the island each year. St Lucia is one of the few Caribbean islands to show consistent, although slowing, growth in tourism. Europeans, who stay longer than Americans, are now the largest and fastest growing segment of the market, making nearly 40% of the total compared with 36% North Americans. There are over 3,000 hotel rooms, of which the eight all-inclusive resorts of the 12 major hotels account for almost half. Further expansion is taking place with a new Hyatt hotel in the north of the island and a 350-room hotel and marina to be built by the Jamaican Superclubs chain, is planned for the south, near Hewanorra airport. Small hotels and restaurants have suffered a reported 75% drop in business since the growth of all-inclusives. The Atlantic Rally for Cruisers was changed from Barbados, its original venue, to Rodney Bay, St Lucia in 1990 and this brings revenue of about US$2 mn to the tourist industry. Cruise ship passengers have also shown steady increases. Although the number of calls has fallen, larger ships accounted for the rise.

Culture

There is a good deal of French influence. Most of the islanders, who are predominantly of African descent (though a few black Caribs are still to be found in certain areas), speak Creole/Kweyol, a similar language to French, and in rural areas many people, particularly the older generation, have great difficulty with English. There is a French provincial style of architecture; most place names are French; about 79% of the population are Roman Catholics. The French Caribbean also has an influence on music, you can hear zouk and cadance played as much as calypso and reggae. The Folk Research Centre (see box) has recorded local music. *Musical Traditions of St Lucia* has 32 selections representing all the musical genres, with information on the background of the various styles. *Lucian Kaiso* is an annual publication giving pictures and information on each season of St Lucian calypso. In the pre-Christmas period, small drum groups play in rural bars which sometimes are no bigger than a banana shed. Traditionally, singers improvise a few lines about people and events in the community and the public joins in. The singing is exclusively in Kweyol, wicked and full of sexual allusions. The dance moves also differ from what you see at other events. It is difficult to find out where and when the drums are playing, seek local knowledge. Some announcements are made on Radio St Lucia in the Kweyol programme.

One of the Caribbean's most renowned poets and playwrights in the English language, **Derek Walcott**, was born in St Lucia in 1930. He has published many collections of poems, an autobiography in verse, *Another Life*, critical works, and plays such as *Dream on Monkey Mountain*. Walcott uses English poetic traditions, with a close understanding of the inner magic of the language (Robert Graves), to expose the historical and cultural facets of the Caribbean. His books are highly recommended, including his narrative poem *Omeros*, which contributed to his winning the 1992 Nobel Prize for Literature. In 1997 he published *The Bounty* (Faber & Faber), his first collection of poems since winning the Nobel Prize, full of sadness at the loss of friends but rejoicing in homecoming and his island. Walcott is also a prolific painter, which was his first love, and his watercolours can be found (and bought from his home) on the island. Other St Lucian writers worth reading are the novelists **Garth St Omer** (for instance *The Lights on the Hill*) and Earl Long (an MD in the USA), and the poets Jane King-Hippolyte, Kendal Hippolyte, John Robert Lee and Jacintha Lee, who has a book of local legends.

St Lucia has also produced painters of international renown. **Dunstan St Omer** was born in St Lucia in 1927 into a Catholic family and is best known for his religious paintings. He created the altarpiece for the Jacmel church near Marigot Bay, where he painted his first black Christ, and reworked Castries Cathedral in 11 weeks in 1985 prior to the Pope's visit. St Omer and his four sons have also painted other countryside churches (Monchy and Fond St Jacques) and a quarter of a mile of sea wall in Anse La Raye. **Llewellyn Xavier** was born in Choiseul in 1945 but moved to Barbados in 1961, where he discovered painting. He moved to England in 1968,

☞ *Patois for beginners*

Until recently, Kweyol was not a written language but it has been developed to facilitate teaching.

For people interested in learning a few phrases of Créole, or Kweyol, there is a booklet, Visitors Guide to St Lucia Patois, *available for EC$14 in bookshops, Valmont's Book Salon on the corner of Jeremie and Laborie Streets by the Tourist Office, and Sunshine Books in Gablewoods Mall and Rodney Bay.*

For the more ambitious reader there are traditional story booklets which explain a lot about country life. Short stories are written in a style a child can understand with an English translation at the back. Examples are Mwen Vin Wakonte Sa Ba'w *(I am going to explain it to you), which has a tale for every letter of the alphabet about an animal starting with the same letter, or* Se'kon Sa I Fèt *(know how it is done), a book about farm life. These*

books, part of a series of 8 aimed at a St Lucian readership, are not available in shops. Contact the Summer Institute of Linguistics, Box 321, Vieux Fort, price around EC$5 each.

The Folk Research Centre (PO Box 514, Mount Pleasant, Castries, T4522279, F4517444, open Monday-Friday 0830-1630) preserves and documents the local culture and folklore and has published several books, a cassette (EC$30) and CD (EC$60): Musical Traditions of St Lucia. A Handbook for Writing Creole *gives the main points and features, while a* Dictionary of St Lucian Creole *and* Annou Di-Y an Kweyol, *a collection of folk tales and expressions in Creole and English, accompany it well.*

In 1999 the New Testament was published in Kweyol.

With thanks to Ulrike Krauss.

where he created Mail Art, a new concept in modern art involving many well-known personalities around the world. Galleries in North America and Europe have exhibited his work and his paintings are in many permanent collections. Xavier returned to St Lucia in 1987, where he was shocked by the environmental damage. He has since campaigned vigorously for the environment through his art. *The Global Council for Restoration of the Earth's Environment* is a work created from recycled materials including prints, postage stamps and seals and logos of preservation societies. It is on permanent display at the artist's studio, T4509155 for an appointment.

Other outstanding artists include **Ron Savory**, Ron's Atelier and Framing Co, Vide Bouteille Industrial Park, just past the roundabout at the end of the airport runway (called La Clery junction), T4524412. His rich rainforest scenes and his dancing figures are impressive and he sells collectables, souvenir art, paintings from originals to limited prints to prints, expensive to inexpensive. **Sean Bonnett St Remy** paints wonderful local scenes, village scenes with nostalgic charm and accuracy, he can be contacted at Photographic Images, 42 Brazil Street. **Winston Branch** is splashy, modern abstract, and shows internationally from London to Brazil. He is currently teaching in the USA. **Chris Cox** paints St Lucian birds, such as the parrot and the nightjar. He won an award at the Arts Award ceremony in January 2000 and can be contacted at Forestry. **Arnold Toulon**'s Modern Art Gallery in Bois d'Orange, T4529079, also exhibits local artists including **Cedric George** and **Nancy Cole,** along with his own works. **Alcina Nolley**, an artist and teacher of art, can refer you to many artists and artisans, particularly of the Arts and Crafts Association, T4532338, nolleym@candw.lc

The last week in January is Nobel Laureate Week, with lectures celebrating the two Nobel prize winners produced by the island (Sir Arthur Lewis and Derek Walcott). They were both born on 23 January. Other events include the annual Arts Awards, during which the Cultural Centre is packed. www.stlucia-arts.com is a new website

St Vincent and the Grenadines

St Vincent, and its 32 sister islands and cays which make up the Grenadines, were until fairly recently, almost unknown to tourists except yachtsmen and divers. They remain uncrowded. St Vincent is very picturesque, with fishing villages, coconut groves, banana plantations and fields of arrowroot, of which the island is the world's largest producer. It is a green and fertile volcanic island, with lush valleys, rugged cliffs on the leeward and windward coasts and beaches of both golden and black volcanic sand. The highest peak on the island is La Soufrière, an active volcano in the north rising to about 4,000 ft. It last erupted in 1979 but careful monitoring enabled successful evacuation before it blew. The steep mountain range of Morne Garu rises to 3,500 ft and runs southward with spurs to the east and west coasts. Most of the central mountain range and the steep hills are forested. St Vincent is roughly 18 miles long and 11 miles wide and has an area of 133 square miles, while the Grenadines contribute another 17 square miles all together.

Windward Islands

Ins and outs

There are no direct services from Europe or North America but same day connecting flights are available through Antigua, Barbados and Puerto Rico. *American Eagle* flies from San Juan, Puerto Rico. *LIAT* flies from Antigua, Barbados, Beef Island (BVI), Grenada, Port of Spain (Trinidad), St Lucia, St Maarten, San Juan (Puerto Rico). *BWIA* flies from Barbados and Port of Spain. *Helenair* from Grenada, Trinidad, St Lucia and Union Island; *Air Guadeloupe* from Fort-de-France, continuing to Union Island and Canouan. **Union Island** is reached by *LIAT*, *Helenair*, *Mustique Airways* and *Air Guadeloupe* from Carriacou, Fort de France, Grenada, St Lucia and St Vincent. **Canouan** receives *Air Guadeloupe* flights from Fort de France, St Vincent and Union Island. Inter island charters are also operated by *SVGAIR*, *Mustique Airways* and *Aero Services*, may be economical for a group. **ET Joshua airport**, small and rather chaotic, is two miles from Kingstown. The taxi fare to town is EC$20 (with other fares ranging from EC$15-40 for nearer or more distant hotels set by government); minibus to Kingstown EC$1.50, 10 mins. Frequent and easy minibuses also run east if you need to get to Young Island or Calliaqua. In the Grenadines there is a new airport on Bequia, a new airport on Union Island, a private airport on Mustique and a small, private airport on Canouan. If your luggage is lost en route to St Vincent, obtain a Property Irregularity Report (PIR) from the airline otherwise you will have to keep coming back to the airport to check if it has arrived.
Sea *Windward Lines Ltd* operates a passenger and cargo ferry service on the *MV Windward* from Trinidad on Thu afternoon, arriving St Vincent Fri 0730, departing 1000 for Barbados-St Lucia-Barbados arriving back in St Vincent Mon 0700 and leaving for Trinidad 1600 (occasional visit to Bequia) with a following service to Güiria, Venezuela or Pampatar, Margarita, see page 25. In Kingston, the offices of Windward Lines are up a steep flight of steps from the ferry. You can check bags at the supermarket near the dock while you visit their offices or look for accommodation and save yourself the effort of carrying them.

Getting there
See transport, page 827, for further details

Air Flights within the Grenadines are cheap but prices rise if travelling to or from another country, for example Carriacou or St Lucia. *Mustique Airways* flies daily from St Vincent to Port Elizabeth, Bequia, a five-minute flight, twice daily Mon-Fri to Union Island (20 mins), and also to Mustique. Both Inter-island flights and the ferry can be erratic and sometimes leave early or fail to appear at all. **Sea** If economizing it is worth considering boat travel internationally, for example from Union Island to Carriacou. See page 828. **Road** Minibuses from

Getting around
Check in for flights a good hour before departure

Kingstown leave from the Little Tokyo Fish Market terminal to all parts of St Vincent island, including a frequent service to Indian Bay, the main hotel area; they stop on demand rather than at bus stops. At the terminal they crowd round the entrance competing for customers rather than park in the bays provided. They are a popular means of transport because they are inexpensive and give an opportunity to see local life. No service on Sunday or holidays. On Bequia, buses leave from the jetty at Port Elizabeth and will stop anywhere to pick you up, a cheap and reliable service. **Car** Driving is on the left. A local driving licence, costing EC$40, must be purchased at the airport, the police station in Bay Street, or the Licensing Authority on Halifax Street, on presentation of your home licence. However, there is no need to pay if you have an International Driving Permit and get it stamped at the central police station. There are limited road signs on St Vincent. **Cycling** is rewarding but be careful in the north, which is a drug producing area. The ride between Layon and Richmond is a strenuous four hours one way, but absolutely spectacular. Expect long, steep hills and lots of them.

St Vincent

Not to scale

Temperatures the year round average between 77°F and 81°F (25-7°C), moderated by the **Climate** trade winds; average rainfall is 60 inches on the coast, 150 inches in the interior, with the wettest months May to Nov. Best months to visit are therefore Dec to May. You can expect a shower most days, though. Low season is Jun to mid-Dec.

Flora and fauna

St Vincent has a wide variety of tropical plants, most of which can be seen in the **Botanical Gardens**, where conservation of rare species has been practised since they were founded in 1765. There you can see the mangosteen fruit tree and one of the few examples of *spachea perforata*, a tree once thought to be found only in St Vincent but now found in other parts of the world, as well as the famous third generation sucker of the original breadfruit tree brought by Captain Bligh of the *Bounty* in 1793 from Tahiti. Other conservation work taking place in the gardens involves the endangered St Vincent parrot, *Amazona guildingii*, which has been adopted as the national bird. An aviary, originally containing birds confiscated from illegal captors, now holds 12 parrots. In 1988 the first parrot was hatched in captivity and it was hoped that this was the first step towards increasing the number on the island, estimated at down to only 500. This mostly golden brown parrot with a green, violet, blue and yellow-flecked tail, spectacular in flight, is found in the humid forests in the lower and middle hills on the island. The main colonies are around Buccament, Cumberland-Wallilabou, Linley-Richmond and Locust Valley- Colonarie Valley. Their main enemy is man, who has encroached into the forest for new farming land and exploited the bird's rarity in the illegal pet trade, but they have also suffered severely from hurricanes and volcanic eruptions such as in 1979. They are protected now by the Wildlife Protection Act, which covers the majority of the island's birds, animals and reptiles and carries stiff penalties for infringements. A parrot reserve is being established in the upper Buccament Valley.

Another protected bird unique to St Vincent is the whistling warbler, and this, as well as the black hawk, the cocoa thrush, the crested hummingbird, the red-capped green tanager, green heron and other species can be seen, or at least heard, in the Buccament Valley. There are nature trails starting near the top of the Valley, passing through tropical forest, and it is possible to picnic. The **Vermont Nature Trail** can be reached by bus, from the market square in Kingstown to the road junction in Peniston near the *Emerald Valley Hotel and Casino*; the sign for the trail is not clearly marked. It is a long walk through the village to the trail, but rewarding in the views of village and rural life. If travelling by car, look for the Vermont Nature Trail sign about one mile past Questelles. The car park, at 975 ft, is close to the Vermont Nature Centre. Get a trail map from the information hut on the right. A guide is not necessary unless you want scientific information as you walk along this marvellous trail. El Roy is a recommended tour guide with an extensive knowledge of the flora and fauna in the area. There is a rest stop on the trail, at 1,350 ft, and a Parrot Lookout Platform at 1,450 ft. It is a beautiful trail, through thick forest and is probably the best place to see the St Vincent parrot. Be prepared for rain, mosquitoes and chiggars, use insect repellent. Anyone interested in nature trails should visit the Forestry Department (in the same building as the Land and Survey Department), who have prepared official trail plans, published in conjunction with the Tourism Department. A pamphlet details the Vermont Nature Trails, Wallilabou Falls, Richmond Beach, Trinity Falls, Falls of Baleine, Owia Salt Pond and La Soufrière Volcano Trails. The tourist office may also have a supply of pamphlets.

Diving and marine life

The underwater wildlife around St Vincent and the Grenadines is varied and beautiful, with a riot of fish of all shapes and sizes. There are many types and colours of coral, including black coral at a depth of only 30 ft in places. On the New Guinea Reef

Essentials

Documents All visitors must have a passport and an onward, or return, ticket. Nationals of the UK, USA and Canada may enter for up to six months on proof of citizenship only. As well as the three countries already mentioned, citizens of the following countries do not need a visa: all Commonwealth countries, all the EU countries (except Eire and Portugal), Chile, Finland, Iceland, Liechtenstein, Norway, Switzerland, Sweden, Turkey, Uruguay, Venezuela. You will be asked where you will be staying on the island and will need a reservation, which can be done through the Tourist Office at the airport, before going through immigration (or you can make one up). If you are only given entry of a few days and want to stay longer, extensions are easily obtained for EC$20.

Customs 200 cigarettes, or 50 cigars, or 250 grams of tobacco, and 40 fluid ounces of alcoholic beverage may be imported duty free.

Currency The East Caribbean dollar, EC$.

Departure tax There is a departure tax of EC$30, or US$12.50.

Ports of entry (Own flag) Wallilabou, on the northwest coast, Kingstown, Bequia (police station), Mustique and Union Island (airport, EC$10 weekdays during working hours, EC$25 overtime, holidays and weekends). Yachtsmen often anchor at Blue Lagoon or Young Island and bus/taxi to Kingstown to complete customs and immigration formalities. Fees are EC$10/US$4 per person (EC$25 on Saturday on Union Island) and charter yachts are charged US$2 per feet per month. For an exit stamp, go to the airport customs and immigration one day before departure.

Anchorages On Bequia the local businesses cater to the boating community, delivering water, fuel, laundry, beer and groceries. Men and boys meet yachts in the northern St Vincent anchorages and ask to assist in tying stern line to a tree or offer other services. EC$7 is the current fee for tying up; other services negotiable. Others meet boats in Bequia, Union and the Tobago Cays, offering to supply bread, ice, vegetables, fruit, lobster, or conch (lambi) as well and selling T shirts and jewellery. They can take 'no' for an answer, but will return if you say 'maybe tomorrow'. Anchorages at Wallilabou, Young Island, Petit Byahaut, Blue Lagoon, Bequia, Palm (Prune) Island, Mustique, Canouan, Mayreau (Salt Whistle Bay and two others), Tobago Cays, Union Island (Clifton, Frigate Island, Chatham Bay), Petit St Vincent. **Marinas** at Caribbean Charter Yacht Yard, Lagoon Marina, Bequia Slipway, Anchorage Yacht Club on Union Island. **Moorings** at Young Island, Blue Lagoon, Friendship Bay, Union Island, Palm Island, Petit Byahaut (US$10 fee is deducted if

(Petit Byahaut) you can find three types of black coral in six different colours. The coral is protected so do not remove any. There are 10 marine protected areas including the northeast coast and the **Devil's Table** in Bequia, **Isle de Quatre**, all **Mustique**, the **east coast of Canouan**, all of **Mayreau**, the **Tobago Cays**, the whole of **Palm Island**, **Petit St Vincent** and the surrounding reefs. Spearfishing is strictly forbidden to visitors and no one is allowed to spear a lobster. Buying lobster out of season (1 May-30 September) is illegal as is buying a female lobster with eggs. Fishing for your own consumption is allowed outside the protected areas. Contact the Fisheries Department for more information on rules and regulations, T4562738.

There are facilities for **scuba diving**, **snorkelling**, **deep sea fishing**, **windsurfing** and **waterskiing**, with instructors for novices. There is reef diving, wall diving, drift diving and wrecks to explore. The St Vincent reefs are fairly deep, at between 55 to 90 ft, so scuba diving is more rewarding than snorkelling. Dive sites include **Bottle Reef**, **the Forest**, **the Garden**, **New Guinea Reef** and **the Wall**. In Kingstown Harbour there are three wrecks at one site, the *Semistrand*, another cargo freighter and an ancient wreck stirred up by Hurricane Hugo, as well as two cannons, a large anchor and several bathtubs from the old wreck. **Bequia** is also considered excellent, with a leeward wall and 30 dive sites around the island and nearby, reached by boat *you have dinner), Mustique (pay at Basil's Bar, EC$40). For possibilities of crewing on yachts, check the notice board at the Frangipani Yacht Services, Bequia.*

Hours of business *Shops: 0800-1200, 1300-1600 Monday-Friday (0800-1200 only, Saturday); **government offices**: 0800-1200, 1300-1615 Monday-Friday; **banks**: 0800-1200 or 1300 Monday-Friday, plus 1400/1500-1700 on Friday. The bank at the Airport is open Monday-Saturday 0700-1700.*

Official time *Atlantic Standard Time, four hours behind GMT, one hour ahead of EST.*

Voltage *220/240 v, 50 cycles, except Petit St Vincent and Palm Island, which have 110 v, 60 cycles.*

Media *Newspapers The Herald is daily and contains news from wire services, including pages in French, Italian, Spanish et cetera. Three newspapers, The Vincentian, Searchlight and The News, are published weekly. The News is editorially independent and by far the best.*
Radio *Four radio stations: AM 705kHz, Nice FM 96.3, Hitz FM 107.3, WE FM 99.9. Weather can be heard on SSB weather net 4001 at 0800, 8104 at 0830.*
TV *Two TV stations and Krib cable (26 channels).*

Tourist offices overseas *UK 10 Kensington Court, London W8 5DL, T020-79376570, F020-79373611.*
USA: 801 2nd Avenue, 21st floor, New York, NY 10017, T212-6874981, 800-7291726, F212-9495946 and 6505 Cove Creek Place, Dallas, Texas, 75240, T214-2396451, 800-2353029, F214-2391002.
Canada: Suite 504, 100 University Av, Toronto, Ontario M5J IV6, T416-9719666, F416-9719667.
Martinique: Karib Tourism Department, WID, Marketing and Promotion Office, 122 1er rue Victor Hugo, Fort-de-France 97200, T0596-638686, F0596-638886.

Clothing *Wear light, informal clothes, but do not wear bathing costumes or short shorts in shops or on Kingstown's streets.*

Laundry *Call on VHF, or phone, for Daffodils or several other companies to come and pick up. Laundrymat is available with several washers and dryers if you wish to do it yourself.*

Public holidays *1 January, Discovery and National Heroes Day (22 January), Good Friday and Easter Monday, Labour Day in May, Whit Monday, Caricom Day and Carnival Tuesday (in July), August Bank Holiday first Monday in August, Independence Day (27 October), Christmas Day and Boxing Day.*

---

within 15 minutes. The **Devil's Table** is good for snorkelling as well as diving. Other dive sites are *M/S Lirero*, the Wall off West Cay, the Bullet, the Boulders and Manhole. The best snorkelling is found in the Tobago Cays and Palm Island. There is snorkelling and diving around most of the other islands with at least one dive shop on each inhabited island. As well as the specialist companies, many of the hotels offer equipment and services for their guests and others.

There is a network of dive shops, some of which we list here: *Dive St Vincent* (Bill **Dive centres** Tewes) at Young Island Dock, PO Box 864, T4574714, F4574948, www.divest vincent.com, NAUI, PADI certification courses, camera rental, trips to Bequia and the Falls of Baleine; also on St Vincent are *Dive Fantasea*, at Villa Beach, offering dives around St Vincent and tours to the Grenadines, also snorkelling, T457-4477, F4575577, fantasea@ caribsurf.com

On the other islands are: *Friendship Divers*, near Bequia Beach Club on Friendship Bay, SSI and CMAS instruction, open daily, German and English speaking staff, T/F4583422, diveresidence@caribsurf.com; *Sunsports* at the Gingerbread complex has PADI/NAUI diving, sunfish and tennis (T4583577, F4573031, sunsport@carib surf.com). *Dive Paradise, Friendship Bay Hotel*, Bequia, T/F4583563, F4573115, www.paradisebequia.com, two dive boats, waterskiing, German and English speaking staff, no credit cards; *Grenadines Dive* (Glenroy Adams), at *Sunny Grenadines Hotel*, Clifton, Union Island, T458-8138, F4588122, gdive@caribsurf.com, VHF 16/68, rendezvous service in Tobago Cays and surrounding islands; *Blueway International*, at *Tamarind Beach Hotel*, instruction, rentals, boat trips and rendezvous service, T4588044, F4588851, VHF16, cantbh@caribsurf.com. Some operations offer 'yachties' discounts. A two-tank dive costs around US$90, snorkellers US$20, full scuba equipment rental US$45, open water certification US$435.

Beaches and watersports

St Vincent has splendid, safe beaches on the leeward side, most of which have volcanic black sand. The windward coast is more rocky with rolling surf and strong currents. All beaches are public. Some are difficult to reach by road, but boat trips can be arranged to the inaccessible beauty spots. Sea urchins are a hazard, as in many other islands, especially among rocks on the less frequented beaches. Nearly all the inhabited islands of the Grenadines have at least one beach, and often many more, some fringed with palm trees, others without any sun protection. As elsewhere in the Caribbean, the windward side is too rough for swimming, with heavy surf, while the leeward side of the islands has calm water, excellent for swimming, snorkelling or windsurfing. *Paradise Windsurfing*, Bequia, has five different locations and offers different levels of instruction, call Basil Cumberbatch, T4583222.

Sailing   Sailing is excellent, indeed it was yachtsmen who first popularized the Grenadines and it is one of the best ways to see the islands. You can take day charter boats, easily arranged through hotels, or charter your own boat. There is a variety of boats for skippered day charters. Talk to the operators about size and predicted wind conditions if you are inclined towards seasickness. The large catamarans are usually quite stable so that you will hardly know you are on a boat, but they take quite large groups. On Bequia the *Friendship Rose* schooner, T4583202 (0800-1700), 4583090 (1700-2000), F4573071; the 60 ft catamaran, *Passion*, highly recommended, US$60 for day trip to Mustique Tuesday, Thursday, US$75 to the Tobago Cays Wednesday and Sunday, US$75 to St Vincent and Falls of Baleine Friday, snorkelling and fishing gear on board, all drinks and excellent rum punch included, T4583884, F4573015, passion@caribsurf.com; *Pelangi* at *Hotel Frangipani*, T4583255, frangi@caribsurf.com; the *Quest*, a 44 ft CSY yacht offers day or long-term charters, T4583917; *Wind and Sea* in Clifton on Union Island offers day cruises, visiting Palm Island, Mayreau and the Tobago Cays with snorkelling and drinks included, T4588647.

Bareboat and crewed yachts are available through the Anchorage Yacht Club, Union Island, T4588221; *Barefoot Yacht Charters* (Blue Lagoon), have an American Sailing Association (ASA) sailing school and is the longest established charter company, T4569526, F4569238, www.barefootyachts.com; *Blue Water Charters* is at the *Aquatic Club*, Villa, T4561232, F4562382; *Nicholson Yacht Charters* for over 70 crewed yachts, T460-1530, in USA T800-6626066, F617-6610554. *Moorings*, *VPM* and *Star Voyager* have their base at Bougainvilla, Clifton, Union Island.

Yacht races include the **Bequia Easter Regatta**, in which there are races for all sizes and types of craft, even coconut boats chased by their swimming child owners or model sailing yachts chased by rowing boats. Everyone is welcome and there are crewing opportunities; you may find yourself crewing alongside the Prime Minister. There are other contests on shore and the nights are filled with events such as dancing, beauty shows and fashion shows. The centre of activities is the *Frangipani Hotel*, which fronts directly on to Admiralty Bay. The Canouan Yacht Race is in August.

Other sports   Many of the more expensive hotels have **tennis** courts but there are others at the Kingstown Tennis Club and the Prospect Racquet Club. On Bequia, tennis is offered at three hotels: *Friendship Bay*, *Spring* and *Plantation House*. *Sunsports* at the

Cricket Grenadine style

Cricket is played throughout the Grenadines on any scrap of ground or on the beach. In Bequia, instead of the usual three stumps at the crease, there are four, and furthermore, bowlers are permitted to bend their elbows and hurl fearsome deliveries at the batsmen. This clearly favours the fielding side but batsmen are brought up to face this pace attack from an early age and cope with the

bowling with complete nonchalance. Matches are held regularly, usually on Sundays, and sometimes internationals are staged. In Lower Bay v England, which Lower Bay usually wins, the visitors' team is recruited from cricket lovers staying in the area. Ask at De Reef; it is best to bat at number 10 or 11.

Gingerbread complex offers tennis and other sports. **Squash** courts can be found at the *Cecil Cyrus Squash Complex* (St James Place, Kingston, reservations T4561805), the *Grand View Beach Hotel* and the *Prospect Racquet Club*. **Horse riding** can be arranged at the *Cotton House Hotel*, Mustique and at the *Emerald Equestrian Centre* in Queensberry. Trail rides go up from the beach into the forest and mountains, T4587247, F4567578. Spectator sports include **cricket** (Test Match cricket ground at Arnos Vale, near the airport), **soccer**, **netball**, **volleyball** and **basketball**. Pick up games of basketball are played on St Vincent after 1700, or after the heat has subsided, at the Sports Complex behind the airport. Everyone is welcome, although it can get very crowded and there is only one court, arrive early. There is also a court in Calliaqua (same times), but it is right on the street. Players beware, fouls are rarely called, although travelling violations are. No one is deliberately rough but overall the game is unpolished, unschooled but spirited. For fun **running**, the Hash House Harriers meet on Sunday afternoon, contact Joe Sheridan, T4571310 (day) or 4584119 (night).

Kingstown

The capital, Kingstown, stands on a sheltered bay where scores of craft laden with fruit and vegetables add their touch of colour and noisy gaiety to the town. However, much land has been reclaimed and continuing dock works shield the small craft from sight, except at the north end of the bay. Looking inland from the bay, the city is surrounded on all sides by steep, green hills, with houses perched all the way up.

Sights

The Market Square in front of the Court House is the hub of activity. Market day is Friday and Saturday and very colourful with all the produce spread out on sacks or on makeshift tables. A new covered market has been built to replace the outdoor affair and make it more hygienic, extending from Upper Bay to Halifax Street. The shopping and business area is no more than two blocks wide, running between Upper Bay Street and Halifax Street/ Lower Bay Street and Grenville Street. There are quite a lot of new buildings, none of them tall. The government financial services building in front of the police station is large, modern, concrete and not particularly pretty. A Fish Market, built with Japanese aid, was opened in 1990 near the Police Headquarters. This complex, known as Little Tokyo, has car parking facilities and is the point of departure for minibuses to all parts of the island. It has a strange little turret which looks like a guard tower. The War Memorial, flanked by two small cannon, is being preserved. On Halifax Street at the junction with South River Road is the Old Public Library, an old stone building with a pillared portico. It is being renovated with French aid and will be the Museum of St Vincent. Alliance Française is in the basement. There are public toilets to the rear.

Around Market Square

The jetty At the jetty where the boats for the Grenadines berth, you can see island schooners loading and unloading, all of which is done by hand. The men throw crates from one to the other in a human chain; the whole business is accompanied by much shouting and laughter. When the banana boat is in dock, the farmers queue in their pick-ups to unload their boxes of bananas, and the food and drink stalls on the road to the Reception Depot do good business.

Cathedrals Kingstown has two cathedrals, St George's (Anglican) and St Mary's (Catholic). **St George's**, parts of which date from 1820, has an airy nave and a pale blue gallery running around the north, west and south sides. There is an interesting floor plaque in the nave, now covered by carpet, commemorating a general who died fighting the Caribs. Other interesting features include a memorial to Sir Charles Brisbane (1772-1829) who captured Curaçao and a miniature of the action. Plaques to the rich and the good line the walls, nearly all of which were carved in London. A lovely stained glass window in the south transept was reputedly commissioned by Queen Victoria on the death of her grandson. She took exception to angels in red rather than the traditional white and it was put into storage in St Paul's Cathedral. It was

Kingstown

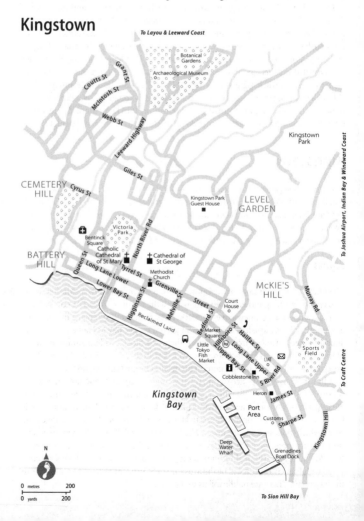

brought to St Vincent in the 1930s. **St Mary's** is of far less sober construction, with different styles, Flemish, Moorish, Byzantine and Romanesque, all in dark grey stone, crowded together on the church, presbytery and school. Building was carried out throughout the 19th century, with renovation in the 1940s. The exterior of the church is highly decorated but the interior is dull in comparison. There are pleasant, shaded courtyards outside with fish ponds in them. The Methodist church, dating from 1841, also has a fine interior, with a circular balcony. Its construction was financed largely through the efforts of freed slaves. There is a little bell tower at the south end, erected in 1907.

In Kingstown the Botanical Gardens just below Government House and the Prime Minister's residence are well worth a visit (for a description see above under Fauna and flora). Established in 1765, they are the oldest in the Western Hemisphere. In the Gardens, there is a very interesting **Archaeological Museum** of Amerindian artefacts, some of which date from about 4,000 BC. The most spectacular exhibit is the bat effigy. Outside is a collection of shrubs which may have been planted in a Carib garden. Anyone interested in St Vincent history, flora or fauna should talk to the curator, Dr Earle Kirby (Doc); he is very knowledgeable and friendly. Unfortunately, the museum is badly neglected and only open Wednesday morning 0900-1200 and Saturday afternoon 1500-1800. Dr Kirby is elderly and not always at the museum. Occasionally he will open the museum and give a personal tour for especially interested visitors. The Nicholas Wildlife Complex has parrots, agouti, Barbados Green Monkey and St Vincent Parrot, but not very well housed. The Gardens themselves are open 0600-1800 daily. They are about a 20-minute walk from the market square: go along Grenville Street, past the cathedrals, turn right into Bentinck Square, right again and continue uphill to the gate. Or take a bus, EC$1 from the terminal. You will be approached by guides who can explain which plant is which, very useful, otherwise you may miss some important plants and trees. There are notices specifying the official tour rates, so make sure you agree a price beforehand.

Botanical Gardens

Fort Charlotte (completed 1805) is on the promontory on the north side of Kingstown Bay, 636 ft above sea level, 15 minutes' drive out of town (EC$1.50 from bus terminal to village below, if you ask the driver he might take you into the fort for EC$1-2, worth it if it is hot). Although the fort was designed to fend off attacks from the sea, the main threat was the Black Caribs and many of its 34 guns (some of which are still in place) therefore faced inland. The gatehouse, 1806, was where Major Champion of the Royal Scots Fusiliers was killed on 13 October 1824 (see plaque in St George's Cathedral) by Private Ballasty. The murderer was executed at the scene of the crime. In the old barrack rooms, a series of paintings shows the early history of St Vincent. Painted by William Linzest Prescott in 1972, they suffer from poor lighting and their condition is deteriorating. There is also a coast guard lookout which controls the comings and goings of ships entering the port. Ask the guard to point out landmarks to you. Below, the ruins of a military hospital can be seen, as well as a bathing pool at sea level on the end of the point, used when the fort housed people suffering from yaws. The National Trust and the Caribbean Conservation Association (CCA) are proposing to develop Fort Charlotte as part of an Eastern Caribbean plan for historic military sites, with an Interpretive Centre, gift shop and museum. The National Trust of St Vincent and the Grenadines, PO Box 752, T4562591, has further information.

Fort Charlotte
The views of Kingstown & surroundings are spectacular. On a clear day the Grenadines & even Grenada are visible

Around the island

The highest peak on the island, La Soufrière volcano, rises to about 4,000 ft. In 1970 an island reared itself up out of the lake in the crater: it smokes and the water round it is very warm. Hiking to the volcano is very popular, but you must leave very early in the morning and allow a full day for the trip. About two miles north of Georgetown

La Soufrière & Mount St Andrew

(van from Kingstown to Georgetown EC$4, you can ask the driver to make a detour to the start of the trail for an extra charge) on the Windward side you cross the Dry River, then take a left fork and walk/drive through banana plantations to where the trail begins. A local guide is recommended, although not essential, always useful for carrying food and water as well as ensuring you do not get lost. It takes about three hours to reach the crater edge and it is a strenuous hike along a marked trail, the first three miles are through the Rabacca plantation, then up, along Bamboo Ridge and all the way to the crater's magnificent edge; the top can be cloudy, windy, cold and rainy, take adequate clothing and footwear. There is an alternative, unmarked and even more challenging route from the Leeward side starting from the end of the road after Richmond, but you will need a guide. After crossing a river delta, turn right into a ravine and climb; it will take about four hours. Guided tours usually on Tuesday and Thursday, about US$20-35, guides provide and carry drinks. If you want to avoid organized tours, a guide can be obtained in Georgetown. One such is Benjamin Hudson, who lives opposite Sadoo's Grocery. Leave an extra set of clothes in the van in case you get wet through. Take water and insect repellent.

An easier climb is up **Mount St Andrew**, near Kingstown. A tarmac track runs up to the radio mast on the summit of the peak, at 2,413 ft, passing first through banana and vegetable gardens and then through forest. There are no parrots but otherwise virtually all the species of birds which can be found on the Vermont Nature Trail. It is particularly good for the Antillean crested hummingbird and black hawks. The view from the summit covers the Grenadines and the Vermont and Mesopotamia valleys. To reach the track either take a van running along the Leeward Highway and ask to be put down at the junction with the Mount St Andrew road, or start your walk in Kingstown.

The Leeward coast There are few good roads, but cars, including self-drive, can be hired and most of the beauty spots are accessible by road. The Leeward Highway is a dramatic drive, passing through Questelles and Layou. Much of this road has been improved to **Barrouallie** (pronounced Barrelly), a small whaling village. This drive along the west coast towards La Soufrière should not be missed; it has been described as a 'tropical corniche'. There are lush valleys and magnificent seaviews. It is a very crumpled landscape. The road was upgraded significantly in 1993. The drive from Kingstown to the end of the road at Richmond takes about two hours.

The road leaves Kingstown and initially heads inland. There are views down into Campden Park Bay, where the East Caribbean Group of Companies has a deep water port complex and flour mill. The road passes through the small village of Questelles before rejoining the coast briefly at Buccament Bay and down into Layou where there are a few excellent examples of gingerbread houses.

There are some interesting **petroglyphs** and **rock carvings** dating back to the Siboney, Arawak and Carib eras. The best known are just north of Layou, carved on a huge boulder next to a stream. They can only be visited on payment of US$2 for the owner, Mr Victor Hendrickson to open the gate to the fenced off area. Ask the local children to show you his house and then the petroglyphs for a tip, well worth a visit.

Passing Mount Wynne and Peter's Hope, **Barrouallie** is the next village of any size. Here there is a petroglyph dated at 800 BC in the yard of the Anglican secondary school. The road also passes through the remains of a sugar mill (the furnace chimney is still standing) and then heads inland from the popular anchorage at Wallilabou Bay. A stone gateway marks the entrance to the **Wallilabou Falls** (Wally-la-boo). You can swim here but the falls are not much more than a spurt (2 m at the most). There are no changing rooms here. On the opposite side of the road is a nutmeg plantation. You can get there by car or by bus from Little Tokyo Fish Market to Barrouallie and walk from there.

The road goes inland along the Wallilabou valley before quickly rising over the ridge into the North Leeward district. From here onwards all the villages are clearly marked with good road signs. The pipeline from the hydroelectric scheme follows the road and is most visible at the aptly named Spring Village. Another pretty beach is reached at Cumberland and the road climbs quickly to Coulls Hill with perhaps the best view on the coast. The road through Chateaubelair (restaurant with nice deck, use their facilities to change for a swim and have a snack), skirting Petit Bordel with small islands offshore to **Richmond** and Wallibou beach is most attractive. However, in 2000 the road was washed out before Richmond, so check locally before setting out. There are some beach facilities at Wallibou.

Another set of falls, also on the Leeward side, is 20 miles north of Kingstown; **Petit Wallibou Falls** are a double waterfall in a very remote region and you can bathe at the bottom of the second waterfall. To get there, go through Richmond (if the road is repaired) and turn right up the side road beside the Richmond Vale Academy; follow this road for one mile, it then turns into a track for two miles. At the river the top of the waterfall is on your left. There is a steep climb on the left hand side of the waterfall to reach the pool where you can swim. **Trinity Falls** are 45 minutes' walk from Richmond in the Wallibou Valley, set deep in a canyon in the rainforest. The only known hot springs are in the canyon, having appeared since the last volcanic eruption. The road has been badly eroded and it is best to park about 40 minutes' walk from the car park, except that there is a lot of loose gravel and you may fall. From the car park it is another 45 minutes' walk to the Falls (reasonable physical fitness required), through lovely rainforest. There is a sign down the river warning about undertow, but note that this also applies to the pool by the Falls. The current is very strong, swimmers have been sucked under and the sides are steep, with nothing to hold on to. In addition, the wind erosion has loosened boulders which are now potentially dangerous.

A boat trip to the falls of **Baleine** (on the northwest coast) is recommended. Wading ashore and for a few minutes up a river which originates on Soufrière, you come to the falls. At their base are natural swimming pools. It is possible to reach the falls on foot, but the easiest way is to take an excursion by motor boat (for example with Dive St Vincent), which includes a stop for snorkelling, and a picnic lunch, for US$35-40. Sea Breeze Nature Tours uses a 36 ft auxillary sloop, not recommended if you get seasick, otherwise nice, includes snorkelling stop, rum punch but no lunch, Captain Hal Daize is an authority on the bottle-nosed dolphin and may find a school of them to watch, recommended, T4584969, seabreeze@vincy.com

The Queens Drive takes you into the hills south of Kingstown and gives splendid views all around. The Marriaqua Valley with its numerous streams is particularly beautiful. In the Valley, beyond Mesopotamia (commonly known as Mespo), the lush, tropical gardens of Montreal are worth a visit; anthuriums are grown commercially there. **The Windward coast**

The road meets the **Windward Highway** at Peruvian Vale. It gets progressively drier as the road goes north hugging yellow sandstone cliffs which contrast with the white waves surging in towards the black volcanic beaches. A number of banana packaging stations are passed especially around Colonarie. There is a particularly impressive view of the coast just after the Black Point tunnel. The tunnel is 350 ft long and was constructed by Colonel Thomas Browne using Carib and African slaves in 1815. It was blasted through volcanic rock and the drill holes are still visible. It provided an important link with the sugar estates in the north. **Georgetown** is almost like a ghost town, with one or two quite well maintained houses, the rest haven't been painted for years. It is an economically depressed area since the sugar mill closed a few years ago. The houses are covered by black volcanic grit which gives it a very gloomy feel. A number of houses have been abandoned. There are lots of churches. The Anglican church is a miniature of St George's Cathedral in Kingstown.

The road to **Sandy Bay** (beyond Georgetown), where St Vincent's remaining Black Caribs live, is now good, however you have to cross the Dry River, a jumble of rocks, grit, rubbish and dead wood swept down from the mountains above, which sometimes is not dry and therefore not passable. Sandy Bay is poor but beyond it is an even poorer village along a rough dirt road, **Owia**. Here is **Salt Pond**, a natural area of tidal pools filled with small marine life. The rough Atlantic crashes around the huge boulders and lava formations and is very picturesque. The villagers have planted flowers and made steps down to the Salt Pond area. There is also an arrow-root processing factory which can be visited. Past Owia is **Fancy**, the poorest village on the island, also Black Carib and very isolated, reached by a rough jeep track which makes a pleasant walk. A project to bring electricity to the northern villages is under way with French financial assistance. Baleine Falls (see above) are a two mile hike from here around the tip of the island, rugged and not recommended for the unadventurous. Fishing boats can be hired in Fancy to collect you (do not pay in advance).

The southeast of the island is drier and has different vegetation and birdlife. Take a van running to Stubbs and alight at the post office by the Brighton road junction. Walk into Brighton village and find a guide who can lead you to see, among others, the mangrove cuckoo, smooth-billed ani, broad-winged hawk and green heron. When tidal conditions are right it is possible to cross to Milligan Cay. To see seabirds in the bay visit early morning or late afternoon.

Young Island A tiny, privately-owned islet, 200 yds off St Vincent. Pick up the phone at the crossing to see if you will be allowed over. **Fort Duvernette**, on a 195-ft high rock just off Young Island, was built at the beginning of the 19th century to defend Calliaqua Bay. To visit it, arrangements must be made with the hotel, who will provide a guard to accompany you. The 100 steps up to the fort have been partially washed away by hurricanes. There is a lovely lagoon swimming pool, surrounded by tropical flowers. **LL** *Young Island Resort*, P O Box 211, T4584826, F4574567, www.youngisland.com; all accommodation in cottages (MAP), yachts are US$500-650 per day, no children 15 January – 15 March, part sailing and honeymoon packages available. The Thursday noon buffet for US$12 is highly recommended. A three-course meal costs about US$40 in the evening.

Essentials

Sleeping

Government tax of 7% on hotel rooms; most add a 10% service charge; a/c is not generally available, it is often worth asking for a fan

Camping is not encouraged. There are no organized campsites

Kingstown On Upper Bay St, **B** *Cobblestone Inn*, PO Box 867, T4561937, F4561938. Upstairs in a building which used to be a sugar and arrowroot warehouse, a/c, mostly quiet but avoid room 22, noisy from street below, rooms good. Recommended. Nearby, at junction with South River Rd, is **C** *Heron*, PO Box 226, T4571631, F4571189, also once above a warehouse (now above a screenprinting shop and bookshop). Popular with business visitors, but has recently lost a lot of its class, set-menu food in restaurant, a/c, TV lounge, the place for a well-earned bacon and egg breakfast after crossing from Bequia on the early boat. **C** *Haddon*, PO Box 144, Grenville St, T4561897, F4562726, stargarage@caribsurf.com Good food, helpful, a/c, tennis courts nearby, car hire available. **LL-L** *Camelot Inn*, T4562100, F4562233. Originally the governor's residence and the oldest guest house on the island, but refurbished 1996 with 22 luxury rooms and 2 honeymoon suites, Camelot theme rigorously carried through with *King Arthur's Restaurant*, the Knight's room, etc, very upmarket, pool, tennis, gym, beauty salon, free transport to beach. **C** *Kingstown Park Inn*, PO Box 1594, T4572964, F4572505. Bed and breakfast, 8 rooms, fans, a/c in 1 room, bar and restaurant, car rental. **D-E** *Bella Vista Inn*, behind *Camelot*. 7 rooms, 3 with private bath, fans, run by Nzinga Miguel and her daughter Cleopatra, friendly, homely atmosphere, breakfast EC$10, dinner on request EC$15. **D** *Leslie's Guest House*, Kingstown Park, T4562863, 1 min from *Camelot*. 10-min walk downhill to town, shared bathroom, clean, cool, nice garden, large veranda, Leslie Waldron very friendly and helpful. **Close to Kingstown: AL** *Tropic Breeze Hotel*, T4584618, F4564592, widco@caribsurf.com 12 double rooms with balconies, 6 a/c. **B** *New Montrose Hotel*, PO Box 215, T4570172, F4571233, newmontrosehotel@caribsurf.com 25 rooms, kitchenettes, balcony, TV, phone, view of Kingstown and Grenadines, walking distance from Botanical Gardens.

Villa Point and Beach and Indian Bay (3 miles from town) **LL-AL** *Grand View Beach*, PO Box 173, Villa Point, T4584811, F4574174, www.grandviewhotel.com 19 rooms, 1st class, pool, tennis, squash, fully-equipped gym, snorkelling, excursions arranged, restaurant. **L-AL** *Sunset Shores*, PO Box 849, T4584411, F4574800, www.sunsetshores.com 32 rooms, a/c, TV, sunfish, snorkelling gear, pool, table tennis, dining room, bar. **AL** *Villa Lodge Hotel & Breezeville Apartments*, PO Box 1191, Villa Point, T4584641, F4574468, villalodge@ caribsurf.com 10 rooms and 10 apartments overlooking Indian Bay, discounts for longer stay, a/c, fans, TV, pool with lovely view, restaurant, bar, 10 mins from airport. **AL-A** *The Lagoon Marina and Hotel*, PO Box 133, Blue Lagoon, T/F4584308, lagnan@caribsurf.com 19 rooms with lovely view, run by Vincentians, Richard and Nancy Joachim, also 1-bedroom and 3-bedroom apartments, yacht charter US$275-400 per day, US$1,400-2,800 per week, full service marina, bar, restaurant, nice pool with slide, scuba diving, windsurfing. **A-B** *Beachcombers Hotel*, PO Box 126, T4584283, F4584385, beachcombers@ caribsurf.com Small, family-run, includes breakfast, laundry service, restaurant and bar. **A-C** *Seasplash Apartments*, T4561725, F4562191. 5 mins from beach. **B-C** *Belleville Apartment Hotel*, PO Box 746, T4584776, F4562344. 8 self-contained apartments or 2-bedroomed suite. **B-C** *Paradise Inn*, PO Box 1286, T4574795, F4574221, paradinn@caribsurf.com Rooms or apartments, beach, restaurant, bar, laundry service, a/c or fans, helpful and friendly staff, view of Young Island, on bus route to Villa, special rates for senior citizens and church groups. **B-D** *Coconut Beach Inn*, T/F4574900. Nice, clean, comfortable rooms, beautiful seaview, good restaurant (see below). **B-C** *Casa de Columbus*, PO Box 993, T4584001, F4574777, www.casadecolumbus.com Hotel on beach, nice verandah, good snorkelling just outside the hotel, daily or weekly rates, 2 bedroomed apartments available, sleep 3-4, a/c, kitchenettes, restaurant, watersports nearby. **B** *Rosewood Apartment Hotel*, 3 mins from Kingstown, T4575051, F4575141, rosewood@caribsurf.com 7 new 1-bedroom apartments with view of Grenadines. **C** *Sky Blue Beach Apartments*, T4574394, F4575232. Self-contained a/c apartments, 2 mins to beach. **C** *TranQuillity Beach Apartment Hotel*, PO Box 71, Indian Bay, T/F4584021. Excellent view, kitchen facilities, fans, TV, laundry service, clean, friendly, very helpful owners, Mr and Mrs Providence, delicious meals if given a few hours notice. **B-C** *Umbrella Beach*, PO Box 530, T4584651, F4574930. 9 double rooms with kitchen, bath, balcony, nice, simple, opposite Young Island. **C-D** *Trottie's Apartments*, near Blue Lagoon, T4584486, F4564060, jemt@caribsurf.com 1 bedroom, view of Caribbean and Grenadines. **B** *Canash Beach Apartments*, T4569147, F4587147. 6 fully furnished self-contained apartments. Other guest houses: **E** *Sea Breeze Guest House*, Arnos Vale, near airport, T4584969. Cooking facilities, 6 rooms with bath, no credit cards, noisy, friendly, helpful, bus to town or airport from the door. At Ratho Mill: **C** *Ridgeview Terrace Apartments*, PO Box 176, T4561615, F4572874, 200 yds from Blue Lagoon Beach. 5 apartments overlooking yacht basin and Grenadines, a/c, kitchens, balconies, daily maid service.

Leeward coast LL *Petit Byahaut*, T/F4577008, VHF68, www.outahere.com/petitbyahaut, set in a 50-acre valley. No TV or phones, luxury 10 ft x 13 ft tents with floors, queen-sized bed, shower, toilet, sink, sitting area and hammock in each tent, includes all meals, snorkelling, sail and row boats, kayaks, hiking, airport and water taxi transfer, 3 night minimum stay, scuba diving from beach or kayaks included but diver certification and first dive checkout (US$50) required, guided dives US$40 per person, you can hire the whole resort for 14 people, access only by boat, diving and snorkelling good in the bay, ecological and conservation emphasis, solar powered. **E** *Bambareaux Beach Complex*, Layou, T4587789. Bungalows with cooking facilities, about 1 km northwest of town on gravel road along the coast, off main road.

Peniston Valley A-B *Emerald Valley Resort & Casino*, PO Box 1081, T4567824, F4567145. 12 cottages, a/c, kitchenettes, 9-hole golf course, poolside restaurant, tennis.

Windward coast A-B *Argyle Nature Resort*, PO Box 1639, T4580992, F4572432. 10 rooms, fans, TV, phone, restaurant, pool, natural jacuzzi, horse riding, short walk to beach or petroglyphs. *Ferdie's Footsteps*, on the main street in Georgetown, T4586433. Food and accommodation. *Stage's Hideout*, Langley Park, Georgetown, T4576975. Often booked solid. In the very northern tip of the island you can find lodging with the *Stay Family*, **F** pp, very basic, not very clean, meals available. Travel with caution in the north because of drugs growing.

Eating **Kingstown** is improving with new restaurants offering better choice for dining out. The better restaurants, eg the *French Restaurant*, are in the beach area several miles east. *Vee-Jay's* restaurant on Lower Bay St is friendly and offers good local food, open Mon-Sat 1000-1900, Fri until late, also **Vee-Jay's Rooftop Diner & Pub** on Upper Bay St, T457-2845/1395, above Roger's Photo Studios. Open Mon-Sat from 0900, sandwiches, rotis etc for lunch, good local juices, dinner by reservation only, cocktail bar, entres EC$12-45, great steel band. *The Attic*, West Indian/European, multi-screen sports broadcasts, a/c, open 1100 until late. *Bounty Restaurant and Art Gallery*, T4561776. Breakfast and lunch, patties, rotis, pizza, Mon-Fri 0800-1700, Sat 0800-1330. *Knight's Room Dining*, English-style castle with deluxe table style service at *Camelot Inn*. *Kingston Park Inn*, T4572964. West Indian/Continental, intimate family owned inn. *Rainbow Palace*, West Indian fast food, Grenville St, T4561763. Open Mon-Fri 0800-1630, Sat 0800-1400. For genuine West Indian food and local company *Aggie's Bar and Restaurant* on Grenville St, T4562110. Superb, open Mon-Sat from 0900, Sun 1700-2400, Fri happy hour 1600-1800. *Harbour View* upstairs on corner of Bay St and Egmont St. Not bad, open late. *Basil's Bar and Restaurant* (see below) has a branch underneath the *Cobblestone Inn*, in Upper Bay St, T4572713. Buffet 1200-1400 for hungry people, EC$32, acceptable but not startling, open from 0800, pleasant for an evening drink and a chat. *Cobblestone Roof Top Restaurant*, belonging to the *Cobblestone Inn*, T4561937. West Indian lunches and hamburgers, open Mon-Sat 0700-1500, good place for breakfast, as is the *Heron Hotel* (see above).

Fast food At the bus station (Little Tokyo) you can buy freshly grilled chicken and corn cobs, good value and tasty. Cafés on the jetty by ferry boats serve excellent, cheap, local food, eg salt cod rolls with hot pepper sauce. On market days fruit is plentiful and cheap, great bananas. Takeaway food from *Pizza Party*, T4564932/9, in Arnos Vale by the airport. Delivery and takeaway until 2300, no credit cards. *Chung Wua*, Upper Bay St, T4572566. Open Mon-Sat 1100-2230, Sun 1700-2200, Chinese eat in or takeaway, no credit cards, from EC$10. For fast food, *KFC* have 2 branches, Upper Bay St and corner of Melville and Grenville Sts.

Villa area *The French Restaurant*, T4584972. VHF Channel 68, open Mon-Sat 0900-2130, prices EC$40-85 for main course, lobster from the tank, lovely beach view. The *Lime Restaurant & Pub* on the waterfront at Villa, T4584227. A casual menu and a dinner menu, reasonable prices, open 0930-2400. *Beachcombers* on Villa Beach, T4584283. Light fare and drinks, very casual, pizzas, samosas, burgers, popular with children, good value, or à la carte menu, open air, food 0700-2200, bar open later, happy hour 1700-1830. *Mariners' Inn*, view of Young Island. *Slicks*, T4574337. VHF68, moderate prices, building decorated with artwork of owner and other local artists. *The Aquatic Club*, T4584205. West Indian and international, lunch 1100-1400, dinner 1800. *Paradise Restaurant*, T4574795. In hotel, offers local food and occasional Fri night barbecues with live music. The adventurous should try *Papa Spoon's Rasta Ranch* on the Callaquia playing field for inexpensive local, all natural food served in calabash bowls. The *Coconut Beach Inn* on Indian Bay has a good restaurant and rooms to let (see above), West Indian specialities, sandwiches, fish and chips etc, open daily from 1000, dinner by reservation only before 1500, entrées, EC$10-45. *Villa Lodge Hotel* is a good place to eat, not cheap but wonderful piña colada. *Sunset Shore Restaurant*, overlooking Young Island, T4584411 for reservations. International, full English, West Indian or continental breakfast, open 0730-2130, barbecue Wed, Sat, Sun brunch 1200-1500, credit cards. *Surfside Beachbar/Restaurant*, T4575362. Informal Continental/West Indian, pizza and seafood, 1000-2200, closed Mon. *Barefoot*, T4569902. International, part of Barefoot Yacht Charters, waterfront pub-style restaurant with yachtsmen's specials and light meals available on the verandah, dinghy dock.

Cumberland Bay *Stephens Hideout*, T4582325. West Indian and seafood, restaurant on Leeward Highway, Beach Bar on the bay, call ahead for made to order meals or picnic on beach, open 0900-2230, no credit cards, tours arranged. *Wallilabou Anchorage*, T4587270. Caters mainly for yachties, mooring facilities, West Indian specialities.

Several hotels have live music some evenings. *Emerald Valley Casino*, T4567824. Call for **Nightlife** transport, closed Tue. *Basils Too*, T4584205. Offers lunch, dinner and dancing on Villa Beach by Young Island. Check for happy hours at bars for lower-priced drinks, snacks and often entertainment. *Aquatic*, in Villa (see restaurants). Is the main nightspot on the island, admission EC$20, more if there is a live band, which there sometimes is at weekends. In Kingstown, *Touch Entertainment Centre*, T4571825. Opened its dance hall in 1993, run by the Vincentian band, *Touch*. *The Attic*, T4572558, at the corner of Melville and Grenville Sts, upstairs from *KFC*. Nightly live entertainment, jazz, karaoke, dancing, large screen video, music bar open 1200 till late, restaurant open Mon-Sat for lunch 1100-1430. Other nighttime places are *Veejays* and *Harbour View*, both on Upper Bay St and *Dano's* on Grenville St. *Russell's Cinema*; *Cinerama*, T4856364. 3 screens, every night. Also *Cinerama* in Georgetown, Thu-Sun.

St Vincent's carnival, called **Vincy Mas**, is held in the last week of *June* and the 1st week of **Festivals** *July* for 10 days. In 2000 Vincy Mas celebrated its 23rd anniversary. Mas is short for masquerade, and the 3 main elements of the carnival are the costume bands, the steel bands and the calypso. During the day there is J'Ouverte, ole mas, children's carnival and steel bands through Kingstown's streets. At night calypsonians perform in 'tents', there is the King and Queen of the bands show, the steel bands competition and Miss Carival, a beauty competition with contestants from other Caribbean countries (a talent contest, a beauty contest and local historical dress). Thousands of visitors come to take part, many from Trinidad. From *16-24 December*, there is a **Carolling Competition** and **Nine Mornings Festival**, during which, for 9 mornings, people parade through Kingstown and dances are held from 0100. There is also an art and craft exhibition.

Kingstown market (do not take photos of the vendors) and Bequia have excellent fresh **Shopping** vegetables and supermarkets. Grocery and wine availability is improving, with several gourmet provisioning spots catering to yachts and guests staying on the island; *Standard Grocery*, Lower Middle Street, Kingstown, T4561553; *CK Greaves Co Ltd*, Upper Bay Street, Kingstown and Arnos Vale; *The Gingerbread Shop* and *Gourmet Shop* (Bayshore Mall). *Sunrise Supermarket*, opposite airport at Arnos Vale, T4571074. One of the best in the Caribbean, very well stocked. *Midway*, near cricket field in Arnos Vale, T4565430. Open Mon-Sat 0730-2100, Sun 0730-1200, wide selection and delivery service, provisions for yachts.

The St Vincent Philatelic Society on Bay Street, between Higginson Street and River Road, sells stamps in every colour, size and amount for the novice and collector alike. Service is helpful but slow in this second floor warehouse, complete with guard. *The Artisans Art & Craft Centre*, Bay Street, T4562306. Upstairs in the Bonadie Building, sells handicrafts from about 70 artisans around the country, open Mon-Fri 0900-1630, Sat 0900-1300. For handicrafts, resort wear and books, *Noah's Arkade*, Blue Caribbean Building, Bay Street, Kingstown (T4571513, F4569305), and at the *Frangipani* on Bequia (T4583424). Other bookshops: *Wayfarer*, beneath the *Heron Hotel*.

Chris and Jazelle Patterson of *Dolphin Tours* (Ebony and Ivory Ltd), have been recommended for **Tour operators** giving comprehensive tours of Bequia and St Vincent, PO Box 1, Bequia, T4583345, 4573205.

Road Bicycles: From *Sailors Cycle Centre*, T4571712, http:\\Vincy.com/ **Transport** Sailor's.html Middle St, owned by Trevor 'Sailor' Bailey, who also operates Sailor's Wilderness Tours for hiking and biking. On Bequia, *Lighthouse*, T4583084. Dennis Murray rents **motor bikes** on Bequia, T457-2776/9113. The alternative to a bike is to rent a **Moke** or **Mule jeep** that will seat 4-6 people.

Bus Fares start at EC$1, rising to EC$2 (Layou), EC$4 (Georgetown on the Windward coast), to EC$5 to the Black Carib settlement at Sandy Bay in the northeast (this is a difficult route,

Windward Islands

though, because buses leave Sandy Bay early in the morning for Kingstown, and return in the afternoon). The number of vans starting in Kingstown and running to Owia or Fancy in the north is limited. The best way is to take the early bus to Georgetown and try to catch one of the two vans running between Georgetown and Fancy (EC$10). To get to Richmond in the northwest take a bus to Barrouallie and seek onward transport from there. It is worthwhile to make a day trip to Mesopotamia (Mespo) by bus (EC$2.50).

Car hire   If you do want to travel round St Vincent, it is better to rent a car, or hire a taxi with driver for EC$40 per hour. Note that the use of cars on the island is limited, so that only jeeps may be used to go right up Soufrière or beyond Georgetown on the east coast. Charges at *Kim's* (T4561884, F4561681, stevekim@caribsurf.com) for example are: EC$100 per day for a car, with restrictions on where you drive in the north, EC$125 for a jeep, 60 miles free per day, EC$1 per mile thereafter, weekly rental gives one day free, EC$1,000 excess deposit in advance, delivery or collection anywhere on the island, phone from airport for collection to save taxi hassle, credit cards accepted. Among other agencies (all offering similar rates and terms) are *Ben's* T4562907, F4572686, *David's* T4564026, F4564026, *Star Garage* T4561743, F4562726, *UNICO* T4565744, F4565745.

Taxi   Taxi fares are fixed by the Government but you must check it with the driver first to avoid overcharging. Late at night and early morning fares are raised. Kingstown to Airport EC$20, Indian Bay EC$25, Mesopotamia EC$40, Layou EC$40, Orange Hill EC$80, Blue Lagoon EC$35, airport to Young Island EC$20, airport to Blue Lagoon EC$25. Hourly hire EC$40 per hour. *Vibie Taxi* recommended, T4565288, 4565781, helpful. *Young Island Taxi Association* can be reached through Young Island on VHF 68. *Chevi Taxi* is recommended.

Sea   From Kingstown to Bequia, MV *Admiral 1* sails at 0900 and 1900 Mon-Fri, returning 0730 and 1700; 0700 returning 1700 on Sat, 1 hr; MV *Admiral II* (passengers and cars) sails at 1030 and 1630 Mon-Fri (1230 on Sat), returning 0630 and 1400 (0630 on Sat), 1 hr journey, EC$10, EC$12 at night and weekends (both vessels run by Admiralty Transport Co Ltd, T4583348 for information); if you travel under sail, be prepared to get wet from the spray as the crossing is often rough, *Bequia Eagle* (cars and passengers) and *Maxann O* (island schooner) sail at 1230, returning 0630 Mon-Fri, 1¼ hrs.

MV *Barracuda* sails on Mon and Thu from Bequia (0600) for Kingstown, then returns (1030) to Bequia, continuing (1145) to Canouan, Mayreau, arriving in Union Island at 1545; on Tue and Fri she returns to St Vincent via Mayreau, Canouan and Bequia, leaving Union Island at 0630, arriving St Vincent 1200. On Sat she departs St Vincent at 1000 for Canouan, arriving 1430, then sails via Mayreau to Union Island, returning to St Vincent at 2230. All times are approximate, depending on the amount of goods to be loaded. There are 3-4 cabins, two of which are used by the crew but you can negotiate for one quite cheaply if you need it. The *Barracuda* is the islands' main regular transport and carries everything, families and their goods, goats and generators; she rolls through the sea and is very cheap, for example Bequia-Union EC$15, Union-Canouan EC$12, Canouan-Mayreau EC$8; the trip can be highly entertaining but note that the timetable is very unreliable.

Fishing boats sail from Ashton, Union Island to Carriacou 0700, 1 hr, days vary according to demand and weather, returning Carriacou-Union Island from Hillsborough Pier, 1300, EC$15. Frequent boat trips are organized, ask at hotels, take your passport even though not strictly necessary and expect thorough searches of you luggage at Customs and Immigration. For other services, check at the Grenadines dock in Kingstown. There are often excursions from Kingstown to Bequia and Mustique on Sun. Fares from Kingstown to Bequia EC$10, EC$12 at night and weekends, Canouan EC$13, Mayreau EC$15 and Union Island EC$20. From Bequia you can take a boat trip to Mustique for US$40 per person by speedboat from Friendship Bay or by catamaran from Port Elizabeth, ask at Sunsports at *Gingerbread*. Throughout the Grenadines local power boats can be arranged to take small groups of passengers almost any distance. If possible try to ensure that the boat is operated by someone known to you or your hotel to ensure reliability. Prices are flexible. Do not expect a dry or comfortable ride if the sea is rough.

Airlines *LIAT*, Halifax Street, Kingstown, T4571821 for reservations, airport office T4584841, on Union Island T4588230; *Mustique Airways*, PO Box 1232, T4584380, F4564586; *SVGAIR*, PO Box 39, Blue Lagoon, St Vincent, T4575124, F4575077, www.svgair.com, air taxi service to Barbados, Martinique, St Lucia and within the Grenadines; *British Airways*, T4571821. **Banks** *Barclays Bank Plc*, *Scotia Bank*, *Canadian Imperial Bank of Commerce*, *National Commercial Bank* of St Vincent, all on Halifax Street, Caribbean Banking Corporation, 81 South River Road, Kingstown, and at Port Elizabeth, Bequia. *Barclays Bank* has a branch on Bequia; *National Commercial Bank* has branches at ET Joshua airport, Georgetown, Barrouallie, on Bequia and Union Island and agencies at Layou and Chateaubeleair. On Canouan, *National Commercial Bank*, T4588595, open Mon-Thu 0800-1300 or 1500, Fri 0800-1500 or 1700, depending on the bank. When you cash TCs you can take half in US dollars and half in EC dollars if you wish. Lots of banks have 24-hr ATMs, but they will not necessarily accept your card. **Embassies & consulates** *UK*, British High Commission, Grenville Street, Box 132, Kingstown, T4571701 (after hours T4584381), F4562750; *Netherlands* Consulate, in the East Caribbean Group of Companies building in Campden Park, T4571918; *China*, Murray Road, T4562431; *Venezuela*, Granby Street, T4561374; *France*, Middle Street, Box 364, Kingstown, T4561615; *Italy*, Queen's Drive, T4564774. **Communications** Post: Halifax Street. Open 0830-1500 (0830-1130 on Sat, closed Sun). *St Vincent Philatelic Services Ltd*, General Post Office, T4571911, F4562383; for old and new issues, World of Stamps, Bay 43 Building, Lower Bay Street, Kingstown. **Telephone:** operated by Cable and Wireless, on Halifax Street; there is a 5% tax on international phone calls. Phone cards and fax available. Portable phones can be rented through *Boatphone* or you can register your own cellular phone with them upon arrival, T4562800. The international code for St Vincent is 784, followed by a seven-digit local number beginning with 45. From many cardphones you can reach USA Direct by dialling 1-800-8722881. **Medical facilities** *Kingston General Hospital*, T4561185. Emergency T999. **Tourist information** Local tourist office: *St Vincent and the Grenadines Department of Tourism*, Finance Complex, Bay Street, PO Box 834, Kingstown, T4571502, F4562610, www.grenadines.net, open Mon-Fri 0800-1200, 1300-1615; if the office downstairs is closed during working hours (has been known), go upstairs to the Ministry, where they are most helpful; helpful desk at ET Joshua airport, T4584379, hotel reservation EC$1; on Bequia (at the landward end of the jetty), T4583286, open Sun-Fri 0900-1230, 1330-1600, Sat morning only; on Union Island, T4588350, open daily 0800-1200, 1300-1600. There is a desk in the arrivals hall at the Grantley Adams airport on Barbados, open daily from 1300 until 2000 or the last flight to St Vincent (T4280961). This is useful for transfers to LIAT after an international flight. The Tourist Office and the Hotel Association publish *Escape*, a good magazine on the islands giving details of accommodation, restaurants and shopping as well as articles of interest. Bequia publishes its own brochure, *Holiday Bequia*, and Mustique Airways also has a magazine. **Maps:** a map of St Vincent, 1:50,000 (and Kingstown, 1:10,000), EC$15, is available from the Ministry of Agriculture, Lands and Survey Department, Murray Road. In 1992 the Ordnance Survey (Southampton, UK) brought out a new tourist map of St Vincent, 1:50,000, with insert of Kingstown, 1:10,000, double sided with Grenadines on the reverse, with text panels giving information, walks etc.

Directory

Windward Islands

The Grenadines

The Grenadines, divided politically between St Vincent and Grenada, are a string of 100 tiny, rocky islands and cays stretching across some 35 miles of sea between the two. They are still very much off the beaten track as far as tourists are concerned, but are popular with yachtsmen and the 'international set'.

Bequia

Named the island of the clouds by the Caribs (pronounced Bek-*way*), this is the largest of the St Vincent dependencies with a population of about 5,000. Nine miles south of St Vincent and about seven miles square, Bequia attracts quite a number of tourists, chiefly yachtsmen but also the smaller cruise ships and, increasingly, land-based tourists. Tourism is becoming much more important as more cruise ships stop and the number of yachts increases. More hotel rooms and apartments are being added. The island is quite hilly and well-forested with a great variety of fruit and nut trees. Its main village is **Port Elizabeth** and here Admiralty Bay offers a safe anchorage. Boat building and repair work are the main industry. Experienced sailors can sometimes get a job crewing on boats sailing on from here to Panama and other destinations. For maps and charts (and books) go to Iain Gale's Bequia Bookshop, which is very well stocked. The nearest beach to Port Elizabeth is the pleasant Princess Margaret beach which shelves quickly into the clear sea. There are no beach bars to spoil this tree-lined stretch of soft sand. At its south end there is a small headland, around which you can snorkel to Lower Bay, where swimming is excellent and the beach is one of the best on the island. Local boys race their homemade, finely finished sailing yachts round the bay. In the village is *Kennedy's Bar*, a good place to watch the sunset with a rum punch. Further along is *De Reef*, whose bar and restaurant are the hub of much local activity.

Away from Port Elizabeth the beaches are empty. Take a taxi through coconut groves past an old sugar mill to **Industry Bay**, a nice beach surrounded by palms with a brilliant view across to Bullet Island, Battowia and Balliceaux where the Black Caribs were held before being deported to Roatán. Some luxury homes have been built at the north end of the bay. Food and drink available at the *Industry Beach Bar*. A short walk along the track leads to **Spring Bay**, to the south, where there is a beach bar (may be closed). Both beaches are narrow with shallow bays and a lot of weed, making them less good for swimming and snorkelling. North of Industry is **Old Hegg Turtle Sanctuary** in the northeast corner of the island. Not to be missed, an extremely worthwhile conservation project founded and maintained by a

St Vincent & the Grenadines

Beguian to save the hawksbill turtle. EC$10 donation warmly welcomed to maintain the facilities and feed the turtles.

The walk up **Mount Pleasant** from Port Elizabeth is worthwhile (go by taxi if it is too hot), the shady road is overhung with fruit trees and the view of Admiralty Bay is ever more spectacular. There is a settlement of airy homes at the top, from where you can see most of the Grenadines. By following the road downhill and south of the viewpoint you can get to **Hope Bay**, an isolated and usually deserted sweep of white sand and one of the best beaches. At the last house (where you can arrange for a taxi to meet you afterwards), the road becomes a rough track, after half mile turn off right down an ill-defined path through cedar trees to an open field, cross the fence on the left, go through a coconut grove and you reach the beach. The sea is usually gentle but sometimes there is powerful surf, a strong undertow and offshore current, take care. **Friendship Bay** is particularly pleasant, there is some coral but also quite a lot of weed, a taxi costs EC$15, or you can take a dollar bus (infrequent) in the direction of Paget Farm, get out at Mr Stowe's Store (EC$1.50) and walk down to the bay (you may have to ring for a taxi at one of the hotels to get back, though).

The tourist office by the jetty (very helpful) can help you arrange a visit to the cliffside dwellings of Moon Hole at the south end of the island, where a rocky arch frames the stone dwelling and the water comes up the front yard. At **Paget Farm**, whale harpooning is still practised from February to May (the breeding season) by a few fishermen who use two 26-ft long cedar boats, powered by oars and sails. If you can arrange a trip to **Petit Nevis**, to the south, you can see the whaling station and find out more about Bequia's whaling tradition. Despite pleas from conservationists, in both 1998 and 1999 a humpback mother and calf were harpooned off Bequia.

Hotels and guest houses L-AL *The Old Fort*, on Mount Pleasant, T4583440, F4573340, oldfort@caribsurf.com A 17th-century French built fortified farmhouse, probably oldest building on Bequia, magnificent views, idyllic restaurant (must book), animals in spacious grounds include donkeys, kittens, peacocks, pool with view of 25 islands, beach within

Sleeping

Bequia

■ Sleeping	3 Frangipani	6 Old Fort
1 Bequia Beach Club	4 Friendship Bay	7 Plantation House
2 De Reef Apartments	5 Julie's Guesthouse	8 Spring on Bequia

Windward Islands

walking distance, 5/6 rooms, also available as a rental villa to sleep 10-14, excursions, diving, boat trips arranged. Highly recommended. Call Otmar Schaedle, multilingual. **LL-L** *Friendship Bay*, PO Box 9, T4583222, F4583840. Lovely location, but in need of renovation, no bar or evening meal at restaurant, plumbing temperamental, boat excursions, water and other sports facilities, friendly, jump-up at beach bar, Sat night. **A-C** *Blue Tropic Apartments*, Friendship Bay, T4583513, F4573074. Newly built, 10 rooms, view of bay, restaurant, bar, free bikes, beach mats and sun chairs. **L** *Bequia Beach Club*, Friendship Bay, T4583248, F4583689. 10 rooms, restaurant, bar, diving, windsurfing, tennis nearby, day sails, weekly barbecues. **LL-AL** *Spring on Bequia*, T4583414, F4583305, on a bay to the northeast of Port Elizabeth. Part of a 200-year-old working plantation, 10 rooms, pool, tennis, bar, restaurant, beach bar. In Port Elizabeth itself, **L-C** *Frangipani*, PO Box 1, T4583255, F4583824. Cheaper rooms share bathroom, on beach, pleasant, bar, terrible sandflies and mosquitoes in wet season, mosquito net provided. **L-B** *Gingerbread*, PO Box 1, T4583800, F4583907, www.begos.com/gingerbread Added new luxury apartments with kitchens overlooking Admiralty Bay, old apartments at lower rates. 1-bedroomed with kitchen and bathroom, restaurant and bar upstairs, café downstairs, dive shop, tennis, waterskiing, international phone calls 0700-1900 in upstairs office of restaurant, attractive, friendly. **F** *Mitchells*, overlooking harbour (above Bookshop, go round the back and seek out the owner), includes morning coffee, but 10 more if you are staying only 1 night, cooking facilities available, good, cheap, basic. **C-D** *Julie's Guest House*, T4583304, F4583812. 19 rooms with bath and shower, turn right by the police station, mosquito nets in rooms, good local food, good cocktails in noisy bar downstairs, meeting place for travellers to form boat charter groups. **LL** *Plantation House Hotel*, PO Box 16, T4583425, F4583612, planthouse@caribsurf.com Rebuilt after 1988 fire, on beach at Admiralty Bay, tennis, swimming pool, watersports, Dive Bequia dive shop, cottages or rooms, all MAP, honeymoon packages etc, entertainment at weekends. **E** *The Old* **Fig Tree**, PO Box 14, T4583201. Restaurant with basic rooms, shared or private bath, meals extra (good), friendly, on extremely narrow beach. **A-B** *Keegan's Guesthouse*, T4583254, F4573313. Lovely position on Lower Bay, 11 rooms, also apartments US$365-490 per week, and **A-B** *Creole Garden Hotel*, T/F4583154, at Lower Bay above Corner Bay and Lower Bay beach, MAP, bath, porch, refrigerator.

Apartments to rent **B-C** *Island Inn Apartments*, T4573433/4583706, F4573431, Friendship Bay. 6 1-2 bedroomed apartments, run by Bequian Val Lewis, fully equipped, excellent facilities and maid service, 2 mins from beach. **B-C** *The Village Apartments* in Belmont, PO Box 1621, Kingstown, T/F4583883, tvabqsvg@caribsurf.com Overlooking Admiralty Bay. Studio, 1 or 2-bedroomed apartments. **C-D** *Hibiscus Apartments*, Union Vale, T4583889, F4573388. 4 units, kitchenettes, laundry service, scooters and bike hire. **B** *Bay View Apartments*, Friendship Bay, T4583248, F4583689. 8 self-contained apartments, beach, windsurfing. **B** *De Reef Apartments*, Lower Bay, T4583484, F4573103. 1 bedroom. **A-C** *Kingsville Apartments*, Lower Bay, T4583932, F4583000. 1-2 bedrooms.

Eating Apart from hotel restaurants, *Mac's Pizza* on Belmont Beach, T4583474, is recommended. Very popular, get there early or reserve in advance, even in low season, also takeaways, try the lobster pizza, pricey but covered with lobster, don't add other ingredients. *Le Petit Jardin*, Back St, T4583318. French and international, open daily 1130-1400, 1830-2130, reservations preferred, EC$30-85 for entrées. *Harpoon Saloon*, T4583272. Happy hour 1700-1800, wide ranging menu, moderate prices, managed by Vincentian, Noel Frazer, steel band some nights. *Whaleboner*, T4583233. Food fresh from their own farm, EC$5-65, open Mon-Sat 0800-2200, Sun 1400-2200. *Daphne's*, just off the main street, T4583271. Cooks excellent créole meals to eat in or takeaway, no credit cards. *Dawn's Créole Tea Garden*, Lower Bay, at the far end, T4583154. Open from 0800, breakfast, lunch and dinner, good home cooked food, fairly expensive, must book for dinner. The *Gingerbread Café* has sandwiches and snacks all day, open 0700-1800, also *Gingerbread BBQ*, outdoors on bayside 1200-1500, and *Gingerbread Restaurant & Bar*, T4583800, upper floor of *Gingerbread* complex, overlooking Admiralty Bay. Open 0800-2130, reservations recommended in season for dinner, West Indian and international, live music 3 nights a week. *Green Boley* on the beach a bit south, T4583247. Local fast food to EC$20. *Maranne's* at the *Green Boley Bar* for ice cream and other frozen desserts EC$2-10. *The Old Fig Tree*, T4583201. Fish and chips, rotis, pizza, fresh food. *Timberhouse*, on hill overlooking Port Elizabeth, T4573495. Closed Sun, reservations suggested. *Porthole*, T4583458. Local creole dishes, rotis, Mexican, fish. *De Bistro*, local creole dishes. *Julie and Isolde's Guest House*, T4583304. Inexpensive local dishes, reservations suggested. *Bequia Café*, large plate lunch of local food for EC$10. *T and G Restaurant*, good reasonably priced Creole cooking. Over S & W Grocery is a small local snackette. *Schooners* own jetty, happy hour 1730-1830, fresh or frozen dinners for yachties. *De Reef*, Lower Bay. If you rent a locker note that all keys fit all locks, lovely position, popular with yachties, set meals and bar snacks, the place for Sun lunch. The *Frangipani* has sandwiches and snacks all day, slow service but friendly and you have a good view to look at, Thu night barbecue, buffet, steel band. At Lower Bay, *Coco's Place*, T4583463. Friendly pub and local kitchen, live music Tue, Fri. *Fernando's Hideaway*, T4583758. Local style fresh food, dinner Mon-Sat, special "goat water" soup. *Theresa's*, T4583802. Colourful local restaurant with gourmet West Indian food, vegetarian, Mon night international buffet when restaurant and "host" provide character as well, Sun in season live jazz band from 1430. *Keegan's*, T4583530. Inexpensive 3 course local dinners and bar snacks all day. At Friendship Bay *Spicy and Herby*, T4583222. Bar with swing seats.

There are small supermarkets in Port Elizabeth (limited choice of meat), S & W, Knights, Shoreline and 2 deli-type shops, with improving selection of groceries and beverages; Doris's, Schooners, Dieter's; fish is sometimes on sale in the centre by the jetty although a new fish market is being built, fruit and vegetable stalls by the jetty daily, frozen food and homemade bread from *Doris*, also *Daphne's* for homemade bread. Fresh bakeries also from *Mac's Pizzeria, Harpoon Saloon, Gingerbread Coffee Shop* and *Whaleboner*.

Nightlife

Jump ups on Tue at *Plantation House*, Thu at *Frangipani* with barbecue and steel band, Tue and Sat at *Harpoon Saloon* with steel band, occasionally at *De Reef*, sometimes Sat night at *Friendship Bay*, string band several nights a week at *Gingerbread*. Check bars for happy hours. There is something going on most nights either at Admiralty Bay or Friendship Bay, check locally. Bands play reggae music in the gardens of several hotels, popular with residents and tourists.

Shopping

There are several marine stores & fishing tackle shops here

Crab Hole, T4583290. Overlooking Admiralty Bay is a boutique where silk screened fabrics are made downstairs and sewn into clothes upstairs, open 0800-1700 Mon-Sat in season, closing earlier out of season. Bequia has lots of boutiques: *Solana's, Almond Tree, Island Things, Local Color, Melinda's, Sprotties*, the *Garden, Whaleboner* and numerous T-shirt stands by the waterfront. Also don't miss Mauvin's and Sargeant's model boat shops, where craftsmen turn out replicas of traditional craft and visiting yachts. *Bequia Bookshop* in Port Elizabeth, run by Iain Gale, who keeps an excellent stock of books, maps and charts, T4583905. See also under St Vincent page 827.

Transport

Air **J F Mitchell Airport**, named after the Prime Minister, has been built on reclaimed land with a 3,200-ft runway, a terminal and night landing facilities, at the island's southwest tip. Residents view it as a mixed blessing. The island's infrastructure and hotel accommodation is inadequate to handle greater numbers of tourists. **Road** For about US$45, you can take a taxi around the island. You can also rent Honda scooters (and bicycles) from an agency between the bookstore and the National Commercial Bank for US$10 per hour or US$30 per day, but you need to get the police to verify your licence. Cycling is really enjoyable, lots of hills but not too steep and not a lot of traffic, great views and beaches scattered all over the island. **Taxi**: on Bequia, taxis are pick-up trucks with benches in the back, brightly coloured with names like 'Messenjah', call them by phone or VHF radio. **Sea** Water taxis scoot about in Admiralty Bay for the benefit of the many yachts and people on the beach, whistle or wave to attract their attention, fare EC$10 per trip. There are day charters to other islands (see above, Beaches and watersports). Bart has trips to the Tobago Cays and one other island with snorkelling, swimming, breakfast, lunch and all drinks on the *Island Queen*, US$75 per person, attentive, friendly service, hotel pick-up, beautiful scenery, recommended. For those arriving on yachts, there are anchorages all round either side of the channel in Admiralty Bay, Princess

Windward Islands

Margaret Beach, Lower Bay, Friendship Bay and off Petit Nevis by the old whaling station. Bequia Slipway has dockage, some moorings are available.

Directory **Medical facilities** *Bequia Casualty Hospital*, Port Elizabeth, T4583294. See also under St Vincent, page 829. **Tourist information** Information booth at the entrance to the main wharf.

Mustique

Lying 18 miles south of St Vincent, Mustique is three miles long and less than two miles wide. In the 1960s, Mustique was acquired by a single proprietor who developed the island as his private resort where he could entertain the rich and famous. It is a beautiful island, with fertile valleys, steep hills and 12 miles of white sandy beach, but described by some as 'manicured'. It is no longer owned by one person and is more accessible to tourists, although privacy and quiet is prized by those who can afford to live there. There is no intention to commercialize the island; it has no supermarkets and only one petrol pump for the few cars (people use mopeds or golf carts to get around). Apart from the private homes, there are two hotels, one beach bar, a few boutiques, shops, a small village and a fishing camp. All house rentals are handled by the Mustique Company, which organizes activities such as picnics and sports, especially at Easter and Christmas. Radio is the principal means of communication, and the airstrip, being in the centre of the island is clearly visible, so check-in time is five minutes before take off (that is after you've seen your plane land).

There is sailing, diving, snorkelling and good swimming (very little waterskiing). Riding can also be arranged or you can hire a moped to tour the island. The main anchorage is Brittania Bay, where there are 18 moorings for medium sized yachts with waste disposal and phones. Take a picnic lunch to Macaroni Beach on the Atlantic side. This gorgeous, white sand beach is lined with small palm-thatched pavilions and a well-kept park/picnic area. It is isolated and wonderful. Swimming and snorkelling is also good at Lagoon Bay, Gallicaux Bay, Britannia Bay and Endeavour Bay, all on the leeward side.

Basil's Bar and Restaurant is *the* congregating spot for yachtsmen and the jet set. Snorkelling is good here too. From it there is a well-beaten path to the *Cotton House*

Mustique

Hotel, which is the other congregating point. There is an honour system to pay for moorings at *Basil's Bar*, EC$40 a night, EC$20 second night. Johanna Morris has a group of shops: *The Pink House, The Purple House, Johanna's Banana, Treasure Fashion, Basil's Boutique* and *Across Forever*.

Since the island has no freshwater, it is shipped in on Mustique Boats *Robert Junior* (T4571918) and the *Geronimo*. Both take passengers and excursions on Sunday (EC$10, two hour trip).

LL *Cotton House*, T4564777, F4565887, cottonhouse@caribsurf.com A 20-room refurbished (by Oliver Messel) 18th-century cotton plantation house built of rock and coral, is expensive, pool, tennis, windsurfers, sailfish, snorkelling, all complimentary, horseriding and scuba diving available, sailing packages tailor made. Smaller, less expensive **LL** *Firefly House*, T4563414, F4563514, www.mustiquefirefly.com All 4 rooms with view overlooking the bay, bed and breakfast. 50 of the private residences are available for rent, with staff, from US$2,800 per week in summer for a 2-bedroomed villa to US$13,000 per week in winter for a villa sleeping 10. Contact *Mustique Villa Rentals*, in the UK, T01628-583517, or the *Mustique Company Renters Office* by the airstrip on Mustique, mailing address PO Box 349, T4584621, F4564565, or *Resorts Management Inc*, The Carriage House, 201½ East 29th St, New York, NY 10016, T212-6964566, F212-6891598.

Sleeping

Basil's Bar and The Raft, T4584621 for reservations. For seafood and nightlife, open from 0800, entrées EC$10-75. Locals' night on Mon with buffet for EC$35 excluding drinks and dancing, Wed is good. On Sat go to the *Cotton House*. Reservations required at the *Cotton House* and *Firefly*. Up the hill from *Basil's* is the local *Piccadilly* pub, where rotis and beer are sold, and pool is played; foreigners are welcome, but it is best to go in a group and girls should not go on their own. You can buy fresh fish, conch (lambi) and lobster from local fishermen.

Eating
Mustique has a good, small grocery

Union Island

The most southerly of the islands, Union Island is 40 miles from St Vincent and only three miles long by one mile wide with two dramatic peaks, Mount Olympus and Mount Parnassus. Arrival by air is spectacular as the planes fly over the hill and descend steeply to the landing strip. The road from the airport to Clifton passes a mangrove swamp which is being used as a dump prior to filling it in to get rid of mosquitoes and enable building to take place. A walk around the interior of the island (about two hours Clifton-Ashton-Richmond Bay-Clifton) is worth the effort, with fine views of the sea, neighbouring islands, pelicans and Union itself. It has two settlements, **Clifton** and **Ashton** (minibus between the two, EC$2), and the former serves as the south point of entry clearance for yachts. The immigration office and customs are at the airport, so if you arrive by boat you check in at the *Yacht Club* and the airport. For visiting yachts there are anchorages at Clifton, Frigate Island and Chatham Bay, while the *Anchorage Yacht Club* marina has some moorings. The *Anchorage Yacht Club* seems to be full of French people. The barmen are slow and sometimes rude.

A good reason to visit Union Island is to arrange day trips to other islands or to find a ride on a yacht to Venezuela towards the end of the season (May-June). Fishing boats make the one-hour trip to Hillsborough on Carriacou (EC$15, leave Ashton at about 0730, ask locally for days as they vary, *MV Jaspar* twice a week, Monday and Thursday 1200 form Hillsborough, return from Union Island Tuesday and Friday around 0600, captain takes you through immigration procedures, which can take an hour), which can be a bumpy ride. Expect to have your bags thoroughly searched on arrival at Customs and Immigration at Hillsborough. Day trip boats to other islands leave from Clifton around 1000 and are all about the same price, EC$120, including lunch. Yannis Tours at the *Clifton Beach Hotel* arranges tours to the nearby **Tobago Cays** (see below), Palm Island, Petit St Vincent and other small islands. You may be able to join a group flying in from Barbados. They have a comfortable catamaran, which is recommended if the sea is a bit rough. Alternatively, you can hire a local such as Carlos (his name is painted on the side of his boat) to take you in a smaller boat wherever you want to go. This is recommended if the sea is calm so that you can spend the maximum time snorkelling at the Tobago Cays. Boats come and go, but there should be plenty of choice.

The beach at **Chatham Bay** is beautiful and deserted, but not particularly good for swimming as there is a coral ledge just off the beach. Snorkelling and diving are good though. It is one of the last undeveloped anchorages in the Grenadines. An area at the north end of the bay has been allocated for a hotel development and a road is planned over the mountain from Ashton to Chatham Bay, but at the moment you still have to walk 30 minutes along a footpath through the bush from the end of the road just above Ashton down to the bay. A large tourist development is planned for Union Island, with a luxury hotel, 300-berth marina, golf course and villas but is stalled because of financial difficulties.

Sleeping **L-B** *Anchorage Yacht Club*, Clifton, T4588221, F4588365. Full marina service, French restaurant, terrace bar, steel band or piano music, room, cabana or bungalow, plane and yacht charters, agents for *LIAT* and *Air Martinique*. **A-E** *Clifton Beach Hotel and Guest House*, T/F4588235. Rooms, cottages, apartment, rather dilapidated and run down but comfortable nonetheless, MAP available, restaurant, a/c, water and ice for boats, laundry service, bike, car and jeep rental. **A** *Sunny Grenadines*, T4588327, F4588398. MAP, reductions sometimes offered if business is slack, 5 mins' walk from airport, adequate rooms, laundry service, bar quite lively, food very good, boats can tie up at jetty, charter yacht centre. **E** *Lambi's Guest House*, Clifton, T/F4588349/4588359. A/c, restaurant, bar, lively steel band every night. **A-C** *The Cays Apartments*, PO Box 748, Richmond Bay, T4574090, F4574266. 5 studio apartments, self-contained, maid service.

Eating Food is expensive in all the shops and stalls as it has to be imported, but there is a good French-run shop at Clifton for food and drink, visit it before sailing to the Tobago Cays. *Clifton Beach* hotel has a good restaurant and bar. The *Anchorage* restaurant has been criticized for serving bland, overpriced food, the occupants of the shark pool are given food rejected by customers. *Eagle's Nest Entertainment Center*, has a bar with light snacks. *Lambis Restaurant*, casual, lively place with excellent steel band most nights, get there by 1800 for the happy hour. *T & N*, upstairs bar, light meals, good rotis. *Sydney's Bar & Restaurant*, T/F4588320, VHF 16, Clifton, towards the airport. Owned by Sydney, who handpaints

Union Island

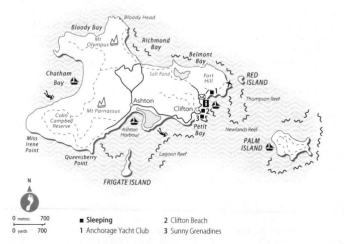

■ Sleeping	**2** Clifton Beach
1 Anchorage Yacht Club	**3** Sunny Grenadines

T-shirts for sale in Tobago Cays, and run by Marin from Munich, local meals, snacks, seafood crêpes, pasta, happy hour 1800-1900, two for one, also guest house. *Jennifer's Restaurant*, West Indian food at reasonable prices, music at weekends. *Boll Head Bar* in centre of town for West Indian food. *Grenadines Pub*, between *Sunny Grenadines* and *Grenadines Dive*, private dock with water and ice available, Grenadine's top chef prepares West Indian food. Most places have a happy hour 1800-1900, with half price drinks, good value.

At Easter on Union Island there are sports, cultural shows and a calypso competition. Also on Union Island, in **May**, is the *Big Drum Festival*, an event which marks the end of the dry season, culminating in the Big Drum Dance, derived from African and French traditions. It is also performed on other occasions, for weddings or launching boats and even in times of disaster.

Festivals

Bougainvilla Complex on Union Island offers *Grenadines Vine Shop*, T4588289. There are 2 *Lambis* supermarkets, *Grand Union* will deliver to the dock, and 4-5 smaller groceries sell fresh produce and hardware.

Shopping

See under St Vincent, page 829. **Communications** Phone calls can be made via cardphone at *Anchorage Hotel*, the airport or in town. USA direct operator can also be reached by dialling 1-800-8722881 and credit card calls or operator assisted calls can be made. **Tourist office** T88350.

Directory

Windward Islands

Canouan

A quiet, peaceful, crescent-shaped island 25 miles south of St Vincent, with very few tourists and excellent reef-protected beaches. The beach at the *Canouan Beach Hotel* is splendid with white sand and views of numerous islands to the south. There are no restaurants outside the hotels and only basic shops. The main anchorage is Charlestown (bank, grocery), Grand Bay, with Corbec and Rameau Bays as possibilities. In settled weather, South Glossy and Friendship Bays make possible anchorages, with excellent snorkelling. Diving and snorkelling are good at all these anchorages and on the reefs on the windward side. Dive trips can be arranged through Blueway International. A recommended day trip is to the Tobago Cays, Mayreau or Petit St Vincent,

Canouan

0 metres 500
0 yards 500

■ **Sleeping**
1 Canouan Beach Hotel

depending on the weather and conditions, on the *Canouan Beach Hotel* 35-ft catamaran, EC$100 with lunch and drinks, non-hotel guests are permitted to make up numbers if the boat is not fully booked. There is an airstrip. A Swiss company, Canouan Resorts Development Ltd, has leased 1,200 of the island's 1,866 acres in a US$100 mn development plan. A road has been built for the new, exclusive development, *Carenage Bay*, at the north end of the island and makes a good walk with wonderful views of the project where some of the luxury homes are under construction. In the centre of the development is an old church that will be restored as part of the project. An 18-hole golf course will be ready for opening soon. Off the main road on the Windward side of the island behind a long reef is a beautiful beach. There are hiking trails within the resort; get a trail map from the hotel. At the beginning of 2000 there was a political furore when residents mounted road blocks in protest at being denied access to beaches in the north, previously open to the public via public roads.

Sleeping **LL** *Carenage Bay Resort & Golf Club*, T4588000, F4588885, info@canouan.com 178 rooms/suites, luxury, casino, on 800 acres, has taken over the northeast of the island, golf, diving, gym, health club, sailing, windsurfing, tennis, yacht charters, 4 restaurants, 3 bars. **LL** *Canouan Beach Hotel*, PO Box 530, T4588888, F4588875, joenadal@caribsurf.com Has developed the south part of the island with deluxe bungalows as well as the main building, nudist beach, all-inclusive. **LL** *Tamarind Beach Hotel and Yacht Club*, T4588044, F4588851, cantbh@caribsurf.com 42 rooms, MAP, 2 restaurants, watersports, scuba diving at extra charge, golf course, long dock for dinghies, yachties welcome to use bar and restaurant, excellent conch creole appetizers, moorings rather rolly, more comfortable sleeping to anchor in north corner of bay. They also provide water, ice, bread, showers, maildrop and message service to yachties and charter boats. You are recommended to phone in advance to book rooms. **AL** *Villa le Bijou*, Mme Michelle de Roche, T4588025. MAP, on hill overlooking town, superb views, friendly, helpful, showers, water and ice for yacht visitors, no credit cards. **A-B** *Anchor Inn Guest House* in Grand Bay, T4588568. George and Yvonne offer clean and basic accommodation, for double rooms, MAP, packed lunches available, no credit cards; also possible to rent houses.

Mayreau

A small privately-owned island with deserted beaches and only one hotel and one guest house, though there is a plan to develop tourism. You can reach it only by boat. Once a week, however, the island springs to life with the arrival of a cruise ship which anchors in the bay and sends its passengers ashore for a barbecue and sunburn. In preparation for this, local women sweep the beach and the manchineel trees (poisonous) are banded with red.

Sleeping & eating **LL** *Salt Whistle Bay Club*, T4588444, F4588944, contact by radio, VHF h 16, boatphone 4939609, T613-6347108, in UK T0800-373742. 10 rooms, MAP, yacht charters and picnics on nearby islands), **B-C** *Dennis' Hideaway* (5 rooms). Good food and drinks at reasonable prices can be found at *Dennis' Hideaway*. *J & C Bar and Restaurant*, has the best view of the harbour with soft music, boutique, room for a large group, good lobster, fish and lambi, for parties of four and over the captain's dinner is free; *Island Paradise*, everything is prepared fresh, good lobster, fish and curried conch, half price happy hour 1800-1900, barbecue Friday with local band, free ride up the hill, skipper's meal free with more than three for dinner. There is a payphone in the village with an overseas operator for credit card calls.

Tobago Cays

The Tobago Cays are a small collection of islets just off Mayreau, protected by a horseshoe reef and surrounded by beautifully clear water. The beaches are some of the most beautiful in the Caribbean and there is diving and snorkelling on Horseshoe reef and wall. There are day charters out of St Vincent, Bequia and Union

Island. Anchor damage, together with over-fishing and removal of black coral has led to the death of some of the reef; hard coral lies broken on the bottom. The cays have now been declared a wildlife reserve and visitors are asked to take care not to damage marine resources. Although the Tobago Cays are crowded with charter boats, liveaboard boats or day charter catamarans, the reef is slowly coming back to life. Mooring buoys have been put in to prevent anchoring on the reef. Parrot fish, grouper, trunkfish, snapper and other reef fish, including a 6-ft nurse shark, can now be seen again. There are free moorings inside Horseshoe reef for day charter boats or dinghies, and anchorages west of Petit Rameau in the cut between Petit Rameau and Petit Bateau, or to the south of Baradel. You can shop at your boat or on the beach. Ice, fresh fish, lambi, lobster, T-shirts, even French designer clothes.

Petit St Vincent

Locally referred to as PSV, this is a beautiful, privately-owned, 113-acre island with one of the Caribbean's best resorts, the *Petit St Vincent* (rates vary during the year from US$510d to US$800d, FAP, includes room service and all facilities, plus 10% service and 7% tax, closed September/October, no credit cards). The island is owned and managed by Hazen Richardson, with help from his wife, Lynn, a staff of 80 (for 44 guests) and seven labradors (who seem to be in charge of entertainment). Accommodation is in 22 secluded cottages, there is a tennis court, fitness track and a wide range of watersports (sunfish, hobie cats, windsurfers, yacht day sails, snorkelling) is available, T4588801, F4588428. You can have room service (especially nice for breakfast) or eat in the central building. Once a week dinner is moved to the beach with music from a local band. Communication with the administration is done with coloured flags hoisted outside your cottage. Picnics can be arranged on the tiny islet Petit St Richardson. US reservations: PSV, PO Box 12506, Cincinnatti, Ohio 45212; T513-2421333 or 800-6549326, F513-2426951. The island can be reached by the resort's launch from Union Island. The resort will charter a flight from Barbados to Union Island for US$130 per person one way, children half price. The one anchorage is off the bar and restaurant, protected by a reef. The bar is open to visiting yachties or charter boats and reservations can be made for dinner if space is available. There is a credit card pay phone for

Mayreau & the Tobago Cays

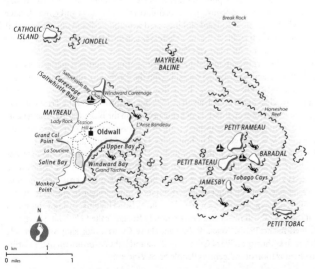

international calls. You can snorkel and dive off the Mopion and Punaise sandbar islands to the northwest, where moorings are available.

Palm Island

Also known as Prune Island, is another privately-owned resort, about a mile from Union Island, with coral reefs on three sides. The island was developed by John and Mary Caldwell, after they had made several ocean voyages. John is the author of *Desperate Voyage*, a book describing his first ocean crossing; he sailed from the USA to Australia to meet Mary, with virtually no experience. The boat was demasted, wrecked on a reef and John was stranded on an island and forced to eat slime off the bottom of the boat until he was rescued. The Caldwells later arranged to lease this swampy island from the St Vincent government and their family still runs the resort.

There are four beaches, of which the one on the west coast, Casuarina, is the most beautiful. **LL** *Palm Island Beach Club*, apartments and individual bungalows, T4588824, F4588804, palm@caribsurf.com (full board, no credit cards). The *Sunset Bar* is a casual bar and restaurant open to yachties and passengers of small cruise ships. Water purchase is possible for yachts, moorings available. Sailing, windsurfing, scuba diving, snorkelling, fishing, tennis, health club all available for guests; a dive master is also available to accompany yacht visitors, snorkelling and diving is usually on the Mopion and Punaise sandbar islands. There is a 10-minute launch service from Union Island. Shared charter flights can be arranged on *Mustique Airways* from Barbados to Union Island, where you will be met.

Background

History

By the time Columbus discovered St Vincent on his third voyage in 1498, the Caribs were occupying the island, which they called Hairoun. They had overpowered the Arawaks, killing the men but interbreeding with the women. The Caribs aggressively prevented European settlement until the 18th century but were more welcoming to Africans. In 1675 a passing Dutch ship laden with settlers and their slaves was shipwrecked between St Vincent and Bequia. Only the slaves survived and these settled and mixed with the native population and their descendants still live in Sandy Bay and a few places in the northwest. Escaped slaves from St Lucia and Grenada later also sought refuge on St Vincent and interbred with the Caribs. As they multiplied they became known as 'Black Caribs'. There was tension between the Caribs and the Black Caribs and in 1700 there was civil war.

In 1722 the British attempted to colonize St Vincent but French settlers had already arrived and were living peaceably with the Caribs growing tobacco, indigo, cotton and sugar. Possession was hotly disputed until 1763 when it was ceded to Britain. It was lost to the French again in 1778 but regained under the Treaty of Versailles in 1783. However, this did not bring peace with the Black Caribs, who repeatedly tried to oust the British in what became known as the Carib Wars. A treaty with them in 1773 was soon violated by both sides. Peace came only at the end of the century when in 1796 General Abercrombie crushed a revolt fomented the previous year by the French radical Victor Hugues. In 1797, over 5,000 Black Caribs were deported to Roatán, an island at that time in British hands off the coast of Honduras. The violence ceased although racial tension took much longer to eradicate. In the late 19th century, a St Vincentian poet, Horatio Nelson Huggins wrote an epic poem about the 1795 Carib revolt and deportation to Roatán, called *Hiroona*, which was published in the 1930s. Nelcia Robinson, above Cyrus Tailor shop on Grenville Street, is an authority on Black Caribs/Garifuna and is the co-ordinator of the Caribbean Organization of Indigenous People on St Vincent.

Milton Cato 1915-1997

Milton Cato was a key figure in the development of democracy and independence in St Vincent and the Grenadines. From a poor family, he pulled himself up through a scholarship to grammar school, and after serving in the Canadian Volunteer Army in the War, was called to the bar in 1949. He returned from London to set up business in Kingstown and became involved in politics, then in its infancy, with plantation workers only recently having won the vote. In 1955 he founded the St Vincent Labour Party (SVLP), and when St Vincent became part of the West Indian Federation, he went in 1958 to Trinidad as one of his island's representatives. After the collapse of the Federation he entered St Vincent's parliament in 1961 and led the SVLP to victory in the 1967 elections, becoming Chief Minister. In 1969 he participated in the negotiations which gave the island the status of Associated Statehood. He remained in power, with a brief interlude in 1972-74, and led St Vincent into independence in 1979. In the general elections of that year the SVLP won 11 of the 13 seats in the newly independent House of Assembly. However, economic stagnation and natural disasters, together with allegations of corruption, hit the popularity of Cato's government and the SVLP was defeated in the elections of 1984 which brought James Mitchell to power. Milton Cato retired a year later, shunning honours or public recognition of his service to his country, and died on 10 February 1997.

In the 19th-century labour shortages on the plantations brought Portuguese immigrants in the 1840s and East Indians in the 1860s, and the population today is largely a mixture of these and the African slaves. Slavery was abolished in 1832 but social and economic conditions remained harsh for the majority non-white population. In 1902, La Soufrière erupted, killing 2,000 people, just two days before Mont Pelée erupted on Martinique, killing 30,000. Much of the farming land was seriously damaged and economic conditions deteriorated further. In 1925 a Legislative Council was inaugurated but it was not until 1951 that universal adult suffrage was introduced.

St Vincent and the Grenadines belonged to the Windward Islands Federation until 1959 and the West Indies Federation between 1958 and 1962. In 1969 the country became a British Associated State with complete internal self-government. Government during the 1970s was mostly coalition government between the St Vincent Labour Party (SVLP) and the People's Political Party. In 1979 St Vincent and the Grenadines gained full independence, but the year was also remembered for the eruption of La Soufrière on Good Friday, 13 April. Fortunately no one was killed as thousands were evacuated, but there was considerable agricultural damage. In 1980 Hurricane Allen caused further devastation to the plantations and it took years for production of crops such as coconuts and bananas to recover. Hurricane Emily destroyed an estimated 70% of the banana crop in 1987.

The general elections held in June 1998 were won for the fourth successive time by the National Democratic party (NDP), which has held power under Prime Minister James Mitchell (Sir James after receiving a knighthood in the 1995 New Year Honours list) since 1984. The NDP won eight of the 15 seats in the House of Assembly, compared with 12 previously, and its share of the vote fell. The remaining seats were won by the United Labour Party (ULP), led by Vincent Beache. Mr Beache called for new elections within nine months because the ULP won 54.6% of the vote compared with only 45.3% for the winning NDP. Later in the year Ralph Gonsalves was elected leader of the ULP on the resignation of Mr Beache, who retained his position as leader of the opposition in the House of Assembly until October 1999.

The Government has often been criticized for its handling of the economy and for failing to deal with drug trafficking and health and education issues. US officials believe that offshore banks in St Vincent are being used to launder drugs money and that the southern Grenadines are a transshipment point. Marijuana is grown in the hills of St Vincent. A US eradication exercise in December 1998 was announced with enough warning to allow farmers to get in an early harvest. By mid-1999 the hills were green again with a new crop. Farmers protested that they had no alternative crop to grow. In January 2000 another crop eradication drive, backed by US Marines, destroyed over three million marijuana seedlings, one million mature plants and 14,000lbs of cured marijuana. One man was killed near Barrouallie.

Political tensions in 2000 were defused by the mediation of the Caribbean Community (Caricom). Conflict arose when the government introduced a bill to increase pension and gratuities for members of parliament which was passed by the House of Assembly in April. The ULP, trade unions and other organizations organized strikes and called for the government's resignation. The Caricom agreement, signed in May, called for general elections to be bought forward by two years and held no later than end-March 2001. A Caricom mission will oversee the elections. Sir James Mitchell (69) announced he would step down as leader of the NDP in August 2000. Two members of the ULP, Stanley John and Ken Boyea, resigned from the party when they faced disciplinary hearings in May. They had planned to start a new political party while still members of the ULP.

The people About a quarter of the people live in the capital, Kingstown and its suburbs. 8% live on the Grenadines. Sixty-six percent of the population is classed as black and 19% as mixed, while 2% are Amerindian/black, 6% East Indian, 4% white and the remainder are 'others'.

Government St Vincent and the Grenadines is a constitutional monarchy within the Commonwealth. The Queen is represented by a Governor General. There is a House of Assembly with 15 elected representatives and six senators. Sir James Mitchell has called for constitutional reform, but no action has been taken.

The economy

The St Vincent economy is largely based on agriculture and tourism, with a small manufacturing industry which is mostly for export. The main export is bananas, the fortunes of which fluctuate according to the severity of the hurricane season; in 1990 the volume rose to 79,586 tonnes, the highest ever, but in 1991-93 the crop was reduced because of drought. Drought again affected the 1994 crop which was then hit by Tropical Storm Debbie and exports fell to 30,933 tonnes. The sector used to contribute about 60% of export revenues and the fall in prices brought about by the new European banana policy has hit hard. The Banana Growers Association is in debt and has been attempting to cut costs, but launched a EC$50 mn programme to rehabilitate and improve 3,200 acres of banana land by 1997. Investment has also taken place in irrigation and packing sheds. Quality, prices, planting and production all recovered strongly in 1998. Nevertheless, the Government is encouraging farmers to diversify and reduce dependence on bananas with incentives and land reform. About 7,000 acres of state-owned land is being split up into 1,500 small holdings.

Arrowroot starch is the second largest export crop, St Vincent is the world's largest producer; the Government increased production by raising the area sown from 140 acres in 1990 to 1,200 acres by 1996. Arrowroot is now used as a fine dressing for computer paper as well as the traditional use as a thickening agent in cooking. Other exports include coconuts and coconut oil, copra, anthurium lilies, orchids, sweet potatoes, tannias and eddoes. Over half of all exports are sold to the UK.

Fishing has received government promotion and substantial aid from Japan. In 1998 Japan gave the island a grant of 776 mn yen (about EC$4.5 mn) for the construction of fishery centres in Kingstown and elsewhere, having previously granted EC$12 mn in 1996 for construction of jetties and fish refrigeration facilities in St Vincent, Canouan and Bequia, 72 mn yen (about US$7 mn) for a coastal fisheries development project and 916 mn yen for the national fisheries development plan.

St Vincent emerged as the largest flag of convenience in the Caribbean, with 521 ships on its register in 1990. In 1991 about 100 more were added as a direct result of the Yugoslav conflict, most of which came from Croatia and Slovenia. However, ships carrying the Vincentian flag have a poor record for safety, second only to Romania. Between 1990-92, 16.5% were detained by European port officials for unseaworthiness.

Tourism in St Vincent and the Grenadines is important as a major employer and source of foreign exchange. Expansion is limited by the size of the airport and the Government has encouraged upmarket, often yacht-based tourism. A plan to extend the airport runway to take jumbo jets is under discussion with possible finance from Taiwan, France and Kuwait. Stopover tourist arrivals are around 60,000 a year. Visitor expenditure is about US$50 mn a year.

Healthy economic growth was recorded in the 1980s: government receipts grew faster than spending, investment in infrastructural development was promoted and social development projects such as schools and hospitals received foreign concessionary financing. In the 1990s growth slowed as the banana industry faced considerable difficulties but, apart from 1994 when zero growth was registered, rates have remained positive.

Grenada

Grenada is described as a spice island, for it produces large quantities of cloves and mace and about a third of the world's nutmeg. It also grows cacao, sugar, bananas and a wide variety of other fruit and vegetables. Some of its beaches, specially Grand Anse, a dazzling two-mile stretch of white sand, are very fine. The majority of the tourist facilities are on the island's southwest tip, but the rest of the island is beautiful, rising from a generally rugged coast to a spectacular mountainous interior. The highest point is Mount St Catherine, at 2,757 ft. The island seems to tilt on a Northeast-Southwest axis: if a line is drawn through ancient craters of Lake Antoine in the Northeast, the Grand Étang in the central mountains and the Lagoon at St George's, it will be straight. Northwest of that line, the land rises and the coast is high; Southeast it descends to a low coastline of rias (drowned valleys). The island is green, well forested and cultivated and is blessed with plenty of rain in the wet season. Grenada (pronounced "Grenayda"), the most southerly of the Windwards, has two dependencies in the Grenadines chain, Carriacou and Petit (often spelt Petite) Martinique. They, and a number of smaller islets, lie north of the main island. The group's total area is 133 square miles. Grenada itself is 21 miles long and 12 miles wide.

Ins and outs

From Europe Scheduled flights from London, Gatwick, via Tobago twice a week with *British Airways*. *JMC* also flies twice a week with its year round charter service. *Condor* flies from Munich once a week via Tobago. **From the USA** *BWIA* flies from Miami and New York via Port of Spain, Trinidad. *American Airlines* fly daily from Miami. *Air Jamaica* and Delta have a joint operation from New York and Montego Bay; Air Jamaica also flies from Baltimore. **From the Caribbean** *BWIA* connects Grenada with Barbados and Trinidad. *LIAT* flies to Grenada from Antigua, Barbados, Dominica, Martinique, Guadeloupe, St Maarten, Tortola, Trinidad, St Lucia, St Vincent, San Juan and Tobago. *Helenair* flies from St Vincent, St Lucia and Trinidad. *Air Caribbean* also flies from Trinidad. *Airlines of Carriacou* connect Grenada with Carriacou and Union Island, flying several times a day from 0715 to 1720. Several companies operate charters to Grenada from Europe, the Caribbean and North America. The **Point Salines airport** is five miles from St George's: taxis only, fixed rates as advertized to St George's, EC$30 (US$14), 15 mins; EC$25 (US$10) to Grand Anse and Lance aux Épines. Journeys within a one-mile radius of the airport EC$7 (US$2.75). Add EC$10 (US$3.75) to fares between 1800 and 0600. However, if

Getting there
See transport, page 861, for further details

Getting there
See transport, page 861, for further details

Windward Islands

you start walking down the road towards St George's, you will find that the taxi changes into a bus and will pick you up for much less (only feasible with light luggage). If you are energetic, it takes an hour to walk to Grand Anse, longer to St George's.

Getting around

Driving is on the left. Be prepared for no road signs, no indication which way the traffic flow goes (just watch the other cars) & few street names

Buses run to all parts of the island from the Market Square and the Esplanade in St George's; on the Esplanade look for the signs in the square, ask around. Fares are EC$1 within St George's, EC$3 to Grand Étang, and EC$4.50 to Grenville and EC$5 to Sauteurs. There is also a regular bus service between Grenville and Sauteurs. The last buses tend to be in mid-afternoon and there are very few on Sun. **Cars** can be rented from a number of companies for about US$55 or EC$150 a day, plus US$2,500 excess liability and 5% tax (payable by credit card). You must purchase a local permit, on presentation of your national driving licence, for EC$30/US$12; a local permit is not

Grenada

required if you hold an international driving licence. Maps are often not accurate, so navigation becomes particularly difficult. Also be careful of the deep storm drains along the edges of the narrow roads. **Bike** rentals can be arranged with Ride Grenada, T4441157. Bike parts, but no repairs, at Ace Hardware, Lagoon Rd, south end. Cycling is good around Grenada, with accommodation conveniently spaced. The ride between Sauteurs and Victoria is peaceful with spectacular views. From Gouyave to St George's via Grand Etang is difficult but rewarding with some steep hills in the beautiful forest reserve and small, friendly communities. Allow 5-6 hrs.

The average temperature is 26°C. December and January are the coolest months. **Climate** The rainy season runs from June to November. In November 1999, the west coast of Grenada was hit badly by Hurricane Lenny and was declared a disaster area, as was the west coast of Carriacou and the whole of Petit Martinique. Sea walls collapsed, taking coastal roads with them, cutting off some villages, while floods hit harbour front restaurants in St George's and beach hotels at Grand Anse. Damage was estimated at US$100 mn. Winter (high) season prices come into effect from 16 December to 15 April. The tourist season is at its height between December and March, although visitor numbers also pick up in July and August.

Flora and fauna

A system of national parks and protected areas is being developed. Information is available from the Forestry Department, Ministry of Agriculture, Archibald Avenue, St George's. The focal point is the **Grand Étang National Park**, eight miles from the capital in the central mountain range. It is on the transinsular road from St George's to Grenville. The Grand Étang is a crater lake surrounded by lush tropical forest. A series of trails has been blazed which are well worth the effort for the beautiful forest and views, but can be muddy and slippery after rain. The **Morne Labaye** nature trail is only 15 minutes' long, return same route; the shoreline trail around the lake takes 1½ hours and is moderately easy; much further, 1½ hours' walk, is **Mount Qua Qua**. The trail then continues for an arduous three hours to **Concord Falls**, with an extra 30-minute spur to **Fedon's Camp** (see page 853). From Concord Falls it is 25 minutes' walk to the road to get a bus to St George's. These are hard walks (Mount Qua Qua, Fedon's Camp, Concord): wet, muddy, it rains a lot and you will get dirty. Take food and water. A guide is not necessary.

An interpretation centre overlooking the lake has videos, exhibitions and explanations of the medicinal plants in the forest. Leaflets about the trails can be bought here for EC$2 each. There is a bar, a shop and some amusing monkeys and parrots. The Park is open 0830-1600, entrance US$2, closed Saturday but there are some stalls open selling spices and souvenirs. There is overnight accommodation at Lake House, T4427425 or enquire at forest centre, also for camping.

The high forest receives over 150 inches of rain a year. Epiphytes and mosses cling to the tree trunks and many species of fern and grasses provide a thick undergrowth. The trees include the gommier, bois canot, Caribbean pine and blue mahoe. At the summit, the vegetation is an example of elfin woodland, the trees stunted by the wind, the leaves adapted with drip tips to cope with the excess moisture.

Apart from the highest areas, the island is heavily cultivated. On tours around the country look for nutmeg trees and the secondary product, mace, cloves, cinnamon, allspice, bay, tumeric and ginger. In addition there are calabash gourds, cocoa, coffee, breadfruit, mango, paw paw (papaya), avocado, and more common crops, bananas and coconuts. Sugar cane is used to make rum at three distilleries. Many of the spices can be seen at the Douglaston Estate or the Nutmeg Co-operatives in Gouyave or Grenville. Laura's Spice and Herb Garden, near Perdmontemps in St David's, has samples of herbs and spices grown in their natural habitat.

In the northeast, 450 acres around **Levera Pond** was opened as a National Park in 1994 (US$1 entrance). As well as having a bird sanctuary and sites of historic interest, Levera is one of the island's largest mangrove swamps; the coastal region has

Leatherback turtles come ashore here in Apr, May & Jun

☞ *Essentials*

Documents *Citizens of the UK, USA and Canada need only provide proof of identity (with photograph) and an onward ticket (but note that if you go to Grenada via Trinidad, a passport has to be presented in Trinidad). For all others a passport and onward ticket are essential, though a ticket from Barbados to the USA (for example) is accepted. Departure by boat is not accepted by the immigration authorities. Citizens of certain other countries (not the Commonwealth, Caribbean – except Cuba—, South Korea, Japan and most European countries) must obtain a visa to visit Grenada. Check before leaving home. When you arrive in Grenada expect to have your luggage examined very thoroughly. It may take you at least 45 minutes to get through passport control and customs. You must be able to give an accommodation address when you arrive.*

Currency *East Caribbean dollar: EC$2.70 = US$1.*

Departure tax *For stays of over 24 hours, departure tax is EC$50, (EC$25 for children 2-12). EC$10 airport tax is charged on departure from Lauriston Airport, Carriacou.*

Ports of entry *(Own flag) Hillsborough on Carriacou, Grenada Yacht Services at St George's, Spice Island Marina, Prickly Bay. No port fees for clearing in or out of Prickly Bay or St George's during normal working hours, Monday-Thursday 0800-1145, 1300-1600, Friday until 1700, overtime charges will apply outside those hours. On Carriacou, anchor in Tyrrel Bay and take bus, EC$2, to Hillsborough, charges EC$20 port fees during most times. Four crew and/or passenger lists, ships stores and health declaration, port clearance from the last country and valid passports. Monday-Thursday 0800-1145, 1300-1600, Friday until 1700. To clear out of the country take the boat to Prickly Bay (where they can see the boat), and four copies of the crew list. Firearms must be declared. Seal in a proper locker on board or*

take to an official locker on shore to be returned on departure. Yachting fees on Grenada are: less than 50 feet US$10, 50-100 feet US$12.

Anchorages *Halifax Harbour (may have smoke from garbage burning), St George's Lagoon (security problems noted), True Blue Bay, Prickly Bay, Mount Hartman Bay, Clark's Court Bay, Port Egmont, Calivigny Harbour, Westerhall Bay. Hog Island can be used as a day anchorage; government and coast guard uncertain about overnight use; occasionally clear out all boats but then don't come back for a while. Can dinghy to Lower Woburn from Mount Hartman or Hog Island to catch bus, EC$2, to St George's, otherwise taxi from Secret Harbour. Prohibited anchorages : Grand Anse Bay, Prickly Bay, Pingouin (Pink Gin) Beach, Point Salines, Tyrrel Bay (Carriacou), Mangrove Lagoon, the entire inner Lagoon. The outer Lagoon is prohibited to yachts and other liveaboard vessels. The Mangrove Lagoon may only be entered to shelter from a hurricane. Marine weather for Grenada and the Windward Islands on VHF Ch 6 at 1000.*

Marinas *Grenada Yacht Services in St George's Lagoon (T4402508) is being redeveloped with a new hotel, villas et cetera, see below. Spice Island Marine Services in Prickly Bay (Lance aux Épines), T444-4257/4342, F4442816, has a small boatyard with bar, restaurant, ship's store, laundry and mini-market, where boats can be stored or repaired on land as well as stern-to-dock, fuel and water. The Moorings Secret Harbour base in Mount Hartman has stern-to-docks, fuel and water, a mini-mart with basic food and drink, Rum Squall bar, will hold message/fax and mail for yachties, T4444548, F4444819. Day charter services, bareboat or with captain, from the marina. Carriacou Yacht Services in Tyrrel Bay provide mail, phone, fax and message service to yachts, as do The Studio, next to Alexis Supermarket. Plans are in hand for a marina at Clark's Court as well as a* controversial multi-million dollar resort with a championship golf course located on Hog Island. Controversy involves displacing local farmers and fishermen as well as losing a yacht anchorage and the environmental impact of constructing a causeway to connect Hog Island with the mainland.

Hours of business *Banks: 0800-1300 or 1400 Monday-Thursday; 0800-1200 or 1300, 1430-1700 Friday.* **Shops**: *0800-1600 Monday-Friday, 0800-1300 Saturday.* **Government offices**: *Monday-Friday 0800-1145, 1300-1600, closed Saturday.*

Official time *Atlantic Standard Time, 4 hours behind GMT, 1 ahead of EST.*

Voltage *220/240 volts, 50 cycles AC.*

Media Newspapers *There are no daily papers, only weeklies, including* Grenadian Voice, Indies Times, Grenada Guardian, The National, *and* The Informer.
Radio *There are four radio stations, on AM 535 kHz, AM 1440 kHz, FM 90 kHz and FM 101.7 kHz.*
Television *There are two television stations but many hotels have satellite reception. Cable TV is being installed.*

Tourist offices overseas *Austria c/o Discover the World Marketing, Stephans Platz 6/3/7, 1010 Vienna, T512-868640, F512-868660, discover_vie@compuserve.com*
Canada 439 University Av, Suite 930, Toronto, Ontario MSG 178, T416-5951343, F416-5958278, assoc@thermrgroup.ca
Germany Uhlandstrasse 30, 53340 Mechenheim, T02225-947507, F02225-947508.
UK 1 Collingham Gardens, Earls Court, London SW5 0HW, T020-73705164/5, F020-72440177, grenada@compuserve.com
USA 800 2nd Avenue, Suite 400K, New York, NY 10017, T212-6879554, 800-9279554, F212-5739731, gbt@caribsurf.com

Clothing *Casual, lightweight summer clothes suitable all year. Bathing costumes not accepted off the beach.*

Laundry *Tangie's Laundry & Dry Cleaning Service, Sugar Mill Roundabout, St George's, T4444747, next to the* Sugar Mill Night Club, *pick up and delivery service. Also Super Kleen, T4408499, Henry's Safari Tours, T4445313, and Spice Island Marina, T4444257.*

Safety *On the Carenage in St George's, you may be pestered for money, particularly after dark, but it is no more than a nuisance. Lagoon Road, however, does appear to be unsafe at times. Unemployment and drug abuse are serious problems; more than three quarters of the prison population have been sentenced for drug related crimes. Night police patrols have been introduced in hotels and beach areas. In the countryside people are extremely helpful and friendly and there is no need anywhere for anything other than normal precautions against theft. If visiting St George's it is best to pick a day when there are no cruise ships in port, to avoid hassle from vendors and touts. Carriacou is generally safe, despite smuggling. However two Swedish tourists were murdered on Paradise Beach in 2000 in the middle of the day, which just proves you can never be too careful. Locals were shocked and a man was quickly apprehended.*

Public holidays *New Year's Day (1 January), Independence Day (7 February), Good Friday and Easter Monday, Labour Day (1 May), Whit Monday (in May/June), Corpus Christi (June), August holidays (first Monday and Tuesday in August) and Carnival (second weekend in August), Thanksgiving (25 October), 25 and 26 December.*

Communications *The international code for Grenada is 473. See page 861 for further details.*

coconut palms, cactus and scrub, providing habitat for iguana and land crabs. There are white beaches where turtles lay their eggs and, offshore, coral reefs and the Sugar Loaf, Green and Sandy islands (boat trip to the last named on Sunday, see Ferries). You can swim at Bathway but currents are strong at other beaches. The coast between Levera Beach and Bedford Point is eroding rapidly, at a rate of several feet a year. South of Levera is **Lake Antoine**, another crater lake, but sunken to only about 20 ft above sea level; it has been designated a Natural Landmark.

On the south coast is **La Sagesse Protected Seascape**, a peaceful refuge which includes beaches, a mangrove estuary, a salt pond and coral reefs. In the coastal woodland are remains of sugar milling and rum distilleries. To get there turn south off the main road opposite an old sugar mill, then take the left fork of a dirt road through a banana plantation. Close to the pink plantation house (accommodation available), a few feet from a superb sandy beach, is *La Sagesse* bar and restaurant, good food, nutmeg shells on the ground outside. Walk to the other end of the beach to where a path leads around a mangrove pond to another beach, usually deserted apart from the occasional angler, fringed with palms, good snorkelling and swimming, reef just offshore.

Marquis Island, off the east coast, can be visited; at one time it was part of the mainland and now has eel grass marine environments and coral reefs. Nearby is **La Baye Rock**, which is a nesting ground for brown boobies, habitat for large iguanas and has dry thorn scrub forest. It too is surrounded by coral reefs.

To see a good selection of Grenada's flowers and trees, visit the **Bay Gardens** at Morne Delice (turn off the Eastern Main Road at St Paul's police station, the gardens are on your left as you go down). It's a pleasant place with a friendly owner; the paths are made of nutmeg shells. In the capital are the rather run down **Botanic Gardens**.

Grenada is quite good for birdwatching. The only endemic bird is the Grenada Dove, which inhabits scrubby woodland in some west areas. In the rainforest you can see the emerald-throated hummingbird, yellow-billed cuckoo, red-necked pigeon, ruddy quail-dove, cocoa thrush and other species, while wading and shore birds can be spotted at both Levera and in the south and southwest. The endangered hookbilled kite (a large hawk) is found in the Levera National Park and nowhere else in the world. It uses its beak to pluck tree snails (its only food) out of their shells. A pile of shells with holes in them is evidence that a kite ate there. Watch also for the chicken hawk. Yellow-breasted bananaquits are very common.

There is little remarkable animal life: frogs and lizards, of course, and iguana, armadillo (tatoo) and manicou (possum), all of these are hunted for the pot. One oddity, though, is a troop of Mona monkeys, imported from Africa over 300 years ago, which lives in the treetops in the vicinity of the Grand Étang. Another import is the mongoose.

Diving and marine life

Dive sites The reefs around Grenada provide excellent sites for diving. A popular dive is to the wreck of the Italian cruise liner, *Bianca C* which went down in 1961. Other dive sites include **Boss Reef**, **the Hole**, **Valley of Whales**, **Forests of Dean**, **Grand Mal Point** (wall dive), **Dragon Bay** (wall dive) ends at Molinière, **Happy Valley** (drift with current to Dragon Bay). Three wrecks from cargo ships off Quarantine Point, St George's, are in strong currents. Molinière reef for beginners to advanced has a sunken sailboat, the *Buccaneer*; Whibble Reef is a slopey sand wall (advanced drift dive); Channel reef is a shallow reef at the entrance to St George's with many rusted ships' anchors; Spice Island reef is for resort dives and beginners as well as the wrecks *Red Buoy*, *Veronica L* and *Quarter Wreck*. Dive sites around Carriacou include **Kick Em Jenny** (a submarine volcano), **Isle de Ronde**, **Sandy Island**, **Sister Rocks** (to 100 ft, strong currents), **Twin Sisters** (walls to 180 ft and strong currents), **Mabouya Island**, **Saline Island** (drift dive). The reef suffered some damage in 1999 from Hurricane Lenny, but the diving here is still good.

Dive companies change locations and resort affiliations rapidly, but there is usually one at any of the larger resorts. *Dive Grenada* is at *Allamanda Beach Resort*, T4441092, F4445875, www.divegrenada.com, PADI courses, wreck dives for experienced divers, night dives, snorkelling. *Eco Dive and Trek* at *Coyaba Beach Resort*, in Grand Anse, offers PADI courses, snorkelling, kayak and sunfish instruction, also home of Grenada's Turtle Conservation Project, T4447777, F4444808, www.scuba divegrenada.com *Sanvics Watersports, Grand Beach Resort*, is an all-inclusive operation with trips to islands, T4444371, F4445227, sanvics@caribsurf.com *Scuba Express* at *True Blue Inn*, has a custom designed dive boat with groups limited to 10 and a fully equipped dive shop, T4442133, F4440516, www.scubaexpress-grenada.com *Scuba World* at the *Rex Grenadian*, T/F4443864, scubaworld@caribsurf.com *1st Spice Divers Grenada*, at *Secret Harbour* and *the Moorings*, Lance aux Epines, T4441126, F4441127, www.spicedivers.com, operate from a pier at Mount Hartmann Bay with a 30 ft boat, courses offered in English, Dutch, German, French and Spanish, run by Peter and Gerlinde Seupel, quality personal attention. *Spice Island Diving* is at the *Spice Island Beach Resort*, T4443483, F4445319, www.spicebeachresort.com On Carriacou both dive operations are German speaking: *Tanki's Watersport Paradise*, at L'Esterre Bay, Carriacou, T4438406, F4438391, www.cacounet.com/paradise, and *Carriacou Silver Diving* at Main Street, Hillsborough, T/F4437882, www.scubamax.com, run by Max and Claudia Nagel, an enthusiastic German couple who have been on the island since 1993, two boats, very professional.

A basic scuba dive costs about US$40 per person, a two-tank dive is US$75, equipment rental US$10, resort course US$75, snorkelling trips US$16-20; dive packages and open water certification are available. Several charter boats doing day trip sailing excursions also offer scuba equipment. The nearest recompression chamber is in Barbados or Trinidad, both 30 minutes by air ambulance. Members of the Grenada Scuba Diving Association all carry oxygen on board their boats.

Snorkelling equipment hire costs about US$12 for three hours, sometimes for a day; again, there are plenty of opportunities for this. Glass-bottomed boats make tours of the reefs. The *Carriacou Islander* is a 35-ft motor catamaran with an observation window which can be raised or lowered as required and cruises around Carriacou and Petit Martinique.

Humpback whales can be seen off Grenada and Carriacou during their migrations in December-April. Pilot whales and dolphins are also found in Grenadian waters (see *Whale and Dolphin Watching* by Erich Hoyt at the beginning of this book). Contact Mosden Cumberbatch (see below) for whale watching tours, he has a power catamaran especially designed for whale watching, US$50 including sandwiches and drinks for lunch, five-hour trip. The Kido Ecological Research Station on Carriacou also organizes whale and dolphin watching on the catamaran, *Houkule'a*, which has hydrophones, T/F4437936 kido-ywf@caribsurf.com They are actively involved in restoring a mangrove system in the northern part of Carriacou and offer guided group tours to view the Petit Carenage Mangrove Restoration project. Volunteers are sometimes needed.

Beaches and watersports

There are 45 beaches on Grenada. The best are in the southwest, particularly **Grand Anse**, a lovely stretch of white sand which looks north to St George's. It can get crowded with cruise passengers, but there's usually plenty of room for everyone. Beach vendors have a proper market with 78 booths, washroom facilities, a tourist desk and a jetty for water taxis, to prevent hassling on the beach. **Morne Rouge**, the next beach going southwest, is more private, has good snorkelling and no vendors. There are other nice, smaller beaches around **Lance aux Épines**. The beaches at **Levera** and **Bathway** in the northeast are also good.

Windsurfing, waterskiing and **parasailing** all take place off Grand Anse beach. Windsurf board rental about US$7 for 30 minutes, waterskiing, US$15 per run, parasailing US$25. The *Moorings' Club Mariner* Watersports Centre at *Secret Harbour*, T4444439, F4444819, has small sail boats, sunfish, windsurfing, waterskiing, speedboat trips to Hog Island including snorkelling. Inshore sailing on sunfish, sailfish and hobiecats is offered by Grand Anse and Lance aux Épines hotels and operators. Rates are about US$10 for 30 minutes for sunfish rental.

Day sails **Sailing** in the waters around Grenada and through the Grenadines, via Carriacou, is very good. Sheltered harbours, such as Halifax Bay on the Leeward coast, can be found and there are marinas on the south coast. First Impressions (formerly Starwind Enterprises) has two catamarans accommodating 35 people for all types of charters, day, overnight, sunset, call Mosden Cumberbatch, T4403678, US$50 per person day sail, snorkelling included, US$15 sunset cruise. *Carib Cats*, T4443222, offer full-day, snorkelling or sunset cruises. *Catch the Spirit*, T4444753, sanvics@caribsurf.com, offer customized trips for snorkellers, divers or fishermen. *Firefly* is a 38 ft sloop available for day sails or charters, T4438625, studio@caribsurf.net The *Moorings Secret Harbour* Watersports Centre has skippered charters at US$25 per person half day, US$50 per person whole day, minimum four people, T4444439. Trips go to Carriacou, Sandy Island, Calivigny Island and Hog Island, or up the coast, stopping at beaches for barbecues or reefs for snorkelling. There are lots of other companies offering day sails, no shortage of choice. On Carriacou the *Silver Beach Resort* has a catamaran, *Afoxe*, for day sails, US$50 including lunch.

On the first weekend in August the **Carriacou Regatta** is held, which has developed into a full-scale festival, with land as well as watersports and jump-ups at night (T4437930). **La Source Grenada Sailing Festival** is held annually in January-February with several races and regattas, organized by the Grenada Yacht Club, T4402500. Other races include the True Blue Inn Pursuit Yacht Race in February (T4442000), the Bank of Nova Scotia Yacht Race in March, the Venezuela Independence Day Regatta in July, the Grand Anse Yacht Race in September (T4403050) and Grand Anse Match-Yacht Racing in October (T4403050). In November an end-of-hurricane-season yacht regatta sponsored by Carib Beer is timed to coincide with Beach Fest, a weekend of beach parties and watersports (T4403050).

Fishing **Deep-sea fishing** can be arranged through *Grenada Yacht Services, Bezo Charters*, call Graham or Ian (T443-5477, westrum@caribsurf.com), *Evans Chartering Services*, call Bob or Jill (T4444422, bevans@caribsurf.com) and Tropix (T4404961). At the end of January each year, Grenada hosts **The Spice Island Game Fishing Tournament**, T4402198 for information.

Other sports **Cricket**, the island's main land sport, is played from January to June. The locals play on any piece of fairly flat ground or on the beaches. **Soccer** is also played. Hotels have **tennis** courts and public courts are found at Grand Anse and Tanteen, St George's. There is a nine-hole **golf** course at the Grenada Golf and Country Club, Woodlands, above Grand Anse; the club is open daily 0800 to sunset, but only till 1200 on Sunday (T4444128). **Volleyball** can be played at the Aquarium Beach Club after snorkelling on the reef. It is a fun spot on a secluded beach just below Point Salines off the airport road, T4441410. **Hiking** is excellent, if muddy, in the Grand Étang National Park (see above, Flora and Fauna and below, Around the Island). An annual international **triathlon** is held in January, with a 1 km swim along the Grand Anse beach, a 25 km bicycle race to the airport, St George's and back to the hotel, then a 5 km run to the Carib brewery and back in individual and relay style. For information, contact Paul Slinger, PO Box 44, St. George's, T4403343. **Horseriding** can be arranged with The Horseman, St Paul's, St George's, for lessons or trail riding, T4405368.

A National Stadium is being built outside St George's, for completion in 2000 but already in use, which will be used for cultural events and exhibitions as well as sports, and have shops, offices, restaurants and bars. Sports facilities will include an international football and athletics stadium with a capacity for 15,000, a test match cricket ground and a cycle track.

St George's

St George's is one of the Caribbean's most beautiful harbour cities. The town stands on an almost landlocked sparkling blue harbour against a background of green and hazy blue hills, with its terraces of pale, colour-washed houses and cheerful red roofs. The capital was established in 1705 by French settlers, who called it Fort Royale. Much of its present-day charm comes from the blend of two colonial

St George's

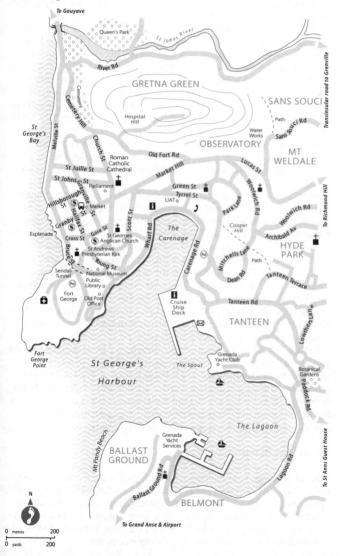

cultures: typical 18th-century French provincial houses intermingle with fine examples of English Georgian architecture. Unlike many Caribbean ports, which are built around bays on coastal plains, St George's straddles a promontory. It therefore has steep hills with long flights of steps and sharp bends, with police on point duty to prevent chaos at the blind junctions. At every turn is a different view or angle of the town, the harbour or the coast. The tourist board publishes a booklet, *Historic Walking Tour of St George's*, which is recommended.

The Carenage runs around the inner harbour, connected with the Esplanade on the seaward side of Fort George Point by the **Sendall Tunnel**, built in 1895. There is always plenty of dockside activity on the Carenage, with food, drinks and other goods being loaded and unloaded from wooden schooners. It is planned to redevelop St George's harbour, moving the cruise liner dock from the mouth of the Carenage to a point further down the southwest coast. The Carenage would then be left to small shipping and all the shopping would be duty-free. So far, a small promenade and shelter have been built.

The small **National Museum**, in the cells of a former barracks, in the centre of town (corner of Young and Monckton Streets) is worth a visit; it includes some items from West Africa, exhibits from the sugar and spice industries and of local shells and fauna. ■ *US$1, open Mon-Fri 0900-1630, Sat 1030-1300, T4403725*. **Fort George** (1705) on the headland is now the police headquarters, but public viewpoints have been erected from which to see the coast and harbour. Photographs are not allowed everywhere. Some old cannons are still in their positions; tremendous views all round. Just down from the Fort is St Andrew's Presbyterian Kirk (1830) also known as Scot's Kirk. On Church Street are a number of important buildings: St George's Anglican Church (1825), the Roman Catholic Cathedral (tower 1818, church 1884) and the Supreme Court and Parliament buildings (late 18th, early 19th century). St George's oldest religious building is the Methodist Church (1820) on Green Street.

The **Public Library** is an old government building on the Carenage which has been renovated and stocked with foreign assistance. In this part of the city are many brick and stone warehouses, roofed with red, fish tail tiles brought from Europe as ballast. A serious fire on 27 April 1990 damaged six government buildings on the Carenage, including the Treasury, the Government Printery, the Storeroom and the Post Office. Restoration work has been carried out. Also on the Carenage is a monument to the Christi Degli Abbissi, or Christ of the Deep, moved from the entrance to the harbour, which commemorates "the hospitality extended to the crew and passengers of the ill-fated liner", *Bianca C*. It stands on the walkway beside Wharf Road. The Market Square, off Halifax Street (one of the main streets, one steep block from the Esplanade), is always busy. It is the terminus for many minibus routes and on Saturday holds the weekly market.

Just north of the city is **Queen's Park**, which is used for all the main sporting activities, carnival shows and political events. It is surrounded by a turquoise palisade. From **Richmond Hill** there are good views (and photo opportunities) of both St George's and the mountains of the interior. On the hill are Forts Matthew (built by the French, 1779), Frederick (1791) and Adolphus (built in a higher position than Fort George to house new batteries of more powerful, longer range cannon), and the prison in which are held those convicted of murdering Maurice Bishop.

Around the island

The southwest From the Carenage, you can take a road which goes round the Lagoon, another sunken volcanic crater, now a yacht anchorage. It is overlooked by the ruins of the *Islander Hotel*, which was taken over by the revolutionary government and subsequently destroyed in the intervention. Work has now started on a new hotel and five-star yachting complex which will have 300 luxury rooms, 200 villas and restaurants and cafés along the waterfront, to be in operation by 2000.

Carrying on to the southwest tip you come to **Grand Anse**, Grenada's most famous beach. Along its length are many hotels, but none dominates the scene since, by law, no development may be taller than a coconut palm. A side road leads round to the very pleasant bay and beach at Morne Rouge, which is away from the glitz of Grande Anse. There is a good view across Grande Anse to St George's from the little headland of **Quarantine Point**. From Grand Anse the road crosses the peninsula to the Point Salines airport and the Lance aux Épines headland. The road to Portici and Parc à Boeuf beaches leads to the right, off the airport road; follow the signs to *Groomes* beach bar on Parc à Boeuf (food and drink available). Portici beach is virtually deserted, with good swimming despite a steeply shelving beach and excellent snorkelling around Petit Cabrits point at its northeast end. On **Prickly Bay** (the west side of Lance aux Épines) are hotels, the Spice Island Marina and other yachting and watersports facilities. Luxury homes take up much of Lance aux Épines down to Prickly Point. There is a glorious stretch of fine white sand, the lawns of the *Calabash Hotel* run down to the beach, very nice bar and restaurant open to non-residents, steel bands often play there. **Hog Island**, just off Mount Hartman Point, is being developed as a luxury *Ritz Carlton* resort, with 225 rooms and an 18-hole golf course, not likely to open before 2000, see **Marinas**, page 846. The project has met with some controversy. Friends of the Earth have criticized the lack of a proper environmental study, pointing to the devastation likely to the habitat of the Grenada dove, which is concentrated in that area.

From the Point Salines/Lance aux Épines crossroads you can head east along a road which snakes around the south coast. At **Lower Woburn**, a small fishing community (which can be reached by bus from St George's), you can see vast piles of conch shells in the sea, forming jetties and islets where they have been discarded by generations of lambie divers. Stop at *Island View Restaurant* or a local establishment, *Nimrod and Sons Rum Shop*. Yachtsmen visit this spot to sign the infamous guest register and to be initiated with a shot of Jack Iron rum (beware, it is potent!). Past Lower Woburn is the **Clarks Court Rum Distillery** (tours available with rum sales, tip the guide). It is a steam driven operation, unlike the river Antoine water wheel system. Any number of turn-offs, tracks and paths, go inland to join the Eastern Main Road, or run along the rias and headlands, such as Calivigny, Fort Jeudy, Westerhall Point or La Sagesse with its nature reserve (see above). Many of Grenada's most interesting and isolated bays are in the southeast, accessible only by jeep or on foot; taxi drivers can drop you off at the start of a path and you can arrange to be picked up later. The East Coast road from Westerhall to Grenville is being upgraded from a dirt to a concrete road, which makes driving difficult in parts.

The west coast road from St George's has been rebuilt with funds from the government, the Caribbean Development Bank, the EEC and USAID. It is good all the way to Industry. Only the section from Industry to Sauteurs has particularly rough patches but it is fine in an ordinary car with care. **The west coast**

Beauséjour Estate, once the island's largest, is now in ruins (except for the estate Great House). On its land are a Cuban-built radio station, a half-completed stadium and squatters; the owners and the government cannot agree on the estate's future. Beyond Beauséjour is Halifax Bay, a beautiful, sheltered harbour.

At Concord, a road runs up the valley to the First **Concord Falls** (45 minutes hot walk from the main road or go by car, driving slowly, children and vendors everywhere), where you can pay US$1 to go to a balcony above the small cascade. The Second Concord Falls are a 30-minutes' walk (each way), with a river to cross seven times; a guide will charge EC$20 but there is no need for one, the path has been improved and security at the lower falls has stopped occasional thefts, but it is slippery when wet. You should not swim in the pools as they are part of the island's water supply. Three hours further uphill is **Fedon's Camp**, at 2,509 ft, where Julian Fedon (see page 868) fortified a hilltop in 1795 to await reinforcements from Martinique to assist his rebellion against the British. After bloody fighting, the camp was captured; today it is a Historical Landmark. It is possible to hike from Concord to Grand Étang in five hours, a hard walk, wet and muddy but rewarding (see page 845). The trail is hard to spot where it leaves the path to the upper falls about two thirds of the way up on the left across the river. There is no problem following the trails in the opposite direction.

North of Concord, just before Gouyave, is a turn-off to **Dougaldston Estate**. Before the revolution 200 people were employed here in cultivating spices and other crops. Now there are only about 20 workers, the place is run down, the buildings in disrepair, the vehicles wrecked. Still, you can go into a shed where bats fly overhead and someone will explain all the spices to you. Samples cost EC$3 for a bag of cinammon or cloves, EC$2 for nutmeg, or there are mixed bags; give the guide a tip.

Gouyave, 'the town that never sleeps', is a fishing port, nutmeg collecting point and capital of St John's parish. At the Nutmeg Processing Station, you can see all the stages of drying, grading, separating the nutmeg and mace and packing (give a tip here too). The husks are used for fuel or mulch and the fruit is made into nutmeg jelly (a good alternative to breakfast marmalade), syrup or liquor. The Station is a great wooden building by the sea, with a very powerful smell. A tour for US$1 is highly recommended. Gouyave is the principal place to go to for the Fisherman's Birthday festival. On the last Friday in every month from May-December, Gouyave is open to tourists on a grand scale, with tours and walks during the day. In the evening the main street is closed to traffic, there is food, drink and music and dancing.

The north Just outside Victoria, another fishing port and capital of St Mark's Parish, is a rock in the sea with Amerindian petroglyphs on it (best to know where to look over the parapet). The road continues around the northwest coast, turning inland before returning to the sea at **Sauteurs**, the capital of St Patrick's parish, on the north coast. The town is renowned as the site of the mass suicide of Grenada's last 40 Caribs, who jumped off a cliff rather than surrender to the French (see page 867). Sauteurs celebrates St Patrick's Day with a week of activities in the arts, crafts, food and drink. Behind Sauteurs is McDonald College from whose gate there are marvellous views out to sea, with the Grenadines beyond the town's two church towers, and inland to cloud-covered mountains. In March Sauteurs celebrates St Patrick's Day with a week of events, exhibits of arts and crafts and a mini-street festival.

From Sauteurs a road approaches **Levera Bay** (see above) from its west side. Turn left at *Chez Norah's* bar, a two-storey, green, corrugated iron building (snacks available); the track rapidly becomes quite rough and the final descent to Levera is very steep, suitable only for four-wheel drive. A better way to Levera approaches from the south. The road forks left about two miles south of Morne Fendue, passes through river Sallee and past Bathway Beach. The river Sallee Boiling Springs are an area of spiritual importance; visitors are inspired to throw coins into the fountain while they make a wish. Swimming is good at the beautiful Levera Beach and there is surf in certain conditions. Do not swim far out as there is a current in the narrows between the beach and the privately-owned Sugar Loaf Island. Further out are Green and Sandy Islands; you may be able to arrange a trip there with a fisherman who keeps his boat on Levera Beach.

Morne Fendue plantation house offers accommodation and serves lunch for EC$40, including drinks; good local food and all you can drink, T4429330, reservations essential. The house, owned by Betty Mascoll MBE, is full of atmosphere (although some of the plaster and stucco work is in poor shape), and the driveway ends in a flowerbed full of poinsettias. St Patrick's is an agricultural region, comparatively poor and marginal.

The east coast On the east side of the island, Amerindian remains can be seen on rock carvings near **Hermitage** (look for a sign on the road) and at an archaeological dig near the old **Pearls airport**. Apparently it's so unprotected that lots of artefacts have been stolen. The airport is worth a quick visit to see the two old Cuban and Russian planes and the duty-free shop, a ghost town, although the runway is well used for cricket, biking and social encounter in general. An excursion can be made to Lake Antoine (see above) with, nearby, the **River Antoine Rum Distillery**, driven by a water mill, the oldest in the Caribbean (guided tours, T4427109). The only modern equipment is the lock for government control. Try the 151° proof rum, they sell all by the bottle. The **Dunfermline Rum Distillery** can also be visited. There are no organized tours but the staff will show you around and explain the process.

Grenville is the main town on the east coast and capital of St Andrew's Parish, the largest parish in Grenada with a population of about 25,000. It is a collection point for bananas, nutmeg and cocoa, and also a fishing port. You can tour the Nutmeg Cooperative Processing Station, US$1, with samples of nutmeg and mace (tip the guide). There are some well-preserved old buildings, including the Court House, Anglican Church, police station and Post Office. Saturday is market day, worth seeing. Weavers turn palm fronds into hats, baskets and place mats.

The Rainbow City Festival is held here at the beginning of August, with arts and crafts displays, street fairs, cultural shows and a 10 km road race. Funds are being raised to restore and convert the old Roman Catholic church into a library, museum, art gallery and cultural centre. Construction of the church began in 1841 and was used as a church until 1915, when mosquitoes finally triumphed over worshippers. From 1923-1972 it was used as a school, but then abandoned.

Two miles south of Grenville are the **Marquis Falls**, also called Mount Carmel Falls, the highest in Grenada. Trails are being improved, with signposts and picnic areas. Marquis village was the capital of St Andrew's in the 17th and 18th centuries. Nowadays it is the centre of the wild pine handicraft industry. Historical sites nearby are Battle Hill and Fort Royal. From here boats go to Marquis Island (see above).

Mount St Catherine can be climbed quite easily, contrary to popular opinion, although in places it is a climb rather than a walk. There are several routes, perhaps easiest from Grenville. Take a minibus to the Mount Hope road, this is a four-wheel drive track which becomes the path up the mountain. It takes about two hours from leaving the minibus. A guide is not necessary. Do not go alone, however, and do not go if you suffer from vertigo. Do not take chances with daylight. For information on this and anything else, contact Mr and Mrs Benjamin at Benjamin's Variety Store, Victoria Street, Grenville. If they do not know the answer they will know someone who does. Mrs Benjamin is on the Tourist Board. Telfer Bedeau, from Soubise, is the walking expert, and can be contacted on T4426200.

The interior

The transinsular, or hill road, from Grenville to St George's used to be the route from the Pearls airport to the capital, which all new arrivals had to take. Now it is well-surfaced, but twisty and narrow. The minibus drivers on it are generally regarded as 'maniacs'. To give an idea of the conditions, one bend is called 'Hit Me Easy'. The road rises up to the rain forest, often entering the clouds. If driving yourself, allow up to 1½ hours from Levera to St George's and avoid the mountain roads around Grand Étang in the dark, although the night-time sounds of the dense jungle are fascinating. Shortly before reaching the Grand Étang (full details above), there is a side road to the St Margaret, or **Seven Sisters Falls**. They are only a 30-minute walk from the main road, but a guide is essential, or else get very good directions. After Grand Étang, there is a viewpoint at 1,910 ft overlooking St George's. A bit further down the hill is a detour to the **Annandale Falls** which plunge about 40 ft into a pool where the locals dive and swim. Tourists are pestered for money here, for diving, singing, information, whether requested or not. If coming from St George's on Grenville Road, fork left at the Methodist Church about half way to Grand Étang.

The peaks in the southeast part of the Grand Étang Forest Reserve can be walked as day trips from St George's. **Mount Maitland** (1,712 ft), for instance, is a pleasant morning out. Take a bus from the Market Place to Mardigras, or if there is none, get off at the junction at St Paul's and walk up. At the Pentecostal (IPA) church, turn left and immediately right. The paths are reasonably clear and not too muddy, but shorts are not recommended and long sleeves are preferable. The walk takes less than an hour each way and there are good views from the top over both sides, with some hummingbirds.

Mount Sinai (2,306 ft) is not as spectacular as Mount St Catherine, nor as beautiful as Mount Qua Qua, but is not as muddy either. Take a bus from St George's to Providence, then walk up (two hours) the particularly lovely (and friendly) road to Petit Étang and beyond, where the road turns into a track in the banana fields. The path up the mountain is hard to spot; it begins behind a banana storage shed and must be closely watched. The terrain is a bit tricky near the top. There is a path down the other side to Grand Étang. Local opinions differ over how badly you would get lost without a guide as the paths are no longer maintained.

The highest point in the southeast is known on the Ordnance Survey map as South East Mountain (2,348 ft), but to locals as Mount Plima (Plymouth?). You can get up to the ridge, from where there are fine views, but both this summit and the nearby Mount Lebanon are inaccessible without a guide and machete. Here too it used to be possible to descend to Grand Étang but it is difficult now. For this area take a bus from St George's to the junction for Pomme Rose and walk up through the village. Mayhe Hazard lives near the top of the village and is the local expert on the trails (traces). He is good company and may be prepared to guide in the area; he will certainly show you the trail to the ridge, which you could never find alone.

Essentials

Sleeping
Hotel rooms are subject to a 10% service charge & 8% tax on accommodation, food & beverages

Grenada is particularly well served with good, mid-range, small hotels and guest houses, only a selection of which we print here. The Tourist Board has a brochure of *Intimate Inns of Grenada*, which lists many of them. Although large-scale tourism is starting to be developed, most of the hotels are still small enough to be comfortable and friendly even if they do cater for package tours. The majority of hotels are in the Grand Anse area, with several around Lance aux Épines. In St George's there are more guest houses than hotels

St George's C *Tropicana Inn*, Lagoon Road, T4401586, F4409797, tropicana@cpscarib net.com 20 double rooms, bath, a/c, some with patio, cater to business as well as vacation traveller, family run, overlooks marina, on bus route.

Grand Anse LL-AL *Allamanda Beach Resort and Spa*, PO Box 27, St George's T4440095, F4440126, siesta@caribsurf.com 52 rooms, a/c, fans, pool, fishing, boating, bar, café, restaurant, games room, scuba diving and watersports, tennis, massage, gym. **L-AL** *Coyaba*, PO Box 336, St George's, T4444129, F4444808, coyaba@caribsurf.com Popular with package tours, but very comfortable, lots of facilities, 70 rooms on 5½ acres, three are wheelchair accessible, large pool with swim-up bar. **LL-AL** *Grenada Grand Beach Resort & Convention Centre*, PO Box 441, St George's, T4444371, F4444800, higda@caribsurf.com 186 rooms and suites, a/c, garden view, or beachfront, suites or rooms, many facilities, restaurant pricey, open 0700-2300, being expanded 1998-99 to add 50 suites, golf course, swimming pool and 800-seat conference centre. **LL** *Spice Island Beach Resort*, PO Box 6, St George's, T4444258, F4444807, spiceisl@caribsurf.com US$2.5 mn expansion and renovation programme in 2000 with rebuilt reception area. Ocean front suites, garden view, or pool suite, no children under 12 in pool suites, no children under five in winter, all inclusive available on request, lots of sports and other facilities on offer, fitness centre, health spa. Shared facilities with sister property, **L-AL** *Blue Horizons Cottage Hotel*, PO Box 41, St George's, T4444316, F4442815, blue@caribsurf.com 32 rooms, a/c, fan, games room, parking, pool, TV, phone, its *La Belle Créole* restaurant is one of the island's best. **LL-A** *The Flamboyant*, PO Box 214, St George's, T4444247, F4441234, flambo@caribsurf.com 61 units in rooms, suites and cottages, EP, TV, phone, pool, free snorkelling equipment, at the end of Grand Anse, lovely views, steep walk down to beach, quite a walk to bus stop. **B-C** *South Winds Holiday Cottages and Apartments*, Grand Anse, PO Box 118, St George's, T4444310, F4444404, cdavid@ caribsurf.com Monthly rates on request, 1-2 bedrooms, a/c or fan, cable TV, radio, electric mosquito killer, large kitchen, terrace or balcony, simple but clean, good restaurant, friendly staff and dogs, 5-10-min walk from beach, good view, also car hire.

Morne Rouge **AL-B** *Gem Holiday Beach Resort*, PO Box 58, T4443737, F4441189, gem@ caribsurf.com Rooms vary in quality, one or two-bedroomed apartments, lovely beach, good position but hot, a/c nice and cool, enjoyable beachside lounge also popular with locals, restaurant limited. **L-A** *True Blue Inn*, P O Box 308, St George's, T4442000, F4441247, trueblue@caribsurf.com, between Grand Anse and Point Salines airport. Small and friendly, owner-managed cottages and apartments, kitchenettes, pool, dock facilities, boat charter available, restaurant and bar.

Point Salines **LL-L** *Rex Grenadian*, PO Box 893, St George's, T4443333, F4441111, grenrex@caribsurf.com 212 rooms, a/c, fans, gym, pool, tennis, two beaches, watersports, scuba diving, six restaurants and bars, conference facilities, five rooms for handicapped guests. **LL** *La Source*, PO Box 852, T4442556, F4442561, lasource@caribsurf.com 100 rooms, all-inclusive, steep hike to some rooms, pool, nine-hole golf course, health and leisure facilities, haphazard scheduling of treatments so partners not always done simultaneously, beaches not as good as Grand Anse, limited availability.

Lance aux Épines **LL** *Calabash*, PO Box 382, St George's, T4444334, F4445050, calabash@ caribsurf.com Winner of a prestigious Golden Fork award for quality of food and hospitality, probably the poshest hotel on Grenada, 30 suites, eight with private pool, 22 with whirlpool, expensive, MAP including breakfast in suite, afternoon tea and dinner, on beach, nice grounds, tennis, games room, health and beauty facility. **LL-AL** *Twelve Degrees North*, PO Box 241, St George's, T/F4444580, 12degrsn@caribsurf.com. 10 apartments with maid/cook, laundry, no children under 15, very private, tennis, pool, snorkelling, windsurfing, sunfish all included. **LL-AL** *Secret Harbour*, PO Box 11, St George's, T4444439, F4444819, secret@ caribsurf.com. 20 luxury rooms, chalets built into the rock face overlooking the harbour, private, wonderful views, pool, friendly, steel band at times, no children under 12 accepted, this is a Club Mariner Resort and bareboat or crewed yacht charters are available from the marina. **L-A** *Coral Cove Cottages*, PO Box 487, St George's, T4444422, F4444718, coralcv@ caribsurf.com Several, lovely, well-equipped cottages, beautiful view of Atlantic, 15 mins walk to Lance aux Epines, own beach and jetty, good snorkelling, pool, very private, great for children. **B-C** *Villamar Holiday Resort*, PO Box 546, St George's, T4444716, F4441341. 20 rooms near Grand Anse and Prickly Bay, a/c, kitchenette, TV, phone, patio, one and two bedroom suites for families, business or single travellers, children under 12 sharing free, monthly/group rates on request. *Holiday Haven*, PO Box 364, St George's, T4440808, F4444343, above a cove on Prickly Point. 2-3 bedroomed villas, a/c, TV, phone, modern, square design, weekly rates available.

South coast **AL** *Petit Bacaye*, on bay of same name, PO Box 655, Westerhall PO, T/F4432902, hideaways@wellowmead.u-net.com Thatched self-catering cottages, one or two-bedroom, includes tax and service, breakfast and snacks at beach bar, fisherman call daily, catch can be cooked to order, reef and own islet 200 m offshore, jeep and guide hire arranged, sandy beach round the bluff. **AL-C** *La Sagesse Nature Centre* (see page 848), St David's, PO Box 44, St George's, T/F4446458, lsnature@caribsurf.com 8 rooms, small, excellent, perfect setting, an old plantation house on a secluded, sandy bay (the sea may be polluted in the rainy season, seek the hotel's advice), child-friendly, good restaurant, excursions.

Guest houses **St George's** **D** *Mitchell's Guest House*, H A Blaize Street, T4402803. Central, nine double and two single rooms with fan, breakfast on request, downstairs rooms dark and not very private, no towels, town noises, ability to sleep through cock crowing essential. **D** *St Ann's Guest House*, Paddock, beyond Botanic Gardens (some distance from centre), T4402717. Includes excellent breakfast, friendly, entrance forbidden to 'prostitutes and natty dreds', meals (communal), EC$20, good value, a bit difficult to sleep because of dogs and roosters, take ear plugs. **E** *Yacht's View*, Lagoon Road, T4403607. Cheap but noisy and frequently without water or fans, 9 rooms, 5 bathrooms, 4 kitchens. **E** *Lakeside*, at the end of Lagoon Road going towards Grand Anse, T4402365 (Mrs Ruth Haynes). View over yacht marina, helpful, cooking facilities, drinks available, mixed reports. **Grand Anse C** *Roydon's*, T/F4444476. EP or MAP, helpful staff, fans, private bathroom, very nice even if a bit over-priced, next to a busy street, good restaurant, 10 mins' walk from beach. **Grenville C** *Grenada Rainbow Inn*, PO Box 923, St Andrew's, T4427714, F4425332, rainbowinn@ grenadaexplorer.com 15 rooms or apartments, buses stop outside, organic food, earthen oven for barbecue. A few miles north at **Dunfermline** is **E** *Sam's Inn*, T4427853/7313. Use of kitchen, hot water, balconies, country setting, small store close by, Mrs Ellen Sam is very friendly owner. **Morne Fendue C** *The Plantation House*, see page 854, T4429330. Breakfast included, good base for exploring the north, including Bathway beach and the Carib jump at Sauteurs. **Victoria D** *Hotel Victoria*, on the waterfront. Basic rooms but nice location. **Gouyave E** *Patino's*, at the end of the town on the waterfront above a small bar. Does not look like a guest house so you may have to ask for directions, but worth the effort. Two-bedroom apartments with kitchens, Patino is very friendly, lived in Canada. Good base for nutmeg factory and Concord Falls.

Villas and apartments There are many furnished villas and apartments available for rent from various agents, daily or weekly rental. **D** *RSR Apartments* on Lagoon Road, Springs PO, St George's, T4403381, F4408384, bastjo@hotmail.com Recommended for good value, 1 or 3 bedroom apartment, kitchen, living room, bathroom, veranda, guard at night, also cockroaches, bus into town.

Camping Camping is not encouraged as there are no facilities, but it is permitted in the Grand Etang National Park and in schools and church grounds on Carriacou.

Eating

Rum punches are excellent. Be sure to try the local sea-moss drink (a mixture of vanilla, algae & milk)

Grenada's cooking is generally very good. Lambi (conch) is very popular, as is callaloo soup (made with dasheen leaves), souse (a sauce made from pig's feet), pepper pot and pumpkin pie. There is a wide choice of seafood, and of vegetables. Goat and wild meat (armadillo, iguana, manicou) can be sampled. Nutmeg features in many local dishes, try nutmeg jelly for breakfast, ground nutmeg comes on top of rum punches. Of the many fruits and fruit dishes, try stewed golden apple, or soursop ice cream. There are three makes of rum, whose superiority is disputed by the islanders, *Clark's Court*, *River Antoine* and *Westerhall Plantation Rum*, made by Westerhall Distilleries. All three can be visited for a tour and sampling of rum and products for sale. Several readers have endorsed Westerhall Plantation Rum for its distinct flavour and aroma. The term 'grog', for rum, is supposed to originate in Grenada: taking the first letters of 'Georgius Rex Old Grenada', which was stamped on the casks of rum sent back to England. Grenada Breweries brew *Carib Lager*, *Guinness* and non-alcoholic malt beers.

There is quite a wide choice of restaurants, apart from the hotels mentioned above, and you are recommended to eat the local dishes, which are very good. Tax of 8% and service of 10% is usually added to the bill. Unless stated otherwise, restaurants below are in **St George's**. *Nutmeg*, on the Carenage above the Sea Change Book Store (T4402539). Delicious local dishes and its own famous rum punch, very popular, but avoid if you do not want to see turtle on the menu, open Mon-Sat 0800-2300, Sun 1600-2300. *Rudolph's*, also on the Carenage (T4402241). Entrées EC$18-50, but good, local and international food, in friendly pub atmosphere, excellent rum punch, open Mon-Sat 1000-2400. *Portofino*, on the Carenage. Italian about US$20 for meal and drink, nice place, witty proprietor, T4403986. *Tropicana*, on the Lagoon, T4401586. Popular, Chinese and local food, good, entrées from EC$10-45, excellent egg rolls and rotis, vast portions. Recommended. Seating inside or out on covered patio, barbecues, open 0730-2400, reservations recommended in high season, also takeaway rotis and Chinese. *Mamma's*, Lagoon Road. Multifarious local foods which the conservation-minded may not want to try (famous for wild meat dishes when in season but you don't always know what you are getting, you may not be told until you've finished that there is no wild game that night), need to book, T4401459, full dinner EC$45 1930-2100, bar open until 2400. *Patrick's*, also on Lagoon Rd, is reported even better, with a greater variety and interesting combinations of local foods, breadfruit salad and green papaya salad are outstanding. *Ebony*, Victoria Street, Grenville. Unique local dishes in relaxed setting, another place where you might find things like turtle on the menu, snacks and entrées, no credit cards, T4427325. *Blue Orchid Restaurant and Bar*, Grand Anse, T4440999. Family night specials on Thu and Fri, bring your own alcoholic beverages. On Melville Street, near waterfront taxi stand, *Deyna's*, T4406795. New, modern, good local food at local prices, and lots of it, rotis, excellent coffee, open Mon-Sat 0800-2100, Sun 1000-1600, crowded at lunch. Recommended. *Pitch Pine Bar*, Esplanade, T4401976. Fun place on the waterfront for a drink or meal, curry mutton, fish broth.

At the St George's end of Grand Anse is *Coconut Beach Restaurant*, T4444644. With excellent French creole food and fruit juices and punches, barbecues and live music Wed, Fri, Sun evenings in high season, open 1000-2200. *Fish 'n' Chick*, at Sugar Mill roundabout, T4444132. Barbecue and grilled fish and chicken, local fast food and takeaway. *Joe's Steakhouse*, T4444855. Steak and seafood restaurant and bar, Le Marquis complex, USDA steaks, marinated and grilled with Caribbean touch. *Beachside Terrace*, at the *Flamboyant Hotel*, T4444247. Big buffet and steel band Wed in season, good, very cheap Sun barbecue lunch, geared towards families. The *Cot Bam Beach Bar* on Grand Anse in front of *Coyaba* (approach by road at night) has good food, cheap, limited menu, locals drink here from morning onwards and are keen conversationalists. *Kentucky Fried Chicken*, Granby Street and Grand Anse, and *Pizza Hut* outlets are in this area. *Tabanca at Journey's End*, near *The Flamboyant*, T4441300. Excellent food, a mixture of Grenadian and international, run by an Austrian, her coffee is superb, open 1700-2300, live music weekly after 2100, closed Tue. *La Boulangerie* at Le Marquis Mall, Grand Anse, T4441131, French bakery and coffee shop with baguettes, croissants, sandwiches, pizza and roast chicken, good picnic food, free delivery, open Mon-Sat 0800-2100, Sun 0900-2100. *Brown Sugar Restaurant*, above *South Winds Holiday Cottages* in Grande Anse, T4442374. Panoramic view of Grand Anse Bay and St George's Harbour, complementary transport, vegetarian and children's meal available, overpriced, steel band on Tue, Fri, good musicians on Sun, open 1800-2300. *Bad Ass Café*, Le Marquis Complex, Grand Anse, T4444020. Mexican, burgers, baked potatoes, sandwiches, salad bar, open 1100-1400. *Aquarium Restaurant*, T4441410, Point Salines Beach. Open 1000-2300 except Mon, Sat volleyball, Sun lobster barbecue, showers, toilets, snorkelling offshore, good food, lobster, fish, steak, sandwiches, live music and buffet from 1900 first Sat in month, dinner reservations requested. *Red Rooster*, Lance aux Épines, T4444855. Offers takeaway and delivery to hotel area for chicken and local food. *Cicely's*, Calabash Hotel, Lance aux Épines, T4444334. Reservations required, dinner 1900-2300, award winning restaurant overlooks Prickly Bay, entrées EC$40-60. *Red Crab*, Lance aux Épines, T4444424. Excellent local seafood and international, entrées from EC$25, fabulous steak dinner EC$60, live music Mon, Fri in season, darts Wed nights. *Choo Light*, next door, T4442196. Chinese, good service, food and prices, also takeaway, open Mon-Sat 1100-1500, 1800-2300, Sun and holidays 1700-2300. *Island View Restaurant and Nightclub*, Clark's Court Bay, Woburn, T4441878, VHF 16. Open 1000-2300, casual games room with pub food, pool tables, pinball machine etc, disco from 2200 Fri and Sat, dinghy dock, boat outings arranged with food and drinks. *Petit Bacaye*, on bay of same name. Fresh fish, fishermen's catch cooked to order.

See above for *Morne Fendue* plantation house restaurant, good local food and drinks, lunch EC$40, reservations essential, T4429330. *La Sagesse* (see page 848 and 857) terrible service reported, fresh lobster, grilled tuna, outdoor restaurant, beautiful location, walk it off afterwards, good hiking over the mountain, T4446458 for reservations which are recommended, especially for dinner, US$28 for return transport, lunch, guided nature walk with exotic fruit tasting, dinner packages available, entrées EC$15-50. *Mount Rodney Estate*, St Patrick's. Open for lunch 1200-1400 Mon-Fri, reservations essential, EC$45 set price, T4429420.

Bars

Happy hours at marinas: *Boatyard Bar* at Prickly Bay Marina. 1730-1830, TV and live music several times a week in season, also good food at the Yacht Club. *Rum Squall Bar* at Secret Harbour Marina. Inexpensive weekly barbecue and daily happy hour 1600-1700. *Grenada Yacht Club* in St George's. Happy hour Wed, Fri, Sat 1800-1900, yachtsmen and others welcome, great place to sit and watch the boats entering the lagoon (and see if they are paying attention to the channel markers or run aground). *Casablanca Sportsbar*, Grand Anse. Games, pool, snooker, large TV.

Festivals **Easter** is a time for lots of events, both religious and otherwise. There are dinghy races from Grand Anse to the Yacht Club, a kite flying competition at the old Pearls airport, with music, food and drink, and other activities.

Carnival takes place over the 2nd weekend in *August*, although some preliminary events and competitions are held from the last week in July, with calypsos, steelbands, dancing, competitions, shows and plenty of drink. The Sunday night celebrations, Dimanche Gras, continue into Monday, J'Ouvert; Djab Djab Molassi, who represent devils, smear themselves and anyone else (especially the smartly dressed) with black grease. On Monday a carnival pageant is held on the stage at Queen's Park and on Tuesday the bands parade through the streets of St George's to the Market Square and a giant party ensues. For information on playing Mas with a band contact Derrick Clouden (T4402551) or Wilbur Thomas (T4403545) of the Grenada Band Leaders Association. During Carnival it is difficult to find anywhere to stay and impossible to hire a car unless booked well in advance.

Also in *August*, over the first weekend, are the **Carriacou Regatta** (see above) and the **Rainbow City cultural festival** in Grenville which goes on for about a week.

Throughout the island, but especially at Gouyave, the **Fisherman's Birthday** is celebrated at the end of *June* (the feast of Saints Peter and Paul); it involves the blessing of nets and boats, followed by dancing, feasting and boat races. **Independence Day** is *7 February*. Grenada holds a **Spice Jazz Festival** in *May or June*, with lots of music, cooking, sports.

Nightlife The resort hotels provide evening entertainment, including dancing, steelband and calypso music, limbo, etc. There are not a great many discothèques and nightclubs outside the hotels and low season can be very quiet. The Boatyard at the marina on L'Anse Aux Epines Beach has bands playing Wed and Fri nights with dancing; *Castaways*, L'Anse Aux Epines, T4441250, restaurant from 1700-2200 and disco from 2200; *007* is a floating restaurant and bar on the Carenage, opposite the fire station, T4405656, with a Spanish and creole cuisine and karaoke on Wed, Fri, Sat and Sun nights; *Dynamite Disco* at the Limes on Grand Anse Beach has weekend parties; *Fantazia 2001 Disco* on Morne Rouge Beach, T4444224, from 2130 Fri and Sat dancing and *Cultural Cabaret*, cover charge, *Golden Oldies* Wed; *Le Sucrier*, in the Sugar Mill at Grand Anse roundabout, Wed-Sat 2100-0300, DJs or live music. The *Regal Cinema* is off Lagoon Road, next to *Tropicana*, movies nightly at 2030, EC\$5 for double feature. The *Marryshow Folk Theatre* in the University of the West Indies building on Tyrrel Street, has concerts, plays and special events.

Shopping Grenada prides itself on its spices, which are ideal souvenirs. They are cheaper in the supermarket than on the street or in the market. They can be seen in preparation on tours to the Nutmeg Processing Station, or visit Laura's Spice & Herb Garden near Perdmontemps to see them growing. Arawak Islands Ltd make a range of spices, sauces, herbal teas, candied nutmeg pods, perfumes, soap, bath goodies and massage oils, scented candles and incense sticks; factory and retail outlet on the Upper Belmont Road between Grand Anse and St George's, T4404577, open Mon-Fri 0830-1630, mail order also available, PO Box 432, T/F4443577, www.arawak-island.com *De la Grenade Industries* make nutmeg jams, jellies, syrups, sauces and drinks, available in supermarkets and groceries, PO Box 788, St George's, T4403241, F4407626, www.delagrenade.com *The Grenada Co-operative Nutmeg Association* purchases nutmeg from its membership of 7,000 farmers and markets it worldwide. It sells nutmeg oil in 15 ml and 30 ml bottles, PO Box 160, St George's, T4402117, F4406602, gcnanutmeg@caribsurf.com *The Yellow Poui Art Gallery* sells Grenadian paintings and is worth a visit, above *Gifts Remembered* souvenir shop on Cross Street. *Spice Island Perfumes* on the Carenage sells perfumes and pots pourris made from the island's spices, as well as batiks, T-shirts, etc. *Grenada Craft Centre* on Lagoon Road, next to the *Tropicana Inn* houses Grenadian craftspersons selling jewellery, pottery, batik, wood, basketry and T-shirts. *Art in Grenada*, gallery, on second floor Grand Anse Shopping Complex. *Batik Art Factory* on Young Street, see batik being made by deaf and handicapped women, sign language greatly appreciated if you know how. *White Cane Industries* on the Carenage adjacent to the Ministry of Health, featuring a wide variety of arts and crafts made by skillful blind Grenadians. You can purchase straw and palm wares, and items in wood. There is duty-free shopping at the airport and on the Carenage for cruise ships.

St George's Bookshop is on Halifax Street; *The Sea Change Book and Gift Shop* is on the Carenage, beneath the *Nutmeg* bar, it has *USA Today* when cruise ships come in. Good supermarkets include *Foodland*, on Lagoon with dinghy dock; *Food Fair* in St George's with dinghy tie up; *Food Fair* in Grand Anse; *Matheson's Supermarket*, open daily from 0800, will deliver to yachts.

Taxi Fares are set by the tourist board. On Grenada, taxis charge EC$4 for the first 10 miles **Transport** outside St George's, then EC$3 per mile thereafter (an additional EC$10 charge is made after 1800 and before 0600). From St George's Pier it is US$3 to the city or Botanical Gardens, US$12 to L'Anse aux Épines. A taxi tour of Grenada costs about US$40-55 per person for a full day or US$15 per person per hour. Island tours of Carriacou cost the same as on Grenada. A recommended driver is Leroy Wilson (VHF 16/68, T4431171, pager 4417089), good local history, driving and hiking tours (Seven Falls, Hot Springs); also Christopher Greenidge, T4447334. Taxis and buses are heavily 'personalized' by the drivers with brightly coloured decorations and names like 'Rusher with Love' or 'Danny Boy', while large speakers blast out steel bands or reggae music; taxi drivers will adjust the volume on request. A **water taxi** service runs from in front of the *Nutmeg* restaurant, St George's to the Grand Anse beach. **Hitchhiking** is quite easy though the roads are not very good.

Car hire Companies in St George's include *Spice Island Rentals* (Avis), Paddock and Lagoon Road, T4403936; *Dollar Rent-a-Car*, airport, T4444786, F4444788; *David's*, at the airport and several hotels, T4443399; *McIntyre Bros*, cars and jeeps, T4443944, F4442899, macford@caribsurf.com; *Maitland's* (who also rent motorcycles), Market Hill, T4444022, also an office at the airport which is often open for late arrivals when others are closed; *C Thomas and Sons,* cars, minibuses, jeeps, T4444384, mixed reports. We have received reports that daily rates quoted over the phone are not always honoured when you pick up the car; check that the company does not operate a three-day minimum hire if you want a rate for one day only, this often applies in high season.

Airlines *LIAT*, The Carenage, St George's, T4402796/7 (4444121/2 Point Salines, 4437362 Carriacou); **Directory** *British Airways*, T4402796; *BWIA*, The Carenage, St George's, T4403818/9 (T4444134 at airport); *American Airlines*, T4442222; *Aereotuy*, T4444732/6, F4444818; *Airlines of Carriacou*, T4443549, 4441475; *Helen Air*, T444-2266/4101, on Carriacou T4438260; *Air Europe*, T4445678; *JMC*, T4402796; *Martin Air*, T4444732.

Banks *Barclays Bank* (branches in St George's-Halifax Street, Grand Anse, Grenville and Carriacou), T4403232; *National Commercial Bank of Grenada* (Halifax Street and Hillsborough Street, St George's, Grand Anse, Grenville, Gouyave, St David's, Carriacou), T4403566; *Scotiabank* (Halifax Street, St George's), T4403274, branch at Grand Anse; *Grenada Bank of Commerce* (Halifax and Cross Street, St George's, and Grand Anse), T4404919; *Grenada Co-operative Bank* (Church Street, St George's, Grenville and Sauteurs), T4402111. They do not exchange European currencies other than sterling.

Communications Post: the General Post Office in St George's is at Burns Point near the pier, south of the Carenage, open 0800-1600 Mon-Fri, only postage stamps are sold during the lunch hour, 1200-1300. Villages have sub-post offices. Telephone: *Cable & Wireless Grenada Ltd*, T4401000, gndinfo@caribsurf.com, with offices on the Carenage, St George's, operates telephone services, including USA Direct and calls to USA on Visa card, etc, at a fee, facsimile, telex, telegraph and cellular phones. Payphones take coins or phone cards, available at outlets near payphones. Home Direct Service can be made from any phone, if you have a credit or telephone charge card, and is available to the UK through BT Direct and to Canada through Teleglobe. Credit card holders and Visaphone card holders' access number is 1-800-8778000 for domestic and international calls. If you dial 1-800-8722881 at any public phone (no coin required), you get through to AT and T. A call to the UK costs approximately EC$37.50 for 5 mins. Grentel Boatphone provides mobile cellular phone service.

Embassies & consulates *The British High Commission* is at 14 Church Street, St George's, T440-3222/3536, F4404939. *The Venezuelan Embassy* is at Archibald Avenue, St George's, T4401721/2. *USA*, Lance Aux Epines Stretch, St George's, T4441173, F4444820, usemb_gd@ caribsurf.com; *Republic of China*, Archibald Avenue, T4403054; *Netherlands*, Grand Etang Road, St George's, T4402031; *Guyana*, Gore Street, St George's, T4402189; *Sweden*, T4401832; *France*, Honorary Consul, 7 Lucas Street, T4406349; *European Community*, Archibald Avenue, T4403561; *Spain*, Honorary Consul, T4402087; *Turkey*, Honorary Consul, T4402018.

Medical facilities St George's General Hospital is at Fort George's Point. There is also Princess Alice Hospital in Grenville, Princess Royal Hospital in Carriacou and the private St Augustine Medical Centre. Black Rock Medical Clinic in Grand Anse Shopping Centre has 24-hr emergency service. For an ambulance, T434 in St George's, T724 in St Andrew's and T774 on Carriacou. SunSmile Dental Care Clinic at Grand Anse offers dental treatment Mon-Sat and emergency care.

Tourist information Local tourist office: Grenada Board of Tourism, Box 293, Burn's Point, St George's, T440-2279/2001/1346, F440-6637, www.grenada.org. 0800-1600, very helpful. There is also a cruise ship office, T4402872, and tourist office at the airport, helpful, hotel reservation service, T4444140. The Grenada Hotel Association is at Ross Point Inn, Lagoon Road, PO Box 440, St George's, T4441353, F4444847, www.grenadahotelsinfo.com. **Local travel agents:** all in St George's: *Grenada International Travel Service*, on Church Street (American Express representative), T4402945; *Huggins Travel Service*, the Carenage, T4402514 and many others. For guided hikes contact Telfer Bedeau in the village of Soubise on the east coast; you must ask around for him (or T4426200 or see if the Tourism Department can put you in touch). Edwin Frank, from the Tourism Bureau, T4435143, does guided tours at weekends, US$20 per person island tour, very knowledgeable on history, politics, geography, people, fauna, hiking etc, recommended and much better than an untrained taxi driver. Dennis Henry, of *Henry's Safari Tours* (T4445313, F4444460, VHF channel 68, safari@caribsurf.com) conducts tours of the island and is very well informed on all aspects of Grenada. Henry's also services yachts, dealing with laundry, gas, shopping etc. *Arnold's Tours*, Archibald Avenue, T4400531, F4404118, offers similar services to Henry's, also recommended, but in German as well. Clinton 'Guava' George, of *Clinton's Taxi Service*, T4444095, 4419648, knows a lot about Grenadian geography, politics and biology and gives a well-informed, fun tour of the island. *Adventure Jeep Tours* (T4445337, F4445681, www.grenadajeeptours.com) have all-terrain vehicles for good views, also hiking. *Sunsation Tours* is very knowledgeable and recommended, bilingual guides are available for half or full day tours, PO Box 856, St George's, T4441656, 4441594, F4441103. Organized tours usually take in St George's and/or most of the island including plantation tours, Concord waterfall, the Nutmeg Processing Station, National Parks, the river Antoine Rum Distillery, Lake Antoine and the Marquis Waterfall. Most tour agencies are happy to tailor a tour to suit you. **Maps** Grenada National Parks publishes maps and trail guides, worth having for the Grand Étang National Park and related walks. The Overseas Surveys Directorate, Ordnance Survey map of Grenada, published for the Grenada Government in 1985, scale 1:50,000, is available from the Tourist Office, from the Lands and Surveys Department in the Ministry of Agriculture (at the Botanic Gardens) and from shops for EC$10.50-15 (it is not wholly accurate). Also available from Ordnance Survey, Southampton, are two separate sheets, North (1979) and South (1988) at 1:25,000 scale.

Carriacou

Population: 5,000 *Carriacou (pronounced Carr-ycoo) is an attractive island of green hills descending to sandy beaches. It is much less mountainous than Grenada, which means that any cloudy or rainy weather clears much quicker. Efforts are being made by the Government to curb contraband and drug smuggling in Carriacou, but a lot comes in around Anse la Roche, where there are picturesque smugglers' coves. Hurricane Lenny caused severe damage in 1999 because of the tidal surges it brought to the west side of the island. The waves undermined a small part of the seafront road in Hillsborough and part of the road. Tyrell Bay was washed away. With an area of 13 sq miles, it is the largest of the Grenadines. It lies 23 miles northeast of Grenada; 2½ miles further northeast is Petit Martinique, which is separated by a narrow channel from Petit St Vincent, the southernmost of St Vincent's Grenadine dependencies.*

Air Carriacou's airport is **Lauriston**, a EC$10 taxi ride from Hillsborough, EC$20 from Mount Pleasant. Disconcertingly, the main road goes straight across the runway. A fire engine drives out from Hillsborough to meet incoming flights, bringing the Immigration Officer, who clings to a platform at the back in Keystone Cops fashion. Every day *LIAT* and *Airlines of Carriacou* fly frequently between Grenada and Carriacou: US$50 return, half that one way (flying time is 12 mins). **Sea** *Osprey Lines*, T4408126, F4439041, osprey@grenadines.net, operate a hovercraft service, the *Osprey Express,* from Grenada to Carriacou (and Petite Martinique), journey time 1½ hrs, twice a day except Wed, EC$40 one way, EC$75 return, bicycles EC$20, a day trip is possible if you take the 0900 crossing (0800 on Sun). A ferry (*Alexia II, Alexia III, Adelaide B*) also sails from the Carenage, St George's to Hillsborough, Carriacou, Tue 0930, Wed 1000, Fri 1100, Sat 0800, Sun 0700, returning Mon 1000, Wed 0930, Thu 1000, Sat 0900, Sun 1700, EC$20 one way, EC$ 30 return, 3-4 hrs. Cargo boats leave from the other side of the Carenage for mthe *Osprey Express*, normally EC$20, bicycles EC$10 or free, usually daily but enquire locally for days and times. In heavy seas you may be better opting for a schooner, which despite being smaller, ride the waves better than the larger boats which may make you seasick, said to be worse going to Carriacou than coming back. Be prepared for incredibly loud reggae/rap music. Times are sub-ject to change and you must check. There are also unscheduled services between these islands; by asking around you might be able to get a passage on one. Carriacou is 1 hr by boat from Union Island; fishing boats leave irregularly, enquire locally, fare about EC$15 between Hillsborough and Ashton. *MV Jaspar* (small private boat) twice a week, captain is required to take you through all immigration procedures.

Buses cost EC$1 for one mile, EC$2 for more than that; Harvey Vale to Windward EC$4. The same van may be a taxi and cost US$10, ask for "bus" and be prepared to wait. Cycling is rec-ommended, the traffic is very light. Many of the roads are in very poor repair, giving the sem-blance of off-road cycling. Potential for lots of flat tyres in the dry season as there is an abundance of cacti.

Getting there
See transport, page 866, for further details

Getting around

Windward Islands

Carriacou

Carriacou's capital is **Hillsborough** and has a population of about 600. On the one hand, the islanders display a strong adherence to their African origins in that the annual Big Drum Dances, which take place around Easter, are almost purely West African. The Tombstone Feasts are unique. On the other hand, French traditions are still evident at L'Esterre and there is a vigorous Scottish heritage, especially at **Windward**, where the people are much lighter skinned than elsewhere on the island as a result of their Scottish forebears. Windward used to be the centre for the craft of hand-built schooners but in recent years the boat builders have moved to Tyrrel Bay. Begun by a shipbuilder from Glasgow, the techniques are unchanged, but the white cedar used for the vessels now has to be imported from Grenada or elsewhere. The sturdy sailing vessels are built and repaired without the use of power tools in the shade of the coconut palms at the edge of the sea. To demonstrate the qualities of these local boats, the Carriacou Regatta was initiated in 1965. It has grown into the major festival described above.

The local painter, Canute Calliste, has his studio at L'Esterre. His naive style captures the scenes of Carriacou (kite flying, launching schooners, festivals). He is also an accomplished violinist and performs the quadrille, a dance which is part of the island's cultural heritage.

The **Carriacou Historical Society Museum** on Paterson Street in Hillsborough has exhibits from Amerindian settlements in the island and from later periods in its history; the woman who runs it is the daughter of Canute Calliste, and can tell you about the Arawak ruins on the island. ■ *Mon-Fri, 0930-1600, Sat 1000-1600.* There are also ruined plantations. On Hospital Hill, Belair, northeast of Hillsborough, there is an overgrown old sugar Mill, stunning views. There is good walking on the back roads and the woods are teeming with wildlife such as iguanas.

There are interesting underwater reefs and sandy islets with a few palms on them, ideal for snorkelling and picnicking. **Sandy Island** is a tiny, low-lying atoll in Hillsborough Bay off Lauriston Point, with a few palm trees for shade, safe and excellent swimming and snorkelling, take food, drink and plenty of suntan lotion. Boat from Paradise Beach, five minutes, or from Hillsborough EC$60, 30 mins each way, pick a day when the islet is not swamped with boat loads of cruise ship visitors. Alternatively try **White Island**, a similar islet in Manchineel Bay off the south coast, ask for boats at *Cassada Bay Hotel*. Visitors should see the oyster beds at **Tyrrel Bay** where 'tree-oysters' grow on mangrove roots. Tyrrel Bay is a favourite anchorage for the many yachts which visit the island. There is a yacht club with rooms available, food, drink and a slightly small tennis court.

A beautiful beach is **Anse La Roche**, which faces west and has a spectacular view across the strait to the mountains of rugged Union Island. Snorkelling is good, particularly among the rocks at the side. Walk from Bogles along the dirt road heading northwards, past the *Caribbee Inn* and forking right at Honey Hill House; after about 30 mins the road starts to rise, turn left at the large tree which overhangs the track and follow a narrow path through the woods to a ruined farmhouse. The path leads to the right, through bushes; keep to the downhill side of the open slope, bear right down a steep slope leading through more trees to the beach. Take food and drink, there are no facilities and few people, about 45-min walk each way. We have received reports that it is very easy to get lost finding Anse La Roche beach and it might be easier to take a water taxi there. Very peaceful, watch the yachts rounding the headland on their way to anchorage; at night turtles swim ashore to lay their eggs. The **Kido Ecological Research Station** is near Anse La Roche and High North Park, where you can go birdwatching, hiking, cycling, whale watching and even volunteering for one of the conservation projects (see page 865). Kido is actively trying to restore the mangroves on the north coast, T/F4437936, kido-ywf@caribsurf.com

Instead of turning off the track to Anse La Roche, carry on walking northwards; the well-shaded, grassy road rounds Gun Point with lovely views of the Grenadines. A path leads down (opposite a mauve-painted house) to the beach at **Petit Carenage Bay**, which has coarse, coral sand, good swimming and modest surf in some conditions. Returning to the road, Windward is a few minutes walk further on, a few shops and local bars. The Caribbean coast is spectacular in places and a walk from Windward to Dover, then following the coast road until it becomes a dirt road leading to Dumfries, is very pleasant and secluded.

It is advisable to use insect repellent on the beaches, especially in the rainy season. At night it is best to use a mosquito net.

Hotels A-B *Silver Beach Hotel*, T4437337, F4437165, silverbeach@grenadines.net 16 rooms or apartments, simple but attractive, though for a longer stay a cheaper rate can be negotiated with the owner, good, helpful, child-friendly, offers showers and transport to yachts in Tyrrel Bay, own catamaran, *Afoxe*, for day sails. **A-B** *Cassada Bay Resort*, Belmont, T4437494, F4437672, cassada@caribsurf.com Rooms in cabins, use of private island, fitness room, use of watersports equipment, mini-cinema room. **LL-AL** *Caribbee Inn*, Prospect, T4437380, F4438142. Lovely but isolated setting on promontory above the sea, small room, also suites, villa, expensive food, snorkelling off stoney beach, 40 mins' walk to excellent beach, out of town.

Guest houses   A-C *Bogles Round House*, T/F4437841. 3 cottages built by long-term travellers Kim and Sue Russell around their round house, self-contained, sleep 2-3, no service or tax, discounts available, located away from the main tourist areas, 50 ft yacht options, dive charter, bare boat, captained. **A-C** *Green Roof Inn*, Seaview, T/F4436399, greenroof@ caribsurf.com On hillside overlooking sea, Swedish run, 10 mins north of Hillsborough, 3 double rooms with private bathroom, 1 single and 1 double with shared bathroom, adjoining rooms for family suite, extra beds available, mosquito nets, fans, sea view or garden view, airport/jetty transfers and breakfast at 0800 included, restaurant (see below), sandy area in front of hotel for swimming and long sandy beaches on both sides of the hotel a couple of minutes away, day trips arranged. **B-D** *Bayaleau Point Cottages*, Windward, T/F4437984, goldhill@caribsurf.com. 4 lovely, well-equipped wooden, painted cottages, very clean, beautiful view, own little beach, good snorkelling, owners helpful, friendly, food and drink on request, good for children. Highly recommended. **C** *Patty's Villa*, Main St, Hillsborough, T4438412. Beautifully restored West Indian house, 2 apartments, sleep 2, mosquito net, fan, kitchen, bathroom, garden. **C** *Scraper's*, Tyrrel Bay, T/F4437403. Local restaurant and 7 rooms, with or without a/c, corresponding pricing, 2-bedroomed cottages available, close to bay, cheaper for locals. **C-D** *Peace Haven Guest House*, south of pier, Main St, Hillsborough, T4437475. Basic, small but good rooms, share small kitchen and bathroom, contact Lucille Atkins, very friendly and helpful, on the seafront a few hundred yards south of the jetty, also apartments, sometimes water shortages. **D-F** *Ade's Dream*, T4437317, F4438435, adesdea@caribsurf.com, north of pier, Main St, Hillsborough. 23 rooms or apartments, own kitchenette or share large kitchen, very clean, run by hard working and friendly Mrs Mills (good reports), supermarket downstairs open daily. **D** *Millies Guest House*, Main St, Hillsborough, T4437310, F4438107. Room or 1-, 2-, or 3-bedroomed apartments with kitchen, bathroom/shower, fans, a/c, ocean view, also Millie's Yacht Charter for exploring other islands. **E** *Sand's Guest House*, T4437100, between Hillsborough and the airport. Quiet, basic but clean, across the road is a nice beach, 11 rooms, with or without shared kitchen and bathroom, or apartment. **D-E** *Kido Ecological Research Station*, guest house for ecotourists and animal protection and wildlife rehabilitation centre, rescued turtles, barn owl, Mona monkey and other transient residents, T/F4437936, http://members.aol.com/ ywf/home/kido.html (see page 864). On a forested ridge on the northwestern coast near Anse La Roche, 2 bedrooms in main house, large pagoda for groups, fans, mosquito nets, screens, Italian and West Indian vegetarian food with fish, guided environmental tours and cultural exchange programmes for groups, private access to Sanctuary Bay, 5 mins down steps, or 20-min trail through High North Park to Anse La Roche, or swim from one to the other (marine snorkelling trail), 55-ft catamaran for sailing and whale watching, turtle nesting monitoring (Apr-Dec), minibus from Hillsborough to Bogles, US$0.70, then 15-min walk up lane to Kido Station, or taxi US$10.

Sleeping
Out of season the island is quiet. Not all the hotels are open

Windward Islands

Villa and apartment rental LL-C *Down Island Ltd*, Villa Rental Agents, T4438182, F4437086, uskabder@caribsurf.com. **C** *Alexis Luxury Apartment Hotel*, Tyrrel Bay, T/F4437179. Weekly rentals. **D** *Grammas Apartments*, Main and Patterson Streets, Hillsborough, T4437255, F4437256; and others, ask at tourist office.

Eating The **market** near the pier in Hillsborough comes alive on Monday when the produce is brought in. Food is limited in variety, especially fresh vegetables, but according to season you can get onions, tomatoes, potatoes, cucumbers etc from Grenada. 'Jack Iron' rum (180° proof) is a local hazard, it is so strong that ice sinks in it. It is distilled in Barbados but bottled in Carriacou; it costs around EC$10 per bottle and is liberally dispensed on all high days and holidays (fairly liberally on other days too).

There are some basic local bar/restaurants but they often run out of food quite early or close in the evenings, check during the day if they will be open for dinner; finding meals is particularly difficult at weekends. Several small bars and restaurants in Tyrrel Bay which do takeaways and other services such as emails and faxes for visiting yachts. *Scraper's*, Tyrrel Bay, T4437403. Very good lunch but not much atmosphere, Mr Scraper and his family are very hospitable. *Roof Garden*, misleading name, near Market Hall, Hillsborough, T4437204. Clean and friendly but limited choice. *Hillsborough Bar*, Main St. Attractive place for a drink, Eddie uses fresh fruit juices in his cocktails (strong) and won't serve rum punches if he hasn't any fresh limes, meals can be ordered the day before. *Poivre et Sel*, Tyrell Bay, above Alexis Supermarket, difficult to find, T4438390, VHF 16. Excellent French food, French chef, try the lobster crêpe, a nice change from West Indian, lively meeting place for the local French community. *Callaloo by the Sea*, Hillsborough, T4438004. Entrées EC$16-50, plenty of choice, good value despite upmarket appearance, open daily, closed Sep. *E & A's*, very close to the pier. Good local cooking, ask for a large plate of vegetables. *Talk of the Town*, in Hillsborough. Cheap and good. Try the full moon barbecue at *Paradise Inn*, Paradise Beach. *Cassada Bay Resort* in the southeast, T4437494, VHF 16. Good for a meal or drink, good food and wonderful sunset view, friendly, open 0800-2200 for food, bar from 1000 until late. *The Caribbee Inn at Prospect*, north of Hillsborough, T4437380. Candlelit dining in country house hotel, creole cooking, homemade bakeries, set dinner EC$65 at 1900, reservations only. The *Silver Beach Resort* is good for breakfast, snacks and lunch, quiet out of season, slow service in evenings, dinner EC$40-60, transport (and showers) available for yachtsmen from Tyrrel Bay. *The Green Roof Inn*, on hillside overlooking the sea, 10 mins' walk north of Hillsborough, T4436399. On second floor veranda with spectacular views of Hillsborough bay and sunset, roof, but no walls, Swedish chef, mainly seafood, lobster, barracuda, swordfish, Caribbean ingredients with European preparation, open Tue-Sun for dinner, lunch on request. The ice cream parlour just round Tyrell Bay after *Scrapers* (on the part where the road is damaged) is recommended. *The Nest Inn*, at Gun Point, a small local bar, is run by Mr Fleary, who spent 30 years in London before returning home.

Nightlife There is a good jump-up every Fri after mass at Liz' Refreshment, Tyrrel Bay, with excellent DJ.

Festivals Carriacou celebrates its carnival at the traditional Lenten time, unlike Grenada. It is not spectacular but it is fun and there is a good atmosphere. In Aug is the Carriacou Regatta (see above). The Parang takes place in mid-Dec and runs over 3 evenings (Fri-Sun) from about 2100-0200 at the Tennis Club in Hillsborough (entrance EC$20 per night). It is a musical celebration: local groups perform on Fri, Sat is the most lively night with visiting Calypsonians and performers from Grenada and other islands judged by visiting dignitaries, and Sun is comedy day, with in-jokes likely to be lost on visitors.

Transport **Road** Buses go from Hillsborough to Bogles, Windward (EC$2) and to Tyrrel Bay. A bus also goes from the airport to Windward (EC$1.50). The normally excellent service goes to pieces if it is wet. There are also plenty of **taxis**, or you can hire a **car**. John Gabriel, T4437454; Martin Bullen, T4437204. Jeep hire is available for EC$100 per day or less for a week. **Sea** **Water taxis** to beaches cost EC$60-100 depending on the length of the journey. Alternatively, just walk around. Fishing and sailing trips from Hillsborough pier or ask at hotels. **Yachts** can be hired by the day from Tanki's diving base near the airport; ask for Captain Dennis. The studio, next to *Alexis supermarket* on Tyrrel Bay, T/F4438625, VHF 16, has yachts, charter service, email and internet access, mail drop, bookswap, bar, coffee shop, music, closed Sun, small and pleasant.

Airline offices See page 861. **Banks** *Barclays Bank* and *National Commercial Bank* have branches on Carriacou. These, the government and customs offices, post office and the commercial centre are around the pier in Hillsborough. **Hospitals** See page 861.

Directory

Petite Martinique

Petite Martinique is the only offshore island from Carriacou on which people live, about 900-1,000 of them, descended from French fishermen, Glaswegian ship-wrights, pirates and slaves. Its area is 486 acres, rising to a small, volcanic peak. The principal occupations are boatbuilding and fishing. There is a dock with fuel, water, ice and other yachting supplies. There was excitement in 1997 when the government proposed to build a house for 12 Coast Guard personnel in the campaign against drug smuggling. Hundreds of people, about half the population, turned out to demonstrate against the arrival of government surveyors and clashed with armed police and the Special Services Unit.

Population: 800

Water taxis are available from Windward on Carriacou. The *Osprey Express* and the other ferries call here after Hillsborough coming from St George's, and the mail boat from Carriacou calls on Monday, Wednesday and Friday. Accommodation at **E** *Sea Side View Holiday Cottages*, T4439007, F4439210, one two-bedroomed and two one-bedroomed, self-contained cottages near beach, supermarket and boutique. **E** *Miracle Mart Guest House*, T4439065, F4439022, jhingram@caribsurf.com Three rooms, four beds, fan, kitchen, restaurant. *Palm Beach Restaurant and Bar*, menu emphasizes seafood, good roti, free water taxi service for those anchored in Petit St Vincent, Monday-Saturday 1000-2200, Sunday 1400-2200, T4439103, VHF 16.

Background

History

When Columbus discovered the island on his third voyage in 1498, it was inhabited by Caribs, who had migrated from the South American mainland, killing or enslaving the peaceful Arawaks who were already living there. The Amerindians called their island Camerhogue, but Columbus renamed it Concepción, a name which was not to last long, for shortly afterwards it was referred to as Mayo on maps and later Spaniards called it Granada, after the Spanish city. The French then called it La Grenade and by the 18th century it was known as Grenada. Aggressive defence of the island by the Caribs prevented settlement by Europeans until the 17th century. In 1609 some Englishmen tried and failed, followed by a group of Frenchmen in 1638, but it was not until 1650 that a French expedition from Martinique landed and made initial friendly contact with the inhabitants. When relations soured, the French brought reinforcements and exterminated the Amerindian population. Sauteurs, or Morne des Sauteurs, on the north coast, is named after this episode when numerous Caribs apparently jumped to their death in the sea rather than surrender to the French.

The island remained French for about 100 years, although possession was disputed by Britain, and it was a period of economic expansion and population growth, as colonists and slaves arrived to grow tobacco and sugar at first, followed by cotton, cocoa and coffee. It was during the Seven Years' War in the 18th century that Grenada fell into British hands and was ceded by France to Britain as part of a land settlement in the 1763 Treaty of Paris. Although the French regained control in 1779, their occupation was brief and the island was returned to Britain in 1783 under the

Windward Islands

Treaty of Versailles. The British introduced nutmeg in the 1780s, after natural disasters wiped out the sugar industry. Nutmeg and cocoa became the main crops and encouraged the development of smaller land holdings. A major slave revolt took place in 1795, led by a free coloured Grenadian called Julian Fedon (see page 853), but slavery was not abolished until 1834, as in the rest of the British Empire.

In 1833, Grenada was incorporated into the Windward Islands Administration which survived until 1958 when it was dissolved and Grenada joined the Federation of the West Indies. The Federation collapsed in 1962 and in 1967 Grenada became an associated state, with full autonomy over internal affairs, but with Britain retaining responsibility for defence and foreign relations. Grenada was the first of the associated states to seek full independence, which was granted in 1974.

Political leadership since the 1950s had alternated between Eric (later Sir Eric) Gairy's Grenada United Labour Party (GULP) and Herbert Blaize's Grenada National Party. At the time of independence, Sir Eric Gairy was Prime Minister, but his style of government was widely viewed as authoritarian and corrupt, becoming increasingly resented by a large proportion of the population. In 1979 he was ousted in a bloodless coup by the Marxist-Leninist New Jewel (Joint Endeavour for Welfare, Education and Liberation) Movement, founded in 1973, which formed a government headed by Prime Minister Maurice Bishop. Reforms were introduced and the country moved closer to Cuba and other Communist countries, who provided aid and technical assistance. In 1983, a power struggle within the government led to Bishop being deposed and he and many of his followers were murdered by a rival faction shortly afterwards. In the chaos that followed a joint US-Caribbean force invaded the island to restore order. They imprisoned Bishop's murderers and expelled Cubans and other socialist nationalities who had been engaged in building a new airport and other development projects. An interim government was set up until elections could be held in 1984, which were won by the coalition New National Party (NNP), headed by Herbert Blaize, with 14 seats to GULP's one in the legislature. After the intervention, Grenada moved closer to the USA which maintains a large embassy near the airport, but on 1 December 1999 diplomatic relations with Cuba were restored and embassies were opened in St George's and Havana.

Further reading on this era of Grenada's history includes: *Grenada: Whose Freedom?* by Fitzroy Ambursley and James Dunkerley, Latin America Bureau, London, 1984; *Grenada Revolution in Reverse* by James Ferguson, Latin America Bureau, London, 1990; *Grenada: Revolution, Invasion and Aftermath* by Hugh O'Shaughnessy, Sphere Books, London, 1984; *Grenada: Revolution and Invasion* by Anthony Payne, Paul Sutton and Tony Thorndike, London, Croom Helm, 1984; *Grenada: Politics, Economics and Society*, by Tony Thorndike, Frances Pinter, London 1984, and many others.

In 1987, the formation of a new opposition party, the National Democratic Congress (NDC), led to parliamentary changes. Further divisions within the NNP preceded Mr Blaize's death in December 1989; his faction, led by Ben Jones, became the National Party, while the New National Party name was retained by Keith Mitchell's faction. In general elections held in 1990, each of these parties won two seats while the NDC, led by Nicholas Brathwaite (formerly head of the interim administration), won seven. The GULP gained four seats.

In 1991 the Government decided to commute to life imprisonment the death sentences on 14 people convicted of murdering Maurice Bishop after world wide appeals for clemency. Amnesty International and other organizations have appealed for the release of Mrs Phyllis Coard, one of the 14 convicted, on grounds of ill-health following years of solitary confinement. She was allowed to go to Jamaica for cancer treatment in 2000, but has not been pardoned.

In February 1995 Mr Brathwaite retired and was succeeded by George Brizan. General elections were held in June 1995. The NDC campaigned on its economic stabilization policies, but faced keen opposition from the NNP, led by Keith Mitchell, and GULP, led by Sir Eric Gairy. The NNP (32.7% of the vote) won eight seats, the NDC five (31.1%) and GULP two (26.8%), so Keith Mitchell became Prime Minister. Sir Eric Gairy failed to win a seat. In December 1995, Grenada's eighth political party, the Democratic Labour Party (DLP), was launched by Francis Alexis, former deputy leader of the NDC, thereby reducing the NDC to four seats. In June 1997, Prescott Williams launched the Grenada Progressive Party, aimed to appeal to women and young people. Sir Eric Gairy died in August 1997 and GULP split into two factions. In a much postponed election in April 1998, Herbert Preudhomme was elected leader, after many accusations of fraud and recounts.

The most recent general elections, in January 1999, were an unparalleled victory for the NNP, which won all 15 seats with 62% of the vote. The opposition parties were too numerous and weak to provide an effective challenge, although the NDC received 24% of the vote. Keith Mitchell was sworn in for a second term as Prime Minister. The Government intends to act more vigorously against increasing crime, particularly where weapons and drugs are involved, and is considering the resumption of executions for murder (last carried out in 1978). The announcement was criticized by the regional human rights movement, Caribbean Rights.

In 2000, a Truth and Reconciliation Commission was established to investigate events in 1976-91. The inquiry was expected to take six months and cover the last three years of Gairy's authoritarian rule, the New Jewel Movement revolution in 1979, the establishment of the People's Revolutionary Government, the bloodshed of October 1983, the US invasion, the trial and subsequent reprieve from exection in 1991.

Government

Grenada is an independent state within the Commonwealth, with the British monarch as Head of State represented by a Governor General (Daniel Williams since 1996). There are two legislative houses, the House of Representatives with 15 members. and the Senate with 13 members. The Government is elected for a five-year term.

The economy

Structure of production

Agriculture accounts for about 12% of gdp. According to a 1995 agricultural census the number of farmers has fallen to 11,871, from 15,319 in 1961, with the area of prime farming land falling from 61,000 to 31,000 acres in the same period. The major export crops are nutmeg, bananas and cocoa; nutmeg and mace together account for about 14% of all exports and Grenada is a leading world producer of this spice. International prices for nutmeg collapsed in the mid-1990s but new projects have come on stream (for example a nutmeg oil distillation plant began operations in 1994 which will produce 30 tons a year from 300 tons of defective nutmeg). Production of nutmeg and mace fell in 1998.

Banana exports have fallen because of labour shortages and inconsistent quality and quantity but account for about nine of exports. Cocoa exports (15% of the total) were hit by the loss of Grenada's main customer because of overstocking, and a mealy bug infestation which spread to 93% of cocoa fields in 1996. Both cocoa and nutmeg growers receive funds from the European Community commodity price funds (Stabex). There is also some cotton grown on Carriacou and limes are grown on both Carriacou and Grenada. Sugar cane is grown in the south of Grenada but efficiency is not high. Most of the rest of farming land is devoted to fruit and vegetables for export as well as domestic consumption, such as yams, eddoe, sweet potatoes, tannia, pumpkin, cassava, pigeon peas and maize.

Manufacturing is also mostly processing of agricultural produce, making items such as chocolate, sugar, rum, jams, coconut oil, honey and lime juice. There is a large brewery (majority owned by Guinness) and a rice mill. There are 10,000 acres of forest, of which three-quarters are owned by the Government which is undertaking a reafforestation programme to repair hurricane damage. Fishing is a growing industry, involving about 1,500 people and contributing 16% of exports. Japan financed the construction of fishing centres in Gouyave and Grenville, a jetty and fish processing plant near St George's.

Recent trends The economy suffered from the uncertainties surrounding the Bishop murder and the US invasion, but confidence has gradually returned and investment has picked up. The main area of expansion has been construction, led by tourism, which has benefited from the airport expansion started with Cuban assistance by the Bishop administration. Stopover visitors and cruise ship passengers have risen steadily as new hotels and facilities have been built. The yacht charter business has also expanded considerably. Room capacity should exceed 2,500 by 2000. Tourism revenue reached EC$169 mn in 1998, up from EC$159 mn in 1997. Cruise ship arrivals were likely to be down in 2000, however, when Carnival announced in November 1999 that it was ending calls to Grenada. It claimed that the landing fee of US$3 per person and environmental levy of US$1.50 were excessive. Carnival previously accounted for about half of the annual income of EC$9 mn from cruise passengers.

Despite buoyant tourism, Grenada has considerable financial imbalances and unemployment is a problem at 14% of the labour force. Imports are six times the value of exports and tourism revenues are insufficient to cover the trade deficit. During the 1990s the Government has engaged in selective debt rescheduling, a reduction in the number of public employees, the sale of certain state assets and an overhaul of the tax system. The IMF approved a structural adjustment programme to allow Grenada to seek credits from other multilateral agencies. By 1994 economic growth began to pick up, the fiscal position had improved, allowing the Government to consider greater capital spending. After three years of structural adjustment the Government announced a new economic programme aimed at producing annual growth of 3% in 1994-96. Fiscal policy was to remain tight, but public sector investment would rise. Positive results were recorded and gdp growth rose steadily. Construction is still providing the main impetus for growth, with several huge tourism projects being built, but investment in telemarketing and data processing is expected to help absorb a large number of the unemployed generating 1,000 jobs in 2000.

A 1999 IMF report criticized the Government for obtaining economic growth at the expense of deteriorating public finances and increasing the current account deficit. However, no new taxes were proposed in the 1999 budget and capital spending on infrastructure (roads, airport expansion, cruise ship terminal, water supply), was set to increase.

Culture

The population of some 98,400 (of which 5,726 live on Carriacou and Petit Martinique) is largely of African (85) or mixed (11) descent. In contrast to other Windward Islands which have had a similar history of disputed ownership between the French and English, the French cultural influence in Grenada has completely died out. Nevertheless, it is a predominantly Catholic island, though there are Protestant churches of various denominations, and a Baha'i Centre. Many people who emigrated from Grenada to the UK are returning to the island and are building smart houses for their retirement which are in stark contrast to the tiny, corrugated iron shacks which are home to many of their countrymen. The population is very young; 38% are under 15 years old and nearly 26% are in the 15-29 years' age bracket.

Barbados

17

Barbados

Barbados is flatter, drier, and more prosperous than other islands in the Caribbean and so tourists who come here looking for the 'untouched' Caribbean are in for a disappointment. There are no volcanoes or rain forests, and hardly any rivers, but there are plenty of white sand beaches and lots of pleasantly rolling countryside with fields of sugar cane, brightly painted villages, flowering trees and open pastures. The island is probably better equipped with infrastructure and reliable tourist services than anywhere else to the south of Miami on this side of the Atlantic. It is 21 miles long and 14 miles wide, lying east of the main chain of the Leeward and Windward islands.

Essentials

Before you travel

Documents

Work permits are very difficult to obtain; regulations are strictly enforced

Visitors from North America, Western Europe, Commonwealth African countries, Argentina, Venezuela, Colombia, and Brazil need a **passport** but no **visas**. US visitors may get in on a driving licence, but the immigration officers are not keen on this form of documentation. Visitors from most other countries are usually granted a short stay on arrival, and tourist visas are not necessary. Officially, you must have a ticket back to your country of origin as well as an

Barbados

■ **Sleeping**
1 Sam Lord's Castle
2 Villa Nova

▲ **Other**
1 Andromeda Gardens
2 Animal Flower Cave
3 Banks Brewery
4 Barbados Zoo Park
5 Barclays Park
6 Clapham, Harry Bailey Observatory
7 Codrington College

8 Cotton Tower
9 Drax Hall
10 East Point Lighthouse
11 Farley Hill House & Wildlife Reserve
12 Flower Forest
13 Folkestone Marine Museum, Underwater Park & St James Church
14 Four Square Rum Factory
15 Garrison
16 Graeme Hall Swamp

17 Gun Hill Signal Station
18 Harrisons Cave
19 Morgan Lewis Mill
20 Mount Gay Distillery
21 Portvale Sugar Factory
22 St John's Church
23 St Nicholas Abbey
24 Sunbury Plantation House
25 The Aquatic Centre
26 Turners Hall Woods
27 Tyrol Cot
28 Welchman Hall Gully

onward ticket to be allowed in. Immigration officers do check. You will also need an accommodation address on arrival, they do not check your reservation but if you say you do not know where you will be staying, you will be sent to the back of the queue and 'helped' to select a hotel at least for one night.

State the maximum period you intend to stay on arrival. Overstaying is not recommended if you wish to re-enter Barbados at a later date. Extending the period of stay is possible at the Immigration Office, Careenage House on the Wharf in Bridgetown (T4269912) but costs US$12.50 and is fairly time consuming. When visiting the Immigration Office, which is open from 0830-1630, you will need to take your passport and return ticket. Tickets are inspected quite carefully.

Money

Currency The currency unit is the Barbados dollar, which is pegged at B$2.00 for US$1.00. Banks will of course charge a small commission on this rate. Many tourist establishments quote prices in US dollars, if you are not careful a hotel room may end up costing twice as much as you bargained for. Banks will only change the US dollar, Canadian dollar, sterling, and Deutschmark. Other currencies they will not exchange. **Credit cards** are accepted in the large resorts, their use is now widespread.

Banks ***Barclays Bank***, the ***Royal Bank of Canada***, ***CIBC Caribbean Ltd***, ***Scotiabank***, ***Caribbean Commercial Bank***, ***Barbados Mutual Bank*** and ***Barbados National Bank*** all have offices in Bridgetown. The first five also have branches in the main south and west coast tourist centres. Opening hours for banks are 0800-1500 Monday to Thursday, and 0800-1300 and 1500-1700 on Friday. ***Caribbean Commercial Bank*** in Hastings and Sunset Crest is also open on Saturday from 0900 to 1200. The ***Barbados National Bank*** has a branch and a bureau de change at the airport; the latter is open from 0800-2400, but inaccessible unless you are actually arriving or departing. All banks now have cash machines (Cirrus: Visa and Mastercard) at most branches which you can use with a credit card after hours. Banking facilities in ***JB's*** and ***Big B Supermarkets*** are open 1000-1900 Monday-Thursday, 1000-2000 Friday, 1000-1500 Saturday.

Getting there

Air

Flights to Barbados are heavily booked at Christmas & for Crop Over

From North America ***BWIA*** and ***American Airlines*** fly from New York, Washington DC and Miami daily; ***Air Jamaica*** flies from New York and Baltimore; ***Air Canada*** flies from Montréal and Toronto. ***BWIA*** also flies from Toronto. **From Europe** ***British Airways***, ***Virgin Atlantic*** and ***BWIA*** have several flights a week from London. ***Concorde*** has a scheduled service in winter. ***Condor*** have weekly flights from Frankfurt. There are also lots of charter flights which are usually cheaper and recommended if you are staying only on Barbados. **From South America** ***Liat***, ***Surinam Airways*** and ***BWIA*** from Georgetown, Guyana; ***Aeropostal*** from Caracas via Margarita; ***Suriname Airways*** from Paramaribo. **From Caribbean Islands** Connections with Caribbean islands are good, from Antigua (***Liat***, ***British Airways***, ***BWIA***), Dominica (***Liat***, ***Air Guadeloupe***), Fort-de-France, Martinique (***Liat***, ***Air Guadeloupe***), Grenada (***Liat***, ***BWIA***), Kingston, Jamaica (***BWIA***), Montego Bay (***Air Jamaica***), Pointe-à-Pitre, Guadeloupe (***Liat***), Port of Spain, Trinidad (***BWIA***, ***Liat***, ***Air Caribbean***), St Lucia (***Liat***, ***BWIA***, ***Air Jamaica***), St Maarten (***Liat***, ***BWIA***), St Vincent (***Liat***, ***BWIA***), San Juan, Puerto Rico (***Liat***, ***American Eagle***), Tobago (***Liat***, ***Condor***) and Tortola, BVI (***Liat***). Eastern Caribbean Express flies to the Eastern Caribbean islands.

Check different airlines for inter-island travel, the Trinidad route is particularly competitive, ***British Airways*** often has good offers between Barbados, Antigua and St Lucia and a comfortable plane. It is usually worth organizing ticketing at the start of your journey so that Barbados appears as a stopover rather than as the origin for any side trips you make.

Several companies run mini-cruises based on Barbados. The cruise ship passenger tax is US$8.50

Sea ***Windward Lines Limited*** run a weekly passenger/car/cargo ferry service: Trinidad – St Vincent – Barbados – St Lucia – Barbados – St Vincent – Trinidad – Güiria (or every other week to Pampatar, Margarita), see pages 25 and 27 for schedules and fares. **To Venezuela** is especially good value as you see several islands and have somewhere to sleep on the way. Restaurant on board. Seasickness pills available, payable in almost any currency. There are a few

Touching down

Departure tax There is a departure tax of B$25, not payable if your stay is for less than 24 hours.

Embassies Australian High Commission, Bishop's Court Hill, T4352843. **Belgian** Consulate, Rockley Resort, T4357704. **Brazilian** Embassy, 3rd Floor, Sunjet House, Fairchild St, T4271735. **British** High Commission, Lower Collymore Rock, St Michael, PO Box 676, T4366694, F4365398. **Canadian** High Commission, Bishop's Court Hill, St Michael, T4283550. **Colombian** Embassy, Dayrells Rd, T4296821. **Cuban** Embassy, Collymore Rock, T4352769. **Danish** Consul, c/o Yankee Garments, T4244995. **Dutch** Consul, c/o Chickmont Foods, T4188000. **French**, Hastings, Christ Church, T4356847. **German**, Banyan Court, Bay St, St Michael, T4271876. **Guatemalan Embassy**, 2nd Floor, Trident House, Broad St, T4353542, F4352638. **Israeli** Consul, T4264764. **Italy**, T4371228. **Norwegian** Consul, T4297286. **People's Rep of China**, Golf View, Rockley, T4356890. **Swedish** Embassy, Branckers Complex, Fontabelle, St Michael, T4274358. **US** Consular Section, Alico Building, Cheapside, Bridgetown, T4364950. **Venezuelan** Embassy, El Sueño, Hastings, Christ Church, T4357619.

Official time Atlantic Standard Time, 4 hours behind GMT, 1 ahead of EST.

Voltage 120 volts (American standard) and 50 cycles per second (British standard). Some houses and hotels also have 240-volt sockets for use with British equipment.

Safety Bridgetown is still much safer than some other Caribbean cities but crime rates have increased. Local people are now more cautious about where they go after dark and many no longer go to Nelson St or some other run-down areas. Baxters Rd, however, is generally quite safe although the former attracts prostitutes while the latter attracts cocaine addicts (paros). Take care when walking along deserted beaches and watch out for pickpockets and bag snatchers in tourist areas. Families with small children to care for at night rarely notice any crime and have commented on how secure they felt on Barbados. If hiring a car, watch out for people who wash the vehicle unasked and then demand US$5. Police have patrols on beaches and plain clothes officers around some rural tourist attractions.

sunbeds on the upper deck, so you could sleep under the stars or bring a hammock. Barbados is not well served by small inter-island schooners. You may be able to get a passage to another island on a yacht, ask at the harbour or at the *Boatyard* on Carlisle Bay. Mooring facilities are available at the Shallow Draft next to the Deep Water Harbour, or there are calm anchorages in Carlisle Bay.

Touching down

Airport information

Notice board on left, as you come out of arrivals, lists taxi fares

The airport is modern and well equipped. Clearing Immigration can be a problem and it can take an hour to clear a 747. If three 747s arrive together expect delays. There is a *Liat* connection desk before Immigration. There is a helpful Tourism Authority office, *Barbados National Bank* (very slow), (bureau de change in the arrivals and departure areas is open from 0800-2400), a post office, car hire agencies and quite a wide range of shops (good for stocking up on film or alcohol even if just going on a day trip) including an Inbound Duty Free Shop (very useful, saves carrying heavy bottles on the plane). *The Voyager* restaurant is fairly expensive. Across the car park there are two lively rum shops, one of which does snacks; the shop in the gas station is open when terminal shops are closed, selling food, papers etc. Taxis stop just outside customs. Check the notice board on the left as you come out of arrivals, as it gives the official taxi fares. Talk to the dispatcher if necessary. Drivers may attempt to charge more if you haven't checked. There is a bus stop just across the car park, with buses running along the south coast to Bridgetown, or (over the road) to the *Crane* and *Sam Lord's Castle*.

Airline offices The *Liat* office is at St Michael's Plaza, St Michael's Row (T4366224). *BWIA* (T4262111), *British Airways* (T4366413), are all on Fairchild St. *American Airlines*

Barbados

Tourist offices overseas

Benelux, Weekenstroo Public Relations, Breiterlaan 298, 2596 Den Haag, T3170-3280824, F3170-3280838, benelux@barbados.org

Canada, 105 Adelaide St W, Suite 1010, Toronto, Ontario, M5H 1P9, T416-2149880, toll-free 1-800-268 9122, F416-2149882, canada@barbados.org/canada

France, c/o Tropic Travel, 8-10 Rue St Marc, 75002 Paris, T33-0142365118, F42365119, france@barbados.org

Germany, Staatliches Fremdenverkehrsant Barbados, Neue Mainzer Strasse 22, D-60311 Frankfurt/Main, T069-24269630, F069-230077, germany@barbados.org

Italy, 20145 Milano, Via Gherardini 2, T0233105841, F0233105827, italy@barbados.org

Sweden, Skeppsbron 22, 1130 Stockholm, T460-84115066, F84115067, sweden@barbados.org

UK, 263 Tottenham Court Rd, London W1P 0LA, T020-76369448/9, F6371496, btauk@barbados.org

USA, 800 Second Ave, New York, NY 10017, T212-9866516/8 or toll-free 800-2219831, F212-5739850, btany@barbados.org; 150 Alhambra Circle, 10th Flr, Coral Gables, FL 33134, T305-4427471, F305-5672844, bt@miami@barbados.org; 3440 Wilshire Blvd, Suite 1215, Los Angeles, CA 90010, T213380 2198/9, toll free 800-2219831, F213-3842763, btla@barbados.org

The Barbados Embassy in **Caracas** (Quinta Chapaleta, 9a Transversal, Entre 2 y 3 Avenidas, Altamira, T582-391471, F323393) can also provide tourist information.

(T4284170) has offices at the airport. **Virgin Atlantic** is in Hastings, T7447477.

Local tourist office The Barbados Tourism Authority has its main office in Harbour Rd, Bridgetown (T4272623, F4264080, www.barbados.org). There are also offices at the deepwater harbour (T4261718) and the airport (T4280937). The BTA publishes a useful annual *Sports and Cultural Calendar*, which gives information on what to see throughout the year and the addresses of sporting organizations. Two good sources of information are *Visitor* and the *Sunseeker*, published fortnightly and distributed free by Barbados's two daily newspapers. *Sunseeker* has an amazing listing of every possible club and society, down to Progressive Balloon Dance and Clay Pigeon Shooting. If you want to meet fellow Soroptimists, Rehabilitation Therapists, Astronomers or Girl Guides...there you go. Also lists where to worship, entertainment and daily events. *Simply Barbados* is a free glossy magazine with articles on culture, profiles, environment, business etc. *Ins and Outs of Barbados*, also free, is published annually, a glossy with lots of advertising and distributed by hotels. *Exploring Historical Barbados*, by Maurice Bateman Hutt, is quite good but it was published in 1981.

Tourist information

Local tour agencies Bus tours *L E Williams* (T4271043, US$50-65 day tour, has a sign up in the bus: 'no 10 percent service charge is paid with the tour price', heavy pressure selling of tapes, limited drinks from bar), **Bartic tours** (T4285980), **Sunflower Tours** (T4298941), **International Tour Services** (T4284803), **Bajan Tours** (T/F4372389, cheaper and better value than some, no pressure on tipping, US$32.50 per half day, US$50 full day including lunch), **Island Safari** (T4325337, tour is with 4WD Landrovers so can get to some less accessible beaches, US$40 per half day, US$57.50 full day with lunch, US$90 land and sea tour), **Adventureland** (T4293687, also 4WD and same price) and **Blue Line** (T4239268, tours for US$25-55, including entrance fees to sites visited). Longer tours generally include lunch at the *Atlantis Hotel* in Bathsheba. A criticism of the tours with some companies is that it can take 1½ hours to pick up everyone from hotels and those further north do not get the full tour through Bridgetown and Holetown. If there are 4 of you, it is more flexible to take VIP tours in a limousine with Sally Shearn, T4294617, US$40 per hour, minimum 4 hours, a variety of tours or design your own, admission charges not included. The Transport Board also does a round the island tour by bus on Sunday, aimed mainly at locals and costing only US$5, to the fury of the higher priced competition; book ahead and take your own picnic. **Grenadine Tours**, T4358451, and **Caribbean Safari Tours**, T4275100, do day tours to Grenadines and other islands, with yacht charter if you want. The latter is at the *Ship Inn*, St Lawrence.

Media   **Newspapers**   *The Advocate*, also publishes *The Sunday Advocate* and *Sunseeker* (fortnightly) tourist magazine, see above. *The Nation* (publisher also of *Sunday on Saturday, Sunday Sun, The Visitor* tourist fortnightly and *Barbados Business Authority*, Monday, US$0.50). *Broad Street Journal* is a free business weekly. **Radio**   *CBC Radio*, medium wave 900 kHz; Voice of Barbados, medium wave 790 kHz; BBS, FM 90.7 MHz; Love FM, FM 104.1 MHz; Radio Liberty, FM 98.1 MHz, FAITH 102 FM. **Maps**   Ordnance Survey Tourist Maps including Barbados in the series, 1:50,000 scale with inset of Bridgetown 1:10,000.

Religion   Barbadians are a religious people and although the main church is Anglican, there are over 140 different faiths and sects, including Baptists, Christian Scientists, Jews, Methodists, Moravians and Roman Catholics. Times of services can be found in the *Visitor* and *Sunseeker*.

Getting around

Air   **Helicopters**   For those who want to make a lot of noise buzzing around the island, *Bajan Helicopters* do tours from US$75 per 20 minutes, US$125 per 30 minutes right round the coastline. The heliport is near the deep water harbour at Bridgetown, T4310069.

Car   The island is fairly small but it can take a surprisingly long time to travel as the rural roads are
Petrol costs US$1 narrow and winding. The Adams Barrow Cummins highway runs from the airport to a point
per litre. The speed between Brighton and Prospect, north of Bridgetown. This road (called the ABC, or industrial
limit is 55 mph. access highway) skirts the east edge of the capital, giving access by various roads into the city.
Drive on the left Roads into Bridgetown get jammed morning and afternoon. Office hours are 0830-1630 and at either end of the day traffic is diabolical. Drivers need a visitor's driving permit from Hastings, Worthing, or Holetown police stations (cost US$5). You will need this even if you have an International Driving Licence. Car hire companies usually sort it out for you.

Car hire   This is efficient and generally reliable. A medium sized car will cost on average US$105 per day, US$400 per week. Mini-mokes are fun but not recommended in the rainy season. *Sunny Isle Motors*, Dayton, Worthing, T4357979; *Stoutes Car Rentals* (T4354456/7, F4354435) are particularly helpful, and will arrange to meet you at the airport if you telephone in advance; *L E Williams* (T4271043) has slightly lower rates for some vehicles; *Regency Rent-a-Car*, 77 Regency Park, Christ Church, T4275663, F4297735, free pick up and delivery. *Wander Auto Rentals & Taxi Services Inc*, T4354813, T2304817 (mobile). Other companies are listed in the Yellow Pages. There are often discounts available (including free driver's permit) and tourist magazines frequently contain 10% vouchers.

It is also possible to hire a light motorcycle or a bicycle: motor scooters about US$45 per day, US$205 per week, bicycles US$12.50 per day, US$50 per week, although there will also be a deposit to pay. Fun Seekers, Rockley Main Rd, T4358206. Cycling is best on the east coast, but traffic is heavy everywhere and rush hour from 1600 makes cycling unpleasant almost anywhere on the island.

Bicycle & motorcycle

Buses are cheap and frequent, but also crowded. There is a flat fare of B$1.50 (B$1 for schoolchildren in uniform) which will take you anywhere on the island. Around Bridgetown, there are plenty of small yellow privately-owned minibuses and route taxis with ZR numberplates; elsewhere, the big blue and white Mercedes buses (exact fare required or tokens sold at the bus terminal) belong to the Transport Board. Private companies tend to stick to urban areas while the public buses run half empty in rural areas. Almost all the routes radiate in and out of Bridgetown, so cross-country journeys are time-consuming if you are staying outside the city centre. There is a City Circle route, clockwise and anti-clockwise round the inner suburbs of Bridgetown which starts in Lower Green. Terminals for the south: Fairchild St for public buses, clean, modern; Probyn St, or just across Constitution River from Fairchild St for minibuses; further east by Constitution River for ZR vans. Terminals for the west: Lower Green for public buses; west of Post Office for minibuses; Princess Alice Highway for ZR vans. During the rush hour, all these terminals are chaotic, particularly during school term. On most routes, the last bus leaves at midnight and the first bus at 0500. There are two routes from the airport: Yorkshire buses go straight to Bridgetown, others go along the south coast past the hotels to Bridgetown. Make sure you get the right one.

Bus

However, travelling by bus can be fun. There are some circuits which work quite well; for example: **1.** Any south coast bus to Oistins, then cross country College Savannah bus to the east coast, then direct bus back to Bridgetown; **2.** Any west coast bus to Speightstown, then bus back to Bathsheba on the east coast, then direct bus back to Bridgetown.

Out of town bus stops are marked simply 'To City' or 'Out of City'. For the south coast ask for Silver Sands route.

Taxis are expensive. There are plenty at the airport, the main hotels, and in Bridgetown. There are standard fares, displayed just outside "arrivals" at the airport, and are also listed in the *Visitor* and the *Sunseeker*. Between the airport and any point north of Speightstown, US$27.50, to Holetown, US$19, to Bridgetown Harbour US$15, to Garrison US$12, to Oistins US$8; between the city centre and *Sam Lord's Castle* US$19, to Oistins US$10, Dover US$9; between *Sandy Lane* and Oistins US$18. Fares are quoted also by mile (US$1.25) or kilometre (US$0.75) but there are no taxi meters. You may have to bargain hard for tours by taxi but always agree a fare in advance. Rate per hour is US$16. Vehicles which look like route taxis but with ZM numberplates, are taxis plying for individual hire, and will charge accordingly. **VIP limo services** (T4294617) hire a vehicle with driver for a whole-day tour at a cost of US$150 for up to four persons.

Taxi
Up to 5 people can travel for 1 fare

Keeping in touch

The General Post Office Headquarters is in Cheapside, Bridgetown and there are District Post Offices in every parish. Collections from red post boxes on roadsides. Local postal rates are US$0.25 for priority, US$0.20 non-priority. Airmail rates to North America US$0.60 or US$0.25, to Europe US$0.70 or US$0.35, to the Caribbean US$0.45 or US$0.25. There is an express delivery service of 48 hours worldwide: to the Caribbean US$14-18, USA US$23, Europe US$28. A Philatelic Bureau issues first-day covers four times a year.

Post

Calls from a pay phone cost 25 cents for three minutes. Otherwise local calls are free. Many business places will allow you to use their telephone for local calls. International calls can be made from most hotels or (more cheaply) from Barbados External Telecommunications (Wildey). Faxes can also be sent from and received at BET's office by members of the public. BET has a public office on the Wharf in Bridgetown for international calls and facsimile. Phone cards are available for US$5, 10, 20, 30 from phone company offices, Cave Shepherd or Super

Telephone
International phone code: 246

Centre supermarkets; a cheaper way of making overseas calls than using hotel services, and can be used on most English-speaking islands except Trinidad, Jamaica, Guyana, Bahamas.

Food and drink

Food Fresh fish is excellent. The main fish season is December to May, when there is less risk of stormy weather at sea. Flying fish are the national emblem and a speciality with two or three to a plate. Dolphin (dorado, not a mammal in spite of its name) and kingfish are larger *steak-fish*. Snapper is excellent. *Sea eggs* are the roe of the white sea urchin, and are delicious but not often available. Fresh fish is sold at the fish markets in Oistins, Bridgetown and elsewhere in the late afternoon and evening, when the fishermen come in with their catch. *Cou-cou* is a filling starchy dish made from breadfruit or corn meal. *Jug-jug* is a Christmas speciality made from guinea corn and supposedly descended from the haggis of the poor white settlers. Pudding and *souse* is a huge dish of pickled breadfruit, black pudding and pork.

Drink Barbados rum is probably the best in the English-speaking Caribbean, unless of course you
Malibu, the rum & come from Jamaica, or Guyana or … It is worth paying a bit extra for a good brand such as
coconut drink, now VSOP or Old Gold, or for Sugar Cane Brandy, unless you are going to drink it with Coca Cola, in
also in a lime flavour, which case anything will do. A rum and cream liqueur, Crisma, has now been introduced,
comes from popular in cocktails or on the rocks. The Malibu Visitor's Centre runs a tour, US$7.50, luncheon
Barbados tour, US$27.50 and a special day pass, US$37.50. *Falernum* is sweet, slightly alcoholic, with a hint of vanilla. *Corn and oil* is rum and falernum. *Mauby* is bitter, and made from tree bark. It can be refreshing. *Sorrel* is a bright red Christmas drink made with hibiscus sepals and spices; it is very good with white rum. Banks beer has Bajan Light and other beers; they do brewery tours Tuesday, Thursday 1000-1300, call in advance T4292113. Rachel Pringle Brewery produces Tiltman Beer. Water is of excellent quality, it comes from inland springs.

Shopping

Street vendors are very Prices are generally high, but the range of goods available is excellent. Travellers who are
persistent but generally going on to other islands may find it useful to do some shopping here. If coming from
friendly even when you another Caribbean island there are strict controls on bringing in fresh fruit and vegetables,
refuse their wares because of the mealy bug infestation.

   The best stocked **supermarket** is *JB's Mastermart* in Wildey. *Big B* in Worthing and *Supercentre* in Oistins and Holetown are also good, and are easier to reach by public transport. Also in Holetown is the *Gourmet Shop* selling a lot of luxuries. *Emporium* in Holetown and Worthing has a good selection of wines and luxury foods. *Patisserie Flindt*, Holetown, *Savoy*-trained chef makes delicious (expensive) French pasties, cakes and chocolates (US$5 for a chocolate mousse, US$1.50 for one chocolate), very good coffee, good for a light meal. Food is not cheap but generally most things are available and good quality. Supermarkets are now open on Sundays 0900-1300. *Big B* in Worthing is open 0800-1900 Monday-Tuesday, 0800-2000 Wednesday-Saturday, 0900-1300 Sunday, photocopying available. *Julie'N* on the corner of Rendezvous and Highway 7, satisfactory. Large new *Julie'N* hypermarket on St Barnabas Highway, corner of Highway 5, and in Rendezvous, typically American with wide range of surrounding shops, usually provides free transport back home with shopping within three mile radius, which include some south coast hotels. Julie'N also has the biggest supermarket in central Bridgetown, north side of bridge opposite Treasury Building.

   Duty-free shopping is well advertised. Visitors who produce passport and air ticket can take most duty-free goods away from the store for use in the island before they leave, but not camera film or alcohol. Clothing is significantly cheaper duty-free, so don't go shopping without ticket and passport. Cameras and electrical goods may be much cheaper in an ordinary discount store in the USA or Europe than duty free in Barbados. A duty-free shopping centre for cruise ship passengers in Bridgetown inside the deep water harbour: the *Bridgetown Cruise Terminal* has 21 shops, hand carts selling crafts, 13 chattel houses selling T shirts etc, car hire, bicycle hire, dive shop, agency to arrange horse riding, outlet for tours off the beaten track, two fast food restaurants, steel band twice a day plus other entertainment.

Broad Street is dominated by enormous **jewellers**: *Colombian Emeralds, Diamonds International, Diamonds in Paradise, Jewelers Warehouse* and *Little Switzerland. The Art Foundry* (Heritage Park, Foursquare, St Philip, Monday-Friday, 0900-1700, T4180714), have paintings, sculpture, prints, photographs, installation art and craft for sale. The *Verandah Art Gallery* (Bridgetown, Monday-Friday 0900-1630, Saturday 0900-1300, T4262605) has a reasonable selection with some Haitian art and temporary exhibitions. The *Barbados Gallery of Art*, Bush Hill, The Garrison, St Michael, T2280149, sells prints and has exhibitions. *Medford Craft Village*, Barbarees Hill, has wooden carvings etc. Other good displays of craft items are at *Pelican Village* on the Princess Alice Highway near the harbour, where you can watch artisans at work. *Red Clay Pottery* and *Fairfield Gallery* just outside Bridgetown sells very good ceramics, T4243800. *Earthworks & Potters House*, Edgehill Heights No 2, St Thomas, T4250223, for ceramics, also has small restaurant/café. There is also a street market in Temple Yard where Rastafarians sell leather and other goods.

Bookshops are much better stocked than on other islands. *The Cloister* on Hincks St, T4262662, probably has the largest stock and sells Footprint Handbooks. *The Book Place* on Probyn St specializes in Caribbean material and has a good secondhand section. *Brydens* and *Cave Shepherd* also have a good selection. Also *Roberts Stationery*, *The Book Shop*, *The Bookstop*.

Camera repairs Louis Bailey in Da Costa Mall in Broad St is well-equipped, expensive. Professional Camera Repair, Room 1, Collins Building, Broad St, Bridgetown, T4267174. **Film processing** Graphic Photo Lab in Worthing is quick and efficient. Recommended for slides and enlargements. Be prepared to wait a day or two for slides wherever you go. Fast film processing at Cave Shepherd and at Photo Finish, which has Worthing, Broad St and Sunset Crest branches.

Holidays and festivals

New Year's Day, Errol Barrow Day (21 January), Good Friday, Easter Monday, National Heroes Day (28 April), Whit Monday (1 May), Emancipation Day (1 August), Kadooment Day (first Monday in August), Independence Day (30 November), Christmas Day and Boxing Day. **Public holidays**

Crop Over is the main festival (**1 July** to **7 August 2000**), with parades and calypso competitions over the weekend leading up to Kadooment Day (the first Monday in August), and calypso 'tents' (mostly indoors though) for several weeks beforehand. The celebrations begin with the ceremonial delivery of the last canes on a brightly-coloured dray cart pulled by mules, which are blessed. There is a toast to the sugar workers and the crowning of the King and Queen of the crop (the champion cutter-pilers). The bands and costumes are a pale imitation of what Trinidad has to offer but even Trinidadians now take Barbadian calypso seriously. The big crowd is on the Spring Garden Highway outside Bridgetown Monday afternoon, which has roadside music and places selling drinks for two weeks before Kadooment. Next to the Highway there is Festival village, an area for open-air parties with live music, small entry fee. Baxters Road Mall runs for a couple of weekends beforehand; the road is closed off for fried fish, music and beer. Some related activities take place in July. For more information contact the National Cultural Foundation, T4240909, http://barbados.org/ cropover.htm.

Festivals

For a diary of events & festivals see http://barbados. org/eventcd.htm

The Holetown Festival (**13** to **20 February 2000**, contact Alfred Pragnell, T4356264), commemorating the first settlers' landing in February 1627, and the *Oistins Fish Festival* at Easter (**22** to **24 April 2000**, contact Dan Carter, T4273272), celebrating the signing of the Charter of Barbados and the history of this fishing town, are much less elaborate. There are competitions and a big street party with music goes on until late at night. Many villages will also hold a 'street fair' from time to time.

NIFCA, the *National Independence Festival of Creative Arts* is a more serious affair, with plays, concerts and exhibitions in the four weeks before Independence on **30 November**. The *Holders Season* (**14 March** to **1 April 2000**), is a fairly new, but already popular, festival started in 1992 with a season of opera, Shakespeare, cabaret and sporting events such as cricket, golf and polo. Performances are staged outdoors at Holders, an old plantation house. Contact Carol Walcott, T4326385, F4326461 for details.

Barbados

Congaline Carnival is held in late **April**, finishing with a Mayday jump up in the streets from Garrison Savanna to Spring Garden. Bajan and other Caribbean music. Contact the National Cultural Foundation, T4240909.

There is a jazz festival held usually the second week of **January**, contact Gilbert Rowe, T4374537) and for lovers of Gospel music the Gospel Fest is held in **May** (contact Adrian Agard, T4307300.

Diving and marine life

Scuba diving to the reefs or the wrecks around the coast can be arranged with *Underwater Barbados*, *Coconut Court Hotel*, Hastings, or Carlisle Bay Centre, Bay St, St Michael, T/F4260655; *West Side Scuba Centre* at *Sunset Crest Beach Club*, Holetown, T/F4322558, putnam@ sunbeach.net *Hightide Watersports*, T/F4320931, hightide@sunbeach.net, at the *Boatyard* and *Sandy Lane Hotel*. *Exploresub*, St Lawrence Gap T4356542, F4284674, x-sub@ caribsurf.com *Carib Ocean Divers* at *Royal Pavilion* and *Glitter Bay*, T4224414. *Blue Reef Water Sports* at *Glitter Bay* T4223133. *Reefers and Wreckers* at *Kings Beach* T4225450; *Roger's Scuba Shack*, *Boatyard*, Bay Street, T2463483, and several others. These companies also offer PADI diving courses, equipment rental and other facilities such as snorkelling. The only BSAC accredited school (also PADI and NAUI courses) is *Coral Isle Divers* on the Careenage in Bridgetown, T/F4319068, coralis@caribnet.net, who use a 40-ft catamaran dive boat. The Barbados Sub Aqua Club, a branch of the British Sub Aqua Club (BSAC) meets at 0800 on Sunday at the *Boatyard Pub* on the waterfront on Bay St, Bridgetown. They do not hire out equipment but if you have your own they are most welcoming to members from other branches, T4216020, Rob Bates. One of their groups dives for old bottles on a reef just offshore where ships have anchored for some 350 years. There is a recompression chamber at St Anne's Fort, T4278819, or tell the operator if there is an emergency. A new offering is Snuba, when you have a mask and air tube and can go deeper than snorkelling without the hassle of scuba, US$35, T4359037.

For those who want to see the underwater world without getting wet, the *Atlantis Submarine* is at Shallow Draft Harbour, T4368929, day and night dives at US$80, children aged four to 12 half price. The tour starts with a short video and then you go by bus to the deep water port or join the launch at the Careenage. The boat takes about 10 minutes to get to the submarine, sit at the front to be first on the sub, an advantage as then you can see out of the driver's window as well as out of your own porthole. Two divers on underwater scooters join the submarine for the last 15 minutes, putting on a dive show. Booking is necessary, check in 30 minutes before dive time, whole tour takes one and a half hours. The *Atlantis Seatrec* (same phone numbers as submarine, US$35) is a reef observation craft with large windows below deck and waterline giving you a snorkeller's view of the reefs. There are also video monitors to watch as a diver films the reef.

Beaches and watersports

Beaches There are beaches along most of the south and west coasts. Although some hotels make it hard to cross their property to reach the sand, there are no private beaches in Barbados. The west coast beaches are very calm, and quite narrow, beach erosion is a serious worry and the Government's Coastal Conservation Unit is trying to sort it out. A swell can wash up lots of broken coral making it unpleasant underfoot. The south coast can be quite choppy. The southeast, between the airport and East Point, has steep limestone cliffs with a series of small sandy coves with coconut trees, and waves which are big enough for surfing. **Bottom Bay** is currently *the* place to go. Be careful on the east side of the island, currents and undertow are strong in places. Don't swim where there are warning signs, or where there are no other bathers, even on a calm day. **Bathsheba**, on the east coast, is quite spectacular, with wonderful views. Some hotels sell day passes for the use of their facilities: pool, showers, deck chairs, etc. Work on the new *Sandals Resort* at **Paradise Beach** has been shelved and the site is for sale. Meanwhile, with no hotel, the beach is beautifully deserted. Go to north end of Spring Gardens Highway, then up west coast road Highway 1 for about half a mile, then turn sharp left. Drive down to Batts Rock Beach, walk south to get to Paradise Beach.

Beach vendors now have a licence, plastic stalls, and a blue and yellow uniform shirt. Unscrupulous cocaine and sex vendors still operate but are more subtle in their approach than in the past.

There are a large number of **motor and sailing boats** available for charter by the day or for shorter periods. *Tall Ships Incorporated*, T4300900, tallships@sunbeach.net, runs *Excellence I* and *II*, *Irish Mist*, *Tiami* and *Spirit of Barbados* catamarans, *Harbour Master* and *Jolly Roger* (the last two being boozy fun cruises), US$61.50, except *Jolly Roger*, US$55. *Ocean Mist*, 60-ft power catamaran, also four-day trip to Grenadines, or eco-marine heritage cruise with hotel transfers, lunch, snorkelling, Sunday-Thursday 0930-1530, T4367639. *Stiletto* catamarans, T2313829, *Cool Runnings* catamarans, T4360911, *Small Cats*, T4216419, *Kool Kat*, T4209507, *Why Not*, T2303792, *Ocean Rebel*, T4287192, *Heat wave*, US$62 for lunch/snorkel/cruise, T4237871, *Gallivanter* (sports fishing), T4374044, *Calypso Charters*, T4267166, *Secret Love*, T4321972, lunch and snorkelling US$49 per person, sunset snorkelling cruise US$37.50. *Limbo Lady*, Patrick and Yvonne Gonsalves take no more than eight people on their 48-ft yacht and give you a really good day/evening out, with snorkelling, fishing, sunset cruise with delicious canapés, Cava and singing by Yvonne, who plays the guitar, T4205418, F4203254. Others are moored in the Careenage in Bridgetown, with a telephone number displayed. Most are equipped for fishing and snorkelling, and will serve a good meal on board. Rates and services offered vary widely. The big sailing event is the Mount Gay/Boatyard Regatta, held in late May, contact the Barbados Yachting Association, T4356494. The Barbados Sailing and Cruising Club has its clubhouse and facilities at Aquatic Gap, St Michael, T4264434, and welcomes visitors. A second Atlantic Rowing Race starts in Tenerife in October 2001, finishing in Barbados, with 32 teams signed up by mid-1999. **Glass-bottomed boats** can be hired from several private operators along the west coast.

Deep sea fishing can be arranged with *Blue Jay Charters*, T4222098 (competitive prices, discounts offered), *Blue Marlin*, *Idyll Time*, T4364322, 4356669, *Barracuda Too*, T4267252, *Canon II*, T4246107, *Billfisher II*, T4310741 or *Honey Bea III*, T4285344. The Barbados Game Fishing Association (230 Atlantic Shores, Christ Church, T4222016, Julie Packer, Secretary) runs an international tournament in April.

The south coast is good for windsurfing and the International Funboard Challenge is held in March. The Barbados Windsurfing World Cup is in January. The best surfing is on the east coast and the Barbados International Surfing Championship is held at the Soup Bowl, Bathsheba, in late November. Contact the Barbados Windsurfing Association at Silver Sands, T4287277, or the Barbados Surfing Association, Roger Miller, T4265837

Skyrider Parasail, T4350570 and *Ultimate High,* T2314386 for **parasailing**. **Jetskis** are allowed only on certain beaches: Brown's and Brandon's near Bridgetown, Dover on south coast, Mullins on west.

Sailing *(margin)*

Fishing *(margin)*

Windsurfing *(margin)*

Barbados *(margin)*

Other sports

Ask the tourist office for the Sports and Cultural Calendar, which has lots of information about what is on and who to contact in all possible areas of sport. Contact the National Sports Council, Blenheim, St Michael, T4366127, for information on any sport not mentioned below.

Athletics A multi-purpose gymnasium is part of the Sir Garfield Sobers Sports Complex at Wildey, St Michael, T4376016. Badminton, bodybuilding, boxing, basketball, gymnastics, handball, judo, karate, netball, table tennis, volleyball and weightlifting, plenty of changing rooms and showers and also sauna and massage rooms, a medical room and warm-up/practice area. Adjacent is the Aquatic Centre, with an Olympic-size **swimming** pool, tennis courts, hockey, football and cricket pitches outside.

Bridge The Sun, Sea and Slams International Bridge Festival is held in October and ordinary players get a chance to play against people like Zia Mahmood of the *Guardian*'s bridge column plus other big stars. Call Barbados Bridge League. They have a duplicate game Mon, Wed, 0900 (T4357441), Thu 1930, Fri 0900, Sat 1430 (T4293189, 4293724).

Cricket Lots of village cricket all over the island at weekends. A match here is nothing if not a social occasion. For information about the bigger matches at Kensington Oval phone the Barbados Cricket Association, T4361397.

Cycling Contact the Mountain Bike Association, Wayne Robinson, T4310419, or Robert Quintyne, T4293367.

Draughts and **dominoes** are played to a high standard. Join a rum shop match at your peril. Barbados has the current world champion draughts player, Suki King.

Golf There are five courses, the best and most prestigious of which has traditionally been Sandy Lane, where work is going on to build two new 18-hole courses in addition to nine holes of the original courses on 600 acres of former sugar cane land next to the hotel, T4322946/4321311/4321145. However, a new 18-hole, par 72, course at Royal Westmoreland Golf and Country Club, St James, T4224653, has opened and this will soon have 27 holes spread over 480 acres on a hilly site in St James with views over the west coast. To play here you must be staying in one of the villas or at a hotel with an access agreement. Members can use the hotel's beach club facilities five minutes drive away. Construction of 350 villas around one of the nine-hole loops has now started, three club houses, a swimming pool and five tennis courts. The *Almond Beach Village* was built next to the 9-hole Heywoods course in the northwest, T4224900, there is also an 18-hole course at Belair, near *Sam Lords. Rockley* has no clubhouse and is not highly rated, nine holes, T4357880. The Barbados Academy of Golf is at Balls in Christ Church, T4207505/6, open 0600-2200. There are a putting green, driving range, 18-hole mini course (fun for families, not serious golfers), lessons and balls (US$6 per bucket). Durants course (nine holes) will reopen early 2000. The Barbados Open Golf Championship is held in December.

Gym The Universal Gym in Hastings is good, with reasonable equipment, aerobic classes and weights at moderate prices. Other gyms are World Gym near Bussa roundabout on ABC Highway and not easy to reach, except by car; and West One at *Sunset Crest* near Holetown on west coast.

Hockey is played on an astroturf hockey pitch at Wildey, near Sir Garfield Sobers Gymnasium. The Banks International Hockey Festival is held in August (19-26 August 2000, 19-25 August 2001) with 37 local teams and 26 from overseas. Hockey Federation T4299430.

Horseracing At the Garrison on Saturday for most of the year. Again, this is something of a social occasion. The Sandy Lane Gold Cup Race, held in March, features horses from neighbouring islands. For information on race meetings phone Barbados Turf Club, T4263980.

Motor racing on the circuit in St Philip. There is off-road karting at Bushy Park Race Circuit, St Philip, Monday-Saturday 1030-1700. The Barbados Rally Club, T4387068.

Polo Barbados Polo Club near Holetown, St James, T4321802. National and international matches are played at Holders Hill between September and March, every Saturday at 1400.

Riding There are eight riding schools offering beach and/or country rides. Some do not give instruction and cater for pleasure riding only. Congo Road Riding Stables, T4236180, one-hour ride including lift to and from hotel is US$25, beginners or advanced; also Brighton Stables on west coast, T4259381; Beau Geste Stables, St George, T4290139, Tony's Riding School, St Peter, T4221549, Caribbean International Riding Stables, St Joseph, T4331453, Trevena Riding Stables, St James, T4326404 and Big C Riding Stables, Christ Church, T4374056. The Barbados Equestrian Association, Stacey Phillips, T4379314.

Road tennis is also a local game with defined rules, played with a low wooden 'net' on some minor (and some main) roads. The World Road Tennis Series is held at the end of November.

Running The Run Barbados Series is held in early December and is comprised of a 10 kilometre race and a marathon. Contact Morris Greenidge at the Barbados Tourism Authority, T4272623.

Squash *Rockley Resort* has two courts, T4357880, Barbados Squash Club, Hastings, three courts, T4277193, *Casuarina Hotel*, T4283600. Squash Racquets Association, Craig Archer, T4242612.

Tennis There are good courts at *Royal Pavilion* and *Glitter Bay* (Peter Burwash Tennis Centre at Royal Westmoreland Golf Course). *Paragon*, T4272054, *Rockley Resort*, T4357880, *Sam Lord's*, T4237350, *Crane Hotel*, T4326220.

The National Trust

The National Trust runs an Open House programme of visits to interesting private houses on Wednesday afternoons from January to April every year (B$15, children 5-12 half price, B$6 for members of foreign National Trusts, see below, Boyces Garage do a tour plus entrance for B$35, T4251103. A National Trust Heritage passport is available: pick up a free booklet and get it stamped at Andromeda Gardens (B$12), Welchman Hall Gully (B$11.50), Sir Frank Hutson Sugar Museum (B$15), Tyrol Cot (B$11.50) and then you get free admission to Gun Hill, Bridgetown Synagogue, Arbib Nature trail and Morgan Lewis. The National Trust Headquarters is at Wildey House, Wildey, open 0800-1600,

T4369033, 4262421, which houses the Trust's collection of antique furniture and the Euchard Fitzpatrick and Edward Stoute photography collections. The Duke of Edinburgh Award Scheme (Bridge House, Cavans Lane, Bridgetown, T4369763) and National Trust joint scheme also arrange early Sunday morning walks to places of historical and natural interest. There is a reciprocal free entry to National Trust Properties for members of the National Trust in the UK, Australia, New Zealand, Fiji and Zimbabwe. The same arrangement applies to members of the National Trust for Historic Preservation in the USA and the Heritage Canada Foundation.

Walking The most beautiful part of the islands is the Scotland District on the east coast. There is also some fine country along the St Lucy coast in the north and on the southeast coast. Walking is straightforward. The Ordnance Survey, Southampton, UK, produces a map of Barbados in its tourist map series, 1:50,000 scale with 1:10,000 inset of Bridgetown available from the Public Buildings in Bridgetown, from the museum, in the airport and from some bookstores in town. There is a particularly good route along the old railway track, from Bath to Bathsheba and on to Cattlewash. The National Trust, together with the Duke of Edinburgh Award Scheme, T4262421, organizes walks at 0600 on a Sunday morning and sometimes at 1530 or 1730 (depending on season) on Sunday afternoon. Details are usually printed in the *Visitor* and *Sunseeker* magazines. Their walk to Chalky Mount in the Scotland District has been recommended.

Water Polo is played at the Barbados Aquatic Centre, where visitors are welcome to join in practice sessions with the team, which is sponsored by the local beer company, Banks. Training is every Monday and Wednesday at 1830, while matches are played every Saturday at 1400. Call Stephen Lewis, T4296767 (work), 4286042 (home).

Bridgetown

The capital, Bridgetown, is on the southwest corner of the island. The city itself covers a fairly small area. It is busy and full of life. There are no really large buildings except Tom Adams Financial Centre, which houses the central bank. The suburbs sprawl most of the way along the south and west coasts, and quite a long way inland. Many of the suburban areas are very pleasant, full of flowering trees and 19th-century coral stone gingerbread villas. There are two interesting areas, downtown Bridgetown with National Heroes Square on the north side of the Careenage and the historic area at Garrison.

Getting there You can get a bus or taxi from the airport to Bridgetown. **Getting around** Minibuses and route taxis run around the capital, cheaply and efficiently, but terribly slow in rush hour. See page 878 for details.

Ins & outs

Sights

National Heroes Square was until 1999 called Trafalgar Square, with a statue of Lord Nelson, sculpted by Sir Richard Westmacott and predating its London equivalent by 36 years. It has recently been the subject of some controversy as it was thought to link Barbados too closely with its colonial past. First Nelson was turned through 180° so that he no longer looked down Broad Street, the main shopping area, but now he is to be removed, when a suitable home can be found. The square is now celebrating 10 official national heroes, including Sir Grantley Adams. There is a memorial to the Barbadian war dead and the fountain commemorates the piping of water to Bridgetown in 1861. To the north is the Parliament Building. Built in 1872, the legislature is an imposing grey building with red roof and green shutters. Built in gothic style, the clock tower is more reminiscent of a church. You can walk between the buildings (providing you are correctly dressed).

Take the northeast exit out of National Heroes Square along St Michael's Row to reach the 18th-century **St Michael's Cathedral**. It has a fine set of inscriptions and a single-hand clock. The first building was consecrated in 1665 but destroyed by a hurricane in 1780. The present cathedral is long and broad with a balcony. It has a fine vaulted ceiling and some tombs (1675) have been built into the porch. Completed in 1789, it suffered hurricane damage in 1831. If you continue east, you reach **Queen's Park**, a pleasant, restful park just outside the city centre. **Queen's Park House** is now a small theatre and art gallery. There is a small restaurant and bar, which does a good lunch and a buffet on Friday.

The **synagogue** is an early 19th-century building on the site of a 17th-century one, one of the two earliest in the Western hemisphere. The original synagogue, was built in the late 1660s by Jews fleeing Recife, Brazil, who heard that Oliver Cromwell had granted freedom of worship for Jews and gained permission to settle in Barbados. The tomb of Benjamin Massiah, the famous circumciser of 1782 lies on the left hand side of the graveyard, just inside the entrance. Recently painstakingly restored, it is now used for religious services again and is open to visitors. It is supported by only 16 families now. ■ *Mon-Fri, 0900-1200, 1300-1600.*

Bridgetown

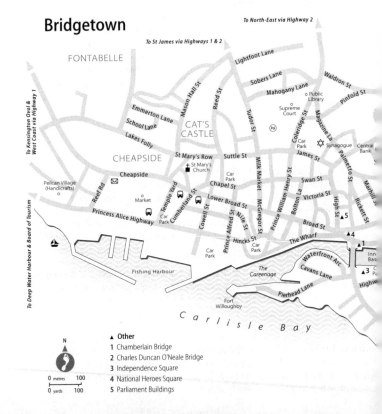

▲ **Other**
1 Chamberlain Bridge
2 Charles Duncan O'Neale Bridge
3 Independence Square
4 National Heroes Square
5 Parliament Buildings

The area south of James St is good for **street markets**. A whole range of goods can be bought along Swan St and Boulton Lane, good fruit and vegetables as well as leather goods. Street music is sometimes performed. This is in marked contrast to the large shopping malls and department stores on Broad St. Here you will find a whole range of sophisticated shops catering for tourists (see page 880). The Government plans to ban traffic from Broad St as part of a plan to regenerate the city centre. More developments are planned along by the Careenage where old warehouses are being converted into restaurants, discos, smart shops. Multi-storey car parks, a marina and port expansion are also part of the US$25mn project.

The **Harry Bailey Observatory** in Clapham is not far from Banks Brewery. A chance for northern visitors to look at the Southern Hemisphere stars. ■ *T4261317. Fri nights 2030-2330.*

The **Mount Gay Visitor Centre** at Brandons, St Michael, does a very good 45-minute tour of the blending and bottling plant, with an exhibition of rum, rum tasting and shop near the deep water port in Bridgetown on the Spring Garden Highway. For their distillery tour, see page 890. ■ *T4258757. B$12, or a special luncheon tour B$50. 0900-1600 Mon-Fri.* The **Malibu Visitors' Centre**, Brighton, St Michael, is near the West India Rum Refinery. The adjacent beach has watersports. ■ *T4259393. US$6 for tour, US$27.50 tour with lunch. Mon-Fri 0900 with the last tour at 1545.* **Banks Brewery** has a tour and also do a 'beer trail', whereby you get your card stamped in participating bars and restaurants around the island. With five stamps you get a free brewery tour, 15 get you a T-shirt. ■ *T4292113. US$5 adults, US$2.50 children 10-15, no children under 10, proceeds to charity. Tour on Tue and Thu 1000 and 1300.*

A short bus ride from town is **Tyrol Cot**, built in 1850, home of Sir Grantley Adams. There is a Heritage Village with craftwork on sale, plus chattel-house museum, gardens and restaurant in the old stables. Run by the National Trust. ■ *T4242074. US$5.75, children US$2.90. Mon-Fri 0900-1700.*

The Garrison Area

Cross the Careenage by the Charles Duncan O'Neale Bridge (one of the bus terminals and market area are just to the west) and follow Bay St around the curve of Carlisle Bay. You will pass St Patrick's Cathedral (Roman Catholic), the main government offices with St Michael's Hospital behind it before reaching the historic Garrison area. From here you can visit **Fort Charles** on Needham Point (turn right at the Pepsi plant). The fort was the largest of the many which guarded the south and west coasts. It now forms part of the gardens of the *Hilton Hotel* (being rebuilt). Only the ramparts remain but there are a number of 24 pounder cannons dating from 1824. There is a military cemetery here and the Mobil oil refinery was the site of the naval dockyard. Built in 1805, it was subsequently moved to English Harbour, Antigua. The buildings were then used as barracks before being destroyed in the 1831 hurricane.

To East Coast via Highways 3, 4 & 5

Harrison's College

Crumpton St

Roebuck St

Garnet St

Church St
St Michael's Cathedral

St Michael's Row

LIAT

Constitution River

Market

Bus Terminus

Fairchild St

BWIA

Jordan Lane

Probyn St

Nelson St

King William St

Beckwith St

Queen St

Spruce St

Vine St

Wellington St

Queens Park

Queens Park

Constitution Rd

Queen's College

River Rd

To Hospital, Wildey & Southeast via Highway 6

To Garrison, Rockley, Oistins & Airport via Highway 7

Carry on up the hill to the **Garrison Historical Area**, which contains many interesting 19th-century military buildings, grouped around the Garrison Savannah. There are numerous buildings surrounding the parade ground, now the six furlong race course. These were built out of brick brought as ballast on ships from England. They are built on traditional colonial lines, the design can be seen throughout the Caribbean but also in India. Painted bright colours, some now contain government offices. There are several memorials around the oval shaped race course, for instance in the southwest corner, the 'awful' hurricane which killed 14 men and one married woman and caused the destruction of the barracks and hospital on 18 August 1831 and outside the Barbados Museum in the northeast corner to the men of the Royal York Rangers who fell in action against the French in Martinique, Les Saintes and Guadeloupe in the 1809/10 campaign.

Across the road is **St Anne's Fort** which is still used by the Barbados defence force. You cannot enter but look for the crenellated signal tower with its flag pole on top. It formed the high command of a chain of signal posts, the most complete of which is at Gun Hill (see below). The long, thin building is the old drill hall. **The Main Guard**, overlooking the savannah, has a nice old clock tower and a fine wide verandah. It has been turned into an information centre and houses exhibits about the West Indian Regiment. The Garrison Secretary of the Regiment, Major Michael Hartland, T4260982, is here. Outside is the **National Cannon Collection** which he created, an impressive array of about 30 cannon, some are mounted on metal 'garrison' gun carriages (replaced with wooden ones during action as they were prone to shatter). There are also a number of newer howitzers, dating from 1878. Major Hartland welcomes visitors but he is still creating a Regimental museum, so make an appointment first.

The **Barbados Museum** is housed in the old military prison on the northeast corner of the savannah. Based on a collection left by Rev N B Watson (late rector of St Lucy Parish), it is well set out through a series of 10 galleries. It displays natural history, local history (in search of *Bim*), a fine map gallery including the earliest map of Barbados by Richard Ligon (1657), colonial furniture (Plantation House Rooms), military history (including a reconstruction of a prisoner's cell), prints and paintings which depict social life in the West Indies, decorative and domestic arts (17-19th century glass, china and silver), African artefacts, a children's gallery and one to house temporary exhibits. The museum shop has a good selection of craft items, books, prints, and cards. The *Café Musée* under the trees in the museum courtyard is a delightful place for a drink or for lunch. ■ *T4270201/4361956. US$5.80 for adults, US$2.90 for children. Mon-Sat 0900-1700, Sun 1400-1800.* Library available for research purposes. ■ *US$10 for visitors, US$5 for locals, plus VAT. Mon-Fri 0900-1300.*

The **Barbados Gallery of Art**, at the top of Bush Hill, across the savanna from the museum, has a collection of paintings and visual arts from Barbados and the Caribbean. ■ *T2280149. US$2.50 adults, US$1 children, Tue-Fri, Sat US$1 adults, children free. 1000-1700.* **George Washington House**, close by, is where he stayed in 1751. The National Trust has launched an appeal for restoration funds.

Nearby there are stables for the race course. The Barbados Turf Club holds meetings on Saturday during three seasons (January-March, May-October and November-December). The biggest one being the Sandy Lane Gold cup held in March. Races go clockwise. A good place to watch is from the Main Guard. At other times, it is used as a jogging course for people in the mornings, when you can see the horses being exercised, or on weekday evenings. There is also rugby, basketball, etc, played informally in the Savannah, go and see what is going on on Sunday afternoons. There is a small children's playground in one corner. Later, at night, prostitutes parade here.

Also near Garrison is **Mallalieu Motor Collection**, with a Vanden Plas Princess, Wolseley and Lanchester. ■ *T4264640, US$5.*

Around the Island

Being the most easterly island and extremely difficult to attack, there are few defensive forts on Barbados. Instead the great houses of the sugar growing plantocracy give the island its historic perspective and most of its tourist attractions. Many parish churches are also impressive buildings. The island is not large but it is easy to get lost when driving. Deep gullies cut in the coral limestone which is the surface rock over most of the island. These are often full of wildlife and plants but make travelling around very confusing. It sometimes helps to remember that the island is divided into 11 parishes named after 10 saints, Christ Church being the eleventh. A good map is essential. The bus service is cheap and efficient and recommended even for families with small children.

The west coast

The mass development of the west coast was carried out only recently. The beaches are easily eroded and can be covered with broken coral after storms. Pre-war, the area was regarded by the local Bajans as unhealthy. They preferred to go for their holidays to the east coast. Nowadays, the road north of Bridgetown on Highway 1 is wall to wall hotels. Highway 2a runs parallel inland and goes through the sugar cane heartland, with small villages and pleasant views.

Holetown today is a thoroughly modern town but was the place where the earliest settlers landed on 17 February 1627. The Holetown monument commemorates Captain John Powell claiming the island for England. Initially named Jamestown, it was renamed Holetown because of a tidal hole near the beach. It was quite heavily defended until after the Napoleonic Wars. Little trace of the forts can be seen now. Well worth visiting is **St James Church**. Originally built of wood in 1628, it was replaced by a stone structure in 1680. This building was extended 20 ft west in 1874 when columns and arches were added and the nave roof raised. You can see the original baptismal font (1684) under the belfry and in the north porch is the original bell of 1696. Many of the original settlers are buried here (although the oldest tombstone of William Balston who died in 1659 is in the Barbados Museum). Church documents dating to 1693 have been removed to the Department of Archives. It was beautifully restored between 1983-86.

Holetown

On the beach at the back of the church is the post office and also the **Folkestone Park and Marine Reserve**. Here you can snorkel in a large area enclosed by buoys. The reef is not in very good condition but there are some fish. Snorkelling equipment for hire as are glass bottomed boats which will take you over the reef to two small wrecks further down the coast. A diving platform about 100 yds offshore allows you to snorkel over the wrecks. There are toilets and a shower here. ■ *The small museum is open Mon-Fri 1000-1700. Slide shows are held about every hour. US$1.*

The **Portvale Sugar Factory** (best in the crop season, February to May) and **Sir Frank Hutson Sugar Machinery Museum** inland has an exhibition on the story of sugar and its products. ■ *T4320100 to check. US$7.50 when factory is running Feb-May, US$4 the rest of the time, children half price. 0900-1700, Mon-Sat.*

Follow the coast road and glimpse the sea at Gibbes and Mullins Bays to reach Speightstown where William Speight once owned the land. An important trading port in the early days, when it was known as Little Bristol. Speightstown is now the main shopping centre for the north of the island. There are several interesting old buildings and many two-storey shops with Georgian balconies and overhanging galleries (sadly many have been knocked down by passing lorries). The Lions Club building (Arlington) is 17th-century, built very much on the lines of an English late medieval town house. No longer occupied, it is rapidly becoming derelict, but well worth a look.

Speightstown
Pronounced Spitestown or Spikestong in broad dialect

Barbados

The National Trust runs the **Arbib Nature & Heritage Trail**, starting in Speightstown. There are routes of 5½ kms and 7½ kms, starting from St Peter's church. ■ *US$7.50, reservations T4262421. Wed, Thu, Sat, 0900-1430.*

In 1996 construction started on a marina at Heywoods Beach just north of Speightstown, known as Port St Charles. The US$60mn project will include 145 residential units, restaurants, a yacht club and watersports as well as have a capacity for nine mega-yachts and 140 yachts on completion in 2000. The first houses have already been sold, with prices ranging from US$0.4mn to US$1.8mn; homeowners are allowed to bring in a boat duty free to this upmarket development.

St Lucy

The road north of Speightstown is mercifully free of buildings and there is a good sandy beach on **Six Men's Bay**. Go through Littlegood Harbour and notice the boat building on the beach. The jetty you can see is at Harrison Point. You are now entering the unspoilt (apart from Arawak Cement Plant) parish of St Lucy. Almost any of the roads off Highway 1b will take you to the north coast, at first green and lush around Stroud Point but becoming more desolate as you approach North Point. The northwest coast, being slightly sheltered from the Atlantic swells, has many sandy coves (Archers Bay). The cliffs are quiet and easy to walk. You may spot turtles swimming in the sea.

The **Animal Flower Cave** at **North Point** is a series of caverns at sea level which have been eroded by the sea. The animals are sea anemones. There are various 'shapes' in the rock which are pointed out to you. ■ *The main cave can be closed due to dangerous seas, so T4398797 around 0930 to enquire. US$1.50(US$1 if you cannot see full cave). The floor of the cave is very stony and can be slippery.*

Following the rocky coast, turn into the semi-abandoned *North Point Surf Resort* (park outside the wall to avoid being charged for parking, the buildings are half ruined now, and there is an enormous empty swimming pool) where you can walk around the Spout, which has lots of blow holes and a small, rather dangerous beach.

Good walks along the cliffs can be enjoyed, for instance from River Bay to Little Bay along the Antilles Flat, but beware as there is no shade and there are shooting parties during the season. If driving, several back roads go through the attractive communities of Spring Garden and St Clements. At Pie Corner you can rejoin the coast and visit **Little Bay**. This is particularly impressive during the winter months with the swell breaking over the coral outcrops and lots of blowholes. Note the completely circular hole on the north edge of the Bay. If you climb through this natural archway in the cliff, there is a big, calm pool, just deep enough to swim between the cliffs and a line of rock on which the enormous waves break and send up a wall of spray. Wear shoes to stop your feet getting cut to pieces on the sharp rock.

At **Paul's Point** is a popular picnic area. If the ground looks wet park at the millwall by the Cove Stud Farm as it is easy to get bogged down. You will get a good view of **Gay's Cove** with its shingle beach (safe to swim in the pools at low tide) and beyond it the 240-ft high **Pico Teneriffe**, a large rock (almost in the shape of Barbados and named by sailors who thought it looked like the mountain on Teneriffe in the Canaries) on top of a steeply sloping cliff. The white cliffs are oceanic rocks consisting of myriad tiny white shells or microscopic sea creatures. The whole of the coast to Bathsheba is visible and it is easy to see the erosion taking place in Corben's Bay. Indeed you get an excellent impression of the Scotland District, where the coral limestone has been eroded. The whole of this coast between North and Ragged Points has been zoned, no further development will be allowed along the seafront.

The **Mount Gay Rum Distillery** is reached off the road between the St Lucy church junction and Alexandra. ■ *Tours Mon-Fri at 1100 and 1400. They also have a visitor's centre in St Michael (see page 887).*

The Scotland District

Just to the northwest is **St Nicholas Abbey** which is approached down a long and impressive avenue of mahogany trees. Dating from around 1660, it is one of the oldest domestic buildings in the English-speaking Americas (**Drax Hall**, St George, open occasionally under the National Trust Open House programme, is probably even older). Three storied, it has a façade with three ogee-shaped gables. It was never an abbey, some have supposed that the 'St' and 'Abbey' were added to impress, there being lots of 'Halls' in the south of the island. Visitors are given an interesting tour of the ground floor and a fascinating film show in the stables behind the 400-year-old sand box tree. Narrated by Stephen Cave, the present owner and son of the film maker, its shows life on a sugar plantation in the 1930s. You will see the millwall in action and the many skilled workers from wheel wrights to coopers who made the plantation work. The importance of wind is emphasized. If the millwall stopped the whole harvest came to a halt as the cane which had been cut would quickly dry out if it was not crushed straight away. The waste was used to fuel the boilers just as it is today in sugar factories. There is a collection of toy buses and lorries in the stables.

Going back down the steep Cherry Tree Hill you come to the National Trust-owned **Morgan Lewis Mill**, a millwall with original machinery which the National Trust is attempting to restore to working condition. More funds are needed to finish the job. You can climb to the top of it. Note the 100-ft tail, this enabled the operators to position the mill to maximize the effect of the wind. It is on a working farm. ■ *T4227429. US$5. Mon-Sat, 0900-1700.* On the flat savannah at the bottom of the hill is a cricket pitch, a pleasant place to watch the game at weekends.

The **Barbados Wildlife Reserve**, established with Canadian help in 1985, is set in four acres of mature mahogany off Highway 2. It is an excellent place to see lots of Barbados green monkeys close up. Most of the animals are not caged, you are warned to be careful as you wander around the shady paths as the monkeys can bite. They have a collection of the large red-footed Barbados tortoise. Also (non-Barbadian) toucans, parrots and tropical birds, hares, otters, opossums, agoutis, wallabies, porcupines, and iguanas. You can observe pelicans and there is a spectacled caiman (alligator) in the pond. The primate research centre helps to provide farmers with advice on how to control the green monkeys who are regarded as a pest. The animals are fed near it at about 1600. The centre has also developed a nature trail in the neighbouring Grenade Hall Forest, ask for further details. An early 19th-century signal station next to Grenade Hall Forest has been restored. The wonderful panoramic view gives you a good idea of its original role in the communications network. ■ *T4228826. US$11.50, children half price. Daily 1000-1700. Café and shop. Getting there: bus from Bridgetown, Holetown, Speightstown or Bathsheba.*

Farley Hill House, St Peter, is a 19th-century fire-damaged plantation house; a spectacular ruin on the other side of the road from the Wildlife Reserve, set in a pleasant park with views over the Scotland District. There is a large number of imported and native tree species planted over 30 acres of woodland. ■ *T4223555. US$1.75 per vehicle. Daily 0830-1800.*

From Farley Hill it is possible to walk more or less along the top of the island as far as **Mount Hillaby**, through woods and then canefields. However, it helps to know where you are going as the paths have a mind of their own and losing them can be uncomfortable. You will see plenty of monkeys on the way and good views.

The Atlantic Parishes

The five-mile East Coast Rd, opened by Queen Elizabeth on 15 February 1966 affords fine views. From Belleplaine, where the railway ended, it skirts Walker's Savannah to the coast at Long Pond and heads southeast to **Benab**, where there is **Barclays Park**, a good place to stop for a picnic under the shady casuarina trees. A walk up **Chalky Mount** has been recommended for the magnificent views of the east coast, easily reached at the end of the bus line from Bridgetown. If you ask locally for the exact path you are likely to be given several different routes. Walk down through the meadows to Barclays Park for a drink when you come down. There is no paved road. Staff in the café will know times of buses to either Bathsheba or Speightstown. The East Coast Rd continues through **Cattlewash**, so named because Bajans brought their animals here to wash them in the sea, to Bathsheba.

The tiny hamlet of **Bathsheba** has an excellent surfing beach (see page 882). Guarded by two rows of giant boulders, the bay seems to be almost white as the surf trails out behind the Atlantic rollers. Surfing championships are often held here. A railway was built in 1883 (but closed in 1937) between Bridgetown and Bathsheba. Originally conceived as going to Speightstown, it actually went up the east coast to a terminus at Belleplaine, St Andrew. The cutting at My Lady's Hole, near Conset Bay in St John is spectacular, with a gradient of 1:31, which is supposed to have been the steepest in the world except for rack and pinion and other special types of line. The railway here suffered from landslides, wave erosion, mismanagment and underfunding so that the 37-mile track was in places in very bad condition. The crew would sprinkle sand on the track, the first class passengers remained seated, the second class walked and the third class pushed.

Above the bay at Hillcrest (excellent view) are the **Andromeda Gardens**. Owned by the Barbados National Trust, the gardens contain plants from all over Barbados as well as species from other parts of the world. There are many varieties of orchid, hibiscus and flowering trees. ■ *T4339261. US$6, children US$3. Every day, 0900-1700. The Hibiscus Café at the entrance is a useful place to stop for refreshment. The Atlantis Hotel is a good place for lunch especially on Sunday (1300 sharp) when an excellent buffet meal containing several Bajan dishes is served. Almost an institution and extremely popular with Bajans, so book ahead.*

From Bathsheba you can head inland to **Cotton Tower signal station** (National Trust owned. Not as interesting as Gun Hill). Then head south to Wilson Hill where you find Mount Tabor Church and **Villa Nova**, another plantation Great House (1834), which has furniture made of Barbadian mahogany and beautiful gardens. It was owned by the former British Prime Minister, Sir Anthony Eden, and until 1994 was part of the National Trust's heritage trail. It has now been bought by Swiss investors who are opening it as a five-star country resort hotel, T4361710, F4361715. You can continue from here via Malvern along the scenic **Hackleton's Cliff** (allegedly named after Hackleton who committed suicide by riding his horse over the cliff) or via Sherbourne (**F** *Coconut Inn*, two-room guest house run by Geoff and Terry Browne, who also do excellent Bajan lunches) to Pothouse, where **St John's Church** stands with views over the Scotland District. Built in 1660 it was a victim of the great hurricane of 1835. There is an interesting pulpit made from six different kinds of wood. You will also find the grave of Fernando Paleologus "descendant of ye imperial line of ye last Christian emperors of Greece". The full story is in Leigh Fermor's *The Traveller's Tree*.

At the satellite tracking station turn off to **Bath**. Here you will find a safe beach, popular with Barbadians and a recreation park for children. It makes a good spot for a beach barbecue and a swim.

Codrington College is one of the most famous landmarks on the island and can be seen from Highway 4b down an avenue of Cabbage Palm trees. It is steeped in history as the first Codrington landed in Barbados in 1628. His son acted as Governor for three years but was dismissed for liberal views. Instead he stood for parliament and was elected speaker for nine years. He was involved in several wars against the French and became probably the wealthiest man in the West Indies. The third Codrington succeeded his father as Governor-General of the Leeward islands, attempted to stamp out the considerable corruption of the time and distinguished himself in campaigns (especially in taking St Kitts). He died in 1710, a batchelor aged 42, and left his Barbadian properties to the Society for the Propagation of the

Gospel in Foreign Parts. It was not until 1830 that Codrington College, where candidates could study for the Anglican priesthood, was established. From 1875 to 1955 it was associated with Durham University, England. Apart from its beautiful grounds with a fine avenue of Royal Palms, a huge lily pond (flowers close up in the middle of the day) and impressive façade, there is a chapel containing a plaque to Sir Christopher Codrington and a library. There are plans to develop it as a conference centre. You can follow the track which drops down 360 feet to the sea at the beautiful Conset Bay. ■ *US$2.50. Getting there: you can take the Sargeant St bus as far as Codrington College, then walk 7 miles back along the Atlantic Coast to Bathsheba.*

At **Ragged Point** is the automatic **East Point lighthouse** standing among the ruined houses of the former lighthouse keepers. There are good views north towards Conset Point, the small Culpepper island, and the south coast. Note the erosion to the 80-ft cliffs caused by the Atlantic sweeping into the coves.

The centre

Northeast of Holetown and reached from St Simon's Church are **Turners Hall Woods**, a good vantage point. It is thought that the wood has changed little to that which covered the island before the English arrived. The 50-acre patch of tropical mesophytic forest has never been clear-felled (although individual trees were often taken out). You can walk over the steep paths here and see many species, ranging from the sandbox tree to Jack-in-the-box and the 100-ft locust trees supported by massive buttresses. The island's first natural gas field was here and the main path through the wood is the remains of the old road.

On Highway 2, take the Melvin Hill road just after the agricultural station and follow the signs to the **Flower Forest**, a 50-acre, landscaped plantation, opened in 1983 with beautifully laid out gardens. Dropping downhill, the well-maintained paths afford excellent views over the valley to the east coast. To the west you can see **Mount Hillaby**, at 1,116 feet the island's highest point (see above for walking from Farley Hill). It too contains species not only from Barbados but also from all over the world, they are beautifully arranged with plenty of colour all year round. There is a *Best of Barbados* shop, cafeteria and toilets. Good information sheet. ■ *T4338152. US$7, children 5-16 half price. Daily 0900-1700.*

Close by and to the south on Highway 2 is **Welchman Hall Gully**, a fascinating walk through one of the deep ravines so characteristic of this part of Barbados. You are at the edge of the limestone cap which covers most of the island to a depth of about 300 feet. There is a small car park opposite the entrance (despite the sign to the contrary). Maintained by the National Trust, a good path leads for about half a mile through six sections, each with a slightly different theme. The first section has a devil tree, a stand of bamboo and a judas tree. Next you will go through jungle, lots of creepers, the 'pop-a-gun' tree and bearded fig clinging to the cliff (note the stalactites and stalagmites); a section devoted to palms and ferns: golden, silver, macarthur and cohune palms, nutmegs and wild chestnuts; to open areas with tall leafy mahogany trees, rock balsam and mango trees. At the end of the walk are ponds with lots of frogs and toads. Best of all though is the wonderful view to the coast. On the left are some steps leading to a gazebo, at the same level as the tops of the cabbage palms. ■ *T4386671. US$6, children B$6. Daily, 0900-1700.*

Roads in this area are often closed by landslides & circuitous routing may be necessary

Harrison's Cave nearby has an impressive visitors' centre which has a restaurant (fair), shop and a small display of local geology and Amerindian artefacts. You are taken into the cave on an electric 'train'. The visit takes about 20 minutes and you will see some superbly-lit stalactites and stalagmites, waterfalls and large underground lakes. There is a guide to point out the interesting formations and two stops for photo-opportunities. Interesting as it is, it is all rather overdone, you have to wear hard hats (to prevent complaints of bumped heads) and serviettes (to catch the drips) on your head despite the fact that the caves are totally stable. ■ *T4386640.*

The Easter Rebellion

The 1816 Easter Rebellion was an uprising by slaves who thought (incorrectly) that William Wilberforce had introduced a bill in the English parliament granting slaves their freedom. It was thought by the slaves that the Barbados plantation owners were denying them this freedom. Despite destroying a large acreage of cane fields, no owners or their families were killed and the uprising was quickly crushed by the West Indian Regiment. Several hundred slaves were killed in battle or hanged afterwards, including the best-known leader, an African called Bussa, and Washington Francklyn, a free man of mixed race who was thought, probably erroneously, to have planned the rebellion. 123 slaves were exiled to Sierra Leone.

Daily 0900-1600. US$12.50, children US$5. Getting there: the bus from Bridgetown to Chalky Mount stops near Harrison's Cave and the Flower Forest.

If you take Highway 2 heading to Bridgetown you will pass **Jack-in-the-Box gully**, part of the same complex of Welchman Hall Gully and Harrison's Cave. **Coles Cave** (an 'undeveloped' cave nearby, which can easily be explored with a waterproof torch or flashlight) lies at its north end.

At **Gun Hill** is a fully restored signal tower. The approach is by Fusilier road and you will pass the Lion carved by British soldiers in 1868. The road was built by Royal Scot Fusiliers between September 1862 and February 1863 when they were stationed at Gun Hill to avoid yellow fever. The signal station itself had its origins in the slave uprising of 1816. It was decided that a military presence would be maintained outside Bridgetown in case of further slave uprisings. It was also intended for advance warning of attack from the sea. The chain of six signal stations was intended to give very rapid communications with the rest of the island. The hexagonal tower had two small barrack rooms attached and would have been surrounded by a pallisade. They quickly lost importance as military installations but provided useful information about shipping movements. Informative guides will explain the workings of the signal station and point out interesting features of the surrounding countryside. You will not necessarily get the same story from all the guides. ■ *T4291358. US$5 (children half price), guide book US$1. Mon-Sat 0900-1700.*

Near Gun Hill is the **Francia Plantation**, house and gardens are open to the public, with old furniture, maps and prints. ■ *T4290474. US$4.50. Mon-Fri 1000-1600.*

Orchid World, at Groves, St George, is a 6½-acre orchid garden under the same management as the Flower Forest. ■ *T4330306. US$7. 0900-1700.*

The southeast coast

The area around Six Cross Roads was where the Easter Rebellion of 1816 took place (see box). You can visit one of the great houses (Oughterson Plantation House is no longer in operation). Turn north at Six Cross Roads for **Sunbury Plantation**. Some 300 years old, the house is elegantly furnished in Georgian style, much of it with mahogany furniture, and you can roam all over it as, unusually, there is access to the upstairs private rooms. In the cellars, you can see the domestic quarters. There is a good collection of carriages. The house and museum were damaged by fire in 1995 but have been restored and opened again. ■ *T4236270. US$6. 1000-1630 every day. There is a restaurant in the courtyard. A 5-course plantation house dinner with all the trimmings costs US$75 per person for groups of 15 or more.*

Take the road to Harrow and Bushy Park to reach the **Barbados Zoo Park**. The zoo is very small but has expanded from a bird garden and more animals have slowly been added, these now include tapirs, armadillos, agoutis, several types of monkey and a zebra. Vikki, a small monkey, is a great favourite with children as she will stroke their hands. You are given bread and encouraged to feed the ducks.

Sam Lord's Castle on the southeast coast is the site of an all-inclusive hotel. It is high on the list of tourist attractions because of the reputation of Sam Lord who reputedly lured ships onto Cobbler's Reef where they were shipwrecked. There is supposed to be a tunnel from the beach to the castle's cellars to facilitate his operation. The proceeds made him a wealthy man although the castle was supposed to have been financed from his marriage to a wealthy heiress. The castle is not particularly old or castle-like, being in fact a regency building. Unfortunately the rooms are poorly lit making it difficult to appreciate the fine mahogany furniture or the paintings. Note the superb staircase, you are not allowed upstairs. Wander down to the cove where there is a good example of a turtlecrawl, a salt water pond enclosed by a wall. Here turtles were kept alive until wanted for the kitchen. Today the hotel, in conjunction with the Barbados Wildlife park, keeps a few hawksbill turtles, a shark and a congor eel. ■ *US$5 entrance charge (children US$2.50) even though the hotel reception forms part of the 2 rooms open to the public.*

Foursquare Rum Factory and **Heritage Park**, in an old sugar factory, with sugar machinery, craft market, pottery, bottling plant, folk museum, pet farm, pony stables and Foundry Art Gallery. ■ *T4201977. US$6 adults, children half price. Rum punch and miniature included. Mon-Thu, 1000-1800, Fri-Sat 1000-2100, Sun 1200-1800.*

Crane Bay, southwest of Sam Lord's Castle, is worth a detour. It is a pleasant cove overlooked by 80-ft cliffs. *Crane Hotel* often charges for admission, but it is worth it for a drink and the spectacular view over the bay from the cliff top restaurant.

The south coast

Oistins, the main town in the parish of Christ Church, was named after Edward Oistine, a plantation owner in the area. It was important in colonial times as the place where the 'Charter of Barbados' was signed in 1652, giving the island to the Commonwealth Parliament. It is now the main fishing port. Christ Church parish church overlooks the town and is notable for its cemetery containing the Chase Vault. When the vault was opened in 1812 for the burial of Colonel Thomas Chase, the lead coffins were found scattered around inside. It happened again in 1816, 1817, 1819 and 1820, whereupon the coffins were removed and buried separately in the churchyard.

Graeme Hall Swamp, Worthing, near St Lawrence Gap, has 80 acres of wetland and mangroves around a lake. It is a natural habitat for birds and there are 18 resident species and 150 migrants. A boardwalk is open to the public but the rest is to be a bird sanctuary for scientific research only. Three endangered Caribbean duck species are found here.

The largest expanse of inland water in Barbados

Essentials

Super luxury Most of these are on the west coast and cost over US$300 a night. The 330-room *Almond Beach Village*, T4224900, F4220617, on the old *Heywoods Resort* site, with its 161-room sister resort, *Almond Beach Club*, T4327840, F4322115, 4 miles away. The all-inclusive *Almond Beach Village*, www.almondresorts.com is on 30 acres of land with a 9-hole golf course, 1 mile of beach, 9 pools, 4 restaurants, shops, watersports centre, nightclub and children's play areas, families or couples welcome. *Sandy Lane*, being rebuilt with temporary closure until end-2000, astronomical room rate, expanding with construction of private villas, 2 new 18-hole golf courses in addition to original 9-hole course, state-of-the-art spa, T4321311, F4322954. *Glitter Bay*, T4224555, F4221367, and *Royal Pavilion*, T4225555, F4223940, are very smart, next to each other in 30-acre grounds, www.cphotels.ca One is 'Spanish Colonial Style', the other a pink palace. Perhaps better value to stay elsewhere and visit for a drink or afternoon tea, but well worth looking at, the guests as spectacular in some cases as the (faultless) interior design and landscaping, tennis, fitness centre, swimming pools, beauty salon, watersports and boutiques also on offer at one or other of the sister

Sleeping

Most accommodation offered is very pleasant, if not particularly cheap. 15% VAT is levied on hotel services

Barbados

hotels. Elegant Resorts has four beachfront properties within 5 miles, guests may use the facilities of all four and there is a free water taxi between them: *Colony Club*, T4222335, F4220667. 97 colonial-style rooms and suites, in 7 acres of palms, ponds and free form pool with swim up bar. *Crystal Cove*, T4322683, F4328290. 88 rooms and suites, also with pools and gardens, swim up bar through waterfall. *Tamarind Cove*, T4321332, F4326317. 165 rooms each with 2 beds. *Coconut Creek*, T4320803, F4320272. 53 rooms with 2 beds, pool, tennis. Elegant Resorts also own *Turtle Beach Hotel*, a new resort on the south coast, St Lawrence Gap, T4287131, F4286089. All-inclusive, 167 rooms. **LL-AL** *Sand Acres Hotel*, T4287141, F4282524 and its sister resort, *Bougainvillea Beach Resort*, Maxwell Coast Rd, T4180900, F4180995, www.wheretostay.com Luxurious rooms with facilities for self-catering, efficient and helpful staff, not as expensive as some in this category. *Settlers Beach*, Holetown, St James, T4223052, F4221937, www.barbados.org No children in February, pool, on beach, and *Treasure Beach*, Paynes Bay, T4321346, F4321094, both Unique Hotels, in UK T0800-373742. *Lone Star Motel*, next to restaurant of same name, T4190599, F4190597, www.thelonestar.com 4 huge rooms, uncluttered, simple mahogany furniture building was originally a garage built in 1940s by Romy Reid, who ran a bus company and called himself the Lone Star of the west coast, then it was a nightclub and then a house, owned by Mrs Robertson, of the jam company, who waterskied offshore until her late 80s. *Cobblers Cove*, St Peter, T4222291, F4221460, www.barbados.org 40 rooms, small and exclusive, run by Hamish Watson, wins lots of awards, high proportion of repeat business. *Coral Reef Club*, Holetown, St James, T4222372, F4221776, www.barbados.org Member of Elegant Resorts of Barbados and Prestige Hotels, London, lovely landscaped gardens, lawn running down to sea, cottage style, very highly regarded; also in Holetown, under same management, *Sandpiper Inn*, T4222251, F4221776, www.barbados.org Family-run, with award-winning restaurant, delicious but expensive food, both have large grounds and are on long beach.

Also on the west coast, good but not as luxurious, **LL-AL** *Casuarina Beach Club*, St Lawrence Gap, T4283600, F4281970, www.bajan.com On beach, 180 rooms, pool, tennis. **LL-L** *Grand Barbados Beach Resort*, Aquatic Gap, convenient for Bridgetown, EP, T4264000, F4292400. 133 rooms and suites. **LL-AL** *Kings Beach Hotel*, at Mullins Bay, T4221690, F4221691 or 0932-849462 in the UK or 800-2231588 in the USA, facilities for children and the handicapped. **LL-AL** *The Savannah*, between Garrison Savannah and beach, T2283800, F2284385, savannah@caribsurf.com 21 rooms in recently renovated historic building, antique furniture, each room different, earth-friendly bathroom goodies, special Caricom rate, recommended for business visitors. **LL** *Villa Nova*, east coast, opening date uncertain for this restored and converted mid 19th-century plantation house, former home of Lord Avon (British Prime Minister Sir Anthony Eden), country house hotel, polished hardwood floors, antique furniture, 800 feet above sea level, cool breeze, in 14 acres of gardens with monkeys, only 17 suites, height of luxury.

Near the airport **LL-A** *Crane Beach*, T4236220, F4235343, www.crane.com Fairly near the airport, but definitely a taxi ride away, spectacular cliff top setting, good beach, and good pool, tennis, luxury prices and usually fairly quiet with only 18 rooms, but they are planning an extra 250 units. **L-B** *Silver Sands Resort*, Christ Church, T4286001, F4283758, www.barbados.org 20 minutes' drive from airport, on the sea at South Point, rooms spacious and well-equipped, good service, food dull, good beach but take care swimming, waves strong and high, good for surfing but children and weak swimmers should use the pool. **C** *Shonlan Airport Hotel*, T4280039, F4280160. 14 rooms, 11 bathrooms, some rooms with kitchenette, very mixed reports, noisy, nowhere near a beach, but only a mile from the terminal, although the taxi fare makes it no cheaper than a guest house further away.

Good value **LL-A** *Sandy Beach Island Resort*, Worthing, T4358000, F4358053, www.fun barbados.com 128 rooms, wide beach, enough sand for volleyball etc, calm water with reef just offshore, 2-bedroom suites with kitchen and living room perfect for families. **L-A** *Sandridge*, 1 mile from Speightstown, T4222361, F4221965. Good-sized rooms or family apartments with cooking facilities, north-facing balconies overlook pool, friendly staff and management, watersports free for guests, good value barbecue evenings, excellent for families. **AL-A** *Time Out at the Gap*, St Lawrence Gap, T4205021, F4205034. 76 rooms, aimed at sports and nightlife age group, pool. **L-AL** *Blue Horizon Apartment Hotel*, Rockley, T4358916, F4358153, bluehrzn@gemsbarbados.com 120 rooms, all have balconies.

Apartments and guest houses **L-C** *Chateau Blanc Apartments*, First Av, Worthing, T4357518, F4357414, www.barbados.org Good value studios, well-equipped but old kitchen facilities, friendly management, also has one to two bedroomed apartments on beach front. **AL-A** *Woodville Beach Hotel*, Hastings, T4356694, F4359211, www.barbados.org Studio apartment, 1 or 2-bedroom. **AL-A** *Worthing Court Apartment Hotel*, Worthing, T4357910, F4357374, www.ndlc.com Studios or one-bedroom connecting apartments, very pleasant, discounts for airline staff, food not so good. The Hotel School, in Marine House, has reopened as **AL-B** *Pommarine Hotel*, T2280900, F2280907. 21 rooms, student run, excellent value. **A-C** *Angler Apartments*, Derricks, T/F4320817, www.barbados ahoy.com. Owners live on premises, priority given to service, friendly, informal, family orientated, restaurant, freshly made Caribbean dishes, will prepare special meals on request, some home-grown vegetables. **A-C** *Fred La Rose/Bonanza/Venice Gardens*, Dover, T4289097, F4283924, www.sunbarbados/lodgings/bonanza.cmf Studio, 1 or 2 bedrooms, helpful, quite convenient but not too clean. There are several other cheap places to stay in this area, all within walking distance of each other. **A-C** *Little Paradise* in Paradise Village, Black Rock, north of Bridgetown on Princess Alice Highway, T4243256, F4248614. 1-bedroom apartment, or 2 bedrooms, a/c, fridge, very pleasant. **A-C** *The Nook Apartments*, Dayrells Rd in Rockley, T/F4276502. Apartments with pool, maid service, clean, secure, convenient for shops and restaurants, discounts for airline staff and Caricom residents. **B-C** *Meridian Inn*, Dover, T4284051, F4206495, www.barbados2000.com Studios, kitchenettes, balconies, daily maid service, beach, credit cards. All these are well served by the south coast bus routes. **B-C** *Roman Beach Apartments*, Enterprise, T4287635, F4300406. Friendly, comfortable studios, on beautiful beach. **C** *Melrose Beach Apartments*, Worthing, T4357985, F4357984. Good location, 14 units, a/c available. **C** *Tree Haven*, Rockley, T4356673, F4366673. A short bus ride from the centre of town, excellent studio apartments opposite the beach, very clean, helpful and friendly owner. **C-D** *Miami Beach Apartments*, Enterprise Drive, Christ Church, T/F4285387. Kitchen, 1-2 bedroom, living room, veranda, TV, phone, 2 minutes from small, clean beach, 3 minutes to main road and minibus route. **C-E** *Antoine's*, Maxwell Main Rd, Christ Church, T4204463, F4283988. 2 double rooms with shared bath and 1 room with private bath and cooking facilities, excellent restaurant. **D-E** *Cleverdale*, Fourth Av, Worthing, T4281035, F4283172, karibik@sunbeach.net 4 rooms, with shared or private bathroom, close to beach, breakfast room, living room, kitchen, veranda and barbecue for guests to share, clean and good value, also internet access and help with finding alternative accommodation, run by Europeans, Brigitte Taylor and Heidrun Rice. **E** *Pegwell Inn*, Oistins, T4286150. Good for shops and airport buses, not brilliant for beaches. **E** *Shells Guest House*, First Av, Worthing, T4357253, F4357131. With breakfast, good value, well run, good location, 6 rooms with fan, 5 bathrooms, TV room, excellent food in restaurant. **E** *Angle House*, Upper Bay St, Bridgetown, T4279010, near *Grand Barbados*. Clean, central, convenient, nothing special.

"Getaways" **B** *Atlantis*, Bathsheba, T4339445. On the east coast, with a spectacular setting, good food, pleasant, family-run hotel but a little run down, owned by Enid Maxwell, who started the hotel with her late father in the 1940s. **AL-A** *Edgewater Inn*, Bathsheba, T4339900, F4339902. Pool overlooking sea, quiet and out of the way, popular with Venezuelans. Also at Bathsheba, the *Round House Restaurant* has four rooms. **AL-A** *Sea-U*, guest house, T4339450, F4339210, http://axses.com/ency/bta/hotels/seau.ctm 4 spacious rooms, run by nice German lady, evening meal US$15, breakfast US$5. **LL** *Sam Lord's Castle*, T4237350, F4236361. Built round a cliff-top plantation house with some fairly spurious pirate legends attached, all-inclusive. Good Sunday buffet, 3 swimming pools, and outdoor bars where they serve the drinks in plastic cups.

Barbados

Villa rental Agents and property managers including *Alleyne*, *Aguillar* and *Altman*, the most upmarket and a Christie's affiliate, T4320840. *Realtors Limited*, Riverside House, River Rd, St Michael, T4264900, F4266419. *Bajan Services Ltd*, Seascape Cottage, Gibbs, St Peter, T4222618, F4225366. *Rival Enterprises Ltd*, Flamboyant Av, Sunset Crest, St James, T4326457, F4322422, rival@caribsurf.com 1-bedroom apartments to 3-bedroom villas in gardens, **LL-B** in season, cheaper in summer, well located, close to restaurants and shops as well as beach. Weekly rates for a small villa on the beach start at US$800 in the summer but can be twice the price in the winter, plus tax. If staying for a while, try the small ads in the *Advocate* and *Nation*. Ordinary apartments to let can be rented furnished for about US$400 a month which could work out cheaper even if you do not stay that long. If possible get a Bajan who knows the island well to help you.

YMCA One **F** hostel at Pinfold Street, Bridgetown, T4263910/1240 which can accommodate 24 people, dormitory beds or single rooms, breakfast B$3.50, lunch B$4.

Eating Barbados has a very wide range of places to eat. The price range in a restaurant for a main course is US$12-40, but in cheap places you can get a filling meal for US$5. There is a good listing in the *Visitor*.

Expensive The two smartest places are now: *Lone Star*, T4190599, with caviar bar on west coast, lunch US$15-3,000, wonderful setting, beach level, plenty of space, not ruinous if you choose carefully; and *Emerald Palm*, also on west coast, T4224116. *Ile de France* in Settlers Beach, T4223245. French managed and very good. *La Maison*, Holetown, T4321156, award winning restaurant in beautiful setting on beach, gourmet but rather pretentious, US$20-40 main course for dinner. *The Mews*, 2nd St, Holetown, T4321122. Quite expensive but superb food, Austrian chef cooks mix of local and French dishes, very pretty house, tables on balcony or interior patio. Recommended. *Olives*, T4322112. Mediterranean/Caribbean. Recommended. *Kitchen Korner*, T4322684. Same owner. *Peppers*, T4327549. Jamaican, Dominican. *Sakura*, T4325187. Japanese. *Town House*. *Sitar*, Indian. *La Terra*, T4321099. Same owners as *Olives* and better than *Baku Brasseries*, T4322258, same building, different owners. *The Restaurant*, the only bit of *Sandy Lane* complex to stay open, very good. *Bagatelle*, St Thomas, T4216767, reopened with Richie Richings, excellent reports but up for sale, elegant, inland. *The Treasure Beach Hotel*, T4321346. Some of the best food on the island at US$50 a head. *The Fathoms*, Paynes Bay, St James, T4322568. Always good, especially the oriental lobster stirfry, good value, beautiful at night in gardens overlooking beach under shade of large mahogany tree, also delightful at lunchtime, open all day every day, recommended for service as well as food. *Nico's Champagne Wine Bar*, T4326386, on the west coast, closed Sunday. Paul Owen's *The Cliff*, Derricks, St James, T4321922. Worth the prices for a glimpse of the décor, stunning desserts, attractive and delightful meal, another recommended as the best food on the island, sushi bar and separate grill planned, innovative food. *Carambola*, St James, T4320832. Gone downhill, badly cooked frozen fish, off-hand management but pretty setting but you may see rays swimming by. *Il Tempio*, T4322057. Italian. *Bourbon St*, T4244557. Jazz theme, cajun cooking. *Brown Sugar*, Aquatic Gap, Bay St, St Michael, T4267684. Buffet lunch B$22, dinner, regional specialities, rather overrated. *Champers*, in Hastings. *Shak Shak* in Rockley, T4351234. *David's Place*, also on waterfront, in Worthing, T4359755. Very good with better service and friendlier, reasonable prices. *Bellini's*, T4357246. Italian menu, not just spaghetti and pizza. *Pisces*, T4356564. Much larger, also on St Lawrence Gap, good fish dishes, an excellent vegetarian platter and a perfect waterfront setting, but deals with tour reps have increased their custom at the cost of quality and comfort. *Fishing Boat*, fish, but not as good as Pisces. *Josef's*, T4356541/4283379. On St Lawrence Gap, small, delightful, is well used by Barbadians, you need to book well ahead, arrive early and have pre-dinner drinks on the lawn with the sea lapping the wall a few feet below you. *Masquerades*, T4356134. Indian food Friday and Saturday. *Jeremiah's*, Maxwell Coast Rd. *Club Enigma* in Hastings. *Boucan* in *Savannah Hotel*, by Garrison, T2283800. *Ile de France*, Holetown, T4223245. French.

Mid-range On the west coast, *Mango's by the Sea* in Speightstown is good value. *Jambalayas*, T4356581. Lively, range of dishes from wider Caribbean including Hispanic. *Mullins Beach Bar*, just south of Speightstown has good menu (very good pepperpot and jerk chicken), loud, fun, overcrowded but great food, reasonably priced, best lunchtime but get there early, also good at sunset, worth a visit to see the *trompe l'oeil* monkey murals. At Holetown, *Ragamuffins*, T4321295. *Angry Annie's*, *Raffles*, (African atmosphere), *Tam's Wok*, *Rum Barrel*, *Min's Chinese*, *TML Bar*, *Joan's Deli & Bar*, *Cocomos*, T4320134, right on beach, service and food recommended, nice atmosphere. *Fronds Vegetarian* at Edgehill St Thomas, T4252020. Linked to the Future Centre, which promotes sustainable development, closed Monday, reservations only. In Bridgetown, *The Boatyard* in Bay Street, full of divers and friends at weekends, food unimportant. *Waterfront Café* on the Careenage, T4270093, interesting food, plenty to look at and a good social centre in the evenings, closed Sunday. Also on the Careenage, *Rusty Pelican*, T4367778. On the south coast, *39 Steps*, T4270715, on the coast road near the Garrison is well run and lively, lunchtimes and evenings, closed Sunday, imaginative blackboard menu and choice of indoors or balcony, opened by Josef, previously of restaurant of that name, see below, popular, so book at weekends. *Jeff Mex*, for Mexican food, at 33 Broad St, Bridgetown, open 1000-1700, T4310857. *Pom marine Hotel*, in Marine House (T4275420), a hotel school, does an excellent lunch at certain times of year, and a smarter evening meal on Tuesday, also drinks and snacks in the evening when they are running courses for bar staff. *Fat Andy's*, *Bubba's Sports Bar*, (US football and other sports on giant screens). *Lucky Horseshoe Saloon and Steak House*. *The Lamplighter* at junction of Rendezvous and Highway 7, next to *Palm Garden Court Hotel*, same management, owned by British woman and her Bajan husband, new, small, attractive gardens, enjoyable. *Kolors*, *Sandy Beach Hotel*. Buffet Monday, Thursday afternoon and Sunday lunch. *Shells*, very good food at reasonable prices. *Red Rooster*, T4353354, opposite *Coconut Court*, Hastings. *Carib Beach Bar* at Worthing, near former *Rydal Waters Guest House*, T4358540, has inexpensive meals and drinks, barbecue and music twice a week, excellent rum punches, happy hour 1700-1800 Monday-Friday, great fun even if you are not eating. *Sand Dollar*, St Lawrence Main Rd, T4356596, mid-range. *Café Sol*, very popular, Mexican American. *McBrides*, Irish. *Ship Inn*, Captain's carvery, T4356961, lunch buffet US$13, evening buffet US$21. *B 4 Blues*, Canadian. *Steak House St Lawrence*, with salad bar. *Whistling Frog*, T4205021, in *Time Out in the Gap* hotel, pub sports bar with Bajan flavour, lively. *Boomers* in St Lawrence Gap has quite good fast-food type dishes in a restaurant-type setting. *Flamers*, St Lawrence Gap, T4180607. Near Bathsheba on east coast, new. *Roundhouse* on cliff, good, lovely restored location, overlooks sea, ask for breadfruit chips.

Cheap Island wide fast food from *Chefette* chain with 9 branches and increasing variety, salad bars at Holetown, Rockley and Warrens (ABC Highway) branches only, good value steak, fish meals, etc, pizza delivery T4366000; and *Pizzaz*, Fontabelle and Holetown, for deliveries, T42-PIZZA, also sells fried chicken. *Pizza Man Doc* has six branches and does deliveries. *Chicken Barn*, Bay Street and Worthing (big portions if you're hungry). For those who like that sort of thing there are several *Kentucky Fried Chickens*, although for vegetarians the salad bars here and at the *Chefettes* (see above) have been recommended. West Coast places include *Fisherman's Pub* in Speightstown, good meal for US$5 and right on seafront. In Bridgetown you have *Port Hole*, Fontabelle, friendly bar near Board of Tourism Office, good solid lunch for B$11. *The Food Court* in the Imperial Plaza, Bridgetown, has veggie and salad bar sections as well as Chinese, creole, etc. *Pink Star*, in Baxter's Road, open late. On the south coast, the *Light and Power Canteen*, on Bay St and at Spring Gardens which are open to the public and do a huge traditional lunch; in Worthing on the main road opposite the Plantation supermarket, the *Roti Hut* is cheap but nasty, nothing like rotis on Trinidad. *St Lawrence Pizza Hut*, T4287152. In Oistins there are lots of evening and late night places by the fish market selling fried fish and other meals, like Baxters Rd. The fish fry by the road is best on Friday but at least one vendor is operating most nights. In the east, the *Pot and Barrel*, good inexpensive pizzas, just outside *Sam Lord's Castle*, worth a try. *Barclays Park Beach Bar* on the east coast does rum punch and light meals (closed after 1830). Good reports about *Sand Dunes* at Belleplaine and *Little Edge*, Bathsheba (T4339900), for breakfast and lunch.

Generally, eating out in Barbados is not cheap. Buffets are good value. Unlimited food for a fixed price, usually lunchtime only, certain days only. Try **Colony Club** (buffet by the beach on Sunday B$25) or **Sam Lord's. Atlantis Hotel** in Bathsheba has an enormous Sunday buffet, which is the place to try for traditional Barbadian cooking at its best (filling). Get up early and do a National Trust Sunday morning walk to work up an appetite.

Entertainment **Cinemas** One cinema in Bridgetown (Globe); Vista cinema on south coast, US$4-5, plus a drive-in not far from the south coast.

Dances For something less glossy and more Bajan, it might be worth trying one of the dances which are advertized in the *Nation* newspaper on Friday. People hire a dance hall, charge admission (usually US$2.50), provide a disco, and keep the profits. There are very few foreigners, but the atmosphere is friendly, and the drinks a lot cheaper than in the smarter nightclubs. Unfortunately, there have been a few fights at 'Dub' fêtes and they are no longer as relaxed as they were.

Rumshops **Baxters Rd** in Bridgetown used to be the place to try but fewer people go there now. The one roomed, ramshackle, rumshops are open all night (literally), and there's a lot of street life after midnight, although you might get pestered by cocaine addicts. Some of the rumshops sell fried chicken (the **Pink Star** is recommended, it has a large indoor area where you can eat in peace and the place also has clean lavatories) and there are women in the street selling fish, seasoned and fried in coconut oil over an open fire. Especially recommended if you are hungry after midnight. The Government plans to upgrade Baxters Rd as a tourist attraction. **Nelson St** rumshops are really houses of ill repute but have amazing larger-than-life naif paintings on the outside. Interior upstairs bar décor is a curious mix of girlie pix, flourescent pontilliste and lifesize portraits of politicians. **Oistins** also has rumshops, better than Baxters Rd on Friday and Saturday, fish and a small club, US$2.50 entry, where they play oldies. Also recommended is **Fisherman's Pub** in **Speightstown**, lots of music on Friday (no entry charge) otherwise fairly good all week. They also serve good cheap meals, lunchtime and evenings.

If you drink in a rumshop, rum and other drinks are bought by the bottle. The smallest size is a mini, then a flask, then a full bottle. The shop will supply ice and glasses, you buy a mixer, and serve yourself. The same system operates in dances, though prices are higher; night clubs, of course, serve drinks by the glass like anywhere else. Wine, in a rumshop, usually means sweet British sherry. If you are not careful, it is drunk with ice and beer.

Nightclubs There are quite a selection. Most charge US$12.50 for entry on 'free drinks' night. It's worth phoning in advance to find out what is on offer. There are live bands on certain nights in some clubs. Most do not get lively until almost midnight, and close around 0400. Some have a complicated set of dress codes or admission rules, which is another reason for phoning ahead.

After Dark, St Lawrence Gap, recently redecorated, huge selection at the bar, very lively. Others are **Harbour Lights**, T4367225, lots of tourists and expats, open-air on the beach, local and disco music, crowded on Wednesday, US$12,50 entry covers drinks Wednesday, Friday, no cover charge Sunday or Thursday, beach party on Monday. **The Boatyard**, T4362622, is the sailor's pub in front of the anchorage at Carlisle Bay, Bay St, free drinks on Tuesday, very lively, popular with landlubbers too. **The Ship Inn** in St Lawrence has a big outdoor area and is often packed, especially at weekends and when there is a live band. Also **Reggae Lounge** in St Lawrence Gap. The **Waterfront Café** has jazz and steel pan most nights. The beach bars can be lively (see listings above), but pick your night. **Bubba's Bar** in Rockley has 10-ft video screen plus 10 other TVs for watching sports while you drink. **Coach House**, Paynes Bay, St James, T4321163. **Adriana's Entertainment Centre**, Queen St, Speightstown, T4190126. **Casbah**, in Holetown, same building as *La Terra* and *Baku* restaurants, is billed as 'European style' and 'Moroccan themed', free drinks Thursday, Latin beat Wednesday.

Party cruises The **Jolly Roger** run 4-hr daytime and evening cruises along the west coast to Holetown, near the Folkestone Underwater Park (where the fun and games take place) from the deepwater harbour. The drinks are unlimited (very). There is also a meal, music, dancing, etc, US$55 for the dinner cruise. On daytime cruises, there is swimming and snorkelling. The *Harbour Master*, which unlike the other cruises pulls up on the beach, 100 ft long, 40 ft wide with four decks, see above, Sailing.

Shows The *Visitor* has a fairly full listing. Some of the better ones are: Tropical Spectacular Dinner Show at the *Plantation Restaurant* US$75 with dinner, Wednesday and Friday, starts 1830, show and drinks US$37.50, T4285048. *1627 And All That*, Tyroll Cot, Thursday, 1830, US$57.50, colourful show, bar, hors d'oeuvres, buffet dinner, tour of 17th century market place and cultural village, steel band, complimentary transport, T4281627, 4296016 to book.

Theatres There are several good semi-professional theatre companies. Performances are advertized in the press. It is usually wise to buy tickets in advance. Most people dress quite formally for these performances.

Background

History

There were Amerindians on Barbados for upwards of a thousand years. The first Europeans to find the island were the Portuguese, who named it 'Os Barbados' after the Bearded Fig trees which grew on the beaches, and left behind some wild pigs. These bred successfully and provided meat for the first English settlers, who arrived in 1627 and found an island which was otherwise uninhabited. It is not clear why the Amerindians abandoned the island, although several theories exist. King Charles I gave the Earl of Carlisle permission to colonize the island and it was his appointed Governor, Henry Hawley, who in 1639 founded the House of Assembly. Within a few years, there were upwards of 40,000 white settlers, mostly small farmers, and equivalent in number to about 1% of the total population of England at this period. After the 'sugar revolution' of the 1650s most of the white population left. For the rest of the colonial period sugar was king, and the island was dominated by a small group of whites who owned the estates, the 'plantocracy'. The majority of the population today is descended from African slaves who were brought in to work on the plantations; but there is a substantial mixed-race population, and there has always been a small number of poor whites, particularly in the east part of the island. Many of these are descended from 100 prisoners transported in 1686 after the failed Monmouth rebellion and Judge Jeffrey's 'Bloody Assizes'.

The two principal political parties are the Barbados Labour Party (BLP) and the Democratic Labour Party (DLP). A third party is the National Democratic Party (NDP), but it is no longer very active. The Democratic Labour Party held office in 1986-94. Economic difficulties in the 1990s eroded support for the government. The Prime Minister Erskine Sandiford narrowly lost a vote of confidence in June 1994, and stood aside for his Finance Minister David Thompson, who led the party into a general election on 6 September. The BLP won the elections with 19 seats, compared with eight for the DLP and one for the NDP. Mr Owen Arthur, then 44, an economist, became Prime Minister and took on the portfolios of Finance and Economic Affairs. In the January 1999 general elections, the BLP was returned with an overwhelming vote of confidence. It won 26 of the 28 seats, while the DLP won the other two. The NDM did not contest the elections.

Geography

Most of the island is covered by a cap of coral limestone, up to 600,000 years old. Several steep inland cliffs or ridges run parallel to the coast. These are the remains of old shorelines, which formed as the island gradually emerged from the sea. There are no rivers in this part of the island, although there are steep-sided gullies down which water runs in wet weather. Rainwater runs through caves in the limestone, one of which, Harrison's Cave, has been developed as a tourist attraction. The island's water supply is pumped up from the limestone. In the Scotland District in the northeast, the coral limestone has been eroded and older, softer rocks are exposed. There are rivers here, which have cut deep, steep-sided valleys. Landslides make agriculture and construction hazardous and often destroy roads.

Government

Barbados has been an independent member of the Commonwealth since November 1966. The British Monarch is the Head of State, represented by a Governor General. There is a strong parliamentary and democratic tradition. The House of Assembly is the third oldest parliament in the Western Hemisphere and celebrated its 350th anniversary in 1989, although voting was limited to property owners until 1950. There are 21 senators appointed by the Governor General, of whom 12 are on the advice of the Prime Minister, two on the advice of the Leader of the Opposition and seven at his own discretion to reflect religious, economic and social interests. 28 single-member constituencies elect the House of Assembly.

A 1998 Commission on the constitution chaired by a former BLP leader and Attorney General, Sir Henry Forde QC, recommended abolition of the monarchy, with the Governor General replaced by a ceremonial president, changes in the composition of the Senate, and replacement of the London-based Privy Council as final appeal court by a Caribbean Court of Justice.

The economy

Structure of production There are few natural resources and sugar is still the main crop but many producers have abandoned the land, while trying to get planning permission for golf courses or housing developments. The factories and most estates are under the management of the Barbados Agricultural Management Co.

There is some export-oriented manufacturing and an expanding offshore financial sector with a good reputation. There is a well-established service sector, and a wide range of light industries which produce mainly for the local, regional, and North American markets. Manufacturing is the second largest foreign exchange earner. Informatics is a growing business, employing over 2,000 people. There is a small oil industry. Barbados National Oil Company's onshore field in St Philip produces enough for local requirements (although it is refined overseas). There is also enough natural gas for piped domestic supply to urban and suburban areas. Conoco has an offshore exploration programme which has yielded promising preliminary results.

By far the main foreign exchange earner is now tourism, which accounts for 15% of gdp and employs 10,300 people. In 1998, 512,397 tourists, 36% of whom came from the UK, the single largest market, stayed in Barbados and 506,610 cruise ship passengers also visited. Total tourist expenditure was US$750.5mn in 1997. In that year there were 12,138 beds on the island, of which 10,008 were in hotels, 168 in guest houses and 1,962 in apartments.

Recent trends Since 1993 the economy has been expanding rapidly, with increasing tourist arrivals, recovery in the sugar industry and strong growth in the off shore financial sector. Construction has been boosted by investment in new hotel projects, housing and infrastructure (such as the US$73mn south coast sewerage project). Economic growth averaged 4% a year in 1994-98 and unemployment fell to 10.2% in 2000 from its peak of 26.2% at the start of 1993. The introduction of VAT at the start of 1997 was outstandingly successful as a revenue earner, cutting the fiscal deficit from 3.4% of gdp in 1996 to 0.7% in 1997. This allowed the prime minister to remove VAT from essential foods in his September budget, which in turn produced a dramatic drop in retail prices.

Tourism projects planned or in progress include a complete rebuilding of the *Barbados Hilton* and *Sandy Lane* properties and 14 smaller projects which are expected to add 680 new rooms. Plans are also being developed for the site of the former oil refinery, between the *Barbados Hilton* and *Grand Barbados* hotels on the south coast. A beachfront site which was to be a Sandals resort is now for sale.

Barbados currently has no hotels with more than 330 rooms, and the only major hotel chain represented is Hilton International. The emphasis on small scale tourism may be an advantage in the British market, but has held back sales in North America. The redevelopment of the former refinery site and the long-delayed Sandals project are expected to address this problem.

Culture

The people

Barbados has a population of 265,000. This is more than any of the Windwards or Leewards, and is considered enough to make the island one of the 'big four' in the Caribbean Community. With population density of 1,596 per square mile in 1997, Barbados is one of the most crowded countries in the world.

Because Barbados lies upwind from the main island arc, it was hard to attack from the sea, so it never changed hands in the colonial wars of the 17th and 18th centuries. There is no French, Dutch, or Spanish influence to speak of in the language, cooking or culture. People from other islands have often referred to Barbados as Little England, and have not always intended a compliment. Today, the more obvious outside influences on the Barbadian way of life are North American. Most contemporary Barbadians stress their Afro-Caribbean heritage and aspects of the culture which are distinctively 'Bajan'. There are extremes of poverty and wealth, but these are not nearly so noticeable as elsewhere in the Caribbean. This makes the social atmosphere relatively relaxed. However, there is a history of deep racial division. Although there is a very substantial black middle class and the social situation has changed radically since the 1940s and 50s, there is still more racial intolerance on all sides than is apparent at first glance.

Literature

Two Barbadian writers whose work has had great influence throughout the Caribbean are the novelist George Lamming and the poet Edward Kamau Brathwaite. Lamming's first novel, *In The Castle Of My Skin* (1953), a part-autobiographical story of growing up in colonial Barbados, deals with one of the major concerns of anglophone writers: how to define one's values within a system and ideology imposed by someone else. Lamming's treatment of the boy's changing awareness in a time of change in the West Indies is both poetic and highly imaginative. His other books include *Natives Of My Person*, *Season Of Adventure* and *The Pleasures Of Exile*.

Brathwaite is also sensitive to the colonial influence on black West Indian culture. Like Derek Walcott (see under St Lucia) and others he is also keenly aware of the African traditions at the heart of that culture. The questions addressed by all these writers are: who is Caribbean man, and what are his faiths, his language, his ancestors? The experience of teaching in Ghana for some time helped to clarify Brathwaite's response. African religions, motifs and songs mix with West Indian speech rhythms in a style which is often strident, frequently using very short verses. His collections include *Islands*, *Masks* and *Rights Of Passage*.

Heinemann Caribbean publish the *A to Z of Barbadian Heritage* which is worth reading. Macmillan publish *Treasures of Barbados*, an attractive guide to Barbadian architecture.

Trinidad and Tobago

18

Trinidad and Tobago

Trinidad and Tobago are only just off the coast of Venezuela, yet they share little of the culture of South America. The people are a cosmopolitan mix of African, East Indian, Chinese, white and Syrian and their music, cuisine, culture, society and politics reflect the amalgamation of those races through conflict and harmony. Trinidad's carnival is world famous and attracts thousands of visitors but its wealth comes from oil, gas and manufacturing rather than tourism and so its beaches remain empty and unspoilt. Beach tourism has been developed on the smaller, sister island of Tobago, where hotels are spreading around the coastline, but there are still glorious bays and coves and resorts are low key. Both islands have a large area of protected rainforest, home to a huge array of flora and fauna, and birdwatching is a major attraction. Together the islands have more species of birds than any other Caribbean Island, the variety being South American rather than West Indian.

Essentials

Before you travel

Documents   **Passports** are required by all visitors. **Visas** are not required for visits of under three months by nationals of most Commonwealth countries, West European countries, Argentina, Brazil, Colombia, Israel, Iceland and Turkey; holders of OAS passports; for US citizens for visits up to three months; and for Venezuelans for stays of up to 14 days. Some Commonwealth citizens do need visas, however; these include Australia, New Zealand, India, Sri Lanka, Nigeria, South Africa, Uganda, Tanzania, and Papua New Guinea. A visa normally requires 48 hours' notice. A waiver for those with no visa can be obtained at the airport, but it costs TT$50. Entry permits for one to three months are given on arrival; a one month permit can be extended at the immigration office in Port of Spain (at 67 Frederick St). This is a time-consuming process, so try and get a three-month entry permit if planning a long stay. Business visitors are allowed to work without a work permit for one month in each calendar year.

Only those coming from an infected area need a yellow fever inoculation certificate   Even though you may not get asked for it all travellers need a **return ticket** to their country of origin, dated, not open-ended, proof that they can support themselves during their stay, an address at which they will be staying in Trinidad (the tourist office at the airport can help in this respect). A ferry ticket to Venezuela has often satisfied immigration officials instead of a full return ticket to your own country. People going to Venezuela can obtain a tourist card (free of charge) at the BWIA office; this means buying a return ticket but this can be refunded or changed if an alternative ticket out of Venezuela is later purchased.

Customs   Duty-free imports: 200 cigarettes or 50 cigars or 250g tobacco, one litre wine or spirits, and TT$1,200 worth of gifts. Perfume may not be imported free of duty, but may be deposited with customs until departure. Passengers in transit, or on short visits, can deposit goods such as liquor with customs at the airport and retrieve it later free of charge.

Money   The **currency** is the Trinidad and Tobago dollar, TT$. Notes are for TT$1, 5, 10, 20 and 100.
See page 22 for latest exchange rate   Coins are for 1, 5, 10, 25 and 50 cents. The Trinidad and Tobago dollar, fixed at TT$2.40 = US$1 since 1976, was devalued to TT$3.60 = US$1 in December 1985, then to TT$4.25 = US$1 in August, 1988 and finally floated in April 1993.

    Travellers' cheques and major **credit cards** are accepted almost everywhere on Trinidad. On Tobago there are no **banks** outside Scarborough; travellers' cheques are changed by large hotels but if you are travelling to the northern end of the island make sure you have enough TT$ as not everyone accepts US$. All banks charge a fee for cashing travellers' cheques, some more than others, so check first. Banks generally will not change Venezuelan or other South American currencies. On departure you can change TT$ back into US$ at *First Citizens Bank* at Piarco, open until 2200, but they charge US$10 minimum fee. Better to use small amounts of TT$ in the duty free shops.

Climate   The climate on the islands is tropical, but, thanks to the trade winds, rarely excessively hot.
Humidity is fairly high. Trinidad & Tobago are outside the hurricane belt   Temperatures vary between 21° and 37°C, the coolest time being from December to April. There is a dry season from January to mid-May and a wet season from June to November, with a short break in September. It can rain for days at a stretch but usually falls in heavy showers.

Getting there

Air   **From North America** *Air Canada* and *BWIA* from Toronto to Port of Spain. *BWIA* and *American Airlines* from Miami and New York to Port of Spain. *Air Caribbean* flies to Miami and will shortly be introducing services to New York, Orlando and Toronto. **From Europe** *BWIA* from London to Port of Spain. *British Airways* from London Gatwick to Tobago. Several charters, including *JMC* (was *Air Caledonian*) from London Gatwick to Tobago and *Condor* from Frankfurt and Munich. **From South America** To Port of Spain, *Aeropostal* from Caracas via Porlamar, *BWIA* from Caracas daily; *BWIA*, *Air Caribbean* and *Suriname Airways* from Georgetown, Guyana; *Suriname Airways* from Paramaribo. **From**

Caribbean *BWIA*, *Liat*, *ALM*, *Air Caribbean*, *American Eagle* and *Helenair* connect Trinidad and Tobago with other Caribbean islands including Antigua, Barbados, Curaçao, Grenada, Jamaica (Kingston), St Lucia, St Maarten, St Vincent, San Juan, Puerto Rico. *Air Caribbean* operates the domestic shuttle Trinidad-Tobago. *BWIA* launched a new regional service in 1999, *BWee Express*, with new 50-seat Havilland Dash-8 aircraft, with flights from Trinidad to Tobago, Grenada, St Lucia and St Vincent.

Ferries   A weekly 250-passenger and cargo ferry service run by *Windward Lines Limited*   **Sea** sails from Trinidad **to Güiria, Venezuela** alternating with a ferry **to Margarita (Pampatar)**, every other week, with 12 hours in Margarita. It then it sets off **for St Vincent, Barbados** and **St Lucia**, see pages 25 and 27 for schedules and fares. Check in two hours before departure in Trinidad (one hour in other ports). The schedule is printed in two daily newspapers, times vary depending on the Güiria or Margarita crossing, occasionally there is a stop in **Bequia**, everything stops for Carnival in Trinidad. For information and tickets contact Global Steamship Agencies Ltd, Mariner's Club, Wrightson Rd, PO Box 966, Port of Spain, T6242279, 6252547, F6275091. Cabins, aircraft seats and convertible berths are available. Every Friday morning a boat carrying racing pigeons leaves **for Güiria, Venezuela.** Contact Francis Sagones, T6320040; or talk to Siciliano Bottini in the Agencia Naviera in Güiria for sea transport in the other direction. Fishing boats and trading vessels ply this route frequently and can often be persuaded to take passengers. Be careful to get your passport stamped at both ends of the journey. A Trinidadian, Adrian Winter Roach, travels at least once a week with his boat *El Cuchillo*, and charges US$60 one way, US$100 return, he can be contacted in Venezuela through the Distribuidora Beirut, Calle Valdez 37, Güiria, T/F81677. Lots of shipping lines have a service going north, go **to Queen's Wharf** and ask to speak to the captains. **For Guyana**, try Abraham Shipping Company Ltd, 10 Abercromby St, T6241138/1131, they handle 90% of the Guyana and Suriname trade.

Yachts   **Chaguaramas, Trinidad**, and **Scarborough, Tobago** are the ports of entry. In   *Crew will be admitted* Chaguaramas, take the boat to the customs dock (open 24 hours, overtime 1600-0800 and   *for 90 days; a 90-day* weekends and holidays) to clear on arrival in Trinidad and fill in combined Customs and   *extension costs US$30* Immigration form. Overtime for after hours, weekends and holidays is high, so it pays to arrive   *per person* during normal working hours.

Departure by sea   Clear out with Customs and Immigration. Pay port fees of US$8 for each month that the boat was in Trinidad and Tobago waters. To go from one island to the other clear out with Immigration and in on the new island. Clear Customs only when making final departure from the country. New arrivals must be signed aboard the vessel as crew by Immigration in Chaguaramas.

Departure by air   Boats can be left in storage; yacht yards will help with paperwork, present it to Customs and clear with Immigration within 24 hours of departure for exemption from departure tax. When returning to Trinidad by air, go to third party line at airport to get paperwork to take with baggage to Chaguaramas Customs to clear. Arriving outside office hours leave boat parts for weekday review. Arriving guests should have return ticket and letter to Trinidad Immigration stating vessel name and official number.

Marinas   The Trinidad marinas are all west of Port of Spain along the coast to Chaguaramas.   *There has been a huge* **Trinidad and Tobago Yacht Club** (TTYC), Bayshore, T/F6374260, a private club, leases   *increase in facilities* members' slips to visiting yachts when available, 60 in-water berths, security, restaurant, bar,   *in the 1990s,* laundry. **Point Gourde Yachting Centre**, T6275680, F6254083, opened 1996, 65 in-water   *principally to take* berths, full service marina. **Trinidad and Tobago Yachting Association** (TTYA),   *advantage of* Chaguaramas, PO Box 3140, Carenage, T/F6344376, a private members' association with   *Trinidad's location* moorings and anchorage available to visiting yachts, full service haul out yard, 15-ton marine   *outside the* hoist, moorings, repair shed, bar, laundry. **Power Boats Mutual Facilities**, Chaguaramas, PO   *hurricane belt* Box 3163, Carenage, T6344303, F6344327, haul-out and storage, 50-ton marine hoist, 23 in-water berths, boat storage, marine supplies, fibreglass repairs, welding, woodworking,

Touching down

Departure tax *There is a TT$75 exit tax payable in local currency, or US$15, plus a TT$25 security fee. Passengers in transit do not have to pay, but are required to obtain an 'exempt' ticket from the departure tax window before being allowed through to the immigration officers on the way to the departure lounge. Visitors leaving by sea pay the departure tax to the shipping agent. Your immigration card must be presented on departure. See also page 909.*

Business hours *Government offices: 0800-1600, Monday-Friday.* **Banks:** *0800-1400, Monday-Thursday, 0800-1200, 1500-1700, Friday Some banks have extended hours until 1800.* **Businesses and shops:** *0800-1600/1630, Monday-Friday (shops 0800-1200 on Saturday). Shopping malls usually stay open until about 2000, Monday-Saturday.*

Communications *The international phone code is 868. See pages 938 & 950 for further details.*

Official time *Atlantic Standard Time, 4 hours behind GMT, 1 hour ahead of EST.*

Voltage *110 or 220 volts, 60 cycles AC.*

Weights & measures *Trinidad and Tobago have gone metric, so road signs are given in kilometres, but people still refer to miles.*

Clothing *Beachwear is for the beach. In the evening people dress more smartly but are less formal than, for example, the Bahamians.*

Tipping *If no service charge on bill, 10% for hotel staff and restaurant waiters; taxi drivers, 10% of fare, minimum of 25 cents (but no tip in route taxis); dock-side and airport porters, say 25 cents for each piece carried; hairdressers (in all leading hotels), 50 cents.*

---

apartments, grocery, restaurant, laundry. **Peake Yacht Services**, Chaguaramas, T6344423, F6344387, full service marina, 150-ton marine hoist, capable of beams to 31ft, 21 in-water berths, boat storage, 10-room hotel, restaurant, Mini-Mart, laundry, skilled maintenance, recommended. **Industrial Marine Services** (IMS), Chaguaramas, T6344328, F6344437, full service haul-out and storage yard, 70-ton marine hoist, paint shop, chandlery, sail maker, fibreglass repair, welding, woodworking, sandblasting, restaurant, laundry. **Crews Inn Marina**, Chaguaramas, Tardieu Marine will lift and dry storage. **Humming-bird Marina** has a restaurant. For groceries there is **Hi-Lo** at Crews Inn as well as many small shops, restaurant and bank with ATM. All locations charge a fee to anchored boats for use of shoreside facilities.

Touching down

Airport information

Trinidad **Piarco International** is 16 miles southeast of Port of Spain. Try to avoid overnight connections here. Airline schedules ensure that it is possible to arrive at Piarco after the check-in counters have closed until next morning, so you cannot go through to the departure lounge. *Sky cap* has 24-hour left luggage service. There is a restaurant upstairs which is open 24 hours. There is seating under three covered areas but it is not comfortable for an overnight wait. If you are in transit always check that your bags have not been off-loaded at Piarco, most are not checked through despite assurances. To eat at the airport, there is the *Pizza Boys* restaurant upstairs in the terminal building and a variety of fast food outlets downstairs, including *KFC*. Indian delicacies, like 'doubles' or roti, can be had at informal food stalls to the right as you exit the terminal. If intending to take the bus to Piarco airport, allow plenty of time to ensure arriving in time for checking in. Note that a new terminal was due to open in September 2000 (as we went to print), which is expected to improve service in all areas.

Tobago **Crown Point airport** is within walking distance of the hotels in the southwest. Crown Point airport is also uncomfortable for a long wait, often with no food available after you have been through immigration control. There are a few shops, snack bars and a bank with an ATM outside the terminal building but only a small duty free inside.

· ·

Tourist offices overseas

Overseas offices all have up-to-date hotel lists

Canada *RMR Group, Taurus House, 512 Duplex Ave, Toronto, M4R 2E3, T416-4858724, F416-4858256.*

Germany *Basic Service Group, Am Schleifweg 16, D-55128, Mainz, T49-06131-73337, F06131-73307.*

Italy *Ian Rocks, Via Sant Allessandro 688, Caronno Pertusella, 21042 VA, T392-96451070, F96564870.*

UK *Mitre House, 66 Abbey Rd, Bush Hill Park, Enfield, Middlesex, EN1 2RQ, T020-83501009, F020-83501011, anna@ttg.co.uk*

USA *Keating Communications, 350 Fifth Ave, New York, NY10018, T1-888-595-4TNT, 212-7602400, F212-7606402. Press information, 331 Almeria Av, Coral Gables, F1-33134, T305-4444033, F305-4470415.*

TIDCO's website is www.tidco.co.tt, tourism-info@tidco.co.tt Another website is www.visittnt.com

· ·

Airlines offices *BWIA* is at 30 Edward St (T6252470, 6255866/8, F6252139), opens for reservations at 0800; be prepared for a long wait, particularly for international tickets. BWIA at Piarco airport, T6693000 (open later than Edward St office); also at Carlton Centre, San Fernando, T6579712/6485, and at Crown Point airport, Tobago, T6398741/2. *Air Caribbean* for flights between the two islands, 1 Richmond St, T6232500, F6238182. *American Airlines*, 90 Independence Square (T6235008, F6690261, Piarco, T6644838/47312). *Air Canada* is at 88 Independence Square (T6252195, F627304, at Piarco T6644065). *LIAT*, 30 Edward St, T6252470, at Piarco airport T6645458, on Tobago at Crown Point airport, T6390484. *Suriname Airways*, Cruise Ship Complex, Wrightson Rd, T6274747.

There is a 15% VAT on airline tickets purchased in Trinidad & Tobago

Local tourist office *The Tourism and Industrial Development Company of Trinidad and Tobago Ltd (TIDCO)*, 10-14 Phillips St, 3rd Floor, Port of Spain, T6231932, 623-INFO, F6233848 is the sole tourism agency. Lists of hotels, restaurants, tour operators, monthly schedule of events, maps for sale etc. *Piarco Tourist Bureau* (at the airport), T6645196, helpful with hotel or guest house reservations for your first night. You can also buy maps of Trinidad and Port of Spain here. In Tobago the *Division of Tourism* is in Scarborough, NIB Mall, there is a kiosk, and the head office is on the third level, next to *Buddy's Restaurant* (T6392125, F6393566), or at Crown Point airport, T6390509. *TIDCO Tobago* is at Unit 12, TIDCO Mall, Sangster's Hill, Scarborough, T6394333, F6394514. *The National Carnival Commission* is at 82-84 Frederick St, Port of Spain, T6238867.

Tourist information

The people of both islands are, as a rule, very friendly but several areas are no longer safe at night, especially for women. To the east of Charlotte St, Port of Spain becomes increasingly unsafe. Laventille and East Dry River are to be avoided. Central Port of Spain is fairly safe, even at night, as there are plenty of police patrols. Care must be taken everywhere at night and walking on the beach is not safe. Stick to main roads and look as if you know where you are going. The incidence of theft has risen sharply. Avoid the area around the port or bus terminal except when making a journey. A favourite local saying is 'Tobago is Paradise, Trinidad is New York'. Take care accordingly but do not underestimate crime in Tobago. We have received reports of theft and muggings on the Pigeon Point road and parts of Scarborough are known to have crack houses. Do not walk in the Turtle Beach area after dark. Soft top jeeps are at risk of theft. Leave nothing in them. If there is no safe where you are staying take your valuables (passport, tickets etc) to a bank in Scarborough; the *Royal Bank* charges US$12 for two weeks. Women alone report feeling 'uncomfortable', particularly if they look like a tourist. Male prostitution has become a problem in Store Bay. HIV exists.

Safety

Trinidad & Tobago

Where to stay

See pages 931 & 945 for further details

Hotels There are many hotels on the islands and the better known ones are expensive, but there are very good guest houses and smaller hotels which are reasonable. Information about accommodation can be obtained from the Tourism and Industrial Development Co (TIDCO). Their office at Piarco airport is helpful. VAT (15%) is charged by all hotels and in most a 10% service charge is added to the bill. Some, like the *Hilton*, add a 2% surcharge. For bed and breakfast in private homes contact *Trinidad and Tobago Bed and Breakfast Co-operative Society*, PO Box 3231 Diego Martin, T/F627-BEDS. **Camping** On Trinidad it is unsafe and is not recommended. Try the Boca Islands to the west. On Tobago, it is possible near the Mt Irvine beach. Ask the taxi drivers for advice on where to camp.

Getting around

Air *Air Caribbean* flies the Trinidad to Tobago route offering seven to eight daily flights; the crossing takes 20 minutes and costs US$75 return, for visitors, even standby. Departures, however, are often heavily booked at weekends and holidays, particularly Christmas and afterwards (at other times tickets can be bought the day before, even standby).

Road
Driving is on the left and the roads are narrow and winding

On Trinidad the Uriah Butler Highway and Solomon Hochoy Highway are good dual carriageways from Port of Spain south to San Fernando, but other roads are not of such a high standard. On Tobago the roads are good in the south but badly maintained further north. There are lots of pot holes in Scarborough and traffic weaves about all over the place to avoid them. The road between Charlotteville and Bloody Bay is for four-wheel drive vehicles only and then only in the dry season. Mountain bikes are fine on these roads if you can stand the hills and the heat. International and most foreign driving licences are accepted for up to 90 days, after that the visitor must apply for a Trinidad and Tobago licence and take a test. Visitors must always carry their driving document with them. Do not leave anything in your car, theft is frequent. Be careful where you park in Port of Spain, police are diligent and will tow the car away. It costs US$17 to retrieve it.

Car hire
Some companies only rent for a minimum of 3 days

Rental can be difficult on **Trinidad**, particularly at weekends, because of heavy demand. Best to make reservations in advance. Several companies do not accept credit cards, but require a considerable cash deposit. Small cars can be rented from US$30 a day upwards, unlimited mileage, check tyres before driving off. Deposit varies from company to company, as does method of payment, book in advance. Insurance costs US$1. Many companies have offices at the airport. Car rental firms are numerous and include: *Auto Rentals Ltd*, Uptown Mall, Edward St, Port of Spain (623-7368), *Piarco* (T6692277), and at Cruise Ship Complex, 1 D Wrighton Rd (T6248687). *Bacchus Taxi and Car Rental*, 37 Tragarete Rd (T6225588). *Lord Calloo*, 100 la Paille Village, Caroni (T/F6695673), helpful, check tyres. *Singh's*, 7-9 Wrighton Rd (6254247) and at airport (T6455417, F6643860). *Southern Sales and Service Co Ltd*, El Socorro Extension Road, San Juan, T6275623-4 (24-hr service), recommended. *Autocenter Ltd*, 6 Ariapita Av, T6284400. *Econo Car Rentals*, 191-193 Western Main Rd, T6228072, one of the cheapest. If you prefer an executive limousine, contact *Executive Limousine Service*, 70 Sackville St, Port of Spain, T6252624. Also on **Tobago**: *Auto Rentals Ltd*, Crown Point Airport (T6390644, F6390313). *Peter Gremli Car Rental*, Crown Point, T6398400. *Rodriguez Travel*, Clark Trace, Bethany, T6398507. *Banana Rentals* at *Kariwak Village*, cars and jeeps, US$21 per day, scooters US$10 per day (deposit US$60), **bicycles** US$4 per day (T6398441/8545). *Suzuki Jeep Rental* (and small cars), and *Cherry Scooter Rental* at *Sandy Point Beach Club* (scooters and deposit cheaper than Banana). *Tobago Travel*, P O Box 163, Store Bay Rd, Crown Point (T6398778/8105, F6398786), *Baird's*, Lower Sangster Hill Rd (T6392528). *Rollock's Car Rental Service*, Lowlands (T6390328, after hours T6397369), US$48 per day, recommended. *Hill Crest Car Rental Service*, 47 Mt Pelier Trace, Scarborough, T/F6395208. *Thrifty Car Rental*, Turtle Beach Hotel, T6398111 and other agencies. Excellent bike shop, *Geronimo's Cycle and Sport Ltd*, 15 Pole Carew St, Woodbrook, Port of Spain, T6222453, owned and managed by former professional cyclist, Gene 'Geronimo' Samuel. On Tobago, bike repairs and parts at *Numeral Uno* hardware store in Carnbee, a good contact for joining local riders for some fun road riding.

In **Trinidad**, the word 'taxi' includes most forms of public transport. The word 'travelling' means going by bus or taxi rather than by private car. Buses are run by the *PTSC*. They are big and cheap, also slow, irregular and dirty. However, the PTSC also has newer air-conditioned buses, Express Commuter Service (ECS), with a/c lounge for waiting passengers, on main routes from Independence Square to Arima, Chaguanas, Five Rivers and San Fernando, also from Arima to Sangre Grande. These are not quite so cheap, faster and more comfortable, US$1 to San Fernando. The PTSC office is located at the remodelled South Quay railway station, called City Gate, and is the main terminal for both buses and maxi taxis. You can get information showing how to reach the various sights by bus.

Bus
On all routes, you must purchase your ticket at the kiosk before boarding the bus; you may have to tender the exact fare

On **Tobago** all buses originate in Scarborough. Schedules are changed or cancelled frequently. Buses are every hour between Crown Point (airport) and Scarborough, TT$2. They originate in Scarborough on the hour and get to Crown Point about 25 mins later. Buy tickets from the grey hut outside the airport building where timetable is posted. Also an express bus to Scarborough, TT$2, ticket from souvenir shop, not hut as for the other bus. Bus Scarborough-Plymouth hourly on the hour, return on the half hour, half-hourly in busy times, via Carnbee, Buccoo junction, Mt Irvine and Black Rock. To Charlotteville 7 buses a day, TT$8, first one at 0430, 1½ hrs and then return. Also some maxis on this route. On Tobago, route taxis charge TT$4 and leave from Republic Bank in Scarborough. The Crown Point Airport route is the best, every 15-30 mins, 0530-1830; Black Rock route is fair, every 30 mins Monday-Friday 0530-2030, every 60-75 mins Saturday and Sunday until 2000. Route taxis to Charlotteville start from Burnett Square, TT$9-10 depending on whether vehicle is minibus or car, 1-1½ hrs. The route taxi system is difficult for the foreigner, being based on everyone knowing every car and therefore where it is going.

Agree on a price before the journey and determine whether the price is in TT or US dollars. Taxis are expensive, although route taxis (similar to colectivos) are very cheap. These cannot be distinguished from ordinary taxis, so ask the driver. They travel along fixed routes, like buses, but have no set stops, so you can hail them and be dropped anywhere along the route. During rush hour it is not easy to hail them, however, and in general it takes time to master how they work. Be warned that route taxis are not covered by insurance so you cannot claim against the driver if you are involved in an accident. There are also 'pirate' taxis with the P registration of a private car, which cost the same as the ordinary taxis, although you can sometimes bargain with the drivers. 'Ghost' taxis accept fares and drive off with your luggage as well – be warned. Be careful if hitching on Tobago as the cars that stop often prove to be pirate taxis.

Taxi
Look for cars with first letter H on licence plates (no other markings)

Route taxi In Port of Spain most sedan taxis (saloon cars, often rather beat up) set off from Chacon St, but those for St Ann's and St James leave from Woodford Square, for Carenage

Trinidad & Tobago

from St Vincent and Park Streets, for the Diego Martin area from South Quay, and for Maraval, Belmont and Morvant from Duke and Charlotte Streets. Fares in town US$0.50, further out US$0.75. If you are in a hurry you can pay for any remaining empty seats and ask the driver to go. They will also go off-route for a little extra but going off route to the *Hilton* costs US$7. They are the only means of transport on some suburban routes, such as to St Ann's, and in rural areas away from main roads. Travelling to remote areas may involve three or more taxis, not really a problem, just ask where the next one stops. Major routes run all night and are amazingly frequent during the day, others become infrequent or stop late at night. St Christopher's taxis or airport taxis are taxis as understood in most countries. Some are smarter and more comfortable than route taxis. St Christopher's operates from the main hotels. Take a taxi if you have a complicated journey, or you have heavy baggage, or it is raining. At night it can be a lot cheaper than getting robbed.

Maxi-taxi These are minibuses which cover longer distances than route taxis; they are frequent and go as fast as the traffic will allow, often a bit faster. They are colour coded (yellow for Diego Martin and west, red for east, green for San Fernando, brown or black for maxis which start in San Fernando and travel south from there) and they set off mostly from South Quay except the Carenage and Chaguaramas maxis, which start from Green corner on St Vincent and Park Streets (Globe cinema) and Maraval maxis, which start from Oxford and Charlotte Streets. Check exact route before starting, eg east taxis are either 'San Juan' or 'all the way up' the Eastern Main Rd to Arima, or 'highway', which is faster and runs closer to the airport but misses places like Tunapuna and Curepe. Fares start at US$0.30 and run to Arima, US$1; to Chaguanas, US$1; to San Fernando, US$1.75. If you are worried about being overcharged, pay with TT$10 and look as though you know how much change to expect, but drivers are usually very helpful and friendly.

Sea

Taking the ferry is very time consuming; it is a lot less hassle to fly

Boats: M/V *Panorama* from Port of Spain to Tobago once a day at 1400 Monday-Friday and 1100 on Sunday and public holidays, no crossings on Saturday; return crossings from Scarborough at 2300 Monday-Friday and Sunday. The crossing is supposedly five hours. Hammocks can be slung at night; the a/c is very cold, locals take a blanket. The trip can be rough. Tickets are sold at the Port Authority (T6392417) on the docks, US$8-10 return, cabin for two US$13 when available, children under 12 half price, under three free, office hours Monday-Friday 0700-1500, 1600-1800, 1900-2200 (buy passage in advance, everyone will recommend you to queue at 0800, but 1000 is usually early enough). You need a boarding pass and not just a ticket before you can board.

Keeping in touch

Media

Newspapers and books The main daily papers are the *Daily Express*, the *Trinidad Guardian* and *Newsday*. The *Mirror* on Friday and Sunday has interesting investigative journalism. The *Independent* is a weekly, on Wednesday. *Trinidad and Tobago Review* is a serious monthly. *Tobago News* is weekly. There are several racier weekly papers which appear on Friday or Saturday. *Punch, Bomb, Heat* and *Blast* are sensational tabloids, not to be missed by the visitor who wants the gossip. There is a local "yachtie" newspaper *The Boca*. The official visitor's guide, *Discover Trinidad and Tobago* is published twice a year and distributed free to all visitors by TIDCO and through hotels. There are three book-length guides including *Trinidad and Tobago, An Introduction and Guide*, by Jeremy Taylor (Macmillan 1991). **Radio** ICN Radio (610 AM), Radio Trinidad (730 AM), Music Radio (97 FM), 98.9 Yes FM, WABC (103 FM), ICN Radio (100 FM), Radio 95 FM, Radio Tempo (105 FM), Radio 96.1 FM, Rhythm (Radio 95.1 FM), Radio 1CN (91.1 FM), Sangeet (106.1 FM), Love Radio (94.1 FM), Gem Radio (93 FM), Central Radio (90.5 FM), Power (102 FM). **Television** Three local TV stations: TTT, CCN TV and The Information Channel (government-owned), and up to 45 different US cable channels, depending on which area you are in.

Food and drink

A wide variety of European, American and traditional West Indian dishes (these include pork souse, black pudding, roast sucking pig, sancoche and callaloo stews, and many others) is served at hotels and guest houses. Some also specialize in Créole cooking. There is also, of course, a strong East Indian influence in the local cuisine and also lots of Chinese restaurants. Seafood, particularly crab, is excellent. The many tropical fruits and vegetables grown locally include the usual tropical fruits, and sapodillas, eddoes and yam tanias. The variety of juices and ice creams made from the fruit is endless. Coconut water is refreshing, usually sold around the Savannah, Port of Spain. For those economizing, the *roti*, a chapatti pancake which comes in various forms, filled with peppery stew, shrimp or vegetable curries, is very good. The best place for *roti* is Patraj at 159 Tragarete Rd, Port of Spain. *Buss up shut* (shut means shirt) is a paratha, or Indian bread accompaniment to curries. *Pelau*, savoury peas and rice and meat cooked with coconut and pepper, is also good, but when offered pepper sauce, refuse unless you are accustomed to the hottest of curries or *chili* dishes. Try also *saheena*, deep-fried patties of spinach, dasheen, split peas and mango sauce. *Pholouri* are fritters made with split peas. *Buljol* is a salt fish with onions, tomatoes, avocado and pepper. *Callaloo* is a thick soup based on dasheen leaves. *Doubles* are curried chick peas (channa) in two pieces of fried bara bread. *Pastelles*, eaten at Christmas, are maize flour parcels stuffed with minced meat, olives, capers and raisins, steamed in a banana leaf (known as *hallacas* in Venezuela). A *hops* is a crusty bread roll. If you go to Maracas Bay, have *shark-and-bake*, a spicy fried bread sandwich of fried shark with a variety of sauces such as tamarind, garlic, *chadon beni*. Dumplings are a must on Tobago, particularly good with crab. The shopping malls offer a variety of places to eat, including Créole, Indian, Chinese, etc. On Tobago there are lots of small eating places, clean and nice, where you can get a freshly cooked meal and a beer for US$3-4 per person.

Food

A local drink is *mauby*, like ginger beer, and the rum punches are recommended. Fresh lime juice is also recommended; it is sometimes served with a dash of Angostura bitters. Local beers are *Carib* ("each bottle tastes different") and *Stag* ("the recession fighter"), both owned by the same company which also brews *Heineken* and *Guinness*. A nice place to drink Guinness is the *Cricket Wicket*, in Tragarete Rd, opposite the Queen's Park Oval. There are lots of rums to try, many of which deserve better than to be swamped with punch or coke.

Drink

Holidays and festivals

New Year's Day, **Carnival** Monday and Tuesday, before *Ash Wednesday* (not officially holidays but everyone regards them as such), **Spiritual Shouter Baptist Liberation Day** (*30 March*), **Good Friday**, **Easter Monday**, **Indian Arrival Day** (*30 May*) celebrating the arrival of Indian labourers in 1845, **Corpus Christi**, **Eid ul-Fitr** (changes according to religious calendar), **Labour** or **Butler's Day** (*19 June*), **Emancipation Day** (*1 August*), **Independence Day** (*31 August*), Divali (depends on religious calendar), **Christmas Day**, **Boxing Day**.

Public holidays

All Souls' Day (*2 November*) is not a holiday, but is celebrated. The Hindu festival of **Divali** is a holiday, but **Puagwa** (*February/March*) is not. Similarly, of the Moslem festivals, **Eid ul-Fitr** is a public holiday, but **Eid ul-Azha** and **Yaum um-Nabi** are not (all fall 10 to 11 days earlier each year).

Special events

Trinidad Carnival takes place officially each year on the two days before Ash Wednesday which marks the beginning of the Christian season of Lent. In practice, the festivities start well in advance, with the Mas' camps abustle, the calypsonians performing most nights of the week and the impressive Panorama finals taking place with the competing steelbands at the Queen's Park Savannah stadium the week before Mas' proper. Band launching parties, where band leaders show off their costume designs, are held before Christmas. Calypso 'tents', where calypsoes are played, start in Jan. Try SWWUT Hall on Wrighton Rd, De Luxe

Carnival
See also page 956

See also page 956

Trinidad & Tobago

Cinema on Keate St and Spektakula on Henry St. Panyards start practising even earlier; visiting one is usually no problem. Amoco Renegades are at 17a Oxford St, Port of Spain; Exodus is at St John's Village on Eastern Main Rd, St Augustine; Witco Desperadoes is at Laventille Rd, Port of Spain. There are parties most of the time from then on. The biggest public fetes at Spectrum, previously Soca Village near the National Stadium, may have a crowd of 20,000 or more. Getting a ticket in advance or arriving early (eg 2130) saves a struggle at the door; most go on until 0400-0500.

Panorama steel band finals are held a few nights before Dimanche Gras. Parties on Sunday start early. The Dimanche Gras show at the Savannah that night is unmissable. There are two main carnival shows for children: the Red Cross Kiddies Carnival one week before carnival proper, and the school-based children's carnival the following Saturday. On Carnival Monday, the festivities start with 'J'Ouverte' at 0200, which involves dressing up in the cheapest and most outlandish disguises available ('old mas'), including mud, which will inevitably be transferred to the spectators. In the afternoon is the Parade of Bands at the Savannah, featuring the very large and colourful bands, portraying a wide sweep of historical and cultural events. Though the Savannah is the main venue, on both Carnival Monday and Tuesday the bands are required to appear before the judges at other locations, including Independence Square and Victoria Square.

Tickets for all National Carnival Commission shows (about US$10 for most events) are sold at the Queen's Park Savannah, where the shows are held. You can join one of the Mas' camps by looking in the newspaper for the times and locations of the camps. If you are early enough you can get a costume which will allow you to participate in one of the 'tramps' through town. The Tourist Office (see Essentials) has a list of names and addresses of the bands to whom you can write in advance to organize a costume. Fair-skinned visitors should avoid the skimpy costumes. You will be 2 full days in the hot sun and sun block lasts about 5 mins. There is a lot of alcohol consumed during the road marches but there are no drunken brawls. Police are much in evidence on the streets. Note that it is illegal to sell tapes of carnival artists but 'bootleg' tapes are inevitably sold on the streets. If you have the strength, don't forget Last Lap, which means jumping up with a steel band around Port of Spain to squeeze the last ounce out of the festival, prior to its official end at midnight on Tuesday.

The Hosay, or Hosein Festival, commemorating the murder of two Moslem princes, starts 10 days after the first appearance of the new moon in the Moharrun month of the Moslem calendar. Colourful processions, hauling 10-to 30ft-high miniature temples of wood, paper and tinsel, start the next day, heralded by moon dancers and accompanied by drum-beating. The main celebrations are in St James, west of Port of Spain. There is also a Hosay celebration in Cedros in South Trinidad. Many strict Muslims disapprove; lots of beer and rum is consumed. Also celebrated is the Moslem festival of Eid-ul-Fitr, to mark the end of Ramadan. Two principal Hindu festivals are Puagwa, or Holi, the colour, or spring, festival on the day of the full moon in the month of Phagun (Feb/Mar), and Divali, the festival of lights, usually in the last quarter of the year. At Puagwa everyone gets squirted with brightly coloured dyes (abeer); strict Hindus have their doubts about some of the dancing styles. Divali is more of a family affair and involves a lot of rather good food in Indian homes. On 29 August in Arima the feast of St Rose of Lima is celebrated; the parish church is dedicated to her. Descendants of the original Amerindians come from all over the island to walk in solemn procession round the church (see below, *Arima*).

Tobago There is a carnival but it is very quiet compared with Trinidad's. On Easter Monday and Tuesday, there are crab, goat and donkey races at Buccoo Village. The Tobago Heritage Festival lasts for the second fortnight of July, with historical re-enactments, variety shows and parades.

Flora and fauna

The rainforests of the Northern Range running along the north coast and the wetlands on the east and west coast are more extensive, more dense and display a greater diversity of fauna and flora than any other ecosystems in the Caribbean. Trinidad combines the species of the Caribbean chain from Jamaica to Grenada with the species of the continental rainforests of South America. The Forestry Division of the Ministry of Agriculture, Land and Marine

Resources (Long Circular Rd, St James, Port of Spain, T6227476, contact them for information on guided tours and hikes) has designated many parts of Trinidad and Tobago as national parks, wildlife reserves and protected areas. On Trinidad, the national parks are the Caroni and Nariva Swamps, Chaguaramas, and Madamas, Maracas and Matura in the north range of hills.

The variety of fauna on Tobago is larger than on other similar sized islands because of once being attached to South America. It is home to 210 different bird species, 123 different butterfly species, 16 types of lizards, 14 kinds of frogs, two dozen species of snakes (all of them harmless), and it has some spectacled caymans at Hillsborough Dam. The best place to see one of the world's most beautiful birds, the blue crowned Mot Mot, is in the Grafton Wildlife Sanctuary, where they are fed daily at 1600 at the abandoned Copra House.

Trinidad's wetlands are unparalleled by any other Caribbean island. There are mangrove **Wetlands** swamps, fresh swamps, grassy fresh water marshes, palm marshes and water-logged savannah land, covering 7,000 acres of the Central Plain. A permit from the Forestry Division is necessary for trips into restricted areas such as the Nariva Swamp and Bush Bush Island in the Aripo Scientific Reserve; 72 hours' notice is required, best to visit with a guide who can arrange it for you.

The **Nariva Swamp**, the largest freshwater swamp in Trinidad is a Wetland of International Importance under the Ramsar Convention. It contains hardwood forest and is home to red howler monkeys and the weeping capuchin as well as 55 other species of mammal of which 32 are bats. Birds include the savannah hawk and the red-breasted blackbird. A tour by kayak is recommended (T6247281 or 6292680) as it permits the sighting of wildlife not possible on a motor boat. You paddle silently across fields of giant water lilies, through channels in thick forest of mangroves and towering silk cotton trees with monkeys and parrots chattering overhead and exotic butterflies fluttering around you. Catch the dawn for seeing most birds and other wildlife. The **Caroni Swamp** is usually visited in the late afternoon as it is the roosting place of scarlet ibis and egrets. You go out through mangroves into a lagoon where the boat's engine is turned off so that you can quietly watch the birds. No permit is necessary, see below, Around the island.

The slopes of the Northern Range are covered with forest giants like the silk cotton trees, **Rainforests** which carry creepers and vines and the thick forest canopy of mahogany, balata, palms and flowering trees like the poui and immortelle which provide cover and maintain a cool, damp environment no matter the heat of the day. There are organized bus tours to places like Chaguaramas National Park or the Asa Wright Nature Reserve (where in turn there are further tours for ornithologists), or you can find a guide for a day's hike tailored to your interest in ecology or adventure.

The **Northern Range Sanctuary**, Maracas, or El Tucuche Reserve, is a forest on the second highest peak, at 3,072 feet, covering 2,313 acres. It contains some interesting flora, such as giant bromeliad and orchids, as well as fauna, including the golden tree frog and the orange-billed nightingale-thrush. There are several hiking trails, the most popular of which is from Ortinola estate; guides can be hired. The 7-mile trek to the peak takes five hours through dense forest; the views from the top are spectacular; for information contact the Field Naturalists' Club (see below). Walking alone is not recommended in the northern hills, join a group or at least walk with someone who knows the (often badly defined) trails well.

There are seven natural landmarks, three of which are described below (Blue Basin, the Pitch Lake and the Devil's Woodyard) and others include Tamana Hill in the central range, and Galera Point in the northeast. 12 areas are scientific reserves (eg Trinity Hills, Galeota Point and the Aripo Savannas); 12 are nature conservation reserves: the Asa Wright Centre is described below, but also Cedros Peninsula and Godineau Swamp in the southwest, Manzanilla in the east and Valencia. The **Trinity Hills Wildlife Sanctuary** lies west of Guayaguayare and was founded in 1934. Its forests are home to a large variety of birds, monkeys, armadillos and opossums. Permission to visit must be obtained from the Petroleum Company of Trinidad and Tobago (Petrotrin) in Pointe-a-Pierre.

The **Valencia Wildlife Sanctuary** covers 6,881 acres and contains at least 50 species of birds including antbirds and tanagers. Several mammals live here: deer, wild pig, agouti, tatoo.

Trinidad & Tobago

Near Valencia is the Arena Forest, one of ten recreation parks, while five areas have been designated scenic landscapes (Blanchisseuse, Maracas and Toco-Matelot on the north coast, Cocos Bay on the Atlantic, and Mount Harris on the Southern Rd, south of Sangre Grande). Permission to visit certain forests and watershed areas must be obtained from the Water and Sewerage Authority (WASA), Farm Rd, Valsayn, St Joseph. Their ponds often serve as home to caymans and a variety of waterbirds and are easily accessible off the main highway east of Port of Spain. Although about 46% of the island remains forested, there is much concern about the loss of wildlife habitats.

On Tobago, apart from two national parks (Buccoo Reef and the virgin and secondary forests of east Tobago), there are the Goldsborough natural landmark, the Kilgwyn scientific reserve, the Grafton nature conservation area, the Parlatuvier-Roxborough scenic landscape, and three recreation parks (including Mount Irvine). At the **Grafton Bird Sanctuary** the blue crowned mot mots are fed at 0800 and 1600 at the Old Copra House. They are not tame enough to be hand fed but it is still a spectacular sight. Many of the small islands off the coasts of the two larger ones are reserves for wildlife and are important breeding grounds for red-billed tropic birds, frigate birds, man-o-war and other sea birds (for instance Saut d'Eau, Kronstadt Island and Soldado Rock off Trinidad, and Little Tobago, see below, St Giles and Marble Islands off Tobago).

Many flowering trees can be seen: pink and yellow poui, frangipani, cassia, pride of India, immortelle, flamboyant, jacaranda. Among the many types of flower are hibiscus, poinsettia, chaconia (wild poinsettia – the national flower), ixora, bougainvillea, orchid, ginger lily and heliconia. The Horticultural Society of Trinidad and Tobago (PO Box 252) has its office on Lady Chancellor Rd, Port of Spain, T6226423.

The islands boast 60 types of bat, and other mammals include the Trinidad capuchin and red howler monkeys, brown forest brocket (deer), collared peccary (quenk), manicou (opossum), agouti, rare ocelot and armadillo. A small group of manatee is being protected in a reserve in the Nariva Swamp. Caymans live in the swamps. Other reptiles include iguanas and 47 species of snakes, of which few are poisonous: the fer-de-lance, bushmaster and two coral snakes.

The aboriginal name for the island of Trinidad was Ieri, the land of the hummingbird

Trinidad and Tobago together have more species of birds than any other Caribbean island, although the variety is South American, not West Indian. No species is endemic, but Tobago has 13 species of breeding birds not found on Trinidad. Most estimates say that there are 433 species of bird, including 41 hummingbirds, parrots, macaws, the rare red-breasted blackbird, the nightingale thrush and the mot mot. There are also 622 recorded species of butterfly. The most accessible bird-watching sites are the Caroni Bird Sanctuary, the Asa Wright Centre, the Caurita Plantation and the Wild Fowl Trust, all described elsewhere in this chapter.

Recommended is *A Guide to the Birds of Trinidad and Tobago*, by Richard ffrench (Macmillan Caribbean), with introductory information on rainfall, the environment and vegetation as well as birds. *Birds of Trinidad and Tobago*, also by Richard ffrench (M Caribbean Pocket Natural History Series) is a shorter guide with colour photos of 83 of the more common species. *Birds of Trinidad and Tobago – A Photographic Atlas*, by Russell Barrow (MEP Trinidad, 1994) is the most recent bird book.

Those interested can also contact the Trinidad Field Naturalists Club, PO Box 642, Port of Spain (T6248017 evenings only, walks on Sunday). *The Trinidad and Tobago Field Naturalists' Club Trail Guide*, by Paul Comeau, Louis Guy, Ewoud Heesterman and Clayton Hull, was published in 1992, 288 pages on 48 trails, difficult to obtain. ffrench and Bacon's *Nature Trails of Trinidad*, first published in 1982 has been revised by Dr Victor Quesnel and reissued by SM Publications Ltd under the auspices of the Asa Wright Nature Centre. Each October Trinidad and Tobago hold Natural History Festivals to foster understanding of the islands' flora and fauna.

Diving and marine life

Coral reefs flourish almost all round the island

The waters around Tobago are becoming known as an unspoilt diving destination and several dive shops have started operations in the last few years. Every known species of hard coral and lots of soft corals can be found, and there is a huge brain coral, believed to be one of the world's largest, off Little Tobago which you can see on a glass bottom boat tour. The

Guyana current flows round the south and east shores of Tobago and supports a large variety of marine life. Dive sites are numerous and varied, there are walls, caves, canyons, coral gardens and lots of fish. There is exciting drift diving but it is not recommended for novices. The only thing better than racing past dancing sea fans at three knots is to do it again at five knots. You are swept along the coral reef while, high above, manta rays flap lazily to remain stationary in the current as they sieve out the plankton. Snorkelling is also excellent almost everywhere, with good visibility. Some of the most popular sites are Arnos Vale, Pirate's Bay, Store Bay, Man O'War Bay and Batteaux Bay. In 1997 a new site was added, with the sinking of the *Scarlet Ibis*, renamed the *Maverick*, a 350ft roll-on/roll-off ship. This artificial reef lies 100ft deep on a sandy bed and already coral is growing and schools of fish are being attracted to the wreck.

The only really safe place for diving off Trinidad is in the channels called the Bocas, between the islands off the northwest peninsula (The Dragon's Mouth). However, the currents are cold, so protective gear is essential. Contact the Diving Association of Trinidad, or Twin-Island Dives, Maraval.

The leatherback **turtle** nests March to September on several beaches on Trinidad (Matura, Fishing Pond on east coast, Paria, Tacaribe and Grand Riviere on north coast) and Tobago (Great Courland Bay known as Turtle Beach, Stonehaven Bay, Bloody Bay and Parlatuvier), up to eight times a season, laying 75 to 120 eggs each time about 10 days apart. Incubation is 60 days. Turtle watching tours are organized by the Asa Wright Nature Centre and others.

Aquamarine Dive Ltd (Keith and Alice Darwent) is at *Blue Waters Inn*, Speyside, T6604341,   **Dive centres**
F6394416, amdtobago@trinidad.net *(Blue Waters Inn* tends to be full throughout the year so book early.) This is a five-star PADI facility, dives are around Little Tobago and all escorted by at least two dive masters because of the currents. Full range of courses available. *Man Friday Diving,* Charlotteville, T/F6604676, mfdiving@tstt.tt, covers the area from Charlotteville to Speyside. Other dive operators include *Ron's Watersports and Dive Centre*, Main Rd, Charlotteville, (in Trinidad) T6730549 (in Tobago) T6604941, www.opus.co.tt/ron, diving the Speyside and Charlotteville areas, dives start at US$35 with tank and weights, cheaper for more dives; *Black Rock Dive Centre*, Grafton Beach Resort, Black Rock, T6390191, F6390030, and *Le Grand Courlan*, T6399667, F6399292, legrand@trinidad.net There are several more people involved in diving, fishing and other watersports, who are not listed here. A single tank dive costs on average US$35, night dives US$45, PADI Open Water course US$300, rental of BCD and regulator US$6-7, mask, fins and snorkel US$8-10.

Beaches and watersports

The best beaches on Trinidad are on the north coast and the views from the coastal road   **Beaches**
are spectacular as you drive through forest and look down on sandy bays and rocky promontories. Close to Port of Spain **Maqueripe Bay** has a sheltered beach. **Maracas Bay**, 10 miles/16 km from the capital, has a sheltered sandy beach fringed with coconut palms; despite small waves there can be a dangerous undertow here and at other beaches and drownings have occurred, do not swim far out and watch the markers. Lifeguards are on duty until 1800 at weekends and holidays; there are changing rooms, showers etc, car parking and cabanas for beach vendors. Try 'shark-and-bake', shark meat in a heavy fried dough, a Maracas speciality, or the 'shark and bread', a roll with shark meat in it, very tasty, especially after a drinking session at 0300, sold all along the beach. *Maracas Bay Hotel* opened in 1996 and a few people rent out basic rooms in the village, ask at the small shop. There are buses to Maracas Bay running every four hours (but they can be irregular) from the bus terminal. Easy at weekends but less frequent during the week. Difficulties in catching the bus have led travellers to recommend car hire or taxis: from Port of Spain costs US$25 or there is a pick-up 'route taxi' service from the centre of town, TT$10. Another method is maxi-taxi to Maraval then four-wheel drive jeep to Maracas, irregular, get back in good time. The jeep may go right into Port of Spain but do not rely on it.

Next to Maracas Bay is **Tyrico Bay** (surfing, lifeguard, another horseshoe-shaped beach with a dangerous undertow and sandflies). **Las Cuevas**, also on the north coast (like Maracas Bay there are changing rooms, showers, lifeguards, surfing is good here but beware of the sandflies in the wet season), is a picturesque bay with fishing boats moored at one end. It can get crowded at weekends but is empty during the week. **Blanchisseuse** beach has a sweet water lagoon where the river runs into the sea and the place is kept clean by the owners of *Cocos Hut* restaurant who are establishing a 28-acre nature reserve on the banks of the river. There are lots of birds but also mosquitoes and sandflies. Leatherback turtles come on to Blanchisseuse beach in the nesting season but most of the eggs are eaten by dogs. At the northeast end, near Toco, are a number of bays, including **Balandra** for good bathing. For Toco, get an express bus or highway maxi to Arima, then route taxi to Sangre Grande, then taxi to Toco.

Further down, the Atlantic coast from Matura to Mayaro is divided into three huge sweeping bays, with palm trees growing as high as 200ft in some places. Of these bays **Mayaro** and **Manzanilla** both have beautiful sandy beaches, but be careful of the Atlantic currents, swimming can be dangerous. There are several beach houses to rent at Mayaro, heavily booked in peak holiday periods, some are poor, check beforehand. Manzanilla has new public facilities and one hotel. From nearby Brigand Hill Lighthouse, a TSTT signal station, you can get a wonderful view of the east coast, the Nariva Swamp and much of Trinidad. Light patches of green are rice fields encroaching on the swamp. In the southwest, near La Brea and the Pitch Lake is the resort of Vessigny. The southwest, or Cedros, peninsula is a three-hour car trip from Port of Spain to the unspoilt beaches and miles of coconut palm plantations. Generally, the beaches are difficult to get to except by taxi or car.

For boat trips to the islands north and west of Port of Spain T6228974, Elton Pouchet, US$75 for one to three people.

Tobago is noted for its beaches, two of the best being only minutes from the airport: **Store Bay**, popular with locals, lots of vendors, food stalls and glass bottom boats; and **Pigeon Point**, a picture postcard beach fringed with palms with calm, shallow water protected by **Buccoo Reef**. You have to pay to use the beach (TT$10), but you get changing facilities, umbrellas and beach bars. Here also there are lots of glass bottom boats going out to Buccoo Reef and a catamaran for coastal tours and swimming in the **Nylon Pool**, a shallow area offshore. Other good beaches on the leeward side of the island are **Stone Haven Bay, Mount Irvine Bay** and **Courland Bay**, one of the longest. All have resort hotels and watersports. **Englishman's Bay** is another lovely bay, with the forest coming down to the beach and a river running into the sea. The east-coast is more rugged and windswept, with cliffs and coves carved out by the Atlantic Ocean. **Hillsborough Bay**, just outside Scarborough, has a glorious long beach with overhanging palms, but the sea is dangerous because of rip tides. Do not swim there. **Big Bacolet Bay**, also known as Minister Bay, is great for surfing, body surfing and boogie boarding, but watch out for the currents. In the northeast, **King's Bay** has a beach bar, toilets and huts for shade. There is a signpost to the beach, almost opposite the track to King's Bay Waterfall. **Speyside** and **Charlotteville** both have protected bays, from the former you can take glass bottom boat trips to **Little Tobago** with bird-watching, walking and snorkelling included (about US$12.50) and from the latter you can walk to Pirate's Bay through the forest. Snorkelling is good on the reef here.

Sailing Yachting has become big business in Trinidad and there are now several marinas attracting custom from other islands more at risk from hurricanes. Provisioning is excellent and there are boat repair and maintenance facilities; local teak costs a fraction of US prices, workmen are highly skilled, services are tax free and spare parts can be imported duty free. Marinas have both dry storage and stern-to docks (see Yachting essentials, Marinas). Facilities have been built at Courland Bay, Tobago, to attract the yachting crowd.

Every July/August, there is a power boat race from the Trinidad and Tobago Yacht Club (TTYC), Trinidad to Store Bay, Tobago. The Trinidad and Tobago Yachting Association (TTYA) (www.ttya.org/ayw/index.html) sponsors Carnival Fun Race and a weekly racing programme in winter and spring. Each year Tobago has a sailing week in May, sponsored by Angostura and Yachting World Magazine; many crewing possibilities, lots of parties.

Charters can be arranged, for deep sea fish such as blue marlin, sailfish, tuna, wahoo offshore, **Fishing** king fish, barracuda, Spanish mackerel, African pompano, grouper, snapper in coastal waters, or bonefish and tarpon in the mangroves and flats. Prices for deep sea fishing are around US$250 per four hours, US$400 per eight hours, maximum six people and for bonefishing US$150 per four hours, maximum three people. On Tobago contact Capt Gerard 'Frothy' De Silva, Friendship Estate, Canaan, T6397108. He has a custom built, 38ft sports fishing boat, *Hard Play*, and two 23ft skiffs for flats fishing. The annual International Game Fishing Classic is held in February/March, the Kingfish Tournament is in June and a Funfish Tournament is in November. Contact the Trinidad and Tobago Game Fishing Association, T6245304, for information.

For **surfing** or **windsurfing**, contact the Surfing Association of Trinidad and Tobago, T6374533, and the Windsurfing Association of Trinidad and Tobago, T6592457.

Kayaking (including tuition) is available at many hotels on Tobago or at the Chaguaramas Kayak Centre run by Merryl See Tai, 500m after the Alcoa dock, just before Pier One. You can hire kayaks for use in the bay or go on excursions along the coast, up rivers or to the Bush Bush Sanctuary in the Nariva Swamp. Walking tours and overnight expeditions also arranged, T6337871, 6803480, 6292680 (home).

Cricket is very popular. Test matches are played at Queen's Park Oval, west of Queen's Park **Other sports** Savannah, Port of Spain; take a cushion, sunhat/umbrella, whistle (!) and drinks if sitting in the cheap seats. It is a private club but a friendly gate guard might let you in for a look around. For information, ring Queen's Park Cricket Club, T6222295/3787. Hockey and soccer are also played at the Oval (Football Association T6245183/7661). Also played are rugby, basketball, cycling and marathon running.

There is **horse-racing** at Santa Rosa Park, Arima, about 15 km outside Port of Spain. Horse-hire near Fort George.

Swimming at the *Hilton Hotel*, US$4 (US$2 children), *Cascadia Hotel* (chutes and waterslides, very busy at weekends and holidays) or *La Joya* at St Joseph, check first for availability, T6621184; see below for swimming and **golf** at St Andrews (Moka) Golf Club (T6292314); there are five other golf clubs on Trinidad, including a nine-hole public course at Chaguaramas (T6344349); squash, Long Circular Mall, T6221245, 0600-2200 (0900-1700 Saturday), US$3 for 40 mins, advance booking essential.

Tennis: Trinidad Country Club Maraval, T6223470/2111/2113, temporary membership, advance booking necessary, also at *Hilton Hotel*, Tranquility Square Lawn Tennis Club (T6254182) and public tennis courts at Princes Building Grounds, Upper Frederick St (T6231121). The *Cascadia Hotel*, Ariapita Rd, St Ann's has two **squash** courts with seating for 100 spectators per court, tennis courts, sauna and **gym** with lots of equipment and facilities, open for non-members, 0600-2100 Monday-Friday, 0900-1700 Saturday, T6233511. Squash also at Pelican Squash Club, *Pelican Inn*, Cascade, T6374888, equipment for hire, and at Body Works Squash Courts, Long Circular Mall, T6221215.

On Tobago, **golf** and **lawn tennis** at Mount Irvine Bay, T6398871: green fee US$20 per day, tennis US$3 in day, US$6 at night. Squash at *Grafton Beach Resort*, 0800-2200, US$9.50 for 45 mins including court, ball and racket rental. Black Rock has a basketball league in late August, early September; you can play before or after the games. At the *Turtle Beach Hotel* it is possible to play **volleyball**. For **hiking**, **bird-watching** on and off-shore, contact the very knowledgeable naturalist, David Rooks, PO Box 58, Scarborough, T6399408.

Trinidad

Trinidad, the most southern of the Caribbean islands, lying only seven miles off the Vene-zuelan coast, is one of the most colourful of the West Indian islands. It is an island of 1,864 square miles, traversed by ranges of hills, the northern and southern ranges, running roughly east and west, and the central range, running diagonally across the island. Apart from small areas in the northern, forested range which plunges into the sea on the north coast, the main peaks of which are Cerro del Aripo (3,083 ft) and El Tucuche (3,072 ft), all the land is below 1,000 ft. The flatlands in central Trinidad are used for growing sugar cane. There are large areas of swamp on the east and west coasts. About half the popula-tion live in the urban east-west corridor, stretching from Chaguaramas in the west through Port of Spain to Arima in the east. Trinidad is separated from the mainland of South America by the Boca del Dragón strait in the northwest (Dragon's Mouth) and Boca del Serpiente in the southwest (Serpent's Mouth), both named by Columbus.

Trinidad

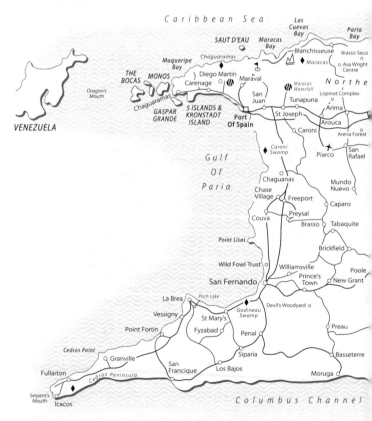

Port of Spain

Port of Spain lies on a gently sloping plain between the Gulf of Paria and the foothills of the Northern Range. The city has a pleasant atmosphere, with many new buildings constructed in the last few years and older ones now being better maintained. It is full of life and an exciting city to spend time in. The streets are mostly at right-angles to one another; the buildings are a mixture of fretwork wooden architecture and modern concrete, interspersed with office towers. Within easy reach of the port are many of the main buildings of interest.

Population: 51,000

Ins and outs

The taxi fare from **Piarco airport** to Arouca is US$7 and to the centre of Port of Spain is US$20, to Maraval US$24, Diego Martin US$27, San Fernando US$31 (50% more after 2200). Taxi despatchers find taxis for new arrivals, ask to see the rate card for taxi fares to different places. Unlicensed taxis outside the main parking area charge less, depending on the volume of business. Public transport is much cheaper. To get to Port of Spain walk out of the airport and cross the road to catch a route taxi (see page 913), destination Main Rd, or, rather better if slower, go a bit further to Arouca (US$0.30). Then take a route taxi or maxi taxi from the junction into Port of Spain (US$0.90). Coming back to the airport do the same in reverse.

Getting there
Population: 51,000 (350,000 including suburbs) See page 912 for further details

Trinidad & Tobago

People are very helpful if you need to ask. There is a direct bus, US$0.30, 45 mins to one hour, from the airport to Port of Spain bus station (catering) for airport workers, leaving City Gate terminal 0630 and 0700, returning from Piarco 1515 and 1545 only. Tickets not available at the airport. From the central bus terminal at the old railway station you will have to walk to Independence or Woodford Square for a route taxi for your ultimate destination. This is not advisable at night, especially if carrying luggage. Take a taxi.

You can see most of the sights of Port of Spain by walking around the town centre. For further afield, however, there are taxis, buses, route taxis and maxi taxis.

Getting around

Sights

On the south side of **Woodford Square**, named after the former governor, Sir Ralph Woodford, is the fine Anglican Cathedral Church of the Holy Trinity (consecrated 1823), with an elaborate hammer-beam roof festooned with carvings. It was built during Woodford's governorship (1813-28) and contains a very fine monument to him. **The Red House** (completed 1907) contains the House of Representatives, the Senate and various government departments. It was the scene of an attempted overthrow of the Robinson Government by armed black Muslim rebels in July 1990. The rebels held the Prime Minister and several of his Cabinet captive for five days before surrendering to the Army (see box, page 953). On the west side of the Red House, at the corner of St Vincent and Sackville Streets, can still be seen the skeletal remains of the former Police Headquarters, which the rebels firebombed before launching their assault on the Red House. The first Red House on this site was, ironically, destroyed by fire in 1903 during riots over an increase in water rates. On the opposite side of the Square to the Cathedral are the modern Hall of Justice (completed 1985), Central Library and City

Port of Spain

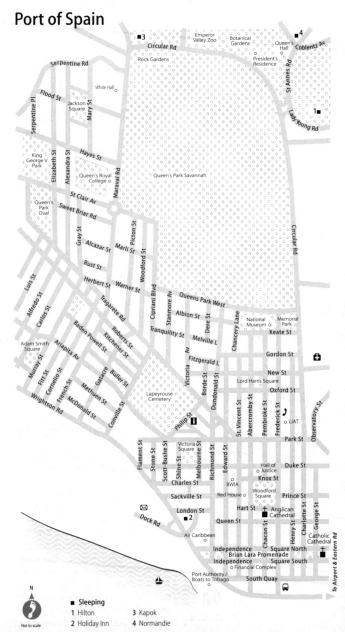

N
Not to scale

■ **Sleeping**
1 Hilton
2 Holiday Inn
3 Kapok
4 Normandie

Hall (1961), with a fine relief sculpture on the front. The Square is Trinidad's equivalent to Speaker's Corner in London's Hyde Park.

On **Independence Square** (two blocks south of Woodford Square) are the Roman Catholic Cathedral of the Immaculate Conception, built on the shore-line in 1832 but since pushed back by land reclamation, and the Salvatori building at the junction with Frederick St. The central area of Independence Square, from the cruise ship complex to the Cathedral, has been made into an attractive pedestrian area, known as Lara Promenade in honour of the Trinidadian cricketer and former West Indies captain, Brian Lara. Behind the Cathedral is Columbus Square, with a small, brightly-painted statue of the island's European discoverer. South of Independence Square, between Edward and St Vincent Streets is the financial complex, two tall towers and Eric Williams Plaza, housing the Central Bank and Ministry of Finance. Also, a little to the south of the square is the old neo-classical railway station, now known as City Gate, a transport hub for taxis and buses travelling between Port of Spain and eastern Trinidad.

To the north of the city is **Queen's Park Savannah**, a large open space with many playing fields and a favourite haunt of joggers. It was the site of Trinidad's main race-course for decades, until racing was centralized in Arima. In the middle of the Savannah is the Peschier cemetery, still owned and used by the family who used to own the Savannah. Below the level of the Savannah are the Rock Gardens, with lily ponds and flowers. Opposite are the **Botanic Gardens**, founded in 1818 by Sir Ralph Woodford. There is an amazing variety of tropical and sub-tropical plants from Southeast Asia and South America, as well as indigenous trees and shrubs.

Adjoining the Gardens is the small **Emperor Valley Zoo**, dating from 1952, which specializes in animals living wild on the island. It has a number of reptiles, including iguanas, four species of boas and the spectacled caiman. ■ *0930-1800, no tickets after 1730, adults TT$4, children 3-12, TT$2.* Also next to the gardens is the presidential residence: a colonial style building in an 'L' shape in honour of Governor James Robert Longden (1870-74). Just off the Savannah (on St Ann's Rd) is Queen's Hall, where concerts and other entertainments are given.

There are several other Edwardian-colonial mansions along the west side of Queen's Park Savannah, built in 1904-10 and known as the **Magnificent Seven** (after the film of the same name). From south to north, they are Queen's Royal College; Hayes Court, the residence of the Anglican Bishop; Prada's House, or Mille Fleurs; Ambard's House, or Roomor; the Roman Catholic Archbishop's residence; White Hall, which has regained its status as the Prime Minister's office; and Killarney, Mr Stollmeyer's residence (now owned by the Government). Apart from Hayes Court, which was built in 1910, all were built in 1904. A walk along the north and west sides of the Savannah can be made in the early morning (before it gets too hot), arriving outside Queen's Royal College as the students are arriving and the coconut sellers are turning up outside. The Anglican Church of All Saints at 13 Queen's Park West is also worth a visit; its stained glass windows are recently restored. Knowsley, another 1904 building, and the spanking new headquarters of the BP Amoco Oil Company, formerly the historic *Queen's Park Hotel* (1895), both on the south side of the Savannah, are interesting buildings too. For a history of Port of Spain buildings, with illustrations, read *Voices In The Street*, by Olga J Marrogordato (Inprint Caribbean Ltd 1977).

Just off the Savannah, at the corner of Frederick and Keate Streets, is the small **National Museum**, in the former Royal Victoria Institute. It has sections on petroleum and other industries, Trinidad and Tobago's natural history, geology, archaeology and history, carnival costumes and photographs of kings and queens, and art exhibitions (including a permanent exhibition of the work of the 19th-century landscape artist, M J Cazabon, see further page 956). ■ *Entry free.*

Away from the city centre, to the west of Port of Spain, is the suburb of St James where in Ethel St is a large new Hindu temple, the Port of Spain Mandir. On the waterfront is the San Andres Fort built about 1785 to protect the harbour.

Trinidad & Tobago

Around the island

There are pleasant drives in the hills around with attractive views of city, sea, and mountains. Go up Lady Young Rd, about two miles from Savannah, to a lookout 563ft above sea level (not on a taxi route, but some cars take this route from the airport), by Lady Chancellor Rd to a look-out 600ft above sea level (not always safe, even by car) and to the Laventille Hills to see the view from the tower of the shrine of Our Lady of Laventille. From **Fort George**, a former signal station at 1,100ft, there are also excellent views. To reach it take the St James route taxi from Woodford Square and ask to get off at Fort George Rd. From there it is about one hour's walk uphill passing through some fairly tough residential territory. The fort was built around 1804 and formerly called La Vigie. Although it was never used to defend the island, in times of danger people from Port of Spain brought their valuables up here for safe keeping. From Fort George you can also continue on foot on a rough road up to the telecommunications masts at the top of the hill, from where there are views down to Port of Spain, over to Venezuela and across the northern hills.

Chaguaramas　Midway along the Western Main Rd to Chaguaramas a road runs off to the north, through the residential area of Diego Martin. The **Blue Basin** waterfall and natural landmark, on the Diego Martin river, is off this road, about a five-minute walk along a path from the town. (If you do leave your car to visit the fall, leave nothing of value in it. You are also advised to visit the falls in a group of five or six people if possible to avoid being robbed.) At River Estate, by Diego Martin, is a waterwheel which was once the source of power for a sugar plantation.

The Western Main Rd, with many pretty views, especially of the Five Islands, runs on past West Mall in Westmoorings, where there is a large new residential development and the Chamber of Commerce on the waterfront. From here the road continues along the coast past the Trinidad and Tobago Yacht Club (TTYC) (opposite Goodwood Park where the rich live) and to **Carenage**, where there is a remarkable little church, St Peter's Chapel, on the waterside. The Alcoa transhipment facility is next and then you are into Chaguaramas, on the bay of the same name. On your left is Pier One, a small marina with restaurant and entertainment facilities, popular at weekends, and further along is Chagville, a public beach opposite the Chaguaramas Convention Centre, where political parties hold their annual delegates' meetings. This area used to belong to the US navy 1945-64 but is now under the control of the Chaguaramas Development Authority (CDA). This statutory body is developing

Trinidad northwest

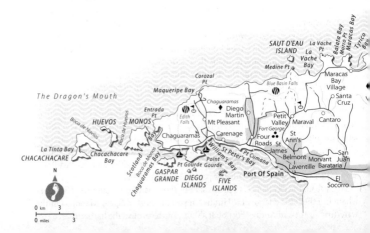

the area with a mix of tourism, recreational and marine related industries. Chaguaramas was the focus of international attention in May 1999, when the Miss Universe pageant was held there at the old heliport opposite the Convention Centre.

Further along the coast road, the **Chaguaramas Military History and Aviation Museum** (PO Box 3126, Carenage, T6344391) has exhibitions of VE Day and Trinidad's role in both world wars with intricate models as well as relics. ■ *Entry through military checkpoint, TT$10 adults, TT$5 children, T6344391, knowledgeable staff.* Next you come to the Yachting Association, Power Boats, Peake's and Industrial Marine Services (IMS), all offering services to the yachting clientele and the area is packed with boats stacked on land or in the water. ■ *Buses from Port of Spain to Chaguaramas run about every 30 mins, TT$2.*

From Chaguaramas you can sometimes get a launch (known locally as a *pirogue*, expect to pay US$25 round trip although locals pay about TT$15) to **Gaspar Grande**, one of the islands offshore, on which are the **Gasparee Caves**. ■ *TT$5.* Try to get a *pirogue* with a canvas shade as these are used to dealing with tourists and are likely to be more reliable. The Gasparee Caves are certainly worth a visit. It is about a 20-minute boat ride from the Crews Inn marina. The landing stage is at the west end of Gaspar Grande which has many weekend homes. The caves are about 15 mins from the landing stage (no facilities or drinks) up a good path through woods, quite steep in places and hot. The caves are locked and it is necessary to have a guide from the house at the end of the path (drinks available). The complex of caves is large but you are only shown one, with good steps leading down and naturally lit from a blow hole. There is a beautiful lake (tidal) at the bottom with stalactites which the guide will light. Some of the path around the cave is quite slippery. Despite what the boatman may tell you, there is now no swimming allowed in the cave. Be prepared for a wait at the landing stage as despite all assurances, a number of boatmen will not wait for you, preferring to return to the island and then come back to pick you up (which they usually do). Don't be afraid to ask another boatman to take you back, you will of course have to pay again though. As well as going to the caves, ask the boatman to take you across to **Scotland Bay**. There are excellent views of the other islands making up the Dragon's Mouth. This is much frequented by boats and yachts at the weekend but is virtually deserted during the week and makes an ideal place for a picnic. Good swimming here. **Monos Island**, at the west tip of Trinidad, has many deep caves and white sandy beaches, popular with more affluent Trinidadians.

Trinidad & Tobago

The north coast

North of Port of Spain is **Maraval**, just beyond which is the 18-hole St Andrews golf course at **Moka** (there is also a swimming pool, US$3 for non-members). The North Coast Rd branches left off Saddle Rd (which runs through Maraval back over the hills to meet the Eastern Main Rd at San Juan), leading to Maracas Bay, Las Cuevas and Blanchisseuse (see page 919). There is a lookout point on the road to Maracas Bay at the *Hot Bamboo Hut*, where a track goes steeply down to *Timberline* (see page 934). The stall-holder can call the toucans in the forest, take binoculars to see them fly close and answer him. It is possible to walk to Maracas from Port of Spain in about three hours, best to take a maxi or route taxi to Maraval to avoid the traffic and then hike from there. The

Northern Range locations for hiking are best reached from the coastal villages, where there are small hotels, guest houses and restaurants.

East of Port of Spain The east corridor from Port of Spain is a dual carriageway and a priority bus route through the industrial and residential suburbs. At **St Joseph**, which was once the seat of government, is the imposing Jinnah Memorial Mosque. North of St Joseph is the Maracas Valley (nothing to do with Maracas Bay), which has a 300 ft waterfall about two miles from the road. Get a Maracas Valley taxi from St Joseph and ask where to get off.

This is the oldest Benedictine complex in the Caribbean Further east, high on a hill, is **Mount St Benedict** monastery, reached through St Johns Rd in St Augustine. Although the monastery was founded by a Belgian, the first Benedictine monks came from Bahia, Brazil, in 1912. It started with a tapia hut but construction of the main building on Mt Tabor began in 1918. The monastery has a retreat, lots of educational facilities, a drug rehabilitation centre, a farm and a guest house and is popular with birdwatchers and walkers. There are marvellous views over the Caroni Plain to the sea. A minibus from Port of Spain to St Augustine takes 40 minutes, TT$5. There are several good, cheap Chinese restaurants in **Tunapuna**, the town after St Augustine, and a wide variety of fruits in the market.

A little further along the Eastern Main Rd, the Golden Grove Rd branches south to Piarco international airport. If you turn north at this point (Arouca) a road winds 10 km up into the forested mountains to the **Lopinot Complex**, an estate built by the Comte de Lopinot (see page 951) at the turn of the 19th century. Originally called La Reconnaissance, it is now a popular picnic spot and destination for school trips; there is a small museum. There is a bar across the road, open 'anyday, anytime'.

High on a ridge in the Maracas Valley are the only known Amerindian petroglyphs (rock drawings) in Trinidad, known as the **Caurita** drawings. They are probably Arawak and show a series of faces with curving lines indicating limbs. To get there it is a stiff climb of one to 1½ hrs in the valley, with access from the main cross roads between San Juan and Tunapuna.

Arima *Population: 26,000* Arima is the third largest city, 25 km east of Port of Spain, reached by bus or route taxi. It has a small but interesting Amerindian museum at the Cleaver Woods Recreation Centre, on the west side of town housed in a reproduction Amerindian long house, entrance free but donations welcome. In Arima there is a group of people who regard themselves as descendants of the original Amerindians of the area, although there are none left of pure blood. They have a figure head Carib queen and call themselves the **Santa Rosa Carib Community**, although it is not clear whether they are of Carib, Arawak or other Amerindian descent. West of the church in the centre of town is the Santa Rosa Carib Community Crafts Centre selling traditional crafts: cassava squeezers, serving trays, carvings etc. The Catholic church has good stained glass windows. At the end of August there is an annual religious procession where the image of Santa Rosa de Lima is carried from the church and paraded through the streets, very picturesque and interesting.

Northeast of Arima From Arima the road runs either to Toco at Trinidad's northeast tip (which is well worth a visit though its rocky shore defies bathing) or, branching off at Valencia, to the east coast.

The **Hollis Reservoir** can be visited with a permit from WASA (see page 918). There are a number of short, well-marked trails through beautiful forest and birdwatching is rewarding. From the Valencia junction (avoid the road to Sangre Grande) drive about 1½ km and turn left after a small church into Quarrie Rd. Continue north until you reach a WASA pump house, where the guard on duty inspects permits. You can park here or drive along the Quarrie River to the dam where parking is also available.

At **Galera Point**, reached off the road which goes to Toco, over a rickety wooden bridge, there is a small, pretty lighthouse. If you arrive before 1530 it is often open and you can climb to the top for a breathtaking view from the ramp.

The **Salibea Waterfall** is also near Toco. At the Toco 14-mile post, cross the bridge and turn left immediately after the 14¼-mile post into the Salibea/Matura Trace. Follow a 20-minute, rather rough drive and park in front of two houses. Walk 15 minutes along the trail, turn left at the junction, continue about 10 minutes to a second junction where the path narrows on the right going slightly uphill into Mora Forest. Keep on the trail, crossing first a small stream and then a larger river. Ten minutes later at another junction you may bear right over a small hill or walk upstream. Either will get you to Salibea Waterfall and pool in 10 minutes. The pool is 6m deep and recommended for good swimmers. There is a picnic area or continue by car to the *Mount Plaisir Estate Hotel*, on a wide, sandy beach, where lunches are served at midday.

About 8 miles north of Arima, off the Blanchisseuse Rd, you can get (by car or taxi from Arima, US$7, the driver should wait for you, or a warm 2½ hour walk up hill through lovely forests) to the **Asa Wright Nature Centre**, an old plantation house overlooking a wooded valley and a must for bird-lovers. The Nature Centre now owns 700 acres of forest (not all of which are at the centre) and the annual Christmas bird count usually numbers 161-186 (1990-94) species. There is a beautiful man-made pool where you can swim, a network of trails and guided tours. Sit on the verandah and watch the hummingbirds. Take binoculars. The rangers are very knowledgeable and can tell you about the plants and insects (easier to see) as well as the birds. The rare oil-birds in Dunstan Cave (also called Diablotin Cave) can only be seen if you stay more than three nights; their numbers had dwindled but 138 were counted on 1994 bird count day. Field trips for guests are also organized to the Caroni Swamp, Nariva Swamp, Aripo Savannah, Arena Forest and Blanchisseuse, while turtle watching tours are also offered to the east and west coasts during leatherback nesting season March-September. ■ *The centre is open daily 0900-1700 (PO Box 4710, Arima, T6674655, F6670493 for booking, or in the USA, Caligo Ventures, 156 Bedford Rd, Armonk, NY 10504, T914-2736333, 800-4267781, F914273-6370). US$6 per person tour and coffee/tea, US$10.50 including buffet Sun lunch, US$6.50 including weekday lunch, or you can just have sandwiches on the verandah, see below for accommodation. It is wise to give 48 hrs notice of your visit. The centre publishes a newsletter, The Bellbird.*

This road carries on to Blanchisseuse. A nine-mile (14 km) walk from the road are the **Aripo Caves** (the longest system in Trinidad) with spectacular stalagmites and stalactites (in the wet season, June to December, a river runs through the caves). Oilbirds can be seen at the entrance. Only fully equipped spelunkers should venture beyond the entrance. To get there, turn at Aripo Rd off the Eastern Main Rd, turn right at the four-mile post, over the bridge into Aripo village. Keep left, continuing uphill to a wide bend to the left where you may park off the road and begin the walk uphill. After a couple of minutes turn left at the small house. After a further 10 minutes take the trail to the right of the junction and to the left at the next junction, continuing uphill along the river. At a shelf of rock there is a well-cleared trail away from the river. Keep to this trail heading north until the top of the hill. Go downhill five minutes to the stream which leads into the cave. Do not enter without a flashlight, rope and other equipment. A knowledgeable guide is recommended.

Blanchisseuse has a population of about 3,000 and is divided between the Upper Village and Lower Village, with the Arima road being the dividing line. There is a post office, health centre, RC Church, government offices and police station in Lower Village, while Upper Village has the school, recreation field and several wood and leather artisans. Sandals are good value at around US$13; find Lloyd, who has a workshop in Blanchisseuse and a shop in Maracas. All this part of the coast is very beautiful with the forest coming down to the sea. You can hike east all along the coast from here, starting at the 100-year-old Silver Bridge just outside the village. It reportedly takes three days and a guide is recommended, ask Fred (at *Laguna Mar*) or Barbara Zollna (at *Zollna House*) to arrange it.

This town was named after the washerwomen who did their laundry in the Marianne River

Trinidad & Tobago

From Arima you can take a (rare) bus, or hitchhike, to Brasso Seco and Paria (though the latter does not appear on some maps). From here the trail runs to **Paria Bay**, which is possibly the best beach on the island, about eight miles/13 km, ask directions, or see the Tourism and Industrial Development Co (TIDCO) *Sites (trail guide)* book for the route. There is a primitive shelter on the beach but no other facilities so take provisions with you. At the beach, turn right to get to the bridge over the Paria River, from where it is a five-minute walk inland to the spectacular Paria waterfall. Another path from the beach leads west to Blanchisseuse (seven miles/11 km), where the track forks; take the fork closer to the shore if you want to continue along the coast to Las Cuevas (see page 920).

South of Port of Spain Driving south from Port of Spain you see rice fields, herds of water buffalo, buffalypso (bigger animals, selectively bred for meat), Hindu temples and Moslem mosques. There are boat trips to the **Caroni Bird Sanctuary**, the home of scarlet ibis, whose numbers are dwindling as the swamp in which they live is encroached upon. The boats leave around 1600 so as to see the ibis returning to their roost at sunset. It is a spectacular sight and is recommended even for those who do not consider themselves bird watchers. Egrets, herons and plovers can also be seen. Bus or route taxi from Port of Spain or San Fernando to Bamboo Grove Settlement no 1, on the Uriah Butler Highway, from where the boats leave, TT$2.50 or TT$5 respectively. Maxi taxi (green bands) from Independence Square. Ask to be dropped off at the Caroni Bird Sanctuary. Arrange return transport in advance, it is impossible to hail a bus in the dark. There are two boat operators in the swamp: *Moodoo Tours* and *Winston Nanan* (T6451305), US$10, group rates available, although a visitors' centre is under construction and an entrance fee may be imposed. Nanan rarely guides now and not all his boatmen are informative; enquire at the Asa Wright Centre for more detailed tours. Tour operators in Port of Spain offer tours, usually on Nanan's boats. Take mosquito repellent and if possible a cold bag with drinks, although Nanan sells drinks on board, repellent is essential when you get off the boat at the end of your trip.

San Fernando
Population: 60,000
San Fernando on the southwest coast is a busy, hot city, as yet not spoilt by tourism but spoilt by just about everything else and not especially attractive. An expressway connects Port of Spain with San Fernando, making it a 30-minute drive (one hour by taxi). In its neighbourhood are the principal industrial-development area of **Point Lisas** and the **Pointe-a-Pierre** oil refinery. Within the oil refinery is the 26-hectare **Wild Fowl Trust**, a conservation area with two lakes and breeding grounds for many endangered species. Many birds bred in captivity are later released into the wild. There is a Learning Centre with a small archaeological exhibition and shell collection. ■ *1000-1700, Sat 1200-1600, Sun 1030-1800, T6375145, Ms Molly Gaskin or Mrs K Shepard on T6624040, call 48 hrs in advance to get permission to enter the compound (there are many entrances, it can be confusing).*

A famous phenomenon to visit on the southwest coast near San Fernando is **Pitch Lake**, about 47 ha of smooth surface resembling caked mud but which really is hot black tar; it is 41 m deep. It has been described by disappointed tourists, expecting something more dramatic, as looking like a parking lot, although others have pointed out that it is parking lots that look like the Pitch Lake. If care is taken it is possible to walk on it, watching out for air holes bubbling up from the pressure under the ooze. In the wet season, however, most of the area is covered with shallow fresh water. The legend is that long ago the gods interred an entire tribe of Chaima Indians for daring to eat sacred hummingbirds containing the souls of their ancestors. In the place where the entire village sank into the ground there erupted a sluggish flow of black pitch gradually becoming an ever-refilling large pool. It provides a healthy, though recently decreasing, item in Trinidad's export figures. It can be reached by taking a bus from Port of Spain to San Fernando (US$1 by air-conditioned express, by route taxi it costs US$1.75) and then another from there to La Brea (US$0.75).

Insist on a professional guide, who should report to the security guard before taking you around, as locals who pose as guides harass tourists for large tips. Agree on a price in advance as there are no fixed rates. Sometimes there are crowds of guides who are difficult to avoid, but on the other hand it is difficult to understand the lake without explanation. Pompei, trained by the Tourist Board, is recommended, he is tall and stout.

East of San Fernando, near Princes Town, is the **Devil's Woodyard**, one of 18 mud volcanoes on Trinidad. This one is considered a holy site by some Hindus (it is also a natural landmark). It last erupted in 1852 and the bubbling mud is cool.

On the coast is the fishing village of **Moruga**, which is reached by a fascinating drive through the Trinidad countryside. Every year around the middle of July they have an unusual celebration of Columbus' 1498 landing on the beach. Fishing boats are decked out as caravels, complete with the red Maltese cross. Columbus, a priest and soldiers are met by Amerindians (local boys, mostly of East Indian and African extraction); after the meeting everyone retires to the church compound where the revelry continues late into the night.

The south coast

The **Karamat Mud Volcano**, Moruga, erupted in 1997. Thick mud spurted 50 m high, killing one man, burying animals alive and engulfing houses, leaving 100 homeless. Seek local advice before visiting. From Penal Rock Rd proceed west to the 8-mile post. On the right head down Haggard Trace driving south until the Moruga West oil field gate. Enter on the road and continue left for 1 mile. Pass a series of tank batteries, No 7, on the left, and continue to an oil pump on the right. Take the side road for 400 yds. Park near the oil pump at a well-head. Do not take the side track into the forest road. Continue up hill.

It is quite difficult to get beyond Arima and San Fernando by bus, but there are route taxis, privately-operated maxi taxis, or you can hire a car or motorcycle.

Essentials

If you intend to stay in Trinidad for carnival, when prices rise steeply, you must book a hotel well in advance. Some are booked a year ahead. If arriving without accommodation arranged at Carnival time, the tourist office at the airport may help you to find you a room with a local family, though this like hotels will be expensive. You will be lucky to find anything.

Sleeping
VAT of 15% will be added to your bill

Port of Spain area   (hotels) **LL-L** *Hilton*, on a rise at the corner of Lady Young and St Ann's Rds, Northeast Queen's Park Savannah, T6243211, F6244485, hiltonpos@wow.net   Public areas and pool deck are on top and 394 rooms and 25 suites on lower levels, facilities for the disabled, view and breeze from pool level excellent, all facilities, restaurants, bars, eating by the pool is not expensive, non-residents can eat/swim there, tennis, badminton, gym, conference centre, ballroom, executive suite, frequent entertainment. **LL-B** *Cascadia*, 67 Ariapita Rd, St Ann's, T6240940, F6278046, up in the hills. 68 rooms, children under 12 free, rooms and suites vary, nice pool, chutes and waterslide (TT$25 for non-guests to use pool), sports facilities including squash, tennis, gym, sauna, conference facilities, *Coconuts Club* disco, restaurant, bar, busy at weekends. **L** *Holiday Inn*, Wrightson Rd (PO Box 1017), T6253366, F6254166, holidayinn@trinidad.net, in the business centre. All facilities very nice, friendly but poor breakfast service.

AL-A *Chaconia Inn*, 106 Saddle Rd, Maraval, T6288603, F6283214. 31 rooms, pool, restaurant. **AL-A** *Kapok*, 16-18 Cotton Hill, St Clair, Northwest Queen's Park Savannah, T6226441, F6229677, in USA T800-74, in UK T0800-951000, stay@kapok.co.tt   95 rooms, a/c, TV, phone etc, good, friendly, comfortable, light, big windows, some studios with kitchenette, try to get room on upper floors for good view and away from traffic noise, excellent *Tiki Village* restaurant with Chinese and Polynesian cuisine, small pool, gym, facilities for meetings, computer room, shopping arcade. **AL-B** *Normandie*, off St Ann's Rd, at the end of Nook Av (No 10), T6241181, F6240108, normandie@wow.net   53 standard, superior and loft rooms, a/c,

Trinidad & Tobago

reduced rates for businessmen, swimming pool, in a complex with craft and fashion shops, art gallery and restaurants, comfortable, nice furnishings, wooden floors, good restaurant, outdoor theatre and *Breakfast Shed* for lunch.

B *Caribbean Condo Villas*, L40 Majuba Cross Road, Petit Valley, T6320113. Apartment accommodation with kitchenette and cable TV available. **B-C** *Hosanna Hotel*, 2 Santa Margarita Circular Rd, St Augustine, T6625449, F6625451. 18 rooms, restaurant, jacuzzi, pool, all credit cards. **C** *Tropical Hotel*, 6 Rookery Nook Rd, Maraval, T6225815, F6224249. A/c, pool, maid service, bar and restaurant attached, short walk from the Savannah, friendly, helpful. **C-D** *The Cove*, PO Box 3123, Carenage, T6344319. The only seaside resort in Chaguaramas, pool, seaside bathing, maid and laundry, kitchenette, access to golf, one 3-bedroom apartment **B**, breakfast US$6, lunch/dinner US$10.

Below US$20 a night are few & far between in the capital & some are not recommended by TIDCO

Port of Spain area (guest houses) **B** *Ville de French*, 5 French Street, Woodbrook, T6227521. Guest house, 12 rooms. **C** *Alicia's Guest House*, 7 Coblentz Gardens, St Ann's, T6232802, F6238560. 17 rooms, all different, some dark, some cheap, all a/c, fan, TV, phone, fridge, family rooms, suites, small pool, jacuzzi, exercise machine, meals available, excursions organized. **C** *Par-May-La's Inn*, 53 Picton St, T6282008, T/F6284707, parmaylas@ trinidad.net Specially convenient for carnival and cricket, double or triple rooms with bathroom, a/c, TV, phone, some cheap singles, facilities for the disabled, family run by Bob and Pamela Gopee, friendly, helpful, parking, complimentary continental breakfast, full American breakfast, or local cuisine with roti, evening meals on request, credit cards accepted. Nearby the same family has 15 apartments, **C** *Sun Deck Suites*, 42-44 Picton Street, T6229560. A/c, with cooking facilities, sleep 2/3. **C** *Pelican Inn*, 2-4 Coblentz Av, Cascade, T/F6276271. 14 rooms, pub, squash court. **C** *The Bight*, Lot 5, Western Main Rd, Chaguaramas, T6344389, F634387. 10 rooms, sports bar, marina, nearby beach and golf course. **C** *Trini House*, 5A Lucknow St, St James, T/F6287550. 3 rooms, includes breakfast, English, German, Italian and French spoken by owner Michael Figuera, pan tuition. **C-D** *Kitty Peters*, 26 Warren St, breakfast extra, immaculately clean, hot water showers, fans, quiet area, friendly. **C-D** *Valsayn Villa*, 34 Gilwell Rd, Valsayn North, T/F6451193. Very large, modern, private house with beautifully furnished rooms and lovely garden, or fully furnished villas **B** and up, in one of the safest residential areas, close to university, 15 mins from airport, 20 mins by bus from down town Port of Spain, excellent home-cooked Indian meals available.

D *Fondes Amandes Guest House*, 9B Fondes Amandes Road, St Anns, T6247281. CP, accommodates 6, pool. **D** *Halyconia Inn*, 7 First Av, Cascade, T6230008, 6246481. Kitchenette, exercise facility. **D** *ML's Gingerbread House*, 25 Stone Street, Woodbrook, T6253663, F6224415, mark@wow.net Run by Mona Lyndersay, Victorian house with turrets, fretwork and jalousies, antique furnishings, fruit and flower garden, featured on 1994 postage stamp, 3 double rooms with bathrooms, breakfast included, other meals on request, varied cuisine, excursions arranged. **D** *La Calypso Guest House*, 46 French St, Woodbrook, T6224077, F6286895. Ask for room at back or high up for less noise, clean, safe, efficient, kitchen, helpful, jacuzzi, car hire available, breakfast US$3, pool at their other guest house. **D** *Fabienne's Guest House*, 15 Belle Smythe St, Woodbrook, T6222773. 8 rooms, pool, within walking distance of National Stadium. **D-E** *Copper Kettle Hotel*, 66-68 Edward St, T6254381. Central, good value, clean, safe, hot and dingy rooms with shower, price depends on whether you have a/c, friendly and helpful staff, good restaurant.

E *Scott's Guest House*, 5 Pomme Rose Av, Cascade, T6244105. Friendly, safe area, can be booked from airport. **E** *The Abercromby Inn*, 101 Abercromby St, T6235259, F6276658, aberinn@carib-link.net 17 rooms, a/c, TV, phone, laundry facilities, some large and some very small economy rooms, clean, no food, have to order from outside, 5 mins' walk to Queen's Park Savannah, karaoke lounge. **E** *Mardi Gras Guest House*, 134A Frederick St, T6272319. Price rises in carnival week, with private bath, dining room, bar. **E** *Schultzi's Guest House and Pub*, 35 Fitt St, Woodbrook, T/F6227521. Includes breakfast, kitchen, hot shower, mixed reports, helpful owner, Lisa Nichol-Yeates, transport available to airport or dock. **E** *The New City Cabs Guesthouse*, 33 St Ann's Rd, St Ann's, T6236443. Cheap. **E** *Pearl's Guest House*, 3-4 Victoria Square East, T6252158. Access to kitchen, can prepare own meals, laundry room, very friendly, family home from home, excellent location for Carnival. **E** *Bullet Guest House*, 6 Park St, central. Clean and safe, does not raise prices during carnival. **E** per person *YWCA*, 8a Cipriani Blvd, T/F6276388. Women only, rooms with 2 beds, fan, breakfast included. **F** *Hillcrest Haven Guesthouse*, 7A Hillcrest Rd, Cascade, T6241344 prices rise to **C** during Carnival. Minimum stay 6 nights, use of kitchen facilities, mixed reports. **F** *Royal Guest House*, 109 Charlotte St, T6231042, in front of gas station. Coffee shop next door owned by same family, shared bathroom, good beds, friendly, safe.

Near the airport **A** *Bel Air International*, Piarco, by the airport, T6644771/3, F add ext 15, belair@tstt.net.tt Small room, overpriced, typical airport hotel, swimming pool, good bar and restaurant (expensive breakfast) but noise from planes. **B** *Pax Guesthouse*, Mt St Benedict, Tunapuna, T/F6624084, pax-g-h@trinidad.net. Built 1932, original furniture made by monks, 18 rooms, popular with birdwatchers, 147 species of bird on estate, donkey trails into forest, rooms have high ceilings, no a/c necessary, one family room, most share showers, simple but wholesome food, lovely view of central Trinidad as well as of occasional monk. **B** *LeSportel Inn and Nature Tours*, Centre of Excellence, Macoya Rd, Tunapuna, T6633902-4. Part of massive football complex sponsored by FIFA, 34 a/c rooms, pool, transport into Port of Spain nearby. **C** *Sadila House*, run by Savitri and Dinesh Bhola, Waterpipe Rd, Five Rivers, Arouca, T6403659, F6401376, close to airport. 3 rooms, breakfast included, credit cards accepted, weekly and group rates available, a/c, TV. **D** *Airport View Guesthouse*, St Helena Junction, Piarco airport 1.5 km, T6643186. Convenient, a/c, hot water, double rooms have 2 double beds, breakfast US$5, restaurant nearby serving American style food. **D-E** *The Caribbean Lodge*, 32 St Augustine Circular Rd, Tunapuna, T6452937, (15-30 mins to Port of Spain by bus on the priority route). Shared or private shower, a/c, comfortable, laundry facilities, breakfast room.

Arima **LL-L** *Asa Wright Nature Centre*, 7½ mile mark, Blanchisseuse Rd, Arima, PO Box 4710, Arima, T/F6674655 or in USA, Caligo Ventures, 156 Bedford Rd, Armonk, NY 10504, T914-2736333, 800-4267781, F914-2736370. Price includes all meals, rum punch, tax and service, 2 main house rooms colonial style, high ceilings, wooden furniture and floors, fan, bathroom, 24 standard rooms and bungalow in gardens, all designed to be private and secluded, facilities for the disabled, verandahs for birdwatching, 80% of guests in high season are birdwatching groups. **C** *Chateau Guillaumme*, 3 Rawle Circular, Arima, T6676670, joanwilliam@yahoo.com Run by Matthew and Joan William, 2 double and 2 triple rooms, bathroom, very clean, lower price for long stay, airport transfers, very helpful. **E** *Alta Vista*, up the road from *Asa Wright*, no phone on premises but T6298030, F6293262 for reservations. 6 self-contained wooden cabins, meals with advance notice, attractive swimming pool made by damming a stream, verandah overlooking forest, nice waterfall along a trail, TT$10.

Maraval **B-C** *Zollna House*, 12 Ramlogan Terrace, La Seiva, Maraval, T6283731, F6283737. Owned by Gottfried (Fred) and Barbara Zollna, small guest house, food varied with local flavour, special diets catered for, breakfast and dinner US$6 and US$12 per person respectively,

Barbara is very knowledgeable about Trinidad and knows all about B&B places. **C** *Carnetta's House*, 28 Scotland Terrace, Andalusia, Maraval, just off Saddle Rd, T6282732, F6287717, carnetta@trinidad.net. Children under 12 free, prices double during carnival, a/c, all rooms different sizes, some fridges, some kitchenettes, TV, phone, ironing board, carpets, family room, laundry, nice gardens, grow some produce, meals on request, parking, family atmosphere, videos for TV, lots of repeat business, maxi taxi will drop you at gate for extra US$0.50, run by Carnetta and Winston Borrell, the same couple own **C** *Carnetta's Inn*, 99 Saddle Rd, Maraval, T6225165/2884. 14 rooms in 2 adjacent properties, all rooms with mini-fridge, most with kitchenette, single, double, triple and connecting rooms, TV, a/c, phone, internet access, *Bamboo Terrace* restaurant serves local cooking, Shipwreck Bar for special cocktails. **C** *Monique's Guest House*, 114-116 Saddle Rd, Maraval, T6283334, F6223232, Moniques@carib-link.net, on way to golf course and north coast beaches. Easy access from city, maxi taxi US$0.50, 10 rooms in main house, 10 more over the hill, large rooms, different sizes sleep 4/5, a/c, TV, phone, some kitchenettes, good food in restaurant, clean, attractive, facilities for the disabled, Monica and Michael Charbonné are helpful and hospitable. **C** *Villa Maria Inn*, 48A Perseverance Rd, Haleland Park, Maraval, T6298023, F6298641, villmar@tstt.net.tt 20 rooms, bar, golf course within walking distance, games room pool, dance floor. **C-D** *Jireh's Guesthouse*, 109 Long Circular Rd, Maraval, T6282337, 6221915, www.trinidad.net/jireh Kitchenette

It can be hard to get a hotel room on the N coast in the low season when many places shut; self-catering may be difficult with few shops, no bank, no car rental

North coast AL *Timberline*, includes breakfast, dinner, tax and service, T6382263 for reservations. 2 large rooms in former manager's house on old cocoa plantation, a few cabins, very basic, rustic, mainly used by religious groups, on peninsula, fantastic sea views, track down to secluded beach, peaceful, isolated, vegetarians catered for. See page 927 for position.

    Maracas L-AL *Maracas Bay Hotel*, T6691914, F6691643, west of beach. Includes breakfast and dinner, 36 a/c rooms with shower, each with porch overlooking bay, clean but rather characterless and spartan, nature trails, watersports.

    Blanchisseuse B *Vista del Mar*, Paria Main Rd, Blanchisseuse, c/o Cheryl/Robert Lall, Lensyl Products Ltd, Western Industrial Estate, Trincity, T662-7534/3626, lensyl@trinidad.net. 2 self-contained apartments. **B-C** *Laguna Mar Nature Lodge*, at milepost 65½ just before suspension bridge over Marianne River. *Cocos Hut* restaurant attached, owned by Fred Zollna, close to beach and lagoon, see Beaches and watersports, 10 rooms with 2 double beds, bathroom, jogging trail, write c/o Zollna House, 12 Ramlogan Terrace, La Seiva, Maraval, or T6283731, F6283737. **C** *Second Spring*, 13 Damier Village, Blanchisseuse, PO Box 3342, Maraval, T6643909, F6234328. Cottage or 3 studios including breakfast and service, at milepost 67¾, rustic, comfortable, in gardens on clifftop with wooden walkway, spectacular views of coast, beaches in walking distance, restaurant 5 mins' walk, owned by Ginette Holder who is friendly and hospitable, excellent value. **C** *Surf's Country Inn*, Lower Village. Good restaurant on hill above coast road, 3 rooms including breakfast, owners plan 6 cabanas to sleep 4, nice furnishings, picturesque, small beach below, T6692475. **C** *The Almond Brook*, Upper Village, Paria Main Rd, Blanchisseuse, T6420476. 2-bedroomed cottage on beach and 'couples retreat' up the hill, both same price but latter includes breakfast. **B** *Mount Plaisir Estate Hotel*, Hosang St, **Grand Riviere**, on bay of same name on north coast, T6708381, F6804553, info@mtplaisir.com 10 beachfront rooms, breakfast, nature trails, restaurant. *Matura Beach*, Grand Riviere. A wonderful place to stay in small open-air rooms, mosquito nets provided, that open onto the turtle watching beach.

Balandra Bay At milepost 23 on the Toco Main Rd, north of Balandra Bay is Mr Hugh Lee Pow's **E** *Green Acres Guest House*, on a farm backed by the ocean. 3 good meals a day included, very kind and restful. *Manzanilla Calypso Inn*, ¼ mile off main road where road joins beach, on Calypso Rd at south end of Manzanilla, T6685113, T6685116. The only hotel, run by Meena Singh and her daughter Arisa, 10 motel-style rooms, large dining room overlooking scenic part of the beach, meals on request, nice place.

Mayaro on the southeast coast has beach houses to rent but check their condition, some are unacceptable. **C** *Azee's*, at 3½ mile mark Guayaguayare Rd, Grand Lagoon, Mayaro,

T6309140, F6304619. 5 rooms, restaurant, not quite respectable. **C-E** *Harry's*, Grand Lagoon, south end of Mayaro. Right on beach (plastic litter), nice grounds, rather peculiar building, apartments range in size from tiny room with double bunk bed, kitchenette, bathroom, a/c, TV, to larger units, some with verandahs, watch out for TT$50 service charge. **C** *Mrs Paria's*, guest house, just beyond the BP/Amoco compound. Self-contained room, TV, breakfast, beautiful modern home.

San Fernando There is not a lot of choice, **B** *Royal Hotel*, 46-54 Royal Rd, T6524881, F6523924, royal@tstt.net.tt A/c, kitchenette, lovely hilltop garden. **AL-B** *Tradewinds*, 38 London St, St Joseph Village, San Fernando, T6529463, F6538733. 13 rooms, kitchenette, bar, restaurant. **AL** *Farrell House Hotel*, Southern Main Rd, Claxton Bay, near San Fernando, T6592230, F6592204. A/c, swimming pool, kitchenette, restaurant, good view of the Gulf of Paria, popular with visiting oil men. **D** *Mikanne Hotel and Restaurant*, 15 Railway Av, Plaisance Village, Pointe-a-Pierre, T/F6592584. 13 rooms, a/c, private bath, meal plans, TV on request, pleasant, convenient for oil refinery and Wild Fowl Trust. At La Brea near the pitch lake is a hotel called *The Hideaway*, some rooms a/c, OK but not for the faint hearted, rooms available for 3, 12 or 24 hrs.

The Bed and Breakfast Cooperative of Trinidad and Tobago, Cruise Ship Complex, Wrightson Rd, Port of Spain, T6272337, lists a number of establishments in Port of Spain, the suburbs, Carenage, Tunapuna, Arima and Blanchisseuse. If arriving by boat, the Seaman's Mission, opposite the immigration office, has been helpful in finding hotel rooms.

Port of Spain At the main hotels where you can expect to pay US$15 in a nice setting with imaginative menus, eg *Tiki Village* in the *Kapok Hotel*, T6226441. Serves good Polynesian and Chinese food, nice Chinese lunchtime buffet. The *Hilton* Sunday brunch buffet is good value at TT$66 plus 15% VAT and 10% service and use of pool, the food here is of an international standard but breakfast is uninspiring often with stale bakeries despite popularity as business meeting place. *Rafters*, 6 Warner St, Newtown, T6289258. Pasta, burgers, salads or more elaborate local and seafood, good, bar and restaurant have different menus. Recommended. In the *Normandie* complex, Nook Av, *La Fantasie*, for fine dining, T6241181, and *Café Trinidad*, lovely baking smell, good for breakfast or tea, both pricey. Also outside, *The Breakfast Shed*, see below, women come from the main location to serve lunch. *Boticelli* at the City of Brand Bazaar, Valsayn, T6458733. *Apsara*, an Indian restaurant at the Grand Bazaar shopping complex just outside Port of Spain. *Le Chateau de Poisson*, 30 Ariapita Av. Specializes in seafood, T6226087. *Veni Mangé*, 67A Ariapita Av, T6244597. Small, friendly, good food include vegetarian dishes. Open Mon-Fri 1130-1430, dinner Wed only 1930-2230. *Il Colosseo*, 47 Ariapita Av, T6233654. Good Italian food. *Tamnak Thai*, 13 Queens Park East, T6250647. First attempt to introduce Thai food into Trinidad, with chefs imported from Bangkok. *Roxan's*, Corner Ariapita Av and O'Connor St, Woodbrook, T6224425. A new Arabic restaurant closer to the downtown area. *Nouvelle Creole*, corner of Ariapita and Corinth, Woodbrook. Well-prepared, nice formal service, in elegantly restored gingerbread house, about TT$70 for lunch including beer and coffee. *Kam Wah*, 74-76 Maraval Rd. Developing a reputation as not just another Chinese restaurant. *Little Lisbon*, Long Circular Rd. Brought Portuguese food to Trinidad. *The Rotisserie*, Long Circular Rd. *The Swan Chinese Restaurant*, Maraval Rd. Smart, but good value restaurants including *Woodford Café*, 62 Tragarete Rd. Open 1100-2200, Mon-Sat, Creole fare, US$4-6, T6222233. At 6 Nook Av is *Solimar*, T6246267. International, reasonable prices, good service, outdoor dining, excellent food, reservations advisable and essential at weekends. *Ali Baba*, T6225557, on first floor level in Royal Palm Plaza shopping mall on Saddle Rd, Maraval. Open-air dining with a roof, Arabic and other dishes, US$10 and upwards, excellent service, popular, run by a Lebanese, Joe. Nearby, in the *Royal Palm Suite Hotel* is the *Buccaneer's Cove* restaurant, specializing in international and local food, T6285086, and next door is the *A Pang* Chinese restaurant, T6227212. *Gourmet Club*, upstairs at Ellerslie Plaza, Maraval, T6285113. Italian, expensive but good, nice decor, open 1100-2300 weekdays, Saturday 1800-2300. *Café Gordon*, 39A Gordon St, T6275514. Breakfast 0730-1100, lunch 1100-1500, small, pleasant, Indian-owned,

Eating

different lunch menu every day with choice of 2 dishes, usually TT$10. If you've a yen for the best pepper shrimps in the Caribbean, the Chinese *Hong Kong City Restaurant*, 86A Tragarete Rd, is the place, good food but rather snooty service. *Asian Moon*, 37 Henry St, Port of Spain, T6232467. Another of the many Chinese restaurants, its attraction is its central location. *Davises*, 100 Oxford St, T6250144. Specializes in 'new island cuisine', combining classical gourmet cooking with fresh local ingredients. *Jenny's* on the Boulevard, 6 Cipriani Blvd. Wide variety of dishes, but try the crab back. *Buccoo Rouge*, Level 2, West Mall, Westmoorings, T6324072. Good French cuisine and seafood.

Fast food outlets including *Mario's Pizza Place*, Tragarete Rd and other outlets are average to awful. *Joe's Pizza*, St James. Good, also other Italian dishes. *Pizza Burger Boys*, Frederick St, and Ellerslie Plaza, Boissiere Village, Maraval (for takeaway T6282697, best of its type, will deliver to boatyards and marinas). The first *Pizza Hut* opened in Curepe but the largest one in the world is *Pizza Hut Roxy*, which used to be a cinema, central. *Kentucky Fried Chicken* in most cities and towns, better than you might expect. *Royal Castle*, 49 Frederick St and other locations throughout Trinidad. Chicken and chips with a local flavour. All along Western Main Rd in St James there are lots of cafés, snack bars and restaurants, all reasonably priced, lots of choice. The *Pelican Inn*, Coblenz Av, Cascade. Serves food, but is mainly a pub, hugely popular (late arrivals at the weekend have to park 600m away). *New Shay Shay Tien*, 81 Cipriani Blvd, T6278089. Recommended. *Singho*, Level 3, Long Circular Mall, St James, T6282077. Chinese food. *Valpark*, Valpark Shopping Plaza, Churchill Roosevelt Highway, Curepe, T6624520. Also Chinese. *De Backyard*, 84 Picton St. Local dishes. *Golden Palace*, 212 Southern Main Rd, Marabella, T6586557. Also Chinese, very good. *Imperial Garden*, Highland Plaza, Glencoe, T6636430. 'Authentic' Chinese food. Also *China Palace II*, Ellerslie Plaza, Maraval, T6225866. For Chinese food in San Fernando, try *Soongs Great Wall*, 97 Circular Rd, T6522583, round the corner from the *Royal Hotel*. Very good, the distinctive, Trinidadian version of Chinese food. At the cruise ship harbour, *Coconut Village*, good food, cheap. *Breakfast Shed*, opposite *Holiday Inn* and sometimes called *Holiday Out*, a big hall with several kitchens where locals eat, US$2.50 for very substantial lunch with juice. *Hot Shoppe* has by far the best rotis, see Food. Next to the Maraval Rd branch, the jerk chicken/jerk pork places have good, spicey Jamaican-style food. The **Town Centre Mall** and **Voyager Mall** on Frederick St have indoor halls with a varied and good selection of stands selling cheap food of different nationalities during the day, seating in the middle. **Colsort Mall** is similar but not so good. *Willie's Ice Cream*, branches in Arima, Montrose, Mid Centre Mall, Coffee St, Marabella and Tunapuna, and franchises in other places, tropical fruit flavours. If you like good bagels and speciality breads, try *Adam's Bagels*, 15A Saddle Rd, Maraval, or 34 Henry St, Port of Spain, T62-BAGEL.

Chaguaramas *Pier One*, T6344472, F6344556. Like country club, restaurant, conference facilities, family club, marina, seafood, live entertainment at weekends, open 1100-2300, popular at weekends, pool, kayaks, dinghies, fishing area. *Anchorage*, Point Gourde Rd, T6344334. For seafood, open 1100-2400 Mon-Sat, dancing, live entertainment some evenings, popular with yachties. *Pisces*, TTYC. Moderately priced local food and special nights, call for reservations. *Windjammers*, TTYA. Fast food and inexpensive local dishes after sailing with TTYA members. *The Bight*, Peake's, bar and restaurant with outdoor dining overlooking the Chaguaramas anchorage.

North coast *Timberline*, T6382263, off the coast road to Maracas. Renovated cocoa house on promontory, down very steep track, gourmet local food, grow own herbs and some fruit and vegetables, path down to small beach, very peaceful, lovely view, lots of wildlife, accommodation available. At **Blanchisseuse**, *Surf's Country Inn*, North Coast Rd, T6692475. Good value, delicious meals, beautiful setting, changing rooms available. *Cocos Hut*, also on coast road at Mile 65½ by Marianne River. Small, friendly, no menu, but usually a choice of fish or meat dishes, slow service but all food freshly cooked; both these restaurants offer rooms. For afternoon tea (and other meals by reservation) *Pax Guesthouse* on Mt St Benedict, above Tunapuna. Where tea is a tradition and all the bread, cakes, jam, honey etc are handmade by the monks, wholesome and tasty, lovely views of Trinidad from patio. *The Grand Bazaar*, near Caroni Bird Sanctuary. Has good, authentic Indian food. *Baha's on the Bay*, Western Main Rd, Carenage, T6372222. International cuisine. *Bougainvillea*, 85 Rivulet Road, Brechin Castle, Couva, T6364837. Chef claims to specialise in 'American, Italian, Spanish, Creole, Chinese and seafood delights'.

Bars and clubs Trinidad abounds in evening entertainment. Monday local song and dance at the *Hilton* is less authentic in atmosphere than the steel band concerts on Friday at the same venue. Entrance US$2. For those wishing to visit the places where the local, rather than tourist, population go, anyone in the street will give directions. Though the atmosphere will be natural and hospitality generous, it will not be luxurious and the local rum is likely to flow. *Chaconia* on Saddle Rd has live music on Friday and Saturday. *Moon Over Bourbon Street*, West Mall, has a cocktail lounge and live local entertainment at weekends. The *Bel Air* near the airport has live entertainment on Saturday night. Other discos and clubs including *Cascade Club*, music for dancing on Friday and entertainment on Saturday, near *Normandy Motel*, St Ann's. *The Anchorage*, Point Gourde Rd, live bands Friday, Saturday, also at *Pier One* and the *Base*, just opposite, *Small Boats*, Chaguaramas. *The Parrot*, Grand Bazaar, Uria Butler Highway, Valsayn. *The Golden Star*, Store Bay, good disco, the *Upper Level Club*, West Mall, Westmoorings. *The Attic Pub*, Shoppes of Maraval, Saddle Rd. *Club Coconuts* in *Cascadia Hotel*, St Ann's, disco, popular with young people. *Chameleon*, Valpark Shopping Plaza, Valsayn. *MOBS Two*, Chaguaramas. *The Pickle House*, Abercromby St, orange building, different types of music on different nights, New Orleans jazz, rhythm and blues, local music, Latin American and panang in the run up to Christmas. *The Tunnel*, 89 Union Rd, Marabella near San Fernando and in Chaguanas. For spicier entertainment, go to the *International* (Wrightson Rd). *Mas Camp Pub*, Woodbrook. Nightly entertainment including calypso and steel band, best place to see live calypso out of season (cover charge usually US$2). The Silver Stars Steel Orchestra (formed in the 1950s) can occasionally be seen in rehearsal (check beforehand) at the Panyard, 56 Tragarete Rd, Newtown, Woodbrook, Port of Spain. Silver Stars plays at local parties, cruise ships or on the beach, workshops for individuals or groups can be arranged, contact Michael Figuera, T/F6287550. For late drinking and music, *Pelican* (down hill from *Hilton*), 2-4 Coblentz Av, Cascade, T6247486. Lively, good crowds especially Fri, Sat, open from 1800. Also lively, *Smokey and Bunty's* in St James.

Theatres *Queen's Hall*, 1-3 St Ann's Rd; *Little Carib*, White and Roberts Streets; *Central Bank Auditorium*, Eric Williams Plaza, Edward St. In San Fernando, *Naparima Bowl* reopened after a lengthy period of renovation; the folk theatre of the South National Institute of Performing Arts (T6535355). See press for details of performances. See Culture section in Background, page 957.

Cinemas Two cinemas: **Globe** and **Strand**, at Park Plaza on Park St and Tragarete Rd. Another cinema, **De Luxe,** at north end of Frederick St. They are very cheap and occasionally show something good. Audiences are audibly enthusiastic, particularly for sex and violence.

Most shops take US dollars at a reasonable exchange rate. The main Port of Spain shopping areas are Frederick St, Queen St, Henry St and Charlotte St (fruit and vegetables), less exciting but pleasanter than Long Circular Mall at the junction of Long Circular Rd and Patna St, St James, West Mall, Cocorite, Port of Spain, Ellerslie Plaza on the way to Maraval, close to Savannah. Purchases can be made at in-bond shops in Port of Spain and at the airport. There is a huge selection of duty-free shops, accessible to both arriving and departing passengers, selling everything, including computers.

Markets offer wide varieties of fruit. Handicrafts can also be purchased at markets. In Port of Spain there is a craft market in Independence Square with leather, hand painted T-shirts etc. There are also street vendors on Frederick St and elsewhere. Crafts also at East Mall on Charlotte St and at the cruise ship complex. There are several kilns in the Freeport area, turn off the Uriah Butler Highway before the Hindu temple for Chase Village where most of the pottery is unpainted; the potters sell it on to others for decoration and glazing. Good quality local pottery in a variety of designs is available from Ajoupa Pottery, owned by Rory and

Nightlife
St James is normally livelier at night than Port of Spain

Shopping
Bargains can be found in fabrics, carvings, leather & ceramics

Trinidad & Tobago

Bunty O'Connor. You can get it in Port of Spain but a wider selection can be viewed at their kiln at Freeport, central Trinidad; T6225597 at Port of Spain shop at Ellerslie Plaza, or T6730604 at kiln/factory. Batik can be bought at many places including the Ajoupa pottery shop at Ellerslie Plaza. Althea Bastien, a designer and batik maker, has a shop at her house, 43 Sydenham Av, T6243274, difficult to find. The Central Market is on the Beetham Highway. Do not purchase turtle shell, black coral, or other protected, shell items.

For music, try *Crosby's Music Centre*, 54 Western Main Rd, St James, or *Rhyner's*, 54 Prince St, Port of Spain. Production costs are a problem and despite being the main music outlets in this island of music they frequently have no stock. Also *Arcade Record Store*, Castries Rd, Scarborough, will make tape compilations to your specification.

For bookshops *Metropolitan Books*, Colsort Mall, has a good selection; *R I K Services Ltd*, Queen St, Port of Spain, and 104 High St, San Fernando, mostly school books; *Ishmael M Khan and Sons*, 20 Henry St, Port of Spain. Black literature at *Afrikan World Books* and *Kultural Items*, Park Plaza on Park St and St Vincent St, T/F6272128, good selection, history, contemporary issues. There are second hand bookshops in Town Centre Mall and various side streets. Generally the selection is poor, particularly for Caribbean novels which is disappointing in a country with such a long literary tradition.

Directory **Banks** In Port of Spain: *Republic Bank Ltd* (formerly Barclays, gives cash on Visa card), 11-17 Park St, T6254411, F6230371, also at airport, very slow, open 0800-1100, 1200-1400, on Fri 0800-1200, 1500-1700. *Royal Bank of Trinidad and Tobago*, 3B Chancery Lane, T6234291. *Bank of Nova Scotia*, Park and Richmond Sts, T6253566. *Citibank*, Queens Park East, T6251040. *Citicorp Merchant Bank*, same address, T6233344. *Western Union Money Transfer*, Uptown Mall, Edward St, Port of Spain, T6236000, and 10 other locations in Trinidad and Tobago. Banks in the West and Long Circular Malls are open until 1800. Peake's Yacht Yard has a branch with a 24-hour cash machine and a teller from 0900-1400.

Communications **Post**: TT Post, now a corporation being run by New Zealanders, has its main office on Wrightson Rd, Port of Spain, and is open 0800-1600, Mon-Fri. Stamps for Europe TT$3 upwards. **Telephone:** The main *Telecommunications Services of Trinidad and Tobago Ltd* (TSTT) office on Frederick St operates international telephone and fax. The service for international calls has improved greatly, with direct dialling to all countries. The fax service shuts from 2300 Sat to 2300 Sun and on public holidays except for 'life or death' messages. This means no faxes for 3 days over Carnival. Phone cards are available for TT$15, 30, 60, or 100 plus 15% VAT, from TSTT offices, banks, airport, cruise ship complex etc. Home Direct Service for AT&T, Sprint and MCI available from TSTT, Cruise Shop Complex in Port of Spain, TTYC, TTYA and Peake's Yacht Yard. In Tobago, at airport and TSTT office. **Internet** Cyber cafés: *Interserve* (near West Mall), *Mariner's Office* (Crews Inn Marina), *New Hope Computing*, Sweetbriar and Maraval Rd (provides drinks with hourly computer time rental).

Embassies and consulates (Port of Spain), **Brazilian** Embassy, 18 Sweet Briar Rd, St Clair (T6225779, F6224323). **British** High Commission, 19 St Clair Av, St Clair, T6222748, F6224555, a very smart, modern building, its upper floors have an excellent view over Queen's Park Oval. **Canadian** High Commission, 3-3A Sweet Briar Rd, St Clair (T6226232); US Embassy, 15 Queen's Park West (T6226371/6, F6285462), 0700-1700. **Danish** Consulate, 20-22 Tragarete Rd, T6251156, F6238693. **Dutch** Embassy, Life of Barbados Building, 69 Edward St, PO Box 870, T6251210/1722, F6251704. **French** Embassy, 6th floor, Tatil Bldg, Maraval Rd, T6227446, F6282632. **German** Embassy, 7-9 Marli St, PO Box 828 (T6281630/2, F6285278). **Guayanese** Consulate, 3rd floor, Park Plaza, Corner of Park and St Vincent Streets, T6271692, F6233881. **Jamaican** High Commission, 2 Newbold St, St Clair, T6224995/7, F6289180. **Japanese** Embassy, 5 Hayes St, St Clair, T6226105/5838, F6220858. **Venezuelan** Embassy, 16 Victoria Av (T6279823/4), 0900-1300, 1400-1600, Consulate at same address, T6279773/4, visa section only open mornings. Changes of address, and other representatives, can be checked at the Ministry of External Affairs, T6234116/60.

Hospitals There are hospitals in Port of Spain, San Fernando, and Mount Hope, as well as several district hospitals and community health centres. The Port of Spain General Hospital is at 169 Charlotte St, T6232951. Recommended doctors are Dr Harry N Singh, Main Rd, Kelly Village, Caroni, T6691854 and Dr Pham Van Cong, 195c Western Main Rd, Cocorite, T6228972.

Tourist information Local tour operators *Trinidad and Tobago Sightseeing Tours*, run by Gunda Busch-Harewood, 12 Western Rd, St James, T6281051, F6229205. Pleasant and quite reliable, will arrange accommodation and car hire and has a representative on Tobago (Margaret Hinkson, T6397422, F6229205). Gunda also offers evening tours and is a good contact for liming, parties etc. She uses *in Joy Tours* who run sightseeing tours, deep sea fishing, panyard visits etc, T6337733, F6228974. *The Travel Centre Limited*, Level 2, Uptown Mall, Edward St, Port of Spain, T6235096, F6235101 (PO Box 1254) is an American Express Travel Service Representative. *The Davemar Reservations Agency*, 2 Aylce Glen, Petit Valley, T6377583, run by Marjorie Cowie, can arrange accommodation in hotels, guest houses or self-catering and organize sightseeing tours. Walking tours, cave exploration, horse riding in the Northern Range, kayaking expeditions and other trips off the beaten track can be arranged with *Caribbean Discovery Tours Ltd*, 9B Fondes Amandes Rd, St Ann's, T6247281 run by Stephen Broadbridge together with Merryl See Tai of the Kayak Centre, T6292680 (see page 921), camping (in basic-luxury tents or cabins) or lodging in guest houses arranged for longer trips, tailor-made tours. Roger Neckles, a local bird photographer, runs specialist minibus tours for birdwatchers. *Banwari Experience Ltd*, 64 Prince St, Port of Spain, T624-TOUR, F6751619, banwari@tstt.net.tt, run by Andrew Welch, offers cultural and nature tours, hiking, history, birdwatching, carnival.

Tobago

Tobago is not as bustling as Trinidad but tourism is booming. Nevertheless, it is ideal for those in search of relaxation. The tourist area is concentrated on the southwest end and about six miles from the capital, Scarborough. There are small hotels and guest houses scattered all around the island, however, offering peace and quiet in beautiful surroundings. The forest on the central hills provides a spectacular backdrop for the many horseshoe bays around the coast and there is good walking, sailing and diving. Tobago is 26 miles long and only nine miles wide, shaped like a cigar with a central 18-mile ridge of hills in the north (the Main Ridge, highest point 1,890 ft) running parallel with the coast. These northeast hills are of volcanic origin and the southwest is flat or undulating and coralline. The population is concentrated in the west part of the island around Scarborough. There are small farms but the main ridge is forested and quite wild. The climate is generally cooler and drier, particularly in the southwest, than most parts of Trinidad.

Scarborough

Getting there On Tobago, taxi fares are clearly displayed as you leave the airport: to Crown Point US$6, Pigeon Point US$7, Scarborough US$10, Mt Irvine, Roxborough US$33, Speyside US$40, Charlotteville US$45. **Getting around** Scarborough is small enough to walk around, but for trips to the suburbs or further afield.

*Ins & outs
See page 912 for
further transport
details*

Sights

In Scarborough itself the **Botanic Gardens** on the hill behind the Mall are worth a visit. There are also some interesting buildings, such as the House of Assembly on James Park (built in 1825), and Gun bridge, with its rifle-barrel railings. New development has included a new deep water harbour and cruise ship terminal. Scarborough Mall is modern, concrete and rather tatty but most activity is around here: the tourist office, post office, library and bus station as well as the market, where you can find local varieties of fruit and vegetables, clothing, meat and fresh coconut water. There are banks on Main St. Just off Main St, George Leacock has turned his home into a museum, quite interesting.

*The town is pleasant
but perhaps not worth
an extended visit*

Above the town is **Fort King George**, which is well-maintained and has good views along the coast. This fort reflects the turbulent history of the Caribbean.

Building commenced in 1777, continued under the French in 1786 (Fort Castries), renamed Fort Liberté in 1790 after the garrison revolted, recaptured by the British in 1793, returned to France in 1801 and when the island was ceded to Britain in 1802, it was named Fort King George in 1804. It was decommissioned in 1854. There are two of artist Luise Kimme's huge wooden figures in the middle of the parade ground which are very attractive. You can visit her workshop on Sunday but its best to ring first, T6390257.

At the Barrack Guard House is the **Tobago museum**, with an excellent display of early Tobago history including Amerindian pottery, shells, military relics, maps and documents from the slave era. ■ *Mon-Fri, 0900-1700, doors close 1630, adults US$0.50, children US$0.15.* The gardens are attractive and well kept and there are excellent views over Scarborough. There are a number of historic buildings here which can be seen apart from the museum. Buildings include the Officers' Mess, the Magazine (almost hidden under an enormous silk cotton tree), the Bell Tank (still with water in it and an amazing echo), a fine arts centre which has displays by local artists as well as a permanent exhibition. A number of cannon mounted on metal garrison gun carriages can also be seen. At the same location is a hospital through which you have to drive to get to the fort.

Tobago

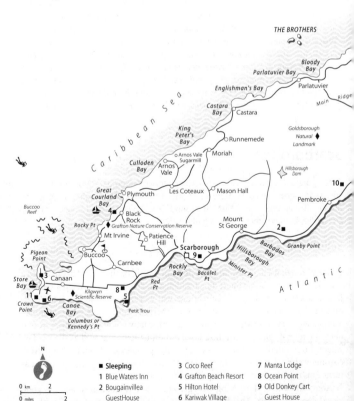

■ Sleeping	3 Coco Reef	7 Manta Lodge
1 Blue Waters Inn	4 Grafton Beach Resort	8 Ocean Point
2 Bougainvillea	5 Hilton Hotel	9 Old Donkey Cart
GuestHouse	6 Kariwak Village	Guest House

Around the island

If you are driving around Tobago, the 1:50,000 map, usually available from the tourist office in Scarborough, at US$3.50, is adequate, although note that many of the minor roads are only suitable for four-wheel drive. If you are hiking, get the three 1:25,000 sheets, not currently available in Tobago but obtainable from the Lands and Survey Division, Richmond St, Port of Spain, or a good map shop abroad. It is possible to walk anywhere. There is book of trails.

East from Scarborough

Off the coastal road you can go to the Forest Reserve by taking a bus from Scarborough to **Mount St George** and then walking or hitching to **Hillsborough Dam**. The lake is the drinking water supply for the island so no swimming, you may find a man to take you on the lake in a rowing boat. It is a lovely forest setting. A four-wheel drive vehicle is necessary if you want to drive but walking there is recommended. From there continue northeast through the forest to **Castara** or **Mason Hall** on an unpaved, rough road. A guide is not necessary, there is only one path. Birdwatching is excellent (oropendulas, mot-mots, jacamans, herons) and there are cayman in the lake, but look out for snakes (none of them poisonous). Alternatively, take a taxi to Mason Hall (ask the taxi to drop you at the road for the Hillsborough dam) and walk to Mount St George via Hillsborough Dam, which is easier walking as the track is on the level or downhill, about nine miles. By Mount St George (Tobago's first, short-lived principal town, then called George Town) is **Studley Park House** and **Fort Granby** which guards Barbados Bay.

The road continues through **Pembroke** and **Belle Garden** and nearby is **Richmond Great House**, now a hotel. It has a lovely view but is not as 'great' a house as some of the plantation houses on other islands. **Roxborough**, the island's second town, also on the Windward coast, is worth a visit. The **Argyll River** waterfalls near Roxborough comprise four beautiful falls with a big green pool at the bottom, a 10-minute walk upstream from the road which can be very muddy. You can't miss them because of all the rather overpriced and pushy guides standing in the road.

A good walk is the road from Roxborough to Parlatuvier and Bloody Bay through the Main Ridge Forest Reserve. There is hardly any traffic and you go through singing forests with masses of birds (early morning or late afternoon is the best for spotting great numbers) including cocricos, collared trogon, mot-mots, jacamans, humming birds. After the five-mile marker is a semi-circular trail in the forest called Gilpin's Trace. There are great views from the hut at the top of the road. If you walk Gilpin's Trace and want to try other, lesser known trails, Kelton

ST GILES OR
MELVILLE
ISLAND

North
Pt

Man
O'War
Bay

Corvo Pt

Charlotte
-ville

nse Fourmi

Eastern Tobago NP

GOAT IS

Pigeon
Peak

1

7

Speyside

Tyrrel's Bay

orest   Reserve

LITTLE
TOBAGO

Delaford

oxborough   King's Bay
Waterfall

Pedro Point

King's
Bay

rgyll
aterfalls

Queen's
Bay

Belle Garden

Prince's Bay

RICHMOND ISLAND

Ocean

10 Richmond Guest
House
11 Tropikist

Trinidad & Tobago

Thomas is a recommended guide, contact him through the airport information centre. Wordsworth Frank is also good, he runs glass bottom boat tours too. Beyond Roxborough is **King's Bay**, with waterfalls near the road in which you can swim. These are sometimes dry, however, so a refreshing swim cannot be guaranteed.

Speyside & Little Tobago From the fishing village of Speyside you can visit Little Tobago, a forested islet off the northeast coast, and sanctuary for birds. There are wild fowl and 58 species of other birds, including the red-billed tropic bird found here in the largest nesting colony in the north Atlantic. Boats across cost US$12.50 (includes a guided tour of the islet and snorkelling). There are lots of glass bottomed boats and fish and coral to see, boatmen will find you (see page 920). Go early in the morning to see the birds. If you want to camp, you are supposed to have prior permission from the Forestry Division at Studley Park, T6394468. They also have a rudimentary camp on the main ridge by the Roxborough-Parlatuvier road, which can be used by arrangement. At Speyside, you can sling a hammock near the government centre on the beachfront. It is well-lit but it may be windy. A night-guard might keep your belongings under lock.

From Speyside you can climb **Pigeon Peak**, at about 1,900 ft the highest point on the island. There are two routes up the hill through the forest, the shorter one is steeper than the longer, so both take about three hours. There is also a track on the Speyside Road from Charlotteville, 100m on the right before the turning to Flagstaff Hill. This is suitable for a four-wheel drive to begin with. After about 30 mins' walk you clamber down into a stream bed and up again, from where it becomes a rough, steep path through old banana plantations and then woodland. There is no trouble following the path here, there are even markers cut into or painted on to trees, and there are many birds. However when the ground becomes flatter it becomes confusing. A guide therefore is essential and Lebeque Jack has been recommended. Remember there are lurid, yet true, tales of tourists being lost up here for days. The actual summit is above the woodland, through grass and small shrubs, and has a trig point. From the top you can see the north and south coasts and offshore islets.

Charlotteville A trip to Charlotteville in the northeast is recommended. There are maxi taxis from Scarborough (TT$10, three a day but not on Saturday, when the Adventist drivers do not work, for the return journey you can arrange to be picked up). Magnificent

Scarborough

Buccoo: Goat-racing centre of the world

Think of famous sports arenas around the world: Lords and cricket, Twickenham and rugby, Henley and rowing and the name of Buccoo doesn't loom large. But Buccoo is the goat-racing centre of the world. The Buccoo Goat Race Festival was started in 1925 by Samuel Callendar and has had several venues around the village before the current purpose built track behind the beach facilities at Buccoo was constructed in 1985. Easter Tuesday was chosen because Good Friday and Easter Saturday were already taken for marble pitching, Easter Sunday for the Moravian Love Feast and Easter Monday for horse racing.

The course is about 100 metres long and there is a maximum of 10 goats per race. Each jockey has to wear the silk of the goat's owner, white shorts and bare feet. Jockey and goat proudly walk around the ring with Mr Patterson giving the crowd helpful guidance on the form before walking down to the start (highly amusing and more so as the afternoon goes on and the rum flows). There is betting but it is all rather discreet. The goats are then loaded into the starting stall (accompanied by much banter from the commentators perched precariously in the judges' box). A yellow flashing light signifies that they are under

starters orders, the gates flip open and the race is on. Goats lead with the jockey running behind holding the goat on a short length of rope. This is no gentle jog, the goats are very fast and the jockeys give Linford Christie a good run for his money. Of course the jockey has little control over his goat and the best fun is had when the goat suddenly veers across the other runners. The finish is often chaotic with all 10 runners nearly ending in the grandstand at the end of the course. This may be one reason why the race was moved from the Battery. The closeness of the cliffs overhanging the sea made it unpopular. The races are often very close and the judges may be called on to study video evidence before declaring the winner.

The afternoon is interspersed with various cultural events and the occasional crab race. Huge sound rigs on the street above the course compete with each other and sometimes drown the commentators. If you are lucky the Prime Minister will attend. Rum and beer flow and the whole day is topped off by an enormous jump up until late into the night.

Patrick Dawson

Trinidad & Tobago

views are afforded on the way and the village itself is on a fine horse-shoe bay with a good beach, lifeguard, good swimming and snorkelling and two dive shops. The Americans erected a radio tracking station in the Second World War on Flag Staff Hill high overlooking Charlotteville (take the rough track off the main Speyside-Charlotteville road about one kilometre). There are several seats and a bandstand here. Half way along the rough road to Flagstaff Hill there is a cattle path to the right. Follow this as it descends and curves to the left. Near the bottom it meets another, wider trace (trail). Turn left and this will eventually bring you back to Charlotteville. It is a pleasant, shaded walk. From Charlotteville, it is a 15-minute walk to **Pirate's Bay**, which is magnificent and unspoilt and good for snorkelling. Also adjacent is **Man O'War Bay**. **Campbellton Bay** is a 30 to 40-minute walk from Charlotteville (ask locally for directions) through dense forest to a secluded beach, mostly used only by fishermen. It is fairly easy to hitch a ride from Charlotteville to Speyside.

The road between Charlotteville and Plymouth along the Caribbean coast has been improved but four-wheel drive is needed for part of the way and then only in dry weather, or in summer, maybe. Best on a mountain bike or on foot. The stretch between L'Anse Fourmi and Charlotteville is usually impassable and a notice says you travel at your own risk (work has been abandoned on road improvements, supposed to be completed sometime). You are much better off on foot and it is a wonderful hike. In fact hikers are opposed to any paving of the road. The views are worth the trouble with lots of lovely bays beneath you. Get a taxi to L'Anse Fourmi and walk (a comfortable four hours) along the track to Corvo Point, Hermitage (bush rum for sale), Man O'War Bay and Charlotteville. There terrain is undulating. Bird

The north coast

life is plentiful, including parrots, and you may see iguanas. The stretch of road between L'Anse Fourmi and Moriah is smooth, traffic is light and it is very picturesque. Take water with you.

At the southwest end of the island there are many hotels and resorts. The Crown Point area is developing rapidly and parts feel like a building site, with associated litter. At **Store Bay** are the ruins of small **Milford Fort**, and brown pelicans frequent the beautiful but crowded beach, which is a good place to watch the sunset. The fort was once Dutch (Bella Vista) but was overrun by the Indians. The British maintained a small battery here but it is now no more than a nice garden. **Pigeon Point** has the island's most beautiful beach, clean and with calm water, though US$2 is charged for adults and US$0.50 for children for admission as the land is private; a wall has been built to stop you walking along the foreshore and groynes built by the owners have caused beach erosion. There are huts, tables and benches, lockers, bars, shopping, boat hire and watersports. It is another good place to watch the sunset.

From **Mount Irvine Bay**, where there is an attractive, palm-fringed championship golf course (the hotel of the same name has a good beach – surfing) you can walk up to **Bethel** (about two miles), the island's highest village, for excellent views across the island. Another beach which is well worth a visit is **Turtle Bay**.

The main town on this coast is **Plymouth**, with **Fort James** overlooking **Great Courland Bay** (site of the Courlander settlement in the 17th century). Destroyed several times, the present fort was erected in 1800. Also here is the Latvian Monument, designed by a local artist, it was erected in 1976 and represents "Freedom". A much-quoted attraction in Plymouth is the enigmatic tombstone of Betty Stevens (25 November 1783), which reads: "She was a mother without knowing it, and a wife, without letting her husband know, except by her kind indulgences to him."

Hidden in the forest some miles from **Arnos Vale** is the **Arnos Vale Sugarmill**, dating from 1880; a recommended excursion, it is possible to hitchhike. The Arnos Vale Waterwheel Park has a small museum, gift shop, restaurant and stage where shows are put on. It is difficult to continue along this coast by public transport, Plymouth to Parlatuvier is not a recognized route. You have to go instead via Roxborough, with a lovely journey from there through the forest. Check that there is transport back in the afternoon as there is nowhere to stay in Parlatuvier.

The small village of **Castara** on the coast can be seen in 10 minutes but is a pleasant place to visit. There is a small bay with a sandy beach and a snorkelling reef, or a 10-minute walk inland will take you to an easily accessible waterfall. Eating places are readily available and there is accommodation.

Buccoo Reef   Glass-bottomed boats for visiting this undersea garden leave from Pigeon Point, Store Bay and the larger hotels nearby. Boats may be cheaper if hired from Buccoo Village. The charge is US$6 for 2 to 2½ hrs, with shoes and snorkel provided; wear swimming costume and a hat. Longer trips with barbecue cost around US$20, worth it if you eat and drink plenty. The dragging of anchors and greed of divers have tarnished the glory of this once marvellous reef, though, and you may prefer to make the trip to Speyside where there are also glass bottomed boat trips over a pristine reef. Elkhorn and other corals have been badly damaged by snorkellers and divers walking on them. The reef is now protected by law; it is forbidden to remove or destroy the corals or other marine life. Boat trips also include the **Nylon Pool**, an emerald-green pool in the Caribbean. Boats leave between 0900 and 1430, depending on the tide. Be selective in choosing which boat – and captain – you take for the trip; some are less than satisfactory (Selwyn's *Pleasure Girl* has been recommended, so has Archie and Mala's *Come to Starcheck*, others include Hew's Tours, Hewlett Hazel, T6399058, F6397984, Kenneth Christmas, Buccoo Reef Cooperative, Buccoo Point, T6398582, or after 1900, T6398746). From Scarborough to Buccoo by bus is TT$2. Taxis also go to Buccoo.

Essentials

Tobago Plantations, T6371025, www.tobagoplantations.com is a new 750-acre development around Petit Trou Lagoon which, when completed will have a hotel, villas, condominiums bungalows, 18-hole championship Jack Nicklaus golf course, marina, shopping centre, wildlife refuge and tropical fruit plantation. In 2000 the 200-room *Tobago Hilton* will open as part of the development, all rooms with seaview and no more than 30m from white, sandy beach.

Sleeping
There are many cheap guest houses & many people take in visitors; ask at any village store

Near Crown Point LL *Coco Reef*, PO Box 434, T6398571, F639-8574, cocoreef-tobago@ trinidad.net, in North America T800-2211294. Modelled on a Bermudan hotel, peach and white walls, red roof, 96 rooms, 20 suites, 17 garden villa suites, 3 villas, on man-made beach, pretty view of Pigeon Point, height of luxury, several restaurants, small pool, conference facilities, spa, gym, tennis, shops, dive shop, sail boats, close to airport and in main hotel area. Beyond Pigeon Point is **AL** *Lagoon Lodge*, Bon Accord, T6398555, F6390957. Approached down poor track, isolated, split level cabins sleep 2 adults and 2 children, fully equipped, TV, music, phone, fan, a/c, airy, comfortable, ideal for self-catering, owner provides fruit, eggs, milk, maid/cook available, set in 4 acres of gardens with chickens, peacocks, rhea, boardwalk through mangroves to sea lagoon, jetty with hammock, kayak and sailboat, very private, tranquil. Mosquitoes in wet season. Turn right out of the airport and take the first right for **AL-A** *Kariwak Village*, PO Box 27, T6398545/8442, F6398441, kariwak@tstt.net.tt Very nice, compact rooms in cabins, restaurant with excellent food, no beach, small pool, no radios or TV, meeting facilities, owners involved in the arts, exhibitions held here, yoga and therapy, retreats. **AL-B** *Tropikist*, PO Box 77, Crown Point, T6398512, F6390341. 33 a/c rooms with balcony, pool, loungers, large lawn, swings, restaurant overlooks sea, small beach but not suitable for swimming, painted white with lots of bougainvillea, right by airport. **A-C** *Belleviste Apartments*, Sandy Point, T/F6399351, bellevis@tstt.net.tt 20 self-contained apartments, kitchenette, pool, near airport.

B *Jimmy's Holiday Resort*, Store Bay, T6398292, F6393100. Apartment, bars, eating places, shops nearby. **B-C** *Arthur's By The Sea*, Crown Point, T6390196, F6394122, arthurs@trinidad.net Kind and helpful, a/c, pool, 4 min walk from safe beach. **B-C** *Conrado Beach Resort*, Milford Extension Rd, between Store Bay and Pigeon Point, T6390145. Price including breakfast, beach front, standard or superior rooms, some small, some with balconies, TV, phone, some roadside view, priced accordingly, restaurant on beach for breakfast, inside for night-time, good snorkelling offshore on small reef, fishing boats moored outside, family owned, excellent service. **B-C** *Crown Point Beach Hotel*, PO Box 223, T6398781/3, F6398731, crownpoint@trinidad.net Studios and cabins, pool, *Best of Thymes* restaurant, excellent food. **B-C** *Sandy Point Village*, T6398533, F6398534. 44 large rooms and suites, some split level, TV, kitchenette, balcony, quiet a/c, in pleasant gardens, pool, beach rooms under restaurant open on to sea, poor beach, most people go to Store Bay, airless disco in basement, *The Deep*, music goes on until early hours. If you turn right out of the airport, and take the first right, you come to **D-E** *Store Bay Holiday Resort*, T6398810, F6399733. 5 min walk, do not be fooled by taxi drivers who will charge US$5 for the ride, about the cheapest in this area, self-catering only, 16 apartments, clean, well-furnished, kitchen, gardens, night time security guard, small pool, friendly, good value. Close by is **B-C** *Toucan Inn*, PO Box 452, T6397173, F6398933. Includes tax and service, African style huts, good food and entertainment.

C-D *Coconut Inn*, Store Bay Local Rd, Bon Accord, T6398493, F6390512. 6 rooms, 10 self-contained apartments, pool. **C-D** *Jetway Holiday Resort*, 100m from airport terminal, T/F6398504. Can be noisy until after 2200, 9 pleasant self-contained units with cooking facilities, friendly, helpful, a few min walk to Pigeon Point and Store Bay. A bit further from the main road is **C-D** *Golden Thistle*, T6398521, F6397060, clyde@trinidad.net. Quiet location, 36 rooms around pool, lawn or neither, single storey, a/c, TV, phone, bath tub and shower, functional but dark, no atmosphere. **C-D** *James Holiday Resort*, Crown Point, T/F6398084. Standard room or apartment, **L2** 3-bedroom apartment maximum 12 people, car and jeep rental, credit cards accepted, 2 min walk from airport, a/c, shower, TV, patio or balcony, res-taurant. **C-D** *Surf Side Holiday Homes*, Milford Rd Extension, Store Bay, T6393521, F6284707, www.trinidad.net/surfside 30 self-contained apartments, a/c, walking distance to beaches. **D** *Serenity Apartments*, 14 Centre St, Canaan, T639-0753/2370, F6390753, serenapt@tstt.net.tt Run by Miss Selma Alfred, 5 double and triple rooms with bathroom, kitchenette, a/c, balcony, daily cleaning, 2 min walk to buses, evening meals by arrange-ment, airport pick-up, tours arranged. **E** *Plaza 2*, Milford Rd, Canaan. No kitchen facilities, away from the beach but buses stop outside. **E** *Spence's Terrace*, Crown Point, T6398082. Room, kitchenette, bathroom, balcony, new and fresh. Recommended. **F** *Balgobin & Dorris Guest House*, and taxi service, John Gorman Trace, Milford Rd, Crown Point, T6397328. 15 min walk from airport and beach, nice, clean rooms with bathroom and cooking facilities, mosquito nets on windows, fan, quiet and safe, friendly owners. There are lots of guest houses and small hotels along the road between the airport and Pigeon Point. **F** *Lewis Villa*, T6398022. Small units with kitchen, good value. **F** *Classic Resort Guest House*, walk straight out of airport turn left at junction and follow road round, past Milford Fort, following signs for Sandy Point, T6390742. Double room with kitchen and lounge with TV, friendly.Near beach and airport, Spence is helpful, car rental available.

Lowlands area **AL-B** *Palm Tree Village*, Little Rockly Bay, Milford, T6394347, F6394180. A/c, 18 2-4-bedroom villas or 20 hotel rooms, kitchenettes, pool, small beach, quite smart but lacking atmosphere, nightclub attached, tennis, fitness centre, conference room, horse. **AL-C** *Ocean Point*, Milford Rd, Lowlands, T/F6390973, www.ocean point.com Studios sleep 3, suites fit 5, dive packages available, a/c, TV, pool, sundeck, 2 min walk from sea, trans-port needed, family-run, friendly. Recommended. In USA T800-6924094, UK T020-87414894. On the same road, **B-C** *Hampden Inn Guest House*, Lowlands Post Office, Milford Rd LP 171, T/F6397522. B&B, German spoken, standard or superior rooms all on ground floor, ham-mocks, large bathrooms, restaurant/bar, bike hire, TV, dive packages, no pool. **B** *Coral Reef*, T6392536, F6390770, PO Box 316. 17 rooms, 18 apartments, 30 years old and showing it, basic, dark corridor, no view, hard beds, old carpets, pool, a/c. **C** *Viola's Place*, Birchwood Tri-angle, Hampden, T/F6399441, violasplace@hews-tours.com 14 self-contained rooms, kitchenette, pool, airport pick-up.

Mostly guest houses or CPs **Scarborough** Highly recommended is *Glenco Guest House*, Glen Rd, Scarborough (rates negotiable according to length of stay), clean, basic, mosquitoes, no fans, breakfast, T6392912. About ½ mile south of Scarborough is the **B-C** *Old Donkey Cart House Resort*, 73 Bacolet St, T6393551, F6396124. Run by Gloria Jones-Knapp, 2 min from beach on hillside with seaview. Includes breakfast, tax and service, charming rooms in old house or apart-ments in new building, restaurant, good food, pool. **B** *Horizons Tobago Apartments*, 89 Bacolet Point, T/F7091648, www.toben.com 1 and 2-bedroomed apartments, a/c, large pri-vate pool, good amenities. 10 min drive from Scarborough is **C** *Ocean View*, John Dial, T6396796. Recommended. Under same management is **C** *Windy Edge*, Concordia, 12 min drive from the harbour. 600 ft above sea level overlooking the Atlantic and the Caribbean, spacious grounds, quiet, highly recommended, includes breakfast, evening meals by arrangement US$25-30, route taxis pass by, T6395062. **D-E** *Della Mira Guest House*, 36 Bacolet St, PO Box 203, T6392531, F6394018, on outskirts of town, below road. Seaview, 14 rooms, restaurant, pool. **D** *Miriam's Bed and Breakfast*, or *Federal Villa*, Crooks River, T6393926. 3 rooms, shared bath, fan, modest but clean and comfortable, 7-min walk to harbour, run by friendly and helpful Miriam Edwards, secretary of the Bed and Breakfast Association. **E** *Sea Breeze Motel*, Milford Rd, Scarborough, T6396404. Spot-lessly clean, bathroom, TV, on seafront west of the port, recommended as base for tour-ing. **E-F** *Hope Cottage*, Calder Hall Rd, corner of Ottley St, not far from hospital, T6392179, F6397550. 15 rooms, 3 with private bathroom, fan, pleasant, kitchen can be used, mini-market nearby, spacious public rooms, bar, restaurant, verandah, homely, peaceful, popular with students, entrance between 2 tamarind trees, brought from India and planted when original house was built in early 19th century.

Contact the **Association** c/o *Federal Villa*, 1-3 Crooks River, Scarborough, T6393926, F6393566, or the Tourism Development Authority on Tobago; the brochure lists 14 properties, mostly in the southwest or near Scarborough, about US$25d.

Windward coast L-A *Blue Waters Inn*, Batteaux Bay, Speyside, T6604341, F6605195, bwi@bluewatersinn.com An isolated and delightfully unsophisticated hotel, 38 rooms, 1-2 bedroom bungalows and self-catering units, caters for people who want to sit on the beach, bird watchers and divers, includes tax and service, dive packages with Aquamarine Dive on site, tennis, very pretty bay, no other development, view of Little Tobago. **L-B** *Manta Lodge*, Windward Rd, Speyside, PO Box 433, Scarborough, T6605268, F6605030, info@mantalodge.com. 22 standard, superior or loft rooms, rather sterile, loft has no view, a/c essential as hot under roof, superior rooms, though cheaper are better, with balcony, view and more air, small pool, bar, restaurant, caters mainly to divers, packages available with Tobago Dive Experience. **L-B** *Richmond Great House*, T/F6604467 (see page 941), overlooking Richmond Bay. Lovely, airy, quiet, colonial elegance, polished wood floors, suites in main house or newer rooms downstairs, pool, owned by Professor of African history. **A-B** *The Speyside Inn*, Windward Rd, Speyside, T/F6604852, speysideinn@trinidad.net 6 rooms, 2 cabins, lovely airy rooms, nicely furnished, excellent value, tax and large breakfast included with home made breads, dinner by reservation only, small beach across road, view of Little Tobago, close to *Jemma's* restaurant. **C-E** *Bougainvillea Guest House*, by Fort Granby, Studley Park, T6602075, F6602133. Includes breakfast and airport transfer, owned by Hilton McFarlane who also lectures in medicine at UWI, beautiful location on hillside overlooking bay, lots of birds, fruit trees, stress free, all rooms different, some small, some family rooms, some shared bathrooms, some new rooms, beach 3 min walk, small pool. **C** *Paradise Villa*, Pembroke Main Rd, Pembroke, T6644933. 2 rooms, kitchen, dining room. One **F** guest house in Roxborough, ask for Mrs Carter, Police Station Rd, 2 rooms, kitchen, shower, quiet, friendly.

Charlotteville B *Man O'War Bay Cottages*, T6604327, F6604328, pturpin@tstt.net.tt 10 cottages, sleep 4, minmum 2 nights, spacious, well-equipped kitchen, right on beach with tropical gardens behind, barbecue facilities, expensive shop with limited range, check your bill carefully. **C-E** *Cholson's Chalet* has rooms or 1-3 bedroomed apartments separated from the beach by the road, contact Hewitt Nicholson (T6392847) or Pat Nicholson (T/F6398553), the price sometimes rises after you have moved in. **D** *Morre's*, Bellaire Rd, Charlotteville, T6604799, contact Susan Simon. 4 double rooms, 1 2-bedroom self-contained apartment, all with kitchen facilities. **E** Mrs May Williams has ground floor apartment, 2 rooms sleep 6, communal kitchen, bathroom, house faces jetty, between 2 shops painted blue, quite pleasant. **E** Marshall and Michelle Jack (twins), 13A Pirates Bay Rd, T6605923, 6604419. Shared bathroom, no soap or towels but very clean, use of good kitchen, so close to sea that you could jump in from window, so don't stay there if the noise of the sea keeps you awake. **F** *Alyne*, very friendly, clean, comfortable. Ask around for private accommodation, it is available, eg Mrs McCannon's house in Bellaire Rd, not luxury but OK. For rooms or small houses to rent try asking in *Phebe's Ville View* restaurant, see below.

Castara L-AL *Cuffie River Nature Retreat*, Rennemede, T/F6789020, cuffiriv@tstt.net.tt 10 rooms, lounge bar, jacuzzi, hot tub. **D-E** *The Naturalist Beach Resort*, Castara Village, T6395901, F6605357, natural@trinidad.net 5 rooms, beach nearby, snorkelling. **E** *Blue Mango*, T6392060. Owned by friendly Colin Ramdeholl, simple but charming, good walking and swimming nearby, eating places in the village.

Culloden Bay LL *Footprints Eco Resort*, T6600118, F6600027, www.footprint secoresort.com Set in 62 acres of nature reserve, 2 villas, 4 studio apartments and honeymoon retreat, more planned, all on stilts, well-equipped, palm roofs, wooden, solar powered with a/c, jacuzzi, great views over sea, good fixed menu, salt water pools at low tide, good snorkelling on reef, guests encouraged to plant a tree, very noisy corcico birds at dawn calling across the valley, Mia Persad and staff willing to take you around if you have no transport. You get to it from Golden Lane which passes the enormous silk cotton tree that is supposed to be the grave of Gan' Gan' Sarah.

Arnos Vale L-AL *Arnos Vale Hotel*, PO Box 208, T6392881, F6393251. 38 rooms, beautiful surroundings in tropical forest, great birdwatching, Mot Mots and other birds come to be fed at 1600, afternoon tea-time, hospitable, dive shop, new 30-room complex being built at site of old water wheel. **D** *Arnos Vale Vacation Apartments*, Arnos Vale Road, Plymouth, T/F6391362, trade-info@tidco.co.tt Run by Victor Forde, 1-2 bedroom apartments, kitchen, large living room area, fully furnished, beautiful garden with fruit trees and tropical birds, transport to airport, car hire available.

Plymouth LL-L *Mount Irvine Bay Hotel and Golf Course*, PO Box 222, T6398871, F6398800. Rooms, suites or garden cottage, luxury furnishings, TV, phone, pool, beach, sauna, gym, mediocre food at *Sugar Mill* restaurant, tennis, gardens of 16 acres. **LL-L** *Grafton Beach Resort*, PO Box 25, Stonehaven Bay, Black Rock, T6390191, F6390030, grafton@trinidad.net 108 rooms, luxury. Highly recommended. A/c, pool, TV, friendly and efficient service, good food at restaurants, breakfast recommended, excellent beach front location, facilities for the disabled. **LL** *Le Grand Courlan* is its sister resort next door, T6399667, F6399292, legrand@trinidad.net 78 luxury rooms, 10 1-bedroom suites, 8 garden rooms with jacuzzis, all have phone, fan, a/c, hairdryers, minibar, handsome furnishings, shops, pools, restaurants, business centre, health spa, fully equipped gym, very upmarket compared with other hotels on Tobago. Next door is **LL** *Plantation Beach Villas*, Stonehaven Bay Rd, Black Rock T6399377, F6390455, villas@wow.net 6 villas each with 3 bedrooms, verandah, maid service, pool, beach bar. **LL** *Sanctuary Villa Resort*, Grafton Estate, PO Box 424, T6399556, F6390019, www.sanctuaryvillas.com, just inland. Luxury villa development, 42 room hotel planned, fantastic views across island to Pigeon Point and Buccoo Reef from hill, bordered by 260-acre bird sanctuary. **AL** *Rex Turtle Beach Hotel*, PO Box 201, Plymouth, T6392851, F6391495. 125 rooms, overlooking garden, railings on upper floor balconies unsafe for children, pool, on beach, tennis, a/c, service and management good, Sunday West Indian buffet highly recommended, especially the curried crab. **AL-D** *Cocrico Inn* and *Courland Bay Villa*, T6392961, F6396565, cocrico@ tstt.net.tt 16 rooms, kitchenette or 4-room villa and apartment, restaurant, swimming pool, friendly, clean, excellent meals, laundry service. **C** *Turtle View Residence*, 32-33 Courland Estate, Black Rock. 8 rooms. **C-E** *King Solomon's Mine Holiday Resort*, T6392545. Owned by Leroy Solomon, at the end of George St off Shelbourne St where buses run, rooms or apartments, kitchen, beautifully furnished, good view from upstairs balcony, popular with Germans. **B** *Adventure Eco Villas*, Arnos Vale Road, T6393839. Advertised as an 'adventure farm and nature reserve' to appeal to eco-conscious travellers. **B** *La Belle Creole*, Mt Irvine, PO Box 372, T6390908. Run by Mrs Gerhild Oliver, English, German, French and Italian spoken, right by golf course, 5 min walk from beach, bed and breakfast, dinner on request, queen sized beds. *Massiah's Cottage*, Mt Irvine. Reasonable rates, T6394444 after 1600, owner works for Liat. **B-C** *Golf View Apartments* , Buccoo

Junction, Mt Irvine, T/F6390979. 15 apartments, 6 rooms, pool. **B-C** *Old Grange Inn*, PO Box 297, Buccoo Junction, Mt Irvine, T6390275, F6399395, grangeinn@trinidad.net 18 rooms, pool, restaurant, bar, a/c. **B-D** *Blue Horizon*, Jacamar Drive, Mt Irvine, T6390432/3, F6395006. 14 self-contained rooms, kitchenette, pool. **D** *Villa Fords*, Sherwood Park Trace, Carnbee, T6390113. 3 self-contained apartments, 1 room. **E** *Green Acres*, Daniel Trace, Carnbee, T6398287. Clean rooms with shower, safe, some with kitchens, includes breakfast, delicious local food, friendly family, US$4-5 taxi service. Highly recommended. **E** *Michael Baker's* apartments, Daniel Trace, Carnbee, T6398243. Owner is chief of lifeguards and singer. **E-F** *Rolita Tea Hut*, Old Grange Rd, Mt Irvine, opposite *Blue Horizon*. Small guest house run by Roy and Pat Cousins, rooms with shower and WC, pool, meals available 0700-2100 daily, also lunch boxes, 20 min walk from beach. T6397970. In Buccoo on Battery St, **F** *Aunty Flo's*, T6399192. Nice, friendly, run by Mrs Flora Howie, very little maintenance, plumbing erratic. **F** *Tante Loo*, Plymouth. Basic but friendly guest house run by sons of Tante Loo, who died in 1991.

Around Store Bay and Crown Point There are a number of restaurants, many have tables outside near the beach. The *Beach Bar* has music all day on Sat, and a barbecue from 2000-2400, for US$17 per head for drinks and small portions of fish and chicken, poor value unless you drink a lot. *Miss Jean's*, US$2 and less for all kind of 'ting', a full meal with drinks for 2 costs less than US$10, crab and dumplings are a speciality but the crabs are woefully small because of overfishing. *Best of Thymes*, now at *Crown Point Beach Hotel*. Good food, red snapper recommended, Indian influences. *Miss Esme*, T6388323. Flying fish and bake. *Golden Star*, Crown Point, T6390873. Restaurant and bar, lobster thermidor and grilled king fish in creole sauce. *Copratray*, Store Bay Local Rd, Bon Accord. Fri night barbecue a speciality. *Taj Terrace*, corner Pigeon Point Rd and Store Bay Rd, T6399020. One of the few Indian restaurants on Tobago. *Eleven Degrees North*, Store Bay Rd, Crown Point, T6390996. Food served on tables claimed to be works of art. *Dillon's Seafood Restaurant*, Crown Point, T6398765. Open daily from 1800 except Mon, good food and service, though a little expensive. The restaurant at the *Kariwak Village* has interesting, excellent food and drinks, good salads, excellent punches, well served. Nearby is *Golden Spoon*, junction of roads to Scarborough and Pigeon Point, T6398078. Open for breakfast, lunch and dinner, local dishes. *Arthur's By The Sea*, Crown Point, T6390196, for local and Italian food. *Bonkers*, at Store Bay Local Rd, Crown Point, T6397173. Serves creole food, live music, popular. *Eleven Degrees North*, Crown Point. Fashionable bar and restaurant, live music Thu. *Joy's*, in Buccoo. Small, friendly, good local food for US$3.50, barbecue on Wed for US$2.50. *La Tartaruga*, Buccoo Bay, T6390940. Italian restaurant café-bar, PO Box 179, excellent Italian food, limited menu, expensive, reservations essential. *Papillon*, Bucco Junction and Mt Irvine, T6399773. Local and seafood dishes.

Patinos, Shirvan Rd, T6399481. Run by Kenneth and Marcia Patino with their son as chef, excellent food, delicious West Indian platter at lunchtime, evening steel band once a week, reservations needed. Good accommodation also. *The Starting Gate*, Shirvan Rd. Good food, pool and table football. *Shirvan Mill* on Shirvan Rd. Specializes in seafood and steaks, expensive and romantic, T6390000. *Arnos Vale Waterwheel*, Franklyn Rd, Arnos Vale. Caribbean food, T6600815. The *Cocoa House*, Footprints Eco Resort, Culloden Bay, Culloden, T6600118. Good Caribbean seafood.

The main hotels have good restaurants, worth eating at even if you're not staying there, eg *Tamara's*, Coco Reef Resort. Exceptional cuisine but expensive. *Neptune Seafood*, Grafton Beach Resort. Excellent. *Leandro's Mediterranean Bistro*, Le Gran Courlan, Black Rock, T6399667. Offers Mediterranean pasta, seafood. *The Pinnacle*, Le Gran Courlan. Good. *The Ocean View*, Grafton Beach Resort. Good.

The *Black Rock Café* on Black Rock main road, T6397625. Recommended for very good food, slow service, very busy. *Under the Mango Tree*, Black Rock. Very tasty local food, US$17 for full meal. *The Seahorse Inn*, next to Grafton Beach Resort. Excellent dinners, extensive menu. *Peacock Mill*, Friendship Estate, Canaan, T6390503. Restaurant and bar in old sugar mill with lots of peacocks wandering around and coming to be fed at around 1700, their squawks accompany the jazz sometimes featured outdoors under the trees. *Indigo*, 2 Horseshoe Ridge, Pleasant Prospect, Grafton, T6399635. Local and foreign dishes.

Eating

Most of the food from the huts on the beach is reheated

Trinidad & Tobago

Charlotteville *Phebe's Ville View*, Charlotteville. Nice view of the bay, very good and cheap meals, try the prawns if available, dumplings and curried crab also recommended, very friendly, rooms and apartments for rent at reasonable prices, Phebe also has a laundry and special prices for people on yachts. *Gail's*, Charlotteville, on seafront as you walk to Pirate's Bay. Breakfast and dinner, no lunch, all fresh, very tasty, delicious vegetables and salad, Gail is a genius with fish, very friendly.

Speyside *Jemma's Sea View*, Speyside, T6604066, on a tree top platform by the beach. Good, filling lunch or dinner, fixed menu but 2 choices, TT$40, slow service, nice atmosphere, no alcohol and closed Saturday (Adventists), you can get hassled here for boat trips. *The Fish Pot*, *Blue Waters Inn*, T6602583. Sea food, as name implies.

Scarborough The *Blue Crab*, at the corner of Main St with Fort St, Scarborough, T6392737. Specializes in local food, very good lunch but slow service, reasonable prices, nice view over harbour. *Kings Well Inn*, corner Burnette and Carrington Streets, T6393883. Run by Kim and Cheryl Cleveland, famous for bake and buljol and homemade ginger beer. *Rouselles*, Bacolet St, T6394738. One of the best, seafood, short but excellent menu, very busy Saturday. *La Laconda*, 73 Bacolet St, T6393551. Local and international cuisine in tropical garden atmosphere. *Old Donkey Cart*, Bacolet, T6393551. Good food, European wines, nice shady garden setting or in old house if it is raining, closed Wed except Dec-Apr. *De Bamboo Bar & Restaurant*, Milford Rd, Scarborough, next to *Sea Breeze Motel*. Recommended, lobster good value, 3-course meal US$20. *Buddies Café* in the Mall, Scarborough. Is reasonable, T6393355. *Pizza Boys*, opposite the Customs House near the port in Scarborough. Pizzas, burgers, chicken and doughnuts.

Nightlife Though not as lively as Trinidad, Tobago offers dancing in its hotels. The Buccoo Folk Theatre gives an attractive show of dancing and calypso every Thu at 2100. There is a *Tobago Folk Performing Company*. In Scarborough, *El Tropical* is a club frequented mostly by locals. It has a live show every Sat night at about 2330. Also *JG's Disco*, nightly. *Michael's Bar*, Black Rock, recommended for friendly evening entertainment. The *Starting Gate Pub*, Shirvan Rd, is recommended. Look in on the entertainment spots in the Crown Point area – *Copra Tray* at Store Bay Local Rd; *The Deep*, Sandy Point Village and *Toucan Inn* & *Bonkers*, Store Bay Local Rd. There are also the *Golden Star*, Milford Rd, Store Bay and *The Lush*, Shirvan Rd, Store Bay. Don't miss Sunday School on Buccoo Beach, a big party starting early every Sunday evening with live music, followed at about 2300 by a DJ playing until early in the morning. Entertainment is available every night of Tobago Race Week, mostly at Crown Point but also at *Grafton Beach* or *Grand Courlan* hotels.

The **cinema** in Scarborough is good value, US$1.10 for two films, but the audience can be a bit noisy. On a quieter level, the Public Library in Charlotteville is stocked with all the literature in the English language you ever wanted to read and some German books too.

Shopping On Tobago, you can get excellent handicrafts at the *Cotton House*, Bacolet St, just outside Scarborough (taxi US$2.50), batik studio, high standard, pictures and clothes at reasonable prices. They also have an outlet at Sandy Point. Local batiks also at the *Backyard*, Milford Rd, Crown Point and locally produced artefacts at *Shore Things*, Pigeon Point Rd. *Francis Supermarket* at Crown Point is not particularly well stocked but is open Monday-Saturday 0800-1800, Sunday and holidays 1000-1400. The main supermarket is *Penny Savers* on main road at Milford, good range including pharmaceuticals, open long hours and holidays, has ATM (blue machine).

Directory **Banks** On Tobago, there are no banks or ATMs in the north of the island. ATMs can be found at the airport, *Penny Savers Supermarket* on Milford Rd and in Scarborough. Known locally as 'blue machines', they accept Visa, Plus, Mastercard and Cirrus. **Communications Telephone** There is a TSTT telephone office in Scarborough. Home direct service for AT&T, Sprint and MCI available from TSTT office and at the airport. **Hospital** Scarborough (T6392551). **Tourist information** Local travel agents *AJM Tours* at the airport, T6390610, F6398918, day trips on Tobago and to Margarita, Angel

Falls, Grenada and the Grenadines. Peter Gremli is a recommended tour guide, friendly, knowledgeable and popular. Taxi drivers have set rates for sightseeing tours and can be more flexible than an organized tour. A day tour on Trinidad can include the Asa Wright Centre and the Caroni Swamp with sightseeing along the way. See also page 938.

Background

History

Trinidad was discovered by Columbus and he claimed it for Spain on his third voyage in 1498. Whether he named the island after the day of the Holy Trinity, or after a group of three hills that he spied from the sea is in dispute. At that time there were at least seven tribes of Indians living on the island: the Arawaks, Chaimas, Tamanaques, Salives, Chaguanes, Quaquas and Caribs, the last being divided into four sub-groupings, the Nepoios, Yaios, Carinepagotos and Cumanagotos. The peaceful Arawaks were the majority and lived in the south part of the island, having originally come from the upper regions of the Orinoco river. The north part was populated by Indians of the Carib strain from the Amazon area who were aggressive and warlike. It was their hostility which prevented successful colonization until the end of the 17th century when Catalan Capuchin missionaries arrived. However, European diseases and the rigours of slavery took their toll on the Indian population and by 1824 there were only 893 Indians left on Trinidad. Today there are none.

Columbus' arrival

The first Spanish governor was Don Antonio Sedeño who arrived in 1530 but who failed to establish a permanent settlement because of Indian attacks. In 1592 the governor, Don Antonio de Berrio y Oruna, founded the town of San José de Oruna (now St Joseph). It was destroyed by Sir Walter Raleigh in 1595 and not rebuilt until 1606. In 1783 a deliberate policy to encourage immigration of Roman Catholics was introduced, known as the Royal Cedula of Population, and it was from this date that organized settlement began with an influx of mostly French-speaking immigrants, particularly after the French Revolution. Many also came from St Lucia and Dominica when these islands were ceded to Britain in 1784, others came with their slaves from the French Caribbean when slavery was abolished and from Saint Domingue after the war of independence there (eg the Compte de Lopinot, whose house in Lopinot has been restored, see page 928).

Spanish rule

British rule in Trinidad began in 1797 when an expedition led by Sir Ralph Abercromby captured the island. It was later ceded to Britain by Spain in 1802 under the Treaty of Amiens. (VS Naipaul's *The Loss of El Dorado* is a fascinating, if pessimistic, account of the early Spanish settlement, Sir Walter Raleigh's raid, and the early years of British rule). At this time large numbers of African slaves were imported to work in the sugar fields introduced by the French until the slave trade was abolished in 1807. After the abolition of slavery in 1834, labour became scarce and the colonists looked for alternative sources of workers. Several thousands of immigrants from neighbouring islands came in 1834–48, many Americans from Baltimore and Pennsylvania came in 1841, Madeirans came seeking employment and religious freedom and were joined by European immigrants, namely the British, Scots, Irish, French, Germans and Swiss. There was also immigration of free West Africans in the 1840s, but by 1848 this had ceased as conditions improved in their own countries. In 1844 the British Government gave approval for the import of East Indian labour and the first indentured labourers arrived in 1845 (Indian Arrival Day, 30 May, is now a public holiday). By 1917, when Indian immigration ceased, 141,615 Indians had arrived for an indentured period of five years, and although many returned to India afterwards, the majority settled. The first Chinese arrived in 1849 during a lull in Indian immigration. Initially these were men only and this

British rule

Trinidad & Tobago

naturally encouraged intermarriage, but later arrivals included women. In 1866 the Chinese Government insisted on a return passage being paid, and this put an end to Chinese immigration. Persistent labour shortages led to higher wages in Trinidad than in many other islands and from emancipation until the 1960s there was also migration from Barbados, Grenada and St Vincent.

Colonial Tobago

Tobago is thought to have been discovered by Columbus in 1498, when it was occupied by Caribs. He is said to have called the island 'Bella Forma'; the present name is a corruption of tobacco, which the Caribs used to grow there. In 1641 James, Duke of Courland (in the Baltic), obtained a grant of the island from Charles I and in 1642 a number of Courlanders settled on the north side. In 1658 the Courlanders were overpowered by the Dutch, who remained in possession of the island until 1662. In this year Cornelius Lampsius procured Letters Patent from Louis XIV creating him the Baron of Tobago under the Crown of France. After being occupied for short periods by the Dutch and the French, Tobago was ceded by France to Britain in 1763 under the Treaty of Paris. But it was not until 1802, after further invasions by the French and subsequent recapture by the British, that it was finally ceded to Britain, becoming a Crown Colony in 1877 and in 1888 being amalgamated politically with Trinidad. By some reckonings Tobago changed hands as many as 29 times because of its strategic importance and for this reason there are a large number of forts.

Dr Eric Williams

The first political organizations in Trinidad and Tobago developed in the 1930s, when economic depression spurred the formation of labour movements. Full adult suffrage was introduced in 1946 and political parties began to develop. In 1956, the People's National Movement (PNM) was founded by the hugely influential Dr Eric Williams, who dominated local politics until his death in 1981. The party won control of the new Legislative Council, under the new constitutional arrangements which provided for self-government, and Dr Williams became the first Chief Minister. In 1958, Trinidad and Tobago became a member of the new Federation of the West Indies, but after the withdrawal of Jamaica in 1961 the colony, unwilling to support the poorer members of the Federation, sought the same rights for Trinidad and Tobago. The country became an independent member of the Commonwealth on 31 August 1962, and became a republic within the Commonwealth on 1 August 1976. Dr Williams remained Prime Minister, his party drawing on the support of the majority African elements of the population, while the opposition parties were supported mainly by the Indian minority.

Defeat of the PNM

In 1986, the National Alliance for Reconstruction (NAR) ended 30 years' rule by the PNM which had been hit by corruption scandals, winning 33 of the 36 parliamentary seats in the general election. Six NAR members defected in 1989 to form the United National Congress (UNC), led by former Deputy Prime Minister, Basdeo Panday. The popularity of the Prime Minister, A N R Robinson, was extremely low and he was seen as heading an uncaring administration which alienated voters by its economic policies of cutting the public sector and other costs.

Return of the PNM

General elections were held on 16 December 1991, bringing another about turn in political loyalties. Patrick Manning, of the PNM, led his party to victory, winning 21 seats, while the UNC won 13 and the NAR was left in the cold with only the two Tobago seats. Elections for Tobago's House of Assembly, in December 1992, gave the NAR 11 seats and the PNM one seat, the same as in the previous assembly. By mid-term the Government was suffering from unpopularity and lack of confidence. Its economic policies were blamed for higher unemployment, lack of growth and rising crime. However, the opposition was not strengthened by the formation of three new parties, which were likely to split any anti-Government vote. The National Development Party (NDP) was launched in 1993 by Carson Charles, former leader of the NAR, after he failed in a second bid for the party's leadership. The Republic

Jamaat-Al-Muslimeen

On 27 July 1990 Trinidad was shaken by an attempted overthrow of the Government by a Muslim fundamentalist group, the Jamaat-al-Muslimeen, led by the Imam Yasin Abu Bakr. The rebels held the Prime Minister, A N R Robinson, eight of his Cabinet and other hostages, until their unconditional surrender on 1 August. A total of 23 people were killed in the disturbances and about 500 were injured (including the Prime Minister) during the bombing of the police headquarters, the takeover of the parliament building and TV station and subsequent rioting. Despite a promise of an amnesty, 114 Jamaat members were arrested and charged with offences including murder and treason. After taking their case to the courts their appeal was heard in 1992 and the amnesty was reinstated, leading to the release of prisoners. The Government's appeal against the decision was turned down by the High Court in 1993. It then turned to the Privy Council, which heard its case in 1994. The Judicial Committee of the Privy Council ruled that the amnesty was not valid, because the Muslimeen breached its conditions when they continued to hold hostages and make demands for four days after the amnesty was granted instead of ending their insurrection immediately. The Muslimeen will therefore receive no compensation for wrongful imprisonment but neither can they be rearrested and charged for offences committed during their rebellion.

Party (RP) was formed by the late Nello Mitchell, a former general secretary of the PNM, after he was expelled from the PNM for gross disrespect of the party. Third, Yasin Abu Bakr, leader of the Jamaat-al-Muslimeen, formed the National Vision Party in 1994. Two PNM MPs and one UNC MP died, causing by-elections to be held in 1994. One seat was won by the PNM, the two others by the UNC. The UNC, NAR and NDP announced a joint platform in July 1994, which led to the resignation of the leader of the NAR, Selby Wilson. At the end of 1994 another new party, the Movement for Unity and Progress, was set up by a former UNC MP, Hulsie Bhaggan.

UNC Government

In 1995 the economy began to improve and the Prime Minister took a gamble in calling early general elections to increase his majority. His tactic failed, however, when the UNC and the PNM both won 17 seats. Although the PNM received 48.8% of the vote compared with 45.8% for the UNC, Basdeo Panday formed an alliance with the NAR, who again won the two Tobago seats, and he was sworn in as Prime Minister on 9 November 1995. A lawyer and trade union leader, he was the first head of government of Indian descent. By February 1996 the PNM was reduced to 15 seats after defections from the party attributed to a lack of leadership. Both MPs became independents but immediately accepted government positions.

Greater autonomy for Tobago was anticipated as a result of the coalition with the NAR. Parliament passed a bill to amend the constitution allowing a constitutional role for the Tobago Assembly, which will now be responsible for state lands, town and country planning, customs and excise, housing, education and statistics. However, it still does not have legislative powers. In the December 1996 elections for the Tobago House of Assembly, the NAR won 10 seats, the PNM one and an independent one. Following the election of ANR Robinson to the presidency (see below) his seat in the House of Representatives fell vacant. A by-election was won by the NAR. The second NAR Tobago seat was lost to the NAR when the holder defected and became an independent. The PNM member lost his position as Minority Leader in the Assembly in February 2000, when Deborah Moore-Miggins, who had been elected as an Independent in December 1996, formed her own People's Empowerment Party (PEP). Elections are expected by the end of 2000.

Trinidad & Tobago

The people

Trinidad has one of the world's most cosmopolitan populations. The emancipation of the slaves in 1834 and the adoption of free trade by Britain in 1846 resulted in far-reaching social and economic changes. To meet labour shortages over 150,000 immigrants were encouraged to settle from India, China and Madeira. Of today's population of approximately 1,276,000, about 40% are black and 40% East Indian. The rest are mixed race, white, Syrian or Chinese. French and Spanish influences dominated for a long time (Catholicism is still strong) but gradually the English language and institutions prevailed and today the great variety of peoples has become a fairly harmonious entity, despite some political tension between blacks and those of East Indian descent. Spanish is still spoken in small pockets in the north mountains and French patois here and there. Catholics are still the largest religious group but Hindus are catching up fast. The Anglican Church and Methodists are also influential. There are many evangelical groups. Spiritual Baptists blend African and Christian beliefs; the women wear white robes and head ties on religious occasions. They can be seen performing the sea ceremony on the coast to the west of Port of Spain late on Sunday nights. Most East Indians are Hindu, some are Muslim, others have converted to Christianity, particularly Presbyterianism (Canadian Presbyterian missionaries were the first to try converting the Indian population). Tourism plays a small role in Trinidad's economy. In the 1960s and 1970s the official policy was to discourage tourism, and although this has now changed, visitors are still a rarity in some parts of the island, big hotels are set up for business visitors and some tourist services may be lacking. Nevertheless, Trinidadians are genuinely welcoming to strangers.

Tobago's population, mainly black, numbers about 51,000. The crime rate is catching up with Trinidad's but the people are still noticeably helpful and friendly. Tourism is a major source of income here and considerable investment has gone into hotels and infrastructure in the last few years; even a *Hilton Hotel* is being built.

Government Trinidad and Tobago became a republic within the Commonwealth on 1 August 1976 under a new constitution which provides for a President and a bicameral Parliament comprising a 31-seat Senate and a 36-seat House of Representatives. Tobago has its own 12-seat House of Assembly, which runs many local services. In February 1997 the first contested presidential election was won by ANR Robinson, the former prime minister and leader of the NAR. He was sworn in for a five-year term, succeeding Noor Hassanali, who retired after serving two terms. The electoral college which voted for the president is made up of the House of Representatives and the Senate.

The economy

Structure of production Petroleum and petroleum products dominate the economy, providing about a quarter of gdp, one fifth of government current revenue and three quarters of foreign exchange earnings. Three quarters of oil production comes from marine fields. Production is around 123,000 barrels a day but proven reserves are enough to last only 11 years. There is one refinery, at Pointe-a-Pierre, the other at Point Fortin having been mothballed. The island has substantial proven reserves of natural gas of 21.30 trillion cu ft, producing about 1.4 billion cu ft daily in 2000. These are used as a basic raw material for the production of petrochemicals such as methanol and ammonia and the provision of electric power throughout the country. New plants will raise annual methanol capacity to 2.97 million tonnes by 2001 and ammonia capacity to 3.45 million tonnes, making Trinidad and Tobago the world's largest exporter of both. Trinidad is rich in mineral deposits including asphalt from the pitch lake at La Brea on the southwest coast, gypsum, limestone, sand, gravel, argillite and fluorspar, but apart from the asphalt, which is used for road surfacing, they are not well developed.

The soil in Trinidad is remarkably rich and the first settlers had no difficulty in raising a variety of crops, with tobacco, sugar and cocoa being the major exports. Today, however, agriculture contributes 2.1% of gross domestic product and employs only 8.8% of the labour force. Agricultural exports have been broadened to include citrus fruits, coconut oils and flowers, and diversification of the traditionally sugar-based agriculture of the Caroni area with rice, pawpaw, other fruit and vegetables has led to improvements in supplies for the domestic market. Sugar production and exports grew in the early 1990s, but declined from 1994 because of poor weather.

Unemployment is most acute in the 15 to 19 age group, where about 43% are out of work. The crime rate has increased noticeably since the 1970s, particularly serious crimes and murders, many of which are related to drugs and gang killings.

A concerted attempt is being made to diversify the economy and lessen the dependence on petroleum. Tourism is becoming an important source of foreign exchange and the Government is actively promoting both islands abroad. Earnings from incoming tourism now comfortably exceed expenditure by Trinidadians abroad, thanks to a recession-induced slowdown in holidays abroad and increased visitor revenues. Stayover arrivals were 214,722 in 1999. Tobago now has just under 2,000 hotel rooms available, following an expansion in construction and more are planned, notably a 200-room Hilton hotel. The Government hopes that 3,600 more hotel rooms will be constructed in Trinidad (1,400 at present) and 1,200 more in Tobago by 2005. A new cruise ship complex was opened in August 1989 at Port of Spain. A similar terminal has been constructed in Tobago as part of the Scarborough harbour re-development project.

Recent trends Dependence on oil has led to wide fluctuations in the rate of economic growth, with the 1970s a period of rapid expansion and rising real incomes as oil prices soared, and the 1980s a decade of declining output and falling wages as the oil market retrenched. The recession in the oil industry exposed structural imbalances in the rest of the economy and the inability of agriculture, manufacturing or services to counter its effects.

Assistance was sought from the IMF in the context of debt rescheduling agreements with the Paris Club of creditor governments and with commercial banks. The Government also turned to the World Bank, the Inter American Development Bank and Japan for the new lending to support structural adjustment of the economy. Proceeds from the sale of state enterprises were to be used to reduce the outstanding external debt of US$2.4bn. The second standby agreement expired on 31 March 1991 and the Government did not seek a third IMF programme.

From 1990 the economy did begin to grow slowly after seven consecutive annual declines in gdp but it contracted again in 1992 and 1993. A liberalization of some foreign exchange controls in 1992 led to an easing of liquidity constraints and a return of some capital held overseas. In April 1993 the TT dollar was floated, with an initial depreciation of 26 to TT$5.75 = US$1, and a consequent rise in the rate of inflation, but then stabilized. By late 1996 and into 1997, the TT$ began depreciating again, crossing the TT$6 = US$1 threshold and reaching TT$6.27 = US$1 by the second quarter, largely because of an import surge, but since then it has stabilized. The economy was also liberalized in other ways, for example by lowering import tariffs, abandoning quotas, progressively reducing the tax rate and selling state companies to private investors. Foreign investment began to increase in 1995–96, led by inflows from the USA. Gdp increased by 6.9% in 1999, the highest level since the 1970s and far in excess of the average of 3.5% over the last 5 years. Growth was led by the energy sector which benefited from a resurgence in the oil price and the commencement of LNG production.

Culture

The most exciting introduction to the vivid, cosmopolitan culture of this Republic is, of course, Carnival, or 'De Mas', as locals refer to the annual 'celebration of the senses'. Background reading is a help for a visit at any time of the year. Some authors to investigate are CLR James, Samuel Selvon, Shiva Naipaul, all now deceased, as well as Shiva's more famous brother, VS Naipaul. Also, the historian and past prime minister Dr Eric Williams, Earl Lovelace and newcomer Valerie Belgrave (whose *Ti Marie* has been described as the Caribbean *Gone with the Wind*). Although the tradition of performance poetry is not as strong here as in, say, Jamaica (calypso fulfils some of its role), the monologues of Paul Keens-Douglas, some of which are on album or cassette, are richly entertaining and a great introduction to the local dialect or patois.

Alongside a strong oral/literary tradition goes a highly developed visual culture, reflecting the islands' racial melange. The most obvious examples are the inventive designs for the carnival bands, which often draw on craft skills like wire bending, copper beating, and the expressive use of fibreglass moulds. Fine painters and sculptors abound, too, although the only good galleries are small and commercial and located primarily in Port of Spain. Michel Jean Cazabon, born 1813, was the first great local artist (an illustrated biography by Aquarela Gallery owner Geoffrey MacLean is widely available). Contemporary work to look out for, often on the walls of the more enlightened hotels, restaurants and banks, includes paintings by Emheyo Bahabba, Pat Bishop, Isaiah Boodhoo, Francisco Cabral, LeRoy Clarke, Kenwyn Crichlow, Boscoe Holder and the fabled, controversial Mas' designer Peter Minshall, who designed the opening ceremony for the 1992 Barcelona Olympic Games (thousands twirled silk squares in one sequence) and the Atlanta Games in 1996.

Jewellery and fashion designers also figure strongly in the life of these islands, with exceptionally high standards of work demonstrated by jewellers like Barbara Jardine, Gillian Bishop and Rachel Ross. The doyenne of the fashion business is the gifted Meiling, but attractive original clothing by a growing number of native fashionmakers can be found in boutiques and shopping centres.

Carnival This extraordinary fête (see page 915 for dates etc) is considered by many to be safer, more welcoming to visitors and artistically more stimulating than its nearest rival in Rio de Janeiro. Commercialization is undermining many of the greatest Mas' traditions, but some of the historical characters like the Midnight Robber and the Moko Jumbies can be glimpsed at the Viey La Cou old time Carnival street theatre at Queens Hall a week before Carnival and often at J'Ouverte (pronounced joo-vay) on Carnival Monday morning and in small, independent bands of players. But it's a great party, enlivened by hundreds of thousands of costumed masqueraders and the homegrown music, calypso and steelband (usually referred to as 'pan').

Calypsonians (or kaisonians, as the more historically-minded call them) are the commentators, champions and sometime conscience of the people. This unique musical form, a mixture of African, French and, eventually, British, Spanish and even East Indian influences dates back to Trinidad's first 'shantwell', Gros Jean, late in the 18th century. Since then it has evolved into a popular, potent force, with both men and women (also children, of late) battling for the Calypso Monarch's crown. This fierce competition takes place at the Sunday night Dimanche Gras show at the Queens Park Savannah, which in turn immediately precedes the official start of J'Ouverte at 0400 on the Monday morning, marking the beginning of Carnival proper. Calypsonians band together to perform in 'tents' (performing halls) in the weeks leading up to the competition and are judged in semi-finals, which hones down the list to six final contenders. The season's calypso songs blast from radio stations and sound systems all over the islands and visitors should ask locals to interpret the sometimes witty and often scurrilous lyrics, for they are a fascinating introduction to the state of the nation. Currently, party soca tunes dominate although some of the commentary calypsonians, like Sugar Aloes, are still heard on the radio. There is also a new breed of 'Rapso' artists, fusing calypso and rap music. Chutney, an Indian version of calypso, is also becoming increasingly popular, especially since the advent of radio stations devoted only to Indian music. Chutney is also being fused with soca, to create 'chutney soca'.

Pan music has a shorter history, developing this century from the tamboo- bamboo bands which made creative use of tins, dustbins and pans plus lengths of bamboo for percussion instruments. By the end of the Second World War (during which Carnival was banned) some ingenious souls discovered that huge oil drums could be converted into expressive instruments, their top surfaces tuned to all ranges and depths (eg the ping pong, or soprano pan embraces 28 to 32 notes, including both the diatonic and chromatic scales). Aside from the varied pans, steelbands also include a rhythm section dominated by the steel, or iron men. For Carnival, the steelbands compete in the grand Panorama, playing calypsoes which are also voted on for the Road March of the Year. Biennally, the World Steelband Festival highlights the versatility of this music, for each of the major bands must play a work by a classical composer as well as a calypso of choice. On alternate years the National Schools Steelband Festival is held, similarly in late October/early November. A pan jazz festival is held annually in November, with solos, ensembles and orchestras all emphasizing the versatility of the steel drum. TIDCO organized a World Beat festival for the first time in October 1999, featuring Caribbean and international artistes. It plans to make it an annual event.

Other musical forms in this music-mad nation include **parang** (pre-Christmas). Part of the islands' Spanish heritage, parang is sung in Castillian and accompanied by guitar, cuatro, mandoline and tambourine. For the Hindi and Muslim festivals, there are East Indian drumming and vocal styles like chowtal, which is particularly associated with Puagwa in early March.

Throughout the year, there are regular performances of plays and musicals, often by Caribbean dramatists, and concerts by fine choirs like the Marionettes Chorale, sometimes accompanied by steelbands. There is a lot of comedy but some serious plays too, see press for details. Theatres include the Little Carib Theatre (T6224644), Space Theatre (T6230732), the Central Bank Auditorium (T6230845) and Queen's Hall (6241284).

In short, Trinidad and Tobago boast some of the most impressive artists to be found anywhere in the region, and visitors can enjoy that art throughout the year, although many of the now internationally recognized performers tour abroad during the summer months.

Trinidad & Tobago

The Venezuelan Islands

19

The Venezuelan Islands

When the Spaniards landed in East Venezuela in 1498, in the course of Columbus' third voyage, they found a poor country sparsely populated by Indians who had created no distinctive culture. Four hundred years later it was still poor, almost exclusively agrarian, exporting little, importing less. The miracle year which changed all that was 1914, when oil was discovered near Maracaibo. Today, Venezuela is one of the richest countries in Latin America and is one of the largest producers and exporters of oil in the world.

Venezuela has 72 island possessions in the Caribbean, of which the largest and the most visited is Isla de Margarita. This island, and two close neighbours, Coche and Cubagua, form the state of Nueva Esparta. Most of the other islands are Federal Dependencies (whose capital is Los Roques) stretching in small groups of keys to the east of Bonaire. Two other sets of islands are incorporated in the national parks of Morrocoy (west of the country's capital, Caracas) and Mochima, east of Caracas.

Essentials

Before you travel

Documents Entry is by **passport** and **visa**, or by passport and **tourist card**. Tourist cards (*tarjetas de ingreso*) are valid only for those entering by air and are issued by most airlines to visitors from: Andorra, Antigua and Barbuda, Argentina, Australia, Austria, Barbados, Belgium, Brazil, Canada, Chile, Costa Rica, Dominica, Denmark, Finland, France, Germany, Ireland, Italy, Iceland, Japan, Liechenstein, Luxembourg, Lithuania, Malaysia, Mexico, Monaco, Norway, Netherlands, New Zealand, Paraguay, Portugal, St Kitts/Nevis, St Lucia, San Marino, St Vincent, South Africa, Spain, Sweden, Switzerland, Taiwan, Trinidad and Tobago, the UK, Uruguay and the USA. They are valid for 90 days with, theoretically, two extensions of 60 days each permissible, at a cost of US$25 each (alternatively leave the country and re-enter). Overstaying your 90 days without an extension can lead to arrest and a fine when you try to depart. *DIEX* offices in many cities do not offer extensions – best to go to *DIEX*, Av Baralt on Plaza Miranda in Caracas, T4832744, take passport, tourist card and return ticket; opens 0800, passport with extension returned at the end of the day.

If you enter the country overland, it is safest to obtain a multiple entry visa in advance. In theory, this may not be necessary, but in practice you may well be asked for it. Apply to a Venezuela consulate prior to arrival. For a tourist visa, you need one passport photo, passport valid for six months, references from bank and employer, onward or return ticket, completed and signed application form. The fee in the UK is £22 (costs vary from country to country). Transit visas, valid for 72 hours are also available, mostly the same requirements and cost (inward and onward tickets needed). *DIEX* in Caracas will not exchange a transit for a tourist visa. It appears that you cannot get a visa in advance in the USA (although a one year, multiple-entry visa is available in advance from 455 Market St, San Francisco, open Monday-Friday, 0900-1300, with US$ cash and letters of reference from your bank and employer), or Canada, so to apply for an overland visa in Colombia or Brazil you need: passport, one photo and an onward ticket. In Manaus you also need a yellow fever inoculation certificate. A tourist card issued by *Viasa* in Bogotá is only valid for arriving in Caracas by air from Bogotá, not if you travel overland. To extend a visa for one month, in any city, costs about US$25 (passport photo needed). Consuls may give a one-year visa if a valid reason can be given. To change a tourist visa to a business visa, to obtain or to extend the latter, costs £42 in UK. Visas to work in Venezuela also cost £42 and require authorization from the Dirección General Sectorial de Identificación y Control de Extranjeros in Caracas. Student visas require a letter of acceptance from the Venezuelan institution, proof of means of support, medical certificate, passport photo, passport and £42. It generally takes two days to issue any visa. Tourist visas are multiple entry within their specified period.

NB Carry your passport with you all the time you are in Venezuela as the police mount frequent spot checks and anyone found without identification is immediately detained (carrying a certified copy for greater safety is permissible, though not always accepted by officials). Border searches are very thorough and there are many military checkpoints in military areas, at which all transport is stopped. Have your documents ready and make sure you know what entry permits you need; soldiers may be unfamiliar with regulations for foreigners. Do not lose the carbon copy of your visa as this has to be surrendered when leaving the country.

Customs You may bring into Venezuela, free of duty, 25 cigars and 200 cigarettes, two litres of alcoholic drinks, four small bottles of perfume, and gifts at the inspector's discretion. New items to the value of US$1,000 may be brought in.

Money **Currency** The unit of currency is the bolívar, which is divided into 100 céntimos (owing to devaluation, céntimos were not in use early 2000). There are coins for 5, 10, 20, 50, 100 and 500 bolívares, and notes for 5, 10, 20, 50, 100, 500, 1,000, 2,000, 5,000 and 10,000 bolívares. There is a shortage of small coinage and small notes: many shops round up prices unless you have small change or notes.

People are reluctant to take 5,000 & 10,000 bolívar notes because these denominations are frequently forged

Touching down

Departure tax *Passengers on international flights pay an exit tax of approximately US$30 payable in bolívares or dollars. Minors under 12 years of age do not pay the exit tax. There is a 1% tax on the cost of all domestic flights, plus an airport tax which varies according to the airport.*

Business hours *Banks: open from 0830 to 1530, Monday to Friday only.* **Government offices**: *hours vary, but 0800-1200 are usual morning hours. Government officials have fixed hours, usually 0900-1000 or 1500-1600, for receiving visitors. Business firms generally start work about 0800, and some continue until about 1800 with a midday break.* **Shops**: *0900-1300, 1500-1900, Monday to Saturday. Generally speaking, Venezuelans start work early, and by 0700 everything is in full swing. Most firms and offices close on Saturday.*

Official time *Atlantic Standard Time, four hours behind GMT, one hour ahead of EST.*

Voltage *110 volts, 60 cycles, throughout the country.*

Weights & measures *Metric.*

Hotel price grades **LL** *over US$150;* **L** *US$100-150;* **AL** *US$ 66-99;* **A** *US$46-65;* **B** *US$31-45;* **C** *US$21-30;* **D** *US$12-20;* **E** *US$7-11;* **F** *US$6 and under.*

Tourist offices overseas
Germany *Im Rheingarten 7, D-53225 Bonn, T0049228-400920, F0049228-400922, www.botschaft-venezuela.de*
UK *56 Grafton Way, London W1P 5LB, T020-73876726, F020-73833253, www.venezlon.demon.co.uk*
USA *1099 30th St, NW, Washington DC 20007, T1-202-3422214, F3426820, www.embavenez-us.org*

Tipping *Taxi drivers are tipped if the taxi has a meter (hardly anywhere), but not if you have agreed the fare in advance. Usherettes are not tipped. Hotel porters, US$0.50; airport porters US$0.50 per piece of baggage. Restaurants, between 5% and 10% of bill.*

Safety *Cameras and other valuables should not be exposed prominently. In Caracas, carry handbags, cameras etc on the side away from the street as motor-cycle purse-snatchers are notorious. Hotel thefts are becoming more frequent.*

Exchange To convert unused bolívares back into dollars upon leaving, you must present the original exchange receipt (up to 30% of original amount charged); only banks and authorized *casas de cambio* can legally sell bolívares. *Casas de cambio* may change travellers' cheques more readily than banks, but they always insist on seeing a passport and may also insist on proof of purchase. *Ital Cambio* seems to be the most fastidious; they may even take your photo. Commission charges vary but several institutions change Thomas Cook travellers' cheques without commission, eg *Ital Cambio*, *ABN Amro Bank* and *Banco Provincial*. Visa and Mastercard transactions offer good rates. *Corp Banca* is affiliated with American Express, no commission, some branches cash personal cheques from abroad on an Amex card. *Banco Unión* and *Banco Mercantil* (not all branches) handle Visa and ATM transactions, including cash advances and Banco Mercantil handles Mastercard. *American Express* assistance T02-2084922; *Mastercard* T8001-2902; *Visa* T8001-2169.

Since 1997, it has become very difficult to change dollars cash or travellers' cheques in Venezuela. Visitors are strongly advised to use Visa or Mastercard. If changing money in hotels, do not take sterling or any other European currencies. Have money sent to you by telex and not by post, which can take weeks. Rates of exchange in hotels are generally poor.

NB It is quite common for tour companies not to accept credit cards, other than for flights, so you will need cash or travellers' cheques for buying tours.

Tropical, with little change between season. **Climate**

Getting there

Air **From Europe** *British Airways* fly from London to Simón Bolívar, the international airport for Caracas three times a week direct. There are also services from Paris (*Air France*), Amsterdam (*KLM*), Madrid (*Iberia*), Frankfurt (*Lufthansa*), Rome (*Alitalia*), and Lisbon (*TAP*). **From North America** Direct flights with *American Airlines* (New York, Dallas, Miami), *Delta* (Atlanta), *United Airlines* (Miami, Chicago), *Continental* (Houston, New York) and *Servivensa* (Miami, New York). Also from Miami, *Aeropostal*. **Within the Caribbean** *Aeropostal* have services from Port of Spain (daily except Sunday and Wednesday to Caracas), while *BWIA* flies daily. *Air France* flies from Guadeloupe and Martinique on Sunday. *Cubana* flies twice a week, *Aeropostal* five times a week from Havana. From Aruba to Caracas: *ALM*, *Servivensa* and *Air Aruba* daily, *Aeropostal* and *Avior* three a week; to Las Piedras/Punto Fijo on the Paranaguá Peninsula, *Servivensa* daily. From Curaçao to Caracas: *ALM* daily, *Aeropostal* four a week, *Avior* three; to Las Piedras, Santa Bárbara three a week (if you have no onward ticket from Curaçao, you must buy a return).

Sea **Ports of entry** Do not try to clear Customs and Immigration without an agent in commercial port, well worth the fee. Get your tourist card at a Venezuelan embassy before arriving, although if you arrive during a major storm officials may make an exception. The time a yacht may stay in Venezuelan waters is to be increased from six to 18 months. **Security** During the busy hurricane season security problems increase; thieves arrive by night in boats with bolt cutters and fast engines and steal dinghies, motors and other items left on deck. Best security is in marinas. Porlamar even has trouble with swimmers during the day. Fewer problems in the outer islands of La Blanquilla, La Tortuga, Los Roques, Los Aves and Los Testigos, but trouble reported in coastal anchorages eg Cumaná, Mochima, Morrocoy, Puerto La Cruz. Take all precautions possible.

See pages 25 & 976 for details of Windward Lines & other ferries

Touching down

Airport information To avoid overbooking the Government obliges airlines to post a passenger list, but it is important to obtain clear instructions from the travel agent regarding confirmation of your flight and checking-in time. Passengers leaving Caracas on international flights must reconfirm their reservations not less than 72 hours in advance, it is safer to do so in person than by telephone; not less than 24 hours for national flights (if you fail to do this, you lose all rights to free accommodation, food, transport, etc if your flight is cancelled and you may lose your seat if the plane is fully booked). Beware of counterfeit tickets; buy only from agencies. If told by an agent that a flight is fully booked, try at the airport anyway. International passengers must check in two hours before departure or they may lose their seat to someone on a waiting list. Handling charge for your luggage US$0.50.

Airport facilities 28 km from Caracas, near the port of La Guaira: **Maiquetía**, for national flights, **Simón Bolívar** for international flights, adjacent to each other (5 min walk – taxis take a circular route, fare US$2.25; airport authorities run a shuttle bus between the two every 10 minutes from 0700). **NB** Following the storms at the end of 1999, which damaged the airport and its surroundings, some international flights were diverted to the city of Valencia and many internal flights were using Charallave airport, south of Caracas. Many facilities close on 1 January, including duty and money exchangers. Several *casas de cambio* open 24 hours (*Italcambio*, good rates, outside duty-free area; also *Banco Industrial*, branch in international terminal and another, less crowded, in baggage reclaim area). If changing TCs', you may be asked for your purchase receipt; commission 2½%. There are cash machines for Visa, Amex and Mastercard. Pharmacy, bookshops, basement café (good value meals and snacks, open 0600-2400, hard to find; cafés and bars on 1st floor viewing terrace also good value), tourist office (see below). No official left luggage; ask for Paulo at the mini bar on the 1st floor of international terminal. Look after your belongings in both terminals. Direct dial phone calls to USA only, from AT&T booth in international departure lounge. CANTV at gates 15 and 24, open 0700-2100, long-distance, international and fax services. When several flights arrive close together there are long queues for immigration.

From airport to Caracas Taxi fares from airport to Caracas cost US$18 minimum, depending on the quality of the taxi, the part of city, or on the number of stars of your hotel, regardless of distance. Overcharging is rife and taxi drivers can be aggressive in seeking passengers. Fares are supposedly controlled, but it is essential to negotiate with the drivers; find out what the official fare is first. After 2200 and at weekends a surcharge of 20% may be added, you may get charged up to US$40. Drivers may only surcharge you for luggage (US$0.50 per large bag). If you think the licensed taxi driver is overcharging you, make a complaint to Corpoturismo or tell him you will report him to the Departamento de Protección del Consumidor. The airport shuttle bus (blue and white with "Aeropuerto Internacional" on the side) leaves from east end of terminal, left out of exit (in the city, under the flyover at Bolívar and Av Sur 17, 250 m from Bellas Artes metro, poorly lit at night, not recommended to wait here in the dark), regular service from 0700 to 2300, bus leaves when there are enough passengers; fare to international terminal US$3.50. The bus is usually crowded so first time visitors may find a taxi advisable.

Always allow plenty of time when going to the airport, whatever means of transport you are using: the route can be very congested (two hours in daytime, but only 30 minutes at 0430). Allow at least two hours checking-in time before your flight. Airport bus or *por puesto* to airport can be caught at Gato Negro metro station.

Local tourist office *Corpoturismo*, Apartado 50.200, Caracas, main office for information is *Unatur*, floor 35, Torre Oeste, Parque Central, T5749553/5765696. The tourist office at the international airport has good maps, helpful; some English spoken, open 0700-2400; tourist office at national terminal open 0700-2100. When manned both offices are useful, will book hotels, reconfirm flights, English spoken, better service than the Corpoturismo office in the city. Two useful websites are: www.chevere.com and www.infoguia.net

Tourist information

The Venezuelan Islands

Where to stay

Hotels Fairmont International, Torre Capriles, Planta Baja, Plaza Venezuela, Caracas, T7828433, F7824407, will book hotel rooms both in Caracas and in other towns, where they have 102 hotels on their books. All, except luxury class hotels charge officially controlled prices. **Camping** In Venezuela camping is a popular recreation, spending a weekend at the beach, on the islands, in the *llanos* and in the mountains. It is not, however, possible at the roadside. If camping on the beach, for the sake of security, pitch your tent close to others, even though they play their radios loud.

See box on page 963 for details of hotel price grades

Getting around

Most important places are served by *Avensa, Servivensa* and *Aeropostal. Aereotuy, Aserca* (recommended) and **Santa Bárbara** fly to a variety of destinations. Internal airlines offer special family discounts and student discounts, but this practice is variable (photocopies of ISIC card are useful as this allows officials to staple one to the ticket). Sometimes there is little difference between 1st class and tourist class fares.

Avensa/Servivensa operate an airpass, which must be bought outside Latin America or the Caribbean. It is valid for 45 days and passengers must buy a minimum of four coupons. No route may be flown twice in the same direction. Economy class only; children pay 67% and infants 10% of the adult fare. Prices are by Zone: Caracas to Aruba, Bonaire or Curaçao US$55; Caracas-Miami (but not Barquisimeto or Maracaibo-Miami), Caracas-Bogotá US$80; Caracas-Quito US$160; Caracas-Lima US$180; Caracas-Mexico City US$200; any internal Venezuelan flight US$40 (except Canaima US$60).

Air

Beware of overbooking during holiday time, especially at Caracas airport

All visitors to Venezuela can drive if they are over 18 and have a valid driving licence from their own country; an international driving licence is preferred. If you have an accident and someone is injured, you will be detained as a matter of routine, even if you are not at fault. Do not drive at night if you can help it (if you do have to, do not drive fast). Carry insect spray if you do; if you stop and get out, the car will fill with biting insects. Self-drive tours, and fly-drive

Car

are available, the latter through *National Car Rental*, which has a wide network of offices.

There are five grades of gasoline: 'normal', 83 octane; 87 octane; 89 octane; 91 octane; and 'alta', 95 octane. Gasoline costs on average US$0.10-0.16 a litre; diesel costs US$0.10 a litre. Service stations are open 0500-2100, Monday-Saturday, except those on highways which have longer opening hours. Only those designated to handle emergencies are open on Sunday. In the event of breakdown, Venezuelans are usually very helpful. There are many garages, even in rural areas; service charges are not high, nor are tyres, oil or accessories expensive, but being able to speak Spanish will greatly assist in sorting out problems. Carry spare battery water, fan belts, an obligatory breakdown triangle, a jack and spanners. Some cars have a security device to prevent the engine being started and this is recommended. The best road map is published by *Lagoven* and a similar version by *Corpoven* but at twice the scale and with a very good street plan of Caracas on the back, available from most service stations (not just Lagoven's), latest edition 1995, US$2. The best country map is published by *ITM*, Vancouver BC, Canada, by the late Kevin Healey. There is an automatic US$20 fine for running out of fuel.

Bus   Buses are relatively cheap, but the quality of long-distance travel varies a lot. There are numerous services between the major cities. The colectivo taxis and minibuses, known in Venezuela as *por puesto*, seem to monopolize transport to and from smaller towns and villages. Outside Caracas, town taxis are relatively expensive.

Sea   You can also charter a yacht and visit the Venezuelan islands. A Venezuelan captain must be on
See page 964 for   board, even on a bareboat charter. He knows the rules, regulations and places to go, which
arriving by yacht in   makes it easier. A recommended yacht is *El Gato*, Captain Pinky can be contacted through
your own vessel   Cumanagoto Marina. A typical 12-day cruise starts from the mainland with a downwind sail to Los Testigos for a few days of relaxation, snorkelling or diving, then to Juan Griego, on north coast of Margarita with a night in a hotel, on to La Blanquilla to visit two beautiful, white sand beaches, spending the night ashore in tents, and back to Margarita. Charters can be designed to suit your needs, day sails or longer.

Keeping in touch

Post   *Ipostel*, the national postal service, has improved greatly. They now offer an international express mail service (EMS), which guarantees delivery in 2-3 days depending on destination. It costs from US$20 for up to 1 kg. *Ipostel* also offer EEE, which is a domestic express service, guaranteeing delivery next day. An alternative to *DHL* and other courier companies is *Grupo Zoom*, who sell A5 or A4 envelopes for international postage, guaranteed delivery in 3-4 days, cost US$10-15.

Telephone   All international and long distance calls are operated by *CANTV* and can be dialled direct.
International   Major cities are linked by direct dialling (*Discado Directo*), with a three-figure prefix for each
phone code: 58   town in Venezuela. There are *CANTV* offices for long-distance and international calls. Collect calls are possible to some countries, at least from Caracas, though staff in offices may not be sure of this. Most public phones on prepaid *CANTV* cards in denominations of 3,000 and 5,000 bolívares. Buy them from *CANTV* or numerous small shops bearing the *CANTV* logo, or a scrap of card reading "Si! hay tarjetas!" They are also sold by street vendors. Make sure they are still in their clear plastic wrapper with an unbroken red seal. Many small shops impose a 25% handling charge and *tarjetas* may be out of stock. When making international calls from a public booth, ensure that it has a globe symbol on the side. International calls are cheaper with a *tarjeta*, minimum needed B$5,000, but you get little more than a minute to Europe. To make an international call, dial 00 plus country code, etc. Canada direct: 800-11100. For UK, BT Direct, 800-11440 (BT chargecard works from any phone). For collect calls to Germany T800-11490. International calls are charged by a series of bands, ranging from about US$1 per minute to USA and Canada, to US$2 to UK, to US$2.15 (a 40% was announced in March 2000). There are various reduced and economy rates according to band. Fax rates are as for phones.

Food and drink

There is excellent local fish (*pargo* or red snapper), crayfish, small oysters and prawns. Of true **Food**
Venezuelan food there is *sancocho* (a stew of vegetables, especially yuca, with meat, chicken *Venezuelans*
or fish); *arepas*, a kind of white maize bread, very bland in flavour; toasted *arepas* served with a *dine late*
wide selection of relishes, fillings or the local somewhat salty white cheese are cheap, filling
and nutritious; *cachapas*, a maize pancake (soft, not hard like Mexican *tortillas*) wrapped
around white cheese; *pabellón*, made of shredded meat, beans, rice and fried plantains
(vegetarian versions available); and *empanadas*, maize-flour pies containing cheese, meat or
fish. At Christmas only there are *hallacas*, maize pancakes stuffed with chicken, pork, olives,
etc boiled in a plantain leaf (but don't eat the leaf). A *muchacho* (boy) on the menu is a cut of
beef. *Ganso* is also not goose but beef. *Solomo* and *lomito* are other cuts of beef. *Hervido* is
chicken or beef with vegetables. *Contorno* with a meat or fish dish is a choice of chips, boiled
potatoes, rice or yuca. *Caraotas* are beans; *cachitos* are *croissants* of bread. *Pasticho* is what the
Venezuelans call Italian *lasagne*. The main fruits are bananas, oranges, grapefruit, mangoes,
pineapple and papaya. **NB** Some Venezuelan variants of names for fruit: *lechosa* is papaya,
patilla is water melon, *parchita* passion fruit, and *cambur* a small banana. A delicious sweet is
huevos chimbos – egg yolk boiled and bottled in sugar syrup.

Venezuelan rum is very good; recommended brands are *Cacique*, *Pampero* and *Santa Teresa*. **Drink**
There are four good local beers: *Polar* (the most popular), *Regional* (with a strong flavour of
hops), *Cardenal* and *Nacional* (a *lisa* is a glass of keg beer; for a bottle of beer ask for a *tercio*);
Brahma beer (lighter than *Polar*), is imported from Brazil. There are also mineral waters, gin and
good, local wine. The Polar brewery has joined with Martell (France) and built a winery in Carora.
Wines produced are 'Viña Altagracia' and 'Bodegas Pomar'. 'Bodegas Pomar' also produces a
sparkling wine in the traditional champagne style. Liqueurs are cheap, try the local *ponche
crema*. The coffee is very good (*café con leche* has a lot of milk, *café marrón* much less, *cafe negro*
for black coffee, which, though obvious, is not common usage in the rest of Latin America).
Visitors should also try a *merengada*, a delicious drink made from fruit pulp, ice, milk and sugar; a
batido is the same but with water and a little milk; *jugo* is the same but with water. Fruit juices
are very good. A *plus-café* is an after-dinner liqueur. Water is free in all restaurants even if no food
is bought. Bottled water in *cervecerías* is often from the tap; no deception is intended, bottles are
simply used as convenient jugs. Insist on seeing the bottle opened if you want mineral water.
Chicha de arroz is a sweet drink made of milk, rice starch, sugar and vanilla.

Holidays and festivals

There are two sorts of holidays, those enjoyed by everybody and those taken by employees **Public holidays**
of banks and insurance companies. Holidays applying to all businesses include: 1 January,
Carnival on the Monday and Tuesday before Ash Wednesday (everything shuts down
Saturday-Tuesday; make sure accommodation is booked in advance), Thursday-Saturday of
Holy Week, 19 April, 1 May, 24 June (the feast day of San Juan Bautista, a particularly popular
festival celebrated along the central coast where there were once large concentrations of
plantation slaves who considered San Juan their special Saint; some of the best-known
events are in villages between Puerto Cabello and Chuspa, to the east, such as Chuao, Cata
and Ocumane de la Costa), 5 July, 24 July, 12 October, 25 December. Holidays for banks and
insurance companies include all the above and also: 19 March and the nearest Monday to 6
January, Ascension Day, 29 June, 15 August, 1 November and 8 December. There are also
holidays applying to certain occupations such as Doctor's Day or Traffic Policeman's Day.
From 24 December-1 January, most restaurants are closed and there is no long-distance
public transport. On New Year's Eve, everything closes and does not open for a least a day.
Queues for tickets, and traffic jams, are long. Business travellers should not visit during Holy
week or Carnival.

The Venezuelan Islands

Health

Water in all main towns is heavily chlorinated, so safe to drink, although most people drink bottled water. Medical attention is good. State health care is free and said to be good (the Clínica Metropolitana in Caracas has been recommended). A doctor's consultation costs about US$10. On the coast from Cumaná east precautions against vampire bat bite are warranted since they can be rabies-carriers. Lights over hatches and windows are used by local fishermen to deter bats from entering boats and shore cabins. If bitten seek medical advice. Some rivers are infected with bilharzia and in some areas there are warning signs; check before bathing. Protection against mosquito bites is advised as dengue fever has been present since 1995.

Further reading

GAM, the monthly *Guía Aérea y Marítima de Venezuela*, gives details of all flights into and within the country, but also of hotels, travel agents, car hire, etc. The *Guide to Venezuela* (925 pages), by Janice Bauman, Leni Young and others, in English (freely available in Caracas) is a mine of information and maps, US$11. *Elizabeth Kline's Guide to Camps, Posadas and Cabins/Guía de campamentos, posadas y cabañas in/en Venezuela* is published every other year and gives a comprehensive survey of these establishments. (Apartado 63089, Caracas 1067-A, Venezuela, T02-9451543, ekline@cantv.net).

For information on the **national parks** system, and to obtain necessary permits to stay in the parks, go to Instituto Nacional de Parques (Inparques), Museo de Transporte, Edificio Sur, Avenida Rómulo Gallegos, Parque del Este (exit Parque del Este metro opposite park, turn left, office is a few hundred metres further on up a slight incline), T2841956, F2344238, Caracas, or to the local office of the *guardaparques* for each park (www.marnr.gov.ve/).

Isla de Margarita

Isla de Margarita is in fact one island whose two sections are tenuously linked by the 18 km sandspit which separates the sea from the Restinga lagoon. At its largest, Margarita is about 32 km from north to south and 67 km from east to west. Most of its people live in the developed eastern part, which has some wooded areas and fertile valleys. The western part, the Peninsula de Macanao, is hotter and more barren, with scrub, sand dunes and marshes. Wild deer, goats and hares roam the interior, but four-wheel drive vehicles are needed to penetrate it. The entrance to the Peninsula de Macanao is a pair of hills known as Las Tetas de María Guevara, a national monument covering 1,670 ha.

Ins and outs

Getting there
See transport, page 975, for further details

Air Airport del Caribe General Santiago Mariño (PMV), between Porlamar and Punta de Piedra is comfortable and modern and has the international and national terminals at either end. Bus from Plaza Bolívar, US$1, taxi US$10. There are many flights a day from Caracas, with *Servivensa, Aeropostal, Laser, Avior* and *Air Venezuela*, 45 mins flight; tickets are much cheaper if purchased in Venezuela in local currency. Reservations made from outside Venezuela are not always honoured. As well as flights to Venezuelan destinations, *Aeropostal* also flies to Barbados and Port of Spain, 5 times a week. **Sea** There are also ferries from Puerto La Cruz and Cumaná in Venezuela, and the *Windward Lines* service to Trinidad, Barbados, St Lucia and St Vincent.

Getting around
Car hire is a cheap way of getting around

Por Puestos serve most of the island, leaving mainly from the corners of Plaza Bolívar in Porlamar. Fares: to Punta de Piedra (from 4 blocks from Plaza Bolívar, towards sea-front), US$0.75, to the ferry terminal US$0.85; to La Asunción, US$0.35, from Calle Fajardo, half a block from Igualdad; to Pampatar, US$0.25; to La Restinga (from La Marina y Mariño), US$1, El Agua (from corner of Guevara and Marcano), US$0.65; Juan Griego, US$0.65. Several offices at the airport. The roads are generally good and most are paved. A bridge connects the two parts. Sign posts are often poorly-positioned. It is best not to drive outside Porlamar after dark. Beware of robbery of hired vehicles. Check conditions and terms of hire very carefully for your liability.

The climate is exceptionally good, but rain is scant. Water is piped from the mainland but water trucks also deliver to resorts to keep up with demand. **Climate**

Flora and fauna

Despite the property boom and frenetic building on much of the coast and in Porlamar, much of the island has been given over to natural parks. Of these the most striking is the **Laguna La Restinga**. Launches provide lengthy runs around the mangrove swamps, but they create a lot of wash and noise. The mangroves are fascinating, with shellfish clinging to the roots. The launch will leave you on a shingle and shell beach (don't forget to arrange with your boatman to collect you), and you can rummage for shellfish in the shallows (protection against the sun essential). Flamingoes live in the lagoon.

There are mangroves also in the Laguna de las Marites Natural Monument, west of Porlamar. Other parks are Las Tetas de María Guevara, Cerro el Copey, 7,130 ha, and Cerro Matasiete y Guayamurí, 1,672 ha (both reached from La Asunción). Details of Inparques, the national parks office, are given on page 968.

By boat from Porlamar you can go to the Isla de los Pájaros, or Morro Blanco, for both bird-spotting and underwater fishing. In Boca del Río there is a Museum of the Sea.

Diving and marine life

The Venezuelan Islands are fast becoming new dive destinations with sites found off Margarita, La Blanquilla, Los Testigos, Las Frailes and Los Roques. There is good snorkelling and diving off Cubagua on a sunken barge and a ferry with cars still inside. At Farallón, near Pampatar, there is an underwater religious statue, large brain coral, large sea fans and large fish, including barracuda, in about 12 m of water. La Macura is a rock patch where holes in boulders are home to large, colourful parrotfish. Los Frailes, eight small islands northeast of Margarita are ideal for current dives and rich underwater life including moray eels, barracudas and oysters.

Beaches and watersports

Apart from the shopping, what attracts the holidaymakers from Venezuela and abroad are the beaches: long white stretches of sand bordered by palms, but rather hot, with little shade (sunscreen essential). Nude sunbathing is forbidden. Topless bathing is not seen, except at some resort pools and beaches, but the tanga (*hilo dental* – dental floss) is fairly common.

In Porlamar, the main beach suffers from its popularity: calm shallow water, pedalos for hire, windsurf classes; but that by the *Bella Vista*, although crowded with foreign tourists, is kept clean. For a more Venezuelan atmosphere go northeast to Pampatar, which is set around a bay favoured by foreign yachtsmen as a summer anchorage; jet skis for hire on a clean and pretty beach. A scale model of Columbus' *Santa María* is used for taking tourists on trips. A fishing boat can be hired for US$20 for 2½ hours, four to six passengers; shop around for best price, good fun and fishing.

The beaches on the eastern side are divided into ocean and calm beaches, according to their location in relation to the open sea. The former tend to be rougher (good surfing and windsurfing) and colder. Windsurfing instruction and equipment rentals can be found. Water is uniformly clear and unpolluted. It is still possible, even in high season, to find practically deserted beaches. Restaurants, *churuatas* (bars built like Indian huts), sunshades and deckchairs are becoming widespread. (Hire charges are about US$1.50 per item.)

Other sports   **Golf** can be played at the *Isla Bonita Golf and Beach Hotel*, where there is an 18-hole, par 72 course in the Valle Pedro González, T657111, open to all. **Horse riding** is organized through the desert, mountains and beaches of the Peninsula de Macanao and the wilderness area of Cabatucán, beginners welcome, T819348.

Porlamar

Phone code: 095
Population: 85,000

Most of the hotels are at Porlamar, 20 km from the airport and about 28 km from **Punta de Piedra**, where most of the ferries dock. It has a magnificent cathedral. At Igualdad y Díaz is the Museo de Arte Francisco Narváez. The main, and most expensive, shopping area is Avenida Santiago Mariño; better bargains and a wider range of shops are to be found on Gómez and Guevara. The centre of the city is crowded with cars and shoppers, while to the east there is continuing, apparently chaotic development of big holiday hotels and condominiums, separated by vast areas of waste ground and construction sites. Costa Azul is the main *urbanización*, served by a long strip of featureless sand known as Playa Moreno. At night everything closes by 2300; women alone should avoid the centre after dark. Porlamar has many casinos, all of which lack legal status. Note that in Porlamar there is a Calle Mariño and an Avenida Santiago Mariño in the centre.

Ferries go to the **Isla de Coche** (11 km by 6 km), which has over 4,500 inhabitants and one of the richest salt mines in the country. They also go, on hire only, to **Isla de Cubagua**, which is totally deserted, but you can visit the ruins of Nueva Cádiz (which have been excavated). Large catamarans take tourists on day sails to Coche.

Isla de Margarita

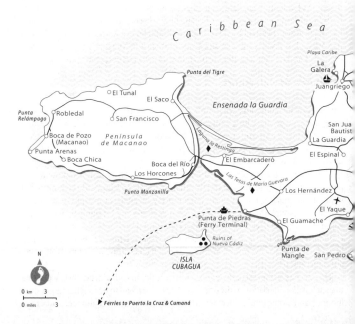

Around the island

The capital, La Asunción, is a few kilometres inland from Porlamar. It has several **La Asunción** colonial buildings, a cathedral, and the fort of Santa Rosa, with a famous bottle dun- *Population: 16,660* geon. ■ *Mon 0800-1500, other days 0800-1800.* There is a museum in the Casa Capitular, and a local market, good for handicrafts. Nearby are the Cerro Matasiete historical site, where the defeat of the Spanish on 31 July 1817 led to their evacuation of the island, and the Félix Gómez look out in the Sierra Copuy.

Between La Asunción and Porlamar are the Parque Francisco Fajardo, beside the Universidad de Oriente, and **El Valle del Espíritu Santo**. Here is the church of the Virgen del Valle, a picturesque building with twin towers, painted white and pink. The Madonna is richly dressed (one dress has pearls, the other diamonds); the adjoining museum opens at 1400, it displays costumes and presents for the Virgin, including the "milagro de la pierna de perla", a leg-shaped pearl. A pilgrimage is held in early September. Proper dress is requested to enter the church.

Throughout the island, the churches are attractive: fairly small, with baroque towers and adornments and, in many cases, painted pink.

Pampatar has the island's largest fort, San Carlos Borromeo (built 1662 after the **Pampatar** Dutch destroyed the original fort), and the smaller La Caranta, where the cannon *Population: 10,590* show signs of having been spiked. Visit also the church of Cristo del Buen Viaje, the Library/Museum and the customs house. There is an amusement park to the south-west of Pampatar, called Isla Aventura, with ferris wheel, roller coaster, water slide, dodgems etc. ■ *Fri and Sat, 1800-2400, Sun, 1700-2400, and more frequently in peak holiday season. Entrance in peak season is US$5 adults, US$3.35 children, includes all rides; in low season entrance is US$0.50 and each ride US$0.30-0.60.* The beach at Pampatar is picturesquely circled with palm trees and kiosks selling local fresh fish from the fishing fleet anchored in the bay. Limited local services and watersports.

Restaurants and services crowded at weekends. La Caracola beach has an ultralight airport, kiosks, beachchairs. Bella Vista, near town, is calm, with restaurants and services.

On the eastern coast is **Playa Guacuco**, **East coast** reached from La Asunción by a road through the Guayamurí reserve: a lot of surf, fairly shallow, palm trees, restaurant and parking lot; excellent horseriding here or up into the hills, US$30 for two hours, contact Harry Padrón at the ranch in Agua de Vaca, or phone travel agent on 611311. Before Punta Cabo Blanco are **El Cardón** and **Puerto Fermín**/El Tirano (Lope de Aguirre, the infamous conquistador, landed here in 1561 on his flight from Peru), El Caserío handicrafts museum is nearby. Beyond the point is **Parguito**: long and open, strong waves, best for surfing, full public services.

Playa El Agua, 45 minutes by bus from Porlamar is 4 km of stone-free white sand with many *kioskos*, which have palm-leaf shade areas. The sea is very rough for children, but fairly shallow (beware the strong cross current when you are about waist deep). This is the most popular beach on the island and at Venezuelan holiday times it is over-crowded. At other times it is ideal for sunbathing and walking; the fashionable part is at the southern end; the northern end is popular with younger people, is less touristy, has fewer facilities, and less shade. It is possible to see the island by Ultralight from here at weekends. Contact Omar Contreras, T095-617632 or José-Antonio Fernández T095-623519, English spoken. There is bungee jumping, parasailing and most watersports. Activities abound at weekends in peak season. **El Humo** is less crowded and well-known, with deeper water and stronger currents, but it is a nice beach.

Manzanillo (population: 2,000) is a picturesque bay between the mountains. The water gets deep rather suddenly, fishing huts, fish sold on beach, apartments, expensive restaurant, **Playa Escondida** at the far end.

North coast The coast road is interesting, with glimpses of the sea and beaches to one side, inland vistas on the other. There are a number of clifftop look-out points. The road improves radically beyond Manzanillo, winding from one beach to the next. **Playa Puerto la Cruz** (the widest and windiest beach) adjoins **Pedro González** (population: 3,700), with a broad sweeping beach, running from a promontory (easy to climb) to scrub and brush that reach down almost to the water's edge (ask for Antonietta Luciani at *Restaurant Pedrogonzález*, she has an apartment to rent,

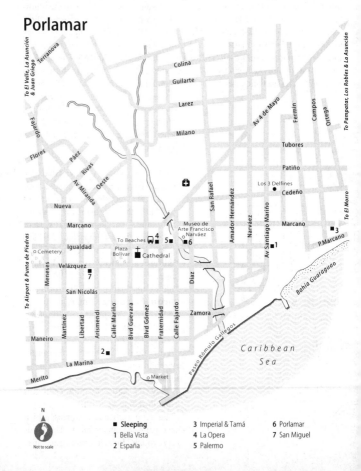

Porlamar

■ **Sleeping**
1 Bella Vista
2 España

3 Imperial & Tamá
4 La Opera
5 Palermo

6 Porlamar
7 San Miguel

N
Not to scale

US$40 per day, sleeps six, well-equipped, and recommended, as is her restaurant).

Further west is **Juan Griego** bay and town (population: 8,300), a small, sleepy town whose picturesque bay is full of fishing boats, drawn up on the narrow beach or moored offshore. The little fort of **La Galera** is on a promontory at the northern side, beyond which is a bay of the same name with a narrow strip of beach, more fishing boats and many seafront restaurants. La Galera is a good place to watch the famous Juan Griego sunset. **Playas Caribe**, north of La Galera, has beach restaurants, palm trees, some deserted caverns at the south end and the water is usually rough.

South of Juan Griego, the road goes inland to **San Juan Bautista** (a pleasant colonial town ringed by hills; *por puesto* from Juan Griego), then to Punta de Piedra, the ferry dock, see below (a pleasant stretch through cultivated land and farms at regular intervals; *por puesto* Juan Griego to ferry). Due south of San Juan is **El Yaque**, near the airport and the mouth of the Laguna de las Marites. This is an international windsurfers' hangout. It has flat water and windy conditions. Surf boards can be hired at the *Club El Mistral*, good service, very helpful and friendly, half day costs US$30. It is being rapidly developed with small hotels, but it suffers from aircraft noise and lacks public transport (taxi from Porlamar, US$8). The hinterland around El Yaque is very bleak.

Near San Juan is Fuentedueño park which has special walks. A branch goes northwest to La Guardia at the eastern end of La Restinga. The dyke of broken sea-shells stretches to the Peninsula de Macanao: on its right a spotlessly clean beach, on its left the lagoon. At the far end are many little restaurants and a cluster of fisher-men's huts with landing stages from which the launches make trips into the laby-rinth of canals and mangroves in the lagoon (US$14 per boat taking five passengers; bus from Porlamar harbourfront US$1, ask driver to drop you off).

Inland from Juan Griego

This western part of the island is quite underdeveloped, although it is hardly an untouched paradise. Some of the beaches are highly regarded: Manzanilla, Guayaconcito, Boca de Pozo, Macanao, Punta Arenas (many fishermen live here, have a lunch of fresh fish after your watersports) and Manglanillo. Harbour at Chacachacare. El Tunal is a shadeless, isolated beach near a small fishing village. La Pared has one fish restaurant with an excellent setting to watch the sunsets.

Peninsula de Macanao

Essentials

La Asunción B *Ciudad Colonial*, La Margarita, T423086. Upmarket, pleasant. **D** *de la Asunción*, Unión, 2 blocks from Plaza Bolívar, T420902. With bath, a/c, TV, fridge (rooms with balcony cost more but face noisy road, rooms without window cost less).

Sleeping
See page 963 for hotel price grades

Pampatar AL *Flamingo Beach*, T624822, F620271. 5-star, all-inclusive, food, drinks, enter-tainment, service, taxes, casino, good value. **C** *Residencial Don Juan*, with bath and fan, apartments sleeping 6 are available, bargain over price.

Porlamar The following are all recommended. **LL** *Hilton*, Costa Azul, T624111, F620810. Sailing dinghies for hire (ask for special rates when booking). **AL** *Bella Vista*, Av Santiago, T617222, F612557. Swimming pool, beach. **AL** *Dynasty*, T621411, F625101. Opposite *Hilton*, nice restaurant, pool. **A** *Stauffer*, T612911, F618708. Large rooms, excellent service and res-taurant, bar on roof, casino being added. **A** *Marbella Mar*, Av Principal y Calle Chipichipi, T624022, F624488. Clean rooms, friendly, especially with children, free bus service to the beach. **B** *Aguila Inn*, Narváez, 500 m north of centre, T612311, F616909. Clean, swimming pool, restaurant. **B** *Colibrí*, Av Santiago Mariño, T616346. New rooms, **D** in older rooms, both with bath, a/c, TV. **B** *Imperial*, Av Raúl Leoni, Vía El Morro, T616420, F615056. Best rooms in front have balcony, clean, comfortable, safe, a/c, good showers, triple rooms available, Eng-lish spoken. **D** *La Opera*, Igualdad entre Blvd Gómez y Fraternidad. Clean. **D** *Porlamar*, Igualdad y Fajardo, T630271. Clean, good restaurant and video bar La Punta, a/c or fan, hot

The Venezuelan Islands

water, friendly. **E** *Brasilia*, San Nicolás. Quiet, clean, nice new rooms at back. **E** *Domino*, La Libertad 7-40. With fan or a/c, basic, friendly. **E** *España*, Mariño 6-35, T612479. Cold shower, very clean, friendly, good breakfast, fan. **E** *Malecón*, Marina y Arismendi, T635723 .Seaview from front rooms, the Mexican owner, Luis and his wife are very helpful and generous. **D** *Palermo*, Calle Igualdad, opposite cathedral. Friendly, clean, best rooms on top floor with views of plaza. **D** *Robaldar*, Igualdad, near Libertad. Shower, a/c, TV, friendly. Cheaper places on Maneiro. **E** *Tamá*, next to *Imperial*. Gringo place with basic rooms, OK, excellent restaurant and atmosphere, bar is German-run, lots of languages spoken. Many others around Plaza Bolívar (eg **E** *San Miguel*, good value).

Playa El Agua AL *Lagunamar*, a few kilometres north of Pampatar, T620711, F621445. Occupies a vast spread of flat coastland, 9 pools and 6 restaurants. **A** *Casa Trudel*, T/F490558. 4 rooms with bath, bed and breakfast, homely atmosphere, with bath (Dutch/Canadian owners), no young children, evening food service, barbecue once a week, 5 mins' walk from beach. **A** *Trudel's Garden Vacation Home*, Calle Miragua, T/F490558. 6 large, 2-bedroom houses set in a beautiful garden, 200 m from beach, fresh towels daily, fully-equiped kitchens, for reservations by post write to Dan and Trudy O'Brien, Apdo 106, Isla Margarita, 6301, Parlamar, Venezuela. **B** *Residencias Miramar*, Av 31 de Julio-Carretera Manzanillo, esq Calle Miragua, 3 mins from beach, 1 min from supermarket. Family-run, self-catering apartments, comfortable, barbecue, clean. **D** *Hostería El Agua*, Av 31 de Julio Vía Manzanillo, T48935. Contact Sarah Studer, English, French, German and Italian spoken, clean bathroom, good beds, fan, fridge, laundry facilities, 4 mins' walk from beach. **A** *Pelican Village*, northern end. Small group of bungalows, satellite TV, pool, restaurant, bar, German run, quiet. An un-named chalet park next to the *Miragua Club Resort*, self-catering, all facilities, very welcoming, no price but "usually cheaper than *Miramar*".

Manzanillo A *Hotel Karibek*, overlooks the sea. Wonderful view, quiet rooms, extremely clean, balcony, bath, fan, swimming pool, bar and restaurant adjacent, breakfast provided, easy taxi ride to other beaches. **B** *Pahayda Vilas*, nice apartments, large rooms, 2 baths for 4 people, sign at main road. 100 m further on towards Playa Azul, beach house with rooms to let and German-owned restaurant, good food.

Juan Griego B *El Yare*, El Fuerte, T530835, 1 block from beach. Some suites with kitchen, owner speaks English. **C** *Nuevo Juan Griego*, next to beach. English spoken, very popular, expensive restaurant. **D** *Aparthotel y Res El Apurano*, C La Marina y El Fuerte, T530901. Friendly, English speaking manager, 2-bedroom apartments with bath, hot water, a/c, but no utensils or towels (because of theft). **D** *Hospedaje El Caney*, Guevara 17, T514-3875345, F514-6823774. With bath, patio, kitchen facilities, pleasant. **D** *Patrick's*, El Fuerte, next to *Hotel Fortín*, T/F534089. French-run, a/c rooms with fine sunset views, excellent restaurant and bar. **E** *Residencia Carmencita*, Calle Guevara 20, T55561. A/c, private bath. **E** *Fortín*, a/c, cold water, opposite beach, most rooms have good views, good restaurant and tables on the beach. **E** *La Posada de Clary*, Los Mártires, T530037. Several others. Also cabins for 5 with cooking facilities US$20.

El Yaque B *California*, T014-951907, F950908. 46 rooms, small pool.

Isla del Coche *Coche Speed Paradise*, Playa da Punta, T0149-9527226. 48 rooms, more under construction, windsurfing, sandsurfing, swimming, weekend buffet recommended, beautifully landscaped with desert paths, shells, rocks and driftwood, pool can be used by yachties during the week, see the macaws being 'watered' in the afternoon. *Isla de Coche*, T991431. 23 rooms, older resort, pool, windsurfing.

Eating Porlamar *Doña Martha*, Velázquez near Hernández. Colombian food, good, inexpensive. *El Punto Criollo*, Igualdad near *Hotel Porlamar*. Excellent value, good. *Rancho Grande*, Guevara, near Playa El Agua bus stop. Colombian, good value. Recommended. *El Pollo de Carlitos*, Marcano y Martínez. Nice location, live music most nights, good food and value.

Bahía bar-restaurant, Av Raúl Leoni y Vía El Morro. Excellent value, live music. *Los 3 Delfines*, Cedeño 26-9. Seafood. Recommended. *La Isla*, Mariño y Cedeño. 8 fast food counters ranging from hamburgers to sausages from around the world. *Dino's Grill*, Igualdad y Martínez, T642366. Open 0700-1400, buffet lunch, indoor/outdoor seating, grill, homemade sausages, wood-fired pizza oven, cheap, friendly, good service. Recommended. On 4 de Mayo: *El Picadilly*, good cheap lunch, and *Dragón Chino*, great Chinese food.

Pampatar *El Farallón*, excellent seafood restaurant beside Castillo. Seafood soup recommended, bowl of shellfish and meal on its own. Also beach restaurant *Antonio's* and *Trimar*, seafood.

Playa El Agua *Restaurant El Paradiso*, southern end. Rents out cabins, small but comfortable. *Kiosko El Agua*, helpful, English spoken. *Posada Shangri-Lá* is recommended, *Casa Vieja*, seafood, *La Dorada*, French owned by Gérard and Hilda, with good beach view, good value. Many beach restaurants stay open till 2200.

Juan Griego *Restaurant Mi Isla* is recommended. *Viña del Mar*, opposite *Hotel Fortín*. A/c, attractive, excellent food. *Juan Griego Steak House*, same building as *Hotel El Yare*. Good value. Recommended. Also *El Buho*. French-owned pub. *Viejo Muelle*, next door. Good restaurant, live music, outside beach bar.

Many on the island, including **16-26 March** at Paraguachí (*Feria de San José*); **27 July** at Punta de Piedra; **31 July** (Batalla de Matasiete) and **14-15 August** (Asunción de la Virgen) at La Asunción; **8-15 September** at El Valle; **4-11 November** at Boca del Río, **4-30 November** at Boca del Pozo; **5-6 December** at Porlamar; **27 December-3 January** at Juan Griego.

Festivals
See map for locations

Porlamar *Mosquito Coast Club*, behind *Hotel Bella Vista*. Disco with genuine Venezuelan feel, good *merengue* and rock music, bar outside. Also does excellent Mexican meals (beware of overcharging on simple items like water). Discothèque for singles, *Village Club*, Av Santiago Mariño. Recommended for good music with a variety of styles but expensive drinks, cover charge. *Doce 34*, Av 4 de Mayo. 2 dance floors. Highly recommended. Nightlife is generally good, but at European prices.

Nightlife

Porlamar Besides all duty-free shops, *Del Bellorín*, Cedeño, near Santiago Mariño. Good for handicrafts. Artisans display crafts in the evening on 4 de Mayo. Good selection of jewellery at *Sonia Gems*, on Cedeño. Many other places on the main street are overpriced. When purchasing jewellery, bargain hard, don't pay by credit card (surcharges are imposed), get a detailed guarantee of the item. Designer clothes are cheap in many places, especially on Blvd Guevara, Blvd Gómez, Calles Igualdad and Velázquez; cosmetics and perfumes also good value.

Shopping

Supertours, Calle Larez, Quinta Thaid, T618781, F617061. Tours of the island and elsewhere. *Zuluoga Tours*, San Nicolás entre Arismendi y Mariño No 16-40. Helpful. Ask travel agents about excursions on the sailing catamaran, *Catatumbo*, recommended.

Tour operators

Air *Avensa* on Calle Fajardo, Porlamar, T617111, airport 691021. *Aereotuy* (LTA) has a fleet of small planes for trips to national parks, eg Canaima, Los Roques, Delta del Orinoco and Isla La Blanquilla. It operates *posadas* on Los Roques as well as 3 large charter catamarans. T095-632211 (Porlamar), F617746, or in Caracas T02-7638043, F7625254.

Transport
Aug & Sep are vacation months: flights & hotels are fully booked

Road Bus: several bus companies in Caracas sell through tickets from Caracas to Porlamar, arriving about midday. Buses return from Porlamar from terminal at Centro Comercial Bella Vista, at bottom end of Calle San Rafael (it takes about 4 hrs). By car from Caracas to the ferry terminal. **Car hire**: *Ramcar*, at airport and *Hotel Bella Vista*, recommended as cheap and reliable, non-deductible insurance (as do *Hertz* and *Avis*); others on Av Santiago Mariño. In all cases check the brakes. Scooters can also be hired from, among others, *Maruba Motor Rentals*, La Mariña (English spoken, good maps, highly recommended, US$16 bike for 2, US$13 bike for 1). Motor cycles may not be ridden between 2000 and 0500. **NB** There are

The Venezuelan Islands

service stations in towns, but check the gauge on the fuel pump carefully: overcharging is common. **Taxi**: taxi fares are published by the magazine *Mira* but are not uniformly applied by drivers. If you want to hire a taxi for a day you will be charged US$10-15 per hour. Always establish the fare before you get in the car. There is a 30% surcharge after 2100.

Sea Ferry (very busy at weekends and Mon) **From Puerto La Cruz**, to Margarita (**Punta de Piedra**): Conferries, Los Cocos terminal, T677221, and *Meliá Hotel*, Puerto La Cruz, T653001, to Margarita, 4 a day between 0800 and 0100 each way (extras at 0400 and 1600 at busy times), 5 hrs, passengers US$12.50 one way 1st class, US$8.50 2nd (in enclosed middle deck with limited views), children and pensioners half price, cars, US$25. A new fast ferry, *Margarita Express*, takes 2 hrs, US$20. Ferries not always punctual. **From Cumaná**, Conferry Terminal, Cumaná Puerto Sucre, T311462, ferries at 0700 and 1600 to Margarita, returning 1000 and 2000, US$7.50 one way for passengers. A ferry from Punta de Piedra to Coche sails Mon-Fri, 1600, returns 1730, Sat and Sun, 0800 and 1730, returns 0530 and 1730.

Windward Lines, www.infinetworx.com/windward (see page 25) sails to Pampatar, Isla Margarita every other week (Tue) from Trinidad, leaving again on Wed at 1800, arriving in Port of Spain on Thu and continuing to St Vincent, Barbados and St Lucia. TCs can be changed on board at good rates. Contact Windward Lines agent, Julio César Acosta, Acosta Asociados, T081-657393, 094-820058, or mobile 0149-9948115, grupoacosta@cantv.net efficient, speaks English, ensures immigration/customs goes smoothly. He sells tickets under a canopy on the quay some hours before the ferry sails. Immigration and customs sit next to him. **Yacht**: on arrival, take your dinghy to Vemesca (Venezuelan Marine Supply) in Porlamar which is the main anchorage. Clear in and out at the Port Captain's office. It can be very crowded in hurricane season and rolly with southeast winds. Lock up the boat, dinghy and motor as thefts are common. A few boats stop in Pampatar, and Juan Griego makes a good stopping point when coming from La Blanquilla. On Isla de Coche by *Paradise Speed* (move close to ferry dock at night and stay out of way of fishermen), El Saco, Cubagua. Dinghy thefts and other security problems at Porlamar, Coche and Cubagua. Fuel and water at Porlamar dock, fuel but no water at Juan Griego. Occasionally possible to get a slip at Concorde marina. Supplies at Vemesca and several local marine stores.

Directory **Banks** *Casa de cambio* at Igualdad y Av Santiago Mariño. Also *Cambio La Precisa*, Maneiro entre Mariño y Blvd Guevara. Good rates. Banks are open 0830-1130, 1400-1630. There are often long queues. Don't change money with street people, you will be short changed. **Tourist office** A tourist information booth on 4 de Mayo has map, coupon booklet, *La Vista* tourist magazine. Travel agencies can also provide a tourist guide to Margarita. An outspoken and well-informed English-language newspaper, *Mira*, is published on the island; the editor/publisher acts also as an inexpensive tour guide; Av Santiago Mariño, Ed Carcaleo Suites, Apdo 2-A, Porlamar (T095-613351). The best map is available from Corpoven.

Islas Los Roques

Prices are higher than the mainland & infrastructure is limited but the islands are beautiful & unspoiled

Islas Los Roques lie 150 km north of Caracas; the atoll, of about 340 islets and reefs, constitutes one of Venezuela's loveliest national parks (225,153 ha). There are long stretches of white beaches and almost 20 km of coral reef with crystal-clear water ideal for snorkelling (best at the southern part of the archipelago) and diving. There are many bird nesting sites (eg the huge gull colonies on Francisqui and the pelicans, boobies and frigates on Selesqui); May is nesting time at the gull colonies. For more information write to La Fundación Científica Los Roques, Apdo No 1, Av Carmelitas, Caracas 1010, T326771. The islands are best visited midweek as Venezuelans swarm here on long weekends and at school holidays (low season is Easter to July). Average temperature 29°C with coolish nights. You will need strong sunblock as there is no shade. Park entry US$15.

Many of the islands' names are contractions of earlier names: eg Northeast Cay is Nordisqui, 'Sarky' comes from Sister Key, 'Dos Mosquices' from Domus Key, where there are sea turtles and a Marine Biology Centre researching the coral reef and its ecology.

Gran Roque is the main and only permanently inhabited island. The airport is here, as is the national guard, three grocery stores, public phones, medical facilities, a few restaurants and accommodation. There is nowhere to change travellers' cheques. Park Headquarters are in the scattered fishing village (*Population*: 900). You can negotiate with local fishermen for transport to other islands: you will need to take your own tent, food and (especially) water. Gran Roque's main beach was washed away in a hurricane in late 1999. The offshore coral was unaffected. **Madrisqui** has nine summer houses. **Francisqui** is three islands joined by sandspits, with calm lagoon waters to the south and rolling surf to the north. For windsurfing, *Happy Surf*, Francisqui.

Gran Roque
Phone code: 02

Eola is a yacht, fully equipped, with cabins, chartered for US$120 per day, all inclusive, highly recommended as a worthwhile way of getting some shade on the treeless beaches. Run by Italians Gianni and Jaqueline. Also *Desmid*, T014-9159001, and *Floating Village*, T016-66327730. This is one of the least visited **diving** spots in the Caribbean. You can arrange packages to stay ashore in a lodge and/or on board a sailing yacht and dive daily. *Sesto Continente Dive Resort*, on the edge of the village, T/F0149-241853, ask for Jakob, Saul (speaks English) or Hugo, very kind people, two dives cost US$60, the boat is comfortable, recommended. Also *Reef Divers*, T0149-141616, F02-7510704, hpina@telcel.net.ve, recommended, English, French and Italian spoken. Boca del Medio is an easy dive east of the island chain in clear, shallow water of about 10-15 m, with a great variety of coral, fauna and flora. Piedra de la Guasa is a 10-25 m underwater cliff where you can see grouper, snapper, barracuda, horse-eye jack etc. Olapa de Bavusqui are caves where you can observe sharks and a variety of crustaceans. At Boca de Cote there are spectacular cliffs dropping to 55 m with lots of different fish and coral. Cayo Sal is an impressive site with cliffs and caves filled with multicoloured sponges and black coral. At Noronoqui there is a labyrinth of antler coral and at Nordesqui there are a few shipwrecks and many lobsters.

Diving & marine life

Gran Roque **AL** *Canto de la Ballena*, on the seafront, T518225. Full board, excellent food, relaxed, fans, can pay with travellers' cheques. **AL** per person *Posada Bora La Mar*, T2843891. 4 basic rooms, with bathroom and ceiling fan, run by María Agustí, good food. There are many other posadas, ranging from **D** per person to **LL**. These include: *Las Palmeras* and *Natura Viva*, both have 15 double or triple rooms with bathroom and fans, and are run by Aerotuy T02-7638043, F02-7625254, or Porlamar T065-632211. **B** per person *Posada de Judith*, 3 comfortable rooms with bathroom, 3 meals; and *La Mecha*, 2 rooms with bathroom, 3 meals and transport to the other cays; both are run by Judith Campagna de Puig, T2713660, who also runs *Campamento Lilo*, where lodging is what nature provides and you eat what you catch, also organizes activities. **B** per person *Gremary*, 11 basic rooms, the oldest *posada* on the island, some with bathroom, lunch and transport extra, run by Gregorio Romero, T/F3372765.

Sleeping & eating
See page 963 for details of hotel price grades

Cayo Francés One *posada*, **A-B**, T02-7930694, F7939579. Full board including drinks, good food, friendly staff, nice beach, snorkelling gear, water and light 24 hrs, fan, bargaining possible if you stay for several days; also hammock sites and camping. *Crasqui*, on Cayo Crasqui, contact *Sun Chichi* hotels, T02-9935866, F916549. 25 double and triple cabin-style tents, with primitive communal bathrooms, interesting construction, water from desalination plant, all-inclusive, meals, beach activities, drinks.

Camping You need a permit from Inparques, T02-2347331, F02-2344238 in Caracas, or the office in Gran Roque. Tiny but irritating biting insects in the calmer months can make camping miserable.

The Venezuelan Islands

Transport **Air** Flights from Maiquetía or Porlamar. *Chapi Air* from Maiquetía at 0800, returning at 1600, US$110. *Aereotuy* (T02-7638043, F7625254) fly from Maiquetía 3 times a day. 2-day package (return flight, accommodation, meals, drinks, catamaran excursion with snorkelling and diving equipment), from US$300 per person (one-day from Margarita US$150). **Sea** If you arrive by yacht, Los Roques are not a port of entry, although you may stay 14 days if exit clearance from the previous country lists Los Roques on the way to an official port.

Other Venezuelan Islands

Islas Los Testigos are the first islands approached by yachts coming from Grenada or Trinidad. This is a protected area where spearfishing and scuba diving are forbidden. You can fish with a hand-line from a yacht or buy fish and lobster in season from any of the 150 fishermen who live on the islands. There is a vast colony of frigate birds and large sand dunes can be found on the windward side of the major island. There is no airport or ferry. No official clearance is given, the coastguard officer stands by VHF16 and can give temporary clearance, usually up to 48 hours. Also worth mentioning are the **Archipelago of Las Aves**, west of Los Roques, where fishing and diving are good. There are no commercial enterprises and the islands are visited mostly by yachts travelling between Venezuela and Bonaire.

 La Tortuga is Venezuela's second largest island, lying west of Margarita. It is a low, dry island with wonderful beaches, good snorkelling, gorgeous water and a week's worth of anchorages. Visit **Los Palaquemos** by dinghy, an offshore reef with a few visible rocks. The small airstrip is used by small planes from Caracas at weekends. Further out are **La Blanquilla** and **La Orchila** (a military installation, do not land), both with coral reefs. La Blanquilla can be reached as a day trip from Margarita with Línea Turística Aereotuy (LTA). It has a secluded white sand beach with crystal clear water and excellent snorkelling. While it lacks palm trees, shade can be found in caves along the shore. You can swim into underwater caverns while snorkelling. Most yachts anchor at Playa Yaque. Americano Bay is just north of Playa Yaque and has white sand beaches, clear water, good snorkelling and is a lovely spot to watch the sunset from the deck of a yacht. About 500 km north of Margarita, at the same latitude as Dominica, is **Isla de Aves**, 65 sq km of seabirds (sooty and brown noddy tern, frigate birds, gulls) surrounded by crystal clear water. The island is also a nesting site of the endangered green turtle. There is a Venezuelan coast guard station.

Much closer to the mainland are two areas of reefs and islands which have been designated national parks. There is no way to get to them other than by spending time in Venezuela itself.

Parque Nacional Morrocoy

The national park of Morrocoy comprises hundreds of coral reefs, palm-studded islets, small cosy beaches and calm water for water-skiing, snorkelling, and skin-diving. The park is reached from Tucacas in the south and Chichiriviche in the north. With appropriate footwear it is possible to walk between some of the islands. The largest, cleanest and most popular of the islands is **Cayo Sombrero** (busy at weekends); even so it has some deserted beaches, with trees to sling a hammock. **Playuela** is beautiful and better for snorkelling (beware of mosquitoes in the mangrove swamps), while **Playa del Sol** has no good beach and no palm trees. **Bocaseca** is more exposed to the open sea than other islands and thus has fewer mosquitoes. **Cayo Borracho** is one of the nicest islands. **NB** Much of the coral in the park was destroyed in 1996 and the potential for scuba diving has fallen greatly. Beginners will still get good value for money but there isn't much to interest advanced divers.

 Adjoining the park to the north is a vast nesting area for scarlet ibis, flamingoes and herons, the **Cuare Wildlife Sanctuary**. Most of the flamingoes are in and around the estuary next to Chichiriviche, which is too shallow for boats but you can walk there or take a taxi. Birds are best watched early morning or late afternoon.

You may **camp** on the islands but must first make a reservation with Inparques (national parks), T8008487, 0800-2000 Mon-Sun; reserve at least 8 working days in advance giving all details; US$2.50 per person per night, 7 nights maximum, pay in full in advance (very complicated procedure). Very few facilities and no fresh water; Cayo Sombrero and Paiclas have restaurants, Boca Seca has a small café (closed Mon); Sombrero, Playa Azul and Paiclas have ecological toilets. At weekends and holidays it is very crowded and litter-strewn (beware rats).

Sleeping

From Tucacas Prices per boat range from US$20 return to Paiclas to US$40 return to Cayo Sombrero (maximum 7 per boat). Ticket office is to the left of the car entrance to the park. Recommended boatmen are Orlando and Pepe. **From Chichiriviche** Prices per boat vary according to distance; eg, US$10 to Cayo Muerto, US$35 to Cayo Sombrero. A 3-4 hr trip is US$50 per boat; 5-6 hr trip US$70 (maximum eight per boat); bargaining possible. There are two ports; one close to the centre and Playa Sur. The latter has a ticket system which is supposed to guarantee that you will not be cheated and that you will be picked up on time for return trip.

Transport
Playa Sur is not safe after dark; muggings reported

Tucacas

Tucacas is a hot, busy, dirty and expensive town, with lots of new building in progress, where bananas and other fruit are loaded for Curaçao and Aruba.

Phone code: 042
Population: 15,100

The only accommodation within the park is **AL** per person *Villa Mangrovia* on the Lizardo Spit between Tucacas and Chichiriviche. 3 rooms, good service, reservations through *Last Frontiers*, UK, T01844-208405, or *Journey Latin America*, UK, T0181-7478315. **B** *Hotel Manaure*, Av Silva, T831683. A/c, hot water, clean, good restaurant. **D** *La Suerte* on main street. Very clean, a/c, **E** with fan, with small shop. **E** *Las Palmas*, with shower, fan, kitchen and laundry facilities, helpful, cheap boat trips to islands. Opposite is **E** *La Esperanza*. Fan, with bath, fridge, clean, German owner arranges trips to islands. Cheap accommodation is difficult to find, especially in high season and at weekends, hotels are generally more expensive than elsewhere in Venezuela. *La Entrada*, good, cheap meals for US$2, open weekday lunchtime only. **Camping** Gas available in Tucacas or Puerto Cabello for camping in the Park.

Sleeping & eating
See page 963 for details of hotel price grades

Diving equipment can be hired from near the harbour. *Submatur*, Ayacucho 6, T830082, F831051, owner Mike Osborn, 4 day PADI course US$330, 1 day trip 2 dives US$65 (US$45 with own equipment); also rents rooms, fan and cooking facilities.

Sport

Guilica, 2 blocks up from *Hotel La Esperanza* on Av Principal, T/F830939. Tours to islands, also bird watching. *Valadero Tours*, round corner from *Hotel La Esperanza*. Tours to islands and mainland destinations, fax service, will reconfirm flights.

Tour operators

Frequent *por puesto* from Valencia, US$5, bus US$2.50. Coro, US$5. Bicycles can be hired in town.

Transport

Banks *Banco Unión*, cash advance on credit cards only. Hotels and travel agents will change money but at very low rates, if they have enough cash.

Directory

The Venezuelan Islands

Chichiriviche

Population: 7,000 A few kilometres beyond, towards Coro, is the favourite, and hence expensive, beach resort of Chichiriviche, which gets very crowded at holidays and weekends.

Sleeping & eating

See page 963 for details of hotel price grades

Hotels A *La Garza*, Av Principal, T86711. Attractive, pool, restaurant, full board, cheaper without, comfortable, popular, post box in lobby, daily collections, changes cash. **A** *Náutico*, T86024. Friendly, clean, including breakfast, dinner and trip to islands, good meals, fans, popular. **A** *Parador Manaure*, Mariño T86121, F86569. Sharing apartments for 5, clean, small pool, fully-equipped kitchen. **B** *Villa Marina*, T86503. Aparthotel, good, clean, safe, pool. **B** *La Puerta*, out of town, next to the port, T86621. Very clean, nice bar and restaurant, helpful owners. **C** *Capri*, Zamora, T86026, near docks. Shower, fan or a/c, clean, pleasant Italian owned, good restaurant and supermarket. **C** *Villa Gregoria*, Mariño, 1 block north of bus stop. With bath, clean, fan, laundry facilities, very friendly, Spanish run. **D** *Residencial Linda*, 1 block from docks. Italian owners, friendly, helpful, use of kitchen. **D** *Posada La Perrera*, Riera, near centre, 150 km from bus stop. Quiet, fan, clean, laundry facilities, patio, hammocks, luggage stored, Italian owner, tours arranged, very good. **D** *Residencial Delia*, Mariño 30, 1 block from *Gregoria*, T86089. Including breakfast, 4 double rooms, shared bath, clean, organizes tours, very friendly. **E** *Posada Alemania*, Cementos Coro, T850912. German-run, runs tours, rents snorkel gear, 200 m from Playa Sur, nice garden. **E** pp *Morena's Place*, Sector Playa Norte, 10 mins' walk from the bus stop, T/F850936, cvanmarcke@vln1186.ve.mbr.com Beautifully decorated house, fan, hammocks, helpful hosts, English spoken.

Sports

Diving *Centro de Buceo Caribe*, Playa Sur. Runs PADI courses for US$360, 1 day diving trip US$65, rents equipment, rooms for rent, **D**, with cooking facilities. *Aqua-Fun Diving*, Casa El Monte, El Sol, Virgen del Valle, T86265. Run by Pierre and Monika who speak German, English, French and Spanish, high quality dive equipment, PADI courses from beginner to pro level, excursions for divers with certification card (US$40-65 per person, US$30-55 with own equipment), 2 double rooms to rent, **D**, including breakfast, with fan.

Tour operators

Valadero Tours, 2 blocks from Banco Industrial on opposite side. Tours to islands US$16-19 per person, and to other parts of the country. Cheaper tours available with *Morrocoy Tours*, behind gas station near *Hotel La Garza*, or from *Ulrich's Lodge* restaurant on main street towards port.

Transport

Buses To Puerto Cabello, frequent *por puestos*, 2 hrs, US$3.50. Direct buses from Valencia or take bus from Morón to Coro and get out at turnoff, 1½ hrs, US$1.75.

Directory

Banks *Banco Industrial*, opposite bus terminal on main street. The only bank in the state of Falcón which changes dollars cash, open 0930-1530. *Valadero Tours* (see below) may change cash and TCs at very poor rates.

Mochima National Park

Puerto La Cruz

Venezuela's second Caribbean coastal national park is Mochima, 55 km from the port of Puerto La Cruz. This city is 320 km, five hours east of Caracas. It is the main commercial centre in this part of the country, especially for oil, but is also a popular holiday centre with good watersports and yachting facilities. The park itself also includes the mainland coast between Los Altos and Cumaná. The beaches and vistas of this stretch of the coast are beautiful. Since both Puerto La Cruz and Cumaná are ferry terminals for Margarita, Mochima can easily be incorporated into a visit to this part of Venezuela.

Isla de la Plata

The easiest island to reach is Isla de la Plata, yet another supposed lair of the pirate Henry Morgan. It has a white sand beach, and clear waters which are ideal for snorkelling. There are food and drink stalls, but take drinking water as there is none on the island. Also take a hat and sunscreen. It's about 10 minutes by boat to the island.

Further away, and larger, are the **Chimana islands** with beautiful beaches (Grande, Sur, del Oeste), in the waters around which there is snorkelling and good scuba diving. The islands are very popular and consequently are badly littered. All have restaurants, snack-bars and thatched shelters for hire.

Other islands in the vicinity are Monos (also good for scuba diving), **La Borracha**, **El Borracho** and **Los Borrachitos**, and **Caracas de Oeste** and **Caracas del Este**. All are in sheltered waters and are easy to explore by boat.

Other islands

Three companies offer trips to the islands: *Transtupuerto*, on Paseo Colón opposite *Hotel Diana*, T667138, trips to closest islands (Islas Chimanas and Las Borrachas) for US$8, day tour around several islands with stops US$30-40, includes snorkelling equipment and soft drinks; *Transporte Turístico Virgen del Valle*, offers similar deals (food extra); *Transtupaco*, next to *Hotel Meliá*, no tours, they act as a taxi to the islands.

Transport
Boat trips to the islands are cheaper from Santa Fe or Mochima (see below)

Alternatively, you can reach the islands with the *Embarcadero de Peñeros*, on Paseo Colón, behind the *Tejas Restaurant*. Departures from 0900-1000, return at 1600-1630; US$6 per person. Tourist office in Puerto La Cruz, *Coranztur* (Paseo Colón opposite *Hotel Diana*, T688170, open Mon-Fri 0800-1200, 1400-1730) provides tour operators for day trips to various islands for swimming or snorkelling; 6-hr trip to four islands costs US$15 per person,

The Venezuelan Islands

Puerto La Cruz

To Cumaná & Parque Nacional Mochima

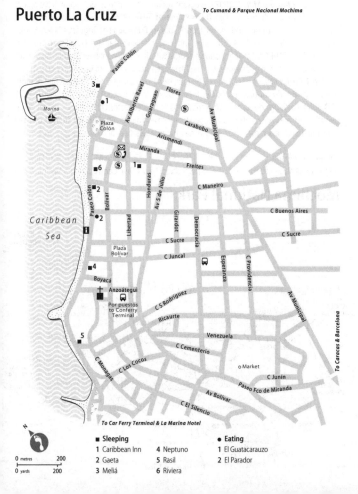

■ Sleeping
1 Caribbean Inn
2 Gaeta
3 Meliá
4 Neptuno
5 Rasil
6 Riviera

● Eating
1 El Guatacarauzo
2 El Parador

0 metres 200
0 yards 200

To Car Ferry Terminal & La Marina Hotel

including drinks. The islands to the east (Isla de Plata, Monos, Picuda Grande and Chica and the beaches of Conoma and Conomita) are best reached from the port at **Guanta** (taxi from town, or *por puesto* from Freites between Av 5 de Julio and Democracia, and ask to be dropped off at the Urb Pamatacualito).

Santa Fe

Phone code: 093

Further east from Puerto La Cruz is Santa Fe, larger and noisier than Mochima, but a good place to relax. The attractive beach is cleaned daily. It has a market on Saturday.

Sleeping & eating
See page 963 for details of hotel price grades

B *Playa Santa Fe Resort and Dive Center*, T014-7733777, Santafe@telcel.net.ve, renovated *posada* with various rooms and suites, laundry service, restaurant under construction, owner Jerry Canaday speaks English, diving trips US$65, transport to beaches, mountain bike rental. **C** *Café del Mar*, T210009, 1st hotel on beach, fan, very clean, good restaurant, tours to islands US$5-10 per person, also to Gran Sabana, Orinoco Delta, owner Matthias Sauter, German spoken. **C** *Siete Delfines*, on beach, T/F093-314166, **D** without breakfast, safe, fan, terrace where you can cook, excellent food, bar, great atmosphere, laundry service, secure, recommended, ask here for information, diving courses (US$65), waterskiing, windsurfing in Dec, paintball, beach games, owner Ricardo Piuzzi speaks German, English, Italian and some French. **D** *Bahía del Mar*, T210073, pleasant rooms with fan, upstairs rooms have a cool breeze, French and English spoken. **D** *Las Palmeras*, T014-7736152, behind *Cochaima*, new, fan, room for 5 with fridge and cooker, French spoken. **D** *Posada Los Angeles*, T014-7755445, also new, with fan, room for 4 with fridge and cooker, Italian restaurant. **D** *La Sierra Inn*, near *Café del Mar*, T014-933116, comfortable rooms with fans, self-contained garden suite with fridge and cooker, run by Sr José Vivas, English spoken, helpful, tours to islands from US$10 per person. **E** *Cochaima*, on beach, run by Margot, noisy, popular, fan, next to restaurant of same name, safe. **E** *El Portugués, Sr Julio César*, last *posada* on beach, cooking facilities, very helpful. **F** *Posada Lodging*, opposite *Club Naútico*, basic, shared bath. Other places to eat: *Club Naútico*, fish and Venezuelan dishes, open for lunch and dinner. *Los Molinos (Julios)*, open all day from 0800, beach bar serves sandwiches, hamburgers, beer and cocktails.

Sports **Diving** *Explosub*, *Hotel Meliá*, PO Box 4784, Puerto La Cruz, T653611, T/F673256. Efficient, helpful, will dive with 1 person, US$75 per 2 dives. *Lolo's Dive Centre*, Guanta Marina, Bahía

Mochima National Park

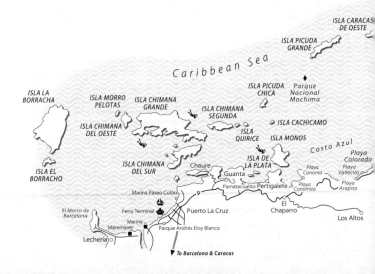

de Guanta, T683052, F682885, or contact Eddy Revelant, cellnet 0149-801543. Experienced, English spoken, collect you from hotel and provide lunch, US$60 per 2 dives, 2-3 person minimum, 4-day PADI course US$300. Hotels and travel agents organize trips. The nearest recompression chamber is on Isla Margarita. In Mochima: *Rodolfo Plaza* runs a diving school for beginners and hires equipment, also walking and canoeing trips around Mochima; contact him in Caracas (Los Palos Grandes, Av Andrés Bello entre 3a y 4a transversal, T02-9612531). *Francisco García* (2 doors down from Rodolfo), also runs a diving school (PADI courses) and shop, T093-932991. *Fantasea Dive Center*, T/F210073, scuba24@ hotmail.com, PADI courses all levels, including 4-day PADI certification course US$300, also basic **D** accommodation.

Por puesto at 0600 and bus to Cumaná (US$1.75), and Puerto La Cruz (US$1.40). It is sometimes difficult to get the bus from Puerto La Cruz to stop at Santa Fe, *por puesto* may be a better bet, US$2, 1 hr, or taxi, US$23 including wait. Jeep, boat or diving tours available. Francisco is recommended for boat trips, he can be found a few houses to the west of the *Cochaima*. Fishermen offer similar trips but their prices are extortionate. Boat trips to Playas Colorada or Blanca cost US$10 per person; better to hire your own boat for half the price, or hitch down the road to Colorada. Ask for Thomas, he has a boat and will take you wherever. **Transport**

Mochima town

The small, colourful weekend resort of Mochima, beyond Santa Fe, is 4 km off the main road, hitching difficult. The sea is dirty near the town. Boats to nearby beaches, such as Playa Marita and Playa Blanca, and around the islands, US$12-15, depending on the distance (up to six people). Arrange with the boatman what time he will collect you.

C *Posada Gaby*, at end of road with its own pier next to sea, T014-7731104, F093-330462, a/c or fan, breakfast available, lovely place, take guests to islands for US$6-7 per person. **D** *Posada Mochimero*, on main street in front of *Restaurant Mochimero*, a/c or fan. **D** *Villa Vicenta*, Av Principal, T014-9935877, basic rooms with cold water, owner Otilio is helpful. **E** *Posada Beatriz*, T014-7732262, run by Sr Juan Remez, fan, use of kitchen. Sr César Bareto rents rooms for 2 and house for 4 or more, **D**. Also ask Sra Milagros Cova, whose properties all have bed linen and kitchen utensils, Doña Cruz, or Mama Inés. **Sleeping**

ISLA CARACAS DEL ESTE — Las Playuelas — Playa Blanca — Playa Marita — Península de Manare — Bahía Mochima — ISLA VENADO — Ensenada Tigrillo — Mochima — Cerro Aceite Castillo — Punta Gorda — Golfo de Santa Fe — Playa Santa Cruz — Santa Fe — Playa Los Hicacos — To Cumaná (approx 20 km)

0 km 3 / 0 miles 3 / N

A highly recommended restaurant is *El Mochimero*, on waterfront 5 mins from jetty, lunch and dinner. *Brisas de Mochima*, at the end of the main road behind the statue, fish dishes, lunch and dinner. *Dulce y Salado*, next to jetty, delicious *pastelitos* and *empanadas*, homemade cakes and juices. *Mi Compay*, close to jetty, hearty breakfasts, *arepas*, juices and coffee. **Eating**

From Puerto La Cruz, the trip can be organized by taxi, US$40 including the journey home. Buses do not travel between Santa Fe and Mochima, *por puestos* can be taken, bargain hard on the price, US$15-21 is reasonable. Once in Mochima it is very difficult to find a taxi, you should arrange to be picked up again by the same driver if just staying for 1 day. Bus to Cumaná, 1400, US$1.40. **NB** At Christmas, Carnaval and **Transport**

The Venezuelan Islands

Easter this part of the coast becomes extremely congested, so patience is needed as long queues of traffic can develop. Robbery may be a problem, but if you take care and use common sense, the risk is minimal. It can also become littered and polluted, especially on the islands. Camping on the islands in Mochima national park is not advisable.

Background

History

Christopher Columbus made landfall on the nearby Paria Peninsula in August 1498. Two years later, a settlement had been established at Santiago de Cubagua (later called Nueva Cádiz) to exploit the pearls which grew in its waters. Cubagua became a centre for pearling and for slavery, as the local Indians were used, under appalling duress, to dive into the oyster beds. By 1541, when Santiago was destroyed by an earthquake and tidal wave, the pearl beds had been almost exhausted, but the Greek word for pearl, *margarita*, was retained for the main island of the group.

Margarita, and the nearest town on the mainland, Cumaná, were strongholds of the forces for the independence of South America from Spain. Between 1810 and 1817, the island was the scene of revolts and harsh Spanish reprisals. The liberator Simón Bolívar declared the Third Republic, and was himself declared Commander in Chief of the Liberating Army, at Villa del Norte (now Santa Ana) in 1816. After the war, the name of Nueva Esparta (maintaining the Greek allusion) was conferred in recognition of the bravery of Margarita in the struggle. Subsequent events have been nothing like so heroic, with life revolving around fishing and small agriculture. After a regeneration of the the pearl industry at the end of the 19th century, it has gone into decline, the oyster beds having all but disappeared through disease.

The economy

The island's tourism boom began in 1983, largely as a result of the fall in the value of the bolívar and the consequent tendency of Venezuelans to spend their holidays at home. Margarita's status as a duty-free zone has also helped. Venezuelan shoppers go in droves for clothing, electronic goods and other consumer items. Gold and gems are good value, but many things are not. There has been extensive building in Porlamar, with new shopping areas and Miami-style hotels going up. A number of beaches are also being developed. All-inclusive resorts and timeshare are expanding on the northeast corner of the island and there is a glut of hotel rooms and apartments. The island's popularity means that various packages are on offer, sometimes at good value, especially off-season.

Local industries are fishing and fibre work, such as hammocks and straw hats. Weaving, pottery and sweets are being pushed as handicraft items for the tourists. An exhibition centre has been opened at El Cercado, near Santa Ana, on Calle Principal, near the church.

20

Netherland Antilles, the ABC Islands

*The Netherlands Antilles consist of the islands of Aruba ,
Bonaire and Curaçao, popularly known as the 'ABCs' (60-80
km off the coast of Venezuela outside the hurricane belt), and
the '3 S's': Sint Eustatius (Statia), Saba, and the south part of
Sint Maarten (St-Martin) in what are generally known as
the Leeward Islands (880 km further north in the hurricane
belt). Because of the distance separating the north islands
from the other Dutch possessions, the 3 S's are described in a
separate section earlier in the Handbook.*

*There is some confusion regarding which islands are
Leeward and which are Windward: locals refer to the ABCs
as 'Leeward Islands', and the other 3 S's 'Windward', a
distinction adopted from the Spaniards, who still speak of the
Islas de Sotavento and de Barlovento with reference to the
trade winds.*

*Each island is different from the others in size, physical
features, the structure of the economy and the level of
development and prosperity.*

Bonaire

Population: 14,190

Bonaire is the least densely populated of the islands and the inhabitants are mostly of mixed Arawak, European and African descent. They are a very friendly and hospitable people. The island is quiet, peaceful and very safe. As in Curaçao and Aruba, Dutch is the official language, Papiamento the colloquial tongue, and Spanish and English are both widely spoken.

Ins and outs

Getting there **Air** *KLM* flies from Amsterdam once a week in a joint operation with *ALM*, although this may change from a direct service to going via Curaçao. *Martinair* offers a direct service. If you are a diver and it is specified on your airline ticket, *KLM* will allow you an extra 10 kg baggage allowance for diving equipment (regular allowance 20 kg tourist class, 30 kg business class) without incurring overweight charges. If you fly with *ALM* you are entitled to a free return flight to Curaçao as part of your ticket. *ALM* (in association with *United Airlines*) flies from Aruba, Curaçao, Atlanta, Miami and several other places via Curaçao (eg Caracas,

Bonaire

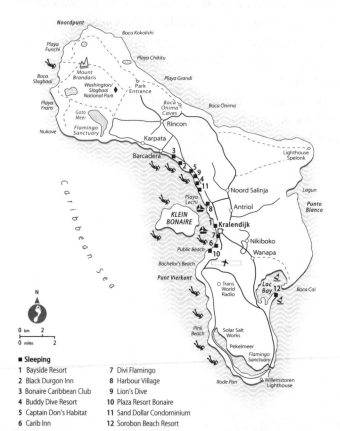

■ **Sleeping**
1 Bayside Resort
2 Black Durgon Inn
3 Bonaire Caribbean Club
4 Buddy Dive Resort
5 Captain Don's Habitat
6 Carib Inn
7 Divi Flamingo
8 Harbour Village
9 Lion's Dive
10 Plaza Resort Bonaire
11 Sand Dollar Condominium
12 Sorobon Beach Resort

Essentials

Documents *See page 1002.*

Departure tax *There is a departure tax of US$6 (NAf 10) on local flights and US$20 (NAf 36) on international flights.*

Hours of business *Shops are open 0800-1200 and 1400-1800, Monday-Saturday, or until 2100 on Friday, and for a few hours on Sunday if cruise ships are in port. Supermarkets are open 0800-2000 and some on Sunday 1100-1400.*

Voltage *127 volts, 50 cycles. 220 volts available at some resorts.*

Tipping *10-15% in restaurants, which is often added automatically to the bill. Tax is 10%. Dive shops 10%.*

Radio *The news is broadcast in Dutch on Voz di Bonaire, FM 94.7 MHz, Monday-Saturday on the hour 0700-1800. Transworld Radio broadcasts in English on 800 KHz MW daily 0700-0830, 2200-2400, news 0700 Monday-Friday, 0800 and 2200 daily, 2300 Saturday and Sunday; Caribbean weather forecast 0730 Monday-Friday, 0800 Saturday and Sunday. Radio Nederland, 6020 KHz at 0630, 6165 and 15315 KHz at 2030, 9590 and 11720 KHz at 2330. The Papiamento broadcast is on 97.1 FM.*

Tourist offices overseas
Canada *RMR Group Inc, Taurus House, 512 Duplex Avenue, Toronto, Ontario, M4R 2E3,*

T416-4844864, 800-8266247, F416-4858256.
Europe *Interreps BV, Visseringlaan 24, 2288 ER Rijswijk, The Netherlands, T31070-3954444, F31070-3368333, interrep@interrep.demon.nl*
USA *Adams Unlimited, 10 Rockefeller Plaza, Suite 900, New York, NY 10020, T212-9565912, 800-2662473, F212-9565913, lisa@adams-pr.com*
Venezuela *Flamingo Representaciones, Yazmín Pérez de Ramírez, Av Humboldt, Edif Humboldt, Piso 1 Apt 5, urb Bello Monte, Caracas, T9534653, F9511625.*

Bonhata, *the Bonaire Hotel and Tourist Association, also promotes the island, T7175134, F7178240, PO Box 358.*

Public holidays *New Year's Day, Good Friday, Easter Monday, Queen's Birthday and Rincon Day (30 April), Labour Day (1 May), Ascension Day, Bonaire Day (6 September), Christmas Day and Boxing Day. Carnival takes place over about six weeks from the end of January to the beginning of March, with parades, jump-ups and the election of King and Queen of the Carnival and 'Prince and Pancho'. Several days are devoted to the Tumba festival, a Tumba being a winning song. Carnival is organized by the Fundashon Karnival Boneiru (Fukabo). Dates for the main adult parade are 25 February 2001, 10 February 2002, 2 March 2003, 22 February 2004, 6 February 2005.*

Netherland Antilles, the ABC Islands

Kingston, Maracaibo, St Maarten, San Juan, Santo Domingo). *Air Aruba* flies from Aruba, Bogotá and Medellín. *Air Jamaica* flies from Chicago and Montego Bay. The Venezuelan airline, *Avior*, which provides commuter services to most cities in Venezuela, has a flight from Caracas to Bonaire Sun, Wed and Fri, arriving in Bonaire at 1830 and returning at 1900, 19 seats, about US$120 return, tickets can be booked with *Bonaire Air Services* at the airport or in Kralendijk. **Sea** There is no regular ferry service from Venezuela but a coaster, *Don Andrés*, makes a weekly run from Muaco, La Vela. You have to contact the captains direct, try the *capitanía* or the maritime agency 2 blocks from the Plaza Bolívar. It is a long journey, heavy seas, not recommended for the seasick or women.

There is no regular bus, but a so-called 'autobus' passes at certain places in town and takes you to the street or place you want to go for a few guilders. There are taxis at the airport but they are difficult to find around the island. Taxis do not 'cruise' so you must telephone for one, T7178100. The best way of getting about is to hire a car, scooter or mountain bike. Distances are not great but the heat is. Some hotels have a shuttle service to town. Hitching is fairly easy.

Getting around
See transport, page 998, for further details

Flora and fauna

The old salt pans of Pekelmeer, needed by the Salt Company, posed an ecological problem: Bonaire has one of the largest Caribbean flamingo colonies in the Western Hemisphere, and these birds build their conical mud nests in the salt pans. Pleas from wildlife conservationists convinced the company that it should set aside an area of 56 ha for a flamingo sanctuary, with access strictly prohibited. The birds, initially rather startled by the sudden activity, have settled into a peaceful co-existence, so peaceful in fact that they have actually doubled their output and are now laying two eggs a year instead of their previous one. There are said to be over 15,000 flamingoes on the island, and they can be seen wading in Goto Meer Bay in the northwest, in the salt lake near Playa Grandi, and in Lac Bay on the southeast coast of Bonaire, feeding on algae which give them their striking rose-pink colour. It is an impressive sight to witness the flamingoes rising from the water in the evening as they prepare to overnight in Venezuela.

There are also two smaller bird sanctuaries at the Solar Salt Works and Goto Meer. At Pos'i Mangel, in the national park, thousands of birds gather in the late afternoon. Bronswinkel Well, also in the park, is another good place to see hundreds of birds and giant cacti. The indigenous Bonaire Green Parrot can be seen in the Park and at Onima. About 190 species of birds have been found on Bonaire as well as the flamingoes. An annual Birdwatching Olympics and Nature Week is held in September, with prizes for those who spot the greatest number of species.

There are lots of iguanas and lizards of all shapes and sizes. The big blue lizards are endemic to Bonaire, while the Anolis, a tree lizard with a yellow dewlap, is related to the Windward Islands Anolis species rather than to the neighbouring Venezuelan species. The interior has scant vegetation but the enormous cacti provide perching places for yellow-winged parrots. The most common mammal you are likely to see is the goat, herds of which roam the island eating everything in sight except the cacti.

Diving and marine life

The least developed and least populated of the ABC islands, Bonaire has a special appeal to devotees of the sea, whose treasures are unsurpassed in the Caribbean. Surrounding the island are coral reefs harbouring over a thousand different species of marine creatures. Bonaire is outside the hurricane belt, but in November 1999 Hurricane Lenny produced a surge which damaged the top reef and knocked over many coral heads while wiping out many beaches in the south. Shore diving from *Habitat* south to past the *Sand Dollar* was badly affected. However, there are still lots of fish and with little rain and no run-off, visibility of 30 m or more is assured all year around. The Bonaire Marine Park is working with Cargill, the salt company, to improve shore diving access at all the southern sites. Ranked as one of the three top dive spots in the world, and number one in the Caribbean (followed by Grand Cayman Island and Cozumel), Bonaire is a leader in the movement for preservation of underwater resources and around the whole island is a protected marine park from the high water mark down to 60 m. Two areas have been designated marine reserves, with no diving allowed; along Playa Frans, north to Boca Slogbaai, and west of Karpata. Lac Bay is also part of the Marine Park because of its mangroves and sea-grass beds and has been designated a recreation area but no more hotels will be allowed. Stringent laws passed in 1971 ban spearfishing and the removal of any marine life from Bonaire's waters. It is a serious offence to disturb the natural life of the coral reefs, and the local diving schools have set up permanent anchors in their dive spots to avoid doing any unwarranted damage. With about 600 dives a day, conservation is essential. You are requested not to touch the coral or other underwater life, such as sea horses; not to move anything to create a better photo, not to feed the fish, as it is not natural and encourages the more aggressive species; not to drop litter, particularly plastic which does not decompose and can be harmful to sea creatures, and not to kick up sand with your fins as it can choke and kill the coral. All qualified divers are required to do a check out dive before they can do any diving, whether from the shore or a boat. Advanced buoyancy courses are available free of charge and are highly recommended for divers to train you to keep horizontal along the reef and limit fin damage to coral. Several sea turtles can be seen around Bonaire but they are rare. If you see one, in the water or on a beach, report the sighting to the Sea Turtle Conservation Bonaire (STCB), or contact the Bonaire Marine Park, T7178444, www.bmp.org The STCB has a network of volunteers for turtle watching and conservation. They are working on protecting nesting sites on both Bonaire and Klein Bonaire, some of which will be fenced. STCB launched a newsletter in December 1999, for information stcb@bonairelive.com Every month an underwater clean up is organized by *Green Submarine*, Kaya Playa Lechi, T7172929, to clear all the rubbish washed up by the sea. Divers are usually requested to bring their own tanks and air, but dive shops may provide complimentary tanks if you ask. Snorkellers are also welcome.

On the east side of the island there is a shelf and a drop-off about 12 m from the shore down to a 30 m coral shelf and then another drop down to the ocean floor. The sea is rather rough for most of the year although it sometimes calms down in October or November. Along the west side of the island there are numerous dive sites of varying depths with wrecks as well as reefs. The most frequently dived sites include, **Calabas Reef**, **Pink Beach**, **Salt City**, **Angel City** and the **Town Pier**. There are also several sites for boat dives off Klein Bonaire, just 1½ km from Kralendijk. The *Bonaire Marine Park Guide* is recommended and can be obtained from dive shops or from the Foundation National Parks Bonaire, STINAPA Bonaire, PO Box 368, info@stinapa.org

Snorkelling is recommended at **Nukove**, **Boca Slagbaai**, **Playa Funchi**, **Playa Benge**, **Windsock Steep** and **Klein Bonaire**. Dive boats usually take snorkellers along when dive sites are close to shore, about US$12 for two-hour trip with divers on one tank. A guided snorkel programme has been started, offering training and marine education with experienced guides. Ask the tourist office for its brochure.

According to the Year 2000 Reader Survey carried out by *Rodale's Scuba Diving Magazine*, four of Bonaire's dive resorts were voted into the top 15 best in the world. *Buddy Dive Resort* (5th), *Captain Don's Habitat* (7th), *Sand Dollar* (9th) and *Plaza Resort Bonaire* (15th) were the most successful, while *Sand Dollar Dive and Photo* were named the 4th most popular dive operator and *Sand Dollar Resort* was voted the second most popular dive resort in the world. The main schools are *Dive Bonaire* (T7178285, F7178238, at the *Divi Flamingo*), *Buddy Dive* (T7175080, F7178647, www.buddydive.com), *Habitat Dive Center* (T7178290, F7177346), *Dive Inn Bonaire* (T7178761, F7178513, next to the *Sunset Inn*), *Sand Dollar Dive and Photo* at the *Sand Dollar Condominium Resort* next to *Den Laman* restaurant (T7175433, F7175252, sand$dive@bonairenet.com, rebuilt after Hurricane Lenny in 1999), *Great Adventures Bonaire* and *Great Photo Adventures* (T7177500, F7177507) at the *Harbour Village Beach Resort*, with instruction in several languages, *Bon Bini Divers* at the *Coral Regency Resort* (T7175425, F7174425, www.bonbinidivers.com). *Green Submarine* at Playa Lechi 24 (T/F7172929, dive@greensubmarine.com) is run by Antillean Eric Groenhart and courses are taught in Dutch, English, German and French. *Blue Divers* (T7176860, F7176865, www.bluedivers.com), next to *Palm Studios*, is Swiss and Belgian owned, English, German, Dutch, French and Spanish spoken, shore diving and equipment rental, excellent guided dives with Bonairian Franklin Winklaar, who has been diving the reef for over 20 years, helping the likes of the late Jacques Cousteau. Prices are competitive, ranging from US$25-50 for a two-tank dive if you have your own equipment. Add a 10% service charge on most diving and 5% sales tax on all training courses and rentals. All packages include tank, air, weights and belt; equipment rental varies, US$6-11 for a BC jacket, US$6-11 for a regulator, US$6-10 for mask, snorkel and fins. Camera and other equipment rental

Dive centres

Netherland Antilles, the ABC Islands

widely available (*Sand Dollar Dive & Photo Shop*, T7175433, *Photo Tours*, T7175353 ext 328, F7175363). All dive operations are well equipped and well staffed with a good safety record. If booking a package deal check whether their week-long dive packages include nightly night dives, or only one a week. For less experienced divers it is worth choosing a dive boat which keeps staff on board while the leader is under-water, in case you get into difficulties. In the case of reasonably experienced divers, some dive masters do not always get into the water but stay on board. Shore diving is available nearly everywhere.

There is a US$10 per person levy for maintenance of the marine park which has to be paid only once every calendar year. You will be given a marine park tag. There is a recompression chamber at the San Francisco Hospital Emergency Room. An Annual Dive Festival is held in June.

Beaches and watersports

Bonaire is not noted for its beaches; the sand is usually full of coral and rather hard on the feet, and those on the leeward coast are narrow. Beaches in front of some hotels have been helped with extra sand. However, they do offer peace and quiet, and you will not get pestered by people trying to sell you things. Recommended are **Sorobon** (a private, nudist resort where non-guests pay US$10 for admission), **Lac Bay** which has an area of mangroves at the north end of the bay, and in the northeast **Playa Chiquito**. Be careful at Playa Chiquito, or Chikitu, there is a memorial plaque there for good reason. The surf is strong and it is dangerous to swim but it is pleasant for sunbathing. Another reasonable, but shadeless beach is **Pink Beach**, south of Kralendijk, past the **Salt Pier**, the water is shallow and good for swimming but the strip of sand is narrow and gritty. In the Washington-Slagbaai National Park are two attractive bays: **Playa Funchi**, which is good for snorkelling, but has no sand and no facilities so the area is very smelly, and **Boca Slagbaai**, which is popular with tour boats for snorkelling and you can see flamingoes wading in the salinja behind the beach. At the latter, there are clean toilets and showers in a restored 19th-century house and salt barn (ask the attendant to open them for you) and drinks and snacks are available. A very pleasant break in a hot and sweaty tour round the national park. Fishing, sailing, windsurfing and waterskiing are all popular as an alternative to div-ing, which is what most people come to Bonaire to enjoy.

Fishing You can charter a fishing boat through your hotel and arrange half or full day trips with tackle and food included. Bonaire has good bonefishing and also deep sea fish-ing. Two independent charter companies are *Piscatur*, run by Captain Chris Morkos, T7178774, F7174784, half day US$275 for four people, US$425 full day in 30-ft diesel boat, or US$125 half day for two people, US$225 full day in 15-ft skiff; and *Slamdunk*, a 30-ft Topaz, T7175111 Captain Rich at the Marina, same rates but for six people. Captain Freddy, T7175661, F7175662, has a boat for charter which can be equipped for fishing, or you can cruise to the Venezuelan Islands. Captain Bob, T7177070, F7177071, also does fishing charters, half or full day, with his boat *Its About Time*. Fishing boats with diving gear can be chartered from Club Nautico, Kaya Jan NE Craane 24, T7175800, F7175850. There is an annual Bonaire Interna-tional Fishing Tournament, held at the end of March, which attracts participants from throughout the Americas.

Sailing The annual Bonaire Sailing Regatta is held in mid-October. This has grown into a world class event with races for seagoing yachts, catamarans, sunfishes, windsurfers and local fishing boats. The smaller craft compete in Kralendijk Bay, while the larger boats race round Bonaire and Klein Bonaire. Held over five days, the event attracts crowds and hotel reservations need to be made well in advance. For information call the Regatta office, T7177425, F7175576. There is also an annual Nautical Race in November for small boats. At the end of the year Aquaspeed organizes a sailing boat race event with competitions for windsurfing, sunfish, centaur and fishing boats, starting from in front of the Regatta House in Playa, contact Elvis Martinus, T7172288. Speed races are held in Kralendijk Bay. The Marina at *Harbour Village* is the only facility of its kind in Bonaire. There are 60 slips for boats up to 110 ft with showers, laundry, fuel, waste disposal etc, and has a 120-ton syncrolift and supply shop for repairs.

Day sails Sailing trips with snorkelling and beach barbecue, often on Klein Bonaire, or sunset booze cruises, from US$25 per person plus 10% service, are offered on *Samur* (PO Box 287, T7175592, F7176677, samur@bonairelive.com), a 56-ft Siamese junk built in Bangkok in 1968, based at the *Sand Dollar Dive and Photo*, with pick up service from most resorts. Others include *Oscarina*, a 42-ft cutter, T09-5601340, F7178240, *Insulinde*, T09-5601340 and *Paranda*, T7172450. Several charter yachts offer trips as far as the Venezuelan islands, eg *Sea Witch*, cell phone 09-560 7449, F7177359, kroon@bonairenet.com, PO Box 348, dive gear on board, maximum of four guests on the 56-ft ketch; *Woodwind* is a 37-ft trimaran offering sailing and snorkelling around Bonaire, cell phone T09-5607055, F7178238. Bonaire Boating, T7175353 ext 505, F7175622, www.abc-yachting.com, have charter boats and offer day sails, motorboats and a 3-day package to Islas las Aves with diving equipment. They can also take you big game fishing, snorkelling, kayaking and sunset sailing. Their Watersports & Adventure Centre is at the *Caribbean Court Resort*. Baka de Laman offers a watertaxi service, T09-5607126, F7172568.

Windsurfing Conditions are ideal for windsurfing with winds of 15-25 knots in December-August and 12-18 knots in September-November. On the leeward side offshore winds allow you to sail to Klein Bonaire. At Lac Bay on the windward side of the island where the water is calm and shallow, there is a constant onshore wind. The bay is about 8 sq km but a coral reef just outside the bay breaks up the waves. However, the adventurous can get out of the bay at one end where long, high waves enable you to wave ride, jump or loop. *Jibe City* (closed September, T7175233, F7174455, www.jibecity.com) run by Ernst Van Vliet, is a BIC/TIGA Centre and has the latest models and Gaastra sails with retail shop and *Hangout Bar*. Lessons from US$45 per hour, rentals from US$55 per day, US$265 per week. *The Place*, managed by Elvis Martinus, is also on Lac Bay, T7172288, F7175279. Windsurfing rentals and instruction are available on both sides of the island along with kayak, sunfish, mini speed boats, water skiing, sea biscuit rides, small hobie cat, waterscooters, waterskiing, hydrosliding and paddle boats. Many dive shops rent kayaks, quite a good way of getting to Klein Bonaire without a boatload of other people. Jibe City rents kayaks for a whole (US$30 single kayak, US$35 double) or half day (US$20/25) or a couple of hours (US$10/15). *Sand Dollar Dive & Photo* offers courses, guided trips and rentals of various models of sit-in or sit-on-top kayaks. *Discover Bonaire* (see page 1000) has courses and tours for sit-in and sit-on kayaks. A full-day guided trip is US$90, half day US$50, sunset excursion US$35. Rental is US$10 per hour, US$45 per day for a single kayak, US$15 and 50 for a double kayak.

Other sports There are **tennis** courts at the *Divi Flamingo Beach Resort*, open 0800-2200, T7178285 and the *Harbour Village Beach Resort*; *Sand Dollar Condominium Resort*, open 0900-2100, T7178738. There is also **horse riding** but little else in the way of land based sports. Kunuku Warahama has horses and playgrounds for the children as well as lots of other animals. Lunch and dinner also available, T7175558. **Walking** and **birdwatching** are popular in the Washington/Slagbaai National Park, particularly climbing up Mount Brandaris. **Cycling** is popular and tours are organized or there is a cycling trails map if you want to go it alone. In May a Mountain Bike Challenge Race is held and in October a Mountain Bike speed challenge race. Also in May there is a two-day 80-km road race and a 5-km fun run, just two of several **running** events held during the year. A **bridge** club, Ups and Downs, meets at the *Hotel Rochaline*, T7178286, welcomes guest players, enroll before 1400, play starts 1930.

Kralendijk

Population: 1,700 Kralendijk, meaning coral dike, the capital of Bonaire, is a small, sleepy town with colourful buildings one or two storeys high. It is often referred to locally as simply 'Playa', because of its historic position as the main landing place.The town is just a few blocks long with some streets projecting inland. In 1999 a seaside promenade project was completed along the Playa section of Kralendijk, which will eventually be extended south to the *Divi Flamingo* hotel. Most of the shops are in the small Harbourside Shopping Mall and on the main street, the name of which changes from J A Abraham Boulevard to Kaya Grandi to Breedestraat. The **Museum** (Department of Culture), Sabana 14, houses snippets of folklore, archaeology and a shell collection. ■ *Weekdays 0800-1200, 1300-1700, T7178868*. The small **Fort Oranje** has been renovated and now houses the Bonairean court of justice as well as a permanent archaeological collection with items found during the renovation. There is a plaza called **Wilhelminaplein**, in which stands a monument to the Bonairens who were killed in the Merchant Marines in the Second World War, and a **fish market** built like a Greek temple. Stop in at the **Bonaire Art Gallery**, Kaya LD Gerharts 10, run by Bonnie Kerr. Most of the artwork is made on the island and there is a thriving culture of drift-wood art. Personal exhibitions are held November-

Kralendijk

N

Not to scale

■ Sleeping
1 Club Nautico
2 Divi Flamingo Beach Resort

3 Rochaline
4 Sunset Inn & Dive Inn

To Airport & Willemstoren

April. The most famous artist living on Bonaire is Vgo. He is best known for his image of a barracuda with a heart and his artwork is represented worldwide.

Around the island

Hire a car if you do not want to go on an organized tour. The island can be toured in a day if you start early but it is more pleasant to do a north tour on one day and a south tour another. Take food and drinks, there are rarely any available along the way, and aim to picnic somewhere you can swim to cool off.

North of Kralendijk the road passes most of the hotels, past the Water Distillation Plant along the 'scenic' road, which offers several descents to the sea and some excellent spots for snorkelling along the rocky coastline. The first landmark is the radio station which has masses of aerials. Note that the road is one-way, do not turn round, but beware of pot holes and watch out for lizards sunbathing. At the National Parks Foundation building you can turn right on a better road to **Rincon**, climbing to the top of the hill for a steep descent and a good view of Rincon and the Windward coast. Alternatively, continue along to the Bonaire Petroleum Company where the road turns inland to Goto Meer Bay, the best place to see flamingoes, on another road to Rincon, Bonaire's oldest village where the slaves' families lived. Past Rincon is a side road to the **Boca Onima** caves with their Arawak Indian inscriptions. Indian inscriptions in several caves around the island can still be seen, but they have not been decyphered.

The north

The road leading north from Rincon takes you to Washington/Slagbaai National Park, which occupies the north portion of the island, about 5,460 ha, and contains more than 190 species of birds. The park was set up in 1969. ■ *Daily 0800 to 1700 (no entry after 1500). NAf 5, US$3, children up to 15 NAf 0.75. Bicycles only on guided tours as per park rules, arrangements must be made in advance for bike entry. Toilet at the entrance. Bring food and water.* There is a small museum of local historical items opposite the office and a room with geological explanations, bird pictures and a shell collection behind the office. No hunting, fishing or camping is permitted. You can choose to drive a 34-km or a 24-km tour, the roads being marked by yellow or green arrows. You will get a route map when you pay to get in. The road is dirt, rough in parts, and the long route can be very hot and tiring unless you make several stops to swim and cool off. It is possible to drive round in an ordinary car but many car rental agencies prohibit the use of their cars and four-wheel drive is preferable. Allow plenty of time as once you have chosen your route you have to stick to it. Even the short route takes a minimum of two hours. Check your spare tyre before you start. *Cycle Bonaire* is now permitted to take cycling tours into the park but other two-wheeled transport is not allowed. Guided hiking excursions up Mount Brandaris (260 m, the island's highest point) and hiking trails have been marked. Do not expect much variation in vegetation, the overall impression is of miles of scrub and cactus, broken only by rocks or salinjas. You can drive to Goto Meer on the longer route but you can get a better view from the observation point outside the Park. The return to Kralendijk inland through the villages of **Noord Salinja** and **Antriol**.

Washington/ Slagbaai National Park

The tour south passes the airport and Trans World Radio's towering 213 m antenna which transmits three million watts, making it the hemisphere's most powerful radio station. Its shortwave broadcasts can be picked up in almost any part of the world. The coastal area south of Kralendijk is being heavily developed for tourism with construction of time share apartments, villas and hotels. The salt pier dominates the view along the coastal road and the salt pans are a stunning pink/purple colour. Further on are the snow-white salt piles and the three obelisks: blue, white, and orange, dating from 1838, with the tiny huts that sheltered the slaves who worked the saltpans. The roofs start at waist level and it is startling to think of men

The south

Netherland Antilles, the ABC Islands

sharing one of these structures. Remember the flamingoes are easily frightened, so move quietly if near them.

At the south tip of the island is **Willemstoren**, Bonaire's lighthouse, which dates from 1837. Pass Sorobon Beach and the mangrove swamps to **Boca Cai** at land-locked **Lac Bay**, with its clear water excellent for underwater exploration. The extensive seagrass beds and surrounding mangroves are an important nursery for marine creatures. What seem to be snow-capped hills from a distance are great piles of empty conch shells left by the local fishermen at Boca Cai. Near the Sorobon Resort is the Sea Hatch Bonaire shrimp farming project. Take the road back to Kralendijk through the village of **Nikiboko**.

Essentials

Sleeping

The tourist office has an extensive list, including apartments & villas, properties approved by Bonhata

High season rates (16 Dec to 2 weeks after Easter) are roughly double low-season rates in the more expensive hotels; the cheaper ones tend to charge the same all year round. August is 'family month' with lots of good deals. Dive packages are available at most resorts. A US$5.50 or US$6.50 per person per night government tax and 10-15% service charge must be added. All the hotels with on site dive shops, and some others besides, offer dive packages which give better value than the rack rates listed here. In addition there are lots of apartments and condos for rent, not mentioned here. Ask the tourist office for details.

South of Kralendijk A-C *Sunset Inn*, Kaya L D Gerharts 22, T7178291, F7178118. Only 7 rooms, some rooms with kitchenettes, bicycle rental, across the road from the sea, within easy walking distance of town, next to Dive Inn dive shop. **LL-AL** *Divi Flamingo Beach Resort & Casino*, J A Abraham Blvd 40, T7178285, F7178238, in USA 800-3673484, F919-4192075, www.divibonaire.com Totally renovated in 2000, 145 units, standard rooms or more luxurious, is on a small artificial beach, snorkelling or diving just off the beach is excellent, tennis, pools, jacuzzi, dining is outdoors. Next door is **L-A** *Bruce Bowker's Carib Inn*, J A Abraham Blvd 46, T7178819, F7175295, PO Box 68, bruce@caribinn.com Rooms, apartments and 3-bedroom house, a/c, cable TV, pool, dive shop. **LL-AL** *Plaza Resort Bonaire*, J A Abraham Blvd 80, T7172500, F7177133, info@plazaresortbonaire.com 200 rooms, suites and villas, diving, tennis, racquet ball, watersports, casino, pool, beach, striving to be 5-star resort. Using all the same facilities is **LL-L** *Port Bonaire Resort*, a condo-resort, villas and apartments, on waterfront, no beach, pool. **LL-AL** *Caribbean Court Bonaire* , J A Abraham Blvd, T7175353, F7175363, www.caribbeancourt.com 21 apartments, 1-3 bed-rooms, overlooking canal, close to airport, Dutch colonial style, fully equipped, Bonaire Boating has its Watersports & Adventure Centre here, dive packages available, use dive facilities at *Plaza Resort Bonaire*.

Kralendijk B-C *Hotel Rochaline*, Kaya Grandi 7, T7178286, F7178258. 10 rooms, a/c, functional, bar facing sea, restaurant. Popular and often full is the **B-C** *Palm Studios* attached to Blue Divers Diveshop on Kaya den Tera 2, T7176860, F7176865, www.bluedivers.com 10 rooms, a/c, common shower and kitchen, big garden, clean, cosy, pool, recommended for budget travellers/divers. **B-C** *Blue Iguana*, Kaya Prinses Marie 6, T/F7176855. 7 rooms, bed and breakfast, walking distance of seafront and shops.

North of Kralendijk LL *Bayside Resort*, Kaya Jan NE Craane 24, T7175800, F7175850. Short walk to town, 1-bedroom suites sleep 4, 2-bedroom penthouses sleep 6, fully equipped, balconies overlooking charter boats; **LL** *Harbour Village Beach Resort and Marina* on Playa Lechi, Kaya Gob N Debrot 72, PO Box 312, T7177500, F7177507, www.harbourvillage.com Renovated in 2000, rooms, suites and villas, a/c, cable TV, restaurants, bars, fitness centre, Peter Burwash tennis centre, pool, spa, private beach, 64-slip and mega-yacht marina and dock, dive shop, and non-motorized watersports, upmarket resort, look out for promotional packages but make sure you get what is on offer, eg car hire, also watch out for extra charges such as incoming phone calls and check your bill carefully. **LL-L** *Sand Dollar Condominium Resort*, Kaya Gobernador N Debrot 79, T7178738,

F7178760, T1800-2884773, PO Box 262, sanddollar@bonairenet.com, 76 apartments, a/c, rocky shoreline, tennis, pool, sailing, sport fishing, bicycle and kayak rental, Sand Dollar Dive and Photo. **L-AL** *Buddy Beach and Dive Resort*, PO Box 231, Kaya Gob N Debrot 85, T7175080, F7178647, www.buddydive.com, 68 rooms and apartments all with sea views, a/c, kitchen, pool, Buddy Watersports Center. **LL-AL** *Lions Dive Hotel Bonaire*, Kaya Gob N Debrot 91, T7175580, F7175680, www.bonairenet.com Suites and apartments some sleep 6, diving with Bon Bini Divers, pool, sundeck. **LL-AL** *Captain Don's Habitat*, Kaya Gob N Debrot 103, T7178290, F7178240, in USA T800-3276709, F305-3712337, 93 rooms, cottages and nice villas of differing standards, well laid out seafront bar and restaurant, dive packages, family packages, special excursions for children during their family month every August, pool, dive shop with world's youngest snorkelling instructor, mountain bike rental. A little further along the coast is **AL-C** *Black Durgon Inn/Pilot Fish Apartments*, Kaya Gobernador N Debrot 145, T7175736, F7178846, 8-room inn, 1-bedroom apartments, 2/3-bedroom villa, with view of Klein Bonaire, relaxing, non-commercial, a/c, cable TV, dive shop. Right by the radio masts is **B-C** *Bonaire Caribbean Club*, PO Box 323, T7177901, F7177900, www.bonairecaribbeanclub.com 20 rooms, good view from *Hill Top Bar and Restaurant*, bicycles and snorkelling gear for rent, caves nearby, good walking.

Windward coast **LL-L** *Sorobon Beach Resort*, at Lac Bay, T7178080, F7176080, sorobon@bonairenet.com Clothes optional, 30 chalets on the beach, restaurant for hotel guests, small shop for self-catering, free trips to town for shopping daily, massage, yoga, snorkelling, kayaks, windsurfing. **LL-AL** *Lac Bay Resort*, Kaminda Sorobon 64, T7178198, F7175686. In protected nature area, studios, apartments and 3-bedroom villa, good view from *Oasis* restaurant and bar.

International food at the major hotels varies on different nights of the week with barbecues **Eating** or Indonesian nights, etc. Main courses in the upper-priced restaurants are about US$12-20, but several restaurants do bar snacks if you want to economize. All food is imported, so even fruit and vegetables in the market are not cheap. Conch is recommended, either fried or in a stew, as is goat stew. You may not want to try iguana soup, which may also be on the menu. If you want to eat lobster, check where the restaurant gets its supplies, some lobster fishermen are reported to be unauthorized and disapproved of by divers and conservationists.

There are over 60 restaurants on this small island, so we print only a selection. The hotels mostly offer good restaurants with fine views over the sea. *Rum Runners at the Reef* at *Captain Don's Habitat*, T7177303. Breakfast, lunch and dinner with theme nights, eg Bonairean food, Mexican or barbecue, with live music some nights. *Captain Wook's Marina Bar & Grill*, T7177500, one of the restaurants at the *Harbour Village* marina. Tex-Mex specialities and you can use the cascade pool and outdoor pool table. *It Rains Fishes*, at the *Bayside Resort*, T7178780. Dinner only, special 3-course menu for NAf30.

In Kralendijk, *Rendez-Vous*, Kaya L D Gerharts 3, T7178454. Dinner, seafood specials, vegetarian choice, good vegetables, small and friendly, *The Grillroom* is an extension, with charcoal grill and salad bar, dinner only, both closed Sun. *Mona Lisa*, on Kaya Grandi, T7178718. Closed Sun, bar and restaurant, interesting, imaginative food, Dutch chef enjoys discussing the menu, expect to pay NAf 25-35 for main course, friendly service, popular. *Shamballa*, next to *City Café* in Kralendijk. Mexican décor, live music and a mix of food from tapas and sushi to Caribbean grill, popular with locals. *Mi Poron*, Kaya Caracas 1, a block from Roman Catholic Church, T7175199. Many antiques, welcoming patio, daily specials, authentic *krijollo* restaurant, open 1200-1400, 1800-2200. *Croccantino*, Kaya Grandi 48, T7175025. Italian, in historic town house, a/c dining room or garden dining, open daily for lunch and dinner. *Capriccio*, Kaya Isla Riba I, T7177230. Closed Tue, Italian, homemade pasta, pizza, lunch and dinner. *The Dome*, in the town centre. Sports bar and restaurant with sandwiches, cakes, coffee and juices, satellite TV with sport and results from Europe and the USA. *Beefeater*, Kaya Grandi 12, T7177776. Open from 1600 daily, steak and seafood, local specialities, pricey, small. *Zeezicht*, Kaya JNE Craane 12, T7178434. On the waterfront, does breakfast, lunch and dinner, sandwiches and omelettes as well as fish, steak, pasta and some Indonesian, open daily. A cheap place to eat is *Ankertje*, Kaya C E B Hellmund 17, T7175216. View nothing special, overlooks the small industrial harbour, dinner only, family meals. In La Terraza shopping mall there is a pizza bar, *Cozzoli's Pizzeria*, T7175195. For fast food, breakfast, lunch and dinner, owner Simon Brandsma is a master baker from Holland and his fresh bread, croissants and tarts are recommended. South of town, just past *Carib Inn* is *Richard's Waterfront Dining*, J A Abraham Boulevard 60, T7175263. American owner, happy hour 1700-1900, dinner 1830-2230, closed Mon, seafood and steak specialities. *Blue Moon*, Kaya CEB Hellmund 5, T7178617, hans@bonairenet.com On waterfront, set menu or à la carte, French and international, open for food 1800-2200, happy hour 1700-1830, closed Wed. *Den Laman Seafood Restaurant*, at the roundabout near the northern hotels, T7178955. Open for lunch and dinner, lots of fresh fish and lobster. *Maiky Snack Kaminda*, New Amsterdam 30, T09-5670078. An out-in-the-country spot to get home-made local food, soup, main dish and drink US$8.50, dinner only.

There are lots of Chinese restaurants. *Mentor's*, Kaya Korona 140, T7174999. Lunch and dinner, cheap, large portions of Chinese food. *Great China*, Kaya Grandi 39, T7178886; *Shanghai Bar Restaurant*, Kaya L D Gerharts 17, T7178838, all open for lunch and dinner. As in the other Dutch Antilles, Indonesian food is good and popular. *Bali Indonesian*, Kaya Grandi 23, T7174779. Upstairs in La Terraza Shopping Center in Kralendijk, open for dinner Tue-Sun, traditional dishes, rijsttafel and vegetarian dishes. *Old Inn*, on J A Abraham Blvd opposite *Plaza Resort*, T7176666. Indonesian Rijsttafel a speciality, also steak, fish and children's menu, dinner only, closed Wed. There are also a couple of Surinamese restaurants: *Surinaamse Bar Restaurant*, Kaya A Cecillia 31, T7172127 and *Spanhoek*, Kaya L D Gerharts, T7176686.

On the windward side of the island, *Beachclub Kontiki* next to the *Lac Bay Resort*, T7175369, kontiki@bonairelive.net Seafood, steaks, salads and wide variety of international cuisine, friendly, casual, beautiful view, Caribbean décor, open 1200-1500, 1830-2200, closed Mon. The beach bar, *Hang Out*, at Jibe City is recommended for rest and regaining energy for windsurfing, good food, drink, shade.

Water Comes from a desalinization plant and is safe to drink. Take water with you on excursions. Do not, however, wash in or drink water from outside taps. This is *sushi* (dirty) water, treated sufficiently for watering plants but nothing more.

Nightlife
Not well developed but there are a few places

Check schedule of Bonaire's *Weekly Happenings* update at tourist office. *Paradise Disco* is at Kaya LD Gerharts 11, T7177345. *Karel's Beach Bar* has a live band, Kaya K Craane 12, from 2200 Fri and Sat. *Harbour Village Beach Resort* has a mariachi band on Sat night at its *Compadres Mexican Grill* restaurant. There are casinos at the *Divi Flamingo Beach Resort* (open 2000 except Sun, T7178285) and *Plaza Resort* (T7172450). There is a **cinema** on Kaya Prinses Marie, *The Movies Bonaire*, T7172400, www.InfoBonaire.com/cinema, for what's on, usually closed Mon and Tue.

Shopping

Bonaire is not a major shopping centre, though some shops do stock high quality low duty goods. Sales tax is 5%. The *Harbourside Shopping Mall* contains small boutiques and a 1 hr photo processing shop, *Kodalux*, T7178123. *Photo Tours* at *Plaza Resort Bonaire*, also offers full underwater facilities and equipment rental. Local arts and crafts are largely sea-based and fabrics. The state owned *Fundashon Arte Industri Bonairano* and the privately owned *Caribbean Arts and Crafts shop* are both in Kralendijk for souvenirs. See also the *Bonaire Art Gallery*, Kaya LD Gerharts 10. A local music group, Piedra di Boneiru, which plays on local, native instruments, has recorded 2 CDs, available locally, of Bonairean and Antillean songs. The largest supermarket is *Cultimara*, T7178278, with groceries and some household goods, or there are several minimarkets. *Sand Dollar Grocery*, open daily, is located in a small plaza in front of the *Sand Dollar Beach Club* along with *Lovers Ice Cream Parlour*. Near the *Divi Flamingo* a turning opposite leads to *Joke's* grocery and mini-market.

Transport **Air** Flamingo airport (BON) can accommodate 747 jumbo jets with a runway of 2.4km, but currently aircraft are much smaller.

Road Bicycle Available to rent from most hotels' front desks. *Cycle Bonaire/Discover Bonaire,* has TREK 21 speed bicycles and offers rentals, sales, repairs and guided tours. Bike rental is US$15 per day or US$75 per week, plus 5% sales tax, while guided excursions are US$40 half day including drinks and US$65 whole day including lunch but not including bike rental. Also *Hot Shot*, see above, and *Bonaire Boating*, T7175353, ext 505, F7175622, and some hotels. *Discover Bonaire* (see page 1000) has tours through the kunuku and Washington/Slagbaai National Park. The roads in the south are flat and in good condition but there is no shade and you would need lots of water and sun screen. In the north it is more hilly and the roads are not so good. For mountain bikers there are lots of unpaved trails and goat paths. Either way cycling is hot, hard work.

Car hire *A B Car Rental* at the airport, PO Box 339, T7178980, F7175034. *Budget*, T7174700, F7173325. *Sunray Car Rental*, at the airport, T7175230. *Trupial Car Rental*, Kaya Grandi No 96, T7178487. *Avis*, J A Abraham Blvd 4, Kralendijk, T7175795, F7175793. There are nearly a dozen other companies not listed here, plenty of choice, many have offices in the hotels. At the busiest times of the year, it is best to reserve a car in advance. Four-wheel drive vehicles are not easy to find, there are not many on the island, and it is best to order one in advance. Most cars are manual, not automatic. There are pickups and minivans for divers wanting to carry gear around for shore diving. Some companies prohibit the use of ordinary cars on unmade roads and in Washington/Slagbaai Park. There is a government tax of US$4 per day plus 2% on the rental fee. The speed limit in built-up areas is 33 kph, outside towns it is 60 kph unless otherwise marked. Many of the roads in Kralendijk and the north of the island are one-way. There are 4 filling stations, open Mon-Sat 0700-2100. The Kralendijk station is also open Sun 0900-1530.

You must have a driver's licence held for at least 2 years. Minimum age for car rental varies between agencies from 21-26

Motorcycle Small motorcycles can be rented from US$12 a day; *Hot Shot Scooter and Cycle Rental,* Kaya Bonaire 4, T/F7177166; *Bonaire Boating*, T7175353 ext 505; *Cycle Bonaire/Discover Bonaire*, T7177558, *De Freeweiler*, T7178545; *Macho Scooter Rentals*, T7172500. Prices are high compared with car rental and there are several inconveniences: the tanks are small and filling stations are few and far between, and you are not allowed into Washington/Slagbaai National Park.

Taxi Drivers carry list of officially approved rates, including touring and waiting time, but be sure to agree a price beforehand.The short trip from the airport to the *Divi Flamingo Beach Resort* is US$8.50; fares increase by 50% from midnight-0600. Taxis have TX on their licence plates. Taxis are available at the airport but do not cruise for business elsewhere. To call a taxi, T7178100 for the taxi stand at the airport.

Airlines *ALM*, T7178500. *KLM*, T7178300. *Air Aruba*, T7177880, 7177890. *Servivensa*, T7178361. **Directory** **Banks** Open 0800 or 0830-1530 or 1600, Mon-Fri, a few close for lunch. All have ATMs. TCs and credit cards are widely accepted. *ABN Amro*, T7178417, F7178469; *Maduro & Curiel's Bank (Bonaire) NV*, T7177249, F7172645, with a branch in Rincon, T7176266; *Antilles Banking Corporation Bonaire*, T7174500, F7174510; *Banco di Caribe NV*, T7178295, F7175153. **Communications** Telephone Direct dialling to the USA with a credit card is available at the airport and at Telbo in town. The international code for Bonaire is 599, followed by a 7-digit number beginning with 717. For information on services, contact Telbo, T7177000, F7175007. To rent a cellular phone, T09-5692244/6999. **Internet:** *De Tuin eetcafe* is a cybercafe on Kaya L D Gerharts 9, T7172999, for internet access, lunch and dinner. There is also public email at the Harbourside Mall. Internet service providers are BonaireLive!, T7175180, F7175181 and BonaireNet, T/F7177160, **Post:** J A Abraham Blvd, Kralendijk, on the corner of Plaza Reina Wilhelmina opposite the ABN bank, open 0730-1200, 1330-1700 for stamps and postage, 1330-1600 for money orders etc. Airmail to the USA and Canada is NAf1.75 for letters, NAf0.90 for postcards. There is also Express Mail and Federal Express Mail. Rocargo Services, T7178922, F7175791, is the FedEx and cargo agent. **Medical facilities** The Hospitaal San Francisco in Kralendijk has 60 beds, T7178900. There is an air ambulance for emergency evacuation and a recompression chamber for scuba diving accidents. The emergency phone number is T191. There is a dentist at Chirino Dental Clinic, T7178106. Opticians at *Optica Antillana*, T7178815, and *Ram's Optica*, T7175612. For hearing aids and dentures, *Oraid Hearing Instruments*, T7178850.

Netherland Antilles, the ABC Islands

Places of worship Roman Catholic, San Bernardo Church, Kralendijk, T8304, Our Lady of Coromoto, Antriol, T7174211, or San Ludovico Church, Rincon; United Protestant Church, T7178086; Evangelical Alliance Mission, T7176245; Jehovah's Witnesses, Antriol; New Apostolic Church, Nikiboko, T7178483; Seventh Day Adventist Church, T7174254. **Tourist information** Local tourist office Kaya Simón Bolívar 12, Kralendijk, T7178322, F7178408, www.InfoBonaire.com The Bonaire Hotel and Tourism Association (Bonhata) is at T7175134, F7178534, info@bonhata.org The Bonaire tourist map shows all the dive and snorkelling sites around the island as well as the best bird watching places. *The Official Roadmap with Dive Sites* is available in some shops and adequate for most purposes. It gives a good street plan of Kralendijk, dive sites and points of interest on Bonaire and Klein Bonaire, but tends to indicate as 'beach' areas which are rocky cliffs. **Local travel agents** *Bonaire Tours*, T7178778, F7174890, head office Kaya L D Gerharts 22, for large or small groups, 2 hr north or south tour, half or full day Washington Park tour, day trip to Curaçao. *Bonaire Nature Tours* for small groups, maximum 7 people, 0900-1800, led by Dutch biologist/dive instructor, Klaus Bakker, tours can be tailor-made, T/F7177714. *Chogogo Tours* cater for small groups, T/F7174435. Taxis have fixed prices for sightseeing tours. *Discover Bonaire*, Kaya Gob N Debrot 79, PO Box 262, T7175252, F7177690, www.discover bonaire.com, for kayaking, nature tours, guided snorkelling and mountain biking, tours plus 10% service. *SeaCow Watertaxi*, T/F7172568, trips to Klein Bonaire Mon-Sat, US$10 per person. Sunset and evening cruises Tue, Fri, Sat, US$20, and snorkel trips. *Bonaire Travel & Tours*, Lourdes Mall, between *Mundo Musikal* and *Harmony Gift Shop/Bonaire Art*, T7174343, F7175060, run by Natasja Statie-Gerharts, is Bonaire's newest agency. **Useful addresses** Immigration, T7178000. Central government main number, T7175300. Police, T7178000. Stinapa and Bonaire Marine Park, T7178444.

Background

Geography

Bonaire, second largest of the five islands comprising the Netherlands Antilles, is 38 km long and 6½-11½ km wide and 288 km square. It lies 80 km north of Venezuela, 50 km east of Curaçao, 140 km east of Aruba, outside the hurricane belt. The south part of the crescent-shaped island is flat and arid, much of it given over to the production of salt. The north end of the island is more hilly, the highest point being Mount Brandaris, and is a national park. There is little agriculture and most of the island is covered in scrub and a variety of cacti, many of which reach a height of 6 m. Despite its lack of natural resources, it is, however, known as 'Diver's Paradise', for its rich underwater life and is also valued by bird watchers. The windward coast is rough and windy, while the leeward coast is sheltered and calm.

Klein Bonaire, a small (608 ha), flat, rocky and uninhabited islet 1 km off Bonaire's shores, is frequented by snorkellers and divers. It has sandy beaches but no natural shade and only a few shelters used by tour boats. In 1868 the Dutch government sold the plantation island to Angel J Jeserun and it remained in private hands until 30 December 1999, when it was sold to Bonaire for 9.3 million Dutch guilders by the Klein Bonaire Development Corporation (KBDC), who had owned it since 1971. Finance for the purchase was conditional upon the island becoming a nature reserve. For details contact the Foundation Preservation Klein Bonaire, www.kleinbonaire.org, whose president is Bruce Bowker. Stinapa and the FPKB will be drawing up and implementing a management plan.

The economy

Bonaire has a fairly diversified economy with salt mining, oil trans-shipment, a textile factory, rice mill and radio communications industry. The Antilles International Salt Company has reactivated the long dormant salt industry, which benefits so greatly from the constant sunshine (with air temperatures averaging 27°C and water 26°C), scant rainfall (less than 560 mm a year), and refreshing trade winds. A shrimp farm started operations in 1999. Sea Hatch Bonaire is near Sorobon and will offer tours and farm-raised shrimp.

However, for foreign exchange, the island is overwhelmingly dependent on tourism, even if it is highly specialized. The USA is the largest single market, followed by the Netherlands (26%), Aruba (6.6%) and Venezuela (6.6%). The Venezuelan market has shrunk because of that country's economic difficulties, as well as stiff competition from Miami. Divers are the main category among stayover visitors (44% of the total), although their proportion of the total has fallen as the attractions of windsurfing and birdwatching have been publicized more widely. Accommodation for tourists is split fairly evenly between hotels and condominiums or villas, amounting to about 1,100 rooms and still growing. Financial assistance for the development of tourism has been provided by the EU, which has financed the expansion of the airport and development of other infrastructure. Cruise ship tourism is a controversial issue and there has been much debate locally on the increase in the number of calls from 18 ships in 1998-99 to 61 ships in 1999-2000.

Curaçao

Curaçao, the largest of the five islands comprising the Netherlands Antilles, lies in the Caribbean Sea 60 km off the Venezuelan coast, outside the hurricane belt. The landscape is barren, due to low rainfall which makes for sparse vegetation consisting mostly of cactus thickets, and although it is not flat, the only significant hill is Mount Christoffel in the northwest, which rises to a height of 375 m. On a clear day you can see Aruba, Bonaire and Venezuela from the top. Deep bays indent the south coast, the largest of which, Schottegat, provides Willemstad with one of the finest harbours in the Caribbean. On the island cactus plants grow up to 6 m high, and the characteristic wind-distorted divi divi trees reach 3 m, with another 3 m or so of branches jutting out away from the wind at right angles to the trunk. The population is truly cosmopolitan, and 79 nationalities are represented, of whom 16% were born outside the Netherlands Antilles.

Population: 170,000

Ins and outs

From Europe *KLM* flies direct from Amsterdam several times a week and has connecting flights to Guayaquil and Quito. *Condor* flies from Cologne/Bonn. **From North America** There are flights from New York and Tampa with *Air Aruba*, and from Miami with *American Airlines*. *ALM* flies from Miami and Washington DC. **From South America** *SAM* flies from Bogotá; *Air Aruba* flies from Bogotá and Medellín; *ALM*, *Servivensa*, and *Aeropostal* fly from Caracas; *ALM* also flies from Valencia and Maracaibo and *Servivensa* from Las Piedras and Maracaibo, Venezuela. *Surinam Airways* fly from Paramaribo. **From the Caribbean** from Aruba (*Air Aruba*, *ALM*), Bonaire (*ALM*, *Air Aruba*), Havana (*Cubana*), Kingston (*ALM*), Port au Prince (*ALM*), Sint Maarten (*ALM*), San Juan (*ALM*), Santo Domingo in the Dominican Republic (*ALM* and *Aeropostal*), Panama City (*Aeropostal*) and Port of Spain (*ALM*).

Getting there
Curaçao is very well served by airlines but the companies & their routes change frequently so check the latest flight guide

There are collective taxis, called buses, and identified by an AC prefix on their licence plates, which charge about US$1 anywhere. *Konvoois* are big buses which run to a schedule and serve outlying areas of Curaçao. There is a terminal at the post office by the circular market in Punda and another near the Rif Fort in Otrabanda. There are about 4 car rental agencies at the airport, all the offices are together so it is easy to pick up price lists for comparison. One or two companies usually have desks in each of the major hotels. Look in local tourist literature or newspapers for news of special deals on offer, there is lots of choice. There have been problems with unsafe cars, inadequate insurance and licensing. Those listed in the transport section are considered reputable. Taxis are easily identified by the signs on the roof and TX before the licence number. There are taxi stands at all hotels and at the airport, as well as in principal locations in Willemstad.

Getting around
See transport, page 1017, for further details

Essentials

Documents All visitors must have an onward ticket to a destination outside the Netherlands Antilles and a confirmed room reservation before arriving. Tourists may stay for up to three months with a valid passport. Those intending to stay more than 90 days must apply for a visa. US citizens do not need a passport; a birth certificate, alien registration card or naturalization papers are sufficient. Canadians must have a valid passport or birth certificate. Transit visitors and cruise ship visitors must have proof of identity for a 24-hour, or less, stay on the island. Immigration procedures at the airport are quick and easy.

Money The currency is the guilder, divided into 100 cents. There are coins of 1, 2½, 5, 10, 25, 50 cents and 1 and 2½ guilders, and notes of 10, 25, 50, 100, 250 and 500 guilders. Old and new coins are in circulation.
Exchange The exchange rate is US$1=NAf1.77 for bank notes, NAf1.79 for cheques, although the rate of exchange offered by shops and hotels ranges from NAf1.75-1.80. Credit cards and US dollars are widely accepted.

Departure tax There is an airport tax of US$6 on departure to the Netherlands Antilles or US$20 to Aruba or other destinations. This must be paid at a separate kiosk after you check in.

Official time Atlantic Standard Time, 4 hours behind GMT, 1 hour ahead of EST.

Voltage 127/220 volts AC, 50 cycles.

Tourist offices overseas *Argentina:* Paraguay 880, 1st floor of 7 (1057), Buenos Aires, T541-3115965/2488, F541-3128849. *Germany:* Arnulfstrasse 44, D-80335 Munich 2, T4989-598490, F4989-5504045. *Holland:* Vasteland 82-84, 3001 BP Rotterdam, PO Box 23227, T3110-4142639, F3110-4136834, ctbenl@wirehub.nl *UK:* Axis Sales and Marketing, 421a Finchley Road, London NW3 6HJ, T0171-4314045, F0171-4317920. *USA:* 475 Park Avenue South, Suite 2000, New York, NY10016, T212-6837660, 1800-2703350, F212-6839337, curacao@ix.netcom.com; 330 Biscayne Blvd, Suite 808, Miami, FL33132, T305-3745811, 800-4458266, F305-3746741. *Venezuela:* Torre la Previsora, Local No 3, Planta Baja, Av las Acacias con Bolívar, Urb las Caobos, PO Box 63345, Caracas, T602-7814622, F602-7826582.

Safety There is a drugs problem in Willemstad and you are advised to be careful in Otrabanda at night and avoid the outer stretches of Pietermaai even by day (crack houses). If strangers stop you on the street asking 'alles goed?' (everything OK?) be assured that they are not enquiring after your mood.

Health The climate is healthy and non-malarial; epidemic incidence is slight. Rooms without air-conditioning or window and door screens may need mosquito nets during the wetter months of November and December and sometimes May and June, and, although some spraying is done in tourist areas, mosquitoes are a problem. Some anti-mosquito protection is recommended if you are outdoors any evening. Beware of a tree with small, poisonous green apples that borders some beaches. This is the manchineel (manzanilla) and its sap causes burns on exposed skin.

Public holidays New Year's Day, Carnival Monday (February), Good Friday, Easter Monday, Queen's Birthday (30 April), Labour Day (1 May), Ascension Day, Flag Day (2 July), Christmas on 25 and 26 December.

Diving and marine life

The waters around Curaçao contain a wide variety of colourful fish and plant life and several wrecks (*Superior Producer*, near the water distillation plant, and a tugboat in Caracas Bay) which have foundered on the coral reef just offshore. The reef surrounds the island and consists generally of a gently sloping terrace to a depth of about 10 m, then a drop off and a reef slope with an angle of about 45°. The coral formations are spectacular in places and there are many huge sponges; one in Boca Sta

Martha is so big it is known as 'the double bed'. There are lots of fish and you are likely to see barracuda, moray, eels, spiny lobsters, turtles, manta rays and maybe sharks. Underwater visibility averages 24 m and water temperature varies between 24-27°C. There are lots of opportunities for successful underwater photography.

Scuba diving is very popular in Curaçao and many of the large resort hotels have dive shops on site. They have been encouraged by the establishment in 1983 of the Curaçao Underwater Park managed by the Netherlands Antilles National Parks Foundation (Stinapa), which stretches from the *Princess Beach Hotel* to East Point. The park extends out from the shore to a depth of 60 m and covers 600 ha of reef and 436 ha of inner bays.

Over 40 permanent mooring buoys for boats have been placed at dive sites along the south coast as part of Stinapa's programme for sustained utilization of the reef. A few of the sites can be dived from the shore (West Point, Blauwbaa, Port Marie, Daaibooi, Vaersen Bay, San Juan, Playa Kalki), but most of the coastal strip is private property and boat dives are necessary. The *Guide to the Curaçao Underwater Park*, by Jeffrey Sybesma & Tom van't Hof, published in 1989 by Stinapa and available in bookshops locally, describes the sites and discusses conservation. For independent divers and snorkellers without a boat there is the *Complete Guide to Landside Diving and Snorkelling Locations in Curaçao*, by Jeffrey Sybesma and Suzanne Koelega, including a map with the sites and roads to them. No harpoons or spear guns are allowed and make sure you do not damage or remove coral or any other sea creatures.

Dive centres

There are many dive operators, not all of which are mentioned here, and it is worth shopping around before booking a package deal. The *Curaçao Diving Operators Association (CDOA)* standardizes safety regulations and should be contacted if you have any complaints or suggestions. Most operators offer a single boat dive for around US$30-35, a two-tank dive for US$55-60 and snorkelling trips including equipment for about US$15-20, but check when booking whether 10% service is included in the quoted price. *Underwater Curaçao* (T4618131, F4657826) at the *Lions Dive Hotel* next to the Seaquarium is one of the larger operations with two dive boats for 20 divers each and two scheduled dives a day. It has a large air station, equipment rental, a retail shop and offers several courses. *Curaçao Seascape* at the *Sheraton Curaçao Resort*, T4625000, is also good. *Princess Divers*, T4658991, F4655756, has three dive boats and offers snorkelling, boat dives, shore dives, PADI courses, photo equipment. Standards were reported to have declined somewhat in 2000 but new ownership of the hotel may result in improvements. *Eden Roc Dive Centre* is at the *Holiday Beach Hotel*, and is a PADI five-star facility, T4628878. *Marlies' Coral Cliff Diving* at Santa Martha Bay (PO Box 3782, T8642822, F8642237) has a deliberately sunk airplane in shallow water just offshore for divers and also offers introductory or certification courses and package deals, also windsurfing US$10 per hour, with sunfish, hobiecats and pedalboats available, prices not including 10% service. *Habitat Curaçao* is an offshoot of *Captain Don's Habitat* in Bonaire, at Rif St Marie, offering PADI, NAUI and SSI courses, boat dives, shore dives, snorkelling, photography, all equipment available for rent, lots of package deals, T8648800, F8648464. *Sami Scuba Centre Dive School Wederfoort* has been in operation since 1966, very friendly, reputable, mostly shore dives, the drop starts 25 m from dive centre; a six-day package including air, weights and no tank limit, costs US$120, a PADI open water course is US$257, accommodation and restaurant available, contact Eric and Yolanda Wederfoort, Marine Beach Club, St Michielsbaai, T8884414, F8692062, www.divewederfoort.com. Out at Westpoint and Playa Kalki are *All West Diving and Adventures*, T8640102, offering courses, boat dives, introductory dives (US$30) and equipment for rent. Students are given preferential rates.

Seaquarium

The Seaquarium, southeast of Willemstad, just beyond the *Lions Dive Hotel*, has a collection of undersea creatures and plants found around the island, which live in channelled sea water to keep them as close as possible to their natural environment.

The Seaquarium was built in 1984, the lagoons and marina being excavated so as to leave the original coastline untouched and do minimal damage to the reef offshore. A new attraction is the shark (lemon and nurse) and animal (turtles, stingrays) encounter programme, good for photography, US$55 for diving (no previous experience necessary), US$30 snorkelling. Good quality photos of visitors feeding the sharks are offered at US$25 for 12. ■ *0830-1700. US$13.25, children under 15 US$7.50, after 1600 US$3 and US$1.50 respectively. T4616666.* There is a restaurant, snack bar and shops selling shells and coral in marked contrast to the conservation efforts of the Underwater Park administration. The Seaquarium can be reached by bus marked Dominguito from the post office at 35 minutes past the hour (except for 1335), which passes the *Avila Beach Hotel*.

The *Seaworld Explorer* is a cruising underwater observatory, not a submarine, you sit in the hull and look out of the windows as the vessel moves along the wall. The boat leaves from the *Curaçao Caribbean*, 1030, one-hour trip, US$29, children US$19, T4628833.

Beaches and watersports

There are several nice beaches on Curaçao. The northwest coast is rugged and rough for swimming, but the southwest coast offers some sheltered bays and beaches with excellent swimming and snorkelling. Windsurfing, waterskiing, yachting and fishing are available at resorts. Many of the beaches are private and make a charge per car (amount depends on day of the week and popularity, US$3-6) but in return you usually get some changing facilities, toilets and refreshments. Public beaches are free but most have no facilities and some are rather dirty and smelly round the edges. Topless sunbathing is not recommended on public beaches but is tolerated on private beaches.

Heading south out of Willemstad are the two small, artificial beaches at the *Avila Beach Hotel*, where non-residents pay an entrance fee. The sand is imported and the

Curaçao

sea is not calm enough to see much if you snorkel but the breakwaters make it pleasant for swimming. You can get to the beach at **Piscadera Bay** near the *Sheraton* hotel by catching one of their shuttle buses from beside the Rif Fort in Otrabanda. Southeast of Willemstad, by the *Princess Beach Hotel*, the *Lions Dive Hotel* and the Seaquarium (see above), is a 450 m, man-made beach and marina with all watersports available. It can be crowded and noisy with music; motorized watersports are all down one end. ■ *0830-1800. Entrance to the beach is US$2.25. Showers and toilets. Mambo Beach Club for night-time entertainment.* Past the Seaquarium is a residential area and private beach on **Jan Thiel Bay**, good swimming and snorkelling, entrance NAf6 per car, changing facilities, drinks and snacks. **Santa Barbara** located at the mouth of Spanish Water Bay on the Mining Company property, is a favourite with locals. ■ *Open 0800-1800. Entrance US$2.25 per person. Changing rooms, toilets and snack bars. You can take a bus from the post office, get off at the Mining Company gate and hitchhike down to the beach, or take a taxi, it is too far to walk.* Across the bay, which is one of the island's beauty spots, is the Curaçao Yacht Club, with a pleasant bar. There are four yacht clubs in Spanish Water.

Travelling northwest from Willemstad heading towards Westpoint, there are lots of coves and beaches worth exploring. A left turn soon after leaving town will take you to **Blauw Bay**, good for snorkelling but a Curasol development is under construction and the beach is now closed, or to **St Michiel's Bay**, a fishing village and tanker clearing harbour (free). **Daaibooibaai**, south of St Willibrordus is a public beach and gets very crowded on a Sunday. Further up the coast, **Port Marie** (private, charge per car) is sandy but there is no shade. There is a little restaurant and dive area to change, rinse off equipment etc. **Cas Abao beach** has pretty with good snorkelling and diving from shore in beautiful clear water. ■ *Changing facilities, showers, shade huts, lounge chairs cost US$3, US$3 per car per day, US$5 at weekends and holidays, snacks and beverages.* **San Juan**, a private beach with lots of coral is off to the left of the main Westpoint road down a poor track, entrance fee charged. **Boca Sta Martha**, where the *Coral Cliff Resort* is located, is quiet with nice sea. ■ *Beach entrance US$4.50 for non-residents, no pets or food allowed on the beach, some shade provided.* **Lagun** is a lovely secluded beach in a small cove with cliffs surrounding it and small fishing boats pulled up on the sand. It is safe for children and good for snorkelling. ■ *There are facilities and some shade from trees. Some buses pass only 50 m from the beach.* **Jeremi**, a public beach with no charge, is of the same design, slightly larger sandy beach with a steep drop to deep water and boats moored here, protected by the cliffs. Further up the coast, **Knip** is a more open, larger, sandy beach again with cliffs at either end. Many people rate this the best beach on the island, but the stairway down to the beach was destroyed by the storms of 1999. There are some facilities here and it is very popular at weekends when there is loud music and it gets crowded and noisy. **Playa Abau** is big, sandy, with beautiful clear water, surrounded by cliffs. ■ *Some shade provided, toilets, well organized, popular at weekends and busy.* Nearing

Netherland Antilles, the ABC islands

the west tip, **Playa Forti** has dark sand and good swimming. There is a restaurant on the cliff top overlooking the sea which gets very busy at weekend lunchtimes. The beach at **Westpoint** below the church is stoney and littered, the only shade comes from the poisonous manchineel trees. Fishing boats tie up at the pier but bathers prefer to go to Playa Forti. Beyond Westpoint is **Kalki beach** which is good for snorkelling and diving as well as bathing. Westpoint is the end of the road, about 45 minutes by car or one hour by bus from Otrabanda, US$1.

Day sails Many charter boats and diving operators go to **Klein Curaçao**, a small, uninhabited island off East Point which has sandy beaches and is good for snorkelling and scuba diving, a nice day trip with lunch provided. The most popular charter boat is *Waterworld* which leaves at 0900 from the Seaquarium Marina for Klein Curaçao day trips (US$18) and to Banda Abou, sunset, snorkelling or party trips on request; motor boat takes 100 passengers and departures sometimes depend on whether there is a cruise ship in port, T4656042. Other companies include *Mermaid*, T5601530, *Second Chance*, T7671579, *Miss Ann*, T7671579 and *Bounty*, T5601887. There are snorkel, snorkel-picnic and sunset trips with the *Vira Cocha* daily from the Seaquarium marina, maximum 22 passengers, T5600292. There are also day sailing trips from Willemstad up the coast with barbecue lunches at, for example, Port Marie, for about US$55, to the East End with lunch at Santa Barbara, and weekend sailing trips to Bonaire, accommodation on board, for about US$225. One such sailing ship is the 120 ft *Insulinde*, T5601340, shore T8688710, F4616633, www.insulinde.com, beautiful trip, including lunch but not drinks. Deep sea fishing charters can be booked with *Second Chance* T7671579, *Curaçao Seascape* T4625000, *Speedy* T7675195 and Hemingway T5620086.

Sailing The Curaçao International Sailing Regatta is held in January with competitions in three categories, short distance (windsurfers, hobie cats, sunfish etc), long distance (yachts race 112 km to Klein Curaçao and back) and open boat (trimarans, catamarans etc race 32 km to Spanish Water and back), all starting from the *Santa Barbara Beach Resort*. For details, contact the *Lion's Dive Hotel*, T4618100. The Sami Sail Regatta in April is organized by the fishing village of Boca St Michiel. The International Blue Marlin tournament is held in March. The Yacht Club is at Brakkeput Ariba, z/n, T7673038 or contact Mr B van Eerten, T7675275. *Sail Curaçao* has sailing courses, rentals and boat trips, also surfing lessons, T7676003.

Other sports *Rancho Alegre*, T8681181, does **horse riding** for US$20 per hour, including transport. *Ashari's Ranch* offers horses for hire by the hour inland (US$20), or 1½ hours including a swim at the beach (US$30), open 1000-1900, Groot Piscadera Kaya A-23, T8690533, beginners as well as experienced riders, playground for children. There is **bowling** on the island, *Curaçao Bowling Club*, Chuchubiweg 10, T7379275, six lanes, US$11 per hour, reservations advised. The Curaçao Golf and Squash Club at Wilhelminalaan, Emmastad, has a 10-hole sand **golf** course open 0800-1230, green fee US$15 for 18-hole round, and two **squash** courts, US$7, open 0800-1800, T7373590. *Santa Catharina Sport and Country Club*, T7677028, F7677026, has six hard **tennis** courts, a **swimming** pool, bar and restaurant. The large hotels have tennis courts: the *Holiday Beach*, *Marriott* and the *Princess Beach* have a pro.

Willemstad

Willemstad, capital of the Netherlands Antilles and of the island of Curaçao, is full of charm and colour. The architecture is a joyous tropical adaptation of 17th-century Dutch, painted in storybook colours. Pastel shades of all colours are used for homes, shops and government buildings alike. Fanciful gables, arcades, and bulging columns evoke the spirit of the Dutch colonial burghers.

Population: 140,000

The earliest buildings in Willemstad were exact copies of Dutch buildings of the mid-17th century, high-rise and close together to save money and space. Not until the first quarter of the 18th century did the Dutch adapt their northern ways to the tropical climate and begin building galleries on to the façades of their houses, to give shade and more living space. The chromatic explosion is attributed to a Governor-General of the islands, the eccentric Vice-Admiral Albert Kikkert ('Froggie' to his friends), who blamed his headaches on the glare of white houses and decreed in 1817 that pastel colours be used. Almost every point of interest in the city is in or within walking distance of the shopping centre in **Punda**, which covers about five blocks. Some of the streets here are only 5 m wide, but attract many tourists with their myriad shops offering international goods at near duty-free prices. The numerous jewellery shops in Willemstad have some of the finest stones to be found anywhere. There is a red and white trolley train which takes 60 passengers around the streets of Punda several times a day.

Markets

The **Floating Market**, a picturesque string of visiting Venezuelan, Colombian and other island schooners, lines the small canal leading to the Waaigat, a small yacht basin. Fresh fish, tropical fruit, vegetables and a limited selection of handicrafts are sold with much haggling. Visit early in the morning. In the circular, concrete, public market building nearby there are straw hats and bags, spices, butcheries, fruit and vegetables for sale, while in the old market building behind, local food is cooked over charcoal and sold to office workers at lunchtime.

Synagogue

Nearby on Hanchi Snoa, is one of the most important historical sites in the Caribbean, the **Mikvé Israel-Emanuel synagogue**, which dates back to 1732, making it the oldest in continuous use in the Western Hemisphere. In the 1860s, several families broke away from the Mikvé Israel congregation to found a Sephardi Reform congregation which was housed in the Temple Emanuel (1867-1964) on the Wilhelminaplein. In 1964, however, they reunited to form the Mikvé Israel-Emanuel congregation, which is affiliated with both the Reconstructionist Foundation and the World Union for Progressive Judaism. The big brass chandeliers are believed to be 300 years older than their synagogue, originating in Spain and Portugal, their candles are lit for Yom Kippur and special occasions. The names of the four mothers, Sara, Rebecca, Leah and Rachel are carved on the four pillars and there are furnishings of richly carved mahogany with silver ornamentation, blue stained glass windows and stark white walls. The traditional sand on the floor is sprinkled there daily, some say, to symbolize the wandering of the Israelites in the Egyptian desert during the Exodus. Others say it was meant to muffle the sound of the feet of those who had to worship secretly during the Inquisition period. ■ *Services are held Fri 1830 and Sat 1000. Dress code for men is coat and tie and ladies equally conventional. Normally open 0900-1145 and 1430-1645, free.*

In the courtyard is the **Jewish Cultural Historical Museum**, occupying two restored 18th-century houses, which harbours an excellent permanent exhibition of religious objects, most of which have been donated by local Jewish families. There are scrolls, silver, books, bibles, furniture, clothing and household items, many 18th-century pieces and family bequeathments. Two circumcision chairs are still in use. Outside are some tombstones and a ritual bath excavated during restoration work. A small shop sells souvenirs, the Synagogue Guide Book and *Our Snoa*, papiamento for Synagogue, produced for the 250th anniversary in 1982. *Sephardim: The Spirit That Has Withstood The Times*, by Piet Huisman (Huisman Editions, The Netherlands, 1986) is an interesting illustrated account of the Sephardic communities of the Caribbean and the Americas, setting them in their historical context. Available in the synagogue shop and bookshops in town. Unfortunately, for those who want deeper research of the Jewish families, the *History of the Jews of the Netherlands Antilles*, by Isaac south and Suzanne A Emmanuel, two volumes, is no longer in print. ■ *Museum T4611633, F4611214. Open the same hours as the Synagogue, closed Jewish and public holidays. US$2, children US$1.*

Jewish cemetery West of the city, on the Schottegatweg Nord, is one of the two Jewish cemeteries, Bet Chayim (or Beth Haim), consecrated in 1659 and still in use. There are more than 1,700 tombstones from the 17th and 18th centuries, with bas-relief sculpture and inscriptions, many still legible. It is a little out of the way but well worth a visit. It is also a fine example of what atmospheric pollution can do, as the tombstones have suffered from the fumes from the surrounding oil refinery.

Fortkerk This 18th-century Protestant church, located at the back of the square behind **Fort Amsterdam**, the Governor's palace, still has a British cannonball embedded in its walls. It is not as large as the synagogue museum, but well laid out, with some interesting items, eg original church silver and reproductions of old maps and paintings of Curaçao. Note the clock in the ceiling of the church and make sure you are shown the still-functioning rain water cistern inside the church. It was once the main source of fresh water for the garrison. ■ *Mon-Fri 0900-1200, 1400-1700. US$2/NAf3, children US$1, you get a guided tour of the church and the associated museum. T4611139, F4657181.*

Willemstad orientation

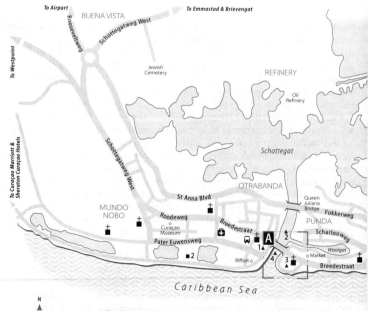

Relate map:
A. Willemstad centre,
page 1010

Not to scale

■ **Sleeping**
1 Avila Beach
2 Holiday Beach
3 Trupial Inn

▲ **Other**
1 Brionplein
2 Ferries

Two forts, **Rif Fort** and **Water Fort** were built at the beginning of the 19th century to protect the harbour entrance and replace two older batteries. All that is left of Rif Fort is a guard house dating from about 1840 but you can walk on the walls and eat at the restaurants in the vaults. The Water Fort Arches have been converted to house shops, bars and restaurants.

Forts

The **Maritime Museum** opened in 1998 in a 1729 colonial mansion on the Waaigat inlet near the Floating Market. It has permanent and temporary exhibitions of marine history relating to Curaçao and the Caribbean, with video presentations and multimedia displays. The museum has its own boat for tours of the harbour and ferrying cruise ship passengers and a harbourside café and gift shop. ■ *van Brandenburg, T4652327. Mon-Sat 1000-1700, admission US$8.50 for adults, US$4.50 for students and children under 12.* Another good museum in this area relating to Willemstad's maritime and trading history is the **Kura Hulanda**, with exhibits of the slave trade, tracing it back to the capture of slaves in Africa, their trans-Atlantic crossing and eventual sale as commercial goods. ■ Klipstraat 9, T4621400, F4621401, www.kuruhulanda.com

Museums

The **Philatelic Museum** is on the corner of Keukenstraat and Kuiperstraat in a recently restored building which is the oldest in Punda (1693). There is a comprehensive permanent display of Dutch Caribbean stamps, plus temporary exhibitions. ■ *Mon-Fri, 0900-1200, 1330-1700, Sat 1000-1500, admission US$2 or NAf3.50 for adults, NAf1.75 for children. T4658010, F4617851.*

The Central Bank of the Netherlands Antilles owns and operates a **Numismatic Museum**, Breedestraat 1, Punda, with a collection of coins and notes from the Netherlands Antilles and some from other countries, as well as a display of precious and semi-precious gemstones on loan from a local collector. ■ *Mon-Fri 0830-1130, 1330-1630. Free. T4613600, F4615004.*

The Octagon, Simón Bolívar's sisters' house where Simón Bolívar stayed during his exile in Curaçao in 1812, is near the Avila Beach Hotel reached down a small road off Penstraat just before you get to the hotel. The building is in need of some repair work and looks neglected although there is an attendant (make sure his dogs are chained). There is one octagonal room downstairs, with some manuscripts, pictures and books, and a similar one upstairs, with a bed and some furniture; not much to see unless you are a Bolívar aficionado. ■ *Closed lunchtimes.*

There are often special exhibitions in the World Trade Centre which are worth looking out for. These may include collections from museums in Holland or elsewhere. ■ *T4636105.*

3 Fort Amsterdam
4 Queen Emma Bridge

The swinging **Queen Emma bridge** spans St Anna Bay, linking the two parts of the city, Punda and Otrabanda (the latter means 'the other side' in Papiamento, and people tend to refer to 'Punda' and 'Otrabanda' rather than 'Willemstad'). Built on 16 great pontoons, it is swung aside some thirty times a day to let ships pass in and out of the harbour. The present bridge, the third on the site, was built in 1939. While the

Bridges

Netherland Antilles, the ABC Islands

bridge is open, pedestrians are shuttled free by small ferry boats. The bridge is closed to vehicular traffic.

The new **Queen Juliana** fixed bridge vaults about 50 m over the bay and connects Punda and Otrabanda by a four-lane highway. Taxis will often offer to stop at the bridge so you can get a panoramic view and photo of Willemstad on one side and the oil refinery on the other. Although you can reach it on foot it is not open for pedestrians; the wind and the way it shakes will explain why.

Otrabanda

Parts of **Otrabanda** are gradually being restored and there are many old houses here, both small, tucked away down alleys, and large mansions or town houses. The Belvedere, an Otrabanda landmark, was restored in 1992-93. Breedestraat is the main shopping street, the **Basilica Santa Ana**, founded in 1752 and made a Basilica in 1975 by Pope Paul VI, is just off here. The houses fronting on to the Pater Euwensweg, the highway heading west along the coast, once overlooked the Rifwater lagoon, now reclaimed land. Along St Anna Bay, past the ferry landing, is **Porto Paseo**, a restored area with bars and restaurants, popular on Friday evenings when there is music and dancing, or you can just sit and admire the view. The old hospital has been restored and is now the *Hotel and Casino Porto Paseo*. A new cruise ship pier has been built at Otrabanda for liners too big to reach the existing terminal in Willemstad harbour.

On the outskirts of Otrabanda, on van Leeuwenhoekstraat, is the **Curaçao Museum**, founded in 1946 (housed in an old quarantine station built in 1853) with a small collection of artefacts of the Caiquetio Indian culture, as well as 19th and 20th century paintings, antique locally-made furniture, and other items from the colonial era. Labels are inadequate and the hand-out leaflets only partly make up for this. In the basement there is a children's museum of science, but it is limited and rather outdated, almost a museum piece in itself. On the roof is a 47-bell carillon, named The Four Royal Children after the four daughters of Queen Juliana of the Netherlands, which was brought from Holland and installed in 1951. Lots of explanatory leaflets

Willemstad centre

■ **Sleeping**
1 Otrabanda   2 Porto Paseo   3 Van der Valk Plaza

are given out at the museum, with a suggested route map. ■ *Daily, except Sat, Mon-Fri 0900-1200 and 1400-1700, Sun 1000-1600. US$2.25/NAf5.30, US$1.25/NAf2.60 for children under 14. T4623873, F4623777.*

Another area within walking distance of Punda and worth exploring, is **Scharloo**, across the Wilhelmina bridge from the floating market. A former Jewish merchant housing area, now under renovation, there are many substantial properties with all the typical architectural attributes; note the green house with white trimmings known as the Wedding Cake House at Scharlooweg 77. Under a five to 10 year plan to restore the buildings, companies or government departments take them over for use as offices in many cases. Reading matter of architectural enthusiasts includes the expensive but magnificently illustrated *Scharloo – a 19th-century quarter of Willemstad, Curaçao: historical architecture and its background*, by Pauline Pruneti-Winkel (Edizioni Poligrafico Fiorentino, Florence 1987), and a more general collection of essays with illustrations, *Building up the Future from the Past: Studies on the Architecture and Historic Monuments of the Dutch Caribbean*, edited by Henry E Coomans and others (De Walburg Pers, Zutphen, the Netherlands, 1990).

Scharloo

The **S E L Maduro Library** is at the **Landhuis Rooi Catootje**, the site, in 1954, of the Round Table Conferences which led to the Statuut between the Dutch Kingdom and its Caribbean territories. The library, in the beautifully restored landhuis, contains all manner of things Caribbean and the conference table still stands in the dining room. ■ *Open by appointment but well worth the effort, T7375119. Take the Rond minibus from Punda and ask to be let off next to the chicken factory, a site better known to most drivers than the house itself.*

Around the island

The restored country estate houses, or *landhuizen*, emerge here and there in the parched countryside. Not all of them are open to the public but it is worth visiting some of those that are. Set in 503 ha in the east part of the island is **Brievengat**. Its exact date of construction is unknown, but it is believed to date from the early 18th century. It was used in the 19th century to produce cattle, cochineal and aloe, but a hurricane in 1877 devastated the plantation and the house which were gradually abandoned. Shell later took over the property to extract water from the subsoil, but in 1954 when it was in a state of ruin Shell donated it to the Government who restored it to its former grandeur. The windows and the roof are typical of the local style but unusual are the arches extending the length of the house and the two towers at either side, which were once used to incarcerate slaves. ■ *Daily 0915-1215, 1500-1800, entrance US$1.10, children half price, bar and snacks, live music on Wed and Fri and often on Sun, check beforehand, open house on Sun 1000-1500 with folklore show at 1700 on last Sun of the month. T7378344. Take the bus marked Punda-Hato from Punda at 15 mins past the hour and get off at the Sentro Deportivo Korsou.*

Chobolobo, at Salinja, came into the Senior family in 1948 and Senior & Co make the Curaçao liqueur here, using a copper still dating from 1896 and the original Valencia orange known locally as Laraha. The clear, orange, amber, red, green and blue are for cocktails and all taste the same; others are chocolate, coffee, rum raisin. Chobolobo is worth visiting, but if you resist the temptation to buy Senior & Co's products you will find them cheaper in the duty free lounge at Hato Airport although they occasionally run out of some brands. The original Curaçao Liqueur can only be purchased on the island. Copy cats are exported from Holland etc. ■ *Mon-Fri 0800-1200, 1300-1700. Free and visitors may taste the liqueur. T4613526.*

Near the Hato international airport on Rooseveltweg, are the **Hato Caves** which contain stalactites and stalagmites, a colony of long nose bats and pools among spectacular limestone formations. There are also some Caquetio rock drawings believed to be 1,500 years old. ■ *Guided tours every hour, the last one at 1600, 1000-1700, adults US$4, children US$2.75. T8680379, F8688114.*

Jan Kok is the oldest landhouse on the island, dating from 1654 and overlooking the salt flats where flamingoes gather. ■ *1100-2100 high season and 1100-1900 on Sun low season. Bar and restaurant, guided tour Tue, Thu 0900-1300 through the salt pans and the landhouse. T8648087. Take the bus marked Lagun and Knip from the Riffort, Otrabanda, at half past the even hour in the morning or half past the odd hour in the afternoon.* **Santa Martha**, built in 1700 and restored in 1979, is used as a day care centre for the physically and mentally handicapped but is open to visitors. ■ *Mon-Thu, 0900-1200, 1300-1500, Fri 0900-1200, if you call in advance, T8641559.* **Ascension**, built in 1672 and restored in 1963, is used by Dutch marines stationed on the island.■ *First Sun of the month 1000-1400 only. T8641950. Local music, handicrafts and snacks. Take bus marked Westpunt from Otrabanda (see below).* **Landhuis Kenepa** or **Knip**, near the beach of the same name, is a restored 17th-century landhouse where there was a slave rebellion in 1795. It has a collection of antique furniture and an exhibition about the Kenepa people. ■ *T8640244, F640385. On the same bus route as Jan Kok.*

The Christoffel Park covers an area of 1,860 ha in the west of the island, including Mount Christoffel at 375 m, which was formerly three plantations. These plantations, Savonet, Zorgvlied and Zevenbergen, are the basis for a system of well-marked trails, blue (9 km), green (7½ km or 12 km) and yellow (11 km), and there is a red walking trail up Mount Christoffel which takes about four to five hours there and back. You can see a wide range of fauna and flora, including orchids, the indigenous *wayacá* (*lignum vitae*) plant, acacias, aloe, many cacti, calabash and the tiny Curaçao deer. The ruins of the Zorgvlied landhouse can be seen off the green route. The Savonet route takes you to the coast and along to Amerindian rock drawings, painted between 500 and 2,000 years ago in terracotta, black and white. In this area there are also two caves (take a strong torch), one of which is about 125 m long and you have to crawl in before you can stand up (lots of bats and lots of guano on the ground) and walk to the 'white chamber'(stalactites and stalagmites) and the 'cathedral'.

The 17th-century **Savonet Plantation House** is at the entrance to the park on the Westpoint road, but it is not open to the public. However, several outbuildings are used. There is a small museum with archaeological exhibits, Guided tours are available, special walks at dawn or dusk are organized at random, check in the newspapers, evening walking tours to see the Curaçao deer, maximum eight people, reservations essential. You can rent mountain bikes and horses in the park, T8640363. Stinapa publishes an excellent *Excursion Guide to the Christoffel Park, Curaçao*, by Peer Reijns, 1984, which is available at the Park administration. A basic map of the trails is also provided. The bus Otrabanda-Westpunt passes the entrance to the park. Rancho Alfin at the park also does tours, including night trips, sunrise trips and a romantic package for honeymooners, T8640363, 5608229. ■ *Museum. Mon-Sat 0800-1600, Sun 0600-1500. T8640363. Park. From 0800 Mon-Sat, NAf35 per person, admission to the mountain side closes at 1400 and to the ocean side at 1500, although you can stay in until later. On Sun the park opens at 0600 and closes at 1500, no admittance after 1300 and 1400 for inland or sea routes.*

Behind Spanish Water Bay on the south coast rises **Mount Tafelberg**, where phosphate mining used to take place.

Essentials

Sleeping

There is a 7% government tax & 10% (sometimes 12-15%) service charge to be added to any quoted room rate & many hotels add an extra US$3 per day energy surcharge

New hotel, villa or timeshare developments are springing up all over Curaçao. Several huge resorts are planned around Knip beach, Lagun, Cas Abao, Piscadera, Parasasa, Cornelis Bay and Jan Thiel. Be prepared for construction work. Many hotels have no hot water taps, only cold. This is because the water pipes in Curaçao are laid overground, the water in them being warmed by the sun during the day and cold at night. Time your shower accordingly.

Willemstad (hotels) **AL** *Plaza Hotel and Casino* in the *Van der Valk* chain, on Punda seafront, T4612500, F4616543, www.plazahotelcuracao.com Very central, huge tower dominates the skyline by the fortress walls, price per room includes service, tax, breakfast, bargain for a cheaper rate for several nights, popular with the Dutch, good food, recently renovated, shops, restaurants, diving, boat excursions, 2 private aircraft with instructor, fishing, child care. **AL** *Otrabanda Hotel and Casino*, on Breedestraat just by the bridge in Otrabanda, T4627400, F4627299, or reservations through *International Travel & Resorts*, New York, T800-2239815, F212-2511767, or in Holland, *Holland International*, T70-3957957, F70-3957747. Excellent location, good for business travellers, standard rooms small but comfortable, single rooms available, suites are larger rooms with sofas, coffee shop and restaurant with good view of Punda and floating bridge, includes excellent buffet breakfast and guided tour of Otrabanda on Wed, pleasant service, pool,. Also very central is **LL-AL** *Hotel and Casino Porto Paseo*, de Rouvilleweg 47, T4627878, F4627969. Room or 2-bedroom suite, includes breakfast, swimming pool, dive shop, in attractive restored old hospital. **C-D** *Pelikaan Hotel*, Lange Straat 78, T4623555, F4626063. In the heart of Otrabanda, newly rebuilt, small, comfortable, clean, 40 rooms, a/c, restaurant. Further west along the main road is the **L-AL** *Holiday Beach*, T4625400, F4625409, reservations through ITR. Currently full of US Airforce personnel moved from base closed in Panama, concrete block on a manmade beach, but convenient, 10 mins' walk to shops and restaurants, 200 rooms in need of decoration, a/c, phone, TV, new casino, videogame room and banks of gaming machines, mediocre food at high prices, pool, tennis, dive shop on site, conference rooms. 15 mins' walk east of the centre is the family-owned **L-AL** *Avila Beach*, Penstraat 130, PO Box 791, T4614377, F4611493, http://avilahotel.com Built in 1811 as Governor's residence but most rooms in an old hospital wing, small and with no sea view, very popular, always full, cool reception area, service friendly but slow, no pool, lovely bar shaped like a ship's prow on the beach, great for evening cocktails, pleasant outdoor dining, live music Wed. A new extension has been built in an attractive colonial style, **LL-L** *La Belle Alliance*, the other side of the pier (bar and restaurant, *Blues*, excellent fish, meat not so good, live jazz Thu, Sat, closed Mon) on another man-made beach, 40 hotel rooms, and some apartments, all rooms and suites with sea view, conference facilities and ballroom, tennis, both the beaches are protected by breakwaters and have imported sand for pleasant swimming. **A-B** *Trupial Inn*, Groot Davelaarweg 5, T7378200, F7371545. In residential area, 74 rooms, a/c, newly decorated, nice, pool, restaurant, tennis, open air bar, entertainment, shuttle bus to downtown, suites available. **C** *Hotel San Marco*, Columbusstraat 5, Punda, T4612988, F4616570. 89 rooms, completely renovated, a/c, TV, safe, clean, excellent value. **D** *Mini-Hotel Mauric*, Oranjestraat 60, T/F4657214.

Willemstad (guest houses and apartments) The tourist board's main office at Pietermaai 19 has a very large list of guest houses and apartments (not all of which it recommends) including some cheap hotels such as **E** *Estoril*, Breedestraat 181, Otrabanda, T4625244. In Scharloo, **D-E** *Park*, on Frederikstraat 84, T4623112. Bath and fan, not nice, noise from road, fleas, not clean enough, both *Estoril* and *Park* cater to 'short stay' visitors, not recommended. **E** *Mira Punda*, Van de Brandhofstraat 12. Near floating market, fan, cold water, clean, private bath, in restored mansion, bar downstairs has lots of local colour. **C** *Bon Auberge*, Hoogstraat 63-65, T4627902, F4627579. Dutch owned, friendly, clean, conveniently located in Otrabanda close to shops and transport, 23 rooms, hot water, some have a/c, others fans, not all have bath, 4 good apartments for US$200 per week. A nice small hotel is **D** *Buona Sera (Bonacera) Inn*, Pietermaai 104, T4618286. On the road to the Bolívar museum, not a very safe area, 16 rooms, sleeps 1-4, a/c, private bathroom, recently built seaview restaurant and bar, plans to create small beach, family-run, friendly, English, Dutch, Spanish, French and Papiamento spoken. **C** *Bramendie Apartments*, Bramendieweg 103, in Dominguito, T4655337. 10 apartments with kitchenette, porch, TV, a/c, phone with deposit, car rental, good discount for long stay. **C** *Douglas Apartments*, Salinja 174, PO Box 3220, T4614549, F4614467. A/c, cots available, towels and linen provided, kitchenettes, a/c, phone, fax facilities, on 1st floor of shopping gallery, bus stop outside. Outside town, **C** *Wayaca Apartments and Bungalows*, Gosieweg 153, T7375589, F7369797. A/c, TV, phone, supermarket, launderette, tennis, minimum 1 week, car rental can be included; houses also available usually on weekly basis or longer. **C** *Art and Nature Inn*, 17 Valkensweg, T8682259. 10 mins' drive from Willemstad, bungalow with kitchenette and bathroom, each of 12 studios is decorated with murals, mosaics and paintings by the proprietor, Geerdine Kuypers, an internationally known artist, speaks 6 languages, great hostess, 5-min drive to supermarket.

Netherland Antilles, the ABC Islands

East of Willemstad On Dr Martin Luther King Boulevard is the **LL-AL** *Princess Beach Resort and Casino*, 600 m from the Seaquarium on a narrow beach, T7367888, F4614131, www.princessbeach.com Change of ownership meant renovation work in 2000, aiming to upgrade to 5-star complex, may become *Radisson* or *InterContinental*. Pools, restaurants, bars, shops, 341 rooms and suites make this the biggest resort on the island, popular, food good at all 3 restaurants, newly constructed conference centre, dive packages available, fitness centre with massage, good entertainment. Next door is the **AL** *Lion's Dive*, T4618100, F4618200, http://lionsdive.com Attractive, not high rise, wooden balconies give it style but needs renovating, poor plumbing, 72 rooms, TV, small pool, unlimited use of Seaquarium, dive shop on site, dive packages available, fitness centre, windsurfing, restaurant, nice atmosphere, friendly staff, helpful service, caters for hard-core diving fraternity, courtesy bus to town. **LL-A** *Seru Coral*, Koral Partier 10, T7678499, F7678256. A new resort in the east part of the island, in the middle of nowhere but great restaurant, nice pool, nice studios, apartments and villas, 3 miles from beach, 18 from airport, 9 miles from town. *Santa Catharina Sport & Country Club*, same ownership, T7677028, F7677026. Tennis, fitness centre, football pitch, pool, restaurant, bar, with studios, suites and bungalows all with kitchenettes, phone, TV, terrace overlooking northeast coast.

West of Willemstad Along the coast are **C** *El Conde Hotel*, Roodeweg 75, near hospital, T/F4627611. Some rooms noisy, basic, 7 rooms, a/c. **LL-L** *Curaçao Marriott Beach Resort and Casino* , next to the International Trade Centre, Piscadera Bay, PO Box 6003, T7368800, F4627502. 248 luxury rooms and 34 suites, very comfortable, excellent service, 2 children under 12 sharing room free, this upmarket resort, built in Dutch colonial style is on a private beach and offers a freeform pool, whirlpools, tennis, fitness centre, kids programme, watersports, casino, conference facilities. **LL-L** *Sheraton Curaçao*, T4625000, F4625846. 194 rooms and suites, totally renovated, now beautiful, private beach, pool, scuba, watersports, fitness centre, casino. **AL** *Piscadera Bay Resort*, T4626303, F4625962. 94 semi-detached bungalows for 2-4 people, beach with dive shop and bar/restaurant, monthly rental can be arranged. Two minutes from the airport is **B** *Holland*, T8688044, F8888114. 45 rooms, a/c, TV, phone, business services, restaurant, pool, car rental, casino, diving. **B** *Bulado Inn*, in Boca St Michiel fishing village, Red A'Weg, T8695731, F8695487. Family run, new, very nice, good value, call and check for deals, 17 a/c rooms, all ocean view, restaurant, bar, pool, nicely landscaped, tennis, meeting rooms, car rental, parking, 10 mins walk from beach. **LL-B** *Habitat Curaçao*, linked to *Captain Don's Habitat* in Bonaire, at Rif Baai, T5607263, F7371331. 76 suites and cottages, pool, restaurant, bar, beach, free town shuttle bus, dive centre, lots of packages available. **C** *Landhuis Cas Abao*, T8603525, F8649460. Dates from 1751, rebuilt 1993, stylish, rooms vary but have good views, secluded beach, minimum stay 4 days, no credit cards, beautiful area, restaurant closed in evenings and owners leave premises after 1900, long drive to find a decent evening meal. **LL-B** *Coral Cliff*, resort and casino on Santa Marta Bay, PO Box 3782, T8642666, F8641781. Quiet beach, nice sea, some shade provided, entrance US$4.50 for non-residents, sprawling, concrete block hotel, rooms or suites, good sea view from restaurant on hill, dive shop on premises, excellent diving from beach, watersports, mini golf, horse riding arranged, free airport pickup, shuttle service to town. **B-C** *Bahia Inn*, near Lagun beach, PO Box 3501, T8684417. Small, basic, adequate, several beds in each room, building work all along this coastal road. At Westpoint, **A-C** *All West Apartments*, T4612310, F4612315, dive shop attached, T8640102, F8640107, allwest@cura.net A/c studios and apartments, caters to individuals, adventure diving, PADI courses, boat and shore diving, small scale. **C-D** *Jaanchie Christian's*, T8640126. Popular restaurant with 4 rooms to let, a/c, bathroom, breakfast included, double beds, can fit extras in, usually full, phone for reservation.

Camping *Brakkeput*, adjoining Spanish Waters, Arowakenweg 41A, PO Box 3291, T674428. School parties catered for, sports fields, showers and toilets, tents available, US$1.25 per person overnight with minimum charge US$18.75, cheaper for youth organizations. Camping is allowed on some beaches, but there are no facilities and you have to bring your own fresh water supplies.

Native food is filling and the meat dish is usually accompanied by several different forms of carbohydrate, one of which may be *funchi*, a corn meal bread in varying thickness but usually looking like a fat pancake (the same as *cou-cou* in the Eastern Caribbean). Goat stew (*stoba di kabritu*) is popular, slow cooked and mildly spicey (milder and tastier than Jamaican curry goat), recommended. Soups (*sopi*) are very nourishing and can be a meal on their own, grilled fish or meat (*la paria*) is good although the fish may always be grouper, red snapper or conch (*karkó*), depending on the latest catch; meat, chicken, cheese or fish filled pastries (*pastechi*) are rather like the *empanadas* of South America or Cornish pasties. While in the Netherlands Antilles, most visitors enjoy trying a *rijsttafel* (rice table), a sort of Asian *smørgasbørd* adopted from Indonesia, and delicious. Because *rijsttafel* consists of anywhere from 15 to 40 separate dishes, it is usually prepared for groups of diners, although some Curaçao restaurants will do a modified version of 10 or 15 dishes.

A selection of European, South American (mostly Chilean) and Californian wines is usually available in restaurants. Curaçao's gold-medal-winning Amstel beer, the only beer in the world brewed from desalinated sea water, is very good indeed and available throughout the Netherlands Antilles. Amstel brewery tours are held on Tue and Thu at 1000, T4612944 for information. Some Dutch and other European beers can also be found. Fresh milk is difficult to get hold of and you are nearly always given evaporated milk with your tea or coffee. Curaçao's tap water is excellent; also distilled from the sea.

Willemstad One of the most highly regarded restaurants in Willemstad is *The Wine Cellar* on Concordiastraat, T4612178. Owned by chef Nico Cornelisie, a master rotisseur, in small old house, only 8 tables, chilly a/c, very good food but unexciting wine list, local fish and meat (ostrich) particularly good, reservations recommended, closed Sun. *Alouette*, in a restored house, Orionweg 12, T4618222. Very popular, reservations recommended, French-style food, low-calorie or vegetarian meals available, comparatively small menu but changed frequently, except for the goat cheese crêpe which is such a favourite it is a permanent fixture, excellent food and service, attractive decor, open 1200-1430, 1900-2200, later at weekends. *Mi Kalbas*, de Ruyterkade, opposite post office, T4621010. Very good food, local specialities and international menu, full bar, run by former food and beverage manager at *Princess Beach*. *Larousse*, also in an old house on Penstraat 5, almost opposite the *Avila Beach*, T4655418. French menu with local and imported North Sea fish, quiet, open 1800-2400, closed Mon. *Fort Nassau*, reservations T4613450. Spectacular location with a panoramic view from the 200-year old fort, American-style menu using local ingredients, open Mon-Fri 1200-1400, Mon-Sun 1830-2300. *De Taveerne*, in an octagonal mansion, Landhuis Groot Davelaar, T7370669. Beef and seafood, à la carte menu, antique furnishings, closed Sun. *Bistro Le Clochard*, in the Rif Fort walls overlooking the harbour, T4625666/4625667, www.bistroleclochard.com. French and Swiss cuisine, choose fresh local fish rather than imported, open Mon-Fri 1200-1400, 1830 onwards, Sat evenings only, open Sun in Dec-Mar. *La Pergola*, in the Waterfort Arches, T4613482. Serves Italian food, fish, pizza, terrace or a/c dining, open 1200-1400 Mon-Sat, 1830-2230 daily. *Grill King*, in the Waterfort Arches, T4616870. Friendly and has good international food, open Mon-Sat 1100-2300, Sun 1700-2300. There are several restaurants in the Arches, nice variety, pleasant location, good for a meal or just drinks. Some other moderately priced yet good restaurants include *Fort Waakzaamheid*, T4621044. Lovely sunset views from the terrace on top of the fort, which is on a hill above Otrabanda, medieval atmosphere, restaurant and tavern, good food and menu, open daily 1200-1400, 1800-1030, reservations suggested, dinner US$15-20. *Tasca Restaurant Don Quijote*, Gosieweg 148, T7369835. Spanish, seafood and daily specials, good paella, takeaway, happy hour 1700-2000, open weekdays 1700-0100, closed Tue. *Green Mill*, Salinja Galleries, T4658821. Lunches or dinners, happy hour Mon-Thu 1800-1900, Fri 1700-1830, menu with good variety. *Café con Leche*, behind cinema. Cuban-Curaçaoan, daily specials, moderately priced, fish, chicken, good desserts. *Cactus Club I*, Van Staverenweg 6, T7371600, in the Mahaai area. Tex Mex food, fun atmosphere, blended and frozen cocktails, local dishes also available, service with a smile. *Cactus Club II* on the beach at the Seaquarium, T4651265. *Hook's Hut*, between *Marriott* and *Sheraton* hotels Thatched tiki hut bar and restaurant next to the sea, good drinks and ambience, food OK.

Eating
10% service is added to the bill in restaurants but an extra 5% is appreciated

Netherland Antilles, the ABC Islands

For an Indonesian meal it is best to make up a party to get the maximum number of dishes but this is not essential. The *Indonesia*, Mercuriusstraat 13, T4612606. Wonderful Javanese food specializing in 16 or 25-dish rijstaffel, essential to book, often several days ahead, open 1200-1400, 1800-2130 daily, dinner only on Sun. *Mambo Beach* , at the Seaquarium, T4618999. Wed Indonesian buffets. *Surabaya* in the Waterfort Arches, T4617388. Has good food but overpriced and no hot plates to keep it warm, vegetarian menu too, open Tue-Fri 1200-1400, Tue-Sun 1800-2300.

The best place to try local food in Willemstad is the old market building beyond the round concrete market tower by the floating market, here many cooks offer huge portions of good, filling local food cooked in huge pots on charcoal fires, at reasonable prices, choose what you want to eat and sit down at the closest bench or one of the nearby tables having first ordered, takeaway available, very busy at lunchtimes, the best dishes often run out, make sure you have the right money available. The best restaurant for local food is *The Golden Star*, Socratesstraat 2, T4618741. Informal, friendly, plastic table cloths, fun, TV showing American sport, home cooking, very filling, goat stew washed down by a couple of Amstels recommended, popular with locals and tourists, open daily 1200-2300, live music Sat 1900-2300, takeaway available.

On the Westpoint road, opposite the entrance to the Christoffel Park, is *Oasis*, T8640085. Seafood and creole dishes but also offering chicken and ribs, open 1200-2400, weekends 1030-0300, dinner served until 2100, dancing afterwards. *Playa Forti*, atop a cliff overlooking beach of same name, wonderful view, very popular lunchtime at weekends, Colombian and local dishes. Further along the road in Westpoint is *Jaanchie's*, T8640126. Another weekend lunchtime favourite with local families although no sea view, huge, filling portions, see the bananaquits eating sugar, parties catered for, takeaway service, bus stops outside for return to Willemstad,.

A good fish restaurant is *Pisces*, at the end of Caracasbaaiweg, T4672181. Reservations recommended. *El Marinero*, Schottegatweg Noord 87B, T7379833. Moderately priced seafood dishes, lunch 1200-1500, dinner 1830-2330. *Fisherman's Wharf*, Dr Martin Luther King Blvd, close to *Princess Beach*, T4657558. Very good seafood, lunch and dinner. *Seaside Terrace*, T4618361. Little beachside restaurant near *Princess Beach Hotel*, more like a snack stand but great fresh, huge, lobster for US$28, as well as seafood of all kinds as well as chicken, pork etc, and a US$7 barbecue on Sun with live entertainment, a few tables to watch sunset, open 1000-2200 Tue-Sun. *Octopus*, Marinebadplaats, St Michielsbay, T8881244. Fresh fish, local food, bar, restaurant and terrace by the sea, run by Eric and Yolanda Wederfoort, see Diving and marine life. Chinese food at *Ho Wah*, Saturnusstraat 93, T4615745. *Ham Yuen*, Fokkerweg 25, T4613462. Locals' favourite Chinese food. *Sawasdee*, Van Eyck V Voorthuyzenweg 5, near Curaçao Museum, T4626361. Thai restaurant, takeaway available, open 1830-2200.

For drinks, snacks or cheap lunches, *Downtown Terrace*, also in Gomezplein, T4616722. You can hear the chimes from the Spritzer and Fuhrmann bells, great selection of Belgian beers. There is plenty of fast food to cater for most tastes, including pancake houses, and *Pizza Hut* at Pietermaiplein prides itself on having won awards. *Domino's Pizza*, on Schotlegatweg Oost 48, T7366555. 12 in pizzas from US$9.60, delivery service. *Denny's*, attached to side of *Holiday Beach Hotel*, T4625232. Good food at good prices, some local dishes, takeaway available, is open 24 hrs. Late night fast food, local fashion, can be found at truk'i pans, bread trucks which stay open until 0400-0500 and sell sandwiches filled with conch, goat stew, salt fish and other Antillean specialities. Great fruit shakes at *Trax's*, a van at the Otrabanda side of the Queen Emma bridge. Wonderful home made ice cream, large variety, at *Vienna Ice Café*, on Handelskade in Punda.

Nightlife K-Pasa is a weekly dining and entertainment guide, widely available, www.k-pasa.com For 'night-owls', there are casinos. All the large hotels have them, with many gaming tables and rows and rows of fruit machines, open virtually all hours. There are many nightclubs and discothèques, several of which are in the Salinja area: *Façade* (Lindberghweg 32-34, T4614640, open 2200-0400 except Mon and Thu, happy hour on Fri from 1800) and *Club 99* (Lindbergweg) are favoured by wealthy locals of all ages, you will not be let in wearing jeans or trainers and they have airport-style metal detectors at the door; *Infinity* is at Fort Nassau, open Fri and Sat, 2100-0200, T4613450; *Havana Club* (formerly *the Pub*) is at Salinja 144; for all-night music and dancing, *La Paix* and *De Fles* (the *Flask*) have been recommended for salsa and merengue, you may be the only foreigner there, take local currency; in Otrabanda, *Rum Runners* is recommended for cocktails and harbour view. *The Music Factory*, Salinja 131, T4610631. Open Mon-Sat 1700-0300, Fri live music, Sat DJ, special drinks nights with half-price brand names 2200-2400. On the Seaquarium beach is the *Mambo Beach Club*, a good nightspot with happy hour and dancing Sun, restaurant during the week, T4618999. The Centro Pro Arte presents concerts, ballets and plays. *Mirage*, a 'gentlemen's club', has a show for men only Wed 2300 and Sat midnight, T8681170. *Classy Lady*, adults only, T4625250. **Cinema** *The Movies Curaçao*, T4651000, www.themoviescuracao.com shows recent releases. While on the subject of entertainment, one of the most bizarre sights of Curaçao, not dealt with in the tourist brochures, is the government-operated red-light area. Close to the airport, it resembles a prison camp and is even guarded by a policeman.

Curaçao, Aruba and Bonaire all hold the traditional pre-Lent **carnival**. On the *Sunday*, a week before, is the children's parade. Curaçao's main parade is on the Sunday at 1000 and takes 3 hours to pass, starting at Otrabanda. The following Monday most shops are closed. On the Monday at 1500 there is a children's farewell parade and there is a **Farewell Grand Parade** on the *Tuesday* evening when the Rey Momo is burned. **Festivals**

Several music festivals are held throughout the year. You can hear *tumba* around carnival time. Contact the Curaçao Jazz Foundation, T4658043, for details of the May and November jazz festivals and the Festival Center, T7376343, for details of *salsa* (August) and *merengue* (May) festivals. For the **Golden Artists Music Festival** in *October*, T4655777.

Open on Sunday morning and lunchtimes if cruise ships are in port. Weekday opening is 0830-1200 and 1400-1800. The main tourist shopping is in Punda (see above) where you can pick up all sorts of duty-free bargains in fashion, china etc. *Arawak Craft Products*, Mattheywerf 1, Otrabanda, T4627249, F4628394, near cruise ship dock and ferry, tiles, reliefs of Dutch style houses and other ceramics, you can watch the potters and artists and even make your own, *Arawak Art Gallery* upstairs, open 0900-1800, on Sunday also if cruise ship in dock. **Shopping**
Willemstad's jewellery shops are noted for the quality of their stones

Bookshops *Boekhandel Mensing* in Punda has a limited selection of guide books and maps. Larger and more well stocked bookshops are out of the centre of Willemstad. *Mensings' Caminada* and *Schottegatweg and Van Dorp* in the *Promenade Shopping Centre*, good maps and guide book section. *Van Dorp* shops are also located in most large hotels; they stock *Footprint Handbooks*. The public library is a modern building in Scharloo, cross the bridge by the floating market, turn right along the water and it is on your left. *The Reading Room* has books in Dutch, English, Spanish, French and Papiamento, T4617055.

Road Bus To the airport get a bus marked Hato from Punda at 15 mins past the hour from 0615 to 2315, or from Otrabanda at 15 mins past the hour from 0615 to 2320, returning on the hour, usually full. Buses to Westpunt leave from Otrabanda on the odd hour, last bus 2300, return on the even hour. Buses and minibuses to Dominguito (the Seaquarium) and Caracas Bay run from Punda. A bus marked Schottegat runs from Punda via the Octagon Bolívar Museum, the *Trupial Inn Hotel*, the Curaçao Golf and Squash Club, the Jewish cemetery and the Curaçao Museum to Otrabanda. The Lagun and Knip bus route leaves Otrabanda at half past the even hour in the mornings and on the odd hour in the afternoons via the Curaçao Museum, the University, Landhuis Jan Kok, Santa Cruz beach, Jeremi beach, Lagun Beach and Bahia beach, returning from Knip on the alternate hour. While the service in and around Willemstad is efficient, the service to Westpunt is erratic and planning is needed to avoid getting stranded. The standard city bus fare is NAf1 with no apparent time-tables or bus stops, very passenger-friendly and recommended. Outside town you may get charged a variety of fares, particularly on minibuses. Check beforehand or ask what others are paying. **Transport**

Netherland Antilles, the ABC Islands

Car hire Companies include *Budget* (best rates, ask for specials or coupons), *Europcar/ National*, *Avis*, *Caribe Rentals*, *Dollar Rent a Car*, *Star Rent a Car*, *Vista Car Rental*. Prices start at about US$35 daily, unlimited mileage, includes insurance, deposits from US$250; jeeps, minimokes, buggies, scooters and bikes also available. Foreign and international driving licences are accepted. Traffic moves on the right.

Taxi It is not always possible to get a taxi to the airport early in the morning or late at night so if you are going to a night club arrange your taxi in advance (sometimes the driver will turn up a little early and join you on the dance floor). Taxis do not have meters but fares are fixed. Fares from the airport to *Holiday Beach*, US$15, *Van der Valk Plaza* or *Avila Beach* US$18, *Lions Dive* US$20, *Coral Cliff* US$27. Airport displays taxi fares to main hotels. Try and pay in guilders as taxi drivers do not always have the right change for dollars. Fares for sightseeing trips should be established at beginning of trip, the usual price is US$20 for the 1st hour and US$5 for each subsequent 15 mins. Tipping is not strictly obligatory. The high price of taxis is a common complaint. Taxis do not always go looking for business and it can be difficult to hail one. Best to telephone from a hotel lobby or restaurant/bar, one will arrive in a couple of mins. For taxi fares or complaints T8690747, or go to a taxi stand and just get into an empty car, the driver will then turn up. Drivers do not always know the area as well as they should, even restaurants can sometimes be tricky for them to find. The rear windows of many taxis do not work, which makes the car uncomfortable in the hot climate. Courtesy vans operated by the hotels can be more comfortable.

Sea The ferry from Venezuela is reported to be back in action, but we had no details as we went to press. It is also possible for the adventurous and persistent to get a boat from Muaco at La Vela. You have to contact the captains direct as the practice of taking passengers is discouraged. Try Nelson García (T6522533) of *Carmen Reynely* or Douglas Zavala (T378268) of *Trinidad II* (neither speaks English). The *capitanía* is not much help, try the maritime agency 2 blocks from Plaza Bolívar for help in contacting captains. The journey takes 9 hrs, head seas all the way, not for the seasick, not recommended for women.

Directory **Airlines** *ALM* (T8695533) has an office in Gomezplein in Punda where you can pay your departure tax and avoid the queues at Hato Airport. There is also an ALM office in the International Trade Centre and at the airport. *ALM* often has flights at rather unsociable hours, tends to lose luggage and is jokingly known in Dutch as 'Altijd Laat Maatschappij', the Always Late Company. *KLM* (T4652737) offices are also at Gomezplein. *American Airlines* at the airport; *Avianca*, T8683659. *Servivensa*, T8680538. *TAP Air Portugal*, T8686395. *Air Aruba*, T8683777/5707/-3659. *Aeropostal*, T8882818. *Pelican Air*, T4628155, does helicopter tours of the island. **Banks** *ABN-AMRO Bank*, *Antilles Banking Corp* , *Maduro & Curiel Bank* on Plaza Jojo Correa, T4611100, *Banco di Caribe* on Schottegatweg Oost, T4616588. Banking hours are 0800-1530 Mon-Fri. At the airport the bank is open 0800-2000 Mon-Sat, 0800-1600 Sun. ATMs at *ABN-AMRO Bank* and *Maduro & Curiel Bank* (Visa, Mastercard and Cirrus, issuing either US$ or NAf). **Communications Telephone**: All American Cables & Radio Inc, Keukenstraat; Kuyperstraat; Radio Holland NV, De Ruytergade 51; Sita, Curaçao Airport. Prepaid phone cards are available for international calls from Antelecom, Belvédère House, T124. Telephone rates abroad are published in the telephone book, but beware if phoning from a hotel, you can expect a huge mark up, check their rates before you call. To Europe, US$3.05 per minute, to the USA US$1.60, to Australia and Africa US$5.55, to the Netherlands Antilles US$0.55, Central America US$3.90, Venezuela US$1.10, Leeward and Windward Islands US$1.75. There are other companies offering lower rates, so shop around, eg TSI charges US$0.70 per minute to the Netherlands, US$0.50 to the USA (T8696590, 5601988) and Amtel charges US$0.61 and US$0.49 respectively (T7375327, 4610304). For **internet access**, there is a cybercafé in the Salinja Galleries. The public library has 2 public internet terminals. **Medical facilities** The 550-bed St Elisabeth Hospital is a well-equipped and modern hospital with good facilities including a coronary unit and a recompression chamber (T462-4900). For emergencies, T110 (hospital), 112 (ambulance). The **Sentro Mediko Santa Rosa**, at Santa Rosaweg 329, is open 7 days a week, 0700-0000, laboratory on the premises. **Places of worship** Curaçao has always had religious tolerance and as a result there are many faiths and denominations on the island. Details of services can be found in the official free guide, *Curaçao Holiday*, which lists Anglican, Catholic, Jewish, Protestant and other churches. Anglican Church, Leidenstraat; Holy Family Church (Roman Catholic), Mgr Neiwindstraat, Otrabanda; Methodist Church, Abr de Veerstraat 10; Mikvé Israel – Emanuel

Synagogue, Hanchi Snoa 29, Punda; Ebenezer Church of the United Protestant Congregation, Oranjestraat; Christian Heritage Ministries (Evangelical), Polarisweg 27, Zeelandia; Church of Christ, 40 Schottegatweg West; Church of God Prophecy (Ecumenical), Caricauweg 35. **Tourist information** Local tourist office The main office of the *Curaçao Tourism Development Bureau* is at Pietermaai 19, Willemstad, PO Box 3266, T4616000, F4612305. There is an information office on Breedestraat, east of Hendrikplein, and at the airport, www.curacao.com/tourism. *The Curaçao Hotel and Tourism Association (CHATA)* is at Kaya Junior Salas 1, T4651005, in down town Punda, offering helpful information, assistance in finding a hotel, brochures, maps, etc. There are also several Visitor Information Centres dotted round Willemstad and some booths sponsored by resort hotels, which have irregular hours. *Members of Curaçao Hospitality Services* look after the parking lots and are trained in first aid and how to give directions. **Local travel agents** One of the best island tours available is with *Casper Tours*, T5610721/4653010, informative, fun, covers east to west, 0900-1600 including lunch at a local restaurant for US$35 (cruise ships' tours from US$15) in a/c mini buses, English, Dutch and Spanish spoken. *Taber Tours*, http://curacao.com/tabertours (branch at airport and at many hotels) do a variety of tours, usually in large Greyhound type buses. *Old City Tours* do a walking tour of Otrabanda, 1715-1900, US$5.55 including a drink, T4613554. *Dornasol Tours*, T8682735, highly recommended local guide with minibus, full or half day eco-tours by biologist and historian Lies van de Kar, English, Dutch, German and Spanish spoken, also tours of Jewish sites. **Maps** Curoil nv publishes a good road map with a satellite photo of the island with superimposed information, town street plans and an excellent index, available in Mensing and other bookshops. **Useful addresses** Police and fire: T114.

Background

The economy

Curaçao has a more diversified economy than the other islands, yet even so, it suffered severe recession in the 1980s and unemployment is around 13% of the labour force. The major industry is the oil refinery dating back to 1917, now one of the largest in the world, to which the island's fortunes and prosperity are tied. Imports of crude oil and petroleum products make up two thirds of total imports, while exports of the same are 95% of total exports. That prosperity was placed under threat when Shell pulled out of the refinery in 1985, but the operation was saved when the island government purchased the plant, and leased it to Venezuela for US$11 mn a year. Despite the need for a US$270 mn reconstruction, principally to reduce pollution, the Venezuelan company, PDVSA, signed a 20-year lease agreement which came into effect in 1995, ending its previous system of short term operating leases. Bunkering has also become an important segment of the economy, and the terminal at Bullenbaai is one of the largest bunkering ports in the world. The island's extensive trade makes it a port of call for a great many shipping lines.

Coral reefs surrounding the island, constant sunshine, a mean temperature of 27°C (81°F), and refreshing trade winds lure visitors the year round, making tourism the second industry. Curaçao used to be a destination for tourists from Venezuela, but a devaluation of the bolívar in 1983 caused numbers to drop by 70% in just one year and several hotels had to be temporarily taken over by the Government to protect employment. A restructuring of the industry has led to a change of emphasis towards attracting US and European tourists, as well as South Americans, and numbers have now increased. Stayover visitors are around 225,000 a year, while cruise ship passengers are at a similar level. Cruise visitor numbers have been boosted by the arrival of the megaship *Rhapsody of the Seas*, which carries 2,000 and calls 26 times a year. A new cruise ship pier in Otrabanda will further increase arrivals. The single largest market for visitors to Curaçao is Holland, with 30% of stayover arrivals, followed by the USA with 15% and Venezuela with 14%. Most rooms are in top grade hotels, with only a few in guest houses, but self-catering apartments, time share and condominiums are growing fast. There are about 2,500 hotel rooms, with more planned to be built. Diving has been promoted and Curaçao now registers about 10,000 visiting divers a year. A dive improvement programme is being funded by the EC together with a beach improvement programme and a visitor information programme.

A third major foreign currency earner, the offshore financial sector, saw its operations severely curtailed in the 1980s. Once a centre for booking the issue of Eurobonds because of its favourable tax laws, the repeal of witholding tax in the USA in 1984 eliminated Curaçao's advantages and virtually wiped out the business. A second blow came with the cancellation by the USA, followed by similar action by the UK, of its double taxation treaty. These changes have led to greatly reduced income for the island's Government, although the offshore centre is actively seeking new areas of business, including captive insurance and mutual funds, in a highly competitive market. There are 61 banks, of which only 14 are licenced to carry out domestic business, the rest are offshore. After the crisis of the mid-1980s, assets in the offshore banks have risen steadily again.

Aruba

Like Curaçao and Bonaire, Aruba has scant vegetation, its interior or cunucu is a dramatic landscape of scruffy bits of foliage, mostly cacti, the weird, wind-bent divi divi trees and tiny bright red flowers called fioritas, plus huge boulders, caves and lots of dust. Aruba is the smallest and most westerly of the ABC group lying 25 km north of Venezuela and 68 km west of Curaçao.

Ins and outs

Getting there   **From Europe** *KLM* has direct flights from Amsterdam, going on to Lima, in a joint operation with *Air Aruba*. *Martinair* has a charter flight from Amsterdam. **From North America** Atlanta (*Delta*), Baltimore (*Air Aruba*), Fort Lauderdale (*TWA*), Hartford (*American Airlines*), Houston (*Continental*), Miami (*American Airlines, Air Aruba*), Minneapolis (*Sun Country Airlines*), New York (*American Airlines, Air Aruba*), Philadelphia (*Air Aruba*), Tampa (*Air Aruba*) and Washington DC (*American Airlines*). There are also many charter services from Boston, Chicago, Cleveland, Detroit, Hartford, Los Angeles, Philadelphia, Minneapolis, Pittsburgh and Toronto, mostly in the winter season. Scheduled services from Canada involve a change of plane in Miami. Charter service from Canada is available through *Air Canada, Royal Air, Canada 3000* and *Skyservice* on a seasonal basis. **From South America** Lots of flights from Venezuela: Barcelona, Caracas, Las Piedras, Maracaibo, Porlamar and Valencia with *Air Aruba, ALM, Servivensa, Aeropostal, Aserca* and *Santa Barbara Airlines*. From Colombia, *Air Aruba* and *Avianca* fly from Bogotá and Medellín. *KLM* from Lima. **From the Caribbean** From San Juan with *American Airlines, TWA* and *ALM*, as well as frequent flights from Bonaire and Curaçao with *ALM* and *Air Aruba*. *Aeropostal* from Santo Domingo.

Getting around   Beware of aggressive local drivers. Driving is on the right and all traffic, except bicycles, coming from the right should be given right of way, except at T junctions. Good maps are available at petrol stations. You must have a valid foreign (held for at least 2 years) or international driver's licence and be at least 21 to rent a car. Requirements vary between companies with a minimum age of 21-25 and a maximum of 65-70.

See transport, page 1033, for further details

Climate   Aruba is out of the hurricane belt and the climate is dry. The hottest months are August-October and the coolest are December-February, but the temperature rarely goes over 32°C or below 26°C. A cooling trade wind can make the temperature deceptive. Average rainfall is 51 cm a year, falling in short showers during October-December.

Flora and fauna

Aruba has 48 different types of native trees, 11 of which are now very scarce and in some cases have only 5 examples left. The loss of native trees is due to wood cutting, changing weather and marauding goats. A tree planting programme is under way and negotiations with goat owners are in progress to keep them out of protected areas. About 170 species of birds can be found on Aruba, and about 50 species breed on the island but if you include the migratory birds which come in November-January the total rises to around 300 species. The most common birds are the trupiaal (with its bright orange colours), the chuchubi, the prikichi (a little parrot) and the barika geel (the little yellow-bellied bird you will find eating the sugar on the table in your hotel). The shoco, a burrowing owl, is endangered. An interesting site to see waterfowl is the Bubali Plassen, opposite the Olde Molen. Here you can often find cormorants, herons and fish eagle. Brown pelicans can be found along the south

As well as various kinds of lizards, Aruba has large iguanas, that are hunted to prepare a typical Arubian soup

shore. Two kinds of snakes can be found on Aruba: the Santanero, a harmless little snake (however, be careful when you pick it up, because it defecates in your hand) and the not so harmless rattle snake. Aruba's rattle snake, the cascabel, is a nearly extinct unique subspecies and does not use its rattle. Rattle snakes live in the triangular area between the Jamanota, Fontein and San Nicolas. The best place to go looking for rattle snakes, if you really want to, is the area south of the Jamanota mountain. In the unlikely event that you get a bite from a rattle snake, go immediately to the hospital. They have anti-serum.

The **Arikok National Park** covers a triangle of land between Boca Prins and San Fuego and bounded on the east by the sea as far as Boca Keto. After decades of discussion the plan converts 17% of the island into a protected park area. Work is

Netherland Antilles, the ABC Islands

Aruba

California Lighthouse · California Dunes
Arashi Beach · Tierra del Sol Golf Course
Malmok Beach & Antilia – German Wreck · Seroe Gerard Gold Mine
Hadikurari · Salinja Cerka · Boca Cura
Palm Beach
Caribbean Sea
De Olde Molen · Noord · Chapel of Alto Vista
Eagle Beach · Santa Anna Church · Boca Mahos
Bubali Bird Sanctuary · Gold Mill ruins
Bushiribana o · Andicouri · Noordkaap
Druif Beach · Ponton · Paradera · Gold Mine o · Natural Bridge
o Ayó
Casibari - Rock formations
Oranjestad · Hooiberg
Bucuti Yacht Club · Jucuri · Santa Cruz · Arikok NP · Dos Playa
Paarden Bay · Mahuma · Boca Prins
Aruba Nautical Club · Frenchmans Pass & Gold Mill ruins · Fontein Cave
Spanish Lagoon · Jamanota · Guadirikiri Caves
Pos Chiquito · Huliba Cave · Rincon
Mangel Halto Beach · Aruba Golf Club
Savaneta · Boca Grandi
Caribbean Sea · Commanders Bay · San Nicolas
Lago Refinery
Rodgers Beach · Seroe Colorado
Baby Beach · Colorado Point

N
Not to scale

Essentials

Documents US and Canadian citizens only require **proof of identity**, such as passport, birth certificate, certificate of naturalization, with photo ID if not using a passport. Other nationalities need a **passport**. Those who need a **visa** include citizens of Afghanistan, China, Cuba, Dominican Republic, Iraq, Iran, Cambodia, Korea, Libya, Mauritania, Mongolia, Burma, Syria, Vietnam, Peru, Haiti, Albania, Croatia, Serbia and Bosnia, unless they are legally residing in a country whose citizens do not need a visa. A return or onward ticket and proof of adequate funds are also required for all visitors. Dogs and cats are permitted entry if they have a valid rabies and health certificate but, no pets are allowed from South or Central America. Check with your hotel to see if they are allowed to stay.

Customs People over 18 are allowed to bring in one fifth of liquor, 200 cigarettes, 50 cigars and 250 grammes of tobacco.

Currency Aruba has its own currency, the Aruban florin, not to be confused with the Antillean guilder, which is not accepted in shops and can only be exchanged at banks. The **exchange rate** is Afl1.77=US$1, but shops' exchange rate is Afl1.80. US dollars and credit cards are widely accepted, even on buses, and the Venezuelan bolívar is also used. ATMs dispense only Aruban currency.

Voltage 110 volts 60 cycle AC same as USA.

Departure tax Aruba Passenger Facility Charge is US$20, or Afl36. If flying out to the USA, you will clear US customs and immigration in Aruba, which saves you time at the other end (US Immigration, T831316). There are two terminals for international and US-bound flights, with restaurants, duty-free shops and other services.

Tourist offices overseas **Argentina**, Av Córdoba 859 Piso 8, Buenos Aires 1054, T/F54-11-3118053, 3152015. **Brazil**, Rua Cel

Joaquim Ferreira Lobo, 314-04544-150, São Paulo, T5511-8227033, F8299916. **Canada**, 86 Bloor Street West, Suite 204, Toronto, Ontario M5S 1M5, T416-9751950, F416-9751947, toll free 800-268 3042, ata.canada@toaruba.com **Colombia**, Calle 114, No 9-45, Oficina 701, Torre B, Teleport Business Park, Bogotá, T571-6292879, F6292902.
The Netherlands, Schimmelpennincklaan 1, 2517 JN, Den Haag, T70-3566220, F3604877, ata.holland@visitaruba.com
USA, 199 Fourteenth Street, NE, Suite 2008, Atlanta, GA 30309-3688, T404-8927822, F404-8732193, ata.atlanta@toaruba.com; I Financial Plaza, Suite 136, Fort Lauderdale, FL 33394, T954-7676477, F7670432, ata.florida@toaruba.com; 401 Wilmette Av, Westmont, IL 60559, T603-6631363, F6631362, ata.chicago@toaruba.com; 12707 North Freeway, Suite 138, Houston, TX 77060, T281-87-ARUBA, F281-87278725, ata.houston@toaruba.com; 1000 Harbor Blvd, Ground level, Weehawken, NJ 07087, T201-3300800, F3308757, toll free (800) TO ARUBA, ata.newjersey@visitaruba.com
Venezuela, Centro Ciudad Comercial Tamanaco, Torre C, Piso 8, Oficina C-805, Chuao, Caracas, T582-9591256, F9596346, ata.venezuela@visitaruba.com

Clothing Swim suits are not permitted in the shopping area. Most casinos require men to wear jackets and smart clothes are expected at expensive restaurants, otherwise casual summer clothes worn all year. Public nudity of any kind is illegal although topless sunbathing is tolerated on most resort beaches.

Public holidays New Year's Day, GF Betico Croes Day (25 January), Carnival Monday (beginning of February), Flag Day (18 March), Good Friday, Easter Sunday and Easter Monday, Queen's Birthday (30 April), Labour Day (1 May), Ascension Day (May), Christmas Day, Boxing Day.

continuing to provide trails, clean up and upgrade the park, clearing litter and reconstructing benches and a stairway built at Fuerte Prins in the 1960s. The three centres will be linked by trails for cars and walkers. Arikok Centre contains the 184.5 m Arikok hill, the second highest point in Aruba. Prins Centre in the northeast includes the former Prins Plantation, the functioning Fontein Plantation and the Fontein Cave. The Jamanota Centre in the south includes the 189 m Jamanota hill, the highest point the island, and the old gold mining operation at Miralamas. The Spanish Lagoon area is also included. www.arubanationalparks.com

Diving and marine life

Visibility in Aruban waters is about 30 m in favourable conditions and snorkelling and scuba diving is very good, although not as spectacular as in the waters around Bonaire. A coral reef extends along the west side of the island from California reef in the north to Baby Beach reef in the south, with dives varying in depth from five to 45 m. There are lots of dive sites suitable for beginners where you can see morays, grouper, eagle rays, manta rays and sting rays, as well as lobsters, parrot fish, angel fish and others. The coral is in good condition and varied. The northwest of the island has fields of seagrass which attract leatherback turtles during the nesting season and are home to hawksbill, green and loggerhead turtles all year. The other side of the island is only for experienced divers as there are strong currents and it is often rough. Organized boat trips regularly visit two wrecks worth exploring, although they can get a bit crowded. One is a German freighter, the *Antilla*, which was scuttled just after the Second World War was declared and is found in 20 m of water off Malmok beach on the west coast. You can see quite a lot just snorkelling here as parts of the wreck stick up above the water. Snorkelling boat trips usually combine Malmok beach and the wreck. The other wreck is nearby in 10 m of water, the *Pedernales*, a flat-bottomed oil tanker which was hit in a submarine attack in May 1941, while ferrying crude oil from Venezuela to Aruba. Only the central part of the tanker remains, the US military took away the two end pieces, welded them together and made a new ship which was used in the Normandy invasion. The Aruba Watersports Association recently sunk a DC-3 aeroplane near the *Pedernales*, to be another wreck dive site only 10 m deep. Be very careful not to touch anything underwater; not all the dive masters bother to warn you of the dangers of fire coral and hydroids. An annual Aruba Perrier Reef Care Project takes place over a weekend in June or July when everyone gets together to preserve the underwater environment and clean up debris and pollution from the main dive sites and beaches. Local dive operators help out and local hotels provide refreshments.

Dive centres There are several scuba diving operations and prices start from about US$35 for a single tank dive. Snorkelling from a dive boat varies from US$10-22. *Aruba Pro Dive* is at about five resorts, T825520, F877722, but tries to keep groups small at an average of six divers. *Red Sail Sports*, L G Smith Blvd 83, PO Box 218, T861603, F866657, and at hotels, sailing, snorkelling, diving with PADI, SSI, IDEA, HSA certification courses, windsurfing, waterskiing, hobie cats etc, accommodation packages available, this is a large, reputable international operation and an expensive one. Others include *Pelican* (PADI, NAUI, SSI, T872302, F872315), *Unique Sports of Aruba* (PADI, T/F860096, uniquesports@visitaruba.com), *SEAruba* (T/F838759), who offer diving in the southeast and to Venezuela, *Native Divers* (IDD, PADI, T/F864763), *Dax Divers* (PDIC, T/F851270) and *Dive Aruba* (PADI, T827337, F821817). For further information on dive sites, dive operators and marine news contact the Aruba Tourism Authority or visit the website, www.scuba.aruba.com

Atlantis Submarines operate a two-hour trip, including the boat ride to the Atlantis VI, which descends to 30 m and explores the *MI Dushi I* and *Morgenster* shipwrecks or the *Sonesta* aeroplane wreck.

Beaches and watersports

There are good, sandy beaches on both sides of the island although fewer on the east side which is rough and not so good for swimming. Travelling north along the west coast from Oranjestad an excellent road takes you to the main resort areas where nearly all the hotels are gathered. **Druif Beach** starts at the *Tamarijn Aruba Beach*

Of the 3 ABC islands, Aruba stands out as having the best beaches, all of which are public & free

Netherland Antilles, the ABC Islands

Resort, extending and widening along the coast to the sister hotel, the *Divi Aruba*, with good windsurfing. At the *Manchebo* there is a huge expanse of sand, often seen in advertisements. North of here is **Eagle Beach** where the 'low rise' hotels are separated from the beach by the road, and then **Palm Beach** where the 'high rise' hotels front directly on to the beach. These three sandy beaches extend for several kilometres, the water is calm, clear and safe for children, although watch out for watersports and keep within markers where provided.

A residential area and the new golf course stretches up from Arashi to the lighthouse and the coast is indented with tiny rocky bays and sandy coves, the water is beautiful and good for snorkelling, while shallow and safe for children. It is also a fishing ground for the brown pelicans. At night they normally sleep in the shallow water close to the lighthouse. A little way after the lighthouse there is a very spectacular place where high waves smash against the rocks at a small inlet. There is a blow hole, where water sometimes spouts up more than 5 m.

At the other end of the island is **Seroe Colorado**, known as 'the colony', which used to be a residential area for Exxon staff but is currently used as temporary housing. You have to enter the zone through a guard post, but there is no entrance fee and no hindrance. There are two west facing beaches here worth visiting. **Rodgers Beach** has a snack bar, showers, yachts and is protected by a reef but is in full view of the refinery. **Baby Beach**, on the other hand, is round the corner, out of sight of the refinery, in a lovely sandy bay, protected by the reef, nice swimming and snorkelling, very busy on Sunday, with toilets but little shade. **Sea Grape Grove** and **Boca Grandi**, on the east coast of the south tip has good snorkelling and swimming, being protected by a reef, and is popular with tours who come to see the largest elkhorn coral. Experienced windsurfers come here to wave jump. The prison is near here, remarkable for the pleasant sea view from the cells. Other beaches on the east side of the island are **Boca Prins**, where there are sand dunes, and further north from there, reached by a poor road, is **Dos Playa** where there is good surf for body surfing. The beach here is closed to vehicles because of nesting turtles. The landscape is hilly and barren because of serious overgrazing by herds of goats. **Andicouri** is also popular with surfers, note that you may not approach it through the coconut grove which is private property, there are signs to direct you the right way.

Virtually every type of watersport is available and most hotels provide extensive facilities. Activities which are not offered on site can be arranged through several tour agencies such as *De Palm Watersports*, T824545, *Pelican Watersports*, T831228 and *Red Sail Sports*, T824500. Watersports companies are too numerous to mention in further detail, but you can hire jetskis, waterskis, wave runners, banana boats, snorkelling equipment and other toys. Parasailing can be done from the high-rise hotels. Glass bottomed boat trips from various locations are around US$20-25, but can be more for a sunset cruise.

Windsurfing North of Palm Beach is an area of very shallow water with no hotels to break the wind, known as Fisherman's Huts, which is excellent for very fast **windsurfing**. Surfers from all over the world come here to enjoy their sport and professionals often come here for photo sessions. Although speeds are high and there is a strong offshore wind, surfing is quite safe and there are several rescue boats to get you back if the wind blows you to Panama. This beach is called **Malmok** (south end) or **Arashi** (north end) and there are many villas and guest houses across the road which cater for windsurfers. There are several operators of high quality: *Roger's Windsurf Place*, L G Smith Blvd 472, T/F861918, www.rogerswindsurf.com, windsurf packages available, boards and accommodation; *Sailboard Vacation Windsurf Village*, L G Smith Blvd 462, T862527, boards of different brands for rent. For information about the Aruba Hi-Winds Pro/Am boardsailing competitions, contact ATA Special Events, T823777 ext 239, www.hiwinds.aruba.com They usually take place in June. At the same time a Windsurfing Festival combines a consumer trade show, with all the latest gear, and music and food on the beach.

Several yachts and catamarans offer cruises along the coast with stops for snorkel- **Day sails**
ling and swimming. A morning cruise often includes lunch (about US$40-50), an
afternoon trip will be drinks only – and then there are the sunset booze cruises
(about US$20-30). The largest catamaran is Red Sail Sports' *Fiesta*, which carries 90
passengers, while its sister ship, *Balia*, a 53-ft racing catamaran, does all the usual
cruises and is available for private charter at US$450 an hour, minimum two hours,
T864500; *Pelican I* is a 50-ft catamaran running along the west coast from Pelican
pier; *Wave Dancer*, another catamaran, departs from *Holiday Inn* beach, T825520;
Octopus is a 40-ft trimaran, departing from *Holiday Inn* pier, is also available for private charter, snorkelling and sailing cruises, US$20-35, T833081; *Tranquilo*, a yacht,
can be contacted through Mike, its captain T847533, tranquilo@visitaruba, or *Pelican Tours* T831228. *Mi Dushi* is an old sailing ship built in 1925 which starts cruises
from the *Aruba Grand Beach Resort* pier, morning and lunch US$45, snorkelling
and sunset US$27.50, sunset booze cruise US$25, pirate sails and beach party
US$40, T823513/828919.

Near Spanish Lagoon is the Aruba Nautical Club complex, with pier facilities offer- **Sailing**
ing safe, all-weather mooring for almost any size of yacht, plus gasoline, diesel fuel,
electricity and water. For information, write to PO Box 161, T853022. They also
organize an annual 'catch and release' deep sea fishing tournament every October. A
short sail downwind from there is the Bucuti Yacht Club with clubhouse and
storm-proofed pier providing docking, electricity, water and other facilities. Write
to PO Box 743. A Catamaran Regatta is held annually in November in front of the
Palm Beach hotels, with competitors from the USA, Europe and Venezuela. For
information contact the Aruba Tourism Authority, T823777. Also in November is
the Seaport Yacht Race with races from Havana to Seaport Marina, around the
island and from Punto Fijo in Venezuela. For details contact Mr Henk Grim at the
Seaport Marina, T839190, F839197.

Over a dozen charter boats are available for half or whole day deep sea fishing. The **Fishing**
tourist office has a list so you can contact the captain direct, or else go through *De
Palm Tours*. Whole day trips including food and drinks range from US$350-480,
depending on the number of people on board. A deep sea fishing tournament is held
in October at the Aruba Nautical Club, T853022 for information.

Golf In 1995 the 18-hole, par 71, Tierra del Sol Golf Course opened near the light- **Other sports**
house, designed to fit in with the natural landscape and with the sea on two sides. A
community of homes and villas has also been designed to blend in with the surrounding vegetation with a full-service clubhouse, swimming pool, golf practice range and
tennis and fitness complex. It took over 30 years to get the golf course built because of
difficulties with the barren landscape and the lack of water. Many hotels are signing up
for preferential rates for their guests, otherwise contact Tierra del Sol on T860978,
F860671. There is a nine-hole golf course with oiled sand greens and goats near San
Nicolas, golf clubs for rent US$6, green fee US$10 for 18 holes, US$7.50 for nine holes,
T842006, Saturday and Sunday members only, open daily 0800-1700. At the *Holiday
Inn* is an 18-hole mini-golf course. A mini golf course called Adventure Golf has been
built opposite *La Cabana*, close to Bubali, in a nice garden.
　　There are **tennis** courts at most major hotels. The *Aruba Racquet Club* is at Rooi
Santo 21 in the Palm Beach area and has eight lit courts, an exhibition centre court,
pro shop, pool, aerobics classes, fitness centre, bar and restaurant. Open 0800-2300,
for reservations, T860215. There is usually an international tennis tournament in
September. **Horseriding** at *Rancho El Paso*, Washington 44, near Santa Ana
Church, T873310, Paso Fino horses, daily rides except Sunday, one hour through
countryside, US$15, or two hours part beach, part *cunucu*, US$30. The National
Horse Fair, a three-day international competition for Paso Fino horses is held here
in April. *Rancho Dalmari* also has Paso Fino horses and offers 2½ hours rides with

snorkelling, daily at 0900 and 1500, a/c transport from your hotel included, T860239. *Rancho del Campo* takes riders into the national park, 2½ hours, 0930 or 1530, US$45 including transport and snorkelling, T820290.

Bowling The Eagle Bowling Palace at Pos Abou has 16 lanes, of which six are for reservation, open 1000-0200, US$9 from 1000-1500, US$10.50 from 1500-0200, US$1.20 shoe rental, T835038; also three racquetball courts available. There is an international bowling tournament in April, T826443 for details, and an international youth tournament in July. Wings Over Aruba, at the airport, T837104, F837124, has a pilot school, with sightseeing **flights**, aerial photography, aircraft rental; sightseeing in a seaplane US$130 per 30 minutes, trial flying lesson US$120 per 90 minutes. **Sailcarts** available at a special rink not on the beach, Aruba Sailcart N V, Bushiri 213, T836005, open 0900-sunset, US$15 per 30 minutes for a single cart, US$20 per 30 minutes for a double cart. **Drag races** are held several times a year at the Palo Marga circuit near San Nicolas, call the Aruba Racing Association, T841315. **Triathlons** and **marathons** are held periodically, contact the tourist office for details or IDEFRE, JG Emanstraat, Oranjestad, T824987, F836478.

Sky diving is now available in Aruba with *Sky Dive Aruba*. Beginners can do a tandem jump from 10,000 ft to a drop zone near the Fisherman's Huts on the salt pans on the northwest coast. An early morning jump is US$195 and afternoon US$215. There are plans to cater for certified jumpers and those who want to get their TAFF certification.

Oranjestad

Population: 21,000

Oranjestad, the capital of Aruba, is a busy little freeport town where 'duty-free' generally implies a discount rather than a bargain. The main shopping area is on Caya G F (Betico) Croes, formerly named Nassaustraat, and streets off it. Many of the buildings in the colourful Antillean style are actually modern and do not date from colonial times as in Willemstad, Curaçao.

There is a small museum in the restored 17th-century Fort Zoutman/Willem III Tower, Zoutmanstraat. ■ *Mon-Fri, 0900-1200, 1330-1630, entrance US$1.15.* *T826099.* Named the **Museo Arubano**, it contains items showing the island's history and geology, with fossils, shells, tools, furniture and products. It is not particularly well laid out, the displays are unimaginative and old-fashioned but it is still worth going if only to see the building. The fort, next to the Parliament buildings, opposite the police station, dates from 1796 and marks the beginning of Oranjestad as a settlement. Built with four guns to protect commercial traffic, in 1810-1911 it sheltered the government offices. The tower was added around 1868 with the first public clock and a petrol lamp in the spire, which was first lit on King Willem III's birthday in 1869 and served as a lighthouse. The Fort was restored in 1974 and the tower in 1980-83. The **Archaeological Museum** on J E Irausquin 2-A, is small, but cleverly laid out in three parts, Preceramic, Ceramic (from 500 AD) and Historic (from 1500-1800 AD when the Indians used European tools). The two main sites excavated are Canashitu and Malmok and most objects come from these. The descriptions are in English and Papiamento, easy to read and educational. There are some interesting publications available in English. Recommended, the best museum in the ABCs. ■ *Mon-Fri 0900-1630. T828979.* A numismatic museum, **Mario's Worldwide Coin Collection**, also known as the **Museo Numismatico**, Zuidstraat 27, not far from Fort Zoutman and the Central Bank of Aruba (where it is possible to buy specimen sets of Aruba's extremely attractive coins) has a large collection of coins from over 400 countries and coins from ancient Greece, Rome, Syria and Egypt. A bit cramped, but with a lot of fascinating material, the museum is run by the daughter of the collector, Mario Odor; donations welcomed. ■ *Mon-Fri, 0730-1200, 1300-1600.* There is an extensive collection of shells at **De Man's Shell Collection**, Morgenster 18, T824246 for an appointment. The **Cas di Cultura**, Vondellaan 2, has concerts, ballet, folklore shows and art exhibitions, T821010.

Gasparito Restaurant/Art Gallery has an exhibition of Aruban art for sale and display, Gasparito 3. ■ *0900-2300 daily. T867044.* Galeria Eterno, Emenstraat 92. Also exhibits local artists. ■ *Mon-Fri 1000-1700 or by appointment. T839484, F839575.*

Around the island

The landscape is arid, mostly scrub and cactus with wind blown divi divi (watapana) trees and very dusty. Flashes of colour are provided by bougainvillea, oleanders, flamboyant, hibiscus and other tropical plants. You will need a couple of days to see everything on offer inland without rushing. The Esso Road Map marks all the sites worth seeing and it is best to hire a car (four-wheel drive if possible, but not essential) as you have to go on dirt roads to many of them and there is no public transport. Tour agencies do excursions, about US$20-28 for a half day tour of the island, see page 1035.

Traditional Aruban houses are often protected from evil spirits by 'hex' signs molded in cement around doorways & surrounded by cactus fences

The village of **Noord** is known for the **Santa Anna Church**, founded in 1766, rebuilt in 1831 and 1886, the present stone structure was erected in 1916 by Father

Netherland Antilles, the ABC Islands

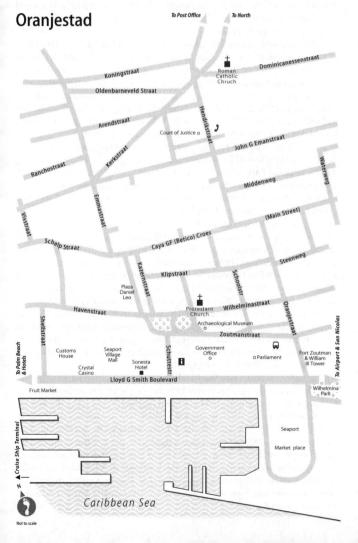

Oranjestad

Not to scale

Thomas V Sadelhoff, whose portrait is on the twelfth station of the Cross. It has heavily carved neo-Gothic oak altar, pulpit and communion rails made by the Dutchman, Hendrik van der Geld, which were the prize work shown at the Vatican Council exhibition in 1870. They were then housed in St Anthony's Church at Scheveningen in Holland, before being given to Aruba in 1928. The church is popular for weddings, being light and airy with a high vaulted ceiling and stained glass windows. ■ *Services are held Mon, Wed and Fri at 1830, Sat at 1900 and Sun at 0730 and 1800.* Not far from Noord on the north coast is the tiny **Chapel of Alto Vista**, dating from 1952 but on the site of the chapel built by the Spanish missionary, Domingo Antonio Silvester in 1750. It is in a spectacular location overlooking the sea and is so small that stone pews have been built in semi circles outside the Chapel.

Also on the north coast are the ruins of a gold mine at **Seroe Gerard** and a refinery at **Bushiribana** in a particularly bleak and sparsely vegetated area. The machinery at the mill, right on the coast, was damaged by sea spray and moved to Frenchman's Pass in 1824. A partly paved road leads to the natural bridge where long ago the roof of a cave collapsed, leaving only the entrance standing. It is actually fairly low and not as spectacular as tourist brochures would have you believe. There is a souvenir shop and you can get snacks here.

Inland, extraordinary rock formations can be seen at **Casibari** and **Ayó**, where huge, diorite boulders have been carved into weird shapes by the wind. At Casibari steps have been made so that you can climb to the top, from where you get a good view of the island and the Haystack. There is a snack bar and souvenir shop. Ayó does not have steps, you have to clamber up, but a wall is being built up around the rocks to keep out the goats. There are some Indian inscriptions. Toilets, a snack bar and souvenir shop are planned. The 541 ft **Hooiberg**, or Haystack, has steps all the way up. Very safe, even with children, the view is worth the effort.

At the village of **Santa Cruz**, just southeast of the Haystack, a cross on top of a boulder marks the first mission on the island. Travelling east from here you pass the **Arikok National Park**, where there are some well laid out trails for easy, but hot, walking. There are some interesting rock formations, indigenous fauna and flora and Amerindian art. See Flora and fauna above. The road leads to Boca Prins (dune sliding) and the **Fontein** cave. Work has been completed to restore the Amerindian drawings in the cave, clean up the more recent graffiti and install a car park and picnic benches. The cave is open to visitors during daylight hours only. There is a large chamber at the entrance, with natural pillars, and a 100 m tunnel leading off, halfway down which are Indian paintings. Despite the desolation of the area, there is a well near the caves with brackish water, which a Japanese man uses to cultivate vegetables for the Chinese restaurants on the island. Further along the coast are the **Guadirikiri** caves, two large chambers lit by sunlight, connected by passages and pillars, with a 100 m tunnel, for which you need a torch. Bats live in this cave system. The road around the coast here is very bumpy and dusty, being used by quarry trucks. A third cave, **Huliba**, is known as the Tunnel of Love. Again, no entry fee but helmets (US$2.50) and torches available. The walk through the tunnel takes 20-30 minutes with a 10-minute return walk overground.

The road then takes you to **San Nicolas** where there is a strong smell of oil. The Lago Oil Refinery (Exxon) was built in 1928 and was the largest refining plant in the world during the Second World War, when it supplied the allies. The effect on San Nicolas was dramatic. It drew immigrant workers from 56 countries and the community thrived. However, after the war a steady decline set in. After the closure of the oil refinery in 1985, San Nicolas was a ghost town, but now that Coastal Oil has taken over the refinery, activity is beginning to pick up. Old wooden houses are being demolished and new concrete houses built instead. A landmark is *Charlie's Bar*, which has been in operation since 1941; a good place to stop for refreshment to see the souvenirs hanging everywhere. Efforts are being made to rejuvenate the town and attract tourism.

Returning northwest towards Oranjestad you pass through Savaneta, where the Dutch marines have a camp. Turn off to the left to *Brisas del Mar*, a good seafood restaurant open to the sea, very popular. At Pos Chiquito, a walkway leads through mangroves to *Isla di Oro*, a restaurant built like a ship where there is dancing at weekends and pedalos and watersports. A little further on a bay with shallow water and mangroves is ideal for snorkelling beginners. The view is not spectacular but you can see many colourful fish. **Spanish Lagoon**, once a pirates' hideout, is a seawater channel, at the mouth of which is the Aruba Nautical Club and the water desalination plant. At the other end is a bird sanctuary where parakeets breed and the ruins of the Balashi gold mill dating from 1899, where the machinery is better preserved than at Bushiribana. There is quicksand in the area around the bird sanctuary, so it is not advisable to walk there. Nearby is **Frenchman's Pass** where the French attacked the Indians in 1700. From here you can turn east again to drive up **Jamanota**, at 189 m the highest elevation on the island.

Essentials

Glittering luxury hotels jostle for space along Druif Bay, and Eagle and Palm beaches. At the end of the 1990s nearly all the resorts along this hotel strip added rooms or upgraded existing facilities. Decent, cheap accommodation is now very difficult to find. The Aruba Apartment Resort and Small Hotel Association (ARASA) members offer accommodation at less than US$100 but to get a double room at that price at one of the large hotels you will have to negotiate a package deal in advance. Summer rates are substantially less than high season winter rates (16 Dec-15 Apr).

Sleeping
A 17.66% tax/service charge must be added; some hotels also add a US$1.50-5.75 per day energy surcharge

Around Oranjestad Closest to the airport, but only a 10-15 min walk into town, is the **LL-AL** *Caribbean Town Beach Resort*, L G Smith Blvd 2, T823380, F832446. Convenient for business travellers, 63 rooms and suites built round a pool, children under 18 sharing free, large rooms, most with kitchenette, oceanside rooms are cheaper than pool side as they overlook the road but a/c reduces traffic noise, Surfside beach club and watersports centre across the road. In Oranjestad on the waterfront is the **LL-AL** *Aruba Marriott Resort*, at Seaport Village, L G Smith Blvd 9, T836000, F825317, www.arubasonesta.com Deluxe highrise, 300 rooms, Seaport Village shops and Crystal casino on the premises. Also **LL-L** *Aruba Marriott Suites*, at Seaport Village, at L G Smith Blvd 82, by Seaport Market place. 250 1-bedroom suites, pools and small beach, no beach at the hotel but guests may use a private island reached by motor launch from the hotel lobby which has watersports and all facilities, even a private honeymooners' beach, the only drawback being that the island is right at the end of the airport runway. Just outside town to the west in a rather unattractive industrial area immediately after the free zone, is the **L-AL** *Bushiri Beach Resort*, L G Smith Blvd 35, T825216, F826789, www.bushiri.com A 150-room all-inclusive, often booked solid, reserve in advance, price per person, child discounts, indoor and outdoor kids activities, on man-made beach, gym, table tennis, lots of activities, good reputation for food.

Punta Brabo Beach The low-rise resort hotel development starts on Punta Brabo Beach, Druif Bay, all hotels are on the beach and offer swimming pools, tennis, watersports, shops, restaurants etc: **LL** *Tamarijn Aruba Beach Resort*, J E Irausquin Boulevard 41, T824150, F834002, www.tamarijnaruba.com One of the Divi hotels, all-inclusive, rates fluctuate monthly, highest at Christmas, 236 rooms, beachfront, but not much beach, watersports, land sports, resort is next to Alhambra Bazaar and Casino, shares facilities with **LL** *Divi Aruba Beach Resort Mega All-inclusive*, next along the beach at J E Irausquin Blvd 45, T823300, F834002, www.diviaruba.com 203 rooms and suites, honeymoon packages, all-inclusive, windsurfing, tennis, pool. *Divi Village*, at J E Irausquin Blvd 47, T835000, F820501. 132 apartments and free form pool. Next is the **L-AL** *Manchebo Beach Resort*, J E Irausquin Blvd 55, Manchebo, T823444, F832446, www.manchebo.com Run by Best Western, 71 rooms with balcony or terrace, dive shop and windsurfing on huge expanse of beach. **LL-AL** *Bucuti Beach Resort*, J E Irausquin Blvd 55-B, T831100, F825271, www.bucuti.com Attractive design, pleasant resort, 63 rooms, some with kitchenette, some suites, balconies, sea view, fitness centre, business centre. **LL-AL** *Casa del Mar*, J E Irausquin Blvd 51-53, Punta Brabo Beach, T827000, F826557, www.casadelmar-aruba.com 147 luxury 2-bedroom (time- share) apartments on the beach and 1-bedroom suites not on the beach, rather boring architecture, children's playground, gamesroom, tennis, pool, minimarket, laundromats. **LL-AL** *The Aruba Beach Club*, same address, T823000, F834871, mshipabccdm@setarnet.aw shared facilities, 131 rooms with kitchenette, for up to 4 people, family orientated.

Eagle Beach LL-AL *La Cabana*, J E Irausquin Blvd 250, T879000, F875474, www.lacabana.com Massive resort, 803 studios and suites, tennis, squash, fitness centre, waterslide, children's pool and playground, casino and condominiums. **LL-AL** *Amsterdam Manor*, J E Irausquin Blvd 252, T871492, F871463, www.amsterdammanor.com Low-rise, pleasant, 72 painted Dutch colonial style studios and apartments with sea view, kitchen, pool, bar and restaurant. **LL-AL** *La Quinta*, J E Irausquin Blvd 228, T875010, F876263. Timeshare with rentals, 54 apartments with kitchenette, pools, tennis.

Palm Beach After the sewage treatment plant and Pos Chiquito the road curves round Palm Beach where all the high rise luxury hotels are. All have at least 1 smart restaurant and another informal bar/restaurant, some have about 5, all have shops, swimming pools, watersports, tennis and other sports facilities on the premises and can arrange anything else. Hotels with 300 rooms have casinos. The first one is **LL-AL** *Aruba Phoenix Beach Resort*, J E Irausquin Blvd 75, T861170, F861165, www.diviphoenix.com The name reflects the fact that this hotel was once the *Aruba Royal*, abandoned but resurrected by Divi, 101 a/c studios and apartments, fitness centre, 2 pools, jacuzzi, watersports. **LL-L** *Wyndham Aruba Beach Resort and Casino*, J E Irausquin Blvd 77, T864466, F863403. 444 rooms, behind it is the restaurant *De Olde Molen*, an imported windmill around which **LL-A** *The Mill Condominium Resort* has been built, J E Irausquin Blvd 330, T867700, F867271. 200 rooms and suites with kitchens, sauna, excercise room, tennis, 2 pools, beach club membership across the road. **LL-L** *Aruba Grand Beach Resort & Casino*, T863900, F861941. 200 rooms and suites, Olympic size swimming pool. The oldest hotel along here is the renewed and extended **LL-L** *Radisson Aruba* , J E Irausquin Blvd 81, T866555, F863260, arubasales@radisson.com Covers 14 acres, 372 rooms and suites, not all with sea view, new pool area with 2 freeform pools, tennis, fitness centre, games room, watersports, conference centre, resort spa, golf putting, usual luxury facilities. **LL-L** *Allegro Resort Aruba*, J E Irausquin Blvd 83, T864500, F863191. 421

Northwest coast

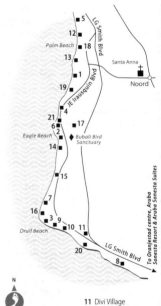

N

Not to scale

■ **Sleeping**
1 Allegro Resort Aruba
2 Amsterdam Manor
3 Aruba Beach Club
4 Aruba Grand Beach Resort & Casino
5 Aruba Marriott Resort & Stellaris Casino
6 Aruba Phoenix Beach Resort
7 Bucuti Beach Resort
8 Bushiri Beach Resort
9 Casa del Mar
10 Divi Aruba Beach Resort Mega All-Inclusive

11 Divi Village
12 Holiday Inn Aruba Beach Resort & Casino
13 Hyatt Regency Aruba Beach Resort & Casino
14 La Cabana
15 La Quinta
16 Manchebo Beach Resort
17 Mill Condominium Resort & De Olde Molen Restaurant
18 Playa Linda Beach Resort
19 Radisson Aruba
20 Tamarijn Aruba Beach Resort
21 Wyndham Aruba Beach Resort & Casino

rooms and suites with sea view and balcony, full service, deluxe, Red Sail diving and watersports on site. The next hotel along is the **LL** *Hyatt Regency Aruba Beach Resort & Casino*, J E Irausquin Blvd 85, T861234, F865478. 360 rooms and suites, designed for a luxury holiday or for business meetings and incentive trips, built around a huge 3-level pool complex with waterfalls, slides and salt water lagoon, in beautiful gardens, health and fitness centre, Red Sail diving and watersports, very popular, great for children or business travellers, always full. **LL** *Playa Linda Beach Resort*, J E Irausquin Blvd 87, T861000, F863479, www.playalinda.com A timeshare resort of suites and efficiencies, health club, games room. **LL-AL** *Holiday Inn Aruba Beach Resort & Casino*, J E Irausquin Blvd 230, T863600, F865165, www.holidayinn-aruba.com 600 rooms with balcony, dated concrete block style, pools, tennis, diving, casino, lots of other facilities. **LL** *Aruba Marriott Resort and Stellaris Casino*, L G Smith Blvd 101, T869000, F860649. 413-room hotel next to the *Holiday Inn*, lots of facilities and luxuries, *Vela Windsurf Centre*, *Red Sail Watersports*.

Apartments and guest houses The Aruba Tourism Authority publishes a list of apartments and guest houses. Weekly or monthly rates are more advantageous. If you arrive at a weekend the tourist office in town will be shut and you cannot get any help except at the airport. In the district of Noord, **C** *Cactus Apartments*, Matadera 5, Noord, T822903, F820433. **C** *Coconut Inn*, Noord 31, T866288, F865433. 40 a/c studios and 1-bedroom apartments, TV, balcony, kitchenette, pool, near beach. **B-C** *Turibana Plaza Apartments*, Noord 124, T867292, F862658, turibana@setarnet.aw *Roger's Apartments*, windsurfing packages only, L G Smith Blvd 472, PO Box 461, Malmok, T861918, F869045. **LL-A** *Boardwalk Vacation Retreat*, Bakval 20, Noord, T866654, F861836, www.theboardwalk-aruba.com Right by the *Marriott*, 150 m to the beach, 1 or 2-bedroom casitas with living room and kitchen, hammocks, fans, a/c, well-equipped, nice furnishings, mini market, pool with jacuzzi, gardens with flowering plants, palm trees and hummingbirds. *Windsurf Village*, L G Smith Blvd 462, *The Boulevards*, L G Smith 486, and *The Edges Guesthouse*, L G Smith Blvd 458, all run by Sailboard Vacations Windsurf Villages, windsurfing packages only, T862527, F861870. **A-C** *Vistalmar*, Bucutiweg 28, T828579 daytime, T847737 evenings, F822200. One-bedroom apartments with car run by Alby and Katy Yarzagaray, friendly, wooden jetty for swimming and sunbathing, near airport, laundry facilities. Also Mr and Mrs Kemp, **C** *A1 Apartments*, Pagaaistraat 5, T828963, F834447, a1apts@visitaruba.com Fully-furnished a/c rooms with kitchenette, 10-15 mins walk from main shopping centre and public beach at *Bushiri Beach Hotel*.

Camping Permit needed from police station, on Arnold Schuttrstraat, Oranjestad, who will advise on locations. It can take 10 days to get a permit and you must have a local address (ie hotel room). The permit costs one Afl4 stamp and it appears you can camp anywhere.

With few exceptions, meals on Aruba are expensive and generally of the beef-and-seafood **Eating** variety, but you can get some excellent food. Service charge on food and drinks is 15% at the hotels but at other places varies from 10% to 15%. Most tourists are on MAP at the hotels, many of which have a choice of formal or informal restaurants. The Aruba Gastronomic Association (AGA) has a dine around programme at 27 restaurants.

For Aruban specialities, *Gasparito*, Gasparito 3, T867044. Aruban and seafood, wins awards for cuisine, open daily except Wed 1700-2300, art gallery attached exhibiting Aruban works. *Mi Cushina*, Noord Cura Cabai 24, T848335. Aruban and seafood, open 1200-1400, 1800-2200, closed Thu, recommended, on road to San Nicolas, about 1 mile from San Nicolas. *Brisas del Mar*, Savaneta 222A, T847718. Seafood specialities, right on the sea, cool and airy, recommended, reasonable prices, open 1200-1430, 1830-2200. *La Nueva Marina Pirata*, at Spanish Lagoon, T827372. Seafood and Aruban dishes, open 1800-2300, Sun 1200-2300, closed Tue, follow the main road to San Nicolas, turn right at *Drive Inn*. The hotels have some very good gourmet restaurants, but outside the hotels the best French restaurant is *Chez Mathilde*, Havenstraat 23, T834968. Open for lunch and dinner, expect to pay over US$25 per person. *Boonoonoonoos*, Wilhelminastraat 18A, T831888. Open Mon-Sat

1100-2230, Sun 1700-2230, has French and Caribbean specialities and the average price is around US$15. *Villa Germania*, Seaport Market Place, T836161. German food for breakfast, lunch and dinner, open 0800-2200. *Twinkle Bone's*, Turibana Plaza, Noord 124, T869806. Open 1800-2300, prices around US$18, prime rib, singing chefs and waiters. Several Argentine restaurants serving steak, seafood and Argentine specialities, *El Gaucho*, Wilhelminastraat 80, T823677. Open 1130-1430, 1800-2300. *The Buccaneer*, Gasparito 11 C, T866172. Decorated as a sunken pirate's ship with aquariums, seafood, open Mon-Sat from 1730, no reservations. *Qué Pasa?*, Schelpstraat 20, T833872. A good, cheap and intimate restaurant in the centre of Oranjestad, open 1800-0400, Italian/international.

Several Oriental restaurants, *Astoria*, San Nicolas, T845132. Chinese, open 1130-2300, indoor and outdoor dining, low prices. *Warung Djawa*, Wilhelminastraat 2, T834888. Serves Indonesian and Surinamese food, open Mon-Fri, 1130-1400 for weekday rijstafel buffet lunch, and Wed-Mon 1800-2300, all you can eat, many recommendations. For Japanese food try *Sakura* , Wilhelminastraat, 4, T824088, *Sake House* , Caya Betico Croes 9, T830405, or *Benihana* , Sasakiweg, T826788.

La Paloma, Noord 39, T874611. One of the many Italian restaurants you can choose from, open 1800-2300, closed Tue, Northern Italian and seafood. *Charlie's Bar*, Zeppenfeldtstraat 56, San Nicolas, T845086, is good for Aruban light meals, open 1200-2130, bar until 2200. *Café The Paddock* on L G Smith Blvd near *Wendy's*, T829021. Outside seating, very good, great saté, inexpensive for Aruba, Amstel on draught and the *daghap* (dish of the day) for Afl 14.50. *The Plaza Café* at the Seaport Market Place, T838826, has a nice terrace and you can get a good, reasonably priced meal there. The *Coco Plum* on Caya Betico Croes 100, T831176, serves a good meal and refreshing fruit juices on a terrace. There is a wide array of fast food outlets, including *Burger King, Kentucky Fried Chicken, McDonalds, Wendy's, Taco Bell, Dunkin Donuts, Subway* and *Domino Pizza*. For night owls in need of food the white trucks (mobile restaurants) serve local food and snacks from 2100- 0500 at around US$5, located at Wilhelmina Park, the post office and the courthouse.

Nightlife The major attraction is gambling and there are 11 casinos on the island. Hotels must have 300 rooms before they can build one; those that do usually start at 1100 and operate 2 shifts. A few are open 24 hrs. Arubans are allowed in to casinos only 4 times a month. Some casinos also offer dancing and live bands. The place to be for a disco night out is *Visage*, at L G Smith Blvd 54. Other discothèques including *Blue Wave* on Shellstraat, T838856; *Chesterfield Nightclub*, Zeppenfeldtstraat 57, San Nicolas, T845109; and plenty of others in hotels or elsewhere. The *Seaport Cinema* in Oranjestad has 6 screens showing US films. The *Drive-In Theatre* in Balashi occasionally shows European or Latin American films.

Festivals The most important festival of the year is *Carnival*, held from the Sunday two weeks preceding Lent, starting with Children's Carnival. There are colourful parades and competitions for best musician, best dancer, best costume etc. The culmination is the Grand Parade on the Sun preceding Lent. Other festive occasions during the year include *New Year*, when fireworks are let off at midnight and musicians and singers go round from house to house (and hotel to hotel); *National Anthem and Flag Day* on *18 March*, when there are displays of national dancing and other folklore, and *St John's Day* on *24 June*, which is another folklore day: 'Derramento di Gai'. For visitors who do not coincide their trip with one of the annual festivals, there is a weekly Bonbini show in the courtyard of the Fort Zoutman museum on Tuesday 1830-2030, US$3, music, singing and dancing, interesting but overenthusiastic MC, bartenders from hotels mix cocktails and special drinks. The programme is altered every week, so those on a 2-week holiday do not sit through the same thing twice. Local dance music, such as the fast, lively *tumba* is very influenced by Latin America. Arubans are fond of *merengue*. Throughout the year there are several different music and dance festivals. The *International Theatre Festival* takes place every other year; for information contact CCA, Vondellaan 2, T821758. There is also a *Dance Festival* in *October* at the Cas de Cultura, for information T/F830223.

In addition to Caya G F (Betico) Croes shopping areas include the Port of Call Market Place, **Shopping**
Seaport Village Mall, Harbour Town, The Galleries, Strada I and II and the Holland Aruba Mall.
A wide range of luxury items are imported from all over the world for resale to visitors at cut
rate prices. Liquor rates are good, but prices for jewellery, silverware and crystal are only
slightly lower than US or UK prices. There is no sales tax. There are also local handicrafts such
as pottery and artwork, try *Artesanía Arubiano*, on L G Smith Blvd 178, opposite *Tamarijn
Hotel*, T837494, or ask the Institute of Culture, T821010, or the Aruba Tourism Authority,
T823777, for more information. *Galeria Harmonia*, Main St, St Nicolas, exhibits and sells
local artists' work, T842969. Bookshops include *Van Dorp* in Caya G F (Betico) Croes is the
main town centre bookshop. The light and airy *Captains Log* in the new Harbour Town
development has a few books and reading material but is mostly souvenirs. Many bookshops in the hotels have some paperbacks.

Road Bus The bus station is behind Parliament on Zoutmanstraat. Route 1 starts in San   **Transport**
Nicolas and runs through Oranjestad via the hospital to Malmok, Mon-Sat, 0455-2255 hourly,
returning from Malmok on the hour, journey time 55 mins. Route 2 also runs from San
Nicolas on a slightly different route to Oranjestad and Palm Beach, more or less hourly,
0525-2200. Route 3 runs between Oranjestad and San Nicolas, 0550-2030 and Route 4 runs
from Oranjestad through Noord to Palm Beach almost hourly on the half hour. There are also
extra buses running between Oranjestad and the *Holiday Inn* (schedules available at the
hotels and the tourist office). One-way fare is US$1. Otherwise there are 'jitney cars' which
operate like colectivos; the fare is US$1.25. A jitney or bus from Oranjestad to San Nicolas will
drop you at the airport.

Car hire There are some 23 car hire companies. *Airways* (Sabana Blanco 35, T821845, airport T829112), *Hertz* (L G Smith Blvd 142, T824545, airport T824886), *Avis* (Kolibristraat 14,
T828787, airport T825496), *Budget* (Kolibristraat 1, T828600, airport T825423), *Dollar*
(Grenedaweg 15, T822783, airport T825651) and *Toyota* (L G Smith Blvd 114, T834832, airport T834902) have offices in Oranjestad and at the airport. Many companies also have desks
in the hotels. Prices begin at US$35 daily, US$215 weekly, with unlimited mileage. Often
when you rent a 4WD vehicle (recommended for getting to beaches like Dos Playa) you cannot take out all risks insurance.

Motorcycle A rental 50cc moped or scooter costs around US$30 a day, a 250cc motorcycle
US$40, a Harley Davidson SP1100 US$90 and insurance is US$8-15 a day, depending on the
size of engine. *Big Twin* rents Harley Davidson, T839322, F828660. *Pablito's Bikes Rental*, L
G Smith Blvd 228, T878300, F870042, at *La Quinta Beach Resort*, Eagle Beach, men's, ladies,
children's **bicycles**, US$3 per hour, US$8 half day, US$12 per 24 hrs. Other companies
include *Donata*, T878300, F870707, *Dream Cycles*, T824329, F838199, *George*, T825975,
Nelson, T866801, *New York*, T863885, *Semver*, T866851 and *Ron's* T862090.

Taxi Telephone the dispatcher at Pos Abao 41 behind the Eagle Bowling Palace on the   *Taxis do not*
Sasaki road, T822116. Drivers speak English, and individual tours can be arranged. Ask for flat   *have meters*
rate tariffs. From the airport to Oranjestad is US$9, to the low rise hotels US$12 and to the
high rise hotels US$14 per taxi, not per person, maximum 4 passengers.

Sea Boat The harbour is 5 mins walk from the town, there are a tourist information centre
and some souvenir shops which open if a cruise ship is in. A fruit boat leaves once a week for
Punto Fijo, Venezuela; check with Agencia Marítima La Confianza, Braziliëstraat 6 (T823814),
Oranjestad. There used to be a ferry to Venezuela, check with Rufo U Winterdaal, Eman
Trading Co, L G Smith Blvd 108, Oranjestad (PO Box 384), T821533/821156, F822135, Tx5027.

Airline offices Airline offices for all airport lines T824800. *American Airlines*, T822700. *Air Aruba*,   **Directory**
T836600. *ALM*, T838080. *Avianca/SAM*, T826277. *KLM*, T823546/7. *Viasa*, T836526. *Servivensa*,
T827779. *Aeropostal*, T837799. *Vasp*, T825995.

Netherland Antilles, the ABC Islands

Banks *ABN/AMRO Bank*, Caya G F (Betico) Croes 89, T821515, F821856, at the Port of Call shopping centre (close to the harbour where the cruise ships come in) on L G Smith Blvd; ATMs at these offices and at Sunday Plaza Building, L G Smith Blvd 160 and Dr Horacio Oduber Hospital, for Cirrus or Mastercard. *Aruba Bank NV*, Caya G F (Betico) Croes 41, T821550, F829152, and at L G Smith Blvd 108, T831318. *Banco di Caribe NV*, Caya G F Croes 90-92, T832168, F834222. *Caribbean Mercantile Bank NV*, Caya G F (Betico) Croes 51, T823118, F824373, ATM for Cirrus or Mastercard here and also at Palm Beach 48 (Noord), Zeppenfeldstraat 35 (San Nicolas), Santa Cruz 41 (Santa Cruz), L G Smith Blvd 17, Seaport Village Mall. *Interbank*, Caya G F (Betico) Croes 38, T831080, F837152. *First National Bank*, Caya G F (Betico) Croes 67, T833221, F821756. *Western Union Money Transfer Service*, T824400. *American Express* representative for refunds, exchange or replacement of cheques or cards is *SEL Maduro & Sons*, Rockefellerstraat 1, T823888, open Mon-Fri 0800-1200, 1300-1700. *Aruba Bank*, *Caribbean Mercantile Bank* and *Interbank* are Visa/Mastercard representatives with cash advance. Aruba Bank at the airport is open daily 0800-1600 except on official holidays.

Communications **Post:** The Post Office at J E Irausquinplein is open 0730-1200, 1300-1630. Postal rates to the USA, Canada and the Netherlands are Afl 1.40 for letters and Afl0.60 for postcards. Letters to Europe Afl 1.50, postcards Afl 0.70. Collectors can subscribe for new issues by contacting the Philatelic Service, T821900, F827930. **Telephone:** Modern telephone services with direct dialling are available. Aruba's country and area code is 297. Hotels add a service charge on to international calls. The ITT office is on Boecoetiweg 33, T821458. Phone and fax calls, email and mariphone calls at Servicio di Telecommunicacion di Aruba (Setar), at Palm Beach opposite *Hyatt Regency Aruba Beach Resort*, in Oranjestad just off the Plaza and next to the Post Office Building at Irausquinplein, Oranjestad. Email services at some hotels are complimentary for guests: *Bucuti, Casa del Mar/Aruba Beach Club, Hyatt*. **Internet:** There is an internet café at Royal Plaza Mall, Oranjestad, with access for US$7 per 30 mins. The local television station is Tele-Aruba, but US programmes are also received.

Embassies & consulates **Brazil**, E Pory Ierlandstraat 19, T821994. **Chile**, H de Grootstraat 1, T821085. **Costa Rica**, Savaneta 235-B, T847193. **Denmark**, L G Smith Blvd 82, T824622. **Dominican Republic**, J G Emanstraat 79, T836928. **Germany**, Scopetstraat 13, T821767. **Honduras**, Bilderdijkstraat 13, T821187. **Italy**, Caya G F Betico Croes 7, T822621. **Liberia**, Windstraat 20, T821171. **Panama**, Weststraat 15, T822908. **Peru**, Waterweg 3, T825355. **Portugal**, Seroe Colorado 73, T846178. **El Salvador**, H de Grootstraat 1, T821085. **Spain**, Madurostraat 9, T823163. **Sweden**, Havenstraat 33, T821821. **Venezuela**, Adriane Lacle Blvd 8, T821078.

Laundry *Wash 'n' Dry Laundromat*, Turibana Plaza, Noord. *Hop Long Laundromat*, Grensweg 7, San Nicolas. *Dakota Laundry*, Amandelstraat 3, Oranjestad. *Aruba Laundromat*, Hendrikstraat 30, Oranjestad.

Medical facilities All the major hotels have a doctor on call. There is a well-equipped, 280-bed hospital (Dr Horacio Oduber Hospital, LG Smith Blvd, T874300, F873348) near the main hotel area with modern facilities and well-qualified surgeons and dentists. Posada Clinic Aruba, L G Smith Blvd 14, T820840, F835664, offers haemodialysis service, multilingual staff, reservations 3 months in advance, modern equipment. Labco Medical and Homecare Service, Cabuyastraat 6A, Ponton, PO Box, 1147, T825541, F826567, 24-hr service, free delivery, rents items such as wheelchairs, crutches, bedpans etc to visitors. The emergency telephone number for the Ambulance and Fire Department is 115. Also for ambulance in Oranjestad, T821234 and in San Nicolas, T845050. Air Ambulance, Mr Rupert Richards, T829197, F835664. Drinking water is distilled from sea water and consequently is safe. The main health hazard for the visitor is over-exposure to the sun. Be very careful from 1100-1430, and use plenty of high factor suntan lotion.

Places of worship A wide range of churches is represented on Aruba, including Catholic, Jewish and Protestant. There are Methodists, Baha'i, Baptists, Church of Christ, Evangelical, Jehovah's Witnesses and 7th Day Adventists. Check at your hotel for the times of services and the language in which they are conducted.

Tourist information **Local tourist offices** *Aruba Tourism Authority*, L G Smith Boulevard 172, Oranjestad, PO Box 1019, near the harbour, T823777, F834702, www.aruba.com Also at airport (open daily until about 1900, helpful for accommodation) and cruise dock. Staff are friendly and efficient. The *Aruba Hotel and Tourism Association*, LG Smith Boulevard 174, PO Box 542, Oranjestad, T822607, F824202. They have a hotline for complaints and compliments, T839000, Mon-Fri 0900-1700, answering machine at other times. Their official guide is the annual *Aruba Experience*, which is also on

the internet, www.aruba-experience.com Another very good site on Aruba is www.visitaruba.com
Local travel agents *De Palm Tours*, L G Smith Blvd 142, PO Box 656, T824400, F823012,
www.depalm.com, also with offices in many hotels, sightseeing tours of the island and excursions to
nearby islands or Venezuela. Their Mar-Lab Biological Tour, US$25 including a visit to Seroe Colorado,
and snorkelling at Boca Grandi. *Aruba Transfer Tours and Taxi*, PO Box 723, Pos Abou z/n, T822116.
Julio Maduro, *Corvalou Tours*, T821149, specializes in archaeological, geological, architectural,
botanical and wildlife tours, a mine of information on anything to do with Aruba, strongly
recommended. For a combination 6-hr tour with lunch, US$35, call archaeologist Egbert Boerstra,
T841513, or Julio Maduro, or Private Safaris educational tour, T834869. Mr Boerstra has been involved
in excavation work at Ser'l Noka, Malmok, Savaneta, Tanki Flip and Canashito and has worked with the
project to establish the Arikok National Park. There are lots of companies offering tours of the island by
minibus with a swimming and snorkelling stop at Baby Beach, about US$30 per person.

Background

History

Archaeologists have discovered that there were two waves of Amerindian migration
to Aruba. The first came from present day Venezuela about 4,000 years ago. They
were semi-nomadic, living in family groups of 10-15 people and lived on what they
could gather from the sea: fish, conch, turtle eggs and turtle meat. A second group,
the Caquetios, arrived much later, around 1000 AD, and were different physically,
linguistically and culturally. Their villages have been discovered around the island,
including Tanki Flip, Savaneta and Santa Cruz. Both peoples shared the northwest
coast, now the hotel strip, where evidence has been found of their fishing activities.
The Caquetios were also farmers and it is believed that the island was much greener
before woodcutting, aloe farming and grazing animals were introduced. Santa Cruz
was the seat of the provincial cacique, or chief. He ruled over the island's village
chiefs but was himself subordinate to a mainland chief who governed Aruba,
Bonaire, Curaçao and coastal Venezuela. A strict hierarchy was maintained, with
status reflected in the size of your house, your body decorations and your burial.

The people

Aruba is one of the very few Caribbean islands on which the Indian population was
not exterminated although there are no full-blooded Indians now. The Aruban
today is a descendant of the Caquetio Indians, with a mixture of Spanish and Dutch
blood from the early colonizers. Alonso de Ojeda was the first European to set foot
on Aruba in 1499. There was no plantation farming in Aruba, so African slaves were
never introduced. Instead, the Indians supervised the raising of cattle, horses, goats
and sheep, and their delivery to the other Dutch islands. They were generally left
alone and maintained regular contact with the mainland Indians. The last Indians to
speak an Indian language were buried in urns about 1800; later Indians lost their language and culture. When Lago Oil came to Aruba many workers from the British
West Indies came to work in the refinery in San Nicolas, leading to Caribbean English becoming the colloquial tongue there instead of Papiamento. Of the total population today of about 84,200, including some 40 different nationalities, only about
two-thirds were actually born on the island. The official language here, as in the
other Netherlands Antilles, is Dutch, but Papiamento is the colloquial tongue. English and Spanish are widely spoken and the people are extremely welcoming. The
crime rate is low and there are very few attacks on tourists.

The economy

Gold was discovered in 1825, but the mine ceased to be economic in 1916. In 1929,
black gold brought real prosperity to Aruba when Lago Oil and Transport Co, a

subsidiary of Exxon, built a refinery at San Nicolas at the east end of the island. At that time it was the largest refinery in the world, employing over 8,000 people. In March 1985 Exxon closed the refinery, a serious shock for the Aruban economy, and one which the Government has striven to overcome. In 1989, Coastal Oil of Texas signed an agreement with the Government to reopen part of the refinery by 1991, with an initial capacity of 150,000 barrels a day, but despite plans to increase it, present capacity is only about 140,000 b/d.

Aruba has three ports. San Nicolas is used for the import and transshipment of crude oil and materials for the refinery and for the export of oil products. There are also two sea-berths at San Nicolas capable of handling the largest tankers in the world. Oranjestad is the commercial port of Aruba, and it is open for day and night navigation. In 1962 the port of Barcadera was built to facilitate shipment of products from Aruba's new industrial zone on the leeward coast.

The economic crisis of 1985 forced the Government to turn to the IMF for help. The fund recommended that Aruba promote tourism and increase the number of hotel rooms by 50%. The Government decided, however, to triple hotel capacity to 6,000 rooms, which it was estimated would provide employment for 20% of the population. Hotel construction has expanded rapidly and marketing efforts have attracted investors and visitors from as far afield as Japan. By 1990 tourist accommodation in 15 major high rise and low rise hotels reached 3,326 rooms, with many more available in small hotels, guest houses and apartments. Nevertheless, by 1992 the Government was facing a financial crisis because of state guarantees totalling NG516 mn for three hotel projects which had run into financial difficulties and on which work had ceased: the 466-room *Beta Hotel* (NG170 mn), the 376-room *Eagle Beach Hotel* (NG186 mn) and the 411-room *Plantation Bay Hotel* (NG160 mn). Although the Dutch government provided a loan for the hotels' completion in 1992, the Aruban government now faces heavy interest and principal repayments for 15 years to banks. These will be funded by unpopular higher excise duties, petrol prices and import duties. In mid-1993, the *Plantation Bay Hotel* was sold to the Marriott chain. In 1995 its opening raised the total to 6,626 rooms in hotels, a figure which rose to 7,103 by 1996. By 2000 nearly all the hotels had undergone alterations, adding rooms or upgrading existing facilities. Total employment in tourism absorbs 35% of the workforce.

The economy is now overwhelmingly dependent on tourism for income, with around 650,000 stayover visitors a year, producing revenue of US$600 mn. Over half of tourists come from the USA; the next largest country of origin is Venezuela. A further 250,000 passengers arrive on cruise ships.

Efforts are being made to diversify away from a single source of revenues into areas such as re-exporting through the free trade zone, and offshore finance. Aruba is still dependent on the Netherlands for budget support and the aim is to reduce the level of financial assistance. New legislation has been approved to encourage companies to register on the island by granting tax and other benefits. Regulations are generally flexible and unrestricting on offshore business, although efforts are being made to ensure an efficient level of supervision.

There is no unemployment on Aruba and labour is imported for large projects such as the refinery and construction work. Turkish guest workers came to help get Coastal started and Philippinos work in the high rise hotels. The Government is encouraging skilled Arubans to return from Holland but is hampered by a housing shortage and a consequent boom in real estate prices.

Background to the ABC islands

History

The first known settlers of the islands were the Caiquetios, a tribe of peaceful Arawak Indians, who lived in small communities under a chieftain or a priest. They survived principally on fish and shellfish and collected salt from the Charoma saltpan to barter with their mainland neighbours for supplements to their diet. There are remains of Indian villages on Curaçao at Westpunt, San Juan, de Savaan and Santa Barbara, and on Aruba near Hooiberg. On each of the ABC islands there are cave and rock drawings. The Arawaks in this area had escaped attack by the Caribs but soon after the arrival of the Spaniards most were forcibly transported from Curaçao to work on Hispaniola. Although some were later repatriated, more fled when the Dutch arrived. The remainder were absorbed into the black or white population, so that by 1795, only five full-blooded Indians were to be found on Curaçao. On Aruba and Bonaire the Indians maintained their identity until about the end of the 19th century, but there were no full-blooded Indians left by the 20th century.

The islands were encountered in 1499 by a Spaniard, Alonso de Ojeda, accompanied by the Italian, Amerigo Vespucci and the Spanish cartographer Juan de la Cosa. The Spanish retained control over the islands throughout the 16th century, but because there was no gold, they were declared 'useless islands'. After 1621, the Dutch became frequent visitors looking for wood and salt and later for a military foothold. Curaçao's strategic position between Pernambuco and New Amsterdam within the Caribbean setting made it a prime target. In 1634, a Dutch fleet took Curaçao, then in 1636 they took Bonaire, which was inhabited by a few cattle and six Indians, and Aruba which the Spanish and Indians evacuated. Curaçao became important as a trading post and as a base for excursions against the Spanish. After 1654, Dutch refugees from Brazil brought sugar technology, but the crop was abandoned by 1688 because of the very dry climate. About this time citrus fruits were introduced, and salt remained a valuable commodity. Much of Curaçao's wealth came from the slave trade. From 1639-1778 thousands of slaves were brought to Willemstad, fed with funchi and sold to the mainland and other colonies. The Dutch brought nearly half a million slaves to the Caribbean, most of which went through Curaçao.

Wars between England and the Netherlands in the second half of the 17th century led to skirmishes and conquests in the Caribbean. The Peace of Nijmegen in 1678 gave the Dutch Aruba, Curaçao, Bonaire and the three smaller islands in the Leeward group, St Eustatius, Saba and half of St Martin. Further conflicts in Europe and the Americas in the 18th century led to Curaçao becoming a commercial meeting place for pirates, American rebels, Dutch merchants, Spaniards and créoles from the mainland. In 1800 the English took Curaçao but withdrew in 1803. They occupied it again from 1807 until 1816, when Dutch rule was restored, during when it was declared a free port. From 1828 to 1845, all Dutch West Indian colonies were governed from Surinam. In 1845 the Dutch Leeward Islands were joined to Willemstad in one colonial unit called Curaçao and Dependencies. The economy was still largely based on commerce, much of it with Venezuela, and there was a ship building industry, some phosphate mining and the salt pans, although the latter declined after the abolition of slavery in 1863.

In the 20th century the economy prospered with the discovery of oil in Venezuela and the subsequent decision by the Dutch-British Shell Oil Company to set up a refinery on Curaçao because of its political stability, its good port facilities and its better climate than around Lake Maracaibo. In 1924 another refinery was built on Aruba, which brought unprecedented wealth to that island and the population rose. The Second World War was another turning point as demand for oil soared and British, French and later US forces were stationed on the islands. The German invasion of Holland encouraged Dutch companies to transfer their assets to the

Netherlands Antilles leading to the birth of the offshore financial centre. After the War, demands for autonomy from Holland began to grow.

Government

The organization of political parties began in 1936 and by 1948 there were four parties on Curaçao and others on Aruba and the other islands, most of whom endorsed autonomy. In 1948, the Dutch constitution was revised to allow for the transition to complete autonomy of the islands. In 1954 they were granted full autonomy in domestic affairs and became an integral part of the Kingdom of the Netherlands. The Crown continued to appoint the Governor, although since the 1960s this has gone to a native-born Antillian. Nevertheless, a strong separatist movement developed on Aruba and the island finally withdrew from the Netherlands Antilles in 1986, becoming an autonomous member of the Kingdom of the Netherlands, the same status as the whole of the Netherlands Antilles.

The Netherlands Antilles now form two autonomous parts of the Kingdom of the Netherlands. The main part, comprising all the islands except Aruba, is a parliamentary federal democracy, the seat of which is in Willemstad, Curaçao, and each island has its own Legislative and Executive Council. Parliament (Staten) is elected in principle every four years, with 14 members from Curaçao, three from Bonaire, three from Sint Maarten and one each from Saba and St Eustatius.

A new Government of the five-island federation was sworn in in June 1998. Suzanne Römer, of the Partido Nashonal di Pueblo (PNP) is the Prime Minister, at the head of a six-party coalition cabinet, with 13 of the 22 seats, Within the coalition, the PNP has three seats, the Partido Laboral Krusado Populat (Curaçao) three seats, the Frente Obrero de Liberashon (Curaçao) two seats, the Democratic Party (Sint Maarten) two seats, the Partido Democratico Bonairiano (Bonaire) two seats, and the Windward Islands People's Movement (Saba) one seat.

In Aruba the last general election was held on 29 July 1994. The Arubaanse Volkspartij (AVP) won 10 of the 21 seats and formed a new government led by Prime Minister Heny Eman. The People's Electoral Movement (MEP) won nine seats. The Organisashon pa Liberashon de Aruba (OLA) won two seats and joined in a coalition with the AVP.

Separate status for some or all of the islands has been a political issue with a breakaway movement in Curaçao and St Maarten. The Netherlands Government's previous policy of encouraging independence has been reversed. The Hague has been trying to draw up a new constitution governing relations between the Netherlands, the Antilles Federation and Aruba. A round-table conference was held in 1993 to establish the basis for future relations including financial support but ended without any decision on Aruba's desire to cancel proposals for independence in 1996, Curaçao's demand for *status aparte* and future relations of the islands with the Netherlands if the Federation collapses.

In November 1993 a referendum was held in Curaçao on its future status within the Federation. The Government was soundly defeated when the electorate unexpectedly voted to continue the island's present status as a member of the Antillean federation (73.6%), rejecting the other options of separate status (11.9%), incorporation in the Netherlands (8.0%) and independence (0.5%).

Referenda were also held on the other islands, Saba, Statia, St Maarten and Bonaire with the aim of restructuring the Antilles. The vote in October 1994 was overwhelmingly in favour of the status quo, with 90.6% support in Statia, 86.3% in Saba, 88.0% in Bonaire and 59.8% in Sint Maarten.

Footnotes

21

Footnotes

Index

V

W

Y

Footnotes

Maps

Footnotes

Sales & distribution

Footprint Handbooks
6 Riverside Court
Lower Bristol Road
Bath BA2 3DZ England
T 01225 469141
F 01225 469461
E Mail info@
footprintbooks.com

Australia
Peribo Pty
58 Beaumont Road
Mt Kuring-Gai
NSW 2080
T 02 9457 0011
F 02 9457 0022

Austria
Freytag-Berndt Artaria
Kohlmarkt 9
A-1010 Wien
T 01 533 2094
F 01 533 8685

Belgium
Craenen BVBA
Mechelsesteenweg 633
B-3020 Herent
T 016 23 90 90
F 016 23 97 11

Canada
Ulysses Travel Publications
4176 rue Saint-Denis
Montréal
Québec H2W 2M5
T 514 843 9882
F 514 843 9448

Europe
Bill Bailey
16 Devon Square
Newton Abbott
Devon TQ12 2HR. UK
T 01626 331079
F 01626 331080

Denmark
Nordisk Korthandel
Studiestraede 26-30 B
DK-1455 Copenhagen K
T 3338 2638
F 3338 2648

Scanvik Books
Esplanaden 8B
DK-1263 Copenhagen K
T 33 12 77 66
F 33 91 28 82

Finland
Akateeminen Kirjakauppa
Keskuskatu 1
FIN-00100 Helsinki
T 09 12141
F 09 121 4441

Suomalainen Kirjakauppa
Koivuvaarankuja 2
01640 Vantaa 64
F 08 52 78 88

France
L'Astrolabe
46 rue de Provence
F-75009 Paris 9e
T 1 42 85 42 95
F 1 45 75 92 51

VILO Diffusion
25 rue Ginoux
F-75015 Paris
T 01 45 77 08 05
F 01 45 79 97 15

Germany
GeoCenter ILH
Schockenriedstrasse 44
D-70565 Stuttgart
T 0711 781 94610
F 0711 781 94654

Brettschneider
Fernreisebedarf
Feldkirchnerstrasse 2
D-85551 Heimstetten
T 089 990 20330
F 089 990 20331

Geobuch Gmbh
Rosental 6
D-80331 München
T 089 265030
F 089 263713

Gleumes
Hohenstaufenring 47-51
D-50674 Köln
T 0221 215650

Globetrotter Ausrustungen
Wiesendamm 1
D-22305 Hamburg
F 040 679 66183

Dr Götze
Bleichenbrücke 9
D-2000 Hamburg 1
T 040 3031 1009-0

Hugendubel Buchhandlung
Nymphenburgerstrasse 25
D-80335 München
T 089 238 9412
F 089 550 1853

Kiepert Buchhandlung
Hardenbergstrasse 4-5
D-10623 Berlin 12
T 030 311880

Greece
GC Eleftheroudakis
17 Panepistemiou
Athens 105 64
T 01 331 4180-83
F 01 323 9821

India
Roli Books
M-75 GK II Market
New Delhi 110048
T (011) 646 0886
F (011) 646 7185

Israel
Geographical Tours
8 Tverya Street
Tel Aviv 63144
T 03 528 4113
F 03 629 9905

Italy
Librimport
Via Biondelli 9
I-20141 Milano
T 02 8950 1422
F 02 8950 2811

Netherlands
Nilsson & Lamm bv
Postbus 195
Pampuslaan 212
N-1380 AD Weesp
T 0294 494949
F 0294 494455

Norway
Schibsteds Forlag A/S
Akersgata 32 - 5th Floor
Postboks 1178 Sentrum
N-0107 Oslo
T 22 86 30 00
F 22 42 54 92

Tanum
PO Box 1177 Sentrum
N-0107 Oslo 1
T 22 41 11 00
F 22 33 32 75

Olaf Norlis
Universitetsgt 24
N-1062 Oslo
T 22 00 43 00

Pakistan
Pak-American Commercial
Zaib-un Nisa Street
Saddar
PO Box 7359
Karachi
T 21 566 0418
F 21 568 3611

South Africa
Faradawn CC
PO Box 1903
Saxonwold 2132
T 011 885 1787
F 011 885 1829

South America
Humphrys Roberts
Associates
Caixa Postal 801-0
Ag. Jardim da Gloria
06700-970 Cotia SP
Brazil
T 011 492 4496
F 011 492 6896

Southeast Asia
APA Publications
38 Joo Koon Road
Singapore 628990
T 865 1600
F 861 6438

Spain
Altaïr
Balmes 69
08007 Barcelona
T 93 3233062
F 93 4512559

Bookworld España
Pje Las Palmeras 25
29670 San Pedro Alcántara
Málaga
T 95 278 6366
F 95 278 6452

Libros de Viaje
C/Serrano no 41
28001 Madrid
T 01 91 577 9899
F 01 91 577 5756

Sweden
Hedengrens Bokhandel
PO Box 5509
S-11485 Stockholm
T 8 6115132

Kart Centrum
Vasagatan 16
S-11120 Stockholm
T 8 111699

Lantmateriet Kartbutiken
Kungsgatan 74
S-11122 Stockholm
T 08 202 303
F 08 202 711

Switzerland
Artou
8 rue de Rive
CH-1204 Geneva
T 022 311 4544
F 022 781 3456

Office du Livre OLF SA
ZI 3, Corminboeuf
CH-1701 Fribourg
T 026 467 5111
F 026 467 5466
Schweizer Buchzentrum
Postfach
CH-4601 Olten
T 062 209 2525
F 062 209 2627

Travel Bookshop
Rindermarkt 20
Postfach 216
CH-8001 Zürich
T 01 252 3883
F 01 252 3832

USA
NTC/ Contemporary
4255 West Touhy Avenue
Lincolnwood
Illinois 60646-1975
T 847 679 5500
F 847 679 2494

Footprint travel list

Footprint publish travel guides to over 120 countries worldwide. Each guide is packed with practical, concise and colourful information for everybody from first-time travellers to travel aficionados . The list is growing fast and current titles are noted below. For further information check out the website **www.footprintbooks.com**

Andalucía Handbook
Argentina Handbook
Bali & the Eastern Isles Hbk*
Bangkok & the Beaches Hbk*
Bolivia Handbook
Brazil Handbook
Cambodia Handbook
Caribbean Islands Handbook
Chile Handbook
Colombia Handbook
Cuba Handbook
Dominican Republic Handbook*
East Africa Handbook
Ecuador & Galápagos Handbook
Egypt Handbook Handbook
Goa Handbook
India Handbook
Indian Himalaya Handbook*
Indonesia Handbook
Ireland Handbook
Israel Handbook
Jordan Handbook*
Jordan, Syria & Lebanon Hbk
Laos Handbook
Libya Handbook*
Malaysia Handbook
Myanmar Handbook
Mexico Handbook
Mexico & Central America Hbk
Morocco Handbook
Namibia Handbook
Nepal Handbook
Pakistan Handbook

Peru Handbook
Rio de Janeiro Handbook*
Scotland Handbook
Singapore Handbook
South Africa Handbook
South American Handbook
South India Handbook*
Sri Lanka Handbook
Sumatra Handbook
Thailand Handbook
Tibet Handbook
Tunisia Handbook
Venezuela Handbook
Vietnam Handbook

* available autumn 2000

In the pipeline – Turkey, London, Kenya, Rajasthan, Scotland Highlands & Islands, Syria & Lebanon

Also available from Footprint
Traveller's Handbook
Traveller's Healthbook

Available at all good bookshops

Will you help us?

We try as hard as we can to make each Footprint Handbook as up-to-date and accurate as possible but, of course, things always change. Many people write to us - with corrections, new information, or simply comments.

If you want to let us know about an experience or adventure - hair-raising or mundane, good or bad, exciting or boring or simply something special - we would be delighted to hear from you. Please give us as precise information as possible, quoting the edition number (you'll find it on the front cover) and page number of the Handbook you are using.

Your help will be greatly appreciated, especially by other travellers. In return we will send you details about our special guidebook offer.

Write to Elizabeth Taylor
Footprint Handbooks
6 Riverside Court
Lower Bristol Road
Bath
BA2 3DZ
England
or email cih2001_online@footprintbooks.com

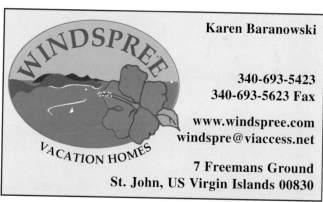

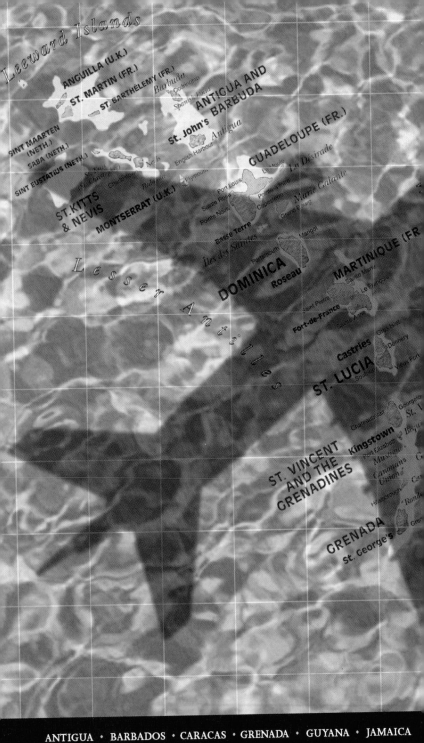

Leeward Islands

ANGUILLA (U.K.)
ST. MARTIN (FR.)
ST. BARTHELEMY (FR.)
Barbuda
St. Codrington
Spanish Point
SINT MAARTEN (NETH.)
SABA (NETH.)
SINT EUSTATIUS (NETH.)
ANTIGUA AND BARBUDA
St. John's
Antigua
English Harbour
GUADELOUPE (FR.)
La Désirade
ST. KITTS & NEVIS
Charlestown
Redonda
Plymouth
MONTSERRAT (U.K.)
Port Louis
Sainte Rose
Pointe Noire
Pointe-à-Pitre
Basse-Terre
Marie Galante
Grand Bourg
Îles des Saintes
Marigot
Lesser Antilles
Portsmouth
DOMINICA
Roseau
Sainte Marie
MARTINIQUE (FR.)
Saint Pierre
Le François
Fort-de-France
Sainte Anne
Gros Islet
Castries
Dennery
ST. LUCIA
Vieux Fort
Soufrière
Georgetown
Chateaubelair
St. V
Port Elizabeth
Bequia
Kingstown
Mustique
Canouan
Union
ST. VINCENT AND THE GRENADINES
Hillsborough
Ronde
GRENADA
St. George's

ANTIGUA · BARBADOS · CARACAS · GRENADA · GUYANA · JAMAICA
LONDON · MIAMI · NEW YORK · ST. LUCIA · ST. MAARTEN · ST. VINCENT
TORONTO · TRINIDAD & TOBAGO · WASHINGTON DC

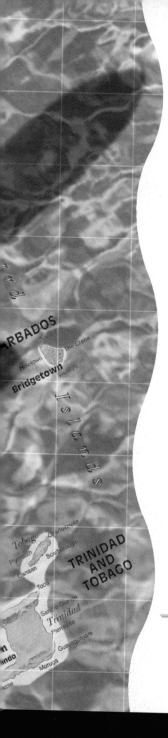

One truly West Indies Airline has the Caribbean covered

BWIA, the airline that truly reflects the heart and soul of the West Indies, offers you a daily schedule of flights from Heathrow to a host of Caribbean destinations.

Our wide-bodied jets, with a new livery that reflects the spirit of the West Indies, offers you an in-flight comfort, service and style that comes with a typical Caribbean smile. To further whet your appetite, the finest Caribbean food and drink provide a true taste of the West Indies from the moment you board the plane.

For more information about the one truly West Indian airline that has the Caribbean covered, telephone, visit our website at www.bwee.com or see your Travel Agent.

BWIA
West Indies
AIRWAYS

SHARING OUR WARMTH WITH THE WORLD

BECAUSE NOBODY KEEPS TRACK OF TIME DURING THEIR HOLIDAYS...

WE'RE 24 HOURS ALL INCLUSIVE

CoraL

HOTELS & RESORTS

DOMINICAN REPUBLIC

CORAL HAMACA
BEACH HOTEL & CASINO
Boca Chica

CORAL COSTA CARIBE
BEACH HOTEL & CASINO
Juan Dolio

CORAL CANOA
BEACH HOTEL & SPA
Bayahibe

TEL. (809)562.6725   FAX (809) 562.0660 www.coralhotels.com e-mail: coral.h@codetel.net.do

Caribbean Islands

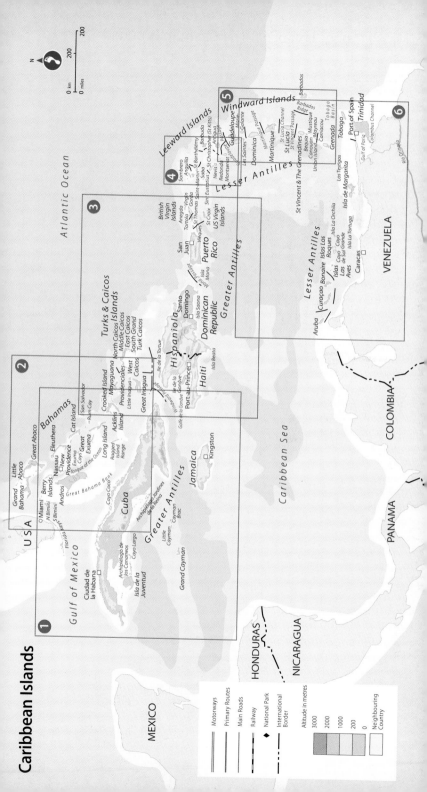

Map legend:

- Motorways
- Primary Routes
- Main Roads
- Railway
- National Park
- International Border
- Neighbouring Country

Altitude in metres

- 3000
- 2000
- 1000
- 200
- 0

N

| 0 km | 200 |
| 0 miles | 200 |

Map panels

① ② ③ ④ Leeward Islands ⑤ Windward Islands ⑥

Atlantic Ocean

Caribbean Sea

Gulf of Mexico

Countries and regions

MEXICO

USA
O Miami
Florida Keys

Bahamas
Grand Bahama, Little Abaco, Great Abaco, Berry Islands, Eleuthera, Nassau New Providence, N Bimini, S Bimini, Andros, Cat Island, San Salvador, Rum Cay, Exuma, Great Exuma, Long Island, Crooked Island, Acklins Island, Ragged Island Range, Mayaguana, Providenciales, Little Inagua, Great Inagua, West Caicos, Tongue of the Ocean, Great Bahama Bank

Cuba
Ciudad de la Habana, Isla de la Juventud, Archipiélago de los Canarreos, Cayo Largo, Cayo Coco, Archipiélago Jardines de la Reina, Little Cayman, Cayman Brac, Grand Cayman

Greater Antilles

Jamaica
Kingston

Turks & Caicos
North Caicos Islands, Middle Caicos, East Caicos, South Caicos, Grand Turk Caicos

Hispaniola
Île de la Tortue, Île de la Gonâve, Golfe de la Gonâve, Canal de la Tortue, Presqu'île du Nord-Ouest, Haiti, Port-au-Prince, Dominican Republic, Santo Domingo, Isla Saona, Isla Beata

Puerto Rico
San Juan, Mona Passage, Isla Mona, Isla de Vieques

British Virgin Islands
Anegada, Virgin Gorda, Tortola, St Thomas, US Virgin Islands, St John, St Croix

Leeward Islands
Sombrero, Anguilla, Saint-Barthélemy, Sint Maarten / Saint-Martin, Saba, Sint Eustatius, St Christopher (St Kitts), Antigua, Barbuda, Redonda, Nevis, Montserrat, Guadeloupe, Grande-Terre, Les Saintes, Marie-Galante

Windward Islands
Dominica, Martinique, Martinique Passage, St Lucia Channel, St Lucia, St Vincent Passage, St Vincent & The Grenadines, Bequia, Mustique, Canouan, Mayreau, Union Island, Carriacou, Grenada, Barbados, Barbados Ridge, Tobago Basin, Tobago

Lesser Antilles

Trinidad
Port of Spain, Gulf of Paria, Columbus Channel

VENEZUELA
Caracas, Los Testigos, Isla La Orchila, Isla de Margarita, Islas Los Roques, Cayo Grande, Islas Las Aves, Isla de Sola, Isla Tortuga, Aruba, Curaçao, Bonaire

COLOMBIA

PANAMA

NICARAGUA

HONDURAS

Map 1 Cuba, Jamaica & the Cayman Islands

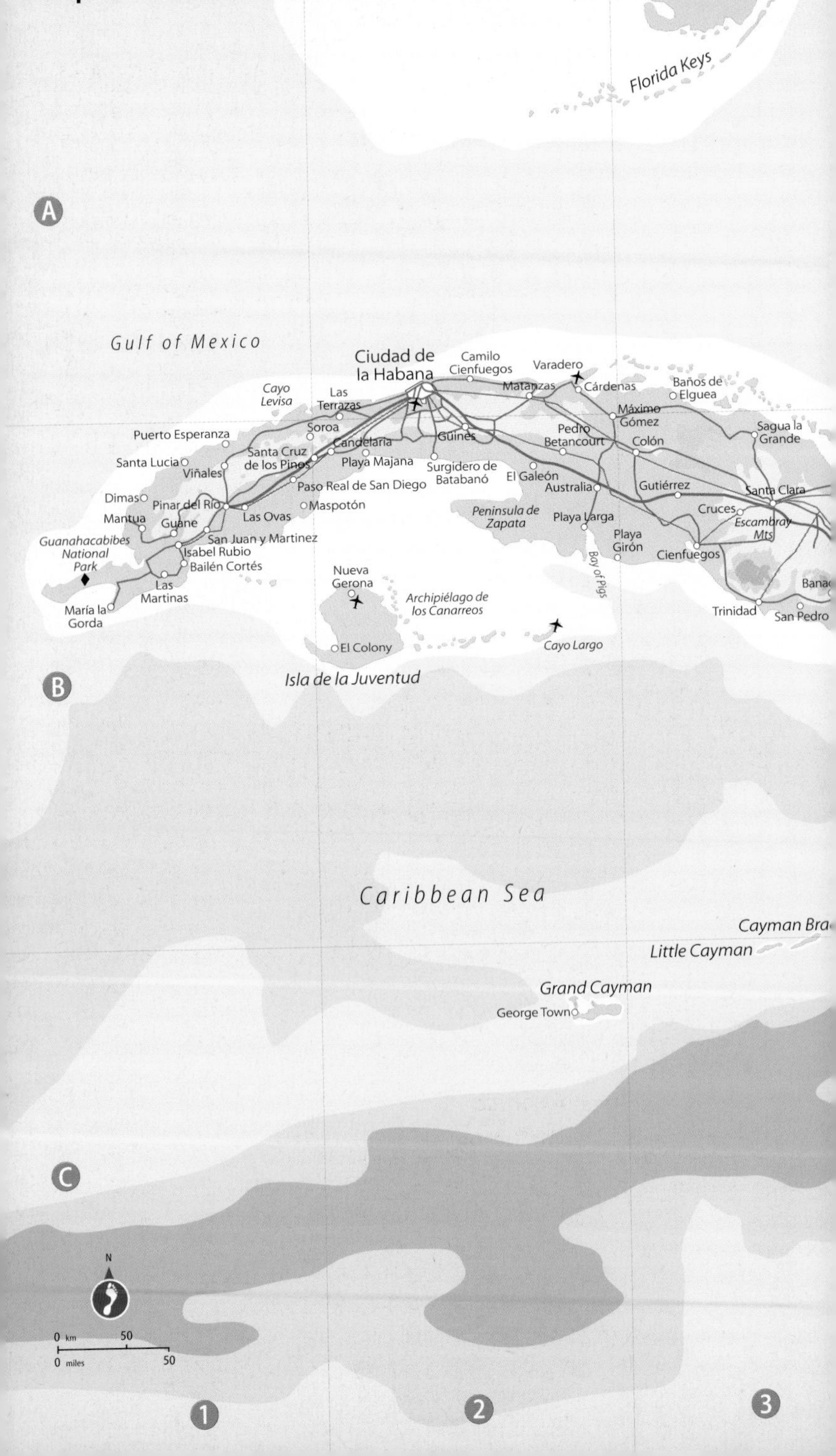

USA

Florida Keys

A

Gulf of Mexico

Cayo Levisa

Ciudad de la Habana

Camilo Cienfuegos

Varadero

Cárdenas

Baños de Elguea

Las Terrazas

Matanzas

Máximo Gómez

Sagua la Grande

Soroa

Puerto Esperanza

Candelaria

Güines

Pedro Betancourt

Colón

Santa Lucía

Santa Cruz de los Pinos

Playa Majana

Viñales

Paso Real de San Diego

Surgidero de Batabanó

El Galeón

Gutiérrez

Santa Clara

Dimas

Pinar del Río

Maspotón

Australia

Cruces

Mantua

Guane

Las Ovas

Península de Zapata

Playa Larga

Escambray Mts

San Juan y Martinez

Playa Girón

Guanahacabibes National Park

Isabel Rubio

Bailén Cortés

Cienfuegos

Banao

Nueva Gerona

San Pedro

Las Martinas

Archipiélago de los Canarreos

Trinidad

María la Gorda

El Colony

Cayo Largo

Isla de la Juventud

Bay of Pigs

Caribbean Sea

Cayman Bra

Little Cayman

Grand Cayman

George Town

N

0 km 50

0 miles 50

B

C

1

2

3

N

0 km   40

0 miles   40

Atlantic Ocean

A

Arthur's Town

Alligator Point

Cat Island

New Bight

Old Bight

Hawks Nest Point

Port Howe

Cockburn Town   San Salvador

B

Rum Cay

Port Nelson

Great Exuma

George Town

Stella Maris

Little Exuma

Long Island

Deadman's Cay

Clarence Town

Samana Cay

Landrail Point   Colonel Hill

Crooked Island   Richmond

Long Cay

Bight of Acklins   Goodwill

Ragged Island Range

Acklins Island

Mayaguana

Abraham's Bay

C

Salina Point

Castle Island

Mayaguana Passage

Little Inagua

Land and Sea Park

Great Inagua

Bahamas National Trust Park

Lake Rosa

Guardalavaca

Matthew Town

4   5   6

Map 3 Hispaniola, Puerto Rico, Turks & Caicos Islands & the Virgin Islands

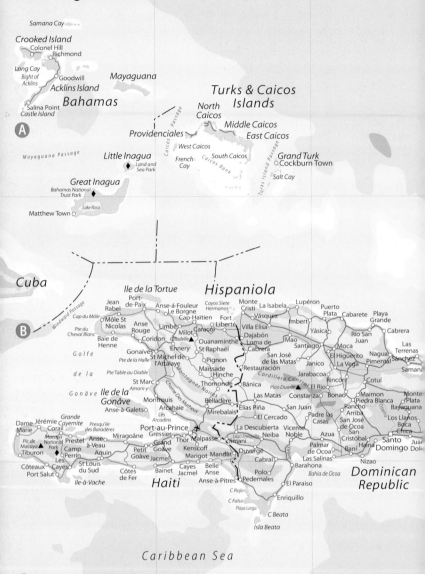

Samana Cay

Crooked Island
Colonel Hill
Richmond

Long Cay
Bight of
Acklins
Goodwill
Acklins Island
Mayaguana

Bahamas
Salina Point
Castle Island

Turks & Caicos
Islands

North
Caicos
Caicos Passage
Providenciales
West Caicos
Middle Caicos
East Caicos

Mayaguana Passage
Little Inagua
Land and
Sea Park
French
Cay
South Caicos
Caicos Bank
Grand Turk
Cockburn Town

Great Inagua
Bahamas National
Trust Park
Lake Rosa
Salt Cay
Turks Island Passage

Matthew Town

Cuba

Ile de la Tortue
Hispaniola

Jean
Rabel
Port-
de-Paix
Anse-à-Fouleur
Le Borgne
Cap Haitien
Monte
Cristi
La Isabela
Luperón
Puerto
Plata
Cabarete
Playa
Grande

Cap du Môle
Pte du
Cheval Blanc
Môle St
Nicolas
Anse
Rouge
Limbé
Caracol
Fort
Liberté
Villa Elisa
Imbert
Yásica
Río San
Juan
Cabrera

Baie de
Henne
Coridon
Milot
Ehnery
St Raphaël
Dajabón
Loma de
Cabrera
Mao
Santiago
Moca
El Higüerito
Nagua
Pimentel
La Vega
Las
Terrenas
Sánchez

Golfe
Gonaïves
Ste Michel de
l'Attalaye
Ouanaminthe
Pignon
San José
de las Matas
Janico
Jarabacoa
Rincón
Cotuí
Samana

de la
Pte de la Halle
Maïssade
Hinche
Restauración
Bánica
Pico Duarte
El Rio
Bonao
Maimón
Piedra Blanca

Gonâve
Pte Table au Diable
St Marc
Thomonde
Belladère
Las Matas
Constanza
Rancho
Arriba
Los Llanos
Bayaguana
Monte
Plata

Ile de la
Gonâve
Montrouis
Arcahaie
Mirebalais
Elías Piña
San Juan
Padre las
Casas
San José
de Ocoa
San
Cristóbal
Boca
Chica

Dame
Marie
Jérémie
Grande
Cayemite
Presqu'île
des Baradères
Les
Arcadins
La Descubierta
El Cercado
Vicente
Noble
Azua
Bani
Haina
Santo
Domingo

Corail
Pic de
Macaya
Macaya
National
Park
Prestel
Miragoâne
Port-au-Prince
Gressier
Thor
Malpasse
Lago Enriquillo
Neiba
Palmar
de Ocoa
Las Salinas
Nizao

Tiburon
Camp
Perrin
Anse-
à-Veau
Petit
Goâve
Grand
Goâve
Kenscoff
Marigot
Mandat
Duvergé
Cabral
Barahona
Bahía de Ocoa

Côteaux
Les
Cayes
St Louis
du Sud
Aquin
Jacmel
Cayes
Jacmel
Belle
Anse
Polo
El Paraíso

Port Salut
Ile-à-Vache
Côtes
de Fer
Bainet
Anse-à-Pitres
Pedernales
Enriquillo

Haiti
C Rojo
C Falso
Playa Larga
C Beata

**Dominican
Republic**

Isla Beata

Caribbean Sea

Atlantic Ocean

Las Galeras
Cayo Levantado
Sabana de la Mar
El Valle
Hato
Mayor
Miches
El Seibo
El Macao
Bávaro
Ramón
Santana
Higüey
Punta Cana
La Romana
San Pedro
de Macoris
Bayahibe
Boca del
Yuma
Isla Saona

Mona Passage
Isla Mona

*Punta
Boninquén*
Jobos
Arecibo
Dorado
San
Juan
Isla
Verde
Luquillo
Quebradillas
Manati
Aguadilla
Juncos
Fajardo
Ceiba
Añasco Beach
Mayagüez
San
Sebastián
Utuado
Aibonito
Caguas
Humacao
Adjuntas
Coamo
Patillas
Yabucoa
Boquerón
Guánica
Ponce
Santa
Isabel
Guayama
*Punta
Jagüey*

**British Virgin
Islands** *Anegda*
The Settlement
Road *Virgin
Town Gorda*
Charlotte *Tortola*
St Thomas Cruz Bay
Culebra Amalie *St John*
Dewey
Vieques
Esperanza
**US Virgin
Islands**

St Croix
Christiansted

Puerto Rico

N

0 km   50
0 miles   50

4   5   6

Map 4 Leeward Islands

Anegada Passage

Sombrero

A

Dog Island

Anguilla

Scrub Island

The Valley

Island Harbour

Blowing Point

Saint-Martin

Marigot

Sint Maarten

Philipsburg

Gustavia

St Barthélémy

Atlantic Ocean

Saba

B

Sint Eustatius

Oranjestad

Mt Liamuiga

St Christopher (St Kitts)

Mt Verchilds

Basseterre

Newcastle

Charlestown

Nevis

Redonda

Barbuda

Codrington Lagoon

Codrington

Long Island

Guiana Island

St John's

Parham

Antigua

English Harbour

Montserrat

Chances Peak (Volcano)

Plymouth

Caribbean Sea

Leeward Islands

C

Guadeloupe Passage

N

0 km 20

0 miles 20

Guadeloupe

Basse-Terre

1   **2**   **3**

Map 5 Windward Islands

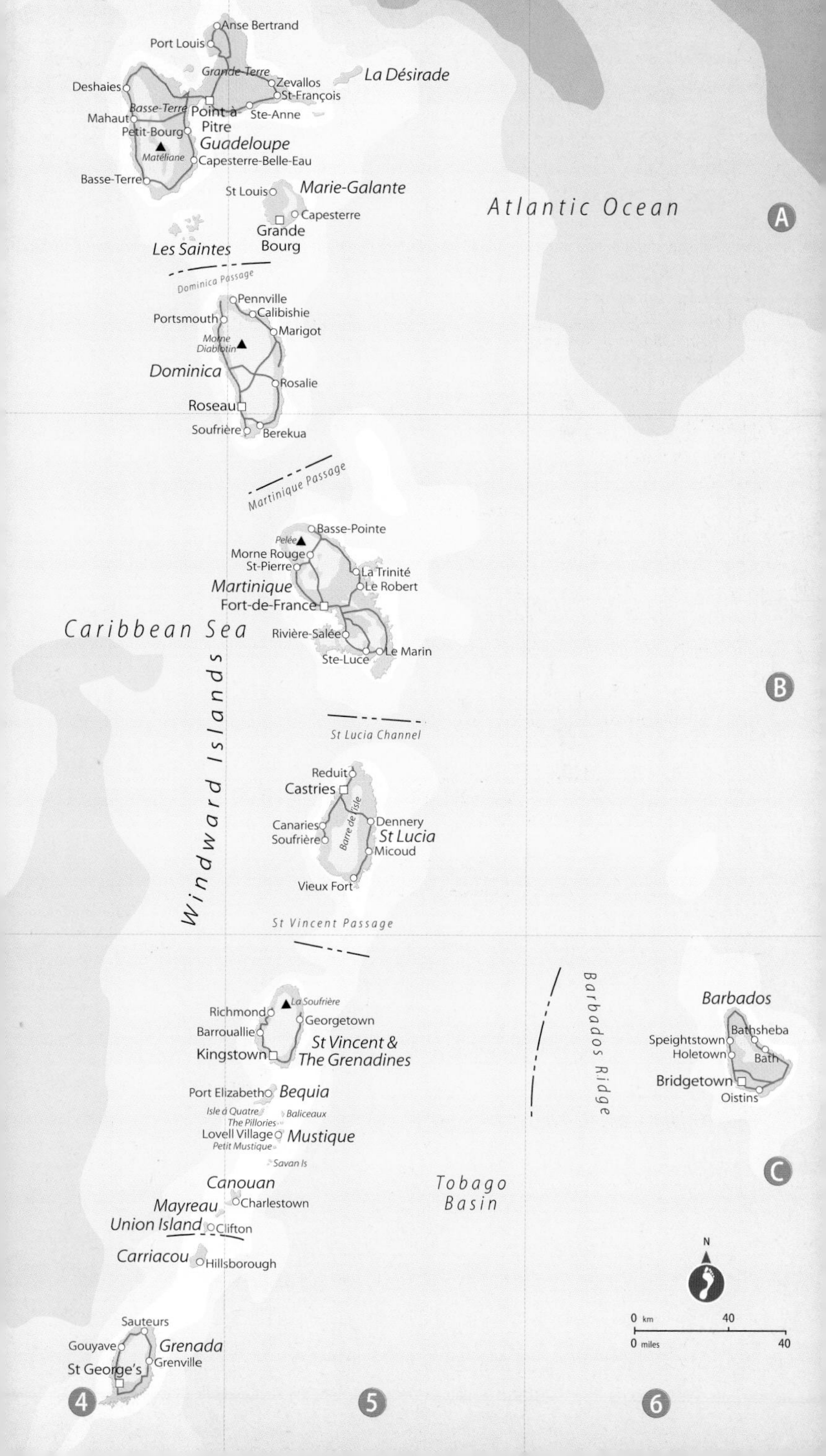

Anse Bertrand
Port Louis
Grande-Terre
Zevallos
St-François
La Désirade
Deshaies
Basse-Terre
Point à Pitre
Ste-Anne
Mahaut
Petit-Bourg
Guadeloupe
▲ *Matéliane*
Capesterre-Belle-Eau
Basse-Terre
St Louis
Marie-Galante
Capesterre
Grande Bourg
Les Saintes

Atlantic Ocean

A

Dominica Passage
Pennville
Calibishie
Portsmouth
Marigot
▲ *Morne Diablotin*
Dominica
Rosalie
Roseau □
Soufrière
Berekua

Martinique Passage

Pelée ▲
Basse-Pointe
Morne Rouge
St-Pierre
La Trinité
Le Robert
Martinique
Fort-de-France □
Rivière-Salée
Le Marin
Ste-Luce

Caribbean Sea

Windward Islands

B

St Lucia Channel

Reduit
Castries □
Canaries
Barre de l'Isle
Dennery
Soufrière
St Lucia
Micoud
Vieux Fort

St Vincent Passage

▲ *La Soufrière*
Richmond
Georgetown
Barrouallie
St Vincent &
The Grenadines
Kingstown □
Port Elizabeth
Bequia
Isle à Quatre • *Baliceaux*
The Pillories
Lovell Village
Mustique
Petit Mustique
Savan Is
Canouan
Mayreau
Charlestown
Union Island
Clifton
Carriacou
Hillsborough

Barbados Ridge

Barbados
Speightstown
Bathsheba
Holetown
Bath
Bridgetown □
Oistins

C

Tobago Basin

N

0 km 40
0 miles 40

Sauteurs
Gouyave
Grenada
St George's □
Grenville

4

5

6

Map 6 Lesser Antilles & Trinidad

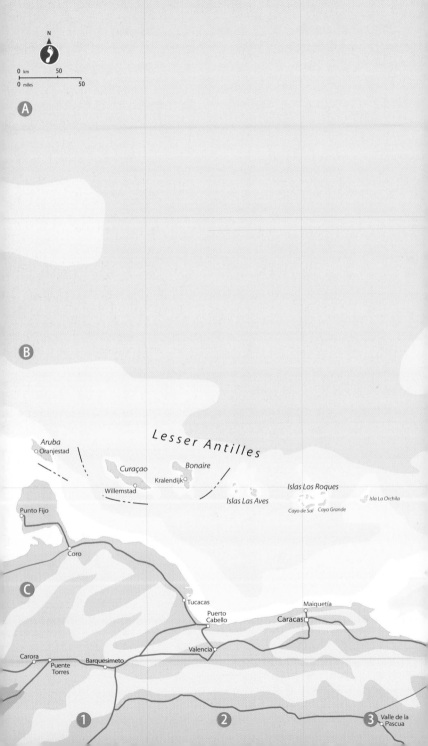

N

0 km 50
0 miles 50

A

B

Lesser Antilles

Aruba
○ Oranjestad

Curaçao
Willemstad ○

Bonaire
Kralendijk ○

Islas Los Roques
Islas Las Aves
Cayo de Sal Cayo Grande

Isla La Orchila

Punto Fijo ○

C

Coro ○

Tucacas

Puerto
Cabello

Maiquetía

Caracas ○

Carora ○
Puente
Torres

Barquesimeto ○

Valencia ○

Valle de la
Pascua

1

2

3

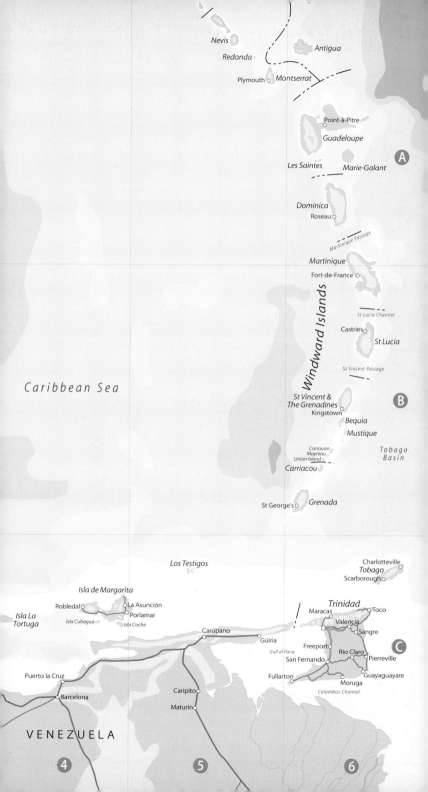

What the papers say

"The most complete, up-to-date information on the islands."
Travel & Leisure

"Top marks for the travel-proof cover. But there is more that is good – text is short, sharp, to the point and accurate. A hit"
Escape Magazine, UK

"Footprint - no-nonsense, succinct, authoritative guides."
National Geographic Traveler

"Anyone on the prowl in the Caribbean should use this as their bible."
Caribbean Beat, BWIA

"Your book is the only one to mention Haiti, which is what we were looking for. It is a shame that the other books only mention the 'touristy' places. Your book is excellent."
AB, Canada

Awards
Wanderlust Readers' Award for Top Guidebook Series
Bronze Award
Literati Club
Outstanding Achievement

Website
www.footprintbooks.com
Take a look for the latest news, to order
a book or join our mailing list.

Acknowledgements

Associate editor
Ben Box turned his attention to contemporary Latin American affairs in 1980, beginning a career as a freelance writer. During his frequent visits to the region he has travelled extensively in the Caribbean. He also edits the Footprint South American Handbook and other titles.

Specialist contributors
Several specialists have helped provide information for the **Essentials** section including:

Watersports by Rosie Mauro, formerly of Barbados
Scuba diving and **Hurricanes** by Martha Watkins Gilkes, a freelance diving journalist based in Antigua and author of *The Scuba Diving Guide to the Caribbean* (Macmillan)
Windsurfing by Nicolette Clifford, formerly based in Tortola, British Virgin Islands
Walking by Mark Wilson, currently based in Trinidad
Cricket by Jeremy Cameron
Cycling by Patricia Thorndike de Suriel of Iguana Mama, in the Dominican Republic
Flora and Fauna and **Responsible Travel** by Mark Eckstein with additional information from Mark Wilson
Whale and dolphin watching by Erich Hoyt, consultant for the *Whale and Dolphin Conservation Society*, marine ecologist and author of 12 books including *The Whale Watcher's Handbook*, *Collins Whales and Dolphins* and *Seasons of the Whale*
Sailing by Kathy Irwin, an experienced sailor from Heath, Texas
Health by Dr David Snashall, presently Senior Lecturer in Occupational Health at the United Medical Schools of Guy's & St Thomas' Hospitals in London and Chief Medical Advisor of the British Foreign and Commonwealth Office.

Correspondents
We are most grateful to all our regular and not so regular correspondents in the Caribbean region:

Antigua and Barbuda Martha Watkins Gilkes
Bahamas Deby Nash
Barbados Mark Wilson
Cayman Islands Tedde Thompson
Cuba Siân Oram and Juan Carlos Otaño
Curaçao Nan Elisa
Dominica Steve McCabe
Dominican Republic Sarah Cameron would like to thank all those who helped during her trip to the Dominican Republic in 2000, particularly Carlos Batista at the Secretariá de Estado de Turismo, Dania Goris in Santo Domingo, Daniela Wenger in Las Terrenas and Patricia Thorndike in Cabarete, all of whom have also helped to update the text
Haiti Hilde Skogedal
Jamaica Robert Kerr

Martinique Graham Norton and Jacques Bajal at the Office Départemental du Tourisme de la Martinique
St Kitts and Nevis Maria Vendiese James
St Lucia Annette Blackburn
Trinidad and Tobago David Renwick
Turks & Caicos Islands Kathi Barrington
US Virgin Islands Martha Watkins Gilkes

Thanks also go to Nigel Gallop (music, Puerto Rico), John Alton (*Strand Cruise and Travel Centre*, London), Frank Bellamy and the staff of *Caribbean Experience* (London), Rod Prince (*Caribbean Insight*, London) and the many Tourist Offices in Europe and the Caribbean who provided much information and answered our queries. In addition, Amanda George did an invaluable job of checking websites.

We are very grateful to all the travellers who have written to us over the last year:

D L & D C Baker, UK; Pam Bernard & friends, Canada; Ria & Freek Biersteker, Netherlands; Jenny Boland, UK; Jeremy Cameron, UK; Nicole Champagnol; Nicole Charles, UK; Mariam Cherian, UK; Krystyna Danielsson, Sweden; Richard Day, Haiti; Niclaes Didier, Belgium; Jane Eiseley, USA; David Elak, Germany; Robert Euler, Canada; Louise Friend, UK; Natasja Frijlink, Netherlands; Tanja Gilb, Germany; Victoria Holt; Christina Hotz, Switzerland; Heinz Lauber, Austria; Josefine Laviolette, UK; Pavlos Mastiki; Bruce Miller, USA; Doris Mosimann, Switzerland; Pierre Musson, USA; Arash Nouri; Sian Oram; Maj Brit Pedersen, Denmark; Scott A Rasmussen, Puerto Rico; Ray; Elizabeth Ann Reed, USA; Jochen Reidi; Simone Ronckers, Netherlands; Clare Santry, UK; Yossi Schwartz, Israel; Grethel Suarez, Cuba; Dave Upton, Australia; Janet Valbuena, UK; Hilde Van Mederkassel, Belgium; Marc Verhoef; Martin Wanner, Switzerland; Margaret Wardlow, UK; Vaughan Wastling, UK; Gregoary Williams, USA; Sarah Wright, UK; Bruce Young; Peter Zartner.